WORLD AUTHORS

1970-1975

Biographical Reference Books from
The H. W. Wilson Company

American Reformers

Greek and Latin Authors 800 B.C.–A.D. 1000
European Authors 1000–1900
British Authors Before 1800
British Authors of the Nineteenth Century
American Authors 1600–1900
Twentieth Century Authors
Twentieth Century Authors: First Supplement
World Authors 1950–1970
World Authors 1970–1975
World Authors 1975–1980

The Junior Book of Authors
More Junior Authors
Third Book of Junior Authors
Fourth Book of Junior Authors and Illustrators
Fifth Book of Junior Authors and Illustrators

Great Composers: 1300–1900
Composers Since 1900
Composers Since 1900: First Supplement
Musicians Since 1900
American Songwriters

Nobel Prize Winners

World Artists 1950–1980

World Film Directors: Volumes I, II

WORLD AUTHORS

1970-1975

A Volume in the Wilson Authors Series

Editor
JOHN WAKEMAN

Editorial Consultant
STANLEY J. KUNITZ

THE H. W. WILSON COMPANY
New York 1980

93-416

First Printing 1980
Second Printing 1985
Third Printing 1989

Printed in the United States of America

Library of Congress Cataloging in Publication Data
Main entry under title:

World authors, 1970–1975.

(The Authors series)
Includes bibliographies.
1. Literature, Modern — 20th century — Bio-bibliogra-
phy. 2. Literature, Modern — 20th century — History
and criticism. I. Wakeman, John. II. Series:
Authors series.
PN451.W3 1980   809′.04 [B]   79-21874
ISBN 0-8242-0641-X

Sosnora on page 780 are from *Post-War Russian Poetry* edited by Daniel Weissbort (Harmondsworth, Eng.: Penguin, 1974)

The lines from "A Natural Grace" by C. K. Stead on page 783 are from *Whether the Will Is Free* (Auckland, NZ: Paul's Book Arcade, 1964)

The lines by C. K. Stead on page 783 are from *Crossing the Bar* (Auckland, NZ: University Press, 1972)

The lines from "In the Mountains" on page 794 are from *Sleeping With One Eye Open* (Boston: Stone Wall Press, 1964) copyright © 1964 by Mark Strand

The lines from "Eating Poetry" and from "Keeping Things Whole" on page 794 are from *Reasons for Moving* (New York: Atheneum, 1968) copyright © 1963, 1964, 1965, 1966, 1967, 1968 by Mark Strand

The lines from "The Untelling" on page 795 are from *The Story of Our Lives* (New York: Atheneum, 1973) copyright © 1971, 1972, 1973 by Mark Strand

The lines from "Camping in the Valley" by James Tate on pages 799–800 are from *Camping in the Valley* (Chicago: Madison Park Press, 1968)

The lines from "Absences" on page 800 are from *Absences* (Boston: Little, Brown, 1972) copyright © 1970, 1971, 1972 by James Tate

The lines from "Manhood End" on page 810 are from *The Owl in the Tree* by Anthony Thwaite (Oxford: Oxford University Press, 1963) copyright © 1963 by Oxford University Press

The lines from "The Sofas, Fogs, and Cinemas" on page 814 are from *Iliad of Broken Sentences* (London: The Bodley Head, 1967) copyright © 1967 by Rosemary Tonks

The lines from "Perplexity" by Miguel Torga on page 817 are from *Selections from Contemporary Portuguese Poetry* (Irvington-on-Hudson, NY: Harvey House, 1966) copyright © 1966 by Harvey House

The lines from "Presence" by U Tam'si on page 832 are from *Brush Fire* (Ibadan: Mbari Publications, © 1964, 1957).

The lines from "The Dead" by U Tam'si on page 832 are from *Selected Poems* (Atlantic Highlands, NJ: Humanities, 1970)

The lines from "Leda" on page 834 are from *To See, To Take* (New York: Atheneum, 1973) copyright © 1964, 1965, 1966, 1967, 1968, 1969, 1970 by Mona Van Duyn

The lines from "We Rigged Up a Theatre" by Yevgeny Vinokurov on page 845 are from *The War Is Over* (Chester, PA: Dufour, 1976)

The lines from "I" by Yevgeny Vinokurov on page 845 are from *The New Russian Poets 1953–1968* (New York: October House, 1966) copyright © 1966, 1968 George Reavey

The lines from "Coins and Coffins" on pages 846–847 are from *Coins and Coffins* (Hawk's Well Press, 1962) copyright © 1962 by Diane Wakoski

The lines from "I Have Learned to Live With My Face" on page 847 are from *The Motorcycle Betrayal Poems* (New York, Simon & Schuster, 1971) copyright © 1971 by Diane Wakoski

Page 853. Use of "A Flamingo's Dream" and "From Persian Parables" by Aleksander Wat, from *Postwar Polish Poetry: An Anthology*, by Czeslaw Milosz. Copyright © 1965 by Czeslaw Milosz. Used by permission of Doubleday and Company, Inc.

The lines from "Dead Water" by Wen I-to on page 855 are from *The White Pony* (New York, John Day Co., 1947) edited by Robert Payne copyright © 1947 by the John Day Co.

The lines by Sándor Weöres from "A fogak tornaca" on page 857, from "The Last Parasol" on page 858, and "Moon and Farmstead" on page 859 are from *Sándor Weöres and Ferenc Juhász: Selected Poems* (The Penguin Modern European Poets, 1970) (Harmondsworth, Eng.: Penguin, 1970) copyright © 1970 by Sándor Weöres; translation copyright © 1970 by Edwin Morgan. Reprinted by permission of Penguin Books Ltd.

"After moon sun" by Sándor Weöres on page 858 is from *Books Abroad*, Winter 1969, vol. 43, #1. Copyright © 1969 by the University of Oklahoma (Norman, OK: University of Oklahoma Press)

The lines from "If the Night Could Get Up and Walk" on page 864 are from *An Ear in Bartram's Tree: Selected Poems 1957–1967* by Jonathan Williams (Chapel Hill: University of North Carolina Press, 1969) copyright © 1962, 1969, by Jonathan Williams. The University of North Carolina Press, 1969, for the Contemporary Poetry Series.

The lines from "The Island" by George Woodcock quoted on page 880 are from *Imagine the South* (Pasadena: Untide Press, 1947) copyright © 1947 by Untide Press

The lines from "Poem at Thirty" by John Warren Woods, quoted on page 882 are from *On the Morning of Color* (Bloomington: Indiana University Press, 1961) copyright © 1961 by Indiana University Press

PREFACE

THIS BOOK is the latest in The Wilson Authors Series, which began with Kunitz and Haycraft's *British Authors of the Nineteenth Century* (1936) and includes among other titles *Twentieth Century Authors* (1942) and its supplement and *World Authors 1950–1970* (1975). Since the present work does not update biographies of authors dealt with elsewhere in the Series, it is called a companion rather than a supplement to the preceding volumes.

In the selection of subjects, this volume follows the general policies of the Series. Most of the 348 authors included here are "imaginative" writers — poets, novelists, dramatists — of literary importance and/or of exceptional popularity. There are also a number of philosophers, historians, biographers, critics, scientists, journalists, and others whose work seemed of sufficiently wide interest, influence, or literary merit.

The majority of these 348 writers came to prominence between 1970 and 1975. However, we have also included several whose reputations were made earlier, but who were omitted from previous volumes in the Series because of a lack of biographical information, or because their work was not then familiar to readers of English. This is no longer a very significant criterion, thanks to the vast increase in translations from all languages.

About a fifth of the authors in this book have provided autobiographical articles. These have been reproduced without alteration (except of course those that have been translated from foreign languages, where accuracy has been sought even at the cost of elegance). Nothing conveys so well the precise flavor of the writer's literary character and voice.

As with *World Authors 1950–1970*, critical comment is fuller than in the earlier volumes in the Series, but abides by the same principle, attempting not "an independent appraisal but . . . a fair summation of representative critical response." Beyond this, we have quite often offended against what used to be called the New Criticism by suggesting connections between an author's life and the kind of books he writes. Some artists achieve or suffer an emblematic status, so that their lives, no less than their books, provide clues to the social or moral or psychological mechanisms of their time and place. We have frequently gone beyond a chaste recital of events and dates to record information or anecdotes that seem to us illuminating or suggestive in these terms.

The editorial notes were written by specialists in the literatures concerned and checked by independent researchers; they were later updated and checked again. Errors inevitably remain, but fewer, it is hoped, than are usually to be expected in a work of this scale. (The same claim was made in the preface to *World Authors 1950–1970* and seems to have been justified, since remarkably few errors have been reported to us. Those that have will be corrected in the next printing.)

In general, the book is intended for students and common readers (though some of the autobiographical articles, at least, will be of interest to scholars as well). We have therefore striven for simplicity in such vexed matters as pseudonyms and the transliteration of foreign names. In transliterations, for example, we have preferred the forms made familiar by trade publishers to the daunting constructions urged upon each other by warring specialists. The bibliographies are equally utilitarian. The lists of Principal Works are intended to include all of an author's published books in English (with dates of *first* publication) but usually not magazine pieces, contributions to symposia, etc. The lists of writings *about* an author and his work are selective when there is a great deal of such material, relatively full when there is not.

In the text, foreign titles are followed by an English version of the title and a date in parenthesis. The date is that of the first publication of the original work. The English title appears in roman type if we have supplied the translation; in italics if the book has actually been translated and published under that title; in quotation marks if it is a poem, story, or other short piece translated and published under that title in a magazine or collection. Dates given for plays in the text are usually specified as dates of writing or of first *production*; dates given in the bibliographies are dates of first *publication*.

One scholarly reviewer of *World Authors 1950–1970* found it "without a rival among single-volume works" in its field, and several readers have paid it the almost equally welcome compliment of saying that they use it as a bedside book, dipping into it not for instruction but for pleasure. The kindest thing we heard of it was said by an old teacher, who remarked that no book he knew gave him a clearer sense of literature as a single republic. We have tried to insure that this companion volume will perform the same functions.

If it does, most of the credit belongs to our distinguished contributors, many of whom have earned international reputations as authorities on one or another of the world's literatures. Their names are listed below.

J. W.
June 1979

CONTRIBUTORS

Diane Ackerman
Konstantin Bazarov
Valerie Cossey
Charles Gibbes
Susan Green
Michael Hamburger
Eric Homberger
Erik Korn
Catharine L. Mastny
Robert Maurer

R. P. Meijer
Gerald Moore
Alastair Niven
Gavin Orton
Giovanni Pontiero
Martin Seymour-Smith
C. H. Sisson
William Walsh
Irving Wardle
Paul West

KEY TO PRONUNCIATION

ā āle

â câre

a add

ä ärm

ē ēve

e end

g go

ī īce

i ill

K German ch as in *ich* (iK)

N Not pronounced, but indicates the nasal tone of the preceding vowel, as in the French *bon* (bôN)

ō ōld

ô ôrb

oi oil

o odd

o͞o o͞oze

o͝o fo͝ot

ou out

th *then*

th thin

ū cūbe

û ûrn; French eu, as in *jeu* (zhû), German ö, oe, as in *schön* (shûn), *Goethe* (gû tə)

u tub

ü Pronounced approximately as ē, with rounded lips: French u, as in *vu* (vü); German ü, as in *Gefühl* (ge fül´)

ə the schwa, an unstressed vowel representing the sound that is spelled
a as in sofa
e as in fitted
i as in edible
o as in melon
u as in circus

zh azure

´ = main accent

A NECROLOGY OF AUTHORS
WILL BE FOUND AT THE END OF THE BOOK

*ABELL, KJELD August 25, 1901–March 5, 1961), Danish dramatist, was born in Ribe, Jutland, the son of Peter and Susanne Abell. His father was a schoolteacher. A Max Reinhardt production of Strindberg's *Ghost Sonata* was his introduction to the excitements of the modern theatre. Abell studied for a time at the Academy of Art in Copenhagen, then switched to economics at Copenhagen University. He graduated in that subject in 1927 but, reacting against his bourgeois upbringing and deciding that the theatre was his true métier, went off to Paris and then London to work as a commercial artist and stage designer. Abell returned to Denmark in 1930 and became a stage designer at the Danish Royal Theatre in Copenhagen. He had his first major success there in 1931 with a series of widely acclaimed designs for George Balanchine's Russian Ballet, and himself wrote a ballet in 1934. Abell's interest in the techniques of theatrical presentation and his delight in innovation are very evident in his own work, which relies a great deal on visual effects.

This was true of his first play, *Melodin der blev vaek* (1935, translated by F. Sinclair and R. Adam as *The Melody That Got Lost*), an episodic comedy using music, masks, dummies, and apparitions, among other theatrical devices. It tells the story of a Chaplinesque "little man" who eases the tedium of office work by humming a little song. The melody is lost when Larsen gets married and settles down to Danish middle-class respectability—a state which is evoked in the play with terrifying precision and considerable wit. Larsen and his wife eventually set out to rediscover the lost melody, finding it in the possession of a child and an ordinary workingman, among others. The play, in which critics saw the influences of Jean Giraudoux, Brecht, and Erich Kästner, was an immediate success, widely translated and produced. According to a reviewer in the *Times Literary Supplement,* it was enjoyed as much for "the wholly irreverent way the author had treated the established theatrical conventions" as for "the exuberant iconoclasm of his social thinking."

Abell returned to the attack on the narrowmindedness and inertia of his own class in *Eva aftjener sin barnepligt* (Eve Does Her Childhood Service, 1936), an expressionist comedy in which the mother of mankind, pining for the childhood she never had, steps out of a picture in a museum and endures an appalling middle-class upbringing until Adam rescues her and puts her adopted family on trial. The family is condemned to live as a family portrait in the museum (where they will feel at home) while Adam and Eve go out

*â′ bəl

KJELD ABELL

Danish Information Office

to rediscover creation: "The world isn't a museum—every day it's as fresh and new as when Adam first saw a hen lay an egg."

In the plays that followed Abell altered the emphasis of his attack to excoriate the moral passivity of the middle classes, their unwillingness to soil their hands with the dirty but essential work of fighting for humane values in a fascist age. This point is made most tellingly in *Anna Sophie Hedvig* (1939, translated under the same title by Hanna Astrup Larsen), which many critics regard as Abell's best play. A respectable family is discussing the virtues of appeasement when a visiting maiden aunt, a schoolteacher named Anna Sophie Hedvig, reveals that she has killed a colleague—a petty tyrant who was attempting to seize power in the school. Mousy and insignificant though she appears to be, Anna has nevertheless been prepared to commit murder in defense of civilized values. At the end of the play she is seen standing beside a Spanish Republican soldier facing Franco's firing squad: the soldier's cause is hers. "It's no use being 'all right'—the others are fighting with quite different weapons—and here we sit being 'all right'—but for whose benefit? Only for the sake of our own consciences—have we the right to do that, while our world is being destroyed?"

Similar problems are considered in *Judith* (1940), a modern reinterpretation of the biblical story of Judith and Holofernes. In Abell's version Judith has a middle-class conscience; she is the "priestess with the clean hands" who is only with great difficulty persuaded to assassinate Holofernes. In the end it is a woman of the people—a brothel-keeper—who does the deed.

1

Dronning går igen (1943, translated by J.F.S. Pearce as *The Queen on Tour*) presents an actress, appearing as the Gertrude of *Hamlet*, defending herself against accusations of murder. This play was produced during the German occupation of Denmark, and its exhortations to active resistance are necessarily somewhat obliquely expressed, but it is notable for its praise of the theatre as "part of living life" and a force for individual development and social change.

Abell had expressed similar views in an essay published in 1939: "Is not the real essence of the theatre that it sets the imagination of each one of us in motion and makes us come to grips with the world and form a personal view of existence? Is not the cinema a picture of the world, while the theatre can allow us to *create* a picture of the world?" Life and theatre met in 1944 when Abell stopped a performance at the Royal Theatre in Copenhagen to announce that the dramatist Kaj Munk, a symbol of Danish resistance, had been found dead in a ditch near the German headquarters at Silkeborg. Abell himself then went underground and joined the Resistance. His play *Silkeborg* (1946) is a tribute to the movement.

It is generally agreed that Abell's postwar plays are inferior to his earlier work—excessively verbose, irritating in their surface flippancy and contrived ambiguity, and, to quote B.G. Madsen, "frequently lapsing into tortuous cerebral tirades held together (when they *are* held together) by a disconcertingly capricious logic." *Dage på en sky* (1947, translated by E. Bredsdorff and A.I. Roughton as *Days on a Cloud*) is about a scientist who, horrified by his contribution to atomic war, throws himself out of his plane. His suicide is interrupted when he lands on a cloud that is already occupied by an assembly of Greek gods and goddesses. They discuss his obligations to society while he wonders whether or not to open his parachute. In the end he is persuaded to shoulder his responsibilities and return to life to fight on the side of humanity.

Den blå pekingeser (The Blue Pekinese, 1954) is also about a character contemplating suicide —a middle-class woman of the sort that appears so often in Abell's plays, spoiled, irresponsible, selfish, but full of anguish at the meaninglessness of her life. She has to learn that she is part of the human community and can only live as part of a whole: "The whole—it stands over men like the sky, binds us together, liberates us." Abell's late plays also include an expressionist study of Hans Christian Andersen (1955), and *Kameliadamen* (1959), a version of Dumas's

novel *La Dame aux Camélias* in which Dumas himself appears.

Abell's "baroque, luxuriant, and often child-like capacity for make-believe" owes a great deal to Andersen. There are times, in the opinion of one critic, when the fantasy element in the plays "ceases to contribute anything to the central poetic idea and instead becomes an exhibit in itself, a form of spectacle." This is so in *Skriget* (The Scream, 1961), a play which operates on several levels at once, mingling talking birds, the everyday world, the surreal, and the biblical to make Abell's usual points about the sterility of the middle class, and the vitality and openness of workers and children. Its elaborate and lavish fantasy, in the opinion of a critic in the *Times Literary Supplement*, fails to disguise the "creaking ordinariness" of much that is said.

Abell is considered the "chief architect of Danish poetic drama," and remains, with Kaj Munk, the most important Danish dramatist of the time. He also wrote ballets and revues, articles and sketches, poems, and the excellent children's book *Paraplyernes oprør* (Revolt of the Umbrellas, 1937). *De tre fra Minikoi* (1957, translated by A. I. Roughton as *Three From Minikoi*), a novel inspired by Abell's visit to China, is also an absorbing compendium of his thoughts on art, politics, and life in general. Abell was married in 1927 to Grete Kock-Petersen. In 1960, a year before his sudden death, he was elected to the Danish Academy.

The novelist and dramatist H. C. Branner wrote of Abell that "as a friend he was loyal to the point of sacrifice, and generous beyond all measure, but he was also tyrannical, moody and incalculable. Nobody was more conscious than he of his responsibilities as a human being, but nobody could so drive his fellow beings to despair as he could. . . . This terribly honest artist was vain as few others are; this fierce aggressor was himself sorely vulnerable."

PRINCIPLE WORKS IN ENGLISH TRANSLATION: *Plays*—The Melody That Got Lost, 1939; Anna Sophie Hedvig *in* Gustafson, A. (ed.) Scandinavian Plays of the Twentieth Century, 1944, *and in* Corrigan, R.W. (ed.) Masterpieces of the Modern Scandinavian Theatre, 1967; The Queen on Tour *in* Bredsdorff, E. (ed.) Contemporary Danish Plays, 1955; Days on a Cloud *in* Sprinchorn, E. (ed.) The Genius of the Scandinavian Theatre, 1964. *Novel*—Three From Minikoi, 1960. *Other*—The Soul of the Theatre (essay) *in* Corrigan, R.W. (ed.) Masterpieces of the Modern Scandinavian Theatre, 1967.

ABOUT: Claudi, J. Contemporary Danish Authors, 1952; Gassner, J. and Quinn, E. (eds.) The Reader's Encyclopedia of World Drama, 1969; Gustafson, A. (ed.) Scandinavian Plays of the Twentieth Century, 1945; Kristensen, S.M. (ed.) En bog om Kjeld Abell, 1961; Marker, F.J. Kjeld Abell, 1976; Penguin Companion to Literature 2, 1969; Schyberg,

F. Kjeld Abell, 1947; Sprinchorn, E. (ed.) The Genius of the Scandinavian Theatre, 1964. *Periodicals*—Scandinavian Studies August 1961; Theatre Arts Monthly November 1936; Times Literary Supplement January 18, 1963.

French Cultural Services

MARCEL ACHARD

*"ACHARD," MARCEL (pseudonym of Marcel Auguste Ferréol) (July 5, 1899–September 4, 1974), French dramatist and film scenarist, was born at Sainte-Foy-lès-Lyon, in the Rhone Valley, and educated at the Institution Rollin at Caluire-et-Cuire. He was the son of a farmer. Achard announced at the age of seven that he intended to become a dramatist, and his first puppet play was produced at school when he was ten. His fascination with the theatre, the circus, the pantomime and the whole spirit of the *commedia dell'arte* persisted and developed during his adolescence. A volume of early poems, *La Muse pérégrine* (The Wandering Muse), published in 1924, showed that verse was not his true métier.

Achard began his career as a schoolteacher at Vaulx-en-Velin (1916-1918), but immediately after World War I entered the Paris theatrical world as a prompter at the Théâtre du Vieux-Colombier (1919-1920). His first play, *Celui qui vivait sa mort* (The One Who Lived His Death), appeared without success in 1922, but *Voulez-vous jouer avec moâ* (Would You Like to Play With Me) was a triumph, and established him at once. This bittersweet circus-ring farce, with clowns for characters, is distinguished by the charm and wit of its dialogue, which was always Achard's forte. The author himself played a leading role in the first production, at Charles Dullin's Théâtre de l'Atelier in 1924. It remains one of the three or four most effective of his fifty-odd plays.

La Vie est belle (Life Is Beautiful), first performed in 1928, introduces a character (here named Charlemagne) who was to appear in various guises in many of the later plays—a lovable wanderer who imposes his own poetic fantasies on the prosaic people he encounters. Louis Jouvet played a similar Pierrot-like role in *Jean de la lune* (John of the Moon, 1929), perhaps the most popular of all Achard's plays. In the teeth of the evidence, Jean calmly persists in his belief in the frivolous Columbine's fidelity, and in this way eventually wins her absolute devotion. This theme—that idealism and fantasy have their own wisdom, and do not always lose their battle with human (and especially female) frailty—recurs repeatedly in Achard's plays. *Jean de la lune* was twice filmed, the second version being directed by the author in 1948.

Rather more serious in its intentions was *La*
*a chär'

Belle Marinière (The Beautiful Bargewoman), also staged in 1929. This relatively realistic study of what happens when a bargewoman falls in love with her husband's best friend was marred, it was thought, by inappropriately fanciful dialogue. After that, with few exceptions, Achard seems to have been content to shine as one of the principal decorations of the French boulevard theatre, exploiting with great skill the humor, the pathos, and the improvisational techniques associated with the *commedia dell'arte*.

Contemporary critics find Achard's tendency to whimsy cloying, and his work has gone out of fashion since World War II. It is true that the content of his plays scarcely developed after about 1928, but his technical mastery is not to be despised, and he introduced some interesting innovations. *La Femme en blanc* (The Woman in White, 1933) uses a cinematic flashback technique, in which the protagonist narrates past events that are enacted while he describes them. In *Le Corsaire* (1938), actors making a film about a pirate find strange parallels between their lives and his, in a manner reminiscent of Pirandello. Achard was unsurpassed in his ability to create, through dialogue, an illusion of reality in a sea of fantasy, and more substantial dramatists, like Jean Anouilh, have learned from him in this respect.

Several of Achard's later plays have been translated into English: *Auprès de ma Blonde* (1947) was adapted by S. N. Behrman as *I Know My Love; Patate* (1957), a comedy about an irascible eccentric, was translated by Felicity Douglas as *Rollo*; and *L'Idiote* (1960), a comedy-thriller, was called *A Shot in the Dark* in Harry

Kurnitz's English version. The author was married in 1925 to Juliette Marty. A Commander of the Légion d'honneur, he was elected to the Académie Française in 1959. He was president of the Cannes International Festival in 1958 and 1959 and of the Venice Festival in 1960.

PRINCIPAL WORKS IN ENGLISH TRANSLATION: I Know My Love, 1952; Rollo, 1960; A Shot in the Dark, 1962.

ABOUT: Bourdet, D. Pris sur le vif, 1957; Brisson, P. Le théâtre des années folles, 1943; Lalou, R. Le théâtre en France depuis 1900, 1961; McGraw-Hill Encyclopedia of World Drama, 1972; Penguin Companion to Literature 2, 1969; Smith H. (ed.) Columbia Dictionary of Modern European Literature, 1947; Surer, P. Le théâtre français contemporain, 1964; Who's Who in France, 1973-1974. *Periodicals* —Romanic Review XVII 1926; Times (London) September 6, 1974; Yale French Studies Winter 1960 (Achard issue).

Royal Netherlands Embassy

GERRIT ACHTERBERG

*ACHTERBERG, GERRIT** (May 20, 1905–January 17, 1962), Dutch poet, was born in Neerlangbroek, the son of a farmer. He worked for some years as a primary-school teacher and as a civil servant, but thereafter devoted himself exclusively to poetry. Achterberg was the finest of the poets who wrote for *Criterium* (Criterion), an influential journal established in Amsterdam in 1940. The *Criterium* poets were a diverse group, sharing no particular literary or political creed. And in fact Achterberg, who lived a retiring life in the village of Leusden, central Netherlands, belonged to no movement, took no part in literary politics, wrote no criticism or reviews. He gave his life to the exploration in poetry of a single theme: the death of the beloved and the search for some way in which she and the poet might be reunited.

This theme was introduced in Achterberg's first volume, *Afvaart* (Departure), published in 1931 when he was twenty-six. The poet sails past "the last city," the last stronghold of reality, into a world in which the separation might be negated. Six years later, in December 1937, Achterberg killed the woman with whom he was lodging and wounded her sixteen-year-old daughter. As a result he spent six months in custody and some time in mental institutions.

In this tragic way, Achterberg gave reality to the theme that obsessed him. What is strange is that this had no apparent effect on his poetry. Paul Rodenko, writing in *Delta* (Summer 1958), suggests that "the death of the beloved is for Achterberg not so much a biographical fact as an elemental truth, a dimension of human existence as such, of which the actual death of the beloved is simply a confirmation." It is in poetic

*ak′ ter berk

terms an emblem both of human mortality and of the imperfection of all human relationships— "of the unbridgeable gap which separates the 'I' from the other. [Achterberg's] . . . is in the last analysis poetry of the fundamental isolation of man."

In *Eiland der Ziel* (Island of the Soul, 1939), as in the first book, the possibility of reunion with the beloved is viewed optimistically, as something that might well be accomplished by the power of poetry: the word will breach the walls of the city of death. However, in *Dead End,* which followed in 1940, optimism turns to despair, and the imperfections of poetry and the inadequacy of the poet become the dominant motifs, as they are in "Misgeboorte" (Miscarriage): "By poetry possessed,/ by demons violated,/ the words rot/ at their birth,/ and song becomes offal for dogs." The struggle for communication in these dark poems makes heavy demands on language, and they are characterized by irregular syntax, neologisms, and unusual words or words used in an unfamiliar sense—Achterberg believed that centuries of corrupt usage had robbed language of its original precision and power, and many of his experiments were attempts to return words to their primal innocence.

Achterberg was married in 1946 to Johanna Catherina van Baak, and at about this time he achieved a precarious psychological balance which he defended against anyone or anything that might upset him emotionally; his poetry reflected this new stability. The prosody of his early verse was often irregular, using alliteration and frequent stresses in a constantly changing rhythmic scheme. The imagery was not particularly rich, and what there was derived mostly from nature. In his postwar work Achterberg shows an increasing interest in form, especially the sonnet, and a wide and often startling use of imagery derived from the sciences and other specialized disciplines.

This innovatory use of imagery went along with the development of Achterberg's conception of his theme. In *Limiet* (Limit, 1946), the dead beloved is imagined disintegrating into various, and often new, elements. Achterberg seeks metaphors for this process in the fields of chemistry, physics, geography, photography, and linguistics. Other areas of knowledge are explored in later volumes, in search of images which might coincide with and preserve the state of being of the beloved, dispersed as she is imagined to be throughout the cosmos. In *Energie* (Energy, 1946), physiology was introduced, as were topography, cartography, arithmetic, and the theory of relativity; in *Sphinx* (1946), archaeology and philosophy; in *Doornroosje* (Sleeping Beauty, 1947), economics and law; in *Spel van de Wilde Jacht* (Play of Wotan's Chase, 1957), magic and folklore. *Hoonte* (1949), which contains some of the relatively few poems in which Achterberg deviated from his obsession, is notably lacking in this kind of imagery, and this tends to confirm the assumption that he employed these specialized tools only in the service of his central theme.

Achterberg's role in his poems is that of an Orpheus seeking to rescue his beloved from death and to give her immortality in the poem, which to him was the true reality. Paul Rodenko points out that for Achterberg, "the word is not primarily meaning, nor even sound, but energy" —that he set out to combine words in such a way as to "attain a certain net-tension to which the life-force of the beloved can be connected, so that she becomes 'live' in the poem": in Achterberg's words, "Any connection, any switch will do/ whatever language it is taken from,/ as long as it is in the proper tension." The beloved "you" addressed in Achterberg's poetry had from the beginning a more than specifically biographical connotation, and increasingly came to stand for an indefinable complex of ideas, including love, death, poetry, beauty, God, and the absolute.

In Dutch literary criticism, it was for a time customary to regard Achterberg as a poet outside the tradition. In spite of his modern diction, his preoccupation with the alchemical power of the word was ascribed to an "archaic-primitive mentality," and some critics have gone so far as to approach his work from a purely anthropological point of view. In fact, it is more fruitful to see him in relationship to such poets as Leopold, Roland Holst, Marsman, and particularly Novalis (with his conviction that Sophie could return to him after her death). Achterberg's belief that "the word must exist/ which coincides with you" is also reminiscent of Novalis's *"geheimes Wort."*

Paul Rodenko says that his pursuit of the beloved led Achterberg "to a titanic poetry which attempts to force its way into the utmost secrets of heaven and hell, matter and infinity, with the powerful weapon of language," and that his "remarkable energetic materialism. . . . lends to his whole *oeuvre* a quality of sur-real tension which strikes the reader again and again like an electric shock." Especially on account of its use of imagery and its orphic emphasis on the power of the word, Achterberg's poetry has been regarded as the beginning of a new era in Dutch poetry. When in the early 1950s a number of young poets grouped themselves together as "Experimentalists," they singled out Achterberg as one of the very few of the previous generation whose work had opened up new perspectives. In 1949 Achterberg was awarded the National Prize for Literature. His poems have been collected in four volumes of *Cryptogamen* (1946-1961) and in *Verzamelde Gedichten* (1963).

PRINCIPAL WORKS IN ENGLISH TRANSLATION: *Poems* in Barnouw, A.J. (ed.) Coming After: An Anthology of Poetry From the Low Countries, 1948; Delta (Netherlands) Summer 1958; Odyssey Review 1 1961.

ABOUT: Aafjes, B. Gerrit Achterberg: De dichter van de Sarcophaag, 1944; Bakker, B. and Middeldorp, A. (eds.) Niew kommentaar op Achterberg, 1966; Fokkema, R.L.K. Varianten bij Achterbergm 1973; Loggem, M. van Oorsprong en noodzaak, 1950; Ruitenberg-de Wit, A.F. Formule in de morgenstond, 1968; Seymour-Smith, M. Guide to Modern World Literature, 1973; Sierksma, F. (ed.) Commentaar op Achterbergm 1948. *Periodicals*—Delta (Netherlands) Summer 1958.

ADAMS, RICHARD (GEORGE) (May 9, 1920–), English novelist, was born near Newbury in Berkshire, the son of Evelyn Adams, a country doctor, and the former Lilian Button. He was sent away to a preparatory school when he was eight, and then to Bradfield College in Berkshire, where he was initially unhappy but ended as head boy. Adams served in the airborne forces during World War II and afterwards read history at Worcester College, Oxford, graduating in 1948. The same year he married Elizabeth Acland, an expert on the history of ceramics, and entered the civil service. At the time of his early retirement in 1974 he held a senior post in the Department of the Environment as assistant secretary in charge of the clean air section. His office, according to Elizabeth Dunn, was "away

© 1979 by Jill Krementz

RICHARD ADAMS

modeled on Adams's wartime commanding officer, and leads "by persuasion, not bluff and bullying." Other members of the party possess exceptional ingenuity or prowess in battle, and there is a clownish rabbit to entertain them, a bard to inspire them with tales of the rabbit folk hero El-ahrairah, and the seer Fiver to warn them of dangers to come. And there is no lack of dangers on this journey—from human beings and their machines and poisons, from other animals, and from other rabbits—especially from General Woundwort, a fascistic monster whose followers have surrendered their individual freedoms in exchange for military security. The heroes find their promised land, make a desperately dangerous raid on Woundwort's warren for does, and then fight a great pitched battle with the General's forces for the survival of their community.

The rabbits in *Watership Down* have a folklore and a mythology, and they converse with one another—in English, mostly, but with a peppering of terms from a "snuffly domestic vocabulary" called Lapine that includes terms like *silflay* (going up to feed), *hraka* (droppings), and *tharn* (paralysis induced by fear). They have a conception of past and present, they plan and work together to solve their problems, and they enlist allies (including a seagull and a mouse) to help them against their many *elil* (enemies). Although the book incorporates much rabbit lore culled from R. M. Lockley's factual *The Private Life of the Rabbit* (1966), it remains a fantasy and was originally published as a children's book, though its American publisher (who paid $800,000 for it) offered it as a novel for adults. It was an immediate and enormous success in both countries, and in Britain received both the *Guardian* award for children's fiction and the Carnegie Medal.

The book's reviewer in the London *Times* greeted it with "trembling pleasure," and other critics were reminded of C. S. Lewis, Tolkien, A. A. Milne, Kenneth Grahame, and even Swift. Whether or not it should be read as an allegory was much disputed, but the majority of reviewers seemed to feel that its only message was an admirable but unexceptional plea for ecological common sense. What no one disputed was that *Watership Down* was a splendid adventure story, original in conception but reassuring in its celebration of such old-fashioned virtues as honor, courage, and loyalty, and with excellent accounts of action and descriptions of natural phenomena. Janet Adam Smith called Adams "a master of menace and suspense" with a sensibility like that of Thomas Hardy, though she regretted that the seagull and mouse were made

from the administrative mainstream of the Department, lined with Victorian prints and edged with pot plants." From 1952 to 1975 Adams and his wife lived with their two daughters, Julia and Rosamond, in Canonbury, in the Islington area of London. They also owned a weekend cottage on the Berkshire Downs. In 1975 the family moved to the Isle of Man, a British tax-haven.

Before his sudden success, Adams was an amateur naturalist and a devoted student of literature, but wrote nothing more imaginative than departmental reports. He was determined that his daughters should share his love of poetry and drama, and from the time they were five or six used to take them to see productions at the Royal Shakespeare Theatre in Stratford-on-Avon. To entertain the children during these long automobile journeys, Adams made up stories about the rabbits and other animals of the Berkshire Downs. His daughters were insistent that he should write these tales down, and the eventual result was a coherent narrative of more than four hundred pages. Completed in the mid-1960s, *Watership Down* was rejected by several agents and publishers but finally appeared in 1972 under the imprint of a small publishing house and in an edition of two thousand; two years later something approaching a million copies had been sold in Britain and the United States.

At the beginning of *Watership Down,* a Berkshire rabbit warren and most of its inhabitants are destroyed in the building of a housing development. A small party of yearling bucks escapes, thanks to the clairvoyant runt Fiver, and sets out in search of a new warren. Hazel, a natural leader, finds himself in command of the party; he is

to "talk in that pidgin lingo that foreigners used to speak in simple-minded books and plays." Selma G. Lanes praised the book as a "glorious paean to man's (or rabbit's) resilience, to the instinct for survival against all odds," though she objected to Adams's "pervasively callous attitude towards females and mating," for which she found no justification in Lockley's more scientific study of rabbit behavior. *Watership Down* seemed to Richard Gilman "a delightful book, at times an affecting one," but in his opinion it lacked the "high wit and imaginative force" of *Alice in Wonderland* and the lyricism of *The Wind in the Willows,* and was "a good deal less than the 'classic'—with the implication in the word of settled universal appeal—that British commentators have so reflexively proclaimed it." Nevertheless, as some reviewers had predicted, the book established something of a cult, and many admirers made pilgrimages in the steps of Hazel and his friends over the few miles of Berkshire countryside so precisely charted by Adams. An animated film of the novel was written, directed, and produced by Martin Rosen, and released in 1978.

Richard Adams himself has said that he is not "a believer in messages in fiction," and in his second book he set out to write "a Rider Haggard story, full of blood, ghosts, darkness, mysterious religion on a mysterious island." Whatever his intentions, however, *Shardik* (1974) was quite certain to be taken as an allegory. It is set in an imaginary but human world, the Beklan Empire, which has fallen into the hands of conquerors. Its former rulers, the Ortelgans, have degenerated into primitive tribesmen who worship the bear-god Shardik. When a great bear is driven from the forest by fire, the Ortelgan hunter Kelderek, "a simple, foolish fellow," takes him to be Shardik. The bear is captured by Kelderek and the priestesses of the bear-cult, and with "god" at their side, the Ortelgans reconquer the decadent metropolis of Bekla. Kelderek, enthroned as king, is soon corrupted, and tries to repair the country's war-shattered finances by such wicked expedients as the sale of licenses to slavers. Shardik himself is drugged, exploited, and neglected, but eventually escapes into the wilderness. Kelderek goes after him but falls into the hands of Genshed, a sadistic dealer in child-slaves, and is close to death when Shardik appears, kills Genshed, and dies himself. Kelderek begins again as governor of a strip of wilderness where, with the help of the slave children redeemed by Shardik's sacrifice, he proceeds to create an ideal state.

This very long book had its admirers: A writer in the London *Sunday Times Magazine* thought that Adams had performed the almost impossible trick of following a first success "with another as triumphant. . . . As he did in *Watership Down,* although very differently, he has created an entire civilization. He makes splendid use of classical form, yet his phenomenal imagination, his language and imagery make it a completely original work." Alison Lurie, pertinently drawing attention to a Jungian analysis once undergone by Richard Adams, found *Shardik* of great interest as "a possible ecological allegory" which "can also be read as a study in the psychology of religion," as well as a "brilliant and frightening novel." But such almost unequivocal enthusiasm was rare in the reviews of *Shardik.* Victoria Glendinning conceded "a certain Technicolor magnificence in some of the set pieces" but was troubled by the fact that Genshed's sadism is described at length while the physicality of love is not, and concluded that the book is robbed of distinction by Adams's "new and apocalyptic rhetoric. He is unable to release or forgo a metaphor, or to let a sentence die a natural death." Paul Zweig also found "scenes of remarkable power, which invariably focus on the bear itself," but thought that the novel's human characters "are rarely more than pulp magazine figures of the crudest sort"; it seemed to Zweig that an "amateurish quality" pervaded the book, a "brave attempt" that finally fails.

There was an equally mixed critical reception for *The Plague Dogs* (1977). Two dogs escape from ARSE (Animal Research, Scientific and Experimental), a government research station in the English Lake District where they have been tortured in the interests of science (or of status-seeking scientists). As a result of brain surgery, the terrier Snitter tends to get muddled. He finds it hard to distinguish between dream and reality but, like Fiver in *Watership Down,* is gifted with flashes of insight and precognition; on occasion he utters perfectly rhymed eight-line verse stanzas with the refrain: "Beyond the notebooks and the knives/ A lost dog seeks a vanished man." The mongrel Rowf is a simpler character, big and strong, but terrified of water because he has been repeatedly "drowned" and revived. In order to survive, the dogs kill a sheep and decide to go "wild," tutored by a rakish fox who speaks a thick local dialect. Snitter accidentally causes a man's death and the dogs are suddenly outlaws. When a whiz-kid reporter discovers that they might also be carriers of bubonic plague, the panic becomes nationwide, the dogs are debated in Parliament, and paratroopers join the hunt. Defeated and ready for death, Snitter and Rowf swim out to sea towards their mythical Isle of Dog. When all seems lost they are rescued by two of Adams's real-life heroes, R. M. Lockley and the naturalist Sir Peter Scott, who happen to be sailing by, and everyone who should lives happily ever after.

Patric Dickinson wrote that Adams "has moved from simple romance through the mysticism of *Shardik* to this would-be satire which degenerates into soap opera. *Watership Down* came from the heart; this pretentious farrago comes solely from the head, and he has not the excuse of Snitter, either. It is likely to disappoint many of those who have taken the author seriously." It did not disappoint Naomi Lewis, for one. Writing in the London *Observer,* she said that this was the real successor to *Watership Down:* "A wholly contemporary story, it involves a quest; it has its visionary, and a powerfully evocative English landscape. But—perhaps by the chance of its subject and its main characters—it is a much more effective novel, more tense, disturbing and concentrated, with Adams's really kindling theme, the animal-man situation, more basic to the whole. . . . As an escape yarn it is outstanding. The political interludes . . . smell richly of the dark side of comedy. . . . It is an uneven work, changing in mood from one day's writing to the next. But at best it's better than anything that the author has done before."

Adams is the co-author of *Nature Through the Seasons* (1975), in which his subjective account of seasonal changes in the English countryside is accompanied by Max Hooper's scientific explanations of the same phenomena. In *The Tyger Voyage* (1976) Adams tells in verse the story of two tigers who sail away from Edwardian England, are shipwrecked, and after many adventures are rescued by gypsies and returned home. Most reviewers were less impressed by the story than by Nicola Bayley's "luminous paintings of soft furry tigers." *The Ship's Cat* (1977), another story in verse, is "a robust Elizabethan adventure" illustrated by Alan Aldridge. Richard Adams was writer-in-residence at the University of Florida in 1975 and at Hollins University, Virginia, in 1976. His recreations include folk songs, chess, fly-fishing, and travel.

According to an interviewer in *Publishers Weekly,* Adams is "feisty, rather pugnacious, with a very keen sense of his own . . . value, extraordinarily talkative and utterly unsentimental—though at the same time subject to swift tears" (as he demonstrated when he read aloud during a café lunch in New York the "Anthem for Doomed Youth" by Wilfred Owen, a copy of whose poems he always carries in his pocket). "What you need is self-discipline," he told another interviewer. ". . . I'm shocked by the products of the new permissive education, they're a scruffy lot. I demand obedience from my children, I've been written about as a domestic tyrant, but we don't think so here [at home]." But he has also said, of these children to whom *Watership Down* is dedicated: "It's essential that parents keep their children company. . . . Money and presents have got nothing to do with it. There should never be any doubt at all that you love their company and you like being with them." It is an article of faith with him, implicit at the end of his first book, and explicit at the end of the second, that "children are the future."

PRINCIPAL WORKS: Watership Down, 1972; Shardik, 1974; (with Max Hooper) Nature Through the Seasons, 1975; The Tyger Voyage, 1976; The Ship's Cat, 1977; The Plague Dogs, 1977; The Watership Down Film Picture Book (captions by Adams), 1978.

ABOUT: Contemporary Authors 49–52, 1975; Who's Who, 1977; Wintle, J. and Fisher, E. Pied Pipers, 1975. *Periodicals* —Christian Science Monitor June 25, 1975; Commonweal December 23, 1972; Current Biography October 1978; Guardian March 29, 1973; National Review April 26, 1974; New Republic March 23, 1974; May 3, 1975; New York Review of Books April 18, 1974; June 12, 1975; New York Times September 5, 1974; New York Times Book Review March 24, 1974; June 30, 1974; April 27, 1975; May 4, 1975; Newsweek April 28, 1975; Observer September 29, 1974; November 17, 1974; September 25, 1977; Publishers Weekly April 15, 1974; Saturday Review May 31, 1975; Times (London) November 8, 1974; September 22, 1977; Times Literary Supplement December 8, 1972; November 15, 1974; December 6, 1974; September 30, 1977.

ADCOCK, (KAREEN) FLEUR (February 10, 1934–), New Zealand poet, writes: "I was born in New Zealand in 1934; my mother was the granddaughter of immigrants from Northern Ireland, and my father, who had arrived in the country from Manchester at the age of ten, had spent his adolescence on a remote farm and become, among other things, a school-teacher— for the time being. In 1939 we travelled to England, where we spent the war years. My sister and I went to nine or ten schools and acquired a succession of English accents; my father completed his Ph.D. in psychology. In 1947 he obtained a position at Victoria University, in Wellington, and suddenly we were required to become a New Zealand family once again.

"I didn't find it easy. I'd left a country where even bread was still rationed for one oozing, it seemed, with cream, butter and meat. I was romantically addicted to English trees and wild flowers, foreign languages, old coins and William Morris. I couldn't play tennis; I could barely swim. I found a nation of well-fed, sports-crazy extroverts; and the Welfare State. It struck me as cosy, carefree, insular and deprived. It still does. But it was not the cultural

FLEUR ADCOCK

in five years I'd bought a house in the same North London street and seen my first British collection of poems, *Tigers,* published by Oxford University Press. Two more have since followed.

"My style has naturally changed over the years, in the usual direction of greater freedom and less formality—which doesn't indicate less care in the writing, but simply a different kind of care, more attention to the heard or spoken rhythms of language rather than to shapes on the page. This no doubt arises partly from the experience of reading poems aloud to an audience; but I continue to respect syntax and structure, and would not deliberately write anything merely for performance: the basic permanent artefact is the printed poem, and it should stand up to considered study. I have never been prolific; I write slowly or in intermittent bursts, and feel satisfied—indeed, relieved—if at the end of a year I've produced half a dozen poems which seem worth retaining.

"Apart from a healthy ration of problems, frustrations, occasional disasters and occasional ecstasies, my life is ordered and regular: work, domestic activities, friendships, as much travel as I can find time for (to Ireland and Europe, once to Nepal, and recently to New Zealand for the first time since I left.) I should like more leisure to read and to write; but as things are I try to live with my eyes and ears open and my senses aware and to listen for the phrases or rhythms inside my head which may become poems."

Fleur Adcock is the daughter of Cyril Adcock —a professor of psychology, as her note above implies—and the former Irene Robinson. After her "nine or ten schools" in England she attended Wellington Girls' School and Victoria University, where her father taught, receiving her M.A. in classics with first-class honors. She went to the University of Otago at Dunedin in 1958 as an assistant lecturer in classics, and remained there (1959-1961) as an assistant librarian. It was then that her poems began to appear in such journals as *Landfall* and the *New Zealand Listener.* A year followed at the Alexander Turnbull Library in Wellington, and in 1963, as she says, with two marriages behind her, she returned to England. She became an assistant librarian at the Foreign and Commonwealth Office in London, where she is now in charge of the research department.

The Eye of the Hurricane, though it did not appear until she was settled in England, was published in New Zealand and made up mostly of poems written there. James Bertram in *Contemporary Poets* found evidence in these poems

desert it's been called: I made friends; I grew to love Wellington with its hills, bays and old wooden houses; I discovered other landscapes, other parts of the islands; I pumped my grandparents and great-aunts for family history; I read a lot of books.

"At eighteen I married a poet, Alistair Campbell, and we had two sons—Gregory (born 1954) and Andrew (born 1957)—before it became apparent that I'd have to complete my growing-up alone or not at all. I obtained a divorce and went off, with baby Andrew, to Dunedin. The only qualification I had was a degree in classics, and so I taught at the university for a year before changing over, rather gratefully, to a job in the library there and training as a librarian.

"I'd always written poems—little verses at the age of six, sonnets about woods and sunsets at twelve, adolescent imitations of Auden and Eliot at the appropriate stages. In Dunedin, helped perhaps by new discoveries in literature, sufficient solitude, and several emotional shocks, I advanced further in the craft. I began to publish occasionally in magazines, and eventually got a volume together (it appeared, after some delays, in 1964).

"Meanwhile in 1962 I made a brief and ill-considered second marriage; and in early 1963 I settled my affairs as best I could and sailed to England with my younger son. London was initially exciting but very soon home; I can't seriously imagine living anywhere else. I acquired a job in a government library and a room in East Finchley. The temporary block or displacement in my writing caused by the transition disappeared, and I began to find my voice, or a series of voices, once again. I found my feet, too: with-of an "inherited interest in psychology . . . sharpened by early classical studies," and of the influence of such poets as Yeats, Graves, and Auden, whom Fleur Adcock admires because (as she wrote in Charles Doyle's *Recent Poetry in New Zealand*) they "have written in strict verse-forms with no lack of grace, passion or precision." Bertram praised the "compactness of form" in Fleur Adcock's own first collection, the "crispness of phrase and skilful selection of detail in short poems which do not neglect the natural surface of things, but constantly turn inward to explore or illuminate the clash of deeply involved personal relationships." Some of these qualities are illustrated in "Comment," quoted here in its entirety:

> The four-year-old believes he likes
> Vermouth; the cat eats cheese;
> And you and I, though scarcely more
> Convincingly than these,
> Walk in the gardens, hand-in-hand,
> Beneath the summer trees.

Many of the poems in *The Eye of the Hurricane* are reprinted in *Tigers* (1967), together with work written after her return to England. These new poems, like the old, are primarily about people—about the poet's relationships with others as wife, lover, or mother—but the collection includes some excellent dramatic lyrics drawing on myth or folklore, as well as poems making interesting use of animal symbolism, and fantasies derived from the poet's dreams (and from her nightmares).

One such fantasy, "Gas," was among the most discussed of the poems in her next volume, *High Tide in the Garden.* "Gas" is a long poem in which gas falls on a village, bringing death to some, duplication to others, who find themselves dividing into two, then four, then eight—and long for "what death there is." Most reviewers were impressed by this mysterious vision of what one understood as "the discovery of the inescapable flexibility of identity in a world deprived of meaning." Douglas Dunn found this a powerful poem, but thought the collection's best piece the "calm and gently written 'Country Station' . . . in which everything is right":

> First she made a little garden
> of sorrel stalks wedged among
> some yellow-brown moss cushions
>
> and fenced it with lolly sticks
> (there were just enough); then she
> set out biscuit-crumbs on a brick
>
> for the ants; now she sits on a
> deserted luggage trolley

> to watch them come for their dinner.
>
> It's nice here—cloudy but quite warm.
> Five trains have swooshed through, and one
> stopped, but at the other platform.
>
> Later, when no one is looking,
> she may climb the roof of that
> low shed. Her mother is making
>
> another telephone-call (she
> isn't crying any more).
> Perhaps they will stay here all day.

A fourth collection, *The Scenic Route,* includes a number of vignettes and reflections inspired by the author's visits to Nepal, to Northern Ireland, and home to New Zealand.

James Bertram finds the poet's special distinction in her avoidance of "any trace of cosiness or sentimentality: in her poetry she is always alert, feline, and formidably self-possessed." However, a reviewer in the *Times Literary Supplement* regards the latter quality as grounds for complaint: "Fleur Adcock's poems have a well-bred, genteel air about them, even though their point is often deliberately to ruffle this fastidious control by introducing elements of nightmare and fantasy"; her occasional pedantries, intended to be faintly self-parodic, "also seem to betray a genuine distance from experience . . . a slightly precious self-consciousness."

Opinions differ equally regarding her generally conventional and disciplined style. While some critics find her unadventurous in language and form, others, like Margaret Byers in *British Poetry Since 1960,* think it her chief virtue that she refuses "to let form become disrupted by strong emotion." Margaret Byers, who is reminded by Fleur Adcock's work of the American writer Elizabeth Bishop, thinks her best poems are "those deft considerations with a slightly academic ring, like 'Notes on Propertius 1.5,' or the gentle ironies which get beyond quiet satire to miniature tragedies of self-deceit or frustration . . . Transitions are her forte: she falls from the present, apparent security of a human relationship to a sleep where her loneliness is reaffirmed by nightmare and she wakes solitary. The present is forever undermined by the accretions of the past and the uncertainties (and the one certainty, death) of the future. . . . Her least successful poems so far seem to me to be the love poems; the strongest, those where textures, objects, things solid and present, blur into the recurrent dream, the garden, the nightmare, and re-emerge altered by the experience."

Fleur Adcock has received a number of prizes and awards, including the Wellington Festival

Poetry Prize (1961), an award from the New Zealand State Literary Fund (1964), the Buckland Award (1967-1968), the Jessie MacKay Prize (1968 and 1971), and an Arts Council publication grant (1971). Her sister is the novelist Marilyn Duckworth.

PRINCIPAL WORKS: The Eye of the Hurricane, 1964; Tigers, 1967; High Tide in the Garden, 1971; The Scenic Route, 1974.

ABOUT: Abse, D. (ed.) Corgi Modern Poets in Focus No. 5, 1973; Contemporary Authors 25-28 1st revision, 1977; International Who's Who in Poetry, 1974-1975; McQueen, H. and Cox, L. (eds.) Ten Modern New Zealand Poets, 1974; Schmidt, M. and Lindop, G. (eds.) British Poetry Since 1960, 1972; Vinson, J. (ed.) Contemporary Poets, 1975. Periodicals—Encounter May 1972; Poetry April 1973; Times Literary Supplement July 23, 1971.

*"ADORNO," THEODOR W(IESEN-GRUND) (September 11, 1903–August 6, 1969), German philosopher, sociologist, musicologist, and critic, was born in Frankfurt. He was the son of Oscar Wiesengrund, a wealthy Jewish wine merchant from whom he inherited a taste for the finer things of life. His mother, from whom he acquired his passion for music, was the former Maria Calvelli-Adorno, a highly successful professional singer, herself the daughter of a German singer and a French army officer of Genoese ancestry. Adorno's sister became an accomplished concert pianist. Beginning in the 1930s, Theodor Wiesengrund-Adorno dropped the first part of his name, thereafter signing himself Theodor W. Adorno.

Adorno's childhood was exceptionally happy. He went to school and then to the university in Frankfurt, studying philosophy, musicology, psychology, and sociology. His family's position and his own abilities gained him entry into the intellectual and cultural elite of Frankfurt, while his father's patient financial support during his prolonged studies gave him a security possessed by few of the intellectuals who grew up in the Weimar Republic. He earned his doctorate in 1924 with a dissertation on Husserl's phenomenology, then temporarily deserted philosophy for music.

In 1925 Adorno went to study under Alban Berg in Vienna, where he also came to know Schönberg, Webern, and others who helped to shape modern music. Arthur Koestler remembers him at this time as "a shy, distraught, and esoteric young man with a subtle charm." Koestler and even Alban Berg found his intense intellectuality disconcerting and, though Adorno later lost his shyness, he always remained a formidable cultural elitist.

*a dorn′ o

German Information Service

THEODOR ADORNO

Adorno soon recognized that his own compositions, mainly quartets and lieder, lacked inspiration. It has been suggested that in this profound disappointment, above all, is to be found the key to what is hermetic, ambivalent, and even impenetrable in his writings. During the years in Vienna, however, writing in various avant-garde journals, Adorno began to establish himself as a critic of music. Before long it was clear that his abilities in this field were enough to insure his fame. His thinking was influenced by the musical traditions of Vienna, but showed little interest in any composer prior to Beethoven. Equally at home with Mahler and the twelve-tone compositions of Schönberg, Berg, and Webern—all of whom he championed —his familiarity with the technical problems of composition gave his writings a professionalism beyond the resources of most critics. He also possessed an extraordinary gift for determining the precise position of a new work in the context of musical history as a whole. Thomas Mann employs his exegesis of Beethoven in Chapter VIII of Doktor Faustus.

The social value of music was a central concern in Adorno's criticism—for example, he disapproved of Stravinsky's neoclassical "objectivism" but praised Schönberg for reflecting in his music the unresolved dissonances of contemporary society. Popular music he regarded as a tool of the establishment, helping to reconcile the masses to their fate, and his hostility extended even to jazz, about which he knew very little. Adorno's essays on music will fill eight volumes in his collected works, and some of them have been translated in Prisms: The Philosophy of Modern Music (dealing mainly with Schönberg and Stravinsky), and *Introduction to the Sociology of Music.* He has been described as perhaps the only philosopher of modern music "to be taken seriously by musicians."

As his reputation as a music critic grew during the 1920s, Adorno began to turn his attention to literary criticism and aesthetic theory as well. In these fields he was much influenced by Walter Benjamin, whom he had met at the University of Frankfurt in 1923. In 1928 Adorno returned to Frankfurt, where until 1931 he edited the musical journal *Anbruch,* for which he had begun to write in Vienna. At the same time he resumed his philosophical studies, receiving his *habilitation* (right to lecture) in 1931, with Paul Tillich as his sponsor. His thesis, a study of the aesthetic theories of Kierkegaard, was published in 1933 and like all his work was found complex in its thought and abstruse in its style. It was during this period that his friendship with Max Horkheimer and the rise of Nazism combined to complete Adorno's commitment to Marxism, and to involve him with the Frankfurt Institut für Sozialforschung (Institute for Social Research).

The Institute had been founded in 1923 by Felix J. Weil, a wealthy student of political science, as a center for Marxist studies. World War I and its aftermath had raised in the minds of West European left-wing intellectuals grave doubts about their ideals and assumptions. The Institute was to undertake a fundamental reexamination of Marxist theory in an attempt to understand past errors and prepare for future action. It entered its most productive phase in 1930, when Max Horkheimer became its director. Under Horkheimer, the Institute concentrated mainly on researches into the structure and development of authority, the emergence and influence of mass culture, and the nature of Marxism itself, drawing on psychoanalysis and the techniques of sociology as well as on Marxist dialectics. Horkheimer always stressed the synoptic and interdisciplinary nature of the Institute's work, which attracted the large and varied talents of Walter Benjamin, Erich Fromm, Herbert Marcuse, Karl Korsch, Karl Wittfogel, and Franz Neumann among others. Other luminaries were more loosely or temporarily connected with the Institute, so there developed what is often spoken of as the "Frankfurt School." Much of the Institute's work was published in its journal, *Zeitschrift für Sozialforschung*—often after such exhaustive evaluation and criticism by other members that it amounted almost to a collective production.

Martin Jay in his history of the Institute, *The Dialectical Imagination,* says that Adorno's views resembled Horkheimer's in that "his thought was always rooted in a kind of cosmic irony, a refusal to rest somewhere and say finally, Here is where truth lies." Adorno did not at first join the Institute, but through his friendship with Horkheimer and others soon began to influence the development of its policies and its *Kritische Theorie.* Critical Theory is a corpus of philosophy and social theory deriving from a deep distrust of closed philosophical systems and expressed mainly through critiques of other philosophies. Its exponents point out that human beings are taught to communicate by their parents, authority figures who present the child with all kinds of irrational ideologies in the very process of teaching it rational discourse. The child grows up in a context of traditions, myths, and authority structures which are seldom rationally examined and tend to be built into the individual's thought processes.

If human knowledge and understanding are to advance, the Critical Theorists argue, it is necessary for us to analyze and emancipate ourselves from institutionalized power relations and ideologies. This is particularly difficult in modern capitalist societies, which by their very nature insulate people from an awareness of exploitation, and in which the enormous influence of the mass media militates against any kind of divergent thinking. Marxist dialectics, unifying theory and practice, had offered a technique that might overcome the domination of the nonrational, but by the 1920s Marxism, as Jeremy Shapiro puts it, was drying up "into a mixture of positivist social science, religious dogmatism, and compulsion neurosis." This is why the Critical Theory of the Frankfurt School looks back to the roots of Marxist thought in Kant and Hegel. It provides a probing and undogmatic technique—not a philosophical system but a "a gadfly of other systems." It has been an important force in the revitalization of West European Marxism in the postwar years and (through Marcuse and others) has greatly influenced the New Left in the United States.

When Hitler came to power in 1933, Horkheimer and many of his colleagues left Germany. The Institute continued its work for a time in Geneva and then, after 1934, in the United States, where it was at first affiliated with Columbia University in New York. Adorno did not accompany his friends. In 1934 he went briefly to Paris, then to Merton College, Oxford University (1934–1937), where he worked on a critique of Husserl's philosophy, later developed into a book, *Zur Metakritik der Erkenntnistheorie* (1956). During these years he made occasional visits to Germany, where he maintained a residence. He was married in 1937, in London, to Gretel Karplus. In 1938 Adorno joined the Institute in the United States, serving as head of music study with Paul Lazarsfeld's Princeton Office of Radio Research (1938–1941). In 1941, when Horkheimer moved to Los Angeles, Adorno (who had been increasingly at loggerheads with Lazarsfeld) joined him there. They became part of a brilliant community of exiles that included Thomas and Heinrich Mann, Bertolt Brecht, and Alfred Döblin.

The "philosophical fragments" Adorno wrote in collaboration with Horkheimer in 1942–1944 were published in 1947 as *Dialektik der Aufklarung* (translated by John Cumming as *Dialectic of Enlightenment*). It shows how Critical Theory had shifted its emphasis during the Nazi years, retaining much of the Marxian analysis but progressing from a critique of capitalism to one of Western civilization as a whole. In similar mood are the epigrammatic paragraphs written by Adorno alone in 1944–1947 and assembled in *Minima Moralia* (1951, translated under the same title by E.F.N. Jephcott). It is a more personal book than its predecessor, and full of striking perceptions, mostly illuminating ways in which the good life is being defeated—the subtitle is "Reflections From Damaged Life." For example, Adorno writes that individuals have become so subordinated to the material needs of society that "in many people it is already an impertinence to say 'I' ".

In both books, according to Jeremy Shapiro, "the rationality of Western civilization is seen as a fusion of domination and technical rationality, bringing all of external and internal nature under the power of the human subject. In the process, however, the subject is swallowed up, and no social force analogous to the proletariat can be identified that will enable the subject to emancipate itself." Shapiro, who believes that these two books already "rank as classics of twentieth-century thought," says that "many themes that have come to dominate the social thought of recent years are already presented by Horkheimer and Adorno in these works, usually with greater depth and subtlety than among our own contemporaries"—they saw man's denial of his oneness with nature as the source of all subsequent inadequacies of civilization "long before ecology had become a catch-phrase of the day."

In 1945 Adorno became co-director of the Institute's most important research project in the United States, leading in 1950 to the publication of *The Authoritarian Personality*. Leaning heavily on Freudian theories of the structure of personality, and involving interviews with over two thousand people, this study sought to identify and analyze the personality traits and family backgrounds that predispose individuals to antidemocratic and fascist views. It had a mixed and rather emotional reception when it was published in America during the McCarthy period, but it is now universally recognized as "one of the key works of modern empirical social science." It is the subject of a volume of essays, *Studies in the Scope and Method of The Authoritarian Personality*, edited by Richard Christie and Marie Jahoda (1954), in which it is described as unique in "its combination of content, method and theory," and as the starting point for a "vast number of later studies."

The Institute returned to Frankfurt in 1949. "Disillusioned with the Soviet Union," writes Martin Jay, "no longer even marginally sanguine about the working classes of the West, appalled by the integrative power of mass culture, the Frankfurt School traveled the last leg of its long march away from orthodox Marxism." The Institute shed its political connections and became a leading center of academic sociology. Adorno was named assistant director of the Institute in 1950 and codirector in 1955. When Horkheimer retired in 1958, Adorno succeeded him as director, holding the position of professor of philosophy and sociology at the Johann Wolfgang von Goethe University in Frankfurt into which the Institute was incorporated. He returned to the United States in 1952–1953, primarily to retain his American citizenship. During that period he served as director of the scientific branch of the Hacker Foundation in Beverly Hills, studying the new medium of television and the persistent popularity of astrology.

Adorno published a stream of books and essays during the 1950s and 1960s—on Wagner and Berg and Mahler, on music in general and the sociology of music, on literature, on Hegel, and on Heidegger, whom he harshly attacks in *Jargon der Eigentlichkeit* (1964, translated by Knut Tarnowski and Frederic Will in *The Jargon of Authenticity*). Adorno's projected aesthetics, dictated during the 1960s and published as the seventh volume of his collected works, is not only unfinished but, according to its reviewer in the *Times Literary Supplement,* "grey and verbose," with many false aphorisms, and "uncomfortably close to . . . McLuhan; it is only occasionally illuminated by flashes of perception." In 1961, at the annual conference of the German Sociological Association, Adorno expressed his opposition to logical positivism in a debate with Karl Popper and a prolonged and important controversy developed. A number of the relevant papers and essays have been collected in the volume translated as *The Positivist Dispute in German Sociology.*

In these same postwar years, the Frankfurt Institute passed through another phase, reflecting the fact that the structure of capitalism (and thus the dialectic of history) had changed decisively, and that the industrial working class was no longer the definitive negation of capitalism. This led to an attempt to root the dialectic in an absolute method of negativity, as in Adorno's *Negative Dialektik* (1966, translated by E. B. Ashton as *Negative Dialectics*). According to Shapiro, "the idea of negative dialectics is the idea of critical thought so conceived that it cannot be co-opted into the apparatus of domination. Its central notion, long a focal one with Horkheimer and Adorno, is that the original sin of thought is its attempt to eliminate all that is other than thought, the attempt by the subject to devour the object. . . . It is this reduction that makes thought the accomplice of domination. *Negative Dialectics* rescues the 'preponderance of the object,' not through a naive epistemological or metaphysical realism but through a thought based on differentiation, paradox, and ruse: a 'logic of disintegration.' " *Negative Dialectics* is regarded by many critics as Adorno's masterpiece, an affirmation and defense of reason against the dark forces of the irrational. Jeremy Shapiro, though he agrees that it is "an important document in contemporary thought," thinks that it stands as "a monument to the end of a tradition: the tradition of the individual subject as the locus of criticism. . . . Adorno's supposed masterwork, despite the brilliance of its conceptual analyses, turns into an old-style juxtaposition of what is living and dead in German Idealism, devoid of the wealth of analysis of individual experience and cultural phenomena of his other work."

As his work suggests, Adorno was a sad and often anguished man, whose most quoted saying is "no poetry after Auschwitz." In the late 1960s, shortly before his sudden death in Switzerland in the summer of 1969, he was deeply distressed by savage demonstrations at Frankfurt against him and his political theories by Maoist and anarchist students. Apart from this, and his time of exile, his life was quiet and uneventful. During his last years he became something of an oracle, whose views were sought by the mass media on topics ranging from the reform of higher education to the merits of a Wagner festival at Bayreuth.

Adorno's writings are very exacting for even the most sophisticated reader, characterized according to one critic by "a sometimes dazzling, sometimes bewildering juxtaposition of highly abstract statements with seemingly trivial observations." He has his moments of clarity and fine phrasing, but often his prose is muddied by a "wearisome display of dialectical fireworks"— by his "willed obscurity and disdainful pride." Martin Jay writes that he "combined a rigorous philosophical mind with a sensibility more aesthetic than scientific," and others have suggested that his passionate defense of reason—his insistence in the face of war and holocaust that the world could be made intelligible—was inspired partly by his own horrified fascination with the irrational. He is said to have looked "exactly as you would imagine a very absentminded German professor." Derwent May described him as "an invigorating and noble mind—a pure specimen of the 'chaste intolerance' he himself recommends, like some Leavis of the Rhine."

PRINCIPAL WORKS IN ENGLISH TRANSLATION: Memorandum: Music in Radio, 1938; (with others) The Authoritarian Personality, 1950; The Stars Down to Earth: The Los Angeles Times Astrology Column: A Study in Secondary Superstition, 1957; Prisms, translated by Samuel and Shierry Weber, 1967; (with Hanns Eisler) Composing for the Films, 1971; (with Max Horkheimer) Dialectic of Enlightenment, 1972; (with others) Aspects of Sociology, translated by J. Viertel, 1972; Negative Dialectics, 1973; The Jargon of Authenticity, 1973; The Philosophy of Modern Music, translated by Anne G. Mitchell and Wesley V. Blomster, 1973; Minima Moralia: Reflections From Damaged Life, 1974; Introduction to the Sociology of Music, translated by E.B. Ashton, 1976; (with others) The Positivist Dispute in German Sociology, translated by Glyn Adey and David Frisby, 1976. *Essays in* Arato, A. and Gebhardt, E. (eds.) The Essential Frankfurt School Reader, 1978.

ABOUT: Boyers, R. (ed.) The Legacy of the German Refugee Intellectuals, 1972; Bräutigam, B. Reflexion des Schönen—Schöne Reflexion, 1975; Buck-Morss, S. The Origin of Negative Dialectics, 1977; Hughes, H.S. The Sea Change, 1975; Jablinski, M. Theodor W. Adorno, 1976; Jay, M. The Dialectical Imagination, 1973; Kaiser, G. Benjamin: Adorno: Zwei Studien, 1974; Lichtheim, G. From Marx to Hegel, 1971; O'Neill, J. (ed.) On Critical Theory, 1976; Oppens, K. (and others) Über Theodor W. Adorno, 1968; Ransom, J.C. Beating the Bushes, 1972; Sauerland, K. Adornos Ästhetik des Nichtidentischen, 1975; Slater, P. Origin and Significance of the Frankfurt School, 1977; Tar, Z. The Frankfurt School, 1977; Zeugnisse: Theodor W. Adorno zum sechzigsten Geburtstag, 1963. *Periodicals*—Books Abroad Spring 1970; Commentary June 1950, March 1951; New York Times August 7, 1969; Times (London) August 7, 1969; Times Literary Supplement September 28, 1967; March 9, 1973; October 4, 1974.

*"ALAIN" (pseudonym of Émile-Auguste Chartier) (March 3, 1868–June 2, 1951), French philosopher and essayist, was born at Mortagne-sur-Perche (Orne), the son of a well-to-do veterinarian. He took his pen name from another writer from Normandy, the fifteenth-century poet Alain Chartier. According to his intellectual autobiography *Histoire de mes pensées* (His-

*a laN'

French Cultural Services

ALAIN

tory of My Thoughts, 1936), he was a devout Catholic up to the age of twelve, but during the next three years all belief left him, never to return.

Alain was educated at the *lycée* of Vanves (later Lycée Michelet) on the outskirts of Paris. There he became a disciple of Jules Lagneau, an intellectualist philosopher who, like his pupil, is remembered as a great teacher. Exceptionally gifted, Alain could have made his mark in science, music, or several other fields, but chose to study philosophy and literature at the École Normale Supérieure. He passed his *agrégation* (competitive teaching examination) in 1892, and began his career as a teacher of philosophy at the *lycée* of Pontivy.

By 1894, when the Dreyfus case divided France into two camps, Alain had taken up a new post in the town of Lorient. He was passionately interested in politics, and defended Dreyfus in a series of articles in *La Dépêche de Lorient*. He continued thereafter to contribute from time to time to newspapers as well as to philosophical journals, and in 1901 published his first book, a study of Spinoza.

Alain taught at the Rouen *lycée* in 1900-1902, and the following year went to Paris—to the Lycée Condorcet, to the Lycée Michelet, and finally to the Lycée Henri IV. He taught philosophy there from 1909 to 1935, inspiring and influencing many brilliant young people, among them Simone Weil, André Maurois, the polemical critic Henri Massis, and the novelist Jean Prévost. John Weightman has written that "Alain, from all accounts, was a quite remarkable personality. His pupils nicknamed him *l'Homme,* which means in French both '*the*

man' and 'Man,' as if he had achieved within himself the philosophical ideal of the fusion of the particular with the universal."

In 1903 Alain began to contribute a regular weekly article to a Rouen newspaper, *La Dépêche de Rouen.* After three years of this he began to find the weekly column a heavy strain and decided to try his hand at shorter but more frequent contributions, which would better suit his aphoristic style and allow him "to make amends immediately for a botched article." Between February 1906 and the outbreak of World War I in 1914, Alain wrote a short essay every day for *La Dépêche de Rouen,* setting out his thoughts on politics, current affairs, philosophy, aesthetics, literature, and any other subject that caught his interest. He settled down each evening with two blank sheets of paper; when they were filled the piece was done, and would be published the next day unrevised.

Montaigne, to whom Alain is often compared, named the literary form he created the *essai;* in a similar spirit Alain called his short pieces *propos,* a word that can mean among other things an informal conversation, or something proposed. A *propos* typically begins with a brief anecdote, a precise bit of information, or a literary quotation, which in the space of a few hundred words is then reflected upon from various illuminating and unconventional angles, until an abrupt final sentence draws from what has gone before some general conclusion or moral lesson which is often both pungent and unexpected. The effect is rather like that of a fable or a parable, or even, at times, of a prose poem. Alain was a liberal humanist in the skeptical Cartesian tradition of French rationalism, and his mind was original and inquiring, unencumbered by conventional prejudices and distrustful of established authority. His prose is clear and readable, enlivened by aphorisms and paradoxes—Richard Pevear describes it as "abrupt, elliptical, and gnomic."

Over three thousand *propos* appeared in *La Dépêche de Rouen,* and after World War I about two thousand more were published in various journals, including *Les Libres Propos,* a weekly founded by one of Alain's former students. From time to time they were collected in book form under such titles as *Les Cent un Propos d'Alain* (A Hundred and One Propos of Alain, five vols., 1908-1928), *Les Propos d'Alain* (The Propos of Alain, two vols., 1920), *Propos sur le bonheur* (Propos on Happiness, 1925), *Propos sur l'éducation* (Propos on Education, 1932), *Propos d'économique* (Economic Propos, 1935).

Though he was forty-six when World War I began in 1914, Alain immediately volunteered.

15

He served in the ranks as a signaler, and was wounded in 1917. The intense antimilitarism of his book, *Mars, ou la guerre jugée* (1921, translated by D. Mudie and E. Hill as *Mars, or The Truth About War*) is therefore that of a moralist who had studied his subject at first hand. He argues that the root cause of all wars is the pernicious urge to wield power over others, and in *Le Citoyen contre les pouvoirs* (The Citizen Against the Authorities, 1926) he urges the citizen to combat the tendency of all those in power to extend and overreach their authority. There is no good government, Alain maintains, but democracy is better than most because it provides the best means of curbing the lust to power.

These two are among Alain's longer works. Another such—a guide to the understanding of the fine arts—is *Le Système des Beaux-Arts* (1920), in which he advances a doctrine resembling the Parnassian theory of art for art's sake or the poetic theories of Paul Valéry (on whose *Charmes* and *La Jeune Parque* he wrote commentaries). His taste in the visual arts was towards classicism—he wrote a book about Ingres—and he himself painted. He was also a good pianist and wrote on music in *La Visite au musicien* (1927), in which the musician visited is Beethoven.

Alain distrusted abstract philosophical systems, so that, though he was a critic of ideas rather than of literature, he tended to draw on literary rather than philosophical texts as a starting point for his own reflections. He declared in *Avec Balzac* (With Balzac, 1937) that he had learned more from that novelist than from any philosopher or critic. He also profoundly admired Stendhal, of whom he published a study in 1935, and in a later *propos* described in terms that might be applied to Alain himself: "Tyrants great and small fear the scandalous example of this man who had a great style and respected nothing. Stendhal is not in the least civic-minded. He doesn't take the gods of politics seriously, whether they are called state or country. His gods are courage, honor, love, friendship."

Despite his loss of faith Alain was not antireligious, though in *Propos sur le christianisme* (Propos on Christianity, 1924) and *Propos sur la religion* (Propos on Religion, 1937) he discusses religion in human rather than supernatural terms. "Religion is like a fairy tale, which, like all fairy tales, is full of meaning. And no one ever asks if fairy tales are true," he says in *Les Dieux* (1934, translated by Richard Pevear as *The Gods*). This book, which he regarded as his masterpiece, is a poetic meditation whose four sections correspond to what Alain considered to be the four main stages in the development of the world's religions, culminating (in his opinion) in Christianity. John Weightman, reviewing the English translation in 1975, wondered if it would "do anything at this point to establish Alain as an important writer with the English-speaking public. Even in French, I fear, the genre may not be quite successful, because the poetry often veers in the direction of noble fine-writing, while the thought is perhaps neither extended nor inventive enough to provide a really vital contribution to the subject."

There has always been a marked contrast between the lack of interest in Alain's work abroad and his enormous reputation in France, where he was the *cher maître*, the much loved and influential teacher of so many intellectuals. André Maurois, who called him "our Montaigne and our Socrates," wrote: "There are not a few of us in the world who think that Alain was, and remains, one of the greatest men of our time—I would not hesitate to say, the greatest." But Wallace Fowlie observes that "in recent years, Alain has been succeeded by newer masters, by men like Malraux and Sartre. To the younger readers in France his wisdom seems overprudent, and his optimism unjustified in a world which appears to so many thinkers on the verge of catastrophe."

Alain was married in 1947 to Gabrielle Landormy. He was awarded the Grand Prix National des Lettres in 1951, in which year he died at Le Vésinet, near Paris. In his old age, crippled by arthritis, Alain wrote: "There is a way of singing which shows that one is not afraid, and which reassures the world of men."

PRINCIPAL WORKS IN ENGLISH TRANSLATION: Mars, or The Truth About War, 1930; Alain on Happiness, 1973; The Gods, 1975.

ABOUT: Bénézé, G. Généreux Alain, 1962; Bridoux, H. Alain, 1964 (in French); Cottrell, R.D. *introduction to* Alain on Happiness, 1973; Dictionnarie de Biographic Française, 1959; Fowlie, W. The French Critic 1549-1967, 1968; Fowlie, W. A Guide to Contemporary French Literature, 1957; Gontier, G. Alain à la guerre, 1963; Halda, B. Alain, 1963 (in French); Maurois, A. Alain, 1949 (in French); Maurois, A. Hommage à Alain, 1952; Park, J. (ed.) The Culture of France in Our Time, 1954; Pascal, G. Alain, 1946 (in French); Pascal, G. La pensée d'Alain, 1957; Penguin Companion to Literature 2, 1969; Pevear, R. *introduction to* The Gods, 1975; Robinson, J. Alain, 1958 (in French); Smith, H. (ed.) Columbia Dictionary of Modern European Literature, 1947; Solmi, S. Il pensiero di Alain, 1930. *Periodicals*— Books and Bookmen September 1975; Observer June 22, 1975; Times Literary Supplement September 5, 1975.

ALDISS, BRIAN W(ILSON) (August 18, 1925–), English science fiction writer, novelist, critic, editor, and journalist, writes: "I was born

© Jerry Bauer

BRIAN W. ALDISS

in a small market town, East Dereham, Norfolk, England, where I was wild and free until boarding school closed in on me. My family exiled itself from Norfolk when I was twelve; we moved to Devon, the other end of the country. My sister and I groaned at our middle-class life; our delight was unbounded when a distant relation, searching among some genealogical tables, announced that we had some French blood in our veins. It seemed to dilute our dullness.

"During that period, I discovered permanent interests which were not particularly popular in our level of society: art, science, prehistory, and social injustices (through the novels of Émile Zola). With a canny grasp of scholarliness and commerce which has never left me, I used to lecture on dinosaurs to my fellow pupils in prep school for one penny per head—though I don't remember anyone ever paying me.

"In the second world war, I volunteered to serve before I was of an age to be conscripted. Many years later, during the Vietnam War, I sat in a bar in California listening to students discussing ways of dodging the draft, and reflected on how attitudes had changed—whether for better or worse.

"I served in the Far East, returning home after almost four years in 1947. Those years, spent in India, Burma, Assam, Sumatra, Malaya, and Hong Kong, meant a great deal, and will always remain valuable. My kitbag contained Palgrave's *Golden Treasury* and science fiction magazines.

"Back in what was then called Civvy Street, I got myself a job of work in an Oxford bookshop and set about writing. One does foolish and sensible things, turn and turn about, I find; I

foolishly strove to be a poet but, within a year or two, I sensibly saw that I had no gift for poetry. Then I became a science fiction writer—and sensibly I have persisted in that folly. My first book was a comedy of ordinary life, though; its jokes have gone a bit stale but it still retains its happiness. Of that I'm proud; I have had to strive to be happy. One of my reservations about sf is that it makes such an ideal vehicle for misery; in other respects it is grossly, maddeningly, underrated, and remains a literary medium full of potential.

"I never had to struggle with rejection slips. Faber & Faber wrote to request me to write the first book; they proved staunch publishers through some twenty books; then they started rejecting. By the time my first book was accepted, I was married. That marriage lasted some while but not for ever. Two valued children were born from it, Clive and Wendy. I was married in 1965 to Margaret Manson; we also have two valued children, Timothy and Charlotte. We live comfortably.

"A writer's life makes dull reading, however satisfying it may be to the man himself. Look: this morning was so fine that, after taking the children to school, my wife and I decided to forget work and walk on the downs above Wantage, which we did. It was beautiful and free. No reader could be excited by such a peaceable diversion: the tumults of fiction are all.

"My writing is altering—but I could claim that after almost every novel. Britain is undergoing rapid change; its sane institutions are being eroded by the weaknesses in systems shaken by high inflation; no-one can say what things will come to pass in the near future. The insidious threat of Communism gathers strength, often operating through well-intentioned bodies like trade unions. After holding socialist beliefs for many years, one is challenged by the perception that it was not enough to be well-meaning, and that views which seemed enlightened at the time may have assisted in the general escalation towards disaster. Under such circumstances, an author's subject matter and approach is forced to change.

"I believe that writers should have a wisdom detached from the market place; but it is in the market place that wisdom is tested.

"While speaking of gloomy times ahead, I hope to write fewer stories prophesying doom; in most cases, such fiction—Orwell's *1984* is a rare exception—merely weakens a reader's will. Besides, as Byron is reputed to have said, 'Is not the past of the human race gloomy enough for you, without supping upon the imaginary horrors of its future?' I may concentrate more on humour, the sort of black humour in my novels *The Hand-Reared Boy, A Soldier Erect, Barefoot in the Head,* and *Frankenstein Unbound.* Well, there is still time. My latest novel, *The Malacia Tapestry,* has much in it in the way of dark wit. It is today in my agent's hands, on its way to my British and American publishers. Well, that is always a highly desirable and optimistic situation. (I centre this autobiographical note about this special ordinary day, so that it can be mounted in the museum case of *World Authors,* to do duty for the butterfly days to come before a new edition . . .)."

Brian Aldiss, one of the most admired and most successful of British science fiction writers, is the son of Stanley and Elizabeth May (Wilson) Aldiss. He was sent away to boarding school at the age of eight—Framlingham College in Suffolk and West Buckland School in Devon—an experience that made him feel "exiled from home" and had "a great alienating effect." As a boy, he stumbled upon copies of American pulp science fiction magazines, *Amazing* and *Astounding,* on the counters of the local Woolworth's. From there he progressed to H.G. Wells, whose speculations on the nature of man and society in *The Island of Doctor Moreau* and *The Time Machine* haunted his imagination.

After army service from 1943 to 1947, most of the time with the Royal Signal Corps, Aldiss settled in Oxford, as he says, and for eight years worked as a bookseller while writing in his spare time. His first published novel, *The Brightfount Diaries* (1955), drew on his experiences in the book trade, and was found "amusing but not particularly original." Aldiss, who had published his first science fiction story in July 1954 in *Science-Fantasy,* won third prize in a science fiction competition organized by the London *Observer* in 1956. The same year he abandoned bookselling to become a full-time writer. *Space, Time and Nathaniel,* Aldiss's first collection of short stories, appeared in 1957. Many short stories and several novels followed in such magazines as *Nebula, Science-Fantasy, Fantasy and SF,* and *New Worlds,* quickly bringing him critical recognition and a wide audience in both England and the United States.

Aldiss's fiction depends less upon technological inventiveness than upon curiosity about human nature, and how it might respond to the extreme danger and stimuli of imaginary worlds. His early novel *Non-Stop* (1958), which has been translated into thirteen languages, is a powerful and often moving example of this kind of concern. It is set inside a vast spaceship containing a disturbing landscape of huge structures, appar-

ently built by men but now overrun by a hydroponic jungle. The hero and his companions struggle through the jungle toward the control room, encountering on the way hostile tribes, aliens, and intelligent rats, and being forced to face their own natures, their failures. Finally they make the wrenching discovery that the ship is a kind of quarantine prison maintained perpetually in orbit about the earth, and that its inhabitants are the victims of an ancient bureaucratic decision.

The artificial society of the ship presents an alternative world, less complex than our own, which nevertheless obliges readers to question their own social structures and the nature and degree of their own freedoms. A strength of the book is the intensely realized setting; yet that strength seemed to one critic to reflect "the breakdown of plot and the failure of some genuinely narrative gesture, subverting the classical story-telling function of novels into an illicit poetic one which substitutes objects and atmosphere for events and actions." Many of Aldiss's later novels and stories have been similarly criticized for a lack of narrative drive and similarly praised for the excellence of their settings and atmosphere.

His writing changed direction during the 1960s, largely under the influence of his close connection with Michael Moorcock's *New Worlds* magazine; his writing has reflected an increasing interest in the history and criticism of science fiction, and in the development of experimental forms. Notable among these experiments are *Report on Probability A* and *Barefoot in the Head,* which mingle social speculation with the material of fantasy. The latter is a fable set in an England of the future, in the time of the Acid Head War. Its subject is the dissolution of reality after a foreign power (Kuwait) has attacked Europe with aerosol bombs containing psychedelic drugs. To express that dissolution, Aldiss uses an experimental narrative style punctuated by verse, word-play, and an increasing distortion of word and image. The book displays striking verbal energy, but the critics greeted it with uncertainty, describing it as self-conscious and pretentious. It was undoubtedly influenced by the French *nouvelle roman* of Robbe-Grillet and Butor, and the film techniques of Resnais's *L'Année Dernière à Marienbad.*

After this, Aldiss has said, "I felt that I had written myself out of science fiction," and, like his exemplar H.G. Wells, he turned to works of social and literary criticism and to the novel of social comedy. In the diaristic *The Shape of Further Things* he makes a very personal statement of his fears for the future and about the possibility of rescuing human potentialities from the stifling grasp of technology. In the same book he explores the links between science fiction and other literary forms, and this is also a valuable aspect of *Billion Year Spree,* which has been called "the best single critical history of science fiction yet published."

At the same time, Aldiss ventured into social comedy with two "fictional autobiographies," *The Hand-Reared Boy* and *A Soldier Erect,* which were welcomed by reviewers as funny, boisterous, and improper. They evoke with a touch of nostalgia the English provincial society in which Aldiss grew up in the 1930s, and India and Burma in the 1940s when Aldiss, like his hero Horatio Stubbs, served in the British army. As the punning titles suggest, sex and particularly masturbation receive a great deal of attention in both books, but it seemed to a reviewer in the *Times Literary Supplement* that "events are described too coolly to offer the sly stimulus of pornography," and most critics greeted with pleasure the promise that there would be more books about the adventures of Stubbs. A third volume in the series, *Rude Awakening,* appeared in 1978.

The Malacia Tapestry (1976), which Aldiss mentions above, was something of a departure— something between science fiction and a historical novel. Malacia is a rich city-state reminiscent of Renaissance Venice, but rigidly opposed to any kind of change, and to any development in art or technology that might lead to change. The hero, Perian de Chirolo, is an out-of-work actor whose ambition for social advancement (and the hand of the rich and beautiful Armida) involves him in some dangerous experiments. He agrees to perform in a series of tableaux for the inventor of a process resembling color photography. All kinds of splendid adventures follow, and Perian is close to fulfilling all his ambitions when the Galileo figure is denounced. "Somewhere in this entertaining farrago," wrote Neil Hepburn, "there is a serious novel crying to be understood. But the questions—about class, authority, wealth, the effect of all of them on the capacity to feel, the weight of the past, the problem of change—are asked in a trite way, and never answered. It is best, perhaps, just to enjoy the continuous pleasure of reading Mr. Aldiss's prose, looking at the illustrations by Tiepolo and Maggiotto with which the text is adorned, and being struck by his felicitous invention of fantastications which never jar with the milieu he is describing."

Brian Aldiss was serving in the Far East when Hiroshima was bombed. For him, the atomic bomb symbolizes the "overwhelming workings of science and technology, applied science, in our lives." Aldiss has called himself a nihilist and an extremist, one who knows that "the state of the world is permanently wrong," that there can be no lasting happiness. Against that grim realization Aldiss, who lives contentedly in an old village near Oxford, sets the pleasures of "travel and introspection," of family, of the English countryside, and above all of his writing; for "we live in a universe which is a desert of human life. . . . The artist's duty is to love and create hope, which can be done even through despair."

Aldiss was literary editor of the Oxford *Mail* from 1958 to 1969, and since 1964 has edited the critical journal *SF Horizons.* He was the first president of the British Science Fiction Association (1960-1965) and served as chairman of his local branch of the Conservation Society in 1968-1969. He became vice-president of the Stapledon Society in 1975, and in 1976-1977 was joint president of the European Science Fiction Committees. Aldiss received the Hugo Award in 1962, the Nebula Award in 1965, and the Ditmar Award as the best contemporary science fiction writer in 1970; the British Science Fiction Association voted him Britain's most popular science fiction writer in 1969. He is an amateur painter and collects watercolors.

In 1959 H. H. Holmes called Aldiss "a cock-eyed poet and prophet in love with humanity and with words"; ten years later "William Atheling" (James Blish) wrote that he was "perhaps the most thorough, disciplined professional ever to concentrate his gifts upon science fiction." His main fault, in the opinion of a reviewer in the *Times Literary Supplement,* is that "his imagination sometimes soars beyond his intellectual control. . . . But he belongs to the select band of those whose prose is original and a delight to read."

PRINCIPAL WORKS: *Novels*—The Brightfount Diaries, 1955; Non-Stop, 1958 (U.S., Starship); Equator, 1961 (U.S., Vanguard From Alpha, 1959); The Interpreter, 1961 (U.S., Bow Down to Nul, 1960); The Primal Urge, 1961; The Male Response, 1961; Hothouse, 1962 (U.S., The Long Afternoon of Earth); The Dark Light Years, 1964; Greybeard, 1964; Earthworks, 1965; An Age, 1967 (U.S., Cryptozoic!); Report on Probability A, 1968; Barefoot in the Head, 1969; The Hand-Reared Boy, 1970; A Soldier Erect, 1971; Frankenstein Unbound, 1973; The Eighty-Minute Hour: A Space Opera, 1974; The Malacia Tapestry, 1976; Rude Awakening, 1978; Enemies of the System, 1978. *Short Stories*—Space, Time and Nathaniel, 1957 (U.S., revised as No Time Like Tomorrow); The Canopy of Time, 1959 (U.S., revised as Galaxies Like Grains of Sand); The Airs of Earth, 1963 (U.S., revised as Starswarm); Best SF Stories of Brian Aldiss, 1965 (U.S., Who Can Replace a Man?); The Saliva Tree, 1966; A Brian Aldiss Omnibus, 1969; Intangibles, Inc., 1969 (U.S., revised as Neanderthal Planet); Brian Aldiss Omnibus 2, 1971; The Moment of Eclipse, 1971; The

Book of Brian Aldiss, 1972 (U.S., revised as The Comic Inferno, 1973); Last Orders, 1977. *Nonfiction*—Cities and Stones: A Traveller's Jugoslavia, 1966; The Shape of Further Things, 1970; Billion Year Spree: A History of Science Fiction, 1973; Science Fiction Art, 1975. *As Editor*—Penguin Science Fiction, 1961; Best Fantasy Stories, 1962; More Penguin Science Fiction, 1963; Yet More Penguin Science Fiction, 1964; Introducing Science Fiction, 1964; The Space Opera Series: Space Opera, 1974; Space Odyssey, 1975; Evil Earths, 1975; Galactic Empires (2 vols.), 1976. *As Editor with Harry Harrison*—Nebula Award Stories 2, 1967; Farewell Fantastic Venus!, 1968 (U.S., All About Venus); Best SF 1967, 1968, 1969, etc.; The Astounding/Analog Reader, 1973; Hell's Cartographers, 1975; Decade: The 1940s, 1975; Decade: The 1950s, 1976; Decade: The 1960s, 1977.

ABOUT: Atheling, W. More Issues at Hand, 1970; Contemporary Authors 5-8 1st revision, 1969; International Who's Who, 1977-78; Ketterer, D. New Worlds for Old, 1974; Lundwall, S.J. Science Fiction, 1971; Manson, M. Item Forty-Three: Brian Aldiss 1954-1962 (bibliography), 1963; Tuck, D.H. (ed.) The Encyclopedia of Science Fiction and Fantasy, 1973; Vinson, J. (ed.) Contemporary Novelists, 1972; Who's Who, 1977; Wilson, C. The Strength to Dream, 1962. *Periodicals*—Books and Bookmen July 15, 1970; Extrapolation May 1970; Foundation 6 1974, 9 1975; Guardian May 24, 1969; August 6, 1971; SF Horizons 1 1964; Science Fiction Studies Fall 1973.

"ALYAGROV" *See* JAKOBSON, ROMAN

*AMICHAI, YEHUDA (1924–), Hebrew poet, novelist, short story writer, and dramatist, was born in Würzburg, Germany. In 1936, three years after Hitler came to power, his family emigrated to Palestine. They settled in Jerusalem, and Amichai completed his secondary education there, graduating from Bet Sefer Maaleh. In World War II he served with the Jewish Brigade in the British Army. He also fought in the Palmakh (Striking Force) of the Israeli Army during the 1948 War of Independence, and he is still a sergeant-major in the reserve. After the war Amichai continued his education at the Hebrew University. He lives in Jerusalem, teaching Hebrew literature and Bible in secondary schools. He is married, and has one son. Amichai, whose adopted Hebrew name means "my people lives," lost his religious faith when he was fifteen. Adam Gillon suggests that this loss left him with the feeling that he had rejected "not only God but also his beloved father, and in a larger symbolic way, the Jewish people." And indeed, a sense of loss pervades Amichai's poetry, along with an acute awareness of time. "Time is a key word if not a central image in Amichai's work," Gillon says, "for it enables him to achieve an artistic distance from which he can view himself, Israel, and the world."

Amichai began to publish his poetry in magazines in the late 1940s, and his first collection

*am' ēκ ī

YEHUDA AMICHAI

appeared in 1955, *Akhshav u-ve-yamim Aherim* (Now and in Other Days). Its appearance has been said to mark the emergence of a new school of Hebrew poets, who set out to transform their ancient and highly literary language into a medium capable of describing contemporary attitudes, contemporary relationships, modern wars. Amichai used as the language of poetry the Hebrew that was actually being spoken around him—that had been created by the exigencies and traumas of the birth of the new state —not excluding colloquialisms and slang, and the words coined for the artifacts and processes of the new technology. As Michael Hamburger has said, Amichai "cannot take his language for granted. For one thing, it was not his first language; and the language itself is an historical anomaly, like other languages that have not grown continuously and organically, but have been preserved, revived and modernized with a high degree of deliberateness. Amichai's awareness of that peculiarity is inseparable from the historical awareness that distinguishes all his work." Thus Amichai writes in "National Thoughts" (translated by Assia Gutmann in *Poems*):

> To speak, now, in this tired language
> Torn from its sleep in the Bible—
> Blinded, it lurches from mouth to mouth—
> The language which described God and the
>   Miracles,
> Says:
> Motor car, bomb, God.

In tackling the problems involved in using the contemporary Hebrew vernacular as a poetic language, Amichai was aided by his familiarity with modern poetry in German and English. He has also experimented with many of the traditional forms of English and European poetry—the quatrain, the sonnet, the elegy, and the lyric. Thus his second collection, *Be-Merhak Shtei Tikvot* (Two Hopes Away, 1958), includes a sequence of sonnets, like this one, "Here We Loved," where the almost Shakespearean rhyme scheme is imitated in Ruth Finer Mintz's translation for *Modern Hebrew Poetry,* along with Amichai's characteristically conversational diction and use of assonance:

My father was four years at their war
And did not hate or love his enemies.
But I know that he, already there,
Formed me daily out of his tranquilities.

They were so very few that he could pick
Between the bombs and smoke
And put them in his tattered sack
With the remains of mother's hardening cake.

Nameless dead he gathered in his eyes,
Numerous dead he gathered for me so
That I might love them, in his glances recognized,

And not die like them by terror taken . . .
He filled his eyes with them, he was mistaken:
To all my battles I must go.

Amichai's third book, *Ba-Ginnah ha Zibburit* (In the Park, 1959), was followed by his collected poems, *Shirim 1948-1962,* and then by *Akhshav ba-Ra'ash* (Now in the Turmoil, 1968). All of his verse shows a flair for paradox and a delight in striking and unusual imagery. And just as his diction juxtaposes literary Hebrew and the contemporary vernacular, so his imagery is full of biblical and traditional allusions which are then challenged, sadly or ironically, by startling anachronisms. For example, in "A Sort of Apocalypse," translated by T. Carmi in the *Times Literary Supplement* (October 29, 1976), Amichai begins with a reference to a traditional biblical image of serenity: "They shall sit every man under his vine and under his fig tree and none shall make them afraid":

The man under his fig tree telephoned the man
  under his vine:
"Tonight they will surely come.
Armour the leaves,
Lock up the tree,
Call home the dead and be prepared."

Many of Amichai's poems are nostalgic exercises in spiritual autobiography, contrasting the

hopes of his childhood with the harsh realities of the present. This is so of one of his best-known poems, "Yad Elohim ba-olam," translated by Leon Yudkin in *Escape Into Siege* as "The Hand of God in the World":

The hand of God is in the world
Like the hand of my mother in the entrail of
  the slaughtered chicken
On the Sabbath eve.
What does God see through the window
Whilst his hands are plunged into the world?
What does my mother see?

My pain has already aged;
And it has borne two generations of similar pains.
My hopes have erected white estates
Far from the stress within me.
My girl has forgotten her love on the pavement
Like a bicycle.

Yudkin examines this poem in some detail in *Escape Into Siege,* analyzing the wealth of striking images on which its success depends. Amichai's facility at making images seems excessive at times and even self-defeating to some critics, who urge him to exercise a little more austerity, especially in his lyric poetry. Similarly, Yudkin criticizes the collection *Ve-lo 'almenat lizkor* (And Not in Order to Remember, 1971) for "dangerous symptoms of mannerism taking over in his poetry." But this volume and the later *Me-ahore kol zeh mistater osher gadol* (Behind All This Hides Great Happiness, 1974), in which love takes a central place in Amichai's poetry, nevertheless confirmed his status as Israel's best-known living poet.

Amichai has been widely translated, and several volumes of his poetry have appeared in English. Leon Wieseltier in his review of *Songs of Jerusalem* (1973) wrote that the poet "demands of himself an unrelenting transparency, a self-consciousness which is a form of sustained vulnerability in the face of experience." He "constructs his poems by balancing one moment against the next, by forcing the many dimensions of his life upon one another in the hope that the life itself will emerge whole. . . . Amichai's experience of the world is above all an experience of its intractability, and the strenuous resistance of his situation to his will. There is thus a powerful tactile element in his poems' imagery. . . . Amichai's muse is resiliency, and personal courage"; he has "achieved a kind of precarious peace within the oscillations of happiness and sadness that constitute his life, and out of this peace rises the elemental lyricism of his poetry." It seemed to M. L. Rosenthal that many of the best poems in the later volume of translations called *Amen* (1977) dealt with "the joys and disasters of love. The themes of sexual power gone awry and of lost relationships and broken marriage darken the book with a bitterness matching its pain at all the death and suffering in Israel's wars, so much so that the two sets of feeling merge inseparably.... This is a harshly lovely, exhilarating, depressing book."

The confrontation between past and present, Europe and Israel, which is explored in so many of Amichai's poems also provides the theme of his first novel, *Lo me-Akhshav, lo mi-Kan* (1963, translated by Shlomo Katz as *Not of This Time, Not of This Place*). Joel, an Israeli archaeologist, goes back to his German birthplace in search of the person he had been there, and in a spirit of revenge; this journey is described in a first-person narrative. But Joel is in a schizoid condition, and this is expressed with disturbing literalness in repeated shifts to a third-person narrative, parallel to the first, in which he remains in Israel and has an affair with an American woman, Patricia. The two stories echo one another, and are linked in various ways—for example by the presence in the narrator's hometown of Patricia's husband, who is making a film about the Holocaust. And the narrator, torn between a desire to revenge himself on the Germans and guilt at having survived, finds his sense of identity further threatened when he is repeatedly mistaken for others, including the former Nazi commandant: "I came here to take vengeance and to know the truth, but the more I examined the men who committed all these atrocities and the places of horror the more I sank down into the knowledge of my own self." In the end the German Joel returns to Jerusalem, while the Jerusalem Joel is killed by a landmine on Mount Scopus—a relic of previous battles, an irrelevance "not of this time, not of this place."

Both the content and construction of the novel excited some controversy in Israel, but its English translation was received with considerable interest and admiration. Amos Elon wrote that the "much shortened [English] version ... loses some of the extraordinary poetic force of the original," but "it still reads much better because it is more concise." Christopher Wordsworth found the style "embarrassingly numinous and ecstatic," but Anthony West called it "a very moving and troubling novel ... Amichai writes with great affective power, both of the glittering structure of self-exculpation that the Germans of the guilty generation have succeeded in erecting on the site of mass graves and desecrated temples and of the ghost-haunted, sun-drenched anti-Germany that the ex-victims have created for themselves. One tastes to the full in his pages the experience of being lost, and of loss that comes from the realization that the world cannot be remade in the image of one's desire."

A second novel appeared in 1971 as *Mi yitneni malon* (O That I Had a Lodging). It is narrated by an Israeli poet in New York, where he at first works for the Jewish Agency, trying to get Israeli immigrants back to Israel. But, though "filling in forms protects one from despair," bureaucracy fails to satisfy his need to find meaning and purpose in his life, and his sense of absurdity is scarcely alleviated when he puts his poetic skills to work as a writer of jingles for a manufacturer of underwear. Once again, the principal criticism of the book was its surfeit of poetic images, which, as Leon Yudkin wrote, "get carried away by their own exuberance, and are not specially linked either to sense or to context."

Amichai has also written a number of plays. *Massa le-Nineveh* (1962), a retelling of the Jonah story, was staged by Habimah in 1964. *Pa'amonim ve-Rakkavot* (translated as "Bells and Trains" in *Midstream,* October 1966) won first prize in an Israeli competition for radio plays. The author has also received the important Shlonsky Prize and two Acum prizes. He was visiting poet at the University of California at Berkeley in 1971.

PRINCIPAL WORKS IN ENGLISH TRANSLATION: *Poetry*—Selected Poems, translated by Assia Gutmann (limited edition), 1968; Poems, translated by Assia Gutmann, 1969; Selected Poems, translated by Assia Gutmann and Harold Schimmel with the collaboration of Ted Hughes, 1971; Songs of Jerusalem and Myself, translated by Harold Schimmel, 1973; Amen, translated by the author and Ted Hughes, 1977. *Poems* in Birman, A. (ed.) An Anthology of Modern Hebrew Poetry, 1968; Burnshaw, S. (and others, eds.) The Modern Hebrew Poem Itself, 1965; Carmi, T. (ed.) Penguin Book of Hebrew Verse, 1977; Mintz, R.F. (ed.) Modern Hebrew Poetry, 1966; Silk, D. (ed.) Fourteen Israeli Poets, 1976; Times Literary Supplement October 29, 1976. *Novels*—Not of This Time, Not of This Place, translated by Shlomo Katz, 1968. *Plays*—Bells and Trains in Midstream October 1966. *Stories* in Burnley, J. (ed.) Penguin Modern Stories 7, 1971.

ABOUT: Encyclopaedia Judaica, 1971; Hamburger, M. *introduction to* Selected Poems, 1971; Yudkin, L. Escape Into Siege, 1974. *Periodicals*—Books Abroad Spring 1972; Commentary May 1974; Judaism 4 1965; New York Times Book Review August 4, 1968; July 3, 1977; New Yorker May 3, 1969; Poetry May 1970; Times Literary Supplement October 29, 1976.

ANDRADE, CARLOS DRUMMOND DE *See* DRUMMOND DE ANDRADE, CARLOS

Biblioteca Nacional

OSWALD DE ANDRADE

*ANDRADE, (JOSÉ) OSWALD DE (SOUZA) (January 11, 1890–October 22, 1954), Brazilian poet, novelist, dramatist, critic, and literary activist, was born in São Paulo. He was the son of José Oswald Nogueira de Andrade and the former Inez Henriqueta da Souza. Andrade was educated at the São Bento gymnasium (1903-1908) and graduated in law from the University of São Paulo (1909-1911 and 1917-1919). He did not practice as a lawyer but gravitated very early to a career in journalism. When he was twenty-one Andrade visited Europe, where in Paris he met a number of avant-garde writers, particularly those associated with Marinetti's short-lived futurist movement, the urban and technological spirit of which deeply influenced and excited him.

In 1912 Andrade returned to São Paulo. There, with the expressionist painter Anita Malfatti, the sculptor Victor Brecheret, and others, he set to work to revitalize Brazilian art. His program was two-pronged and in certain respects apparently self-contradictory. On the one hand he wanted to celebrate in a futurist spirit the industrial and technological sophistication of São Paulo; at the same time he advocated "primitivism"—a return to his country's roots in the Indian Brazil of pre-colonial times.

This proposed fusion of technology and nativism was a difficult task. Though it can be argued that it rests on a paradox rather than a contradiction, it was over-idealistic and (in accordance with Andrade's youthful ebullience) somewhat frenetic. The climax of his efforts came in the so-called Modern Art Week of São Paulo in 1922, in which his (unrelated) name-

*un drä' dē

sake Mário de Andrade also played an active part.

This festival of avant-garde painting, sculpture, and literature enraged polite opinion (which favored the sonnet and representational art) and gained the Modernists the attention they needed. The Brazilian Modernists never formed anything so close-knit as a single school of writers, but the Modern Art Week set off a chain of experimental literary and artistic explosions which found different outlets in different parts of the country. The generation of major and original talents that included Carlos Drummond de Andrade, Manuel Bandeira, and Cecília Meireles could not have emerged without it.

Oswald de Andrade continued to contribute in various ways to this cultural revolution. His 1924 collection of poems *Pau Brasil* (Brazilwood) contained a manifesto calling for a Brazilian poetry that would influence Portuguese verse instead of being influenced by it (and this has happened), and for a socialism that would not suppress artistic autonomy. In the course of time, somewhat though never wholly subdued, he gave increasing attention to the "primitivist" part of his program (and complained that he had discovered the wrong manifesto in Paris—Marinetti's instead of Marx's). His *Revista de Antropofagia* (Cannibalism Review), launched in 1928, celebrated Brazil's Indian past and attacked a Catholic-fascist group (the "Green-Yellow") which had arisen among some of his former collaborators. C.L. Hulet has called Andrade "the most potent yeast in the Modernist loaf, always impatient, anxious, fidgety, forever getting something going, keeping the literary pot boiling."

Typical of Andrade's own ironic, epigrammatic poems is this one, here translated by L.S. Downes:

> When the Portuguese arrived
> It was raining cats and dogs
> So he clothed the Indian
> What a pity!
> Had it but been a sunny morning
> The Indians would have undressed
> The Portuguese.

Some critics maintain that Andrade did his most substantial work in prose—notably in his comic and parodic novel *Memórais Sentimentais de João Miramar* (Sentimental Reminiscences of João Miramar, 1924), and the revealing autobiography *Un Homem sem Profissão* (A Man Without Profession, 1954). *Marco Zero* (Zero Mark, 1943-1945), an uncompleted trilogy on modern Brazilian life which he called a "mural novel," contains passages of brilliant observation. C. L. Hulet says that Andrade wrote "a fragmented, staccato, swift-moving prose that recalls a movie projected at a speed faster than normal. The main characters [in his novels], all marginal and maladjusted, are often well drawn and compelling; however, the tension is not well maintained." Andrade also wrote a number of plays on political themes.

Oswald de Andrade was a famous figure in his lifetime because of his crucial contribution to Brazilian Modernism; his own poetry and prose have generally been regarded as intelligent, amusing, but minor. Samuel Putnam called him the "enduring playboy of Brazilian letters" and Wilson Martins said he was "the Cocteau of our Modernism," all of whose work "is made up of flashes of genius lost in a heavy mass of halting composition." This view has been challenged in recent years, especially by Haroldo de Campos, who enthusiastically introduced Andrade's collected poems, *Poesias Reunidas,* in 1966. Another critic has said that "the virtue of his poetry is the economy with which he suggests the complexity of Brazil," and his capacity for concentration and understatement has undoubtedly influenced younger poets, especially Drummond de Andrade. Andrade was married to Maria Antonieta d'Alkmin, and had two children.

PRINCIPAL WORKS IN ENGLISH TRANSLATION: *Poems in* Bishop, E. and Brasil, E. (eds.) An Anthology of Twentieth-Century Brazilian Poetry, 1972; Downes, L.S. An Introduction to Modern Brazilian Poetry, 1954; Neistein, J. (ed.) Poesia brasiliera moderna: a bilingual anthology, 1972.

ABOUT: Campos, H. de *introduction to* Memórias Sentimentais de João Miramar, 1964 *and to* Poesias Reunidas, 1966; Franco, J. The Modern Culture of Latin America, 1970; Hulet, C.L. Brazilian Literature, 1975; Martins, W. The Modernist Idea, 1970; Nist, J. The Modernist Movement in Brazil, 1967; Penguin Companion to Literature 3, 1971; Seymour-Smith, M. Guide to Modern World Literature, 1975; Who's Who in Latin America Part VI 1948.

*ANTOKOLSKY, PAVEL (GRIGORYE-VICH) (July 1, 1896–October 1978), Russian poet and theatrical producer, writes (in Russian): "I am four years older than the twentieth century, and in July 1976 was eighty. I remember much more than I can find room for here. I remember how as an eight-year-old boy I first arrived in Moscow from St. Petersburg with my parents, and heard the newsboys crying out the tragedies of Tsushima [the defeat of the Russian fleet in the great naval battle of the Russo-Japanese war] and the death of Chekhov. A year later, in December 1905, in the alley beside the house where we lived, a barricade went up, though the following morning it was smashed down by the czarist forces. Thus history was involuntarily breaking into my childhood—

*ant o kol′ sky

PAVEL ANTOKOLSKY

though time didn't go at anything like the pace to which we have become accustomed towards the end of the century. At the edge of the great city heavy locomotives mournfully called to each other, and in the mornings they were joined by the factory hooters. At high school I was a rather mediocre pupil, though I loved the literature and Latin lessons. At the beginning of the war I was a negligent student in the law faculty, but secretly dreaming of the theatre, so that in my second university year I threw up public and Roman law for dramatic studies organized in one of Moscow's backstreets by Evgeny Vakhtangov.

"Apart from what I put into acting, all my excess spiritual energy went entirely into poetry. And poems poured out of me as if from a pump. I had to find my own personality. This was helped by two circumstances. The first was the appearance of Alexander Blok. Through his poetry I came to understand the significance of *metaphors,* like some magic power, transforming the world. Even more important and vital was my meeting in 1918 and friendship with Marina Tsvetaeva. She was four years older than I. From her I first heard not just praise of my poetry, but shrewd appraisal of it. Marina divined in me the same sort of workman that she was herself, and I understood that we weren't gods baking pots, that besides such high-flown matters as inspiration and ecstasy there was simple, daily work. So my poetic life began.

"In 1921 my verses were first published in an almanac edited by Valery Bryusov. Within a year my first book of poems was published, and others followed. But my connection with the theatre was not broken, and in 1923 I went abroad, to Sweden and Germany, with the Vakhtangov company. Postwar, hungry, fearful Berlin made the strongest impression on me and proved to be the starting-point for many future searches and discoveries. The times were fervent, and youth at its height. While still with the Vakhtangov Studio I wrote romantic plays, one of which was staged, though the stage was so small that it was in Shakespeare's words "only fit for a cockfight." Later, in the Vakhtangov Theater, I staged Schiller's *Kabale und Liebe,* and then in the automobile works in Gorky, with the young people of the Komsomol, I put on *The Marriage of Figaro, Romeo and Juliet,* Ostrovsky's *The Forest,* and also a series of contemporary plays.

"A distinct generation announced itself ineluctably as belonging to those times—the generation of the 1920s with which by the will of history our Soviet poetry began. Without seeking each other we met far from accidentally, as comrades-in-arms of the same age—Bagritsky and Tikhonov became my friends; sometime later, because they were younger, we were joined by Lugovskoy, Svetlov, Kirsanov. It seems obvious that each decade of our century had its own distinctive coloration, its own uniqueness, its own musical role in the world orchestra. This is true of the 1930s, 1940s, 1950s, and so on right up to today. For me personally this meant that as a poet I should serve as trumpeter and propagandist of the history being created before our eyes and in some degree by each of us. For a poet this is enough, in order to change and grow as they say "to full knowledge."

"In the 1940s I worked hard as a journalist and as a war correspondent in the army: War imposes heavy responsibilities. And I was to suffer irreparably tragic losses. In 1942 my eighteen-year-old son died bravely in action. In the new year of 1968 my wife Zoya Bazhanova, my beloved sweetheart and lifelong friend, suddenly died. As is well known, though tragedy may be a traumatic experience which can turn a man inside out, in the end one has to bow to it as a shattering lesson in the triumphant process of life. Such a conclusion is not just optimism. In general optimism is a trivial world view—just as is pessimism. Like two mirrors they face each other, one on the right, one on the left—that is all!

"Throughout all my years I have continued to travel through the immense spaces of our motherland and beyond her borders. From Paris to Peking, from Stockholm to Vietnam, from Novosibirsk or Tomsk to Yugoslavia—immense distances. But it isn't geographical space that characterizes the contemporary artist's life. For there is also a fourth dimension—TIME in its mysterious nature. My travels through time exceed all my other travels. For I dare to assert that I was beside Robespierre on the eve of the Ninth Thermidor in the fourth year of the Republic, that in the fifteenth century I lived in poverty with François Villon and perished with him. And earlier, in the fourth century, I was with Diocletian in Triclinium. And if one speaks of immemorially distant centuries, then I remember meeting Nefertiti in the fourteenth century B.C. I am only afraid that all this may sound suspiciously like the fraudulent mystifications of an old Cagliostro. It's simply a matter of the poet's talent for reincarnation. There are no other secrets.

"Here I may finish, though I have left many things unsaid. They remain on my conscience, though this is lightened by the fact that I have told everything in my books. Contemporary life is characterized by record speeds, accelerating ever faster and faster, which is why each separate life is nothing but a fragment, cut short in mid-sentence."

———

Antokolsky's father, Grigori, was a lawyer; his grandfather, Mark Antokolsky, a celebrated Russian Jewish sculptor famous for his bronzes and marbles on historical themes. The family was a cultured one, and Pavel Antokolsky early developed his interest in theatre, poetry, and painting, and an abiding sense of community with the Western European cultural heritage. He entered the law faculty of Moscow University in 1914, but the following year, as he says, abandoned his legal studies to join Vakhtangov's Students' Dramatic Studio as an actor, though he soon discovered a greater talent for producing plays and for writing them. In 1917, without losing contact with Vakhtangov, he served for a while with the militia and in the housing department of the Moscow Soviet. After the Revolution he worked in various Moscow theatres before rejoining Vakhtangov's company, which, from being an offshoot of Stanislavsky's Moscow Art Theatre, had developed into a separate company, the National Arts Theatre.

Antokolsky was a poet steeped in history and in literature. Many of the poems in his early collections *Stikhotvoreniya* (Poems, 1922), *Zapad* (The West, 1926), and *Tretya kniga* (The Third Book, 1927), were inspired by his travels with Vakhtangov in Western Europe, and his impressions of the sites of great historical events. Others deal with Pushkin and Gogol, and the author's reactions to Shakespeare and his plays. His empathy for the past—his "poet's talent for reincarnation"—is evident in several long poems

25

and verse plays inspired by certain crucial moments in human history, such as *Robespierre i Gorgona* (Robespierre and the Gorgon, 1930) and *Kommuna 1871* (The Commune of 1871, 1932). One of his major works of this period was *François Villon* (1934), in which a romantic portrait of Villon as questing wanderer is set against a realistic background of French medieval life.

Dramatic and colorful as these early works are in content, they are in their conception the work of a powerful analytical intelligence. And in manner they are economical and restrained, showing in their disciplined forms and verbal precision the influence not only of such Acmeist poets as Mandelstam and Akhmatova, but of French and English models. It is hardly surprising that Soviet critics of the 1930s often attacked Antokolsky as a typical example of Western orientation in Soviet literature, placing him in "the ranks of the aesthetes," and saying that he was "estranged from Soviet reality."

But such collections as *Deystvuyushchiye litsa* (Dramatis personae, 1932) and *Bolshiye rasstoyaniya* (Great Distances, 1936) do contain poems on everyday contemporary themes. Antokolsky had always wanted to provide art for the people, and in the early 1930s he was prominent among the members of the Vakhtangov company who organized local theatre in the factories and collective farms of the Gorky district. Antokolsky left the Vakhtangov in 1934 to devote himself to literature. The work he produced between then and World War II included *Koshchey* (1937), in which Koshchey the Immortal, villain of many Russian folk tales, becomes a symbol of capitalism in a modern political allegory, and *Pushkinsky god* (The Pushkin Year, 1938), a collection of poems on themes from Russian life and literature.

After Hitler's invasion of Russia in 1941 Antokolsky applied for membership in the Communist Party, though this was not granted until 1943. As the Germans advanced towards Moscow he was among the writers who were evacuated, in his case to Kazan on the Volga, where he became a war correspondent and also directed a front-line theatre. The war brought a new note into his poetry, and the sufferings of his country inspired a profuse outpouring of lyric poetry in the collections *Polgoda* (A Half-Year, 1942), *Zhelezo i ogon* (Iron and Fire, 1942), and *Tretya kniga voyny* (The Third Book of War, 1946). "The Ballad of the Boy Who Remained Unknown" (1942), which was based on a real incident, tells the story of a boy whose mother and sister had been murdered by the Nazis. As the Germans retreated from his town, he hurled a hand grenade into the car carrying the SS generals. Though the boy's name and subsequent fate remained unknown, the story was carried with great pride through the fighting front. Rosemary Heath's translation accompanies Prokofiev's setting of the poem in the Melodiya recording EMI ASD 2947.

Antokolsky's major poem of the war, his most famous single work, is the long poem *Syn* (Son, 1943), a lament on the death of his only son, killed in action as a pilot in 1942. It expressed with profound feeling and great sensitivity the sense of loss shared by most people in a country whose resistance to the Nazis cost twenty-five million lives. The poem was awarded a Stalin prize in 1946, but the further expression of this bereavement in the cycle *Nevechnaya pamyat* (Ephemeral Memory, 1946) was criticized for "decadence, aestheticism, and formalism." Antokolsky went on to sublimate his grief, becoming, as an editor and critic and in his work for the literary seminars of the Writers' Union, a father-figure to the new generation of young poets. Another of his long poems on crucial historical events, *1848*, was published in the centenary of that year of revolutions—partly in answer to his critics. *V pereulke za Arbatom* (In an Alley Behind the Arbat, 1955), about a country boy who goes to Moscow and becomes a construction worker, is a testament to the whole generation that came through World War II and rebuilt the society the war had shattered.

In *Masterskaya* (Workshop, 1958) Antokolsky describes art as "formation which knows no completion," and poetry as a struggle to find a path to self-expression which thus becomes a liberation of the spirit. A recurrent theme in his own poetry is the relationship between man and time, and this subject is discussed in many of the essays collected in *Poety i vremya* (Poets and Time, 1957) and *Puti poetov* (Paths of the Poets, 1965). *Sila Vietnama* (The Strength of Vietnam, 1960) is a poetic travel journal, and *O Pushkine* (About Pushkin, 1960) combines poems and ballads on Pushkinian themes with critical analysis of Pushkin's own works.

The collections *Vysokoe napryazheniye* (High Tension, 1942) and *Chetvertoye izmereniye* (The Fourth Dimension, 1964) resume in verse Antokolsky's musings on art and time, on time's power over man, and man's attitude to time. One critic wrote of the latter collection: "Maturity and depth of thought combine in this work, not only with the original presentation and the unobtrusive technical accomplishment of the work, but also with the depth of feeling. ... The superiority of Antokolsky's late lyrics over all his previous work is witness to his continual spiritual growth and increasing mastery of his craft."

Antokolsky received a number of awards and medals, and was elected several times to the board of the Union of Soviet Writers. He produced five volumes of French poetry in translation, and became a devoted translator of the poetry of the Caucasus and Central Asia after his first visits there in the late 1930s. Antokolsky was an enthusiastic amateur painter, and was said to be an exquisite reader of verse, his own and that of others.

PRINCIPAL WORKS IN ENGLISH TRANSLATION: *Poems in* Bosley, K. (and others, eds.) Russia's Other Poets, 1968; Kunitz, J. (ed.) Russian Literature Since the Revolution, 1948; Markov, V. and Sparks, M. (eds.) Modern Russian Poetry, 1966; Obolensky, D. (ed.) The Penguin Book of Russian Verse, 1962; Ogney, V. and Rottenberg, D. (eds.) Fifty Soviet Poets, 1969.

ABOUT: International Who's Who, 1977-78; Lavrin, J. A. Panorama of Russian Literature, 1973; Slonim, M. Soviet Russian Literature, 1964; Struve, G. Russian Literature Under Lenin and Stalin, 1961. *Periodicals*—Portraits of Prominent USSR Personalities 1, 1968.

*ANTONÍOU, DEMÉTRIOS I(OÁNNIS)

(April 10, 1906–), Greek poet, was born in Beira, Mozambique, then Portuguese Southeast Africa. His family, which comes from Cássos, in the Dodecanese Islands, has bred generations of sea captains, and Antoníou has followed the tradition.

He spent the first three years of his life in Suez and then traveled with his mother in Egypt and Europe. When he was about six years old he was brought to Athens, where he completed his early education. He studied briefly at the University of Athens but left to become an apprentice and later a navigation officer on Greek cargo vessels, sailing all over the world before joining his first passenger ship, the *Akropolis*. During World War II he served as second in command of a torpedo ship which was sunk by the Germans just before their occupation of Greece. After the war he served as staff captain and then as captain of the cruise ships *Achilles* and *Agamemnon*, sailing throughout the Mediterranean, to the Canary Islands, and down the West Coast of Africa.

Antoníou's poems, which began to appear in magazines in the 1930s, brought him the friendship of the late Nobel prizewinner George Seferis, a diplomat with whom he would endlessly discuss Greek poetry whenever and wherever in the world their paths crossed. Seferis, who died in 1971, described Antoníou's habit of filling his cabin "with empty cigarette boxes, covered with

*an ton ē' ōō

verses on every available surface. 'My bottles in the sea,' he used to call them. One day I remember his whispering to me, between orders to the helmsman, his verses. We had our course fixed towards the moon. The sea was calm and Greece was sleeping. Nothing disturbed this rhythmical abolition of time."

These short lyrics seek always what Antoníou calls the "specific gravity of expression." Dense and elliptical in content, laconic in diction, they are capable, as Kimon Friar says, of "slanting suggestions, nebulous half-meanings, disturbing overtones." They convey not so much the sailor's easy nostalgia as the purposeful meditation on the past possible to a man alone on vast sea voyages:

I recalled the signal's greeting
as you sighted us from four miles away
when we returned after many years. . . .

We brought you no more than stories
of distant places, memories
of precious things, of perfumes.

Do not seek their weight upon your hands;
your hands should be less human
for all we held in exile;
the experience of touch, the struggle of weight,
exotic colours
you should feel in our words only
this night of our return.

Obstacle to what
the mast that told you
of our return?

(from "Obstacle to What?", translated by Edmund Keeley and Philip Sherrard)

Apart from his poems about music and about poetry itself—both important themes in his work—Antoníou's verse is rooted in his experience of the sea: long voyages to exotic lands, memories of far-off places, the sadness of parting, the torment and loneliness of exile, the joy and agony of return:

Should we turn back?
—sorrow waits for us in the past:
what you failed to exhaust on journeys,
baring your heart—
Yet for one return
you rave,
moments when you gave away all
for an unrepenting wisdom!

(from "Should We Turn Back?"
translated by Edmund Keeley and
Philip Sherrard)

These are the themes which echo also in the

poetry of Seferis, but the exile of which Seferis writes is humanity's tragic estrangement from a spiritual home. As Keeley and Sherrard have said, what Antoníou conveys is something much more personal—"the feeling of loss in the wanderer who longs for the distant homeland . . . and the commitment to remembrance that his wandering compels. It is, in one sense, a national state of mind . . . the experience of exile is among the more typical for the contemporary Greek. This is what gives Antoníou's personal metaphor a broader dimension, a larger significance; his mood becomes to an extent generic, his statement of it a contemporary definition."

For many years, Antoníou's reputation rested on forty-three short poems, published first in periodicals and collected in book form in 1939 and 1954. In 1967 however he published *Indhíes* (The Indies), a long free verse poem of 1,040 short lines. Less tightly compressed than the short lyrics, with a clear narrative line, the poem is nevertheless a metaphysical one. It takes the form of a letter to the poet's family, and was begun during the winter of 1933-1934, during a visit of Antoníou's ship, the *Peleus,* to the villages of Masoulipatam and Kalingapatam in the Bay of Bengal.

The principal theme of *Indhíes* is the conflict between primitive and technological cultures, of which the young officer becomes aware on New Year's Eve, when the coolies loading his ship are given whiskey and burst into barbaric songs and dances in honor of their god Rama. Later the dancing of a little girl named after Rama's wife Sita brings him a moment of revelation; feeling that he has been visited by the goddess herself and returned to the dark origins of mankind, he becomes mystically aware of the fluidity of time. In the words of Kimon Friar, "this poem, with its strange beauty, its organic metrical structure, its sparse language yet exotic coloring, is unique in modern Greek literature, the fruit of long contemplation and an almost agonized dedication to craft."

Antoníou lives now in semi-retirement in Athens, and gives much of his time to collecting and studying the flora of Greece. He has remained a bachelor, reportedly in obedience to the Greek custom that a man should not marry before his sisters have been given in matrimony; Antoníou has three sisters, only one of them married. A reticent and retiring man despite his courtly manners, he rarely entertains at home, preferring, it is said, to meet his friends in the Athenian literary cafés.

Speaking of Antoníou's poetry, Seferis wrote: "Endless days, just as there is no end to the coal loaded under a leaden light, days spent on the bridge between sea and sky, as the ship rolls and struggles in the waves; seaports with all the bitterness of harbors, with the disenchantment of a desire finally accomplished after forty days of effort and hardship; smiles of exotic places, lighting up momentarily, like the dawn of our native island—all these shades and colors, which we either see instantly or may never see at all, are to be found in the poetry of our seafaring friend. They are to be found just as we might find them if we were reading them in the pages of a logbook, or if we were suddenly to see under the light, looking through a door that had been left open, the face of a sailor, solemn and submissive, as the ship carries us away from the things we love."

PRINCIPAL WORKS IN ENGLISH TRANSLATION: *Poems in* Barnstone, W. (ed.) Modern European Poetry, 1966; Friar, K. (ed.) Modern Greek Poetry, 1973; Keeley, E. and Sherrard, P. (eds.) Six Poets of Modern Greece, 1960.

ABOUT: Dimaras, C. A History of Modern Greek Literature, 1973; Friar, K. (ed.) Modern Greek Poetry, 1973; Gianos, M.P. Introduction to Modern Greek Literature, 1969; Keeley, E. and Sherrard, P. (eds.) Six Poets of Modern Greece, 1960; Politis, L. A History of Modern Greek Literature, 1973; Seferis, G. On the Greek Style, 1966.

*ANWAR, CHAIRIL (July 26, 1922–April 28, 1949), Indonesian poet and translator, was born in Medan, East Sumatra, where his family, of Minangkaban descent, had moved from Djakarta. Education was extremely expensive in the Dutch East Indies (now Indonesia), and the fact that Anwar completed his elementary education and a further two years of Dutch lower middle school suggests that his family was ambitious for him and at least moderately prosperous. He was an exceptionally intelligent student, mixed well with his peers, and had a passion for books, which he seems to have been able to read in English and German as well as Dutch and Indonesian.

In 1940 Anwar left Sumatra. He told friends that his father, who had abandoned his mother for another woman, had stopped sending money for his education. Anwar went with his mother to Djakarta, where he spent the remainder of his brief and dissolute life. The longest period of work he ever seems to have done was the three months he spent on the editorial board of the magazine *Gema Suasana* (Echoes From Everywhere), and even then he seldom appeared at the office.

"I'm a poet," Anwar said, and when he was not writing he was drinking, escorting his girlfriends to dances and parties and movies, endlessly talking in the coffeehouses or the streets.

*chī′ ril an′ wär

CHAIRIL ANWAR

His exhibitionism was extreme: friends remember him taking a prostitute to a city park to see what sex would be like in public, or declaiming the poems of Emily Dickinson from the back of an open car. This reckless dissipation ruined Anwar's mother, who sold her possessions to pay for his extravagances, and destroyed the poet's own health. He seems nevertheless to have been a popular figure at many levels of Djakarta society—as welcome to a night's lodging in the homes of the wealthy and prominent as he was with the prostitutes under the city's innumerable bridges. "When I die," he said, "I don't want it to be in a bed. I want to die in the middle of the street."

According to H. B. Jassin, Anwar was "a thin pale youngster, careless of his appearance. His eyes were red, and very wild, but they always appeared thoughtful; his movements were slow, as if utterly indifferent. . . . In his ideals, in his movements, and in his actions themselves, he stabbed, cut, and smashed old notions, leading some of his friends to think him ignorant, unaware of custom, a kind of bandit, characterizations he himself thought an honor and necessary in order to influence his slower friends into revolutionary ways."

Anwar's vagabond and self-destructive way of life was above all an anguished response to the horrors of life. "Here I am," he exclaims, "a wild beast,/ cut off from his companions." At another level, the anarchic behavior of Anwar and his friends reflects the traumatic collapse of values brought about by the Japanese occupation of Indonesia in 1942. The Dutch, their language, and the Western social cultural patterns they had imposed, were swept aside with an ease that called into question everything the Indonesians had been taught to believe.

Accounts differ as to Anwar's response to the occupation (as they do about so much else in his life). He certainly welcomed the opportunity it brought to "free ourselves from the old system that has weakened our nation"—to create "the new, the fully alive Indonesian man"—and he admired the courage and military prowess of the Japanese. It seems equally clear that he came to resent and hate the brutality of the invaders and the censorship they imposed. What is not certain is what he did about the situation. One source says that he did not join those who fought against the Japanese, and promptly betrayed what he knew about the resistance when the Japanese arrested and briefly tortured him. Another source says just as unequivocally that at the end of the war, when British and Dutch forces landed in Djakarta, Anwar was fighting with the nationalist forces.

Whatever the facts may prove to be regarding Anwar's personal behavior, there is no doubt that out of the excesses, the humiliations, and the self-explorations of the years in Djakarta came the finest poetry yet written in Indonesian. Anwar said that "from the time I was fifteen years old I've headed for only one goal: art." His early poems were written under the romantic and idealistic influence of the *Pudjangga Baru* (New Writer) movement of the 1930s, which did much to transform the Indonesian language (a form of Malay) into a literary medium. Later he learned from such Dutch expressionists as Marsman and Slauerhoff, and from Rilke (all poets whom he translated). He destroyed his juvenilia and turned violently against the *Pudjangga Baru,* dismissing its products as "utterly bland." In 1943 he wrote, "Till now our art has been thin, superficial. No more of the old farts. No more gentle breezes of *that* kind!"

"Diponegoro" (1943), which expresses with great vitality his socialistic and patriotic fervor, was the first of his poems to attract widespread attention. He did not become well known as a writer until some years later, when he emerged as the leader of the Angkatan Empatpuluh Lima. It was in the hands of this movement—"the Generation of '45"—and above all of Anwar himself, that Indonesian flowered as a modern literary language.

No collection of Anwar's poetry appeared until after his death. His output consists of only about seventy-five short poems, most of them published in *Deru Tjampur Debu* (Cries in the Dust, 1949), and in *Kerikil Tadjam* (Sharp Gravel) and *Jang Terampas dan Jang Putus* (The Plundered and Broken), which appeared together as a single volume in 1949. His work includes love poems, revolutionary poems, poems about art and about his struggles with religious faith, poems of disgust at his own compulsive lechery, and poems of regret or defiance at the prospect of death. Many are addressed to "Ida"—probably his friend Ida Nasution, a journalist.

"In art," Anwar wrote, "vitality is the chaotic initial state; beauty the cosmic final state." He achieved a new and vital kind of poetry, and successfully imported modernism—in the form of compression, complex symbolism, and ambiguity—into Indonesian poetry. He was a master of technique and of his language, which is full of problems for the poet—including the treacherous ease with which it rhymes. Anwar said: "I will scrape and dig into *every word* as far as I can get, right down to the essence of the word, to the substance of the image"; that is what he did, as B.S. Oemarjati has shown in her linguistic study of his poetry. The miracles that Anwar performed with the Indonesian language cannot be shown in translation, but something of his quality is evident in "Jang Terampas dan Jang Luput," one of his last poems, which appeared under several titles. The reference to Karet is to the cemetery there:

Darkness and a passing wind rake me.
I shiver, and so does the great room where the one
   I want is lying.
The night sinks in, the trees are as dead as columns
   of stone.

At Karet, at Karet (where I go next), the cold wind
   blows just as noisily.

I'm tidying my room, and my heart, in case you
   come
And I can set free a new story for you;
But now it's only my hands that move fiercely.

My body is quiet and alone, the tale and the time
   go stiffly, icily by.

> (translated as "The Captured and the Freed"
> by Burton Raffel and Nurdin Salam)

Anwar appears to have published little prose, the few works in this form in the collection comprising only one or two speeches, a radio talk, and some letters.

When Anwar died of typhus at the age of twenty-seven, he was also suffering from syphilis, tuberculosis, and cirrhosis of the liver. He left a wife, the former Hapsah Wiriaredja, whom he had married in 1946, and a daughter who was crippled by inherited disease; he had, in effect, abandoned them years earlier. Towards the end

of his life, struggling to pay medical bills, Anwar sometimes signed his own name to a poem which he had only translated. When these plagiarisms were discovered after his death, there was a storm of literary (and political) outrage and an attempt (by "socialist realists" and others) to discredit all his work. The attempt has failed, and Anwar is now regarded as Indonesia's greatest writer and the founder of modern Indonesian poetry.

PRINCIPAL WORKS IN ENGLISH TRANSLATION: Selected Poems, translated by Burton Raffel and Nurdin Salam, 1963; The Complete Poetry and Prose of Chairil Anwar, translated by Burton Raffel, 1970; The Complete Poems of Chairil Anwar, translated by Liaw Yock Fang with H.B. Jassin, 1974.

ABOUT: Budiman, A. Chairil Anwar, 1976; Jassin, H.B. Chairil Anwar: Pelopor Angkatan 45, 1956; McVey, R.T. (ed.) Indonesia, 1963; Oemarjati, B.S. Chairil Anwar: The Poet and His Language, 1972; Penguin Companion to Literature 4, 1969; Raffel, B. introduction to Complete Poetry and Prose, 1970; Raffel, B. The Development of Modern Indonesian Poetry, 1967; Teeuw, A. Modern Indonesian Literature, 1967.

*"**ARGHEZI, TUDOR**" (pseudonym of Ion Theodorescu) (May 20, 1880–July 14, 1967), Romanian poet, essayist, and novelist, was born in Bucharest, of a peasant family which had moved to the capital from Carbunesti. His parents wanted a civil service career for him and made considerable sacrifices to send him to secondary school in Bucharest. However, at the age of fourteen he ran away from home after a quarrel with his father, earning his living as a suburban court official, clerk, and stonemason's assistant.

At the age of sixteen he published his first poems in the magazine *Liga Ortodoxă* (The Orthodox League), edited by Alexandru Macedonski, who was regarded as the father of Romanian symbolism. Macedonski hailed the young poet (then writing as Ion Theo) for his audacity and brilliant success in breaking with the banal imagery and conventional versification of the time. After this precocious success Arghezi continued to scrape a living at various casual jobs—as a copyist and then as an assistant chemist in a sugar factory—until at the age of twenty he encountered the first of the moral and spiritual crises which were to recur throughout his life.

Feeling a need to "look for God," Arghezi in 1899 entered the monastery of Cernica. His four years as a monk left him with "numerous reminiscences of spiritual elevation but also many memories of squalor and debasement." After this experience he returned to Bucharest and re-entered the literary world, editing with his
*är gä′ zē

TUDOR ARGHEZI

friend V. Demetrius a weekly review, *Linia Dreaptă* (The Straight Line). Towards the end of 1904 he went abroad, working as a salesman, watchmaker's apprentice, and stonemason in France and Switzerland.

Returning to Romania in 1910, Arghezi soon became known as a chronic polemicist, making enemies on all sides. He contributed to many journals and founded several of his own, beginning with the violently pacifist *Cronica* (The Chronicle). After World War I he was imprisoned for a time for having contributed to the pro-German *Gazeta Bucureștilor* during the occupation, but upon his release continued his dual career as polemicist and poet with unabated fury.

Though he was profoundly interested in social and moral problems and deeply dissatisfied with the contemporary state of the world, Arghezi had no coherent ideology but veered from one solution to another, advancing each new theory with the same fiery conviction. He was not really a social or political thinker at all, for, as Dumitru Micu points out, his polemics were closely linked to his creativity: "The two poles of the writer's sensibility—his power to love (covering the whole gamut of feeling from tenderness to frenzy) and his capacity to hate tenaciously—are equally prominent in both his verse and prose. . . . The aspiration that characterizes Arghezi's entire creation is in his journalistic writings more openly and explicitly focused upon social problems."

The Romanian critic E. Lovinescu early noted the "characteristic complexity of Arghezian psychology: a Faustian personality, harboring not just two souls, but a battlefield of the contradictory principles of modern man." His dramatic, frenzied, theatrical, richly metaphorical poetry reflects his vitality and his spiritual unrest—his Faustian yearning to know and understand human destiny, the torment of a soul longing, in a world that shelters "snakes and evil," to find the key to a pure, absolute, untarnished existence. Like Baudelaire, whose work he translated and by whom he was greatly influenced, his poetic sensibility swings between the two poles of "spleen" and "idéal," between Satanism and a longing for the infinite.

It was not until he was forty-seven that his first collection of poems appeared in book form as *Cuvinte potrivite* (1927), a title which refers to Arghezi's notion of poetry as "perfectly matched words." The book immediately became a center of controversy, intensely admired by some and as violently repudiated by others. It established Arghezi at once as a poet of immense originality of thought and sensibility, expressing himself in equally unexpected and striking imagery. These poems show his powerful tensions, his "heavenly anguish," his violent alternations between extremes of faith and denial, prayer and blasphemy: "My real sin/ Is much more grave and unpardonable;/ With my bow I had tried/ To topple you, God!"

Arghezi's religious dilemma is powerfully expressed in the famous sequence of "Psalmi" (Psalms) in *Cuvinte potrivite,* in which the poet explores modern man's relationship with God:

Running with the wind, on my horse, like a Prince
  Charming,
I have roamed all over the country and its forests,
but when I reached the mountains, scarred by
  ravines,
I found I was unable to conquer their peaks. . . .

I have pursued You through poetry, words and
  syllables,
or dragging myself down on my hands and knees,
servile and humble; the effort, I thought,
would make You accept me at least out of pity.

Throughout my life I have tried to snatch an hour's
  talk with You,
But You would always hide as soon as I appeared.
When I grope at your doorway with my sad and
  whispered prayer
I always find chains, bolts and bars.

Angry in front of such obstacles, I feel an urge to
  destroy them,
but I realise I would, in this case, have to destroy
  You first.

    (from "Psalm" translated by Roy MacGregor-
    Hastie)

In 1930 Arghezi published two remarkable novels. *Icoane de lemn* (Wooden Icons) draws upon his experience of the monastic life, which is presented as an inferno of sodomy and moral infection. *Poarta neagră* (The Black Gate) deals in similar terms with the suffering and degradation he experienced during his postwar period of imprisonment. Prison was also the inspiration for his second volume of poems, *Flori de mucigai* (Flowers of Mildew, 1931), whose title is an oblique reference to Baudelaire's *Les Fleurs du mal.* Written "with the nails of the left—the devil's—hand," *Flori de mucigai* is at the opposite pole from the idealistic aspirations of *Cuvinte potrivite,* seeking perverse beauty in the depravity of the human dregs who mildew within the "House of the Dead."

The collection *Cărticică de seară* (Booklet for the Evening, 1935) exhibits yet another face of Arghezi's poetry, reflecting in its quieter celebrations of nature a pantheistic sense of intimate correspondence between the macroscopic and microscopic worlds, where the spider constructs "labyrinths of raw silk by the same laws that underlie the construction of the universe." The same vision of cosmic communion is expressed in *Hore* (Round Dances, 1939), where the image of the poet-gardener in touch with the fertile mysteries of the earth becomes part of a conception of art as play. The world here is viewed through the mind and spirit of a child, in joyful and exuberant verses which do indeed resemble those chanted during a round dance.

Dumitru Micu has described Arghezi as "undeniably the greatest writer for and especially about children in Romanian literature," and his stories of his own children, Miṭura and Baruṭu, were collected in *Cartea cu Jucarii* (The Book of Toys, 1931). Many of his poems were also about his children, like "Cîntec de adormit Miṭura," translated by Roy MacGregor-Hastie in his *Anthology of Contemporary Romanian Poetry* as "Lullaby for Mitsura":

> God—build her a little house,
> in a corner of the farmyard,
> no higher than a flower,
> narrow as an ear of corn.
>
> In her courtyard, a tiny puddle,
> with a raft of matches
> strong enough to bear her fragment
> of Your sky and infinity. . . .
>
> And give her a box of paints
> and a lot of Chinese paper.
> While she splashes the paper
> let her daub Your glory, too.
>
> And when everything is ready,
> Papa will move in with her.

Tablete din ṭara de Kuty (Tablets From the Land of Kuty, 1933) is by contrast a savagely satirical anti-utopian novel. It was quickly followed by other novels—the autobiographical *Ochii Maicii Domnului* (The Madonna's Eyes, 1934) and *Cimitirul Buna-Vestire* (The Cemetery of the Annunciation, 1936). Meanwhile, throughout the 1930s, Arghezi continued to pour out articles and pamphlets attacking the corruption of Bucharest society, the church, and the government with its fascist sympathies. During World War II he was imprisoned, with many other writers, artists, and intellectuals, in the "poets' concentration camp" at Tirgu Jiu.

Recognition came with the change of government after the war. Arghezi received the National Poetry Prize for the first time in 1947. But as Romania was transformed into a socialist state, he went through a spiritual crisis which silenced him from 1947 to 1954. His uncertainties were resolved by the time he published *1907* (1955), a cycle of poems dealing with the 1907 peasant uprising which shows him identifying himself with the aims and aspirations of his communist fellow prisoners at Tirgu Jiu. Another poem cycle, *Cîntare omului* (Song of Man, 1956) has been described by George Ivașcu as "the supreme Arghezian incantation, a synthesis of syntheses," in which "the poet, seeing the whole universe transformed into an immense workshop, eulogizes the technical progress of mankind." He was awarded the State Prize for Poetry in 1956.

Eight further poetry collections followed, including *Cadente* (Cadences, 1965), *Silabe* (Syllables, 1965), *Ritmuri* (Rhythms, 1966), and *Noaptea* (Night, 1966). But the work of Arghezi's seventh decade, much of it a pagan invocation of nature, darkened by growing presentiments of death, lacks the anguished intensity of his earlier work, even when, as in *Poeme noi* (New Poems, 1963), it once more deals with the old opposition between the ideal and the real. During these last years the aging writer, once so scandalously controversial, was firmly established as the greatest Romanian poet since Eminescu. Like Baudelaire, whose work he translated superbly, he could say in "Testament": "Out of the mold, out of the mud and slime/ I made beauty in a new image of truth." His own poetry has been widely translated, into Italian by Quasimodo, into Spanish by Alberti, and into more than twenty other languages. A selection appeared in English in 1976, translated by Michael Impey and Brian Swann. According to Roy MacGregor-Hastie, it was left to Arghezi "to refine the language of Romanian poetry and

give it both a Romanian and a universal quality.
. . . His life spanned virtually the whole history
of what we think of as Romanian literature.
. . . He gave a sense of continuity to the evolution
of a Romanian literary tradition, and set his own
milestones to mark the stages of that evolution."

PRINCIPAL WORKS IN ENGLISH TRANSLATION: Selected Poems, 1976. *Poems in* MacGregor-Hastie, R. (ed.) Anthology
of Contemporary Romanian Poetry, 1969.

ABOUT: Cassell's Encyclopaedia of World Literature, 1973;
Crohmălniceanu, O.S. Tudor Arghezi, 1960 (in Romanian);
Micu, D. Opera lui Tudor Arghezi, 1965 (translated into
English as Tudor Arghezi, 1965); Penguin Companion to
Literature 2, 1969; Vianu, T. Arghezi, poet al omului, 1964.
Periodicals—Books Abroad Winter 1969; Times Literary
Supplement August 26, 1977.

© 1974 by Vivian Frankel

MARGARET ATWOOD

ATWOOD, MARGARET (ELEANOR)
(November 18, 1939–), Canadian poet, novelist,
and critic, writes: "I was born in Ottawa, Ontario, in 1939, two months after the outbreak of
World War II. Six months later I was taken by
my family to a lake in northern Quebec (remote
then, accessible now), and for the next eleven
years I alternated this way between the bush
(first in Quebec, then on the northern shore of
Lake Superior, then Quebec again) and various
cities—Ottawa, Sault Sainte Marie, Toronto. I
did not spend a full year in school until I was in
Grade Eight. I began to write at the age of five—
poems, 'novels,' comic books and plays—but I
had no thought of being a professional writer
until I was sixteen. I entered Victoria College,
University of Toronto, when I was seventeen
and graduated in 1961. I won a Woodrow Wilson Fellowship to Harvard, where I studied Victorian literature, and spent the next ten years in
one place after another: Boston, Montreal, Ed-
monton, Toronto, Vancouver, England, and Italy, alternately teaching and writing.

"I had my first poem accepted for professional
publication when I was nineteen. It took me a
while to discover modern Canadian poetry because the literary culture at that time in Canada
was largely underground: authors were published in small editions and not generally known.
This changed during the next decade, when I
was becoming active as a poet and prose fiction
writer. At the beginning of the sixties there was
only a handful of magazines and indigenous
publishing houses; at its end there were many,
and writers had become public figures.

"I and many other members of my generation
were part of this expansion. Because of our beliefs and the extraordinary amount of blood and
energy that sustaining a Canadian literary culture in the face of U.S. domination required,
many of us also did time as publishers, and I
served a three-year sentence with the House of
Anansi in Toronto. It was during this period
that I wrote *Survival,* which was originally intended as the first beginner's guide to Canadian
literature but which turned into a treatise of
sorts on the case for nationalism. It caused a
certain amount of uproar, which has always
puzzled me, as it seems to me merely to state the
obvious. Largely because of it, I became a combination target and cult figure, and began to feel
a rather pressing need for privacy. I now live on
a farm in southern Ontario, where I'm still not
finding as much time to write as I'd like. When
I'm not writing or thinking about it, I play with
my young daughter (born in May 1976), work in
the garden or go canoeing, when I can. Writing
is still my main occupation or obsession, but
should I find myself with nothing new to try or
say I will stop without regret and do something
else."

Margaret Atwood is one of the three children
of Carl Edmund Atwood, an entomologist, and
the former Margaret Killam, a dietitian. It was
because of the nature of her father's work that
she grew up partly in the sparsely settled "bush"
country of Northern Ontario and Quebec—an
experience that has been of critical importance
in her writing. At Victoria College she came
under the influence of the critic Northrop Frye,
the principal of the college. *Double Persephone,*

her first small book of poems, was published in 1961 in Toronto, and showed her debt to the mythopoeic school associated with Frye, and to the poet Jay Macpherson, another of her teachers at Victoria College.

Radcliffe gave her her M.A. in 1962 and there followed a year of graduate study at Harvard and then a year or two of spare-time writing and casual employment—cashier, waitress, market researcher—during which period she also tried her hand as a film scenarist. She was a lecturer in English at the University of British Columbia, Vancouver, in 1964-1965, and then returned to Harvard (1965-1967) for further graduate work. In 1967-1968 she was an instructor in English at Sir George Williams University, Montreal, in 1969-1970 she taught at the University of Alberta, and in 1970-1971 she traveled in England, France, and Italy.

The Circle Game, her first important collection, was published in 1964 and appeared in a revised edition in 1966, when it received the Governor-General's Award as the year's best book of verse. These "astonishingly assured" poems seemed to John Robert Colombo close to "confessional" verse, "but they also have an interesting and impersonal dramatic strain, especially when writing about the geography and history of Canada." In 1967, Canada's Centennial Year, Margaret Atwood won the Centennial Commission's poetry competition with a group of poems later included in *The Animals in That Country.* The spare, unrhymed, unmetered poems in that 1968 collection center on the mystery of human identity, and the unbridgeable gap between the world of feeling and that of materialism, status, and power. The ugly evidence of the primacy of materialism and greed is found everywhere, in our despoliation of nature and of one another. Mona Van Duyn found these poems deeply distrustful of the human mind itself: "the word, the imagination, even the poem. . . . A pencil, even in the hands of a poet, is a 'cleaver'; what is completely captured by the poem dies."

The same themes are explored in Margaret Atwood's witty and mildly surreal first novel, *The Edible Woman.* A young woman, thoroughly conditioned by her materialistic society, sets her sights on a rising young lawyer, succeeds in becoming engaged to him, and then inexplicably loses her appetite for food. It is the emotional cannibalism of her role in an artificial society that sticks in her throat, and she is cured by a strange little ritual at the end of the book. She bakes a cake modeled in the shape of a woman— her artificially "normal" self—and offers it to her fiancé. He refuses this strange offering, but

she consumes it and returns to health. George Woodcock thought the novel "full of verbal and situational wit, and as a comedy of manners it has to be read in detail for all its social ironies to be observed. It uses very capably . . . the element of fantasy that has become so important a component of the New Fiction."

The insights into human relations and the peculiar nature of Canadian society that emerge in Margaret Atwood's early work have been clarified and deepened in what has followed. *Power Politics* (1971) is a sequence of poems about a love affair, offered as an exemplar of all "victor/ victim patterns, with their endless variations of pose, accusation, complicity and subversion of the human." The woman is used by the man as fall guy in a series of roles that society requires of him but that are remote from his true nature—

> the hinged bronze man, the fragile man
> built of glass pebbles,
> the fanged man with his opulent cape and boots

Starved of reality in this fundamentally sadomasochistic game, love dies:

> You refuse to own
> yourself, you permit
> others to do it for you:
>
> you become slowly more public,
> in a year there will be nothing left
> of you but a megaphone. . . .
>
> or you will be slipped under
> the door, your skin furred with cancelled
> airmail stamps, your kiss no longer literature
> but fine print, a set of instructions.
>
> If you deny these uniforms
> and choose to repossess
> yourself, your future
>
> will be less dignified, more painful, death will be
>   sooner,
> (it is no longer possible
> to be both human and alive): lying piled with
> the others, your face and body
> covered so thickly with scars
> only the eyes show through.

Helen Vendler called this "a plain explicit poetry, perfectly sure of itself" and "glistening with terse bright images, untentative, closing like a vise," in a book which "moves almost unwillingly, but relentlessly, through a brilliant schema of unflagging suspense and pitches of drama."

In *Survival,* Margaret Atwood's "thematic guide to Canadian literature," she concludes that Canadian writers have tended to draw characters who end as victims—of their society, of American power, of their own weakness, or, most often, of their harsh climate and landscape. If American literature is characterized by a frontier spirit of risk, adventure, and ultimate triumph, Canadian literature centers on mere survival. There is an element of complicity in this national habit of mind, an immature willingness to accept the role of victim rather than struggle for self-respect and self-definition.

It is this theme that she dramatizes in *Surfacing,* one of the most discussed of recent Canadian novels. The unnamed narrator, her lover Joe, and a married couple leave the city and go to her family's cabin on a remote lake in Quebec, where her botanist father has disappeared. The heroine pretends that she has left her husband and child; in fact she is running away from a failed love affair and an abortion. She is a failed artist; Joe is a failed potter; the married couple, who seem so emancipated and well-adjusted, are failed rebels, their social attitudes borrowed from the Americans they profess to hate. All of them are numbed by the self-deceptions imposed by their society, incapable of true feeling.

The heroine has been estranged from her parents for a long time. At the cabin, surrounded by the symbols and artifacts of her childhood, she begins to look for clues to the nature and identity of her parents, embarking on a long journey—an archetypal quest—back to her beginnings. As she becomes increasingly obsessed with her search for identity, she becomes progressively estranged from her companions, haunted by apparitions of her lost child, aware of the indigenous spirits of the place. Diving in the lake, she finds the bloated body of her father, curled like a fetus; he had fallen into the water while photographing mysterious Indian paintings on the cliffs and, weighed down by his cameras, had drowned.

The heroine's submergence in the lake, among the floating deadheads of memory, and the encounter with her dead father-child, are traumatic. She enters a period of shamanistic possession (which her companions regard as a nervous breakdown). For a time she lives naked and alone on an island in the lake, stripped of all falsities, surviving like a wild animal on roots and mushrooms, in the presence of gods. Then, as George Woodcock has put it, "the delirium that in a dual sense is panic passes away from her. Then she returns to a consciousness beyond beasthood, beyond the animistic world of primitives and children." She has surfaced after a necessary submergence, and is ready to return to the city, and to live more honestly and bravely: "This above all, to refuse to be a victim. . . . give up the belief that I am powerless."

In terms of the argument introduced in *Survival,* the novel bitterly attacks the attitude to nature that Margaret Atwood identifies as American—that nature is to be struggled with, destroyed, and defeated. Nor, she suggests, is passive survival enough; human beings are part of nature, and cannot live fully and wholly until they have been initiated into it, and learned to respect its mysteries. Francine du Plessix Gray wrote that "the female religious vision" presented in this novel "marks the surfacing . . . of a future tradition of religious quest in women's novels," and that its "singular prophetic power makes it, for me, one of the most important novels of the twentieth century."

Some of Margaret Atwood's readers were disappointed when her next novel, *Lady Oracle* (1976), turned out to be closer in weight to *The Edible Woman* than to *Surfacing.* Its narrator is Joan Foster, best known as the colorless wife of a radical graduate student named Arthur. What Arthur doesn't know is that she is also Louisa K. Delacourt, prolific author of costume Gothics like "Terror at Redmond Grange," a generous sample of which is provided. Nor does Arthur know about her obese and miserable adolescence, or her poet lover, Royal Porcupine, who stages avant-garde exhibitions featuring run-over animals. This intricate secret life threatens to emerge when Joan, experimenting with automatic writing, produces "Lady Oracle," a volume of inspirational poesy in the manner of Rod McKuen. Condemned to fame and threatened with exposure, she fakes her own death and escapes to Italy, where she settles down to write a wholly honest account of her life. Katha Pollitt complained that the book left too many questions unanswered, and that instead of the myths and archetypes of *Surfacing,* it offers "the stock figures and pat insights of a certain kind of popular feminist-oriented fiction." However, Doris Grumbach found "many kinds of pleasure in the book," and thought that the physical manifestations of love had "not been captured so well and so humorously since Mary McCarthy's early novels and short stories and the recent work of Alison Lurie."

You Are Happy is another collection of poems, ranging "from the personal to the mythological, from the negative aspects of love to the joyously positive ones." Helen Vendler wrote that Margaret Atwood here attempts "a new indifference and a new humility in her chronicle of the relations between man and woman," in "poems so neat and silent that they move in space like an invisible invasion, descend, pierce the mind and leave a wound." The author herself says that she finds herself in these later poems "less concerned about the relationships between men and women than I am about those among women (grand-mother/mother/daughter, sisters) and those be-tween cultures."

Margaret Atwood's *Selected Poems* appeared in Canada in 1976 and in the United States in 1978. Carolyn Forche in her review wrote that "for this poet, the snow that settles overnight, silently, obscuring even the little that was known of the land itself is the flesh that has settled on her bones. The civilization she confronts is one that has tacked itself to a continent: an overlay of roads taped to the earth. . . . [Her] *Selected Poems* (1966-1974) is a chronicle of her preoccu-pation with surfaces. She rubs windows into the ice, takes a razor to the glass, etches her poems across mirrors and 'a bland madness of snows.' Her language carves—and the instrument used is tonally blunt, laconic, as incisive as suits the purpose. What emerges is a bare outline: runner tracks on the ice, white scars on the body, an engraving on the shell of things, attempting to suggest the pattern of some internal order." Carolyn Forche finds it "lamentable that her voice so often indulges itself, meandering through these narratives with a stridency and submission to intention that preclude any power of language itself to issue its mysteries"; it is therefore interesting to learn that Margaret At-wood thinks of poetry as an aural activity rather than a "rational" one. In an interview in the New York *Times Book Review* (May 21, 1978), she told Joyce Carol Oates that her poems "usu-ally begin with words or phrases which appeal more because of their sound than their meaning, and the movement and phrasing of a poem are very important to me. I tend to conceal rhymes by placing them in the middle of lines, and to avoid immediate alliteration and assonance in favor of echoes placed later in the poems. For me, every poem has a texture of sound which is at least as important to me as the 'argument.' "

According to Paul Delany, Margaret Atwood has "brought into sharp focus for Canadian lit-erary intellectuals the problem of their country's cultural identity in the seventies. . . . [Atwood] has thereby outsoared her previous status as a widely respected younger poet . . . she has become the literary standard-bearer of a resur-gence of nativism and nationalism in Canada, eclipsing established Canadian writers of more cosmopolitan outlook such as Mordecai Richler, Leonard Cohen and Irving Layton." Jay Walz

has called her the "impatient, talented leader of a coterie of Canadian writers."

The author was assistant professor of English literature at York University, Toronto, in 1971-1972, and writer-in-residence at the University of Toronto in 1972-1973. In 1971-1973 she was an editor and member of the board of directors at the House of Anansi Press, Toronto. She is a member of the Canadian Civil Liberties Associa-tion (and was a member of its board of directors in 1973-1975). Her awards include the E.J. Pratt Medal (1961), the President's Medal from the University of Western Ontario (1966), and *Po-etry*'s Bess Hokin Prize (1974), and she has two honorary doctorates. She calls herself a "pessi-mistic pantheist" in religion, a William Mor-risite in politics. She has been married, and now lives on a farm near Alliston, Ontario, with the novelist Graeme Gibson, by whom she has a daughter. The parody of a gothic romance in *Lady Oracle* suggests an interest in popular art forms, and there was further evidence of this in 1978 when Margaret Atwood tried her hand at a comic strip in the Toronto *Globe's* magazine *Weekend*—an autobiographical sequence in a style reminiscent of Jules Feiffer.

PRINCIPAL WORKS: *Poetry*—Double Persephone, 1961; The Circle Game, 1964 (revised 1966); Talismans for Children, 1965; Kaleidoscopes: Baroque, 1965; Speeches for Doctor Frankenstein, 1966; The Animals in That Country, 1968; (with others) Five Modern Canadian Poets, edited by Eli Mandel, 1970; The Journals of Susanna Moodie, 1970; Procedures for Underground, 1970; Power Politics, 1971; You Are Happy, 1974; Selected Poems, 1976. *Novels*—The Edible Woman, 1969; Surfacing, 1972; Lady Oracle, 1976. *Criticism*—Survival: A Thematic Guide to Canadian Litera-ture, 1972.

ABOUT: Contemporary Authors 49-52, 1975; Gibson, G. (ed.) Eleven Canadian Novelists, 1973; Kostash, M. (and others) Her Own Woman, 1975; Vinson, J. (ed.) Contempo-rary Novelists, 1976; Vinson, J. (ed.) Contemporary Poetry, 1975; Who's Who in America, 1976-1977; Woodcock, G. (ed.) Poets and Critics, 1974. *Periodicals*—Atlantic April 1973; Canadian Forum February 1970; January 1973; November-December 1974; Canadian Literature Spring 1974, Winter 1976; Commonweal September 7, 1973; Na-tion June 28, 1971; March 19, 1973; New York Times April 24, 1973; New York Times Book Review October 18, 1970; March 4 1973; August 12, 1973; April 6, 1975; September 26, 1976; May 21, 1978; Poetry July 1972; Publishers Weekly August 23, 1976; Time October 26, 1970; Times Literary Supplement October 26, 1973; July 15, 1977.

AUROBINDO, SRI. *See* GHOSE, AUROBIN-DO

AUSTIN, J(OHN) L(ANGSHAW) (March 26, 1911–February 8, 1960), English philosopher, was born in Lancaster, the son of Geoffrey Lang-shaw Austin, an architect, and the former Mary Bowes-Wilson. He was educated at Shrewsbury

Ramsey & Muspratt, Oxford

J. L. AUSTIN

early age of forty-eight, he was the most powerful single influence on the development of philosophy at Oxford. This was partly because of the originality and critical rigor of his lectures, which were always well attended. The journalist Ved Mehta, who sat in on one of them, describes Austin as "a tall and thin man, a sort of parody on the dessicated don. His face suggested an osprey. His voice was flat and metallic, and seemed to be stuck on a note of disillusion." And after describing how Austin dismantled a passage from the work of another philosopher, A. J. Ayer, Mehta goes on: "I was told that Austin performed like this day after day, mocking, ridiculing, caricaturing, exaggerating, never flagging in his work of demolition, while the sceptical undergraduates watched, amused and bemused, for behind the performance—the legend—there was the voice of distilled intelligence. Austin's trenchant remarks on philosophers would make a small volume of cherished quotations."

Even more than in his formal lectures, however, Austin's influence was transmitted through his regular Saturday morning discussions, attended by many of the Oxford philosophers (with some conspicuous exceptions like Isaiah Berlin, who found Austin's approach uncongenial). Austin distrusted the sort of traditional philosophy in which general questions were asked and great speculative metaphysical systems built up. He believed that many of the traditional problems of philosophy might disappear if the words, idioms, and metaphors in which these problems are discussed were properly defined and understood. Austin did not maintain that elucidation of the forms and concepts of ordinary language should be the last word in philosophical arguments, but he did insist that "it *is* the *first* word," and said that "we are using a sharpened awareness of words to sharpen our perception of, though not as the final arbiter of, the phenomena."

What Austin and his associates did was systematically to collect a list of words and phrases applicable to a given area of discourse, and then to make up "stories" in which these words and phrases were used in such a way as to illustrate differences—sometimes very subtle differences—in their meaning and common usage. Austin believed, according to the *McGraw-Hill Encyclopedia,* that "any distinction which has become fixed in everyday language, surviving centuries of use and succeeding in the competition with alternative distinctions, may well be thought to point toward some real distinction in experience." The "stories" would be discussed, and, if there was sufficient agreement, the group

School and was a classical scholar at Balliol College, Oxford University, where he won the Caisford Prize (1931) and obtained a first-class honors degree in *literae humaniores* (1933). Austin spent the whole of his professional life at Oxford. He was a fellow of All Souls College from 1933 to 1935, and then went to Magdalen College as a fellow and tutor in philosophy.

During the 1930s, Austin established himself as an authority on the philosophy of Leibniz and did a great deal of work on Greek philosophers, especially Aristotle. His own thought during this period was largely critical, and when World War II began in 1939 he had published only a single philosophical paper. Austin served in the Intelligence Corps during the war. Beginning in 1944 he was attached to Supreme Headquarters, Allied Expeditionary Forces. According to the *McGraw-Hill Encyclopedia of World Biography,* Austin "displayed an extraordinary talent for analyzing and relating vast numbers of facts about the capacities of the enemy. . . . prior to the Normandy invasion he was the chief organizer of all the intelligence available to the Allied armies," and "he more than anybody else was responsible for the life-saving accuracy of the D-Day intelligence." Austin reached the rank of lieutenant-colonel, and in 1945, in recognition of his services, he was made an Officer of the Order of the British Empire and an Officer of the (American) Legion of Merit, and was awarded the Croix de Guerre.

Austin resumed his post at Magdalen in 1946, and in 1952 became White's Professor of Moral Philosophy—a university rather than a college appointment. In fact, from the time of his return to Oxford until his death from cancer at the

would prepare an account of the meaning of the terms used and their interrelationships. It was hoped that in this way the group, and its successors, would eventually arrive at a sort of supergrammar, a catalog of all the possible functions of words.

Austin regarded this painstaking cooperative technique as one which might make a science of philosophy, but admitted that "like most sciences, it is an art." He himself brought to the technique he had developed an ingenuity, subtlety, and wit unmatched by any of his associates. Austin's critics (and sometimes Austin himself) seem divided as to whether "ordinary language philosophy" is "really philosophy," or preparation for a systematic and empirical study of language. J. O. Urmson states that Austin had no philosophy; only a technique which "lent itself rather to a set of quite independent inquiries."

Austin once said: "I had to decide early on whether I was going to write books or to teach people how to do philosophy usefully," but G. J. Warnock has remarked that Austin was unhappy that he had written so little. In fact, his books were all published posthumously, and only seven papers appeared during his lifetime. All of these are included in *Philosophical Papers* (1961), along with three others, one of which had been given as a broadcast talk and the other two read to learned societies. In the first paper, "Are There *A Priori* Concepts?," Austin begins quite typically by saying that "I still do not understand what the question before us *means*: and since I hold, nevertheless, no strong views as to how it should be answered, it seems best to occupy myself primarily in discussing its meaning." This discussion reveals his mistrust of the terminology of other philosophers—he thought that many philosophical controversies are needlessly protracted and indecisive because philosophers who think they are disputing about a matter of substance are often doing no more than using a term in different ways. In the second paper, "The Meaning of a Word," he argues that this is in fact "a spurious phrase"; there can be no general answer to the question "what is the meaning of a word?", only specific answers about the meaning of specific words.

Austin was also interested in the assumptions underlying the traditional problem of free will, and two of the papers in this book are important contributions to the philosphical study of human action, responsibility, and freedom. In the first, "A Plea for Excuses," Austin maintains that it is a mistake to suppose that actions may be divided neatly into the free and the unfree. For example, an action may be performed "carelessly," "inadvertently," "absent-mindedly," or

"aimlessly," and these are all significantly different, and clearly relevant to the traditional problem of the freedom of the will. Austin goes on to suggest that if philosophers thoroughly investigated these and other such notions, they might completely dispose of the question of free will— a claim which few other philosophers have been able to accept. Similarly, in "Ifs and Cans," he tackles some traditional difficulties in ethics by examining the peculiarities of the verb *can*, and goes on to express the hope that if the joint labors of philosophers, grammarians, and other students of language could result in the birth of a "true and comprehensive *science of language*," then we might rid ourselves of one more traditional philosophical problem "in the only way we ever can get rid of philosophy, by kicking it upstairs."

Much of Austin's work is destructively critical of traditional philosophy, but he made a number of original and positive contributions, including the theory to which he devoted his radio talk on "Performative Utterances" (1956). In this he opposes the extreme application of the verification principle of the logical positivists, according to which a statement which is neither analytic nor empirically verifiable may be dismissed as meaningless. Austin points out that many utterances do not set out to be statements of fact in this sense, but are intended to influence people in this way or that, or simply to let off steam. Or they may be what he calls "performative utterances"— like the "I do" in the marriage ceremony, and the similar "I bequeath," "I christen," "I name"—in which to say the words is to perform the action.

Austin elaborated on this idea when in 1955 he delivered the William James lectures at Harvard University. The lectures, later revised and published as *How To Do Things With Words* (1962), are largely devoted to a consideration of the way in which to *say* something is to *do* something. In any speech-act he distinguishes the locutionary element—what is actually said—from two others. The illocutionary element is the kind of speech-act the sentence performs, such as warning or ordering. And the perlocutionary element is its effect—whether the warning is heeded or the order obeyed. Some philosophers regard the doctrine of illocutionary forms as Austin's principle positive contribution.

Another set of lectures, first given at Oxford in 1947 and much revised in subsequent years, was published posthumously as *Sense and Sensibilia* (1962), after being reconstructed from Austin's manuscript notes by G. J. Warnock, the Oxford philosopher who became custodian of his papers. In these lectures Austin attacks the phenomenalist theory of perception advanced by the logical positivist philosophers, according to which the significant content of all beliefs about the material world must be interpretable in terms of private, individual, sense-experiences, so that to talk of an objective external world is not to talk of the unobservable causes of our sensations, but is to talk of these sensations, actual and possible, themselves.

The work is in fact mainly a criticism of A. J. Ayer's second book, *The Foundations of Empirical Knowledge* (1940). But again Austin approaches the subject through language, arguing that much philosophical discussion of such problems as perception was condemned to inconclusiveness or irrelevance because it was conducted in technical language—"sense datum," "material object," etc.—which, having been used uncritically, had obscured vital differences in the phenomena which were the subject of conflicting theories. Once again Austin insists on the need for the sort of "new beginning" that he believed might proceed from a critical examination of such crucial words as "look," "appear," "seem," "illusion," and "delusion." Thus his detailed examination of the systematic ambiguity of the word "real" shows the lack of clarity in the claim that what we perceive is not reality but appearance.

Austin's services were much in demand as an administrator: in 1949-1950 he was junior proctor of his university, and in 1952 he was appointed a delegate of the Oxford University Press, serving as chairman of its finance committee from 1957 until his death. He was elected a Fellow of the British Academy in 1958, and was president of the Aristotelian Society in 1956-57. In 1958 he went as a visiting professor to the University of California at Berkeley, and by 1960 he had decided to leave Oxford, where he had already reached the summit of his influence, and move permanently to Berkeley, an intention which was cut short by his death. His immense influence on the philosophy of English-speaking countries is universally acknowledged. Williams and Montefiore write that "the truth is that in spirit and tone, it is not so much the Wittgensteinian mode that prevails in contemporary British writing, as that which earlier we identified with Austin and Moore: it is a certain academic dryness, a deliberate rejection of the literary and dramatic, that is for the most part the style of this philosophy. Critics who are oppressed by these characteristics tend to ascribe them to some sort of intellectual cowardice, a failure of nerve in face of the more challenging aspects of experience."

G. J. Warnock has said: "Like Wittgenstein, Austin was a genius, but Wittgenstein fitted the popular picture of a genius. Austin, unfortunately, did not. Nevertheless, he did succeed in haunting most of the philosophers in England, and to his colleagues it seemed that his terrifying intelligence was never at rest. Many of them used to wake up in the night with a vision of the stringy, wiry Austin standing over their pillow like a bird of prey. Their daylight hours were no better. They would write some philosophical sentences and then read them over as Austin might, in an expressionless, frigid voice, and their blood would run cold." H.L.A. Hart in the *Dictionary of National Biography* agrees that Austin "was often reserved in manner and on occasion formidable," but goes on: "He had great native courtesy, gaiety, and charm, and much manifest benevolence, especially for his pupils." P. F. Strawson thought him "one of the kindest men in the university."

Austin's deep distrust of general ideas and systematic theories and his dedication instead to detailed and piecemeal inquiry and exhaustive researches into language tended during his lifetime to be taken as authoritative, though critics of linguistic philosophy found this resistance to general theorizing particularly objectionable. However, P. F. Strawson, one of the British philosophers who along with Sir Isaiah Berlin, Sir Karl Popper, and Stuart Hampshire has been associated with a revival of interest in general ideas and systematic philosophy, has suggested that "the pull of generality was felt by Austin himself, who before he died, was beginning to work out a general classificatory theory of acts of linguistic communication."

PRINCIPAL WORKS: Philosophical Papers, 1961; How To Do Things With Words, 1962; Sense and Sensibilia, 1962. *As Translator*—Foundations of Arithmetic, by G. Frege, 1955.

ABOUT: Ayer, A.J. The Central Questions of Philosophy, 1973; Ayer, A.J. The Problem of Knowledge, 1956; Dictionary of National Biography 1951-1960; Edwards, P. (ed.) The Encyclopedia of Philosophy, 1967; Fann, K.T. (ed.) Symposium on J.L. Austin, 1969; Graham, A. J.L. Austin: A Critique of Ordinary Language Philosophy, 1978; McGraw-Hill Encyclopedia of World Biography, 1973; Magee, B. (ed.) Modern British Philosophy, 1971; Mehta, V. Fly and the Fly-Bottle: Encounters With English Intellectuals, 1963; O'Connor, D.J. (ed.) A Critical History of Western Philosophy, 1964; Warnock, G.J. English Philosophy Since 1900, 1958; Who Was Who, 1951-1960; Williams, B. and Montefiore, A. (eds.) British Analytical Philosophy, 1968. *Periodicals*—Analysis April 1967; British Academy Proceedings 1963; Illustrated London News February 20, 1960; Listener April 7, 1960; December 10, 1970; January 14, 1971; Mind April 1961, January 1964, April 1965, January 1966, January 1968, July 1969, January 1971, July 1971, April 1972, October 1972, January 1974; Philosophical Quarterly April 1964, April 1966, July 1968, October 1975; Philosophy April 1964, January 1974; Times Literary Supplement February 9, 1962.

*AWOONOR, KOFI (NYIDEVU) ("AWOONOR-WILLIAMS, GEORGE")

(March 13, 1935–), Ghanaian poet, novelist, critic, translator, and dramatist, was born in the village of Wheta, in the Volta Region of Ghana (then the Gold Coast), the son of Atsu and Kosiwo Awoonor. His father is a trader and storekeeper; his mother's family farms around the inland village where he was born. The poet grew up mainly in the old coastal town of Keta, situated on a narrow sandbar between the Atlantic and the Keta Lagoon. This was a thriving fishing and trading post, as well as an early center of German administration and missionary activity. The Ewe people, to whom Awoonor belongs, are split among three African nations as a result of successive boundary changes following the breakup of the old German colony of Togo in 1914-1918.

KOFI AWOONOR

Thomas Bennett

In the manner of colonial times, Kofi Awoonor was brought up under the name George Awoonor-Williams and so published his early poems, but he resumed his African personal names in the late 1960s. He was educated at Keta Presbyterian School, Zion College, and Achimota School before going on to the University College of Ghana in 1957, the year of Ghana's independence. In 1959 he was awarded the Gurrey Prize for the best original work in English. After completing his degree in English literature, Awoonor became a lecturer in English at the University of Ghana (1960-1963), then a research fellow and lecturer in African literature at the University's Institute of African Studies. It was at this time that he began his research into the traditional culture and poetry of the Ewe. He also published several early poems of his own in the Ghanaian literary journal *Okyeame* (Spokesman), of which he was an editor, as well as in the rising African journals *Black Orpheus* (Ibadan, Nigeria), and *Transition* (Kampala, Uganda). Awoonor later founded and was chairman of the Ghana Playhouse, where he wrote, acted in, and produced plays for the stage, radio, and television.

Awoonor left the Institute in 1964 to become managing director of the newly-founded Ghana Film Industry Corporation and during the next two years was actively engaged in film production. He also made several journeys with government delegations, visiting Russia and Eastern Europe, Cuba, Indonesia, Japan, Ceylon, and China. Although Awoonor was critical of several aspects of the Nkrumah regime in Ghana, he probably saw its overthrow in February 1966 as a retrograde step and a fresh opening for imperialism in Africa. In September 1967 he re-

*a wōō′ nor

signed from the Film Corporation and went to University College, London, as a Longman Fellow. In 1968 he received the M.A. degree there in English language and modern linguistics before moving to the University of California as a visiting scholar. After a year in California, Awoonor went to the Stony Brook campus of the State University of New York, where he earned his Ph.D. in 1972 with a thesis on the influence of the oral tradition on selected literatures of Africa. At Stony Brook he became successively assistant professor, associate professor (from 1974), and chairman of the department of comparative literature. He also held visiting professorships at Queens College, New York, and at the University of Texas (1972-1973).

The prevailing note in all Awoonor's work is one of grief; it is the deep cry of the dirge that he learned from his Ewe poetic masters: "Let us return to the magic hour of our birth/ for which we mourn" (*This Earth, My Brother*). His has been a leading voice in that generation of Africans who have sought to rediscover the injured roots trampled upon or overturned by their predecessors in their haste to adopt Western ways. And *Rediscovery* is the title given by Awoonor to his first collection of poems, published in 1964. From his earliest work, Awoonor has steadily addressed himself to this task, and from the first he has apprenticed himself far more to the rich poetic and musical tradition of the Ewe than to such exotic influences—important to his African contemporaries—as Eliot, Pound, Hopkins, Yeats, or Dylan Thomas.

We may see the evidence of this apprenticeship in such early poems as "Songs of Sorrow" and "Song of War," published by Awoonor in 1961. These are more or less transliterations into English of funeral dirges and battle songs of the great Ewe dirge poet Vinoko Akpalu, who flourished among the Anlo Ewe in the years between 1920 and 1960 and whose songs were widely known in Eweland. A slightly later poem, "My God of Songs Was Ill," published in *Night of My Blood,* shows how completely Awoonor places himself within the tradition of the Ewe poet, or *heno*:

> Go and tell them that I crossed the river
> While the canoes were still empty
> And the boatmen had gone away.
> My god of songs was ill
> And I was taking him to be cured.
> When I went the fetish priest was away
> So I waited outside the hut
> My god of songs was groaning
> Crying. . . .

Most Ewe poets believe that all their songs are gifts from a god of songs, or *hadzivodoo,* who sings within them and must be cared for and propitiated. The fetish hut here might be the very one that stood within his maternal grandfather's compound in Wheta when Awoonor was a boy, and when the household constantly resounded to the songs of the gods Yewe and Da worshipped by his family. Paul Theroux, in his review of *Rediscovery,* pointed out how certain words and phrases recur from poem to poem in Awoonor's work, and said that he "extends his rhythms by extending the lines into other poems. . . . He is not 'writing the same thing'. . . . but enlarging his theme by repetition in depth." This technique, as Gerald Moore has said, is a common feature of the Ewe dirge tradition.

Far from concealing this debt to tradition, Awoonor has written extensively about it in his major critical work, *The Breast of the Earth.* He has also collected and translated the work of the three greatest living Ewe dirge singers in his book *Guardians of the Sacred Word,* which includes a valuable critical introduction. Awoonor had found this distinctive path towards an English poetic style of his own when the majority of his West African poetic contemporaries were borrowing heavily from the alien poets they had encountered at university. This independence of approach must owe something not only to the strength of Ewe poetic tradition, but to the presence within Awoonor's maternal household of so many practitioners of it, including his own mother, aunt, and uncle. Although the whole tendency of his missionary education, started at the age of four, was to turn him away

from his heritage, it remained inviolable within his memory and sensibility. The desire to become an artist thus automatically guided him into the role of the *heno,* "the guiding spirit, the voice and expression of the force . . . of the word which is still a sacred phenomenon, at all levels of human conduct" (*Guardians*).

The short lyrics collected in *Rediscovery* show Awoonor already adopting this prophetic role, calling on his generation to recognize its abandonment of the ways and shrines of their people in a headlong, indiscriminate pursuit of modernity. Here, the grief of the traditional *heno* for human mortality, the poverty and loneliness of old age, becomes a threnody for the impending death of a whole culture: "On the sacred hearth with the neglected embers / The cock offering has fluttered and gone" ("The Years Behind"). But Awoonor does not seek for cultural purity. He welcomes a blending of what is vital in the new alien influences with the mainstream that comes to him from the past:

> My life's song falls low among alien peoples
> Whose songs are mingled with mine;
> And the tuneful reverberate is reborn
> Reborn on the tabernacle of my father's temple.

> (from "The Years Behind")

Alongside these more public utterances run the poet's private anguish and his struggle to apprehend the nature and meaning of rebirth. The sudden death of his cousin and childhood companion Dede at the age of twelve was followed by funeral ceremonies from which he was excluded, and then by a visionary moment of reunion with her when she rose like a mermaid from the sea to join him. The death of his brother from typhoid a few years later redoubled the urgency of this search for a more meaningful resurrection than that accessible to him in Christian teaching, a resurrection which would be a rebirth into the tribe and a reunion with his origins:

> The funeral drums beat from the eastern houses.
> Where lies our salvation? You asked.
> We do not need any salvation.
> Does our end lie on this beginning shore?

> . . . . And in the season of search
> When discoverers land on far off shores
> And the others who took the big boats return
> We shall find our salvation here on the
>   shore, asleep.

> (from "Salvation")

41

This theme is central to Awoonor's deeply moving and original novel, *This Earth, My Brother,* which is intimately linked with the development of his poetry. The contrasted styles in the novel's linked chapters, which juxtapose realistic prose narrative with intense poetic reverie, reflect the divided sensibility of the hero, Amamu, who has abandoned the communal culture of Keta for a life of individual aggrandisement as a lawyer in Accra. Only at the end of the book, when he walks out of that meaningless life and returns like a pilgrim to the "beginning shore" of his homeland, does he become reunited with himself and his visionary companion Dede. Emile Snyder wrote in *Saturday Review* that this novel, "fusing the language of history and of poetry, represents one of the most significant attempts in any literature today to reconcile man with himself."

In the same year as Awoonor's first novel appeared *Night of My Blood,* in which several short poems, republished from *Rediscovery,* were placed with a number of new poems, longer and more ambitious than anything he had attempted before. Here Awoonor fully achieves the scope of the Ewe dirge, with its developing theme constantly coiling back on itself to gather up the choral refrain, in such key poems as "I Heard a Bird Cry" and "Night of My Blood." The former, written before Awoonor left Ghana in September 1967, in his most passionate appeal to his generation:

> But who will release the prisoners?
> And break the poor-man's hunger?
> I was there when they released the prisoners.
> I heard tears of anguish
> And the agony of the hungry.
> Let the earth keep silent
> And let us hear!
>
> The deaf ran home that day
> Shaking their heads.
>
> Hush! I heard a bird cry.

Night of My Blood announced Awoonor's full maturity as a poet and was followed shortly afterwards by works establishing him as a critic of great power and originality. *The Breast of the Earth* (1975) is the most important contribution yet made to establishing the relationship between African oral tradition and the new literatures created in languages derived from Europe. It is a work of great scope, written with sustained passion, insight, and wit. Its observations on African oral culture in general are reinforced by Awoonor's detailed study of Ewe poetic tradition in the anthology *Guardians of the Sacred Word,* published in the previous year.

Nineteen seventy-three brought the publication of a new book of poems, *Ride Me, Memory,* deriving their inspiration mainly from Awoonor's American experience. Here the predominant mood is satirical and ironic, corresponding to the bitter sarcasm of the *halo* or drum of abuse in Ewe tradition. The poet has fallen among strangers and sings of his exile:

> This is the parched grass's desire
> for those grey waters
> of rivers
> far from the graveyards of the clan
> the festival music fled,
> low moans of slaughtered rams
> tramplings of strangers
> inherited the earth.
> And I, Awoonor, the dropsied
> seed from ancient loins
> wander here where there is winter
> birdsong and a yellow moon.
>
> ("To Those Gone Ahead")

Even the reference here to the poet by his own name is a device more familiar in Ewe than English poetry. Likewise the deep yearning towards the natal earth, the earth where his birth cord lies buried and which lies ever waiting to regather him, is a theme characteristic not only of Awoonor's poetry but of the whole tradition which he serves and enriches. No full-length study of Awoonor's extensive and important work had appeared down to 1978, though it has been very widely read and has been translated into French, Russian, Chinese, and German.

Awoonor, a short, stocky man, is married and has three children. Associates at Stony Brook remember him for his "reserved British ways" which "melted at parties among trusted friends or when reciting his poetry in the tonal chant of his native Ewe dialect." One of his students said of him that "he had the ability to make people seem special. He could take the basic disenfranchised Long Island student and make him feel human." While teaching at Stony Brook, Awoonor lived with relatives in the Bronx but often took visiting friends to fish on Long Island Sound and on one occasion borrowed a colleague's backyard to slaughter and roast an entire goat.

In 1975 Awoonor returned to Ghana as senior lecturer in the English department at Cape Coast University. In November 1975, amid rumors of an abortive coup against the regime of Colonel I. K. Acheampong, Awoonor was arrested and held for many months without charge or trial. In February 1976 the poets Louis Simpson and Stanley Kunitz visited the Ghanaian Embassy in Washington to express concern over the arrest and were told that Awoonor had been detained "for questions of national security." Amnesty International, P.E.N., and the Union of Writers of the African Peoples all involved themselves in the case, pressing for information about the reasons for Awoonor's arrest and the conditions under which he was being held. At last, in August 1976, Awoonor was brought to trial, charged with harboring the ringleader of an alleged anti-government plot. Awoonor agreed that he had given lodging to Brigadier Kojo Kattah, a friend from childhood, but said he did not know that Kattah was wanted by the authorities. He was found guilty, and in October 1976, after almost a year in custody, was sentenced to twelve months' imprisonment. This sentence appears to have been no more than a gesture, however, since Awoonor was pardoned immediately after it was delivered, and released. He returned to Cape Coast University, where he is now an assistant professor of English. He lists his interests as jazz, tennis, African herbal medicine, and politics.

PRINCIPAL WORKS: *Poetry*—Rediscovery, 1964; Night of My Blood, 1971; Ride Me, Memory, 1973. *Novels*—This Earth, My Brother, 1971. *Plays*—Ancestral Power *and* Lament *in* Pieterse, C. (ed.) Short African Plays, 1972. *Nonfiction*—(as editor, with G. Adali-Mortty) Messages: Poems From Ghana, 1970; (as translator and editor) Guardians of the Sacred Word, 1974; The Breast of the Earth, 1975.

ABOUT: Awoonor, K. The Breast of the Earth, 1975; Beier, U. (ed.) Introduction to African Literature, 1967; Contemporary Authors 29-32 1st revision, 1978; Duerden, D. and Pieterse, C. African Writers Talking, 1972; Herdeck, D.E. African Authors, 1974; International Who's Who, 1978-79; Lindfors, B. and others (eds.) Palaver, 1972; Moore, G. (ed.) African Literature and the Universities, 1965; Moore, G. The Chosen Tongue, 1969; Vinson, J. (ed.) Contemporary Poets, 1975; Wästberg, P. (ed.) The Writer in Modern Africa, 1967 (Uppsala); Who's Who in African Literature, 1972; Zell, H.M. and Silver, H. (eds.) A Reader's Guide to African Literature, 1972. *Periodicals*—Africa January 1968; Ariel January 1975; Benin Review June 1974; Matchbox (Amnesty International) Summer 1976; New York Review of Books September 23, 1971; New York Times February 22, 1976; February 25, 1976; August 25, 1976; September 6, 1976; New Yorker November 13, 1971; Okike April 1975; Times (London) October 23, 1976; Transition 41 1972.

*AYCKBOURN, ALAN (April 12, 1939–), English dramatist, was born in London, the son of Horace Ayckbourn, a musician, and the former Irene Maud Worley, whose parents had been music hall entertainers. He was uprooted from the suburbs by his mother's remarriage to a bank manager, and the rest of his childhood

*āk' bôrn

ALAN AYCKBOURN

Alec Russell

was spent in following his stepfather from branch to branch of his bank through a succession of temporary homes in Sussex. He was educated at Haileybury School and the Imperial Service College (1952-1957).

Ayckbourn's mother was a writer and magazine editor, and his first ambition was to be a journalist. At Haileybury, this was displaced by acting, thanks largely to a French teacher who directed the school's plays and took them on foreign tours. Through this connection, when he left school, Ayckbourn became an assistant stage manager with Donald Wolfit's touring company. Then, through what he calls the "Mafia of stage managers," he moved on to the Connaught Theatre in Worthing and the Leatherhead Theatre in Surrey, where he started acting, and finally to the Library Theatre, Scarborough, in Yorkshire. There—as a leading actor, playwright, and later as director of productions—he has remained, apart from the years between 1965 and 1969 when he worked as a drama producer for the British Broadcasting Corporation in Leeds.

The Library Theatre, Scarborough, and its companion theatre, the Victoria, Stoke-on-Trent, were the creation of the late Stephen Joseph, a theatre-in-the-round pioneer with a puritanical faith in artistic self-sufficiency. Joseph liked the simplest possible staging, and he liked his actors to write. "I owe it to him," says Ayckbourn, "that he first threw the gauntlet down and said, 'Write a play.'" Under the pseudonym of Roland Allen, he began writing farces aimed at the seaside vacation crowds who made up the bulk of the Scarborough audiences. From the start, therefore, he was producing material for a familiar group of actors working within given stage limitations towards a production on a fixed date. With his actor's loathing of minor roles, it was very much to Ayckbourn's taste to write small-cast plays; and he says that Scarborough gave him a "marvellous training in the economies of writing: how to make a crowd out of a few people, how to use off-stage characters, and how to be ingenious in the theatre."

One early product of this discipline was *Mr. Whatnot,* a farce, much of it mimed, about a dumb piano-tuner disrupting a stately home when he falls in love with the owner's daughter. Of its original in-the-round production in 1963, Stephen Joseph said: "It was written for performance without scenery and changed scene frequently, including several journeys—across acres of garden, down dark passages and even in speedy vehicles along the highway. Real properties, phoney properties and mime properties all enriched the scene, ranging from a genuine steering wheel to represent the car, to an entirely imaginary piano that was played furiously. Here actors found unending opportunities for creating the substance of reality from the merest hint of its existence." The result reminded more than one reviewer of a Marx Brothers movie.

Mr. Whatnot reached London in 1964, but it was not until 1967, with the West End production of *Relatively Speaking,* that Ayckbourn really arrived. The piece was an instant and long-running success, widely translated and produced all over the world, and it catapulted the author into the role he has since prolifically sustained as Britian's most popular entertainment playwright.

Relatively Speaking is a four-character piece about a young man who turns up at the country house where his girlfriend's ex-lover lives with his wife, believing the couple to be his girl's parents; the girl herself then arrives to wind up the affair and retrieve her letters. Out of this slender situation the whole play is unraveled. There are no supporting characters, no subplot, no larger meaning. The action is strictly a game of misunderstandings played between two innocents and two people who are in the know. The characters are as flat as cardboard and whatever personal traits they do possess are introduced only in so far as they assist the game. Anyone less guileless than Greg, the boy, would have smelt a rat; anyone less polite than the upper-middle-class couple would have asked him who he was. Ayckbourn judges to a hair's breadth how much obtuseness the spectator will tolerate and the latest moment for saving the play from caving in. The effect, as the *Times* said, is like watching "a house of cards, always just escaping

collapse." By applying a maximum inventiveness to the minimum of material and allowing himself nothing to fall back on, Ayckbourn achieves a kind of cosmic escapology in which the laughs arise from seeing the guilty parties breaking out of a series of apparently hopeless situations. "It does not hurt," Ayckbourn says, "to write one well-made play. *Relatively* was a mechanical piece, but nobody can ruin it. It just goes on ticking to the end like a clock."

In *How the Other Half Loves* (1969) he set himself another seemingly impossible task: a piece of elaborate sexual intrigue with all the characters sharing the same stage environment. The set consists of two living rooms merged together, one grand and the other not. We are at home both with the Fosters (company director level) and the Philipses (skilled employee level). Each of the husbands is attempting an affair with the other's wife, and each hits on the same alibi, which involves asking a hapless couple called the Featherstones to dinner. In actual time, the dinners take place on two successive evenings; in stage time, they take place simultaneously, so that when Featherstone is deluged with stew at one address he is drenched by a leaky ceiling at the other. The ingenuity of this scene drew well-earned critical comparisons with Goldoni's *The Servant of Two Masters.*

Critics of Ayckbourn at this point in his career were apt to patronize him as a virtuoso technician with nothing to say. John Russell Taylor, writing in 1971, sets the tone: "If Ayckbourn looks certain to remain, at best, one of our most reliable light entertainers, there are, after all, many worse things to be." Ayckbourn began to challenge this view in his next comedy, *Time and Time Again* (1971), which invited laughter as much for its acknowledgment of pain as for its mechanical manipulation of incident. The play exhibits his usual skills—for example, a love scene in which one of the participants is also taking part in a cricket match—and its main character, Leonard, is another passive agent of farcical chaos (like Greg and Mr. Featherstone); but this time the audience is also invited to ask why Leonard's wife turned him out, why he ditched his teaching job to become a gardener. And after building him up as a sympathetic ironist and giving him two acts to demolish his boorishly self-important brother-in-law, the play finally turns against him, revealing him, as one reviewer wrote, as "a walking compendium of rueful malice—and a quite poignant illustration of that deep reluctant indifference to everything and everybody which lays waste more of us than is usually realised."

If some reviewers were disconcerted by this

unexpectedly chilly turn of events, they were again won over by *Absurd Person Singular* (1972), whose comedy is a direct expression of pain and desperation. Another six-character piece, it consists of three successive Christmas parties given by each of the couples in turn. It moves from the suburban house of the Hopcrofts (lower middle class), to the apartment of the Jacksons (professional middle class), and finally to the residence of the Brewster-Wrights (upper middle class). Financial greed rather than sex is the class solvent in this case, and the play works like a seesaw, charting the rise of the go-getting Sidney Hopcroft at the expense of his architect and bank manager acquaintances, until the curtain falls on a scene of enforced jollity in which he is literally calling the tune.

Technically, Ayckbourn's masterstroke in this play is to use a series of kitchen settings and evoke the parties with off-stage voices (including the growls of a ferocious dog standing guard over the kitchen door). The comedy stems partly from social anxieties, like the Hopcrofts' panic when they run out of tonic water. But the real caliber of the piece appears in its farcical second act, which the mutely desperate Eva Jackson spends in vain attempts to kill herself while the others busy themselves with cleaning the cooker in which she means to gas herself, repairing the ceiling light by which she considers hanging herself, and using her suicide notes as scribbling paper.

A long-running success in Europe and North America, this play was followed by *The Norman Conquests* (1974), which marks Ayckbourn's current limit in technical wizardry and won both the *Evening Standard* award and the *Plays and Players* award as the best new play of the year. Norman is an unenthusiastic assistant librarian (elsewhere described as "a gigolo trapped in a haystack") and the action follows his incompetent efforts to seduce two girls during a weekend family house-party. This situation would seem hardly to contain enough material for one comedy, but *The Norman Conquests* consists of three full-length plays, all covering roughly the same stretch of time and running in any order. Each is set in a different part of the premises: *Table Manners* in the dining room, *Living Together* in the living room, and *Round and Round the Garden* in the open air. Sometimes the plays diverge in time, sometimes they coincide, so that the sighting of a flying tin of cookies in one play will be overheard off-stage in another, and Norman's threat to frighten the invalid mother will be matched elsewhere by the news that he has gone upstairs vowing to wrap the telephone wire around her neck.

Norman is another of Ayckbourn's wild cards —the one character who tries to act out his escapist fantasies in a family who are immobilized by a middle-class sense of responsibility. They comprise the fullest gallery of what Ayckbourn calls the "English limbo characters" who populate all his plays. Drawn, as he acknowledges, from recollections of his Southern childhood, they represent a once wealthy class now fallen on lean times and substituting petty rules of conduct for the moral imperatives of the past. *The Norman Conquests* bristles with characters who have sublimated their passions into keeping the house tidy or devising board games and who set tremendous store by place settings for dinner and how the coffee is poured out. The naked miseries of *Absurd Person Singular* are absent from the trilogy, but by demonstrating how easily primary human feelings can be stifled by pointless daily routines, its comedy exploits a vein of insistent melancholy.

If Ayckbourn is to be believed, all these huge commercial successes were written with only his Scarborough audience in mind. The title of a nonexistent play is announced, and in the last week before rehearsal "I just go hell for leather and write the play in about three days." *The Norman Conquests* took him ten days. "I can't work any other way. Unless I see my play announced I won't write it." He departed once from this method in the Wodehouse musical, *Jeeves,* which he and Andrew Lloyd-Webber wrote for a London opening and which ranked as the West End's most spectacular flop of 1975. Ayckbourn has not repeated this experiment, and his subsequent work has all originated in Scarborough.

Absent Friends (1975), another party comedy, presents a reunion of six old friends, one of whom has lost his fiancée in a drowning accident. The point is that the condoling guests care very little for each other and least of all for the bereaved Colin—another of Ayckbourn's thick-skinned innocents, blithely unaware of the effect he has on other people. The humor derives from the sight of private hostilities and unhappiness breaking into an occasion when everyone is supposed to be on his best behavior. "That it fails to raise many laughs," wrote Irving Wardle, "is due to Ayckbourn's own lack of sympathy with everyone on stage." *Confusions* (1976) consists of five playlets featuring human communication as a switchboard permanently blocked with crossed lines, and displaying the usual combination of anguish and ingenious craftsmanship.

In 1977 Ayckbourn received the cultural imprimatur of a production at the National Theatre in London, where *Bedroom Farce* explored the havoc that can be wrought by two thick-skinned and self-absorbed people whose marriage is (not suprisingly) on the rocks. Trevor and Susannah peddle their misery around the three-bedroom set, leaving generous helpings of it with Trevor's parents, his married exgirlfriend, and a couple of friends who are trying to give a party. Brilliantly directed by the author in collaboration with Peter Hall, the play seemed to some reviewers less wintry than other recent pieces, and an unsurpassed demonstration of Ayckbourn's talent as a virtuoso technician and comic gymnast.

It is the other Ayckbourn, whom Irving Wardle calls "the bleak anatomist of the marriage trap," who predominates in *Just Between Ourselves* (1977), a study of two marriages in which feeling has been stifled by the petty rules of suburban etiquette. "It is beginning to look," Wardle wrote, "as though the entire Ayckbourn opus amounts to a single Balzacian epic on the fears and miseries of English suburbia." But Victoria Radin complained that "Ayckbourn's minimalist, self-consciously elegant form creates only collections of behaviour, and omits the messy bits that might blur the outline but bear some resemblance to people. If his play tells of a whimper, it tells it by a whimper." A third new Ayckbourn play reached London in 1978– *Ten Times Table,* in which the suppressed hostilities within a small-town committee find an outlet in the historical pageant they meet to prepare.

Ayckbourn, for the time being, has staked out his ground. He is not, for all the sharpness of his social observation, a conscious social critic (though this has been claimed for him). Nor, for all his comic gifts, is he a witty writer. Unlike his wise-cracking transatlantic opposite number, Neil Simon, he builds his laughs entirely from the response of character to situation. At the same time (like Simon) he is showing increasing dissatisfaction with simply turning out funny plays, and his recent work shows a consistent intention to achieve comedy through more restrained means than the farcical set-pieces which he has come to find too easy. The disadvantage for the audience is that where Ayckbourn's lightweight early entertainments conveyed a strong sense of affection even for his most obnoxious characters, in his later and more serious plays the affection seems increasingly to have been displaced by contempt.

Ayckbourn's masters include Congreve, Oscar Wilde, and Chekhov; he says that he was influenced when he began to write by Terence Rattigan and Noel Coward, and later, quite heavily, by Pinter. Brian Connell has described Ayckbourn as "a burly man, with thinning brown hair, hazel eyes, and a mobile, actor's face," who "speaks jerkily and vehemently, like one of his characters." The author was married in 1959 to Christine Roland, and has two sons. His recreations include music, cricket, and astronomy. In *Contemporary Authors,* Ayckbourn compares himself with the passive Leonard in *Time and Time Again* and says: "I have never made any decisions, they have always been made for me. . . . I could look back on my life and say I planned it that way, but I didn't plan to be an actor, nor a director, nor a writer."

PRINCIPAL PUBLISHED WORKS: Relatively Speaking, 1968; Countdown *in* Mixed Doubles, 1970; Ernie's Incredible Illucinations (for children) *in* Durband, A. (ed.) Playbill One, 1969 (and published separately in 1977); How the Other Half Loves, 1972; Time and Time Again, 1973; Absurd Person Singular, 1974; The Norman Conquests, 1975; Absent Friends, 1975; Confusions, 1977; Three Plays (Bedroom Farce, Absurd Person Singular, Absent Friends), 1977; Just Between Ourselves, 1978.

ABOUT: Contemporary Authors 21-24 1st revision, 1977; International Who's Who, 1977-78; Joseph, S. Theatre in the Round, 1967; Taylor, J.R. The Second Wave, 1971; Vinson, J. (ed.) Contemporary Dramatists, 1977; Who's Who, 1977; Who's Who in the Theatre, 1977. *Periodicals* —Daily Telegraph Magazine February 21, 1975; Encounter December 1974; Guardian August 7, 1970; August 14, 1974; New York Times October 11, 1974; October 20, 1974; Observer February 13, 1977; Plays and Players September 1975; Sunday Times Magazine (London) February 20, 1977; Times (London) January 5, 1976.

BAILEY, PAUL (February 16, 1937–), English novelist and critic, was born in Battersea, London, the son of Arthur Oswald Bailey, a garbage collector, and the former Helen Burgess. Apart from some years of wartime evacuation as a very small child, Bailey grew up in Battersea, "in a house familiar to devotees of working-class fiction: two-storeyed, with an outside lavatory." All the same, "proud of their children, proud of their small, tidy homes, the neighbours of my childhood formed a genuine community." Bailey himself was known as "The Professor" or "Bleeding Macbeth" because "I read more books than were good for me and had ideas 'out of my class.' " From 1948 to 1953 Bailey attended Sir Walter St. John's Grammar School in Battersea, and thereafter until 1956 trained at the Central School of Speech and Drama in London. From 1956 to 1963 he worked as an actor, appearing on television, in repertory at Stratford, at the Royal Court Theatre, and elsewhere. He had no great success in the theatre, however, and was employed as a salesman at Harrods, the famous London department store, when he settled down seriously to write.

His first novel, *At the Jerusalem,* appeared in

PAUL BAILEY

Mark Gerson, courtesy Jonathan Cape

1967 and was an immediate success. An account of life in a home for elderly women, it is a simple tale, lucidly and tersely written, yet with subtle overtones and undertones. It is told in three parts, of which the first describes Mrs. Gadny's arrival at the Jerusalem, a dreary converted workhouse. She is a shy, simple, gentle woman, distressed by the false jollity and lack of privacy at the Jerusalem, and in the second section she recalls the circumstances that brought her there —the death of her beloved daughter, the subsequent brief stay with her stepson and his wife, who had not wanted her. And there are memories of her marriage to a man who had never come to terms with the death of his first wife, and happier recollections of her early days as a housemaid. The third part of the novel is an account of Mrs. Gadny's rejection of the world in which she finds herself, her proud descent into madness, culminating in a memorable outburst at another inmate's ninetieth birthday party. In the end she is sent to "another home in Kent"— a mental hospital.

The novel seemed to some critics superior to Muriel Spark's *Memento Mori,* which is also set partly in an old people's home—more truthful and compassionate, and without her "fey delight in the macabre." Malcolm Page in *Contemporary Novelists* thought that Bailey sometimes sneers "too patly" at values and behavior he despises, but praised the way in which the novel makes the reader face—"in a way that is often painful and frightening—the pathos, vulgarity and indignity of being old, and the way in which the elderly are treated." *At the Jerusalem* was for many critics the outstanding new English novel of 1967, and it brought Bailey the Somerset

Maugham Award and an award from the Arts Council. Peter Buckman called it "pitilessly good."

Trespasses, which followed three years later, is a more experimental novel, composed in short passages which, though they are not chronologically arranged, convey the story of a man's life and his most important relationships, and what he thinks of as his manifold trespasses against others. We are given an account of Ralph Hicks's childhood and schooldays, his grief at his father's death and his resentment of his possessive mother, his courtship of and marriage to a woman who commits suicide, and his own subsequent breakdown. Hicks himself is the main narrator, but other first-person passages are attributed to his homosexual friend Bernard Proctor, or to Hicks's mother. And the entries in this balance sheet of "trespasses" are arranged in sections headed "Her" (about Hicks's wife), "Him" (about Proctor), "Then," "Here," and so on. *Trespasses* is about indignity, sadness, and mess, but at the end of it Hicks can hope— thanks to the complex exercise in recollection and self-understanding that the novel comprises —to "become a man."

Because of its technique, the novel has a somewhat staccato quality, but this is much modified by Bailey's great skill in the placing of apparently random elements and effects, and his actor's ear for dialogue; Derwent May praised his "avoidance of gimmickry or pretentiousness in his very original experimental technique." An American critic, Joseph Catinella, wrote that Bailey had failed to dramatize alienation "in significant human terms," and Derwent May similarly thought that he had given us Hicks's problems "without a complete sense of the person." But, May went on, "the treatment of his minor characters is vigorous and thorough and their message clear: understanding and tolerance given in a degree which approaches love . . . is the only answer." Here, as in his first novel, Bailey's "principal strength lies in the way he causes a small world to radiate wider and graver implications." It seemed to May that *Trespasses* "both moves and excites," establishing Bailey in "a firm place among the best of the younger [English] novelists."

A Distant Likeness (1973) is more melodramatic. Inspector Frank White is cracking up under several kinds of pressure, including the desertion of his wife and the frustration of interrogating a wife-murderer who won't speak ("the distant likeness" is between the murderer and the policeman). When in a moment of near-breakdown White hands the psychopath a knife, hinting that he might kill himself, a warder is nearly murdered instead, and White's career ends. The technique resembles that of *Trespasses* —short, cryptic passages from White's "stream-of-consciousness," flickering between past and present and from place to place, character to character.

When the silent prisoner is given a notebook and pencil, he writes only: "No more words." A reviewer in the *Times Literary Supplement* thought this "a significant and intended reference . . . to a problem which is patently besetting Mr. Bailey, though he may himself see it less as a dilemma than as a challenge: how to say as much as possible in an ever-contracting space." But where in *Trespasses* Bailey's "terse, allusive technique seemed justified by the situation . . . here, with the extension of this method to the point where reading becomes a case of mere 'puzzling out,' it seems wilful and precious." Other critics disagreed, though few seemed to like this novel as well as its two predecessors (an exception was Francis Wyndham, who found it "entirely satisfying as a work of art"). Malcolm Page wrote that "at first glance the novel is irritatingly slight and allusive, but ultimately Bailey brings the reader into unusually intimate contact with Inspector White." One incident found unconvincing by all the critics who noted it is White's homosexual encounter between interrogations—this is a theme that Bailey has attempted in each of his novels, though never with much success.

The narrator of *Peter Smart's Confessions* (1977) is an unsuccesful actor whose latest attempt at suicide has failed—he swallowed an insufficient quantity of the tranquilizers intended for his wife's Pekingese. His confessions make it perfectly clear why Peter Smart might wish to be almost anywhere but in this world, but are rescued from tedium and self-pity by his wry humor and his talent for mimicry (of art journalism, romantic fiction, and the purpler kind of verse drama, as well as of the speech habits of his colleagues and associates). Jane Miller commented that "the history . . . [Smart] writes for himself is composed of the sounds of voices, obsessional, lunatic and monotonous ones, often wonderfully funny and idiosyncratic, and always impervious to his own. . . . At its best . . . this is a black and serious comedy, of a kind Paul Bailey has always known how to write, and which here is able to inform and explain a complex account of a life."

Besides the four novels, Bailey has also written a film version (not yet used) of *At the Jerusalem,* and several plays. One of these, *A Worthy Guest,* was produced in Newcastle in 1973 and in London the following year. *At Cousin Harry's,*

an early radio play, was broadcast in 1964. Bailey works as a reader for Jonathan Cape, who publish his novels, and has done a good deal of broadcasting and book reviewing. He lives in London and is unmarried. He received an award from the Author's Club in 1970, and the E.M. Forster Award (U.S.) in 1974, and is one of the most respected English novelists of his generation. Bailey admires the fiction of Italo Svevo and Henry Green but thinks that he has been more inspired by painting than by literature, and mentions Rembrandt, Masaccio, Piero della Francesca, and Giotto. He lists his recreations as tennis, reading, and opera, and says that he values his anonymity. He is a socialist and an agnostic.

PRINCIPAL WORKS: At the Jerusalem, 1967; Trespasses, 1970; A Distant Likeness, 1973; Peter Smart's Confessions, 1977.

ABOUT: Contemporary Authors 21-24 1st revision, 1977; Ross, A. (ed.) Living in London, 1974; Vinson, J. (ed.) Contemporary Novelists, 1976. *Periodicals*—Books and Bookmen August 1967; Contemporary Literature Summer 1972; Library Journal April 15, 1967; Listener July 6, 1967; April 30, 1970; June 14, 1973; London Magazine October 1967; July-August 1970; New Statesman June 2, 1967; April 17, 1970; New York Times Book Review May 21, 1967; Observer May 28, 1967; Saturday Review March 6, 1971; Spectator April 18, 1970; Stand 2 1967; 2 1968; Times Literary Supplement June 8, 1967; April 16, 1970; June 29, 1973; May 27, 1977.

BAINBRIDGE, BERYL (MARGARET) (November 21, 1934–), English novelist and dramatist, was born in Liverpool, Lancashire, and grew up in a small, overcrowded house near the sea, about twelve miles from the city. She is the daughter of Richard Bainbridge, a salesman, and the former Winifred Baines. In an interview she said: "My mother was lower middle class, my father was working class. I found visiting his family very interesting, but my mother always made clear that her family came from higher up in the class structure and that she looked down on his people." Elsewhere she has said that "there were very few people who got on well with my mother," but that she herself adored her; she remembers her "buying me little exercise books and sharpening my pencils for me. I was always writing. Reading was encouraged when I was younger, but as I grew older it was frowned upon."

The household was dominated by the moods of her father, "a bad-tempered, morose man" who nevertheless "used to read me Dickens as a child and tell me stories." He had not always been a salesman, but according to his own account had dealt in diamonds, shipping, cotton, and property before bankruptcy had ended his

BERYL BAINBRIDGE

high-flying days: "He was a proud man and a failure according to his own lights"; also, rather surprisingly, a lifelong socialist. Periods when he was cheerful and amusing would end without warning in an outburst of violent rage, followed by sullen withdrawal. It is not surprising that Beryl Bainbridge's "earliest memories are of fear and anxiety." By the time she was ten, "hearing his voice raised against my mother, I was in the habit of hurling myself through the scullery door and leaping on his back" to bring him "crashing to the floor." At about this time she began a secret notebook in which she plotted her father's murder. He died when she was seventeen, and afterwards she began to see him in a different light. "My mother then turned on me as I grew up and began to have other interests of my own. Then I would remember back into the past and be able to understand better what his point of view had been at that time."

Her books have drawn a great deal on her memories of this household and of other members of her family: "All my childhood was spent with people who were disappointed. They'd married the wrong person, failed in business, been manipulated by others." She says that her father, hating the present, "faced backwards. In doing so, he created within me so strong a nostalgia for time gone that I have never been able to appreciate the present or look to the future. ... Continually I try to write it down, this sense of family life. For it seems to me that the funny noises we make with our mouths, or the squiggles that we put on paper, are only for ourselves to hear, to prove there's someone there."

Beryl Bainbridge was educated at Merchant Taylors', a well-known private school in Liver-

pool, and at a ballet school in Tring, Hertfordshire. Presumably she herself paid for this expensive education, since she was a child actress. Her career seems to have begun when she was in her early teens, and between then and 1960 she performed on radio and in a series of repertory companies in Liverpool, Windsor, Salisbury, London, and Dundee. She was married in 1955 to Austin Davies, a painter, and had three children—a son and two daughters—before the marriage ended in 1959.

She began to write seriously when her first baby interrupted her stage career. A newspaper story about two schoolgirls who had committed murder gave her the idea for her first novel, which she completed and began to send around to London publishers in the late 1950s. One of them wrote to inform her that her central characters were "repulsive beyond belief" and that one scene in the book was "too indecent and unpleasant even for these lax days." The manuscript was subsequently misplaced by another publisher, and it was not until 1972, when she had already published two other books, that this first novel appeared as *Harriet Says.* . . . It tells the story of two schoolgirls growing up in a seaside town near Liverpool just after World War II. The nameless narrator is a plump and unattractive girl of thirteen, somewhat in the power of the cool and sophisticated Harriet. Pursuing "experience," they interest themselves in Mr. Biggs, a middle-aged neighbor whom they call the Tsar. They follow him about, spy on his marital lovemaking, write about him in their secret diaries. Biggs notices their interest and guiltily reciprocates it. It is the fat narrator who eventually seduces him and who, with a weapon provided by Harriet, kills Mrs. Biggs when she arrives home too early one evening.

Some reviewers found the novel pointless—a muted and arbitrary "exercise in perversity." This was a minority opinion, however, Gail Godwin thought that the book "certainly ranks in content with the more celebrated thrillers of corrupt childhood, but it has literary and psychological virtues as well. The architecture of its narrative would have satisfied Poe: every incident advances the design. The language, though simple, often has the effect of poetry." And it seemed to a reviewer in the *Times Literary Supplement* that "until the horror of the last pages, the two girls are very funny in their seriousness of purpose. . . . But when all their nonsense becomes real, it is very alarmingly real to us: the way in which Harriet now emerges as devilish follows logically everything she has already been shown to be, though there was much comedy in that. The book is tightly written, full of spiky thoughts and unexpected pockets of exactly reproduced feeling. . . . It is a very good first/third novel indeed."

The first of Beryl Bainbridge's novels in order of publication was *A Weekend With Claud* (1967), in which a group of friends go to stay with another, an antique dealer in the country. A gunshot is heard and Shebah, an elderly Jewish woman, is slightly wounded. This incident, as Karl Miller says, "is told and retold by members of this circle of friends—Maggie, Shebah, the self-assured Victorian Norman, as he's nicknamed—and a sense of the separateness of each one of them is conveyed. . . . In this novel especially, the storytelling can be hard to follow, and the reader stumbles over a profusion of rare words that somehow seem doubtfully spelled. And yet none of this appears to matter very much, and the tactical successes are frequent and cherishable. In its best episodes, the book is wonderfully alert to the flow of feeling between the friends, to the accesses of hostility, to the bitter humor which envelopes its losses and departures."

Another Part of the Wood, which followed a year later, is a rather similar book, though longer and more densely constructed. George, who owns an estate in North Wales and is preoccupied with the sufferings of the world, is visited by friends—the pretentious Joseph, who is divorced; his small son; and his girlfriend Dotty, of whom he wishes to rid himself. The extreme and tragic incident which occurs in most of Beryl Bainbridge's novels is provided in this instance by the death of Joseph's son who, thanks to adult irresponsibility, takes a fatal dose of sleeping tablets. The author has explained that in her novels she is "committing to paper, for my own satisfaction, episodes that I have lived through. . . . I have used the device of accidental death because I feel that a book has to have a strong narrative line. One's own life, while being lived, seems to have no obvious plot and is therefore without tension."

The Dressmaker, called *The Secret Glass* in the United States, is equipped with an unaccidental and gruesome death, but otherwise draws more directly even than usual on her family memories of "people who were disappointed." It is set during World War II in Liverpool, where Rita, aged seventeen, lives in respectable but very dreary poverty with her two aunts. They are the dressmaker Nellie, whose narrow prudery and sense of martyrdom dominate the household, and Marge, "a foolish girl of fifty years of age" who had once been married and is potentially flighty. Rita falls in love with a sullen and illiterate young GI but alienates him when, responsive

to her conditioning, she tries to "improve" him. He turns his randy attention to Aunt Marge, who succumbs. This outrage against the sanctity of her wretched family is more than Nellie can bear, and the stage is set for a denouement which had for some reviewers an almost classical inevitability, though to others the horrors of this conclusion seemed "like a last-minute frill tacked onto a straitjacket." The *Guardian's* reviewer called the novel "a triumph of atmosphere and economy with pent thoughts and cramped emotions that whisper frantically on when the book is shut," and Karl Miller agreed that it was "a triumphant success. . . . A magnificent book."

In 1970 Beryl Bainbridge worked for a time as a cellar woman in a London wine-bottling plant where most of the workers were Italian immigrants. The firm's employees once went on an outing to Windsor, and this excursion provided the basis for *The Bottle Factory Outing,* winner of the *Guardian* fiction prize in 1974. The novel begins as farce and ends in macabre tragedy when Freda, the large and domineering English beauty who has organized the outing, is mysteriously killed (there are grounds for disbelieving the confession of Rossi, the lecherous factory manager). Freda's body, adorned with plastic tulips, is quietly disposed of in a sherry-cask. It is Freda's friend Brenda, the born loser, demoralized by politeness, who in the end seems best equipped as a survivor. Lorna Sage thought the book was really about how Freda's "full-bodied, banal, technicolour fantasies of culture and romance get worked out in sinister black and white. . . . The writing is done with unwavering concentration. . . . and though there is a kind of pity in the writing, there's a much stronger sense of sheer fixated curiosity." Jonathan Raban also thought that "Miss Bainbridge's prose style is so exactly attuned to the dislocated mental world of her characters that the novelist is able to pass herself off more as an eavesdropper than as an artificer." But it seemed to Raban that "this accuracy, control and perfect pitch" was achieved by Procrustean methods: "One might say that her characters are simply the sort of people who are untroubled by thoughts . . . who are capable of only the most vestigial feelings. . . . Or one might accuse Miss Bainbridge of depriving them of the right to think and feel in order to construct a world simple enough to be contained by that pure, lucid but underprivileged prose." *Sweet William* (1975) is a portrait of a charming, ambiguous, and destructive womanizer and of Ann, who has his child—one of those "deprived and exploited women" who, as Frank Kermode says, are probably the author's main interest: "Ann herself . . . [is] emancipated from her lower-middle-class background but without much change—a victim of sexual freedom rather than of sexual bondage." The novel has been filmed.

Anne Tyler has suggested that these early novels, skillful as they are, "required a peculiar kind of distancing: the reader felt a need to deny any connection with characters so extreme." This was not the case, she thought, with *A Quiet Life* (1976), "a combination of Beryl Bainbridge's two special strengths—her knack for depicting ingrown worlds (people entangled at close quarters, bitter and desperate, gnawing away at each other) and her ability to pounce on the startlingly comic underside of the most hopeless situation." Thus a girl threatening suicide pauses to comment on the large bosom of a passer-by; a man dying of a heart attack hears his wife worrying that his boots will ruin the carpet, and gives a little snicker. The man who dies is a bankrupt afraid that his wife has a lover; what kills him is the discovery that she spends her evenings reading romances at the local railroad station because "she can't stand being in the same room as him." And he receives this intolerable information from his seventeen-year-old son Alan, the novel's narrator, who in this way joins the ranks of Beryl Bainbridge's unpunished murderers—unpunished except by the dreadful narrowness of the existence to which they are condemned at birth. "The novel itself is quiet," wrote Julia O'Faolain, "a feat of concealed craft. It is hard to deal with semi-articulate people without either short-changing them or boring the reader, and it must have been harder still to tell the story through the consciousness of someone as fact-shy as Alan. Miss Bainbridge turns the disability into a tool. Alan's flinching apprehension speeds the pace and gives it a lifelike rhythm."

Edward Freeman in *Injury Time* (1977) invites a married couple to dinner at the house of his mistress Binny Mills, this risky project being a concession to Binny's wish to share in his social life. The evening is interrupted first by the arrival of Binny's friend Alma, hopelessly drunk, then by a party of bank robbers on the run, who hold the dinner guests as hostages and wickedly misuse them. The novel explores, as black comedy, the various responses of the various guests to their plight. The result had its admirers, but some reviewers were disappointed and to Katha Pollitt it read "like a trivializing of Miss Bainbridge's best work, almost like self-parody." It nevertheless brought her the 1977 Whitbread Award.

Frank Kermode, reviewing novels by Ruth Prawer Jhabvala, Nadine Gordimer, Philip Larkin, and Beryl Bainbridge, thought the latter "probably the most gifted of these novelists. . . . It is an odd and in a muted way fantastic talent, as is perhaps necessary in modern English writers who want to escape the rather stifling conditions of normal contemporary competence." Kermode suggests that the violence that ends so many of Beryl Bainbridge's novels "is little more than a gesture with which the disgust heaped up in the course of accumulating lacerating details, the pain of all the accurately depressing dialogue, is swept off the page. Though they are sometimes funny, and often very compassionate, Bainbridge's novels cannot really bear themselves." It bothers some critics that (as Michael Irwin puts it), her characters "are subject to a good deal of physical and emotional humiliation. . . . Having invented these sad beings the author punishes them with apparent relish." Irwin thought that she at times reveals "such shrewd sympathy that she is clearly capable of work of much greater scale and warmth. It would be interesting to see her attempt a more expansive project, even at some sacrifice of her characteristic wit and technical neatness."

Since then Beryl Bainbridge has attempted "a more expansive project," a historical fantasy called *Young Adolf* (1978), bringing it off with no sacrifice whatever of wit and neatness. She says that when she was eleven, at the end of World War II, she went with her school to see the unexpurgated films of the death camps at Belsen. This had "a profound effect" on her mind, and throughout her adolescence she read everything she could find on the death camps. Later, she tried but failed to write a book about the persecution of the Jews: "By this time, life—as my father would have phrased it—had put the boot in and I had fewer feelings." Her interest was revived by a visit to Israel in 1977 and when she came home she started to read Robert Payne's biography of Adolf Hitler. There she learned of the possibility that Hitler might have visited England as a young man—might indeed have lived for a time in Liverpool, the city whose character and recent past obsess her. Further researches confirmed that Hitler's half-brother Alois had settled in Liverpool in 1910, working as a waiter and razor salesman. He had married an Irish girl, Bridget, and had a son. In November 1912 Adolf Hitler arrived to visit them. He was twenty-three, "penniless, travelling with false papers, and on the run from being drafted into the Austrian army." The circumstances of this visit and Hitler's wretched state of mind were fully documented in Bridget's diary: "He had no friends, no money and no future. . . .

[Bridget] said his clothes were a disgrace and he lay on her sofa all day with his face turned to the wall." What intrigued Beryl Bainbridge was that history had so ignored the visit. She decided that her novel "had to deal with young Adolf in Liverpool and his involvement in such ludicrous and embarrassing situations that he would never, in the whole of his life, breathe a word of his visit to anyone."

The result was very warmly praised. The novel shows Hitler gradually acquiring his characteristic style. Someone gives him a brown shirt. He combs his hair over one eye to hide a cut and plans to grow a moustache. He steals a library book, lies, raves about racial purity. "Yet," according to Diane Johnson, "there is something likable about his continued hope for his own small life in the face of a world that despises him, there is something dignified in his self-regard, something commonplace enough in his powerlessness and capacity for self-deception. In England, catastrophe attends him, he is confused, wretched, isolated, absurd." After five months, his half-brother buys him a ticket back to Germany. He is to go to Munich, where Alois's landlord, Mr. Meyer, has some political contacts "that could prove useful to Adolf." They put him on the train and Meyer remarks: "It is a pity he will never amount to anything." Diane Johnson wrote that the novel is not "a dramatization of known events—it is an invention of another kind, a feat of imagination and craft, without definition. Whatever the real facts of Hitler's life, we believe this account in part because of its manner, detailed and confident, and because it does not insist too stridently in foreshadowing the later reality. . . . The novel's time is told so absorbingly, and with such authority, that we lose our power to hold the future in mind." Young Adolf, "depressed, hungry, pitiful, driven to expedients, is very like a character in a novel by Beryl Bainbridge"; and like all her novels, this one is "a mosaic of personal interpretations" by characters who misinterpret, misunderstand, or see too little. "When the characters seem comic to the reader, it is because they seem comic to each other, not to the author, who is virtually invisible in all her work." Similarly, "by being only partially perceived, the horror which underlies and threatens in all her narratives seems mere daily horror. The characters have no overview. Young Adolf is the author's "most ambitious treatment yet of the serious concern and conviction that underlie her comedy."

There was an excellent reception for Beryl Bainbridge's first television play, Tiptoe Through the Tulips (1976), a portrait of a "dowdy, lifedented" woman, "variously ridiculous and tragic in her yearnings, variously silly and wise in her relationships, variously vulnerable and strong in her struggle to survive." Two more plays for television followed in 1977, The Warrior's Return and It's a Lovely Day Tomorrow. In 1971–1973 the author worked as a clerk for Gerald Duckworth Ltd., the firm that has published her more recent novels. She lists as her recreations "painting and sleeping," but her paintings find purchasers and are something more than a hobby. Naive in style, they are often "another expression of her interest in the past"—an interest whose ambivalence is evident in such paintings as one of Napoleon in splendid regalia, accompanied by a woman apparently unaware that she is quite naked.

Anna Quindlen, who interviewed Beryl Bainbridge for the New York Post, says that she "looks like a child—small, bony face, big eyes, bangs. . . . Her voice is childlike, breathy and small." The author said in 1976 that for more than a decade she had spent the bulk of her time sequestered at home with her children, writing late at night when they were in bed. She lives "a very insulated life. The only person I ever read is Graham Greene. . . . I don't read other people because I don't want to copy them. Because I was in the theatre, I tend to mimic." She lives in the Camden Town area of London, in a house full of Victorian bric-a-brac and old furniture, and says that she would "like to have lived in Victorian times. Women knew where they were then." She describes herself as a lapsed Catholic and a socialist.

PRINCIPAL WORKS: A Weekend With Claud, 1967; Another Part of the Wood, 1968; Harriet Said . . ., 1972; The Dressmaker, 1973 (U.S., The Secret Glass); The Bottle Factory Outing, 1974; Sweet William, 1975; A Quiet Life, 1976; Injury Time, 1977; Young Adolf, 1978.

ABOUT: Contemporary Authors 21–24 1st revision, 1977; Vinson, J. (ed.) Contemporary Novelists, 1976; Who's Who, 1978; Writers Directory, 1976–1978. Periodicals—Christian Science Monitor April 28, 1977; Encounter February 1975; National Observer April 9, 1977; New Republic May 24, 1975; March 25, 1978; New Review November 1977; New York Post March 27, 1975; New York Review of Books May 16, 1974; July 15, 1976; New York Times March 17, 1976; March 1, 1978; New York Times Book Review September 30, 1973; September 15, 1974; March 20, 1977; February 26, 1978; Observer October 27, 1974; October 5, 1975; Publishers Weekly March 15, 1976; Times (London) March 17, 1976; November 4, 1978; Times Literary Supplement October 6, 1972; November 1, 1974; October 3, 1975; October 8, 1976; September 30, 1977; November 3, 1978; December 1, 1978; Washington Post June 21, 1975.

BAKER, RUSSELL (WAYNE) (August 14, 1925–), American humorist, political commentator, and journalist, was born in Loudoun

United Press International

RUSSELL BAKER

County, Virginia, the son of Benjamin Rex Baker and the former Lucy Robinson. He served with the United States Naval Reserve in 1943-1945 and received his B.A. from Johns Hopkins University in Baltimore in 1947. Unlike John Updike, who set out to be a humorist and wound up as a novelist, Russell Baker the humorist decided at college that he wanted to write serious fiction: "The novel still had a certain cachet. Hemingway was still climbing into the ring with Tolstoy, and Norman Mailer was going to the mat for the sixth time with the Bitch Goddess." The gnomes of the publishing industry did not share Baker's conviction that he could write a better novel than *All the King's Men,* and in the end he was forced to conclude that they were right.

In 1947, meanwhile, when he left Johns Hopkins, a friend found him a job as a police reporter on the Baltimore *Sun.* After two years as a rewrite man, Baker was promoted to the hotel circuit, reporting after-dinner speeches and menus, until in 1952 the *Sun* made him its London correspondent. After a year there, Baker told Israel Shenker in an interview for the New York *Times Book Review,* he made "one of the basic errors of my life. I gave up one of the great jobs in journalism—London correspondent—to go to the White House. There's nothing worse than being a White House correspondent; it's the nadir. . . . I sit in the White House lobby with all these great names in journalism. Merriman Smith. Nobody's doing anything. People reading detective novels. Sleeping. Breathing. Then the big story comes: Eisenhower is taking a vacation. Off we go to Denver for eight weeks."

At the invitation of James Reston, Baker left the *Sun* in 1954 and joined the New York *Times,* hoping to make his escape from the White House. A few months later he was back in Washington, where he served a further seven-year stretch. In the 1960 Presidential campaign Baker followed the two main contestants alternately and claims that he preferred to cover Nixon. Shenker explains that "Baker came from the old tradition that when you covered a candidate you were supposed to hate him"; he couldn't hate Kennedy and this made him uneasy. "I'm a terrible softy on most politicians," Baker says, "and I'm terribly fond of them. They're among the few people in America who still work, live by their wits, have no job security, endure brutal hours, and show great ingenuity even when they're thieves."

Some of this feeling comes through in Baker's first book, *An American in Washington* (1961), a guide to the peculiar mores and customs of the capital, "dedicated to easing tensions between the United States of America and the District of Columbia." The visitor to Washington is told how to upstage a congressional committee, made aware of "the supreme importance of lunch in the city's social fabric," and advised on the importance of name-dropping and the art of obfuscation. One reviewer found the style difficult, "overcrowded with metaphors, and only fairly successful in its humor," but most readers were both instructed and entertained. Sidney Hyman wrote that "the needle hits its mark without touching any bones en route precisely because Mr. Baker appears to be such a staunch defender of the manners and morals he jabs."

All the same, by 1962 Baker was thoroughly bored and frustrated and thinking of moving back to the Baltimore *Sun.* To keep him, the *Times* agreed to let him write a regular column. The proposal was that he should take over "Topics of the Times," which ran on the editorial page and was written, Baker alleges, largely by copyboys. He had something different in mind. "My conception was to keep it casual," he says. "I'd always been very interested in what the *New Yorker* did in 'The Talk of the Town,' and I thought we could do it with advantage. . . . I wanted to keep sentences short and use Anglo-Saxon words. I wanted to say not 'utilize' but 'use.' The *Times* had imposed a silly Latinate sound on itself, and when my casual approach appeared . . . it was considered humor. If people tell you long enough you're writing humor, you begin to do it."

Russell Baker's "Observer" column appears in the New York *Times* opposite the editorial page each Friday, Sunday, and Tuesday, and ranges from sharp political satire to what he calls "a casual, convivial conversation with my reader." There is no store of prepared columns; each piece is written two days before it appears. "The whole point is not to think about it until you do it," he told Shenker. "In this line everything is spontaneity. If you thought consciously it would drive you crazy. . . . Once in a while I get an idea for a piece in advance, and it's almost always a bad piece. The important thing is to get it started. I'll often put a piece of paper in the typewriter and decide the paper doesn't want to be written on, so I'll throw it away and take another piece of paper. . . . When I finish the piece I take it home and listen to my wife reading it aloud to see if she picks up the rhythm. If she doesn't, I'll adjust it. My wife has a great common denominator ear."

The "Observer" column, which brings Baker twelve or thirteen hundred letters a year, has provided the makings of several books, beginning in 1964 with *No Cause for Panic.* "Baker's method is irony rather than whimsy, sarcasm rather than ranting," Gerald Gottlieb wrote in his review. "His material is the entire United States of America and his talent is of matching size. He is capable of parody, poetry, galloping fantasy, wistful poignancy, and the simple sneer. . . . Testy, inventive, sardonic, he polishes off his book with a glorious gabble of disdain for television. All is suffused with a realistic intelligence, a cold humor, and an even colder irony—not the least of which resides in the title."

There was a suitably grateful response to Baker's next collection, *All Things Considered* (1965), and a more serious press for *Our Next President* (1968). The latter is not drawn from the "Observer" column but is an account of the 1968 Presidential campaign and election written well before the event. Thanks to the vote-grabbing prowess of Governor Wallace, according to Baker's prognostications, neither President Johnson, campaigning for re-election with Robert Kennedy as running mate, nor the Lindsay-Tower opposition can secure a majority. The House is deadlocked and eventually installs as acting President the Vice-Presidential candidate of the party which controls the Senate—Robert Kennedy. Parts of the book appeared before publication in the *Saturday Evening Post,* and Pierre Salinger noted that one immediate effect had been "a study by the Senate of what it would do in such an eventuality. . . . The view emerged that the Senate would have to do just what Baker suggests." E.D. Canham in the *Christian Science Monitor* suggested that Baker "may have performed what some will regard as a great public service. . . . [He] may have prevented the chain of events he so vivaciously describes."

Poor Russell's Almanac, another collection of "Observer" pieces, was published in 1972 and generally admired. "At his best," R.Z. Sheppard wrote, "Baker fills his allotted space . . . with bizarre, often bleak fantasies about human foolishness. At his second best, he holds a funhouse mirror up to the nature of the consumer state. . . . [The author] is a fine stylist whose columns frequently unfurl to defend the language against corruption."

Baker was married to Miriam Nash in 1950 and has a daughter and two sons. He has described himself as looking like a novelist and/or "a decaying boy. Tall. Six foot two. A little like the young Gary Cooper, shy and charming. You can tell by looking at me that I used to be skinny, but now I am running to fat. Slouchy. Pot-bellied. Round-shouldered." As all this suggests, Baker, like most humorists, is inclined to melancholy. He says he "can contemplate the H-bomb with equanimity" because "mankind is probably incidental to the great scheme of things. . . . I'm more upset by signs of my own decay, and I go about life with a great deal of self-pity. The moments I feel good are when I'm not feeling depressed. . . . The metronomic quality of a columnist's life is like Chinese water torture. FridaySundayTuesday, FridaySundayTuesday. That stretches out in front of me till I'm sixty-five. I don't see how anybody with less zest for life than Joe Alsop keeps himself from going out of the window." He does not agree with those who say that humor is dying, though, and cites as examples to the contrary his friend Art Buchwald, Woody Allen, Donald Barthelme, Roger Angell, Art Hoppe, and "of course, Perelman."

PRINCIPAL WORKS: An American in Washington, 1961; No Cause for Panic, 1964; All Things Considered, 1965; Our Next President, 1968; Poor Russell's Almanac, 1972.

ABOUT: Who's Who in America, 1976-1977. *Periodicals—* Book Week May 16, 1965; April 7, 1968; Christian Science Monitor March 28, 1968; Editor and Publisher August 16, 1969; Esquire April 1976; New York Times Book Review March 17, 1968; January 30, 1972; Publishers Weekly January 24, 1972; Saturday Review November 14, 1964; Time January 17, 1972; November 6, 1972.

BASU, BUDDHADEV *See* BOSE, BUDDHADEVA

BAZIN, ANDRÉ (April 18, 1918–November 11, 1958), French film critic and theoretician, was born in Angers. His family moved to La Rochelle when he was five, and he received his early schooling there and later at Versailles. In 1938 he gained admission to the École Normale Supérieure de Saint-Cloud, studying literature with the intention of becoming a teacher. He

ANDRÉ BAZIN

passed his qualifying examination brilliantly but was prevented by his stammer from securing a teaching post. Instead he worked with Travail et Culture, an organization which encouraged cultural activities among workers.

In 1939 Bazin was drafted into the army. His friend Guy Leger has described the intense interest in the cinema they developed as an escape from the "phony war": "He was already attracted to the study of the true value of the cinematic image as well as to the historical and social aspects of cinema. ... What had been for me up to then only a pastime now began to appear, under the tutelage of André, a product of the age of the image, something that needed study if one was to savor its true flavor and understand its real significance; to make out its true language and to discover its objective laws."

During the war Bazin was a member of the Maison des lettres, an organization devoted to the welfare of young students. There he founded a film club, which showed movies banned by the German occupation forces for political reasons. At the end of the Occupation, he became the film reviewer of *Le Parisien Libéré*, developing a new approach to film criticism based on a conception of the cinema as an art form characterized by its capacity for objectivity. His writing was always remarkable for his ability to convey his ideas to a wide readership without condescension or over-simplification, and he became a regular contributor to *L'Écran Français, Esprit,* and *L'Observateur.* Bazin was also appointed director of cultural services at the Institut des Hautes Études Cinématographiques.

La Revue du Cinéma, which he established in 1947, became in 1950 *Les Cahiers du Cinéma,*

founded by Bazin with Jacques Doniol-Valcroze. This rapidly became the best known of serious French film magazines and one of the most influential in the world. Here Bazin gathered around himself a group of brilliant young critics who have demonstrated that the cinema is an art form worthy of the same kind of serious study as literature or the theatre. Notable among them were François Truffaut, Jean-Luc Godard, Eric Rohmer, Claude Chabrol, and Jacques Rivette, all of whom later turned to film-making, creating the French *nouvelle vague* (New Wave). Bazin is indisputably "the theoretician and spiritual father" of that explosion of creative energy in the cinema.

The techniques developed by the *nouvelle vague* directors grew out of Bazin's central preoccupation with the film image as an objective representation of reality. He distinguished between this use of the camera and films in which reality is deliberately manipulated or distorted by lighting, acting, or the montage technique, which he abominated. He excoriated the theatricality of Fritz Lang and other German Expressionist directors and maintained that directors like Sergei Eisenstein, the great exponent of montage, did not *show* an event but evoked it, an entirely different matter. Depth of focus was of prime importance in achieving the effect he sought, of bringing the spectators' responses to an image closer to their responses to reality. For similar reasons Bazin favored long takes, natural lighting, and naturalistic acting. The film-makers he most admired included Robert J. Flaherty, Erich von Stroheim, Carl Dreyer, the Italian Neo-realists, and, above all, Jean Renoir: such directors, he claimed, used the technical resources of the cinema not to subvert the image but to simplify and purify it.

However, despite the rigidly systematic nature of his theories, Bazin was catholic and generous in his response to actual films and film-makers. He praised Eisenstein's *Battleship Potemkin* for its realism, and found so much to admire in the work of that baroque expressionist Orson Welles that he wrote a book about him, in collaboration with Jean Cocteau. Bazin's eclecticism often led him to oppose the more dogmatic enthusiasms of his younger colleagues on *Les Cahiers du Cinéma.* A particular bone of contention was their ardent advocacy of the *auteur* theory, which argues that the worth of a film can be judged by the extent to which the director has imprinted his personality upon it. This theory, too narrowly interpreted, led to fulsome praise of many inferior but idiosyncratic Hollywood films.

Bazin's essays on montage, the *auteur* theory,

the ontology of the photographic image, eroticism in the movies, the work of various directors, and the nature of cinema in general were collected in the four volumes of *Qu'est-ce que le cinéma?* published between 1958 and 1965; a two-volume selection has been translated by Hugh Gray as *What Is Cinema?* These essays have been widely acclaimed for the breadth of Bazin's esthetic and historical learning, his sociological and psychological insight, and his talent for striking directly to the heart of an issue. Leo Braudy has called him "the most important contemporary film critic and theorist, constantly invoked, praised and argued with. . . . He has the great critic's gift of speaking about a specific work in terms that enlighten you not only about the work but also about the entire context of its art." Pauline Kael wrote that Bazin "has a genius for argument. His great gift is that the argument does not stay on the page; the reader fights back. . . . He gets involved in a running battle that is an extraordinary, elating experience. . . . *What Is Cinema?* joins that small company of books on movies that do not exploit interest in movies but intensify it."

Bazin also wrote a study of Vittorio De Sica and began one of Jean Renoir, which was unfinished when Bazin died. It was prepared for publication on the basis of his notes by François Truffaut, who considers it "the *best* book on the cinema, written by the *best* critic, about the *best* director," and asks the reader to consider it "unfinished in the manner of *A Day in the Country,* which is to say that it is sufficient to itself and, even in its fragmentary state, the finest portrait of Jean Renoir ever written." Two further collections of essays, one on the "cinema of cruelty" and the other on the cinema of the Occupation and the Resistance, were published in 1975, with introductions by Truffaut.

Bazin was a practicing Catholic with left-wing political views, much influenced by the existentialism of Jean-Paul Sartre. His convictions are seldom explicit in his work, but they are implicit there, as they were in his conduct. François Truffaut, who maintains that Bazin rescued him from delinquency and the reform school, virtually adopting him in 1948, says that subsequently "every pleasant thing that happened in my life, I owed to him."

Bazin lived in Nogent, just outside Paris, with his wife, his small son, and a host of strange pets, among them a chameleon, a parrot, squirrels, tortoises, and a crocodile. He suffered from a long illness, his health deteriorating daily until his death at the age of forty. According to Truffaut, "his chronic physical ill health was paralleled by his constantly surprising moral strength. He would borrow money aloud but lend it with a whisper. In his presence everything became simple, clear, and aboveboard. Since he considered it wicked to ride in a four-seater car all alone, he often picked up three other people at the bus stop in Nogent. . . . Whenever he and his wife and small son went away for a few weeks he would look about among his friends for a couple not as comfortably housed to whom he could lend his house, and then find someone to lend his car to."

Jean Renoir wrote: "I loved him because he belonged to the Middle Ages. . . . The frail figure of Bazin, withered with sickness, was like Pascal's 'thinking reed.' For me, he was the incarnation of one of the saints in the Cathedral of Chartres who project a luminous and magical vision through their stained-glass representations. . . . Clothes looked different on Bazin. They were the same clothes one saw on other people, but on him they lost their contemporary appearance. The anachronism of his outward appearance was neither a protest nor a revolt, nor, least of all, an esthetic declaration. It was involuntary. It identified him as an aristocrat before he opened his mouth, and he was not even aware of it. His little beret perfectly suited the frail figure of the reformer of the French cinema. I will never forget it."

PRINCIPAL WORKS IN ENGLISH TRANSLATION: What Is Cinema? vol. 1, 1967; vol. 2, 1971; Jean Renoir, translated by W. W. Halsey and William H. Simon, 1973; The Cinema of Cruelty, 1977; Orson Welles, translated by Jonathan Rosenbaum, 1978.

ABOUT: Andrew, D. André Bazin, 1978; Graham, P. The New Wave, 1967; Gray, H. *introductions to* two volumes of What Is Cinema?, 1967, 1971; Renoir, J. *forewords to* What Is Cinema?, 1967 *and to* Jean Renoir, 1973; Sarris, A. The Primal Screen, 1973; Sitney, P.A. Film Culture, 1971; Truffaut, F. Films in My Life, 1978 *and forewords to* What Is Cinema? vol. 2, 1971 *and to* Jean Renoir, 1973; Tudor, A. Theories of Film, 1970; Wollen, P. Signs and Meaning in the Cinema, 1969. *Periodicals*—Cahier du Cinéma January 1959; Film Quarterly Spring 1971, Summer 1972, Spring 1973; New Statesman December 1, 1967; New York Times Book Review September 10, 1967; September 9, 1973; Sight and Sound Summer-Autumn 1958-1959, Winter 1958-1959, Spring 1968, Winter 1974-1975; Yale Review October 1968.

BELL, DANIEL (May 10, 1919–), American sociologist, journalist, and editor, was born in New York City, the son of Benjamin Bolotsky and the former Anna Kaplan. He grew up on the Lower East Side where his parents, Polish-Jewish immigrants, worked in the garment industry. Bell's first language was Yiddish; he did not begin to learn English until he went to school at the age of six, but once started his progress in the language was astonishing. By the time he was

DANIEL BELL

thirteen he was reading Marx and Mill and expounding their theories as a soapbox orator for the Socialist party. He graduated from high school at sixteen and entered the City College of New York.

City College and the Depression both contributed to Bell's political education. His contemporaries at the college included the sociologists Seymour M. Lipset and Nathan Glazer, the critic Irving Howe, and the writer Irving Kristol. All were, like himself, of immigrant background, and all became part of the anti-Communist left. Bell joined the Young People's Socialist League although, skeptical of political dogma, he says that he thought of himself even then as a socialist with a small s.

Bell concentrated mainly on sociology and ancient history at City College. He received his B.S. in sociology in 1938 and went on to do graduate work at Columbia University. It was then, in 1939, that he began to write articles for the *New Leader.* He contributed regularly to the magazine until 1941 and then, exempted from military service on medical grounds, served as its managing editor until 1945, when for a short time he held the same post with the magazine *Common Sense.*

From 1945 to 1948 Bell was an instructor in the social sciences at the University of Chicago. In the latter year he was asked by *Fortune* magazine to write a memorandum on its coverage of labor-management relations, and performed this task so well that he was invited to join the magazine's staff as labor editor. Bell retained that post for ten years, and also served from 1952 to 1958 as a part-time lecturer in sociology at Columbia. *The New American Right* (1955), edited by Bell,

is a collection of essays by sociologists and historians on the postwar growth of conservative political groups; it was revised and expanded in 1963 as *The Radical Right.*

In 1956 Bell took an eighteen-month leave of absence from *Fortune* and went to Paris to organize two international academic seminars for the Congress for Cultural Freedom. He finally left *Fortune* in 1958 for a year at Stanford University as a fellow of the Center for Advanced Study in the Behavioral Sciences, and then returned to Columbia to teach sociology as an associate professor and to complete work for his doctorate, which he received in 1960. The same year he published *The End of Ideology,* the work which established his reputation as a writer and social thinker.

Bell was already well known as an immensely prolific journalist and reviewer—so prolific, indeed, as to inspire the suspicion that there might be more than one person writing under his name. *The End of Ideology* collects sixteen of his essays studying, among other subjects, the diminished militancy of the American labor movement, the bureaucratization of capitalism, the notion of the "power elite," the failure of American socialism and, in general, "the exhaustion of political ideas in the fifties." The book was widely recognized as an important contribution to the understanding of complex changes in contemporary society. Arthur Schlesinger Jr. wrote that "the fusion of journalistic skill and sociological knowledge" in Bell's work "makes him one of the most rewarding of contemporary commentators on American society." The book has become something of a classic in contemporary social thought.

However, Bell's evident metamorphosis from socialist to liberal moderate did not please his more radical associates. Dennis Wrong, the editor of *Dissent,* described Bell in that journal as a "centrist" who was "uncommonly knowledgeable" about the American economy but avuncular in his treatment of political and social issues. Bell, in reply, cheerfully accepted the "centrist" label but insisted, as he had in his book, that idealism was not enough: "A utopia has to specify *where* one wants to go, *how* to get there, the costs of the enterprise, and some realization of, and justification for, *who* is to pay."

The Reforming of General Education (1966) was the result of a year-long study of undergraduate education in relation to social change in the United States. Attacking the trend towards early specialization in undergraduate programs, Bell called for a return to the traditional values of a general education—for "four years of unforced maturation" and a renewed emphasis on humane studies. The shortening of under-graduate programs, he maintained, would pro-duce highly trained but intellectually im-poverished specialists. Bell also suggested that unrest on college campuses was partly attributa-ble to the early application of "organizational harness," and that liberal studies could moder-ate the "tension between technocratic and apocalyptic moods which wrack the university."

H. D. Aiken wrote that Bell's "pluralistic ac-count of methods of inquiry and learning is a pearl of greatest price. But when one looks close-ly, he continues to wear the stigmata of the ra-tionalist and the academician for whom knowing *about* things, rather than knowing them ever more appreciatively and discriminat-ingly, is the main achievement to be hoped for from the higher forms of learning." W. C. Booth thought that the book had "a few obvious faults," but called it "the most valuable study of the intellectual structure of college education since the Harvard *Redbook* and Chicago's *Idea and Practice of General Education.* . . . It de-serves to be studied, and built upon, and studied again. Everyone who is even remotely concerned with education must work his way through this lively, sane, learned argument if he is to earn the right to be heard, as it were, on the other side." The book brought Bell the Borden Medal of the American Council on Education.

Bell had become a full professor at Columbia in 1962 and was chairman of the sociology de-partment at Columbia College from 1959 to 1969. The uprising of Columbia students in 1968 provided him with direct experience of the "apocalyptic mood" described in *The Reforming of General Education*. Bell played an important role in the negotiations between students and administrators. He strongly disapproved of some of the tactics adopted by the students, but helped to create the student-faculty senate and to draw up guidelines for the reform of educa-tional policy.

Meanwhile, in 1965, Bell had become chair-man of the Commission on the Year 2000, estab-lished by the American Academy of Arts and Sciences to assemble information on the likely shape of American society at the turn of the century. This kind of social forecasting has been among Bell's abiding interests, and he believes that "the function of prediction is not, as is often stated, to aid social control" but on the contrary "to widen the spheres of moral choice." Some preliminary speculations were published by the Commission as the summer 1967 issue of *Daedalus* and in book form the following year as *Toward the Year 2000*. Among other things con-tributors predicted that by the end of the twen-

tieth century world population will have in-creased by fifty-five percent and the American national income by one hundred percent; the use of leisure time will have become a major prob-lem, and Americans will experience a greatly increased sense of alienation and depersonaliza-tion—unless people, forewarned by these in-formed guesses, choose "to change to a different path."

The Coming of Post-Industrial Society is an-other "venture in social forecasting" in which Bell discusses the new and complicated patterns of conflict and compromise among technocrats, the managerial elite, the military, politicians, and trade union leaders; and the growing tension between equality and meritocracy. He draws at-tention to "the codification of theoretical knowl-edge" which increasingly shapes innovation in science, technology, and social policy, modify-ing the operation of corporate capitalism. Ar-nold Beichman thought this "one of the most important works of social analysis to appear for some time," but Bert Cochran considered that "key components of the theory do not hang to-gether," and Norman Birnbaum wrote: "[This] is not an elegant book. Its chapters are loosely strung together, laden with often unfocused eru-dition; it lacks theoretical drive, and its argu-ment is repetitive—not all of it consistent. Bell's prose is cumbersome—although fortunately not obscure—and the text is labored, even dutiful, as if a lesson had to be gotten through. His range of reference is impressive—from Plato to Ivan Illich, with very little left out in between. This scholarly apparatus is impressive, but it is entire-ly disproportionate to the weight of his argu-ment."

The Cultural Contradictions of Capitalism, a sequel, followed in 1976. The central contradic-tion of which Bell writes derives from capital-ism's hunger for expanding markets. Pressing more and more "for increased consumption, for buying now and paying later," capitalism (in M. C. Beardsley's summary of the argument) generates "a new, non-Puritan, non-Protestant-work-ethic morality that sets less and less value on thrift and on rationality—the virtues that are necessary to keep the productive system going." This irresponsible and antirational mood is fur-ther encouraged by contemporary art and cul-ture, high and low. Bell believes that this rift is harmful to individuals, who are denied any sin-gle and clear-cut notion of what they should properly expect of themselves, of others, and of society; he maintains also that this "radical dis-junction" enters increasingly into many issues of public policy. It bothered some reviewers that Bell offered no convincing remedy for the disease he had diagnosed, and F. E. Manuel in the *New Republic* called the book jaundiced and murky, "something between a potpourri and a mishmash of essays." A majority of critics, however, shared the opinion of the *Atlantic*'s reviewer, who found the work "ambitious, far-reaching, and challenging at every turn. . . . a model of clarity and relentless intelligence."

Daniel Bell left Columbia in 1969 and went to Harvard University as professor of sociology. In 1965, in collaboration with Irving Kristol, he had established *The Public Interest,* a quarterly designed to provide the kind of informed and objective analysis of public issues he had advocated in *The End of Ideology.* Bell and Kristol were co-editors of the magazine until 1973, when Bell relinquished that post, claiming pressure of work and denying that his resignation had been prompted by the attacks of socialist critics, to whom *The Public Interest* sometimes read like an organ of the New Conservatism.

Bell has served on the President's Commission on Technology, Automation, and Economic Progress (1964-1966) and as chairman of the Government Panel on Social Indicators (1966-1968). He is a fellow of the American Academy of Arts and Sciences and of the American Sociological Association, a member of the Council on Foreign Relations and the Century Association. He serves on the editorial boards of the *American Scholar* and *Daedalus.* From 1957 to 1961 he was a member of the board of directors of the American Civil Liberties Union. Bell has honorary degrees from Grinnell College and Case Western Reserve University.

The author has been married three times: to Nora Potashnik in 1943, to Elaine Graham in 1949, and to Pearl Kazin in 1960. He has a daughter by his first marriage and a son by his third. An energetic and voluble man, his principal hobby is cooking, which he has described as "the perfect moral act, complete free will. You can put in as many herbs as you like. But in order to know what you've got, you must taste the consequences."

PRINCIPAL WORKS: The End of Ideology, 1960; The Reforming of General Education, 1966; The Coming of Post-Industrial Society, 1973; The Cultural Contradictions of Capitalism, 1976. *As Editor*—The New American Right, 1957 (revised as The Radical Right, 1963); Towards the Year 2000, 1968; (with Irving Kristol) Confrontation: The Student Rebellion and the Universities, 1969; (with Irving Kristol) Capitalism Today, 1971.

ABOUT: American Men of Science, 1968; Contemporary Authors 1-4 1st revision, 1967; Horowitz, I.L. (ed.) The New Sociology, 1964; Who's Who in America, 1976-1977. *Periodicals*—American Journal of Sociology July 1974; At-

lantic March 1976; Book Week May 22, 1966; Christian Science Monitor July 5, 1973; Commentary April 1976; Contemporary Sociology March 1974; Encounter May 1974; Journal of Aesthetics Winter 1976; Journal of Higher Education December 1966; Life May 12, 1967; Nation July 30, 1973; New Republic September 15, 1973; September 22, 1973; March 20, 1976; New York Review of Books October 20, 1966; November 3, 1966; September 26, 1968; October 18, 1973; June 24, 1976; New York Times March 20, 1969; June 3, 1973; New York Times Book Review July 17, 1966; February 1, 1976; New York Times Magazine April 9, 1967; Saturday Review April 16, 1966; Science April 4, 1975; Teachers College Record November 1966.

BELL, MARVIN (HARTLEY) (August 3, 1937–), American poet, was born in New York City and grew up in Center Moriches, Long Island. He is the son of Saul Bell and the former Belle Spector. Marvin Bell received his B.A. at Alfred University, New York, in 1958. He went on to Syracuse University, but left the same year when he married Mary Mammosser. That marriage ended very quickly and painfully, and Bell made a second marriage in 1961 to Dorothy Murphy. He has two sons, Nathan and Jason.

Bell continued his education at the University of Chicago (M.A., 1961) and in the Writers' Workshop at the University of Iowa (M.F.A., 1963). For the next two years he served in the U.S. Army as a lieutenant, and in 1965 he began his teaching career as a visiting lecturer at the Iowa Writers' Workshop. Bell returned to Iowa the next year as an assistant professor of English and has remained there, becoming an associate professor in 1969 and professor of English in 1975.

The two poems in Bell's first pamphlet of verse, *Poems for Nathan and Saul* (1966), are "The Manipulator," a moving tribute to his Russian Jewish father, and "Pieces," a harrowingly frank documentary about his first wife's mental illness and the birth of his first son:

> My first wife feared
> gas and the night,
> and feared the two
> would suck her inside
> out, if she relaxed.
> Everyone needed
> the help she needed,
> she guessed, and she was wrong. . . .
>
> I tried to afflict her
> with affection,
> I tried making her
> knuckle under.
> I tried to let her go
> crazy, and it worked.

Both poems from this first pamphlet are reprinted in *Things We Dreamt We Died For,* pub-

BELL

Erik Borg

MARVIN BELL

gant, full of ingenious word-play and rhythm-play, but lacking inner urgency."

The Escape Into You (1971) is a sequence of fifty-four eighteen-line poems, each made up of three six-line stanzas in the manner of John Berryman's *Dream Songs.* Reviewers agreed that these were more personal than most of Bell's earlier poems, more urgent and intense in mood, richer in texture, denser in imagery, "a non-stop emotional and spiritual striptease." Donald Justice praised the book, which he called "a diary without dates, fragments of a story without any names, part of a life":

I'm in a phone booth in Saratoga Springs.
The water tastes awful, but very helpful.
You aren't answering, whatever I'm asking.
I'm asking right now why you aren't answering.
It's pleasure, pain, or just love of quiet.
You're not answering; I've got coins for nothing.

(from "Light Poem")

Vernon Young wrote of this collection that Bell's "craftsmanship is confident and his intelligence is in the foreground. Even so, there is a prickly something not assimilated, a source of rancor that remains, in a context ostensibly ironic, as a gust of the uncouth, a drive to savage himself or to appear tougher than his work." Young says that in these poems the speaker gives thanks to Eros for diverting him from despair, but "feeding on flesh brings only a sour taste to the narrator which he tries unsuccessfully to identify with ecstasy." And Richard Howard thought this sequence the product of "the rage to make poetry."

Howard felt very differently about *Residue of Song* (1974), which persuaded him that Bell has "a considerable [poetic] estate on his hands, or within his reach." There are many poems in this collection, as in earlier ones, about Bell's father, and about his own fatherhood. Howard believes that "this chain-of-generations is what has always bound Bell closest to his gift, the links in the family romance he finds so indissoluble. ... This tremendous sequentiality of Bell's admits very few gaps ... when they occur, the world appears to stop" and he "writes poems to keep things going.... until we reach the hospital or heaven or maybe just the next hideout, the escape into you. It would be folly to say I understand these poems, many of them. ... Bell is in search of those psychosomatic dangers not yet registered by poetry, even by his own; and the search does him honor, if there's little comfort, and a great deal of menace in it." And he quotes: "Did I forget what's closest to my heart?/ Ache, peril, fissure, clot and blast." Daniel Halpern

lished the same year, together with another fine poem about his father, some love lyrics, and a tender portrait of his son, observed while assigning names to Halloween pumpkins. This was followed by Bell's first full-length collection, *A Probable Volume of Dreams.* It was the 1969 Lamont Poetry Selection of the Academy of American Poets, and brought him both the Bess Hokin Prize and the *Virginia Quarterly Review*'s Emily Clark Balch Prize.

Peter Elfed Lewis, writing in the British review *Stand,* was impressed above all by the variety and versatility of this collection: "The quality of the poetry is uneven, but the range of subject-matter, emotion and tone is extraordinary. Bell writes about things personal and public, about love, marriage, divorce, children, politics, war, Jews, America, about dreams and nightmares and realities"; and he ranges from an absolute simplicity of manner to allusive complexity, from detailed realism to surreal fantasy, from the elegiac to the "wryly comic" or the "hilariously funny."

While recognizing the "dark, even sinister, undertones" beneath the surface humor of much of Bell's poetry, Lewis found his jokiness and his penchant for puns and word-play at times irritatingly inappropriate. Geof Hewitt in *Contemporary Poets* agreed, complaining that in too many of these poems "the throw-away line undercuts the poem, and a tension is created between Bell the poet and Bell the entertainer." Hayden Carruth confessed in his review that he had been one of the Lamont Poetry Selection judges, and had not voted for Bell because his "poems seem *too* accomplished: striking and ele-

wrote: "Marvin Bell may be one of our funniest poets; he is one of our most tragic, and most intelligent."

Bell was editor of the Iowa magazine *Statements* in 1959-1964, poetry editor of *North American Review* in 1964-1969, and poetry editor of *Iowa Review* in 1969-1971. He was a visiting professor at Oregon State University in the summer of 1969, and at Goddard College, Vermont, in the summer of 1972. He taught at the Bread Loaf Writers' Conference in 1973-1975.

PRINCIPAL WORKS: Poems for Nathan and Saul (pamphlet), 1966; Things We Dreamt We Died For, 1966; A Probable Volume of Dreams, 1969; The Escape Into You: A Sequence, 1971; Woo Havoc (pamphlet), 1971; Residue of Song, 1974; Stars Which See, Stars Which Do Not See, 1977.

ABOUT: Contemporary Authors 21-24 1st revision, 1977; Lee, A. (ed.) The Major Young Poets, 1971; Malkoff, K. (ed.) Crowell's Handbook of Contemporary American Poetry, 1973; Vinson, J. (ed.) Contemporary Poets, 1975; Writers Directory 1976-1977. *Periodicals*—Hudson Review Summer 1967, Spring 1970, Winter 1971-1972; Kenyon Review 1 1970; Massachusetts Review Autumn 1970; Nation February 2, 1970; New Republic March 29, 1975; North American Review March 1967; January 1968; Parnassus Fall-Winter 1972; Poetry December 1967, May 1971, August 1972, September 1975; Shenandoah Summer 1971; Southern Review Spring 1970; Stand 4 1972; Virginia Quarterly Review Winter 1972, Spring 1975; Western Humanities Review Summer 1970.

BELL, QUENTIN (CLAUDIAN STEPHEN) (August 19, 1910–), English art historian, critic, and biographer, was born in London, the second son of the art critic Clive Bell and the former Vanessa Stephen, sister of Virginia Woolf. He grew up in Bloomsbury, and toddled among the giants of the Bloomsbury group of liberal intellectuals, which remains one of the most discussed (and gossiped about) of all English intellectual cliques. "Bloomsbury" was a set of brilliant, talented, and influential friends who came to live in or near that district of London just before World War I. They shared a certain earnestness in pursuit of "the good, the true and the beautiful" and a "comprehensive irreverence" for sham that shocked many of their contemporaries. The group included (besides Quentin Bell's parents), Virginia and Leonard Woolf, the iconoclastic biographer Lytton Strachey, the economist John Maynard Keynes, and the art critic Roger Fry, as well as a number of equally colorful lesser talents.

Quentin Bell was educated at Leighton Park, a Quaker school at Reading, and became a painter, sculptor, and potter. Though he is nowadays better known as a writer and critic, he has never abandoned these other pursuits, and had a number of exhibitions between 1935 and 1977. Bell

QUENTIN BELL

Chatto & Windus

served from 1941 to 1943 in the political warfare executive, and after the war published his first major book, *On Human Finery* (1947), an extended essay on the social significance of fashion. Bell maintains that fashion is specifically a Western phenomenon, and one that has emerged only during the last four centuries as a product of the rivalry between the aristocracy and an ambitious and wealthy middle class. He bases his thesis on Thorstein Veblen's *The Theory of the Leisure Class,* maintaining that along with Veblen's "conspicuous consumption," "conspicuous leisure," and "conspicuous waste," the leisure class has practiced "conspicuous outrage" in defiance of "sartorial morality." At this point, wrote one reviewer, Bell "steps out of economics into erotics; he passes from the world of Marx into the world of Freud." Although some critics thought the book attached too little importance to aesthetic and subjective factors in the development of fashion, most admired it as a scholarly and readable contribution to a neglected subject. Raymond Mortimer found that "the thought is so clear, the humour so appetisingly dry, that I am compelled to recommend the book urgently." There was a new edition, substantially revised and "greatly enriched," in 1976. Bell draws just as heavily on Veblen in his introduction to *Those Impossible English* (1952), a collection of old photographs assembled by Helmut and Alison Gernsheim to illustrate the fashions, habits, ideas, aesthetics, and morals of English society between 1850 and 1950.

In 1952 Bell was appointed a lecturer in art education at King's College, Newcastle, then part of the University of Durham. The "service degree" of Master of Arts was conferred upon him in 1957 by the University of Durham, and in 1959 he went to the University of Leeds as a senior lecturer and head of the department of fine art. He remained at Leeds for eight years, in 1962 becoming Professor of Fine Art.

In *The Schools of Design* (1963), Bell turned his attention to the history of his own profession, surveying the development of academies of fine art since the Renaissance, and going on to consider in detail the troubled history of the first state-supported art schools, established in England during the second quarter of the nineteenth century. He discusses the feuds, the financial troubles, and the inner workings of the state schools, illuminating above all the doctrinal struggles of the time between those who wanted academies of high art and those who favored schools of industrial design. The book was found "as entertaining as it is illuminating," and there was much praise also for the clarity and conciseness of *Ruskin* (1963), a brief account of the critic's life and work in which Bell presented the heretical theory that Ruskin's later writings, far from being inferior to his early work, were in fact ahead of their time, foreshadowing some of the most advanced doctrines of the twentieth century.

The lectures Bell delivered in 1964-1965 as Slade Professor of Fine Art at Oxford University were published in 1967 as *Victorian Artists*. They deal with English painting between John Constable's death in 1837 and Roger Fry's Post-Impressionist Exhibition of 1910, which ushered in the era of modernism. The book was very harshly reviewed by Timothy Hilton, who complained of the "elisions of argument, the blurring of problems, the interdisciplinary doodling that characterise Professor Bell's meandering course through nineteenth-century English art. As art history, the book displays a serious lack of balance." This was a minority opinion, however, and most critics shared the view expressed by *Choice*'s reviewer, who called it "intelligently and charmingly written, rich with information and anecdote, scholarly but in no way ponderous."

After a year as Ferens Professor of Fine Art at the University of Hull (1965-1966), Bell went to the University of Sussex as Professor of the History and Theory of Art, a post he retained from 1967 until his retirement as Emeritus Professor in 1975. In 1968, meanwhile, he had drawn upon family documents and photographs, and his own recollections, to provide a brief account of the evolution and influence of the Bloomsbury group, with portraits of some of its members. Disinclined "to act as Clio's chambermaid," Bell offered not intimate revelations

or gossip but an examination of the ideas and ideals that characterized Bloomsbury, even though these were "almost impalpable, almost indefinable." He concluded that the group was "a conglomeration of individualists rather than a society moving toward a definite objective," but that all of them believed that "it was . . . absolutely necessary, if charity were to survive in the world, that reason should be continually awake." Angus Wilson called the book "a remarkable juggling feat, in which reasoned criticism is modified with inner light and natural personal prejudice with a fine if markedly academic objectivity." And Leonard Woolf, the group's most prominent survivor, described it as "a clear and concise account," judicious, entertaining, and of "sound intelligence."

It was Woolf who had meanwhile encouraged Bell to embark upon a biography of Virginia Woolf, providing him with much unpublished material including family letters and the twenty-seven manuscript volumes of her diaries. *Virginia Woolf: A Biography* appeared in 1972, with an introduction in which Bell explained his "purely historical" purpose in providing "what will, I hope, be a clear and truthful account of the character and personal development of my subject." He had not attempted a critical discussion of his aunt's work, he said, because "even if I had the equipment for such a task I should not have the inclination; I have found the work of the biographer sufficiently difficult without adventuring in other directions. . . . To know the psyche of Virginia Woolf, and this is what she is in effect asking of a biographer, one would have to be either God or Virginia, preferably God. Looking from outside one can go no further than what I have called the outline, and for the rest one may guess . . . but never for one moment allowing oneself to forget that this is guesswork and guesswork of a most hazardous kind."

In fact, as the reviewers recognized, Bell's "guesswork" was based on much better information than is usually the case in biographies. Not only had he been given access to a great deal of privileged documentary material, he had grown up at the heart of his subject's highly exclusive milieu, and as a favorite nephew had even joined with her in writing and illustrating some of her fanciful biographies of friends and relations; he is mentioned in the preface to *Orlando* as "an old and valued collaborator in fiction." Critics agreed, however, that this intimacy had not been allowed to preclude objectivity, and that Bell remains "frank, where frankness is needed," not shrinking from judgment "even where . . . his own parents are concerned."

Such controversy as the book aroused centered on Bell's decision to avoid literary criticism. Michael Rosenthal asked "how satisfactory can the biography of a writer be if the author is unwilling (or unable) to grapple with the crucial facts of her imaginative life? In clearly distinguishing what he is doing from what literary critics do, Bell fosters an artificial distinction that has the unfortunate effect of impoverishing his own work." Other reviewers, pointing out that Mrs. Woolf's books had already been anatomized in an endless stream of critical studies, agreed with William Maxwell, who wrote that "what is interesting at this point, what one wants to know about and has always wanted to know about, is . . . Leslie Stephen's high-strung, overimaginative youngest daughter." William Abrahams likewise commended "Bell's major achievement" in restoring " 'the daily-ness' of Virginia Woolf's life, from which, in accord with the unknowable laws of genius, her work sprung." And indeed the critical verdict was overwhelmingly favorable. The book was praised for its brevity and selectivity, its admirable prose, and its avoidance of amateur psychoanalysis. It was called "a model of tact and self-effacement" and "a work of great distinction, rich in insight and understanding . . . likely to be *the* biography for quite some time." It received both the James Tait Black and the Duff Cooper memorial prizes for biography.

Reading *Virginia Woolf,* wrote William Maxwell, "one begins to sense gradually . . . [Quentin Bell's] personality—truth-loving, ironic, masculine, sensitive, an aesthete, amused at confusion in others while not permitting it in himself, and with a horror of long-windedness and of any other kind of sprawl." The author was married in 1952 to Anne Popham, who having worked with her husband for ten years in his research for *Virginia Woolf* is now editing the novelist's diaries. The Bells, who live in Sussex, have one son, Julian, and two daughters, Virginia and Cressida. Quentin Bell is a fellow of both the Royal Society of Arts and the Royal Society of Literature. He served as a member of the National Council for Diplomas in Art and Design in 1962, and on the National Advisory Committee on Art Education in 1967. From 1948 to 1952 he was chairman of the Lewes (Sussex) Divisional Labour Party. He has contributed regularly to the *Listener* since 1951.

PRINCIPAL WORKS: (ed.) Essays, Poems, and Letters of Julian Bell, 1938; On Human Finery, 1947 (revised edition 1976); (with Helmut and Alison Gernsheim) Those Impossible English, 1952; The True Story of Cinderella, 1957; The Schools of Design, 1963; Ruskin, 1963; Victorian Artists, 1967; Bloomsbury, 1968; Virginia Woolf: A Biography, 1972.

ABOUT: Academic Who's Who, 1975-1976; Contemporary Authors 57-60, 1976; Who's Who, 1978. *Periodicals*—Atlantic February 1973; Commentary August 1973; New Statesman November 24, 1967; June 16, 1972; October 20, 1972; New York Review of Books February 8, 1973; November 25, 1976; New York Times Book Review March 17, 1968; November 5, 1972; New Yorker February 3, 1973; Saturday Review December 9, 1972; Times Literary Supplement July 25, 1968; June 30, 1972; November 12, 1976; Yale Review March 1973.

*BENJAMIN, WALTER ("Detlev Holz," "C. Conrad") (July 15, 1892–September 26, 1940), German literary, art, and cultural critic and philosopher, was born into a wealthy Jewish family in a fashionable part of Berlin. He was the son of Emil B. Benjamin, an art dealer and antiquarian. His parents were aggressively proud of their achievements and possessions, gained in a non-Jewish society. Walter Benjamin himself, shy and awkward both as a child and as a man, was in constant if cautious rebellion against his parents' complacency and "anti-Semitism." In his teens Benjamin was sent to Haubinda, a rural educational establishment, and there met the educational reformer Gustav Wyneken. From 1910 to 1914 he was active in Wyneken's youth movement, publishing his first articles in its magazine *Der Anfang* and rising to the presidency of the Berlin Free Student Association. He broke with the movement in 1914 because of its acceptance of World War I.

At various times in his life, and often simultaneously, Benjamin very nearly committed himself to both Zionism and communism. Though in the end he found it necessary to keep his options open, and chose neither Moscow nor Jerusalem, both were important in the shaping of his ideas. John Berger says "he was at one and the same time a romantic antiquarian and an aberrant Marxist revolutionary. The structuring of his thought was theological and Talmudic; his aspirations were materialist and dialectical." His long flirtation with Zionism began as early as 1913 and was intensified by his meeting in 1915 with Gershom Scholem, who was to be his most loyal friend. Scholem went to Eretz Yisrael in 1923 and became the greatest modern scholar of the Kabbalah. Benjamin toyed all his life with the idea of following Scholem to Israel but did not—perhaps primarily because his emotional and intellectual roots were in classical and West European humanism.

Benjamin embarked on a conventional academic career not because he particularly wanted one but to pacify his father, on whom he was financially dependent. Beginning in 1912 he studied philosophy and literature at the universities of Berlin, Freiburg, and Munich, moving to

*ben' yam ēn

WALTER BENJAMIN

Bern, Switzerland, in 1917. The same year he was married to Dora Kellner, but they soon separated. Benjamin obtained his doctorate at Bern in 1919 and returned to Berlin the following year. His father would probably have supported him until he obtained a full professorship, but academic success eluded him. Benjamin was hopelessly impractical—quite unable to cope with the ordinary exigencies of everyday life, let alone the ruthless infighting of academic careerism. And his ineptitude was compounded by the bad luck that haunted him all his life, and which he personified as the *bucklicht Männlein*—the "little hunchback" he had encountered as a child in a familiar German folk poem.

The *bucklicht Männlein* insured that even his first great success worked against him. In 1924 Benjamin sent his essay, "Goethe's 'Elective Affinities,' " to Hugo von Hofmannsthal, who recognized it as an "absolutely incomparable" masterpiece and published it in two sections in *Neue Deutsche Beiträge* (1924–1925). Hannah Arendt found this essay "of unique stature in the general field of German literary criticism and the specialized field of Goethe scholarship," and George Steiner has said that Benjamin comes closer here than anywhere else in his work "to revealing something of his own radical, anguished comprehension of love." However, the essay constituted a damaging attack on the ideology of the intellectual circle around Stefan George, then establishing itself as a powerful force in the academic world. At the time of its publication, its most telling effect was to confirm Benjamin's reputation as an unreliable eclectic.

At about the same time, Benjamin submitted his doctoral thesis at the University of Frank-

furt. If it had been accepted he would have gained his *habilitation* (right to lecture) and begun his academic career, but it was not accepted and some critics have expressed a certain sympathy with the Frankfurt professors who rejected it. The thesis was called *Ursprung des deutschen Trauerspiels*. The only major work by Benjamin to appear in his lifetime, it was published in Berlin in 1928 and was translated fifty years later by John Osborne as *The Origin of German Tragic Drama*. It begins with a "cognitive-critical prolegomenon" of daunting opacity, employing a "mystical terminology" drawing on the vocabulary of intellectual history and aestheticism from Hegel to Croce, as well as the methods of Talmudic and Kabbalistic exegesis which Benjamin had learned from Scholem. This "visionary hermeneutic" is then applied to German allegoric political martyr-dramas of the seventeenth century to show among other things how the *Trauerspiel,* concerned with "the inconsolable quality, the desolation of earthly life," differs from the transcendental and elevating nature of classical tragedy. "Idea crowds on idea in bewildering provocation," wrote George Steiner, "and the monograph ends with an unsurpassed anatomy of allegory."

It seemed to Steiner that the work is "profoundly riven by Benjamin's ambivalence towards the whole academic convention. Benjamin performs the motions of textual exegesis, of learned citation, of 'source-study' with a certain clenched intensity." Frank Kermode goes further, suggesting that the book is both an academic thesis "and a parody of it, an occasion for attacking academic scholarly method while reveling in all the footnotes and put-downs proper to the genre. Benjamin says, probably with little truth, that he wrote it in a café, using a seat close to the jazz band." He also boasted that "the writing consists largely of quotations —the craziest mosaic technique imaginable." At any rate, the thesis was rejected and the gates of German academe were closed to Benjamin, who thereafter was regarded by most of his contemporaries as a failure. He became something like a nineteenth-century *littérateur* (though without the private income that should go with the role). The ironic fact is that the unstructured, uncommitted, and generally unhappy life he led may have been essential to the development of his unique kind of critical vision. John Berger writes that his photographs "show the face of a man rendered slow and heavy by the burden of his own existence, a burden made almost overwhelming by the rapid instantaneous brilliance of his scarcely controllable insights."

It was in the mid-1920s that Benjamin came

closest to joining the Communist Party, after indoctrination by the Russian actress and director Asja Lacis. A visit to Moscow in 1926–1927 failed to complete his conversion but probably added to his father's disapproval and disappointment. Denied an independent income, he was forced to live with his parents until 1930, when they died. In the same year he and his wife, by whom he had a son, were finally divorced.

No one knows precisely how Benjamin managed to live after 1930. He published articles in several newspapers, among them *Vossische Zeitung, Literarische Welt,* and *Frankfurter Zeitung,* and made translations of Baudelaire and (in collaboration) of Proust. He also wrote important essays on Proust, Karl Kraus, Baudelaire, Kafka, and Brecht, though some of these appeared only posthumously. Apart from *Ursprung des deutschen Trauerspiels,* the only books that appeared during his lifetime were his dissertation *Der Begriff der Kunstkritik in der deutschen Romantik* (The Concept of Art Criticism in German Romanticism, 1920) and *Einbahnstrasse* (One-Way Street, 1928), a collection of aphorisms, epigrams, and maxims. *Berliner Kindheit um Neunzehnhundert* (A Berlin Childhood Around 1900), written in the late 1930s, did not appear until 1950.

Benjamin never completed "Passagenarbeit," the book he regarded as his *magnum opus.* It was to be a massive Marxist study of Paris, considered architecturally, sociologically, culturally, and psychologically as the quintessential locus of mid-nineteenth-century capitalism. To quote a critic in the *Times Literary Supplement,* Benjamin saw that "the modern city is the defining locus of imaginative life, that the industrial city . . . has literally restructured our inner landscape and the habitat of our dreams"; he regarded "nineteenth-century Paris and a Baudelaire sonnet as related elements in the anatomy and myth of capitalism." Benjamin had come to think of "the work of literature as a *product* specific to the modes of production in a given society," and he proposed to work this notion out in relation to the poetry of Baudelaire. His Marxism "is a recognition of the vital reciprocity between matter and feeling, between human experience and the available and expressive syntax."

An important part of Benjamin's always inadequate income came from the Institut für Sozialforschung (Institute for Social Research) in Frankfurt, of which Theodor Adorno, an early disciple, was a prominent member and later director. Beginning in 1935 Benjamin received a small but regular stipend as a research associate of the Institute, and a number of his essays appeared in the Institute's journal *Zeits-chrift für Sozialforschung.* When Hitler seized power in 1933 the Institute migrated to the United States. At the same time Benjamin left Berlin and went to Paris, a city that was immensely congenial to him, as was French literature and culture. He was able to take with him the "most important half" of his fine library, said to be the only material possession of any value that he ever owned. During his years in Paris, Benjamin sold some articles to German periodicals (writing under pseudonyms), and as "Detlev Holz" edited *Deutsche Menschen,* an anthology of letters published in Switzerland in 1936. The Swiss publisher promptly went bankrupt and the edition was not distributed. It was discovered in a cellar in 1962, just as a new edition came off the press in Germany. Exacerbating such characteristically bad luck with characteristic shyness, Benjamin failed to exploit his contacts in Paris with Gide, Charles du Bos, and others.

All the same, Benjamin was not entirely wretched in Paris. He loved to roam the city in the manner of a *flâneur*—stroller, idler—a significant figure in his writings, receptive to every apparent trifle. At such times, he wrote, "the true picture of the past flits by. The past can be seized only as an image which flashes up at the instant when it can be recognized and is never seen again." He speaks of losing one's self in a city "as one loses one's self in a forest. . . . Then signposts and street names, passers-by, roofs, kiosks or baths must speak to the wanderer like a cracking twig under his feet in the forest." Frank Kermode says "this is how Benjamin worked with the arts also. Nothing justifies his genius so obviously as his writing about Paris; boulevard, iron arcade, Art Nouveau speak to him, the improbable connections are made, and we are thinking not about a single object but about a whole culture."

Benjamin met Bertolt Brecht in 1929 and during the 1930s they became close friends. Although Benjamin was not willing to leave Paris and settle in Denmark, where Brecht was then living, they visited each other frequently. Stanley Mitchell says they were alike in "their cast of mind, manner of speech, fondness for image, parable, allegory, aphorism. . . . [and possessed] a similar historical imagination and a similar humanism." In this friendship, as Hannah Arendt remarked, "the greatest living German poet met the most important critic of the time, a fact that both were fully aware of." It was under Brecht's influence that Benjamin crystallized his idiosyncratic form of Marxism, his notion of the writer as a producer of commodities, and his fondness for *das plumpe Denken*—"crude thinking"—which, Hannah Arendt says, partly accounts for his frequent use of proverbs and everyday idioms and his ability "to write a prose of such singularly enchanting and enchanted closeness to reality."

Most critics nowadays consider that his discussions and correspondence with Brecht enabled Benjamin to bring his ideas into focus, though some maintain that his "pre-Marxist" writings contain profounder insights. At the time, Gershom Scholem and Adorno considered Brecht's influence on their friend "disastrous." Adorno blamed Brecht for the undialectical nature of Benjamin's use of Marxist categories, though dialectical thought was essentially alien to Benjamin in any case. In November 1938 Adorno rejected the first version of an important essay on Baudelaire that Benjamin had submitted to *Zeitschrift für Sozialforschung.* Thereafter Benjamin felt that he was living on borrowed time, and that Adorno and the Institute, the only "material and moral support" of his life in Paris, might at any moment desert him.

Benjamin's *bucklicht Männlein* seemed increasingly in control of things in the last two years of his life. In the winter of 1939–1940 he left Paris for a "safer" place—with characteristic incompetence choosing Meaux, a troop center, and one of the few dangerous places in France. When France fell he made his way via Marseilles to the town of Port Bou, on the Franco-Spanish border. He was at last, very reluctantly, on his way to the United States. His precious library had been confiscated by the Gestapo and he was suffering from a cardiac condition. On September 26, 1940 he learned that his group of refugees was to be returned to France and probably handed over to the Gestapo. He died that night of an overdose of morphine. The next day the border officials relented, and his companions were allowed to proceed to Portugal. "It is only for the sake of those without hope that hope is given to us," he said once.

Almost all of Benjamin's work has survived. Georges Bataille hid some of his papers in the Bibliothèque Nationale and the material confiscated by the Gestapo later surfaced in East Germany. Fifteen years after his death, a two-volume collection of his writings was published in Germany as *Schriften,* edited by Theodor Adorno. Two volumes of letters followed in 1966, and the same year there appeared a collection of his essays on Brecht. The publication of his *Gesammelte Schriften* began in 1972 and his work has been widely translated, bringing him the posthumous fame that, as Hannah Arendt said, is "the lot of the unclassifiable ones, that is, those whose work neither fits the existing order

nor introduces a new genre that lends itself to future classification."

According to Hannah Arendt, "the only world view that ever had a decisive effect" on Benjamin was Goethe's. He shared Goethe's belief in the existence of an *Urphänomen,* an archetypal phenomenon, "a concrete thing to be discovered in the world of appearances in which 'significance' and appearance, word and thing, idea and experience, would coincide. The smaller the object, the more likely it seemed that it could contain in the most concentrated form everything else." This is why Benjamin's imagination was always caught not by abstract ideas but by objects, like the two grains of wheat in the Musée Cluny on which someone had inscribed the whole of the *Shema Israel.* He sought, as he says, "to capture the portrait of history in the most insignificant representations of reality, its scraps, as it were."

Something similar lies behind his passion for quotations, which he collected tirelessly and which play a central role in his writings—his dream was to compose a book entirely of quotations. He used quotations in order "to plumb the depths of language and thought . . . by drilling rather than by excavating," assembling and juxtaposing his fragments into a sort of surrealistic montage that would enable the past to speak directly to the present with as little subjective comment and explanation as possible. He believed that there was a God-given ultimate language, "a language of truth, the tensionless and even silent depository of the ultimate secrets which all thought is concerned with." Hannah Arendt says that in all his literary studies his basic approach was "not to investigate the utilitarian or communicative functions of linguistic creations, but to understand them in their crystallized and thus ultimately fragmentary form as intentionless and noncommunicative utterances of a 'world essence.' "

These ways of thinking are, of course, essentially poetic, and in his writings Benjamin relied less on dialectical argument than on images and metaphors whose validity is emotionally perceived. A famous example is his image of the "angel of history," who has his face "turned toward the past." What we see as a chain of events, *"he sees [as] one single catastrophe which keeps piling wreckage upon wreckage and hurls it in front of his feet. The angel would like to stay, awaken the dead, and join together what has been smashed to pieces. But a storm is blowing from Paradise"* and "irresistibly propels him into the future to which his back is turned, while the pile of ruins before him grows skyward. What we call progress is *this* storm."

Some regard Benjamin as the greatest philosopher-critic of the century. Frank Kermode values him mainly for his "informed eye": the way in which "a poem, a picture, something seen in a city's streets—a prostitute at her window, perhaps—takes its place in a network of correspondences, and the object is transformed." Kermode wrote that "the Coleridge of the *Notebooks* is as near a parallel as one can get for the range of perception, the breadth of reading, the willingness to engage the occult and take on any metaphysical task necessary to the explanation of the things of the world." Benjamin is still the subject of an *"odium theologicum* generated by personal and political dissent over the true meaning of his works" which a critic in the *Times Literary Supplement* finds "as repellent as any in modern intellectual debate." The same critic writes: "List Peirce, Croce, and Benjamin, and you have named those moderns who have added anything fundamental to the philosophy of forms, to our understanding of the interactions between art and meaning. . . . He was a Kabbalist at heart, a virtuoso of secrecy and allegoric detour; he was, at very nearly the same moment, an intellectual persuaded of the need for action, for plain statement, for mass education. . . . His integrity in regard to philosophic thought was absolute," and if he showed himself willing to compromise to retain Adorno's financial support, it is because "in addition to being a critic of genius, a reader of consciousness comparable to Proust, Walter Benjamin was a human being. Just more so than most."

PRINCIPAL WORKS IN ENGLISH TRANSLATION: Illuminations: Essays and Reflections, translated by Harry Zohn, 1968; Understanding Brecht, translated by Anna Bostock, 1973; Charles Baudelaire: A Lyric Poet in the Era of High Capitalism, translated by Harry Zohn (with Paris, Capital of the Nineteenth Century, translated by Quintin Hoare), 1973; Reflections, translated by Edmund Jephcott, edited by Peter Demetz, 1978; The Origin of German Tragic Drama, translated by John Osborne, 1978.

ABOUT: Adorno, T.W. Prisms, 1967; Adorno, T.W. (and others) Über Walter Benjamin, 1968; Arendt, H. *introduction to* Illuminations, 1968; Bachmann, D. Essay und Essayismus, 1969; Berger, J. The Look of Things, 1971; Boyers, R. (ed.) The Legacy of the German Refugee Intellectuals, 1972; Guenther, H. Walter Benjamin und der humane Marxismus, 1974; Kaiser, G. Benjamin-Adorno: Zwei Studien, 1974; Leo Baeck Institute Year Book X, 1965; Scholem, G. Walter Benjamin, 1975; Tiedemann, R. Studien zur Philosophie Walter Benjamins, 1965; Unseld, S. (ed.) Zur Aktualität Walter Benjamins, 1972; Usinger, F. Tellurium, 1960; Wiesenthal, L. Zur wissenschaftstheorie Walter Benjamins, 1973; Witte, B. Walter Benjamin, 1976. *Periodicals*—Atlantic March 1969; Commentary September 1969; Commonweal August 22, 1969; Mercure de France July 1952; New Republic December 14, 1968; New Statesman September 7, 1973; New York Review of Books December 18, 1969; October 12, 1978; New York Times Book Review July 30, 1978; New Yorker October 19, 1968; Times Literary Supplement August 22, 1968; January 8, 1971; December 14, 1973; October 25, 1974.

BERGER, JOHN (PETER) (November 5, 1926–), English novelist, art critic, essayist, film writer, and translator, was born in Stoke Newington, London, the son of S.J.D. Berger, O.B.E., M.C., and the former Miriam Branson. He studied at the Central School of Art and the Chelsea School of Art, both in London, and served for two years in the Oxford and Buckinghamshire Light Infantry (1944-1946). Berger was for a time a professional painter, exhibiting at the Wildenstein, Leicester, and Redfern galleries in London, while earning his living as a teacher of drawing. He began his career as an art critic on the London left-wing weekly *Tribune,* and went on to become art critic of the *New Statesman,* a position which he held for ten controversial years.

A collection of Berger's *New Statesman* pieces was published in 1960 as *Permanent Red: Essays in Seeing,* appearing in the United States two years later with the less conspicuously socialist title of *Towards Reality.* The Kirkus reviewer noted that Berger was a Marxist who "rides the 'wave of the future' with seriousness and sensitivity; to many of his persuasion he undoubtedly seems a prophet. To anyone else, a rather genteel and gullible propagandist." But Aaron Bohrod said there was "no question that Berger is one of the most thoughtful and provocative art critics of the day," and M. E. Landgren wrote: "One may disagree with Berger on many points and find some of his judgments somewhat summary, but he commands the respect of those who appreciate criticism with substance. His estimates of Picasso, Matisse, Léger, and Lipchitz are superb."

Richard Wollheim in his review discussed Berger's art criticism as a whole, and at some length, saying that Berger "contrives to write in a way that seems far superior to anything else of its kind in the field." He seems to Wollheim to possess three major assets: "He writes exceptionally well: the sentences race on with great fluency, without there ever being a trace of slackness or pomposity. The style is colloquial and direct, the epithets are generally sparse, and the metaphors contemporary: all the better to set off the occasional passage where a suppressed romanticism breaks out and issues in descriptions of a more elaborate or evocative kind. This is rare modern prose." Wollheim credits Berger also with "a most effective and deadly wit," and a willingness to relinquish the status of gentleman amateur and to "grub around" in his criticism

JOHN BERGER

"with ideas and appearances." But Berger's critical approach does not seem to Wollheim "specifically Marxist" and indeed Wollheim finds his theories muddled. What Berger looks for in a work of art is that it should "increase our awareness of our own potentiality" and in this way "help or encourage men to know and claim their social rights"; Wollheim does not agree that these criteria are necessarily interrelated and says, moreover, that "from his theory of criticism no theory of art follows."

Berger argues, according to a reviewer in the *Times Literary Supplement,* that "the nature of all art is an attempt to define and render unnatural the distinction between the actual and the possible, to express the inadequacy of the given state of things, sometimes with horror, sometimes by presenting the desirable ideal." This idea is pursued in the polemical work *The Success and Future of Picasso* (1965), in which Berger attacks Picasso for valuing his own genius more than what it created. He allows Picasso only two "valid" periods: the Cubist (1907-1914), when he was truly "revolutionary," if only intuitively so; and the period between 1931 and 1943 when Picasso was "involved in a passionate love affair, and many of his best works were sexual in inspiration and content." Berger's attack aroused resentment—particularly the suggestion that Picasso should have "visited India, Indonesia, China, Mexico or West Africa" on the grounds that the "world Communist movement, with its internationalism and (at least at rank-and-file level) its true fraternal sense of solidarity, was ideally suited" to enable him to "travel on the terms he needed . . . [as] a

seer searching for his unique people in whose name he might speak."

"The dilemma that burdens these pages," wrote one critic, "is that of Mr. Berger himself, who knows that Moscow is wrong to condemn the art of Picasso as 'decadent' but cannot bring himself, as Éluard, Aragon and others did, to give expression to his intuitive convictions." The book was also attacked for some errors, but Berger's praise of the achievements he does allow Picasso was found highly illuminating, and the book was called unusual, engaging, and stimulating. Here as elsewhere, Berger's urgent sense of engagement with his material was generally felt to transcend his theoretical Marxism, which was almost universally regarded as being essentially humanistic.

Berger's next book seemed to be of a very different kind. This was *A Fortunate Man: The Story of a Country Doctor* (1967), illustrated with photographs by Jean Mohr. It is a portrait of a physician who practices in a rural area of England called "the Forest." In a series of vignettes or "stories," Dr. Sassall is shown as the guide, mentor, and friend of his patients, who are presented less as individuals than as members of a rural community. "Sassall" is the pseudonym of an actual doctor whom Berger obviously likes and greatly admires. But Berger's thesis is that this man is "fortunate" and satisfied in his work only by the "miserable standards" of our wretched capitalist society; the book is as political as anything Berger has written.

Many reviewers who shared or ignored Berger's political views found the book moving and "beautiful," but one in the *Times Literary Supplement* felt that the reader never gets to know Sassall: "One has very little idea of what he is really like. For even with his central figure Mr. Berger is interested less in the man than in his relation to the community." S. K. Oberbeck wrote that this "intense, probing narrative" is an account of "Sassall's struggle to come to terms with the metaphysics of his profession. . . . the relationship of doctor and patient, the role of the doctor in society, the psychological transformation Sassall underwent to become the kind of doctor he is. . . . [However,] Berger's explanations of Sassall's personal and psychological growth sometimes become hard to follow." Miles Burrows evidently agreed; the book, he said, "is rambling, diffuse, at times risks confusion and sentimentality, but is never patronizing, and seldom oversimplified . . . Berger respects Sassall with a puzzled, almost mystical feeling, and tries to evaluate his life and work from some ultimate standpoint, which leads him into difficulties."

Berger returned to his own kind of art criticism in *Art and Revolution* (1969). Here he faces, as squarely as he ever has, the artistic problems confronting the Marxist who is more or less disenchanted with the Soviet experiment. The book examines the predicament of the Russian sculptor Ernst Neizvestny, Berger's exact contemporary, whose work elicited Khrushchev's public wrath. What Berger wanted to achieve was a demonstration of how a particular artist, working in an environment inimical to his talent, has been able, by endurance, to produce an art which "reveals and expresses an essential part of the experience being lived by millions of people, more especially millions in the three exploited continents" (Asia, Africa, and South America—Berger does not seem to consider that any European communist countries are exploited).

Many reviewers objected that Neizvestny's sculptures were not good or important enough to sustain the book's argument, and Berger was also accused of presenting a distorted view of modern Russian art—Hilton Kramer wrote that "the mixture of art, historical fact and ideological fiction is sometimes breathtaking. . . . [Berger] writes extremely well, but he has . . . about as much faith in the disinterested artistic intelligence as the party hacks he seeks to educate. With friends like Mr. Berger, the underground artists of the Soviet Union will need no enemies." But Peter Levi, in a letter to the *Times Literary Supplement,* pointed out that "this book is critical in the development of John Berger's writing," and that Berger, almost singlehandedly, had made art criticism in Britain a "life-giving and humanly serious subject"; many who disagree with Berger's political views would accept the truth of this judgment.

In the essays collected in *The Moment of Cubism* (1969), Berger maintains, as Douglas Brown wrote, that "the 'moment' of Cubism is the supreme moment in twentieth-century art" —that the Cubist painters were "almost unconsciously and for a short period in the grip of a profound intuitive understanding of the modern world, what it was, and what it promised." For Berger, Cubism is the only form of modern art which reflects the possibility of "a transformed world," and he laments the abandonment of the Cubist "journey." The book also includes some "extremely vivid and moving" studies of individual painters and paintings, and essays on museums and their function, portrait painting, photography, and the capitalistic approach to works of art as "desirable property."

Meanwhile, in the late 1950s and early 1960s,

Berger had established a second reputation as the author of three polemical novels. The first of these, *A Painter of Our Time* (1958), is a fictional exploration of Berger's preoccupation with the relationship between art and politics. The central figure is a gifted Hungarian emigré painter who cannot make a living in London because he is not fashionable, and the book bristles with sketches of greedy dealers and venal critics. When success does at last seem imminent, Janos Lavin has to consider the terms on which it is offered, and weigh these against the implications of events in Hungary, where his friend Laszlo, a Communist like himself, has been executed (and later "rehabilitated"). Goronwy Rees admired it as a portrait of an artist and of "a man at work," but concluded that Berger "has few if any of the gifts of the novelist"; other readers disagreed, and found the book vividly written, witty, and often perceptive.

Berger's concern with commercialism and exploitation is extended to the traffic in human suffering in *The Foot of Clive* (1962), set in the men's ward of a general hospital. And in *Corker's Freedom* (1964) he turns to the question of employment itself. This book, which Berger has called "partly a film scenario and partly a historical document," is the most accomplished of his early novels. Maggie Ross wrote that it was "basically a series of suburban interior monologues in which each character is given free rein to voice his innermost thoughts." Corker, an elderly and "ordinary" man who runs a small employment agency, is continually at odds with himself. The novel is an account of the momentous day on which he decides to leave his bullying sister and set up house at the agency. Towards the end, while delivering a travel talk at the local church hall, Corker's "several selves come together," as one reviewer put it, and "the whole man speaks." Maggie Ross described as "tedious" the novel's "interminable use of an explanatory thought-stream in which nothing is left unsaid," but found the book as a whole "fascinating." Berger, she concluded, "is a writer of honesty and power whose ideas tend to proliferate to such an extent that the solidity of the main design becomes obscured. I hope he will again attempt to fight the battle of the inarticulate man in a story less complexly rich."

The most discussed of Berger's books, and arguably the fullest statement of his position, is *G.* (1972), of which the author said "I do not know whether it will be eventually categorised as an essay, a novel, a treatise, or the description of a dream." It gives an account of the short life of G., born in Paris in 1887, the bastard son of an Anglo-American heiress and an Italian merchant. Raised by his incestuous aunt and uncle on an English farm, expensively educated, G. is first seduced, at the age of fourteen, by his aunt. We see him next in 1910, a wealthy Don Juan with an interest in aviation. He is in Switzerland to witness the attempt by his Peruvian friend Chavez to fly over the Alps. Chavez, a prototypical cubist and surrealist antihero, makes the flight but crashes for no apparent reason upon attempting to land. G., involved in various sexual conquests, is indifferent to his friend's death, as he is to everything except being "alone with a woman." In the end, he is equally indifferent to his own equally random death—he is killed in Trieste, where he has been mistaken for a spy, on the eve of Italy's entry into World War I. The novel is dedicated to "Anya and her sisters in Women's Liberation."

A reviewer in the *Times Literary Supplement* spoke of Berger's "attempt to translate Cubism into literary terms by employing and rather over-taxing many of the devices used in recent years by Sarraute, Sollers, Butor and the other novelists who have said farewell to naturalistic certainty and divinely certified mimesis. Mr. Berger's entire narrative is broken up into hundreds of double-spaced sections, some of them constituting only a single line or phrase, thus deliberately exposing the hiatus between conception and achievement." The same writer points out that G., "the seducer who apparently treats females as objects, in reality invests them with self-determination. In one of his many discursive passages, Mr. Berger further explains: 'The stranger who desires you and convinces you that it is truly you in all your particularity whom he desires, brings a message from all that you might be to you as you actually are'. . . . Mr. Berger's hostility towards private property, particularly as it affects works of art, quite legitimately extends to woman-as-property. The role of woman in G.'s society merely exemplifies the general social structure, so that G. himself can be regarded as an anarchist revolutionary."

Almost all of its reviewers took G. very seriously, though not all of them thought it had succeeded in its large intentions (or agreed what these were). Leo Braudy compared it to John Fowles's *The French Lieutenant's Woman* to the latter's disadvantage, saying that G. is "a complex novel of ideas that sets off in the reader meditations about sex, history and the nature of the novel that could never have been excited by the flaccid ironies and self-important complacencies of John Fowles's work"; its characters, settings, ideas and form are intricately related— "a kind of interdependency that great novels always exhibit." Shirley Toulson, noting that G.

was written "more in the form of a film script than an orthodox work of fiction," wrote that "Berger has set himself the vast task that Tolstoy undertook: that of depicting how each one of us is history in that we are both monumentally shaped by events and, in small measure, by the mere act of inhabiting our skins, influence their course." Arnold Kettle called it "the most interesting novel in English I have read for a good many years." Francis Hope, like some other critics, was less enthusiastic, saying that Berger had written "a bizarre combination of fiction, reconstructed history, social theory and sexual rumination. . . . had it set up in sections rather than paragraphs . . . appropriated some passages from Collingwood, Saint-Just . . . and others . . . and thrown in two drawings of male and one of female genitalia—not to titillate, but to, as it were, illustrate the difficulties of using words to describe experiences beyond words." Hope did not find the result "shatteringly experimental," but he thought it a "bold venture" which should be applauded, though he was not sure "what else one should applaud."

In the closest reading the novel has yet received, the reviewer in the *Times Literary Supplement* wrote that "G. is a work which raises questions of great critical interest. It does not, however, always succeed in fashioning convincing connexions, whether casual or structural. . . . Mr. Berger's dilemma . . . is that of the *intellectual* who is *also* an artist. . . . And although the painter's eye might seem to be Mr. Berger's most distinctive characteristic as a writer, it would probably be more useful to regard the intellectual's fierce analytical intelligence and seriousness of moral purpose as his true point of departure. Certainly G., which is almost totally devoid of humor, is fundamentally an exploration of morality." Berger has "a high talent for set-scenes and dialogue of a conventional kind," but, estranged from naturalism and its assumptions, has no regard for these conventional skills: "He may be right. But the modern writer must either yield some territory to the dramatic heritage of fiction or risk alienating his readers in the wrong way. To emphasize that the failings of G. are the result of a rich endowment of talents and of a bold, experimental intelligence which distrusts the safe, mediocre and provincial, is not to explain these failings away. One comes away from G. as from many modern paintings: provoked and stimulated, yet baffled and faintly resentful."

G. won the Booker Prize (£5,000) and the *Guardian* fiction prize (£210) in 1972, and the James Tait Black Memorial Prize (£400) in 1973. In his Booker Prize acceptance speech,

Berger attacked as imperialists the sponsors of the prize, Booker McConnell Ltd., an international company whose interests range from cane sugar production to retailing. He announced his intention of giving half the money to the Black Panther movement because "they resist . . . the further exploitation of the oppressed; and because, through their black people's information centre, they have links with the struggle in Guyana, the seat of Booker McConnell's wealth." He would use the remainder of the money "to write a further book about the eleven million migrant workers in Europe and their families." This was published in 1975 as *A Seventh Man*, with photographs by Jean Mohr, providing (along with much else, including a Marxist polemic against capitalism and speculations on the nature of the self) a portrait of a typical migrant worker drawn "often in an acutely sensitive and moving way." A powerful and inventive dramatization of the book by Adrian Mitchell was staged in London in 1976.

Berger has also written a number of notable film scenarios in collaboration with the Swiss director Alain Tanner. *La Salamandre* (The Salamander, 1971) studies Rosemonde, a young woman who has had an illegitimate child, drudged for her uncle, and now works in a factory. According to Stanley Kauffmann, Rosemonde is "a thoroughly contemporary young human being, teased by a consumer society into aspirations she can't fulfill, standards without resonance or sanity. . . . The film shows her moving . . . from clumsy attempts at conformity to a break-out" into a more spontaneous life-style. Two journalists who interview her (and sleep with her) eventually abandon the idea of making a television program about her: "They have touched more than they are able to deal with." *Le Milieu du Monde* (1974), released in the United States as *The Middle of the World*, records in a rather Brechtian style the rise and fall of a love affair between a zealous and ambitious Swiss politician and another of Tanner's anarchic and free-spirited heroines. *Jonah Who Will Be Twenty-Five in the Year 2000* is set in Geneva, where eight young people try in various more or less eccentric ways to solve the problems brought to general consciousness by the political upheavals of 1968. Pauline Kael wrote that the film "sees hope and renewal in all their methods," which range from organic farming and Rousseauist education to physical fulfillment and gambling: "The film honors precisely that 'lunatic fringe' that the Marxists have always derided." It received the New York Critics' Prize for the best scenario of 1976. Vincent Canby has called Berger and Tanner "one of the most interesting filmmaking teams in Europe today."

In collaboration with Anna Bostock, Berger has translated Brecht's *Poems on the Theatre* and *Helene Weigel*, as well as *Return to My Native Land* by Aimé Césaire, the left-wing poet and politician from Martinique. Berger has contributed to many magazines and newspapers in Britain, Europe, and the United States, and has worked a great deal on television, notably in two much-admired series of programs about art on Granada TV and one on the BBC. The latter, called *Ways of Seeing*, gave rise to a book of the same title. The author is married, with two children, and has lived in London, Paris, and Switzerland. Michael Ratcliffe has said that "although he possesses considerable, underused gifts of narrative and humour, John Berger is still not what one would call a natural novelist. With four novels behind him, he remains primarily a critic and cultural historian who (rightly) regards his criticism and his history as equally work 'of the imagination' as his fiction, and who carries into all his writings a restless and sometimes scintillating sense of context and cross-reference." Berger received the George Orwell Memorial Prize in 1977.

PRINCIPAL WORKS: *Fiction*—A Painter of Our Time, 1958; The Foot of Clive, 1962; Corker's Freedom, 1964; G., 1972. *Art Criticism*—Marcel Frishman, 1958; Permanent Red: Essays in Seeing, 1960 (U.S., Towards Reality, 1962); The Success and Future of Picasso, 1965; Art and Revolution: Ernst Neizvestny and the Role of the Artist in the U.S.S.R., 1969; The Moment of Cubism, 1969; Selected Essays and Articles: The Look of Things (ed. by N. Stangos), 1971 (U.S., The Look of Things); Ways of Seeing, 1972. *Other*—A Fortunate Man: The Story of a Country Doctor, 1967; A Seventh Man: A Book of Images and Words About the Experience of Migrant Workers in Europe, 1975. *As Translator* (with Anna Bostock)—Poems on the Theatre by Bertolt Brecht, 1961 (republished as The Great Art of Living Together: Poems on the Theatre by Bertolt Brecht); Helene Weigel: Actress, by Bertolt Brecht, 1961; Return to My Native Land by Aimé Césaire, 1969.

ABOUT: Vinson, J. (ed.) Contemporary Novelists, 1976; Who's Who, 1978. *Periodicals*—Book Week July 9, 1967; Books and Bookmen September 1972; Cambridge Quarterly Winter 1967, Autumn 1970; Chicago Sunday Tribune March 18, 1962; Commonweal July 11, 1969; Encounter June 1961; Guardian October 5, 1971; July 29, 1976; Nation September 4, 1967; New Republic July 1, 1972; October 7, 1972; New Statesman May 5, 1967; February 28, 1969; December 1, 1972; New York Review of Books November 30, 1972; New York Times October 24, 1976; New York Times Book Review May 25, 1969; September 10, 1972; Newsweek June 26, 1967; New Yorker October 18, 1976; Observer June 11, 1972; July 26, 1977; Spectator June 10, 1972; Times (London) November 24, 1972; March 5, 1973; Times Literary Supplement March 19, 1964; August 19, 1965; January 27, 1966; May 25, 1967; May 1, 1969; May 8, 1969; June 12, 1969; June 9, 1972; November 24, 1972.

"BERRINGTON, JOHN." *See*
BROWNJOHN, ALAN

*BETTELHEIM, BRUNO (August 23, 1903–), American psychologist, is descended from a Hungarian Jewish family which has produced many famous rabbis and physicians. He was born in Vienna, the son of Anton Bettelheim and the former Paula Seidler. Bettelheim was educated at the Reform Realgymnasium in Vienna, matriculating in 1921. He points out (in *The Informed Heart*) that the First World War made a profound impact on the formative years of Viennese intellectuals of his generation, whose "personal crisis of adolescence" was aggravated by the collapse of the Austro-Hungarian empire and the postwar social and economic chaos. "Since this adolescent crisis took place in Vienna against a family background of assimilated Jewish bourgeoisie, the influence of Freud and his teachings soon made itself felt." Bettelheim underwent psychoanalysis for several years, mainly for help with personal problems, and without at first intending to become an analyst, but became interested enough to specialize in psychology and philosophy at the University of Vienna, where he received his Ph.D. in 1938. When the Nazis occupied Austria in 1938 he was arrested and sent to concentration camps in Germany, first to Dachau and afterwards to Buchenwald. This experience was to have a profound impact on his later thought and work. In 1939 he was released and allowed to emigrate to the United States.

In America Bettelheim worked for the next two years as a research associate with the Progressive Education Association at the University of Chicago, and from 1942 to 1944 he was an associate professor of psychology at Rockford College in Illinois. He became an American citizen in 1944 and the same year moved to the University of Chicago as assistant professor of educational psychology, becoming associate professor in 1947 and full professor in 1952. On joining the Chicago faculty in 1944 he was also appointed principal of the university's Sonia Shankman Orthogenic School, a residential laboratory school devoted to the education and treatment of a small group of six- to fourteen-year-old children with special problems. They were all of average or above-average intelligence but suffered from severe emotional disorders that had not responded to treatment in other clinics.

Much of Bettelheim's writing has sprung from his work on the psychology of emotionally disturbed children, for whose treatment he has de-

*bet′ tel him

© 1979 by Jill Krementz

BRUNO BETTELHEIM

veloped new techniques. But he has also used his own experience as a Jew in Nazi concentration camps as a basis for studying the way people meet stress and as a jumping-off point for studying the psychological aspects of racial prejudice. He first attracted attention with an article called "Individual and Mass Behavior in Extreme Situations," published in the *Journal of Abnormal and Social Psychology* (October 1943), which set out to examine "the concentration camp as a means of producing changes in the prisoners which will make them more useful subjects of the Nazi state." This pioneer study of the effects of Nazi terror on personality, and of human adaptability to the stress of concentration camp life, won immediate and widespread recognition. It was reprinted in the magazine *Politics* and then in pamphlet form, by order of General Eisenhower becoming required reading for all United States military government officers in Europe.

Dynamics of Prejudice (1950), written in collaboration with Morris Janowitz, is a psychological and sociological study of racial prejudice based on interviews with GI veterans in the Chicago area, examining the ways in which their anxieties and their environments affected their attitudes and aggravated their hostility towards minority groups such as Negroes and Jews. The book has come to be regarded as a key work in this field. It was reprinted as part of the later book *Social Change and Prejudice* (1964), in which the original sociological and psychological findings are reassessed in the light of both social changes and developments in theory over the intervening years.

In *The Informed Heart: Autonomy in a Mass*

Age (1960), Bettelheim compares the deliberate attempt to break down normal human behavior in concentration camps with other forms of stress in modern societies that can threaten or destroy the individual's sense of identity. The basic theme of the book is the importance of preserving this personal autonomy and integrity. Bettelheim explores the sense of identity among prisoners of the Nazis, showing that for the *political* prisoners "who had expected persecution by the SS, imprisonment was less of a shock because they were psychically prepared for it"; they had something to believe in and were able to react to their terrible fate quite differently from prisoners who had no such convictions. The "non-political middle-class prisoners (a minority group in the concentration camps) were those least able to withstand the initial shock. They were utterly unable to understand what had happened to them and why. More than ever they clung to what had given them self-respect up to that moment." The sense of identity and self-esteem of the average member of this group rested on the props of social position and prestige, and when these were taken away he or she collapsed morally.

Bettelheim argues that the pressures of modern mass society, with its powerful conditioning mechanisms, can produce similar effects. He provides a sketch of his own background and experiences to show how these shaped his own search for ways to preserve the dignity and worth of human life, and his belief that despite society's stresses, self-realization can be achieved: "Our hearts must know the world of reason, and reason must be guided by an informed heart." B. H. Stoadley found the book "insightful, often brilliant, and frequently uneven," and Melvin Seeman wrote: "Though there is deep concern about the 'higher integration' that our changed environment calls for, there is very little answer to the problem of autonomy." Maurice Richardson also had reservations, finding himself less than fully convinced by Bettelheim's analogy between concentration camp life and the life of the present-day western subtopian man; nevertheless, he wrote, "his book gives you the impression of being lit from within by a humanist glow." In this book and elsewhere, Bettelheim sternly condemns the Jewish masses for failing to resist the Nazis.

A series of four books as well as many articles stem directly from Bettelheim's work at the Orthogenic School. *Love Is Not Enough* (1950) describes this unique laboratory school and the methods devised there to help disturbed children who have failed to respond to other treatment. The title is meant to suggest that though loving care is essential in returning a psychotic person to mental health, it must be underpinned by a consistent therapeutic philosophy, carefully applied. The book illustrates this principle by describing how the school handles everyday occurences with each child as they happen. Bettelheim believes that the study of abnormal psychology can teach a great deal about the functioning of the normal mind, and similarly, that the reactions of disturbed children to the shortcomings in their upbringing can throw light on the rearing of normal children. Here too, he argues, love is essential but not enough—parents must make deliberate efforts to "create a setting in which both their own legitimate needs and the needs of their children can be satisfied with relative ease." He concludes with the hope that "the experience gained at the school . . . may contribute to the greatest art of all—how to live a socially useful and emotionally satisfying life."

Bettelheim followed this "convincing and challenging" account of the school's general educational and therapeutic philosophy with the detailed case histories of four of its most seriously maladjusted children in *Truants From Life* (1955). Though the four were very different in personality and in their particular pathological conditions (severe delinquency, anorexia, institutionalism, and childhood psychosis), all were so severely disturbed that they were completely unable to function in society. Bettelheim describes their rehabilitation in detail, stressing that often the turning point was brought about by what might be seen as "momentous trifles." The book pursued the argument of *Love Is Not Enough* by showing how a unified philosophy, and an institution based on it, can be successful in restoring mental health in widely diverse cases. Some reviewers found the book too long, but it was generally welcomed. J. J. Farrell observed that "each of these children is unique, and their stories reveal something of that wonderful uniqueness which is a part of human nature. The account of how these children were restored to society is inspiring. Here are real success stories."

In the third book on the work of his school, *The Empty Fortress* (1967), Bettelheim presents a detailed discussion of therapeutic results in cases of infantile autism, a very severe psychosis whose victims withdraw into a self-oriented fantasy world excluding external reality. Bettelheim suggests that autistic behavior results from an infant's conviction that it has no control over its environment; some persistent disparity between the infant's needs and the mother's ability to satisfy them prevents the child from developing

73

a sense that his acts can get results. The book includes accounts of how autistic children were treated at Bettelheim's clinic, but a reviewer in the New York *Times Book Review* pointed out that besides being "a passionate, lucid account of these children . . . it is also a pioneering analysis of far wider scope—an attempt to explain the mysterious process by which all personality, healthy or disturbed, is formed."

In *A Home for the Heart* (1974), Bettelheim extends his argument to consider the whole idea of the mental hospital, from physical setting to staff training, arguing that the methods he has used so successfully in the Orthogenic School "can and must be applied to the treatment of all mental patients requiring residential treatment." He stresses that although the Orthogenic School was best known for its work with children, it had in fact broadened its scope to include some adolescents and young adults until it was treating about fifty patients at any given time, with an age range of six to twenty-six. Bettelheim's revolutionary therapy is one that relies on the dynamics of human relations, involving total cooperation between patients and staff. Treatment does *not* consist of regular, routine analytical sessions. Instead, the psychiatrist regards the patient as part of his own life, lives close by, is available day and night, and often receives as much as he gives from the mutual understanding and trust which is the basis of the school's concept of healing: "A person who is extremely insecure emotionally, such as the psychotic person, is as dependent psychologically on those who take care of him (in whose power he is) as the child is on his parents."

Not all of Bettelheim's books deal with disturbed children. *Dialogues With Mothers* (1962) records thirty-three discussions with mothers of normal children, led by the author, covering a wide range of specific problems in rearing children. It was hailed as a valuable and sometimes controversial contribution to the literature of child guidance and parent education. M. B. Hoover said of it: "All sessions reproduced in the book center around the problems of parents with children under six. But that should not limit the volume's audience, since the value of the discussions hinges not on the specific difficulties considered but on the way in which Dr. Bettelheim helps a mother achieve empathy with her child and insight into how her attitudes are affecting her thinking and actions . . . It is an unusual attempt to go a step beyond Spock."

The Children of the Dream (1969) is a controversial analysis of the communal rearing of children in Israeli kibbutzim, examining the difference in personality and basic attitudes resulting from this procedure. It is admittedly a personal and impressionistic account, based on only seven weeks of a fieldwork, mainly in one kibbutz; Naomi Shepherd concluded that "he is unable to judge whether the kibbutz education achieves the desired results precisely because he is unable to relate it to Israeli society as a whole." But Bettelheim's experiences with disturbed children have made him a severe critic of many middle-class American child-rearing practices, so that he was in a good position to suggest that some accepted traditions of education and family organization might usefully be reexamined in the light of experience derived from the kibbutz life-style. *Symbolic Wounds: Puberty Rites and the Envious Male* (1952) calls for a revised approach to Freud that would incorporate more recent knowledge.

Human fears and longings have been objectified all over the world in folk tales, and in *The Uses of Enchantment: The Meaning and Importance of Fairy Tales* (1976), Bettelheim studies such tales as fables of identity, symbolic representations of a child's struggle with his or her own desires and fears on the road to adult sexuality and independence: "Each fairy tale is a magic mirror which reflects some aspects of our inner world, and of the steps required by our evolution from immaturity to maturity." Each tale briefly and pointedly displays some "existential dilemma" in a way that helps a child to come to grips with his most difficult problems in their most essential form—problems of his own animality, his longing for power, his sexual desires and anxieties, his sense of dangers from within and without. In Bettelheim's Freudian interpretation, all the wicked stepmothers and fairy godmothers are, simply, Mother; the kings and hunters and even wolves are all Father; the two little pigs who are eaten in "The Three Little Pigs" are discarded stages in the development of the third—the only—pig; the witch's house and the parental home in "Hansel and Gretel" are two aspects of the same place.

However various, these stories are all images of trial successfully overcome, offering a sense of possibility and hope. Similar interpretations of folk tales have of course been made previously by both Freudian and Jungian psychoanalysts. But John Updike observed: "What is new, and exciting, is warmth, humane and urgent, with which Bettelheim expounds fairy tales as aids to the child's growth, which he understands as a growth through conflicts, the chief conflict being Oedipal." Bettelheim emphasizes the range of possible responses of children of different ages and sexes to the same tale. He also compares different versions of the old stories, preferring for example, the brutal folk version of Cinderella collected by the brothers Grimm to the prettier and more literary but psychologically less "necessary" version of Perrault, with its fairies and pumpkins. Bettelheim stresses that the stories should be presented without "explanation," allowing the listener to respond to the unspoken significances subconsciously. He argues that if the child is allowed to be his own interpreter, these tales will speak directly to his desperate isolation and unarticulated anxieties: "The fairy tale is therapeutic because the patient finds his own solutions, through contemplating what the story seems to imply about him and his inner conflicts at this moment in his life." *The Uses of Enchantment* brought Bettelheim both a National Book Award (1977) and the National Book Critics Circle award in criticism (1976). Elizabeth Janeway in her review wrote that "Bettelheim combines a capacity for lucid speech with a mind of rare strength and subtlety. . . . He is a natural parabolist, capable of seeing the universe in a grain of sand and passing the vision on."

From 1963 until his retirement in 1973, the author was Stella Rowley Professor of Education at the University of Chicago, and professor of psychology and psychiatry, as well as director of the Orthogenic School. Bettelheim is a fellow and diplomate of the American Psychological Association and a fellow of the American Orthopsychiatric Association. He was a founder member of the National Academy of Education, and belongs to the American Philosophical Society, the American Sociological Association, the American Association of University Professors, and the Chicago Psychoanalytic Society. Bettelheim was married in 1941 to Gertrud Weinfeld, a social worker. They have three children, Ruth, Naomi, and Eric.

PRINCIPAL WORKS: Love Is Not Enough: The Treatment of Emotionally Disturbed Children, 1950; (with Morris Janowitz) Dynamics of Prejudice, 1950; Symbolic Wounds: Puberty Rites and the Envious Male, 1952; Truants From Life: The Rehabilitation of Emotionally Disturbed Children, 1955; The Informed Heart: Autonomy in a Mass Age, 1960; Paul and Mary: Two Case Histories from Truants From Life, 1961; Dialogues With Mothers, 1962; Social Change and Prejudice, 1964; The Empty Fortress: Infantile Autism and the Birth of Self, 1967; The Children of the Dream, 1969; A Home for the Heart, 1974; The Uses of Enchantment, 1976.

ABOUT: Bettelheim, B. The Informed Heart, 1960; Current Biography, 1961; Des Pres, T. The Survivor, 1976; Fromm, E. The Anatomy of Human Destructiveness, 1973; International Who's Who, 1978–79; Who's Who in America, 1976–1977. *Periodicals*—American Journal of Sociology May 1961, July 1969; Conservative Judaism Spring 1970; Harper's June 1976; Harvard Educational Review Fall 1967; Nation April 1, 1961; National Review May 10, 1974; New Republic March 4, 1967; May 24, 1969; New Statesman March 17, 1961; September 25, 1969; New York Review of Books July 15, 1976; New York Times February 12, 1950; September 17, 1950; New York Times Book Review October 8, 1961; April 6, 1969; March 17, 1974; May 23, 1976; New York Times Magazine January 11, 1970; Saturday Review July 8, 1961; April 18, 1964; May 15, 1976; Times Literary Supplement October 9, 1969; Yad Vashem Studies 8 1970.

BIRNEY, (ALFRED) EARLE (May 13, 1904–), Canadian poet, novelist, and critic, writes: "My parents worked a small stock ranch and vegetable farm in a remote area of central Alberta. Our only close neighbors, two miles away, were Piegan Indians, who did not encourage visitors. An only child, I saw other children at Sunday School at the flagstation (pop. 50). Between the long savage winters I was a Wordsworthian boy, solitary and independent; my playmates were the barnyard birds and animals, the minnows in our creek. The pathless firwoods around me were magical presences; invisible creatures drummed and hooted, partridge and owl, and sometimes a lynx mewed. When the September snows came, my father would make the hundred-mile train journey to the city of Calgary (pop. 50,000) to earn, at his old trade of housepainting and paperhanging, the necessary cash the ranch never supplied. Then my mother tended the stock, with what little help I could give, in temperatures as low as 55 below zero Fahrenheit. I learned to read with my mother's help, from her Bible and the weekly farm paper, and a bowdlerized Burns.

"When I turned seven my father sold the ranch and set up at his trade in the village of Banff, high in the Rockies. Here I took my grade schooling and tried to become a social animal. But now the wilderness rose to peaks a mile above me, and the winter ice sometimes lay bare for miles along the town's river. I flubbed at hockey, became a speed skater, learned to fish and to climb mountains. World War One came; my father volunteered as a stretcher-bearer and was whisked to France. My mother boarded tourists and I sold newspapers and worked as a butcher's boy. Two years later my father came back, a shell-shock case, unable to work at his trade. A grateful government found him another sub-marginal farm, this one in a fruit valley in British Columbia, where I had my high schooling. At fifteen I started wandering, working first as a farm laborer and axeman, then by turns a bank clerk, surveyor's rodman, pick-and-shovel laborer, mountain guide, fossil collector. At eighteen I had enough money to try a year at British Columbia's university in Vancouver. By dint of scholarships, and summer wages, variously, as a housepainter, mosquito control fore-

EARLE BIRNEY

man and weekly newspaper editor I made it through to the B.A. In the process I stopped wanting to be a geological engineer, explorer and author, and settled for teaching English.

"The next eight summers I drilled Vancouver's 'repeating' freshmen in Composition (at $300 a summer) and in the first four winters, in substitution for my unwritten poems, wrote marginalia in thousands of sophomore essays at the universities of Toronto and California, to make another $700 and pay my fees through the M.A. to the brink of the Ph.D. But the Depression caught me with my doctoral thesis unfinished and I was lucky to find an instructor's job in the University of Utah, and even luckier when I was fired three years later for supporting a miners' strike broken by state troops and Silver Shirt vigilantes. The only job I had in sight was a ten-dollar-a-week one as a professional revolutionary in New York, but along came a telegram from the Royal Society of Canada offering me a $1500 scholarship to the University of London to complete my doctoral thesis on Chaucer.

"I made the money last two years, by working my passage from Vancouver to England on a freighter, and living in a working-class area of East London. Half the time went to completing the thesis, in the British Museum, the other half as an activist in the Independent Labour Party, speaking in London squares and on streetcorners, writing for the Left press, travelling through Britain organizing unemployed groups, and interviewing Trotsky in Norway.

"In 1936 I received my Ph.D. at the University of Toronto and was appointed to their staff in English. Six more years slipped by. I served as literary editor and reviewer for the *Canadian*

Forum, published revised sections of my thesis in the usual learned publications, and until 1940, continued to write and work for the radical press. The war which, as a Marxist, I had long predicted, had arrived, and I was caught up in it. From 1940 to 1942 I continued teaching in the daytime and in evenings trained, and trained others, for infantry. Then I volunteered for overseas duties with the Canadian Army and spent the next three years in Britain, Belgium and Holland. Before I left, however, I set down quickly a group of poems I had been long intending to write. Their locale was largely the western wilderness in which I had spent my early years. They appeared as a book which was awarded the Governor-General's medal for the best collection of poetry published that year in Canada. I came back from the wars with a second collection, which was similarly honored.

"From then on, though I was to put in twenty more years as a professor, I believed myself to be a poet, certainly, and a man of letters, hopefully. I found the need of the novel form, to write out what I wanted to say about the Second World War and about my activist radical days. I have also written a good deal of radio and television drama, two books attacking traditional concepts of education in literature, and a few short stories and travel articles. For the last thirty years I have been increasingly involved in both sound and concrete poetry and in the presentation of slides and readings to carry my own experimentations to as wide a public as possible. In addition to semi-annual tours of my own country, I have been able, with the help of the Canada Council, to read Canadian poetry to audiences through Latin America and the West Indies, Britain, Africa, South Asia, Australia and New Zealand. I have just recently returned from my third (and last) round-the-world reading tour. Although my *Collected Poems* came out this year, I am projecting a new book of verse, and several prose books for publication before 1980."

Birney is the son of William B. Birney and the former Martha Robertson. His father, who came from Leighton Buzzard in England, arrived in Alberta in 1880 and was for some years a prospector before he turned his hand to farming. The family settled in the mountain village of Banff in 1911 and Earle Birney began his formal education there, as he says, in a school which had "a library full of Everymans and Henties, and . . . teachers who took time to interest us in reading." When his father returned from the war, the family moved to the Kootenay region of British

Columbia, where Birney attended Creston High School.

He entered the University of British Columbia in 1922, intending to become an engineer, but switched to English and graduated in 1926 *magna cum laude*. As he explains above, poverty and political activism so interrupted and prolonged his education that ten more years passed before he received his doctorate from the University of Toronto, where he remained as an instructor, then assistant professor of English, from 1936 to 1942.

"I was so all-fired clear-cut political in the thirties," Birney says, "that I regarded the writing of poetry as a treacherous withdrawal of energy from the class struggle." Consequently though he had begun to write in the 1920s, it was not until the late 1930s when he was settled at the University of Toronto that his poems began to appear with any regularity—many of them in *Canadian Forum*, of which he was literary editor from 1936 to 1940. His first collection, *David*, was published in 1942, when he was thirty-eight. The title piece is a long narrative poem about a boy, climbing in the Rockies, whose older companion is desperately injured in a fall. The boy must decide whether or not to try to save him, or to allow him to die as he wishes.

The poem is written in interlinked quatrains of subtly assonantal four- and five-stress lines. Its diction has been called "strong, active and violent," with images drawn largely from warfare and animal ferocity. Immensely popular, and widely regarded as a minor classic, "David" has been praised for the "solidity of its design, the truth of its drama, the remarkable suggestiveness of the glacier imagery and the mountain-climber's language."

Other poems in the book more directly reflected Birney's radical political commitment and, in their form and language, his academic training in Old and Middle English literature. "Anglo-Saxon Street," for example, is according to one critic "an ingenious adaptation of Old English alliterative verse to modern squalid urban subject matter." All the same Paul West, while finding much to admire in these early poems, complained of a lack of synthesis between their fundamentally philosophical content and their "tent-pegging" detail.

From 1943 to 1945 Birney served with the Canadian Army's Infantry Personnel Selection Service, ending the war as major-in-charge of personnel selection in the Northwest Theatre. Back in Canada, he was for a year supervisor of European foreign language broadcasts for Radio Canada in Montreal. He then resumed his academic career as professor of medieval English literature (1946–1963) and then as head of the department of creative writing (1963–1965) at the University of British Columbia. He was editor of *Canadian Poetry Magazine* in 1946–1948 and of *Prism International* in 1964–1965.

Now Is Time, his second collection, appeared in 1945 and deals with the war, rehabilitation, and Birney's hopes for a more loving and reasonable postwar society. One critic wrote that "a strong sense of optimism pervades the book in which, with a Chaucerian attention to the detail of contemporary life, Birney resumes his role as Canadian chronicler." The same might be said of *The Strait of Anian,* though here it was thought that the humanist affirmations were growing somewhat half-hearted and skeptical. *Trial of a City* comprised, along with a dozen new poems, a mordant satirical verse play in which various witnesses are called to decide whether the city of Vancouver (and, by implication, mankind in general) should be saved or damned.

Most critics agree that Birney's verse reached maturity in *Ice Cod Bell or Stone* (1962). Paul West regards this volume as Birney's finest achievement, in its best poems tellingly combining "pastiche of raw vernacular" with "cool meditation studded with vivid detail." The collection includes a dozen poems about Mexico, and others set in the Far East—India, Japan, Thailand, and elsewhere—like this exuberant and life-affirming account of a Japanese boy with a kite:

> tall in the bare sky and huge as Gulliver
> a carp is rising golden and fighting
> thrusting the paper body up from the fist
> of a small boy on an empty roof higher
> and higher in the winds of the world.
>
> (from "A Walk in Kyoto")

Paul West would disagree with those who regard Birney as primarily a chronicler of the Canadian scene, maintaining that it is precisely the Canadian poems in this volume that are the least successful—a fact that (using Birney's own phrase) he attributes to Canada's "lack of ghosts":

> We French, we English, never lost our civil war,
> endure it still, a bloodless civil bore;
> no wounded lying about, no Whitman wanted.
> It's only by our lack of ghosts we're haunted.

George Woodcock has called Birney a "sharply intellectual" and also "critical" poet, because "the stylistic criticism embodied in the form of his poems is matched by the social and moral criticism embodied in the content." This critical faculty is applied to Birney's own work when, as he often does, he revises his poems in accordance with his own changing views about his experience of life and the forms in which these views may best be expressed.

Woodcock finds the poetry Birney wrote during the early 1960s the "most congenial"—that "in which he combines his topographical flair with his sense of history and his power of conveying the immediacy of present experience." This judgement is, perhaps, a tacit rejection of Birney's experiments with sound and concrete poetry. The poet himself explains his interest in these forms by saying (in *Contemporary Poets*) that he believes poetry to be "both an oral entertainment and a visual notation." It is characteristic of him that, even in his seventies, he should "hope to remain responsive—but eclectic—in relation to contemporary change and experimentation."

Paul West writes that Birney is, like Chaucer, "voracious for the detail of contemporary life and yet, while musing on and exposing foible, lunging after ghosts, the miraculous or the shining timeless. . . . The method is compactly allusive, as if he wants to transform everything. And the key to Birney's power . . . is his urge towards myth." Another critic, writing in the *Times Literary Supplement,* suggests that "Birney may be the single important living poet strongly influenced by Chaucer. . . . no poet draws upon a richer vocabulary—literary and colloquial, archaic and ephemeral, scientific and common. Few poets can handle so wide a range of rhythm patterns so expressively. Even fewer have Birney's skill in dramatizing an action or anecdote. His ability to capture every level or variety of English speech is at least as rare. Only his ironic humour belongs to many modern poets," of whom few share "that immense sympathy with the suffering and the voiceless which gives Birney his authority." But he "seldom grants himself the respect he deserves . . . one finds him isolating the humorous persona of his work from the lyric inner self," though "it is only when the two elements are connected that Birney's highest powers can be felt."

Turvey (1949) is subtitled "a military picaresque" and the novel was, Birney says, "written out of things that happened to me, or stories told to me, during the Second World War." Private Thomas Leadbeater Turvey is a Canadian GI, naive and enthusiastic. He is eager to fight his country's enemies but never sees one, instead finding himself enmeshed in one bureaucratic muddle after another. He returns joyfully in the end to civilian life, his irrepressible individuality undiminished. Reviewers were reminded of Hašek's *Good Soldier Schweik* and, though Turvey has none of Schweik's peasant cunning, the novels have in common a faith in the eventual victory of the individual over "the inhumanity of mass organization." Admired for its "wholly convincing comic unity," the novel brought Birney the Stephen Leacock medal for humor in 1950.

Down the Long Table, which followed in 1955, is equally satirical but more serious. Professor Gordon Saunders is a Canadian teacher in the United States. While under investigation by a tribunal closely resembling the House Un-American Activities Committee, he remembers the events and circumstances which brought him into and out of the Communist Party and a period of social militancy in Vancouver in the 1930s. The vividness of the novel as a social and historical document and its command of colloquial speech patterns were much admired, but it seemed to George Woodcock that it was "divided by conflict between the historical impulse to reconstruct authentically time past and the fictional impulse to establish a self-consistent imaginary world." Birney says that he regards his short stories as "extensions of my work as a poet. More relaxed in style than my best-known poem 'David', they are nevertheless equally symbolic in technique, and unified around a two-person relationship and a definitive action."

Birney was writer-in-residence at the University of Toronto in 1965–1967 and at the University of Waterloo, Ontario, in 1967–1968. In 1968 he went to the University of California, Irvine, as Regents Professor in Creative Writing. He received a Borestone Mountain award for poetry in 1951 and the Lorne Pierce Medal in 1953. He has an honorary doctorate from the University of Alberta and is a Fellow of the Royal Society of Canada. Birney was married in 1940 to Esther Bull and has one child, William.

PRINCIPAL WORKS: *Poetry*—David and Other Poems, 1942; Now Is Time, 1945; The Strait of Anian, 1948; Trial of a City and Other Verse, 1952; Ice Cod Bell or Stone, 1962; Near False Creek Mouth, 1964; Selected Poems: 1940–1966, 1966; Memory No Servant, 1968; The Poems of Earle Birney, 1969; Pnomes, Jukollages and Other Stunzas, 1969; (with others) Five Modern Canadian Poets, edited by Eli Mandel, 1970; Rag and Bone Shop, 1971; (with others) Four Parts Sand: Concrete Poems, 1972; What's So Big About Green?, 1973; The Bear on the Delhi Road (selected poems), 1973; Collected Poems (two volumes), 1975; The Rugging and the Moving Times, 1976; Alphabeings & Other Seasyours, 1976. *Novels*—Turvey, 1949; Down the Long Table, 1955. *Essays*—The Creative Writer, 1966; The Cow Jumped Over the Moon: The Writing and Reading of Poetry, 1972. *As Editor*—Twentieth Century Canadian Poetry, 1953; (with Margerie Bonner Lowry) The Selected Poems of Malcolm Lowry, 1962; (with Margerie Bonner Lowry) Malcolm Lowry's Lunar Caustic, 1968 (first published in Paris Review 29 1963).

ABOUT: Contemporary Authors 1-4, 1st revision, 1967; Davey, F. Earle Birney, 1971; International Who's Who, 1978–79; International Who's Who in Poetry, 1977–1978; Klinck, C.F. Literary History of Canada, 1965; Nesbitt, B. (ed.) Critical Views on Earle Birney, 1974; New, W.H. Articulating West, 1972; Pacey, D. Ten Canadian Poets, 1958; Percival, W.P. (ed.) Leading Canadian Poets, 1948; Phelps, A.L. Canada Writes, 1951; Robillard, R. Earle Birney, 1971; Silvestre, G. (and others) Canadian Writers, 1967; Vinson, J. (ed.) Contemporary Novelists, 1976; Vinson, J. (ed.) Contemporary Poets, 1975; Woodcock, G. Odysseus Ever Returning, 1973. Periodicals—Ambit Summer 1965; Canadian Forum July-August 1971, September 1972; Canadian Literature Summer 1962, Autumn 1966, Winter 1967; English Autumn 1962, Autumn 1965, Summer 1967; Guardian October 26, 1973; Journal of Commonwealth Literature July 1967; Lugano Review 1 1975; Northwest Review Spring-Summer 1965; Outposts Autumn 1965, Spring 1974; Saturday Review October 9, 1965; Times Literary Supplement October 26, 1973; West Coast Review October 1970 (bibliography).

Thomas Victor © 1979

PAUL BLACKBURN

BLACKBURN, PAUL (November 24, 1926– September 13, 1971), American poet, translator, and editor, was born in St. Albans, Vermont, the son of William Blackburn and the former Frances Frost, a poet and novelist. Blackburn attended New York University for a time and then, after two years in the United States Army, went on to the University of Wisconsin (B.A., 1950). It was then that he read the *Cantos* of Ezra Pound and through them developed an interest in Provençal poetry. He pursued his Provençal studies as a Fulbright student at the University of Toulouse (1954–1955), remained there for another year as a lecturer, and then lived for almost two years (1956–1957) in Spain and Morocco. Blackburn was fluent in French and Spanish, and moderately so in Catalan, Portuguese, Italian, and German. Returning to New York, a city he loved, he worked at various jobs —for a time as a printer—and in 1959 joined Funk & Wagnalls as an associate editor of the *New International Yearbook,* a post he retained until 1962.

Blackburn listed among his sources and influences "the work of Ezra Pound and William Carlos Williams, Robert Graves' *White Goddess,* and many of my contemporaries." It was through a correspondence with Pound that he came to know Robert Creeley, Charles Olson, Cid Corman, Jonathan Williams, and others who in one way or another shared his approach to poetry and his intense interest in technique. Some of his early work appeared in Corman's magazine *Origins* and Creeley's *Black Mountain Review,* and Blackburn is often discussed as if he had been a member of the Black Mountain or

"projectivist" school of poetry with which these poets were associated. He himself denied this, and said rather that the sort of work that interested him started in the early 1950s "with Olson, Creeley, Corman, myself, and then the people at Black Mountain picked it up, and apparently the movement came to some sort of explosion with the San Francisco Renaissance."

In the same interview, in David Ossman's *The Sullen Art* (1963), Blackburn explained his approach to prosody: "What goes into the poem, especially in the last ten years, is very much a matter of speech rhythms and of natural, rather than forced rhythms. That is why a poem may very well seem to have no obvious structure whatsoever. . . . It just doesn't work out that simply, because the rhythms that you start with and that you have to resolve are very often irregular in themselves, or are more highly charged, simply because they are the way we speak." All the same, a poem "must tie together as a musical unit—however irregular it looks on the page, and even if it sounds almost free-form. . . . like any piece of music, it needs resolution."

Blackburn's debt to William Carlos Williams is evident in this emphasis on natural speech rhythms and was noted by Frederick Eckman in his review of Blackburn's first book, *The Dissolving Fabric,* published by Robert Creeley's Divers Press in Majorca in 1955. Eckman found these poems mostly "fragmentary perceptions cast in delicate, free rhythms. They wear an idiomatic surface, beneath which rests an ironic sophistication." It is interesting that in this early work the reviewer sensed a certain conflict between the idiomatic diction adopted by Blackburn and "a tendency, usually restrained before it becomes very apparent, toward a kind of rhetoric—repetition, parallelism, dramatic close—that is anathema to the Williams esthetic."

Brooklyn-Manhattan Transit followed in 1960, *The Nets* in 1961, and *Sing-Song* in 1966, all small collections from small presses. Many of these poems were first heard in Lower East Side coffeehouses in the readings which became institutionalized as the Poetry Project, St. Mark's Church. By its nature, Blackburn's poetry benefits from being read aloud, and he used a variety of typographical devices in his books in an attempt to insure that the pace and pauses he intended would be followed by other readers:

Rise at 7:15
study the
artifacts
    (2 books
    1 photo
    1 gouache sketch
    2 unclean socks
perform the neces-
sary ablutions
    hands
    face
    feet
    crotch)
even answer the door with good grace, even
if it's the light & gas man
announcing himself as "EDISON!
Readjer meter mister?"
For Christ sake yes
read my meter
Nothing can alter the euphoria
The blister is still on one finger
    There just are
some mornings worth getting up
    & making a cup
of coffee that's all

        ("Good Morning Love!")

It may have been the unorthodox rhythms and appearance of his usually highly accessible poetry that delayed its general acceptance, but by the early 1960s the quality of his work was widely recognized by other poets. Paul Carroll is quoted by David Ossman as saying: "I don't suppose any poet of our age handles a single line, a stanza, a whole poem with his grace and skill," and Gilbert Sorrentino spoke of the "great staggering sweetness of hopeless futility" in his verse —its "wry, flat statement of the world, ah God, what a hopeless place it is, after all."

The Cities (1967) was the first of Blackburn's books to come from a major publisher. The dominant motif, according to M.L. Rosenthal, was of "the speaker going through the motions of living, thinking, and sensing the passing moments in the wake of a broken marriage":

Dried green leaf on the door
Blackened leaf below it

Under that a metal leaf, blackened also
Below that the leafy ace of clubs

Outside the window the tree I thought a friend
has undressed all its branches & is ugly to me

Returning home defenseless. . . .

        (from "The Quarrel")

From this central motif, Rosenthal said, the poems lead out in various directions—"humorous, sensuously recreative of the concrete outside world, speculative (especially about sex and love and their contemporary meaning or, rather, the way we are changing our experience of them), and collagist."

The last collection to appear during Blackburn's short lifetime was *In. On. Or About the Premises* (1968). Here, as elsewhere, he writes about barrooms, subways, Bowery derelicts, the city of New York, and what one reviewer delicately called "the jobs of ingestion, elimination and coition." When Blackburn writes of the outcasts of his city, he speaks in their own accent and idiom, quite without condescension or self-congratulation, with a compassion that was found "at once generous and alarming." Charles Stein thought that the witty surfaces of these "fast-paced, open-form poems . . . belie a darker, almost desperate content."

Paul Blackburn died of cancer in 1971, when he was forty-four. A great deal of his poetry remained uncollected at the time of his death, and several posthumous volumes have appeared—*Early Selected y Mas* (1972), *Halfway Down the Coast* (1975), and *The Journals* (1975). In an affectionate review of the last two in *The Nation*, Michael Stephens said that Blackburn wrote "poems of life without apology, without posturing. . . . Many unaware writers and critics failed to discern the complex forms, the sly intelligence, the reserved elegance of that lyrical gift. . . . Blackburn was socially and literally accessible as lesser poets, and yet he was cut from the fabric of genius." *The Journals* is a chronicle in poetry and prose of the years from 1967 to 1971. "As the book progresses," Stephens wrote, "the idea of death is superseded by the daily elements of physical decline and the actuality of dying. This book is remarkable for many reasons, among which are the maturity of Blackburn's poetry and poetics, the energy and intelligence of the writing, and the human courage informing every utterance. *The Journals* presents consummate Blackburn. The book culls deep intelligence, vast energy which refuses to wane with cancer, experience, and boldface energy. As the book presents new hope for poetry, it simultaneously breaks new ground for prose. Novelists of the future should read this work."

Blackburn became poetry editor of *The Nation* in 1962, and was associate editor of the *World Scope Encyclopedia Yearbook* in 1963-1965. He was poet-in-residence at the Aspen Writers' Workshop in the summer of 1965 and a staff member there in 1966-1967, when he was also poet-in-residence at the City College of New York. He lectured at CCNY in 1968, before going to the State University College at Cortland, New York. His translations included a volume of Spanish poetry, *Proensa,* the Spanish epic *El Cid,* two volumes of short stories by Julio Cortázar, and a collection of poems by Picasso.

M.L. Rosenthal wrote that Blackburn was "a gentle, affectionate person with devoted friends all over the country." Michael Stephens, similarly, said that he "knew Ezra Pound ... Black Mountaineers, New York poets, and just plain folk who enjoyed, like Blackburn, booze, beer, cigarettes and conversation." The poet was married three times—to Winifred Gray McCarthy, to Sara Golden, and to Joan D. Miller—and had one son, Carlos.

He was "so naturally, so humanly a poet," according to Rosenthal, "that to read him is to tune in at once, intimately, on our own inner selves. . . . The poems are always immediate. They isolate a situation or atmosphere or mood and let the poet's aroused and varied feelings play over it. . . . Blackburn was probably our finest poet of city life since Kenneth Fearing. He knew the lingo and tempo of New York. . . . His voice is often a sounding board for the whole sense of a New York moment," but he could also "sense the absolute stillness of a moment in the Spanish countryside, the perplexity of anyone's articulateness before the stunning dilemmas of existence, the triumph of joy at the incongruity of things under the most dismaying literal conditions." Joseph Wilson similarly speaks of Blackburn's "lyric wonder before the real," and says: "Blackburn's poems finally 'come alive' for the ear and eye and mind; they *are* an experience with all the personal meanings of any situation."

PRINCIPAL WORKS: Poetry—The Dissolving Fabric, 1955; Brooklyn-Manhattan Transit: A Bouquet for Flatbush, 1960; The Nets, 1961; Sing-Song, 1966; The Reardon Poems, 1967; The Cities, 1967; In. On. Or About the Premises, 1968; Early Selected y Mas: Poems 1949-1966, 1972; Halfway Down the Coast, 1975; The Journals, edited by Robert Kelly, 1975. Translations—Proensa, 1953; Poem of the Cid, 1966; End of the Game (stories) by Julio Cortazar, 1967; Hunk of Skin (poems) by Pablo Picasso, 1968; Cronopios and Famas (stories) by Julio Cortazar, 1969; Peire Vidal (poems), 1972.

ABOUT: Contemporary Authors 33-36, 1973; Leary, P. and Kelly, R. (eds.) A Controversy of Poets, 1965; Malkoff, K. (ed.) Crowell's Handbook of Contemporary American Poetry, 1974; Murphy, R. (ed.) Contemporary Poets of the English Language, 1970; Ossman, D. The Sullen Art, 1963; Penguin Companion to Literature 3, 1971; Rosenthal, M.L. The New Poets, 1967. Periodicals—Contemporary Literature Spring 1972; New York Times September 15, 1971; New York Times Book Review August 11, 1974; Poetry October 1956, May 1969.

BLOOM, HAROLD (July 11, 1930–), American literary critic, was born in New York City, the son of William and Paula (Lev) Bloom. He was educated at Cornell University, where he received his B.A. in English in 1951, and at Yale, which gave him his Ph.D. in 1955. The same year Bloom began his teaching career at Yale and he has remained there, becoming an assistant professor in 1960, associate professor in 1963, and professor of English in 1965. Since 1974 he has been De Vane Professor of the Humanities.

Harold Bloom has become well known as an interpreter of the tradition of Romanticism in both English and American literature, and especially in poetry. He has put forward a view of literary history and its relation to creative originality quite antithetical to that of T. S. Eliot, who in his commitment to Christian orthodoxy, classicism, and conservatism had rejected the Romantic emphasis on visionary poetry of the individual imagination in favor of the metaphysical and religious poetry of the seventeenth century. Bloom on the contrary argues for the centrality of Romanticism as the major English poetic line.

Bloom's early books are powerful studies of the major Romantic poets. He sees Shelley as a prophetic and religious poet whose passionate convictions happen to be agnostic, and in *Shelley's Mythmaking* (1959) he places at the very heart of Shelley's poetry its mythopoeic power. Shelley, drowned at twenty-nine, made no single poem that shows all his powers working together, but in the most important of his completed poems, *Prometheus Unbound,* he "shares with Blake and Wordsworth an ambition to replace *Paradise Lost.*" Bloom's approach to myth-making is largely through the neo-Hasidic religious mythopoeism of Martin Buber, with its vocabulary of I-Thou and I-It relationships—Bloom describes myth-making as "the confrontation of life by life, a meeting between subjects, not subjects and objects." The *Keats-Shelley Journal* said of the book that "the figure emerging from this study is a rather more vital one than is generally to be found in Shelley criticism: a genuine visionary struggling to overcome his human limitations. Bloom's book is bound to affect

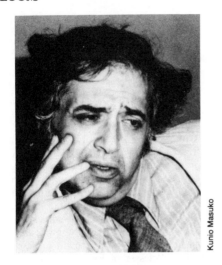

Kunio Masuko

HAROLD BLOOM

subsequent analyses of Shelley's art." The *Times Literary Supplement* was scathing, however, complaining that Bloom's interpretation of Shelley involved "the omission of *Adonais,* and such other essential poems as do not fit it."

Bloom further develops the themes of Romantic myth-making and the relationship between nature and imagination in *The Visionary Company: A Reading of English Romantic Poetry* (1961, revised edition 1971). This is a detailed account, with prose paraphrases, of all the major poems of the six great English Romantic poets—Blake, Wordsworth, Coleridge, Byron, Shelley, and Keats—as well as some minor poets like Beddoes and John Clare. Bloom tries throughout to isolate certain persistent themes, symbols, and attitudes in Romantic poetry: "The poetry of the English Romantics is a kind of religious poetry, and the religion is in the Protestant line, though Calvin and Luther would have been horrified to contemplate it. . . . there are at least two main traditions of English poetry, and what distinguishes them are not only aesthetic considerations but conscious differences in religion and politics. One line, and it is the central one, is Protestant, radical, and Miltonic-Romantic; the other is Catholic, conservative, and by its claims, classical." And Bloom concludes: "The central desire of Blake and Wordsworth, and of Keats and Shelley, was to find a final good in human existence itself."

As he was soon to show, Bloom is very much concerned with the ways in which poets influence one another, and it seemed to R. O. Preyer that, while "there is little in the way of critical evaluation" in the book, the reader "is directed instead toward a tissue of correspondences, analogies, analogues, and similarities." Preyer called the result "perceptive, irritating, repetitive, and even profound," and other critics agreed. One in the *Times Literary Supplement* found Bloom's prose "often tortured and obscure, sometimes downright absurd," though "embedded in [the] paraphrases, and often impeded by them, are critical judgments of validity and worth." As a companion volume to this study Bloom produced the anthology *English Romantic Poetry* (1961), which John Holmes described as "a necessary, intelligent, and ample collection."

Blake's Apocalypse (1963), a study of William Blake's major prophetic books, was followed by Bloom's interpretation of a twentieth-century Romantic, W. B. Yeats. Bloom begins by saying that "Yeats was a poet very much in the line of vision; his ancestors in English poetic tradition were primarily Blake and Shelley, and his achievement will at last be judged against theirs." Therefore, though the book provides a detailed account of Yeat's complicated mythic system, Bloom relates his poetry not to the esoteric traditions the poet himself invoked, but to his ancestors in the English Romantic tradition. A critic in *Library Journal* wrote: "This study is significant both as criticism and as criticism of Yeats. It is also going to be highly controversial; Bloom is either adulated or scorned as a critic, there is no moderate view. Here his prose is typically dense and tangled, his methodology typically impeccable. . . . a major study which will influence critical thought in many areas and will cause great debate among scholars and lovers of Yeats."

The Ringers in the Tower: Studies in Romantic Tradition (1971) is a collection of Bloom's essays reprinted from magazines, anthologies, and paperback introductions of the previous decade. The "Romantic tradition" here ranges from Blake to such contemporary American poets as Allen Ginsberg and A. R. Ammons. Though their occasions had been so different, these essays are like all of Bloom's work variations on a small group of themes. Margaret Lebowitz spoke of their emphasis "on Blakean and Coleridgean motifs of metaphysical idealism and on a psychoanalytically conditioned sensitivity to 'violence,' " and praised Bloom for his "clarity and astonishing insight." *Choice,* on the other hand, found the book "long on subjective 'interpretations' and comparisons . . . , short on style and literary analysis. . . . Bloom generally leaves his ringers dead."

There followed four books in which Bloom enunciated an ambitious, original, and characteristically controversial theory of poetry and how it is created. In *The Anxiety of Influence* (1973) he lays out the essence of this theory: "Poetic influence—when it involves two strong, authentic poets—always proceeds by a misreading of the prior poet, an act of creative correction that is actually and necessarily a misinterpretation. The history of fruitful poetic influence, which is to say the main traditions of Western poetry since the Renaissance, is a history of anxiety and self-serving caricature, of distortion, of perverse, willful revisionism without which modern poetry as such could not exist." Even critics who jibbed at Bloom's concept of misreading recognized the force of his claim that the history of poetry is in part the history of the struggle between great poets and their great precursors—that Blake defined his own genius in the struggle to free himself from Milton's dominating influence and to "rewrite" *Paradise Lost.* It may be argued that the same sort of creative conflict or tension existed between Virgil and Homer, Dante and Virgil, Milton and Spenser, Wordsworth and Milton. In Freudian terms, as Bloom puts it, this creative conflict is like the necessary conflict between the son and the father (which often involves a stage when the son denies the father's paternity). Bloom's model for this conflict is the struggle of Satan against God in *Paradise Lost,* and he goes on to describe half a dozen ways in which poets exploit and "revise" the work of their "precursor angels" in the attempt to clear a space for themselves.

Few critics were wholly convinced by this startling book, and most were irritated by some aspects of it, but Reed Whittemore thought it "should be one of the most discussed books of literary criticism for the last three hundred years." John Hollander, pointing out that Bloom has always been more of an interpreter than an explainer, called the book "aphoristic, dense, allusive, and more than a little outrageous. It is far from being a handbook of criticism, and remains theoretical in that it makes demands of a critical method without specifying how they are to be met. After being debated and mulled over, it may turn out to embody what is after all a theory of American poetry. The American imagination in its anxiety about the precursor, Europe, suggests itself as an exemplary image throughout. . . . In any case, this remarkable book has raised profound questions about where in the mind the creative process is to be located, and about how the prior visions of other poems are, for a true poet, as powerful as his own dreams and as formative as his domestic childhood."

In *A Map of Misreading* (1975) Bloom sets out to show how his theory of misreading or "mis-

prision" works in practice, dealing at some length with Browning's "Childe Roland," and examining the influence of Milton and of Emerson on their literary heirs. A number of readers found, as Michael Wood did, that "a vision as large as this is a lot larger than I need," but commended the "sheer care for poetry" which the book demonstrated. E. W. Said wrote: "Bloom is the most rare of critics. He has what seems to be a totally detailed command of English poetry and its scholarship, as well as an intimate acquaintance with the major avantgarde critical theories of the last quarter century. . . . Yet for Bloom this gigantic apparatus, to which he has assimilated Freudian theory and the Kabbalistic doctrines of Isaac Luria, a sixteenth-century Jewish mystic, is no mere scholarly baggage. Since it is the essence of Bloom's vision that every poem is the result of a critical act, by which another, earlier poem is deliberately misread, and hence rewritten, it follows also that Bloom's sense of the poems he has read is intensely combative, constantly experienced, actively felt. This is polemical criticism at its fiercest and most brilliant."

The third book in Bloom's tetralogy is *Kabbalah and Criticism* (1975), in which he explains the sources and techniques he uses in his criticism, and reveals the extent of his debt to Freud, Nietzsche, Vico, Emerson, and above all to the great scholars and interpreters of the Kabbalah —he maintains that the doctrines of Isaac Luria and others provide "a dialectic of creation astonishingly close to revisionist poetics." John Hollander enjoyed "the condensed, often wild, frequently humorous and good natured tone of this little book," but others found it difficult and idiosyncratic. There was an equally mixed response to the final book in this group, *Poetry and Repression* (1976). Here Bloom discusses the poet's struggles with his own psyche as well as continuing his examination of poetry as "a psychic defense against poetic parents." This time there were objections to Bloom's kabbalistic and "formidably arcane" critical vocabulary (though Helen Vendler pointed out that "Bloom has always wanted a theology to support his literary theory," as in his early use of Martin Buber, and wants "to see whether we possess other ways of interpreting the cosmos besides our Platonic and Aristotelian ones"). There were complaints also about the "violence" of his critical approach, in which, Christopher Ricks wrote, "critics rail; figures of speech murder; effects battle; poetry menaces and must assault. . . . [and] poets have to be made up to take part in this lurid melodrama." For some critics, all the same, Bloom's theories were interesting enough to surmount these annoyances.

Another collection of his critical essays was published in 1976 as *Figures of Capable Imagination*. All of them deal in one way or another with what Bloom acknowledges to be his "obsessive subject"—that "literature itself is founded upon rivalry, misinterpretation, repression, and even plain theft and savage misprision." This was followed by *Wallace Stevens: The Poems of Our Climate* (1977). A study of this poet was to be expected from Bloom, who had earlier described Stevens as "the legitimate heir" of the aspirations of the Romantic poets. The book is not only an interpretation of Stevens's work but a sustained application of Bloom's own theory of literary history. The first chapter is a brief survey of American Romanticism from Emerson to Stevens, explaining the dialectic of Fate, Freedom, and Power which Bloom uses throughout. And in the final chapter he develops the interpretative method he has been using, which he calls "poetic crossing," into a coherent theory of the ways in which poems produce meaning. These "crossings" are representative moments of crisis. For Bloom the exemplary poem in post-Enlightenment literature is "the Wordsworthian crisis poem," which turns obsessively upon the poet's fear that he has lost his imaginative power. Other crises are the struggle with the death of love and the facing of death itself, all of which Bloom traces in particular poems by Stevens. Denis Donoghue, who found "wonderful perceptions" in the book, also had a number of reservations, including the fact that "Bloom presents literary history since the Enlightenment as one story and one story only, a struggle of gods and demiurges."

Bloom received a Fulbright fellowship in 1955, Yale's John Addison Porter Prize in 1956, the Newton Arvin award in 1967, a Guggenheim fellowship in 1962–1963, and the Melville Cane Award in 1970. He has an honorary doctorate from Boston College. The author has taught as a visiting professor at the Bread Loaf Summer School (1965–1966), at the Hebrew University in Jerusalem (1959), and the Society for Humanities at Cornell University (1968–1969). He was married in 1958 to Jean Gould and has two children, Daniel and David. Hilton Kramer dismisses Bloom as the author of numerous works "of supererogatory obfuscation"; Christopher Ricks says: "Harold Bloom once had an idea, now the idea has him." But it seems to John Hollander that Bloom "has helped to make the study of Romantic poetry as intellectually and spiritually challenging a branch of literary studies as one may find."

PRINCIPAL WORKS: Shelley's Mythmaking, 1959; The Visionary Company: A Reading of English Romantic Poetry, 1961; Blake's Apocalypse: A Study in Poetic Argument, 1963; Yeats, 1970; The Ringers in the Tower: Studies in Romantic Tradition, 1971; The Anxiety of Influence: A Theory of Poetry, 1973; Kabbalah and Criticism, 1975; A Map of Misreading, 1975; Poetry and Repression, 1976; Figures of Capable Imagination, 1976; Wallace Stevens: The Poems of Our Climate, 1977. *As Editor*—English Romantic Poetry, 1961; (with John Hollander) The Wind and the Rain, 1961; Poetry and Prose of William Blake, 1965; (with F.W. Hilles) From Sensibility to Romanticism: Essays Presented to Frederick A. Pottle, 1965; Literary Criticism of John Ruskin, 1965; Selected Poetry of Shelley, 1966; Marius the Epicurean, by Walter Pater, 1970; Romanticism and Consciousness: Essays in Criticism, 1970; Selected Poetry of Coleridge, 1972; The Romantic Tradition in American Literature (33 volumes), 1972; (with Lionel Trilling) Romantic Poetry and Prose, 1973; (with Lionel Trilling) Victorian Prose and Poetry, 1973; (with Frank Kermode, John Hollander, and others) Oxford Anthology of English Literature, 1973; Selected Writings of Walter Pater, 1974.

ABOUT: Borklund, E. Contemporary Literary Critics, 1977; Contemporary Authors 13–16 1st revision, 1975; Who's Who in America, 1976–1977. *Periodicals*—Guardian April 19, 1962; Hudson Review 28 1975; New Republic February 10, 1973; January 24, 1975; June 11, 1977; New York Review of Books April 17, 1975; February 19, 1976; September 15, 1977; New York Times Book Review March 4, 1973; April 13, 1975; June 12, 1977; August 21, 1977; Poetry October 1970, August 1973, December 1977; Times Literary Supplement August 21, 1959; April 20, 1962; March 12, 1971; June 25, 1976; March 11, 1977; Yale Review June 1959, March 1971, December 1971, Autumn 1977.

*BOBROWSKI, JOHANNES (April 9, 1917–September 2, 1965), German poet, novelist, and short story writer, was the son of a railroad official. He was related to the novelist Joseph Conrad, whose mother was a Bobrowska. He was born in Tilsit, now a Russian town renamed Sovetsk, then a German border town in East Prussia. But he grew up, as he said, "on both sides of the River Memel," for he spent part of his boyhood—a very significant part—on his grandfather's farm in Lithuania. In 1928 he went to school in Königsberg, where he experienced a sharp contrast between "the patriarchal closed-in-ness of village life" and the sophistication of a city with a notable literary, musical, and philosophical past.

In 1938 Bobrowski moved with his family to Berlin, where he began to study the history of art, becoming particularly interested in the German Baroque. In 1939 he was conscripted into the army. Having tried to paint and then to compose, he wrote his first poems as a soldier in Latvia in 1941. He was captured in 1945, and remained as a prisoner of war in Russia until 1949, for part of the time doing forced labor as a miner in the Donets region. Returning to Germany, he settled in East Berlin as a reader for

*bob rov′ skė

JOHANNES BOBROWSKI

Bobrowski is the poet not only of a geographical but of a historical borderland, thronged with legends, with the ghosts of former inhabitants, with echoes of the ancient Balto-Slav nature cults. In "Sarmatian time" there is no clear division between past and present, and the perspective stretches back to the beginning of time, to the

> Image of the hunter, conjuration,
> animal-headed,
> painted in the icy
> cave, in the rock.
>
> (from "Village," translated by
> Ruth and Matthew Mead)

And so the German soldiers at Lake Ilmen in 1941, gazing on "Wilderness. Against the wind./ Numb," are aware of the immensity of both space and time:

> The wolf crossed the clearing.
> Listens for the bells of winter.
> Howls for the enormous
> cloud of snow.
>
> (from "Lake Ilmen, 1941,"
> translated by Ruth and
> Matthew Mead)

Verlag Lucie Groszer and then for the Union Verlag, a publishing house connected with the Lutheran Church. Bobrowski was himself a Lutheran but practiced an unorthodox kind of Christian socialism—what he called an "ideology of the poor," strongly influenced by the Sermon on the Mount.

Bobrowski was at the most obvious level a nature poet, though his landscapes are always peopled by figures. And although his writing is rarely directly autobiographical, the circumstances of his life are deeply relevant to it. He said once that his choice of theme was like a war wound: "I began to write near Lake Ilmen in 1941 about the Russian landscape, but as a foreigner, a German. This became [my] theme. ... the Germans and the European East—because I grew up around the river Memel, where Poles, Lithuanians, Russians and Germans lived together, and among them all the Jews—a long story of unhappiness and guilt, for which my people is to blame, ever since the days of the Teutonic Knights. Not to be undone, perhaps, or expiated, but worthy of hope and honest endeavor in German poems."

It is part of Bobrowski's achievement to have given his personal East Prussian background an archetypal quality, so that his vision of human suffering acquires the broadest geographical and historical perspective. His poems appeared in three collections, *Sarmatische Zeit* (Sarmatian Time, 1961), *Schattenland Ströme* (Shadowland Streams, 1962), and *Wetterzeichen* (Storm Signals, 1966). They are set mostly in the partly historical, partly mythical and imaginary land of Sarmatia, the steppe country between the Vistula and the Volga.

A reviewer in the *Times Literary Supplement* wrote that Bobrowski's poetry "is beautifully lyrical, and yet impersonal, oracular in the manner of Hölderlin. The perceptions are enacted in language that is stark, dynamic, and almost invariably concrete, outstanding for its nervous strength and its total precision. Like his prose, it is dense in the sense of being radically condensed and richly allusive. By invoking a river or village he evokes a whole world and a whole tradition. His work is occult, but hardly ever obscure, and his artistry has the 'hiddenness of all perfect things.' " This is true not only of the diction but of the rhythms and structures of his poems, which are usually free but have behind them a haunting sense of stricter measures, so that the vast landscapes in which they are set seem to have been captured in an invisible net.

The hidden significance of these landscapes is revealed in dramatic images that reconstruct relationships man has destroyed or neglected. "Pruzzian Elegy," for example, is a brilliant evocation of the Old Prussian people, exterminated by the Teutonic Knights, whose language yet survives in place-names and whose past is resurrected in the songs of old women and the sounds of nature:

Names speak of
a stamped-out people, hillsides,
rivers, often still lustreless,
stones and roads—
songs in the evening and legends,
the rustle of lizards names you
and today, like water in the marsh,
a song, poor
with grieving. . . .

(translated by Ruth and
Matthew Mead)

"Dead Language" shows how two languages, German and Old Prussian, coexist and need each other. The extinct Old Prussian is no longer intelligible without the clues provided by modern German; yet this, the language of rationality and narration, is also dead because it has forgotten how to express the brotherhood of man and nature. So in bringing together his two "dead" languages, Bobrowski revitalizes both, while at the same time—and with extraordinary economy—suggesting the need for *nachbarschaft* or "neighborliness," a concept which emerges memorably from some of his love poems. This is the basic theme of Bobrowski's stories, collected in *Boehlendorff und andere* (Boehlendorff and Other Stories, 1965), *Mäusefest* (Mouse Feast, 1965), and *Der Mahner* (The Exhorter, 1968), which are also imaginative recreations of the whole way of life of that pastoral folkworld of Eastern Europe which was disrupted by the Nazis.

Levins Mühle (1964, translated by Janet Cropper as *Levin's Mill*), the first of Bobrowski's two novels, is set in a Prussian village in 1874, when the Germans were increasingly imposing their own culture on the local population. It describes the struggle between the narrator's grandfather, a rich German miller who charges a fee for grinding the Polish peasants' corn, and the Jew Levin, who puts good money in their pockets by buying it from them before grinding it in his own small mill. Grandfather Johann regards Levin as a threat to society, the Kaiser, and his own wealth, and when Levin's mill is destroyed no one doubts that Johann is responsible. The Jew tries to obtain justice but fails, inevitably, and wanders off into Russia.

Bobrowski's characters, shaped by historical forces beyond their control, are far from being lay figures. Johann, for all his scheming, is an endearing old rogue, and his victory is a Pyrrhic one, for he too is forced to leave the village. As one reviewer observed, "humour and irony save the novel from ponderous political or moral allegory. . . . and it is a delightful complement to [Bobrowski's] lyrical evocations of East European landscapes and figures."

A second novel, *Litauische Claviere* (Lithuanian Pianos, 1966), is about two German musicians planning a German-Lithuanian opera that will express the totality of a divided community, and thus help to bring the two nations together. Their project is set against the tragic background of two days in 1936 (the year Hitler refused a nonaggression pact with Lithuania), when a traditional Lithuanian folk festival coincides with a Nazi rally and racial tensions flare into violence. The libretto of the opera, which deals with the life of an eighteenth-century Lithuanian poet, is used to relate the events of 1936 to the past. This novel, completed only a few weeks before Bobrowski's premature death, suffers from the fact that characterization is subservient to thesis. It was nevertheless found moving in its idealism and both distinguished and original.

Bobrowski died of peritonitis, leaving a widow and four children, just as his works were beginning to receive the acclaim of a much wider audience than his small circle of ardent admirers. Apart from a few poems which appeared in a magazine during the war and have not been reprinted, his first publication was a group of poems published in 1955 in an East German magazine edited by Peter Huchel, whose influence Bobrowski has acknowledged. These poems also had an enthusiastic reception when some of them appeared in a West German anthology in 1960, and Bobrowski's work was thereafter published in both East and West Germany. It brought him a number of important awards, including the Heinrich Mann prize from the East German Academy of Arts, the Swiss Charles Veillon prize, and the coveted prize of the Gruppe 47 in West Germany.

His reputation has continued to grow, and he is widely regarded now as the most considerable postwar lyric poet to write in German. When a selection of his poems appeared in English as *Shadowland,* Bobrowski was hailed by Theodore Weiss as "obviously one of the few genuinely new voices of our time, able to absorb and possess some of its major horrors in altogether *human* work; he suggests some of the hope poetry holds out to our shattering age."

PRINCIPAL WORKS IN ENGLISH TRANSLATION: *Poetry*— Shadowland: Selected Poems, translated by Ruth and Matthew Mead, 1966; Johannes Bobrowski and Horst Bienek: Selected Poems, translated by Ruth and Matthew Mead, 1971; From the Rivers: Selected Poems, translated by Ruth and Matthew Mead, 1975. *Poems in* Bridgewater, P. (ed.) Penguin Book of Twentieth Century German Verse, 1963; Hamburger, M. (ed.) East German Poetry, 1972; Keith-Smith, B. Johannes Bobrowski, 1970; Middleton, C. (ed.) German Writing Today, 1967; Prawer, S. S. (ed.) Seventeen Modern German Poets, 1971; Schwebell, G.C. (ed.) Contemporary German Poetry, 1964. *Fiction*—Levin's Mill, 1970; I Taste Bitterness (short stories), translated by Marc Linder, 1970; The House in the Meadow, translated by Moya Gillespie (for children; adaptation of Samuil Marshak's Terem-teremok), 1970.

ABOUT: Flores, J. Poetry in East Germany 1945-1970, 1971; Gumpel, L. "Concrete" Poetry From East and West Germany, 1976; Hoefert, S. West-Östliches in der Lyrik Johannes Bobrowskis, 1966; Keith-Smith, B. (ed.) Essays on Contemporary German Literature, 1966; Keith-Smith, B. Johannes Bobrowski, 1970; Prawer, S.S. (ed.) Essays in German Language, Culture and Society, 1969; Wolf, G. and Rostin, G. (eds.) Johannes Bobrowski: Selbstzeugnisse und Beiträge über sein werk, 1975. *Periodicals*—Forum for Modern Language Studies 4 1966; Germanic Review January 1966; Times (London) September 4, 1965; Times Literary Supplement September 21, 1962; January 14, 1965; September 30, 1965; September 22, 1966; April 20, 1967; February 22, 1968.

Mark Gerson

EDWARD BOND

BOND, (THOMAS) EDWARD (July 18, 1934–), English dramatist, was born in the London suburb of Holloway, the son of Florence Kate (Baker) and Gaston Cyril Bond. They were a displaced rural working-class couple, Bond's father being a farm laborer who had moved to London during the Depression in search of work. Bond's childhood was disrupted by wartime evacuation, first to Cornwall and then to his mother's parents in East Anglia; when he left secondary modern school at the age of fifteen it was, he says, with "no formal education at all."

There followed a variety of jobs in factories and offices, with a prolonged spell as law clerk in a firm of London solicitors and two years national service with the British army in Germany. By this time he had become a habitual writer. Like Harold Pinter, Bond began as a poet and was converted to the theatre by a Shakespearean performance by Donald Wolfit. But it was not until the 1960s (with some fifteen unperformed plays behind him) that his work reached the public. It did so through his membership in the Writers' Group attached to the Royal Court Theatre in London, whose director, William Gaskill, describes Bond as "a classic case of a writer who has come directly to us without coming through an agent, and who was nursed over a very long period."

Bond's apprenticeship came to an end in December 1962 with the performance of *The Pope's Wedding* as one of the Royal Court's Sunday evening productions without décor. The play's central character is Scopey, a young East Anglian farm worker. The girl he marries looks after an old hermit, Alen, who lives in a hut outside the village. Scopey visits the place and becomes obsessed with Alen. He loses his wife and job, and moves into the hut to feed, protect, and finally destroy the old man.

Bond developed his craft through conscientious study of other writers, and *The Pope's Wedding* shows the influence of Samuel Beckett and Harold Pinter, both of whom are fascinated by the enigmatic figure of the old vagrant or social outcast. "What I wanted to do," Bond says, "was to get inside the image and see what it was all about. That is what Scopey does in the play, and in the end he kills a man and wears his clothes in order to find out. And of course there's nothing there." Whatever its derivation, the play spoke with Bond's own voice and exhibited characteristics common to all his work, proceeding entirely by enactment and leaving spectators to deduce the characters' feelings from terse exchanges of fact and intention. The language of Scopey's companions has a stunted authenticity, and their behavior is taken straight out of the fields and the streets. Stealing a girl's handbag, kicking a ball about, stoning an old man's cottage: this is how they are. And the disconcerting thing for middle-class audiences was to be shown this kind of life without any implied judgment from the author—none, that is, that did not also apply to the whole system in which they live.

The same qualities dominated Bond's next play, *Saved*, whose premiere at the Royal Court in November 1965 occasioned the biggest furor in the history of that combative theatre. There were angry walkouts by the public and torrential abuse from reviewers (with the notable exceptions of Penelope Gilliatt, the *Observer*'s reviewer, and Laurence Olivier, who championed the play in the same newspaper). After a clampdown by the censor, the theatre was successfully prosecuted for staging the work even to club audiences. A teach-in, letters to the press, and questions in the House of Commons, led to a revival of the play in 1969. Recantations poured in, and the consensus was that a formidable talent had been savagely misjudged.

Saved owed its notoriety to a short scene in the first half showing a baby being stoned to death by a gang of boys. Those who hated the play took the view that this brutal scene represented a new and intolerable affront to common humanity enacted in the name of art. It was left to Ronald Bryden in the *New Statesman* to point out that Bond "is out to rub our noses in the fact that the real new poor are the old poor plus television, sinking deeper into a form of poverty we do not yet recognize—poverty of culture." The really dreadful thing, many critics felt, was not the baby-stoning scene but the climate of moral attrition pervading the whole play—the sense that casual violence and the numbing of human feeling are all that can be expected in so brutalizing an environment. Although Bond's name has often been associated with a taste for violence, he has repeatedly denied any personal obsession with it. "It is the common involvement with violence that is relevant. Even if I had such an obsession, it wouldn't help to explain Auschwitz or the H-bomb site at Lakenheath."

Like *The Pope's Wedding, Saved* shows a working-class boy detaching himself from aimless and inarticulate friends, and involves him in a short-lived sexual attachment, an Oedipal relationship, and the destruction of an innocent creature. The differences are that *Saved* is set not in the countryside but in the brick desert of South London, and that its hero, Len, is a helper rather than a destroyer. Jilted by his girl, he stays around to be of use to her family, and by the end has begun to establish in their household a precarious oasis of humanity. For that reason, Bond has described the play as "almost irresponsibly optimistic."

Having struck this blow for working-class naturalism, the author next swung to the other end of the social scale, which is depicted with even greater savagery in *Early Morning*—a piece originally banned by the censor before its eventual clandestine appearance at the Royal Court in March 1968. Set in the court of Queen Victoria, this Goyaesque farce gets briskly under way with an intrigue between Disraeli and the Prince Consort to assassinate the monarch and give the throne to Prince Arthur (alleged Siamese twin of the Prince of Wales.) However, the plan misfires when the Consort drinks poisoned champagne from the slipper of Florence (alias Freddie) Nightingale, with whom the Queen is having a lesbian affair. After a general massacre,

the cast ascend to heaven as cannibalistic immortals, and the world of political gangsterdom dissolves into the image of people literally eating each other. "The events of this play," Bond states, "are true." And in a symbolic sense perhaps they are. Bond's choice of the Victorian age to illustrate such a statement underlines his belief that the greater the respectability of a society the more shelter it affords for corruption. "The play is extremely funny," according to B. A. Young, but he criticized its lack of organization and suggested that "what emerges from it, apart from the comedy, is no more than a generalized feeling of indignation against humanity for being so horrible."

Nineteen sixty-eight also saw the Coventry premiere of *Narrow Road to the Deep North,* a Brechtian piece prompted by one of the travel sketches of the seventeenth-century Japanese poet Matsuo Basho. Another stylistic departure for Bond, it did much to free him from his reputation for deliberate shock tactics. England appears only tangentially, in the figures of a colonialist and his Bible-thumping wife ("You Westerners are so inscrutable," observes one of the Japanese); the main story concerns the journey of Basho, the poet protagonist, to seek *satori* in the Deep North, and his return home, where he is swept up in a rebellion against a local tyrant. "Terse, formal dialogue of great effectiveness," wrote one critic, portrays "the ebb and flow of savagery as rival factions war for mastery of the city." Everything hinges on Basho's initial decision to continue his pilgrimage at the cost of leaving a child abandoned, perhaps to die, on the road: after Basho has sacrificed humanity to spirituality, the enlightenment he achieves seems unconvincing, and the abandoned infant survives to become the tyrant Shogo.

Edward Bond is above all a moralist, who views Western society as a self-created hell. Violence, for all its prominence in his work, "is not in itself a danger to any species." In his view, the real danger lies in educational indoctrination, politics, religion, technology, and the other means by which human capacities are lopped or twisted to fit the procrustean bed of civilization. For this reason the figure of the child—the still unmutilated newcomer about to be fed into the killing machine—occupies a central place in his writings. "People are not born violent by nature," Bond says, "the natural condition in which people are born is love, the aptitude for loving and being loved. . . . children are made competitive, aggressive—society does not control the beast in men, it makes men animals in order to control them."

His main problem has been to convey his vision of society as a legalized atrocity to a public who see it as perfectly normal. Hence his use of Brechtian "alienation" techniques, and his practice of dismantling protective national myths, as in *Early Morning* and in his next play, *Lear* (Royal Court, October 1971). This is a post-Auschwitz reworking of the legend, burning up its Shakespearean source material in the opening scenes. Lear's kingdom is reduced to civil war when his elder daughters (renamed Bodice and Fontanelle) make political marriages with his two deadliest enemies and convert a peasant Cordelia into an equally ruthless leader of the insurgents. There is a killing and an execution in the first few minutes, and thereafter the toll of enormities mounts at a rate unusual even for Bond: besides the shootings, bayonetings, and deafenings (with Bodice's knitting needles), there is a scene in which Lear is strapped into a surgical throne and crownlike head-cage so that his eyes can be efficiently extracted.

Ranging the countryside in ragged incognito, Lear remains his arrogantly insulated self up to the moment of blinding. At that point the mantle of Oedipus falls on him and he begins his real moral education. Bond describes him as a child growing up: "Lear is protected in his court cradle until he's an old man, and suddenly he's born." Helen Dawson thought it "one of the most powerful plays to have emerged in years . . . Bond has remarkably captured the spirit of the original and transferred it to our time. He leads us into a world where natural instincts are perverted in the name of the common good, or moral codes, or law and order, or the national interest. . . . it is unmistakably the work of a visionary craftsman."

Having dealt thus with Shakespeare's greatest play, Bond discovered a similar pattern in Shakespeare's own life in *Bingo,* which opened at the Northcott Theatre, Exeter, in November 1973 and moved to the Royal Court in August 1974, with John Gielgud in the lead. Subtitled "Scenes of Money and Death," the piece concerns Shakespeare's retirement as a Stratford property-owner, and takes its cue from the historical fact that he signed an agreement with local landowners indemnifying him against any loss that might arise from their attempt to enclose the common fields—thus siding with the rich against the poor who stood to lose much from enclosure. The assumption is that he has coined his talent to achieve financial security ("Thank God we're not thatched!") and now discovers the worthlessness of the prize. Having quit the savageries of London for rural peace, he finds the horrors coming home to roost. Estranged from a family who have had his money

but not his love, he can hardly bear to set foot in the house; and when he tries to help a beggar girl who comes to his garden, the result is that she is arrested and hanged for fire-raising. Hopelessly compromised in the system he has tried to escape, Shakespeare commits suicide, with his daughter Judith hammering on the bedroom door for his will. Money, throughout the play, excites the characters like a whiff of fresh blood.

Direct violence hardly appears in *Bingo,* and there is even some humor, as when Ben Jonson arrives to touch his old rival for a loan ("Your recent stuff's been pretty peculiar. Tell me, what was *A Winter's Tale* about?"). But it is a bleaker work than its companion piece—as Ronald Bryden wrote, "a passionately cold, powerfully unforgiving play." Like Lear, Bond's Shakespeare has been cocooned from experience through the exercise of a special and privileged power; but where Lear awakens to understanding and a final positive action, Shakespeare only shrivels into taciturn despair. "There is compassion," wrote Harold Hobson, "but it is a compassion that reckons itself helpless; there is the recognition of right, but it is right that there is no possibility of achieving. This is a play, memorably poetic and mysterious, in which the despair is total." Both *Bingo* and *Lear* are extraordinary textual achievements, as they invite the most audacious comparison available in English, yet are in no way diminished by their Shakespearean echoes.

Between these two Shakespearean exercises there appeared Bond's one full-scale comedy, *The Sea* (Royal Court, May 1973)—in its own way another remarkable linguistic feat. The setting here (perhaps drawing on Bond's memories of wartime Cornwall) is a coastal village in the early years of the century, and the play's first gesture is to establish the polarity of society and nature, showing a rigidly structured little community perched on the elemental brink. The piece opens with a drowning in a tremendous storm and then retires into a dingy draper's shop where two ladies are dallying over curtain material. That scene defines the pecking order of Mrs. Rafi, the queen of local society, her much-bullied companion Jessica, and Hatch, the obsequious little draper whose orders she has so often canceled in the past; by the end of the scene it has generated emotions to match the storm. Jessica wishes her mistress dead while the humiliated Hatch finds an outlet for his hatred in delusions of an invasion from outer space.

The confined setting enables Bond to compose a complete society in miniature, with Mrs. Rafi at the tip of the pyramid and, at the base, the peasants whom Hatch leads on loony surveillance patrols of the beach in search of UFOs. There is also a separate group consisting of the drowned man's friends, and an old shanty-dweller (recalling Alen in *The Pope's Wedding*) who, contemplating the poisonous village community, says: "We're becoming the strange visitors to this world." Each group has its own style. With Mrs. Rafi and her court the tone is one of high-stepping farce, as when she rehearses the neighborhood ladies in an Orpheus drama and has herself ferried over the Styx to the tune of the Eton Boating Song. The peasants mumble in local dialect, while the lower-middle-class Hatch retains the manner of an ultra-respectable petty official, even when roaming the beach knife in hand. The message, as in *Saved*, is that when personal freedom is frustrated it is forced into an ugly secondary channel, but now the social spectrum is much wider. As Bond puts it: "My plays like to keep an eye on what's happening down the street."

In *The Fool* (Royal Court, November 1975), Bond presents another literary protagonist, viewed for once with sympathy. The subject is John Clare, laborer, militiaman, poet, and long-term inmate of the Northamptonshire lunatic asylum. The play, which spans fifty years of Clare's life, with a cast of some thirty speaking parts, opens at the time of the hunger riots after Waterloo. The young Clare is taking part in a Christmas mummers' play outside the door of a local aristocrat. Two scenes on, the starving actors have become rioters. They seize the local parson, strip him ("Where you stole that flesh, boy?"), and propose to flay him, for which they are arrested. Clare, pursuing his beloved at the time of the assault, sees his friends' death-sentences commuted to deportation. He subsequently enjoys his brief spell as the pet of literary London, but reverts to impoverished obscurity, chained to a hard-tongued wife whom he cannot support, before being committed to the asylum by one of his former patrons.

From first to last Clare remains a passive character, which accounts for the bewilderment with which some reviewers responded to the play. Technically there is nothing more difficult than the creation of a passive hero, but Clare comes movingly to life as soon as the point is grasped that he is a poet and nothing else: his writing illuminates a world that he can neither understand nor deal with when he lays down his pen. In that sense, the title is to be taken literally. In *Theatre Quarterly* for Spring 1976, which contains several articles about *The Fool*, Martin Esslin reviewed the play's reviews and found them, with few exceptions, totally inadequate. He himself thought the play "undoubtedly will,

in due time, be regarded as a major work by one of the century's greatest playwrights."

The three relatively minor pieces that followed in 1976 were received with less interest. *Stone* was written at the invitation of Gay Sweatshop in London as a contribution to a series of lunchtime plays on homosexual themes. It is an allegory, dealing with oppression in general, in which a man's seven golden talents are tarnished by exposure to the capitalist system. Another allegory, *Grandma Faust,* in which Uncle Sam tries to gain the soul of a black man, was described by Bernard Levin as a piece of "mindless agitprop." *The Swing,* written for the "A-A-America" season at the Almost Free Theatre in London, was less dismissively reviewed. Set in Kentucky in 1911, it begins with the murder of a black man by an audience which has paid to witness this spectacle. It goes on to deal with issues as apparently diverse as sexual frustration, economic violence, the social effects of electricity, and racial persecution.

The Swing had a mixed reception. One critic called it "a powerful, baleful, concentrated play," but Ned Chaillet in the London *Times* wrote that Bond "mishandles the American idiom, indulges in turgid anti-Americanism and freely throws in anachronistic speech when it suits him. There is power but no glory in *The Swing.*" It seemed to Chaillet that in these three plays "an opaque personal mythology of violence and its economic causes too frequently obscures the stories he is telling" and that "more than taking himself seriously . . . [Bond] is taking himself oracularly."

There was a general critical feeling that Bond had returned to his full stature in *The Bundle* (1978). It begins at the same point as *Narrow Road to the Deep North,* with the poet Basho setting out in search of enlightenment, refusing to succor an abandoned infant. This time "the bundle" grows up to be not a tyrant but Wang the liberator, who leads a successful uprising against a bloodsucking landowner, and teaches the peasants to tame the river that regularly floods their land. Wang is shown to be more decisive and more ruthless than Basho in pursuit of what he deems the good: Basho passes by an abandoned baby but Wang throws one into the river, because "we have not earned the right to be kind." Discussing the play with Victoria Radin, Bond said: "I felt I wanted to take the subject one stage further. It's very difficult to do good. It has nothing to do with the simple welling-up of fine emotions. People who imagine they do good can be immensely destructive and rapacious people. I would like to think that the play explores this mask of hypocrisy." Bond regards *The Bundle* as his first "answer" play, after a series of what he calls "problem" or "historical analysis" plays. "The answers should be simpler, and if not, the questions should be harder and less manipulable. I'm very pleased about this. It gives me a whole lot to do."

Irving Wardle found a divided viewpoint in this "complex and marvellously written play"; it seemed to him that, in view of Bond's radical and activist argument, the selfish aesthete Basho "ought to be as discredited as the intellectuals in Brecht's *Turandot,* but he is not. Bond shows him as a great poet, a man of iron self-discipline, and a genuine seeker for the truth." Robert Cushman disagreed, finding "the drift of the play" against Basho. Cushman's own main reservation was that the play seemed to him one-sided—the landowner's cruelty is highly visible, but "the process of Wang's revolt is unconvincingly bloodless, just as its outcome is unconvincingly idyllic. . . . In theory [Bond] endorses cruelty in a good cause: in practice he fails to present it." Nevertheless, Cushman wrote, *The Bundle* "has the force and the onward movement of a tidal wave. It communicates narrative joy [and]. . . . returns us to the weight and rhythm of epic theatre. . . . More than once, Mr. Bond seems to be learning from Brecht, and bettering the instruction."

Edward Bond is widely regarded as the most important British playwright to emerge during the 1960s. Robert Cushman says that "the best of Mr. Bond's writing has matchless stage presence; his carved prose must be the envy and the goal of half the playwrights in Britain." And Frank Marcus has written that "with the single exception of Samuel Beckett, I know of no other contemporary dramatist whose work is so imbued with a sense of tragic destiny." Bond is nevertheless a lonely figure on the English theatrical scene. His stage career has been confined for the most part to short runs at the Royal Court. The abuse he originally suffered from reviewers has changed to wary respect, but no manager has been tempted to present his work commercially. In the United States, his work has fallen on equally stony ground. Violence apart, his plays repel the "entertainment" public by putting them morally on the spot. It is not enough to offer aesthetic approval: a change of heart is also demanded of the audience. Bond's best public is on the Continent, particularly in West Germany, where the importance of his work was instantly recognized and where there exists a tradition of political drama, as well as stages more adequate than the cramped Royal Court for mounting the plays on a fittingly large scale.

Bond is the author or co-author of several films, including Nicolas Roeg's *Walkabout* (adapted from a novel by James Vance Marshall), *Nicholas and Alexandra,* and Antonioni's *Blow-Up.* He received the George Devine Award in 1968 and the John Whiting Award in 1969, and is an advisory editor of *Theatre Quarterly.* A slight, shy, round-faced, mild-seeming man who could still pass for a solicitor's clerk, Bond lives in an isolated Cambridgeshire village with his Viennese wife, the critic Elisabeth Pablé, whom he married in 1971. He is an anarchist and an atheist. Bond told a *Guardian* interviewer: "My work amounts to self-education through plays. If you follow the development of the plays you will see the typical twentieth-century man, worried about society, and searching for some way to live personally, and to find a society which can go on existing."

PRINCIPAL PUBLISHED WORKS: Saved, 1966; Narrow Road to the Deep North, 1968; Early Morning, 1968; The Pope's Wedding and Other Plays (includes "The Sharpeville Sequence," comprising Black Mass, written for the Anti-Apartheid Movement, and two short stories, Mr. Dog *and* The King With Golden Eyes), 1971; Lear, 1972; The Sea, 1973; Bingo (*published with* Passion, a play written for the Campaign for Nuclear Disarmament), 1974; The Fool (*published with* We Come to the River, libretto to a score by Hans Werner Henze), 1976; A-A-America (includes Grandma Faust, The Swing, and Stone) 1976; The Plays of Edward Bond: 1 (Saved, Early Morning, The Pope's Wedding), 1977; The Bundle, 1978; Theatre Poems and Songs, 1978.

ABOUT: Contemporary Authors 25–28 1st revision, 1971; Coult, T. The Plays of Edward Bond, 1978; Crowell's Handbook of Contemporary Drama, 1971; Current Biography 1978; Esslin, M. Brief Chronicles, 1970; McCrindle, J.F. (ed.) Behind the Scenes, 1971; Marowitz, C. Confessions of a Counterfeit Critic, 1973; Scharine, R. The Plays of Edward Bond, 1976; Taylor, J.R. Anger and After, 1969; Taylor, J.R. The Second Wave, 1971; Trussler, S. Edward Bond (Writers and Their Work), 1976; Vinson, J. (ed.) Contemporary Dramatists, 1973; Who's Who, 1977. *Periodicals*—Drama Autumn 1975; Encounter December 1971; Gambit 17 1970; Guardian September 29, 1971; November 24, 1976; Listener July 22, 1976; New Society November 25, 1965; December 11, 1975; New Theatre Magazine 2 1967; New York Times January 2, 1972; August 25, 1974; November 9, 1975; Nova June/July 1969; Observer October 3, 1971; December 2, 1973; November 23, 1975; July 18, 1976; January 15, January 22, 1978; Opera July 1976; Plays and Players October 1970; Sunday Times (London) May 27, 1973; November 18, 1973; November 25, 1973; August 18, 1974; October 31, 1976; Theatre Quarterly January-March 1972, Spring 1976; Times (London) May 23, 1973; August 15, 1974; November 19, 1975; October 28, 1976; November 25, 1976; January 16, 1978; Times Literary Supplement January 15, 1970; August 30, 1974; Transatlantic Review Autumn 1966.

*BONTEMPS, ARNA (Arnaud Wendell Bontemps) (October 13, 1902–June 4, 1973), American novelist, poet, biographer, editor, dramatist, and writer for children, was born in Alexandria,

*boN tomp

ARNA BONTEMPS

Louisiana, the son of Paul Bismarck Bontemps and the former Marie Carolina Pembrooke. His father, grandfather, and great-grandfather were all brick masons; his mother, who died when he was twelve, was a schoolteacher until her marriage.

When Arna Bontemps was three years old the family left the South and moved to Los Angeles. He grew up there, working his way through school as a newsboy, gardener, postal clerk, and jubilee singer. He attended San Fernando Academy from 1917 to 1920, and gained his B.A. at Pacific Union College in 1923. In that year, having abandoned earlier plans for a career in either medicine or music, he accepted a teaching post at the Harlem Academy and went to New York to "see what all the excitement was about."

"The excitement" was that upsurge of black creativity known as the Harlem Renaissance, a movement in which Bontemps was soon a prominent participant, along with such writers as Langston Hughes, Jean Toomer, Countee Cullen, and Claude McKay. Bontemps's seven years in New York were richly rewarding for him. His first published poem appeared in W.E.B. Du Bois's *Crisis* in 1924, and for two consecutive years (1926 and 1927) he won the Alexander Pushkin Prize for Poetry presented by the left-wing magazine *Opportunity.* In 1927 he also received the *Crisis* poetry prize. Bontemps was married to Alberta Johnson in 1926.

God Sends Sunday, Bontemps's first novel, was published in 1931. Influenced, it was thought, by Carl Van Vechten's *Nigger Heaven* in its emphasis on sex and fast living, it tells the story of Little Augie, a diminutive black jockey

whose phenomenal luck lifts him to wealth and fame but in the end depraves and destroys him. Set in the 1890s, "in the sporting world of race-track men and gamblers, of jazz and the shimmy, of fights and razor carvings," it was generally praised for its vigor and economy, and for the unsentimental objectivity of its portrayal of black people and their way of life; several critics commented enthusiastically on the novel's complete avoidance of "race consciousness."

In *The Harlem Renaissance Remembered,* Bontemps describes that flood of creativity and its subsequent effects on established white culture as "a more exciting and perhaps more telling assault on oppression than the dreary blood-in-the-streets strategy" of the post–World War I race riots in American cities. But the Harlem Renaissance was short-lived, one of the casualties of the 1929 stock market crash. The hopeful young writers, composers, and artists had to disperse in search of jobs. Bontemps decided that it was time for him to return to the South and secured a teaching post at Oakwood Junior College, Huntsville, Alabama. There, surrounded by the misery and suffering of the Depression, he found the material for such stories as the much-anthologized "A Summer Tragedy," which brought him the *Opportunity* short story prize in 1932. Twelve of Bontemps's short stories were collected in *The Old South* (1973)—"stories of the South of the sharecropper and the colored laundress and the itinerant preacher," as one reviewer wrote, "stories of great humor and resourcefulness and feeling."

Research during this period into slave narratives, and the evidence they provided of the slaves' will to freedom, determined the subject of Bontemps' second novel, *Black Thunder* (1936). Another factor was the proximity of the Scottsboro trials, which provided for Bontemps "a prologue to what happened to my thinking and . . . encouraged me to go ahead with some such statement as *Black Thunder.*" A dramatization of the Gabriel Insurrection, an abortive slave revolt near Richmond in 1800, the novel sought to boost Afro-American morale and pride in the black heritage, and was the first full-length novel to make black violence against white society its main theme. Gabriel Prosser was captured and eventually hanged, but his assertion that the act of rebellion had made him a free man would, Bontemps hoped, inspire other oppressed black people.

The novel is made up of short chapters each written from the point of view of a single character. Robert Bone thought this "a technique especially suited to the presentation of complex historical events" and was reminded of John Dos Passos. Other critics admired the book's restraint and detachment, and the realism of the characterization—neither Prosser nor his companions are stereotypical proletarian heroes. "Bontemps's success," wrote J. O'Brien, "lies in his ability to draw upon folklore and folk idiom. . . . Motivated by many of the same concerns as the realistic writers of the 1930s," he "avoids their limitations by turning to myth and history as the true subjects of his novels," and derives his vivid and simple style from the oral tradition of the slave narratives. A. B. Spingarn called it "the best historical novel written by an American Negro."

In 1935 Bontemps and his family moved back North to Chicago. He taught there for three years before taking up a fellowship at the graduate library school of the University of Chicago. Shortly before he received his M.A. in 1943 he went to Fisk University, Nashville, Tennessee, as chief librarian, a post he retained until 1964.

Bontemps's third novel, *Drums at Dusk* (1939), again drew on the subject of slave insurrection—Toussaint L'Ouverture's successful revolt in Haiti. The theme is explored as much from the point of view of the French as from that of the rebels and, according to J. O'Brien, restates the premise of the preceding novel—that history itself is the determining factor in the success or failure of attempts to change society. *Drums at Dusk* is a more romantic story than *Black Thunder,* and some critics thought that this element had been allowed to overshadow the revolutionary message. Robert Bone complained of "crude melodrama," saying that Bontemps "embroiders his narrative with all of the sword-play, sex, and sadism of a Hollywood extravaganza."

Discouraged by such criticism, Bontemps wrote no more novels. In the introduction to a later edition of *Black Thunder,* he expressed his hopes of influencing future generations by writing for children: "I was in no mood merely to write entertaining novels. . . . And I felt that black children had nothing with which to identify." His stories for young people, praised by Sterling Brown for their "sincere and informed sympathy," include *Popo and Fifina* (written in collaboration with Langston Hughes, 1932), *You Can't Pet a Possum* (1934), *Sad-Faced Boy* (1937), *Lonesome Boy* (1955), and three tall tales written with Jack Conroy. Bontemps's history book for children, *The Story of the Negro* (1948), won the Jane Addams Children's Book Award.

Although it was as a poet that Bontemps first made his name, *Personals* (1963) is the only collection of his poems, most of which are scattered in periodicals of the 1920s (though they have been reappearing in a number of recent anthologies). The sharp awareness of black history that informs his prose is there also in his verse, as in "A Black Man Talks of Reaping":

I have sown beside all waters in my day.
I planted deep, within my heart the fear
That wind or fowl would take the grain away.
I planted safe against this stark, lean year. . . .

Yet what I sowed and what the orchard yields
My brother's sons are gathering stalk and root
Small wonder then my children glean in fields
They have not sown, and feed on bitter fruit.

According to A. P. Davis, Bontemps's poems combine "traditional religious imagery and a concern with the black man's history, his culture, and his present life of unfulfilled dreams in a land of promises." Many are protest poems, "but the protest is oblique and suggestive rather than frontal." There is a "sad, brooding quality" about even his love poems. Sterling Brown similarly called Bontemps's verse "meditative, couched in fluent but subdued rhythms."

A prolific writer, Bontemps's versatility was amply demonstrated over the years. His nonfictional works include biographies of Frederick Douglass, George Washington Carver, and Booker T. Washington, and he edited the autobiography of W. C. Handy (*Father of the Blues,* 1945). He also collaborated with Jack Conroy on a study of black migration from the Southern states to the North, *They Seek a City* (1945). Other ventures included anthologies of black American poetry and folk lore, of slave narratives, and of English and American poetry. Bontemps wrote several plays, among them *Creole* (written with Schuyler Watts) and *Careless Love* (with Langston Hughes). With the help of Countee Cullen, Bontemps adapted his novel *God Sends Sunday* into a play and then into a musical, *St. Louis Woman.* With songs by Johnny Mercer and Harold Arlen, it ran for over a hundred performances on Broadway in 1946.

Although he relinquished his post as chief librarian at Fisk in 1964, Bontemps stayed on for two more years as acting librarian. In 1966 he moved back to Chicago, where for the next three years he taught literature at Chicago University. In 1969 he was appointed lecturer and curator at the James Weldon Johnson Afro-American Collection at Yale. He returned to Fisk in 1971 as writer-in-residence, and the following year was appointed honorary consultant in American cultural history to the Library of Congress. He received two Guggenheim fellowships (1949 and 1954), and two Rosenwald fellowships (1938 and 1942), and had honorary doctorates from Morgan State College in Baltimore, and Berea College, Kentucky.

Bontemps died in 1973, while working on his autobiography. He and his wife had two sons and four daughters. A man of "quiet aspect and sensitive features," Bontemps's leisure interests included literature, sport, and the theatre. Abraham Chapman has said that he was a central figure in the creation, dissemination, and teaching of black American literature. His friend Jack Conroy and others have spoken of the support and encouragement he gave to young black writers. He remained optimistic about the future of race relations in the United States, regarding the struggle between black and white as a "spectacular" in which the curtain was about to rise on the "third act." "It was men like Bontemps," wrote A. G. Simms, "who tilled the soil which nourished black nationalism. . . . He anticipated in his career every facet of liberation—even the return to the South developing today."

PRINCIPAL WORKS: *Fiction*—God Sends Sunday, 1931; Black Thunder, 1936; Drums at Dusk, 1939; The Old South (short stories), 1973. *Poetry*—Personals, 1963. *Children's Fiction*—(with Langston Hughes) Popo and Fifina, Children of Haiti, 1932; You Can't Pet a Possum, 1934; Sad-Faced Boy, 1937; (with Jack Conroy) The Fast Sooner Hound, 1942; (with Jack Conroy) Slappy Hooper, the Wonderful Sign Painter, 1946; Chariot in the Sky: A Story of the Jubilee Singers, 1951; (with Jack Conroy) Sam Patch, the High, Wide, and Handsome Jumper, 1951; Lonesome Boy, 1955; Mr. Kelso's Lion, 1970. *Nonfiction*—(with W.C. Handy) Father of the Blues, 1941; We Have Tomorrow, 1945; (with Jack Conroy) They Seek a City, 1945 (republished as Anyplace But Here, 1966); The Story of the Negro, 1948; The Story of George Washington Carver, 1954; (with Langston Hughes) The Book of Negro Folklore, 1958; Frederick Douglass: Slave, Fighter, Freeman, 1959; One Hundred Years of Negro Freedom, 1961; Famous Negro Athletes, 1964; Young Booker: Booker T. Washington's Early Days, 1972. *As Editor*—Golden Slippers: An Anthology, 1941; (with Langston Hughes) The Poetry of the Negro: 1746-1949, 1949; American Negro Poetry, 1963; Great Slave Narratives, 1969; Hold Fast to Dreams: Poems Old and New, 1969; The Harlem Renaissance Remembered, 1972.

ABOUT: Baker, H.A. Black Literature in America, 1971; Bone, R.A. The Negro Novel in America, 1965; Brown, S.A. The Negro in American Fiction, 1937; Chapman, A. (ed.) Black Voices, 1968; Contemporary Authors 1-4, 1st revision, 1967; Current Biography, 1946; Davis, A.P. From the Dark Tower, 1974; Dreer, H. American Literature by Negro Authors, 1950; Gloster, H.M. Negro Voices in American Fiction, 1948; Hopkins, L.B. More Books by More People, 1974; Kunitz, S.J. and Haycraft, H. (eds.) Junior Book of Authors, 1951; O'Brien, J. (ed.) Interviews With Black Writers, 1973; Rollins, C. Famous American Negro Poets, 1965; Warfel, H.R. American Novelists of Today, 1951; Vinson J. (ed.) Contemporary Poets, 1970; Who's Who in America, 1974-1975. *Periodicals*—American Libraries December 1974; Harper's April 1965; Library Journal July 1973; September 1973; Library Quarterly July 1944; New York Times June 6, 1973; Phylon 4 1950; Saturday Review December 9, 1961; July 14, 1962; Time June 18, 1973; Wilson Library Bulletin October 1973.

*BORDEWIJK, FERDINAND ("Ton Ven") (October 10, 1884–April 28, 1965), Dutch novelist and short story writer, was born in Amsterdam, where his father ran a banking office. In 1894 the family moved to The Hague. Bordewijk studied law at the University of Leiden and in 1913 became a barrister. After a year with a life insurance company he went into practice as a barrister in Rotterdam and later in Schiedam. For a time he also taught law at a commercial college.

Victor van Vriesland, in his book on Bordewijk, quotes from a letter the author wrote him in 1946: "I do not think that a life devoted to literature would satisfy me. I can only write in the evenings and on Sundays, and not even then all the time. On the other hand, any hour of the day will do. I can start writing at any moment of the day, but I can also interrupt it at any moment and then take up the thread again at any given time. It was not as simple as that when I began, but writing is a craft in which one can train oneself, as in any other craft. Moreover, it is a hobby; practicing the law, which I like greatly, is the main thing for me."

Bordewijk always presented himself in this way, as an amateur writer, but there is nothing amateurish about his work. He began to publish comparatively late and made a false start with a volume of poems, *Paddenstoelen* (Toadstools), published in 1916 under the pen name of Ton Ven. In the following years he produced three volumes of short stories, all entitled *Fantastische Vertellingen* (Fantastic Tales, 1919, 1923, 1924). These dark stories give evidence that Bordewijk was familiar with the work of Edgar Allan Poe; they are no less obsessed with terror and annihilation, but there is none of the hysteria sometimes present in Poe's tales. As Adriaan van der Veen wrote in *Delta* (Spring, 1958), Bordewijk's style is "cool, hard, and matter-of-fact" and his stories never entirely lose touch with reality. Instead, reality "is inflated grotesquely, fantastically, until it attains demonic proportions." There was a stronger element of fantasy in the two short novels that followed in the early 1930s. *Blokken* (Blocks, 1931) is an account of the rise and fall of a modern, perhaps communist, state, which is destroyed by the disparity between utopian ideals and human weakness.

*bor' də vek

Royal Netherlands Embassy

FERDINAND BORDEWIJK

Knorrende Beesten (Grunting Animals, 1933) is a bizarre story about motor cars.

These first works enjoyed a *succès d'estime,* but it was not until Bordewijk published *Bint* in 1934 that his reputation was fully established. He was fifty years old by then, but the novel had all the freshness and energy usually associated with the work of a young writer. It is set in a school like the one in which Bordewijk had taught. Bint, the headmaster, regards progressive educational theories as inimical to the order that he prizes. He struggles to impose absolute discipline but fails, just as the utopians in *Blokken* had failed, because human beings cannot be made to conform to abstract notions of perfection.

Bint is a relatively realistic novel, but its realism is often larger than life and at times borders on surrealism. Adriaan van der Veen has pointed out that in Bordewijk's work, "chaos and annihilation are terrifying possibilities, but as long as there is a balance of power, total destruction can be averted. The disturbance of that balance of power is the leading theme of many . . . of Bordewijk's works of fiction." In *Bint* it is the headmaster, with his obsessive authoritarianism, who disturbs this delicate balance.

An equally formidable character, the brothel keeper Mrs. Doom, seeks to dominate events in *Rood Paleis* (The Red Palace, 1936). Greedy and aggressive, she disturbs the balance between matriarchal commercialism and "aristocratic" male privilege, and as a result her brothel goes up in flames, symbolizing the destruction of the nineteenth century values it embodies. Bordewijk's style in these novels is terse, spare, and amused, and conspicuously lacking in descrip-

tive passages—qualities which established him as the foremost representative of the "Neue Sachlichkeit" (New Objectivity) in Dutch literature.

In *Karakter* (1938, translated by E. M. Prince as *Character*), Brodewijk returned to the theme of discipline. It portrays a father who tries to develop his son's character by ruthlessly obstructing him in every possible way and at every opportunity. Though the father is still considerably larger than life, there is a notable swing in this novel towards everyday reality and a more conventional style, a tendency which continued in such later books as *Eiken van Dodona* (The Oaks of Dodona, 1946), *Bloesemtak* (Branch of Blossoms, 1955), and *De Doopvont* (The Baptismal Font, 1952). Whether embodied in freaks and monsters or in ordinary human beings, the threat of terror and chaos is never far away in Bordewijk's work.

The author was married in 1914 to the composer Johanna Roepman. During the bombing of The Hague in 1945 his entire library was lost, as was the manuscript of his wife's translation into English of *Bint*. After the war Bordewijk continued to live in The Hague and, with his son as his partner, to practice law in Schiedam, until his death at the age of eighty. In 1953 he received the P.C. Hooft Prize—the Dutch national prize for literature.

PRINCIPAL WORKS IN ENGLISH TRANSLATION: Character: A Novel of Father and Son, 1966.

ABOUT: Dubois, P.H. Over F. Bordewijk, 1953; Seymour-Smith, M. Guide to Modern World Literature, 1973; Vriesland, V.E. van. F. Bordewijk, 1949. *Periodicals*—Delta (Netherlands) Spring 1958; Writing in Holland and Flanders 2 1957, 15 1963.

*BOSE, BUDDHADEVA (November 30, 1908–), Indian poet, critic, novelist, and short story writer, was born in Comilla, East Bengal. He received his M.A. in English literature at Dacca University, where he emerged as a leader of the kallol movement, a group of gifted young Bengali writers who were quickly thought of as ultra-moderns. This was partly because of their views on sex and society (Bose was at this time a pronounced Freudian) and their interest in the life of poor laborers and craftsmen rather than in more traditional poetic subjects. But they were also breaking with traditional style and language, and Bose, a prolific writer from the beginning, was soon involved in controversy with Rabindranath Tagore, the great poet who dominated Bengali literature. He attacked not Tagore's own work but his influence on some

*ba' shoo

other young poets who (as he wrote in *An Acre of Green Grass*) "have had the dubious luck of being born Rabindranath's contemporaries. . . . I do not know that any single poet in history so completely permeated the language and the literature of his country and his time as Rabindranath in his later years. Inevitably and rightly, young poets were steeped in him; but what was neither inevitable nor right was that many, instead of journeying with him and in him, were led to use him as an anchor. For these it was impossible not to imitate Rabindranath, and it was impossible to imitate Rabindranath. Thus the illusion grew that one could achieve Rabindranath's sweetness by jingling a large enough number of rhymes, and his almost ethereal tenderness by plunging headlong into sentimentality."

Ever since his modernism first created a furor in Bengali literature Buddhadeva Bose has been a progressive and controversial figure—as recently as 1970, according to Dorothy Blair Shimer, he was convicted by a Calcutta magistrate "apparently for political reasons" on charges of obscenity. He has defended his position in innumerable articles and essays, and as editor of the journal *Pragati* (Prosperity) in Dacca, which during its short lifetime provided an outlet for much progressive Bengali writing. After moving to Calcutta in 1931 he became coeditor of the highly influential literary magazine *Kavita* (Poetry), a quarterly which from its founding in 1935 until its closure in 1961 provided a standard of excellence for Bengali poetry. His critical review of modern Bengali literature in *An Acre of Green Grass* (1948), published in English in Bombay, shows him to be a learned, penetrating, and sensitive critic, as well as a tough and polemical one.

Though he has been an extremely prolific writer of poetry, novels, and stories, very little of his work has been translated into English. Perhaps the main reason for this is that there is a strong poetic element even in his prose, for his gifts are essentially lyric. He achieved fame as a poet in early youth, and since then has published many volumes in Bengali, a representative selection from which appears in *Srestha kavita* (Best Poetry, 1957). The author himself made this adaptation of "The Hilsa," quoted here from *The Literary Review:*

July has come to the skies, Bengal is numbed with rain.
On darkening Meghna's shores the slender palms
Grow dim like wraiths of smoke; and Padma,
   gorger of green

Villages, pounces upon a bank where an ancient house,
Still as a painted scene, awaits extinction.

Murky is midnight, the river crooked.
Ah the little boats, tossing in the torrent!
And who are those, half-naked, with taut and dripping
   muscles
Flinging nets of hunger, tugging at heavy ropes?
They are those who feed us, so I've heard.

At the end of the night the black, blind wagons of
   Goalundo
Are loaded with gleaming hills of silver,
Bright harvest of the water, hilsas by the hundred,
Daring sport of streams, slaughtered, dead.

Morning comes to Calcutta, unkempt and busy,
Like wives of clerks who stalk from bed to kitchen,
Where now the mustard smites, and the keen air
   spreads
The twanging joy of hilsa, hissing hot on ovens.

Dorothy Blair Shimer comments that "this poem is filled with religious and regional meaning in its references to the hardy hilsa fish which, like the salmon, against great odds swims upstream to spawn. The Meghna gathers the waters of the great Ganges and Brahmaputra Rivers before emptying into the Bay of Bengal, while the Padma (a small river apparently given to monsoon flooding) enters the Ganges just above the Meghna. The Goalundo Ghat, or river landing, is near the joining of India's two most sacred streams—the Ganges and the Jumna. So, the everyday business of reaping the river's harvest is rooted in religious meaning, as, in reality, is the life of every devout Hindu."

Since his first novel, *Sara,* appeared in 1930, Buddhadeva Bose has published over forty more, including *Kaler putul* (Puppet of Time, 1946) and *Bipanna bismay* (Precarious Surprise, 1969). His subjects are intimate and personal, and most of his early novels are fundamentally autobiographical, with few characters and a hero who is essentially the poet himself; cultured and sophisticated but also cynical, he is unable to change society and so mocks its faults. Bose's works show the influence not only of Freud but of D. H. Lawrence, whose attempt to subordinate reason to instinct and passion is in accord with Bose's own theories, though not necessarily with his temperament, which has been called essentially intellectual. Humayun Kabir suggests that Bose's egocentricity and misogyny have prevented him from creating fullblooded subsidiary characters, and that his essentially lyric gifts do not equip him to dramatize situations and characters through the flow of events. In Kabir's view Bose has not yet written a novel fully worthy of his undoubted talent.

In his short stories Buddhadeva Bose has found an ideal medium for exploring every aspect of contemporary Bengali society, a culture whose basic values and beliefs have been changing rapidly under the pressures of the modern world and the problems of poverty, malnutrition, and overcrowding, the failure of nationalism, and the tragedy of partition. Typical of his stories is "Hatasha" (Despair), about a graduate from a respectable but impoverished family who finds it impossible to get a job. Or "The Birth of Beauty" (translated by Lila Ray in *Broken Bread*), which begins with three schoolboys finding a parcel in the street. A crowd gathers, speculating about its contents, and disperses hastily after deciding it is a bomb; the eldest boy says despairingly: "Everybody gone! Nobody did anything! That's why we are a slave nation!" But the youngest boy, left to guard the parcel, takes it home and finds inside a huge wooden doll, an ancient and highly realistic model of a dancing girl. His mother is at first filled with puritanical disgust at this shameless object and wants it destroyed. But gradually she becomes more and more fascinated by it, and when its owner advertises for its return she demands a huge price. Even then, her husband has to wrest the doll away from her. It represents for her a discovery of beauty, which she now sees in her son as well. "Where Bubu had stood sunshine lay beside a dark patch of shade. It was beautiful."

In 1967 one of Buddhadeva Bose's plays, *Tapasvī o Tarangini,* received the award of the Sahitya Akademi of New Delhi, India's academy of letters, and in 1970 he was named by the President of India a "lotus-jewel" of the nation. He is universally regarded as one of the leading writers of contemporary Bengal, who as a critic and translator as well as a creative writer has played a crucial role in the shaping of Bengali literature in the period after Rabindranath Tagore, and has also influenced Indian writing in other languages. From 1956 to 1963, when he resigned "for political reasons," he was the first chairman and professor of the comparative literature department of Jadavpur University in Calcutta. He has lectured in Europe and Japan and spent a year in the United States as a visiting professor at Pennsylvania College for Women (1953-1954).

PRINICPAL WORKS IN ENGLISH AND ENGLISH TRANSLATION: An Acre of Green Grass: A Review of Modern Bengali Literature, 1948; (editor) An Anthology of Bengali Writing, 1971; Rain Through the Night, translated by C.B. Seely, 1973. *Poems in* Chatterjee, D. (ed.) Modern Bengali Poems, 1945; Kabir, H. (ed.) Green and Gold, 1960; Shimer, D.B. (ed.) Voices of Modern Asia, 1973; Kenyon Review 11 1949; Partisan Review Summer 1955. *Stories in* Ray, L. (ed.) Broken Bread: Short Stories of Modern Bengal, 1957; Dial 3 1960; Pacific Spectator 7 2 1953.

ABOUT: India Who's Who, 1970; Kabir, H. The Bengali Novel, 1968; Penguin Companion to Literature 4, 1969; Prusek, J. (ed.) Dictionary of Oriental Literatures 2, 1974; Seymour-Smith, M. Guide to Modern World Literature, 1973; Shimer, D.B. (ed.) Voices of Modern Asia, 1973; Who's Who of Indian Writers, 1961.

*BOTTRALL, (FRANCIS JAMES) RONALD (September 2, 1906–), English poet and critic, writes: "Umberto Saba used to say that he was thirty years behind the times because he was born in 1883 in Trieste and brought up there. Similarly I feel that I lost twenty years by being born in 1906 in the mining town of Camborne in West Cornwall. My parents, my grandmother and my aunt—I had three mothers and one father—were all strict Wesleyan Methodists. From fourteen to eighteen I was a Sunday-school teacher and organist and often accompanied my father on his preaching appointments. He was a clerk in a local coal and timber firm. During World War I, I was mainly taught mathematics, physics and chemistry. I did not hear a symphony concert or a concert of chamber music until I went to Cambridge in 1925 and I had only crossed the borders of Cornwall once, in 1924, when I went with other boys from Redruth County School to the British Empire Exhibition at Wembley.

"When I got to Cambridge, few people could understand the Cornish dialect I spoke. Hoping to read Classics, I taught myself Greek, but I found that, in order to get a scholarship, I had to read English. My early years as a university teacher and, later, administrator, took me to Helsinki, Princeton, Singapore and Florence. I worked in the British Air Ministry during the first part of World War II and in October 1941 went to Sweden to start the British Council's work there. Then to Rome, London, Rio de Janeiro, Athens and Tokyo, where I finished my career as Cultural Counsellor of the British Embassy. Later I worked from 1963 to 1965 for FAO, Rome, in which city I eventually retired. From 1964 to 1974 I was the principal reviewer of contemporary Italian literature and Scandinavian literature and history for the *Times Literary Supplement.*

"My restricted upbringing and subsequent extensive travel provided me with unusual contrasts of experience and variations of living. These contrasts oppose each other or resolve themselves in my poetry. The first contrast was between the great cliffs overlooking the stormy

*bot' rəl

RONALD BOTTRALL

"From January 1952 to January 1972 I wrote about thirteen poems. In February 1972 I started writing rapidly and have not stopped since. I cannot explain this barren period or the fruitful one which I am now experiencing, but I do know that I could not have begun to write again if I did not possess a considerable technique. In the course of my work I have used almost every known metrical form and one or two unknown ones. I believe that ability to use these forms is invaluable and if a poet does not have it he is technically inferior and handicapped to that extent, however good a poet he may potentially be."

Atlantic and the derelict engine-houses in the distressed mining area of Camborne-Redruth, but I did not describe my upbringing at length until I wrote 'Talking to the Ceiling' in 1972. Of course, the sea, the coast of Cornwall, the farms and farmland (I lived next door to a farm and two-and-a-half miles from the sea) do persist through my poetry, but they are countered by impressions and images gathered from continual travelling around the world.

"One thing has been constant. I have always written to please my very exacting self. I have never published a line that I did not wish to publish and I have never written poetry for the purpose of making money.

"My interests in the other arts are in this order: music, painting, architecture, sculpture and drama. This is in a way unfortunate, because while music is the art most closely allied to poetry, the abstract notation in which it is expressed makes it far harder to incorporate into poetry than painting, architecture, sculpture and drama. However, I have, I think, succeeded occasionally in writing poems which convey something of the power of music.

"I suppose that it is fairly accurate to say that in one's early formative years, when one begins to write poetry, themes present themselves with remarkable facility and so do situations which seem suitable for poetry, but one hasn't got the technique to deal with them. Then one arrives in mid-career, at a point where these things coalesce and the poet has the technique to present them in the best possible way. As one grows older, the technique is there, but the themes come more rarely and the situations do not crop up when they are needed.

As an undergraduate at Cambridge in the late 1920s, where Bottrall was a contemporary of William Empson, Charles Madge, and Kathleen Raine, among other notable young poets, a brilliant future was expected for him. He graduated in 1929 with distinguished first-class honors in the English Tripos, and subsequently contributed to F. R. Leavis's famous Cambridge critical journal *Scrutiny*. Leavis regarded Bottrall as the most able and promising poet of his generation and warmly praised his technical skill, his intelligence, and his grasp of the contemporary scene.

Leavis was by no means alone in his admiration and expectations for Bottrall. T. S. Eliot in 1932 referred to him as one of the four best young English poets, and the subsequent neglect of his work has scandalized admirers as discriminating and diverse as Anthony Burgess, Eugenio Montale, Francis King, Martin Seymour-Smith, Robert Graves, Charles Tomlinson, and G. S. Fraser. No doubt Bottrall's reputation has suffered from his championship by Leavis, an influential but controversial figure, and also from the fact that he was never elected to the literary "cabinet" of young writers which W. H. Auden gathered around himself in the 1930s.

All the same, some part of the explanation for his failure to redeem his early promise must be sought in the poetry itself. Bottrall (who wrote very perceptively on Ezra Pound in *Scrutiny*) has said that Pound's *Hugh Selwyn Mauberley* was the greatest influence on his early work, and this may be seen in a poem like "Un Bel Homme du Temps Jadis" from *Farewell and Welcome:*

Eager to embrace every fresh manifestation
Of intellectual and political snobbery,
He was nevertheless too watchful for the revelation
To outlast more recent and more successful jobbery.

His material home was a neutral country,
His stock-in-trade litmus paper,
His spiritual home a Laodicean chantry,
His badge a chameleon couchant on a cloud of vapour.

Careful to avoid undisciplined enthusiasm,
He always watched for the week-end reviewers
Before committing himself to a criticism
Of new works by even solidly established
    authors. . . .

But this, as Martin Seymour-Smith has pointed out, is only one of "a number of distinct
manners, ranging from the Blakean through the
satirical to the loosely anecdotal. . . . shock, the
utmost candour and humour co-exist, and the
result is a bewildering versatility: his poems may
be bizarre . . . anecdotal or cryptic." This tends
to discourage reviewers, who prefer a poet who
can be more tidily pigeonholed, as does the fact
that Bottrall's poems contain few great single
lines but must be read in their entirety if their
meanings and virtues are fully to be grasped.
Moreover, Bottrall has always been readier than
most poets to include inferior occasional poems
in his collections, giving the impression of great
unevenness.

In any case, Bottrall is not an easy poet. He
is complex, learned, and allusive. He knows thirteen languages well, and is not averse to echoing
the manner or even the phrasing of any of those
foreign poets whom he admires for remaining
true to their vocations in an age that he deplores,
both for its vulgarity and its technology. Among
those whose influences have been absorbed into
his own resolutely English poetry are Eugenio
Montale, Antonio Machado, Alexander Blok,
Constantine Cavafy, Fernando Pessoa, Yeats,
and César Vallejo.

G. S. Fraser wrote in 1970 that Bottrall's
"natural fluency makes it hard for him to eliminate and condense. Nor is there any final
philosophy of life in this poetry except that of
the sceptical, disabused, but always eager and
curious spectator and critic of life, an urbane
critic coupled with a lyrical celebrator." In 1974,
however, after reading *Poems 1955-1973*, Fraser
felt constrained to modify this judgment, especially in the light of the long autobiographical
poem "Talking to the Ceiling"—"a poet's late
assertion of the sacredness of roots . . . a kind of
counterblast to *The Waste Land.*" Charles Tomlinson speaks in rather similar terms of a tension
in Bottrall's work "between naturalness and
rootless sophistication, between locality and
what he calls urbanality," but Tomlinson also
finds "throughout Bottrall's best poems a moral
resistance [which] eludes definition because by
its nature it is protean, not fixed, flowing power-

fully in to fill the vacuum it abhors." And he
finds a hint of its "mode of operation" in a poem
like "One Cornishman to Another," addressed
to the primitive painter Alfred Wallis:

When there came trawling over the blue bay
Ships with the energy of tackle and gear
Drawing wealth from depths you saw them hounds
    at play
Moving because of the lissom and sheer
Ripple of thew and muscle
Interlocking as timbers in a trim vessel.

The work Bottrall has produced during the
extremely fruitful period that began in 1972 includes the most concentrated poems he has ever
written (among them some highly cryptic poems
reminiscent of Vallejo), as well as a powerful
sequel to "Talking to the Ceiling" called "Aun-
tie Mabel." When these new poems are collected, Bottrall may at last take the central position
on the English poetic scene that many feel is
properly his.

The author, the son of Francis and Clara Bottrall, was a Foundress' Scholar of Pembroke
College, Cambridge. He began his career as Lec-
tor in English at the University of Helsinki, Fin-
land (1929-1931). In 1931-1933 he held a
Commonwealth Fund Fellowship at Princeton
University, in 1933-1937 he taught as Johore
Professor of English at Raffles College, Sin-
gapore, and for a year after that was assistant
director of the British Institute in Florence. In
1939 Bottrall became secretary of the School of
Oriental and African Studies at London Univer-
sity, a post which he retained throughout World
War II, while serving as a civil servant in the Air
Ministry (1940-1941) and with the British
Council in Sweden (1941-1944). After the war,
as he says, he represented the British Council in
Italy (1945-1950). In 1950-1954 he was the
Council's controller of education, based in Lon-
don, serving thereafter in Brazil (1954-1956),
Greece (1957-1959), and Japan (1959-1961),
where he was also Cultural Counsellor to the
British Embassy in Tokyo.

Bottrall has a son by his 1934 marriage to
Margaret Smith, well-known under her married
name as a scholar and critic. They were divorced
in 1954 and Bottrall made a second marriage in
that year to Margot Samuel. He left Rome in
1977 and since then has been living in Cairo,
Egypt. The author received an O.B.E. in 1949,
became a Knight of the Order of St. John of
Jerusalem in 1972, a Grand Officer of the Italian
Order of Merit in 1973, and a Knight of Malta
in 1976. He was awarded the Syracuse Interna-

tional Literary Prize in 1954 and is a Fellow of the Royal Society of Literature.

A large, good-looking man, Bottrall has in recent years been troubled by deafness (see his poem "Occlusion") and a complicated asthmatic condition. The writing of poetry, which he finds irresistible, makes him unwell (he calls this his "Simenon syndrome," because the Belgian novelist has abandoned writing on account of a similar affliction); in "Overplus" Bottrall says: "My lungs are a palimpsest/ On which my earlier writing/ is faintly visible./ More writing may mean death./ But too much writing is a bad thing/ Anyhow." A renowned and energetic anecdotalist, Bottrall is possessed of a seemingly inexhaustible knowledge of the most famous writers (of all nationalities) of his time.

PRINCIPAL WORKS: *Poetry*—The Loosening, 1931; Festivals of Fire, 1934; The Turning Path, 1939; Farewell and Welcome, 1945; Selected Poems, 1946; The Palisades of Fear, 1949; Adam Unparadised, 1954; Collected Poems, 1961; Day and Night, 1974; Poems 1955-1973, 1974. *Nonfiction*—Rome (Art Centres of the World series), 1968. *As Editor*—(with Gunnar Ekelöf) T.S. Eliot's Dikter i Urval, 1942; (with Margaret Bottrall) The Zephyr Book of English Verse, 1945; (with Margaret Bottrall) Collected English Verse, 1946.

ABOUT: Bergonzi, B. (ed.) The Twentieth Century, 1970; Contemporary Authors 53-56, 1975; Daiches, D. (ed.) British and Commonwealth Literature, 1971; Daiches, D. The Present Age, 1958; Fraser, G.S. The Modern Writer and His World, 1953; International Who's Who, 1977-78; International Who's Who in Poetry, 1974-75; Leavis, F.R. New Bearings in English Poetry, 1932; Orr, P. (ed.) The Poet Speaks, 1966; Seymour-Smith, M. Guide to Modern World Literature, 1973; Seymour-Smith, M. Who's Who in Twentieth-Century Literature, 1976; Sitwell, E. *introduction to* Collected Poems, 1961; Vinson, J. (ed.) Contemporary Poets, 1975; Who's Who, 1978. *Periodicals*—Birmingham Post May 3, 1975; London Magazine June-July 1975; Sunday Telegraph (London) April 6, 1975; Times (London) April 10, 1975.

*BOUTENS, PETER CORNELIS** (February 20, 1870–March 14, 1943), Dutch poet, translator, and scholar, was born in Middelburg, on the island of Walcheren. His parents were strict Protestants, but when he was a boy the stifling pressures of the church alienated him from conventional religious belief, and ill health made him retire into himself. Against his father's wishes he studied classical literature at the University of Utrecht, gaining a doctorate of letters in 1899 with a dissertation on Aristophanes. For five years he was a teacher of Latin and Greek at a boy's preparatory school at Voorschoten, near Leiden. But by 1904 the success of his early poetry allowed him to devote himself entirely to literature, and he settled in The Hague, leading

*bou′tənz

PETER CORNELIS BOUTENS

a quiet bachelor life. He died during the Nazi occupation.

His first book of poems, *Verzen* (Verses, 1898) had an introduction by the leading critic Lodewijk van Deyssel, who brought Boutens immediate recognition with his praise: "Here is no longer reality with feeling, but feeling rendered by means of reality." The influence of the "Tachtigers" (the Generation of 1880) led Boutens in these early poems to impressionism, but he clearly had already the makings of a symbolist; the sensuous impressions, vividly though they are conveyed, are emblems of his own insights and feelings. Boutens used an impressionist technique to express subjective spiritual experiences in poetry whose "every word is a symbol of profound significance."

In early books like *Praeludiën* (Preludes, 1902) his mystical perceptions were often enigmatically expressed. But in *Stemmen* (Voices, 1907), *Vergeten Liedjes* (Forgotten Songs, 1909), and *Carmina* (Songs, 1912) he achieved a more direct classical style and an absolute mastery of rhythm and form. His poems are organized in strict stanza patterns, but, as the Dutch poet Albert Verwey has pointed out, his rhythms and line lengths are varied with a confident freedom that enables him to incorporate extremely complex images in poems which somehow remain richly melodious.

Boutens is a poet of nature and solitude, passionately sensitive to the distinctive beauty of the Dutch landscape. Nevertheless, for him nature is a parable that in moments of inspiration becomes transparent, revealing a larger reality. His pagan conception of life unites a Platonic philosophy and Hellenistic spirit in the pursuit of the true, the good, and the beautiful, which he invokes and celebrates in *Lente-maan* (Spring Moon, 1916), *Liederen van Isoude* (Songs of Isolde, 1921) and *Zomerwolken* (Summer Clouds, 1922). His later collections, *Bezonnen verzen* (Thoughtful Poems, 1931), *Honderd Hollandsche kwatrijnen* (One Hundred Dutch Quatrains, 1932), and *Tusschenspelen* (Interludes, 1942), are marked by more concrete imagery and a deepened national feeling.

His most famous and popular work is *Beatrijs* (Beatrice, 1908), which has been reprinted over fifty times. This is a free adaptation of a medieval Dutch legend about a nun who returns to the world for a time because of her love for a knight. During her absence a statue of the Virgin Mary comes to life to replace her, though the nuns discover this only after Beatrice's death, when the knight arrives as an old pilgrim to ask for a grave beside hers in the convent church. Despite its ballad form, the poem is very modern in its fusion of musical color and symbolism, and the psychological deftness of the inner mother-child relationship between Mary and Beatrice.

Boutens also wrote a play in Middle Dutch verse, *Alianora,* for the University of Leiden's 325th anniversary in 1910, and an open-air drama, *Middelburg's overgang* (The Capture of Middelburg), which was performed in that city's market square in 1924. He had read very widely in German, French, and English as well as classical poetry, and had a remarkably retentive memory for verse. Boutens has been called the best translator of his generation in Holland, and he was responsible for notable Dutch versions of works by Homer, Aeschylus, Sophocles, Sappho, Plato, Omar Khayyám, Goethe, Novalis, Louise Labé, Rossetti, and Oscar Wilde, among others. His *Verzamelde Werken* (collected works) were issued in seven volumes between 1943 and 1954. He served for many years as chairman of his country's national society of authors.

PRINCIPAL WORKS IN ENGLISH TRANSLATION: *Poems in* Barnouw, A.J. (ed.) Coming After, 1948; Columbia University, The Great Literature of Small Nations VIII, 1929; Grierson, H. J. C. (ed.) The Flute, 1949; Snell, A. L. (ed.) Flowers From a Foreign Garden, 1902; Weevers, T. The Poetry of the Netherlands, 1960; Adam July 1949.

ABOUT: Binnendijk, D.A.M. Een protest tegen de tijd, 1965; Grierson, H.J.C. Two Dutch Poets, 1936; Penguin Companion to Literature 2, 1969; Smith, H. (ed.) Columbia Dictionary of Modern European Literature, 1947; Weevers, T. The Poetry of the Netherlands, 1960.

*BOYE, KARIN (MARIA) (October 26, 1900– April 23, 1941), Swedish poet and novelist, was
*bô′ yə

KARIN BOYE

born in Gothenburg, the daughter of a withdrawn and somewhat unstable engineer, Fritz Boye, and his imaginative wife, the former Signe Liljestrand. A gifted and introspective girl— "tautly emotional, rigorously honest"—Karin Boye became interested in Buddhism in her teens but was later converted to a somewhat puritanical form of Christianity. She abandoned Christianity in its turn and as a student at the University of Uppsala became a leading member of the Clarté movement, a group of left-wing idealists.

Martin Seymour-Smith has suggested that hers remained nevertheless an essentially religious nature, and that she was only a "desperate and reluctant Marxist." In any case, her revolutionary zeal was never purely political. She was one of the founders in 1931 of the avant-garde periodical *Spektrum,* which devoted issues to such subjects as Functionalism and—Karin Boye's special interest—psychoanalysis. Early literary influences included the semi-mystical romantic poet Vilhelm Ekelund and T. S. Eliot, whose *The Waste Land* Karin Boye helped to translate for publication in *Spektrum.*

Her own poetry was much less esoteric than these activities might suggest, and its simplicity and directness, its subtly haunting rhythms, earned it considerable popularity. Her technical skill was already evident in her first collection, *Moln* (Clouds, 1922), where severely disciplined verse forms give shape and structure to a rather strained and diffuse idealism.

Gömda Land (Hidden Lands, 1924) is equally idealistic but more equivocally so. In this second volume, Karin Boye holds up the ideal of the ascetic warrior, indifferent to personal comfort, happy only in battle; but she is also aware of the negative aspects of such selfless dedication, acknowledging that chaos and indiscipline are perhaps essential to human development. In a famous poem, the author contrasts the steadfast Aesir (gods), the guardians of masculine honor and tradition, with the devious and mercurial Elves, who rule over the deeper, more instinctive, and feminine forces in nature and the human psyche.

In *Härdana* (The Hearths, 1927), Karin Boye describes her own struggle to overcome a defensive rigidity:

> Armed, erect, and clad in mail,
> I walked forth—
> But the mail was made of fear
> and of shame. . . .
> Spring appears in winter's regions
> where I froze.
> I will meet the powers of life
> weaponless.
>
> (translated by Gavin Orton)

At this point in her career, the influential critic Hagar Olsson welcomed her work as the first sign of a genuine renewal in Swedish poetry.

Eight years were to pass before Karin Boye published her next collection. *För trädets skull* (For the Tree's Sake, 1935) showed much greater depth and maturity than her earlier verse, and a tendency to more irregular rhythms and verse patterns, in keeping with the poet's increasing identification with the instinctual rather than the rational in nature. A central symbol of the pain and yet the necessity of growth and change is the tree, with its sure slow growth, its final hesitation ("Of course it hurts when buds burst"), and its triumphant flowering.

Karin Boye's reputation as one of the most arresting and original of modern Swedish poets was confirmed by the posthumous publication of *De sju dödssynderna* (The Seven Deadly Sins, 1941). The uncompleted title poem considers the problem of good and evil in the light of modern psychoanalysis. Influenced perhaps by T.S. Eliot's *Murder in the Cathedral,* it takes the form of a cantata in which man stands before God's throne and defends his sins. In Lust he has sought a glimpse of divine ecstasy; his Pride has been his refusal to admit failure; his Sloth has been a tense waiting for spiritual enlightenment. Above all, he has sought unity: "All that is scattered and divided/longs to be made whole."

This poem has been seen as an expression of the author's own state of mind in her desperately troubled last years. For although her poetry is cool, precise, and lucid, striving to express harmony, in her life she remained hopelessly divided. She was married in 1929-1932 to Leif Björk but was bisexual—a source for her of much unhappiness. She had an intensely emotional nature, often at war with her sharp critical intelligence. Above all, perhaps, she was a passionate humanitarian reduced to despair by the gross inhumanities of the 1930s in Europe. After several abortive attempts, she ended her own life, alone in a winter forest at Alingsås. Not only for this reason, she reminds the English-speaking reader of Sylvia Plath.

Karin Boye also published five novels and a number of short stories. *Astarte* (1931) and other novels of the early 1930s, which focus on particular moral and psychological problems, and rather self-consciously employ expressionist techniques, have been found somewhat lifeless and abstract. More successful is *Kris* (Crisis, 1934), based on the author's own early religious crisis, and *För lite* (Too Little, 1936), which describes the creative failure of a once promising writer imprisoned in petty domesticity.

Her best novel is *Kallocain* (1940, translated by G. Lannestock under the same title). Written at a time when Nazism seemed to be triumphing in Europe, it is a passionate protest against all totalitarian dogma, and has been compared, in its intensity and horror, with Orwell's *1984*. A politically indoctrinated scientist, Leo Kall, discovers the pale green drug Kallocain, under whose influence people reveal their innermost thoughts and deepest feelings. From his experiments with it, he learns, at first with shocked dismay and then with increasing sympathy, that people's wishes have nothing to do with the creation of a World State, however perfectly it may satisfy their physical needs. Instead they have visions of growing into harmony with nature, and yearn for spiritual ecstasy with a thirst that can only be quenched from the deep, mystical springs of life.

This affirmation of human richness, made in the face of the brutal simplifications of totalitarianism and of her own anguish, is central to an understanding of Karin Boye's work. Her life is summed up in the striking phrase from one of her own poems which Margit Abenius chose as the title for her biography of her lifelong friend: "drabbad av renhet"—"struck down by purity."

PRINCIPAL WORKS IN ENGLISH TRANSLATION: *Novel*—Kallocain, 1966. *Poems* in Swenson, M. (ed.) Half Sun, Half Sleep, 1967; Life and Letters October 1949.

ABOUT: Abenius, M. Drabbad av renhet, 1950; Abenius, M. and Lagercrantz, O. (eds.) Karin Boye: minnen och studier, 1942; Gustafson, A. A History of Swedish Lterature, 1961; Penguin Companion to Literature 2, 1969; Seymour-Smith, M. Guide to Modern World Literature, 1973; Smith, H.

(ed.) Columbia Dictionary of Modern European Literature, 1947.

BRADBURY, MALCOLM (STANLEY) (September 7, 1932–), English novelist, critic, dramatist, poet, and humorist, writes: "I was born in Sheffield, England, of lower-middle-class background. My father worked as a railway clerk. I grew up in suburban London and then, after the outbreak of war, we moved to Sheffield —for the bombing, as it turned out; and then to safer Nottingham. Here I went to grammar school. I was a beneficiary of the 1944 Butler Education Act—a rather miserable one, since I had a solitary temperament and a heart condition. However it was undoubtedly the long periods spent in the library while others played games that encouraged me to read, and then write. I began writing stories for the local *Nottinghamshire Guardian* (where D.H. Lawrence, to me the *other* Nottingham writer, had published), and comedy sketches for the BBC—it seemed a high art-form at the time, and I have always been fascinated by comedy and soon afterwards started writing for *Punch*. When, in 1950, I went to University College, Leicester, a redbrick, to read English, I hoped to become a writer—a rather self-consciously provincial or regional one—and I started my first novel, *Eating People Is Wrong*, set in just such another English provincial university. University for me, a first-generation student, was a great intellectual excitement; I was surprised, then attached, and have been in university environments ever since. University was freeing to me, and embodied values that excited me; the novel I wrote was about the liberalism of personal relations that I found there—a comedy about its virtues and its limitations. After graduating, I became a research student, first in London, then in the United States, writing theses and rewriting the novel; I am a dedicated rewriter. In 1959, I married, got my first university teaching post, and published the novel, which proved a critical success, and is now being reissued in England.

"Since then I have been teaching and writing together, an interesting but hard connection to make, partly because there is little time for writing, partly because my critical interest is in fiction and it sometimes wages war with my practice. I have written much criticism—books on Forster and Waugh, both of whom influenced me, on the social context of modern English literature, and the state of the novel *(Possibilities)*. But I managed another novel in 1965, *Stepping Westward*, about a key myth of the time—the English writer going to the States in hope of liberation from English provincialities

MALCOLM BRADBURY

and encountering an alternative, more political liberalism. The strain between liberal individuality and history with its process and imperatives was the theme; the manner is again comedy, a liberal comedy with realistic inclinations. The central character, James Walker, is a 'soft' English liberal who meets a harder, more political version in the machinations of Bernard Froelich, an American professor who tries to use him, to plot his life.

"This interest in plotters and the designs they seek to impose on liberal contingency became the theme for a third novel, which developed into *The History Man,* published in 1975 and granted a Royal Society of Literature Award. If the two previous books are comic liberal realism, this is not; historical imperatives seemed to me over time to have increased, man seemed to me to live in a much more history- and fashion-centred world, unable to perpetuate continuous values; I felt the need for a harder, more exact, less generous form, a more precise economy of telling. The book, about a radical couple, the Kirks, in 1972, replaying the liberation stories of 1968 in a lowered situation, is told largely in the present tense, is set in an immediate world of things, of hard modern places; the time span is condensed, and the novel limits the possibilities of humanistic awareness or action, as I think the world does. It is a saddened book, but still a comedy. The path toward it is visible in the stories and parodies of my collection *Who Do You Think You Are?;* the stories grow harder, more precise, more concerned with technique and composition, language and the power of plots over time, and the parodies clear the air of styles toward which I had tended in my earlier writing.

"I have also written two collections of humour, half a volume of poems; there are several radio plays, a number of contributions to the television satire programme *That Was the Week That Was*, and lately I have been writing television plays: *The After-Dinner Game* (with Chris Bigsby); a second play under a pseudonym; a third yet to be made, when the economics permit; a fourth, *Missing Time*, about the distance between 1956, the year of Suez and Hungary, and the economic-crisis present-day. I am, like the character Stuart Treece, the central figure of *Eating People Is Wrong*, a professor of literature, which says something about the power of fantasy. My novels are all set in universities, because that is my central experience; but they are not, I believe, campus novels, rather novels about self-aware intellectuals capable of irony and doubt, concerned with the issues of change and liberation, the problems of humanism, and so might well have been in other settings. My interest in technique and stylistic precision grows, and the rhythm of my writing, from liberal comedy in the fifties to something more exact, experimental and bleak in the seventies, seems to me a significant rhythm of modern stylistic change. I now live in Norwich, married, with two children, furiously chasing all the writing, teaching, and critical work I want to do."

———

Bradbury graduated from University College, Leicester, in 1953, and received his M.A. in English in 1955 from Queen Mary College, London. He was a research student at Indiana University (1955-1956) and the University of Manchester (1956-1958), and in 1958 worked for a time at Yale with a junior fellowship from the British Association for American Studies. These researches brought him his doctorate in American studies from Manchester in 1963. Meanwhile, Bradbury had begun his teaching career as a staff tutor in Hull University's extramural department (1959-1961). From 1961 to 1965 he was an English lecturer at the University of Birmingham, and in 1965 he moved to the School of English and American Studies at the University of East Anglia at Norwich, where he has remained as lecturer (1965-1967), senior lecturer (1967-1969), reader (1969-1970), and (since 1970) professor of American studies.

Eating People Is Wrong (1959), the novel that Bradbury began as an undergraduate at Leicester, is an amiable satire of British academic life at a provincial university. Professor Treece has an unsuccessful affair with a neurotic senior colleague, then a happier one with a research student, Emma, a sensible, intelligent, but by no

means extraordinary girl who is also loved by an undergraduate, Louis Bates. Bates tries to kill himself when Emma rejects him, and many critics thought Bradbury's compassionate and sensitive handling of this brilliant but immature character the best thing in the book. Bates is the kind of young man who might be produced by any higher cultural sub-group, and this tends to bear out Bradbury's repeated assertion that what he writes are not really "campus" novels— "any intellectual milieu might do as well." This first novel, like its successors, has less to do with, say, university politics than with Bradbury's stated preoccupation with "problems and dilemmas of liberalism and . . . moral responsibility."

A satirical novel about postwar British academia, *Eating People Is Wrong* could scarcely escape comparison with Kingsley Amis's *Lucky Jim:* David L. Parkes thought it "more broadly comic and less sharply satirical . . . Professor Treece is a kind of successful Jim Dixon." Bradbury's second novel, *Stepping Westward* (1965), about a British writer in the United States, likewise invoked comparisons with Amis's *One Fat Englishman*. James Walker, a novelist from Nottingham University, goes as writer-in-residence to a Midwestern university, where he is bewildered by America and American academic life and exploited by a scheming and ambitious colleague. Discovering that he is expected to take a loyalty oath, Walker lights out for Mexico, an action that has far-reaching effects for the faculty and the students, and eventually for himself.

Most reviewers found the satire in *Stepping Westward* exaggerated and the characters caricatures, but enjoyed the result nevertheless. Bernard McCabe wrote: "Within this very funny book Mr. Bradbury proposes a serious novel about freedom and community and friendship's inevitable failures. The result is interesting, but too schematic and analytical to be really successful. The comedy works, though, thanks to Bradbury's artful writing. . . . This sort of slapstick should have its cheerful audience. The model is early Evelyn Waugh, a happy mingling of satire and fantasy." A critic in the *Times Literary Supplement*, who thought that the novel was overburdened with detail and needed a sharper sense of focus, praised it all the same as a *vade mecum* for visitors to the United States: "Every situational joke, every classic encounter is exactly and wittily exploited. The dialogue is often marvellously acute, the tricks of American speech expertly 'bugged.' "

The History Man (1975) is an altogether tougher piece of work, though still a comedy. Howard Kirk has progressed from a background of "vestigal Christianity and inherited social deference" to become a sociology don at a new university. He is politically radical, sexually predatory, and a bully. His wife Barbara is an equally representative contemporary figure: she describes herself as "just a person, trapped in the role of wife and mother," and greets nervous guests at her famous parties with questions about their contraceptive methods. Kirk is presented as "the treacherous comic embodiment of Hegelian inevitability," convinced that history is on his side, and on the side of all his moral and political irresponsibilities.

As Bradbury explains above, *The History Man* is "told largely in the present tense [and] set in an immediate world of things." Indeed, his endless catalogue of possessions, elaborately described, reminded some reviewers of Robbe-Grillet and the French "new novelists." It seemed to Hilary Spurling that "things tend to take over on a scale which suggests mounting moral uneasiness: it is as though the monstrous regiment of fixtures and fittings which enclose, and perhaps helped to produce, Howard had somehow become too much for his creator." Michael Ratcliffe had no such misgivings about this tendency, and also commended Bradbury's choice of the present tense—"a perfect ironic device for a history of existentially humourless professionals for whom no other element of time is conceivable since they have murdered the Past to bring in the Future now: It is the Now mode for the Now people. . . . Witty, aggressive and richly observant, *The History Man* is one of the best novels of the year." Margaret Drabble evidently agreed, saying that Bradbury had written a novel "that raises some very serious questions about the nature of civilization without for a moment appearing pretentious or didactic—a fine achievement."

The seven short stories collected in *Who Do You Think You Are?* all have academic settings and, Philip French wrote, reflect Bradbury's "commitment to a basic liberal humanism." The same book contains eight parodies—of Angus Wilson, Iris Murdoch, J. D. Salinger, and Alan Sillitoe among others. French, who particularly enjoyed the Sillitoe piece, concluded that Bradbury had established himself as a major parodist, though another critic thought that these exercises were more in the nature of tributes to the authors concerned than true parodies. Bradbury has also written a number of skillful and amusing plays and revues, mostly in collaboration with other writers, for the stage and for radio and television. The television play *The After-Dinner Game* (1975), written with Christopher Bigsby (lecturer in American literature at the University of East Anglia), introduced some of the characters in *The History Man,* and was described by Michael Ratcliffe as "brilliant."

Professor Bradbury is one of those who maintain that literary studies have become too specialized, too rigidly confined by the new orthodoxy of close textual analysis. He believes that sociology can be "an enabling discipline allowing new insights and means to develop in literary study." In *The Social Context of Modern English Literature* (1971) he employs sociological concepts to examine "the ecology of modern writing in England." The result seemed to a reviewer in the *Times Literary Supplement* to have "a strange abstract quality which constantly frustrates the reader's expectations," leaving him "stuck with the problem" of "marrying" sociology to literary studies. The book was found useful, nevertheless, as a statement of a pressing and important problem, and for "Professor Bradbury's intelligent openness of approach."

This same openness and flexibility of approach was commended in *Possibilities,* a collection of essays on the state of the novel. Though critics would have preferred to see "a properly detailed study of the contemporary English novel," this book, it was thought, "despite some uncertainties in pitch and proportion, helps to maintain and advance the kind of civilised, informed discussion about the possibilities of the novel which we need." Bradbury has written a monograph on Evelyn Waugh for a series of studies of twentieth-century writers, and is the co-editor with Eric Mottram of the volume devoted to American literature in the *Penguin Companion to Literature.*

The author was a fellow of the American Council of Learned Societies in 1965 and a visiting fellow of All Souls College, Oxford, in 1969. In 1972 he went as a visiting professor to the University of Zurich, and in 1977-1978 spent two months at Yaddo, the writers' colony in New York State. Bradbury is said to be genial, amusing, and relaxed in manner, and is liked by most of his students as a stimulating, undogmatic, and dedicated teacher. According to *Who's Who,* he has no recreations. His wife Elizabeth is a part-time librarian at the University of East Anglia and also writes for the radio.

PRINCIPAL WORKS: *Fiction*—Eating People Is Wrong, 1959; Stepping Westward, 1965; The History Man, 1975; Who Do You Think You Are? (stories and parodies), 1976. *Poetry*—(with Allan Rodway) Two Poets, 1966. *Humor*—Phogey! or, How to Have Class in a Classless Society, 1960; All Dressed Up and Nowhere to Go: The Poor Man's Guide to the Affluent Society, 1962. *Criticism*—Evelyn Waugh (Writers and Critics series), 1964; What Is a Novel?, 1969;

The Social Context of Modern English Literature, 1971; Possibilities: Essays on the State of the Novel, 1973. *As Editor*—Forster: A Collection of Critical Essays, 1966; E.M. Forster's A Passage to India: A Casebook, 1970; (with Eric Mottram) U.S.A., volume 3 of The Penguin Companion to Literature, 1971; (with David Palmer) Victorian Poetry (essays), 1973; (with James McFarlane) Modernism (Pelican Guide to European Literature), 1976.

ABOUT: Contemporary Authors 1-4 1st revision, 1967; Vinson, J. (ed.) Contemporary Novelists, 1976; Who's Who, 1977. *Periodicals*—Books and Bookmen February 1976; Daily Telegraph July 30, 1977; Encounter December 1973, February 1976; New Leader March 15, 1976; New York Times Book Review February 8, 1976; New Yorker May 3, 1976; Reporter September 8, 1966; Saturday Review May 21, 1966; Sunday Times Magazine (London) January 15, 1978; Times (London) November 6, 1975; Times Higher Education Supplement (London) November 14, 1975; March 5, 1976; Times Literary Supplement August 5, 1965; October 8, 1971; August 10, 1973; November 7, 1975.

MELVYN BRAGG

BRAGG, MELVYN (October 6, 1939–), English novelist, film and television writer, writes: "I was born just after the war broke out in a small town, Wigton, in Cumberland. My father at that time was a fitter at a local aerodrome; my mother did part-time jobs including cleaning and postal delivery work. Although I was an only child, we lived with my grandmother and various uncles and I was in effect brought up in a large adult family.

"My father soon went into the Royal Air Force. He like my mother had grown up in a family of eight children. He had a number of jobs as a labourer, as a boot boy, as a mechanic, etc.; he was to go on to be a bookmaker, a publican and at present is running a sweet shop with my mother. Both of them were born in Cumberland, both have extensive families remaining in Cumberland, although a surprisingly high percentage of these families has emigrated to Australia, New Zealand and Tasmania.

"Wigton had a population of about four thousand. It had a big factory and yet farms came right into the middle of the town. It had both industry and agriculture, was busy as a market centre, and a local focus for churches, banks, schools, shops, and festivals.

"I went to a local primary school and at eleven won a scholarship to the local grammar school. At eighteen I won a scholarship to Wadham College, Oxford, where I read modern history and eventually took an M.A. During this time I would describe my life as very normal and average for the period. Mid-century England went through a great social change which may have seemed greater at the time than it does in retrospect. The fact is that material benefits accrue steadily to that part of the working class that I belonged to and this gave us all the opportunities to do what our parents had only dreamed of—staying on at school, going to university, travelling, and enjoying leisure for periods longer than a Sunday.

"I was in the choir in the Church of England from the age of six and until the age of eighteen was a regular church attender and if it is possible to tease out influences on one's work I would claim that the Bible, especially the Psalms, and the Book of Common Prayer, and Hymns Ancient and Modern mean more to me than anything else I read.

"I read a lot although there were very few books in the house. One was not encouraged to read although, unlike some, I was not actually driven away from it. I played a lot of sport, went to dances, etc.—normal childhood in a busy town in the mid-century. I had no real conviction that I wanted to become a writer until I went to Oxford. There, in the gentle depression of adolescent academic life, I found that making up stories was something which I could be absorbed in more fully and with more satisfaction that anything else. It took me about six years, through into my twenties, until I would claim even to friends that I was a writer. During that time I worked at the BBC as a producer and was fortunate enough to work with some excellent directors and writers. I left the BBC when my second novel was published and since then I have been a freelance writer, supplementing my living by occasional film scripts and since 1973 by a steady output of BBC programmes.

"I feel that in the last ten years I have managed to clear the ground and organise myself so that I can now begin to write what I wanted to write fifteen years ago. I have felt a commitment to documenting my background, that of my parents and grandparents. I have set most of my novels in Cumberland because of a love for the place and again because of a commitment to putting it into print. At the moment I feel the weight of unwritten books about what has happened to me since I left my hometown exactly half my lifetime ago."

Rodney Pybus, writing in *Stand* in 1970, noted that all of Melvyn Bragg's novels up to that time had been concerned with life in Cumberland, and the "struggle of people who either have to make their living from the land or try to escape from it. The landscape of Cumberland, predominantly harsh and wild compared to that treated in fiction by George Eliot or Thomas Hardy, is always a solidly felt presence in these books; it provides not only a background . . . but a yardstick against which his characters can and must measure themselves, a presence of nature which moulds and sometimes dominates the characters. . . . The books also chronicle implicitly (for the most part) man's changing relationship to the countryside as industry and technology advance."

For Want of a Nail (1965), Bragg's first book, chronicles the years between eleven and seventeen in the life of Tom Graham, who because of his parents' lack of concern and understanding fails to develop his exceptional abilities; there are signs of hope at the end of the novel in Tom's recognition of his own ignorance and sterility. A poignant if imperfect novel, it introduces several motifs that recur in Bragg's later books, including the boy's close relationship with his grandfather and the unsettling effects of the family's move from country to city in Cumberland.

John Foster, in *The Second Inheritance* (1966), is a Cumberland farmer's boy in love with an aristocratic girl who will go to bed with him but will not accept him as a husband; his "second inheritance" is the self-knowledge and assurance he derives from conquering his passion. Some readers found the book indigestibly solid, but Ian Fleming thought that when Bragg "writes directly out of what he evidently cares about—the local countryside, the helpless tyranny of parents, the anguished silences of adolescence—he can blaze up most impressively." Somewhat similar themes are explored in *Without a City Wall* (1968).

The Hired Man (1969), one of the most admired of Bragg's novels, is set in the years between 1898 and 1920, and centers on John Tallentire, a landless farm laborer, moody and vaguely ambitious. The social upheavals of those years drive Tallentire and his wife from the countryside to the city, when Tallentire finds work as a coal miner. Rodney Pybus has referred to the defining importance to Bragg's characters of work, and especially work on the land, and quotes this passage about Tallentire: "It was not so much that he put everything into his work as that he looked to the work to put everything into him. Labour was his school, his opportunity, the stuff of his imagination and increasingly the object to which his senses reached. He attacked it, and wanted his blows returned, to go harder, daring it to give him limits."

Pybus sees in this passage an example of "an earnestness of endeavour" in Bragg's writing "which sometimes overreaches itself until it starts to blunt the power of observation and creative intelligence . . . a tendency to 'describe' rather than 'make' " (the quoted passage in fact leads into a most vividly enacted account of Tallentire ploughing with a pair of horses). Pybus also finds it "odd that Bragg can display such vigorous, authentic writing and at the same time with apparent insensitiveness clumsily inject lumps of social history . . . into the book, so that the veins of the story become temporarily clogged." All in all, however, Pybus, like many other critics, admires in Bragg's prose "a strength and solidity with nothing flimsy, whimsical or sentimental, and . . . an honesty and decency in the handling of his themes which does seem to be engendered by the substance." This and other novels have evoked comparisons with Hardy, with George Eliot, and above all with the earlier work of D. H. Lawrence.

A Place in England (1970), a sequel, describes what happens after John Tallentire's son Joseph loses his job as a footman in a rich household in 1930—his struggle to survive and raise a family, his service in World War II, and his success as landlord of a pub. A reviewer in the *Times Literary Supplement* pointed out that Joseph's son Douglas "works in the London film and television world, and writes novels about Cumberland —just as Mr. Bragg does. . . . Through the character of Douglas, the author discusses some of the difficulties involved in 'using' his own people. . . . One of the difficulties is that of Thomas Hardy, and it results in a kind of 'awkwardness' of style, like Hardy's—often an awkwardness with positive merit. There is a conflict between dialogue and narration which expresses a tension between two styles of language and living."

Ted Johnson, the narrator of *The Nerve* (1971), lives alone in London, where he is a teacher, but comes from Cumberland (like his successful friend Rod, a television producer and novelist of whom he is guiltily envious). The novel is an account of Johnson's nervous breakdown (or breakthrough, as it may turn out to be)—an "accomplished study of urban neurosis." Bragg returned to his Cumberland setting in *Josh Lawton* (1972), a sort of "modern pastoral" about a farm boy, a talented athlete of surpassing sweetness and innocence, whose marriage to an empty-hearted local beauty leads to catastrophe. In her review Shirley Toulson concluded that "Bragg has proved an ability to maintain a consistent yet dynamic vision of a region: what is more, he can show how the accidents of economic and physical geography shape the course of the families who live there. . . . He builds a solid, workable structure for his stories, with a tragic necessity linking beginning to middle, middle to end. His concern is with those aspects of goodness, which even if they come under the umbrella of moral custom, remain independent of it."

Rosemary Lewis, the passionate, intelligent, and willful heroine of *The Silken Net* (1974), is a Cumberland girl, half-French, who dreams of a life of cosmopolitan elegance and tries to impose her vision on the simple countryman she marries. Ronald Blythe wrote that "the curious atmosphere of [the] post-war, pre-inflation years is perfectly evoked. . . . The earthy-husband, civilised-wife theme has been extended in this calm, deep novel into a whole new range of emotions and responses. The sense of lives running parallel with major social transitions of which they are unaware, or to which they are indifferent, is remarkable. But most attractive of all is the book's open-heartedness, its serious intention and a certain ingenuousness in the way it treats its themes."

Speak for England (1976) is an oral history of Bragg's home town of Wigton. It reproduces interviews with over sixty residents, young and old, and of every social class—farmers, farm laborers, factory workers, war veterans, shopkeepers, miners, a solicitor, a trade unionist, a nun, a doctor, and so on. Reviewers found a certain amount of unavoidable repetition in these recollections, which seemed to most readers illuminating and interesting, reminiscent of Ronald Blythe's *Akenfield*. Bragg's own comments on his interviewees and what they say were liked less well. While reviewers shared his delight at the improved economic situation of the working class in Wigton (and in England in general), some questioned his conviction that living standards would and should continue to rise. However, as Norman Nicholson wrote, "the author's social and political beliefs need not have concerned us . . . had they not led him to intrude unnecessarily into his own book, to push himself forward with a strident, hectoring man-

ner quite out of keeping with the modest matter-of-factness of the other speakers. It is hard to understand why one who has written so well elsewhere should have lapsed into prose so clotted, cluttered and sharp-tempered. . . . Mr. Bragg seems almost to have tried to ruin his own book, though fortunately he has not succeeded. The sheer compelling interest of so much of the material cannot be shouted down."

Bragg is also the author or co-author of film scenarios for Karel Reisz's *Isadora,* Ken Russell's *The Music Lovers,* and Norman Jewison's screen version of *Jesus Christ Superstar.* His script for Russell's television film about Debussy brought him a Writers' Guild Award, and he has also written notable television documentaries about George Orwell and about the dialects of England. He provided the book for Alan Blaikley and Ken Howard's New Orleans musical *Mardi-Gras* (1976), producing according to Irving Wardle "a most scrupulous pastiche: not only the local references, and general grasp of the language, but in distinct revivalist and French-American speech rhythms."

In the early 1970s Bragg made a new reputation as a television interviewer and program presenter (especially in the fields of art and literature), in these roles conveying the unusual impression that he is more anxious to learn from his guests than to display his own superiority. His BBC/TV book program *Read All About It,* which is both intelligent and lively, is said to be almost wholly Bragg's creation. He has received the Rhys Memorial Prize (1968), the Northern Arts Association Prose Award (1970), and the Silver Pen Award (1970), and is a Fellow of the Royal Society of Literature. Since 1969 he has been a member of the Arts Council's Literary Panel.

In the *Times Literary Supplement* for October 15, 1971, in an article called "Class and the Novel," Bragg discussed some of the difficulties he faced when he began to write: "The novel appeared to be the fictional parish magazine of the cultivated middle classes: at one and the same time I detested its exclusiveness and could not wait to become a subscriber." He says it "took a long time for me to imagine that the foreground of the novel could be occupied by people who did a hard day's work." He has come to believe that "class in writing can well become more overt and writing may benefit from it. Politics is begging to be fleshed in fiction, and meeting that demand may be necessary proof of the essential relevance of the novel today."

Melvyn Bragg is the son of Stanley Bragg and the former Mary Parks. In 1961, his last year at Oxford, he was married to Marie-Elisabeth

Roche, daughter of the Rector of the Sorbonne, who was working in Oxford as an *au pair* girl. She died in 1971. Bragg, who has a daughter by his first wife, was married again in 1974 to Catherine Mary Haste, a writer. He lists his recreations as walking and books. According to an article about him in the *New Statesman*, Bragg is "a man of serious ambition, deeply interested in television and its future, yet by no means dependent on his present success. Friends of long standing see him as largely unaltered by fame: he is a likeable and kindly man, cautious and resilient, with much natural charm, who admits to an egocentricity which few who know him rush to deny."

PRINCIPAL WORKS: *Novels*—For Want of a Nail, 1965; The Second Inheritance, 1966; Without a City Wall, 1968; The Hired Man, 1969; A Place in England, 1970; The Nerve, 1971; Josh Lawton, 1972; The Silken Net, 1974; Autumn Manoeuvres, 1978. *Nonfiction*—Speak for England: An Essay on England 1900-1975, 1976. *Other*—A Christmas Child, 1976.

ABOUT: Contemporary Authors 57-60, 1976; Vinson, J. (ed.) Contemporary Novelists, 1976; Who's Who, 1977. *Periodicals*—Guardian April 30, 1971; Kenyon Review 127 1971; Listener September 4, 1975; New Statesman April 8, 1977; Observer March 21, 1976; July 11, 1976; Stand Summer 1970; Sunday Times (London) August 18, 1974; Sunday Times Magazine (London) November 28, 1976; Times (London) July 15, 1976; Times Literary Supplement October 15, 1971; June 2, 1978; August 20, 1976.

BRASCH, CHARLES (ORWELL) (July 27, 1909–May 19, 1973), New Zealand poet and editor, was born in Dunedin, the son of Henry Brasch (or Brash, as he preferred to style himself) and the former Helene Fels. Both parents were of Jewish origin, though neither was a practicing Jew. His mother, a sensitive and gifted woman, died when he was four, and he was never at ease with his father, a lawyer and a self-made man intent on financial and social success. Brasch was educated at Waitaki Boys' High School and at St. John's College, Oxford (1927-1931), where he read modern history and contributed to *Oxford Poetry*. After his graduation he returned to New Zealand, worked for a few unhappy months in his grandfather's warehouse, and then, after a showdown with his father, escaped back to England. He lived mostly in London but traveled in Europe, the Near East, Russia, and the United States, and worked for three seasons with the Egypt Exploration Society on the excavations at Amarna. Brasch later taught at an English school for disturbed children. Rejected for military service on medical grounds, he spent most of the war years in London as a civil servant in the Foreign Office,

CHARLES BRASCH

serving also as "an earnest if somewhat awkward member of the Home Guard."

Although he was an expatriate for so long, Brasch's literary career was always closely bound up with his native country. Most of his books were published there and, though some of his early poems did appear in John Lehmann's *New Writing* and *Penguin New Writing* in England, he was at the same time contributing to the New Zealand journals *Phoenix* and *Tomorrow*.

During the 1930s Brasch made two visits home, and both of his first two volumes of poetry, *The Land and the People* (1939) and *Disputed Ground* (1948), have at their core a group of poems about New Zealand. The titles of these books indicate Brasch's central theme: the relationship between the natural grandeur of New Zealand and the crass settlers who have occupied the land without ever imaginatively possessing it, any more than they comprehended the native culture of the Maoris, which they destroyed:

The plains are nameless and the cities cry for
  meaning,
The unproved heart still seeks a vein of speech
Beside the sprawling rivers, in the stunted
  township,
By the pine windbreak where the hot wind blows.

At another level, the colonizer's sense of guilt, disharmony, and unease in his still-alien land are used to reflect the common condition of man in the universe, and also the poet's private search for a solution to his own sense of inadequacy and failure. This is a heavy freight of meaning to load upon poems which are on the face of them mostly nature lyrics, and it is not surprising that Brasch's early work, in particular, was found excessively abstract, tentative, and obscure, though often strikingly beautiful in sound and tone.

The pursuit of a reconciliation between "the root of nature and the flower of man" is quite explicitly worked out in Brasch's allegorical verse drama *The Quest,* published in London by the Compass Players in 1946. Here the Shepherd, repeatedly frustrated in his search for this harmony, announces: "I have described a circle round the earth/ And reached my starting place,/ And I am ready for that which awaits me there."

And indeed Brasch did return to his "starting place," late in 1945, there to launch and edit New Zealand's best and longest-lived literary journal, *Landfall,* the first issue of which appeared in March 1947. Another ten years passed before he published his third collection of poetry, *The Estate.* That volume shows him coming gradually to terms with his country and himself, discovering areas of repose in friendship and in art. The process continues in *Ambulando* (1964), in which Brasch experiments with a more personal and colloquial diction, and most happily in the last collection published during his lifetime, *Not Far Off* (1969), which expresses a new gaiety of spirit.

Even in the more hopeful poems of his last years, Brasch's tone is always more questioning than assertive, his verse sparing of metaphor and without strong accents. His range was limited and his talent was not robust, but it was real, and his skill (or instinct) in the use of such devices as half rhymes, internal rhymes, and consonance was exceptional. He also employed a kind of "syntactical rhyme," in which statements are knit together by grammatical parallels. His best poems achieve great beauty of cadence. *Home Ground,* the posthumous collection published in 1974, seemed to James Bertram "the most moving of all his books, and the one in which ... [his] elusive personal and poetic character ... emerges most clearly." It includes a group of poems written during the last few weeks of his life, when he was dying from Hodgkin's disease, these characteristically controlled, self-deprecating, and generous lyrics, Bertram wrote, "have the special poignancy of the last poems of Rilke and D.H. Lawrence."

Whatever conclusion posterity may reach about Brasch's poetry, he is assured of a place in New Zealand literary history by his editorship of *Landfall,* which he made into one of the best literary journals in English. E. H. McCormick has described it as "a magnificent achievement, every number testifying to the editor's impartiality, his skill, his standards of taste and judgement. The beautifully printed, scrupulously edited volumes, illustrated and analysed and indexed, merit nothing but gratitude and respect." To the principal criticism leveled against *Landfall*—that it was inhospitable to experimental writing—McCormick replies that the magazine "could have been different only by sacrificing its main source of strength, the principles of its editor."

According to his obituary in the London *Times,* "Brasch's independence, personal, political and artistic, gave him a unique position in the community." He was a staunch supporter of liberal causes, a generous but discriminating patron of young painters, and a benefactor of the Hocken Library and of the University of Otago, where he taught for a time and which conferred on him an honorary D. Litt. Brasch translated poems by the Punjabi poet Amrita Pritan, Sergei Yesenin, and Peter Huchel. Before his death, he launched a new series of books under the imprint Square and Circle in which writers and artists were to collaborate, the first volume being illustrated by the Maori artist Ralph Hotere. He was "the generous friend and self-effacing critic of many writers and artists." What his friends valued in him, according to James Bertram, "behind the polite diffident manner and the clear, beautifully articulated speech, was a nature of great warmth and sweetness, of strong impulsive loyalties running beneath a cool, slightly dry exterior. . . . He was a passionate man who had learnt to be patient, a disciplined romantic."

PRINCIPAL WORKS: *Poetry*—The Land and the People, 1939; Disputed Ground: Poems 1939-1945, 1948; The Estate, 1957; Ambulando, 1964; Not Far Off, 1969; Home Ground, edited by Alan Roddick, 1974. *Drama*—The Quest, 1946. *Essays*—Present Company, 1966. *As Editor*—Landfall Country: Work From "Landfall," 1947-1961, 1962. *As Translator*—Black Rose, by Amrita Pritam, 1967 (New Delhi); (with Peter Soskice) Poems by Esenin, 1970.

ABOUT: Bertram, J. Charles Brasch, 1977; McCormick, E.H. New Zealand Literature, 1959; Murphy, R. (ed.) Contemporary Poets of the English Language, 1970; Penguin Companion to Literature 1, 1971; Wilkes, G.A. and Reid, J.C. The Literatures of Australia and New Zealand, 1970. *Periodicals*—Islands Spring 1973; Spring 1975; Landfall December 1948; September 1957; March 1965; December 1969; September 1972; New Zealand Listener October 16, 1964; June 11, 1973; Times (London) May 24, 1973.

BRATHWAITE, (L.) EDWARD (May 11, 1930–), West Indian poet, dramatist, historian, critic, and editor, began in 1976 to sign himself Edward Kamau Brathwaite. He was born in Bridgetown, Barbados, the son of Hilton Brath-

EDWARD BRATHWAITE

waite and the former Beryl Gill. He attended Harrison College, Barbados, and in 1950 went with a Barbados Scholarship to Pembroke College, Cambridge University. Brathwaite received an honors degree in history in 1953, and remained in Cambridge to earn his Certificate of Education (1955).

From England Brathwaite went to Africa, serving from 1955 to 1962 as an education officer in Nkrumah's Ghana. He established a children's theatre there, and himself wrote several plays for children. For a year during this period (1956–1957) he acted as United Nations Plebiscite Officer in Togoland. He was married in 1960 to Doris Welcome and has a son, Michael Kwesi Brathwaite. After an exile of twelve years, Brathwaite returned to the West Indies as resident tutor in the extramural department of the University of the West Indies at St. Lucia (1962–1963), at the same time broadcasting and producing features, talks, discussions, and poetry programs for WIBS (Windward Island Broadcasting Service). In 1963 he went as a lecturer in history to the University of the West Indies at Kingston, Jamaica. There he has remained, apart from the three years at the University of Sussex in England (1965–1968) which brought him his D. Phil. in 1968. He is now senior lecturer in history at the University of the West Indies.

Brathwaite's poetry had been appearing, mainly in the West Indian magazine *Bim,* since 1950. But he writes in *Contemporary Poets* that his early verse, up to about 1965, "had no real centre. The 'centre' is connected with my return to the West Indies in 1962 after twelve years absence ... I had, at that moment of return, completed the triangular trade of my historical origins. West Africa had given me a sense of place, of belonging; and that place and belonging, I knew, was the West Indies. My absence and travels, at the same time, had given me a sense of movement and restlessness—rootlessness. It was, I recognized, particularly the condition of the Negro in the West Indies and the New World." These feelings and discoveries provide the theme of Brathwaite's most important work—the trilogy of long poems initially published separately and collected into a single volume in 1973 as *The Arrivants.*

The first poem in the trilogy, *Rights of Passage,* appeared in 1967, and draws on Brathwaite's own travels to evoke what one critic called "the theme of the West Indian, modern and ancestral, in slavery, emigrating, suffering, resilient but melancholy." Gordon Rohlehr thought that the poem's intentions were even more ambitious—that it was "an attempt to review the situation of the black man in the Third World by appreciating what he has been able to create in spite of centuries of exile [and deracination]." Brathwaite says that "the tone, the cadence and above all the *organisation*" of his long poems, and especially this one, owe a great deal to T. S. Eliot. This is the only European influence on his work that he is prepared to acknowledge. He had also learned a great deal from jazz, in "the way the lines are broken, the phrasing, etc." But he thinks that the most important influence "was perhaps the West Indian novelists who from the very beginning have been putting the speech of our people into our ears; in contrast to our poets who have, on the whole, been very concerned with 'English' poetic complexities."

A reviewer in the *Times Literary Supplement* wrote that Brathwaite in *Rights of Passage* relies "on a stridency that after almost ninety pages leaves one poleaxed"; his theme is potentially "striking and exciting," but the author's "technique and verbal control do not match his ambition." Gerald Moore disagreed: "The hurrying movement of the verse itself, with its breathless lines and densely-packed assonances, perfectly contains the urgent quality, driven but aimless, which Brathwaite imparts to the journey that has carried negroes to every part of the world to labour in the enterprises of other men." The poem was in any case "the first sustained attempt to appropriate West Indian cadences and musical rhythms for the purposes of poetry," and brought Brathwaite international recognition.

Masks (1968), the trilogy's second volume, is both an elegy for the disintegration of the tribal system and a dramatic recreation of Brath-

111

waite's own pilgrimage to the forest empire of Ashanti from which his ancestors were taken as slaves. This experience is evoked with such intensity, wrote Gerald Moore, "as to make it a representative West Indian experience of homecoming," even though, at the end, the pilgrim—"masked" because he is in search of his identity—does not find what he seeks, and must turn away to tread again "the dark path" of exile. The poem opens and closes with rhythms and phrases based upon the Akan drum language, the language in which the drummer prepares and sanctifies the wood, skin, and sticks of his drum:

> There is a quick
> stick grows in the for-
> est, blossoms twice year-
> ly without leaves;
> bare white branches
> crack like light-
> ning in the harm-
> attan. . . .
>
> From this stripped tree
> snap quick sticks for
> the festival. Its wood,
> heat-hard as stone,
> is toneless as a bone.
>
> (from "The Two
> Curved Sticks of
> the Drummer")

"In the end," wrote Hayden Carruth, "his seeking was, and had to be, a failure, as he acknowledges, but it produced magnificent poetry." And it seemed to Gerald Moore that "*Masks* stands as the most impressive and complete work yet produced in the literature of the black revenant who finds in Africa something less than a real homecoming, but something infinitely more than failure and disappointment."

Brathwaite himself says of *Masks* that the influence was "Ghanaian traditional verse, history and mythology," and that it contains not a single image "that refers to an idea or object *outside* the West African context. This is not necessarily a good thing. And I didn't set out to achieve this. It's simply that having finished the poem, I realized that that's what had happened. But it's rare and a moment to be thankful for, when a writer can attain this kind of autonomy. I got it by wearing a mask. What I'm trying to do in *Islands* [the final poem in the trilogy] is attain the same kind of autonomy without the mask. Folk speech, folk rhythms, the faces of myth, the faces of history; ritual, above all; the way the landscape makes us pray; the kinds of gods it invokes, it evolves."

Jerome Cushman, for one, felt that Brath-

waite had achieved the kind of autonomy he sought in *Islands:* "Brathwaite knows who he is, and that is why his poetry sings in two worlds, the here and now and the time of his ancestors. . . . When he speaks of identity his words crackle and the rhythms pulsate, engaging our sensibilities, our feelings, and our respect." Another reviewer, in the *Virginia Quarterly Review,* wrote that "*Islands* moves from the African 'discovery' of the New World through a rediscovery of archetypal forms to a final vision of spiritual and racial wholeness. Through it all the verse is controlled by a consciousness exalted with the recognition of the old gods, but alert also to the particulars of life in the modern world."

Discussing the trilogy as a whole, William Walsh says that Brathwaite "is the poet as prophet, missionary, propagandist"; *The Arrivants* "attempts to dramatize not just the pain but the wound to being and the damage to human nature, caused by the deracination of the Negro soul. This immense theme trawls through the history of Africa, the West Indies, Britain, and America. It is impelled on a tide of extraordinary energy and sustained by remarkably rich rhythmic resources. There are patches, as there would be in any long poem, which are flat and perfunctory, but also moments of considerable power and intensity. One's reluctance to acknowledge it as a major work comes from one's sense of its failure to cohere and from one's feeling of its conceptual generation, so that one ends by recognizing the huge theme, the considerable powers, the endless ambition, and the final disappointment." Hayden Carruth, who warmly praised "the density, variety, wisdom, and fervor" of Brathwaite's poems, their vigor and (in spite of everything) their optimism, evidently felt no such disappointment. Brathwaite's recording of the entire trilogy has been greatly admired, and it deserves to be judged, at least in part, as a dramatic work.

The most notable of Brathwaite's historical and ethnological studies is his doctoral thesis, *The Development of Creole Society in Jamaica* (1971), which studies a Caribbean plantation during fifty years of slavery, 1770–1820. "To Mr. Brathwaite," wrote one reviewer, "[these] fifty years were of crucial importance for the direction and limitation of Jamaican creole identity. . . . In his carefully researched chapters on the political establishment and their ideas, on the culture and stratification of each of the population groups, and on the social changes in the period under discussion, Mr. Brathwaite gives us a lively picture, free of stereotype and cliché, of a society whose cultural and social ambivalence and divisiveness have proved to be more persistent than its (formally) colonial status."

Brathwaite was founding secretary of the influential Caribbean Artists' Movement in 1966, and since 1970 has been editor of its magazine *Savacou,* published in Mona (Kingston), where he lives. *Savacou,* named after the bird god of the vanished Arawaks, has been called "the most challenging and ambitious of the many new journals now appearing in the Caribbean." Brathwaite received a poetry bursary from the British Arts Council in 1967, and the same year won a prize in the Camden (London) Arts Festival. *Islands* brought him the Cholmondely Award, and in 1972 he received a Guggenheim fellowship and a City of Nairobi fellowship; the Bussa Award followed in 1973. He read his work at the Poetry International Festivals in London in 1969 and 1971.

PRINCIPAL WORKS: *Poetry*—Rights of Passage, 1967; Masks, 1968; Islands, 1969; (with others) Penguin Modern Poets 15, 1969; Panda No. 348, 1969; The Arrivants, 1973; Other Exiles, 1975; Black & Blues, 1976; Mother Poem, 1977. *Plays*—Four Plays for Primary Schools, 1963; Odale's Choice: A Play for Schools, 1967. *History*—Folk Culture of the Slaves in Jamaica, 1970; The Development of Creole Society in Jamaica, 1770–1820, 1971; Caribbean Man in Space and Time, 1974; Contradictory Omens: Cultural Diversity and Integration in the Caribbean, 1974. *As Editor* —Iouanaloa: Recent Writing From St. Lucia, 1963; The People Who Came, 1–3, 1968–1972.

ABOUT: Contemporary Authors 25–28 1st revision, 1977; Moore, G. The Chosen Tongue, 1969; Savacou Bibliographical Series 2, 1973; Vinson, J. (ed.) Contemporary Poets, 1975; Walsh, W. Commonwealth Literature, 1973. *Periodicals*—Bim July-December 1970; Books and Bookmen May 1967; Caribbean Quarterly September-December 1971, June 1973; Critical Quarterly Summer 1970; Cuadernos Americanos September-October 1972; Hudson Review Summer 1974; Jamaica Journal September 1968; Library Journal March 15, 1970; New Statesman April 7, 1967; Pan-Africanist 1 1971; Poetry April 1969; Times Literary Supplement February 16, 1967; August 15, 1968; June 30, 1972; November 14, 1975; Universitas March 1969; Virginia Quarterly Review Summer 1967, Autumn 1968, Spring 1970; West Indies Bulletin December 1971.

*BRAUDEL, FERNAND (PAUL) (August 24, 1902–), French historian, was born at Lunéville (Meuse), the son of Charles Braudel, a school headmaster, and of the former Louise Falet. Braudel has himself described his birthplace as an important influence on his historical thought; Lunéville is on the north-eastern French plain, near the German border—for centuries a zone of confrontation between Latin and Germanic civilizations, the frontier of repeated French continental expansion and contraction. Braudel's work has been an attempt to grasp the importance of such "unchanging (or at least

*brö del

Marcel Amson

FERNAND BRAUDEL

very slowly changing) conditions which stubbornly assert themselves over and over again."

Braudel was educated at the Lycée Voltaire and in the Faculté des Lettres of the University of Paris, where after graduating he went on to take a doctorate. He began his teaching career in 1924 at the Lycée Constantine in Algiers. It was during his eight years there that he discovered his great theme of the Mediterranean in history, and began the researches to which he has devoted his life. Though this was the final period of unchallenged French domination in North West Africa, Braudel's vision of history is post-imperial, shaped by his analysis of the failure of French imperial ambitions and of the intellectual dogmas underlying colonialism.

In 1932 Braudel returned to Paris, where for the next three years he taught at the Lycée Condorcet and the Lycée Henry IV. He was married in 1933 to Paule Pradel, by whom he has two daughters. After two years at the University of São Paulo in Brazil, Braudel took up a post at the École Pratique des Hautes Études in Paris, where he taught from 1937 until the outbreak of World War II in 1939. Braudel served as an army lieutenant on the Maginot Line, was captured, and spent the remainder of the war years as a prisoner in Germany—an ordeal not without advantages for him, offering as it did an opportunity for prolonged and concentrated thought. In 1945 Braudel resumed his post at the École Pratique des Hautes Études, where he has remained, in 1956 becoming president of the École's economic and social sciences section. That unique institution, which has become the center of historical, economic, and anthropological studies in France, has itself had a profound impact on Braudel's thought, cross-fertilizing his own ideas with those of equally original thinkers from other fields, including the structural anthropologist Claude Lévi-Strauss. Since 1949 Braudel has also served as professor of modern history at the Collège de France, and in 1963 he became administrator of the Maison des Sciences de l'Homme.

Fernand Braudel has had immense influence not only as a writer and a teacher, but as editor of the review *Annales,* originally founded by Lucien Febvre and Marc Bloch to propagate their own view of history. The *Annales* school, of which Braudel has been the leader since Febvre's death, rejects the conception of history in which man is seen as the master of his destiny, progressing slowly but steadily towards some spiritual, political, or technological millenium. Against this linear interpretation of history, the *Annales* school asserts the importance of the limitations which nature imposes upon man and his fragile social, economic, and cultural institutions. These historians maintain that to understand any society, we must begin by studying its geographical setting, climate, and resources. They are therefore less interested than other historians in the history of individual nations, and find it more profitable to study a whole geographical region or even a whole continent. As Richard Mowery Andrews puts it, the *Annales* historians "would agree with modern historians that human beings are their own puppeteers, but they would insist that the dance of the puppets and the gestures of the fingers commanding them move within the strict confines of a physical space, obey fixed impulses, and submit to barely visible forces of tradition rarely understood or even acknowledged by the participants. Ironically, these historians are often castigated as 'reactionary' by modern historians of both liberal and Marxian allegiances, whose own moral and intellectual canons are those of the eighteenth and nineteenth centuries."

The most solid single monument of this historical school is the profoundly innovative study of the Mediterranean with which Braudel made his reputation: *La Méditerranée et le monde méditerranéen à l'époque de Philippe II* (1949), whose second, revised edition of 1966 has been translated by Siân Reynolds as *The Mediterranean and the Mediterranean World in the Age of Philip II* (volume 1, 1972; 2, 1973). The first volume is a "geohistorical" account of an area ranging from the Sahara to the Baltic, from the Atlantic to the Black and Red Seas, showing how the two great basins of the Mediterranean, east and west, came to produce in the sixteenth century the two hostile empires of Catholic Spain and Muslim Turkey. In this account, as one critic explained, "wars, politics, and diplomacy are subordinated to basic social and economic factors, to geography and climatology, and to such . . . problems as the barriers of distance, the lines of land and sea communications, the nature, provisioning, and commerce of cities, or the . . . inflationary effects of Sudan gold, American silver, and the price revolution."

"Politics merely followed the outline of an underlying reality," Braudel writes. "These two Mediterraneans, commanded by warring rulers, were physically, economically, and culturally different from each other. Each was a separate historical zone." And in the second volume of his great work he analyzes in these terms the rise and decline of the two territorial empires, showing that in this instance the "underlying reality" was "the decline of material existence, of the decadence one after another of Turkey, the whole of Islam, Italy and the Iberian supremacy, as older historians would say, or, as today's economists would put it, of the malfunctioning and collapse of its vital sectors (public finance, investment, industry, shipping)." In the Mediterranean, "in both the long and short term, agricultural life was all-important. Could it support the burden of increasing population and the luxury of an urban civilization so dazzling that it has blinded us to other things?" The population of the Mediterranean almost doubled between 1300 and 1600, and the influx of gold and silver stimulated only the privileged summits of the Mediterranean economy: agriculture could not support these burdens, the gulf widened between rich and poor, between the declining east and the west, and the anxious élites in their bloated empires were propelled towards confrontation. The battle for supremacy was won by Spain at Lepanto in 1571. Spain herself turned towards the Atlantic after that, but power was already beginning to shift from her to northern Europe, the Europe of the modern era.

Braudel rejects the theories of Erich Weber, Spengler, and Toynbee concerning the inevitable rise and fall of civilizations as too simple and too sweeping, arguing that a new explanation of this process "has to be built from the basic structures of every particular case." And this is what his history does for the Mediterranean. The *Annales* historians have been accused of "dehumanizing" history, of replacing the clash of human protagonists with geography, time, and economics; no such criticism can be leveled at Braudel's masterpiece, whose "geographical and economic landscapes," as J. H. Plumb has written, "are alive with human beings, individuals as well as communities" and in which "he is as concerned to distinguish the beliefs, superstitions, social attitudes as well as the economic activities of his mountain folk from those of the plain and cities."

Indeed the work has been universally acclaimed for its depth, scope, originality, and erudition as "a work of great seminal influence regarded since its first appearance . . . as the chief masterpiece of the contemporary French historical school," and as "probably the most significant historical work to appear since World War II." J. H. Elliott has remarked that "no other book I know of illustrates more graphically the way in which historical writing has been renovated in our own times by contact with other disciplines—geography, economics, and the social sciences." Plumb finds it almost unequaled as "an intellectual and scholarly tour de force," and goes on: "Each paragraph is not only erudite, but more often than not pierced with novel insights, at times of such daring that Braudel, who is personally present on every page, rapidly warns the reader not to take them as anything but tentative suggestions." And according to Naomi Bliven, "what he offers, then, is not answers but approaches. His deepest concern . . . is the contrast between, on the one hand, the brevity of human lives and events (a war, a flood, a drought, a depression) that can be so decisive for individuals and, on the other hand, the very long periods (centuries, indeed) it takes for societies to develop or to change in any important way."

Civilisation matérielle et capitalisme (1967, translated by Miriam Kochan as *Capitalism and Material Life 1400-1800*), the first volume of a projected two-volume work, turns to a more general theme, the emergence of modern industrial capitalism. This first volume describes conditions in the precapitalist world, showing once more how from about 1500 onwards the rapid increase in populations began to outstrip the production of goods, leading to extreme disparities between the living standards of rich and poor. Working his way through an analysis of diet, homes, and clothing throughout the world, Braudel goes on to discuss technology, money, and towns—the three major motors of progress. Technological advance and the development of a sophisticated credit system were both prerequisites of capitalism, and both, as Braudel shows, were created by or for the merchant communities of certain medieval towns, all of them in northern Europe. The "capitalist spirit" of these cities produced the Industrial Revolution, the era of "pre-capitalism, which is the source of all the economic creativeness of the world" but

also of "all the most burdensome exploitation of man by man."

Most reviewers had reservations about the book, though most admired it. J. H. Plumb spoke of "the excess of factual errors, occasional dubious and portentous generalisations, a cloudy overall structure, and the omission of what for many historians are the critical agents of change," but praised Braudel's "vivid and exciting style" and said that "again and again he strengthens the conviction that this is the way history will go, and must go." Keith Thomas noted that in dealing with non-European countries Braudel "remains heavily dependent upon the impressions of a few European travelers. . . . Nevertheless Braudel's book splendidly vindicates the cause of comparative history, for many of his most striking conclusions arise directly from his taking so broad a view. . . . His work leaves a profound impression of vitality, imagination, sensibility, and infinite curiosity."

Fernand Braudel is generally regarded as one of the greatest living historians, and his influence in contemporary French intellectual life compares with that of Lévi-Strauss. He is an officer of the Légion d'Honneur, a Commandeur de l'Ordre National du Mérite, and holds honorary degrees from many universities in Europe and the United States. He is a member of the Haut Comité de la Langue Française and of the commission on diplomatic archives.

PRINCIPAL WORKS IN ENGLISH TRANSLATION: The Mediterranean and the Mediterranean World in the Age of Philip II: Volume 1, 1972; Volume 2, 1973; Capitalism and Material Life, 1400-1800, 1973; Afterthoughts on Material Civilization and Capitalism, translated by Patricia M. Ranum, 1977 (lectures delivered at Johns Hopkins University in 1976).

ABOUT: International Who's Who, 1976-1977; Perkin, H. (ed.) History: An Introduction for the Intending Student, 1970; Who's Who in Europe, 1972; Who's Who in France, 1977-1978. *Periodicals*—Choice April 1974, June 1974; Economist November 10, 1973; History June 1974; Nation February 16, 1974; New Statesman June 15, 1973; New York Review of Books May 3, 1973; December 13, 1973; New York Times Book Review December 31, 1972; November 10, 1974; May 18, 1975; New Yorker April 1, 1974; Times (London) May 23, 1977; Virginia Quarterly Review Spring 1973, Spring 1974; Yale Review June 1974.

BRAUTIGAN, RICHARD (January 30, 1933–), American novelist, poet, and short story writer, was born in Tacoma, Washington, and grew up in the Pacific Northwest. This, and the fact that he is married and has a child, is all the biographical information he has published.

Brautigan's poetic prose has been taken more seriously than his verse, which Robert Adams finds "rather like the more playful poems of

John Fryer

RICHARD BRAUTIGAN

e. e. cummings. There are lots of lively small poems on small occasional topics; considerable charm, a nicely understated wit." And Adams offers by way of example "The Return of the Rivers":

All the rivers run into the sea;
yet the sea is not full;
unto the place from whence the rivers come,
thither they return again.

It is raining today
in the mountains.

It is a warm green rain
with love
in its pockets
for spring is here,
and does not dream
of death. . . .

A slow rain sizzles
on the river
like a pan
full of frying flowers,
and with each drop
of rain
the ocean
begins again.

The first of Brautigan's novels to be published was *A Confederate General From Big Sur* (1964). The narrator, Jesse, and his new friend Lee Mellon, retire to Big Sur. There, aided by girls and marijuana, they improvise a short-lived Eden which may or may not be more desirable than the violent and greedy life exemplified in the book by the insane millionaire Roy Earle. The novel, composed in fragmentary short chapters and offering an infinite choice of endings, greatly

irritated some New York reviewers. Philip Rahv, for example, called it "pop-writing of the worst kind, full of vapid jokes and equally vapid sex-scenes. . . . The only connection with the Confederacy is that one of the young men fraudulently claims descent from a general in the Civil War. And what is so terribly funny about that remains the author's secret." For Tony Tanner, on the other hand, it "manages to combine fleeting reminiscences of the obvious attritions of the Civil War with the less obvious attritions of life on the California coast today," though "the book is the reverse of didactic." Arthur Gold was most impressed by Brautigan's use of language, "which is consistently more inventive and delicate than you could expect from one of the so-called 'beats.' "

Trout Fishing in America, which followed in 1967, is a plotless ramble around America past and present, stuffed with jokes, anecdotes, and parables. The title is the name of a legless alcoholic and also of a cheap hotel; it represents a state of mind, a revolutionary slogan, an idea of what America was like before they began to make trout into steel in Pittsburgh and before the waterfalls and trout streams wound up in the Cleveland Wrecking Yard.

"Yes," I said. "I'm curious about the trout stream you have for sale. Can you tell me something about it? How are you selling it?"

"We're selling it by the foot length. You can buy as little as you want or you can buy all we've got left. A man came in here this morning and bought 563 feet. He's going to give it to his niece for a birthday present," the salesman said.

"We're selling the waterfalls separately of course, and the trees and birds, flowers, grass and ferns we're also selling extra. The insects we're giving away free with a minimum purchase of ten feet of stream."

"How much are you selling the stream for?" I asked.

"Six dollars and fifty cents a foot," he said. "That's for the first hundred feet. After that it's five dollars a foot."

"How much are the birds?" I asked.

"Thirty-five cents apiece," he said. "But of course they're used. We can't guarantee anything."

The book was found both funny and poignant, playful and serious, profound and absurd—"a narrative that denies, episode by episode, the form and language of the pastoral." An English reviewer in the *Times Literary Supplement* wrote that Brautigan's style is one "of fine simplicity and economy. His sentences, whether soberly informative or wildly hallucinatory, are seldom troubled by dependent clauses. He has a fondness for similes, both strikingly apt and superbly irrelevant. His heritage, in homage or parody, is completely American: there are echoes of Mark Twain, Hemingway, and Sherwood Anderson, even of Erskine Caldwell and the Steinbeck of *Cannery Row*. And his flashing incongruities and rambling *non sequiturs* probably owe less to European surrealism than to Hollywood silent comedies, and the general ethos of 'psychedelic California.' An American manner for American matter: a slender American classic."

From the beginning, some reviewers had found reasons to doubt that the whimsical "alternative society" evoked in Brautigan's novels was meant to represent an ideal; such doubts increased with publication of *In Watermelon Sugar* (1968). Its nameless narrator is the standard Brautigan hero—open, innocent, naively optimistic, an invulnerable Beat Candide. When he was nine, some tigers helped him with his arithmetic and ate up his parents. The tigers regretted the latter action but explained that it was "a thing we have to do," and the narrator acquiesced. Now he lives in California, in the beautiful and gentle community of iDEATH, and everything is perfect until he stops sleeping with Margaret and starts sleeping with Pauline. This makes Margaret jealous, and she begins to spend her time with a gang of anachronistically fierce and drunken thugs led by someone named in-BOIL. He believes that the utopian iDEATH is only a figment of its inhabitants' imaginations: "You're all at a masquerade party," he tells them. "The tigers were the true meaning of i-DEATH." To prove his point he and his gang hack themselves to death with their knives, and then Margaret hangs herself from an apple tree. The narrator is very sad about this but is at a loss to understand her despair, and is in any case more interested in the contents of his potato salad.

Thomas A. Vogler has suggested that the Brautigan hero is a figure of the "old American Adam reborn," ignoring evil and surviving catastrophes without even being aware of them, though the evil and the catastrophes are all too obvious to the reader over his shoulder. And whether the Brautigan hero is truly innocent, or strangely self-lobotomized, is always ambiguous: "We take the juice from the watermelons and cook it down until there's nothing left but sugar, and then we work it into the shape of this thing that we have: our lives." Robert Adams wrote that *In Watermelon Sugar* is "a beautiful American book, a kind of *Our Town* in depth, with the ancient American problem (can we conceivably be as sincere and as innocent as we pretend

without also being filthy liars and hideously cruel?) at the heart of it."

The Abortion (1971) is a less fantastic and in some ways a less ambitious novel. Its hero works in a San Francisco library that accepts manuscripts from aspiring writers, regardless of quality, but never lends out books. He is perfectly content with his small world until he falls in love with the frantically attractive Vida, and they have to make an odyssey to Mexico to procure an abortion for her. The America they see on the way is not to their taste, and when the narrator returns to San Francisco with Vida and his friend Foster the library has changed hands, so he has to settle for becoming a cult hero of the younger generation instead of a librarian. But he makes a very good adjustment and is soon contented once more. The question that the book never asks (so the reader does) is whether he ought to be quite so cozy, in view of what has happened to him and to his friends and to his country.

Brautigan's subsequent novels include *The Hawkline Monster* (1974), subtitled "A Gothic Western," which it more or less is, and *Willard and His Bowling Trophies* (1975), subtitled "A Perverse Mystery," which involves a search for the missing trophies, murder, and the tragedies of perverse sex. In *Sombrero Fallout* (1976), a famous humorist begins a story but discards it unfinished. The fragment in the wastebasket grows into an epic of American machismo which rumbles along under its own steam, accompanied by passages from the stream-of-consciousness of the neurotic author, and from his Japanese ex-girlfriend's dream of childhood. Brautigan's short stories have been collected in *Revenge of the Lawn,* and reminded Sara Blackburn of William Saroyan in their "simplicity, humor, surrealism, nostalgia, and bittersweetness." Josephine Hendin wrote that these stories comprise a single vision of "people who have drowned their feelings and live underwater lives. . . . Going underwater, underground, inside, Brautigan's people live with no passionate attachment to anyone or any place, and never permit themselves to feel a thing. . . . *Revenge of the Lawn* is not Brautigan's best book. But it has the Brautigan magic—the verbal wildness, the emptiness, the passive force of people who have gone beyond winning or losing to an absolute poetry of survival."

Brautigan has become as great a campus idol as Hesse, Tolkien, Vonnegut, or the hero of *The Abortion,* "admired for his tenderness toward human vulnerability, for his pose of the *faux naïf,* for his air of sweet inexpressible sadness." How seriously he should be taken as a literary phenomenon is a matter of opinion. L. J. Davis thinks "it may be a sign of the times (or something) and it is certainly a symptom of the current state of American fiction that some critics doggedly persist in treating Brautigan as if he were a Joseph Conrad instead of an Art Buchwald. . . . Brautigan will give no one bad dreams. He is sorry for us and he is fun to read. When one has said that about him, one has said about all there is to say." For Neil Schmitz, on the other hand, "far from being the self-indulgent poet of the counterculture . . . Brautigan is instead an ironist critically examining the myths and language of the pastoral sensibility that reappeared in the 1960s." Perhaps the most sensible view is the one expressed by Thomas A. Vogler, who is left with the feeling that "any response to so understated a form of art risks overstatement."

PRINCIPAL WORKS: *Fiction*—A Confederate General From Big Sur, 1964; Trout Fishing in America, 1967; In Watermelon Sugar, 1968; The Abortion: An Historical Romance 1966, 1971; Revenge of the Lawn: Stories 1962-1970; 1971; The Hawkline Monster: A Gothic Western, 1974; Willard and His Bowling Trophies: A Perverse Mystery, 1975; Sombrero Fallout: A Japanese Novel, 1976; Dreaming of Babylon, 1977. *Poetry*—The Return of the Rivers, 1957; The Galilee Hitch-Hiker, 1958; Lay the Marble Tea, 1959; The Octopus Frontier, 1960; All Watched Over by Machines of Loving Grace, 1967; The Pill Versus the Springhill Mine Disaster (Poems 1957-1968), 1968; Rommel Drives on Deep Into Egypt, 1970; Loading Mercury With a Pitchfork, 1976; June 30th, June 30th, 1978.

ABOUT: Acton, J. (and others) Mug Shots, 1972; Contemporary Authors 53-56, 1975; Cook, B. The Beat Generation, 1971; Malley, T. Richard Brautigan (Writers for the Seventies), 1972; Tanner, T. City of Words, 1971; Vinson, J. (ed.) Contemporary Novelists, 1976; Vinson, J. (ed.) Contemporary Poets, 1975; Who's Who in America, 1974-1975. *Periodicals*—Book World January 11, 1970; Bulletin of Bibliography January 1976; Critique 2 1971, 1 1974; Life August 14, 1970; Modern Fiction Studies Spring 1973, Autumn 1974; New American Review 11 1971; New Republic September 20, 1975; New York Review of Books April 22, 1971; New York Times Book Review February 15, 1970; March 28, 1971; January 16, 1972; Saturday Review June 12, 1971; December 4, 1971; October 10, 1976; Times Literary Supplement August 14, 1970; April 1, 1977; TriQuarterly Winter 1973.

"BRIAO, FERNANDES DE." *See* OATES, JOYCE CAROL

BROCK, EDWIN (October 19, 1927–), English poet and novelist, writes: "I have never known *why* a working-class South London boy with practically no formal education and no background of reading decided, at the age of eighteen, that he would become a poet. Nor do I know why, thirty years later, poetry continues to be a constant and central factor in his life. I

EDWIN BROCK

can, however, remember *when* and *where* it happened.

"The Where was HMS Tamar, a grim Victorian naval barracks in the Wanchai district of Hong Kong. The When was 1946, the year after the Japanese had surrendered a helpless fire-blackened island to the Allies.

"It was the year when millions of people without country or home were standing in queues all over Europe; it was the year when military policemen tried to impose an unworkable 'no fraternisation' rule on restless womanless troops; the year when Britain slipped straight from wartime shortages to postwar austerity without noticing the difference.

"At that time, in Tamar, a huge fan clanked hopelessly above the head of a fair-skinned youth who pulled his damp shirt away from a back covered in prickly heat, impetigo and the blue stain of gentian violet. Sweat, boredom and sexual frustration were the deepest of his war wounds. His hand reached for the battered paperbacks beside his bunk, and took the only one unread: *The Penguin Book of Modern Verse*. He flipped its pages dully and uncomprehendingly. There seemed no rhyme or reason for any of the words. They looked at him like a sign saying: 'Keep off. This is not for the likes of you.' Who, he wondered, do these bastards think they are?

"Only one poem stopped him: T. S. Eliot's 'Rhapsody on a Windy Night.' Perhaps it was because he had been away from the streetlamps, the cat in the gutter and the smell of chestnuts roasting on streetcorners for so long that the images stirred a self-pitying nostalgia. Whatever the reason, the poem stayed in his mind and,

118

some days later, prompted him to try something strange and unexpected: he wrote a poem.

"That anecdote is written in the third person because the boy now seems too far away to have any connection with myself. Yet some things, some tastes and attitudes towards writing, have remained over the years. And though I read that Penguin anthology today with more understanding, much of the irritation remains; and, often, it is for the same kind of reasons. A great deal of modern English poetry seemed to me then, intuitively, and seems today, more consciously, to come from a private set-apart world called Eng. Lit.: a world of good taste, verbal competence and well-groomed academic intelligence. In this world, the vulgarity and warm, often sloppy sentiment which were part and parcel of my life were missing. So were the words I used to express them. For one thing, nobody ever seemed to use the pronoun I: that one-letter word seemed as forbidden then as the naughty four-letter ones.

"For some years after leaving the Navy I tried to write a pastiche of the poems which were then appearing in the intelligent weeklies. Occasionally one was taken by a little magazine, but for the most part, predictably and rightly, they were rejected.

"Again, I can remember the exact moment when I found my own voice. I was wearing a policeman's uniform, patrolling a beat in southeast London. A poem was making itself felt, nibbling persistently at the edge of my mind. After living with it for a while, I propped myself up in a police 'phone box and scribbled down some words about the day my father died. It was the first time I had thought of writing a purely autobiographical poem, and the words came simply, easily and, I hope, honestly. I could not believe it was a poem and, reading it through, thought: that's a rough sketch for a poem; tomorrow I'll work on it. But when tomorrow came I realised I could not change a line without losing whatever it was I had caught on the page. So I shrugged and sent the draft-poem to the *Times Literary Supplement,* which was then at the top of my list of 'periodicals I'd most like to appear in.' Very quickly it was accepted and I was asked for more.

"That happened nearly twenty years ago and, eight collections of poetry later, whatever personal style I have achieved has grown directly from that poem. It amuses me now (no it doesn't, it irritates me!) to hear myself called 'confessional,' as though I have followed in the footsteps of those American poets whose 'new' style earned them that label. For much as I now admire *Life Studies,* I had not, at the time of writing about my father's death, heard the name Lowell, nor had I read a single living American poet.

"But I can understand the confusion. Today I read all the American poetry which comes my way, and find, in the aggression of an Alan Dugan or the quiet sensitivity of a James Wright, the immediacy I could not find in that Penguin anthology thirty years ago.

"Dugan, Wright and others make poetry which seems as necessary to them as food and air. If I gave it a label, I would call it a poetry of self-definition, and I would accept that label for the thing I stumbled upon in that police box in that backstreet in the mid-fifties. It is as though today our environment changes so quickly, so profoundly and, often, so nightmarishly, that every poem must be, among other things, an act of redefinition: as though the poet who wrote yesterday has no relevance for today.

"Therapy? Sorcery? I don't know. But for me it is an exciting way of using words, and is the only kind of poetry I want to read or write.

"For the rest of this autobiographical note: I was born in London in 1927, have been a sailor, clerk, journalist, policeman and adman, have married twice and have three children. Everyone seems to find those kind of facts necessary."

———

As he complains above, Brock's "poetry of self-definition" has been labeled by many critics "confessional." And, as he allows, this is not difficult to understand:

> My mother says a dead wasp still
> may sting; that spiders I have slaughtered
> will avenge, and all the puffed up toads
> of Christendom may make my soul a
> torment at its end.
>
> My family garden's full of broken
> bones, and burning bodies smoulder in
> my weeds; the guilt that glistens here
> I will atone; I sow the blight
> that bites the tails of seeds. . . .

This is from "A Desperate Kinship," one of the poems in *An Attempt at Exorcism* (1959), Brock's "sometimes romantic, often fanciful, always personal" first book. Dylan Thomas was the most obvious influence on these informal and conversational poems, it was thought, and "magic, not logic, is what [Brock's] poetry seeks to demonstrate, if not define. . . . That is to say, what he wants to evoke is a different order of reality, not the world of common experience . . . but that particular sort of private experience for which there are no direct or easy equivalents.

... An Attempt at Exorcism is a book both to praise and to arouse expectation."

The poet's father, prematurely dead, his embittered mother, his quietly despairing wife, his wry or bitter sense of remorse: these themes, introduced in the first collection, are resumed in the two sonnet sequences that make up *A Family Affair* (1960), which was written, Brock says, to prove to himself that he could handle the traditional forms.

The sense of guilt grows more pervasive, more wretched and self-abasing, in the collection which established Brock's reputation, *With Love From Judas* (1963). These poems record the break-up of the poet's first marriage. In an interview given the following year, Brock admitted that "a large streak of masochism entered into his motivation" in writing poetry, which "seemed to him like scratching oneself to make sure one bleeds," but which also provided a cheap substitute for psychoanalysis. And so the poet confesses his wife's infidelity, his own hypocrisy and meanness of spirit, and the irreparable harm he believes he has done to "the two children who live on me," wringing a painful lyricism from the most ordinary language and banal betrayals. In "A Last Poem to My Wife," he writes with disgust of his wife's religious beliefs:

Soon you will return to your belief in witches,
but there will be no need to burn you:
nobody may live long with the cancer of a dying god.

Peter Porter maintains all the same that Brock is a confessional poet only in the religious sense of the term, and says that "he recalls the past half as a fallen Christian and half as a worldly masochist, so that lyricism and harshness are accommodated in the same work."

There was a great deal of praise also for *The Portraits and the Poses* (1973). The "Portraits" in this book are earthy and low-keyed sketches of other people. In the "Poses" section, Brock confronts his world (and God's) with a bewildered honesty that is frequently both troubling and moving. God preoccupies him, but is found wanting: to be God, he thinks, is "an uncomfortable way/ to make a living." And he compares human suffering with Christ's in "Curriculum Vitae":

always I measured his pain
with the burning children and
their burned mothers who
had had no god to forsake them
whose death was permanent

in a London street and not
a long weekend in
a Mediterranean cave.

If Brock finds himself guilty and God inadequate, he has equally hard things to say about human violence and heartlessness, and some of his best poems are those of ironic social comment, like "Five Ways to Kill a Man" and "Song of the Battery Hen":

I have the same orange-
red comb, yellow beak and auburn
feathers, but as the door opens and you
hear above the electric fan a kind of
one-word wail, I am the one
who sounds loudest in my head. ...

God made us all quite differently,
and blessed us with this expensive home.

Brian Swann has noted that "the determinedly dour attitude" of Brock's verse "leaves a number of flat lines and poems in its wake. Brock possesses no real image-making power, but he conquers by his thrust and insistence. The updated Hardyesque plain diction humps its way through, growling and complaining." In fact, Brock's technique, uneven in his first books, has grown steadily more skillful and economical, and he has in recent years achieved interesting effects with a very short line of between two and five syllables. The American influence on his verse has increased, and much of his recent work has appeared in American journals or (in book form) under American imprints. Peter Porter, acknowledging that Brock is "one of the few English poets whose cadences can be heard by Americans," believes that "his aesthetic has little in common with any of theirs. His ear is perhaps the first to come fully alive in South London: he sees Dulwich in a light as unreal as Samuel Palmer's over Shoreham"; although it is "couched in popular form, Brock's recent poetry is among the most intensely felt of its time."

All this is evident in the "long thin poems" collected in *The Blocked Heart* (1975), in which Alasdair Maclean noted "an increasing concern with the metaphysical" along with "the blood and screaming," but which left Elaine Feinstein feeling that "sometimes his images, and his whole relation to daily life, are just too easy," so that "we resent the facility that turns true pain into clever verse." Brock's selected poems, published as *Song of the Battery Hen* (1977), had a generally respectful reception, and Vernon Scannell called Brock "the spokesman of the tough, undeceived but spiritually hungry, the hard case with a heart that refuses to ossify. He suffers but he is resolved to survive."

The Little White God (1962), Brock's only novel to date, is about a London policeman who has a love affair with the wife of a criminal whom he has put in jail—a relationship which costs him his career and perhaps his marriage. The story itself was thought "machine made," but with enough vitality to complement the novel's admirable documentary aspect, its "harsh, wry realism." *Here, Now, Always* (1977), the author's autobiography, employs both prose and verse in its episodic narrative. Scannell called it "a rather odd, frequently moving, and almost always diverting book. . . . a balanced, sombrely tinted portrait of a particular man in a particular place and time. . . . The prose is mainly admirable, supple and sinewy, having little truck with metaphor and abstractions but focusing sharply on the objects themselves, the tastes, sounds, sights and smells of childhood."

Brock's father was an electrician, often away from home, who was killed in a road accident when the boy was ten; he never felt very close to his mother. Brock served in the Royal Navy from 1945 to 1947, and was an editorial assistant on a trade paper from 1947 to 1951, when he joined the Metropolitan Police. He had by then become a frequent contributor to *Poetry Quarterly*. In 1958, when his poems began to appear in the *Times Literary Supplement,* a story about the "policeman poet" was published in the *Daily Express.* This troubled Brock's superiors, but led to the publication of his first book. Brock left the police in 1959 to become an advertising writer—with Mather and Crowther (1959-1963), J. Walter Thompson (1963-1964), Masius Wynne-Williams (1964), and S. H. Benson, whose creative group Brock headed from 1964 to 1972. Since then he has worked freelance for Ogilvy, Benson, and Mather. He has been poetry editor of *Ambit* since 1961. Brock, who is said to look "more like a professional football player than a poet," now lives in Norfolk. He has two children by his first marriage, which began in 1959 and ended in 1964, and one by his second marriage (1964).

PRINCIPAL WORKS: *Poetry*—An Attempt at Exorcism, 1959; A Family Affair: Two Sonnet Sequences, 1960; With Love From Judas, 1963; (with Geoffrey Hill and Stevie Smith) Penguin Modern Poets 8, 1966; Fred's Primer: A Little Girl's Guide to the World Around Her, 1969; A Cold Day at the Zoo, 1970; Invisibility Is the Art of Survival: Selected Poems, 1972; The Portraits and the Poses, 1973; Parox-ISMS, 1974; I Never Saw It Lit, 1974; The Blocked Heart, 1975; Song of the Battery Hen: Selected Poems 1959-1975, 1977. Novel—The Little White God, 1962. Autobiography—Here, Now, Always, 1977.

ABOUT: Brock, E. Here, Now, Always, 1977; International Who's Who in Poetry, 1974-1975; Pryce-Jones, A. *introduction to* Invisibility Is the Art of Survival, 1972; Rosenthal, M.L. The New Poets, 1967; Thwaite, A. Poetry Today: 1960-1973, 1973; Vinson, J. (ed.) Contemporary Poets, 1975. *Periodicals*—Guardian May 21, 1964; Times Literary Supplement November 13, 1959; October 26, 1962, January 30, 1976; March 25, 1977.

BROWN, GEORGE MACKAY (October 17, 1921–) Scottish poet, novelist, short story writer, dramatist, and essayist, writes: "I was born in the small fishing-port of Stromness in the Orkney Islands. I have since only left the islands to attend Edinburgh University and for brief holidays in Scotland. You might say there is a deep attachment to Orkney, though it is not rooted in ancestry: neither my father's name (Brown) nor my mother's (Mackay) is Orcadian.

"I am fortunate to live in a community of farmers and fishermen and tradesmen. A writer should know the people he writes about over a period of years and even of generations; this is possible in a small community like Orkney. There are stories attached not only to living men and women, but to their great-grandparents. This is the way that legend takes over from gossip.

"The islanders have always been great story-tellers. That art is very much under threat now, since the advent of newspapers and television. But I remember fine story-tellers in my childhood. To me the story was an essential part of life.

"There is a strong element of ritual in my work—the deliberate working to a pattern. Without such set forms life is a meaningless drift. Here in Orkney the labour and the ritual are one. On the farms especially—not so much now, with mechanisation, as formerly—one sees the slow deliberate working to a fixed end: ploughing, sowing, harrowing, the green and the gold corn, reaping, gathering into barns, threshing, winnowing, milling, at last the bread and the ale. That kind of work was very hard, but all the same everyone on a farm was part of this meaningful pattern that was essential to life. The bleakness and the labor were clothed in beauty.

"The sea rhythms were more dangerous and swift and dramatic. But the ritual element was there too, on a more primitive level. The fisherman even had a special vocabulary that he used at sea; as if a mis-spoken word could overwhelm him. Indeed many of these men never knew when they set out in the morning whether they would return. To move from the hunter to the seed-man was to enter a safer more meaningful ceremony.

"And yet the Orkney crofts were so small,

Patrick Hughes

GEORGE MACKAY BROWN

ing and the occasional poem. If I had had to actually work hard on a farm or a fishing-boat, or in a shop or office, the seed might have died in me.

"Another fortunate event was my close contact, over two or three years, with the older Orkney poet Edwin Muir. Under his praise and encouragement, any talent I had burgeoned and bloomed. Even then I might have done nothing about it, but Edwin Muir (unknown to me) sent a group of my poems to the Hogarth Press. So *Loaves and Fishes* came to be published. Since then I have been in the nurturing and patient hands of the same publishers.

"The winds of poetry blow where they list. In windless periods I would idly turn out a story, to pass the time. To my surprise the Hogarth Press liked the manuscript of *A Calendar of Love* (short stories); reviews were good; and so I discovered that after all I was perhaps better at narrative prose than verse. Good fortune again; many poets, myself included, lose their talent in middle age. I have a great fund of unwritten stories to warm my old bones.

"It sometimes happens that an image can alter the whole course of a writer's work. St. Paul is not my favourite saint, but his phrase about the seed falling into the earth and dying, in order to bring forth its proper fruit, seemed to me when I chanced on it to explain the whole of life; especially when I saw all around me the ploughs and corn-stalks and barns—"the orient and immortal wheat." The same simple majestic imagery, the ritual of bread, led me into the Catholic Church, rather than any moral impulse, or theological enquiry or persuasion.

"I lead a quiet reserved rather lonely life, without spouse or family. As an existence it has its drawbacks, but on the whole I think fortune has been kind to me, here also. I can work regularly and in peace, with only the trivial anxieties of a bachelor to distract me.

"I have lately been afflicted with a mild nervous trouble called, vaguely, agoraphobia. It keeps me from travel and large cities. Fortunately, neither the one nor the other is necessary to me. Here in Orkney there is enough character and stuff of legend to keep me going for another few years yet."

many of them, that the ploughman had to be a fisherman too. It is not without significance that two of my books are called *Loaves and Fishes* and *Fishermen With Ploughs*.

"All my work is a kind of celebration—if it comes off—of the lives of farmers and fishermen in the only community I know well.

"I was fortunate too in that I had this writing talent, for otherwise I would be an utterly useless member of society. There is nothing else I can do.

"I was born into a poor but reasonably happy and secure family. My father was a postman and a part-time tailor. My mother came from the Highlands of Scotland and was a Gaelic-speaker. Some people have noted a 'mystical element' in my work which, they claim, is alien to the Orcadian outlook. I admit it, and hope that at its best it might enhance my writing, here and there. This mystical Celtic strain must come from my mother.

"I was the youngest of five children.

"At school, where my performance was ordinary in every subject, I discovered by accident that I could write essays and compositions better than anybody else in the class.

"Like nearly all authors, I began by writing poetry. I wrote my first poem at the age of eight or nine in the middle of a summer field while the milk-horse drew his clanging cart up the road. It was a poem in praise of Stromness. My parents praised it when I showed them the scrap of paper. It must, of course, have been awful.

"My life as a writer has been full of fortunate turns. My health was uncertain from adolescence on; I was absolved from work for long periods; and I filled these gaps of time with read-

George Mackay Brown is the son of John and Mary (Mackay) Brown. He attended Stromness Academy and in 1951, at the age of thirty, resumed his education at Newbattle Abbey College, in Midlothian, Scotland, where Edwin Muir was then warden. He left Newbattle Abbey in 1953, returned in 1956, and then went on as a mature student to Edinburgh University, where he read English (M.A., 1960), and did postgraduate work on Gerard Manley Hopkins (1962-1964). The influence of Muir's measured blank verse and myth-creating vision is evident in Brown's early poetry, along with echoes of Hopkins, Yeats, Dylan Thomas and, above all, the icy simplicities of the Scandinavian sagas.

His first book, *The Storm*, published in 1954 by the Orkney Press, included a sequence of sometimes rather prosaic free verse portraits of Brown's fellow Orcadians, and a powerful poem on Orkney's patron saint, Magnus the Martyr. Muir found in the collection a quality of grace which, as Alexander Scott has suggested, characterizes all of Brown's writings—an unsentimental recognition of the charity and compassion, human as well as divine, which ameliorates and sometimes illuminates the darkness and cruelty of life.

Loaves and Fishes and *The Year of the Whale* contained poems almost exclusively concerned with what one critic called "the ancient simplicities and sanctified rituals of life in Orkney"—the past and present of the farmers and fishermen, their work and their dreams, customs and faiths, loves and deaths. There followed two small books from small presses, and then *Fishermen With Ploughs*, a cycle of poems about the colonization of Orkney from Norway by voyagers fleeing from starvation and disease after the death of their god Balder, and the community's slow evolution. When *Poems New and Selected* appeared in 1971, Maurice Wiggin wrote: "Pitched high, grave, elegiac, austere, the 'saga voice' of George Mackay Brown is not tuned to the modern ear. Or the other way round. Yet such is the power of his purity, the persuasion of his meticulous craftsmanship, that he rings truer than many 'modern' poets. He is certainly one of the most considerable artists writing now in verse."

In his short stories, Brown writes with the same kind of spare directness and ballad-like stylization about the same characters and themes—Saint Magnus the Martyr, a girl (a modern martyr) who becomes an alcoholic because she cannot otherwise bear the cruelty and anguish she sees all around her, a Viking sea captain, a young soldier who slowly apprehends his own death by hearing gossip of it among the living, the evils of progress and puritanism. It seemed to some critics that (as J. R. Frakes put it) Brown was striving too self-consciously in his first collection of stories and sketches "towards a runic style, manipulating refrains and incremental repetitions, folk rhythms and local idiom. Full of crafty tinkers, lobster creels, kirkyards and hayforks, these stories exploit local color instead of extending it into a more universal art."

Frakes was one of those who welcomed with enthusiasm the far more incisive and effective stories in *A Time to Keep*, of which another reviewer wrote that Brown "is here going further than the thorough and compassionate understanding of a people that has always distinguished his best work . . . and writing with immense resourcefulness and power." Jacky Gillott, reviewing *The Sun's Net* (1976), said that "these tales illustrate the author's power to write from the central meeting point of religion, legend, and superstition. His people are at their best when they are figurative shapes . . . the more representational he makes them, the closer he comes to the specific and the present moment, the less compelling he is."

Brown's dislike of the modern world of technology and materialism provides a recurrent theme in all his work. It is critical in *Greenvoe*, his first novel, which evokes an Orkney village in "rolling prose-poetry" that reminded one reader of Dylan Thomas's *Under Milk Wood*. Switching his narrative from lobsterman to squire, from farmer to ferryman, Brown weaves a richly detailed impression of a way of life that has taken a thousand years of history and myth to create—and that in the end is threatened by a plague of government officials determined to incorporate the island into an Early Warning System. A number of reviewers found this technological invasion a contrived and unconvincing conclusion to a novel which was otherwise almost universally admired for its humor, sensitivity, and unsentimental poetry.

In his second novel Brown returned to the story of the twelfth-century Earl of Orkney who became St. Magnus, and whose murder by his ambitious cousin was followed by a period of peace and sound rule that gave his death the quality of sacrifice. This unorthodox novel is composed of prose passages, verse, a section in dramatic form, and one that jumps forward in time to describe a modern martyrdom in a concentration camp. "Despite the story, the Christian moral and the linking symbolism," wrote one reviewer, "the book remains an assemblage of brilliant fragments, nothing ever less than superbly observant, and arresting, yet oddly unsatisfactory when put together."

Orkney Tapestry is also an "interweaving of poems and prose, myth and history, anecdote and legend," but a portrait of the islands rather than a novel about them, like *Letters From Hamnavoe*, a collection of essays and articles. Brown's play *A Spell for Green Corn* was performed on radio in 1967 and staged in 1970 in

123

Edinburgh, where another play, *Witch,* had appeared the year before. His adaptations for television of three of his short stories were broadcast in 1971. Brown received an Arts Council award for poetry in 1965 and the Society of Authors travel award in 1967. *A Time to Keep* brought him both the literature prize of the Scottish Arts Council and the Katherine Mansfield Menton Prize. His verse appears in several anthologies of modern Scottish poetry and a number of his poems on St. Magnus and on other themes have been set to music by Peter Maxwell Davies. The author became an O.B.E. in 1974. He lives very modestly in a small modern house overlooking the harbor at Stromness, where he knows everyone.

The three television plays broadcast in 1971 upset some of Brown's fellow Orcadians, who feared that they would damage the tourist industry; it is true that, as Raymond Gardner said in a *Guardian* interview, Brown's work conveys "an overriding sense of loss, both moral and physical," and that he does not like what Progress has done to his world. Some critics have maintained that these attitudes, together with his 1961 conversion to Catholicism and his geographical isolation, impose damaging limitations on his work. But Maurice Wiggin suggests that "in his narrowness lies his strength. He is not narrow in the ordinary sense of provincial—his theme is nothing narrower than the total span of human possibility—but as an Orcadian writing in and out of the Orkneys he manages to generate intense energy by compressing the spring of impulse tight within the narrow limits of locality (and legend). He fires not a scattergun but a crossbow: the bolt flies short, but hard and true."

PRINCIPAL WORKS: *Poetry*—The Storm, 1954; Loaves and Fishes, 1959; The Year of the Whale, 1965; Fishermen With Ploughs, 1971; Poems New and Selected, 1971; (with Iain Crichton Smith and Norman MacCaig) Penguin Modern Poets 21, 1972; Winterfold, 1976. *Short Stories*—A Calendar of Love, 1967; A Time to Keep, 1969; Hawkfall, 1974; The Two Fiddlers: Tales from Orkney (for children), 1974; The Sun's Net, 1976; Pictures in the Cave (for children), 1977. *Novels*—Greenvoe, 1972; Magnus, 1973. *Play*—A Spell for Green Corn, 1970. *Other*—An Orkney Tapestry, 1969; Letters From Hamnavoe, 1975.

ABOUT: Contemporary Authors 21-24 1st revision, 1977; International Who's Who in Poetry, 1974-1975; Vinson, J. (ed.) Contemporary Novelists, 1976; Vinson, J. (ed.) Contemporary Poets, 1975. *Periodicals*—Guardian October 13, 1971; Listener April 17, 1967; Observer July 4, 1976; Sunday Times (London) August 22, 1971; May 28, 1972; Times Literary Supplement November 18, 1965; February 16, 1967; August 27, 1971; September 4, 1969; September 27, 1974; August 13, 1976; March 25, 1977.

BROWN, STERLING (ALLEN) (May 1, 1901–), American poet and critic, was born in Washington, D.C., where his father was a professor at Howard University's School of Religion. As Robert O'Meally says, Howard was then "a center (if not *the* center) of the black intellectual world." As a boy, Sterling Brown met Alain Locke, Kelly Miller, and Montgomery Gregory, and heard W.E.B. Du Bois and Booker T. Washington speak at Lincoln Temple, his father's church. The families of Jean Toomer and Paul Laurence Dunbar were friends.

Brown's early interest in poetry was stimulated by his mother, an excellent reader. He was educated at public schools in Washington and later at Williams College, Massachusetts (B.A., 1922) and Harvard University, where he gained his M.A. in 1923. From 1923 to 1926 he taught at Virginia Seminary and College, Lynchburg, Virginia, and there followed two years at Lincoln University, St. Louis, Missouri (1926–1928), and one year at Fisk University, Nashville, Tennessee (1928–1929). In 1929, continuing family tradition, Brown joined the faculty of Howard University, where as professor of English he conducted courses in American civilization for more than thirty years. Brown has been a key figure in black American culture, and not only as a writer and teacher. He served as editor on Negro Affairs for the Federal Writers' Project from 1936 to 1939, and in 1939 joined the staff of the Carnegie Corporation's study of the Negro in America, directed by Gunnar Myrdal, the conclusions of which were published as *An American Dilemma* in 1944.

Long before that, Sterling Brown had made his name as a poet with the publication in 1932 of *Southern Road*. Though he is often associated with the "Harlem Renaissance" of the 1920s, Brown did not share the urban orientation of the movement. A "poet of the soil," he was drawn to the rural South, its dialects and black folklore, as he had come to know them as a young teacher in Virginia, Missouri, and Tennessee. In those days, Brown says, he learned as much from his students as they did from him. According to Robert O'Meally, "he was fascinated by the talk and the songs of his students and their parents; they were intrigued by this lanky, athletic professor who took seriously the local lore. The students brought to class local champion singers and talkers ... [like] Luke Johnson, whom Brown paid a quarter for every song he would write down." One student introduced Brown to the blues, and he began what is now an important collection of blues and jazz, on which he has become an authority.

Scurlock Studio

STERLING BROWN

In the South, O'Meally says, Brown "became increasingly aware of black language as often ironic, understated and double-edged." He decided that "he would try to render black experience as he knew it, using the speech of the people." It was this above all that characterized *Southern Road*. In these poems the black people are depicted as victims not only of the whites, but of all that surrounds them—the land, the elements, and their own fear, ignorance, and credulity. Whereas earlier poets had used the folk idiom humorously or contemptuously, Brown uses it to convey the whole range of black experience—bitterly, for example, in "Old King Cotton":

> Ole King Cotton,
> Ole Man Cotton,
> Keeps us slavin'
> Till we'se dead an' rotten. . . .
>
> Starves us wid bumper crops
> Starves us wid po'.
> Chains de lean wolf
> At our do'.

Elsewhere, Brown portrays the impact of urban life upon immigrants from the South, the yearning to return to the roots, and (in "Children's Children") the young ghetto black's loss of his folk heritage, the lasting truths of the old songs:

They have forgotten, they have never known,
Long days beneath the torrid Dixie sun
In miasma'd rice swamps;
The chopping of dried grass, on the third go round
In strangling cotton;
Wintry nights in mud-daubed makeshift huts,
With these songs, sole comfort.

The young laugh at these songs, "deep buried beneath the weight/ of dark and heavy years," yet:

> When they hear
> Saccharine melodies of loving and its fevers,
> Soft-flowing lies of love everlasting;
> Conjuring divinity out of gross flesh itch;
> They sigh
> And look goggle-eyed
> At one another.

The theme of racial protest is most evident in the later poems in the collection, like "Master and Man," which denounces the exploitation of black agricultural workers, and "Sam Smiley," about a black veteran of World War I who discovers that while Americans of all colors can be first-class citizens in war, the rules are different in peacetime. *Southern Road* has its comic aspects, best seen in the poems which describe the adventures of the fast-talking ne'er-do-well Slim Green. This sort of humor, effective as a vehicle of protest, was abandoned by Brown as he turned more and more to overt protest in the poetry he wrote after *Southern Road,* most of it in conventional English, like "Southern Cop":

> Let us forgive Ty Kendricks,
> It was in darktown. He was young,
> His nerves were jittery. The day was hot.
> The nigger ran out of the alley,
> And so he shot. . . .
>
> Let us pity Ty Kendricks.
> He has been through enough.
> Standing there, his big gun smoking,
> Rabbit-scared, alone;
> Having to hear the wenches wail
> And the dying nigger moan.

John Henrik Clarke regards Brown as "the dean of American Negro poets," and Léopold Senghor has described Sterling Brown and Langston Hughes as "the most Negro" poets in American literature. The publication of *Southern Road* elicited almost unanimous praise from the critics. "On every page there is 'race,' " wrote a critic in the New York *Times,* "but it is 'race' neither arrogant nor servile. There is pathos, infinite pathos; but everywhere there is dignity that respects itself. There is neither moaning nor sentimentalizing, but a frank facing of reality. Moreover, there is everywhere art." A more recent critic, David Littlejohn, while he finds Brown's irony sharp, his ideas exciting, feels that "he lacked, unfortunately, any real organic verbal skill, so his poetry still resides more in his ideas, in the effects of underplayed indirection, than in the total achievement." But "it was right for the time, and it remains a strong indictment."

Although he continued to contribute poetry to various magazines, Brown became increasingly preoccupied in the 1930s with the literary image of the black people of America, and in 1937 he published *Negro Poetry and Drama* and *The Negro in American Fiction.* Brown's importance as a scholar of black writing rests primarily on these two books, which criticize not only the white authors who had fixed the black stereotype in the American mind but also those authors of the Harlem Renaissance who portrayed black life in only its extreme and distorted forms. *Negro Poetry and Drama* traces the development of black poetry from the self-conscious writers of the eighteenth and nineteenth centuries, through folk and dialect poetry, to the black poets of the 1930s. In dealing with drama, where black people were more often created characters than creative playwrights, Brown focuses mainly on changes in their portrayal, from subsidiary roles in early plays to those of central significance in the 1930s.

The same theme is scrutinized more closely in *The Negro in American Fiction.* Brown postulates seven black stereotypes in American literature and argues that these evolved at the dictates of social policy. "When slavery was being attacked . . . southern authors countered with the contented slave; when cruelties were mentioned, they dragged forward the comical and happy-hearted Negro." Similarly, "in Reconstruction, when threatened with such dire fate as Negroes' voting, going to school, and working for themselves . . . southern authors added the stereotype of the brute Negro." Even at the time of publication "much social policy demands that slavery be shown as blessed and fitting, and the Negro as ludicrously ignorant of his own best good." To counteract these harmful images, Brown believed that "the final interpretation of Negro life must come from within." The new black American writer must seek to create a sense of racial pride through a rediscovery of Africa and its culture and a celebration of the heroes of black American history; black people must be portrayed in their environment, not merely as outsiders in a white-dominated society. A central element of the new writing should be protest—propaganda should be fought with propaganda, though "propaganda, however legitimate, can speak no louder than the truth. Such a cause as ours needs no dressing up."

Brown's essay "A Century of Negro Portraiture in American Literature," published in *Massachusetts Review* (Winter 1966), brought his findings up to date. Three years later, *Negro Poetry and Drama* and *The Negro in American Fiction* were reissued in a single-volume edition, with a preface by Robert Bone. For Bone, Brown's essays are not "by modern critical standards, penetrating. . . . Rather they are comprehensive surveys in the field of iconography, tracing . . . the changing image of the Negro. Their real focus is the sociology of literature, the politics of culture . . . the uses and abuses of the image-making function in society. . . . Brown demonstrates that the American literary imagination has been obsessed with the figure of the Negro, and that with honorable exceptions our literary heritage is racist to the core." Emanuel and Gross in *Dark Symphony* credit Brown with having been "greatly responsible for the knowledge that most Americans have of the Negro past." The desire to make a wider public aware of the depth and scope of black literature clearly inspired the anthology *The Negro Caravan* (1941) of which Brown was co-editor. This book has been described as a classic of its kind, making available a rich selection of spirituals, blues, work songs, ballads, and folk tales from the nineteenth and twentieth centuries. Brown has published only one other verse collection since *Southern Road,* a volume of narrative poems called *The Last Ride of Wild Bill* (1975).

Sterling Brown was a Guggenheim Fellow in 1937–1938. He has made occasional forays from Howard University to teach as a visiting professor at New York University, Atlantic University, Vassar College, and the University of Minnesota. Robert Bone has commented that Brown's refusal to repudiate his black heritage was not the customary decision for a man of his background, a "child of the misnamed black bourgeoisie." Always an integrationist, he has succeeded, according to Bone, in transcending racial chauvinism in all its forms. Brown is said to be a gifted raconteur, humorist, and mime.

PRINCIPAL WORKS: *Poetry*—Southern Road, 1932; The Last Ride of Wild Bill and Eleven Narrative Poems, 1975. *Poems in* Chapman, A. (ed.) Black Voices: An Anthology of Afro-American Literature, 1968; Bontemps A. and Hughes L. (eds.) The Poetry of the Negro, 1949; Johnson, J.W. (ed.) The Book of American Negro Poetry, 1959. *Nonfiction*—Negro Poetry and Drama, 1937; The Negro in American Fiction, 1937 (published together in 1969 with a preface by Robert Bone); (editor, with others) The Negro Caravan, 1941. *Essay in* Emanuel, J.A. and Gross, T.L. (eds.) Dark Symphony, 1968.

ABOUT: Brawley, B.G. Negro Genius, 1937; Contemporary Literary Criticism 1, 1973; Cunard, N. Negro Anthology, 1934; Davis, A.P. From the Dark Tower, 1974; Dreer, H. American Literature by Negro Authors, 1950; Emanuel, J.A. and Gross, T.L. Dark Symphony, 1968; Wagner, J. Black Poets of the United States: From Paul Laurence Dunbar to Langston Hughes, 1973. *Periodicals*–Black Scholar

March 1977; Ebony October 1976; New Republic February 11, 1978.

BROWNJOHN, ALAN (CHARLES) ("John Berrington") (July 28, 1931–), English poet, novelist, and critic writes: "I was born and brought up in a south-east London suburb poised exactly, and almost determinedly, between the upper working- and lower-middle classes. Doggedness, in its moral respectability and its hard-working attitudes, was its principal hallmark, and when doggedness no longer needs to be applied (as it was, for example, in the depression years of the 1930's, my own childhood) to maintain one's position, it tends to produce what the sociologists term 'upward mobility.'

"To the surprise of its headmaster and staff, my very modest grammar school began to show symptoms of upward mobility in the postwar years. My own sixth form began to produce not only Civil Service clerical officers, deputy bank managers and small insurance executives, but dons, doctors, lawyers, advertising men and writers. I suppose I am a product of this social shift, a poet living in turn in Putney, Chelsea and Hampstead, lecturing in a college for young teachers, and speaking south-east English with a covering of Oxford cadences and intonations.

"I think of myself as primarily concerned, as a writer, with: watching the shifts in the social and cultural fabric of England in my time, interpreting the interrelation of private living and public events, offering didactic comment on the changing state of things, issuing warnings, and finding hope in a depressing world. All of this is predictable from my background, I think; a background infinitely concerned with the intricacies of the English class structure, jealous of its private concerns, nonconformist (in respectable ways) in its politics, and censorious about changes it didn't like. I regard myself as labouring to *universalise* all this in significant statements in my writing, in the firm belief that if you are good enough you can 'universalise' out of much more constricted social situations than my own—and adhering to another strong item of faith: that English culture and institutions (using the terms in their widest sense) still have more to offer the world at large than most other cultures, with the possible exception of the Scandinavian, and that the English language is still the finest vehicle for placing these things at the disposal of civilisation, even in our (happily) post-imperial and (dismally) intra-European situation. I am implying that England should be giving what it can in this situation, not taking what it can grab!

ALAN BROWNJOHN

I like to see myself as a wry kind of English puritan, mostly abstemious in habits, extreme in my tenacity of rigorous political positions (a socialist of the only sort worth being in England: on the left of the Labour Party, loathing doctrinaire Marxism only less than Right-wing Labourism). I am atheist in (ir)religion, sceptical of all intellectual and artistic nonsense and pretentiousness, an enemy of all philistine materialism—especially commercial culture, believing that the greatest social and cultural disaster in my time has been the commercialisation of the British broadcasting media.

"For a definition of poetry I take a personal, unpretentious, non-mystical formulation: that it is 'words to which one wishes to give particular importance.' The kind of importance, personal and public, which I have in mind will have been implied by the foregoing list of beliefs.

"I regard few things in life as funny, but *those* things are intensely funny; so I think of myself as having an intense sense of humour.

"For the personal record: I have been twice married, with one son by my first marriage. I enjoy giving public readings of my verse, and do it only too often for my physical and mental health. I love music (hoping that that term will define itself when I say that the only *near*-music I am passionate about is modern jazz). I am temperamentally inclined to depression, using depression as a substitute for physical illness. And, although allergic to them and unable to own one, I like cats—and would ban dog ownership in towns, as I believe they do in Iceland."

To the characteristically clearsighted and exact account above should be added the useful

127

note Alan Brownjohn contributed to *Contemporary Poets of the English Language* (1970): "I write, with no preconceptions at all as to how I *should* write or what the result will be, in a variety of forms. Tight verse forms are certainly among these, but I suppose that a heavily-stressed free verse is my basic manner. So far, the themes of love, and human relationships, probably predominate—sometimes placed in the context of a society which I intrinsically dislike —hence the emphasis various critics have placed on both the 'domestic' and the 'social' in my verse. I can't think of any surprising or unusual influences—just the major names which one admires in the verse of all periods. But I believe poetry needs to change and adapt to changes in society, and much of my recent personal thinking about the art is concerned with this."

Alan Brownjohn was one of the earliest and most faithful members of the now defunct "Group"—an open and fluid assemblage of poets who met weekly during the 1950s and early 1960s to discuss each other's work. Brownjohn was represented in *A Group Anthology* (1963), along with Edward Lucie-Smith, Peter Porter, George MacBeth, Peter Redgrove, and others. These poets, according to Lucie-Smith, had in common only the belief that "the process by which words work in poetry is something open to rational examination." By and large the Group also showed a greater interest in social and political problems than the so-called "Movement," which preceded it, and some Group poetry was characterized by a certain brutality of theme and manner.

This brutality is entirely absent in Brownjohn's work, but the social concern is not; Peter Porter has said that England has "no more potent and inventive social poet." Brownjohn's method is satirical. He "works for the fair society," Porter says, "by dissecting the foolishness and indecency of the existing one," often choosing "to look at minor failures of taste and nerve and deduce wider issues from them." His tone of voice is quiet, colloquial, but exact to the point of hesitancy—"like a Larkin who has thought more but felt less," as Anthony Thwaite puts it.

Brownjohn's early poems indeed seemed to some reviewers too subdued and undramatic, too fussily precise in their accounts of human pretension and hypocrisy; one critic complained of "a language that takes no delight in itself," which must be "read and re-read before its low faint tone reaches you." Others have from the beginning admired the scrupulousness and intelligence of Brownjohn's work, finding in his restraint a proper expression of his compassionate but uncompromising moral seriousness, and like

Anthony Thwaite valuing the way his "sensitive decorum bides its time and works itself into the memory more tenaciously than some poets who make a showier assault."

A new clarity and directness has been evident in Brownjohn's later verse, and *Warrior's Career* (1972) was generally felt to mark a major advance in confidence and variety. A reviewer in the *Times Literary Supplement* wrote that the poems in this collection "search out hypocrisies, evasions, the complexities of human relationships and the oddities of change almost in a spirit of social hygiene. What they have to say is troubled and humane; the means by which they say it is reflective and steady":

We used to be some self-absorbed people living
In a compromised age, about twenty years
    ago. We hated it, it
Was a terrible age, and underneath
    we liked it in a way, it
Was because it gave us the chance
    to feel like that.

Now it has all changed, and we are older,
And we hate the age completely,
    not nearly so
Entranced with our hatred. But now
    there are lots of younger
People entranced with hatred of this
    terrible age,

While underneath they like it in a
    way, because
It gives them the chance to feel like
    that. We ourselves feel lost
Because we can't tell them they are
    compromised like us,
That being hard for the self-absorbed
    to see.

                    (from "Palindrome")

These poems range from urban vignettes to an extremely funny calypso about King Arthur, from a witty inquiry into fashionable attitudes to pollution to "Pastoral," about a fox-hunt on the moon:

In all these men and women pride was burning
to have this ceremony in such a place:
The air-locked air smelt grand, the beasts were
    sprightly,
The clothes were filled with arrogance and grace.

The faces, just as furious and paltry
As were their ancestors' before their births,
Joyed at the springy touch of lunar pastures
As had those solid forebears on the earth's . . .

A Song of Good Life (1975) was also welcomed

by most of its reviewers. It begins with a series of satirical but not uncompassionate vignettes, mostly in verse, illustrating the preoccupations and desperations of actresses, executives, married graduates, monarchs, disc jockeys, and other *dramatis personae* of life in the early 1970s. This is followed by a short play, also concerned to make audible the false notes in the contemporary "song of good life," and then by a section of odes and genre poems. Whether Brownjohn is writing about a radio tower, an office party, or a new highway out of London, it seemed to Peter Porter that "he can make the reader see not just the immediate squalor of each but the further dimension of shabbiness they lead to. He uses irony very differently from most modern poets: he winds it round his subjects in coils of syntax hardly less elaborate than Henry James's." Porter found this collection not a departure for Brownjohn "but an admirable consolidation and his best book to date." Alasdair Maclean, on the other hand, regretted the amount of attention Brownjohn gives to satirical and "public" poems, admiring him most when he "now and then forgets about executive-bashing and sets out, with easy skill and a pleasant tone of wry melancholy, to describe some inner landscapes."

Brownjohn's Beasts is a book of poems for children, "crammed full of observation and ideas," and *To Clear the River* is a novel for young people, describing ten days in the lives of two teenagers in a provincial town: Strongly attracted to each other, they yet hold back, the boy out of inexperience, and girl because she fears that reality may destroy her idealistic fantasies. "The doubts, the suspicions and the difficulties of adolescence are admirably conveyed," wrote one reviewer, "and if the end is inconclusive this is because for most of us life does not make neat patterns." Brownjohn is the *New Statesman's* poetry critic and has also contributed poems and/or reviews to the *London Magazine,* the *Observer, Encounter, Ambit,* and other major British journals, and to the New York *Times* and the *Southern Review* in the United States.

The author is the son of Charles Brownjohn, a printer, and the former Dorothy Mulligan. He was educated at Brockley County School and Merton College, Oxford University, which gave him his B.A. in 1953, his M.A. in 1961. Formerly a schoolteacher, he has since 1965 been senior lecturer in English at Battersea College of Education. His work has often been featured on BBC radio and television programs. Brownjohn was a member of the Wandsworth Borough Council in 1962-1965, and was once a unsuccessful Labour candidate for Parliament, but is no longer an active politician. He has served as chairman of

the Poets' Workshop in London (1970–1971) and as a member of the council and the executive committee of the Poetry Society (1967–1969). He became a member of the Literature Panel of the Arts Council of Great Britain in 1968, and has been chairman of the Panel since 1973. Alan Brownjohn's first wife was the poet Shirley Toulson; they were married in 1960 and divorced in 1969. He made a second marriage in 1972 to Sandra Willingham, a teacher.

PRINCIPAL WORKS: *Poetry*—Travellers Alone (entire issue of Artisan 5), 1954; The Railings, 1961; The Lions' Mouths, 1967; Sandgrains on a Tray, 1969; (with Michael Hamburger and Charles Tomlinson) Penguin Modern Poets 14, 1969; Brownjohn's Beasts (for children), 1970; Warrior's Career, 1972; A Song of Good Life, 1975. *Novel*—(as "John Berrington") To Clear the River, 1964. *Nonfiction*—Philip Larkin (Writers and Their Work series), 1975. *As Editor*—First I Say This, 1969; (with Seamus Heaney and Jon Stallworthy) New Poems 1970–1971, 1971.

ABOUT: Contemporary Authors 25–28 1st revision, 1977; International Who's Who in Poetry, 1974–1975; Raban, J. The Society of the Poem, 1971; Schmidt, M. and Lindop, G. (eds.) British Poetry Since 1960, 1972; Thwaite, A. Poetry Today, 1973; Vinson, J. (ed.) Contemporary Poets, 1975. *Periodicals*—Ambit October 1975; London Magazine October 1969; Observer (London) November 16, 1975; Times Literary Supplement February 16, 1967; October 23, 1969; December 15, 1972; January 30, 1976.

BUKOWSKI, CHARLES (August 16, 1920–), American poet, short story writer, and novelist, writes: "I was born in Andernach, Germany. My father was with the Army of Occupation and my mother was a native of Germany. I was brought to America at the age of two. We soon moved to Los Angeles, where I have lived most of my life. I am largely self-educated, although my education does include two years at Los Angeles City College. I began to roam the country soon afterwards, subsisting on menial jobs which included janitor, gas station attendant, guard, dishwasher, shipping clerk, warehouseman, receiving clerk, foreman, truck driver, mailman, stock boy, post office clerk, parking lot attendant. I also worked in a dog biscuit factory, a fluorescent lighting factory, and a slaughterhouse, was a member of a railroad track gang, and also worked for the American Red Cross. I saw most of the cities and had about one hundred jobs. Much of the time I starved while trying to write, limiting myself to one candy bar a day while writing four or five short stories a week. Often I had no typewriter and handprinted most of my work, sending it to the *Atlantic Monthly, Harper's* and the *New Yorker.* It all came back.

"Finally, at the age of twenty-four, I had a story accepted by Whit Burnett's *Story* magazine. I had another accepted by Caresse Crosby's

BUKOWSKI

CHARLES BUKOWSKI

Portfolio. I began drinking heavier than usual, stopped writing, and simply drank. This continued for ten years, during which time I lived with some women who were as desperate as I. It ended with a series of massive hemorrhages and I was in the charity ward of the Los Angeles County General Hospital. After being misplaced in an underground cavern ("he was downstairs and his papers passed over him upstairs") I was given twelve pints of blood and twelve pints of glucose. I refused an operation which I was told I would need or that I would die. I was also told that if I ever took another drink that I would die. They lied to me twice.

"After coming out of the hospital I managed to find a job and an apartment. I came home from the job each evening and drank huge quantities of beer and began writing poetry. I wrote sixty poems in two weeks and had no idea of what to do with them. I found a list of poetry magazines and one was in Wheeler, Texas. I thought, ah, there's an old woman down there who lives in a vine-covered cottage and raises canaries; these poems should jiggle her panic meter. I dropped them into the mailbox and forgot about them. I got back a very thick letter proclaiming me as a 'genius.' That sounded all right. I wrote back. The entire issue of the magazine *(Harlequin)* was given over to my work. We continued to correspond. She came out to visit me. She was a quite handsome blonde girl. We married and went back to Texas where I found that she was a millionairess. The marriage lasted two-and-one-half years.

"I continued to write, had luck. I even got back to the short story, placed quite a number of them with the *Evergreen Review;* my books of

poems came out, about one a year from various sources, the main being Loujon Press editions. I began a column, "Notes of a Dirty Old Man," which started with the underground newspaper *Open City* and was later picked up by *Nola Express* and the L.A. *Free Press.* The stories also came out in book form via the Black Sparrow Press and City Lights. I quit working at the age of fifty (I mean working for somebody else) and wrote my first novel, *Post Office,* in twenty nights using twenty pints of whiskey, thirty-five six-packs and eighty cigars. Black Sparrow published it. I have since been writing and surviving on my writing. John Martin of Black Sparrow was a great aid to me. He promised me $100 a month for life whether I ever wrote anything or not. What other writer ever had such luck?

"I have not much liked the writing of the centuries; I found it very staid and stilted, very near to false except in certain isolated instances. This helped keep me at it. I liked Céline's *Journey,* Villon, Neruda, early Hemingway, Salinger, all of Knut Hamsun, Fedor Dos and not much else. I still don't like much else. I'm still writing, mostly underground and hardly rich, just the way it should be. I like to play the horses once or twice a week, I like classical music, beer, I'm a romantic, a softy, I like the boxing matches and the one or two good women I have known have lifted me quite high above the rooftops.

"In 'Works About,' forgive me, there have been any number of reviews, articles, a book and a bibliography, but it's all in the closet behind this wall here and if I went in there and tried to find it all I'd begin to sweat and get very unhappy, and I know that you just don't want me to do that. Thank you, and forgive my typing and my spelling; I was never too much interested in that."

Bukowski began to emerge as a hero of the underground in the early 1960s. In 1964 Kenneth Rexroth praised him as a poet of alienation and a writer of real substance, and in 1966 the New Orleans *Outsider* magazine voted him its "outsider of the year." Since then the literary establishment, which he has persistently ridiculed, has begun to take him affectionately if somewhat gingerly to its bosom. He is the subject of an admiring critical biography by Hugh Fox, and his poetry has been enthusiastically praised in France by Sartre and Genet.

It was as a poet that he first attracted attention. Dabney Stuart has said that his "energetic, tough, and unnerving" poems are "written out of a driving necessity for expression"; that they are "a battleground on which Bukowski fights for his life and sanity" with "words and wit and sour bitterness":

> wax museums frozen into their best sterility
> are not bad, horrible but not bad. the
> cannon, think of the cannon. and toast for
> breakfast the coffee hot enough you
> know your tongue is still there. three
> geraniums outside a window, trying to be
> red and trying to be pink and trying to be
> geraniums. no wonder sometimes the women
> cry, no wonder the mules don't want
> to go up the hill. are you in a hotel room
> in Detroit looking for a cigarette? one more
> good day. a little bit of it. and as
> the nurses come out of the building after
> their shift, having had enough, eight nurses
> with different names and different places
> to go—walking across the lawn, some of them
> want cocoa and a paper, some of them want a
> hot bath, some of them want a man, some
> of them are hardly thinking at all. enough
> and not enough. arcs and pilgrims, oranges
> gutters, ferns, antibodies, boxes of
> tissue paper.
>
> (from "Something for the Tonts, the Nuns,
> the Grocery Clerks, and You")

Bukowski refers above to the stiltedness and near falseness he finds in the literature of the past; he claims that he has no use at all for conscious craftsmanship, and sets down his generally autobiographical poems as they come to him, without revision. In manner they most resemble Whitman, though in fact Bukowski's range is wider than he pretends—some of his most effective work, for example, is reminiscent of the "automatic writing" of the surrealists:

> regard me in high level of terror
> as the one who pulled down the shades
> when the president stopped to shave
> enthralled by the way the Indian turned
> through darkness and water and sand. . . .

Bukowski output is generous in quantity and uneven in quality, but at their best his poems powerfully convey the impression, as William Corrigan has said, of "the spoken voice nailed to paper." Commenting on this remark, Dabney Stuart wrote that the world Bukowski inhabits "reduces the poet to an ineffectual isolation. Sometimes he almost whines. . . . The American language, as Bukowski hears it, can be nailed to paper rather easily. But to give it form or, better still, discover a form of it, is another thing. . . . Escapists don't write great poetry."

Hugh Fox has spoken of Bukowski's "dark, negative world view . . . that hangs on from day to day, seeking out the ugly, the broken, the destroyed, with no hope (or desire) for any kind of 'ultimate' salvation." It is indeed "the ugly, the broken, the destroyed"—drunks, madmen, whores, and gamblers, the denizens of shabby apartments and squalid Los Angeles barrooms —whom he celebrates in his poetry. The same milieu provides the sad heroes and heroines of his fiction, which has on the whole been taken more seriously by establishment critics than his verse.

His first novel, *Post Office*, is a lightly reworked account of his years of hard labor with the Los Angeles post office—of bullying superiors, nagging citizenry, hard drinking, easy sex, and brilliantly executed escapes to the racetrack. A reviewer in the *Times Literary Supplement* found it a brave and vivacious book, genuinely melancholy and also convulsively funny—a "loser's string of anecdotes" which, however, lacks the connections that might have made it more than the sum of its parts. This hard-luck story is continued in *Factotum* (1976). Bukowski, disguised this time as Henry Chinaski, presents himself, as Richard Elman says, "flat out from his opening sentences, plucky but woebegone, a careerist of lousy odd jobs and one night stands in the backwaters of our great American cities." Elman found this "sensitive, moving, amusing narrative," purged of literary mannerisms and self-advertisement, a great improvement over the "goosed-up" prose of Bukowski's early fiction.

Bukowski's short stories are similar. Thomas R. Edwards, writing in the *New York Review of Books* about the large collection called *Erections, Ejaculations, Exhibitions and General Tales of Ordinary Madness*, says that these stories "make literature out of the unfashionable and unideological tastes and biases of an average Wallace voter." Edwards concludes that Bukowski "comes off best at anarchist satire in a plastic world—drinking and foul-mouthing himself into disgrace in cocktail lounges, on airliners, and at college poetry readings, showing up at a high-society Zen wedding as the only guest who's put on a tie and brought a present . . . mistaking long-haired boys for girls, caught between secret pleasure and horror at the knowledge that his poems are known and admired by some of the *cognoscenti*. For all his dedication to the old role of the macho artist . . . Bukowski has a bit of the softy, the man of sentiment, the gull in him, happily for his art; he knows as well as we do that history has passed him by and that his loss is ours too, and in some of these sad and funny stories his status as a relic isn't wholly without its sanctity."

The author has provided a record of his operation for hemorrhoids in *All the Assholes in the World and Mine.* Robert Wennersten visited him in Los Angeles in 1974 and says that he is a "broad, but not a tall man." He was "dressed in a print shirt and blue jeans pulled tight under a beer belly. His long, dark hair was combed straight back. He had a wiry beard and moustache, both flecked with grey." Hugh Fox describes him as "sagging, broken down, melting"—apparently on the verge of collapse. Yet there is also "aboslute clarity and control of his mind," and he is a man of such good will, generosity, and courage that Donald Newlove was prompted to call him, in the *Village Voice,* "the only *beloved* underground poet I've heard of." Bukowski has one daughter, Marina Louise, by his 1955 marriage to Barbara Fry. Talking to Robert Wennersten about his drinking, he said that it "joggles you out of the standard of everyday life, out of everything being the same. It yanks you out of your body and your mind and throws you up against the wall. I have the feeling that drinking is a form of suicide where you're allowed to return to life and begin all over the next day."

PRINCIPAL WORKS: *Poetry*—Flower, Fist and Bestial Wail, 1959; Longshot Poems for Broke Players, 1961; Poems and Drawings, 1962; Run With the Hunted, 1962; It Catches My Heart in Its Hands (new and selected poems, 1955-1963), 1963; Cold Dogs in the Courtyard, 1965; Crucifix in a Deathhand, 1965; At Terror Street and Agony Way, 1968; Poems Written Before Jumping Out of an Eight-Story Window, 1968; (with Philip Lamantia and Harold Norse) Penguin Modern Poets 13, 1969; The Days Run Away Like Wild Horses Over the Hills, 1969; Fire Station, 1970; Mockingbird Wish Me Luck, 1972; Burning in Water, Drowning in Flame, 1974; Women, 1978. *Novels*—Post Office, 1971; Factotum, 1976. *Short Shories*—Confessions of a Man Insane Enough to Live With Beasts, 1965; Notes of a Dirty Old Man, 1969; Erections, Ejaculations, Exhibitions and General Tales of Ordinary Madness, 1972; South of No North: Stories of the Buried Life, 1973; Life and Death in the Charity Ward, 1974. *Other*—All the Assholes in the World and Mine, 1966; A Bukowski Sampler, edited by Douglas Blazek, 1969. *As Editor* (with others)—Anthology of L.A. Poets, 1972.

ABOUT: Acton, J. (and others) Mug Shots, 1972; Contemporary Authors 17-20 1st revision, 1976; Dorbin, S. A Bibliography of Charles Bukowski, 1969; Fox, H. Charles Bukowski: A Critical and Biographical Study, 1969; Penguin Companion to Literature 3, 1971; Vinson, J. (ed.) Contemporary Poets, 1975; Writers Directory, 1976-1978. *Periodicals*—Americas February 1964; London Magazine December 1974-January 1975; New York Review of Books October 5, 1972; New York Times Book Review July 5, 1964; August 8, 1976; North American Review Fall 1969; Northwest Review Fall 1963; Outsider 3 1963 (Bukowski issue); Poetry July 1964; Times Literary Supplement November 29, 1974; Today April 1966; Village Voice November 14, 1974.

*BULATOVIĆ, MIODRAG (February 20, 1930–), Yugoslav novelist, short story writer, and dramatist, was born in a tiny village near Bijelo Polje in Montenegro, the son of Milorad and Milica (Culilković) Bulatović. At the age of eleven he saw his father, a forest ranger, killed by a brother-in-law over a property dispute, and World War II added further scars to his childhood. Brought up in extreme poverty, he escaped into a wandering life. He was treated for starvation in hospitals and jailed twice for vagrancy. He snatched a little schooling, but it was not until the age of sixteen that he read his first full-length book. Bulatović was immediately seized by a passionate urge to write: "in prose as well as in verse I described my life, the tragedy of my family, and the fate that seemed to await me. I wrote and I cried; I cried and I wrote."

He quickly established himself with his first book of stories, *Djavoli dolaze* (The Devils Are Coming, 1955), and the novel *Vuk i zvono* (The Wolf and the Bell, 1958). They introduced his highly individual style—symbolic and disjointed and full of black humor—and his perennial theme: the increasingly pitiless violence of the world, in which people must struggle fiercely to realize themselves.

The novel *Crveni petao leti prema nebu* (1959, translated by E.D. Goy as *The Red Cock Flies to Heaven),* which appeared in many languages, brought him world renown. The action takes place during a summer day when a peasant wedding is being celebrated by drunken villagers. Among those watching their antics are the last of a proud patriarchal family, who tries to bring himself to acknowledge his illegitimate son; the various outcasts of this Breughelesque community; and a Muslim youth who carries with him his sole possession, a red cockerel, the symbolic firebird or phoenix which alone is able to rise above the filth and squalor of human life.

While many critics, like one in the *Times Literary Supplement,* hailed it as an imaginative tour de force, others were distressed. Stoyan Christowe credited the author with "an abundance of creative imagination," but called the book "nothing more than a succession of cruelties, torments, brutalities, horrors, and depravities. . . . The scenes the author describes could happen in a nightmare—but the novel is not meant to be a fantasy. Perhaps the author intended his macabre wedding-feast as a symbol of our times—but there is so much symbolism in these pages that, in the end, there is no symbolism at all." In contrast Angus Wilson wrote that

**boo la' to vich

MIODRAG BULATOVIĆ

"Bulatović's supreme achievement . . . is to have taken his peasant's experience of life and made it into a living Breughel, to have created in words a terrifying and beautiful genre scene."

His second novel, *Heroj na magarcu* (1965, translated by E. D. Goy as *Hero on a Donkey*), involved Bulatović in a major scandal when it was published in the magazine *Savremenik* (Contemporary). It is a savagely satirical picture of a small town in Montenegro in 1943, occupied by unheroic Italians who live in a state of unending terror, which they relieve by drunkenness and by ever more daring forays into the delights of sex. The "hero on a donkey" not only runs a popular bar-*cum*-brothel, specializing in obscene pictures, but also conceives of himself as an embryonic partisan hero. He becomes the central figure in a novel concocted by one of the army officers, who sets about the tricky task of molding his hero's activities into myth. The Yugoslav authorities, outraged by Bulatovic's vision of war as pornography, prevented publication of the work in book form, but it was rapidly translated into many other languages. The *Times Literary Supplement* found it "a good humored, robust, anti-heroic . . . Schweiklike piece of satirical writing."

Although the "hero on a donkey" dies in that novel, he is resurrected for a series of picaresque adventures in *Rat je bio bolji* (translated by B. S. Brusar as *The War Was Better).* The earlier novel was still largely realistic, but here, as Joseph Hitrec pointed out, the author "zeroes in on the *outré,* the flagrant and monstrous in contemporary experience, and does it with a will that for sheer invention and energy might leave a Genet or a Burroughs exhausted. In this 'higher real-

ity,' to use Bulatović's own phrase, dislocation is the norm." V. D. Mihailovich called it "a first-class surrealistic trip backward into the war and postwar days, an emotional circus complete with atrocities, absurdities and dementia. . . . Bulatovic uses the war in the Balkans as a pretext to mock war in general and to show what it does to man. . . . [The novel is] an eloquent and important protest against the failures of modern civilization. Moreover its sheer zaniness and heady flights of fantasy make this . . . a delight to read."

The play *Godo je došao* (1966, translated as *Godot Has Come*) begins where Beckett stops. "My impression," writes Bulatović, "was that the world was not as Beckett showed it: it was far worse." Whereas Beckett's mysterious Godot may represent the frail hope for a better future cherished by men imprisoned in an indifferent universe, in Bulatović's play Godot actually arrives, and proves to be only a baker who throws flour in everyone's faces. The play received its premiere in Germany in 1966, where it was praised for the author's ability to create scenes of powerful grotesquerie and for his willingness to grapple with some of the fundamental problems of contemporary experience, but criticized for excessive profanity and clowning.

Bulatović has become the best known internationally of all the younger Yugoslav writers, especially in France and Germany, where his frequent brushes with authority have made him a celebrity. His Yugoslav critics have been sharply divided: some admire him as the most original among his contemporaries, though still not fully in control of his gifts; the upholders of "socialist realism," however, reproach him for wasting his talent on nightmares and accuse him of nihilism, cynicism, and pornography.

The author lives in Ljubljana with his wife, the former Vera Milovanović, whom he married in 1955. "Engaging and loquacious," according to Western visitors, Bulatović lists his personal interests as "travel, contacts with ordinary people, avoidance of fools, scoundrels, and careerists of all kinds." He says that he feels "almost physically, the approach of death—horrible and sickening—but I want to write some sincere and human books. Will I ever finish the novel of my family, the poem on liberty and my people, the novel of sad laughter, which I intend to write?"

PRINCIPAL WORKS IN ENGLISH TRANSLATION: The Red Cock Flies to Heaven, 1962 (England, The Red Cockerel); Hero on a Donkey, 1966; The War Was Better, 1972. *Stories in* Johnson, B. (ed.) New Writing in Yugoslavia, 1970; Lenski, B. (ed.) Death of a Simple Giant, 1965; New Writers 2, 1962; Atlantic December 1962.

BULLINS

ABOUT: Contemporary Authors 5-8, 1969; International Who's Who, 1977-78; Kadić, A. Contemporary Serbian Literature, 1964; Penguin Companion to Literature 2, 1969. *Periodicals*—New York Herald Tribune Book Review November 25, 1962; Times Literary Supplement May 4, 1962; December 15, 1966; Tulane Drama Review Spring 1967.

BULLINS, ED (July 2, 1935–), American dramatist, was born in Philadelphia, Pennsylvania, the son of Edward Bullins and the former Bertha Queen. His mother, a power machine operator, brought him up in a North Philadelphia slum. Bullins played guard and tackle on sandlot football teams and joined a street gang called the Jet Cobras. Ferguson Junior High was outside the Cobras' territory, "so most times I had to fight my way to school and fight my way back." He dropped out of high school when he was seventeen, and for a year ran numbers, sold bootleg whiskey, and did janitorial and other jobs. From 1952 to 1955 he served in the U.S. Navy, becoming lightweight boxing champion of his ship while serving in the Mediterranean.

The Navy gave Bullins the time and the opportunity to read, and when he went home to Philadelphia he joined an adult high school program. What else he did at that time he has not revealed, but in 1958 he decided that it would be expedient for him to get out of town. He went off to California and began part-time studies at Los Angeles County College. It was then that he began to write, turning out his first stories, essays, and poems. Some of these were published in *Citadel,* a college magazine which he himself founded. From the beginning his work showed signs of the psychological insight, the wit, and the ear for dialogue that were to characterize his plays.

Bullins began to write for the stage in 1964, when he moved to the San Francisco Bay Area and joined a creative writing program at San Francisco State College. He found that he took easily to dramatic form. "It hit the right notes in me," he says. "When I began writing plays I really became interested in people—in dealing with them. Playwriting is an exact craft. You can't fool around. You can't have too much fat on the horn. The best plays are like poems." It was in 1964 that Bullins saw *The Dutchman* and *The Slave,* a double bill by Imamu Amiri Baraka, and was profoundly encouraged to find that Baraka, already an established dramatist, "was dealing with the same qualities and conditions of black life that moved me." Bullins's own first play, a one-act "nonsense drama" called *How Do You Do,* was published in 1965. In it two black people, Roger and Dora, vent on each other the frustrations imposed on them by white society.

ED BULLINS

"The play consists mainly of word music and seesaw shifts in the relationship of the black couple," wrote Charles Marowitz. "But during these shifts, insights, like white hot coals, glower out of the play's hearth, illuminating murky corners of the white mind."

Finding it difficult at first to secure production of his plays, which were often unorthodox in form and improper in language, Bullins formed his own company of black actors. They performed his plays and those of Marvin X and other black dramatists in rented lofts and in bars and coffeehouses. *Clara's Ole Man,* one of the best-known of Bullins's early one-act plays, was staged in 1965 at the Firehouse Repertory Theatre in San Francisco. It is a cautionary tale about a young man who hopes to bed the beautiful Clara when her "ole man" is away, and is shocked to find that the person who so dominates Clara is a gross and corrupt woman. The play was revived off-Broadway in New York in 1968, when Peter Bailey called it "a no-holds-barred, sock-it-to-'em portrayal of life among black tenement dwellers in a South Philadelphia slum."

Caught up in the black revolutionary fervor of the mid-1960s, Bullins served briefly as cultural minister of the Black Panthers and was one of the founders of Black House, the Panthers' Bay Area headquarters. He left the movement in 1967, when a clash between its political and cultural wings left him permanently disillusioned with political ideologies (though not with black militancy). The same year, 1967, Bullins left California and went to New York, where he joined the New Lafayette Theatre then being launched in Harlem by Robert Macbeth. He served the New Lafayette first as resident dramatist and later, beginning in 1971, as associate director, and says the theatre both "inspired and sustained" him. From 1968 to 1972 he also conducted a writers' workshop there, and edited the magazine *Black Theatre*.

Meanwhile, Bullins's own reputation was spreading far beyond the New Lafayette and the black community. Excerpts from his play *A Son, Come Home* were shown on National Educational Television in 1968. The same year this play was performed off-Broadway at the American Place Theatre with two other Bullins one-acters, *Clara's Ole Man* and *The Electronic Nigger,* and the latter was also given a lunchtime production in London. Set in a Southern California community college, it centers on a science-obsessed black student who constantly interrupts his creative writing class with irrelevant scientific data, systematically destroying the bookish instructor. It seemed to reviewers both funny and sharply observed. *The Gentleman Caller* is a much darker play, an allegory about the suicidal decadence of white society that ends with a black maid killing her white employer; it was staged in 1969 at the Brooklyn Academy of Music.

By this time Bullins had embarked on what Jack Kroll has called "one of the most extraordinary projects an American playwright has ever attempted"—a cycle of twenty plays intended to provide a dramatic history of black people in America in the twentieth century. The cycle begins with *In the Wine Time* (1968), which like most of the plays Bullins produced at this time had its first production at the New Lafayette Theatre. It is a rather Odetsian portrait of a black family in Harlem: the drifter Cliff Dawson, his embittered and exhausted wife, and their young nephew Ray. Cliff and his wife have very different ideas of what Ray should be and do, trying to fulfill through him their own frustrated hopes; in the end the contest is decided by the casual violence of the ghetto. *Choice*'s reviewer thought this Bullins's best play to date, praising in particular his use of the "pungent, frequently poetic language of the streets." Cliff Dawson reappears in the next play in Bullins's Twentieth Century Cycle, *In New England Winter,* produced at the New Lafayette in 1969 and at the Henry Street Playhouse in 1971. Here Cliff, recently released from prison and separated from his wife, plans a bank robbery with some other small-time criminals. The complicated plot left some reviewers confused.

Steve Benson, the central character in *The Duplex,* is Cliff's younger half-brother. Steve (who is sometimes taken to be Bullins's spokes-

man and *alter ego*) is an altogether more serious and thoughtful man than his brother. We encounter him in this play as a young student living in a run-down rooming-house in southern California and immersed in a troubled love affair with his landlady. With this play, wrote John M. Reilly, "the theme of the cycle is fully established: the difficulties of love, and by implication group solidarity, and the complicity of people in disabling themselves. . . . [Steve Benson] hesitates between submission to the anodynes of alcohol and sex and the resolution to direct his own life. The forces for submission are so powerful that hesitation seems the only plausible action for him in the brief time of the play, for even if he strikes out on his own he must hurt others. It is a situation worthy of the blues, and it is part of Bullins' genius that he disavows either a strictly sociological or psychological presentation. He conveys clearly enough the fact that his characters are subject to socially caused conditions; yet his sympathy for them is so great, his identification with them so strong, that he rejects either a portrayal of them as victims or the easy sentiment of pity."

First seen at the New Lafayette in 1970, *The Duplex* was revived at the Forum Theatre of Lincoln Center in 1972 in a production that Bullins denounced as a "darkie minstrel show." Knowing the propaganda value of controversy, Bullins often sends out combative letters and statements in order "to cause a play in the real world. They set a tone. They let people know where I'm coming from." Most critics felt that his denunciation of the Lincoln Center production was a gambit of this sort rather than a serious complaint. John Simon, at any rate, failed to find anything "seriously wrong with the direction or anything seriously right about the play itself." Edith Oliver, on the other hand, called it Bullins's most ambitious play "and, in spite of some weaknesses, his best so far," and this was the majority opinion. Catharine Hughes wrote that "it is a mixture of styles, from farce to tragedy, a play that works within its own definition of theatre (and mine)."

Like its predecessors in the cycle, *The Fabulous Miss Marie* (New Lafayette, 1971) focuses on a character introduced briefly in the preceding play, in this case a former nightclub dancer, earthy, tough, and witty. A jazz group playing on stage and asides to the audience are among the vaudeville devices employed in the play, which *Variety* found "dramatically sound," holding "a clear, precise mirror up to important aspects of contemporary black life. There is not a false or wrong character." Other plays in the cycle include *Home Boy,* which reached off-

135

Broadway in 1976 and features songs with lyrics by Bullins and music by Aaron Bell, and *The Corner,* a short piece examining a moment of decision in Cliff Dawson's early life.

Not all of Bullin's recent plays have been conceived as part of his Twentieth Century Cycle. *The Pig Pen* (American Place Theatre, 1970) puts on stage a booze-drug-and-sex party in the course of which the guests learn of the assassination of Malcolm X. It had its admirers, but George Oppenheimer condemned it roundly as "theatrical anarchy by a group of non-actors in a non-play, noisy, ugly, meaningless and unbearably dull." *Goin' a Buffalo,* staged (and filmed) at the New Lafayette in 1968 and revived at the WPA Theatre in New York in 1972, is set in Los Angeles, and examines the futile lives and misguided ambitions of Pandora, a black prostitute, and two ex-cons—her husband, Curt, and his friend Art.

House Party, which has music by Pat Patrick and lyrics by Bullins, brings on stage one at a time a company of nine actors, each of whom presents a variety of monologues and character sketches—portraying for example Josephine Baker's maid, a Harlem mother, a black politician, drama critic, woman poet, dope-dealer. Walter Kerr called it a "cavalier collage" by "a writer who hasn't bothered to roll up his sleeves," but Edith Oliver was impressed: "By the time the troupe is through, every aspect of black life—bleak and joyous, sexual, social and private—appears to have been covered in one way or another. Mr. Bullins' writing has never been stronger; his irony, his understanding, his ability to catch a whole life in a single speech or song lyric, and his mocking, parodic humor have never been more apparent."

There was a great deal more praise than criticism for *The Taking of Miss Janie,* a companion piece to *The Pig Pen,* involving a number of the same characters. It examines the effects on individual relationships of the erosion of the political idealism of the 1960s, the gradual fading of the belief that a new era of social justice and progress was beginning. The play begins and ends with the rape by a black poet of a condescending white woman who has always insisted that their friendship must remain platonic. First produced in 1974 at the New Federal Theatre in New York, it transferred the following year to the Mitzi Newhouse Theatre, Lincoln Center, and won the New York Drama Critics' Circle Award as the best play of the season as well as two Obie awards. Bullins's subsequent plays include *Jo Anne!* (1976), a mingling of fact and fantasy based on the case of Joan Little, a young black prisoner charged with the ice-pick murder of her white jailer, and *I Am Lucy Terry* (1976), written for young people, which uses words, music, and dance to tell the story of America's first black poet. *Sepia Star* (1977), a musical about a rhythm-and-blues singer, was written in collaboration with a white composer, Mildred Kayden, who also worked with Bullins on *Storyville,* produced earlier at the University of California, San Diego.

A collection of Bullins's early short stories was published in 1971 as *The Hungered One,* and moderately well received, though it attracted less attention than his novel *The Reluctant Rapist* (1973). This follows the vicissitudes of Steve Benson in the late 1940s and early 1950s, drawing some of its scenes and themes from Bullins's plays, and using a technique which enables him to present Benson's past and present simultaneously. "To commit rape," Benson says, "is to commit oneself to one's own death," so (he argues) he "gambles with death" for all the women he rapes. J. H. Bryant thought that "Steve Benson the rapist is a metaphor of Ed Bullins the playwright," who "rips, tears, rapes ... blows apart black life. . . . There are long passages of reflection, and there are references to books and authors. But this isn't a philosophical novel. It is a novel of the felt texture of living, especially of living black."

Financial problems closed the New Lafayette Theatre in 1973. The same year Bullins was playwright-in-residence at the American Place Theatre, and in 1975 he became unit coordinator at the New York Shakespeare Festival Theatre's writers' workshop. He was editor of a special black dramatists' issue of *Drama Review* (Summer 1968) and of the two anthologies *New Plays From the Black Theatre* and *The New Lafayette Theatre Presents.* He has taught at Dartmouth and Fordham, and has been a visiting lecturer at Talladega College in Alabama and other colleges. He was a Guggenheim fellow in 1971 and received Rockefeller grants in 1968, 1970, and 1972. Bullins won a Drama Desk–Vernon Rice Award for "outstanding achievement in the off-Broadway theatre" in 1967–1968 and an Obie Award in 1971. He has an honorary doctorate (1976) from Columbia College, Chicago.

The author is five feet six inches tall and "his middle is slowly getting away from him into a paunch." He is said to have "small, coolly observant eyes and a round, fleshy face." Bullins, who likes to vary his image, is sometimes clean-shaven and sometimes bearded; in the same spirit, he sometimes shaves his head. Jervis Anderson, who wrote his *New Yorker* profile, says that Bullins rarely smiles, but is soft-spoken, "easy-going and unassertive" in manner. He is married to the former Trixie Warner, a native of Montserrat in the British West Indies. They live in the Bronx and have children, but Bullins, who refuses to discuss his private life, does not say how many. He lists as his favorite recreations "traveling and womanizing."

According to an article in *Current Biography,* Bullins had by 1977 written more than fifty plays. He believes that black writers have "revolutionized the American theatre" and he is himself "in the forefront of American playwrights of the black experience. . . . He has written of—and for—ordinary black people, resilient ghetto dwellers of the urban North, in a language that is harsh, sometimes obscene, but touched with lyricism." He is "sure of his skill and ambitious to be included one day among the most important playwrights America has ever produced." John M. Reilly says that Bullins's plays "have been characterized variously as 'theatre of reality' (that is his own term), 'revolutionary drama,' and 'surnaturism.' Each description has validity, but the most meaningful term for Bullins's work may be 'nationalist.' On one level the nationalism appears in a rejection of white American bourgeois culture. More profoundly, though, Bullins's plays are nationalist in the same way that Black music is nationalist. Like the blues writer, Bullins uses common life—troubles related to finding love or coping with frustration—as subject, the popular idiom for expression." Several critics have praised his "extraordinary ability to make an audience feel that it is catching the characters unaware in the act of living." Bullins himself says: "It's very strange that some people will say that I'm a raving radical and others will say that Bullins doesn't stand for anything. . . . We are not protesting to whites. We are having a discourse, a discussion, a dialogue between black and black, writers and the audience."

PRINCIPAL PUBLISHED WORKS: *Plays*—How Do You Do: A Nonsense Drama, 1967 (*also in* Black Dialogue July-August 1965); In New England Winter (*in* New Plays for the Black Theatre, edited by Ed Bullins, 1969); Five Plays (Goin' a Buffalo; In the Wine Time; The Electronic Nigger; A Son, Come Home; Clara's Ole Man), 1969 (*in* England, The Electronic Nigger and Other Plays); State Office Building Curse (*in* Drama Review September 1970); The Duplex: a Black Love Fable in Four Movements, 1971; The Gentleman Caller, 1971 (*also in* Illuminations 5, 1968); Four Dynamite Plays (It Bees Dat Way; Death List; The Pig Pen; Night of the Beast), 1971; The Corner (*in* Black Drama Anthology, edited by Woodie King and Ron Milner, 1972); Dialect Determinism (*in* Spontaneous Combustion, edited by Rochelle Owens, 1972); The Theme is Blackness: The Corner and Other Plays (contains fifteen plays by Bullins, some of them very short), 1973; The Fabulous Miss Marie (*in* The New Lafayette Theatre Presents, edited by Ed Bullins, 1974). *Fiction*—The Hungered One: Early Writings, 1971; The Reluctant Rapist, 1973. *Poetry*—To Raise the Dead and Foretell the Future, 1971. *As Editor*—New Plays from the Black Theatre, 1969; The New Lafayette Theatre Presents, 1974.

ABOUT: Contemporary Authors 49–52, 1975; Current Biography, 1978; Hatch, J.V. Black Image on the American Stage, 1970; Vinson, J. (ed.) Contemporary Dramatists, 1977; Who's Who in America, 1976–1977; Who's Who in the Theatre, 1977. *Periodicals*—Ebony September 1968; Nation November 12, 1973; National Observer August 9, 1971; New York Times September 22, 1971; November 4, 1973; May 11, 1975; May 18, 1975; August 19, 1977; New York Times Book Review June 20, 1971; September 30, 1973; New Yorker June 16, 1973; November 5, 1973; Newsday July 27, 1975; Newsweek March 20, 1972; Times Literary Supplement February 12, 1971; Washington Post August 21, 1976.

BYRNE, JOHN KEYES. *See* "LEONARD, HUGH"

CABRAL DE MELO NETO, JOÃO. *See* MELO NETO, JOÃO CABRAL DE

*CABRERA INFANTE, GUILLERMO ("G. Cain") (April 22, 1929–), Cuban novelist and short story writer, writes: "I was born in Gibara, a small city on the Northern coast of Cuba's Oriente Province (not far from where both Batista and Fidel Castro were born), the second child and first son of Guillermo Cabrera, a journalist, and Zoila Infante, a local Communist beauty. (My parents were to become in fact, barely five years later, founders of the Partido Comunista, providing their offspring with enough CP antibodies to be effectively vaccinated against revolutionary measles for life—a reactionary feat in itself if one takes into account that none other than Vladimir Ilyich Ulyanov [Lenin] was born on the same date!) At twenty-nine days old I went to the movies for the first time with my mother and at three years old I was able to read films better than books, which I couldn't read till I was four: this fact marked my life forever, even more so if you consider that I taught myself to read by concentrating on deciphering the captions in the balloons in *Dick Tracy* and *Tarzan.* I studied at a Quaker school and when I was twelve my family emigrated to the capital, Havana becoming my greatest adventure: life in a big city. Being extremely poor I managed to study in high school and at the school of journalism, while working at the same time in a medley of jobs. Before graduating, in 1952, I was imprisoned and later fined for publishing a short story with four-letter words *in English.* In 1953-1954 I started writing a movie column under the pseudonym of G. Cain in *Carteles* magazine, of which I became fiction editor in 1957. After the Revolution, in 1959, I briefly

*ca brâr' a in fan' tã

CABRERA INFANTE

Utermohlen

GUILLERMO CABRERA INFANTE

held several official posts but more significantly to me, I founded *Lunes,* a cultural magazine and literary supplement of *Revolución,* the semi-official newspaper. I edited it until the magazine was banned by the Government in 1961. I first married in 1953 and had two daughters, Ana and Carola; then I got a divorce in 1961 (a decisive year: the year of the Bay of Pigs invasion) and married again to Miriam Gómez, a young actress. In 1960 I published my first book, *Así en la paz como en la guerra,* a collection of short stories which, translated into French, was nominated in 1962 for the Prix International de Littérature. The same year I was officially sent to Brussels as cultural attaché. In 1963 I published *Un Oficio del Siglo XX,* a collection of movie reviews. The next year I was promoted to *chargé d'affaires* in Belgium and my novel, *Three Trapped Tigers,* won the prestigious Spanish prize Joan Petit-Biblioteca Breve. In 1965 I traveled to Havana to my mother's funeral and due to some political scheming I was retained in Cuba for four months before being allowed to leave the country, this time without any official job and for good. My novel was banned in Spain (where I lived for a year, 1965-1966) and was not published until 1967, when I was already living in London, earning a living by writing articles (in Spanish) and doctoring film scripts (in English). One of those scripts was made into a lousy film in 1968. In 1970 I went to Hollywood, where a screenplay of mine was made into a successful film, titled *Vanishing Point,* and written under the pseudonym of Guillermo Cain. In 1971 I got a Guggenheim Fellowship for creative writing. In 1972, while writing the script of *Under the Volcano,* I suffered a serious nervous

breakdown—and came out of it by writing and re-writing several books almost at the same time: *Vista del Amanecer en el Trópico, O,* and *Exorcismos de Esti(l)o,* published in Spain, respectively and after the first book was again banned by the Spanish censorship, in 1974, 1975, 1976. I must add that all my books are considered forbidden fruits in Cuba. I am at the moment writing a very long novel, *Cuerpos Divinos,* which I will stop for a while to do some more screenwriting. I must also add that I consider my novel *Three Trapped Tigers,* its American version, a book written in English more than a translated one. My second book to appear in the USA, *View of Dawn in the Tropics,* is an effort to destroy the myth of (Cuban) History by creating histories which contain the historical passages as capsules of language, another translation of life into literature."

Although Cabrera Infante claims above to have been "effectively vaccinated against revolutionary measles" in infancy, he did in fact contribute in various ways to the overthrow of the Batista dictatorship. According to his own account in Rita Guibert's *Seven Voices,* he helped to edit the then clandestine magazine *Revolución,* transported arms, and gave refuge to terrorists and revolutionaries in his Havana home. Disillusionment set in not long after Castro seized power in 1959; it became complete with the suppression in 1961 of *Lunes,* which in Cabrera Infante's view represented "the most liberal cultural faction within the revolution." Later in 1961, when he was sent to Brussels as cultural attaché, he felt himself to be "a more or less official exile." Since then he has come to regard his exile as permanent. In Cuba, he believes, Castro has turned "paranoia . . . into a political system," creating a Stalinist police state.

Most of the work he has so far published deals, however, with the last years of the Batista regime. It was during these years that he wrote all but one of the fourteen stories collected in his first book, *Así en la paz como en la guerra* (In Peace As In War, 1960). These stories form a coherent picture of Cuban life during the 1950s among the middle classes, where "the contradictions seem more glaring." His themes—the loss of virginity, racial discrimination, adultery—are colored by his awareness of the human misery, corruption, and injustice all around him. And these vignettes of a fragile society are interspersed with fifteen trenchant and uncompromising sketches of brutality, violence, and death as purveyed by Batista's thugs.

The counterpoint established between the stories and the sketches suggests very pointedly the connection between the breakdown of values in individual relationships and the impersonal machinery of political tyranny outside. The author's uninhibited frankness, his use of colloquial speech inflections, and his constant alternation between humor and tragedy, all foreshadow the manner and tone of his masterpiece *Tres tristes tigres* (1967, translated as *Three Trapped Tigers*). It should be made clear that it was an earlier and much more overtly political version of this novel which received the Joan Petit-Biblioteca Breve prize in 1964; it was rewritten in its present form when Cabrera Infante became convinced of the incompatibility of literature and politics.

Tres tristes tigres (generally known as *TTT*) established Cabrera Infante as one of the most original and witty novelists to have emerged in Latin America. It has no plot in the accepted sense, but develops from a carefully structured collage of monologues, some spoken and some written in letter form, in the vernacular of Havana in the late 1950s. The principal speakers are a group of young men: Códac (a photographer), Eribó (a *bongosero* or drummer), Silvestre (a writer), Arsenio Cué (a television actor), and the shadowy Bustrófedon (an oral poet, who leaves behind when he dies tape recordings of his linguistic experiments). Their confessions and conversations reconstruct a prerevolutionary Havana of nightclubs, alcohol, drugs, jazz, bolero singers, homosexuals, bisexuals, whores, and gangsters, its authenticity reinforced by a scrupulous regard for topographical detail.

A long and extremely ambitious novel, *Tres tristes tigres* (the title is from a treacherous tongue twister) functions on several levels. It forms an intimate and deeply nostalgic diary of the nocturnal adventures and discussions of a group of friends—of their efforts, as David Gallagher put it, "to clutch a sort of private solidarity, to make a defiant private stand. That stand is composed of inexhaustible humor, of a relentless effort to keep the party going." But humor is "a fragile weapon. . . . against sadness, against mediocrity, against the limitations of an underdeveloped island," and the novel is also an indictment of those limitations, a portrait of Cuba as a society at the end of its tether, a grotesque parody of European and North American civilization.

Cabrera Infante says that *TTT* "started from the concept of oral literature, of writing derived from speech and the voice"—that it carries out "acts of terrorism against the established Spanish language" in its attempts to render the "spoken Cuban" of the streets. Cabrera Infante finds in the street talk of bus drivers and whores

an authenticity and vitality that for him is lacking in the elegant periods of high literature. To that extent *TTT* is a novel about literature—about how a novel should be written—and it supplies, by way of contrast with its own procedures, parodies of seven distinguished Cuban writers, each of them describing with self-conscious artistry the death of Trotsky.

The novel is also (the author insists) "a joke lasting for about five hundred pages," packed with puns, anagrams, palindromes, paradoxes, tongue twisters, number games, "spanglish," and pastiches, and with typographical errors which are allowed to impose their own perverse logic on what is said and done. The last word of the novel (and its subject, the author claims) is *traditori*—"traitors"—and this refers, no doubt, to political treason, to the treason of the writer against the reality he seeks to capture, and perhaps to the treacherous distortions of the critics into whose hands the book must fall. Interesting comparisons have been made between *TTT* and the *Satyricon* of Petronius, Sterne's *Tristram Shandy*, and *Alice in Wonderland*, and, nearer home, with the labyrinthine fantasies of Jorge Luis Borges, whom Cabrera Infante looks to as "our Gogol and our Pushkin rolled in one."

Tres tristes tigres was rendered into English by the author in collaboration with Donald Gardner and Suzanne Jill Levine and published in 1971 as *Three Trapped Tigers*. As he says above, Cabrera Infante regards the English version as a recreation rather than a translation of the original. He says that "narrative in the traditional sense was not vital to the book" and "I was more interested in the tempo, the beat and rhythms of writing and speech than in finding equivalent versions in words. . . . I acted as jury, prosecution, and defense of my text, and the translation was the true culprit. Thus I sentenced parts of the book to disappear or reappear at my summons, or condemned them to oblivion according to a judgment that always seemed to the translator obscure, strange, inexplicable. . . . This form of poetic justice can never betray the original book." The result seemed to David Gallagher "one of the most inventive novels that has come out of Latin America" and one of the funniest books to have appeared in Spanish since *Don Quixote;* "it has savagely refreshed an often portentously solemn heritage."

Rita Guibert, who interviewed Cabrera Infante in 1970, describes him as a man "of medium height, with spectacled, dark eyes, rather long straight black hair and a mustache drooping down to his bearded chin. . . . [He] talks at breakneck speed, but his talk is a feast of words." Cabrera Infante says that his position among Latin American writers is "one of absolute independence and therefore great isolation." He is an anti-utopian and a skeptic, who believes that "not a single corpus of irrefutable ideas exists," and says that "like all skeptics I feel drawn to stoicism." His skepticism obviously extends to such intellectual fashions as Structuralism—asked for his opinion of Lévi-Strauss he pretended to believe that the French anthropologist was the manufacturer of jeans. He regards "literature as a game, a complicated game, abstract and concrete at the same time, taking place in a physical plane—the page—and on the various mental planes of memory, imagination, and thought." He would like his contribution to the contemporary novel in Spanish to be judged as "the shaky foundations of a future movement to disrespectfulness."

PRINCIPAL WORKS IN ENGLISH TRANSLATION: Three Trapped Tigers, 1971. *Stories in* Cohen, J.M. (ed.) Latin American Writing Today, 1967; Cohen, J.M. (ed.) Writers in the New Cuba, 1967. *As translator*—Dubliners, by James Joyce, 1972.

ABOUT: Benedetti, M. (and others) Literatura y arte nuevo en Cuba, 1971; Franco, J. Spanish American Literature Since Independence, 1973; Gallagher, D.P. Modern Latin American Literature, 1973; Guibert, R. Seven Voices, 1973; Lafforgue, J. (ed.) Nueva Novela Latino americana, 1969; Monegal, F.R. El Boom de la Novela Latino americana, 1972; Monegal, F.R. El Arte de Narrar, 1968; Ortega, J. La Contemplación y la Fiesta, 1969; Ortega, J. Relato de la Utopia, 1973; Ortega, J. (and others) Guillermo Cabrera Infante, 1974; Sánchez-Boudy, J. La Nueva Novela Hispano americana y Tres Tristes Tigres, 1971; Schwartz, K. A New History of Spanish American Fiction, 1971; Souza, R.D. Major Cuban Novelists, 1976.

"CAEIRO, ALBERTO." *See* PESSOA, FERNANDO

CAGE, JOHN (September 5, 1912–), American composer and writer, was born in Los Angeles, California, the only child of John Milton Cage and the former Lucretia Harvey. His father was an electrical engineer well known as an inventor, and the family moved about a great deal as his fortunes waxed and waned. John Cage attended schools in Ann Arbor and Detroit before graduating in 1928 from Los Angeles High School (where he was class valedictorian), and entering Pomona College, Claremont, California. In 1930, losing interest in college, he sailed for France, where he spent six months studying architecture under a young and very modern architect named Goldfinger. "To be an architect, one must devote one's life solely to architecture," Goldfinger said one day to a

JOHN CAGE

friend, and Cage, overhearing this, explained that there were too many other things to do, and left.

Cage had had piano lessons as a child and in Paris was accepted as a pupil by Lazare Lévy. He took only two lessons: "I could see that his teaching would lead to technical accomplishment, but I wasn't really interested in that. Meanwhile he sent me to a Bach festival, where I finally discovered Bach—you can imagine how delighted I was over that! On my own, I went to a concert of modern music by the pianist John Kirkpatrick, who really got me interested in modern music. He played Stravinsky, Scriabin, and some other things. . . . I began spending a lot of time playing as much of this music as I could on the piano."

Still unready to devote himself exclusively to any one of the arts, Cage spent the next year wandering through Europe, writing poetry, painting, and composing: "My attitude then was that one could do all these things—writing, painting, even dancing—without technical training. . . . The trouble was that the music I wrote sounded extremely displeasing to my own ear when I played it." Cage had thus traveled a good deal, both geographically and intellectually, before he returned to Los Angeles in the fall of 1931 and decided that music was his vocation.

Cage took a job as a gardener in a Santa Monica auto court, supplementing his income by selling tickets door-to-door for lectures by himself on modern painting and music—lectures which he prepared week by week as he went along. Seeking information about Arnold Schönberg, he contacted a disciple of the composer, the pianist Richard Bühlig, who was sufficiently impressed to take him on as a pupil. Cage developed a rigidly structured method of composition not unlike Schönberg's serialism, though using not twelve tones but twenty-five. In 1933 he went to New York to study harmony and composition with Henry Cowell at the New School for Social Research and with Adolf Weiss, a former pupil of Schönberg's. The following year he returned to California and studied for two years with Schönberg himself—"a magnificent teacher, who always gave the impression that he was putting us in touch with the musical principles."

At this time Cage was earning his living at various casual jobs—as a dishwasher, as a researcher, and in a Los Angeles craft shop. One day in 1935 a young art student came into the shop who, though she left without speaking to him, deeply impressed Cage. On her second visit Cage invited her to dinner and during the meal asked her to marry him. She was Xenia Andreyevna Kashevarova, one of the six striking and talented daughters of a Russian Orthodox priest from Juneau, Alaska. They were married in June 1935 and divorced ten years later. In 1936 Cage went as a dancing-class accompanist and composer to the Cornish School, Seattle, where he remained until 1938, later moving east to teach at the Chicago School of Design (1941–1942).

During the 1930s, Cage developed new forms of percussion music altogether unique in tone. Critics seeking the sources of his highly original approach to music cite the composer's own temperament, the influence of oriental ideas, especially Zen Buddhism (which Cage studied with D. T. Suzuki and Alan Watts), the theory of Dadaism, and the example of such composers as Varèse, who, in Cage's words, "fathered forth noise into twentieth-century music." Cage argued that whereas music in the past had been a matter of consonance opposed to dissonance, in the immediate future it would be a matter of so-called musical sounds opposed to noise. In 1938, the better to illustrate and apply his theories, Cage invented his "prepared piano" by putting bolts, pieces of rubber, bamboo slats, and other objects between the strings of an ordinary concert piano, transforming it into a sort of percussive orchestra rather like an Indonesian gamelan orchestra.

The young dancer and choreographer Merce Cunningham seized on Cage's compositions as the musical equivalent of his own ideas about ballet, and Cage served as Cunningham's musical director from 1944 to 1966. Conventional members of the musical establishment were naturally horrified by Cage's experiments, but

their importance was recognized in 1949 when he received a Guggenheim fellowship and an award from the National Academy of Arts and Letters for "extending the boundaries of music." In 1952 Cage "open[ed] the doors of music to the sounds which happen to be in the environment" with the famous *4' 33"*, in which a pianist sits motionless at the piano for four minutes, thirty-three seconds, the only sounds being those made by the audience (including its protests). From 1955 to 1960 Cage taught composition at the New School for Social Research in New York.

Cage's first book, written in collaboration with Kathleen Hoover and published in 1959, was a study of the American composer Virgil Thomson written "with warmth and with discrimination." This was followed in 1961 by *Silence,* collecting lectures and essays produced over a period of twenty years, some of them highly experimental in manner. Cage writes about Satie and Varèse, the history and future of experimental music in the United States, ballet and ballet music, and the young artist Robert Rauschenberg. The latter collaborated with Cage and Cunningham in their ballets and in such events as *Theater Piece,* the famous pioneer "Happening" they organized in 1952 at Black Mountain College (where Cage taught summers in 1948–1952). The collection also includes the "stories-in-a-paragraph" that make up Cage's autobiography, and many jokes and anecdotes that have nothing to do with music.

The book had an ecstatic reception, even from many critics who disliked Cage's work and influence as a composer, and some recognized that these writings had been composed with as much skill and originality as his music. Nicólas Slonimsky called Cage "a master of verbal expression, who juggles with words and lines in free verse with amazing skill, and in total disregard of all literary conventions." Commending in particular the "numbing and haunting" piece called "Lecture on Nothing," Slonimsky drew attention to the influence of Gertrude Stein "in the relentless hammering on recurrent words and syllables until the verbal structure begins to crumble. . . . *Silence* is a wonderfully stimulating compendium of outrageous nonsense that makes a lot of sense."

Again and again in these pieces Cage ponders the purpose of music and of art in general, and in one of them he describes the revelation that came to him in the late 1940s, when he asked a young Indian student what she had been taught at home was the purpose of music. She replied that her teacher had said that the function of music was to "to sober and quiet the mind, thus rendering it susceptible to divine influence." Cage writes: "I was tremendously struck by this. And then something really extraordinary happened. . . . [A colleague] came across a statement by the seventeenth-century English composer Thomas Mace expressing the same idea in almost exactly the same words. I decided then and there that this *was* the proper purpose of music. In time, I also came to see that all art before the Renaissance, both Oriental and Western, had shared this same basis, that Oriental art had continued to do so right along, and that the Renaissance idea of self-expressive art was therefore heretical."

This startling idea led Cage to the conclusion that art is or should be "purposeless play . . . not an attempt to bring order out of chaos nor to suggest improvements in creation, but simply to wake up to the very life we're living, which is so excellent once one gets one's mind and one's desires out of the way and lets it act of its own accord." From here it is only a step to Cage's pursuit of the complete depersonalization of creativity, through a "will-less" state of contemplation, or through the use of chance procedures like throwing dice, or allowing the imperfections in a piece of manuscript paper to decide the placing of notes. The listener to music produced in these ways is not to "attempt to understand something that is being said, for, if something were being said, the sounds would be given the shapes of words. Just an attention to the activity of sounds."

Increasingly, Cage's works have been major environmental extravaganzas, like his "Musicircus," in which all the musical talents of a particular area are invited to play anything they choose at the same time and place. Cage was also one of the first to use the new medium of magnetic tape to make electronic music, attracted by the random effects it makes possible. In 1951 he organized a group of musicians and engineers to experiment with the medium, and in 1958 spent four months at the Studio di Fonologia in Milan, where he recorded *Fontana Mix.* Cage was a fellow of the Center for Advanced Studies at Wesleyan University in 1960–1961, composer in residence at the University of Cincinnati in 1967, and research professor at the Center for Advanced Studies, University of Illinois, in 1967–1969. At Illinois he collaborated with Lejaren Hiller to produce his most elaborate work, *HPSCHD,* which employs seven harpsichords, fifty-two computer-generated tapes, and fifty-nine amplifiers and speakers, as well as forty movies and over six thousand slides dealing with manned space flight.

A Year From Monday, a second collection of lectures and essays, appeared in 1967, and included "diaries" for the three years beginning in 1965—long essays, each a "mosiac of ideas, statements, words, and stories." This collection suggested to Calvin Tomkins that Cage was "less and less interested in composing music and more and more interested in improving society." And certainly these pieces do show a significant change of attitude—less insistence on withdrawal and "will-lessness," and a growing belief that the author should bring his private thought processes out into the new electronic world "where our central nervous system effectively now is." Howard Junker thought that this book lacked "the mystic fervor . . . with which *Silence* challenged the comforts and constraints of musical tradition," but Michael Kirby was profoundly impressed and wrote: "It must be said that John Cage demonstrates in an unpretentious, subtle and forceful way the profound spiritual basis of avant-garde art."

Cage's writings between 1967 and 1972 were published in 1973 as *M,* a title arrived at with the help of *I-Ching,* the Chinese "book of changes." Indeed the whole book is organized around words and names beginning with M, and Cage's observations, insights, and quotations are arranged in a sequence also decided by *I-Ching.* The collection contains four more annual "diaries," together with dadaistic poems and verbal games, and a "Mushroom Book" in which Cage discourses learnedly on the collecting and cooking of fungi, another of his passions. The book as a whole shows that the author's interest in social philosophy has continued to increase at the expense of his interest in music. To his old heroes like Buckminster Fuller Cage now adds new ones like Mao Tse-tung. Donal Henehan wrote that "there is a good deal in *M* that will strike some readers as trivial or worse. . . . [But] under the robes of the Zen priest, the dice-throwing shaman, the chaos-embracing composer and the poet of noble savagery, we have no trouble finding John Cage the apostle of know-how and benign technology. . . . He preaches artistic and social anarchy, but always with a cheerful humor and a practical man's concern for the society he must continue to live in."

Notations (1969), compiled by Cage with Alison Knowles, is a collection of reproductions of musical manuscripts donated by over two hundred and sixty composers, with comments by the composers and the compilers. "This handsome book," as one reviewer called it, "an amazing and inexhaustible treat," was part of a fundraising scheme for a foundation through which Cage helps musicians and other artists. Cage himself received a grant from the Thorne Music

Fund in 1967–1969. He was elected to the National Institute of Arts and Letters in 1968. He has put "know-how and benign technology" at the service of happenstance by employing a computerized *I-Ching* in such recent compositions as *Renga With Apartment House 1776,* commissioned for the Bicentennial by the National Endowment for the Arts and the Boston Symphony Orchestra.

Cage's disciples among younger American composers include Earle Brown and Morton Feldman, and his interest in chance procedures has been a decisive factor in the growth of aleatory music, but it is probably true to say that his ideas have been more influential than his music. As Robert Hughes has remarked, "if it can be said that advanced art in America through the '50s and early '60s had one single native guru, that man was Cage: at once the most avant-garde and the most transparent of composers, the Marcel Duchamp of music, the man who erected combinations of silence and random sound into an aesthetic strategy in order to give art the inclusive density of life." Arnold Schönberg described Cage as "not a composer, but an inventor—of genius," while Virgil Thomson maintains that his "aim with music, like Samson's in the pagan temple, has long been clearly destructive." Aaron Copland believes that Cage "is really interested in the experimental attitude, not in creating great eternal masterpieces but in amusing himself on the highest level with new notions concerning music."

According to Calvin Tomkins, Cage "gives the impression of one who finds his own life a continually delightful and surprising affair." In spite of his gray beard, he looks considerably younger than he is. Cage has not remarried, and since 1954 has lived alone and very modestly in a small cottage in the Gate Hill cooperative community in Stony Point, New York. He was one of the founders in 1962 of the New York Mycological Society.

PRINCIPAL LITERARY WORKS: (with Kathleen Hoover) Virgil Thomson, 1959; Silence: Lectures and Writings, 1961; A Year From Monday, 1967; (as editor, with Alison Knowles) Notations, 1969; M: Writings 1967–1972, 1973.

ABOUT: Contemporary Authors 13–16 1st revision, 1975; Current Biography, 1962; Ewen, D. Composers of Tomorrow's Music, 1971; Ewen, D. (ed.) Composers Since 1900, 1969; Ewen, D. The World of Twentieth Century Music, 1968; International Who's Who, 1977–78; Kostelanetz, R. (ed.) John Cage, 1970; Kostelanetz, R. Master Minds, 1969; Salzman, E. Twentieth Century Music, 1967; Scholes, P.A. (ed.) The Oxford Companion to Music, 1970; Tomkins, C. The Bride and the Bachelors, 1965; Vinton, J. (ed.) Dictionary of Twentieth-Century Music, 1974; Who's Who in America 1976–1977; Yates, P. Twentieth Century Music, 1967. *Periodicals*—American Scholar Spring 1968; Antioch

Review Summer 1962; Art and Architecture May 1962; Christian Science Monitor December 14, 1961; Commonweal January 12, 1962; Guardian June 14, 1976; Hi Fi November 1972; Music December 1976; New Republic January 6, 1968; New York Times February 14, 1960; October 12, 1976; July 17, 1977; New York Times Book Review January 21, 1968; September 23, 1973; New Yorker February 24, 1973; Newsweek December 25, 1967; Perspectives of New Music Spring 1963, Spring-Summer 1968; Quarterly Journal of Speech April 1962; Reporter February 4, 1960; Saturday Evening Post October 19, 1968; Saturday Review January 30, 1960; Time November 29, 1976; Village Voice October 15, 1967.

"CAIN, G." *See* CABRERA INFANTE, GUILLERMO

"CAMPOS, ÁLVARO DE." *See* PESSOA, FERNANDO

*CAPETANAKIS, DEMETRIOS (January 22, 1912–March 9, 1944), Greek poet and critic who wrote mainly in English, was born in the port of Smyrna (now Izmir), where his father was a doctor. He began school in Smyrna, but in 1922, when the Greeks were driven out of the city during the Greco-Turkish war, he moved with his family to Athens. He studied law, philosophy, and political and social science at Athens University, and while still a student published four Greek poems and a drama, *Mia Thiella* (A Storm), in the periodical *Nea Zoi* (New Life) in 1933.

He has been described by Linos Politis as "an unquiet spirit, gifted with subtlety of feeling and open to every vibration, able to take to any new environment." In 1935 he went to Germany to study philosophy under the existentialist Karl Jaspers at Heidelberg, and there came in contact with the disciples of Stefan George. That poet's aesthetic ideals had for a time a considerable influence on Capetanakis, reflected in his doctoral thesis *Liebe und Zeit* (Love and Time, 1936). (His admiration for George subsequently gave way to revulsion—he came to regard him as one of "the chief spiritual corrupters of German youth.") When Capetanakis returned to Athens in 1937 he continued to publish philosophical and aesthetic essays, including *Mithologia tou oraiou* (Mythology of the Beautiful) and a Greek translation of *Liebe und Zeit* as *Eros kai khronos* (1939). Since his death these essays in Greek have been collected as *Dokimia* (Essays, 1962).

In 1939 Capetanakis came to England with a British Council scholarship to continue his studies at Cambridge. He moved to London in the fall of 1941 to work in the Greek Department of Information in exile, and thus entered a wider literary and political world where he made many

*kap et an ä′ kēs

143

CAPETANAKIS

Hans Wild

DEMETRIOS CAPETANAKIS

friends among well-known literary figures. He was especially close to John Lehmann, Edith Sitwell, and William Plomer. Capetanakis fell in love with England and its language, "the poetic language *par excellence,*" and began to write poetry in English. He used the language with extraordinary power and originality, and with a clarity and delicacy which were essentially Greek. His first English poem appeared in *Penguin New Writing* in 1942, and other poems of his, as well as the literary essays he wrote in English, were subsequently published in various numbers of *New Writing* and *Daylight.*

As William Plomer said of him: "With his romantic temper he was particularly drawn to melancholy and passion, especially the incandescent passion that may burn like a jet in a circumscribed environment or a frustrated heart, or that bursts out in desperate acts or in the creation of enormous myths, or in confession transmuted into art. Hence his interest in Dostoievsky, Rimbaud, Stefan George or Emily Dickinson, the fascination exerted upon him by the Brontës, his quick response to a mention of a picture by Géricault or a poem by Christina Rossetti, his knowledge of Proust and Balzac ... his eagerness to know every detail of some private or public tale of a contemporary *crime passionel.*" Thus his first English poem, "Detective Story," with its deceptive simplicity of form and statement:

The stranger left the house in the small hours;
A neighbour heard his steps between two dreams;
The body was discovered strewn with flowers;
Their evenings were too passionate, it seems.

They used to be together quite a lot;

The friend was dressed in black, distinguished looking
The porter said; his wife had always thought
They were so nice and interested in cooking.

And this was true perhaps. The other night
They made a soup that was a great success;
They drank some lager too and all was right.
The talk, the kisses and at last the chess.

"It was great fun!" they said; yet their true love
Throbbed in their breasts like pus that must be freed.
The porter found the weapon and the glove,
But only our despair can find the creed.

Capetanakis' sixteen published poems in English were all written in the middle of the war, and everything he produced was, as John Lehmann put it, "the fruit of long, arduous struggles of mind and spirit." He wanted to make his poems "cryptic messages with hints of what to hope and how to live." These poems, with their disturbing undertones of tragedy, grew from his passion to grasp the deepest truth—of his own experience or that of others—in imaginative symbols. It is this passionate integrity, John Lehmann suggests, which leads him at times to "a certain repetitiveness in argument and an excessive bareness of statement." Lehmann records that Capetanakis used to say that "in some unexpected way, the war physically was not frightening enough; but that, metaphysically, for any one who cared to think, what was happening was so disturbing that poetry of a high order must come out of it. To have death standing continually next to one is certainly no situation to breed conventional thoughts, but rather such lines as Demetrios wrote in his best-known, most extraordinary poem 'Abel.' "

And then he chose the final pain for me.
I do not blame his nature: he's my brother;
Nor what you call the times: our love was free,
Would be the same at any time; but rather

The ageless ambiguity of things
Which makes our life mean death, our love be hate.
My blood that streams across the bedroom sings:
"I am my brother opening the gate."

About eighteen months before his death, when he had been ill for some time, but before it was discovered that he had leukemia, Capetanakis passed through a crisis of despair— of agony of spirit at his own condition, the war, and the suffering of his country, and doubts concerning his powers as an artist. This crisis, from which he somehow emerged with renewed hope and confidence, transformed his whole outlook on life and death. It is reflected in his last poem, "Lazarus":

This knock means death. I heard it once before
As I was struggling to remember one,
Just one thing, arguing in my fever for
Help, help. Then the door opened, yet no Son

Came in to whisper what I had to know
Only my sisters wetted me with tears,
But tears are barren symbols. Love is slow,
And when she comes she neither speaks nor hears:

She only kisses and revives the dead
Perhaps in vain. Because what is the use
Of miracles unheard-of, since instead
Of trying to remember the great News

Revealed to me alone by Death and Love,
I struggled to forget them and become
Like everybody else. I longed to move
As if I never had been overcome

By mysteries which made my sisters shiver
As they prepared the supper for our Friend.
He came and we received him as the Giver,
But did not ask Him when our joy would end.

And now I hear the knock I heard before,
And strive to make up for the holy time,
But I cannot remember, and the door
Creaks letting in my unambiguous crime.

Apart from his own original poems, Capetanakis also made English translations of the Greek poets Seferis, Elytis, and Prevelakis.

Edith Sitwell said that his gifts as poet and critic seemed to her equally great: "They were of strange profundity," because "he did not remain a thing apart from the element he explored. He *was* the element itself." This receptiveness was described as a "strange x-ray power" by John Lehmann: "he entered into your mind and heart with an uncanny power of imaginative understanding [because] he had certain very profound and unusual feelings about the meaning of life and what was valuable in it."

His critical studies have the same quality of intimate engagement, very different from the academic detachment of the literary expert, for they too were the fruit of long, arduous struggles of mind and spirit—struggles very often with Capetanakis' own problems of philosophy and belief, worked out in his reflections on the work of other writers. These critical essays show an existentialist concern with the absurdity of human existence, with death and nothingness. As he expressed it at the end of his essay on Rimbaud: "Nothingness might save or destroy those who face it, but those who ignore it are condemned to unreality. They cannot pretend to a real life, which if it is full of real risks, is also full of real promises."

Capetanakis died of leukemia at Westminster Hospital in London at the age of thirty-two. John Lehmann compares him with other poets who died young: "If Demetrios Capetanakis had lived, even if only for one or two more years, he would have been able to complete a cycle of work, already planned, which revealed itself more remarkable and beautiful with every advance he made." Apart from their original periodical publications, his English poems and essays appeared in *Demetrios Capetanakis: A Greek Poet in England* (1947), which John Lehmann edited. Several of his poems have since been set to music by the American composer Ned Rorem.

PRINCIPAL WORKS IN ENGLISH: Demetrios Capetanakis: A Greek Poet in England, ed. by John Lehmann, 1947.

ABOUT: Deutsch, B. Poetry in Our Time, 1963; Grigson, G. (ed.) Concise Encyclopedia of Modern World Literature, 1963; Lehmann, J. (ed.) Demetrios Capetanakis: A Greek Poet in England, 1947; Lehmann, J. I Am My Brother: Autobiography II, 1960; Lehmann, J. The Ample Proposition: Autobiography III, 1966; Penguin Companion to Literature 2, 1969; Politis, L. A History of Modern Greek Literature, 1973; Press, J. Rule and Energy, 1963. *Periodicals*—New Writing and Daylight Autumn 1944.

*CARDENAL, ERNESTO (January 20, 1925–), Nicaraguan poet, was born in Granada, Nicaragua, the son of Rodolfo Cardenal and the former Esmeralda Martinez. He was educated at a Jesuit college there, and went on to study humanities at the University of Mexico (1944-1948) and at Columbia University in New York (1948-1949), subsequently spending two years in Europe.

Cardenal was a member and leader of the Nicaraguan "generation of 1940," and his verse represented from the beginning a reaction against an escapist and too-subjective literary tradition. Whether he was writing love lyrics or calls to revolution against the Somoza dictatorship, he sought for lucidity and objectivity—a poetry that would "reach the people" and that would be characterized by an interest in the hard facts and prosaic realities of everyday life in Central America. These early poems began to appear in newspapers and magazines in the 1940s—his more revolutionary work in the influential Mexican journal *El corno emplumado* (The Plumed Horn). His first book of poems, *La ciudad deshabitada* (The Deserted City) was published in 1946, and followed a year later by *Proclama del conquistador* (The Conqueror's Proclamation).

At Columbia Cardenal was introduced to the poetry and theories of Ezra Pound, a discovery which has been decisive in the development of his own work. Cardenal shares Pound's convic-

*car dā nal'

ERNESTO CARDENAL

tion that poetry can be discovered in every aspect of human experience, from economics and politics to history and philosophy, and that the structures of poetry can assimilate statistical data, newspaper articles, fragments of letters, historical chronicles, lampoons, anecdotes, and an assortment of other elements traditionally considered alien to poetic expression. He has also incorporated into his own work Pound's "ideogrammic method," which derives from the belief that general concepts are most meaningfully expressed though a cluster of particulars. Just as the Chinese ideogram for *red* combines characters meaning "rose," "cherry," "rust," and "flamingo," Cardenal will use two or more specific images (priest/Mercedes Benz) to suggest the general notion that he wishes to convey (corrupt clergy).

All of these Poundian devices were evident in *Epigramas* (Epigrams), a collection of poems published in 1961 but written in the early 1950s, when many of them circulated clandestinely. The book comprises thirty-four translations from Catullus and thirty-nine from Martial together with forty-nine original poems—the latter ranging from love poems to abrasive political satires. The theory of poetry advocated and practiced by Cardenal and his followers he has called *"exteriorismo"* (exteriorism), and defined as a "poetry created from the elements of the external world all around us. Poetry created from happenings, from people and objects. Poetry in this genre can absorb day to day realities, places we know, the . . . names of people of flesh and blood, even their dates and statistics if necessary. . . . It is a poetry which owes something to Walt Whitman but much more to the poets of

China and Japan. Any poet writing in this vein must express his feelings through the images of the external world like those poets of primitive civilizations. It is the poetic language of the Bible and Homer and of all the radical verses ever written."

After his return to Nicaragua in 1952, meanwhile, Cardenal had become deeply involved in revolutionary politics. Many of his friends were killed after the failure of "Conspiración de Abril," the abortive attempt in April 1954 to overthrow Anastasio Somoza. The dictator was in fact assassinated in 1956 and Cardenal, though personally uninvolved on this occasion, was lucky to escape arrest.

There followed for Cardenal a prolonged emotional and spiritual crisis, in the course of which he experienced a religious conversion. In 1957 he entered the Trappist monastery of Our Lady of Gethsemani, in Kentucky, where he became a novice under the spiritual direction of Thomas Merton. After two years, the rigors of the Trappist regime proved too much for his health. He continued his studies at the Benedictine monastery of Santa María de la Resurrección at Cuernavaca, in Mexico, and in 1961 moved on again to a seminary in Colombia.

Hora (Hour), published in 1960, was completed before his conversion. This long poem, now regarded as a classic of revolutionary literature, deals with the sorrows of Nicaragua as a banana republic and dictatorship and, according to a critic in the *Times Literary Supplement,* "greatly extended Cardenal's range, bringing in two further Poundian features: cross-cutting from source to source, and the use of deliberately prosaic passages to contrast both with lyrical evocations of nature and the epic treatment of heroic events." Vivid memories of the poet's own participation in revolution emerge:

In May the malinches bloom in the streets of
    Managua.
But April in Nicaragua is the month of death.
In April they killed them.
I was with my comrades in the April rising
and I learned how to use a Rising machine-gun.

As a Trappist novice at Gethsemani, Cardenal was forbidden to engage in secular writing, an act of self-renunciation which he cheerfully accepted as Merton had done before him. He did, however, draw on the spiritual diary he kept there in the writing of *Vida en el amor* (translated by Kurt Reinhardt as *To Live Is To Love*), a mystical work in prose which was completed at Cuernavaca but not published until 1970, when it appeared with a preface by Merton. The book, which has had a great deal of influence on progressive Latin American Catholics, is in its doctrine reminiscent of Augustinian neoplatonism but in spirit closer to a Franciscan vision of a world sustained by love.

Brief jottings made at Gethsemani were later worked up into the taut lyrics of *Gethsemani, Ky.* (1960). Robert Márquez has said that after Cardenal's conversion his main themes remained unchanged—"his repudiation of a world ruled by greed, institutionalized violence, and the concept of private property—but to these was added the mystic love of God. The poet's vision becomes at once more tender and more apocalyptic." The religious poems in *Gethsemani, Ky.* resemble his earlier work in the simplicity of their imagery and their emphasis upon external detail (in contrast to the abstractions and "inner perceptions" of much religious verse): "Spring has come to the Trappist cemetery/ to the cemetery once more green with sprouting grass/ its iron crosses laid out like seeds." The poems in *Salmos* (1969, translated by Emile G. McAnany as *Psalms of Struggle and Liberation*) are like socialist Sermons on the Mount: "Be not impatient if you see them make many millions/ Their commercial transactions are as the wheat of the fields. . . ."

The same direct criticism of human greed and debased values is to be found in *Oración para Marilyn Monroe y otros poemas* (A Prayer for Marilyn Monroe and Other Poems, 1965), in which the title poem is an elegy of overwhelming pathos and compassion. The actress's suicide is seen as a symbol of the spiritual emptiness and collective guilt of modern man:

She only acted out the script we gave her
—the script of our own sad lives—and it was an
   absurd script.
Forgive her Lord and forgive us too, for our
   twentieth century
and this colossal Super-Production in which we
   have all collaborated.
She was hungry for love and we offered her
   tranquillizers.

(translated by Robert Pring-Mill)

Another work written or at least begun at Cuernavaca was *El estrecho dudoso* (The Uncertain Passage, 1966), a long epic poem describing the political and social evolution of Central America from the Spanish conquest to the beginning of the seventeenth century (and commenting indirectly on the equally bitter present). It offers a view of the past which has much in common with Pablo Neruda's in *Canto general,* though of course without Neruda's antireligious bias, and makes much use of carefully reworked documentary material.

In 1965, Cardenal was ordained into the priesthood in Nicaragua. The following year he founded a small religious community on a remote island in the Solentiname Archipelago in Lake Nicaragua. The community pursues a way of life based on a primitive form of Pauline Christianity. It observes no strict rule but is organized rather like a commune or colony where religious, artisans, craftsmen, and intellectuals work side by side in silent fellowship.

Homenaje a los indios americanos (Homage to the American Indians, 1969) brings together poems written over a period of some fourteen years, celebrating the simplicity and sense of community that could be found in the Amerindian past in such a way as to constitute an implied criticism of contemporary capitalism. The collection includes poems, increasingly intricate in structure, on Mayan, Incan, and North American Indian themes.

Notable among Cardenal's more recent works are "Coplas a la muerte de Merton" (1969), his elegy for Thomas Merton, and *Oráculo sobre Managua* (1973), in which he strives to reconcile the image of a benevolent God with the devastation by an earthquake of Managua, the Nicaraguan capital, on Christmas Eve. *En Cuba* (1972, translated as *In Cuba*) is a prose account of Cardenal's three-month visit to Cuba in 1970, when he was persuaded to leave Solentiname to serve on the jury of a poetry contest. His view of Castro's Cuba is largely sympathetic—he has been called "a perceptive but curiously naive observer of the Cuban scene."

Cardenal has defined his mission as that of a revoluntionary man of God who interprets the teachings of Christ as essentially political, social, and radical. Christ and Gandhi are his two great exemplars in this nonviolent struggle against evil and injustice (though in his opinion both would always have opted for violence rather than cowardice). Cardenal is one of those who believe that the Roman Catholic Church has a vital role to play in redressing the social inequalities and political injustices of the nations of Latin America. This is very evident in *El Evangelio en Solentiname* (1975, translated by Donald M. Walsh as *The Gospel in Solentiname*). The book is a collection of twenty-nine tape-recorded conversations about the Gospels between Cardenal and the fishermen and farmers of Solentiname in which Jesus is seen as a liberator come to deliver the poor from oppression, and Herod is identified with the dictator Somoza. "This is 'Marxian Christianity,' " wrote T. C. Hunt, "not as abstract theory but gropingly, movingly articulated by poor people."

In recent years most of Cardenal's work, first

published in magazines and in slim volumes in various Latin American countries, has appeared in definitive editions in Mexico and Buenos Aires. He is generally regarded as a major poet, "probably the most stimulating Latin American poet to have emerged since 1950." His work is immensely popular and has had great influence.

PRINCIPAL WORKS IN ENGLISH TRANSLATION: The Psalms of Struggle and Liberation, 1971; To Live Is To Love, 1972; Homage to the American Indians, translated by Monique and Carlos Altschul, 1973; In Cuba, translated by Donald D. Walsh, 1974; Marilyn Monroe and Other Poems, translated by Robert Pring-Mill, 1975; The Gospel in Solentiname (England, Love in Practice), 1976; Apocalypse and Other Poems, edited and selected by Robert Pring-Mill and Donald D. Walsh, 1977. Poems in Caracciolo-Trejo, E. (ed.) Penguin Book of Latin American Verse, 1971; Carpentier, H. and Brof, J. (eds.) Doors and Mirrors, 1972; Márquez, R. (ed.) Latin American Revolutionary Poetry, 1974; New Directions 17 1961; Review (Center for Inter-American Relations) Fall 1973, Winter 1974; Twentieth Century 177 1968, 178 1969.

ABOUT: Arellano, J. E. Eight Nicaraguan Poets, 1967; Benedetti, M. Los poetas communicantes, 1972; Contemporary Authors 49-52, 1975; Franco, J. Spanish American Literature Since Independence, 1973; Ojeda, J. P. Ernesto Cardenal 1975. Periodicals—Times Literary Supplement July 12, 1974.

*"CARMI, T." (pseudonym of Carmi Charny) (December 31, 1925–), Hebrew poet and translator, was born in the Bronx, New York City, the son of Bernard Charny and the former Anna Aichenbaum. Apart from three years spent in Tel Aviv as a child (1931-1934), he grew up in New York. His father was a teacher of Hebrew, and that was the language spoken in his home. Carmi received his B.A. in 1946 from Yeshiva University, New York, and the same year, after some postgraduate work at Columbia, went to France, working there for about a year in orphanages for refugee children and studying at the Sorbonne.

In 1947 Carmi settled in Israel. He served from 1947 to 1949 in the Israel Defense Forces, fighting on the Jerusalem front during the 1948 War of Independence and afterwards serving as a captain in the air force. From 1949 to 1951 he studied at the Hebrew University in Jerusalem; since then he has earned his living as an editor, translator, and teacher. Carmi edited the biweekly literary journal Massa from 1952 to 1954, and the bilingual literary quarterly Orot in 1955. In 1957-1961 he was a children's book editor with the Sifriyat Hapoalim publishing house in Tel Aviv and in 1963-1971 did similar work for another Tel Aviv publisher, Am Oved.

Carmi had published some early poems in Hebrew while still in the United States, and his first book was published in Israel in 1951 as Mum va-Halom (Blemish and Dream). These lyrics,

*kar' mē

Pieter van der Meer

T. CARMI

"modern" and conversational in style, original and concrete in their imagery, nevertheless draw on every level of literary Hebrew. Unlike those Hebrew poets who came to Israel from the horrors of wartime Europe, Carmi's awareness of the Holocaust is, with notable exceptions, more implicit than explicit in his verse, which is mainly concerned to probe his own inner self and his personal relationships. M. L. Rosenthal writes that "Carmi's finely responsive and resilient personality stamps his poems with a pervasive anticipation of discovery. ... He is one of those who, in the midst of tragic life, and themselves committed to humane loyalties, still insist on savoring whatever life genuinely has to offer."

En Perahim Shehorim (There Are No Black Flowers, 1953) takes its title from Karl Marx's essay on literary style: "The essential form of the spirit is gaiety and light, and you make shadows its only manifestation; it must be dressed only in black and yet there are no black flowers." These poems draw on Carmi's experiences working with orphaned refugees in a dilapidated French chateau where bamboos grew in a grotto. This exotic scene is repeatedly invoked in "René's Songs" (translated by R. F. Mintz in Modern Hebrew Poetry), spoken by a child who remembers the death of his brothers, sisters, and parents in the concentration camp crematorium. He calls the directress of the orphanage Lo-Imi ("not my mother"—a term of rejection derived from the Bible):

Bright-haired am I, my face and body white.
Bright as my mother's hair;
White as my father's silence;
The day he ascended in the smoky chariots,

Why did Lo-Imi whisper in the frosty light that hour!
—René, you are the black flower. . . .

This collection was followed by *Sheleg bi-Yerushalayim* (Snow in Jerusalem, 1956) and *Ha-Yam ha'Aharon* (The Last Sea, 1958), for which Carmi received the important Shlonsky Prize. *Nehash ha-Nehoshet* (The Brass Serpent, 1961) contains a cycle of poems whose starting-point is the Biblical story of the brass serpent made by Moses as a charm against snakebite. *The Brass Serpent* (1964), the volume of translations made by Dom Moraes in collaboration with the author, contains selections from this and from earlier books. It includes one of Carmi's most discussed poems, "To a Pomegranate Tree," in which the poet struggles helplessly to rid himself of an overmastering symbol:

Get away from here, get away,
Go visit other eyes.
I wrote about you yesterday.

Green, I said
To your branches bowing in the wind
And red red red
To the still drops of your fruit
And I brought your root to light,
Your moist, dark, stubborn root.

So now you don't exist.
Now you block off the day
And the yet unrisen moon.

Come, my love, and see. . . .
Have a look at this odd tree:
His blood's in my eyes, on my hands, on my head
And he still stands where he stood.

Harold Schimmel has shown (in *The Modern Hebrew Poem Itself*) that in Hebrew the entire poem is an incantatory celebration in which first the tree and then the poet's new love are seen possessing his whole being. And M. L. Rosenthal regards this as typical of Carmi's preoccupation "with the way passionately regarded external reality invades his own very nature. Like an Israeli Lawrence, he has his pomegranate personify a world of fierce knowledge, blood-drenched, sexual and intractable."

Carmi's later collections include *Ha'Unikorn Mistakel ba'Mar'ah* (The Unicorn Looks in the Mirror, 1967), *Tevi'ah* (The Claim, 1967), and *Hitnatslut ha-Mehaber* (Author's Apology, 1974). A selection of his poems and translations from the years 1951-1969, published in 1970 as *Davar ehad* (Another Version), brought him the Brenner Prize in 1972. Christopher Ricks, who particularly admires Carmi's "ripely sardonic love poems," has said that in his more philo-

sophical and mystical pieces the poet "is fascinated by the problem of the point at which tradition becomes inertia, or endurance becomes stubbornness." James Dickey writes that, though Carmi's work "wells up from the Old Testament, he is no throwback to Biblical diction and Biblical rhetoric. He is modern without losing the sense of being rooted in human concerns that have lived in many generations of men before him. This gives his poems great depth as well as great continuity, and allows him to cherish and revel in his own individuality."

An extremely prolific and accomplished translator, Carmi has shown a special interest in the theatre. He has made Hebrew versions of Sophocles' *Antigone,* Shakespeare's *Midsummer Night's Dream,* and Farquhar's *Beaux' Stratagem,* along with many plays from the contemporary repertoire that he has helped to bring to the Israeli stage, including that of the Habimah National Theatre in Tel Aviv, where he served as a member of the repertoire committee in 1958-1960. He has translated Christopher Fry's *The First Born,* Edward Albee's *The Zoo Story,* John Osborne's *Look Back in Anger,* Brendan Behan's *The Hostage,* Lillian Hellman's *The Little Foxes,* Edgar Lee Masters' *Spoon River Anthology,* Tom Stoppard's *Rosenkrantz and Guildenstern Are Dead,* Brecht's *Herr Puntila,* Michel de Ghelderode's *Pantagleize,* and André Obey's *Noé.* He has also translated into Hebrew a selection of poems by the Turkish poet Nazim Hikmet, and has made English translations of much Hebrew poetry and of Leah Goldberg's play *Lady of the Manor.*

Carmi was co-editor with Stanley Burnshaw and Ezra Spicehandler of *The Modern Hebrew Poem Itself* (1965), a notable bilingual anthology which provides a prose commentary on each poem and an indication of its pronunciation in Hebrew. Carmi has also edited a more orthodox (and more comprehensive) bilingual anthology of Hebrew poetry from Biblical to modern times, *The Penguin Book of Hebrew Verse* (1977). The author was Ziskind Visiting Professor of Humanities at Brandeis University in 1970, attached to the departments of English and Near Eastern Jewish Studies. In 1973 he was adjunct associate professor at the Institute of Arts and Communications at Tel Aviv University, where from 1971 to 1973 he lectured on problems of translation in the department of general literature. From 1971 to 1974 he was editor-in-chief of *Ariel,* a quarterly review in English of the arts and letters in Israel, and from 1974 to 1976 he was a visiting fellow at the Oxford Centre for Postgraduate Hebrew Studies in England, at the same time conducting seminars in the history of

Hebrew poetry at the Oriental Institute in Oxford and at the School of Oriental and African Studies in London.

The author has lectured and given poetry readings at many universities and poetry festivals in Europe, Britain, and the United States, and in 1977 he was poet in residence at the Hebrew University, Jerusalem. He received a commission (1966) and a fellowship (1968) from the National Translation Center at Austin, Texas. He has also had grants from the Lucius N. Littauer Foundation (1969), the Israel Matz Foundation (1971), the Arts Council of Great Britain (1974), and the Jewish Memorial Foundation (1975). In 1973 he received the Prime Minister's Award for literature. Carmi has been married twice, in 1951 to Shoshana Heiman and more recently to Tamara Rikman. He has two children.

PRINCIPAL WORKS IN ENGLISH AND ENGLISH TRANSLATION: *Poetry*—The Brass Serpent, translated by Dom Moraes in collaboration with the author, 1964; Somebody Like You, translated by Stephen Mitchell, 1971; (with Dan Pagis) Selected Poems, translated by Stephen Mitchell, 1976. *Poems in* Birman, A. (ed.) An Anthology of Modern Hebrew Poetry, 1968; Burnshaw S., Carmi, T., and Spicehandler, E. (eds.) The Modern Hebrew Poem Itself, 1965; Carmi, T. (ed. and tr.) The Penguin Book of Hebrew Verse, 1977; Mintz, R.F. (ed.) Modern Hebrew Poetry, 1966; Silk, D. (ed.) Fourteen Israeli Poets, 1976; Modern Poetry in Translation July 1971. *As Editor*—(with Stanley Burnshaw and Ezra Spicehandler) The Modern Hebrew Poem Itself, 1965; The Penguin Book of Hebrew Verse, 1977.

ABOUT: Contemporary Authors 13-16 1st revision, 1975; Encyclopaedia Judaica, 1973; Rosenthal, M.L. *introduction to* Selected Poems, 1976. *Periodicals*—Books Abroad Spring 1972; Hebrew Book Review 4 4 1974; Nation April 2, 1973; New Statesman November 27, 1964; New York Times Book Review November 21, 1965; Times Literary Supplement November 19, 1964; October 29, 1976.

*CASTANEDA, CARLOS (December 25, 1925–), Peruvian-born anthropologist, gives in his books and interviews a colorful account of his life which has been strongly disputed. According to this account, he was born at São Paulo, Brazil, on December 25, 1935, into a well-known family of Italian descent whose surname was not Castaneda. His young and immature parents left him to be raised until he was six on his maternal grandparents' chicken farm in isolated Brazilian backcountry. There followed a "hellish year because I was living with two children," before his mother's early death. He was then placed in a Buenos Aires boarding school where his father, an aloof professor of literature, seldom visited him. In 1951, when he was sixteen, he emigrated from South America, and settled with a foster family in Los Angeles.
*cas tan ä′ da

It was not until 1959 that he changed his name legally to Castaneda.

However, in the early 1970s, when Castaneda's books had made him famous, an investigation sponsored by *Time* magazine arrived at a substantially different story. United States immigration records revealed that Carlos César Arana Castaneda, a Peruvian fitting the author's description, had entered the country in 1951. The son of César Arana Burungaray, a goldsmith, and Susan Castaneda Navoa, he had been born on Christmas Day 1925 in Cajamarca, Peru, where he had attended school until the family moved to Lima in 1948. After graduating from the Colegio Nacional de Nuestra Señora de Guadalupe, he studied painting and sculpture at the National School of Fine Arts in Lima. Castaneda pursued different interests in the United States. Between 1955 and 1959 he studied psychology at Los Angeles City College, and in 1962 he received a B.A. in anthropology from the University of California at Los Angeles, where he studied intermittently between 1959 and 1971. Confronted with these contradictory accounts of his life, Castaneda shrugs them off: "To ask me to verify my life by giving you my statistics, is like using science to validate sorcery. It robs the world of its magic and makes milestones out of us all."

Castaneda received his graduate training in the specialized anthropological field of ethnomethodology, a system of cultural analysis pioneered by one of his UCLA professors. Eager to "do a good job of being an academic," and realizing that "if I could publish a little paper beforehand, I'd have made it," he embarked upon a study of the medicinal plants used by the Indians of the southwestern United States. Pursuing his researches in Arizona in the summer of 1960, he encountered Don Juan Matus, an aged Yaqui Indian locally famous as a visionary sage and sorcerer. Don Juan was instructed by Mescalito, the spirit of the peyote plant, to choose Castaneda as his disciple and to train him as a "man of knowledge."

This sorcerer's apprenticeship went on intermittently—in Arizona and later in Sonora, Mexico—over a period of five years, and involved the ritualized consumption of peyote and other hallucinogenic plants. Near the end of this time, Castaneda found himself beginning to perceive reality in terms unacceptable to Western thinking and science—to treat the extraordinary creatures and experiences of his hallucinatory states as real, and normal experience as illusory. Fearing total psychic breakdown, he abruptly broke off his relationship with Don Juan in the autumn of 1965.

Some months later, Castaneda organized his notes about this experience into a master's thesis. The work begins with a narrative account of his dealing with Don Juan, and this is followed by a technical "structural analysis" of the sorcerer's beliefs. The manuscript was taken up by the University of California Press, which published it in an edition of two thousand copies in June 1968 as *The Teachings of Don Juan: A Yaqui Way of Knowledge*. It immediately aroused intense interest, not only among scholars but within the hippie counterculture; reprinted as a paperback, it became a major best-seller. "Its effect," Douglass McFerran wrote, "was almost as unbelievable as the more magical incidents that Castaneda describes. Discovered by the generation turned on to drugs by Timothy Leary and turned off to more traditional outlooks by the war in Vietnam, Castaneda's drug-using Don Juan became a folk hero whose impact was all the stronger for the fact that, unlike the Maharishi or any other cult founder of the period, he solicited no new followers."

Most reviewers found Castaneda's "structural analysis" ponderous, stilted, or even sophomoric, but many were full of praise for the skill with which he had described his relationship with Don Juan—a relationship which seemed to Edmund Leach "at once intimate yet tense, as between Moby Dick and Ahab, God and Job, or any psychoanalyst and his patient." Dudley Young, however, found the book "unsatisfactory because it falls uneasily between ethnography, spiritual autobiography, and travel literature," and, while some anthropologists welcomed it as the prototype of an exciting new form, others took Castaneda to task for concentrating so unprofessionally on his own experiences, rather than what they might reveal about the Yaqui way of life. And there were a few who denied that the book was a work of science at all, suggesting that Castaneda had combined his extensive knowledge of Indian and desert lore with the skills of a novelist to produce a new *Gulliver's Travels*.

In 1968 Castaneda returned to Mexico to present Don Juan with *The Teachings*. Further experiences of "non-ordinary reality" followed, and are described in *A Separate Reality: Further Conversations With Don Juan* (1971). Ted Hughes thought this a different kind of report from the first book, whose "real vitality . . . radiated from the painful, rather brilliantly recorded defeat and near-collapse of Castaneda's scientific, rational ego." In the second book, "he is no longer preoccupied with defending his outraged reason. Now he is trying to experience for himself the incomprehensible dynamics and

reality of Don Juan's world. . . . Castaneda becomes the guinea-pig hero of a modern quest as the weird glamour of the hypnotic, manipulating, profound, foxy old Indian carries him, with his notebooks and tape recorder, into regions where the words 'rational' and 'scientific' are violently redefined."

Journey to Ixtlan (1972) concentrates on certain mental and physical exercises Castaneda had undertaken during his apprenticeship but had not described in the earlier books. These exercises had not involved the use of psychedelic plants, and he had only gradually come to comprehend their significance as he advanced in wisdom. Robert Hughes wrote that this account of "grueling desert marches and arduous disciplines, apparitions and struggles in fog and bright sunlight, as well as some mind-wrenching magic tricks, makes hypnotic reading." And it seemed to Paul Riesman that Castaneda's first three books, "taken together . . . form a work which is among the best that the science of anthropology has produced."

However, some doubtful and dissenting voices were raised against *Journey to Ixtlan,* and more against the fourth volume in the series, *Tales of Power* (1974). This is based on Castaneda's experiences in 1971 and 1972, when he and another apprentice were exposed to even more extreme assaults upon reason by Don Juan and another sorcerer, Don Genaro. Elsa First, noting the development of Castaneda's style from "the factual precision of the first book to the lunatic extravagance of this last," was undismayed: "Castaneda is doing to his audience exactly what Don Juan and Don Genaro do to Carlos from the moment they begin rambunctiously teasing him out of his wits with the possibility that he is seeing their 'doubles'. In teaching his readers to 'believe without believing,' Castaneda enlarges his achievement as the chronicler of ancient methods for restructuring the sense of reality. He has brought us closer to understanding the teaching behind all the magic. In Don Juan's words, 'Life in itself is sufficient, self-explanatory, and complete.' "

Philip Toynbee responded rather less kindly. He had read *The Teachings of Don Juan* with "passionate interest and excitement" until he had been told that nobody except Castaneda had ever seen Don Juan and that there were strong reasons for believing that the book was largely a work of pure imagination"; if that were so, it seemed to Toynbee "a fabrication of the same order as Lewis Carroll's or Hans Andersen's: at best of the same order as Bunyan's." In Toynbee's opinion, however, the later books "mark an increasing decline in Castaneda's ambiguous powers. There is the grim sound of barrels being scraped as we read ... [the] last two volumes: they are repetitive to a degree, and they use a vocabulary so inflated that the 'wonders' Castaneda continues to describe now seem perfectly commonplace pieces of storytelling, interlarded with banal philosophical statements of a kind which is entirely familiar to any student of Western philosophy. ... I have no doubt at all that he began to inflate and dress up his experience even in his first book, and that he has continued to do so, with a more and more febrile exhaustion of his inventive resources, in every subsequent volume." There was a similarly mixed response to *The Second Ring of Power* (1978), in which Castaneda encounters Don Juan's women disciples.

Whether Carlos Castaneda is an inspired anthropologist, as some continue to regard him, or what William Kennedy called him, "a superb but flawed novelist," he has become a rich man: over four million copies of his books were in print in September 1975. In spite of widespread misgivings within the profession, he received a doctorate in anthropology from UCLA in 1973 with a thesis embodying the text of *Journey to Ixtlan.* He still attends meetings on ethnomethodology, but has taught for only one academic quarter. This was at the University of California at Irvine where, he later remarked, his students "looked like they were just waiting for me to crack up."

Castaneda is a small man who dresses conservatively—"a man in a Brooks Brothers suit, armored against the future." A former schoolmate remembers him as "witty, imaginative, cheerful, a big liar and a real friend," but Castaneda is obliged to live nowadays as a virtual recluse, dividing his time between his Los Angeles apartment and a beach house near Malibu, hounded by "very strange people" who "expect something that I can't give at all." He says that he does not use drugs and that he would have been afraid to touch peyote except under instruction. Castaneda told an interviewer that he often writes for up to eighteen hours a day: "I try to live the way Don Juan demands, using all my strengths and efficiency. The result is I work my head off."

PRINCIPAL WORKS: The Teachings of Don Juan: A Yaqui Way of Knowledge, 1968; A Separate Reality: Further Conversations With Don Juan, 1971; Journey to Ixtlan: The Lessons of Don Juan, 1972; Tales of Power, 1974; The Second Ring of Power, 1978.

ABOUT: Contemporary Authors 25-28, 1st revision, 1977; De Mille, R. Castaneda's Journey, 1976; Drury, N. Don Juan, Mescalito and Modern Magic: The Mythology of Inner Space, 1978; Holroyd, S. PSI and the Consciousness

Explosion, 1977; Noel, D.C. (ed.) Seeing Castaneda: Reactions to the "Don Juan" Writings of Carlos Castaneda, 1976; Silverman, D. Reading Castaneda: A Prologue to the Social Sciences, 1975; Who's Who in America, 1976-1977. *Periodicals*—America February 26, 1977; American Anthropologist April 1969, August 1972; Christian Century March 21, 1973; March 28, 1973; Commonweal September 17, 1971; April 6, 1973; Harper's February 1973, September 1974; Nation February 10, 1969; Natural History June 1971; New Republic November 16, 1974; New Statesman January 14, 1972; New York Review of Books June 5, 1969; New York Times Book Review September 29, 1968; October 22, 1972; October 27, 1974; January 22, 1978; May 7, 1978; Observer May 11, 1975; Psychology Today September 1974; Publishers Weekly November 20, 1972; Religious Studies December 1975; Seventeen February 1973; Time November 6, 1972; March 5, 1973; Times Literary Supplement June 15, 1973.

*CAUTE, (JOHN) DAVID (December 16, 1936–) English historian, novelist, dramatist, and essayist, writes: "Although both of my parents were born in England, none of my grandparents were. My father's parents were French and Irish Catholics; my mother's were Jews from Austria (her father was a rabbi and a talented composer, Asher Perlzweig). My father was an army dentist, which accounts for the fact that I spent the first month of my life in Egypt, where he was then stationed. My mother graduated in physiology and later lectured in nutrition. It was she who brought me up because my father, sadly, was usually posted to some remote part of the world, and then, after the war, after a brief reunion, he died when I was eleven.

"My schooling was academic and middle-class. After four years at the Edinburgh Academy I transferred, at the age of thirteen, to a boarding school, Wellington College, Berkshire. After winning a scholarship in modern history to Wadham College, Oxford, I spent eighteen months in the army, serving in the Gold Coast Regiment in the colony which a year later, in 1957, became the independent state of Ghana. It was out of West African experiences that my first novel, *At Fever Pitch,* was written.

"After studying history at Wadham under such tutors as Lawrence Stone, A. F. 'Pat' Thompson, John Hale, John Cooper, and Christopher Hill, I was elected a fellow of All Souls College, Oxford, where I remained for six years until in 1965 I resigned in protest against that stubborn institution's refusal to admit students. Having spent a graduate year at Harvard as a Henry Fellow in 1960-1961, I returned to America in 1966 as visiting professor at New York University and Columbia. I taught at Brunel University from 1967 until 1970, when I decided to devote myself full-time to writing.

"My first marriage, to Catherine Shuckburgh,

*cōt

DAVID CAUTE

effectively ended in 1966, and we were divorced four years later. Edward and Daniel are the sons of that marriage. By my second wife, Martha Bates, I have two daughters, Rebecca and Anna.

"I work in a number of fields—too many, perhaps. I do not want to open up any fundamental questions about my writing here, preferring not to discuss the meaning of my work in a few words. However, it is fair to say that there runs throughout my novels and plays a strong tension between the intellectual and imaginative sides of my nature, with the former too dominant in my opinion. Deep inside me resides the middle-class respect for scholarship as something worthy, as work, and the distrust of art as something slightly frivolous and recreational. When I write history I feel myself to be respectably married, but when I give time to novels and plays I play truant with a mistress. No one has ever articulated such an outlook in my presence, so I attribute it to early psychological self-conditioning, and to the fact that my institutional life, my honours and awards, my career, were linked to my role as historian. Although my first novel picked up two prizes, it was written during an Oxford term, in broad daylight, when I should have been *working,* and therefore generated a good deal of guilt. I feel at ease with a novel or play, whether as writer or reader, only at night."

David Caute is an unusual figure among contemporary British writers on two counts: he is a professional historian as well as a novelist and dramatist, and his plays and novels are "public" or didactic, written from the point of view of a democratic socialist.

His first novel, *At Fever Pitch* (1959), is about

a young British officer, Michael Glyn, doing his national service in an African country in process of achieving self-government. Among its themes are the uneasy balance between the outgoing British authorities and the nationalists; the snobbery, drunkenness, and general awfulness of Glyn's brother officers; the rise of a local African leader; and Glyn's own sexual ambivalence. Most reviewers thought that this was too much to have attempted in two hundred and fifty pages, and found the book unbalanced and at times overheated, but it was praised for some brilliant scenes, for its insight into the minds of a large cast of characters, black and white, and for its "atmosphere of urgent truth." V. S. Naipaul wrote that "the limitations of Mr. Caute's experience cannot be hidden," but that he had "applied a genuinely creative imagination to his African experience," and had "written an interesting and intelligent novel." It brought him both the Rhys Memorial Prize and an award from the London Authors' Club.

Comrade Jacob, which followed in 1961, is a historical novel about the Diggers—a sect of early agrarian communists who in Cromwell's England alarmed the government and greedy landowners by appropriating and cultivating common land in Surrey. Bernard Bergonzi found "something shadowy about the substance of this novel"—a greater concern with debate than with drama. Although he admired Caute's portrait of Gerrard Winstanley, the Diggers' visionary leader, Bergonzi concluded that this "well-written and highly intelligent book" was an honorable failure. Naipaul disagreed, calling this a far better book than its predecessor, and a reviewer in the *Times Literary Supplement* thought it "a remarkable, and moving, evocation of a stirring and significant experiment" by "a scholar of some assurance and brilliant representational imagination." Beyond that, Caute has said, the novel was intended as an indirect comment on present-day communism. His first play, *Songs for an Autumn Rifle,* was a "fringe" production at the Edinburgh Festival the same year, 1961. A rather unsophisticated piece of playmaking (shaped, the author later remarked, "in the spirit of banal realism"), it examines the effect on Briitsh Communists of Russia's brutal suppression of the 1956 Hungarian uprising.

Caute's first work of historiography was *Communism and the French Intellectuals* (1964). Working from published sources, he examined the activities and motives of many of the important writers, philosophers, historians, artists, and intellectuals who joined the French Communist Party, or actively supported it, between 1914 and 1960. The book was universally admired for its lucidity and good judgement, the thoroughness of its documentation, and its freedom from both condescension and sentimentality. E. J. Hobsbawm was impressed by the way it "controverts a characteristic 1950s view that ... [Communist parties] could attract only the deviant, the psychologically aberrant, or the seeker after some secular religion." *The Left in Europe Since 1789* (1966), which examines the "parallels and contradictions that have marked the history of left-wing movements in Europe since the French Revolution," was received with somewhat less excitement, but on the whole favorably. There was on the other hand a harsh reception for Caute's third novel, *The Decline of the West* (1966), dealing with intrigue in a newly independent African state. Christopher Ricks called it "a bad best-seller, its characters mere contrivances and its talk vacuously ideate, which nevertheless writes about such real horrors (gladiators, torturers) that we cannot but be gripped at times."

An ambitious experiment followed in The Confrontation, a trilogy comprising a play and a novel about an English don named Steven Bright, and an essay supposedly written by him. All three books are concerned with the question of political commitment. The trilogy's first volume is the play, *The Demonstration,* in which Bright is professor of drama at an English university. He is rehearsing with his students a play he has written about the Pentagon peace march; they insist on substituting one of their own ("The Demonstration") about their own experience of repressive authority in the university. As Ronald Hayman says, "we are often jerked from one level of theatrical reality to another, when, for instance, a scene between the Women's Dean and a student turns out to be a scene between two students, one of whom is playing the Women's Dean but can come out of character to make comments on her." Conversely, when the long-awaited performance of Bright's play is broken up by a "police raid," he accuses the police superintendent of "method acting" because he carries a genuine identity card but finds (when he cannot pull off the superintendent's moustache) that the repressive raid is real, or at any rate "real."

In the novel *The Occupation,* volume three in the trilogy, Bright is winding up a year as a visiting professor in New York. His affair with a student ends and his office is invaded and occupied by radical and violent students—or he imagines it is: it is deliberately unclear how much of the novel's action takes place only in Bright's disturbed mind. Bright, as one reviewer rather alarmingly put it, faces "the essential dilemma of the aging academic liberal, forced to confront the breakdown of his political, social and moral certainties, of his control over his domestic and sexual life, and, finally, perhaps, of his mind."

"Bright's" essay *The Illusion* discusses politics, the theatre, and the novel. Its principal argument, elegantly and eloquently expressed, is against those Marxist critics who decry all literary modes but "socialist realism." Caute/Bright maintains on the contrary that modernist tendencies in literature, including the cult of the irrational, can and should be reconciled with socialist intentions. The trilogy's play and novel can thus be read as attempts to apply the principles advocated in the essay; and indeed both raise modernist doubts about the accuracy of distinctions between "fantasy" and "reality," about the authority and omniscience of the author, and about the viability of the literary forms of which they are examples.

The trilogy left John Weightman with the impression that Caute "is emotionally on the side of student 'revolutionaries,' but sees the intellectual weakness of their position, and is thus trapped in a Hamlet-like oscillation. He projects this oscillation into Steven Bright ... but lacks the literary skill to turn him into a representative hero or anti-hero of our time. He is not much more than a ragbag of miscellaneous reading and personal hang-ups, relieved by an occasional aphorism." Another reviewer found these "confessional" books "both original and courageous," but like Weightman thought that they failed as literature: "Their continuity, rhythm, tone, use of metaphor and references are similar to those used in conversation. Sentences, scenes, appeals—all are characterised by a fluency which engulfs life and gives it a regular, undifferentiated brilliancy."

The Fellow-Travellers (1973) is a witty and provocative study of the many Western intellectuals who, between 1926 and 1956, declared their sympathy with Stalinism without becoming Communists—among them Gide, Shaw, Sartre, Romain Rolland, Theodore Dreiser, and Sean O'Casey. What they had in common, Caute believes, was a combination of gullibility and latent authoritarianism. This is one of the most admired of Caute's books—"a valuable, even remarkable exercise in intellectual history." Neil McInnes wrote that Caute "marshals his immense cast in successive scenes that are only roughly in chronological order, and repeatedly zooms in on one of them for a close-up. This keeps the reader engrossed, allows some useful repetition of key themes, and leaves the impression of familiarity with a vast chunk of intellectual history. . . . he has written a book of more enduring importance than he allows."

A collection of Caute's essays and reviews was published in 1974 as *Collisions*. It includes among other pieces his much-discussed denunciation of All Souls College, originally published in *Encounter* at the time of his resignation, and an account of the 1965 Oxford Teach-in on Vietnam, of which Caute was the co-organizer, as well as notable essays on Czechoslovakia and Israel and studies of Sartre, Malraux, and Lucien Goldmann. "Dr. Caute," wrote a reviewer in the *Times Literary Supplement,* "is a very impressive literary critic, perhaps partly because he does not see himself as one. He sees himself as a creative writer defending fellow-writers such as Flaubert, Malraux or Robbe-Grillet against critics like Sartre and Goldmann who try to explain them away." The same reviewer suggested that Caute, as a creative writer, is too self-aware, and that "his true vocation is that of a critic rather than a novelist."

Caute's third play, given a try-out production in London in 1973, is *The Fourth World.* It is a rather surprising departure, a play dealing less with social issues than with the personal problems of its principal character. This is Simon Feather, a leftist English novelist on the American university gravy train. His situation is rather like that of Steven Bright in *The Occupation*: his marriage is over, his mistress has rejected him, and so has his publisher. Irving Wardle wrote that Caute, "not previously my idea of a laugh, has extracted an intellectually supercharged comedy from these dispiritingly banal events, and he has done so largely by inventing a form that really answers the demands of the material. His most conspicuous move is to split his hero in half: treating Eliot's 'man that suffers' and 'mind that creates' as two independent characters. Thus, while Simon I is bawling plaintive obscenities up at Ilse's window and having his case rifled by passing New York cops, Simon II is standing languidly by observing the indignities and occasionally taking over when things get really dangerous."

David Caute has also written a play for radio, *Fallout* (1972), and one for television, *Brecht and Company* (1976). His other works include a monograph on Frantz Fanon and a perceptive account of a visit to Cuba. He says in *Contemporary Novelists* that "perhaps the tension between man's private and public existences is the central 'problematic' of my thinking and writing. Nowadays I'm more preoccupied by questions of literary form than I used to be. Another thing: it scarcely used to occur to me that I owed my readers an occasional smile or even laugh, but

I'm learning now to open the cage on humour a bit, to let it out, to be unashamedly frivolous if I feel like it. So far the response has been encouraging."

PRINCIPAL WORKS: *Novels* —At Fever Pitch, 1959; Comrade Jacob, 1961; The Decline of the West, 1966; The Occupation, 1971. *Published Plays*—The Demonstration, 1970. *Nonfiction*—Communism and the French Intellectuals, 1914-1960, 1964; The Left in Europe Since 1789, 1966; Fanon, 1970; The Illusion, 1971; The Fellow-Travellers: A Postscript to the Enlightenment, 1973; Collisions: Essays and Reviews, 1974; Cuba, Yes?, 1974; The Great Fear: The Anti-Communist Purges Under Truman and Eisenhower, 1978. *As Editor*—Essential Writings of Karl Marx, 1967.

ABOUT: Cole, C.R. and Moody, M.E. (eds.) The Dissenting Tradition, 1975; Contemporary Authors 1-4, 1st revision, 1967; Hobsbawm, E.J. Revolutionaries, 1973; O'Brien, C.C. Writers and Politics, 1965; Vinson, J. (ed.) Contemporary Dramatists, 1973; Vinson, J. (ed.) Contemporary Novelists, 1976; Who's Who, 1977. *Periodicals*—Commentary March 1965; Commonweal May 14, 1965; English Historical Review April 1967; Guardian July 22, 1971; Listener July 22, 1971; September 5, 1974; Nation December 21, 1964; June 27, 1966; National Review January 5, 1973; April 13, 1973; New Statesman February 14, 1959; July 10, 1964; May 12, 1965; September 23, 1966; November 28, 1969; July 23, 1971; January 19, 1973; March 1, 1974; New York Times Book Review October 4, 1964; October 9, 1966; April 8, 1973; March 19, 1978; Saturday Review October 8, 1966; Spectator May 12, 1961; Sunday Telegraph July 25, 1971; Sunday Times (London) November 23, 1969; Times (London) July 22, 1971; March 13, 1973; September 14, 1978; Times Educational Supplement (London) August 27, 1971; Times Literary Supplement February 13, 1959; May 19, 1961; October 22, 1964; September 8, 1966; November 3, 1966; December 2, 1971; July 6, 1973.

"CHAPMAN, WALKER." *See* SILVERBERG, ROBERT

CHARNY, CARMI. *See* "CARMI, T."

CHARTIER, ÉMILE-AUGUSTE. *See* "ALAIN"

*CHAUDHURI, NIRAD C(HANDRA) (November 23, 1897–), Indian memoirist, historian, and social critic, was born into a liberal Hindu family, the second son of a lawyer, in the small Bengal country town of Kishorganj. His childhood and youth are described in *The Autobiography of an Unknown Indian* (1951). It gives a lovingly and densely detailed account of his parents, their ancestral villages, and the intense, enfolding life of their extended families, but remains a sweeping indictment of their way of life.

Chaudhuri received his B.A. at Calcutta University, but was forced by illness to abandon his postgraduate work in history. He has nevertheless studied English and English literature as

*choud' hŏŏr ē

155

thoroughly as Bengali, European history as thoroughly as Asian. He was active among Tagore's literary following in Calcutta in the 1920s, and has spent most of his life since then in Delhi as an editor, journalist, broadcaster, and government employee. Chaudhuri has served as assistant editor of *The Modern Review* (Calcutta), as secretary to Sarat Bose (leader of the Congress Party in Bengal), and as a commentator on All India Radio. He has contributed to the London *Times,* the *Times of India, Atlantic Monthly, Encounter,* and many other newspapers and magazines, Eastern and Western.

The Autobiography of an Unknown Indian appeared when Chaudhuri was in his fifties. If he was unknown when he wrote it, he was very soon afterwards famous and, in some quarters, notorious. Provocatively dedicated to the British Empire, the book dismisses as a "superannuated folly" the notion that Hindu civilization can be revived by nationalism, Gandhiism, or anything else, and maintains that if India is to become anything more than an "archaeological site" it will have to set about creating "an Indian version of European civilization in our own interest, for our private use and in order to keep ourselves within the pale of civilized life."

The violence and arrogance of Chaudhuri's strictures outraged many of his readers, Indian and Western, and tended to obscure the harsh truth of much of what he said. Other readers showed less interest in the doctrine propounded by the book than in the personality it evoked. As William Walsh has said, "it is written in a masculine, confident English of long, balanced sentences . . . an idiom which is distinctly late-Victorian in flavour." The story of the formation of Chaudhuri's character is also the story of the impact of Britain on India, and the gradual transformation of that ancient culture under the influence of European concepts of God and nationalism, freedom and duty. Walsh regards the book as "the most significant single discursive work to be generated by the love and hate of Indian-British relationships."

Five weeks which Chaudhuri spent in Britain in 1955 as the guest of the British Broadcasting Corporation produced *A Passage to England* (1959), in which he puts down the impressions he received from his belated first visit to his spiritual home. Less aggressive than the *Autobiography,* the book was admired for the freshness and wit of the author's response to what he actually saw and experienced, but found deluded and sentimental in its generalizations about the political, economic, and religious underpinnings of the British way of life.

In *The Continent of Circe,* which received the Duff Cooper Memorial Prize, Chaudhuri resumes the theme of his first book. His thesis is that the Hindus are of European stock, Aryans from Mitannian-Mesopotamia, who colonized India and were corrupted and denatured by the subcontinent's climate and geography. It is this stupefying environment that must be conquered if the Hindus are ever to achieve the sense of history and communal destiny that alone will rescue them from Circe's cave. Chaudhuri draws on linguistics, history, the Sanskrit epics, and much characteristically jaundiced observation of contemporary Indian society in support of his theories, and his scholarship was admired even by those who were unconvinced by his arguments or irritated by his fanaticism.

The great German Vedic scholar Max Müller, who taught at Victorian Oxford and became a British Privy Councillor, is the subject of Chaudhuri's *Scholar Extraordinary* (1974). There was a great deal of praise for the book's "lucid, readable, yet vivid style," but again something like outrage at Chaudhuri's passionate conviction that the only hope for humanity lay in a return to the values of Müller's world—not excluding its parental harshness, its devotion to the most crippling kinds of self-denial, its morbidity and snobbery. Angus Wilson, who found himself somewhat repelled, was all the same "delighted by a skill that can combine and reveal the inner qualities of German romanticism, Victorian Oxford, and Hindu liberal theism all in one engrossing narrative." A substantial "political and psychological essay" on Clive of India followed in 1975. John Grigg wrote that, "without producing any new evidence, or even re-reading the documents on which other lives have been based, Mr. Chaudhuri has subjected Clive's career to his own very distinctive, culturally bifocal, vision."

Chaudhuri has also written *The Intellectual in India,* a booklet published in a series called Tracts for the Times, and *To Live or Not To Live!* (1970), "an essay on living happily with others." One of the most discussed of his magazine articles, published in *Encounter* (April 1957), disparages E. M. Forster's *A Passage to India* and plumps for Kipling's *Kim,* with its mystique of empire, as "the finest story about India in English." The article is reprinted in *Rudyard Kipling* (1972), a symposium edited by John Gross. Chaudhuri is regarded in India as one of the sharpest native critics of Hindu society, and says that for twelve years his work was tacitly banned by the government.

The author is a small, dapper man, just over five feet tall. Revisiting England in 1970, he complained that Oxford had undergone a disastrous change: "It is full of the lower middle class. It distresses me to walk on the streets at midday when these people do their shopping." At home, he entertains frequently in his Delhi flat, which is hung with Turner and Constable reproductions. He says that he has largely lost his taste for Indian music, preferring Mozart, and that he rarely goes to sleep at night without "first reading a chapter from Miss Austen or Miss Brontë." Chaudhuri describes himself as "a priggish compound of a Roundhead and a Victorian," and seems to William Walsh "a character of genuine and singular individuality, by turns arrogant, despairing, feverish, complacent, melancholy, but always faithfully Indian and saltily himself."

PRINCIPAL WORKS: The Autobiography of an Unknown Indian, 1951; A Passage to England, 1959; Continent of Circe, 1965; The Intellectual in India, 1967; To Live or Not To Live! 1970; Scholar Extraordinary: The Life of Professor the Rt. Hon. Friedrich Max Müller, P.C., 1974; Clive of India: A Political and Psychological Essay, 1975.

ABOUT: Greenberger, A.J. The British Image of India: A Study in the Literature of Imperialism, 1880-1960, 1969; International Who's Who, 1977–78; Naik, M.K. and others (eds.) Critical Essays on Indian Writing in English, 1968; Parry, B. Delusions and Discoveries, 1972; Penguin Companion to Literature 1, 1971; Verghese, C.P. Nirad C. Chaudhuri, 1973; Walsh, W. Commonwealth Literature, 1973. *Periodicals*—Atlantic July 1966; Commonweal June 17, 1966; Economist December 4, 1965; Encounter January 1966; Listener November 20, 1975; Nation December 15, 1951; New Statesman November 5, 1965; June 27, 1959; New York Herald Tribune Book Review November 25, 1951; New York Times Book Review May 1, 1966; New Yorker November 12, 1960; Observer November 17, 1974; Spectator November 16, 1951; Times Literary Supplement July 31, 1959; December 2, 1965; December 27, 1974.

CHOMSKY, (AVRAM) NOAM (December 7, 1928–), American linguist and political essayist, was born in Philadelphia, Pennsylvania, the elder son of a Hebrew scholar, William Chomsky, and the former Elsie Simonofsky. Chomsky's father emigrated from his native Russia in 1913, taught at Gratz Teachers College and Dropsie College in Philadelphia, and earned a considerable reputation as a scholar. When Noam Chomsky was ten years old he read the proofs of his father's edition of a thirteenth-century work, *David Kimhi's Hebrew Grammar,* in this informal manner learning something of the principles of historical linguistics. Chomsky was educated at the Oak Lane Country Day School and Central High School, Philadelphia, from which he graduated in 1945. He went on to the University of Pennsylvania, where he studied linguistics, mathematics, and philosophy, but was distract-

NOAM CHOMSKY

ed from his academic studies by his passionate interest in the Middle Eastern political developments that led to the establishment of the State of Israel. He had intended to go to Palestine himself, but under the influence of Zellig Harris, professor of linguistics at Pennsylvania, who shared his political interests, Chomsky decided to continue his formal education and to major in linguistics. He received his B.A. in 1949.

While Robert Sklar has described Zellig Harris as "the most rigorous practitioner of the linguistic methodology Chomsky was to overthrow," George Steiner has argued that Harris "initiates the new linguistics in his *Methods in Structural Linguistics* (1951)" because in it "certain key notions of grammatical depth and transformation were first set out." Chomsky himself agrees that "Harris's book was extremely important, both to the field and to me personally (I learned structural linguistics from it as an undergraduate, proofreading it, in 1947). However, it contains nothing about 'grammatical depth' or 'transformation.'"

In fact, Chomsky says, "most of the ideas on generative grammar that I later worked out" were contained in the descriptive generative grammar of modern Hebrew with which Chomsky earned his M.A. at Pennsylvania in 1951. This work, which he had begun as an undergraduate at Harris's suggestion, set out "to find a system of rules which would enable you to characterize all of the sentence structures in the language." Meanwhile, in 1950-1951, Chomsky had begun his career as an assistant instructor in linguistics at Pennsylvania, for a time teaching Hebrew also at the Mikve Israel School in Philadelphia. In 1951 he began four more years of graduate study under a junior fellowship in the Society of Fellows at Harvard University. His dissertation on "Transformational Analysis" brought him a Ph.D. degree in linguistics from the University of Pennsylvania in 1955, and the same year he joined the faculty of the Massachusetts Institute of Technology as assistant professor of modern languages and linguistics.

Because of their unorthodoxy, Chomsky's manuscripts were at first rejected by linguistic journals and publishers. His first book, *Syntactic Structures,* was eventually published in the Netherlands in 1957, when he was still only twenty-nine. It marks the beginning of the Chomskyan revolution in linguistics, which has been called a "Copernican" revolution: not only has it revolutionized the scientific study of language; it also has far-reaching implications for the understanding of human nature and the study of human cognitive processes. In the 1950s linguistics had been in the doldrums, particularly in America, and Chomsky's first book was almost instantly recognized as a work of profound importance, in which linguistics could be seen to take a new turning. Chomsky's contribution was twofold. First, he questioned the goals towards which linguistic theory was oriented, and redefined the aims and functions of a grammar. And secondly he specified the form that this new grammar should take: that it should be *transformational.*

In the empiricist or "structuralist" or "Bloomfieldian" school of linguistics in which Chomsky was trained, language was viewed in behaviorist terms as a system of habits established by conditioning—a child learns to talk much as a rat learns to press a bar to get food. The empiricists deliberately restricted themselves to concerns which could be treated with scientific precision and rigor—they largely ignored semantics, and concentrated on the analysis of the units of phonology and syntax. In this way they hoped to arrive at procedures which would enable a linguist, given a body of material in an unknown language, to correctly analyze the grammar of that language.

Although Chomsky's first book reflected his "Bloomfieldian" training, he broke away from the empiricists at several important points. He insisted that the behaviorist theory of language learning failed to account for the *creativity* of speech—the way in which young children are able to master the complex grammatical rules of their native language, and are then able to produce and understand an indefinitely large number of sentences that they have never heard before. He maintained, moreover, that "a linguistic theory should not be identified with a manual of useful procedures," but instead should provide general principles for choosing between alternative grammars. And he stipulated that an ideal grammar would be one that provided rules and conditions which, applied to a given language, would generate all the sentences of which the language was capable—and only *sentences* (not strings of nonsense).

Chomsky goes on in *Syntactic Structures* to examine three alternative kinds of grammar—three different "models for the description of language." He deals with them in order of complexity, shows the first two to be unsatisfactory, and explains his preference for a third, which he initiated and which he calls "transformational grammar." This depends upon the fact that a particular string of words may be organized into an immense variety of sentences by the application of a relatively few "transformational rules." For example, such a string may yield "The man opened the door," "The man did not open the door," "Did the man open the door?," "Was the door opened by the man?," and so on and on. Transformational grammar, which is too complex to describe here, does meet Chomsky's own requirement that a grammar should be able to generate all the sentences of which a language is capable, though in its present form it is too general, and not sufficiently exclusive of non-sentences.

Considering its importance, *Syntactic Structures* is a brief and relatively informal book. However, it draws upon a great deal of highly technical research which preceded its publication and which was described in *The Logical Structure of Linguistic Theory,* a long monograph that was made available in mimeographed form in 1955 and finally published in 1975. John Lyons, in his book about Chomsky in the "Modern Masters" series, suggests that "Chomsky's most original, and probably his most enduring, contribution to linguistics is the mathematical rigor and precision with which he formalized the properties of alternative systems of grammatical description. . . . He has greatly extended the scope of what is called 'mathematical linguistics' and opened up a whole field of research, which is of interest not only to linguists, but also to logicians and mathematicians."

Transformational grammar was extensively studied, discussed, and argued over, and in 1965, in *Aspects of the Theory of Syntax,* Chomsky published a "Mark II" grammar incorporating a number of modifications. The most important of these was the inclusion of semantics as an integral part of grammatical analysis, and the new distinction between the "deep" (i.e., logical) structure of a sentence, and its "surface" (i.e., grammatical) structure. In *Topics in the Theory of Generative Grammar* (1966) Chomsky gives a concise account of his revised grammar, and replies to some of his critics. Meanwhile, Chomsky had become an associate professor at MIT in 1958 and a full professor in 1961. Since 1966 he has been Ferrari P. Ward Professor of Foreign Literatures and Linguistics there.

In *Cartesian Linguistics* (1966), Chomsky resumes his arguments against behaviorism and the empirical philosophy underlying it, and aligns himself with such rationalist philosophers as Descartes; he believes that human beings perceive and interpret the external world in terms of certain innate ideas, and that they are endowed with faculties which enable them to act as free agents, rather than as mechanisms wholly at the mercy of their environment. In his opinion, children are born with a grasp of certain universal principles which govern the structure of all human languages; unlike the "Bloomfieldians," who regard linguistics as purely descriptive, Chomsky sees it as the linguist's task to determine these universal principles, which must surely throw much light on the structure and predispositions of the human mind. Similar themes are explored in *Language and Mind* (1968), based on the Beckman Lectures Chomsky delivered at the University of California in 1967, and containing the clearest statement of his philosophy of language.

Chomsky's regard for the unique capacities of human beings relates his views on language closely to the political concerns which have increasingly dominated his writing since the 1960s. He had always been intensely interested in politics, and his views, formed in what he calls "the radical Jewish community in New York," always tended towards socialism or anarchism. But it was only in 1965 that disillusionment with the Vietnam war made him a leading political activist and critic of American foreign policy. He became a member of the steering committee of RESIST, took part in demonstrations like the 1967 protest march on the Pentagon, and taught undergraduate courses in political and social change. At the same time he emerged as an eloquent anti-war spokesman in articles published in such journals as *Mosaic*, the *New York Review of Books, Ramparts,* and *Liberation.*

A number of these polemical essays were collected in 1969 in *American Power and the New Mandarins,* a book dedicated to "the brave young men who refuse to serve in a criminal war." It is a powerful indictment of American involvement in the war, and of the "new mandarins"—those liberal intellectuals and social scientists who provide themselves with ideologi-

cal justifications for serving giant corporations and the federal government, and the academics who defend or fail to oppose America's attempt to impose its own conception of law and order on other countries by force. Some of the book's reviewers were among the "new mandarins" attacked in it, and the critical reception was mixed. J. G. Harrison thought it the work of "a brilliant and incisive thinker," while another reviewer accused Chomsky of "moral hubris." *Problems of Knowledge and Freedom* (1972) contains Chomsky's Bertrand Russell Memorial Lectures, given at Trinity College, Cambridge University, in 1971. They bring together Chomsky's two major preoccupations, reverting to his linguistic theories concerning human creativity, and going on to attack what he regards as the illicit domination of free spirits by governments and large corporations.

In collaboration with Howard Zinn, Chomsky edited Volume 5 of the Gravel edition of the Pentagon Papers, which was published in 1973 together with a selection of critical essays and an index to Volumes 1-4. Chomsky himself offered a critique of the Pentagon Papers in his long essay "The Backroom Boys," of which the *Times Literary Supplement* said: "His basic theme is not only superlatively well documented, but essentially convincing ... if, as seems certain, America's mission in Vietnam was based on a total misreading both of the global situation and of American interests, then it is essential that the men and traditions which made that misreading possible be exposed and renounced, and the conduct of United States foreign policy put into better hands."

"The Backroom Boys" was published in England together with two other essays in a volume of that title; in the United States it appeared as part of a larger collection of essays, *For Reasons of State* (1973). This collection widens the debate to include many other issues besides American involvement in Vietnam—civil disobedience, the function of the university, anarchism, psychology and ideology, and language and freedom. Sheldon S. Wolin wrote that "Chomsky displays those qualities which exemplify the finest traditions of intellectual responsibility and which have rightly earned for him the gratitude of those who have long regarded the Vietnamese war as an abomination. He is relentless in tracking down official lies and exposing hypocrisy and moral indifference in the high places where the war was conceived and executed. Yet the passion of Chomsky's indictment is always controlled, and while he is harsh toward his opponents, he is never unfair or arrogant." Wolin nevertheless finds Chomsky "unimpressive as a radical thinker. . . . Stated simply, Chomsky's political writings are curiously untheoretical. . . . His apparent assumption is that politics is not a theoretical subject."

There was also, and predictably, much criticism of *Peace in the Middle East?* (1974), in which Chomsky returns to his earliest political interests, when as a young man he hovered on the fringes of left-wing Zionist groups in New York. He had then opposed Jewish statehood and favored some form of binationalism for Arabs and Jews. In this collection of speeches and articles he still rejects the State of Israel as being based on repression and the expulsion of the Palestinians, and wants it replaced by a federation. Some Zionist critics dealt harshly with the book, while Bernard Avishai found it "so timely . . . that one wishes that it were better." It seemed to Avishai that these essays are burdened with an unrealistic idealism—that "Chomsky's sustained attack on 'Zionist' impediments to 'brotherhood' detracts greatly from his otherwise valuable and periodically prophetic observations about Israeli society. So, too, does the way he uses the principle of socialist binationalism as a *deus ex machina* that could resolve the conflict." Michael Walzer wrote that "at crucial points the essays reveal only a skillful evasiveness and it is very hard to say what Chomsky thinks."

Chomsky returned to linguistics in *Reflections on Language* (1975), which John Sturrock called "a hawkish restatement of Chomsky's rationalism." For Chomsky, Sturrock wrote, "language is still a cause, as Vietnam was once a cause and as injustice in general still is. It is a cause which seems to have lost some of the drive and the favor it used to have, and this may explain the note of what sounds rather like bad temper in the present essays. . . . Chomsky is the one living linguist with a mind large enough to coordinate within it linguistic issues and social ones, and it is this which makes him such an honorable, sympathetic figure. It is all the sadder, then, to find him arguing so sweepingly here from one set of issues to the other, as if the establishment of rationalist linguistics was somehow an early step on the road to Utopia."

George Steiner describes Chomsky as "an exhilarating thinker, possessed, as was Spinoza before him, by a passionate appetite for unity, for complete logic and explanation. There is a common bond of monism in Chomsky's desire to get at the root of things, be they political or linguistic. But it might be, to advance a cautionary platitude, that neither politics nor language is quite like that. Unreason and the obstinate disorder of local fact may prove resistant to the claims of either political justice or formal logic." And indeed, in recent years, a great deal of serious and telling criticism of transformational linguistics has appeared. But John Lyons concludes his monograph on Chomsky with these words: "I personally believe, and very many linguists share this belief, that even if the attempt he has made to formalize the concepts employed in the analysis of language should fail, the attempt itself will have immeasurably increased our understanding of these concepts and that in this respect the 'Chomskyan revolution' cannot but be successful."

Chomsky was a National Science Foundation fellow of the Institute for Advanced Study at Princeton in 1958-1959 and a research fellow at the Harvard Center for Cognitive Studies in 1964-1965. He has taught as a visiting professor at Columbia University and at the University of California (Los Angeles and Berkeley). In 1969 he went to England to give the Shearman Lectures at University College, London University, and the John Locke Lectures at Oxford University. Chomsky received a Guggenheim fellowship in 1971-1972, and has honorary doctorates from half a dozen universities in the United States, Britain, and India. He has served as a council member of the International Confederation for Disarmament and Peace, is a fellow of the American Association for the Advancement of Science, and a member of the American Academy of Arts and Sciences, the National Academy of Sciences, the American Academy of Political and Social Science, the Linguistics Society of America, the American Philosophical Society, the Aristotelian Society of Great Britain, and other professional bodies. A slim, brown-haired man, five feet ten inches tall, Chomsky was married in 1949 to Carol Schatz, and has two daughters and a son. Mrs. Chomsky's 1968 Harvard doctoral thesis on *The Acquisition of Syntax in Children From Five to Ten* was published in 1970 and warmly praised.

PRINCIPAL WORKS: Syntactic Structures, 1957; Current Issues in Linguistic Theory, 1964; Aspects of the Theory of Syntax, 1965; Topics in the Theory of Generative Grammar, 1966; Cartesian Linguistics: A Chapter in the History of Rationalist Thought, 1966; Language and Mind, 1968; (with Morris Halle) The Sound Patterns of English, 1968; American Power and the New Mandarins, 1969; At War With Asia, 1970; Chomsky: Selected Readings, edited by J.P.B. Allen and Paul Van Buren, 1971; Studies on Semantics in Generative Grammar, 1972; Problems of Knowledge and Freedom, 1972; For Reasons of State, 1973 (in England published as two volumes: For Reasons of State *and* The Backroom Boys); Peace in the Middle East? Reflections on Justice and Nationhood, 1974; The Logical Structure of Linguistic Theory, 1975; Reflections on Language, 1975.

ABOUT: Aitchison, J. General Linguistics, 1972; Bach, E. An

Introduction to Transformational Grammars, 1964; Bolinger, D. Aspects of Language, 1968; Cohen, D. Psychologists on Psychology, 1977; Contemporary Authors 17-20 1st revision, 1976; Current Biography, 1970; Dinneen, F.P. An Introduction to General Linguistics, 1967; Greene, J. Psycholinguistics, 1973; Hiorth, F. Noam Chomsky, 1977; Hockett, C.A. The State of the Art, 1967; Leiber, J. Noam Chomsky, 1975; Lyons, J. Introduction to Theoretical Linguistics, 1968; Lyons, J. Chomsky, 1970; Palmer, L.R. Descriptive and Comparative Linguistics, 1972; Robins, R.H. A Short History of Linguistics, 1967; Robinson, I. The New Grammarians' Funeral: A Critique of Noam Chomsky's Linguistics, 1975; Steiner, G. Extraterritorial, 1970; Thomas, O. Transformational Grammar and the Teacher of English, 1966; Who's Who in America, 1976-1977. *Periodicals*—Christian Science Monitor April 3, 1969; Commentary May 1969; Journal of Linguistics 3 1967; Language 33, 1957; Listener May 30, 1968; Nation September 9, 1968; New Republic April 19, 1969; October 24, 1974; New Society January 9, 1969; May 29, 1969; New York Review of Books June 29, 1972; January 23, 1975; New York Times October 27, 1968; New York Times Book Review March 16, 1969; January 9, 1972; September 30, 1973; October 6, 1974; February 15, 1976; New York Times Magazine May 5, 1968; New Yorker November 15, 1969; Newsweek August 26, 1968; Times Literary Supplement June 18, 1970; March 31, 1972; July 7, 1972; November 24, 1972; December 21, 1973; February 14, 1975; November 21, 1975; September 10, 1976; Virginia Quarterly Review Summer 1969.

CHOU SHU-JEN. *See* "LU HSÜN"

CLARK, JOHN PEPPER (April 6, 1935–), Nigerian dramatist, poet, and critic, was born at Kiagbodo, in the Ijaw country of the Niger Delta, Southern Nigeria, into a large polygamous family. His father, Clark Bakederemo, is the seventh in line of succession to the founder of Kiagbodo, and an important officiant in the religious ceremonies of the Main clan of the Western Ijaw people. Clark's mother died in his infancy, and he was brought up by his maternal grandmother in the Urhobo area, some hundred miles from Kiagbodo. His father fetched him home when he was six, and he went to school with his older brothers in the nearby town of Okrika, where the boys lived in the school compound. From 1948 to 1954 Clark attended Warri Government College, Ughelli, and from there he went on to University College, Ibadan (now Ibadan University). He graduated in 1960 with honors in English. Clark began writing poetry early, and while at Ibadan founded the influential poetry magazine *The Horn,* in which many young Nigerian poets published their early work.

Moving to Lagos, Clark began his career as a government information officer (1960–1961) and then joined the staff of the *Daily Express* as an editorial and feature writer (1961–1962). His first play, *Song of a Goat,* was produced in Ibadan in 1961 and published the same year, and his first book of poems followed in 1962, published

JOHN PEPPER CLARK

World Literature Today

like the play by the Mbari Writers and Artists Club in Ibadan.

In 1962 Clark went to the United States with a Parvin Fellowship to study at Princeton University. The experience was an unhappy one, and Clark never completed his year there. The story of his frustrations is told in the bitter memoir *America, Their America* (1964). "The ferocity of his anti-Americanism," wrote William Walsh, "is obviously to be accounted for in part by American race-relationships and part by his own truculence of temperament, in part by conventional socialist intellectual categories. . . . He arrived with his national irritabilites prickly and distended and in spite of his cultivation and generosity of spirit, he flays America and the Americans so totally and with such consuming fury that in the end the energy of his writing becomes a vapid routine."

Returning to Nigeria, Clark went with a research fellowship to the Institute of African Studies at Ibadan, undertaking research into the heroic sagas of the Ijaw people. Clark made a complete recording and transcription of the seven-day *Ozidi* drama cycle of Orua, and began work on an English adaptation and abridgement of the saga. Another product of these researches was the film *Tides of the Delta,* made with Frank Speed. In 1964 Clark joined the English department at Lagos University, where he is now professor of English.

Adrian A. Roscoe considers that, as a poet, Clark has as yet "no settled style"; he gets "an impression of good material inadequately controlled and organised." Martin Tucker, similarly, says that Clark's poetry "can be brilliantly lyric or merely adequately imitative." The long poem "Ivbie," published in *Poems* (1962), contains some of Clark's freshest and most deeply-felt writing. It draws deeply on his childhood among the dark creeks of the Delta, as do such well-known short poems as "For Granny From Hospital," in which he recalls:

> ... the loud note of quarrels
> And endless dark nights of intrigue
> In Father's house of many wives.

Another early poem, "Night Rain," has been particularly admired for its sharp and vivid imagery. It describes the poet's experience of waking among his brothers during a heavy storm, in a mud-and-thatch house that affords scant shelter:

> What time of night it is
> I do not know
> Except that like some fish
> Doped out of the deep
> I have bobbed up bellywise
> From streams of sleep
> And no cocks crow. ...

The Nigerian critic N. J. Udoeyop, discussing this poem, wrote: "It is through submission to nature's power that man's soul becomes indestructible. The smooth, easy harmonious rhythm of the poem is an adequate vehicle for conveying the sense of harmony which we can attain through identification with nature. This smooth rhythm becomes more striking at the moment of self-identification in a way which almost suggests a ritual dance":

> So we'll roll over on our backs
> And again roll to the beat
> Of drumming all over the land,
> And under its ample soothing hand
> Joined to that of the sea
> We will settle to sleep of the
>   innocent and free.

In general, Clark has remained very much a poet of particular moods and experiences, whose poetry stands or falls by the power of its imagery, rather than by any sustained argument or idea. However, the collection *Casualties* (1970), written during the Nigerian Civil War, gains a certain unity from its overall concern with that tragedy and its note of somber concern. The joyful spontaneity of much of Clark's early work is absent, but the best of these poems have a new strength and simplicity, derived from compassion for all the victims of the fratricidal struggle:

> Show me a house where nobody has died
> Death is what you cannot undo
> Yet a son is killed and a daughter is given. ...
> Earth will turn a desert
> A place of stones and bones
> Tears are founts from the heart
> Tears do not water a land
> Fear too is a child of the heart
> Fear piles up stones, piles up bones
> Fear builds a place of ruin.

> (from "Dirge")

Some of Clark's best poetry is contained in his plays, all of which are in a highly stylized free verse. As a dramatist, he inclines towards a tragic view of man mastered and destroyed by a fate which is beyond his comprehension or control. Thus Zifa in *Song of a Goat* loses his virility and his wife Ebiere, in her frustration, seduces Zifa's younger brother Tonye. Overcome with guilt, Tonye hangs himself, and Zifa, shamed and grief-stricken, walks into the sea. The chorus of villagers which comments on this grimly simple story was taken by some critics to be an anomalous borrowing from Greek drama, but Clark has pointed out that this theatrical convention is native to the Ijaw drama also. *Song of a Goat* is perhaps the most admired of Clark's plays, and Martin Esslin, though he found the play "not quite convincing," added that "the stark, timeless and almost placeless simplicity of the language invests the trivial event with the dignity of near tragedy." Clark's fellow-dramatist Wole Soyinka was reminded of Lorca, and called this a play of "contained, poetic violence." He went on: "We encounter human beings whose occupation and environment are elemental, visceral. Flood and ebb affect their daily existence, their language, their spectrum of perception." And he quotes these lines:

> There, another blow
> Has been dealt the tree of our house, and see
> How the sap pours out to spread our death. I
> Believe it now, now I believe it. White ants
> Have passed their dung on our rooftop.

The Masquerade (published 1964) suggested that Clark had embarked upon a kind of Nigerian *Oresteia,* showing how the malevolent fate which had destroyed Zifa's family in the first play implacably pursues the second generation. A stranger has won the hand of a beautiful girl in a Delta fishing village. The marriage is in progress when it is revealed that the stranger is Tufa, Ebiere's illegitimate son by Tonye. Tufa and his bride are both killed by the girl's outraged father, and her mother goes mad with grief. Martin Esslin praised "the highly sophisticated simplicity" of the play's language and wrote: "The atmosphere of relentless doom is so strong; the father, Diribi, acts with such utter conviction, that I, for one, was carried along." Anthony Graham-White, however, found the play full of unassimilated Shakespearean echoes, and complained of a sense of arbitrariness and of "the author pushing beyond what a short play will bear."

In *The Raft,* published in 1964 and adapted as a radio play in 1966, four men are floating downriver on a raft over which they have no control, and all four are eventually swallowed by the river. Gerald Moore has praised the consistency and locally-rooted strength of the play's imagery, and William Walsh writes that it is in this play that Clark's "considerable talent has been beautifully organized and set free. . . . The raft is as important here as in *Huckleberry Finn.* The river is a shaping, unifying form, as well as a natural force. As in *Huckleberry Finn* it represents life unconstrained by artifice, and value uncomplicated by pretence." Esslin felt that this particular work would have been more effective "as a realistic play in realistic prose," but acknowledged that "a very ambitious objective—the raft as an image of human life and man's dependence on his fellow men and sheer chance —is very boldly and imaginatively pursued."

Ozidi, Clark's adaptation of the Ijaw drama cycle, was published in 1966. His first full-length play, it resembles his earlier works, according to Anthony Graham-White, in that it deals with "a curse upon a family, bizarrely bloody events, a son obliged to pursue a fate determined by his father." More loosely structured than its predecessors, simpler and less "literary" in its language, it is also more optimistic in its conclusion, since Clark has modified the traditional fate of the vengeful hero so that, instead of being carried off by the Smallpox God, he finally triumphs over him, leaves magic and revenge behind, and assumes the full stature of heroic man. Clark's plays have been widely performed in Africa ever since 1961 and he is established as one of the most important contemporary black dramatists. Margaret Laurence has suggested that he suffers "from an insufficient knowledge of theatre. Too much action takes place offstage, and there are too many speeches which are stilted, with feelings or even events being declaimed rather than actually happening. . . . But what he does have is a poetic fluency which, when it is going well, goes very well indeed, and an intense desire to enquire into the rituals of destiny."

The most notable of Clark's critical writings is the volume of essays published in 1970 as *The Example of Shakespeare.* He writes perceptively about the Nigerian traditional drama and has much of interest to say about various literary attempts to render African vernacular speech into English—he himself seeks to convey the quality of African speech through the selection of appropriate imagery, rather than through experiments in grammar or word-order. Elsewhere in the collection he displays an intense interest in prosody, especially alliteration and stress—devices which he met in the work of his early master, Gerard Manley Hopkins, and which, as he points out, also occur in the Udoje poetry of the Nigerian Delta. A reviewer in the *Times Literary Supplement* spoke of "the curious mixture of penetration, petulance, and originality of response which distinguishes his prose," and found his critical writing "free from academic jargon or heaviness," though it "does sometimes lack clarity"; the book was welcomed "as a contribution to the slender body of African literary criticism, and as bringing some illumination to the practice of one of its most talented poets."

Clark returned to the United States in 1975–1976, spending a year at Wesleyan University's Center for the Humanities. He is married to the theatre artist Ebun Clark, and has two children.

PRINCIPAL WORKS: *Poetry*—Poems, 1962; A Reed in the Tide, 1965; Casualties: Poems 1966-1968, 1970. *Plays*—Song of a Goat, 1961; Three Plays (Song of a Goat, The Masquerade, The Raft), 1964; Ozidi, 1966. *Prose*—America, Their America, 1964; The Example of Shakespeare, 1970.

ABOUT: Beier, U. (ed.) Introduction to African Literature, 1967; Cartey, W. Whispers From a Continent, 1971; Contemporary Authors 65–68, 1977; Duerden, D. and Pieterse, C. (eds.) African Writers Talking, 1972; Herdeck, D.E. African Authors, 1974; Laurence, M. Long Drums and Cannons, 1968; Lindfors, B. (and others, eds.) Palaver, 1972; Moore, G. African Literature and the Universities, 1965; Moore, G. The Chosen Tongue, 1969; Penguin Companion to Literature 4, 1969; Roscoe, A.A. Mother Is Gold, 1971; Tucker, M. Africa in Modern Literature, 1967; Udoeyop, N.J. Three Nigerian Poets, 1973; Vinson, J. (ed.) Contemporary Dramatists, 1977; Vinson, J. (ed.) Contemporary Poets, 1975; Walsh, W. Commonwealth Literature, 1973. *Periodicals*—Black Orpheus 20 1966, 2 1968; Books Abroad Summer 1970; Nigeria Magazine 89 1966.

*CLAUS, HUGO (MAURICE JULIUS) (April 5, 1929–), Belgian poet, novelist, dramatist, and screenwriter, was born in Bruges, Belgium, and educated at various boarding schools and colleges. He worked as a house painter, migrant agricultural worker, actor, night watchman, and in various other casual jobs before becoming a full-time writer. Claus has traveled widely in Europe, especially in France and Italy, and has lived in Ghent, Amsterdam, and Paris.

*clous

163

Belgian Consulate

HUGO CLAUS

His 1953 marriage to the actress Elly Overzier and his later relationship with Sylvia Kristel brought him into contact with the theatre and film worlds, on which he has drawn in several of his novels and stories.

Claus made his name as an innovator in Flemish fiction with his first novel, written when he was only nineteen and published in 1950. *De Metsiers* (The Metsier Family), about a defeated and degenerating Flemish farming family, centers on the feverish romance between the retarded son Yannie and his half-sister Ana. The book's structure is clearly derived from Faulkner's *As I Lay Dying,* but it has a terse power of its own, and introduces a motif which is developed further in Claus's later work—a nostalgia for the innocence of youth and an aversion to adult seediness and corruption. The novel, which brought Claus the Leo J. Krijn prize, has been translated by George Libaire as *The Duck Hunt.* Dan Wickenden noted that it was "presented turn and turn about by each of its leading figures," and "told in a series of staccato, stripped-down interior monologues." A critic in *Saturday Review* thought it communicated "little more than a diffuse mood of apathy and despair," but most American reviewers admired the book.

At the same time, Claus was establishing himself as one of the most talented of the experimental and socially engaged young Flemish poets gathered around the magazine *Tijd en Mens* (Time and Man, 1949-1955), of which Claus was an editor. For young people like Claus just after the war, writes Eugene van Itterbeek, "there was a sense of disillusionment and resistance, and at the same time a conviction that poetry was capable of contributing in its own way to moral renewal. It was also the time when the younger generation in Flanders became acquainted with surrealism and existentialism, largely as a result of the cirtical writings of Jan Walravens. Hence the remarkable situation that *Tijd en Mens* combined an existentialist world view and a surrealist poetic." Both elements are discernible in a poem like "Compos Mentis," translated here by James S. Holmes:

. . . A few times, in the distance,
we heard the frogs and the mountain kings.

Sometimes, as I mingled myself with a lady,
the vinegar-and-gall was not so nearby.
Sometimes, although we're sicknesses for one
    another,
another is a velvet animal in fetters. . . .

Whoever wants to search for me (don't search, it's
    a shy disease)
whoever wants to direct his zoomer at me, will
find nothing in this spongy portion of flesh
but a renegade who has made shift for himself
in the human zoo with bad rhymes, ridiculous
    stepping stones
to support himself on his voice. . . .

Claus was one of the poets presented in 1951 in Simon Vinkenoog's epoch-making anthology *Atonaal* (Atonal). His reputation was established by *Tancredo Infrasonic* (1952), which showed the influence of Dylan Thomas in its surrealist imagery, and by the more rational poems of *De Oostakkerse Gedichten* (Poems From Oostakker). Eugene van Itterbeek suggests that the lyric source of Claus's poetry lies in his sense of "the organic bond between the poet and the earth." He is the only Flemish poet, according to the same critic, "who has remained true to the revolutionary spirit of 1950," though in fact he nowadays writes relatively little verse: "By keeping silent as a poet, almost as a matter of principle, Claus implicitly announces that poetry, as a form of individual expression, can no longer be a genuine means of social communication."

In Claus's second novel, *De Hondsdagen* (The Dog Days, 1952), the theme of the loss of innocence becomes dominant. Often in his fiction, the main character is torn between two women: an older one to whom he is bound, and a younger one, usually just on the threshold of womanhood, who personifies his own lost youth and to whom he is irresistibly drawn. In *De Hondsdagen,* Philip hesitates between Lou, who is expecting his child, and the adolescent Bea, whom he searches for after she has run away from boarding school. Similarly, in the later novel *De Koele*

Minnaar (The Cool Lover, 1958), Edward tries to escape from the adult world when he rejects Carla, a married woman with whom he is traveling. He becomes deeply involved with a young starlet, but loses her to a lesbian actress. In these novels youth and purity cannot be recaptured and both Philip and Edward, for all their struggles, are imprisoned for life in the soiled adult world.

Claus himself regards his next novel, *De Verwondering* (Wonderment, 1962) as a turning-point in his work. The conflict between innocence and maturity is still present, but it is intricately interwoven with many other themes. The story centers on a schoolteacher, a weak man, profoundly insecure, who becomes involved with a group of war criminals. These people have adopted as their hero a certain Crabbe, a Flemish former SS man. The schoolteacher becomes so enmeshed in this cult, identifies so deeply with Crabbe, that in the end he surrenders his own frail identity and becomes insane. By fusing reality and hallucination, repeatedly shifting the point of view, widening and narrowing the focus, Claus has constructed a novel of many-leveled complexity—an allegory about an everyman lost in the labyrinth of his own personality. The book enjoyed great critical and commercial success, though a few readers complained that its complexity was artificial and imposed, and that the story was overloaded with literary, artistic, and mythological allusions.

No such charge could be leveled against *Omtrent Deedee* (About Deedee, 1963), a tense and succinct account of a family reunion. This gathering is an annual ritual, held to commemorate the death of the mother, but, under the influence of drink, pent-up suspicions, jealousies, and lusts break loose, and the reunion gradually degenerates into a drunken orgy. Even Deedee, the priest, who has always been the family's moral and intellectual model, loses his self-control and shows himself to be as corrupt and perverted as the rest.

In *Omtrent Deedee,* as in Claus's first novel, the events are seen from the point of view of one character after another. The same technique is employed in *Schaamte* (Shame, 1972), which examines the corruption of a Belgian television team who are filming a passion play on a Pacific island. *Schaamte* almost reads like a film script, consisting largely of dialogue linked by narrative bridges, with description pared to the absolute minimum. Subsequent novels include *Het Jaar van de Kreeft* (The Year of the Cancer, 1973), which is as detailed as *Schaamte* is terse, and *Jessica!* (1977), which harks back to the complexity and the symbolic overtones of *De Verwondering.*

Claus was already well established as a novelist and poet when he began to write for the theatre, and he was from the beginning as successful in the new medium as in the others. His first play, which brought him the triennial Belgian State Prize for Drama in 1955, is *Een Bruid in de Morgen* (A Bride in the Morning), which centers on the relationship between a brother and a sister. The theme is reminiscent of *De Metsiers,* but here the relationship is a very delicate and poetic one. When the naive and hypersensitive young man succumbs to his scheming mother's plans to marry him off, his sister kills herself. The play, published in 1955, was produced in Holland by the Dutch director Ton Lutz before it was seen in Belgium. Because of the close friendship and sympathy that have grown up between Claus and Lutz, most of Claus's plays have had their premieres in Holland.

Het Lied van de Moordenaar (The Song of the Murderer, 1957), is about a gang of robbers whose idolized leader brings about their downfall when he falls in love with a baroness. It was not liked either by the critics or the public, but Claus's reputation was repaired and enhanced by *Suiker* (Sugar, 1959) a naturalistic play set among Flemish border workers harvesting sugar beets in northern France. A prostitute seeks salvation in her love for the simple-minded worker Kilo, and by the end of the play, in spite of the machinations of her jealous former lover, it actually looks as if she and Kilo might be happy together. The potential sentimentality of this theme is largely avoided, thanks to the play's bittersweet humor. One critic, who was reminded of Tennessee Williams by the mingling of realism and poetry in Claus's early plays, went on: "But everything he writes is dominated by a verbal magnificence which sometimes weakens his plays," as when he puts excessively literary speeches into the mouths of brigands or agricultural laborers.

Suiker was followed by a string of relative failures. These included the farce *Mama, Kijk, Zonder Handen!* (Look, Ma, No Hands!, 1959); *De Dans van de Reiger* (The Heron's Dance, 1962), later filmed, and described as "a fairly amusing philosophical tale about romantic love lost in the jungle of human eroticism"; a lavish and spectacular version of the Till Eulenspiegel legend (1966); and *Het Goudland* (The Gold Country, 1966), a dramatization of an adventure story by Hendrik Conscience which flopped completely. Claus's *Thyestes,* adapted from Seneca, had a mixed reception. Claus returned to naturalism in *Vrijdag* (Friday, 1969). Though its underlying structure may mirror the Roman Catholic mass, as Claus has indicated, this is a precisely observed and convincing representation of the emotions of a Flemish laborer who returns home after a prison sentence for incest. It is the most successful and probably the most enduring of Claus's plays.

Claus has also published art and literary criticism, has translated Georg Büchner, Cyril Tourneur, Dylan Thomas, and others, and has written a number of screenplays. He received the French Lugné-Poe prize in 1955. His other awards include a second triennial Belgian State Prize for Drama (1967), the Henriëtte Roland-Holst prize, also for drama (1965), and the triennial Belgian State Prize for Poetry (1971). Claus is generally regarded as the leading Flemish writer of his generation.

PRINCIPAL WORKS IN ENGLISH TRANSLATION: The Duck Hunt, 1955 (republished in England as Sister of Earth, 1966); Friday (play), translated by the author and Christopher Logue, 1972; Karel Appel, Painter, translated by Cornelis de Dood, 1962. *Story in* Krispyn, E. (ed.) Modern Stories From Holland and Flanders, 1973. *Poems in* Delta (Netherlands) Spring 1970, Spring 1971.

ABOUT: Belgian Review. The Contemporary Novel, 1966; Belgian Review. The Contemporary Theatre, 1970; Cassell's Encyclopedia of World Literature, 1973; Dupuis, M. Hugo Claus, 1976; Fleischmann, W.B. (ed.) Encyclopedia of World Literature in the Twentieth Century, 1967; Goovart, T. Het geclausureerde beest, 1962; Roey, J. de, Hugo Claus, 1964; Seymour-Smith, M. Guide to Modern World Literature, 1973; Weisgerber, J. Hugo Claus: Experiment en Traditie, 1970. *Periodicals*—Delta (Netherlands) Spring 1971; New York Times January 5, 1955; Writing in Holland and Flanders 17 1964.

"CLIFFORD, FRANCIS" (pseudonym of Arthur Bell Thompson) (December 1, 1917–August 24, 1975), British suspense novelist, wrote: "I was born in Clifton, a residential suburb of Bristol, Gloucestershire, England. My mother, Agnes Evans, was Welsh and French, and I am the youngest of her three children. My father, George Bell Thompson, was one of two sons of a west country Church of England clergyman, and the grandson of another. He and my mother settled in South London when they married, my father then being in the oil industry.

"He died early in 1919, so I cannot remember him, but photographs show him as a tall, slim, rather frail-looking man. He had, I am told, a lively sense of humour and a practical bent. His death left my mother with little money and the burden of three children to support. The strain on her was considerable and unremitting and she died when I was eight years old of a cerebral haemorrhage; her dying I can vividly recall.

FRANCIS CLIFFORD

"My sister, brother and I were cared for by various aunts and uncles in north and south London. It was an unhappy time for us all, pervaded by the sense of loss. I was luckier than the others because a place was secured for me as a boarder at Christ's Hospital, that unique and most wonderful of English public schools. Academically, I was a late developer; certainly I excelled there only on the playing field. After seven otherwise undistinguished years I began a period of training in the London office of a Far East merchant, eventually going out to Burma to work in the rice trade.

"Again, I was lucky, being just in time to experience and observe something of the flavour of the British Raj, so soon to be swept away. Less than two years after my arrival in Rangoon the war in Europe had begun and I had volunteered for, and been commissioned into, the Burma Army.

"The war which the Japanese then let loose was a major turning point in my life. That I survived at all was a miracle, and though scarred by the horrors there are areas of my makeup which were awakened and given lasting existence by the trauma of events. In late 1943 I was invalided home to Britain, where I was privileged to spend the remainder of the war in the headquarters of the Special Operations Executive.

"I was married for the first time soon after returning home. There is one child, a son, but the marriage failed. Shortly afterwards I was received into the Roman Catholic church, life—then and now—seeming meaningless without faith. In 1955 I married for the second time and, as before, there is one son. Throughout the years of this marriage we have lived at various times in Spain and Ireland and we have travelled fairly widely, mainly in Europe.

"When the war ended I did not return to the Far East: instead I began work as a London-based industrial journalist. For twelve years I edited a newspaper and magazine in the steel industry. I also started writing fiction in my spare time—short stories to begin with, then a novel. This was in the early fifties and my Irish wife—still my best critic—was the person who guided and encouraged me.

"Since 1960 I have been a fulltime writer, and have managed to survive. Inevitably, one or two of the earlier novels have an autobiographical basis. Several have been filmed. Throughout I have concentrated on suspense, my belief being that only when a character is at the end of his (or her) tether—emotionally, physically, spiritually or financially—does his true nature emerge.

"I write slowly. I don't think I am a natural writer. I neither type nor dictate. And the longer I continue as a novelist the more I go along with T. S. Eliot's reference to 'the intolerable wrestle with words and meanings, in which every new attempt is a wholly new start and a different kind of failure.' "

———

As he says, Clifford was commissioned in the Burma Rifles at the beginning of World War II and eventually joined Force 136, conducting sabotage in Japanese-occupied territory. He survived a thousand-mile trek back to the Allied lines, an ordeal which permanently affected his health, and spent the rest of the war with the Special Operations Executive. He left the army with the rank of major and a Distinguished Service Order.

Honour the Shrine (1953), his first novel, draws on his wartime experiences, being narrated by a wounded British saboteur, the only survivor of a successful mission, who is hidden behind enemy lines and nursed back to health by a heroic Catholic priest. In the end, when the narrator is flown to safety, the priest elects to remain behind, facing certain death. The book was called "extremely promising, above all in the sincerity and simplicity of the telling," and in the air of authenticity conveyed by its accounts of the suspense preceding the mission, the nightmare of the action itself, and the narrator's fears of capture during the long wait for rescue.

It was Clifford's descriptions of action that most impressed reviewers of *The Trembling Earth,* set in a Spanish village where a mixed trio of men struggle to preserve the church and its bell, shifted from its moorings by an earthquake.

Overdue deals with the aftermath of a plane crash in the Arizona desert, *Act of Mercy* describes a young English couple's attempt to succor the hunted ex-president of a Latin American republic, and *A Battle Is Fought To Be Won,* which returns to the theme and setting of *Honour the Shrine,* was admired as "a dramatisation of the terrible dilemma of the sensitive individual who knows he is afraid of the horrors of war, but is equally afraid of the censure of his fellows." These and subsequent novels were sometimes found hackneyed in their themes, but showed an increasing skill in characterization and description, and in the development of suspense. Several reviewers were reminded by Clifford's style and his religious preoccupations of Graham Greene, though one remarked that "his ability does not extend to making metaphysical speculation convincing."

Act of Mercy was filmed by Warner Brothers in 1962, and *The Naked Runner* in 1966, with Frank Sinatra playing the part of a former spy who is forced, on pain of his son's life, to act as an assassin for East German intelligence. *The Naked Runner* was a best-seller, and this and its sale to the movies ended the hardships of Clifford's first years as a freelance writer. He never achieved the massive popularity of an Ian Fleming, but a large public enjoyed his novels as exciting adventure stories, and a smaller one valued their moral seriousness and scrupulous craftsmanship. Anthony Boucher, who had found "almost every conceivable cliché of glib fiction" in *Overdue* (1957), had arrived at a very different opinion of Clifford's work by 1965, when he reviewed *The Third Side of the Coin,* a novel about an embezzling bank teller who finds a kind of redemption as the result of his involvement in a Spanish earthquake. "The more one reads of Francis Clifford," Boucher wrote, "the more one respects him as one of the really good writers in that genre of the suspense story which borders on the straight mainstream novel. . . . The quake sequences are a triumph of vivid visualization; and the story, as is usual with Clifford, is as strong as its presentation is quiet and underplayed."

Admiration for Clifford's work continued to grow steadily. When he died suddenly of a heart attack at the age of fifty-seven, his obituarist in the London *Times* called him "a suspense novelist who took the genre to an altogether new stature. . . . His books were as far removed from most suspense writing as fine brandy is from common wine." His belief that the true nature of a person emerges only when he is at the end of his tether is reminiscent of Conrad, but in fact he had more in common as a writer with John

Buchan. Clifford twice received the Silver Dagger of the Crime Writers Association, for *Another Way of Dying* in 1970 and for *The Grosvenor Square Goodbye* in 1975.

PRINCIPAL WORKS: Honour the Shrine, 1953; The Trembling Earth, 1955; Overdue, 1957; Something to Love, 1958; Act of Mercy, 1960; A Battle Is Fought To Be Won, 1960; Time Is an Ambush, 1962; The Green Fields of Eden, 1963; The Hunting Ground, 1964; The Third Side of the Coin, 1965; The Naked Runner, 1966; All Men Are Lonely Now, 1967; Another Way of Dying, 1969; The Blind Side, 1971; A Wild Justice, 1972; Amigo, Amigo, 1973; The Grosvenor Square Goodbye, 1974 (U.S., Goodbye and Amen); Drummer in the Dark, 1976; Ten Minutes on a June Morning, 1977 (short stories).

ABOUT: Contemporary Authors 53-56, 1975. *Periodicals* —New York Times August 30, 1975; Times (London) August 29, 1975; October 1, 1977; Times Literary Supplement January 9, 1976.

LEONARD COHEN

© 1978 by Fred W. McDarrah

COHEN, LEONARD (NORMAN) (September 21, 1934–), Canadian poet, novelist, and songwriter, was born in Montreal. He is the son of Nathan B. Cohen, a prosperous clothing manufacturer, and the former Marsha Klinitsky. Cohen, whose father died when he was nine, grew up in the fashionable Montreal suburb of Westmount. He began to write poetry at fifteen, when "the city began to jump at me," and learned to play the guitar at a socialist summer camp when he was sixteen. "I used it as a courting procedure," he told one interviewer. "Probably I got down on my knees to serenade a girl. I was shameless in those days." A year or two later he was playing his own first songs in one of Montreal's Mountain Street cafés. Graduating from Westmount Secondary School, Cohen went on to McGill University, where he majored in English, won the MacNaughton Prize in creative writing, and graduated with a B.A. in 1955.

Let Us Compare Mythologies, Cohen's first collection of poems, appeared a year later in 1956. *The Spice-Box of Earth* followed in 1961 and *Flowers for Hitler* in 1964. These poems, and Cohen's way of life, established him as an *enfant terrible* in the genteel world of Canadian literature. After a half-hearted apprenticeship to the family clothing business, and an equally unenthusiastic year of law studies at Columbia University in New York, Cohen went to Europe in 1959. Thereafter he divided his time between Montreal, the small Greek island of Hydra, and travels in many parts of the world. In 1961, Cohen went to Cuba at the time of the Bay of Pigs invasion, but found himself unable to decide which side to fight on. One result of this expedition was the poem called "The Only Tourist in Havana Turns His Thoughts Home-

ward." Cohen made no secret of his experiments with LSD and other drugs, or his devotion to alcohol and sex. His income at this time seems to have been limited to a small inheritance and the proceeds from his books, together with grants from the Canada Council in 1960 and 1961, and the Quebec Prize for Literature in 1964.

George Woodcock has pointed out that almost all of the images and allusions in Cohen's first two poetry collections have their origins in classical mythology, medieval romance, or the Bible. These two books, moreover, seemed to Al Purdy "absolutely conventional in metre and form. They gain distinction from other people's poems through a heavy sensuality, sometimes almost cloying, integral in nearly everything he wrote." It was the content rather than the manner of these early poems that so outraged conventional opinion, but won Cohen a large and ever-growing following among young people in Canada and the United States.

Sandra Djwa, in an essay collected in George Woodcock's *Poets and Critics,* identifies Cohen as "a black romantic"—a decadent poet who seeks revelation through extreme and self-destructive experience, and says with Baudelaire: "Through the unknown we'll find the new." She writes that "in Cohen's work this possibility of a new revelation is specifically associated with the myth of descent culminating in the creating of art. In ... *Let Us Compare Mythologies,* the structural myth is that of the death of the poet-god Orpheus and the possibility of his resurrection in art. Like Eliot's *Waste Land* the book moves through cycles of winter death followed by spring rebirth, and the poet-victim as a part of this cycle moves between the extremes of innocent and destructive love. In terms of the controlling Orpheus myth, the figure of the beloved woman suggests Eurydice while the madwoman evokes the Bacchanals. . . . The rationale for this disintegrative experience is explicit in the poem 'Story.' Only by allowing the madwoman full sway is it possible for the poet as victim to find his place in art: 'to understand one's part in a legend.' "

"It is this myth of art," Sandra Djwa goes on, "which seems to provide the basic structure in Cohen's work. . . . In *The Spice-Box of Earth* this longing for the old lost ideals is re-worked in terms of a neo-Hassidic myth. No longer able to accept a despotic God, the poet as priest is forced beyond Genesis into a desolation that is 'unheroic, unbiblical.' " He finds that "neither religious belief nor physical love can fill up the void between 'a ruined house of bondage and a holy promised land.' This reconciliation of the spirit is only to be found in the fairy-tale land of art."

The descent into evil is pursued to its logical conclusion in *Flowers for Hitler,* in which, Djwa says, influenced by Genet among others, "Cohen takes the blackness of the human capacity for evil and from it attempts to extract the flowers of art." In these poems, Cohen insists that the irrational evil of monsters like Hitler and Eichmann must be seen and acknowledged as part of the ordinary human personality: "I wait/ for each one of you to confess." When we recognize and confess that such wickedness is in all of us, and immerse ourselves in it, it may be seen to possess a strange kind of beauty—poems may grow "like butterflies on the garbage" of life. In other poems in this volume, Cohen makes the extermination camps an occasion for black humor: "Peekaboo Miss Human Soap/ Pretend it never happened." George Woodcock thinks that these poems about the Holocaust represent "Cohen's only real attempt to emerge from his romantic inner self and face the actual modern world," but other critics were divided as to whether they should be read as bitterly satirical comment on "the banality of evil" or attempts to secure a *frisson* at any cost.

Flowers for Hitler contains a one-act play, "The New Step," and is more experimental in its use of verse forms than its predecessors. Nevertheless, Woodcock believes that Cohen is distinguished from other members of "the present *avant-garde* of Canadian poets" in that "he is naturally the most conservative, in techniques and sentiments alike." All of his books, whatever the "structural myth" that controls their general tenor, also contain love lyrics of great skill and charm, like "In Almond Trees Lemon Trees" from *Parasites of Heaven:*

> In almond trees lemon trees
> wind and sun do as they please
> Butterflies and laundry flutter
> My love her hair is blond as butter
>
> Wasps with yellow whiskers wait
> for food beside her china plate
> Ants beside her little feet
> are there to share what she will eat
>
> Who chopped down the bells that say
> the world is born again today . . . .

In 1963 Cohen published his first novel, *The Favorite Game,* a largely autobiographical story about the adolescence of a rich Montreal Jewish boy, Lawrence Breavman, his love affairs, and his development as a poet. An episodic work, shifting back and forth in time, it contrasts the ephemeral nature of Breavman's love affairs with the stability of his friendship with the "bronze and squint-eyed Krantz," and the intensity of his feeling for Martin. The latter is a mathematical prodigy—a "divine idiot" who dies horribly, crushed by a bulldozer, while obsessively killing and counting mosquitoes in a swamp.

Woodcock says that "Martin represents the other pole to profane love in Cohen's world. He is . . . of the company of the saints, those exalted and obsessed ones to whom Cohen is ever drawn." Most reviewers found the novel insubstantial, immature, and even trivial, but unanimously recognized its promise. Daniel Stern wrote: "It is clear from the first page that we are in the hands of a genuine poet. The method is oblique, lyrical and condensed. The childhood flirtations, the death of a father never really understood, the whining and self-pity of the mother, the oceanic emotions of adolescence—all are sharply etched with original mastery and wit. It is pleasant proof that conventionality of material need never dictate conventional treatment."

Beautiful Losers (1966), Cohen's second novel, had a much greater impact. The book is in three parts. First, the masturbatory musings of "I" about his Indian wife Edith, who has killed herself, and F., the megalomaniac politician who has been the lover of both Edith and "I," and who dies of syphilis. Secondly, the "Long Letter From F," now dead—a fantasy about F.'s journey with Edith to Argentina, where they enjoy a prolonged sexual orgy and meet Hitler in disguise. Lastly, "Epilogue in the Third Person," in which "I" retreats to a tree house and immerses himself in the study and contemplation of the life of Catherine Tekakwitha (1656-1680), a Mohawk Indian saint, and learns to combine within himself F.'s debauchery and the saint's self-mortification.

John Wain admired *Beautiful Losers* as both "a personal tragedy and a judgement on Canadian life. . . . Mr. Cohen has a real theme, the frightening vacuum of modern Canada and the Canadian's uncertainty as to who he is and where his allegiances lie, both historically and in the present." George Woodcock, on the other hand, called it a "tedious book. The burlesque element is overdone; the pop art use of comic strips and junky advertisements already seemed old hat by the time of publication; the savage sexual comedy, inverting Cohen's normal sexual sentimentality, ceases quickly to amuse." Whatever the critics made of it, however, *Beautiful Losers* was taken up by Cohen's young readers with such enthusiasm that within three years half a million copies had been sold.

And Cohen soon afterwards moved into a different dimension of popularity as a folk-rock singer and composer. Over the years he had gone on writing songs, mainly for the pleasure of his friends. In the mid-1960s he met the American singer Judy Collins, who liked his songs and began to perform them. In 1967 he himself appeared at the Newport Folk Festival and at two concerts in New York's Central Park, and the same year did an immensely successful program on CBS/TV. His first recording was released in 1968, and he was very soon an international star with an audience of millions, ranked with Bob Dylan and John Lennon.

Not everyone applauded Cohen's apotheosis, however, or agreed that he was "the intellectual's pop singer." Literary critics who had thought of him as a rising star in the small firmament of Canadian poetry seemed to regard this development as a betrayal, and dealt harshly with his songs and their effect on his poetry. George Woodcock, for example, wrote that the songs "represent an extension *in extremis* of the sentimentality that was implicit in the best of Cohen's love poems; with the total surrender to sentimentality comes the disintegration of structure, of imagery, of intellectual content, of true emotion. As in the less successful of Cohen's earlier poems, one knows that it is not real love that is being sung about, or a real world, and the never-land that Cohen has created with his guitar and voice is precisely what attracts the masses, who, in this age as in any other, are inveterate escapists."

Most critics believe that Cohen's later poetry shows a decline in quality. John Robert Colom-

bo wrote of *Parasites of Heaven* (1966) that its author "is phenomenally talented . . . but diminishing returns set in at the point . . . [when Cohen] became a nationally known poetic showman and celebrity." In spite of his "natural ear for language" and his "brilliant lines and breath-taking metaphors," the book seemed to Colombo slight in substance and ruined by "mawkish posturing." George Woodcock agreed that "popularity has rotted the sense of craftsmanship and weakened the selective faculty" in "the glib, shallow and self-imitative statements of loneliness that have become characteristic of Cohen's poems in his present phase. . . . These pieces . . . may appear successful when used as neutral vehicles for the emotions a singer superimposes; they have nothing of their own."

The Energy of Slaves (1972) fared little better, though some critics found more honesty and restraint in these poems, and welcomed a new willingness to try out unorthodox forms. A writer in the *Times Literary Supplement* called this poetry "for people who do not know much about poetry and have no intention of learning more. . . . Prosy, inexpert, uncompelling, the poems get through love, loneliness, war, torture, self-doubt, poignant incidents, worldly wisdom, anger, regret, and so on and so forth, with the rapidity of a pulp-fiction writer thumbing through his file index cards." Calvin Bedient likewise thought that "you have to be plugged into Universal Compassion to get the slightest jolt from these poems," and Tom Wayman complained of Cohen's "unlimited contempt" for the women to whom many of the poems are addressed.

"Reading through Cohen's work," writes Sandra Djwa, "we become aware of an unsatisfied search for an absolute." His dominant theme is "the relationship between experience and art, and more specifically the suggestion that the value of experience is to be found in the art or 'beauty' distilled from it." Djwa believes that the work Cohen has published since 1964 has sacrificed "organic growth and original discovery to a pre-determined formula," and is limited also by "the increasingly self-conscious attitude of the poet as persona in relation to the codification of his central myth." George Woodcock writes that Cohen is "a fine craftsman, in a somewhat decorative manner," but complains of a shallowness of feeling, even in the love lyrics, which proceeds, he suggests, from a "solipsism that underlies all his writings."

Cohen received a doctorate from Dalhousie University in 1971. According to *Current Biography,* he has lived "fairly steadily" since 1960 with Marianne, a Norwegian woman, and with

Axel, her son by a previous marriage. The author is "dark, brooding, *sotto voce,*" and is or was a chain-smoker. His "unsatisfied search for an absolute" has led him to Eastern philosophies, vegetarianism, and astrology, as well as to drugs; he believes that "there is really a power to tune in on. It's easy for me to call that power God."

PRINCIPAL WORKS: *Poetry*—Let Us Compare Mythologies, 1956; The Spice-Box of Earth, 1961; Flowers for Hitler, 1964; Parasites of Heaven, 1966; Selected Poems, 1956-1968, 1968; Leonard Cohen's Song Book, 1969; (with others) Five Modern Canadian Poets, 1970; The Energy of Slaves, 1972. *Novels*—The Favorite Game, 1963; Beautiful Losers, 1966.

ABOUT: Contemporary Authors 21-24 1st revision, 1977; Current Biography, 1969; Davey, F. (ed.) From There to Here, 1960; Gnarowski, M. (ed.) Leonard Cohen: The Artist and His Critics, 1976; Morley, P. The Immoral Moralists, 1972; Ondaatje, M. Leonard Cohen, 1970; Sylvestre, G. and others (eds.) Canadian Writers, 1966; Vinson, J. (ed.) Contemporary Novelists, 1976; Vinson, J. (ed.) Contemporary Poets, 1975; Woodcock, G. Odysseus Ever Returning, 1973; Woodcock, G. (ed.) Poets and Critics, 1974. *Periodicals*—Bulletin of Bibliography July 1974; Canadian Forum July 1967; Canadian Literature Autumn 1961, Winter 1965, Summer 1967, Autumn 1967, Spring 1974; Commonwealth Literature June 1973; Delta November 1961; Guardian August 29, 1970; Life June 28, 1968; London Magazine August-September 1975; Look June 10, 1969; McCall's January 1969; Maclean's Magazine October 1, 1966; New Leader May 23, 1966; New York Review of Books April 28, 1966; New York Times April 26, 1966; New York Times Book Review May 8, 1966; February 18, 1973; Observer June 23, 1974; Saturday Night November 1963, February 1968; Tamarack Review Summer 1966; Time September 13, 1968; Times Literary Supplement October 11, 1963; April 23, 1970; September 18, 1970; September 25, 1970; January 5, 1973; Vogue August 1, 1969.

COLES, ROBERT (MARTIN) (October 12, 1929–), American psychiatrist, sociologist, and novelist, writes: "My parents met in Boston in the middle 1920s. My father had come from Yorkshire, England; he is from a Jewish family that has been in England for many generations: Sephardic, from Spain originally. He came to America to become an engineer at the Massachusetts Institute of Technology. Earlier in this century engineers were messianic figures of sorts —Herbert Hoover, 'the great engineer' who fed the hungry and promised to make (technological) sense of the industrial West's problems. My mother came to Boston from Sioux City, Iowa; she is the daughter of an Episcopal minister. (At this writing, 1975, they are both very much alive and well.) She went to college in the Boston area and their encounter and marriage was, of course, fateful for my brother (a professor of English at the University of Michigan) and me, but a living example, I suppose, of how the improbable

ROBERT COLES

William W. Anderson

becomes the actual. I have long been suspicious of all ideologies, including the one I had to submit to for a while, psychoanalytic orthodoxy. My parents' lives provide an excellent witness, I believe, to the continuing mystery and power of what the novelist George Eliot called 'unforeseen circumstances.' Theirs has been a marriage of the rational and the intuitive; the skeptical and the deeply religious. It has been a good, happy marriage, over fifty years long.

"My life has been unremarkable. I was born and grew up in Boston. I went to Harvard, majored in English, wanted to write, put aside a thoroughly unpromising, short-lived career as a student who wrote poems and short stories for a long, demanding, exhausting career in medicine. At Harvard I wrote an essay on William Carlos Williams, whom I got to know some before he died. His poetry and prose continue to mean a lot to me—joined as they were to his extended medical practice, given up only when he was old and felled by a stroke. I wanted to be a pediatrician, but was not tough enough for the children's good, and maybe (in view of the career I did pursue) my own. *Faute de mieux* I moved toward psychiatry and psychoanalysis, and eventually, child psychiatry. Years of training and personal anaylsis made me grateful for a certain side of Freud, for his daughter Anna, both brilliant and possessed of common sense and decency (a combination never to be taken for granted), and for Erik H. Erikson. But when I had finished my various hospital residencies and a period of prolonged and guided introspection (psychoanalysis) I was quite ready for something else than an unremitting loyalty to an office, a hospital, a clinic.

"By chance I was in the South when the civil rights struggle burst upon America in the late 1950s, and I chose to stay there and begin what has turned out to be a life's work: an effort to understand how children and their parents of various backgrounds come to terms with historical change as it happens to unfold for them. The result: three volumes of Children of Crisis, with two more about to come, dealing with Indian, Eskimo, and Chicano children (volume four) and well-to-do children (volume five). While I have done what is perhaps best called 'social and psychological observation' in that often-mentioned (by anthropologists and others) 'field,' I have not let go an interest in certain writers and their work, as opposed to their childhood experiences. And I have not let go, either, a continuing interest in certain religious and ethical issues—and in a few of those twentieth-century writers who have taken those issues most significantly (as I see it) to heart. My 'heroes,' if one is allowed them, probably tell as much about my own values, concerns, loyalties and commitments as any further wordiness on my part would: James Agee, George Orwell, Dorothy Day, Walker Percy, Georges Bernanos, Flannery O'Connor, Simone Weil. And finally there have been my wife, Jane Hallowell Coles, and our three sons: Robert Emmett, Daniel Agee, Michael Hallowell. I started doing my work and writing it up after I was married, and I am quite certain that were it not for the abiding, sustaining presence of my wife and children, I would not have been able to do what little I have done in the way of documenting how certain American children, sometimes against great odds, struggle to live out honorable lives."

The novelist Walker Percy has described Robert Coles as "that rarest of creatures, the social scientist who keeps his theory and his ideological spectacles in his pocket and spends his time listening to people and trying to understand them. Like Freud he is humble before the facts. . . . He treads a narrow path between theorizing and novelizing and emerges as what in fact he is: physician, and a wise and gentle one. He is doctor to the worst of our ills."

Coles, the son of Philip Winston Coles and the former Sandra Young, grew up as part of "a comfortable, bookish and musical" family but, according to his brother, has always been "a predominately inward person," shy and rather solitary. Coles went to Boston Latin School and received his A.B. in 1950 at Harvard, where he played for the Adams House tennis team, edited the *Harvard Advocate,* and wrote for the *The Crimson.* After Harvard, as he says, he put aside

his literary ambitions. He went to the College of Physicians and Surgeons at Columbia University, became an M.D. in 1954, and then began his "long, demanding, exhausting career in medicine."

He interned at the University of Chicago clinics (1954-1955) then served as a resident in psychiatry at Massachusetts General Hospital (1955-1956), McLean Hospital, Belmont, Massachusetts (1956-1957), and the Judge Baker Guidance Center, Roxbury Children's Hospital, Massachusetts (1957-1958). In 1955-1958 he was also a teaching fellow at Harvard Medical School. For the next two years Coles served in the United States Air Force, becoming chief of the neuropsychiatric service at Keesler Air Force Base, Biloxi, Mississippi, with the rank of captain. He returned to the Judge Baker Guidance Center with a fellowship in child psychiatry in 1960-1961. At the same time (1960-1962) he was a member of the psychiatric staff at Massachusetts General Hospital, psychiatric consultant to the Lancaster Industrial School for Girls in Lancaster, Massachusetts, and a clinical assistant in psychiatry at Harvard University Medical School.

By then, according to a cover article about Coles in *Time* (February 14, 1972), he had begun to fear that in psychiatry "he would lose a larger vision of what life is about, that in dwelling too much on the mind, the mind would become abstracted from the body, from the neighborhood, from the society and . . . everydayness." In 1961 he published an article bitterly criticizing his profession, claiming that psychiatrists and psychoanalysts had cut themselves off from all but a very few wealthy clients of their own social and educational standing. This was one of the factors which led him to the work he then undertook; another, according to *Time,* was a deep-rooted belief, inspired partly by the King James Bible, in a "vision of redemptive possibility living side by side with the possibility for betrayal and tragedy." Coles is according to his friend Erik Erikson "a very religious man, but not churchy."

As he notes above, Coles had become interested in the civil rights struggle in 1958. From 1961 to 1963 he was based in Atlanta, Georgia, as a research psychiatrist with the Southern Regional Council, studying the psychological effects of school desegregation. Coles interviewed hundreds of those involved in the desegregation campaign, white and black, in towns and in rural areas. It was the tape recordings of these interviews, edited and shaped for clarity, rhythm, and point, which formed the basis of the first volume of Children of Crisis (1967), subtitled "a study of courage and fear." The book is illustrated with drawings made at Coles's request by the small children among his interviewees—drawings which often expressed more than the children could put into words about their attitudes and anxieties regarding the people in their daily lives.

The result seemed to John Dollard extraordinary: "One sees and feels the dreadful, wonderful, disorderly process as it was emotionally experienced by participants ... from both sides." The book brought Coles the Anisfield-Wolf Award in Race Relations from *Saturday Review,* the Family Life Book Award from the Child Study Association of America, the Four Freedoms Award from B'nai B'rith, a *Parents' Magazine* Medal, the Hofheimer Prize for Research from the American Psychiatric Association, and the Ralph Waldo Emerson Award from Phi Beta Kappa, whose selection committee commented: "These case studies, presented with a meticulous concern for significant detail and with a compassionate understanding of man at his noblest and vilest, add a psychiatric and psychoanalytic dimension to the usual social, economic, and political analyses of one of the, perhaps *the,* crucial issues of our society." Mary Ellman in her review noted that there was in the book "no conscious effort to disguise the complexity of the issue, and no pretense that psychiatric examination is the sufficient or even the most nearly sufficient method of its solution. On the contrary, what emerges from the book is the inadequacy of the psychiatric mode. . . . Still, in the discussion of such unchartered lives, a professional or clinical terminology might have had the advantage of precision. In its absence here, a certain blandness of diction, an ethical simplism, becomes apparent."

What followed was not another psycho-social study but a story for children, *Dead End School,* into which, one reviewer wrote, Coles "pours his understanding of the courage and fear involved in getting an education in a ghetto school." Another children's story, *The Grass Pipe,* appeared in 1969, and two other novels have followed. In 1963, meanwhile, Coles had become, as he has remained, a research psychiatrist with the Harvard University Health Services, and had turned his attention to the plight of migrant workers. He studied the migrants for seven years as they followed the harvests north from Florida. One of the first results of these investigations was *Uprooted Children: The Early Lives of Migrant Farm Workers,* developed from Coles's 1969 Horace Mann Lecture.

The same studies produced *Migrants, Share-croppers and Mountaineers* (1972), the second volume of Children of Crisis, which describes in turn "the lives of the children of migrant pickers, sharecroppers and poor whites in Appalachia," and goes on to delineate representative social and economic communities, and such local types as the Bossman, the Teacher, the Sheriff, and the Preacher, ending with general comments on the rural experience. The third volume in the series, *The South Goes North,* appeared at the same time and deals with black and white families who had exchanged rural poverty in the South for urban squalor in the North. As in the first volume, Coles's information is based on hundreds of interviews, from which he quotes generously. "I have not handed out questionnaires or asked anyone to say 'yes' or 'no' or 'maybe' to anything," he said. "Rather I have gone to certain homes week after week, until it has come to pass that I have known certain families for years. Nor have these men and women and children been 'patients' or 'special' in any particular way. They have been Mr. George Wallace's average man in the street."

In these books, according to *Newsweek's* reviewer, "his families speak, often for half-a-dozen pages at a stretch, and out tumble the knots and tensions of real life, full of passion, ambiguity, ignorance and gritty wisdom born of the sheer need to survive just a little while longer. And the results read like verbal documentaries in which the camera, sound-track and editing equipment are all lodged in the expanding sense of a 'participant-observer' named Robert Coles." The social scientist David Riesman sees Coles's principal contribution as "anti-stereotype. Policemen are not pigs, white Southerners are not rednecks, and blacks are not all suffering in exotic misery. What he is saying is, 'People are more complicated, more varied, more interesting, have more resiliency and more survivability than you might think'." Marge Piercy has praised the lucidity of Coles's prose and says: "His writing is clean and sensitive, with at times a Biblical wash to it. His ear is open to the intent of the speaker. He writes clearly because he would be ashamed to take refuge in jargon." These volumes brought Coles the Pulitzer Prize, and a number of other awards—the Weatherford Prize, the Lillian Smith Award, and the McAlpin Medal. The only serious criticism made of them is one voiced by J. J. Conlin, who thought that the author had produced "great social descriptive documents," but lacked "a good social or sociological framework for viewing the social systems that he has depicted."

Coles published many articles between May 1967 and August 1975, and wrote or co-authored twenty-five books. *Erik H. Erikson* is a study of the development of Erikson's thought as shown in his books, and was found at times "embarrassingly laudatory." *The Middle Americans* applied the interview technique of Children of Crisis to describe the views and life-style of some working-class families "whose small devices for enduring life decently, no matter what, . . . [Coles] deeply admires," and *The Old Ones of New Mexico* deals similarly with a group of elderly Spanish-speaking rural New Mexicans. *Farewell to the South,* a collection of articles forming a postlude to the first volume of Children of Crisis, includes one essay in which Coles "candidly explains not only his own motivations for taking up what was to become a life's work but also the particular hazards that he, as a psychiatrist trained to spot instances of psychopathology, faces in dealing with 'normal' people." The interest in "certain religious and ethical issues" which Coles mentions above is evident in *A Spectacle Unto the World,* an account of the *Catholic Worker* movement founded by Dorothy Day and Peter Maurin, with photographs by Jon Erikson (who also illustrated *The Middle Americans*).

Coles's 1973 Page-Barbour Lectures at the University of Virginia examined the fiction of James Agee (who has influenced his own style), Elizabeth Bowen, and George Eliot—writers whose novels, he believes, lend themselves to his effort to understand the problems of childhood and human development. The lectures, which demonstrate wide reading in theology and philosophy, as well as fiction, were revised and published as *Irony in the Mind's Life.* Coles makes a similar approach to literary criticism in *William Carlos Williams: The Knack of Survival in America,* in which he seeks to demonstrate that Williams's art anticipated and was superior to later work in the behavioral sciences on the lives of the American working class. It was generally admired, though Helen Vendler complained that Coles was "simply transforming literature into a vehicle for his own propaganda" —his own "theories of art, psychiatric practice, and social attitudes."

The author has retained his appointment as a research psychiatrist with the Harvard University Health Services, and has been a lecturer in general education there since 1966. He is a member of the boards of the Field Foundation, the Institute of Current World Affairs, the American Freedom From Hunger Foundation, the National Rural Housing Coalition, and the Twentieth Century Fund, and a member of the National Sharecroppers Fund and the National Advisory Committee on Farm Labor, as well as of the American Psychiatric Association, the American Orthopsychiatric Association, the Group for the Advancement of Psychiatry, and Phi Beta Kappa. He serves on the editorial boards of the *American Scholar, Contemporary Psychoanalysis,* and *Child Psychiatry and Human Development,* and is a contributing editor of *New Republic.* Coles is a Fellow of the American Academy of Sciences. An Episcopalian, he is independent in his politics. Coles received an Atlantic Grant in 1965, in support of his work on Children of Crisis, and a National Educational Television Award in 1966 for his contribution to outstanding programming. He lists his recreations (though it is surprising that he has time for any) as tennis and skiing.

According to *Time,* his prodigious output has already established Coles as "the most influential living psychiatrist in the United States." His testimony helped to launch the hunger crusade in the South in 1967, has influenced health planning for mine workers, helped to preserve the migrant health program when it was about to be ended by Congress in 1970, and has done much else to bring deprived groups into the mainstream of society, and to "depolarize a divided society." *Time* says that Coles "has performed one of the most difficult and important feats of all: to criticize America and yet to love it, to lament the nation's weaknesses—its 'greedy, monopolistic, avaricious and sordid sides'— while continuing to cherish its strengths." The black psychologist Kenneth Clark believes that Coles's presence on the national scene "keeps morality, decency and justice alive."

PRINCIPAL WORKS: *Nonfiction*—Children of Crisis: A Study of Courage and Fear, 1967; Still Hungry in America, 1969; The Image Is You, 1969; (with Maria Piers) Wages of Neglect, 1969; Uprooted Children: The Early Lives of Migrant Farm Workers, 1970; Teachers and the Children of Poverty, 1970; (with others) Drugs and Youth: Medical, Psychiatric and Legal Facts, 1970; Erik H. Erikson: The Growth of His Work, 1970; The Middle Americans, 1970; The Geography of Faith: Conversations Between Daniel Berrigan, When Underground, and Robert Coles, 1971; Migrants, Sharecroppers, and Mountaineers (Volume II of Children of Crisis), 1972; The South Goes North (Volume III of Children of Crisis), 1972; Farewell to the South, 1972; A Spectacle Unto the World, 1973; The Old Ones of New Mexico, 1973; The Darkness and the Light, 1974; The Buses Roll, 1974; Irony in the Mind's Life: Essays on Novels by James Agee, Elizabeth Bowen, and George Eliot, 1974; William Carlos Williams: The Knack of Survival in America, 1975; The Mind's Fate: Ways of Seeing Psychiatry and Psychoanalysis, 1975; Eskimos, Chicanos, Indians (Volume IV of Children of Crisis), 1978; Privileged Ones (Volume V of Children of Crisis), 1978; *with* Jane Hallowell Coles: Women of Crisis, 1978. *Fiction*—Dead End School, 1968; The Grass Pipe, 1969; Saving Face, 1972; Riding Free, 1973; Headsparks, 1975. *Poetry*—A Festering Sweetness, 1978.

ABOUT: Contemporary Authors 45-48, 1974; Current Biography, 1969; Who's Who in America, 1976-1977. *Periodicals*—America August 30, 1975; Book Week May 21, 1967; Bulletin of the New England Council of Child Psychiatry May 1975; Christian Science Monitor June 29, 1967; March 2, 1972; August 16, 1972; Commentary November 1967; August 1972; Commonweal October 27, 1972; Daedalus Winter 1974; Modern Medicine Magazine June 15, 1975; Nation July 24, 1972; National Review August 10, 1971; September 26, 1975; New York Review of Books September 28, 1967; December 18, 1969; March 9, 1972; November 13, 1975; New York Times Book Review November 22, 1970; February 13, 1972; August 6, 1972; January 22, 1978; June 11, 1978; New York Times Magazine March 26, 1978; Newsweek January 17, 1972; Psychology Today November 1975; Saturday Review June 17, 1967; Time February 14, 1972; July 15, 1974; Times Literary Supplement May 9, 1968.

"CONRAD, C." *See* BENJAMIN, WALTER

COOVER, ROBERT (LOWELL) (February 4, 1932–), American novelist, short story writer, and dramatist, was born in Charles City, Iowa, the son of Grant and Maxine (Sweet) Coover. The family left Iowa when Coover was nine years old but, he says, "in our drifting around in the Mid-West we were never far away. . . . When I got away from the area after college, I never wanted to return. . . . [But] almost everything I've written has been done out of the country."

Coover attended Southern Illinois University, Carbondale, in 1949-1951, and received his B. A. at Indiana University in 1953. From 1953 to 1957 he served in the U.S. Navy, emerging with the rank of lieutenant. He was "a student of sorts" at the University of Chicago in 1958-1961 and received his M.A. there in 1965. For several years, Coover and his wife, Pilar Sans-Mallafré, lived in Tarragona, Spain, her home town. Subsequently, Coover taught at Bard College in New York State (1966-1967), at the University of Iowa (1967-1969), at Columbia (1972), Princeton (1972-1973), Virginia Military Institute (Autumn 1976), and at the University of Barcelona (Autumn 1977). He has also been writer-in-residence at Wisconsin State University (1968) and Washington University, St. Louis (1969).

Contemporary fiction, Coover believes, should draw upon "familiar mythic and historical forms," but it should do so in order "to combat the content of those forms and to conduct the reader. . . to the real, away from mystification to clarification, away from magic to maturity, away from mystery to revelation." In *The Origin of the Brunists* (1966), Coover's method is to show what happens when form is allowed to supplant content, mystery to supplant revelation. Justin Miller, a newspaper editor, investigates a new religious sect, the Brunists. An amalgamation of fundamentalists

ROBERT COOVER

and theosophists, devoted numerologists counting the days to the apocalypse, they have drawn together around an enigmatic messiah named Giovanni Bruno, only survivor of an Appalachian mine disaster. Miraculous occurrences contribute to the development of a new religion in a way that parallels the growth of Christianity. By the end of the novel, Brunism has been emptied of divine inspiration; it will nevertheless flourish for centuries—a corpse held up by an almost indestructible framework of ritual, mythology, and self-deception, by "the everlasting lust for perpetuity and stage directions."

This first novel was taken very seriously by the reviewers, though most found it flawed. Emile Capouya decided that Coover had "attempted to revive the naturalistic novel for serious literary purposes by grafting onto it fantastic, surreal, and hysterical elements. . . . He is perfectly conscious of naturalism's deficiencies and inadequacies. He tries to make up for them with rant, brutality, portable apocalypse, and an attitude toward his characters that oscillates between prayerful absorption and contempt. The scenes in the mine are excellent. . . . but his story does not convince us that it takes place in the real world."

J. Henry Waugh in *The Universal Baseball Association* is a middle-aged accountant with a weakness for liquor and B-girls, but a genius for games. His masterpiece is a form of baseball, which he plays night after night at his kitchen table, alone with his dice and his score cards. The players in this "paper league," Red Smith wrote, "are as Henry made them, mostly boozy, lecherous and selfishly scheming, and they constantly intrude on his other life." Henry's imaginary baseball association has its own history, which resembles the real history of baseball, and parodies the Biblical version of the story of man; J. H. Waugh is also Yahweh, author of the universe.

Coover's point, M. F. Schulz has suggested, is that the Judeo-Christian notion of an orderly, meaningful cosmos is no more convincing than Henry's belief in an orderly, meaningful baseball association. He concentrates a great deal on rules, averages, and statistics, but he cannot always resist the temptation to tamper with the rituals he has invented: "For all the pretence at order and pattern subsumed in the statistics, irrational chance and personal whim, not without its inference of solipsistic idealism, actually direct the results."

It was Coover's third book that firmly established his reputation. *Pricksongs and Descants* is a collection of twenty short pieces, in a variety of more or less experimental modes. Here as elsewhere in his work, wrote Jackson I. Cope, "Robert Coover's vocabulary, the sheer sense of power in the word, is luxurious, and his control over it manifest in the sure play of a number of styles: ballad, colloquial, ritualistic, parodic, apocalyptic." There are retellings of Biblical stories, like an account from Joseph's point of view of the Virgin Birth, parodies or pastiches of other writers, stories based on (but questioning the premises of) familiar fairy tales, brief parables, stories which are revised as they go along to reveal a whole gallery of possible outcomes of a given situation. In "The Babysitter," *all* of the fantasies provoked by the presence in one household of an attractive young babysitter interact with her own fantasies and also with the fantasy world of the television to raise a variety of questions about the nature of reality. William H. Gass called this "a book of virtuoso exercises: alert, self-conscious, instructional, and show-off."

The Public Burning (1977), a horrified satire on the American way, is set in New York, Washington, and California during the first year of the Eisenhower Administration, and ends with the saturnalian public execution in Times Square of Julius and Ethel Rosenberg. Along the way we are provided with an appalling panorama of the nation in 1952, and meet among others the garrulous Yankee peddler Uncle Sam, his elusive enemy The (Communist) Phantom, and Vice President Richard Nixon. Coover's Nixon, obscene in his increasingly feverish sexual fantasies about the doomed Ethel Rosenberg, nevertheless seemed to some readers the most sympathetic character in the book—desperately accident-prone (and eventually sodomized by Uncle

Sam), he does at least feel some imaginative sympathy for the Rosenbergs, and is brought to life as a complex mixture of absurdity and pathos.

Paul Gray in *Time* called the novel an "overwritten bore," diminishing historical characters into pasteboard grotesques, "a protracted sneer." T.R. Edwards agreed that the book was "considerably too long and repetitious," and demurred at Coover's "thoroughgoing contempt for our politics and folkways," but pointed out that "all vigorous satire is simplistic and excessive" and concluded that this novel was "an extraordinary act of moral passion." Some other reviewers were almost unstinting in their praise; Thomas LeClair in the *New Republic,* for example, considered it "too important a book—too total and significant a vision—to be denied by taste or ideology. . . . It is by stretching fact past 'faction' to myth that Coover obviates history and makes [this] a major achievement of conscience and imagination."

Coover's views have also found expression in several short plays. "Love Scene" is about a godlike stage director and his unsuccessful attempt to animate an onstage Adam and Eve beyond merely mechanical eroticism. In "Rip Awake," Rip Van Winkle worries about the Revolution: did it really happen, and if so and he missed it, does he need one of his own? "The Kid" is a deadly second look at the heroic myth of the Wild West, and "A Theological Position" dwells on the Virgin Birth and its alternatives in a cynical age.

A pensive and agile writer, as much indebted to Durkheim and Lévi-Strauss as to the Bible and Cervantes, Coover addressed himself to the last in his prologue to *Pricksongs and Descants:* "We, too, suffer from a 'literature of exhaustion'. . . . We seem to have moved from an open-ended, anthropocentric, humanistic, naturalistic, even . . . optimistic starting point, to one that is closed, eternal, supernatural (in its soberest sense), and pessimistic. The return to Being has returned as to Design, to microscopic images of the macrocosm, to the creation of Beauty within the confines of cosmic or human necessity, to the use of the fabulous to probe beyond the phenomenological, beyond appearances, beyond randomly perceived events, beyond mere history. . . . But these probes are above all . . . challenges to the assumptions of a dying age, exemplary adventures of the Poetic Imagination, high-minded journeys toward the New World and never mind that the nag's a pile of bones."

Coover received the William Faulkner Award in 1966 and a Creative Arts Award from Brandeis University in 1969, when he was also awarded a Rockefeller grant. He held Guggenheim fellowships in 1971 and 1974. Coover is fiction editor of the *Iowa Review.* He has published some verse in magazines, and has made a documentary film, *On a Confrontation in Iowa City* (1969). Coover and Pilar Sans-Mallafré were married in 1959 and have three children. They now live in England.

PRINCIPAL WORKS: *Fiction*—The Origin of the Brunists, 1966; The Universal Baseball Association, Inc., J. Henry Waugh, Prop., 1968; Pricksongs and Descants, 1969; The Water Power (unpublished chapter from The Origin of the Brunists), 1972; The Public Burning, 1977. *Plays*—A Theological Position (also includes The Kid, Love Scene, Rip Awake), 1972. *As editor*—(with Kent Dixon) The Stone Wall Book of Short Fiction, 1973.

ABOUT: Contemporary Authors 45-48, 1974; Gado, F. (ed.) First Person, 1973; Gass, W. Fiction and the Figures of Life, 1971; Scholes, R. Structuralism in Literature, 1974; Schulz, M.F. Black Humor Fiction of the Sixties, 1973; Vinson, J. (ed.) Contemporary Novelists, 1976; Who's Who in America, 1976-1977. *Periodicals*—Book Week October 9, 1966; Book World July 7, 1968; Bulletin of Bibliography July 1974; Critique 3 1969; Nation December 8, 1969; New American Review 11 1971; New Republic August 17, 1968; September 17, 1977; New York Times Book Review September 25, 1966; July 7, 1968; October 19, 1969; August 14, 1977; Newsweek May 15, 1972; Partisan Review Winter 1973; Saturday Review October 15, 1966; August 31, 1968; September 17, 1977; Time June 28, 1968; August 8, 1977.

CORREIA DA ROCHA, ADOLFO. *See* "TORGA, MIGUEL"

CORSO, (NUNZIO) GREGORY (March 26, 1930–), American poet, was born in Greenwich Village, New York City, the son of Fortunato Corso and the former Michelina Colonni. His mother died when he was eleven and he grew up in a succession of foster homes and institutions. "Grammar school is the extent of my formal education," he says; "the streets of New York City (age twelve) to the youth detention homes and Catholic boys' homes and the Tombs (city prison) and Bellevue mad ward (age thirteen–fourteen); to the streets again, to my first journey outside New York, Vermont, to a Vermontian boys' home, to escape, to Vermont prison (Windsor, age fourteen–fifteen); to New York City again and streets and Tombs again and streets and Tombs again (I never stayed less than three months at a time, petty charges but no one to bail me); to Clinton prison for three years (age 16–19) and then my hard-knocked education commenced."

In fact it was in prison that Corso began to read seriously. After his release he worked as a manual laborer (1950–1951), then on the Los Angeles *Examiner* (1951–1952), then as a merchant seaman, sailing on Norwegian vessels

Howard Smith

GREGORY CORSO

(1952–1953). It was during this period that he began to write poetry. Returning to New York, he met Allen Ginsberg ("I found a good poet in the Village," Ginsberg wrote to Neal Cassady in January 1952), who enthusiastically praised Corso's poems. Ginsberg showed them to the poet Mark Van Doren, then professor of English at Columbia University, who also encouraged Corso. For three years, from 1954 to 1956, Corso was at Harvard—not as a student but staying with friends in Eliot House. He says: "I could live like I did at Harvard because I did not know what Harvard was, and as for formal education, attended, though I was free to, no classes there, only visited MacLeish's class once, because he was a poet—most of my time was spent with my student friends on the banks of the Charles, drinking beer and talking about the great philosophers and the future."

Meanwhile, Corso's poems were appearing in magazines—first the *Harvard Advocate,* then in little magazines associated with Allen Ginsberg and the other Beat writers, especially Jack Kerouac and William Burroughs, who had become his friends. *The Vestal Lady on Brattle,* a pamphlet of Corso's verse financed by his friends at Harvard and Radcliffe, was published in Cambridge in 1956. These poems, mostly about humanity threatened by death, or nature, or society, were written in what Reuel Denney called a "jive-surrealist tone of voice." Denney thought that Corso "cannot balance the richness of the bebop group jargon from which his manner cleverly derives with the clarity he needs to make his work meaningful to a wider-than-clique audience." Other critics, including Malcolm Cowley, were impressed.

In 1956 Corso joined Ginsberg and Kerouac in San Francisco. There he gave his first poetry reading before moving on to Mexico for a few months, then to Washington, D.C., where he spent Christmas with Randall Jarrell and his family. Corso says that Jarrell, then Poetry Consultant to the Library of Congress, influenced him a great deal—less in "the mechanics of verse" than in "the mechanics of being." The whole of 1957 and 1958 were spent in Europe and Corso says "I wrote my best work during these years and tried for the first time various drugs."

Gasoline, his second collection, appeared in 1958 with an introduction by Ginsberg in which Corso is associated with Shelley, Apollinaire, Lorca, and Mayakovsky: "Corso is a great word-slinger, first naked sign of a poet, a scientific master of mad mouthfuls of language. He wants a surface hilarious with ellipses, jumps of the strangest phrasing picked off the streets of his mind." Bruce Cook wrote that the most successful poems in the volume were the shorter pieces, "most of them made up of bits of nostalgia and simple, though very precise, description. . . . Corso shows an uncanny ability in some of these shorter poems to touch reality directly with language." Other poems, "at once despairing and ecstatic," announcing apocalypse but hoping for salvation, showed the influence of Ginsberg and, through him, of Whitman:

> I have known the strange nurses of Kindness,
> I have seen them kiss the sick, attend the old,
> give candy to the mad!
> I have watched them at night, dark and sad,
> rolling wheelchairs by the sea!
>
> (from "But I Do Not Need Kindness")

When Corso returned to the United States at the beginning of 1959, he says, "I found myself known to people I never knew—the Beat Generation was on its way." Corso, the ex-con turned poet, had his share of the adulation and the notoriety that the life-styles and the literary shock tactics of the Beats invited. In 1960 he left again for Europe "so that I might get back to my-ownself and write and not get caught up in the frankensteination of beatnikry that soon ensued; also I did not like reading the same poems over again—it was either making it as an entertainer or as a poet—but Europe was no longer the same, I was this here Beat poet, and my old self suffered the loss of its mangled identity. Fame is a bitter business when you find yourself the object of examination, when you find you have no money to take an occasional refuge by."

The Happy Birthday of Death, published in this same hectic and demoralizing year, was the most warmly received of Corso's early books. One critic thought that Corso had recovered his balance and was writing in a more natural conversational idiom in this collection, which seemed to another writer to contain some of the most personal and moving poems written since World War II. One of these was "Marriage," a funny and touching poem which has become the best known of Corso's works, and which brought him the Longview Award. In it the poet considers the pros and cons of marriage, runs through a list of possible girls (and their families), and contemplates the horrors of the wedding itself:

> Everybody knowing! I'd be almost inclined not to
>   do anything!
> Stay up all night! Stare that hotel clerk in the eye!
> Screaming: I deny honeymoon! I deny honeymoon!
> running rampant into those almost climactic suites
> yelling Radio belly! Cat shovel!
> O I'd live in Niagara forever! in a dark cave
>   beneath the Falls
> I'd sit there the Mad Honeymooner
> devising ways to break marriages, a scourge of
>   bigamy
> a saint of divorce.

"But there's got to be somebody," he concludes, switching without warning to a minor key:

> Because what if I'm sixty years old and not
>   married,
> all alone in a furnished room with pee stains on my
>   underwear
> and everybody else is married! All the universe
>   married but me!

Corso presented himself as a naïf, a primitive, but as critics read more of his work they began to describe it in traditional literary terms. They saw that he made extensive use of surrealistic techniques, and that there were quite serious literary pedigrees for his nonsense writing, and for the work he produced out of hallucinatory experiences. Geoffrey Hartman noted that Corso was an "authentic singer" in the visionary tradition of Blake, while G. S. Fraser was reminded of Marinetti by Corso's shock tactics. All the same, he was frequently reprimanded for his lack of artistic control, his refusal to interest himself in diction and versification.

Many of the qualities of Corso's verse, good and bad, proceed naturally from his approach to the art. In *Poets on Poetry* he remarks that he lost all his early poems—a suitcase full—in a bus terminal in Miami Beach: "I never felt badly about it because I felt myself to be inexhaustible —like I had a great big supply of this stuff called poetry. The only care I took, and maybe not even that so well, was not to lose the poet. As long as I had the poet I would have the poems." And in the same essay he says: "A saving grace and a disturbing handicap it is to speak from the top of your head, putting all trust in your self as truthsayer. I write from the top of my head and to write so means to write honestly, but it also means to write clumsily. No poet likes to be clumsy. But I decided to heck with it, as long as it allows me to speak the truth. If the poet's mind is shapely then the poem will come out shapely."

Corso's decision "to rely upon himself as both medium and message," wrote Richard Howard, "rather than upon an imposition of shapeliness within the conventions of written communication, may be due to his higher loyalty to the art, or to his lack of insight as an artist. . . . All of Corso's poems are hasty productions, untimely ripped and never quite free of the shreds and shrieks of selfhood; in fact, he rejoices in a certain fakery, the suggestion that out of the anthology of Being he has never quite chosen, never really made his commitment to anything more than infinite potentiality." This seems to Howard a matter of great regret, since he believes that in Corso's poetry, for all "its vulgarities and distractions and boastings, there lie, disparate, yearning for union and the release of choosing, the elements of a giant art."

Long Live Man, which contains a number of lyrics inspired by Corso's travels, appeared in 1962, after which he published nothing of any great importance until 1970, when *Elegiac Feelings American* appeared. This long and complex poem was praised by Bruce Cook for "the beautifully sustained high seriousness of its diction. There is nothing of the bombast or facetiousness of his early work. *Elegiac Feelings American* is a poem of great maturity and (something never before felt in Corso's work) power. It is the work of a man who has at last made a fundamental choice, an artist."

Corso has also written an amusing autobiographical novel, *The American Express,* one or two plays, and *The Minicab War,* in which the poet (with some assistance from Anselm Hollo and Ron Haworth) parodies, among others, T.S. Eliot, John Betjeman, and George Barker. He taught in the English department at the State University of New York, Buffalo, from 1965 to 1970, and has appeared in two films, Peter Whitehead's *Wholly Communion* and Andy Warhol's *Touch.* Corso's 1963 marriage to Sally November ended in divorce, and he was married again in 1968 to Belle Carpenter. He has two daughters, one by each of his marriages.

PRINCIPAL WORKS: *Poetry*—The Vestal Lady on Brattle and Other Poems, 1955; Gasoline, 1958; The Happy Birthday of Death, 1960; Long Live Man, 1962; Selected Poems, 1962; (with Lawrence Ferlinghetti and Allen Ginsberg) Penguin Modern Poets 5, 1963; Elegiac Feelings American, 1970. *Fiction*—The American Express, 1961. *Other*—(with Anselm Hollo and Ron Haworth) The Minicab War, 1961; (as editor, with Walter Höllerer) Junge Amerikanische Lyrik, 1961; That Little Black Door on the Left (screenplay) *in* Pardon Me Sir, But Is My Eye Hurting Your Elbow?, edited by Bob Booker and George Foster, 1968.

ABOUT: Ball, G. (ed.) Allen Verbatim, 1974; Charters, A. Kerouac, 1973; Contemporary Authors 5–8 1st revision, 1969; Cook, B. The Beat Generation, 1971; Gifford, B. (ed.) As Ever: The Collected Correspondence of Allen Ginsberg and Neal Cassady, 1977; Howard, R. Alone With America, 1969; Knight, A. and K. (eds.) The Beat Diary, 1977; Malkoff, K. Crowell's Handbook of Contemporary American Poetry, 1973; Nemerov, H. (ed.) Poets on Poetry, 1966; Parkinson, T. (ed.) A Casebook on the Beat, 1961; Vinson, J. (ed.) Contemporary Poets, 1975; Who's Who in America, 1976–1977; Wilson, R. A Bibliography of Works by Gregory Corso 1954–1965, 1966. *Periodicals*—Critical Quarterly Summer 1963; Horizon Winter 1969; Kenyon Review Spring 1963; Listener December 27, 1962; London Magazine April 1961; Partisan Review Fall 1960; Poetry October 1956, December 1958, November 1960; Thoth 1971.

CRAFT, ROBERT (LAWSON) (October 20, 1923–), American musician and writer, was born in Kingston, New York, the son of Raymond Craft and the former Arpha Lawson. He served with the U.S. Army Medical Corps in 1943-1944. Craft was educated at the Juilliard School of Music (B.A., 1946) and studied with Pierre Monteux. By his early twenties, Craft was established as a progressive young conductor with a pronounced flair for contemporary music, particularly that of the second Viennese school of Schönberg, Alban Berg, and Anton Webern. From 1947 to 1950 he conducted the Chamber Art Society of New York, which with Stravinsky and Serge Koussevitsky as sponsors gave a dozen important concerts at Carnegie Hall and elsewhere in New York. He was a devoted admirer of Stravinsky, sometimes hitchhiking as far as Washington, Philadelphia, or Boston to attend the composer's concerts and rehearsals.

In 1948 Craft wrote to Stravinsky about the possibility of performing the *Symphonies of Wind Instruments* at one of the New York concerts, and Stravinsky offered to conduct it himself, without any fee. This led to the first meeting between Craft and Stravinsky in Washington, D.C., on March 31, 1948. This meeting (at which W. H. Auden was also present, delivering his completed libretto for the opera *The Rake's Progress*) was the prelude to a long, important,

ROBERT CRAFT

vinsky's creativity. The composer seems at the time of his early association with Craft to have reached a critical moment in his creative life; the completion of *The Rake's Progress* had apparently exhausted his neoclassical vein, and he was temporarily at a loss. The twelve-tone serial music of Arnold Schönberg was anathema to him, the high priest of tonal music, and was indeed a more or less forbidden topic in the house. But Craft's able and knowledgeable advocacy of serialism in after-dinner sessions when they relaxed and listened to recordings had its effect: the result was the last and most surprising of all Stravinsky's creative metamorphoses, into the serial composer of such late masterpieces as *Agon, Threni,* and *Requiem Canticles.*

The literary partnership between Stravinsky and Robert Craft which began at the time of the composer's seventy-fifth birthday had produced, before his death ten years later, six books jointly signed by the two men: *Conversations With Igor Stravinsky* (1959), *Memories and Commentaries* (1960), *Expositions and Developments* (1962), *Dialogues and a Diary* (1963), *Themes and Episodes* (1966), and *Retrospectives and Conclusions* (1969). The last three all contained lengthy extracts from Craft's diaries (though these were omitted from the English edition, which combined the final two books as *Themes and Conclusions,* credited to Stravinsky alone).

These books contain Stravinsky's anecdotes and reminiscences about growing up in Russia, accounts of how his works came to be written, his views on such collaborators as Diaghilev, Nijinsky, and the painters of the Russian ballet, and unpublished letters to him from these and other musicians, artists, and writers. Stravinsky's ferocious criticisms of contemporary music, conductors, performers, and very much else are mixed with program notes, prefaces, reviews, and wrathful letters to editors. While the first book was built up mainly on the interview principle—questions by Craft, answers by Stravinsky—over the years the collaboration developed and changed. Although most of what is said in the later books was still attributed to Stravinsky, its manner grew increasingly elegant, elaborate, and witty—grew increasingly to resemble the style which Craft has since used in writings under his own name.

Pointed questions in musical circles have led to the admission that certain recordings attributed to Stravinsky were in fact conducted entirely by Craft; in just the same way a fierce controversy has raged around the nature of their literary collaborations. Craft has been accused in Lillian Libman's *And Music at the Close* of using the aging composer "as a ventriloquist's dummy

and controversial association. The two men found themselves immediately in such rapport that Craft was invited to stay in Stravinsky's house in Hollywood, and to advise him on the pronunciation and accentuation of Auden's words as the composer wrote the music for *The Rake's Progress.* Craft was also to organize Stravinsky's manuscripts (and the catalog he compiled was eventually published as an appendix to Eric Walter White's *Stravinsky,* 1965).

In 1949 Craft returned to New York to resume his work with the Chamber Art Society, but it was not long before this enterprise collapsed, no doubt because its programs were so far ahead of popular taste. Craft rejoined Stravinsky in Hollywood, and for the rest of the composer's life served as his assistant, his librarian, his literary and musical amanuensis, his trusted link with the always alien world of America. The association gradually developed into one closer even than friendship, as Craft came to share the work and leisure of the household, the constant travels, and even the domestic problems. Stravinsky and his second wife Vera were childless, and for the last twenty years of the old man's life Craft was in effect their adopted son.

He was also a musician of exceptionally acute intelligence, with a special love and understanding of Stravinsky's own works. Many of the concerts and recordings conducted by the composer in his last years were only possible because he trusted Craft to conduct the rehearsals, he himself taking the baton only for the actual performance or recording session. An even greater achievement, it has been argued, was Craft's decisive contribution to the final phase of Strais used, to express Robert's views on music and other matters." And Craft has conceded that "towards the end the words were more mine than his, but he approved"—that "Stravinsky spoke and I put the words together. I don't say they were his words. But it's this or nothing, just as it is with Aristotle's *Poetics,* which were not written by Aristotle but by a grade-B student. I'm the grade-B student here."

Craft has since said that he is writing something "that explains it all. Maybe I should have said it at the time, but I'm sorting all this out now and will tell it." This has not protected him from much bitter criticism, like Hans Keller's "considered prejudice against Mr. Craft's approach to the truth." The degree of deception involved and the reasons for it will continue to be debated—whether Craft was motivated by financial greed or by a perverse kind of arrogance or by something much less ugly. Lillian Libman herself, Craft's principal accuser, has said: "I loved Stravinsky very much, but Bob needed him and loved him more deeply in a different way. He came to live Stravinsky's life for him. One of my last recollections is of Bob sitting with him, holding Stravinsky's hands and guiding his fingers over the page of a book. He was forcing him to stay alive. That's what to remember. That's why Bob did what he did."

Stravinsky: The Chronicle of a Friendship (1972) was Craft's first book entirely under his own name. These extracts from his diaries are not so much the history of a friendship as a tribute to Stravinsky's indomitable courage throughout the long physical decline of his last years, when, equipped with what amounted to a private pharmacy, he tirelessly circled the globe, conducting, recording, giving interviews, and scintillating in dinner-table conversations with the likes of T. S. Eliot, Isaiah Berlin, Genet, Matisse, Giacometti, and the Kennedys. Craft indulges to the full a weakness for cultural name-dropping and a talent for thumbnail character-assassination. There is much day-to-day trivia about travel itineraries and hotel suites, some carefully written travelogues, and an ironic account of Stravinsky's return after forty-eight years of exile to his native Russia, and his rediscovery of and abasement before the mystery of his Russianness.

The book had a very mixed reception, some reviewers dismissing it as slick, egotistical, and superficial, revealing little about Craft's relationship with Stravinsky, others praising it with the greatest possible warmth. "Reading this marvellous book," wrote Peter Heyworth, "I came better to understand the qualities of mind and character that had enabled Craft to become, and

remain, an essential part of Stravinsky's life. (Vera Stravinsky has said that he was the only friend of her husband to have disagreed with him and survived)." Craft's diaries (of which only about a third appear in this book) will presumably be further utilized as source material for the official biography of Stravinsky which Craft has now undertaken: "It's going to take ten years to write his biography. Unfortunately it will have to be written by me. Nobody else can do it."

Since Stravinsky's death Robert Craft has been a regular writer and reviewer in such journals as the *New York Review of Books,* and a selection of these writings appeared in 1974 as *Prejudices in Disguise.* Though the articles cover a wide range of musical subjects, nearly a quarter of them relate to Stravinsky, and many of them show the influence of the composer's very positive and extreme views on music and its functions, including his puritanical rejection of any suggestion that music might have expressive meaning. Craft's own intelligence, waspish humor, and flair for aphorism are well demonstrated in such articles as the one dissecting the contradictions in Adorno's philosophy of music, and another effectively demolishing Leonard Bernstein's *Mass.* David Cairns found it a "stimulating collection" which "confirms the impression of a mind of uncommon clarity and intelligence" as against the "earlier, superficial image of Robert Craft the appendage of Stravinsky."

Paul Horgan in his book *Encounters With Stravinsky* described Craft's "almost inaudible but precise speech," and said that the author was "neatly made, pale in countenance, with dark hair, and eyes like cloves set behind black-framed spectacles. He had an engaging smile which he could combine with a little twist of frown which imparted social earnestness to the trivial, and helped to spare him thought, for which he had an abundant capacity, but only for matters of consequence. . . . His hands were mostly in motion, shaping towards himself little hollow gestures of nervous preoccupation or of longing for escape." Robert Craft has won both the Grand Prix du Disque and the Edison Prize for his recordings of music by Stravinsky and Varèse, and is well known for his recordings of Baroque music by Monteverdi, Gesualdo, Schütz, and Bach, as well as of the serial music of Schönberg, Berg, and Webern. He lectured at the Dartington School in England in 1957 and at the Princeton Seminar on contemporary music in 1959.

PRINCIPAL WORKS: Stravinsky: The Chronicle of a Friendship, 1948-1971, 1972; Prejudices in Disguise: Articles, Essays, Reviews, 1974; Current Convictions: Views and Reviews, 1977. *With Igor Stravinsky*—Conversations With Igor Stravinsky, 1959; Memories and Commentaries, 1960; Expositions and Developments, 1962; Dialogues and a Diary, 1963; Themes and Episodes, 1966; Retrospectives and Conclusions, 1969 (in England, published in abridged form, together with Themes and Episodes, as Themes and Conclusions).

ABOUT: Contemporary Authors 9-12 1st revision, 1974; Horgan, P. Encounters With Stravinsky, 1972; Libman, L. And Music at the Close, 1972; White, E.W. Stravinsky: The Composer and His Works, 1965. *Periodicals*—Books and Bookmen January 1973; Economist November 11, 1972; Encounter March 1973; Hi Fi November 1972; Listener October 26, 1972; Music and Musicians September 1972, December 1972; Nation June 15, 1970; New Republic January 10, 1970; New Society November 9, 1972; New York Times June 15, 1972; July 21, 1972; March 3, 4, 1972; New York Times Book Review July 7, 1974; Newsweek January 19, 1970; July 17, 1972; Observer November 5, 1972; Spectator November 25, 1972; Time January 19, 1959; December 19, 1969; June 26, 1972; September 18, 1972; Times (London) October 19, 1972; Times Literary Supplement December 22, 1972.

Charné

HARRY CREWS

CREWS, HARRY (EUGENE) (June 7, 1935–), American novelist, was born in Alma, Georgia, the youngest son of Ray Crews, a farmer, and the former Myrtice Haselden. He has written a moving account of his family and their neighbors, and of growing up in the dire poverty of the rural South, in *A Childhood: The Biography of a Place* (1978). Crews served in the U.S. Marine Corps from 1953 to 1956, emerging as a sergeant, and then entered the University of Florida, Gainesville, which gave him his B.A. in 1960, his M.S. (Ed.) in 1962. For the next six years, Crews taught English at the Junior College of Broward County, Fort Lauderdale. In 1968 he returned to the University of Florida as assistant (later associate) professor of English.

His "strange and haunting" first novel, *The Gospel Singer,* appeared the same year. The corrupt evangelist of the title tours the boondocks, dogged by a traveling freak show which plays to the same audiences and (it is implied) appeals to the same degraded tastes. A celebrity in the world of "white-trash Hochkultur," the spurious savior from Enigma, Georgia, has installed his family there in a seventy-thousand-dollar house that they share, as ever, with their pigs. Similarly defiled is the evangelist's relationship with his first convert, MaryBell Carter, an Enigma girl whom he has subsequently systematically corrupted, and who is eventually murdered by a young black with a religious mania. When the novel opens the murderer is in the county jail, awaiting the lynch mob, while the sick and crippled of the region await the return of the Gospel Singer, billed to appear that very night. Several reviewers detected the influence of Flannery

O'Connor in this "gripping story of the devastating effect of pseudo-religion upon a community of ignorant, superstitious, poor whites," but R. P. Nelson was reminded rather of "a sort of religious *Catch-22,* moving back and forth from reality to fantasy to make the point that when man worships man rather than God, he not only worships in vain; he courts disaster."

The hills themselves are naked in *Naked in Garden Hills* (1969), the land destroyed by phosphate mining. Only a few bizarre derelicts scratch a living in this Florida desert. The novel describes what happens when Dolly, an embittered virgin, sets up a lewd tourist trap and tries to wrest control from the Fat Man, engulfed in flesh and greed, who owns the dead land. R. W. Henderson complained that the novel's "overwhelming climax, which outstrips the obscenities and indecencies which permeate the book, is significant in that tourists, presumably average Americans, are deeply involved. The conclusion is that American society is rotten to the core." Henderson, allowing that Crews was a gifted writer, objected that he sought to make his point "by caricature rather than by characterization," in a "monstrous degradation of the human spirit." Jean Stafford reacted quite differently, however: "Macabre and slapstick, howlingly funny and as sad as a zoo, ribald, admonitory, wry and deeply fond, [this book] lives up to and beyond the shining promise of Mr. Crews's first novel. ... It is southern Gothic at its best, a Hieronymus Bosch landscape in Dixie inhabited by monstrous, darling pets."

More such pets inhabit the old people's home in Cumseh, Georgia, which is the setting of *This Thing Don't Lead to Heaven* (1970), Crews's third novel in as many years. It is about the struggle of two old women (life and death?) for the tiny body and overblown soul of a midget masseur called Jefferson Davis Munro, and is peopled with such other oddities as a giantess who writes for the confession magazines, a fanatical salesman of cemetery plots, and a Cuban voodoo woman. The novel offended and disgusted some reviewers, one of whom called Crews "a none-too-clever puppeteer" guilty of "the cheapest kind of god-playing." Even Guy Davenport, who considers the author "a comic novelist of magnificent gifts," thought that he might be writing too fast: "Were this new novel not in the neon glare of its predecessors, it would stand out as an extraordinary novel. Alas, it begins to be repetitious, and gluts the imagination." The following year, undaunted, Crews offered *Karate Is a Thing of the Spirit.* It fared little better than its predecessor, striking some readers as sentimental as well as mannered and bizarre.

Car (1972), which takes as its text America's suicidal love affair with the automobile, began a recovery in Crews's reputation. Herman Mack, a Florida car salvager anxious for fame, announces his intention of eating a brand-new Ford Maverick at the rate of half an ounce a day. His family, the media, and all America observe this feat with a mixture of emotions, most of them unattractive. True love wins out in the end—an unprepared denouement which for Jonathan Yardley spoiled an otherwise "exceedingly funny" book, containing "flash after flash of genuine brilliance." But *Newsweek* praised Crews as "a satirist who's not afraid of blood," and called "this gruesomely funny fifth novel . . . his best yet."

There was a more mixed response to *The Hawk Is Dying* (1973), an ambitious novel about a middle-aged Georgia "boy" whose attempt to gain total dominance over a bird of prey no doubt reflects the struggle between technological man and nature. Rowe Portis praised Crews's ear for Georgia dialect and thought that this novel, "more lucid, more intense than . . . [his] recent work," could "only enhance his already considerable reputation"; Sara Blackburn, on the other hand, found it "a somehow shrill, self-righteous, smoothly-designed display of emptiness, hopelessness, despair."

But there was little but praise for *The Gypsy's Curse* (1974), which is narrated by Marvin Molar, a legless mute who walks on his hands, balances on one finger for the entertainment of Cub Scouts and garden parties, and reads Graham Greene. Marvin lives at the Fireman's Gym in Tampa, Florida, with old Al Molarski (whose skull was permanently crushed by a Hudson

Hornet), and two punch-drunk fighters. All is well, or at least better than might be expected, until the accursed Hester moves in, bringing destruction. The *New Yorker* wished that Crews "hadn't wasted so much talent on such silly, penny-novel mawkishness," but most reviewers were impressed. One wrote in *Library Journal* that "Crews' people are always questing for a faith, a meaning in a lopsided world, and usually with little success. That they seem impossible but turn out as real as grit is the way of Crews, who traps us and punches up the truth in good old Flannery O'Connor style." *Choice's* reviewer found the book "finally no more than a tour de force," but said that it "yields considerable pleasure in the reading because Crews does this sort of thing just about flawlessly."

Most critics now seem agreed that the mirror Crews holds up to life is a distorting one, but brilliantly polished; that he is absolute master of the genre of "comic Southern Gothic" he has invented. This is nowhere clearer than in *A Feast of Snakes* (1976), set during the annual festival in Mystic, Georgia. The day's delights begin with the crowning of the high-school Rattlesnake Queen, continue with pit-bull championship dog fights, and end with a rattlesnake roundup. Along the way, a black girl emasculates Mystic's sheriff with a razor, the losing dog is kicked to death, and Joe Lon Mackey, his years of glory as an athlete ended by domesticity, runs amok with a shotgun. Jerome Charyn wrote of the "incredible beauty" of Crews's descriptions of the rattlers, which draw the reader "into a dreamworld of primitive shapes, anxieties and ideas" in this "dangerous book." P. D. Zimmerman, similarly, was disturbed by the author's "ugly knack for making the most sordid sequences amusing, for evoking an absolutely venomous atmosphere, unredeemed by charity or hope. . . . When Joe Lon goes on a gunning spree at the end of this fantastic, ghastly, funny book, he is acting as Crews's cleansing agent, scouring the earth in the hope that something a little better might grow."

Harry Crews received an award from the American Academy of Arts and Sciences in 1972. His short stories, thus far uncollected, have appeared in *Sewanee Review* and *Georgia Review.* He was married in 1960 to Sally Thornton Ellis, and has two sons.

PRINCIPAL WORKS: The Gospel Singer, 1968; Naked in Garden Hills, 1969; This Thing Don't Lead to Heaven, 1970; Karate Is a Thing of the Spirit, 1971; Car, 1972; The Hawk Is Dying, 1973; The Gypsy's Curse, 1974; A Feast of Snakes, 1976; A Childhood: The Biography of a Place, 1978.

ABOUT: Contemporary Authors 25–28 1st revision, 1971;

CRICHTON

Who's Who in America, 1976–1977. *Periodicals*—Atlantic Monthly April 1973; Best Sellers February 15, 1968; Choice October 1974; Christian Century March 13, 1968; Library Journal January 1, 1968; February 1, 1968; April 1, 1969; April 15, 1970; February 1, 1972; January 15, 1973; April 1, 1974; June 15, 1976; National Review April 2, 1970; New Republic March 31, 1973; New Times November 13, 1978; New York Times Book Review April 13, 1969; April 26, 1970; April 25, 1971; February 27, 1972; March 25, 1973; June 23, 1974; September 12, 1976; New Yorker July 15, 1974; Newsweek March 6, 1972; August 2, 1976; Shenandoah Summer 1974; Time September 13, 1976; Times Literary Supplement January 11, 1974; World April 24, 1973.

MICHAEL CRICHTON

*CRICHTON, (JOHN) MICHAEL (October 23, 1942–), American novelist, writes: "I was born in Chicago, Illinois. During World War II, I lived with my mother and younger sister in Fort Morgan, Colorado, a town of three thousand where both my parents had been raised. After the war, my father, a naval officer, got a job as a newspaper editor and my family moved to New York. I grew up in Roslyn, a suburb of New York City.

"I had always been a rather sickly child. In contrast to my more robust younger brothers and sisters, I was not fond of sports. I preferred to spend hours in my basement with my electric trains. I was a good student and I always had a scientific bent. It is a quirk of fate that I never burned down the house with my various experiments. I planned to be an astronomer when I grew up.

"When I was twelve, I began to grow rapidly. This aggravated my thinness. At thirteen, I was six feet, seven inches tall and weighed one hundred and twenty-five pounds. My awkward appearance increased my sense of isolation. I took up basketball, more or less in self-defense. Success in sports helped me feel better about my height.

"My father encouraged good writing. I recall he would occasionally quote from Fowler at the dinner table. When I was fourteen I wrote my first published article, a travel piece in the New York *Times*. I was paid sixty dollars. I was sufficiently encouraged to make endless submissions to all sorts of magazines over the next three years. Nothing was ever published.

"When I was seventeen I went to Harvard. It was a very exciting time. John Kennedy was President and half the faculty was in Washington; I was very conscious of living in Kennedy's old dormitory. I studied anthropology and decided to become a physician. I graduated *summa cum laude* and won a travelling fellowship for a year abroad. I spent part of that year teaching a course at Cambridge University. I also began

*cri′ tən

writing thrillers under a pseudonym, John Lange, to earn money for medical school.

"After four years at Harvard Medical School I had no desire to be a doctor. I published a book under my own name, *The Andromeda Strain,* and then spent a year at the Salk Institute in La Jolla, California. Here I wrote a book of nonfiction, *Five Patients.* Then my marriage dissolved and I moved to Los Angeles, where I pursued my interest in writing and directing films. I consider my work directing to be as important as writing books. I don't see much real difference between the two activities."

Michael Crichton, who has been accused of "launching an entertainment epidemic," wrote his first book, *Odds On,* when he was a twenty-three-year-old undergraduate at Harvard. It was published the following year under the pen name of John Lange. A stream of Lange adventure-suspense novels followed, most of them paperback originals.

The Lange books, written during vacations and truancies from Harvard Medical School, were churned out, often at the rate of 10,000 words a day, primarily to help with expenses. But they also taught Crichton his trade as a writer, and the best of them are more than potboilers, exhibiting his tendency to use fiction to sweeten the pill of some social or political thesis. *Binary,* for example, deals with a mad millionaire's plot to wipe out the President, the 1972 Republican Convention, and incidentally the entire city of San Diego with stolen nerve gas. It was praised for its skillfully maintained suspense and called "a neat puzzle, in which good and evil, in the form of an introspective government agent and the millionaire, play on each other's weaknesses." A postscript, presented as a think-tank recommendation to the U.S. government, urges specific changes in existing procedures to prevent the theft of such appalling weapons.

Crichton brings a similar technique to bear on the question of abortion in *A Case of Need,* published as by Jefferey Hudson (a pseudonym borrowed by the tall author from a famous seventeenth-century dwarf). A Boston obstetrician, who for reasons of conscience sometimes performs abortions, is cited by a teenager dying from the effects of a botched operation which he did not perform. He is charged with murder, and pathologist John Berry turns detective in an attempt to clear him. An afterword discusses the case for and against abortion. Greatly admired for its tight plotting and sense of drama, the novel received the Edgar award of the Mystery Writers of America, and has been filmed as *The Carey Treatment.*

It was, however, *The Andromeda Strain,* Crichton's first novel under his own name, which made him famous. An unmanned NASA research satellite, recalled after mysteriously jumping its orbit, lands near a remote town in Arizona. It has been contaminated in space by a lethal micro-organism which promptly kills all but two of the town's inhabitants. A team of four variously qualified scientists is assembled in an immensely sophisticated laboratory beneath the Nevada desert, and the book describes, with a mass of wholly convincing scientific and technical detail, their frantic battle to prevent the extinction of all life on earth.

Alex Comfort, conceding that the story was "a very skillful and well-observed piece of fake actuality," found it "mere scientific pornography," ministering to "our need for fear." Most reviewers, however, had little but praise for the book. It seemed to Webster Schott, for example, "a reading windfall—compelling, memorable, superbly executed. Everything hangs on plot, and the plot is inspired. . . . It transmits intelligence. It expands our knowledge of the world we live in." *The Andromeda Strain* was a major bestseller, was selected by the Book-of-the-Month Club and the Literary Guild, and was made into a very successful movie.

Crichton, who sees *The Andromeda Strain* as an updating of H. G. Wells's *The War of the Worlds,* has pointed out that *The Terminal Man,* which followed, is a new version of the Frankenstein theme. It is about Harold Benson, a psychomotor epileptic subject to fits of extreme violence. In an attempt to control this condition, his doctors implant miniature electrodes in his brain and connect them to a computer which monitors his brainwaves. When a seizure is imminent, the electrodes stimulate the brain's pleasure centers and the fit is averted. What the doctors overlook in their hubris is that their patient will enjoy this stimulation and seek more of it. Benson involuntarily initiates more seizures until the blocking mechanism is overriden; a computerized homicidal monster takes to the streets.

Some reviewers thought this horrifying story (which is characteristically supplemented by a page of brain x-rays and a long annotated bibliography) the best of Crichton's books to date, and like its predecessor it was a Book-of-the-Month Club selection. But Theodore Sturgeon, while praising Crichton's expertise in medicine, psychiatry, administration, police procedure and especially computer technology, complained that his characters were "hard to know and . . . impossible to care about. . . . Dr. Crichton's verisimilitude locks itself to technology, not especially to living. . . . One regrets that so careful a piece of work should thereby remove itself from art into the area of entertainment."

The Great Train Robbery is a very different kind of novel—an account, set in 1855, of the theft by London gangsters of £12,000 in gold bullion meant for the British Army in the Crimea. It had a mixed reception, one reviewer finding it padded to the point of impenetrability with "unassimilated and dubious research," another relishing it as "a charming, diverting summer tale," stuffed with "little essays and digressions on Victorian trains, slang, technology, burial customs—even a gratuitous summary of the Sepoy Rebellion."

Dealing, which Crichton wrote in collaboration with his younger brother Douglas under the pseudonym Michael Douglas, is both a lively story about a pot-pushing Harvard undergraduate and a tract in favor of the legalization of marijuana. It has been filmed. This was followed by a second historical novel, *Eaters of the Dead,* purporting to be an Arab traveler's diary of his involuntary stay with a Viking band in A.D. 922. Ibn Fadlan, having been kidnapped by the Norsemen, helps them to combat the Neanderthal cannibals who are devouring the inhabitants of King Rothgar's mead hall (a role ascribed to the monster Grendel in *Beowulf*). Meanwhile he observes his captors from a position of immense cultural superiority, and carefully records their social eccentricities, their tastes in food, drink, and sex. Crichton adds an introduction, editorial insertions, footnotes, an appendix, and a bibliography. There were some complaints about the thinness of Crichton's "computer prose" and the poverty of his imagination, for which the pseudo-academic paraphernalia seemed to most readers little compensation.

Crichton is also the author of *Five Patients*, a lucid and entertaining nonfictional book about the practice of medicine in the United States, based on what he saw at the Massachusetts General Hospital as a medical student, and on a very great deal of research. R. A. Sokolov explained that "each of the five chapters begins with an actual case and then broadens out to discuss how that individual patient's hospital experience represents larger medical and social issues. . . . the reactionary role of the American Medical Association, for example, is devastatingly documented." In 1970, when *Five Patients* was published, Crichton was named medical writer of the year by the Association of American Medical Writers.

Prepared, it seems, to try his hand at almost any kind of writing, Crichton in 1977 published a monograph about the painter Jasper Johns to accompany the Johns retrospective at the Whitney Museum in New York. Crichton is a Johns collector and enthusiast rather than an expert, and his book had a startlingly mixed reception. Hilton Kramer said "it reads as if he had taken a crash course in the history of art . . . in order to produce one of the most ludicrous exercises in the annals of pretentious puffery to come out in a long time. . . . It is a scandal for a museum to sponsor work of this kind." On the other hand, the New York *Times Book Review* called it "the most charming and readable art book in recent years, a 'popular' text in the best sense of the word."

The author is the son of John Henderson Crichton, who was president of the American Association of Advertising Agencies and was formerly executive editor of *Advertising Age,* and Zula (Miller) Crichton. Crichton was writing scripts for puppet shows in the third grade, and long short stories in the sixth. He received his A.B. from Harvard in 1964 and then, as he says, went to Europe on a $3,000 travel fellowship. It was in 1965, during this European trip, that he was married to Joan Radam, who grew up with him in Roslyn. They were divorced in 1970.

In 1970, while he was at the Salk Institute in California, Crichton spent a day or two a week observing Robert Wise's direction of the screen adaptation of *The Andromeda Strain.* He has since put what he learned into practice by directing an ABC/TV movie of *Binary;* an extremely interesting and original science fiction screenplay of his own, *Westworld;* and his adaptation of Robin Cook's medical thriller *Coma.* Crichton, who enjoys diving, tennis, movies, and driving fast cars, finds time to read some three hundred books a year. This human dynamo is said to have an unexpectedly "easy, rambling manner." He was six feet nine inches tall when he stopped growing, and with his extraordinarily youthful face struck one interviewer as looking like "a fifteen-year-old boy standing on a chair." Crichton lives in Hollywood Hills, in a house designed by Richard Neutra, and accommodating paintings by Oldenburg, Rauschenberg, Warhol, Stella, and Lichtenstein, as well as Jasper Johns.

PRINCIPAL WORKS: *As Michael Crichton*—The Andromeda Strain, 1969; The Terminal Man, 1972; The Great Train Robbery, 1975; Five Patients (nonfiction), 1970; Westworld, 1974; Eaters of the Dead, 1976; Jasper Johns (nonfiction), 1977. *As "John Lange"*—Odds On, 1966; Scratch One, 1967; Easy Go, 1968; Zero Cool, 1969; The Venom Business, 1969; Drug of Choice, 1970; Grave Descend, 1970; Binary, 1972; Overkill, 1972. *As "Jefferey Hudson"*—A Case of Need, 1968. *With Douglas Crichton as "Michael Douglas"*—Dealing: Or, the Berkeley-to-Boston Forty-Brick Lost-Bag Blues, 1971.

ABOUT: Contemporary Authors 25-28 1st revision, 1971; Current Biography, 1976; Goodrich, D.L. Horatio Alger Is Alive and Well and Living in America, 1971; Hutchinson, T. Horror and Fantasy in the Movies, 1974; Johnson, W. (ed.), Focus on the Science Fiction Film, 1972; Riley, C. (ed.) Contemporary Literary Criticism 2, 1974; Who's Who in America, 1976-1977. *Periodicals*—Book World June 8, 1969; Guardian January 16, 1971; Life March 3, 1972; New York Times June 15, 1970; December 18, 1977; New York Times Book Review June 8, 1969; April 25, 1976; December 4, 1977; Time May 8, 1972; Vogue September 1973.

CRICHTON SMITH, IAIN. *See* SMITH, IAIN CRICHTON

*CRNJANSKI, MILOŠ (October 26, 1893–), Yugoslav poet, dramatist, novelist, and journalist, was born at Csongrád, in Hungary. He is the son of Thomas Crnjanski, a notary, and the former Mary Vujitsch. In 1914 he was drafted into the Austro-Hungarian army and fought in Galicia, an experience that left a lasting imprint on his personality and writing. He returned from the war in 1918 an intense Serbian nationalist. Crnjanski graduated from the University of Belgrade in 1920, and also studied at the universities of Vienna, Paris, and Berlin.

His poems first appeared in the magazine *Savremenik* (Contemporary) in 1917, and *Lirika Itake* (Lyrics of Ithaca) followed in 1919. Crnjanski proved from the outset a highly individual lyric poet, original both in form and theme. According to Ante Kadić, "he did not strive to be either a conscience or a guide to his generation; he wrote his personal journal; his transient loves, passions and other attachments are given in elegiac, highly emotional verses."

*tsrn yan' ski

MILOŠ CRNJANSKI

Crnjanski's verse has been called expressionist —"often obscure, irregular, disrupted, but yet personal, poetic, yielding and revolutionary, tender and violent . . . European on the surface but only Serbian underneath." Like all his work it conveys a sense of the rootlessness of modern man—what Predrag Palavestra has called "a tragic projection of man's lonely restlessness and painful alienation in a world without hope and intimacy," expressed often as "a yearning for a distant, better and more perfect world, for imagined places of eternal purity, harmony and peace."

The same elegiac quality is evident in his allegorical poetic drama *Maska* (Mask, 1918), and in his fictionalized prose diary *Dnevnik o Čarnojeviću* (Journal of Charnoyevich, 1921). Crnjanski turned increasingly to prose in the late 1920s, notably in his historical novel *Seobe* (Migrations, 1929), a powerful account of the great influx of Serbs into Vojvodina in the seventeenth century to escape from Turkish oppression. This novel, which received the Serbian Academy Prize, confirmed Crnjanski's reputation as the most outstanding figure in Serbian letters during the 1920s. Many years later it was extended into a trilogy, the second and third volumes appearing in 1957 and 1965.

Crnjanski's activities during the prewar years were by no means limited to literature. He taught history at the University of Belgrade in 1922-1927 and wrote for the newspaper *Politika* (1922-1924). His interest in politics and travel then led him into the diplomatic service, beginning with a year as cultural attaché in the Yugoslav legation in Berlin (1928-1929). In 1930-1935 he was back in Belgrade, teaching at the university, and writing for the newspaper *Vreme,* in which he supported the royalist cause and attacked the extreme left. Returning to diplomacy, he served as press attaché in Berlin (1935-1938) and then as press counselor in Rome (1938-1941). What he saw as a diplomat and traveler in Europe are recorded in *Ljubav u Toskani* (Love in Tuscany, 1930) and *Knjiga o Nemačkoj* (Book About Germany, 1931). Criticized for historical inaccuracies, these books are poetic evocations of places and events rather than conventional travelogues.

From 1941 to 1945 Crnjanski served as press counselor with the Royal Yugoslav Government's legation in wartime London. At the end of the war he was, or felt, unable to return to Tito's Yugoslavia. He remained in England for over twenty years, becoming a British citizen in 1951, when he also received a Diploma in Foreign Affairs from the University of London.

During these unhappy and disillusioned years of exile, he worked as a journalist, writing as "C. R. Mill," but continued to publish his books in Yugoslavia. These included a play, *Konak* (The Palace, 1958), a tragicomedy about the assassination of King Alexander, and the second and third volumes of his *Seobe* trilogy. His *Odabrani stihovi* (Selected Poems) was published in Paris in 1954. Sometimes attacked in the Yugoslav press as "the dead poet" and "the defeatist," he retained the affection and respect of the young Serbian poets, whom he has greatly influenced and who regard him as one of the principal architects of modern Serbian literature. His collected works were published in Belgrade in 1966, and late in the 1960s he returned to Yugoslavia.

The themes of migration, exile, and alienation are as constant in Crnjanski's writing as in his life. The long novel *Roman o Londonu* (A Novel About London, 1971) centers on the life of a Russian prince who, as an impoverished emigré in London, approaches old age and considers how to end his life honorably while he still has strength, dignity, and self-respect. The book was warmly praised as a penetrating account of both the psychology and the sociology of exile.

Crnjanski has been married since 1921 to the former Vida Ruzic, a maker of costumes for dolls.

PRINCIPAL WORKS IN ENGLISH TRANSLATION: *Poems in* Lavrin, J. (ed.) An Anthology of Modern Yugolsav Poetry, 1962; Tabori, P. (ed.) The Pen in Exile, 1954-1956. *Story in* Slavonic Review January 1945.

ABOUT: Contemporary Authors Permanent Series 1, 1975; Kadić, A. Contemporary Serbian Literature, 1964; Penguin

DAGERMAN

Companion to Literature 2, 1969. *Periodicals*—Books Abroad Autumn 1972.

*DAGERMAN, STIG (HALVARD) (October 5, 1923–November 4, 1954), Swedish novelist, short story writer, dramatist, and poet, was born in his paternal grandparents' farm house outside the village of Älvkarleby, about a hundred miles north of Stockholm. He was the illegitimate son of a quarryman named Helmer Jansson, and Helga Andersson, a telephone operator. His mother left the farm soon after he was born and Dagerman was raised by his grandparents—generous, deeply religious people with whom he spent a happy childhood. When he was twelve he went to Stockholm to live with his father and stepmother. It was a world, according to Michael Meyer, "of working-class people trying to become bourgeois, farmers being slowly turned into townsmen." Dagerman himself was all his life "a countryman trying uneasily to adapt himself to town life, and he never succeeded; for him, happiness ended when he left his grandfather's farm."

When Dagerman was sixteen, his grandfather was murdered in one of his own fields by a madman, and Dagerman's grandmother died of shock a few weeks later. He tried to write a poem about the tragedy and, though he tore up the result in disgust, this seems to have been the beginning of his interest in writing. Some years of bitter loneliness followed, during which Dagerman became involved in Syndicalist politics, and took over the editorship of an anti-fascist youth newspaper. In 1943 he married Anne Marie Götze, an eighteen-year-old German refugee whose parents had fought in the Spanish Civil War, and had subsequently been imprisoned by the fascists. Dagerman learned from this refugee family to regard with contempt the bourgeois complacency which characterized Swedish life. In 1944-1945 he served as cultural editor of the Syndicalist magazine *Arbetaren* (Workmen), and he remained a Syndicalist—though never a rigid or dogmatic one—all his life.

It was in 1944 also that Dagerman met the leaders of the *fyrtotalisterna* movement—"the writers of the 1940s"—whose ranks he soon joined, serving on the editorial committee of their important and influential review *40-tal.* This movement, which included Karl Vennberg and Erik Lindegren, was united in its sense of guilt at Sweden's wartime neutrality, its disillusionment with "systems" (such as Marxism), and its admiration for Eliot, Kafka, Faulkner, and the Swedish poet Gunnar Ekelöf. Dagerman

*dä′ ger mən

STIG DAGERMAN

Swedish Consulate

always believed (even in his own eventual despair) that politics must be an art of the *im*possible: this implied, for him, that human beings must confront their terror of existence and work through it before they can overcome it. This Nietzschean theme pervades Dagerman's work, in which existential terror fights an ultimately losing battle with faith.

His most explicit statement of this theme occurs in his first novel, *Ormen* (The Snake) which appeared in 1945 when he was only twenty-two. This evocation of a young man's obsessive fear of the menace of the outside world is presented with an intensity and authority that established Dagerman at once as a prodigy of extraordinary brilliance and as the brightest star in Swedish letters. It was followed by *De dömdas ö* (The Isle of the Damned, 1946). This modern morality, in which seven castaways are made to represent that number of deadly sins, is as intense and stylistically brilliant as *Ormen,* but relatively abstract, weighed down by its symbolism.

The story collection *Nattens lekar* (1947, translated by Naomi Walford as *The Games of Night*) is widely regarded as his finest work. Fear and the struggle to master it are again the dominant themes, but these stories derive balance and a degree of detachment from an element of dark and satirical humor. The title story is about an unhappy child who pretends that he is invisible and can wish himself anywhere he cares to go. As Martin Tucker wrote of the English version, "darkness makes all of Dagerman's characters whole, while light destroys them. . . . Yet his stories are ultimately not depressing. Perhaps the source of his strength lies in his style, which is spare and unadorned.

. . . His vision remains hard and unflinching—a search for beauty undefiled by the compromises of reality."

"Den dödsdömde" one of the bleakest stories in this collection, was adapted by Dagerman under the same title as his first and most powerful play. A husband has been condemned to death for murdering his wife, who in fact died at the hands of her lover. The public executioner falls ill, the real murderer confesses, and the husband finds himself transformed from an object of loathing to one of sentimental pity. He is left with nothing but scorn for the callousness of the people he lives among—their readiness to decide his fate in accordance with labels they have almost casually tied to him. Dagerman's message here is what it always is—that each man must face and master his own fear, having no one else to rely upon. This theme is developed in an Expressionist style and with great theatrical virtuosity. The play was immensely successful when it was first produced in 1947, though some critics have complained that it has one mood only—of terror and despair—and that ethical concerns are to some extent allowed to override psychological accuracy. It has been translated by Alan Blair as "The Condemned."

In his subsequent work Dagerman tried to move in the direction of greater realism, with mixed results, but with powerful effect in the novel *Bränt barn* (1948, translated by Alan Blair as *A Burnt Child*). This gripping study of a young man pathologically fixated on his mother is written in short staccato sentences and with the extreme objectivity of a case history. *Bröllopsbevär* (Wedding Pains, 1949) is an equally powerful study of social degradation and defeat, set in the author's native village.

Neither of these novels enjoyed the same acclaim as their predecessors, nor did Dagerman repeat his initial success in the theatre. He wrote two psychological plays, *Skuggan av Mart* (Shadow of Mart, 1948) and *Ingen går fri* (No One Is Free, 1949), the latter based on *Bränt barn*. In *Streber* (The Upstart, 1949) he attempted social realism, capturing very accurately the flavor of a particular working-class milieu but (as in other works) allowing his acute insight into character to be distorted by extraneous—in this case political and Syndicalist—considerations. In 1947 Dagerman published an incisive travel book about postwar Germany, *Tysk höst* (German Autumn).

After 1949 Dagerman became depressed and creatively "blocked." He could not finish the novel *Tusen år hos Gud* (A Thousand Years With God) and was dissatisfied with his dramatic work for radio. His second marriage in 1953

to the distinguished actress Anita Björk failed to release him from this condition. A year later, when he was thirty-one and living just outside Stockholm, he drove his car into his garage and closed the doors, dying of carbon monoxide poisoning. He was survived by his wife and an eight-year-old son. Dagerman's suicide has been attributed variously to his feeling that he could no longer meet the high expectations of his public and to a pathological sense of guilt and despair. Perhaps his death may be compared to that of the Italian novelist Pavese, who felt that people would be happier without him, but whose work shows how profoundly he cared about them.

A selection of Dagerman's satirical and mainly political topical verse appeared posthumously in 1954 as *Dagsedlar,* and there were more poems as well as short stories in *Vårt behov av tröst* (1955), which also included the moving sketch of his childhood translated in *The Games of Night.* His despairing and surrealist love poem, "Birgitta Suite" (1950), was published in English translation in *Poetry* (January 1964).

The ambiguous epitaph that Dagerman proposed for himself was: "Here lies a fallen Swedish author. Forget him often." It is clear that he will not be forgotten. What he achieved, so young, in a period of ten years, is as Alric Gustafson has said "without a Swedish parallel and is the more astonishing because of the originality of its conception and the variety and range of its form." Another critic has said of him that "he has come to stand out almost as the incarnation of that tortured period [of the 1940s], a symbolic figure whose death seemed to confirm the conception of the poet as the martyr to his vision."

PRINCIPAL WORKS IN ENGLISH TRANSLATION: *Fiction*—A Burnt Child, 1950; The Games of Night, 1959. *Play*—The Condemned *in* Gustafson, A. (ed.) Scandinavian Plays of the Twentieth Century, third series, 1951.

ABOUT: Gustafson, A. A History of Swedish Literature, 1961; Gustafson, A. *introduction to* Scandinavian Plays of the Twentieth Century, third series, 1951; Henmark, K. En fågel av eld, 1962; Lagercrantz, O. Stig Dagerman, 1958 (in Swedish); Meyer, M. *introduction to* The Games of Night, 1959; Penguin Companion to Literature 2, 1969; Svanström, R. Stig Dagerman: några minnesbilder, 1954. *Periodicals*—Books Abroad Spring 1955; Delta 11 1957; New Republic November 13, 1961.

"DANIEL, LAURENT" *See* TRIOLET, ELSA

DAVIS, OSSIE (December 18, 1917–), American dramatist, was born in Cogdell, Georgia, the son of Kince Charles Davis, a railroad construction engineer, and the former Laura Cooper.

© 1978 by Fred W. McDarrah

OSSIE DAVIS

The oldest of five children, he grew up in Waycross, Georgia, and attended Central High School there. "Some of the sweetest memories I have are of my father telling us stories," he said years later. "It gave us a chance to laugh at the world." Ossie Davis has continued to laugh at the world, though this has never prevented him from taking it very seriously: in 1935 he and a friend tried their best to get to Africa, so that they could fight alongside the Ethiopians against Mussolini.

Graduating the same year from high school, Davis hitchhiked up to Washington, D.C. and entered Howard University, aided by a National Youth Administration Scholarship. There he joined the Howard University Players, an experimental laboratory for black drama. His ability was recognized by the co-founder of the Players, Dr. Alain Locke, who encouraged him to consider a career as a dramatist. Impatient for glory, Davis left Howard at the end of his junior year and went to New York City, beginning his apprenticeship to the theatre with the Rose McClendon Players in Harlem. Davis learned his craft the hard way, as a sweeper, scene painter, and bit player for McClendon productions in Harlem basement theatres, churches, and union halls, at the same time scratching a living as a janitor, shipping clerk, or garment district handcart pusher, and sometimes spending the night on a park bench.

In 1942 Davis was inducted into the United States Army, which shipped him out for much of the war to Liberia, West Africa. After serving for a time as a surgical technician in the Army Medical Department, he was transferred to Special Services and wrote, produced, and per-

formed in a variety of entertainments. Released at the end of the war, he secured his first starring role on Broadway in Robert Ardrey's *Jeb,* which opened at the Martin Beck Theatre on February 21, 1946, and closed nine performances later. This disappointment was mitigated by encouraging reviews for Davis's own performance, and the fact that the production had introduced him to Ruby Wallace, a young actress who played under the stage name of Ruby Dee. The following year they toured together in Philip Yordan's *Anna Lucasta,* with Davis as Rudolf and Ruby Dee in the title role, and at the end of 1948 they were married.

The following decade was a busy one for Ossie Davis as an actor, though most of his roles were minor ones. He appeared as Trem in James Reach's *The Leading Lady,* Stewart in Garson Kanin's *The Smile of the World,* Lonnie Thompson in Sklar and Peters's *Stevedore,* Jacques in Joshua Logan's *The Wisteria Trees* (an adaptation of Chekhov's *The Cherry Orchard*), the Angel Gabriel in a revival of Marc Connelly's *Green Pastures,* Jo in Kaufman and Ferber's *The Royal Family,* and Cicero in the musical *Jamaica,* among other parts. In 1959 he took over from Sidney Poitier the role of Walter Lee Younger in Lorraine Hansberry's *A Raisin in the Sun.* His motion picture credits for this period include parts in *No Way Out* (1951), *Fourteen Hours* (1951), and *The Joe Louis Story* (1953), and in 1955 he had the title role in a Kraft Television Theatre production of Eugene O'Neill's *The Emperor Jones.*

Davis had by no means abandoned his ambition to write for the theatre, however. He attended a course on the subject at Columbia University in 1948, and in the next few years found time to write a number of plays, including several that he produced under the sponsorship of the Retail Drug Workers Union in honor of Negro History Week. The first of his plays to attract attention was *Alice in Wonder,* a one-acter centering on a black woman whose husband is asked by the television company that employs him to go to Washington and testify against a fellow singer, a black militant. First performed at the Elks Community Theatre in Harlem in 1952, it was produced in an expanded version the following year as *The Big Deal* at the Yugoslav Hall on West 41st Street. "Mr. Davis," wrote a reviewer in the New York *Times,* explores "many ideas which, undoubtedly, are agitating members of his race. However, he has not quite managed to harness his ideas to human beings, with the consequence that he has created more of a tract than a play."

During the 1954-1955 season, Ossie Davis

had worked as stage manager for Howard Da Silva's *The World of Sholem Aleichem,* and it was then that he began the writing of his best-known play, *Purlie Victorious.* He said afterwards that he had "felt right at home" during that season. "Sholem Aleichem's people were my people. They thought they had problems? Well, I wanted them to look inside *my* closet." Purlie Victorious Judson is a black preacher with a golden (or at least gilded) tongue. Returning to rural Georgia after a long absence, he launches a devious plot to secure a $500 inheritance belonging to a dead cousin from Cap'n Cotchipee, everyone's caricature of a white plantation owner of the old school. With this money he hopes to reclaim and restore as his church the ramshackle barn known as Big Bethel.

Purlie Victorious, with Ossie Davis and Ruby Dee in leading roles, opened at the Cort Theatre in September 1961 and ran for two hundred and sixty-one performances. C.W.E. Bigsby called it "a series of satirical portraits"—of black zealots as well as white bigots—constituting "a vivid parody of the racial situation." There was something like universal praise for the play's "scintillating" dialogue and its "skillfull deflation of demagogic language." Henry Hewes wrote that "behind the surface effect of the comedy, one cannot help but admire Mr. Davis's benevolent persistence in carrying out with a certain amount of success the writing of a cheerful comedy about a subject that cries out for rancor," while Louis D. Mitchell described the play as "a series of irresistible mirrors in which men are forced to see the folly of hatred, the insanity of bigotry, and the fruitlessness of racial-supremacy theories."

Some critics, however, thought humor an unsuitable medium for Davis's message, and Edith Oliver contended that he had used "humor to distort the truth rather than to point it up." It seemed to her that "if what the Negro in the South was really up against were dopey old cartoons like Cap'n C., then segregation could be ended in twenty minutes." The author himself has said that the play's whole point "is to prove that though the hour is late, there is still time for one more laugh—from the belly as well as the heart. Segregation . . . is an abomination to the human spirit and a shame upon the face of the earth. . . . And yet, looking at the world through Negro-colored glasses as I am forced to do every day of my life by segregation—what else can I do but laugh? It's absurd." Davis also wrote the original book for the musical *Purlie* (1970) and starred in a screen version of the play, released in 1963 as *Gone Are the Days* and rereleased (more successfully) as *Purlie Victorious.*

The only other work Davis has written for the theatre is *Curtain Call, Mr. Aldridge, Sir,* a thirty-minute reading dealing with the career of Ira Aldridge, the nineteenth-century black Shakespearean actor. This piece, commissioned by the Ira Aldridge Society, was presented in 1963 at the Henry Hudson Hotel in New York. Since then, Davis's success as an actor and nightclub entertainer has overwhelmed his career as a dramatist. His most notable performances include his portrayal of Johannes in Howard Da Silva's Broadway hit *The Zulu and the Zayda* in 1965 and of the handyman in NBC/TV's semidocumentary *Teacher, Teacher* in 1969 (which brought him an Emmy award from the National Academy of Television Arts and Sciences). His numerous movie roles range from that of the black Roman Catholic priest in *The Cardinal* (1963) to the educated runaway slave in *The Scalphunters* (1968) and a Jamaican soldier in *The Hill* (1964). In the late 1960s and the 1970s Davis has made himself a new reputation as a film director with *Cotton Comes to Harlem* (1969), *Kongi's Harvest* (1970), and *Black Girl* (1972).

"A real artist must . . . stand up and be counted," he said in a *Variety* interview, "when he sees a man—or a civilization—going down the road with a gun at his back." A member of the NAACP, the Urban League, the Student Nonviolent Coordinating Committee, and the Southern Christian Leadership Conference, he has served on CORE's advisory board, and was master of ceremonies for the March on Washington in August 1963. His eulogy for the black nationalist Malcolm X attracted nationwide attention. In 1975 Davis served as North American Zone Chairman for the Second World Black and African Festival of Arts and Culture. He received an award from Long Island University in 1963 for "outstanding contributions to the theatre," the Frederick Douglass Award in 1970, and the Paul Robeson Citation in 1975.

Ossie Davis is a tall, energetic man with a resonant baritone voice. He and his wife have two daughters and a son. They live in New Rochelle, New York, and Davis teaches Sunday school at the Grace Baptist Church in Mount Vernon. He still thinks of himself primarily as a writer, and says it is to his "eternal shame" that his body of written work "isn't as large as I'd like it to be."

PRINCIPAL PUBLISHED WORKS: Purlie Victorious, A Comedy in Three Acts, 1961; (with Peter Udell and Philip Rose) Purlie: A Musical, 1971; Curtain Call, Mr. Aldridge, Sir *in* Reardon, W. R. and Pawley, T.D. (eds.) The Black Teacher and the Dramatic Arts, 1970.

191

DAVISON

ABOUT: Abramson, D.E. Negro Playwrights in the American Theatre, 1967; Bigsby, C.W.E. (ed.) The Black American Writer, 1969; Biographical Encyclopedia and Who's Who of the American Theatre, 1966; Black American Writers, Past and Present, 1975; Current Biography, 1969; Funke, L. Curtain Rises: The Story of Ossie Davis, 1971; Living Black American Authors: A Biographical Directory, 1973; Mitchell, L. Black Drama, 1967; Notable Names in the American Theatre, 1976; Oliver, C. and Sills, S. Contemporary Black Drama, 1971; Vinson, J. (ed.) Contemporary Dramatists, 1973; Whitlow, R. Black American Literature: A Critical History, 1973; Who's Who in America, 1976-1977; Who's Who in the Theatre, 1977. *Periodicals* —America December 9, 1961; Ebony February 1961, March 1962; Life December 6, 1963; Nation October 14, 1961; New Republic November 6, 1967; New Yorker October 7, 1961; New York Times May 5, 1968; Saturday Review October 14, 1961; Time October 6, 1961; Variety October 27, 1965.

© 1979 by Jill Krementz

PETER DAVISON

DAVISON, PETER (HUBERT) (June 27, 1928–), American poet and memoirist, writes: "I was born in Manhattan. Though I have spent only three or four years of my life there, the city has always seemed like home—the sort of home you leave in order to run away to sea. My mother, Natalie Weiner, was a New Yorker and never felt altogether happy anywhere else. A vibrant, beautiful woman, she was a great giver —to her friends, her family, later on her colleagues in Democratic reform politics. In 1926 she married Edward Davison, a precocious, enthusiastic, young British poet/critic/lecturer whom she had met eighteen months earlier in London, where her wealthy parents had sent her to forget another man.

"My father had grown up in poverty without a father in the slums of South Shields in Yorkshire. He left school at twelve to support his mother and joined the Royal Navy, lying about his age, when he was sixteen, at the outbreak of World War I. Afterwards, at Cambridge, he was regarded by some as a promising postwar aspirant to the laurels of Rupert Brooke. Certainly he possessed a superb lyric gift, a magical voice, a preternatural memory for the sounds and sequences of English poetry; but, sadly, his life long outlasted his talent.

"Though we often moved during my childhood, I grew up principally in Boulder, Colorado (where my father was a professor of English for eight years), with the Rocky Mountains rising behind the little college town and the Great Plains stretching in front of it. Each summer my parents jointly directed a writer's conference, where from the age of seven I encountered heroes like Robert Frost, Ford Madox Ford, Robert Penn Warren, Wallace Stegner, Katherine Anne Porter, Ralph Hodgson, and such younger writers as Jean Stafford and Robert Lowell. I had been a sickly child, but the Colorado climate instilled a permanent zest for the outdoors.

"In 1943 my father was called away to his second war, this time in the American army. My mother and sister and I soon followed him to Washington, where he worked in the Pentagon. My mother took a job in the Office of War Information. During vacations from my Colorado Springs boarding school I too held jobs in Washington, once as a page in the U.S. Senate. I entered Harvard in 1945 as a scholarship student and studied history and literature under I. A. Richards, W. J. Bate, Howard Mumford Jones and others. My friends at Harvard tended to be musicians, and I spent much time singing in choirs, choruses, and operettas. When I went to my father's college at the English Cambridge for a year of graduate study on a Fulbright scholarship, my friends were mostly writers and actors.

"Returning to New York in 1950, I fell by happy accident into a job as first reader for Harcourt, Brace, but I had only barely begun to learn the publishing trade when I was called into the Army for the Korean war, two years of frustrating stateside service in a bizarre little propaganda unit called the Second Loudspeaker and Leaflet Company. In 1953 I returned to New York and for another two years learned all I could about book publishing. A palace revolution at Harcourt, Brace coincided with a profound personal revulsion against New York, and I fell, by another happy accident, into a job with Harvard University Press, in Cambridge, Massachusetts, where I have lived ever since 1955.

"Putting New York behind me turned out to be difficult, both literally and psychically. Within a couple of years, and not without psychiatric help, I began at last to write poems, long my most intimate aspiration. The expected difficulty of editing other people's work while writing my own proved not to be a deterrent. By 1959 my poems and poetry reviews were being published regularly in *The Atlantic Monthly* (for whose book-publishing department I had gone to work in 1956) and other magazines in America and Britain.

"In 1963 my first collection of poems, *The Breaking of the Day* (a title which refers to Jacob's struggle with the angel), won the Yale Series of Younger Poets competition. A second book of poems, embodying a perennial conflict between the images of city and island, followed the first by two years. A third, more introspective, came four years after that. In 1964 I had become Director of the Atlantic Monthly Press, an editorial responsibility which seemed to intensify editing and poetry alike. Now in 1971 I had spent twenty years in book publishing and was growing stale. I took a year's sabbatical in Rome to embark on a retrospective self-analysis in prose called *Half Remembered.*

"After returning to the *Atlantic* in 1972, I finished a fourth volume of poems under the title *Walking the Boundaries,* which also included a selection from my earlier work. Since that publication I have written little prose and have conducted various outridings toward simplicity, flexibility, and force in my poems. In 1972 I was named poetry editor of the *Atlantic.*

"I have led a quirky and problematical life, in which my wife and children have been my point of balance, as publishing has been vital to my external life and poetry to my inner world. How could such a divided existence be recommended? It has given me a life too full of work and not enough of play. If my imaginative life somewhat follows that of Edwin Muir, my poetry has been most deeply influenced by Robert Frost, master of polarity, and Thomas Hardy, master of intensity. Balancing acts please nobody, but perhaps I can justly boast of being a better publisher than other poets and a better poet than other publishers."

Davison's first book, *The Breaking of the Day,* was as he says the 1964 selection in the Yale Series of Younger Poets. Dudley Fitts, who at that time edited the series, was "impressed by the range and depth of these poems, and by the generous human candor that sparks them," and Josephine Jacobsen agreed, though she found the more abstract poems in the collection uneven in quality. The volume includes two sequences of autobiographical poems—the title sequence

about Davison's Jewish mother and Christian father, who left him firm in neither faith, and "Not Forgotten," about his mother's death from cancer. James Schevill admired the unselfpitying compassion of these sequences, and their direct and colloquial style, finding in these and other poems "that ability to move deeply into an experience and transform it with brilliant technical control that is the mark of the real poet. This is a strong first book, and Peter Davison takes his place with the important young poets in the country."

To Davison, as he writes above, his native New York "has always seemed like home—the sort of home you leave in order to run away to sea." The conflict this implies is central to his second collection, *The City and the Island,* in which images of the island as what is private and lonely—dream, nightmare, art, imagination— are contrasted with images of the city as what is known, public, and worldly. In "Lunch at the Coq d'Or," for example, the speaker describes a business lunch at a restaurant where "Each noon at table tycoons crow/ And flap their wings around each other's shoulders":

> I know my man. Purdy's a hard-nosed man.
> Another round for us. It's good to work
> With such a man. "Purdy," I hear myself,
> "It's good to work with you." I raise
> My arm, feathery in the dim light, and extend
> Until the end of it brushes a padded shoulder.
> "Purdy, how are you? How you doodle do?"

Davison's expert and varied technique, the polish and urbanity of his tone, and his Audenesque skill in "reviving and reappraising myth and legend" were widely recognized. Some reviewers could see not much more in these poems than technical virtuosity, but Phoebe Adams found "both city and island ... full of unexpected images and meanings," and W.J. Smith thought that these "graceful lines have at times a resonant intensity that is rare." The more introspective poems in *Pretending to Be Asleep* attracted relatively little attention, though Phoebe Adams praised them as "the loot of a borderer's raids into the territory between wish and truth, imagination and reality, dream and waking."

A selection from these books was published with twenty-five new poems in *Walking the Boundaries,* which appeared in England as well as in the United States. A reviewer in the *Times Literary Supplement* complained of too many generalized feelings, too little engagement with experience, too much colorless language, but another British reviewer, the poet John Fuller, responded very differently. "What an assured talent is here unveiled," he wrote. "There seems to be little that Davison can't accomplish within the Frost/Jarrell tradition he is largely working in. The earlier poems have a fine singing line, sure-footed rhythms and a well-directed variety and form. There are monologues, confessions, ratiocinations, erotic mythologies, much sympathy and intelligence and surprising imaginative leaps." There was a similar reception for the more recent collection called *A Voice in the Mountain,* which was said to contain so many good poems "that a few minor, over-academic failures are scarcely noticed."

Davison's "retrospective self-analysis" *Half Remembered* throws much light on his poetry. It is primarily an account of his relationship with his strong-willed parents—his rebellion against their domination and the long journey from resentment to compassion which brought him to maturity. Helen Bevington wrote: "The remarkable impact of Peter Davison's tale lies in the telling. . . . The scrutiny is close, the story is clearly true, of a life more than half remembered: it was lived, it is relived in all its flounderings, all the random searchings for answers to the conundrum of self."

Peter Davison's Colorado Springs boarding school was the Fountain Valley School, of which he was a trustee from 1967 to 1975. He graduated from Harvard A.B., *magna cum laude* and Phi Beta Kappa, in 1949, and spent the following year in England at St. John's College, Cambridge. The author was married in 1959 to Jane Auchincloss Truslow and has two children. Davison was a member of the advisory board of the National Translation Center in 1965-1968. He is a Democrat.

PRINCIPAL WORKS: *Poetry*—The Breaking of the Day, 1964; The City and the Island, 1966; Pretending to Be Asleep, 1970; Walking the Boundaries: Poems 1957-1974, 1974; A Voice in the Mountain, 1977. *Autobiography*—Half Remembered: A Personal History, 1973.

ABOUT: Contemporary Authors 9-12 1st revision, 1974; Davison, P. Half Remembered, 1973; Fitts, D. *foreword to* The Breaking of the Day, 1964; Murphy, R. (ed.) Contemporary Poets of the English Lanuguage, 1970; Who's Who in America, 1976-1977. *Periodicals*—London Magazine August-September 1974; New Republic October 7, 1974; New Statesman April 26, 1974; July 5, 1974; New York Times Book Review September 16, 1973; Times Literary Supplement June 21, 1974; February 10, 1978.

DE FILIPPO, EDUARDO. *See* FILIPPO, EDUARDO DE

MICHEL DEGUY

***DEGUY, MICHEL** (May 23, 1930–), French poet and philosopher, was born in Draveil, near Paris, the son of Jacques Deguy and the former André Pémartin. His father is or was an industrialist whose own father had helped to introduce modern metallurgy into Japan. Deguy's childhood memories include "golden" vacations in grandparental homes in Brittany, the Loire Valley, and on the Mediterranean; there are also darker recollections, including the execution during the German occupation of his uncle, Charles Deguy.

Deguy was educated at the Lycée Pasteur in Neuilly and the Lycée Louis-le-Grand in Paris, from which he graduated in both literature and philosophy. Immediately after the war he traveled extensively in Western Europe, hitchhiking in Germany, Sweden, Italy, and Spain, before going on to complete his education at the Sorbonne. He graduated in philosophy in 1953 and the same year was married to Monique Brossollet; the couple now have three children, Sylvie, Nicolas, and Marie-Armelle. Deguy began his career as a teacher in the cities of Nantes, Arras, and Beauvais, returning to Paris in 1960 as a professor of philosophy and French literature in various *lycées*. Since 1969 he has taught French literature at the University of Paris at Vincennes. He is also a reader for the French publishing house Gallimard, one of the directors of the review *Critique,* and a regular contributor to the *Nouvelle Revue française.*

Les Meurtrières (The Murderesses), Deguy's first collection of poems, appeared in 1959 while he was teaching in the provinces. This was followed in 1960 by *Fragment du cadastre* (Frag-

*də gē'

194

ment of a Survey), which won the Prix Fénéon. It is a sort of artistic autobiography, mainly in verse, which is at the same time a meditation on language and poetry. Deguy is fascinated by language, its triumphs and failures, and has been much influenced by linguistic philosophy:

"Well yes . . . I mean . . . of course . . . you
 understand . . ."
Speech arrives late—a long life
is needed for the brevity of art!

No it hasn't been too good; never gathered enough.
We held each other's hands in vain.
Our friend has changed his tongue.
The lips of one near were moving, inaudible.
A sister was watching as if we had not lived
 together.
A woman was hailing to be seen, greatly
 reproachful.

("Speaking," translated by Anthony Rudolf)

Deguy received the Prix Max Jacob for his next collection, *Poèmes de la Presqu'île* (Poems of the Peninsula, 1961), which includes a section of prose-poems about Brittany. *Biefs* (Millraces, 1964) also includes both prose-poems and poems in verse, many of them very brief. These first four books were widely admired for their technical versatility and for their originality—the freshness of Deguy's vision of the relationships between people, and between people and the world they live in. Critics found traces of an assortment of poetic influences—of Mallarmé, Valéry, René Char, and especially of Saint-John Perse. Deguy also shares some of the theories put forward by Philippe Sollers and other writers associated with the magazine *Tel Quel,* who are intent on "desacralizing" literature—treating it as a craft or a job rather than as an "inspired" or personal mode of expression. In fact, Deguy served on *Tel Quel*'s editorial committee in 1962–1963, but was expelled after a year, perhaps because he remained too independent in his thinking, believing as he does that poetry is too important to be left to linguists and philosophers.

In 1963 or 1964 Deguy met the Chilean poet G. Iommi, and participated with him and others in the "Améréïde" artistic expedition to Latin America, from Tierra del Fuego to Bolivia. And with Iommi he founded the *Revue de Poésie* (Poetry Review), of which seven issues appeared between 1964 and 1971. One famous issue (May 1, 1968) consisted entirely of blank pages for readers to write on themselves, just as the walls of Paris were being written on during the student upheavals of that time. Other issues of the *Revue*

de Poésie were devoted to foreign poets, including Hölderlin, Góngora, Dante, and Pindar, and Deguy collaborated in translations of all of these poets. He has also translated (in collaboration) Heidegger's critical study of Hölderlin's poetry.

Deguy is the master of a bewildering variety of poetic techniques, styles, and moods. According to G. D. Martin, this is especially obvious in the collection *Ouï Dire* (Hearsay, 1966), where "Deguy's startling virtuosity as a poet can be seen at its best: he makes his vocabulary draw on every facet of experience . . . and yet achieves poetry, for one feels his most outrageous comparisons are always 'right' and exact":

I miss you but now
Not more than those I do not know
I invent them piercing with your face
The earth that was rich in worlds
(When every king steered an island
Towards esteem for his wealth (birds'
Ash, manganese and salamander)
And castaways federated the shores)

Now I miss you but
Like those I do not know
Whose impatience I imagine with your face
I have thrown your teeth to dreams
I have used you, cold-shouldered you

Vestal virgins bring back to the Pacific
Its water steams after the faithful's departure
The ocean foams like a mongol child on his pillows
Hairy carcass curled up in the salt gully
A sea-lion blasphemes Poseidon

I do not miss you more than those
I do not know now
Orphic you have become I have thrown
Your dismembered absence into several vales
You have turned me into a guest I know
Or I invent.

("Prose," translated by Anthony Rudolf)

Actes (Acts, 1966) and *Figurations* (Representations, 1969) are essentially essays on poetry combined with illustrative poems, a characteristic fusion of poetry and poetics. In his subsequent work, Deguy has been increasingly concerned with relationships within language itself, with the poem's search "for a more profound poem/ Another below this one. . . ." C. A. Hackett writes that this "quest is as stimulating to follow as that of Mallarmé, the chief of many exemplars which include Plato, Dante, Vico, Pound, and Wittgenstein. Deguy is seeking not only to return to the source of language, to its 'innocence,' but also to reassemble fragments of our cultural heritage in order to obtain a coherent and total view of poetry and language. He is aware that in this century of technology, and the 'planétarisation' of uniformity and boredom, the threat to poetry has become so grave that it must strive to 'reprendre son bien' not merely from music, as Mallarmé had recommended, but from all disciplines and fields of activity."

G. D. Martin believes that this quest has taken Deguy into "rarified regions" where "not everyone will follow him, but the fact remains that his is the contemporary poetic genius most lavishly endowed"—of the French poets of his generation, Deguy "has perhaps the greatest range, as well as the most brilliant and experimental output." In Anthony Rudolf's opinion, Deguy's "strategic importance in the battleground which is French poetry lies in the undoubted fact that he is as brilliant and erudite as any scholar or critic, yet avoids, even transcends, mere scholarship and criticism, and in books and essays and lectures and of course poems has produced the most profound reappraisal of tradition and poetic praxis (e.g. on the nature of metaphor) of anyone in France actually writing poetry that can still be distinguished from other texts."

Deguy has taught as a visiting professor at Johns Hopkins University, Baltimore; the State University of New York at Buffalo; the University of California at Los Angeles; and the University of Perth in Australia. He has published studies of the work of the sixteenth-century French poet Joachim Du Bellay and of Thomas Mann, a writer with whom he clearly has great imaginative sympathy. He has read his poetry in North and South America, and in several European countries. *Reliefs* (1975) is a collection of essays, interviews, and discussions—"untidy fragments," G. D. Martin calls them, "in which Michel Deguy questions himself or is questioned by others," revealing "his real concern for, and tentative confidence in, poetry as a mode of knowledge—or rather as a mode of inquiry into what lies at knowledge's outer frontier."

PRINCIPAL WORKS IN ENGLISH TRANSLATION: *Poems in* Martin, G.D. (ed.) Anthology of Contemporary French Poetry, 1972; Taylor, S.W. (ed.) French Writing Today, 1968; Taylor S.W. and Lucie-Smith, E. (eds.) French Poetry Today, 1973; London Magazine August-September 1972; Modern Poetry in Translation 16 1973; Poetry Review Spring 1972; Stand 2 1966.

ABOUT: Hackett, C.A. New French Poetry, 1973; Jaccottet, P. L'Entretien des muses, 1968; Meschonnic, H. *preface to* Deguy's Poèmes 1960-1970, 1973; Quignard, P. Michel Deguy, 1975. *Periodicals*—Cahiers du chemin April 1971, January 1974; Critique February 1966, March 1968, April 1970, January 1974; Lettres nouvelles February-March 1974; Nouvelle Revue française February 1967; Times Literary Supplement April 2, 1976.

DELANY, SAMUEL R(AY) (April 1, 1942–), American science fiction writer, was born in New York City, the son of Samuel Ray Delany and the former Margaret Boyd. He was educated at the Bronx High School of Science and studied for two years at the City College of New York, where he served for a time as poetry editor of the literary magazine *Prometheus*. Delany says his youth was divided between his parents' house in Harlem and their country home in Hopewell Junction, New York. His early ambition to become a writer of speculative fiction was reinforced in 1962 by the success of his first novel, *The Jewels of Aptor,* written when he was only nineteen. Set like many of its successors in a world devastated by atomic cataclysm, it tells of a quest for power-wielding "jewels" in a manner described in *Analog* as "outrageously fantastic, romantic and gorgeously implausible . . . full of fantastic bits and glimpses of bizarre beauty, of horror that has a cleaner side, with a denouement that lifts the story out of itself."

This early promise was confirmed over the next five years, when Delany published almost two novels a year, most of them dealing with more or less conventional science fiction themes but distinguished by an original and poetic use of imagery and language. *Captives of the Flame* (1963), *The Towers of Toron* (1964), and *City of a Thousand Suns* (1965)—the trilogy later published in one volume as *The Fall of the Towers* —is an epic of sweeping imaginative scope which critics compared favorably with Frank Herbert's *Dune* and similar works by Isaac Asimov. It is an account of the desperate plight of the Empire of Toromon, humanity's last refuge. Toromon has survived the Great Fire and is protected by a radiation barrier from the poisoned wastes surrounding it, but is then threatened from without by foreign conquerors and the malevolent if insubstantial Lord of the Flames, and from within by a berserk computer.

Other products of this early period include *The Ballad of Beta-2* (1965), about a journey to the stars spanning several generations, and *Empire Star* (1966), a thoughtful and often funny novel which reminded some critics of *Huckleberry Finn*. It tells the story of Comet Jo, a boy raised in a rigid and limited culture, and shows how his blinkered perceptions are gradually extended and enriched by his travels in other parts of the universe, and his encounters with such multifaceted characters as Jewel, the "crystallized Tritovian" who is the novel's narrator, and Muels Aranlyde, the anagrammatic analog of the novel's author.

The relativity of perception is also a central concern in *Babel-17* (1966), in which the poet

Rydra Wong is entrusted by the Earth Alliance with the vital and perilous mission of deciphering the language of invading aliens. After many adventures, intellectual and otherwise, Rydra masters Babel-17, and finds that language is indeed thought—that Babel-17, dangerously booby-trapped as it is, embodies and endows her with an understanding of the nature of things far in advance of human perceptions. The novel received the 1966 Nebula Award of the Science Fiction Writers of America, and Delany was praised for his "rampaging talent [which] mesmerizes the reader with the thunderous, luminous world he has created." It seemed to a British reviewer that Delany's "great feat is his invention of truly *future* people . . . fantastic creatures that are human, yet vastly alien . . . [who] can be compared to the people of the mighty Norse sagas, raw, stormy, colourful, larger than life."

During the fall of 1965 and the spring of 1966, Delany traveled in Europe and the Middle East. *The Einstein Intersection,* written during this period and published in 1967, brought him a second Nebula Award and established him as one of America's major science fiction writers. This brilliant short novel evokes a future world in which the laws of physics have been subtly altered by some cosmic catastrophe. "The central subject of the book," Delany has said, "is myth. This music is so appropriate for the world I float on. I was aware how well it fitted the capsulated life of New York. Its torn harmonies are even more congruent with the rest of the world." In particular, he sought to probe the "musical essence" of the Orpheus legend, asking: "Did Orpheus want to live after he lost Eurydice the second time? He had a very modern choice to make when he decided to look back."

The protagonist Lo Lobey is a member of an alien race which has settled on the post-Einsteinian world, assuming human shape and striving to recover the wider culture of its predecessors, but hampered by inaccurate information. Seeking to recreate mankind's ancient myths, Lo Lobey becomes Orpheus, otherwise known as Ringo, searching for his dead love (Eurydice, La Friza), a lovely deaf-mute with telekinetic gifts. In the course of his quest he encounters the Dove, the beautiful woman incarnate; Green-eye, a ritual victim; Spider, the embodiment of treachery; and Bonny William (alias Kid Death), the red-headed killer who represents Pluto, Satan, and Billy the Kid. *Analog's* reviewer found Delany's ecumenical borrowings from ancient myth, the New Testament, and Hollywood westerns and romances "beautifully intricate and gloriously mystifying."

There is a similar shuffling of vastly different cultures and mythologies in *Nova* (1968), which draws on medieval Grail legends in a story about the struggle between two families in the Pleiades Federation and the Draco Empire. The novel suggests that twentieth-century skepticism will be mocked at in a more truly sophisticated era by characters who put their faith in fortune-telling and the Tarot pack. Delany collected another Nebula in 1967 for his short story "Aye, and Gomorrah," while his novella "Time Considered As a Helix of Semi-Precious Stones" brought him both a fourth Nebula in 1969 and a Hugo Award from the World Science Fiction Convention in 1970. At that point Delany "retired" to write his *magnum opus,* making his "work-in-progress seem more interesting than most published novels," according to one critic.

Dhalgren, published in 1975, is nearly nine hundred pages long. It employs a science fiction theme, but otherwise makes no concessions to the conventions of the genre. Indeed, it seems to owe most to the influence of James Joyce—for example in its circular structure and its many mythological allusions. It presents a highly sophisticated but deliberately vague and distorted tapestry of life in the "autumnal" American metropolis of Bellona, where an unspecified disaster has destroyed the city's social structure and modified the space-time continuum itself, and where the few remaining inhabitants have arrived at a new kind of semi-anarchical community. A young newcomer—a drifter known variously as Kidd, kid, and the Kid, who may or may not be the insane William Dhalgren—arrives in Bellona. He becomes the lover simultaneously of a boy and a girl, takes over the leadership of a youth gang, and is made the city's poet laureate. His reactions to all this, and to a large cast of other characters, are described (often several times, with variations) in a series of notebooks which are presumably (but not certainly) the book called *Dhalgren.*

"If the book can be said to be about anything," wrote Gerald Jonas, "it is about nothing less than the nature of reality." In it, "the premonitions of subatomic physics and cosmology are given flesh. The universe, as experienced by an ordinary person from day to day, no longer follows the old rules. Presumably, there are some rules, but they are not understood yet, and there is no assurance that men can ever know them." The novel's texture, Jonas goes on, "is dense and intricate, totally unlike anything else in science fiction. . . . The characters and events in *Dhalgren* are observed through a microscope: conversations go on and on; the smallest actions are analyzed and reanalyzed." Unfortunately, it is "precisely the kind of book that most people turn to S.F. to get away from. Its virtues are apparent; but it is a chore to read."

After this, *Triton,* the more accessible and entertaining (but not less serious) novel that followed in 1976, was received by the reviewers with some relief, and praised especially for its characterization. Set on one of the moons of Neptune in the year 2112, it imagines a world whose inhabitants have almost unlimited freedom for self-expression—who can change sex or religion as readily as they change their clothes. The story centers on Bron, whose problem is that he cannot decide what self he wants to express. Jonas called this Delany's "most controlled and therefore his most successful experiment to date. . . . First and foremost, *Triton* is a novel of manners—those of a rich and complex society in which the avowed highest good is the free expression of each individual's personality. . . . By the end of the book, Bron's despair has reached almost Kierkegaardian proportions. While mercilessly anatomizing that despair, Delany also manages to suggest the ecstasies of fulfillment that await those who overcome their fear of freedom."

Samuel Delany was married in 1961 to the poet Marilyn Hacker, with whom he founded the avant-garde science fiction magazine *Quark.* He wrote and directed the film *The Orchid.* Between novels, Delany has worked as a shrimp fisherman, as a folksinger, and in 1975 as the visiting Butler Professor of English at the State University of New York at Buffalo. He and his wife, who have one daughter, have lived in New York, San Francisco, and London.

While writing *The Einstein Intersection,* Delany described his writing technique as "the meticulous process of overlaying another filigree across the novel's palimpsest. . . . The designs keep going, taking your eyes up and out of yourself." Gerald Jonas has called him "the most interesting author of science fiction writing in English today," and Judith Merril says that he has "a mytho-poetic power comparable only to that of Sturgeon, Ballard, Vonnegut, and Cordwainer Smith." According to T. A. Shippey in *Contemporary Novelists,* "Delany combines his own strengths, wide suggestion and preoccupation with the craft of writing, with those of the traditional science-fiction novel—fertility of invention, skill at analysing political, social, and technological factors . . . [He] shows his gift for making highly abstract points without losing the sense of individual reality: in William James's terms, he is both tough- and tender-minded." Delany himself believes that the vision "science

fiction tries for" is very close to "the vision of poetry, particularly poetry as it concerned the nineteenth century Symbolists. No matter how disciplined its creation, to move into an unreal world demands a brush with mysticism. Virtually all the classics of speculative fiction are mystical."

PRINCIPAL WORKS: The Jewels of Aptor, 1962 (unabridged edition 1968); Captives of the Flame, 1963 (revised as Out of the Dead City, 1968); The Towers of Toron, 1964; City of a Thousand Suns, 1965; The Ballad of Beta-2, 1965; Empire Star, 1966; Babel-17, 1966; The Einstein Intersection, 1967; Nova, 1968; The Fall of the Towers (the Toromon trilogy: Captives of the Flame, The Towers of Toron, City of a Thousand Suns), 1970; Driftglass: Ten Tales of Speculative Fiction, 1971; Dhalgren, 1975; Triton, 1976; The Jewel-Hinged Jaw, 1978 (essays).

ABOUT: Reginald, R. (ed.) Contemporary Science Fiction Authors, 1975; Tuck, D.H. (compiler) The Encyclopedia of Science Fiction and Fantasy, 1974; Vinson, J. (ed.) Contemporary Novelists, 1976; Wollheim, D.A. The Universe Makers, 1971. *Periodicals*—Extrapolations May 1969; New York Times Book Review February 16, 1975; March 28, 1976.

*DELIBES (SETIÉN), MIGUEL (October 17, 1920–), Spanish novelist, writes (in Spanish): "I was born in Valladolid—a provincial capital in northern Castile—and graduated in law, commerce and journalism. At present I combine my literary activities with a professorship of history at the School of Commerce in Valladolid and a directorship of the Valladolid daily *El Norte de Castilla* (Northern Castile), which is the second oldest daily paper in Spain. My literary vocation came late, since my first artistic inclinations were towards drawing and modeling. I was twenty-five before I wrote my first article, and twenty-six when I wrote my first novel, *La sombra del ciprés es alargada,* which won the Nadal Prize in 1947. In this, as in all the Spanish novels of the time, the pessimism and despair stemming from the Spanish Civil War are evident. It's a novel of initiation into which I poured my preoccupation with death, which would later be one of the most obsessive constants, along with nature and childhood, of my narrative work.

"In these confused times, when the concept of the novel is being weakened, I believe the necessary elements of a novel to be a man, a landscape, and a passion. These elements, interlocking in a time, give us a story. This story is for me the essence of a novel. This is not to deny the novel all possibility of evolution, since each of its elements—construction, style, characters, narrative tempo—can be modified, transformed, subjected to all sorts of experiments, as long as it is employed to relate something. This

*de lě′ bes

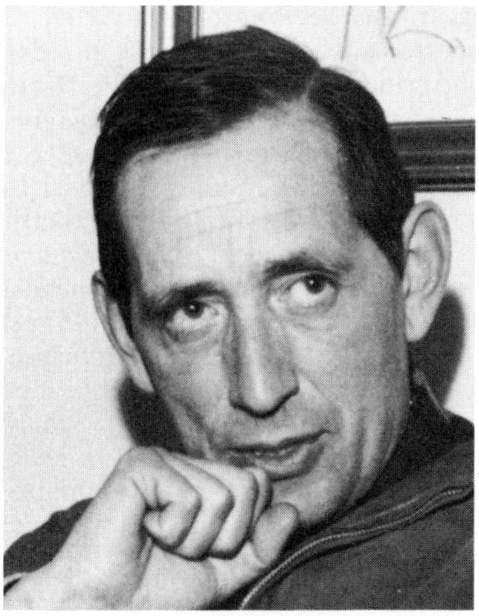

MIGUEL DELIBES

means that my own narrative work springs from men, not ideas, that for me the novel continues to have the purpose of explaining the human heart.

"Throughout my work runs a preoccupation with saving humanity from the frustrations caused by ignorance, incomprehension, politico-social organization and violence. In this sense—without considering myself a revolutionary writer—I have taken the part of the weak, of the marginal. This adds a moral ingredient to my writing which has been pointed out by several critics.

"On February 2, 1973 I was elected a member of the Royal Academy of the Language. I have given lectures in all European countries, and a course on the contemporary Spanish novel at the University of Maryland."

Delibes has lived for almost the whole of his life in his birth place, Valladolid, and that city and its province of Castile serve as the background for most of his novels. These tend to be about ordinary people in simple environments, for as an author he is resolutely provincial: "I enjoy the isolation and provincial life. I never thought my physical presence was necessary to conquer Madrid. Some people have suggested that my books are not really universal because I deal with provincial ambiences. I do not believe that the importance and universality of a work require a given density of population."

The writer's grandfather Frédéric-Pierre Delibes, a nephew of the French composer Léo Delibes, was an engineer who came to Spain to direct the construction of a railroad to Santander and settled there. His son, the writer's father Alonso Delibes Cortés, married María Setién, a native of Burgos, and moved to Valladolid, where for many years he held a professorship of mercantile law at the School of Commerce. The family was a conservative Catholic one in which religion and morality, home and domestic life, were highly important. But the father was also a passionate, dedicated hunter who transmitted his enthusiasm to his son. Hunting has been Delibes's own lifelong hobby, the subject of two nonfiction books—*La caza de la perdiz roja* (Hunting the Red Partridge, 1963) and *El libro de la caza menor* (Small Game Hunting, 1964)—as well as an important theme in his fiction.

Delibes's other major preoccupations also stem from his childhood. He was, he recalls, an anxious and withdrawn boy, very dependent on the warmth and affection of his family, and extremely devout. His vacations were spent in a mountain village where his grandparents owned a house—the setting of *El camino*—and the town-country dichotomy runs through his novels, in which the city as the embodiment of the most deplorable aspects of "progress" and the mass society contrasts with the natural and individualistic world of the country. Delibes's close relationship with his father is also reflected in the importance of parent-child relationships in the novels. Even his obsession with death proceeds, it seems, from his childhood dread of his father's death.

When the Civil War broke out in 1936 Miguel Delibes was still too young for military service. After studying for a time at the School of Commerce he enlisted as a volunteer in Franco's navy (1938-1939), serving briefly on the cruiser *Canarias* (though it is said that after the war he took considerable risks in aiding Republican political prisoners as they were released from local jails). His father was approaching retirement age and was anxious that Miguel should succeed him at the College of Commerce. In 1939 Delibes accordingly began a period of intensive study in Valladolid, Bilbao, and Madrid to prepare himself for this role, earning degrees in law, commerce, and journalism, and working for six months in a bank to gain practical experience. He had not yet begun to write, but by the age of twenty was supplementing his income as a cartoonist for *El Norte de Castilla,* beginning a long association with that newspaper. In 1945 he duly succeeded his father as professor of mercantile law at the College of Commerce, where he subsequently taught cultural history as well.

Delibes was married in 1946 to Ángeles de Castro. His studies had by this time interested him in the problems of literary self-expression and he decided to try his hand at a novel. This was *La sombra del ciprés es alargada* (The Cypress Casts a Long Shadow, 1948), which received the valued Nadal Prize—he has said that he would not have continued to write if it had not. The gloomy shadow of the cypress, found in every Spanish churchyard, conveys the central idea of the book. It tells the story of a boy who adopts his tutor's warped philosophy of indifference, seeking to avoid the risk of loss and pain by denying himself love or any kind of emotional commitment. Despite himself, he does eventually fall in love and marry, and his worst fears seem to be confirmed when his wife is accidentally killed before his eyes. His emergence from grief as the result of a religious conversion has been seen as a weak, poorly motivated, and unconvincing ending.

Aún es de día (It Is Still Day, 1949), partly perhaps in response to such criticism, reverses the psychology of the central character. For here the deformed dwarfish boy, cruelly mocked by society, retains an indestructible optimism quite unjustified by his bitter circumstances. And as he struggles to rise above these and make his life one of true Christian charity, he discovers in his darkest moment the possibility of achieving beauty through the spirit.

In these two early novels the narrative was clogged by long passages of sometimes unconvincing introspection, and there was a general air of "portentous solemnity." All this had disappeared in *El camino* (1950, translated by John and Brita Haycraft as *The Path*). Here, as Philip Polack says, instead of "long descriptions and introspections, things happen and people talk and their characters and relationships and reactions grow out of the events and the talking." The novel is simply a picture of life in a mountain village as seen by an eleven-year-old boy, Daniel, who is about to go away to boarding school in the city. He spends his last night in his native village sleeplessly reliving his childhood, and on this thread is hung a whole string of anecdotes—about the amiable village priest, the waspish spinster who scours the fields at night for sinners, and above all the narrator's own exploits in the company of his two closest friends. The idyll is harshly tested when one of the boys dies, but glows with warmth and humor by contrast with the anticipated restraints of the city. It remains Delibes's most popular and perfect novel, a small classic.

Several of his later books have a similar simplicity and looseness of structure, like the two novels which are presented as excerpts from the diary of Lorenzo. He is a devoted hunter whom Delibes sees as an example of "the uncontaminated Spaniard, a product of sun and wind, a braggart and yet controlled, long on talking and shorter on deeds, vehement and dreamy, lazy and critical, but at the same time fair in love . . . noble in principles and loyal to his friends." *Diario de un cazador* (Diary of a Hunter, 1955) won the Miguel de Cervantes National Literature Prize and was selected by several critics as their "book of the year." Like *El camino* it is little more than a string of anecdotes—about hunting, about the illness and death of Lorenzo's mother, the ups and downs of his romance with Anita—but in its easy vernacular style it beautifully conveys the flavor of ordinary Spanish rural life. In the sequel, *Diario de un emigrante* (Diary of an Emigrant, 1958), Lorenzo and Anita try their luck in Chile, but within a year are back home in Valladolid.

Mi idolatrado hijo Sisí (My Adored Son Sisí, 1954) is a much more ambitious and tightly plotted novel. Spanning a period of some thirty years ending with the Civil War, it recreates a whole epoch in the history of Valladolid, setting the changing scene with excerpts from newspapers at the head of chapters, as John Dos Passos did in *U.S.A.* In essence, it is an attack on birth control and the tendency toward small families, telling the story of an only son's destruction of his father's hopes for him. The adored son Sisí is denied nothing and by early adolescence is engaged in every available vice. Drafted into Franco's forces, he is attracted to a devout and innocent girl. Just as he seems to be undergoing a change of heart, he is transferred through his father's influence to a less dangerous zone, where he is promptly killed. The father belatedly decides to have another son and turns to his former mistress, only to find her already pregnant—by, of course, Sisí. Himself the father of seven children, Delibes dedicated the book to his seven brothers and sisters, and said he wrote it "to combat Malthusianism" and echo the Biblical command: "Be fruitful, multiply and replenish the earth."

From 1952 to 1958, retaining his post at the College of Commerce, Delibes served also as subdirector of *El Norte de Castilla,* and in 1958 became its editor, imparting to the newspaper his own Christian socialist ideology. According to Janet Díaz, he made *El Norte*'s Sunday supplement "El caballo de Troya" (The Trojan Horse) the most daringly progressive journal in Franco's Spain. Pressure against the newspaper mounted in Madrid, and in 1963, when reprisals were threatened against Delibes's friends and associates, he was forced to relinquish the editorship, though he has continued to serve on its board.

Delibes's particular concerns, reflected in the

articles and essays collected in such books as *Un año de mi vida* (A Year of My Life, 1972), are the desperate circumstances of the Spanish poor, and the need for a better ecological balance. As he said in his speech on being admitted to the Royal Academy of the Language in 1975: "The present direction of progress does not suit me; by that I mean that it makes me uneasy to see how technical development is pursued at the cost of man and that the technology-nature equation is formulated in a spirit of competition. . . . When we look carefully, we can see that twentieth-century man has learnt only how to compete and the day when we shall all be capable of going somewhere together is forever retreating into the distance."

These values are asserted in all of Delibes's work, and his criticism of society, though mild in comparison with that of his contemporary Camilo José Cela, is central to such novels as *La hoja roja* (The Red Leaf, 1959), which deals with the problems of old age, and received the Premio Juan March, and *Las ratas* (The Rats, 1961). The water rats in the latter are an essential element in the diet of some of the cave dwellers in a desperately backward Castilian village. Deprivation and isolation produce primitive mentalities like that of el Tío Ratero, the cave dweller who hunts and sells the rats. Philip Polack called this "a bitter but very beautiful book."

Later works such as *El príncipe destronado* (The Dethroned Prince, 1973), *Las guerras de nuestros antepasados* (The Wars of Our Ancestors, 1975), and above all *Parábola del náufrago* (Parable of the Shipwrecked Man, 1969) show Delibes experimenting with new techniques and structures. *Parábola* is a Kafkaesque fantasy about the total crushing and dehumanization of the few who dare to be different. Delibes has also produced many short stories in collections such as *La partida* (The Departure, 1954) and *Siestas con viento sur* (Siestas With the Southern Breeze, 1957), which won the Fastenrath Prize. He has traveled very widely, and has published a number of books about his impressions of the countries he has visited, including *USA y yo* (1966, translated by Alfred Johnson as *Smoke on the Ground*), and *La primavera de Praga* (Springtime in Prague, 1968), a sympathetic account of the Czech experiment in democratic socialism.

Delibes is one of the most admired and popular of living Spanish novelists. According to Philip Polack, "it is the patient, sober exploration of universal themes . . . that makes Delibes' novels much more than trivial records of a few isolated human beings in their humdrum environments. . . . the Spanish scene is surveyed with a rare blend of sympathy and humour, of detachment and deep emotion." Janet Díaz says that Delibes is a man "of mercurial temperament, sad and high-spirited by turns"; he has "become more liberal with the years and progressively more disillusioned with reigning conditions in [Franco's] Spain."

PRINCIPAL WORKS IN ENGLISH TRANSLATION: The Path, 1960; Smoke on the Ground, 1972.

ABOUT: Amor Vázquez, J. and Kossoff, R. *introduction to* El camino (Holt scholastic edition), 1960; Brown, G. G. A Literary History of Spain: The Twentieth Century, 1972; Chandler, R.E. and Schwartz, K. A New History of Spanish Literature, 1961; Contemporary Authors 45-48, 1974; Díaz, J.W. Miguel Delibes (Twayne's World Authors), 1971; López Martínez, L. La novelística de Miguel Delibes, 1973; Pauk, E. Miguel Delibes, 1975; Polack, P. *introduction to* El camino (students' edition), 1963. *Periodicals*—Hispania December 1963; Spain August 1975; Vida Hispánica Summer 1965; Times Literary Supplement February 17, 1961.

DICKINSON, PETER (December 16, 1927–), English writer of detective stories and children's books, was born in Livingstone, Northern Rhodesia (now Zambia). He is the son of Richard Sebastian Willoughby Dickinson, a colonial civil servant, and the former Nancy Lovemore. Dickinson's parents returned to England when he was seven. He grew up there, and was educated at Eton College. There followed a "chaotic period" as a conscript in the British army (1946-1948) before Dickinson went on to King's College, Cambridge. He received his B.A. in 1951.

While he was still at Cambridge, Dickinson's tutor asked him if he would care to join the staff of *Punch,* the venerable British humor magazine. He did so in 1952 and worked there until 1969, serving as assistant art editor, and then as assistant editor in charge of beauty care and agriculture (which, as he says, at least brought him free hot-water bottles and garden fertilizers). He also contributed verse to the magazine, and for a time reviewed detective stories.

Then it occurred to Dickinson that he was approaching forty and was less than a household name. "There is this extraordinary feeling," he says, "when all one's contemporaries are brigadiers and bishops, that if one doesn't start being go-go, one will be went-went." He stopped reviewing detective stories and settled down to write one. It was to incorporate a strange image which had come into his head: "I had a picture of a tribesman lying dead on a bare floor in a room in London, with a lamp at his feet and a wake going on around him, and from that I got this corking idea which you could hardly go wrong with, provided you could make up a tribe realistically."

Not everyone would agree that "you could

PETER DICKINSON

Fay Godwin ©

posed to make a routine investigation of the sad suicide of an old family retainer, but he soon comes to believe that there is more to this simple tragedy than meets the eye.

Both the critics and the general public have warmed to Jimmy Pibble. Dickinson described him as "an elderly, intelligent man, refreshing in that he is clearly not a great lover, not a strong personality but fairly easily browbeaten. . . . Likeable, unintentionally cuddly. . . . I suppose he is like what a fairly unambitious man would like to think of himself as, towards the end of his working life; honourable but having resigned himself to the fact that he is not the tops."

In *The Seals,* published in 1970, and called *The Sinful Stones* in America, Pibble visits a small Hebridean island to investigate the activities of a strange monastery where Sir Francis Francis, a nonagenarian scientist of genius, is a guest or possibly a prisoner. And *Sleep and His Brother,* which followed a year later, is even more remarkable in its concerns. Thanks to the machinations of more ruthless and ambitious colleagues, Pibble has lost his job at the Yard, and is struggling to adjust himself to early retirement. He becomes involved with the problems of the McNair Foundation, a charity which exists to care for the victims of cathypynia. This is a rare and fatal disease afflicting children, who become obese, sleep a great deal, and are mentally retarded, but have by way of compensation certain gifts of a parapsychic nature. Along with these strangely appealing children we are introduced to a pair of doctors with problems of their own, and a rich Greek philanthropist. "There is murder in the offing," wrote the *New Yorker*'s reviewer. "The cathypynics whimperingly sense it, and so, irresistibly, do we." One critic found the book diffuse and disappointing, but most shared the opinion of "Newgate Callendar," who thought it a virtuoso performance: "It is not so much that [Dickinson] is an unusually fine prose stylist. Even more, he has the ability to suggest, to leave things unsaid, and over his books hangs a suspended cloud that can scare the reader."

Pibble's retirement is interrupted again in *The Lizard in the Cup* (1972). This drew even warmer praise from the pseudonymous Callendar, who wrote: "The book is not only a travelogue about one of the Greek islands, and a basic introduction to drug traffic. It is about people. Dickinson is one of the most natural and literate of mystery writers. His people talk as people really talk; they have understandable motivations; and each person emerges as a believable character in his own right. But Dickinson never forgets that

hardly go wrong" with Dickinson's idea, but certainly he did not. It concerns the last surviving members of the Ku tribe, who have been brought to England from New Guinea by the wealthy daughter of a missionary, and installed in a house in London. The Ku headman is murdered, and Inspector Pibble of New Scotland Yard finds his inquiries hindered by the immense cultural gap between himself and the tribesmen, who in spite of their impeccable English subscribe to values and religious beliefs remote from his own. He has to become an amateur anthropologist before he can begin to approach a solution to the crime.

The book, called *Skin Deep* in Britain and *The Glass-Sided Ants' Nest* in the United States, was published in 1968 and universally admired. *Library Journal* called it "a compassionately written first novel of surprising dimension," and *Critic* thought it "one of the most offbeat detective stories to appear in a number of years. The sleuth is a semi-hero who stands halfway between 'Handsome' West and Inspector Dover, both in charm and intelligence. Mr. Dickinson . . . may fudge just a little in his solution, but the fascination of a tribal murder in the heart of London is so great that you won't really mind."

Skin Deep received the Gold Dagger award of the Crime Writers' Association as the best mystery of 1968, and Dickinson carried off that honor again in 1969 with *A Pride of Heroes,* called *The Old English Peep Show* in the United States. Jimmy Pibble, now a superintendent, goes to Herrings, an English stately home which has been turned into a highly successful tourist trap by its owners, Sir Richard and Sir Ralph Clavering, a brace of aged war heroes. Pibble is sup-

he is writing a mystery story. There is plenty of action and the plotting is impeccable."

The Green Gene (1973) is not a detective story but an exercise in science fiction and social satire, with an even less heroic and confident hero than Jimmy Pibble. This is Mr. Humayan, an Indian technical expert who has been brought to Britain to investigate the "Celtic gene" which is turning a subordinated and increasingly rebellious section of the population bright green. Humayan, a nervous, sensitive, and deeply insecure man, gets himself dangerously involved, politically and sexually, with the green revolutionary forces, but eventually triumphs over his problems with a mixture of cowardice and verve.

"If we were asked which modern writer could pull off a detective story based on anthropology and psycholinguistics," wrote one reviewer of *The Poison Oracle* (1974), "the answer could only be Peter Dickinson." Wesley Morris is a rather reclusive scholar who works as palace zoo-keeper in a small Arabian sheikdom. His principal interest is in teaching his intelligent chimpanzee Dinah to communicate, using colored plastic chips, but he is also intrigued by the sheikdom's primitive marsh-dwellers, whose language has no construction for cause and effect. When an oil-motivated assassination threatens the marshmen's way of life and the very structure of the state, Morris finds himself (and Dinah) unavoidably involved in the effort to identify the assassin. "It is hard to praise this book too highly," said a writer in the *Times Literary Supplement.* "The interweaving of strands, all intrinsic, each of its own story-telling value, is brilliant. Characterization is more than adequate, and not least of Morris himself, a kindly man of low sexual drive but intense devotions. ... There is no intention of asking us to accept this as a serious novel of art and insight. Instead, it is a model of the highest weight a detective story can bear."

There was very nearly equal enthusiasm for *The Lively Dead* (1975), in which the aristocratic but socially conscious Lydia, landlady of a run-down rooming house in Kensington, is interrupted in her campaigns against dry rot and bureaucracy by two pickled corpses, a turbanned thug, the police, and a Russian spy. "How delicious it is," wrote H.R.F. Keating, "to enter once more the wild Dickinsonian world, to slide into its warm and piquant depths and wriggle with pleasure as if in some transcendent bubble-bath all tiny expected ticklings yet one solid and equal scented substance. ... events, spies, frighteners and zaniness begin from page one and mount in liveliness and genuine suspense . . . to the end. Characters are splen-

did, skyhigh improbable but always rooted in simple truth. Description, of both scenes and happenings, is wonderfully skilful (a Sunday taxi buzzes along 'like a bluebottle in an empty kitchen'). . . . Dickinson has something to say. Here, illustrated by every extraordinary individual who stalks the pages, is a voice reminding us not to dream of imaginary and empty futures but to acknowledge and welcome the force of life as it shows itself here and now, thrusting 'its green blade through.' "

This triumph was followed by yet another in *King and Joker* (1976), "an irresistibly entertaining fantasy predicated on the idea that the Duke of Clarence, the oldest son of Edward VII, did not die of pneumonia but survived to marry Mary of Teck and succeed to the throne." The British royal family, thus altered, and democratized on the Swedish model, is troubled by a series of foolish practical jokes which cease to be even mildly amusing when the king's cousin is found murdered. It seemed to P.D. Zimmerman that "Dickinson has created the wholly believable character of a princess whose loss of innocence is more intriguing than the detective work that surrounds her. . . . Few detective stories offer enlarging experiences. But in his heroine Dickinson captures both the adolescent state of mind—with its preoccupations about identity and half-right notions of adult behavior—and the royal state of mind, with its oscillations between public posturing and private conflict."

The technique which Dickinson uses in this novel of looking at the action through a child's eyes is one that he has used to excellent effect in his books for children. His work in this field, which some critics consider even better than his adult thrillers, began with the "Changes" trilogy—*The Weathermonger, Heartsease,* and *The Devil's Children*—of which the second and third volumes were both Junior Literary Guild selections. These stories are set in an England of the near future which has abruptly reverted to medieval bigotry; machinery has come to be regarded as the work of the devil, and those who understand it as witches. Dickinson's subsequent work for children includes fantasies set in contemporary Wales, sixth-century Byzantium, and Baghdad, all of them praised in the highest terms. *The Blue Hawk* (1976), a "magnificent tale" with "fascinating political and philosophical overtones," brought him the Guardian Award for children's fiction in 1977. Dickinson takes his children's books just as seriously as his crime fiction, "although they are easier to write, as it is easier to cook a good breakfast than a good dinner."

Peter Dickinson has four children of his own

by his 1953 marriage to Mary Rose Bernard. He lives with his family in the North Kensington district of London, and describes himself as "leftish" in politics, and a "lapsed Anglican." Catherine Stott, who interviewed him for the *Guardian,* says that his personal style "is true-blue aristocratic camp . . . one of those elegant anachronisms who use Wodehousian words such as *rum, corking* and *fubsy* in a deep fruity voice, and have a habit of throwing back their heads to laugh, bred long ago from the squirearchical habit of associating too closely with horses. The camp bit enables him to flatter himself outrageously while retaining his charm."

Asked why his writing career started so late, he said: "I think there is a strong element of lying fallow; that there is an awful lot of stuff which you happen to know which is lying around in your mind in a rather untidy way. People who start being brilliant writers at twenty simply haven't got the store of rather trivial experience that I have, and the oddities of knowledge, even if they have gone up the Orinoco in a canoe. This is what does give the reader an impression of richness, and I always try to give them more than their money's worth." In the same *Guardian* interview, Dickinson said that he had "read practically no modern fiction. I am, in a highbrow sense, almost illiterate . . . not totally since I've read everything by anyone who's dead . . . I like plots and stories and well-made plays. I dream in plots, and have been known to wake up shouting, 'I simply will not dream these dreadful clichés.' " And in *Contemporary Authors* he writes that he is "fascinated by anything old, no matter how ugly. Enjoy manual labour, the English language, argument, time, dotty hypotheses. Concerned about social justice and the maiming of the future. My books come if I'm lucky, and I don't like talking about them for fear it will spoil my luck."

PRINCIPAL WORKS: *Adult Fiction*—Skin Deep, 1968 (U.S., The Glass-Sided Ants' Nest); A Pride of Heroes, 1969 (U.S., The Old English Peep Show); The Seals, 1970 (U.S., The Sinful Stones); Sleep and His Brother, 1971; The Lizard in the Cup, 1972; The Green Gene, 1973; The Poison Oracle, 1974; The Lively Dead, 1975; King and Joker, 1976. *Juvenile Fiction*—The Weathermonger, 1968; Heartsease, 1969; The Devil's Children, 1970; Emma Tupper's Diary, 1971; The Dancing Bear, 1972; The Iron Lion, 1972; The Gift, 1973; The Blue Hawk, 1976; Annerton Pit, 1977. *Miscellaneous*—Chance, Luck and Destiny, 1975; (as editor) Presto! Humorous Bits and Pieces, 1975.

ABOUT: Contemporary Authors 41-44, 1974. *Periodicals*—Guardian February 8, 1971; Library Journal October 1, 1968; March 1, 1969; May 1, 1976; New York Times Book Review April 13, 1969; May 9, 1971; May 14, 1972; November 2, 1975; New Yorker June 12, 1971; Newsweek August 9, 1976; Times Literary Supplement March 14, 1968; June 26, 1969; April 16, 1970; February 26, 1971;

April 12, 1974; December 5, 1975; April 2, 1976; April 30, 1976.

DIDION, JOAN (December 5, 1934–), American novelist, essayist, journalist, and film scenarist, was born in Sacramento, California, the daughter of Frank Reese Didion and the former Eduene Jerrett. Her family has lived for five generations in the Central Valley and California is very important to her and in her work, though she says that "all that is constant about the California of my childhood is the rate at which it disappears." Joan Didion received her B.A. from the University of California, Berkeley, in 1956. The same year she won *Vogue's* Prix de Paris, after which she joined the magazine as an assistant feature editor (1956-1963). It was at this time that she met John Gregory Dunne, who was then on the staff of *Time,* and whom she married in 1964. Joan Didion has also served as a contributing editor of *National Review* and has written for a variety of other magazines, including *Mademoiselle, Holiday,* and *American Scholar.* She has shared a *Saturday Evening Post* column with her husband and has collaborated with him on several screenplays, including *The Panic in Needle Park,* the movie version of her novel *Play It As It Lays,* and Barbra Streisand's version of *A Star Is Born.*

Run River (1963), her first novel, is set in the Sacramento Valley and is perhaps about that lost paradise, in the sense that the falling-apart of its listless heroine and her marriage seems to reflect the physical and spiritual spoliation of the Great Valley. Lily Knight McClellan has been married for nineteen years to a wealthy ranch owner, Everett McClellan, whose ruling passion is a sense of order. It may be this that drives Lily to go to bed with men she doesn't much care for (she herself has no idea why she does this), or (as Alfred Kazin suggests) the habit may be "the expression of a deep personal fright." In any case, Everett's sense of order obliges him in the end to murder one of Lily's lovers and then kill himself.

Even critics who thought it a pity that Joan Didion should have concerned herself with such tiresome characters agreed that this was "a beautifully told first novel," full of wit, imagination, and promise. Many thought the novel more than promising, Robert Maurer, for example, asserting that "even in this first novel there seems to be nothing technically that she cannot do." And for Alfred Kazin, *Run River* remains the best of Joan Didion's books so far—less "smart" than its successors, but with a greater emotional depth and "seriousness," and with an authenticity derived from "Lily's moral and

Mary Lloyd Estrin

JOAN DIDION

physical fragility, her *not* knowing, her *not* being on top of things, her almost accidental love affairs. . . . the involuntary unacknowledged strength of [Joan Didion's] sensibility, the really arresting thing, is seen not in the clear cold eye, the writer's famous detachment, the perfect sentences . . . but in the sense of fright, of something deeply wrong. No, the center is not holding."

The same chilling sense of vacancy, of "inner space" as a center that cannot possibly hold, predominates in the essays, columns, and articles collected in *Slouching Towards Bethlehem* (1968). Some of these pieces deal with the author's eight years in New York, which she dislikes; many with the decline and fall of Sacramento and California, which she loves; others with Joan Baez, Howard Hughes, backstage Hollywood. The famous title piece, a record of interviews with "flower children" in the Haight-Ashbury district of San Francisco, caused her so much pain, she said, that "for twenty and twenty-one hours a day I drank gin-and-hot-water to blunt the pain and took Dexedrine to blunt the gin." One reviewer found a "theatrical touch" in some of these essays that reminded him of Walter Winchell or Jim Bishop, but most critics thought them brilliant—alert, lucid, economical, and powered by an acutely sensitive moral sense that links the author more with the new journalism than the old. C.H. Simonds called the book "a fragmentary chronicle of the breakings-up of society, civilization and her own world; and of her search for a niche in the rubble." Melvin Maddocks wrote that "a substantial element of spiritual biography is present in these pieces of wary skepticism.

Though she has a journalist's weakness for converting her themes into 'myths,' 'dreams,' and 'folk' symbols, she is an original observer and even better, an original thinker."

Play It As It Lays, Joan Didion's second novel, followed in 1970. Maria Wyeth, a young actress, lives in Hollywood. She drives the freeways around Los Angeles for hours on end in an attempt to escape a past that includes two failed marriages, a string of casual affairs, the birth of a brain-damaged daughter, an unwanted abortion, and a friend's suicide. Acknowledging that she is living in a world quite without meaning for her, where "nothing applies," Maria breaks down, and is institutionalized. At the end of the book she stoically resumes her life.

The novel, accreting around Maria Wyeth in desolate, one-line sentences, disappointed a few of its reviewers; they thought it a routine book by a good writer and objected that it seldom moved beyond clichés or archetypes and, even when it did, did so in a prose which tended "to posture like a figure from a decadent period of art, whose fingers curl toward an exposed heart or draped bosom swelling with suspect emotion." There were those who found Maria less interesting than the author herself, whose own individuality is forever on the verge of burying itself in her nostalgic image of the Central Valley, as if she were more a piece of California than a woman. But most reviewers seemed to share the opinion of John Leonard, who concluded on this evidence that "there hasn't been another American writer of Joan Didion's quality since Nathanael West. She writes with a razor. . . . A pool of blood forms in the mind. Meditate on it, you are both frightened and astonished. When was the wound inflicted?" The novel was filmed by Frank Perry in what Pauline Kael (who had found the book "ridiculously swank") called the "high-class-whorehouse style."

Kazin made the interesting suggestion that her sense of style "is as much a display of manners in the old sense as is her special blend of elegance and despair." The English critic Jacky Gillott, reviewing Joan Didion's next novel, at first found her prose infuriatingly mannered, which is not the same thing. *A Book of Common Prayer* (1977) is narrated by Grace Strasser-Mendana, the North American widow of a wealthy and powerful planter in Boca Grande, a small Central American republic on the verge of revolution. Grace had been trained as an anthropologist, and the subject she seeks to describe with cool scientific precision is Charlotte Douglas, a woman very different from herself. Jacky Gillott swung "from rage to admiration" as she began to appreciate the "stunning skill"

205

with which "Miss Didion eludes her own re- morseless brief by bringing the extraordinary ac- tivity and character of Charlotte to life under this reductionist gaze."

Charlotte is a version of the Didion heroine or anti-heroine (the question is debatable); at any rate she is a woman who fails numbly at things, including two marriages. Her daughter, whom she loves, is wanted by the FBI for terrorism. Hoping to encounter her, Charlotte goes to Boca Grande: "In a certain dim way she believed that she had located herself at the very cervix of the world, the place through which a child lost to history must eventually pass." Waiting there, she busies herself with vaccination and birth control programs, plans to organize a film festi- val and to open a boutique. She is shot dead during a coup d'état, and never does encounter her daughter, but some readers thought she had at last encountered herself.

Russell Davies found "a heavy throb of disil- lusionment in the verbal texture of the book, its patterns of call-signs and repetitions, which do, at odd moments, resemble the *sotto-voce* recita- tion of private and habitual prayers." (The au- thor herself has said that technically the novel is "almost a chant. You can read it as an attempt to cast a spell or come to terms with certain contemporary demons.") Whether the "heavy throb of disillusionment" is Grace's or Char- lotte's or Joan Didion's is not clear, and greatly exercised and divided the reviewers. Many saw in Charlotte no more than a victim of the times, but Russell Davies discerned "a weird stoicism, a sort of hormonal obstinacy . . . which we are left wishing to account for. And perhaps to ad- mire." (The author had "wanted to do a decep- tive surface that appeared to be one thing and turned color as you looked through it.") The book has been much discussed and praised.

Joan Didion lives with her husband and her daughter Quintana in Trancas, just over the line from Malibu, in a beach-cliff house overlooking a private stretch of the Pacific coast. She is a Republican and an Episcopalian and says that she is "quite religious in a certain way," with "a very rigid sense of right and wrong." She is also "very attached to certain forms," and for this reason admires elegance and likes to cook and sew. She writes, she says, "entirely to find out what I'm thinking, what I'm looking at, what I see and what it means. What I want and what I fear."

According to Alfred Kazin, "the Dunnes are a most successful writing couple and definitely a couple. Though Joan Didion has frequently de- scribed herself in print as a creature on the verge of divorce, breakdown, and catastrophe . . . the fact is that she is an extraordinarily successful and professional young woman who would seem to have 'life by the tail.' " And yet, Kazin says, she is "a very vulnerable, defensive young wom- an whose style in all things is somehow to keep the world off, to keep it from eating her up. . . . The thinness, the smallness, the inescapably alarmed fragility of the woman is probably the most important physical element surrounding her and perhaps explains the impending sense of catastrophe that informs so much of her work."

PRINCIPAL WORKS: *Novels*—Run River, 1963; Play It As It Lays, 1970; A Book of Common Prayer, 1977. *Essays*— Slouching Towards Bethlehem, 1968.

ABOUT: Contemporary Authors 5-8 1st revision, 1968; Cur- rent Biography, 1978; Kazin, A. Bright Book of Life, 1973; Vinson, J. (ed.) Contemporary Novelists, 1976; Who's Who in America, 1976-1977. *Periodicals*—American Scholar Winter 1970-1971; Christian Science Monitor May 16, 1968; Commonweal November 29, 1968; Harper's August 1970, December 1971; Ms February 1977; National Review May 7, 1963; June 4, 1968; New York Herald Tribune Books May 12, 1963; New York Review of Books August 9, 1970; April 28, 1977; New York Times July 21, 1970; New York Times Book Review July 21, 1968; August 9, 1970; December 5, 1976; April 3, 1977; Newsweek August 3, 1970; March 21, 1977; Publishers Weekly October 9, 1972; Time August 10, 1970; March 28, 1977; Times Liter- ary Supplement July 8, 1977; Vogue October 1, 1972.

DOCTOROW, E(DGAR) L(AURENCE) (January 6, 1931–), American novelist, was born in the Bronx, New York City, the son of David R. Doctorow, who ran a music store, and the former Rose Buck, a pianist—"old-fash- ioned social democrats" who were both second- generation Russian immigrants. Although, as Doctorow told an interviewer, there was "never any money," he has happy memories of his bar mitzvah, visits to the theatre, summer camps, and ball-playing in the streets around Eastburn Avenue. Doctorow decided early on that he wanted to write. At the Bronx High School of Science he worked on the literary magazine, *Dynamo*, and then went on to Kenyon College in Gambier, Ohio, where he did some acting and majored in philosophy. After graduating in 1952, Doctorow spent a year at Columbia Uni- versity, working for an M.A. that he never ac- quired.

In 1953 Doctorow began two years in the U.S. Army Signal Corps, after which he returned to New York and supported himself with a variety of jobs, including stints as an airlines reserva- tions clerk, as a reader for Columbia Pictures, and as an editor at New American Library, while writing in his spare time. He stayed on at New American Library, and was a senior editor there from 1959 to 1964, when he moved to Dial

© 1979 by Jill Krementz

E. L. DOCTOROW

Press as editor-in-chief. In 1968 he became Dial's vice-president and publisher as well, and in this phase of his career sometimes put in twenty hours a day, drafting his first two novels while working as an editor with such writers as Norman Mailer, James Baldwin, and Richard Condon.

Welcome to Hard Times (1960), Doctorow's short first novel, was an attempt to make valid use of what he called "a disreputable genre," the Western. Working with "cheap materials of a nonliterary kind," he was "interested in the counterpoint of what I was doing and what the reader might expect me to do." In the course of a single day, a badman destroys the town of Hard Times, casually and with shocking brutality. The weak mayor, Blue, does nothing until the killer has gone; then he patiently rebuilds his town and founds a famous whorehouse there. The badman returns and once more reduces Hard Times to a smoking ruin, but this time Blue fights back and kills the Man From Bodie, though he is mortally wounded himself. The novel is clearly a parable. Wirt Williams, who was reminded of Conrad's *Heart of Darkness,* thought its primary theme is "that evil can only be resisted psychically: when the rational controls that order man's existence slacken, destruction comes. . . . [Doctorow's] book is taut and dramatic, exciting and successfully symbolic." Another critic, commenting on the novel's 1975 reissue, drew attention to the author's "profound sense of American myth and his marvelous sensitivity to American materials"— qualities rigorously excluded from MGM's 1967 screen version, which Doctorow called "the second worst movie ever made," but which never-

theless helped him make the down payment on his house in New Rochelle, New York.

Another popular myth, "the myth of the monstrous visitation," was borrowed from science fiction as the basis for *Big as Life* (1966), in which two gigantic human figures appear in New York harbor, towering naked and stinking over the skyline. The city panics, the social order disintegrates, moral chaos reigns, but in the end "Doctorow's dead-pan manner . . . turns from satire to tenderness and human concern," and there are hopeful signs that humanity will make a fresh start. The book had a mixed reception, the author thought, because "the general reader dismisses it as science fiction, and the science fiction buffs are furious because it isn't science fictiony enough—I have departed from the formula." But those who liked it liked it very much.

By 1969 Doctorow was so heavily involved in his work for Dial Press that he was neglecting his own writing. He left the publishing business and went as writer-in-residence to the University of California at Irvine (1969–1970), where he finished his third novel, *The Book of Daniel* (1971). Daniel Lewin, a disoriented graduate student at Columbia, is the son of socialist parents who had been executed in the early 1950s for conspiring to steal atomic secrets for Russia. This book, which Daniel is supposed to be writing in lieu of a thesis, describes his increasingly "diffuse, apocalyptic, hysterical" efforts to arrive at the truth about his parents, about himself in relation to them, and about his younger sister's struggle to recover her sanity. Daniel is defeated. Even when he flies to California and confronts the man whose testimony convicted his parents, there is no satisfaction; the old man is senile and kisses Daniel on the head in the heart of Disneyland.

The Book of Daniel was obviously inspired by the execution of Ethel and Julius Rosenberg, which Doctorow regards as "a major political crime of the 1950s." He has said however that he did no research into the Rosenberg case, and that his novel is less about the Rosenbergs than about the "idea" of the Rosenbergs. One reviewer complained of Doctorow's (or Daniel's) "exaggerated sense of irony" and "corny sideswipes," but Stanley Kauffmann called the book "the political novel of our age," and David Caute wrote that "line by line [Doctorow] wrenches from the reader the tribute of absolute assent and recognition: yes, it is, it was exactly like that. . . . This novel represents a marvelous marriage of the intellect and the imagination." It enjoyed a notable *succès d'estime,* was nominated for the National Book Award, and found its way onto college reading lists.

P. S. Prescott called *The Book of Daniel* "a purgative book, angry and more deeply felt than all but a few contemporary American novels. . . . a ferocious feat of the imagination." It left Doctorow creatively drained, so that for months after its completion he wrote nothing—could think of nothing, indeed, to write about. But eventually, sitting at his desk in his 1906 house in New Rochelle, he was seized by an idea—an image of a visit to that house, shortly after it was built, by the escape artist and magician Harry Houdini. This unaccountable but promising notion was soon joined by other images of America in the years before World War I and jogged along by haphazard research in histories, biographies, and picture books of the period. The result was *Ragtime* (1975), which Doctorow says was "a happy, easy book to write—it didn't fight me."

Three elements are interwoven in *Ragtime:* the lives of a wealthy New Rochelle family whose money comes from the manufacture of American flags, bunting, and fireworks; the destruction of an immigrant family by poverty; and the story of Coalhouse Walker, a black ragtime musician who is turned by prejudice and suffering into a violent militant—a bomber and murderer who seizes the great library of J.P. Morgan before being killed. These more or less fictitious characters (some unnamed, except as Father, Mother, The Little Girl, etc.) are involved by events with an assortment of historical personages, among them Houdini, Emma Goldman, Carl Jung, Henry Ford, and Harry K. Thaw, who murdered Stanford White for love of the demimondaine Evelyn Nesbit. No attempt is made to distinguish between historical events and invented ones, and Doctorow, who "used to know" which were which, but has forgotten, doesn't much care: "Let's just say that *Ragtime* is a mingling of fact and invention—a novelist's revenge on an age that celebrates nonfiction." Thus, we have Emma Goldman administering a massage to Evelyn Nesbit, J. P. Morgan discussing reincarnation with Henry Ford, Sigmund Freud concluding that America is "a gigantic mistake," among many other impudent and entertaining ploys in a game of "what if?"

George Stade wrote that "the rhythm of the sentences and events in this novel is the verbal equivalent of ragtime. The left hand pounds out the beat of historical change. It modulates from the Wasp to the immigrant to the black families as through the tonic, dominant, and subdominant chords upon which the right hand builds its syncopating improvisations. These are variations on themes provided by representative figures and events of the time. . . . [This] is an anti-nostalgic novel that incorporates our nostalgia about its subject. It is cool, hard, controlled, utterly unsentimental, an art of sharp outlines and clipped phrases. Yet it implies all we could ask for in the way of texture, mood, character and despair." Roger Sale had reservations: he found Doctorow "excellent in vignettes and short passages" like those that occupy most of the first half of the novel, less successful in the second half, which concentrates on the martyrdom of Coalhouse Walker—"story makes his history predictable and easy just as politics makes Dos Passos's history predictable and easy in *U.S.A.*" Sale's conclusion is that *"Ragtime* may not be an entirely successful book, but the writer who can do this, and as well as Doctorow has, need set no limits on what he can do next." British reviewers were on the whole less impressed, and Philip Howard thought it a "pretentious and vulgar" book which had been "mistaken for another pretender to the title of the Great American Novel." By and large, however, *Ragtime*'s reviews ranged from the enthusiastic to the ecstatic. It was a major bestseller and a Book-of-the-Month Club Selection, won an award from the National Book Critics Circle, and was optioned by the film producer Dino De Laurentiis. The paperback rights were sold for nearly two million dollars.

Since 1971 Doctorow has taught creative writing at Sarah Lawrence College. He received a Guggenheim fellowship in 1972 and has had grants from the American Academy of Arts and Letters and the National Institute of Arts and Letters. A play, *Drinks Before Dinner,* was staged at the Public Theater in December 1978.

Doctorow has been described as looking "faintly messianic, like the Cézanne head of Achille Emperaire," a tall, "gentle man with worried brown eyes" and a "grayspeckled beard which he explores incessantly as he frets from question to question." He was married in 1954 to Helen Setzer, a drama student from Hickory, North Carolina, whom he met at Columbia. They have two daughters and a son. Doctorow's leisure interests include contemporary poetry and "movies, tennis, family fights."

PRINCIPAL WORKS: *Novels*—Welcome to Hard Times, 1960; Big as Life, 1966; The Book of Daniel, 1971; Ragtime, 1975. *Play*—Drinks Before Dinner, 1978.

ABOUT: Contemporary Authors 45–48, 1974; Current Biography, 1976; Who's Who in America, 1976–1977; Who's Who in the World, 1971–1972. *Periodicals*—American Scholar Winter 1975–1976; Atlantic January 1976; Book Week July 10, 1966; Choice November 1966; Commentary October 1975; Commonweal December 19, 1975; Encounter February 1976; Guardian March 10, 1972; January 19, 1976; National Review August 15, 1975; New Republic July

5, 1965; June 5, 1971; April 10, 1976; New Statesman January 23, 1976; New York Post July 9, 1966; August 31, 1971;
July 12, 1975; New York Review of Books August 7, 1975;
New York Times July 23, 1967; February 27, 1974; September 26, 1976; New York Times Book Review September 25,
1960; July 6, 1975; Newsweek June 7, 1971; July 14, 1975;
Publishers Weekly June 30, 1975; Saturday Review July 17,
1971; July 26, 1975; Sunday Times (London) January 18,
1976; Time July 14, 1975; Times Literary Supplement February 18, 1972; January 23, 1976.

"DOMINIC, R.B." *See* **"LATHEN, EMMA"**

*DONOGHUE, DENIS (December 1, 1928–),
Irish literary critic and scholar, was born at Tul-
low, in County Carlow, Eire, the fourth child of
Denis Donoghue, a policeman, and the former
Johanna O'Neill. He was educated at University
College, Dublin, where he received his B.A. in
1949, his M.A. in 1952, and his Ph.D. in 1957.
Donoghue began his career in 1951 as an administrative officer in the Irish Government's
Department of Finance, but in 1954 he returned
to University College, Dublin, as an assistant
lecturer, and with two interruptions has taught
there ever since, becoming a college lecturer in
1957, and professor of modern English and
American literature in 1965. In 1962-1963 he
was a visiting scholar at the University of Pennsylvania, and in 1964-1965 he was a university
lecturer at Cambridge University and a fellow of
King's College, receiving a second M.A. from
Cambridge in 1965.

A number of apparently contradictory influences appear in Donoghue's work—most obviously of two critics, Yvor Winters and Kenneth
Burke, and two poets, Yeats and Wallace Stevens. It is as if these figures represent opposing
poles between which the magnetized needle of
Donoghue's critical sensibility oscillates. He is
essentially an eclectic critic, drawn as much
by the sturdy puritanism, conservatism, and
antiromanticism of Winters as by the irrationalism, quasi-Marxism, volatility, and versatility of
Kenneth Burke; Yeats's sensuality attracts him
as much as Stevens's aestheticism.

Donoghue's first book was *The Third Voice*
(1959), a study of modern British and American
verse drama treating Eliot and Yeats as crucial
figures, but also discussing the work of Christopher Fry, Cummings, Auden, MacLeish,
Pound, Wallace Stevens, and Richard Eberhart.
Reviewers thought that the book conveyed a
sense of excitement when Donoghue discussed
Eliot's contribution, but was otherwise uncompelling, though always "safe and sane" in its
judgments.

There was a quite different response to *Connoisseurs of Chaos,* which followed after a long

*don' o hū

DENIS DONOGHUE

interval in 1965. This is a study of ten American
poets: Whitman, Frederick Goddard Tucker-
man (whose neglected virtues Winters trumpet-
ed to the world), Melville, Emily Dickinson, E.
A. Robinson, Frost, Roethke, J. V. Cunningham
(also from the Winters stable), Robert Lowell,
and Stevens himself. The title is taken from one
of Stevens's poems, and his presence pervades
the book. All ten poets are seen in the light of
Stevens's vision (or Donoghue's sense of it); as
Donoghue declares: "Stevens first invents God
and thereafter plays all his parts."

G. S. Fraser noted in his review that the
book's "predominant terms of discussion are order and chaos, the poet's 'blessed rage for order'
in a world where 'God, nature and man are out
of tune.' " The result seemed to Fraser "a major
contribution to the study of American poetry,"
though he found Donoghue "strenuous" rather
than "transparently lucid" in his argument, and
thought that he "sometimes obscures or mis-
directs rather than clarifies the issues." Graham
Thom wondered whether "for all the ingenuity
and delight" there "was really any direction at
all: isn't Mr. Donoghue simply using Stevens to
give an artificial sense of coherence to his own
mental chaos?" He felt that Donoghue, whom
he called a "sometimes acute critic," might be
too ambitiously philosophical, and suggested
that he concentrate more on his subjects and less
on the construction of a philosophy of poetry.

However, *The Ordinary Universe,* which followed in 1968, was also philosophically ambitious, and aroused a very lively interest.
Donoghue's argument here is at bottom religious, though not explicitly so, and the influence
of Winters is apparent. He is concerned to de-

fend art which celebrates life, "the world's body," against the formalism of modern criticism, the alienation and despair of modern literature. And he develops his argument through studies of Tennyson and Hopkins, Eliot and Yeats, Stevens and W. C. Williams, O'Neill and Bellow, Pound and Lawrence.

Graham Hough admitted that he had in the end rather lost the thread of this argument, and thought that Donoghue "obeys two impulses as a critic—one to submit himself with candour and humility to works that he admires; the other to uphold his own scale of values. In writing of modern literature he does not find it easy to bring them together; they alternate rather than combine." Nevertheless, "both those who accept and those who refuse Mr. Donoghue's argument will still want the conversation to continue." Donald Davis, praising Donoghue as a "model polemicist" of "independent judgement and fair-mindedness," nevertheless found "surprising faults in two main elements: taste and interpretation. . . . If the texts, when scrutinised, do not reveal what this author claims they do, a reader must be sadly credulous to believe the argument they are designed to support. . . . A close study of *The Ordinary Universe* maintains one's respect for Professor Donoghue's gifts while weakening one's trust in his new book." There was a great deal of praise for Donoghue's energetic but "conspicuously civilised" style, his wide reading, and his capacity to illuminate individual texts: "The reader is admitted to a discourse whose witty allusiveness sometimes makes quite heavy demands on his alertness of mind."

Donoghue's "critical introduction" to Jonathan Swift, published in 1969, was in fact rather more than that, demanding from the reader some familiarity with Swift's work and his times. The author had set out to question the assumption "that irony is the key to Swift," and had produced, in Kenneth Burke's opinion, "an expert presentation of the profuse inventiveness that enlivens Swift's stylistic tactics." However, a writer in the *Yale Review* found this "a curiously flat and reductive account of Swift," and one in the *Times Literary Supplement* was puzzled as to "why so well-mannered and logical a discourse should prove so difficult. It may be that there is too great a disparity between the polished lecturer's tone and the gritty information and argument in which he courageously involves himself. . . . [or] there is perhaps lacking a sustained vision of Swift's genius to pull the book together. Every chapter nevertheless says something new and something profound."

A pamphlet about Emily Dickinson followed —one of the University of Minnesota's series—

and then a brief study of Yeats. The latter was a by-product of a larger venture, which Donoghue subsequently abandoned. In 1970 he had entered into an agreement with the Oxford University Press and Senator Michael Yeats— Yeats's son and literary executor—to write an "authorized biography" of the poet. In 1973 he withdrew from this, explaining in an article in the *Times Literary Supplement* that Senator Yeats had given permission to other scholars to edit and publish certain unpublished Yeats manuscripts, and that he believed the term "authorized biography" should imply the "withholding of manuscript material in my favour." Senator Yeats replied politely and regretfully, pointing out that Donoghue had not asked for such guarantees in 1970, and that he could hardly rescind permissions already given. Donoghue's short study of Yeats in the Fontana Modern Masters series suggests that Senator Yeats had been right to lament the author's abandonment of a full biography. Donoghue had performed "a tricky job magnificently," wrote a reviewer in the *Times Literary Supplement.* He did not persuade everyone that Yeats was "a representative modern man," but many consider this study the best introduction to the poet.

The T. S. Eliot Memorial Lectures that Donoghue delivered in 1972 at the University of Kent were published in 1973 as *Thieves of Fire*: they represent his most ambitious undertaking. He had taken the Prometheus myth as the basis for his lectures, and Graham Martin and other critics called the book itself "Promethean." For Donoghue, the "Promethean writer" is the "versatile giant" that "starts with an incorrigible sense of its own power, and seeks in nature only the means of its fulfillment" (the "it" is deliberate and significant). He recalls the distinction made by the art critic Adrian Stokes between the "carver" of stone, who searches for a form imprisoned in the stone and given by nature, and the "modeller" who seeks to impose his own truth on the stone. In *The Ordinary Universe,* Donoghue confesses, he had "set out a preference for . . . the carving side. But I found myself fending off the versatile giants. . . . On the present occasion, I mean to bring the different traditions more closely together, and to attend to one without banishing the other." There is no clear evidence that Donoghue has changed his own mind in favor of the "modellers," but he has certainly treated his Prometheans—Milton, Blake, Melville, Lawrence—with far greater sympathy than in the past.

The *Times Literary Supplement*'s reviewer called this a daring book and "a very fine performance" which "justifies its extravagance," though he found Donoghue more conventional on the novelists than on the poets he deals with: "Prose is too lucid, too accessible, to be exciting to him." John T. Hall thought that Donoghue had missed an opportunity by not treating the myth of Prometheus comprehensively enough, and criticized him for a tendentious and "not over-informed" selection from its variants, and for his habit of taking "any fact which is grist to his mill—regardless of whether it is important in its own context or not." But the general verdict was that Donoghue had a fascinating mind, and one critic suggested that he had and should use the capacity to express himself creatively as well as critically.

The seven essays collected in *The Sovereign Ghost* (1977) contemplate the uses of the imagination, whose "essential power . . . is the power of making fictions and making sense of life by that means." The imagination, Donoghue suggests, "is the name we give to the mind when it is prepared, if feeling requires it, to see everything change except itself. . . . Imagination would then mean the act of a mind determined to keep open every possibility of creation, freedom, play, and pleasure." He considers in these terms the work of Shakespeare, Pope, Wordsworth, Henry Adams, Henry James, Allen Tate, and T. S. Eliot, among others. In the title essay, Donoghue defends his notion of the imagination against the structuralist interpretation, in which the imagination is not sovereign but is an entity to be defined by the language it uses; Donoghue rejects the "implication that the subject is merely the sum of its occasions." He says: "If I were required to make a leap of faith, only one leap being allowed, I would aim for the Romantic assumption which features imagination and subjectivity as primary terms." This collection seemed to Michael Wood "very alert and engaging work, attuned to theory but not lost in it," while George Core went so far as to call the book "the most inclusive anatomy of the imagination since Coleridge."

Denis Donoghue was music critic of the *Irish Times* in 1957, and director in 1960 of the first Yeats Summer Festival. He is a member of the board of the Abbey Theatre, Dublin, and has served as president of the Irish Association of Civil Liberties and as a member of the international committee of the Association of University Professors of English. Donoghue has been a visiting professor at Harvard, UCLA, and the University of Edinburgh. He received a fellowship in 1963-1964 from the American Council of Learned Societies. The author was married in 1951 to Frances Rutledge. They have eight children and live in Mount Merrion, Dublin.

Donoghue is a powerful and somewhat controversial teacher. He has been described as "scrupulous, testy and admirably solemn: a wise moralist in a world his gravity makes frivolous." Some find him humorless; others playful. It is very generally regretted that his Yeats biography is not to be completed, but most students of literary criticism still expect him to write a major book.

PRINCIPAL WORKS: The Third Voice: Modern British and American Verse Drama, 1959; Connoisseurs of Chaos: Ideas of Order in Modern American Poetry, 1965; The Ordinary Universe: Soundings in Modern Literature, 1968; Jonathan Swift, 1969; Emily Dickinson, 1969; Yeats, 1971; Thieves of Fire, 1973; The Sovereign Ghost: Studies in Imagination, 1977. *As Editor*—The Integrity of Yeats, 1964; (with J.R. Mulryne) An Honoured Guest: New Essays on W.B. Yeats, 1965; Jonathan Swift: A Critical Anthology, 1971; Memoirs: Autobiography—First Draft Journal of W.B. Yeats, 1973; Seven American Poets From MacLeish to Nemerov: An Introduction, 1975.

ABOUT: Academic Who's Who, 1975-1976; Contemporary Authors 17-20 1st revision, 1976. *Periodicals*—Christian Science Monitor September 5, 1968; Economist July 20, 1968; Hudson Review Spring 1966, Autumn 1970; Kenyon Review Autumn 1959; New Republic May 9, 1970; New Statesman July 5, 1968; March 8, 1974; New York Review of Books April 14, 1977; New York Times Book Review November 28, 1965; April 24, 1977; Sewanee Review October 1977; Southern Review October 1976; Times Literary Supplement May 26, 1966; October 3, 1968; April 2, 1970; March 17, 1972; February 16, February 23, December 21, 1973; March 1, 1974; Yale Review March 1970.

*DONOSO, JOSÉ (October 5, 1924–), Chilean novelist and short story writer, was born in Santiago. He has provided a vivid account of his childhood and youth in *Review 73* (Fall 1973), describing himself as the son of "a physician more addicted to horse racing and to playing cards than to his profession, with the result that visible means of support were slender." His mother, a pretty and amusing woman, belonged to the ne'er-do-well branch of the *nouveau riche* family that owned the newspaper *La Nación*. In this raffish and chaotic household, the upbringing of the infant José was entrusted largely to the family maid, Teresa Vergara.

In 1929, the family moved into a house in the old section of Santiago, where Donoso's father served as resident physician to his three widowed, wealthy, and bedridden great aunts, who lived there with their respective retinues of servants and relations. Donoso and his younger brother Pablo grew up rapidly in this bizarre microcosm of Chilean society, surrounded by complaisant servant girls, romantic aunts, and mad cousins. Their world from an early age was one of late hours, parties, music, and visits to the theatre and the Russian opera. An English gov-

*don ōs′ ō

211

DONOSO

© 1979 by Layle Silbert

JOSÉ DONOSO

erness hired to provide some formal education and discipline soon resigned in despair.

In bleak contrast to the hothouse atmosphere of Donoso's home life were the spartan rigors of The Grange, an English day school in Santiago in which he was enrolled in 1932. He found the homework, compulsory games, and *esprit de corps* imposed by the school altogether depressing, and for the rest of his life avoided all forms of group activity. Home became as disagreeable as school when their father ordained that Donoso and his brother should be toughened up with boxing lessons. Donoso retreated into a world of hypochondria, daydreams, and books—Jules Verne, Dumas, romantic biographies, and such fashionable novelists as Somerset Maugham, Huxley, Pearl Buck, and Margaret Mitchell. He began himself to write, in his early teens completing a play in imitation of Hugo's *Hernani.*

After frequent truancies, Donoso finally left The Grange in 1943 without a degree. He played the role of the young man-about-town, moving restlessly from one job to another, until in 1945 he decided it was time to see something of the world outside Santiago. Donoso went south to Magallanes, where he worked for a time as a shepherd, subsequently roaming the pampas of Patagonia, and making the acquaintance of sailors and stevedores in Buenos Aires. Returning to Santiago in 1947, he completed his English studies at the University of Chile's Pedagogical Institute, and in 1949 went with a Doherty Foundation scholarship to Princeton University, an experience he recalls with nostalgia and gratitude. Donoso hitchhiked throughout the United States, where he published his first short stories in English, and also visited Mexico and Central America.

Returning to Santiago in 1952, Donoso became professor of English conversation at the Catholic University of Chile. The imaginary illnesses of his youth now became a reality. Donoso is a chronic sufferer from stomach ulcers and depression, conditions which have been alleviated but not cured by years of psychoanalysis. In 1955, however, with financial help from his friends, he published his first book, *Veraneo y otros cuentos* (Summertime and Other Stories). Donoso's short stories often deal with children and adolescents, showing how their awakening perceptions and instinctive curiosity lead remorselessly to their first confrontations with evil and unhappiness. Social concern, where it appears, is focused on the ambiguous relationship between an enervated bourgeoisie and their servants—a complex game of mutual blackmail and emotional tyranny. Donoso perceives similar ambiguities in the most ordinary situations—adolescent friendships, marriage, the dependence of old age—and evokes them with a delicacy and poignancy rare among contemporary Latin American writers. *Veraneo* was highly praised by the critics and awarded Santiago's Municipal Prize.

In 1957, despite family disapproval, Donoso threw up his job and went off to live with a fisherman's family in Isla Negra in order to complete his first novel, *Coronación* (1957, translated by Jocasta Goodwin as *Coronation*), also published with financial help from the author's friends. It brings together and develops many of the themes introduced in Donoso's short stories. A senile nonagenarian is cared for by two elderly and devoted maids, and by her grandson, Don Andrés, a middle-aged bachelor. All of these characters are in various ways sexually repressed and psychologically inadequate, imprisoned in their claustrophobic household by their fears of the changing world outside. The arrival of Estela, an attractive young peasant girl, brings a dangerous breath of real life into this hermetic fantasy world, and it collapses. The novel ends on a note of *grand guignol*: the old woman lies deranged and dying, robed like a queen, while the servants drink themselves insensible, Estela's boyfriend tries to rob the house, and Don Andrés, rejected by Estela, raves in anguish. *Coronación* was awarded the William Faulkner Prize in 1962 as the best Chilean novel of the quinquennium. "It is life against death," wrote a reviewer in the *Times Literary Supplement,* "but the issues are tragically confused. Señor Donoso holds fast to the fact of death and it is this which gives his surrealistically comic and shocking climax its power and the novel its quality."

Donoso was becoming increasingly active as a journalist and in 1959, after another visit to Argentina, he joined the staff of the Santiago journal *Revista Ercilla,* where he worked until 1964. In 1960 he received the Chile-Italia prize for journalism. Donoso was married in 1961 to María Serrano. The following year he and his wife attended a writers' congress at the University of Concepción, where Donoso met and made friends with Carlos Fuentes and Pablo Neruda. There followed a period of about two years when Donoso lived in Mexico, reviewing for *Siempre,* and completing the novel *Este domingo* (1966, translated by Lorraine O'Grady Freeman as *This Sunday*) and the novella *El lugar sin límites* (1966, translated by Suzanne Jill Levine and Hallie D. Taylor as *Hell Has No Limits*).

Este domingo centers on the events of a single day in the lives of a middle-aged, middle-class couple, Alvaro and Chepa Vives. Like all of Donoso's characters, they are the prisoners and victims of their social roles, but both have attempted to cross social barriers in search of some *raison d'être.* Alvaro recalls his affair with the servant Violeta—a relationship in which he gained a sense of life through her degradation. Chepa is a do-gooder, in love with the convict for whom she has secured a parole. The threads are tied with dramatic irony when the released convict murders Violeta. Pursuing her protegé, Chepa is destroyed by a horde of brutalized children—much like those to whom she has extended her self-serving charity. Alexander Coleman wrote that "the descriptions of rituals in the family home are richly and lovingly done . . . but the author never glosses over the lurking sense of brutality and repressed sexuality. . . . Donoso's cool and biting intelligence demonstrates once again that he is one of the major novelists now writing in Latin America."

El lugar sin límites deals similarly with relations between rich and poor, master and servant. It was published in English translation along with short novels by Carlos Fuentes and Severo Sarduy in *Triple Cross* (1972), and was universally regarded as the best of the three pieces. "Almost imperceptibly," wrote Bruce Allen, "its garish set pieces become a vivid microcosm of a society in collapse. A superb piece of work that far outshines its companions, it lends the welcome weight of recognizable reality to the collection."

In 1966-1967 Donoso taught creative writing at the University of Iowa's Writers' Workshop. His health was still poor and, deciding that teaching was not compatible with writing, he went to Spain to devote himself to *El obsceno pájaro de la noche,* a novel on which he had been working intermittently for years. In 1968 he was back in the United States, teaching at Fort Collins, Colorado, when he became desperately ill and underwent an emergency operation for a hemorrhaging ulcer. Still convalescent, he returned to Spain and began a total rewrite of *El obsceno pájaro de la noche.* The completed novel was launched in Latin America with immense publicity and subsequently appeared in Spain in an expurgated edition. Foreign translations quickly followed, and an English version by Hardie St. Martin and Leonard Mades was published in 1973 as *The Obscene Bird of Night.*

This novel, which is Donoso's masterpiece, takes its title from a passage in a letter written by Henry James senior to his sons: "The natural inheritance of every one who is capable of spiritual life is an unsubdued forest where the wolf howls and the obscene bird of night chatters." The book's central image derives from a scene witnessed by Donoso while waiting one day at a traffic light in the center of Santiago: a large grey car halted at the light "with a chauffeur in uniform, very erect, *à la* White Russian *emigré* style . . . sturdy, very handsome, very good. And I look behind him, and the back seat is occupied by only one person: a little monstrous dwarf, with his whole face done entirely by plastic surgery."

The novel's narrator is Humberto, devoted servant of the wealthy landowner Jerónimo Azcoitía. Humberto has come to the end of his life as porter in a convent where the Azcoitías send their unwanted relatives, servants, and furniture. He recalls the past, when he served as tutor and keeper to "Boy," Jerónimo's monstrously deformed heir, who is hidden away on a remote country estate, surrounded for his comfort by a court of freaks. Humberto, who stood in for Jerónimo on his wedding night, and replaced him as a target for the mob during an election campaign, has also surrendered his sexual organs and his powers of speech and hearing so that the aging aristocrat may be reinvigorated. In the end, Humerto takes his revenge on the Azcoitías by murdering Jerónimo's late-born bastard, before he himself dies in the fire which destroys the convent and all it stands for.

El obsceno pájaro de la noche, much longer than Donoso's earlier novels, has been described as a book of magnificent disorder. It is basically an interior monologue with dialogues inserted— a monologue in which it is not always easy to know who is speaking, for Humberto plays many roles. The reader soon finds himself struggling for solid ground in a rising tide of theses and antitheses, assertions and contradictions, sudden metamorphoses and changes of direction, where nothing is constant but ambiguity. The dual vision of Donoso's previous books broadens: master-servant, virgin-prostitute, beauty-monster, God-Satan are all shown to be interrelated aspects one of another. The book is full of echoes of the legend of the Blessed Inés, a rich and beautiful girl cloistered in a convent when it was thought that she must be either a witch or a saint.

Many interpretations of the book are possible. A reviewer in the *Times Literary Supplement* concluded that Humberto represents the figure of the writer, who "is always being shaped and used by the creatures of his imagination. He is parasitic on society, he is exploited by it and is its victim." Donoso himself acknowledges that the novel marks an entirely new departure in his work and says: "I think that the theme of the monsters corresponds perhaps to a caricaturization, a parody, if you wish, of my whole previous narrative work, and upon parodying it there is a kind of desire to discard it: that aristocratic world which I have taken seriously up till now in my novels. . . . One of my great terrors, and which is perhaps the reversal of the aristocratic world which I spoke about in my earlier novels, is the terror of destitution, of abjection, of non-existence, of being reduced to nothing, of the being who is eliminated, of the exploitation of man by man. The theme doesn't interest me in the social sense at all; I'm interested in the exploited human being, but both in the destroyed and the destroyer—one of my great psychoanalytical fantasies."

Robert Coover, reviewing the English translation, wrote that "the story line is like a great puzzle with everything in it from burlesque to romance, magic to murder, often bizarre, yet always—for Donoso is himself possessed by an astonishingly agile imagination—invested with a vibrant, almost tangible reality. . . . along with everything else, this is a book about an author being driven mad by the book he is trying to write, by this effort to struggle against metamorphosis and the elusiveness of the 'real,' to confront his own monsters and cope with the paradoxes of metaphor, to alleviate his fear of extinction by the creation of 'an enchanted present' without suffocating himself in his own imagination, and to pursue intransigently the impossible synthesis of all that that imagination contains. Rarely have we been brought so close to this process." Michael Wood has placed the book with Cortázar's *Hopscotch* and García Márquez's *One Hundred Years of Solitude* as one of "the major modern novels of the subcon-

tinent"—all of them "metaphors for [the] vast, encompassing unreality" of Latin America.

Three less ambitious books by Donoso appeared in English in 1977. The nine stories collected in *Charleston*, translated by Andrée Conrad, deal for the most part with lonely people who escape from their prosaic lives into fantasy, or into dependence on enchanting children or pets. R. Z. Sheppard called these "modern ghost stories in which the reader may recognize phantoms of himself," but Anatole Broyard thought that "Donoso cannot seem to get up much impetus in the space of a short story." *Sacred Families,* also translated by Andrée Conrad, contains the three novellas published in Spain as *Tres novelitas burguesas* (1973). In "Chattanooga Choo-Choo," a Spanish playboy obliterates his mistress's face every night with vanishing cream, regularly recreating her for the sake of novelty; she responds to this male chauvinism by detaching and hiding his genitalia. The implication is that these "beautiful people" are no more than the sum of their parts, just as the smug couple in "Green Atom Number Five" have fashionable possessions instead of feelings. Bourgeois greed and emptiness are also satirized in "Gaspard de la Nuit," about a teenage boy's visit to his divorced mother.

Broyard found "a rather touristic and anthropological detachment" in these stories, and attributes this quality to the fact that Donoso now lives in Spain. "He sounds like a man without a country or a history of his own. . . . In his novellas, the language is meager, fussy, deracinated and marred by clichés. Perhaps in moving from Chile to Barcelona he lost his tongue." It was to escape the parochialism of Chilean literature, with its old-fashioned insistence on social realism, that Donoso moved to Spain, as he explains in *Historia personal del "boom"* (1972). This brief and largely subjective account of Latin American fiction in the 1960s has been translated by Gregory Kolovakos as *The Boom in Spanish American Literature*. Donoso and his wife have a daughter.

PRINCIPAL WORKS IN ENGLISH TRANSLATION: Coronation, 1965; This Sunday, 1967; Hell Has No Limits *in* Triple Cross, 1972; The Obscene Bird of Night, 1973; Charleston and Other Stories, 1977; Sacred Families, 1977; The Boom in Spanish American Literature, 1977. *Stories in* Cohen, J.M. (ed.) Latin American Writing Today, 1967; Flakoll, D.J. and Alegria, C. (eds.) New Voices of Hispanic America, 1962; Howes, B. (ed.) The Eye of the Heart, 1973; Triquarterly Anthology of Contemporary Latin American Literature, 1969; Américas February 1959; Mexican Life June 1960.

ABOUT: Forster, M.H. (ed.) Tradition and Renewal, 1975; Franco, J. The Modern Culture of Latin America, 1970; Franco, J. Spanish American Literature Since Independence, 1973; International Who's Who, 1977-78; Penguin Companion to Literature 3, 1971; Schwartz, K. A New History of Spanish American Fiction, 1971; Vidal, H. José Donoso, 1972. *Periodicals*—Books Abroad Spring 1975; Current Biography 1978; Nation March 11, 1968; June 11, 1973; New York Review of Books August 4, 1977; New York Times Book Review March 14, 1965; November 26, 1967; June 17, 1973; June 26, 1977, Review 73 Fall 1973; Saturday Review March 13, 1965; July 9, 1977; Time June 27, 1977.

DORN, EDWARD (MERTON) (April 2, 1929–), American poet, novelist, and essayist, was born in the prairie town of Villa Grove, Illinois, and educated at the University of Illinois, Urbana. He subsequently took some courses at Eastern Illinois University, which was where he first heard of Black Mountain College, the experimental educational community or "anti-university" in North Carolina.

Dorn went to Black Mountain first in 1950 or 1951. At that time, he told Roy K. Okada in *Contemporary Literature,* "I didn't have any aesthetic values. I was a work-scholarship student. I had learned how to print, working on the hometown newspaper, and so part of the possibility of my being there was that I could run the Black Mountain printing shop. It was a small shop and they did their own programs for dances and a little bit of poetry. It was all new to me. . . . For one thing, I don't believe I'd ever met a person from the eastern part of the United States. A lot of people were from New York. The information they had all came into me as a flood."

After a year Dorn left Black Mountain "and wandered around the west—that was the first big odyssey I made. And I got to understand that there was the west than Route 66, which led to L.A. I spent some time in Wyoming and wandered up eventually to Washington and worked in the woods and met loggers who had been Wobblies or were old enough to have known people who were. And I met some people in the woods who had been trained by Marxist unions."

In 1954 Dorn returned to Black Mountain College. It was then that he came under the crucial influence of the poet and scholar Charles Olson, rector of the college in its last years, from 1951 to 1956, and aesthetician of "projective verse." This theory of poetry, drawing on the ideas and practice of Pound, W.C. Williams, and others (not all of them poets), is anti-academic and anti-rational. It calls for open forms (since "form is never more than an extension of content") and for "composition by field"—rapid juxtapositions of words and phrases, and of perceptions, creating their own field of energy without logical transitions or discursive analysis. The

R. Rusk

EDWARD DORN

poetic line is conceived of as a structure not of regular meter but of syllable and the individual breath.

Olson's own poems, it has been said, "make precise statements of personal experience given meaning in a discriminated historical and geographical context"—that of Gloucester, Massachusetts. Olson's influence sharpened Dorn's interest in the American West—"in what will identify the west in some big conceptual sense," and in the interaction there between man and landscape. He asked Olson what he should read on the subject and received the sixteen-page annotated reading plan published in 1964 as *A Bibliography on America for Ed Dorn*—a list of books "that give a sense of beginnings, in the American frontier, and of very ancient things carried on, Babylon and Sumeria behind the Old Testament, Semitic place names in Homer."

Dorn's own poems began to appear in the 1950s in Robert Creeley's *Black Mountain Review* and elsewhere. The Black Mountain poets for many years shunned the normal commercial channels of publication and publicity, and Dorn has continued to do so, so that recognition has come very slowly. His first collection, *The Newly Fallen* (1961), seemed to its few reviewers uncertain in structure and colored by too many undigested influences, but individual in tone and capable of conveying difficult intellectual arguments in its search for "fresh ways to order chaos." It also included some splendidly lyrical love poems—a form in which Dorn has continued to excel—like this "Song":

> . . . Thus days go by
> and I stand knowing her hair

215

in my mind as a dark cloud, its presence
straying over the rim of a volcano
of desire, and I take something
so closed as a book
into the world where she is.

There was dawning recognition of Dorn's fundamental concerns in reviews of *Hands Up!* (1964). Thomas Clark was struck by the breadth of his vision, in which "vertical sections of land and 'miles deep/ fossil ranges . . . the backyard/ of our eternity' are held against the ground image of property owners and autodealers whose sole measurement is the division of the superficial." Dorn's "syntax, line structure, even punctuation," Clark wrote, "here register gestures of thought that disclose both the poet's way of perceiving and the world's fashion of perceiving itself. So the verse holds a freshness of the *experience* of thought, that honesty. Everyone ought to read this book."

When he left Black Mountain Dorn taught for some years at Idaho State University, Pocatello, where he edited the magazine *Wild Dog*. In 1965 he went to England, teaching and studying there until 1968 as a visiting professor of American literature at the University of Essex. *From Gloucester Out* (1964), the first of three successive books originally published in England, is a long poem in homage to Olson's Gloucester poems, in which Dorn investigates the importance for the poet of a grasp on locality—a place from which to view the world beyond. Eric Mottram regards this poem as a turning point for Dorn, "in which 'projective verse' methods were extended personally."

The same skill in the management of varied materials and free but complex forms is evident in *Idaho Out* (1965). The British poet and critic Donald Davie believes that the "standpoint" which Dorn is "concerned to investigate is not characteristically a fixed point [like Olson's Gloucester], the point where roots are sunk; it is a moving point, the continually changing standpoint of a man who is on the move across continents and oceans." And in *Idaho Out* we see the poet driving from Idaho to Montana and back again, "his standpoint changing as he moves, yet conditioned by the terrain it moves through and over, as much as by the consciousness which occupies the moving point." A. Alvarez was impressed by the poem's "anarchic, footloose vitality," and its feeling for the West. It was republished, with others on related themes, and some love poems and nature poems, in *Geography* (1966). Not all of the poems in this collection were as successful as *Idaho Out*—in some of them, it was thought, their colloquialisms and

"natural" speech rhythms, their "prosy manner and chopped-up lines work against [Dorn's] deeper feelings," concealing his "real humanity and strength."

Dorn set out "to locate another hemisphere" in *The North Atlantic Turbine* (1967), containing poems written during his years in England. That country both attracted and repelled him (though he is never more harsh about those aspects of England that he dislikes than he sometimes is about America). Some critics regretted Dorn's tendency to "slam his reader over the head with politics" at this stage in his career. One of the most admired pieces in the book was "Oxford," a long poem in which, according to Donald Davie, "concern for locality and 'locating,' so far from leading to localism or regionalism, lends itself on the contrary to vast and rapid panoramas." It was in England, Dorn says, that "the distance in perspective made me realize that I was a western poet. I mean a poet of the west— not by nativity but by orientation . . . I could feel that geography. I was impelled westward." At the same time, *The North Atlantic Turbine* marks the end of his commitment to locality and the beginning of his interest in "that non-spatial dimension, intensity"—his move from "worrying about working out a location to a spiritual address."

Perhaps the best poem in that collection is "An Idle Visitation." This reappeared as the first hundred and five lines of *Gunslinger,* the long multi-volume comic epic in which, it is generally agreed, Dorn has found his "spiritual address." The four books of *Gunslinger* were published in a single volume in 1975 as *Slinger*. Slinger himself is the archetypal Westerner, but also pagan sun-worshipper and solar deity. Other characters include Hughes Howard (representing "a kind of primitive, entrepreneurial capitalist . . . dinosaur"), the brothel keeper Lil, persons called Heidegger, Parmenides, and Lévi-Strauss, and one named "I," who

is costumed as the road manager
of the soul, every time
the soul plays a date in another town
I goes ahead to set up
the bleachers, or book the hall
as they now have it,
the phenomenon is reported by the phrase
I got there ahead of myself
I got there ahead of my I
is the fact
which not a few anxious mortals
misread as intuition. . . .

("I" dies in the poem, in line with Dorn's conviction that the ego has had its day.)

One reviewer in the *Times Literary Supplement* thought that *Gunslinger* did no more than mix "the banalities of endless, desultory colloquialism with pretentious whiffs of 'philosophy,'" but this was distinctly a minority view. *Gunslinger* has been acclaimed by Robert Duncan as "one of *the* poems of the era, of the one we are going into, of the era *Gunslinger* begins to create for us." Thomas McGuane calls it "a fundamental American masterpiece" and Michael McClure "an act of white magic." "At once comic and profound, narrative and piercingly lyrical," wrote Donald Davie, "the form and idiom of *Gunslinger* transcend completely the programmes of Black Mountain, just as they transcend (dare one say?) any programme so far promulgated or put into practice in Anglo-American poetry of the present century."

Dorn's prose works include a highly subjective response to Charles Olson's *Maximus Poems,* and a "first-rate novel of life on the land in the American North-west," published in 1965 as *The Rites of Passage* and republished in 1971 as *By the Sound. The Shoshoneans* (1966) is the product of a journey Dorn made through Idaho, Utah, and Nevada in 1965 with the photographer Leroy Lucas to investigate the plight of the Indians of the Basin-Plateau; most reviewers found it well-intentioned but chaotic, aimless, and silly in its free-associational argument.

Dorn was visiting poet at the University of Kansas in 1968–1969. He returned to the University of Essex in 1974–1975, settled for a time in San Francisco, and then went as poet-in-residence to Kent State University, Ohio, where he taught courses in writing and in the literature of the American West. He is married and has children. With his wife Jennifer, the engraver Michael Myers, and the printer Holbrook Teter, he has produced the remarkable newspaper (or broadsheet, or anti-newspaper) *Bean News,* in which appears some of his more directly social poetry. Dorn received grants from the National Endowment for the Arts in 1966 and 1968, and held a D.H. Lawrence Fellowship in 1969.

PRINCIPAL WORKS: *Poetry*—The Newly Fallen, 1961; Hands Up!, 1964; From Gloucester Out, 1964; Idaho Out, 1965; Geography, 1965; The North Atlantic Turbine, 1967; Gunslinger, Book I, 1968; Gunslinger, Book II, 1969; Gunslinger, Books I and II, 1970; Twenty-Four Love Songs, 1969; The Midwest Is That Space Between the Buffalo Statler and the Lawrence Eldridge, 1969; The Cosmology of Finding Your Spot, 1969; Songs: Set Two, a Short Count, 1970; Spectrum Breakdown: A Microbook, 1971; A Poem Called Alexander Hamilton, 1971; The Cycle, 1971; The Hamadryas Baboon at the Lincoln Park Zoo, 1972; Gunslinger, Book III: The Winterbook Prologue to the Great Book IV Kornerstone, 1972; Recollections of Gran Apachería, 1974; Slinger, Books I, II, III, IV, 1975; The Collected Poems 1956-1974, 1975. *Novel*—The Rites of Passage: A Brief History, 1965 (republished as By the Sound, 1971). *Short Stories*—Some Business Recently Transacted in the White World, 1971. *Other*—What I See in the Maximus Poems, 1960; (with Michael Rumaker and Warren Tallman) Prose I, 1964; The Shoshoneans: The People of the Basin-Plateau, 1966. *As Translator (With Gordon Brotherston)*—Our Word: Guerrilla Poems From Latin America, 1968; Tree Between Two Walls, by José Emilio Pacheco, 1969; Selected Poems of César Vallejo, 1976.

ABOUT: Dodsworth, M. (ed.) The Survival of Poetry, 1970; Leary, P. and Kelly, R. (eds.) A Controversy of Poets, 1965; Malkoff, K. Crowell's Handbook of Contemporary American Poetry, 1973; Ossman, D. (ed.) Sullen Art, 1963; Penguin Companion to Literature 3, 1971; Vinson, J. (ed.) Contemporary Poets, 1975. *Periodicals*—Athanor Winter 1973; Contemporary Literature Summer 1974; Hudson Review Winter 1967–1968; Michigan Quarterly Review Spring 1967; New Republic April 24, 1976; Poetry February 1962, November 1965, October 1966, March 1969; Stand 8 1966; Times Literary Supplement January 27, 1966; September 4, 1970.

DOUGLAS HOME, WILLIAM. *See* HOME, WILLIAM DOUGLAS

"DOUGLAS, MICHAEL." *See* CRICHTON, MICHAEL

DRABBLE, MARGARET (June 5, 1939–), English novelist, dramatist, and critic, writes: "I have made several attempts to force myself to write an autobiographical sketch, but find it more or less impossible to write about myself. So, in brief: I was born into a family which enjoyed literature, writing came naturally to me, and I turned to writing novels as soon as I married and had graduated from university. I wrote my first three novels while expecting my three children, thereby disproving, to myself at least, the theory that one kind of creativity displaces another, and the notion that pregnant women cannot think because they have lapsed into a vegetable state (or an animal state). Inevitably my first novels are circumscribed by the limits of my own experience: they are all written in the first person, from the woman's point of view, and are concerned with the female experience. As the children have grown older, I have been able to extend my range a little, but not much: I am now more able to travel, to meet people from different social groups, and to do research. But my material is still, necessarily, limited by family considerations, as well as enriched by them.

"I was born in the north of England, but like most of my family have moved south. Most of my adult life has been lived in London, with visits to Stratford-upon-Avon, where my hus-

Fay Godwin

MARGARET DRABBLE

band was acting in the Royal Shakespeare Theatre, and to Paris, where I took the children on a Travel Award for some months in 1966. I lead essentially a domestic life, which I enjoy very much. It is also a bourgeois life. I enjoy daily activities in the home, enjoy working for radio and television because it is sociable, sit on committees because I think I ought, and because they offer a view of a largely masculine world otherwise denied to most women. In my life, I try to preserve a balance between work and home, and have been very lucky to find a career which enables me to have my cake and eat it. I am by no means a recluse, but I dislike invasions of my privacy, perhaps because with a family one gets so little of it. I have a room in town where I go to work, because writing at home, for men or women, is constantly interrupted.

"In my work, I try to confront the problems that confront me. The worse the problem, the more interesting the book. The problems used to be personal ones—how to combine marriage and work, for example—but I now find myself increasingly interested by and able to tackle more general subjects: the guilts and anxieties of British society, an individual's relationship with his own and his country's past. I have always been deeply interested in the interaction of fate and free will, accident and determination, and most of my novels, if not all of them, concern this theme. I much admire Freud (whose anti-feminism seems to me a historical and sociological accident) and have, I think, been much influenced by his writings on the theme of free will and self-discovery. One could say that each book is a process of discovery, about oneself and the world outside. I write to find out, as I read to

find out: I have no particular definable message that I could abstract from the books themselves. Writing is certainly a therapeutic process, though it can also be more than that: it is also a seeking for new patterns, new models, a new future.

"There is a book on my work by Valerie Grosvenor Myer, called *Puritanism and Permissiveness* (Vision Press) which seems to me to analyse very accurately the peculiar influences of the heritage I received."

Margaret Drabble is the daughter of John Drabble, a circuit judge until his retirement in 1973 who is himself an author, and the former Kathleen Marie Bloor, who had been a teacher of English. Like her elder sister Antonia (the novelist and critic A.S. Byatt), Margaret Drabble was born in Sheffield and educated at the Mount School, a famous Quaker boarding school in York. Both at school and in her "very tolerant, liberal, middle-class" family she encountered "moral pressure, not punishment." She has continued to accept most of her parents' values and also agrees with the "principles of a lot of Quaker theory . . . That men are equal and that there is the light of God in every man and that all people are one in the sight of God—I believe all that."

An exceptionally able student, Margaret Drabble went on with a major scholarship to Newnham College, Cambridge, where she read English and was also notably successful as an undergraduate actress. She left Newnham in 1960 with a brilliant first-class honors degree, and the same year married the actor Clive Swift, a Cambridge contemporary. For a year both she and her husband were members of the Royal Shakespeare Company, after which she relinquished the stage in favor of babies and novels.

Her first book, *A Summer Bird-Cage,* appeared in 1963. It is narrated by Sarah, newly graduated from Oxford, as she contemplates the marriage her more cynical and beautiful sister has made for money, and wrestles with her own conflicts. The novel is highly contemporary in its concerns, traditional in its manner—intelligent, morally serious, subtle and sensitive in its probing into motive, witty and well-mannered in its prose. Most of its reviewers were delighted by it. Walter Allen thought it "very close to the grain of immediate contemporary life," and said "we shall be lucky if the year produces another first novel as good."

Unadventurous as she is in matters of technique, Margaret Drabble, as Bernard Bergonzi has pointed out, has "devised a genuinely new kind of character and predicament." The protagonists of most of her novels are "young women who are not merely intelligent, educated, more or less attractive, and sharply observant. They are also mothers, and their involvement with their children cuts sharply across their concern with a career and their desire for emotional freedom." This is the situation of Emma in *The Garrick Year* (1964). She has a shaky marriage to a rising young actor, a hunger for excitement, a lover, and two small children. Her attempt to sort out her priorities during a drama festival in Hereford forms the substance of the novel. Her dilemma is resolved when her daughter falls into a river and Emma dives in to save her—a total immersion in the maternal instinct which apparently reconciles her to her life and her self.

The conflict between children and career is dramatized very directly and tellingly in *The Millstone* (1965). Rosamund, a dedicated and puritanical young scholar, is momentarily distracted from her thesis on the Elizabethan sonnet by a young man, and finds herself pregnant. She astonishes her academic friends by deciding to have the baby and raise it alone, and does so, learning a great deal in the process about herself, about life, and about the other women who attend the same ante-natal clinic in a poor part of London. Rosamund never entirely overcomes her puritanism, but critics agreed that she is presented to us with a "compassion and humanity" that had been lacking in the two earlier novels, and with a completeness that is all the more remarkable in that she is the book's narrator, so that we know about her only what she herself tells us. This was generally recognized as Margaret Drabble's first fully mature novel, and it has remained the most popular of them. It was serialized in a women's magazine and by the BBC, and a film version was made from the author's own scenario (called *A Touch of Love* in England, *Thank You All Very Much* in the United States).

The two novels that followed had a more mixed reception, and seemed to Bernard Bergonzi "embarrassing and unconvincing over long stretches." There is some justice in this as a criticism of *Jerusalem the Golden* (1967), about a young graduate climbing away from a lower-middle-class background via an affair with a married man. *The Waterfall* (1969) is a different matter, however, and some critics consider this the author's most achieved work of art. Jane, the narrator, is another victim of the Puritan conscience which so preoccupies Margaret Drabble. Having driven away her husband by her coldness, she flings herself into an adulterous affair in a deliberate effort to free herself from her puritanism. Torn between self-disgust at the de-

ceit and selfishness this involves, and an instinctive conviction that it is her only hope of salvation, she becomes literally schizoid. This is reflected in the form of the novel, which is narrated alternately in the third person (representing Jane's super-ego) and the first person (id). Jane never reconciles these two aspects of her character, but the reader is left with the feeling that her hard-won freedom to love is worth the mental agony it cost.

There was a general feeling that the male characters in this novel were far less convincing than the female—a criticism often made of Margaret Drabble's books. Some reviewers had other reservations, and Maureen Howard called it "intellectually topheavy" and "bleak and uninventive" in its manner. It seemed to Valerie Grosvenor Myer, on the other hand, that the "apparent shapelessness" of the novel "is transcended by an art which creates a coherent and beautiful pattern out of incoherence and contradiction. This is achieved by a developing pattern of qualifying statements about what has been said before, structural parallels and interlinked patterns of imagery. . . . The artistic strength of *The Waterfall* lies both in its technical skill and in its honesty. It shows us Jane winning through, painfully, to a rejection of puritanism while still acknowledging its force. . . . This is Margaret Drabble's neatest exposition of her central concern, and paradoxically the most conclusive in its dramatised recognition that there is no true solution to the conflict between instinct and morality."

"The conflict between instinct and morality" is also the theme of *The Needle's Eye,* which appeared in 1972 after a rather longer interval than usual. Rose Vassiliou, a rich English woman divorced from her mercurial Cypriot husband, is driven by conscience to give away all she has to build a school in Africa (where it is soon destroyed by civil war). She settles with her three children into a life of near poverty in a decaying area of London. When her husband tries to take the children from her, she turns for help to Simon Camish, a socialist lawyer who finds Rose's odd combination of moral seriousness and scattiness more attractive than his wife's pursuit of the sweet life. They fall as nearly in love as their regretful moralities permit. In the end, Rose returns to her husband, doing her duty "in the dry light of arid generosity." The novel, as Valerie Grosvenor Myer says, "is a severe indictment of the unnecessary suffering caused by 'life-denying' Evangelicism, from which Rose has to make a partial escape. . . . she recognises that in withdrawing from society, from 'community,' she was wrong, but her

219

return to marriage, love and duty brings no happiness either."

Myer believes that the need for community at all levels of human life is the central theme of *The Needle's Eye,* and she makes a convincing case for this view in her study of Margaret Drabble. None of the novel's other critics perceived as much, but they were virtually unanimous in their admiration for it. A writer in the *Times Literary Supplement* called it "a very ambitious, marvellously written, morally admirable book." Joyce Carol Oates wrote: "Though I have admired Miss Drabble's writing for years, I will admit that nothing she has written in the past quite prepared me for the depth and richness of [this book.]"

The Realms of Gold (1975) received more moderate praise. Its heroine, divorced and the mother of four children, is a distinguished archaeologist who is drawn home from a conference in Africa when her maiden aunt dies of starvation, a tragedy eagerly publicized by the newspapers as evidence of family neglect. The title refers both to the heroine's archaeological discoveries and the memories she shares with her family. Reviewers found the book untidy and occasionally slow, but valued it nevertheless for its "old-fashioned pleasures, not least an implicit moralizing that leaves one persuaded that on the whole it is wiser to be nice than nasty, even to oneself." Lorna Sage thought that in this novel Margaret Drabble, like her heroine, "cheerfully accepts the frayed uncertain boundaries of her vision and her sympathy, and really enjoys herself."

The Ice Age (1977), being a more ambitious novel, had a more mixed press. It is, as one reviewer put it, "a bold attempt to describe and diagnose England's present ills, and to assess her chances of recovery." When the book begins, Anthony Keating, a television producer turned property speculator, is recovering from a heart attack and facing bankruptcy, while Len Wincobank, the working-class tycoon who drew him into the business, is in prison. Keating's lover, Alison Murray, is in an East European country where her teenage daughter is awaiting trial for dangerous driving. Kitty Friedman, a friend of Alison and Anthony, is in hospital, having lost a foot in an I.R.A. bombing incident in Mayfair. These variously injured, inadequate, but on the whole well-meaning people reflect at considerable length on the condition of England, and are themselves representative of that condition.

Some critics, like Michael Irwin, thought that this was *all* they were—that "their illustrative function is so dominant as almost to deprive them of independent fictional life." Anthony

Thwaite could scarcely have disagreed more, calling this "a continuously readable, continuously surprising book, with the widest and most deeply searched set of characters Margaret Drabble has yet attempted." And Donald Davie was embarrassed, less by the novel's unequivocal, unironic patriotism, than by the fact that her characters "don't get from me, nor I reckon do they deserve from anyone, the affection and respect that Margaret Drabble asks for on their behalf, and seems confident of getting. . . . *The Ice Age* is an embarrassing book, and it betrays more than its author intended about the present state of England and the English. It is, though, a brave and bold book, one that English men and women can be grateful and even, though awkwardly, proud of."

Margaret Drabble has published a number of short stories. Her play *Bird of Paradise* was produced in London in 1969, and she has also written a television play, *Laura* (1964). Her *Wordsworth* (1966) is a brief introduction for students, but her main nonfiction work is a critical biography of Arnold Bennett, the product of many years' research. Convinced that Bennett had been undervalued since his death, she set out to rehabilitate his reputation, writing "in a partisan spirit, as an act of appreciation." A number of reviewers thought that this would have been a better book if she had asked some harder questions about Bennett, as a man and a writer, and Frank Kermode dealt harshly with her, suggesting that she had become "temporarily tone-deaf," producing prose that was "so badly written, so offensive to the inner ear" that he broke off at one point to reassure himself "that she can do better when she's trying." The book nevertheless gave great pleasure to many readers and indeed, as Kermode said, "had a rapturous reception in England." One critic wrote that "Miss Drabble's book has made me reconsider the whole question of decency, sincerity and lack of pretension as yardsticks of imaginative literature," and perhaps that was her principal intention.

Margaret Drabble's marriage has now been dissolved, and she lives with her three children in London. She received the John Llewellyn Rhys Memorial Award in 1966, the James Tait Black Memorial Prize in 1968, and the E. M. Forster Award in 1973. She has an honorary doctorate from the University of Sheffield (1976). Since 1969 she has lectured to adults at evening classes at a London college. Margaret Drabble is small, slim, and attractive, dresses carefully, and is extremely well-liked and popular as a television "personality." She votes Labour and says that she is preoccupied "not very hopefully" with equality and egalitarianism. She occasionally takes part in political demonstrations, though she is uncertain of their value. None of her books is about feminism, she says, "because my belief in the necessity for justice for women . . . is so basic that I never think of using it as a subject." She is "absolutely staggered" by the number of people who read her books, and would like to think it is because "there are an awful lot of people like me."

PRINCIPAL WORKS: *Novels*—A Summer Bird-Cage, 1963; The Garrick Year, 1964; The Millstone, 1965 (also published as Thank You All Very Much); Jerusalem the Golden, 1967; The Waterfall, 1969; The Needle's Eye, 1972; The Realms of Gold, 1975; The Ice Age, 1977. *Short Stories*—Penguin Modern Stories 3, 1969 (with others). *Criticism*—Wordsworth, 1966; Arnold Bennett, 1974. *As Editor*—(with B.S. Johnson) London Consequences: A Group Novel, 1972; Lady Susan, The Watsons, Sanditon, by Jane Austen, 1974; The Genius of Thomas Hardy, 1975; (with Charles Osborne) New Stories 1, 1976.

ABOUT: Contemporary Authors 13-16 1st revision, 1975; International Who's Who, 1977-78; Myer, V.G. Margaret Drabble: Puritanism and Permissiveness, 1974; Vinson, J. (ed.) Contemporary Novelists, 1976; Who's Who, 1977. *Periodicals*—Books and Bookmen September 1969; Contemporary Literature Summer 1973; Economist July 13, 1974; Encounter September 1974; Guardian April 13, 1967; April 1, 1972; Library Journal June 1, 1972; Nation October 23, 1972; New Statesman March 29, 1963; July 17, 1964; September 10, 1965; March 31, 1972; September 26, 1975; New York Review of Books October 5, 1972; October 31, 1974; November 27, 1975; November 10, 1977; New York Times Book Review April 4, 1965; November 23, 1969; June 12, 1972; September 1, 1974; November 16, 1975; New Yorker December 16, 1972; December 23, 1974; January 12, 1976; Observer September 28, 1975; September 4, 1977; Saturday Review November 15, 1975; Sunday Times (London) July 8, 1973; Sunday Times Magazine (London) August 6, 1967; November 16, 1969; Times (London) March 27, 1972; September 23, 1975; Times Literary Supplement April 12, 1963; July 23, 1964; September 23, 1965; May 22, 1969; March 31, 1972; July 12, 1974; September 26, 1975; September 2, 1977.

DREXLER, ROSALYN (SELMA) (November 25, 1926–), American novelist and dramatist, was born in New York City, the daughter of George Bronznick, a pharmacist, and the former Hilda Sherman. She describes herself as self-educated. Rosalyn Drexler has worked as a waitress, a playground director, and a masseuse, and was at one time a professional wrestler, appearing as "Rosa Carlo, the Mexican Spitfire." She was married in 1946 to the painter Sherman Drexler and has two grown-up children, Rachel and Denny. The writers who have influenced her most, she believes, are Nathanael West and the Brazilian novelist Machado de Assis.

The theatre was Rosalyn Drexler's first love, and she carried off an Obie Award with her first off-Broadway production, the underground musical comedy *Home Movies,* which put one

ROSALYN DREXLER

critic in mind of an unexpurgated Marx Brothers movie." She began it "just to amuse herself" at a time when she was housebound with a young child. Staged in 1964 at Judson Poets' Theatre, with music by Al Carmines, it delighted its audiences and most of its reviewers (though Gerald Weales objected to what he called its "tone of chi-chi camp").

Dr. Fraak, amiable hero of *The Line of Least Existence* (1967), is an analyst, a former pusher and pimp. He is pursued by the "bottle-shaped bohunk" Pschug, who is eager to kill him for seducing his daughter, the beautiful Ibolya. Pschug also epitomizes the perpetual immigrant to whom the United States is always *terra incognita*. His concern for Ibolya is misplaced—she enjoys sex and enjoys just as much the gifts Fraak exchanges for this commodity. In the end, Fraak cheerfully signs himself and his wife into a mental hospital, and Pshug goes along too. Arthur Sainer found "a sense here of the old-fashioned, well-made play . . . where things in the end are patched up, where no real harm is done. What has been done is almost solely to the spectator, not to the characters. The spectator has been battered by the epigram, the pun, the metaphor." It is not really a "well-made play," however: "Diversion is one of the major traits of the Drexler comedies, so ingrained that it ceases to be diversion and becomes a motif within a generally bizarre pattern. The mainstream is thus colored by a lurching series of tributary streams which appear and disappear unexpectedly and rapidly. The narrative operates like a Marx Brothers film where Groucho's nose for the prurient takes him on unexpected journeys."

The Line of Least Existence gave its title to a

221

collection of six short Drexler plays published in 1967. There is a great deal of sex and violence in these absurdist pieces: the sex, as Sainer says, "is open, blatant, a little bizarre—and genial. No mystery, no sense of the erotic. Sex is for buddies"; the violence is mostly in the language, which reminded critics of *Ubu Roi* as well as *King Lear.* Jack Kroll, reviewing the collection in *Newsweek,* identified Rosalyn Drexler's obsessive theme as "the total dissonance that occurs whenever living creatures find themselves in any sort of relationship." Michael Smith wrote in the *Village Voice* that "few contemporary playwrights can equal Mrs. Drexler's verbal playfulness, fearless spontaneity, and boundless irreverence; few, in fact, share her devotion to pure writing."

Much the same qualities, naturally, appear in the author's novels. The first of them, *I Am the Beautiful Stranger* (1965), is presented as the diary of Selma Silver, a teenager growing up in the Bronx of the 1930s, recognizing strong yearnings to be an artist, and purveying unorthodox sex to older men. It disturbed reviewers who are disturbed by such things but was praised by others for its deftness and its charm, its unhackneyed depiction of the bittersweet rigmaroles of adolescence, and most of all for its astringency. Richard Gilman thought it so likely "that this wayward, subtly liberating and wholly original novel will be praised for the wrong reasons that I feel obliged to deal first with the prospective idolators. . . . The book stands entirely outside both pop literary sex and that genre of canny, youthful disaffection . . . which *The Catcher in the Rye* established. . . . Above everything, . . . [Selma] has to find out about the delusions, exploitations and reputed wonders of sex. . . . In one of Selma's epigrams she remarks that 'to be alive is also to fall down.' Nothing better illustrates the achievement in style—simple, pared, casual but with amazing resonance—or the imaginative solidity of this bold, light, enormously replenishing book."

Melissa Johnson in *One or Another* (1970), married to a right-wing gym teacher and deeply bored, fantasizes her way from the beauty parlor of the Great Northern Hotel to Yellowstone Park and war-torn Nigeria. She also has an affair with one of her husband's students, but he winds up in the asylum and Melissa is driven in the end to say: "I'm going back inside my head." It seemed to Jack Kroll that "in these lives madness is no longer a possibility—it is a note in their chord of being that automatically sounds with every breath they draw. . . . What counts now is the delicate new apotheosis, a new transcendence that accepts the mad world as the

only human habitat, while plotting shrewdly against its madness. Few writers have been able to suggest this new transcendence. Mrs. Drexler is one of them: funny, scary, preternaturally aware, she is at the exact center where the new sensibility is being put together cell by cell." William Hjortsberg was reminded by this "very funny book" of Molly Bloom's recollections of Gibraltar in *Ulysses,* and also of Kafka—not only the austerity of his style but "the bizarre juxtaposing of abnormalities, the hard edges and latent guilt."

To Smithereens (1972) stirs together the sleazy world of "lady wrestlers" and the tired chic of "the plastic New York art scene." The wrestler is a frank, witty, and naive girl named Rosa Rubinsky; she takes up with Paul Partch, an aging masochist who crushes cockroaches because they remind him of his mother and who abandons art criticism in favor of writing pulp for a wrestling magazine. Rosa is not exactly average herself—she defines her private norm as making a stag movie with a dwarf and says her Shangri-La is a hotel lobby "where you don't have to stay . . . where you can stop to rest, or lean and think." Most reviewers shared Sara Blackburn's admiration for the author's "marvelous talent for taking this kind of material and imbuing it with qualities of great warmth and wicked satire, pathos, and a haunting aura of nostalgia for a world most of us have never known." Sally Kempton called it a feminist novel and a novel about self-definition as well as "a domestic comedy, a collage of ideas about art, a treatise on sexual fantasy, and the best account of the wrestling scene I've ever read."

"What I wear determines who I am. . . . I once wore a tiger-striped night-gown and clawed a man to death," says Helen Jones, eponymous heroine of *The Cosmopolitan Girl. Cosmopolitan* magazine is not the only American institution satirized in this novel, in which we learn of Helen's love for her talking dog Pablo and Pablo's fight for civil liberties as well as Helen's difficulties with Albert, her mother's pyromaniac companion, and the right-wing radio host Joe, who completes their troubled ménage. Sara Sanborn thought that Rosalyn Drexler's set pieces— "newspaper clippings, radio interviews, beauty advice—are among the delights of the book; her one-liners are memorable: 'Most of Daddy's friends were young and in an advanced state of inner peace.' " *Library Journal*'s reviewer decided that the novel began promisingly and that "Drexler uses dirty words with delirious grace," but it seemed to him that "about a third of the way through the satire gets blurry and the book becomes unglued and uninteresting. It appears that lack of focus and discipline are wasting Drexler's gifts." It seems unlikely that Rosalyn Drexler is much attracted by discipline; she remains a paragon of the virtues she has elected, and an "absolute original."

The author has received two grants from the Rockefeller Foundation, the *Paris Review* prize for humor (1966), and a Guggenheim fellowship (1970). She is a member of the New Dramatists' Committee (New York), New York Theatre Strategy, the Dramatists' Guild, P.E.N., and Actors' Studio. Her leisure interests include painting, sculpture, and singing. *She Who Was He,* a play produced in New York in 1973, was a startling departure from her earlier work. Set in pre-Biblical times, it was called "lofty and even autumnal in tone"—a work in which "ephemeral hijinks had given way, at least for the moment, to the eternal seriousness of myth."

PRINCIPAL PUBLISHED WORKS: *Novels*—I Am the Beautiful Stranger, 1965; One or Another, 1970; To Smithereens, 1972; The Cosmopolitan Girl, 1975. *Plays*—The Line of Least Existence, and Other Plays (Home Movies, The Investigation, Hot Buttered Roll, Softly and Consider the Nearness, The Bed Was Full), 1967; The Investigation; and, Hot Buttered Roll, 1969; Home Movies *in* Poland, A. and Mailman, B. (eds.) The Off Off Broadway Book, 1973.

ABOUT: Poland, A. and Mailman, B. (eds.) The Off Off Broadway Book, 1973; Vinson, J. (ed.) Contemporary Dramatists, 1977; Who's Who in America, 1976-1977. *Periodicals*—Atlantic Monthly April 1975; Books and Bookmen June 1967; Book World March 19, 1972; Library Journal February 15, 1972; April 1, 1975; Massachusetts Review Winter 1972; Nation August 31, 1970; New York Review of Books August 10, 1972; New York Times Book Review June 13, 1965; June 5, 1970; June 28, 1970; February 27, 1972; March 30, 1975; Newsweek April 1, 1968; June 1, 1970; March 10, 1975; Village Voice March 28, 1968.

*DRIEU LA ROCHELLE, PIERRE-EUGÈNE (January 3, 1893–March 16, 1945), French novelist, short story writer, poet, and literary and political essayist, was born in Paris. The family, whose name was Drieu, had retained the nickname "La Rochelle" given to his paternal great-grandfather, an officer in the wars of the Revolution and the Empire. Pierre-Eugène seems as a child to have seen little of his father and to have been most deeply attached to his maternal grandmother. She encouraged in him an enthusiasm for Rousseau and for Napoleon, and fostered his dreams of military glory while overprotecting him.

His family—Catholic, bourgeois, and nationalist—had social ambitions beyond their income. They sent him at the age of eight to a

*drē û'

PIERRE-EUGÈNE
DRIEU LA ROCHELLE

NRF – Roger Parry

private school, Sainte-Marie de Monceau—conducted by the order of Marists. He lost his religious faith when he was about fourteen and indeed seems always to have found it difficult to believe in anything, especially himself. In *État-Civil* (Vital Statistics, 1921), which he later called a "curiously premature autobiographical essay," he portrays himself as a melancholy and solitary youth, full of doubts about the future of France, and rejecting the decadent past to which he nevertheless feels himself to belong: "I was born too old, in a world which—I want to believe it with a desperate fanaticism—will be tomorrow very young again."

Drieu's ambitious family wanted him to have a career in diplomacy. When he was sixteen he was sent to England, living with a family there to improve his grasp of the language. The following year he entered the École Libre des Sciences Politiques. He was an exceptionally able student but unaccountably failed his final examinations in 1913—one of many such unexpected failures and disappointments in his life.

For Drieu, the outbreak of World War I seemed to offer a chance to burn away his own and his country's self-doubts—a hope shared by Montherlant, Giraudoux, and Apollinaire, among other writers and intellectuals. Drieu was wounded three times, earned several decorations and citations for bravery, and achieved the rank of sergeant. He saw as much as anyone of the squalor, horror, and monotony of war but retained a romantic and mystical sense of exultation in its heroism and cathartic suffering, and in the comradeship and loyalty to authority he found in the trenches.

It is this exultation that predominates in his first book, *Interrogation* (1917), a collection of often bombastic war poems which celebrate the life of action in Nietzschean and anti-rationalist terms, and even express admiration for the strength of the German war machine. Maurice Barrès, who had influenced Drieu almost as much as Nietzsche, called it the best book of poems to come out of the war, and it had immense success, making its young author's reputation overnight. Another book of war poems, considerably less lyrical in tone, was published in 1920 as *Fond de cantine* (Bottom of the Footlocker). The short stories in *La comédie de Charleroi* (translated by Douglas Gallagher as *The Comedy of Charleroi*), which appeared years later in 1934, also dwell on the dark side of the war. All the same, the title story, in which Drieu draws on his experiences at the battle of Charleroi in 1914, clearly evokes the sense of power and fulfillment he found while taking part in a bayonet charge.

In 1919 Drieu was married to Colette Jeramec, a medical student, partly of Jewish descent, who was also an heiress. They were divorced in 1922 but Frédéric Grover, in *Drieu la Rochelle and the Fiction of Testimony,* suggests that this marriage provided for his financial needs, freeing him to pursue a literary career. Thereafter Drieu was involved more or less permanently in a series of more or less passionate love affairs, interrupted in 1927-1929 by a second marriage to Alexandra Sienkiewicz.

World War I, which brought him success, fame, and an interlude of moral certainty, was the high point in Drieu's life; things never seemed so clear or so hopeful again. Grover writes that "Drieu represents in himself various experiences critical to recent French literature— the ineradicable trauma of World War I, the romantic revolt of surrealism, the political commitment to extremist parties, and finally a desperate preoccupation with decadence in general and the fate of France in particular." A close friend of Louis Aragon, he was during and just after the war strongly attracted by the nihilism of dadaism and surrealism, but quarrelled publicly with his friends when Aragon and others became Communists. For many years after that Drieu, an elitist who thought the proletariat was a myth, struggled to retain his ideological independence.

During the postwar years Drieu sought an explanation of his own emotional, sexual, and intellectual problems through an examination of the times—and an understanding of contemporary social and moral disorders through self-analysis, encouraged in this by those who saw in

him a witness for his generation. *Mesure de la France* (1922) is a grim appraisal of the postwar condition of his country—its political disarray, spiritual bankruptcy, and frantic hedonism. Drieu went on to announce and welcome the collapse of Western civilization in *Les Derniers Jours,* a political magazine written entirely by himself and Emmanuel Berl, which survived for seven issues in 1927. In *Le Jeune Européen* (The Young European, 1927), *Genève ou Moscou* (1927), and *L'Europe contre les patries* (Europe Against the Fatherlands, 1931) Drieu, the passionate patriot, pinned his hopes for the future on a federated Europe, rising regenerate from the ashes of nationalism.

Drieu's novels and short stories, like his political essays, are never far from autobiography, just as his fictional heroes embody his own preoccupations and weaknesses, his restless search for some course of action which might redeem him and his society. The stories collected in *Plainte contre inconnu* (Complaint Against Nobody, 1924) characteristically combine bitter social satire and pitiless introspection. Drieu's friend the dadaist writer Jacques Rigaut once called him a *valise vide* (empty suitcase), and this is the title of one of these stories, a study of a typical product of the 1920s. In this exemplary young man "the attributes of personality were broken or perverted. The mind created every morning and devoured before evening its daily fad. . . . Any violent notion was good provided it gave the sensation of energetic stir: negation, paradox, illogicality, contradiction, all the possible combinations of abstract thought, which are not more numerous than those of love." He considers suicide, but fears that even this ridiculous act might seem too large, too serious, unless it could be accomplished with proper indifference: "On going to bed, instead of turning the light off, absent-mindedly I make a mistake and press the trigger."

Rigaut himself committed suicide in 1929, and this inspired Drieu's novel *Le Feu follet* (1931, translated by Richard Howard as *The Fire Within* and by Martin Robinson as *Will o' the Wisp*). It presents from within the thoughts and actions of Alain Leroy as he visits his friends in various milieux of his diseased society, searching for some reason why he should not kill himself. Having considered what life has to offer, he concludes that "to die is the finest thing you could do, the most positive, the most you could do." The novel was made into a powerful film by Louis Malle.

Alain Leroy decides that suicide is the correct course for a man of action in a society without values. Not all of Drieu's questing intellectuals find so clearcut a remedy. Gille, in *L'Homme couvert de femmes* (The Man Covered With Women, 1925), is distracted from his search for salvation by his obsessive need for women—a questing hero landlocked on Circe's island. Gille is still questing and still lost in *Drôle de voyage* (Strange Journey, 1933), which indicts not only postwar sexual mores but political, religious, and artistic decadence. The old beliefs and values of Western civilization were exhausted and must be replaced with new ones, Drieu believed; the war had proved that. Those who clung to the old ways were lost, like the Catholic journalist Blaquans in *Blèche* (1928), a novel which seemed to Frédéric Grover a precursor of the existentialist novel, traditional in form, but preparing "the new climate of sensibility for the existentialist hero, the hero of the absurd." *Une Femme à sa fenêtre* (1930, translated by P. Kirwan as *Hotel Acropolis*) is set in Greece and explores the rivalry of two men, a leftist and a rightist, for the same woman. It was filmed nearly fifty years after it was written by the French director Pierre Granier-Deferre from a screenplay by Jorge Semprun.

By the time he published *Gilles* in 1939, Drieu thought he had found a solution for himself and for Europe. This ambitious novel presents a panoramic view of the twenty years from 1917 to 1937 through the memoirs of its hero, who is all of Drieu's heroes rolled into one—the Don Juan, the surrealist, the soiled idealist seeking a way out of his decadent society, the man of ideas who wants desperately to be a man of action. He learns to live by facing death for Franco in the Spanish Civil War, and discovers joy in the comradeship of fascist soldiers with bodies like Greek gods'.

Drieu, although he refused for years to join any political party, had become increasingly interested in the conflicting claims of communism and fascism, in the early 1930s visiting both Germany and Russia to study the two movements. By 1934 he had come down on the side of fascism, though he always insisted on the right of the intellectual to preserve a certain skepticism. His reasons for choosing fascism were characteristically complicated. He believed that capitalism must be reformed along socialist lines and thought that fascism would destroy capitalism, providing a shortcut to this end. He hoped that French fascism would breed not a crude dictatorship but an elite of leaders, physically, mentally, and morally healthy, who would be able to contain and reduce European decadence, and form a bulwark *against* the fascist dictatorships of Germany and Italy. In 1936 he joined Jacques Doriot's anticommunist Parti Populaire Fran-

çais, explaining his motives in *Avec Doriot* (With Doriot, 1937). He left the PPF, disillusioned, in 1938, but never ceased to call himself a fascist.

Drieu became increasingly disenchanted with German fascism during the late 1930s, concluding that Hitler was giving up the possibility of European unity "in order to substitute for it the summary and brutal notion of the hegemony of Berlin." When Germany invaded France he at first decided to escape to England or, failing that, to commit suicide. Instead he threw in his lot with the invaders, accepted the editorship of the *Nouvelle Revue Française,* and turned it into a collaborationist journal. Alastair Hamilton has offered several reasons for this *volte-face*—Drieu's hunger to participate in large events, his excited admiration for the efficiency with which the Nazis had raped France, and his hope that the strength and virility of Germany might after all save Europe.

This hope dimmed, like all of Drieu's hopes, as the war and the occupation proceeded. In 1942, nevertheless, he rejoined Doriot's PPF, by then one of the most odious collaborationist organizations in France. Drieu's dreams had turned into nightmares once too often, and it seems clear that he deliberately committed himself to failure and ignominy. He was all the same one of the least fanatical of the prominent collaborators, using his slight influence with the Germans to secure the release of Jean Paulhan and others who had been arrested (including his first wife Colette Jeramec). After the beginning of 1943 he spoke with increasing frequency of suicide, which had always obsessed him. He developed an interest in Oriental mysticism, and advised his friends against political commitment.

In November 1943 Drieu visited Geneva (where, as he later pointed out, he could have remained in safety). He returned to France however and in August 1944, two weeks before the Allied liberation of Paris, he took an overdose of Luminal. Saved by the unexpected return of his housekeeper, and recovering in a hospital, he slashed his wrists but again failed to kill himself. It was after this that he wrote *Récit secret* (1951, translated by Alastair Hamilton as *Secret Journal*), in which he writes with considerable detachment and serenity about his life and about suicide, the end to which he believed his whole existence had been directed. He also began a novel, *Mémoires de Dirk Raspe*. Inspired by the life of Vincent van Gogh, it is also a portrait of the artist Drieu might have become. Unfinished as it is, it is regarded by some critics as his masterpiece.

In March 1945 Drieu, who had been staying

at Colette Jeramec's house, returned to Paris, where Resistance tribunals were executing collaborators. On March 15 he learned that he was to be tried, and the following morning he was found dying, having swallowed three tubes of Gardenal and turned on the gas. He died in this way to escape trial, humiliation, and likely execution; because he had failed; because suicide had always seemed to him one of the few honorable and unequivocal actions available to the intellectual, an escape hatch from the ivory tower.

Another reason for Drieu's suicide was his horror of old age. Tall, slim, and elegant, he was still attractive to women, but he had begun to lose his hair and his teeth, and these signs of decline appalled and disgusted him. According to Alastair Hamilton, he gave in person and in his writings the impression of "a mocking, frivolous, egocentric individual who affected boredom and played, coldly and pitilessly, with people and ideas"; in practice, in his actual dealings with people, "he was affectionate, compassionate and generous." His hatred of the society he lived in, and his urge to destroy it, have been seen as reflections of his own self-loathing.

Drieu la Rochelle was an accurate, vigorous, and often moving recorder of his times but, as Hamilton says, "mediocrity was his obsession. He feared it and he ran towards it." Aldous Huxley, who knew him well, thought him "an outstanding example of the strange things that happen when a naturally weak man, whose talents are entirely literary, conceives a romantic desire for action and a romantic ambition for political power." To Henri Peyre he seemed "one of the most pathetic veterans of World War I and perhaps the most characteristic writer of a French lost generation; he embodied all the dreams and disappointments of his country between the two World Wars. He could have been the equal of Malraux. He almost was. But his loss of nerve, his own determination to go down in decay and self-inflicted death cut short his own rich promise."

PRINCIPAL WORKS IN ENGLISH TRANSLATION: *Fiction*—Hotel Acropolis, 1931; The Fire Within, 1961; Will o' the Wisp, 1966; The Comedy of Charleroi (stories), 1973. *Nonfiction*—Secret Journal and Other Writings, 1973.

ABOUT: Andreu, P. Drieu la Rochelle, 1952 (in French); Field, F. Three French Writers of the Great War, 1975; Kunnas, T. De la Rochelle, Céline, Brasillach et la tentation fasciste, 1972; Grover, F.J. Drieu la Rochelle, 1962 (in French); Grover, F.J. Drieu la Rochelle and the Fiction of Testimony, 1958; Hamilton, A. *introduction to* Secret Journal, 1973; Mabire, J. Drieu parmi nous, 1963; Penguin Companion to Literature 2, 1969; Seymour-Smith, M. Guide to Modern World Literature, 1973; Vandromme, P. Pierre Drieu la Rochelle, 1958 (in French). *Periodicals*—Books Abroad 1 1967; Times Literary Supplement September 21, 1973; University of Toronto Quarterly January 1945.

DRUCKER, PETER F(ERDINAND) (November 19, 1909–), American economist and management consultant, was born in Vienna into a family, originally Dutch, that had published bibles and other religious books in Holland in the seventeenth century (Drucker in Dutch and German means "printer"). His father, Adolph Drucker, was a high official in the Austrian civil service until 1923, when he resigned to establish a private practice as an international lawyer. Adolph Drucker also had strong cultural interests, and was one of the founders of the music festival at Salzburg. An outspoken liberal, he fled from Hitler's invasion of Austria in 1938 and became professor of international economics at the University of North Carolina, later taking a similar post in Washington, D.C., and on retirement taught European literature at the University of California. Although Peter Drucker speaks admiringly of his father he says: "He and I were totally different people. We never saw anything—events or people—the same way, never shared any interest. Yet we were very close and had tremendous respect for each other." His mother, formerly Caroline Bond, had been one of the first women in Austria to study medicine. Drucker says he is "very much *her* son. Where my father had principles, she had perception. Till the last years of her life, when she was very ill, we always understood each other without having to discuss anything."

Peter Drucker was educated in a gymnasium (secondary school) in Vienna until 1927, and for a year and a half gained practical experience as a junior clerk in export houses in England and in Hamburg before studying law at the University of Frankfurt, receiving his LL.D. in 1931. While studying in Frankfurt he worked in the local office of an American banking firm and as an editor and writer on a newspaper, the *Frankfurt General Anzeiger*. In 1930, while still a student, he began to teach international law and constitutional history at the university. Drucker became known as a bold thinker but as one within the conservative tradition, and this led the Nazis to offer him a post in the Ministry of Information when they came to power in 1933. His answer was his first book, a brief monograph on the political writings of a nineteenth-century conservative philosopher. This was *Friedrich Julius Stahl: Konservative Staatslehre und geschichtliche Entwicklung* (Friedrich Julius Stahl: Conservative Political Theory and Historical Change, 1933), which with its emphasis on constitutional government and the rule of law, as

PETER F. DRUCKER

well as on the fact that Stahl was Jewish by birth, amounted to an anti-Nazi manifesto. The book passed censorship, but after a few weeks in which it attracted widespread attention it was banned. In April 1933 Drucker left Germany for England, where he took a job in a merchant bank. After four years there he was offered a job as American correspondent for a group of British newspapers, and sailed for the United States, where he also became an American adviser to British banks.

Drucker's varied economic and journalistic work in Germany had given him an inside view of the disastrous political and economic events that led to Hitler's takeover. He applied his insights in his first full-length book, *The End of Economic Man* (1939), which analyzes the causes of the rise of fascism and the failure of established institutions, and argues the case for a new economic and social order. Drucker maintains that the systems of government by which the world has been run, whether capitalistic or socialistic, have been rooted in the assumption that human beings generally act in accordance with their economic interests. Man has been Economic Man, his values economic values, and hopes of a more decent world order have been sought through the satisfaction of economic needs. Economic Man had now been killed by totalitarianism, which was not the beginning of a new order, only the result of the total collapse of the old. As John J. Tarrant has observed, "it is unlikely that many of those who now celebrate Drucker as 'Mr. Management' are aware that he was once proclaiming the doom of capitalism." Contemporary reviewers welcomed the book as one of "the most challenging and penetrating

analytical studies of the totalitarian state that has appeared in this country," and called it "brilliantly written," though some readers thought that Drucker was too negative, too scornful of established institutions, of economics and the capitalist system. But he believed that some new concept was urgently needed, and his next books were attempts to forge a philosophy by which he felt free men could live and grow.

In 1940 Drucker accepted a teaching post at Sarah Lawrence College in Bronxville, New York. From 1942 to 1949 he was professor of philosophy, government, and religion at Bennington College in Vermont and in 1950 he moved to New York University's Graduate Business School as professor of management. During World War II he had spent considerable time in Washington working on intelligence about German industry and also applying himself to problems of wartime production. But in his writing he was exploring the basic questions faced by industrial societies in peace as well as war. In his previous book he had urged the need for a new world order, and *The Future of Industrial Man* (1942) offers his vision of the new society, exploring the question of whether individual freedom can be preserved in industrial society. He begins by emphasizing the dominant role of industry in the war, which in his view was being fought largely between the industries of the contending nations. Postwar society would inevitably be an industrial one, and "no society can function as a society unless it gives the individual member social status and function, and unless the decisive social power is legitimate power." Drucker claims that while civilization is now fixed on an industrial base, government and international relations continue to rest on preindustrial customs and techniques. He examines the mercantile societies of the past, and also the speculations about a dehumanized industrialized future offered by writers and film-makers like Fritz Lang (in *Metropolis*) and Charlie Chaplin (in *Modern Times*).

It was thought that Drucker had not really solved the problems he had set himself, and which have continued to occupy him—how the individual is to be given status and function, and how the corporate power of the ruling managerial class is to be made legitimate (a critical question for him, since as the subtitle of the book tells us, his is "A Conservative Approach"). Henry Hazlitt described the book's style as "a combination of a German mysticism and a popular magazine looseness ... a brilliant blur," but it seemed to W. H. Chamberlin that Drucker "possesses a fund of historical and economic knowledge; his mind does not follow conventional grooves; his style eschews the cliché and achieves frequent paradoxes and occasional profundity." Jacques Barzun found the book worthy of the careful study "that our scholars reserve for authors who have been dead a thousand years."

Much of Drucker's career has been as an independent management consultant, advising hundreds of businesses, government agencies, public service institutions, state and city governments, and the national governments of America and several foreign countries. He always works alone, without a staff. For his first consultancy, he was retained to conduct a massive study of General Motors. This provided the basis for his next book, *Concept of the Corporation* (1946), an account of the methods used by General Motors as it grew from a small company to an industrial giant. It displeased the management of the firm, who thought they had been unfairly criticized, but reviewers regarded the book, whose main thesis is that big business is the representative institution of American society, as pro-business. The study has acquired the status of a classic, and the concepts it embodies have been adopted over the years by many other large corporations, including competitors of General Motors such as Ford. John J. Tarrant sees the book as completing "the trilogy in which Drucker laid out his blueprint for the new order. He had proclaimed the end of Economic Man. He had envisioned the rise of Industrial Man. He had focused on the corporation as the essential institution of the new society. Now—what was the institution like? What should it be like? How could it be run?"

The central thesis of Drucker's *The New Society* (1949) is that mass production in American industry is bringing about a new social order, the first of its kind in history. Here he pulls together the threads of his earlier books and offers a comprehensive picture of the way he believes the world will work in the latter part of the twentieth century, with everyone working together freely and peacefully for the good of their corporation and so of their community, which would be a harmonious industrial society. Though Drucker has been widely regarded as the ideologist and apologist of American capitalism, the industrial utopia he envisaged did not conform with any received system, capitalist or communist. Many considered his ideas unworkable, and the industrial psychologist Douglas McGregor wrote: "People today are accustomed to being directed, manipulated, controlled in industrial organizations and to finding satisfaction for their social, egoistic and self-fulfillment needs away from the job. . . . Genuine 'industrial citizenship' . . . is a remote and unrealistic idea, the meaning of which has not even been considered by most members of industrial organizations."

The Practice of Management (1954) is a helpful guide to the powers and responsibilities of managers and to ways of increasing productivity and performance, with examples drawn from the histories of Sears Roebuck, General Motors, Ford, IBM, Chrysler, and other American corporations. One of the ideas Drucker puts forward is "management by objectives"—shifting the focus from processes to goals. Though this technique has been widely accepted, few companies have been prepared to go as far as Drucker has urged in giving managers the freedom to control themselves, a policy which is vitally important in Drucker's eyes: "What the business enterprise needs is a principle of management that will give full scope to individual strength and responsibility, as well as common direction to vision and effort, establish teamwork, and harmonize the goals of the individual with the commonweal." Leo Teplow called this "probably the most stimulating and thoughtful book in the overall management field" by an author who "writes as brilliantly as he thinks."

America's Next Twenty Years (1957) is a collection of essays in which Drucker analyzes trends in population changes and their possible implications for education, government, and economics. The key to his approach to planning and forecasting is here concisely explained: "The major events that determine the future have already happened—irrevocably." Drucker projected his prophecies further in *Landmarks of Tomorrow* (1959), which he called "a report on the new post-modern society." In it he discusses the accelerating rate of change and the speed with which principles once universally accepted are nowadays discarded, so that the concepts and disciplines that direct our lives today were largely unknown fifty years ago. Change is accepted as normal, and we no longer look for the one right and permanent solution. Yet we still need to understand how all the disparate patterns of "physical, biological, psychological and social order" are meaningful as reflections of a larger unity—we need a concept of the whole that will enable us to understand ourselves and what is happening to us, and so give us more control over our lives. Technology needs social and cultural foundations, and Drucker's hope as a Christian is for a return to spiritual values. According to John J. Tarrant: "Many Drucker-watchers come upon such eloquent tributes to the values of the spirit as strange, coming as they do from . . . [a] man who is capable of the most hard-headed pragmatic observations and analyses. This is a side of Drucker that is not easy to fit in with a large body of his work and with the conventional view of the man. Nonetheless, it is Drucker."

A more hard-headed book followed in 1964. This was *Managing for Results*, a practical re-evaluation of industrial marketing practices in which Drucker argues that growth is the function and contribution of business, and the reason for its existence. In *The Effective Executive* (1967) he makes a systematic study of the essentials for executive success. The result had a mixed but generally favorable reception. Reviewers thought that it contained much good advice but also a good deal of "trivia, historical inaccuracies, misinterpretations, and non-sequiturs."

In his next book Drucker returned to the examination of the kind of changes currently visible in society, politics, and economics, and those likely to occur in the near future. *The Age of Discontinuity: Guidelines to our Changing Society* (1969), is a manifesto for action, or as Drucker calls it an "early-warning system," asking "what must we do today to shape tomorrow?" Drucker begins by noting fundamental changes affecting this kind of forecasting, which in the past meant extrapolating from present trends. This is in large degree no longer possible, Drucker says, since there have been advances in technology and the sciences of such magnitude as to make the future highly unpredictable. We are no longer dealing with continuities but discontinuities, and the book's four parts deal with four major areas of discontinuity: the explosive growth of new technology, which will result in major new industries while rendering obsolete existing major industries and big businesses; the change from an "international" economy, in which separate nations are the units, to a "world" economy which cuts across national boundaries; the fact that in modern industrial societies many of the most important economic and social tasks are performed not by individuals or families but by institutions—religious, educational, business, and governmental.

For Drucker, the most important area of discontinuity is the growth of knowledge based on mass education. This he regards as the crucial resource of both the economy and society. Just as the Industrial Revolution replaced muscle-power with skill, according to Drucker, so now knowledge will become essential to the performance of functions formerly requiring skill. And the elevation of knowledge to this central role calls for profound changes in the way we learn, work, and govern ourselves. "No one needs to be told that our age is an age of infinite peril," Drucker writes. "No one needs to be told that

the central question we face with respect to man's future is not what it shall be, but whether it shall be. If we do not survive, the concerns of this book will, of course, perish with us. But if we do survive, its concerns will become our tasks. They are humdrum tasks, tasks of patching the fabric of civilization rather than of designing a new garment for a 'New Adam.' They are tasks of today, and not tasks for 'the Year 2000.' But they are the tasks to which we have to address ourselves to deserve tomorrow."

In *The Unseen Revolution* (1976), Drucker argues that a revolution had over the previous twenty-five years been quietly transforming the United States into the first truly socialist nation, the vehicle for this revolution being the remarkable growth of employee pension funds, which by 1985 "will own at least fifty percent of the equity capital of American business." Drucker goes on to discuss the implications of this trend. Most critics tended to share the opinion of Steven Wecker, who found this "a provocative, if not particularly persuasive, book." Jason Epstein maintained that the development was less revolutionary than it seemed—Drucker believes that "he has identified a greatly expanded American *rentier* class consisting of retired employees in whose interest he can once more defend American corporate practice as he has done in his many previous books on the subject. . . . Astute readers will quickly see that in other respects too Drucker's pension fund socialism is much the same as capitalism."

Drucker has contributed essays and articles to a wide range of periodicals, and several collections of these have been published, including *Technology, Management and Society* (1970) and the similar volume published in Britain as *Drucker on Management* (1970); *Men, Ideas and Politics* (1971) which covers a broad spectrum of subject matter, including a commentary on Kierkegaard; *Management: Tasks—Responsibilities—Practices* (1974); and *People and Performance: The Best of Drucker on Management* (1977), in which Drucker comments: "The emphasis throughout this book is on people and performance. For this is what management is all about. Indeed, if there is one right way to define management it is as the work and function that enables people to perform and to achieve." According to John J. Tarrant, "Drucker's preeminence as the analyst of institutions and the architect of the craft of management is almost universally accepted." *Adventures of a Bystander* (1979) is a collection of sketches of some of the eminent and extraordinary people Drucker has known. According to a reviewer in *Publishers Weekly,* "he writes with wit and spirit—and

DRUMMOND DE ANDRADE

sometimes with exaggeration—about Sigmund Freud, Henry Luce, Alfred Sloan, Buckminster Fuller, and Marshall McLuhan, as well as about remarkable friends and acquaintances of his Viennese boyhood, Frankfurt and London in the 1930s, and America during the Depression and World War II."

For over twenty years Drucker was professor of management at the Graduate Business School of New York University, where in 1972 he was named Distinguished University Lecturer; he retired in 1976 as professor emeritus. Since 1971 he has also been Clark Professor of Social Science at the Claremont Graduate School, Claremont, California, where he now lives. Drucker received the German Hegemann Prize in 1965, and has honorary degrees from universities in the United States, Britain, Japan, and Switzerland. He is a fellow of the International Academy of Management, the American Association for the Advancement of Science, and the American Academy of Management. In 1965–1966 he was president of the Society for the History of Technology. He has been an American citizen since 1943. A large man, six feet tall and heavy-set, Drucker is a collector of Japanese art and a former amateur mountain climber. He was married in 1937 to Doris Schmitz, a physicist, and they have three daughters, Kathleen, Cecily, and Joan, and a son, Vincent. Asa Briggs once observed that Drucker "has three outstanding gifts as a writer on business—acute perception, brilliant skill as a reporter, and unlimited self-confidence."

PRINCIPAL WORKS: The End of Economic Man, 1939; The Future of Industrial Man: A Conservative Approach, 1942; Concept of the Corporation, 1946 (in England, Big Business); The New Society, 1949; The Practice of Management, 1954; America's Next Twenty Years, 1957; Landmarks of Tomorrow, 1959; Managing for Results, 1964; The Effective Executive, 1967; The Age of Discontinuity, 1969; Technology, Management and Society, 1970; Drucker on Management, 1970; Men, Ideas and Politics, 1971; Management: Tasks, Responsibilities, Practices, 1974 (revised as An Introductory View of Management, 1977); The Unseen Revolution, 1976; People and Performance, 1977; Management Cases, 1977.

ABOUT: Contemporary Authors 61–64, 1976; Current Biography, 1964; International Who's Who, 1978–79; Tarrant, J.J. Drucker: The Man Who Invented the Corporate Society, 1976; Who's Who in America, 1976–1977. Periodicals —Business Week February 9, 1974; Nation's Business March 1974.

*DRUMMOND DE ANDRADE, CARLOS (October 31, 1902–), Brazilian poet, journalist, critic, and short story writer, was born in the small town of Itabira, in the iron-mining state of Minas Gerais, a harsh and rocky region where

*drū mond' də un drä' də

Biblioteca Nacional

CARLOS DRUMMOND DE ANDRADE

life is often hard, narrow, and fanatically devout. He was the ninth child of Carlos de Paula Andrade, a landowner, and Julieta Augusta Drummond de Andrade, who was of Scottish descent. Drummond de Andrade spent his childhood on the family estate, and received his early education in Itabira. He was a delicate child who developed an early love of literature and a precocious interest in writing. In 1918 he entered the Jesuit Colégio Anchieta at Nova Friburgo. He was intensely homesick, felt that he was being harshly treated, and became increasingly rebellious until, after two years, he was expelled.

In 1920, the family moved to the state capital of Belo Horizonte, where Drummond de Andrade joined the other aspiring young writers who met at the Alves bookshop or the Cafe Estrêla. At twenty he won a literary competition with a short story called "Joaquim do Telhado" (Roof-top Joaquim). The following year he enrolled at the University of Minas Gerais to begin the study of pharmacy, though he continued to devote much of his time to writing and reading. During this period Drummond de Andrade began a correspondence with the much-loved Brazilian poet Manuel Bandeira that lasted until Bandeira's death in 1968. He also established friendships with other writers and artists associated with the early phase of Brazilian Modernism, among them the French poet Blaise Cendrars and Modernism's two principal pioneers, Mário de Andrade and Oswald de Andrade.

Drummond de Andrade was married to Dolores Morais in 1925, when he also collaborated in the founding of the short-lived but important Modernist journal *A Revista* (The Review). The same year, he graduated with a degree in pharmacy, promptly deciding against any such career. By 1926 he was teaching geography and Portuguese in the Ginásio Sul-Americano in Itabira, but soon joined the staff of the *Diário de Minas* (Minas Daily) where he became chief editor before transferring to the editorial staff of the official state newspaper *Minas Gerais* (1930-1932). The birth of his daughter Maria Julieta added an important new dimension to his life.

Meanwhile, Drummond de Andrade was contributing to the polemics which accompanied the Modernist renewal of Brazilian art and letters in the 1920s. In the first issue of *A Revista* he wrote: "The excessive output of criticism prevalent in the period before 1914 led to abuses at the other extreme, namely an attitude of complete apathy and indifference on the part of artists and writers when confronted with the phenomena of the visible world. A plethora of aesthetic doctrines culminated in *Dadaism* and the confusion of the Tower of Babel was repeated. Now the artist and writer finds himself shunning all abstract theories in order to pursue reality with unblemished hands." In the second issue of the same journal, he called upon his fellow artists to express an authentic spirit of nationalism and even primitivism in their work, avoiding the slavish imitation of foreign cultures.

The extent to which he had himself transcended the avant-gardism of the early Modernists was apparent in *Alguma Poesia* (Some Poetry), which in 1930 ushered in the second phase of Brazilian Modernism. These lyrics, startlingly devoid of rhetoric or any kind of literary attitudinizing, deal in the simplest language with the comfortably humdrum realities of life—usually of the provincial life the poet knows best: "The sea does not interest me/ But I have seen the lake . . . / The lake is big and also tranquil . . . / I have not seen the sea/ But I have seen the lake." ("Lagoa").

The apparent naivety of these verses is deceptive; their simplicity only half disguises a highly sophisticated, ironic, often disquieting sense of what Mário de Andrade has called *vida besta* (absurd life): "Stop!/ Life has come to a halt/ or was it an automobile?" ("Cota Zero"). The same collection included "No Meio do Caminho" (In the Middle of the Road):

In the middle of the road there was a stone
there was a stone in the middle of the road
there was a stone
in the middle of the road there was a stone

I will never forget that event
in the life of my exhausted retina
I will never forget that in the middle of the road
there was a stone
there was a stone in the middle of the road
in the middle of the road there was a stone.

(translated by Martin Seymour-Smith)

Martin Seymour-Smith has said of this poem (which caused something of a furor among purists and reactionary critics) that it is "a perfect—and a characteristically perfectly casual—statement of one aspect of the modern situation. The proper path is blocked: we must go one way or another, but we remain obsessed with the obstacle. For Drummond de Andrade, life itself is an 'impossible' idea. . . . He is deeply concerned with the process of writing poetry, and with its 'impossibility'; his own manner is lyrical (as if in direct contrast to his minute metaphysical and phenomenological investigations), humorous, relaxed; he distrusts and ironically uses language to question its own capacities. He is a fascinating poet because the surface of his work is a deliberate refutation of his intellectuality."

Brejo das Almas (Swamp of Souls), which followed in 1934, is a darker collection, less content to be merely descriptive, harsher in its comments on human isolation, including the poet's own: "I have lost the tram and all hope/ I return home looking pale/ The road is useless and there is not a car in sight to run me over." ("Sonêto da Perdida Esperança"). The same year, 1934, Drummond de Andrade moved to Rio de Janeiro as personal adviser to the Minister of Education, Gustavo Capanema. In Rio he became involved in new editorial commitments, and six years passed before the publication of his next book of poems.

World War II had begun when *Sentimento do Mundo* (Grief of the World) appeared in 1940, and this accounts for the change of mood in this collection. The childhood games and provincial gardens of Drummond de Andrade's early poems seemed irrelevant in the face of catastrophe, and his verse now sadly records the world's follies and disorders, the reckless wickedness of politicians and industrialists, finding hope only in the ideal of working-class solidarity. Similar work was collected in *Poesias* (Poems, 1942) and *A Rosa do Pove* (The Rose of the People, 1945), which includes a long tribute to "the man of the people, Charlie Chaplin." The famous poem "José" from *Poesias* has been described as "one of the most Brazilian of all modern poems, and so popular as to have become a national institution." José is a human symbol of Brazil and all its heartbreaking problems: "Key in hand/ you'd like to open the door—/ there's no door;/ you'd like to drown in the sea./ but the sea's dried up. . . ."

In 1945 Drummond de Andrade left the Ministry of Education to become head of the history section of the Office of the National Historical and Artistic Heritage. He remained there until his retirement in 1962, in 1954 becoming also the historian of the Rio daily *Correio da Manhã* (Morning Mail). Meanwhile, such volumes as *Poesia até Agora* (Poetry to Date, 1948) and *Claro Enigma* (Bright Enigma, 1951) show Drummond de Andrade gaining absolute mastery of his technical resources and his highly personal style.

In these collections, and more definitely in the books that followed during the 1950s, the anguish of the war years gives way to a new serenity of spirit; the reader receives the clear impression of a man who has come to terms with himself and the world. Social commitment is still strong in *Fazendeiro do Ar* (Planter of Air, 1954), but the overall tone is much more relaxed: once a socialist, Drummond de Andrade no longer believes that injustice and suffering can be cured by political activism. In "A Distribuição do Tempo" (The Distribution of Time), he writes: "One minute, one minute of hope/ then all is over. And all belief/ in problems has disappeared. All that remains is calm/ decision hovering between death and indifference." A similar note of acceptance can perhaps be found in "Elegia" (Elegy), with its ambiguous confidences: "I have gained (lost) my day. And that cold thing (also known as night) descends." The collection also includes a number of poems evoking scenes and people from the poet's past, as does *Lição de Coisas* (The Lesson of Things, 1962), which shows a renewed interest in technique.

Drummond de Andrade is also the author of a number of inventive and ironic prose chronicles, critical essays, short stories, and other prose works, of great interest in themselves and for the light they throw on his development as a poet. He has also translated extensively from French prose and drama—Molière, Balzac, Laclos, Maeterlinck, and Proust—and, from the Spanish, García Lorca's play *Doña Rosita La Soltera*. His own work has attracted a great deal of attention abroad, and translations have appeared in England and the United States, in France, Spain, Sweden, Czechoslovakia, Germany, Argentina, and Chile.

John Nist has spoken of Drummond de Andrade's "creative dedication to an unattainable perfection which demands from him a personal

humility that operates by the tactics of irony and humor," and calls him "the most meditative lyricist in modern Brazilian literature. . . . Drummond in his honesty to the word has become, with both courage and humility, the much-needed and much-admired professor of aesthetics to the younger Brazilian writers." Drummond de Andrade is the most important poet of the second phase of Brazilian Modernism, which began with him. "Temperamentally reserved and shy, a true introvert," he is, according to Nist, "the most admired intellectual of his generation" in Brazil.

PRINCIPAL WORKS IN ENGLISH TRANSLATION: In the Middle of the Road, translated by John Nist, 1965. *Poems in* Bishop, E. and Brasil, E. (eds.) An Anthology of Twentieth Century Brazilian Poetry, 1972; Caracciolo-Trejo, E. (ed.) The Penguin Book of Latin American Verse, 1971; Cohen, J.M. (ed.) Latin American Writing Today, 1967; Fitts, D. (ed.) Anthology of Contemporary Latin-American Poetry, 1942; Nist, J. (ed.) Modern Brazilian Poetry, 1962; Pontiero, G. (ed.) An Anthology of Brazilian Modernist Poetry, 1969. *Story in* New World Writing 14 1958.

ABOUT: Andrade, M. de. Aspectos da Literatura Brasileira, 1959; Brasil, A. Carlos Drummond de Andrade, 1971; Brotherston, G. Latin American Poetry, 1975; Costa Lima, L. Lira e Antilira, 1968; Costa Lima, L. Três marcos da poesia brasileira, 1967; Downes, L.S. (ed.) Modern Brazilian Poetry, 1954; Huler, C.L. Brazilian Literature, 1975; International Who's Who, 1977-78; Martins, H. A Rima na Poesia de Carlos Drummond de Andrade, 1968; Moraes, E.de. Drummond, rima, Itabira, mundo: ensaio, 1972; Nist, J. The Modernist Movement in Brazil, 1967; Penguin Companion to Literature 3, 1971; Pontiero, G. (ed.) An Anthology of Brazilian Modernist Poetry, 1969; Sant'Anna, A.R. de. Drummond, 1972; Seymour-Smith, M. Guide to Modern World Literature, 1973; Teles, G.M. Drummond, 1970; Who's Who in Brazil, 1948.

"DRUMMOND, WALTER." *See* SILVERBERG, ROBERT

DUNN, DOUGLAS (EAGLESHAM) (October 23, 1942–), Scottish poet, editor, and critic, is the son of William Douglas Dunn, whom he has described as a "worker," and the former Margaret McGowan. Dunn was born at Inchinnan, Renfrewshire, in southwest Scotland, and educated in the nearby city of Paisley, at Renfrew High School and Camphill School. Leaving school when he was seventeen, Dunn went to work as a library assistant at the Renfrew Public Library in Paisley (1959-1962), at the same time studying at the Scottish School of Librarianship. He qualified as an Associate of the Library Association in 1962, and from 1962 to 1964 worked in the Andersonian Library at the University of Strathclyde, Glasgow, before spending two years in the United States as a librarian at the Akron Public Library, Ohio. He was married in

DOUGLAS DUNN

November 1964 to Lesley Balfour Wallace, an art gallery administrator.

In 1966, after a short spell in charge of the chemistry department library at the University of Glasgow, Dunn went to the University of Hull to read English, graduating with first-class honors in 1969. From 1969 to 1971 he was an assistant librarian at the Brynmor Jones Library, University of Hull, working under Philip Larkin, who is the Brynmor Jones Librarian as well as one of Britain's most distinguished poets. Since then Dunn has earned his living as a freelance editor and literary journalist; he regularly reviews poetry for the monthly magazine *Encounter*. More recently he has tried his hand as a dramatist, and a television play, *Ploughman's Share,* and a radio play, *Scotsmen by Moonlight,* were both performed in the late 1970s.

Dunn's first book, *Terry Street,* appeared in 1969 and established him at once. A Poetry Book Society choice, it also brought him an award from the Scottish Arts Council. The poems it contains were written while Dunn was studying at the University of Hull and living in Terry Street itself, a Hull slum. He says that "Terry Street became for me a place of sad sanity. It was an alternative to the gaudy shams everywhere, a cave under a waterfall. But in thinking of Terry Street like this I was probably kidding myself into believing there could be a place not entirely of this age and yet handy enough to it for purposes of observation. . . . I began to feel strange and lost, as though I was trying to inflict loneliness on myself and I came to dislike Terry Street, and left it."

It bothered some critics that Dunn had written about the life of the street not as a participant

but as an observer. "He has been in there," Anthony Thwaite wrote, "like a Disney cameraman parked up a palm-tree with his head disguised as a coconut: he has shot the stuff and he has got it out. The results are distinguished in a prize-for-reporting sort of way," but in many poems "the work is about as close as a patently gifted poet can go to the banal." This effect arose "out of a determination concerning what poetry should not be"—it should not be cheaply romantic or lyrical—and this determination Dunn shared with Philip Larkin, the most obvious influence on poems like "Winter":

Recalcitrant motorbikes;
Dog-shit under frost; a coughing woman;
The old men who cannot walk briskly groaning
On the way back from their watchmen's huts.

But Thwaite acknowledges that, even when Dunn seems to be "just flatly describing something," there is "a guarded quirkiness, an obliqueness, a hesitant cadence" quite different from Larkin's "finished and final quality." And many critics had none of Thwaite's reservations. "These people," it seemed to Dannie Abse, "are not patronised or devalued as human beings. On the contrary, Mr. Dunn's fine achievement is to see what is dignified and potential, even beautiful, in this human ungainliness," and to celebrate "ordinary, everyday, simple actions." The second part of *Terry Street* contains some poems in a more playful vein, in which, as Abse says, Dunn "moves further away from the familiar and ordinary," taking "vigorous risks" with success:

The bed breathes its choir of springs as I move.
I see her face like a face beneath the water,
Such is the moonlight of Canada.

(from "Insomnia on Roetzel's Island")

Dunn is well aware of these two aspects of his work and nature. In 1970 he wrote: "I'm on a train that puffs between two stations. One is Romantic Sleep, the other is Social Realism. If I ever get off the train, I don't know which station it will be at." And, of course, his critics are divided as to which station he *should* get off at, as they showed in their reviews of *The Happier Life* (1972). The poems here in Dunn's more romantic, irrational vein were applauded by some and damned by others, like Anthony Thwaite, who called them "ambitious failures, spoiled by different kinds of literary self-consciousness." Thwaite thought that "the real strengths of the new book are developments of the *Terry Street* vein," and that "best of all are the longer, ruminative, sharply ironical but still tender poems that one might call moralising odes" like the title poem, which Thwaite quotes as "eloquent testimony of how far Douglas Dunn has come from the creaking bedsprings of Terry Street":

> And though I change, and sunlight's never
> The same again, or woods so dark,
> And active generations cry, "Forget, forget!"
> These are the fields of love and death,
> And cannot change, were meant to be
> Forever there distortedly,
> The fixed and visionary part of me.

Thwaite wrote in 1973 that "the regret, nostalgia and wry self-observation Dunn's poems transmit I find more directly moving than any [other] new work," and *The Happier Life* brought its author a Somerset Maugham Award. But the same book drew a rather startlingly harsh review from the Scottish critic Maurice Lindsay, who alleged that Dunn does no more than "snipe and sneer at everything that comes within the range of his cleverness. . . . [Success] is not to be found through sneering envy, in denigrating the daily concerns of ordinary people." Lindsay's verdict was that "Dunn doesn't really like people much," and it may have been this criticism that inspired the harsh self-appraisal of "I Am a Cameraman" in Dunn's third book, *Love or Nothing* (1974): "They suffer, and I catch only the surface./ The rest is inexpressible, beyond/ What can be recorded. You can't be them." Dunn goes on in the same poem to the apparently despairing conclusion that "Life tells the biggest lies of all,/ And draws wages from itself," and he speaks of "The poem that shrugs off every word you try./ The music no one has ever heard."

The tendency to priggishness, the "dangers of diffuseness and flatness," and the technical carelessness that had troubled some reviewers of *The Happier Life* were found also in *Love or Nothing*, which nevertheless had many admirers, was a Poetry Book Society Choice, and received the Geoffrey Faber Memorial Prize. This collection, whose main themes included memories of childhood, exile (from Scotland) and return, and the artist's difficulty in depicting reality, demonstrated to Roy Fuller that Dunn "can be a rewardingly observant and unobvious poet." But James Fenton found his vioce "less certain" in these poems, and Fuller thought that "the virtues of the book are overwhelmed by its slackness of execution. . . . Something has gone seriously amiss with Mr. Dunn's working methods, all the more sad since the persona behind them is patently sentient and humane."

Dunn would presumably not accept this criticism—or rather would not accept that it *is* a criticism—since he says that he would no longer count himself "among the camp of the traditionalists, seeking elegance for its own sake, or trying to live up to a 'standard'. . . . A poem should live for the day." This change of attitude perhaps reflects his conversion to Marxism in the mid-1970s. Douglas Dunn, "a chubby little figure" according to James Fenton, is a member of the Writers' Action Group, whose aim is the implementation of a fair Public Lending Right, under which royalties would be paid to authors when their books are borrowed from public libraries. His recreations include playing the clarinet, listening to music, and writing short stories.

PRINCIPAL WORKS: *Poetry*—Terry Street, 1969; (with others) Poetry: Introduction 1, 1969; (with others) Modern Poets in Focus 1, edited by Dannie Abse, 1971; Backwaters (pamphlet), 1971; The Happier Life, 1972; Love or Nothing, 1974. *As Editor*— New Poems 1972-1973: The P.E.N. Anthology, 1973; A Choice of Byron's Verse, 1974; Two Decades of Irish Writing: A Critical Survey, 1975.

ABOUT: Abse, D. (ed.) Modern Poets in Focus 1, 1971; Contemporary Authors 45-48, 1974; Thwaite, A. Poetry Today, 1960-1973, 1973; Vinson, J. (ed.) Contemporary Poets, 1975. *Periodicals*—Encounter February 1975; English Summer 1971; Listener August 9, 1973; London Magazine October 1969; August-September 1972; New Statesman December 6, 1974; Poetry July 1975; The Review Spring-Summer 1972; Spectator July 22, 1972; Stand 2 1970; Times Literary Supplement November 20, 1969; June 9, 1972; January 31, 1975.

ELKIN, STANLEY (LAWRENCE) (May 11, 1930–), American novelist and short story writer, was born in New York City, son of Phil Elkin, a salesman, and Zelda (Feldman) Elkin. He attended neighborhood schools and went on to the University of Illinois, Urbana (1948-1960), where he received his B.A. (1952), M.A. (1953), and Ph.D (1961). He served in the U.S. Army from 1957 to 1959. Since 1960 he has been with the English department of Washington University, St. Louis, becoming professor of English in 1969.

Elkin's short stories began to appear in magazines in the 1950s, and his first novel, *Boswell,* was published in 1964. As a boy, Boswell is singled out by a celebrated psychiatrist and advised to make of himself the personification of the *persona* who is *grata,* and he does—especially after discovering mortality during an incarnation as a professional wrestler engaged in a bout with the Angel of Death. With monomaniacal zeal, he pursues the great and famous, from the world's richest man to the prototypical international revolutionist, from a Nobel-winning anthropologist to an Italian *principessa.* He asks no more than the privilege of reflecting a beam or

STANLEY ELKIN

© 1979 by Jill Krementz

(1967), which made it clear that he was to be considered something more than an entertainer. Its hero, Leo Feldman, ultimate salesman, "artist of the marketplace," is jailed for purveying from the basement of his department store "favors" which are inimical to organized society—illegal abortions, narcotics, black market babies, guns for would-be assassins. In the strange prison to which he is consigned, the rules laid down by Warden Fisher are complex and arbitrary, and Feldman alone (in a company of murderers, rapists, thieves) is designated "a bad man." Peculiar events ensue: he is thrown into solitary (where he learns a lot about the value of life), then resurrected to attend the Warden's party and to have intercourse with the Warden's wife, ending the night in a switched-off electric chair. Finally he is submitted to a Kafkaesque trial by the Warden and the other prisoners, and executed—but not before he has uttered a great, all-embracing affirmation of life.

A Bad Man is a disturbing book as well as a very funny one. Raymond M. Olderman in *Beyond the Wasteland* wrote that it "takes away the last toehold of reality—the distinction between good and evil—and leaves us in total doubt that anything ordinary exists." R. Z. Sheppard welcomed it as "one of the year's most substantial and stylish novels," and other reviewers recognized it as the work of a satirist who was also a "bleak absurdist and a deadly moralist, with a brisk and busy imagination." But Daniel Stern, acknowledging that "the prose, dialogue, and imagery are brilliant," found in the end that "the sympathy I should have felt for the hero and his human predicament was submerged beneath the pratfalls, the metaphysical gags and their significance."

There was, if anything, a warmer reception for *The Dick Gibson Show,* which followed in 1971. Gibson is an itinerant radio man in love with the medium, a disc jockey, announcer, anchorman, and talk-show host in many small towns, winding up with the show of his dreams, a nighttime phone-in program. Participants in Gibson's radio shows seem impelled by their invisibility and the strange passivity of their host to treat him as a father confessor, pouring out to him their bizarre, ludicrous, sad, or ugly secrets—a woman dying in pain, a druggist out to win the love of a Super-Kotex user, a ten-year-old millionaire alone in the world, the last caveman—all must be heard.

The theme of the novel, according to one reviewer, is that of *The Great Gatsby*—"the failure of life to become myth." As Dick Gibson says, talking on compulsively after the show is over: "Well, ladies and gentlemen, there is no astrolo-

two of their glory—of fawning at the feet he knows only too well are made of clay. "So eccentric a character," wrote a reviewer in the *Virginia Quarterly Review,* "offers unlimited opportunities to set him off as a foil against more or less conventional types, and in the process to expose their pretensions," but the narrative, "suffering from unreasonable length and the requirements of its picaresque form, bogs down into a series of *longueurs.*" Robert Maurer also had reservations, but brightened up to note that Elkin "writes marvelously well. Humor explodes in bursts. Scenes crackle with gusto and imaginative fertility, and his people pop off the page with overabundant flesh."

Boswell, like all of Elkin's novels, shows a raconteur's delight in the tall tale, the gag, the set piece; and it is not surprising to find him thoroughly at home in the short story form. The nine stories collected in *Criers and Kibitzers, Kibitzers and Criers* (1966) range from fantasy and a kind of grotesque pathos to broad ethnic humor—what *Library Journal* called the "Oy veh school" of modern Jewish fiction. John Thompson found something like sadism in Elkin's tendency to create wretched characters for no better purpose than to bedevil and destroy them, but a reviewer in *Choice* wrote delightedly of Elkin's "outrageous images, fresh and unexpected happenings. It is a jumpy, staccato prose, intentionally uneven, often erupting with rapier suddenness. A striking feature of the stories is their rapid pace, the reader's awareness of their constant forward motion . . . [which] minimizes setting and encourages a narration of rather than a dramatization of events."

It was Elkin's second novel, *A Bad Man*

gy, there's no black magic and no white, no ESP, no UFOs. Mars is uninhabited. The dead are dead and buried. Meat won't kill you and Krebiozen won't cure you and we'll all be out of the picture before the forests disappear or the water dries up. Your handwriting doesn't indicate your character and there is no God. All there is . . . are the strange displacements of the ordinary." "The strange displacements of the ordinary," wrote a reviewer in the *Times Literary Supplement,* "form the novel's substance and provide its logic. It's a fascinating, brilliantly organized and rewardingly mysterious performance: continuously entertaining, often funny, touching and always demanding."

By common consent, the best of the three novellas collected in *Searches and Seizures* (1973) was "The Bailbondsman," a portrait in considerable depth of an aging Cincinnati bondsman of Phoenician descent, a "seedy monster," according to Thomas R. Edwards, "who is all the same fascinated by mystery, Faustianly concerned to 'know things' and finally shaken by the recognition that crime is the only mystery his education and experience have allowed him to get close to. . . . In its mastery of clashing tones and expectations, its secure attachment of a powerful but sometimes erratic imagination to a particular and troubling human case, 'The Bailbondsman' may be the finest work yet of this immensely gifted writer . . . it shows that an art founded on aggression, on assaults against the reader's habits of association and sense of good manners, can be both wrenchingly funny and oddly moving."

Edwards, who suspects that Elkin has been more praised than read, believes that "no American novelist tells us more about where we are and what we're doing to ourselves." David P. Demarest, writing in *Contemporary Novelists,* says that "technically the brilliant qualities of Stanley Elkin's fiction are imagery and anecdote or vignette. . . . Elkin's style is often 'dense' with imagery—an almost over-richness that itself becomes part of what the novels are saying. . . . The comic effect is central and continuous, but it is typically founded on qualities that, in the last analysis, are not funny at all—the grotesque, the ugly, the deflationary. In fact a fundamental theme of Elkin's fiction is physical waste, mortality. . . . comedy is palliative or defensive, a willingness, even a need, to laugh at failure's inevitability. . . . Despite differences in detail and nuance, Elkin's novels are thus variations on a single theme: given mortality, the ego's need . . . is the only human motive that demands no justification."

Mortality is never far away in *The Franchiser*

(1976), whose hero discovers that he has multiple sclerosis. Ben Flesh is a collector of business franchises, a passive, simple, amiable man who lives without wife or hearth, cruising the highways that connect his empire of Howard Johnsons, Mister Softees, and Holiday Inns. His only family is an adoptive one of eighteen variously freakish people, most of whom come to grief in appropriately freakish ways. Ben himself, as Michael Wood wrote, "his franchises tied up in a failing Travel Inn, his America caught in a galloping financial crisis, his nerves all haywire from multiple sclerosis, talks a lot, weeps a lot, and ends the book happy, grateful that he isn't all the lamentable other things that he might have been—remaining only, Elkin suggests . . . the lamentable thing he is."

In Wood's opinion, the novel is about identity and its erosion—about the homogenization of America by people like Ben, the homogenization of people (symbolized in Ben's adoptive family, which is made up of twins and triplets)—the way "things look like other things" and seem increasingly to *be* like other things. "In spite of the element of overkill in the prose," and the fact that Elkin "is funny without being comic," Wood thought this "a very good novel indeed." John Leonard wrote that "the plot founders. The texture, however, is exact, the sense of motion and of place, the jostling of ghosts and dreams in a room or in the imagination. . . . *The Franchiser* is the best of Elkin's novels because throughout it he sustains and controls his metaphor; he grapples with, and mostly subdues, his vagaries."

Elkin has been a visiting lecturer at Smith College (1964-1965) and a visiting professor at the University of California, Santa Barbara (Summer 1967) and the University of Wisconsin (Summer 1969). In 1957 and 1975 he taught at Yale. Elkin received the Longview Foundation Award in 1962, the *Paris Review* prize for humor in 1965, a Guggenheim Fellowship in 1966, a Rockefeller Fellowship in 1968, and grants from the National Endowment for the Arts (1972) and the National Institute of Arts and Letters (1974). He was married in 1953 to Joan Jacobson and has three children. Asked to comment on his work in *Contemporary Novelists,* he said that he didn't know what to say: "What I like best about it, I suppose, are the sentences. What I like least about it is my guess that no one is ever moved by it."

PRINCIPAL WORKS: *Novels*—Boswell: A Modern Comedy, 1964; A Bad Man, 1967; The Dick Gibson Show, 1971; The Franchiser, 1976. *Short Stories*—Criers and Kibitzers, Kibitzers and Criers, 1966; The Making of Ashenden, 1972 (U.K. only); Searches and Seizures, 1973 (U.K., Eligible

Men). *Play*—The Six-Year-Old Man *in* Esquire 1969. *As Editor*—Stories From the Sixties, 1971.

ABOUT: Contemporary Authors 9-12 1st revision, 1974; Guttman, A. The Jewish Writer in America, 1971; Lebowitz, N. Humanism and the Absurd in the Modern Novel, 1971; Olderman, R. Beyond the Waste Land, 1972; Penguin Companion to Literature 3, 1971; Tanner, T. City of Words, 1971; Vinson, J. (ed.) Contemporary Novelists, 1976; Who's Who in America, 1976-1977. *Periodicals*—Book Week June 21, 1964; Book World October 22, 1967; March 7, 1971; Choice October 1966; Commonweal December 8, 1967; Library Journal November 15, 1973; Nation November 27, 1967; August 28, 1976; New Republic November 24, 1973; New York Review of Books February 3, 1966; January 18, 1968; March 21, 1974; August 5, 1976; New York Times Book Review July 12, 1964; January 23, 1966; October 15, 1967; February 21, 1971; October 21, 1973; June 13, 1976; Newsweek April 19, 1971; Paris Review Summer 1976; Publishers Weekly October 22, 1973; Saturday Review August 15, 1964; January 15, 1966; November 18, 1967; May 29, 1976; Time October 27, 1967; March 1, 1971; Times Literary Supplement October 22, 1964; August 27, 1971; December 13, 1974; Virginia Quarterly Review Autumn 1964.

HARLAN ELLISON

ELLISON, HARLAN (JAY) (May 27, 1934–), American science fiction writer, novelist, editor, and critic, was born in Cleveland, Ohio, the son of Louis Laverne Ellison and the former Serita Rosenthal. He spent a restless and unruly childhood in Painesville, Ohio, thirty miles east of Cleveland, where he attended grade school and high school. At the age of thirteen he ran away and worked with a traveling carnival until private detectives returned him to his parents. Six months later he left home again and for a time was a logger in Ontario, Canada.

In 1949 his father died and Ellison and his mother moved to Cleveland, where he graduated from East High School and, at about the same time, discovered science fiction. He became a founder member of the Cleveland Science Fiction Society, published in the club magazine, and eventually took it over. Through this magazine, and through fan activities, he met many leading science fiction writers, some of whom encouraged him in his own literary ambitions.

Meanwhile, Ellison scraped a living in a variety of casual jobs. It is claimed that, before he was eighteen, he had worked as a tuna fisherman, itinerant crop picker, bodyguard, dynamite truck driver, short-order cook, cab driver, lithographer, and brush salesman. He also acted from time to time at the Cleveland Play House.

From 1954 to 1955 Ellison attended Ohio State University, where a creative writing instructor assured him that he had no talent. Ellison replied in terms which ended his university career. He moved on to New York, where he was among other things a bridge painter and a Times Square book salesman. For ten weeks he lived in the Red Hook district of Brooklyn, joining a street gang called the Barons to gather material later used in his first novel *Rumble,* in two collections of short stories, and in the autobiographical *Memos From Purgatory.* It was at this time that Ellison sold his first short stories and this encouragement released a great burst of activity. During 1956 and the early part of 1957 over a hundred of his stories and articles appeared in a wide range of pulp magazines. Ellison was drafted into the army in 1957 and is said to have narrowly escaped court-martial on three occasions before his honorable discharge in 1959. The same year his first (1956) marriage ended in divorce.

For the next two years, Ellison moved between New York and Chicago. He edited *Rogue Magazine* (1959-1960), helped to establish the Regency line of paperbacks (1960-1961), and continued to pour out great quantities of stories and articles for pulp magazines of all kinds— science fiction, western, detective, "true confession," and men's. In 1961 he published the novel *Rockabilly,* a study of a monstrous rock singer, the culture that has produced him, and the entourage that exploits and finally destroys him. Here, as elsewhere in his writings, Ellison refers to real places and people in order to endow his story with an air of immediacy and authenticity. Despite its clumsy and overblown style, the novel is a serious social statement, expressing the revulsion against racial prejudice, violence, and materialism that permeates Ellison's later and more mature work.

Encouraged by his first movie sales, Ellison moved in 1961 to California, where he has remained. His first years there were difficult ones,

237

bringing periods of considerable poverty and a second marriage and divorce as Ellison, supporting himself with his pulp fiction, struggled to break into television and feature films. Success came slowly, with contributions to such television series as *Route 66, The Alfred Hitchcock Hour,* and *The Untouchables,* and a jackpot of seven scripts for *Burke's Law.* The turning point in Ellison's career came in 1962, when his short story collection *Gentleman Junkie* was enthusiastically reviewed in *Esquire* by Dorothy Parker.

Ellison's reputation was confirmed by his editing of the enormous and now famous anthology of science fiction stories and fantasies, *Dangerous Visions* (1967), and its two equally important successors. The three anthologies contain original stories, all of them experimental in style or content, both by established writers in the field and by unknowns. The volumes also contain tens of thousands of words by the editor, commenting upon the authors, the stories, himself, his society, and writing in general. In his introduction to the first volume, Ellison wrote: "The millenium is at hand. We are what is happening." He fully intended the trilogy to shatter the taboos and conventions of speculative fiction, and it has done so. It is universally recognized as a seminal influence in the development of "New Wave" science fiction, and has been adopted as a standard text in over two hundred colleges and universities.

Ellison's own writing has grown in technical accomplishment during the years he has spent on the *Dangerous Visions* trilogy, and his view of the world has darkened. He believes, as he has explained in the prefaces which are a feature of his books, that such phenomena as "random violence, mass madness, the rape of our planet" and the "gaggingly hideous" manifestations of racial prejudice cannot be explained in rational terms. In some of his stories he has attributed them to the machinations of a new order of gods, who have come into being because they are what the world now believes in. The first of these was the Paingod, introduced in *The Paingod and Other Delusions* (1965), who has the "forever task of dispensing pain and sorrow to the myriad multitudes of creatures that inhabit the universe," and who is necessary because beauty and pleasure cannot exist without their opposites.

In recent years, Ellison has become the most honored of all science fiction writers: he has received six Hugo awards from the annual World Science Fiction Convention, and two Nebula awards from the Science Fiction Writers of America, as well as the Edgar Allan Poe award of the Mystery Writers of America. Not everyone, it should be said, takes his literary achievements as seriously as does the science fiction fraternity. The twenty-two "racy" stories in *Love Ain't Nothing But Sex Mispelled,* only some of which are speculative fictions, were harshly reviewed by Richard Rhodes. The best of these stories seemed to Rhodes no more than "competent writing about authentic people." He thought the book "only pretends toughmindedness: it reeks with fear," offering a Grand Guignolesque vision of the human condition in which "abortions inevitably end in hemorrhage and death ... a bitch-goddess's soul takes up residence in a slot machine; an aspiring young author's favorite girl turns out to be a lesbian voyeur.... Ellison usually doesn't describe; he flails. He sets up his characters with minimal sympathy and then batters them down at each story's end."

The most generally admired of Ellison's books to date is *Deathbird Stories,* in which he added to his dark pantheon of contemporary deities gods of the freeway, of the ghetto, of Freudian guilt, of business, of street violence, and of machinery. Phoebe Adams found these stories almost unreadably horrible, but concluded that they never quite reach that point "because the fantasy is an ingenious projection and perversion of recognizable reality." Gerald Jonas in the New York *Times Book Review* wrote that "the stories offer a mixture of overheated hype and genuine concern for the human condition. ... There are times ... when Ellison raises excess and pretension to a form of art." The Hugo-winning title story is an overwhelming fable in which the world's sufferings end in the darkness of the Deathbird's merciful wings. Jonas called this "a compendium of every trick Ellison has ever pulled, every artistic sin he has ever committed: I found it genuinely moving."

Ellison writes regularly for the movies and for television, and in the latter medium has three times won the Writers Guild of America's award for Most Outstanding Script. For two-and-a-half years he wrote a weekly television column for the Los Angeles *Free Press* under the title "The Glass Teat," and two collections of these pieces have appeared in book form; a regular column of personal reminiscence and comment later ran for two years in the same newspaper and in the Los Angeles *Weekly News.* Ellison has also written about the movies in *Cinema* and has reviewed records and music in *Jazz Guide, FM,* and elsewhere. He reviews science fiction in the Los Angeles *Times,* and has lectured on that and other subjects at over three hundred colleges and universities. He has taken part in numerous demonstrations in support of civil rights and pacifism.

The author's third marriage in 1965 to Lory Patrick lasted only forty-five days. Since the death of his dog Ahbhu, who figures prominently in two award-winning stories, he has lived alone. Ellison is a short, energetic, thrusting man, dark-haired, blue-eyed, with a pale, youthful face. His instincts are iconoclastic, his manner frequently outrageous. He is both liked and disliked with passion. Isaac Asimov has described him as "a giant among men in courage, pugnacity, loquacity, wit, charm, intelligence—indeed in everything but height." His early work includes much that is hurried and clumsy, but he deserves the reputation he has achieved since the mid-1960s. Such much-reprinted and prize-winning stories as " 'Repent, Harlequin!' Said the Ticktockman" (1966), "I Have No Mouth and I Must Scream" (1967), and "The Beast That Shouted Love at the Heart of the World" (1968) are moving fables of suffering and human defiance.

PRINCIPAL WORKS: *Novels*—Rumble (reprinted as Web of the City), 1958; The Man With Nine Lives, 1960 (revised as The Sound of a Scythe, 1976); Spider Kiss, 1961; Rockabilly, 1961; Doomsman, 1967; Demon With a Glass Hand (novelization of television script), 1967; Kill Machine, 1967; (with Edward Bryant) Phoenix Without Ashes, 1975. *Short Stories*—The Deadly Streets, 1958; A Touch of Infinity, 1960; The Juvies, 1961 (reprinted as Children of the Streets); Gentleman Junkie and Other Stories of the Hung-Up Generation, 1961; Ellison Wonderland, 1962 (reprinted as Earthman, Go Home); Paingod and Other Delusions, 1965; I Have No Mouth and I Must Scream, 1967; Perhaps Impossible, 1967; From the Land of Fear, 1967; Love Ain't Nothing But Sex Mispelled, 1968; The Beast That Shouted Love at the Heart of the World, 1969; Over the Edge, 1970; (with others) Partners in Wonder, 1971; Alone Against Tomorrow, 1971 (U.K., All the Sounds of Fear); The Time of the Eye, 1974; Approaching Oblivion, 1974; Deathbird Stories, 1975; Strange Wine, 1978. *Nonfiction*—Memos From Purgatory, 1961; The Glass Teat: Essays of Opinion on Television, 1970; The Other Glass Teat, 1975. *As Editor*—Dangerous Visions, 1967; Again, Dangerous Visions, 1972; The Last Dangerous Visions, 1975.

ABOUT: Contemporary Authors 5-8 1st revision, 1969; Gunn, J. Alternative Worlds, 1975; McCaffrey, A. Science Fiction, Today and Tomorrow, 1974; Who's Who in America, 1976-1977; Wollheim, D.A. The Universe Makers, 1972. *Periodicals*—Collage October-November, 1960; Colloquy May 1971; Esquire January 1962; Manchester Guardian Weekly July 4, 1963; National Review July 12, 1966; May 7, 1968; New Worlds 5 1973; New Yorker September 16, 1967; Publishers Weekly February 10, 1975; SF Commentary September 1, 1974; Swank April 1974; Times Literary Supplement January 14, 1977.

ERIKSON, ERIK H(OMBURGER) (June 15, 1902–), American psychoanalyst, was born in Frankfurt, Germany, the only child of Danish parents who separated before he was born. When he was three, his mother, the former Kar-

ERIK H. ERIKSON

la Abrahamsen, married Dr. Theodor Homburger, a Jewish pediatrician in Karlsruhe. The boy grew up there, believing himself to be Homburger's son. Rejected as a Jew by his anti-Semitic German classmates, Erikson was called "the goy" at synagogue because of his Nordic features: it is scarcely surprising that he was a mediocre student at the Karlsruhe Humanistisches Gymnasium. Eventually his mother and stepfather told him of their "loving deceit," and he learned that his father had been a non-Jewish Dane. He later changed his name to Erikson, retaining "out of gratitude" the "H" of his stepfather's name as a middle initial. Erikson has in recent years been accused by Marshall Berman and others of evading or denying his Jewishness—an accusation against which he has been vigorously defended by many others, including Karolyn Gould and Mark Gerzon.

When he left the *gymnasium,* Erikson says that he regarded himself as "an artist . . . a European euphemism for a young man with some talent, but nowhere to go." In fact, he wandered for a time in the Black Forest, drawing, reading, and making notes, then went for a year to an art school in Karlsruhe. Two years followed at the Kunst-Akademie in Munich, where he concentrated on etching and woodcuts. After living for a time in Florence, Erikson returned in 1927 to Karlsruhe. He was preparing himself for a career as an art teacher when he received a letter that changed his life.

The letter was an invitation from an old friend, Peter Blos, to help him establish an experimental school in Vienna for the children of patients and acquaintances of Sigmund and Anna Freud. Erikson promptly joined Blos in

Vienna, where the school flourished. The young man was soon accepted by the Freuds for training as an analyst, and was himself analyzed by Anna Freud. He worked as a child analyst at the Vienna Psychoanalytic Institute, achieving full membership there in 1933. At the same time he qualified as a Montessori teacher.

After Hitler came to power in Germany, Erikson migrated via Denmark to the United States, where he went into private practice as Boston's first child analyst, serving also as a consultant at the Massachusetts General Hospital, the Judge Baker Guidance Center, and the Harvard Psychological Clinic. According to *Current Biography,* "a powerful influence was exerted on Erikson by the Cambridge intellectual community, anthropologists Margaret Mead, Ruth Benedict, and Gregory Bateson and psychologists Henry Murray and Kurt Lewin." In 1936 he shelved his doctoral studies in psychology at Harvard for a full-time research position at the Yale University Institute of Human Relations, teaching concurrently at the Yale Medical School (1936-1939), first as an instructor, later as an assistant professor in psychoanalysis. In 1938 he joined the anthropologist Scudder Mekeel in an innovative field study of the child training methods used by the Sioux Indians of South Dakota's Pine Ridge Reservation.

As academic recognition grew, Erikson moved in 1939 to San Francisco, where he conducted his own practice, did training analysis for the San Francisco Psychoanalytic Institute, and participated in a major study of normal child development at the University of California's Institute of Child Welfare at Berkeley. Analysis of Nazi propaganda and of information gained from prisoners of war formed part of his government service during World War II. "Hitler's Imagery and German Youth," published in *Psychiatry* in 1942, shows how skillfully Hitler used imagery evoking common childhood experiences to win the affection and loyalty of the German people. A very different society is discussed in another monograph of the period, *Observations on the Yurok: Childhood and World Image* (1943), based on a field study of the Yurok Indians of northern California, undertaken with the anthropologist Alfred Kroeber.

Erikson's own youthful experiences had predisposed him to an interest in the individual's sense of identity, and the way in which this may be affected by social conditions and pressures. These concerns underly much of his early work, and took on new significance shortly after World War II when he was working with emotionally disturbed veterans at San Francisco's Mount Zion Hospital. "Most of our patients," he wrote

later, " . . . had neither been 'shellshocked' nor become malingerers, but had through the exigencies of war lost a sense of personal sameness and historical continuity. They were impaired in that central control over themselves for which, in the psychoanalytic scheme, only the 'inner agency' of the ego could be held responsible. Therefore, I spoke of a loss of 'ego identity.'" Other work of this period explored the concept of group identity, and analyzed the limited identity roles open to black Americans.

His conviction that psychoanalysis could contribute to a better understanding of "the vicissitudes of normal life" led Erikson to an intense study of the complex interactions between the epigenetic self and society. In 1950 he published *Childhood and Society,* in which he asserted that Freud's psychosexual developmental stages are paralleled by eight psychosocial ones covering the entire lifespan from infancy to maturity and requiring of the ego continual re-establishment and social orientation. William K. Hubbell noted in his review that Erikson "explores childhood anxiety and response patterns cross-culturally in Negro, Yurok, and Sioux as well as [white] American childhood; in Germans through Hitler's imagery in *Mein Kampf;* in Russians through an engrossing analysis of an early Russian film on Maxim Gorky's childhood. Placing these studies within a Freudian framework, he derives a persuasive theory of ego identity, integrity, and security." It impressed Hubbell that the book called for the "mutual regulation" of children and parents, and he called it "an exciting, humane, and authoritatively scientific study," as well as "a chastening lesson in how to write a book" for social scientists given to "polysyllabic jargonizing." A reviewer in the *American Sociological Review* thought that Erikson had failed to test his hypothesis "on an adequate sample of cultures," but praised his "intuitive genius, uncommon empathy with children, and artistic skill." The work has become one of the most widely used textbooks in its field, and is perhaps the most admired of all Erikson's books.

A non-Communist who objected on principle to the loyalty oath required of him at the University of California, Erik Erikson left there in June 1950 to join the senior staff of the Austin Riggs Center in Stockbridge, Massachusetts. To balance his work there with mentally disturbed adolescents from wealthy families, he commuted regularly to Pittsburgh to treat disturbed children from less affluent backgrounds at the University of Pittsburgh School of Medicine and at the Arsenal Health Center, where he worked with Dr. Benjamin Spock.

During the 1950s Erikson continued to study and reflect upon the subject of identity, by which he means, according to one interpreter, "a basic confidence in one's continuity in the midst of change." What Erikson called the "identity crisis" is that stage in human development when the sense of identity is more or less painfully emerging. Normally occurring in adolescence, the identity crisis is for some people—especially some creative people—a prolonged and agonizing process. Erikson was greatly interested in this phenomenon, particularly as it had affected men of exceptional talent, and in 1958 he published his first full-length "psycho-historical" work, *Young Man Luther: A Study in Psychoanalysis and History*. Focusing on Luther's famous seizure in the Erfurt Monastery choir, the book sought to show how childhood experiences, notably his father's strictness, had precipitated this crisis—and how in combating it, Luther freed himself and his followers from the rigidity of medieval Catholicism.

The book was discussed and admired by social scientists, historians, and theologians alike. There was some criticism—complaints about excessive wordiness, an insufficient consideration of economic and political factors during the Reformation, and a too personal interpretation of Luther's scatological language. But these seemed minor flaws compared with Erikson's unique combination of historical study and clinical analysis. "There is not one single 'wild interpretation' in it!" Y. A. Cohen exclaimed in *American Anthropology*. Clyde Kluckhown observed: "*Young Man Luther* has the sustained quality of genuineness; it is wholly the author's own rather than a contrived amalgam of the thought of others. Even those who, in company with the present reviewer, are not persuaded by every step in the argument cannot fail to have a rich experience with substance and in integrity." Reinhold Niebuhr called the work "a very profound study."

Retaining his consultantship at the Austin Riggs Center, Erik Erikson returned to Harvard as professor of human development and lecturer in psychiatry from 1960 until his retirement ten years later. His prolific writings in the 1960s included essays and lectures on the connections between psychic and social development and on such contemporary problems as youth dissidence, political protests, racism, and women's status in American society. A collection of these papers appeared in book form as *Insight and Responsibility: Lectures on the Ethical Implications of Psychoanalytic Insight* (1964). The critical response was generally positive, but Paul Pickrel thought these pieces "better in detail

than in general," and Lionel Abel found "not a unified position but something like a hodge-podge. In these lectures urging responsibility and insight, there is not one single insight I could responsibly call true or even useful." There was a mixed reception also for the papers reshaped as the chapters of *Identity: Youth and Crisis* (1968). While S. H. Miller wrote that the book "ministers to wisdom," Chandler Brossard thought that "what is more important than [Erikson's] bad logic and Olympian disengagement from human reality, is his apparent unawareness of the profound difference between, and mortal conflict of, Identity and Being. And this reveals the totality of what I feel is his conservatism."

Erikson's participation in a seminar on the human life cycle held in Ahmedabad, India, in 1962 inspired his much-honored psychohistorical biography, *Gandhi's Truth: On the Origins of Militant Nonviolence* (1969). Following the pattern established in *Young Man Luther*, the book discusses the Indian leader's development—in R.A. Gross's phrase—"as a man, a political strategist and thinker and a modern saint." It shows how Gandhi's life and India's social and political history merged during the 1918 textile workers' strike in Ahmedabad when Gandhi first used the tactic of fasting, thus inaugurating nonviolent civil disobedience against the British.

Irving Howe called *Gandhi's Truth* a combination of "psychoanalytic probings, historical narrative, the insights of a keen old bird, all entwined in an illusion of unity and decorated with a gorgeous dialectic." Joseph Featherstone found it "a difficult, brilliant, immensely rewarding book, written in passion and yet in fits and starts, full of second thoughts, asides, private meditations and doubts, and even an open letter to the Mahatma, attacking his narrow self-righteousness, especially in personal and family matters." Anthony Storr remarked that it fully justified "the still dubious activity of applying psychoanalysis to biography." The book received both the Pulitzer Prize and the National Book Award in the field of biography. Erikson, who had dedicated the work to Martin Luther King, gave the thousand-dollar NBA prize to "men and women who are working and suffering for causes that Gandhi would have considered his own."

Erikson's Jefferson Lectures, delivered in 1973 under the auspices of the National Endowment for the Humanities, were expanded and published as *Dimensions of a New Identity* (1974). George Stade referred to them as "his sane, humane and wry musings on the crooked byways of our national character," and thought it "good to be in his company," in spite of "the inconclusiveness of Erikson's meanders." *Life History and the Historical Moment* (1975) collects a number of previously published essays from the 1960s and early 1970s, on subjects ranging from abortion and birth control to Erikson's own identity crisis.

Toys and Reasons (1977), based on the 1972 Godkin Lectures at Harvard, is the most admired of Erikson's recent books. It explores "the life-and-death importance of human make-believe," and especially the instinctive human need to ritualize experience. Erikson pays close attention to the way in which children play, showing that this is "the infantile form of the human propensity to create model situations in which aspects of the past are re-lived, the present represented and renewed, and the future anticipated." Ritualization can also be harmful, however: we are all of us "familiarized by ritualization with a particular version of human existence"—that of our own culture; this fortifies our sense of identity, but leads us to regard the rest of mankind as alien and inferior. Erikson also examines what Rosemary Dinnage summarizes as "a new tendency to play strenuously at being playful, with the help of drugs or alcohol if necessary; but also, in the political field, an insidious spread of vicious game-playing in high places." On the other hand, he does not ignore the benign playfulness of artistic and scientific creativity. Anthony Storr wrote that "Erikson has never quite parted company with psychoanalysis . . . but his view of fantasy is much closer to Jung's than to Freud's, in that he emphasizes its value and is interested in its prospective implications. . . . Erikson's writing is highly compressed and rather turgid . . . But this is a rich and stimulating book."

The author was married in 1930 to Joan Mowat Serson, a teacher and writer with a master's degree in sociology. The Eriksons live in Tiburon, California, and have three grown children—Kai, a sociologist, Jon, a photographer, and Sue, a social anthropologist. Erikson is a member of the National Academy of Education, a fellow of the American Academy of Arts and Sciences, and a life member of the American Psychoanalytic Association. He has honorary degrees from Yale, Brown, Loyola, and other universities, but dislikes and generally declines such honors. He received the Milanese Foneme Prize in 1969, the Aldrich Award from the American Academy of Pediatrics in 1971, the Montessori Medal from the American Montessori Society in 1973, and the McAlpin Research Award from the National Association for Mental Health in 1974. A fellow of Stanford University's Center for Advanced Studies in the Behavioral Sciences in 1962 and 1965, he was the Davie Lecturer at Cape Town in 1968, and the Godlein Lecturer at Harvard in 1972. Since 1972 he has been senior consultant in psychiatry at Mount Zion Hospital in San Francisco.

Marshall Berman has given this summary of Erikson's achievement: "Erik Erikson is probably the closest thing to an intellectual hero in American culture today. He has added striking new phrases to our language—'life cycle,' 'identity crisis,' 'inner space,' 'psychohistory'—words that signify new ways to interpret and confront our lives. As a psychoanalyst he has played with children and unraveled marvelous hidden depths and resonances in their play. He has evoked the joy and dread of adolescence with a rare vividness and sympathy, and disclosed new dimensions of meaning in experiences we thought we knew all too well. In his many case histories he has shown us people in their full actuality. . . . He has used his splendid literary gifts to make the basic Freudian family drama more credible and compelling than ever, by showing how it works in a variety of radically different worlds. . . . His work on personal and familial 'identity crisis' in the fifties predicted and analyzed incisively the tragic social and political identity crisis that would overwhelm all America in the sixties; we can find here some of the most trenchant cultural criticism American culture has ever known. Finally, since the appearance of *Childhood and Society* in 1950, Erikson has given us glimpses and intimations of a vision, a beautiful myth of the organic unity and wholeness of life."

PRINCIPAL WORKS: Childhood and Society, 1950; Young Man Luther: A Study in Psychoanalysis and History, 1958; (as editor) Youth: Change and Challenge, 1963 (republished in 1965 as The Challenge of Youth); Insight and Responsibility: Lectures on the Ethical Implications of Psychoanalytic Insight, 1964; Identity: Youth and Crisis, 1968; Gandhi's Truth: On the Origins of Militant Nonviolence, 1969; In Search of Common Ground: Conversations with Erik H. Erikson and Huey P. Newton, 1973; Dimensions of a New Identity, 1974; Life History and the Historical Moment, 1975; Toys and Reasons: Stages in the Ritualization of Experience, 1977.

ABOUT: Alexander, F. and others (eds.) Psychoanalytic Pioneers, 1966; Auden, W.H. Forewords and Afterwords, 1973; Browning, D.S. Generative Man: Psychoanalytic Perspectives, 1973; Capps, D. and others (eds.) Encounter With Erikson, 1977; Coles, R. Erik H. Erikson: The Growth of His Work, 1970; Current Biography, 1971; Evans, R. Dialogue with Erik Erikson, 1967; Friedenberg E.Z. The Dignity of Youth and Other Atavisms, 1966; Johnson, R. A. Psychohistory and Religion, 1977; Lasch, C. The World of Nations: Reflections on American History, Politics, and Culture, 1973; Roazen, P. Erik H. Erikson: The Power and Limits of a Vision, 1976; Ruether, R.R. (ed.) Religion and Sexism: Images of Woman in the Jewish and Christian Traditions, 1974; Schultz, D. Theories of Personality, 1976; Who's Who in America, 1977-1978. *Periodicals*—American Anthropology June 1960; Book World July 27, 1969; Harper's August 1968, April 1970; Mental Hygiene July 1971; Nation December 7, 1964; September 22, 1969; New Republic October 3, 1964; October 18, 1969; June 8, 1974; June 14, 1975; Newsweek August 10, 1964; August 18, 1969; December 21, 1970; New Yorker November 7, 1970; November 14, 1970; New York Herald Tribune Book Review November 16, 1958; New York Review of Books November 20, 1969; October 16, 1975; New York Times Book Review March 31, 1968; September 14, 1969; November 22, 1970; May 19, 1974; March 30, 1975; May 4, 1975; April 10, 1977; New York Times Magazine April 5, 1970; Scientific American April 1970; Time November 30, 1970; March 17, 1975; Yale Review March 1959.

Peter Fisher

MARTIN ESSLIN

ESSLIN, MARTIN (JULIUS) (June 8, 1918–), British drama critic, radio writer, and translator, was born in Budapest, Hungary, the son of Paul Pereszlenyi and the former Charlotte Schiffer, just as the Austro-Hungarian Empire was collapsing at the end of World War I. He was educated at a *gymnasium* in Vienna and at Vienna University, where he graduated in English and philosophy, and studied theatrical direction at the Reinhardt Seminar of Dramatic Art. In 1938, just as he was about to begin his theatrical career, Hitler occupied Austria and Esslin as a Jew was forced to flee.

After a year in Brussels, Esslin settled in England, becoming a British citizen in 1947. He joined the British Broadcasting Corporation in 1940 and was employed by the Corporation for thirty-seven years. Beginning as a scriptwriter and producer in the BBC's European Services (1941-1955), he became in 1955 assistant head of the European Productions Department. In 1961 he switched to the radio drama department as assistant head, and from 1963 until his retirement in 1977 he was the BBC's head of radio drama. Over the years, he has translated many foreign plays for radio and adapted novels and other works for the medium, as well as writing radio features on political, social, and literary subjects. It is probably true to say, all the same, that Esslin is most widely known as a drama critic.

His first book was a study of Bertolt Brecht, a writer whom he was particularly well equipped to interpret to the English-speaking world because of his own experience of the rise of Hitler and his training in the German theatre. *Brecht: A Choice of Evils* (1959), which has also appeared as *Brecht: The Man and His Work,* was published only three years after Brecht's death, when it seemed to Esslin "quite clear that in the case of politically so controversial a figure as Brecht an antidote to the formation of legends, on the left as well as on the anti-Brechtian right, was urgently wanted."

The "choice of evils" that Brecht faced arose out of the fact that he was deeply involved in all the problems and issues of his age, and committed as much politically as artistically: "Brecht was a Communist, he was also a great poet. But while the West liked his poetry and distrusted his Communism, the Communists exploited his political convictions while they regarded his artistic aims and achievements with suspicion. ... Brecht's importance, moreover, transcends his significance as a dramatist, poet, or amusing personality. He is above all an epitome of his times: most of the cross-currents and contradictions, moral and political dilemmas, artistic and literary trends of our time are focused and exemplified in Brecht's life and its vicissitudes." The book was found ambitious, thoughtful, and authoritative, and Kenneth Tynan described it as "a brilliantly perceptive study of the most ambiguous and perpetually fascinating figure of the twentieth century European theatre." Professor Idris Parry called it "an outstanding work of criticism. It is hard to imagine that a better psychological study of Brecht will ever be possible."

Although Brecht was at this time known outside Germany almost solely as a dramatist and theatrical reformer, Esslin's study also dealt with his work as a lyric poet and a prose writer. And in *Bertolt Brecht* (1969), one of the Columbia Essays on Modern Writers, Esslin notes how Brecht's image in the English-speaking world has been distorted by the translation of so few of his poems, essays, and stories in comparison with his plays: "It may sound heretical today, but may well be true nevertheless, that posterity might attribute greater importance to Brecht's poems and some of his short stories than to his work as a dramatist." This essay also discusses Brecht's dread of being condemned to "classic" status—his desire that his work should be an active agent for genuine social and cultural progress. And Esslin ends by asking whether the efforts of writers like Brecht *can* change social conditions, concluding that they can do so "only indirectly: by changing man's sensibility, the atmosphere, the moral climate that surrounds him."

Martin Esslin's best-known book is *The Theatre of the Absurd* (1961), whose title became such a catch-phrase that the author subsequently complained about the thoughtless use of a term that, "coined to describe certain features of certain plays in order to bring out underlying similarities, has been treated as though it corresponded to an organized movement." Esslin himself applied the term to the work of Beckett, Adamov, Ionesco, Genet, and their followers, whose plays are "not intended to tell a story but to communicate a pattern of poetic images." Such writers create myths whose apparently surrealistic logic reflects the existential predicament of the individual in a universe without God or any sort of ordering principle. All the same, "concerned as it is with the ultimate realities of the human condition, the relatively few fundamental problems of life and death, isolation and communication, the Theatre of the Absurd," Esslin wrote, "however grotesque, frivolous, and irreverent it may appear, represents a return to the original, religious function of the theatre."

Seeking to evoke the absurdity of the human condition and the limitations of the rational approach, these dramatists begin by rejecting traditional concepts of character and plot. It was the eschewal of these familiar conventions that so confused the critics and sophisticated audiences who first saw such plays—an effect which Esslin contrasts with the deep and immediate impact made by a performance of Beckett's *Waiting for Godot* on the inmates of San Quentin Penitentiary, who had fewer preconceptions about what a play should be. Revised editions of *The Theatre of the Absurd* appeared in 1968 and 1974, and in his 1968 preface Esslin comments on the speed with which Beckett's best-known play had achieved the status of an "all too easily understood modern classic." In these later editions Esslin extended his discussion to include a number of younger Absurdist dramatists, and also the barbed, vigorous, but surreal political plays of Slawomir Mrozek, Vaclav Havel, and other Polish and Czech writers. It seemed to Esslin (but not to all of his readers) that these Eastern European plays reflected the influence not only of Ionesco and Beckett, but also of Brecht, whose epic political theatre had seemed the very antithesis of the Theatre of the Absurd. Reviewers of the first edition of Esslin's book welcomed it as "an extremely valuable and well-shaped guide," though A. Alvarez praised it more faintly as "a useful but lumbering trudge" and "a good, if somewhat nagging guide"; it remains the standard work on its subject.

Some of Esslin's articles, interviews, and prefaces were collected in *Reflections: Essays on Modern Theatre* (1969), an enlarged edition of which appeared in Britain in 1970 as *Brief Chronicles: Essays on Modern Theatre*. Here Esslin continues his discussion of the Theatre of the Absurd, of Brecht, and of the new East European dramatists. He also ranges back to figures like Ibsen and Pirandello who are among the founders of the contemporary theatre, as well as considering some more recent playwrights not discussed in his earlier books. In a final section on "the future of the theatre" he looks at such general trends as violence, nudity, and improvisational theatre, and also considers contemporary English drama in relation to the mass media, in which Esslin has of course been heavily involved for most of his working life: "That the development of the electronic mass media has already produced a fundamental revolution in man's modes of perception, his sense of time and space, his manner of communication and perception of ideas is, for me at least, beyond a doubt. And that such a change will, of necessity, have far-reaching consequences for literature and drama also strikes me as self-evident." *Brief Chronicles* was praised by O. M. Sorensen as an important and purposeful collection, but seemed to Victor Burg marred by haste and a weakness for overgeneralization.

The Peopled Wound: The Work of Harold Pinter (1970), is a study produced with some assistance from Pinter himself, who checked the factual material and allowed Esslin to read his unpublished work, including his early novel, *The Dwarfs*, and a complete but discarded play, *The Hothouse*. Esslin was thus able to offer an analysis not merely of Pinter's established dramatic oeuvre but of all his work, including his early poetry and his film scripts. The criticism most often made by those who disagree with Esslin is that he is too prone to psychological and philosophical interpretations, and his conclusion that Pinter's plays are fundamentally about "alienation" and "non-communication" was opposed by Richard Gilman: "Judgements of this kind which rise from theories of literature instead of full encounter with it, are never able to account for the fact that, as in Pinter's case, the works themselves are not alienated, succeed in establishing certain kinds of identity and are capable—which is precisely the miracle—of communication." But most critics accepted Esslin's basic premise that Pinter's work is essentially lyric and poetic and hence psychologically internal. T. E. Luddy wrote: "This exhaustive and challenging analysis is thoroughly convincing. . . . One of Esslin's strongest assets has always been his sensitivity to language, and his analysis of 'Pinterese' as a poetic and dramatic medium in the tradition of Chekhov is superb." The playwright John Mortimer wrote that "his is not only by far the best critical appraisal of Harold Pinter plays, it contains many pages I read with real excitement for their discoveries about modern dramatic writing. When Mr. Esslin makes a generalization it is new and stimulating."

An Anatomy of Drama (1976) is a collection of eleven radio talks written for Britain's Open University, intended as a general introduction to dramatic theory. It asks: "What is it that drama can express better than any other medium of human communication?" In answer, Esslin defines drama as a collective ritual producing a powerful and direct crowd reaction, as distinct from the private experience of reading. The theatre is thus "the place where the nation thinks in public in front of itself." The same year, Esslin published a monograph in the Modern Masters series on Antonin Artaud, the tormented prophet of "total theatre." The book provides a careful account of Artaud's life, maintaining that despite his record of almost continual failure and aberration, he nevertheless remains a vitally important figure as the theoretician of a liberalizing theatrical revolt which demonstrated the limitations of language and of rationality, paving the way for such developments as the Theatre of the Absurd.

Martin Esslin was married in 1947 to Renate Gerstenberg, and has a daughter. He was awarded the title of professor by the Austrian President in 1967, and received an O.B.E. in 1972. Esslin was visiting professor of theatre at Florida State University from 1969 to 1976, and since 1977 has served (for two quarters each year) as professor of drama at Stanford University in California. He is a member of the British Arts Council, and has served as chairman of the Arts Council Drama Panel, as well as advisory dramaturge to the Royal Shakespeare Company. Esslin lists his recreations as reading and book collecting.

PRINCIPAL WORKS: Brecht: A Choice of Evils, 1959 (also published as Brecht: The Man and His Work); The Theatre of the Absurd, 1961; Reflections: Essays on Modern Theatre, 1969 (in England, Brief Chronicles: Essays on Modern Theatre); Bertolt Brecht (Columbia Essays on Modern Writers), 1969; The Peopled Wound: The Plays of Harold Pinter, 1970 (revised as Pinter: A Study of His Plays, 1973); An Anatomy of Drama, 1976; Artaud, 1976. *As Editor*—Samuel Beckett: A Collection of Critical Essays, 1965; Absurd Drama, 1965; The Genius of the German Theatre, 1968; Three Eastern European Plays, 1970. *As Translator*—(with Renate Esslin) All Change and Other Plays, by Wolfgang Bauer, 1973.

ABOUT: Who's Who, 1978. *Periodicals*—Chicago Sunday Tribune April 3, 1960; Christian Century July 13, 1960; December 8, 1965; Christian Science Monitor September 30, 1969; Choice March 1966; Commonweal June 10, 1960; Nation September 1, 1960; New Statesman November 28, 1959; November 27, 1970; New York Review of Books December 17, 1970; New York Times Book Review March 20, 1960; January 23, 1966; September 13, 1970; Theatre Arts June 1960; Times Literary Supplement November 6, 1959; July 23, 1970; July 6, 1973; December 17, 1976; Yale Review June 1960.

FARB, (STAN) PETER(S) (July 25, 1929–), American writer on natural history and anthropology, journalist, and novelist, was born in New York City, the son of Solomon and Cecelia (Peters) Farb. He received his B.A. *magna cum laude* at Vanderbilt University, Nashville, Tennessee, in 1950, and then joined the staff of *Argosy* magazine as feature editor (1950-1952). In 1953 he left *Argosy* to become a freelance writer and researcher in the natural history of North America and related fields, publishing his articles in *Reader's Digest* and many other magazines.

His first book, *The Living Earth,* appeared in 1959. It is, as the title suggests, a nontechnical study for the layman of the soil and of the small lives inhabiting it, their relationships and strange adaptations. Based on wide reading and on interviews with many scientists pursuing research in various aspects of soil biology, it had a mixed but generally favorable reception. A reviewer in the *Christian Science Monitor* wrote that Farb had employed no tricks of rhetoric, but had let "his own honest excitement about the secrets of the soil and the life it nurtures communicate itself through clear, precise prose which at times reads like poetry. . . . Rarely has one small book shed so much light on the natural wonders all around us." Other readers had reservations, however; one thought that the book covered too much ground with insufficient care and thoroughness, and another that Farb at times "plunges fearlessly into subjects beyond his depth."

A half-dozen books appeared between 1959 and 1963, some of them for children, on such varied subjects as insects, hydrology, and forests. During the same period Farb was a regular columnist for *Better Homes and Gardens.* In

Nancy Crampton

PETER FARB

1960-1961 he served as editor-in-chief of Panorama, a Columbia Broadcasting System publishing project, and in 1964 he went to New York City's Riverside Museum (now closed) as curator of American Indian cultures, remaining there until 1971. In 1966-1971 he acted also as a consultant to the Smithsonian Institution in Washington.

Meanwhile, in 1963, Farb had his first major success as a writer with *Face of North America: The Natural History of a Continent,* a historical account of the factors that went to produce the varied and spectacular scenery of America. Helen Henley found it a useful reference book and a great deal more besides: "With its relaxed, essay-like style, it can be read right through with considerable pleasure, leading the reader on by a thread of underlying excitement about what is going on all around him, too often unnoticed. It has also some of the suspense of a well-built narrative." Harold Borland called it "one of the best books about outdoor America ever written." *Face of North America,* a best seller, was a selection of the Book-of-the-Month Club and of the Outdoor Life Book Club, and was presented by President Kennedy to the heads of a hundred foreign governments. A condensed and simplified edition for young readers appeared in 1964.

Ecology, an excellent introduction to the interrelationship between living organisms and their physical environment, with a strong conservationist bias, was followed by *The Land and Wildlife of North America,* and then by *The Land, Wildlife, and Peoples of the Bible,* in which, using the Bible as his chief source, Farb interprets ancient events and observations in

the light of what is now known about the Holy Land's anthropology, botany, geology, climatology, and zoology.

Farb's work at the Riverside Museum led in 1968 to another major book, with a suitably impressive title, *Man's Rise to Civilization as Shown by the Indians of North America From Primeval Times to the Coming of the Industrial State.* It describes ten American Indian societies, beginning with the Shoshonean hunters of the Great Basin, and proceeding through increasingly complex societies to the highly evolved Aztec state. It goes on to discuss what is known about the histories of these societies, and ends with a painful account of the subjugation of the Indians by European settlers. *Man's Rise to Civilization* was selected by no less than four book clubs, and it seemed to R.F. Murphy quite natural that it should have had this kind of success. He thought that the book would nevertheless annoy serious students of the subject because Farb's "asides on theoretical questions . . . show a gift for providing simple and unitary answers where none are possible. . . . This should not, however, deter the reader who wants to learn something about the American Indian and anthropology, for the ethnography is accurate and interestingly presented."

Farb's interest in linguistics is evident in *Man's Rise to Civilization,* and in *Word Play* he provides an illuminating and entertaining popular account of current linguistic theories, including structural linguistics and "body language." Some of the games that people play with language are exemplified in Farb's novel *Yankee Doodle,* in which Benjamin Pennyman, last of an illustrious family, reflects upon the social, political, and individual ills of the country his ancestors helped to create. This stream-of-consciousness novel, strongly influenced by James Joyce, is full of puns, parodies, dialect, and satire. It greatly amused some readers but Paul Theroux considered that in his first novel, like Henry James in some of his last fictions, Farb "chews more than he bites off."

In 1971, when he left the Riverside Museum, Farb went to Yale as a visiting lecturer. In the same year he served as a judge on the National Book Awards committee, and became a fellow of Calhoun College (1971-1975). The extraordinary breadth of his interests is shown by the wide range of societies to which he belongs. He is a fellow of the American Association for the Advancement of Science and of the Society of American Historians, a former secretary of the New York Entomological Society, and a former board member of the Allergy and Asthma Foundation of America. He is also a member of the

American Anthropological Association, the Ecological Society of America, the Society for American Archaeology, the Society of Magazine Writers, Phi Beta Kappa, and the P.E.N. Club. He has edited Harper's North American Nature series since 1964, in which year Secretary of the Interior Stewart Udall described him as "one of the finest conservation spokesmen of our period." His books on natural history have set something of a sales record for works in this field. Farb was married in 1953 to Oriole Horch, a museum director, and has two sons.

PRINCIPAL WORKS: Living Earth, 1959; The Story of Butterflies and Other Insects, 1959; The Story of Dams: An Introduction to Hydrology, 1961; The Forest, 1961; The Insects, 1962; The Story of Life: Plants and Animals Through the Ages, 1962; Face of North America: The Natural History of a Continent, 1963; Ecology, 1964; The Land and Wildlife of North America, 1964; (with John Hay) The Atlantic Shore, 1966; The Land, Wildlife, and Peoples of the Bible, 1967; Man's Rise to Civilization as Shown by the Indians of North America, 1968; Yankee Doodle (novel), 1970; Word Play: What Happens When People Talk, 1973; Humankind: A Status Report on Our Species, 1978.

ABOUT: Contemporary Authors 13-16 1st revision, 1975; Who's Who in America, 1976-1977. Periodicals—Book World November 24, 1968; October 25, 1970; Canadian Forum March 1969; Christian Science Monitor February 28, 1963; Natural History May 1974; New York Times Book Review November 17, 1968; Saturday Review October 19, 1968; Time December 13, 1968; February 18, 1974.

FARMER, PHILIP JOSÉ (January 26, 1918–), American novelist, science fiction writer, and biographer, writes: "I was born in North Terre Haute, Indiana, next door to the birthplace of Theodore Dreiser and Eugene V. Debs. As far as I know, Terre Haute has erected no statues to any of us. I was the oldest of five children and descended on my father's side from pioneer stock of English, Irish, Scotch, and Dutch descent. They were doctors, engineers, mechanics, and farmers, and many were Christian Scientists. This may explain my attraction to, and repulsion from, mysticism. My great-grandfather Dooley was a Civil War veteran. He once told me that he had known a Revolutionary War veteran who had in turn known Voltaire. This has always given me a sense of the continuity of life; I felt as if Voltaire had said 'Hello' to me across the centuries. My mother was descended from a Kansan of English and Cherokee ancestry and a native of Thuringia, Germany, who fled religious persecution.

"Moved to Peoria, Illinois in 1922 and have spent most of my life in a city whose name is synonymous with rusticism. This is only appropriate for a Farmer. Married Bette Virginia Andre in 1941 and have a son and daughter and four grandchildren.

PHILIP JOSÉ FARMER

Don Fanzo, courtesy Chilton Book Co.

"In junior high school, while taking Spanish, I added the accent mark to Jose (my grandmother's name bestowed upon me at birth) and so hispanicized and masculinized it. The change is legitimate, and it does add a certain note of distinction to an otherwise drab name.

"Like most writers, I've held a variety of jobs, ranging from water-boy for a streetcar repair crew to electromechanical technical writer for the space-defense industry. I've never played a piano in a whorehouse, much to my regret.

"If we are what we eat, we are also what we read. As a very young boy, I read the Oz books, Grimm and Andersen, Gulliver's Travels, Mark Twain, Homer's Odyssey, The Three Musketeers, Edgar Rice Burroughs, A. Conan Doyle, H. G. Wells, The Prisoner of Zenda, Jack London's Klondike and South Seas tales, the Bible, and the Book of Mormon. I still read these, but later strong influences were Joyce, Dostoievsky, and Henry Miller. And of course I was steeped in childhood and adolescence in the pulps, the Shadow, Doc Savage, Argosy and Blue Book magazines, and all the science fiction publications. My childhood was, in the main, a happy one, busy, reading, playing, hiking into the nearby rural areas.

"I entered the University of Missouri in 1936, but the Depression, war, and marriage strung out my attendance of college. Not until 1950 did I graduate (B.A. in English literature at Bradley University). In the meantime, I had sold my first story to Adventure magazine. This was in 1945. The Saturday Evening Post would have taken it if I would have cut out a drunk scene; I refused. I did not write much between 1945 and 1950, but in 1952 I sold a short novel, The Lovers, to

Startling Stories magazine. This is now reckoned in science fiction history as a tabu-breaker. It broke the barriers of the mature use of sex in pulp-magazine science fiction. The editors of the two top magazines in the field had previously rejected it on the grounds that it sickened them and would be sure to offend their readers. Three succeeding stories of mine were rejected by these two for the same reasons. Today, the stories would offend scarcely anyone, but at that time they were considered outrageous and daring. However, they still read well and are considered classics in their genre.

"From 1956 to 1969 I wrote manuals, brochures, and advertising for the space-defense industry. After being laid off a month before the first moon landing, I became a full-time fiction writer. I left Los Angeles for my hometown because the *I Ching,* three times running, advised me to stay in the city and be a hero or retire to the country and be a sage. I chose the latter, and sager, course.

"After forty-one books and sixty-three short stories, most of them science fiction, I plan to finish up in this field in the next three years. Then, on to mystery and mainstream. I want to write a long serious novel on the science fiction world and a comic novel based on my experiences in the space industry. Of recent years my writings have been guided by precepts from Heraclitus, Virgil, and the Preacher: you can't step into the same river twice; character determines destiny; easy is the descent into hell; consider thy latter end, my son, and be wise."

The author is the son of George Farmer, an electrical power engineer, and the former Lucile Jackson. Although his childhood was a happy one, and he was a notable school athlete, Farmer was troubled by an acute sense of inferiority, and sought relief from it in the fantasies and adventure stories he lists above. The first issue of *Science Wonder Stories,* published in June 1929, converted him instantly to the science fiction pulp magazines, and at about the same time he began to write as avidly and rapidly as he read, churning out epic fantasies about Roman soldiers and Viking heroes. A long time was to pass before any of his stories was published.

Farmer entered the University of Missouri in 1936, as he says, leaving the following year without a degree. Thereafter for twenty years he earned his living in a variety of non-literary jobs, including a spell in the United States Army Air Force as an aviation cadet (1942-1943), and eleven years working in various capacities for a steel company in Bartonville, Illinois. He was a technical writer for General Electric from 1956

to 1958 and for Motorola from 1959 to 1969, since when he has been a full-time writer. Despite this experience, Farmer's fiction has always depended less upon technological speculation than upon human problems: "I'd like to see us explore space," he has said, "but I don't think we have to. People are more important than rockets."

"O'Brien and Obrenov," the first of his stories to be published, appeared in *Adventure* magazine in 1946, but was followed by a long hiatus when he wrote little and sold nothing. In 1951, after reading an account of ant parasites, Farmer wrote *The Lovers.* It is set on a planet inhabited by insects that have taken on the appearance of women, and breed by mating with human males. They die in pregnancy, thus conveniently providing a corpse on which the larvae can feed. This notion is used as the background to the tragic love story which one famous editor rejected as "nauseating." *The Lovers* appeared in the April 1952 issue of *Startling Stories* and, according to Sam Moskowitz, "fathered a brief but traumatic revolution" in science fiction. The revolution was the introduction of sex into a field traditionally "surpassed in prudery only by the Frank Merriwell stories."

For a few years after *The Lovers* appeared, the science fiction pulps featured a spate of stories on sexual themes. This soon ended, but the genre has never fully recovered its primal innocence. Farmer's own contributions to the trend have included "Mother" (1953), a literal working-out of Freudian ideas centering on cave-like organisms which are in fact gigantic carnivorous wombs; "Moth and Rust" (1953), revised and published in book form as *A Woman a Day* (1960); and "Strange Compulsion" (1953). In 1953 Farmer received the first of the awards later known as "Hugos" (and accepted it with a lecture on "Science Fiction and the Kinsey Report"); he has received that honor twice more since then.

As many of Farmer's stories deal with religion and mysticism as with sex, and there is a series of them about the space priest Father John Carmody. The comic novel *Flesh* mixed the two modes in a story about a religious cult, on a pastoral and matriarchal Earth of the future, which elects as its messiah (and ritual sacrifice) a man of prodigious sexual prowess. Even more central to Farmer's reputation are the moving stories of *Strange Relations* (1960), in which the longings of alien beings are presented in human and humane fashion.

Another part of Farmer's output borrows characters from the imaginative literature in which he immersed himself as a boy. He has published series of stories and heavily researched "biographies" of Tarzan and of Lester Dent's Doc Savage, and in *A Feast Unknown* matches these two heroes in an extraordinary battle of lust and violence which some reviewers found both terrifying and morbid. The three "Riverworld" books have as major characters Lewis Carroll's Alice, Sir Richard Burton, Hermann Goering, and Mark Twain, and *The Wind Whales of Ishmael* carries the Pequod into an alternative universe after the shipwreck at the end of *Moby Dick.* When Kurt Vonnegut invented a character named Kilgore Trout, a science fiction writer and author of *Venus on the Half-Shell,* Farmer caused considerable confusion by publishing under that pseudonym a novel of that title.

The most admired of Farmer's books have been those in the "Riverworld" series. In the first of these, *To Your Scattered Bodies Go,* all the human beings who have ever lived are resurrected along the banks of a great river upon an artificially created world. The makers of this universe of apparently random yet numerically symmetrical riverside states are the "Ethicals," physically like men but technologically far more advanced. Their motives are uncertain, but there is speculation both in this book and in its sequels, *The Fabulous Riverboat* and *The Dark Design,* that the Riverworld is a scientific experiment with humanity, for the purpose of which man's past, present, and future have been mixed. In positing an alternative world, Farmer invites speculation about our own.

Some reviewers have criticized Farmer's interest in sexuality and abnormal psychology as "pornographic," but Sam Moskowitz has defended him against such charges, calling him "one of the prime movers of modern science fiction"—a writer whose stories are "scientifically based on biology which happened to involve sex." Admitting that Farmer's work is uneven, and can be undisciplined, wordy, and in poor taste, Moskowitz concludes that "at his best, he ranks at the very top of the writers to emerge in science fiction during the decade of the fifties. No single new author of that era even approaches him in strength, originality, and fecundity of ideas."

Farmer is said to be a gregarious, soft-spoken, kindly man, "a walker of streets, a drinker of coffee, a smoker of cigarettes, a lover of grandchildren." He has listed among his interests linguistics (which he studied for a postgraduate year at Arizona State University in 1961-1962), the works of Sir Richard Burton, Homer, the Mycenean age, and the creation of coats of arms for fictional characters.

PRINCIPAL WORKS: The Green Odyssey, 1957; Flesh, 1960; Strange Relations (short stories), 1960; A Woman a Day, 1960 (republished as The Day of Timestop, 1968); The Lovers, 1961; The Celestial Blueprint (short stories), 1962; The Alley God (short stories), 1962; Fire and the Night, 1962; Cache From Outer Space, 1962; Tongues of the Moon, 1964; Inside Outside, 1964; Dare, 1965; The Maker of Universes, 1965; Night of Light, 1966; The Gates of Creation, 1966; The Gate of Time, 1966; Riders of the Purple Wage, 1967; A Private Cosmos, 1968; The Image of the Beast, 1968; A Feast Unknown, 1969; The Stone That Awakens, 1970; Cosmos, 1970; Love Song, 1970; Lord Tyger, 1970; Down in the Black Gang (short stories), 1971; To Your Scattered Bodies Go, 1971; The Fabulous Riverboat, 1971; Time's Last Gift, 1972; Tarzan Alive, 1972; Doc Savage, His Apocalyptic Life, 1973; The Book of Philip José Farmer (short stories), 1973; The Other Log of Phileas Fogg, 1973; Timestop!, 1973; The Wind Whales of Ishmael, 1973; Hadon of Ancient Opar, 1974; (as editor) Mother Was a Lovely Beast: Fiction and Fact About Humans Raised as Animals, 1974; (as "John H. Watson") The Adventure of the Peerless Peer, 1974; (as "Kilgore Trout") Venus on the Half-Shell, 1975; Behind the Walls of Terra, 1975; Flight to Opar, 1976; The Dark Design, 1977; The Lavalite World, 1977.

ABOUT: Contemporary Authors 1-4 1st revision, 1967; Ellison, H. (ed.) Dangerous Visions, 1967; Fiedler, L. in The Book of Philip José Farmer, 1973; Lundwall, S. J. Science Fiction, 1972; Moskowitz, S. Seekers of Tomorrow, 1966; Sadoul, J. Histoire de la Science Fiction Moderne, 1973; Tuck, D. H. (ed.) The Encyclopedia of S.F. and Fantasy, 1973; Versins, P. Encyclopédie de l'Utopia, 1973; Wollheim, D. The Universe Makers, 1971. Periodicals—Science Fiction Review 14, 15 1975.

*FEIFFER, JULES (January 26, 1929–), American cartoonist, dramatist, and novelist, was born in the Bronx, New York City. He is the son of David Feiffer, who worked as a salesman, as a dental technician, and in various other jobs, and the former Rhoda Davis, a fashion designer. Feiffer made an early start on his career as a cartoonist. At the age of five he won a gold medal in a contest sponsored by Wanamaker's department store in New York with a drawing of Tom Mix in action, and by the time he was six he had no doubt that he was the best cartoonist in the business. Among his competitors, he most admired Will Eisner, creator of *The Spirit,* and Milton Caniff *(Terry and the Pirates),* who did their own writing and "fashioned quite a believable world on the comic page." Feiffer told Robin Brantley that "what was important to me from the beginning was telling a story and creating characters."

Feiffer attended grade school in the Bronx and then passed "a miserable four years" at the James Monroe High School in the same borough, enjoying art classes but nothing else. Nothing about the Bronx appealed very much to Feiffer: "I always thought it was some dreadful mistake that I was living there," he told Brant-

*fī′ fer

John Olson

JULES FEIFFER

ley. "I should have been living in the Manhattan of the movies I saw as a kid." He was not a rebellious child, however: "I assumed I was outnumbered from the start, so I went underground for the first twenty years of my life. I observed, registered things, but commented as little as possible."

Graduating from high school, Feiffer applied to New York University but found he was half a credit short. He had already begun classes at the Art Students League in New York (1946), and he continued his studies in drawing at Pratt Institute (1947–1948 and 1949–1951), at the same time picking up any work he could with comic strip artists. Will Eisner employed him on and off between 1946 and 1951, at first paying him ten dollars a week to erase pencil marks and ink in cartoons. "Eisner didn't trust me with drawings," Feiffer says. "I was clumsy. I got it by hacking away at it. There are still those who think my style is lousy." In fact, he "got it" well enough by 1949 to ghostscript some episodes of *The Spirit* and to create his own cartoon strip, *Clifford,* which ran in six Sunday newspapers until 1951, when Feiffer was drafted.

In the army, "treated with open contempt by one form of authority or the other," he for the first time in his life felt "free to hate . . . back." Serving in New Jersey with a Signal Corps cartoon animation unit, Feiffer began to express his feelings in cartoons of his own. It was in this way that he came up with the character of Munro, a four-year-old boy who, thanks to a bureaucratic foul-up, is drafted into the army. Munro made his mark later, but in 1953, when his creator returned to civilian life, no one was interested. Feiffer went from job to job or lived on unem-

ployment insurance while undergoing psychoanalysis, drawing, and trying "to write great things." He worked for a comic book publisher, made slide films, and designed booklets for a commercial art firm. In 1956 he took some of his cartoons to a struggling weekly newspaper in Greenwich Village. The people there actually liked his work, and Feiffer became a regular contributor—unpaid—to the *Village Voice.*

Feiffer probably contributed as much to the success of the *Voice* as that newspaper did to his own. *Sick, Sick, Sick,* his first volume of *Voice* cartoons, was published in April 1958. It caught on at once, selling one hundred and fifty thousand copies in the first three years. It was in 1958 also that the London Sunday *Observer* began to publish Feiffer's *Village Voice* strip, and soon it was syndicated. A second volume of the cartoons, *Passionella,* appeared in 1959 and followed the example of its predecessor by becoming a best-seller. *Passionella* introduced the infant soldier Munro, who went on to glory as the subject of a Rembrandt Films animated cartoon, winner of a 1961 Oscar as the best short-subject cartoon of the year. It was in the midst of all this excitement, in 1961, that Feiffer was married to Judith Scheftel, a Warner Brothers production executive. They have one daughter, Kate.

The unique character of Feiffer's work was recognized in 1962 when he received a Special George Polk Memorial Award. There is little action in a Feiffer cartoon, and there are no gags. His situations are taken from life as it is anxiously lived by the college-educated urban middle-class in America today. His characters are Greenwich Village intellectuals and artists, admen and television executives and businessmen, politicians and political activists, lovelorn students and army generals, whites and blacks, men and women—all of us, in fact, emotionally famished, egocentric, guilt-ridden, and woebegone as we are, struggling and failing to get ourselves loved, or admired, or understood by everyone or someone, if it is only ourselves. The perceptions are generally those of psychoanalysis, and the technique most often is to let the character exhibit his bland or formidable public mask, and then to strip it away to reveal the cringing morsel it is meant to hide.

Gilbert Millstein sees Feiffer "alone and unafraid in a world made of . . . just about all of the intellectual shams and shibboleths to which our culture subscribes"—a world in which he "moves lightly, pinking, piercing, bludgeoning, sneering when the occasion demands, pitying when he must pity." Kenneth Tynan once categorized him as "the best writer now cartooning," and called his characters "the explainers." This last phrase evidently pleased Feiffer, for it turned up as the title of his third collection of cartoons in 1960, and a year later as the name of a wry satirical revue, Feiffer's first work for the stage, which opened in Chicago at the Second City in May 1961. A one-act play followed a month later at the Festival of Two Worlds in Spoleto, Italy. This was *Creeping Arnold,* about a man in his thirties who reverts to crawling when his septuagenarian parents have another child. It is a situation that would look perfectly at home in a Feiffer cartoon, and whether or not his literary works are in fact only extended cartoons has been much debated, not least by Feiffer himself.

At any rate, finding that his weekly cartoon strip kept him busy for only four or five hours a week and did not allow him to investigate the themes that interested him in any depth, Feiffer tried his hand at several literary forms in the early 1960s. His first novel, *Harry, the Rat With Women,* was published in 1963. Harry is extremely beautiful, and passes his days celebrating this fact and basking in the love of others until, in a moment of aberration, he gives some flowers to his wife. A pimple appears on his perfect nose, but Harry does not heed this warning. He becomes more and more generous, more and more concerned for others, less and less beautiful. In the end he is a very ugly paragon of goodness and compassion, and dies. "The fable darkens toward the end, as the author tries to extract meanings of a somber kind," wrote Saul Maloff. "Though funny passages abound and brilliant vignettes spill over one another, he has by this time laughed himself out of the possibility of implication: the tone has been fatally set. What we are left with, for all the wit and adroitness of comment, is fable untransformed —vintage Feiffer cartoons, unillustrated."

For Feiffer, as for so many others, the 1960s were a time of political awakening. He attacked the Vietnam War in his cartoon strip in 1963 (and believes that he was the first cartoonist to do so). And, though he is "not a group man" and always felt "terribly shy politically" he spoke at peace demonstrations in Washington and participated in Vietnam read-ins. He also testified on behalf of Lenny Bruce at the latter's obscenity trial in 1964. By the mid-1960s, Feiffer "was in a mood of black despair about the country and where it was going. . . . I felt terribly old and very bitter about the future of this country and my future in it." It was in this mood that he wrote his first full-length play, *Little Murders,* a black comedy about urban violence. The Newquists live barricaded in their apartment, so inured to the mayhem in the streets that they hardly bother to glance outside when the shooting begins. In the end, the daughter is killed by a shot through the window and the family, led by the daughter's photographer boyfriend, begin to gun down passing pedestrians at random. Along the way, the play takes pot-shots at American conformity, sexual hangups, religious fanaticism, and other Feiffer targets.

Little Murders opened on Broadway in 1967 and closed a week later, though it brought Feiffer recognition from the New York drama critics as the most promising playwright of the season. Produced in London the same year by the Royal Shakespeare Company, it was rapturously received and voted the best foreign play of the year. A critic in the *Times Literary Supplement* wrote that "the mean, bullying, conforming father, the cheerful, stupid, hysterical mother, and the jokey, epicene son are extremely funny and diabolically accurate; but most brilliant of all is the relationship between the all-American daughter, overgrown, over-masculine, overconfident of winning every fight, and the laconic, ingrown photographer, who won't fight at all until she is murdered." It seemed to this critic that *Little Murders* was more than a long Feiffer cartoon: "There are sequences of dialogue where the protagonists do leap self-defeatingly from one untenable extreme to another, very much like people in a Feiffer strip, but he has also succeeded in writing in fully theatrical terms. . . . Every scene is realized three-dimensionally." The play was revived in New York in 1969 and under the direction of Alan Arkin was this time successful, winning both the Obie Award and the Outer Critics' Circle Award. It was later filmed.

The Unexpurgated Memoirs of Bernard Mergendeiler (1967) is a one-act dialogue between a newly acquainted man and woman, in bed together, who are hopelessly inhibited until they find that they both consider sex dirty. The play is based on cartoon characters, as is *Feiffer's People,* produced in Edinburgh and London in 1968 and in Los Angeles in 1971. At this point in his career as a dramatist, Feiffer seemed to have acquired a more devoted following in Britain than in the United States. *God Bless* (1968) is a savage satirical attack on the accommodation of American liberals to the status quo, a statement of Feiffer's absolute political disillusionment, in which we are told that betrayal has always been "the radical's only way to be taken seriously." It seemed to American critics a rather boring political tract, failed in New Haven, and never reached New York. On the other hand Ronald Bryden, reviewing the London production the same year, wrote: "There's practically no action, only talk, but what talk it is. . . . The distinction and delight of the play is the way it nets all the fluttering ideas of the moment, pins them down and scrutinises them, with the cool, critical intelligence of a historian writing a decade from now. . . . Yet few contemporary plays give so passionate a sense of commitment. Every line breathes appalled love for the anguished nation it scarifies." It seemed to Bryden "marvellous: as dazzling an extravaganza of pure ideas as any since Shaw's *On the Rocks,* which I take to be its model, and easily the funniest, most literate and farsighted new play to reach London this year." Kenneth Tynan disagreed with its premises, but concluded that "nothing in London is better worth disagreeing with."

Another despairing satire followed in 1970, *The White House Murder Case,* which has the United States fighting a war in Brazil and using nerve gas, while back at the White House a cover-up plan is mounted and the President's lady is murdered. Some found it an uneasy mixture of drama and politics, but it was generally well reviewed and received an Outer Critics' Circle Award. The movie *Carnal Knowledge* appeared in 1971, directed by Mike Nichols from Feiffer's scenario. It follows the sexual adventures and disasters of two men, from college to middle age, and was a financial and critical success, though some reviewers were disturbed by its heroes' evident hatred of the women in their lives.

It was in 1971 also that Feiffer began work on his play *Knock, Knock.* He finished it the following year, but for various reasons it was not until 1976 that it opened off-off-Broadway at the Circle Repertory Company theatre. It was an immediate success, the best received of all Feiffer's plays, and soon moved uptown to the Biltmore Theatre. His earlier stage works, he says, had been thesis plays: "I had in mind what I wanted to say, then created the characters and the situation to say it." By 1971, he "simply wanted to have a good time. I was worn out by evangelizing. . . . everybody knew everything already, everybody knew how bad it was, you couldn't disturb or shock or create new discontent. . . . The point now is to start working out ways of living a life within all this. Is it possible to exist in a world . . . where despair is the basic theological value in society . . . ? And my answer is, as impossible as it all is, the alternative is impossible. The alternative is death and, after all these years of effort, that's hardly an answer."

This new spirit of existential affirmation is very evident in *Knock, Knock,* which is about "the necessity for hope and change"—about "living out your life with some hope . . . reinventing it if necessary." Two middle-aged men live together in a little house in the woods. Cohn is practical and realistic; Abe a dreamy philosopher. One day, in the course of a discussion about such things, Cohn rubs a lamp to prove that genies do not exist, nor wishes come true. A genie appears, Cohn's wishes come true, and anything becomes possible. Abe disappears and Joan of Arc enters to announce that the sky has fallen and everyone can therefore go straight to heaven. Later on, Joan (who was formerly Cinderella but didn't care for the role) asks for a mountain to move and gets one large rock through the window and another by special messenger. The play is full of puns, jokes, and old comedy routines: "Knock, knock." "Who's there?" "Joan." "Joan who?" "Joan ask me no questions and I'll tell you no lies." Walter Kerr wrote that the play is "about reality, illusion, life, death, the proper way to eat spaghetti and the faith that moves mountains." He thought it "gaily, giddily, overflowingly improvisational," but also oddly touching at times and "surprisingly substantial in some subterranean way."

Hold Me!, a "delectable" cabaret-style revue based on some of Feiffer's cartoons, was staged in 1977. The same year he published his second novel, *Ackroyd,* about a neurotic young man who sets himself up as a private eye, assuming the name of Agatha Christie's murderee, Roger Ackroyd. His first client, a sportswriter who becomes a famous novelist, needs an analyst rather than a detective, since all his fears—that his wife is unfaithful, that his friends are stealing his book ideas, etc.—turn out to be paranoid delusions. No one is stealing anything from him except, eventually, Ackroyd, who is badly in need of an identity, and winds up with his client's wife, son, mistress, and craft. Most critics found the book witty and original at times, but uneven and too long.

Feiffer has been described as "a tall slim man with a paunch and a light, monklike fringe of hair." He has been separated from his wife since 1971. Friends say that the affirmative quality which appeared in *Knock, Knock* is evident in his private life as well, and that he has become less competitive and sharply witty in social situations. His cartoons are less preoccupied with politics than they used to be, concerned more with personal themes. Feiffer's strip now appears in over a hundred newspapers, in the United States and abroad. He says: "The more I write plays, the more important the cartoon becomes. . . . It reaches more people, affects more lives than the plays ever will."

PRINCIPAL PUBLISHED WORKS: *Plays*—Creeping Arnold, 1963 (*also in* Best Short Plays of the World Theatre, 1958–1967, edited by Stanley Richards, 1968); Little Murders, 1968; The Unexpurgated Memoirs of Bernard Mergendeiler (*in* Collision Course, edited by Edward Parone, 1968); Dick and Jane (*in* Oh! Calcutta!!, edited by Kenneth Tynan, 1969); The White House Murder Case (*with* Dick and Jane), 1970; Carnal Knowledge (screenplay), 1971; Knock, Knock, 1976. *Novels*—Harry, the Rat With Women, 1963; Ackroyd, 1977. *Cartoon Collections*—Sick, Sick, Sick, 1958; Passionella, and Other Stories, 1959; The Explainers, 1960; Boy, Girl, Boy, Girl, 1961; Hold Me!, 1963; Feiffer's Album, 1963; The Unexpurgated Memoirs of Bernard Mergendeiler, 1965; The Penguin Feiffer, 1966; Feiffer on Civil Rights, 1966; Feiffer's Marriage Manual, 1967; Feiffer on Nixon: The Cartoon Presidency, 1974. *Other*—(editor) The Great Comic Book Heroes, 1965; Pictures at a Prosecution: Drawings and Text from the Chicago Conspiracy Trial, 1971.

ABOUT: Contemporary Authors 17–20 1st revision, 1976; International Who's Who, 1978–79; McCrindle, J.F. (ed.) Behind the Scenes, 1971; Newquist, R. Counterpoint, 1964; Vinson, J. (ed.) Contemporary Dramatists, 1977; Who's Who in the Theatre, 1977. *Periodicals*—Harper's Magazine September 1961; Horizon November 1961; Life September 17, 1965; Mademoiselle January 1961; New Republic May 14, 1977; New York Times February 1, 1976; New York Times Book Review January 11, 1959; New York Times Magazine May 16, 1976; Newsweek November 13, 1961; November 22, 1965; March 7, 1977; Saturday Evening Post October 3, 1964; Time February 9, 1959; May 26, 1961; Village Voice April 13, 1967; May 4, 1967.

IRVING FELDMAN

FELDMAN, IRVING (MORDECAI) (September 22, 1928–), American poet, writes: "I was born in Coney Island and lived there until I was seventeen. I specify Coney Island because it has pleased me to think I hail from a place so different, small, and celebrated—just as all of us there felt ourselves lucky to be its natives. Its elements continue to fill my mind: the warm, sociable, and various crowds of Boardwalk and beach, our carnival sideshows and freakshows, parades, and fireworks, our ample ballfields, our crowded immigrant streets (crowded, too, with the unemployed of the Great Depression) that seemed to a child an endless market day and fair, the long views and cosmic intimations of sea and sky, salt smell and waves and flotsam on the beach, and mysteries of the horizon with the great passenger liners departing and the excursion boats floating in rich with music and lights like incredible birthday cakes; and, even, on the bay side of the Island, rotting piers and hulks and legends of bootleggers and the Revolutionary War.

"I attended the City College of New York and, later, Columbia University. In 1954 I went to teach at the University of Puerto Rico, where I met and married my wife, the sculptor, Carmen Alvarez Feldman. Our son, Fernando, was born in 1956. I have taught since 1964 at the State University of New York at Buffalo, and have lived on several occasions and for several years in France and Spain."

The English critic Anthony Thwaite wrote of the poems in *Works and Days* that they "cover the whole span of the Jewish temper and experience, from mystical exultation to harsh incisive satire, from poems which tremble on the edge of frivolous whimsy to others which brood long and hard on the problems of a race both chosen and rejected." There was an element of "rowdy low-comedy wit" in some of Feldman's Brooklyn poems which was enjoyed by some, though not all, of his reviewers:

To be Chosen—that means having only one part.
But if I'm Elect, why all this fat around my heart?
Why was I born in Brooklyn with the lower
    middle-classes?
Is that a hero's place? Was Moses freckled? Samson
    wear glasses?

(from "The Wandering Jew—The Wailing Wall")

Most critics, however, reserved their warmest praise for the more dramatic poems in which Feldman, turning to the Jewish past or classical mythology, spoke not in his own contemporary and antiheroic accents but in the persona of Prometheus, Adam, or Abraham, and in a voice that was called "plangent, even solemn," though never rhetorical or sentimental.

These two voices—the wry and the plangent—are fused in some of the poems in Feldman's second book, *The Pripet Marshes,* most notably in the title poem and "To the Six Million," two long elegies on the victims of Nazi brutality:

Survivor, who are you?
Ask the voices that disappeared,
The faces broken and expunged.
I am the one who was not there.
Of such accidents I have made my death.

(from "To the Six Million")

Richard Howard, who thought that the mythological impersonations of Feldman's first book had been a kind of self-concealment or camouflage, found a "wonderful courage" in "To the Six Million," where Feldman "accepts the burden laid upon him by his unparticipating history, an acceptance unmediated by myth or personation, a self-acceptance." The same collection included "Artist and Model," a series of poems after pictures by Picasso which was much praised for its precision. Elsewhere in the book some reviewers found a certain loss of tension, "a tendency to blur, to admit too much."

Feldman's range widened in *Magic Papers*, where, for example, he observes the behavior of lovers on the Brighton Beach local, or a girl dressing hornpout for a meal, reflects upon his wife's nightmares or his own childhood, in poems "generally long, generally low-pitched." Richard Howard spoke of the disquieting "accent of wisdom" in these poems, and "a gravity that pinions the mind. It is not a gravity alien to wit, or even to fun, and it is wonderfully nimble in tracing a figure. Still, it is a gravity which is heavy with grief":

Oh why is the soul sent on errands
in the dark?
with its list
of names, its fist of pennies,
its beating heart?

(from "To Waken You
With Your Name")

R.W. Flint, reviewing *Lost Originals* (1972), called it "a strong book from one of our best poets." It seems to Flint that Feldman is "something like a Malamud in verse, equally given to dream and elegy, to the whole wry fable-making post-Talmudic tradition and to those rituals of kitchen, bed and street that engender his acid-etched visionary lyrics." The collection disappointed Henry Taylor, however, who found it "marred by a puzzling unevenness," and John Thompson, who was left "with the sense that I have been listening to a tired voice speaking with a generally sour distaste in the absence of real occasion."

There was a mixed reception also for *Leaping Clear* (1976), another wide-ranging collection in which the title poem describes Feldman's cir-cumambulation of his city "of a dreamy Sabbath afternoon" (the quotation is from *Moby Dick*). A reviewer in *Library Journal* wrote that "Feldman inherits and extends the tradition of American city poets, like Whitman, who look for the beauty in the ugliness. Hart Crane comes quickly to mind. The obstacles to transcendence are immense, however: the poverty of the city, indifferent and cruel bureaucracies, the universal diaspora of peoples that characterize our life, in a word, the sense of distance from the beginnings of things. These beginnings—'the wilderness,' 'the sabbath,' 'the lost sea-space'—are little more than notions, fragments of lost thought. Feldman brings to his perception of the city the quasi-religious force of Wordsworth, Hart Crane, Stevens." John Thompson, on the other hand, was no more impressed by this collection than by its predecessor, and Gilbert Sorrentino called Feldman "not a poet but a self-parodist," with an "astonishing insensitivity to language."

The poet is the son of William and Anna (Goldberg) Feldman. He received his B.S.S. in 1950 from CCNY and his M.A. in 1953 from Columbia. Feldman began his teaching career as an instructor in English at the University of Puerto Rico (1954–1956), taught at the Université de Lyons in France in 1957–1958, and then went to Kenyon College as assistant professor of English (1958–1964). Since then he has taught English at the State University of New York at Buffalo, as an associate professor until 1968 and thereafter as professor. Feldman received the Kovner Memorial Award of the Jewish Book Council in 1962 for *Works and Days*, and has had grants or fellowships from the Ingram Merrill Foundation (1963), the National Institute of Arts and Letters (1973), and the Guggenheim Foundation (1973).

PRINCIPAL WORKS: Works and Days, 1961; The Pripet Marshes, 1965; Magic Papers, 1970; Lost Originals, 1972; Leaping Clear, 1976.

ABOUT: Contemporary Authors 1–4 1st revision, 1967; Howard, R. Alone With America, 1969; Vinson, J. (ed.) Contemporary Poets, 1975; Who's Who in America, 1976-1977. *Periodicals*—Commentary July 1962; Midstream September 1965; April 1972; Modern Poetry Studies Winter 1973; New York Times Book Review August 15, 1965; November 22, 1970; February 25, 1973; Parnassus Spring-Summer 1974; Poetry September 1973; Saturday Review January 6, 1962; July 3, 1965; Spectator November 3, 1961.

FERGUSON, HELEN. *See* KAVAN, ANNA

FERRÉOL, MARCEL AUGUSTE. *See* "ACHARD," MARCEL

EDWARD FIELD

FIELD, EDWARD (June 7, 1924–), American poet, was born in Brooklyn, New York and says that he is the son of "humble Jews from Russia and Poland." He grew up in Lynbrook, Long Island, and was educated at Lynbrook public schools and at New York University, where he studied liberal arts but left without a degree. During World War II he served with the Eighth Air Force (1942-1946) as a navigator in heavy bombers, and it was at this time that he began to write poetry. After the war he lived for a year and a half in Europe. His early poems were published in *Poetry Quarterly* (England) and *Botteghe Oscure* (Italy), and he was later a frequent contributor to *Evergreen Review.* Returning to the United States in 1948, Field worked in a warehouse, in art reproduction, as a machinist, and for some years as a clerk-typist in various offices. Performing with amateur groups gave him a hankering after a stage career, and, after studying with Vera Soloviova, he was for a time a moderately successful actor, securing some leading roles in summer stock.

Field's first book of poems, published in 1963, was *Stand Up, Friend, With Me.* It won the 1962 Lamont Award, given by the Academy of American Poets for a collection of poems in manuscript, and brought Field a Guggenheim Fellowship in 1963. These forty-three poems, most of them recording "a restless, cocky, hardbitten Manhattan existence," were greatly enjoyed. R.W. Flint, noting affinities with the Beat poets in Field's colloquialisms and raffish humor, thought that he was in fact "only a random tourist in Beatdom"—that "this stubbornly secular, romantic–anti-romantic, self-mocking poet" was really closer to "the rational comedy

of Heine than to the vatic style of Ginsberg: Heine out of Cummings out of Delmore Schwartz."

This excerpt from "Unwanted" demonstrates the characteristic Field manner:

. . . . I wish someone would find my fingerprints somewhere
Maybe on a corpse and say, You're it.

Description: Male, or reasonably so
White, but not lily-white and usually deep-red

Thirty-fivish, and looks it lately
Five-feet-nine and one-hundred-thirty pounds: no physique

Black hair going gray, hairline receding fast
What used to be curly, now fuzzy

Brown eyes starey under beetling brow
Mole on chin, probably will become a wen

It is perfectly obvious that he was not popular at school
No good at baseball, and wet his bed.

His aliases tell his history: Dumbell, Good-for-nothing,
Jewboy, Fieldinsky, Skinny, Fierce Face, Greaseball, Sissy.

Warning: This man is not dangerous, answers to any name
Responds to love, don't call him or he will come.

And Field is scarcely more reverent or poetical in a fundamentally serious piece like "Ode to Fidel Castro," in which he urges his muse to tickle him now and then "For I am going to write on World Issues/ Which demands laughter where we most believe."

Richard Howard, noting the influence on these poems of Whitman and Cavafy, commended them for "their extreme resistance to the habitual conventions of literature." He said that Field had produced "a canon of successful poems without meter, without rhyme, without music, without images," purveying instead a particular hedonistic vision of life "to which the poet is so accountable that he relies on his entire identification with it to speak for him."

There was a similarly delighted reception for *Variety Photoplays,* in which Field writes about movies and movie stars, and muses with a mixture of nostalgia and irony on the disparity between reality and the Hollywood fantasies he grew up with. Howard thought these "long prosy grumbles and bitchings" somewhat more wry and resigned than the poems in Field's first book, but Chad Walsh found him still "deeply involved in the human drama." It seemed to Walsh that Field's "poetic asceticism" made many effects unattainable for him: "His gain is a kind of lean, stripped-down power and ability to speak the direct words of a common humanity."

Field ventured into startlingly different territory in *Eskimo Songs and Stories*, which he selected and adapted from material collected by the Danish explorer Knud Rasmussen, who lived for a time among the Netsilik Eskimos. Reviewers agreed that Field, working his poems up from literal English translations, had captured with great clarity and force not only the harshness of Arctic life but its excitement, humor, and "sense of celebration." The new poems collected in *A Full Heart* (1978) had a mixed press. M. L. Rosenthal complained of Field's "cultivation of a familiar speech without tension or change, and his utterance of mountains of 'prophetic' clichés, about Jews and the poor and England and Israel and whatnot," but praised half-a-dozen pieces in the collection, including two poems of "homosexual assertiveness," in which "the bargain-price guru disappears and a human being of troubled depths becomes visible and audible."

Field has received the Shelley Memorial Award of the Poetry Society of America. He has read his poetry at the Library of Congress, the New York YMHA, and many American colleges, and nowadays relies for his income mainly on these readings and occasional teaching stints at poetry workshops. He wrote the narration for the award-winning documentary film *To Be Alive*, commissioned by Johnson's Wax for the New York World's Fair in 1965–1966.

PRINCIPAL WORKS: Stand Up, Friend, With Me, 1963; Variety Photoplays, 1967; (as editor and adapter) Eskimo Songs and Stories, 1973; A Full Heart, 1978.

ABOUT: Contemporary Authors 13–16 1st revision, 1975; Crowell's Handbook of Contemporary American Poetry, 1973; Howard, R. Alone With America, 1969; Vinson, J. (ed.) Contemporary Poets, 1975. *Periodicals*—Atlantic December 1963; Christian Science Monitor July 3, 1963; Commentary August 1963; Kenyon Review Fall 1968; Nation November 9, 1963; New York Review of Books November 23, 1967; New York Times Book Review May 14, 1978; Saturday Review October 26, 1963.

*FILIPPO, EDUARDO DE (May 24, 1900–), Italian dramatist, poet, film-maker, television writer, and librettist, writes (in Italian): "I was born in Naples on May 24, 1900 from the union of Eduardo Scarpetta, the greatest Neapolitan actor, writer, producer, and comedian of the time, and Luisa de Filippo, unmarried. It took

*fil ē′ pó

EDUARDO DE FILIPPO

me some time to understand the circumstances of my birth, for in those days children lacked the quickness and audacity they have today, so that it came as a great shock to me when at the age of eleven I realized that I was the 'son of an unknown father.' The morbid curiosity of the people around me certainly didn't help me to achieve a mental and emotional balance. On the one hand I was proud of my father, to whose theatrical company I had belonged—though at irregular intervals rather than full time—first as an extra and then as an actor, ever since I had made my stage debut at the age of four in the costume of a little Japanese in a parody of the operetta *The Geisha*. On the other hand the constant scandalmongering, gossip, and backbiting painfully oppressed me. I felt rejected, or merely tolerated, and ridiculed simply because I was 'different.'

"However, I have by now understood for a long time that talent will make its way and nothing can stop it, and indeed that it will grow and develop more exuberantly when its possessor is considered 'different' by society. In fact such a person will end by wanting to be truly different, and his powers will multiply, his thoughts be in continual effervescence, his body will not know fatigue, until he has attained the goal he has set himself. All this, however, I didn't yet know, and my 'difference' weighed on me to the point where I finished by leaving my mother's home and my school and setting out into the world alone, with very little money in my pocket, but with the firm intention of finding my own way. I must stress, however, that this had to be the way I had already and always chosen: the theatre, which had become and is everything for me.

"It is futile to talk of the difficulties, the privation and hunger: anyone who wishes to be free to pursue an ideal will always encounter periods of difficulty and wretchedness. Nevertheless, if you have inside you the splendor of an ideal that you know you can serve worthily, you can put up with anything. For some years I did everything: extra, scene-shifter, stage director, character actor; then, little by little I made a name as an actor and also as a writer and producer. I wrote my first comedy, a one-act piece called *Farmacia di turno* (Pharmacy Open on Alternate Sundays) in 1920; my first official production was the staging of a musical comedy, E. L. Murolo's *Sorrento gentile,* in 1922; but how many sketches and scenes had I written, how many unsigned productions had I staged in the preceding years.

"After having been in several different sorts of theatrical company, in 1931 I formed my own Compagnia Umoristica I De Filippo, in which my sister Titina and my brother Peppino also took part. Our triumphal debut was with one of my own comedies, *Natale in casa Cupiello* (Christmas at the Cupiellos), and for years we passed from one success to another all over Italy. In 1944, Peppino left the company. Meanwhile the war was coming to an end, and with it the twenty years of fascist rule. At last I was able to change my style of writing; during the fascist era I was forced to conceal social reality beneath the grotesque and the absurd in order to avoid censorship. But now I could speak clearly and try out the theatrical form at which I had always aimed, that tragicomedy which is indeed among the most ancient of all theatrical forms: an ideal (rather than realistic) correspondence between life and spectacle, that is to say a fusion, at times harmonious, at times strident and jarring, of laughter and tears, of the grotesque and the sublime, of drama and comedy—abandoning that stage artifice which makes a sharp division between farce and tragedy.

"I asked myself: 'Why should the theatrical public have to do nothing but laugh, or nothing but cry, for two hours? Why should the audience of, say, Molière be able to accept his tragic comedies—or comic tragedies—and today's audience not be able to?' And the answer that I gave myself to these questions was just one: 'There *isn't* any valid reason; there is only a custom that has now become traditional for such an artificial division.' I then wrote *Napoli milionaria* (Millionaire Naples), founded a new company called Il Teatro di Eduardo, and, encouraged by the enormous success of this new

genre, have continued for thirty years to write and perform a score of comedies which are now known and staged all over the world. It isn't easy to sum up an artistic life that has been so long and so crowded (I work not only in the theatre but in cinema, television, and radio; I have built a theatre in Naples, and formed another company, La Scarpettiana, that I have directed, though without acting in it, for some years; I have written poems, stories, and essays): everything seems important and nothing appears indispensable, so that at a certain point you don't know whether you have said too much or too little. ... In the end, the one thing that really matters in the life of an artist is the future, since to dwell on the past may hinder the creative impulse."

Almost all of Eduardo de Filippo's plays are set in his native city of Naples, and most are written in Neapolitan dialect, or a diluted form of it, though like Pirandello he has also translated his dialect plays into standard Italian. A great deal of the life of the Italian theatre depends even today on dialect drama, which still flourishes in Venice and Genoa as well as in Naples, often combined with improvisation in the tradition of the *commedia dell'arte.* Neapolitan vaudeville and music-hall shows, which Filippo saw as a boy, included many sketches centered around the escapades of Pulcinella, the cunning rogue of the *commedia dell'arte,* who gradually evolved into the stock figure of the *piccolo borghese,* the lower-middle-class rogue of Neapolitan comedy. The great writer-director-actor in this tradition, until his death in 1925, was Filippo's father, Eduardo Scarpetta, who wrote and acted in about a hundred Neapolitan comedies. Scarpetta's three illegitimate children by Luisa de Filippo all joined their father's famous acting company as children, and became leading actors while still adolescents.

When Eduardo de Filippo left home he first joined the company of L. Carini as utility man, character actor, and author, then moved on to other companies, collaborating with other writers in sketches and one-act plays, many of them farces like his father's, in the *commedia* tradition of the vaudeville theatre. In the 1930s he met Pirandello and was influenced by such basic Pirandellian ideas as the fine division between illusion and reality, and the idea of a fiction that is created as an evasion of life, but comes to assume an autonomy of its own—though in Filippo's plays such themes are treated not tragically but with the zest and gusto of the Neapolitan folk tradition.

The more sophisticated comedies he wrote

under Pirandello's influence formed the staple repertoire of the Humorous Theatre that he established with his brother Peppino and his sister Titina in 1931. These include their opening play, *Natale in casa Cupiello* (Christmas at the Cupiellos, 1931), which rather bitterly contrasts reality and illusion in a story about a childishly naive man who encounters evil in a setting of colorful misery. This was followed by *Sik-Sik l'artefice mago* (Sik-Sik the Magic Craftsman, 1930), *Gennariello* (1932), and *Uomo e galantuomo* (Man and Gentleman, 1933), among other triumphs. Success in the movies followed almost at once with such films as *Tre uomini in frak* (Three Men in Tails, 1932), *Sono stato io!* (I Did It!, 1937), and *In campagna è caduta una stella* (A Star Is Fallen in the Countryside, 1942).

In 1945 Filippo was reported by the Rome newspaper *Il cosmopolita* as saying of these early plays that in them "I wanted to show the world of plot and intrigue and interest: the adulterer, the gambler, the superstitious, the slothful, the fraudulent. All part of a recognizable, definable Neapolitan way of life, but a way of life belonging to the nineteenth century. In those plays I kept alive a Naples which was already dead in part, and in part was covered up and hidden by the 'paternalistic' care of the fascist regime. . . . The new century, this twentieth century, did not come to Naples until the arrival of the Allies; the second world war here, it seems to me, made a hundred years pass overnight. And if so much time has passed, then I need to write of other things, and condition my acting accordingly."

And it was with his more profound tragicomedies of the postwar years that Filippo achieved an international reputation and appeal. These plays are set in a Naples which is undergoing the crisis of war, the overthrow of fascism, the Allied occupation, or the slow and painful return to normality. They evoke the moral confusions but also the desperate lust for life of the times, along with the greed and cunning that have been bred into the *piccolo borghese* by centuries of oppression, and a profound concern for the family.

Luciano Codignola has this to say of Filippo's characters: "Whatever their class, sex, age, and culture they share one characteristic: a profound lack of motivation hardly hidden by a certain liveliness in their attitudes which corresponds to the southern veneer, to the Neapolitan color. . . . A Filippo character appears always to be acted upon, always the object and never the subject of passions. . . . What forces these characters into such misery, and what keeps them there? . . . It is first of all a radical mistrust of social institutions and values. . . . The family is the only institution that they heed and acknowledge, the only buffer between the individual and a social power which has systematically destroyed all those institutions which in other countries have become instruments of mediation." Filippo had introduced this theme in *Natale in casa Cupiello* as early as 1931, and he returned to it with a sense of urgency when the war and its aftermath threatened the institution of the family. Since then, Codignola writes, the principal theme in all of his plays has been the family, and "the ways in which the institution survived in a new situation, resisted all pressures, and finally prevailed."

All of these concerns are evident in the first of Filippo's plays in his new manner, *Napoli milionaria* (Millionaire Naples, 1945). It begins with the city still in the hands of the fascists, and tormented by Allied bombing. During an air raid Gennaro, a streetcar conductor, loses his way and winds up in a German labor camp. When he returns after a year he finds that his wife has grown rich in the flourishing black market and is living with another man, while his daughter has become a prostitute and his son a car thief. But neither Gennaro's wounded pride and desire for revenge nor his wife's greed can prevail against the strength of the family ideal, and Gennaro is able to restore the situation to its former status simply by taking advantage of his prestige as head of the family. This immensely popular play also achieved worldwide success as a film. Giorgio Prosperi, writing in 1971 after a triumphant revival in Rome, said: "After all, what are the three acts of *Napoli milionaria* if not three moments of Italian life, which all of us have passed? As the war drew towards its end, great hopes; the war over, a false euphoria, followed, as was inevitable, by a bitter awakening. It is still amazing that Eduardo should have been able to portray these three moments with simple characters and natural dialogue which, as the years pass, do not lose the strength of unaffected simplicity."

Filumena Marturano (1946, translated under the same title) is a comedy of family life and is often considered Filippo's masterpiece. Filumena had been a Naples prostitute. Twenty-five years before the play begins she had been taken from a brothel by the rich playboy Domenico Soriano, who had kept her as his mistress and then as his devoted and exploited housekeeper. When she discovers that he is about to marry a young woman, Filumena pretends to be dying, and thus tricks Soriano into marrying her. She quickly "recovers" and reveals that she has adopted this desperate ruse in order to give a name to her three grown sons, of whose existence Soriano had been quite unaware. Enraged, he annuls the marriage, but he is haunted by Filumena's further revelation that he is the father of one of the boys—and her refusal to tell him which one. In the end, the claims of the family take precedence over Soriano's personal desires. He remarries Filumena, legally and voluntarily, and, after struggling unsuccessfully to identify one or other of the young men as a chip off the old block, he accepts all three of them as his sons.

Filumena has been almost universally regarded as one of the greatest female characters in Italian theatre, with her deep attachment to the values of the family and her profound sense of a natural justice which has little to do with the mere formalities of law. Eric Bentley has said that "a plot summary could hardly suggest the kind of fun and pathos Eduardo gives to the story. . . . One enjoys, above all, the fine blend of comedy and drama, the naive pathos, the almost seriousness of what might easily be ludicrous." The play was filmed under its original title in 1950, with Filippo as the rich playboy and his sister Titina in the title role. Bentley remarked of it that "Eduardo is one of those stage actors whose magic cannot penetrate celluloid: on the screen it is impossible to see much more than competence in this man whom Gordon Craig, as report has it, considers the finest living actor." At any rate, in 1964 the play was again filmed, this time under the title *Matrimonio all' italiana (Marriage Italian Style),* and with Sophia Loren and Marcello Mastroianni in the leading roles enjoyed spectacular success all over the world.

Another popular play of this period that was successfully filmed was *Questi fantasmi* (1946, translated by Marguerita Carrá and Louise H. Warner as *Oh, These Ghosts*), in which an innocent husband takes his wife's nocturnal lover for a benevolent ghost who leaves him money on the table. The husband has been forced by poverty to accept an apartment that is said to be haunted, but his conviction that it *is* haunted saves him from actual tragedy. It is a drama of illusion and reality treated in a manner much lighter than that of Pirandello. The young wife fails to realize that her husband has accepted his fantasy as reality, believing instead that it is greed for the money which leads him to accept dishonor, and despising him all the more. But her lover, with whom she had been planning to run away, does realize the truth, and is so touched by it that he departs for ever—however empty it may be, the marriage will survive. The theme of *Le voci di dentro* (Inner Voices, 1948), is that dreams may project our capacity for good or evil. Alberto dreams that the Cimmaruta family have murdered his friend, and the dream is so vivid that when he awakes he denounces them to the police. The friend turns out to be still alive, but the various members of the family, far from reproaching Alberto as he expects, come and accuse one another of the crime—his dream was an intuition of what they were capable of.

After the war, Eduardo de Filippo bought the ruins of the ancient Teatro San Ferdinando, built in Naples by the Bourbons in 1700 but reduced to rubble by Allied bombing. He rebuilt it at his own expense, reopening it in 1954 with a splendid production of an old play by Antonio Petito, the most famous Pulcinella of the nineteenth century. Both of his companies, La Scarpettiana and Il Teatro di Eduardo, have since performed there, as well as at many other theatres all over Italy. In 1955 Il Teatro di Eduardo presented *Questi fantasmi,* with Filippo himself in the leading role, at the Sarah Bernhardt Theatre in Paris as part of that year's Paris Festival. In 1962 the company made a three-month tour of Europe—Budapest, Warsaw, Moscow, Leningrad, Vienna, and Antwerp—presenting plays by Pirandello and by Eduardo de Filippo, including *Napoli milionaria, Filumena Marturano, Questi fantasmi,* and *Il Sindaco del Rione Sanità* (1960, translated as *The Local Authority*), a grotesque but extremely interesting comedy about the death of an old Mafia boss. In 1973 the company went to London to present *Napoli milionaria* as part of Peter Daubeny's World Theatre Season.

In his book *My World of Theatre* (1971), Daubeny describes a visit to Eduardo (as he is universally called) "in his small apartment in the chic Parioli district of Rome, where he lived surrounded by china plates, cups and saucers. He presented a melancholy detached figure who seemed, like so many great actors, to have become a victim of his own comic inventiveness, which had drawn him subconsciously into the miseries of life. He seemed far more interested in his collection of English bone china than any visit to London. . . . I left this kindly, inscrutable and unsmiling host among his glittering display of porcelain." Daubeny also writes at length about Eduardo's brother Peppino, whose company he had brought to London's World Theatre Season in 1964, and who has also written numerous plays, in which he appears himself as a great comic actor and master of mime.

In 1973 Britain's National Theatre presented a production by Franco Zeffirelli of another of Eduardo de Filippo's plays, *Sabato, domenica e lunedì* (1960, translated by Keith Waterhouse and Willis Hall as *Saturday, Sunday, Monday*), with Laurence Olivier, Frank Finlay, and Joan

Plowright among the cast. It is one of the author's many studies of family life, the central idea here being the way all the family trudge through the working week longing for the weekend, only to end up in a flaming row over the all-important Sunday lunch. Olivier played the old grandfather, a retired hatter whose lust for hats amounts almost to a sexual deviation. His son Peppino owns a men's clothing shop and heads a large and quarrelsome family in the bosom of which, over Sunday lunch, he accuses his wife of infidelity with the accountant next door. It emerges that she is not unfaithful to him—only resentful of his insults to her cooking.

Irving Wardle observed that "throughout the family we see similar possibilities for trivial resentments to smash relationships. . . . de Filippo's style is expansive, designed to give character precedence over plot; but its design consistently shows people, encased within the closed family world, pulling in different directions. And the comedy generally comes where two or more egoisms collide. 'I'm not going to be made to look a fool in my own house,' announces Peppino, donning a hat recently stretched by his father so that it almost comes down to his nose." After a solid year of success in London, a new production of this play with a different cast failed in New York: "I did not recognize this saraband of shouting, circus gags and hysteria as mine," said the rueful author, after seeing the dress rehearsal. *Filumena,* a British production of *Filumena Marturano,* followed in 1977. Like *Saturday, Sunday, Monday* it was directed by Zeffirelli, translated by Waterhouse and Hall, and starred Joan Plowright. It was even more warmly received than its predecessor, and called more believable and more moving.

There have been several editions in Italian of collections of some of Eduardo de Filippo's more than fifty plays, including a four-volume collection which assembles the early comedies as *Cantata dei giorni pari* (Cantata for Even Days) and the later tragicomedies as *Cantata dei giorni dispari* (Cantata for Odd Days), the two titles referring to the popular superstition that even-numbered days are lucky and odd-numbered days unlucky. His poetry includes the highly acclaimed volume *Il paese di Pulcinella* (Naples, Home of Pulcinella, 1951), *O Canisto* (1971), and *Le Poesie di Eduardo* (1975). For Italian television he wrote the serial story *Peppino Girella* (1962), and some of his many opera productions have had great success abroad, including Donizetti's *Don Pasquale* at the Edinburgh Festival and Rossini's *Barbiere di Siviglia* in Berlin. His many prizes and awards include the Premio

Internazionale per il Teatro (1972), the London *Evening Standard* Award for the best play of the year (1972), and the Premio Internazionale per il teatro Luigi Pirandello (1975). He received an honorary doctorate from the University of Birmingham in 1977.

Luciano Codignola has said of Filippo that "if you write in dialect, even diluted dialect, there are certain topics that cannot be discussed. Italian dialects lack a sufficient vocabulary . . . to talk in terms of modern psychology, political thought, or sociology . . . These limitations of dialect are also the limitations of de Filippo's theatre." To appreciate Filippo's work, according to Thornton Wilder, "one must truly love theatre—not the well-shaped play, not the picture of relatively superficial custom and manner, not the heated unfoldment of patterns of idealized heroism and villainy—but the 'show' of the people, by the people, for the people. . . . How sad his plays are: the weight of humanity." And the English critic Robert Cushman has remarked of Filippo's acting style that he is "the soberest of comedians. He has a gift for simply existing on stage, with minimum effort and maximum intensity, which no British actor can match."

PRINCIPAL WORKS IN ENGLISH TRANSLATION: Saturday, Sunday, Monday, 1974; Three Plays by Eduardo de Filippo (The Local Authority, Grand Magic, Filumena Marturano), translated by Carlo Ardito, 1976; Filumena Marturano *and* Son of Pulcinella *in* Corrigan, R. (ed.) Masterpieces of the Modern Italian Theatre, 1967; Oh, These Ghosts! *in* Tulane Drama Review Spring 1964.

ABOUT: Anderson, M. and others (eds.) A Handbook of Contemporary Drama, 1972; Bentley, E. In Search of Theatre, 1953; Bentley, E. What Is Theatre?, 1969; Crowell's Handbook of Contemporary Drama, 1971; Daubeny, P. My World of Theatre, 1971; Gassner, J. and Quinn, E. (eds.) Reader's Encyclopedia of World Drama, 1969; International Who's Who, 1978-79; Ivask, I. and Wilpert, G. von (eds.) World Literature Since 1945, 1973; McGraw-Hill Encyclopedia of World Drama, 1972; Matlaw, M. Modern World Drama, 1972. *Periodicals*—Modern Drama December 1973; Observer October 30, 1977; Theatre Arts May 1955; Times (London) November 2, 1973, November 4, 1977; Tulane Drama Review Spring 1964.

FINKEL, DONALD (October 21, 1929–), American poet, was born in New York City, the son of an attorney, Saul Finkel, and the former Meta Rosenthal. He was educated at Columbia University, where he was Phi Beta Kappa, receiving his B.A. in philosophy in 1952, his M.A. in literature in 1953. He began his career as an instructor in English at the University of Iowa (1957-1958), and taught at Bard College, New York, in 1958-1960, when he edited the *Shasta Review.* Since 1960 he has been poet-in-residence at Washington University, St. Louis, Missouri. He has lived intermittently in Mexico.

Joseph Pirone

DONALD FINKEL

"The Clothing's New Emperor," Finkel's first collection, appeared in *Poets of Today VI* in 1959. It contains a number of poems about the writing of poems, some about bullfighting, many drawing on mythological characters—Midas, Theseus, Bluebeard, Jacob, Orpheus, and others—and a long poem called "The Hunting of the Unicorn: A Tapestry in Five Acts." Richard Howard, who has written very perceptively about Finkel's poetry in *Alone With America* and elsewhere, detects signs of strain in this "truculent indenture to the myths of recurrence," this "commitment to periodicity," pointing out that "though the forms are closed, the rhymes are generally slant, and the jumpy lines consort awkwardly with sense units."

It is Howard's belief that "the escape from myth into individuality" is "the prime compulsion of Donald Finkel's poetry" and he finds support for this theory in the demythologizing poems in *Simeon* (1964). The title sequence of sixteen poems comprises a wittily deprecating account of the saint's elevation by Simeon's all too human brother (and *alter ego?*), and there are robust, witty, often slangy poems about (for example) Christ and Dionysus, fairy tales and snake charmers, marriage and the female pudenda. In these poems, Howard writes, "the preoccupation with an absolute—eternity, recurrence, transfiguration—is dismissed, definitively mocked, or acknowledged to be beyond the poet's grasp."

This development continues in *A Joyful Noise* (1966), where, Howard maintains, "Finkel's purpose is to establish the poem in a world without myth, on the surface." R.J. Mills also observed a process of demythologization in these funny, bawdy, and satirical poems, "populated with fat clowns, mock Arabian Nights figures, Jewish saints, and the like." And Joseph Bennett found something new in the collection—"startling, sudden flowers of language, newly minted metaphors." Both Bennett and Lucien Stryk thought that Finkel was at his best in short lyrics like "Hands," where as Stryk says he shows an exceptional ability to "invest the abstract with body":

The poem makes truth a little more disturbing,
like a good bra, lifts it and holds it out
in both hands. . . .

Lately the world you wed, for want of such hands,
sags in the bed beside you like a tired wife.
For want of such hands, the face of the moon is
    bored,
the tree does not stretch and yearn, nor the groin
    tighten.

Devious or frank, in any case,
the poem is calculated to arouse.
Lean back and let its hands play freely on you:
there comes a moment, lifted and aroused,
when the two of you are equally beautiful.

As if in response to suggestions that his style was "somewhat too febrile to make the long poem fully accessible to him," Finkel produced one in *Answer Back* (1968). "Episodic in its ecstasy, insistently abrupt and goofy," it is essentially a series of meditations on such large themes as nature, sexual love, and living in America, divided into six sections and interspersed with quotations from (for example) Fred Hoyle, Whitman, Heraclitus, and Lenny Bruce. Finkel is an amateur speleologist, and cave exploration is used as a metaphor for other kinds of investigation—into the human mind, the human past. Stryk allows that *Answer Back* has "its real felicities and triumphs. . . . Full of extraordinary juxtapositions . . . and fearing nothing, the poem accomplishes one thing certainly: it gives the reader a strong sense of the man behind it—his loves, fears, hates, hang-ups."

Answer Back seemed to Richard Howard a "launching-pad for the explosive, or at least exploded, poems in *The Garbage Wars* (1970), in which the poet's voice "is raised, or rather plunged, in a song of destruction celebrating the surrender of selfhood . . . the descent into that furnace where identity itself is shucked off and Eros released and realized. These poems are a devout submission to primary experience. . . . Consistently Finkel urges himself to let go, to drop: 'open your deepest passages to the flame'. . . . It is not what meets the eye that

261

matters here, but what meets ear: Finkel's convulsive, splintered utterances in which punctuation is replaced by blanks, are the harangues of a man likely to be saved from drowning, if at all, by letting himself loose. If the poems look jagged on the page, their cadence—for Finkel is a master of phrasing, 'breathing all I have in and out'—is a true one, music not only of water but of earth and air and fire, elemental music."

In the winter of 1970 Finkel accompanied a scientific expedition to Antarctica. He records and meditates upon that experience in *Adequate Earth* (1972), another vivid, witty, and thoughtful long poem using the collage technique of *Answer Back.* Helen Vendler, reviewing *A Mote in Heaven's Eye,* the collection that followed in 1975, wrote: "Finkel has as he has always had an authentic rhythm, a colloquial and jeering tone, a surrealist humor and a gift of childlike diminution of life to cartoon dimensions. But these tricks are laid aside for a harsher outline in his recent poems about Mexico, beautiful and clearly seen."

Finkel has served as consultant in prosody to the Random House Dictionary, and was visiting professor at Bennington College in 1966-1967. He received the Theodore Roethke Memorial Prize in 1974, and his other awards include *Poetry Northwest*'s Helen Bullis Prize (1964), a Guggenheim fellowship (1966), and grants from the Ingram Merrill Foundation (1972) and the National Endowment for the Humanities (1973). Finkel was married in 1956 to the poet and novelist Constance Urdang, and has two daughters and a son. He is a member of the Antarctican Society and the Cave Research Foundation.

PRINCIPAL WORKS: The Clothing's New Emperor *in* Poets of Today VI, 1959; Simeon, 1964; A Joyful Noise, 1966; Answer Back, 1968; The Garbage Wars, 1970; Adequate Earth, 1972; A Mote in Heaven's Eye, 1975; Going Under/ Endurance, 1978.

ABOUT: Contemporary Authors 23-24 1st revision, 1977; Howard, R. Alone With America, 1969; Vinson, J. (ed.) Contemporary Poets, 1975; Who's Who in America, 1976-1977. *Periodicals*—New York Times Book Review December 20, 1964; September 4, 1966; November 22, 1970; September 7, 1975, Poetry July 1965, November 1966; Saturday Review August 24, 1968.

FLEXNER, JAMES T(HOMAS) (January 13, 1908–), American biographer and historian, was born in New York City, the son of Simon Flexner and the former Helen Thomas. His father, a distinguished pathologist and bacteriologist, was the first director of the Rockefeller Institute for Medical Research (1904-1935), and was famous for his studies of poliomyelitis, dys-

JAMES T. FLEXNER

entery, and meningitis. An uncle, Abraham Flexner, was a well-known educator who directed the Institute of Advanced Study at Princeton from 1930 to 1939. James Flexner graduated in 1925 from the Lincoln School of Teachers College, Columbia University, and four years later received his B.S. *magna cum laude* from Harvard. The same year, 1929, Flexner joined the New York *Herald Tribune* as a reporter. After three years there he left to serve as executive secretary (1931-1932) of the Noise Abatement Commission established by New York City's Department of Health. He has been a freelance professional writer ever since.

Flexner's first book, *Doctors on Horseback* (1937), contains biographical studies of seven American pioneer doctors. It was found "virtually devoid of technical errors," and impressed Mary Ross as an example of "the all-too-rare kind of biography which has both the concreteness and vigor of fiction and the ring of authenticity." It was followed by another exercise in medical biography, *William Henry Welch and the Heroic Age of American Medicine* (1941), written by Flexner in collaboration with his father. The product of almost eight years of research into "Popsy" Welch's voluminous correspondence and writings, this massive study not only details the life of the great pathologist and medical pioneer himself but describes nearly three hundred years of his family's history. E.L. Keyes called it "the best history we have read of the birth of medical science in these United States."

Finding many Americans "woefully ignorant about the development of their own culture," James Flexner has concentrated much of his attention since the late 1930s upon "aspects of our cultural heritage which have been either forgotten, or because seen altogether in a European light, misunderstood." Seeking to recreate "the past both in terms of personality and events," he has produced almost a dozen books which interweave biography and cultural or art history. *America's Old Masters* (1939), his first venture into this field, comprises biographical sketches of the first four American artists to achieve international fame: Benjamin West, John Singleton Copley, Charles Willson Peale, and Gilbert Stuart.

This was followed over the next twenty years by a series of books tracing the history of American painting since early colonial times. *American Painting: First Flowers of Our Wilderness* (1947) discusses the products of the pre-Revolutionary period up to 1774 in their social and cultural context. *American Painting: The Light of Distant Skies* (1954) deals similarly with the years between 1760 and 1835, and *That Wilder Image* (1962) considers "the painting of America's native school from Thomas Cole to Winslow Homer." Not surprisingly, the "resounding opinions" Flexner expressed in these books did not win universal agreement, and Hilton Kramer, reviewing *That Wilder Image,* complained of Flexner's "refusal to look at the paintings themselves with the heightened vision of our time, or indeed, with anything approaching modern sophistication." Kramer was also dissatisfied with Flexner's style, which he found "gentlemanly and unemotional, full of interesting facts and dull observations, and in the end not really equal to the excitement of the material." But most critics welcomed and admired the series—above all for the way American painting is shown to be the organic product of a new kind of society and environment. *First Flowers* seemed to J.C. Long "a superb book," and to the *New Yorker* "the most thorough-going study of American colonial painting generally available." Oliver Larkin wrote of *The Light of Distant Skies* that "those colleagues who challenge some of Mr. Flexner's evaluations and qualify some of his assertions will nevertheless appreciate the vigor and general cogency of his interpretation of a period." And *That Wilder Image* brought Flexner the Francis Parkman Prize.

Flexner, who has also written monographs on Copley, Gilbert Stuart, and Winslow Homer, and an excellent *Short History of American Painting,* has not limited himself to art history. *The Traitor and the Spy* (1953), about Benedict Arnold and John André, seemed to one reviewer the most carefully researched and searching version of the story so far published; another critic, agreeing that this was "a sharply woven, colorful study, marked by assiduous research," thought it lacked "the deep penetration that could have made it a more permanent contribution." There was also a somewhat mixed reception for *Mohawk Baronet* (1959), a biography of Sir William Johnson, the frontiersman, general, and statesman who colonized the Mohawk Valley in New York.

In the course of his researches for all these books, Flexner told an interviewer, "I kept running into [George] Washington in all kinds of strange connections, and he never turned out to be the kind of person I'd read about. So I said 'One of these days, when I'm old and gray, I'll write a life of Washington.' Then Little Brown asked me to write a life of Washington, and I decided I was old and gray." The one-volume biography that Flexner had planned grew into four volumes which occupied him for twelve years. He said later that "people who write biographies of Lincoln have it easy. Lincoln had a public career of about twelve years, and John Wilkes Booth gave the books an easy end. Washington had a public career from the age of twenty until he died at sixty-seven." Flexner set out to reveal Washington's character through his responses to the endless challenges of his life, portraying him "in all his fallibility and also in all his greatness" as America's "indispensable man." He later observed that "there have been in all history few men who possessed unassailable power who used that power so gently and self-effacingly for what their best instincts told them was the welfare of their neighbors and all mankind."

George Washington: The Forge of Experience appeared in 1965, and dealt with Washington's early life, his education, and his military career up to the outbreak of the American Revolution. *George Washington in the American Revolution* followed in 1968, and *George Washington and the New Nation,* carrying the story up to the end of Washington's first Presidential term, in 1970. The last six years of the President's life are considered in *George Washington: Anguish and Farewell* (1972). A one-volume abridgement of the biography appeared in 1974 as *Washington: The Indispensable Man.*

Reviewers of the four volumes were almost unanimous in their admiration for Flexner's indefatigable research, his "intimacy" with a man who had few intimates, and the balance of his portrait, which avoids both the hero worship of nineteenth-century biography and modern cynicism. Bruce Bliven praised Flexner's "systematic, stylish, profound, and perfectly convincing" account, adding that his "scholarship and accuracy are a marvel, but instead of covering everything, like a giant grass cutter, he steers straight for the incidents that reveal the man." Arthur Cooper wrote that Flexner's "serviceable prose and meticulous detail combine to create a vivid and wholly human Washington. . . . Flexner does a better job than any previous historian in exposing the private George Washington concealed within the historical monument."

In 1973 Flexner received both the National Book Award for the fourth volume of his Washington biography, and a special Pulitzer Prize citation for the biography as a whole. His 1978 account of Alexander Hamilton's youth, emphasizing the formation of the statesman's character, won generally favorable reviews. In a New York *Times* interview Flexner offered a clue to his success as a "non-academic" historian: "I think a great many historians establish an ideal series of values and then criticize the people they are writing about on the basis of these values without realizing what *they* would do if they were there." An advantage of being a biographer, he says, "is that you can strain to understand someone bigger than you are, while a novelist can't spell out anyone bigger than himself."

James Flexner was married in 1950 to Beatrice Hudson, a singer, and has a daughter. He has written several television plays, and is a prolific contributor to magazines and newspapers, and a popular lecturer. He has served as a consultant for Colonial Williamsburg (1956-1957) and on the advisory committee for *The Papers of George Washington,* and is a trustee of the New York Public Library. An active member of P.E.N., he was president of its American center in 1954-1955 and honorary vice-president in 1963-1966. In 1975-1976 he was president of the Society of American Historians. Flexner received a grant from the Library of Congress in 1945 and a Guggenheim fellowship in 1953.

PRINCIPAL WORKS: Doctors on Horseback: Pioneers of American Medicine, 1937; America's Old Masters: First Artists of the New World, 1939; (with Simon Flexner) William Henry Welch and the Heroic Age of American Medicine, 1941; Steamboats Come True: American Inventors in Action, 1944 (republished as Inventors in Action, 1962); American Painting: First Flowers of Our Wilderness, 1947; A Short History of American Painting, 1950 (also published in paperback as The Pocket History of American Painting); John Singleton Copley, 1948; The Traitor and the Spy: Benedict Arnold and John André, 1953 (revised 1975); American Painting: The Light of Distant Skies (1760-1835), 1954; Gilbert Stuart, 1955; Mohawk Baronet: Sir William Johnson of New York, 1959; That Wilder Image: The Painting of America's Native School From Thomas Cole to Winslow Homer, 1962; George Washington: The Forge of Experience (1732-1775), 1965; The World of Winslow Homer (1836-1910), 1966; George Washington in the American Revolution (1775-1783), 1968; George Washington and the New Nation (1783-1793), 1970; Nineteenth Century American Painting, 1970; George Washington: Anguish and Farewell (1793-1799), 1972; Washington: The Indispensable Man, 1974; (with Linda Bantel Samter) The Face of Liberty, 1975; The Young Hamilton, 1978.

ABOUT: Contemporary Authors 1-4 1st revision, 1967; Who's Who in America, 1976-1977. *Periodicals*—New York Times April 15, 1973; May 8, 1973; New Yorker March 10, 1973; July 3, 1978; Partisan Review February 1949; Publishers Weekly June 1, 1946.

*FOLLAIN, JEAN (RENÉ) (August 29, 1903–March 9, 1971), French poet, critic, and memoirist, was born in the village of Canisy, in Normandy, the son of Albert Follain and the former Berthe Heussebrot. The family had generally produced either teachers or lawyers; his father was the former and Jean Follain became a lawyer. He attended the local Collège de Saint-Lô and received his legal education at the University of Caen. Follain worked as an advocate in the Paris courts from 1927 to 1951, and was a district judge at Charleville from 1951 until his retirement in 1963.

His earliest poems appeared in provincial magazines, but in the late 1920s he became associated with the group around the review *Sagesse,* which included such figures as Max Jacob and André Salmon. Though a difficult poet, Follain was in no sense a surrealist, and his connection with that movement was tenuous. His first collection, *La Main chaude* (The Warm Hand), appeared in 1933, and other volumes followed steadily every year or two, including *Chants terrestres* (Terrestrial Songs, 1937), *Usage du temps* (The Uses of Time, 1943, which included a selection from earlier volumes), *Les Choses données* (The Things Given, 1952), *Territoires* (Territories, 1953), *Objets* (Objects, 1955), and *Poèmes et Proses choisis* (Selected Poems and Prose, 1961).

Follain's style scarcely changed over all those years, though his mastery of it increased, and his perceptions deepened. His brief quiet poems return constantly to the countryside of his childhood, but not in ordinary nostalgia. "When I speak of the past," he said, "it is precisely to place it in the present, it is to give it back its life in the present, since the past has a contemporary life; it is to place it back in the present time, and in the general time, if you will, in absolute time."

Many of Follain's poems and prose poems focus on everyday utensils and objects—like Francis Ponge, he is a "poet of the object." Follain eschews rhetoric and even metaphor, believing that the function of poetry is "to name things, to make them exist in their very vibran-
*fo laN'

JEAN FOLLAIN

Serge Gavronsky has attempted a more specific account of the way in which Follain achieves his effects. "Each poem," Gavronsky says, "has a relatively simple architecture that affects the voice, the shape and the content. He has perfected a syntax that plays with unexpected breaks, forcing the doubling back of the lines, as a pivotal end-of-the-line word appears to qualify both what has preceded and what is about to come. This ambiguity, this muted violence which reflects the content, is often accomplished through a gender or a pronoun which allows him to move, imperceptibly, from one level to the next, imposing a high degree of concentration on the reader." Follain himself said that he strove for "a poetry of concentration" in which "there is a tightening of the text, a great value attached to the poem itself, a sort of verbal incantation rather well controlled but which must maintain itself as an incantation."

cy, if one can say that, in their fleetingness." As Serge Gavronsky has written: "He awakens the past to play a new role in the present, and lets the reader perceive through the craftsmanship of the poem itself, as if a veil had been lifted, the very essence of Time momentarily incorporated in the object." This can be seen even in translation in a poem like "The Man Who Stuffed Birds":

> The taxidermist sat
> before the pink throats
> wings green or mauve
> of his songbirds
> dreaming of his mistress
> with a body so different from
> but sometimes so close to
> that of the birds
> that it seemed to him
> strange. . . .
>
> (translated by
> Bernard Waldrop)

Patricia Terry has pointed out that here, as in all of Follain's poetry, "no magical patina of music or brilliance of imagery serve to break down the barriers of the rational. Everything is accomplished by a precision in the choice and placing of the simplest words. Metrical formality is replaced by subdued rhythms which construct, out of unpretentious phrases, statements which the reader, like the taxidermist, finds both convincing and strange. That strangeness is the real subject of the poem. . . . Follain is almost entirely absent from his own work. The mute surfaces of objects and events, detached from the flux and exhibited in his poems, are made to reveal themselves as signs of a larger order."

Follain, who was married in 1934 to Madeleine Denis, traveled widely after his retirement, visiting Japan (1958), Latin America (1960), and the United States (1966). He produced a study of Peru and a dictionary of slang, as well as several volumes of memoirs. One of the finest of these is the posthumous *Collège* (1974), which deals with his secondary studies during World War I at the Collège de Saint-Lô. It radiantly brings to life not only the self-effacing, thoughtful young pupil but also his classmates and teachers. It is a book written without strain, reflecting a tranquility that had been earned by a lifetime of much deep and uncluttered reflection and meditation. Like all of Follain's work, it "paints the invisible through the visible."

It was in fact Follain's memoirs that first brought him a wide reputation and readership, though his stature as a poet was increasingly recognized. He received a number of prizes for his work—the Mallarmé in 1939, the Blumenthal in 1941, the Capri in 1958, and the Grand Prix de Poésie de l'Académie Française in 1970. He was a Chevalier of the Légion d'Honneur.

PRINCIPAL WORKS IN ENGLISH TRANSLATION: Transparency of the World: Poetry of Jean Follain, translated by W.S. Merwin, 1969. *Poems in* Aspel, A. and Justice, D. (eds.) Contemporary French Poetry, 1965; Barnstone, W. (ed.) Modern European Poetry, 1966; Gavronsky, S. (ed.) Poems and Texts, 1969; Taylor S.W. and Lucie-Smith, E. (eds.) French Poetry Today, 1971.

ABOUT: Aspel, A. and Justice, D. (eds.) Contemporary French Poetry, 1965; Barnstone, W. (ed.) Modern European Poetry, 1966; Cardinal, R. (ed.) Sensibility and Creation, 1977; Dhôtel, A. Jean Follain, 1956 (in French); Gavronsky, S. (ed.) Poems and Texts, 1969; Jaccottet, P. L'Entretien des muses, 1968; Taylor, S.W. and Lucie-Smith, E. (eds.) French Poetry Today, 1971; Who's Who in Europe, 1964-1965.

*FORSSELL, LARS (HANS CARL ABRA-HAM) (January 14, 1928–), Swedish poet and dramatist, was born in Stockholm, the son of Dr. Arne Forssell and the former Lisa Falke. His father was a state archivist and Conservative member of parliament. Lars Forssell began his university education in the United States, at Augustana College, Illinois (B.A., 1948), and continued it at Uppsala, where he graduated in 1952. He was married in 1951 to Kerstin Hane.

Forssell's first book of verse, published when he was only twenty-one, was *Ryttaren* (The Rider, 1949), a work that like much Swedish poetry of the time was grimly disillusioned, full of literary allusions, and written in highly abstract and metaphorical language. It was warmly received by the critics, especially Erik Lindegren, who gave it a full-page review. Forssell (who published a translation of *Cantos I-XVII* in 1959), appears to have been influenced particularly by Pound and his theory of masks, and in his early verse adopts a number of personae, most often that of the clown or jester. His notion of the clown figure owes something to the character created by Charlie Chaplin, the subject of a monograph by Forssell published in 1953.

The clown is the central figure in *Narren* (The Fool, 1952). This collection, which in its tone was found reminiscent of Eliot's *Sweeney Agonistes,* includes the savagely funny harlequinade "Narren som tillhörde sina bjällror" (translated by Harry G. Carlson as "The Fool Attached to His Bells"). The Fool is desperately afraid of dying, but pretends to be dead to escape his creditors, who nevertheless strip him of his clothes, his dignity, and his bells: "The bells deceived me/ they were faithful." This touching and ridiculous antihero is the first in a long line of Forssell characters who are isolated from their fellows by a fear of life and of death, unable to give or receive love. Another such "disengaged man" (in Harry G. Carlson's phrase) is the bourgeois intellectual whose persona Forssell assumes in the verse collection *F.C. Tietjens* (1954). This elusive contemporary figure, uncommitted to anything except the search for his own identity, and treated with sarcasm and ridicule, is clearly modeled in part on the poet himself.

Forssell is a poet of extraordinary versatility, as he showed in *Telegram* (1957). This volume contains poems in the modernistic and esoteric manner of his first books, along with others in a great variety of styles and modes, including some that draw (but always with some kind of twist or reservation) on nursery rhymes and oth-

*fôsh el'

LARS FORSSELL

Swedish Information Service

er popular forms. Forssell writes a beautiful and romantic poem about freedom, then depreciates it by calling it "Lettre sentimentale." On the other hand, he can mock at one of his own obsessional fears in the prose sketch "A. A. Milne in Memoriam," where Christopher Robin tries in vain to explain the nature of death to the immortal Winnie-the-Pooh.

In *En kärleksdikt* (A Love Poem, 1960), Forssell speaks for the first time without disguise in lyrics that are simple and deeply felt; sensual, but always tender. The collection *Röster* (Voices, 1964), however, is anything but simple. Its most important section is a suite of poems about the dancer Nijinsky, his progress into madness, and his "marriage with God": "This wave of tenderness/ from nothingness to nothing."

Beginning with *Ändå* (Nevertheless, 1968), Forssell's poetry has been mainly concentrated on political problems, and particularly the relationship between rich and poor. In the poem "Vita di Gesualdo" he describes the composer of madrigals whose delicate music contrasts with his personal cruelty, and whose wealth is an affront to the poverty around him: "He was sixteenth-century Europe/ And Europe with her cruel daughter/ the Countess d'Amerigo/ he still is." *Oktoberdikter* (October Poems, 1971) is dominated by a group of poems about Lenin, "Uljanov." In simple but striking language Forssell portrays Lenin as the matter-of-fact revolutionary who regrets the lives lost in the revolution but sees no alternative: "We have no need of cheerful prophecies/ We have no need of cataclysmic visions/ We need bread."

Försök (Attempts, 1972) was written almost entirely in a single night as a reaction to renewed American bombing in Vietnam. Forssell sees individuals as being powerless to influence events, like fish trapped in nets, but he has himself pointed out that the title can be read in Swedish as an imperative: Try! This faintly optimistic line of thought is continued in *Det möjliga* (The Possible, 1974). Love may seem impossible, political freedom may seem impossible, but Forssell takes as a symbol of hope the great trees he has seen in Zimbabwe (Rhodesia) and the patient Africans sitting under them: "All love awaits its time/ and outwaits even impossibility/ under the mighty tree."

Forssell is one of the most admired of contemporary Swedish poets, whose versatility is both his greatest strength and his most serious handicap, leading him at times to write too facilely and glibly. His reputation as a dramatist has grown more slowly. His plays, according to a critic in the *Times Literary Supplement,* "have by and large defied categorization, hovering between the ponderously lyrical and the topical and satirical, and the response of the public and the critics has been slow and bewildered. . . . It has seemed as if the whimsical and theatrical antics of Mr. Forssell's stage creations have been alien to the mainstream of the Swedish theatre—too European, too 'stagey' in their reliance on traditions of vaudeville and music-hall artistry."

Kröningen (1956, translated by Harry G. Carlson as *Coronation*) is a retelling of the story of Alcestis and Admetus, with Admetus presented as a whining antihero incapable of comprehending his wife's sacrifice of her life for his. In the short one-act play *Charlie McDeath* (1961, translated by Carlson under the same title), the "disengaged man" is a ventriloquist, so afraid of real life that he exchanges roles with his dummy. This play was presented as a curtain-raiser to *Mary Lou* in a program which opened in 1962 at the Stockholm Municipal Theatre, bringing Forssell his first resounding theatrical success, and critical praise as "a renovator in Swedish drama." *Mary Lou* itself, set in a Cologne radio station near the end of World War II, is about "Axis Sally" from Illinois, "a fascinating study of loneliness, neurosis, and betrayal" that benefited from a fine performance by Ingrid Thulin in the title role.

Söndagspromenaden (1963, translated by Carlson as *The Sunday Promenade*) is about a flamboyant grocer in a small Swedish town who sets off into a make-believe world that places no burdens on his emotional resources. Every Sunday morning he leads his family and friends on a promenade around his dining room table, paying imaginary visits to romantic places, until his escapist fantasies collapse under the weight of real life (and death). Carlson thought the play contained too many ideas for any of them to be satisfactorily worked out, but praised it nevertheless for its "shining, stinging imagery, wonderful humor . . . and bold, exciting theatricality."

Forssell is also the author of two historical plays, *Galenpannan* (1964, translated by Carlson as *The Madcap*), a somewhat Brechtian portrait of King Gustav IV in exile, and *Christina Alexandra* (1968), a study of the Swedish queen in the form of a dream play. He has also translated a number of foreign plays, and in *Borgaren och Marx* (The Bourgeois and Marx, 1970) has adapted Molière's *Le bourgeois gentilhomme* into an ironic entertainment in which the ambition of the middle-class hero is to be not a nobleman but lefter than the Left. According to Carlson, Forssell believes that "the day is not far off when everyone with even a grain of conscience . . . will be compelled to be a traitor against all ideologies." He has "tried to think of the betrayer as a new kind of hero, but the figure resists such treatment." All the same, Carlson believes, Forssell has dramatized with increasing effectiveness "the painful posture of the disengaged man, who is faced with the knowledge that although commitment to faith and love may be intellectually absurd, they are vital to his emotional well-being."

One of Forssell's most notable successes as a dramatist came in 1970, when his play *Show* (otherwise known as *Geten*—The Goat) was produced by Ingmar Bergman. It is a haunting tragicomedy about an entertainer who is clearly modeled on the American satirist Lenny Bruce, though the character also possesses qualities reminiscent of earlier Forssell antiheroes—the clown, Admetus, Chaplin, and Nijinsky. A reviewer in the *Times Literary Supplement* wrote that "the constant harassment and persecution of the itinerant artist is well depicted in a barely contained atmosphere of frenzied hysteria. . . . What is less convincing is the choice of Lenny Bruce as a persona for Mr. Forssell's special interests, his views on the artist as a tragic embodiment of the sufferings of mankind. For the Goat is also the scapegoat: caught between the forces of society he cannot and will not understand and his 'kids', the young radical followers who ultimately discard him as obsolete."

Forssell has also written film scripts, cabaret entertainments, and song lyrics, and has been active as a journalist and essayist. He was elected a member of the Swedish Academy in 1971.

PRINCIPAL WORKS IN ENGLISH TRANSLATION: *Plays*—Five Plays (contains The Sunday Promenade, Mumbly Bungler, The Fool Attached to His Bells, Charlie McDeath, The Coronation), 1964; The Madcap *in* Modern Nordic Plays (Sweden), 1973; Charlie McDeath *in* Literary Review Winter 1965-1966. *Poetry*—Nijinsky *in* For W.H. Auden, 1972; *poems in* Allwood, M.S. (ed.) Twentieth Century Scandinavian Poetry, 1950; Fleisher, F. (ed.) Eight Swedish Poets, 1963.

ABOUT: Crowell's Handbook of Contemporary Drama, 1971; Gassner, J. and Quinn, E. (eds.) The Reader's Encyclopedia of World Drama, 1969; Lagercrantz, O. Svenska lyriker, 1961; Penguin Companion to Literature 2, 1969; Printz-Påhlson, G. Solen i spegeln, 1958. *Periodicals*—Scandinavian Studies February 1965; Times Literary Supplement September 10, 1971.

Jerry Bauer

MICHEL FOUCAULT

*FOUCAULT, MICHEL (October 15, 1926–), French philosopher, psychologist, and cultural historian, was born in Poitiers, the son of a doctor, Paul Foucault, and the former Anne Malapert. He became one of that intellectual elite admitted to the École Normale Supérieure in Paris, studying philosophy there and later at the Sorbonne. Foucault received his *licence* in philosophy in 1948 and in psychology in 1950; a diploma in psychopathology followed in 1952. His doctoral thesis was on the novelist Raymond Roussel, and this was published in book form in 1963. Beginning in 1960, Foucault taught philosophy and French literature at the universities of Lille, Uppsala, Warsaw, Hamburg, Clermont-Ferrand, São Paulo, and Tunis. In 1968 he became a professor in the University of Paris at Vincennes, and in 1970 he was appointed to the chair of the history of systems of thought at the Collège de France.

Foucault gained his reputation as a cultural historian of great ability and originality with his first book. This appeared in 1961 in two editions, one called *Folie et déraison: Histoire de la folie à l'âge classique,* the other called simply *Histoire de la folie à l'âge classique.* (The latter title was also applied to an abridged edition published in 1964). The book, which won the Medal of the Centre de le Recherche Scientifique on its publication in 1961, has been translated by Richard Howard as *Madness and Civilization: A History of Insanity in the Age of Reason.* Foucault's style —elegant, arrogant, scintillatingly brilliant—is flamboyantly difficult. Edgar Z. Friedenberg commented on the "glistening but astonishingly opaque intellectual texture which is fashionable in French philosophical discourse," while praising the brilliance and profundity of the book.

In recent years the question of madness and

*fōo kō'

how to define it has become the center of an intense debate. Foucault makes a major contribution to this by documenting (mostly from original sources) the strikingly different ideas about insanity peculiar to medieval times, the Renaissance, and the modern period. In the Middle Ages insanity was accepted as a part of everyday life, and fools and madmen walked the streets without restraint. The Renaissance loaded them aboard "Ships of Fools," which crisscrossed the seas and canals of Europe so that towns thus purged of insanity might enjoy a comic sideshow when foreign lunatics docked at their harbors. It was only in the eighteenth century, when derangement began to be considered a threat, that asylums were built and walls erected between those described as insane and the rest of humanity. To show how each age viewed insanity, Foucault argues, is also to show how its culture defined itself—where it placed its limits, what sort of behavior was socially tolerable. Language is critically important here, since the ability or failure to conduct what we consider to be rational discourse is one of the principal tests we apply in differentiating between those who are like ourselves, and therefore acceptable, and those who are alien and "other."

The insane asylum originated in the same social and intellectual upheavals which produced the modern hospital, and it is the rise of clinical medicine—and the implications of that rise— which Foucault discusses in *Naissance de la clinique: une archéologie du regard médical* (1963, translated by A.M. Sheridan Smith as *The Birth of the Clinic: An Archaeology of Medical Perception*). Foucault describes this book, in terms which could be applied to his whole *oeuvre,* as "an attempt to apply a method to the confused, understructured and ill-structured domain of the history of ideas."

And here again Foucault is seeking to identify "a mutation in discourse"—one which accompanied the transformation of the old "medicine of symptoms" into an empirical "medicine of organs," where what mattered was accurate observation and description. The structural change was "indicated—but not, of course, exhausted—by the minute but decisive change whereby the question: 'What is the matter with you,' with which the eighteenth century dialogue between doctor and patient began (a dialogue possessing its own grammar and style), was replaced by that other question: 'Where does it hurt?,' in which we recognize the operation of the clinic and the principle of its entire discourse."

In recent years we have begun to move from this purely somatic medicine toward another mutation in discourse with the increasing realization that illness may be psychosomatic. So, Foucault argues, medicine has not only a methodological but also an ontological importance in the constitution of the so-called human sciences: for a time man believed he could put himself on a slab and view himself as an object, while still retaining all the privileges of a sovereign consciousness. Like the Structuralists, Foucault is fundamentally concerned with linguistics, with how changes in medicine illustrate the way in which "the whole relationship of signifier to signified at the level of experience is redistributed." Theodore Zeldin, who wrote that "there is so much in this book ... that it is impossible to do more than hint at its interest," went on: "Foucault's importance is that he has boldly attempted to create a new method of historical analysis and a new framework for the study of the human sciences as a whole."

This new method of historical analysis is applied to other subjects in *Les mots et les choses* (1966, translated as *The Order of Things: An Archaeology of the Human Sciences*). This does for biology, language, and money what the earlier books did for insanity and disease, showing how differently each age conceives them. Biology, linguistics, and economics developed only recently out of the less "scientific" earlier studies of natural history, grammar, and wealth. Hunting below the surface of human activity for patterns and currents unperceived at the time, Foucault seeks the *"épistème"* which made possible these great revolutions in the human sciences. An *épistème* Foucault defines as "an epistemological space specific to a particular period." Frank Kermode suggests that the term refers to the *"unconscious* of knowledge, the network of resemblances and discontinuities that constitutes a systematic constraint on what, at a given period, may be said to be the case."

In his preface, Foucault describes the book's germination; he read a story by Jorge Luis Borges that refers to a "certain Chinese encyclopaedia" in which "animals are divided into: (a) belonging to the Emperor, (b) embalmed, (c) tame, (d) sucking pigs, (e) sirens, (f) fabulous, (g) stray dogs, (h) included in the present classification, (i) frenzied, (j) innumerable, (k) drawn with a very fine camelhair brush, (l) et cetera, (m) having just broken the water pitcher, (n) that from a long way off look like flies." Foucault's laughter, he writes, "shattered all the familiar landmarks of my thought—*our* thought. . . . In the wonderment of this taxonomy, the thing we apprehend in one great leap, the thing that, by means of the fable, is demonstrated as the exotic charm of another system of thought, is the limitation of our own." And so he was led into the speculations about our systems of ordering, and the nature of changes in them, that make up this book.

In analyzing these changes, Foucault demonstrates his belief that our own current intellectual life and systems of scientific thought are built on assumptions profoundly taken for granted, and normally not exposed to conscious inspection, yet likely in time to be discarded. And he shows that this is just what has happened to the similar unexamined assumptions on which were based the "knowledge" of earlier periods of Western thought. For example, "words and things" were related in Renaissance thought by supposing a universal system of correspondence (macrocosm and microcosm, earth and sky, planets and faces). Particular sympathies and similarities within this overall system were supposed to be indicated by signs or signatures of affinity, so that aconite was used to treat eye diseases because the seed of the plant resembles an eyelid. Words themselves, Foucault suggests, were regarded as an extension of this natural language, and "glittered in the universal resemblance of things."

With the seventeenth-century scientific revolution, this system of correspondence was swept away and replaced by a different method of thought which relied on measurement and the relating of one thing to another as steps in an orderly system. This dramatic discontinuity Foucault sees as laying down a new stratum in the archaeology of science, illustrating "the fact that within the space of a few years a culture sometimes ceases to think as it had been thinking up till then and begins to think other things in a new way."

Maurice Cranston observed in his review that "Foucault is likely to be remembered less for his positive philosophical theories than for his critical ideas. Wherever his books have been published they have helped to undermine confidence in established forms of psychology and the other social sciences." Jean Piaget, who in his *Structuralism* discusses *Les mots et les choses* at some length, argues that Foucault is not positive enough: "Skeptical epistemologies have a real function, that of raising new problems by undermining easy solutions. What we would want of Foucault is, accordingly, that he prepare the way for a second Kant to reawaken us, along with himself, from dogmatic slumbers. In particular, we would expect the author of a work with such revolutionary intentions to offer a constructive critique of the human sciences, an intelligible account of the new-fangled notion of *épistème,* and an argument that would justify his restrictive conception of structuralism. But we are disappointed on all three counts. Beneath the cleverness there are only bare affirmations and omissions and it is up to the reader to make connections and to construct arguments as best he can." (It should be said that Foucault emphatically denies that he is a structuralist: "In France certain half-witted 'commentators' persist in labelling me a 'structuralist.' I have been unable to get it into their tiny minds that I have used none of the methods, concepts, or key terms that characterize structural analysis.") Most critics—even those who disagreed with the book—recognized that it was a major work of exploratory thought and analysis, conceptually very rich and challenging. It has been hailed as one of the most important French contributions to philosophy since Sartre's early work.

Foucault's next book, *L'Archéologie du savoir* (1969, translated by A.M. Sheridan Smith as *The Archaeology of Knowledge*), discusses and seeks to justify the "archaeological" method of interpretation he had used in his earlier books. Unfortunately new terminology proliferates in a text that is highly abstract and involuted, and most critics found it very difficult to understand. Peter Caws remarked that "as the subject matter of Foucault's writing has become more diffuse its style has become more intricate, not to say contorted. Never a man to use one word where five will do . . . Foucault has, confronted with the genuinely difficult task he has set himself . . . produced an extravagantly and self-indulgently rhetorical text full of asides on his own development, other people's reactions to his work, and so on." An appendix to the American edition of this book contains "The Discourse on Language," a translation of Foucault's important inaugural lecture as professor at the Collège de France.

Moi, Pierre Rivière, ayant égorgé ma mère, ma soeur et mon frère (1973) was translated by Frank Jellinek as *I, Pierre Rivière, Having Slaughtered My Mother, My Sister, and My Brother . . . : A Case of Parricide in the 19th Century.* Here Foucault returns to the study of madness through the story of a brutal crime in a small French village. The first part of the book contains the actual documents of the case in the words of the participants—judges, witnesses, doctors, lawyers. At the center of the story is the haunting and amazingly articulate memoir of the killer himself, a twenty-year-old Norman peasant who in 1835 killed his mother, sister, and little brother with a pruning hook. Having thus "delivered [his] father from all his tribulations," he then took refuge in the forest, living on plants and roots for a month before giving himself up. The final part of the book reprints a number of papers given at Foucault's Collège de France seminar on the case.

Torn between implacably hostile and perpetually warring parents, Pierre Rivière had developed a classical schizoid personality, and a crucial factor in the case was the question of his sanity, about which contemporary medical opinion was sharply divided. Before his fate could be decided he had to be described and defined, but all the experts involved in the case had their own separate terminologies and terms of reference, creating "a battle among discourses and through discourses." When the balance was finally struck, the murderer was neither executed nor treated, but was consigned to an ordinary prison, where a few years later he hanged himself. Dr. Thomas Szasz has described the book as "a spell-binding account—not only of the murder of a family by a 'madman,' but also of the murder of free will and responsibility by the mad-doctors. A glimpse into the birth of the psychiatrization of law, the medicalization of crime, and the therapeutization of justice."

Surveiller et punir: Naissance de la prison (1975, translated by Alan Sheridan as *Discipline and Punish: The Birth of the Prison*) focuses on the French penal system from the mid-eighteenth to the mid-nineteenth centuries, showing how physical assaults on the criminal—torture, mutilation, and execution—gave way to imprisonment, surveillance, and suspension of rights. Foucault writes that the apparently more humane penal system created at this time inaugurated the modern "scientific-judiciary complex where the power to punish props itself up, receives its justifications and its rules, extends its efficacity and conceals its exorbitant singularity"

—he argues, in other words, that the modern penal system is a tool of class domination, separating the criminal from the body of the working class so as to reduce proletarian solidarity and protest. Many reviewers recognized the book's importance without entirely accepting its thesis. David J. Rothman called it "the most accessible of Foucault's writings, the most straightforward in prose and argument, the most cultural in orientation," and Bruce Jackson wrote that "one finishes ... [this work] burdened with new insight and old despair: the problems are as serious as one thought, but the reasons far more complex, the solutions far more distant." A collection of essays by Foucault and interviews with him has been published as *Language, Counter-Memory, Practice.*

Foucault plans a series of six volumes on the history of sexuality and the psychiatric discovery of it. The first volume appeared in 1976 as *Histoire de la sexualité, Volume 1: la volonté de savoir* (translated by Robert Hurley as *The History of Sexuality, Volume 1: An Introduction*). Here Foucault relates how the growth of Puritanism and the Counter-Reformation abolished the natural attitude towards sex that had prevailed in medieval Europe, bringing about the prohibition of sexual expression all over the Western world. The reason for this denial of sexuality is usually given as the rise of the self-denying, energy-conserving, disciplined European bourgeoisie. However, in this "tough and exasperating little book" Foucault approaches these events in a different way, through an account of the development of an inquisitorial attitude towards sexual matters on the part of those in power. This begins with the detailed questions laid down for the confessor to ask of the penitent in the seventeenth-century French church, continues through the attitudes of parents, nurses, and schoolmasters during the eighteenth and nineteenth centuries, and does not exclude the clinical rigor of the psychoanalytic interview. Far from bringing genuine liberation, Foucault maintains, Freud and his successors have substituted a science of sex for the art of love.

Despite frequent criticisms of the obscurity of Foucault's style, critics have almost unanimously agreed with Professor Christopher Lasch "that Foucault's work is indispensable for cultural historians, amply rewarding the effort required to understand it." He has in the late 1960s and the 1970s achieved the sort of dominant place in French thought once held by Sartre. Foucault writes frequently for French newspapers and reviews, is an editor of *Critique,* and since 1973 has been director of the monthly review *Zone des tempêtes.*

PRINCIPAL WORKS IN ENGLISH TRANSLATION: Madness and Civilization: A History of Insanity in the Age of Reason, 1965; The Birth of the Clinic: An Archaeology of Medical Perception, 1973; The Order of Things: An Archaeology of the Human Sciences, 1970; The Archaeology of Knowledge, 1972; Discipline and Punish: The Birth of the Prison, 1977; Language, Counter-Memory, Practice: Selected Essays and Interviews, 1977; The History of Sexuality, Volume 1: An Introduction, 1978. *As Editor*—I, Pierre Rivière, Having Slaughtered My Mother, My Sister, and My Brother ... : A Case of Parricide in the Nineteenth Century, 1975.

ABOUT: Elders, F. (ed.) Reflexive Water, 1974; Piaget, J. Structuralism, 1971; Simon, J.K. (ed.) Modern French Criticism, 1972; Who's Who in France, 1977-1978. *Periodicals* —Atlas September 1966; Book World February 14, 1971; Choice March 1974; Christian Century June 16, 1965; Christian Science Monitor March 15, 1978; Commentary October 1965; Encounter June 1968, December 1976; History and Theory 12 1973; 13 1974; Horizon Autumn 1969; Modern Language Notes January 1963; Nation July 5, 1965; July 5, 1971; January 26, 1974; March 4, 1978; New Republic March 27, 1971; November 10, 1973; January 26, 1974; New Society June 16, 1977; Newsweek January 25, 1971; New Statesman June 4, 1971; December 7, 1973; New York Review of Books August 12, 1971; May 17, 1973; January 26, 1978; New York Times Book Review August 2, 1965; February 28, 1971; October 22, 1972; February 24, 1974; May 18, 1975; February 19, 1978; March 26, 1978; Partisan Review 4 1975, 3 1976; Times Literary Supplement October 6, 1961; July 2, 1970; June 9, 1972; February 1, 1974; Yale French Studies 49 1973; Yale Review December 1972, March 1974.

FRANCIS, DICK (October 31, 1920–), Welsh thriller writer, memoirist, and journalist, was born in Tenby, Pembrokeshire, in South Wales, and was famous as a jockey long before he became a writer. Both of his parents came from Pembrokeshire. His father, George Francis, was a notable jockey, show jumper, and rider to hounds who during Dick Francis's childhood was manager of W. J. Smith's hunting stables at Holyport, near Maidenhead in Berkshire. His mother, the former Molly Thomas, was the daughter of a farmer who was also a passionate huntsman. Dick Francis learned to ride as naturally (and almost as soon) as he learned to walk. He rode in his first hunt when he was seven, and was soon winning prizes as a show jumper. He never had any other ambition than to become a jockey and, regarding anything that kept him away from horses as a waste of time, was a reluctant pupil at Maidenhead County Boys' School.

In 1938, Francis's parents established their own stables near Wokingham, in Surrey, and the boy worked there until 1940, when he joined the Royal Air Force. After two or three miserable years as an airframe fitter, his monthly request for transfer to flying duties wore down official resistance. He was trained as a pilot, flew both fighters and bombers on noncombat duties, and

FRANCIS

DICK FRANCIS

left the RAF in 1946 with the rank of Flying Officer.

It was only then, when he was twenty-five, that Francis was able to fulfill his childhood ambition to become a jockey. Too tall for flat-racing, he began his career as an amateur steeplechase jockey (and secretary) to George Owen, a former jockey who had retired to farm and train horses in Cheshire. Immensely successful as an amateur, Francis became a professional National Hunt jockey in 1948, and for ten years was one of the best and best-liked of British riders. He was Champion Jockey in 1953-1954, when he won seventy-six races, but never achieved his other great ambition, which was to win the Grand National. He very nearly did so in 1956 on the Queen Mother's horse Devon Loch but, as every British racing enthusiast knows, the horse unaccountably fell, fifty yards from the winning post.

This profound disappointment contributed to Francis's decision to leave racing before his age and his many injuries began to affect his performance. For ten years he had broken one or two bones in every racing season; his collarbone had been broken twelve times, and his left shoulder was so badly dislocated that it slipped out of its socket in certain positions. Francis "hung up his boots" in February 1957. He was immediately offered three jobs, and accepted all of them, becoming an official judge (an extraordinary honor for an ex–professional jockey), a race commentator, and a racing journalist. This last activity developed out of a suggestion from the London *Sunday Express* that the former Champion Jockey should put his name to a few ghost-written articles about his profession; Francis asked if he could try writing them himself, his articles were accepted, and he went on to serve for sixteen years as the *Sunday Express*'s racing correspondent.

"I never really decided to be a writer," Francis says. "I just sort of drifted into it." His first book was his autobiography, *The Sport of Queens,* which was published with considerable success in 1957. Francis now thinks it is a "rather elementary" work, but most reviewers share the opinion of A. J. Hubin, who wrote: "The story of Dick Francis is here, as alive as those blowing stallions he rode to victory." If his first book had not been a success, Francis would never have written another. As it was, finding that "jockeys can earn more than journalists," and seeking ways to enlarge his income, he set to work on a thriller. He says that "whatever I now know about writing I learnt from the discipline of working for a newspaper. . . . Writing a novel proved to be the hardest, most self-analysing task I had ever attempted, far worse than an autobiography: and its rewards were greater than I expected."

Dead Cert was published in January 1962 and sold well from the start, though it was not much reviewed. Dick Francis had an even greater success with his second novel, *Nerve* (1964), in which Rob Finn, a young steeplechase jockey, finds himself involved in a mysterious tragedy at the Dunstable races. Anthony Boucher wrote that "mysteries-by-the-famous normally reveal a great amount of information on the celebrity's special field and a minimal amount of aptitude for creating a novel. But a notable exception to this rule is Dick Francis. . . . [who] here tackles the difficult form of the suspense novel without a murder, and indeed without an overt crime. . . . The author constructs his suspense so skillfully, builds his characters so firmly and, in short, writes so well that one's reaction is not, 'How can a great jockey write such a good novel?' but rather, 'How can such an excellent novelist know so much about steeplechasing?' Whatever his past fame, Dick Francis is now well on his way to celebrity status purely as an unusually intelligent suspense novelist."

For Kicks (1965) is an ingenious story about an almost undetectable method of fixing races, and the young Australian breeder who poses as a stable lad to unmask the fixer. It brought Francis the Silver Dagger Award of the Crime Writers' Association, and seemed to one reviewer a winner "as a puzzle, as a thriller, as a novel of milieu, and as an essay in character . . . with a grand final surprise lurking after the plot seems to be concluded." There were slightly cooler reviews for *Odds Against* (1965), which seemed to one critic "at times long-winded and stiff," but *Flying Finish* (1966), about a repressed young peer who wins self-respect by battling against skulduggery in the racehorse transport business, was called "a beautifully tense thriller, painfully suspenseful and original as well." Henry Grey's psychological difficulties in this novel are characteristic—as Edmund Crispin says, each of Francis's narrator-heroes "is near sunk under some disastrous emotional handicap (crippled or penniless or divorced, or supporting an ailing wife, or practising journalism) before the villains start mercilessly homing in on him."

Franciscan thrillers have continued to appear at the rate of one a year, and by and large have continued to delight both fans and critics. *Blood Sport* (1967) was a well-observed first try at a novel with an American setting, and *Forfeit* (1968), whose hero is a sportswriter with a paralyzed wife, brought Francis the Edgar Allan Poe Award of the Mystery Writers of America. The combination of flying and racing that Francis explored in *Flying Finish* is used again with equal success in *Rat Race* (1970), of which one reviewer wrote: "It becomes repetitious to call each new Dick Francis mystery his best yet, but what are you going to do when the man just insists on getting better and better with each book?" In *Smokescreen* (1972) an English stuntman–movie star goes to South Africa to find out why a dying friend's horses don't win their races, and winds up very nearly dead himself, while *Slayride* (1973) has a Norwegian setting. *In the Frame* (1976) was something of a departure, featuring a hero whose only connection with horses is that he paints them for a living. A murder close to home takes him off to Australia in pursuit of a ring dealing in stolen art works and the result was found "as supremely competent as any of [Francis's] books—well-written, lively, fast and exciting."

Dick Francis was married in 1947 to Mary Brenchley, who helped him with his grammar and punctuation when he was a novice writer, and still helps him with his plots. Francis and his wife like to visit the places in which he sets his books and, accompanying him in a horse transport plane while he was researching *Flying Finish,* she fell in love with flying. She has since qualified as a pilot, has written a *Beginner's Guide to Flying,* and occasionally chauffeurs Francis (who never bothered to get a civilian licence) in the plane they own. They live at "Penny Chase," the house they built in Berkshire from Francis's earnings as a jockey, and have two grown sons, one of whom has followed in his father's stirrups as a steeplechase jockey and trainer. The author is a well-built man of average height who, with his much-broken nose, crooked teeth, and "rawhide" cheeks looks like "a middleweight fighter who quit the ring comfortably in time and has stayed trim by habit." Francis still rides for exercise at a friend's racing stables, and also enjoys boating and tennis.

James Fox has suggested that "the real fascination to be picked from the Francis thrillers is the way they put over, sometimes unconsciously, the closed-in, hierarchical world of racing. Conservative to his boots ... Dick Francis writes in homage to this military attitude to rank and position that you find on the turf." *The New Yorker,* by contrast, finds the Francis books "very gallant stories," and Edmund Crispin attributed their success to their author's "natural-born skill in yarn-spinning ... his plain, lucid, strong prose style," and "his ingenuity in finding out more crimes to do with horses than the entire real-life criminal fraternity could dream up in a hundred years." A reviewer of *Slayride* likewise commended "the always compulsive storytelling and inventive plotting, the good English, and the gentle but stalwart morality" which "make Mr. Francis most people's present first choice as crime writer."

PRINCIPAL WORKS: *Autobiography*—The Sport of Queens, 1957. *Fiction*—Dead Cert, 1962; Nerve, 1964; For Kicks, 1965; Odds Against, 1965; Flying Finish, 1966; Blood Sport, 1967; Forfeit, 1968; Enquiry, 1969; Three to Show (containing Dead Cert, Nerve, Odds Against), 1969; Rat Race, 1970; Bonecrack, 1971; Smokescreen, 1972; Slayride, 1973; Knockdown, 1974; High Stakes, 1975; Across the Board (containing Flying Finish, Blood Sport, Enquiry), 1975; In the Frame, 1976; Risk, 1978.

ABOUT: Contemporary Authors 5-8 1st revision, 1969; Francis, D. The Sport of Queens, 1957; Who's Who, 1978. *Periodicals*—Atlantic March 1969; Book World February 1, 1968; April 30, 1972; Christian Science Monitor July 17, 1969; Guardian July 28, 1973; Harper's July 1964; Life June 6, 1969; National Review August 24, 1971; New Republic July 26, 1976; New Statesman February 28, 1964; New York Times Book Review April 5, 1964; March 21, 1965; April 3, 1966; June 18, 1967; March 16, 1968; March 16, 1969; July 26, 1970; March 14, 1971; May 21, 1972; February 25, 1973; February 17, 1974; July 13, 1975; June 13, 1976; New Yorker March 15, 1969; Publishers Weekly January 8, 1968; Saturday Review August 1, 1970; Sports Illustrated March 25, 1968; Time May 22, 1972; March 5, 1973; Times Literary Supplement December 8, 1966; December 31, 1971; January 18, 1974; October 31, 1975.

FRASER, LADY ANTONIA (August 27, 1932–), English biographer, historian, novelist, and children's writer, was born in London into a distinguished Catholic-Socialist family. Her father is Francis Aungier Pakenham, who became the seventh Earl of Longford in 1961; he began his career as a historian and subsequently distinguished himself as a politician who served in Labour governments both before and after

David Montgomery, Sunday Times Magazine

LADY ANTONIA FRASER

inheriting his peerage, as a social reformer, and as an ardent campaigner against pornography. Lady Antonia's mother, the Countess of Longford, is the former Elizabeth Harman; she is famous for her biographies of Wellington and of Queen Victoria.

The oldest of eight children, Lady Antonia grew up in a house which was "knee-deep in books and the discussion that revolved around them." Her brother Thomas and her sisters Rachel and Judith have all published books. She spent her early childhood in Oxford, where her father was then teaching, and attended the Dragon School there. At the age of eight she chanced upon a biography of Mary, Queen of Scots, in the Oxford Public Library and was immediately and permanently fascinated, reading everything she could find about Mary and playing out scenes from her tragic life with her younger siblings in supporting roles. Her interest in history, thus aroused, was encouraged during her years at St. Mary's Convent, Ascot. From there she went on to Lady Margaret Hall, Oxford University, receiving her degree is history in 1953.

For three years after leaving Oxford Lady Antonia worked as an editor in the London publishing house of Weidenfeld and Nicolson, and during this period wrote two children's books for the Heirloom Library—retellings of the legends of King Arthur and of Robin Hood. Reissued fifteen years later, they had a mixed reception, some reviewers finding them admirably vigorous and colorful, others calling them melodramatic, "with the swashbuckling eighteenth-century flavor of earlier historical films and romantic novelettes."

In 1956 Lady Antonia put aside her literary career and her family's political convictions to marry the Conservative politician Hugh Fraser, a wealthy Scot who has served as Secretary of State for Air. Rich, witty, and stunningly beautiful, Lady Antonia was soon established as one of London's most brilliant and fashionable hostesses, a setter of fashion and darling of the society columns. The fact that she owned a hundred white dresses (a predilection she shares with Mary Stuart) was reported as breathlessly as the details of her journey by mule through Ethiopia. She was a contributing editor of the British *Vogue* and herself became, as she reflected some years later, "a press creation—the result of a lot of friends who are journalists, a London telephone number, an obliging nature and too little sense that these things can eventually snowball."

Lady Antonia's life was never entirely frivolous, however. She joined her husband in election campaigns, bore him six children, and became increasingly involved in their upbringing. One result of this was a little book about dolls, published in 1963. It whetted her appetite for historical research and led to her *History of Toys* (1966), an ambitious and lavishly illustrated study in which she examines the aesthetic, commercial, psychological, and sociological aspects of the subject, discussing examples from ancient Egypt to the present, but giving most emphasis to the toys of eighteenth- and nineteenth-century England. A reviewer in *Library Journal* said that "the text continually and brilliantly links past and present, drawing on art, verse and memoirs to make a point." Naomi Bliven was equally impressed, and wrote that, though "a history of toys must be a summary," Antonia Fraser "does not write hurriedly. She describes, she reports, she chats. Without giving the reader the irritating feeling of being instructed, she imparts an enormous amount of information."

Sometime in the mid-1960s, Elizabeth Longford let it be known that she was considering a biography of Mary, Queen of Scots; with her own mother threatening to preempt the subject dearest to her heart, Lady Antonia was spurred into action and promptly secured a contract from Weidenfeld and Nicolson. Her family, she says, were amused—"they thought I was going to write a trashy book." Determined then to "prove I was more than just a pretty brain," she plunged "into as many published and unpublished sources as I could discover, taking as my starting-point Mary's own letters and the calendars of state papers." After two years of research in English, French, and Scottish archives and libraries—an investigation for which she first had to teach herself to read sixteenth-century Scots—she published her six-hundred page biography in 1969.

Mary, Queen of Scots was warmly and universally praised as an immensely readable rehabilitation of a figure much obscured by prejudice, inaccuracy, and the "cobwebs of fantasy." *Time*'s reviewer wrote that "her Mary emerges neither as a Jezebel nor as a saint, but as a high-spirited woman who was brave, rather romantic, and not very bright. ... The narration—grave, fluent, never intrusive—lets the details speak for themselves." J. P. Kenyon agreed that "Lady Antonia avoids the temptation to romanticize an inherently romantic and tragic story, and her tense, muscular narrative generates a flow which carries the reader on unwearying to the end. It is as definitive a life as we shall get." Jean Stafford thought that Lady Antonia had "so lucid a manner of presenting history that she succeeds in almost completely clarifying the muddied maelstrom in which Europe and the British Isles were thrashing," but on this point C. V. Wedgwood was less impressed, finding the treatment of the period's political, economic, and religious upheavals "enough to make the sequence comprehensible but never deep enough to explain the significance of the forces with which Mary had to contend." But, she added, "it seems churlish to complain that something is missing in a book which is so full of interesting detail and so rich in human interest." It became an international best-seller and brought its author the James Tait Black Memorial Prize for biography.

Thus encouraged, Lady Antonia next embarked on an even more ambitious task—a "humanizing" biography of Oliver Cromwell. The research, which included visits to battlefields and other important Cromwellian sites, took four years, and produced an even larger book than its predecessor. It was published in 1973 as *Cromwell: Our Chief of Men* (*Cromwell: The Lord Protector* in the United States), and had a generally favorable press, though most critics expressed some reservations. Several thought that the book lacked historical background and depth, and one complained that the author had drawn too credulously on historical legend and folk history to fill out the skimpy information available about Cromwell's early life. But a reviewer in the *Times Literary Supplement* wrote that "on Oliver Cromwell's family connections, and especially on his attitude towards his children and other near relatives, Lady Antonia's aims are triumphantly vindicated. ... Extreme skill is evident also in the analysis of Cromwell's character." If Lady Antonia sometimes goes beyond the evidence in her discussion of Cromwell's thoughts and feelings, "on some aspects of his career, new evidence has been brought to bear and fresh questions have been asked." Paul Johnson also had reservations, but concluded that "as a portrait of a man it is a genuine work of art: complete, subtle, understanding and convincing."

King James VI of Scotland, I of England (1974) is Antonia Fraser's own contribution to the Kings and Queens of England series, of which she is the general editor. This relatively brief but handsomely illustrated biography concentrates, as the series demands, on the more popular and personal aspects of James's life; within these limits, it was generally considered "a successful portrait, making a superficially repulsive and often misunderstood figure rather more accessible and sympathetic."

Lady Antonia has also edited *The Lives of the Kings and Queens of England* (1975), a collection of biographical sketches by eight different writers. The sixteenth-century love poems she had encountered during her work on Mary and James inspired her to put together a collection of *Scottish Love Poems* and this in turn led to her much-praised anthology of *Love Letters. Quiet As a Nun* (1977), Lady Antonia's first work of fiction, is a thriller about a television reporter, Jemima Shore, and her investigation into the unusual death of a former schoolfriend who had become a nun. It was generally well received and was very successfully adapted for television. Jemima Shore reappears in *The Wild Island* (1978), caught up in a neo-Jacobite plot in the Scottish Highlands. A reviewer in the *Times Literary Supplement* thought that Jemima seemed more interested in her elegant clothes than in the desperate intrigues going on around her, but called this "pleasant and amusing entertainment, civilized and well-written."

Lady Antonia is tall, slim, and beautiful, with blond hair and blue eyes. She is much in demand as a broadcaster on radio and television, and as a lecturer, and has written a number of radio plays. In 1975 she was cited by the actress Vivien Merchant in her divorce proceedings against her husband, the playwright Harold Pinter. Lady Antonia was herself divorced by Hugh Fraser the following year. The author was a member of the Arts Council of Great Britain in 1970-1972 and in 1974-1975 served as chairman of the Society of Authors. She enjoys the opera, the ballet, and the theatre, and is an enthusiastic swimmer and tennis player, but the only recreation she bothers to list in *Who's Who* is "life."

PRINCIPAL WORKS: *Biography*—Mary, Queen of Scots, 1969; Cromwell: Our Chief of Men, 1973 (U.S., Cromwell:

The Lord Protector); King James VI of Scotland, I of England, 1974. *Fiction*—Quiet As a Nun, 1977; The Wild Island, 1978. *For Children*—King Arthur and the Knights of the Round Table, 1955. *Other*—Dolls, 1963; A History of Toys, 1966. *As Editor*—Scottish Love Poems: A Personal Anthology, 1975; The Lives of the Kings and Queens of England, 1975; Love Letters, 1976.

ABOUT: Current Biography, 1974; International Who's Who, 1978–79; Who's Who, 1978. *Periodicals*—Book World November 16, 1969; Christian Science Monitor November 28, 1973; Life February 20, 1970; National Review December 12, 1973; New Republic December 15, 1973; New Statesman May 16, 1969; June 8, 1973; New York Review of Books November 6, 1969; November 15, 1973; New York Times November 5, 1966; New York Times Book Review November 23, 1969; March 1, 1970; October 28, 1973; June 2, 1974; March 30, 1975; New Yorker December 3, 1966; January 14, 1974; August 11, 1975; December 27, 1976; Newsweek August 11, 1975; Observer January 21, 1968; Saturday Review–World December 23, 1973; Time October 17, 1969; November 5, 1973; December 27, 1976; Times Literary Supplement July 3, 1969; July 20, 1973; April 18, 1975; May 5, 1978; Virginia Quarterly Review Spring 1974; Washington Post November 2, 1969; Yale Review March 1974.

GEORGE MAC DONALD FRASER

FRASER, GEORGE MacDONALD (April 2, 1925–), Scottish novelist, short story writer, film scenarist, historian, and journalist, writes: "My parents, a Scottish doctor and nursing sister, agreed with Dr. Johnson that the best sight a Scot ever sees is the high road to England—at least, they agreed with him as far as Carlisle, where they settled after the First World War. I was sent to Carlisle Grammar School, where I performed so indifferently that they decided to send me to Glasgow Academy, where my examination showing was, if anything, worse. However, I did win two prizes, for English and general knowledge, learned to play Rugby and cricket with cunning if not enthusiasm, received a cup for throwing the cricket ball, read impressive quantities of historical fiction, and became probably the only Laertes in theatrical history to defeat Hamlet—admittedly, only at a rehearsal. These qualifications were not considered sufficient for entrance to the medical faculty of Glasgow University, and I went into the army, a willing conscript, in 1943. I was occasionally a lance-corporal, served as an infantryman with 17th Indian Division of XIVth Army in Burma, and was finally commissioned in the Gordon Highlanders.

"After the war I was a sports and general reporter with the *Carlisle Journal,* where I married Kathleen Hetherington, a reporter from another paper. We went to Canada together, and after a brief period in Toronto where I almost sold a set of encyclopedias to a man with a broken washing-machine, we got jobs as reporters in Saskatchewan. After a year we came home, our first son was born, and I worked as a report-

er and sub-editor on the *Cumberland News* before we moved to Glasgow in 1953. On the *Glasgow Herald* I was variously on sports, parliamentary, and foreign news sub-editing, leader-writing and feature-writing, before becoming features editor, and deputy editor from 1964 to 1969. Our daughter and second son were born in 1953 and 1957 respectively.

"I had been writing on and off since the age of five, and thanks to my wife's encouragement I persevered in the hope of becoming a novelist; my first book, *Flashman,* was published in 1969, and I gave up newspaper work and devoted myself to being a free-lance author."

Harry Flashman entered English literature as the bully and "bad influence" in Thomas Hughes's tribute to the British public school system, *Tom Brown's Schooldays* (1857). In that novel he is very properly expelled from Rugby by the great Dr. Arnold. George MacDonald Fraser has been inspired to speculate about the career that might follow these disgraceful beginnings, and in this way has created not only a splendid comic character but a knowledgeable satire on the moral pretensions and hypocrisies of Victorian society.

Flashman appeared in 1969 and purported to be the first installment of his shameless memoirs, covering the years between 1839 and 1842, but written many years later in old age. They give Flashman's own version of his expulsion from Rugby, and his subsequent entry into Lord Cardigan's 11th Light Dragoons. Parted by his inveterate cowardice from this crack regiment, he is sent to the North West Frontier and is caught up in the appalling blunders of the first Afghan

War (1842). After ignominious surrender, all the British troops involved in that disaster perished in the retreat through India, the only survivor being a certain Dr. Brydon. In Fraser's account, Flashman also survives, thanks to his genius for self-preservation and his skill as a seducer, and emerges from the debacle a national hero.

Harry Flashman is a coward, a liar, and a cheat, but he has no illusions about himself, and in his memoirs at least is disarmingly frank. The reader warms to him, not least because many of the historical and imaginary characters around him behave little better while paying lip-service to high Christian ideals. The novel was universally praised, both as a "highly entertaining *jeu d'esprit*" and for the accuracy of its historical detail, though one critic objected mildly that Flashman falls "too easily into the attitudes of a mid-twentieth-century con-man."

Having established his character, Fraser went on to exploit him with much-applauded skill. In *Royal Flash,* Sir Harry (as he has now become) blunders his way through various battles, plots, and boudoirs as an officer of the Horse Guards, compounding the Schleswig-Holstein Question, and avoiding disaster by a mixture of luck and cynical cunning. *Flash for Freedom!* takes him to the United States, and *Flashman at the Charge* involves him in the Crimean War (he accidently leads the charge of the Light Brigade, is captured by Cossacks, escapes by sled, and foils the Czar's plan to overrun India, enjoying the favors of an international cast of remarkable women along the way). "Fraser has done a wondrous thing," Peter Andrews wrote in his review of this novel. "By making his principal character into the ultimate anti-hero, Fraser has brought back the old-fashioned English adventure novel for those of us who wouldn't ordinarily read them." *Royal Flash* was filmed in 1975 from the author's own scenario.

In 1970, meanwhile, Fraser had published *The General Danced at Dawn,* in which he draws on his own experiences as a young officer in the Gordon Highlanders. These nine stories are all narrated by Lieutenant Dand McNeill, newly commissioned in a Highland regiment during the years just after World War II, when the regiment is returning home from service in India via North Africa. Martin Levin thought that "some of the entries would require a native reader for full appreciation. . . . Others are more universally the stuff of good-humored military fiction: of missions unaccomplished, obstacle courses failed, and snafus from Jerusalem to Edinburgh." Another reviewer decided that Fraser's "insistent emphasis on clannish camaraderie might be more moving were his plots less weak and predictable . . . and were his moments of modest truthfulness not bluffly outshouted by a tone of unconvincing heartiness." There was a generally warmer reception for *McAuslan in the Rough,* a second collection of stories employing the same formula, centering this time on the exploits of Private John McAuslan, "the dirtiest soldier in the world"—the regimental idiot who somehow always comes through in a pinch. "Mr. Fraser's command of tones and turns of phrase is compellingly right," one reviewer concluded, and "a whole cast of characters" is "memorably caught by a vividness of presence and voice."

Sir Harry Flashman, KB, VC, rides again in *Flashman in the Great Game,* surviving the horrors of Meerut, Cawnpore, and Lucknow to be prayed over by General Havelock, haunted by the ghost of Dr. Arnold, and in the end to make a very good thing out of the Indian Mutiny. "The joke has been splendidly established," one reviewer wrote, "but even the best of jokes wears thin; for any Flashman aficionado a moment comes when the belly-laughs subside and the story-teller's mantle—Buchan, Hope, Masters —envelops him and sweeps him away." Richard Usborne was also reminded of Buchan, and went on: "As [Flashman's] chronicles progress he is finding it harder and harder to convince me that he is the thoroughgoing bounder and cad that his author wants him to be and that he himself blatantly insists he is." Usborne, who said that he longed to fault Fraser on a fact, but could not, thought this the best of his books so far.

The Steel Bonnets is not a novel but a factual study of the "borderers"—the raiders, cattle thieves, and protection racketeers on either side of the Anglo-Scottish border who preyed on each other and feuded continually until they were stopped by the lawful and more efficient brutalities of James I early in the seventeenth century. The distinguished historian Hugh Trevor-Roper called it "a splendid book, both scholarly and readable, accurate and alive, documented and well written. It is the only work I know which imposes form on the anarchy of Border history, and gives life to that form. . . . This is a book which a historian can envy." Apart from *Royal Flash,* Fraser has written screenplays for *The Three Musketeers* (1974), *The Four Musketeers* (1975), and *The Prince and the Pauper* (1977).

George MacDonald Fraser lives with his wife and children at Baldrine on the Isle of Man. A "sentimental Presbyterian," he is "firmly opposed to all party politics." He lists his recreations as "snooker, picquet, talking to wife, history, singing."

PRINCIPAL WORKS: *Novels*—Flashman: From the Flashman Papers, 1839-1842, 1969; Royal Flash, 1970; Flash for Freedom!, 1971; Flashman at the Charge, 1973; Flashman in the Great Game, 1975; Flashman's Lady, 1977. *Short Stories*—The General Danced at Dawn, 1970; McAuslan in the Rough, 1974. *History*—The Steel Bonnets: A History of the Anglo-Scottish Border Reivers, 1971.

ABOUT: Contemporary Authors 45-48, 1974; Who's Who, 1977. *Periodicals*—Book World June 29, 1969; September 6, 1970; May 14, 1972; Guardian August 22, 1970; National Review August 3, 1973; New York Times Book Review October 26, 1969; October 18, 1970; May 20, 1973; November 11, 1973; Sunday Times (London) October 31, 1971; Time August 27, 1973; Times Literary Supplement June 12, 1969; October 8, 1971; April 7, 1972; December 21, 1973; May 31, 1974; November 28, 1975.

DANIEL FUCHS

FUCHS, DANIEL (June 25, 1909–), American novelist, short story writer, and film scenarist, writes: "I was born on Rivington Street, the New York City East Side, fragrant with hopes and desires. We moved over to Brooklyn, landing after a while in the Williamsburg section, also fragrant etc. Well, they were wonderful places. I dream about them and have pleasant times walking along similar streets in neighborhood sections, unknown to me by name, in Milan, Rome, Paris, London. The odd thing is I lived on Rivington Street for all of five days and in Williamsburg for all of twelve years, a short period of time for one of my great age (1909–). It is mother to me.

"I've been in California on and off (with time out for the war and some other trips) for forty years. People think you're sly when you say good things about Hollywood and the movies. No, it was lots of fun—the studio life, the movie people, the terrain itself—the great spaces, the beaches, the deserts, the hills, the plants and flowers. It was an idyllic place to raise my sons; of course, they're grown now, no longer ours, and my wife and I are getting pretty wrinkled. ... You can best get the feel of what the place was like through Peter Viertel's novels, *The Canyon* and *Bicycle on the Beach,* and in Robert Parrish's new book, *Growing Up in Hollywood.* I sincerely love those other cities I mention above but find I always hanker to get back to Los Angeles, to feel the brute sun on my back.

"I've written three Williamsburg or Brooklyn novels, still in print at present in the Equinox-Avon edition; a collection of short stories titled *Stories* in tandem with three other short story writers; a number of short stories, some in anthologies, most of them not; a novel, *West of the Rockies;* and many movies."

As he says, Fuchs spent the first twelve years of his life in the slums clustered around the foot of the Williamsburg Bridge in Brooklyn, the home then of the poorest New York Jews. Irving Howe wrote in *Commentary* (July 1948) that "it was the cramped and harried life of this slum that was to be decisive, even traumatic, in shaping Fuchs's career as a writer.... All of Fuchs's novels are dominated by a sense of place—the sense of place as it grasps a man's life and breaks him to its limits."

Fuchs was educated at the Eastern District High School in Brooklyn and the City College of New York. From 1930 to 1937, in the thick of the Depression, he taught without tenure in New York elementary schools as a "permanent substitute," earning six dollars per working day, nothing during vacations and holidays. It was during this period that he wrote the three Brooklyn novels—"a miniature *comédie humaine,*" Irving Howe called them—that have ever since retained the admiration and affection of so many critics and common readers.

Summer in Williamsburg (1934), written during summer vacations from P.S. 225 in Brighton Beach, was published when Fuchs was twenty-four. In a cinematic montage of short scenes, it immerses the reader in the heat and smells of a Williamburg summer while he watches a dozen more or less defeated immigrants struggle noisily to accommodate their minds, tongues, and high Judaic principles to the ugly realities of American slum life. The novel centers on an aspiring young writer, Philip Hayman, and on his family and friends and girlfriends. Philip is driven by the mysterious suicide of a neighbor, Sussman, to confront the choices open to him as a product of the ghetto. At one extreme is Philip's uncle Papravel, a pious racketeer who knows "there is still a God over America" when sabotage and murder bring him the transit monopoly he covets; at the other is Philip's father, honest, kind, but desperately poor. Philip decides that "people in tenements lived in a circle without significance, one day the duplicate of the next until the end, which occurred without meaning"; finding himself in a trap from which there is no escape, but eschewing self-pity, he lapses into "dignified passivity."

The novel's first reviewers in 1934 thought it fresh and vigorous, honest and powerful, if immature in its unrelenting cynicism. When the book was reissued in 1961 (along with the rest of the "Williamsburg trilogy"), critics found its episodic structure unsatisfactory, its dependence on dialogue excessive (though the talk was "acoustically true and psychologically revealing"). The book was saved, it was thought, by Fuchs's "wry and disenchanted tenderness" for his characters, and by the "self-sustaining vitality" of his determination to see them afresh.

Homage to Blenholt, which followed two years later, is a neater and funnier novel, though not more optimistic. Max Balkan and his friends Munves and Coblenz are young misfits trying in their different ways to enrich their lives and escape from the Williamsburg trap. Max is a meek and timid dreamer, a *schlemiel* hero scheming to become a Wall Street Tamburlaine. He models himself on Blenholt, the late and great Commissioner of Sewers—a crooked diabetic politician who has died of a surfeit of candy. Max makes a pilgrimage to his hero's funeral, is beaten up when it turns into a riot, and then discovers that the most promising of his financial inspirations (bottled onion juice) has been on the market for years. He and the scholarly Munves resign themselves to Williamsburg, marriage, and a steady job. Max's mother rejoices at this decision but his father, an old actor who had once played Hamlet in Yiddish in Melbourne and now carries a sandwich board, recognizes in her "earthy guffaws the clamorous demands of the world, its insistant calls for resignation and surrender, and he knew now that Max would never be the same again." Another dream has died, another escape from Williamsburg has been cut off, "but all the same the evening sun that day went down on time."

Irving Howe regards this as Fuchs's best novel, allowing free play to "his true gift, which was for an exuberant if slightly embittered comedy, a mocking play with daydreams, a marvelous twisting of Yiddish rhythms as these came to inhabit and haunt American speech. The book rocks with zest and energy." Irwin Shaw, writing in *Rediscoveries* (1971), found that something of the novel's impact had faded for him,

"but the dramatic gift is still there, the scenes are constructed with sure-handed skill, the tangle of many lives is confidently handled, the feel of a vanished society is transmitted, heightened but not betrayed by fantasy."

The despairing note on which *Homage to Blenholt* ends carries over into *Low Company* (1937), the grimmest and most violent of the trilogy. It centers around a soda parlor in "Neptune Beach" owned by the man of property Spitzbergen, who also rents out the apartments used by Shubunka, an independent brothel operator, physically grotesque but intelligent and gentle. When the syndicate moves in on Shubunka's business, he turns for help to Spitzbergen, but is refused. "Business is business," says Herbert Lurie, the sympathetic dress store owner. "It's the same goddamed thing in my line, only a little less lousy." Shubunka is almost killed and leaves town. Spitzbergen is murdered in a stickup by the compulsive gambler Karty, who is himself beaten almost to death by his brothers-in-law after he embezzles their money and loses it on the horses. The violence spreads to affect people who have played no part in all this vice, but the novel suggests that no one is innocent—all our lives are interwoven, whether we like it or not. Herbert Lurie comes to understand how evil had infected the dingy characters around him "and, further, how miserable their own evil rendered them. It was not enough to call them low and pass on."

A more ambitious and skillful book than its predecessors, *Low Company* is tighter in structure and richer in characterization. Irving Howe nevertheless enjoyed it less, feeling that in it Fuchs had largely withdrawn his sympathy from his characters, and that his comic gift had become subservient to the demands of the well-made novel. It seemed to him to have "neither the earnest bewilderment of *Summer* nor the high-pitched humor of *Homage,*" and Alfred Kazin likewise missed the passion of Fuchs's earlier "autobiographical prose poetry of the tenements." Not everyone shared these views, however, and Richard Elman recently referred to *Low Company* as Fuchs's masterpiece.

Irving Howe thinks of *Homage to Blenholt* as "a high-spirited attempt to delay or evade the problem of choice," while *Low Company* "marks an acceptance of the burdens of commonplace reality." This, Howe speculates, may have been the reason for the abrupt termination of Fuchs's career as a novelist—the "grim and ironic appreciation of the power of the commonplace, everything in daily existence that erodes ambition and spirit." Fuchs's own explanation is that he decided "to become rich." He says that the

Williamsburg novels "didn't sell—four hundred copies, four hundred, twelve hundred. The reviews were scanty, immaterial. The books became odious to me." Like many other "proletarian" novels of the 1930s, they were attacked for expressing too little political commitment, or too much.

A fourth novel was put aside half-finished and turned into short stories. More stories followed, after which, according to John Updike, Fuchs turned his attention to gambling, and with considerable success. Then the stories began to sell to such journals as *Collier's* and *Saturday Evening Post,* and Fuchs was offered a thirteen-week movie contract. He left P.S. 225, seen off at the station by his former pupils, and went to Hollywood, where the thirteen weeks have stretched to forty years. The best known of his screenplays are *Love Me or Leave Me* (which brought him an Oscar in 1955), *Panic in the Streets* (1957), and *Jeanne Eagels* (1957). He also adapted his third novel, *Low Company,* into an "interesting but unsuccessful" B movie called *The Gangster.*

Allen Guttman believes that Fuchs was the first American Jewish writer "to take apart the world of Sholom Aleichem's Kasrilevka and to reconstruct it on the sidewalks of New York." Howe says that he has written "some of the most winning fictions we have about American Jewish life. His scope narrow but his tone pure, Fuchs was that rarity, a 'natural' writer with a gift for spontaneous evocation and recall." Stanley Edgar Hyman considered that Fuchs's "true tradition is that of Nathanael West and Henry Roth in the 1930s, the symbolists and fantasists, a tradition he shares with many of the finest young writers of our time. He is best when he is most bold and imaginative, most garish and grotesque . . . Fuchs was never quite bold *enough,* never really understood his literary heritage, never achieved a firm center for his sprawling natural history. His talent is considerable, and his later works might have been the triumphs that bits of these books promise."

In fact, apart from a handful of stories in the *New Yorker* and elsewhere, Fuchs published no more fiction until 1971, when his fourth novel appeared, thirty-four years after the third. This was *West of the Rockies,* which one reviewer called "a vigorous, but formless distillation of three decades of accumulated movieland impressions." Although the locale has changed the people are the same, scarred and self-pitying, driven by similar anxieties and compulsions. The aging movie star Adele Hogue, much-married and high-strung, runs away from the picture she is making and hides in a Palm Springs hotel.

Assigned to bring her back is Burt Claris, an agent with whom she has been having an affair. The hotel is owned by Fannie Case, whose husband Harry, a former lover of Adele's, has continued to take care of her in times of trouble. The action of the novel is provided by the attempts of this foursome to resolve the complexities of their relationships.

There was some praise for the novel's "pure" and "professional" style, but the book as a whole seemed to most reviewers a sad disappointment, superficial and dull, though the *Times Literary Supplement* admired its realism, and the skill with which the "notion of dependence and muted anguish" was developed. In his review in the New York *Times Book Review,* Richard Elman called the book self-righteous, nostalgic, and frustrating, complained about its "highly adjectival prose," and wondered if Fuchs's "failure to elicit my feelings meant he was not in touch with his own." He urged Fuchs to "try again with all the very real talent that he can summon, all that exertion of imagination and mind and feeling he has shown here only in glimpses."

Fuchs put down some of his own thoughts about Hollywood in *Commentary* (February 1962), where he describes his working relationship with directors and producers in the movie capital during his early years there. He refuses to join in the general denigration of Hollywood as it was then, defending it instead as "the best, most solid creative effort of our decades." What the "gaudy company, rambunctious and engrossed" produced in "those sun-filled, sparkling days, was a phenomenon, teeming with vitality and ardor, as indigenous as our cars or skyscrapers or highways, and as irrefutable."

Daniel Fuchs was married in 1932 and has two sons. In 1962 he received a grant from the National Institute of Arts and Letters.

PRINCIPAL WORKS: *Novels*—Summer in Williamsburg, 1934; Homage to Blenholt, 1936; Low Company, 1937 (in England, Neptune Beach); Three Novels (Summer in Williamsburg, Homage to Blenholt, Low Company), 1961 (republished as The Williamsburg Trilogy, 1972); West of the Rockies, 1971. *Short Stories*—(with others) Stories, 1956.

ABOUT: Guttmann, A. The Jewish Writer in America, 1971; Hyman, S.E. Standards: A Chronicle of Books for Our Time, 1966; Madden, D. Proletarian Writers of the Thirties, 1968; Madden, D. (ed.) Rediscoveries, 1971; Penguin Companion to Literature 3, 1971; Seymour-Smith, M. Guide to Modern World Literature, 1973; Vinson, J. (ed.) Contemporary Novelists, 1976. *Periodicals*—Books February 23, 1936; February 14, 1937; Commentary July 1948, July 1961, February 1962; Harper's July 1971; New Republic May 15, 1971; New Statesman August 8, 1936; New Yorker November 11, 1961; October 23, 1971; New York Times November 18, 1934; February 23, 1936; February 28, 1937;

New York Times Book Review June 13, 1971: July 18, 1971; Time September 1, 1961.

*FUGARD, ATHOL (HAROLD LANNI-GAN) (June 11, 1932–), South African dramatist, was born in the village of Middelburg in the semi-desert Karoo region of Cape Province, where his parents ran a small general store. He is the son of Harold Fugard, English-speaking, "possibly of Irish descent," and an amateur jazz pianist, and the former Elizabeth Magdalene Potgieter. His mother, an Afrikaner, was still alive in 1974, "seventy-eight and as big as a mountain." Fugard told an interviewer that she had shared his own gradual emancipation from racial prejudice and was "a magnificent monument to decency."

In the mid-1930s, when Fugard was still very young, his parents sold their store and moved to Port Elizabeth, where the author has lived for most of his life and set many of his plays. He has described it as "an almost featureless industrial port on the Indian Ocean" with a population of half a million—black, white, Indian, Chinese, and Coloured (the South African term for people of mixed black and white parentage). Port Elizabeth "is also very representative of South Africa in the range of its social strata, from total affluence on the white side to extremest poverty on the non-white." As a ten-year-old boy, steeped in the bigotry of his class and kind, Athol Fugard once spat in the face of a black man. He attributes the depth of his passion for social justice to this incident: "I cannot talk about it to this day. I bear the guilt."

After leaving high school, Fugard studied motor mechanics at Port Elizabeth Technical College. He found this not much to his liking, and in 1950 went on with a scholarship to read philosophy and social anthropology at the University of Cape Town, where his principal recreation was boxing. Believing that a degree might condemn him to an academic career, he left the university in 1953, in the last half of his final year. He equipped himself with £20 and ten tins of sardines, and spent six months hitchhiking up through black Africa to Port Sudan. There he signed on as the only white crew member of a tramp steamer bound for the Far East. For the next two years Fugard traveled widely as a merchant seaman, almost entirely in the company of blacks and Orientals. This experience was an important element in his gradual awakening to the wickedness of apartheid.

By the time Fugard returned to South Africa in 1956, he was intent on writing "the great South African novel." However, the same year

*fōō′ gärd

ATHOL FUGARD

he married an actress named Sheila Meiring and, he says, "following her around from rehearsals to auditions and then watching from the wings, I became more and more involved in theatre." (Sheila Meiring, on the other hand, has established herself as one of South Africa's most admired and interesting novelists and poets.) In 1958 Fugard worked for six months as a clerk in the Fordsburg Native Commissioner's Court in Johannesburg, an experience which completed his conversion into an enemy of apartheid. All South African blacks over the age of sixteen are required to carry passbooks which strictly limit their movements, permitting them to enter only specified urban areas at specified times, and then solely "to minister to the needs of the white man." The Fordsburg Court existed mainly to try infringements of the pass laws, and Fugard saw there "more suffering" than he "could cope with." He says: "We sent an African to jail once every two minutes. It was the ugliest thing I have ever been a part of. I think my basic pessimism was born there, watching that procession of faces and being unable to relate to any of them."

It was then that Fugard made his first black friends, and began to visit them in the black townships. *No-Good Friday,* his first full-length play, portrayed the squalor and hopelessness of life in one such township. With Fugard himself playing the part of a priest, and an inexperienced amateur cast, it was performed in 1958 before white audiences in private houses, and well received. It was the beginning not only of Fugard's career as a dramatist but of his predilection for small-scale and semi-amateur productions with an element of improvisation, as distinct from the glossy professionalism of the commercial theatre.

By the end of 1958 Fugard had left the Fordsburg Court and joined the National Theatre Organization as a stage manager. In 1959, while working for this white segregated institution, Fugard completed his second play, *Nongogo,* about a mine workers' prostitute, and presented it "wherever and whenever possible" with an equally segregated black cast of five. Though these early plays are apprentice pieces, they introduce, in their concern with deprived characters dreaming of a better existence, a theme that pervades Fugard's work. *Nongogo,* moreover, already shows some progress towards the simplicity of presentation that has become his hallmark.

Seeking a broader experience of theatre, Fugard and his wife left South Africa in 1959 and went to London. Unable to find work in the theatre, Fugard earned his living as a cleaner while Sheila Meiring became a typist. They fared only a little better during a visit to Holland. What cash they could spare, however, was spent on theatre tickets, and they were able to witness and to learn from the renewal of vitality in British and European drama at that time, and the redirection of dramatic form by such writers as Samuel Beckett and Harold Pinter. They were still in London on March 21, 1960, when seventy-two demonstrators against the pass laws were massacred by police in Sharpeville, near Johannesburg. The government tightened its restrictions on the anti-apartheid movement, and an exodus of white liberals began. At that point, Athol Fugard and Sheila Meiring bought one-way tickets and flew home because "it wasn't the time to be away."

The Blood Knot, Fugard's first mature play and still perhaps his best-known work, was also the first he wrote after his return to South Africa. It studies the relationship between two Coloured half-brothers—the light-skinned and guilt-ridden Morrie, and the envious, dark-skinned Zach—living in a slum on the outskirts of Port Elizabeth. Writing on behalf of the illiterate Zach, Morrie begins a correspondence with a woman named Ethel, discovering too late that she is white. When Ethel asks to meet Zach, the brothers spend their savings on new clothes for Morrie, who can pass for white and is to go in Zach's place. The dangerous meeting is averted when Ethel becomes engaged to someone else, but Morrie's wearing of the smart new suit plunges the brothers into unfamiliar roles, and their acting out of the fears and hatreds implicit in the color bar brings them close to actual violence. The play was first performed in October 1961 at the Rehearsal Room, a theatre club

sponsored by the African Music and Drama Association in Johannesburg, with Zakes Mokae as Zach and Fugard playing Morrie, as he did during part of the play's New York run in 1964. This powerful indictment of the crippling emotional effects of apartheid was surprisingly well received in South Africa, where some critics thought that the conflict between the two brothers only demonstrated the wisdom of "separate development" for blacks and whites.

In 1961, when *The Blood Knot* was first staged, it was still possible in South Africa, as Fugard says, "for a black man and a white man to appear on the same stage before a mixed audience, provided the management of the theatre involved was prepared to let this happen." The following year, when major plays by Robert Bolt and Harold Pinter were being performed in South Africa by whites only, Fugard wrote an open letter to British dramatists asking them to make it a condition, when granting performance rights to their plays, that all audiences be nonsegregated. The letter provoked heated public discussion and led to a continuing boycott of South African theatre by English-language dramatists in other countries. This had not been Fugard's intention and he has opposed the boycott, believing that access to foreign ideas and art is essential if South Africa is ever to achieve a civilized society.

It was in 1962 also that Fugard was asked by a deputation of five men of the Xhosa tribe if he would help them to form a theatre company. Reluctant as he was at first, he did not feel able to refuse, and the Serpent Players came into existence in the Port Elizabeth township of New Brighton. The company has been harrassed by the authorities from the beginning. Three members were arrested in 1964 and the following year new government restrictions prevented Fugard from attending a Serpent production in a black township. In 1967 Fugard's passport was withdrawn. In spite of all this, and the fact that the company has little money, and is made up of amateur actors able to rehearse only after work and before curfew, the Serpent Players became the first successful non-white theatre company in South Africa. Unable to perform publicly before white or mixed audiences, it has taken productions of Fugard's plays, and also works by Brecht, Genet, Strindberg, and Sophocles, into black townships all over South Africa, and has toured successfully abroad.

Fugard's next play, *People Are Living There* (1963), centers on the blowzy landlady of a seedy rooming house in a poor white district of Johannesburg. Deserted by her lover, she invites her three lodgers to celebrate her fiftieth birthday with a party that ends, as one critic wrote, in the "uneasy peace of mutual contempt." Jack Kroll, reviewing the American opening at the Repertory Theatre of Lincoln Center three years later, wrote: "The play takes a while to get going, but once it finds traction it moves with power, scarifying humor, and dramatic effectiveness in its portrait of marginal people in a dispirited society." It was followed by *Hello and Goodbye* (1965), in which a neurotic young man and his prostitute sister meet after a long separation at the funeral of their father, an old Afrikaner railroad worker. It was seen at the Sheridan Square Playhouse in New York in 1969, and had a not very enthusiastic reception as a rather static and old-fashioned psychological drama reminiscent of Eugene O'Neill. Marilyn Stasio called it "a considerably flawed work . . . salvaged by the complexities of its two characters and their interaction, and by their sure and forceful language, rather than by its dramatic action, which is minimal."

It was Fugard's next play that established him as an important dramatist. This was *Boesman and Lena* (1968), a long one-acter about two Coloured vagrants who wander from one condemned shanty-town to another across the South African wilderness, wrangling, drinking, scavenging. We encounter them in an area of wasteland on the banks of a river and receive from their conversation a sense of the meaningless repetitiousness of life that reminded some critics of the work of Samuel Beckett. Boesman accepts his life, bolstering his self-respect by beating Lena; she is less brutalized by her circumstances and relies more on alcohol to numb her sense of outrage. The impossibility of any real contact between human beings is dramatized in Lena's tentative encounter with a derelict old black who speaks no English. *Boesman and Lena* ran for a year in New York in 1970–1971, and it seemed to Tom Prideaux that "as a play-builder, Fugard is so skilled that his audience, even after living through such a grim evening, still reaches the end with a sense of emotional uplift, of having touched greatness." In response to a petition signed by four thousand people, Fugard's passport was returned to him in time for him to attend the London production of the play in 1971. *Statements After an Arrest Under the Immorality Act* (1972) returns to the subject of interracial love which Fugard had introduced in *The Blood Knot,* demonstrating the appalling intrusiveness of South Africa's sex laws in an intensely dramatic series of episodes.

Some of Fugard's plays incorporate material improvised by members of the Serpent Players out of their own life experiences, in a way that owes a great deal to the work of the Polish director Jerzy Grotowski. The best-known of these experiments are *Sizwe Bansi Is Dead* and *The Island,* both of which were devised by Fugard in collaboration with John Kani and Winston Ntshona. Sizwe Bansi is a slow, simple countryman who goes to Port Elizabeth to find a job. Being illiterate, he is unaware that his passbook bears a stamp that utterly disqualifies him for any such enterprise, making him not only unable to provide for his family but liable to arrest and imprisonment. Sizwe is apprised of these facts by his city-slicker friend, and they go out to get drunk. The situation is saved when they chance upon the corpse of a black man with proper credentials, and Sizwe reluctantly exchanges his identity for that of the dead man. This play, which is always liable to change slightly in performance in spontaneous response to a given audience, was performed all over South Africa in 1972 by the Serpent Players, who the following year took it to theatres in England, Scotland, Wales, and Ireland. At the end of the same year it was presented in repertory at the Royal Court Theatre in London, and in 1974 it moved to the Ambassadors Theatre in the West End, London's Broadway. The British critics were unanimous in their praise, voting it the best play of 1973, and there was no less enthusiasm when it was seen in New York the following year. The play begins with an enormously long monologue by John Kani as a small-time photographer, who describes among other things a day in the South African Ford factory where he once worked. This monologue seemed to some reviewers too long, but others agreed with Russell Davies, who called it "a masterpiece of self-revelation, subversive mimicry, and desperate energy." Clive Barnes thought that the evening was "like a train gathering speed. The play, the theme, the performances gradually took over, and the sheer dramatic force of the piece bounced around the theatre like angry thunderbolts of pain."

The Island is often played in tandem with *Sizwe Bansi Is Dead,* and both have benefited from brilliant performances by Kani and Ntshona. In *The Island* they appear as friends serving sentences on Robben Island, where South Africa's black political prisoners are kept. The two men do not talk politics, however; the play centers, often comically, but finally with great power, on their rehearsals of a version of the *Antigone* of Sophocles for a prison concert. John (the actors use their own names in the play) is the smart one, and has great difficulty in driving the plot of the *Antigone* into Winston's head. Their friendship is threatened by the news that John is soon to be released, while Winston will serve life, but they are drawn together again in opposition to another prisoner, who is unfairly favored by the authorities. The play ends with their performance of the *Antigone* as a magnificent parable of injustice and resistance. Brendan Gill preferred *The Island* to its companion piece as "being more nearly an autonomous work of art and less a work of propaganda, however lofty a purpose that propaganda may be." And he called the final *Antigone* scene "a moment of theatre so pure and so touching that one's heart threatens to stop." In New York both plays were nominated for Tony Awards for best play, best actor, and best director, and in fact John Kani and Winston Ntshona jointly won the "best actor" award.

Fugard speaks of these two plays as "the child" of Kani and Ntshona, and says that he did not feel that he had "the right or privilege to change the words. Their truth eclipses my esthetics. For them to discover an opportunity to articulate their anger in a society that conspires to make them deaf and dumb and blind has had a profound effect on their lives." Fugard has not continued his collaboration with them, however, explaining in 1974: "I want to live privately with paper. I don't want to look for a common denominator with another imagination. . . . I'm so impatient now—to be private again, to go on journeys I can make only by myself." The first product of this decision was *Dimetos,* a play commissioned for the 1975 Edinburgh Festival and based on a classical myth mentioned by Albert Camus in his notebooks. More obscure and mystifying than any of Fugard's other plays, it deals with the dilemma of an artist who fears the loss of his powers if he cuts himself off from his own society, but who in conscience cannot lend that society his support. It was coolly received by critics in Edinburgh and again in London a year later, when Paul Scofield played the lead in a revised version. Michael Billington called it "woozily imprecise," and said it was "so busy being primal and mythic that it forgets to be dramatic."

Fugard has also written a television play (dealing rather surprisingly with a motor race) and several screenplays. He provided the scenario for Ross Devenish's film version of *Boesman and Lena,* and appeared in it with Yvonne Bryceland, an actress who has been especially associated with his work. He also wrote the screenplay for and starred in Devenish's *The Guest at Steenkampskraal* (1977), a study of the naturalist and anthropologist Eugène Marais, who is regarded as the founder of South African literature, and his last despairing attempt to cure himself of morphine addiction. Fugard is a small

man, wiry, bearded, and ascetic-looking. In his manner he is intense and restless, fidgeting endlessly with a pipe, a cigarette, or worry beads. He lives with his wife and their daughter Lisa in a bungalow outside Port Elizabeth overlooking the Indian Ocean, where he likes to fish, study the birds, and skin-dive to harpoon eagle-rays.

"What's happening in the world, good people?" asks Sizwe Bansi. "Who cares for who in this world? Who wants Who?" In one way or another this question is asked in all of Fugard's plays, giving them a general human significance even while they remain deeply committed to the predicament of South Africa. He admits to feeling despair about his country, and in "bearing witness" to what he sees there, he is aware of a profound ambivalence—a sense that "all human beings are in some sense victims," so that he cannot deny his compassion even to the white South Africans who have created the society in which they are imprisoned along with the blacks. "My main feeling is one of confusion," he told an interviewer in 1971. "I am a classic example of the guilt-ridden impotent white liberal of South Africa." The sense of humor which in spite of everything persists in his work rests upon a kind of existentialism close to that of Camus. Recognized as South Africa's foremost playwright, and a dramatist of world stature, Fugard has been called "the conscience of his country."

PRINCIPAL PUBLISHED WORKS: The Blood Knot, 1963; Hello and Goodbye, 1966; The Occupation (*in* Ten One-Act Plays, edited by Cosmo Pieterse, 1968); Boesman and Lena, 1969; People Are Living There, 1969; The Coat (published with The Third Degree by Don MacLennan), 1971; Three Port Elizabeth Plays (The Blood Knot, Hello and Goodbye, Boesman and Lena), 1974; Statements: Two Workshop Productions Devised by Athol Fugard, John Kani, and Winston Ntshona—Sizwe Bansi Is Dead and The Island; and a New Play, Statements After an Arrest Under the Immorality Act, 1974; (with John Kani and Winston Ntshona) Sizwe Bansi Is Dead and The Island, 1976; Dimetos and Two Early Plays (No-Good Friday and Nongogo), 1977; Boesman and Lena and Other Plays (The Blood Knot, People Are Living There, Hello and Goodbye), 1978.

ABOUT: Current Biography, 1975; Encyclopaedia of Southern Africa, 1973; International Who's Who, 1978–79; Vinson, J. (ed.) Contemporary Dramatists, 1977; Who's Who, 1978; Who's Who in the Theatre, 1977. *Periodicals*—Guardian July 17, 1971; Listener December 5, 1974; London Magazine February-March 1972; New York Post November 30, 1974; New York Sunday News December 8, 1974; New York Times December 3, 1974; December 17, 1974; Observer July 18, 1971; January 6, 1974; Theatre Quarterly Winter 1977–1978.

FULLER, JOHN (LEOPOLD) (January 1, 1937–), English poet and critic, was born at Ashford, Kent, the only child of Roy Fuller and the former Kathleen Smith. His father, a lawyer,

JOHN FULLER

is also one of the most distinguished English poets of his generation—an intellectual poet, fond of cerebral solutions, devoted to W. H. Auden and "intelligibility." John Fuller, though he has found his own style, has inherited some of these tendencies.

He was educated at St. Paul's School in London (1949–1955). After national service in the Royal Air Force (1955–1957), during which he published his early poems in magazines (especially the now defunct *Truth*), he read English at New College, Oxford University, from which he graduated as a B.A. in 1960 (M.A., 1964; B.Litt., 1965). In his last year at Oxford he won the Newdigate Prize for poetry and the following year, 1961, he published his first collection, *Fairground Music.* The critic A. Alvarez, who thought it one of the most promising first books by a young poet he had seen for many years, was reminded of the early work of Thom Gunn, finding "the same slightly bewildered surge of [imaginative] energy, the same determination to force both poetic and logical coherence on his material, the same awareness of his own talent." Not all the reviewers were quite so impressed, however, and there were complaints of immaturity and comparisons with Rupert Brooke as well as with Gunn, Wallace Stevens, and Auden.

After a short period as a freelance writer, living in Oxford, John Fuller went as a visiting lecturer to the State University of New York at Buffalo (1962–1963). He was an assistant lecturer at the University of Manchester from 1963 until 1966, and since then he has been a fellow and tutor of Magdalen College, Oxford.

From his time as an Oxford undergraduate,

Fuller was a close associate of the group of poets and critics who founded the "little magazine" *the Review* (which in 1973 was transformed into the larger and less generally admired *New Review*). Many of the poets favored by its editor, Ian Hamilton, were, like Hamilton himself, "miniaturists"—authors of highly compressed short poems reminiscent of Japanese *haiku.* Fuller was never a miniaturist, but many of the poems he has published in magazines have appeared in *the Review* or in the *Times Literary Supplement,* of which Hamilton was formerly the poetry editor.

The qualities Hamilton admires in Fuller are rationality, subtlety, coherence, and the deliberate eschewal of sentiment—as Hamilton once characteristically remarked, speaking of the difference between Fuller's first book and his second: "We've saved him from that." And it was indeed in *The Tree That Walked* that Fuller began to find the voice he wanted his select audience to hear:

> Dead rain breeding life. The acres heave.
> Everywhere sap stiffens into bark
> And I am sick for something to believe.
> Kneading an untuned piano in the dark
> Beneath the flooded window, I can grieve
> Approximately to the printed mark.
> I know my orders to the very breve.
>
> And I pretend the piano keys are stones
> On which emotion lying like a wreath
> Gives order to the necessary bones.
> In love and pain we only show the teeth.
>
> (from "Alive and Dead")

It was a voice that did not wholly satisfy everyone. Stephen Wall, praising the technical accomplishment in these poems, and the control of complex thought processes, found them "oddly tangential to some of the central commonplaces of human feeling. The impression of a rooted reticence has something to do with the sense of powers not only excellently under control but also sometimes too tightly restrained."

Fuller has maintained this reticence in subsequent collections, all of them demonstrating an Augustan versatility and an intensely intellectual virtuosity. The virtuosity seemed self-defeating to one reviewer of "The Labours of Hercules," a sonnet sequence in *Cannibals and Missionaries* written in a progressive Hungarian form of stultifying difficulty. But this was called the only failure in a collection that in places struck a slightly surreal note: "The perfect technique now reflects a disturbed world, making these his most impressive poems to date." *Epistles to Several Persons,* which followed, is a

285

group of five allusive, topical poems written to five friends in the difficult "standard habbie" stanza form favored by Robert Burns. These two volumes were published together in the United States as *Poems and Epistles*. *The Mountain in the Sea* contains poems set in a remote part of Wales where Fuller spends part of each year. This deft and witty verse is also "moral" in the sense that it attempts to define a way in which a man may maintain a proper, meticulous (and by implication socially valuable) observation of his world.

John Fuller's statement that he has "never felt that there was any inherent virtue in powerful feelings and simplicity," and that poetry "has greater duties" than honesty, is characteristic, and sums up the feature of his work that has attracted the hostility of some critics. Fuller will continue to be a controversial poet, an anti-romantic of considerable accomplishment, a true heir of the eighteenth century and of the later Auden. Where his approach will (or can) lead remains to be seen. But it is to him above all that neo-Augustan intellectuals will look for work of real substance, for he—almost alone—has demonstrated that he has the necessary seriousness and the technical equipment.

The author has also produced some cleverly fanciful verse and a novel for children, and has written song lyrics and libretti for the composer Bryan Kelly. His full exegesis of Auden's poetry and his short critical examination of the sonnet are generally regarded as meticulous and impeccable. Fuller is devoted to riddles and puzzles, and since 1971 has edited a formidable annual collection of these, *Nemo's Almanac*, founded in 1892. He is also the founder of the small Sycamore Press, which he and his wife run from Oxford. His literary prizes include the Richard Hillary Memorial Prize (1961), the E.C. Gregory award (1965) and, for *Epistles to Several Persons*, the Sir Geoffrey Faber Memorial Prize (1974).

In 1960 Fuller was married to Cicely Martin, by whom he has three daughters. Asked to contribute an autobiographical statement to this book, he replied, "Such an exercise ought to be a distillation of something already confronted and realised: I don't believe I have reached such a point." This decision illustrates the fundamental seriousness that even his severest critics acknowledge.

PRINCIPAL WORKS: *Poetry*—Fairground Music, 1961; The Tree That Walked, 1967; The Art of Love, 1968; Cannibals and Missionaries, 1972; (with Peter Levi and Adrian Mitchell) Penguin Modern Poets 22, 1973; Epistles to Several Persons, 1973; Poems and Epistles, 1974; The Mountain in the Sea, 1975; A Bestiary, with woodcuts by Brigitte Hanf,

1975; Bel and the Dragon, 1977 (the Oxford Prize Poem on a Sacred Subject). *Songs, Musical Plays and Libretti*—Herod Do Your Worst: A Nativity Opera, 1968; Half a Fortnight, 1973; The Spider Monkey Uncle King, 1974. *For Children*—Squeaking Crust (poems), 1974; The Last Bid (novel), 1975. *Nonfiction*—A Reader's Guide to W.H. Auden, 1970; The Sonnet (The Critical Idiom series), 1972. *As Editor*—(with J. Mitchell) Light Blue Dark Blue, 1960; Oxford Poetry, 1960; (with Harold Pinter and Peter Redgrove) New Poems 1967, 1968.

ABOUT: Contemporary Authors 21–24 1st revision, 1977; International Who's Who in Poetry, 1974–1975; Thwaite, A. Poetry Today 1960–1973, 1973; Vinson, J. (ed.) Contemporary Poets, 1975. *Periodicals*—The Review Spring-Summer 1972; Times Literary Supplement August 10, 1967; January 18, 1974.

FULLER, R(ICHARD) BUCKMINSTER (July 12, 1895–), American architect, inventor, engineer, mathematician, cartographer, philosopher, poet, educator, environmentalist, and world planner, describes himself as "a comprehensive anticipatory design-science explorer." A scientific optimist who puts his faith in the potentialities of a vastly expanded technology, he likes to think of himself as "a citizen of the twenty-first century," but draws from his ancestry and family traditions a strong sense of continuity with the past. He was born in the Boston suburb of Milton, Massachusetts, the second of the four children of Richard Buckminster Fuller, a successful merchant dealing in tea and leather, and of Caroline Wolcott (Andrews) Fuller. On his mother's side his ancestors include Roger Wolcott, a governor of the colony of Connecticut, while members of the Fuller family had first settled in New England in the 1630s. His paternal ancestors include his great-aunt, Margaret Fuller, the noted feminist, reformer, and transcendentalist critic. Buckminster Fuller's own philosophy of synergetics —viewing the part in relation to the whole—and his essentially religious belief in the benign order of nature and the universe, have obvious affinities with New England transcendentalism.

"I was born cross-eyed," Fuller writes in the autobiographical essay which begins his book *Utopia or Oblivion*. "Not until I was four years old was it discovered that this was caused by my being abnormally far-sighted. My vision was thereafter fully corrected with lenses. Until four I could see only large patterns, houses, trees, outlines of people with blurred coloring. While I saw two dark areas on human faces, I did not see a human eye or a teardrop or a human hair until I was four. Despite my new ability to apprehend details, my childhood's spontaneous dependence only upon big pattern clues has persisted." Along with his two sisters, Leslie and

R. BUCKMINSTER FULLER

Rosamund, and his brother Wolcott, he grew up in the comfortable surroundings of the family home. He was educated at Milton Academy, where he did well in science and mathematics, and in 1913 he entered Harvard University, where four generations of Fullers had enrolled since the Reverend Timothy Fuller joined the Class of 1760.

Fuller began his freshman year "puerilely in love with a special romantic Harvard of my own conjuring," but he was uneasy in the socially stratified atmosphere he found there and contributed to an already strong family tradition of dissent by getting himself expelled not once but twice. On the eve of midterm exams he was suddenly impelled to outdo Harvard's big spenders, and squandered his tuition and allowance on a lavish party in New York for Marilyn Miller and the entire chorus line of the Ziegfeld Follies. After his expulsion for this spree he spent several months in 1914 as an apprentice mechanic at a textile mill owned by a cousin. Having thus supposedly demonstrated his reliability, he was readmitted to Harvard, only to be finally and irrevocably expelled in 1915 as generally irresponsible.

Dumped on the labor market without a degree, Fuller had to take what jobs he could get. From 1915 to 1917 he worked for Armour and Company in New York, first as a meat lugger and later as a cashier. Joining the U.S. Navy in 1917 he took a three-month officer training course at Annapolis, and then served as a commander of crash boats at the Navy flying school at Newport News, Virginia. His first two practical inventions, both designed to prevent pilot drownings, were a seaplane rescue mast and

boom and a "jet stilt" vertical-takeoff aircraft. Fuller left the Navy in 1919 with the rank of lieutenant, junior grade.

During the early months of his service, on July 12, 1917, he had married Anne Hewlett, the daughter of a well-known architect, James Monroe Hewlett. The same year Fuller made what he now called a Grand Strategy Decision by starting his Chronofile. As a boy, while his brother had collected geological specimens, Buckminster Fuller had collected any piece of paper with his name on it: letters, postcards, bills, school reports, programs. He now decided to file all this material chronologically, to make up a unique document of the life of one twentieth-century man. "Beginning in 1917, I determined to employ my already rich case history, as objectively as possible, in documenting the life of a surburban New Englander, born in the Gay Nineties (1895)—the year automobiles were introduced, the wireless telegraph and the automatic screw machine were invented and x-rays were discovered; having his boyhood in the turn of the century; and maturing during humanity's epochal graduation from the inert, materialistic nineteenth century into the dynamic, abstract twentieth century." By 1960 the Fuller Chronofile already amounted to two hundred and fifty volumes, and it has gone on growing at an accelerating rate ever since.

Fuller returned to Armour and Company in 1919, working in New York until 1922 as an assistant export manager. He then moved on to become national sales manager of the Kelly-Springfield Truck Company, which went out of business after three months. Fuller's father-in-law had invented and patented a substitute for the common brick which he called the "Stockade Block," and in 1922 Fuller helped to establish, and develop machinery for, the Stockade Building System. He served as president of the company until 1927, when he was ousted by the stockholders, who held him responsible for its lack of success. This led to the great crisis of his life.

After the death of his four-year-old daughter Alexandra in 1922 Fuller had plunged into sustained depression and heavy drinking. In 1927, jobless and stigmatized as a failure in top management, he found himself stranded in Chicago with his wife and their newborn second daughter, Allegra. Fuller came close to suicide at this "critical detonation point," but in a lakeside dialogue with himself he turned his life around. He recognized that if he committed suicide all his remarkably diverse experience would perish too, and he emerged from the crisis with a new sense of destiny and mission. Giving up all thought of an ordinary business career, Fuller moved with his family to a small apartment in a Chicago slum, where he settled down to "search for the principles governing the universe and help advance the evolution of humanity in accordance with them." The result was a work called first *4D,* and later *4D Time Lock,* a comprehensive essay on man's evolutionary functioning in the universe, and its support by a Design Science. This manifesto, which contains in embryonic form all of Fuller's fundamental ideas, was privately printed in 1928 in two hundred copies which the author sent off to two hundred recipients "deemed to be a fully representative group of altruistic thinkers."

One of Fuller's basic premises is that human nature cannot be reformed, as religious and political thinkers have so often hoped, and that it is not human beings but their environment which must be changed if society is to be improved. From this conviction has flowed a series of designs for revolutionary structures which would further his goal of "finding ways of doing more with less to the end that all people—everywhere—can have more and more of everything." Most of these designs never got beyond the stage of models—for instance the twelve-decked, hexagonal, 4-D (fourth dimensional) luxury apartment block or "living machine," designed to be light enough to be carried into place by dirigibles (which would first drop a bomb to make the excavation). Other projects were a prefabricated modular bathroom, and the Dymaxion House, which was intended to be hung from a pole.

The most conspicuous legacy from this period is in fact the word *dymaxion,* coined by a publicist from words he heard Fuller use frequently—*dynamism, maximum,* and *ions*—which became Fuller's property and for years his trademark. He sank his inheritance in the three-wheeled, rear-engined, streamlined Dymaxion car, which, though it never actually got into production, did achieve three handmade prototypes. Leopold Stokowski helped by buying one of these, but another was involved in a fatal accident which generated unfavorable publicity and thus proved fatal to the car also.

Fuller had embarked on an enterprise that Peter Blake has described as an attempt "to reinvent every single item in his environment, from his own spectacles to mathematics, geography, the English language, anthropology, the reutilisation of scrap metal, diets, socialism and bathroom plumbing." His structures were based on a geometry that utilized triangles, circles, and tetrahedrons rather than rectangles and planes. His Dymaxion Air-Ocean World Map projects the whole globe onto a flat surface with minimal

distortion, avoiding the grotesque disproportion at the poles of the commonest map projection, Mercator's; it is therefore uniquely suitable for such purposes as indicating shortest air routes, and is the only cartographic projection of the world ever to be patented.

The inventor meanwhile formed companies to promote these conceptions—the 4D Company of Chicago (1927–1932) and the Dymaxion Corporation of Bridgeport, Connecticut (1932–1936). In 1936–1938 he worked as assistant to the director of research and development of the Phelps Dodge Corporation, and in 1938–1940 was technical consultant to *Fortune* magazine. From 1942 to 1944 he served the U.S. Government as chief of the mechanical engineering section of the Board of Economic Warfare, and in 1944 he was special assistant to the deputy director of the U.S. Foreign Economic Administration. Fuller's Dymaxion Development Unit, a portable military emergency shelter constructed of corrugated steel and fiberglass, was produced for the armed forces early in World War II. He then launched what promised to be a lucrative invasion of the postwar housing market with his Dymaxion Dwelling Machine Corporation, which he founded in 1944 to develop his prefabricated Wichita House. Two prototypes were actually assembled, but once again the grand design collapsed for lack of money. Fuller then turned his attention from the house as a whole to its shell, developing his spherical geometry to devise the geodesic dome. These now-familiar domes are so constructed that a load applied to any part of the dome is borne by the structure as a whole, and this makes it possible to build extremely large structures which are both very light and very strong. The first sizable geodesic dome, fifty feet in diameter, was built at Black Mountain College, North Carolina, in 1948, and during the 1950s Fuller was commissioned to design and build many hundred-foot or two-hundred-foot domes, as well as one more than three hundred and eighty feet in diameter for the Union Tank Car Company at Baton Rouge, Louisiana, which became the largest clear-span structure then in existence. Fuller has been president since 1949 of Geodesics, Inc.

The geodesic dome was Fuller's breakthrough, the solid commercial success which, as Hugh Kenner puts it, "drew the royalties that set him free to buzz round the world evangelizing. Its fame, moreover, elicited the invitations to come and evangelize." Not that this rhetorical energy was new—Kenner labels him in an earlier phase the "Dymaxion Messiah." For though Fuller has tirelessly bombarded the public with artifacts and inventions, the most important thing for him has always been the concepts and ideas motivating them, and it was increasingly clear to him that his true vocation was to raise the consciousness of his contemporaries as a writer and lecturer.

In fact, Fuller's first collection of essays, *Nine Chains to the Moon,* was in general apathetically received in 1938, though it was praised by Albert Einstein. Only when it was reissued in 1963 did it begin to establish itself as a Fuller classic, adumbrating as it does most of the component ideas of his "comprehensive anticipatory design science"—the conviction that the environment must be changed if society is to be improved; the recycling of resources in order to "do more with less"; the elimination of scarcity; and, above all, the "creative control, or streamlining of society, by the scientific-minded (the right-makes-mightist)." The title was chosen "to encourage and stimulate the broadest attitude towards thought" and to emphasize the smallness of our universe compared with our imagination—if all the people of the world were to stand upon one another's shoulders, they would make nine complete chains between the earth and the moon, and "if it is not so far to the moon, then it is not so far to the limits—whatever, whenever or wherever they may be."

Informed that one of his technical papers was incomprehensible, Fuller's response was to read it aloud "in spontaneously metered doses," watching for expressions of comprehension from the listener and then intuitively measuring out the next portion. He was discovering that he thought aphoristically, in discrete "energy packets"; retyped this way, his thoughts came to look like poetry. In 1940 his thoughts coalesced into several books of verse, which however remained unpublished for over twenty years. They include the three-hundred-page *Untitled Epic Poem on the History of Industrialization* (first published in 1962), which divides the history of the United States into two parts, the first treated briefly as the "Great Experiment" in political innovation, the second more fully as "Industrialization." The work was described in *Time* magazine as a "gas-filled balloon advertising the glories of technocracy," but admired by R. F. Sayre for the way in which Fuller "experiments with language as a technology and with different ways of getting a new technology into a new language." Typical is the passage on mutual trust expressed in the figure of a mail sorter on an express train, who works:

with muttered faith that
the engineer is competent
that the switchmen are not asleep,

that the track walkers are doing their job,
that the technologists
who designed the train and the rails
knew their stuff....

Other poems dating from 1940 include "Machine Tools" (partly written for *Fortune* magazine) and the collection *No More Secondhand God* (1963), which besides prose-poems expressing Fuller's personal philosophy also contains expositions of his Dymaxion Energetic Geometry. Many critics commented on the obscurity of its style, one in *Christian Century* saying that "his private jargon renders much of what he has to say virtually unintelligible. We vote for the domes. He's singing songs of God, but not for us." The *Times Literary Supplement* observed that "the poems and essays in this book are a mixture of naivety, shrewd sense and complete nonsense. All of them show signs of wide intellectual activity.... In this book we are given the opportunity to see the kind of thinking from which his activity springs. Some of it is sound, some of it is crazy." And Harold Taylor found "an extraordinary momentum to Buckminster Fuller's thinking. He is a man incapable of developing only one idea at a time. His ideas stream from him in clusters as he talks two, three or even seven hours at a stretch, one idea suggesting its successor, one cluster of ideas creating new clusters, some ideas expressed in words of his own invention, at times in a syntax of intolerable complexity and almost complete opacity."

Fuller found an operational basis for the constant round of lectures, conferences, and consultations that he calls his "toings and froings" when in 1959 Southern Illinois University offered him a position as a research professor. Its campus at Carbondale became home for his growing staff and the ever-increasing body of documents in the Fuller Chronofile. A talk on the expansion of physical facilities in higher education delivered to the university's Campus Planning Committee was the basis of the book *Education Automation* (1963). In it he applies his theories to the comprehensive planning of the campuses of the future, making the maximum use of automation and electronic aids. Opinions of it have varied from the dismissive view that "most of the book is devoted to polysyllabic gabble on non-educational matters, including much anecdotal autobiography," to a belief that it contained the seeds of the educational revolution of the late 1960s. Fuller has always been the enemy of specialization, and the book includes stirring calls for a new generation of "comprehensive designers."

Many of Fuller's ideas are expressed most clearly in the essays collected in *Ideas and Integrities* (1963), whose "spontaneous autobiographical disclosures" give a useful account of the development of his thought. Peter Blake wrote that each page of the book "is, in a sense, a statement of a contemporary problem, followed by a series of incisive, unexpected, wildly imaginative questions. The genius of Richard Buckminster Fuller is that he knows exactly what questions to ask, and in which order. What makes him more than a walking computer is his humanity and his imagination. For whether he likes it or not, Bucky is, above all, an artist and a poet."

As Fuller zoomed from campus to campus during the 1960s and 1970s his books sold especially well among the young, who shared his concern with pollution, conservation, the humane distribution of resources, and environmental design. Not all of his views have been welcomed by the counterculture, however, or even by old-fashioned liberals, some of whom were appalled by the suggestion that the world should be administered by a technocratic elite in *Operating Manual for Spaceship Earth* (1969). Theodore Roszak compared Fuller with Marshall McLuhan as "a great bamboozler: a combination of Buck Rogers and Horatio Alger. . . . He manages to lay hamhandedly on the line most of the tacit assumptions of the technocratic mentality. . . . To be sure, 'General Systems Theory,' the form of technical expertise Fuller recommends for the better piloting of 'Spaceship Earth,' is intended to be ambitiously broadgauged: the very antithesis of the myopic specialization which is Fuller's *bête noire*. The prospectus sounds intriguing, but the social realities behind GST are bound to be unappealing to those who have sentimental attachments to participative and communitarian politics. This form of elitist brains-trusting—an outgrowth of wartime operations research—is apt to be the essential component of the technocracy's *machine à gouverner*."

In his introduction to the essays and lectures collected in *Utopia or Oblivion* (1969), Stephen Mullin compares Fuller with a sputnik orbiting the earth as a twinkling symbol of technological salvation. Here again Fuller calls for accelerating industrialization under the benevolent despotism of artist-scientist environmental designers, for industry is continually increasing the performance per weight of the world's resources, doing "more with less," the formula which lies at the root of his design science. It seemed to Konstantin Bazarov that there was little to choose between Fuller's utopia and oblivion: his

"fundamental fallacy is that he merely provides technological solutions to technologically-posed problems, which is what led to the world being in such a mess in the first place. He never thinks of human beings as people with emotions, wishes, desires and beliefs, but suggests instead that the planet can be run by an elite group of benevolent designers who will produce a favourably designed environment which will allow man to be as successful as the hydrogen atom. What the measure of success of a hydrogen atom is he doesn't tell us, but since they are all alike and none of them is alive I can't say I have much desire to compete with them."

In spite of such objections, Fuller's reputation and influence have continued to grow. In 1970 he was described by Patrick O'Donovan in the London *Observer* as "America's answer to Leonardo." Between 1954 and 1975 he was awarded thirty-nine honorary degrees, ranging from Doctor of Arts at the University of Michigan, to Doctor of Humane Letters at Brandeis, Doctor of Engineering at Notre Dame, and Doctor of Science at McGill. He received thirty gold medals and other awards of merit during the same period. Fuller is a Fellow of the American Academy of Arts and Sciences and of the World Academy of Art and Science, a member of the National Institute of Arts and Letters and of the National Academy of Design, and a Benjamin Franklin Fellow of the Royal Society of Arts in England. He is a member or fellow of some thirty professional societies, American and foreign. Books about him proliferate, and James Meller has edited an anthology of his writings under the title *The Buckminster Fuller Reader* (1970). *I Seem To Be a Verb* (1970), assembled by Jerome Agel and Quentin Fiore (who also designed Marshall McLuhan's whimsical *The Medium Is the Massage*), takes its title from a typical Fuller poem:

> . . . I am not a thing—a noun.
> I seem to be a verb—
> an evolutionary process—
> an integral function of the universe,
> and so are you.

The new poems that make up *Intuition* (1972) center on the distinction between Mind and Brain. Described by one reviewer as "a collection of verse-essays in future-think, written partially in English, partially in space-speak," these poems express one of Fuller's fundamental ideas, summed up thus in the publisher's note: "That humanity is suffering from a kind of cosmic near-sightedness, an inability to comprehend universal principles, due to concentration on special 'parts.' Only by using our whole minds—our intuition, as well as our reason—will we be able to fulfil our unique role in the universe." Emile Capouya found "evidence throughout this book that Buckminster Fuller is indeed exquisitely sensitive to certain forms of beauty—the poem 'Intuition' is a kind of hymn composed for the launching of a sailing vessel. But framing seemly, shapely speech is not among his gifts."

Fuller's most ambitious work is *Synergetics: Explorations in the Geometry of Thinking* (1975), assembled in collaboration with E.J. Applewhite. *Synergy* is another word used by Fuller to express one of his basic concepts: start with parts, and when they come together they will interact unexpectedly to make a whole that is greater than the sum of its parts—like a watch or an airplane. Only by starting with wholes can you hope not to be fooled, and this means identifying very large trends, and ultimately starting with the experience of what Fuller calls *Universe,* with a capital *U.* This must be discovered partly through science and partly through intuition, for it is not a collection of things but a harmonious, all-embracing set of relationships, which can only be expressed in number, the metaphysical counterpart of physical reality. It is number which permits the artist-scientist-designer to understand Universe and imitate it in his own creative work. And so *Synergetics* expounds in detail the elements of Fuller's "energetic geometry" based on the tetrahedron, to become a sort of illustrated summary of Fuller's gospel, or as O. B. Hardison puts it, "a comprehensive gathering, a kind of *summa theologica* of Fuller's mathematics, philosophy and design theories . . . a remarkable book. Probably no reader will go through it from cover to cover; but all readers who spend the time needed to overcome its threshold difficulties will be generously rewarded. It is the legacy of a man who has had a powerful impact on the twentieth-century imagination." Hardison called this "a major work whose implications will be debated, acclaimed, questioned, and, in some cases, attacked for years to come." *And It Came to Pass—Not to Stay* (1976), a collection of seven verse-essays conveying the essence of Fuller's social and political philosophy, was called "a genuine vision from a genuine visionary."

Fuller left Southern Illinois University after a wave of student unrest in 1970 had helped to force the resignation of its president. In 1972 he was named World Fellow in residence at the University City Science Center, Philadelphia, an institution maintained by a consortium of thirty universities, colleges, and hospitals in the area. Here he has access to laboratories, storage space, and computers, and teaches at each of the schools that sponsored him there—the University of Pennsylvania, Bryn Mawr, Swarthmore, Haverford, and the Science Center itself. In 1972 the Design Science Institute, a nonprofit organization based in Washington, DC, was established to perpetuate Fuller's ideas and designs.

The author returned to Harvard in 1961–1962 as Charles Eliot Norton Professor of Poetry, and he has held many other academic appointments, including the R. Buckminster Fuller Chair of Architecture at the University of Detroit (1970). Though he did not formally qualify as an architect until 1974, Fuller designed the United States Pavilion at Expo 67—the Montreal World's Fair—and he has since designed banks, concert halls, and theatres, among other buildings. In 1971 he worked with Indian officials on the final plans for a coordinated jet airport system for the cities of New Delhi, Bombay, and Madras.

Buckminster Fuller is a small man, only a little over five feet tall. He has a large head, crew-cut white hair, and blue eyes magnified by heavy lenses; he wears hearing aids in both ears. He dresses formally, but has been found "immediately charming," and "a man of remarkable humility." Fuller lives with his wife in an apartment thirty stories above Philadelphia, overlooking the Delaware, though even in his eighties he is still often away on his "toings and froings"; he has so far circled the globe thirty-nine times, "never as a tourist." Every year he spends the entire month of August at the family vacation home on Bear Island, Maine, where he keeps his forty-foot yacht *Intuition.* Here he may be joined by his daughter Allegra, who is married to the film director Robert Snyder, and his two grandchildren, Alexandra and Jaime. From an octogenarian vantage point he sees his life as neatly coincident with the grand patterns of innovation, beginning "on the Victorian side of our present world technology" and extending into the age of lunar exploration.

PRINCIPAL WORKS: 4D, 1928 (reprinted 1972 as 4D Time Lock); Nine Chains to the Moon, 1938 (reprinted 1963); Untitled Epic Poem on the History of Industrialization, 1962; Education Automation, 1963; Ideas and Integrities: A Spontaneous Autobiographical Disclosure, 1963; No More Secondhand God, 1963; What I Am Trying to Do, 1968; Operating Manual for Spaceship Earth, 1968; Utopia Or Oblivion, 1969; The Buckminster Fuller Reader, edited by James Meller, 1970; (with Jerome Agel and Quentin Fiore) I Seem To Be a Verb, 1970; The World Game, 1971; Intuition, 1972; Buckminster Fuller to Children of Earth, 1972; Earth, Inc., 1973; (with E.J. Applewhite) Synergetics: Explorations in the Geometry of Thinking, 1975; And It Came to Pass—Not to Stay, 1976.

ABOUT: Applewhite, E.J. Cosmic Fishing: An Account of Writing Synergetics With Buckminster Fuller, 1977; Close, G.W. R. Buckminster Fuller, 1977; Current Biography, 1976; Hatch, A. Buckminster Fuller: At Home in the Universe, 1974; Kenner, H. Bucky, 1973; McHale, J. R. Buckminster Fuller, 1962; Marks, R.W. The Dymaxion World of Buckminster Fuller, 1960; Marks, R.W. (ed.) Richard Buckminster Fuller, 1963; Robertson, D.W. Mind's Eye of Buckminster Fuller, 1974; Rosen, S.M. Wizard of the Dome, 1969. *Periodicals*—Architectural Design December 1972; Architectural Forum October 1963, January 1972; Arts Review September 1970; Book Week January 26, 1964; April 27, 1969; Christian Century May 8, 1963; Christian Science Monitor May 10, 1972; Commentary October 1973; Horizon Summer 1968; Life February 26, 1971; Nation September 1, 1969; June 15, 1970; New Republic June 10, 1972; New Statesman February 27, 1970; New York Times Book Review July 28, 1963; April 20, 1969; June 29, 1975; New York Times Magazine April 23, 1967; July 6, 1975; New Yorker October 10, 1959; January 8, 1966; March 13, 1971; Newsweek July 13, 1959; August 5, 1963; April 21, 1975; Observer February 22, 1970; Playboy February 1972; Readers Digest November 1969; Saturday Evening Post March-April 1973; Saturday Review May 2, 1970; June 24, 1972; February 1973; Spectator March 7, 1970; Time January 10, 1964; May 11, 1970; February 19, 1973; Times Literary Supplement September 6, 1963; August 6, 1964; September 11, 1969; Wall Street Journal April 8, 1975.

ERNEST J. GAINES

GAINES, ERNEST J. (January 15, 1933–), American novelist and short story writer, was born in Oscar, Louisiana—in that southern part of the state where French settlement in the eighteenth century has left its mark in the names of places and people, in certain traditions and attitudes, and in the survival of a "Cajun" minority and language. Gaines is the oldest of twelve children of Manuel Gaines, a laborer, and the former Adrienne Colar. Raised on a plantation in Point Coupée parish, some twenty-five miles from Baton Rouge, he spent much of his youth working in the sugar cane and cotton fields. Gaines read little or nothing as a boy, but he comes "from a long line of storytellers" and made his own first attempts at narrative when at twelve and thirteen he put on short plays in church. An important figure in his childhood was his crippled great-aunt Augusteen Jefferson, who could not walk and therefore crawled about her house, taking care of her own cooking, washing, sewing, and gardening without a trace of self-pity. A fictionalized portrait of her appears in Gaines's first novel, and some of her quality is incorporated in his best-known creation, Miss Jane Pittman.

When Gaines was fifteen his mother left Louisiana and joined her second husband, a merchant seaman, in Vallejo, California, about thirty miles from San Francisco. Gaines followed her to Vallejo, where he attended high school and junior college and discovered the pleasures of reading in the public library. He wrote his first novel at the age of sixteen. Gaines served from 1953 to 1955 in the U.S. Army and afterwards settled in San Francisco, where he has lived ever since. He attended San Francisco State College on the GI Bill (1955-1957), receiving his B.A. in 1957, and publishing his first stories in the college magazine. In 1958-1959 he studied at Stanford University on a Wallace Stegner Creative Writing Fellowship. Intent, he says, upon mastering "the art of writing (which I'm sure will take the rest of my life)," he has been a full-time writer since 1959, when he had his first success, receiving the Joseph Henry Jackson Award for his short story "Comeback."

"The artist is the only free man left," Gaines said once. "He owes nobody nothing—not even himself. He should write what he wants, when he wants, and to whomever he wants. If he is true, he will use that material which is closest to him." Gaines himself has done so, writing almost exclusively about the blacks and whites of rural Louisiana. He is a politically conscious but not a militant writer, preferring "to get down all that black people do, plus the violent, militant thing." A recurrent theme in his work is the conflict between militant or simply ambitious young blacks and their more passive and tradition-bound elders.

This is the theme of *Catherine Carmier* (1964), a rewritten version of his unpublished first novel with a structure borrowed from Turgenev's *Fathers and Sons*. In it a college-educated young black returns from California to be reunited with his beloved great-aunt, aware that he will never again be able to share her values and the traditions of his childhood. *Catherine*

Carmier was not much noticed, but there was a generally favorable reception for Gaines's second novel, *Of Love and Dust,* which followed in 1967. Set in Louisiana in 1948, it tells the story of Marcus, a young black who, while awaiting trial for murder, is bonded out for field work on a local plantation. The brutal Cajun overseer, Sidney Bonbon, enraged by Marcus's open contempt, works him almost to death. Marcus, refusing to be broken, responds by courting Bonbon's black mistress. Rebuffed by her, he turns his attention to Bonbon's forlorn blond wife, seduces her, and takes her with him when he makes his hopeless attempt to escape north. The novel's narrator, Jim Kelly, knows that Marcus is doomed and at first hates him for disturbing the status quo, but comes gradually and grudgingly to admire his courage.

Sara Blackburn called this "a serious, powerful novel. . . . Kelly's transition from cynical don't-rock-the-boatism to something else takes place over a series of exciting and beautifully realized scenes, some of them funny. . . . [Gaines] is a writer of terrific energy; his characters have a dimension and authenticity that makes us know and care about them. It takes a lot of nerve to write a novel like this today, and a lot of skill to bring it off. Mr. Gaines has plenty of both." Other reviewers were more equivocal in their praise. Robert Granat found "some vivid scenes and fine portraits" as well as "occasional technical awkwardness" and an "undergraduate" quality. James Lea also found weaknesses in technique, but concluded that Gaines had "succeeded where many others of his race and generation have failed: he has written a book about Negroes and whites as just plain people, sharing equally the blame for maintaining a worn-out tradition."

The five short stories collected in *Bloodline* (1968) feature such diverse black protagonists as an eight-year-old boy visiting a dentist in the city, a roughneck youth spending a night in jail, the bastard nephew of a white plantation owner challenging convention, and a proud old woman forced to resettle after a bombing. There was much praise for Gaines's ability "to create living characters and to set them against a rich and vivid background," and for his "marvelous ear for speech rhythms, content, and dialect." The most arresting of these stories, several critics agreed, was "A Long Day in November," in which a small boy, son of a cane-plantation worker, describes how his gadabout father's obsession with an old car led to his parents' separation, and how the car was eventually burned as a kind of sacrificial offering to bring about a reconciliation. Marilyn Sachs, reviewing

an expanded version of this story published as a novella in 1971, said that "Ernest Gaines, maybe because he is black, and can see people moving under their skins, has written . . . about a black family, and has made them sound like people."

The Autobiography of Miss Jane Pittman appeared in 1971 and established Gaines as one of the most admired black writers in America. The novel purports to be the tape-recorded life story of a centenarian black matriarch. Ticey, as she had been first called, was born into slavery. Freed toward the end of the Civil War, she was renamed Jane Brown by a passing Yankee corporal, joined a band of black refugees traveling to Ohio, survived a Klan ambush, and settled down to work on a Louisiana plantation. She made a good marriage to Joe Pittman, a black cowboy, and adopted Ned, son of a dead friend, who grew up to be a fighter for black freedom and black education. Ned was murdered by a hired killer, and Miss Jane turned for strength and comfort to God. Sixty years later another young freedom fighter came into her life, and he too was gunned down by white men. It was at his death that Miss Jane joined the civil rights movement and, at the age of one hundred and nine, set off to demonstrate against segregated water fountains.

Jerry Bryant called the book "an epic poem" which is "literally . . . an account of Jane's life" and figuratively "a metaphor of the collective black experience." Geoffrey Wolff, similarly, was reminded of *The Odyssey* by the way Jane's travels "manage to summarize the American history of her race." Other reviewers singled out for praise Gaines's mastery of black and Cajun dialects, his "wit and wrath, imagination and indignation, misery and poetry," and his use of fable, myth, and folk tale to further and deepen the narration. Melvin Maddocks wrote that this "is not hot-and-breathless, burn-baby-burn writing. Unlike apocalyptic novelists, Gaines does not make the revolution happen by surreal rhetoric. He simply watches, a patient artist, a patient man, and it happens to him. When Jane, disobedient at last, walks past her plantation owner to take part in a demonstration, a code goes crack, as surely, as naturally as a root pushing up through concrete." Alice Walker said that Gaines is "mellow with historical reflection, supple with wit, relaxed and expansive because he does not equate his people with failure." An adaptation of the novel, broadcast over CBS/TV, won the 1974 Emmy award for the best drama special of the year.

Gaines was writer in residence at Denison University, Granville, Ohio, in 1971. He received a grant from the National Endowment for the Arts in 1966. Jerry Bryant believes that Gaines's special contribution to American literature is his successful resolution of the conflict between the demands of art and the demands of black politics: "No American novelist, either white or black, has been able to harmonize these discordant notes. . . . No novelist, that is, before Gaines."

PRINCIPAL WORKS: Catherine Carmier, 1964; Of Love and Dust, 1967; Bloodline (short storeis), 1968; The Autobiography of Miss Jane Pittman, 1971; A Long Day in November, 1971; In My Father's House, 1978.

ABOUT: Chapman, A. (ed.) New Black Voices, 1972; Contemporary Authors 9-12 1st revision, 1974; Living Black American Authors, 1973; Major, C. The Dark and Feeling, 1974; O'Brien, J. (ed.) Interviews With Black Writers, 1973; Tooker, D. and Hofheins, R. Fiction! Interviews With Northern California Novelists, 1976; Vinson, J. (ed.) Contemporary Novelists, 1976; Who's Who in America, 1976-1977. *Periodicals*—Biography News October 1974; Christian Science Monitor June 3, 1971; Nation February 5, 1968; April 5, 1971; Negro Digest November 1967; New York Times Book Review November 19, 1967; May 23, 1971; June 11, 1978; Newsweek June 16, 1969; May 3, 1971; Saturday Review January 20, 1968; August 17, 1968; May 1, 1971; Southern Review January 1974; Time May 10, 1971.

GARDNER, JOHN (CHAMPLIN) (July 21, 1933–), American novelist, biographer, short story writer, poet, scholar, and translator, was born at Batavia, New York, the son of John Champlin Gardner and the former Priscilla Jones. He recieved his undergraduate education at De Pauw University (1951-1953), graduating with a B.A., then spent some time in 1955 at Washington University, St. Louis. He went to the State University of Iowa with a Woodrow Wilson Fellowship in 1955, receiving his M.A. there in 1956, his Ph.D. in 1958. Teaching appointments followed at Oberlin College, Ohio (1958-1959), Chico State College (1959-1962), and San Francisco State College (1962-1965). In 1965 he became professor of English at Southern Illinois University, Carbondale, making brief excursions as visiting professor to the University of Detroit (1970-1971), Northwestern University (1973), and Bennington College (1975). He left Southern Illinois in 1976 and now teaches at the State University of New York in Binghamton.

In an interview published in J.D. Bellamy's *The New Fiction,* Gardner said: "I think I use the stylistic tricks of Chaucer more than those of any living man." He also acknowledges the influence of Melville and of Walt Disney. Elsewhere he has dismissed the fiction of Samuel Beckett as "pretty paltry stuff intellectually" compared with that of John Galsworthy, and placed himself behind the banners of Socrates, Christ, and Tolstoy. As he explains in *On Moral*

Nancy Crampton

JOHN GARDNER

Fiction (1978), the modern writer's preoccupation with alienation and despair, the modern elevation of form over content, seems to him treacherous. Art, he believes, should enlarge our sympathies, should celebrate and affirm, redefining for each new generation what it is to be human. And he indicts as "either trivial or false" practitioners such contemporary idols as Bellow, Mailer, Vonnegut, Heller, Didion, and Barth.

Gardner's own first novel was *The Resurrection* (1966), in which a philosophy professor dying of leukemia hunts through his stock-in-trade for some significant source of hope. He finds no consolation in philosophy, but some in the precarious survival of the culture of which it is a part. The book was found tautly ruminative, deft in its characterization, and skillful in its handling of such devices as interior monologue and tense-switching, but so littered with philosophical tags that it becomes "a kind of seminar."

The Wreckage of Agathon, which followed in 1970, is a satire set in ancient Sparta during the Helots' revolt against the lawgiver Lycurgus. Jailed for sedition along with his young disciple Peeker, a foul-minded and incorrigibly opinionated seer called Agathon ("the good") ruminates among the rats upon the militaristic state in which he lives and is dying, and the slim chances of survival within it of learning, tolerance, and humanity. If these qualities do survive, Gardner implies, even in ancient Sparta (or modern America), it is because of the irreducible irreverence and humanity of such reprobates as Agathon.

The conflict between freedom and order has

been the theme of all the novels that Gardner has published since, though he has usually placed himself on the other side of the argument. He does so in *Grendel* (1971), which is a reworking of the Anglo-Saxon heroic poem *Beowulf* from the point of view of the man-eating monster slain by Beowulf. In Gardner's version, Grendel is undone by his love for the order and beauty of human poetry, which condemns him to self-consciousness and vulnerability. Gardner's Grendel *is* a monster, a force for evil and chaos, but in his witty self-disgust, his disarming love of language, his longing for acceptance by the creatures he is fated to destroy, he is "a great, complex character." A reviewer in the *Times Literary Supplement* summed up the book as "a subtle and comic exploration of what evil is, told by its unwilling embodiment. It is fiercely ugly and inventive, and very good."

About *The Sunlight Dialogues* (1972), "a vast, clotted meditation on the laws of the universe as demonstrated in upper New York State," opinions varied. Set in Gardner's hometown of Batavia, the novel consists of ostensible exchanges, really monologues, between Taggert Hodge, the Sunlight Man, a half-crazy, anarchic magician, fallen son of Batavia's patriarch, and Fred Clumly, the aging, puzzled, ordinary, charitable police chief who must put him away if order and law are to survive. Gardner has said of the Sunlight Man that he "imagines all the possibilities of the world . . . [but] finds no order, no coherence in it. He's a wild romantic poet with no hope of God. The two characters who have the most imagination in the novel are Clumly and Mrs. Clumly, because they can see into other people's minds."

"Long, many-stranded, allegorical," wrote Victor Howes, "*The Sunlight Dialogues* is a rich broth unevenly cooked, with hard carrots and watery potatoes. By turns comic, satiric, symbolic, it is also by turns flat, prosaic, over-explicit. Unlike the material of *Grendel,* its separate parts do not fuse into an imagined whole. . . . The reader senses the presence of Jungian archetypes, sun-signs, hermetic lore, 'huge cloudy symbols of a high romance' . . . but long before the story grinds to a halt on page 673, the reader has begun to ask himself 'Which way did the magic go?' " This view was shared by some other reviewers, but as many inclined to the opinion expressed by Tony Tanner: "It is a major fictional exploration into America, no less. . . . And without abandoning its fictional promises, it draws us into a sobering meditation on the possible shapes of our immediate future. It tells no lies yet ends with a refusal to accept despair. It does all this at the same time as it

involves us in an absorbing and intricately interwoven story. This is a great deal for any one novel to do, and it should be recognized immediately for what it is—a very impressive achievement." And it seemed to Thomas R. Edwards that Gardner knows his Middle America "as well as any novelist we've had, not excepting Updike, the early Cozzens, or even Faulkner."

Jason and Medeia, which followed, has been called "perhaps the first fully serious narrative poem in English since *The Ring and the Book.*" It is a retelling in blank verse of the story of Jason and the Argonauts, from the world-weary viewpoint of a modern professor of medieval literature who is John Gardner himself. Frank D. McConnell in *Contemporary Novelists* wrote that the poem manages "to present the legend as a version of the conflict between permanence and change, civilization and the chaotic forces of love underlying—and sometimes destroying—the civilization they create." Morris Dickstein concluded that Gardner "is a prolific and learned writer of amazing virtuoso dexterity, but with little power of judgment or depth of inspiration," whose books "all have the willed brilliance of the born overachiever." Melvin Maddocks, on the other hand, thought that Gardner had succeeded brilliantly: "Applying his first-class imagination with maximum risks, he has, like his characters, worked a desperate and glorious venture."

Nickel Mountain (1973) is an almost equally startling departure from the common run of contemporary fiction, a gentle and entirely straightforward "pastoral novel" about "the survival of plain human goodness." The "knottily constructed" stories collected in *The King's Indian* resume the themes and the "fiendishly mixed forms" of Gardner's other novels, and the long title story was called in *Library Journal* "a high point in Gardner's fiction thus far . . . a portmanteau (Poe, Melville, Coleridge, Dickens, other influences) tall-tale, a sea/detective story fleshed out with spiritualism and mesmerism, biblical typology, and sardonic philosophical relativism." In the opinion of Alan Friedman, "collages or not, bamboozling or not, his ventriloquial fictions do suddenly grow nerves and breathe with an awesome, independent life."

Paul Gray wrote that in Gardner's short stories "one situation constantly recurs . . . traditionalist meets anarchist; an inherited past must defend itself against a plotless future." The same may be said of all Gardner's fiction, which is why Frank D. McConnell calls him a "postmodernist"—one committed to a new insistence on "the civilizing nature of art, a re-founding of the City of Man so efficiently destroyed between

[Joyce's] *Ulysses* and Pynchon's *Gravity's Rainbow.* And if the phrase makes any sense, then in this as in other respects Gardner is the first and most continually interesting of the 'postmodernists.' "

This view received further support in Gardner's next novel, *October Light,* which offers "two stories for the price of one." It is set in Vermont, where James L. Page, a foul-tempered old farmer, locks his octagenarian widowed sister in her bedroom in a fit of rage. An enlightened old lady—a late convert to the women's movement and the sexual revolution—she stubbornly refuses to come out again and stays there for days, surviving on apples from the attic and reading the only book she can find, a battered paperback novel called *The Smugglers of Lost Souls' Rock.* This story (which Gardner assembled in collaboration with his wife) is a "trashy" fantasy with Faustian echoes about marijuana smuggling and UFOs in the American West. It is quoted at length in *October Light,* so that the story unfolds for the reader just as it does for the old prisoner in Vermont. She is fascinated by the fantasy, which evokes a "permissive" and disorderly society that is anathema to her brother.

It was generally regarded as a tribute to Gardner's skill that the reactionary and cantankerous Page retains the reader's interest and sympathy and, in the revelations near the novel's close, achieves an almost tragic stature. Critics differed a great deal about the value of *The Smugglers of Lost Souls' Rock:* Robert Towers called it a "boring and exasperating farrago" which "seriously wounds the novel as a whole," while Edwin Morgan found it compulsive reading and said that Gardner had used it "very cunningly in relation to his two main characters." *October Light* seemed to Morgan "a rich, witty, and generally very entertaining book," and Towers, in spite of several quite serious reservations, found it nevertheless "a lavishly talented, often impressive work, clearly his best book since *Grendel.*" It received the 1976 fiction award of the National Book Critics Circle.

Though he is best known for his fiction, Gardner has acquired a very considerable reputation as a scholar with studies of the construction of the Wakefield Cycle of miracle plays and of Christian poetry in Old English, and translations into modern English of *Gawain and the Green Knight,* the alliterative *Morte Arthure,* and other Middle English poems. His modernizations of the Gawain-poet's works were said by a reviewer in *Choice* to "retain the original tone, most of the original texts, much of the alliteration, and many of the other poetic devices and stanzaic forms" in translations that would "appeal to eager undergraduates and their teachers more than do most older translations."

The Life and Times of Chaucer was welcomed as "popular literary biography of the highest order." Though the facts of Chaucer's life are relatively well documented, he never wrote about himself "except jokingly and trivially," and in building up his portrait of the man and the world he lived in Gardner draws on his extensive knowledge of the politics, philosophy, social life, and literary atmosphere of the period, and, when knowledge fails, on his own "novelist's imagination." "Fortunately," wrote Christopher Lehmann-Haupt, "Mr. Gardner has a wonderful imagination for this sort of work: it is alive in history, bristling with facts and opinions." This was the commonest reaction to the book, though Gabriel Josipovici found himself "very conscious of having Gardner's Chaucer, rather than Chaucer himself."

There was also a good deal of praise for *The Poetry of Chaucer,* published almost simultaneously and also intended for the nonspecialist. Gardner's principal thesis in this chronological study is that Chaucer was much influenced by Nominalist philosophy, and drew from this the idea that truth is relative and that "quite possibly, there can be, in the end, no real communication between human beings." It was this opinion, Gardner suggests, that accounted for the inferiority of Chaucer's late poetry—it was *deliberately* bad, an almost Absurdist "art of bad art." There were few takers for this theory, and Charles Muscatine criticized Gardner's "inveterate passion for sensing, finding, digging out and playing with analogy" as "far fetched and, finally, cold." John Gardner is also the author of a number of well-received children's books that reflect his interest in mythology and folklore.

Gardner held a Danforth fellowship in 1970-1973. He received a grant from the National Endowment for the Arts in 1972, and a Guggenheim fellowship in 1973. He told J.D. Bellamy that he is not nearly as prolific as he appears to be, but is publishing in quick succession works written over a period of fifteen years when he could find no publisher. He has identified *Nickel Mountain* and *The Sunlight Dialogues* as early works, *Grendel, The King's Indian,* and *Jason and Medeia* as more recent. Bellamy describes Gardner as "a well-built man of medium height with light collar-length hair and very light eyes." He lives on a farm and smokes a churchwarden pipe. The author was married in 1953 to Joan Louise Patterson, and has three children.

PRINCIPAL WORKS: *Fiction*—The Resurrection, 1966; The Wreckage of Agathon, 1970; Grendel, 1971; The Sunlight

Dialogues, 1972; Jason and Medeia (novel in verse), 1973; Nickel Mountain: A Pastoral Novel, 1973; The King's Indian: Stories and Tales, 1974; October Light, 1976. *Nonfiction* —The Construction of the Wakefield Cycle, 1974; The Construction of Christian Poetry in Old English, 1975; The Life and Times of Chaucer, 1977; The Poetry of Chaucer, 1977; On Moral Fiction, 1978. *For children*—Dragon, Dragon, 1975; Gudgekin, the Thistle Girl, 1976; The King of the Hummingbirds, 1977; In the Suicide Mountains, 1977; A Child's Bestiary, 1977. *As editor and translator*—The Complete Works of the Gawain-Poet in a Modern English Version, 1965; The Alliterative Morte Arthure, The Owl and the Nightingale, and Five Other Middle English Poems, in a Modernized Version, 1971. *As editor*—(with Lennis Dunlap) The Forms of Fiction, 1962; (with Nicholas Joost) Papers on the Art and Age of Geoffrey Chaucer, 1967.

ABOUT: Bellamy, J.D. (ed.) The New Fiction, 1975; Current Biography, 1978; Vinson, J. (ed.) Contemporary Novelists, 1976; Who's Who in America, 1976-1977. *Periodicals*— American Scholar Winter 1974-1975; Atlantic March 1973, May 1977; Book Week July 17, 1966; Christian Science Monitor September 9, 1971; December 20, 1972; January 30, 1974; Commonweal March 1, 1974; Library Journal October 15, 1974; Nation May 21, 1973; June 15, 1974; National Review February 23, 1973; February 28, 1975; New Republic December 7, 1974; New York Review of Books December 30, 1971; October 19, 1972; October 4, 1973; February 20, 1974; March 21, 1974; April 28, 1977; New York Times September 4, 1971; March 23, 1977; New York Times Book Review November 15, 1970; September 19, 1971; December 10, 1972; July 1, 1973; December 9, 1973; December 15, 1974; December 26, 1976; December 25, 1977; Newsweek December 24, 1973; April 10, 1978; Saturday Review of the Arts January 1973; Time November 9, 1970; January 1, 1973; July 16, 1973; December 31, 1973; Times Literary Supplement November 22, 1974; August 17, 1977.

*GARNEAU, HECTOR DE SAINT-DENYS (June 12, 1912–October 24, 1943); French-Canadian poet and diarist, was born in Montréal, the son of Paul Garneau and the former Hermine Prévost. The family was a wealthy and distinguished one; Hector's great-grandfather, François-Xavier Garneau (1809–1866), was an eminent Canadian historian; he was also a poet, as was Hector's grandfather, Alfred Garneau. The boy spent a happy childhood on his family's large estate at Sainte-Catherine-de-Fossambault, near Québec. He grew up with his cousin Anne Hébert, who lived nearby, and who has become one of the most distinguished of French-Canadian poets and novelists.

Garneau was educated in Montréal at the Jesuit Collège Sainte-Marie—in 1924–1925 he studied for a time at the École des Beaux Arts but then returned to the Collège. A devotee of all the arts, Garneau was also handsome, strong, and healthy. In 1928, however, he suffered an attack of rheumatic fever, which left him with a damaged heart. Another bout of serious illness followed in 1933, putting an end to his education.

*gär nō′

In 1934 Garneau had an exhibition of his paintings at the Montreal Art Gallery, and the same year he and a friend founded the review *La Relève* (The Relief), which was inspired by the eclectic neo-Catholicism and "personalism" then current in France. For a time Garneau contributed art criticism to *La Relève,* but he had already begun to withdraw for long periods to Sainte-Catherine-de-Fossambault. He spent most of his last years there, wrestling with a series of psychological and religious crises similar to those experienced by Anne Hébert and by his close friend Jean le Moyne, editor of his posthumous works. Edmund Wilson considers that the work of all three is haunted by the claustrophobic atmosphere of the ancestral mansion: isolated, dark, and stifling, with family relationships "ingrown to the verge of incest."

Certainly Garneau was tormented by a puritan conscience, and a shyness "amounting to a fear of a loss of identity." He also felt keenly the dearth of culture in Montréal and in Canada in general, and in his *Journal* complains at length about the lack of concerts and art exhibitions, the general absence of taste. The *Journal,* published posthumously in 1954, has been one of the most influential documents in modern Canadian literature. Written as a seris of *pensées,* it deals with the anguished years between January 1935 and January 1939.

In the *Journal,* as C.R.P. May has written, "pages of moral introspection follow pages which relate his experience of music and art to general aesthetic theories about the artist's possession of reality, but these are complementary aspects of a very articulate treatment of the crisis of maturity. The adult world of responsibility demands a different courage from that which the child needs to explore and possess the world through his imagination." Other passages deal with French-Canadian nationalism, on which Garneau writes subtly and humanely; with suicide, on which he dwells at length; and with the symbolism he used in his poetry. Many critics consider that the *Journal* and Garneau's letters to his friends (*Lettres à ses amis,* 1967) contain the clearest thinking to be found in all modern Canadian literature, though Edmund Wilson disagreed, finding his prose often "groping" and "entangled," opaque with "undefined abstractions" and "unparticularized allusions."

Almost all of Garneau's poetry was written during the same few years that the *Journal* covers. Mordechai Richler has said that the single slim volume he published in his lifetime, *Regards et jeux dans l'espace* (Gazes and Games in Space, 1937), "initiated the whole modern movement in French-Canadian poetry"—was the first book "to make full and unashamed use of free verse rhythms and techniques." A second small collection, *Solitudes,* is included in the *Poésies complètes* (1949).

Garneau's poetry is metaphysical and introspective. It explores, often elliptically and haltingly, memories of childhood and the apparently uncorrupted beauty of nature in a search for a kind of innocence that can be reified in experience. But adult experience Garneau found to be vulgar, sinful, and mediocre; hence his anguish:

> I am a bird-cage
> Bone-cage
> With a bird
>
> The bird in his bone-cage
> It is death who makes his nest
>
> When nothing happens
> You hear his wing-ruffle
>
> And after a burst of laughter
> If you suddenly stop
> You hear his coo
> Deep down
> Like a tiny bell. . . .
>
> Wouldn't he love to fly away
> Is it you who holds him back
> Or me
> Or what
>
> He can only escape
> When he's eaten me all
> My heart
> My source of blood
> My life
>
> In his beak will be my soul.
>
> (from "Cage d'oiseau,"
> translated by
> Miranda Britt)

Garneau is a quintessentially French-Canadian representative of the French Catholic tradition evident in the tormented work of Georges Bernanos, whose novel about an adolescent suicide, Mouchette, provided the context for Garneau's final meditations on suicide in the last pages of his *Journal.* The "spiritual suicide" represented by his last four years of total silence has been called an "ultimate, desperate appeal to the grace of God."

It is not certain how he died. One night after visiting a friend, he took a canoe to an island where he was building a camp and where, perhaps, he had a heart attack. His partly frozen body was found the next morning among the trees.

Garneau is regarded in Canada with reverence, particularly among the young. The mystery of his death—the possibility that he took his own life—only adds to his stature as a tragic hero. There is a film about his life which ends with a shot of an empty canoe. As a person he was, according to Edmund Wilson, "sensitive and reflective and of an extreme scrupulosity of conscience." He was the first really important French-Canadian poet after the ill-fated Émile Nelligan (mad from the turn of the century until his death in 1941), and his small output—showing as much awareness of Rilke as of Rimbaud and Claudel, yet startlingly original and disturbing—is still the subject of intensive study.

PRINCIPAL WORKS IN ENGLISH TRANSLATION: Nine Poems, translated by J. Beaupré and G. Turnbull, 1953; Journal, translated by John Glassco, 1962; Complete Poems, translated by John Glassco, 1975; (with Anne Hébert) Selected Poems, translated by F.R. Scott, 1962; *Poems in* Roy, G.R. (ed.) Twelve Modern French Canadian Poets, 1958.

ABOUT: Ellis, M.B. De Saint-Denys-Garneau: art et réalisme, 1949; Fortier, L. Le drame spirituel de Saint-Denys-Garneau, 1952; Kushner, E. Saint-Denys-Garneau, 1967; Légaré, R. L'aventure poétique de Saint-Denys-Garneau, 1957; Oxford Companion to Canadian History and Literature, 1967; Penguin Companion to Literature 1, 1971; Wilson, E. O Canada, 1967.

---

*GATSOS, NIKOS (November 25, 1911; some sources give December 6, 1914–), Greek poet, lyricist, and translator, was born in Asea, in Arcadia, where his family owned land and where he attended primary school. At the age of eleven he went to Tripolis, capital of the Peloponnese, to enroll in the gymnasium there. When he was sixteen he moved with his family to Athens, where he completed his high school education and entered the University, studying classics, philosophy, and history from 1932 to 1936 (though he did not take his degree until many years later). In 1935-1936 he spent almost a year in Paris and in southern France.

His early influences came from Greek, French, and later from English literature. During the late 1930s, he became one of the highly talented group associated with *Ta Nea Grammata* (New Letters), an Athens literary journal that was responsible for establishing many of the writers who have dominated recent Greek poetry, Seferis and Elytis among them. The single volume of verse, *Amorgos,* that Gatsos published in 1943 with the encouragement of this group fully substantiated his early promise. (It was reprinted in 1964.)

*gats′ os

The volume's long title poem, on which Gatsos' reputation rests, refers not to the Aegean island of Amorgos, but to an abstract notion of unattainable beauty and perfection. "Amorgos" is said to have been written in a single night, using the surrealist method of automatic writing developed by André Breton—a method that accords very well with Gatsos' Heraclitean belief that the essence of art, as of life, is flux, relativity, and conflict.

The poem is in six parts, written variously in free verse, in quatrains of fifteen-syllable lines, in prose, and in the classical diction of the *katharevousa*. "Amorgos" juxtaposes life and death, love and war, beauty and horror, in a tone of gentle reverie, and in surreal images that are presented with such quiet assurance that the reader is almost persuaded that he is on the verge of full comprehension. The dark images refer to the fear of old age and death, to violence and battle, and in a muted way to the circumstances of the Axis occupation of Greece. The images of hope come mostly from nature—flowering trees, the evening star, the sea. And the extreme juxtapositions of the poem's content are reflected in its manner, which draws as readily on popular songs as on classical mythology, in language which fuses the traditional and the colloquial:

Among the branches of an osier I see the innocent
    shirt of your childhood drying
Take it, a flag of life, to make a shroud for death
And may your heart yield not
May your tears fall not on this implacable earth
As once on the icy wastes rolled the tear of a
    penguin
To complain is useless
Life will be everywhere the same, with a flute of
    serpents in a land of phantoms
With a song of thieves in a forest of fragrance
With a knife-blade of sorrow in the cheeks of hope
With the yearning of spring in the innermost heart
    of an owlet
If only a plow may be found and a keen-edged
    scythe in a joyful hand
If only there blossom
A bit of grain for the holidays, a little wine for
    remembrance, a little water for the dust.

(translated by Kimon Friar)

"Amorgos," violently attacked by the traditionalists when it first appeared, was received with delight by the young. It has since become one of the most discussed, analyzed, and translated of modern Greek poems. Edmund Keeley and Philip Sherrard said of the book that "it was more impressive in quality than any first volume of poems since Seferis's *Turning Point*, published twelve years earlier. . . . The poem offered not only a new voice but a new possibility for extending the permissable language of poetry."

This possibility Gatsos has left to others to explore. He had written only a handful of poems before "Amorgos," and he has written only a handful since. Instead he has supplemented a small income by working for the Greek radio service, by translating the poems and plays of others, and by writing extraordinary and sometimes surreal lyrics for the songs of such popular Greek composers as Mikis Theodorakis, Manos Hadzidhakis, and Stavros Xarhakos. His translations include versions of plays by Tennessee Williams, Eugene O'Neill, Strindberg, Archibald MacLeish, Lope de Vega, Genet, and Lorca, and of poems by Eliot and Spender, among others.

There have been many attempts to explain Gatsos' silence after his single extraordinary and influential outburst in "Amorgos." (He himself treats the poem ambiguously, sometimes discussing it very seriously, sometimes implying that it was no more than a fanciful game.) Kimon Friar has suggested that Gatsos "is the classic example of what happens to the creative mind when it permits theory to supersede practice"—that his notion of what the perfect poem should be is so intimidating as to inhibit even the attempt to create it.

Gatsos' one passion apart from poetry is gambling, and he rarely leaves Athens except to visit the Corfu or Rhodes casinos. Normally he confines his travels to a daily excursion between his home in the Fokíonos Négri district and Floca's cafe-restaurant in central Athens, where he holds court among the writers, artists, and composers who come to him for advice and good conversation and, as Friar says, "to benefit from one of the best critical minds in Greece today."

PRINCIPAL WORKS IN ENGLISH TRANSLATION: *Poems in* Barnstone, W. (ed.) Modern European Poetry, 1966; Friar, K. (ed.) Modern Greek Poetry, 1973; Keeley, E. and Sherrard, P. (eds.) Four Greek Poets, 1966; Keeley, E. and Sherrard, P. (eds.) Six Poets of Modern Greece, 1960; Fulbright Review Fall 1964; New Directions 13, 1951; Poetry October 1964.

ABOUT: Friar, K. (ed.) Modern Greek Poetry, 1973; Gianos, M.P. Introduction to Modern Greek Literature, 1969; Keeley, E. and Sherrard, P. (eds.) Six Poets of Modern Greece, 1960; Politis, L. A History of Modern Greek Literature, 1973. *Periodicals*—New Directions 13, 1951; Poetry October 1964.

*GATTO, ALFONSO (July 17, 1909–March 8, 1976), Italian poet, was born in Salerno, the son of Guiseppe Gatto and the former Erminia Albirosa. He came from a Calabrian seafaring fam-
*gat′ tō

299

ily: "My grandfather had sailing boats in the port of Reggio Calabria ... before the earthquake [which razed the town in December 1908]." The family was poor, and though after going to school in Salerno Gatto did attend the University of Naples in 1926-1929, economic difficulties forced him to leave without a degree. For the next few years he led a restless life, holding a variety of jobs—clerk, teacher, proofreader, and finally journalist and art critic. In 1936 he was arrested by the Fascist authorities and imprisoned for six months in San Vittore jail in Milan.

Gatto was an editor of or contributor to several major Italian magazines and newspapers, in Milan, Florence, and Rome, including *Milano-Sera, Settimana, Unità,* and *Epoca.* But a crucial experience was founding in 1938 his own literary periodical, *Campo di Marte,* which he and the novelist Vasco Pratoline co-edited. Their enthusiasm for foreign literature soon incurred the wrath of the Fascist censor, and led to the magazine's suppression in 1939 after only nine months. Afterwards, during the war, both Gatto and Pratolini took an active part in the partisan underground, and Gatto is regarded as "il poeta della Resistenza"—the poet of the resistance. He left the Communist Party in 1951 in protest against its stifling of debate in the postwar years, but remained a socialist.

The sensuous poems in his earliest collection, *Isola* (Island, 1932) are little more than colorful evocations of landscapes and moods—melancholy, despairing, ecstatic—expressing his exuberant southern temperament. Later he developed greater depth and control along with a more complex diction in the hermetic and even the surrealist manner, in *Morto ai paesi* (Dead in the Villages, 1937). However, Carlo Golino has pointed out that Gatto's "surrealistic idylls," as these compositions have been called, "are actually continual attempts to clarify his own moral problems, to discover new forms adaptable to his strongly musical bent."

During the 1940s, his increasing social awareness and sense of moral commitment brought him to a plainer style, especially during the period when he was active in the resistance. The poems in *Il capo sulla neve* (The Head in the Snow, 1946) relive some of the intensely dramatic moments of war and liberation. One of the most poignant of them is "Anniversario" (Anniversary):

I remember those days:
In the unpredictable morning, what woke us was the fear
Of being left alone, I heard the sky
like a dead voice. And already the light

abandoned by the dying on the window-panes
touched my forehead; on my hair
it left traces of its eternal sleep.
No human cry was heard—only the snow—
and all were alive behind that wall
merely to weep, and silence
drank in torrents the weeping of the earth.

Oh, Europe frozen to her heart
will never again grow warm: alone with the dead
who love her eternally, she will be white
without boundaries, united by the snow.

(translated by Giovanni Pontiero)

These poems of war and resistance culminate in the collection *La storia delle vittime* (The Story of the Victims, 1966), for which Gatto received the Viareggio Prize in 1966. The "victims" here are not merely those of fascism, but represent the whole history of human sorrow; the poems form a great manifesto, demanding the restoration of dignity to "insulted human nature." In his preface, Gatto explained what the collection's subtitle, *poesie delle resistenza* (poems of resistance), meant to him: it is the poet's duty to make himself the voice of humanity, to call constantly for a "revolution which will have man as its center."

Much of his later poetry, as in *La madre e la morte* (The Mother and Death, 1959) concentrated on the theme of death. But according to the *Times Literary Supplement* the "core of moral urgency and creative inspiration is more or less missing" from the poems he published after the mid-1960s. In these he experimented with new verbal and stylistic techniques and with new patterns of visual and musical analogy: "Now, in his latest verse, he casts himself in the role not so much of a poet, as of a painter in words. What he offers, therefore, is a complex of images and impressions, projected onto an ever-shifting canvas of landscape and scenery. In doing this he shows considerable virtuosity and ingenuity and he almost always succeeds in producing a brilliant visual transcript of what he thinks and feels as well as of what he watches and perceives."

Gatto also published several studies of contemporary Italian artists and some other prose works, including *La sposa bambina* (The Child Bride, 1943) and *Carlomagno nella grotta* (Charlemagne in the Grotto, 1962). In the latter, as a southerner himself, he seeks for the real spirit of the Italian South, painting a portrait which is "pitiless, dark and without hope," but "nevertheless fascinating, and above all truthful." The author received a number of literary prizes in addition to the Viareggio, including the San-Vincent in 1948, the Marzotto in 1954, and the

Bagutta in 1956. In 1976 he appeared as a Communist writer in Francesco Rosi's hotly debated film *Cadaveri Eccellenti (Illustrious Corpses),* based on a novel by Leonardo Sciascia about a series of political murders. Shortly afterwards he was killed in a road accident.

PRINCIPAL WORKS IN ENGLISH TRANSLATION: *Poems in* Caetani, M. (ed.) An Anthology of New Italian Writers, 1951; Golino, C. (ed.) Contemporary Italian Poetry, 1962; Lind, L. R. (ed.) Twentieth-Century Italian Poetry, 1974; Singh, G. (ed.) Contemporary Italian Verse, 1968; Trevelyan, R. (ed.) Italian Writing Today, 1967.

ABOUT: Bo, C. Nuovi studi, 1946; De Robertis, G. Scrittori del Novecento, 1940; Dizionario Enciclopedico della Letteratura Italiana, 1966; Pacifici, S. A Guide to Contemporary Italian Literature, 1962; Penguin Companion to Literature 2, 1969; Pento, B. Alfonso Gatto, 1972. *Periodicals* —Books Abroad 1 1956, 3 1963, 4 1967; La Fiera Letteraria July 4, 1954; December 25, 1955; Times (London) March 10, 1976; Times Literary Supplement, December 18, 1970.

EUGENE D. GENOVESE

---

*GENOVESE, EUGENE D(OMINICK) (May 19, 1930–), American historian, was born in Brooklyn, New York, the son of Dominick F. Genovese, a dock worker, and Lena (Chimenti) Genovese. At New Utrecht High School he gravitated toward children of "left-wing families," and at seventeen he joined the Communist Party, becoming an active organizer for the Communist front group, American Youth for Democracy. Genovese was expelled from the Communist Party after three years, accused of being "anti-Semitic, anti-Negro, and a Browderite right-wing deviationist." He later explained to a New York *Times Magazine* interviewer that "the real reason for my expulsion was I zigged when I was supposed to zag. Actually, I should have been expelled because I was violating party discipline."

Receiving his B.A. from Brooklyn College in 1953, Genovese soon afterwards served for ten months in the U.S. Army before being discharged on account of his former Communist Party membership. Graduate studies in history followed at Columbia University, where he earned his M.A. in 1955, was a Richard Watson Gilder fellow in 1957-1958, and received his Ph.D. in 1959. His dissertation topic, "The Agricultural Reform Movement in the Slave South," reflected his growing interest—first expressed in an undergraduate honors paper—in studying slave economy as one aspect of a social process.

Genovese began his career as an instructor and assistant professor at Brooklyn Polytechnic Institute. He taught here from 1958 to 1963, when he went to Rutgers University as assistant

*je nō vā′ zə

professor (1963-1965) and associate professor (1965-1967). At Rutgers Genovese touched off a widespread debate about academic freedom when, in a campus teach-in speech on April 23, 1965, he declared: "I do not fear or reject the impending Vietcong victory in Vietnam. I welcome it." A heated campaign to secure his discharge in the end failed, the university adminstration and many of Genovese's colleagues sturdily maintaining that his position in the history department depended not upon his political opinions but upon his reputation as a scholar. In 1967 Genovese moved on to Sir George Williams University in Montreal as professor of history, and two years later he became professor of history and chairman of the history department at the University of Rochester, where he has remained. He is said to be a "dynamic" and very popular lecturer, and to have "a genius for organization."

Eugene Genovese describes himself as a "Neo-Marxist" who, rejecting mechanistic determination, aims at liberating the Marxist philosophy of history from its burdensome and sterile past. He remains fully committed to the Marxist principle that all of the great qualitative strides in social development can best be explained by the growth, polarization, and conflict of social classes. In 1971 he wrote: "The Marxian interpretation of history constitutes a way— the most fruitful way, in my experience—of seeing history as a process and of binding the past to the future: not in the sense of providing a basis for prediction (we may leave that to astrologers), but in the sense of suggesting the contours both of that which is possible and of disasters to be avoided." He disapproves of (but does not al-

ways avoid) sweeping theoretical pronouncements, favoring instead the sort of painstaking
and detailed investigations demonstrated by
such English Marxists as Christopher Hill and
E. J. Hobsbawm. Genovese has also been influenced by the Italian Communist leader Antonio Gramsci, whom he regards as "the
greatest Western Marxist theorist of our century."

The Political Economy of Slavery (1965),
Genovese's first book, jolted the American historical profession. In these essays he analyzes
the economy, culture, and ideals of the Southern
slaveholders, and argues that slavery, while
economically ruinous, gave the antebellum
South a uniquely patriarchal and aristocratic social system and civilization distinct from—and
indeed hostile to—the bourgeois capitalism of
the rest of the United States. It was this "fundamental antagonism between modern and pre-
modern worlds" rather than economic factors
that prevented the Southern ruling class from
relinquishing slavery and made the Civil War
inevitable. This view was attacked from both
right and left, but many critics recognized and
commended the book's objectivity and scholarship. One of these was Martin Duberman, who
went on: "This is not to say that the book is
faultless, only that its faults cannot be directly
linked to its author's ideology." Duberman
thought that the work suffered from over-com-
pression but concluded: "There is no doubt that
[this] is an important book, and ... both its
major and minor themes are impressively and
persuasively stated."

Of the two essays in *The World the Slaveholders Made* (1969), the first relates slavery in the
American South to other modern slaveholding
and serfholding societies in Europe, the West
Indies, and the continental Americas, while the
second centers on the social philosophy of
George Fitzhugh, the Virginia apologist for slavery: both seek to show that the various paths to
abolition taken in the Americas can be interpreted in terms of class rather than race. J. H.
Plumb wrote that "Genovese argues his thesis
with a subtlety and breadth of scholarship that
we have now come to expect in his work. ... the
book sparkles with originality and it is a most
important contribution to the swelling historiography of slavery."

In Red and Black (1971), a collection of historical and topical essays, was followed in 1974
by *Roll, Jordan, Roll,* Genovese's eight-hun-
dred-page study of "the world the slaves made"
—the product of twelve years of "obsessional"
research into plantation records, family papers,
slave narratives, and travelers' reports. It pro-

vides a detailed and rounded view of an entire
society as it shaped and was shaped by the institution of slavery, and it brings out very forcefully the critical importance of Christianity in the
rise and fall of that society. As David Brion
Davis put it, "religion served as the touchstone
for both the masters' paternalism and the slaves'
independence of soul," and it "became the major
battleground for psychological control."

"The author carefully and meticulously examines every participant in the slavery enterprise," wrote Norman Lederer, "never ignoring
the humanity of all concerned and the ambiguity
of the roles which all parties to the institution
had to play." David Brion Davis called this "the
most profound, learned and detailed analysis of
Negro slavery to appear since World War II.
... Genovese's great gift is his ability to penetrate the minds of both slaves and masters, revealing not only how they viewed themselves
and each other, but how their contradictory perceptions interacted. . . . For Genovese, the
'story' of slave life is a testament of the power
and perseverance of the human spirit under conditions of extreme oppression." C. Vann Woodward thought the book a notable example of
traditional historiography, Marxian only in incidental (but important) ways; he concluded: "If
this is a fair sample of Marxist history (and, alas,
I am afraid it is not) then American historiography could do with a good bit more of it." It
brought Genovese the Bancroft Prize.

Genovese was a social science research fellow
in 1968-1969 and a fellow of Stanford University's Center for Advanced Study in the Behavioral Sciences in 1972-1973. He taught as a visiting
professor at Columbia in 1967 and Yale in 1969,
and serves on the editorial boards of the *Journal
of Social History* and *Dialectical Anthropology*.
In the opinion of J.H. Plumb he has "established
himself without question as one of the leading
historians of the South. In Genovese, America
has a Marxist historian in every way as gifted
and as subtle as Hill, Hobsbawm, or Soboul, and
at times just as opaque." The author is a well-
built man, impeccably tailored, with slightly
graying black hair. He and his third wife, Elizabeth Fox-Genovese (who also teaches history at
Rochester), are said to give "superb dinner parties."

PRINCIPAL WORKS: The Political Economy of Slavery: Stud-
ies in the Economy and Society of the Slave South, 1965;
The World the Slaveholders Made: Two Essays in Interpre-
tation, 1969; In Red and Black: Marxian Explorations in
Southern and Afro-American History, 1971; Roll, Jordan,
Roll: The World the Slaves Made, 1974. *As editor*—The
Slave Economy of the Old South: The Selected Essays of
Ulrich B. Phillips, 1968; (with Laura Foner) Slavery in the

New World: A Reader in Comparative History, 1969; The Slave Economies, 1973; (with Elinor Miller) Plantation, Town, and County: Essays on the Local History of American Slave Society, 1974; (with S.L. Engerman) Race and Slavery in the Western Hemisphere: Quantitative Studies, 1975.

ABOUT: Who's Who in America, 1976-1977. *Periodicals—* Book Week November 21, 1965; Book World January 4, 1970; Commentary July 1966, October 1970, January 1975; Nation November 22, 1965; January 19, 1970; National Review May 5, 1970; September 10, 1971; New Republic November 9, 1974; New York Review of Books February 26, 1970; August 12, 1971; October 3, 1974; New York Times Book Review December 14, 1969; September 29, 1974; New York Times Magazine December 19, 1965; Newsweek July 14, 1976; Saturday Review December 6, 1969; Science and Society Spring 1969; Southern Review October 1974; Studies on the Left July-August 1966.

GERMAN, DANIEL. *See* "GRANIN," DANIEL

GHOSE, AUROBINDO (usually known as Sri Aurobindo) (August 15, 1872–December 5, 1950), Indian poet, religious philosopher, and mystic, writing in English, was born in Calcutta. His father, Dr. Krishnadhan Ghose, was a Government Civil Surgeon, while his mother, Swarnalata Devi, was a daughter of Rishi Rajnarain Bose, one of the great men of the nineteenth-century Indian renaissance which was cradled in West Bengal. But Dr. Ghose, having himself attended Aberdeen University, wanted his children to have a wholly European education. At the age of five Aurobindo Ghose was sent to the Loretto Convent School at Darjeeling, and in 1879, when he was seven, his parents took him to England along with his two older brothers (one of whom, Manmohan Ghose, also became a poet) so that the children could grow up uncontaminated by Asian ways and ideas.

After living for some years with a family in Manchester, where he was educated privately, Aurobindo Ghose entered St. Paul's School, London, in 1885. A brilliant classical scholar, he won a scholarship from St. Paul's to King's College, Cambridge, where he gained first-degree honors in the classical tripos at the end of his second year. He had spent fourteen years in England, where apart from Greek and Latin he had read much English poetry and learned German and Italian. He also had some knowledge of Sanskrit. But he had been cut off from his native Bengali and unlike Rabindranath Tagore he wrote little in that language, most of his work being in English.

Graduating from Cambridge, he returned to India in 1893 and entered the service of the Maharajah of Baroda, where he remained until 1906. He was employed in various departments

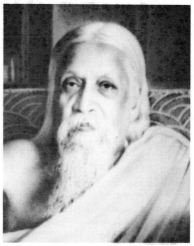

Sri Aurobindo Ashram

AUROBINDO GHOSE

of the Baroda administration, but finally gravitated towards Baroda College. He taught French for a time and ultimately became professor of English and vice-principal. During these years, according to Srinivasa Iyengar, "Sri Aurobindo fast achieved the feat of re-nationalizing himself. His mind had returned from 'Sicilian olive-groves' and 'Athenian lanes' to the Shore of the Ganges, to Saraswati's domains. He gained a deeper insight into Sanskrit and Bengali, and cultivated besides Marathi and Gujerati." He also wrote a great deal during his years at Baroda, including such poems as *Songs to Myrtilla* (1895) and the long narrative poem *Urvasie* (1896).

But Aurobindo had also become passionately interested in the Indian nationalist movement and in 1906 he left Baroda for Calcutta, the center of revolutionary politics, where he became editor of a new English-language daily, *Bandemataram.* In 1907 he was arrested by the British on account of articles he had published, but was acquitted at his trial. He was arrested again in 1908 in connection with the Muzzaferpore bomb outrage, and though in the end he was once more acquitted, he was detained in Alipur jail throughout the protracted trial. Aurobindo had already been practicing yoga, and it was in prison that he had the mystical experience—a vision of Narayana (Vishnu)—that changed his entire outlook and indeed transformed his life.

No longer interested in conventional politics but feeling the profound pull of the spiritual life, Aurobindo left Calcutta early in 1910 and retired to Pondicherry. Here he lived in seclusion for the rest of his life, earning world recognition as a philosopher and mystic and founding an ashram (a religious center) with the help of another spiritual quester, Madame Mirra Richard, now known as The Mother.

At Pondicherry Aurobindo sought a new interpretation of the yogic teachings through which India might find national rebirth. Many of his philosophical writings were originally published in *Arya,* a monthly review published between 1914 and 1921 for the benefit of his growing army of disciples. The tone of these essays, with titles like "The Synthesis of Yoga," "Secrets of the Veda," "The Ideal of Human Unity," "The Human Cycle," is according to William Walsh "one which is peculiarly mystical and evasive, constantly escaping the grapple of the ordinary Western mind." Aurobindo himself, in a letter written in 1930, carefully differentiated between the philosophical systems of West and East. In Western metaphysics, thought and logic have been regarded as the supreme instruments of knowledge, and "even spiritual experience has been summoned to pass the tests of the intellect, if it is to be held valid." In the yoga of the Indian saints the position has been just the reverse: "The first rank has always been given to spiritual intuition and illumination and spiritual experience" and "even when one begins with thought, the aim is to arrive at a consciousness beyond mental thinking."

Aurobindo's ideal was neither personal immortality nor release from self into Nirvana, the bliss of Brahma, but the establishment of a Divine Life here on this earth. And in the three volumes of his major work *The Life Divine* (1939–1940), he sought to work out the central tenets of his philosophy. His point of departure is that "the earliest pre-occupation of man in his awakened thoughts . . . is also the highest which his thoughts can envisage. It manifests itself in the divination of Godhead, the impulse towards perfection, the search after pure Truth and unmixed Bliss, the sense of secret immortality. . . . Today we see a humanity satiated but not satisfied by victorious analysis of the externalities of Nature preparing to return to its primaeval longings. The earliest formula of Wisdom promises to be its last—God, Light, Freedom, Immortality."

The goal of Aurobindo's world-transforming yoga is "supermanhood." He aims by cultivation of the spirit to move through mind into "supermind" and a direct apprehension of Being. Westerners have restlessly sought happiness through materialism and Easterners often through extremes of asceticism, but Aurobindo repudiates both of these contrasting attitudes, maintaining that both are severely partial ver-

sions of reality. True Self is to be won by a spiritual consciousness which "links the highest to the lowest through all the mediating terms and achieves an indivisible whole." And just as evolution has already released life and mind in matter, the great powers of higher consciousness, of the concealed godhead within each person, may also be released and become part of terrestrial existence.

Aurobindo was a prolific poet in English, his range extending from romantic lyrics to long epics in blank verse. But his poetry can only be fully understood in the context of his yoga, for it too was meant as a bridge between the divisions and discords of the present life and the future Life Divine. Thus in the blank verse plays in *Collected Poems and Plays* (1942), he finds mythical correlatives for his philosophy in the legends not only of ancient India—*Vasavadutta* —but also of Greece *(Perseus the Deliverer),* Scandinavia *(Eric),* Syrian romance *(Rodogune),* and in a tale of Baghdad in the days of Haroun al Rashid *(The Viziers of Bassora).* In all these plays a heroine doomed by her beauty is redeemed by the power of love, which can defy death as Perseus does in rescuing Andromeda from the dragon. Apart from these five full-length plays, his mastery of blank verse is seen in such narrative poems as *Urvasie,* in which again indomitable love gains a victory over death.

His major poetic work is the 24,000-line blank verse "cosmic epic" *Savitri,* on which he worked for fifty years before the first volume was published in 1946. In one of the episodes of the ancient Hindu *Mahabharata,* Savitri is the wife whose unflinching devotion and spiritual strength rescue her husband from death. This ancient legend is transformed by Aurobindo to embody his own teachings, becoming an epic of the evolving soul, of mind transformed into "supermind" and earth-nature transcended by "supernature." The girl Savitri becomes the great World-Mother, the vessel of the immortal spirit, while nevertheless remaining also the agonized wife confronting her husband's Death:

Something stood there, unearthly, sombre, grand,
A limitless denial of all being
That wore the terror and wonder of a shape.
In its appalling eye the tenebrous Form
Bore the deep pity of destroying gods. . . .
His shape was nothingness made real, his limbs
were monuments of transcience and beneath
Brows of unwearying calm large godlike lids
Silent beheld the writhing serpent, life.

Savitri wins her trial of strength with Death, her bewildered husband is restored to her, and then:

Night, splendid with the moon dreaming in heaven
In silver peace, possessed her luminous reign.
She brooded through her stillness on a thought
Deep-guarded by her mystic folds of light,
And in her bosom nursed a greater Dawn.

The gifted Indians who wrote poetry in English at the turn of the century were handicapped by their failure to find a natural and easy mode of experssion, and modern critical opinion is divided about Aurobindo's importance as a poet, because of his archaic idiom and the obscurity of his theme. Thus William Walsh, claiming that "the importance of Aurobindo Ghose belongs rather to the history of ideas and of religion than literature," writes that his verse "all shows colossal energy, moral earnestness, benevolence, a sense of the vastness and continuity of human experience, but it all seems, too, deficient in the self-propelling life of genuine poetry."

Aurobindo claimed that the Vedic mantra was the natural medium for mystic poetry, and in his view the "future poetry" would more and more approximate the mantra, minimizing, if not wholly eliminating, those middlemen the intellect and the senses. And his lyric poems do effectively convey his own mental outlook and its feeling of vast horizons, as in "Ocean Oneness":

Silence is around me, wideness ineffable;
White birds on the ocean diving and wandering;
A soundless sea on a voiceless heaven—
Azure on azure—is mutely gazing.

Identified with silence and boundlessness
My spirit widens, clasping the universe
Till all that seemed becomes the Real,
One in a mighty and single vastness.

Someone broods there nameless and bodiless,
Conscious and lonely, deathless and infinite,
And, sole in a still eternal rapture,
Gathers all things to his heart for ever.

To many of his contemporaries, Aurobindo was a giant. Romain Rolland saw him as the foremost of Indian thinkers, who synthesized the genius of Asia and the genius of Europe, who held in his hand "in firm unrelaxed grip, the bow of creative energy." When he died he was buried on the grounds of his own ashram, but for four days his body lay in state, reposing "in a grandeur of victorious quiet," honored by thousands upon thousands of pilgrims.

PRINCIPAL WORKS: Sri Aurobindo Birth Centenary Library (complete works in thirty volumes), 1970–1972; The Essential Aurobindo, edited by Robert A. McDermolt, 1973. Ear-lier Publications: Poetry and Plays—Poems, 1941; Collected Poems and Plays, 1942; Poems, Past and Present, 1946; Savitri: A Legend and a Symbol, 1950; Last Poems, 1952; Ilion: An Epic, 1957; Vasavadutta: A Dramatic Romance, 1957; More Poems, 1957; Rodogune (play), 1958; The Viziers of Bassora: A Dramatic Romance, 1959; Eric: A Dramatic Romance, 1960; Selected Poems, 1965. Nonfiction —The Ideal of Human Unity, 1919; The Renaissance in India, 1920; War and Self-Determination, 1920; Thoughts and Glimpses, 1920; Evolution, 1921; The Ideal of the Karmayogin, 1921; The Brain of India, 1921; Essays on the Gita, 1922 (second series, 1926; two series in one, 1966); The Riddle of This World, 1933; Lights on Yoga, 1935; Bases of Yoga, 1936; The Message of the Gita, 1938; The Life Divine (three vols.), 1939, 1940, 1955; The Mother, 1946; Views and Reviews, 1946; Heraclitus, 1947; The Significance of Indian Art, 1947; The Spirit and Form of Indian Polity, 1947; Letters of Sri Aurobindo, 1947–1951; The Synthesis of Yoga, 1948; More Lights on Yoga, 1948; Speeches, 1948; The Doctrine of Passive Resistance, 1948; The Human Cycle, 1949; Science and Culture, 1951; The Message and Mission of Indian Culture, 1951; Integral Education, 1952; The Supramental Manifestation Upon Earth, 1952; The Problem of Rebirth, 1952; Elements of Yoga, 1953; The Mind of Light, 1953; The Future Poetry, 1953; The Foundations of Indian Culture, 1953; Sri Aurobindo on Himself, 1953; On Yoga (two vols.), 1955, 1958; Thoughts and Aphorisms, 1958; A Practical Guide to Integral Yoga, 1958; The Hour of God, 1959; The Future Evolution of Man, 1963; Reason and Beyond Reason, 1963; Man—Slave or Free, 1966; The Destiny of Man, 1969.

ABOUT: Asiatic Society. Sri Aurovinda: Proceedings of a Symposium, 1976; Bhattacharya, P.K. A Scheme of Education, 1952; Bristow, Sir R. Sri Aurobindo, 1950; Chaudhuri, H. Sri Aurobindo, 1951; Chaudhuri, H. and Spiegelberg, F. The Integral Philosophy of Sri Aurobindo, 1960; Chincholhar, L.G. A Critical Study of Aurobindo, 1966; Das, M. Sri Aurobindo, 1972; Donnelly, M. Divine Becoming: The Message of Sri Aurobindo, 1948; Donnelly, M. Founding the Life Divine, 1955; Feys, J. Life of a Yogi, 1976; Ghose, J. Sri Aurobindo, 1973; Ghosh, J.C. Sri Aurobindo, 1929; Gupta, N.K. The Yoga of Sri Aurobindo, 1939; Kapali Sastri, T.V. Sri Aurobindo: Lights on the Teachings, 1948; Langley, G.H. Sri Aurobindo, 1949; Maitra, S.K. The Meeting of the East and West in Sri Aurobindo's Philosophy, 1956; Maitra, S.K. Sri Aurobindo, 1950; Maitra, S.K. Sri Aurobindo and the New World, 1957; Maitra, S.K. Studies in Sri Aurobindo's Philosophy, 1945; Nandakumar, P. Sri Aurobindo, 1972; Pandit, M.P. Dictionary of Sri Aurobindo's Yoga, 1966; Pandit, M.P. Sri Aurobindo: Studies in His Life and Thought, 1957; Pandit, M.P. Sri Aurobindo: A Survey, 1872–1972, 1974; Pearson, N. Sri Aurobindo and the Soul Quest of Man, 1952; Purani, A.B. Life of Sri Aurobindo, 1960; Satprem. Sri Aurobindo, 1974; Sethna, K.D. The Poetic Genius of Sri Aurobindo, 1947; Sethna, K.D. The Passing of Sri Aurobindo, 1951; Singh, K. Prophet of Indian Nationalism, 1963; Smith, J. Pioneer of the Supramental Age, 1958; Srinivasa Iyengar, K.R. Indian Writing in English, 1962; Srinivasa Iyengar, K.R. Sri Aurobindo, 1945; Varma, V.P. The Political Philosophy of Sri Aurobindo, 1960; Walsh, W. Commonwealth Literature, 1973.

*GILLIATT, PENELOPE (ANN DOUGLASS) (March 25, 1932–), English film and theatre critic, film scenarist, novelist, and short story writer, was born in London, one of the two daughters of Cyril and Mary (Douglass) Conner. Her father is a barrister who became head

*gil′ē ət

Strachan

PENELOPE GILLIATT

of commonwealth and foreign relations at the British Broadcasting Corporation. Part of her childhood was spent in Northumberland but in 1942, when she was ten, her parents spearated and Penelope Conner chose to return to London and the blitz to live with her father. She attended Queen's College in Harley Street (1942-1947), and with her father went to concerts, studied languages, and played cello and piano duets. At fifteen she passed the Oxford University matriculation examinations, but she was too young to be admitted and instead spent a year at Bennington College, Vermont (1948-1949), where she was told that she had an IQ of 170.

Returning to London, Penelope Conner began her career in 1950 as a tea-girl and apprentice journalist with an unglamorous magazine group. She subsequently joined the British *Vogue* in a similar capacity, working her way up through the ranks until she became that journal's features editor. She also wrote film and theatre reviews for *Vogue,* and for such other magazines as the *New Statesman,* the *Guardian,* and the *Spectator.* In 1954 she married the distinguished neurologist Roger Gilliatt, M.C., now professor of clinical neurology in the University of London.

Penelope Gilliatt made her reputation initially as film critic for the influential London Sunday newspaper the *Observer,* a post she retained from 1961 to 1967, apart from a year (1965-1966) when by way of a change she served as the *Observer's* theatre critic. In 1967 she went to the United States as guest film critic of the *New Yorker,* and she has resumed that role for six months of every year since. A selection of her film and theatre criticism was published in 1973

as *Unholy Fools: Wits, Comics, Disturbers of the Peace.* "Penelope Gilliatt has always been a maddening critic of theatre and film" wrote a reviewer in the *Times Literary Supplement,* "maddening because she can be so devastatingly accurate and penetrating at some times, and at others so far off target that she does not seem to have bothered to take aim. In her regular film columns, especially, we seem to encounter a split personality: sometimes she knuckles down to a serious appreciation of the work before her . . .; sometimes she merely deploys all the skill of the brilliant journalist to scribble some light entertainment. . . . Every few pages you want to stamp and scream, but it is difficult to put the book down long enough to do so." It is comedy that generally brings out the best in her criticism. She distinguishes "two great classes of comedy, the comedy of dither and the comedy of phlegm." She prefers the latter, which she defines as "someone being placed at the center of chaos," and identifies among its great exponents Buster Keaton, Bea Lillie, and Jacques Tati.

Penelope Gilliatt's first marriage had meanwhile ended, and in 1963 she had married the playwright John Osborne. During the next few years she began to make a new reputation as a novelist and short story writer. Her first book was *One by One* (1965), in which London is attacked by a second great plague: thousands die every week, panic and despair spread. The novel focuses in particular on the situation of a young married couple, Joe and Polly Talbot, who are awaiting the birth of their first child. Joe, a veterinarian, throws himself unstintingly into the battle against the plague, and sends Polly away to safety until after her baby is born. When she returns to London she finds that Joe is becoming increasingly alienated from her and from reality: "I hate nearly everything I see," he says. "I'm not fit to live with." Polly tries in mounting desperation to save him, but he continues to retreat from her and from life, and in the end kills himself.

The novel is an odd mixture of grimness and absurdity, tragedy and satire. It is evidently a parable—an indictment of a sick society, gripped by a disease which makes its victims mad before it destroys them. Robert Maurer has suggested that Joe Talbot, in his consuming rage, was perhaps modeled on John Osborne. Penelope Gilliatt's journal of the plague year describes the catastrophe with great skill but, in the opinion of one reviewer, it is "too much of a rag-bag of protest, comic observation, emotional analysis, fantasy and cleverness—the language is prickly with sharp, self-conscious phrases"—and "does not quite gel into an effective novel. But the passion and intelligence which produced it are far too rare and ambitious for one to wish that it had been written in any other way or to forget the impression it leaves."

A State of Change (1967), Penelope Gilliatt's second novel, describes a series of episodes in the life of a Polish girl, Kakia Grabowski, who settles in London a few years after World War II. She lives for four years with a young television executive, Don Clancy, and then moves on to a similar relationship with Don's married friend Harry Clopton, a doctor. The friendship of these three survives the change of sexual allegiance, Don's disastrous love affair with another woman, and Harry's imprisonment for performing an illegal abortion. The book is more than anything else a record of their sophisticated and often witty discussions with each other and with a succession of modish figures brought on for this purpose—less a novel of character than an instructive and entertaining guide to the social and political attitudes of British intellectuals between about 1949 and 1966.

Penelope Gilliatt's short stories, most of them first published in the *New Yorker,* have on the whole been more unequivocally admired than her novels. Her first collection was published in 1968 as *What's It Like Out?* (and in the United States a year later as *Come Back If It Doesn't Get Better*). "The nine stories are set in England, urban and rural," wrote W.C. Hamlin, "and they investigate variously the disruptive influence of women, the obligation or refusal to get used to the idea of aging, the terror of being unable to cope with the notion that life has some purpose, the maddening reality that it is not the inability but the need to communicate which is one of the most destructive forces in society."

In *Contemporary Novelists* these spare, compassionate, and wryly funny stories were most praised for their creation of "a series of characters all fiercely independent, often caught in the confusion of an ambivalent and paradoxical world, but stoutly insisting on their right to make their own choices and to maintain their individuality." Reviewers were delighted in particular by "The Redhead," a brilliant sketch of a hopelessly ineffective but indomitable woman, and "What's It Like Out?," in which an octagenarian couple, physically enfeebled but intellectually vigorous, run rings around a brash young reporter sent to interview them on the subject of senility. There was similar enthusiasm for *Nobody's Business* (1972)—eight stories and a short play that "come in on the downbeats, not the plump moments of life"; " 'O god, I wish the shops were open,' said the great atheist economist, near tears, to his terror." Something of a

preoccupation with aged, eccentric, but intellectually unquenchable men and women is evident in her third collection, *Splendid Lives* (1977), which Lorna Sage described as "tough-minded and celebratory."

John Spurling once remarked that "the trouble with Mrs. Gilliatt's fiction ... is that the characters are organised on Calvinist principles. The minor characters are analysed, probed and dislodged from their secure perches with considerable skill and enjoyable ferocity; the central characters, the justified sinners, are also analysed but for reasons unexplained by the author remain 'good,' 'true,' 'human.' " It is a complaint that seems to have occurred to no one else, and most reviewers would concur with Anthony Burgess's estimate of her work as being "of great originality," with a peculiar flavor that is recalled "like a rarely consumed but classic dish."

The wit and controlled poignancy of her fiction also distinguishes her work as a film scenarist and as a dramatist for radio and television; she has been called "the first major film critic since James Agee to enjoy distinction as a scenarist." The most notable of her scripts is the one she wrote for John Schlesinger's film *Sunday Bloody Sunday* (1971), which brought her an Oscar nomination and awards from the Writers' Guild (Britain), the Writers' Guild of America, the National Society of Film Critics (U.S.), and the New York Film Critics. *Time*'s reviewer wrote of the film that "its text is sexual, but its theme is nothing less than the nature of affection"; it "must be considered one of the central films of the decade," and "the essential triumph of *Sunday Bloody Sunday* belongs to Scenarist Penelope Gilliatt." She has also written the libretto for an opera called *The Beach at Aurora.*

Penelope Gilliatt has contributed profiles to the *New Yorker* of celebrated film-makers, including Jean Renoir, Woody Allen, Jacques Tati, Luis Buñuel, and Buster Keaton; the essays on Tati and Renoir have developed into books. *Jean Renoir: Essays, Conversations, Reviews* (1975) describes two meetings with the great French director, and discusses his films. The author's "own style and sensibility," it was said, "add much to the feel and flavor of the book because she shares many of her subject's salient virtues: breadth, concision, insightfulness, and an abiding affection for the ambivalence and diversity of humankind."

Titian-haired, pale-skinned, and slender, Penelope Gilliatt, according to *Time,* combines "personal beauty and an intellectual signal that achievers ... [find] irresistible." Her "volatile marriage" to John Osborne ended in 1968, and she lives now with her daughter by that marriage, Nolan, spending nine months of each year in the United States. She received an award form the National Institute of Arts and Letters in 1971, and in 1972 was elected a Fellow of the Royal Society of Literature. She has lectured on writing for the voice and on English and Russian literature at a number of major universities in Britain and the United States, and has worked at the Institute of Pacific Relations in New York. She is greatly interested in the arts of Poland and Czechoslovakia, and is a member of the British Labour Party.

PRINCIPAL WORKS: *Novels*—One by One, 1965; A State of Change, 1967; The Cutting Edge, 1978. *Short Stories*—What's It Like Out?, 1968 (U.S., Come Back If it Doesn't Get Better); (with others) Penguin Modern Stories 5, 1970; Nobody's Business, 1972; Splendid Lives, 1977. *Nonfiction*—Unholy Fools: Wits, Comics, Disturbers of the Peace, 1973; Jean Renoir: Essays, Conversations, Reviews, 1975; Jacques Tati, 1976. *Other*—Sunday Bloody Sunday (screenplay), 1971.

ABOUT: Contemporary Authors 13-16 first revision, 1975; International Who's Who, 1977-78; Vinson, J. (ed.) Contemporary Novelists, 1976; Who's Who in America, 1976-1977. *Periodicals*—Book World July 13, 1969; Books and Bookmen May 1965; Guardian February 19, 1970; National Review August 3, 1973; New Statesman September 22, 1972; July 20, 1973; New York Times October 3, 1971; New York Times Book Review April 7, 1968; June 15, 1969; September 10, 1972; Observer September 24, 1972; Time September 27, 1971; Times (London) October 19, 1978; Times Literary Supplement April 29, 1965; May 25, 1967; September 7, 1973.

GIOVANNI, NIKKI (YOLANDE COR-NELIA GIOVANNI) (June 7, 1943–), American poet, memoirist, and essayist, writes: "I was born in Knoxville, Tennessee, from which my parents moved when I was two months old. I grew up in the suburbs at Cincinnati, Ohio, which when I was growing up was called 'the Valley.' The Valley is about fifteen miles from the city but I was sixteen or seventeen before the Expressway was built so going into town not only felt like a big deal—it was. We finally settled in Lincoln Heights, which sits atop what would have been a beautiful view if the factories hadn't come.

"Every summer my sister and I went back to Knoxville to visit my mother's family, thereby giving me a great love of mountains and water. I should confess, however, that I neither climb nor swim. I just like to look.

"Probably my best known poem is 'Nikki-Roosa,' which is about my childhood. I liked being a child and I have enjoyed growing up. There are, I am learning, problems such as paying bills and meeting deadlines, but that's a part of growing up. One of the amazing things to me

NIKKI GIOVANNI

Betsy Nolan Public Relations

is my parents. They had two children and half the income but they managed. I have one child and twice the resources and I scrape. I try to let my poetry flow among the life rhythms I have known.

"Writing brings me pleasure. I'm delighted that I publish and am absolutely ecstatic that I earn a living in my chosen field, but I'm sure I'd write anyway. I'd just be secretive about it.

"Maybe I should also confess that I don't like doing things like this. There is a certain arrogance about saying I write because it's my tongue and I hope writing expresses my heart. But the heart is ever pumping new blood through an old body. Each beat brings its own ingredients to the head. I guess existentialism with a twinge of pragmatism would be my basic ideology. I also have a great love for history. Somewhere between what was and what is, is what will be. Because of the political turmoil, terms such as justice and truth keep coming up —so the slogans like 'getting the country moving' and 'living up to the great documents.' As long as America continues to hide its sickness the country will remain sick. And all we touch will turn to tin.

"I have no problem with the 'double-vision' and 'dual responsibilities' of which some authors have written. I'm a Black American, a Black poet, a mother (which is universal), and an inhabitant of earth—though not necessarily in that order. I feel strongly that what is good is good for us all. The unnecessary feelings such as greed, racism, indifference, envy must be wiped out. I don't think it will happen soon but mankind must improve as a group on an individual level. There are those who say technology has outstripped mankind though I believe mankind has lagged. We all must go forward.

"I guess it's also fair to admit that my beliefs are only a part of me. But they are the part I prefer to share. Oriana Fallaci said: 'Every person must keep something private'; I try. All public people need to retreat some place both physically and psychically. Especially those whose ideas and state of mind affect other people —which includes all of us. Reflection is a necessary tool for all people and we writers are, I think, reflectors."

Nikki Giovanni is the daughter of Jones Giovanni, a probation officer, and the former Yolande Cornelia Watson, a social worker. Her surname, she believes, "just means that *our* slavemasters were Italian instead of English or French"; "Nikki" is the nickname given to her by her beloved older sister Gary. Though the family were Baptists, she received most of her early education at a Roman Catholic parochial school in Cincinnati. She had a happy childhood, and says that "I was trained intellectually and spiritually to respect myself and the people who respect me. I was emotionally trained to love those who love me." She began to write stories and poems while still a child, and neither she nor her family doubted that she was destined for fame.

At sixteen she was accepted as an early entrant by Fisk University in Nashville. (Her maternal grandfather, John Brown Watson, had been one of the university's first graduates.) Her extreme independence of spirit led to expulsion from Fisk at the end of her first semester. "After knocking around and sponging off my parents for a while," she says, "I went back to Fisk as a woman—not a girl." Returning to Fisk in 1964, Nikki Giovanni wrote for the *Forum* newspaper and joined John Oliver Killens's writers' workshop. Uncowed by her expulsion, she agitated for the reinstatement of Fisk's chapter of the Student Non-violent Coordinating Committee, which was forbidden to operate on campus, and won her case after leading a group of two hundred students to the student council. She graduated in 1967 with honors in history, studied for nine months at the School of Social Work at the University of Pennsylvania, then left, frustrated, to involve herself for a time in black politics in Newark, New Jersey.

Her first book of poems was privately published in 1968, with the help of a Ford Foundation grant. This was *Black Feeling, Black Talk,* on the strength of which the National Foundation of the Arts gave her a grant to attend the School of Fine Arts at Columbia University. She did not stay long enough at Columbia to obtain her master's degree, but she completed a new collection of poems published (with the help of a Harlem Cultural Council grant) as *Black Judgement* (1969). A third collection, *Re:Creation,* followed in 1970. Convinced that "you've got to find a way to make people know you're there," Nikki Giovanni in 1970 established her own publishing corporation, TomNik Ltd., which produced among other items a new and more attractive edition of *Black Judgement.* It was in 1970 also that Giovanni began to establish herself as a personality as well as a writer with her appearances on *Soul!,* a WNET television program devoted to black culture. Through *Soul!* she met Phil Petri, who edited her first two books of poetry for a new one-volume edition published in 1970.

This was the work that first aroused widespread critical interest in Nikki Giovanni's poetry. Alicia Ostriker wrote in *Partisan Review* that the earliest poems here, "written mostly to friends and lovers, reveal an attractive, lively personality, full of youthful exuberance, youthful pride, youthful sexiness and frankness":

Those were barefoot boy with cheek of tan days
And I was John Henry hammering to get in

I was the camel with the cold nose

Now, having the tent, I have no use for it
I have pushed you out

Go 'way
Can't you see I'm lonely

(from "Poem [for BMC No. 2]")

However, as Alicia Ostriker points out, halfway through the book "a change takes place, apparently based on the discovery that one's own politics of joy do not so rapidly alter the universe." Then come poems like the much-quoted "The True Import of Present Dialogue: Black vs. Negro," which asks "Can a nigger kill a honkie/ Can a nigger kill the Man," and also asks "Can you kill the nigger/ in you?" It seemed to Ostriker that the book records "a classical struggle between Love and Duty. Here, as of old, Duty means 'to kill.' " Nevertheless, Nikki Giovanni says: "I try to write about black love," and in her best poems she does so, according to Ostriker "successfully and joyously."

Black Feeling, Black Talk, Black Judgement had a very considerable commercial success, a fact which must be attributed partly to the author's skill and vigor as a publicist. Having given free readings of her work in New York City, Atlanta, Boston, and Detroit, she soon found

309

herself in demand for readings and lectures on college campuses. And in 1971 she became a national figure with the first of several very successful record albums, *Truth Is On Its Way,* in which she reads her poems to an accompaniment of gospel music. *Variety* in its review called Nikki Giovanni "probably the most prominent black poetess in America," whose poems "express the bitterness, pain, frustrations and joys of being black in white America. The poems are masterfully superimposed over the gospel music." The album sold a hundred thousand copies within two years of its publication, and brought its author a flood of invitations to appear at colleges across the country, on major television shows, and at festivals of black culture.

Gemini, a volume of autobiographical and critical essays, was also published in 1971. Many critics enjoyed Nikki Giovanni's recollections of her childhood, which were written, one said, "with wit and the compressed rhythms she brings to her poetry," but most white reviewers found her "exhortations to a black revolution" contradictory, illogical, and sometimes foolish or frenzied. There was a mixed reception also for *Spin a Soft Black Song* (1971), a collection of poems for young children. Nancy Klein found "a combination of casual energy and sudden wit" in these poems, which seemed to her to explore "the contours of childhood with honest affection, sidestepping both nostalgia and condescension." *Library Journal*'s reviewer, on the other hand, thought that "the attempt to emulate childish language" was "painfully evident," and that most of the poems failed "in capturing or conveying feelings of childhood."

The poems collected in *My House* (1972) are grouped into two sections: the "rooms inside," about personal relationships, and the "rooms outside," dealing with the black experience in general. Dorothy Nyren thought that, at her worst, Nikki Giovanni sounded like Rod McKuen, and that there was "not enough black gold here for the price." Most reviewers admired the book, however, and one in *Choice* wrote that these poems "are versatile, funny, touching, gentle, hard-nosed, uncompromising, prejudicial—and real. They pierce the heart. . . . Blacks will identify with these poems, but so will others."

Ego-Tripping (1973), a volume of verse for teenagers, was followed by *The Women and the Men* (1975), containing poems written between 1970 and 1975. The book begins with a group of portraits and other poems about black women. There follows a section of love poems, and then a group of poems about Africa. J. F. Cotter thought the book offered "unfortunate examples of the dangers of success"—that the poet was

"self-consciously determined to speak as a black woman of her African past and of her present love. She fails because the public voice drowns out the private emotion." But Robert McGeehin had nothing but praise for the clarity and honesty of these poems, and *Choice*'s reviewer, who found the book "highly uneven, but with joyous surprises along the way," noted also that the author "has mellowed, at least poetically. She has dropped her honky-hating attacks which marred some of her past work, and has become more optimistic, loving, gentle, concerned."

A discussion with James Baldwin, taped in London in 1971 for the *Soul!* television program, was published in 1973 as *A Dialogue.* Cornelia Holbert wrote that "when a poet turns to prose, when a fine prose writer reveals himself after all a poet, the resulting conversation is a privilege to read. Here are: an effective description of the writer and his task; an acute differentiation between love and lust; a mystical treatment of The Word; an expression of the saving grace of responsibility to children." There was also much praise for *A Poetic Equation* (1974), containing a dialogue between Nikki Giovanni and the older black poet Margaret Walker. "Their differences of opinion, which are many," wrote June Goodwin, "show both a generation difference—Mrs. Walker of the conservative '40's and '50's and Miss Giovanni of the impatient and militant '60's and '70's—and the conflicting philosophies within black culture today. The book is most exciting when the women discuss literature, their own and others."

A similar dialogue with the Russian poet Yevgeny Yevtushenko was published in the first issue (Spring 1972) of *Encore,* on which Nikki Giovanni serves as an editorial consultant and columnist. In 1968 she taught as an assistant professor of Black Studies at Queens College, Flushing, New York, and in 1968–1970 she taught creative writing as an associate professor of English at Livingston College, Rutgers University, New Brunswick, New Jersey. She works for black advancement through such organizations as the National Council of Negro Women. Giovanni holds honorary doctorates from four colleges and universities. She received *Mademoiselle*'s award for outstanding achievement in 1971 and the following year was chosen by *Ladies' Home Journal* as woman of the year.

Nikki Giovanni, who is said to be cool and offbeat in manner, is five feet two inches tall, weighs one hundred pounds, has a short Afro haircut, and usually dresses casually. The author has a son, Thomas Watson Giovanni, who was born in 1969. "I had a baby at twenty-five," she has said, "because I *wanted* to have a baby and

I could *afford* to have a baby. I did not get married because I didn't *want* to get married and I could *afford* not to get married." She is a student and collector of the works of the black novelist Chester Himes, and enjoys painting and making collages, listening to music, and playing Scrabble and whist.

Publishers Weekly has described Nikki Giovanni as "the most oral of the young poets," who "takes her language from house, street and the cadenced repetition of church song." Many critics have drawn attention to the conflict in her work between black militancy and her own loving and optimistic temperament—and between revolutionary stridency and the demands of art. To the distress of her more extremist readers and the satisfaction of most others, she has tended in each successive collection to write less about war and more about love. Martha Duffy has described her as "one of the most talented and promising black poets. She is also one of the most visible, not only because she is beautiful but because she is a shrewd and energetic propagandist."

PRINCIPAL WORKS: *Poetry*—Black Feeling, Black Talk, 1968; Black Judgement, 1969; Re:Creation, 1970; Black Feeling, Black Talk, Black Judgement, 1970; Spin a Soft Black Song (for children), 1971; My House, 1972; Ego-Tripping and Other Poems for Young Readers, 1973; The Women and the Men, 1975; Cotton Candy on a Rainy Day, 1978. *Prose*—Gemini: An Extended Autobiographical Statement on My First Twenty-Five Years of Being a Black Poet, 1971; (with James Baldwin) A Dialogue, 1973; (with Margaret Walker) A Poetic Equation, 1974. *As Editor*—Night Comes Softly, 1970.

ABOUT: Contemporary Authors 1st revision, 1978; Current Biography, 1973; Giovanni, N. Gemini, 1971; Malkoff, K. Crowell's Handbook of Contemporary American Poetry, 1973; Vinson, J. (ed.) Contemporary Poets, 1975; Who's Who in America, 1976–1977. *Periodicals*—America February 7, 1976; Choice March 1973, January 1976; Christian Science Monitor June 4, 1970; June 19, 1974; Ebony February 1972, August 1972; Harper's Bazaar July 1972; Jet May 1972; Library Journal December 15, 1971; June 15, 1972; November 1, 1972; October 1, 1975; Mademoiselle December 1969, January 1972, May 1973, December 1973, September 1975; New York Times April 25, 1969; November 28, 1971; July 26, 1972; New York Times Book Review November 28, 1971; February 13, 1972; September 27, 1974; Newsweek January 31, 1972; May 28, 1973; Partisan Review Spring 1972; Publishers Weekly November 13, 1972; Saturday Review January 15, 1972; Southern Humanities Review Spring 1971; Time April 6, 1970; January 17, 1972; October 3, 1972; Washington Post July 23, 1972; November 18, 1973.

GIPPIUS, ZINAIDA. *See* **HIPPIUS, ZINAI-DA**

GITTINGS, ROBERT (WILLIAM VICTOR) (February 1, 1911–), English poet, biographer, critic, and dramatist, writes: "I was born at

ROBERT GITTINGS

Southsea, the residential area of the naval port of Portsmouth in England. My father, a brilliant medical student, but poor, became a naval surgeon because of the greater security then offered by the Royal Navy. The life consisted of two-year appointments, based on various ports. Hence I had early experience of Portsmouth itself, Plymouth, Chatham, and Harwich, made dramatic by wartime scares, often real, of stray mines lethally approaching their coasts. Yet the really dramatic occurrence of my childhood came in the years 1916 to 1919, when my father was stationed at Rosyth, on the Firth of Forth, and we moved as a family to Edinburgh for those years. The impact of that city was startling, the tall smoky streets with their glimpses of jagged mountains or bright sea, the wild and antique character of the place, the people whose language I could barely understand, and the history I learned at my first small school, a compound of savage pride and brutal conflict. I think this, obscurely, first inclined me to poetry; and secondly, returned to Southsea, where my father left the Navy for a successful shore practice as an opthalmic consultant, another revolution in my personal life, a painful spinal complaint, kept me flat on my back for fifteen months. Hitherto, and happily for all my life after, physically fit and athletic, I found compensation during that enforced stillness in reading poetry, and, in fact, wrote my own first serious poem then. When I was well enough to attend school (1927-1930), my poetry was encouraged by two remarkable men, H.G.C. (now Sir George) Mallaby and A. D. (now Canon) James, both then masters at St. Edward's School, Oxford. The publication of some of my schoolboy poems in a literary magazine led to correspondence with another young poet, Arthur Harris, now universally known as the playwright Christopher Fry, whose friendship and influence have been lasting.

"Though I obtained a scholarship to Jesus College, Cambridge, where I was successively research student, Fellow, and supervisor of studies in history, I now realise I was not really an academic, though I continue to value my historical training and my college associations. The British Broadcasting Corporation, in which and with which I worked for twenty-three years, provided the equivalent for me of an extended Ph.D. course, teaching me research among original sources, clarity and order in my writing and presentation, without suppressing in any way my freedom as a poet, an enlightened regime which I shared, at least for part of those years, with such poets as Louis MacNeice, W. R. Rodgers, Patric Dickinson, and my former college pupil, Terence Tiller. In 1950, another former pupil, A.J.W. Hill, the virtual creator of Heinemann Educational Books, became my publisher for poetry, biography, verse plays and critical works, another very happy association.

"All this, of course, sounds far more smooth and easy than it actually was. There were long periods of doubt, foolish mistakes and personal distress. In particular, there were times of being unemployed, still more of feeling that I was unemployable: a cautious temperament inherited from my father, and the fact that my twenties were spent in the 1930s did not make for confident security. I have also vacillated between various forms of literature (and, perhaps, various forms of life). Though I seem to be known as a biographer, I still think of myself primarily as a poet, who owes his insights in biographical writing about poets such as Keats and Hardy to my own experiences and searchings in poetry. I have never been attached to any literary 'school,' and have what I hope is a fairly catholic use of any technique that seems to fit the poetic experience, dramatic, documentary (I have often blurred the boundaries between biography and poetry here), 'modern' or 'traditional.' In biography, I hope to have made some innovation in my use of widespread non-academic sources and associations: to have considered, perhaps more carefully than some more committed biographers, the whole person. Keats said the poet was like the chameleon, taking the colour of everything it touched. I believe my books and their methods may have encouraged the idea of a chameleon biographer too.

"I enjoy the external rewards and awards, the late-in-life visiting professorships to U.S.A. universities, where I have now many valued friends, and in 1970 the degree of Doctor of Letters of my own university and the CBE. I shall never be without, though, a certain sense of surprise that anyone listens to what I have to say. So much of it—and this applies to both poems and biographies—seems just to be recording the obvious in simple sequence. My wife is an acclaimed biographer, in a slightly different though related field, and our daughter researches in seventeenth century history. Two sons by a previous marriage both have highly individual and different gifts."

Most of the poems in Gittings's first collection, *The Roman Road,* published in 1932 when he was only twenty-one, reflected, it was said, "either a struggle against or a wry acquiescence in" a sense of melancholy and futility—a mood from which the poet was sometimes released by the contemplation of natural beauty. Entirely traditional in form, these poems were admired for their "searching and impersonal candour." There was similar praise for Gittings's blank verse retelling of *The Story of Psyche* (1937), though it was thought that "the deeper tones of imaginative experience are hardly within his compass."

Gittings began to write radio scripts as a freelance during his years at Jesus College, Cambridge (research student and fellow, 1933–1938; supervisor in history, 1938–1940). He joined the BBC as a scriptwriter and producer in 1940. *Wentworth Place,* which appeared in 1950 after a long silence, contained poems scarcely less conventional in form than their predecessors, but considerably more confident and skillful. Gittings's bent for portraiture and narrative emerged clearly in this volume, in poems dealing perceptively and imaginatively with scenes from the life of such personages as Newton, William Cowper, and especially Keats. There were more of these biographical vignettes in *Famous Meeting* (1953).

These and subsequent volumes of Gittings's verse have been praised for their integrity and their disciplined craftsmanship, and Howard Sergeant thinks "it is high time that his poetic talents were properly recognised." All the same, it is not on his poetry or on his accomplished plays and verse plays that his reputation rests. In 1954 he published *John Keats: The Living Year,* an account of the last and most productive twelve months of Keats's short life, September 1818 to September 1819. This was the black year that witnessed the slow death of Keats's brother Tom, the failure of *Endymion,* recurrent financial crises, Keats's desperate passion for Fanny Brawne, and the onset of his own fatal illness. It was also the year in which he completed *Hyperion* and *Otho,* drafted *The Fall of Hyperion,* and wrote among other major poems "The Eve of St. Agnes," "Ode to a Nightingale," "Ode on a Grecian Urn," and "La Belle Dame Sans Merci."

Endlessly examined and re-examined as it had been, there was still much that was mysterious and uncertain about Keats's nature and its relation to his poetry. Misconceptions and misinterpretations had been handed on from one study to another. Focusing down on this single agonized *annus mirabilis,* Gittings reconsidered the existing evidence and looked for more. He consulted the opinions of Keats's friends, visited the places the poet had visited in 1818–1819, studied the books that he had read with such passionate intensity. Thanks to these procedures, and his own "sound and unastonished comprehension of human motives and human behaviour," Gittings was able to identify the origins of many of the settings, opinions, and moods in Keats's last works, to discover a new importance in his little-regarded liaison with Mrs. Isabella Jones, and to reach extraordinarily interesting conclusions about Keats's chameleon-like character. It was, one reviewer wrote, "a revolutionary method of portraiture, the portrayal of a creative living mind reacting day after day in a certain segment of time, and the result is startling."

Various themes undeveloped in *The Living Year* were explored in the essays in *The Mask of Keats,* while *The Keats Inheritance* tells the absorbing and distressing story of a bequest which, if Keats had only known of it, might have released him from all his financial hardships. In *John Keats,* Gittings applied the methods he had developed and perfected in these earlier books to produce "a complete and richly detailed biography, in which the reader is enabled to live with Keats from month to month, almost from hour to hour, his short and strenuous life," and to follow the "symbolic biography" concealed in his poems. The book received the W. H. Smith award of £1,000.

In *The Young Thomas Hardy,* Gittings brough a similar set of tools and techniques to bear on Hardy's life from his birth in 1840 to a point in the late 1870s when he had begun to establish himself as a writer. The book received the Christian Gauss Award. Irving Howe thought it "the richest account thus far of Hardy's childhood, youth and literary beginnings," but regretted Gittings's lack of verbal flair—a criticism that had been made by some reviewers of the earlier books. *The Older Hardy* was, as Samuel Hynes remarked, a "difficult story to write—the downhill side of a long, respectable life, in which the only dramatic events were inner ones." Gittings, Hynes says, concentrates his attention on Hardy's connections with his family and his relations with women, drawing a portrait "made of careful particulars, a domestic rather than a public image. It is an approach that enables Gittings to make full use of his greatest gift as a biographer, his tireless and ingenious pursuit of hidden facts."

The author is the son of Surgeon-Captain Fred Gittings and the former Dora Brayshaw. He was married in 1949 to Joan Grenville Manton, who writes as Jo Manton, his 1934 marriage to Katherine Campbell having ended in divorce. Gittings left the BBC in 1963, and since then has served as a visiting professor at Vanderbilt University, Tennessee (1966), at Boston University (1970), and the University of Washington (1972, 1974, and 1977). His recreations, he says, include most outdoor pursuits except blood sports.

PRINCIPAL WORKS: *Poetry*—The Roman Road, 1932; The Story of Psyche, 1936; Wentworth Place, 1950; Famous Meeting, 1953; This Tower My Prison, 1961; Matters of Love and Death, 1968; American Journey: Twenty-Five Sonnets, 1972; Collected Poems, 1976. *Plays*—The Makers of Violence, 1951; Through a Glass Lightly, 1952; Man's Estate *in* Lehman, L. (ed.) Two Saints Plays, 1954; Out of This Wood, 1955; Love's a Gamble: A Ballad Opera (music by Doris Gould), 1961; Conflict at Canterbury: An Entertainment in Sound and Light, 1970. *Nonfiction*—John Keats: The Living Year, 1954; The Mask of Keats, 1956; Shakespeare's Rival, 1960; The Keats Inheritance, 1964; John Keats, 1968; The Young Thomas Hardy, 1975; The Older Hardy, 1978 (U.S., Hardy's Later Years); The Nature of Biography, 1978. *As Editor:* The Living Shakespeare, 1960; Selected Poems and Letters of John Keats, 1960; (with Evelyn Hardy) Some Recollections, by Emma Hardy, 1961; Letters of John Keats: A New Selection, 1970; The Odes of Keats, 1970; Omniana, by Robert Southey and S.T. Coleridge, 1970. *With Jo Manton*—The Peach Blossom Forest and Other Chinese Legends, 1951; Windows on History (4 vols.), 1959–1961; The Story of John Keats (for children), 1962; Makers of the Twentieth Century, 1968; The Flying Horses, Tales From China, with Verses in the Chinese Style by Robert Gittings, 1977.

ABOUT: Contemporary Authors 25–28 1st revision, 1977; International Who's Who in Poetry, 1974–1975; Vinson, J. (ed.) Contemporary Poets, 1975; Who's Who, 1978. *Periodicals*—Encounter July 1975; Guardian November 7, 1969; New Republic September 7, 1968; New Statesman March 22, 1968; April 18, 1975; New York Times Book Review September 1, 1968; July 6, 1975; Times Literary Supplement March 31, 1950; April 9, 1954; April 11, 1968; April 18, 1975; April 8, 1977; March 10, 1978; November 16, 1978.

GIURLANI, ALDO. *See* "PALAZZESCHI," ALDO

*GLÜCK, LOUISE (ELISABETH) (April 22, 1943–), American poet, was born in New York City, the daughter of Daniel Glück, a business executive, and the former Beatrice Grosby. She

*glik

313

GLÜCK

LOUISE GLÜCK

was educated at Sarah Lawrence College and went on to study poetry with Stanley Kunitz in his workshops at Columbia University, where in 1966 she received the Academy of American Poets' prize. At about the same time she was herself teaching poetry to dropouts in New York City. Louise Glück has a son by her 1967 marriage to Charles Hertz, which ended in divorce. She taught at the Fine Arts Work Center, Providence, Rhode Island, in 1970, and the following year was artist-in-residence at Goddard College, Plainfield, Vermont. In the spring of 1973 she was a visiting lecturer at the University of North Carolina and she has since taught at the University of Virginia.

The poems collected in *Firstborn*, published in 1968 when she was twenty-five, attracted a great deal of attention. "In a typical poem," wrote Robert Boyers in *Contemporary Poets*, "images of corruption and decay are marshalled, but we do not know why they must have any connection with the people presented in the poem." Boyers found evidence that Glück had learned from Lowell and Jarrell as well as Kunitz in these terse and painful poems, which at times have a "stenographic bluntness" that reminded him of Alan Dugan. Lisel Mueller spoke of "diction like a clenched fist, or a muscle-cramp," evoking a poetic world which is "an externalization of intense inner experience".

Whether these poems are autobiographical, as some critics thought, or explorations of experience through assumed personae, as Glück claims, is almost irrelevant. Her poems, as Lisel Mueller says, "are a series of shocks," impressing on us, "over and over, the trauma of being alive, of feeling anything at all. . . . The elemen-

tal physical connections she writes about are, more often than not, realized in her diction." Robert Boyers also found much to admire—individuality, poise, the "casual weaving of dense aural patterns"—but thought that some of these poems were marred by a tendency to melodrama, "the forcing of images to yield more than they can or ought to yield."

This tendency had quite disappeared by the time Louise Glück published *The House on Marshland,* the collection of thirty-five brief poems which followed in 1975 after a long silence. The vision is still of a world tormented by pain, death, and darkness, but the tone is mild, reflective, even lyrical. Helen Vendler thought that the new poems represented a "phenomenal" advance over the old ones; they "are almost dreamy, they drift in a reflection like the moon in a pool (the moon and the pool recur as powerful counters in her private language). . . . I find the family poems unforgettable, like the one simply called 'Poem,' about the parents' marriage as seen by the observant, uncomprehending, helpless child-to-be-poet. . . . A very peculiar power, and a new style, commanding in its indifference to current modes." J. D. McClatchy had no doubt that this was "one of the year's enduring books." He said that Glück had "scoured both her experience and her style, and while one regrets so slim a sheaf, one is grateful for its *achieved* balance." And he quoted in evidence these lines from "For My Mother":

> It was better when we were
> together in one body.
> Thirty years. Screened
> through the green glass
> of your eye, moonlight
> filtered into my bones
> as we lay
> in the big bed, in the dark,
> waiting for my father.
> Thirty years. He closed
> your eyelids with
> two kisses.

Louise Glück had a grant from the Rockefeller Foundation in 1967-1968, and one the following year from the National Endowment for the Arts. In 1971 she received *Poetry*'s Eunice Tietjens Memorial Prize.

PRINCIPAL WORKS: Firstborn, 1968; The House on Marshland, 1975.

ABOUT: Contemporary Authors 33–36, 1973; Malkoff, K. Crowell's Handbook of Contemporary American Poetry, 1973; Vinson, J. (ed.) Contemporary Poets, 1975; Who's Who in America, 1976–1977. *Periodicals*—Kenyon Review 32 1 1970; Library Journal February 1, 1975; Michigan

Quarterly Review Fall 1969; New York Times Book Review April 6, 1975; Partisan Review 36 2 1969; Poetry February 1971; Shenandoah Summer 1970; Virginia Quarterly Review Summer 1975; Yale Review Autumn 1975.

GOLDMAN, WILLIAM (August 12, 1931–), American novelist and screenwriter, was born in Chicago, Illinois, the son of Maurice Clarence Goldman and the former Marion Weil. He received his B.A. from Oberlin College, Ohio, in 1952 and, after two years in the army (1952-1954), resumed his education at Columbia University, which gave him an M.A. in 1956. He was married in 1961 to Ilene Jones and has two children.

Unlike most writers, Goldman has known no other career. His first novel was accepted the summer he finished graduate school and published with considerable success the following year. This was *The Temple of Gold,* about the painful passage to maturity of Raymond Euripides Trevitt, the nonintellectual son of a genteel academic. While his best friend Zock goes on to Harvard, Ray flunks out of college, drinks too much, and is driving the car in which Zock is killed. Searching for the "handle" that will put him in control of his life, Ray enlists in the army, performs a notable act of heroism, and is medically discharged. He marries and goes back to college, but at twenty-one, still scarred by Zock's death, he realizes that the "handle" he is looking for does not exist, and drops out of marriage and college to start life again.

Warren French called it a moving story by "an extraordinarily talented writer obsessed with the problems of young men whose vivid anticipations cannot be realized in a humdrum world." French found the style of the first-person narration exaggerated, and David Dempsey thought the book readable but facile. To Dan Wickenden, however, it seemed "a considerable achievement. Mr. Goldman has worked out his own adroit way of conveying a novel across a considerable span of time; he has devised for his narrator a fresh and vigorous idiom, and he has fulfilled the novelist's basic function of bringing his characters wholly alive and engrossing us in their actions."

Your Turn to Curtsy, My Turn to Bow (1958), which studies the effect on another youth of the self-crucifixion of a football hero and would-be messiah, attracted less attention, but there was a warm reception for *Soldier in the Rain* (1960). Here again the focus is on a young man placed in a situation where larger-than-life characters threaten to overwhelm his half-formed personality. The setting is an army transit camp in the American South near the end of the Korean

Van Williams

WILLIAM GOLDMAN

War, where for a time young Private Metzer comes under the appalling influence of two villainous old veterans—inhabitants of a private world of privilege and security cunningly built up in the interstices of the military machine. The *New Yorker* found the book sentimental, but a reviewer in the *Times Literary Supplement* wrote that the relationship between the two old soldiers is developed "with the comic certainty of an artist who knows how to go slow and is not afraid of admitting death and sorrow," while Paul Scott recommended the novel unreservedly as "funny, lyrical, hard-headed, warm-hearted, sane."

Goldman's first major commercial success came in 1964 with the publication of *Boys and Girls Together,* in which five people assemble in Greenwich Village to stage a play. Each of the five is more or less disturbed—the play's author a dangerously unhappy homosexual, the actress sexually voracious, the producer dominated by his mother—and the novel is an account of their actions and interactions. Reviewers complained variously that this very long book (623 pages) was "sprawling, verbose, and frequently tiresome . . . a monotonous recital of sexual pecadillos and misadventures," and that the characters "relate only to one another, never to the world at large." But Richard Schickel was "grateful for the mitigating verbal skills Mr. Goldman has lavished on his novel; unlike the other authors of giant economy size bids for the best seller list, he has had the wit to skimp on the descriptive passages, use lots and lots of dialogue and keep his sentences short. In addition, he has a solid gift for gag lines, plenty of hairpin curves in his story line and a flair for good old-fashioned melodrama." And as a "bid for the best seller list," *Boys and Girls Together* was immensely successful.

The same year, as "Harry Longbaugh," Goldman published *No Way to Treat a Lady,* a tense (and often funny) tale about a psychopathic killer with a genius for disguise and the Manhattan cop assigned to unmask him (while coping simultaneously with a love affair and a stereotypical Jewish mother). Published as a paperback original, it reappeared as a hardback under Goldman's own name in 1968, tying in with the release of a movie version through which Rod Steiger happily mugged his way as the protean killer.

The Thing of It Is . . . (1967) introduced Amos McCracken, a songwriter who finds that not even a hit musical on Broadway can buy happiness. With their marriage collapsing around them, Amos and his wife make a grand tour of London, Rome, and Venice with their six-year-old daughter Jessica in a vain effort to pick up the pieces. Martin Levin thought that Goldman rarely gets "beneath the surface qualities of Amos and Lila McCracken . . . but he does capture the bottled-up hostility . . . The conversation has the ringing authority of dialogues overheard through motel walls. It compels attention—but it does not linger." McCracken is revisited in *Father's Day* (1971), his marriage dead, his career on the skids, and only his beloved daughter to sustain him. But Father's Day with Jessica turns into a nightmare of small and large mishaps, and when Jessica is injured through his carelessness Amos loses his shaky hold on reality and tries to carry the child off to Florida. Levin called it "a virtuoso performance in which the lightning tempo counter-acts a tendency to cloy," but Sara Blackburn was left with the uneasy feeling that she was being "sold a piece of merchandise that's actually shoddy stuff under a bright exterior."

In *Boys and Girls Together* and the McCracken novels, Goldman wrote about the New York theatrical scene from first-hand experience. His ear for dialogue and skill in construction had led him early into the theatre—which indeed had always interested him, providing the subject for his thesis at Columbia. *Blood, Sweat and Stanley Poole,* written in collaboration with his brother James, was produced in New York in 1961, and the musical *A Family Affair,* written with James Goldman and John Kander, was staged in 1962. Some years later, wanting to try his hand at a nonfictional book, Goldman settled on Broadway as his subject.

The Season (1969) is an evaluation of the 1967-1968 Broadway season, during which Goldman saw every play produced at least once, and conducted interviews with writers, directors, actors, reviewers, scalpers, backers, and actual and potential members of the theatre audience. His book discusses costs, financing, the unions, corruption in ticket-selling, the general uselessness of the critics, the inadequacy of the producers, the mechanics of casting, advertising and public relations, and the feebleness of much of what passes for drama. Needless to say, *The Season* was immensely controversial and wholly pleased almost no one. The commonest response, however, was something close to that expressed by Edwin Newman, who wrote: "Goldman's writing is at times cute and sententious, but generally it is breezy and sharp. The quotes are funny and enlightening. The attitude is pugnacious but open-minded. *The Season* may well be the most informative book about Broadway ever written."

Meanwhile, Goldman had made a new and immensely successful career for himself as a screenwriter. His first screenplay was for *Harper* (1966), the much-admired adaptation of a Ross Macdonald "private eye" novel starring Paul Newman (released in Britain as *The Moving Target*). This was followed by his Oscar-winning original screenplay for *Butch Cassidy and the Sundance Kid* (1969), the most original, successful, and influential Western for many years. Subsequent films have included *The Great Waldo Pepper, The Stepford Wives,* and *All the President's Men.*

Goldman has continued to write novels, though fewer of them than before his success as a screenwriter. *Marathon Man* (1974) is about an American student with two ambitions—to become a great runner and to write a dissertation exonerating his father, a historian driven to suicide by Senator Joe McCarthy. Along the long, hard way he becomes involved with two former Nazi war criminals and learns a great deal about suffering, given and received. Eric Moon found it a "superb thriller" but the novel's "cinematic layout and almost childishly mawkish style" led Gene Lyons "to suppose that this is one of those cases where the screenplay is father to the novel." And indeed *Marathon Man* became another extremely successful film, with a cast that included Dustin Hoffman and Sir Laurence Olivier, and scenes of torture and violence that greatly disturbed some reviewers.

The Princess Bride (1975) is a book of a very different kind, "a witty, affectionate send-up of the adventure-yarn form" in which the wicked Prince Humperdinck seeks to steal the beautiful Buttercup from her childhood sweetheart, thus setting the stage for a drama involving giants, magicians, swordsmen, dungeons, resurrections, and other excitements in short supply in contemporary fiction. In a rather arch introduction, Goldman recalls his boyhood, when his father read him "S. Morganstern's classic tale of true love and high adventure." He explains that, giving the book to his own son, he discovered that his father had wisely skipped the dull parts, and had himself produced this "abridgement," complete with comments (printed in red) explaining what had been cut and why—a device which one reviewer called "a kind of comedic extension of Brecht's distancing effect, alienation to provoke not an intellectual response but an *entertained* response. And it works."

Goldman began his career as a "serious" novelist of exceptional promise, perceptively exploring the problems of idealistic young men in a naughty world. He has become a dazzlingly expert craftsman and entertainer, to the regret of a handful of critics and the delight of thousands of readers and moviegoers. And in the process he has made himself one of the highest paid writers in history. According to *Publishers Weekly,* he received $400,000 for his *Butch Cassidy* screenplay, at that time a record. He was paid $300,000 for *All the President's Men,* $500,000 for the novel and screenplay of *Marathon Man,* and a million dollars for the novel and screenplay of *Magic,* together with a percentage of the profits of some or all of these movies. Goldman is a former editor of *Transatlantic Review.* He says: "I'm not all that crazy about the act of writing, which is probably why I write quickly. The sooner I'm done, the sooner I can go to the movies. Besides movies I like tennis, swimming, mysteries, the New York Knicks, and working out baseball statistics."

PRINCIPAL PUBLISHED WORKS: *Novels*—The Temple of Gold, 1957; Your Turn to Curtsy, My Turn to Bow, 1958; Soldier in the Rain, 1960; Boys and Girls Together, 1964; (as "Harry Longbaugh") No Way to Treat a Lady, 1964 (republished under own name, 1968); The Thing of It Is . . ., 1967; Father's Day, 1971; Marathon Man, 1974; Wigger (for children), 1974; The Princess Bride: S. Morganstern's Classic Tale of True Love and High Adventure: The "Good Parts" Version, Abridged, 1975; Magic, 1976. *Plays* —(with James Goldman) Blood, Sweat, and Stanley Poole, 1962. *Screenplays*—Butch Cassidy and the Sundance Kid, 1969; The Great Waldo Pepper, 1975. *Nonfiction*—The Season: A Candid Look at Broadway, 1969.

ABOUT: Contemporary Authors 9-12 1st revision, 1974; Penguin Companion to Literature 3, 1971; Vinson, J. (ed.) Contemporary Novelists, 1976; Who's Who in America, 1976-1977. *Periodicals*—Books and Bookmen January 1968; Book Week August 2, 1964; Chicago Sunday Tribune October 13, 1957; Commonweal November 29, 1957; Life October 31, 1969; New Leader September 15, 1969; New York Times November 17, 1957; August 31, 1969; September 19, 1969; New York Times Book Review April 14, 1968; September 28, 1969; January 31, 1971; October 27, 1974; New Yorker May 20, 1967; Publishers Weekly June 23, 1969; June 10, 1974; March 15, 1976; Saturday Review October 19, 1957; July 25, 1964; Times Literary Supplement December 9, 1960; Variety August 13, 1969.

*GORBANEVSKAYA, NATALYA (1936–), Russian poet and translator, was born in Moscow. As a child she was an excellent student, but in early adolescence she lost interest in schoolwork, and by the time she entered Moscow University as a student of philology she was restless and often depressed. She developed an acute fear of heights which made it impossible for her to attend physical education classes. In her second year an unhappy love affair drove her to attempt suicide, and soon afterwards she was expelled from Moscow University, partly on account of the "pessimism" and "decadence" of her anguished love poems, which had appeared in the university's "wall newspapers." She went to Kaliningrad to study cinema technology, but returned home after four days. Then and later she hitchhiked to many parts of the Soviet Union. In her letters she describes this method of travel as one of her greatest pleasures and recalls journeys to Leningrad and Estonia. On one occasion she hitchhiked to the Caucasian state of Georgia with a Georgian man she had met, but returned after two weeks: "Not the right man."

In 1956 Natalya Gorbanevskaya re-entered the faculty of philology of Moscow University, having won a place there in a competitive examination; the following year she was again expelled for missing classes. Her restlessness continued during the next year, but in August 1958 she settled down to work as a librarian at the All-Union Book Center, at the same time enrolling as an external student of Leningrad University. Under this double pressure, however, her fear of heights intensified until she could not even go upstairs. She also suffered from insomnia and "a dreadful internal irritability," so that she could not, for example, bear the rustling of paper. At work she spent long periods sitting quite motionless, her hands clenched. In October 1959, after visits to a hospital psychiatrist, she spent two weeks in the Kashchenko psychiatric hospital, an experience she found so dreadful that she swore never to go into a hospital again.

Her son Yasik was born in 1961, and in 1964 she received her external degree from Leningrad University. She went to work at the State Institute of Experimental Pattern Design and Technical Research as a translator and editor of technical information. In January 1968 she was one of the twelve signatories of a letter addressed

*gôr bən yef′ skī yə

to the Chairman of the Moscow Municipal Court, demanding an open trial for the dissident writers Alexander Ginzburg and Yuri Galanskov—Galanskov had edited the 1966 *samizdat* poetry collection *Phoenix,* in which some of Gorbanevskaya's own poems had appeared. (*Samizdat*—literally "self-publishing"—refers to the thousands of typewritten manuscripts that are distributed clandestinely in the Soviet Union, often at great risk, containing material denied official publication.) She also joined in other protests about this trial, and in February 1968 it was she who sent a protest letter signed by one hundred and seventy people to the Soviet leaders.

Later the same month, six months pregnant and suffering from anemia, she was sent to a maternity hospital. She described herself at that time as "a small, dishevelled, shortsighted woman, dressed in the preposterous hospital smock." Gorbanevskaya hated the hospital and its routines. Her insomnia and acute irritability recurred, she could not eat, and she used up "an enormous amount of energy" trying to shut out the conversations of the women around her about their sex lives and their gruesome medical histories. In spite of all this, and the moralistic inquiries from hospital orderlies about her lack of a husband, she desperately wanted her baby and was terrified that they might "drag me off, give me a scrape and then say that the miscarriage began itself." She made desperate efforts to have herself discharged and eventually succeeded, but not before her extreme distress had earned her another week in the Kashchenko psychiatric hospital.

Her second son Oska was born in May 1968, and she took him with her when, on August 25, she and six friends went to the Red Square in Moscow to protest against Russia's invasion of Czechoslovakia. Her companions included the physicist Pavel Litvinov, grandson of the former Foreign Minister, and Larissa Daniel, wife of the writer Yuri Daniel. The seven sat down in the old place of execution in front of St. Basil's Cathedral, and unfurled their homemade banners and a little Czech flag. Bystanders gathered around them immediately, shouting that they were "hooligans" and "parasites." Their banners were torn up and they themselves were punched. After about five minutes two police cars arrived and the demonstrators were bundled in with maximum violence and driven away.

Gorbanevskaya has described the demonstration and its consequences in her prose work *Polden,* a *samizdat* publication in 1970, translated into English by Alexander Lieven as *Red Square at Noon.* A reviewer in the *Times Literary Supplement* called the book "a positive hymn to the courage" of the men and women who made their protest "knowing full well what the consequences would be," and Stuart Hood said it was "an excellent piece of reporting, sometimes ironical but always restrained."

Gorbanevskaya herself was allowed to go free, apparently because of her two young children. Five of the others were brought to trial, charged with slandering the state and "criminal conspiracy." *Red Square at Noon* gives a full account of their interrogation and trial, including in detail the long statements they made in their defense. The book also provides an account of Gorbanevskaya's own psychiatric examination which ended inconclusively, though the notorious Professor Lunts, a colonel in the KGB as well as a psychiatrist, suggested that "the possibility of low profile schizophrenia is not excluded," and recommended that she "should be declared insane and lodged in a penal category psychiatric hospital for compulsory treatment."

In fact, Gorbanevskaya was released and placed under her mother's guardianship. Throughout her friends' trial—a shameless parody of justice—she continued her protests, at home and in foreign newspapers. All five were sentenced to various terms of exile. These events were duly reported in the *Chronicle of Current Events,* a *samizdat* periodical devoted to the recording of such infringements of human rights and legal process, which has appeared in the USSR at fairly regular two-month intervals since April 1968. Natalya Gorbanevskaya, who founded or helped to found the *Chronicle,* told an *Index on Censorship* editor that she was "very, very proud" of this achievement—"more than of my poetry, perhaps more than of the demonstration."

Early in 1969 Gorbanevskaya became a founder-member of the Action Group for the Defense of Civil Rights in the USSR. And on December 24, 1969, when the KGB discovered that she had written *Polden,* she was arrested and sent to Butyrka Prison. The following April a forensic psychiatric examination ended with the conclusion that she was suffering from schizophrenia and the recommendation that she should be sent for compulsory treatment to a psychiatric hospital "of special type." This recommendation was accepted at a special session of the Moscow City Court on July 7, 1970, when she was declared to have committed criminal acts while of unsound mind. She was sent back to Butyrka, then to the special psychiatric hospital in Kazan, where a course of drug treatment was administered. In February 1972 she was released, and returned to live with her mother in Moscow. In December 1975 she was permitted to emigrate to Vienna with her two sons. She now lives in Paris and continues to write poetry.

Although Gorbanevskaya is regarded as one of the most interesting of contemporary Russian poets, only a handful of her poems have been published officially in her own country. The rest of her slender output has appeared there only in *samizdat*—in several collections of her own, and in the important *Phoenix* anthologies of 1961 and 1966. All of these poems were collected in a volume published in 1969 by Possev-Verlag, a Russian émigré publishing house in Frankfurt. And a selection of her poems appeared in English in 1972, edited and translated by Daniel Weissbort. This volume includes a number of appendices: the notes and some of the letters she wrote when she was trying to leave the maternity hospital, the Russian psychiatric reports on her mental condition, letters from Butyrka, a transcript of her trial, and a review of the Russian psychiatric reports by a British psychiatrist who says that in his opinion the behavior described in the reports in neurotic but not schizophrenic. Much of the biographical material in this article is drawn from her letters and notes, and from *Red Square at Noon*.

In Gorbanevskaya's poetry, writes Weissbort, "a near-hysterical shrillness, a staccato beat ... is contained within a taut framework that her flexibility, her poetic skill and energy, enable her to discover anew for each poem." Weissbort is reminded of the poetry of Marina Tsvetaeva, and another frequent comparison is with Sylvia Plath, whom Gorbanevskaya resembles in her preoccupation with suffering, isolation, and impending disaster, her easy and almost affectionate attitude to the idea of suicide:

> Goodbye!—and I am myself amazed
> how bright and cold it grows,
> how the rain stops drizzling.
> Goodbye!—like a little ladleful I spill
> into the broad clear river,
> into the deep gentle Lethe.
>
> (from "Darkness" translated by
> Daniel Weissbort)

Some of her poems are on themes from Russian history, others celebrate places she visited on her hitchhiking trips, and often she turns to nature. Her work is almost always intensely personal and subjective, whatever its theme, and the dominant mood is one of suffering. Not all of her poetry is unhappy, however, as this ecstatic love lyric shows:

> Denying love,
> to be caught in its snare,
> to lift the dark from words
> as hands from the face,
>
> and to see the light explode
> over town and forest,
> like a Kyrie Eleison,
> like a March-day slogan,
>
> and a Mozart chorus
> above the roar of drift-ice,
> like the blissful cold that flows
> down from the white mountains.
>
> (translated by
> Daniel Weissbort)

Natalya Gorbanevskaya is a Christian, and religious imagery plays an important part in her work, as in the following poem, where she compares the pangs of love to the agonies of martyrdom:

> Why talk of disaster or beauty
> when the oblivious body, happy,
> naked as the thief's upon the cross,
> wants to be deceived . . .
>
> And this transcendental merging of passions,
> these clutching hands, this gasping breath,
> are like bones breaking softly on the cross
> and, at the stake, the crackle and the blaze.
>
> (from "Frontier of Light"
> translated by
> Daniel Weissbort)

The pianist Vladimir Ashkenazy, who knew Gorbanevskaya in Russia, told Weissbort that he was impressed above all by "her absolute honesty and sincerity," and by a quality that he called "spirituality." Weissbort says that she "perhaps more than any other poet of her generation, has had the capacity to transmute her suffering into a universal image. . . . Gorbanevskaya has had the immense courage to remain vulnerable."

PRINCIPAL WORKS IN ENGLISH TRANSLATION: Selected Poems, 1972; Red Square at Noon, 1972. *Poems in* Bosley, K. and others (eds.) Russia's Other Poets, 1968; Milner-Gulland, R. and Dewhirst, M. (eds.) Russian Writing Today, 1977; Proffer, C. and E. (eds.) The Ardis Anthology of Recent Russian Literature, 1973; Weissbort, D. (ed.) Post-War Russian Poetry, 1974; Index on Censorship January-February 1977.

ABOUT: Gorbanevskaya, N. Selected Poems, 1972; Gorbanevskaya, N. Red Square at Noon, 1972; Reddaway, P. (ed.) Uncensored Russia, 1972. *Periodicals*—Guardian January 8, 1970; Index on Censorship January-February 1977; Sunday Times February 20, 1972; Times Literary Supplement May 26, 1972.

*"GRANIN," DANIEL (ALEXAN-DROVICH) (pseudonym of Daniel German) (January 1, 1918–), Russian novelist and short story writer, was born and educated in Leningrad, and has spent most of his life there. After graduating from the Leningrad Technical Institute he worked as an electrical engineer at the Kirov Works until the German invasion in 1941. Granin volunteered for the army as a private, and later commanded a tank squadron at the front. He was released towards the end of the war to serve as director of part of the Leningrad electrical power network. He subsequently worked as a research scientist, publishing papers on electrical discharges in gases.

It was not until he was thirty that Granin published his first story, "Variant vtoroi" (The Second Variant, 1949). The novella *Spor cherez okean* (The Quarrel Across the Ocean) followed in 1950 and a volume of short sketches, *Novye druzya* (New Friends), in 1952. With the publication of the novel *Iskateli* (1955, translated by Robert Daglish as *Those Who Seek*), Granin left the engineering profession and became a full-time writer.

Like his other early works, *Iskateli* is a fairly conventional piece of realistic writing which reflects the author's technical background. It describes the struggles of a young engineer, newly appointed as director of an industrial laboratory, to overcome the opposition of entrenched and conservative superiors and to develop an important new piece of electrical equipment. The young hero succeeds because he is a ruthless fighter, but Granin is careful to attribute his victory to the laboratory as a whole: "The time of the lonely individual is coming to an end."

A very different point of view informs "Sobstvennoe mnenie" (1956, translated by Valentin Eyre as "A Personal Opinion"). This novella was published in *Novy mir* at the time of the Thaw, and along with Dudintsev's very similar novel *Not by Bread Alone* it provoked violent controversy. A crusading young scientist wants to publish a paper criticizing a motor invented by an important academician. Minaev, the head of the research institute, is touched by the young man's idealism, which he once shared, but lacks the courage to support him. In the end Minaev finds himself collaborating with other scientific bureaucrats and defenders of the status quo in having the young dissenter posted elsewhere. What outraged Granin's critics was the clear implication that Minaev was not simply a weak individual but the typical product of a system that bred cowardice, temporizing, and hypocrisy.

*grä′nēn

DANIEL GRANIN

The novel *Posle svadby* (After the Wedding, 1957) is concerned with Khrushchev's new agricultural policy, and *Ostrov molodykh* (The Island of the Young, 1962) is a book about Cuba, whose revolution attracted Granin as it did Yevtushenko and other Russian writers. In *Idu na grozu* (1962, translated by Robert Daglish as *Into the Storm*), Granin returned to the world of science. Tulin, a talented and glamorous young "scientific wizard" doing research into weather control, plans an experiment which involves a flight into a thunderstorm. His colleagues are Krylov—awkward and tactless, but tenacious of purpose—and Richard, a zestful young idealist. The experiment becomes a disaster when the party is flown by accident into the very heart of the storm, and the jealous bureaucrat in charge of the party sabotages the apparatus and causes Richard's death. A commission of inquiry forbids further research of this kind, and it is not the brilliant Tulin but the persevering Krylov who fights this decision. The novel was made into a successful film by the director Sergei Mikaelyon.

Idu na grozu draws on the author's own experience of a similar flight, an ordeal which, he has said, revealed to him about the work of Antoine de Saint-Exupéry, whom he greatly admires. This novel, which seemed to some western critics a little naive and schematic in its characterization, was followed by accounts of Granin's travels in East Germany, Australia, and England.

The most admired of Granin's books to date is the short story collection *Kto-to Dolzhen* (Somebody Must, 1970). In the long title story,

Granin continues his exploration of the nature of scientific creativity, and his campaign against the weaknesses of the Soviet scientific bureaucracy—its careerism, inertia, and "shkurnichestvo" (self-seeking egotism). Drobyshev, a successful young research scientist, is approached by an older man, Selyanin, who asks for his help in developing an invention in the face of influential opposition. Drobyshev (who is attracted by Selyanin's young wife) persuades Selyanin to abandon his project, urging his responsibility to his family: "It is immoral to work at the expense of life." In the second half of the story the roles are reversed. Drobyshev has become totally committed to a new area of research and it is his turn to go for help to Selyanin, now affluent and apparently content in a routine job. Selyanin refuses his help but Drobyshev decides to go on alone, because "somebody must." The convincing complexity of the relationship between the two scientists seemed to Keith Armes to mark a great advance in Granin's work.

Kto-to Dolzhen also contains an interesting science fiction story and an essay on the nineteenth-century Russian scientist Vasily Petrov, who is Granin's ideal, a scientist driven not by ambition but by pure curiosity. "Scientists like Petrov," Granin writes, "created the moral climate of science. . . . In them we find present the never-aging measure of purity, disinterestedness, and poetry." Granin is the author (with Igor Talankin) of the film *Choice of Target* (1975), about the development of the atom bomb in the United States, Germany, and the Soviet Union.

Katherine Hunter Blair has contrasted Granin's work with that of such science-oriented Western writers as Nigel Balchin, suggesting that where Balchin uses science merely to add excitement to his plots, it is for Granin an integral and vital element in his drawing of character. She believes that Granin's transmutation of science into art means that Soviet writing "may go further than the West in bridging the gap which C. P. Snow sees between the artist and the scientist." Keith Armes has called Granin "the most prominent Soviet scientific novelist."

PRINCIPAL WORKS IN ENGLISH TRANSLATION: Those Who Seek, 1956; Into the Storm, 1965; A Personal Opinion *in* Stillman, E. (ed.) Bitter Harvest, 1959.

ABOUT: Alexandrova, V. A History of Soviet Literature, 1963; Blair, K.H. A Review of Soviet Literature, 1966; Brown, E.J. Russian Literature Since the Revolution, 1963; Gibian, G. Interval of Freedom, 1960; Hayward, M. and Crowley, E.L. (eds.) Soviet Literature in the Sixties, 1965; Hayward, M. and Labedz, L. (eds.) Literature and Revolution in Soviet Russia 1917-1962, 1963; Prominent Personalities in the U.S.S.R., 1968; Slonim, M. Soviet Russian Literature, 1964; Swayze, H. Political Control of Literature in the U.S.S.R. 1946-1959, 1962. *Periodicals*—New Republic April 22, 1957; Soviet Literature 7 1976; Survey Winter 1974.

GREENBERG, URI ZVI ("Tur-Malka") (October 17, 1898–), Hebrew and Yiddish poet, was born in Bialykamien, Eastern Galicia, then part of the Austro-Hungarian Empire. He was descended on both sides of the family from well-known Hasidic leaders. When Uri Zvi Greenberg was a child his father, a rabbi, moved the family to the city of Lvov (then Lemberg). There the boy received a traditional Hasidic upbringing and education and spent his childhood among some of the poorest and most oppressed Jews of Eastern Europe. He was early embittered by the sufferings of his people.

Greenberg started writing at the age of eighteen, his first Yiddish poems appearing in 1921 in a Zionist weekly, while at the same time his Hebrew poems were published in Palestine. In 1915 he was drafted into the Austrian army; after fighting on the Serbian front, he deserted in 1917. Returning to Lvov, he witnessed the Polish pogroms against the Jews, in which the whole street on which his family lived was demolished—an event that left a profound mark on him and his work.

His first book of poems, which appeared in Yiddish in 1915, shows the beginning of the expressionist tendency that dominates his later verse. In 1920 he went to Warsaw and joined two other progressive young Yiddish poets, Moishe Broderson and Melech Ravich, in publishing a literary journal called *Khalastrie* (The Gang), with which Peretz Markish also became associated. Different in temperament and outlook though they were, these young men were nevertheless united in their rebellion against accepted forms and values, disregarding traditional imagery and making violent experiments with language. The expressionist trend was also reflected in their innovations in typography and design, in which the artists El Lissitzsky and Marc Chagall played important parts. A good example of all these trends is Greenberg's poem *Mefiste* (Mephisto, 1921), which appeared in large album format with a cover of cubist design.

After a year in Berlin (1923) Greenberg emigrated to Palestine in 1924. Here he stopped writing in Yiddish and devoted himself solely to poetry in Hebrew. When the Labor daily newspaper *Davar* was founded in 1925 he became one of its regular columnists, constantly calling for self-realization through pioneering. After the Arab riots of 1929 he broke with the Labor Zionist movement and joined the extreme wing

Encyclopaedia Judaica archives, Keter Publishing

URI ZVI GREENBERG

of the Zionist Revisionist Party, denouncing both the British government and the Zionist leadership for betraying the Zionist dream. His angry poetic response to the bloody events of 1929 was contained in the collection *Ezor Magen u-Neum Ben ha-Dam* (A Protection and the Speech of the Son of Blood, 1930), the title poem of which closes with his statement of the function of the Jew: "To be like a burning bush, body burning in his blood/ Until the extinguisher come."

Thus, though Greenberg became one of the leading Hebrew poets of his generation, he occupied a somewhat isolated position because of his extreme nationalism and right-wing political views. By 1928 he was calling (with himself clearly in mind) for the emergence of a Hebrew Walt Whitman, conceived as the bardic singer of the nation's soul. His concept of Zionism was a religious and mystical one; he regarded it as the means to the fulfillment of the Jewish historical destiny of Messianic redemption and world sovereignty, the Jew in his view being wholly other than the non-Jew, having been elected by God at the beginning of time as a holy instrument of His will. Thus the one overriding theme of all his poetry is Jewish suffering in the Diaspora and Jewish rehabilitation in Israel.

Like the ancient Hebrew prophets, with whom he claims spiritual kinship, Greenberg is merciless in his tirades, condemning, accusing, chastising, and hurling curses on all those who are prepared to compromise. He revived in Hebrew literature the desperate fighting spirit of Masada. His verse is always strident, as he himself recognizes: "How can I, a Jew, who is wild and disheveled and aching, string songs as one

strings pearls." Waxman compares his poetry to "molten lava thrown out of a volcano," while Wallenrod describes him as one "seen marching ahead of the crowd, gesticulating, exhorting." He "stands high on a hill and shouts loud for attention—urging the people on, without tolerance of their smallest transgression."

Greenberg has been criticized as a hollow rhetorician, and his harsh poetry of resentment and defiance has often been censured for its shrillness, violence, and intolerance. Yet it is redeemed by his monumental visions of the Jewish role in history, which connect the religious inheritance and traditional aspirations of the Jewish people with the present as immediate and moving experiences. Thus he takes over such a traditional Jewish theme as the lament over the desecrated condition of Jerusalem, and turns it into the Zionist doctrine of "compulsion," of Zionism as something forced on Jewry by the world's hatred of the Jew:

Ah, well it is that we have forsaken Londons, Parises and New Yorks!
Ah, well it is that we have forsaken Europe and all the splendors,
And have become comrades to all the barefoot who burn in fever and whisper love to the sands and stones in Canaan.

We were compelled to go forth and to leave behind all treasure,
To set only bag upon the shoulder, to go forth with the kit of exile.
We sang songs also like recruits of an army, recruits of the army of the barefoot on the shores of the Mediterranean Sea.
They said: "Fever in Zion consumes its sick."
They said: "The Canaanite attacks upon the road and slays."
They said: "Jackals enter in under the blankets and devour the flesh of the living as he sleeps in his tent."

They said, they said, they said—but we went forth.
We were compelled to go forth. The earth cried out from under our feet, the beds trembled.
We ate, out of shame, the morsel to a satiety unto death.
We drank with a shudder, and we vomited like an adulteress,
And we saw in horror our own likeness in every outstretched figure upon a cross, until the cross and its agony rose up within the life of the spirit.

(from *Jerusalem,*
translated by
Charles A. Cowen)

Between 1931 and 1934 Greenberg again lived in Warsaw, where he was sent by the Zionist Revisionist Party to edit its Yiddish weekly *Di Velt* (The World). When he returned to Palestine in 1936 his attacks on the moderate socialist Zionist leadership became even more vehement, and his vision of the impending Nazi Holocaust was prophetically expressed in such poems as "Migdal ha-Geviyyot" (The Tower of Corpses) in his collection *Sefer ha-Kitrug ve ha-Emunah* (Book of Accusations and Belief, 1937). After the war his powerful laments on the destruction of European Jewry, including his own parents and sister, in the collection of Holocaust poems *Rehovot ha-Nahar* (Streets of the River: The Book of Dirges and Power, 1951) won both the Bialik and Israel prizes for Hebrew literature. In his poetic introduction to this deeply disturbing volume Greenberg sees the Nazi Holocaust as only the latest and most terrible demonstration of the workings of Jewish destiny:

It happened to us yesterday . . . but as though
  generations ago
Encrusted in ancient parchments hidden in bundles
  within pottery jugs
We found this written in blood of black:
There was a flood of Jewish blood, incomparable,
  trembling, the cutting off of Exiles.
Even an angel dips his wings in this blood
  murmuring—no remnant.
In Zion then came the events of Ararat.

Leon Yudkin, who translated these lines, says that his poem "does not attempt to raise the experience on to a pedestal or to distance it; on the contrary, the 'expressionist' revels in the particulars of the moment, piling together precise though emotional descriptions of the horrors in detailed actuality—the tortures and the slaughter. But always the referent is history, the historical function of the Jew, the Jewish myth." Greenberg sees this tragedy as the logical culmination of the long confrontation between the Jews and the Christians, the latter still as thirsty for blood as in the Crusades; the six million dead are an insuperable barrier that must eternally separate the Jew from the non-Jewish world, which is a "burning furnace of hostile gentilism." Even Greenberg's personal and love poetry draws heavily on biblical and kabbalistic concepts and symbols, treating his own experience of life in terms of Jewish mythology.

During the final struggle against Britain for the independence of a Jewish Palestine, Greenberg supported the terrorism of Irgun Zvai Leumi, and after the establishment of the State of Israel he was elected to the Knesset as a member for the Herut Party (1949 to 1951). Robert Alter, summing him up as "a poet of the Holocaust," calls him "a thorough maverick, such an uncompromising extremist in all his aesthetic and ideological positions that there is a strange sort of integrity in the very purity of his oppositionalism. His politics are on the far fringes of the messianic Right . . . and he has denounced as backsliders and traitors all who lack his single-minded dedication to fulfilling the manifest destiny of the Jewish people, which is to triumph by might over its historical enemies, Christianity and Islam." Greenberg remains an important exception to the prevalent modern stance of the poet as the self-absorbed explorer of his own experience, and still strives, as Hebrew poets and prophets for three millennia have done, to speak for a whole people in its historical anguish.

PRINCIPAL WORKS IN ENGLISH TRANSLATION: Jerusalem, translated by Charles A. Cowen, 1939. *Poems in* Leftwich, J. The Golden Peacock, 1939; Mezey, R. The Door Standing Open, 1970; Mintz, R. F. Modern Hebrew Poetry, 1966; Books Abroad Spring 1972; Poetry July 1958.

ABOUT: Burnshaw, S. and others (eds.) The Modern Hebrew Poem Itself, 1966; Encyclopaedia Judaica, 1971; Friedlaender, J. Iyyunim be-Shirat Uri Zvi Greenberg, 1966; Halkin, S. Modern Hebrew Literature, 1970; Kravitz, N. Three Thousand Years of Hebrew Literature, 1972; Liphshitz, A. Uri Zvi Greenberg, Meshorer Adnut ha-Ummah, 1945; Wallenrod, R. The Literature of Modern Israel, 1936; Waxman, A. A History of Jewish Literature, 1960; Yeivin, J. M. Uri Zvi Greenberg, Meshorer Mehokek, 1934; Yudkin, L. Escape Into Siege, 1974. *Periodicals*—Commentary November 1973.

"GRIFFIN, DAVID." *See* MAUGHAM, ROBIN

*****GUARE, JOHN (EDWARD)** (February 5, 1938–), American dramatist, was born in New York City, the son of Eddie Guare and the former Helen Clare Grady. The author says his father was "a nice man, a swell fellow. . . . He worked on Wall Street and *hated* it. He always said: 'Don't get a job. Figure out a way you don't have to work.'" The Guares came from Castle Dunguaire in Ireland, arriving in Vermont in the seventeenth century. The author's family on his mother's side was in show business—his great-uncles Jimmy and Jere Grady ran a touring repertory company from 1880 to 1925, and his uncle Billy Grady was a theatrical agent whose clients included W.C. Fields and Will Rogers, and who became casting director at MGM. When John Guare was eight the family was visited by Uncle Billy, then searching for a boy to play Huckleberry Finn in a proposed film musical. Guare's career might have begun there and then, but he tried so feverishly to impress his uncle that the great man went away convinced that the boy was deranged. This painful episode later found its way into *The House of Blue Leaves*—one of many examples of Guare's gift

*gâr

JOHN GUARE

for finding "the bizarre and comic" in his own experience and turning it, as Thomas B. Markus says, "into material of general and sometimes social and political interest."

Guare was educated at Catholic schools—St. Joan of Arc in Jackson Heights, New York City, St. John's Prep in Brooklyn, and Georgetown University in Washington (B.A., 1960). There followed three years of study under John Gassner at the Yale University Drama School, where Guare was bored and frustrated by the emphasis on traditional structure and logical development in playwriting. He received his M.F.A. in 1963, and began his career (Uncle Billy by then having forgiven him) with MGM in Hollywood. Wretchedly unhappy there, he escaped into the Air Force Reserve, and then went off to Europe. After London and Paris, he told an interviewer in the New York *Post,* he hitchhiked to the Sudan, "speaking to no one" but writing "lots and lots and lots of stuff" in the pocket-sized notebooks he always carries with him. He subsequently returned to Yale Drama School on a fellowship to study screenwriting, and there wrote his first successful plays.

Some of Guare's early short plays had already been produced by then—*Did You Write My Name in the Snow?* at Yale in 1962 and *To Wally Pantoni, We Leave a Cadenza* at the Barr-Albee-Wilder theatre workshop in New York two years later. *A Day for Surprises* (1965) is a romantic fantasy satirizing the sort of librarians who would watch unmoved as a very large stone lion prowled through the premises. *Something I'll Tell You Tuesday* and *The Loveliest Afternoon of the Year* followed in 1966 at Cafe Cino: brief sketches of which the second aroused most

interest. It is a dark absurdist comedy in which a lonely girl's idyllic encounter with a strange young man in the park ends in murder. Guare had his first success with *Muzeeka,* which satirizes bourgeois values as they are represented by vapid "wall-to-wall" music and by American television coverage of the Vietnam War. It was produced in Waterford, Connecticut in 1967 and off-Broadway in New York in 1968, when it brought Guare an "Obie" award, and was later seen at the Edinburgh Festival and in London.

John Grady, another of Guare's great-uncles, had been a policeman in Lynn, Massachusetts. Raiding a brothel one night, he found what he thought was a baby crying; it turned out to be a cantankerous midget named Billy Rhodes, whom John Grady eventually adopted. Guare utilizes this incident in *Cop-Out,* a satire on police power which closed after seven performances on Broadway in 1969. This disaster was later mitigated by the fact that Guare was voted most promising Broadway playwright in *Variety*'s 1970 critics' poll, but at the time he was deeply hurt. He left the country and, according to the New York *Post* interview, spent some time hitchhiking around the Arctic Circle, writing as he went. Another year went into work on a musical version, never completed, of Brecht's *The Exception and the Rule,* planned by Leonard Bernstein and Jerome Robbins as a vehicle for Zero Mostel.

The House of Blue Leaves opened in 1971 at the Truck and Warehouse Theatre in the East Village, New York. It is set in Sunnyside, Queens, and deals with a day in the unenviable life of Artie Shaughnessy, a middle-aged zookeeper who aspires to fame as a Hollywood songwriter. Artie's wife Bananas is insane and his draftee son Ronnie, as eager for glory as his father, intends to go down in history as the man who blew up the Pope (who on the day we are considering is visiting New York). Artie himself plans to ask His Holiness to restore his wife's reason so that he will feel less guilty when he leaves her for his mistress Bunny. Other characters include Artie's friend Billy Einhorn, a producer of bad movies, and a stone-deaf starlet who is Billy's girlfriend.

Henry Hewes wrote that "Guare has personified in Artie the American dream of success and the destructive forces unleashed by the frustration of never achieving it. . . . The play maintains a spirit of savage comedy unmatched here since Peter Nichols's *A Day in the Death of Joe Egg.* . . . Because he buries his frustrations so deep, . . . [Artie's] final, wordless act, the strangling of Bananas, emerges as grotesque and therefore within the black, zany framework of the rest of the proceedings." Hewes went on to say that the play's "delights are so great and its vision so essentially true that I find myself valuing it more highly than any new play this season." Walter Kerr was struck by Guare's technique of introducing a bizarre or funny absurdist image (like the sight of three nuns clambering over the grill outside Artie's apartment) and then providing "a casually rational accounting for it." This technique, Kerr wrote, was worked into "a straightforward narrative of the 'traditional' sort that . . . made us feel for the seedy, hapless, indefatigable fellow as keenly as any normally built play might. Mr. Guare was . . . using the storytelling techniques of standard or Broadway or 'popular' theatre to embrace the wildest extravagances of one branch of the avant-garde, and he was bringing it off." The play earned for Guare a second "Obie" and awards from both the New York Drama Critics' Circle and the Outer Critics' Circle.

There were more awards and another ration of glory for the New York Shakespeare Festival's musical version of *Two Gentlemen of Verona,* adapted by Guare and Mel Shapiro, with music by Galt MacDermot. It also opened in 1971 and received the New York Drama Critics' Award and a "Tony" award as the season's best musical. Most critics welcomed the show's interracial casting and its bold updating of Elizabethan values and assumptions (often with satirical effect, as when we learn that the Duke of Milan keeps an army stationed abroad so that he can campaign for re-election on a platform of "Bring the Boys Home"). Peter Schjeldahl called it a "wild, hilarious, sexy and brazenly high-handed adaptation" and "an evening of goofy and exhilarating theatre in which Shakespeare, while occasionally roughed up a bit beyond the call of duty, is well served in unexpected and significant ways."

Ten years earlier, when he was unknown, Guare had spent a summer on the island of Nantucket, Massachusetts, working as caretaker for an island resident, Mrs. C. L. Sibley. It was reportedly in tribute to Mrs. Sibley that Guare arranged for the tiny Nantucket Stage Company to give his next play its premier in 1973. This was *Marco Polo Sings a Solo,* which eventually reached Joseph Papp's Public Theatre for a brief run in 1977. Set on a Norwegian iceflow, and described by Walter Kerr as "a vaudeville tour of the human condition in the year 1999," it seemed to Kerr "a series of images and acts, more than a coherent play; and some are underbaked and some drag on," though at its best it is "a brilliantly absurdist comedy of ideas."

Elsewhere, Kerr has described Guare as an "accomplished manipulator of verbal conceits" who is "in danger of substituting an undeniable gift of the gab for an interior structure strong enough to propel his plays home." This was a frequent criticism of *Rich and Famous,* staged at the Academy Theatre in Lake Forest, Illinois, in 1974 and at the New York Shakespeare Festival's Newman Theatre in 1976. It chronicles the disasters that befall a young playwright on the opening night of his first produced play: the play flops, and all of the dramatist's former admirers—represented by two actors playing many roles—promptly abandon him. Michael Feingold thought the piece's satirical premise "doesn't bear much examination, largely because Guare's impish sense of fantasy keeps providing corroborative details more germane to Ionesco than to Broadway and its success drive. . . . The resulting event isn't a play, but, as one of Guare's characters says before disappearing into a painting . . . 'What a wonderful bumpinto.' "

Other reviewers of *Rich and Famous* dealt more harshly with the play, as they did with *The Landscape of the Body,* produced at the Public Theatre in 1977. Characteristically combining the bizarre and the brutal, it centers on a young woman who is suspected of the savage murder and mutilation of her own son, and ends by blaming the crime on chance or (some thought) on society in general. Walter Kerr suggested that Guare had failed to provide the audience with sufficient information about the boy's death —information that Guare "as *rational* absurdist, is honor-bound to give us." Nevertheless, Kerr wrote, "John Guare is a high-risk playwright, and I salute him for it"; though he has not yet repeated the success of *House of Blue Leaves,* his "hand is growing firmer, his jovially jaundiced eye keener, as he draws blood with his biggest laughs, turns the palpably absurd into plain common sense. . . . Mr. Guare's knack for retroactively transforming the zany into the alarming, the possibly true, is unique in our time." Thomas B. Markus has described him as "the most successful and promising American playwright to forge to the front of the public's attention since Edward Albee."

Guare is also the author of a television play, *Kissing Sweet* (1969), and collaborated with Milos Forman on the screenplay for Forman's *Taking Off* (1971). He has lectured at New York University and is a member of the Dramatists' Guild Council. Guare has listed among the influences on his work Old Vic productions of Feydeau and Strindberg, and some critics see in his plays an unholy but potent alliance of the farceur and the anguished analyst of domestic

GUÉHENNO

warfare. The author himself says he is drawn to
savage farce "because it's the most abrasive,
anxious form and I'm trying to extend its boundaries because I think the chaotic state of the
world demands it." And anyway, "why
shouldn't Strindberg and Feydeau get married,
at least live together?" Guare says that he is
"very obsessive about work. Work for me is all
voyaging, a kind of emotional serendipity. I
write to get objectivity on things that have happened. Life is the unconscious, writing the conscious."

PRINCIPAL PUBLISHED WORKS: Something I'll Tell You
Tuesday and The Loveliest Afternoon of the Year: Two
Plays, 1967 (these two plays also in Poland, A. and Mail-
man, B. [eds.] The Off Off Broadway Book, 1972); Muzeeka,
1968 (also in Lahr, J. [ed.] Showcase 1, 1970); Cop-Out and
Home Fires: Two Plays, 1968; Cop-Out, Muzeeka, Home
Fires: Three Plays, 1971; Kissing Sweet and A Day for
Surprises: Two Short Plays, 1971 (A Day for Surprises also
in Reynolds, S. [ed.] Best Short Plays of 1970); (with Milos
Forman) Taking Off (screenplay), 1971; The House of Blue
Leaves, 1972; (with Mel Shapiro) Two Gentlemen of Vero-
na, 1973.

ABOUT: Poland, A. and Mailman, B. (eds.) The Off Off
Broadway Book, 1972; Vinson, J. (ed.) Contemporary
Dramatists, 1977; Who's Who in America, 1976-1977;
Who's Who in the Theatre, 1977. Periodicals—Guardian
December 18, 1971; National Observer August 10, 1974;
New York Post February 26, 1971; New York Times March
6, 1971; August 8, 1971; July 9, 1973; August 17, 1975;
February 29, 1976; October 23, 1977; Saturday Review
March 20, 1971; November 20, 1973.

*GUÉHENNO, JEAN (MARCEL JULES
MARIE) (March 25, 1890–), French biographer, essayist, and critic, was born in the old
Breton town of Fougères, the son of Jean and
Jeanne (Girou) Guéhenno. His father was a cob-
bler, and Guéhenno left school at the age of
fourteen to follow the same trade, working for
the next four years in a shoe factory. Many years
later, in Changer la vie (Changing One's Life,
1961) and Carnets du vieil écrivain (Notèbooks
of an Old Writer, 1971), he recalled these early
years of poverty and hardship, which left him
with a sense of shame that he has never been able
to forget. Determined to "change his life," he
devoted his meager leisure to study with such
brilliant effect that at the age of twenty he was
admitted to the École Normale Supérieure. At
the basis of his educational theories is the hard-
won conviction that it is a crime to deny anyone
the culture of which he is capable.

Guéhenno served in the army during World
War I, winning the Croix de Guerre, and began
his teaching career in 1919 at the Lycée de Lille.
He subsequently taught at Sceaux and then in
Paris, at the lycées Buffon, Henry-IV, and Louis-
*gā e nō

French Cultural Services

JEAN GUÉHENNO

le-Grand. It was during these years between the
wars that he began to make his name as a journalist and writer. In the late 1920s he was editor
of the monthly review l'Europe, and in 1934 was
co-founder with André Chamson of the weekly
Vendredi. He also supervised the collection
Écrits for the Librairie Grasset.

His books, like his journalism, reflect his interest in the cultural, social, and political heritage of France, his concern for the poor, and his
involvement with the left-wing Front Populaire
of the 1930s. Journal d'une "révolution" 1937-
1938 (Diary of a Revolution, 1939), for example,
is an account of his own struggle with his impoverished and impoverishing origins, and beautifully depicts the childhood of a poor French boy.
The "revolution" of the title refers to Guéhenno's inner conflicts in his relations with the
Front Populaire. He argues out his dilemma
over the primacy of morality or politics, concluding that the former must be dominant. Although Guéhenno describes himself as a non-
believer, his work reveals a considerable sympathy with Christian views.

During World War II Guéhenno was an active member of the resistance, and he received
the Médaille de la Résistance. He contributed to
Lettres françaises (1942-1944) and published an
attack on the German occupation, Dans la prison (In the Prison, 1944), written under the
pseudonym Cévennes. Guéhenno regards the
fall of France as a physical but not a moral
defeat, and has pointed out that only a minute
percentage of the population was guilty of
treachery or collaboration.

After the war, Guéhenno contributed to Figaro and Figaro Littéraire, while his career as an

educationalist advanced with his appointment as General Inspector of National Education, responsible for literature and grammar. He retained this post from 1945 until his retirement in 1961. Meanwhile, in books like *La France et la monde* (France and the World, 1946), *La Part de la France* (The Role of France, 1949), and *La France et les Noirs* (France and the Blacks, 1954), he developed the theory that France's true mission in the postwar world is cultural, and that in this sphere alone her influence has increased.

Other postwar essays discuss the proper role in France of the universities, popular education, journalism, and other institutions; they reflect his dislike of bureaucracy and of materialism, and an idealistic faith in culture as a potential source of social unity. He has been described in the *Times Literary Supplement* as "a determined anti-specialist whose knowledge must always remain subservient to a dominant concern with the cultural tradition of his country. The particular tradition which . . . [he] represents is that of the Enlightenment; and he defends its principles with a vigour that is proof against every sort of fashionable cynicism and despair."

Guéhenno once remarked that "the whole inclination of my heart is towards Rousseau," and his masterpiece is undoubtedly his three-part biography *Jean-Jacques: en marge des Confessions, 1712-50* (Marginal Notes on the Confessions, 1948), *Jean-Jacques: roman et vérité, 1750-58* (Fiction and Fact, 1950), and *Jean-Jacques: grandeur et misère d'un esprit, 1758-78* (The Splendor and Misery of a Soul, 1952). The work was translated into English in two volumes by John and Doreen Weightman as *Jean-Jacques Rousseau*.

As the title suggests, Guéhenno is concerned more with Jean-Jacques the man than with Rousseau the thinker. Using the *Confessions* and the collected letters as a basis, he attempts in effect to re-experience Rousseau's life, studying his thought "in its process of development and not as a series of results. At no point did I feel that his life was complete and rounded off, any more than he himself had done. I resolved to re-live it day by day, without referring to any of his works or any of his letters or any of the documents until the appropriate time." Peter Gay described this as "an ingenious procedure carried through with complete success," and George Lichtheim noted that even Guéhenno's style, well preserved in the translation, was "plainly fashioned on that of his hero."

Rousseau claimed of himself that he was above all sincere and, though his behavior was in fact often hypocritical, dishonest, and sly,

Guéhenno concludes that he did remain true to his deepest convictions: "The events in which he is involved are not his real life; they are no more than the external manifestations of fate. The real life is more mysterious and more intense. It springs from the soul, which remains impervious to events." Peter Gay in his review concluded that "in more than seven hundred pages, in gratifying detail and with complete lucidity, Guéhenno reenacts Rousseau's life. Rousseau stands before us much as he stood, as it were, before himself."

Guéhenno has been married twice, most recently in 1946 to Annette Rospabé, and lives with his wife in Paris. They have one child. He has received the Prix des Ambassadeurs (1953), the Grand Prix Littéraire de la Ville de Paris (1955), and the Prix Eve Delacroix (1959). He was elected to the Académie Française in 1962, and is a Commander of the Légion d'Honneur. Guéhenno has been sought out by younger writers as a friend and adviser, and has helped many of them through emotional and intellectual crises.

PRINCIPAL WORKS IN ENGLISH TRANSLATION: Jean-Jacques Rousseau, 1966.

ABOUT: Fleischmann, W.B. (ed.) Encyclopedia of World Literature in the Twentieth Century, 1971; International Who's Who, 1977-78; Lichtheim, G. The Concept of Ideology, 1967; Who's Who in France, 1977-1978. *Periodicals*—Livres de France December 10, 1961; Nation February 13, 1967; New Statesman September 16, 1966; New York Review of Books December 29, 1966; Times Literary Supplement October 21, 1939; November 6, 1953; September 24, 1954; June 15, 1967; Yale Review March 1967.

*GUILLEVIC, (EUGÈNE) (August 5, 1907–), French poet who signs his poems with his surname only, was born at Carnac in Brittany, a village famous as the site of row upon row of neolithic stone monuments—menhirs, dolmens, and tomb chambers—extending for some two-and-a-half miles. He was brought up in an impoverished working-class home, the son of a sailor who became a gendarme. Guillevic received his elementary education at Saint-Jean-Brévelay, near Carnac, but in 1919, when he was twelve, his family moved right across France to the Alsatian town of Ferrette (Haut-Rhin), where his father had been transferred. There he continued his education at the Collège in the nearby town of Altkirch. It is notable, as Denise Levertov points out, that "outside of school, Guillevic did not hear French spoken around him, but, in early childhood, Breton, and in adolescence, Alsatian, until he was nearly twenty." Guillevic took his *baccalauréat* in 1925
*gē ye vik'

327

GUILLEVIC

GUILLEVIC

plates his subjects silently and intently, waiting for them to communicate to him their essential nature, and then, very often, relates what he has learned about them to what he knows about man. Thus, in "Mountains," he writes:

> They'll have to be left in their place, left to their
> fate,
> these mountains made of earth,
> yet having the form of breasts,
> and breathing.
>
> They'll have to be left to form that blue forehead
> that we pass in front of—
>
> We with our fury inside us,
> and too much flesh.
>
> (translated by Teo Savory)

and then passed the competitive examination into the civil service. He briefly held a post in the French *faubourg* of the city of Basel in Switzerland before being drafted into the army in 1927 for his military service, first in Besançon, then at Mayence. He settled in Paris in 1935, and spent most of his adult life as an economist in various ministries of the French government—mainly in the Ministry of Finance, where he served from 1946 until his retirement in 1963 as an *inspecteur de l'économie nationale.*

Though he began writing poetry at the age of twenty-two, Guillevic did not publish until he was over thirty, and even then his first collection, *Requiem* (1938), was only a small book brought out by a minor press. His poetry began to receive recognition with the appearance in 1942 of *Terraqué,* which was greeted as "a revelation" by Drieu la Rochelle in an article in *Nouvelle Revue Française.* The title fuses the words for land and water, conjuring up that terraqueous shoreline region where the two elements meet. From the first Guillevic's poetry was highly individual, and his entire output has been unified by his unceasing struggle to bridge what he sees as a tragic gulf between man and nature. His poems are almost always brief, with short lines and direct statements, giving an impression of compactness and density that has often put critics in mind of the rocky landscapes and dour beauty of his native Brittany. Guillevic's avowed purpose in his intensely imagistic poems is to isolate the essences of creatures and things—of birds, animals, flowers, rocks, and stones—and to purge them of the intellectual and emotional assumptions and associations that man has imposed upon them. He contem-

As Savory puts it: "In his poetry the flower, the ant, the blackbird, the rocks—especially the rocks—are only themselves. He has extracted from the things of this world not their meaning to man, or the lessons they might teach, but, as it were, their philosophy of themselves in an alien world peopled by those strange beings, men." Singled out and scrutinized in this way, the commonest objects seem strangely unfamiliar and mysterious.

At the end of 1942, Guillevic became a member of the Comité National des Écrivains, and during the occupation he joined the clandestine Communist party, which played a leading role in the resistance. The poems he published during these years (when he wrote under the pseudonym "Serpières") were collected in *Exécutoire* (Writ of Execution, 1947), which also reprints the contents of three earlier volumes: *Élégies* (1946, translated by Maurice A. O'Meara under same title), *Amulettes* (Amulets, 1946), and *Fractures* (Breakages, 1947). The brevity and concreteness of these poems of the resistance make their effect all the more powerful; the bloody story of the war is told simply through the description of objects and things. Thus in the poetic cycle "Charnier," the charnel-house of the title contains "not more than a hundred" murdered bodies, "all heaped up." And each succeeding poem examines a different aspect of these rotting corpses:

> At one edge of the charnel-house
> lightly in the air, and bold,
>
> A leg—a woman's
> certainly—
>
> A young leg
> in a black stocking

And a thigh,
a real one,

Young—and nothing,
nothing.

(translated by
Teo Savory)

But Guillevic's concentration upon the mechanics and chemistry of murder does not conceal his underlying preoccupation with the meaning of these deaths, or his compassion for the dead. He longs "to put each of them/ into a hole of his own/ Because together/ they create too much silence beside sound."

In the radical climate of postwar French intellectual life, Guillevic's poetry became a vehicle for his Marxist idealism in such collections as *Gagner* (To Earn, 1949) and *Trente et un Sonnets* (Thirty-One Sonnets, 1954). In these poems he turned from free verse to regular and traditional forms, and from an imagistic poetry of intense perception to a more discursive verse of events and social conditions. A number of critics share the view of C.A. Hackett, who wrote that the poems in these collections "have with few exceptions, lost the virtues of their brevity; they are no longer the concise expression of personal feeling, but have become the formulae of a political creed."

At any rate Guillevic, while remaining a committed Marxist, returned to his original inspiration and method in the concise, monolithic poems of a sequence named after his native region, *Carnac* (1961), in which his work regains its previous force and vitality:

Before us,
you were there,

Before the appearance
of timid things

Which got along without you,
abandoned you,

Where eyes were growing.

(translated by Teo Savory)

Savory says of this book that it "makes the poet's approach to his writing clear. When he fills up a whole page with the two lines

A whole system of arithmetic
died in your waves,

it is as though hours and days of contemplative communication with the Brittany shore had gone into these lines. He broods on the natural world until what emerges baffles our own tidier world of symbolic discourse and arithmetical systems. Nouns, the only way we can name things, are, to the nouns themselves, not simple statements but entire galaxies of meaning. Waves defy the mind of man."

In *Sphère* (Sphere, 1963), this poet of elementary matter concentrates his attention on a simple geometric figure (which is, however, also the shape of the world.) His next collection is called *Avec* (With, 1966) because "when one is in the poem one is with some object ... some thing which has been drawn by the poet from the exterior or interior worlds, or above all, from that penumbra where the two spheres mingle." A central group of eight poems with the collective title "Du poète" provides a statement of Guillevic's poetic and philosophic faith, which is profoundly mystical despite the apparent rationalism and materialism of such individual titles as "Éthique," "Dialectique," and "Politique." In *Euclidiennes* (1968, translated by Teo Savory as *Euclidians*) the subject matter is again geometric, and here Guillevic's striving for concision and simplicity reaches its ultimate fulfillment. These brief epigrams are illustrated with geometric shapes, carrying an earlier surrealist idea into a new system of graphic poetry which has some affinity with "concrete" poetry.

Ville (The City, 1969) consists of nearly one hundred and fifty short poems which seek to isolate the essence of various objects and aspects of city life—the streets, sidewalks, windows, gutters, lights, shadows, machines that together make up Paris and its people for the poet. Spire Pitou observed that many readers will see in these short, aggressive poems, each of which moves swiftly to an appraisal of the infringement of things upon people, "a frank evaluation of the human condition in one of the large cities of the world today." Guillevic's next book, *Paroi* (Wall, 1970) seemed to Alexander Aspel "an impressive poem about his consciousness of being in the world." It unfolds a whole dialectic of the poet's relationship to the "wall," which, as one critic wrote in the *Times Literary Supplement,* "is ultimately the whole physical and mental universe apprehended as the barrier which prevents us from entering a half-glimpsed, magnetic, other world beyond. . . . The poem is a kind of comic-tragic monologue, in which diverse tones gravitate around a worried rumination, mulling obsessively over its single problem, turning it—with infinite care and frequent and appealing pedantry—over and over again."

Encoches (Notches, 1971), containing many

short poems on a great variety of themes, was followed by *Inclus* (Enclosed, 1974). This is a long and fragmentary meditation on the art of poetry, in which the poet is seen in many aspects —as Narcissus and Priest, Clown and Craftsman. Guillevic's is a world in which natural objects are wholly themselves; perhaps, as Teo Savory says, "the ultimate conclusion of his work is that man is the only synthetic, the only alien, the only unnatural object? That man is only part of something, and is without complement. Or is the natural world our complement? Our missing part?"

Guillevic has translated or adapted many poems from German, Russian, and Hungarian. Since 1947 he has traveled very widely, visiting Algeria, Tunisia, Czechoslovakia, Hungary, the Soviet Union, Romania, Italy and Belguim. He is married and has two children. Gullevic is a member of the PEN club and the Société des Gens de Lettres as well as of the Union des Écrivains, and serves as president of the Académie Mallarmé. He received the Grand Aigle d'Or de la Poésie in 1973 and the Grand Prix de Poésie of the Académie Française in 1976. He is a Chevalier de la Légion d'Honneur.

A critic in the *Times Literary Supplement* has suggested that "Guillevic is notable above all for having discovered a way of writing genuinely cosmic poetry without the least hint of strained portentousness. Using the simplest of means, in a verse that is sparing of images and normally refuses intensity, in short, sharp phrases that are not 'suggestive' through any of the traditional devices, he manages to convey an apprehension of the universal and the infinite." Denise Levertov calls him an atheist who is "a radically religious poet." When she said this to Guillevic he replied: "Of course. But mine is a religion of earth, not of heaven."

PRINCIPAL WORKS IN ENGLISH TRANSLATION: Guillevic (poems), translated by Teo Savory, 1968; Selected Poems, translated by Denise Levertov, 1969; Selected Poems, translated by Teo Savory, 1974; Euclidians, translated by Teo Savory, 1975; Élégies, translated by Maurice A. O'Meara (bilingual edition), 1976. *Poems in* Alwyn, W. (ed.) An Anthology of Twentieth Century French Poetry, 1969; Martin, G.D. (ed.) Anthology of Contemporary French Poetry, 1972; Taylor, S.W. (ed.) French Writing Today, 1968; Taylor, S.W. and Lucie-Smith, E. (eds.) French Poetry Today, 1971.

ABOUT: Daix, P. Guillevic, 1954; Hackett, C.A. (ed.) An Anthology of Modern French Poetry, 1967; Jaccottet, P. L'Entretien des Muses, 1968; Seymour-Smith, M. A Guide to Modern World Literature, 1973; Tortel, J. Guillevic, 1953; Who's Who in France, 1977-1978. *Periodicals*— Books Abroad Autumn 1964, Autumn 1967, Spring 1968, Winter 1970, Autumn 1970, Winter 1971, Winter 1972, Spring 1972; Times Literary Supplement May 27, 1974.

*GULLBERG, HJALMAR (ROBERT)** (May 30, 1898–July 19, 1961), Swedish poet, was born in Malmö, in southern Sweden. The illegitimate son of a wealthy businessman, he was raised by affectionate working-class foster parents who were quite without cultural pretensions. His own tastes proved to be decidedly intellectual and sophisticated, and he was able to cultivate his interests in literature, drama, and music during a long association with the nearby university town of Lund, first as a student of classics and later as a writer supported by the income from his father's estate.

Gullberg's life in the civilized and sheltered little town was enlivened by regular vacations on the European continent. In 1934 he became literary adviser to the Dramatic Theatre in Stockholm, and he moved to the capital two years later to become head of the Swedish radio's drama department. He served in that influential post from 1936 to 1950. Gullberg was elected to the Swedish Academy in 1940.

From the beginning, his poetry was characterized by a sense of spiritual alienation. Two rather facile collections of verse—*I en främmande stad* (In a Foreign Town, 1927) and *Sonat* (Sonata, 1929) were followed by *Andliga övningar* (Spiritual Exercises, 1932), his first great popular success. All three volumes express a deep distaste for earthly life and a longing for religious salvation in a highly personal style that fuses snatches from popular songs, advertising jargon, phrases from hymns and classical poems, and the banalities of everyday conversation.

What appealed to Gullberg's readers was the extreme contrast between form and content— between grandly classical or biblical themes and their ironic treatment in contemporary and trivial terms. In one poem, the poet is described as God's spokesman, but his role is defined in the language of a legal contract; Christ visits the poet and hangs his crown of thorns on a hatpeg; in an unemotional poem called "Ecstasy," the soul divests itself of the bodily senses like a man taking off his hat and coat. Gullberg's religious preoccupations remain exercises, however— preparations for a spiritual union that he never achieved.

Ecstasies of a more physical kind are described in equally urbane terms in *Kärlek i tjugonde seklet* (Love in the Twentieth Century, 1933). A central group of poems called "Love Story" describes an affair in which "longing and prudery" are replaced by "realistic sex": "Our only law is—birth-control." The detached treatment of passion, the academic vocabulary, and the bizarre rhymes belie the catastrophe of the

*göol' berg

Swedish Consulate

HJALMAR GULLBERG

lovers' parting and the beloved's death.

The tragicomic element in Gullberg's verse is fully developed in *Ensamstående bildad herre* (Cultured Bachelor, 1935), in which the gentle schoolmaster Örtstedt, to his horror, receives a parcel from Königsberg containing *das Ding an sich*—Kant's noumenon. In *Att övervinna världen* (To Overcome the World, 1937), Gullberg returns to religious themes, but now in a much more elevated form of lyrical expression. The world of violence and suffering is symbolized by the Crucifixion in a group of poems called "Place of the Skull"; and the common denominator of humanity is "Cloaca Maxima": "Here the Great Sewer alone is/universal and one." The only hope of salvation lies in withdrawal from the world and the pursuit of absolute values beyond the senses and the intellect.

Some of the patriotic verse that Gullberg wrote in the dark years of World War II is included in *Fem kornbröd och två fiskar* (Five Loaves and Two Fishes, 1942), in which Gullberg seems to have concluded that only divine intervention could halt mankind's descent into chaos and destruction. This apocalyptic volume marked the end of a period in Gullberg's work. He published no more for ten years and his popularity waned. A new generation of readers found his prewar work middlebrow, and Gullberg himself said, "All I had written earlier had become foreign to me."

It was under the influence of Pindar and the Song of Songs that Gullberg made a new start, producing free verse, denser and more highly charged than his earlier work, and marked by vivid and highly-colored imagery. His urbane disillusionment had given way to an almost total skepticism and despair when he published his first postwar collection, *Dödsmask och lustgård* (Death Mask and Pleasure Garden, 1952). The new manner is particularly evident in a group of poems called " Paradise Myth," a counterpart to his prewar "Love Story." It describes how a new love affair can strip away the hardened features of grief, like a death mask, from a relationship that emerges as pristine as that of Adam and Eve—and just as certain to end in exile from Eden. "Dialogue at Dawn" in the same volume sees the poet's work as totally vain and futile but another sequence of poems draws on classical mythology in a defiant celebration of the artist's role, beginning with these magnificent lines on the death of Orpheus: "Singing head driven to sea with its hair's/ black sail hoisted, with extinguished eyes."

Terziner i okonstens tid (Tercets in a Time of Non-Art, 1958) reflects a reaction against the free verse of the earlier collection. Now the sometimes querulous poet upholds the strict discipline and geometry of Dante's cantos, "triangle linked to triangle," against the shapelessness of modern art. In all these postwar poems, Gullberg rejects the hope of religious salvation: "No Hermes fetches and accompanies us,/ no angels from the sky in our day raise us/ up to the Trinity's thrones," he asserts, referring to the two mythologies in which his work is rooted.

In the late 1950s, Gullberg was attacked by a rare and incurable form of creeping paralysis and was for a time completely immobilized, unable even to speak. Out of this excruciating experience he produced some of the intensely personal poems in *Ögon, läppar* (Eyes, Lips, 1959), terse, skeletal "verbal remnants" of moving dignity and simplicity:

> Eyes that observed, wide
> with wonder and intimate.
> Tears to collect. Kisses to lose.
> Lips that know and can be silent.

Gullberg made a temporary recovery, but, faced with a relapse, he decided to end his life, and drowned himself.

In addition to his own poems, Gullberg made magnificent translations from Spanish, from French, and most notably from the Greek of Sophocles, Euripides, and Aristophanes.

PRINCIPAL WORKS IN ENGLISH TRANSLATION: *Poems in* Allwood, M.S. (ed.) Twentieth Century Scandinavian Poetry, 1950; Fleischer, F. (ed.) Seven Swedish Poets, 1963; The Literary Review Winter 1965-1966.

ABOUT: Fehrman, C. Hjalmar Gullberg (in Swedish), 1958; Gierow, K.R. Hjalmar Gullberg (in Swedish), 1961; Gustafson, A. A History of Swedish Literature, 1961; Holmberg, O. Hjalmar Gullberg: en vänbok, 1966; Penguin Companion to Literature 2, 1969; Seymour-Smith, M. Guide to Modern World Literature, 1973; Smith, H. (ed.) Columbia Dictionary of Modern European Literature, 1947. *Periodicals*— Scandinavian Studies 3 1952; American-Scandinavian Review December 1961.

courtesy Professor Stephen G. Nichols, Jr.

RAMON GUTHRIE

GUTHRIE, RAMON (January 14, 1896– November 22, 1973), American poet, novelist, editor, and translator, was born in New York City, the son of Harry and Ella May (Hollister) Guthrie. He had his early education at the Mount Hermon School in Massachusetts in 1912–1914. During World War I, he joined the American Field Service as a volunteer at the age of twenty, serving at Verdun and elsewhere in France, and in the Balkans. In 1917, when the United States entered the war, Guthrie joined the Aviation Section of the Army Signal Corps. He was cited four times for the destruction of enemy planes and received the Silver Star for conspicuous gallantry in action.

Invalided to the south of France during the war, Guthrie became interested in Provençal poetry. In 1919, when he left the Army, he stayed on in France. He attended lectures for a time at the Sorbonne in Paris and then enrolled in the University of Toulouse, where he immersed himself in Provençal literature while studying for his *licence* and doctorate in law (1922). Returning to the Sorbonne (1922-1923), he settled down to write and to paint, joining the circle of American expatriates that included Hemingway, Stephen Vincent Benét, and Sinclair Lewis. He was Lewis's literary confidant for many years, and helped him in his research for *Dodsworth*.

Trobar Clus, Guthrie's first book of poems, appeared in 1924. About a third of the collection consists of lyrics inspired by the old Provençal troubadors, or translations of their work; the remaining poems, on contemporary themes, show the same influence, together with that of the French symbolists and of Ezra Pound. "They have a certain note of boldness, dash and adventure," wrote one contemporary critic, "of irreverence combined with manly vigor; they sing of wine, war and women. . . . Yet they are very modern, especially those couched in bizarre and erratic verse forms, and they display a hardshelled disillusionment such as we find difficult to associate with old romantic far-off times." The *Dial*'s reviewer found not much more than the "peculiar hollow resonance of mock-mediaevalism," but Malcolm Cowley, who thought that Guthrie seemed "impatient with the finer details of technique," concluded that "at times he can write lines so perfect as to make any craftsman proud."

The Provençal troubadors continued to fascinate Guthrie, whose first novel, *Marcabrun* (1926), was a fictionalized account of one of the most famous of them, known in the twelfth century for the boldness and insolence of his songs. A critic in the New York *Times* called it "Rabelaisian in form," but thought that "the very coarseness of the text lends a picturesqueness to the situation that gentler handling would have failed to bring out. . . . A colorful romance whose novelty of presentation makes it absorbing reading."

In 1922, meanwhile, Guthrie had married Marguerite Maurey, and in 1924 he returned to the United States, taking up a post as assistant professor of Romance languages at the University of Arizona (1924–1927). In 1930 he went to Dartmouth College as professor of French and comparative literature, teaching there for over thirty years.

A World Too Old, another volume of poetry, appeared in 1927, and revealed the continuing influence of Provençal poetry. "His rhythmic prose-poem manner," wrote one reviewer, "is, to take the words of one of his own lines, 'clamorous, unreined, carousing' "; J. H. Preston thought that "Ezra Pound has done all this so much better." A second novel, *Parachute* (1928), tells the story of Lieutenant Rickey, wounded in the air service in France, who is hospitalized in a small New York town where he is known as "Tony the Wop." His affair there with a married woman, his friendship with the sardonic Sayles, and their venture into commercial aviation are the principal business of the novel. Guthrie's "special gift for characterization and ironic laughter," it was thought, "sometimes leads him, with his minor characters, into caricature. His style is at times marred by adjectives unrestrained."

After these moderately promising beginnings, Guthrie published relatively little for many years. He settled into his teaching career, earned his M.A. from Dartmouth in 1938, and became known as an authority on Proust (whose complete works he is said to have re-read every year). At the same time he pursued his interest in painting and in Gothic and Romanesque architecture; his paintings were quite widely exhibited, and he wrote art reviews and articles for the New York *Times* and *Herald-Tribune,* the *New Republic, Saturday Review,* and other journals. He returned to Europe and especially to France as often as he could. During World War II Guthrie served with the Office of Strategic Services, often behind enemy lines, in North Africa, Italy, and France.

Meanwhile, he continued to publish poems from time to time in magazines and anthologies. *Graffiti,* his first considerable collection of poetry for over thirty years, was published in 1959. It was not widely reviewed, but greatly impressed some of its readers. Julian Moynahan wrote that "Guthrie shows himself to be a poet in the line of Pound and Ford Madox Ford, heir to the 'better tradition' of European letters and the visual arts from the Provençal bards to Modigliani, and a master of post-Imagist poetic craft. The collection is a treasure house of witty, romantic poems that review modern history, defy God, and praise the saints and heroes of art and thought from an emphatically anti-Fascist posture." M. L. Rosenthal commented that "there is so much gaiety in Guthrie that one almost misses the common, brooding humanity his gaiety leavens":

> Everything about her
> bounced:
> It was like early Spring
> fresh from the Forêt de Chantilly
> coming around a corner at full tilt
> with its arms full of daffodils.
>
> (from "Fragment of
> a Travelogue")

But the "common, brooding humanity" is present, as Rosenthal shows—a "desolate, postcatastrophic quality" exemplified in these lines from "Postlude: For Goya," where the poet, scanning the sky, sees "two skinned bulls, motionless, backed off/ from goring one another." Guthrie is one of those who, having "looked starkly at the Goya-like scene of our generations of war," have yet "steadfastly nourished the impulse to affirm":

> ... after a while
> we will creep forth and search among the crevices
> for seeds and cover them with dust
> and try for tears to quicken them.
> Remember only this is not an end.
> We have won if we can believe
> that this is not an end.
>
> (from "Postlude: For Goya")

The clown or buffoon appears in half-a-dozen of the poems in *Graffiti,* as a representative of fallible humanity, and/or of the poet: "The voice of the Lord spoke out of a whirlwind/ I answered him out of a cyclone cellar." In "The Clown: He Dances in the Clearing by Night," he is the figure of the artist, capable of undoing, if only briefly, what Rosenthal calls "the inexorable oppressions implicit in actual experience":

> The Tyger in the forest stared,
> chin sunk upon his powered paws
> while pirouette and caper dared
> the awesome sinews of the Laws
> his stripèd humors improvise—
> Immutabilities laid down
> by conclaves of eternities—
> *revoked an instant by the Clown.*

Guthrie's next collection came a little more quickly. This was *Asbestos Phoenix* (1969), containing poems that with one or two exceptions had all been written since *Graffiti* appeared. Germaine Brée wrote: "Poetry as voice courses through this volume in rich patterns, a fierce, many-faceted, lyrical discourse of love, pain, rage, joy, memory and desolation. The first response—mine at least—is delight in ... Guthrie's mastery of rhythm, the rare variety and range of the modes of poetic discourse he can adopt, and yet always speak in his own voice directly in the poem." There were some more hesitant reactions, but Brée concluded that this volume "alone would place Ramon Guthrie among the major poets of the midcentury."

Guthrie had retired from Dartmouth in 1963 as professor emeritus. At about the same time he contracted cancer of the bladder, was treated by radiation, and almost died of subsequent hemorrhaging. Fifty-seven blood transfusions and an indomitable will to survive brought him back to health. *Maximum Security Ward,* written mostly under the threat of death between 1964 and 1970, is a long poem about this critical illness and Guthrie's sequestration in the intensive care unit of a typical American hospital, which he compares, as Julian Moynahan says, "with the political prisons and politicized psycho wards of totalitarian states," offering "similar experiences of numbing routine, bloodletting, insomnia, drugging, anxiety and loneliness, and . . . a similar vantage point from which a brave and gifted man can consider things, register his dismay and delight at having lived, and go down singing." Accounts of hospital routine are mixed with the poet's recollections and with the memories of the human species as they are recorded in the ancient myths.

The extraordinary flavor of this "verse novel" was not to everyone's taste, and W.H. Pritchard thought it courageous but unexceptional; he could not understand "why such poetry, and it often seems very minimal poetry, should be compared with Lowell's" (as it was) "nor why it should seem shocking to anyone that Ramon Guthrie's work has been largely overlooked until now." Alexander Laing, on the other hand, called it a seminal work of literature, "an impassioned and anguished, but also rowdy and ribald, testament that all the reasons for despising and despairing of humanity are not quite reason enough." Louis Untermeyer wrote that the poem "is, by turns, tenderly lyrical, even sentimental, and blackly bitter, an amalgam of muffled horror and ribald humor. Provençal idioms nudge contemporary slang, and flaring images jostle a joke. . . . There are, as might be expected in a work of such organized disorganization, gaps and failings. . . . The conjunction of the banal and the bewildering does not always achieve the expected shock . . . but the accumulating strength and intensity of the poem sustain the lapses and carry the occasional overreaching excesses." And the poem seemed to Julian Moynahan the masterpiece of "a magnificent American poet who has been overlooked . . . a deeply, heart-breakingly American book whose importance will become clearer and clearer as time passes."

PRINCIPAL WORKS: *Poetry*—Trobar Clus, 1924; A World Too Old, 1927; Scherzo for a Poem To Be Entitled The Proud City, 1933; Graffiti, 1959; Ramon Guthrie Kaleidoscope, 1963; Asbestos Phoenix, 1969; Maximum Security Ward, 1970. *Fiction*—Marcabrun, 1926; Parachute, 1928. *As Editor*—(with G.E. Diller) French Literature and Thought Since the Revolution, 1942; (with G.E. Diller) Prose and Poetry of Modern France, 1964.

ABOUT: Contemporary Authors 5-8 1st revision, 1969; Rosenthal, M.L. The New Poets, 1967; Vinson, J. (ed.) Contemporary Poets, 1975; Who's Who in America, 1974–1975. *Periodicals*—Dartmouth Alumni Magazine December 1968; Études Anglaises January-March 1957; Nation July 7, 1969; February 15, 1971; New York Herald Tribune November 8, 1959; New York Times November 23, 1973; New York Times Book Review August 3, 1969; January 17, 1971; Publishers Weekly November 24, 1973; Saturday Review December 5, 1970; Washington Post November 24, 1973.

HABERNIG, CHRISTINE. *See* "LAVANT", CHRISTINE

HAILEY, ARTHUR (April 5, 1920–), British-born Canadian novelist and television dramatist, was born in Luton, Bedfordshire, where his father worked as a factory storekeeper. He is the only child of George Wellington Hailey and the former Elsie Wright. An avid reader, Hailey has wanted to be a writer for as long as he can remember. At the age of ten he was sending "incredibly pompous" letters to the local newspaper, and he went on to try his hand at poems, plays, and short stories.

Hailey excelled at English at the Surrey Street elementary school in Luton, but never could get the hang of mathematics; he failed to pass the scholarship that would have enabled him to continue his education, and left school at the age of fourteen, though he subsequently studied typing and shorthand at evening classes. His cavalier approach to arithmetic cost him his first job, as office boy in a real estate agency, and after that he drifted from one office job to another until the outbreak of World War II.

Enlisting in 1939 in the Royal Air Force Volunteer Reserve, he became a sergeant pilot after training in Canada and the United States and ended the war as a flight lieutenant, having served in Europe, the Middle East, and the Far East without ever firing a shot in anger. He was married in 1944 to Joan Fishwick, by whom he had three sons before they were divorced in 1950.

After the war, Hailey worked for a time in the Air Ministry in London, editing the Royal Air Force publication *Air Clues*. In 1947, depressed by the scarcities and controls of postwar life in England, he emigrated to Canada. He settled in Toronto, becoming a Canadian citizen in 1952. Hailey began his new life in Canada as a real estate salesman, but after a few months joined the Maclean-Hunter publishing company, where in 1949 he became editor of a trade journal, *Bus and Truck Transport*. It was there that he met Sheila Dunlop, an English girl who became his second wife in 1951. He subsequently joined a trailer manufacturing company, Canadian Trailmobile Ltd., as sales promotion manager (1953-1956).

Hailey had never abandoned his ambition to become a writer, and during and after the war he had managed to sell an occasional short story. One night in the mid-1950s, returning to Toronto from a business trip to Vancouver in an old DC-4, he began speculating, in a Walter Mittyish way, about what would happen if the airline pilots were suddenly incapacitated, perhaps by

Diane Hailey

ARTHUR HAILEY

food poisoning. Could he, a former fighter pilot, handle such a plane? Hailey got home excited by the dramatic possibilities of this theme, and in a matter of ten days, writing in the evenings and on weekends, he turned the idea into a one-hour play. He knew nothing of television techniques but sent his play, devoid of camera instructions, to the script department of the Canadian Broadcasting Corporation. Nathan Cohen, producer of CBC's General Motors Theatre, recognized its "terrific suspense" and snapped it up. The play was broadcast in April 1956.

Flight Into Danger was sensationally successful on Canadian television, was broadcast in England by the BBC and in the United States over NBC as an Alcoa Hour play. Paramount filmed it as *Zero Hour.* With this evidence of his potential as a writer, Hailey left Trailmobile in May 1956 and set up an advertising agency, Hailey Publicity Services Ltd., with Trailmobile as its major client. This gave him a degree of financial security while he settled down to write. At first he concentrated on television plays, contributing to Westinghouse Studio One, Playhouse 90, U.S. Steel Hour, Goodyear-Philco Playhouse, Kraft Theatre, and various series, and earning awards as the best Canadian television playwright of 1957 and 1958. Among Hailey's contributions to the "golden age" of American television were *Shadow of Suspicion,* about a man falsely accused of murder; *Time Lock,* about a child trapped in a bank vault; *Death Minus One,* about a V-2 bomb activated after lying undetected for years in a London ruin; and *Course for Collision,* in which a plane carrying the President of the United States al-

most collides with a Soviet bomber over the North Pole.

In 1958, at the instigation of a young London publisher, Ernest Hecht of Souvenir Press, *Flight Into Danger* was rewritten as a novel by two English writers working under the joint pseudonym of John Castle. Encouraged by this example, Hailey decided to give the same treatment to his highly successful Studio One play, *No Deadly Medicine.* This hospital drama about an aging pathologist reluctantly accepting displacement by a younger doctor had won an Emmy for its star, Lee J. Cobb, and another for its author. *The Final Diagnosis,* Hailey's novelization of this story, was as successful as the play: it was a selection of the Literary Guild and the *Reader's Digest* Condensed Book Club, sold five million copies in ten languages, and was filmed as *The Young Doctors.* Its critical reception was less than excited but generally favorable—one reviewer complained that Hailey "never really vests his characters with individuality," but concluded that *The Final Diagnosis* was "a fast-paced, polished novel that reads easily, entertains, and informs."

At that point in his career, Hailey turned conclusively from television drama to the novel. His next book, *In High Places,* is a story of politics and diplomacy in which Canada, on the verge of war with the Soviet Union, seeks to incorporate itself into the United States. A Doubleday $10,000 Prize Novel and a Literary Guild selection, it is Hailey's own favorite among his novels but the least successful in terms of sales, presumably because its theme was of relatively little interest to American readers. It was followed by *Hotel,* the first in a so far unbroken series of block-busting best-sellers whose themes are indicated by their laconic titles.

The novel describes what takes place in a luxury hotel in New Orleans during a five-day period in October 1964, focusing on such dramatic events as an attempted rape, a burglary, a racial incident, and a change of management, and involving what Martin Levin called "a large roster of stock wayfarers who have long wandered among the pages of popular fiction." Along the way Hailey delivers in highly palatable form an immense amount of carefully researched information about the hotel industry. The result seemed to Patricia MacManus "a lengthy slice-of-life novel" which would be "a sure thing for the lending-library circuit; a pure gloss finish, the recurring crescendo effects of a cliff-hanger, and enough interesting story-lines to keep even the most plot-addicted readers scurrying to stay abreast of the multi-layered goings-on at the St. Gregory." *Hotel* remained on the American best-seller lists for a year, was published in twenty-two languages, and filmed by Warner Brothers.

Airport applies the same formula to the events of a single night at a large Midwestern airport and inspired two successful movies; *Wheels* gives the Hailey treatment to the Detroit automobile industry (and reportedly made him a million dollars *before* publication); while *The Money-changers* deals with power struggles, scandals, and assorted personal dramas at the "First Mercantile American Bank." Both *The Money-changers* and *Wheels* were serialized on televison.

Hailey nowadays goes about each of his books in the same way. Having chosen his "subject background," he spends something like a year meeting and interviewing people who work in that field, from assembly line workers and bellhops to corporation presidents. He is an excellent interviewer, relaxed and disarming in manner, and scrupulous in the preservation of confidences. He eschews the distracting paraphernalia of notebook or tape recorder, relying on his memory, and dictating detailed notes at the end of each day on what he has learned. The typed-up notes go into a battery of carefully indexed files. "At the end of the year," he says, "I've absorbed through my pores the feeling I want." Then comes a six-month planning period, when Hailey re-reads his notes, sorts them into areas of interest, roughs out the many interlocking story lines that are a feature of every Hailey novel, and begins to visualize the characters who will enact these stories. When planning is finished, he will have a detailed plan of the novel, exhaustive notes on each of the characters, and charts to show time sequences and character interrelationships. There follows the task that Hailey enjoys least—the actual writing of the book, at the strictly maintained rate of six hundred words a day.

No one, least of all the author, would claim that the result is great literature. Hailey's prose is no more than serviceable and his characters are taken from stock to meet the needs of his plots. Nevertheless, as David J. Geherin wrote in *Contemporary Novelists,* "each of his novels is filled with enough information about the subject of his exhaustive research to satisfy the most curious reader; there are enough character types to appeal to the widest possible audience; everything is interwoven into a complex web of plots and sub-plots to satisfy every reader's desire for a good, suspenseful story. . . . Hailey is a good popular novelist. He has learned what his audience expects and his audience knows what to expect from him; the reciprocal arrangement ought to ensure a continuing place for Hailey's novels on the best seller lists for years to come."

Hailey has two daughters and a son by his second marriage. He and his family left Toronto in 1965 and, after four years in the Napa Valley of California, sought relief from American taxation in the Bahamas. They live in the Nassau millionaires' enclave of Lyford Cay in a house built to Hailey's own exacting specifications and crammed with gadgets. Hailey is a non-smoker but a wine and food enthusiast; his house is equipped with a standby generator to insure that his excellent wine cellar will always be maintained at the correct temperature. Sports do not interest him, but he keeps himself in condition with a daily swim and eleven minutes a day of the Canadian Air Force 5BX exercises. His recreations include boating, listening to music, reading, and travel. Although he is an agnostic, Hailey regards the Bible as one of the chief influences on his writing, along with the works of Shaw and Somerset Maugham.

PRINCIPAL WORKS: *Novels*—(with "John Castle") Flight Into Danger, 1958 (U.S., Runway Zero Eight); The Final Diagnosis, 1959; In High Places, 1961; Hotel, 1965; Airport, 1968; Wheels, 1971; The Moneychangers, 1975; Overload, 1978. *Plays*—Close-up on Writing for Television: Collected Plays, 1960; Flight Into Danger *in* Four Plays of Our Time, 1960.

ABOUT: Contemporary Authors 1-4 1st revision, 1967; Current Biography, 1972; International Who's Who, 1977-78; Vinson, J. (ed.) Contemporary Novelists, 1972; Who's Who, 1977; Who's Who in America, 1976-1977; Writer's Digest Yearbook, 1967. *Periodicals*—Maclean's Magazine April 27, 1957; October 1971; Manuscripts 1 1970; Sunday Times Magazine (London) February 27, 1972.

HALBERSTAM, DAVID (April 10, 1934–), American journalist and novelist, was born in New York City, the son of an Army surgeon, Dr. Charles A. Halberstam. His mother, the former Blanche Levy, had been a schoolteacher. She and her two sons followed Dr. Halberstam from one Army post to another across the United States, and David Halberstam remembers it as "a marvelous boyhood of auto trips." He was especially happy in El Paso, where there were horses to be ridden and "polo to be watched at Fort Bliss—the last days of that particular empire." Later, in grammar school at Winsted, Connecticut, Halberstam's classmates included John Bushnell, now of the State Department, and Ralph Nader.

In 1951 Halberstam graduated from Roosevelt High School in Yonkers, New York, where he had been a member of the track team and worked on the school newspaper, and entered Harvard University. At Harvard he became managing editor of the *Crimson* and a part-time

DAVID HALBERSTAM

reporter for the Boston *Globe.* He had already settled on a career in journalism, and after he received his B.A. in 1955 he went south; believing that the racial question would become the central issue in American life, he deliberately set about equipping himself to deal with it authoritatively. He began his career with the West Point *Daily Times Leader* in Mississippi, and from 1956 to 1960 worked on the Nashville *Tennessean,* at the same time contributing articles on race relations and, increasingly, on politics to the *Reporter* and other magazines.

These years in the South provided the background for Halberstam's first novel, *The Noblest Roman* (1961), about the efforts of a Southern bootlegger to buy, kill, or corrupt an inconveniently honest new sheriff. The novel was generally liked for its well-drawn characters, lean prose, and "athletic" action, and for portraying the charm as well as the violence and political skulduggery of small-town life in the South. Jay Milner thought that it had a documentary flavor, enlivened by "a sensitive reporter's skill and eye for detail."

James Reston of the New York *Times* had been impressed by Halberstam's *Reporter* articles, and in the fall of 1960 Halberstam joined the *Times*'s Washington bureau, where he reported on the early days of the Kennedy administration. In 1961 the *Times* sent him to the Congo, where he arrived just in time to cover the United Nations' attempt to end the secession of Katanga. His cables about this "small but very nasty street war" (which he could dispatch only by flying them regularly through the hazardous air space between Elisabethville and Ndola in

Zambia) won him the 1962 Page One Award of the Newspaper Guild of New York.

It was, however, Halberstam's reporting from South Vietnam that made his reputation. The *Times* sent him there in September 1962, and within a month he had begun to accompany Vietnamese troops on military operations in the Mekong Delta, finding his way out "to the boondocks, to isolated posts, to strategic hamlets." The optimism of the official handouts was sharply contradicted by what Halberstam saw in the field—the growing strength of the Vietcong, the Vietnamese army's reluctance to engage the enemy, the disasters publicized as victories. Halberstam decided that it was necessary "to write very frankly" about the deteriorating situation in Vietnam, military and political. He did so, along with a handful of other American journalists.

Their reports were attacked as inaccurate and irresponsible by the Pentagon, the White House, and the Vietnamese authorities. According to Gay Talese, Halberstam became "the most conspicuous *bête noire* of the American State Department and the White House," and President Kennedy personally suggested his transfer to a less sensitive post. After the overthrow of the Diem regime, the widow of Ngo Dinh Nhu said: "Halberstam should be barbecued, and I would be glad to supply the fluid and the match." These cordial suggestions were resisted by the *Times,* and Halberstam's reports from Vietnam brought him the 1964 Pulitzer Prize for international reporting (shared with another Vietnam reporter) and the George Polk Memorial Award. Halberstam also shared with two of his colleagues the first Louis M. Lyons award for reporting the truth as they saw it "without yielding to unrelenting pressures."

Halberstam left Vietnam at the end of 1963 and spent the next year in New York. *The Making of a Quagmire,* an account of his adventures in the Congo and more particularly in Vietnam, and his struggles with officialdom, together with his views on American policy, was published in 1965. A reviewer in the *New Republic* found it "choppily constructed and written in the nondescript style of a journeyman journalist," but Charles Mohr called it "a sensitive and brilliant book." Coinciding as it did with the beginning of the teach-ins against the war, it had, according to Bert Cochran, "an electrifying effect on a new generation of dissenters. It opened the eyes of a wider public to the sordid activities concealed by official fustian."

At the beginning of 1965 Halberstam was assigned to the *Times* bureau in Warsaw, where his insistence on writing what he saw rather than what the Polish government wanted him to see once more earned him official disapproval. In December 1965 he wrote a piece in which he said that the Warsaw government was weak and the Polish people "restless and alienated"; a week later he was ordered out of the country. A more positive result of his Polish assignment was his meeting with Elzbieta Czyzewska, the country's most popular actress, to whom he was married in June 1965. In 1966 he was posted to Paris, where his wife subsequently joined him.

Halberstam was bored in Paris, and increasingly disenchanted with newspaper work in general and the *Times* in particular. Talese says that even after winning his Pulitzer he had difficulties with members of the foreign desk—"he had gone too far, too fast" and some of his colleagues missed few opportunities to question his judgement. If you stay with newspaper work, he wrote at that time, "you hit a point of no return, your talent levels out and diminishes, and . . . you retire without even knowing it." Recalled to New York, Halberstam served there for another year, but in April 1967 resigned from the *Times* to become a contributing editor of *Harper's* under its new editor-in-chief Willie Morris.

Among the articles Halberstam did for *Harper's* were several on Vietnam, which he revisited in 1967, and others on American politics and politicians, including the 1968 Presidential campaign. His second novel, *One Very Hot Day* (1968), describes a crucial day in the life of a company of Vietnamese troops and their American advisers, bringing out very tellingly their varying attitudes and interrelationships. Wilfrid Sheed found "a lot of intriguing information . . . and a mess of anecdotes, editorializing dialogue and atmosphere dialogue stitched together somehow into a story . . . as sharp and comprehensive a look at the war as you could hope to get in the space." *The Unfinished Odyssey of Robert Kennedy* (1969) is a "personal, impressionistic, committed" account of Senator Kennedy's political career and its abrupt end, and *Ho* (1971) a brief biography of the North Vietnamese leader Ho Chi Minh.

Halberstam regarded the Vietnam War as "the worst tragedy to befall this country since the Civil War." In the late 1960s he became preoccupied with the origins of American involvement in Vietnam and the subsequent escalation of the war. He began a study of the high officials of the Kennedy and Johnson administrations—the "architects" of the war—of the times that shaped them and their attitudes and assumptions. Portraits of McGeorge Bundy and Robert S. McNamara had already appeared in *Harper's* when, in March 1971, Willie Morris unexpectedly resigned his editorship in a dispute

between the magazine's "money men" and "literary men." Halberstam resigned with Morris, as did half-a-dozen other senior editors. Thereafter Halberstam freelanced for *Esquire*, the *Atlantic Monthly, McCall's,* and other journals while continuing his study of the nature of power in America.

This was published in 1972 as *The Best and the Brightest* and is essentially a gallery of detailed biographical and psychological studies of Bundy, McNamara, Dean Rusk, Walt W. Rostow, Generals Maxwell Taylor and William Westmoreland, and Presidents Kennedy and Johnson. Halberstam seeks to understand why these able and dedicated men—America's "best and brightest"—dragged the country into the quagmire of Vietnam. He concludes, as one reviewer wrote, "that they became victims of their own brilliance, of hubris, and of the cold war mentality."

The book was based largely on interviews, and Halberstam's consequent inability to document many of his revelations was harshly criticized by Mary McCarthy. Others found his account subjective, confused, or equivocal. But most reviewers shared the opinion of Peter S. Prescott, who called it "a staggeringly ambitious undertaking that is fully matched by Halberstam's performance." Bert Cochran, one of those who thought Halberstam "unclear in his own mind about his basic concepts," nevertheless admired the book's "rich texture woven of inside stuff that connects individuals and decisions, anecdotal detail that blows the breath of life into the musty bureaucratese of memo writers, gossip that adds flash and dazzle." John Barkham predicted that this "brilliant, unsparing" book would "stir the conscience of the next generation if not of this." *The Best and the Brightest* became a Book-of-the-Month Club alternate selection and a bestseller, and in 1973 brought Halberstam the National Book Award for nonfiction and the Overseas Press Club's award.

In *The Kingdom and the Power,* Gay Talese describes Halberstam as he was during his years with the New York *Times:* "He worked best when free to follow his own instincts, to pursue his own ideas without the guidance or resistance of an editor. . . . He was a driven, totally involved reporter who was unencumbered by conventionalism." Some years later, in 1972, Halberstam wrote: "I run faster and harder now than I did ten years ago, chasing my own irrational need for excellence." In 1976, "between treks on the college lecture circuit," he was at work on a study of the power of the media in America—especially the power of television.

Halberstam is a very tall man, athletic in

build, with curly black hair and dark eyes. He and his wife have an apartment on New York's East Side and Halberstam, to his own surprise, has "come to love the city and depend upon it." For relaxation he reads detective novels and thrillers, watches late-night movies on television, and goes fishing in Nantucket.

PRINCIPAL WORKS: *Nonfiction*—The Making of a Quagmire, 1965; The Unfinished Odyssey of Robert Kennedy, 1969; Ho, 1971; The Best and the Brightest, 1972. *Novels*—The Noblest Roman, 1961; One Very Hot Day, 1968.

ABOUT: Current Biography, 1973; Halberstam, D. The Making of a Quagmire, 1965; Talese, G. The Kingdom and the Power, 1969; Who's Who in America, 1976-1977. *Periodicals*—Commentary January 1965; Economist July 14, 1973; Esquire January 1964; Harper's Bazaar August 1972; Nation May 17, 1965; January 8, 1973; National Review February 16, 1973; New Republic May 15, 1965; February 17, 1973; New York Review of Books April 22, 1965; January 25, 1973; New York Times Book Review May 16, 1965; January 7, 1968; November 12, 1972; December 3, 1972; Saturday Review April 10, 1971; Time November 27, 1972; December 22, 1975.

IAN HAMILTON

HAMILTON, (ROBERT) IAN (March 24, 1938–), English poet, critic, and editor, was born in King's Lynn, Norfolk, the younger son of Robert Tough Hamilton and the former Daisy McKay, and grew up in Darlington, Yorkshire. Hamilton originally wanted to be a professional soccer player but had to abandon this ambition after an attack of scarlet fever which, it was feared, had affected his heart. So, he says, "I became a scholarly type . . . sitting in the library all day. The idea was that if you couldn't make it as a terrific footballer you might as well be a terrific intellectual instead." Hamilton lost his prefect's badge at Darlington Grammar School for selling his first magazine, *The Scorpion,* in competition with the official school magazine. "I left school hurriedly after that," he says, "encouraged on all sides."

After two years' National Service (1956–1958), Hamilton went on to read English at Keble College, Oxford University, where his "academic career was so undistinguished it frequently bordered on the disastrous." At Oxford he started another magazine, *Tomorrow* (1959–1960), "a terrible magazine . . . an embarrassment to record," which got him into "enormous debt to the printers." This debt, Hamilton told John Horder, "was one of the main motivations for starting off a new magazine. I mean it couldn't get worse so John Fuller and I and one or two others thought we might as well pile up more debt as anything else. . . . It was sheer lunacy. I didn't even have a job at the time." It was also a quite characteristic decision for Hamilton who, Horder says, "seems to have

gone out of his way to invite one crisis after another."

Hamilton's new quarterly, launched in 1962 when he graduated from Oxford, was *the Review.* It survived for twelve years before its apotheosis into *The New Review,* and became one of the two or three most important "little magazines" devoted to poetry in England. Anthony Thwaite has suggested that the spiritual ancestor of *the Review* was Geoffrey Grigson's *New Verse,* which resembled "in its combativeness, its scalpel-like intelligence, its rough or sly humour, and even its neat and rather austere format." *the Review* regularly gave more space to poetry criticism than to poetry itself, and its intention was nothing less than the reform of English poetry.

Reviewing *the Review* on its tenth birthday, Hamilton wrote in the *Times Literary Supplement* that when his magazine began, "the poetry world—as viewed from an Oxford bedsitter—seemed both sterile and corrupt: sterile in the sense that the prevailing and praised modes were either sub-Movement ratiocinations, mechanical and dull, or the souped-up journalese of the then vigorously self-publicizing Group; corrupt because the kind of reviewing that all this wretched stuff was treated to was insipid and timorous in a way that could only . . . have been engendered by a profound social or careerist terror. With the exception of Alvarez in *The Observer,* the whole metropolitan gang . . . appeared philistine and lily-livered."

"What was needed," it seemed to Hamilton and his friends, "was a magazine that would clear the air, that would be rigorous and polemical, that would rap dunces and hound charlatans." And this *the Review* provided, attacking pretension and incompetence wherever it found them, ruffling feathers on all sides, and pulling handfuls of them from the tails of even such sacred monsters as Ted Hughes and Hugh Mac-Diarmid. This naturally displeased a great many poets and critics: Anthony Thwaite, for example, wrote that "the narrow acerbities of *the Review* have had an effect that goes far beyond its small circulation, but chiefly in the arena of controversy. Those who admire it might say that its main concern is to keep up standards: those who dislike it, that it is brutally destructive and almost wholly negative." Donald Davie regards Hamilton as a talented critic but one whose "historical imagination reaches back no further than 1930," and implies that he had made a deliberate and successful "take-over bid" for English poetry.

Hamilton himself, in his tenth anniversary assessment of *the Review,* wrote that "on the critical side, it seems to me that the most that can be claimed—in terms of *influence*—is that *the Review* has been a useful watch-dog kind of presence. The general level of poetry reviewing . . . is no more honest and purposeful today than it was ten years ago. . . . And if there were, ten years ago, prevailing modes that appeared to us unlovely, today's fashions are by comparison grotesque. . . . On the creative side, I confess to far less gloom. . . . Poets like Michael Fried, Hugo Williams, David Harsent, Colin Falck and (though he writes in a variety of manners) Douglas Dunn have all, it seems to me, written excellent poems which go a long way towards answering *[the Review's]* . . . prescriptions," which were for "a new lyricism, direct, personal, concentrated, a poetry that would prove whatever it proposed."

From 1962 to 1964, Hamilton regularly reviewed poetry in the *London Magazine,* and in 1965, three years after he launched *the Review,* he succeeded Al Alvarez (on the latter's recommendation) as poetry critic of the influential Sunday newspaper the *Observer.* The same year Hamilton became assistant editor of the *Times Literary Supplement,* where he remained until 1973, assigning the poetry and fiction reviews and, much of the time, selecting the poems published by the paper. These posts, together with his writings in other journals and his editorship of *the Review,* made Hamilton a figure of extraordinary power and influence in English poetry. "How successful Hamilton was," wrote Donald Davie, "can be seen by checking how many of the names that now turn up regularly in the . . . [principal British poetry journals] first appeared in the pages of *the Review.*" Davie quotes from John Fuller's long, light-hearted,

Audenesque poem "To Ian Hamilton": "The Fat Men quivered at your glance,/ Careers destroyed by your advance./ Still you are wooed at every chance,/ Like an heiress." John Horder called Hamilton "the most feared poetry reviewer writing since Grigson," and Francis Hope has referred to him as "the Chief Inspector of English poetry."

Discussing the collection of Hamilton's reviews and essays published in 1973 as *A Poetry Chronicle,* Hope wrote that he "is never flashily polemical nor idly malicious; he is in no sense 'against poetry,' though he is, rightly, against some poets. But his criticism sometimes seems a little too like a laboratory test. . . . [and] it seems a limitation that there is no word in this book to suggest that English poetry is an activity . . . with four hundred years of history behind it rather than fifty." However, "what Mr. Hamilton has done is to fight against emptiness and pretentiousness in all its forms. . . . The poetry he likes—direct, concrete, dour, unaffected— may not be the only kind of good poetry going, but it is the kind most worth encouraging now. Without reading him, one cannot understand what modern English poetry is at." Donald Davie says that Hamilton "*has* talent, *has* courage, *has* integrity. . . . He is capable of learning from experience, and changing his mind." Davie feels that Hamilton is limited in perspective and blind to foreign poetries, but that he has all in all been a good influence.

As a poet, Hamilton is greatly admired, although, apart from a small pamphlet of verse that appeared in 1964 and his much-praised contribution to *Poetry: Introduction 1* (1969), he has published only one major collection, *The Visit* (1970), and that of only about thirty short poems. The principal influence on his work is that of Robert Lowell (Donald Davie has suggested that *For the Union Dead* is the standard by which Hamilton measures other modern poets) and he also admires Sylvia Plath, who he says "has everything I simply don't have."

Of his own poems, Hamilton says "they could all, I suppose, be described as dramatic lyrics. That is to say, the reader is offered only the intense, climactic moment of a drama—the prose part, the part which provides the background data, is left to the imagination." Anthony Thwaite says that "the crises, or 'climactic moments,' with which the poems deal are isolated vignettes of dying or death, of mental stress or breakdown, in which the poet is not at the centre of the event but its concerned observer, tied by blood or affection, resigned to hopelessness or guilt. In their brevity (several of them are only six or seven lines long) the poems seem almost refined beyond reticence, stripped down to something so taciturn as to be practically silent, as in 'Curfew' ":

> It's midnight
> And our silent house is listening
> To the last sounds of people going home.
> We lie beside our curtained window
> Wondering
> What makes them do it.

Thwaite speaks of "the risks of evanescent portentousness in this sort of thing . . . the dangers of threadbare banality," and indeed the "minimalist" poetry favored by Hamilton and other *Review* poets has been much ridiculed and parodied by hostile critics. When it succeeds, however, the result is a poem as satisfactory as, say, "Memorial," which has been praised by Martin Dodsworth for its "truth, respect for the language, respect for what it says," and by Michael Fried, who found it "impossible to imagine a poetry more naked in its means or more lyrical in its essence":

> Four weathered gravestones tilt against the wall
> Of your Victorian asylum.
> Out of bounds, you kneel in the long grass
> Deciphering obliterated names:
> Old lunatics who died there.

A writer in the *Times Literary Supplement* has given this account of Hamilton's method: "His regular mode of discourse is in the second person, addressed to the beloved. His flat, declarative sentences suggest exhaustion but make a poignant contrast to the depth of the reactions they deal with. These reactions, by their acuteness, peculiarity, and discontinuity, indicate the strain under which the poet works. Yet, by avoiding direct comment on his own case, he maintains his dignity and privacy. . . . Nothing marks Mr. Hamilton's personal voice more than the muted ironies and small anticlimaxes that suggest an abysmal familiarity with disappointment. . . . To imply the flattening weight of pain upon the beloved, Mr. Hamilton practises a rigorous economy in descriptive detail. Unparticularized hands take up the expressive burden that most poets would assign to vivid features of the face. Less often the head, sometimes the hair, eyes, or lips emerge, quite without specific colour or shape, as if the poet could not bear to look closely. The typical atmosphere is hushed, windless. . . . When the poet does particularize, therefore, the epithets operate with a sudden power of mysterious evocation."

Alan Brownjohn, discussing the varied responses of contemporary poets to the problem of rendering "intimate and profound emotion," says that Hamilton's solution is an original one: he has established "an area where personal feeling can be expressed not only with vividness and fidelity to experience but also with a subtlety and a reticence which do not diminish its force. It is a very private, very individual form of writing; but the emotions are recognisable and universal. . . . As a poet who has helped to keep certain areas of personal sensitivity open at a time when crudity and rhetoric have invaded so much personal verse, his place is assured." And he quotes in evidence an uncollected poem, "Friends":

> "At one moment we wanted nothing more
> Than to wake up in one another's arms."
> Old enemy
> You want to live forever
> And I don't
> Was the last pact we made
> On our last afternoon together.

Among the books Hamilton has edited are an anthology of poems written in World War II and a selection from the work of the Welsh poet Alun Lewis—a notable rehabilitation of the poet Robert Graves thought the best of those who died in the war. *The Modern Poet,* a collection of sixteen essays from *the Review,* was praised for its "ad hoc, wary criticism" and called "the best guide available to recent [British] poetry." There was a genial reception also for Hamilton's *The Little Magazines* (1976), a study of "the most exemplary and memorable" of this century's little magazines and their editors. Hamilton's chosen six are Harriet Monroe's *Poetry,* Margaret Anderson's *Little Review,* T. S. Eliot's *Criterion,* Geoffrey Grigson's *New Verse,* Cyril Connolly's *Horizon,* and the *Partisan Review.* Jeremy Lewis called this a "witty, extremely readable but all-too-brief survey . . . replete with sardonic observations and pleasing anecdotes."

Hamilton left the *Observer* at the beginning of 1970: "Never liking most of the poetry any of the time," he says, "I got fed up with the sound of my own carping voice." Three years later he also resigned from the *Times Literary Supplement,* and in 1974 *the Review* became *The New Review,* with monthly publication, a larger and glossier format, and contributions on a variety of cultural themes, often by journalists rather than literary critics. There has been a bitter running controversy over the amount of money granted to it by the Arts Council, and critics have been divided as to the merits of the new magazine.

The author lectured on poetry at the University of Hull in 1971-1972. He received the E.C.

HANDKE

Gregory Award in 1963 and the Malta Cultural Award in 1974. He has served on the Arts Council's literature panel. Hamilton was married in 1963 to the German-born Gisela Dietzel and has a son. He is a tall man, dark and good-looking; many have seen in him a strong resemblance to the John Donne of the Lothian portrait. In manner he is affable, reticent, and modest; some find him vague, others concise. He seldom expresses strong opinions in conversation, saving these for his criticism.

PRINCIPAL WORKS: *Poetry*—Pretending Not to Sleep (pamphlet), 1964; (with others) Poetry: Introduction 1, 1969; The Visit, 1970. *Criticism:* A Poetry Chronicle, 1973; The Little Magazines: A Study of Six Editors, 1976. *As Editor* —The Poetry of War 1939-1945, 1965; Selected Poetry and Prose of Alun Lewis, 1966; The Modern Poet, 1968; Selected Poems of Robert Frost, 1973; (with Colin Falck) Poems Since 1900, 1975.

ABOUT: Abse, D. (ed.) Poetry Dimension Annual 3, 1975; Schmidt, M. and Lindop, G. (eds.) British Poetry Since 1960, 1972; Thwaite, A. Poetry Today 1960-1973, 1973; Vinson, J. (ed.) Contemporary Poets, 1975; Who's Who, 1978. *Periodicals*—Agenda April-May 1965; Encounter May 1973; English Summer 1971, Autumn 1973; Guardian June 5, 1970; Hudson Review Summer 1965; Landfall March 1954; Listener January 25, 1973; London Magazine September 1970, June-July 1973; New Statesman February 7, 1969; January 12, 1973; Observer January 14, 1973; Poetry June 1961; Poetry Review Autumn 1970; The Review Spring-Summer 1972; Stand 4 1970, 4 1974; Times Literary Supplement January 30, 1969; February 7, 1970; August 11, 1972; March 23, 1973; October 19, 1973.

*HANDKE, PETER (December 6, 1942–), Austrian dramatist, novelist, essayist, and poet, was born in the small town of Griffen in the province of Carinthia, near the Yugoslavian border, where his father worked as a bank clerk. He grew up there, except for the four years between 1944 and 1948 when his family exchanged the lakes and forests of the mountainous Carinthian region for the rubble of Berlin. Handke was educated in a Jesuit seminary and went on to study law at the University of Graz (1961–1965).

Both his Jesuit training and his legal studies had their effect on Handke's habits of thought and literary style. It has been said that his fiction often reads like a legal document, "with dry affirmative clauses qualifying each other and building to a final flawless definition." Handke has recalled how deeply he was affected when he read the totally objective and dispassionate instructions for conducting an execution in a martial-law penal code: "They altered my previous ideas about the literary presentation of dying and death, they altered my ideas about dying and death itself. I then wrote a piece that transposed the law book's method into literature and

*händ′ kə

German Information Center

PETER HANDKE

that in some sentences even consisted of the authentic legal code." This and other prose pieces appeared in the mid-1960s in *manuskripte* and similar magazines devoted to experimental writing.

The year after he completed his studies at Graz, Handke burst upon the literary scene as a novelist, dramatist, and *enfant terrible*. He began with an attack on what had been the most powerful and influential association of German writers, the Gruppe 47, at their meeting at Princeton University in April 1966. Speaking from the floor on the last day of the convention, Handke poured scorn on the discussions and lectures he had attended, their "trifling and idiotic" enslavement to conventional descriptive literature, "the superannuated criticism that accommodates itself to this kind of writing and which registers boredom at every attempt at something different." This attack, delivered with great *éclat* by a writer still in his early twenties, undoubtedly contributed to the decline of the 47 Group. It was the highly-publicized first step in a quite deliberate campaign that has made Handke the most widely read and discussed German-language writer of his generation. His prolific output, in almost every possible genre and medium, has helped to keep him in the public eye, as has his combination of a "pop" image with very serious philosophical concerns, deriving from Wittgenstein's semantic inquiries, from existentialism, and from French structuralism.

Handke's first novel was *Die Hornissen* (The Hornets, 1966), which resembled his earlier prose experiments in its style of dispassionate reportage and evoked comparisons with Robbe-Grillet and other exponents of the French "new

342

novel." In the same year his play *Publikumsbe-schimpfung* (translated by Michael Roloff as *Offending the Audience*) won him immediate acclaim as a dramatist. Handke has said in an interview that he "couldn't stand the pretense of reality" in traditional plays and wanted to startle people into recognizing that the stage and its contents are "artifacts"—their functions are not natural, but decreed by the author and the director. Moreover, the theatre "can make us aware that there are functions of man's power over man that we don't know about, functions that we accept by force of habit," and that these functions are "man-made . . . not all nature-given."

Publikumsbeschimpfung, Handke's first attempt to do "something onstage against the stage," was performed in June 1966 as part of a week of experimental theatre in Frankfurt. Four actors come on stage and tell the audience that the play they are assembled to watch will not take place. Instead they are treated to a discussion of the nature of the theatre, enlivened by a litanistic use of rhythm, the Beatles' music, and assorted sound effects. The discussion then turns to the spectators themselves—their appearance, smell, intelligence, and so on—and they are alternately complimented on their "performance" and insulted. The first audiences to endure this rough handling were both stimulated and charmed, and this "antiplay" has become one of the most popular works in the German repertory (though at a production in Barcelona the audience hurled insults back at the actors, a reaction that must have delighted Handke).

Two more plays, *Weissagung* (translated by Roloff as *Prophecy*) and *Selbstbezichtigung* (translated by Roloff as *Self-Accusation*), were produced in October 1966; the latter is interesting as a first treatment of the theme of *Kaspar.* In *Hilferufe* (translated by Roloff as *Calling for Help*), the cast (which may be of any size) is divided into two groups of speakers. One group speaks a familiar cliché; the other rejects it. Another cliché is offered but is also found inadequate, and the process continues until the listeners hear what they need—the word *help;* according to one critic, "only the word *help* can express meaning for the individual who wants to be free from a life filled with platitudes and clichés." The scenario for this piece is only four pages long—an extreme example of Handke's determination to allow director and participants the maximum freedom in the development of variations and improvisations. Handke called these early plays *sprechstücke* ("speech" or "speaking" plays)—not so much because they are antiplays with a minimum of the delusive paraphernalia of the traditional theatre as be-

cause their very subject is language, and the extent to which language determines and delimits personal identity. This is equally true of Handke's first full-length play, *Kaspar* (1968, translated under the same title by Michael Roloff), which established his international reputation.

Kaspar is based on the true story of Kaspar Hauser, a boy discovered in Nuremburg in 1828 who for the first sixteen years of his life had been hidden away from the world in a closet. Though he had the mental and physical capacities of an adult, he was scarcely better able to talk, walk, or comprehend his environment than a baby. At the beginning of the play, Kaspar flops onto the stage and speaks, over and over again, the only sentence he knows: "I want to be a person like somebody once was." Anonymous Prompters teach him to speak and, with language, Kaspar absorbs the false values and assumptions implicit in it; he becomes an orderly, efficient, and well-adjusted member of a corrupt society. It is clear that, as far as Handke is concerned, this progress from primal innocence to social integration is a fall from grace. "I have been made to speak," Kaspar says. "I have been sentenced to reality." Jack Kroll wrote that "the strong intellectual and dramatic excitement of the play is in watching how the very process of mastering reality leads to Kaspar's alienation from reality. . . . At the end Kaspar is drowning in superfluous, contradictory self-awareness—the true tragic fate of modern man." Stanley Kauffmann was reminded of Samuel Beckett, and concluded that "we have a new dramatist of genuine significance."

Several radio plays and a television play followed, and then the stage play *Das Mündel will Vormund sein* (1969, translated by Roloff as *My Foot My Tutor*), in which two characters, one dominant and the other passive, act out their relationship through ten scenes in total silence— a logical development for a dramatist who so mistrusts language and, most critics thought, "an oddly compelling piece of theatre." Another stage play, *Quodlibet* (1970, translated by Roloff under the same title) was called a "thin and labored one-dimensional practical joke."

Meanwhile, in 1967, Handke had published his second novel, *Der Hausierer* (The Peddler), a murder mystery which Nicholas Hern has called "a collection of those nonsequential, nondescriptive, single-sentence statements that have become the hallmark of Handke's literary oeuvre"—the nonsequential statements being employed in this case to evoke an atmosphere of anxiety and fear. *Begrüssung des Aufsichtsrats* (Welcoming the Board of Directors), a volume of short prose pieces, was also published in 1967.

Handke's first major success as a novelist came in 1970 with *Die Angst des Tormanns beim Elfmeter* (translated by Michael Roloff as *The Goalie's Anxiety at the Penalty Kick*). Bloch, a construction worker who had been a well-known soccer player, loses his job, picks up a girl, murders her, then waits for the police to arrest him. It is a working out of Handke's preoccupation with personal identity and the alienation induced by a failure to reconcile our private inner reality with outward reality—the reality accepted by our society. Bloch's downfall begins with his mistaken interpretation of a gesture, which leads him to believe that he has been fired. After that, he finds himself progressively losing his grip on the rules that govern ordinary conversation and what passes in his society for reality. At one point, near the end, words disappear altogether, to be replaced by meaningless hieroglyphics. Bloch passes into a state of acute paranoia in which every new experience becomes an insufferable intrusion into his consciousness; the apparently motiveless murder follows. The book was generally recognized as the first fully mature novel of a serious artist.

The conventions of drama and of language itself had been called in question by Handke's first plays. In *Ritt über den Bodensee* (1970, translated by Roloff as *The Ride Across Lake Constance*), the question is extended to all forms of communication between one individual and another. The title refers to a ballad well known in Germany about a horseman who unwittingly rides over the frozen Lake Constance in a snowstorm, but drops dead of fright when he discovers what he has done. As Nicholas Hern puts it, the "weird collection of characters" in the play "exist on the thin ice between wakefulness and sleep, reality and imagination, sanity and madness. Their conversations are allusive, inconsistent, full of half-completed anecdotes; their actions are likewise disjointed, as if compiled at random from stock theatrical business. . . . Handke is questioning the assumption that those who conform to set patterns of speech and behavior are sane, and that those who do not are insane." Or, to quote Botho Strauss: "The ride parallels the functioning of our grammar, of our system of coordinating perception and meaning. . . . It is only a provisional, permeable order, which, particularly when, as in Handke's play, it becomes conscious of its own existence, is threatened by somnambulism, schizophrenia, and madness." Even reviewers who were quite unable to understand the play found themselves "oddly, compulsively, interested."

Der kurze Brief zum Langen Abschied (1972, translated by Ralph Manheim as *Short Letter, Long Farewell*) is a partly autobiographical novel set in the United States. It is narrated by a German writer who, arriving at an American hotel, finds this letter from his estranged wife: "I am in New York. Please do not look for me, it would not be nice for you to find me." In his journey through America (and through its mythology), the narrator tries on a series of spurious identities borrowed from books and films. He nevertheless finds everywhere about him reminders of his marriage and its gradual decay—even when he "tries to lose himself in a world of objects and matter-of-factness," one reviewer wrote, "it turns out to be as full of messages as the landscape of hoardings and neon signs through which he moves." He also receives more literal messages from his wife, who is soon threatening his life, and they meet on the west coast in a potentially murderous confrontation. But their separate journeys across their separate Americas have changed them; after an encounter with no less a myth-maker than the film director John Ford, they are able to part in peace.

A reviewer in the *Times Literary Supplement* praised Handke's "understanding of complex relationships and of the half-tones of perception," but thought there were times "when the narrator's cerebral distinctions and minute observations lapse into a rather mechanical mannerism." Stanley Kauffmann wrote that "this short, superbly wrought, understated yet powerful novel can be described, in one aspect, as a scale model of America made with absolute verism but then bathed in a slantwise light that shows the fantasy hidden in the fact. . . . [It is] a book of secrets to which we are made privy, full of sharp visions and of disquieting proportions, disquieting but true." John Rockwell was fascinated by the book but found it "just all very, very cold."

Most criticism of the latter kind was disarmed by *Wunschloses Unglück* (1972, translated by Ralph Manheim as *A Sorrow Beyond Dreams*). A remarkable biography of the author's mother, who died a suicide, it is also a book about the difficulty of writing such a work. Some readers were disturbed by the scrupulous objectivity of Handke's account, but most realized that, as Michael Wood wrote, his "objective tone is a defense against the potential flood of his feelings . . . [and] also an act of piety, an expression of respect: this woman's bleak life is not to be made into 'literature.' " Wood called it "a major memorial to a host of buried German and Austrian lives, the best piece of new writing I have seen in several years." A dramatization by Daniel Freudenberger was staged in New York in 1977 and was well received.

Handke has also published several volumes of poetry, beginning in 1969 with *Die Innenwelt der Aussenwelt der Innenwelt* (translated by Roloff as *The Innerworld of the Outerworld of the Innerworld*). Frank Kermode said of this collection that "Handke's poems are word games . . . much concerned with horror and fright. . . . They are a series of sentences bound together by linguistic and rhetorical devices of the kind that are currently interesting practitioners of 'text-linguistics' or 'discourse-analysis.' Above all they are encounters between the poet, a self-confessed traitor to silence, and his enemy the language." The more personal poems in Handke's third collection, *Als das Wünschen noch geholfen hat* (1974, translated by Roloff as *Nonsense and Happiness*), also deal with the precarious relationship between inward and outward reality; one critic thought them "pretty slack and meandering," and another said they offered "the spectacle of a man enjoying the smell of his own psychological exhalations." They show that for Handke happiness is achieved when these two kinds of experience are in harmony—in that "paradisiac state" in which (as he has described elsewhere) "one wanted only to look, and in which looking itself was a kind of knowledge"; when the most ordinary and everyday things and happenings assume a significance lent to them by the "inner world."

The opposite state, self-alienation that is also alienation from people and things, is the subject of Handke's novel *Die Stunde der wahren Empfindung* (1975, translated by Manheim as *A Moment of True Feeling*). Gregor Keuschnig, married, with one daughter, is a press attaché at the Austrian embassy in Paris. After a nightmare in which he commits a murder, he experiences "a complicated fracture of the mind," and enters a period of crisis in which "nothing makes sense"—in which he feels both violent and vulnerable, and can only marvel at the steadfastness with which others "go through with" their lives. We observe him over a period of forty-eight hours when, his old personality crumbling, and no alternative to hand, he leads "a double life . . . pretending to live as usual." It seemed to Michael Wood that the book echoes Sartre's *La Nausée* more closely than Handke could have realized, only "nausea here is a little too comfortable." John White was also disappointed, finding "an eventual, somewhat meagre epiphanous experience hardly . . . adequate to the intricate build-up," so that the "best parts of the narrative remain (as so often with Handke) the fragmentary images and highly artificial similes

of the hero's reaction to a state of profound disorientation." Stanley Kauffmann, however, praising above all the texture of Handke's "fiercely perceptive account," suggested that he was moving "stunningly and courageously" towards "the novel as poem. . . . Certainly this new book proves further that, in power and vision and range, he is the most important new writer on the international scene since Beckett."

In Handke's long story *Die linkshändige Frau* (1976, translated by Manheim as *The Left-Handed Woman*) the "paradisiac state" predominates, to such a degree that Rudolf Harting was reminded of the almost mystical "other state" described by the Austrian novelist Robert Musil. The book did not escape criticism in Germany, where Handke nevertheless retains a very large audience. He has been much censured by the New Left, and attacked in Hans Magnus Enzensberger's magazine *Kursbuch* for his militant subjectivity and his self-proclaimed preference for the ivory tower (*Ich bin ein Bewohner des Elfenbeinturms*—I Am an Inhabitant of the Ivory Tower—is the title of a collection of essays Handke published in 1972). Considering the personal nature of his themes, and his almost abstract treatment of them in many of his works, his continuing popularity is extraordinary.

Handke himself says that the only thing that preoccupies him as a writer is "nausea at stupid speech forms." And he has explained, without apology, that he writes not for the New Left but for "the bourgeois and late bourgeois . . . since these are people who attend theatre and control society." He is separated from his wife, by whom he has a child. Handke has lived in Düsseldorf, Berlin, and Paris, settled for a time in Frankfurt, where in 1969 he and ten other writers established a cooperative publishing house, and again in Paris, though his Austrian background remains very relevant to his work. He has also traveled widely in the United States. Handke is extremely interested in the cinema; he wrote the scenario of Wim Wender's *Falsche Bewegung* (False Move), and has made his own film version of *Die Linkshändige Frau*. In 1973 Handke was awarded the Büchner Prize, which is Germany's highest literary honor, and he has also received the Gerhart Hauptmann Prize (1967) and the Schiller Prize (1972).

PRINCIPAL WORKS IN ENGLISH TRANSLATION: *Plays*—Kaspar and Other Plays (*with* Offending the Audience *and* Self-Accusation), 1969; The Ride Across Lake Constance and Other Plays (*with* Prophecy, Calling for Help, My Foot My Tutor, Quodlibet, They Are Dying Out), 1976. *Fiction* —The Goalie's Anxiety at the Penalty Kick, 1972; Short Letter, Long Farewell, 1974; A Moment of True Feeling,

1977; The Left-Handed Woman, 1978. *Poetry*—The Innerworld of the Outerworld of the Innerworld, 1974; Nonsense and Happiness, 1976. *Other*—A Sorrow Beyond Dreams, 1975; Three by Peter Handke (*contains* A Sorrow Beyond Dreams; Short Letter, Long Farewell; The Goalie's Anxiety at the Penalty Kick), 1977.

ABOUT: Boa, E. and Reid, J.H. Critical Strategies: German Fiction in the Twentieth Century, 1972; Crowell's Handbook of Contemporary Drama, 1971; Current Biography, 1973; Deutsche Dichter der Gegenwart, 1973; Falkenstein, H. Peter Handke, 1974; Gilman, R. The Making of Modern Drama, 1974; Hern, N. Peter Handke, 1972; Heintz, G. Peter Handke, 1971; Hill, L.M. Language As Aggressor, 1976; McGraw-Hill Encyclopedia of World Drama, 1972; Mandel, S. Group 47, 1973; Rischbieter, H. Peter Handke, 1972; Scharang, M. (ed.) Über Peter Handke, 1973; Schultz, U. Peter Handke, 1973; Ungar, F. (ed.) Handbook of Austrian Literature, 1973; Wer Ist Wer?, 1974/1975; Who's Who in Germany, 1972. *Periodicals*—Drama Review Fall 1970; New Republic February 28, 1970; September 28, 1974; New York Review of Books May 1, 1975; June 23, 1977; New York Times March 22, 1971; New York Times Book Review May 21, 1972; September 15, 1974; April 27, 1975; July 31, 1977; June 18, 1978; Performance September-October 1972; Publishers Weekly September 12, 1977; Sunday Times (London) December 9, 1973; Text + Kritik 24 1969 (Handke issue); Times (London) May 15, 1972; November 13, 1973; Times Literary Supplement April 21, 1972; December 1, 1972; Universitas February 25, 1970.

Ellin Hare

RICHARD HARE

HARE, RICHARD (MERVYN) (March 21, 1919–), British moral philosopher, is the son of Charles Aubone Hare, a paint manufacturer, and the former Louise Kathleen Simonds. He won a scholarship to Rugby School (1932–1937) and another to Balliol College, Oxford. The war intervened, and in 1940, before he had graduated, Hare was commissioned as an officer in the Royal Artillery. The following year he went to Asia, where he served as a lieutenant with the Indian Mountain Artillery. He was captured by the Japanese, and was a prisoner-of-war in Singapore and Thailand from 1942 to 1945. His ideas about moral philosophy were permanently influenced by his experiences in the Japanese prison camps. "A prisoner-of-war community is a society which has to be formed, and constantly reformed, out of nothing," Hare says. "The social values, whether military or civil, which one has brought with one can seldom be applied without scrutiny to this very strange, constantly disintegrating situation." In these artificial communities he came to realize that nothing in society was 'given,' that every man is born with a conscience, and it is in this, rather than in society, that the source of morality is to be found. After the war, Hare resumed his place as a scholar at Balliol, where he graduated in 1947 with a first-class honors degree in *Literae Humaniores*. He remained at Balliol as a fellow and tutor in philosophy for twenty years. He was appointed White's Professor of Moral Philoso-

phy at the University of Oxford in 1966, when he also became a fellow of Corpus Christi College. Hare was married in 1947 to Catherine Verney; they have one son and three daughters.

Hare has pointed out that, since the 1940s, British moral philosophers have devoted most of their work to "questions about the analysis or the meaning of the moral words and the types of reasoning that are valid on moral questions. It may be that some of them were attracted by the intimate theoretical interest of this branch of philosophical logic. . . . But it may surely be said that the greater part, like myself, studied these questions with an ulterior motive: they saw this study as the philosopher's main contribution to the solution of practical moral problems such as trouble most of us. For if we do not understand the very terms in which the problems are posed, how shall we ever get to the root of them?"

For these analytical philosophers, a basic problem in moral philosophy was to define the status of value judgments—what sort of utterance is it to say that something is or is not good? The "emotive theory" developed by A. J. Ayer and C. L. Stevenson in the 1930s maintained that such utterances are merely expressions of the speaker's personal feelings. Hare addressed himself to this argument in his first book, *The Language of Morals* (1952), which he had drafted in the Japanese prison camps. It has been more influential and more widely discussed than any other recent book on ethics.

Hare agrees with Ayer and Stevenson that value judgments cannot be deduced from wholly factual or descriptive premises, but he insists that they express more than the feelings of the speaker—that they are essentially prescriptive rather than descriptive. Value judgments *can* be defended, he points out, though only in the light of the speaker's previously chosen moral standards. Value judgments are therefore not true or false but sincere or insincere; sincere if the speaker behaves in accordance with them. To say that A is good is to appeal to the general principle that all things like A will be good, and it is to assert that A has certain properties by virtue of which it meets the standards applicable to its class. Thus, for Hare, "good" commends a thing so as to guide choice: "It is the purpose of the word *good* and other value-words to be used for teaching standards." A moral utterance must also be "universalizable"—what is right (or wrong) for one person must be right (or wrong) for any similar person in similar circumstances.

These arguments have been criticized by G. J. Warnock, Bland Blanshard, and Alasdair MacIntyre, among others. Warnock for instance comments that it is often not really noticed how *surprising* Hare's view is: "For he is saying, not only that it is for us to decide what our moral opinions are, but also that it is for us to decide what to take as grounds for or against any moral opinion. We are not only, as it were, free to decide on the evidence, but also free to decide what evidence is. I do not, it seems, decide that flogging is wrong because I *am* against cruelty; rather, I decide that flogging is wrong because *I decide to be* against cruelty. And what, if I did make that decision, would be my ground for making it? That I am opposed to the deliberate infliction of pain? No—rather that *I decide to be* opposed to it. And so on."

Similarly, Professor Blanshard writes: "If Mr. Hare met an opponent of the Christian way of life, in which I take it he believes (or, rather, to which he has made a non-rational commitment), he would no doubt set out in his able fashion its doctrines of love, sin, and forgiveness, and its attitudes toward art, sex, and science, exhibiting these as some sort of connected whole. Having done so, he could only say, 'Take it or leave it'. His subscription to the Christian way of life as a whole is neither more nor less reasonable than its rejection; since it is not a judgment but an act of will, it of course does not *follow* from anything that has been presented, nor does his opponent's opposite subscription; and if he wants to change his opponent's attitude, his only recourse, so far as I see, is to psychological pressures."

Hare replies to some of these criticisms in *Freedom and Reason* (1963), a book which grows organically out of his first one, and starts by arguing once more that the essential nature of a moral term is to be both prescriptive and uni-

versalizable. Hare goes on to explain what he thinks the purpose of moral philosophy is: to examine the nature of moral arguments and concepts, so that non-philosophers may be taught to understand what they are doing in discussing moral matters, and may therefore do so clearly and to good effect. Then Hare proceeds to break new ground. In the second part of the book he links his own theory with utilitarianism, and distinguishes between a morality of interests and a morality of ideals, which often leads to fanaticism, since people who are firm believers in ideals are frequently prepared to inflict all sorts of suffering on others for the sake of them. Part III of the book shows Hare's theory applied to a particular moral problem, that of the oppression of people on grounds of racial difference. The *Times Literary Supplement* commented that "the second half of the book is really excellent, and of absorbing interest."

During the early 1970s, Hare put together several collections of previously published essays and papers, beginning with *Essays on Philosophical Method* (1971), which includes his notable Oxford inaugural lecture "The Practical Relevance of Philosophy." *Essays on the Moral Concepts* (1972) begins with an essay on the freedom of the will, which provides a useful account of how Hare's own theory of prescriptivism differs from emotivism. He distinguishes between moral judgments and propaganda, maintaining that moral judgments belong to the same logical category as "advise, order, command, tell," rather than that of "persuade, induce, cause." The connection between prescription and action is the crux of Hare's case. For if imperatives are the logical model for evaluative judgment, agreement cannot depend on discovering true judgments—if a simple imperative like "shut the door" cannot be true or false, neither can a more complex imperative like "suicide is sinful." And the search for a substitute for the truth and falsity test leads to the stress on *sincerity* which marks all Professor Hare's work.

The sincerity of the person making a moral judgment (and of his listener) is crucial in the practical illustrations in the radio talks and lectures collected as *Applications of Moral Philosophy* (1972), which tackle in a clear and nontechnical way such controversial issues as lawful government and political dissent, peace and war, and moral education. The main value of these essays, according to *Choice,* "is to show that, contrary to the belief of some, analytic ethicians are concerned with concrete moral problems, and not just with theoretical linguistic ones." A reviewer in the *Times Literary Supplement* wrote: "One has to acknowledge that

Professor Hare's sober image of the moral philosopher has much to recommend it. It demands no more than ordinary virtue and ordinary intelligence from him; and insofar as it makes unusual demands upon him, it simply insists that he apply the logical expertise he possesses as competently as possible. In face of the frivolity and trendiness of much that passes for moral philosophy, the austerity and rigour of Professor Hare's work are virtues of a high order."

Hare was visiting fellow at Princeton in 1957 and at the Australian National University in 1966, visiting professor at the University of Michigan in 1968, and visiting professor at the University of Delaware in 1974. From 1963 to 1966, while teaching at Balliol, he was Oxford's Wilde Lecturer in Natural Religion. Hare was president of the Aristotelian Society in 1972–1973, and became a Fellow of the British Academy in 1964. He is a foreign honorary member of the American Academy of Arts and Sciences.

Professor Hare's interest in problems of practical ethics is reflected in his work as a member of such bodies as the National Road Safety Advisory Council (1966–1968) and the Church of England's working party on euthanasia (1964–1975). Ved Mehta quotes him as saying: "The most characteristic thing about Oxford philosophy is that we insist on clear thinking. . . . Clear thinking, of course, is especially important in my own field of moral philosophy, because almost any important moral question arises in a confused form when one first meets it. But most of the undergraduates who come up to Oxford are not going to be professional philosophers. . . . I think the most important thing I can do is to teach them to think lucidly—and linguistic analysis is frightfully useful for this. . . . My own hobby is town planning. I read quite a lot of literature, and it's perfectly obvious that immense harm is done . . . because people don't think clearly enough."

According to a critic in the *Times Literary Supplement*, "Professor Hare has always possessed an argumentative style in which a polite and kindly arrogance and a good-humoured contempt for the errors of his critics have been so evident that the least combative might be roused." Ved Mehta found Hare "a little idiosyncratic and somewhat oracular but very approachable." Hare is regarded at Oxford as being somewhat puritanical in his views, Mehta says, but "he is renowned throughout the university for his kindness . . . [and] for his selfless teaching." His recreations include music and gardening.

PRINCIPAL WORKS: The Language of Morals, 1952; Freedom and Reason, 1963; Essays on Philosophical Method, 1971; Practical Inferences, 1971; Essays on the Moral Concepts, 1972; Applications of Moral Philosophy, 1972.

ABOUT: Blanshard, B. Reason and Goodness, 1961; Hudson, W.D. (ed.) New Studies in Ethics, 1974; Lazerowitz, M. and Ambrose, A. Philosophical Theories, 1976; Mehta, V. Fly and the Fly Bottle, 1963; O'Connor, D.J. (ed.) A Critical History of Western Philosophy, 1963; Wallace, G. and Walker, A.D.M. (eds.) The Definition of Morality, 1970; Who's Who, 1978. *Periodicals*—Analysis December 1965, June 1976; Choice March 1973; Christian Century July 3, 1963; Mind April 1963, October 1963, April 1965, July 1968, January 1970, April 1970, October 1971, July 1972; Philosophical Quarterly January 1963, July 1964; Times Literary Supplement April 5, 1963; January 19, 1973.

HARRIS, MARK (November 19, 1922–), American novelist and memoirist, writes: "I was born in Mount Vernon, New York, United States of America, November 19, 1922. My wife and daughter, who have at times in the past played with astrology, tell me that I am a Scorpio. I know that on my birthdate, 1863, Abraham Lincoln delivered his Gettysburg Address.

"My parents were American-born of European descent—German, English, Polish, and Russian. My father, Carlyle Finkelstein, was an attorney. My mother, born Ruth Klausner, never had a professional career of any sort. I have one brother, Henry (a name which has been important in my life); and a sister, Martha.

"I attended the public schools of Mount Vernon. I graduated from our principal city high school in 1940. As a boy, I was fond of reading and of sports, especially baseball, and I think it was because of my relatively small stature that I saw I had no professional future in sports. Therefore I turned more and more to reading, and afterward to writing.

"What influences a life? I see now that perhaps I was born to be a writer. Yet I cannot be sure of the order of things. Does the need to express precede the development of the talent? I do not know. In any case, my opinion is that my being a Jew was the single greatest factor in stimulating my need or desire to write. Discrimination in employment plagued me after my high-school graduation, and in the army, which I entered (not voluntarily) in 1943. My keen sense of words made me extremely sensitive to the irony of contradictions between the American espousal of democracy and, on the other hand, the practice of discrimination. At about this period of my life I dropped my last name (Finkelstein), and employed my middle name as my new last name—Harris.

"The event of name-changing has entered my writing. I perceive now that other crises of my

MARK HARRIS

life have entered my writing, but I am glad that I did not know this when I was writing my early novels: I would have been inhibited if I had known how much I was revealing.

"I was in the army for fifteen months. My service was of no use to the war, but of much to myself, and I believe now that the war was unnecessary. All wars are simply murder for fun and profit. The idea of mankind's war-making tendency has become a major theme in my work, combined with the idea of fatherhood.

"After my military service I found work as a newspaper reporter in Port Chester, New York; in New York City; and in St. Louis. Again, as in the army, the experience was tremendously beneficial to me, if not to the press which employed me. I entered newswork because I thought that that was proper work for a true writer. I soon saw that newspaper work was essentially unrelated to fine writing. By 'fine writing' I mean the writing which explores the possibilities of sensations to their deepest parts. Journalism does not seek to do this.

"Luckily, in 1945 I met Josephine Horen, whom I married in 1946. Her insight into me was greater than my insight into myself, and she urged me to attend college and to become a teacher. I had felt these tendencies in me, too. We attended Denver University and the University of Minnesota. In 1954 I began work as a professor of English at San Francisco State College (now University), and continued elsewhere in subsequent years: Purdue University, the California Institute of the Arts, Immaculate Heart College in Los Angeles, the University of Southern California, and the University of Pittsburgh.

"Mainly I have become a teacher of 'creative writing.' I am a thoroughly introspective person, a student of my own development. I can therefore be useful in guiding students toward their own fulfillment. At any rate I hope to guide them toward their best civilized possibilities. For me, the university life is best. It gives me time to develop my writing and my thought in the only quarter of America I think is habitable. If not for university life in America we would have no intellectual life and no clues that the people of America might ever become more than shopkeepers and manufacturers.

"Henry Adams tells us it is a race against time. Either we shall learn to live with our acceleration or we shall perish. I tell students that the reason I am teaching them is that I hope to make the world safe for my children. My wife and I have three children—Hester Jill, Anthony Wynn, and Henry Adam.

"I have been extremely fortunate. My life and work have been unified. I have felt a tremendous satisfaction in the work itself, and also in the rewards, although I try when I write to think of the work, not of the rewards. I am grateful for the best traditions of America, for they have strengthened me; as for the worst traditions, they supply the indignation necessary to me. I suppose men and women are good and bad wherever they live."

Discussing his work in *Contemporary Novelists* (1976), Harris wrote that "although I am spiritually at the center of my novels. . . . I am disguised as poet or baseball player or professor or historian. I am always a minority person in some sense." In his first novel, *Trumpet to the World,* written during his brief and reluctant army career, the author appears in the disguise of an uneducated black man, Willie Jim—a reader who wants to be a writer. It is not an unhopeful novel and (as Harris says) "we end with the feeling that men of good will can succeed if only they write down their feelings and publish them."

City of Discontent, a colorful and partly fictionalized biography of Vachel Lindsay, was followed by *The Southpaw.* This purports to be the journal of Henry W. Wiggen, a young pitcher for the New York Mammoths whose picturesque way with language reminded reviewers of Ring Lardner. Henry's account of his struggle to succeed in his chosen career without surrendering either his identity or his integrity is both funny and exciting, and offers as well what one reviewer called "a long, serious and penetrating look at American mores and morals." There was even more critical enthusiasm for *Bang the*

349

Drum Slowly, in which Henry is made sadder and wiser by the illness and death of a teammate. This novel, filmed in 1973 from the author's own scenario, was followed by a third but much slighter Wiggen story, *Ticket for a Seamstitch.*

Harris drew more directly on his own experience in *Something About a Soldier,* centering on a young Jewish recruit who becomes a pacifist and a worker for black rights, and in *Wake Up, Stupid,* about a period of crisis in the life of Lee Youngdahl, a teacher who has also been successful as a boxer and a writer. Richard Sullivan found the latter "a bright, funny, occasionally ribald, always engaging novel artfully composed in the old epistolary manner." In *The Goy,* a distinguished midwestern historian—"a Christian cast among Jews" when he goes east—tries but fails to open himself to Jewish warmth and humanity. *Killing Everybody* is something of a departure, a "comedy of urban desperation" recording twenty-four hours in the lives of several ordinary people whose suppressed fantasies of sexuality and violence are allowed to come true.

The preoccupations that run through Harris's novels are also evident in three autobiographical volumes. *Mark the Glove Boy* deals with the 1962 gubernatorial struggle in California between Richard Nixon and Pat Brown, which Harris covered for *Life* magazine. It describes not only what he saw but the writing of his article and his own reactions to the contestants. Tom Wicker praised Harris's insight (though not his article) but G.W. Johnson in *New Republic* complained that the author seemed to find his own soul-states more interesting than Nixon's, and called the book "an exercise in preciosity; or ... bilge." There was a mixed press also for *Twentyone Twice,* a journal of Harris's adventures as a special investigator for the Peace Corps. *Best Father Ever Invented* is a full-scale autobiography. The life it describes so candidly is not a happy one, and this book lacks the optimism of some of the novels. As Roger Sale wrote, Harris's best and best-known work, *Bang the Drum Slowly,* "is a charming, funny, affirming book, and Harris, as he sees himself, has been mostly an acerbic, humorless and corrosive man. Little wonder he hates the terms of his fame, if not the fame itself. Little wonder his autobiography is terribly at war with itself, at once moving, distasteful and inarticulate."

Harris's play *Friedman and Son* was produced by the Actor's Workshop in San Francisco in 1962. He wrote and produced the award-winning documentary film *The Redwoods* (1968). William J. Schafer wrote in *Contemporary Novelists* that Harris's work "is dominated by genial comedy. . . . Sports and games are at the center of the work, especially the social games which are the substance of comedy of manners. . . . Harris's fiction is solidly within this tradition which translates social games into comedy, a comedy which explains our secret lives more clearly than any social or psychological theory."

The author received his Ph.D. in American Studies at the University of Minnesota in 1956. He held a Fulbright professorship at the University of Hiroshima in 1957-1958 and returned to Japan in 1964 as a delegate to the Dartmouth Conference in Kurashiki. In 1963 he was a visiting professor at Brandeis University. He has received grants and fellowships from the Ford and Guggenheim Foundations, the National Institute of Arts and Letters, and the National Endowment for the Arts, and has an honorary doctorate from Wesleyan University (1974).

PRINCIPAL WORKS: *Fiction*—Trumpet to the World, 1946; The Southpaw, by Henry W. Wiggen: Punctuation Inserted and Spelling Greatly Improved, 1953; Bang the Drum Slowly, by Henry W. Wiggen: Certain of His Enthusiasms Restrained, 1956; A Ticket for a Seamstitch, by Henry W. Wiggen: But Polished for the Printer, 1957; Something About a Soldier, 1957; Wake Up, Stupid, 1959; The Goy, 1970; Killing Everybody, 1973; *Play*—Friedman and Son, 1963; *Nonfiction*—City of Discontent: An Interpretive Biography of Vachel Lindsay, 1952; Mark the Glove Boy: or, The Last Days of Richard Nixon, 1964; Twentyone Twice: A Journal, 1966; (with others) Public Television: A Program for Action, 1967; Best Father Ever Invented, 1976. *As editor* —Selected Poems of Vachel Lindsay, 1963.

ABOUT: Contemporary Authors 5-8 (first revision), 1969; Harris, M. Best Father Ever Invented, 1976; Harris, M. *preface to* Friedman and Son, 1963; Harris, M. Mark the Glove Boy, 1964; Harris, M. *preface to* The Southpaw (1963 reprint); Harris, M. Twentyone Twice, 1966; McCormack, T. (ed.) Afterwords, 1969; Vinson, J. (ed.) Contemporary Novelists, 1976; Who's Who in America, 1976-1977. *Periodicals*—Virginia Quarterly Review Autumn 1961; Wisconsin Studies in Contemporary Literature I 1965.

HARRIS, (THEODORE) WILSON (March 24, 1921–), Guyanese novelist and poet, writes:

"I was born in British Guiana (now Guyana) at New Amsterdam at the mouth of the Berbice river. Berbice was one of the three counties of British Guiana in the nineteenth century but it was originally a Dutch Colony established in the early seventeenth century.

"My mother moved from New Amsterdam to Georgetown, Demerara, when I was two years old on the death of my father, who had been a prominent businessman in New Amsterdam.

"She remarried but my stepfather died when I was about seven. He was a member of an expedition into the interior of Guyana in 1928 or thereabouts and he never returned home. There was some uncertainty as to how his death actual-

WILSON HARRIS

ly occurred. Perhaps he was drowned in one of the rivers that run through that profoundly beautiful but hazardous landscape. I remember the shock of the news when my mother received it. Long after when I came to write novels which were set in the Guyana heartland I recalled the death of my stepfather as the first message or intimation I had received of the enigmatic densities and spaces of the Guyana interior.

"The Guyana highlands which run through Roraima (Amerindian name for mother of the waters and the night mountain) are part of the archetypal watershed of the Amazon and the Orinoco and, in some degree, they symbolize an interior that is still mysterious to the Guyanese people, most of whom live along the coastlands facing the Atlantic.

"The population there is composed of people of Indian, African, Chinese and European descent. There is a significant Amerindian presence in the interior (Macusis, Warraus, Wapishanas and others) though the Arawaks live as much on the coast as in the interior.

"My mother was of mixed descent, Arawak, European, African. We lived with her father for several years after the death of her second husband. From him I learnt of Arawak and other antecedents on my grandmother's side, and that my great-grandfather had been a Scot who came to British Guiana as a teacher in the first half of the nineteenth century.

"My grandfather's life spanned a complex and intricate passage in the history of British Guiana. He was born in the middle of the nineteenth century less than a generation after the abolition of slavery. He had been a retired civil servant for

some time when my mother and I went to live with him in the late 1920s. He died in 1937.

"I left Queen's College, Georgetown, to study surveying (cadastral, topographic, hydrographic) and qualified to practise in the early 1940s. I became a government surveyor and led parties into the interior for several years.

"During that time I wrote poems but the major impact of those expeditions seemed to store itself in the imagination and did not profoundly affect the tone of my writing until 1959 when I was living in Britain and wrote *Palace of the Peacock,* the first novel of a Guyana Quartet. It was published in 1960 by Faber and Faber.

"The imaginative intelligence sometimes sleeps on its material before all the elements of profound necessity may cohere into a form of arousal in poem or novel.

"This element of sleep and arousal is a crucial matter because there begins another kind of expedition which seems to be retracing the contours of the past but, in fact, is involved in a mutation of resources, in a new vision, within which new signals, new perspectives, are *seen* in old and new landscapes or investitures of the psyche of tradition.

"It is in this sense that I wrote the Guyana Quartet, culminating in *The Secret Ladder* (1963), upon a ground of the imagination I could not have entered before, and moved on to other novels like *Tumatumari* (1968), *Ascent to Omai* (1970), also set in Guyana, then further on still into *Black Marsden* (1972) and *Companions of the Day and Night* (1975), set in Europe and Mexico.

"My wife is also a writer. She has written lyrics, a libretto and several radio plays. We live in London."

Wilson Harris began, as he says, as a poet, in the magazine *Kyk-over-al,* in *Fetish,* privately printed in 1951, and in the more important collection *Eternity to Season* (1954), also privately printed in Georgetown. Edward Brathwaite places him outside the present mainstream of Caribbean writing in English and finds "his metaphorical perception and expression ... more akin to that of the Martiniquan poet Aimé Césaire and the Cuban writer Alejo Carpentier. His sensibility has been formed by the world of the Guyanese forest and its rivers, its complexities and contradictions":

The world-creating jungle
travels eternity to season. Not an individual artifice
this living moment

this tide
this paradoxical stream and stillness rousing
reflection.

The living jungle is too full of voices
not to be aware of collectivity,
and too swift with unseen wings
to capture certainty.

("Amazon")

In his poetry, Brathwaite writes, Harris "does not concern himself with social conditions, individual problems, the 'historical' colonial past, or a possible or impossible future. His themes are time (into which he subsumes history), creation, separation and unity. His burden is not the Faustian ego but the environmental collective." The same may be said of Harris's fiction, to which he turned conclusively in the late 1950s, abandoning verse.

Harris was thirty-eight before he wrote his first novel, *Palace of the Peacock,* and had already spent some seventeen years as a surveyor (in 1955-1958 as his government's Senior Surveyor in charge of projects). His work involved long journeys of exploration in the wild interior of Guyana—periods of extreme isolation for Harris, who was often the only educated member of his party and was further isolated by his position of authority.

In these years he was a voracious reader, a poet, but above all a thinker. As he himself remarks, "the imaginative intelligence sometimes sleeps on its material." The material accumulated then was to prove abundant when he left Guyana in 1959 to become a full-time writer in England.

An early article like "Art and Criticism" (1951), written during this formative period, indicates the range of his reading and speculation at that time. He was already very much aware of the radical transformations in narrative wrought by the French "new novelists" (particularly Claude Simon) and by short story writers like Isaac Babel. He had also read extensively in modern philosophy. Some of his poems contain in embryo themes later developed in his fiction:

So life discovers the remotest beaches in time
that are always present in action: the interior
walls of being open like a mirrorless pool.

(from "Behring Straits")

After some early experiments in fiction, which he destroyed, Harris came to the conclusion that the true Caribbean novel demanded a "fulfilment of character" rather than the "consolidation of character" found in the traditional realistic novel of relatively stable societies. The writer was involved in a dialogue with the past, and this dialogue must change not only himself, but the past he rediscovers. And since in the Caribbean that past is one of violence, subjugation, invasion, slavery, racial tension, and discrimination, the writer is further involved in overcoming the barriers existing in his own mind and his own upbringing, which prevent him from recognizing and experiencing a common humanity. This is the search for what he calls "a vision of consciousness," and the action of his novels generally tends towards the discovery of such a vision. It often arises from the interaction of two contrasted sensibilities: a limited, complacent, educated, coastland sensibility becomes exposed in the heartland to one that is indigenous, animistic, and in harmony with the untamed natural world (like Stevenson and Kaiser in *Heartland,* Fenwick and Poseidon in *The Secret Ladder*).

Hena Maes-Jelinek suggests that for Harris "humanity is on the whole divided between hunter and hunted, victor and victim, each category remaining self-deceptively confined to its own monolithic role and trying to extend these divisions to nature and society. But Harris denies the genuineness of those categories. He sees in nature and in all forms of human existence an ambivalence of purpose and design that should be given free play . . . omnipresent nature is both perilous and protective. It is also a mirror reflecting man's dual nature, his spiritual states as well as his physical metamorphoses."

In many of the novels, starting with *Palace of the Peacock,* there is a physical journey into the brooding, unknown heart of Guyana. But, tangential to this physical journey and diverging from it, is the psychic journey undertaken in the mind or spirit of the voyager. Within the ever-widening space between these two journeys (or "arrows") the vision of consciousness must be deployed, so that the very meaning of the physical journey (which is a journey also into the past of the land and the race) will be transformed. This is what Harris calls "the quest of phenomenal space rather than phenomenal time." Old selves will be transcended and abandoned like husks, from which the liberated potentialities of man can spring anew. This process can be seen at work in all of Harris's novels, and can be seen to have an effect upon all of his characters.

Harris's autobiographical note above sheds some light on one of the recurring preoccupations of his novels, the idea of a haunted stretch of water, above or below a fall, where a death by drowning has, or might have, occurred. The mystery surrounding the death of his stepfather is transferred by Harris's peculiar imaginative processes to other times and situations. Thus, in *The Eye of the Scarecrow,* the narrator (Harris) pushes his schoolfriend L—— into a canal and nearly drowns him. Later in the same novel the narrator and L—— find themselves on a river bridge in the interior, where L—— has been sent to survey a vanished mining town. There is a vague suggestion that the narrator's father (or the narrator himself?) has drowned L—— in the river below. Or that the narrator (or his alter ego, the Scarecrow) has strangled an Amerindian woman called Hebra. The novel gradually becomes a confessional document addressed to L—— in which the narrator purges these images of guilt flooding in upon him from the past: "All at once I dreamed that it—the accumulative ironies of the past, the virtuous rubbish heap and self-parody of ancestors in death—still sought to warn me not to dig into itself so deep for the classical burden of truth."

The Eye of the Scarecrow also offers an account of that dreaming swoon which often overwhelms Harris's characters and delivers them from the prison of their limited personal past: "I closed my eyes feeling all of a sudden close to sickness: a spinning and sleeping top. The dreaming fit passed. I looked around once again. No one seemed aware that anything had happened. . . . But I experienced once more the resulting chaos I knew, loss of orientation, the unruly pivot around which revolves the abstract globe in one's head. . . . This sensation of helpless upheaval, the stigmata of the void. . . ."

Elsewhere, Harris has described an experience when his surveying boat pulled adrift just above Tumatumari Falls. The crew were in imminent danger of death in the torrent but managed to make their way out. Three years later, in the same spot, the boat pulled adrift again. But this time their anchor fouled the anchor lost in the previous mishap. Harris comments: "It is almost impossible to describe the kind of energy that rushed out of that constellation of images. I felt as if a canvas around my head was crowded with phantoms and figures. I had forgotten some of my own antecedents—the Amerindian/Arawak ones—but now their faces were on the canvas. . . . There was a sudden eruption of consciousness, and what is fantastic is that it all came out of a constellation of two ordinary objects, two anchors."

No wonder that Harris, on his own voyages upriver, was haunted by the ghost of his vanished stepfather and by all that he had represent-

ed in a turbulent, mysterious, hidden world of possibilities. No wonder that no less than five of his novels are concerned in one way or another with the cluster of images rushing out of the anchor incident. Harris's imagination is sparked off by anything suggesting that one event or personality is continually being invaded and altered by another.

His Guyanese material proved richly adequate to inform all of his writing down to 1972. This includes the two volumes of stories, which show an intense interest in Amerindian myth. Since then, Harris's work has begun to incorporate more recent experiences in Mexico and Europe, and to dwell upon moments in which a suppressed cultural pattern erupts through a decaying later one. But it is doubtful whether the particular kind of novelist he is could have been formed by a less enigmatic, complex, and challenging beginning than the one he received in the wild, numinous landscape of Guyana.

Hena Maes-Jelinek writes that "throughout Harris's fiction the creation of consciousness, the opening of new windows on the world, is . . . analogous to the artist's creative act. Each novel is an awakening of consciousness through the medium of language, a language which, economic and highly selective as it is, attempts to convey the immediacy and intercommunicability of all being. Harris refuses to impose a 'false coherency' on the raw material of life." It follows that Harris's novels are sometimes difficult —a reviewer in the *Times Literary Supplement* of *Ascent to Omai* complained that "critics of poetry are more accustomed to this kind of work than are reviewers of novels." Nevertheless, his stature as a major contemporary novelist is indicated by the amount of attention devoted to his work in the Americas and Europe, and his importance in the contemporary Caribbean imagination is evident in the work of such painters as Aubrey Williams and such poets as Edward Brathwaite and Derek Walcott.

Harris, the son of Theodore Wilson and the former Millicent Glasford, has lived in Britain since 1959. In 1968 he attended the National Identity Conference at Brisbane and the UNESCO symposium on Caribbean Literature in Cuba. He was writer-in-residence at the University of the West Indies and at Scarborough College, Toronto University, during 1970, when he also lectured at the State University of New York at Buffalo. The following year he was Commonwealth Fellow in Caribbean Literature at Leeds University. He was a visiting professor at the University of Texas—Austin in 1972 and at the University of Aarhus, Denmark, in 1973. He received grants from the British Arts Coun-

353

cil in 1968 and 1970 and a Guggenheim fellowship in 1973. In 1974 he held the Henfield Writing Fellowship at the University of East Anglia. Harris has been married twice: to Cecily Carew in 1945 and to Margaret Whitaker in 1959.

PRINCIPAL WORKS: *Poetry*—Fetish, 1951; Eternity to Season, 1954. *Fiction*—(The first four titles comprise the Guyana Quartet) Palace of the Peacock, 1960; The Far Journey of Oudin, 1961; The Whole Armour, 1962; The Secret Ladder, 1963; Heartland, 1964; The Eye of the Scarecrow, 1965; The Waiting Room, 1967; Tumatumari, 1968; Ascent to Omai, 1970; The Sleepers of Roraima (stories), 1970; The Age of the Rainmakers (stories), 1971; Black Marsden, 1972; Companions of the Day and Night, 1975; Da Silva da Silva's Cultivated Wilderness and Genesis of the Clowns, 1977. *Nonfiction*—Tradition, the Writer and Society, 1967; Fossil and Psyche, 1974.

ABOUT: Contemporary Authors 65-68, 1977; Fletcher, J. Commonwealth Literature and the Modern World, 1975; Gilkes, M. Wilson Harris and the Caribbean Novel, 1975; James, C.L.R. Wilson Harris: A Philosophical Approach, 1966; James, L. (ed.) The Islands In Between, 1968; Maes-Jelinek, H. The Naked Design, 1975; Moore, G. The Chosen Tongue, 1970; Ramchand, K. The West Indian Novel and Its Background, 1970; Van Sertima, I. Enigma of Values, 1975; Vinson, J. (ed.) Contemporary Novelists, 1972; Vinson, J. (ed.) Contemporary Poets, 1975; Walsh, W. Commonwealth Literature, 1973; Walsh, W. (ed.) Readings in Commonwealth Literature, 1973; Who's Who, 1977. *Periodicals*—Ariel January 1970; Review of the Center for Inter-American Relations Spring 1974; Financial Times February 27, 1975; Journal of Commonwealth Literature July 1969, June 1971, April 1975; Language and Literature (Copenhagen) Autumn 1971; Literary Half-Yearly July 1970; New Letters Fall 1973; New Statesman December 1, 1972; Spectator December 3, 1965; Times Literary Supplement February 15, 1963; July 4, 1968; October 10, 1975; Tribune June 12, 1970; October 16, 1970; World Literature Written in English November 1974.

HARRISON, JIM (JAMES THOMAS)

(December 11, 1937–), American poet and novelist, writes: "I was born in Grayling, in northern Michigan, the second of five children. Throughout my father's adult life he was an agriculturist and conservationist for the federal and state governments. I own a rather uneventful rural childhood—working, swimming, fishing, hunting—which was sadly truncated at age thirteen when my father took a position at Michigan State University and we moved to southern Michigan. It took two decades to comprehend the unhappiness of this move from a basically agrarian culture into the twentieth century.

"Motives in my life seem largely muddled, unexplained, even mysterious, but I think I essentially became a writer at age sixteen when I gave up religion and began reading John Keats, Walt Whitman, Faulkner, Dostoevsky, James Joyce and a few others, but at the particular time these writers were seminal to me. The right book at the right time has a truly biblical power, and

Dan Gerber

JIM HARRISON

one good book drives one on to the next. At nineteen, after a year at college, I ran off to New York City to become a writer though I was soon starved out. At the time I imagined myself to be some sort of marvelous combination of Henry Miller, Rimbaud, Apollinaire and Lord Byron which didn't quite jibe with being a clerk or busboy, though the latter at least assured something to eat.

"This is all to say that there is nothing particularly extraordinary in my life. In those early days in addition to New York, I lived in Boston and San Francisco. I finished college, got married, then worked as a farm laborer, carpenter, hod carrier, salesman. I wanted to be a writer but had no idea quite how to go about it. Then when I was twenty-three my father and one of my sisters died in an auto wreck and death proved to be a teacher, even though death is ineluctably death and nothing else. But after a breakdown I began working very hard and suppose that I haven't stopped since.

"Now I live on a small farm back in northern Michigan where I started. I tried teaching for two years with great unhappiness. Guggenheim and National Endowment fellowships sprung me from universities and since then, for the past seven years, I have made something of a living as a poet, novelist, journalist, and screenwriter. I have two daughters and a lot of animals. I travel a lot for reasons of energy—to get out of ruts—and in recent years I've been to Europe, Russia, Africa, and South America. I spend a great deal of time fly fishing and hunting grouse.

"Most all writing means nothing. I have come to think that if it isn't regarded as a holy calling, an obsession without which one would die, it isn't worth it. Poetry is too important on earth to be trifled with and the impulse behind the novel is little different from poetry. Necessity is the test—whether or not everything you love on earth depends on it.

"During recent years I have taken up with the teaching of the Zennist, Shunryu Suzuki. I'm daily more preoccupied with the novel, remembering Kafka's dictum that a book 'should be an axe for the frozen sea within us.' "

Plain Song was warmly welcomed as a volume of lyrics celebrating, with a "flat rhetoric" reminiscent of William Carlos Williams and with only apparent simplicity, "the object (redbird, rock, young bull, caged wolf) and the experience (county fair, love, being lost)." These were generally short, free-form poems, conversational and idiomatic in diction. Seeking a means of dealing in a more sustained way with a mood or an idea, Harrison experimented in his second book, *Locations,* with "suites" of short poems "related not by a logical narrative but by association," and influenced, it was thought, by Rilke and Apollinaire. Dealing with "landscapes, birds and beasts, a hunter's wandering," he writes, one reviewer said, "heavily, convulsively, as though burrowing through quantities of psychic material—turning it over, sniffing around it. . . . It is as though he wishes to lose himself in the life he is describing."

It was Harrison's third collection, *Outlyer and Ghazals,* that established him. The ghazal is a poem of between five and a dozen couplets popular in Arabic, Persian, and other Eastern literatures since the eighth century. In Harrison's hands the couplets (rather like the short poems in *Locations*) are often complete in themselves, and are given continuity only by a mood or a metrical pattern. He himself said that he had tried in these sixty-five ghazals "to regain some of the spontaneity of the dance, the song unencumbered by any philosophical apparatus, faithful only to its own music."

The book did not please everyone—one reviewer thought that these verses had neither the insight nor the artistry that would qualify them as poetry, and found no more than "a teary and infantile enumeration of the women who have ignored, neglected, or left him." A commoner view was expressed by M. L. Rosenthal, who thought that this bitterly depressed book was redeemed from grimness "by a buffoonery of anguish. . . . an open, volatile atmosphere" and the precision of "a workman who knows just how to use his tools." Rosenthal concludes: "Within each ghazal, and in the ebb and flow and shifting emphasis of the clusters within the

entire sequence, all the poetic faces and voices of Jim Harrison make themselves felt. It is sometimes exasperating, sometimes cheaply facile, often heartbreaking, often exquisitely beautiful as the waves of language and sense-impressions and uncontrollably black moods and randy philosophizing and esthetic balancings sweep over the pages."

One of the most admired poems in the collection is not a ghazal but the insomniac's complaint "Awake":

Limp with night fears: hellbore, wolfbane,
Marlowe is daggered, fire, volts, African vipers . . .

black water, framed by police, wanton wife,
I'm a bad poet broke and broken at thirty-two,
a renter, shot by mistake, airplanes and trains,
half-mast hardons, a poisoned earth, sun will
go out, car break down in a blizzard,
my animals die, fist fights, alcohol, caskets,
the hammerhead gliding under the boat near
Loggerhead Key, my soul, my heart, my brain,
my life so interminably struck with an ax
as wet wood splits bluntly, mauled into
sections for burning.

Letters to Yesenin, which followed, was no more cheerful—was indeed avowedly the work of a poet who had reached an emotional dead end. All the same, these poems seemed to Lawrence Russ in *Contemporary Poets* encouraging, partly because in them Harrison seemed to have found a form that suited his talent—especially his talent for creating a sense of natural speech—and partly because they have "a feel of genuine honesty in contrast to the locker-room honesty of the ghazals."

Wolf, Harrison's first novel, is narrated by Carol Severin Swanson, an extravagantly male nature lover and sexual adventurer. Alone in the Huron Mountains of upper Michigan, he looks back ten years to his twenties, when (as one reviewer put it) "he was at large in the nation, getting women and booze and drugs and brutish jobs and a heightened awareness of the virtues of keeping his own counsel." Swanson's experience of society has proved to him that he is an anachronism, as much a member of a dying species as the wolf of the title—he wants to live, but not in the world as it is. Set in New York, Boston, San Francisco, and many "nameless burgs" in between, the novel seemed to Jonathan Yardley "a raunchy, funny, swaggering, angry, cocksure book" which is at the same time "a poignant, handsomely written self-exploration."

A Good Day to Die is similar—the story of a pilgrimage west made by two "good ole boys" and the girlfriend of one of them, who plan to blow up a proposed dam across the Grand Canyon as an ecological protest. *Library Journal*'s reviewer called it a story "of sexual frustration, drug psychosis, alcoholic dissipation, and inevitable disaster," and thought that "the American ecological and spiritual dilemma is inadequately met with the guerilla mentality presented here."

This was followed by a much quieter novel, *Farmer,* set during the 1950s in a dying agricultural community in Michigan. It is an account of eight months—fall through summer—in the life of Joseph Lundgren, a schoolteacher-*cum*-farmer who finds, in his forties, that he has "neglected to do any of the things most people occupy themselves with." Now, with his mother dead and the local school closed down, he has arrived at a moment of crisis and choice—a watershed considerably muddied by his clandestine affair with a girl student. "What holds . . . [Joseph] together," wrote Webster Schott, "is Michigan, a crusty doctor–hunting partner, and his own sense of man's history. There is no stability in emotions, only needs. Continuity rises from habit, hunting game with his friend, satisfying the demands of animals and land. . . . [Harrison] writes beautifully. He sees life going on and on, its meaning in its pattern. . . . He moves us rather than overwhelms us. He creates an art small except in its grace." Christopher Lehmann-Haupt agreed that in this, the most admired of Harrison's novels to date, he had "finally found a narrative pace to suit his sensibility."

The author, the son of Winfield Sprague Harrison and the former Norma Wahlgren, decided at the age of twelve that he wanted to become a writer. He studied comparative literature at Michigan State University, which gave him his B.A. in 1960, his M.A. in 1964. His most influential teacher was Herbert Weisinger, a mythographer, and he says that he has learned also from Denise Levertov, Robert Duncan, and Louis Simpson, among other poets. His brief and unhappy teaching career was as an assistant professor in the English department at the State University of New York at Stony Brook. Harrison was married in 1960 to Linda King.

PRINCIPAL WORKS: *Poetry*—Plain Song, 1965; Locations, 1968; Outlyer and Ghazals, 1971; Letters to Yesenin, 1973. *Fiction*—Wolf, 1971; A Good Day to Die, 1973; Farmer, 1976.

ABOUT: Contemporary Authors 13–16 1st revision, 1975; International Who's Who in Poetry, 1974–1975; Untermeyer, L. Fifty American and British Poets, 1973; Vinson, J. (ed.) Contemporary Poets, 1975; Who's Who in America, 1976–1977. *Periodicals*—Detroit Free Press April 16, 1972; Library Journal June 1, 1971; September 15, 1973; New York Times Book Review December 28, 1969; July 18, 1971; December 12, 1971; September 9, 1973; October 10, 1976; New Yorker November 5, 1973; Saturday Review December 25, 1971; Stony Brook 1–2 1968.

*HAVEL, VÁCLAV (October 5, 1936–), Czech dramatist and poet, was born in Prague, the son of Václav M. Havel and the former Božena Vavrečkova. His father was a very rich man, owner of large sections of the commercial center of Prague. During the Stalinist period in postwar Czechoslovakia, Havel, as the son of an ex-millionaire, was denied formal higher education. However, while working in a chemical laboratory he was able to study at evening classes, and in 1954 he completed his secondary schooling. From 1955 to 1957 he attended a technical college, and in 1956, when he was barely twenty, Havel published his first essays on poetry and drama. It was not until 1959, after two years of military service, that he was able to find his first job in the theatre, and that was as a stagehand at the Divadlo ABC (the ABC Theatre of Prague). The following year he moved to the famous Divadlo na zábradlí (Theatre on the Balustrade), where he began as stagehand and electrician but soon became secretary, manuscript reader, and, in 1961, *dramaturg* (literary manager and writer-in-residence). Havel retained that post until 1968, and from 1962 to 1967 was allowed to study in the drama department of the Prague Academy of Arts. His monograph on the writer and painter Josef Čapek, elder brother of the more famous Karel, appeared in 1963.

The Theatre on the Balustrade is situated in an ancient town house in the heart of Prague's Old City, and its cramped auditorium has room for barely two hundred seats and a tiny stage. It has nevertheless been an important center of Czech avant-garde drama and mime ever since its foundation in 1958, at a time when the rigidities of the Stalinist period were giving way to more relaxed attitudes. The first artistic director of the Balustrade was Ivan Vyskočil, a brilliantly versatile writer, actor, and producer, in collaboration with whom Havel wrote his satirical first play, *Autostop* (Hitchhiking, 1961).

In 1962 Vyskočil was succeeded as artistic director by Jan Grossman, a drama critic and translator devoted to the "theatre of the absurd." Grossman, Havel, and their associates made the Balustrade into Prague's leading dramatic ensemble, purveying a kind of political theatre in which the influence of such absurdist dramatists as Ionesco is successfully combined with that of the twin tutelary spirits of literary Prague, Kafka and Jaroslav Hašek, author of *The Good Soldier Schweik.* All of Havel's early

*hav' el

VÁCLAV HAVEL

plays had their first productions at the Balustrade and owe a great deal to the experimental spirit and generous teamwork Grossman developed there.

Havel's first solo play was *Zahradní slavnost,* which had its premiere in 1963 and has since been translated into the major European languages—into English as *The Garden Party* by Vera Blackwell, who has translated all of Havel's plays. A reviewer in the London *Times* called it "an inspired satire on the dehumanization of present-day Man, in a world which continually creates pseudo-reality out of meaningless clichés and phrases." Hugo Pludek, a clever young careerist with an unequaled talent for parroting official slogans, surrenders all his humanity and individuality and rises rapidly to become director of both the old "Office for Liquidation" and the more positive "Office for Inauguration," which is intended to replace the old ministry. But this gives rise to all sorts of problems and intrigues, since the Office of Liquidation cannot be officially liquidated except by itself, and the moment it does it will not exist to complete the procedure. In the end a solution to this impasse is found in the creation of a new bureaucratic monster, the Central Office for Inauguration and Liquidation.

Vyrozumění, first staged in 1965 and translated as *The Memorandum,* is another satire directed against social institutions that serve not society but themselves, and again employs a Schweikian situation with Kafkaesque implications. It begins with the bureaucrat Josef Gross reading aloud the memorandum of the title. It is written in Ptydepe, a new artificial language invented "on a strictly scientific basis," and is

quite meaningless to him; nor can he have a translation made without a special application written in Ptydepe. Completely outmaneuvered by his sinister deputy Ballas, Gross is reduced to the rank of Staff Watcher (spy), but regains his position when he persuades Maria, a sympathetic typist, to translate the memorandum, which turns out to contain a devastating critique of Ptydepe. Undaunted, Ballas introduces another and equally fatuous artificial language, and this time Gross knows better than to oppose it. When Maria is dismissed and comes to Gross, he makes an impassioned speech in defence of human values but in the end refuses to help her, pointing out that in saving his skin she had after all broken the rules.

After the British premiere of *The Memorandum,* a *Times* critic wrote: "Havel's achievement is that he has created a play that works very effectively on two levels. On the one hand he amusingly satirizes the idiocies of any bureaucratic system in which form becomes more important than content, regulations more significant than actual communication. But this is also a political play in that it shows that one of the first instincts of an autocrat is to tidy up the variety, color and expressiveness of language." *The Memorandum* "has a wit, elegance and intellectual bite which should earn it a Western popularity at least equivalent to Frisch's *The Fire Raisers,*" by a writer who is "one of the most exciting post-war talents that has appeared in the East European theatre." The *Guardian* called it "a great comedy which deserves classic status." In Britain it has been performed on radio and television as well as on the stage, and when it was produced in New York in the spring of 1968 it won the *Village Voice* award as the best off-Broadway foreign play of the season.

Havel's collection *Protokoly* (Protocols), published in 1966, includes both of these plays, as well as two important essays on the theatre and some of his extremely witty concrete poetry. By that time critics had begun to realize that Havel's absurdist plays were not simply political in their intentions but dramatized an almost universal human condition of alienation, lack of communication, and loss of identity. As Martin Esslin has written, "it would be wrong to interpret Havel's Schweikian dilemmas as mere satire against the idiocy of a local bureaucracy. The bureaucracy depicted by Havel has profound metaphysical features; it also represents the inner, logical contradictions of existence itself, the dilemma inherent in the use of all language (and Havel's logico-linguistic antinomies have much in common with Wittgenstein's critique of language as a vehicle for logic), the antinomies inherent in all rules of conduct."

The truth of this became clearer in Havel's third play, *Ztížená možnost soustředění* (translated as *The Increased Difficulty of Concentration*), which opened at the Balustrade in April 1968, during the hopeful days of the Prague Spring. In this sardonic but very funny play about the role of sex in a dehumanized society the main character, a social scientist, dictates an essay on human values. But what he is saying is heard by the audience in the context of his own moral and emotional chaos, torn as he is between the demands of his wife, his mistress, and his secretary. As it becomes increasingly and farcically difficult to keep the three women apart, his life is further complicated by Puzuk, a computer which has fastened on him as a "random sample" and is programed to measure and classify his identity. It fails miserably in this task, which is hardly surprising, an identity being what the social scientist noticeably lacks. Even his romantic and erotic excesses are less an expression of individuality than a form of escapism. "In such a centre-less, spiritually mechanized life concentration is difficult if not impossible," wrote one critic, "and all experience equally worthless." Produced at Lincoln Center in New York in 1969, the play won an Obie award for "outstanding achievement in the off-Broadway theatre."

Havel had never been a Communist, and during 1968 he joined enthusiastically in the campaign to decentralize and democratize the Czech government, notably in a famous article, "On the Theme of Opposition," in the writers' journal *Literární Listy* (April 4, 1968). Arguing for "moral-political recognition of the non-Communist viewpoint" by the creation of a second, non-Communist political party, he wrote: "Power in the end respects only power, and a government can be made to improve itself only when its existence, and not just its good reputation, is at stake." Havel also spoke out against censorship and joined with other non-Communists in forming a "Club of Engaged Non-Party Members" that sought to become the nucleus of an opposition party.

After the Russian invasion of August 1968, both Havel and Jan Grossman were barred from all public artistic activities, at the Balustrade or anywhere else in Czechoslovakia. In spite of many invitations to continue their work in the West, both decided to remain in their own country. Havel's passport was confiscated in the summer of 1969 by the Husak government. He worked for a time as a laborer in a brewery in Trutnov, Bohemia, but has otherwise continued

to live in Prague, and has remained an active reformist, in spite of continual harassment and repeated arrests. After an amateur production in 1975 of Havel's adaptation of *The Beggar's Opera,* even members of the audience were subjected to police reprisals. In January 1977, many Czech writers, intellectuals, and ordinary working people signed Charter 77, a manifesto describing the failure of the Czech government to observe human and civil rights and calling upon the authorities to honor the pledges made in signing the Helsinki agreement. A wave of arrests followed and Havel, who had been elected one of the Charter's three spokesmen, was taken into custody for the fifth time. In May 1977 he was released, and in October he was brought to trial, charged not in connection with Charter 77 but with "subversion of the Republic" for sending banned material out of the country for publication abroad. He received a fourteen-month suspended sentence.

The plays Havel has written since the crushing of the Czech reform movement are semiautobiographical works reflecting his experience (and his country's) during those years. They have not, of course, been produced in Czechoslovakia, but two of them have been broadcast as a double bill by the BBC's Radio 3, and later staged in London, in translations by Vera Blackwell. *Audience* is set in a small brewery and features a conversation between the Head Maltster and Ferdinand Vanek, a dissident writer forced as Havel was to work as a laborer in the brewery cellars. The Head Maltster sees in this educated and intelligent employee a potential accomplice in his schemes to divert some of the brewery's profits into his own pocket. In their increasingly drunken discussion, the writer refuses to cooperate in the maltster's petty dishonesties, or to solve his political problems by informing against himself.

Audience is an indictment of one aspect of life in a so-called Communist society; *Private View* examines another level of the same society and finds it equally wanting. The same writer, Ferdinand Vanek, visits his friends Vera and Michael in their new apartment, which is crammed with works of art, antiques, and the records and gadgets that Michael has "brought back from the States." Delighted with all this evidence of their own success, appalled that Vanek should work in a brewery when with a little less idealism he could be a journalist, they are bewildered when he walks out on them: "But you haven't seen the electric almond peeler! We were even going to let you watch us making love!" The irony is that Vanek, having kept his integrity, needs nothing else, whereas Vera and Michael, for all their material possessions and fashionable jargon, have nothing of value to themselves or anyone else.

Discussing these two plays, Irving Wardle wrote that "not a trace of personal bitterness disfigures the writing. Havel's instrument remains the cool moral satire, beautifully constructed and brilliantly funny, and autobiographical only because the times happen to have dealt him a dramatic role. . . . The simple idea behind both plays is that the presence of a man who says 'No' is intolerable to those who have accepted the compromises of Czech 'normalization.' "

Havel, who has been described by Martin Esslin as "short, cherubic and outwardly cheerful," is married to the former Olga Šplíchalová. He received the Austrian State Prize for European Literature in 1969. According to a critic in the London *Times*, "no Czech playwright since Karel Čapek forty years ago has had an impact" comparable to his.

PRINCIPAL PUBLISHED WORKS IN ENGLISH TRANSLATION: *Plays*—The Memorandum, 1967 (also *in* Three East European Plays, 1970); The Garden Party, 1969; The Increased Difficulty of Concentration, 1972. *Other*—On the Theme of Opposition *in* Oxley, A. (and others, eds.) Czechoslovakia, 1973.

ABOUT: Crowell's Handbook of Contemporary Drama, 1971; Esslin, M. Brief Chronicles, 1970; Esslin, M. The Theatre of the Absurd, 1974; Gassner, J. and Quinn, E. The Reader's Encyclopedia of World Drama, 1970; International Who's Who, 1977-78; Shub, A. An Empire Loses Hope, 1970. *Periodicals*—Books Abroad Spring 1967, Summer 1972; Index on Censorship January-February 1978; New York Review of Books August 4, 1977; Times (London) April 23, 1975; January 10, 1975; February 21, 1977; March 21, 1977; October 14, 1977; October 19, 1977; Times Literary Supplement March 10, 1972.

*HÁY, GYULA (or in German JULIUS) (May 5, 1900–May 7, 1975), Hungarian dramatist, spent much of his creative life in exile and wrote many of his plays in German. He was born in Abony, a town southeast of Budapest on the Great Hungarian Plain or *puszta.* Háy described Abony as "an overgrown village that had never quite succeeded in becoming a town. Such villages are characteristic of the Great Hungarian Plain. At that time it numbered seventeen thousand inhabitants, but with the exception of an extremely modest center—and even that was without water mains and drainage—every street and every corner of every street looked as if it belonged to some God-forsaken hamlet."

Háy's father was manager and chief engineer of the Gerje and Perje Flood-Control Company, Gerje and Perje being two streams which flowed

*hī

eastwards into the great unruly River Tisza. But the head of the family was undoubtedly grandfather Miska, "a short, thin, silent, pipe-smoking, old, rich, Jewish Hungarian." His house lay just across the street, though apart from land and stock and houses in Abony he also owned an elegant apartment house in Budapest, where he spent the winters. "Although Father had five brothers and sisters, the family fortune remained concentrated right up until 1909 in one hand, a hand as spindly as a mummy's, threaded with blue-black veins, covered with grizzled hairs, and stinking of the cheapest pipe-tobacco its owner—my grandfather—could buy."

When the old man died there was a sizeable inheritance, but Háy's father "refused to give up his job as an engineer. His paternal admonitions were few and far between, but one of them was to the effect that . . . the only guarantee of a solid livelihood was a diploma." His two older sons followed his advice, but Gyula and Kari showed artistic promise. Their father's one great passion was music, and he was a gifted cellist, playing in his younger days in large Budapest orchestras, and also appearing as a soloist. Háy's mother, he wrote, "was a short woman, but her rotundity, clad in the fashions of the turn of the century, gave her a truly imposing presence. She read a great deal—Hungarian, German and French—but most of the books were from the lending library: she never wanted to build up a library of her own. She subscribed to the Parisian magazine *L'Illustration,* which carried a supplement in which a complete play was printed, with photographs of the Paris production. I used to stare at those pictures for hours and hours, dreaming of God knows what non-existent plays."

Háy was educated in the nearby town of Cegléd, the traditional agricultural center of the area. Born in 1900, he was the same age as the century; by the time he and it were eighteen years old, he was caught up in its turbulent political history. His autobiography may be read as the typical case history of a Central European middle-class intellectual who devoted his life to the Communist cause, working for it throughout long years of exile, only to feel hopelessly betrayed by the way in which his dream was realized in his native land: "My father died one summer day in 1934. I was unable to escort him to the grave because I was in prison in Vienna at the time. As a dangerous Communist. My mother died one autumn day in 1958. I was prevented from attending her funeral by the fact that I was serving a term in a Budapest jail. As a dangerous anti-Communist."

When the Austro-Hungarian Empire collapsed after World War I, Hungary declared its independence. In 1918 there was a brief liberal revolution led by Count Károlyi. The eighteen-year-old Háy had just enrolled at the University of Budapest: "Now that everything was suddenly on the move, however, we soon became aware of how meaningless and irrelevant our university studies were." He had been eagerly reading the pamphlets by Karl Marx then published in Hungary for the first time. He became a Bolshevik convert, took part in the demonstrations that led to Béla Kun's Communist revolution, and enthusiastically supported Kun's government during the few months before invading foreign armies crushed it, unleashing the White Terror in which workers, peasants, Jews, and anyone suspected of left-wing sympathies was murdered.

Háy, who had by this time written an unpublished novel, left for Germany to study stage design at the Dresden Academy of Arts and Crafts, and was also apprenticed to the chief designer for the Dresden State Playhouse. After a year he moved on to Berlin, to the college attached to the National Museum of Arts and Crafts, planning sets "for non-existent, haif-worked-out, half-dreamt-up plays." After two years he was asked if he ever tried writing the plays he designed sets for, but Háy was still thinking in terms of novels. In 1923 he went back to Hungary and married his fiancée, Margit. The couple stayed in Hungary for the next six years, living mostly on an allowance from Margit's uncle and Háy's father. Háy wrote two more novels, which remained unpublished in the family home in Abony "until all three were destroyed down to the last scrap of paper when my older brother Max and his family were dragged off to the gas-chamber in 1944."

Meanwhile, in the early 1920s, Háy did manage to publish articles, reviews, and the occasional short story, gradually becoming a moderately well-known figure on the fringe of progressive Hungarian literature, and eking out his allowance with various kinds of commercial and applied art. His son Peter was born in 1925. Háy returned to Berlin in 1929, partly under the influence of the Brecht-Weill *Threepenny Opera,* whose "songs were like a personal greeting from Berlin to me. A greeting—and a reproach for my infidelity." Margit was supposed to follow with Peter, but did not, and the marriage broke up. But at last Háy had found his vocation: "For me, then, there was no longer a shadow of a doubt. I had found my one proper job in life: I *had* to write plays. Nor was I lacking in the conviction that I *could* write plays. As to *why* I wanted to write plays, I was also quite clear about that: to

change the existing social order." Suddenly full of ideas, Háy wrote three plays in quick succession and began sending them off to publishing houses, receiving two or three rejections a week. In the autumn of 1931 all three were accepted by Fischer Verlag, and within two weeks one of them, *Das neue Paradies* (The New Paradise), a comedy of nineteenth-century American socialists trying unsuccessfully to create a Utopia, was in the repertoire of Max Reinhardt's Deutsches Theater in Berlin.

In Berlin Háy met Brecht, but was hostile to his notion of "alienation" in the theatre, seeing this as a rejection of the dramatic element, of first-hand experience, of the "shattering moment" when the actor is transformed into the character he is playing. Háy's own drama grows out of the realist tradition, though his realism is tempered with irony. Martin Esslin, introducing one of his later plays in English, wrote: "Háy shows himself a master of the scrupulously constructed, brilliantly carpentered 'well-made play'. He is a consummate craftsman in the manner of Ibsen, Hauptmann and Shaw."

Many of Háy's plays are historical dramas. *Gott, Kaiser und Bauer* (God, Emperor and Peasant, 1932; Hungarian title *Isten, cszászár, paraszt*) centers on the fifteenth-century confrontation between the Holy Roman Emperor Sigismund and the Czech religious reformer and national leader Jan Hus. Based on careful historical research, it deals with the Council of Konstanz, called on the insistence of Sigismund to heal the shameful schism in the Church which had produced three rival popes. Hus was promised safe conduct by the Emperor, though his sentence had been decided even before the hearings took place, and he was burnt at the stake for refusing to recant opinions he had never held. This treachery precipitated the Hussite wars. The play dramatizes the conflicts in Sigismund's mind as he sends Hus to the stake against his own wishes—powerless, even though an emperor, to save him.

Lavishly produced at Max Reinhardt's Deutsches Theater in December 1932, the play was seen to be not a remote historical exercise but intensely relevant to the contemporary situation —the collapse of the Weimar Republic and the rise of Hitler. Performances began to be disrupted by Nazi rowdies, and an unsigned article in the official evening paper of the Nazi Party, rumored to have been written by Goebbels himself, condemned the play as "an attempt to misrepresent the primal origins of the history of the German people" and described Háy as "an expert at robbing people of illusions." *Gott, Kaiser und Bauer* has come to be regarded as perhaps the best of all the author's dramatic works. Other plays written during this period, though they were not performed till later, include *Der Damm an der Theiss* (The Dam on the Tisza, 1933), a gentle tragedy in which Háy first dealt with a theme central to all his work: the interrelationship of men and the earth. *Der Barbar* (The Barbarian, 1934; Hungarian title *A barbár*), is a short play on the third Roman war against King Mithridates of Pontus, in which that masterful genius is finally defeated by the ruthless professional Pompey.

Some poems by Háy were set to music and sung at Communist gatherings in Berlin by Brecht's wife, Helene Weigel. He also worked with an Agitprop troupe that performed songs and sketches in beer gardens and at election meetings, which were frequent during the death throes of the Weimar Republic. It was with a girl he met in this troupe, Micky, that he left Germany as Hitler rose to power in 1933. They went first to Prague, and then, like many other German refugees, to Vienna. There unmarried couples were not allowed by the police to occupy the same lodging, and Háy and Micky found themselves living apart in a series of temporary rooms (one of them belonging to a young Cambridge undergraduate named Kim Philby, who was then being recruited for his future role as a master spy).

In the dangerous climate of an Austria threatened with takeover by Hitler, Háy continued his political work, editing the duplicated newspaper *Red Banner Over Floridsdorf,* named after the working-class district of Vienna which was to become the scene of the major fighting in the brief civil war of February 1934. Háy was imprisoned for several months, but in late July was released and given a week to leave the country. He says that the most important part of his luggage "took up no more room than my trouser pocket. This was a number of sheets of lavatory paper written closely in pencil—the beginning of the play I had been working on during my last few weeks in prison." This new play, which took two more years to complete, was *Haben* (1936, translated by Peter Háy as *Have;* Hungarian title *Tiszazug*). It is based on actual events in Hungary in the 1920s, at the time of the great land hunger under Horthy's fascist regime, when young peasant wives in the village of Tisza murdered their husbands in a wave of mass hysteria.

Haben was highly praised by Lion Feuchtwanger in a long article. This called forth a rejoinder by Brecht, who pointed out that this was not a Marxist play, as Feuchtwanger assumed, "because a play that describes the greed for property or the spiritual deformations that lie at the origins of property falls short of being Marxist. . . . The Marxist is very much less interested in the fact that somewhere some women get hold of a few farms by marrying and then murdering their owners than in the way in which farms the world over are managed and run." *Haben* had to wait for performance until after the war, when the Hungarian version was produced at the National Theatre in Budapest in 1945; after that it was staged in many Hungarian and German theatres. It has also been widely performed elsewhere, including twice in England.

When he left Vienna Háy went to Zurich. Arthur Koestler, who became his friend during this brief Swiss interlude in 1935, describes him then as "a dark, easy-going young man. He was a Communist by philosophy, but took no interest in politics, paid his party dues as one pays income-tax, and lived entirely for his plays . . . an exile, wandering through Europe with a suitcase full of unperformed plays which represented his capital and his future." At this time, in a double ceremony shared with Arthur Koestler and his bride, Háy married Micky, who was expecting a child—to be called Andrea. The new family's financial situation was precarious, and they depended on what little Háy could earn as a freelance writer, though a Zürich publisher did bring out *Gott, Kaiser und Bauer* in book form. Publication of a Russian translation of the play had been arranged by Lunacharsky, the Russian Minister of Culture, who had seen it in Berlin and had invited Háy to visit the Soviet Union. Lunacharsky died shortly afterwards, but in 1935 the invitation was renewed, and Háy, living in crisis, poverty, and unemployment in a Europe threatened by fascism and war, eagerly accepted.

In Russia, all plans to put his plays into production gradually passed into oblivion. He was commissioned to write a feature film about the German Volga Republic, to be directed by Erwin Piscator, but the film never got made. Nor did a proposed screen version of Háy's play *Haben,* since the great director Eisenstein had to drop this in order to make *Ivan the Terrible.* Háy nevertheless continued to write plays, though with little hope of production. *Der Putenhirt* (The Turkey-Boy, 1938) is a tragicomedy set on the Hungarian plain, while *Gerichtstag* (Day of Reckoning, 1944) is a working-class tragedy set in late Nazi Germany after Stalingrad. Though it "immediately met with Comrade Walter Ulbricht's unqualified disapproval," it was the first play of Háy's to be seen in Germany after the fall of Hitler. The first performance was in the Deutsches Theater in Berlin—the very stage from which *Gott, Kaiser und Bauer* had been driven thirteen years before.

During the last year of the war Háy worked as one of the staff of three of the Hungarian-language "Radio Kossuth," the others being two future leaders of Hungary, Mátyás Rákosi and Imre Nagy. On April 12, 1945 Háy at last left Russia and returned to his homeland and the surviving members of his family. His, he wrote, was "one of the families that had got off fairly lightly"—three dead in Auschwitz or Belsen, and Háy's younger brother Kari seriously ill as a result of his experiences in the death-camp at Bor. Háy was also reunited with the now grown son of his first marriage, Peter, who was about to be ordained as a priest: "The Benedictines had saved Peter and his mother from Auschwitz; they had his loyalty." Háy's marriage to his German wife Micky, who did not speak Hungarian, had been breaking up ever since the victory at Stalingrad had made his return home more likely, and he now took a third wife, Eva.

Háy became a professor at the Academy of Theatrical Art in Budapest. With other writers who had been living in exile, he played an important part in the cultural and political debates of the following years. In the plays he wrote during the Stalinist years immediately after the war, he tended to toe the line of "socialist realism." Thus *Az élet hídja* (1950, translated by Heinz Bernard as *The Bridge of Life;* in German *Die Brücke des Lebens*) shows how workers of superhuman courage and virtue triumph over vile bourgeois intriguers to rebuild the Kossuth Bridge over the Danube during the winter of 1945-1946. In 1951 the play was awarded the highest distinction in Hungarian literature, the Kossuth Prize. The award was announced to Háy by the ruthless director of cultural affairs, József Révai, with the comment: "Now you've written something really smarmy—I can finally give you the Kossuth Prize." The play was shortly afterwards staged in Dresden and at the Unity Theatre in London. But in Berlin, Háy's director and friend Langhoff "took the opportunity of doing the best thing a true friend could have done" by saying that it was a weak play which he did not wish to produce, instead giving the much earlier but still unperformed *Der Putenhirt* (The Turkey-Boy) its first production.

During the thaw following Stalin's death Háy had the courage to face his own record as well as that of Stalinist communism as a whole. This led to a bitter awakening and a search for a new authenticity, reflected in the play *Varró Gáspár igazsága* (Gáspár Varró's Truth, 1955; German title *Gáspár Varrós Recht*). This is a study of a Hungarian village under socialism, centering on the clash that comes when the stubborn honesty of an old swineherd working on a collective farm conflicts with the "higher interests" of the party bureaucrats. One of Gáspár's supporters declares that "those who are trying to protect the state from the truth do not believe in the truth of our social order." This was written during the liberal climate of Imre Nagy's first brief period as prime minister—the author was even able to occupy an office in the Ministry of Justice while he consulted trial records which he needed to make his play authentic. With Nagy's first fall from power the play was promptly banned, even though it had already been printed and was in rehearsal at the National Theatre.

This was in 1955, when Hungarian life was in turmoil; and it was the disillusioned communist writers who created the ferment that led to the 1956 revolution, the Writer's Union providing the main arena of political activity. Háy became very popular and influential as a publicist, a key figure second only to Tibor Déry. The most quoted of the polemical pieces Háy wrote in 1956 was "Why Don't I Like Comrade Kucsera?", published in *Irodalmi Ujság* (Literary Journal) on October 6, 1956. The fictitious Kucsera represented the archetypal party bureaucrat, the wielder of power and exploiter of society: "Kucsera is the great mistake of our history. . . . Kucsera is the know-nothing by conviction and passion who looks down on us from the pedestal of his ignorance. . . . There is no room in history for both Kucsera and us. We have to choose: either Kucsera or humanity. In Kucsera's eyes a lie is not a lie, murder not murder, law not law, and man not human."

According to Noel Barber, this article made Háy "the idol of Hungarian youth." As Arthur Koestler observed: "Literally overnight 'Comrade Kucsera' became a household word like Scrooge or Tartuffe, a national symbol for the little Neros who ruled the country." When the demonstrating masses filled the streets of Budapest in October many of the banners read "Down with the Kucseras!" And as the revolution was crushed by tanks in November, the last voices to be heard over the radio in the Parliament building were those of Gyula Háy and his wife Eva in what Koestler describes as "a touchingly quixotic appeal": "To all writers of the world, to all scientists, academics and leaders of cultural life: Help us! Time is short! . . . Help the Hungarian people! . . . Help! Help! Help!" A few weeks later, during the night of January 19–20, 1957, Háy was arrested. He was sentenced to six years imprisonment, and served three of them before he was released in the amnesty of April 1960. A few years later, he was allowed to leave the country. He went into exile once more, living in Switzerland until his death.

In prison Háy had continued to write, and he emerged with "a sack full of books and papers," among them a play called *Mohács*. Mohács is a small market town on the Danube in the extreme south of Hungary. It commands the southern approaches to both the Hungarian Plain and Transdanubia, where in 1326 the Turkish forces shattered the Hungarian army, bringing the country under the Ottoman yoke for a hundred and fifty years. The play recalls the historical situation which led to this terrible defeat, another occasion when "the West looked on without lifting a finger." The youthful hero King Lajos may be seen as another Imre Nagy, doomed to failure despite his courage, since both internal and international forces are ranged against him.

This is usually considered Háy's best historical drama since *Gott, Kaiser und Bauer*. It was published in a collection called *Királydrámak* (Royal Dramas, 1964), along with other historical plays, including *A ló* (completed 1961, produced 1964, translated as *The Horse;* German title *Das Pferd*). This is a rollicking comedy that satirizes the "cult of personality" by going back to Roman history, when the emperor Caligula raised his horse to the office of consul. It was translated into English by Peter Háy (Eva's son by an earlier marriage), and staged in England at Oxford in 1965. *Attila éjszakái* (Attila's Nights, 1964; German title *Attilas Nächte*), also published in *Királydrámak,* is a loosely constructed tragedy on the "scourge of God," Attila the Hun, whom Háy portrays as a much more humane and intelligent figure than he is in most Western accounts. In the play, Attila's love for a young princess brings about not only his own death but the dissolution of the Hun empire. The first act appears in English translation in *Tri-Quarterly* (Spring 1967).

Háy wrote two plays in his Swiss exile in which he directly confronted Hungary's recent past and the human predicament in totalitarian countries, *Appassionata* (1965) and *Der Grossinquisitor* (The Grand Inquisitor, 1967; Hungarian title *A főinkvizitor*). But his most important reckoning with the past was his autobiography *Geboren 1900* (1971, translated and abridged by J. A. Underwood as *Born 1900*). This sums up his whole experience as a quixotic idealist living in a world of harsh political realities, the saga of his exiles, of his shattering experiences in Stalin's Russia, and the triumphant climax of his life's drama as he metaphorically mans the barricades in the Hungarian revolution, ending in 1960 with his joyful reunion with his wife as he emerges from the last of his prisons. Paul Ignotus sums it up by saying "the completion of this work strikes one as the completion of Háy's life, a drama crowning all those he wrote and acted in, the final drama in which the dramatist faces, last of all, himself. It is a compelling and moving testimony." Arthur Koestler considers Háy "one of the outstanding dramatists of our time" and, hoping that the long overdue translations of at least his major historical dramas will be published soon, predicts "that they will have an impact similar to the belated discovery by the West of Bertolt Brecht—Julius Háy's only rival of comparable stature among playwrights of the European left."

PRINCIPAL PUBLISHED WORKS IN ENGLISH TRANSLATION: Have, 1969; Born 1900, 1974; Attila's Nights (first act only) *in* Tri-Quarterly Spring 1967; The Horse *in* Three East European Plays, 1970.

ABOUT: Barber, N. Seven Days of Freedom: The Hungarian Uprising 1956, 1974; Crowell's Handbook of Contemporary Drama, 1971; Háy, G. Born 1900, 1974; Ignotus, P. Hungary, 1971; Koestler, A. The Invisible Writing, 1953; Matlaw, M. Modern World Drama, 1972; Penguin Companion to Literature 2, 1969. *Periodicals*—Horizon Winter 1975; Times (London) May 9, 1975; Times Literary Supplement November 15, 1974.

HAYDEN, ROBERT (EARL) (August 4, 1913–), black American poet, was born in Detroit, Michigan, and grew up there on St. Antoine Street. He was raised by foster parents—poor people who, he says, worked hard for a living and worked even harder so that he could have the education they lacked. His interest in reading came from his natural mother, who lived in Buffalo and sometimes sent him books. He learned to read at home before he started public school, and wrote his first poems and stories while in grade school. Hayden's sight has always been poor, and in high school he was placed in a sight conservation class where his teachers introduced him to books that made a profound impression on him, among them George Eliot's *Romola* and Hawthorne's *The Marble Faun*—books that "[took me] completely out of the environment I lived in."

After high school there was a period when Hayden, lacking money for college, did various odd jobs but spent most of his time reading and "trying to be a poet." Haunting the public library, he discovered Carl Sandburg and Edna St. Vincent Millay and (through Alain Locke's anthology *The New Negro*) the poets of the Harlem Renaissance: "Countee Cullen ... I read with almost bated breath." By this time Hayden knew that he wanted to be a poet himself,

Timothy D. Franklin

ROBERT HAYDEN

though he was for many years unsure of his talent. Eventually he was able to enroll at Detroit City College, now Wayne State University, where he majored in Spanish.

In 1938, after graduating, Hayden joined the Federal Writers' Project and for two years was in charge of research into black history and folklore in the Detroit area, at the same time doing some part-time work for the black weekly *The Michigan Chronicle*. Louie Martin, editor of the paper, became interested in Hayden's poetry, and in 1940 he established the Falcon Press to publish *Heart-Shape in the Dust*. Hayden himself says that this first collection "was the work of a young poet, and there are echoes of other poets in it. It was full of . . . protest poems, and it was full of poems that were primarily concerned with racial themes. It did quite well."

In fact, though *Heart-Shape in the Dust* clearly reflects the influence of the poets of the Harlem Renaissance, it established Hayden's promise at once, and is now a collector's piece. Its contents range from "Diana," a savage attack on "Southern mythology" in which a white woman's "venereal virginity" costs a black man his life, to Hayden's obituary for his father, which embodies a deeply religious strain that appears often in his work. "Speech" pleads for white workers and black to put aside racial animosities and to recognize that the real enemy of both is exploitative capitalism. The hero of "Bacchanale," one of the many dialect poems in Hayden's early work, announces that he is "gonna git high" because, though he has lost his job and his girl, "there's gotta be joy somewhere/ for a po' colored boy." It is in its way as much a celebration of black courage and endurance as

"Gabriel," a very moving short poem in question and answer form about the last minutes of Gabriel Prosser, who planned a slave insurrection near Richmond, Virginia, in 1800. A.P. Davis wrote that Hayden "crystallizes the heroic defiance and the prophetic implications of Black Gabriel's action . . . and captures in an image the whole thrust of the poem":

> Gabriel hangs
> Black-gold in the sun,
> Flame-head of
> Rebellion.

In 1940, the year that his first book appeared, Hayden was married to his wife Erma, then a teacher in the Detroit public school system. At about this time Hayden left the Federal Writers' Project and in 1941, after a brief stint with the Historical Record Survey, began graduate work at the University of Michigan, Ann Arbor, studying creative writing and play production. One of his courses, on the analysis of poetry, was taught by W.H. Auden. "That was a marvelous experience," Hayden says. "[Auden] . . . would never have won any prizes for pedagogy. But somehow or other he stimulated us to learn more about poetry and even to search ourselves." Auden helped Hayden to get a job in the university library and they never entirely lost touch with each other. In 1941 and again the following year, Hayden received the university's Avery Hopwood Poetry Award. He gained his M.A. in 1944 and stayed on at Michigan with a teaching fellowship for a further two years.

Hayden left the North in 1946 to take up a post as assistant professor of English at Fisk University in Nashville, Tennessee. He and his wife had never encountered legal segregation before and their unhappiness was compounded by the provincialism they found in the South and the absence of a congenial culture. For a time Erma Hayden and their daughter lived in New York so that the girl could attend a progressive school there. Mrs. Hayden, who was interested in working with a modern dance group as an accompanist, studied piano at the Juilliard School. Eventually the Haydens decided that being a divided family was even less desirable than segregated schooling for their daughter, and they were reunited in Nashville. Disagreeable as all this was, jobs were hard to come by, and Hayden taught at Fisk for twenty-two years, becoming an associate professor and, just before he left, a full professor of English. He says: "I taught eighteenth-century literatures and I taught creative writing and I taught Afro-American literatures and I taught all sorts of things. I was advisor to the student publication, *The Herald*. I worked rather closely with young people who were writing and . . . later on I worked with the Fisk newspaper, *The Fawn*."

Just after World War II Hayden and some of his students at Fisk founded the Counterpoise Press. He says: "We wanted to do something to encourage creative writing at Fisk, and we also wanted to encourage Afro-American writers in general. Again, we wanted to get away from the blatantly propagandistic, and we wanted to get away from the out-and-out protest poem, and we were trying in a sense to make an opportunity for ourselves." The first of the three or four pamphlets published in the Counterpoise series was *The Lion and the Archer* (1948), containing poems by Hayden and Myron O'Higgins. It showed that Hayden had moved away from the colloquial and dialect poems of his first collection towards a "denser, more baroque styling" and a more symbolic and metaphysical mode. "I did write about the South, and I did write my reactions to it," he says. "But I guess I wanted to approach those things as an artist and not as a propagandist." *Figures of Time* followed in 1955, also in the Counterpoise series, though printed by a small press in Nashville. It includes some poems written in Mexico on a Ford Foundation grant in 1954–1955.

Julius Lester, a student of Hayden's at Fisk, has described Hayden's "pain and loneliness" in "that miasma of black bourgeois gentility," where no one "had the vaguest notion of what a poet's function was, not that they gave it any thought. Yet, somehow, Hayden continued to believe—in himself and poetry—though no one except his wife and a few students and friends in New York ever cared." It was through the missionary efforts of one of Hayden's friends that his important collection *A Ballad of Remembrance* was published in 1962—not in the United States but in England. It is notable in particular for two long and very powerful poems, "Middle Passage" and "Runagate Runagate," which are recognized to be among Hayden's finest achievements.

"Middle Passage" evokes the horrors of the slave ships—the terrible "voyage through death/ to life upon these shores." It draws with profoundly ironic effect upon contemporary accounts written by the slavers themselves, including an outraged survivor of the *Amistad* mutiny, who describes the slaughter of their captors by "murderous Africans." "Runagate Runagate" is a narrative of escape from slavery along the "underground railroad," skillfully interwoven with snatches of spirituals and passages from contemporary documents. There was particular admiration for the way in which the rhythms in the first section match the desperate plunging flight of the fugitive:

Runs falls rises stumbles on from darkness into
  darkness
and the darkness thicketed with shapes of terror
and the hunters pursuing and the hounds pursuing
and the night cold and the night long and the river
to cross and the jack-muh-lanterns beckoning
  beckoning
and blackness ahead and when shall I reach that
  somewhere
morning and keep on going and never turn back
  and keep on
going. . . .

North star and bonanza gold
I'm bound for the freedom, freedom-bound
and oh Susyanna don't you cry for me

A.P. Davis has remarked that "in very few poets is the change of tone so pronounced as in the Robert Hayden of *A Ballad of Remembrance* when compared with the Robert E. Hayden of *Heart-Shape in the Dust*. The latter shows a young novice poet following, perhaps too closely, models from the New Negro Renaissance. The Hayden of *A Ballad of Remembrance* shows a mature craftsman making use of the diction, the forms, and, unfortunately, some of the obscurity of contemporary verse making." Unlike other black poets of his generation, Davis went on, Hayden had not adopted a "militant, nationalist, anti-Western-tradition stance," but had elevated his ethnic concerns to a higher plane: "He no longer writes old-fashioned protest poems. On the contrary, he plays down the parochial and limiting elements in a given racial situation or incident and, by removing the racial emphasis, he raises the human interest involved."

In the 1960s, when Black Power broke upon the American scene, Hayden had to pay for his eschewal of racial militancy. At a writers' conference held at Fisk in the spring of 1966 he was bitterly attacked as an "Uncle Tom" by the students and by other black writers. It is ironic that the same year *A Ballad of Remembrance* brought him the Grand Prize for Poetry at the First World Festival of Negro Arts in Dakar, Senegal. Julius Lester, who visited Hayden at about this time, says that this honor was not enough to offset his rejection by his own students on his own campus. "When I walked into his house, his first words to me were a tirade against 'the nationalists'. . . . He had always insisted on being known as a poet, not a black poet, and he could be belligerent about it. I listened to him again as he angrily maintained that there was "no such thing as black literature. There's good literature and there's bad. And that's all!"

Some critics evidently agreed, as they showed by their reception for Hayden's *Selected Poems,* which also appeared in 1966. *Choice's* reviewer wrote: "Almost unnoticed, outshouted by more strident poets," Hayden has remained "true always to a quiet, loving and shrewd insight into the world and its inhabitants. *Selected Poems* reveals the surest poetic talent of any Negro poet in America; more importantly it demonstrates a major talent and poetic coming-of-age without regard to race or creed. ... He writes with a stripped down and precise lyricism that lingers in the mind and echoes. A major book of poetry." Another critic made the interesting suggestion that this collection, and Hayden's work as a whole, is dominated by "the tension between dream and reality," which are reflected in the "juxtaposition of more 'refined' Latinate words with the blunter Anglo-Saxon," as in this passage from "Veracruz";

> Here only the sea is real—
> the barbarous multifoliate sea
> with its rustling of leaves
> fire, garments, wind;
> its clashing of phantasmal jewels,
> in lunar thunder,
> animal and human sighing.

Selected Poems was the first book of Hayden's poems commercially published in the United States since *Heart-Shape in the Dust* nearly twenty years earlier. Three more followed during the next five years. *Words in the Mourning Time* (1970) is more contemporary in its concerns than earlier collections, including poems in which, as Hayden's publisher notes, he writes "of King, of Kennedy, of war, riot, hope, despair." Jerome Cushman noted that "the romanticism in Hayden's poetry does not interfere with its toughness of spirit and clarity of vision. His is a sharp, wry wit." The title poem includes Hayden's refusal to accept "evil as deliverance from evil"—his insistence that we must

> Reclaim now, now renew the vision of
> a human world where godliness
> is possible and man
> is neither gook nigger honkey wop nor kike
> but man
> permitted to be man.

The Night-Blooming Cereus followed in 1972 and then *Angle of Ascent: New and Selected Poems* (1975), the most admired of Hayden's books

to date. Michael S. Harper wrote: "Hayden has always been a symbolist poet struggling with historical fact, his rigorous portraits of people and places providing the synaptic leap into the interior landscape of the soul, where prayer for illumination and perfection are focused on the oneness of mankind. Having committed himself to the improvement of language, he has sometimes been falsely accused of timidity of commitment to the black struggle because of his refusal to 'politicize' his work for expedient and transient goals. But it is Hayden's poetry that best captures the Afro-American tradition of the black hero, from the slave narratives and testimonials of Douglass, Harriet Tubman, Sojourner Truth, to musicians and jazz singers such as Bessie Smith, Billie Holliday, Miles Davis. Hayden is the master conversationalist and handler of idiom; his perfect pitch is always pointed toward heroic action and his central images are almost always an embracing of kin. He has never abandoned his people. ... His search for kinfolk is the permanent condition of his poetry and his personality." And Harper quotes by way of example this passage from " 'Mystery Boy' Looks for Kin in Nashville":

> And when he gets to where the voices were—
> Don't cry, his dollbaby wife implores:
> I know where they are, don't cry.
> We'll go and find them, we'll go
> and ask them for your name again.

Hayden finally left Fisk at the end of 1968 and went back North to the University of Michigan, where he has taught ever since. He has served as a visiting professor at the universities of Washington (Seattle) and Connecticut, and at Denison University. In 1971 he was described as "one of the most underrated and unrecognized poets in America." In 1975, however, he was elected a Fellow of the Academy of American Poets, and in 1976 he took a leave of absence from the University of Michigan to serve as poetry consultant to the Library of Congress—the first Afro-American so honored.

Raised as a Baptist, Hayden became a member of the Baha'i faith in 1941. He serves as poetry editor of *World Order,* the Baha'i magazine, and his convictions are evident in many of his own poems. Hayden says: "I believe in the essential oneness of all people and I believe in the basic unity of all religions. I don't believe that races are important; I think that people are important. ... These are all Baha'i points of view, and my work grows out of this vision." According to John O'Brien, Hayden's "contagious energy seems to mark everything that he does, though he admits that he is forever behind in his work. He is warm, comic, and very articulate."

PRINCIPAL WORKS: Heart-Shape in the Dust, 1940; (with Myron O'Higgins) The Lion and the Archer, 1948; Figure of Time, 1955; A Ballad of Remembrance, 1962; Selected Poems, 1966; Words in the Mourning Time, 1970; The Night-Blooming Cereus, 1972; Angle of Ascent, 1975. *As Editor*—Kaleidoscope: Poems by American Negro Poets, 1967; (with D.J. Burrows and F.R. Lapides) Afro-American Literature: An Introduction, 1971; (with J. Phillips and L. Carter) How I Write 1, 1972.

ABOUT: Brown, S.A. and Davis, A.P. The Negro Caravan, 1969; Davis, A.P. From the Dark Tower, 1974; Gibson, D.B. (ed.) Modern Black Poets, 1973; Malkoff, K. Crowell's Handbook of Contemporary American Poetry, 1973; O'Brien, J. (ed.) Interviews With Black Writers, 1973; Phillips, J., Carter, L., and Hayden, R. (eds.) How I Write 1, 1972; Vinson, J. (ed.) Contemporary Poets, 1975; Who's Who in America, 1976–1977; Young, J.O. Black Writers of the Thirties, 1973. *Periodicals*—America February 7, 1975; Choice May 1967; Ebony January 1978; Library Journal January 15, 1968; March 1, 1971; Midwest Quarterly Spring 1974; Negro History Bulletin October 1957; New York Times Book Review November 5, 1967; January 17, 1971; January 24, 1971; February 22, 1976; Poetry July 1967, July 1977; Saturday Review February 11, 1967; May 11, 1968; April 3, 1971.

Horst

SHIRLEY HAZZARD

HAZZARD, SHIRLEY (January 30, 1931–), Australian-born novelist and short story writer, was born in Sydney, the daughter of Reginald Hazzard, a government official, and the former Catherine Stein. Educated at the Queenwood School in Sydney, she accompanied her parents shortly after World War II to Hong Kong, where her father had been assigned, and started work there in the offices of the British Combined Services Intelligence (1947-1948). From that post she went in 1949 to join the staff of the British High Commissioner in Wellington, New Zealand, and in 1951 she became a technical assistant for underdeveloped countries with the United Nations in New York. She was sent on a year's assignment to Italy in 1957—an experience that has been extremely important in her life and in her work—but except for this remained at U.N. Headquarters until 1962.

Several short stories drawing on the people and places she had encountered on her travels appeared in the *New Yorker* in the early 1960s. Encouraged by their warm reception, she resigned in 1962 from her increasingly frustrating post at the United Nations and has been a full-time writer ever since. Her first collection of short stories appeared in 1963 as *Cliffs of Fall.* These ten stories, all of them involving relationships between men and women, and most of them portraits of women unhappily in love, are set variously in Europe and New York.

Stanley Kauffmann wrote scornfully that the author "plunges bravely up to her ankles in all the little currents of domestic crisis that are the native waters of the sensitive school: marital trouble, estrangement, affairs, non-affairs. In the hands of masters . . . these materials can reveal some of the drama still possible in sophisticated life. In lesser hands this kind of writing becomes only a dainty feminine accomplishment, the contemporary equivalent of strumming the spinet or decorating teacups. The net result of Miss Hazzard's book is not to move us, only to demonstrate that she is well-bred." But reviewers less hostile to "the sensitive school" responded very differently. D. M. Wolfe, for example, though he thought the author's talent "unextended," wrote that her "art is rich and glowing in stylistic resources. . . . Her most original stylistic gift is for the deft characterizing abstraction." And Brigid Brophy wrote that "Miss Hazzard is an outstandingly gifted, expert writer, who knows the precisely most economical point at which to make the incision into her highly interesting situations."

The Evening of the Holiday, Shirley Hazzard's short first novel, followed in 1966. Sophie, an English spinster in her thirties, visits Italy and meets Tancredi, an attractive middle-aged architect estranged from his wife. Almost automatically, he sets out to seduce her; eventually, rather wearily, she succumbs. And then, to their astonishment, they find themselves deeply and passionately in love—a brief idyll which ends by mutual consent. *Time*'s reviewer called this a "near-perfect first novel," in which Shirley Hazzard had proved "that she writes like no one except herself. And she proves it by choosing a worn theme that a single sentimental slip could have transformed into a ladies'-magazine romance"—this "unlikely material" yields "a small masterpiece. . . . because her prose is so understated that it forces the reader to become uncommonly attentive." Most reviewers agreed, Laurence LaFore writing that "for readers battered by the explicit, Miss Hazzard's allusions and inferences come not merely as a relief but as a sort of literary triumph. . . . Rarely is emotional power so finely mingled with a writer's perception of meaning and of means."

Eight short stories about life in the lower echelons of the United Nations bureaucracy, first published in the *New Yorker,* were collected as *People in Glass Houses: Portraits From Organization Life* (1967). John Colmer wrote in *Contemporary Novelists* that each of these stories could be read as a separate study, "but because similar characters recur and a single controlling vision illuminates each, they cohere into an amusing but highly serious work of fiction. Two related paradoxes bring the portraits into a single focus. The first is that the attempt to bring new life to the peoples of the underdeveloped countries often destroys not only them but the bureaucrats and technologists themselves, who become the maimed and inhuman servants of a great impersonal machine. The second is that language and reason, the two great servants of truth and reality, become translated into the instruments of power, self-deception and unreality. . . . What gives *People in Glass Houses* its special power is the author's perception that the debasement of language and the dehumanising of man are but different aspects of a single process. Because the cast of characters is representatively cosmopolitan and because even love affairs are moulded by the great administrative machine, no corner of life is untouched." Frederic Raphael was considerably less pleased with the book, however. He said that Shirley Hazzard's satire was "in the tradition of Evelyn Waugh; it reinforces the comfortable despair of the conservative who believes in the folly of aspiration, in the irremediable frailty of man. . . . The United Nations is taken by Miss Hazzard to be a conspiracy of longwindedness. She is pitiless in her exposure. . . . For those who want their own inertia justified and their scorn of international cooperation confirmed, here are eight well-turned placebos."

Shirley Hazzard's second novel, like her first, is set in Italy. *The Bay of Noon* (1970) is narrated by an English woman, Jenny Unsworth, who recalls the time, some fifteen years earlier, when she had spent a year in Naples as a NATO translator. Seeking to escape from an implicitly incestuous relationship with her brother and his wife, she had found herself caught up instead as a

puzzled observer in the moribund affair between Giaconda, a beautiful novelist, and a married film producer, Gianni; when Giaconda finally decided to leave Gianni, it had been Jenny's boyfriend that she ran off with. This betrayal, the time she spends with Gianni in mutual consolation, and above all the city itself, here richly evoked, bring Jenny literally "to her senses," and to the end of innocence. "The language of the novel is elegant and controlled," wrote Elizabeth Dalton, "with a Jamesian tendency to hesitation and qualification in syntax and refinement of diction. . . . the distortion of memory, the search for the true past, is one of its themes. But if Jenny is successful as a voice and style, she is less so as a living character. In action she has a peculiar self-effacing blankness. . . . The novel is like one of the objects that Jenny loves to pick up in the shops and stalls of Naples . . . small, flawed and rather beautiful."

Defeat of an Ideal (1973) is a very different kind of work, an angry "study of the self-destruction of the United Nations," in which the organization's failings, satirized in *People in Glass Houses,* are spelled out in detail. Shirley Hazzard asserts that the United Nations is ineffectual, top-heavy, and controlled by the United States. The Secretariat, she says, discriminates against women, buries its staff in red tape and paperwork, and fails to foster a career-service mentality. The two Secretaries-General under whom she served do not escape her scathing condemnation—Trygve Lie as a bully, a fool, a liar, and a coward; Hammarskjöld for his rudeness and his delusions of sainthood.

The critical response was divided between those who found the book important, idealistic, thought-provoking and splendidly frank, and those who regarded it as little more than hand-wringing inspired by personal bitterness, short of substantive information. Christopher Lehmann-Haupt took a middle position, describing Hazzard's attack as a "tumultuous lover's quarrel" stemming more from concern than enmity. "Her polemic," he wrote, "bitter as it seems, is . . . about the most interesting, encouraging, and hopeful thing to be said about the United Nations in a dozen years or so."

The author was married in 1963 to the writer Francis Steegmuller. They live on New York's East Side, but annually visit Italy, Shirley Hazzard's "adopted home." She has retained her interest in Australian affairs and in 1977 contributed a long account of political, cultural, and economic developments there to the *New Yorker.* She received an award from the National Institute of Arts and Letters in 1966 and a Guggenheim fellowship in 1974.

According to John Colmer, Shirley Hazzard "is essentially an expatriate cosmopolitan writer, deeply rooted in the European literary tradition, much travelled, acutely sensitive to the spirit of place, with a keen eye for national differences, and an acute ear for the words that express and unconsciously betray human values. ... In Shirley Hazzard's fiction, as in the mind of one of her fictional characters, 'poetry and reason meet without the customary signs of struggle'. ... With exquisite delicacy and restraint, she reveals the coexistence of happiness and sorrow in love, the poignancy of misunderstanding and regret, and the consolations of memory. Through the eyes of her very different heroines, all of whom combine intellectual toughness and extreme vulnerability, she presents a world that immediately strikes the reader as both beautiful and true."

PRINCIPAL WORKS: *Fiction*—Cliffs of Fall, and Other Stories, 1963; The Evening of the Holiday, 1966; People in Glass Houses: Portraits From Organization Life, 1967; The Bay of Noon, 1970. *Other*—Defeat of an Ideal: A Study of the Self-Destruction of the United Nations, 1973.

ABOUT: Contemporary Authors 9-12 1st revision, 1974; Geering, R.G. Recent Fiction, 1974; Vinson, J. (ed.) Contemporary Novelists, 1976; Who's Who in America, 1976-1977; Who's Who of American Women, 1975-1976. *Periodicals*—Book World May 3, 1970; Commonweal November 2, 1973; Meanjin December 1970; New Statesman October 25, 1963; New York Times March 25, 1970; March 1, 1973; New York Times Book Review November 10, 1963; January 9, 1966; October 15, 1967; April 5, 1970; New Yorker June 13, 1970; Saturday Review December 28, 1963; Saturday Review of Education April 1973; Time January 14, 1966; Times Literary Supplement October 19, 1967; May 7, 1970; April 20, 1973; Yale Review October 1973.

*HEANEY, SEAMUS (JUSTIN) (April 13, 1939–), Irish poet, was born in the townland of Mossbawn, near Castledawson, County Derry, Northern Ireland, the son of Patrick and Margaret Heaney. He grew up on his father's farm there, stumbling "in his hob-nailed wake" as he ploughed with a team of horses. The eldest of nine children, he was educated at St. Columb's College, Londonderry (1951–1957) and then at Queen's University, Belfast, from which he graduated in 1961 with a first-class honors degree in English. At the university, where he wrote and published his first poems in undergraduate literary magazines, he was a member of the University Gaelic Society and also of a local amateur dramatic society. After a year's training at St. Joseph's College of Education in Belfast, Heaney began his career as a secondary school teacher (1962–1963). In 1963 he returned as a lecturer in English to St. Joseph's College of

*shăm′ us hē′ nē

SEAMUS HEANEY

Nancy Crampton

Education, and in 1966 became a lecturer in English at Queen's University. He taught there until 1972, then for three years was a freelance writer. In 1975 he moved to Eire, where he is head of the English department at Carysfort College, a college of education in Dublin. In 1970–1971 he was guest lecturer in English at the University of California at Berkeley, and he returned there in 1976. Heaney was married in 1965 to Marie Devlin, and has two sons and a daughter. He is a member of the Irish Academy of Letters.

Heaney's first publication was a pamphlet, *Eleven Poems* (1965); the volume *Death of a Naturalist* followed a year later, and attracted immediate and enthusiastic attention. These poems evoke Heaney's rural childhood in Derry, the life of his family there, and the Irish past. Wordsworth grew up "fostered alike by beauty and by fear" and so did Heaney, as Christopher Ricks pointed out: "The beauty he finds in unexpected places—the farm machines glinting in the dark barn, the soft mulch at the bottom of the well." In potatoes:

Flint-white, purple. They lie scattered
like inflated pebbles. Native
to the black hutch of clay
where the halved seed shot and clotted
these knobbed and slit-eyed tubers seem
the petrified hearts of drills. Split
by the spade, they show white as cream.

(from "At a Potato Digging")

The fear was the product of the same intense apprehension of things, as when, in a barn full of sacks of corn, "I lay face-down to shun the fear above./ The two-lugged sacks moved in like

369

great blind rats" ("The Barn"). And in the title poem a schoolboy collecting frogspawn from a flax dam encounters one day a terrible conclave of bullfrogs: "The great slime kings/ Were gathered there for vengeance."

All of the reviewers of these early poems were impressed by the freshness of their phrasing and the fastidious precision with which they caught the look, smell, heft, and feel of things and scenes. Richard Murphy, who says that Heaney began to write poetry under the spell of Gerard Manley Hopkins, observes that he has always been able "to give you the feeling as you read his poems that you are actually doing what they describe. His words not only mean what they say, they sound like their meaning." "Formally simple and conversational, a little clumsy and thick-tongued," these poems were, Robert Fitzgerald thought, "carefully guarded" against the curse of anything so easy as an Irish lilt, indebted more to Joyce than to Yeats. Heaney's work "was and would be incarnational, conceived in an objective and substantial world and embodied in forms respectful of it." But even these mostly personal early poems attempted more than a sensuously exact remembrance of things past. Denis Donoghue (who found some of them marred by youthful overwriting) said that Heaney's poems "are always parables and sometimes revelations." Christopher Ricks wrote: "The deploying of rhymes and half-rhymes, the subtle taking up of hints, the sardonic pitying puns—there can be no doubt about . . . [the poet's] technical fertility, and it gains its reward in a directness, a freedom from all obscurity, which is yet resonant and uncondescending."

Anthony Thwaite had called *Death of a Naturalist* "substantial and impressive," but accused its author of attempting to "hit the required sophistication"; discussing Heaney's second major book, *Door into the Dark* (1969), he found it "impossible to fault the clean language, sensuous delight, concise and modest statements; and I'm sure it's all authentic. But I'm equally sure that the appeal of Heaney's work is of an exotic sort, to people who can't tell wheat from barley, or a gudgeon from a pike." The *Times Literary Supplement* offered a different criticism, complaining that the people in Heaney's poems "are mostly clichés disguised in heroic trappings," but then hastening to add that "nobody in his right mind would deny that Mr. Heaney's is one of the outstanding talents on the scene, or want that talent to settle in its ways too early."

Such bet-hedging criticism apart, there was a general feeling that *Door into the Dark* marked a clear advance over *Death of a Naturalist*—a second step in an important career. Robert Fitz-

gerald found "a shorter line, a more selective eye and ear . . . at work, as for instance to evoke an empty stall and a vanished plow horse" in these lines: "Green froth that lathered each end/ Of the shining bit/ Is a cobweb of grass-dust." And in a poem like "Shoreline," Fitzgerald noted how "the given note more often had a carrying power beyond local matters. . . . Here the visible and audible meeting of land and water all around Ireland, and within Ireland . . . makes a wide scene held long in the mind, long enough to take in images and noises of beachings long ago, echoing finally in Viking and Norman place names. The poet now can work with bare but telling items in prose rhythms quietly spaced and ordered; he commands a style":

> Turning a corner, taking a hill
> In County Down, there's the sea
> Sidling and settling to
> The back of a hedge. Or else
>
> A grey bottom with puddles
> Dead-eyed as fish.
> Haphazard tidal craters march
> The corn and the grazing.
>
> All round Antrim and westward
> Two hundred miles at Moher
> Basalt stands to.
> Both ocean and channel
>
> Froth at the black locks
> On Ireland. . . .
>
> Take any minute. A tide
> Is rummaging in
> At the foot of all fields.
> All cliffs and shingles.
>
> Listen. Is it the Danes,
> A black hawk bent on the sail?
> Or the chinking Normans?
> Or currachs hopping high
>
> On to the sand?
> Strangford, Arklow, Carrickfergus,
> Belmullet and Ventry
> Stay, forgotten like sentries.

In 1969, the year he published *Door into the Dark,* Heaney wrote: "A poet at work is involved in a double process of making and discovery, a process that at the best times is unique, unselfconscious and unpredictable. Every real poem that he makes represents a new encounter with what he knows in himself, and it survives as something at once shed and attained. A poet begins involved with craft, with aspirations that are chiefly concerned with making. He needs a way of saying and there is a first language he can learn from the voices of other poets, dead and alive. To speak of this as apprenticeship is perhaps not completely accurate. It is a mimicry and a posturing that leads to a confidence, a voice of his own that he begins to hear, prompting behind lines he has learned. Once the search to know the voice is over, the next problem is how to use it. Here craft passes into technique, which is the ability to send the voice in pursuit of the self. Technique is dynamic, active, restless, an ever provisional stance of the imagination towards experience. It prospects for secrets and compounds resolutions. It divines and discovers the poet's meaning in and for the world. I began to write poetry in 1963, craft-ridden, but compulsively attracted to those guardians of technique like the water-diviner and the untutored musician, men whose wrists and fingers receive and uncode energies into meanings. To learn their ease and grace in the half-way station between the cellars of the self and the courtyards of the world around them has been and will be my study so long as I continue to write."

The violence that broke out in Northern Ireland in the summer of 1969 filled the courtyards of Heaney's world with suffering and hatred. Thereafter, wrote Anthony Thwaite, as "the grim situation in Mr. Heaney's native Ulster became grimmer, a different kind of poem began appearing above his name in the periodicals— recognisably by the same man, but speaking from the centre of a bitter, and bitterly present, conflict." One such piece appeared as the dedicatory poem in Heaney's third book, *Wintering Out* (1972):

This morning from the dewy motorway
I saw the new camp for the internees:
a bomb had left a crater of fresh clay
in the roadside, and over in the trees

machine-gun posts defined a real stockade. . . .

Is there a life before death?
That chalked up
on a wall downtown.
Competence with pain,
coherent miseries, a bite and sup
we hug our little destiny again.

Thwaite and others wondered why *Wintering Out* contained no more of these "harsh and compassionate new poems," without which the collection "gives the slightly unsatisfactory impression of being a transitional book, skirting round themes he is reluctant to tackle head on." In fact, as Heaney has explained, he wanted to avoid any cheap exploitation of "current events." He concerned himself instead, in a

number of fine, grim poems in *Wintering Out,* with the remote past of Ireland and of man.

In *North* (1975), most critics agreed, Heaney had "pulled all the threads together," finding in the distancing effect of history a way to approach the appalling present. "Here," as a perceptive blurb-writer said, "the Irish experience is refracted through images drawn from different parts of the Northern European experience, and the idea of the north allows the poet to contemplate the violence on his home ground in relation to memories of the Scandinavian and English invasions which have marked Irish history so indelibly." Thus, in "Funeral Rites," even "as news comes in/ of each neighbourly murder," the poet notes how "we pine for ceremony,/ customary rhythms"; he envisages for the newly dead a grand burial in the megalithic tombs at New Grange, and invokes the Icelandic Gunnar, murdered in a blood-feud and still unavenged, but rapt and serene in death.

> . . . When they have put the stone
> back in its mouth
> we will drive north again
> past Strang and Carling fjords
>
> the cud of memory
> allayed for once, arbitration
> of the feud placated,
> imagining those under the hill
>
> disposed like Gunnar
> who lay beautiful
> inside his burial mound,
> though dead by violence
>
> and unavenged.
> Men said he was chanting
> verses about honour
> and that four lights burned
>
> in corners of the chamber:
> which opened then, as he turned
> with a joyful face
> to look at the moon.

It seemed to Robert Fitzgerald "almost startling that the measured progression and elevation of this poem can do nothing for Northern Ireland." Other critics wrote no less admiringly of the cycle of poems in *North* about the Iron Age people whose bodies have been found strangely preserved in the peat bogs of Ireland and Northern Europe, and about the bogs themselves, "a melting grave" in which

> . . . The mothers of autumn
> sour and sink,

ferments of husk and leaf

deepen their ochres.
Mosses come to a head,
heather unseeds,
brackens deposit

their bronze.
This is the vowel of earth
dreaming its root
in flowers and snow,

mutation of weathers
and seasons,
a windfall composing
the floor it rots into.

I grew out of all this
like a weeping willow
inclined to
the appetites of gravity. . . .

(from "Kinship")

Terence Brown writes in *Northern Voices,* his study of Ulster poetry, that "Heaney's sense of landscape combines erotic and religious impulses. . . . So he often writes as if a woman were the landscape, while much of his landscape verse implicitly suggests feminine sexuality and fertility. . . . Irish history too reveals itself in his poetry as a landscape, feminine, protective, preservative, in which man's artifacts and deeds are received in an embracing comprehension." Heaney's imagination is "synthetic and osmotic (in the sense that ideas and intuitions seep across thin membranes to blend with each other)," and the bog poems arise almost organically from the "natural-historical-religio-sexual complex" which is his "central imaginative obsession." Many of the corpses preserved in the bogs were those of people sacrificed to pagan goddesses; Heaney believes that "the fury of Irish Republicanism is associated with a religion like this," and he is able very powerfully to relate the pitiful victims of past and present violence in the name of faith. Brown says that Heaney's "sense of the self and of the poetic imagination is markedly similar to his apprehension of nature and history," and it is interesting that Heaney says of the bog poems that they have "come up like bodies out of the bog of my own imagination." Richard Murphy thinks that "this poetry is seriously attempting to purge our land of a terrible blood-guilt, and inwardly acknowledging our enslavement to a sacrificial myth. I think it may go a long way toward freeing us from the myth by portraying it in its true archaic shape and color, not disguising its brutality."

"These new poems," wrote Anthony Thwaite, "have all the sensuousness of Mr. Heaney's ear-

lier work, but refined and cut back to the bone. They are solid, beautifully wrought, expansively resonant. They recognize tragedy and violence without despairingly allowing themselves to flog human utterance into fragments. . . . This is not only 'mature': it is noble." Martin Dodsworth found the book "unequalled in our contemporary poetry as a testimony to the patience, persistence, and power of the imagination under duress." And Robert Fitzgerald said that, with *North,* "a publicly conducted meditation among the living and the dead," Heaney's "old and new gifts are astringently and powerfully realized. There is no point in avoiding the inevitable comparison. Yeats is hardly a presence in his work . . . but Heaney has heard a spirit music no less distinct than that of his great predecessor."

Heaney received the Eric Gregory Award in 1966, the Cholmondeley Award in 1967, the Faber Memorial Prize and (jointly) the Maugham Award in 1968. The Denis Devlin Memorial Award followed in 1973, and the annual literary award of the American Irish Foundation in 1973–1974. *Door into the Dark* and *North* were choices of the Poetry Book Society and the latter brought Heaney both the W.H. Smith award and the Duff Cooper Memorial Prize. He is almost universally recognized as the foremost in a notable generation of Northern Irish poets that includes Derek Mahon, Michael Longley, and Michael Hartnett. Helen Vendler thinks him "the best poet now writing in Ireland," and Stephen Spender believes that "his is the most striking talent to come out of Ireland since that of the late Patrick Kavanagh." Some critics have gone further, like one in *Poetry* who called him "undoubtedly the most talented younger poet writing in the British Isles," and Martin Seymour-Smith, who thinks Heaney the first "major" figure to have emerged in British poetry since Ted Hughes.

PRINCIPAL WORKS: Eleven Poems, 1965; Death of a Naturalist, 1966; (with Dairo Hammond and Michael Longley) Room to Rhyme, 1968; A Lough Neagh Sequence, 1969; Door into the Dark, 1969; Wintering Out, 1972; The Fire i' the Flint: Reflections on the Poetry of Gerard Manley Hopkins (Chatterton Lecture), 1975; North, 1975. As Editor—(with others) New Poems 1970–1971, 1971; Soundings: An Annual Anthology of New Irish Poetry, 1972; Soundings 2, 1974.

ABOUT: Brown, T. Northern Voices, 1976; Buttel, R. Seamus Heaney, 1975; Dunn, D. (ed.) Two Decades of Irish Writing, 1975; Robson, J. (ed.) Modern Poets in Focus 2, 1971; Thwaite, A. Poetry Today 1960–1973, 1973; Vinson, J. (ed.) Contemporary Poets, 1975; Who's Who, 1978. Periodicals—Commonweal September 25, 1970; Critical Quarterly Spring 1974, Spring 1976; Daily Telegraph February 14, 1976; Encounter September 1966, March 1973, November 1975; Hollins Critic October 4, 1970; Irish Times December 28, 1973; Listener December 7, 1972; November

8, 1973; New Blackfriars March 1973; July-August 1976; New Republic March 27, 1976; New Statesman May 27, 1966; June 27, 1969; February 16, 1973; July 11, 1975; New York Review of Books September 20, 1973; September 30, 1976; New York Times Book Review April 18, 1976; Phoenix January 1971; Poetry November 1970; Southern Review Summer 1969; Times Literary Supplement June 9, 1966; July 17, 1969; March 17, 1972; December 15, 1972; August 20, 1975; Ulster Commentary February 1976.

HEDĀYAT, SĀDIQ. *See* HIDĀYAT, SĀDIK

*HEISSENBÜTTEL, HELMUT (June 21, 1921–), German poet, novelist, radio dramatist, and critic, was born at Rüstringen, near Wilhelmshaven, in North Germany, the son of Hans Heissenbüttel and the former Klara Lorenz. His father was the son of a village carpenter and spent twelve years in the German Navy before taking an office job and becoming a contributor of essays to a local newspaper, Heissenbüttel has attributed some importance to his father's working-class origins and literary interests.

Helmut Heissenbüttel was educated at the Kaiser-Wilhems-gymnasium at Wilhelmshaven, the Realgymnasium at Papenburg, and the Dresden Technische Hochschule. He had to interrupt his education to serve in the German Army, on the Eastern Front, where he was seriously wounded in 1941 losing his left arm. After his discharge from the army Heissenbüttel went to the University of Leipzig and then to the University of Hamburg, studying architecture, the history of art, and German literature—an unusual combination of subjects that points forward to his special preoccupations and practices as a writer. From 1955 to 1957 Heissenbüttel worked in Hamburg as a publisher's reader with Claassen Verlag, and since 1959 he has been chief editor of literary broadcasts with Süddeutscher Rundfunk, the South German radio service, in Stuttgart.

There is a rare consistency in Heissenbüttel's work, partly because his first books did not appear until he was sure of his direction, partly because of the degree of theoretical deliberation that underlies everything he has produced. From the first, he set out to continue the "tradition of the new," linking his practices to those of an earlier avant-garde, especially the Dadaists and Gertrude Stein, but determined to push their linguistic innovations much further by drawing on a great body of new information and speculation about language, including the semantic investigations of Wittgenstein. In his own words, he wanted "to force an entry and become established in a world that still seems to evade language. And the threshold that is

*hīs′ en büt′ el

HELMUT HEISSENBÜTTEL

German Information Service

reached is not that to nothingness, to speechlessness, to chaos (whatever reasons may be invented for the urge to reach such a threshold); it is the threshold to that which is *not yet* sayable."

In his first two books, *Kombinationen* (Combinations, 1954) and *Topographien* (Topographies, 1956), Heissenbüttel's experiments with language are held in check by a certain residue of subjective lyricism—by what Peter Demetz calls "a pensive imagination still concerned with the summer afternoons, little railway stations, and long-forgotten songs of his 'buried childhood,'" as in the poem from *Topographien* called simply "C":

incessantly in the counterflowing streams the same
　faces meet
the loudspeakers talk uninterruptibly
little girls' piano-playing excavates a tunnel through
　the years
the gulls' cry slicing my early dream is still my
　sister
out of the tunnels ascend the illuminated frontal
　planes
woodfiresky of the regions behind
open doors to disconnected railway wagons in the
　November sun
flattened smoke-fields over shunting yards
open-latticed mirror-images in the corrugated iron
　of canals
in this country of canals and bridges
the glistening parallels of the country lying before
　me.

(translated by Christopher Middleton)

But poem "D" begins: "subtract days enumerate annoyances function with precision/ without interest in the interest of the interested/ that less can be achieved with what can be

achieved than when nothing can be achieved."
And step by step and in chronological sequence,
as Demetz says, "the traditional poem, often
represented by echoes of Rilke, breaks apart."
Heissenbüttel's preoccupation, even in these first
books, with abstract spatial relationships on the
one hand—a preoccupation suggesting that of
the architect or engineer—and with purely linguistic and grammatical processes on the other,
lays the foundation for all his subsequent work.
In these early pieces, too, the distinctions between poetry and prose (and indeed between
genres), between one art and another, and between the arts and the sciences, begin to be
called in question.

Heissenbüttel's later works are called "texts"
only. Poetry and prose cease to be distinct
media, and his experiments with words and sentences assume the objectivity of a scientist's experiments. As Peter Demetz has said,
Heissenbüttel is concerned to "combat the rules
of grammar because these imply an ordered
world which has long ceased to exist." For example, he creates word-chains in which (to
quote August Closs) "the words themselves
become autonomous and behave like playful
atoms, turning around themselves. The very
identity of the actual objects becomes illusory,
causality is eliminated and replaced by a pattern
of analogies and associations." Or he may put
whole sentences through various permutations,
as in "Das neue Zeitalter" (The New Age) from
Textbuch V:

when who meets whom and what he says when
  who meets whom and then he says what when
  who calls whom what

when a cold warrior meets a cold warrior and says
  cold warrior when a fellow-traveler meets a
  fellow-traveler and says fellow-traveler when an
  ex-Nazi calls an ex-Nazi an ex-Nazi

when an intellectual calls an intellectual an ex-Nazi
  when an avant-gardist meets an avant-gardist and
  says cold warrior when a non-conformist meets a
  non-conformist and says fellow-traveler. . . .

when he calls him that when he meets him and
  then says that when he meets him and then says
  that

all of them join the Communist Party and live
  happily ever after

(translated by Michael Hamburger)

Again and again, Heissenbüttel has explained
that the function of his work is not so much to
give pleasure—though it usually does—as to reveal the nature and laws of language itself by
pushing it to the limits of the hitherto sayable;
he is pursuing not aesthetic titillation but "radical enlightenment." This enlightenment, it is
true, applies to more than linguistics, since for
all practical purposes language is inseparable
from the uses to which we put it. His work sheds
light on psychological processes, not excluding
subconscious ones, and also on social and political behavior.

Heissenbüttel's various texts in verse and
prose were published in six successive "textbooks" between 1960 and 1967, before being collected into a single volume, *Das Textbuch,* in
1970. In the same year he published what looked
like his nearest approach to a conventional
genre, his long novel *D'Alemberts Ende*
(D'Alembert's End). In fact, its subtitle of "novel" was Heissenbüttel's only concession to the
general reading public, and its reception was as
mixed as that of all this austere writer's works.
Above all, the book incorporated theoretical reflections about language and aesthetics that
made it decidedly an "antinovel," or a novel
perpetually questioning its own procedures and
possibilities. Heissenbüttel's affinity with the
French *nouveau roman* had struck critics even of
his shorter prose pieces in the textbooks, especially those called "quasi-stories." More and
more, he has been interested not in sustaining
fictions for their own sake but in using some of
the conventions of fiction in order to explore the
nature of reality.

It is not surprising that Heissenbüttel has also
excelled as a critic and theorist of the arts, especially of literature, painting, and sculpture. His
work in this field has been collected in the
volumes *Über Literatur* (About Literature,
1966), *Zur Tradition der Moderne* (On the Modern Tradition, 1972), and *Gelegenheitsgedichte
und Klappentexte* (Occasional Poems and
Blurbs, 1973). The occasional poems in the latter show a pervasive sense of fun, as when a
dense wood of words is made up by repeating the
word *Baum* (tree), or a long tendentious title
reminiscent of Peter Weiss is capped by the simple expression of resignation *"achso."* Many of
these poems are addressed to friends—fifty-two
*Marilyn Monroe*s for Richard Lindner, or a collage of musical expressions for Mauricio Kagel.
The "blurbs" are introductions, often in experimental form, to the work of other writers and of
visual artists, whom Heissenbüttel has done
much to help. A reviewer in the *Times Literary
Supplement* found "much wit and wisdom in
Heissenbüttel's aesthetic texts" but thought that
"the true synthesis of aesthetic object and reflection lies in the way in which the texts themselves
embody the very qualities they are analysing in

other media. A sense of formal consciousness is thus transmitted. . . . and, as a result, the occasional becomes the vehicle of something substantial and permanent." The author's correspondence with the literary critic Heinrich Vormweg was published in 1970 as *Briefwechsel über Literatur.*

Heissenbüttel had called *D'Alemberts Ende* "Project No. 1." His "Project No. 2," which followed in 1974, was *Das Durchhauen des Kohlhaupts* (The Splitting of the Cabbage), a volume of "didactic poems" which in fact includes texts originally written as radio plays. Here as elsewhere in his work, genres and media are deliberately confounded, so that they can be transcended in the interests of enlightenment.

Although Heissenbüttel has connections with the "concrete poetry" movement, his practices are unlike those of any other writer in this mode, not only because he has extended his experiments from lyric poetry to narrative fiction and drama, but because his intellectual curiosity and scope set him apart. His seriousness and honesty have won him the respect even of critics basically opposed to the kind of radical innovation in the arts that Heissenbüttel represents; and to which he is dedicated, to the extent of wishing to invent new methods of composition that can be adopted by anyone who has mastered them, much as a new scientific technique is adopted. Yet his work has proved inimitable. Some critics, like Erich von Kahler, have condemned Heissenbüttel's search for generally practicable methods of composition as a dehumanization of art. Others, especially those of the New Left, have attacked him as a "formalist," claiming that his personal commitments are subordinated to his dominant concern with procedures and techniques. In fact, his pursuit of enlightenment is far from being morally or politically neutral, as is clear from such poems as "Das neue Zeitalter." Among other things, he is a satirist and a comic writer of distinction.

Heissenbüttel's particular kind of comedy does not stop short of self-parody, as in his speech on receiving the Büchner Prize:

A speech is a speech.

A speech is a speech is called a speech is a spoken speech that is it must be spoken that is delivered. Only a delivered speech is a speech. An undelivered speech is not a speech but an essay. . . .

At this point I have to interpolate a digression. I really had no idea what I should say here. I knew the occasion for which this speech was to be delivered but the occasion would not turn into

a scheme. The most various points of view the most various advice the most various inquiries were of no avail. The speech I can deliver is a speech about the possible difficulties of a speech. . . .

(translated by Michael Hamburger)

These comic convolutions, too, are not convolutions for the sake of convolutions, but for the sake of truthfulness.

In 1963, Heissenbüttel gave a series of lectures at the University of Frankfurt. He is a member of the Academy of Arts, Berlin, and of the German Academy for Language and Literature, Darmstadt. His work has been widely translated. Heissenbüttel received the Lessing Prize in 1956, the Hugo Jacobi Prize in 1960, and the Büchner Prize in 1969. He was married in 1954 to Ida Warnholz and has two daughters and a son.

PRINCIPAL WORKS IN ENGLISH TRANSLATION: Texts, 1977. Poems and texts *in* Bridgwater, P. (ed.) Penguin Book of Twentieth-Century German Verse, 1963; Hamburger, M. and Middleton, C. (eds.) Modern German Poetry, 1962; Middleton, C. (ed.) German Writing Today, 1967; Dimension 2 1974; Modern Poetry in Translation Spring 1967.

ABOUT: Closs, A. Twentieth Century German Literature, 1969; Demetz, P. Postwar German Literature, 1970; Domin, H. (ed.) Doppelinterpretationen, 1966; Gumpel, L. "Concrete" Poetry From East and West Germany, 1976; Hamburger, M. The Truth of Poetry, 1969; International Who's Who, 1976-77; Mandel, S. Group 47, 1973; Penguin Companion to Literature 2, 1969; Vormweg, H. Die Wörter und die Welt, 1968; Who's Who in Germany, 1972. *Periodicals*—Times Literary Supplement August 17, 1973.

HENNISSART, MARTHA. *See* "LATHEN, EMMA"

HERBERT, FRANK (PATRICK) (October 8, 1920–), American science fiction writer and novelist, was born in Tacoma, Washington, the son of Frank and Eileen (McCarthy) Herbert. Not much information has been published about his early life, except that he attended the University of Washington at Seattle in 1946-1947. Over the next twenty years he worked variously as a professional photographer and television cameraman, radio news commentator, lay analyst, oyster diver, and jungle survival instructor, and more regularly as a newspaper reporter and editor in various West Coast cities, among them Los Angeles, San Francisco, Santa Rosa, and Seattle. In 1956, when he was thirty-six, he published *The Dragon in the Sea,* his first work of science fiction to appear in book form. He says that the genre attracted him because "the luxury of unbridled investigation carries its own ongoing sense of excitement. . . . 'What will I find around the next corner?' "

FRANK HERBERT

The Dragon in the Sea (which has also appeared as *Under Pressure* and *21st Century Sub*) was originally published as a serial in the science fiction magazine *Astounding.* A submarine tug of the fuel-starved future crosses the Atlantic to raid subterranean oil sources in enemy territory, a desperately hazardous assignment which has already caused the loss of a score of other ships. This time, a brilliant psychologist gifted in electronics accompanies the four-member crew in a last-chance effort to detect a possible saboteur among them before disaster strikes again. H. H. Holmes praised "the admirable coherence and plausibility of its technological background," and the way in which it welded "technology to a suspenseful story of espionage and peril." It seemed to Holmes that "if it's less successful in coming to grips with such problems as the place of religion in life and the possible evil of even a just war, at least it's stimulating to see these problems raised in adventure fiction."

This first novel was joint winner in 1956 of the International Fantasy Award and established Herbert as a figure to be reckoned with in modern science fiction. He continued to contribute to the science fiction magazines, with increasing success, and in the 1960s became a full-time freelance writer. All the same, it was not until 1965 that he published his second major novel, the famous *Dune.* On the desert planet Arrakis, life survives only because its inhabitants, the seminomadic Fremen, have developed total ecological awareness, learning how to conserve and recycle every possible trace of moisture, including their own body fluids. The book's hero, Paul Atreides, is forced in his teens to escape into the

desert wastes after his father is killed by rival nobles. Winning acceptance as the Fremen's leader, he overcomes his enemies in battle and creates a vast star empire over which he rules as Muad'Dib, a legendary figure increasingly beset by treachery and conspiracy. Highly successful in terms of sales, *Dune* received the 1965 Nebula Award of the Science Fiction Writers of America as the best novel of the year and in 1966 won the Hugo Award at the World Science Fiction Convention.

Dune Messiah, about the religion that grows up around Muad'Dib, followed in 1969—another huge success which pushed Dune sales to the million-copy mark. The trilogy was completed in 1976 by *Children of Dune,* which deals with the divisive power struggles that follow the death of the great leader, and ranges, as one reviewer noted, "from nitty-gritty palace intrigue and desert chases to religious speculation and confrontations with the supreme intelligence of the universe." Gerald Jonas wrote that this "unlikely combination of old-fashioned space opera, up-to-date ecological concern and breathtakingly ecumenical religiosity" was distinguished from its competitors by "the obsessive quality of Herbert's imagination." He went on: "To read the Dune trilogy is to plunge into someone else's obsession. As in Tolkien's *The Lord of the Rings,* nothing in these books is real, yet everything has a life-or-death importance . . . the reader is held, like Coleridge's Wedding Guest, so that 'he cannot choose but hear,' no matter what his other faculties tell him. On this criterion, I would personally rate the Dune trilogy an unqualified success." Although some critics remained unpersuaded of the epic's literary merit, W.E. McNelly concluded that "its quality may finally convince those who haven't accepted the fact that science fiction can be good."

During the ten years it took him to complete the Dune trilogy, Herbert also wrote and published a number of other and for the most part less remarkable works of science fiction. *The Green Brain,* for example, published in 1966, describes the domination of the earth by a strange mutant life form, while *Destination: Void,* appearing the same year, is a technological and psychological drama set in a spaceship where human minds break down and a computer takes control. *Santaroga Barrier* (1968), like the Dune trilogy, reflects Herbert's passionate interest in ecology. It deals with an isolated valley community whose inhabitants seek to improve their circumstances by controlling both physical and social behavior. Their rejection of material progress and technological innovation in favor of intellectual development solves some problems but creates others, leading to an excessively stable and static society lacking in creativity, personal ambition, and vitality.

The novel *Soul Catcher* (1972) was Herbert's first major venture outside the science fiction field. Its protagonist Charles Hobuhet is an American Indian and anthropologist whose sister is raped and murdered by white men. Transformed by this experience, Hobuhet takes on the role of Katsuk, the incarnation of the spirit of his ancestors, and kidnaps the young son of an important government official to be a ritual sacrifice. "Slowly building tension and creating mood," wrote W. E. McNelly, "Herbert makes his apparently very simple story a crucial search for identity." McNelly found the novel "at once mythopoeic and redemptive," and was reminded of Graham Greene. W. R. Evans agreed that it was on the whole "well written, vital and suspenseful," but thought it "essentially a good long short story that has been drawn out too long."

Frank Herbert has a daughter by his 1941 marriage to Flora Parkinson, which ended in divorce in 1945, and two sons by his second wife, Beverly Ann Stuart, whom he married in 1946. The Herberts live on a six-acre wooded tract in Port Townsend, Washington, where they are conducting an ecological experiment designed to show how life can be maintained at a high level with a minimal energy drain. A recognized expert on ecology, Herbert served in 1971 as a consultant in ecological and related studies to the Lincoln Foundation and to the countries of South Vietnam and Pakistan. He is an active campaigner for the conservation of natural resources, refusing, he says, "to be put in the position of telling my grandchildren: 'Sorry, there's no more world for you. We used it all up.'"

The author was a member of the national World Without War Council in 1970-1973 and since 1972 has served on the board of directors of the Council's Seattle branch. In 1973 he wrote, directed, and filmed a television special, *The Tillers.* Herbert's short stories have appeared in *Collier's, Esquire,* and such science fiction magazines as *Analog* and *Galaxy,* and several collections of them have appeared in book form. He taught at the University of Washington in 1970-1972 and has lectured widely on science fiction and its influence on the future. The first writer to win all three of the major honors offered by the science fiction fraternity—the International Fantasy, Nebula, and Hugo awards—Frank Herbert has enjoyed great and continued success in the field, as the numerous reprints, foreign language editions, and film versions of his books attest.

PRINCIPAL WORKS: *Novels*—The Dragon in the Sea, 1956 (also published as 21st-Century Sub, 1956, and revised as Under Pressure, 1974); Dune, 1965; The Green Brain, 1966; Destination: Void, 1966; The Eyes of Heisenberg, 1966; The Heaven Makers, 1968; Santaroga Barrier, 1968; Dune Messiah, 1969; Whipping Star, 1970; The God Makers, 1972; Soul Catcher, 1972; Project 40, 1973 (also published as Hellstrom's Hive, 1973); Children of Dune, 1976; The Dosadi Experiment, 1977. *Short Stories*—The Worlds of Frank Herbert, 1971; The Book of Frank Herbert, 1973; The Best of Frank Herbert, 1974. *Nonfiction*—(ed.) New World or No World, 1970; Threshold: The Blue Angels Experience (screenplay), 1973.

ABOUT: Aldiss, B. Billion Year Spree, 1974; Allen, L.D. Herbert's Dune and Other Works, 1975; Contemporary Authors 53-56, 1975; Tuck, D.H. (compiler) The Encyclopedia of Science Fiction and Fantasy, 1974; Who's Who in America, 1976-1977. *Periodicals*—New York Times March 11, 1956; New York Times Book Review August 1, 1976.

*HERMANS, WILLEM FREDERIK (September 1, 1921–), Dutch novelist, short story writer, poet, dramatist, and geographer, was born in Amsterdam, the second child of Johannes Hermans and the former Hendrika Eggelte, both of whom were schoolteachers. He attended the venerable Barlaeus Gymnasium in Amsterdam. Growing up during the Depression in a restrictive family atmosphere, Hermans had a joyless childhood, exacerbated by the attentions of a meddling grandmother who lived across the street. His sense of loneliness was intensified by the tragic death of his only sister, who was shot by a cousin shortly after the German invasion of the Netherlands in 1940. All this has left its mark on Hermans's work.

After the war Hermans published his first poems and stories and joined the staffs of the literary reviews *Criterius* (1946-1948) and *Podium* (1949-1950). At about the same time he resumed his education at Amsterdam University, where he studied physical geography. He graduated in 1950 and obtained his doctorate in 1955 with a thesis on the Oesling area of Luxemburg. In 1958 he was appointed reader in physical geography at the University of Groningen. Hermans traveled a great deal during this part of his life—in Canada and the United States as a pulpwood expert; as a geologist in Luxemburg, Sicily, and Scandinavia; and as a special reporter in France, Germany, and Spain. He was married in 1950 to Emelie Henriette Meurs.

When Hermans began to publish in the late 1940s, the frankness with which he presented his unequivocally pessimistic view of life met with widespread opposition, and he was attacked by many as a dangerously jaundiced and negativist writer. After two volumes of poetry, he published his short first novel, *Conserve* (1947),

*hâr' märns

377

WILLEM FREDERIK HERMANS

which showed his potential as an experimental prose writer, "using film techniques to shift time sequences, locality and the positions of the reader and narrator," according to P. K. King.

This was followed by Hermans's first major novel, *De Tranen der Acacia's* (The Tears of the Acacias, 1949). The book is set in Amsterdam in the dreadful last year of the war. The protagonist, Arthur Muttah, has never known his mother and has been neglected by his father. Brought up by a tyrannical grandmother, he lives in an atmosphere of great emotional tension with her and his half-sister Carola, whom he both loves and hates. Muttah is not a defeatist: he struggles to form relationships, to decide where his allegiances should lie, but endlessly fails. His friend Oskar, for example—is he loyal, or self-seeking and callous, a Resistance hero or a traitor? In the end, rejected by his friend, his sister, and his father, Muttah follows his father to Brussels, is rejected again, and dies miserably in a brothel. Some critics were reminded of Céline by the novel's brutal cynicism and scatology.

In *Ik Heb Altijd Gelijk* (I Am Always Right, 1951), Lodewijk returns from two years' military service in Indonesia consumed with contempt for Holland—its smallness, triviality, insignificance, and complacency. He is no less scathing in his religious views, and Hermans was on this account brought to trial, charged with having insulted the Dutch Roman Catholics. In the end the court ruled that a writer cannot be held responsible for the opinions of his characters, and the case was dismissed—much to Hermans's disgust, for he insisted that he was fully responsible for Lodewijk's opinions, which he held to be correct.

The human struggle to force the random absurdity of life into some kind of meaningful pattern is a dominant theme in Hermans's work. The attempt always ends in failure, especially in his early fiction, which most rigorously demonstrates his belief that "writing is the creation of fallacy" by confronting deep emotion with absolute cynicism. "Mankind thinks in terms of an order which does not really exist," Hermans says, "and is blind to the original chaos. There is only one real word: chaos."

This dismal conviction is nowhere more powerfully illustrated than in Hermans's most famous short story, "Het Behouden Huis" (The House of Refuge), first published in 1952 and included in the collection *Paranoia* (1953). The narrator, a Dutchman, is fighting alongside a group of East European partisans against the Germans. Sent on a solitary mission, he finds a deserted but undamaged house, a haven from the madness of war. Then the Germans recapture the town and the narrator rejoins the partisans. During their counterattack he throws a hand grenade into the house: "It was as if it, too, had been play-acting all the time and only now showed itself for what in reality it had always been: a hollow, draughty lump of stone, inwardly full of decay and filth." There is no refuge from chaos.

A similar theme is explored in *De Donkere Kamer van Damocles* (1958, translated by Roy Edwards as *The Dark Room of Damocles*), the most admired of Hermans's novels. It tells the story of Osewoudt, a Dutch Resistance fighter. Osewoudt is not presented as a hero, however, but as an insignificant creature for whom the Resistance offers escape from his tobacconist's shop, his mad mother, and his ugly wife, and makes him the unquestioning tool of his superior officer Dorbeck. As Manfred Wolf writes in *Books Abroad,* Osewoudt becomes "part of a system as ruthlessly totalitarian as the enemy's." Towards the end of the war, Osewoudt is captured by the Germans, but escapes and makes his way to the liberated southern provinces. There he is immediately apprehended by the Dutch, who mistake him for Dorbeck, now revealed as a German agent. All Osewoudt's attempts to clear himself fail—Dorbeck is nowhere to be found, and the evidence that Osewoudt thinks will clear him only makes him look more guilty: "Everything I have done slips through my fingers. The people I have worked with during the war are all dead or gone and even the streets where I used to walk no longer exist. How can this be?" At his wits' end he

Royal Netherlands Embassy

walks out of the prison hospital where he is being held and is shot dead by the guards.

All Osewoudt's actions had seemed to him rational, but in the end each of them can be interpreted in so many ways that all meaning is lost and only the chaos remains. Hermans's portrait of the Resistance was bitterly attacked in some quarters, and Manfred Wolf complained that he had identified so closely with his characters that "we feel much of the time as if we are reading a study of juvenile delinquency by a juvenile delinquent." Other critics, however, found this a gripping and brilliantly constructed novel whose symbolism, for the first time in Hermans's work, seemed to hint at the existence of some moral values. The novel was filmed in France as *Inconnu aux services secrets* (1963) and in England as *The Spitting Image* (1964).

In *Nooit Meer Slapen* (Never Sleep Again, 1966), the central character is a geologist who treks through Finmarken in search of evidence to support his theory of meteorites. Everything fails. He cannot obtain the aerial photographs he needs and when he eventually gets them they prove to be useless; he is frustrated by his inability to draw; he loses his fountain pens; he breaks his pencils; he gets completely lost; finally he has to turn back empty-handed. In spite of this defeat, the novel seemed to P. K. King less nihilistic than the early books, though in it "man is still trying to find himself in a wasteland of few bearings, with memories only of a bogus past."

Three more novels have appeared since then: *Herinneringen van een Engelbewaarder* (Memoirs of a Guardian Angel, 1971); *Het Evangelie van O. Dapper Dapper* (The Gospel According to O. Dapper Dapper, 1973); and *Onder Professoren* (Among Professors, 1975). The second of these is a surrealistic joke and the other two, while they are more realistic, and have their quota of sharp satire, are in a decidedly less gloomy vein than Hermans's earlier novels—at times almost lighthearted in their humor.

Hermans has also written half-a-dozen plays, none of which has made any great impact, and has published four collections of short stories. *Mandarijnen op Zwavelzuur* (Mandarins in Sulphuric Acid, 1964) is a collection of fierce polemical articles in which Hermans pours a stream of highly inventive abuse over the heads of a whole gallery of Dutch writers and academics. A second helping of the same was published in 1977 as *Boze Brieven van Bijkaart* (Bijkaart's Angry Letters). Hermans has also published several highly esteemed geological and geographical works, including his thesis on Oesling (1955), a book about soil erosion (1960), and a travel book about the Netherlands Antilles (1969).

In 1973, after a conflict with the university authorities, Hermans resigned his post at the University of Groningen and with his wife and son settled in Paris as a full-time writer, apparently with no intention of ever returning to the Netherlands: "I do not wish to end my life as gloomily as I started it," he wrote in 1974. This voluntary expatriate is generally regarded as the most important Dutch novelist of the postwar period. In 1977 he was awarded the triennial Dutch State Prize for Literature. Hermans's recreations include experimental photography, collecting rare surrealist books, and making collages.

PRINCIPAL WORKS IN ENGLISH TRANSLATION: The Dark Room of Damocles, 1962. *Story in* Delta 3 1966 *and in* Odyssey December 1961.

ABOUT: Contemporary Authors Permanent Series 1, 1975; Fens, K. De gevestigde chaos, 1966; Janssen, F.A. Over De Donkere Kamer van Damocles van Willem Frederik Hermans, 1976; Morriën, A. De gruwelkamer van Willem Frederik Hermans, 1955; Oversteegen, J.J. Literair lustrum, 1967; Penguin Companion to Literature 2, 1969; Rodenko, P. De sprong van Münchhausen, 1959; Weck, J.G.M. and Huisman, N.S. In contact met het werk van moderne schrijvers, deel 3, W.F. Hermans, 1974. *Periodicals*—Books Abroad Summer 1967; Delta Autumn 1966; Literary Review Winter 1961-1962; London Magazine October 1961; Writing in Holland and Flanders 29 1970.

*HIDĀYAT, SĀDIK (February 17, 1903–April 9, 1951), Persian novelist, short story writer, dramatist, and folklorist, was born in Tehran. He belonged to a wealthy, cultured, and powerful family which had produced many prominent public figures. In 1926 he went to France with a government scholarship to study dentistry but never took a degree, his interest turning instead to the pre-Islamic languages and cultures of Persia. A chronic depressive, he made his first suicide attempt in 1928, throwing himself into the River Marne.

Contact with the literary and intellectual life of France stimulated him to write. He returned in 1930 to Persia, where he worked for a time in the civil service and at the same time entered upon a period of enormous literary activity, publishing among other works his first collections of short stories, *Zindé bi-gūr* (Buried Alive, 1930) and *Se quatré chūn* (Three Drops of Blood, 1932); the novel *Alawiyyé Khānum* (The Lady Aliwiyyé, 1933); the historical drama *Māziyār* (1933); and a study of Omar Khayyām. Hidāyat was, with Jamālzādeh, one of the creators of contemporary Persian prose. He discarded the traditional formalities and elaborate ornamenta-

*hi dä′ yat

tion, and wrote stories about the lives of the common people in a style that employed the diction and rhythms of ordinary speech, but was nevertheless both beautiful and intensely personal. Fiercely anti-aristocratic and critical of the despotic government of Riza Shah, he became the leader of a radical intellectual movement working for political reform and a renaissance in Persian art and literature.

Yet Hidāyat's personal pessimism was deepening, aggravated by drink and drugs. The shadow of death—"the best asylum for pains and sorrows and troubles and the injustices of life"—darkens his writings, especially the novel *Būf-é kūr* (1936, translated by D. P. Costello as *The Blind Owl*), which is generally considered his masterpiece. Unlike his previous stories, which mainly deal with social ills, this novel is a complex web of images whose constant repetition in different contexts reflects the obsessive patterns of the protagonist's mind. He is a recluse, an educated Persian who lives in a miserable hovel on the outskirts of his native city. He scrapes a living by decorating pen cases, always with the same scene—a dancing-girl beckoning to an old man across a stream. Apparently impotent and addicted to drugs and alcohol, the recluse longs for a love and a purity that are hopelessly beyond him. As his poisoned brain breaks down, the characters from the pen case invade his mind. The girl appears to be his wife and at the same time his sister; to be outside his window and in his bed; to be a murdered and dismembered body in his only suitcase, or lying across his chest after he has tried to bury her. Western critics found affinities with Poe, Kafka, Dostoevsky, and the Sartrean hell of *Huis clos,* while André Breton thought the book a surrealist masterpiece. But this distinctively modern existentialist sensibility is expressed through symbols and images whose roots are deep in Persian culture.

Būf-é kūr first appeared in a mimeographed edition in Bombay, where Hidāyat had gone to study Pahlavi (middle Persian) with the Parsees. It was not published in Iran until 1941, after the deposing of Riza Shah, and even then caused a scandal. This was nevertheless a period of renewed hopefulness for Hidāyat, who committed himself to the struggle against imperialism and evolved in his writings towards a more militant humanism and a sharper awareness of the effects of the class system. His particular concern for the position of women in Persia is very evident in his work. Much of his work between 1941 and 1947 was in the form of journalism, satire, and such political lampoons as *Hādji Āgā* (1945), the story of a charlatan, and his most popular book. In 1944 Hidāyat visited Tashkent, in Soviet Uzbekistan, once a center of Old Persian culture. Returning home, he continued work, but the obscurantism of the Iranian authorities had survived the deposing of Riza Shah, and their increasing repression of left-wing organizations threw him back into deep depression. In 1951 he returned to France after an absence of twenty years, and in Paris committed suicide by gassing himself.

In twenty years of literary activity Hidāyat wrote some thirty books, many of them collections of short stories. But he tried almost every genre, and his writings include a few pieces in French, an essay on Kafka, and translations of Kafka, Schnitzler, and Sartre. He was the first Persian writer to recognize the importance of folklore and seriously to research it. Persia was his great love—its people, especially the poor and oppressed, its past and culture, the theology of Zoroaster, the poetry of Omar Khayyām. Preoccupied with the inner life as he was, he nevertheless portrayed a great gallery of Persian types and a panorama of his country's traditions and customs: "No other writer in modern Persia," writes H. Kamshad, "has illustrated and analyzed with such mastery the life of the hungry peasant, the unfortunate beggar, hypocritical preacher, and greedy bazaar trader."

Hidāyat, who never married, seemed an enigmatic figure even to those who knew him best—a lonely, death-haunted, and often despairing man who was also a compassionate and active social reformer. He is unquestionably Persia's greatest modern prose writer and the chief influence on his country's younger authors, and is regarded by many critics as the most original and powerful Persian writer of the past five hundred years.

PRINCIPAL WORKS IN ENGLISH TRANSLATION: The Blind Owl, 1957; Sadeq's Omnibus (short stories), translated by Siavosh Danesh, 1972? (Tehran). *Stories in* Life and Letters December 1949; New Writers and Writing 14, 1978.

ABOUT: Bashiri, I. Hedayat's Ivory Tower, 1974; Cassell's Encyclopaedia of World Literature, 1973; Kamshad, H. Modern Persian Prose Literature, 1966; McGraw-Hill Encyclopedia of World Biography, 1973; Monteil, V. Un Écrivain persan du demi-siècle, 1952; Prusek, J. (ed.) Dictionary of Oriental Literatures, 1974; Rypka, J. History of Iranian Literature, 1968; Seymour-Smith, M. Guide to Modern World Literature, 1973. *Periodicals*—Books Abroad Winter 1967, Spring 1972; Canadian Forum August 1958; Journal of the Iran Society No. 3 1950; Life and Letters December 1949; Middle Eastern Affairs IX 1960; San Francisco July 20, 1958; Times Literary Supplement March 7, 1958.

*HIKMET (RAN), NAZIM (1902–June 3, 1963), Turkish poet, novelist, dramatist, and critic, was born in Salonika, Greece, which was then in Turkish hands. The family was one of considerable influence and importance in the Ottoman empire. His father, Hikmet Bey, was a physician who at the time of Hikmet's birth was serving in Salonika as director of the Turkish press office and consul general. His mother, who greatly influenced him, had had a European education and helped him to understand French literature and Western music. He was introduced to classical Turkish literature at a very early age by his grandfather Nazim Pasha, a noted poet and critic.

When he was fourteen, Hikmet entered the Naval Academy at Heybeliada near Istanbul, where in 1918 he began to publish his first poems. They were stylized in form and conventional in content, full of romantic melancholy and patriotic fervor (the latter exacerbated by the Allied occupation of Istanbul). In 1920 Hikmet was expelled from the Naval Academy for taking part in a strike. He went to Ankara, where Mustafa Kemal was leading the struggle against the postwar dismemberment of Turkey proposed by the victorious Allies.

Hikmet taught for a time in Anatolia and was much influenced by the socialist revolutionaries he met there. The profound admiration he conceived for the Anatolian peasants and his conversion to socialism are reflected in the poems collected in *Anodolu* (Anatolia, 1922). Traveling via Tbilisi (Tiflis) in Georgia, where other Turkish intellectuals had taken refuge, Hikmet reached Moscow in 1921. There he enrolled in the University of the Workers of the East, studying French, physics, and chemistry and developing his Marxist political ideals.

It was at this time also that Hikmet formulated his own style and theory of poetry, influenced primarily by French *vers libre* and by such Russian futurists as Mayakovsky. According to Talât Sait Halman, "free verse with alternations of long and short lines, occasional rhyming, and wide use of alliteration, assonance, and onomatopoeia, a staccato syntax, were to remain the hallmarks of his art and his major influence on modern Turkish poetics."

Hikmet went home in 1924, joined the Turkish Communist Party, and contributed poems and articles to progressive newspapers. In 1925, threatened with imprisonment, he returned to the USSR, where he remained until 1928. Back in Turkey, he collaborated with the Sertel family on the progressive journal *Resimli Ay* (Pictorial Monthly). He was arrested on political charges

*hik′ met

soon after his return and during the next five years was twice imprisoned. In periods of freedom he worked as a film scenarist, and he also wrote a number of plays, of which *Kafatasi* (The Skull, 1932), was the most notable.

Although Hikmet at this time produced some fine love and nature lyrics, much of his verse dealt angrily or satirically with social injustice in Turkey. In spite of this, he was permitted to publish a great deal of work in such volumes as *835 Satir* (835 Lines, 1929), *Varan 3* (The Third One, 1930), *Sesini Kaybeden Şehir* (The City That Lost Its Voice, 1931), *Gece Gelen Telgraf* (Night Wire, 1932), *Portreler* (Portraits, 1935), and *Şeyh Bedreddin Destani* (The Epic of Sheikh Bedreddin). The latter, a lyrical and dramatic account of a fifteenth-century uprising, avoids the polemics that mar some of Hikmet's political poems and is one of his most accomplished works, described by Halman as "a perfect synthesis of substance and form, of diction and drama, of fact and metaphor." These volumes had great influence, and did much to free Turkish poetry from classical forms and meters.

Hikmet's torrential attacks on injustice, declaimed at public meetings with all the force of his charismatic personality, made him a literary hero whom the Turkish authorities could not ignore. In 1938, when Turkey's relations with the Soviet Union were deteriorating, he was arrested and charged before a military tribunal with inciting naval and army cadets to "spread communism." In all probability Hikmet was, as he said, not guilty of sedition but "only concerned with the literary aspects of Marxism and Communism." His trial, long regarded as a legal scandal, is described in A. Kadir's *1938 Harp Okulu Olayi ve Nazim Hikmet* (The 1938 Incident at the Military College and Nazim Hikmet, 1966). At the end of it, he was sentenced to two terms of imprisonment totaling thirty-five years.

Hikmet took up painting in prison, as well as sculpture, weaving, and carpentry. Although his books were totally suppressed, he wrote copiously. The poems eventually collected in such volumes as *Rubailer* (Rubaiyat, 1966) and *Saat 21-22 Şiirleri* (Poems Written Between Nine and Ten at Night, 1965) affirm his belief in the essential beauty of life, his communist sense of fellowship with all mankind, and his sustaining love for his wife Piraye. Much of this prison poetry was written to be heard rather than read—to be memorized and passed around by word of mouth, like the folk songs and street ballads on which it was modeled. Some of it was not much more than doggerel, but Hikmet also wrote some notable lyrics in prison, and at least one long poem of unquestionable quality and importance.

This was *Moskova Senfonisi,* written during World War II, published in Sofia in 1952, and translated by Taner Baybars as *Moscow Symphony.* It is an ironic but deeply humane series of meditations and conversations about the war, death, freedom, and love, centering on the conversion to a sense of human brotherhood of Jedvet Bey, a rich Turkish landowner. Martin Seymour-Smith wrote that "this eloquent poem, full of beautiful and unsentimental feeling, is effective not for its implicit Marxism but for the golden nobility of mind of which it is the embodiment." It was intended as part of a much longer work, *Memleketimden Insan Manzaralari* (Human Landscapes From My Country, 1966-1967). This multi-volume epic of contemporary history has been called a "failure on a grand scale," and Hikmet in the end did not include *Moskova Senfonisi* in it.

In 1949 a world campaign by intellectuals failed to secure Hikmet's release. He went on a hunger strike the following year, and in 1951, in failing health, he was at last freed under the terms of a general amnesty. Later the same year, Hikmet went to the Soviet Union, antagonizing many Turks, including some of those who had campaigned for his release, by leaving his wife and son behind. He spent the rest of his life in Russia, Czechoslovakia, and Poland, and eventually became a Polish citizen, adopting the surname Borzęcki—the name of a family from which one of his ancestors had come.

The poems Hikmet wrote after 1951 were mostly propaganda pieces, of little literary interest or value, but the autobiographical novel *Yaşamak güzel şey bekardeşim* (Life Is Good, Comrade; published in Russian in 1962 and Turkish in 1967, and in Paris as *Les Romantiques* in 1964) is important and revealing. Some of Hikmet's plays were produced in Moscow during the 1950s, among them *Ferhat ile Sirin* (Ferhat and Sirin), a dramatization of a Turkish love legend, and *Who is Ivan Ivanovich?,* a satire on bureaucracy.

Hikmet died in Moscow in 1963, and his works were immediately published in Turkey, for the first time since 1937. His international reputation has grown rapidly, spread by translations into Russian, Azerbaijan Turki, English, Greek, French, Italian, and several Eastern European languages. His work has been much discussed and has earned him comparisons with Lorca, Éluard, and with Pablo Neruda, with whom he shared the Soviet Union's International Peace Prize in 1950. It is believed that he was nominated for the Nobel Prize in the late 1950s.

In his mature poetry, Hikmet always employed Mayakovsky's "stepped line." Taner

Baybars has said that "his awareness of the richness and beauty of colloquial Turkish, combined with this new form, produced an astonishing result. Although he avoided deliberate rhyming his poetry teemed with internal rhymes.... Hikmet used the language as if 'weaving a silk cloth' with immense skill and assurance." In spite of the harshness of life, Hikmet's poetry is full of humanity and of humor—Baybars has pointed out that his Marxism acts in his best work "merely as a vehicle for the expression of deep *human* emotions."

PRINCIPAL WORKS IN ENGLISH TRANSLATION: Poems, translated by Ali Yunus, 1954; Selected Poems, translated by Taner Baybars, 1967; The Moscow Symphony, and Other Poems, translated by Taner Baybars, 1970; The Day Before Tomorrow, translated by Taner Baybars, 1972; Things I Didn't Know I Loved: Selected Poems, translated by Randy Blassing and Mutlu Konuk, 1976.

ABOUT: Kadir, A. 1938 Harp Okulu Olayi ve Nazim Hikmet, 1966; Penguin Companion to Literature 4, 1969; Prusek, J. (ed.) Dictionary of Oriental Literatures, 1974; Twentieth Century Writing, 1969. *Periodicals*—Books Abroad Winter 1969; New York Times June 4, 1963; Times (London) June 7, 1963.

HILL, (JOHN EDWARD) CHRISTOPHER ("K. E. Holme") (February 6, 1912–), English historian, was born in the city of York, the son of Edward Hill, a solicitor, and the former Janet Dickenson. He attended St. Peter's School in York from 1921 to 1931 and read history at Balliol College, Oxford University, receiving his B.A. in 1934, his M.A. in 1938. From 1934 to 1938 Hill was a fellow of All Souls College, Oxford, a fraternity of scholars who have no students or teaching duties to interrupt their researches. Hill did however choose to teach for part of this period, from 1936 to 1938, in a far less privileged institution, as an assistant lecturer in modern history at University College, Cardiff.

In 1938 Hill returned to Balliol as a fellow and tutor in modern history. World War II intervened a year later, and Hill joined the army as a private in the Field Security Police. In 1940 he was commissioned in the Oxford and Buckinghamshire Light Infantry, where he rose to the rank of major, and during the latter part of the war, beginning in 1943, he was seconded to the Foreign Office. Hill returned to Oxford in 1945, resuming his teaching duties at Balliol and later becoming also a university lecturer in sixteenth- and seventeenth-century history. He was Master of Balliol College from 1965 until his retirement in September 1978.

Hill's reputation as one of the most distinguished of living British historians rests on his studies in the history of the English Revolution

Jerry Bauer

CHRISTOPHER HILL

of 1640-1660, which he regards as "the most decisive single event in the whole of English history." Dissatisfied with the traditional view that the upheaval was inspired mainly by religious differences, he has come to view it as the product of a variety of economic and social pressures, and as a catalyst which brought about the transition from medieval to modern English society. His first important essay on the subject appeared in 1940 in *The English Revolution, 1640,* which Hill edited.

Though he has refused to follow a dogmatic sectarian line, Hill remains a Marxist historian and as a young man was a member of the Communist Party. He sought to defend this commitment in *Two Commonwealths,* published at the end of the war in 1945, in which he compared the organization and workings of the political and economic systems of Britain and the Soviet Union. Using the pseudonym K.E. Holme, Hill was identified only as "a young Englishman who is peculiarly well qualified by training and experience to interpret the public life of the Soviets to us in Britain in its actual working and its inner meaning." This was followed in 1947 by *Lenin and the Russian Revolution,* a contribution to the Teach Yourself History series.

Hill's first major monograph, *Economic Problems of the Church From Archbishop Whitgift to the Long Parliament* (1956), explores "the part played by religion in preparing the seventeenth-century revolution." It deals with the wide-ranging and mounting financial difficulties confronting the church between 1583 and 1640. Hill argues that the everyday details of ecclesiastical tithes, impropriations, augmentations, staffing, and legal rights and duties deserve closer atten-

tion from historians, since the church in the early seventeenth century was "not only a religious" but a "political and economic institution of the greatest power and importance." The book was widely discussed and greatly praised. Hugh Trevor-Roper observed that "Mr. Hill occasionally refreshes himself with the Marxist whisky-bottle, but his writing is cool and sober. We may take or leave his generalisations, which he never imposes on us. His facts, and his presentation of them, impose themselves and evoke only gratitude and admiration. The book is a model of scholarship."

Puritanism and Revolution (1958), a volume of journal articles and book reviews, was followed by *The Century of Revolution, 1603-1714* (1961), the fifth volume in The History of England series. Hill had set out to "penetrate below the familiar events" of the century "to grasp 'what happened'—to ordinary English men and women as well as to kings and queens or abstractions like 'society' and 'the state.' " He maintains that England had been transformed into a modern state during this period, in which were shaped the principles of economic progress, firm Parliamentary rule, an imperialist foreign policy, scientific advance, religious toleration, and literary supremacy; the century ushered in "the world of banks and checks, budgets, the stock exchange, the periodical press, coffee-houses, clubs, coffins, microscopes, short-hand, actresses and umbrellas." J.H. Plumb wrote: "It will be a long time before this brilliantly lucid and forcibly argued book is bettered. It makes all the other single-volume, seventeenth-century histories look rather jejeune."

In *Society and Puritanism in Pre-Revolutionary England* (1964), which one reviewer called "a sociological analysis of Puritanism," Hill examines Puritan ideology in the light of the changing structure of English society in the first half of the seventeenth century. He argues that Puritan ideals embodied the attitudes which carried England from the agrarian economy of the middle ages to the capitalistic and industrial economy of modern times. In developing this thesis, he presents the Puritans as members for the most part of a single social class—the small merchants, manufacturers, and artisans whom he describes as "the honest, industrious sort of Englishman."

A reviewer in the *Times Literary Supplement* remarked that Hill in this book writes "so skilfully, and with such modest confidence, that for the moment all other interpretations seem hazy and inadequate. Eventually, of course, the doubts arise. Is it too good to be more than half true?" Lawrence Stone was equally dubious: "It is impossible to deny the force of this massively documented and powerfully argued thesis. One may seriously doubt, however, whether the picture it presents is more than one aspect of a more complex and ambiguous reality. . . . there is no hint that a crucial . . . element in the Puritan movement was the landed gentry and nobility. . . . The cool, rational analysis of Puritanism as a sensible preparation for the new capitalist environment fails to go to the heart of the matter."

Hill also won admiration for his scholarship but less than total agreement with his thesis when he discussed the compatibility of Puritanism and science in his Ford Lectures at Oxford in 1962, later expanded and published as *Intellectual Origins of the English Revolution* (1965). *Reformation to Industrial Revolution: The Making of Modern English Society, Volume 1: 1530-1780* (1967)—Hill's companion volume to E. J. Hobsbawm's *Industry and Empire, 1750 to the Present Day*—was intended mainly for undergraduates but is less a textbook, according to J.P. Kenyon, than a "portrait of two hundred and fifty years." Treading familiar ground, Hill was nevertheless warmly praised in the *Economist* for handling "an immense amount of material with such skill that it is possible to read his account with a growing sense of excitement at the logic and apparent inevitability of events. . . . His genuine concern for the lives of ordinary people enlarges his approach, and also that of his readers."

God's Englishman: Oliver Cromwell and the English Revolution (1970) is a volume of essays on various aspects of Cromwell's role in the religious and political movements of his day. It was found both perceptive and objective in its portrayal of Cromwell as "an unwitting revolutionary, not a willful desecrator or destroyer." Hill's Riddell Memorial Lectures at the University of Newcastle in 1969 were published two years later as *Antichrist in Seventeenth-Century England*; they reexamined the "identification within the Church of England of the Pope with Antichrist, made by Elizabethan Protestants of many different hues." A reviewer in the *Times Literary Supplement* called this "one of Dr. Hill's shortest works, but also one of the most successfully executed and perfectly achieved," demonstrating his "originality of mind . . . his elegance of presentation, clarity of exposition, and force of argument—including, not least, the ability to make a point against himself without surrendering his main positions."

The World Turned Upside Down (1972) is a work of much broader scope, an examination of the economic and religious ideas of such radical movements of the mid-seventeenth-century as the Diggers, the Quakers, the True Levellers, and the Ranters, showing how the English Revolution had touched off debate not only over the values of the old hierarchical society but also over those of the new Protestant ethic. Radical theorists, especially between 1645 and 1653, aimed at a popular "revolt within the revolution" and, until they were crushed by the New Model Army, envisaged an "upside down world" dominated by the least privileged half of English society. Keith Thomas commented that the book "reveals its author's phenomenal grasp of the printed literature of the period and it is written in his usual plain style, direct, concise, even laconic. . . . The work is less a compact monograph than an open-ended and wide-ranging survey, posing many questions to be answered and throwing out many ideas to be challenged. Wry humor and a strong sense of the contemporary immediacy of its message distinguish this book from much academic writing." *The World Turned Upside Down* has been used as the basis of a play of the same title by Keith Dewhurst, first performed in 1978.

A collection of Hill's essays and lectures written mostly between 1961 and 1973 was published in 1974 as *Change and Continuity in Seventeenth-Century England,* providing a representative sampling of his major interests as well as a demonstration of his methodology. Blair Worden found only in one essay "the extraordinary range of learning, and the incisiveness and vitality of exposition, that characterise Hill's best work." The volume had an even harsher reception from J. H. Hexter, who in a lengthy review in the *Times Literary Supplement* castigated Hill for his failure to search as hard as he should for evidence that might weaken or modify his own theses. Hexter went on: "For a historian of great erudition and vivid imagination to fail to do this is for him to fail his colleagues, to place on them a burden that should have been his. Christopher Hill so fails his colleagues. It is too bad." Hill himself might reply, in the terms he once applied to R. H. Tawney, that "part of good history is to *ask* the right questions. By *right* questions, I mean those that produce fruitful answers."

The questions he asks in *Milton and the English Revolution* (1977) lead him to the conclusion that Milton was above all "a profoundly *political* animal," who derived his ideas less from the library than from a "permanent dialogue" with "the plebeian radical thinkers of the English revolution." John Hollander wrote that "this massive, lively and historically learned study evokes the ideological atmosphere in which Milton wrote, both with his left hand, as a polemicist, and his right. Hill's interpretation of the relation between political energies and the sublimest of visions will provoke rewarding discussions for years to come." A reviewer in the London *Observer* prophesied that this "thoughtful and challenging book" would "take its place as Christopher Hill's *magnum opus,*" and Blair Worden called it "as learned, as courageous, and as affectionate as one would expect." Worden was nevertheless one of a number of critics who resisted Hill's determination "to redirect the course of Milton studies," finding "his attempt to cut Milton off from his Humanist roots" both misguided and unconvincing.

In any case, few historians would disagree with Lawrence Stone's assertion that the period of the English Revolution "must now be regarded as 'Hill's half-century,' and for years to come students will be testing, confirming, modifying, or rejecting his hypotheses." As Stone says, "it is given to few historians to achieve such intellectual dominance over their chosen field, for it requires sustained capacity for taking pains in the drudgery of research, a fertile and facile pen, and tremendous imaginative powers. Together, these are the marks of the great historian."

Christopher Hill has one daughter by his 1944 marriage to Inez Waugh and a son and a daughter by his second wife, Bridget Sutton, whom he married in 1956; another daughter is deceased. A frequent contributor to historical and other journals, Hill has served since 1953 as a consultant on the Yale University Press edition of the prose works of John Milton. From 1952 to 1968 he was a member of the editorial board of *Past & Present,* and since 1970 he has been president of the Past & Present Society. A fellow of the Royal Historical Society and since 1966 of the British Academy, he is also an honorary member of the American Academy of Arts and Sciences. He received his D.Litt. from Oxford University in 1965 and has honorary doctorates also from the universities of Hull, East Anglia, and Sheffield.

PRINCIPAL WORKS: (As "K. E. Holme") Two Commonwealths, 1945; Lenin and the Russian Revolution, 1947; Economic Problems of the Church From Archbishop Whitgift to the Long Parliament, 1956; Puritanism and Revolution, 1958; Oliver Cromwell: 1658-1958 (Historical Association pamphlet), 1958; The Century of Revolution, 1603-1714, 1961; Society and Puritanism in Pre-Revolutionary England, 1964; Intellectual Origins of the English Revolution, 1965; Reformation to Industrial Revolution: The Making of Modern English Society, Volume 1: 1530-1780, 1967 (in England subtitled: A Social and Economic History of Britain); God's Englishman: Oliver Cromwell and the English Revolution, 1970; Antichrist in Seventeenth-Century England, 1971; The World Turned Upside Down: Radical Ideas During the English Revolution, 1972; Change and Continuity in Seventeenth-Century England, 1974; Milton and the English Revolution, 1977. *As editor* —The English Revolution, 1640: Three Essays, 1940; (with Edmund Dell) The Good Old Cause: The English Revolution of 1640-1660, 1949; The Law of Freedom and Other Selected Writings of Gerrard Winstanley, 1973.

ABOUT: Academic Who's Who, 1975-1976; Contemporary Authors 9-12 1st revision, 1974; International Who's Who, 1977-78; Mehta, V. Fly and the Fly Bottle, 1962; Who's Who, 1978. *Periodicals*—Economist June 13, 1964; October 14, 1967; November 1, 1972; English Historical Review October 1966; New Statesman September 8, 1956; April 17, 1964; July 31, 1970; August 20, 1971; June 23, 1972; January 24, 1975; New York Review of Books August 26, 1965; February 13, 1969; December 2, 1971; November 30, 1972; March 23, 1978; New York Times Book Review November 3, 1968; October 4, 1970; January 28, 1973; Punch September 13, 1967; Times Literary Supplement February 1, 1957; May 21, 1964; May 20, 1965; November 30, 1967; September 25, 1970; September 3, 1971; August 18, 1972; October 24, 1975.

HILL, GEOFFREY (June 18, 1932–), English poet, was born at Bromsgrove, Worcestershire. He was educated at Fairfield Junior School and Bromsgrove County High School, and in 1950 went to Keble College, Oxford University, where he received a first-class honors degree in English in 1953. Since then he has taught English at the University of Leeds, where he is now a senior lecturer. Although his poetry is widely read and his work is discussed with a seriousness and respect accorded to very few British poets, Hill is a reticent and modest man who usually chooses to publish in "little magazines" like *Agenda* and *Stand* rather than in national weeklies.

From the beginning, when his poems appeared in a Fantasy Press pamphlet in 1952 while he was still an Oxford undergraduate, it was clear that Geoffrey Hill was a highly original poet, with a powerful command of technique, whose work had little in common with any of the contemporary British schools or movements.

His first book, *For the Unfallen,* appeared in 1959 when he was twenty-seven. As one critic later wrote, it "established, with intense care, his credentials: a line packed tight to buckling point, a wide cultural allusiveness, an almost forbidding formality." At that time, expressing his faith in literature, Hill quoted Ezra Pound's remark that "all the values come from our judicial sentences," and Yeats's admission that the verses of his own in which he took greatest pleasure were those in which he "found something hard and cold, some articulation of the image which is the opposite of all that I am in my daily life." Certainly these poems were impersonal, yet, in the way they strained for meaning, they showed a poet of particular and unusual integri-

Alastair Elliott

GEOFFREY HILL

ty—one to whom a right utterance meant more than a striking one:

Love that drained her drained him she'd loved,
    though each
For the other's sake forged passion upon speech,
Bore their close days through sufferance towards
    night
Where she at length grasped sleep and he lay quiet

As though needing no questions, now, to guess
What her secreting heart could not well hide.

These are the first six lines of "Turtle Dove," and, while they are almost clumsily exact, they betoken a type of seriousness that did not characterize the English poetry of the 1950s. One critic found this seriousness disconcerting, and said that "the work was at times so wrought-up that it could hardly speak," but most reviewers were impressed or even awed. William Walsh has called Hill "a poet of pain and economy. His attention is preoccupied with absolutes, with death, God, war, love, time. He has the courage of his subjects, which are not conceived of as the abstractions of reason—they are too thronged and dense for that—but as the stark observations of a collected and suffering soul. . . . Unterrified of grandeur, quite without fashionable glibness or cleverness, almost suspicious of fluency, he sees life as agonisingly under the jurisdiction of tragedy." But:

    . . . By blood we live, the hot, the cold,
    To ravage and redeem the world:
    There is no bloodless myth will hold.

And by Christ's blood are men made free

Though in close shrouds their bodies lie
Under the rough pelt of the sea;

Though Earth has rolled beneath her weight
The bones that cannot bear the light.

from ("Genesis")

It was nine years before Hill published his next major book, *King Log,* called the "fruit of a ferociously self-critical talent." Various critics discovered affinities with Wallace Stevens, René Char, and the Welsh Catholic poet David Jones, among others, and opinions differed as to whether or not Hill had succeeded in an attempt to "write more simply and directly of people." Some thought that he had not—that his poetry had become "disappointingly ingrown," and one writer detected "the dry pain of self-regarding composition" in poems in which Hill sought to express a sense of the agony of someone else (Tommaso Campanella tortured by the Inquisition, Miguel Hernández imprisoned and starved by the Spanish fascists, Robert Desnos in a Nazi concentration camp). Martin Seymour-Smith wrote that warmth in Geoffrey Hill's poetry "is like a dying sun seen through a wall of ice; an impressive barrier of confident, recondite language screens the reader from all human energy." But other readers admired the "sad irony" that characterized many of these poems, and found deep feeling in them. In particular, there was high praise for "Funeral Music," a sequence of eight fourteen-line poems suggested by bloody incidents during the Wars of the Roses in the fifteenth century, in which Hill attempted, he said, "a florid grim music broken by grunts and shrieks":

They bespoke doomsday and they meant it by
God, their curved metal rimming the low ridge.
But few appearances are like this. . . .
'Oh, that old northern business . . .' A field
After battle utters its own sound
Which is like nothing on earth, but is earth.
Blindly the questing snail, vulnerable
Mole emerge, blindly we lie down, blindly
Among carnage the most delicate souls
Tup in their marriage-blood, gasping 'Jesus.'

(from "Funeral Music 3")

"The brooding sombreness of this," wrote Anthony Thwaite, "is not simply pitying and elegiac: it is laced through with ironies, each phrase is delicately poised to re-create (without loose atmospherics or over-colourful images) a precise and horrible scene, of scrupulous interest in itself and beyond itself; a sound 'Which is like nothing on earth, but is earth.' " And William Walsh spoke of "the curiously potent combination of ceremonial richness and animal realism in these extraordinary poems. They spring from and realise a most individual force and they compose an original, compelling body of verse, which wants only volume to qualify as very considerable work indeed."

Mercian Hymns (1971) is a cycle of thirty prose poems. They center on Offa, eighth-century King of the West Midlands, but, as Anthony Thwaite says, "the effort here is not towards the re-creation of the past. . . . The commanding and unifying figure is sometimes the ancient king, sometimes the poet himself in childhood or present manhood: throughout the sequence, the remote past, the recent past and the present are obliquely presented, often within the space of a single section—as is plain from the beginning":

> King of the perennial holly-groves, the riven sand-
>   stone: overlord of the M5: architect of the
>   historic rampart and ditch . . . guardian of the
>   Welsh Bridge and the Iron Bridge: contractor to
>   the desirable new estates: saltmaster:
>   moneychanger: commissioner for oaths:
>   martyrologist: the friend of Charlemagne.
>
> 'I liked that,' said Offa, 'sing it again.'
>
> (from "Mercian Hymns I")

Thwaite was reminded of Eliot's translation of St.-John Perse's *Anabasis* and of David Jones, but said that "really the method and tone are like nothing else in English—complex, rich, many-layered, an intricately worked meditation on history, tradition, order, power and memory, in which the precision of the language and the mysterious reverberations of the past combine to achieve something completely inevitable and true":

> 'Now when King Offa was alive and dead,' they
>   were all there, the funereal gleemen . . .
>
> He was defunct. They were perfunctory. The
>   ceremony stood acclaimed. The mob received
>   memorial vouchers and signs.
>
> After that shadowy, thrashing midsummer
>   hail-storm, Earth lay for a while, the ghost-bride
>   of livid Thor, butcher of strawberries, and the
>   shire-tree dripped red in the arena of its
>   uprooting.
>
> (from "Mercian Hymns XXVII")

William Walsh has pointed out how often in Hill's poems "the ambiguities and the temptations (to facility or indulgence) of the poet's position are as much part of the theme as the explicit subject." This is true of *Mercian Hymns*

in which, moreover, as Michael Hamburger has pointed out, "Hill's descriptions of the activities of Mercia—coining, hammering, carving—are, first of all, the qualities of . . . [his] own poetic technique."

With this book as with its predecessor, the commonest criticism (amid a chorus of praise) was that it lacked "the splash of common life." Hamburger complained of a verbal frugality and stringency producing "a drastic shrinking of tonal diversity—a kind of tight-lipped, poker-faced emotional anonymity." Peter Levi praised it for its "complete exactness" but said it was "like a tree with fruit and branches, perfectly alive, but without leaves." This quality in Hill's poetry has been discussed by C.H. Sisson, who spoke of "this singularly direct mind which, none the less, seems impelled to seek indirect utterance. . . . There is in Hill a touch of Crashaw, which is that of a mind in search of artifices to protect itself against its own passions."

But Michael Hamburger also wrote of *Mercian Hymns* that "each prose-poem is an achieved construct of trimmed, interlocking units, polished without glossiness (both 'kempt and jutting,' like Offa's head on a coin), tense but unstrained, calculatively wrought without seeming synthetic." And Peter Levi has called Hill "the most important, exciting and instructive English poet to have published his first work since the nineteen forties." This view is quite widely held in England, as was evident in the replies to a questionnaire circulated in 1972 by *the Review* to many poets and critics, in which Hill was the writer most often mentioned as a hopeful portent in English poetry. Christopher Ricks, an early champion, says that he "is, in the judgment of some of us, the best poet now writing in England," and Jon Silkin has contributed a very serious and detailed discussion of Hill's work to *British Poetry Since 1960*. There was a similar response in the United States when the contents of Hill's first three books were collected here in 1975 in a single volume, *Somewhere Is Such a Kingdom*. The book appeared with a lengthy introduction by Harold Bloom and received some equally full and thoughtful reviews, notably one by John Matthias in *Poetry* (July 1976). Matthias drew attention to the fruitful tension in Hill's work "between the scholar and the visionary," and concluded that "since the death of David Jones, . . . [he] carries almost alone the burden of maintaining in the teeth of unsympathetic times—and very profoundly too against his own inclination to remain silent—a visionary poetics in England."

Geoffrey Hill received the Eric Gregory Award in 1961, the Hawthornden Prize in 1969, the Faber Memorial Prize in 1970, the Whitbread Award and the Alice Hunt Bartlett Award in 1971, and the Heinemann Award in 1972. Since 1972 he has been a Fellow of the Royal Society of Literature. The author is married and has two children. Of medium height, gentle and unassuming in manner, he is a conscientious teacher, highly regarded by his students. Hill is the author of a "rhythmically virile and speakable" English version of Ibsen's dramatic poem *Brand,* staged at the National Theatre in London in 1978.

PRINCIPAL WORKS: Poems (pamphlet), 1952; For the Unfallen: Poems 1952-1958, 1959; Preghiere, 1964; (with others) Penguin Modern Poets 8, 1966; King Log, 1968; Mercian Hymns, 1971; Somewhere Is Such a Kingdom: Poems, 1952-1971, 1975 (U.S. only): (as adapter) Brand, by Henrik Ibsen, 1978.

ABOUT: Allott, K. (ed.) Penguin Book of Contemporary Verse, 1962; Bloom, H. *introduction to* Somewhere Is Such a Kingdom, 1975; Press, J. A Map of Modern English Verse, 1969; Schmidt, M. and Lindop, G. (eds.) British Poetry Since 1960, 1972; Thwaite, A. Poetry Today 1960-1973, 1973; Vinson, J. (ed.) Contemporary Poets, 1975. *Periodicals*—Agenda Autumn-Winter 1971-1972, Autumn 1975; Contemporary Literature 4 1972; Delta Spring 1972; Illustrated London News August 20, 1966; London Magazine November 1964; New York Review of Books January 22, 1976; New York Times Book Review January 11, 1976; Poetry July 1976; Review March 1969, Spring-Summer 1972; Spectator October 20, 1968; Stand 10 1 1968, 13 1 1971-1972; Times Literary Supplement August 25, 1966; October 31, 1968; August 27, 1971; June 30, 1978; Yale Review Spring 1976.

HILL, SUSAN (ELIZABETH) (February 5, 1942–), English novelist, short story writer, and dramatist, was born in Scarborough, Yorkshire, the late-born only child of R.H. and Doris Hill. She thinks that "only children tend to have a rather more inner world than children with brothers and sisters. I can't remember a moment when I didn't want to write: from the moment the first books really hooked me, I decided I wanted to write my own. I knew I could write better than I did other things." She grew up in Scarborough, a Victorian spa and seaside resort of considerable elegance, and believes that this is why the sea has always held her "like a sort of umbilical cord." It was there also that she first encountered the aged, lonely, and eccentric men and women in retirement who people so many of her stories.

In one of her many published interviews, she has recalled her Scarborough convent school, a very relaxed institution: "I didn't understand maths so I went and asked the Reverend Mother if I could stop. She asked me what I wanted to do instead and when I said read in the library, she said fine." When Susan Hill was fifteen the

SUSAN HILL

family moved to Coventry, a much larger city, where she attended the local grammar school. From there she went to King's College, London University, receiving a first-class honors degree in English in 1963. It was in London that she became a regular concert-goer and developed her deep interest in music, an important element in her work. This was a lonely and unhappy time for her nevertheless. She says that she felt "gauche, immature and bewildered" at King's, and this in spite of the fact that when she went there she had already written and published a precocious first novel and was on this account a minor celebrity.

Encouraged by a letter from Pamela Hansford Johnson, Susan Hill had begun this novel when she was only fifteen, writing in the evenings after she had finished her school assignments. It was completed when she was seventeen and published in 1961 as *The Enclosure.* A story about an actor and his novelist wife whose marriage is breaking up, it seemed to reviewers a work of remarkable maturity for so youthful an author, and earned her a taste of fame as "the English Françoise Sagan." *Do Me a Favour,* written at college, followed in 1963. Its author says it was "very bad, and much worse than the first one," and the critics agreed. For nearly five years after that Susan Hill worked as book page editor of the Coventry *Evening Telegraph,* reviewing every kind of book. "It was good training," she told an interviewer, "but an awful grind. I lived on very little money. All the time I wanted to write a new book, but didn't have time—I seemed to be always reading other people's. After five years of that I was about to resign, and got the sack as a new editor came in. I had nothing else to do, and so I wrote another novel —on an overdraft."

By this time her precocious reputation had been largely forgotten and the new novel was virtually a new beginning, introducing the style and some of the themes associated with her mature work. It was published in 1968 as *Gentleman and Ladies* and was generally recognized as a remarkable achievement for a writer still in her mid-twenties. The gentleman of the title is Hubert Gaily, a middle-aged bachelor living with his mother. Ma Gaily's attendance at Faith Lavender's funeral involves Hubert in the life of the ladies of the small village of Haverstock, including the two surviving Lavender sisters, each convinced that the other is going mad, the self-pitying Alida Thorne and her ancient mother, and Dorothea Shottery, confidante to them all. There was praise for the author's "briskly impressionistic" style and lightness of touch, and Vernon Scannell found "quite a charge of power" in the book, "particularly in the first two-thirds, where Susan Hill takes a brave and honest look at the business of aging and dying, the unconsoling irony of existence. . . . Where she is less successful is in her tendency to overplot and to load her dice: her goodies are pure gold and her baddies are impure unutterables."

A Change for the Better (1969) is a rather similar novel, centering on another middle-aged woman dominated by a selfish mother—so cruelly and rigidly molded that even when her mother dies she is unable to make a new life for herself, and resigns herself to the old one. Jonathan Raban wrote that "Miss Hill has created a stylized, yet brilliantly accurate grammar and vocabulary for her distressed gentlefolk"—for a society which "finds its linguistic correlative in a dialect of sad clichés . . . mean, complaining, platitudinous." The book was generally admired and sold moderately well, though Susan Hill was still "living from hand to mouth." Two grants from the Arts Council bought her time to write the novel that established her.

This was *I'm the King of the Castle* (1970), in which she turns her attention from the sorrows of old age to those of childhood. Edmund Hooper, a disturbed child raised by an unsympathetic father in a gloomy Victorian villa, feels himself threatened when his father hires a housekeeper, a widow with a young son. Edmund defends his territory against this interloper, Charles Kingshaw, with the weapons of terror and intimidation. Tormented past bearing, Charles eventually runs away into the woods. Edmund pursues him, but in the dark pagan woods is overcome by his own terror, so that Charles

becomes for the moment "king of the castle." Meanwhile the oblivious parents, increasingly absorbed in each other, decide to marry. Charles knows then that the battle is lost and drowns himself. It seemed to Stuart Hood that the novel deals "with original sin and the theory that small boys in particular have only to be scratched to reveal the primeval savage. . . . The trouble about the book is that the horrific neuroses—not to say psychoses—from which both boys suffer are unexplained, without etiologies." This was not the reaction of most critics, who found in it "an almost intolerable tension" and passages of both poignancy and horror reminiscent of William Golding's *Lord of the Flies.* It received the Somerset Maugham award.

Strange Meeting, which followed, was a notable—even astonishing—departure. It is an account of the relationship that develops between two young British officers in World War I, showing how Hilliard, the alienated product of a cold and ungiving family, is warmed, opened, and redeemed by his friendship with the loving and beloved Barton. Susan Hill's interest in the Great War had been aroused by hearing Benjamin Britten's *War Requiem* performed at Coventry Cathedral in 1962. That sent her to Wilfred Owen's poetry and later she became "a First World War addict." Preparing the novel, the only one of her books that has required much research, she read "hundreds of books"—memoirs, diaries, poems. A reviewer in the *Times Literary Supplement* said that "with apparent effortlessness and something like photographic exactness Miss Hill describes life in the trenches. . . . Yet this is . . . not a successful novel. It inspires admiration, but the very restraint and precision of the detail manages to undermine the reality of the central relationship, which fades into a fantasy woven round a discoloured photograph of two handsome young Englishmen." Other critics agreed, but *Strange Meeting* was nevertheless the first of Susan Hill's books to achieve large sales.

It puzzled some reviewers and delighted others that the loving friendship between Hilliard and Barton is not presented as homosexual. Neither is that between Harvey Lawson and Francis Croft in *The Bird of Night* (1972), another study of a friendship tempered under extreme stress—the stress, this time, of madness. Croft is a poet and a genius whose mind hovers between innocent elation and uncontrollable despair, and who eventually kills himself. Lawson is a scholar, a dull devoted man who for twenty years lives with Croft and does his best to protect him from the assaults of reality. The relationship is recalled thirty years after it ended by Lawson, an old man waiting for death, badgered by journalists and scholars hoping to wring yet another television documentary or learned paper out of the anguish of England's greatest contemporary poet.

Nothing is harder for a novelist than to portray genius, and Susan Hill in this novel wisely avoids too many "quotations" from Croft's work, relying instead, as one critic pointed out, "on occasional references to public recognition of Francis as a great poet, on extracts from Francis's diary describing the pain of a poem's gestation, and on an assumption that the reader will spot how a midnight walk in a wood in deep snow became the 'well-known' poem about the owl." According to the *Times Literary Supplement,* Susan Hill "writes with very considerable control and power, using the minimum of stylistic elaboration yet suggesting a strongly poetic instinct for precise images: she has also now shown that she is ready to tackle possibly the most risky and unlikely material open to a woman novelist—a depiction of genius, insanity, a tale of two men who loved each other many decades ago, a tale with no sex, no politics, no topicality. Even if we are not wholly convinced of the poet's greatness, this remains a brave and daring novel about madness, and the speculation it raises about the value we put on unbalanced lives is not to be lightly forgotten." In England, the book won the £1000 Whitbread Award and was shortlisted for the £5000 Booker Prize. In the United States it had considerably less impact, for reasons that were discussed by Michele Murray in the "Restorations" series in the *New Republic.* She suggested that American reviewers gave it short shrift because it ignores fashionable themes and attitudes; instead "it is a thoroughly *created* piece of work, a novel wrought of language carefully designed to tell a story drawn, not from the surface of the author's life or fragments of her autobiography, but from the heart of her imagination."

In the Springtime of the Year is also in a sense a study of madness—in this case of the temporary derangement of a young woman whose sense of order and meaning is shattered by the pointless death of her husband. The book, wrote its reviewer in the *Times Literary Supplement,* "follows the fluctuations of her grief from the first trance of anguish, through chafing, irritating heaviness, to—in the end—a glimmering, precarious acceptance.... The whole, year-long process takes place in a countryside that seems at first oppressively quiet and empty. Only gradually do its rhythms begin to assert themselves and make human sense, so that Ruth comes back to life with the return of spring, and

dares to believe that her husband is living too. ... It is the ritual, almost anonymous, aspect of grief that dominates the writing, a pattern of despair and consolation that is as intensely conventional as a pastoral elegy. *In the Springtime of the Year* is a fable about resurrection, and its characters are not really particular people at all." Margaret Atwood, across the Atlantic, found the book weakened by its dialogue, "reminiscent of nineteenth century melodrama or of the radio plays of a bygone era," and dated also in its assumptions, its characterizations, and its resolution, "which has something to do with the heroine's coming out of her own isolation and grief by Helping Others in Trouble.... Still, despite lapses into simple-mindedness ... [it] justifies itself by the intensity of those things it does well: moments of genuine feeling, moments of vision. It is less a novel than the portrait of an emotion, and as this it is poignant and convincing."

Susan Hill has also published two volumes of short stories, of which the first, *The Albatross,* captured the John Llewellyn Rhys award. The same concerns emerge in her stories as in her novels. "The Albatross" itself, for example, is about Duncan, a retarded youth who lives with his invalid mother. She fosters his sense of inadequacy in order to keep him at home and his only real friend is Ted Flint, a fisherman who has lived the free life Duncan can only dream about. Flint offers Duncan work on his boat and takes him to the local pub, giving him a dangerous taste of a grown-up life. When Flint dies at sea Duncan is left without hope. He has a drink by himself at the pub, murders his mother, and sets fire to their house, gaining a few hours of freedom before he is found. A reviewer of the second collection, *A Bit of Singing and Dancing,* wrote that "Miss Hill's stamp is at once recognizable. She is, for instance, preoccupied ... with approaching death, and with the adjustment, or perhaps resignation, that can make old age dignified rather than fearful or petulant. ... Children—and especially those who are set apart from their fellows, who are parentless or sickly or 'not quite right'—have also become significant figures in Miss Hill's private world of suffering. ... Her range is ... remarkable, and half-a-dozen of these tales are better than most that find magazine publication. ... Hardy and Coppard presented their own, very English, world, and it looks as though Miss Hill is well on her way to joining their company."

There has been no less praise for her radio plays, the best known of which, *The Cold Country,* gave its title to a collection published in 1975. It deals with four men trapped in a tent by an Arctic blizzard, and studies the way in which each man's sense of purpose, his social conditioning, and his very identity are stripped away by hardship, isolation, and impending death. A reviewer in the London *Times* called it "an extraordinarily powerful and moving piece of work. . . . The allegory is the more powerful in that it holds up as an adventure story and Miss Hill displays in it her gift, astonishing in a woman, for getting to the heart of a group of men engaged in an activity apparently exclusive to the male. . . . All in all, this is a formidable occasion for radio drama." *Consider the Lilies* (1973), about a botanical garden curator who sees "the middle air" thronged with angels, attracted a good deal of discussion, though some critics found its "flat statement of metaphysics . . . inclined to fall flat." Susan Hill says that "writing a novel is nice, but it's a lonely business; when it's finished, that's it. Writing a radio play is lovely because when it's finished, it's only half there. It's a collaborative thing."

The late 1960s and early 1970s were immensely productive years for Susan Hill. For most of this time she lived alone in a small house in Leamington Spa, not far from her parents' home in Coventry, and here she wrote her short stories and radio plays. Her novels, however, she tackled differently. Every year she spent about eight weeks between January and March in a rented cottage overlooking the sea at Aldeburgh, on the windswept Suffolk coast, working in absolute seclusion. Aldeburgh is a small seaside resort and fishing port of great charm, famous as the home of Benjamin Britten and the setting of the annual arts festival he established there. Britten and his circle were part of the strong attraction Aldeburgh has for Susan Hill, and she and the composer became friends before he died. She says that he influenced her "in a way most writers are only influenced by other writers." Aldeburgh itself has entered into her novels and short stories: "I've tried to get to the bottom of the fascination of the place by writing about it over and over again—describing the beach and the marshes and the countryside around in dozens of different moods."

A small, slight woman, the author seems to her interviewers gregarious, extrovert, and placid (though she says that she is greatly afflicted by psychosomatic illness, especially when she is starting on a new book). She is a practicing Christian, and was for years an active member of the congregation of Coventry Cathedral, every year devoting several weeks before Christmas to organizing the Cathedral's scheme for distributing toys to underprivileged children. She was engaged to the choirmaster of the

Cathedral, a talented musician who died suddenly of a coronary in 1972, shortly before they were to have been married. Her faith—her belief that "the whole of life is made by God and is constantly being created"—was, she says, of great help to her then. In 1975 she was married to Stanley Wells, a Shakespearean scholar and lecturer at Warwick University. They live at Stratford-on-Avon and have one child. At the time of her marriage the author prophesied that she would in future "write less, and it will probably take longer," and this has been the case. Susan Hill plays the piano and the oboe, and lists her recreations as "music, walking in the English countryside, friends, reading, broadcasting." She became a Fellow of the Royal Society of Literature in 1972.

PRINCIPAL WORKS: *Novels*—The Enclosure, 1961; Do Me a Favour, 1963; Gentleman and Ladies, 1968; A Change for the Better, 1969; I'm the King of the Castle, 1970; Strange Meeting, 1971; The Bird of Night, 1972; In the Springtime of the Year, 1974. *Short Stories*—The Albatross, 1971; A Bit of Singing and Dancing, 1973. *Plays*—The Cold Country and Other Plays for Radio, 1975.

ABOUT: Contemporary Authors 33–36, 1973; Ross, A. (ed.) Living in London, 1974; Vinson, J. (ed.) Contemporary Novelists, 1976; Who's Who, 1978; Writers Directory, 1976 –1978. *Periodicals*—Encounter January 1973; Guardian April 4, 1973; Library Journal April 15, 1969; Listener July 12, 1973; National Review April 27, 1973; New Republic February 16, 1974; May 18, 1974; New Statesman January 31, 1969; New York Times Book Review May 27, 1973; January 25, 1974; Nova June 1973; Observer November 26, 1972; Times (London) October 3, 1972; January 15, 1975; Times Literary Supplement February 6, 1969; October 29, 1971; September 15, 1972.

*HIPPIUS, ZINAIDA (NIKOLAYEVNA)

(November 11, 1869–September 9, 1945), Russian poet, novelist, short story writer, essayist, and critic, was born in Belev, in the central Russian province of Tula. She came of an old and noble German family, her ancestor, Baron von Hippius, having emigrated from Mecklenburg to Moscow in the sixteenth century. The name is spelt in Russian with an initial "G," though she herself always transliterated it into the Latin alphabet with an "H." She was the eldest daughter of Nikolai Romanovich Gippius, superprocurator of the St. Petersburg Senate and later chief judge in Nezhin. As a child she traveled much in Russia with her parents, but she was a somewhat sickly girl, whose doctors suspected congenital tuberculosis, and on this account the family settled when she was fifteen in the Crimean health resort of Yalta.

Zinaida Hippius spent only a few months of her childhood at school—at the Kiev Institute for Girls (1877-1878) and later at the Fisher classics school in Moscow (1882). She was oth-
*hip′ e ŏŏs

ZINAIDA HIPPIUS

erwise educated privately by French, English, and German governesses who taught her their languages, and by graduate students and professors who tutored her in music, history, mathematics, and literature. She read avidly, her favorite author being Dostoevsky, whose works were a profound and lasting influence on her. She began to write poetry as a girl, her first volume of verse appearing as *Severny Vestnik* (The Northern Herald) in 1888, when she was nineteen.

On a visit to Tbilisi (Tiflis) in the same year she met the poet and novelist Dmitri Merezhkovsky, whom she married in 1889. She shared her husband's religious and philosophical interests, and their house in St. Petersburg became a salon and second home for the symbolist writers and modernist artists of the time. But in many ways theirs was a marriage of opposites, both in their literary views—they did not care for each other's poetry and constantly "argued and even quarrelled over matters of poetic taste"—and in temperament and physique. He was drab and diminutive; she was tall, slender, and striking, a Pre-Raphaelite beauty with green eyes and flaming red hair. To their circle of young poets, who were all a little in love with her, she was a "Beardsleyan Sataness," as Andrey Bely dubbed her. With her lorgnette and the masculine clothes she sometimes wore she presented an "ultra-decadent" appearance. While Merezhkovsky was known as the Pope or the Delphic Oracle of literature, she was its Circe, esteemed for her charm, wit, and shrewd analytical ability.

Zinaida Hippius rejected the dedication of many of her young admirers to "art for art's sake," maintaining that poetic insight derived from religious intuition and ecstatic vision. In *Zinaida Gippius: An Intellectual Profile,* Temira Pachmuss has analyzed her ideas to present her as a highly original religious thinker. She divided history into three periods—the Old and New Testaments of the past and the Third Testament of the future, in which all antitheses would be reconciled. Seeking to arouse "a new religious consciousness" that would inaugurate this apocalyptic Third Testament Christianity, she was the guiding spirit in the establishment in 1901 of a Religious-Philosophical Society and in the founding of the religious periodical *Novy put* (The New Way).

Her prose is notable for its intellectual power and wit, qualities particularly evident in the literary criticism she wrote under the masculine pen-name Anton Krayny (Anton the Extreme); Andrey Bely compared her attacks on populist writers to a skilled swordsman's assault on an unarmed pugilist. But her critical essays are highly subjective, showing a blind spot toward writers (such as Chekhov) who did not share her religious views. These essays, often taking the form of psychological profiles of authors, were collected in *Literaturni dnevnik* (A Literary Diary, 1911), and later in *Zhivye litsa* (Living Faces, 1925), which includes memoirs of poets, writers, and others she had known, including Blok, Bryusov, Sologub, Rozanov, and Rasputin.

Her most important imaginative work is her poetry, which combines the religious mysticism and decadent aestheticism common to early Russian symbolism with her own characteristic intellectual wit and brilliance. Her poetry has often been criticized as too abstract and intellectual. But D.S. Mirsky called her formally perfect lyrics "so original that I do not know anything in any language that resembles them," and wrote that "from the very beginning she made her verse a wonderfully refined and well-tempered instrument for the expression of her thought. She went on refining it and making it more obedient to every twist and turn of her subtle musings."

Zinaida Hippius was a highly introspective poet who wrote only when she "felt she could not do otherwise," so that her verse is an accurate reflection of her own inner world. Vladimir Markov believes that "future critics may very well someday call Zinaida Hippius the greatest religious poet of Russia because the mainstream of her poetry is nothing but the story of the soul's journey to a complete finding of God." But her idealistic philosophy went with a pessimistic temperament; if the central theme of her early verse is the spirit's struggle to break free of the prison of reality and fly heavenward, her most powerful poems record the defeat of the spirit. Like one of Dostoevsky's characters she alternates between burning faith and a despairing demonolatry, and it is her more hopeless moods which are expressed most memorably.

Her finest poems are collected in the two volumes of *Sobraniye stikhov* (A Collection of Poems, 1904 and 1910), which are full of symbols of evil and sin, a horrifying vision of a Manichean world in which evil triumphs. Her preoccupation with the morbid and demonic, her sense of alienation and of an inability to love, and the opposition in her nature between idealism and perverse sensuality has been called her "Svidrigailov theme," after the character in Dostoevsky's *Crime and Punishment*. The decadent Svidrigailov has his own nihilistic notion of eternity as a dusty bathhouse filled with cobwebs and spiders—an image that Zinaida Hippius develops in her own way in poems like "Psyche" and "Spiders." Her sense of evil and self-hatred are well reflected in "Ona" (She), translated here by Temira Pachmuss:

In her shameless and despicable baseness,
She is gray like dust, like earthly ashes.
And I am dying from this propinquity,
From the indissoluble bond between her and me.

She is rough, she is prickly,
She is cold, she is a snake.
Her disgustingly searing, jagged scales
Have covered me with wounds. . . .

She, stubborn one, coils around me
With her rings, strangling me.
And this dead, and this black,
And this fearful thing is my soul.

Zinaida Hippius's imaginative prose is generally considered inferior to her poetry. The short stories in the early collections *Novye lyudi* (New People, 1896) and *Zerkala* (Mirrors, 1898) are interesting in their rejection of conventional morals and behavior. As Temira Pachmuss puts it, her "men and women almost proudly parade their loneliness and helplessness before the world. They admit that their thoughts are the product of lonely minds and that a better future can become reality only through a miracle. . . . They advocate the Nietzschean philosophy of egoism and pursue personal happiness at the expense of social considerations." This is not true of her later stories and her novels, which express her own social, religious, and political concerns. The Merezhkovskys supported the unsuccessful revolution of 1905, going abroad to France after its failure and returning to St. Pe-

tersburg only in 1909. They believed that the revolution had failed because the intelligentsia had sought personal liberation rather than a truly revolutionary social movement—one that would create the new and more spiritual society they had preached for so long.

This is the theme of the novels that were Zinaida Hippius's most ambitious work, two studies in political psychology in the manner of Dostoevsky's *The Possessed* which were intended as the first and last parts of a trilogy, though the middle novel was left unfinished. In the first, *Chortova kukla* (The Devil's Doll, 1911), we are shown that Yuri Dolgoruky, the would-be angel and apostle of individualism, is really only a puppet of the devil. There is a vacuum in his soul, for his rationalism, devoid of intuition and religious feeling, deprives life of its meaning, and his revolutionary deeds lead only to disaster. Similarly, in *Roman-Tsarevich* (1914), Roman is a lofty idealist who, like many such, can commit any atrocity in the service of his cause.

Of her plays the most successful was *Zelyonoye koltso* (1916, translated by S. S. Koteliansky as *The Green Ring*). It was staged at the Alexandrinsky Theatre in St. Petersburg by Meyerhold, with the eminent actress Maria Savina coming out of retirement to play one of the parts, and in 1922 was produced at the Neighborhood Playhouse in New York. The play's theme is the revolt of the younger generation against empty materialism, and their pursuit of salvation in the creation of a new society with new human relationships and new spiritual values.

Disillusioned as the Merezhkovskys had been by the 1905 revolution, they were aroused to fresh optimism by the February Revolution of 1917. Zinaida Hippius wrote manifestos for the Socialist-Revolutionary party arguing that democracy was a "most profound *religious* idea." But the Bolshevik coup was totally alien to the Merezhkovskys' concept of revolution as a religious renewal, and they soon came to see it as the Kingdom of the Antichrist. In 1919 they fled to Poland, then to Berlin, and on to Paris, where they spent the rest of their lives as part of the circle of *émigré* writers, and where Zinaida Hippius died in 1945, four years after her husband.

In these long years of exile her sense of loneliness and alienation returned with redoubled intensity, but her later poetry includes some magnificent political invective in verse such as "Veselye" (Joy), a powerful lyric written only four days after the Bolshevik coup, in which she predicts the nightmare of autocracy and slavery to come. The essays in such volumes as *Cher-*

naya kniga (The Black Book, 1924) and *Sinyaya kniga* (The Blue Book, 1929) express her violent antipathy to the Soviet regime, and this has of course led to neglect of her work inside the Soviet Union. Leon Trotsky wrote of her that "a hundred years hence the historian of the Russian Revolution will perhaps point out how a nailed boot stepped on the lyrical little toe of a Petrograd lady, who immediately showed the real property-owning witch under her decadent-mystic-erotic covering." But she has been increasingly recognized as a far more talented and important writer than her once more famous husband—as one of Russia's finest poets, and perhaps its greatest religious poet.

Nina Berberova, who first met Zinaida Hippius in Paris when she was nearly sixty, says she then "had poor vision and was hard of hearing; her laugh was her defense; she played with her lorgnette and smiled, pretending sometimes to be more near-sighted, deafer than she was in fact, sometimes asking that something she had understood perfectly be repeated. A constant struggle-and-joke went on between her and the outside world. She (the real she) shielded herself from the real life around and in her with irony, mannerisms, intrigues, affectations." And Berberova sums her up as "one of the remarkable women of this century. . . . Paradoxical, whimsical, often nasty, sometimes charming."

PRINCIPAL WORKS IN ENGLISH TRANSLATION: The Green Ring (play), 1920; Selected Works of Zinaida Hippius, translated by Temira Pachmuss, 1972; Between Paris and St. Petersburg: Selected Diaries of Zinaida Hippius, translated by Temira Pachmuss, 1975; Intellect and Ideas in Action: Selected Correspondence, translated by Temira Pachmuss, 1975. *Poems in* Deutsch, B. and Yarmolinsky, A. (eds.) Modern Russian Poetry, 1921; Markov, V. and Sparks, M. (eds.) Modern Russian Poetry, 1966; Obolensky, D. (ed.) Penguin Book of Russian Verse, 1965; Pachmuss, T. Zinaida Hippius: An Intellectual Profile, 1971; Raffel, B. (ed.) Russian Poetry Under the Tsars, 1971; Selver, P. (ed.) Modern Russian Poetry, 1917. *Essay in* Field, A. (ed.) The complection of Russian Literature, 1971.

ABOUT: Field, A. (ed.) The Complection of Russian Literature, 1971; Maslenikov, O.A. The Frenzied Poets, 1952; Mirsky, D.S. A History of Russian Literature, 1949; Pachmuss, T. Zinaida Hippius: An Intellectual Profile, 1971; Penguin Companion to Literature 2, 1969; Poggioli, R. The Poets of Russia, 1960; Slonim, M. From Chekhov to the Revolution, 1953; Smith, H. (ed.) Columbia Dictionary of Modern European Literature, 1947; Snow, V. Russian Writers, 1946. *Periodicals*—New York Review of Books March 23, 1972.

HOAGLAND, EDWARD (MORLEY) (December 21, 1932–), American essayist and novelist, writes: "I was born in New York City

EDWARD HOAGLAND

and moved with my family at the age of eight to the suburban town of New Canaan, Connecticut, where my parents continued to live until my father's death in 1967. He was a financial lawyer for the Standard Oil Company of New Jersey, and worked in Europe for the State and Defense departments. Except in autobiographical essays, I have not so far dealt much with this social and personal background, but rather with my reaction against it and the fields of force in which, beginning in my late teens, I sought a new life for myself. I wrote documentary novels about the circus, about big-city boxing, about New York City, and went to northern British Columbia to recapitulate in a book what the American frontier must have been like. Then, around 1969, I started writing essays—have done upwards of fifty or sixty by now. In my case, this was somehow a freer form; I couldn't have stopped if I'd wanted to, and no longer feel the same difficulty in taking up as subject matter the life I knew originally—prep school, a wealthy suburb. I continue to cherish ambitions in fiction as well, however, and expect to write more novels, moving between or blending the forms. I have not yet become aware of bumping my head against some sort of ceiling to my talent; the writer's task of exploring his capacities and regions of responsiveness remains a fairly happy one. I seem to be good at writing about animals, for instance, but still, in an unusual juxtaposition, find in myself some of the versatility that went with the old-fashioned vocation of man-of-letters. I'm peripatetic—go about with muskrat trappers at the mouth of the Mississippi and on muleback in the Big Bend of the Rio Grande—and on the whole find life too fine a phenomenon to quite believe it all is coming to an apocalyptic end. I'm married, with a child, and have been married previously."

Cat Man, the first of Hoagland's "documentary novels," was published in 1956, when he was only twenty-four. The book, based on what he had seen during a vacation job with a traveling circus, struck one reviewer as "disgusting," and another as "a study of filth, degradation and violence," but impressed Walter Havighurst as "a tight and scrupulous tale, all developing in one morning on the weedy riverbank at Council Bluffs, though with some back-tracking interchapters. Not a scene is wasted. There is nothing tentative about this first novel. It is written with knowledge, skill, and authority."

Hoagland turned his attention to professional boxing in *The Circle Home.* It describes the hopeless attempt at a comeback made by Denny Kelly, washed up at twenty-nine, and no more successful as a husband and father than as a fighter. Most reviewers were impressed by the force of Hoagland's direct and staccato prose, and by the humor, compassion, and vividness of his account of the sweaty world of trainers, managers, has-beens, and hopefuls. Taliaferro Boatwright went further, calling the book "a carefully structured work of art in which every piece of brilliant exposition . . . is so stunningly, and yet so artfully natural, that its place in the overall design becomes apparent only in retrospection." Granville Hicks, however, commented that "Hoagland makes us believe in Kelly, but he does not interest us in him," and James A. Hart in *Contemporary Novelists* meant something similar when he wrote that many of Hoagland's characters "are so busy learning survival techniques in an uncaring world that their personalities are never fully developed."

The Peacock's Tail, about a bigoted young WASP who discovers himself and reality among the multiracial rejects in an Upper West Side hotel, had a cool reception and, apart from some short stories in such journals as the *New Yorker* and the *New American Review,* Hoagland has so far produced no more fiction.

In 1966 the author went to British Columbia, where he "rode the rivers, followed the trails, and [hampered by his acute stutter] talked to old timers from the gold-rush and homestead eras about their heydays as trappers, prospectors, traders and explorers." *Notes From the Century Before* is his journal of this adventure and of what he thought and felt as he traveled. Geoffrey Wolff wrote: "his journal is about tangles and unrealized ambitions. His and his subjects'. And he understands wonderfully what to make of what he sees and hears. . . . The book has no thesis, and no real moral. . . . Just a strange and beautiful book."

Hoagland turned from this journal to the essay. *The Courage of Turtles* contains fifteen pieces, many of them previously published in the *Village Voice* and other periodicals on subjects ranging from bear hunting, circuses, tugboats, and taxidermy to autobiography—pieces that describe Hoagland waiting for a baby's birth, and evoke his delight in mailing his mutilated draft card to President Johnson. Hoagland says above that he has found the essay "somehow a freer form" than fiction, and Geoffrey Wolff evidently felt that this was so, saying that "Hoagland remarkably combines the observer's clear sense with the self-revealing passion of a man who has been 'bottled up' too long. . . . To read two pages of Hoagland at random, is to know immediately that you are in the hands of a supremely tough-minded man, and a man of perfect honesty. . . . He is a marvelous writer."

The essays collected in *Walking the Dead Diamond River* center on "the lures and pitfalls of isolation versus the attractions and traumas of what passes for civilization." It was as warmly praised as its predecessor for the "clear focus," the "odd and inquisitive particularity" of Hoagland's vision. Alfred Kazin found himself most interested in the persona of the author himself—not an "all-knowing insider" but someone who "is not afraid to sound vulnerable, excited, self-deceiving, gentle." Thomas R. Edwards, reviewing the pieces collected in *Red Wolves and Black Bears* (1976), suggested that Hoagland "sometimes lapses into routine philosophizing," but said that there were passages in this volume "as richly informed with a sense of the strangeness and wonder of American landscapes and folkways as any I can remember."

The author is the son of Warren Hoagland and the former Helen Morley. He was educated at Deerfield Academy and at Harvard, which gave him his A.B. in 1954, and served in the U.S. Army from 1955 to 1957. Hoagland was married in 1960 to Amy Ferrara and, as he says, has a child by his second marriage (1968) to Marion Magid, who is managing editor of the magazine *Commentary.* He has been a part-time teacher since 1963 at Rutgers University, Sarah Lawrence College, the City College of New York, and the New School for Social Research. He received a Houghton Mifflin Fellowship in 1956, a Longview Foundation Award in 1961, a Guggenheim fellowship and the Prix de Rome of the

American Academy of Arts and Letters in 1964, and an O. Henry Award in 1971.

Hoagland feels that Turgenev, especially the *Sportsman's Sketches,* did most to shape his style. He has said that "writers can be categorized by many criteria, one of which is whether they prefer subject matter that they rejoice in or subject matter they deplore and wish to savage with ironies." He is of the first sort, and this is consistent with his claim to be "a brassbound optimist." In spite of his devotion to what remains of the North American wilderness, Hoagland loves crowds and still thinks of himself as "a city rat"—"I will never lose my New Yorker's grimace, New Yorker's squint and New Yorker's speed." He has a home in Greenwich Village and another in Barton, Vermont.

PRINCIPAL WORKS: *Fiction*—Cat Man, 1956; The Circle Home, 1960; The Peacock's Tail, 1965. *Nonfiction*—Notes From the Century Before, 1969; The Courage of Turtles, 1971; Walking the Dead Diamond River, 1973; The Moose on the Wall: Field Notes From the Vermont Wilderness, 1974 (England only); Red Wolves and Black Bears, 1976.

ABOUT: Contemporary Authors 1-4 1st revision, 1967; Vinson, J. (ed.) Contemporary Novelists, 1972. *Periodicals*—Newsweek January 18, 1971; April 2, 1973; Publishers Weekly May 24, 1976; Time April 2, 1973.

HOBSBAWM, E(RIC) J(OHN) (ERNEST) ("Francis Newton") (June 9, 1917–) British historian, was born in Alexandria, Egypt, the son of Leopold Percy Hobsbawm and the former Nelly Gruen. He grew up in Vienna in what he describes in his book *Revolutionaries* as the "Jewish middleclass culture of central Europe after the first world war." His "first political conversation," he recalls, "took place when I was six in an Alpine sanatorium, between two Jewish mother-type ladies. It dealt with Trotsky. ('Say what you like, he's a Jewish boy called Bronstein.')" He felt the strength of political feeling at the age of ten, when Viennese workers burned the Palace of Justice, and again at thirteen when the Nazis won a hundred and seven seats in the Reichstag in the 1930 German general election. Shortly afterwards his family moved to Berlin, where Hobsbawm experienced first-hand the economic and political decay and demoralization that preceded Hitler's seizure of power.

Leaving Germany in 1933, he settled in England, attending St. Marylebone Grammar School in London and then Cambridge University, where he received his B.A. in 1939, his M.A. in 1942, and his Ph.D. in 1951. He served in the ranks with the British army from 1940 to 1946, emerging as a sergeant, and in 1947 went as a lecturer in history to Birkbeck College, University of London; he became reader in history there in 1959, and in 1970 was appointed professor of economic and social history. From 1949 to 1955 he was also a fellow in history of King's College, Cambridge University.

Eric Hobsbawm ascribes to the traumas and upheavals of his youth his commitment to revolutionary politics. Disenfranchised and disillusioned Jewish intellectuals like himself, he explains in *Revolutionaries,* "became either communists or some equivalent form of revolutionary marxists, or if we chose our own version of blood-and-soil nationalism, Zionists. . . . We . . . became revolutionaries not so much because of our economic problems, though some of us were poor and most of us faced an uncertain future, but because the old society no longer seemed visible. It had no perspectives."

Hobsbawm, whom George Lichtheim described as "a Marxist-Leninist, though a very sophisticated specimen of the breed," joined the British Communist Party in the mid-1930s. He rapidly established himself as one of Britain's leading Marxist historians, an authority on the history (and psychology) of revolution, and on the British labor, socialist, and radical movements. Regarding Marxism as "a process of development" rather than a rigid dogma, he has used it, as Sheldon S. Wolin wrote in the *New York Times Book Review,* "as a mode of analysis which is both empirical and humane; critical of capitalism but also of Stalinist repression; and disposed to prefer the 'sensible' over the visionary."

Eric Hobsbawm's first work, *Labour's Turning Point, 1880-1900* (1948), was a collection of extracts from contemporary sources whose reissue in 1974 confirmed its value. In 1959 he published *Primitive Rebels: Studies in Archaic Forms of Social Movement in the 19th and 20th Centuries,* dealing with the little-studied transformation of 'primitive' or 'pre-political' manifestations of rebellion into tighter-knit socialist and communist political parties and trade unions. The first half of the book deals mainly with nineteenth-century Italy and Spain, the second with Britain. Although Hobsbawm discusses the historical background of each movement, its ideology and socio-economic setting, he does not attempt an "exhaustive or definitive" cross-sectional analysis but rather a survey of developmental patterns which might suggest generalizations about human behavior under revolutionary conditions.

Critics generally found this study in social psychology full of curious and fascinating information and perceptive analogies, expressed in a lively and highly readable style. Some objected to the lack of a final synthesis and the restricted range of case examples (Hobsbawm admitted his preference for "some personal contact, however slight, with the people and even the places" he wrote about). But on the whole reviewers agreed with D.M. Smith's comment in the *Spectator:* "Mr. Hobsbawm writes so fairly and with so much understanding and sympathy that many who disagree with him fundamentally will find their own views substantially altered by what he says."

Hobsbawm's contribution to Sir Ronald Syme's History of Civilization series, *The Age of Revolution, 1789-1848,* traces the impact on Europe of what he calls the "dual revolution"—the French Revolution and the British Industrial Revolution—which, he maintains, changed the course of human history more radically than any previous event. He deals broadly with the period's crucial developments—the growth of the factory system, the changing social structure, the decline of the old agrarian order, and new trends in philosophy, literature, science, and the arts—offering not so much a systematic factual account as a series of personal and highly discursive meditations which Theodore S. Hamerow, writing in the *American Historical Review,* called "provocative, penetrating, immensely learned, and at times highly controversial."

Some of the controversy centered on the fact that the book stops short of 1848, thus leaving unanswered the question asked by J. L. Talmon: "Was the nineteenth century the age of Revolution or the century of the *taming of the Revolution?*" Nor did it seem to some readers that Hobsbawm had proved his contention that his two revolutions had pointed in the same direction. A. J. P. Taylor wrote that Hobsbawm's book "is the *Communist Manifesto* transformed with great skill and knowledge into a work of history." There was a mixed reception also for Hobsbawm's second contribution to the series, *The Age of Capital, 1848-1875,* which appeared in 1975. He admitted his personal "distaste, perhaps a certain contempt," for this acquisitive age, and David Landes concluded in his review that "this subject is just not . . . [Hobsbawm's] 'cup of tea.' "

Labouring Men: Studies in the History of Labour (1964) contains eighteen essays of varying length treating aspects of radical, socialist, and labor ideology from the late eighteenth century to World War I. Many of them, originally published as journal articles as far back as the early 1950s, had become standard reading in the field. It seemed to J. F. C. Harrison that Hobsbawm's greatest achievement was "the enviable ease

with which he moves through all sections and periods of the socialist and labor movements, drawing upon enlightening parallels here and suggesting contrary evidence there. . . . The result is that this book is completely free from that platitudinous parochialism that is the bane of so much labor history. Nor does his Marxism degenerate into sectarian dogmatism." The *Times Literary Supplement*'s reviewer agreed that these studies "succeed more often than they fail; and successes of this kind are at the apex of historical achievement." All the same, he found Hobsbawm's eclectic wanderings disturbing: "Time and again these studies tremble on the edge of a new mastery in the discipline of comparative history; but . . . the comparisons are never really worked through. . . . It is to be hoped that Dr. Hobsbawm will not remain satisfied with having suggested so many fruitful themes to other scholars, but will stay long enough with some body of comparative material to press home a major study to his own conclusion."

Industry and Empire: The Making of Modern English Society, Volume II: 1750 to the Present Day (1968)—the companion volume to Christopher Hill's *Reformation to Industrial Revolution: The Making of Modern English Society, Volume I: 1530-1780*—analyzes Britain's economic rise as the first industrialized country, her domination and her decline as a world power. Hobsbawm attributes Britain's decline and her present ailments to her early and prolonged ascendancy as the "world's workshop," as well as to widespread economic changes beyond her control: choosing to postpone fundamental economic readjustments in favor of continued financial and commercial imperialism, she did not come to terms with the realities of her situation until well into the twentieth century.

Eric Hobsbawm's clear mastery of the immense range of complex social changes that took place between the mid-eighteenth-century and the 1960s earned him warm critical praise. Moreover, unlike most Marxist history, wrote Peter Jenkins, the book is "no recital of turgid facts and mechanical interpretations but, on the contrary, is often original in judgment, is elegantly written throughout and, within the terms of its conception, is balanced and fair." A reviewer in the *Times Literary Supplement* commended the work's contemporary relevancy: "It convinces, as no comparable textbook does, that history matters, that our current predicament is inexplicable except within the terms of historical argument, that anatomies of Britain which lack this dimension are thin and insubstantial." He was somewhat less enthusiastic about Hobsbawm's analytic approach, noting that "a high proportion of his facts are expressed in numerical form and sometimes give a spurious impression of hardness and indisputability, whereas in fact they conceal conflicting evidence and evade the need for important qualifications. This is in part the result of his own disposition towards a stern quantitative historical realism." But David Jordan thought the book would become "a standard introduction to a complex and important subject."

In *Captain Swing* (1969), Eric Hobsbawm joined forces with another eminent historian of social unrest, George Rudé, to "examine the movements of social protest that swept the English countryside during the period from 1790 to 1850." They concentrated in particular on the English agricultural rising of 1830, during which the signature of a mythical Captain Swing appeared on many of the threatening letters sent to landowners on behalf of the impoverished laborers, demanding wage increases, food, and an end to the use of agricultural machinery, especially the threshing machine. As Marxists analyzing the "village laborers' revolt," the authors were interested primarily in relating the pattern of agitation, and the savage repression that followed, to the economic and social structure of the time. There was much praise both for Rudé's day-by-day, sometimes hour-by-hour, account of the spread of the riots, and for Hobsbawm's broader generalizations, which—as one critic remarked—displayed "his usual acuteness of perception, his flair for the striking metaphor and his abundant historical imagination."

The same year, Hobsbawm published *Bandits*, his study of the role of outlaws, past and present, as catalysts of rural upheaval and social revolt, examining the conditions that produced and sustained them and the motives that changed them into revolutionary expropriators. Most reviewers agreed that, as one of them said, Hobsbawm writes "with great elegance, a constantly renewed and often startling insight, compassion, and a sympathetic humour. The result is a wise as well as an exciting book, a very valuable addition to the history of mentalities and to that of popular protest."

Revolutionaries (1973) is a collection of essays and book reviews about revolutionary parties, movements, and writers, all bearing more or less on a single central problem—the reconciliation of orthodox Communism with intellectual integrity. The work was hailed as a brilliant analysis of post-World War I revolutionary trends, from Communism in France and anarchism in Spain to guerrilla warfare in Vietnam. Sheldon S. Wolin, writing in the New York *Times Book Re-*

view, found it not only instructive but also of great interest in providing "fascinating glimpses into the complex loyalties of a highly civilized mind dedicated to Communism."

Eric Hobsbawm was married in 1962 to Marlene Schwarz. The Hobsbawms, who live in London, have a son and a daughter. The author has been a visiting professor at Stanford, the Massachusetts Institute of Technology, and Cornell, among other universities. He holds honorary degrees from the University of Chicago and the University of Stockholm. An honorary fellow of King's College, Cambridge, since 1973, and a fellow of the British Academy since 1976, he has also been since 1971 an honorary member of the American Academy of Arts and Sciences. He has served as a council member of the Economic History Society and as vice-chairman of the Society for the Study of Labour History. Hobsbawm, who is fluent in several languages, lists travel as his principal recreation. He is also very much interested in jazz, and in 1959 published *The Jazz Scene* (under the pseudonym Francis Newton), discussing not only the history and stylistic development of jazz but its impact on modern society.

Theodore S. Hamerow, reviewing *The Age of Revolution,* wrote that "for those who know something about the subject Hobsbawm will be fun. They will admire the deftness with which a sharp mind takes things apart and puts them together again, weaving apparently disparate developments into interesting new patterns, enriching a history of well-known events with original insight and apt allusion." J. H. Plumb has welcomed his "salutary, disturbing, critical effect" on British historiography, and David Landes, one of his most outspoken critics, admits that "I love to read Eric Hobsbawm. He knows so much; he reads everything; he translates German poetry into English rhyme; and whatever he writes about, he has something new and important to say."

PRINCIPAL WORKS: Primitive Rebels: Studies in Archaic Forms of Social Movement in the Nineteenth and Twentieth Centuries, 1959 (also published as Social Bandits and Primitive Rebels); The Age of Revolution: Europe, 1789-1848, 1962; Labouring Men: Studies in the History of Labour, 1964; Industry and Empire: The Making of Modern English Society, Volume II: 1750 to the Present Day, 1968 (in England subtitled: An Economic History of Britain Since 1750); (with George Rudé) Captain Swing, 1968; Bandits, 1969; Revolutionaries: Contemporary Essays, 1973; The Age of Capital, 1848-1875, 1975. As *"Francis Newton"*: The Jazz Scene, 1959. As editor—Labour's Turning Point, 1880-1900: Extracts From Contemporary Sources, 1948; Karl Marx, Pre-Capitalist Economic Formations, 1964.

ABOUT: Academic Who's Who, 1975-1976; Contemporary Authors 5-8 1st revision, 1969; Lichtheim, G. Collected

Essays, 1973; Who's Who, 1978. *Periodicals*—American Anthropologist August 1961; American Historical Review July 1963, October 1965; Book World May 4, 1969; March 1, 1970; Economist January 16, 1965; April 19, 1969; September 1, 1973; Encounter September 1963, March 1965; English Historical Review October 1970; New Statesman November 30, 1962; November 27, 1964; May 24, 1968; February 7, 1969; July 27, 1973; November 21, 1975; New York Review of Books February 13, 1969; June 19, 1969; New York Times Book Review November 3, 1968; November 25, 1973; May 9, 1976; Spectator May 29, 1959; Times Literary Supplement July 10, 1959; January 11, 1963; December 21, 1964; February 27, 1969; September 11, 1969; March 26, 1970; August 17, 1973; June 4, 1976.

SANDRA HOCHMAN

HOCHMAN, SANDRA (September 11, 1936–), American poet, novelist, dramatist, and journalist, was born in New York City, the daughter of Sidney Hochman and Mae Barnett (Schumer) Hochman. She was educated at Bennington College (B.A., 1957) and has also studied at the Sorbonne in Paris and at Columbia University. Sandra Hochman began her career as an actress—she was a member of Lee Strasberg's Actors Studio in New York and has appeared in a number of off-Broadway productions. She has traveled widely in Europe and Asia, and has lived in Paris, London, and Athens. Her first marriage, to the violinist Ivry Gitlis, ended in divorce, as did her 1965 marriage to Harvey Leve. She has a daughter, Ariel.

Her first book, *Voyage Home,* appeared in Paris in 1960; her second, *Manhattan Pastures* (1963), won the Yale Series of Younger Poets Award. Dudley Fitts, then editor of the Yale Series, commended in his introduction to that volume the author's "willingness to take risks," her "power to invest the ordinary with the strange," and her "amused (and amusing) control of the delicate forces of diction and rhythm." Not everyone agreed, but Denise Levertov praised her "instinctive rapport with language," saying that "she doesn't strive to impose metaphor on experience; metaphor and myth simply befall her." The danger inherent in this gift, Levertov thought, was that "she can slip too easily from imagination to fancy; she tends to babble-write when she has nothing to say," and needs to "feel her way deeper into what she experiences, to demand of herself more precision." John Logan, noting that the book relies heavily on allusions to literature or travel, liked best the long poem "Ivory and Horn" and the short lyrics "Adam" and "Silence." Pointing out that only five of these forty poems had seen print before, Logan said that there was a good deal of what looked to him like student work in the collection.

The Vaudeville Marriage (1966) was described by one reviewer as a "cycle of monologues" about failure in marriage, isolation in childhood, heartbreak in family relations—dramatic lyrics in which the pain is "both obscured and intensified by the verbal audacities and fresh metaphors each poem presents. . . . Often near-hysteria pulses under the irony or restraint imposed by the monologuist—her phrases clipped and ironic to block off the wild scream of insanity." The book includes a number of poems about clowns and magic and about dreams—the immanence of wonder and mystery in the ordinary is a recurrent theme in Sandra Hochman's work: "We discover whatever mystery we can." Burton Kendle spoke of her "flat, sometimes throwaway delivery" in poems that "make no attempt to seduce with sound effects," and R. J. Clements thought that hers was "a muse with a big-city temperament and speaking the most contemporary Broadway idiom."

Love Poems, privately printed in Hong Kong in 1966, was followed by the travel poems of *Love Letters From Asia* (1968). The poems Sandra Hochman had written between 1960 and 1970 were collected in *Earthworks* (1970). Diane Ackerman was impressed by those dealing with the author's pregnancy and motherhood, and thought that these experiences had brought a sense of continuity to her work, "a verbal ease and sense of order." But it seemed to John Koethe that the author's "major theme and preoccupation—learning how to live—keeps her constantly poised at that point where one's experience becomes charged and baffling but one cannot quite understand why. Thus, we get from this book a picture of a personality progressively maturing but perpetually bewildered." An English reviewer in the *Times Literary Supple-*

ment suggested that these poems "are like the letters of an adventurous friend—she lives an exciting life, but art so often prefers to stay quietly in an upstairs room." The new poems in *Futures* (1974) were liked for "their consistently honest recordings of passion, pain, disappointment," and for their humor, but there were complaints that they were out of focus, self-indulgent, and prosy.

Walking Papers (1971), Sandra Hochman's first novel, had a very much warmer reception. Diana Balooka, the product of battling Jewish parents and three marriages, delivers her vivid, desperate, often very funny monologue at a time when she is divorcing her third husband in the midst of a bad love affair with another man. "This state of affairs," wrote Annie Gottlieb, "becomes the departure point for a search into the self, into the multiple pasts and selves: all the way back, through a bizarre succession of lovers, to the first lovers, the parents, and their divorce, which first divided Diana from herself. . . . Miss Hochman commands a language of trustful and vital recklessness; it takes risks, rushes things with handfuls of words, scores hits in soaring hyperboles. And the book does have the consistence of a poem; a knotted and tangled net of imagery holds it together." In the end, Annie Gottlieb thought (and many readers agreed), "*Walking Papers* both delights and frustrates by its inclusiveness and its fragmentariness. I was dizzy with admiration for Sandra Hochman's ability, first to *name* so much and then to bring remarkably much of it to more than linguistic life. It is the novel's problem that these are sometimes two separate processes. When they are one, when life and language intensify each other, it becomes clear that Miss Hochman has enough of a novelist's gift . . . to have taken on a little less and made more of it."

The two novels that followed did not repeat this success. Lulu Cartwright in *Happiness Is Too Much Trouble* (1976) takes up an important post in Hollywood (as the "token woman") and fights hard to make worthwhile movies in an industry that is interested only in profits. A reviewer in *Publishers Weekly* found that "despite some occasional fine and engaging writing" the novel "winds up a pretty tedious exercise." There was also a rather cool press for *Endangered Species* (1977), which has as its heroine another lonely woman, this time a poet and a member of the "nouveau poor," who from the disadvantage point of her fortieth birthday looks back over a crowded and generally painful sexual and emotional career.

Sandra Hochman is also the author of a story for children, *The Magic Convention* (1971). Her

play, *The World of Günter Grass,* was produced in New York in 1966. *The Year of the Women,* a film which she both wrote and directed, consists mainly of interviews about the feminist movement, interspersed with fantasy sequences about the oppression of women and of artists; one reviewer felt that it featured "a lot more of Miss Hochman than seems absolutely necessary." The author has been poet-in-residence at Fordham University. She has appeared often on radio and television, and has conducted a weekly poetry program over WBAI. In recent years she has been increasingly active as a journalist, writing—often on feminist themes—for such journals as the New York *Times Magazine, Look, Life, Cosmopolitan, Holiday,* and *Esquire.* She is a contributing editor of *Harper's Bazaar.* With the investigative reporter Sybil Wong she wrote *Satellite Spies,* a "sometimes frightening" study of the uses and misuses of satellites.

PRINCIPAL WORKS: *Poetry*—Voyage Home, 1960; Manhattan Pastures, 1963; The Vaudeville Marriage, 1966; Love Poems, 1966; Love Letters From Asia, 1968; Earthworks: Poems 1960-1970, 1970; Futures: New Poems, 1974. *Novel* —Walking Papers, 1971; Happiness Is Too Much Trouble, 1976; Endangered Species, 1977. *For Children*—The Magic Convention, 1971. *Other*—(with Sybil Wong) Satellite Spies; The Frightening Impact of a New Technology, 1976.

ABOUT: Brannum, M. When I Was Sixteen, 1967; Contemporary Authors 5-8 first revision, 1969; Vinson, J. (ed.) Contemporary Poets, 1975; Who's Who of American Women, 1975-1976. *Periodicals*—Critic April 1963; Hudson Review Spring 1972; New York Times November 17, 1965; New York Times Book Review November 3, 1963; January 8, 1967; August 1, 1971; New Yorker April 27, 1963; Newsweek August 9, 1971; Poetry May 1964, April 1972, October 1975; Saturday Review July 3, 1971; Shenandoah Autumn 1963; Times Literary Supplement May 26, 1972; Virginia Quarterly Review Autumn 1963, Winter 1972.

"HOLME, K.E." *See* HILL, (JOHN EDWARD) CHRISTOPHER

HOLROYD, MICHAEL (DE COURCY FRASER) (August 27, 1935–), English biographer, essayist, and novelist, writes: "I was conceived at the Hyde Park Hotel over Christmas 1934 and was born in London, according to my mother, on 27 August 1935; my father thought it was 29 August. It was one of the things over which they did not agree. My mother was Swedish; my father half-Irish, half-English. They had met on the North Sea, and while on water all went well. But they soon struck land, and their divorce was made final during the Second World War.

"I was largely brought up by my paternal grandparents near a place called Maidenhead Thicket in Berkshire. My life was rich in inactivity. I took my grandparents' pace and condi-

Angela Huth

MICHAEL HOLROYD

tion rather than my own—a regime of seventy- and eighty-year olds. Events continued not to come my way to an extent that was positively sensational, and to compensate for this solitary existence I filled my head with book-adventures.

"My father, in more affluent days, had been educated at Eton. My going there was the last nail in the family's financial coffin. The Holroyds had had an interest in some tea plantations, and I was able to see them on television as the battleground for the Chinese invasion of India. Since I could inherit no money now, it was explained to me (except in the form of debts), I studied, on my father's commercial advice, scientific subjects: astronomy, botany, chemistry and other topics for which I had altogether no aptitude. At last I began to argue so hotly against this programme that my father, sensing the possibility of some financial advantage in my tiresome obstinacy, arranged for me to be articled to a firm of solicitors.

"It took two years to establish my unfittedness for the law; after which I passed two peaceful years in the army as a National Serviceman, proving that I was no man of action. By the time I was twenty-three, it seemed generally agreed that I was good for nothing except writing.

"While at the Maidenhead Public Library one day I picked down at random a book by an author called Hugh Kingsmill. What I read gave me the courage to continue trying to write. He offered me something that was no part of the schoolroom, but what went on outside it: what was felt rather than endured. Under his influence I stepped from my own life into other peoples', where there appeared to be more going on.

"My first biography, a labour of love, was of Kingsmill himself. I believe I may claim, without immodesty, that it is not a good book. But I made amends by bringing back into print some of his own writings in *The Best of Hugh Kingsmill.*

"I have written one novel and a volume of essays: and I hope to write more fiction and essays. In my biographies of Lytton Strachey, Augustus John and the authorized Life of Bernard Shaw on which I am at present working, my aim has been to recreate worlds into which readers may enter, where they may experience feelings and thoughts some of which may remain with them after the book is closed. To this extent, I believe biography and the novel have parallel functions. I search for truth through the individual (not through groups), and try to give a literary pattern to the relationship between myself and my subject. I attempt to combine scholarship with story-telling, factual accuracy with narrative power.

"I have always found writing difficult, but there is no rest to be had until I have written."

In spite of Holroyd's claim, his life of the novelist, critic, and biographer Hugh Kingsmill seemed to some readers a very good book. Even so demanding a reader as Malcolm Muggeridge, who knew Kingsmill well, called it "mature and perceptive," and thought that the young biographer had "got the hang of Kingsmill in an almost miraculous way."

All the same, it was Holroyd's *Lytton Strachey* that established his reputation as one of the most able of contemporary biographers. After a year's work, he had almost completed the first version of this book when James Strachey, Lytton's brother and literary executor, decided that Holroyd should be permitted access to the family's gigantic collection of Lytton Strachey letters and papers. It took a further five years to master these thirty thousand "units of correspondence" and complete the twelve-hundred page, two-volume, "critical biography." The publisher's advance was nothing like enough to finance this marathon, and the book owes its existence to a Bollingen Fellowship, the generosity of Holroyd's friends, and his own frugality and determination.

The first volume of the biography describes Strachey's large and cultivated family, his unhappy school days, and the delight and liberation he found at Cambridge, where he acquired the circle of friends and homosexual lovers who were to become the nucleus of the Bloomsbury Group. The second volume deals with Strachey's early failures and disappointments, his bizarre engagement to Virginia Woolf, the fame which followed the publication of *Eminent Victorians,* and his extraordinary relationship with Dora Carrington, who loved and sustained him until he died and then took her own life.

Some readers found Holroyd's style overblown, particularly in the first volume, and many thought that he had taken Strachey's endless succession of more or less anguished love affairs much too seriously and dealt with them in more detail than they were worth. Nevertheless, most critics recognized in the book a fascinating and remarkable achievement. "In addition to a portrait of Strachey," wrote a reviewer in the *Times Literary Supplement,* "Mr. Holroyd gives us a far-ranging survey of the most influential minds of the first three decades of this century. . . . His footnotes are models of accuracy and information. . . . [These] two volumes form a portrait of an epoch in literature which will not be superseded. Clear-cut, comprehensive, highly coloured and convincing, it will be recognized by contemporary readers and by those who come after as a splendid book."

There was no less praise for Holroyd's next major book, his biography of Augustus John. One reviewer wrote that Holroyd "applies to near-contemporary life the industry of a Maurist; he tracks down every birth certificate, discovers and transcribes every letter, reads every related memoir. He has a lively sense of character and he writes in a witty, eloquent style that keeps the reader afloat. Sometimes he overwrites, but this suits his present subject, for John himself wrote an extremely rich, impressive, prose." The reviewers' principal criticism of this book, as of its predecessor, was that it was too long and not sufficiently selective.

Holroyd's novel *A Dog's Life* was published in the United States but, because of libel problems, not in England. It is an account of a single day in the life of a highly eccentric English family—three generations living in the same country house, with their moribund old dog Smith. It provides a rueful view of old age, the pangs of unrequited love, and the emptiness of success, reminded one reviewer of Dickens and another of Chekhov, and was generally enjoyed for its black humor, though one reviewer found it no more than "a vacant exercise in misanthropy." *Unreceived Opinions* is a collection of literary essays and reviews, readable and elegantly amusing. It includes some complaints about the hard lot of the professional writer, and propaganda for a campaign with which Holroyd has been prominently connected, seeking to ensure that authors should benefit financially when their books are borrowed from public libraries.

Holroyd has written interestingly about his craft in the London *Times* (September 14, 1974), suggesting for example that a biographer's life "may have similarities with that of an actor. He must read, learn lines, metaphorically put on the clothes and *become* his subject—know what it is like to think, feel, move about the room like him." Elsewhere he has said that what helps him most in this struggle to apprehend his subjects is the physical fact of their handwriting: "It's like breaking a code, the nearest thing to actual contact."

The author is the only child of Basil Holroyd and the former Ulla Hall. He served in 1973-1974 as chairman of the Society of Authors, and in 1976-1977 was chairman of the National Book League. He is a Fellow of the Royal Society of Literature and has received the Yorkshire Post Prize (1968) and a Winston Churchill Fellowship (1971). Holroyd lives alone in an unfashionable part of London in a small apartment which he cleans himself. "But I'm not a hermit," he told an interviewer, "not by any means. Sometimes I want people. Just once . . . I lived with a girl for two years. It was an experiment that went wrong. . . . But I'm not alone, I have the dead with me, my files on Lytton Strachey and Augustus John: the dead don't interrupt." He lists his recreations as "listening to stories, avoiding tame animals, being polite, music, sleep."

PRINCIPAL WORKS: *Nonfiction*—Hugh Kingsmill, 1964; Lytton Strachey, Volume One: The Unknown Years 1880-1910, 1967; Lytton Strachey, Volume Two: The Years of Achievement 1910-1932, 1968; (ed.) The Best of Hugh Kingsmill, 1970; (ed.) Lytton Strachey by Himself, 1971; Unreceived Opinions, 1973; Augustus John, Volume One: The Years of Innocence, 1974; Augustus John, Volume Two: The Years of Experience, 1975; (with Malcolm Easton) The Art of Augustus John, 1974. *Fiction*—A Dog's Life, 1969.

ABOUT: Connolly, C. The Evening Colonnade, 1973; Contemporary Authors 53-56, 1975; Holroyd, M. Unreceived Opinions, 1973; Muggeridge, M. Tread Softly for You Tread on My Jokes, 1966; Rees, G. Brief Encounters, 1974; Who's Who, 1978. *Periodicals*—Encounter April 1975; Guardian March 2, 1971; Harper's October 1976; New York Review of Books June 6, 1968; New Yorker September 13, 1969; Sunday Times (London) October 27, 1974; Times (London) September 14, 1974; September 25, 1976; Times Literary Supplement February 29, 1968; October 18, 1974.

"HOLZ, DETLEV." *See* BENJAMIN, WALTER

*HOME, WILLIAM DOUGLAS (June 3, 1912–), British dramatist, was born in Edinburgh, Scotland, the fifth of the seven children of Charles Cospatrick Archibald Douglas-
*hūm

Home, the thirteenth Earl of Home, and Lilian Lambton, daughter of the fourth Earl of Durham. In an interview with Sheridan Morley in the London *Times,* he once commented: "I come from a large and eccentric family, or rather two large and eccentric families: on my father's side they were all reasonably traditional land-owning Conservatives, but my mother's lot were once revolutionary Whigs who threw things at kings. I think that's the right sort of mixed background for a playwright, though curiously enough most of my brothers seem to have become ornithologists or Prime Ministers." His oldest brother Alec, the fourteenth Earl of Home from 1951 until October 1963 when he renounced his peerage for life, was Britain's Prime Minister in 1963-1964 and has twice served as Foreign Secretary.

Home grew up on a fifteen-thousand-acre country estate bordering the Tweed River and spent three years at a preparatory school at New Barnet, Hertfordshire, before entering Eton. During vacations his father took him to see the farces of Ben Travers, and Home "can't think of any other playwright I especially admired" in those formative years. He was still at Eton when he wrote his first play; it was about "a housemaster being murdered, but the headmaster took rather a dim view of it and banned it. Then I had a brainwave and offered the leading role to his son, after which the ban was very rapidly lifted. I think that was when I began to learn about being a playwright." At New College, Oxford, where he took a modest Fourth Class honors degree in history in 1934, Home continued to write plays to alleviate his boredom and depression. He later explained in his autobiography *Half-Term Report* (1954) that his "short apprenticeship" gave him "a taste for something less ephemeral than journalism. . . . I wanted to write long, full-length plays and I wanted them to be acted on the London stage. Furthermore I wanted the world to recognize them as plays and myself as a playwright of some note." On the whole, he says, "the family were delighted . . . it made a nice change from the army and the church, which is what usually happened to younger sons of Earls in those days."

In 1935 Home entered the Royal Academy of Dramatic Art. His brief and relatively undistinguished acting career started in 1937, when he played in repertory at the Theatre Royal, Brighton. He first appeared in London later the same year in Dodie Smith's *Bonnet Over the Windmill.* And it was in 1937 also, when Home was still only twenty-five, that his own first play was staged. *Great Possessions,* a drama about two of his Douglas ancestors who had unwittingly walked into a deathtrap, was produced in London at the "Q" Theatre, then transferred to the Duke of York's Theatre in the West End, London's Broadway. The critics found the work generally gloomy but praised the dialogue as "more than promising." *Passing By,* a play about a clergyman's daughter who wanted a divorce, opened in 1940 at the "Q" Theatre and was denied a West End transfer only because of the beginning of the German air offensive.

Although he objected to World War II on political grounds and favored a negotiated peace, William Douglas Home served in the Royal Armoured Corps from 1940 until 1944, reaching the rank of captain. During these years he expressed his views openly, obtaining leaves of absences to stand in several by-elections as a Progressive Independent. He contested the Cathcart Division of Glasgow in April 1942, the Windsor Division of Berkshire in June 1942, and the Clay Cross Division of Derbyshire in April 1944. In June 1944, when the invading Allies were poised to attack Le Havre, the German commander asked if the city's civilians might first be evacuated. This humane request was denied, and Home therefore refused to take part in the attack which followed. He later explained his action in a letter: "I do not believe a negative war aim is worth the bones of one British grenadier. Am I and those who think like me not to be allowed to choose whether to live for our ideals or to die for negative ideals of . . . tired old men?"

Home's idealism cost him a court-martial and a year's prison sentence. He drew on this experience to write *Now Barabbas . . .* (1947), his first critical success. As Henry Raynor says in *Contemporary Dramatists,* the play is "a cleverly worked out study of a prison during the brief time between a condemned murderer's arrival and execution," discreetly indicating "the strains between warders and prisoners, the development of a homosexual friendship, the day-to-day existence of a variety of inadequates and the closeness of the criminal to the average, decent member of society." The play was very warmly praised by most reviewers for its unsentimental power and skillful construction, and was filmed.

Within six months Home achieved his first great commercial success with *The Chiltern Hundreds,* which opened at the Vaudeville Theatre in August 1947 and as "one of the best comedies in town—if not the best" ran for two years. It is the first of several Home plays dealing with the eccentric affairs of the Earl of Lister and his family. Here the Earl's son, by birth and family tradition a Conservative, is moved to run as a Socialist in a by-election for the family seat —much to the dismay of his American *fiancée* who persuades the Listers' butler to stand against him as a Tory. This amiable satire on British political attitudes was inspired, Home says, partly by his family's non-reaction to their butler's announcement that Alec Douglas-Home had lost his parliamentary seat in the 1945 general election: "It occurred to me then that there was something inherently comic in the fact that a family butler should display concern at their heir's defeat in an election, while the family remained indifferent, if indeed they remembered that he had been standing for Parliament at all."

Like most of Home's comedies, *The Chiltern Hundreds* is (to quote Henry Raynor) "smart, brightly fluent, precisely timed to give each snappy answer some appearance of wit, and designed with considerable elegance." Retitled *Yes, M'Lord,* it crossed the Atlantic in 1949, but had a generally cool reception from the New York critics. "The play's weakness," wrote *Time*'s reviewer, "is not so much that it is trivial, as that it grows tiresome; its scenes are all playing twice, including some . . . that shouldn't be played at all. But there are some compensations: some bright nonsensical chatter, some skillful British acting."

Home's next comedy, *Ambassador Extraordinary* (1948), was a disaster—according to his own account it was "hissed off the stage by the gallery critics on the first night." This was the beginning of a "thin time" during the late 1940s and early 1950s when only one of Home's plays met with any real success. This was *The Thistle and the Rose* (1949), not a comedy but a serious historical drama, depicting the death of King James IV of Scotland and the destruction of the Scottish army at Flodden in 1513 as a tragedy marking the end of the age of chivalry and the advent of power politics.

The Earl of Lister, his family, and his butler reappeared in *The Manor of Northstead* (1954), another well-carpentered entertainment in the tradition of *The Chiltern Hundreds,* and in 1955 Home had his second smash-hit with *The Reluctant Debutante,* about the machinations of a London hostess seeking to arrange a suitable marriage for her uncooperative daughter.

Another "thin time" followed, however, precipitated at least in part by the theatrical revolution which began in 1956, when John Osborne's *Look Back in Anger* had its first production at the Royal Court Theatre in London. A new sense of purpose gripped the British theatre, and its serious adherents had no time whatever for the drawing-room comedies and genteel dramas that had for so long filled the West End stages. Home went on as before, saying "I've always been told I'm a very old-fashioned writer and perhaps I am. But I reckon if we still have an eccentric landed gentry, then they should be written about. . . . Feudalism makes me laugh. . . . People think with a name like mine I must also approve of it, which is not necessarily true; I suppose if I were a Wedgwood Benn I'd get my plays staged at the Royal Court."

In fact, Home's touch seemed less certain in this new climate. Boos and shouts greeted the London opening of *Aunt Edwina* (1959), a work of "unadulterated corn" in which Colonel Edward Ryan's practice of dressing and behaving like a woman forces his embarrassed family to pretend that he is an eccentric aunt. Home stubbornly defended this play however, exhausting his savings and finally even selling his car to finance further performances. There was a somewhat more respectful reception for *The Bad Soldier Smith* (1961), an obviously autobiographical drama set in Normandy in June 1944, but *The Cigarette Girl* was described as "unspeakable drivel" and "the most dismal and abysmal heap of rubbish to be mounted in London." The latter play, whose heroine is cruelly prevented from acknowledging her long-lost illegitimate son, closed after six performances in 1962, and Home complained bitterly that "critics attack anything they think comes from the Establishment."

He has fared better since then, however, recovering the loyalty of that large segment of the British theatre-going public that loves a lord and a good laugh, and receiving serious critical attention from Harold Hobson and one or two other senior British reviewers. The recovery began with *The Reluctant Peer* (1964), a further examination of the tribal customs of the Listers inspired by Alec Douglas-Home's renunciation of his peerage in 1963. It ran for nearly five hundred performances, a record easily outmatched by *The Secretary Bird* (1967). Described by J. W. Lambert as "a crisp comic study of middle-aged pain and frustration," this portrait of a failing marriage played for four years at the Savoy Theatre.

The Jockey Club Stakes (1970), which involves "a trio of upper-class geriatrics" in assorted skulduggeries at the racetrack, delighted some reviewers and troubled those, like Harold Clurman, who found themselves unable to "give a damn about any of . . . [the] people." In *Lloyd George Knew My Father* (1972), the placid routine of a retired general is threatened by government plans to build a superhighway across his ancient lawns. His wife announces that she will kill herself if the road goes through and settles down to planning this ultimate protest with businesslike calm. J.W. Lambert found this "a flawed but poignant portrait of upper-class lips at their stiffest," and some reviewers attributed the play's success to the performances of Peggy Ashcroft and Sir Ralph Richardson. Harold Hobson, however, was most intrigued by the play's sub-text—by signs that this eccentric marriage was so rotten at its core that the General would have welcomed his wife's suicide—and called the play a "brilliantly ruthless comedy" in which "the fun offsets dazzlingly the extreme fundamental seriousness.... It is steel that looks like velvet."

Hobson was equally enthusiastic in his comments on the literary and moral quality of *At the End of the Day* (1973), and this time many of his colleagues agreed. This is a high-spirited study of politicians on the night of a general election—ostensibly that of 1970, though the author asks his audience to accept his political opponents not as Harold Wilson and Edward Heath but as characters in a play which he hopes "will stand on its own feet." Charles Lewson in the London *Times* thought it did more than that: "It directs those feet in some delightful capers, running rings around the notion that politics is an adult game."

But there have been times when Hobson's championship of Home's work has seemed to some other London critics positively quixotic. *The Dame of Sark* (1974) is about the annexation of the British Channel Island of Sark by the Germans during World War II and the relationship between the island's feudal ruler and the German commander—two aristocrats who in their courage, chivalry, and sense of honor tower above the meaner spirits around them. Hobson found the play "superb" in "spirit, in writing, and in ... dramatic irony," but Victoria Radin called it "a grossly sentimentalized version of the facts," while Peter Ansorge thought that "some kind of protest is called for when jaded dialogue of this kind occupies the stage for most of a very long evening"; he was puzzled that "a relatively trite piece of theatrical entertainment, deeply entrenched in the wrong kind of sentiment and self-pity, should have been hailed as a kind of breakthrough for 'civilised values.'"

What is beyond dispute is that Home is once more a highly popular dramatist, and an immensely prolific one. In April 1977, Sheridan Morley noted that Home, "whom even twenty years ago many were prepared to write off as the last gasp of Edwardian theatre," would soon have no less than five plays in simultaneous production. These included *The Perch*, opening at

the Pitlochry Festival; a revival of *The Chiltern Hundreds;* and three new plays opening in London: *In the Red, Rolls Hyphen Royce,* and *The Kingfisher.* The first two had short shrift from most critics, but *The Kingfisher,* about an author who is reunited with his first love after an interval of fifty years, seemed to Ned Chaillet "mirthful, affectionate and, in a fading manner, civilized." A New York production opened in 1978 to mixed reviews.

William Douglas Home was married in 1951 to Rachel Brand, Baroness Dacre, daughter of the fourth Viscount Hampden. They have a son and three daughters, and live in Hampshire. Home has written several plays for television and has adapted some of his best-known stage plays for the cinema, including *Now Barabbas ...*, *The Chiltern Hundreds,* and *The Reluctant Debutante.* Among his recreations he counts golf, bridge, and politics—he was an unsuccessful candidate for the parliamentary constituency of South Edinburgh in 1957, standing that time as a Liberal. Home has acted in several of his own plays, and told Sheridan Morley; "I'm still always terribly keen to take over, if any of the cast get ill. I find the backers usually forbid it; God knows why, because I'm very good when I do get the chance. At least I think so: and that's what counts in the end."

A *Theatre Arts* reviewer once described Home as "a thoroughly domesticated British playwright, a sort of poor man's Maugham or Coward, whose mind is in the drawing room but whose heart is strictly hearthside"; Irving Wardle speaks of his "gallant rearguard actions in defence of landed property and the established church." But it seems to Henry Raynor foolish to reject "the type of play of which William Douglas Home is master, because it uses traditional ideas in a traditional form and is resolutely upper class. . . . The theatre is, or should be, a home for all, including those who ask for little more than a pleasant evening out; invariably to provide this in works that are honest, elegantly made and worthy of the attention of fine actors is to give the theatre notable service."

PRINCIPAL PUBLISHED WORKS: *Plays*—Now Barabbas..., 1947; The Chiltern Hundreds, 1949 (U.S., Yes, M'Lord); Master of Arts, 1950; The Thistle and the Rose, 1951; The Bad Samaritan, 1954; The Manor of Northstead, 1955; The Reluctant Debutante, 1956; The Iron Duchess, 1958; The Plays of William Douglas Home (Now Barabbas ..., The Chiltern Hundreds, The Thistle and the Rose, The Bad Samaritan, The Reluctant Debutante), 1958; Aunt Edwina, 1960; The Bad Soldier Smith, 1962; The Reluctant Peer, 1965; A Friend Indeed, 1966; The Secretary Bird, 1969; The Bishop and the Actress, 1969; The Jockey Club Stakes, 1971; Lloyd George Knew My Father, 1973; The Dame of

HOROVITZ

Sark, 1976; Betzi, 1977. *Autobiography*—Half-Term Report, 1954.

ABOUT: Burke's Peerage, 1970; Home, W.D. Half-Term Report, 1954; Lambert, J.W. Drama in Britain 1964-1973, 1974; Vinson, J. (ed.) Contemporary Dramatists, 1977; Who's Who, 1978; Who's Who in the Theatre, 1977. *Periodicals*—National Review December 31, 1963; Newsweek February 5, 1973; Observer October 26, 1975; Sunday Times (London) July 9, 1972; October 7, 1973; September 22, 1974; Theatre Arts December 1956; Time July 6, 1962; September 18, 1972; Times (London) October 4, 1973; April 9, 1977.

HOROVITZ, ISRAEL (ARTHUR) (March 31, 1939–), American dramatist, novelist, and poet, writes: "End of the night, nearing midnight. Soon to be April Fools' Day. I had to move things along. 'Hurry, Mama! Think of all those hungry theatregoers!'

"Some academics feel I might have been a major figure by now, had I waited: had I let nature take its course. I couldn't. I didn't.

"A long hallway. My father, at the smallest spot of it. He calls to me. I run to him, but the hallway lengthens. I run faster. He is always there, always calling. I cannot save him.

"My town, Wakefield, Massachusetts. Baptists all around. Me, circumcised, circumspect, circumlocutory.

"I remember my mother's womb.

"I remember the ordeal and the wondering why.

"I remember my father, at the end of a long hallway.

"I remember my first crib. Turning at the corner-screws with tiny fingers. I remember the crib coming apart, crashing to the reddish pine floor. I remember my relief on hearing my parents curse the crib-screws and not me.

"I remember my first view of my sister as she watched me watching her: wide-eyed staring.

"I remember first learning there had been a brother in the middle, stillborn. Good choice he made. I and my sister had to play.

"I remember my first view of Lake Quannapowitt, the green-red-and-yellow bandstand, the burnt brown grass, the sense of *déjà vu,* the sense of *déjà vu,* the sense of *déjà vu* . . .

"I do not remember standing tall or blonde.

"I remember my first meeting with Richie. His back yard. Our fathers: face-to-face. Serious talk. Concerned words. Apples on their tree and on their ground nearby. I ate one. Richie and I, wide-eyed, staring, three years old.

"I remember my first view of the summer house in South Hamilton, twenty miles down the road from Wakefield, one year later. The stone hearth. The stilts on which the house stood. The swamp, next to it. Fourteen summers to pass there.

ISRAEL HOROVITZ

"My Aunt Alice was the first to let it slip that my father hadn't always driven a truck, but had once been a law student, perhaps two hundred years before. The word was he'd kissed somebody's wife, been expelled, made to drive a truck forever. No one talked intelligibly of any of this. A whisper here and there, but never a real sentence with subject and predicate.

"Years later, law school again. He was fifty now and studied nights, driving his truck, days, to Fitchburg and Lowell, to the paper mills. He bought newspaper in sixteen-hundred-pound bales from his brother, my Uncle Max, and sold them wired together to mill-owners, who recycled the paper. Hard then to understand why people bought paper from which they would manufacture paper. Harder even to understand why they bought rags from which they would extract *better papers.*

"Grown-ups have always seemed to me to be crazy. The range ranged from *deranged* to *lunatic.* Now that I am myself one of them, it is certain I have always been correct in this matter, although I've underestimated the high end of the scale: a lunatic is merely midpoint. A converted Catholic is all the way.

"Riding on the truck, next to him. Two men, on the road together. Up at four a.m., home for lunch. He to sleep until the next ring of the clock. (Manner of speaking here. I remember no ringing clocks. None ever needed.) All to bed at six p.m. Radio played across the hall, from their room. I and my sister, side by side, twin beds, separated by an aisle and a night table, rock maple, on which I split the back of my skull, age six, trampolining from my bed, dreaming of flight and applause.

"I remember my terror at the opening of *The Creaking Door* and my trembling at the mention of the brand Autolite.

"I remember Fibber's closet.

"I remember every inch of Allen's Alley.

"I still know what the Shadow knew . . .

"I remember, years later, meeting Lamont Cranston. He was what my grandmother called 'a little nothing.'

"I remember my grandmother's enormous chest: a perfect pillow to our dozens. She was frightened to count the precise number of grandchildren. No one ever has. We all loved her so.

"My grandfather was small, handsome. He chewed Dentyne and smelled always of cinnamon, which is, at this writing, my favorite spice.

"My grandmother weighed in at between two and three hundred pounds. My grandfather was half her size. When they fished for pickerel together each Sunday, Gram'pa rowed, Gram'ma sat up the back. The bow of their boat was never in the water.

"My father's family always frightened me. They had so many secrets. My mother's family had none.

"My father's father died somewhere in the American West: near Hot Springs, Arkansas. My grandmother (paternal), aunt and cousin were all killed in an airplane crash, going west to bury him, sometime during the year I was born. From the moment of their crash, through my birth, through this day, I am given to tremendous anxiety at the presence of this subject.

"They are all buried together now in Wakefield. There is a cement bench spread across the heads of their graves. (Who sits on it?) My name is carved brightly across its back. As my grandfather and I share the same name, my *full* name has been on his grave since the year of my birth. I remember first seeing his grave and my full name there, when I was four years old. My father stood holding me in his arms. He was crying. We returned to the grave again when I was thirteen, the day before I was *bar mitzvah*ed. My father cried again.

"He cried again on the day the letter came telling him he had passed the Massachusetts' Bar Exam and could stop driving his truck. The letter was stuck in the mail-slot. I knew from the return address it was the letter for which he'd been waiting weeks. I could not get it unstuck. I knew he'd hit me when I told him it was there. I told him. He hit me. He and my mother ripped the letter getting it out of the slot. When they read it, they cried. They hugged and kissed and I knew then that I was an intruder. I took a walk around the lake.

"My father has cried nearly every day for the past five years, since Parkinson's disease froze him completely to his chair. My mother and he stay alone together. It is difficult for me to visit them, and I am ashamed by the difficulty. It is still impossible for me to save him.

"Everyone who was ever born in Wakefield, Massachusetts, has already died, or will eventually die. I have grown to realize that death is a problem that is indigenous to the entire North Shore area of Massachusetts. I feel somehow responsible.

"I remember kicking Miss Norton's leg, by accident, during recess. The bell had rung for us to return to her fourth-grade classroom. We were playing kickball; I was up. She stepped between the pitch and my small boot. It was clearly ironic that she died three months later, and I was to feel directly responsible for her death for the next twenty years of my life.

"I remember caddying for a twenty-nine-year-old man who was named Guy, Myopia Hunt Club, Hamilton, Massachusetts, three summers after Miss Norton's death. Guy Haskell (Haskell was his last name) was shooting rotten golf that day. He sliced his first drive out of sight. He topped a second attempt and the ball fizzled and bobbed mercilessly out of the fairway, into the rough just to our right. I called to him yelling that the ball was lost as well. But I'd lied. While he teed up a third attempt, I scooped the second into my pocket. After nine more embarrassing strokes, Guy Haskell reached the eighth green, where he clutched his chest, lay down and died. Just before the ambulance whizzed his enormous corpse away, I chucked the stolen ball through the back window and heard it fall and roll to a stop inside, somewhere near his saddleshoes.

"Years later, I remember seeing a business executive die in the revolving doors at 666 Fifth Avenue. Other business executives snapped his arm into two dangling halves, as the living heaved together, unclogging their revolving door. I merely retched. The policeman beside me achieved vomit.

"At age seventeen, I wrote my first play and titled it, fittingly enough, *The Comeback*. I have not stopped writing plays since then.

"I have married and divorced a few times. I have learned to love children, mostly mine.

"I live in Paris, whenever I can, because it pleases me to walk in the *6ème, 14ème* and the *1er*. Also because Beckett, Roy, and Ionesco are there and we are friends. Also because my French is inferior to anyone else's French. And that is somehow pleasing.

"I should mention that I used to think I was a Communist.

"I used to be given to having migraine headaches.

"I used to worry that I was not sufficiently educated.

"I have continued to run long distances, nearly every day, since the age of fourteen, with the exception of the years during which I was given to migraine headaches.

"About my writing, I can say little, except to say that I work carefully and use as my main subject all of the above.

"Beyond that, I can say no more."

Horovitz is the son of Julius Horovitz and the former Hazel Solberg. His first novel was rejected when he was thirteen, and at seventeen he settled down to write "a million plays, an embarrassing number. Like a machine, I just cranked them out." By the time he graduated from Harvard in 1961, a few of the million had already achieved some kind of production, beginning with a performance of *The Comeback* in Boston in 1956. A two-year fellowship at the Royal Academy of Dramatic Art in London (1961–1963) was followed by a stint as a stagehand at the Paper Mill Playhouse in Millburn, New Jersey. In 1965 Horovitz returned to London as the first American playwright-in-residence with the Royal Shakespeare Company at the Aldwych Theatre. Among the other jobs he did during the 1960s, he told a *Newsweek* interviewer, was one as a $50,000-a-year adman in New York.

The *annus mirabilis* for Horovitz was 1968, or rather the 1967–1968 season, when he burst upon the New York scene with productions of no less than four of his short plays. The most notable of them, *The Indian Wants the Bronx,* had already been staged in Waterford, Connecticut. An East Indian recently arrived in New York, waiting late at night for a bus to the Bronx, is teased and then roughed up by two bored young hoodlums. At the end of the play, the Indian, beaten and sobbing, and clutching a severed telephone, faces the audience and utters the only English words he knows: "How are you? You're welcome. Thank you. Thank you." Staged at the Astor Place Theatre, and introducing Al Pacino as one of the young men, this production was among the triumphs of the off-Broadway theatre of the 1960s, admired for its dramatic power, the accuracy of its dialogue and social observation, and the skill with which Horovitz reveals the weakness and vulnerability of the young men; Walter Kerr called it "a small miracle of tact."

It's Called the Sugar Plum, which shared the same bill at the Astor Place, is a bitter comedy, "a kind of Jules Feiffer cartoon," in which a

Harvard undergraduate who has accidentally killed a fellow student is first confronted and soon afterwards loved by the dead youth's fiancée. Harold Clurman praised it as "a humorous and kindly observation of the grubby and foolish sexuality characteristic of the hip young, nurtured on a sophistication derived from total ignorance and which expresses itself in the verbiage of pop psychoanalysis." Edith Oliver, who seemed not to find the play at all "kindly," said that the characters' "aimless cruelty and their aimless, solemn fatuity . . . is the most frightening thing about them."

The other two Horovitz plays seen in New York during the 1967–1968 season are allegories. *Line,* first produced in November 1967 by the La MaMa Experimental Theatre Club, examines the ways in which five characters use guile, force, sex, and every other means at their disposal to gain first place in a line that leads nowhere; this "comedy of displacement," as Horovitz calls it, is a vivid parable about the American success myth. *Rats* was first staged as part of *Collision Course,* an anthology of sketches by a number of new writers given at Café Au Go Go; Gerald Weales wrote that this pointed and stylish short piece uses "a quarrel between two rats over a black baby to make an effective comment on the prevailing attitude in the Negro community against protective paternalism from outside."

These four plays between them carried off most of the available off-Broadway theatrical honors—the *Village Voice*'s "Obie," the Vernon Rice–Drama Desk Award, and the *Show Business* Grand Award, as well as the British *Plays and Players* Best Foreign Play Award, and the Jersey *Journal* Best Play Award. *Chiaroscuro,* a one-act play about a black family chemically transformed into whites, had its premiere in July 1968 at Spoleto, Italy, in the Festival of Two Worlds. Later the same year, retitled *Morning,* it appeared on Broadway as part of a triple bill with Terrence McNally's *Noon* and Leonard Melfi's *Night. Time*'s reviewer thought *Morning* the best of the three plays, and praised Horovitz for understanding that "laughter is a release from tension." Clive Barnes likewise lauded "the brilliant Israel Horovitz, who has fantasies where other people keep their thoughts and translates those fantasies into a mockingly careful realism that is ironically thought-provoking. . . . His writing is disturbingly funny, not least while using four-letter words to fantasticated comic effect." Brendan Gill, on the other hand, thought that these three talented writers had all been flagrantly self-indulgent, producing not real plays but "scruffy little high-school sketches."

In *The Honest-to-God Schnozzola,* two desperately insecure American businessmen play sexual dirty tricks on one another in a German bar which is furnished with a whore, a male transvestite, a dwarf, and other emblems of Old World decadence. There are cabaret-style songs, dances, blackouts, tableaux, and asides to the audience—a departure for Horovitz, whose plays (even the allegories) are generally fundamentally naturalistic in style. It brought Horovitz a second "Obie," and confirmed Edith Oliver in her belief that the author "can delineate a character with a flick of a line or a piece of business, he can write dialogue that is dramatic and rings true, and he can explore an atmosphere or state of mind." Other reviewers were less impressed, and Jack Kroll dismissed the piece as "a sophomore's anthology of moist dreams from 'Steppenwolf,' old German flicks and frat-house bull sessions about Brecht," told with a "mad dervishlike flailing of words, images, sounds, shapes, theatrical ploys, pitchman turns—anything to beat, tweak and (genteelly) terrorize the audience into an acceptance of profundity." *Leader,* an expressionist piece about a dictator which appeared in the same program at the Gramercy Arts Theatre, was also called sophomoric, and raucous to boot.

Horovitz's "tragic farce" *Dr. Hero* got somewhat better reviews, but there was a growing feeling that it was time for the author to move on to full-length works—to exercise "his full territorial imperative" as "a stage animal." Nothing or not much loath, Horovitz wrote between 1971 and 1976 a trilogy of three-act plays set in his Massachusetts birthplace and known as "The Wakefield Plays" (with a nod or perhaps wink at the cycle of Yorkshire miracle plays performed under that title since the Middle Ages). Horovitz's trilogy comprises *Alfred the Great, Our Father's Failing,* and *Alfred Dies,* and centers upon four characters: Alfred and his wife Emily, who return to Alfred's hometown after years of prosperity in the big city, and Alfred's former girlfriend Margaret and her husband Will, a truck driver. *Alfred the Great,* the only one of these plays to have been widely performed and reviewed, aroused little enthusiasm. "No doubt," wrote R.M. Buck in *Library Journal,* "Horovitz has been influenced by Beckett, O'Neill, Albee, and Pinter—and that is good; however, this . . . work contains no new vision beyond the basic themes and ideas of these masters of personal fears and terrors—and this is bad."

Though he has not yet written a million plays,

Horovitz continues prolific. The most successful of his recent plays was *The Primary English Class* (1976), in which a nervous and sexually repressed young woman teaching English to a class of foreigners nurses horrifying but totally unfounded fears about their intentions toward her. *Mackerel,* staged by the Folger Theatre Group in Washington, D.C., in April 1978, is a satirical comedy about a greedy, unhappy, all-American family living by the sea near Gloucester, Massachusetts. When a hurricane hurls a gigantic mackerel through the wall of their ramshackle cottage, they believe that their dreams of wealth and glory are about to come true—all the more so when they discover that the fish's flesh turns a cat into a lion. The outcome is sadly different. A highly convincing model of the fish's head, ten feet long and five feet wide and equipped with rolling eyes, was built for the Folger production and attracted a good deal of publicity, but Richard L. Coe thought the model gave an unfortunate air of realism to the fable: "Because *Mackerel* seems like a combination of early Ionesco with *All in the Family* and a dash of Stanley Kubrick, the visibility of its title character seems more hindrance than help to Horovitz's ambitious charade."

Horovitz has also written several television plays and a number of movie scenarios, including *The Strawberry Statement* (1970), which received the Prix de Jury at the Cannes Film Festival in 1970–1971. In his novel *Cappella,* a writer shares a hospital room with the Jew Cappella, whose life has been an unbroken succession of frustrations and sorrows. The separate and mutually uncomprehending monologues of these two are recorded by the writer's blind copyist. Gradually the monologues become less separate, less distinct, until the two men achieve a kind of symbiosis. D. Keith Mano was irritated by the novel's "absurdist affiliations," but a critic in the *Antioch Review* called it "a moving examination of the writer's awkward self-distancing from 'real life,' " using "multiple dramatic monologues to render a 'double' drama. It seems to dramatize a move away from the writer's technical dependence on his own psyche as the one reliable, judicial viewpoint," a development which "has some interest as a dramatist's way of solving crucial fictional problems."

Horovitz has taught playwriting at the Circle in the Square Theatre School, City College, New York University, and Brandeis University. He is a regular contributor to the *Village Voice* and writes a column called "Words From New York" for *Magazine Littéraire,* published in Paris. Horovitz has received grants or fellowships from the Rockefeller Foundation, the

Fulbright Commission, the American Association of Arts and Letters, the National Endowment for the Arts, and the New York State Council on the Arts. He is a member of Actors' Studio, the New Dramatists' Committee, P.E.N., and the Eugene O'Neill Memorial Foundation. The author has been described as "sharp, puckish, deadpan, with eyes that tend toward the woeful." His 1959 marriage to Elaine Abber ended a year later; his 1960 marriage to Doris Keefe lasted until 1972, when they were divorced, and produced three children. Horovitz's recreations include chess, poker, playing the guitar, and "reading Descartes."

Gerald Weales wrote in November 1968 that for him, "the most interesting new development is the emergence of Israel Horovitz." Edith Oliver has commended his ability to capture the atmosphere and the speech rhythms of particular sections of society, and to "turn cruelty, heartlessness, and even suffering into the components of his comedy, as they are of Beckett's." All the same, the excitement that greeted Horovitz's spectacular debut in 1967–1968 has abated somewhat, and Clive Barnes, while acknowledging that he has "a genuine playwright's voice," suggests that "the eloquence with which he says something at times still outweighs the value of what he is saying." Horovitz himself says, "To be a playwright is to write plays. That's all. To the world, it means to write plays, to have them produced, to have them reviewed favorably, and, then, after the first play, and a second, and maybe the third succeeds, they accept you as a playwright."

PRINCIPAL PUBLISHED WORKS: *Plays*—The Indian Wants the Bronx, 1968; It's Called the Sugar Plum, 1968; First Season (containing Line, It's Called the Sugar Plum, The Indian Wants the Bronx, Rats), 1968; Morning (with Noon by Terrence McNally and Night by Leonard Melfi), 1969; Trees, and, Leader: Two Short Plays, 1970; Acrobats, and, Line: Two Plays, 1971 (Line also in Poland, A. and Mailman, B. (ed.) The Off Off Broadway Book, 1973); The Honest-to-God Schnozzola, 1971; Dr. Hero: A Play in Two Acts, 1973; Shooting Gallery, and, Play for Germs: Two Short Plays, 1973; Alfred the Great, 1974; Spared *in* Richards, S. (eds.) The Best Short Plays, 1975; Uncle Snake: An Independence Day Pageant, 1976; Man With Bags, adapted from L'Homme aux valises by Eugéne Ionesco, 1977. *Novels* —Cappella, 1973; Nobody Loves Me, 1975. *Poetry*—Spider Poems and Other Writings, 1973.

ABOUT: Contemporary Authors 33–36, 1973; Crowell's Handbook of Contemporary Drama, 1971; Gottfried, M. Opening Nights, 1970; Kerr, W. Thirty Plays Hath November, 1969; Lewis, A. American Plays and Playwrights of the Contemporary Theatre, 1970; Little, S. and Cantor, A. The Playmakers, 1970; Notable Names in the American Theatre, 1976; Poland, A. and Mailman, B. (eds.) The Off Off Broadway Book, 1973; Vinson, J. (ed.) Contemporary Dramatists, 1977; Weales, G. The Jumping-Off Place, 1969; Who's Who in America, 1976–1977; Who's Who in the

Theatre, 1977. *Periodicals*—Antioch Review November 1973; Nation February 12, 1968; December 16, 1968; March 8, 1971; March 6, 1976; New York Times May 9, 1968; November 29, 1968; April 22, 1969; January 28, 1972; March 22, 1973; April 22, 1973; August 14, 1974; February 17, 1976; February 29, 1976; New York Times Book Review February 25, 1973; New Yorker January 27, 1968; December 7, 1968; May 3, 1969; February 27, 1971; March 1, 1976; Newsweek May 20, 1968; May 5, 1969; Washington Post April 21, 1978.

HSÜN, LU. *See* LU HSÜN

***HUCHEL, PETER** (April 3, 1903–), German poet, is the son of Friedrich Huchel, a civil servant, and the former Marie Zimmerman. He was born in Berlin but spent much of his childhood on his grandfather's farm at Alt-Langerwisch, a village in Brandenburg. He went to school at Potsdam and began his university studies in literature and philosophy at the Humboldt University in Berlin, moving on to Freiburg, then to Vienna, where he studied for a year in 1926. It was then that his poems began to appear in periodicals. In 1928 Huchel went to Paris with two friends, Hans Arno Joachim and Alfred Kantorowicz, obtaining a grant and working as a translator. From Paris Huchel moved on to Brittany, then to the south of France, where he worked for ten months as a farm laborer near Grenoble. After further travels in the Balkans and Turkey 1930–1932, Huchel lived with the same two friends in central Berlin, then for a time in the village of Kladow on the River Havel.

From 1930, Huchel contributed poems and prose to the periodicals *Die literarische Welt* (The Literary World) and *Die Kolonne* (The Column), winning a prize from the latter for a first collection of poems in 1932. This collection was to have been published the following year, but Huchel withdrew it from publication when the National Socialists assumed power; his first book of poems did not appear until fifteen years later. Huchel's early poems were traditional in form, simple and direct in language, and inspired most often by the life he had known in Brandenburg—his childhood dreams and memories and the hard life of small farmers and farm laborers. Nature is described knowledgeably and lovingly, but without either sentimentality or the mysticism associated with the "Naturlyrik" of Lehmann and Loerke. A special sympathy was reserved in these poems for the foreign itinerant workers from Eastern Europe, as in "Polnischer Schnitter" (The Polish Reaper). Such instincts drew Huchel to socialism, though he has never joined a political party. John Flores suggests that his early poetry re-

*hoo′ Kel

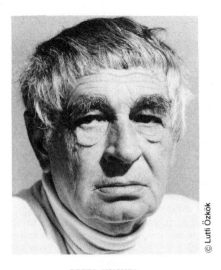

© Lutfi Özkök

PETER HUCHEL

flects "a class-consciousness which is at the same time consciousness of a more fundamental relationship between man and his environment. ... Its two major components are ... the sense of continuity ... between past, present and future activity ... and the seemingly magical harmony between productive human activity and the processes of nature."

During the Hitler regime Huchel was an occasional contributor of plays to the Berlin radio and, briefly, of poems to the periodical *Das innere Reich* (The Inner Realm). In 1940 he became a soldier, but deserted in 1945 and was taken prisoner by the Russians. The poems Huchel had written in the twelve years of Nazi rule but refused to publish were destroyed in Allied bombing raids and had to be reconstructed from memory later. Of his two closest friends, Kantorowicz had emigrated and Joachim had died in a German extermination camp.

Soon after the end of the war, Huchel was transported from a Soviet prison camp to Berlin. From 1945 to 1948 he worked at the Russian-controlled Berliner Rundfunk (Berlin radio station), first as an editor and producer of radio plays, then as artistic director. A house was placed at his disposal in West Berlin, but "for purely private reasons" Huchel moved into a country house at Wilhelmshorst, near Potsdam, which was his home for many years. His first book of poems, *Gedichte,* appeared in East Berlin in 1948 and in West Berlin the following year. The poems Huchel had written during the war were quite different from the nature lyrics of his youth. His landscapes now are ruined and overgrown, nature is seen as horror and decay, and man is as hopelessly corrupted as his envi-

ronment. The uncompleted sequence "Das Gesetz" (The Law), written in the late 1940s, is more optimistic, reflecting Huchel's enthusiasm for the postwar program of land reform in East Germany. But this gleam of hope soon flickered out in Huchel's mounting disillusionment with the East German government and its bureaucracy.

In 1949, however, Huchel became editor of the East German periodical *Sinn und Form* (Meaning and Form). He turned it into the best literary journal in Germany (with the arguable exception of the West German *Akzente)* and the only German forum for distinguished writers from both East and West—his contributors included Paul Celan, Pablo Neruda, Nathalie Sarraute, his friend Johannes Bobrowski, Georg Lukács, Anna Seghers, Brecht, and Sartre. Almost from the start this catholic policy met with criticism in East Germany, and in 1953 Huchel was threatened with dismissal, retaining his post only through the intervention of Brecht. He received various honors from his government, including the East German Fontane Prize in 1955, but attacks continued on both his poetry and his editorial policy. These attacks became more vehement when Huchel began to accept honors and awards from West Germany, and in 1962 he was forced to relinquish the editorship of *Sinn und Form.* He withdrew to his country home, where he lived in isolation and under strict surveillance until 1971. During this period of public disgrace his poems ceased to be published in East Germany and no professional activities were open to him, though he continued to receive an annual stipend as a member of the East German Academy of Arts.

In 1963, meanwhile, Huchel's second book of poems, *Chausseen Chausseen* (Roads Roads) appeared in West Germany, winning him the West German Fontane Prize among other honors. These later poems are rhythmically irregular, almost consistently somber or apocalyptic in mood, and without the framework of argument and rhetoric of the earlier work. Their range of imagery is considerably wider; although the observed and remembered details of country life are still prominent, they now serve to give immediacy to subjects drawn from religion, mythology, history, and literature—as with a number of poems based on Shakespearean characters—more often than from immediate experience. Geographically, too, the later poems range very widely—from China through the Mediterranean world to Western Europe. Huchel's concern, more and more, has been with the timeless archetypes of nature and human life; and these are invoked tragically or elegiacally because their imminent destruction is assumed, as in "Der Garten des Theophrast" (translated by Michael Hamburger as "The Garden of Theophrastus"), a poem addressed by Huchel to his son:

> When at noon the white fire of verses
> Flickering dances above the urns,
> Remember my son. Remember the vanished
> Who planted their conversations like trees.
> The garden is dead, more heavy my breathing,
> Preserve the hour, here Theophrastus walked,
> With oak bark to feed the soil and enrich it,
> To bandage with fiber the wounded bole.
> An olive tree splits the brickwork grown brittle
> And still is a voice in the mote-laden heat.
> Their order was to fell and uproot it,
> Your light is fading, defenceless leaves.

In 1966 Huchel was elected to the West German Academy of Arts and in 1967 his early poems were reissued in West Germany as *Die Sternenreuse* (The Bow-Net of Stars). In 1971, thanks mainly to the intervention of the International P.E.N. Club, Huchel was permitted to leave East Germany. In one of his rare public statements, made in Vienna after his release, Huchel said: "I left a country where for people of my sort the last freedom is solitude, no mail, no traveling, eight years of total isolation: a sad balance, not only for me." Huchel, with his second wife and his son, stayed for a time as guest of honor at the Villa Massimo in Rome, then settled at Staufen in Breisgau, in southern Germany, in a house lent to them by a patron. Various West German and European literary prizes, and poetry readings in many European countries, enabled Huchel to buy a small house in 1974.

Huchel's third collection of poems, *Gezählte Tage* (Days That Are Numbered), had appeared in 1972. A reviewer in the *Times Literary Supplement* wrote that Huchel now "finds himself cast into a spiritual winter from which nature has withdrawn itself and refuses to reveal itself to him." In some of these poems, "the personal intensity of Huchel's vision causes him to express himself obliquely and in a highly condensed form"—almost as if "only alternate lines have actually been printed." The reviewer pointed out affinities between Huchel and both Bobrowski and Robert Frost, and concluded: "What he shares with both is that he is a major poet. . . . [This] may well be the most important volume of poetry to emerge from Germany for some time." A paperback selection of poems was published in 1973 and a collected poems in 1974. Since 1958, translations of Huchel's poetry have appeared in book form in many languages. His correspondence with Hans Henny Jahnn was published in 1974, and in 1975 he edited a selec-

tion of poems by his friend Marie Luise Kaschnitz.

Peter Huchel's poetic career is an extraordinary one, maintained without compromises in the teeth of two totalitarian regimes, and productive of only three slim volumes of poetry over a period of nearly fifty years. Yet from the beginning Huchel's work has found admirers and sponsors, and since 1953, when the first (East German) monograph on his work appeared, he has received a great deal of critical attention in Germany and abroad. Because Huchel has gone his own way, unaffected by fashions or trends, his work has been admired by poets and critics of the most diverse proclivities and age groups, with the exception only of those constrained by exceptionally rigid ideological or aesthetic preconceptions. His own ideological position has been the subject of much speculation and controversy. Huchel has kept silent, sure of his own ground, and refusing to defend or explain it. In a "self-interpretation" of one of his own poems, "Winter Psalm," he wrote: "This text, too, wants to stand for itself and as far as possible assert itself against its interpreters, against possible speculation, elucidations and biographicisms, which is not to say that critics are denied the right to interpret the text by legitimate means and to uncover its distinct layers. To the author, on the other hand, it is very nearly forbidden to distance himself from the linguistic area of his poem to the extent that would be required for a self-interpretation." On the strength of his poems alone, Huchel has established himself as "one of the most courageous and humane of living contemplative poets."

PRINCIPAL WORKS IN ENGLISH TRANSLATION: Selected Poems, translated by Michael Hamburger, 1974. *Poems in* Bridgwater, P. (ed.) Penguin Book of Twentieth-Century German Verse, 1963; Hamburger, M. (ed.) East German Poetry, 1972; Hamburger, M. and Middleton, C. (eds.) Modern German Poetry, 1962.

ABOUT: Closs, A. Twentieth Century German Literature, 1969; Deutsche Dichter der Gegenwart, 1973; Flores, J. Poetry in East Germany, 1971; Hommage für Peter Huchel, 1968; International Who's Who, 1978-79; Keith-Smith, B. (ed.) Essays on Contemporary German Literature, 1966; Mayer, H. (ed.) Über Peter Huchel, 1973; Oxford Companion to German Literature, 1976; Zak, E. Der Dichter Peter Huchel, 1953. *Periodicals*—Times Literary Supplement September 28, 1967; December 29, 1972.

"HUDSON, JEFFERY." See CRICHTON, MICHAEL

INFANTE, GUILLERMO CABRERA. See CABRERA INFANTE, GUILLERMO

*IQBAL, (SIR) MUHAMMAD (November 9, 1877?–April 21, 1938), philosopher and poet, was born at Sialkot in what is now Pakistan but was then the Punjab. According to the [Indian] *Dictionary of National Biography* he was born in 1877, but other sources give a variety of dates, from 1873 to 1878. Iqbal was the son of Sheikh Noor Muhammad, an illiterate but deeply religious man, and of Iman Bibi; his ancestors were Kashmiri Brahmins who converted to Islam.

Iqbal's early education was supervised by Sayyid Mir Hasan, a noted Oriental scholar, and he continued his studies at Murray (Scottish Presbyterian) College in Sialkot, learning Arabic, Persian, and English, as well as Urdu. In 1895 he entered Government College, Lahore (later the University of Lahore), where Sir T. W. Arnold introduced him to Western philosophy. He received his master's degree in philosophy in 1899, graduating first in his class. After serving briefly as MacLeod Reader in Arabic at Oriental College in Lahore, Iqbal returned to Government College as assistant professor of philosophy.

It was at this time that Iqbal, a fluent versifier since childhood, began to make his name as a poet. He wrote in Urdu at first, but learned from the English Romantic poets as well as the Urdu classics. This early verse, mostly lyrical or mystical nature poetry, also reflects Iqbal's youthful interest in the Aligarh movement, whose adherents believed that the Islamic faith could be revitalized by the absorption of Western values and learning. In 1905, in accordance with these views, Iqbal left Government College and went to continue his studies in Europe.

At Trinity College, Cambridge University, Iqbal read philosophy under J.M.E. McTaggart and James Ward, and was greatly influenced by the works of Hegel, Nietzsche, and Bergson. He also attended law lectures at Lincoln's Inn, London, where he was called to the bar in 1908. The same year he received a doctorate from the University of Munich with a thesis published as *The Development of Metaphysics in Persia.* By the end of 1908 Iqbal was back in Lahore, where he practiced thereafter as a barrister at the Chief Court.

What he had seen in Europe had greatly disillusioned him; he could see no hope for India or the world in Western capitalism or the Western greed for power, and he had even absorbed some aspects of Marxist socialism. The Muslim faith seemed to him to offer the best means of national and international salvation, but only if it could be renovated and reformed—purged of the Platonism which he believed had tainted it. Iq-

*ik bäl'

MUHAMMAD IQBAL

bal's religious theories are most fully stated in the lectures published as *The Reconstruction of Religious Thought in Islam,* but it was his poems on the subject that had the greatest impact and influence.

Seeking the widest possible readership among Muslim audiences, Iqbal turned in these long philosophical poems from Urdu to Persian. The first of them was *Asrar-i Khudi* (1915, translated as *The Secrets of the Self*), which sought to replace the passivity and other-worldliness of the Islamic tradition with a dynamic sense of human achievement and potential—of man as God's viceregent on earth:

Thou didst create night and I made the lamp.
Thou didst create clay and I made the cup.
Thou didst create the deserts, mountains, and
  forests,
I produced the orchards, gardens and groves. . . .

(translated by Syed Abdul Vahid)

In *Rumuz-i Bekhudi* (1918, translated as *The Mysteries of Selflessness*), Iqbal describes how the individual should proceed from simple "obedience to the law of life," through study and self-discipline to the state of "divine viceregency," thus fitting himself to take his place in the dynamic and selfless Muslim community Iqbal envisaged as the hope of the world.

These two poems took younger Muslims by storm and account for the knighthood Iqbal received in 1922. The same themes are explored in two volumes of shorter poems published in the 1920s and translated by A. J. Arberry as *The Tulip of Sinai* and *Persian Psalms.* The last and, in literary terms, perhaps the best of Iqbal's major Persian poems was *Javid-Nama* (1932, translated by Arberry under that title and by Mahmud Ahmad as *The Pilgrimage of Eternity*). Structurally inspired by Dante's *Divine Comedy*, it describes a journey around the cosmos with the great Persian poet Jalal al-Din as guide.

The influence of Iqbal's Persian verse has been incalculable, but his work in that language is highly stylized and not infrequently turgid and bombastic. In the 1920s however he returned to Urdu, publishing three major collections: *Bang-i Dara* (The Call of the Road, 1924); *Bal-i Jibril* (Gabriel's Wing, 1935); and *Darb-i Kalim* (The Rod of Moses, 1936). These lyrics, innovative in form and imaginative in content, did much to revitalize the Urdu vernacular as a flexible and modern literary medium.

In 1926, meanwhile, Iqbal had entered politics. He served from 1927 to 1929 as a member of the Punjab legislature and in 1930 became president of the All India Muslim League. In that capacity he called for the amalgamation of the Punjab, the North-West Frontier Province, Sind, and Baluchistan into a single Muslim state —the proposal which led ultimately to the formation of Pakistan. Iqbal is regarded as "the father of Pakistan" as well as his country's national poet, and the day of his death is a solemnly observed national holiday. What E. M. Forster wrote of him in 1946 is still true: "Muhammad Iqbal is a genius and a commanding one, and though I often disagree with him and usually agree with Tagore, it is Iqbal I would rather read. . . . He is one of the two great cultural figures of modern India, and our ignorance about him is extraordinary."

PRINCIPAL WORKS IN ENGLISH TRANSLATION: The Development of Metaphysics in Persia, 1908; The Secrets of the Self: A Philosophical Poem, translated by Reynold A. Nicholson, 1920; The Reconstruction of Religious Thought in Islam, 1934; The Complaint, and, The Answer, translated by Altaf Husain, 1943: Speeches and Statements, compiled by "Shamloo," 1944; Poems From Iqbal, translated by V.G. Kiernan, 1947; The Tulip of Sinai, translated by A.J. Arberry, 1947; Persian Psalms, translated by A.J. Arberry, 1948; The Devil's Conference, translated by Muhammad Ashraf, 1951; Mysteries of Selflessness: A Philosophical Poem, translated by A.J. Arberry, 1953; Complaint and Answer, translated by A.J. Arberry, 1955; The Pilgrimage of Eternity, translated by Shaikh Mahmud Ahmad, 1961; Stray Reflections, edited by Javid Iqbal, 1961; Thoughts and Reflections of Iqbal, edited by Syed Abdul Vahid, 1964; Gulshan-i raz-i jadid (The New Garden of Mystery) and Bandagi namah (Book of Servitude), translated by Bashir Ahmad Dar, 1964; The Guide, 1965; Javid-Nama, translated by A.J. Arberry, 1966; Letters and Writings of Iqbal, edited by B.A. Dar, 1967; The New Rose Garden of Mystery, and The Book of Slaves, translated by M. Hadi Hussain, 1969; A Message From the East (partial translation of Payam-i-mashriq), translated by M. Hadi Hussain, 1971; Rubaiyat of Iqbal, translated by A.R. Tariq, 1973.

ABOUT: Abdur Rahim, K. (ed.) Iqbal: The Poet of Tomorrow, 1968; Ali, S.A. Iqbal: His Poetry and Message, 1932; Beg, A.A. The Poet of the East, 1961; Dar, B.A. Iqbal and Post-Kantian Voluntarism, 1956; Dar, B.A. A Study in Iqbal's Philosophy, 1944; Dictionary of National Biography 1931-1940, 1949; Dictionary of National Biography [of India], 1973; Enver, I.H. The Metaphysics of Iqbal, 1944; Forster, E.M. Two Cheers for Democracy, 1951; Haq, Q.M. and Waley, M.I. Allama Sir Muhammad Iqbal, 1977; Hassan, P.F. The Political Philosophy of Iqbal, 1970; Iqbal as a Thinker: Essays by Eminent Scholars, 1952; Jai Singh, H. The Contribution of Sir Muhammad Iqbal to Modern Islamic Thought, 1954; Khana, Q.K. Aspects of Iqbal, 1938; Krishna, R. Iqbal, 1945; McGraw-Hill Encyclopedia of World Biography, 1973; Malik, H. (ed.) Iqbal: Poet-Philosopher of Pakistan, 1971; May, L.S. Iqbal, 1974; Penguin Companion to Literature 4, 1969; Saiyidain, K.G. Iqbal's Educational Philosophy, 1938; Schimmel, A. Gabriel's Wing: A Study Into the Religious Ideas of Sir Muhammad Iqbal, 1963; Sharif, M.M. About Iqbal and His Thought, 1966; Singh, I. The Ardent Pilgrim, 1951; Sinha, S. Iqbal: The Poet and His Message, 1947; Sud, K.N. Iqbal and His Poems: A Reappraisal, 1969; Vahid, S.A. Iqbal: His Art and Thought, 1959; Vahid, S.A. Studies in Iqbal, 1967; Vahid, S.A. Glimpses of Iqbal, 1974; Waheed, K.A. A Bibliography of Iqbal, 1965.

I-TO, WEN. *See* WEN I-TO

*JACCOTTET, PHILIPPE (June 30, 1925–), Swiss-French poet, was born at Moudon, in the canton of Vaud, in French-speaking Switzerland. He studied at Lausanne University, where he graduated in arts in 1946. He then traveled in Italy and Spain before settling in Paris, where for seven years he represented the Swiss publishing firm of Mermod. Here he became a regular contributor to the distinguished literary periodical *Nouvelle Revue Française* as its poetry critic. In 1953 he moved to the small Provençal town of Grignan (Drôme), where he has established his permanent home. He is married to the painter Anne-Marie Haesler, and has two children.

Since he published his first slim collection, *Requiem,* in 1947 his poetic output has remained limited, and he has made his living from his reviews and as a translator. But as Jean Starobinski points out, all Jaccottet's writings, including his prose works and his translations, reflect poetic creation. He has translated Homer and many Italian poets and novelists, including Carlo Cassola, Eugenio Montale, and Giuseppe Ungaretti, a poet whose purity and perfection of style have clearly influenced his own work. He has also translated the German Romantic poets Novalis and Hölderlin, the prose of Rilke, and the complete works of Robert Musil.

Jaccottet's three prose works, *La Promenade sous les arbres* (The Walk Beneath the Trees, 1957), *Éléments d'un songe* (Elements of a Dream, 1961), and *L'Obscurité* (Obscurity, 1961) explore all sorts of ideas and insights into

*zhak ō tā′

French Cultural Services

PHILIPPE JACCOTTET

creativity in general and Jaccottet's own poetic art in particular. *Éléments d'un songe,* for instance, subtitled "En vivant avec Robert Musil" (Living with Robert Musil), is a series of meditations in which Jaccottet confronts the themes and works of the Austrian novelist and enters into a dialogue with them, setting text against text in pursuit of illumination. A collection of Jaccottet's sensitive critical essays on contemporary French poetry was published in 1968 as *L'Entretien des Muses* (The Discourse of the Muses); his approach is always one of critical empathy with the work before him: "Never has a book of poems been for me a pure object of knowledge, but rather a door opening . . . onto more reality."

Jaccottet's own poetry in early books like *L'effraie et autres poèsies* (The Barn-Owl and Other Poems, 1954) is fairly traditional in both style and content:

This is where I have been trying to lead a life,
in this room of mine, I pretend to love
its table, all the neutral things. . . .
The blackbird stirs a heart-beat in the thick ivy,
the first light sweeps at the retreating shadows.

I too am ready with this sweet acceptance,
that I belong here, that today brings promise.
But for this spider at the foot of my bed,
(from the garden, I suppose) which seems to weave
intent from a body I had almost crushed
the web enshrouding my transparent self.

(from "Interior" translated by
David Pryce-Jones)

But the content of these poems—whether an

impassioned meditation on death such as "Le Livre des Morts" or a lyrical celebration of the wonder (and brevity) of life and love—is always conveyed with an urgent intensity. Each of Jaccottet's collections has marked a significant development in his work towards greater profundity and simplicity—what the editors of *French Poetry Today* describe as "artful simplicity": "The simplicity is a matter of art because, as the translator soon discovers, the poet's effects are very much bound up with the nature, and indeed the structure of the French language." Something of Jaccottet's quality is caught in the following translation of "Dans un tourbillon de neige" ("In a Snow Storm"):

They still ride through the frozen spaces,
Death could not tire them, these few on horses.

They light fires in the snow far apart,
at each gust of wind at least one flickers out.

They're incredibly little, sombre and harassed,
facing the huge, white, gradual misery to be
crushed. . . .

They travel paths worn smooth by the monster's
plodding paws,
perhaps they've made themselves so tiny the better
to give chase?

In the end it's always with the same fist
that we ward off the breath of the foul beast.

(translated by
Edward Lucie-Smith)

This comes from the collection *L'Ignorant* (1958), a title which Jaccottet applies to the poet, meaning in fact not so much ignorance as innocence, a respect for the mystery to which he leaves himself constantly open. What Peter Broome described as Jaccottet's "negative theology" is developed in *La Semaison,* a series of prose notebooks interspersed with poems and prose poems which have been collected in two volumes published in 1963 (covering the years 1954–1962) and 1971 (covering the years 1954–1967). Extracts from both volumes have been published in English as *Seedtime* (1977), in which the prose translations are by André Lefevere, the verse by Michael Hamburger. These observations on art, culture, life, and nature show how his poetry emerges from his response to these fundamental concerns as a part of his search for the central meaning and true nature of things. The notebooks dwell on the need for detachment from self as a precondition of true vision—the unifying vision of poetry, which he defines as an attempt "de concilier ou du moins

415

à rapprocher la limite et l'illimité, le clair et l'obscur, le souffle et la forme" (to reconcile or at least bring closer together the limited and the limitless, the clear and the obscure, inspiration and form). Jaccottet continually stresses the limitations of human understanding—limitations in which the poet must share, for his "negative theology" is an admission of the absence of certainty in life: "A partir du rien. Là est ma loi. Tout le reste: fumée lointaine." (Starting from nothingness. There is my law. All the rest: distant smoke.) And just because nothing is certain and the ultimate remains beyond our reach, Jaccottet commits himself to the accessible realities, striving in his poetry for complete fidelity to his own experience. He has made it his concern, as Alexander Aspel puts it, "to probe the most immediate reality of nature and the changing seasons for bits of simple, elementary truth and its approximation in words that are right."

Jaccottet writes of "ce présent qu'il faudrait saisir comme la flamme"—of needing to seize the present like a flame. And in the brief poems of *Airs* (Airs, 1967), lyrics that are both musical airs and gentle atmospheric disturbances, he does indeed capture the evanescent sensations he receives from nature:

> Each flower is just a little night
> pretending to have drawn near.
>
> But whence its perfume rises
> I cannot hope to enter
> good reason why it stirs me
> and makes me watch so long
> in front of that shut door. . . .
>
> This world is just the crest
> of an invisible fire
>
> (translated by
> Edward Lucie-Smith)

Many of these short poems have qualities similar to Japanese haiku, a form that has influenced a number of contemporary French poets. Jaccottet has described haiku as "poetry *without images,*" finding in these brief, objective poems wisdom and a supreme example of "the absolute effacement of the poet." The quiet poems in *Airs* concern themselves with the eternal themes of beauty, transience, and death—the beauty of nature, of words, and of the human spirit, at once fragile and tenacious. This intimate poetry is nourished by Jaccottet's keen observation of the atmosphere and seasonal changes of the Provençal landscape which he has adopted. And sometimes the poet, in his contemplation of nature, receives brief flashes of illumination in which the antitheses and contradictions inherent in human life are momentarily transcended, as in "Sur les pas de la lune" ("In the Steps of the Moon"):

> Tonight, leaning at the window,
> I saw that the world was weightless,
> and its obstacles were gone.
> All that holds us back in the daytime
> seemed bound to carry me now
> from one opening to the other,
> from within a house of water
> towards something weak and bright
> as the grass I was about to enter,
> fearless, giving thanks for earth's freshness,
> in the steps of the moon I said
> yes and then off I went. . . .
>
> (translated by
> Edward Lucie-Smith)

These moments of illumination are further explored in the poetic prose of *Paysages avec figures absentes* (Landscapes With Absent Figures, 1970), in which Jaccottet contemplates natural scenes, and also paintings, in an attempt to define the revelations they may offer. According to a reviewer in the *Times Literary Supplement,* Jaccottet's "urgent concern for the meaning of landscape . . . and his sense of poetry as illumination, place him, with many of his contemporaries, in a tradition still uninterrupted since the Romantics. . . . Yet this beautiful little book is anything but a late example of an ancient mode. M. Jaccottet renders the spirit of place, through the unemphatic intensity of his prose, in scenes both convincingly and ambiguously mysterious and also richly natural. He is constantly making one see landscape anew, by the rare honesty of a fertile imagination. . . . The softly spoken voice, discreet and appealingly ingenuous, recalling Nerval, strangely reinforces the power of the vision."

Jaccottet is aware that "those lower floors of existence" such as sex and violence have been neglected in his own poetry. He is however a poet with an overwhelmingly affirmative sensibility, whose natural impulse is to relate and connect, and whose choice has been for the heights: "Il n'est pas de poésie sans hauteur." In 1971 his collected verse poems were brought out by Gallimard as *Poésie 1946–1967,* though with significant deletions from and some additions to the original individual collections. The publication of *Poésie* led Virginia A. La Charité to hope that "this highly sensitive and eminently readable poet may now be discovered by a wider audience." And indeed a volume of his poems in translations by Cid Corman, closely following Jaccottet's own selection in *Poésie,* was published in 1974 as *Breathings.* It was warmly welcomed both for the excellence of Corman's translations and for the "luminous watercolors" by the poet's wife which illustrate the book. Professor C. A. Hackett describes Jaccottet as "one of the most sensitive and profound poets now writing in France."

PRINCIPAL WORKS IN ENGLISH TRANSLATION: Breathings, 1974; Seedtime: Extracts from the Notebooks 1954–1967, 1977. *Poems* in Aspel, A. and Justice, D. (eds.) Contemporary French Poetry, 1965; Hartley, A. (ed.) Penguin Book of French Verse 4, 1959; Martin, G.D. (ed.) Anthology of Contemporary French Poetry, 1972; Taylor, S.W. (ed.) French Writing Today, 1968; Taylor, S.W. and Lucie-Smith, E. (eds.) French Poetry Today, 1971; Modern Poetry in Translation 16 1973; Origin April 1970; Poetry August-September 1970.

ABOUT: Clerval, A. Philippe Jaccottet, 1976; Hackett, C.A. (ed.) New French Poetry, 1973; Richard, J.P. Onze Études sur la poésie moderne, 1964. *Periodicals*—Australian Journal of French Studies 1 1968; Books Abroad Spring 1968, Summer 1972, Autumn 1972; Times Literary Supplement February 11, 1972.

JACOBSEN, JOSEPHINE (WINDER BOYLAN) (August 19, 1908–), American poet, critic, and short story writer, writes: "I was born, a premature baby, in Coburg, Canada, where my parents had gone for a summer vacation. I think that maturing healthily from a birth-weight of two-and-a-half pounds was more of a sporting proposition than it now would be. I was told that I was kept in an incubator and fed with a medicine dropper, which gave me, as a child, the unfortunate image of myself as one of those nearly-naked and dreary fledglings which, fortunately, clothe themselves decently later.

"My father, son of an expatriate Irishman, was brought up in Europe, where his family then lived, and where his sister continued to live until her death. He went to college at the University of Heidelberg, then took his medical degree at the University of Bonn. Though he developed a lasting dislike for the Prussian mentality, I think he was happy in his university days; he was an expert fencer, a rock-climber, and captained a bobsled team. He had on his cheek the famous slashes of the Heidelberg duelist. After his parents settled in the United States, he married my mother, his second wife. Until his death of a heart attack, when I was five years old, we lived in New York and on Long Island. My mother was a restless spirit, with very little regard for formal education (though my half-brother went to a boarding-school), and after my father's death we traveled about until I was fourteen. A series of ephemeral governesses taught me noth-

JOSEPHINE JACOBSEN

William L. Klender

ing; nor indeed, in fairness to them, did they try.

"We settled in Baltimore, where my mother's family had many connections, and I went for three years to the Roland Park Country School. Coming into the school with no previous experience whatsoever, at that age, and in a strange city, I should have been dutifully disoriented and miserable. Instead, I was so delighted to find that I could go into the normal classes, and so pleased to be among people of my own age, that these were three extremely happy years.

"I wrote poetry as far back as I can remember, and unfortunately nothing I have subsequently published has brought quite the visceral and voluptuous thrill which struck me when I set eyes on my first published poem, in *St. Nicholas Magazine.* The gold and silver badges which I subsequently won were an anti-climax.

"In my teens, I lived an extremely conventional life, making my debut at Baltimore's Monday German, and strongly cherishing the intention of a career in the theater. I worked in small, and then leading, roles in the Vagabond Theater, the oldest Little Theater in the United States, which at that time gave Baltimore almost the only experimental or foreign plays available to it.

"After meeting Eric Jacobsen, whom I married in 1932, the idea of a theatrical career collapsed; fortunately, I was becoming more and more absorbed in poetry. A small book of early poems was published by the Kaleidograph Press soon after I married. I knew absolutely no one connected with the world of literature, and though my mother's intense joy in reading and her eclectic tastes had given me an appetite for exploration and experiment, I was much too involved in my domestic life to think of myself as a professional writer. Indeed, I remember being secretly amazed when Harriet Monroe accepted for *Poetry* a group of sonnets I had unoptimistically slipped into the mailbox. I continued writing, in a hole-and-corner manner, until my husband left the country, to drive an ambulance with the American Field Service in 1944.

"Partly because I was constantly terrified, I went to work at the small tea-importing firm, the oldest in the country, of which he was president; but I was so unhappy during this period that Mary Owings Miller, the editor of the small but distinguished Contemporary Poetry series, suggested that this would be a good time to throw myself into the preparation of a new book of poems. The result was *For the Unlost.* Not long after this, I began to have the strongest possible craving for the opportunity to work regularly, as a professional writer; but first my husband's absence from home while I had a young son, and after his return, a series of serious illnesses within my family, made any sort of steady schedule highly precarious.

"But gradually, I was working toward spending a larger portion of my time on writing. At the suggestion of Adolphus Emmart, an editor then of the Baltimore *Sun,* I began doing poetry reviews for that paper; Contemporary Poetry published a second book, *The Human Climate,* and my poems began appearing widely.

"But it was only considerably later, and in much part due to my contact with three writers who were also close friends, that I began to have what seemed to me the audacity to consider that what I *was* was a writer. William Mueller, author, at one time chairman of the department of English at Goucher College, and presently head of the Humanities Institute, collaborated with me on two books of criticism, *The Testament of Samuel Beckett,* and *Ionesco and Genet: Playwrights of Silence.* The discipline enforced by producing my share of these two books, and their critical reception, gave me great encouragement. Through Elliott Coleman, poet, and head of the John Hopkins Writing Seminars, I met many poets, and participated in major poetry programs; and my friendship with both of these men and with A. R. Ammons (who, when I first met him, was almost completely unknown, and to whom I felt particularly close, since for long years our work in poetry had been private, self-sustaining, and remote from literary circles) gave me enormous nourishment.

"Then, within seven or eight years, my life swung into a different orbit. My book of poems, *The Animal Inside,* earned me recognition: I was appointed Poetry Consultant to the Library of Congress in 1971, and served there for a second term. I was now, with great suddenness, writing fiction—which I had tried many years before, with mutual dissatisfaction on the part of myself and editors. In one of those abrupt swings, my second story to be published was the only story simultaneously in *The Best American Short Stories* and the *O. Henry Prize Stories,* and wide publishing and anthologizing followed.

"I was in the curious position of having been over fifty-five when I virtually *began* a career of work; this has made many things difficult. On the other hand, in a way I am grateful, as I feel strongly that a force, dammed up, is much more powerful when released; and since I am, in any case, an intensely private person, overly noncompetitive by nature, and happiest working outside of the tight but changing structures of the cliques and schools of poetry, I regret nothing of the long years of a very fitful apprenticeship.

"I feel that working with some success in three related but discrete fields, those of poetry, fiction and criticism, is for me the best possible situation. In my case, fiction and poetry in particular reinforce each other, both working to cross-benefit, and the differing disciplines making for flexibility. In my approach to criticism, of which I have lately done an increasing amount, I try always to have a salutary sense of the fallibility of my dicta, no matter how strongly felt, remembering the history of the criticism of other eras, a history which can most kindly be described as checkered. I am not interested in criticizing the work of writers whose caliber I do not respect, except in the rare case in which one has the opportunity bluntly to attack the specious and self-serving.

"Like all writers, I have lived with the constant question of my relations with the social and political life around me, especially acute at the time of the Vietnamese war; and often I have envied the few whose natural poetic bent enabled them spontaneously to write poetry which spoke eloquently in topical terms—envied them as much as I disliked those who, it seemed to me, often exploited true misery in false poetry.

"Since I believed that the secret which 'sits in the middle and knows' is the core of the poem, I am always reluctant to talk much about my own work. I 'learn by going where I have to go.'

"My great pleasure—inherited from both sides, I suppose—is travel, and now my husband and I do as much traveling as we can, generally a month or so a year. Our summers are spent near our son, a teacher and poet, and his family. It is still true that my steady periods of work are largely limited to our brief travels, and to the weeks I spend, with much gratitude, at the Mac-Dowell Colony and Yaddo.

"I put as much as I could define of my attitude toward poetry into my final lecture at the Library of Congress, 'The Instant of Knowing.' Perhaps I should end with words from those pages: 'The arrangement of the oldest human fact into certain special sounds, in a certain sequence. It is a thing which cannot be argued with. A knowledge of what we already knew, become for an instant so devastatingly fresh that it could be contained no more than a flash of lightning.' "

Josephine Jacobsen's first two books were not much noticed, but there was an approving response to *The Human Climate* (1953). A critic in *Saturday Review* thought it "the work of a poet who is decidedly herself, who speaks her convictions briskly and boldly," and who "feels passionately about the cruelties and the injustices and the hypocrisies of the world." Her idiom was called "direct, incisive, economical," and her approach "while intensely personal . . . is controlled and disciplined. Irony, understatement, the trenchant and telling phrase" are her tools.

However, as she says, it was her fourth book, *The Animal Inside* (1966), published when she was fifty-eight, which brought her general recognition. The poems in this collection range for their subjects from Pennsylvania to Haiti, from starfish and reindeer to death in the family. The title comes from Sir James Frazer's anthropological classic *The Golden Bough:* "The animal inside the animal . . . is the soul" and, though these poems were much praised for the precision of their observation, William Jay Smith noted that Josephine Jacobsen "is never merely pictorial; she is interested in . . . the spiritual motivation of reality."

Laurence Lieberman was impressed by the poet's "power to get outside her own personality and assume the identity of the subject that absorbs her. . . . Even when she deals with death in her family, she cultivates an odd impersonality," but "despite the limited intimacy, there is no loss of intensity. The measured portions of personal involvement allow emotional leeway for her to explore the geography of death with detachment. Especially moving are the poems which illuminate primitive or mythical styles of thought." An example is "Painter in Xyochtl," about the ritual murder of an American painter by a tribe of Central American Indians, a poem "Lawrentian in its authoritative grasp, its sensitivity to the primitive mind." Reviewers of *The Animal Inside* were unanimous in their admiration for the fastidiousness and elegance of Josephine Jacobsen's diction, the range and richness of her stanza forms and rhythmic resources—a sestina on hummingbirds seemed to William Jay Smith one of the best poems in the collection.

That poem reappears in *The Shade-Seller,* which includes substantial selections from the four earlier books, as well as forty-two new poems. One reviewer complained that "too many of the poems seem to be but a superior form of occasional verse," but others found on the contrary an extraordinary capacity for eliciting profound insights into the human predicament from the most commonplace objects and occasions. The new poems in this collection abandon rhyme in favor of blank verse. Many of them, as Peter Meinke wrote, "are travel poems in the best sense: not just accurate descriptions of Greece or Mexico, but rich with implications about the spirit of a particular place, and of the human spirit in general. . . . She is a quiet, deep poet whose quietness contains and controls powerful and often outraged feelings."

Another critic, James Martin, was struck by the way Josephine Jacobsen "helps us see that we belong, that our common interests are more important than our individuality," and he quotes in evidence these lines from her poem "Treaty":

> We can see this. Not even children, playing,
> clean children, unobservant and important,
> can miss the risky tenure of the house,
> can impudently disbelieve the presence:
> mountains, barrancos, flutes, marimbas, drums
> address the multitude whose eyes we bear.
> But now at dusk we do not insist on our
>   knowledge.
> We are quick shadows, but strangers; who need,
>   when all is said,
> a private love, the English language, and a bed.

Eleven of her short stories, which have been much anthologized, were collected in *A Walk With Raschid and Other Stories* (1978). The critical studies of Samuel Beckett and of Ionesco and Genet that she has written with William Mueller have been found intelligent, concise, and readable.

Josephine Jacobsen's late flowering as a poet brought her, a virtual unknown before 1966, to the post of Poetry Consultant to the Library of Congress in 1971—a position as close to that of poet laureate as the United States has to offer. The first woman so honored since Elizabeth Bishop in 1949-1950, she served there for two terms, as she says, and since 1973 has been an Honorary Consultant in American Letters to the Library of Congress. She has served also as a member of the D.C. Commission on the Arts and Humanities, of the National Society of Literature and the Arts, of the women's committee of the Center Stage Association, of the Corporation of the Millay Colony for the Arts, and of a number of Baltimore organizations, including the Citizens' Planning and Housing Association. She has honorary doctorates from Notre Dame and from Goucher College. Josephine Jacobsen's fondness for travel has taken her to Mexico, Guatemala, Venezuela, the Caribbean, France, Italy, Greece, Morocco, Kenya, Tanzania, Portugal, Madeira, Spain, and Canada. She is a Democrat and a Roman Catholic.

PRINCIPAL WORKS: *Poetry*—Let Each Man Remember, 1940; For the Unlost, 1946; The Human Climate, 1953; The Animal Inside, 1966; The Shade-Seller: New and Selected Poems, 1974. *Stories*—A Walk With Raschid and Other Stories, 1978. *Criticism*—(with William R. Mueller) The Testament of Samuel Beckett, 1964; (with William R. Mueller) Ionesco and Genet: Playwrights of Silence, 1968.

ABOUT: Contemporary Authors 33-36, 1973; Who's Who in America, 1976-1977; Who's Who of American Women, 1975-1976. *Periodicals*—Commonweal November 29, 1974; LC Information Bulletin March 18, 1971; New Republic January 4-11, 1975; New York Times Book Review December 11, 1966; Poetry March 1967, May 1975; Saturday Review January 16, 1954.

*JAKOBSON, ROMAN (OSIPOVICH) (October 11, 1896–)

*JAKOBSON, ROMAN (OSIPOVICH) (October 11, 1896–), Russian-American linguist, literary historian, and theoretician, was born in Moscow of Jewish parents, Osip Jakobson and the former Anna Volpert. He was educated at the Lazarev Institute of Oriental Languages of Moscow University, received his diploma in 1918, and began his research in linguistics there (1918-1920). From the outset his work was characterized by that breadth of interest and depth of insight which has allowed him to point the way in several fields: he has been successively one of the pioneers of Russian Formalism, of modern linguistics, and of Structuralism.

When he was still in his teens, Jakobson became closely associated with the group of Futurist poets led by Mayakovsky and Khlebnikov, whose poetry was expressing the prevailing mood of liberation and revolt in the years before the Revolution. Among their linguistic innovations was *zaumny yazyk* ("trans-sense" or "trans-rational" language). This derived from the theory that the sound of a word is deeply related to its meaning, so that a new poetic language could be created which would express ideas and emotions directly through sound, without the distracting associations of ordinary language. Jakobson himself tried his hand at some *zaum* poetry, which he contributed under

*yak′ ob son

ROMAN JAKOBSON

the pseudonym Alyagrov to Kruchenykh's highly eccentric Futurist book *Zaumnaya gniga*. Vladimir Markov in *Russian Futurism* describes "Alyagrov's" poetry as "a conglomeration of known words, word fragments, distorted and invented words, and individual vowels. Stresses are denoted by italicized vowel letters. There is a certain tendency towards internal rhyme, and some deliberate use of unusual letter combinations. On the whole, Alyagrov's *zaum* is original and interesting, but his debut was, unfortunately, his last appearance as a *zaum* practitioner."

Jakobson was later to write important critical accounts of some of the Futurist poets he knew personally. His *Noveyshaya russkaya poeziya* (Recent Russian Poetry, 1921) is primarily a penetrating study of Khlebnikov, though with many incidental insights on Mayakovsky. And Edward J. Brown in his own book on Mayakovsky observes that "probably no one would question the statement that the most interesting critical studies of Mayakovsky are those of Roman Jakobson." These include *O cheshkom stikhe, preimushchestvenno v sopostavlenii s russkim* (On Czech Poetry, Primarily in Comparison With Russian, 1923), which contains the first authoritative analysis of Mayakovsky's verse system; and the famous essay "O pokolenii rastrativshem svoikh poetov" (On a Generation That Squandered Its Poets) in *Smert Vladimir Mayakovskogo* (The Death of Vladimir Mayakovsky, 1930), which comments on the structure and imagery of Mayakovsky's work as a whole.

While the Futurist poets were attacking all traditions and turning literature upside down, the new critical school of Formalists—their most active and convinced supporters—were revolutionizing literary analysis. The Formalists rejected the older sociological and metaphysical approaches to literature, which emphasized its content, and instead considered it primarily from a technical and structural point of view. The development of Russian Formalism was the result of close and intensive intellectual teamwork by a number of linguists and historians of literature. The Moscow Linguistic Circle was founded in 1915 by a group of the university's philology students, including Roman Jakobson. The other main center of Formalism was *Opoyaz* (The Society of Poetical Language), established in Petrograd in 1916 by a group of brilliant critics including Viktor Shklovsky. The Petrograd group was relatively historical in its approach, whereas the Moscow Linguistic Circle was more scientific and produced such studies as Jakobson's "Khlebnikov's Poetic Language" (1919), a paper which foreshadowed many later developments in the linguistic analysis of literature. Formalist criticism continued to flourish in Russia until it was suppressed by the Bolshevik government in the early 1930s; Futurist poetry, with which it shared an iconoclastic spirit and a dynamic notion of form, met the same fate at the same time.

In 1920, however, Jakobson himself had settled in Czechoslovakia. He went there initially as a member of the Russian Red Cross Mission in Prague. Once there, according to a writer in the *Times Literary Supplement,* "with characteristic intellectual curiosity and enthusiasm he plunged into the intellectual life of Prague and soon achieved a position of commanding importance in academic and literary circles." In 1926 he was one of the founders of the Prague Linguistic Circle. The first volume of the *Trauvaux* (Works) of the Circle, jointly produced by the members, was presented at the first conference of Slavic philologists held in Prague in 1929. This book sets out in nine brief theses a program of desirable lines of research in Slavic linguistics, suggesting a radically innovative theory and methodology. The traditional methods of the discipline are criticized as being too concerned with linguistic origins and with the analysis of isolated facts. In their place the theses put the key idea of *structure,* proposing that language should be considered as a functional system which has to be understood in the light of its aim as communication.

These theses are often taken as the formal beginnings of Structuralism—for instance by David Robey in *Structuralism: An Introduction* (1973): "*Structure,* in the *Thèses,* is the structure of the system, the manner in which the individual elements of a particular language are arranged for this purpose in relations of mutual dependence. Since this differs from one language to another, it follows that the separate components of a system can only be understood in the light of the system as a whole, and therefore that the primary object of linguistic study must be the structure of the system itself rather than the individual linguistic fact. It is in this sense that the method of modern linguistics should be, as the *Thèses* suggest, *structural;* and, with slight variations, this has continued to be the basis of the notion of structural linguistics . . . up to the present day."

George Steiner has observed that the Prague Linguistic Circle rapidly became an influential center for the examination of literature in the light of linguistics: "The contributions to current linguistic sensibility made by Jakobson, by N.S. Trubetzkoy, by J.M. Mukařovský, would be difficult to overestimate. It is here that those concepts of structuralism and semiology which are now so fashionable were first set out, and set out with a responsiveness to the genius of poetry and the demands of exact philology which current imitations, particularly in France, often fail to match." Since the members of the Circle collaborated closely, there were many areas of overlap in their work, but Jakobson himself was particularly interested in two main fields: linguistic structure, and literary studies centered on the distinctive features of poetic language.

In the purely linguistic area, Jakobson in his essay "Remarques sur l'évolution phonologique du russe comparée à celle des autres langues slaves" (Notes on the Phonological Evolution of Russian Compared With That of Other Slav Languages, 1929) was among the first to perceive that speech sounds are not atomic entities, but compounds of a small number of universal phonetic properties. In other words, the basic sounds (phonemes) of any language can be classified in terms of a variety of *"traits distinctifs"* (distinctive features), such as whether they are voiceless or voiced, oral or nasal, labial or dental. (A predilection for dichotomies, for the interpretation of linguistic facts in binary terms, is apparent in many aspects of Jakobson's work, and anticipates the binary choices of information theory.)

At this time Jakobson classified the phonemes of different languages primarily in accordance with the nature of their articulation and the particular organs used to produce it—the tip of the tongue, lips, etc. In such later works as *Preliminaries to Speech Analysis* (1952) and *Fundamentals of Language* (1956), Jakobson has described the distinctive features of phonemes in terms of *acoustic* rather than articulatory correlates. This method is of universal application and thus lends itself to Jakobson's most recent work, which has been concerned with the attempt to establish the inherent distinctive features found in all the languages of the world, underlying "their entire lexical and morphological stock."

Jakobson has also published important studies on the way children acquire language, and on the progressive loss of speech in aphasia, a speech disturbance caused by lesions in certain zones of the cerebral cortex. A major contribution to both these subjects was *Kindersprache, Aphasie und allgemeine Lautgesetze* (1941, translated as *Child Language, Aphasia and Phonological Universals*). Here and in later works Jakobson maintains that every child follows the same sequence of acquisition of the distinctive features of his language, a sequence which is reversed in the dissolution of speech in aphasia.

Jakobson, who had received his doctorate at Prague University in 1930, subsequently taught at the Masaryk University in Brno as Professor of Russian Philology (1933-1939). He left Czechoslovakia in 1939 after Hitler's invasion, and spent the next two years in Scandinavia as visiting lecturer at the universities of Copenhagen, Oslo, and Uppsala. In 1941 he settled in the United States, and he has since held professorships at the École Libre des Hautes Études, New York (1942-1946), Columbia University (1943-1949), Massachusetts Institute of Technology (1957–), and Harvard University, where he served from 1949 to 1967 as Samuel Hazzard Cross Professor of Slavonic Languages, Literatures, and General Linguistics, and is now Professor Emeritus. He was married in 1962 to Krystyna Pomorska.

At the Conference on Style held at Indiana University in 1958, Jakobson summed up his view of the main efforts of the revolution in linguistics on the understanding of literature: "The poetic resources concealed in the morphological and syntactic structure of language, briefly the poetry of grammar, and its literary product, the grammar of poetry, have been seldom known to critics and mostly disregarded by linguists, but skilfully mastered by creative writers. . . . All of us here, however, realize that a linguist deaf to the poetic function of language and a literary scholar indifferent to linguistic problems and unconversant with linguistic methods are equally flagrant anachronisms."

In his Russian and Czech periods, Jakobson's writings on literature dealt not only with the characteristics of Futurist and modernist poetry, but with problems of versification and the question of poetic language. The Formalist view of

poetics, imported into Czechoslovakia mainly through Jakobson, was developed there by Jan Mukařovský, who expresses the central issue in the relationship between linguistics and poetics thus: "Is poetic language a special brand of the ordinary language, or is it an independent formation?" Jakobson's answer is given, characteristically, in terms of binary opposition, for crucial to his Structuralist poetics is a basic dichotomy between *metaphor* and *metonymy*. The metaphoric style, in which one object or idea leads to another through their similarity, is typical of lyric poetry and Romantic literary forms; the metonymic, in which one object or idea leads to another through their contiguity, is typical of prose, of epic, and of "realistic" literature in general.

In the essay "Randbemerkungen zur Prosa des Dichters Pasternak" (1936), translated as "Marginal Notes on the Prose of the Poet Pasternak" in Davie and Livingstone's *Pasternak: Modern Judgements* (1969), Jakobson maintains that Pasternak's prose is the characteristic prose of a poet in a great age of poetry, and that this differs markedly from a novelist's prose: "Textbook categories are comfortingly simple: prose is one thing, poetry another. Nevertheless, the difference between a poet's prose and that of a prose-writer, or between the poems of a prose-writer and those of a poet, is very striking. . . . Cases of complete bilingualism are of course undeniable, and when we read the prose of Pushkin or Màcha, of Lermontov or Heine, of Pasternak or Mallarmé, we cannot help being amazed at the command these writers have of the other language; but at the same time we are bound to pick out a foreign note, as it were, in the accent and inner form of their speech. Their achievements in this second language are brilliant sallies from the mountains of poetry into the plains of prose."

Jakobson's contributions to Slavic studies include important essays on the morphology of folktales, building on Vladimir Propp's observation that in all the Russian tales he had studied certain elements were constant even though the stories themselves changed. Jakobson's essay "On Russian Fairy Tales," included in *Russian Fairy Tales* (1945), points out that during the many centuries when Russian written literature was almost entirely subordinated to the church, there grew up a rich oral literature not only of folk tales but of epic and other poetry, whose language was closer to colloquial Russian than was the Church Slavonic of written literature. Jakobson has written a number of brilliant essays on this oral literature. These include a philological study in 1948 of the twelfth-century epic *Slovo o polku Igoreve* (Lay of Prince Igor's Campaign) offering an impressive case for its medieval origin, which had been questioned by some scholars.

Jakobson's major work in poetics in recent years has been a series of structural analyses of poems from different periods and languages, beginning with a study in collaboration with Claude Lévi-Strauss of Charles Baudelaire's "Les Chats" (1962, translated in M. Lane's *Structuralism: A Reader,* 1972). In his introduction, Lévi-Strauss writes: "If a linguist and an ethnologist have seen fit to join forces in their efforts to try to understand what a Baudelaire sonnet is made of, it is because, independently, they have found themselves confronted with complementary problems. The linguist discerns structures in works of poetry which are strikingly analogous to those which the analysis of myths reveals to the ethnologist. For his part, the latter cannot fail to recognize that myths do not consist simply of arrangements of concepts *but* that they are also works of art which arouse in those who hear them (and in the ethnologist himself when he reads them in transcription) profound aesthetic emotions. Is it possible that the two problems are but one and the same?"

In his analysis of the poetic texture of the songs of the medieval Portuguese troubadour Martin Codax, Jakobson writes of his "supreme flair for the innermost ties between sound and meaning," and he has explored the same quality in poems by Dante, Du Bellay, Shakespeare, Blake, Eminescu, Brecht, Pessoa, and other poets. Jakobson's method is to analyze the ways in which members of particular morphological and syntactic classes are distributed among the stanzas of a poem and to discover the symmetrical patterns of distribution which organize a poem by setting the odd-numbered stanzas against the even, the anterior against the posterior, and the central against the peripheral. Against this two major criticisms were leveled in the *Times Literary Supplement* for May 25, 1973—that "by using linguistic categories as he does one can find similar patterns in any text whatsoever and that purely numerical symmetry need not have poetic effects."

The fact remains that Roman Jakobson has made fundamental contributions to both linguistics and literary studies, and important ones to several other disciplines as well—for example to anthropology, directly in his work on Paleosiberian peoples and languages, and indirectly through his influence on Claude Lévi-Strauss and on the development of structural anthropology.

Jakobson has taught as a visiting professor at many universities, including Yale, Princeton, Brown, New York, Brandeis, the Collège de France, and Louvain. He is a member of the American Academy of Arts and Sciences, the British Academy, and of a number of European academies of science. He has served as president of the Linguistic Society of America (1956) and as vice-president of the International Committee of Slavicists and the International Association for Semiotic Studies; he is a member or honorary member of a long and extraordinarily varied list of learned societies. Jakobson was a fellow of the Center for Advanced Study in the Behavioral Sciences in 1958-1959 and 1960-1961, and of the Harvard Center for Cognitive Studies in 1967-1969. In 1965-1969 he was a consultant to the UNESCO Department of Social Sciences, and in 1966-1969 he was a visiting fellow at the Salk Institute for Biological Studies. He received an award from the American Council of Learned Societies in 1960, and another from the American Association for the Advancement of Slavic Studies in 1970. He has honorary doctorates from nearly a score of universities all over the world and is a Chevalier of the Légion d'Honneur. His principal leisure interest is travel.

PRINCIPAL WORKS IN ENGLISH TRANSLATION: Selected Writings (Volume 1: Phonological Studies, 1971; Volume 2: Word and Language, 1971; Volume 4: Slavic Epic Studies, 1966); Slavic Languages: A Condensed Survey, 1955; (with M. Halle) Fundamentals of Language, 1956; (with G. Hüttl-Worth and J.F. Beebe) Paleosiberian Peoples and Languages: A Bibliographical Guide, 1957; (with G. Fant and M. Halle) Preliminaries to Speech Analysis, 1961 (originally published as an M.I.T. Technical Report in 1952); Child Language, Aphasia and Phonological Universals, 1968; Studies on Child Language and Aphasia, 1971; Main Trends in the Science of Language, 1973; Puškin and His Sculptural Myth, 1975; (with Stephen Rudy) Yeats' "Sorrow of Love" Through the Years, 1977; Six Lectures on Sound and Meaning, 1978. *As editor*—(with E.J. Simmons) Russian Epic Studies, 1949; On the Structure of Language and Its Mathematical Aspects, 1961; Slavic Poetics: Essays in Honor of Kiril Taranovsky, 1973; Letters and Notes of N.S. Trubetzkoy, 1975.

ABOUT: Armstrong, D. and Van Schooneveld, C.H., (eds.) Roman Jakobson: Echoes of His Scholarship, 1978; Berberova, N. The Italics Are Mine, 1969; Directory of American Scholars, 1974; Erlich, V. Russian Formalism, 1965; Halle, M. (and others, eds.) For Roman Jakobson: Essays on the Occasion of His Sixtieth Birthday, 1956; Holenstein, E. Roman Jakobson's Approach to Language, 1976; International Who's Who, 1977-78; Lepschy, G.C. A Survey of Structural Linguistics, 1970; Roman Jakobson: A Bibliography of His Writings, 1971; Scholes, R. Structuralism in Literature, 1974; Steiner, G. Extra-territorial: Papers on Literature and the Language Revolution, 1972; To Honor Roman Jakobson: Essays on His Seventieth Birthday (3 volumes), 1967; Vachek, J. The Linguistic School of Prague, 1966; Who's Who in America, 1976-1977. *Periodicals*—Harvard Slavic Studies 1 1953; New Left Review 37 1966; Times Literary Supplement August 3, 1967; May 28, 1970; May 25, 1973.

JOHNSON, B(RYAN) S(TANLEY) (WIL-LIAM) (February 5, 1933–November 13, 1973), English novelist, poet, dramatist, and film-maker, was the son of Stanley Wilfred Johnson, a bookseller's stock-keeper, and Emily Jane (Lambird) Johnson. He was born in London and spent most of his life there, the first six years of it in the working-class district of Hammersmith. With the outbreak of World War II in 1939, he and his mother left Hammersmith for the comparative safety of a small farm near Chobham, in Surrey. In 1941 his mother returned to London and Bryan Johnson joined his school, which had been evacuated to Brotton, near High Wycombe, in Buckinghamshire. In *The Evacuees,* an anthology of personal accounts of the wartime evacuations which Johnson edited, he made it clear that he was profoundly and miserably affected by this separation from his family.

After the war, Johnson completed his education in London schools. He went to work as a bank clerk and later as an accounts clerk until, in 1955, at the age of twenty-three, he entered King's College, London University. He read English and graduated with honors. For a time Johnson was a teacher in a particularly inadequate and violent London high school, an experience on which he drew in *Albert Angelo.* A fervent supporter of the Chelsea Football Club, he also began to establish himself as a highly knowledgeable and literate reporter of soccer football matches.

Johnson was a devotee of such writers as Joyce, Beckett, Sarraute, and Le Clézio; of such film directors as Godard, Resnais, and Antonioni. In *Books and Bookmen* (September 1970), he quoted Nathalie Sarraute's description of literature as a kind of relay race, in which "the baton of innovation" is passed from one generation to the next. He goes on: "Not only has the vast majority of British novelists dropped the baton, but it has stood still, turned back, or not even realized that there is a race."

He himself took up this baton in eight novels, of which the first, *Travelling People,* describes the wanderings up and down Britain of Henry Henry, an ex-clerk with a degree in philosophy. The book, which shifts from impressionistic narrative to interior monologue to passages in dramatic form, and employs visual devices reminiscent of *Tristram Shandy,* was welcomed for its "indications of a real but vagrant talent," but found "irritatingly knowing and self-conscious." Johnson's determined experimentalism continued to trouble his reviewers, most of whom believed that he had the sensibility and the gifts of a first-rate novelist of the traditional sort.

B. S. JOHNSON

Albert Angelo, for example, while rooted in the conventional vicissitudes of an architect obliged to scrape out a living as a relief teacher, includes slotted pages which enable the reader, if he wishes, to look ahead. *Trawl,* set on a fishing boat in the Barents Sea, alternates scenes of trawling with passages in which the seasick narrator hauls up memories that might help him to understand his sense of isolation. This novel, which impressed some readers as an extended prose poem, is one of the most admired of Johnson's books; it nevertheless displeased its reviewer in the *Times Literary Supplement,* who complained of an insistent and inappropriate "echoing of the rhythms of Beckett" and concluded that the author's "dallyings with experiment are irritating because they produce arbitrary gaps in what is elsewhere a coherent story."

In Johnson's next novel, *The Unfortunates,* a writer, brooding on the death of a friend and on the past, goes to a Midlands city to report a football match. The book comes in a box instead of a traditional binding, so that the reader can shuffle its two dozen sections into any order he chooses in emulation of the random movement of the human mind. Most critics lamented the innovation—"more concerned," as Hugh Hebert remarked, "to show how and why the method was wrong in principle than to establish whether it mattered in this particular instance."

House Mother Normal consists of nine interior monologues, eight of them spoken by inmates of a home for the aged during a bizarre social evening, the ninth by their house mother, who will go to any lengths to distract them from the disgusting advances of death. One reviewer, noting that the nine monologues could almost be fitted physically on one another, with exact simultaneity of events, decided however that "the ingenuity of the technique precludes depth of treatment." There were similar reactions to *Christie Malry's Own Double Entry,* which includes some splendidly observed factory scenes in its portrayal of a "Julian Sorel with an adding machine."

Deeply affected by his mother's death from cancer in 1971, Johnson began work on an ambitious trilogy, highly complex in structure, in which he set out to assess the meaning of her life, and of his own life in relation to her and to his wife and children. The first volume, published posthumously in 1975 as *See the Old Lady Decently,* considers the years between his mother's birth and his own. He deals in partly imaginative, partly documentary terms with her early life, and ruminates on the decline of England (the mother country) after World War I, on pre-Christian earth mother cults, and on motherhood in general. As usual, the least traditional parts of the book were least admired by most critics, but the book was generally liked. Valentine Cunningham praised it for "welcoming into fiction . . . the flat, uneducated testimony of the ordinary man," and another reviewer called it "a monument to disciplined love, fretful class consciousness, and femininity." Soon after it was finished, in the winter of 1973, Johnson committed suicide in his Islington flat at a time when his wife and children were away. The trilogy's other two volumes, never written, were to have been called "Buried Although" and "Amongst Those Left Are You," completing the sentence begun in the title of the first volume.

Reviewing *Aren't You Rather Young to be Writing Your Memoirs?,* a collection of prose pieces, a writer in the *Times Literary Supplement* commented that Johnson had "a considerable story-teller's skill, a talent for creating characters who tend to live beyond his control, an ability to write sustained and vigorous prose, a robust and inventive humour. It is all very inconvenient because Mr. Johnson would not have it this way. He is against narrative." Valentine Cunningham, rather similarly, wrote: "The success of B.S. Johnson's anti-novels was that, like Sterne, he managed, in the process of unmaking the art of the novel, also to make novels." The author himself maintained that the novel is of all forms "the most threatened by the media," and said that "where I depart from convention it is because the convention has failed." He was impatient of the majority of his critics, whose "standards are formed by the the reading of the literature of the past, and by definition are

therefore simply not adequate to deal with anything different." And some critics took Johnson's side of the argument, like Anthony Burgess, who once called him "the only living British novelist with the guts to reassess the novel form."

"If a writer's chief interest is in telling stories," Johnson wrote, "then the best place to do it is on television." He made eight films for television, most of them documentaries, and three for the cinema: *You're Human Like the Rest of Them* (1967), *Up Yours Too, Guillaume Apollinaire* (1968), and *Paradigm* (1969). He also wrote several plays for the stage, television, and radio. His poetry seemed to Thomas Kinsella "a remarkably clear and even achievement. It is a poetry that rides mainly on the surface of experience, serious and intelligent, articulating current judgements, the pangs of a broken love affair, etc." Winner of the 1967 Somerset Maugham Award for *Trawl,* Johnson became the first Gregynog Arts Fellow at the University of Wales in 1970. His other awards included the Gregory Award (1963) and the Granada Poetry Prize (1971). *You're Human Like the Rest of Them* won the Grand Prix at both the Tours and the Melbourne festivals of short films in 1968.

From 1964 onwards Johnson was poetry editor of the *Transatlantic Review,* and with Alan Burns founded in 1969 "Writers Reading" to encourage and organize prose readings at colleges and universities. Johnson was married in 1964 to Virginia Ann Kimpton, by whom he had two children. A heavily built man, whose "round face seemed to rest straight on the massive round shoulders," he was "combative but immensely likeable."

PRINCIPAL WORKS: *Fiction*—Travelling People, 1963; Albert Angelo, 1964; (with Zulfikar Ghose) Statement Against Corpses (short stories), 1964; Trawl, 1966; The Unfortunates, 1969; House Mother Normal, 1971; (with others) Penguin Modern Stories 7, 1971; Christie Malry's Own Double Entry, 1973; Aren't You Rather Young to be Writing Your Memoirs? (stories and prose pieces), 1973; See the Old Lady Decently, 1975. *Poetry*—Poems, 1964; Poems Two, 1972; (with Gavin Ewart and Zulfikar Ghose) Penguin Modern Poets 25, 1975. *Plays*—You're Human Like the Rest of Them *in* New English Dramatists 14, 1970. *As Editor*—(with Julia Oman) Street Children, 1964; The Evacuees, 1968; (with Margaret Drabble) London Consequences (a group novel), 1972; All Bull: The National Servicemen, 1973.

ABOUT: Bakewell, M. *introduction to* See the Old Lady Decently, 1975; Bergonzi, B. The Situation of the Novel, 1970; Bradbury, M. (ed.) The Novel Today, 1977; Contemporary Authors 9-12 1st revision, 1974; Gordon, G. (ed.) Beyond the Words, 1973; Johnson B.S. (ed.) The Evacuees, 1968; Vinson, J. (ed.) Contemporary Novelists, 1972; Who's Who, 1973. *Periodicals*—Books and Bookmen September 1970; Critical Quarterly Summer 1969; Guardian March 15, 1969; New York Times Book Review September

23, 1973; Times (London) November 15, 1973; November 13, 1974; May 1, 1975; Times Literary Supplement May 2, 1975.

*JOHNSON, EYVIND (OLOF VERNER) (July 29, 1900–August 26, 1976), Swedish novelist and Nobel Prize winner, was born near Boden, in Norrbotten, Sweden's northernmost province. His father had settled there after working as a laborer on the Lapland iron-ore railroad, but he became mentally ill shortly after his son's birth and the boy was brought up by relatives.

Johnson left school before he was thirteen and worked as a timber floater, sawmill hand, and ditch-digger on the edge of the Arctic Circle, educating himself as best he could by reading, before making his way south to Stockholm in 1919. He was by then involved in trade union and political activities, but his interests turned increasingly to writing. In 1921, destitute and despairing, he left Stockholm and went first to Berlin, then on to Paris. Johnson spent the greater part of the 1920s outside Sweden, mostly in Paris, supporting himself precariously with short stories, newspaper articles, and novels.

He had not found himself, either as a writer or as a person, when he published his first novels. They are all concerned with frustrations and inner conflicts—what Johnson called man's "Hamlet-character"—and reveal the self-taught author's efforts to assimilate the literary and intellectual innovations of the period: Johnson himself acknowledged the influence of Bergson and Freud, Gide, Proust, and Joyce. These novels reflect Johnson's socialist and humanitarian convictions, but also a bitter undercurrent of youthful disillusionment.

Stad i mörker (Town in Darkness, 1926), a conventional but well-written novel, gave the first hint of Johnson's potential, which began to be realized in *Kommentar till ett stjärnfall* (Commentary on a Falling Star, 1929). This bleak picture of human selfishness in a disintegrating capitalist society is presented with considerable sophistication, and includes the first use in Swedish literature of Joyce's stream-of-consciousness technique.

In 1930 Johnson returned to Sweden, his literary reputation already established. He associated himself with the reform politics of the social democrats and moved towards a more positive, less deterministic, attitude to the world. This is clear both from the intricately constructed novel *Bobinack* (1932), with its fascinating title-character—part capitalist, part outsider—and from the more lyrical *Regn in gryningen* (Rain at

*yōn′ son

EYVIND JOHNSON

Swedish Consulate

Dawn, 1933), with its self-mocking primitivism and qualified affirmation of a "more open society."

More important is *Romanen om Olof* (The Novel About Olof, 1934-1937), a four-volume study of adolescence, which takes the form of a powerful and only slightly fictionalized account of Johnson's own harsh struggle for survival and self-realization. Its first volume has been translated by Mary Sandbach as *1914*. The tetralogy is concerned as much with the intellectual as the emotional development of young Olof, from the inarticulate but perceptive fourteen-year-old to the nineteen-year-old strike leader, bloody but unbowed. The novel has established itself as a classic in Sweden, not only as a subtle and imaginative psychological study but also as a record of the rise of an entire section of the population—the underprivileged but talented members of the proletariat.

During World War II, Johnson was one of the most active and outspoken of the Swedish authors who opposed their government's conciliatory attitude towards Germany. He had earlier attacked the Nazi mentality and its Swedish manifestations in *Nattövning* (Night Maneuvers, 1938), and during the war he published a newspaper for the Norwegian Resistance and wrote the lengthy *Krilon* trilogy (1941-1943). The story centers on the estate agent Johannes Krilon and his friends, who are striving for the "possibility of decency" in neutralist Sweden during the war. On another level the book is an intricate allegorical account of man's eternal struggle against evil forces within and without. The novel shows Johnson's technical virtuosity applied with great imagination, deep conviction, and—beneath the structural and stylistic complexities—a fundamentally simple warm-heartedness.

Krilon is a fairy tale, but Johnson maintained that fairy tales could be a more effective way to a true understanding of the world than direct realism. This principle is applied in his next novel, *Strändernas svall* (1946, translated by M.A. Michael as *Return to Ithaca*), in which twentieth-century problems and values are debated in the context of the Trojan War. It is regarded as one of Johnson's most successful novels, admired for his ingenious demythologization of the Homeric legends and the bravura of his language and thought.

Strändernas svall is the first in a series of arrestingly original historical novels which form the most notable part of Johnson's extensive postwar output. *Drömmar om rosor och eld* (Dreams of Roses and Fire, 1949) concerns the seventeenth-century witchcraft trial at Loudon which later attracted the literary attentions of Aldous Huxley and John Whiting. *Molnen över Metapontion* (The Clouds Over Metapontion, 1957) brilliantly interweaves the ancient Greece of the *Anabasis* with a modern story set in a German concentration camp and in postwar Italy, illustrating the persistence of human emotions and human problems throughout history.

Hans nådes tid (1960, translated by E.H. Schubert as *The Days of His Grace*) is set in the swiftly changing Europe of Charlemagne, as seen from one of the nations the emperor enslaves. It is a subtle analysis of the totalitarian spirit—a depressing story of cruelty and despotism, hopeless rebellions, frustrated love, and a pessimism alleviated only by the hope that the idea of freedom will somehow survive. Johnson's preoccupation with time provided him with a more lyrical theme in *Livsdagen lång* (Life's Long Day, 1964). A man and woman meet and are parted over and over again, in eight different but intermerging historical periods. The past is preserved in the present and transmitted to the future: time is a river "where all ages flow abreast." Johnson also published a number of short stories and a series of notable "diaries" embodying travel notes, comments on his work, and thoughtful discussions of the literary process in general.

The author was married twice, in 1927 and in 1940. After World War II he was a member of the Swedish UNESCO delegation in Switzerland, Germany, England, and elsewhere. His personal experiences, his choice of subjects, and his restless experimentalism established him as the most European author of his generation in Sweden. He was elected to the Swedish Academy in 1957 and received the Nordic Council's Literature Prize in 1962. In 1974 he shared the Nobel Prize for Literature with another Swedish novelist, Harry Martinson.

PRINCIPAL WORKS IN ENGLISH TRANSLATION: Return to Ithaca, 1952; The Days of His Grace, 1968; 1914, 1970.

ABOUT: Gustafson, A. A History of Swedish Literature, 1961; Holmberg, O. Lovtal över svenska romaner, 1957; International Who's Who, 1974-75; Orton, G.K. Eyvind Johnson, 1972; Penguin Companion to Literature 2, 1969; Seymour-Smith, M. Guide to Modern World Literature, 1973; Smith, H. (ed.) Columbia Dictionary of Modern European Literature, 1947; Stanford, W.B. The Ulysses Theme, 1963. *Periodicals*—American-Scandinavian Review December 1968; Contemporary Literature Summer 1971; Scandinavica November 1966; Times (London) October 4, 1974.

JONG, ERICA (MANN) (March 26, 1942–) American poet, novelist, and essayist, writes: "For a writer who has so often been accused of autobiography, I seem to have been remarkably reticent about submitting this biographical note. That is because strict autobiography is hard for me. It is easier for me to be utterly candid, to tell the *emotional* truth about an experience when I am not hemmed in by the world of biographical fact. As a novelist, I have written two books *(Fear of Flying* and *How to Save Your Own Life)* that I would rather call self-mythologizing than autobiographical or confessional. While I have drawn on certain obvious details from my own life, I have rearranged and structured, invented and edited, in ways that have nothing to do with 'real' life. I abhor the low level of literary journalism in our own time which causes catch-all terms like 'confessional' and 'autobiographical' to be used instead of a careful reading of a given work. Like all writers, I hate being categorized. I am myself—not a 'confessional poet,' or a 'feminist novelist.' In my fiction, I do identify greatly with writers like Colette, Henry Miller and Proust who mythologized their own lives. But I am also a great admirer of Tolstoy, and would like to grow to the point where I could write one book with the resonance of *Anna Karenina.* I am intrigued by the story, recounted by one biographer, that Tolstoy started out with the conscious wish to portray Anna as a duplicitous and scheming woman who destroys two men, but that as he wrote and rewrote, he became more and more empathic to his heroine and the tragedy of her plight. I am interested in the particular ability of the artist to suspend ego and join with the communal unconscious, the quality that Keats meant when he spoke of Shakespeare's 'negative capability.' I think there is a level of consciousness at which people are

© 1979 by Layle Silbert

ERICA JONG

more like each other than they are different, and if the artist can plumb this level, he or she will find that many people will respond with recognition and gratitude. Whenever I have written about things I thought were more unique and peculiar to me, I have invariably found that dozens of readers wrote to say: 'Me, too!'

"As a poet, I have been influenced by everyone from Chaucer to Keats to Alexander Pope to Byron to Blake to Whitman. Contemporary poets I have loved enormously include Roethke, Jarrell, Plath, Sexton, Neruda, Lowell, Ponge, Cummings and D.H. Lawrence. I tend to devour the entire works of one writer, and then move on, digesting and assimilating the 'influence.' I was lucky to have a good literary education at Barnard College (where they actually gave you a *degree* for reading books like *Don Juan* and *Tom Jones*).

"I tend to be a rather clear writer—no matter what I do. Writers' styles are born, not made, I think. In college I wished to be obscure and Empsonesque (that was the mannerism then), but now I have faced the fact that I am an accessible writer (both in poetry and prose) and that I might as well make the most of it. I would like my work to be a semi-permeable membrane through which feelings, ideas, nutrients pass. While I dislike didacticism, I *do* feel that the writer has an obligation to the audience. It is an obligation to nurture the reader's spirit, to promote self-inquiry and growth, to encourage spiritual daring. A poet-friend once pointed out that many of my poems used the verbs 'learn' and 'teach' and that I seemed to see life as a continual process of self-education. I'll buy that.

"I was born in Manhattan in 1942, grew up on the Upper West Side, played in Central Park, went to P.S. 87 (which was then an old red brick building, smelling of sour milk, on West 77th Street and Amsterdam Avenue), then to Joan of Arc Junior High, Birch Wathen (a private school), and finally to the High School of Music and Art (where my major was art). After that came Barnard College (B.A. 1963); Columbia University (M.A. in eighteenth century literature, 1965); and later some poetry seminars with Stanley Kunitz and Mark Strand at the Writing Division of the School of the Arts, Columbia University (1969–1970). In between, I lived in Heidelberg, Germany for three years (1966–1969), and unfortunately missed the entire period of late sixties madness in the U.S. Nevertheless, in Heidelberg, I first began to write seriously, and it was there that I wrote many of the poems that went into my first book, *Fruits & Vegetables*.

"My childhood was very urban—despite summers in the Berkshires, Fire Island, and much travel abroad. It was only when I first lived in Malibu, California (1974–1975) by the ocean, that I realized how much one needs the presence of nature to balance one's life. But as a child, I don't think I felt at all deprived. I played Indian on the rocks in Central Park, rode my bicycle near the Museum of Natural History, and had a rather greater degree of freedom than kids have today (because there was less fear of random crime in New York). Like most New Yorkers, I naïvely believed that New York was the center of the world.

"I am the middle sister of three, five years younger than Suzanna (Nana) Mann Daou, and five years older than Claudia Mann Oberweger. My mother is a painter, my father an importer of ceramics and giftware (who was at one time a musician and songwriter). My maternal grandparents (who were born in Russia) lived with us during my childhood, and we made up a rather noisy, cynical, talkative, boisterous extended family. My grandfather is a painter who worked in a studio at home during my childhood. I painted by his side when I was very little—and for years thought I wanted to be a painter. Though I never spoke of wanting to be a writer, I always wrote.

"I think I feel happiest and most myself when I am writing, and I can't think of any profession I would rather have. Of course, it's hell at times. Failure is painful for the writer, and success is not less painful. Both neglect and attention create paranoia (which, like insomnia, is the writer's occupational disease). 'Toil, envy, want, the patron and the grave,' seems to apply every bit as much as it did in Samuel Johnson's day. But still, I would rather write than do just about anything else I can think of."

Erica Jong, the daughter of Seymour Mann and the former Edith Mirsky, grew up in a triplex on West Seventy-Seventh Street. "We were smothered with opportunity," she says, "piano lessons, skating lessons, summer camps, art school." She began to write stories when she was ten or eleven, and recalls that her main characters were always men—"I never tried to write about women and I never thought anyone would be interested in a woman's point of view. . . . I wrote about boys in the same way that a black child draws blond hair . . . on the faces in her sketchbook." It was not until she went to Barnard in 1959 that she decided that her métier was poetry. As an undergraduate there, she was Phi Beta Kappa, carried off a Murray Fellowship and other honors, edited the college literary magazine, and produced poetry programs for the campus radio station, earning a reputation as the "class grind." Michael Wertham, the boyfriend who typed up her poems for her, became her first husband.

Graduating in 1963, she taught English at the City College of New York (1964-1966) while studying for her M.A. and completing the course work for a doctorate at Columbia. In 1966 she married Dr. Allan Jong, and from then until 1969 lived with him in Heidelberg. A Chinese-American child psychiatrist, he was running a guidance clinic there for the children of American army personnel. During that period she taught at the University of Maryland's European Division in Heidelberg (1967-1968) and, briefly, sold mutual funds for Bernie Cornfeld's Investors Overseas Service.

The poems she had written in college had been "sonnets and sestinas about unicorns, Venetian paintings, Roman fountains, and the graves of English poets." In Germany, reading Denise Levertov, Pablo Neruda, William Carlos Williams, and Rafael Alberti, and suffering under an acute sense of isolation and alienation, she turned to free verse and more urgent concerns: "I was in psychoanalysis and for the first time was trying to write about my violent feelings about being Jewish in Germany, and my violent feelings about being female in a male-dominated world. I was beginning to be more in touch with my dreams and fantasies. My poems no longer assumed a pseudo-neuter persona. They were frankly female, and that, for the first time, became part of their subject."

Her poems began to appear in such magazines as *Mademoiselle* and *Poetry Journal,* and in 1971, back in the United States, she published her first collection, *Fruits & Vegetables.* In the title sequence, "copulating fruits, heartless onions, and other nonintelligent forms become bawdy, ludicrous, and sometimes pathetic metaphors for human flesh and its autocratic, relentless appetites":

> Goodbye, he waved, entering the apple.
> That red siren,
> whose white flesh turns brown
> with prolonged exposure to air,
> opened her perfect cheeks to receive him.
> She took him in.
> The garden revolved
> in her glossy patinas of skin.
> Goodbye.

This is followed by love poems, poems celebrating sex and sensuality, topical satires, feminist poems, and poems about death, metamorphosis, and the situation of the artist. "The general spirit of the book," according to *Current Biography,* is "that of a feaster at the varied banquet of life, relishing the sweetness without, saddened at the emptiness within." It was received with almost unmixed pleasure. Josephine Hendlin described it as the work of "a brilliant poet of analogies who makes the vibrations of the senses a force that binds us together," and Rozanne Knudsen welcomed Erica Jong as "a dreamy yet graphic, seriously playful, wanton, and earthy addition to the small stock of women poets who celebrate their sex." Karl Malkoff praised the highly pictorial quality of these poems and their "cheerful surrealism"—a surrealism that is "simply a denial of boundaries between subjectivity and objectivity, between the unconscious and the conscious. . . . Ultimately the entire book is directed against the arbitrary categories that separate us from nature, from other human beings, from ourselves."

There were similar poems in *Half-Lives* (1973), but the tone here was often spikier, as in "The Wives of Mafiosi":

> Thinking to take on the power
> > of a dark suit lined with lead
> > of a man with a platinum mouth & knuckles of
> > > brass
> > of a bullet the color of a Ferrari
>
> the wives of Mafiosi stay home
> decanting the Chianti
> like transparent blood. . . .
>
> We too stay home
> & dream of power.
> > We sacrifice the steakblood to the dishwasher.
> > We bring clear offerings of water to the plants.
> > We pray before the baby pictures.

We dream of swallowing bullets
& coupling with money.
　　We dream of transparent armor.
　　We imagine we want peace.
　　We imagine we are different
　　from the wives of Mafiosi.

Helen Vendler wrote of these poems that "her subject is nearly always some form of the double-bind or the Laingian knot. . . . Inside her rigid frames of syntax, a playful metaphorical mind is at work, busy in plentiful invention and little fables. If the whimsical and the bitter sometimes become the petulantly cute, there are nevertheless biting poems about women." And Margaret Atwood read the book, she said, "the way you watch a trapeze act, with held breath, marvelling at the agility, the lightness of touch, the brilliant demonstration of the difficult made to look easy."

Erica Jong had never lost her interest in prose fiction, and by this time had completed two unpublished novels—"God on West End Avenue," written in 1965, and "The Man Who Murdered Poets," set in Heidelberg. These were highly literary works, full of Nabokovian wordplay, and Jong was not satisfied with them: "What I wanted was excess, digression, rollicking language, energy, and poetry . . . Henry Miller or Colette rather than Forster or Bowen." In 1971, in "great trepidation," she set to work on such a novel, basing it on "picaresque adventures that I wanted to use." It was published in 1973 as *Fear of Flying*. Erica Jong had once gone with her husband to a psychoanalysts' convention in Vienna, and it is in this city and situation that she places her restless, fearful, and unfulfilled heroine Isadora Wing. Isadora meets a randy English Laingian and is persuaded to fly from her husband and convention. After two weeks of (frequently unsatisfactory) promiscuity, roaring around Europe in her lover's sports car and in any number of beds, she and her mentor return cheerfully to their respective spouses.

Erica Jong has said that the novel was intended to challenge "the notion that intellectual women must be heads without bodies." *Best Sell* thought it merely "a dull and dirty book" and Paul Theroux in the *New Statesman* denounced the "witless heroine" of "this crappy novel" as "a mammoth pudenda." Needless to say, such criticism did not prevent the novel from becoming a best-seller, and it had its champions—among them Henry Miller, who thought it might very well "make literary history," and John Updike, who admired its "class, sass, brightness, and bite." Updike went on: "Fearless and fresh, tender and exact, Mrs. Jong has arrived non-stop at the point of being a literary personality." And a literary personality she became, endlessly in demand to give lectures and readings, to advise the lovelorn, to be interviewed as a writer, as a feminist, or as an object of prurient speculation. She herself has sometimes seemed more than a little chastened by this spectacle of an intelligent and talented woman fallen among media men: "Sometimes we run too fast/ or trip climbing/ the rotten rungs/ in fame's ladder."

The kind of success her first novel enjoyed may account in part for the relatively hostile reception of her next book of poems, *Loveroot* (1975). A former admirer, Helen Vendler, was clearly unimpressed by her claim to write "in neon sperm across the air," and Robert Kirsch found himself doubting her sincerity. All the same, he thought, "always beyond self-pity, beyond the cheap shots at men, is a lyrical voice of eloquence and splendor. . . . If it means taking Mrs. Jong with all her faults or leaving her, I certainly prefer the former." *Loveroot,* in any case, became one of the very few books of verse ever selected as a Book-of-the-Month Club alternate. The same year her first two poetry collections were republished in one volume, along with an interview and samples of her prose, as *Here Comes, and Other Poems.*

This was followed by Erica Jong's second novel, *How to Save Your Own Life* (1977), in which Isadora Wing flies again. Isadora is by now the author of a scandalous best-seller, *Candida Confesses.* She is persuaded by a Hollywood hustler to adapt it for the movies and as a result does a great deal of shuttling between California and her psychiatrist in New York, finding time nevertheless to experiment with several varieties of sex. In the end she finds happiness and true love in the arms of a young screenwriter, divorces her husband, and settles down to work on a new book. Erica Jong's insistence that she is engaged in self-mythologizing rather than autobiography cut little ice with most reviewers, one of whom suggested that she writes not novels but "breathlessly up-to-date confessional bulletins." However, it seemed to John Leonard that "if Jong wants to write a book on how bad it feels to be an unhappily married celebrity, and to put everyone she knows into it, and to tell us how she cured herself of fragmentation by finding a lover who is also a friend, she's entitled." What bothered Leonard was that "whereas the author of *Fear of Flying* was looking inside her own head, shuffling her fantasies, and with a manic gusto playing out her hand, the author of *How to Save Your Own Life* is looking over her shoulder, afraid that the critics might be gaining on her.

Instead of neat one-liners, she specializes in pious philosophizing. Not insincere, but pious, hectoring, self-important." Martha Spaulding thought that "the continual contrast between Isadora's inward wry defiance and her self-effacing behavior should once again elicit chuckles of rueful recognition from a number of women, for Erica Jong has a knack for describing female guilt and related confining emotions. But that her talent seems to sharpen itself at the expense of husband, friends, and lovers is bound to be distasteful to some readers." Jong herself has explained that she had to return to Isadora Wing, "had to get her out of that stifling marriage, so that she could move up into a position of honesty. I also wanted to show that a woman can have her work and have her man too. I can't think of one female character in literature who has had both her work and her love."

The author has received *Poetry's* Bess Hokin Prize and a fellowship from the National Endowment for the Arts, among other awards. In 1969-1970 she was an instructor in English at Manhattan Community College and she has also served as an instructor in poetry at the YM-YWHA Poetry Center in New York. Erica Jong describes herself as "a left-leaning feminist" and a "non-practising Jew." She is five feet three inches tall, and in 1975 weighed one hundred and thirty pounds. Many interviewers have enjoyed her sunny and ebullient disposition, and one called her "very sexy-looking in a wholesome all-American way. . . . She has fluffy blond hair and blue eyes which peer amused from behind her pink-tinted, oversized prescription glasses." Like Isadora Wing she is now divorced, and lives in Connecticut with Jonathan Fast, son of Howard Fast and himself a writer. Erica Jong is at work on a historical novel set in eighteenth-century England, "an epic story of a woman looking back at her life, from the time she was born in Queen Anne's day, to the romantic poets, all of whom she has known. It will be a literary spoof, a romp. I'm very eager to prove I can write in another genre."

PRINCIPAL WORKS: *Poetry*—Fruits & Vegetables, 1971; Half-Lives, 1973; Loveroot, 1975; Here Comes, and Other Poems, 1975. *Fiction*—Fear of Flying, 1973; How to Save Your Own Life, 1977.

ABOUT: Current Biography, 1975; Jong, E. Here Comes, 1975; Malkoff, K. Crowell's Handbook of Contemporary American Poetry, 1973; Packard, W. (ed.) The Craft of Poetry, 1974; Untermeyer, L. (ed.) Fifty American and British Poets, 1973; Updike, J. Picked-Up Pieces, 1975; Vinson, J. (ed.) Contemporary Poets, 1975; Who's Who in America, 1976-1977. *Periodicals*—Biography News February 1974; May 1975, July 1975; Columbia Forum Winter 1975; Feminist Art Journal Fall 1974; Library Journal August 1971; April 15, 1973; Ms. December 1972, August 1973; Nation June 28, 1971; January 12, 1974; National Review May 24, 1974; New Statesman April 19, 1974; New York May 20, 1974; New York Post January 5, 1974; January 4, 1975; New York Times September 7, 1974; April 29, 1976; New York Times Book Review August 12, 1973; October 21, 1973; November 11, 1973; September 7, 1975; March 20, 1977; New Yorker December 17, 1973; Newsday January 19, 1975; Newsweek December 16, 1974; May 5, 1975; March 28, 1977; Observer Magazine April 24, 1977; Parnassus Spring-Summer, 1974; Publishers Weekly February 24, 1977; Saturday Review December 18, 1971; Time January 20, 1975; Times Literary Supplement August 27, 1971; December 13, 1974; Twentieth Century Literature October 1974; Village Voice September 2, 1971; Vogue October 1975; Washington Post January 12, 1975.

"JORGENSON, IVAR." *See* SILVERBERG, ROBERT

*KAEL, PAULINE (June 19, 1919–), American film critic, was born in Petaluma, California, the daughter of Issac Paul Kael and the former Judith Friedman. The youngest of five children, she was raised on her father's farm in Sonoma County, north of San Francisco. Isaac Kael, a Polish Jew whom she has described as "an agnostic and a movie-goer," lost his farm in the Depression. The family moved to San Francisco, where Pauline Kael graduated from Girls High School in 1936. She majored in philosophy at the University of California at Berkeley, receiving her B.A. in 1940. There followed what she calls a "checkered story" of bohemian living, mostly in San Francisco but briefly in New York, during which she tried her hand at writing plays, made experimental films, and worked at a "crazy-quilt" variety of jobs.

A movie fan since childhood, Pauline Kael dreamed of being a film critic the way other girls dreamed of becoming actresses. Her first review appeared in 1953 in the San Francisco magazine *City Lights*—an appraisal of Chaplin's *Limelight,* which she called "Slimelight." Thereafter she contributed reviews as a freelance to such magazines as *Sight and Sound, Partisan Review,* and *Film Culture,* and wrote regularly for *Film Quarterly.* She also broadcast film reviews (without pay) over Berkeley's Pacifica radio network.

At the same time—from 1955 until the early 1960s—Pauline Kael ran the Berkeley Cinema Guild Theatres, the country's first twin art film cinemas. Her resourceful and imaginative programs included early revivals of W.C. Fields and Mae West, and the Busby Berkeley musicals, and her one-paragraph notes on the films she screened were soon as renowned as the programs themselves. She continued her work as a critic, but told an interviewer in 1966 that she had

*kāl

Jeff Griswold

PAULINE KAEL

received less than $2,000 for ten years of reviewing and had been obliged to earn her keep in such casual jobs as came her way, including stints as a cook, seamstress, and ghostwriter. All this changed in 1965 with the publication of her first book.

This was *I Lost It at the Movies,* a selection of her reviews, broadcasts, and essays dealing mostly with films of the late 1950s and the 1960s. "Miss Kael's interminable shadow-boxing with other reviewers palls after a while," wrote John Simon. "She treats us to liberal doses of autobiography, which is irrelevant when it isn't downright embarrassing. . . . Worst of all, she has an undue love of kitsch and exacerbated suspicion of 'art' films" (like Resnais' *Last Year at Marienbad,* which she called "the snow job in the ice palace"). But "another Pauline Kael emerges" in this "important book," Simon went on; "she is, first of all, an excellent polemicist. . . . Miss Kael has a fine sense for singling out the relevant detail, and, when she is not trying too hard, can be very funny. . . . Above all, Miss Kael has an honorable and exacting notion of what it is to be a critic."

Pauline Kael's attacks on other reviewers and on the pretensions of "art-house" cinema troubled a number of her critics but delighted the general public, who made her book a best-seller. And, whatever their reservations, most critics agreed with John Simon that this was an important book. Richard Schickel was "not certain just what Miss Kael thinks she lost at the movies, but it was assuredly neither her wit nor her wits. Her collected essays confirm what those of us who have encountered them separately over the last few years . . . have suspected—that she

is the sanest, saltiest, most resourceful and least attitudinizing movie critic currently in practice in the United States."

This success led to others, and Pauline Kael moved to New York where her by-line began to appear in such well-heeled mass-circulation magazines as *Life, Holiday,* and *Mademoiselle.* In 1966 she was hired as resident film critic of the glossy women's magazine *McCall's* at a reported salary of $20,000 a year. She was fired six months later, after describing *The Sound of Music* as "the sugarcoated lie that people seem to want to eat." As she told a reporter at the time, she had known all along that "I would sock the ladies right between the ears, but what the hell is the point of writing, if you're writing banality?" A brief stint with the *New Republic* followed in 1967, and in January 1968 she joined the *New Yorker,* where she has remained. Pauline Kael writes the magazine's film reviews during the fall and winter months, Penelope Gilliatt during the other six months of the year. She says that she has never had a contract with the *New Yorker:* "I have a handshake agreement with Bill [Shawn] that he will never change a word without consulting me. I must say, I have no regrets."

Kiss Kiss Bang Bang (1968), her second book, contains movie reviews, essays on Marlon Brando, Orson Welles, and Stanley Kramer, and capsule comments on nearly three hundred films. There is also an account, previously unpublished, of the making of *The Group,* which is offered as an example of what is wrong with Hollywood. F.A. Macklin complained of the author's "continual attacks on other critics" and Mordecai Richler praised her "merciless ability to cut through modish hyperbole and see movies plain"; common readers bought the book in great quantities.

What was new, or had not previously been much noticed, was the interest this book revealed in the sociology of the cinema. Pauline Kael herself wrote, in her review of *Morgan:* "Conceivably it's part of the function of a movie critic to know and indicate the difference between a bad movie that doesn't matter because it's so much like other bad movies and a bad movie that matters . . . because it affects people strongly in new, different ways. And if it be said that this is sociology, not esthetics, the answer is that an esthetician who gave his time to criticism of current movies would have to be an awful fool." David Sterritt concluded that Pauline Kael is "not so much a film critic as she is a movie reviewer . . . who is at least as interested in the psychology of watching films and the sociology of response to films as she is in the works themselves," and whose writings were consequently of little value to those seeking "a thorough understanding of the art of film." Eliot Fremont-Smith, on the other hand, thought it was precisely this that made her work "important and bracing"—that she "relates movies to other experiences, to ideas and attitudes, to ambition, books, money, other movies, to politics and the evolving culture, to moods of the audience, to our sense of ourselves—to what movies do to us, the acute and self-scrutinizing awareness of which is always at the core of her judgment."

Pauline Kael had been commissioned to write a short introduction to *The Citizen Kane Book,* a paperback edition of the script of the 1941 film which some critics regard as the greatest single product of the American cinema. "From being absorbed in the project," she has said, "it became a kind of madness, made all the more strange because I was giving months and months of time to something I couldn't make any money on." The result was a fifty-thousand word essay called "Raising Kane," in which she set out to show that Orson Welles, the film's director, star, and co-author, was far from being its only begetter—that much of the credit for this masterpiece belonged to Herman J. Mankiewicz, for conceiving the film and writing most of the final script, and much to Welles's brilliant cameraman Gregg Toland. An important element in her argument was that Mankiewicz had been acquainted with William Randolph Hearst, on whose life the film was based, and that it was Mankiewicz, not Welles, whom Hearst subsequently chose to ruin in revenge for the film's treatment of his character and personality.

"Raising Kane" appeared in two installments in the *New Yorker* in February 1971, and *The Citizen Kane Book* was published later the same year. It caused a furor, and Pauline Kael's dethronement of the *auteur* theory of the film's creation was strongly rebutted by a number of her colleagues, including Andrew Sarris in the *Village Voice* and Peter Bogdanovich in a long article in *Esquire.* But elsewhere her views won widespread support, and J. A. Avant called the essay "probably the best thing Kael has written, a mixture of journalism, biography, autobiography, gossip, and criticism, carried along by a style so exhilarating that one seems to be reading a new, loose kind of critical biography. . . . It contains an amazing amount of material . . . presented so effortlessly that one doesn't at first realize how difficult most of it must have been to obtain and assemble. Better than anyone else writing about films, Kael understands the difference between ethics and aesthetics and uses this

understanding to illuminate our appreciation of her subject."

Going Steady (1970), collecting Pauline Kael's *New Yorker* reviews for the period between January 1968 and March 1969, seemed to Diana Loercher to confirm her right to be regarded as "one of the most articulate and sensible critics in the field. . . . in a time when the film cult has become one of the most prolific breeding grounds for intellectual snobbery." Charles T. Samuels called her "a splendid critic of acting," and said that "on film lore in general, she is always informative, because of her unique grasp of movies both as business and as social institutions." John Coleman noted with pleasure that she seemed more relaxed than in the past, and that there was "less of that old space-wasting stuff about how lousy and stupid all the other reviewers are." There was equal enthusiasm for *Deeper Into Movies* (1973), containing her *New Yorker* reviews for September 1969 to March 1972, which brought her the National Book Award, in the Arts and Letters category, in 1974.

There were signs of disillusionment in some reviews of *Reeling,* which followed in 1976— suggestions that Miss Kael had succumbed to "a lowbrow view of art and culture." Richard Gilman went so far as to call the book "an amalgam of idiosyncratic opinion, star-gazing, myth-mongering, politics, sociological punditry." And Robert Brustein said that Kael's writing "is becoming larded with hyperbole," much of it applied to ephemeral works and kitsch. However, even Brustein allowed that this is "always an entertaining book, and piece by piece a brilliant one," and admired the author's capacity "to sustain the same keen appetite for celluloid fantasy, the same intense interest in movie stars, as the most avid Hollywood fan."

Pauline Kael is a small woman, brown-haired and blue-eyed. She is "salty" and slightly breathless in speech and is seldom still, giving an impression of great nervous energy. She has been married and divorced several times, and has a daughter, Gina James, who is a dancer and who lives with her in a large, sparsely furnished, dog-infested apartment overlooking Central Park. She avoids press screenings, preferring to go to the movies in the evenings as one member of an ordinary audience: "I consider it immoral to go to the movies in the daytime." She sees six or seven movies a week, waiting for the screen to light up with almost as much enthusiasm as when she was a child and then goes home to work on her review until dawn.

The author is much in demand as a campus lecturer and as a guest on television talk shows.

She has served as a judge at a number of film festivals and in 1970 was chairman of the National Society of Film Critics. She has received a Guggenheim fellowship (1964), the George Polk Memorial Award for criticism (1971), and the Front Page Award of the Newswomen's Club of New York (1974). She holds a number of honorary degrees. Discussing her work as a whole, a writer in the *Times Literary Supplement* tried to define what it was that made Pauline Kael "a better film critic than almost anybody else." He concluded that "the thing that makes her special—makes her a great critic, in fact—is the way her work accumulates into a living body of writing from which a robust aesthetic can be derived, a critique of artistic practicalities can be inferred, and an unsentimental solace taken." Hers is "a body of criticism that can be compared with Shaw's criticism of music and the theatre. Not only is the criticism crucial to the art it treats, but it is capable of surviving the ephemerality of some of its subject matter."

PRINCIPAL WORKS: I Lost It at the Movies, 1965; Kiss Kiss Bang Bang, 1968; Going Steady, 1970; (with others) The Citizen Kane Book, 1971; Deeper Into Movies, 1973; Reeling, 1976.

ABOUT: Contemporary Authors 45-48, 1974; Current Biography, 1974; Murray, E. Nine American Film Critics, 1975; Who's Who in America, 1976-1977; Who's Who of American Women, 1975-1976. *Periodicals*—Book Week April 4, 1965; Book World April 28, 1968; February 23, 1969; February 22, 1972; Christian Science Monitor May 4, 1968; May 21, 1970; Commentary September 1970; Commonweal April 9, 1965; June 28, 1968; Esquire August 1965; Harper's June 1965; Library Journal August 1971; Mademoiselle July 1972; National Review June 4, 1968; March 30, 1973; Newsweek May 30, 1966; May 20, 1968; February 23, 1970; December 24, 1973; June 21, 1976; New York Post May 11, 1966; New York Review of Books March 8, 1973; New York Times May 21, 1968; New York Times Book Review March 14, 1965; May 5, 1968; February 22, 1970; March 7, 1971; October 31, 1971; February 18, 1971; Publishers Weekly May 24, 1971; Saturday Review April 24, 1971; Time July 12, 1968; Times Literary Supplement March 12, 1970; Vogue September, 1973.

KAPLAN, JUSTIN (September 5, 1925–), American biographer, is the son of Tobias D. Kaplan, a manufacturer, and the former Anna Rudman. He was born in New York City and educated there at the Horace Mann School before going on to Harvard for his B.S. (1944) and for three years of postgraduate study in literature (1944-1947).

Kaplan began his career as a freelance writer and editor (1946-1954), working for various New York publishers including Simon and Schuster. In 1954 he was married to the novelist Anne Bernays, daughter of the public relations pioneer Edward L. Bernays. The same year he

JUSTIN KAPLAN

joined the staff of Simon and Schuster as a senior editor, working with such distinguished authors as Bertrand Russell, Nikos Kazantzakis, and Will Durant. "Being at S&S then was a little like playing with the old New York Yankees," Kaplan says, but ultimately he wanted to write books of his own, and in 1959, with "mingled delight and regret," he left Simon and Schuster and New York and settled in Cambridge, Massachusetts. "After I gave in my resignation," Kaplan says, "I felt I was in a sort of limbo for quite a while." He remembers "waking at two o'clock one morning and asking myself, 'What the hell am I doing? I've bought a house here and uprooted my family without anything really definite in sight.' I wondered whether I might be playing a hoax on myself." He was not, as the triumphant success of his first book demonstrated.

It was the art of biography that fascinated Kaplan, and he chose as his first subject Samuel Clemens, "Mark Twain." As his research proceeded, he found that "the biographer dealing with this funny, noble, enigmatic, over-reaching man, who moved effortlessly from laughter to remorse, and from anger to nostalgia, has to come to special terms with his subject. . . . My purpose was not only to explore the mystery of this man but also to respect it." In this he was aided by the availability of much correspondence and other material, published and unpublished, which had not been accessible to earlier biographers.

Mister Clemens and Mark Twain, published in 1966, deals with the years from 1866, when Mark Twain was thirty-one, to 1910, when he died at the age of seventy-five. The book "came from the presses," as one critic remarked, "unmistakably destined for classical status in the field," and it brought Kaplan almost unanimous praise for his scrupulous research, his sense of proportion, and his insight into Mark Twain's life and times. Robert Regan found the biography "crowded almost to the point of bursting its covers with accounts of people, places, and incidents. . . . If the result is occasionally a little chaotic, it reflects in that respect the texture of Mark Twain's life, but most passages . . . succeed brilliantly in bringing order out of an inconceivable mass of significant detail." A. Grove Day wrote that "Justin Kaplan has read all the books and articles, all the letters and notes. . . . He has listened to all the theories but has swallowed none. . . . Mr. Kaplan's objective and discriminating book reads like a good novel. And the plot emerges early. The conflict is the battle between 'Mark Twain'— . . . the exploder of sham—and the success-hunting Samuel Clemens, victim of the 'Gilded Age' that he himself named and satirized. Nowhere does Mr. Kaplan use the word 'schizophrenia,' but his book examines almost clinically the growing gap between the man and his mask." Marius Bewley was impressed above all by Kaplan's "reliable and astute" critical faculty, "his critical understanding of Twain's books." And it seemed to Malcolm Bradbury that "Kaplan gives us a better and deeper Mark Twain than we ever had, a Twain who carried the tensions of the age he lived in and felt his way into the possibilities, and the crudities, of his culture. The place of a mind in a culture is superbly caught, and the narrative remains throughout human and sympathetic while catching it."

Mister Clemens and Mark Twain brought Kaplan the National Book Award in the arts and letters category in March 1967 and the Pulitzer Prize for biography a few months later. Accepting his NBA, Kaplan recalled that "Mark Twain said he hated the past because it was so 'damned humiliating,' hated prying, hated to read over old letters—they 'make my flesh creep,' he said. His biographer is inevitably his enemy, and there were nights during the writing of his book when punishment from beyond the grave seemed perfectly possible. There were also, when this book was finished and its subject laid to rest once again, weeks of a very powerful emotion which I finally recognized as grief." The book's neglect of Mark Twain's early life had been lamented by a number of critics and this deficiency was remedied in *Mark Twain and His World* (1974), which begins the story with Samuel Clemens's birth and childhood in Hannibal, Missouri, but which is otherwise essentially a condensation of the earlier book, rewritten in a more popular style and providing an excellent and highly readable introduction to the subject.

Even before the publication of *Mister Clemens and Mark Twain,* Kaplan had begun the research for his next book (which he explains was "like getting back on the horse *before* you've been thrown"). The new biography was of Lincoln Steffens, the immensely influential turn-of-the-century journalist whom Theodore Roosevelt dubbed "the man with the muckrake" for his investigation and exposure of graft and collusion between politicians and businessmen. Steffens's radicalization from reformer to Christian moralist to Soviet apologist gave him a special interest for Kaplan, since, as he says, "for someone who came to political awareness, as I did, in the McCarthy period, American radicalism was a taboo subject. Now we can look at it squarely without the feeling of being naughty."

Lincoln Steffens was published, appropriately enough, in 1974, at the height of the Watergate scandals, when (as Kaplan noted in an afterword), "muckraking—in its full range of investigation, exposure, and advocacy," had a force and currency it had not achieved "since the high noon of S. S. McClure and his crusaders." Alfred Kazin said that "what Kaplan shows in his excellent book is that Steffens was always more loved than loving, and that he felt such an easy command over people, of every sort, that his own conduct seemed to him duplicitous and required redemption. . . . Steffens projected his life into American history, made his 'outer' life one with the inner life he could not write. This split in himself helped to create a marvelous American myth of purpose. . . . Mr. Kaplan's explanations and corrections of the legend are actually not as destructive as one might expect. And oddly enough, they end up by making Lincoln Steffens just as fascinating as the first readers of . . . [Steffens's] 'autobiography' thought he was." Peter Schrag called this "a brilliant biography of a man and an age—shot through with political and moral contradictions, a weaving together of a vast amount of complicated material. . . . Kaplan has pulled Steffens not only from the shadows of the *Autobiography,* but also from the bowdlerized version of history where most of us first learned about him."

Justin Kaplan, who received a Guggenheim fellowship in 1975-1976, taught English at Harvard in 1969 and in 1973, but says that he "can't teach and write at the same time . . . that's a heroic thing to do." The author and his wife have three daughters. Among Kaplan's leisure activities are walking, swimming, photography, and "aimless attempts to grow grass." Most of the time he is so deeply engrossed in the subjects of his books that, he says, "I write evenings, weekends; I find I become addicted, and I feel guilty when I'm not at work." Kaplan told an interviewer in 1974 that his next biography would be of Walt Whitman. A left-of-center Democrat, Kaplan donated his Pulitzer Prize money to the American Friends Service, declaring his wish "to honor the American tradition of constructive dissent Mark Twain served so nobly, to voice my distress over the course we are following in Vietnam, and to express also my faith and hope that we are capable of devising positive alternatives to that course."

PRINCIPAL WORKS: Mr. Clemens and Mark Twain, 1966; Lincoln Steffens: A Biography, 1974; Mark Twain and His World, 1974. As editor—The Dialogues of Plato, 1948; With Malice Toward Women: A Handbook for Women-Haters, 1952; The Pocket Aristotle, 1956; The Gilded Age, by Mark Twain and Charles Dudley Warner, 1964; Great Short Works of Mark Twain, 1967; Mark Twain: A Profile, 1967.

ABOUT: Bewley, M. Masks and Mirrors, 1970; Contemporary Authors 17-20 1st revision, 1975; Who's Who in America, 1976-1977. Periodicals—Atlantic August 1966, June 1974; Biography News June 1974; Book Week June 26, 1966; Commentary October 1974; Commonweal September 20, 1974; Library Journal June 1, 1966: April 1, 1967; Milwaukee Journal May 5, 1974; Nation July 3, 1967; April 20, 1974; New Republic July 16, 1966; New Statesman July 4, 1975; New York Review of Books September 8, 1966; New York Times March 5, 1967; May 2, 1967; New York Times Book Review July 3, 1966; March 31, 1974; New Yorker September 3, 1966; Newsweek March 20, 1967; Publishers Weekly April 8, 1974; Punch March 1, 1967; Saturday Review June 18, 1966; March 23, 1974; Times Literary Supplement July 4, 1975.

*KAVAN, ANNA (1904–December 5, 1968), English novelist, short story writer, and memoirist, was born Helen Woods in Cannes, France, the daughter of C.C.E. Woods and the former Helen Bright. There is a lack of detailed information about her early life, but what little has been published suggests that her parents were rich, leaving her financially but not emotionally well provided for. It seems that she hardly knew her father, but spent her childhood traveling all over the world with her glamorous and neglectful mother who, divorced or widowed, had made a second marriage to a South African. After the early death of her mother, "the most formidable of all the shadows" that haunt her books, she grew up partly in California and partly in England, where she became an athletic public school girl. According to one account she suffered from tuberculosis as a young woman.

Helen Woods made an early marriage to Donald Ferguson, a well-connected Scot who took her to live in Burma. It was there that she began

*ka van'

ANNA KAVAN

to write. They had a son, Brian, who was killed in World War II. After her divorce from Ferguson she married the painter Stuart Edmonds, "a joyful cricketer and inveterate breeder of bulldogs" with whom she lived in Buckinghamshire and spent some time in various parts of Europe. This marriage was happier than the first, at least in the beginning, but it also ended in divorce.

Meanwhile her books had begun to appear. Her first six novels, written under the name of Helen Ferguson, have been largely ignored by recent critics, but they were taken more seriously when they first appeared. The most admired of them is her third novel, Let Me Alone (1930). It is a portrait of Anna-Marie Forrester, daughter of a reclusive former socialite who teaches her to despise the world before he takes his own life, bequeathing her a lonely adolescence and a hopeless marriage, and a sense of herself as "the exceptional sacrificed to mediocrity." A reviewer in the Times Literary Supplement found the book deeply depressing, but notable for "frequent passages of descriptive skill" and as a sensitive psychological study by "a writer of striking and genuine ability." When it was republished in 1974 it was admired as "a pioneering effort for Women's Liberation." Goose Cross (1936), about an English country village that seems to be populated exclusively by the insane, the suicidal, the criminal, and the degenerate, was praised, with reservations, as the work of a forceful writer with a dark and powerful imagination.

These somber books reflected the author's own state of mind. By the end of the 1930s she had spent periods in mental institutions in Switzerland and England and had become addicted to heroin. The history of her addiction is not clear, but just before the beginning of World War II, when she emerged emaciated but sane from an asylum in Surrey, she acknowledged her dependence by becoming a registered addict (which in England assured her of a regular supply of drugs). At the same time she dyed her auburn hair white-blond and changed her name legally to Anna Kavan—Anna after the semi-autobiographical heroine of *Let Me Alone,* Kavan from Kafka's K.

According to Clive Jordan "the change of name marked nothing less than a change of identity," and this was immediately reflected in her books. "Helen Ferguson's six novels were about distinct characters in recognisable, real situations. With Anna Kavan, we enter a dream-like inner landscape of haunting loneliness, through which obsessively distorted figures from her private life roam in painful clarity."

The first of her books in this new manner was *Asylum Piece* (1940), a collection of sketches of asylum life and snatches of autobiography attributed to a woman whose progressive insanity ends with her death in a Swiss clinic, with an introductory sketch written as by a schoolfriend. A reviewer in the *Times Literary Supplement* wrote that "the subject-matter of these stories is a terrible ambiguity about what is real and what is made more than real by being believed so. What makes Anna Kavan's writing anything but a whining account of her own perpetual nightmare is her extraordinary clarity and her insight: her ability to lay before the reader in simple and exact images the parts of this experience which together confuse and terrify. . . . What is so precisely and movingly caught is the inertia and shame of depression."

That review was written of the 1972 reissue of *Asylum Piece,* but even in 1940 the quality of these sketches was recognized by critics of the caliber of Sir Desmond MacCarthy, Edwin Muir, and L.P. Hartley, and the war years were for Anna Kavan a period of moderate success. She lived for a time in New York, then returned to England to work as a researcher for a military psychiatric unit. In 1942 she became assistant editor of Cyril Connolly's influential magazine *Horizon,* which published several of her stories and reviews.

Change the Name (1941), a novel about a woman whose aloof and day-dreaming egotism borders on the pathological, was not well received. Another volume of short stories, *I Am Lazarus,* was published in 1945, and the autobiographical *The House of Sleep* appeared in the United States in 1947. In her foreword to the latter (published in England the following year

as *Sleep Has His House*), Anna Kavan wrote: "Life is Tension or the result of tension: without tension the creative impulse cannot exist. If human life be taken as the result of tension between the two polarities night and day, night, the negative pole, must share equal importance with the positive day. . . . *Sleep Has His House* describes in the night-time language certain stages in the development of one individual human being." Biographical facts are eschewed in the book, which traces a spiritual development in terms of impressions and dreams that are haunted by a tall pale woman in black: "It is not easy to describe my mother. Remote and starry, her sad stranger's grace did not concern the landscape of the day. Should I say that she was beautiful or that she did not love me? Have shadows beauty? Does night love her child?" Over-fanciful and sometimes artificial, it remains "a testament of remarkable feverish beauty."

After the war, Anna Kavan's reputation declined. In 1956 she was reduced to paying a vanity press £50 to publish her novel *A Scarcity of Love.* Later admired as "a classic fairy-tale novel . . . as grim as Anna Kavan's own life," it was pulped shortly after publication when the publisher went out of business. The Kafkaesque *Eagles' Nest* followed in 1957 and a volume of short stories, *A Bright Green Field,* in 1958. Although Anna Kavan retained the admiration of some discriminating writers, among them Anaïs Nin and Lawrence Durrell, her work made little impact; *Punch* associated her mockingly with the "Horizontal heyday."

It was during this period that Anna Kavan designed the small house in the fashionable Campden Hill district of London where she spent the last ten years of her life. She had a flair for design and formed a limited company to buy, renovate, and sell very profitably a number of other houses in the locality. Her own house, with its overheated rooms, elegant period furniture, and small walled jungle of a garden, was a refuge from the harsh world outside. Her mornings were devoted to writing, and in the evenings she would sometimes entertain friends. Most of them were men; her dislike of women (especially if they were writers) was well known. Faced with such competition at a dinner party she was liable to retreat into reading magazines or to burst into a furious rage; on one occasion she launched a whole duck stuffed with prunes across the table. She herself is said to have been an attractive woman, though not conventionally so, "tall and thin, with . . . strange blue eyes and pale, soft hair," always scrupulously dressed and groomed. The heroines of all her later books have white-blonde hair like her own, and this is referred to obsessively, as a symbol of youth and ethereal beauty.

Her most important visitor was the doctor who had rescued her from a suicide attempt during the war. A European of considerable culture, friend of Bertolt Brecht, talented as a painter and a poet, he became a father figure and her closest companion. When he died in the mid-1960s, she made another unsuccessful suicide attempt. She was by then suffering a great deal from a spinal disease and from a leg badly abcessed by needles, and was worried and humiliated by new and more stringent laws regulating the supply of drugs. Her drug doses increased and her paintings—she had been a talented amateur painter all her life—became more anguished and grotesque, many of them portraying gruesome executions.

In spite of everything, Anna Kavan went on writing, and in 1963, after a long silence, published the novel *Who Are You?* It describes a nightmarish colonial marriage in which the distracted young wife is physically and spiritually raped by her bullying husband, forced to join him in his favorite sport of playing tennis with a live rat as the ball. A stranger known as "Suede Boots" encourages her to escape and, after endless hesitations, it seems that she is about to do so, when (as one critic wrote) "with a sudden jar the needle sticks and a portion of the action recurs, with a different conclusion." Robert Nye called it "a puzzling, disturbing, beautifully written minor piece," and a *Guardian* reviewer thought that it "justifies those of us who feel that Kavan is worth attention. . . . There is a vision at work here which dismays."

The last book to appear during her lifetime was the visionary and beautiful novel *Ice* (1967). The world has entered a terminal ice age, and the heroine moves across it in search of sanctuary, pursued by a man who loves her and who is guided through the frozen wilderness by the gleam of her hair: "astonishing, silver-white, an albino's, sparkling like moonlight, like moonlit venetian glass." For the first time since the 1940s there were signs of renewed and general critical interest in Anna Kavan's work. A *Times* reviewer found it "one of the most terrifying postulations of the end of the world that I have ever come across." The science fiction writer and historian Brian Aldiss voted it the best science fiction novel of the year (which surprised its author). Aldiss, in his introduction to the paperback edition of *Ice,* compares it to the surrealism of Jean Cocteau and Giorgio de Chirico, and finds in the ice "the perfect objective correlative" for Anna Kavan's drug addiction. Jill Robinson, similarly, saw the heroine's search and flight as

"parables of Anna Kavan's fight with herself. She defines, with her imagination, the addict's ambivalence."

Some of her last stories were published posthumously in 1970 as *Julia and the Bazooka* and were received with an intense (if belated) interest. Here, for the first time, she wrote directly about her experience of drugs. Her friend Rhys Davies, in his introduction to the collection, describes the title story as "a most symmetrical example of the art by which this obdurately subjective writer chose elements of her life and transformed them into something rich and strange and basically true." It is about the funeral and cremation of a drug addict killed in wartime bombing. Julia had originally been given her "bazooka" (her syringe) by a tennis coach to improve her game; now "the ashes of the tall girl Julia barely filled the silver cup she had won in the tennis tournament." Jill Robinson, who was reminded of John Fowles and of Kafka, found that these stories could be read together "as an intricately composed psychological novel," in which the pain with which she wrote them "is put into forceful images of powerful compression. . . . Here are the mask-faces for a world she at once runs toward and away from: the doctors; the disapproving women; and the cars. . . . No one has ever evoked as well the love affair one can have with a car." Rhys Davies speaks of her "retreat from the realistic, the tamed, the domestic world," from what she called "that ghastly black isolation of an uncomprehending, solitary, over-sensitive child."

Another posthumous collection, *My Soul in China,* appeared in 1975. The title novella is in Anna Kavan's usual manner; the shorter stories, according to Erik Korn, "take us into a world of zanily overstated apocalypse;" in "Yellow Submarine," an attempted coup by Welsh Nationalists becomes a comic inferno, with "dwarfish green men proliferating in cellars, grandfather clocks; every day there were more of them, they got smaller and smaller." Korn notes that many of these stories are narrated by men, and that they are "often very funny. . . . For the first time, there are glimmerings of an ironic detachment: the escape-hatch unfortunately opened too late."

Anna Kavan died in December 1968. She was found with her "bazooka" in her hand, still full of heroin. Enough of the drug was secreted about the house "to kill the whole street." Rhys Davies wrote of her that "she could not escape from the evil of hopelessness. . . . She did not know, and would not accept when told, that courage was giving her a degree of triumph." Davies believes that her last stories, "their clarity of style, their spurning of sensationalism, and their own code of logic, were another justification of her vision." Taken as a whole, her work is uneven. As Martin Seymour-Smith says, her chief faults are "monotony, a habit of speaking exclusively to herself rather than to the reader, and lapses into sheerly careless writing. But she can crystallise states of mind and being, and at times can detach herself from herself and see herself as she is: sick, afraid, lost and lonely. Then her efforts seem heroic." All of her major works have been brought back into print by her publisher, Peter Owen, who maintains that she was writing thirty years before her time. Since her death she has become something of a cult figure.

PRINCIPAL WORKS: *As Helen Ferguson*—A Charmed Circle, 1929; The Dark Sisters, 1930; Let Me Alone, 1930 (reprinted as by Anna Kavan 1974); A Stranger Still, 1935; Goose Cross, 1936; Rich Get Rich, 1937. *As Anna Kavan*—Asylum Piece (stories), 1940 (reprinted 1972); Change the Name, 1941; I Am Lazarus (stories), 1945; The House of Sleep (autobiography), 1947 (reprinted as Sleep Has His House, 1948); (with K.T. Bluth) The Horse's Tale, 1949; A Scarcity of Love, 1956 (reprinted 1971); Eagles' Nest, 1957 (reprinted 1964); A Bright Green Field (stories), 1958; Who Are You, 1963 (reprinted 1975); Ice, 1967; Julia and the Bazooka (stories), 1970; My Soul in China (stories), 1975.

ABOUT: Aldiss, B. *introduction to* Ice, 1970; Contemporary Authors 5-8 1st revision, 1969; Davies, R. *introduction to* Julia and the Bazooka, 1970; Vinson, J. (ed.) Contemporary Novelists, 1976. *Periodicals*—Daily Telegraph Magazine February 25, 1972; London Magazine February 1970; New York Times December 7, 1968; New York Times Book Review May 11, 1975; Nova September 1967; Times (London) December 6, 1968; Times Literary Supplement December 4, 1930; May 23, 1936; January 28, 1972; April 20, 1973; May 16, 1975.

KEATING, H(ENRY) R(EYMOND) F(ITZWALTER) (October 31, 1926–), English novelist, crime writer, and reviewer, writes: "I was destined to be a writer. My father, a schoolmaster, had always cherished an ambition to achieve authorship and once showed me with pride a piece on keeping rabbits, preserved since his boyhood. When at my christening (at St. Leonards-on-Sea, Sussex) they asked him why my middle forename was spelt with the unusual 'e' he is said to have replied: 'To look good on the spines of his books.' Alas, by the time my first was published he was dead, and in any case, known as Harry, I chose to use my array of initials on the spines.

"Yet it is probably because of that paternal deification of the writer that I think of myself always as a novelist though at the time of setting this down I have two novels only to my name as against sixteen crime stories and I often recall the shade of Conan Doyle persistently considering himself an important novelist in the histori-

Fay Godwin

H. R. F. KEATING

cal mode even to the pitch of attempting to kill off his justly acclaimed Sherlock Holmes. Yet my crime novels are always more novel than crime. Only the first, written at the urging of my wife when I told her that I could not produce a novel since I had nothing to say, is a pure detective story. But, once that was in my hand as a book, patently a device for communicating, I realised that I had at least one thing that I now wanted to tell people, and that the crime story was perhaps a particularly effective way of planting ideas in distant minds since it sugared any pill more lusciously than the mainstream novel, which is always apt to be suspected of didactic intent.

"From this second beginning I discovered with every book more things to say in the next till, partly from a feeling that there were some limits to what could be done with the crime story, I turned in 1971 to a straight novel, *The Strong Man*, long meditated. Another consideration was that my sort of crime story, tending to the subtle in manner, largely eschewing sex and limited in social scope, reaches only a comparatively small public and I wanted a larger one, as well as the financial benefits this could mean— especially as by 1964 I had four children to provide for, though my wife who acts under the name of Sheila Mitchell does not a little of that.

"It was in 1964, however, that I enjoyed one of those strokes of luck so necessary in a writer's career. Seeking a crime story format that would be acceptable in America, I hit on the notion of a detective from India, Inspector Ghote (pronounced Go-tay), whom I thrust upon the Bombay C.I.D. For ten years I wrote books about him without having visited his native land but achieving apparently at least authenticity of atmosphere. In 1975 however I went to Bombay at last, not without fears that the real smells and sordid sights might check for ever the creative flow. Happily the pre-conditioning work of the imagination proved to have inured me in advance, and Ghote lived to see another day."

The author, who is the son of John and Muriel (Clews) Keating, was educated at the Merchant Taylors' School near London (1939-1943). He served in the British Army from 1945 to 1948, achieving the rank of temporary lance-corporal, and then went to Trinity College, Dublin, where he received his B.A. in 1952. Thereafter until 1960 he worked as a newspaper sub-editor—on the Swindon (Wiltshire) *Evening Advertiser* (1952-1955), on the London *Daily Telegraph* (1956-1958), and on the London *Times* (1958-1960). His first detective story appeared in 1959, and the following year he abandoned journalism to become a fulltime writer.

That first book, *Death and the Visiting Firemen,* was set in the ancient cathedral city of Winchester, where vacationing members of the American Institution for the Investigation of Incendiarism, in the course of an Olde English outing by stagecoach, become involved in the murder of a sinister travel agent. The police do their best, but the crime is solved by a thoughtful schoolteacher with the aid of the coachman's young son. A reviewer in the *Times Literary Supplement* found Keating's style "irritating in the extreme, peppered with verbless sentences and staccato stage directions; but behind this mesh of words lies a civilized and unpretentious book with a flavour of its own."

There were similar reactions to the two books that followed—*Zen There Was Murder,* in which a Japanese Zen master teaching in England demonstrates the superiority of Buddhist thought over Western logic by unmasking the killer of one of his students, and *A Rush on the Ultimate,* in which the violent passions unleashed in a croquet tournament lead to murder. Not all of Keating's reviewers were irritated by the style of these first three books; Julian Symons found them "interestingly odd" in their extreme ellipticism, "at times semi-surrealist." Keating's later books have all the same been more ordinary in style, though never less than well-written.

The Dog It Was That Died, which within a Dublin academic setting almost succeeds in combining "a Graham Greene novel with a Chestertonian fantasy," and *Death of a Fat God,* a puzzle with a theatrical background, were followed by the book which brought Keating his first major success and established his reputation. *The Perfect Murder,* as he explains above, introduced Inspector Ganesh Ghote of the Bombay Criminal Investigation Department—a good man, sometimes confused, slightly pompous, often assailed by self-doubts, but determined, intelligent, and awkwardly heroic. Ghote's painstaking attempts to solve the "perfect murder" of the title by orthodox Western police methods are not always appropriate in his eastern and unorthodox society—and are further complicated by the fact that the murder victim turns out to be still alive. The book was called a "charming comedy" which "pokes affectionate fun at the eastern knack of evading issues gracefully." It received both the Golden Dagger award of the Crime Writers Association in Britain, and the Edgar Allan Poe award of the Mystery Writers of America.

There has been much praise for the authenticity of Keating's evocation of the Indian mind and the Indian scene in the Ghote books; it is remarkable that this should have been achieved by someone who had never visited the place. In pursuit of this effect Keating has read a great deal of Indian geography, history, and fiction, subscribes to Indian newspapers, and eavesdrops on Indian immigrants in Britain. He has found not only "a crime story format . . . acceptable in America" but (as he told a *Guardian* interviewer) a setting in which he can locate and resolve personal dilemmas—"an inner landscape where things go wrong"—and an imperfect detective whose triumphs over the odds provide Keating with "a way of asserting his optimism and warding off what he suspects might [really] happen."

Subsequent Ghote books have involved him with the murder of an American philanthropist *(Inspector Ghote's Good Crusade)* and an American physicist *(Inspector Ghote Caught in Meshes),* sent him to an England which turns out to be very different from the place he has dreamed of *(Inspector Ghote Hunts the Peacock),* and added to the long list of thrillers set on a train (the Calcutta Mail in *Inspector Ghote Goes by Train*). Some of these and other Ghote stories have been found short on plot and inadequately motivated, and Julian Symons maintains that "only in *The Perfect Murder* has Keating managed fully to integrate the detective with his criminal problem." All the same, few reviewers of detective fiction have had the heart to complain too seriously about these humane and witty books, and Ghote himself is now firmly established as "one of the great characters of the contemporary mystery novel."

Keating's two mainstream novels are *The Strong Man,* an exciting historical fantasy which

KEMELMAN

is also a pointed political fable, and *The Under-side.* The latter, set in Victorian London, centers on a successful painter who finds himself drawn again and again to the opportunities for gross sexual indulgence available in the capital of the British Empire in its heyday. One reviewer, who found it an impressive and powerful portrait of London's underworld and "a deeply perceptive study of the carnal impulse," advised that its descriptions of the protagonist's sexual adventures, "unsparing and revolting as they are, are not to be undertaken without due warning." Victorian London is also the setting for *A Remarkable Case of Burglary,* a Ghote-less thriller in which the criminal is an upper-class wastrel, a caddish "Raffles." Newgate Callendar called it "an exceptionally smooth piece of work" which "reconstructs an age and brings it to life."

The author reviews crime fiction for the London *Times.* He was formerly also television critic of the *Catholic Herald,* but abandoned this, he says, out of a sense of guilt "because from the moment he took the job his faith rapidly ebbed away." Keating was chairman of the Crime Writers Association in 1970-1971. In *Murder Must Appetize* he provides a knowledgeable and readable survey of "the classic years of the English detective story"—the years leading up to World War II.

PRINCIPAL WORKS: *Crime Novels*—Death and the Visiting Firemen, 1959; Zen There Was Murder, 1960; A Rush on the Ultimate, 1961; The Dog It Was That Died, 1962; Death of a Fat God, 1963; The Perfect Murder, 1964; Is Skin-deep, Is Fatal, 1965; Inspector Ghote's Good Crusade, 1966; Inspector Ghote Caught in Meshes, 1967; Inspector Ghote Hunts the Peacock, 1968; Inspector Ghote Plays a Joker, 1969; Inspector Ghote Breaks an Egg, 1970; Inspector Ghote Goes by Train, 1971; Inspector Ghote Trusts the Heart, 1972; Bats Fly Up for Inspector Ghote, 1974; A Remarkable Case of Burglary, 1975; Filmi, Filmi, Inspector Ghote, 1976. *Novels*—The Strong Man, 1971; The Underside, 1974; A Long Walk to Wimbledon, 1978. *Nonfiction*—Murder Must Appetize, 1975; (as editor) Agatha Christie, 1977.

ABOUT: Contemporary Authors 33-36, 1973; Symons, J. Bloody Murder, 1972; Who's Who, 1978. *Periodicals*—Guardian May 24, 1974; Times (London) January 7, 1971; August 5, 1978; August 24, 1978; Times Literary Supplement August 9, 1974.

KEMELMAN, HARRY (November 24, 1908–), American detective story writer, writes: "I was born in Boston, Massachusetts, my parents having settled there when they first emigrated from Russia. They were rebels against the chassidism in which they had been brought up and, as a result, while our house was generally observant—of the *kashruth* regulations, of Jewish holiday practices—it was not overly religious. But while they were not particularly

William Charles Studio

HARRY KEMELMAN

religious, they were strongly nationalistic and enthusiastic Zionists, and for that reason insistent that their children have a thorough grounding in their religion and history. From about the age of five, therefore, until I was seventeen, I attended various Hebrew schools five days a week, winter and summer, for a couple of hours each day. As a youngster, I naturally resented having to spend my afternoons in a classroom while my friends were free to play outdoors. To add insult to injury, when I was eleven, I was enrolled in a class in Talmud in addition to the Hebrew classes. But I found the subject matter and the way in which it was traditionally taught fascinating and so did not resent this additional burden. We sat around a large table with the learned rabbi at the head, and argued and debated each passage sometimes for days and even weeks, examining every minute facet of the regulation involved. It taught me to think about a subject from all points of view, a method which David Small, the hero of my Rabbi books, uses to good advantage to solve mysteries.

"After attending the Boston public schools, I went to Boston University where I received the A.B. degree in 1930, and then on to the Harvard Graduate School for the Master's degree in 1931. I had decided early on to be a writer, and for that reason I wanted a teaching job, feeling that the small pay would be more than compensated for by the greater leisure for writing it would afford. Unfortunately, the Great Depression of the 1930s had begun and I was unable to get a college teaching position.

"I spent the next year waiting out the Depression—after all the word from the highest authority was that 'Prosperity was just around the

441

corner'—by reading in public libraries and in writing 'Eugene O'Neill and the Highbrow Melodrama,' which was published in the *Bookman*. Since this was the first comprehensive review of O'Neill's plays that was markedly critical, it received considerable attention and I thought I was on my way. But it was twelve years before I published again—the short story, 'The Nine Mile Walk.'

"Since prosperity continued elusive, I went back to the Harvard Graduate School to work for the doctorate. In this second year of graduate study, however, the work was largely philological and involved a pedantic kind of scholarship for which I had little taste. I also got a view of the other side of the academic world where scholarship was not disinterested, but was geared to publication, which in turn was frequently a sycophantic jockeying for academic preferment. Years later I was able to express my dissatisfaction with contemporary graduate study, as well as other developments in education, in *Commonsense in Education*.

"Then followed several years of teaching at various schools, both at the collegiate and high school levels, all of which were at such low pay that I had to hold as many as four teaching jobs simultaneously to make up one inadequate salary. The irony of the situation was that I had gone into teaching for the leisure it would give me, and now what with running from my morning job to my afternoon job, and then on to my evening classes, I had barely time to eat. Hence, when the opportunity presented itself in 1942, I quit teaching and took a federal civil service job and eventually became the Chief Job Analyst and Wage Administrator for the Boston Port of Embarkation, with the responsibility of adjusting and keeping in alignment the salaries of some seven thousand civilian employees.

"Although I enjoyed the work enormously, I chose to leave the service when the war ended since to continue would have meant moving my family—my wife and three children—to Washington, a city for which I had little liking.

"I decided to try my hand once again at writing for a living and rented an office in town so that I could go about it in a businesslike way. It was there that I wrote the Nicky Welt stories for the *Ellery Queen Mystery Magazine* which were later incorporated in *The Nine Mile Walk*. With the first, the title story, the editor offered to buy as many stories based on the same character as I could turn out. But after I had written about half a dozen I lost interest. The stories had attracted some attention since they were the *ne plus ultra* of the armchair detective and I was approached by several publishers to do a book-

length mystery involving Nicky Welt. But I felt that the classical detective story, which was what I was writing, should be a short story and that to give it novel length and treatment would be little more than mechanically stretching the plot.

"We had moved to the small Yankee town of Marblehead twenty miles north of Boston and there I had a chance to observe what I considered an interesting sociological phenomenon—the adjustment of the Jew, that confirmed city dweller, to suburban living, and I wrote '*The Building of the Temple*' on the subject. It was a placid, low-keyed novel and was turned down by a dozen different publishers, each of whom indicated, however, that he was interested in my writing and would like to see my next book.

"But Arthur Fields, who was editor at Crown Publishers at the time, showed a greater perception, I like to think, and invited me to come down to see him. During our discussion he suggested jokingly that if only I could introduce the kind of material I had used in my detective stories the book would be publishable. I laughingly agreed that it would be an interesting combination and we swapped suggestions—not seriously —of detective elements that could be used, as that the temple parking lot would make an ideal place to hide a body.

"When I got back home, however, I took fire at the idea, and working every spare minute, I typed out a first draft of some seventy thousand words in less than two weeks. The story had revolved around a problem of the congregation and a personal problem of its rabbi. By introducing the additional problem of a murder, I was able to tie the three together so that the solution of the murder served to solve the other two. More particularly, I solved my own artistic problem of making a true novel out of a detective story. Arthur Fields accepted it and I spent the next year and a half reworking and rewriting what eventually became *Friday, the Rabbi Slept Late*. The success of the book surprised all of us—Arthur Fields, the publishers, my agent, and myself.

"I am frequently asked—in letters and in casual conversation—how I came to think of a rabbi detective. The truth is I am more interested in the character as a rabbi, involved in explaining the basic tenets of his religion, than as a detective solving artificial problems of crime."

Harry Kemelman explains how he came to combine a novel about "the adjustment of the Jew . . . to suburban living" with a detective story on the classic pattern. He omits to mention that he also incorporated into his first published book the gist of "A Religion for Today," a scholarly unpublished essay on the differences between Judaism and Christianity.

The result was the remarkable hybrid called *Friday, the Rabbi Slept Late*. Rabbi David Small is a stubborn and fiercely honest young scholar who does not please everyone in his conservative congregation in a wealthy suburb near Boston. His contract is up for renewal when the body of a young woman is discovered in the temple grounds and her purse is found in his car. He is not a serious suspect, however, and is soon applying the rigorous logic of a Talmudic scholar to the problem of identifying the murderer, meanwhile explaining the elements of Judaism to the Catholic police chief.

Dorothy B. Hughes found the book "so good it could serve as a pattern of how to write the mystery story. . . . Characters are fresh and true, background material cherishable, and the solution delightfully apt." Anthony Boucher agreed that the murder puzzle was a neat one, and thought that "an even greater delight is the book's depiction of the problems of a temple in a well-to-do Massachusetts suburb and its incidental commentaries on all manner of things Judaic, which should indeed serve as a primer to instruct the gentiles. . . . This could be the most important debut of a detective in recent years." A year after its publication, Dick Schaap reported in *Book Week* that *Friday, the Rabbi Slept Late* had sold some 22,000 copies, "incredible for a first mystery." Kemelman had received $35,000 for the movie rights, and an Edgar award for the best first mystery of the year. The Book-of-the-Month Club had selected the novel as one of its dual alternate selections, rabbis had preached sermons about it, and the book was being translated into five languages.

In *Saturday, the Rabbi Went Hungry*, David Small's intolerant congregation is outraged by the possibility that he may have buried a suicide in the temple's cemetery, and he is obliged to apply his *pilpul* method to determining the real cause of death of the suspect cadaver. Reviewers were agreed that the second novel was as quietly effective, as rich in humor and intelligence, and in "painless ecumenical communication," as the first. Richard Schickel suggested, however, that if Kemelman "has a fault it is a Woukian sincerity in explicating the traditions of Judaism and a trifle too much sweetness in his viewpoint."

Subsequent novels in the series have followed the same pattern, incorporating for the sake of variety such diversions as a visit to Jerusalem which nearly loses Small his congregation back home (in *Monday, the Rabbi Took Off*), and a college murder with overtones of student politics (in *Tuesday, the Rabbi Saw Red*). Kemelman says above that he is more interested in David Small as a rabbi than as a detective, and some reviewers of his recent books have complained that he has given less attention to the mystery element, but the series has established itself "among the very top best sellers in hard covers in the history of the formal detective story."

The Nine Mile Walk collects Kemelman's eight short stories, first published in the *Ellery Queen Mystery Magazine*, centering on Nicky Welt, Snowdon Professor of English Language and Literature at a New England college. Welt, a dryly witty academic, is literally an armchair detective, who (like Rabbi Small) solves his cases not by orthodox police methods but by the rigorous application of pure logic. Here, as in the Small novels, Kemelman does not hesitate to ride his hobbyhorses, and Judith Crist, who found the stories refreshingly original, was left wondering "whether scholarly rivalry, academic advancement and publication in learned journals is motive enough for murder." Anthony Boucher made no such quibbles; he found the collection "a lovely book" whose contents were "among the brightest gems in the literature of pure armchair detection," demonstrating that "their creator has as nice a perception of New England academic life as he has of suburban Judaism."

Harry Kemelman, the son of Isaac and Dora (Prizer) Kemelman, was married in 1936 to Anne Kessin, and has two daughters and a son. He taught from 1964 to 1970 at State College, Boston.

PRINCIPAL WORKS: *Fiction*—Friday, the Rabbi Slept Late, 1964; Saturday, the Rabbi Went Hungry, 1966; The Nine Mile Walk (short stories), 1967; Sunday, the Rabbi Stayed Home, 1969; Monday, the Rabbi Took Off, 1972; Tuesday, the Rabbi Saw Red, 1973; Wednesday, the Rabbi Got Wet, 1976; Thursday, the Rabbi Walked Out, 1978. *Nonfiction*—Commonsense in Education, 1970.

ABOUT: Contemporary Authors 9-12 1st revision, 1974; Who's Who in America, 1976-1977. *Periodicals*—Book Week June 6, 1965; Publishers Weekly April 28, 1975.

KENEALLY, (MICHAEL) THOMAS (October 7, 1935–), Australian novelist, writes: "I was born in New South Wales, Australia. My parents each came from an Irish Catholic family and lived on the north coast of the state at a dairy town called Kempsey. As happens with most writers, a substantial part of my work is bound up with these origins. The sense of exile that comes from growing up in a place that is still a spiritual colony, amongst plants, animals and social forms which had hardly ever been, up to that time, expressed in literature, was some-

THOMAS KENEALLY

thing that emerged inevitably in my early work and in the work of most Australian writers. The excessive mark made by Irish Catholicism on the naive Australian soul was also an early literary preoccupation. Similarly, despite the beauty of that valley, the harsh way the continent dealt with its people. And, above all, the ineluctable fact of the ancient aboriginal race who lived in squalor on the town's verges.

"When my father joined the Australian Air Force in World War II we moved to Sydney and lived in one of its western suburbs. In what happened there a great deal of Australia's past and future was expressed. The Australian forces, my father included, were absent in the Middle East battling for an almost mythical British Empire, while the city teemed with an immense temporary population of American servicemen, forerunners of an immense American investment.

"Even though I attended an Irish Catholic school, the purpose of the state curriculum seemed to be to turn every Australian into loyal children of Britain, and I read no literature there that fitted me for the destiny of being an Australian. The western suburbs of Sydney were short on seasons of mist and mellow fruitfulness.

"Being then devoutly Catholic, as were most of the family, and perhaps sharing with them and with my schoolmates the characteristic, almost tribal, sexual unease, I began studies for the diocesan priesthood. When I left two weeks before ordination, I was still a believer. It was in the next year or so that my wish to be a priest seemed less and less relevant and more and more extraordinary. I worked as a teacher and began to study law. My first short story was published in *The Bulletin,* a weekly journal which histori-

cally had always served as a nursery for Australian writers.

"Writing was a means of dealing with the dislocation which had occurred in my life and beliefs, and of turning myself into a secular person. One summer vacation I wrote a quick, flawed novel, sent it to London and had it published. In 1964 I gave up teaching and took part-time work to finance the writing of another novel, the prescriptive novel about childhood. If those first novels did nothing else, they qualified me for a grant from the Australian government to write a third book.

"This one was concerned with that grotesque penal colony which was Sydney in the 1790s. My purpose was not merely historical, but to show how the brutality of these origins had entered the Australian soul and how little a standing human innocence, as portrayed by the central characters, had in that grotesque though virgin continent. The book was successful, being also published in the United States by Viking Press.

"I found that I could not live modestly from my income as a writer.

"I had by now married and was the father of two small daughters, Margaret and Jane. My wife and I lived with them in a small house in a suburb called Ryde. Here I wrote the farewell piece to my Irish Catholic origins. Inevitably this was a study of the impact of Vatican II on a young Catholic priest of humanist leanings. I was already interested in the study of people, exteriorly of normal lineaments, who live under the onus of a fierce destiny, an extraordinary mission. A book called *A Dutiful Daughter* was a strange fable about a young girl who on reaching puberty turns her parents into creatures that are half bovine. Terrified by what this tells her of her place amongst humans, she hides away with the parents in a farmhouse in a coastal swamp, burdened by her powers but refusing to test their illusion. The idea of onus was carried further in a novel dealing with the stand made in 1900, the year the Australian states federated, by a young aboriginal, and with the vengeance he feels forced and chosen to take on white farm families in New South Wales.

"This book was written in England, where my family and I lived in 1970-1971. A journey to Britain, even as late as 1970, was considered *de rigeur* for Australian writers. Such a journey had for me the benefit of indicating where I belonged.

"Back home again I became involved with Labor Party politics and with the rise of Edward Gough Whitlam to the post of prime minister and his brief but spectacular tenure of it. Perhaps this sharpened my interest in revolutionary figures and in the idea that to be one is partly an act of arrogance and partly victimhood. A result of the idea was a long book on the early career of Joan of Arc, a woman who had about her a little of my own past but whom I saw as a woman savaged by her sense of destiny and her revolutionary role.

"While visiting New York to write a film script, I became aware of the purely commercial benefits that derive from being within reach of publishers. So my family and I lived in New Milford, Connecticut, throughout 1975-1976. During that time I acquired a new American publisher. Harcourt Brace Jovanovich took from me a narrative of events concerning the first young English doctor to be sent to Tito in 1943, and also a more experimental book, involving short sharp scenes and playform dialogue and examining the event of the signing of the Armistice in the forest of Compiègne in November, 1918. 'We are doing for the twentieth century what we did for all of the other youngsters,' says one of the diplomats, 'killing it off in its eighteenth year.'

"This novel and a following one which looked at a grand Antarctic expedition of the Edwardian era, studied the phenomenon of the decline of a civilisation, in this case British civilisation. My Irish forebears, in teaching me certain prejudices against Britain, made Britain seem all the more monolithic. The furious pace of its decline is one of the phenomena of my lifetime and full of illumination.

"My next book, implausible as it seems, is the commentary of an unborn child on his mother's consciousness. His voyage in his mother's waters is a prefigurement of ours towards a new society as well as an echo of a voyage undertaken by one of his ancestors in a benign convict ship travelling to Australia.

"In Australia I've been concerned with an organisation whose aim is a new Australian constitution and a bill of rights. I have also done some work in the burgeoning Australian film industry as actor and script consultant. In 1977 I declined the offer by Queen Elizabeth of the title of Commander of the British Empire for services to literature."

What Keneally calls his "quick, flawed" first novel, *The Place at Whitton* (1964), and his "prescriptive novel about childhood," *The Fear* (1965), were not much noticed, but *Bring Larks and Heroes* (1967) was, as he says, published in New York and London as well as Australia, and enjoyed a considerable success. Corporal Phelim Halloran, a poet and an Irishman of conscience and some learning, accidentally a British soldier,

is posted to the alien and brutal world of Sydney in the late eighteenth century, and there is forced to choose between dutiful wickedness and rebellion; he rebels and is hanged. J. S. Phillipson, noting Keneally's preoccupation with religious questions and his "sense of the grotesque and corrupt," decided that he "had a talent," though he is "scarcely the Australian James Joyce." There was a much more respectful response from *Time*'s reviewer, who was impressed by the sense of tragic inevitability he found in the novel. He went on to say that "Keneally has devised a garbled-Gaelic speech that seems perfectly to fit the character of his protagonist who, like another gifted innocent, Billy Budd, speaks with the tongue of men and angels. . . . This is a high-pitched book, but not only to Australians will the pitch ring true. What Keneally is saying is that out of man's appalling origins, grace and art will come, through courage."

These first three books were most strongly influenced by the novels of Patrick White and the poetry of Dylan Thomas; for his next book Keneally wanted a crisper prose style, and Evelyn Waugh, he says, pointed the way. Father James Maitland in *Three Cheers for the Paraclete* (1968) is an instructor at an Australian seminary who learns that the practice of Christian charity can arouse suspicion and misunderstanding, not least among his superiors at the seminary. Paul Cuneo found the plot ungainly and the title inane, but for him these faults were overwhelmed by the skill with which the author "brings into being the life of the seminary," and by the book's originality and vitality. Hal Porter, a hostile critic, has more regard for this than for Keneally's other early novels, calling it "a brisk and comic chess game of a book. . . . Each move in the game is clear-cut; the prose so well fulfills its purpose that the actors in the comedy take on the semblance of flesh-and-blood creatures."

The Survivor (1969), which quirkily investigates the guilt feelings of Alec Ramsey, survivor of a disastrous Antarctic exploration, was followed by *A Dutiful Daughter* (1971), the "strange fable" Keneally describes above. Hal Porter called this "his most aggressive failure as an artist," and said that "embellishments to the situation (incest, perversion, bestiality, a triple suicide) are dealt with in the coarsely genteel manner which is the one ear-mark of Keneally's style which is otherwise so unjelled that he could be said to have little style at all." A reviewer in the *Times Literary Supplement*, on the other hand, found this "a disquieting novel and in many instances a moving one," and commended the author's skill in "using to his advantage a subject which in less capable hands might have looked merely grotesque, or even ridiculous. . . . The success of the book lies in the way tragedy, black comedy and emotional chaos are made to reside in acts of simple concern." Melvin Maddocks, who thought that Keneally in this novel was "writing like an angel," was one of a number of critics who read the book as a parable about original sin, martyrdom, and redemption.

One of the most praised and commercially successful of Keneally's books followed in 1972, *The Chant of Jimmie Blacksmith.* The novel's hero, modeled on a historical personage, is a mission-educated young aborigine, intelligent and ambitious, who marries a white girl and sets out to make his way in the white world, though he cannot altogether deny the deeper promptings of tribal ritual and magic. Desperately divided, he is then cheated, cuckolded, and persistently humiliated by white people until he accepts his "license to run mad": the outcome is a series of bloody murders on isolated farms and a manhunt. Anthony Thwaite wrote that "Keneally's account of . . . [Jimmie's] hopeless odyssey is exciting and chilling: the battle—with human malevolence, with spiritual fear, with the remorseless natural world—is real. . . . Keneally has many incidental portraits and encounters which add to the rich curiousness of his story" and he "has blended history, psychological insight and epic advantage with great skill." Christopher Porterfield found Keneally's language sometimes overheated, "invoking the pull of blood and the core of blackness in a way that recalls D.H. Lawrence in a rant. But most of the time the novel's intensity arises naturally from the dualities that throb at the center—black and white crime and punishment, civilization and savagery. . . . In the end the reader sees that . . . the tragic contradictions in Jimmie's life are in fact the unresolved agonies out of which a nation is to be created." The novel has been made into a notable film.

Keneally continued his exploration of the notion of "onus"—of a sense of destiny both glorious and tragic—in *Blood Red, Sister Rose* (1974). His Joan of Arc, Carol Stein wrote, "is sharp-tongued and moody, saddened by the knowledge that fulfillment as a woman is not for her, yet proud of her special destiny." This reviewer found the book "a difficult, ironic, intellectually challenging historical novel"; another, in the *Times Literary Supplement,* thought that Keneally "integrates a mass of historical information quite admirably. Yet as we admire we are distracted from the story. His characters are tightly reined: style and situation remain his chief interests, relied upon to establish the credibility of a world which no longer exists, and

anachronism is used to make it accessible to the modern reader."

Dialogue in *Blood Red, Sister Rose* is presented as in the script of a play or a film. The same device is used in *Gossip From the Forest* (1975), Keneally's novel about the 1918 armistice, in which delegations from France, England, and Germany meet, each in a private railroad car, in the forest near Compiègne. The central figure is Matthias Erzberger, the only civilian member of the German delegation—a civilized man forced to bow to the crude and insolent power personified by Marshal Foch. P. S. Prescott called this "a distinguished book that is nothing like most historical novels but seems a fictional meditation on history instead. . . . I hope its intelligence and measured pace will not prevent it from finding an audience." Paul Fussell placed it with books like Solzhenitsyn's *August 1914* that "delineate the past in sympathetic depth and so urge the reader to enter it." It was runner-up for the Booker Prize.

After this modestly experimental and very serious novel, Keneally wrote the first in a series of "entertainments" planned as "a relief from the normal grind of thinking about work in purely artistic terms and trying to produce 'literature.' " *Season in Purgatory* (1976) tells the story (grounded in fact) of a young English surgeon parachuted into Yugoslavia in World War II to help the partisans, and of his love affair with his wily and beautiful assistant. This was praised by Margo Jefferson as a "taut mordant novel" that "moves along at a fast, expertly timed pace. It also manages to be both somber and shrewd about the cost and the value of assorted efforts to preserve life—physically and spiritually—from the concentrated assaults of war. Pelham survives the war to become a pacifist, but also to take up a fashionable and prestigious practice. . . . Keneally . . . perceives astutely that the most wrenching experiences can leave habits of mind and upbringing intact." *Victim of the Aurora* (1977), a novel of equal skill and similar weight, returns to the setting of *The Survivor.* It is a "convincing and powerfully written" account of an Edwardian expedition to the South Pole, a murder, a series of revelations, and a loss of innocence.

Keneally has also written several plays. He has twice received the Miles Franklin Award, given for the best Australian novel of the year, and held Commonwealth Literary Fellowships in 1966, 1968, and 1972. He won the 1970 Australian Bicentenary novel prize, and became a Fellow of the Royal Society of Literature in 1973. As he says, he has done some work in the Australian film industry, and appeared as a hellfire preacher in Fred Schepisi's *The Devil's Playground* (1976). In 1968-1970 he was a lecturer in drama at the University of New England (Australia). Keneally was married in 1965 to Judith Martin. His recreations include swimming, fishing, and Rugby football. Michael Barber describes him as "a genial, mild-spoken man, with none of the patriarchal severity suggested by his dust-jacket portrait."

The demands made by Australian critics on their writers are very intimidating, Keneally says, and this is born out by Hal Porter's harsh comments on his work. Porter calls Keneally "a quick-change artist of undoubted skill" who is "generally an alert entertainer, and dabbles earnestly or mischievously with problems of 'conscience,' the sentimental, limited, and up-to-the-minute conscienceless conscience of present-day trouble-makers. . . . What adds to the observer's uneasiness, and is disconcerting, is to discover, in each successive novel, that the author has not advanced, is merely making an almost wilfully selfconscious break in yet another direction, is starting to wander off into a different sort of formlessness, to reveal a new brand of sloppiness in technique, to invest in other arrangements of clichés, to blur what seems a highly romanticized realism with a coating of symbolism. Perhaps these are the results of Keneally's never working out a detailed plot before starting to write. Perhaps they are the indirect outcome of a deeply embedded uncertainty, a quasi-recklessness."

To this Keneally replies mildly that he would prefer to say that he never writes the same book twice. However, "finding a balance between not writing the same book twice and having a distinctive voice of your own which your small following of readers can trust and know they're always going to hear—that's important too. And I hope I haven't been a quick-change artist in that direction." He acknowledges that he finds it hard to plan a novel beforehand and says, with Frank O'Connor, "I have to write the bloody thing first to see what it's going to be." It is this problem that attracts him to historical themes, which "have a dramatic unity that the present lacks." Hal Porter's opinion of Keneally's work, first expressed in these terms in the 1972 edition of *Contemporary Novelists,* is not shared by most critics; Michael Barber wrote in 1976 that "Thomas Keneally is the leading Australian novelist of his generation, with an international reputation second only to Patrick White's."

PRINCIPAL WORKS: The Place at Whitton, 1964; The Fear, 1965; Bring Larks and Heroes, 1967 (dramatized by the author as Halloran's Little Boat, 1975); Three Cheers for the Paraclete, 1968; The Survivor, 1969; A Dutiful Daughter, 1971; The Chant of Jimmie Blacksmith, 1972; Blood Red, Sister Rose, 1974; Moses the Lawgiver, 1975; Gossip From the Forest, 1975; Season in Purgatory, 1976; Victim of the Aurora, 1977.

ABOUT: Burns, D.R. The Directions of Australian Fiction, 1975; Geering, R.G. Recent Fiction (Australian Writers and their Work), 1974; International Who's Who, 1978–79; Jones, J. and Jones, J. Authors and Areas of Australia, 1970; Kessing, N. (ed.) Australian Postwar Novelists, 1975; Kiernan, B. Images of Society and Nature, 1971; Ramson, W.S. (ed.) The Australian Experience, 1974; Vinson, J. (ed.) Contemporary Novelists, 1976; Who's Who, 1978. *Periodicals* —Commonweal February 1972; Guardian September 1, 1976; Library Journal January 15, 1975; Listener September 9, 1976; Nation November 6, 1972; New York Times Book Review September 12, 1971; January 16, 1972; August 27, 1972; February 9, 1975; April 11, 1976; February 27, 1977; March 26, 1978; Newsweek April 19, 1976; February 7, 1977; Publishers Weekly March 24, 1975; Time August 28, 1972; February 10, 1975; Times (London) October 2, 1975; September 2, 1976; September 5, 1976; September 1, 1977; Times Literary Supplement May 7, 1970; April 23, 1971; October 11, 1974; September 19, 1975; September 3, 1976; October 2, 1977.

KENNEDY, ADRIENNE (LITA) (September 13, 1931–), American dramatist, was born in Pittsburgh, Pennsylvania, the daughter of Cornell Wallace Hawkins, a social worker who became executive secretary of the YMCA, and the former Etta Haugabook, a teacher. She grew up in Cleveland, Ohio, where she attended public schools and began to write furiously in an attempt to block out her sense of being "small, ugly, and inferior." She was no happier at Ohio State University, where she was an indifferent student who switched her major several times before earning a bachelor's degree in education in 1952. A year or two later she moved to New York City, joining creative writing courses at Columbia and the New School for Social Research, and in 1962 becoming a member of Edward Albee's playwriting workshop at the Circle in the Square Theatre. It was a play she wrote for that workshop that brought Adrienne Kennedy her first and, so far, her greatest success.

Funnyhouse of a Negro derived its title from the author's childhood recollections of a Cleveland amusement park where two gigantic laughing white-faced figures stood at the entrance: "My brother and I used to hang around there a lot. It always seemed to me that the white world was doing this, ridiculing the Negro." The fifty-minute, one-act play evokes the tormented last hours of Sarah, daughter of a black father and a white mother, who lives in a boardinghouse with a Jewish poet, and herself writes poems in the manner of Edith Sitwell. Sarah is in love with an idealized dream of European art and white culture from which she feels hopelessly exclud-

447

New York Times /John Sotomayor

ADRIENNE KENNEDY

ed. She professes to hate her father, whom she describes as a messianic black missionary who had taken her mother to Africa, where she lost her sanity, and raped her to produce Sarah, a yellow-skinned misfit in a white world. Alienated from herself and from society, Sarah confronts her nightmares in a variety of assumed personas—as Queen Victoria, as the Duchess of Hapsburg, as Jesus Christ, and as the martyred Congolese leader Patrice Lumumba. And she tries to free herself of her obsession with her father by insisting that she has murdered him. In the end it is herself she kills. It is then revealed that her father is still alive, and is not a failed messiah but simply a black doctor living with a white woman.

Sponsored by Edward Albee, Richard Barr, and Clinton Wilder, *Funnyhouse of a Negro* opened in January 1964 at the Off-Broadway East End Theatre. The New York critics described it variously as surrealistic and expressionistic, and thought it influenced by Tennessee Williams as well as Albee, but most found it strong, arresting, and original. Even some who were confused by its eschewal of linear development—its emphasis on fleeting impressions and fragmented memories—admired its poetic imagery and lyrical dialogue. Howard Taubman called it "a vividly illustrated short story" which digs "unsparingly into . . . the tortured mind of a Negro who cannot bear the burden of being a Negro." A "difficult" play, it almost foundered at the box office, but was reprieved by a donation from Isabel Eberstadt, the daughter of Ogden Nash. It ran for forty-six performances and won the *Village Voice*'s "Obie" award as the most distinguished off-Broadway play of 1964.

The same preoccupations have dominated Adrienne Kennedy's subsequent plays. For example, *The Owl Answers* (1965) has as its protagonist "she who is Clara Passmore who is the Virgin Mary who is the Bastard who is the Owl"—a deeply disturbed Savannah schoolteacher who is the illegitimate daughter of a black cook and a rich white man. Riding the New York subway she endures the taunts of Geoffrey Chaucer, Anne Boleyn, William the Conqueror, and Shakespeare, who symbolize her aspirations to an unattainable white world. Picked up by a black youth, she descends into raving insanity in a Harlem hotel room.

The Owl Answers, originally produced in 1965, first in Westport, Connecticut, then in New York City, was revived in January 1969 at Joseph Papp's Public Theatre in New York as part of an Adrienne Kennedy double bill called *Cities in Bezique.* Its companion piece, *A Beast Story,* is a series of variations on the theme of sexual fear. Clive Barnes saw the program, he said, with "more illumination than pleasure," but found that the plays "wrapped around the mind like strange tendrils." And Walter Kerr reflected: "It is conceivable that this is a kind of theater and that by simply immersing ourselves in it, without asking rational questions of it or trying to force it into some other shape, we might find ourselves clothed by the rain of images, fed by the accumulating overlay. I wouldn't rule the possibility out, any more than I'd wave away Miss Kennedy as a writer: there is a spare, unsentimental intensity about her that promises to drive a dagger home some day."

Glimpses of that promise are visible in all her other plays, which include *A Rat's Mass* (first produced in Boston in 1965, and later in repertory and on tour by Café La Mama) and *A Lesson in Dead Language* (first produced in 1968 at Café Au Go Go in New York). *The Lennon Play: In His Own Write* was Adrienne Kennedy's adaptation of two of John Lennon's books of surreal poems and nonsense stories; first performed by the British National Theatre in 1967 and given in a revised version by the same company in 1968, it parodied, according to Irving Wardle, "every sacred British cow." There was a generally rather cool reception for *An Evening With Dead Essex,* staged in 1974 by the Yale Repertory Theatre. The play is about Mark James Essex, the young black rifleman who murdered a number of people in New Orleans before he himself was killed; he is seen indirectly through the eyes of a director who is putting together a documentary play about Essex. Mel Gussow wrote that "the material is undigested, the impact diluted, but at the end there is a moment that makes one realize how striking the work could be."

The author was married in 1953 to Joseph Kennedy, by whom she has two children, Joseph and Adam; the marriage ended in divorce in 1966. Like some of her characters, Adrienne Kennedy has "always been attracted to the great tradition of English writers and the European way of life," and in 1969 she settled in London for a time. She was back in the United States by 1972, and in 1972–1974 lectured at Yale University. She held a Guggenheim fellowship in 1967, has received grants from the Rockefeller Foundation, the New England Theatre Conference, and the National Endowment for the Arts, and was a Yale Fellow in 1974–1975. She is a collector of letters written by famous people.

Gerald Freeman, who directed *Cities in Bezique,* once wrote that "Adrienne Kennedy is a poet of the theater. She does not deal in story, character and event as a playwright. She deals in image, metaphor, essence and layers of consciousness." Clive Barnes has said much the same thing, adding: "Of all our black writers, Miss Kennedy is most concerned with white, with white relationships, with white blood. She thinks black, but she remembers white. It gives her work an eddying ambiguity." This quality in her work is explained in different terms in *Crowell's Handbook of Contemporary Drama,* which says: "There is a cryptic quality in Miss Kennedy's plays that is both tantalizing and confusing; a deliberate merging of several levels of being so that . . . a character is simultaneously several beings . . . this complexification of character coupled with stylized patterns of action and the frequent use of Catholic religious symbols gives Miss Kennedy's plays the feeling of ritual, pure drama freed from literal representationalism."

PRINCIPAL PUBLISHED WORKS: (with John Lennon and Victor Spinetti) The Lennon Play: In His Own Write, 1968; Funnyhouse of a Negro, 1969 (*also in* Oliver, C.F. and Sills, S. (eds.) Contemporary Black Drama, 1971); Cities in Bezique: The Owl Answers, A Beast Story, 1969 (The Owl Answers *also in* Hoffman, W.M. (ed.) New American Plays 2, 1968); A Rat's Mass *in* Couch, W. (ed.) New Black Playwrights, 1968; A Lesson in Dead Language *in* Parone, E. (ed.) Collision Course, 1968; Sun *in* Owens, R. (ed.) Spontaneous Combustion, 1972.

ABOUT: Abramson, D.E. Negro Playwrights in the American Theatre, 1967; Black American Writers, Past and Present, 1975; Crowell's Handbook of Contemporary Drama, 1971; Harrison, P.C. The Drama of Nommo, 1972; Living Black American Authors: A Biographical Directory, 1973; Mitchell, L. Black Drama, 1967; Notable Names in the American Theatre, 1976; Oliver, C.F. and Sills, S. (eds.) Contemporary Black Drama, 1971; Vinson, J. (ed.) Contemporary Dramatists, 1977; Who's Who in America, 1976-1977. Periodicals—New Yorker January 25, 1964; January 25, 1969; New York Times January 15, 1964; June 20, 1968; July 9, 1968; July 14, 1968; January 13, 1969; January 19, 1969; November 1, 1969; March 18, 1974.

KESEY, KEN (ELTON) (September 17, 1935–), American novelist, was born in La Junta, Colorado, the son of Fred A. Kesey, a dairy farmer, and the former Geneva Smith. The family later moved to Oregon and Ken Kesey went to high school in Springfield. An athletic boy, he swam, fished, and rode the rapids on the Oregon rivers with his younger brother Joe, and learned to box and wrestle. His high school graduating class voted him "most likely to succeed," and at the University of Oregon he was equally prominent and popular—a star in campus plays and on the university's wrestling team.

Graduating with a B.A. in 1957, Kesey went to Hollywood, secured bit parts in two or three movies, then relinquished acting for writing. In 1958-1959 he studied as a Woodrow Wilson Fellow in the graduate writing program at Stanford University, and in 1959 he received an award from the Saxton Memorial Trust. The same year he earned $75 a day as a subject in experiments on the effects of LSD and other hallucinogenic drugs at the Veterans Hospital in Menlo Park, California (thus becoming an accredited acid-head even before Timothy Leary). Afterwards he stayed on at the hospital as a night attendant in the mental ward, an experience which provided the basis for his first and most famous novel, *One Flew Over the Cuckoo's Nest* (1962).

The novel is set in a mental hospital ward ruled by Big Nurse Ratched, who preserves order and discipline by drugging and bullying potential dissidents. Processed for institutional life, cowed, confused, and hopeless, the inmates would rather submit to this treatment than face the challenges of life outside. The narrator is Chief Bromden, a half-Indian who has endured two hundred shock treatments and who is thought to be deaf or catatonic, since he never speaks. Into this orderly hell comes Randle P. McMurphy, a natural anarchist and con man feigning insanity to escape a jail sentence. McMurphy is more of a clown than a crusader, but he is simply unable to bow to Big Nurse's discipline, or to believe that his fellow inmates are less than human, and before long he finds himself leading a revolution. Its success is limited, and McMurphy is not one of the survivors, but in the end Chief Bromden has abandoned his self-imposed silence and found the courage to escape from the hospital.

Chief Bromden personifies not only America's persecuted minorities but a whole way of life—instinctual, pastoral, magic-imbued—which

KEN KESEY

Hank Kranzler

technology has virtually obliterated. And Big Nurse's ward was generally recognized to be a microcosm of the world outside. R. A. Jelliffe called the novel "a parable of life in a world presided over by a tyrannical junta of compulsion and conformity," and admired its "bi-tonal technique of terrible realism in conjunction with a profound and searching parable of government and the governed." Other reviewers were troubled by the combination of tragedy and slapstick —still an unfamiliar technique in 1962—but George Adelman praised the novel as "a boisterous, ribald book" which is also "at times touching and pathetic," and called it "the best novel I have read for a long time."

In fact, the brief reviews that greeted *One Flew Over the Cuckoo's Nest* gave no hint that this was going to become one of the seminal books of the 1960s. In 1975 Pauline Kael wrote, with hindsight: "The novel preceded the university turmoil, Vietnam, drugs, the counter-culture. Yet it contained the prophetic essence of the whole period of revolutionary politics going psychedelic, and much of what it said . . . has entered the consciousness of many—possibly most—Americans." Eric Mottram thinks it one of the most important novels of the post-war years. A play adapted from the book by Dale Wasserman, and starring Kirk Douglas as McMurphy, ran at the Cort Theatre in New York for eighty-two performances in 1963-1964 and was subsequently revived off-Broadway.

Kesey worked for a time as a logger in preparation for writing his second novel, *Sometimes a Great Notion* (1964). This was a complete departure, closer in spirit to Faulkner or Thomas Wolfe than to the black humorists of the 1960s.

Old Henry Stamper, creator of an Oregon lumber empire, has two sons—the raw and truculent Hank, and Lee, who takes after his sensitive, introspective mother, and has gone East to Yale for his education. When the Stamper fortune is threatened by the unions, Lee is called home to Wakonda. The novel centers on the conflict between the two young men, and particularly on Lee's struggle to measure up to the frontiersman prowess of his brother. Lee gains a temporary advantage when he seduces Hank's wife; a brutal fight follows, in which Lee refuses to accept defeat. This Oedipal sequence is his rite of passage into manhood. The quarrel ends, and the novel closes with the two brothers riding the logs together, downriver to market.

Less original than its predecessor in mood and conception, this very long novel was more ambitious and, technically, more experimental. "Device crowds device," wrote a reviewer in *Newsweek.* "Characters sometimes speak in their own right, then in the author's voice; chronology shifts; interior monologues alternate with lyrical hymns to nature, complexity with simplicity." The same writer concluded that the book lacked "a moral and imaginative center" and "ends up as a windy, detailed, mock epic, a barrel-chested counterfeit of life." Julian Moynihan also thought it a "deeply perplexed and ambiguous book," but it seemed to Granville Hicks admirable that Kesey had "succeeded in suggesting the complexity of life and the absence of any absolute truth." Conrad Knickerbocker was also impressed, saying that "what convinces me of Mr. Kesey's virtues as a novelist is his obsessiveness. He views the same basic mysteries again and again, but from different angles. He is never satisfied with surfaces, throwing away revelations that would do less ambitious writers for decades." And Leslie Fiedler took the book very seriously indeed, devoting two and a half thousand words to his review in *Book Week,* and crediting Kesey with "a kind of mythopoeic power not often found in literature these days."

In spite of these encomiums and a 1972 movie derived from the novel, it made little impact and sank into obscurity, while its author went on to become, as Mordecai Richler has observed, "one of that burgeoning band of American writers who are their own most perfect work of art." In the summer of 1964 Kesey and thirteen of his friends—the so-called Merry Pranksters—drove from San Francisco to the New York World's Fair in a 1939 school bus painted in Dayglo colors, and equipped with bunks and a bathtub. This pilgrimage in celebration of the hallucinogenic life-style and the "happenings" the group created along the way were recorded for posterity on film and tape by the Pranksters themselves, and more memorably by Tom Wolfe in *The Electric Kool-Aid Acid Test.* "The sense of communication in this country has damn near atrophied," Kesey said afterwards, "but we found as we went along it got easier to make contact with people. . . . I'd try to let them know we were not against them. If people could just understand it is possible to be different without being a threat." Kesey was back in the news in 1966, when he was arrested twice in California for possession of marijuana. After the second arrest, in October 1966, he jumped bail in San Francisco and fled to Mexico. He and some of the faithful Pranksters spent eight months there before Kesey returned to serve his jail sentence.

The scene changed in 1969, when the prodigal returned to the family farm in Oregon, which his brother had taken care of during Ken Kesey's years of psychedelic riot. The same year Kesey decided at the last moment not to accompany the Pranksters to the Woodstock rock festival, and when the painted bus returned to Kesey's farm they found a sign in the driveway saying simply "No!" A few of Kesey's closest friends have settled near him, but the Merry Pranksters no longer exist, except as a chapter in the history of the hippie counterculture.

Kesey is said to be at work on a third novel, based on his experiences in jail, but so far his only other book is a miscellany called *Kesey's Garage Sale* (1973). It contains a screenplay about Kesey's adventures while on the lam in Mexico, two interviews with him, contributions from Neal Cassady, Hugh Romney, and Allen Ginsberg, and "Tools From My Chest," an account of Kesey's "head tools" (including the Bible, the *I-Ching,* Pogo, Martin Buber, marijuana, William Burroughs, William Faulkner, and the Beatles). In his introduction Arthur Miller wrote that he had found in it "a certain dignity and courage," along with "pages of mawkishness, self-consciousness . . . that sprawled cockiness of American Romance."

Miloš Forman's film version of *One Flew Over the Cuckoo's Nest* was released in 1975, and the following year carried off five Oscars. In spite of the movie's triumphant success, Kesey is unhappy about the adaptation, and no less so that he sold the film rights in 1962 to Kirk Douglas for $28,000. On the other hand, the film's popularity has boosted the book's paperback sales to over four million.

Kesey was married in 1956 to Faye Haxby. They have four children, and live on their farm at Pleasant Hill, near Eugene, Oregon, raising cattle and sheep and growing blueberries. Kesey works the farm by day and writes at night, "into the small hours of the morning." In 1974 *Rolling Stone* magazine sent him to Egypt in search of the "Hidden Pyramid," and since 1973 he has been publishing an "underground" literary magazine, *Spit in the Ocean.* Kesey is a member of the local P.T.A. and heads a project called Bend in the River, concerned with the future of the environment. "The thing about writers," he told an interviewer in 1974, "is that they never seem to get any better than their first work. . . . This bothers me a lot. You look back and their last work is no improvement on their first. I feel I have an obligation to improve, and I worry about that."

PRINCIPAL WORKS: *Fiction*—One Flew Over the Cuckoo's Nest, 1962; Sometimes a Great Notion, 1964. *Other*—Kesey's Garage Sale, 1973; One Flew Over the Cuckoo's Nest (play, adapted by Dale Wasserman), 1974.

ABOUT: Acton, J. (and others) Mug Shots, 1972; Contemporary Authors 1-4 1st revision, 1967; Current Biography, 1976; Olderman, R.M. Beyond the Waste Land, 1972; Penguin Companion to Literature 3, 1971; Strelow, M. and others (eds.) Kesey, 1977; Vinson, J. (ed.) Contemporary Novelists, 1976; Who's Who in America, 1976-1977; Wolfe, T. The Electric Kool-Aid Acid Test, 1968. *Periodicals*—Atlantic August 1964; Book Week August 2, 1964; Books Abroad Spring 1965; Chicago Sunday Tribune February 4, 1962; Commonweal March 16, 1962; Connecticut Review April 1974; Critic August 1964; Critique Fall 1972; Explicator December 1973; Hudson Review Winter 1964-1965; Journal of Popular Culture Winter 1975; Library Journal February 1, 1962; June 1, 1964; November 1, 1973; January 15, 1974; Literature and Psychology 1 1975; Nation February 23, 1974; Newsweek August 3, 1964; New York Herald Tribune Books February 25, 1962; New York Review of Books September 10, 1964; New York Times April 13, 1975; New York Times Book Review February 4, 1962; August 2, 1964; August 18, 1968; October 7, 1973; New Yorker April 21, 1962; Publishers Weekly July 20, 1964; Saturday Review April 14, 1962; July 25, 1964; Time February 16, 1962; July 24, 1964; Washington Post June 9, 1974.

KILLENS, JOHN OLIVER (1916–), American novelist, dramatist, and essayist, was born in Macon, Georgia, where he received his early schooling at Edward Waters College and Morris Brown College, subsequently attending colleges in Atlanta, in Jacksonville, Florida, and in Washington, D.C., before enrolling in the Terrell Law School of Columbia University, New York. He also attended Howard University and New York University. After this northward educational foray, Killens worked from 1936 to 1942 for the National Labor Relations Board in Washington, returning there in 1946 after his army service in the South Pacific. He now lives in Brooklyn, from time to time uprooting himself to serve as writer-in-residence on various campuses. Indefatigably committed to black causes, he has worked for the American Society for African Culture and for the Harlem Writers

© 1979 by Layle Silbert

JOHN OLIVER KILLENS

Guild Workshop, which he founded, and has served as the vice-president of the Black Academy of Arts and Letters and on the executive board of the National Center of Afro-American Artists. Killens has also taught creative writing at the New School for Social Research and at Columbia, where he is an adjunct professor.

Explaining his views in *Black American Writers,* Killens said in 1975 that "art is life and life is art. All art is social, all art is propaganda, notwithstanding all propaganda is not art. The ultimate purpose of art is to teach man about himself and his relationship to other men." Such, in part, is the point of his long, moving, and passionately angry first novel, *Youngblood* (1954), in which a somewhat idealized black family fights to gain and retain its dignity in the town of Cross Roads, Georgia; it is altogether the point of the partly autobiographical novel that followed, *And Then We Heard the Thunder* (1962). This follows the progress of Solly Saunders, a black law student from New York who joins an amphibious regiment in World War II. Determined to be a perfect soldier, Saunders falls foul of Jim Crow prejudice at both Fort Dix and a restricted Red Cross club in the Pacific theater, in the end becoming involved in a race riot in Australia. Nelson Algren thought that Killens's book was "more like a program to which he is a conscientious subscriber" than a novel, but John Howard Griffin disagreed, and praised the book for having "the depth and complexity of lived experience. It calls James Jones to mind, though Killens writes with less technical control and more poetically."

'Sippi (1967) and *Slaves* (1969), his two subsequent novels, went largely unnoticed. *Publish-*

ers Weekly said of the latter that it read like a black version of the "plantation novel": a dignified slave named Luke is sold downriver to "an evil massa" who whips him and makes him work long hours in the cotton fields. "The dialect," the review continued, "is thick and every plantation cliché in the books is used again and again." *Slaves* was adapted as a movie by Killens in collaboration with Herbert J. Biberman and Alida Sherman.

The most admired of Killens's books to date is *The Cotillion; or, One Good Bull Is Half the Herd* (1971). In a combative preface, his narrator dismisses the categories and proprieties of the "well-made" novel—"angles of narration, points of view, objectivity, universality, composition, author-intrusion, sentence structure, syntax, first person, second person. . . . I said, to hell with all that! I'm the first, second and third person my own damn self. And I will intrude, protrude, obtrude or exclude my point of view any time it suits my disposition." And so he does. The story line, such as it is, concerns the efforts of a Harlem matron to install her delicious daughter Yoruba in the upper reaches of black society via the Grand Cotillion, a debutante ball sponsored by a chic black women's club in Brooklyn, the Femmes Fatales (or Fat Tails, depending on who is speaking). Yoruba's ascent is regretfully but lovingly reported by Ben Ali Lumumba (born Ernest Walter Billings), and his account, rendered in "buoyantly evocative and musical" Afro-Americanese, tellingly lampoons the foibles of white socialites and the equally fatuous antics of the blacks who mimic them.

The most amiable as well as inventive of Killens's books, it even has a happy ending, with mother and daughter turning their backs on a second-hand caste system, and coming around to Ben Ali's conviction that black is very beautiful indeed. Indeed, as James R. Frakes wrote, "the outcome is never really in much doubt. The whole laughing, howling, bursting career of the book zooms like a caricature-missile toward the biggest Everlasting Yea since Molly Bloom finally dozed off: Yea to 'the real world,' the black nation, Afro-natural hairdos, dashikis, Negritude. . . . Everything is signified double-forte, and all the dozens are the dirtiest . . . let's say it again—*The Cotillion* is not a 'novel.' And who cares?"

Great Gittin' Up Morning (1972) is a fictionalized account for young people of how Denmark Vesey, a black from Charleston, South Carolina, planned a slave revolt in 1820 and was hanged for it; it found little favor and seemed to one reviewer "overly dramatic and verbose." More festive and grander in manner, *A Man Ain't*

Nothin' But a Man (1975) retells the John Henry legend, vividly creating an interior life for that martyr in man's "struggle against the machine."

Killens's play *Lower Than the Angels* was produced in New York in 1965. He is also the author with Nelson Gidding of the screenplay of *Odds Against Tomorrow,* a 1959 movie starring Harry Belafonte. *Black Man's Burden* was called a "wry commentary on the image white legend has imposed on Negroes. . . . a pastiche of perceptive, sharply delineated vignettes animated by the twin engines of hate and despair." According to Blyden Jackson, Killens began as an ardent integrationist: "Increasingly, it does seem, it has been the 'black is beautiful' theme, even to the extreme of Black Separation, which has governed Killens in his affirmation of his art, as well as . . . in his conduct as a citizen of the world."

Killens is married and has two children. He has been identified by J. Saunders Redding as "one of the small group in whose hands lay the future of black fiction."

PRINCIPAL WORKS: *Fiction*—Youngblood, 1954; And Then We Heard the Thunder, 1962; 'Sippi, 1967; Slaves, 1969; The Cotillion, 1971; Great Gittin' Up Morning, 1972; A Man Ain't Nothin' But a Man, 1975. *Essays*—Black Man's Burden, 1966. *As editor*—The Trial of Denmark Vesey, 1970.

ABOUT: Bigsby, C.W.E. (ed.) The Black American Writer, 1969; Chapman, A. (ed.) New Black Voices, 1972; Rush, T.G. and Myers, C.F. (eds.) Black American Writers, 1975; Vinson, J. (ed.) Contemporary Novelists, 1976; Who's Who Among Black Americans, 1976; Who's Who in America, 1976-1977. *Periodicals*—Atlantic February 1971; Black World 20 1970; Book World March 27, 1966; New York Herald Tribune Books April 14, 1963; New York Review of Books April 20, 1972; New York Times Book Review April 7, 1963; February 27, 1966; January 17, 1971; April 30, 1972; Saturday Review January 26, 1963; March 12, 1966, March 6, 1971.

KLIMENTOV, A. P. *See* "PLATONOV, AN-DREI"

"KNOX, CALVIN M." *See* SILVERBERG, ROBERT

*KOLAKOWSKI, LESZEK (October 23, 1927–), Polish philosopher and writer of plays, stories, and fables, was born in Radom, a town immediately south of Warsaw. He is the son of Jerzy Kolakowski, a publicist, and the former Lucyna Pietrusiewicz. The Germans invaded Poland in 1939, when Kolakowski was still a schoolboy, and he spent most of the period of the occupation reading his way through the large library of the country house where he lived.

*kow a kov' ski

LESZEK KOLAKOWSKI

Judy Metro

Kolakowski finished secondary school after the war, joined the Communist youth organization ZMP (later becoming a party member), and then studied in the philosophical faculty at Lodz University. Even before his graduation in 1950 he was lecturing at Lodz University and publishing philosophical articles. He received his doctorate in philosophy at Warsaw University in 1953.

As a brilliant young Marxist philosopher, Kolakowski taught in 1952-1954 at a Polish Workers' [Communist] Party school in Warsaw, the Institute for the Training of Scientific Workers. He then returned to Warsaw University as a lecturer in modern philosophy, becoming assistant to Professor Tadeusz Kotarbinski and later to Professor Adam Schaff, who was at that time the leading orthodox Marxist spokesman in Poland. He was head of the section of the history of modern philosophy at Warsaw from 1959 to 1968, and professor of philosophy from 1964 until 1968. From 1956 to 1968 he also held a research professorship at the Institute of Philosophy, Polish Academy of Sciences.

Kolakowski began as an orthodox Marxist, chiefly remarkable, according to Edmund Still, "as a precocious doctrinaire." At first he specialized in religious philosophy and history, producing such works as *Szkice o filozofii katolickiej* (Essays on Catholic Philosophy, 1955), a vigorous Marxist polemic against various aspects of mainstream Catholic philosophy. Soon, however, Kolakowski found himself increasingly interested in the rise of Protestant religious thought (a concern unusual in Catholic Poland). While his visits to the West began in 1955 with attendance at an international Thomist congress in Rome, in 1957-1958 he spent several months

453

in France and Holland doing research on the rise of Protestant sectarian movements. His criticism of Catholic theocratic totalitarianism and religious obscurantism continued, but in terms that could be applied just as tellingly to Communist totalitarianism or Stalinist dogma. An important influence on his thought at this time was Spinoza. In 1958, Kolakowski published *Jednostka i nieskończoność: Wolność i antynomie wolności w filozofii Spinozy* (The Individual and the Infinite: Freedom and the Antinomies of Freedom in the Philosophy of Spinoza, 1958). This was both an edition of Spinoza's letters and a major study of a philosopher who believed that freedom of thought was the very essence of a healthy society.

At the same time Kolakowski was publishing essays and articles dealing with more general and immediate ethical and philosophical questions, and these show a similar development from orthodoxy to critical independence. In 1955 he joined the editorial staff of *Po prostu* (Straight Talk), a rebellious weekly run by young Communist intellectuals that played a major part in precipitating the "Polish October" of 1956, which swept Gomulka to power on a wave of reform. Kolakowski was also in 1956-1957 a member of the editorial board of the important liberal weekly *Nowa Kultura* (New Culture), and from 1957 to 1959 he edited *Studia Filozoficzne* (Philosophical Studies).

A collection of the essays Kolakowski had published in such journals before October 1956 appeared in 1957 as *Światopogląd i życie codzienne* (Philosophy and Everyday Life). One Polish reviewer commented that "Kolakowski has made the first attempt at a philosophical analysis of the ideological crisis through which a great part of the Marxist intelligentsia in our country is passing." By this time, Kolakowski was generally recognized as the leading thinker of the "Polish October," and as one of the most important and original Communist writers in Eastern Europe. He had won equally widespread respect for his personal courage and integrity, and his intense moral commitment.

Like many other Marxist "revisionists," Kolakowski at this time was finding much to admire in the thought of the young Hegelian Marx and his theory of alienation. At the same time he came under the influence of Kant and of such contemporary existentialists as Sartre—influences which had their effect on his own treatment of the problems of individual freedom and responsibility. This syncretist amalgam of Marxist, Kantian, and existentialist elements led him towards a humanistic socialism or socialist humanism which offered a direct challenge to the repressive orthodoxy of institutional Communism. Some of the key essays of this phase of Kolakowski's thought have been published in English translation by Jane Zielonko Peel as *Towards a Marxist Humanism* (1968).

The collection includes the long and now famous essay on "Responsibility and History" in which Kolakowski sets out his disillusionment with Marxist certainties about historical progress and stresses that "rules of moral behavior cannot be derived from any theory of historical progress and . . . no such theory can justifiably be used as a pretext for the violation of certain rules of whose validity we are otherwise convinced." Other essays discuss the relation of "institutional Marxism" to politics, maintaining that "the concept of Marxism as a separate school of thought will in time become blurred and ultimately disappear altogether—just as there is no 'Newtonism' in physics, no 'Linnaeism' in botany, no 'Harveyism' in physiology, and no 'Gaussism' in mathematics. This means that what is permanent in Marx's work will be assimilated in the natural course of scientific development." The volume was greatly admired. Sidney Hook found it "rich and suggestive," though "not free from ambiguity," and said that these essays "are both spirited and interesting . . . written in a colorful as well as an incisive style."

Some of these pieces reflect a further development in Kolakowski's views; by about 1959 he was moving into a postrevisionist phase in which his thought centered upon the structure of society, meaning, and culture—so much so that this phase of his work has sometimes been labeled structuralist. His critique of the history of philosophy and of culture and society in general became broader, as is evident in such major works as *Filozofia pozytywistyczna: Od Hume'a do Kola Wiedeńskiego* (1966, translated by Norbert Guterman as *The Alienation of Reason: A History of Positivist Thought*). Some Western reviewers regarded Kolakowski's outline of the philosophical and cultural significance of positivism as not much more than a lucid introduction to the subject for the general reader. Anthony Quinton, for example, wrote that "the story is presented in a rather neutral way. . . . there are occasional Marxist *aperçus* . . . but for the most part this is a thoroughly professional survey." But it seemed to Professor George L. Kline that in this book and in such essays as "Racjonalizm jako ideologia" (Rationalism as an Ideology, 1959) Kolakowski is offering a critique of positivist rationalism, rejecting such fundamental principles of the school as the claim that "only verifiable statements are admissible," and the dismissal of value judgments as mere expressions of feeling.

Kline gives this summary of what he takes to be Kolakowski's own view of philosophy—that it "is the effort to express discursively the content that is expressed in other ways by the plastic arts, literature, religion, and—to some extent—science and political theory. Kolakowski urges study of the manner in which a given world-view (e.g., positivism, existentialism) is reflected in various aspects of culture. Philosophical texts are not 'scientific'; they are 'fragments of human cultural situations and express the reactions of human minds to given needs experienced by men.' Like all other products of human culture, they must be studied by the . . . method . . . of sympathetic value-orientated understanding rather than scientific, value-free explanation."

A notable example of such sympathetic understanding, and the culminating product of Kolakowski's years of research into the religious conflicts of the sixteenth and seventeenth centuries, is *Świadomość religijna i więź kościelna: Studia nad chrześcijaństwem bezwyznaniowym siedemnastego wieku* (Religious Consciousness and the Ties of the Church: Studies in Nondenominational Christianity of the Seventeenth Century, 1965). This is a thorough investigation of heretical and mystical movements in Holland and France, and of the conflict between religious heterodoxy and the orthodoxy demanded by the "totalitarian and theocratic claims of organized Christianity." Again, Kolakowski's findings seemed as relevant to the struggle between revisionist Marxism and institutional orthodoxy as to the religious conflicts he was actually discussing—he concluded that religious movements, as they grow and gather strength, are confronted at a given moment with a choice: they can either organize themselves as churches, impose orthodoxy upon their members, and thus betray their initial inspiration, or they can try to preserve their original purity, at the cost of eventual disintegration.

In 1966 Kolakowski completed another book, *Obecność mitu* (The Presence of Myth), which was set up in type in Warsaw but then banned. (It has since been published in Polish, and French and German translations are planned.) That same year Kolakowski was expelled from the Communist Party on account of a university lecture commemorating the tenth anniversary of the "Polish October," in which he attacked the party hierarchy for failing to fulfill its promises. In 1968, the year of the "Prague Spring," Kolakowski was among the intellectuals denounced by Gomulka, and the attack was followed by his dismissal from his post at the University of War-

saw. Though not Jewish, Kolakowski has a Jewish wife, and the extreme nationalist campaign against "Zionists" forced him too into emigration, though nominally he left to take up a visiting professorship at McGill University in Canada. In fact, after two years at McGill (1969-1970), he accepted a senior research fellowship at All Souls College, Oxford, where he has remained.

Since then Kolakowski has proclaimed his reservations about socialism—not only as it is practised in Eastern Europe but as it is preached by the "New Left" in the West. In 1973 he was one of the organizers of a conference on the subject at the University of Reading. The papers presented there were published as *The Socialist Idea: A Reappraisal* (1974), edited by Kolakowski and Stuart Hampshire. In his own contribution, Kolakowski discusses Marx's "anticipation of socialism as based on the identity of civil and political society" and asks: "Is there any historical connection between the Marxian vision of the unified man and the fact that real communism appears only in totalitarian form, i.e. as the tendency to *replace* all crystallizations of the civil society by coercive organs of the state?"

The same sort of dilemma had of course been central to Kolakowski's earlier studies of utopian religious movements, and he concludes his paper by saying that "the dream of a perfectly unified human community is probably as old as human thought about society. . . . There is no reason to expect that this dream will ever be eradicated in our culture, since it has strong roots in the awareness of a split which humanity has suffered apparently from the very beginning of its existence after leaving animal innocence. And there is no reason to expect that this dream can ever become true except in the cruel form of despotism; and despotism is a desperate simulation of paradise." Kolakowski nevertheless still defends the possibility of thinking in socialist terms, though "we are certainly not allowed to delude ourselves that we hold the secret of the conflict-free society or the key to perfection."

In striking contrast to his scholarly works, Kolakowski has also written plays, stories, and fables which, in the words of Czeslaw Milosz, "display his gifts as a jester in a casual colloquial language." The jester, as Kolakowski explains in one of his essays, is an important figure in his anti-dogmatic, anti-absolutist, anti-monistic philosophy—a strategic persona who can bring "an always active imagination" to the important task of ridiculing every kind of official rigidity and obscurantism, puncturing all inflated or closed systems of thought. *13 bajek z królestwa Lailonii dla dużych i malych* (Thirteen Fables

From the Kingdom of Lailonia for Grown-ups and Children, 1963) is a collection of paradoxical fables built around the opposition of faith and reality. Two of these, "The Humps" and "The Worst Quarrel," have been translated by Maria Rodman in the Kolakowski issue of *Tri-Quarterly* (Fall 1971), which also contains a number of essays and Nicholas Bethell's translation of the play *Zebrak i ladna dziewczyna* (The Beggar and the Pretty Girl). In another play, *Wygnanie z raju* (Expulsion From Paradise, 1961), Adam X Thousand arrives at the Hotel Eden, run by a gentle old Director, and meets Eve. Their life there is carefree but closely supervised, and they are soon bored, until the Vice-Director, a malicious tempter, persuades Eve to accept the key to a forbidden room. Adam and Eve are expelled, but the moral is clearly drawn that freedom without the possibility of choice is no freedom at all—people must be allowed to take responsibility for their own decisions.

Two collections of allegorical tales have been published in English in a single volume called *The Key to Heaven and Conversations With the Devil* in the United States and *The Devil and Scripture* in Britain. *Klucz niebieski, albo opowieści budujące z historii świętej zebrane ku pouczeniu i przestrodze,* originally published in the magazine *Nowa Kultura* in 1957, was translated by Salvator Attanasio in the American edition as *The Key to Heaven: Edifying Tales From Holy Scripture to Serve as Teaching and Warning,* and by Nicholas Bethell in the British edition as *The Key to Heaven.* The lengthy title is an obvious parody of the pious Polish tracts of the Baroque era, and these retellings of seventeen stories from the Old Testament (including the Creation, Noah, Abraham, Saul, Job, Herod, Ruth, Solomon, and Salome) are satirical reinterpretations in the light of dialectical reason. "Each biblical tale," wrote George Gömöri, "has its unconventional moral, or morals, through which Kolakowski demonstrates the relativity of ethics and the uncertainty of truth. Among other things he proves (in the story of Job) that rational behavior in a non-rational context might be more futile than irrational behavior, and that the individual is essentially defenseless when he is confronted with irrational metaphysical demands." A.G. Mojtabai found "a mellow note running through these parables, one of fellowship and complicity in the human condition, of pluralism and tolerance.... Kolakowski has abundant wit and a keen eye for the paradoxes of faith and the moral ambivalences of history."

The second collection of tales, *Rozmowy z diablem* (1965), was translated by Celina Wieniaw-ska and published in America as *Conversations with the Devil,* in Britain as *Talk of the Devil.* It consists of seven conversations in which Satan pits his wits against various mythical and historical figures—Orpheus, Héloïse, Luther, Saint Peter the Apostle, Saint Bernard—and participates in a "Metaphysical Press Conference Given by the Demon in Warsaw, on 20 December 1963." The Devil is a highly subtle and original critical philosopher, opposed both to God's demands for uncritical faith and obedience and man's equally rigid secular ideologies. Ninian Smart sums up the two collections as representing "an ironical and subtle humanism in protest against faith juggernauts. But they testify to a dilemma. Change from tyranny cannot alas be achieved by satire."

In a paper called "Can the Devil be Saved?", delivered at a conference on "The Future of Religion" at Nijmegen University in 1972 and later published in *Encounter* (July 1974), Kolakowski reconsiders the myths that men live by and concludes that men do need a religion "that will help them to move beyond the immediate pressures of life, that gives them insight into the basic limits of the human condition and the capacity to accept them." Yet "we need more than Christianity . . . because the truth of Christianity is as one-sided as any other truth. We need the living tradition of socialist thought which appeals to human forces solely by promoting the traditional values of social justice and freedom. . . . We need a socialism that will help us to understand the complexity of the brutal forces acting in human history and reinforce our readiness to fight against social oppression and human misery." Unfortunately, "we cannot . . . expect a grand synthesis of the different and incompatible traditions which we need. . . . The Eden of human universality is a paradise lost."

Kolakowski was married in 1949 to Tamara Dynenson, a psychiatrist. They have a daughter, Agnes, and live at Headington, near Oxford. The author has taught as a visiting professor at the University of California at Berkeley and is much in demand as a lecturer. He is a member of the International Institute of Philosophy and an honorary member of the American Academy of Arts and Sciences.

According to George Gömöri, "Kolakowski's work abounds in paradoxes and is not exempt from contradictions. The main question asked by his Western critics is whether he accepts the priority of social progress over moral values or *vice versa.* . . . Yet in view of Kolakowski's development in recent years, it is perhaps reasonable to say that he has resolved this dilemma. He is now much closer to Pascal (and in some respects even to Kierkegaard) and more responsive to the essence of authentic existential thought than he has ever been. While postulating an "act of faith" in the possibility of a man-made history, Kolakowski appears to be much less certain about the inevitability and direction of historical progress. ... Most significant perhaps is his insistence that a *classless and free* society is guaranteed neither by science nor by history. For all his recent emphasis on faith and individual responsibility, Kolakowski is a major figure of the Second Enlightenment. This is a movement more limited in its scope than the first, its claims are more modest and it concerns only those huge authoritarian structures which still exist in the middle of our century: the Catholic Church and the Communist Party. ... This might well be the gist of his message: You cannot love *both* truth and authority, you have to choose—without dogmas, often rethinking your own premises. Kolakowski's is a philosophy for grownups."

PRINCIPAL WORKS IN ENGLISH TRANSLATION: *Nonfiction* —Towards a Marxist Humanism: Essays on the Left Today, 1968 (England, Marxism and Beyond); The Alienation of Reason: A History of Positivist Thought, 1969 (England, Positivist Philosophy: From Hume to the Vienna Circle); Husserl and the Search for Certitude (Cassirer Lectures), 1975. *As editor*—(with Stuart Hampshire) The Socialist Idea: A Reappraisal, 1974. *Fiction*—The Key to Heaven and Conversations With the Devil, 1972 (England, The Devil and Scripture). *Miscellaneous*—A Leszek Kolakowski Reader (entire issue of Tri-Quarterly Fall 1971).

ABOUT: Contemporary Authors 49-52, 1975; Kline, G.L. European Philosophy Today, 1965; Labedz, L. *introduction to* Marxism and Beyond, 1969; Milosz, C. The History of Polish Literature, 1969. *Periodicals*—Encounter March 1969, October 1971; Library Journal October 1, 1973; New Republic September 21, 1968; New York Review of Books April 25, 1968; New York Times Book Review September 1, 1968; Saturday Review September 28, 1968; Times (London) October 23, 1978; Times Literary Supplement March 13, 1969; May 3, 1974; March 21, 1975; Times Higher Education Supplement (London) December 7, 1973; Tri-Quarterly Fall 1971.

"KRAYNY, ANTON." *See* HIPPIUS, ZINAIDA

KUMIN, MAXINE (WINOKUR) (June 6, 1925–), American poet, novelist, and author of books for children, writes: "I was born in Philadelphia, Pennsylvania, where my father owned the largest pawnbroking establishment in the city, and I grew up in an environment where status was a preeminent consideration; clothes and possessions and servants reflected one's standard. It was also important to be defined as non-immigrant, non-orthodox Jews, third gen-

MAXINE KUMIN

eration on the paternal side, fifth on the maternal. Oddly enough, because our house stood next door to the Convent of the Sisters of St. Joseph, I was sent for my very early education to parochial school. Thus Jesus entered my life casually but insistently and some of that sanctified passion has stayed in my bones.

"At seventeen, I had the good fortune to go away to Radcliffe College in Cambridge, Massachusetts and burst with a heady sort of relief from the world of hats and gloves and leopard-trimmed coats into Academe. I became an ardent intellectual, espoused leftist causes, got myself investigated by the FBI, discovered the sonnet, chafed uneasily on the itchy, homefront side of World War II and immediately upon graduation was married. A year and a half later, I received my Master's degree; almost simultaneously, the first of our three children was born.

"I returned to the writing of poetry in the despondent middle of my third pregnancy—I had been a closet poet from the age of eight—and little by little, first through the writing of light verse for the slick magazines, and later through the gradual and painful development of style and self, I became a poet. I had no notion of turning to prose until my father died and out of an enormous compulsion I did not understand, I began a story that turned into a first novel. After that, the prose came in spurts, alternating with but never interrupting new collections of poems.

"In some way that is not terribly clear to me, working in prose frees the poet who needs to go underground from time to time. The marvelous density of prose fiction serves as a sort of conduit from the unconscious and brings a sense of discipline and order into my life. In the same way, children's books, almost two dozen of them, begun quite simply as commercial ventures and adding some welcome income to a stringent budget, served as a corrective rein on the creative chaos. The children's stories were invariably playful objects with little ego investment; to write them was a refreshment.

"I have taught in several universities over the years, the subjects ranging from freshman composition through American literature to graduate seminars in the creative writing of poetry. I go on teaching because I still find it a mutually nurturing process. My university affiliation began in the fifties in an era when women were both underemployed and generally mistrusted. Consequently, I was only deemed competent to teach freshman composition to dental technicians and physical education majors. Feminism came to me slowly as social conditions changed and as I dared to develop a sense of my own worth. Then, too, I could not help but observe the struggle of my bright female students to obtain any sort of professional status and to be accorded equality with their male peers. At the same time, our own daughters were striking out in individual directions (lawyer, interpreter), and I empathized with their efforts.

"Everything that happens in the not necessarily remarkable life of the writer is subsumed and reemerges, it is to be hoped, as literature. Looking back through the poems and the novels, I see private experience giving rise to elegy and celebration. I would have to say that the grit of discontent, the acute misery of early and uninformed motherhood worked under my skin to force out the writer.

"Since 1963, I have divided my time between an elderly farm in New Hampshire and our city residence, and much of the energy that went into raising a family has lately gone into the care and feeding of horses and crops. Indeed, the farm itself and the cycle of the seasons have served as the locus for almost all my creative efforts since the land, pond and derelict Colonial house took possession of us. As my belief in the perfectibility of man has eroded before my recognition of human depravity, I find myself digging in ever deeper to accept the natural world. I hope to live out my life on the land, raising horses and turnips and making jam from the wild berries."

The forty short poems in *Halfway* (1961), Maxine Kumin's first collection, were mostly personal—often concerned with the complexities of her relationships with others. They were thought direct, honest, and gentle, and enjoyed for their sometimes sardonic humor. Though some reviewers found these poems moving, and both singly and cumulatively powerful, they seemed to others unambitious, unimportant, and technically uninteresting—evidence perhaps that she had not wholly outgrown the years of "light verse for the slick magazines."

By the time she published *The Privilege* in 1965 her poetic persona was more clearly defined. Richard Moore called her "an accomplished and professional poet of what might be called the Bishop-Lowell-Sexton school" who, "when she has a subject . . . can write moving and memorable poems." Moore particularly admired a series of evocations of childhood, and "some excellently lush love poems" that reminded him of the "Song of Songs." There were also technical advances, and a reviewer in *Choice* wrote that her "clipped, nervous verse line . . . which seems unusually consonantal in sound, proves highly various and adaptable, easily meeting the demands of the sonnet form." The clarity and concreteness of her imagery was also praised, as was her detailed knowledge and close observation of natural phenomena.

There were some darker pieces in *The Nightmare Factory*—along with the "pastoral poems" about cows and horses and "tribal poems" for the author's family—and more of them in *Up Country,* the volume of new and selected poems which brought her the Pulitzer Prize in 1973. Joyce Carol Oates wrote that "Kumin's book acknowledges its debt to Thoreau, though in my opinion Kumin's poetry gives us a sharp-edged, unflinching and occasionally nightmarish subjectivity exasperatingly absent in Thoreau." The following passage from "Pain," a poem written in the hospital, is an example of this subjectivity —and of how far Maxine Kumin has come from the easy charm of her early poems:

. . . Meanwhile pain comes in dressed like a spy.
A bearded spy wearing sneakers and murmuring
    eat!
Eat my quick poison. And of course I nibble the
    edges.
I eat my way to the center of his stem
because something inside it is secret.

At night rowing out to sea on drugs, rowing out
on my little oars, those carefully deployed spoons,
sometimes I think I catch a glimpse of that body
of knowledge. It is the fin of a flying fish.
It is a scrap of phosphorescent plankton
I would take hold of crying, wait!
Thinking, tell me. . . .

Meanwhile I continue putting out to sea
on my little wooden ice cream spoons.
Although I am not a Catholic, the priest has laid

his hand upon me. He has put God into my pain.
Somewhere in my pineal gland He sits and gloats.

As for the lore, I have learned nothing to hand on.
I go out nightly past these particular needles
and these knives.

House, Bridge, Fountain, Gate, containing poems written between 1971 and 1975, offers "a re-examination of . . . [the poet's] life and family connections, of her childhood and motherhood," of a time she spent alone as a poet-in-residence at a Kentucky college, feeling like "the only Jew in town," and of her intense feeling for horses. Helen Vendler complained that the book "suffers from a disease of similes: children 'naked as almonds,' kisses 'like polka dots,' a corset spread out 'like a filleted fish,' someone 'patient as an animal,' a visit 'as important as summer' . . . all inhabit one poem, and the disease . . . becomes mortal as the book continues. The poems . . . have a cheerful will to make the best of things . . . but the whimsy in Kumin gets in my way." On the other hand, it did not bother Victor Howes in the least, and he wrote that "in their nourishment, their closeness of fit, their durable beauty, Mrs. Kumin's poems attest an art nearly invisible."

Her partly autobiographical first novel, *Through Dooms of Love,* is an account of two crucial days in 1939 when a dose of Radcliffe Marxism awakens young Joanna Ferguson to the social implications of her father's trade as "the biggest pawnbroker in Fidelia," New Jersey. Martin Levin called it a "gemlike book," in which the author "enriches her characters' backgrounds with memory and actuality, defining them with luminous brilliance." However, it seemed to an otherwise admiring reviewer in *Library Journal* that the shape and emphasis of the book had been blurred by too much detailed description and meticulous analysis. There was a mixed but generally favorable reception for *The Passions of Uxport,* set in a Boston suburb and telling the story of two marriages in crisis. Those who disliked the book did so because it demonstrates very clearly the erosion in Maxine Kumin's "belief in the perfectibility of man," to which she refers above, and her "recognition of human depravity." Animals play an important part in the novel—dogs, cats, a premature foal, and many dead animals left on the roadside—the latter, one reviewer thought, representing "examples of public and private cruelty."

The Abduction, which followed, was praised as "an intensely moving portrait of a woman," but *The Designated Heir,* about a girl who inherits a fortune and promptly divests herself of it, irritated some reviewers. William McPherson wrote that "Kumin uses a lot of literary devices —sections from . . . [the girl's] Peace Corps journal; symbol and metaphor applied like Band-Aids or perhaps tourniquets—to mask the essential banality of the plot. . . . *The Designated Heir* is a marshmallow of a book—sticky, sweet, and soft in the center, and suitable for roasting." On the other hand Jane Howard, agreeing that Kumin's prose sometimes lapses into coyness, thought that she made up for this with "resonating insights. . . . [This] is not a novel of much action or wide scope, but its texture is a marvel and its people are so vivid that they take up permanent residence in our minds."

Maxine Kumin's books for children, two of them written in collaboration with Anne Sexton, have been generally well received. She is the daughter of Peter Winokur and the former Doll Simon, and was married in 1946 to Victor Montwid Kumin, a consulting engineer. She lives with her family in Newton Highlands, Massachusetts. Maxine Kumin taught at Tufts University as an English instructor in 1958–1961 and again in 1965–1968. In 1971–1972 she taught at Newton College and in 1972 she was a visiting lecturer at the University of Massachusetts. In 1975 she went to Columbia University as an adjunct professor of writing, and the same year was Fannie Hurst Professor of Literature at Brandeis University. From 1961 to 1963 she studied at the Radcliffe Institute for Independent Study. She served as literary consultant to the Central Atlantic Regional Educational Laboratory in 1967–1969. Radcliffe gave her an honorary doctorate in 1976.

PRINCIPAL WORKS: *Poetry*—Halfway, 1961; The Privilege, 1965; The Nightmare Factory, 1970; Up Country, 1972; House, Bridge, Fountain, Gate, 1975. *Novels*—Through Dooms of Love, 1965; The Passions of Uxport, 1968; The Abduction, 1971; The Designated Heir, 1974.

ABOUT; Foremost Women in Communications, 1970; International Who's Who in Poetry, 1974–1975; Shaw, R.B. American Poetry Since 1960, 1973; Ward, M.E. and Marquardt, D.A. (eds.) Authors of Books for Young People, 1971; Who's Who in America, 1976-1977; Who's Who of American Women, 1977–1978. *Periodicals*—Library Journal November 1, 1971; Massachusetts Review Spring 1975; New York Times Book Review November 19, 1972; June 23, 1974; September 7, 1975; Saturday Review March 25, 1972; Virginia Quarterly Review Spring 1971; Yale Review Autumn 1968.

*KUNDERA, MILAN (April 1, 1929–), Czech novelist, short story writer, and essayist, writes (in French): "I was born in Brno, Czechoslovakia. My father, Ludvík Kundera, was a pianist, a pupil and collaborator of the great Czech com-

*ko͞on' de rä

Anne de Brunhoff

MILAN KUNDERA

poser Leoš Janáček. I loved my father, a silent, shy man, very much, and I still love Janáček's music, which was for me the first great revelation of art. Following the example of the Czech avant-garde generation I joined the communist party when I was eighteen, but two years after the definitive victory of communism in Czechoslovakia I was expelled. Seventeen years later, at the crucial 1967 congress of Czechoslovak writers, I gave the opening address, preaching the idea of greater artistic freedom. After the 1968 Soviet invasion this led to the absurd charge that I was a 'counter-revolutionary.' I therefore had to leave my post at the Film Faculty of the Academy of Music and Dramatic Arts, where for over fifteen years I had been a teacher and later assistant professor—my pupils having included such notable cineasts as the directors Miloš Forman, Jiří Menzel and Ivan Passer. My books were withdrawn from all the public libraries. In 1975 I was appointed an associate professor at the University of Rennes, France, where I now live, though retaining my Czechoslovak citizenship.

"My earliest writings were several collections of poetry. I don't have a very high regard for them, or for my first play *The Owners of the Keys* (1962), although that has had some success all over the world. I hadn't discovered my 'own world' until the moment when, at the age of nearly thirty, I began to write the first short stories of the cycle *Laughable Loves,* which was introduced in America by a long preface by Philip Roth. My first novel, *The Joke,* which came out in 1967 in Prague in an edition of one hundred and twenty thousand copies, was published by Gallimard in France in 1968 with an intro-

duction by Louis Aragon. Since then I haven't been able to publish my books in my own country; these therefore appear first in French translation. My second novel, *La Vie est ailleurs,* won the 1973 Prix Médicis for the best foreign novel published in France. This and the preceding novel brought me the friendship of many French intellectuals, whose support at this difficult period of my life has been incomparable and unforgettable.

"The western view of Eastern European literature tends to be a simple division into that of communist propaganda and that of the dissidents who denounce communism. However, the real literature is outside either of these categories. Even though the bizarre drama of politics is often present in my books, their characters aren't taking part in any particular politics, but in other realms—those of humor, irony and imagination. It's in this sense that I don't much like the idea of committed literature. For me the only commitment of the novelist ought to be to oppose the ironic wisdom of the novel to ideological simplifications of every sort."

Kundera at first intended to become a musician, and studied piano with his father and later with Paul Haas and others. In 1948, concluding that this was not his true vocation, he went to study scriptwriting and directing at the Film Faculty of the Prague Academy of Music and Dramatic Arts, where in 1952 he joined the teaching staff. Kundera had begun to write poetry at the age of fourteen and, as he says, his first book was a volume of verse, *Člověk zahrada šira* (Man a Broad Garden, 1953). It reflected humane Communist convictions, but also his interest in surrealism, and it was roundly condemned by the party hacks for its "individualism." This was followed by two more small collections of verse, *Poslední máj* (The Last May, 1955), centering on Julius Fucik, a Czech Communist who was a hero of the anti-Nazi resistance, and *Monology* (Monologue, 1957). The latter, which included a series of confessions by variously lovelorn and frustrated women, sold out soon after publication but was not reprinted for several years because the authorities considered it too brutal, pessimistic, and erotic.

Majitelé klíčů (The Owners of the Keys, 1961), Kundera's first play, was produced in fourteen countries, including the United States and Britain. Set during World War II, it shows how an idealistic student who tries to disassociate himself from the violence of the Czech resistance is forced in the end to abandon his pacifism and join the bloody struggle against the invaders. ("The Owners of the Keys" are all those who withdraw into their private lives, condoning injustice to safeguard their own comfort.) A second play, *Ptákovina, čili Dvojí uši—dvojí svatba* (Double Wedding), which attacked the corruption and hypocrisy of Communist Party officials, was produced in 1968. Kundera also wrote an early critical work, *Umění románu* (The Art of the Novel, 1960), a perceptive study of the highly original Czech novelist Vladislav Vančura, shot by the Nazis in 1942.

But Kundera found his true métier as a sophisticated ironist of carnal love and sexual politics in three volumes of short stories. *Směšné lásky* (Laughable Loves, 1963) contains three stories, in each of which a young man gets his comeuppance through the misfiring of some attempted deceit or stratagem. A young academic, for example, seeking to avoid reviewing a bad essay by a party luminary, accuses the latter of lusting after his girlfriend; he winds up losing the girl, his job, and even his apartment. *Druyh sešit směšných lásek* (The Second Book of Laughable Loves, 1965) contains three more such stories, including "The Hitchhiking Game," a much-praised account of a role-playing sexual game which becomes all too real and revealing. The four stories in *Třetí sešit směšných lásek* (The Third Book of Laughable Loves, 1968) further develop Kundera's themes—the extent to which each of us is the prisoner of his own temperament, the strain this imposes on our relations with others, the illusory nature of our pursuit of happiness through love.

A selection of these stories has been translated by Suzanne Rappaport as *Laughable Loves,* with an introduction by Philip Roth in which he speaks of Kundera's highly classical interest in the planned seduction, and the salutary way in which the most cunningly woven net of sexual intrigue is likely to descend about the plotter. Paul Theroux in his review pointed out that "the stories are bound up with politics, and even when politics is never mentioned, as in 'The Hitchhiking Game,' it enters the story as a kind of fatigue: why else would this pair be behaving like this if it weren't for the fact that their famished imaginations are the result of political frustration?" Theroux wrote that he would be "very surprised if a better collection of stories appeared this year."

Kundera's first novel, *Žert* (1967, translated by David Hamblyn and Oliver Stallybrass as *The Joke*), explores both the generation gap and the ideology gap. The student anti-hero Ludvík sends his politically zealous girlfriend a postcard parodying Marxist slogans ("Optimism is the opium of the people!") and she denounces him.

The careerist Zemanek sees to it that he is expelled from the university and drafted into the army. Years later Ludvík seeks his revenge by seducing Zemanek's wife. By then, however, Zemanek has become a progressive, the hero of his students, and the wretched "joke" turns into a nightmare when his plain and aging wife falls in love with her seducer. The intricate structure of the novel, with four narrators describing the same events from as many viewpoints, allows the multiple ironies of the situation full play. Martin Seymour-Smith called it "at once a satire on the fake communism of the Stalinists, on the opportunists who thrived under it, and on the Czech character itself," and Gavin Millar thought it a "formidable work, grave without sententiousness, delicate without fragility, rich in ideas and feeling."

Oliver Stallybrass, the principal translator of *Žert,* had sought to clarify the novel's narrative line by making certain structural changes. His English publisher wrote to Kundera for his permission and, receiving no reply, incorporated them in the English version published in 1969. Kundera, who had not received the publisher's letters, wrote a furious letter to the *Times Literary Supplement* (October 30, 1969). He said that in Communist Czechoslovakia, even though *Žert* had been held up by the censors for four months, it eventually appeared without a word altered, whereas in the West "scandalous liberties" had been taken with his text. A long correspondence followed and the novel was subsequently republished in a corrected version.

As Kundera says, his second novel *Život je jinde* first appeared in French (and won the Prix Médicis) as *La Vie est ailleurs* (1973, translated by Peter Kussi as *Life is Elsewhere*). It is a remarkable satiric portrait of the artist as a young man. For Jaromil, life means poetry, revolution, and love, but he fails completely in all of these things because he is only a parody of a poet, just as he is only a parody of a revolutionary. The product of a solidly bourgeois background, his rebellion is not truly political but an expression of his attempt to break loose from a claustrophobic relationship with his doting mother. The story is laced with parallels from the lives of such figures as Byron, Rimbaud, Mayakovsky, and Yesenin, revealing by comparison the pathetic and ludicrous dishonesty of Jaromil's ideals. "*La vie est ailleurs*" was one of the slogans adopted by French students during the 1968 upheavals; in Jaromil's terms it means only that life is a dream, a dangerous and irresponsible dream.

In a long interview with A. J. Liehm (published in *The Politics of Culture*), Kundera said "my own youth, my own 'lyrical age' and poetic activity coincided with the worst period of the Stalin era. . . . I got a close look at poets who adorned things which weren't worth it, and I am still able to remember vividly this state of passionate lyrical enthusiasm which, getting drunk on its own frenzy, is unable to see the real world through its own grandiose haze." It is Kundera's distrust and dislike of "narcissistic" romanticism that has brought him from poetry to prose, from lyricism to irony, and that lies behind his savage portrait of Jaromil. The result seemed to J. L. Crain "an altogether extraordinary work, complex, chilling and brilliantly executed. . . . The final wonder is that he has so masterfully succeeded in transforming political passions into a disinterested work of art."

Kundera's third novel, *Valčik na rozloučenou*, appeared in French as *La valse aux adieux* and in English, translated by Peter Kussi, as *The Farewell Party*. It is set in a Czech spa town renowned for its treatment of infertility. After a one-night stand there, the famous jazz trumpeter Klima is informed by Ruzena, a nurse at the spa, that she is pregnant by him. She hopes that he will leave his family for her, but Klima, a notorious womanizer, is also deeply in love with his wife, and he hastens to assure Ruzena that she should have an abortion. Caught up in the ensuing complications are Ruzena's jealous lover, Klima's jealous wife and *her* lover, the doctor in charge of the gynecological clinic (who for the good of humanity fertilizes his patients from his own private sperm bank), and the embittered dissident Jakub, who has reached the dismal conclusion that "there is no difference between the guilty and their victims."

As D.J. Enright wrote, "the turns and counterturns of Czech communism since 1948 form the other strand in Kundera's work, the imprisonments, liquidations, and rehabilitations, the changing orthodoxies, the hopes and disillusionments. This strand is counterpointed with the 'private life,' the hopes and needs, exploitations and treacheries, of sexuality." For Enright, "the counterpointing is so complicated . . . that it is hard to grasp the final significance of this tangled music"; moreover, "the sourness, the glum cynicism consequent upon disenchantment and alienation, come through too sharply, or too repetitively; there is an excess of soul-searching . . . it has the air of a cold-hearted metaphysical puzzle whose terms are either incomplete or not clearly enough set out." A number of other reviewers were similarly disappointed, though Saul Maloff praised the book as "the kind of 'political novel' a cunning, resourceful, gifted

writer writes when it is no longer possible to write political novels."

In Czechoslovakia, Kundera served on the Central Committee of the Writers' Union and the Presidium of the Central Committee, as well as on the editorial boards of the journals *Literárni noviny* and *Listy*. He received the Czechoslovak Writers' Publishing House Prize in 1961 and 1969, the Klement Gottwald State Prize in 1963, and the Writers' Union Prize in 1967. His famous opening address at the 1967 Congress of Czechoslovak Writers, with its powerful advocacy of artistic freedom, has been published in translation in Dusan Hamšík's *Writers Against Rulers* and in *Czechoslovakia,* by Andrew Oxley and others. Kundera was married to Věra Hrabánková in 1963, and lists his leisure interests as boxing, music, and dogs.

In 1977, writing in the British magazine *Index on Censorship,* Kundera offered this defense of the novel: "Since the 1920s, everyone seems to have been writing the obituary of the novel—the Surrealists, the Russian avant-garde, Malraux, who claims the novel has been dead since the time Malraux stopped writing novels, and so on and so forth. Isn't it strange? No one talks about the death of poetry. And yet, since the great generation of Surrealists, I know of no truly great and innovatory work of poetry. No one talks about the death of the theatre. No one talks about the death of painting. No one talks about the death of music. Yet, since Schönberg, music has abandoned a thousand-year-old tradition based on tonality and on musical instruments. Varese, Xenakis . . . I am very fond of them, but is this still music? . . . music may have been dead for several decades, yet no one talks about its demise. They talk about the death of the novel. . . . and this in spite of the fact that the greatest strength of literature over the past fifty years has been in this very sphere—just take Robert Musil, Thomas Mann, Faulkner, Céline, Pasternak, Gombrowicz, Günter Grass, Böll, or my dear friends, Philip Roth and García Márquez. The novel is a game with invented characters. You see the world through their eyes, and thus you see it from different angles. . . . Ideology is a school of intolerance. A novel teaches you tolerance and understanding. . . . Today, when politics have become a religion, I see the novel as one of the last forms of atheism."

PRINCIPAL WORKS IN ENGLISH TRANSLATION: The Joke, 1969; Laughable Loves, 1974; Life Is Elsewhere, 1974; The Farewell Party, 1976. *Story in* Theiner, G. (ed.) New Writing in Czechoslovakia, 1969.

ABOUT: Doležel, L. Narrative Modes in Czech Literature, 1973; Hamšík, D. Writers Against Rulers, 1971; International Who's Who, 1975-76; Liehm, A. The Politics of Culture, 1971; Lombardo-Radice, L. Gli accusati, 1972; Mohrt, M. L'air du large, 1971; Oxley, A. and others. Czechoslovakia, 1973; Roth, P. introduction to Laughable Loves, 1974. Periodicals—Index on Censorship Winter 1975, November-December 1977; New York Review of Books May 21, 1970; August 8, 1974; September 16, 1976; New York Times Book Review January 11, 1970; July 28, 1974; September 5, 1976; January 8, 1978; Times Literary Supplement October 2, 1969.

*LAFORET (DÍAZ), CARMEN (September 6, 1921–), Spanish novelist and short story writer, was born in Barcelona. Her father was an architect, a member of a wealthy Andalusian family of French and Basque stock. Her mother, from a humbler background, had met him while he was teaching in her native Toledo. When Carmen Laforet was two years old, the family moved to the Canary Islands, living in Las Palmas, where her father taught at the Escuela de Peritaje Industrial.

In the autobiographical introduction to Mis páginas mejores (My Best Pages, 1956), she writes nostalgically of her family's happy life on the island; of swimming, sailing, and hiking with her father, a fine sportsman, and her two younger brothers. This idyll was ended when she was thirteen by the death of her mother, a woman of great moral strength whom she dearly loved. Her father remarried and her stepmother seemed to her like the wicked stepmother in fairy tales, except that "fantasy is always poor compared with reality."

Educated in Las Palmas, Carmen Laforet returned to Barcelona in September 1939, just after the end of the Civil War, and enrolled in a liberal arts course at the university. She did not complete the course there, or the legal studies she embarked upon in 1942 at the University of Madrid. Instead she wrote a novel, which won the first Nadal Prize in 1944, had an enormous success in Spain, and brought her an international reputation.

Nada (1945) is about Andrea, an eighteen-year-old girl who, like the author herself, returns full of hope from a childhood and adolescence spent abroad to her native Barcelona. She finds the city physically and spiritually devastated by the Civil War, which continues to smolder in the hearts of the people. The relatives with whom she stays are crippled by shame and guilt, each of them imprisoned in a private hell of despair and striking out in pointless but bitterly destructive quarrels.

This novel, with its harshly unsentimental realism and passionate honesty, and in spite of its immaturities of tone and style, was recognized at once as a landmark in the history of

*la fó ret

Spanish fiction. It has been read variously as a political and as an existentialist novel. E.R. Mulvihill and R.G. Sánchez, in their English introduction to a Spanish edition of Nada, called it "peculiarly the product of its time. It is the voice of a new generation emerging in a country laid waste by civil war, in a world torn by international conflict, and at a time when it seemed that civilization itself might perish. Carmen Laforet here gives expression to the anguished confusion of youth confronted by chaos and seeking a meaning to existence. The heroine well personifies this state of mind, its groping, its fears, and its confusion as she endeavours to comprehend the new world in which she finds herself —a world which had promised so much and seems to offer so little." Nada was translated under that title by Iñez Munos in 1958 and as Andrea by C.F. Payne in 1964.

Carmen Laforet's next book did not appear until 1952, when she published a short novel, La muerta (The Dead Woman). This was followed soon afterwards by La isla y los demonios (The Island and the Demons, 1952). The island is one of the Canary Islands and the demons (which according to superstition live there) symbolize the spirits of frustration and failure that dominate the characters. Like its predecessor, the book centers on a girl's painful development from adolescence to maturity. The author's evocation of the island setting was much praised, as her portrayal of Barcelona in Nada had been, but this novel was thought to lack the intensity and spontaneity of the first.

El Piano (The Piano, 1952), one of several novellas published at about this time, introduced a religious theme which reflected Carmen Laforet's conversion to Catholicism—the faith in which she had been baptized and to which she returned as a result of a mystical experience that she underwent at the end of 1951. This theme is explored more thoroughly in La mujer nueva (The New Woman, 1955), in which a worldly woman, separated from her husband and about to join her lover, rediscovers her faith. Tempted for a time to leave the world and enter a nunnery, she finally returns to her husband.

The novel received the Menorca Prize in 1955 and the Premio Miguel de Cervantes in 1956, but had a mixed reception. One critic called it "discursive, artificial and sentimental," and another wrote: "Were it not widely known . . . that Carmen Laforet has evolved toward a certain type of Catholicism, it would be possible to wonder if the psychological incoherence of the main character and the overwhelming profusion of a vapid religious language are not aimed at a parody." Indeed, most (though not all) critics agree that this and subsequent books, in their sentimentality and lack of intensity, are greatly inferior to her first novel, on which her international reputation rests.

The lives of Carmen Laforet's heroines closely reflect her own experiences; she has acknowledged that her fictional world is intimately linked with her own inner life but denies that any of her books is directly autobiographical. Apart from her fiction, she has written a guide to the island where she grew up, *Gran Canaria* (1961, translated by J. Forrester as *Grand Canary*). The author is married to the literary critic and journalist Manuel González-Cerezales and has five children. She lives with her family near the heart of Madrid.

PRINCIPAL WORKS IN ENGLISH TRANSLATION: Nada, 1958 (also translated as Andrea, 1964); Grand Canary, 1964. *Story in* Flores, A. (ed.) Great Spanish Stories, 1956.

ABOUT: Chandler, R.E. and Schwartz, K. A New History of Spanish Literature, 1961; Illanes Adaro, G. La novelística de Carmen Laforet, 1971; Laforet, C. Mis páginas mejores, 1950; Mulvihill, E.R. and Sánchez, R.G. *introduction to* Nada, 1958; Nora, E. de, La novela española contemporánea, 1958-1962; Northup, G.T. and Adams, N.B. Introduction to Spanish Literature, 1960; Seymour-Smith, M. Guide to Modern World Literature, 1973. *Periodicals—* Books Abroad 1 1953, 1 1956, 4 1956, 1 1958.

*LAING, R(ONALD) D(AVID) (October 7, 1927–), Scottish psychiatrist and pioneer of existential psychoanalysis, was born in Glasgow, the only child of D.P.M. and Amelia Laing. The family was a dour Scottish Presbyterian one: "My father was the only one in his family to marry and, with one possible exception, the only one ever to commit sexual intercourse." In the brief biographical section of *The Facts of Life* (1976) and in various interviews he has described his childhood in a poverty-stricken and violent family living in a three-room apartment in a city housing project.

When he was ten months old his maternal grandmother and his mother's younger sister came to live with the family. But his father's father, who lived just round the corner, never set foot in the apartment after an epic fight just before Laing's birth, in which "Old Pa," then in his fifties, was thrashed and kicked out by his son, Laing's father. For years after this the old man's younger son, Laing's Uncle Jack, sought to even the score: "He'd knock on the door. He'd be let in. Not a word would be spoken. He would take his cap off and his jacket, keeping on his vest; he never rolled up his sleeves. My mother would push the furniture to the side and get out of the room quickly. I went behind the curtains.

*lang

© 1978 by Fred W. McDarrah

R. D. LAING

Then he and Dad would go at it. How many times did that fight take place? Each fight ended when Uncle Jack was down on the floor, couldn't get up, and called enough."

Laing remembers himself as "a very peculiar child" in whom the struggle against "mind control" began early, partly in reaction against the "hard physical beatings" his father gave him at the slightest hint of disobedience, so that at "about five" he was in a state of mental rebellion. "He beat me so hard that he disintegrated my body completely and I really thought he was going to destroy me. And I retreated into a dot . . . a point in space with no dimensions. And I was poised there, and I knew that he hadn't the slightest chance of affecting that. . . . So he never got me." He also completely disavowed his mother's pro-Franco, anti-Semitic views, and indeed had virtually no communication with his parents. "From as far back as I can remember, I tried to figure out what was going on between these people. If I believed one, I couldn't believe anyone else. Especially at the time when my mother, my mother's mother, and my mother's younger sister were all part of the same household. . . . I could not believe all of them, one of them, or none of them, entirely."

As a small boy, Laing was never allowed out alone and had almost no opportunity of mixing with other children until he went to school: "It was almost insufferably delightful. All those creatures like me to play with. And *girls* as well!" Laing has reacted strongly against the false puritanism of his parents' milieu and their repudiation of sex, which was shrouded in guilt and mystery: "I went to a boys' grammar school where there were no girls. At the age of sixteen,

I still had no idea about what we now call the facts of life. . . . My mother and I slept in one room in separate beds, and my father slept in another room. According to both of them, all sexual activity had ceased between them irrevocably before I was conceived. My mother and father still swear they do not know how I was conceived."

As a precocious and sensitive boy surrounded by the most hideous urban industrial squalor in Britain, Laing was determined to escape his origins through either artistic or intellectual achievement. He was interested in writing but was more obviously talented at music, and might well have become a professional pianist had not his father discouraged that aspiration. Instead he devoured all the books within his reach on psychology, philosophy, theology, and the history of ideas. He won a scholarship to a local grammar school, and from there matriculated at the University of Glasgow, studying medicine and graduating as a doctor specializing in psychiatry in 1951.

At that point Laing was conscripted into the army for two years' compulsory national service. His "intolerable" stint as an army psychiatrist confirmed the dislike he had already developed as a student for the prevailing approach to psychosis—the "scientific" approach, which he saw as heartlessly mechanized and bureaucratic, with a degrading tendency to regard the patient as a broken thing to be mended by electric shock treatment or tranquilizers. Laing's own quite different views continued to develop while he worked in the Glasgow Royal Mental Hospital in 1955 and taught in the Department of Psychological Medicine at the University of Glasgow (1953-1956). He then went to London to continue his research at the Freudian-oriented Tavistock Clinic (1956-1960). In the course of his training there in psychoanalysis, he was himself analyzed by Dr. Charles Rycroft, experiencing "the first lifting of the veil—the first detachment from the objects of consciousness in order to look at consciousness itself." In 1960 Laing joined the Tavistock Institute of Human Relations. He has retained his connection with the Institute and in 1960-1967 was also a fellow of the Foundations Fund for Research in Psychiatry, involving himself at the same time in several other institutions and activities.

The psychiatrist Anthony Storr, reviewing *The Facts of Life,* concluded that Laing "is very intelligent, and I suspect that his earliest years were a desert of loneliness, with no one, inside or outside the family, with whom he could establish intimacy." This deprivation left him passionately concerned with questions of birth and

growing up, and precipitated the agonized quest for identity which is his central concern and the basis of all his work. In the course of this existential quest for his own being, Laing has rejected the narrowly empiricist study of external behavior. Instead, he gives both the subtleties and the distortions of human experience their due by talking about what goes on in people's minds and what people do to each other's minds. Dr. Liam Hudson observed in 1972 that "over the last five years, his books have probably had more impact on the minds of intelligent British students than has the rest of psychology put together. . . . His conception of psychology is so remote from the one I pursued in Cambridge that, comparing them, it is hard to believe that they can have even a verbal label—'psychology'—in common. They address different problems, and do so by different routes. One aligns itself with existentialism and phenomenology, attempts to describe the influence of our minds on our actions. . . . The other stems . . . from the English empiricism of Locke and Hume; it sets itself to formulate laws of behaviour rather than of experience."

And Liam Hudson recalls that it was with "delight" and a "sense of revelation" that he himself read Laing's first book *The Divided Self: A Study of Sanity and Madness* (1960), a study of schizoid and schizophrenic persons whose "basic purpose is to make madness, and the process of going mad, comprehensible." Its originality is in examining these forms of insanity in existential terms. Instead of treating schizophrenia as a disease, Laing regards it as "a special strategy that a person invents in order to live in an unlivable situation." In Laing's terms, the schizoid person is an "outsider," estranged both from himself and from society, unable to experience himself or other people as real and substantial. According to Laing, such a person lacks "primary ontological security"; he fears the disintegration and engulfment of the very core of his being, and his abnormal behavior is designed to protect this inner self. Fearing both the destructive effect of the external world upon himself and his own destructive effect upon the world, he develops a "false" self with which to confront that world. Laing writes: "It is only when one is able to gather from the individual himself the history of his self, and not what a psychiatric history in these circumstances usually is, the history of the false-self system, that his psychosis becomes explicable."

Laing stresses that "no one *has* schizophrenia, like having a cold. The patient has not 'got' schizophrenia. He is schizophrenic." The idea that the source of emotional ills might be not within the mind but outside, in the molds that interpersonal relationships force people into, goes back to the American psychiatrist Harry Stack Sullivan. Laing, quoting Sullivan's assertion that the psychotic is more than anything else "simply human," goes on to insist that the therapist "*must* have the plasticity to transpose himself into another strange and even alien view of the world. In this act, he draws on his own psychotic possibilities without forgoing his sanity. Only thus can he arrive at an understanding which must not be purely intellectual but an insight into 'how the patient is experiencing himself and the world.' "

The book received the sort of mixed critical reaction that has greeted all of Laing's books. As Eugene Kennedy observed: "Behaviour therapists who stick to looking at man from the outside may find this book far from congenial. They will label it philosophy or poetry but not science." And Laing's ideas were indeed dismissed by some critics as "existential flights of fancy." But for Marshall Berman *The Divided Self* "vibrates with the excitement of discovery, a discovery that resonates far beyond the hospital gates. Laing is steeped in modern literature and existentialist philosophy. He is aware, and he makes us aware, how much of our whole modern sensibility and awareness is rooted in the radical doubt and anxiety that permeates schizophrenics' whole lives; he evokes the alienation they feel with a vividness that strikes a sympathetic chord in all of us." The same critic drew attention to Laing's "enormous literary gifts . . . his feeling for a patient's language and imagery, his ability to bring an individual human being concretely to life, the clarity and intensity of his style." As Alan Tyson wrote, "it is not perhaps surprising, in view of the widespread distribution of schizoid character traits, that the clinical material of *The Divided Self* evoked a cry of recognition from thousands of readers who felt that the dimensions of their own sense of alienation had been charted for the first time."

Geoffrey Gorer has summed up the impact of Laing's first two books by saying that "it seemed as though a young man was going to make a significant contribution to the dying ranks of British psychiatry. These books were not scholarly in the academic sense, but they did produce new insight into the genesis of some forms of schizophrenia: they moved the debate on the causation of this form of psychosis from the genetic and chemical to the social, and above all the familial setting in which these symptoms could be evoked." Much of the first book discussed the struggle within "the divided self" with unaccept-

ed or unacceptable parts of the personality, but *The Self and Others: Further Studies in Sanity and Madness* (1961) is much more concerned with the ways in which interaction with others can produce pathology.

Laing here makes a deeper exploration of unconscious fantasy, and illustrates his thesis not only from clinical experience but from literature —for instance with studies of the blend of dream, imagination, and reality in Dostoevsky's *Crime and Punishment* and an examination of the murderer Raskolnikov's relations with his mother and sister. His central thesis derives from Gregory Bateson's now classic "double bind" theory: that schizophrenia is a state of mind having its origins in a situation where a person is caught up in a tangle of paradoxical demands in which he cannot possibly do the right thing. A common example is that of a child in a family where there is a power struggle between the parents and the child is faced with impossibly contradictory injunctions; the deranged language that the schizophrenic develops is a logical response to this situation. The book was bitterly attacked by N.N. Holland, who deplored Laing's neglect of "the genetic and chemical factors obviously present" in schizophrenia, and "much more irresponsibly, the agony, nightmare and even suicide so many victims suffer." Marshall Berman also found the book unsatisfactory, and suggested that Laing's indictment of society might strike some readers as "paranoid, even schizophrenic." But many critics welcomed the work, and praised it as a subtle and humane study.

The same theories are pursued and illustrated in *Sanity, Madness and the Family* (1964), written in collaboration with Aaron Esterson. It is a study of eleven women, all of whom had been diagnosed as schizophrenic, and described as deluded, hallucinated, subject to disorders of thought and feeling. Replacing the clinical perspective with a social one, the authors had investigated the women's families rather than their illness, seeking to show that their apparently irrational behavior was in fact entirely sensible given the untenable circumstances in which they had been placed. Again, some critics were delighted by the book, some utterly rejected it, and some sat on the fence, like the reviewer in the *Times Literary Supplement* who called this "a most valuable and stimulating piece of research," but doubted whether the authors' theories were "enough to account for the whole phenomenology of schizophrenia." In their preface to the book's second edition, Laing and Esterson say that they do not dismiss the growing evidence that schizophrenia may be essentially genetic and hereditary, but repeat the question which they say is at the heart of their book: "Are the experience and behaviour that psychiatrists take as symptoms and signs of schizophrenia more socially intelligible than has come to be supposed?"

As Liam Hudson points out, Laing's thought is much more in the European than in the British empiricist tradition, and is greatly indebted to Sartrean existentialism. Convinced of the urgent intellectual importance of Sartre's ideas, but aware that the French writer was known in Britain only by his early works, Laing joined with his fellow-psychiatrist David Cooper to write *Reason and Violence: A Decade of Sartre's Philosophy 1950-1960* (1964). This is a summary of three major works, none of which had at that time been translated into English—*Saint Genet, Questions de Méthode,* and *Critique de la Raison Dialectique.* In his foreword Sartre praises the authors' existential approach to mental illness, expressing his own agreement with their belief that mental illness is a *lived* experience which cannot possibly be understood by a merely *external* approach: "Like you . . . I regard mental illness as the way out that the free organism . . . invents in order to be able to live through an intolerable situation." Henri Peyre praised it as a valuable but "arduous book for philosophers, sociologists, and psychiatrists, and for others who hope to keep abreast of the most pregnant thinking of their time." In *Interpersonal Perception* (1966), written with Herbert Phillipson and A. Russell Lee, Laing discusses techniques, presenting a theory and method of research.

From 1962 to 1965 Laing directed the Langham Clinic, a Jungian psychotherapy center in London, but left after a disagreement over his use of psychedelic drugs. He was also a fellow of the Tavistock Institute of Medical Psychology in 1963-1964, and in 1964-1967 was principal investigator for the Schizophrenia and Family Research Unit of the Tavistock Institute of Human Relations. Meanwhile, in 1964, Laing and his associates founded the Philadelphia Association, a charity concerned to develop practical strategies of social intervention in the light of the theories of Laing and other "anti-psychiatrists." The Association's best-known achievement was the establishment of a therapeutic community at Kingsley Hall in London, where doctors and patients lived together without hierarchical distinctions. This utopian experiment broke up after five years, though offshoots from it survived in the London area. Laing's ideal is a multiplicity of communities where patients, instead of having their symptoms treated with tranquilizers or electric shock, would be free to "go

through" their madness, supported by sympathetic companions who had themselves made the terrifying journey and come out healed. For he has increasingly come to feel that living through psychosis can be a healing and enlarging experience.

The belief that "madness can be a breakthrough, not a breakdown" led Laing to an interest in mysticism and the transcendental, and thence to experiments with hallucinogenic drugs as a means of accelerating transcendental "trips" to the "inner self" for both his patients and himself. His most direct account of personal hallucinogenic experience is the long prose poem "The Bird of Paradise," rich in autobiographical allusions from his Glasgow days onwards, and with lyrical accounts of his visions: "I have seen the Bird of Paradise, she has spread herself before me, and I shall never be the same again. . . . The Life I am trying to grasp is the me that is trying to grasp it."

This poem was published at the end of *The Politics of Experience* (1967), a volume of essays in which he takes a decisive step towards a much more radical and more political vision of modern society as a system that tries to clamp a straitjacket of conformity on every child that is born. From Laing's early view of the schizophrenic as a victim of his own disturbed family, it is only a short step to seeing him as a victim of the perverse values of the society he lives in. This is the characteristic attitude behind all Laing's later work, which reflects an increasingly urgent concern with the sickness of our whole civilization and its alienating and destructive effect upon the individual. The schizophrenic comes to be seen simply as someone who has been unable to suppress his normal instincts and conform to an abnormal society.

Laing writes: "There is little conjunction of truth and social 'reality'. Around us are pseudo-events, to which we adjust with a false consciousness adapted to see these events as true and real, and even as beautiful. In the society of men the truth resides now less in what things are than in what they are not. Our social realities are so ugly if seen in the light of exiled truth, and beauty is almost no longer possible if it is not a lie." In arguing out his basic idea that "humanity is estranged from its authentic possibilities," Laing adopts a prophetic, evangelical, even messianic tone that many critics have found strident and extreme, especially in such famous passages as that in which he declares, "We are all murderers and prostitutes—no matter to what culture, society, class, nation one belongs, no matter how normal, moral or mature one takes oneself to be." Laing for his part complains that his critics ignore "my actual scientific writing . . . [and] the presentations to learned societies where, in a more technical way, I present the material that in a non-technical, non-jargon way I put out in *The Politics of Experience.* That is not meant to be a scientific report in the manner of science."

The Politics of the Family (1971) is a collection of talks which again consider the political aspects of a subject not usually discussed in those terms. Laing's point is that the family is an interpersonal power structure in which the personality is defined and may be deformed by the demands made on it. The critical response was on the whole a disappointed one: Richard Sennett's strongest impression was "that Laing has substituted an easy rhetoric of accusation and condemnation for the struggle to understand people's feelings. . . . Laing can no longer write clearly unless he is showing someone being hurt."

Laing had meanwhile produced a book of a rather different kind in *Knots* (1970). Here he continues to deal with civil war within the family, expressing his views not in discursive prose but in a series of dramatic dialogues or prose poems. Each "knot" is a tangled human situation "that will be vividly, and painfully, familiar to us all," one of those paradoxical patterns of possessiveness, jealousy, or fear that thwart feeling and communication and lead to frustration and sometimes ultimately to madness. Sometimes people are shown tying themselves into knots by circular logic:

There must be something the matter with him
because he would not be acting as he does
unless there was
therefore he is acting as he is
because there is something the matter with him.

In the dialogues the participants are given the names of those clumsy nursery-rhyme characters Jack and Jill:

Jill You put me in the wrong
Jack I am not putting you in the wrong
Jill You put me in the wrong for thinking you put me in the wrong
Jack Forgive me
Jill No
Jack I'll never forgive you for not forgiving me.

"Though the tone is playful and childlike," wrote J.S. Gordon, "the logic is painful and inexorable, and the meaning is many-leveled." Not only did *Knots* become a best seller, like most of Laing's books, but it was also very successfully adapted for performance. As a radio play it was produced by Martin Esslin in 1973 with music by the composer Humphrey Searle. A stage version was conceived and directed by Edward Petherbridge, a founder-member of the Actors Company and was a Fringe hit of the 1973 Edinburgh Festival, whence it graduated to London and New York. Celandine Productions then made a film version with the Actors Company, and this was shown on television and in movie theatres.

Do You Love Me?, a similar "Entertainment in Conversation and Verse," followed in 1976. The conversations are again knotty little exchanges between people, often a rather callous man and a rather anxious woman, who are quite unable to achieve any genuine communication with each other. The verses are often complaints about the domestic trap, and the poet Dannie Abse has suggested that "the performance they require is the backing of cabaret music when they should be sung by some husky-voiced girl showing a lot of silk leg." That is precisely the treatment some of them received in Edward Petherbridge's 1977 stage adaptation.

Laing has continued to publish poetry, including "Three Sonnets" in the *Times Literary Supplement* (July 29, 1977). There is a strong poetic and mythopoeic element also in his partly autobiographical meditations on birth and identity in *The Facts of Life* (1976). The book was described in its own blurb as "rich, disorderly, suggestive, inconclusive and humane," and this seemed fair comment to Anthony Storr, who went on: "Evidently [Laing] feels that to impose form and coherence upon his message would be to distort it. But it would be a disaster if the author of those splendid early books . . . were forever to abandon the attempt to communicate with his fellows in ordinary terms."

The author has five children by his first wife and two by his present wife, Jutta. Laing is a vegetarian, who practices several forms of yoga, and spent most of 1971 and early 1972 meditating under Buddhist and Hindu spiritual masters in Ceylon, India, and Japan. In the autumn of 1972 he made an extensive speaking tour of American college campuses, chiefly to raise funds for the Philadelphia Association, of which he has been chairman since its foundation.

As "psychiatric theoretician, political philosopher and personal guru," Laing seems to J.S. Gordon a figure of the dimensions of "Freud forty years ago." Alan Tyson offers a somewhat different estimate: "It seems to me that the mythopoeic element in Laing is the source both of his diffuse appeal and of the difficulty that is often experienced in getting him into focus. The views that are implied by the impetus of much of Laing's writing (though I am left in some doubt how far Laing still holds them). . . . seem to me romantic myths which contain a strong wishful element and have just enough truth in them to prevent that distressing fact from being easily recognized." Geoffrey Gray has gone further, suggesting that "Laing's literary productions . . . reflect not only the exaggerated view he holds of himself as a visionary, but his utter contempt for ordinary people." But Bruno Bettelheim writes: "As long as psychoanalysis gives men like . . . [Laing] the courage of their convictions; as long as in addition to its 'orthodox' majority it continues to breed such heretics, permits them to continue as psychoanalysts, all is well with psychoanalysis. . . . by responding to the challenge that men like these hurl against the official doctrine . . . psychoanalysis itself will remain alive, because it will be able to reform itself."

PRINCIPAL WORKS: The Divided Self: A Study of Sanity and Madness, 1960; The Self and Others: Further Studies in Sanity and Madness 1961 (revised as Self and Others, 1969); (with D.G. Cooper) Reason and Violence: A Decade of Sartre's Philosophy 1950-1960, 1964; (with Aaron Esterson) Sanity, Madness, and the Family, 1964; (with H. Phillipson and R. Lee) Interpersonal Perception: A Theory and a Method of Research, 1966; The Politics of Experience, 1967; Knots, 1970; The Politics of the Family, 1971; The Facts of Life, 1976; Do You Love Me?, 1976; Conversations with Adam and Natasha, 1978.

ABOUT: Barnett, M. People Not Psychiatry, 1973; Boyers, R. and Orrill, R. (eds.) Laing and Anti-Psychiatry, 1972; Cohen D. (ed.) Psychologists on Psychology, 1977; Collier, A. R.D. Laing: The Philosophy and Politics of Psychotherapy, 1977; Cranston, M. (ed.) The New Left, 1971; Current Biography, 1974; Diehl, D. Supertalk, 1974; Evans, R.I. R.D. Laing, 1976; Friedenberg, E.Z. R.D. Laing, 1973; Hudson, L. The Cult of the Fact, 1972; International Who's Who, 1977-78; Who's Who, 1978; Who's Who in America, 1976-1977. Periodicals—Atlantic January 1971; Book Week July 9, 1967; British Journal of Psychiatry 115 1969; Canadian Forum November 1969; Christian Science Monitor November 19, 1970; Commonweal September 25, 1970; Critic May 1970; Encounter August 1968, February 1972; Esquire January 1972; Essays in Criticism January 1976; Guardian March 27, 1973; November 18, 1976; Life October 8, 1971; Nation May 11, 1970; New Republic May 13, 1967; New Society May 5, 1977; New Statesman November 21, 1969; New York Review of Books February 11, 1971; New York Times Book Review February 22, 1970; December 13, 1970; October 3, 1971; May 30, 1976; New Yorker March 14, 1970; Newsweek December 18, 1972; Observer (London) September 20, 1970; September 16, 1973; April 10, 1977; Partisan Review 1 1974; PMLA March 1976; Saturday Review May 20, 1967; Studies in Black Literature Spring 1976; Studies in Short Fiction Summer 1976; Time February 3, 1967; February 7, 1969; Times Literary Supplement July 2, 1964; July 23, 1964; January 25, 1974; February 14, 1975; November 26, 1976; Vogue September 15, 1969; Yale Review December 1964.

LAMANTIA, PHILIP (October 23, 1927–), American poet, was born in San Francisco and attended elementary and high schools there. He was only fifteen when his poems began to appear in the magazine View, edited in New York by Charles Henri Ford. On the strength of these precocious poems he was welcomed as a surrealist by André Breton, the leader of the movement, who was then living in the United States, and became a contributor to the New York surrealist magazine VVV. At seventeen Lamantia left school to become assistant editor of View. A much-quoted example of Lamantia's early work is "I Am Coming":

> I am following her to the wavering moon
> to a bridge by the long waterfront
> to valleys of beautiful arson
> to flowers dead in a mirror of love
> to men eating wild minutes from a clock
> to hands playing in celestial pockets
> and to that dark room beside a castle
> of youthful voices singing to the moon.
>
> When the sun comes up she will live at a sky
> covered with sparrow's blood
> and wrapped in robes of lost decay.

A collection of the poems Lamantia wrote between 1942 and 1950 was published many years later as Touch of the Marvelous (1966). Tom Clark found them reminiscent of Poe and Hart Crane, of the French surrealists, and above all, in their "mercurial vividness of imagination," of Rimbaud. "This is a very brash and desperate poetry," Clark wrote, "that discovers illumination in the infernal image of violence and pain—or rather recognizes no distinction between illumination and the infernal. . . . The obsessive repetition of images and scenes of violence in so many of them explores dark excitements of the unconscious. The odd correspondences of cruelty and amorousness throw light on a region of torment and delight where no moral structure can exist at all."

With his first published book, Erotic Poems, which appeared when he was only nineteen, Lamantia renounced his affiliation with the New York surrealists, though he remained "essentially a surrealist" in his poetry and in his view of life. Evalyn Shapiro reviewed Erotic Poems rather harshly in Poetry: the reader would find, she warned, "shattered mirrors, the deep twilight of bodies, a nude girl repairing revolvers 'for her criminal midget,' hair, bellies, and so on." She allowed that there were "some quite good images, verses and whole poems in the second-hand surrealist manner." This review, it should

LAMANTIA

PHILIP LAMANTIA

Gerard Malanga

The obsession with pain and cruelty in Lamantia's work gave way in the middle 1950s to a more affirmative imagery, a new preoccupation with human and spiritual love. This is evident in *Ekstasis* (1959), in which, according to Robert S. Sward, Lamantia deals, usually surrealistically, with "religious worship, vision (or revelation), love, damnation, and other themes appropriate to what is essentially religious verse. There is, however, nothing timid, predictable or static about it. That is, Lamantia attempts to use the form, the poem . . . as a means for achieving, for expressing and communicating the discoveries, the revelations that he says are his intention." Sward thought that Lamantia often failed in this intention because of "a simple lack of technique, or control," but that in "Christ," his "most exciting poem," he achieves the "ekstatic breakthrough" that he seeks:

Glory crasht on time . Angel tongues, MAGI •
and burden of the stars . In the FIRE
elliptical HEARTS CONVEX . Impossible
  beauty
CHILD   MARIA   WOMBED   SAVIOR

be said, appeared with an admonitory footnote by Kenneth Burke: "The proportions of this review are not quite satisfactory. There is no mention of the many incidental observations, which I liked greatly. . . ." Samuel Charters, discussing the collection in *Contemporary Poets,* praised its "lyric physicality," its "closeness of physical contact":

The crash of your heart
beating its way through a fever of fish
is heard in every crowd of that thirsty tomorrow
and your trip ends in the mask of my candle-lit
  hair.

> (from "There Are Many
> Pathways to the Garden")

During the late 1940s and the 1950s Lamantia became one of the most influential of the Beat poets, and played an important part in the "San Francisco Renaissance," though in fact he was away from the city a great deal—increasingly a wanderer. In 1953 he was initiated into the Washo Indian peyote rites in Nevada, and he then spent three years in Mexico, living for some time with the Cora Indians of Nayarit. After this experience, Lamantia disposed of all his unpublished earlier verse, though this was later resurrected as *Destroyed Works* (1962). Richard Howard could not decide "whether these litanies were produced by a program of conscious cruelty or the boundless jazz of a drug fantasy, nor can I see that it matters: their effect is that of The Throes—straining for, in, and from ecstasy."

Paul O'Neill described Lamantia as he was at thirty-one in a largely hostile article about the Beats in *Life* magazine, subsequently reprinted in Thomas Parkinson's *A Casebook on the Beat* (1961). O'Neill said that Lamantia, who "can be a delightful conversationalist," was one of the "leading exponents of a Beat cult which believes true poetic effects are best achieved through an 'ecstatic illumination' induced by what Lamantia calls 'the heroic medicines': heroin, opium, mescaline, marijuana, peyote. Lamantia is a tiny, erratic and gentle being with dark hair cropped short along his forehead and a pale, delicate, saintlike face. He has been a heroin addict, although he professes to have kicked the habit by smoking opium for nine months. He is a Catholic and an impassioned student of theology who has convinced himself that the use of drugs to obtain visions does not conflict with the canons of the Church. . . . he lives in fleabag hotels on money doled out by his widowed mother."

A volume of selected poems appeared in 1967, and in 1970 Lamantia published *The Blood of the Air.* John R. Carpenter wrote that Lamantia "has much baggage which comes from wide travel and eclectic reading," and thought that "many readers will not be interested in Lamantia's rites, sacredness, secretness, magic, shrines, castles, and dragons; but I think the freedom he has acquired . . . is in the interest of us all." This freedom of style seemed to Carpenter the most original feature of this "strikingly original book," but he says "there is also an impressive coherence in the personality of the author; this might appear paradoxical since surrealism is often thought to be incoherent in its treatment of reality, yet its aim has always been to make contact with the subconscious and to abolish the inner censorship which forms walls inside the mind. Lamantia's 'beat' poetry of the fifties often struggled for emotional effect. The freedom of the new book comes, I think, from his abandoning this struggle, which wrenched his personality into an alien and conventional form":

> Trees and nonsense bend their songs
> Lips of clouds and kites of pain
> I'm at a shower of windows
> All the houses are made of rain

Lamantia has lived in New York and in the American Midwest, in Tangier and Paris. From 1963 to 1968 he lived mainly in Andalusia, Spain, and in Italy and Greece. Samuel Charters says that Lamantia's work was one of the forces that led to the burst of surrealist poetry in the United States in the 1950s and 1960s, and Eric Mottram notes that "his poems have retained the essential surrealist quality of revealing inner life through explosive images and ecstatic vision." Lamantia himself writes in *Contemporary Poets:* "I understand the power of poetry as the maximum volatile expression of Imagination, a *central power,* relating all levels of conscious and unconscious thought and being. I believe in poetry as a means of unqualified individual liberation. I believe in the poetry of primal melody and the revelation of the mysteries of cosmic being."

PRINCIPAL WORKS: Erotic Poems, 1946; Ekstasis, 1959; Destroyed Works (containing Hypodermic Light, Mantic Notebook, Still Poems, Spansule), 1962; Touch of the Marvelous, 1966; Selected Poems, 1943-1966, 1967; (with Charles Bukowski and Harold Norse) Penguin Modern Poets 13, 1969; The Blood of the Air, 1970.

ABOUT: Parkinson, T. (ed.) A Casebook on the Beat, 1961; Penguin Companion to Literature 3, 1971; Tyler, P. *introduction to* Touch of the Marvelous, 1966; Vinson, J. (ed.) Contemporary Poets, 1975. *Periodicals*—Life November 30, 1959; Poetry April 1947, July 1960, June 1963, May 1967, June 1972.

"LANGE, JOHN." *See* CRICHTON, MICHAEL

LASH, JOSEPH P. (December 2, 1909–), American biographer and journalist, was born in New York City, the oldest of the four children of Russian immigrant parents, Samuel and Mary (Avchin) Lash. He grew up in Morningside Heights, where his parents owned a grocery store. His father died when Joseph Lash was nine and after that, he told an interviewer, it was "rather grim. . . . My mother worked all day in the store, so there wasn't any strong parental hand to guide and counsel us. . . . I was part of the street. There were Irish and Hungarian kids, and a few Jewish kids like myself. I was the smallest guy in the group. It wasn't the easiest life."

Lash was educated at De Witt Clinton High School, where he became book review editor of the *Clinton News,* and at the College of the City of New York, where he was associate editor of *Campus* and where, in 1929, he joined the Socialist party. CCNY gave him his B.A. in English in 1931, and he went on to Columbia University. Lash left Columbia with an M.A. in 1932, in the thick of the Depression. Like thousands with similar qualifications, he could find no work. He campaigned vigorously that year for the presidential candidacy of Norman Thomas, became secretary of the Student League for Industrial Democracy, and edited its journal, *Student Outlook.* He also joined the Association of Unemployed College Alumni and Professional People, rising rapidly to the chairmanship of that body. Lash became increasingly militant in his opposition to the capitalist system, which he held responsible for the miseries and tragedies of the Depression. "I got swept up by the revolution," he has said. "It took me several years to realize that Roosevelt represented a democratic alternative."

During the 1930s, Lash's prominence as a leader of radical youth was such that Richard H. Rovere speaks of him as "the Tom Hayden or Mark Rudd of his generation." In December 1935, when a number of Socialist and Communist youth organizations buried their differences and established the American Student Union, Lash emerged as national secretary of the new coalition, retaining that post until 1939. His first book, apart from small publications for the ASU, was *War, Our Heritage* (1936), a history of student activism and the peace movement written in collaboration with James A. Wechsler, later editor of the New York *Post.*

Lash began to reassess his ideological allegiances during the mid-1930s. In 1937 he resigned from the Socialist party and came close to throwing in his lot with the Communists. The Nazi-Soviet pact of August 1939 disillusioned

JOSEPH P. LASH

© 1979 by Jill Krementz

him, however, as it did many idealistic American radicals, and led to the deep divisions within the ASU that precipitated his resignation in 1940.

Shortly before this, late in 1939, Lash had been called to Washington to testify before the House Committee on Un-American Activities on Communist influence in American youth groups. It was then that he met Eleanor Roosevelt, a sponsor of the American Youth Congress, on the cabinet of which Lash was serving. Mrs. Roosevelt, herself disillusioned by then with the Popular Front, was much impressed by Lash's testimony and the frankness with which he revealed his divided loyalties and ideological doubts. They began a friendship which lasted until her death, and changed the course of Lash's life.

During the next few years, he worked closely with Mrs. Roosevelt in a vain attempt to organize a liberal caucus within the American Youth Congress and the ASU. In 1940, during President Roosevelt's campaign for re-election to a third term in office, Lash served as director of the Democratic National Committee's youth division, and in 1940-1942 as general secretary of the International Student Service, which assisted foreign students visiting the United States. These activities outraged the more radical of his former associates, one of whom called Lash the "bought and paid for elder statesman of the student movement." (This did not prevent the right-wing columnist Westbrook Pegler from attacking him as an unsavory radical, typical of Mrs. Roosevelt's favorites.)

In 1942 Lash entered the United States Army Air Forces as a private. He served in the South

Pacific, received the Air Medal, and was discharged in 1945 with the rank of second lieutenant. Throughout the war he had corresponded regularly with Mrs. Roosevelt and with her close friend Trude von Adam Wenzel Pratt, who had helped him in his efforts to salvage the liberal elements in the American Youth Congress. Lash, whose first marriage (1935-1940) had ended in divorce, was married to Trude Pratt in 1944.

After the war, in 1946, Lash joined Mrs. Roosevelt and others in founding the important anti-Communist liberal organization Americans for Democratic Action. He was director of ADA's New York City branch from 1946 to 1948, at the same time working in Democratic reform politics in the city. In 1948-1950 he was assistant to Elliott Roosevelt, among other things helping him to prepare a two-volume edition of President Roosevelt's letters.

Lash joined the New York *Post* in 1950, writing for that liberal newspaper as United Nations correspondent and specialist in foreign affairs until 1961, when he became an editorial writer. From 1964 to 1966 he was associate editor of the *Post*'s editorial page, under his old colleague James Wechsler. His work at the U.N. led to a friendship with the Secretary-General, Dag Hammarskjöld, whose authorized biographer he became. *Dag Hammarskjold: Custodian of the Brushfire Peace* (1961), was, as Hammarskjöld had insisted, mainly an account of his work at the U.N., dealing only briefly with his early life. It includes an epilogue written after Hammarskjöld's death in 1961. Some reviewers objected that, as one put it, Lash "omits his subject's failures or glosses over them," but most praised it as a faithful and highly readable portrait of a selfless and tireless worker for world peace.

Mrs. Roosevelt died in 1962, and Lash recalled their relationship, especially its early stages in 1939-1942, in *Eleanor Roosevelt: A Friend's Memoir*. Dore Schary wrote that Lash had "kept voluminous personal records ... [and] researched his subject with scholarly thoroughness. Only once or twice does his affection lapse into sugary sentimentality." Trude Lash added to the book a moving account of Mrs. Roosevelt's last days.

It came as no surprise, therefore, when Lash was designated Mrs. Roosevelt's official biographer, and given sole access to his mentor's files in the Franklin D. Roosevelt Library at Hyde Park, New York. Working alone in an old house beside the Hudson, he spent three winters going through her papers to produce his two-volume biography. The first volume, dealing with Eleanor Roosevelt's family history, childhood, youth, and marriage, appeared in 1971 as *Eleanor and Franklin.*

The book was almost universally and comprehensively admired. Richard Rovere called it "exemplary biography . . . perfectly shaped and splendidly written from start to finish. The prose is lucid, spare, and never obtrusive. It is clear from the outset that this is the work of a close friend and admirer, but Lash can nowhere be faulted for sycophancy or indulgence. . . . His portraits of turn-of-the-century life in the Hudson Valley, of early twentieth-century New York, and of Washington during the years of the two world wars are superb. So are his renderings of the dozens of characters who moved in and out of the Roosevelts' lives. But his focus is always sharply on his subject. . . . [This] is biography in the grand manner." *Eleanor and Franklin,* a Book-of-the-Month Club selection in 1971, brought Lash the Francis Parkman Prize of the Society of American Historians, and both the Pulitzer Prize and the National Book Award for biography.

Eleanor: The Years Alone, dealing with Mrs. Roosevelt's life after her husband's death, followed in 1972. It also was a Book-of-the-Month Club choice, and it was scarcely less warmly received than its predecessor, though it was not entirely without its critics. Frank Annunziata in *America,* for example, wrote that the book "contains inordinate direct quotation and [provides] . . . little beyond a triumphant citation of Mrs. Roosevelt's various activities." Most reviewers, however, shared the view of the *New Yorker's* critic, who found it "a no less remarkable achievement" than the first volume in its lucidity and sensitivity, and "a good deal more detailed and analytical in its treatment of public affairs. . . . The author's understanding of the movements [Mrs. Roosevelt] supported is as rich as his understanding of the remarkable human being he celebrates."

Roosevelt and Churchill, 1939-1941 (1976) reexamines the attitudes and policies of the American and British leaders during the years when the United States stood uneasily on the brink of intervention in another European war. It seemed to James Joll that Lash had "written an excellent account, full of shrewd personal and political insights and based on a real command of the sources and an ability to organize his material into a continuously interesting narrative. Much of the story is familiar, but Mr. Lash has added some telling new details from the archives at Hyde Park and in the British Public Record Office. . . . His book not only brings out the difference of temperament between Roosevelt and Churchill, it also tells one much about

the difference between the American and British political systems, between Presidential and Cabinet government." Arthur Schlesinger agreed, calling this "a splendid work—incisive in its analysis, compelling in its narrative, sensitive in its judgments. It is quite worthy of its protagonists—and what more can one possibly say?" It brought Lash the Samuel Eliot Morison Award in 1977.

Mrs. Lash, who came to the United States from Germany in 1931, is a director of the Citizens Committee for Children. The Lashes have a son, Jonathan, and Mrs. Lash also has three children by her previous marriage to Eliot D. Pratt. Joseph Lash enjoys walking, swimming, and fishing. He has maintained his interest in Democratic reform politics in New York, and is a member of the Tilden Democratic Club.

PRINCIPAL WORKS: (with James A. Wechsler) War, Our Heritage, 1936; Dag Hammarskjold: Custodian of the Brushfire Peace, 1961; Eleanor Roosevelt: A Friend's Memoir, 1964; Eleanor and Franklin: The Story of Their Relationship Based on Eleanor Roosevelt's Private Papers, 1971; Eleanor: The Years Alone, 1972; Roosevelt and Churchill, 1939-1941, 1976. *As editor*—From the Diaries of Felix Frankfurter, 1975.

ABOUT: Contemporary Authors 17-20 1st revision, 1976; Current Biography, 1972; Who's Who in America, 1974-1975. *Periodicals*—Atlantic November 1, 1971; Book World October 10, 1971; Commentary February 1972; National Review December 3, 1971; February 4, 1977; New Republic October 16, 1971; January 22, 1977; New York Post March 31, 1966; New York Review of Books November 18, 1971; New York Times May 2, 1972; New York Times Book Review October 17, 1971; July 30, 1972; October 24, 1976; New Yorker October 16, 1971; Saturday Review October 16, 1971; August 19, 1972; Time November 29, 1971; Yale Review March 1972.

"LATHEN, EMMA" (pseudonym of Mary Jane Latsis and Martha Hennissart, who write also as "R. B. Dominic"), American detective story writers, met when they were graduate students at Harvard and discovered a mutual enthusiasm for mystery stories. They have been writing them in collaboration ever since, at the same time carrying on their business careers in Boston. Mary Jane Latsis is an attorney, Martha Hennissart an economic analyst; they have suppressed more detailed information about themselves, aware that potential clients might be discouraged by the prospect of finding their business affairs scrutinized by John Putnam Thatcher.

Thatcher, the unorthodox hero of the Lathen books, is senior vice-president of the Sloan Guaranty Trust—the world's third largest commercial bank and "a jewel in the crown of Wall Street." Seeking only to protect the bank's investments, Thatcher is drawn with welcome regularity into the investigation of crime and potential crime. A courtly and silver-haired widower in his sixties, he is fit, intelligent, and a highly perceptive and unillusioned observer of human nature—"a man," according to the *New Yorker,* "of great charm, bottomless suspicion, and Euclidean squareness." He has another asset in his shrewd and efficient secretary Miss Corsa (whose fan mail, it is said, rivals her employer's).

Thatcher made his debut in *Banking on Death* (1961), in which he investigates an unusual trust fund and a "sound and well-clued murder." Anthony Boucher was pleased to meet this "attractively urbane sleuth," and thought that, though "addicts of violent action may be bored," the "financial involutions" of the case were "clearly and absorbingly presented." Esther Howard found the story marred a little by one obviously planted clue, but otherwise "very nicely and authentically told," and Frances Iles decided rather sniffily that it was "head and shoulders above the usual dreary and deadly portentous American female crime-writers syndicate. . . . a good story, well told, with a good background of banking and big business, good characterisation, and even signs of humour."

There was no doubt about the humor, and even wit, in Lathen's "more than worthy second novel," *A Place for Murder.* The place in question is a well-heeled section of Connecticut, where, as one critic put it, "farming is an amusing way of creating tax losses and murder becomes entangled with such local ceremonies as a civic parade and a dog show." D.B. Hughes was reminded of Josephine Tey and "the best British mystery writers," and called Emma Lathen "the most intriguing mystery-writing woman in our country in at least a decade."

The Sloan employs Clarence Fortinbras, a virtuoso of the adding machine, to look into the shaky financial structure of National Calculating in *Accounting for Murder* (1964). When Fortinbras is found throttled with the cord of his own machine, John Putnam Thatcher must learn the reason why. "Of all books in the general category of mystery," wrote a reviewer in the *Times Literary Supplement,* "the rarest now are the true detective stories, the properly clued intellectual puzzles. . . . In this now recondite field the best currently available is . . . *Accounting for Murder.*"

After an interlude in Detroit in *Murder Makes the Wheels Go 'Round* (1966), Thatcher finds himself involved in the civil rights movement in *Death Shall Overcome,* when a black tycoon tries for a seat on the all-white New York Stock Exchange. Murder is done, shots are fired in West-

chester, and Thatcher winds up on his knees, singing with unaccustomed and undignified gusto the battle-hymns of integration. Boucher in his review wrote that Thatcher "is one of the very few important series detectives to enter the field in the 1960s—a completely civilized and urbane man, whose charm is as remarkable as his acumen. Miss Lathen's . . . scalpel has never been sharper nor her wit more adroit than in this delightfully logical extrapolation of the civil-rights issue to the problem of racial discrimination against a multimillionaire, and Thatcher is splendid in the involuntary and uncomfortable role of a hero of The Movement. Here is (on several levels) a wonderfully rational and pointed novel."

Trade relations between the United States and the Soviet Union are tackled in *Murder Against the Grain* (1967), called "a charming book of classic quality," while in *A Stitch in Time* (1968) Emma Lathen takes her scalpel to the American medical profession, leaving one reviewer with the "burgeoning suspicion" that she is a writer with a social conscience. *When in Greece* (1969) takes Thatcher to the land of lost gods and godlike men, where the Colonels' coup threatens (among other things) a Sloan investment of thirty million dollars. Annette Grant concluded on this evidence that Lathen is "a masterful plotter, an elegant stylist, a comic genius and an old-fashioned purist who never sacrifices logic for surprise effect. . . . This is one of Miss Lathen's funniest and most mischievous books—a delightful and civilized entertainment that leaves no sacred cow unturned."

Thatcher takes in his stride the poisoned takeout chickens of *Murder to Go* (1969), but seemed to some reviewers a little off form in the wilds of New Hampshire, where he investigates the murder of a potential customer in *Pick Up Sticks* (1970). Most of Lathen's fans and critics were fully content with *Ashes to Ashes* (1971), which looks into the disputed closing of a Catholic parochial school in New York and the murder of the leader of the St. Bernadette Parents' League, but there were mixed reviews again for *Murder Without Icing* (1972). "Newgate Callendar" wrote that "if Emma Lathen does not watch out, she too may end up writing by rote. . . . The Lathen style remains smooth, with its quota of urbanity and quiet wit. But, more and more, a gelid cuteness begins to be annoying. Elements of [Richard] Lockridge always have been present in Lathen, but here they are heavily pronounced. Her characters, even the murderers, now tend to be so damned civilized they end up merely icky instead of menacing." Dick Datchery seemed happy enough, however, noting that "Lathen novels are always scrupulously researched and offer readers as a bonus a short course in the subject at hand—in this case professional ice hockey."

And even Newgate Callendar approved of *Sweet and Low* (1974), in which the floors of the Cocoa Exchange run red and Thatcher discovers conservative management practices and private speculation at the sticky center of the murder mystery. With a great deal of solid information under his belt about the cocoa trade, the Lathen reader could next be agreeably instructed in the production and marketing of antique carpets, which form the elegant background to a blood feud (or is it?) within the rich Parajian family in *By Hook or By Crook* (1975). J. G. Harrison found the novel "distinguished, not alone by ingenuity or complexity of plot, but by a high order of literate writing, and . . . strong character drawing, trustworthiness of background, and subtle humor. . . . With gentlemanly, probity-prone John Putnam Thatcher, business brooks no bunkum and finance no finagling, and evildoing is undone with all the singlemindedness of the Protestant work ethic. It is the Racquet Club against the rackets club."

In the opinion of C.P. Snow, "Emma Lathen is probably the best living American writer of detective stories," and Edmund Crispin agrees that her work "has been perhaps the cleverest and most engaging manifestation of detective fiction proper to appear in the last decade; belonging firmly to the Austen tradition, of dry wit and elegant observation touched with farce, it has also in many ways evoked, at any rate in its comic aspect, recollections of another notable female collaboration, that of Somerville and Ross."

Mary Jane Latsis and Martha Hennissart have also written a number of mysteries as "R.B. Dominic," dealing with the exploits of Ben Safford, a young Ohio Congressman. In *Murder Out of Commission* (1976), for example, Safford is caught up in the uproar surrounding a proposed atomic energy plant in a small Midwestern town—an uproar which culminates in the murder of an eminent scientist in a Washington hotel. The novel was well reviewed, but like its predecessors gained nothing like the readership of the Lathen books. "One wonders why," wrote Newgate Callendar. "Safford is a civilized, honest, hard-working Congressman, and the books in which he is featured are written with the Lathen smoothness and charm. There is also a good deal about the ins and outs of Washington." The fact, so far, remains.

PRINCIPAL WORKS: As "*Emma Lathen*"—Banking on Death,

1961; A Place for Murder, 1963; Accounting for Murder, 1964; Murder Makes the Wheels Go 'Round, 1966; Death Shall Overcome, 1966; Murder Against the Grain, 1967; A Stitch in Time, 1968; Come to Dust, 1968; When in Greece, 1969; Murder to Go, 1969; Pick Up Sticks, 1970; Ashes to Ashes, 1971; The Longer the Thread, 1971; Murder Without Icing, 1972; Sweet and Low, 1974; By Hook or By Crook, 1975; Double, Double, Oil and Trouble, 1978. As "*R.B. Dominic*"—Murder, Sunny Side Up, 1968; Murder in High Place, 1970; There Is No Justice, 1971; Epitaph for a Lobbyist, 1974; Murder Out of Commission, 1976.

ABOUT: Encyclopedia of Mystery and Detection, 1976. *Periodicals*—Business Week May 9, 1970; Christian Science Monitor June 4, 1975; Critic September 1971, March-April 1973; Guardian August 10, 1962; Harper's July 1967; New York Herald Tribune Books September 1, 1963; New York Times Book Review December 10, 1961; August 25, 1963; April 3, 1966; October 16, 1966; July 7, 1968; December 27, 1970; March 14, 1971; November 26, 1972; September 22, 1974; New Yorker February 21, 1970; September 9, 1974; Newsweek July 28, 1969; Saturday Review January 30, 1971; Spectator August 3, 1962; Times Literary Supplement April 8, 1965; August 4, 1966; December 21, 1967; August 15, 1968; December 11, 1969; December 26, 1975.

LATSIS, MARY JANE. *See* "LATHEN, EMMA"

LAURENCE, (JEAN) MARGARET (July 18, 1926–), Canadian novelist, memoirist, and critic, was born at Neepawa, Manitoba, the daughter of Robert Harrison Wemyss, a solicitor, and the former Verna Simpson. Her mother died when Margaret was four, and a year later her father married Verna's older sister, also Margaret, a teacher. In 1933 Robert Wemyss died, and the young Margaret and her brother were raised after that by their stepmother, "a clever and loving woman," according to Clara Thomas, and "a great and continuing influence on the life and work of Margaret Laurence." The young Margaret was educated at United College, Winnipeg, Manitoba. Graduating in 1947, she married John Fergus Laurence, an engineer, the same year and worked for a time as a book reviewer for the Winnipeg *Citizen*. John Laurence's career took the couple to England in 1949 and then to Africa—to Somaliland in 1950-1952 and to Ghana in 1952-1957. Returning to Canada, they settled in Vancouver (1957-1962). Since 1962 Margaret Laurence has lived in England but has traveled widely, visiting Greece, Crete, Palestine, India, Egypt, and Spain. In 1969-1970 she returned to Canada as writer-in-residence at the University of Toronto. She has two sons by her marriage to John Laurence, which ended in divorce in 1969.

When the Laurences went to Somaliland in 1950 it was still a British protectorate. John Laurence built a chain of reservoirs which the British government hoped would help the no-

Ian Cameron

MARGARET LAURENCE

madic cattle herders of the Haud Desert to survive the dry season. Traveling with him from one construction camp to the next, Margaret Laurence gradually came to admire the Somali nomads and learned their language. Her first book, *A Tree for Poverty,* was an anthology of Somali poetry and folk stories, published in Nairobi in 1954.

For her first novel, published in 1960, Margaret Laurence drew on her years in West Africa. *This Side Jordan* is set in the Gold Coast a few years before it achieved independence as Ghana. It centers on Nathaniel Amegbe, a shabby, conscientious schoolteacher torn between the Christian-commercial world of the city and the old ways and gods of his tribal childhood. Not everyone was convinced by the novel's "suspiciously sunny conclusion," but it was otherwise very warmly received, praised for the sureness and control of its prose, the authenticity of its setting, and for its "affirmation, without any sentimentality, of the essential dignity of the human personality." Mary Renault called it "a first novel of rare excellence," showing "an impressive sense of the equatorial rhythms: the cruelty, the gay or the wistful resignation, the feckless humor, the splendid hymns."

The ten short stories collected in *The Tomorrow-Tamer* (1963) are also set in West Africa, and also deal, more often than not, with the impact of technology and commerce on a tribal society. They were generally admired, especially for the imaginative sympathy with which the author entered into the minds of her African characters, including young men working on construction crews or soldiering in Western armies. *The Prophet's Camel Bell* (1963) is Marga-

ret Laurence's account of her two years in Somaliland. "She is frank about her own failings," wrote one reviewer, and "charitable with everyone, even those who in some moods she despises. . . . The result, written with a novelist's sense of character and a deft descriptive touch, is a humane and discerning book." It was published in the United States in 1964 as *New Wind in a Dry Land.*

In *The Stone Angel* (1964), her second novel, Margaret Laurence turned from Africa to the outback community of Manawaka, in Southern Ontario—a dismally provincial town no doubt modeled on the one in which she was raised. As versatile and adventurous as ever, she here attempts to portray an old woman, Hagar Shipley, through a "vast senile soliloquy." Stubborn, cunning, and irascible, Hagar is a burden to her sixty-year-old son and his wife, who are scheming to install her in a nursing home. Much of the narrative records Hagar's grim past through a notably skillful use of flashbacks. It was found a compelling if chilling example of contemporary naturalism, but is not wholly negative in its view of humanity. Hagar, as David Blewett writes, "gropes toward the tragic recognition that the enormity of her pride has alienated her from those she loves and has ruined her life. But the winning of self-knowledge enables her to make some restitution and brings her at last a measure of peace."

Another rather bleak study of a lonely woman followed two years later, *A Jest of God,* once again set in Manawaka. Rachel Cameron, thirty-four, a schoolteacher living with her poisonously puritanical mother over her dead father's funeral parlor, tells in her own self-critical way the story of an unhappy love affair and her decision to escape to a less constricted world. Reviewers thought that the crippling conventionalism of small town life had been admirably conveyed, and most were impressed by such set pieces as a macabre funeral and a revivalist meeting. A.N. Jeffares wrote that Rachel's "suddenly awakening and incautious love is unfolded with great skill and sensitivity," and Marilyn Gardner thought that the book reaffirmed Margaret Laurence's "ability to draw, without pathos, life-sized women." The novel, which brought its author the Governor-General's Award in 1967, was filmed as *Rachel, Rachel,* with Paul Newman directing his wife Joanne Woodward in a remarkable and acclaimed performance.

Margaret Laurence's gallery of female studies continued with *The Fire-Dwellers* (1969), in which the sitter for another self-critical self-portrait is Stacey MacAindra, a thirty-nine-year-old housewife with four children and an uncommunicative traveling-salesman for a husband. It is often a painful book but, unlike its predecessors, often a very funny one as well. Though it evokes a familiar and apparently trivial world, the novel gains stature from the honesty and vitality of its heroine. F. W. Watt was one of those who saw it as a tribute to the author's talent "that we get caught in Stacey's experience, find her needs and her weaknesses and her curiously innocent infidelities charming and troubling, and in the end learn to care about her and come to believe that what she thinks and feels and tries to do matters."

The Diviners (1974), written on a grant from the Canadian Council on the Arts, is a more ambitious and experimental novel. Again the setting is Manawaka and the central character is a woman—this time a middle-aged novelist named Morag Gunn, living in an old prairie farmhouse with her eighteen-year-old daughter by a Métis (part-Indian) folksinger. The narrative alternates between Morag's account of her relationship with her daughter, who is about to leave her, and her recollections ("Memorybank Movies") of her own childhood with foster parents—the mother somewhat grotesque, like many of Laurence's female characters, and the father a drunken garbage collector, poetically colorful in his rantings.

Phyllis Bruce thought Morag a character so skillfully drawn as to produce a certain imbalance in the novel, and also found the mother-daughter relationship unsatisfactory; but, she concluded, "these weaknesses are more than compensated for by the memorable gallery of Manawakans that Laurence has created and her sensitive rendering of their joys and tribulations." Patricia Goodfellow was particularly impressed by the book's "masterful" handling of time: "Through blood and legend, Morag embraces the history of the country from its first dour Scottish settlers to the new refugees of her daughter's generation. Many of the characters have a symbolic dimension—the scavenger, the shaman, the diviner, the piper—but Laurence's real power lies in her ability to evoke the precise, familiar emotion: the terror of the orphan, the adolescent's bravado, the rage and self-hatred of the Métis, the vulnerability of the very old, the brittle awareness of the defeated. *The Diviners* adds to an impressive canon of work, rooted deeply and surely in the best traditions of the novel."

A reviewer in the *Times Literary Supplement* of *Long Drums and Cannons* (1968), Margaret Laurence's critical study of six Nigerian dramatists and novelists, wrote that she "sees many

things with a refreshingly new eye, and she interprets these writers with sympathy and sensitivity. . . . Even those who have had little knowledge of Nigerian writers before reading her book will be convinced by her perceptive analysis that this is indeed now a significant part of world literature." The eight short stories in her second collection, *A Bird in the House,* add up to a sensitive and moving account of a Manitoba childhood and adolescence. *Jason's Quest* (1970) is a story for children. David Blewett wrote in 1976 that "Margaret Laurence has emerged in the past few years as a major Canadian writer. . . . In four novels and a collection of interlinked stories she has created the fictional world of Manawaka through which she has distilled her vision of human struggle, isolation, endurance, and ultimate victory. . . . Margaret Laurence is the authentic voice in fiction of Western Canada."

PRINCIPAL WORKS: *Fiction*—This Side Jordan, 1960; The Tomorrow-Tamer (stories), 1963; The Stone Angel, 1964; A Jest of God, 1966 (also published as Rachel, Rachel); The Fire-Dwellers, 1969; A Bird in the House (stories), 1970; The Diviners, 1974. *Other:* (as editor) A Tree for Poverty: Somali Poetry and Prose, 1954; The Prophet's Camel Bell, 1963 (U.S., New Wind in a Dry Land); Long Drums and Cannons: Nigerian Dramatists and Novelists 1952-1966, 1968; Jason's Quest (for children), 1970; Heart of a Stranger, 1976 (travel essays).

ABOUT: Contemporary Authors 5-8 1st revision, 1969; Creative Canada, 1971; Hind-Smith, J. Three Voices, 1975; New, W.H. Articulating West, 1972; Thomas, C. Margaret Laurence (Canadian Writers series), 1969; Thomas, C. The Manawaka World of Margaret Laurence, 1976; Toye, W. (ed.) Supplement to the Oxford Companion to Canadian History and Literature, 1973; Vinson, J. (ed.) Contemporary Novelists, 1976. *Periodicals*—Canadian Forum April 1961, February 1964, July 1964, July 1969, May/June 1974; Canadian Literature Winter 1966; Christian Science Monitor June 12, 1969; March 26, 1970; Harper's July 1964; Kenyon Review Autumn 1964; Library Journal March 15, 1974; Michigan Quarterly Review Winter 1966; New Republic June 20, 1964; New York Times Book Review June 14, 1964; June 23, 1974; Saturday Review December 10, 1960; June 13, 1964; Times Literary Supplement November 4, 1960; September 6, 1963; March 19, 1964; August 11, 1966; May 22, 1969; May 14, 1976.

*"LAVANT," CHRISTINE (pseudonym of Christine Habernig)** (July 4, 1915–), Austrian poet, took her pen name from the Lavant valley in the province of Carinthia, Austria, where she was born and still lives. She was born Christine Thonhauser in the village of Gross-Edling, near St. Stefan, the ninth and last child of a miner. Living in an area of high unemployment, the family had to struggle hard to make a living and two of the children died in infancy. Christine Lavant herself suffered much serious illness during childhood and was left partially and incura-

*lá vant

Austrian Institute

CHRISTINE LAVANT

Rose may also symbolize a human love which lasts beyond death, death itself being seen as a manifestation of mankind's craving for unity with God. The opposite of love is desolation and loneliness, often represented in Christine Lavant's poetry by the childless woman longing for a family, or by the deserted mistress.

Asked for an interpretation of one of her poems, "Die Stadt ist oben auferbaut" (The city is built on high), she wrote: "This poem, like almost all my other poems, is an attempt to express a self-accusation vital to me." What she accuses herself of is despair and indifference, sloth and rebelliousness—the lapses and defeats which Christian mystics have always experienced in their struggle to achieve union with God. And since her humility forbids any reticence, Christine Lavant's poetry is at once visionary and earthy, while her diction idiosyncratically combines Biblical language and rural dialect words. In "Jesus Christus, ich bete und bete" (Jesus Christ, I pray and pray) she tells Christ that he will have to wait for her until she is healed, for poison is in her blood: "My heart has become a trap, set and open,/ and my very thoughts, when they cease to be prayers,/ have turned into snares, crafty and cruel."

An early remark shows how close the religious inspiration of her work brings Lavant to the automatic writing of the Surrealists, though their premises and ends could hardly be more different from hers: "Being able to write comes over me only as a state and then brings to light things which have never been consciously planned either in my head or in my heart. If a plan for such a thing exists at all, it either lies outside me or in a place [inside me] that has remained hidden to my reason until now. As soon as the state recedes, I fall into an uncreative melancholy that no longer desires anything other than death."

Seven years elapsed between the publication of *Die unvollendete Liebe* and her next volume of poems, *Die Bettlerschale* (The Beggar's Bowl, 1956). Others quickly followed, including *Spindel im Mond* (Spindle in the Moon, 1959), *Der Sonnenvogel* (The Sunbird, 1960), and *Der Pfauenschrei* (The Scream of the Peacock, 1962). Her later poetry is less obviously influenced by Rilke, but themes of love, desertion, and self-accusation are still dominant, so that thematically her poems tend to repeat themselves. Moreover, her preference for regular, usually iambic, meters and for rhymed couplets has sometimes been felt to be a limitation. Nevertheless, this mystical, regional, and repetitive writer is regarded by many as the best Austrian

bly blind and deaf. She had only one year of secondary schooling, and has earned her living mainly through knitting and needlework. She was married in 1939 to Joseph Habernig.

Though her work owes some of its power and originality to her lack of formal education—as well as to a social background so unlikely to have produced her that one critic expressed doubts as to her existence—she is by no means a naive poet. On the contrary, she is a highly accomplished writer, versatile enough to have made a name for herself with short stories and radio plays before the publication of the poetry upon which her reputation now rests. Her early poems reveal the influence of Rilke, in their symbolic references (Rose, Angel, Being) and in her use of the theme of a woman deserted by a lover. But she has a natural lyric genius, and her capacity for passionate personal response and musical expression were shown in her first collection, *Die unvollendete Liebe* (The Unfinished Love, 1949), in which she began the consideration of love, both physical and spiritual, that has remained a constant feature of her poetry. Discussing her work in *Symposium,* W. V. Blomster wrote: "Perfect love is a combination of many qualities; its essence, however, is religious. It is a direct manifestation of divine love. At the same time, this love is highly sensual; strong erotic desires demand and deserve satisfaction. The ultimate fulfilment of love lies in the family and the birth of children. These features lie at the core of much of Christine Lavant's poetry."

Love in her poetry is often expressed by the symbol of the Rose, which represents the love of Christ, as well as the love of Mary and of mothers in general. In her later verse, particularly, the

lyric poet now living. The intensity of her vision, the starkness and unpretentiousness of her diction, the vivid physical imagery that makes her a nature poet as well as a religious poet, and her ability to modulate rhythmic monotony by creating a counterpoint of inner tension, have lent strength and distinction to her later collections. In 1954 she was awarded the Georg Trakl prize, and in 1956 the Austrian Förderungspreis der Lyrik.

Her short stories *Das Kind* (The Child, 1948), *Das Krüglein* (The Little Jug, 1949), *Barushcha* (1952), and *Die Rosenkugel* (The Rosebowl, 1956) are largely autobiographical. One of her radio plays, about a schizophrenic girl, has been broadcast in Britain in a translation by Nora Wydenbruck.

Wes Guderian

URSULA LE GUIN

PRINCIPAL WORKS IN ENGLISH TRANSLATION: *Poems in* Hamburger, M. and Middleton, C. (eds.) Modern German Poetry 1910-1960, 1962; Prawer, S. (ed.) Seventeen Modern German Poets, 1971; Schwebell, G. C. (ed.) Contemporary German Poetry, 1964.

ABOUT: Closs, A. Twentieth Century German Literature, 1969; Moore, H.T. Twentieth-Century German Literature, 1967; Ungar, F. (ed.) Handbook of Austrian Literature, 1973. *Periodicals*—Symposium XIX 1 1965.

*LE GUIN, URSULA K(ROEBER) (October 21, 1929–), American writer of science fiction and fantasy, was born in Berkeley, California, the daughter of the distinguished anthropologist Alfred Louis Kroeber and the former Theodora Kracaw. Receiving her B.A. from Radcliffe College in 1951, she pursued graduate studies at Columbia University (M.A., 1952) and in France, where she went in 1953 with a Fulbright fellowship. She was married the same year to Charles A. Le Guin, a historian. She has taught in the French Department at Mercer University, Macon, Georgia and at the University of Idaho, and served for a time as a department secretary at Emory University, Atlanta, Georgia.

Her first three novels are fairly conventional science fiction, all of them dealing with a future "League of All Worlds." In *Rocannon's World* (1966) an "ethnographic surveyor" for the League sets out with his "Abridged Handy Pocket Guide to Intelligent Life-Forms" to study humanoid species on the distant planet Fomalhaut, and becomes involved in encounters of an almost Arthurian kind. Rocannon discovers that rebels are stockpiling weapons on Fomalhaut for an attack on the League, and enlists the aid of local tribesmen in a perilous search for the weapons. Along with the technological gadgetry there are such romantic ele-

*lə gwin

ments as winged windsteeds and a fair lady, and the talk sometimes evokes Malory.

Planet of Exile is about a colony of quarrelsome tribesmen on Gamma Draconis and a girl named Rolery whose desire for freedom, as the author says, "drives her to break right out of her culture-mold: she changes herself entirely by allying herself with an alien self. . . . This small personal rebellion, coming at a crucial time, initiates events which lead to the complete changing and remaking of two cultures and societies." Le Guin goes on: "Jakob is the hero, active, rushing about fighting bravely and governing busily; but the central mover of the events of the book, the *one who chooses,* is, in fact, Rolery. Taoism got to me earlier than modern feminism did. Where some see only a dominant Hero and a passive Little Woman, I saw, and still see, the essential wastefulness and futility of aggression and the profound effectiveness of *wu wei,* 'action through stillness.' "

City of Illusions followed in 1967 and then *A Wizard of Earthsea* (1968), in which the romantic space opera of the first three books gave way to something much more original. Earthsea is an archipelago ruled by benevolent magicians, and the novel describes the sorcerer's apprenticeship of Ged, a bronzesmith's son with a natural talent for wizardry. It is knowing the true and secret names of things that gives the wizards of Earthsea their power over them, but Ged, wilful and arrogant, calls up a spirit too powerful for him. He is almost destroyed by it until he finds the courage to turn and hunt it through all the islands of Earthsea. In a final, terrifying confrontation he understands what in himself created the spirit, and is able to defeat it.

479

Ged's story is continued in *The Tombs of Atuan* (1971), in which he encounters a young priestess dedicated to the powers of darkness and helps her to free herself from bondage to the Nameless Ones and to escape from the subterranean Labyrinth of the Tombs. A reviewer in *The Horn Book* wrote that Ursula Le Guin had "created a successful high fantasy which may be read on a number of levels. But the storytelling is so good and the narrative pace so swift that a young reader may have to think twice before realizing that the adventures that befell . . . [the heroine] were really the experiences that marked the growth of her personality. . . . Somber, but never quite reaching the depths of tragedy, [this] is the story of the transformations that link life and death."

In *The Farthest Shore* (1972), which completes the Earthsea trilogy, Ged reappears as Sparrowhawk, now Archmage of the archipelago. He sets out with the young prince Arren to seek the source of the evil that is blighting their world, encountering such evidence of malaise as a community ruined by drugs and a group of craftsmen turning out trash. Only the sea people, who accept danger and death as part of their lives, retain their moral health. Shirley Toulson, one of the reviewers who had reservations about the book, wrote that it had "an involved and metaphysical cartography, a mass of names of varying degrees of potency, and a syntax leaning heavily on incantation. It may seem grudging to suggest that stripped of these trimmings a pretty run-of-the-mill parable would emerge." Another English reviewer, on the other hand, said in the *Times Literary Supplement* that "at its very simplest level the book is a major adventure yarn: heroic, anguished, desperate, noble, demanding to the uttermost. . . . When she deals with ultimates—the greatest mage, the farthest edge of the world . . .—she carries total belief. . . . The ideas are inescapably there, intrinsic to the whole, and with sure contemporary relevance. The disturbance in Earthsea's equilibrium comes from human greed allied to ill-used human knowledge. . . . After Earthsea lore, with its weight and substance, most other modern fantasies must ring thin."

When the trilogy was published in a single volume in 1977, T.A. Shippey warmly praised it as "not just a story and not just an argument, but the two together, enriched on the one hand by all the archetypes of antiquity and on the other by the equally powerful rationalization-myths of our fathers and grandfathers. . . . It is not an allegory and not a myth. . . . but it *does* challenge comparison with Virgil or Dante or James Frazer, exploring themes which can perhaps now only be treated outside realistic fiction, but doing so with the severity and power of modern rationalism. Mrs. Le Guin . . . is an iconoclastic writer at least as much as a 'mythopoeic' one; but if ever myths were to come again, they would come from creations like her name-imagery, her Shadowland." Published as books for children, the Earthsea novels have acquired a very large following among students and older readers.

In *The Left Hand of Darkness* (1969), an envoy from the space federation of Ekumen visits the remote planet of Gethen (Winter), whose relatively primitive inhabitants are androgynous. For all his sophistication, the envoy is a male chauvinist, and on Gethen, as Curtis C. Smith says, "he learns how difficult it is to think of our fellow humans as people rather than as men and women." Smith called this "a minor classic" in its treatment of androgyny. George Orr in *The Lathe of Heaven,* set in the near future, is alarmed to discover that what he dreams comes true. A psychiatrist uses George's power to solve problems of environmental pollution and overpopulation, but the solutions turn out to be worse than the problems. "When the arrogant dreams and the nightmares have run their course," wrote a reviewer in the *Times Literary Supplement,* "they leave behind a hybrid, shabby world that's learnt humility." D.M. Gilzinger said that the book was "full of familiar themes, including those of the mad scientist as Faust and the invasion of the earth; but the author's graceful prose and extremely strong character portrayal carry this novel beyond the standard science fiction treatment." Theodore Sturgeon agreed that it was "beautifully wrought," and praised its perception and its "profound research" in psychology, cerebrophysiology, biochemistry, and recent work on the role of dreams.

Two imperfect Utopias are compared in *The Dispossessed* (1974): the materialistic society of Urras and the anarchistic world of Anarres. Shevek, the novel's hero, is a physicist who has devised a technique of instant interplanetary communication that could revolutionize life in the universe. When his attempts to develop this technique are frustrated on Anarres by jealousy and suspicion, he goes to Urras, but soon finds that his idea is seized on there not for the benefits it could bring, but as a source of power. "It is very soon apparent," wrote Susan Cooper, that Urras and Anarres "are also the Janus-faces of our own world, and . . . [the] allegorical overtones make fascinating reading. . . . Two time scales interweave in the telling of Shevek's life, so that by the end of the book the end of one thread meets the beginning of the other. It's a perilous device, but Mrs. Le Guin, skillful as always, makes it beautifully illuminate the nature of the hero and his two worlds." Helen Rogan found her characterization "complex and haunting" and her writing "remarkable for its sinewy grace," though another reviewer complained of the book's "unrelieved earnestness."

The seventeen short stories in *The Wind's Twelve Quarters* (1975) are arranged chronologically, and thus illustrate the author's development over a twelve-year period. J. J. Hall wrote that she "is exhilarated less by 'probable causes' than by 'future experience,' less by the gadgetry of the future than by the quality of life and the psychic consequences of social and technological change." The same concerns are evident in *Orsinian Tales* (1976), a collection of short stories which are not science fiction, but which imagine episodes in the everyday life of a nonexistent but typical East European country as it develops from feudalism, through industrial capitalism, to Soviet-dominated Communism. It seemed to Roger Garfitt that Ursula Le Guin had imparted "an extraordinary reality" to her imaginary setting in these stories, which in some respects "belong to an earlier decade. But then they have some old-fashioned excellences, too: descriptive skill, narrative power, and also moral power, a refreshed sense of human dignity."

Very Far Away From Anywhere Else (1976), wrote Sarah Hayes, "has all the trappings of a teenage magazine story," but Ursula Le Guin has transmogrified the stereotype in this "beautifully and intelligently written" book, presenting two young lovers who are "highly precocious misfits" and who decide that, for them, friendship comes before sex. *The Word for World Is Forest* (1977) is a grim parable, obviously relevant to the Vietnam war, about Earthmen who bring defoliation and other benefits of civilization to a primitive planet. Eric Korn said the author "imagines her people, even if they are three foot high, furry, green, and ordered by their dreams, with a firm and extended vision, and writes with a nice balance of delicacy and positiveness." She has also published an essay on fantastic fiction, *From Elfland to Poughkeepsie,* and a collection of poems.

Although in recent years she has made some successful excursions away from science fiction and fantasy, Ursula Le Guin is still best known for her work in these fields, where she is one of the most admired and most honored of contemporary practitioners. She received the Boston Globe–Horn Book award in 1968, Nebula Awards from the Science Fiction Writers' Association in 1969, 1974, and 1975, Hugo Awards from the International Science Fiction Associa-

tion in 1970, 1973, 1974, and 1975, and the Newbery Silver Medal in 1971. In 1973 *The Farthest Shore* brought her the National Book Award. She has taught in writing workshops at Pacific University in Forest Grove, Oregon, at the University of Washington, Seattle, and at Portland State University, Oregon.

The author and her husband have three children, Elisabeth, Caroline, and Theodore, and live in Portland. She says that she gets all her "weird ideas" from reality: "Reality is much stranger than many people want to admit. . . . It doesn't seem probable that one's grandfather was once an egg the size of a pinhead; that leaves eat light; that whales sing in choruses deep under the sea; that when you look at a distant star you are seeing the past; yet all these things are actual—are real."

Gerald Jonas maintains that Ursula Le Guin "writes what might be called anthropological science fiction. First she invents a world, complete with its own flora and fauna, geography and climate. Then she constructs a human society whose customs, technology, politics and religion seem like natural outgrowths of the physical surroundings. Finally she organizes her book around a strong central figure, whose pattern of behavior appears exotic to us but who is considered perfectly normal in that particular society. The result "is a seamless creation" which is "obviously built to last." Another critic has called her the ideal science fiction writer for readers who dislike science fiction, and Tom Hutchinson says: "She is unique. She is legend."

PRINCIPAL WORKS: *Fiction*—Rocannon's World, 1966; Planet of Exile, 1966; City of Illusions, 1967; A Wizard of Earthsea, 1968; The Left Hand of Darkness, 1969; The Tombs of Atuan, 1971; The Lathe of Heaven, 1971; The Farthest Shore, 1972; The Dispossessed: An Ambiguous Utopia, 1974; The Wind's Twelve Quarters (short stories), 1975; Orsinian Tales (short stories), 1976; Very Far Away From Anywhere Else, 1976 (In England, A Very Long Way From Anywhere Else); The Word for World Is Forest, 1977. *Poetry*—Wild Angels, 1975. *Nonfiction*—From Elfland to Poughkeepsie, 1973.

ABOUT: Contemporary Authors 21–24 1st revision, 1977; Contemporary Science Fiction Authors, 1975; Science Fiction Reader Index, 1975; Vinson, J. (ed.) Contemporary Novelists, 1976; Who's Who in Children's Books, 1975. *Periodicals*—America February 7, 1976; Atlantic Monthly December 1975; Book World November 7, 1971; December 19, 1971; Christian Science Monitor November 11, 1971; June 26, 1974; Hollins Critic April 1974; Horn Book April 1971, October 1971, November 1971, December 1972, June 1975; Junior Literary Guild Catalogue September 1972; Library Journal September 15, 1971; October 15, 1972; April 1, 1974; October 15, 1975; National Review February 4, 1972; May 14, 1972; New Republic February 7, 1976; October 30, 1976; New Society November 11, 1976; New Statesman May 25, 1973; New York Review of Books October 2, 1975; New York Times Book Review

LEM

February 18, 1973; October 26, 1975; November 28, 1976; Newsweek November 29, 1971; Science Fiction Studies Spring 1974; November 1975; Times (London) August 5, 1974; Times Literary Supplement June 23, 1972; April 6, 1973; June 20, 1975; October 1, 1976; June 10, 1977; July 8, 1977; July 15, 1977; Yale Review Winter 1976.

*LEM, STANISLAW (September 12, 1921–), Polish novelist and writer of short stories and film scripts, is widely regarded as the leading science fiction writer of Eastern Europe and the Communist world. He was born in Lwów (Lvov, Lemberg) into a doctor's family, and at first intended to follow his father's profession. The medical studies he began at Lvov University in 1939 were broken off by the Nazi invasion in 1941, and during the German occupation he worked as a garage mechanic: "I learnt to damage German vehicles in such a way that it wouldn't be immediately discovered." After the war Lem resumed his medical studies at Lwów (1944–1946), completing them in Kraków at the ancient Jagiellonian University (1946). "At the same time," he says, "I published lyric poems in the Catholic weekly *Tygodnik Powszechny* (Universal Weekly) and as an assistant at the Conservatory attempted to devise psychological tests for assessing the students' talents. I also brought out several essays of a methodological-scientific character in *Zycie Nauki* (The Life of Science), until the Lysenko affair in the Soviet Union. ... After this I abandoned my intention to devote myself to theoretical biology."

Lem has written of his special feeling as a boy for all sorts of old mechanisms—broken bells, alarm clocks, old spark plugs, and "in general for things derailed ... used up, homeless, discarded. ... I would turn some crank or other to give it pleasure, then put it away again with solicitude." This delight in machines and a playful tendency to personify them inform all his work, and along with his knowledge of biology and his extensive reading in science and philosophy seem to have led him naturally to science fiction as a means of expression. The genre has allowed him to incorporate and satirize contemporary beliefs and institutions in his work in a form which has left him comparatively free from political pressure.

In fact, at least one of Lem's early novels, *Czas nieutracony* (Time Not Lost, 1955), is a more or less conventional story about Poland during the Nazi occupation. However, his first major success was the science fiction novel *Astronauci* (The Astronauts, 1951). It was quickly translated into many other languages, including Russian, French, and German, and has since been filmed in East Germany as *The Silent Star*.
*lem

STANISLAW LEM

Franz Rottensteiner

Though Lem's reputation quickly spread throughout Europe, where his books have sold in millions, it was not until 1970 that the first translation into English appeared. This was of *Solaris* (1961, translated under the same title by Joanna Kilmartin and Steve Cox). The most successful of Lem's novels, it gained an even wider audience when it was made into a highly acclaimed film by the Russian director Andrei Tarkovsky and won the Special Jury Prize at the Cannes Film Festival in 1972.

In *Solaris,* as always with Lem, his alien planet is imagined in great detail. Solaris, we learn, has two moons whose gravitational fields are regulated by a colloidal-like sea. There are no continents and apparently no life, though geometric structures of great beauty emanate from the sea, reach maturity, and then die away again, just as living organisms do. Scientists from Earth, studying this strange ocean from a space station hovering on the edge of the planet, have bombarded it with x-rays. As if in retaliation, figures from the past of each of the scientists are materializing from the sea and joining them on the space station. It gradually becomes clear that the Solaris ocean acts as a creating brain, capable of bringing convincingly to life figures from the human subconscious. And for each individual, what materializes is the one person he remembers most guiltily.

A young astronaut, Chris Kelvin, arriving to join the space station, finds it in chaos, pervaded by an atmosphere of unspeakable horror. One of the three scientists there has committed suicide, while the other two have immured themselves with their resident ghosts. For the new arrival Solaris conjures up a girl who had loved him on

Earth, now dead by suicide, but poignantly unaware that she is not real. Czeslaw Milosz sums it up by saying: "The horror of the enigmatic ocean, the nights and days in the station with two moons in the sky, the personal dramas brought from Earth, is such that *Solaris* plunges the reader into dread. The real subject of the book is not man's encounter with a new form of life—the ocean—which escapes his understanding, but his encounter with himself, with his transitory existence. The beautiful geometric structures emanating from the ocean, their growth, maturity, and decay, paraphrase the stages of a human life span, and intensify that anguish within us which is usually veiled by a routine acceptance of the unavoidable."

The same clarity and richness of detail distinguish Lem's accounts of other credible and coherent worlds very different from our own in such novels as *Oblok Magellana* (The Magellan Nebula, 1955) and *Niezwyciężony* (1964, translated by Wendayne Ackerman as *The Invincible*). The latter describes the fate of a huge spaceship from Earth which lands on another world where it is defeated, despite its sophisticated weaponry, by a horde of insectlike mechanisms. As so often with Lem, the system controlling the horde—its "mind"—remains a baffling mystery; like the Solaris ocean, it seems to be a godlike entity, more powerful than the minds of the Earthmen who confront it, and who perceive and suffer but are never able to attain understanding.

Some of Lem's science fiction novels are set on earth and contain elements of the detective mystery. An example is *Śledztwo* (1959, translated by Adele Milch as *The Investigation*), in which a series of bizarre events take place in London. Bodies are missing from their coffins, removed or resurrected. The latest is found in the snow outside a mortuary, but the constable who was supposed to be guarding it is in a coma after running head-on into a car, and cannot say what happened. Lieutenant Gregory, a determined Scotland Yard detective, tries to track down the criminal, but his problems are compounded by a brilliant statistician for whom these ghoulish happenings merely illustrate the indeterminacy of reality. *Katar* (1976, translated by Louis Iribarne as *The Chain of Chance*), is a rather similar mystery, found "high on ratiocination, low on action."

Most of Lem's novels create situations in which man is tested and the ambivalent relationship between man and machine technology examined. Thus *Pamiętnik znaleziony w wannie* (1961, translated by Michael Kandel and Christine Rose as *Memoirs Found in a Bathtub*)

evokes a post-capitalist future in which computers have taken over from the men who created them. The setting is a vast spy center, Pentagon III, buried in the Rocky Mountains and operated by a monstrously complicated and distinctly paranoid computer whose control mechanisms are riddled with devices designed to guard its secrets from a perhaps imaginary enemy. The nameless narrator spends his time hurrying from office to office trying to discover what orders the computer has for him. He is caught up in a maze of incidents that sometimes seem random and sometimes take on a sinister Kafkaesque quality which persuades him that he is being tested, or driven mad, or threatened with death. Lem's other novels include *Eden* (1959), *Powrót z gwiazd* (Return from the Stars, 1961), the autobiographical *Wysoki Zamek* (The High Castle, 1966), and *Glos Pana* (His Master's Voice, 1968).

Lem has also been a prolific writer of short stories, beginning with the collection *Sezam* (Sesame, 1954). Many of these fall into three cycles of stories about recurring characters: Pirx the Pilot, the cosmonaut Ijon Tichy, and a group of robot stories. Ijon Tichy is a naively innocent cosmic traveler in a one-man spaceship whose absurd mishaps and adventures satirize many human beliefs and institutions, as when Tichy, as Earth's delegate to United Planets, has the unenviable task of explaining why the human race should be admitted to the organization. Other stories are simply funny, like the one in which Tichy's ship breaks down and he goes into a time loop to get his Monday self back to help his Wednesday self: the result is a "who's-on-first" routine that one reviewer called "hilarious."

The cycle of stories about Tichy, *Dzienniki gwiazdowe* (1957, translated in part by Michael Kandel as *The Star Diaries*), has gone through many editions, always enlarged, so that it has now grown in Polish to over five hundred pages. Tom Hutchinson describes these comic fables as "a Munchhausen apparatus to accommodate some witty, near Swiftian philosophical razor-slashes." The longest of them is a short novel that has been published separately in English, also in a translation by Michael Kandel, as *The Futurological Congress*. This is an apocalyptic vision of overpopulation in A.D. 1990, with a conference at the Costa Rica Hilton to discuss possible solutions, from "compulsory celibacy, full-scale de-erotization, onanization, sodomization, and—for repeated offenders—castration" to the recycling of human feces into food. Overpopulation has already led to violence and terrorism, and the psychochemical "benignimizers" used to control this turn a revolt into a love-in, from which the narrator is projected fifty years forward in time and finds himself in a chemocratic Utopia, where every human need is satisfied or masked by drugs. Lem (and his translator) has great fun inventing terms ("opinionates," "absolventina," "obliterine") for the delights and horrors of this sardine-packed world.

Michael Kandel was nominated for a National Book Award in 1975 for his translations of this and of *Cyberiada* (1965, translated as *The Cyberiad: Fables for the Cybernetic Age*), amusing stories about two "constructor" robots who perform miracles with odds and ends. These belong to the genre of futurist folktale which Lem had introduced in *Bajki robotów* (Fairytales for Robots, 1964). Some stories from the earlier collection are included in *Mortal Engines* (1977), also translated by Kandel, a volume of stories centering on the activities of robots or computers, and illustrating the relative unpleasantness of human beings. Several of Lem's story collections, such as *Doskonala próznia (*A Perfect Vacuum, 1977), take the form of reviews of nonexistent books, parodying in this way various kinds of literature, various kinds of criticism, and certain contemporary preoccupations. The pseudo-scholarly "Experiment," for example, purports to review a book about the ethics of computer programming by a programmer who has in effect created a universe, and whose moral dilemma is exacerbated by the speculations of his "personoids" about his nature and intentions. Lem's television plays have been collected along with some stories in *Noc księżycowa* (Lunar Night, 1963).

The power of Lem's fiction stems from the depth and scope of his speculative ability, informed as it is by a study of philosophy and a wide range of sciences, from cybernetics to biology. He has written several important speculative nonfiction works, including *Dialogi* (Dialogues, 1957), a series of Platonic dialogues about the philosophy of cybernetics, and *Summa Technologiae* (1964), which tackles futurology and the prospects for cosmic and biological engineering. *Filozofia przypadku* (The Philosophy of Chance, 1968) is an empirical theory of literature, while *Fantastyka i Futurologia* (Science Fiction and Futurology, 1970) is a major critical study of science fiction in two huge volumes. Lem's work is indeed so wide-ranging that he has complained that most critics have tended to treat it piecemeal rather than to see it as a whole —the commercial nature of publishing in the West has meant that his works have been regarded here as a store or kitchen "from which easily

digestible titbits (of a sensational nature) can be sought out and published without their proper context."

Lem has been compared not unfavorably to H.G. Wells, and has been highly praised by such writers as Leslie Fiedler, Theodore Sturgeon, and Ursula Le Guin (though Michael Wood has complained of "tiresome and insistent whimsy" in Lem's work, as well as "an unsteadiness of focus or of inspiration"). He has had a great influence on other writers in Eastern Europe and is one of the most widely translated science fiction writers in the world—into over thirty languages. Lem was one of the founders of the Polish Astronautical Society and the Polish Cybernetics Association, "but withdrew from both when I saw that the institutionalization of such organizations loses more than it is capable of yielding in revelations." Writing of Lem's marriage of imagination and science, Theodore Solotaroff comments: "Lem is both a polymath and a virtuoso storyteller and stylist. Put them together and they add up to genius. . . . Like his protagonists, loners virtually to a man, his fiction seems at a distance from the daily cares and passions, and conveys the sense of a mind hovering above the boundaries of the human condition: now mordant, now arcane, now folksy, now skeptical, now haunted and always paradoxical. Yet his imagination is so powerful and pure that no matter what world he creates it is immediately convincing because of its concreteness and plentitude, the intimacy and authority with which it is occupied. . . . [Lem] is a major writer and one of the deep spirits of our age."

PRINCIPAL WORKS IN ENGLISH TRANSLATION: Solaris, 1970; The Invincible, 1973; Memoirs Found in a Bathtub, 1973; The Cyberiad: Fables for the Cybernetic Age, 1974; The Investigation, 1974; The Futurological Congress, 1974; The Star Diaries, 1976; Mortal Engines, 1977; The Chain of Chance, 1978.

ABOUT: Balcerzak, E. Stanislaw Lem, 1973; Krywak, P. Stanislaw Lem, 1974; Berthel, W. (ed.) Stanislaw Lem: Der dialektische Weise aus Kraków, 1976; Milosz, C. The History of Polish Literature, 1969; Who's Who in the Socialist Countries, 1978. Periodicals—New York Review of Books May 12, 1977; New York Times Book Review August 29, 1976; Science-Fiction Studies July 1977; Sight and Sound Winter 1972–1973, Spring 1973; Times (London) November 11, 1976; Times Literary Supplement December 5, 1975; World Literature Today Autumn 1977.

"LEONARD, HUGH" (pseudonym of John Keyes Byrne) (November 9, 1926–), Irish dramatist, is the son of Annie Byrne, and the foster child of Nicholas Keyes and his wife, the former Margaret Doyle. Nicholas Keyes was a gardener who worked from boyhood to old age in the service of the Jacob family, well-known

Curtis Brown Ltd

HUGH LEONARD

Granada Television. He left Granada in 1963 to become a freelance writer, but did not return to Ireland until 1970, when new legislation made the country a tax haven for writers and artists.

Hugh Leonard is an industrious craftsman, equally at home with the stage, film, and television, whose output comprises an immense quantity of adaptations and much drama criticism as well as original plays. Some of the adaptations are among his most skillful work, such as *Stephen D* (1962), "a consummate piece of stage craft" drawn from James Joyce's *A Portrait of the Artist as a Young Man* and *Stephen Hero*, which brought Leonard his first international success and was followed by stage versions of Flann O'Brien's *The Dalkey Archive* (*When the Saints Go Cycling In*, 1965), Joyce's *The Dead* (1967), and John McGahern's *The Barracks* (1969). In all these, as in his television adaptations of Saki, Maupassant, Simenon, Doyle, Chesterton, Emily Brontë, and Dickens, Leonard functions as a deftly self-effacing servant of the author—every line of *Stephen D*, for example, is taken from Joyce. Speaking of his original work, Leonard says: "Ireland is my subject matter, but only to the degree in which I can use it as a microcosm; this involves choosing themes which are free of Catholicism and politics, both of which I detest and which deprive one's work of applicability outside Ireland."

British audiences who had associated him with the steely Jesuitical intelligence of *Stephen D* were therefore unprepared for the gentle charm of *Madigan's Lock*, his first original play to reach the London stage (1963). An affectionate fantasy about two old Dubliners building a ship in which they plan to sail away to a legendary backwater with a pub that serves free stout for life, this struck the London *Times* reviewer as the work of an Irish J.M. Barrie. *Madigan's Lock* is not a typical Leonard play, but it did introduce him as a writer much concerned with personal memory and detached from the nationalist obsessions of the Irish stage. The early plays show him breaking out of the Celtic shell and cultivating an outsider's perspective on his homeland. Leonard's technical sophistication and alertness to social change reflect a time when Ireland itself was being opened up by foreign industrial investment. And his compulsive productivity suggests a determination not to fall into the trap of romantic inertia which has silenced so many promising Irish artists.

All the same, in its themes of exile, betrayal, and crippling provincialism, his work remains traditionally Irish. The 1960 play *A Walk on the Water* sets the tone. It deals with the reunion of a group of Dubliners who had split up ten years

manufacturers of baked goods, and Leonard grew up in a two-room cottage in Dalkey, a seaside resort a few miles from Dublin. He attended a state school there and went on with a four-year scholarship (1941-1945) to Presentation College, Dun Laoghaire, a Roman Catholic school run by the Presentation Brothers. "I started in the third year," Leonard says, "and stayed into the fourth for three years running because no one bothered to tell me to move on. . . . My marks were so good—small wonder, after three years in the same class—that they offered me free tuition for the remaining two years; but by then I had flogged my school books and had to decline." Instead, leaving school in 1945, Leonard worked briefly in a film rental office and then, in the same year, took a clerical job with the Irish Land Commission.

During his fourteen years with the Land Commission, Leonard was busy as an actor and director with the Commission's amateur dramatic society, which also performed two of his early plays. One of these was *Nightingale in the Branches*, which was accepted in 1956 by the Abbey Theatre, Dublin, when Leonard submitted it under the title *The Big Birthday*. It was then that Leonard first used his pseudonym, borrowing it from a character in an earlier play. Two more professional productions followed: *A Leap in the Dark*, staged at the Abbey in 1957, and *Madigan's Lock* (Globe Theatre, Dublin, 1958). At that point Leonard quit the civil service and embarked on the vastly prolific career which has led Michael Billington to claim him as the best living Irish dramatist. After writing for a time for radio in Ireland, Leonard went to Manchester in 1961 to work as a script-editor for

earlier when their dominant member, Owen, made an English marriage. Returning to Ireland for his father's funeral, Owen recalls the last meeting of his quarrelsome little gang on the old pier where they generally congregated. And he remembers apprehensively the damaging revelations he made then about his friends, betraying those who had trusted him as their father confessor. When they meet, the group welcome Owen as though nothing had happened and allow him to resume his old patronizing manner. At first, the needling tensions of the homecoming seem no more than "the grand old typically Irish custom of expressing friendship through abuse." But as the climax approaches and we begin to learn the full extent of the damage Owen has done, the joking becomes a vengeful cat-and-mouse game that leaves Owen sexually defeated and stripped of his leadership.

There is a great deal of specifically Irish pain, malicious wit, and competition over status in the play; also some melodramatic overwriting. The same elements recur in a better-controlled form in another revenge comedy, *The Poker Session* (1963), which chronicles the return of one Billy Beavis to his family, who had previously driven him into a lunatic asylum and hounded his sister to her death. He unmasks them at a poker party to which he has invited another graduate of the asylum, a middle-aged Dublin hipster who proceeds to let loose all the skeletons in the family closet. The play has the fascination of a detective story, but some critics felt that Billy's grisly family collapses rather too easily under the virtuoso fusillade of Beat language, and that, as R. G. Hogan wrote, "the gimmicky twists of the plot command too much attention," reducing the work to "little more than a crafty melodrama."

Confrontation between the old Ireland and the new continued in *Mick and Mick* (1966), later retitled *All the Nice People,* another study of homecoming and betrayal in which a Dublin girl returns from London and resumes her affair with the man who had jilted her eight years before. Spiritually, she has never left home at all, and it takes a second and more humiliating rejection to kill her illusions and wean her away from her dependence on her stifling middle-class family. Marital disenchantment, one of Leonard's most insistent themes, is vividly expressed in this otherwise facile piece: nothing in the girl's story compares with the scene in which a husband, seeing his pregnant wife fall to the ground, imagines her literally transformed into a grazing cow.

After *The Quick* (1967), a neat satire on the new Ireland in which a dreadful advertising man fights a losing battle to recover his runaway wife

in the V.I.P. lounge of Dublin Airport, Leonard resumed his exploration of the English connection in *The Au Pair Man,* which went on to London, Berlin, and New York after its premiere at the 1968 Dublin Festival. A young Irish debt-collector blunders into the home of a patrician English lady to demand payment for a room divider; once inside he falls under her spell and stays on as an unpaid servant-pupil, acquiring social polish at the price of independence. The house itself, a decaying hovel crammed with expensive furniture and imperial trophies, supplies the play's allegorical dimension. Mrs. Rogers is England and Eugene is Ireland, while the room divider, which alone preserves the crumbling building from collapse, stands for the historic English despoilation of Ireland. The New York *Times* complained that the play was more about props than people, and it is true that the allegory needs the support of a more plausible situation. This is not to deny its precision as a comedy of national manners, and as an object lesson in how the establishment disarms plebeian rebels.

With his return to Ireland in 1970, Leonard re-established contact with his primary material. He achieved his biggest success since *Stephen D* in *The Patrick Pearse Motel* (1971), a satirical farce picking up the threads from Shaw's *John Bull's Other Island* to show the Irish to be fully capable of fouling their own holy places without any help from outside. The title refers to the first in a chain of "Mother Ireland Motels," where the Plough and the Stars flutters over the heated pool and "the best steaks in Ireland" are served up in the Famine Room. "Anyone who has passed through the Shannon Development," the *Times* commented, "will acknowledge the reality of Mr. Leonard's picture." The mechanism of the plot involves an adulterous sextet in midnight trips through the Parnell Room and the deft manipulation of wardrobes and incriminating underwear, as if the Patrick Pearse were the grand hotel of a Feydeau farce. None of these shenanigans distract Leonard from his main target—the Irish *nouveaux riches,* whom he exhibits in sardonic contrast with the motel's caretaker, a veteran of the Easter Rising whom the proprietors dispatch to the mountainside in pouring rain before baring their teeth to the audience in a farewell offer of true Irish hospitality.

In *Da* (1973), Leonard switches from the modern scene to an exercise in "pure autobiography," reworking some of the material from *A Walk on the Water* with a tremendous gain in human understanding and technical resourcefulness. A middle-aged Irish playwright comes home from England to bury his adoptive father and is overwhelmed by memories of the past. But instead of breaking the story into chronological units, the play enters the domain of psychological time, where past and present exist simultaneously. Remembered conflicts, long-rankling humiliations, and unappeased betrayals are externalized into an endless drama unaffected by death or separation. Not only does Charlie re-experience his first job interview and his first attempt to shed his virginity, he also revisits his early childhood and holds acrimonious conversations with himself when young. Returning from the funeral where he has at last disposed of his maddening old father, he finds Da still sitting in his armchair cracking ancient jokes.

The play's tone reflects Charlie's final discovery that the only way of coming to terms with the past is to live with it. The rancorous wit of Leonard's earlier work gives way to an autumnal irony, and all the characters, with the exception of the self-lacerating protagonist, are treated with affectionate respect. Leonard has never written a cleverer play, but its formal ingenuity serves entirely to set up the maximum resonance between past and present, and to release characters like Charlie's dry clerical boss and his infuriatingly loyal father into their own unmanipulated lives. Ion Trewin thought it nothing less than "magnificent" when it appeared as one of Leonard's regular contributions to the Dublin Theatre Festival, and the New York production won both the Antoinette Perry Award (the Tony) and the Drama Critics' Circle Award as the best play of the 1977-1978 season.

Leonard's next Festival production was *Summer* (1974), which preserved the same autumnal mood within a more conventional framework, and which Leonard himself considers the best of his plays. Set on a hillside overlooking Dublin, the piece consists of two picnic scenes separated by a lapse of six years. The people again represent the new Irish prosperity, no longer quite as new as it was. Their vulgarian zest and Leonard's contempt for them have both gone off the boil. His three couples are into early middle age and the past is catching up with them. By the second act, time has also caught up with the idyllic setting, which is about to vanish under the diggers. The same rueful party reassemble, their faces lined a little more deeply with dismay and defeat, their children already snared in the same conformist trap. A gentle watercolor, suspending mood and characters on the barest sketch of a plot, the play moved John Peter in the London *Sunday Times* to describe its author as "the Trigorin of a national drama which doesn't have a Chekhov."

The 1975 Dublin Festival saw the premiere of *Irishmen*, a triple bill including another adultery farce with a cast of Catholic sinners, and a piece *(Nothing Personal)* touching on the post-1969 troubles in Northern Ireland. The last theme is unusual for Leonard and so far he has not returned to it, though veiled references to it can be read into *Time Was*, the full-length play first produced at the Abbey in 1977. Once again the stage is peopled with well-to-do Dublin suburbanites with soured marriages and roving eyes, but now they have moved into a general climate of danger and of yearning for the good old days. Alarmingly, their wish is granted: people are emigrating to the past in droves, with a corresponding migrant traffic into the present. To stem the flow and hush things up, the government has banned the showing of old movies and set up a secret internment camp for the walking dead. This Priestleyan experiment in time travel, conducted with only six principal characters, strains Leonard's ingenuity to the limit, leaving him little attention to spare for meaning or character; the action declines into an uneasy mixture of marital sniping and extravagant farce in a house surrounded by skirmishing Bedouins and U.S. Cavalrymen who periodically break off hostilities for renewed explanations of the time scheme.

Apart from the television adaptations mentioned above, Leonard has written television versions of a number of his own stage plays and is the author of many original television plays (including *Silent Song*, which won the Italia Prize in 1967). He has also contributed episodes to many popular British television series and is the sole begetter of several—perhaps most notably of *Me Mammy*, an extremely funny series about a mother-dominated Irish businessman, his endlessly frustrated English girlfriend, and the old woman herself, with her monstrous collection of plaster saints and her unassailable ignorance and self-righteousness. The movies Leonard has written include *Great Catherine, Interlude, A Portrait of the Artist as a Young Man, Percy,* and *Rake's Progress.* He writes a weekly literary column for the Dublin *Independent* and in 1976-1977 served as literary manager for the Abbey Theatre. "The standard of playwriting in Ireland is abominable," he says. "Everyone in Ireland writes plays, but.... Brian Friel and I are the only ones who live by the pen. ... The literary life is on its last steps. A literary movement in Ireland is when one writer talks to another." A slender, ravaged figure who talks as if he had a train to catch, Leonard lists his recreations as travel, conversation, and driving (or, elsewhere, as chess, travel, and living). He was married in 1955 to Paule Jacquet and has one daughter.

PRINCIPAL PUBLISHED WORKS: *Plays*—Stephen D, 1962; The Poker Session, 1964; All the Nice People (*in* Plays and Players December 1966); The Late Arrival of the Incoming Aircraft, 1968; The Patrick Pearse Motel, 1972; The Au Pair Man, 1975 (*also published in* Plays and Players December 1968); Da, 1975. *Film Scenario*—Great Catherine, 1967.

ABOUT: Hogan, R.G. After the Irish Renaissance, 1968; Rafroidi, P. Aspects of the Irish Theatre, 1972; Vinson, J. (ed.) Contemporary Dramatists, 1973; Who's Who, 1978; Who's Who in the Theatre, 1977; Writers Directory 1976-1978. *Periodicals*—New York Times March 24, 1978; Times (London) August 20, 1977.

LEVIN, IRA (August 27, 1929–), American novelist and dramatist, was born in New York City, the son of Charles Levin, a toy importer, and the former Beatrice Schlansky. He was educated at Drake University, Des Moines, Iowa (1946-1948) and at New York University, where he graduated with an A.B. in 1950. The same year, Levin began his career as a writer for television, contributing plays to NBC's *Clock* and *Lights Out* series, and later to ABC's *U.S. Steel Hour.*

Levin had his first success in 1953, when he was only twenty-four, with the remarkable suspense novel *A Kiss Before Dying.* Its ambitious, charming, and brilliant young villain, Bud Corliss, intent on marrying rich, finds his hopes threatened when Dorothy, his heiress fiancée, becomes pregnant—a circumstance that will probably lead to her disinheritance. He conceives and executes a "perfect" murder, having first secured a "suicide" note by getting her to translate a suitable passage from the Spanish. Just as carefully he studies the tastes and interests of Dorothy's sister Ellen and soon has her hooked as securely as Dorothy had been. But all this elaborate ingenuity is undone by something time-honored and simple and sentimental, and Bud, who had hoped to marry copper, dies horribly in a boiling vat of it.

This first novel received the Edgar Allan Poe Award of the Mystery Writers of America, and was successfully filmed. It was universally praised for the skill and intensity with which the young author had portrayed a profoundly wicked character, and for the ingenuity of its plotting—a source of pleasure, as clever mental play, even at a second reading. James Sandoe called it "the most striking debut of the year," and Anthony Boucher compared Levin with Helen Eustis, saying that he combined "full bodied characterization, subtle psychological exploration, vivid evocation of locale—with strict

IRA LEVIN

Bill Lulow

technical whodunit tricks as dazzling as anything ever brought off."

Levin served with the U.S. Army Signal Corps from 1953 to 1955 and in the latter year had a success of a quite different nature with *No Time for Sergeants,* his stage adaptation of Mac Hyman's novel about an incorrigibly good-natured young hillbilly, Will Stockdale, who is inducted into the U.S. Air Force. A hit on Broadway, it made a star of Andy Griffith and had a cordial reception from the critics, who forgave its beefy inanities for the sake of its unsophisticated, nonconformist generosity. *Time* called it "a fine, boisterous exercise in sustained improbability." It was filmed in 1958 from Levin's own screenplay. For ten years thereafter Levin devoted most of his time to television and to Broadway, though none of the other plays he wrote during the 1950s and 1960s equalled the success of the first.

It was not until 1967 that Levin published his second novel. This was *Rosemary's Baby,* in which a struggling young actor and his wife, in spite of dire warnings, move into the Bramford, a plush old apartment house in Manhattan. The trouble with the Bramford is that it has been the scene of assorted disagreeable activities, including suicide, cannibalism, and witchcraft. An enlightened young couple like the Woodhouses know better than to worry about such primitive nonsense, however, and they are delighted by the cheapness and elegance of their apartment, and the friendliness of the Castavets, their eccentric neighbors. Then Rosemary begins to be troubled by the Castavets' increasing influence over her husband, even though the friendship coincides with an upturn in his career. And she is right to worry, for it is Roman Castavet's intention to impregnate her, with her husband's connivance, with the seed of the Devil himself.

Jane W. Steadman has pointed out in *Contemporary Novelists* that "elaborateness is . . . the chief characteristic of evil in Ira Levin's novels" and that "procedures . . . provide the sustaining interest, even the suspense. . . . combining neatness and system with grotesque and sinister Satanism [or with murder in *A Kiss Before Dying*]. . . . Rosemary uses a scrabble set to work out the anagram which proves that . . . Roman Castavet is really the devil-worshipping Steven Marcato. The month by month details of Rosemary's pregnancy suspend disbelief in her satanic offspring. . . . The forward movement and acceleration of Levin's processes is frequently deliberately interrupted by sudden reversals, single or double, overt or psychological, in which the character, and often the reader, is temporarily disoriented. . . . The effect on the reader of such continual reversals and realignments is a constant uneasiness as to personal safety and moral identity, which produces varying degrees of horror, very successfully in *Rosemary's Baby.*" Most reviewers were indeed most successfully horrified by the novel, but the *Times Literary Supplement* complained that "the conventionality of the protagonists and setting, though rightly emphasized, is of almost uniformly Madison Avenue flavor." And J. J. Hall, reluctant to believe that the book was no more than "devilish fun and games," nevertheless had to conclude that "neither psychology nor religion functions here as anything but plot device." This failing did not prevent the book from becoming a best-seller and (under the direction of Roman Polanski) an immensely successful movie.

Elaborate procedures and routines also play an important role in Levin's third novel, *This Perfect Day* (1970), set in an overorganized Utopia of the future. Seeking to remove himself from total surveillance by computer, the hero Chip (more properly known as Li RM35M4419) has to work out a highly detailed program of his own in order to escape to an island of free spirits and sabotage UniComp's memory banks. Less original than its predecessors, this novel showed too clearly its debts to Huxley and Edgar Rice Burroughs, and suffered from "an anemic uniformity" in characterization which one reviewer attributed to "pulpy prose."

The suspicion that all the local housewives have been murdered and replaced by robots must be common enough in suburbia, but it is more than a suspicion to Joanna, the comely and talented heroine of *The Stepford Wives* (1972), who has reason to believe that the chauvinistic Men's Association up on the hill has similar plans for her. A Literary Guild Selection, condensed by *Reader's Digest,* serialized in the *Ladies' Home Journal,* and eventually filmed, this novel made its author a great deal of money but failed to earn him much in the way of critical esteem. One reviewer enjoyed "a broad current of humor beneath the horrific surface of this little ambush of Women's Lib, life and the pursuit of happiness," but Webster Schott, conceding that Levin has "the magician's touch" and "casts a spell," went on to deny that this achievement was "anything of special note," and added that the book was "written with a grade school vocabulary, a high school version of syntax, and a best-selling author's understanding of what mass audiences want." Levin's forte, said Schott, was "wild ideas. He thinks of a situation. The situation requires bizarre means. The means produce a crisis event. So goes the novel." Similarly harsh things were said about *The Boys From Brazil* (1976), in which Yakov Liebermann strives to uncover a secret cadre of ex-Nazis headed by the former chief doctor at Auschwitz. The *New Yorker* called it "another made-for-the-movies terrorburger," smoothly written and suspenseful, but crippled by "waferthin" characters. It was in fact made into a movie in 1978.

Levin's play *Veronica's Room* (1973) was described in *Time* as "a jigsaw puzzle with too many pieces," but the equally complex thriller *Deathtrap,* which reached Broadway in 1978, was more warmly praised than any of his plays since *No Time for Sergeants,* and seemed assured of success at the box office. Levin has three children by his 1960 marriage to Gabrielle Aronsohn. They were divorced in 1968.

PRINCIPAL PUBLISHED WORKS: *Novels*—A Kiss Before Dying, 1953; Rosemary's Baby, 1967; This Perfect Day, 1970; The Stepford Wives, 1972; The Boys From Brazil, 1976. *Plays*—No Time for Sergeants, 1956; Interlock, 1958; Critic's Choice, 1961; General Seeger, 1962; Dr. Cook's Garden, 1968; Veronica's Room, 1974.

ABOUT: Contemporary Authors 21-24 1st revision, 1977; Vinson, J. (ed.) Contemporary Novelists, 1976. *Periodicals* —Books and Bookmen December 1972; Book World February 15, 1970; Christian Science Monitor May 7, 1970; Library Journal April 15, 1967; February 15, 1970; National Observer June 12, 1967; February 24, 1969; New York Herald Tribune October 18, 1953; New York Magazine November 12, 1973; New York Times October 25, 1953; New York Times Book Review April 30, 1967; February 22, 1970; October 15, 1972; New Yorker November 21, 1953; March 8, 1976; Newsweek March 16, 1970; Publishers Weekly May 22, 1967; Time October 31, 1955; June 23, 1967; November 12, 1973; February 23, 1976; Times Literary Supplement June 1, 1967; Village Voice November 8, 1973.

LEVINE, PHILIP (January 10, 1928–), American poet, writes: "I was born in Detroit, the older of twin brothers. My parents were Russian-Jewish immigrants who had met and married in this country, and settled in Detroit, where my father and grandfather were partners in the auto parts business. Their 'shop' was located near the ball park and the Michigan Central Railroad Depot. The office was filled with typewriters, which I loved, and adding machines, and in the back were grinders and polishers and punch presses, and Black, Mexican, and white men and women working in the terrible din. On weekends my father and grandfather often took my brothers and me to Belle Isle, where they drank beer and talked while we ran among the cool shade trees. One dark morning in 1933 I was awakened by my grandmother, who told me my father had died and I must be quiet. My mother went off to Europe, a young woman in her twenties, in the hope of forgetting her loss, and we were farmed out, first to an aunt and later to friends. She returned, and we moved to poorer and poorer neighborhoods. She went into the gift-shop business in 1935 in Detroit and went broke. There was a sale, and racks of cheap unsold rings in the basement. She went to work running the office for my grandfather, and by 1940 she was able to buy a home on the outskirts of the city. Meanwhile I had come to believe in my father's death—he had not returned as I thought he would—and soon I began to believe in my own, for the country had entered the war and boys from my highschool were enlisting and dying in action. When the war ended, I entered college, Wayne University, with no idea what I wanted to become, and it was there I found writing again. As a boy of fourteen I took long walks and talked to the moon and stars, and night after night I would reshape and polish these talks, but the moon and stars never answered. Now, asked to write by my teachers, I found I could do easily what others could not do, and I grew first to love to write and then to need it. After I graduated college I decided to try writing advertising, and lasted almost a day and became instead a polisher of bearings, a borer of engine blocks, a plater of toilet fixtures, a loader of boxcars, a breaker of old roads. I married badly. Divorced, I took what money I had to Iowa City and the university which had offered me a fellowship in creative writing, which I somehow didn't get. I sat in on the classes of Robert Lowell and then John Berryman, a marvelous teacher, and met a group of exciting and dedicated young writers. I met also the woman I married a year later, Frances Artley, and for the first time since my bad marriage and the nightmare of refusing military service

PHILIP LEVINE

during the Korean War, I was happy. Franny and I lived first in Boone, North Carolina, where she worked costuming a summer drama, and then in Tallahassee where she taught drama and costuming. She had one son, Mark, whom I later adopted. I made no friends there and worked daily at my poetry, which slowly began to come. I began to publish, and when Franny became pregnant I got a job teaching engineers how to write at Iowa. What I taught bored me, I had to hunt for moments to do my own work, and the pay stunk. Our son John, born that first Iowa winter, suffered from asthma, and we were advised to live elsewhere. I got a creative writing grant from Stanford University, the single stipulation that I study with Yvor Winters, who had selected me. I was so underawarded I was soon working at the post office. The priggishness and wealth of Stanford, and Winters' dislike of my poetry, drove me as a writer further into myself and I began to write the first poems that were my own. The next year I got a job teaching at Fresno State College. In the Bay Area they told me Fresno was a town full of cotton pickers—a kind of rural, backwater Detroit, the contempt in their voices said. After I stopped stumbling in the awful summer heat, I began to like the place. I was thirty when I came here, and I'm forty-seven now. There are three sons now, Teddy, being born the first year here, is sixteen now and broader and stronger than I, who have wizened considerably. The trees and flowers and vegetables my wife has nurtured into being have passed into my poetry, the blank skies and semi-tropical summer evenings, the nearby Sierra Nevada mountains with their incredible wealth of spring wildflowers, and Spain where we went to live for two years to escape America. I have been lucky: my work has tunnelled deeper into my childhood and family, into the lives around me when I worked in Detroit ignorant that I lived in the crash and stink of poetry. I didn't publish a book until I was thirty-five and then in an edition of two hundred and twenty. I was over forty before I started to become well known as a poet, too old to be damaged seriously. The cruelty and folly of the Vietnam War dragged me away from my books with fury toward my government and then towards all government. I have no idea where the future will lead, but I am still writing and living among people I love."

Levine is the son of Harry A. Levine and the former Ester Priscol. He received his A.B. from Wayne State University in Detroit in 1950, and then for several years worked as a machinist and in the various other jobs he mentions above. After Wayne State gave him a Master's degree in 1954 he "went off for a year to the mountains of North Carolina and the swamps of northern Florida." He taught English at the State University of Iowa from 1955 to 1957, when he went with a Jones Fellowship in Poetry to Stanford University, and in his unhappiness there, began, as he says, "to write the first poems that were my own." He has been a member of the English faculty at Fresno State College (now the Fresno campus of California State University) since 1958 and professor of English there since 1969.

The poems Levine published in magazines in the late 1950s were already highly accomplished in their handling of a wide range of formal modes, and drew on exceptional resources of language and rhythm. But these technical skills have always seemed less important in his poetry than its content. As Ralph J. Mills says, his verse has been characterized from the beginning by a "driving intensity. . . . a relentless searching through the events of his life and the lives of others, through the particulars of nature," in pursuit of "an unflinching acquaintance with the harsh facts of most men's situation which still confirms rather than denies its validity." Levine struggles to "view life stripped of the vestiges of illusory hope or promise. . . . Committed to a fallen, unredeemable world, finding no metaphysical consolations, Levine embraces it with an ardor, anguish, and fury that are themselves religious emotions."

On the Edge, his first collection, was published in a limited edition in 1963 and as a trade book the following year. These unsettling poems were universally praised for their taut economy and directness, their mastery of traditional verse forms. They are infused with a tragic conviction that to live is to fail, that human dignity decays and courage fails. Yet there are bitter attacks on such cowardice and inhumanity, notably in four monologues attributed to deserters from the French Colonial Army during Algeria's war for independence. Some reviewers thought the book unrelievedly pessimistic, but Robert Dana found a "determination to create something enduring and worthwhile in the face of meaninglessness and defeat." And most critics seemed to agree with Dana that this was a remarkable first book in its "balance of toughness and sensitivity, its courage, its skill in handling a difficult range of subject matter, the clarity embodied in the language, the touches of humor that sting like alum."

There was a greater fluency, versatility, and colloquial intimacy of manner in *Not This Pig* (1968), but no loss of intensity. Ralph J. Mills noted a preoccupation with travel and movement in these poems, many of which "reflect in oblique fashion the vastness of America, the loneliness of individuals," and a determination to find a tongue "for the speechless, the poor, the outcast, the minorities. . . . Though Levine's presence can be felt everywhere in his poems—and indeed some poems are about himself or events of a personal nature—he enters the life around him in America, in Spain, suffers it all himself, and faces his own despair and inner disequilibrium."

Reviewers were struck by "sudden irruptions of the irrational" into some of these poems, and Hayden Carruth quoted an example of this in the extraordinary last lines of "Family Plan":

> The word was that we were getting out
> so at dawn in the burned field
> across from where we'd tried to live
> we gathered our utensils
> and tried to look like soldiers. . . .
> I imagined
> The road we would take, the sudden
> swathes of daisies bowing to the road
>
> and the bees exploding before us
> before we could flinch. I put
> all this in the past tense although it's
> happening now, but how else
> can I make you believe? If I said
> that the ashes in the hair
> of my youngest son make him look like
> a new God born out of fire
> would you think I was nuts? If I said,
> "The car starts, the tank is full,
> and yet we are not going to leave,"
> would it make any difference?

These experiments are pursued more boldly in some of the elliptical, disjunctive, and surreal poems in *Red Dust* and *They Feed They Lion,* reflecting Levine's reading of the Spanish poets Hernandez, Alberti, Neruda, and Vallejo, and of postwar Polish poetry. In the latter collection, Levine returns frequently to the city of Detroit to speak for the "angels"—the despairing and bewildered victims of a technology run mad. The title poem of *They Feed They Lion* seemed to Alan Helms "so urgent and propulsive in voice as to ignore syntax, logical relation, sense. . . . so wholly engaged that it verges on the act of abolishing itself":

> From my five arms and all my hands,
> From all my white sins forgiven, they feed,
> From my car passing under the stars,
> They Lion, from my children inherit,
> From the oak turned to a wall, they Lion,
> From they sack and they belly opened
> And all that was hidden burning on the oil-stained earth
> They feed they Lion and he comes.

Robert Mazzocco has said that in *They Feed They Lion* and in *1933,* which followed, Levine "has become so striking a poet that I'm surprised he's not more highly valued than he is. . . . Levine's is a daunting, brooding art, often without solace. Scorn and sympathy seem to be there in equal measure, 'so much sorrow in hatred,' as he says. The bonds of family, work, class, Levine as householder in America, knockabout wanderer in Spain, the wars of man and nature, wilderness and town—these are the different features of a difficult face, 'human and ripe with terror'—and with knowledge. . . . He can create the sense of a milieu, the sound, feel, geography of a place, a time, a people, the flavor of what's been happening among us and what continues to happen, which seem to me almost totally lacking in most other serious poetry today."

Not everyone was quite so impressed by *1933,* "a sort of litany of the industrial (Detroit) and immigrant (Jewish) backgrounds which formed . . . [Levine] and follow him." Cheryl Walker found too much of it "an exploration of territory already explored" and Richard Harris objected that the book lacked "the conviction of splendor, the just conviction which balances and ransoms the conviction of sordor." *The Names of the Lost* (1976) again moves through "a highly personal landscape in what seems to be an almost penitential act of memory, recording family, friends, the slums and pollution of Detroit, left-wing politics, Spain, Italy, and California." It seemed to James Venit that "not all of these poems earn the full intensity of their emotion, and some falter through a kind of overprotectiveness close to self-pity," but for Jay Parini

Levine's poems "recreate the sense of place and time with a density and specificity all his own," confirming his status "as one of our essential poets."

Robert Pinsky writes that "the power to look around and see and the strength of a living syntax have distinguished Philip Levine's poetry at its best. . . . [but] it must be admitted that Levine's work is uneven and that its failing is the maudlin. I understand the maudlin to be not a degree of feeling or even a kind of feeling, but the locking of tone into a flaw or groove, running there without the capacity for modulation of emotion: a single, sustained whine, piercing but not penetrating." Pinsky finds this "monotony of feeling and repetitiousness of method" increasingly prevalent in Levine's work, but makes his criticism with a sense that the poet "has earned and undertaken the hardness of high standards." The critic might not disagree with Ralph J. Mills when he says that Levine "stands out as one of the most solid and independent poets of his generation—one of the best poets, I think, anywhere at work in the language."

Levine, who says that he has "given up motorcycle racing after creaming self," has traveled widely in recent years. He wrote in *Contemporary Poets* that his major obsessions are "Detroit. The dying of America. Search for communion. Admiration for cactus, pigs, thistles, thorny people who refuse to die." He has received the Joseph Henry Jackson Award (1961), the Chaplebrook Foundation Award for Poetry (1968), *Poetry's* Frank O'Hara Prize (1972), an award from the American Academy of Arts and Letters (1973), a Guggenheim Fellowship (1973), and the Lenore Marshall Poetry Prize (1976).

PRINCIPAL WORKS: On the Edge, 1963; Not This Pig, 1968; Pili's Wall, 1971; Red Dust, 1971; They Feed They Lion, 1972; 1933, 1974; The Names of the Lost, 1976.

ABOUT: Berg, S. and Mezey, R. (eds.) Naked Poetry, 1969; Chapman, A. Jewish-American Writing, 1975; Contemporary Authors 9–12 1st revision, 1974; Engle, P. (ed.) Midland, 1961; International Who's Who in Poetry, 1974–1975; Mills, R.J. Cry of the Human, 1975; Vinson, J. (ed.) Contemporary Poets, 1975; Who's Who in America, 1976-1977. *Periodicals*—American Poetry Review November-December 1972, May-June 1973; Hudson Review Summer 1968; Kayak April 1975; Library Journal October 15, 1976; New York Review of Books April 25, 1968; April 3, 1975; New York Times Book Review July 16, 1972; February 20, 1977; North American Review Autumn 1964; Ohio Review Winter 1975; Parnassus Spring 1975; Partisan Review May 1974, 1 1975; Poetry February 1964, January 1969, July 1972, March 1975; August 1977; Saturday Review March 11, 1972; Southern Review Winter 1972, October 1973; Western Humanities Review Autumn 1972; Yale Review Autumn 1972.

*LÉVY-BRUHL, LUCIEN (April 10, 1857–March 13, 1939), French sociologist, anthropologist, and philosopher, belonged to a Jewish family which came from Metz, in Alsace-Lorraine. He himself was born in Paris and educated in that city, first at the Lycée Charlemagne, where he was known as an exceptionally able student, and then from 1876 in the École Normale Supérieure. He was talented musically as well as academically and thought of becoming an orchestral conductor, but he chose in the end to specialize in philosophy and also took a course in clinical psychopathology. He was awarded his *docteur-ès-lettres* in 1884 for a thesis in Latin which became (in French) his first book, *L'idée de responsabilité* (The Idea of Responsibility, 1884). For a few years after graduating he taught in provincial *lycées,* first in Poitiers (1879–1882) and then in Amiens (1882–1883). There he married the daughter of a diamond merchant, by whom he had three sons. From 1885 to 1895 he taught philosophy at the Lycée Louis-le-Grand in Paris. The rest of his career was spent teaching the history of modern philosophy at the Sorbonne, where he became *maître de conférences* in 1895, assistant professor in 1904, and full professor in 1908. He was a brilliant teacher, and his lectures formed the basis of several of his books, including *La Philosophie de Jacobi* (1894) and his major study of Comte. At the Sorbonne he was a colleague of Émile Durkheim, one of those who established sociology as a separate science. Lévy-Bruhl was influenced by Durkheim, with whom he nevertheless carried on several spirited controversies.

In his early writings, before he began the investigation of primitive thought for which he is now best known, Lévy-Bruhl produced a number of significant works on the history of modern French, German, and English philosophy. Among his studies of German intellectual life are *L'Influence de Jean-Jacques Rousseau en Allemagne* (The Influence of Jean-Jacques Rousseau in Germany, 1887) and *L'Allemagne depuis Leibniz: Essai sur le développement de la conscience nationale en Allemagne 1700–1848* (Germany Since Leibniz: Essay on the Development of National Consciousness in Germany 1700–1848, 1890). There are good brief accounts of various French philosophers in his *History of Modern Philosophy in France* (Chicago, 1890), and he followed this with a major study of the French positivist Comte, *La philosophie d'Auguste Comte* (1890, translated by Kathleen de Beaumont-Klein as *The Philosophy of Auguste Comte).* Lévy-Bruhl finds the origin of Comte's

*lä′ vē brül′

positivism in the mental effervescence of the first generation of the nineteenth century, the urge towards a reorganization of society after the great upheaval of the Revolution and the Napoleonic wars. He argues that Comte had the same aim as the contemporary socialists and the founders of social and religious Utopias, but followed a different path, regarding a new system of philosophy as the indispensable preliminary to any reorganization of society; his originality lay in taking that new philosophy from science. Although Lévy-Bruhl was not himself a positivist, he considered that the positivist spirit had been enormously influential, in history, in poetry, and above all in sociology and psychology: "Contemporary sociology is the creation of Comte; scientific psychology, in a certain degree, has sprung from him. It is not rash to conclude that the Positivist Philosophy expresses some of the most characteristic tendencies of the age."

The most important work of this first phase of Lévy-Bruhl's development is *La Morale et la science des moeurs* (1903, translated by Elizabeth Lee as *Ethics and Moral Science).* Here he maintains that all theoretical systems of morality are doomed to failure, since theory can be applied only to what is, not to what ought to be. Moreover, these absolute moralities—including those of the great religions—fail to take into account the variation of human nature in different civilizations. In this book Lévy-Bruhl lays the foundations of a pluralistic, relativistic sociology, arguing that morals do vary with both time and place, and so should be studied objectively. This was to have important consequences in Lévy-Bruhl's second phase, when he turned from philosophy to write a series of seminal studies of various aspects of nonliterate culture, drawing on accounts by travelers, anthropologists, and missionaries of surviving primitive societies.

Lévy-Bruhl was one of those who tried to draw a sharp distinction between the mentality of "primitive" and "civilized" peoples. This thesis is developed in *Les Fonctions mentales dans les sociétés inférieures* (1910, translated by Lilian A. Clare as *How Natives Think)* and *La Mentalité primitive* (1922, translated by Lilian A. Clare as *Primitive Mentality),* two books that "really make one and the same work in two volumes." Although their brain structure and all their processes of preception are the same as our own, primitive people, he maintained, perceive the external world differently—in contrast to the analytic habit of thought characteristic of the Western mind, primitive thought is a matter of mystical participation in the life of the natural world. He called the primitive mentality "prelogical" because he thought it did not shrink from violating logic, embracing for example the contradiction of regarding a thing as itself and at the same time as something entirely different.

Lévy-Bruhl continued to elaborate this theory in such works as his Herbert Spencer lecture at Oxford, also published as *La Mentalité primitive* (1931), and in *L'âme primitive* (1927, translated by Lilian A. Clare as *The "Soul" of the Primitive*). In the latter he concentrates on primitive belief in various kinds of suprasensible forces as examples of what he calls the "law of participation": that in primitive thought a person may be conceived of as participating in the nature of a thing—from a totem animal to a social group— even to the point of identity.

This sharp distinction between the mentality of primitive and civilized peoples is generally considered to have failed to stand the test of criticism. More recent anthropologists have on the contrary stressed the unity of the human mind and the similarity of its structure in all its manifestations. Lévy-Bruhl's earliest book on this subject provoked a vigorous reply from Durkheim in *Les formes élémentaires de la vie religieuse* (1912, translated as *Elementary Forms of the Religious Life*). Marcel Mauss pointed out that primitive societies are far from being all alike, and other formidable critics included Franz Boas and E. Evans-Pritchard. The latter complained that Lévy-Bruhl had never done any kind of field work and had no experience of primitive peoples, but relied on the books of travelers or missionaries, whose reports were often based on misunderstandings. More recently, the structural anthropologist Claude Lévi-Strauss, who has made an intense study of primitive *conscious* thought, has also dismissed "the false antinomy between logical and prelogical mentality," asserting that "the savage mind is logical in the same sense and the same fashion as ours, though as our own is [so] only when it is applied to knowledge of a universe in which it recognizes physical and semantic properties simultaneously. This misunderstanding once dispelled, it remains no less true that, contrary to Lévy-Bruhl's opinion, its thought proceeds through understanding, not affectivity, with the aid of distinctions and oppositions, not by confusion and participation."

Lévy-Bruhl always examined such objections seriously, and himself revised his ideas in his later work, to the extent of agreeing that both kinds of thought, the rational and the mystical, exist in every human mind, though with one or the other predominating. In the notes he was writing towards the end of his life, which were published posthumously with a preface by Mau-

rice Leenhardt as *Les Carnets de Lévy-Bruhl* (1949, translated by Peter Rivière as *The Notebooks on Primitive Mentality*), he agreed that prelogical and preliterate societies would employ logical thought to meet the practical demands of their environment. He stated that he was prepared to give up the term *prelogical,* and seemed on the verge of agreeing that the acceptance of logical contradictions is not an inherent characteristic of the primitive mentality.

Although Lévy-Bruhl underestimated the rational and empirical elements in the thought of primitive man, he did give anthropology a new understanding of irrational factors in social thought and in primitive religion and mythology. In works such as *Le Surnaturel et la nature dans la mentalité primitive* (1931, translated by Lilian A. Clare as *Primitives and the Supernatural), La mythologie primitive: le monde mythique des Australiens et des Papous* (Primitive Mythology: The Mythic World of the Australians and the Papuans, 1935), and *L'Expérience mystique et les symbols chez les primitifs* (Mystical Experience and Symbols Among Primitives, 1938), he showed that it was possible to discuss the religious ideas and symbolism of primitive peoples in their own terms, rather than merely as evidence of a failure to develop an analytic mode of thought. He was therefore an important influence on contemporaries and juniors who were interested in myth and symbolism, including the psychologist Jung, whose theories of archetypes and the "collective unconscious" have close affinities with Lévy-Bruhl's ideas. Indeed, Jung continued to support the idea that primitive people experienced a mystical participation in the objects of thought after Lévy-Bruhl himself had withdrawn it.

Evans-Pritchard, in a foreword to the 1965 English reissue of *The "Soul" of the Primitive,* sums up the general anthropological attitude to Lévy-Bruhl's work: "Even if ... [his] conclusions about primitive mentality can no longer be accepted quite in the terms in which he set them forth, it is a plain fact that much of the thought of primitive peoples is difficult, sometimes almost impossible for us to understand, in that we cannot follow their lines of reasoning because the underlying assumptions on which they are based, while taken for granted by them, are totally alien to us. So the problem still remains—in his words 'the primitive's thought proceeds along a path in which we find it very difficult to follow it,' as this fascinating book well illustrates."

Born at the time of the second Napoleonic Empire, Lévy-Bruhl was a convinced republican and liberal who became a staunch defender of human rights. His writings on such themes include *L'Idéal republicain* (The Republican Ideal, 1924) and a book examining the causes of the First World War—*La conflagration euro-péenne, ses causes économiques et politiques* (The European Conflagration, Its Economic and Political Causes, 1915). Lévy-Bruhl was related by marriage to Captain Dreyfus, and gave evidence on his behalf in the famous trial. Later he wrote a preface summing up the affair for the 1930 French translation of the notebooks of Colonel Schwartzkoppen, the German military attaché to whom Dreyfus had been wrongly accused of betraying French military secrets. Lévy-Bruhl was also a lifelong friend of the socialist leader, statesman, and historian Jean Jaurès, to whose newspaper he regularly contributed, and of whom he wrote an intellectual biography, *Jean Jaurès: Essai biographique* (1916).

A man of great culture, able to lecture on Turgenev and Flaubert as well as on the primitive mind, Lévy-Bruhl was also very widely traveled, having lectured or attended conferences all over Europe, in the United States (where he was an exchange professor at Harvard in 1919–1920, at Johns Hopkins University in 1926, and at Berkeley), and in Central and South America (Brazil, Paraguay, Bolivia, Argentina). His travels also took him to China, Japan, the Philippines, Java, and Indochina. Lévy-Bruhl was a tall, thin man. Maurice Leenhardt says that "nothing distinguished him from the crowd except for a look that was both assured and searching, with his head slightly inclined, always in a listening position." His second son, Henri Lévy-Bruhl, became a specialist in the sociology of law and wrote many books and papers.

PRINCIPAL WORKS IN ENGLISH TRANSLATION: History of Modern Philosophy in France, 1890; The Philosophy of Auguste Comte, 1893; Ethics and Moral Science, 1905; Primitive Mentality, 1923; How Natives Think, 1925; The "Soul" of the Primitive, 1928; Primitives and the Supernatural, 1935; The Notebooks on Primitive Mentality, 1975.

ABOUT: Cazeneuve, J. Lucien Lévy-Bruhl (translated into English by Peter Rivière), 1972; Cailliet, E. Mysticisme et "mentalité mystique," 1938; Evans-Pritchard, E. *introduction to* reissue of The "Soul" of the Primitive, 1965; International Encyclopedia of the Social Sciences, 1968; Leenhardt, M. *preface to* The Notebooks on Primitive Mentality, 1975; Leroy, O. La Raison primitive, 1927.

*LEZAMA LIMA, JOSÉ (December 19, 1910 –August 9, 1976), Cuban poet, novelist, and essayist, was born in Cuba at the Columbia military barracks, the son of José María Lezama y Rodda, an artillery colonel, and the former Rosa

*les ä′ ma lē′ ma

JOSÉ LEZAMA LIMA

Lima y Rosado. His mother, the daughter of revolutionary exiles, had been brought up in the United States, where her family had lost its fortune helping to finance the Cuban independence campaigns. The poet's birth coincided with the family's move to another military camp (Fortaleza de la Cabaña) and his father's promotion to the directorship of a military academy, the Academia Militar del Morro. His earliest memories were of a world of military discipline, uniforms, parades, and maneuvers, but he recalled his childhood nevertheless as a time of happiness and security.

With the outbreak of World War I, the poet's father volunteered for service with the Allied forces. He died in an influenza epidemic while training at Fort Barrancas, Pensacola, in January 1919. Another child, a girl, was born some months later. In serious financial difficulties, the family joined the Havana household of Lezama Lima's maternal grandmother. The asthma which had begun to affect the boy's health in early infancy became increasingly acute, and troubled him all his life.

In 1920 Lezama Lima entered the Colegio Mimó in Havana, where he revealed a precocious intelligence. He later recalled how his early reading of *Don Quixote* opened up a whole new world to him, "untouched by time or circumstances." In 1926, he proceeded to the Instituto de la Habana, where he matriculated two years later. At about that time he and his mother moved to the Calle Trocadero in Havana where a new chapter began, marked by a deepening bond between the two. Their financial difficulties continued, aggravated by the general atmosphere of gloom and uncertainty associated with the harsh regime of Gerardo Machado (1925-1933). Unemployed, and with the universities closed by the authorities, Lezama Lima immersed himself in reading and meditation. He developed a special interest in the work of the baroque seventeenth-century Spanish poet Luis de Góngora and his contemporaries, as well as in more recent French literature—Rimbaud, Lautréamont, Mallarmé, Valéry, and Proust. By the time Machado was deposed and the universities reopened, Lezama Lima was determined to embark upon a literary career. At the University of Havana he collaborated with other young intellectuals in launching the review *Verbum*. His first book of poetry, *Muerte de Narciso* (Death of Narcissus) was published in 1937.

Lezama Lima completed his university studies in 1938. He found employment first in a lawyer's office, then in the Consejo Superior de Defensa Social (Higher Council for Social Security), in his spare time editing the literary journal *Espuela de plata*. The poems from his first book were republished in 1941 in *Enemigo rumor* (Hostile Sounds), together with much new work—poetry, he called it, "transformed into a hostile presence watching the poet from afar." Lezama Lima's is a hermetic poetry, dense and baroque, evoking "dark pastures," "invisible gardens," and "the great bridge" to a transcendental world beyond the visible one. In "Sonetos a la Virgen" (Sonnets to the Virgin) he identified the two constants in his conception of the creative quest, the interconnected notions of the poetic and the religious. According to Enrique Anderson Imbert, *Enemigo Rumor* "seduced the younger poets, making [Lezama Lima], from that moment, the master. The ascendancy which he exercises over other writers seems to be due to the example of a life monstrously consecrated to literature." Cintio Vitier agreed that this volume placed Lezama Lima at "the center of Cuban poetic life."

In 1943 Lezama Lima established another review, *Nadie parecía* (No One Appeared), this time devoted entirely to poetry, especially on classical and religious themes. He was now living alone with his mother, and critics have written at great length about the extraordinary influence exercised upon the poet by this remarkable woman, whom he venerated. Nineteen forty-four marked a turning point in his career. It was then that Lezama Lima, in collaboration with José Rodríquez Feo, launched *Orígenes* (Origins), which became one of the most important and influential literary reviews of the period for the Cuban avant-garde, receiving contributions from many distinguished foreign writers as well as young Cuban intellectuals, until a disagreement over editorial policy terminated publication in 1957.

Aventuras sigilosas (Secret Adventures), another book of poems, followed in 1945, adumbrating the theme of the mother-muse relationship which became central in the major work that followed. The same year Lezama Lima joined the Dirección de Cultura (Arts Council). A period of frenzied activity and further reading and meditation ensued before the appearance of *La fijeza* (Endurance, 1949), which develops many of the themes and images of *Enemigo rumor*. There were fruitful visits to Mexico and Jamaica in 1949 and 1950.

During the next few years, Lezama Lima devoted himself mainly to criticism. A monograph on the painter Arístides Fernández (1950) was followed by *Analecta del reloj* (Compendium of the Clock, 1953), a volume of essays including two important pieces—"Las imagines posibles" (Possible Images), a partial exposition of the author's poetics, and a highly individual interpretation of Góngora's sensibility.

In 1957 Lezama Lima delivered a series of five lectures at the National Institute of Culture which were published the same year as *La expresión americana* (The Expression of America). They attempt a definition of the Nuevo Mundo [New World] sensibility, which is seen as a subtle merging of Creole and Spanish characteristics—pristine vigor and innocence on one hand, a long, complex, and baroque tradition on the other. The essays in *Algunos tratados en La Habana* (Some Treatises in Havana, 1958) develop Lezama Lima's literary theories, his conviction that the artist must pursue the "eternal enigmas on the other side of things, obscure and remote as well as clear and proximate"—must seek "the reality of the invisible world."

When Fidel Castro's revolution triumphed in 1959, Lezama Lima was appointed director of literature and publications at the National Council for the Arts (Consejo Nacional de Cultura), and from 1959 to 1962 he was a vice-president of the Union of Cuban Artists and Writers, serving also as an advisor to the Cuban Center for Literary Research. His mother died in 1964 and such was the degree of identification between them that it seemed inevitable that his world would collapse. However, as he went on with his work, the poet continued to feel his mother's inspiration and spiritual guidance. Lezama Lima was married in 1965. The following year he dazzled the literary world with one of the most extraordinary novels that has yet appeared in Latin America, the widely acclaimed *Paradiso* (1966, revised 1968, translated under the same title by Gregory Rabassa).

The first half of this enormous novel describes the childhood of the hero, José Cemí (who shares his initials with Jesus Christ). Like Lezama Lima, Cemí is the asthmatic son of a soldier whose "cheerful morning stroll" through life ends when Cemí is still a child, and whose place as head of the family is then assumed with Roman dignity by Cemí's grandmother. The search for the lost father is to occupy the boy throughout the book, which goes on to deal with Cemí's years at school and university, his sexual initiations, his friendships with the calm and balanced Fronesis and the tormented Focíon. Focíon, a homosexual unrequitedly in love with Fronesis, goes mad and is killed by lightning—one of the novel's many violent deaths. Bereft of his friends, Cemí is initiated into wisdom by Oppiano Licario, a mysterious Icarus figure who materializes at crucial moments throughout the book. Indeed, as Jean Franco has remarked, "the world of the fantastic always lies just below the surface of the novel. It can be discovered at any moment by a chance meeting, a sudden juxtaposition of words or events." Even Cemí's asthma attacks become, in the novel, doors into hallucination and fantasy.

The central vision which informs this story is of a prelapsarian state of spiritual wholeness, a state of grace preceding the categorization of things, the separation of the individual from the universal, of imagination from action—a biblical Eden with overtones of Dante's Paradise. As Edmund White wrote, "Cemí must work his way through the immense coordinates of a poetic system before he can hear the tranquil music of the spheres." The novel is also, Michael Wood has suggested, "a huge poem in prose, a personal mosaic of Cuban history," and an act of homage to the poet's mother—an attempt to create a world in which she will shine forever, "to reconstruct, as if in paradise, the angelic, ultimate reality of beings who lie scattered, opaque and dying, about the material world we know."

Paradiso has been called "unrelentingly sexual. . . . charged with bristling erotic energy." It is also a work of much erudition, drawing deeply (if often inaccurately) upon Dante, Pythagoras, Plotinus, St. Augustine, Goethe, Nietzsche, Rimbaud, and Lao Tzu, among many others. One chapter of the book is a dispute between Fronesis and Focíon on the origins of homosexuality which takes the form of a full-scale eclogue or pastoral contest, and the book is full of references to the great hermetic traditions of Egypt, Europe, Asia, and pre-Columbian America.

But what staggered and divided the critics above all else is the novel's reckless verbal extravagance—a Spanish high baroque that has not been equaled since Góngora took it to its wildest extremes in the seventeenth century (though an altogether more moderate baroque is found in the work of another Cuban novelist, Alejo Carpentier). In *Paradiso,* a man strolls to the corner, smoking a cigarette with such enjoyment that he fails to notice the inviting glances of two women on a balcony; in Lezama Lima's terms, this becomes: "Olaya was floating too high, too much held up by those evaporations from the thickness of dusk, wrapped about itself in coils like a python with tattooed scales, interrupting the Talmudic dream with every small initialed arrow, with every cherub that one of its coils wanted to strangle, without succeeding in awakening in him the transfer of his energies, borne to the oven of metamorphosis."

Writing of this sort is a special taste; though one critic maintains that the language is truly the novel's central character, Michael Wood finds it pompous in Spanish, "comic or laborious in English." Wood calls Lezama Lima's compulsive simile-making and periphrases "fussy and self-advertising, mere gesticulation," and cites references to an arrogant cook who is "encased in a silence as impenetrable as Egyptian diorite" and is later found as "hieratic as an Iranian pottery vendor." Wood also complains that Lezama Lima "found no literary form" for either his sense of humor or his irony: "Narrator and characters alike . . . all speak in the same lofty, abstract, erratically imagistic, stylistically undifferentiated jargon. . . . It is a novel written by a certain kind of poet, with all that kind of poet's slavish devotion to the belief that only images matter. All the riches and invention in *Paradiso* have gone into its figurative language, leaving tone, syntax, and the whole craft of prose to fend for themselves."

For Edmund White, on the other hand, *Paradiso* was a novel of great wisdom, and a masterpiece: "Like Proust he is intent upon defeating time and submerging it into the eternity of art, but Lezama has recaptured the historical as well as his own personal past." Severo Sarduy thought that "*Paradiso* constitutes an entire grammar of creation." And Julio Cortázar, another master of labyrinths, wrote: "Lezama Lima is not only hermetic in the literal sense, in so far as the best of his work propounds an apprehension of essences by way of the mythic and the esoteric in all of their historic, psychic and literary forms vertiginously combined within a poetic system in which a Louis XV armchair often serves to seat the god Anubis, but it is also formally hermetic, as much in the candor which leads him to assume that the most heterogeneous of his metaphorical series will be perfectly comprehensible to others, as in the complexity of his *barroquismo.*" Cortázar's statement helps to explain why *Paradiso,* resurrecting an ancient literary mode, should have attracted so much attention among avant-garde writers.

Lezama Lima was said to be "a man of immense personal presence, a compelling conversationalist, possessor of an alarming, eccentric, unfathomable erudition." Jean Franco wrote in 1968 that the author was "a deeply religious man, absorbed in the contemplation of a world outside time. . . . as he talks he rocks himself and smokes his cigar under the portraits of his family and the paintings of his generation. He looks and is the traditional creole—vast, immobile, parchment-colored, asthmatic, still attended by a servant (the Baldovina of the novel) who is now in her mid-eighties." Since *Paradiso* ignores the revolution and contains frank discussion of homosexuality, Lezama Lima was out of favor with Castro's regime after its publication. Plagued by illness, he wrote little in the last years of his life.

PRINCIPAL WORKS IN ENGLISH TRANSLATION: Paradiso, 1974. *Poems in* Caracciolo-Trejo, E. (ed.) Penguin Book of Latin American Verse, 1971; Fitts, D. (ed.) Anthology of Latin-American Poetry, 1942; Tarn, N. (ed.) Con Cuba, 1969; Triquarterly Anthology of Contemporary Latin American Literature, 1969.

ABOUT: Anderson Imbert, E. Spanish-American Literature, 1963; Bravo, A.A. (ed.) Órbita de Lezama Lima, 1966; Franco, J. Spanish American Literature Since Independence, 1973; Goytisolo, J.A. (ed.) Posible imagen de José Lezama Lima, 1969; Menton, S. Prose Fiction of the Cuban Revolution, 1975; Schwartz, K. A New History of Spanish American Fiction, 1971; Souza, R.D. Major Cuban Novelists, 1976. *Periodicals*—Books Abroad Winter 1970; New York Review of Books April 18, 1974; New York Times Book Review April 21, 1974; Review 74 Fall 1974 (special issue on Paradiso); Times Literary Supplement November 14, 1968.

*LIDMAN, SARA (ADELA) (December 30, 1923–), Swedish novelist, dramatist, and social commentator, is the daughter of Andreas Lidman and the former Jenny Lundman. She was born at Missenträsk, Västerbotten, West Bothnia, a remote region in the far north of Sweden where her father was a farmer. Her parents were Lutherans and she was, she says, a "pious child." Her studies at the University of Uppsala were interrupted by persistent tuberculosis, and during these periods of illness she began to write stories of a conventional kind. Later, under the influence of Kierkegaard, Dostoevsky, and the Norrland novelists Stina Aronson and Thorsten

*lid' man

SARA LIDMAN

Swedish Consulate

Jonsson, she discovered her own characteristic tone and area of concern—the problems of guilt and of man's responsibility to his fellows. In her early novels, these concerns are treated in the microcosm of isolated northern farming communities like the one in which she grew up.

Her first novel, *Tjärdalen* (1953), centers as the title suggests upon a tar distillery—a structure that takes a year to build but could provide a valuable source of income for the bitterly poor village, lifting it above the level of mere subsistence. The still is wrecked by a malicious peasant, who is badly hurt in the process. The villagers leave him to die of gangrene—a "collective murder" that raises searching moral questions for Petrus, the peasant who is the conscience of the village, and also for the reader. The novel was an immediate success, according to Harold H. Borland in *Scandinavian Studies,* because it was "so firmly and satisfyingly constructed, and because such a strong individual voice comes through in [Lidman's] style, a warm voice, roughened by dialect in this and the next two novels, and one which makes strange images sound intimate and natural."

Hjortronlandet (Cloudberry Land) followed in 1955. It is set like its predecessor in the 1930s, and in an even more desperately poor northern community. Tracing the tragic destiny of a talented girl in this hopeless society, the novel is less closely knit than *Tjärdalen* but seemed to reviewers to probe more deeply into the complexities of its "cavalcade of differentiated characters." It was selected by the Swedish critics as the best novel of the year, and headed the bestseller list.

Alrik Gustafson ranks these first two novels

with, or above, the "best work of Selma Lager-löf's brilliant early years. . . . Their style is marked by a subtly controlled spontaneity, their humor is sly but warm and profound, their narrative flow is easy, unhurried, quietly lively, their psychological penetration and moral seriousness satisfy every demand of a sophisticated modern reader."

Regnspiran (1958, translated by E.H. Schubert as *Rain Bird*) is the only one of Sara Lidman's novels to have appeared in English. The title refers to the name given in her part of Sweden to the swallow, which is regarded by the peasants there as a magical bird, in touch with the depths of human nature. Linda Ståhl, the novel's central character, shares some of the qualities attributed to the *regnspiran*. The book traces very naturally and convincingly the development of her extraordinary personality, from her difficult childhood and painful adolescence to maturity as a gifted musician, alarmingly perceptive mimic, and ruthless egotist. Linda brings misery and disaster to all who succumb to her strange magnetism, but the reader is never in any doubt that she is herself the victim of circumstances, social and psychological. Harold H. Borland has spoken of the "obsessive, compulsive rhythm and pattern" of the book, which "help to give it its power to unsettle and disturb." *Bära mistel* (Only Mistletoe, 1960) is a sequel in which Linda, in later life, is chained by love, guilt, and her need to atone for her past sins to an unresponsive homosexual.

Sara Lidman has said that by the time she wrote *Regnspiran* she had broken away from the Lutheranism of her parents, but retained "its negative attitude toward man." Her views changed under the influences of Marxism and of what she saw and learned during a sojourn in Africa. She went to South Africa in 1960, was eventually expelled, and in 1962-1964 lived in Kenya. The "true colonial misery" she observed is evoked in *Jag och min son* (My Son and I, 1961)—a novel attacking South African apartheid, staccato with rage—and more successfully in *Med fem diamanter* (With Five Diamonds, 1964).

The latter, set in Kenya at the end of the colonial era, centers on a young Kenyan's struggle to acquire the six goats he needs as bride-price for the girl he loves, making a novel which Ulla Folejewski described as "absorbing—funny, sad, occasionally grotesque." Borland complained that the whites in the novel were mere caricatures, but found in it some of the qualities which had made *Tjärdalen* so satisfying, as "a concentrated study of a small community with an examination in depth of a few characters."

Sara Lidman has now repudiated her early novels because they deal "with the minds of people" and contain "no conception of society." She has turned away from fiction to make herself into a reporter on social conditions. "I'll write stories if I have time," she says, "but my imagination really can't compete with today's reality. Why make up stories when life is so full of fanciful and powerful events? . . . The true problem, for me, is finding the means of presenting social realities." All the same, she continues to be interested in style—in literature rather than propaganda—because "with literature, the reader comes to realize things for himself."

Her new concerns are evident in *Samtal i Hanoi* (1966), the diary of a visit to North Vietnam, where she found grounds for optimism about mankind in a society where "the whole population was united in a common cause." Returning to Sweden, she continued this genre of direct but compassionate reportage in *Gruva* (Mine, 1968), an account of the circumstances of the Lapland iron miners which showed how little industrial democracy really existed in the state-owned mines. Officials called the book exaggerated, but it was totally vindicated when the great Kiruna miners' strike began two years later.

Gruva established Sara Lidman as a central figure in Sweden's current political ferment, and *Newsweek* has described her as "in some ways the most devastating Swedish social critic," active not only as a writer and polemical journalist, but on television and at demonstrations. She profoundly admires Jan Myrdal, and *Gruva* has in fact been compared to Myrdal's *Report From a Chinese Village* in a study by Marianne Thygesen. Lidman believes that Sweden needs not reform but revolution; she says "I'm not a Communist. I don't think I deserve a proud title like that." She is the author of several plays, including *Job Klockmakares dotter* (Job the Clockmaker's Daughter, 1954), *Aina* (1956), and *Marta, Marta* (1970).

PRINCIPAL WORKS IN ENGLISH TRANSLATION: Rain Bird, 1962.

ABOUT: Dahlstedt, K.H. Folkmål i riks-svensk prosadiktning: Några synpunkter med ut-gångspunkt från Sara Lidmans Västerbottensromaner, 1960; Dembo, L.S. and Pondrom, C.N. (eds.) The Contemporary Writer, 1972; Grave, G. Biblicismer och liknande inslag i Sara Lidmans Tjärdalen, 1969; Gustafson, A. A History of Swedish Literature, 1961; International Who's Who, 1977-78; Seymour-Smith, M. A Guide to Modern World Literature, 1973; Thygesen, M. Jan Myrdal og Sara Lidman: Rapportgenren i svensk 60-tals litteratur, 1971. *Periodicals*—Contemporary Literature Summer 1971; Newsweek March 23, 1970; Scandinavian Studies May 1967.

LIFTON, ROBERT JAY (May 16, 1926–), American psychiatrist, was born in Brooklyn, New York. He is the son of a businessman, Harold A. Lifton, and of the former Ciel Roth—both of them second-generation immigrants of Russian Jewish parentage. Encouraged by his family in both social consciousness and educational ambition, Lifton decided while still a boy to become a physician. An exceptional student at Erasmus Hall High School in Brooklyn, he went on with a New York State tuition scholarship for premedical studies at Cornell University (1942-1944), where he was an associate editor of the *Cornell Daily Sun* and a member of the tennis team. Lifton continued his studies at the New York Medical College, received his M.D. in 1948, and for the next year was an intern at the Brooklyn Jewish Hospital.

By this time Lifton had decided to specialize in psychiatry, and from 1949 to 1951 he studied that subject at the Downstate Medical Center in Brooklyn. It was as a psychiatrist that Lifton served in the United States Air Force (1951-1953), spending a year in Japan and six months in South Korea. In Korea he studied the effects of "brainwashing" on American prisoners of war, and this experience confirmed his interest in what has come to be called *psychohistory*—the study of the interrelation between historical events and currents and individual human behavior.

Discharged from the Air Force in 1953 with the rank of captain, Lifton went to Hong Kong, where he was able to interview forty men and women, western and Chinese, who had been brainwashed. He published the results of these investigations in *Thought Reform and the Psychology of Totalism,* concluding that "the emotional scope and power" of Chinese methods of "thought reform" derived from their combination of "external force ... with an appeal to inner enthusiasm through evangelical exhortation." Apart from the psychological issues raised by thought reform in China, the book considers what these procedures imply about the nature of postrevolutionary China. It was widely praised as the work of "a critical and concerned liberal," equipped not only with psychiatric knowledge but with "insights from the social sciences and the results of his eager study of Chinese culture and history." The *Times Literary Supplement* found it "humane and many-sided in its understanding," and C. M. Wilbur in the New York *Times Book Review* thought that it would become "a classic in social science literature because the problems with which it deals so well extend far beyond Communist China in the early 1950s."

ROBERT JAY LIFTON

© 1979 by Jill Krementz

Thought Reform was not published until 1961. In 1954-1955, meanwhile, Lifton taught at the School of Psychiatry in Washington, D.C., and in 1956-1961 was a research psychiatrist at Harvard University, where he was affiliated with the Center for East Asian Studies and also taught classes in the Harvard medical school. In 1961 he went to Yale University to take up an associate professorship sponsored by the Foundations' Fund for Research in Psychiatry. The post has allowed him a great deal of freedom for individual research and he has remained there, becoming a full professor in 1967.

In 1960, while still associated with the Harvard Center for East Asian Studies, Lifton had gone to Japan, where for almost two years he studied the attitudes of students in Kyoto to postwar changes in their society. Though the students could scarcely remember the war, he found them powerfully affected by it and by the bombing of Hiroshima, acutely aware of their country's "extraordinary immersion in death" seventeen years earlier. There followed six months of interviews with seventy-five survivors of the holocaust in Hiroshima itself. Lifton found that the survivors, regardless of class or education, reverted constantly to certain themes—a fear of the physical after-effects of radiation exposure, an intense awareness of death, and a chronic sense of guilt for having survived.

Lifton published his findings in *Death in Life* (1968), a "rackingly painful" book that its reviewer in *Newsweek* found also "genuinely illuminating—both rigorous and imaginative. ... It is one of those rare works destined to bear witness and change the lives of those who read it." It brought Lifton one of the most coveted of

American literary prizes, the National Book Award, as well as the Van Wyck Brooks Award for nonfiction. *Revolutionary Immortality,* also published in 1968, is a psychohistorical account of China's Cultural Revolution. In it, Lifton suggests that Mao, Chou, and other Chinese leaders have a sense of personal involvement in the historical process from which they derive an unconscious sense of personal immortality, and that this, rather than ideology, may have provided the motivation for the Cultural Revolution.

Lifton himself had been "profoundly shocked and emotionally spent" by his Hiroshima interviews and he has said that they were the turning point in his professional and personal life. Thereafter he threw himself with a new sense of commitment into his work for the peace movement, which he had joined in the late 1950s. He is one of the founders of Redress, an organization of concerned professional people, and through it, and his participation in teach-ins and mobilizations, he has fought against the "psychical numbness" which proceeds, in his opinion, from the blind worship of technology. He was particularly outspoken in his opposition to the war in Vietnam, the physical and psychological effects of which he saw for himself when he visited the country in 1954 and again in 1967.

The apocalyptic potentialities of nuclear war, Lifton believes, gravely threaten the human sense of "biohistorical continuity"—the feeling of being part of the great unceasing flow of human history. In *Boundaries* (1970), based on his 1969 lectures for the Canadian Broadcasting Corporation, he argues (in the face of Freudian orthodoxy) that the desire to transcend death is not mere self-delusion but a necessary part of a "formative-symbolic" process which is essential to psychic health. He sees some hope for humanity in the emergence of what he calls "protean man"—the sort of person who in pursuit of his true identity is able to experiment with a whole series of roles, or ideologies, or behavior patterns, discarding without a qualm those that do not satisfy him: "However misguided many of his forays may be, protean man also carries within him an extraordinary range of possibilities for man's betterment, or more important, his survival."

The same year Lifton published *History and Human Survival,* a collection of psychohistorical essays, lectures, and articles on an assortment of widely disparate themes. The collection was marred, it was said, by repetition, by a note of self-congratulation, and by its sometimes "grindingly academic" prose. It nevertheless seemed to many readers an important book, suggesting "directions and even meaning in the seeming chaos around us—our wars, our rebelling youth, our new ability to destroy ourselves." Christopher Lehmann-Haupt found evidence of "an artistic, synthesizing intelligence," able to reconcile apparently opposing forces in recent history and offering a "highly original and bracingly challenging perspective on most of the gut issues of our time."

In *Home From the War* (1973), his most ambitious and radical book, Lifton brings together his ideas about the "psychomythology of war-making." The book is based on "rap sessions" conducted over a period of two-and-a-half years with thirty-five veterans of the Vietnam war, all of them opposed to the war, and briefer sessions with many others. Lifton concluded that the war had placed these men in a "counterfeit universe" in which they were bombarded by the contradictory emotions of anxiety and "psychic numbing," of anger and guilt, leading to a deep sense of frustration and alienation when they returned from the war. Lifton and his colleagues, rejecting professional detachment, had encouraged the men to feel an "animating guilt" about their part in the war, an approach which for many of them proved cathartic. Some reviewers complained about the book's "oracular tone" and "moral arrogance," and Richard Locke, allowing that Lifton is "an enormously gifted clinical observer and interviewer," thought that in this work "imaginative research is debased to moralistic propaganda, high assertion substitutes for nuanced argument, and psychohistory becomes no more than intellectual new journalism." J.G. Gray, on the other hand, found it "fascinating and sophisticated" and "painfully instructive," and *Newsweek's* reviewer concluded that "the themes he pursues are complex and varied and his picture of veterans learning to live with their guilt, learning how to protect one another, silences all complaint."

Lifton is the co-author with Eric Olson of *Living and Dying* (1974), which discusses the problem of finding meaning in life in the face of our knowledge that it must end, and reverts to the notion of "symbolic immortality." This book, intended for laymen and adolescents, had a mixed but generally favorable reception. *The Life of the Self* (1976), subtitled "toward a new psychology," sets out to show how psychology has developed from Freud's "model of instinct and defense to Erikson's model of identity and the life cycle," and proposes a new model based on Lifton's own theories concerning the individual's awareness of death and sense of continuity. Most critics seemed to agree with *Choice's* reviewer, who called it a "loosely organized collection of essays [that] promises more than it delivers." Lifton is a compulsive cartoonist, a habit he describes as "a little more than doodling and a little less than talent"; *Birds* (1969) is a collection of his satirical drawings.

The author is a fellow of the American Academy of Arts and Sciences and has received many honors and awards, including three honorary doctorates. He has acted as a consultant to the Columbia seminars on modern Japanese and Oriental thought and religion (1965–), to the National Institute of Mental Health, and to the New York State Bar Association. As an expert on brain washing, he testified on behalf of Patricia Hearst when the heiress was tried for her part in a bank robbery carried out by the Symbionese Liberation Army.

Lifton was married in 1951 to Betty Jean Kirschner, a journalist and writer whose books include *Return to Hiroshima,* a poetic and moving account for children of the holocaust, and *Twice Born,* about her own life as an adopted child and her search for identity. The Liftons, who have a son and a daughter, divide their time between houses in New York City and Woodbridge, Connecticut, and their summer home at Cape Cod. In spite of his preoccupation with death, Lifton is far from morbid in his attitudes —he told an interviewer that "once you apply yourself to the problem of death, something in you expands a bit and you struggle with it creatively." A tall, lean man, he says that, apart from his cartooning, he relies on sports—especially tennis—and on the humorous imagination of his wife to preserve his sense of balance. He remains one of America's most outspoken critics of war.

PRINCIPAL WORKS: Thought Reform and the Psychology of Totalism: A Study of "Brainwashing" in China, 1961; Death in Life: Survivors of Hiroshima, 1968; Revolutionary Immortality: Mao Tse-Tung and the Chinese Cultural Revolution, 1968; Birds (cartoons), 1969; History and Human Survival: Essays on the Young and the Old, Survivors and the Dead, Peace and War, and on Contemporary Psychohistory, 1970; Boundaries: Psychological Man in Revolution, 1970; Home From the War: Vietnam Veterans—Neither Victims nor Executioners, 1973; (with Eric Olson) Living and Dying, 1974; The Life of the Self: Toward a New Psychology, 1976. *As Editor*—The Woman in America, 1965; America and the Asian Revolutions, 1970; (with others) Crimes of War, 1971; (with Eric Olson) Explorations in Psychohistory: The Wellfleet Papers of Erik Erikson, Robert Jay Lifton, and Kenneth Kenniston, 1975.

ABOUT: Contemporary Authors 17-20 1st revision, 1976; Current Biography, 1973; Who's Who in America, 1976-1977. *Periodicals*—Book World March 24, 1968; Christian Century February 6, 1974; Christian Science Monitor February 29, 1968; Commentary May 1968; Economist January 25, 1969; Encounter January 1969; Nation May 6, 1968; November 9, 1970; New Republic July 28-August 4, 1973; New York Review of Books March 28, 1968; June 28, 1973; New York Times Book Review February 5, 1961; March 31, 1968; June 24, 1973; New Yorker August 3, 1968; Newsweek April 6, 1970; Political Science Quarterly March 1969; Saturday Review February 3, 1968; February 20, 1971; Scientific American June 1968; Times Literary Supplement August 11, 1961; November 7, 1968; April 10, 1969; World Politics July 1969; Yale Review June 1961; March 1969.

LIMA, JOSÉ LEZAMA. *See* LEZAMA LIMA, JOSÉ

*LINDEGREN, (JOHAN) ERIK (August 5, 1910–May 31, 1968), Swedish poet, librettist, critic, and translator, was born in the northern coastal town of Luleå, near the Finnish border. He was the son of an engineer, Ernst Tullius Lindegren, and of the former Alma Elfgren, from whom he is said to have inherited his literary disposition. His father's work took the family south to Malmö in 1916, when the boy began his schooling, and north again three years later when Ernst Lindegren became first engineer in the mining town of Kiruna in northern Lapland, within the Arctic Circle.

In 1921, after a holiday in Germany where he began to read Goethe, Erik Lindegren was sent for his secondary education to Ostersund, in central Sweden, where he stayed with an aunt. In spite of economic difficulties, he went on to study philosophy at Stockholm University, but soon relinquished his studies to devote himself to criticism and poetry. His first book of poems was published as *Posthum ungdom* (Posthumous Youth) in 1935.

During the 1940s Lindegren edited *Prisma,* a magazine devoted to painting, music, ballet, and the theatre. At the same time, Lindegren and Karl Vennberg emerged as central figures among the poets who contributed to the short-lived but influential journal *40-tal* and the representative anthology, edited by Lindegren and Vennberg, called *40-tals lyrik* (Lyrics of the Forties, 1947). This diverse generation of poets, the *fyrtiotalisterna,* shared a sense of disgust at their country's neutrality in the face of Nazism. They also had in common a number of literary influences, including surrealism and the works of Kafka, Eliot, Dylan Thomas, and the Swedish poet Gunnar Ekelöf. The pessimism and the formal disjunctions associated with the *fyrtiotalisterna* are most powerfully exemplified in Lindegren's second book of verse, *mannen utan väg* (1942, translated by R. Bates and L. Sjöberg as "The Man Without a Way").

Written in 1939-1940, the volume was rejected by all the publishers to whom it was offered and was eventually published by the author himself, with the financial assistance of a friend. It

*lin' də grən

Swedish Consulate

ERIK LINDEGREN

consists of a sequence of forty poems built around the central symbol of a man at a cross-roads. Bemused before a signpost which offers too many directions, the man proceeds painfully towards a commitment to action. This potent symbol of the poet's despair and confusion at civilization's collapse into the chaos of Hitler's war is developed in an equally original and appropriate literary form. Each of the book's forty "exploded sonnets" consists of seven nonrhyming couplets. Capitalization, punctuation, and normal syntax are ignored, and lyrical felicities are scorned. Instead the reader is offered discord and cacophony, extreme compression, and verbal and imagistic juxtapositions of visionary and explosive violence, as in this sonnet about the role of the soldier in modern warfare:

to shoot the enemy and roll a cigarette
to flame up and die out like a beacon in a storm

to sit like a fly in the web of interested parties
to believe oneself born unlucky though one is
   merely born

to be a functionary in that which does not function
to be something else or not to be at all

to be fitted as the grey stone into the wall of hatred
and yet to feel contact like the joy of heather. . . .

to doubt that this must be the last time
to affirm everything if only not repeated

to break through and attain a lookout
where lightning stalks to avenge humanity

Slow to achieve acceptance, this most radical of Swedish poetic experiments of the 1940s

became a canonical book for a whole generation of young writers, achieving a status somewhat similar to that in English poetry of Eliot's *The Waste Land.*

Lindegren's subsequent poetry was on the whole less extreme—more resigned and elegiac in mood and more subtle and varied in manner. His delicate associative patterns and complex symbolical sequences have been compared to chamber music, and indeed no modern Swedish poet was more conscious of musicality than Lindegren, whose third book was called *Sviter* (Suites, 1947). Even the deliberate discords of *mannen utan väg* did not exclude a certain musical quality, and nine of the sonnets have been set to music by Karl-Birger Blomdahl. Lindegren also wrote the libretto for Blomdahl's opera *Aniara,* based on Harry Martinson's grim space fantasy, and translated the libretti for Mozart's *Don Giovanni* and Verdi's *Un Ballo in Maschera.*

Death, love, and "the idiotic drama of life" were Lindegren's principal themes, and the pessimistic collection *Vinteroffer* (Winter Sacrifice, 1954) was dominated by images of cold, distance, and petrification. But love, memory, and nature do offer fleeting, fragile visions of a better world, as in the longing, incantatory masterpiece on the transience of beauty, "En sang för Ofelia" (A Song for Ophelia).

Lindegren received the Book Lottery Prize in 1954 and was elected to the Swedish Academy in 1962. His notable translations included versions of Eliot's *Murder in the Cathedral,* and of *Hamlet,* as well as of works by Saint-John Perse, Éluard, Valéry, Faulkner, and Greene. He was married in 1950 to Karen Bergquist, and he died in 1968.

PRINCIPAL WORKS IN ENGLISH TRANSLATION: The Man Without a Way *in* New Directions 21 1969. *Poems in* Allwood, M. S. (ed.) Twentieth Century Scandinavian Poetry, 1950; Bäckström, L. and Palm, G. (eds.) Sweden Writes, 1965; Fleischer, F. (ed.) Seven Swedish Poets, 1963; Literary Review Winter 1965-1966.

ABOUT: Bäckström, L. Erik Lindegren (in Swedish), 1962; Bredsdorff, E. An Introduction to Scandinavian Literature, 1951; Gustafson, A. A History of Swedish Literature, 1961; Printz-Påhlson, G. Solen i spegeln, 1958. *Periodicals—* Books Abroad Autumn 1955, Winter 1975; Scandinavian Studies February 1970.

LLOSA, (JORGE) MARIO (PEDRO) VARGAS. *See* VARGAS LLOSA

"LONGBAUGH, HARRY." *See* GOLDMAN, WILLIAM

LONGFORD, ELIZABETH PAKENHAM (COUNTESS OF LONGFORD)

(August 30, 1906–), English biographer, writes: "I think I became a biographer partly because of my own large family—four girls and four boys—and I wrote short biographies of each one of them every year until they became eighteen. That must have given me a taste for characterisation. I published my first biography when my youngest child Kevin was seventeen. My training had been a mixture of academic and journalistic. I took my degree at Oxford University in classical history and philosophy. The result was to teach me how to argue a point. But it developed my critical faculties out of all proportion to my creative urges. Before university I wrote poetry and stories but never afterwards.

"Luckily it did not matter much, as for the next twenty years I was on and off politics, making speeches, lecturing and three times standing for Parliament as Labour. I had not a burning wish to get in, because of the family problem. I married at twenty-five and my eighth child was born when I was forty-one. The only things I published during those years were political manifestoes and election addresses. They were long-winded and cliché-ridden as these things are. I got out of that style by doing journalism. It was the best training in brevity, and you had to think of the reader. It counteracted my academic tendencies. My politics have always been left-wing. But I don't feel as violent as I did in the 1930s when I lectured to miners and potters living on the dole.

"In those days it was fairly rare for the prosperous to be socialists. But I had learnt a certain minority-mindedness in my childhood home. My mother and father were Nonconformists, my mother being a niece of Joseph Chamberlain, "Radical Joe" as he was called in youth. I was born in Harley Street, the London street of doctors, for my father was an opthalmic surgeon; but also a Unitarian lay preacher. As I was sent to Church of England schools, first day and then boarding, I felt 'different' from the word go. A habit of looking in on things from the outside can be a help in biography.

"I converted my husband to socialism, and he converted me to Catholicism. Though I am not active now in politics, my biographical subjects are moving in a left-wing direction. Having begun with Queen Victoria I am now working on her most astringent critic, Wilfrid Scawen Blunt, a militant anti-imperialist poet, who was imprisoned for holding a proscribed meeting in Ireland. I find writing and the family go well together in harness. This is true of many kinds of writing, though probably not for poets and

ELIZABETH PAKENHAM LONGFORD

perhaps not for novelists. But for my kind it is certainly true. I find that having a large family, now with twenty grandchildren, helps me to identify with my biographical subjects. I aim at a double vision, looking at them from the outside and inside, both at the same time."

Lady Longford is the daughter of Nathaniel Harman and the former Katherine Chamberlain. She was educated at Headington School, Oxford, and at Lady Margaret Hall, Oxford University. The "acknowledged belle of the university," and the star of a succession of student dramatic productions, she demonstrated a more serious side of her nature by beginning her career in 1929 as a Workers Educational Association lecturer at Stoke-on-Trent in the impoverished Midlands. A fellow lecturer there (not entirely by chance, their eldest daughter suggests) was Francis Aungier Pakenham, the second son of the Earl of Longford. They were married in 1931, and Frank Pakenham went on to teach and then to practice politics. He was personal assistant to Sir William Beveridge during World War II, became Baron Pakenham in 1945, and later was Minister of Civil Aviation (1948–1951) and First Lord of the Admiralty (1951). When his brother died in 1961 he succeeded him as Earl of Longford, subsequently serving as Lord Privy Seal (1964–1965) and Secretary of State for the Colonies (1965–1966), and as Leader of the House of Lords (1964–1968). He resigned from the Wilson cabinet in 1968 over the government's decision to defer the raising of the school-leaving age. Lord Longford is these days most widely known as a social reformer and moral crusader whose concerns include Ireland (his family is Irish), religion, penal reform and the plight of ex-prisoners, and pornography; he has written books on all these subjects and on others.

Lady Longford's own political interests, her husband's career, and the raising of their eight children occupied her until she was nearly fifty. However, in 1954–1956 she wrote weekly articles for the London *Daily Express* on the problems and pleasures of bringing up children, and a volume of these was published in 1954 as *Points for Parents,* her first book. *Catholic Approaches,* which appeared under her editorship in 1955, is a collection of essays on "modern dilemmas and eternal truth." Elizabeth Pakenham (as she then still was) next proposed a biography of her greatuncle Joseph Chamberlain but, denied access to his papers, and having already done a great deal of research on the period, she utilized this in a study of Jameson's Raid, part of Cecil Rhodes's abortive attempt to overthrow President Kruger of the Transvaal in 1895.

The first of Lady Longford's books to attract widespread attention was *Victoria R.I.* (1964), published in the United States as *Queen Victoria: Born to Succeed.* This long and detailed biography seemed to J. H. Plumb "easily the best that has yet appeared" and "wonderfully readable," drawing upon Victoria's unpublished journals "to build up an astounding portrait which leaves nothing out." Conor Cruise O'Brien thought it the definitive biography, noting in particular that "Lady Longford, with much art and tact, has 'done' the human interest side of Queen Victoria's life so well that no one else is likely to try it again." Most critics found the political background slightly sketchy, and some of the subordinate characters rather shadowy, but the book was very highly praised by almost all of its reviewers. It enjoyed the "enormous popular success" that had been prophesied for it, and received the James Tait Black Memorial Prize.

Lord Longford is the great-great-nephew of Kitty Pakenham, wife of the Duke of Wellington. This circumstance stimulated Elizabeth Longford's interest in the Duke, but, as she says, "nobody could fail to be interested in Wellington as a character; he was what one means by a character." Three years of research for her two-volume biography involved her in visits to all of Wellington's battlefields except the Indian ones —a necessary exercise because "not being a trained military historian, and never having fired a shot except once at a rabbit," she found it very difficult to visualize battles from maps. There is no shortage of eyewitness accounts of Waterloo and the other great battles of the period, and Wellington himself was a prodigious letter

writer—Lady Longford says "I really nearly did go off my head with all the confusions and contradictions. Sometimes I honestly did think I would blow up and never get it right."

She did not blow up, and her critics thought she got it mostly right. The first volume, *Wellington: The Years of the Sword* (1969), dealt with the great soldier's early life and his military career, ending with the victory at Waterloo, that "damned near thing." The *Economist* thought it "skated too lightly over Wellington's administrative and supply problems," but found the book as a whole sparklingly alive, admirably coherent and compulsively readable." George McDonald Fraser wrote that it had "one fault which Wellington would have spotted at once. It is a damned long book." Even Fraser, however, acknowledged that "Wellington is in there somewhere," and most critics shared the opinion of J.H. Plumb, who called the biography "as vivid, as full of color, as life-enhancing as a Rubens." *Wellington: Pillar of State* (1972) had a similar reception, though not even Elizabeth Longford "could invest Cabinet intrigues over Corn Laws and Catholics with the drama of Ciudad Rodrigo or Talavera." The *Times Literary Supplement* concluded that, "judged by the highest standards, her life of Wellington falls just short of being a work of art, but it is a tribute to her skill that the work should be judged by such standards."

In 1974 Lady Longford published both a "pictorial life story" of Winston Churchill and *The Royal House of Windsor,* "a warm-hearted, sensible appreciation of British monarchs since 1917." Meanwhile, she had turned her attention to Lord Byron, who attracted her "by his honesty, by the enigma of his personality, and by his attempt to get rid of cant." Her relatively short account of his life (in the "Library of World Biography" series) seemed to some readers overly selective, and lacking in color and anecdote, though "a decidedly romantic biography of an archetypal Romantic." A by-product was *Byron's Greece,* for which Lady Longford and the photographer Jorge Lewinski had "retraced Byron's footsteps through Greece" to assemble a book that was called "a judicious balance between travelog and biography."

As Richard Boston has said, "the Pakenham family is so successful, so talented, so glamorous, so numerous, that—like the Kennedy family—they attract a wonder which includes both admiration and jealousy." Apart from Lord and Lady Longford themselves, writers in the family include their eldest daughter, Lady Antonia Fraser, author of notable biographies of Mary Queen of Scots and Oliver Cromwell and more recently of highly popular thrillers, and their eldest son Thomas, who has published an account of the 1798 Irish rebellion. Of their other children, Judith is a poet and Rachel a novelist. A disadvantage of all this is that "the writing Pakenhams," as journalists like to call them, have to read each other's books. "That's the worst thing," Lady Longford says; "giving advice. We have a very strict barter system. If you offer a very long chapter, you have to take two short ones in return. But we do take one another's advice." Asked how she has managed to write so much in spite of all the other demands on her time, she explained: "I don't have a hard and fast line between working and not working. I just work wherever I am when I'm not having to do something else, in the train, on the bus, anywhere."

Richard Boston describes the author as "very charming to meet, very polite and helpful, a good talker, but slightly chilling. She is obviously a strong character and I imagine can be steely when she wants to be. She is not an easy person to get through to and an interview stays on a formal, rather impersonal basis." Lady Longford received a CBE in 1974. She served as a member of the advisory council of the Victoria and Albert Museum in 1969–1975, and she has been a trustee of the National Portrait Gallery since 1968. Her recreations are gardening and reading.

Elizabeth Longford says of the biographer's craft that "one really has to be a historical detective with an immense interest in people and the ability to re-create them in one's own mind as though they were living. . . . A high regard for the truth is absolutely necessary. . . . It is terribly tempting when somebody has said your character smiled, to turn it into 'his loud familiar laugh,' but you mustn't because there is no evidence. I notice that some biographers just have no conscience about that sort of thing." J.H. Plumb regards her as "one of the most accomplished biographers working today. Her art seems almost artless; for the speed and ease with which she can carry one through a long book is deceptive. If one takes any individual page or section, it all looks simple enough—a scene sketched in a few sentences, excellent quotations from the records, a shrewd observation on character here and there and a firm concentration on the story line. But each page, each short section, is a carefully contrived brick in a complex and impressive edifice."

PRINCIPAL WORKS: *As Elizabeth Pakenham*—Points for Parents, 1954; (as editor) Catholic Approaches, 1955 (U.S., Catholic Approaches to Modern Dilemmas and Eternal

Truth); Jameson's Raid, 1960; (with others) The Pakenham Party Book, 1960. *As Elizabeth Longford*—Victoria R.I., 1964 (U.S., Queen Victoria: Born to Succeed; an abridged illustrated edition was published in 1973 in both England and the United States as Victoria R.I.); Wellington: The Years of the Sword, 1969; Wellington: Pillar of State, 1972; Winston Churchill: A Pictorial Life Story, 1974; The Royal House of Windsor, 1974; Byron's Greece, 1975; Byron, 1976 (U.S., The Life of Byron).

ABOUT: Contemporary Authors 5–8 first revision, 1969; Who's Who, 1978. *Periodicals*—Book-of-the-Month Club News March 1970; Economist December 20, 1969; November 11, 1972; October 9, 1976; Guardian November 5, 1969; National Review April 27, 1973; New Republic March 13, 1965; New Statesman September 11, 1964; November 3, 1972; October 22, 1976; New York Review of Books March 11, 1965; May 17, 1973; New York Times March 1, 1970; November 14, 1976; New York Times Book Review January 10, 1965; March 1, 1970; March 18, 1973; New Yorker June 27, 1970; April 21, 1973; Times Literary Supplement October 1, 1964; November 13, 1969; November 17, 1972.

*LORENZ, KONRAD (ZACHARIAS)

(November 7, 1903–), Austrian naturalist and ethologist, was born in Vienna. His father, Professor Adolf Lorenz, was a self-made man who, starting life as the son of a poor harnessmaker, had become a brilliant and pioneering surgeon. It is said that he once charged a Chicago stockyard king a million dollars to cure his daughter of a hip deformity. Adolf Lorenz had married his young assistant, Emma Lecher, and later built a mansion at Altenberg on the Danube, where they had spent their honeymoon. Lorenz Hall, the culmination of Adolf's childhood dreams of becoming *ein grosser Herr,* was a monstrous folly, packed with Roman marbles, vast paintings, and the balustrades of dismantled Viennese bridges, with a magnificent view over the Danube towards the Alps.

Konrad Lorenz was born when his parents were in their forties and his only brother nearly twenty. Fearing that the child might be sickly or retarded, the professor considered abortion but in the end decided to let nature take its course, resolving however that "the newborn child must be fit to stand the extrauterine life or it had better die." Though frail and thin, the boy survived, and grew up at Lorenz Hall in its megalomaniac final form, a bizarre mixture of Baroque and Art Nouveau whose architect ended his life in an insane asylum.

Altenberg was nevertheless an ideal nursery for a future naturalist. The Danube marsh in those days spread several hundred yards inshore from the river bank, with dense willow forests, reeds, and drowsy backwaters. Lorenz described it in 1950 as "an island of utter wildness in the middle of Lower Austria; an oasis of virgin na-

*ló rents

KONRAD LORENZ

ture, in which red and roe deer, herons and cor-morants have survived the vicissitudes even of the last terrible war." It was an idyllic play-ground for the young Lorenz and his childhood friend Gretl Gebhardt, daughter of a neighbor-ing truck farmer. And it was at play that they first observed the curious biological phenome-non of "imprinting," noting that as they splashed around pretending to be ducks, newly hatched ducklings followed them as if they really were their parents. "What we didn't no-tice," Lorenz said at seventy, "is that I got im-printed on ducks in the process. I still am, you know. And I contend that in many cases a life-long endeavour is fixed by one decisive experi-ence in early youth. And that, after all, is the essence of imprinting." The boy's observations of animal behavior were not restricted to crea-tures in the wild, but also extended to such pets as a crocodile and a Madagascar lemur, ravens, cockatoos, the jackdaw colony he established in the attic, and an aquarium stocked with the fish and crustaceans he caught in the Danube.

Lorenz's formal education began at a private school run by an aunt, and at the age of eleven he entered the Schotten-gymnasium. This was one of the best high schools in Vienna, selected because it had a particularly fine science depart-ment, for the boy was expected to become a surgeon like his father and his brother Albert. This parental master plan soon brought Konrad Lorenz into conflict with his father, to whom he had previously been very close, and the tension was increased by his father's determination to separate him from Gretl, his childhood sweet-heart, so that he might make a more "suitable" marriage. The father won the first battle, and in

1922 Konrad Lorenz was sent across the Atlan-tic to study medicine at Columbia University in New York.

At Columbia he came into contact with Thomas Hunt Morgan, who was working on his experiments with fruit flies, and Lorenz has said that "it is one of the major prides of my life that I saw my first chromosome in the microscope of Thomas Hunt Morgan—the father of modern genetics." In other respects, however, Lorenz felt that he was wasting his time at Columbia, since the three pre-medical years there would not be recognized at home. In December 1922 he returned to Austria and entered the University of Vienna as a student, working at the same time as a demonstrator in the anatomy department. One of his students there was Margarethe Geb-hardt—his old friend Gretl. They were married in 1927, and Lorenz graduated the following year as a doctor of medicine.

Lorenz remained at the Anatomy Institute, where he was promoted to assistant (1928–1935). At the same time he studied zoology, receiving his doctorate in that subject in 1933, and pursuing the investigations which were to make him, as Sir Julian Huxley says, "the father of modern ethology." Ethology is the compara-tive study of the behavior of animals in their natural environment, as distinct from behavioral studies conducted under laboratory conditions. Lorenz is not merely a great naturalist, a sort of modern Fabre who has collected a vast amount of new information about birds and fishes; he has also contributed enormously to the way in which scientists approach the study of animal mind and behavior.

But the dominance of the behaviorists in aca-demic psychology was so complete that for many years Lorenz had great difficulty in getting his work accepted as "hard" science, and his early researches were further hampered by a lack of funds. At the beginning of the 1930s he had no animal institute or field station other than the family summer home at Altenberg, where he pursued his studies of jackdaws and geese. His wife Gretl, having given birth to their first two children in the early years of their mar-riage, had then resumed her studies, qualifying as a gynecologist in 1932 and subsequently con-tributing to the family income. In 1937 the Dutch ethologist Niko Tinbergen joined Lorenz for a summer's work on geese at Altenberg, but this relationship was severed the following year, when Austria was annexed by Hitler's Germany. By that time, Lorenz's work was beginning to gain some recognition, and in 1937–1940 he lec-tured at the University of Vienna on both com-parative anatomy and animal psychology. He had become interested in the philosophy of Kant, whose theory of "categorical imperatives" seemed to him close to the biological concept of innate instincts. Various associates managed to secure Lorenz's appointment in September 1940 as professor of psychology at the University of Königsberg in Germany. A third child was born during the academic year the family spent there, but in 1941 Lorenz was drafted into the army, serving as a neurologist in a psychiatric unit and later as a field surgeon.

It militated against the international acceptance of his work that some of Lorenz's most controversial views were first expressed in papers published under the Nazis in the 1930s and 1940s. He claims that he fully realized the evils of the regime "surprisingly late," when in 1943 or 1944 he saw transports carrying gypsies to extermination camps in occupied Poland. In June 1944 he was taken prisoner by the Russians near Vitebsk and sent to a prison camp in Armenia. He was repatriated in February 1948, and carried home two birds in a makeshift cage and a rucksack full of the manuscript he had written during his imprisonment. This was intended to form part of a four-volume standard work on ethology, which has not so far materialized, though the first volume of the completed section was published some thirty years later as *Behind the Mirror*.

Lorenz now had no university position, and it was in these years just after the war that he settled down to write the popular books, enlivened with his own humorous drawings, that have made him famous all over the world. The first of these was *Er redete mit dem Vieh, den Vögeln und den Fischen* (1949, translated by Marjorie Kerr Wilson as *King Solomon's Ring*). Originally commissioned as a book for children, it was equally successful with adults—Elspeth Huxley, for example, called it "the best animal book I've read for years." Full of lively and often extremely funny stories about Lorenz's pets and their behavior, and his relationships with a variety of free-flying wild birds, it is also an irresistibly fascinating introduction to the basic principles of ethology.

It describes how Lorenz's discovery of the rapid and largely irreversible kind of learning now known as "imprinting" arose from his attempts to hand-rear a great variety of birds, including the greylag goose. This is a highly effective way to study those innate behavior patterns that we call instinctive, for if a bird is hand-reared from an incubator egg and has never seen one of its own kind, its behavior must be instinctive rather than learned. In the case of the greylag goose, Lorenz's observations showed

that the newly hatched gosling follows the first moving object that it sees—normally its mother, but in the Altenberg experiment often Lorenz himself: hence the now familiar picture of him taking a morning walk followed by a faithful gaggle of young geese. With mallard ducks, who depend more on hearing than sight, this experiment failed until Lorenz learned to quack like a mother duck—a procedure evoked in another famous drawing, in which the great naturalist is shown crawling about a field, quacking for the benefit of ducklings which are unfortunately hidden by long grass from a group of horrified tourists. Imprinting is an elementary example of a genetically programmed pattern of behavior innate in all members of a species, but dormant until what Lorenz calls a "releasing mechanism" is triggered by some crucial experience.

So kam der Mensch auf den Hund (1950, translated by Marjorie Kerr Wilson as *Man Meets Dog*) discusses, also in popular terms, the ancient and intimate relationship between human beings and dogs. A useful guide for the dog lover, it also, like its predecessor, offers many new insights proceeding from Lorenz's studies. He found that a puppy may become imprinted upon its owner up to a point, but that it will always recognize another dog as a member of its own species, even if it sees one for the first time late in life; unlike the goose, the dog and most other mammals rely mainly on their sense of smell, which is not so easily fooled as sight or hearing. Lorenz also maintains, on the basis of common behavior patterns, that the ancestor of the dog was the golden jackal rather than the northern wolf.

These immensely successful books brought Lorenz's work to the attention not only of the general public but of such scientists as Professor Karl von Frisch, director of the Munich Zoological Institute. He and other influential friends were anxious to provide Lorenz with a field station in Germany, and this project began to be realized at Buldern, near Münster, where in December 1950 Lorenz took charge of a research station for the study of fish, ducks and geese, songbirds, and small mammals, as a subdepartment of the Max Planck Institute. This station was later moved south to Bavaria, where Lorenz went in 1954 as vice-director of the newly established Max-Planck-Institute für Verhaltensphysiologie (Max Planck Institute for Behavioral Physiology) at Seewiesen ("Lake Meadows"). Lorenz served as director of the Institute from 1961 to 1973, making it a place of pilgrimage for zoologists from all over the world.

During his early years at Seewiesen, Lorenz

was writing what was to become his most influential, but also his most controversial book, *Das sogenannte Böse: zur Naturgeschichte der Aggression* (1963, translated as *On Aggression*—by Marjorie Kerr Wilson in the United States and by Marjorie Latzke in England). The German title, which means "the so-called evil," expresses Lorenz's view that "aggression, far from being a destructive principle, is . . . one of the life-preserving functions of the basic instincts." His studies of such animals as the greylag goose had convinced him of the value of aggression—for example in establishing the sexual dominance of the most powerful males, which tend to father strong and healthy young. He distinguishes between true aggression, which is always directed against members of the aggressor's own species, and the actions of a predator like the lion, which attacks other species in response to hunger. True aggression does not threaten the survival of the species, however, because animals in their natural state develop "inherited patterns of restraint"—gestures of submission that appease the aggressor and allow the inferior combatant to escape. Furthermore, according to Lorenz, ritualization and redirection of the aggressive instinct not only establish a hierarchy within a group but actually form strong bonds between individuals: "The bond that holds a goose-pair together for life is the triumph ceremony and not the sexual relations between mates."

It is when Lorenz extends such observations by sweeping analogies to human behavior that psychologists, anthropologists, and even other ethologists have objected, pointing out, for example, that in such animals as the rhesus monkey there is no evidence of pair bonds being founded on ritualized aggression. Even its opponents admitted that *On Aggression* is an immensely readable book, but some thought that this made it all the more dangerous. The psychologist Erich Fromm feared that it would appeal "to the thinking of many people today who prefer to believe that our drift toward violence and nuclear war is due to biological factors beyond our control, rather than to open their eyes and see that it is due to social, political and economic circumstances of our own making." Lorenz himself agrees that aggression in the human species is destructive rather than "life-preserving." In his opinion, this is because human beings, evolving without the deadly natural weapons of many other animals, have never developed instinctive inhibitory mechanisms that would prevent them from killing members of their own species; thus, according to Lorenz, "the invention of artificial weapons upset the equilibrium of killing potential and social inhibi-

tions." In fact, as Lorenz's critics have pointed out, human beings are not the only animals capable of intraspecific killing. Some of his anthropological data have also been questioned, and his principal opponents, the behavioral psychologists, have continued to assert that aggression is a product of environmental factors, not genetic predisposition. All the same, Lorenz's views have been immensely influential, with other scientists and with the very large lay public that devour his own works and other popular studies espousing similar ideas, like Desmond Morris's *The Naked Ape* and Robert Ardrey's *The Territorial Imperative.*

Most scientists now accept that both instinct and learned behavior play their part in determining behavior, but for Lorenz, preoccupied with the importance of instinct, the nature-nurture controversy is very much alive. This is one of the many subjects discussed in the more strictly scientific papers collected in the two volumes of *Über tierisches und menschliches Verhalten* (1965, translated by Robert Martin as *Studies in Animal and Human Behavior*) and in *Antriebe tierischen und menschlichen Verhaltens* (1968, translated by B.A. Tonkin as *Motivation of Human and Animal Behavior*). It is also the theme of a smaller book, *Evolution and Modification of Behavior* (1965), in which he clarifies his position in relation to other schools of behavioral study. Lorenz's denigration of the importance of environment and his emphasis on inherited instinct as the main influence on behavior seem to some colleagues authoritarian and, specifically, right-wing. Criticism of this kind has centered particularly on a 1940 paper in which Lorenz sought to demonstrate that degenerative changes in behavior are brought about by domestication. Part of this paper was seen as an argument for "self-conscious, scientifically-based race policies," though David Snow believes that "the most serious charge that could be upheld was one of political naivety." Lorenz himself has since maintained that his intention had been "to tell the Nazis that domestication was much more dangerous than any alleged mixture of races. I still believe that domestication threatens humanity; it is a very great danger."

This thesis is developed in *Die acht Todsünden der zivilisierten Menschheit* (1973, translated by Marjorie Latzke as *Civilized Man's Eight Deadly Sins*). Overdomestication and overcivilization —the accelerating retreat from the natural—are seen as the main source of such ills as overpopulation, the rape of the environment, and "the waning of all strong feelings and emotion, caused by self-indulgence." Lorenz also fears

509

that the atrophy of instincts favoring the group above the individual, and tolerance towards antisocial elements, will lead to genetic decay in human beings. This book also had a controversial reception, but was welcomed by some critics as a stimulus to thought and argument, raising questions of central importance to the only animal species that is, as Rosemary Dinnage put it, "obliged to create . . . [its] own world."

The first half of the manuscript Lorenz wrote in the Armenian prison camp during World War II was published in Ronald Taylor's English translation as *Behind the Mirror* (1977). R.D. Martin said that the book "represents a search for a natural history of human knowledge, inspired by Lorenz's philosophical approach to ethology. . . . [It is] the clearest summary to date of Lorenz's philosophical standpoint on the observation and interpretation of animal behaviour, including the extrapolation of his views to human behaviour. As such, it is very valuable; as a general philosophical work it leaves something to be desired."

Since 1973 Lorenz has been director of the Department for Animal Sociology in the Austrian Academy of Science's Institute for Comparative Ethology; he administers a small station for the study of tropical fish near his home in Altenberg, and a similar center for the study of geese in the village of Grünau. He is a foreign member of the Royal Society (U.K.), a foreign associate of the National Academy of Sciences (U.S.A.), and a member of many scientific societies. He received the Gold Medal of the New York Zoological Society in 1955, the Vienna City Prize in 1959, the Gold Boelsche Medal in 1962, and the Cino de Duca and the Prix Mondial in 1969. He was awarded UNESCO's Kalinga Prize in 1970, and in 1973 his work was crowned by the award of the Nobel Prize, shared with his fellow ethologists Niko Tinbergen and Karl von Frisch. Professor Tinbergen has said of Lorenz that he "studies animals for their own sake rather than as convenient subjects for controlled testing. . . . He restored the status of observation of complex events as a valid, respectable, in fact highly sophisticated part of scientific procedure. In the process he discovered many hitherto unrecognized principles, and opened up many new, or almost totally neglected, lines of research. Above all, and in essence, he taught very many to look at behavior with the eyes of biologists— he made countless people aware of the fact that the behavior of each species is part of its equipment for survival and reproduction; that it is as much the product of evolution-by-means-of-natural-selection as are, say, the structure of the eye, or the functioning of the digestive organs."

Lorenz is a large man, six feet tall, with pale grey eyes, a grey beard, and thick silver hair. According to Alec Nisbett, his conversation is often "transformed by sheer enthusiasm into a near-monologue that may be brilliant but disconcertingly difficult to respond to. Seemingly arrogant and certainly assertive, he claims humility, and proclaims that a sense of humour is one of man's greatest assets since no one with a sense of humour can be a megalomaniac, or can fail to be humble."

PRINCIPAL WORKS IN ENGLISH TRANSLATION: King Solomon's Ring, 1952; Man Meets Dog, 1953; Evolution and Modification of Behavior, 1965; On Aggression, 1966; Studies in Animal and Human Behavior vol. 1 1970, vol. 2 1971; (with Paul Leyhausen) Motivation of Human and Animal Behavior: An Ethological View, 1973; Civilized Man's Eight Deadly Sins, 1974; Behind the Mirror: A Search for a Natural History of Human Knowledge, 1977.

ABOUT: Contemporary Authors 61-64, 1976; Current Biography, 1977; Evans, R. I. (ed.) Konrad Lorenz: The Man and His Ideas, 1975; Fromm, E. The Anatomy of Human Destructiveness, 1974; Highet, G. Talents and Geniuses, 1957; International Who's Who, 1977-78; Koestler, A. Drinkers of Infinity, 1968; Lorenz, A. My Life and Work, 1936; Montagu, A. (ed.) Man and Aggression, 1968; Nisbett, A. Konrad Lorenz, 1976; Who's Who, 1978. *Periodicals*—Hudson Review 1 1973; New Society April 21, 1977; New Statesman September 23, 1966; New York Review of Books December 15, 1966; April 18, 1974; New York Times Book Review June 19, 1966; New Yorker August 20, 1966; September 10, 1966; March 8, 1969; August 21, 1977; Psychology Today November 1974; Science November 2, 1973; Science News October 20, 1973; Time May 19, 1952; October 22, 1973; Times Literary Supplement January 19, 1967; March 3, 1972; August 30, 1974; February 4, 1977.

*"LU HSÜN" (also rendered as "Lu Xun," "Lu Hsin," "Lusin," etc., pseudonym of Chou Shujen) (September 25, 1881–October 19, 1936), Chinese short story writer, essayist, social and literary critic, and translator, was born in Shaohsing, Chekiang Province, into a family of businessmen and minor officials. Like his two younger brothers, he acquired the foundations of a classical Chinese education in a school maintained by the Chou clan. In the family library he conceived his lasting interest in science, art, folklore, and popular literature. One of his brothers, Chou Tso-jen, also became prominent as an essayist, scholar, and translator.

When Lu Hsün was thirteen, his grandfather, an important bureaucrat and a noted scholar, was arrested for attempted bribery. At the same time his father, Chou Feng-i, became seriously ill. These two events plunged the family into increasing poverty, and Lu Hsün, in the preface to his first collection of stories, recalled his almost daily visits to the pawnbroker to sell clothes and valuables in order to buy medicine. *lōō hsün

During these wretched years, the family was held together by the indomitable spirit of Lu Hsün's mother, a capable country woman who had taught herself to read and who exerted a profound influence on her son. It was her family name of Lu that he adopted as his pen name.

In 1898, shortly after his father's death, Lu Hsün went to Nanking. Until then educated in the traditional Confucian way, he now enrolled at the School of Railways and Mines, graduating in 1901. During his four years in Nanking he read widely in European science, philosophy, and literature, and was particularly excited by the Darwinian theory of evolution. This became an important element in his political and social thought, encouraging him to believe that people were capable of improving themselves and their environment, and that the Chinese, therefore, had it in their power to make their country strong, free of foreign exploitation.

Influenced by the terrible effects of his father's illness, Lu Hsün then decided that he would become a doctor. He obtained a government scholarship to study modern medicine in Japan and in 1904, after two years of language study in Tokyo, he entered the Sendai Provincial Medical School. He retained his interest in Western learning and, seeking to widen the horizons of his countrymen, began to publish popularized articles on scientific subjects in Chinese student magazines.

Lu Hsün spent less than two years at medical school. Seeing in a newsreel the humiliations of his countrymen during the Russo-Japanese War, he became convinced that their spirit was even more in need of healing than their bodies, and settled on a career as a writer and reformer. In 1906, after a brief visit home to submit to an arranged marriage, he returned to Tokyo and began a rigorous study of literature. Most influenced by Nietzsche, Darwin, Gogol, and Chekhov, he published two volumes of European and Russian short stories in translation and launched a short-lived magazine, *New Life*, which expounded Western ideas in classical Chinese.

Returning to China in 1909, Lu Hsün taught science for a year at Hangchow. He was principal of a school in Shaohsing in 1910-1911, and then from 1912 to 1926, with only brief interruptions, he served in the ministry of education in Peking. For some years he abandoned his crusade to rescue China from its spiritual ills. Disillusioned by the apathy of the masses and by what he saw of Peking politics, he immersed himself instead in the study of ancient Chinese inscriptions, carvings, and folk tales, publishing

a number of scholarly collections and commentaries.

His own family's decline into poverty had shown Lu Hsün the dark side of the traditional patriarchal society. To him, the Chinese way of life was compounded of cruelty, greed, complacency, and hypocrisy, and he believed that his compatriots, bemused by the "opium of self-esteem," had become the captives of their own cultural myths, which were cynically fostered by Western imperialists. The Confucian teaching that utopia lay in the past encouraged inertia, and even Sun Yat-sen's 1911 revolution, which swept the exhausted Manchu dynasty from power, was inspired, according to Lu Hsün, by the subconscious slogan Restore the Old.

It was the New Culture Movement of 1917 that aroused Lu Hsün from his own creative apathy, and he enthusiastically embraced its demands for literary realism—for a "literature of the people" written in the spoken vernacular instead of the classical style. His satirical essays, poems, and epigrams began to appear in the movement's magazine, *Hsin ch'ing nien* (New Youth). The Chinese, he wrote, had "never dared to face life," and this had led to a "literature of concealment and deceit." It was "high time for our writers to take off their masks, look life honestly, penetratingly, and boldly in the face, and write of flesh and blood."

To show what could be done, Lu Hsün published in the May 1918 issue of *New Youth* his story "K'uang-jen jih-chi," translated as "A Madman's Diary" and inspired by Gogol's story of the same name. It is an indictment of the genteel jungle of Chinese society, presented through the fantasies of a madman. It is also the first Chinese story that is wholly modern in conception and execution, and it was immediately recognized as a watershed in the development of Chinese literature. "Only today," says the madman, "do I realize that this world in which I have moved about for half a lifetime has been for over four thousand years a man-eating world."

Lu Hsün's masterpiece is the novella *Ah Q chen-chuan* (1921, translated as *The True Story of Ah Q*). The central character, the village odd-job man Ah Q, personifies servility, cowardice, and self-deception, the "diseases of the spirit" of the Chinese people. Ah Q rationalizes every beating he receives as a great personal victory, proudly dubs himself Foremost Self-Belittler, and stumbles gratefully from one disaster to another until he dies at the hands of the executioner, reflecting that "it is in the nature of things that some people should be unlucky enough to get their heads chopped off." The story brought

Lu Hsün national and international fame, and added a term meaning "Ah Q–ism" to the Chinese language.

Lu Hsün published these two stories and a dozen others in *Na Han* (1923, translated as *The War Cry*), and eleven more in *Pang huang* (1926, translated as *Hesitation*). These tautly realistic stories, written in the vernacular, had an immeasurable influence. Many of them are set in Lu Hsün's native Shaohsing, and C.T. Hsia has compared them to James Joyce's *Dubliners:* "Shaken by the sloth, superstition, cruelty and hypocrisy of the rural and town people, whom new ideas would not change, Lu Hsün repudiates his home town and, symbolically, the old Chinese way of life; yet, as in the case of Joyce, this town and these people remain the stuff and substance of his creation."

From 1920 to 1926, retaining his post at the Ministry of Education, Lu Hsün lectured on Chinese literature at National Peking University and elsewhere in the capital. However, his progressive views and his espousal of student causes brought him increasingly into conflict with the authorities. After the massacre of demonstrating students on March 18, 1926, which Lu Hsün called "the blackest day in Chinese history," he was listed as a dangerous radical and forced into hiding. He taught for a few months at Amoy University and then went as academic dean to Sun Yat-sen University in Canton, where the students gave him a hero's welcome. However, in 1927, distressed and disillusioned by the violence which accompanied the continuing student unrest, he left for Shanghai.

Lu Hsün spent the rest of his life in Shanghai with his common-law wife Hsü Kuang-p'ing. He wrote no more stories apart from some satirical versions of traditional tales published in 1936 as *Ku-shih hsin pien* (translated as *Old Tales Retold*). In Shanghai he studied Marxist theory and Soviet revolutionary literature, which he attacked, beginning a public debate with Communist critics. However, sharing with the Communists a belief that China could only be saved by total revolution, as well as a commitment to social realism in literature, he came eventually to support many socialist ideas and ideals. In 1930 he became a leading figure in the newly formed League of Left-Wing Writers and aided the Communist cause in many ways, although his distrust of the Communists' demand for ideological conformity prevented him from joining the Party. Throughout the rest of his life he poured out essays and articles attacking the condition of Chinese society and literature, and in particular the brutalities and oppressive censor-ship of Chiang Kai-shek's Kuomingtang government.

During the last few years of his life, these activities made Lu Hsün a marked man, in constant danger of arrest, protected only by the loyalty of his friends and his enormous personal prestige. After 1933 his work was officially banned and his essays published only clandestinely. It was at this time, nevertheless, that he achieved absolute mastery of the essay form, which in his hands became a witty and impassioned instrument of persuasion, laconic, but as multileveled and rich in implication as poetry.

During the Shanghai years he launched several magazines and produced a stream of translations, seeking always to introduce literature and ideas which he considered important to his country's development. He also wrote poetry, in both vernacular and classical modes. An expert on both Chinese and European woodblock printing, he brought about a revival of the technique, which thanks to him acquired a new importance both as an art form and as an economical method of mass communication and social education.

Geoffrey Grigson's *Concise Encyclopedia of Modern World Literature* gives this account of Lu Hsün and his working methods: "He was a small sardonic man with a heavy black moustache and the air of a ghost who has returned to haunt the world for all the suffering it has brought about. He wrote with extraordinary difficulty, painfully, chipping each word off his breastbone. He would write a line, or simply a few words, and paste them on the wall, and some weeks later another line would be added twenty inches away. Having accomplished so much, he would experiment endlessly until he had filled up that twenty inches. All four walls of the room would be covered with pasted strips, and after many months of work a story of perhaps ten pages would be constructed."

Lu Hsün died of tuberculosis in 1936. He was regarded as the greatest Chinese writer of his day, and as a fearless and uncompromising spokesman for national regeneration. After his death, Mao Tse-tung called him the "giant of China's cultural revolution." He has become something like a legend in China, the subject of innumerable memoirs, biographies, studies, and tributes. His complete works were published in Shanghai in twenty volumes in 1938, and there were supplementary volumes in 1946 and 1952, followed by his collected letters and diaries. A four-volume English-language edition of *Selected Works* was published in Peking in 1956-1960, and in London in 1967.

PRINCIPAL WORKS IN ENGLISH TRANSLATION: The True Story of Ah Q, translated by George Kin Leung, Shanghai, 1926; Ah Q and Others: Selected Stories of Lusin, translated by Chi-chen Wang, New York, 1941; Hesitation, compiled and annotated by Jörgensen, Shanghai, 1946; The War Cry, compiled and annotated by Jörgensen, Shanghai, 1949; Selected Stories of Lu Hsun, Peking, 1954; Chosen Pages From Lu Hsun, the Literary Mentor of the Chinese Revolution, New York (Cameron), 1959; Selected Works, translated by Yang Hsien-yi and Gladys Yang, Peking, vol. 1, 1956; vol. 2, 1957; vol. 3, 1958; vol. 4, 1960 (England, vols. 1-4, 1967); A Brief History of Chinese Fiction, translated by Yang Hsien-yi and Gladys Yang, Peking, 1959; Old Tales Retold, translated by Yang Hsien-yi and Gladys Yang, Peking, 1961; Silent China: Selected Writings of Lu Xun, translated by Gladys Yang, 1973; Wild Grass, 1974. *Stories in* Jenner, W.J.F. (ed.) Contemporary Chinese Stories, 1970; Kyn Yn-Yu, J.B. (ed.) The Tragedy of Ah Qui and Other Modern Chinese Stories, 1930; Snow, E. (ed.) Living China, 1937; Yuan Chia-hua and Payne, R. (eds.) Contemporary Chinese Short Stories, 1946.

ABOUT: Boorman, H.L. (ed.) Biographical Dictionary of Republican China, 1967; Chen, P.H. Social Thought of Lu Hsun, 1976; Ch'en Shou-yi, Chinese Literature, 1961; Chow Tse-tsung, The May Fourth Movement, 1960; Grigson, G. (ed.) Concise Encyclopedia of Modern World Literature, 1963; Hsia, C.T. A History of Modern Chinese Fiction, 1961; Huang Sung K'ang, Lu Hsün and the New Culture Movement of Modern China, 1957; Lai Ming, A History of Chinese Literature, 1964; Ting Yi, A Short History of Modern Chinese Literature, 1959.

Wide World Photos

ALISON LURIE

LURIE, ALISON (September 3, 1926–), American novelist, writes: "I was born in Chicago, Illinois, but moved with my family to New York City when I was four, and a year later to suburban White Plains, where my sister and I grew up in what was then still the country. Our father, Harry Lurie, was a professor of social work and later a social-work executive; our mother, Bernice Stewart, had been a journalist. It has been suggested that I inherited from my father an analytic and satirical attitude towards society, and from my mother the habit of observation and a strong curiosity about other people's lives.

"I was sent to good progressive day and boarding schools with a short and disagreeable interlude at the local public high school. In 1943 I graduated from Cherry Lawn School in Darien, Connecticut; and in 1947 from Radcliffe College, where I majored in English history and literature and wrote a thesis on the relations between the sexes in Jacobean comedy. I also published my first stories, poems, and reviews. After graduation I went to New York and became an editorial assistant for the Oxford University Press.

"In 1948 I married Jonathan Peale Bishop and followed him back to Cambridge [Massachusetts] where he was in the process of getting a graduate degree in English. During the next ten years I worked at various odd (in every sense) jobs, and had two children; I also wrote two novels and many short stories that nobody wanted to publish. By 1956 I had published nothing for seven years and was so much discouraged that I had virtually stopped writing.

"However, in the summer of that year a Boston friend, a poet and dramatist named V.R. Lang, died suddenly. I began to write a memoir of her and of the Poets' Theatre of Cambridge, which she helped to found—not for publication, but to preserve my memory of people and events. Other friends, David Jackson and James Merrill, paid to have a few hundred copies privately printed. A couple of years later, one of these came to the attention of an editor at Macmillan, who asked me if I had written a novel. I sent him the one I was working on, *Love and Friendship,* which he published in 1962.

"In 1957 I moved with my husband and two children to Los Angeles, and in 1961 we moved with three children to Ithaca, New York, where we have been ever since except for sabbatical leaves in London. For the last six years I have taught English part-time at Cornell University. I like teaching; besides, I think that writers who are not geniuses and/or cannot invent a world out of their own heads need some connection with reality, and not just to provide material. (Keeping house will do, but only while your children are small.) For the same reasons, I believe that it is useful as well as agreeable to follow up any passing or permanent interest or hobby. Mine, to date, have included astrology, crisis counseling, folklore, gardening, psychology, stage makeup, sociology, and witchcraft."

Love and Friendship, set in a small New England college, records the comic violence done to good sense when a young faculty wife plunges into self-fulfillment, having an affair with a romantic failure from the music department before climbing back to the safety of her boring marriage. "The plot of this novel is small," wrote William Barrett, "and its world tiny, but Miss Lurie's wit, like Jane Austen's, is wicked and delicious." The comparison with Jane Austen has been made often since then, although she is not one of the authors whose influence Lurie acknowledges; those are Charles Dickens, Christopher Isherwood, Philip Roth, and (most interestingly) Edith Nesbit (1858-1924), English writer of astringent and tough-minded fantasies for children.

Alison Lurie's second novel, equally witty and more assured, takes a young couple from the New England academic background the author knows so well and transplants them (as the author and her family were transplanted) to Los Angeles, the "nowhere city" of the title. The effects of this displacement from Eastern order to Californian chaos, from puritanism to license, are observed with the detachment and precision of a laboratory experiment. Paul Cattleman is briefly bewitched by Haight-Ashbury before returning to the green realities of New England; his frigid wife Katherine is first panic-stricken by Los Angeles, then remade by it—whether for good or ill is a matter of opinion, and the moral judgement is left entirely to the reader.

In its entertaining and highly readable way, *The Nowhere City* poses quite serious questions about the nature of personality and the extent to which "reality" is more real than fantasy. The same themes are pursued in the two novels that followed, *Imaginary Friends* and *Real People.* The first deals with a religious cult in upstate New York—Truth Seekers, who receive enlightenment from outer space—and with the two sociologists who come to study them. This theme seemed to one reviewer "a beautiful, expanding metaphor for innumerable complexities of human relationship." Indeed, the novel satirizes the truth-seeking sociologists as deftly as their dotty subjects, and leaves the reader questioning his own grounds for complacency. *Real People* masquerades as the journal of an extremely sensitive lady writer sojourning in Illyria, an imaginary haven much like the Yaddo artists' colony that has three times harbored Alison Lurie. Janet Belle Smith learns that neither art nor life is quite as "nice" as her short stories had always pretended.

Real People, the thinnest and least compelling of Alison Lurie's novels, was followed by what many thought her best book to date, *The War Between the Tates.* Here, as often before, she uses adultery as a means of exploring moral values, in a story about the descent into sexual skirmishing of an apparently perfectly married middle-aged faculty couple. But in this ambitious novel, the closet warfare between Brian and Erica Tate, and between them and their teenage children, is examined against the background of the real war in Vietnam and such other emblems of the period as the generation gap, liberation movements, campus unrest, drugs, and Eastern religions.

John Leonard complained that the characters "are never permitted to experience their own possibilities, cerebral or visceral," and that "having so severely limited her characters, Alison Lurie seems contemptuous of them." And it appeared to John W. Aldridge that the author was "aware of more than she can imaginatively comprehend." Acknowledging that "hers is an authentic fictional voice," he concluded that "there is also something hobbled and hamstrung about her engagement of experience." Most reviewers, however, were more than content with the faultless prose, the brilliant scenes, the marvelous polish. One writer in the *Times Literary Supplement* called it "a very cool, funny, and didactic tale," and a work of quality, "cabinet-made, with dovetailed joints and secret drawers and marquetry inlays."

The same anonymous critic has discovered something more in Alison Lurie's novels, a faintly visible other dimension, "an allegorical shape. Sometimes, as with the Anna May Mundy/ Anima Mundi character in *Real People,* it has been more obvious than at others. Her first level of analogy is always the academic world or one of its disciplines: *Imaginary Friends* was the book of the sociologist, of the group idea; *Love and Friendship* of the linguistic or philosophical idea; *The Nowhere City* (which had no history) of the historical idea. The parallel between the Tates' private war and political theory is quite explicit; even to see the war as an image of contemporary American society or foreign policy ... would be permissable, though not very fruitful. For the real inspiration of Miss Lurie's entertaining fables is her fascination with levels of truth, with the war between fact and fantasy. ... That pretending is wrong is the moral of all Alison Lurie's books."

PRINCIPAL WORKS: *Novels*—Love and Friendship, 1962; The Nowhere City, 1965; Imaginary Friends, 1967; Real People, 1969; The War Between the Tates, 1974. *Nonfiction* —V.R. Lang: A. Memoir, 1959 (Munich; also published in V.R. Lang: Poems and Plays, 1975).

ABOUT: Contemporary Authors 1-4 (first revision), 1967; Vinson, J. (ed.) Contemporary Novelists, 1976. *Periodicals* —Commentary August 1969; January 1975; New Republic August 10, 17, 1974; New York Review of Books December 7, 1967; August 8, 1974; New York Times Book Review

July 19, 1974; New Yorker October 11, 1969; Publishers Weekly August 19, 1974; Times Literary Supplement February 19, 1970; June 21, 1974.

"LUSIN." *See* "LU HSÜN"

"LU XUN." *See* "LU HSÜN"

MAC A'GHOBHAINN, IAIN. *See* SMITH, IAIN CRICHTON

McAULEY, JAMES (PHILLIP) (October 12, 1917–October 14, 1976), Australian poet and critic, was born at Lakemba, New South Wales. He was educated at Fort Street Boys' High School and the University of Sydney, from which he gained his M.A. and a diploma in education. It seemed to Vincent Buckley, reading some of the poems McAuley wrote as an undergraduate, that he was then "the very type of the Joycean intellectual"—a romantic rebelling, apparently, "against the dour necessities of life itself. It was a rebellion compounded equally of fierceness and irony, of realistic analysis and romantic yearning, of an urge to self-expression and an urge to self-laceration in the very act of expression." From 1938 until 1942 McAuley was a high school teacher. In 1942 he joined the Australian army, serving in the East Indies in education work. The experience he thus gained led to his appointment after the war as Smith Lecturer in Government at the Australian School of Pacific Administration (1946–1960).

In his early twenties, when he was learning from many masters, McAuley was for a time influenced by the then prevailing Jindyworobak Club, whose founder and leading polemicist was the late Rex Ingamells. The Jindyworobak's aim, according to Bruce Elliott, was to introduce a "new respect for the literary and artistic ecology of the country, treating all imported idea-systems as antagonistic to . . . the true, native spirit." They valued romantic spontaneity, linguistic excitement, and "irrationalism." The young McAuley contributed what Elliott has called "electric and memorable" poems to the Jindyworobak anthologies. By 1944, however, he had abandoned his eclecticism and rejected both the Jindyworobaks and the more sophisticated experiments of Dylan Thomas and Henry Treece. He expressed his disenchantment with modernism in one of the most celebrated literary hoaxes of the century.

One afternoon in 1944 McAuley and his friend Harold Stewart concocted sixteen poems by a fictitious poet, Ern Malley, whom they represented as having died (owing to self-neglect) of Graves' Disease at the age of twenty-five. "We produced the whole of Ern Malley's

JAMES MC AULEY

tragic life-work in one afternoon, with the aid of a chance collection of books which happened to be on our desk." Their three rules of composition were that there should be no coherent theme, no care was to be taken with verse technique, and the style was to be fashionably "apocalyptic." "Sweet William," a typical Malley poem, begins:

> I have avoided your wide English eyes:
> But now I am whirled in their vortex.
> My blood becomes a Damaged Man
> Most like your Albion;
> And I must go with stone feet
> Down the staircase of flesh . . .

Max Harris, editor of the magazine *Angry Penguins,* was completely deceived and published all the poems, with an enthusiastic introduction. When the hoax was revealed, Harris was made to look a fool and modernist poetry was mocked all over the English-speaking world. All the same, there was perhaps more verbal energy in Malley's hopelessly inchoate verse than its creators recognized; this aleatory method of composition is now taken seriously by some critics. However, McAuley had made his point. From this time, though he retained his nationalism, he opted for classicism, conservatism, and an uncompromisingly satirical attitude towards modernism.

Under Aldebaran, McAuley's own first collection of poems, appeared two years later. It includes elegant love lyrics, meditations on the meaning of the poet's inner states, harsh satires on modernism in the arts and liberalism in society. Vincent Buckley called it the work of "a mind and sensibility passionate, graceful, and intelligent," but found some of these poems "too self-concerned, too lacking in the more obvious kinds of human sympathy." G. A. Wilkes praised the "natural precision" of the more sardonic poems but, like Buckley, thought it an uneven collection. It seemed to Wilkes, moreover, that the "studious arrangement of the contents, the careful dating . . . the 'Notes' . . . all suggested that McAuley was . . . taking seriously —perhaps too seriously—his own intellectual and poetic development." Nevertheless, *Under Aldebaran* gained its author immediate recognition in Australia as a poet of exceptional gifts. Indeed, some critics maintain that McAuley never surpassed the complexity, grace, and sensuous perception of the best of his early lyrics, like "Envoi":

There the blue-green gums are a fringe of remote
  disorder
And the brown sheep poke at my dreams along the
  hillside;
And there in the soil, in the season, in the shifting
  airs
Comes the faint sterility that disheartens and
  derides.
Where once was a sea is now a salty sunken desert,
A futile heart with a fair periphery;
The people are hard-eyed, kindly, with nothing
  inside them;
The men are independent but you could not call
  them free.

McAuley became a convert to Roman Catholicism in 1952, a development celebrated in his second book, *A Vision of Ceremony* (1956). It includes the polemic and reactionary "A Letter to John Dryden," full of such sarcasms as: "Perhaps you'd choose T. Eliot's mighty line,/ To drift, and flutter, hesitate, opine,/ Hint at meaning, murmur that God knows,/ And gently settle in a soup of prose." But this is exceptional; most of the poems in *A Vision of Ceremony* set out to evoke the poet's new-found sense of harmony, order, and serenity. Wilkes found a "new perceptiveness. . . . a startling clarity born of austerity and self-discipline," though some critics regretted what seemed to them a further loss of warmth and simple humanity.

As a Catholic convert, McAuley hated above all the lack of commitment and certainty he saw all around him in postwar Australia, and the consequent decline of fixed principles in human relations, in politics and society, and in the arts. He expressed these views very vehemently in his poetry, in his essays (like those collected in *The End of Modernity*), and in *Quadrant,* the influential magazine he founded in 1956.

In 1957 McAuley read Patrick White's novel

Voss, and it was this that inspired him to write his one attempt at an epic, *Captain Quiros* (1964). As Wilkes has said, *Voss* challenged the "poets with having allowed their art to fall away from the greater tasks"; McAuley felt that poetry had been "dethroned" by prose and tried to reclaim the throne with a poem conceived as a presentation of a "significant action, examined in all its levels of psychological penetration, pathos, irony, moral and metaphysical meaning." Quiros, whose story is told by his secretary Belmonte, was a late sixteenth-century navigator who set out to claim "Terra Australis" for Catholic Christendom, but failed. The poem is an attempt to demonstrate the superiority of "liturgical" over "secular" literature; the latter is "narrow," according to McAuley, while the "liturgical work" is "limitlessly wide, because of its rigorous concentration on the most universal themes which contain through their simplicity an endless wealth of significance." While some reviewers thought that *Captain Quiros* was "sustained by its dramatic structure," and it was respectfully received, most found it lacking in intensity, and its ardent nationalism was not welcomed by the postwar university generation.

McAuley returned to shorter forms in *Surprises of the Sun* (1969) but seemed to have misplaced his "exquisite lyric gift." A reviewer in the *Times Literary Supplement* found these poems "hotly attitudinizing," and some of the opinions they expressed "of a fatuous stridency calculated to make invention flee and the reader blench," as in this valedictory for Roy Campbell:

He stood against the levelling stampede
And cracked the stockman's whip of his polemic;
He never left his friends or slurred his creed
In times when cowardice grew epidemic. . . .

The same reviewer concluded that McAuley "has always been a first-rate talent with a second-rate message, satisfactory as a poet only when the message is left on one side, with the result that his slighter poems are impeccable and most of his important ones flawed right through." This is a harsh judgment, and most critics would prefer the more moderate one expressed by William Walsh: "Occasionally he falls into a belletristic euphony of an oratorically archaic sort; occasionally his sympathies contract and harden against the world, when the fresh and trembling openness of his fully realized poems is slurred over in an idiom of overmusical, poetic reference. McAuley's poetry shows the conviction of the complex kind, reflective, troubled, caustic, intensely feeling and probingly analytic; but more important than all this is the way one's senses catch in it the tremor of creation and an unfaked individuality of rhythm." He is one of the poets who helped "to extricate Australia from the parochial despotism of the Victorians," and the chief exponent, with his friend A.D. Hope, of the classical tendency in Australian verse.

Despite his outbursts of ill-temper (largely contrived), McAuley was in general a genial, witty, and fair critic. He was temperamentally incapable of judging anything written in free verse, but towards such modernists as Rosemary Dobson and the late Francis Webb, who employ more or less traditional forms, he was both generous and discerning; his *A Map of Australian Poetry* (1964) is a painstaking and invaluable guide to his forebears and successors. He was one of the first Australian critics to suggest reservations about the achievement of Christopher Brennan, in spite of the fact that Brennan was the father of the intellectual, "European" branch of Australian poetry to which McAuley himself belonged; his verdict on Brennan, intelligently and tactfully stated, is now generally accepted. He wrote well on Rilke, whose influence may be seen, well assimilated, in his own best poetry. As A. N. Jeffares wrote of his last published book, *The Grammar of the Real* (1976), his criticism has a "welcome practicality," and is the product of a powerful and wide-ranging mind. His reputation suggests that posterity will not judge him on the strength of his didactic intentions but on what he achieved in spite of them.

In 1960 McAuley became professor of English literature at the University of Tasmania, at Hobart, where he gathered around him many disciples. His magazine *Quadrant,* founded as a quarterly, became a bi-monthly in 1963 under the auspices of the Australian Association for Cultural Freedom; McAuley remained as its co-editor until his death. He had five children by his marriage in 1942 to Norma Abernethy.

PRINCIPAL WORKS: *Poetry*—(with Harold Stewart, as "Ern Malley") The Darkening Ecliptic, 1944 (reprinted as Poems, 1961); Under Aldebaran, 1946; A Vision of Ceremony, 1956; The Six Days of Creation, 1963; James McAuley (selected poems), 1963; Captain Quiros: A Poem, 1964; Surprises of the Sun, 1969; Collected Poems 1936–1970, 1971; Music Late at Night: Poems 1970–1973, 1976. *Criticism*—Poetry and Australian Culture (published with Felons and Folksongs, by R.B. Ward), 1955; The End of Modernity: Essays on Literature, Art and Culture, 1959; C.J. Brennan, 1963 (revised as Christopher Brennan, 1973); A Primer of English Versification, 1966 (U.S., Versification: A Short Introduction); The Personal Element in Australian Poetry, 1970; A Map of Australian Verse, 1975; The Grammar of the Real: Selected Prose 1959-1974, 1976. *As Editor*

—Generations: Poetry from Chaucer to the Present Day, 1969.

ABOUT: Buckley, V. Essays in Poetry, 1957; Dutton, G. (ed.) The Literature of Australia, 1964; Elkin, P.K. (ed.) Australian Poems in Perspective, 1978; Penguin Companion to Literature 1, 1971; Smith, V.B. James McAuley, 1970; Walsh, W. Commonwealth Literature, 1973; Wilkes, G.A. and Reid, J.C. Australia and New Zealand, 1970. *Periodicals* —Horizon Summer 1976; Meanjin September 1971; Overland Autumn 1957; Southerly 3 1947, 3 1957, 4 1969; Times (London) October 18, 1976; Times Literary Supplement April 9, 1976.

McCLURE, MICHAEL (THOMAS) (October 20, 1932–), American poet and dramatist, was born in Marysville, Kansas, the son of Thomas McClure and the former Marian Dixie Johnston. He attended the University of Wichita in 1951–1953 and the University of Arizona in 1953–1954 before receiving his B.A. from San Francisco State College in 1955. He thinks of his college years as "a hermetic period. . . . like a very long silent meditation on forms."

Originally attached to the Bay area of San Francisco in the hope of studying art with Mark Rothko and Clyfford Still, McClure was soon swept up in the vigorous local poetry movement. At college he had written metrical and stanzaic verse in imitation of John Donne and William Blake, but in San Francisco he developed a free, spontaneous, and highly visual style in keeping with his own conception of the role of poetry— one that made lavish use of block capitals, multiple exclamation marks, assorted type sizes, varying line lengths, and a "body-language" of animal growls, howls, and screams. The example and tutelage of Robert Duncan was an important factor in this transition, and McClure has also been greatly influenced by such "prophetic" poets as Blake and Whitman, by Antonin Artaud's concept of "total theatre," and by Eastern philosophy and religion. McClure seems to have arrived quite early in his career at the theories which are illustrated in his published work and explained in his *Meat Science Essays* and elsewhere. He believes that "all life is a single unitary surge, a single giant organism" from which humanity has separated itself by excessive reliance on mentality. If we are not to be overwhelmed by the technology we have created and the destructiveness bred in us by our isolation, we must find our way back to "a mindless purely biological state," and this may be achieved through drugs, Yoga, or trance dancing, through art or through sex. McClure's "spontaneous man" lies in sunlight on the floor of the forest and gives himself completely to his body: "He groans, writhes, twists, denies himself nothing that the sinew and tendons and lungs and

517

MICHAEL MC CLURE

heart request." Although his conscious mind is a "blank field," the stretching man by his actions proclaims that "matter is spirit and the meat is the container. . . . stretching his leg and twisting the muscles of his arms in pleasure creates reason. The pearl gleaming on flesh in the light is an act of reason!"

Robert Duncan and the other practitioners of "projective verse" favor "composition by field" —a poetry that is not logical or analytical but spontaneous, directly reflecting the poet's leaps and changes of feeling, his passing reflections, perceptions, and private associations, however irrelevant they may appear to the "theme" of the poem in hand. The crucial unit of composition in this kind of poetry is the line, which is supposed to vary in accordance with the changing biological rhythms of the poet himself, and especially the rhythm of his breathing. McClure has adopted this approach to poetry and extended it, as was already evident in his first significant collections, *Hymns to St. Geryon* (1959) and *Dark Brown* (1961). These poems were presented as organic extensions of the poet, "the direct emotional statement of the body." A characteristic poem in *Dark Brown* is "Oh Ease Oh Body-Strain Oh Love Oh Ease Me Not! Wound-Bore," which begins:

be real, show organs, show blood, OH let me
be as a flower. Let ugliness arise without care
    grow side by side with beauty. Oh twist
be real to me. Fly smoke! Meat-real, as nerves
              TENDON
Ion, FLAME, Muscle, not banners but bulks as
    we are all 'deer'
and move as beasts. Stalking in our forest
    as these are speech-words!

Mick McAllister wrote in the issue of *Margins* devoted to McClure (March 1975) that "the most startling new thing in *Hymns to St. Geryon* is the plasmic coming to shape of the word and the poem in Hymn I ('The Gesture'). Here projective verse reaches its logical end; the poem becomes 'a body of words'. . . . If the poem is an organism, then the words are the cells of the creature. . . . The poem does not exist on the page; it flows from McClure through the page to the reader and takes its home in the cells of memory in our brains. . . . The physical showing forth, the evocation of tangible presence, in Michael McClure's poetry is his unique skill."

Ghost Tantras (1964) was followed by several minor collections and then by *Star* (1970), one of the most discussed of McClure's volumes of poetry. R. J. Griffin in *The Nation* praised the book's great range and wrote: "The poet has matured without mellowing—'mellow McClure' would be a contradiction in terms. He now manages better than ever a strange conflation of braying self-proclamation and wry self-mockery. . . . Visually his poems stand somewhere between ordinary and shaped poetry. . . . He favors a great variety of line lengths, and ruled lines across the page . . . that work like white space italicized. . . . McClure is no mere manic screamer, nor simply manic here and depressive there. He has never actually written at fever pitch all the time, and *Star* . . . makes clearer than ever his mastery of modulation." Needless to say, some academic critics saw no more in these poems than "rhetorical hysteria" and "bullhorn sloganeering in mad, tall type." J. M. Warner asserted that "McClure is not a poet. . . . He is simply out of control. He reacts to a technological society that has lost sight of the value of the individual and the 'meat' of the body. . . . What is fundamentally wrong with his vision and subsequently his form, is his failure to assume the responsibility of the human being to live and extend what he was born with."

The long poem *Rare Angel* (1974) seemed to David Southern McClure's "purest, most personal work to date." In it, wrote Mick McAllister, "he continues the fleshing out of his vision. The word/cells of the poem are the living particles of an angel-body, organic, representing the unity of history and prehistory, protozoa and star. . . . The poem tracks from mind-world to nature-world, from laughing bluejays to starships; the reader is invited to spread his imagination to fill the volume of the poem. The poem is a river, and we are the river; it flows, and the voices and scenes of the poem flow within it. . . . This is McClure's power: the magic evocation of palpable form, the shaman's recognition of the passionate sensuality of the glacier and star, the intent seriousness of amoeba, planaria, and bee."

September Blackberries, containing poems written between 1968 and 1974, deals most often with what McClure calls "the collision of imploding spiritual values and environmental collapse." This collection, like all of McClure's books, seemed to his admirers important and liberating, though some professional critics remained unliberated. Seamus Cooney, for example, found it typographically strident and said this appearance was not deceptive: "Most of the book is impassioned rhetoric announcing urgent truths, preaching the unity of all forms of life, invoking sacred animals and places. . . . if the result strikes me as the egotistical sublime run rampant, his passionate and sensuous conviction will persuade others. And even resistant readers will enjoy the quieter lyrics."

Karl Malkoff says that McClure thinks of himself as a prophet, but "prophets must make us feel their truths. . . . The question in McClure's case is whether his formal qualities, his sense of free form, are enough to provide the tension that his imagery only occasionally produces." Many of his readers unquestionably do "feel his truths." His poetry, wrote K. C. Power in *Margins,* "shows us that words can become strange & rich again, & that as physical extensions of the body they carry reverberations of the whole history of man's evolution." Eric Mottram has called McClure "one of the most vital and original poets in America, developing some extremely personal forms of typographical, spatial and ejaculatory effects which . . . form a profoundly intimate poetry of love and transcendental experience."

In 1959 McClure began writing for the theatre, and about twenty of his plays have been produced. These are mostly short pieces and resemble his poems in their concerns, in their use of animal noises and "body language," and even in their appearance on the page:

LIFE IS BLASPHEMY, AND ITSELF AN END
IN COLDNESS, IN COLDNESS. OH
all to burst, I shall burst. Free,
    FREE FREE FREE
Oh secret black hunger blossoming to what is
    unseen,
That all is pain reaching to pain, and the
HOT ACT IS A COOLNESS WITHIN IT!

(from *The Blossom; or, Billy the Kid*)

Billy the Kid reappears in the best known of McClure's plays, *The Beard.* First seen at The Committee in San Francisco in August 1965, it reached off-Broadway in New York in 1967, and was subsequently staged in London. When the play opens, two archetypal American figures are seated on golden thrones, Billy and Jean Harlow. The young actress taunts the young killer, confident that he desires her. He replies with an obscenity, she answers with another. "From the moment she answers," wrote the British critic Ronald Bryden, "it is clear they cannot turn back from some sexual encounter, but there is no hurry. . . . the vacancy they inhabit is the eternity of American myth. . . . An hour of patterned, delicate sparring and provocation, deliciously deliberate as the play of foul-mouthed children in a hot, empty hayfield, will pass before he plunges his head into her satin lap in an action so private that it still, apparently, lacks an English name."

Bryden was delighted by the play, and thought it interesting that "in order to claim for America the careless, unbounded possibility of its origins and myths, McClure has had to return to that supposed dead end of the early fifties: poetic drama. . . . To express the larger-than-life ordinariness, McClure has gone back to the theatrical manner, a poetic patterning of clichés, of T. S. Eliot." Eric Mottram received a different impression of the play, seeing Harlow and Billy as "reenactors of destructive rites" finally enabled through sexuality to "regain the *tantra* of men and women as 'mammals and gods and goddesses.' " Others, of course, were less impressed. Harold Clurman found it "not a play to like or to dislike" but "a phenomenon to be understood"; he thought it "inconsequential as art . . . a mockery of sex, a 'milestone' on the road to nonentity." However, a critic in *Newsweek,* noting that the play's language was "without question the 'filthiest' ever heard on a commercial stage in the English speaking nations," concluded that "raising profanity to a comic passion . . . McClure has written a brilliant little monster of a play." The New York production collected two "Obie" awards in 1967.

Eleven of McClure's short plays were collected in *Gargoyle Cartoons* (1971). J. Pyros, writing in *Margins,* characterized them as "odd, kinky, bizarre, confusing, profound," the literary offspring of Ionesco, Dadaism, and the Theatre of the Absurd, cruel in a manner reminiscent of Mack Sennett as well as Artaud: "painless, bloodless, sorrowless." And Arthur Sainer says that McClure's plays "aren't to be seen as much as they're to be tasted, rubbed against, snuggled into, chewed, immersed in." *Gorf,* whose settings include Thebes and the Abyssinian desert, charts a man's journey into myth and his disastrous return to reality. First produced at the

Magic Theatre in San Francisco in 1974, it seemed to one reviewer "not much more than an occasionally humorous collection of alternate theater and counter-culture clichés"—"a deplorably pretentious play," with a "flying purple phallus" for a hero.

McClure has also tried his hand at fiction. The two novellas in *The Mad Cub,* narratives of the drug experience, struck one reviewer as nightmarish but ultimately boring. There was a more respectful reception for McClure's novel *The Adept* (1971). The narrator is Nicholas, a self-absorbed young pusher who sets off into the Arizona desert on his Harley Davidson to do business with a corrupt border guard, and ends by killing him. Like all of McClure's work, this provoked violent antagonism in some critics but impressed others. Sara Blackburn praised "its dazzling descriptions of surface detail, its fascination with sensory preceptions, and its insistence on the value of style rather than story," but went on: "If McClure wants us to understand the beauty of yoga unity and the Nirvana state of oneness with the universe . . . it's strange he's chosen the dealer personality of Nicholas to act it out for us." Josephine Hendin called it "a wild book about a man who adores his body, but hates himself, hates the fact of being full of murder." McClure has also compiled an "as-told-to" account of the life and times of Frank Reynolds, a prominent Hell's Angel.

McClure has taught since 1962 at the California College of Arts and Crafts, where he is now an associate professor. He has received the Magic Theatre Alfred Jarry Award for drama, and grants and fellowships from the National Endowment for the Arts and the Rockefeller and Guggenheim foundations. McClure was married in 1954 to Joanna Keera Kinnison; they have one child, Katherine Jane, and live in San Francisco. A critic in the *Times Literary Supplement* has called McClure a "writer who takes his place with a number of American anti-authoritarians reacting to the threat of organized passive formality." and whose work is "one of the more remarkable achievements in recent American literature, a record of a man's attempt to find the terms he needs for a vital balance, for some kind of homeostasis of body and psyche."

PRINCIPAL PUBLISHED WORKS; *Poetry*—Hymns to St. Geryon, 1959; The New Book: A Book of Torture, 1961; Dark Brown, 1961; Ghost Tantras, 1964; Little Odes, Poems, and A Play, The Raptors, 1969; Star, 1970; Rare Angel (writ with raven's blood), 1974; September Blackberries, 1974; Jaguar Skies, 1975; Antechamber and Other Poems, 1978. *Plays*—The Blossom; or, Billy the Kid, 1967; The Beard, 1967; The Cherub, 1970; Gargoyle Cartoons (contains The Shell, The Pansy, The Meatball, The Bow, Spider Rabbit, Apple Glove, The Sail, The Dear, The Authentic Radio Life of Bruce Conner and Snoutburbler, The Feather, The Cherub), 1971; The Mammals (contains the Blossom, The Feast, Pillow), 1972; Gorf, 1976; The Masked Choir *in* Performing Arts Journal August 1976. *Fiction*—The Mad Cub, 1970; The Adept, 1971. *Nonfiction*—Meat Science Essays, 1963; Freewheelin' Frank, Secretary of the Angels, as told to Michael McClure by Frank Reynolds, 1967. *As Editor*—(with James Harmon) Ark II/Moby 1, 1957; (with David Meltzer and Lawrence Ferlinghetti) Journal for the Protection of All Beings, 1961.

ABOUT: Action, J. (and others) Mug Shots, 1972; Allen, D.M. The New American Poetry, 1960; Clements, M. (ed.) A Catalogue of Works by Michael McClure, 1956–1965, 1965; Contemporary Authors 21–24 1st revision, 1977; Kherdian D. Six Poets of the San Francisco Renaissance, 1967; Leary, P. and Kelly, R. (eds.) A Controversy of Poets, 1965; Malkoff, K. (ed.) Crowell's Handbook of Contemporary American Poetry, 1973; Meltzer, D. (ed.) San Francisco Poets, 1971; Penguin Companion to Literature 3, 1971; Vinson, J. (ed.) Contemporary Dramatists, 1977; Vinson, J. (ed.) Contemporary Poets, 1975; Who's Who in America, 1976-1977. *Periodicals*—Book World August 15, 1971; Choice September 1977; Christian Century January 17, 1968; Library Journal May 1, 1974; Margins March 1975; Nation November 13, 1967; July 20, 1970; New Republic December 2, 1967; Newsweek November 6, 1967; New York Times Book Review June 20, 1971; Poetry August 1962; Saturday Review November 11, 1967; Time November 3, 1967; Times Literary Supplement March 25, 1965.

McGUANE, THOMAS (FRANCIS III) (December 11, 1939–), American novelist and screenwriter, was born of prosperous Irish stock in Wyandotte, Michigan, the son of a manufacturer, Thomas Francis McGuane, and the former Alice Rita Torphy. Looking back on his childhood, McGuane recalls his maternal grandmother's house as "a through-the-looking-glass place . . . full of people who really valued wise-cracks and uncanny stories," and uncles who were "fantastic storytellers." These were promising beginnings for a writer, but then came a boarding school where McGuane's early literary efforts were discouraged (except by one friend who had read all of Proust by the time he was twelve). Things picked up again at Michigan State University, where McGuane received his B.A. in English in 1962. He went on to the Yale School of Drama (M.F.A., 1965) and then, in 1966, to Stanford University as a Wallace Stegner Fellow in creative writing. His short stories have appeared in such journals as *TriQuarterly, Fiction,* and *Esquire,* and he has written on boats and fishing for *Sports Illustrated.* The books he most admires include Burton's *Anatomy of Melancholy, The Unfortunate Traveller* by Thomas Nashe, and the novels of Swift, Wyndham Lewis, and Céline: what they have in common, as he says, is "the comic exaggeration and excesses of language carried to an almost hallucinogenic degree."

McGuane's central theme, as Thomas R. Ed-

Laurie McGuane

THOMAS MC GUANE

wards points out, is "the perilous testing of man against man, the bonding of male aggressions in a violent rivalry that may also be a mode of understanding and even love. . . . Clearly this is Hemingway country. Not just the he-man pleasures of McGuane's men but even the locales of the novels. . . . McGuane's bias is aristocratic, and this marks a limitation (though scarcely a flaw) in his art thus far. His heroes are young men of family, with money behind them, who *choose* not to participate in privilege. Yet below them McGuane can find little but the plastic-and-neon 'Hotcakesland' of commercialized America, where . . . the imagination of death—the only thing left of meaning after the loss of God, country and family—is safely muffled by the consumer goods that swaddle us."

Much of this is already evident in McGuane's first novel, *The Sporting Club* (1968). The setting is a venerable and exclusive hunting and fishing club up in Michigan, where the stolid and conscientious John Quinn meets his old friend Vernor Stanton. The bored and doom-ridden Stanton is a disappointed idealist who treats the world "like the shit it is," and entertains himself as best he can with travel, practical jokes, and assorted troublemaking. Disgusted by the aristocratic poseurs who run the Centennial Club, he gradually involves Quinn in his plans to disrupt the place. Thanks to their machinations, the haughty manager is fired and replaced by Earl Olive, a slob from "Hotcakesland" who floods the club's chaste woodland preserve with fornicating motorcyclists, and is challenged by Stanton to a duel with plastic bullets. Olive loses and ignobly retaliates by dynamiting the club's dams and hunting lodges. Stanton, having

achieved all he set out to do, ends the novel as owner of the wrecked Centennial Club, but insane.

Joyce Carol Oates wrote that "a sense of dizziness, of speed, of a peculiarly cerebral combination of drollery and sadism will carry the reader some distance. . . . An accelerating plot and apparently straight passages of trout-fishing will carry some readers a further distance. . . . But in the end . . . [the novel] promises more than it gives." All the same, Oates praised McGuane's ear for dialogue and his "light, fashionably cool touch," and called him "that notorious and difficult creature—a writer of promise." Other reviewers were bored by the trout-fishing, found the characterization turgid and sketchy, and Stanton's high jinks ultimately as unattractive as the suave jocks they are directed against. But Sara Blackburn was reminded of *The Great Gatsby* by "this tight, funny, elusive and aristocratic novel . . . this hard, wry, thoughtful tale," and she called McGuane "one of the most original and interesting young novelists to have appeared in a long time." The novel was filmed in 1971.

The Stanton role passes in *The Bushwhacked Piano* (1971) to another young lunatic, Nick Payne. Nick's madness, in which he murders a neighbor's piano, is a by-product of his discovery of mortality. This shocking recognition leads him to disassociate himself from the squalid society in which he has been living, and the novel becomes a picaresque as Nick lights out from "a Stonehenge of gas pumps" in search of something more real—love, America, or himself. He pursues his rich girlfriend, a photographer, to her parents' ranch in Montana; becomes a bronco rider; teams up with C. J. Clovis, a multiple amputee and con man seeking to make his fortune by recruiting bats in the battle against mosquitoes; and fights to the finish against Wayne Codd, an appalling, cliché-spouting cowboy. In the end, exhibited in his ex-girlfriend's first photography show as "a cautionary monument of the failed life," Nick feels that he has made his point.

"McGuane is a writing fool," wrote Geoffrey Wolff, who found the book reminiscent of J.P. Donleavy's *Ginger Man;* it "is a trove of pleasures, and no man I'd care to drink with would dislike it." Jonathan Yardley didn't dislike it, but had reservations: "Because it flows so smoothly, it seems effortless—but McGuane's prose is constructed with the greatest care and precision. . . . His social criticism is no less acute. . . . His problem is not style without substance, for he has plenty of both, but condescension to many of his secondary characters. He conveys a poignant awareness of the general shabbiness of the human condition: it is when he gets down to individual particulars that he is less persuasive." Paul West called the author "a clinician of the ephemeral on behalf of self-styled nature lovers."

Thomas Skelton, the hero of *Ninety-Two in the Shade* (1973), is another *non serviam* dropout. He is hitchhiking home to Key West, burned out by drugs, nauseated by politics, exasperated by "declining snivelization," to become a fishing guide: "Simple survival at one level and the prevention of psychotic lesions based upon empirical observation of the republic depended on his being able to get out on the ocean." His new career runs into an obstacle named Nichol Dance, a brilliant guide who resents competition and warns him off with a cruel practical joke. When Skelton, in retaliation, burns Dance's boat, the latter promises to kill him if he ever tries to guide again. Both are men of what Dance calls "credence"—who in a world that offers little worth believing in, believe in keeping their word and "following through" on what they undertake. So, although Skelton admires Dance and Dance is fond of Skelton, the tragic outcome is determined: "Dance shot him through the heart anyway. It was the discovery of his life."

"That last sentence," as Thomas R. Edwards says, "reads several ways: death is indeed a once-in-a-lifetime discovery, maybe what Skelton was looking for all along, maybe the discovery of his life at the instant of its loss, and I suppose that 'his' could point also to Dance, recovering what otherwise would remain lost if the act weren't done." Edwards' only serious reservation about the novel was McGuane's lack of sympathy for characters "who fall short of his own intelligence, intellectual sophistication and toughness." Walter Clemons had another complaint—that despite "unexpected, complex ironies, the relation of Skelton and Dance is too laconic and abstract to achieve quite the classic fatality McGuane aims for" in this "very fine book."

Paul West, who thinks that McGuane's novels have been overrated, finds in them solid vindication of Alfred Kazin's assertion that American absurdists, "unlike the Europeans who invented the term because they have a quarrel with existence . . . have merely realized the limitations of our own power." To Thomas R. Edwards, however, he seems "an important as well as a brilliant novelist, one of our most truthful recorders of a dreadful time," who like Mailer and Pynchon "makes the page, the paragraph, the sentence itself a record of continuous imaginative activity, the capturing and organizing of the bits and pieces a deteriorating culture throws up"—a master of "the brave play of language at the brink of inexpressible horror."

McGuane is also the author of three notable screenplays: *Rancho Deluxe* (1975), *The Missouri Breaks* (1975), and the movie version of *Ninety-Two in the Shade* (1975), which he himself directed. He received the Rosenthal Award of the National Institute of Arts and Letters in 1972. McGuane was married in 1962 to Portia Rebecca Crockett and has a son, Thomas Francis IV. The author divides his time between the family home (and his three boats) at Key West and seven hundred acres in Montana, but says that he is "pretty rootless." A "suntanned outdoorsman," he is "tall, lean, with strong facial features," and an enthusiastic student of natural oddities, from bats to tropical hardwoods.

PRINCIPAL WORKS: *Novels*—The Sporting Club, 1968; The Bushwhacked Piano, 1971; Ninety-Two in the Shade, 1973; Panama, 1978.

ABOUT: Contemporary Authors 49-52, 1975; Vinson, J. (ed.) Contemporary Novelists, 1976; Who's Who in America, 1976-1977. *Periodicals*—America May 15, 1971; Atlantic Monthly September 1973; Book World May 2, 1971; Christian Science Monitor January 19, 1969; Commonweal October 26, 1973; Critique 1 1975; Fiction International 4–5 1975; Library Journal March 15, 1971; Nation April 14, 1969; New Times October 30, 1978; New York Review of Books June 23, 1973; December 13, 1973; New York Times Book Review March 23, 1969; March 14, 1971; July 29, 1973; New Yorker September 11, 1971; June 23, 1973; Newsday April 12, 1971; Newsweek April 19, 1971; July 23, 1973; Saturday Review March 15, 1969; March 27, 1971; Time August 6, 1973; Times Literary Supplement August 21, 1969.

McNALLY, (MICHAEL) TERRENCE (November 3, 1939–), American dramatist, was born in St. Petersburg, Florida, and grew up in Corpus Christi, Texas. He is the son of Hubert McNally, who "made Schlitz the best-selling beer in Corpus Christi," and the former Dorothy Katharine Rapp. They were "terrific" parents, McNally says, and his childhood seems to have been a very happy one. He thinks that "the biggest influence on my imagination as a child was *Kukla, Fran and Ollie,* which was really a theatre show that happened to be transmitted through television." At twelve he became an opera addict, thanks to a nun at his parochial school. "My youth was a little like *American Graffiti,*" McNally told Guy Flatley. "Driving around Mac's Drive-In in our cars, going to the beach and drinking beer. But there was also listening to the Saturday afternoon broadcast of the opera and reading poetry, and not being made to feel a freak for it. In high school, there was an English teacher—Maureen McElroy—

TERRENCE MC NALLY

United Press International

rifice of a new victim invited into the sanctuary each evening, but. . . . *It* comes in the end." McNally's achievement in this play, Weales thought, "is that he manages to convey the pain of his characters despite their nastiness, which is often very funny." Other critics have pointed out that this "parable about placating evil with evil" had "uncomfortable national parallels." The play was well received in Minneapolis but in New York in 1965, with a different cast and director, it failed totally. Wilfrid Sheed called it "the most overtly homosexual play yet seen on Broadway" and (incidentally) "a bad play" and John Simon voted it "the prize horror of the season." McNally nearly gave up and went home, but instead stayed in New York as assistant editor of *Columbia College Today,* an alumni magazine (1965–1966).

A Guggenheim fellowship in 1966 encouraged McNally to try again, and the result was *Next,* a one-acter about a middle-aged misfit who is mistakenly inducted into the army and subjected to a humiliating physical by a gruesome female sergeant. He fends her off with a string of ironic or anarchic jokes, and then turns on her (and the society she represents) with savage indignation. The play did moderately well in Westport, Connecticut, in 1967, and was rewritten for Elaine May's off-Broadway production in 1969 (by which time several of McNally's early plays had been seen in New York). John Simon wrote: "I would never have thought that he had a play like *Next* in him. I was clearly wrong, and I couldn't be happier about it." It seemed to Harold Clurman that McNally's "worthy" intention had been "to launch an exacerbated attack on the mechanics of a civilization which is taken as an acceptable, because inescapable, norm. The flaw—though it should be emphasized that this sketch is one of McNally's better efforts—is that the farcical opening fails to anticipate the final onslaught. One is uncertain whether the stronger impulse is the author's impulse to be as funny as hell or to vent his spleen. The result is a discomfiting uncertainty of style." The play, with McNally's friend James Coco in the lead, nevertheless ran for seven hundred performances. McNally has acknowledged his debt to Elaine May, who taught him "that plays are about what people do, not what they say, that dialogue is only the tip of the iceberg. And she taught me to write *people* instead of symbols. Audiences come to the theatre to find out about the people on stage, not to be lectured by Terrence McNally on the social and political state of America."

In *Sweet Eros* (1968) a sad young man abducts a girl with a view to rape. He ties her to a chair

who took several of us under her wing. She had a *salon,* and we would go to her house after school and drink Cokes and she would tell us things about Shelley and Shakespeare."

McNally majored in English at Columbia University (1956–1960), where he was Phi Beta Kappa, wrote a varsity show, and was awarded an Evans Traveling Fellowship (1960). He received his B.A. in 1960, and then went home to Corpus Christi to start his career as a journalist. This had been a long-standing ambition, but it was feature writing that attracted him and "my jobs were always straight news stories." Disenchanted with newspaper work, he sent an early play to Mollie Kazan, who found it promising but thought he needed practical experience in the theatre. Thanks to her, McNally returned to New York in 1961 as stage manager at the Actors' Studio. Later the same year he was hired as tutor to the teenage sons of John Steinbeck, and accompanied the novelist and his family on a round-the-world tour (1961–1962). From 1963 to 1965 he wrote film criticism for *The Seventh Art,* turning out plays in his spare time. Among the many close friendships he formed in the New York theatre world during these years was one with Edward Albee, his roommate for three years.

And Things That Go Bump in the Night, the first of McNally's plays to be produced, opened at the Tyrone Guthrie Theatre in Minneapolis in February 1964. Gerald Weales has described the play as a "destruction parable in which a bizarre family group attempt to save themselves from *It,* the nameless fear outside their basement sanctuary. . . . Ruby and her two children choose evil and attempt to survive through the ritual sac-

and harangues her while stripping her naked. This early sample of stage nudity caused a considerable furor—in fact, McNally says, "I don't think the audience really *heard Sweet Eros*—the news story overwhelmed what the play was trying to say." McNally's other short plays of the late 1960s include *Tour, Botticelli* (first performed on television in 1968), *¡Cuba Si!* (in which a woman revolutionary encamped in Central Park tries but fails to arouse the United States to revolution), *Witness, Noon* (about an assortment of sexual perverts confronting each other's hangups), and *Bringing It All Back Home,* a savage sketch of contemporary callousness. They consolidated the author's reputation as one of the most prolific, accomplished, and successful of the contemporary dramatists writing for off-Broadway and the collegiate and regional theatres.

Where Has Tommy Flowers Gone?, a two-act play staged at the Yale Repertory Theatre and then at the Eastside Theatre in New York, had a fairly cool reception. Edith Oliver called it "an anthology of brief incidents—straight scenes, put-ons, monologues, and flashbacks—that portray, or at least illustrate in a tangential way, the life and attitude of one Tommy Flowers, cutup, freeloader, and stagestruck rebel against society, and that also, taken together, make up a kind of dossier of his disenchantment with just about everything." Homeless and jobless in New York, Flowers survives by a combination of theft and charm, adopts a sheepdog and a destitute old actor, and falls in love with a beautiful cellist. The piece ends in betrayal and disaster. Edith Oliver concluded that parts of the play are clever and very funny, with many telling scenes and "sharp, immediate, characterizations," but "as social satire, it is too diffuse for anything that has so little to project except an attitude of revulsion —and even that attitude and its targets are shopworn."

This was followed by what many critics regard as the best of McNally's plays to date, *Bad Habits,* which was first performed at the John Drew Theatre in Easthampton, New York, was subsequently seen off-Broadway, and wound up at the Astor Place Theatre in February 1974. *Bad Habits* is actually two one-act plays, "Ravenswood" and "Dunelawn," set in two different but equally expensive and insane mental institutions. In the first the inmates are advised by Dr. Jason Pepper that the way to emotional health is through untrammeled indulgence in nicotine, alcohol, sex, and any other bad habits that appeal to them. Dunelawn is in the care of the saintlike Dr. Toynbee, who (as Clive Barnes put it) "talks in a kind of cultivated gibberish"

and absolutely proscribes all the indulgences that Pepper prescribes. Barnes concluded that McNally "is an unusual American comic playwright. He is not especially witty in the American comedy tradition. The lines that get the biggest laughs are never jokes as such, but simply summing up on situations. McNally hardly writes plays at all. He takes a comic situation . . . and populates it with real people, or, at least, real cartoon people. Perhaps he is like a terribly sharp and incisive *New Yorker* cartoonist—and perhaps you do have to be on his particular wavelength of satirical lunacy to love his awareness of human absurdity."

The most discussed of McNally's subsequent plays was *The Ritz,* which began life at the Yale Repertory Theatre in January 1974 as *The Tubs.* It extracts a good deal of humor from the plight of a Cleveland garbageman in New York who, in flight from his Mafia brother-in-law, seeks refuge in a bathhouse that turns out to be full of manic homosexuals. It was filmed in 1976 from McNally's screenplay by Richard Lester.

In 1973 McNally held a CBS fellowship in creative writing at the Yale School of Drama. He received an Obie award in 1974 and a grant in 1975 from the National Institute of Arts and Letters. *Apple Pie,* a program comprising *Botticelli, Tour,* and *Next,* was televised in January 1969. Much interviewed during the run of *Bad Habits,* McNally was described by Guy Flatley as looking like "a slightly fallen, thirty-four-year-old cherub . . . vaguely southern-sounding," with close-cropped hair and "baby-blue eyes," whose own bad habits include cigarettes and alcohol. (McNally says he once gave up smoking for a year, but "my whole life became not smoking. I wrote next to nothing and lost all my friends.") McNally lives in Greenwich Village with a cairn terrier named Charley. According to Flatley he is "slim of build and has never been married or institutionalized. Or even been to a shrink." McNally says that he has "always been envious of playwrights who give interviews in which they make profound statements about their plays. But I just don't think that way. Obviously, *Bad Habits* is commenting on certain psychiatric practices, and I'd be curious to know how psychiatrists view the plays. What I really hope, though, is that I've created characters people will laugh with and be touched by. That's how I approach plays—through characters." He acknowledges the influence of Shakespeare, Mozart, Beckett, Pinter, and a number of contemporaries, including Edward Albee.

PRINCIPAL PUBLISHED WORKS: And Things That Go Bump in the Night, 1966; Apple Pie: Three Plays (Tour, Next,

Botticelli), 1968; Next, 1969; (with Israel Horovitz and Leonard Melfi) Noon *in* Morning, Noon, and Night, 1969 (also *in* Richards, S. [ed.] Modern Short Comedies, 1970); Sweet Eros, and Witness: Two One-Act Plays, 1969; Tour *in* Parone, E. (ed.) Collision Course, 1969; Sweet Eros, Next, and Other Plays (with Botticelli, ¡Cuba Si!, Witness), 1969; ¡Cuba Si!, Bringing It All Back Home, Last Gasps: Three Plays, 1970; Where Has Tommy Flowers Gone?, 1972; Whiskey, 1973; Bad Habits, 1974; The Tubs, 1974; The Ritz and Other Plays (with Bad Habits, Where Has Tommy Flowers Gone?, And Things That Go Bump in the Night, Whiskey, Bringing It All Back Home), 1976.

ABOUT: Contemporary Authors 45–48, 1974; Crowell's Handbook of Contemporary Drama, 1971; Poland, A. and Mailman, B. (eds.) The Off Off Broadway Book, 1972; Simon, J. Uneasy Stages, 1975; Vinson, J. (ed.) Contemporary Dramatists, 1977; Weales, G. The Jumping-Off Place, 1969; Who's Who in America, 1976-1977; Who's Who in the Theatre, 1977. *Periodicals*—Commonweal May 21, 1965; New York Post May 25, 1974; New York Times January 24, 1971; March 10, 1974; Times (London) February 12, 1974.

© 1979 by Jill Krementz

JOHN MC PHEE

McPHEE, JOHN (March 8, 1931–), American journalist, was born in Princeton, a university town in central New Jersey, and has spent most of his life there. He is the son of Harry Roemer McPhee and the former Mary Ziegler. His father, a doctor, included among his patients several U.S. Olympic teams as well as athletes from Princeton University, and partly for this reason sport has always been important to John McPhee. At the Princeton public schools he excelled at basketball and at English, and he recalls with particular gratitude a high school teacher who demanded three rigorously organized compositions a week. Most summers were spent canoe-tripping in Vermont at Keewaydin, a camp where McPhee eventually became a counselor. He finished high school in Princeton and then spent a year at Deerfield Academy, a prep school in Massachusetts, where his prowess at basketball is still remembered. He entered Princeton University with the class of 1953.

McPhee played basketball in his first year at Princeton, and throughout his four collegiate years appeared regularly on *Twenty Questions,* a popular television and radio program on which a panel (whose token student member he was) sought to identify mystery objects by deductive logic. He also contributed to the *Princeton Tiger,* the *Nassau Literary Magazine,* the *Daily Princetonian,* and the *Princeton Alumni Weekly.* He had already decided that he was going to be a writer, and even then had set his sights on the *New Yorker,* though the stories and poems and articles he sent there from college all came back to him. While at the university, McPhee wrote his first, and so far his only, novel, a partly au-

tobiographical story called "Skimmer Burns," which he was allowed to submit in lieu of a senior thesis.

Receiving his B.A. in English in 1953, McPhee spent a postgraduate year at Cambridge University and toured the British Isles with a university basketball team. Back in Princeton, he tutored for a time at a local school and then went to New York to begin a not very successful career as a freelance writer. He had not found a publisher for his novel and he settled down to try his hand as a television dramatist. "Each morning," he told an interviewer, "I would thread my bathrobe sash through the spokes of the chair and tie myself in. This was the only way I could work because I just couldn't accept my situation." Between 1955 and 1957 he sold three plays to the *Robert Montgomery Presents* television show and then gave up. He joined *Time* magazine, writing on films and plays and sometimes books, producing cover stories on show business celebrities, and winding up as an associate editor.

McPhee was with *Time* from 1957 to 1964, and found the work well-paid, demanding and soul-destroying. Meanwhile he continued to knock at the doors of the *New Yorker,* which in 1963 opened to admit a single article—an account of a basketball game McPhee had once played in the Tower of London. Encouraged, he offered a profile of Bill Bradley, the great Princeton and later professional basketball star. When the editors demurred, he wrote them a five-thousand-word letter describing the article, wringing from them no more than a promise to read the piece. The completed profile, seventeen thousand words long, was delivered in December

1964 and published the following month. McPhee was soon afterwards invited to join the *New Yorker* as a staff writer. This means that the magazine gives him a quarterly retainer and pays most of his expenses in exchange for a first option on everything he writes. He chooses his own subjects and follows his own working methods, and any piece that the *New Yorker* rejects he is free to sell elsewhere. It is an arrangement that fills most journalists with hopeless envy.

Virtually all of McPhee's books first saw the light as articles or series of articles in the *New Yorker*. They deal with a varied assortment of subjects which have one thing in common—that McPhee is interested in them, and in many cases has been interested in them since childhood. His first book, *A Sense of Where You Are* (1965), was an extended version of his profile of Bradley. Rex Lardner found the book "immensely well-written, inspiring without being preachy," and providing "the clearest analyses of Bradley's moves, fakes and shots that have appeared in print." This was followed by *The Headmaster* (1966), a profile of Frank Boyden, headmaster of Deerfield Academy. About the only serious criticism leveled at these two books was that McPhee had been guilty of hero-worship—that he had said "all the good things that might have been said" about his subjects and "few of the bad."

After two books growing directly out of McPhee's own experience came one that developed more chancily. He became intrigued by the fact that orange juice changes color during the winter, and he went down to Florida to investigate this phenomenon, thinking to put together a short piece on oranges. "I went into an orange grove down there," he says, "and found a hundred and forty Ph.D.s studying oranges. There was a library nearby with fifty thousand items on oranges." He ended up with a book-length report *(Oranges,* 1967) on the botany, history, and distribution of the orange, and the beliefs and superstitions that have grown up around it. A reviewer in *Harper's* said that McPhee "writes like a charm, and without being cute, gimmicky, or in any way dull, he just tells you a lot about oranges. . . . It's a delicious book, in a word, and more absorbing than many a novel."

One of the most admired of McPhee's books followed—*The Pine Barrens* (1968). Edward Hoagland called it "a direct loving look at the people and social and natural history of the piney belt of New Jersey, beginning with a chatty old bachelor cranberryman whom we meet lunching on raw onions. It's boyish but masterful." Others praised McPhee's ear for the speech forms of the local "pineys," and his skill in cap-

turing the special atmosphere of this unlikely (and now threatened) wilderness. *A Roomful of Hovings* (1969) collects five relatively short and extremely variegated *New Yorker* profiles—of Thomas Hoving, director of the Metropolitan Museum in New York; Euell Theophilus Gibbons, an expert on living off the land; Carroll W. Brewster, an M.I.T. Fellow who has worked for an African government; Robert Twynam, keeper of the tennis greens at Wimbledon; and Temple Fielding, author of travel guides to Europe. McPhee's special regard for people who have made themselves masters of some craft or area of knowledge is nowhere more evident than in this collection, which had a reception as mixed as its contents. *Time* rather rancorously identified McPhee as "a classicist in technique" but "a romantic in his tastes," who goes on the assumption "that gestures add up not only to personality but to character"—"a hip George Apley"—while J. H. Plumb accused him of a "surface glitter" that made for "immense readability" but obscured the truth behind the facts. Pamela Marsh decided that McPhee "ought to be a bore. . . . With a bore's persistence he seizes a subject, shakes loose a cloud of more detail than we ever imagined we would care to hear on any subject—yet somehow he makes the whole procedure curiously fascinating."

Turning from Wimbledon to Forest Hills, McPhee produced in *Levels of the Game* (1969) an account of the semi-final match between Arthur Ashe and Clark Graebner in the 1968 U.S. Open Tennis Championship. Stroke-by-stroke descriptions of key games are interspersed with flashbacks into the childhood, family background, and formative experiences of the two stars. It seemed to C.F. Ruffin that McPhee "so varies and paces his style that he holds the reader by his sheer technical skill. . . . He exercises such restraint—balancing Graebner with Ashe and Ashe with Graebner—that it would seem that the book should end in a tie. But Ashe is black. And he emerges as the underdog, gets most of the cheers, works hard for his win, and wins. . . . [This] isn't just a tennis book . . . [it] is a compact sociology." *Life* thought it might be "the best tennis book ever written."

In 1969 McPhee took his family to live for a while in the small Hebridean island of Colonsay, where his ancestors had come from. His account of what he saw and heard there was published in 1970 as *The Crofter and the Laird,* a mixture of sociology and shrewdly selected gossip that was universally praised for its unsentimental honesty, "visual precision and . . . grace of language." McPhee had resisted the temptation to see his Colonsay characters as stereotypes, and he does the same in *Encounters With the Archdruid* (1971). This pits a revered conservationist, David Brower of the Sierra Club and Friends of the Earth, against three of his "natural enemies." He is shown in argument with a mining engineer in the Glacier Peak Wilderness of Washington State; with a real estate developer on an island in South Carolina; and with Floyd Dominy, dam builder and Commissioner of Reclamation, in a river canyon in Colorado. Brower's opponents are all honorable men, and tend to view him with more sadness than anger as one for whom a "bit of unused wilderness" is more important than people's legitimate material needs. There is not much doubt in the end that McPhee is on Brower's side but, as John Hay wrote, "anyone looking for good and evil, heroes and villains, moral lessons, and so on, will go away scratching his head."

Wimbledon (1972), which combines some of McPhee's tennis articles with photographs by Alfred Eisenstaedt, was followed by a sortie into less familiar territory in *The Deltoid Pumpkin Seed* (1973). It describes the efforts of a small group of dedicated amateurs to build and fly a computer-designed "aerobody," a huge cargo carrier rather like a rigid dirigible. After assorted trials and travails, and the expenditure of one-and-a-half million dollars, the "big orange thing with no wings" completed a successful test flight before it was shelved for lack of commercial or government support.

"McPhee's writing is both precise and imaginative," wrote Richard Frede. "This is not a funny book, but humor is recurrent. It is contextual humor, pertinent but nèver gratuitous. ... McPhee explains technical detail very well when necessary. And he can do with technical detail what a poet will do with nuance and indirection, and to the same effects." His book "is suspenseful reading. It is serious reading as well."

McPhee penetrates an even more arcane world in *The Curve of Binding Energy* (1974), but one of universal significance. The book is a profile of the nuclear physicist Theodore B. Taylor, who has worked on atomic bomb minaturization and believes that a small bomb could be made by terrorists. To prove his point, Taylor describes some of the steps that an individual, or a group of conspirators, would follow in making a nuke. A. D. Foley in the *Bulletin of Atomic Science* called the result "a collection of gossip and sensationalism," but agreed that "a nuclear device could be built by determined amateurs." Other reviewers were impressed by McPhee's ability to reduce technical jargon to plain English, and C. A. Horwitz found the book "a

compelling, frightening, necessary study of a situation that almost certainly will lead to disaster unless adequate controls are instituted; and ... an equally fascinating portrait of a brilliant, humane man dedicated to battling the demons he helped to unleash upon the world."

Pieces of the Frame (1975) is a collection of magazine articles. Most of them record various journeys, including one to the shores of Loch Ness and another down the wild Chattahoochee River into the heart of downtown Atlanta in the company of a passionately committed environmental biologist and Governor Jimmy Carter. There is an exciting piece about quarterhorse racing and a curious one in which McPhee explores Atlantic City in terms of the game of Monopoly, which has immortalized the names of the city's now decaying streets. Edward Hoagland said in his review that "McPhee writes about people whose company he enjoys ... and one has the sense always with him of a man at a pitch of pleasure in his work, a natural at it, finding out on behalf of the rest of us how some portion of the world works."

The portion of the world he explicates in *The Survival of the Bark Canoe* (1975) is that of Henri Vaillancourt, self-taught master of an almost lost art. Using two of Vaillancourt's bark canoes, McPhee journeyed with him and another friend through the Maine woods, following a route once taken by Thoreau (and discovering in the process that Vaillancourt, a genius in his canoe yard, was neither amiable nor competent as a wilderness companion). Another canoe trip, this time in Alaska, is described in *Coming Into the Country* (1977), which also contains an essay about a search by helicopter for a site on which to build a new Alaskan capital, and another about a stay of some months in a tiny Alaskan settlement on the Yukon River. A number of reviewers thought this the best of McPhee's books; Edward Hoagland wrote that here he "introduced a new generosity of tempo to his work, a leisurely artfulness of organization he has not had before," and called the book "a species of masterpiece."

William L. Howarth, in his introduction to *The John McPhee Reader,* gives a detailed account of McPhee's working methods. After prolonged and exhaustive interviewing and whatever travel his subject calls for, he returns to his office on Nassau Street, Princeton, and transcribes his handwritten notes to produce perhaps a hundred typed sheets. These he reads and re-reads, looking for areas he needs to flesh out with research at the Firestone Library across the street from his office. More typed pages accumulate. The notes are then broken down into topics and sorted into file folders, one for each topic. An index card is made for each folder, and the cards are shuffled and reshuffled until the topics are arranged in what seems to McPhee the best possible order. The notes in the first file are themselves sorted into logical order, and he is ready to start typing his first draft. During this stage, which may last for about two weeks, he spends twelve hours a day at his office, with time out for some hard physical exercise—tennis, squash, or racquet ball. Actually, he says, he averages only two or three good hours of work a day while he is shaping the first draft—"the rest of the time I wander around in here going nuts, trying to bring it all into focus."

McPhee, who has twice been nominated for the National Book Award, teaches a semester seminar on "The Literature of Fact" as Ferris Professor of Journalism at Princeton University. Interviewers have described him as "handsome, lean, muscular and bearded," and as a shy man who treasures his privacy but has nevertheless learned to mix well with the great range of people his work involves him with, and who has "a talent for friendship." He was married in 1972 to Yolanda Whitman, a horticulturist, and has four daughters. Edmund Fuller says of McPhee that "he has a boundlessly diversified range of curiosity, a gift for portraiture which enables him to capture real people as memorably as any novelist does his imaginary ones, honesty and accuracy beyond what is common in journalism, and a Balzacian zest for the details of what things are and how they work." McPhee calls himself "fundamentally . . . a working journalist," and Fuller says that "he is a journalist who writes of fact with that full measure of literary, stylistic distinction which some associate only with fiction or poetry."

PRINCIPAL WORKS: A Sense of Where You Are: A Profile of William Warren Bradley, 1965; The Headmaster: Frank L. Boyden, of Deerfield, 1966; Oranges, 1967; The Pine Barrens, 1968; A Roomful of Hovings and Other Profiles, 1969; Levels of the Game, 1969; The Crofter and the Laird, 1970; Encounters With the Archdruid, 1971; Wimbledon: A Celebration, 1972; The Deltoid Pumpkin Seed, 1973; The Curve of Binding Energy, 1974; The Survival of the Bark Canoe, 1975; Pieces of the Frame, 1975; The John McPhee Reader, edited by William L. Howarth, 1976; Coming Into the Country, 1977.

ABOUT: Contemporary Authors 65–68, 1971; Howarth, W.L. introduction to The John McPhee Reader, 1977. Periodicals—Book World August 15, 1971; Bulletin of Atomic Science October 1974; Christian Science Monitor February 1, 1969; December 24, 1969; July 8, 1970; New Republic July 11, 1970; July 5–12, 1975; January 7, 1978; New York Times July 9, 1974; June 22, 1975; New York Times Book Review November 2, 1969; July 29, 1973; November 27, 1977; December 18, 1977; Saturday Review March 29, 1969; Scientific American September 1974; Time January 31, 1969; Wall Street Journal August 11, 1971; July 14, 1975; January 12, 1976; November 30, 1977.

MACPHERSON, (JEAN) JAY (June 13, 1931–), Canadian poet, writes: "I was born in London, spent the war years in Newfoundland, attended highschool and college in Ottawa, where my mother was one of the early members of the National Film Board. After a year in London, where my father still lives, and another in Montreal, I came to Victoria College, University of Toronto (fall of 1953) as a graduate student in English, and have remained there teaching ever since.

"I write lyric verse, when I am so fortunate as to be able to, but I have no theories to express or comment to make: I read almost none, except by friends. My main reading is nineteenth-century fiction, the area of my thesis topic (subtitled 'Some Conventions of Nineteenth-Century Romance'); my other main interest is mythology, particularly classical. At age nine in Newfoundland I found myself in a house with one other Jean and a class with five; hence I took advantage of a late christening to add the 'Jay' by which I had become locally known; but my gender remains female. I have never been married, nor wished to be.

"The move to Canada was made too early for my consent to be relevant, but on the whole it has worked out well for me and my brother. I owe a great deal to my schools and teachers (the latter I shan't enumerate)—the Maria Grey Preparatory in London; the extraordinary programming the BBC did for dispersed children the first year of the war; Bishop Spencer College in St. John's, Newfoundland; Carleton University in at least some respects; Victoria College in Toronto—a family that sang and read aloud and made the reading and writing of poetry part of our normal life—and perhaps above all the blessing of having become literate before the rise of TV."

Jay Macpherson's first short pamphlet, *Nineteen Poems,* was published in Majorca in 1951 by Robert Graves, who revived his Seizen Press imprint for the purpose. She spent some months in Majorca that year and was for a time influenced, though uneasily, by Grave's non-Christian mythological ideas as expressed in *The White Goddess* and *The Greek Myths.* He for his part regarded her as the most promising young poet he had encountered since World War II.

Subsequently, after a year at University College, London (1951–1952), and another at McGill, Jay Macpherson went to Victoria College, Toronto. There she came under the more

JAY MACPHERSON

Oxford University Press, Canada

In these poems there are echoes of ballads, carols, songs, hymns, and nursery rhymes, of George Herbert, W. S. Gilbert, and William Blake. The book, divided into six sections, moves according to Northrop Frye "from a 'poor child' at the centre of a hostile and mysterious world to an adult child who has regained the paradisal innocent vision." The themes of redemption, and of the relationship between redemption and art, are illustrated by reference to a great range of mythical and literary figures, among them Eve, Mary Magdalene, the Queen of Sheba, Endymion, Adonis, Adam, and Noah.

Frye found the book "completely successful within the conventions it adopts." Munro Beattie wrote that "the diversity of tones, within so consciously limited a range of metres and stanzas, is astonishing. But the supreme achievement of the book is the enhancement of significance in individual poems by the interplay within a whole network of references and counter-references." *The Boatman* was as popular with general readers as with academic critics; it has been five times reprinted, and was reissued in 1968 with seventeen additional poems as *The Boatman and Other Poems*.

A central figure in *Welcoming Disaster,* which followed in 1974 after a long silence, is a decrepit teddy bear, addressed as "Ted, glum chum" or "Tadwit" in poems that are surprisingly free of the whimsy which this conceit appears to threaten:

permanent influence of Northrop Frye, critic, teacher, Episcopalian priest and, as Mordecai Richler has expressed it, "Canada's keeper of standards." This influence was one of those evident in *O Earth Return* (1954), a sequence which received the E. J. Pratt prize and which she later incorporated in the collection that established her reputation, *The Boatman* (1957), winner of the Governor-General's literary award.

The Boatman reflects the experience of gaining a Christian certainty, Protestant in nature, that is neither facile nor glib. A. J. M. Smith has called the book "a subtly organised suite of lyrics, elegiac, pastoral, epigrammatic, and symbolist, which utilizes the traditional forms of quatrain and couplet with great metrical virtuosity and a remarkable flair for the presentation of serious philosophical and, indeed, religious themes in verse that is sometimes beautifully lyrical and sometimes comic . . . and sometimes both at once." There are, for example, two Eurynome poems in the book. One, from "O Earth Return," is serious:

> In the snake's embrace mortal she lies,
> Dies, but lives to renew her torment,
> Under her, rock, night on her eyes.
> In the wall around her was set by one
> Upright, staring, to watch for morning
> With bread and candle, her little son.

The other, from the section called "The Plowman in Darkness," begins:

> Come all old maids that are squeamish
> And afraid to make mistakes,
> Don't clutter your lives up with boyfriends:
> The nicest girls marry snakes.

> Lo! My Tadwit
> He became:
> Nose though hard and
> Look though dim,
> Friendly substi-
> tute for Him.
> Is love haunted?
> To receive
> What another
> Needs to give
> Always, somewhat,
> Looked at square,
> Filling in for
> Those not there?

This is from "Substitutions," and provides an example of the highly original, subtle, dramatic, and punning style of these sometimes sinister and disturbing poems. *Welcoming Disaster* shows a considerable development in both technical skill and emotional depth, for while the learning is still there, it no longer conceals (as it did in *The Boatman*) the anguish of more personal experience.

Jay Macpherson is the daughter of James

Ewan Macpherson and the former Dorothy Hall. She received her B.A. from Carleton College in 1951, her B.L.S. (Bachelor in Library Science) from McGill in 1953, and her M.A. (1955) and Ph.D. (1964) from the University of Toronto. As she says above, she has taught at Victoria College (now University) since 1953— as teaching fellow, lecturer, assistant professor and, since 1967, associate professor of English. She can wear as austere a mask as did the late Marianne Moore, but is regarded as an excellent and demanding teacher and as a wry, humorous, and sophisticated personality.

PRINCIPAL WORKS: *Poetry*—Nineteen Poems, 1951; O Earth Return, 1954; The Boatman, 1957; Welcoming Disaster: Poems 1970-1974, 1974. *Nonfiction*—Four Ages of Man: The Classical Myths, 1962.

ABOUT: Contemporary Authors 5-8 1st revision, 1969; Creative Canada, 1971; International Who's Who in Poetry, 1974-1975; Klinck, C.F. Literary History of Canada, 1965; Oxford Companion to Canadian History and Literature: Supplement, 1973; Seymour-Smith, M. Guide to Modern World Literature, 1973; Vinson, J. (ed.) Contemporary Poets, 1975. *Periodicals*—Canadian Literature Winter 1960; Saturday Night July 20, 1957; University of Toronto Quarterly July 1958.

*MAIS, ROGER (August 11, 1905–June 21, 1955), Jamaican novelist, short story writer, poet, dramatist, and journalist, was born in Kingston, Jamaica, into an upper-middle-class family. He spent his childhood on a remote farm in the Blue Mountains of eastern Jamaica, and had a puritanical upbringing from his sternly religious father. When he left school he settled in Kingston, where he lived for most of his life, working variously as a journalist, a civil servant, a publisher, a photographer, and a painter. From time to time he would disappear back into the country, and for a while he tried his hand as a planter. In this way he became familiar with every aspect of Jamaican life and thought.

According to Jean Creary in *The Islands in Between,* Mais's "integrity towards his principles was absolute and uncompromising. An ugly *objet d'art* could move him to an act of physical destruction. He might fight a man whose ideas he considered mean or dishonest." His friend John Hearne says that "any small disagreement of ideas on subjects he held to be important quickly became a mortal combat which he fought with dedicated ruthlessness. And any quiet, accidental gathering of a few friends was quite likely to evolve, under his pressure, into a monumental debauch. . . . He was a prodigal spender. Everything that he possessed—energy,

*māz

Institute of Jamaica

ROGER MAIS

talent, money when he had it, his entire capital of affections—was always used furiously."

Though it is as a novelist that Mais is best remembered, he began his writing career as a poet, dramatist, and short story writer. His play *Atalanta in Calydon* was produced in Kingston in 1950 and, though he had little success in the theatre, there is a marked dramatic element in much of what he wrote, including his novels. Mais's volume of short stories, *Face,* was privately printed in 1942, at a time when there was no firm in Jamaica that existed solely to publish books, and scarcely any Jamaican fiction being written. Martin Seymour-Smith regards Mais as the best Caribbean poet of the 1930s: "His free verse and his manner show that he fully realized that Caribbean verse, to achieve anything beyond 'local colour,' must break free of sunlight, sea—and the Victorian poetical poesy. . . . Clearly he had read the imagists, and his poetry has a sharpness otherwise entirely lacking in the West Indian poetry of the period."

At a time when Jamaicans of his class simply did not discuss the life of the common people, Mais wrote with passionate indignation about life in the Kingston slums. The National Movement that brought Jamaica to independence was another preoccupation, and he was a member of Manley's Peoples' National Party from its inception. According to Jean Creary, "he influenced both people and the social climate of the country. . . . Penal and social reform both are indebted to his vision and his anger." Mais wrote from first-hand knowledge about the penal system. In 1944, when Winston Churchill asserted that the liberation of the colonies would not follow World War II, Mais replied in his famous article

"Now We Know," and received a six-month jail sentence for fomenting sedition.

In 1952 Mais left Jamaica and went to Europe, living for a year in France and two years in England. He gave his reasons in "Why I Love and Leave Jamaica," one of the documents reprinted in the Roger Mais Supplement to the Jamaican journal *Public Opinion,* speaking contemptuously of his society's "loss, or lack of values," its "want of personal integrity . . . [and] absence of spirit." His first novel, *The Hills Were Joyful Together,* was published in England in 1953, when he was forty-eight.

Edward Brathwaite has pointed out the strong dramatic element in the book, which relies heavily on dialogue, and is set for the most part on a single "stage." This is a "yard" in a West Kingston slum—a sunbaked courtyard used as an informal community center by the residents of the long, low, crowded tenements surrounding it. The yard has its philosopher, the Rastafarian barrow-pusher Ras, but most of the residents seek to escape their degradation and misery through drink, gambling, sex, or crime. The most attractive of the escapists are Surjue, a lawless young man who has retained his own kind of integrity and courage, and Surjue's woman Rema, whom he deeply loves. Surjue is involved by his crony Flitters in a burglary and is taken by the police. In prison, Surjue is tormented by sadistic warders and by anxiety about Rema. He tries to escape and is shot dead.

Jean Creary acknowledges "grave weaknesses" in the novel—"a sameness in the exploration of character," a tendency to prolixity, sentimentality, and over-writing. But, she goes on, Mais's "weaknesses come from the same source where lie his strengths—from his innocent yet potent awareness of himself and of his environment. There is no cautious glancing at other models, no anxiety to conform to decorum. He wrote what he felt, urgently. . . . Mais drew the mystical element in his writing from the rhythmical, figurative style of both Bible and Jamaican *patois.* He used words to reach behind the symbols of language and objects to the nameless reality beyond symbols . . . so that when in Mais words fail, the reader is usually left not with a sense of emptiness, but of vision outreaching vocabulary." Kenneth Ramchand was impressed by the novel's strong sense of life: "Instinctive love, sex, violence, and impulsive generosity, cunning and simplicity, sensitivity and grossness, are pitched to the highest intensity in that little world." And William Walsh spoke of Mais's "Dickensian indignation at the appalling situation of the poor."

Brother Man (1954) is also set in the Kingston slums and is also dramatic in conception, being written in five "acts," with the comments of bystanders providing a kind of chorus at the beginning of each act. In other respects, the novel is very different from its predecessor, concentrating as it does on only four main characters and cutting rapidly from one fragment of action to another in an almost cinematic manner. The central characters are the saintly Brother Man, a developed version of Ras in the first novel; Minette, whom he has rescued from teenage prostitution; the lecherous Papacito; and Papacito's jealous lover Girlie. Brother Man fails to notice that Minette loves him in a more than daughterly fashion, and cannot believe that he is in danger from the mob to whom his sanctity is a reproach. In the end, after he has been stoned, beaten, and fouled by the mob, Brother Man recovers his faith in the arms of Minette.

The critics have been more than usually divided about the quality of this novel. Brathwaite and Ramchand agree that the portrayal of Brother Man himself is inadequate, and the latter goes on to suggest that the "extended parallel between the life and crucifixion of Christ and that of Brother Man" leads to "the introduction of arbitrary visions and apparitions, miracles, naive moralizing . . . and an unfortunate pseudo-Biblical prose," while "the conflict which ought to have been localized in the characters registers only as an uncertainty of intention in the author." But Jean Creary found the book daring in conception and largely successful, while Martin Seymour-Smith called it "one of the few successful accounts in modern fiction of a Christ-like figure. Bra' Man's followers reject him, but he is saved by sexual love. This portrait of a holy man is neither Christian nor Reichian—but it is convincing and original."

Black Lightning (1955), Mais's last published novel, is set in the lush rural Jamaica of the author's childhood. Jake, a blacksmith and sculptor, is carving a statue of Samson, whom he regards as a symbol of man's strength and Faustian independence. Jake prizes independence above everything else, and resents his need even for his wife Estella—a need that becomes all the more painful when she leaves him for another man. Jake's suffering and his growing insight are reflected in the statue, which changes under his hands into "what it wants to be"—a portrait of the blinded Samson, leaning on a little boy. And then Jake is forced into the same kind of helpless dependence when he is blinded by lightning. For a time he allows himself to be looked after by his housekeeper and his friend Amos, but such a life is intolerable to him, and in the end he commits suicide. Jake dies in a wood where all the trees are in flower, and this "pattern of renewal after destruction" is also implicit in the burgeoning love story of Glen and Miriam, with which the novel ends.

Kenneth Ramchand thinks this the best of Mais's books, attaining "a genuine tragic vision." A fourth novel, "In the Sight of the Sun," was never completed. In 1955 it was discovered that Mais had cancer. He went home to Jamaica, and died there three months later. Jean Creary says that "the impact of his personality still lives on, imprinted on the memories of his many friends and enemies from all ranks of society." For his contribution to the island's political development, Mais was posthumously awarded the Order of Jamaica.

PRINCIPAL WORKS: Face and Other Stories, 1942 (Jamaica); The Hills Were Joyful Together, 1953; Brother Man, 1954; Black Lightning, 1955; The Three Novels of Roger Mais, 1966.

ABOUT: Cassell's Encyclopedia of World Literature, 1973; Dathorne, O.R. Caribbean Verse, 1967; James, L. (ed.) The Islands in Between, 1968; Jones, J. and J. Authors and Areas of the West Indies, 1970; Moore, G. The Chosen Tongue, 1969; Penguin Companion to Literature 1, 1971; Ramchand, K. The West Indian Novel and Its Background, 1970; Seymour-Smith, M. Guide to Modern World Literature, 1973. *Periodicals*—Journal of Commonwealth Literature December 1966; Public Opinion (Jamaica) June 10, 1966 (Mais Supplement).

MAJOR, CLARENCE (December 31, 1936–), American novelist, poet, and critic, writes: "On my father's side, my great grandfather, Ned Major, was born around 1860. My great grandmother's name has been misplaced in memory. My grandfather, George Major, was born in 1883 at Smiths Station, Lee County, Alabama. He married Anna Jackson, an adopted child, born in 1882 in either Clark County or Oglethorpe County, Georgia. Her foster mother's name was Edith Jackson. Her real father, Berry Jewel, her real mother, Rebekar. Anna Jackson Major was a sturdy woman who lived to be eighty. Mother of six children, two boys, four girls. During the 1900's, 1920's, 1930's, the family lived in various places throughout Georgia and Alabama. My father was Anna's youngest son. He was born in 1910 in Atlanta. His name is the same as mine.

"My mother was born Inez Huff in April 1919 in Lexington, Georgia, Oglethorpe County. Two brothers: Robert Lee, born 1910, and William Henry, Jr., circa 1908; three sisters: Luvenia, circa 1907, Serena, 1915, and Sally Mae, 1912. Henry Huff, my mother's father, was the son of a judge and himself a successful architect. Many of the wood-frame houses in Lexington were built by him. At some point before 1906, he married Ada Bronner, my grandmother. Ada,

CLARENCE MAJOR

born in 1888, was among the second set of children of Lucy Depree Mills Bronner, born a slave, in 1857. With her first husband, George Mills, 1852, the children were: George, 1870, Lizzie, 1872, Joseph, 1874, and Ella, 1876. This marriage ended and Lucy married Beb Bronner. Aside from Ada, there were five others—years of birth unknown. Names: Sara, Eugene, Allen, Mary Willie and a mysterious male child, born in 1910, who died at age one.

"The offspring of these relatives—hundreds of them—my aunts, uncles, cousins, nephews and nieces—now live all over the United States. One made a career of the Army and is now an officer. Several became clerical workers. I know of at least two who became pharmacists. One lawyer. An automobile mechanic. A printer, a typesetter. Several teachers.

"My mother and father divorced when my sister Serena and I were about five and six. My mother moved to Chicago and my father remained in Atlanta, where he became a successful businessman. We went along with our mother to Chicago but visited our father in Atlanta during the summer.

"My mother married Halbert Ming in 1949. My second sister, Cassandra, was born in 1950.

"I attended a variety of schools, among them the Art Institute of Chicago, the Armed Forces Institute (while in the Air Force), the New School for Social Research, Norwalk Community College, Indiana University's School of Continuing Education (correspondence), and the University of the State of New York at Albany where I earned a B.A.

"I started writing seriously when I was twelve. I wrote novels, stories, poems. I was also painting and drawing a lot. In elementary school, at Forestville, and at Phillips and Dunbar I was well known for having won many prizes in art contests. Some teachers singled me out for special treatment and I began to strut around like I thought I owned the world. I won a scholarship to the Art Institute but didn't stay with it. I gave up painting for many years, devoting almost all my time to fiction and poetry. I have only recently returned to painting. I had my first one-person show at Sarah Lawrence College in 1975.

"I was a lecturer at Sarah Lawrence College from 1972 to 1975; I also lectured at Brooklyn College, the City University of New York, off and on between 1968 and 1975. I served as a writer-in-residence at Aurora College, in Aurora, Illinois, and at Wisconsin State University at Eau Claire. In Harlem I taught writing for the Harlem Education Program at the New Lincoln School, and in Brooklyn's Brownsville for the Center for Urban Education. I also taught in various high schools in New York through Teachers and Writers Collaborative. I've taught in various adult education programs at Queens College, the City University of New York, and at the School of Continuing Education, New York University.

"When I was around twenty I started publishing my own magazine, *Coercion Review*. It was irregular and when it became too much of a business, taking me from my own writing, I dropped it. But while it was going I published some good writers, among them Kenneth Patchen, Henry Miller, and Lawrence Ferlinghetti.

"I've also held various editorial positions, some more demanding than others. Some consisted of only having my name listed in the publication as a corresponding or associate editor.

"I worked briefly as a research analyst, researching the effects of riot news coverage on blacks and whites in Milwaukee and Detroit in 1967.

"Between times I read my fiction and poetry and lectured at Yale, Columbia, Vassar, and over a hundred other universities, colleges, high schools, churches, and art centers.

"Travels: over most of the United States, Canada, Mexico, Italy, England, France, Spain, Jamaica, the Bahamas, Haiti, and the Dominican Republic.

"In my writing I am trying to disrupt tradition, to get closer to what I really want to do. I consider all my books—eleven of them—works-in-progress. I don't feel, though, that there has to be one big book. I am trying to discover a way to use tradition in the most personal and demanding way I can manage."

Clarence Major is an immensely serious, prolific, and ambitious writer. He himself published his first pamphlet of verse, *The Fires That Burn in Heaven,* in 1954 in Chicago, while he was at the Art Institute there. After that, his poems appeared with increasing frequency in a great range of magazines, as he records in his meticulously compiled bibliography. A second verse collection, *Love Poems of a Black Man,* appeared in 1965 and *Human Juices* in 1966, both published in Omaha by Major's own Coercion Press.

However, the first of his books to attract much attention was a novel, *All-Night Visitors* (1969). John O'Brien called it "both a daring innovation in form ('the universe is not *ordered,* therefore I am simply pricking the shape of a particular construct, a form, in it') and an experimental perspective on self-identity. Fragmented, disengaged, and terrified, Eli Bolton tries to reshape the chaos of his experience by affirming his body ('This thing that I am—it is me. *I* am it. I am not a concept in your mind, whoever you are!'). His immersion into sex, however, can lead him in two directions: it can bring him back into the 'ancient depths of myself, back down to some lost meaning of the male,' or it can lead to more depersonalization and separation. The novel, loose and episodic, catalogues the gestures of violence that occur without warning and threaten even the rudimentary pockets of meaning that Eli Bolton can discover. The novel ends uncertainly, as he makes his first real contact with people by inviting a mother and her dispossessed family into his apartment."

Discussing this book with O'Brien in *Interviews With Black Writers,* Major said it was an attempt to deal with "the great self-hatred that's so embedded in Christian teaching"; the novel was one he "had to write in order to come to terms with [his] own body." For Eli Bolton, living in a violent world over which he has no control, sex "is a means of expression and, at times, a weapon." Asked about a surreal and nightmarish quality in the book, Major said he had discovered early on that his theme could not be handled by traditional means or "in a smooth symphonic fashion. I needed short broken chapters, little twisted episodes." *All-Night Visitors* has been translated into Italian and German.

Major's anthology *The New Black Poetry* also appeared in 1969 and greatly enhanced his growing reputation. *Choice's* reviewer found Major's introduction "an incredibly sloppy piece of prose" but admired his selection of poems, the best of which expressed with vigor and imagination "the crisis and drama of the late 1960s." Jerome Klinkowitz called it "the first and still the strongest of the anthologies" concerned with the new renaissance in black literature and Kenneth Rexroth said it was "by far the broadest and best balanced and least sectarian of any of the new collections." There was much praise also for Major's *Dictionary of Afro-American Slang* (1970), which briefly defines more than two thousand five hundred terms and phrases, in many cases citing the period of their greatest vogue. The *Quarterly Journal of Speech* described it succinctly as "Admirable. Well done. Timely. Helpful. Enjoyable."

Swallow the Lake (1970) is a collection of poems in which, wrote Jerome Cushman, Major "writes about his people in the city with a passionate but controlled lyricism. While his language is sometimes harsh and street oriented, the prevailing tonality of the poetry is quiet, almost philosophical. He knows about the desperate young men and women of his generation and he delineates with tender honesty their struggle to keep things together. More literary than polemical, his work shows exciting promise." Frank MacShane in *Poetry* was also impressed: "Major's poems often betray the struggle he is going through and document his attempt to make a resonant statement. He does not want to be just another Black protest poet, a role unworthy of his talent. And so he experiments; and as often as not he fails. The lines of his verse are disjointed; he plays with shapes and punctuation: at this point his work is tentative. But it should be understood that this struggle is being carried on at an advanced level and that it is brought on by a dissatisfaction with simple formulae." Daniel Jaffe also felt a sense of struggle in this collection, a battle against "coming up abstract. Underneath the pulsing of these poems are an abrasive irony and a tearing sense of human groping." Another critic called this poetry "with the resistant, angular surface of tumbled brick."

This considerable collection was followed a year later by another, *Symptoms and Madness,* in which Stephen Stepanchev found "an astonishing ability to assimilate miles and miles of ordinary reality." A slimmer volume, *Private Line,* was published in England in 1971 and there have been two collections since then, *The Cotton Club* (1972) and *The Syncopated Cakewalk* (1974). The latter brought Major the Pushcart Book Prize, but neither was very much noticed and critical interest in the mid-70s shifted to his fiction.

Major's second novel, *NO* (1973), is even more radically experimental than the first. George Davis called it "a nightmare about a young man who is losing his wife. Moses Westby's nightmare centers on the childhood experiences that rendered him incapable of satisfying his wife sexually. In a cryptic style full of oddly indented paragraphs, varying sized print and italics," Major evokes Westby's first sexual encounters and also the traumas deriving from early toilet training and from his experience of racism in the rural South of his childhood. Davis found that it took several readings before he could follow the story line but "when the code is broken, we discover a life twisted by castration and mutilation fears, and a mind filled with images of feces, blood, urine, racism, sex organs and death. All the characters are imprisoned by these images. In fact, we learn little else about them. They act out strange, sometimes macabre, dramas. They either torture Westby or fornicate with him; sometimes the two acts are indistinguishable." Davis wondered where Major would find readers "for this brave but often confusing work."

It seemed to John O'Brien that *NO* "tries to destroy and at the same time gain a new perspective on language, time, and personality. . . . [Major] purposely mingled and confused the slang of the various decades of the twentieth century in order to break down the limits imposed by realistic fiction. He also merged characters so that it is sometimes impossible to recognize whether it is the hero or his father. The purpose of all this is to help in tracing an awakening mind as it moves through its earliest sensual awareness in childhood and finally blossoms into full consciousness at a bullfight, where the hero faces mutilation and death. And in following this mind, Major is not concerned whether or not the 'action' of the novel takes place in the imagination or in the real life of the character. . . . *NO* moves beyond the first novel in insisting that the self is a phenomenon of language and the imagination rather than of actual experience, time, and place. . . . By placing his fear of death in a ritualistic story about a bullfight, the character transcends that fear. At this point art and life make contact; art becomes a vehicle through which life can be ordered and given significance." Major says of this book that, though it is not autobiographical, "its roots are very deep in my emotional life." He did not plan the novel but typed it quite spontaneously onto a long roll of teletype paper: "It was very easy to do, because it was a story that I had been trying to write since I was twelve."

Clarence Major appears undisguised as one of the characters in his next novel, *Reflex and Bone Structure* (1975), an investigation into the connections between artists and what they create. According to Bruce Allen, "Black 'actress' Cora Hull, her two lovers, and the author mix together in a backward-forward sequence of stopped paragraphs. . . . His people's activities intersect with Major's fears of the ends to which he's shaping their destinies (including the possibility of murder). This is truly the fiction of open-ended possibility, grounded in powerful ambiguities. Is Cora the author's real woman, imaginatively projected into 'testing' fantasies? —or a purely literary creation which ensnares his mind and feelings? And: does the novel end in violent wreckage because art *demands* finalities?" A critic in the New York *Times Book Review* said the book was "like the free fall before the parachute opens: an exhilarating trip, with a new view at every turn."

A collection of Major's essays, book reviews, and interviews was published in 1974 as *The Dark and Feeling: Black American Writers and Their Work*. Judy Mimken wrote that this "is not a book of literary criticism, but a personal expression of what it feels like to be a black writer in America. While the writing is sometimes diffuse and there is some bitterness, generally Major approaches his subjects with intelligence and perception." Another reviewer found in it "long overdue insights into the position of the black writer," and Norman H. Pearson said he knew "of no better guide to what is so significantly going on in the creation of a fully American literature in our own time."

Clarence Major began his education in Chicago public schools. A James Nelson Raymond Scholarship took him to the Chicago Art Institute in 1952–1954 and he studied at the Armed Forces Institute in 1955–1956, for the next two years serving as a records specialist in the Air Force. From 1960 to 1966 Major was editor of his own magazine, *Coercion Review*, during this period writing regularly also for *Proof* and the *Anagogic and Paideumic Review*. His brief stint as a research analyst was with the Simulmatics Corporation in New York City in 1967. The same year he taught in the Harlem Education Project's Writers' Workshop and was a drawing instructor at the Upper Manhattan branch of the YMCA. As he says above, he began teaching at Brooklyn College in 1968 and at Sarah Lawrence in 1972. He subsequently resumed his own education and is a graduate of the University of the State of New York, Albany. Major taught as an assistant professor at Howard University in 1975–1976 and at the University of Washington in 1976. In 1977 he became an associate professor at the University of Colorado. He has also taught at the University of Maryland (Spring 1976) and the University of the State of New York, Buffalo (Summer 1976) as a visiting assistant professor, and, as he says, has been writer-in-residence at several institutions. From 1973 to 1976 he was a columnist in the *American Poetry Review* and he is now a contributing editor of that magazine and of *Dark Waters*. Major is a member of the Modern Language Association, the American Association of University Professors, P.E.N., and the Fiction Collective (which published *Reflex and Bone Structure*). He won a number of art contests as a child and more recently received awards from the New York Cultural Foundation and the National Council on the Arts. He is married to Sharyn Jeanne Skeeter.

In his essay "A Black Criterion" (*Black Voices*, 1968), Major urged black writers to break away from Westernized literary structures. Five years later he told John O'Brien that he no longer thought there was or should be any kind "of all-encompassing black aesthetic . . . Black writers today should write whatever they want to write and in any way they choose to write it. No style or subject should be alien to them." This readiness to admit to a radical change of viewpoint is quite characteristic of Major, who as O'Brien says is "careful to note that his ideas about his work and the writing of fiction are tenuous and temporary. . . . He rereads his own work very critically and is anxious to point out what he thinks are its weaknesses." His willingness to reassess his work and his own convictions as he himself develops is related to that willingness to question all "realities" which underlies everything he writes: "I don't think reality is a fixed point around which theories adjust. Reality is anything *but* a fixed point." For Major, O'Brien suggest, "the self is really a non-existent thing, or something that is in a constant state of becoming. Moses in *NO*, for instance, *is* all the things that happen to him and all the ways that people look at him." Major says: "I suppose writing comes from the need to shape one's experience and ideas. Maybe it assures us a future and a past. We try to drive away our fears and uncertainties and explain the mystery of life and the world." Tom Weatherly has suggested that Major's poetry "is not a search for identity, it is identity in process."

PRINCIPAL WORKS: *Novels*—All-Night Visitors, 1969; NO, 1973; Reflex and Bone Structure, 1975. *Poetry*—The Fires That Burn in Heaven, 1954; Love Poems of a Black Man, 1965; Human Juices, 1966; Swallow the Lake, 1970; Symptoms and Madness, 1971; Private Line, 1971 (England only); The Cotton Club, 1972; The Syncopated Cakewalk, 1974. *Nonfiction*—Dictionary of Afro-American Slang, 1970 (In England, Black Slang: A Dictionary of Afro-American Talk); The Dark and Feeling: Black American Writers and Their Work, 1974. *As Editor*—The New Black Poetry, 1969.

ABOUT: Black American Writers Past and Present, 1975; Contemporary Authors 21–24 1st revision, 1977; International Who's Who in Poetry, 1977–1978; Klinkowitz, J. The Life of Fiction, 1977; O'Brien, J. (ed.) Interviews with Black Writers, 1973; Redmond, E.B. Drum Voices, 1976; Vinson, J. (ed.) Contemporary Poets, 1975; Who's Who in America, 1978–1979. *Periodicals*—Carolina Quarterly Spring-Summer 1976; Chicago Review 3 1974; Library Journal November 15, 1970; February 1, 1971; March 15, 1972; June 1, 1974; January 15, 1976; Negro Digest October 1969; December 1969; New York Times Book Review July 1, 1973; Nickel Review December 12, 1969; Parnassus Spring-Summer 1975; Poetry August 1971; Saturday Review April 3, 1971; Virginia Quarterly Review Winter 1971.

"MALLEY, ERN." *See* McAULEY, JAMES

*MANDELSTAM, NADEZHDA (YAKOVLEVNA)** (October 31, 1899–), Russian memoirist and translator, was born in Saratov, a city on the Volga, the daughter of Yakov Khazin. Her mother was a physician and both parents, she says, were "nice, highly educated people"; her brother Evgeni also became a writer. Nadezhda Khazina learned French, German, and English from governesses who "were all parson's daughters," and traveled widely with her family in Western Europe. She went to school in Kiev and stayed there to study art with the cubist-futurist painter Alexandra Exter. A fellow student and one of her closest friends was Ilya Ehrenburg's future wife Lyuba.

It was in the spring of 1919, soon after the Revolution, that Nadezhda Khazina first met the poet Osip Mandelstam, who was then living in Kiev. He went away to the Crimea soon afterwards, but returned to Kiev in 1921, when they were informally married. She explains in her memoirs that "we ... bought ourselves a couple of blue rings for a kopek apiece near the Mikhailov monastery, but as our wedding was secret, we did not put them on our fingers. He carried his in his pocket, and I put mine on a chain and wore it hidden in my bosom. ... Who would then have thought that we would stay together until the end of his life?"

The classicist Mandelstam hated the Revolution and its consequences—"this wolfhound age"—and in June 1921 the couple left Kiev and went as refugees to the Caucasus. After six months in Tbilisi (Tiflis), they returned to Kiev to obtain a marriage certificate and then went on to Moscow. There they remained during the 1920s and early 1930s, earning a living as translators while Mandelstam produced the work which has since established him as one of the major Russian poets of the twentieth century. As Isaiah Berlin said, "his poetry, although its scope was deliberately confined, possessed a

*man′ dəl shtam

NADEZHDA MANDELSTAM

purity and perfection of form never again attained in Russia."

In November 1933 Mandelstam wrote a sixteen-line satire that referred to Stalin as the "Kremlin mountaineer" and "peasant-slayer" and read it aloud to a small circle of friends which included Pasternak and Ehrenburg. One of the group betrayed him and on May 13, 1934, while Mandelstam was at home with his wife and their close friend the poet Anna Akhmatova, the secret police burst into their apartment in search of the poem. Mandelstam was arrested and subjected to a two-week interrogation which left him unbalanced and ill. He and his wife were then sent into exile for three years, first to Cherdyn in the Urals and then to the city of Voronezh in the center of European Russia.

In Voronezh, unable to find work and forbidden to publish, they were desperately poor and hungry, evicted from one miserable lodging after another. They were forced to depend largely on donations from such friends as dared to acknowledge their existence (as Akhmatova, for example, unwaveringly did). Although in Voronezh he several times gave way to spells of insanity, Mandelstam continued to write, producing under almost impossible circumstances two notebooks of poetry, including some of his finest work. In May 1937 the Mandelstams were allowed to return from exile to Moscow. Still without a home or work, still dependent on the charity of friends, they were hardly better off than they had been in Voronezh. But much worse was to come. In May 1938, Mandelstam was arrested again and sentenced to five years in a labor camp for "counter-revolutionary activities." Later that year he wrote to her: "I am,

536

physically, rather badly off. I am totally exhausted and emaciated, and almost unrecognizable, but I do not know whether there is any sense in sending clothes, food and money. But try it anyway. I am very cold without winter clothes." The parcel she sent him was returned to her, marked "The addressee is dead." There were rumors that Mandelstam had survived—that he lived on in the Arctic mines, that he died during the war, that he became "a demented old man of seventy who had once written poetry in the outside world" and was known in the camps as "The Poet." Most probably he died in a transit camp near Vladivostok in December 1938.

Exiled once more from Moscow, Nadezhda Mandelstam worked in factories, then as a teacher of English, in provincial towns all over the Soviet Union: Strunino, Kalinin, Muinak, Dzhambul, Tashkent, Ulyanovsk, Chita, Cheboksary, Vereya, Tarusa, and Pskov. Throughout those homeless years, under constant surveillance, she made it her duty and central purpose to preserve Mandelstam's unpublished poems, hiding many copies of them, smuggling copies abroad, and, in case these expedients failed, committing all of them, with their variants, to memory. Thanks entirely to this singular effort, virtually all of her husband's poetry and prose survives and has been published abroad.

In 1956, when she was in her late fifties and serving as head of the English department at the Chuvash Teachers' Training College in Cheboksary, Nadezhda Mandelstam earned the degree of *Kandidat nauk* (roughly equivalent to a Ph.D.) in English philology. A few years later her husband's poems began to appear in Soviet journals, and his rehabilitation began. In 1960 she was allowed to return to Moscow, where she was provided with a small apartment and a Writers' Union pension. It was then that she settled down to write her memoirs.

The first volume, *Vospominaniya,* reached the West in 1970, when it was translated by Max Hayward as *Hope Against Hope*—it is still "underground" literature in the Soviet Union. It deals with the whole period of her marriage, but concentrates on the ordeal of the last four years of Osip Mandelstam's life. This large book tells much more than a personal story; it records the fate of a whole literary generation and of an entire people, arguing that the insane excesses of Stalin's last years were only possible because of the "mass capitulation of the intelligentsia" in the 1920s. It also provides a detailed and sensitive account of Mandelstam's methods of composition which throws great light on the creative process itself. "I have a feeling," Nadezhda Mandelstam writes, "that verse exists before it is composed. . . . The whole process of composition is one of straining to catch and record something . . . relayed from an unknown source. . . . The last stage of the work consists in ridding the poem of all the words foreign to the harmonious whole which existed before the poem arose." And the book describes the author's struggle to preserve her husband's poetry, "my battle with the forces of destruction, with everything that conspired to sweep me away, together with the poor scraps of paper I managed to keep."

It is her victory against "programmed oblivion," George Steiner thought, that gives this appalling record of terror, suffering, and murder its air of "constant celebration, a quiet triumph." Steiner's unqualified praise of the book was echoed by many other critics. Guy Davenport wrote that "the beautifully paced plot of these memoirs, in which digression and anecdote flow with rhythmic ease in and out of a progression of rising suspense, is itself an allusion to the brilliant school of writers in which Mandelstam was one of the most inventive." A. Alvarez called it "a marvelous book, creative and sardonic, full of subtle details about Russian behaviour, about literary life, colleagues and enemies, about the deviousness and cruelty of the secret police, bureaucrats and informers, and about the strategies of survival and endurance. It also contains, in the chapters on her husband's poems, his reading, and his method of composition, some of the most perceptive writing I have ever read on the poetic process itself." Anselm Hollo concluded that the author "is certainly one of the great women in this century."

The book's central chapter was omitted from the English translation "because it would make little sense for a reader unable to read Mandelstam's verse in Russian." It focuses on the process by which certain themes and images may give rise to several related poems, and illustrates this process by reference to poems from the "Voronezh Notebooks." This section has been translated by Donald Rayfield and published separately as *Chapter 42,* along with the relevant poems in both Russian and English. Mandelstam's discussions of poetic creativity with Akhmatova are recalled in "a brief essay—memoir" originally published in a Russian émigré journal in 1972 and translated by Robert A. McLean as *Mozart and Salieri.* The book, which includes vignettes of the pre-Soviet artistic milieu, was found "meandering but provocative."

The second volume of Nadezhda Mandelstam's memoirs, *Vtoraya kniga* (1972)—literally "second book"—was translated by Max Hayward as *Hope Abandoned* (the title puns sadly on the fact that Nadezhda is the Russian word for "hope"). It is complementary as well as supplementary to the first book, giving a very frank, detailed, and loving account of the Mandelstams' early years together and extraordinarily candid portraits of such friends as Akhmatova, as well as describing the author's life after her husband's death. It also develops her thesis concerning what she calls the "mass capitulation of the intelligentsia." As Alex de Jonge put it: *"Hope Against Hope* described the terror. *Hope Abandoned* explains it, and this can be even more harrowing. It is a profound analysis of emerging totalitarian mediocrity, the story of sheer terror building a nation of toadies and idiots."

But this volume had a considerably more mixed reception than its predecessor. A number of critics pointed out serious errors in Nadezhda Mandelstam's recollections, showing how her somber generalizations proceed from incidents that could not possibly have occurred as she says they did—for example, in a vignette about the novelist Tynianov, whose views she also seriously misrepresents. Robin Milner-Gulland suggested that "the trouble lies, perhaps, in the very strength of personality that made this book possible (and whose self-explanation incidentally is the chief unifying theme running through it.) Mrs. Mandelstam has an outstanding gift for political rhetoric: fine when she is nailing down second-raters and toadies, annoying when she preaches at us and generalises for paragraphs at a time, dangerously unfair when she despises and misrepresents other points of view. . . . All this flaws her argument, particularly in so far as it involves a blanket condemnation of her intellectual generation and the culture of the 1920s. . . . Such faults will not seriously misdirect the ordinary reader, who will doubtless skip the cultural infighting and exercise his commonsense about bitchiness. . . . Best of all is to keep a sharp eye open for special pleading while enjoying the book's considerable merits." The poet Joseph Brodsky concluded that she had done nothing less than "hold a Day of Judgment on earth for her age and its literature." Max Hayward's translation of both volumes has been greatly admired, though Simon Karlinsky complained that he had "toned down the brilliance and verbal exuberance of Mrs. Mandelstam's Russian style."

A journalist who visited Nadezhda Mandelstam in 1973 says that she is a small person with "the figure of an old, slovenly charwoman," and "lacklustre" light blue eyes; she chain-smokes cigarettes, though her doctor has long since forbidden them. Her apartment was badly lit and very untidy, but full of flowers, which she had come to love in her "last days of living." She said that her priest "always tells me that I may not commit suicide. My heart is very weak and old and that is now my only hope; suicide is not for me. I hope that I shall die soon. I believe that then I will see my husband somehow. My only hope: my weak heart. My only confidence: that reunion."

PRINCIPAL WORKS IN ENGLISH TRANSLATION: Hope Against Hope, 1970; Chapter 42, 1973; Mozart and Salieri, 1973; Hope Abandoned, 1974.

ABOUT: Mandelstam, N. Hope Against Hope, 1970; Mandelstam, N. Hope Abandoned, 1974. *Periodicals*—Book World November 8, 1970; Books Abroad Winter 1971; Books and Bookmen April 1974; Christianity Today July 29, 1977; Economist March 23, 1976; Encounter August 1971; Guardian May 27, 1971; March 21, 1974; Harper's July 1971; Nation October 5, 1970; November 16, 1974; National Review December 29, 1970; New Republic February 2, 1974; New Statesman May 28, 1971; March 22, 1974; New York Review of Books January 27, 1972; February 7, 1974; New York Times Book Review October 18, 1970; January 20, 1974; New Yorker December 26, 1970; February 18, 1974; Newsweek March 29, 1971; January 28, 1974; Observer Review May 23, 1971; Poetry July 1974; Saturday Review November 28, 1970; January 24, 1976; Sunday Telegraph March 17, 1974; Sunday Times (London) May 6, 1973; Time January 18, 1971; January 14, 1974; Times Literary Supplement July 2, 1971; Vogue January 15, 1971.

MARCUS, STEVEN (December 13, 1928–), American literary critic and social historian, was born in New York City, the son of an accountant, Nathan Marcus, and of the former Adeline Gordon. He was educated at Columbia University, where he received his B.A. in 1948, his M.A. in 1949, and a Ph.D. in 1961. In 1949, after leaving Columbia, he studied for a time at the Kenyon School of Letters and the same year went to Indiana University as a teaching fellow. He was a lecturer in English at the City College of New York from 1950 to 1952, when he went to England on a Fulbright scholarship, pursuing his interest in nineteenth-century English literature and culture at Pembroke College, Cambridge University. Marcus spent two years at Pembroke, in his second year acting as a supervisor, then returned to the United States for two years of Army service (1954-1956). When he left the Army he returned to Columbia University, where he has remained, as an instructor (1956-1961), assistant professor (1961-1963), associate professor (1963-1966), and professor of English (1966–).

Dickens: From Pickwick to Dombey (1965) was planned as the first volume of a two-volume work, though the second volume has yet to appear. It sets out to explain Dickens's development as a novelist during the first half of his

STEVEN MARCUS

career and takes the form of an analysis in chronological order of his first seven novels, relating them "to each other, to the course of Dickens's life and thought, and to the culture to which they belong." Marcus brought to bear on his material a detailed knowledge of early Victorian society as well as of the Victorian novel, and wrote predominantly as a Freudian. The result was warmly praised, though most reviewers thought that it flagged in some chapters. One reader concluded that Marcus was at his best in relating the psychological stresses in Dickens's character to his achievement in the novels, and *Encounter* called the book "an immensely informed, patient, and scrupulous critical analysis and paraphrase," though it found Marcus prolix and unincisive in his use of language. G.S. Fraser wrote that "we see Dickens almost like Baudelaire, as a great nineteenth-century poet of the city, using art as a prophylactic against madness. . . . Mr. Marcus will enable us to reread the earlier novels with a new intelligence, with a new sense of continuing pattern, a deepening and enrichment of theme."

That Marcus's interest in Victorian England went beyond its literature to its psychology and sociology was clear in this first book, and he turned more directly to these concerns in *The Other Victorians* (1966), his study of pornography and sexuality in mid-nineteenth-century England. Marcus had been invited to write the book by the Institute of Sex Research, using the Institute's library and archives, and he had examined these texts, it was agreed, at microscopic range and with the insight of a first-rate literary critic, a social and intellectual historian, and a psychoanalyst. He studies the views of the Vic-

torian sexologist Dr. William Acton and the researches of the bibliographer of pornography "Pisanus Fraxi" (Henry Spencer Ashbee), and analyzes in some detail *My Secret Life,* the sexual autobiography of a wealthy and anonymous Victorian. There is a conspectus of typical pornographic novels, a glance at the profuse literature of flagellation, and the book ends with general observations about the role of pornography in the Victorian world.

Marcus, wrote F. C. Crews, had "taken the social and psychological preconceptions" of his book on Dickens, "and applied them with rigor and sensitivity"; though he tended at times to become a little portentous in his pronouncements, Marcus had written "a work of lively historical sympathy." Harold Lancour found the book "an often pathetic, sometimes amusing account of human nature stripped to its barest emotions and appetites," and John Simon, while objecting mildly (for him) to the limitations imposed by Marcus's Freudianism, thought the book "full of useful insights . . . . Marcus illustrates cogently how the writings he deals with supplement and, in a sense, explicate the Victorian novel which had to keep mum about sex; indeed, his cross-references to Victorian fiction and other nineteenth-century literature are among the most valuable contributions of his book."

Engels, Manchester, and the Working Class, which appeared after a long silence in 1974, illuminates another corner of Marcus's large subject area. It is a study of Friedrich Engels's first important book, *The Conditions of the Working Class in England in 1844.* Engels, the co-founder of Marxism, was the son of a German textile manufacturer who sent him to England to study the Manchester cotton mills. Marcus analyzes Engels's book and the conditions that combined to produce it—Manchester itself, center of the first industrial revolution; the climate of the time; the writings of Victorian social critics; and Engels's own background and nature. *The Conditions of the Working Class,* as Marcus shows, is unique in the Marxist canon in that it can be read not only for its content but as a work of literature—one worthy to be set alongside the writings of Dickens and Carlyle.

A reviewer in the *Times Literary Supplement* found Marcus's book "a remarkable work of literary criticism, with history brought in by a side wind," but thought Marcus "less convincing when he writes of Engels as a man. Psychology raises its head." It seemed to Asa Briggs that Marcus's technique was most effective "when he is dealing not with . . . big themes but with the texture of a narrative or of an argument. . . . his footnotes, too, are explorations in themselves, and there are enough cross-references to the work of other writers . . . to keep future scholars as busy as Manchester cotton spinners. His ending, offered 'in place of a conclusion,' is surely the starting point of another study by himself."

Representations (1976) collects essays Marcus had written over a period of twenty years—essays sharing "a concern with the reciprocal relationship between literature and society," with the ways in which literature "refers to, refracts, and is a part of the real world." One reviewer found particularly useful the essays on Waugh, on Kipling, on George Eliot, and above all on the historical novel since 1814, with its drift towards the anthropological; another was interested by Marcus's attempt to use the tools of literary analysis on such nonliterary texts as a Freudian case history and an account of the Irish famine.

Marcus has served as an associate editor of the *Partisan Review.* He held a Guggenheim fellowship in 1967-1968, and in 1972-1973 was a fellow of the Center for Advanced Study in the Behavioral Sciences. He was married in 1966 to the sociologist Gertrud Lenzer.

PRINCIPAL WORKS: Dickens: From Pickwick to Dombey, 1965; The Other Victorians: A Study of Sexuality and Pornography in Mid-Nineteenth-Century England, 1966; Engels, Manchester, and the Working Class, 1974; Representations: Essays on Literature and Society, 1976. *As Editor*—(with Lionel Trilling and Ernest Jones) The Life and Work of Sigmund Freud, 1961; The World of Modern Fiction (two volumes), 1966.

ABOUT: Contemporary Authors 41-44, 1974; Hoggart, R. Speaking to Each Other (volume one), 1970; Who's Who in America, 1976-1977. *Periodicals*—Book Week July 3, 1966; Commentary November 1966, November 1974; Commonweal May 14, 1965; Encounter May 1966; Harper's October 1966; Nation June 29, 1974; New Republic September 3, 1966; New Statesman October 4, 1974; New York Review of Books March 11, 1965; August 18, 1966; May 30, 1974; New York Times Book Review May 16, 1965; April 28, 1974; March 21, 1976; Times Literary Supplement October 25, 1974, October 22, 1976.

MARSHALL, *PAULE (April 9, 1929–), American novelist and short story writer, was born in Brooklyn, New York, a child of parents who had immigrated from Barbados shortly after World War I. Educated at Brooklyn College, where she graduated *cum laude* and Phi Beta Kappa in 1953, she has worked as a librarian and journalist. In 1953-1956, as a staff writer for *Our World,* she traveled widely in South America and the West Indies, and since then has spent long periods, writing, in both Barbados and Grenada. She was married in 1950 to Kenneth E. Marshall, by whom she has a son; they were

*pôl

divorced in 1963. She received a Guggenheim fellowship in 1961 and the Rosenthal Award of the National Institute for Arts and Letters in 1962. A Ford Theater Award followed in 1964, a grant from the National Endowment for the Arts in 1966, and a Creative Arts Public Service Fellowship in 1974. Not prolific, she has gained steady attention with each book.

Brown Girl, Brownstones (1959), her first novel, explores the growing-up of Selina Boyce, the daughter of immigrants from Barbados, in a run-down section of Brooklyn. Impeded by an adoring father who cannot adjust to big-city life and who dreams of affluence on a couple of inherited acres back in Barbados, and a mother who is willing to compromise with the American materialistic ethos, Selina becomes another haunted American, Caribbean at heart but willing to think her way into a future of her own making. The book lovingly records the cadences and idioms of Barbados, almost an oral pastoral among the harsher sounds of Brooklyn. Praised for its freshness and vigor, its "crowded, resounding" canvas, its way of loading a bittersweet portrait of an era with "rebellion and tears," it nevertheless struck some reviewers as uneven, perhaps because Selina's parents are in clearer focus than Selina herself; their lives are lived out, whereas hers, told almost autobiographically, has only just begun.

Paule Marshall's next book, *Soul Clap Hands and Sing* (1961), was a quartet of short novels called "Barbados," "Brooklyn," "British Guiana," and "Brazil," in each of which an aging man confronts himself in the context of his relationship with a woman. Each concludes that he has sacrificed unique potential for some protective, socially sanctioned formula. While the *New Yorker* found these "beautifully worked" stories superficial, the *Kirkus* reviewer thought that Marshall had "suddenly expanded a private sense of race and color into an enormously wide, almost mystic, sense of the shimmering chiaroscuro of life itself. . . . The complexity and range of meanings is dazzling." Ihab Hassan particularly admired "Brazil," a sharp yet moving account of a famous comedian about to retire, and wrote: "Paule Marshall . . . allows her poetic style to be molded in each case by the facts of her fiction; she has escaped the clichés that must doubly tempt every Negro author writing today; and she has given us a vision, precise and compassionate, of solitary lives that yet participate in the rich, shifting backgrounds of cultures near and remote."

The Chosen Place, The Timeless People (1969) is the most ambitious of Paule Marshall's books so far, a long novel about an American social research team studying the "backward" folk of a Caribbean island. The sexually ambivalent heroine, Merle Kinbona, "part saint, part revolutionary, part obeah-woman," an island native educated in England, stands between Europe and Africa, between myth and reform, rich and poor, black and white—a veritable crossroads of a woman. When the research team arrives, led by a troubled Jewish anthropologist with a patrician second wife, Merle readily fits out its members with roles: Saul becomes her lover, a relationship which on balance benefits both of them; his assistant, a spineless statistician, becomes the representative of all that is most dehumanizing and dehumanized in the technological society; and Saul's wife Harriet, who kills herself when she finds that he can prefer a black woman, is unmasked as a racist. "Ultimately," as John M. Reilly observes, "the theme . . . is political. Not the politics of parliaments, nor even of parties, but the politics that grows from knowledge that the configurations of character and the complex relationships of love or resentment gain their shape from historical cultures." In the long run, what matters most to the islanders is not Saul's well-meaning intervention, but the cult of Cuffee Ned, who once led a briefly successful local uprising: something generated from within, not imposed from without—and something perhaps necessarily violent.

The Chosen Place, The Timeless People is an old-fashioned novel, complex, committed, and long enough for the reader to follow its characters through crucial decisions and metamorphoses. Some found the portrayal of the white characters unacceptably thin, and that of Merle Kinbona larger than life; opinions varied also regarding the quality of the novel's prose, which seemed ponderous to one reviewer, "trim and sprightly" to another. But that the novel was in any case "a high achievement" was almost universally recognized. Robert Bone, who thought the author's most impressive feat had been "the transformation of politics and history into ritual and myth," went so far as to call the book "the best novel to be written by an American black woman, one of the two important black novels of the 1960s . . . and one of the four or five most impressive novels ever written by a black American."

Paule Marshall lives in New York and teaches creative writing as an adjunct professor at Columbia University. She likes to cook and specializes in Barbadian dishes.

PRINCIPAL WORKS: Brown Girl, Brownstones, 1959; Soul Clap Hands and Sing, 1961; The Chosen Place, The Timeless People, 1969.

ABOUT: Baskin, W. and Runes, R.N. (eds.) Dictionary of Black Culture, 1973; Chapman, A. Black Voices, 1968; The Ebony Handbook, 1974; The Negro Handbook, 1966; Schraufnagel, N.C. The Black American Novel, 1973; Smythe, M. (ed.) Black American Reference Book, 1976; Vinson, J. (ed.) Contemporary Novelists, 1976; Writers Directory 1976-1978. *Periodicals*—Booklist October 15, 1959; September 15, 1961; Book World December 28, 1969; Chicago Sunday Tribune October 1, 1961; Christian Science Monitor January 22, 1970; Critical Quarterly Summer 1971; Guardian August 15, 1960; Kirkus Reviews July 1, 1959; July 15, 1961; Library Journal September 1, 1959; September 15, 1969; New Statesman October 2, 1970; New York Times Book Review October 1, 1961; November 30, 1969; New Yorker September 19, 1959; September 23, 1961; Saturday Review August 29, 1959; September 16, 1961; Times Literary Supplement August 19, 1960.

MAUGHAM, ROBIN (i.e. Lord Robert Cecil Romer Maugham, 2nd Viscount) (May 17, 1916–), English novelist, short story writer, dramatist, memoirist, and travel writer, writes: "I was born the only son of Frederick Herbert and Helen Romer Maugham, both of whom belonged to families which were distinguished as lawyers. I admired my father—much as one might admire some venerable monument such as the Albert Memorial. I adored my mother; and I was fascinated by my uncle William Somerset Maugham, who had escaped from the call of being a lawyer to become a celebrated writer.

"When I was sent to a preparatory school at which I was very homesick, I began my secret literary rebellion at the age of nine by writing a novel, all of five hundred words long, called *The Ioki of Egypt,* the story of a mummified Egyptian princess who came to life in a collector's vault. The tale caused such havoc to my friends in the dormitory that it was banned by the Matron.

"At thirteen I was sent to Eton, where I found little satisfaction except in editing my first magazine, called *Sixpenny* from its price, and in playing the piano. At eighteen, in Vienna, where I was studying the piano, I wrote my first play, *Thirteen for Dinner.* It was produced at the A.D.C. Theatre, and made me £50 during my first year at Trinity Hall College, Cambridge, which I enjoyed greatly, though I resented having to study law during my last year. Relations with my father grew worse when I became a socialist, took a spare-time job in the Cambridge juvenile employment office, and visited the East End of London to examine slum conditions. By then my father was Lord Chancellor of England.

"The war in 1939 put an end to my law studies. I joined up as a trooper, and a year later was commissioned as an officer in the Fourth County of London Yeomanry. I fought in tanks in the Eighth Army in the Western Desert until I was wounded in the head by shrapnel in 1942. While I was in various hospitals for head injuries, a

ROBIN MAUGHAM

wise doctor suggested that I should—as a form of occupational therapy—write an account of my experiences as a tank commander. The account was published in 1945 under the title *Come to Dust.* It was immediately acclaimed by the critics. It is still in print today in England.

"My head injury had given me retrogressive amnesia: I could remember little of the law I had learned—though at the end of the war I was a barrister. In 1947 I published my first novel, *The Servant,* which annoyed my father because he thought it obscene, and annoyed my uncle Somerset Maugham because the New York *Times* review hailed it as 'a masterpiece' and added the fatal words: 'written with a skill and speed the author's uncle might well envy.' However, the novel was a success, and I decided to become a professional writer.

"In all I have written twenty-five books. Four of them (including *The Servant,* which was brilliantly directed by Joseph Losey) have been made into successful films. In 1958 I became haunted by the plight of slaves in Africa, many of whom were smuggled into Arabia to be sold like cattle. So I travelled with another journalist by Land Rover from Dakar to Timbuktu where we lived in a small mud house, and in the Sahara close to the River Niger we bought a slave from his Tuareg master for a sum equivalent to £37, in order to prove that slavery existed, and then liberated him. When my father died and I inherited his title, I made slavery the subject of my maiden speech in the House of Lords. I have been interested to expose slavery ever since that period, but, alas, it still exists.

"Though I have lived away from England for much of my life because I found that being

abroad lent me detachment as a writer, I was very fortunate in maintaining a close relationship with my three sisters: all three were older than I was; two are still living. My eldest sister, Kate Mary Bruce, who died fourteen years ago, was a novelist and playwright who entertained famous literary figures such as Hugh Walpole, Elinor Glyn and H. G. Wells in her home at 79 Cadogan Square. The elder of my two surviving sisters, Honor Earl, is a well-known portrait painter. Diana Marr-Johnson, the youngest, is a novelist who has also recently taken up painting. We do enjoy a happy and unusually close relationship.

"I was glad I wrote my autobiography *Escape From the Shadows* because it rid me of the three 'shadows' who were haunting me. I enjoyed writing the sequel *Search for Nirvana.* But I have not found any permanent abode. I have sold my villa in Ibiza; I am still not certain where I shall end my days."

———

Come to Dust, Robin Maugham's thinly fictionalized account of his experiences as a tank commander in World War II, captured just the right note of excitement, exuberance, and pride among Britons anxious in the postwar gloom to relive their days of glorious sacrifice. Richard Dimbleby called it "as good a piece of war reporting of the intimate kind as I've ever read." Graham Greene commented: "I know of no other book which gives the outsider so vivid and particularized a sense of this form of fighting," and it seemed to Robert Henriques "the real stuff: factual, but sometimes visionary. . . . tough, bitter, disillusioned, tender, disclosing again and again the compassion and brotherly love that deepen as men get closer to combat."

This success and the temporary financial independence it brought combined oddly with retrogressive amnesia to direct Maugham from a legal to a literary career. From 1946 to 1950 he traveled extensively in the Middle East and Northern Africa to research a series of books— *Nomad* (1947), *Approach to Palestine* (1947), *North African Notebook* (1948), and *Journey to Siwa* (1950)—in which he mingled travel impressions, political speculations, and reminiscences about his service in 1943 with British Intelligence in the Middle East (before his deteriorating health and memory caused him to be invalided out of the army). G. G. Stevens called *Nomad* "a useful contribution to a sound philosophy of relations between East and West. . . . made with good temper, wit, and candor." Freya Stark, in her review of *Journey to Siwa,* wrote: "Robin Maugham is one of the young writers whose travels in Africa and Arabia we hail with pleasure because of the pleasure with which he himself has undertaken them: his books have that primary quality in books of travel—the atmosphere of a journey that would have been undertaken if it were never to have been written about at all."

The Servant (1948), Maugham's first novel and, in the opinion of some critics, his best, is a short book about the ambiguous relationship between a wealthy young man and his butler. Barrett looks after Tony very well indeed; he sees to it that he has everything he wants; he even pimps for him. Thus cocooned, Tony's already weak character is steadily eroded, and his dependence on Barrett grows, until in the end it is hard to say which is the servant and which the master. One reviewer wrote that "in the simplicity of its style, the skill of its construction and the unpleasantness of its theme ... [it] resembles a story by the more famous Mr. Maugham." James Stern called it "a minor work of art," but Diana Trilling, who thought it "maintains the tension of the best thrillers," objected that the novel "carries no overtones, though its theme might have been used to suggest many." Overtones, especially social ones, were introduced in Joseph Losey's 1963 film version, which had a script by Harold Pinter. Maugham's own stage adaptation was published in 1972.

Another and more positive sortie across the British class barrier is explored in *Line on Ginger* (1949), in which a young lawyer is impelled, by a sense of comradely responsibility close to love, to track down and rescue from a life of crime a working-class member of his old regiment. "Plotting is the thing Mr. Maugham does best," wrote N. L. Rothman. "He tells his tale with deceptive ease, he illumines it with meticulously chosen bits of dialogue. Everything contributes, everything builds toward the planned effect. There isn't a wasted word and certainly there is no time for boredom. Yet I derived no pleasure from the tale ... I was repelled by the writer's marked disinterest in his characters. Mr. Maugham has no intention of ever getting mixed up personally or emotionally with the people he writes about." James Stern found the book "as readable and exciting as any thriller," but said it suffered from "one of the author's principal virtues: speed. . . . There are gaps in the whirlwind, often slick narrative which make the reader wish to raise questions."

Another budding lawyer bent on reform is the hero of *The Rough and the Smooth* (1951), but Mike Thompson's protegée is not the threatened innocent she appears, and he is ensnared, damaged and very nearly destroyed by the encounter. William Pfaff found in this novel more than

"the glossy good intentions" of its predecessors: "Maugham is very smooth and very serious. He is not being clever here, he is talking about good and evil, honor and suicide, the varieties of corruption"; but "slickness, plottiness, still occasionally intrude. Characters have no life outside their courses of action; that is to say the reader has no peripheral understanding of any of the characters."

Similar reservations have been expressed about most of Maugham's novels. *Behind the Mirror* (1955), in which a British film writer is sent on a delicate mission to Tanganyika, was called "a deftly written study in psychopathology" but lacked conviction for some reviewers. *The Man With Two Shadows* (1958) draws on the author's own experiences in a story about a British secret agent in North Africa who is suffering from the effects of a head wound. A fascinating study of a "man in creepy conflict with a part of his own mind," Rex Lardner called it, and it was admired for its "swift yet sparing evocation of the exotic," and its "ingenious, exciting, and extremely fast-moving plot," even though its hero seemed to some readers only superficially observed.

The Slaves of Timbuktu (1961) is an account of the three-thousand-mile journey Maugham made in 1958 in order to prove that the traffic in slaves continues in North Africa. The book is written in diary form, and is mostly a reissue of a series of articles first published in the sensational Sunday newspaper *The People,* with the addition of quotations from the writings of earlier explorers. One reviewer suggested that Maugham had tried to substitute "the strange and the exotic ... for structure and meaning," but the book had its admirers.

In 1955 the twenty-five passengers aboard the seventy-ton *Joyita* disappeared during a voyage from Western Samoa to the Tokelau Islands. Intrigued by this mystery, Maugham went to the South Pacific and followed up such clues as there were, even purchasing the derelict vessel itself. *The Joyita Mystery* (1962) describes his investigations and presents an ingenious and plausible solution. *November Reef,* published the same year, reworks the incident into an effective suspense novel about an imaginary yacht whose crew and passengers are abducted by a megalomaniac idealist to repopulate his island utopia. After this exotic interlude Maugham returned to more characteristic concerns in *The Green Shade* (1966), a "nice read" about the tumultuous relationship between a middle-aged film director and a young girl.

Somerset and All the Maughams (1966), regarded by some as the author's most substantial book, traces his ancestors back into the seventeenth century and includes personal reminiscences of Maugham's father, the former Lord Chancellor, and of his Uncle Willie—William Somerset Maugham. Kate McQuade thought the book "tells you more about the Maughams than a reasonable person would want to know," but others found it fascinating—especially its remarkably frank revelations about Somerset Maugham, who is "drawn with all his warts, with all his distasteful perversities," and who in his old age reminded Francis King of one of Swift's Struldbrugs—"creatures damned . . . to an everlasting life of drooling misery." There is more of the same in *Conversations With Willie* (1978), which recalls Robin Maugham's visits to his uncle between 1935 and 1965.

"Robin Maugham," writes Burton Kendle in *Contemporary Novelists,* "creates marketplaces, often in exotic locales, for sexual transactions of all varieties"—especially "the pursuit by older men of often deceitful, sometimes innocent, girls and boys. . . . The impulse causing some men to pursue the young may be . . . 'fiercely intense passion' or . . . a perverse pedagogical drive . . . but, ultimately, Maugham's older protagonists seek a lost childhood fantasy or companion, a lost aspect of the self, or a lost opportunity for life. . . . What threatens to defeat all Maugham's work is a style inadequate to his conceptions."

This is the case, Kendle maintains, in "Maugham's most ambitious book, *The Second Window* (1968), which elaborately develops the pervasive themes of his work." The novel is built around the confessions of Martin Yorke, who holds himself responsible for the death of a comrade in battle, the madness of his mistress, and the suicide of a friend, and who once participated in the corruption of a thirteen-year-old girl in Kenya. Charles Miller thought that Maugham had "painted a disturbingly vivid portrait of a derailed personality," but that in the end "Yorke comes off much less a bastard than a bore." And Burton Kendle wrote that the book "suffers not only from [its] florid and ultimately prudish style, but also from the unwieldy structuring of a series of flashbacks. Perhaps because it attempts a more straightforward probing of motive than does *The Servant,* but falters on the verge of frankness, *The Second Window* misses both the subtle treatment of ambiguous human relationships of the earlier book and real sexual honesty."

Meanwhile, in *The Wrong People,* published in 1967 as by "David Griffin" and later in a revised version under his own name, Maugham had essayed for the first time an overtly homosexual theme. The novel is about a teacher at a British juvenile correction center who is blackmailed into furnishing a rich homosexual in Morocco with one of his pupils. *Library Journal*'s reviewer commented that "as a yarn of suspense it lacks convincing excitement; as a sexual novel it always seems to fade out at the crucial moment; and as a study in characterization it ends hopelessly muddled." Another novel about homosexuality, *The Link* (1969), is a speculative account of the nineteenth-century Tichbourne Case, while *The Last Encounter* (1972), which purports to be the last journal of General Gordon of Khartoum, suggests that repressed homosexuality accounts for the paradoxes in that hero's bizarre personality; this last was found a plausible, absorbing, and thoroughly professional novel.

An "intense desire to rid myself of the ghosts from the past which still haunt me" led Maugham in 1972 to publish his autobiography, *Escape From the Shadows,* in which he analyzes his relations with his father, whom he feared, and with his Uncle Willie, and explains the development of his own homosexuality. Maugham describes himself as "one quarter journalist and three quarters writer," and as "overshadowed, queer and alcoholic"; he goes on: "I should have been a complete failure. To this day, I am still surprised when the critical or financial success of one of my novels, plays or films . . . would seem to suggest that I am a success." He believes that "the main impulse which moves a writer is the desire to tell the truth . . . to purge himself by placing on paper once and for all the passions of his body and the inclinations of his heart." The book was on the whole coolly reviewed for its "pedestrian and sometimes meaningless prose" and "vaguely Victorian" sexual descriptions, though there was gratitude for an occasional "touching and memorable scene well told." The autobiography is continued in *Search for Nirvana* (1975).

Maugham's subsequent novels include *The Barrier* (1973), a love story set amid the social rigidities of a military post in India under the Raj, and adorned with five sonnets "in the style of the period" by John Betjeman; *The Sign* (1974), in which a young contemporary of Christ is exploited for political purposes by Joseph of Arimithea; and *Knock on Teak* (1975), a humorous account of the adventures of a writer strongly resembling the author. *Lovers in Exile* (1977) is a collection of four novellas. Maugham is also the author of a number of plays and screenplays. "Though his recent novels repeat the stylistic and formal weaknesses of his earlier work," writes Burton Kendle,

"Maugham has for thirty years, with commendable persistence, explored the sexual intrigue and attendant pain that underlie all human endeavour."

The author resents the comparisons critics frequently make between his work and Somerset Maugham's: "We write differently anyhow. I'm almost fifty years younger and I belong to a generation with a very different outlook," he told a *Guardian* interviewer. All the same, "I learnt a lot from him. To take writing seriously: you are a writer, whether or not you are writing, twenty-four hours a day. It's a very professional business." Beverly Nichols, in *A Case of Human Bondage,* quoted a remark Somerset Maugham once made about his nephew: "I suppose we must grant Robin a touch of g-g-genius. And I suppose that if it hadn't been for me his genius would have been more widely recognised."

PRINCIPAL WORKS: *Fiction*—The Servant, 1948; Line on Ginger, 1949; The Rough and the Smooth, 1951; Behind the Mirror, 1955; The Man With Two Shadows, 1958; November Reef: A Novel of the South Seas, 1962; The Green Shade, 1966; (as "David Griffin") The Wrong People, 1967 (revised edition, under own name, 1970); The Second Window, 1968; The Link: A Victorian Mystery, 1969; The Last Encounter, 1972; The Black Tent and Other Stories, 1972; The Barrier, 1973; The Sign, 1974; Knock on Teak, 1975; Lovers in Exile (novellas), 1977. *Published Plays*—Mr. Lear, 1963; (with Philip King) A Lonesome Road, 1959; Odd Man In (adaptation of play by Claude Magnier), 1958; Enemy!, 1971; The Servant, 1972. *Nonfiction*—Come to Dust, 1945; Approach to Palestine, 1947; Nomad, 1947; North African Notebook, 1948; Journey to Siwa, 1950; The Slaves of Timbuktu, 1961; The Joyita Mystery, 1962; Somerset and All the Maughams, 1966; Escape From the Shadows, 1972; Search for Nirvana, 1975; Conversations With Willie, 1978.

ABOUT: Contemporary Authors 9-12 1st revision, 1974; Vinson, J. (ed.) Contemporary Novelists, 1976; Who's Who, 1978. *Periodicals*—Christian Science Monitor June 16, 1966; Commonweal September 7, 1951; Gay News September 10 and 24, 1974; Guardian March 15, 1961; December 29, 1969; July 19, 1974; Jeremy September 1969; Library Journal June 1, 1966; April 1, 1971; MD December 1969; New Statesman May 12, 1961; April 8, 1966; October 11, 1968; New York Times February 20, 1949; September 9, 1951; May 31, 1959; New York Times Book Review May 9, 1971; Newsweek May 9, 1966; Observer April 23, 1978; Saturday Review April 8, 1950; September 8, 1951; September 21, 1968; Times Literary Supplement November 18, 1955; December 5, 1958; June 2, 1961; April 7, 1966; April 14, 1972; October 20, 1972.

*MEDAWAR, SIR PETER (BRIAN) (February 28, 1915–), British biologist and essayist, is the son of Nicholas Medawar, a British businessman, and the former Edith Muriel Dowling. He was born in Rio de Janeiro, Brazil, where his father had business interests, but was brought to England when he was four years old. He was educated at Marlborough College, the famous "public school" in Wiltshire, and at Magdalen

*mé də wə

Caroline Garland

SIR PETER MEDAWAR

College, Oxford University, graduating with a first-class honors degree in zoology. As an undergraduate he had begun some original research into the growth of tissues and in 1935 he was awarded the Christopher Welch Scholarship and a senior Demyship (scholarship) of Magdalen College so that he could continue his investigations at Oxford's Department of Pathology, working under Sir Howard Florey. At the same time he studied the mathematical computation of growth and change in animals. It was during this period, in 1937, that Medawar was married to Jean Shinglewood Taylor, a zoologist like himself. Medawar's study of embryonic growth patterns brought him the Edward Chapman Research Prize in 1938, and the same year he became a fellow by examination of Magdalen College.

Though he retained his Magadalen fellowship until 1944, Medawar spent some time during the war in Scotland, studying the problems of tissue transplants at the Burns Unit of the Glasgow Royal Infirmary. Blood transfusion and antibiotics had made it possible for military casualties with very extensive burns to survive. However, as Medawar learned from the Unit's director, Sir Harold Gillies, no way had yet been found of ameliorating the disfigurement of the most serious cases. As Medawar says, "the most obvious treatment was to graft the burnt areas with skin from voluntary donors. . . . But Gillies was the first to explain to me that this ambition was absolutely hopeless, because skin grafted from one human being to another simply sloughed off as a result of the 'graft rejection' reaction that everyone knows of nowadays in the context of kidney transplants."

545

Seeking a solution to this problem, Medawar at first experimented with ways of "stretching" the supply of skin from unaffected parts of the patient's own body, which could be grafted onto burnt areas and not rejected. Skin was made into a kind of "soup" of living cells and applied as a dressing, or frozen and sliced into very thin layers. None of these methods prevented the disfiguring puckering of the skin that is the long-term consequence of severe burns.

Eventually, with a subsidy from the Medical Research Council and the assistance of a brilliant plastic surgeon, Thomas Gibson, Medawar began his investigations into the reasons for the body's rejection of tissues transplanted from another organism. In experiments involving rabbits and mice as well as humans, and the grafting of peripheral nerves as well as skin, he came to the conclusion that the body rejected "foreign" tissues because of differences in each individual's immunological pattern. Although graft rejection was thus an immunological process, it did not seem to depend on the formation of antibodies, as when the body musters its defenses against infection. The effective agents in the rejection of transplants (and probably of tumors as well) appeared to be small blood cells, the lymphocytes. An extremely important by-product of these researches was the production of a concentrated form of fibrinogen, a biological "glue" used to join severed nerve endings in skin grafts and other kinds of surgery. These researches led in 1949 to Medawar's election as a Fellow of the Royal Society, one of the highest distinctions available to a British scientist.

Most of this pioneering work on cell-mediated immunity was carried on at Oxford where, in addition to his research program, Medawar maintained a full teaching schedule. He relinquished his Magdalen fellowship in 1944 to go to St. John's College in the same university as senior research fellow and university demonstrator in zoology and comparative anatomy. In 1946 he returned to Magdalen (as fellow by special election) but the following year he went to Birmingham University as Mason Professor of Zoology.

Continuing his research at Birmingham Medawar began to work with Sir Macfarlane Burnet of the University of Melbourne, an authority on influenza, leukemia, and viral diseases. In 1949, Burnet had begun to study individual immunological patterns and reactions, using the work of Medawar and others as a starting point. Burnet found evidence that immunological patterns were not inherited but developed in the embryo, full immunological maturity being acquired gradually after birth. It seemed to him possible that tissues from another organism introduced into the embryo during this formative stage would alter the immunological pattern in such a way that tissues from the same donor could later be grafted onto the mature organism and not rejected. Medawar took up this idea, beginning his research at Birmingham and continuing it, with a team of assistants, at University College, London, where in 1951 he was appointed Jodrell Professor of Zoology and Comparative Anatomy.

Experiments with mice confirmed Burnet's thesis, demonstrating that immunological tolerance could be acquired and that "foreign" tissues could be grafted successfully on laboratory animals. This was not the case with humans, since although tissues from another human might be introduced into an individual embryo, there would be no way of insuring that the same donor would be available if a skin graft should be necessary years or decades later. Nevertheless, Medawar had proved that the "rejection reaction" could be overcome in some circumstances and could theoretically be overcome in others. The prevailing view that "anything foreign must be harmful" was decisively defeated, with an incalculable effect on the morale of surgeons and scientists working in this field. The importance of this achievement was recognized in 1960 when the Nobel Prize for Medicine and Physiology was awarded jointly to Medawar and Burnet. The prize citation described the discovery of the tolerance phenomenon as "a major breakthrough in the field of immunology" that had opened "a new chapter in experimental biology, with several problems of great medical importance laid open to attack." And indeed, much research and many important advances in transplantation surgery and related fields have followed.

In 1962 Medawar became director of the National Institute for Medical Research at Mill Hill, London, a post he retained until a stroke in 1971 enforced his early retirement. At the Institute he continued his own researches into the immunological aspects of organ transplantation and in 1975 said that in retrospect these nine years seemed to him probably the best in his life—immunology had become and still was the most exciting and fastest growing area of modern medical science. He himself devoted most time to work on antilymphocytic globulin, which blocks the operation of cell-mediated immunity and so suppresses the rejection reaction. He believes it has a potentially important role in the treatment of diseases associated with immunological disturbances—perhaps even multiple sclerosis. Since his retirement from the

National Institute (of which he became Director Emeritus in 1975), he has continued his researches at the Medical Research Council's clinical research center at Northwick Park, on the outskirts of London. In 1977 he became Professor of Experimental Medicine at the Royal Institution.

Medawar's first book was a collection of essays published in 1957 as *The Uniqueness of the Individual,* and "dealing essentially with various aspects of laboratory studies of physiology that bear on evolutionary problems." Medawar's subjects included aging, "natural death," and the theories of the French naturalist Lamarck. It was agreed that he had dealt with difficult subjects in lucid and often witty prose and had brought a "Darwinian breadth of philosophy" to his speculations.

Two years later Medawar's name spread to a wider public when he delivered the BBC's 1959 Reith Lectures on "The Future of Man." Published in 1960 under the same title, the lectures drew on contemporary research in demography, genetics, and evolutionary theory to suggest ways in which human beings might increase their ability to control their own evolution. Issues considered included population growth, aging, and the impact of modern medicine on natural selection. Medawar's ideas were often provocative—for example, he predicted the problem of overpopulation at a time when informed opinion had not yet relinquished the belief that the human population of the Western world was in decline. The content of these lectures was found "difficult enough to keep one at full stretch yet not to discourage," and there was universal admiration for Medawar's skill in making scientific ideas accessible to a lay audience. The book was called "a brilliant attack on 'social Darwinism' in its cruder forms and on the excessive claims of the proponents of eugenics." For Jonathan Miller it "demonstrated with wit and verve how the subtle reciprocal effects between the social and the biological yield the unique flux of human change. Throughout runs the urgent call for a humane solution to the biological dilemmas."

Despite the specialized nature of his own researches, Medawar has always been attracted to the wider problems of scientific method and the philosophy of science. "What kind of act of reasoning leads to scientific discovery and the enlargement of the understanding" is a recurrent theme in *The Art of the Soluble* (1967). These eight essays and reviews include a piece on Karl Popper, whom Medawar greatly admires, and others on Herbert Spencer, D'Arcy Thompson, Arthur Koestler, and Teilhard de Chardin. It is

scientific research that Medawar regards as "the art of the soluble," and he has no time for those who introduce transcendental considerations into what he regards as a strictly practical pursuit—his attack on Teilhard was described by A. J. Ayer as devastating, and by another critic as "the rudest review of the century." For that matter, Arthur Koestler was sufficiently displeased by Medawar's review of his *The Art of Creation* to write a letter of protest; it appears in this volume along with Medawar's rejoinder.

Not surprisingly, this controversial collection had a mixed press. G. G. Simpson called it a "hodgepodge" with "little unity beyond the fact that the diverse bits are all products of the same mind—a brilliant one, whose least products can never be called trivia" and whose outspoken attacks are "diverting even for those who do not share" his views. Liam Hudson found something "oddly defensive" in these essays, "as though their author felt, after all, that he might be missing something," while Morton White thought Medawar "much less original and certainly less impressive" on general topics than when he confined himself to biology. Nevertheless, Medawar's prose seemed to White "as sharp and witty as that of any scientist writing in English today" and his "great gift for explaining biology to laymen" comparable with that of T. H. Huxley.

"Hypothesis and Imagination," one of the essays in *The Art of the Soluble,* introduced a theme developed in Medawar's 1968 Jayne Lectures, published the following year as *Induction and Intuition in Scientific Thought.* The lectures set out "to explain what is wrong with the traditional methodology of 'inductive reasoning,'" relating this to contemporary thought with examples drawn from the biological sciences. Medawar allows that induction has its proper place, but maintains that "we cannot browse over the field of nature like cows at pasture." He believes that scientific inquiry advances mainly by what he calls the hypothetico-deductive method—the scientist begins with "an imaginative preconception of what might be true" and at once exposes this hypothesis to critical analysis to find out whether or not his preconception corresponds with reality. Medawar himself acknowledges that there is nothing very original in this view, but John Ziman thought that it could bear repetition in "this clear, incisive, and elegant formulation."

The Hope of Progress (1972) is another collection of essays and lectures, two of them of some importance. Medawar's 1968 Romanes Lecture considers the relationship between science and literature in the search for truth, and argues that literature is willing to accept a criterion of truth less rigorous than science's. (The book includes a reply by John Hollander, suggesting that the sort of truths perceived and conveyed by great writers may correspond more closely to reality than any amount of exact scientific reportage of actual but insignificant phenomena.) "On the Effecting of All Things Possible," the last piece in the collection, defends science against the attacks of those who fear its capacity to change human life and the natural order, and asserts that scientific inquiry provides grounds for optimism about humanity's capacity to improve its environment and itself. "To deride the hope of progress," Medawar writes, "is the ultimate fatuity, the last word in poverty of spirit and meanness of mind." There are also essays on psychoanalysis, on the work of the National Institute for Medical Research, on J.D. Watson's *The Double Helix,* and on "positive eugenics"— the attempt to apply the principles of animal stockbreeding to human beings (a notion which Medawar attacks on scientific as well as moral grounds).

John Kendrew thought that Medawar's prose style resembled Bertrand Russell's—it was "conspicuous for elegance and lucidity, and the flow of his argument has a civilized quality characteristic of the best writing in the humanities." Most reviewers agreed, but most had some reservations about this "marvellous book." One critic in the *Times Literary Supplement* thought that if scientific progress really meant the "effecting of all things possible" it would have to include such horrors as nuclear weapons and the use of "the automated battlefield against South-East Asian peasants: Is this the progress which it is the ultimate fatuity to deride? Certainly Sir Peter would not argue that it is. But it is necessary to ask what is the origin of his blindness to the real nature of the challenge to science, which is a claim that the essential method of scientific thought inevitably leads to a rejection of much that is of most value in human experience, to a denial of values, of beauty, of humane qualities in general." And Alex Comfort, otherwise full of praise, wrote that what seemed to be missing from Medawar's "overall view of Man . . . is the awareness that the contents of the human black box are a part of the substrate, as well as the agent, of science and the identification of truth— he still writes as if his own mind as a thinker wasn't part of the environment about which he thinks."

Medawar's next book was written in collaboration with his wife. *The Life Science* (1976) attempts in twenty-four short chapters a critical synoptic view of the whole field of modern biolo-gy and its social implications, working "down from evolutionary theory to molecules and up again to behaviour and the future path of human intelligence." The *Economist's* reviewer concluded that as a concise guide to biology it was superb, but that the "same conciseness when drawing philosophical implications" left "an unsatisfied impression of over-brevity." Other critics agreed that the book was highly condensed and demanding, and several also complained of its intellectual arrogance—what Stephen Jay Gould called "a cavalier assurance that gives the book a faintly pontifical or establishmentarian odor—too many 'it-cannot-be-denied-that's for my taste, too much dismissal by ridicule." However, Gould thought that while the book had not quite succeeded in capturing all of biology, he had "never read a more noble attempt." And Barbara Ward wrote: "the clarity with which Peter and Jean Medawar have brought together in manageable compass—and with an excellent glossary and cross references—the sheer scale of the scientists' new knowledge, new insights and new sense of interconnectedness makes *The Life Science* an indispensable book for the concerned citizen."

The author served on the British Medical Council committee investigating the hazards of nuclear radiation (1955–1956), on the Agricultural Research Council (1952–1962), on the University Grants Committee (1955–1959), and on the Royal Commission on Medical Education (1965–1968). He was president in 1968–1969 of the British Association for the Advancement of Science. Medawar is an honorary fellow of many British and foreign learned societies and academies in the fields of science, medicine, surgery, pathology, and philosophy, and has honorary degrees from (at the last count) fifteen universities in Britain and abroad. Medawar became a Commander of the Order of the British Empire in 1958 and his knighthood followed in 1965. In 1972 he was named a Companion of Honor, an award given sparingly to British scientists and artists of the greatest distinction.

Sir Peter and Lady Medawar live in Hampstead, London, and have two sons and two daughters. The author is extremely tall, with dark eyes and wavy hair. He attends operas and concerts for recreation, and reads extensively in modern philosophy. Alex Comfort has said of him that "few if any chimera-killers since Heracles have had Medawar's style and range . . . and even if he does not pursue the whole of the phenomenological field he has a unique and important inability to write or tolerate nonsense which has few parallels in scientific-philosophic writing. Add to this a beautifully lucid and humorous style, which can cut down to a sentence what most philosophers say in a page (and indicate its flaws in doing so) and Medawar remains one of the obligatory sources for people who attempt to write about science."

PRINCIPAL WORKS: The Uniqueness of the Individual, 1957; The Future of Man, 1960; The Art of the Soluble, 1967; Induction and Intuition in Scientific Thought, 1969; The Hope of Progress, 1972; (with J.S. Medawar) The Life Science: Current Ideas of Biology, 1976.

ABOUT: Current Biography, 1961; International Who's Who, 1978–1979; Riedman, S.R. and Gustafson, E.T. Portraits of Nobel Laureates in Medicine and Physiology, 1963; Robinson, D. Miracle Finders, 1976; Who's Who, 1978; Who's Who of British Scientists, 1971–1972. *Periodicals* —American Anthropologist October 1961; Christian Century May 17, 1961; Economist January 29, 1977; Encounter September 1967; Guardian April 13, 1972; Harper's February 1977; Nature December 12, 1959; New Society May 4, 1967; April 27, 1972; February 3, 1977; New Statesman February 17, 1967; February 18, 1977; New York Review of Books October 26, 1967; July 14, 1977; New York Times Book Review May 22, 1977; Observer March 13, 1977; Saturday Evening Post October 1, 1960; Saturday Review March 1, 1958; August 1, 1964; Science November 4, 1960; October 13, 1967; November 7, 1969; Science News May 22, 1976; Science News Letter October 29, 1960; Scientific American April 1957, December 1960; Spectator May 6, 1960; April 29, 1972; Time October 31, 1960; Times (London) February 24, 1975; Times Literary Supplement November 25, 1960; May 11, 1967; October 30, 1969; June 23, 1972; Vogue January 1, 1972.

*MEIRELES, CECÍLIA (November 7, 1901– November 9, 1964), Brazilian poet, critic, essayist, and dramatist, was born in Rio de Janeiro, the daughter of Carlos Alberto de Carvalho Meireles and the former Mathilde Benevides. Her father died three months before she was born, her mother three years after. Cecília Meireles grew up in her grandmother's house in Rio—a childhood of "silence and solitude" that left her with a permanent sense of isolation but also nurtured her imagination and a hunger to communicate. She was a brilliant child, an able versifier by the age of nine.

Cecília Meireles attended normal school in Rio from 1913 to 1916, and in 1917 became a primary school teacher. This was by no means the end of her own education, however; she went on to study many languages and literatures, educational theory and method, music, folklore, Oriental civilizations, and much else—indeed she never ceased to study. When she was eighteen, she published *Espectros* (Specters), a collection of seventeen sonnets, elegantly made in the Parnassian manner, about various historical personages. In 1922 she married the painter Fernando Correia Dias.

Her next two books, *Nunca mais . . . a Poema*

*mã re′ lesh

dos Poemas* (Never More . . . and Poem of Poems, 1923) and *Baladas para El-Rei* (Ballads for the King, 1925), included lyrics in free verse, but most of her poems were still largely traditional in form and rooted, at this point, in French symbolism. Nevertheless, as Giovanni Pontiero has said, in these misty and melancholy poems of nostalgia and renunciation "the individual quality of Meireles' poignant lyricism and her mastery of technique are already evident," though sometimes marred by a weakness for abstractions and a certain rhythmic monotony.

It was at about this time that Meireles became associated with the modernist poets in Rio centered around the magazine *Festa* (Festival, 1927–1929 and 1934–1935). They turned her attention to Portuguese poetry, whose symbolism is very different from French symbolism because it incorporates the complex concept of *saudade* (yearning). The *Festa* poets' modernism was of a more balanced and thoughtful kind than that advocated by the futurists and avant-garde extremists of São Paulo, whose Modern Art Week in 1922 had thrown Brazilian culture into ferment. Indeed, the Rio group's modernism has been described as a "dynamic traditionalism." Their precepts included *velocidade* (speed of expression rather than wildness of form), *totalidade* (no form of reality to be excluded), *brasilidade* (attention to the nature and customs of Brazil), and *universalidade* (universality). All of these elements are visible in *Viagem* (Journey, 1939) and later collections, except *totalidade* —an essentially Platonic poet can hardly be called a realist, even though she never ignored or evaded the truth.

Meireles regarded *Viagem* as her real poetic beginning. In these poems she had for the most part expunged the sentimentality that sometimes weakened her early work, overcome her tendency to monotony of tone and rhythm, and curbed her preference for abstract nouns, without smothering the "deep elemental emotion," the sense of loneliness and loss, that gives her poetry its peculiar plangency. *Viagem,* which received the award of the Brazilian Academy, established her as the most talented and accomplished of the *Festa* poets.

In 1934 Cecília Meireles visited Portugal, where she lectured on Brazilian literature at the universities of Lisbon and Coimbra, and from 1935 to 1937 she taught at the newly founded Federal University in Rio as professor of Luso-Brazilian literature, lecturing also on comparative literature and Oriental history and philosophy. In 1940 she went to the University of Texas as a visiting professor of Brazilian literature and culture.

MELO NETO

In *Vaga Música* (Wave Music, 1942) and *Mar Absoluto* (Absolute Sea, 1945) her poetry continued to develop in virtuosity and range, and there is a growing preoccupation with the sea—an image, it has been suggested, of "the plastic fluidity and the adaptability of her interior personality." But Meireles was a devout, though not an obtrusive, Catholic. Martin Seymour-Smith says that "her universe is an ordered one, in which all depends on God," while a French critic has it that her pessimism is concealed by a "reinvented" world, "where the quotidian is transfigured by the cosmic plan."

Though an exponent of "pure poetry"—and Brazil's most distinguished—she nevertheless subsumes, within this, religious, mystical, and nationalistic themes. Thus E. Caracciolo-Trejo's assertion that "her work has no social, political or racial references, but is purely lyrical" is slightly misleading; *Romanceiro de Inconfidência* (Ballad of Perfidy, 1953) is certainly lyrical, modeled as it is on the fifteenth-century Spanish romances, but her subject matter is explicitly the abortive Brazilian rebellion of 1789, and the book is, as J. T. Boorman has said, a "model of controlled, intelligent and subtle poetic nationalism."

In the later part of her life Cecília Meireles traveled extensively, lecturing on Brazilian subjects in Asia (she had taught herself both Hindu and Sanskrit), Latin America, the United States, and Europe. Her encounters with other cultures influenced her work, and her journeys themselves provided the themes of many of her later poems. This tireless woman also wrote a number of plays, books for children, notable essays, and influential literary criticism. She was a prolific contributor to Brazilian periodicals and newspapers, and served for a time as education editor of Rio's *Díario de Notícías.* Among her translations are works by Maeterlinck, Lorca, Anouilh, Ibsen, Tagore, Rilke, Virginia Woolf, and Pushkin. She had three daughters by her first husband, after whose death she made a second marriage to Heitor Grillo. One of her daughters became a well-known actress.

Although Cecília Meireles affected, and was affected by, many of the literary movements of her time, she always remained a poet "who lived on the edge of literary schools," and retained, as Giovanni Ponteiro has said, her "preference for abstractions, the cult of incorporeal beauty, her own highly individual view of reality, and the use of musical and pictorial effects." Her poetry discovers serenity, but never eschews the existential difficulties which prevent its attainment —rather, it seeks, in the tradition of *saudade,* to neutralize the anguish of these difficulties by demonstrating their evanescence, fluidity, and ambiguity. In "Destiny" (here translated by L.S. Downes) she wrote:

> A shepherdess of clouds, with empty face
> I follow after figures of deceit,
> Keeping night watches on the eternal plains
> Which turn and turn beneath my unshod feet.

Cecília Meireles was a Catholic Platonist whose poetry "sings," and John Nist has said that she is distinguished from other major figures of Brazilian modernism by the universality of her concerns.

PRINCIPAL WORKS IN ENGLISH TRANSLATION: *Poems in* Burnshaw, S. (ed.) The Poem Itself, 1960; Bishop, E. and Brasil, E. (eds.) An Anthology of Twentieth-Century Brazilian Poetry, 1972; Caracciolo-Trejo, E. (ed.) Penguin Book of Latin American Verse, 1971; Downes, L.S. An Introduction to Modern Brazilian Poetry, 1954; Nist, J. (ed.) Modern Brazilian Poetry, 1962.

ABOUT: Martins, W. The Modernist Idea, 1970; Nist, J. The Modernist Movement in Brazil, 1967; Penguin Companion to Literature 3, 1971; Ponteiro, G. *introduction to* An Anthology of Brazilian Modernist Poetry, 1969; Twentieth Century Writing, 1969; Who's Who in Latin America Part VI 1948.

*MELO NETO, JOÃO CABRAL DE (January 9, 1920–), Brazilian poet, was born in Recife in Northeastern Brazil, the son of Luiz Cabral de Melo and Carmen Carneiro Leão. The descendant of illustrious families settled in Pernambuco and Paraíba, he is related to several other distinguished Northeastern writers, notably the poet Manuel Bandeira and the sociologist Gilberto Freyre. Raised a Catholic, Melo Neto lost his faith at the age of thirteen or fourteen. "The smallest and the ugliest" in his family, he says that "poetry became my crutch." Melo Neto moved to Rio de Janeiro in 1942, and in 1945 passed the examinations for entry into the Brazilian diplomatic service. His career as a diplomat has taken him to Spain, England, France, and Switzerland. His residence in various Spanish cities marked a particularly fruitful period for the poet and led to a lifelong interest in Spain, its people and culture. In 1952 he was arbitrarily dismissed from his post by the Getúlio Vargas administration but he appealed through legal channels and was eventually reinstated. When Jânio Quadros briefly assumed the presidency in 1960, Melo Neto was appointed to a senior administrative post at the Ministry of Agriculture.

Melo Neto is generally considered to be the most brilliant figure to emerge from the so-called

*mä' lŏŏ nä' tŏŏ

JOÃO CABRAL DE MELO NETO

Manchete. from Pictorial Parade

1945 Generation of Brazilian modernists. In fact, it may be more accurate to regard him as a poet marginal to contemporary literary movements. While the 1945 Generation reacted to the histrionics and strident nationalism of earlier modernists with a deliberate return to traditional forms, Melo Neto was developing his own synthesis and refinement of the more constructive phase of Modernism associated with Murilo Mendes and Carlos Drummond de Andrade. Like Manuel Bandeira, whose work he greatly admires, Melo Neto is both artist and theorist. He is deeply indebted to the Luso-Brazilian poetic heritage and has acknowledged the influence also of Valéry, Ponge, and Marianne Moore.

Something of Marianne Moore's gentle irony and deceptive simplicity can be seen in the dreamlike poems of Melo Neto's first book, *Pedra do Sono* (Stone of Sleep, 1942), together with a playful delight in free and often surreal associations of words and images, and early signs of a profound interest in the poetic process: "The liquid voices of the poem/ beckon to crime/ with a revolver./ They speak to me of islands/ which even dreams/ cannot reach."

There is a deeper concern with the mysteries of poetic creation in *O Engenheiro* (The Engineer, 1945), in which the poet puts away his toys and takes up the tools of his craft with an urgent sense of their importance: "The entire night, the poet/ at his desk, trying/ to save from death the monsters/ germinated in his inkwell." Henceforth, he is to build poems as an engineer builds bridges, ignoring emotional overtones and vague intuitions, rigorously pursuing a kind of Platonic vision of an elemental essence beneath the surface of things; his intention, like Éluard's, is

"to make-see." His diction, always austere, is no longer let free to make its own connections, but scrupulously analyzed, purged of irrelevant associations, mathematically pure and precise. It shows, according to Melo Neto himself, "only the indifferent perfection of geometry, like magazine reproductions of Mondrian, seen from a distance."

With *Psicologia da Composição* (Psychology of Composition) and *Fábula de Anfion e Antiode* (The Fable of Amphion and Antiode), published together in 1947, the poet is at the height of his creative powers. Words, disengaged from their "dictionary situation," are scrutinized as vital clues to an essential reality. Even where Melo Neto chooses to reflect his perplexities in surreal juxtapositions of images, subjective emotional overtones are eliminated: clouds become "hair/ rising like rivers . . ./ statues in flight/ at the edge of the sea;/ light fauna and flora/ of countries of wind." In his conscious flight from the "impure" shadows of the subconscious, Melo Neto concentrates upon the enduring, sharply focused images of stone, sun, tree, and desert.

These are the aesthetics the poet continues to refine in *Uma Faca só Lâmina* (A Knife Entirely Blade, 1955) and *Quaderna* (Four Spot, 1960). The Spanish dancer of "Estudos para uma Bailadora Andaluza" in *Quaderna* may be a paradigm of the artist in the tension of concentration:

> As she taps
> her head, attentive, inclines,
> as if trying to hear
> some indistinct voice.
> There is in this curved attention
> much of the telegraphist
> attentive so as not to lose
> the message transmitted.

> (translated by Giovanni Pontiero)

In "A Palo Seco" (Unaccompanied Song), Melo Neto reminds the reader that he sings "in a desert exposed to sunlight," its shapes and sounds defined beyond ambiguity. "Unemphatic and impersonal" by choice, his poetry is all the same neither inhuman nor unplaced, deriving its insights from human responses that have been distilled rather than suppressed.

A Educação pela Pedra (Education by Stone, 1966) marks the culmination of the poet's quest for an irreduceable reality. The cold and mineral solidity of stone is set against the fluid and mutable, the clear and open against the opaque and closed, the offensive against the defensive in a brilliant counterpoint of key symbols which seeks to locate truth by a process of triangulation, as in "Os Vazios do Homem" (The Emptiness of Man): "Man's empty fullness like a sack/

551

filled with sponges, filled with emptiness:/ man's emptiness, or swollen emptiness,/ or the emptiness that swells of being empty."

Melo Neto draws most of his imagery from the landscape of his native Pernambuco—its countryside, its towns, and the River Capibaribe. *O Cão Sem Plumas* (The Featherless Dog) probes the river's "dense presence" with surrealist images of association and transformation, but there is also an element of social awareness in the closing section of the poem:

> That river
> is dense
> like denser reality.
> Dense
> because of its dense landscape,
> where hunger
> extends its battalions of secret
> and intimate ants.

(translated by Giovanni Pontiero)

The poverty and privations of the inhabitants of the drought-afflicted Northeast provide the theme for what is probably Melo Neto's best-known work, the dramatic poem *Morte e Vida Severina* (The Death and Life of a Severino, 1956). Based on the traditional Pernambucan Nativity Plays, it has been performed on tour in Brazil and abroad by a group of students from the Catholic University of São Paulo, and was singled out for praise at the International Student Drama Festival in Paris in 1961. Severino tells his story without passion or artifice, in language deliberately impoverished to match the deprivation it describes:

> There are lots of Severinos
> and we are exactly alike:
> exactly the same big head
> that's hard to balance properly,
> the same swollen belly
> on the same skinny legs,
> alike because the blood
> we use has little color

(translated by Elizabeth Bishop)

The same unsparing frankness, tinged with a compassionate irony, can be found in the Northeastern sketches in *Dois Parlamentos* (Two Parliaments) and *Serial,* both published in 1961 as part of *Terceira Feira* (Third Fair). Contemplating a cemetery in Pernambuco, the poet muses:

> It is more practical to be buried
> in graves dug in the ground:
> under the sun here, more than graves
> they are ovens of cremation.
> . . . But in lime-strewn graves

nothing is purified:
everything is lost in the earth,
in the form of a soul, or nothing.

(translated by Giovanni Pontiero)

In a manifesto written jointly in 1954 with Mário da Silva Brito and Péricles Eugênio da Silva Ramos, Melo Neto urged fellow poets to resist the temptations of hermeticism in favor of a poetry addressed to ordinary people. In fact, beneath the apparent simplicity of his own work there are profound lessons to be learned about modern priorities in the making of poetry. Translations of Melo Neto's work began to appear during the early 1960s in all the major European languages. His *Poesias Completas* appeared in 1968, and he has been well served by discerning critics. Eduardo Portella has described him as an "anti-poet" who offers "no emotion that is not thought out, no single word that does not introduce a concept, no cadence that does not come as an exact and naked sound." His highly individual technique of conceptual creativity has exercised enormous influence over a new generation of experimental poets, including the pioneers of concrete poetry.

Selden Rodman has described the author as "a small, almost emaciated man with taut features, deep-set, shadow-lined eyes, wiry black hair peppered with white, the fleshy nose too large for the face and disfigured with a cross-shaped pockmark at the tip." He is characterized by an "acute and humorous self-awareness." Melo Neto was married in 1947 to Stella Barbosa de Oliveira.

PRINCIPAL WORKS IN ENGLISH TRANSLATION: The Rebounding Stone, translated by A.B.M. Cadaxa, 1967. *Poems in* Bishop, E. and Brasil, E. (eds.) An Anthology of Twentieth Century Brazilian Poetry, 1972; Caracciolo-Trejo, E. (ed.) The Penguin Book of Latin American Verse, 1970; Cohen, J.M. (ed.) Latin American Writing Today, 1967; Downes, L.S. (ed.) An Introduction to Modern Brazilian Poetry, 1954; Nist, J. (ed.) Modern Brazilian Poetry, 1962; Pontiero, G. An Anthology of Brazilian Modernist Poetry, 1969. Morte e Vida Severina (partial translation) *in* Encounter September 1965.

ABOUT: Brotherston, G. Latin American Poetry, 1975; Coutinho, A. An Introduction to Literature in Brazil, 1969; Franco, J. The Modern Culture of Latin America, 1970; Nist, J. The Modernist Movement in Brazil, 1967; Penguin Companion to Literature 3, 1971; Pontiero, G. An Anthology of Brazilian Modernist Poetry, 1969; Rodman, S. Tongues of Fallen Angels, 1974.

*MEZEY, ROBERT (February 28, 1935–), American poet, was born in Philadelphia, the son of Ralph Mezey and the former Claire Mandell. He studied poetry with John Crowe Ransom at Kenyon College, Gambier, Ohio

*mez′ ē

LaVerne H. Clark

ROBERT MEZEY

(1951–1953) and then spent two years in the United States Army. Resuming his education at the University of Iowa (1956–1960), he received his B.A. in 1959. He went on to Stanford University, California, in 1960–1961, holding a poetry fellowship there in 1961.

Mezey subsequently taught as an instructor at Western Reserve University, Cleveland (1963–1964), and at Franklin and Marshall College, Lancaster, Pennsylvania (1965–1966). In 1967–1968 he was an assistant professor at Fresno State University, California, but was fired, he says, "for free speech and other crimes." (But the publication by some of Mezey's students and fellow professors at Fresno of *Favors,* a selection of his poetry, suggests that he inspired an extraordinary amount of loyalty and liking there.) There have been other posts at "various other colleges, trouble in many, combination of public and private insanity." Since 1976 Mezey has taught as an associate professor of English at Pomona College, in Claremont, California. He has also worked as a probation officer, psychology technician, social worker, and advertising copywriter. In 1964 Mezey lived for a time in Mexico with his wife, the former Ollie Simpson. They were married in 1963 and have three children, Eve, Naomi, and Judah.

For a person apparently so recalcitrant, Mezey's early poems were surprisingly conventional in form, showing the influence of his teachers—Ransom at Kenyon, Paul Engle at Iowa, and especially Yvor Winters at Stanford. A small collection, *Berg-Goodman-Mezey,* was published in England in 1957 and *The Wandering Jew* followed from an Iowa publisher in 1960. The latter is a thirty-three-stanza exercise in religious autobiography, recording the author's youthful certainty, adolescent doubt, and eventual loss of faith, and the sense of negation and emptiness this brought. The poem was said to be at its best when it was most concrete, rather too long, but promising.

The Lovemaker (1961), which received the Lamont Poetry Selection Award, established Mezey's first reputation, as an assured and talented manipulator of traditional forms. John Woods was left with the impression that Mezey "holds his major issues—love and its losses, faith and flesh—at arm's length, where they are weighed equally with his interest in form." Woods was struck by Mezey's "coolness" and James Dickey, though he thought that Mezey wrote very well and was not entirely "schoolgelded," found his ideas uninteresting and his commitment to experience "not deep and passionate enough, however much he may talk about passion." Peter Michelson admired Mezey's enlistment "on the side of craftsmanship. . . . He always sets himself the stern task, the disciplinary form—the acrostic, the sestina, the sonnet, the epigram, the translation, the couplet, the conceit, the variant rhyme and so on." But Michelson also thought that Mezey's characteristic attitude was one of "wariness" and found the last section of the book dominated by a mood of negation, "emotionally and morally passive in the face of . . . [his] loss of religious tradition."

Many of the poems in *White Blossoms* (1965) deal "with the effects of absence, of loss, of the collapse of a relationship—evidently one triggering experience": a "note of complaint [which] brings cohesiveness to the collection, and accumulates intensity as it recurs." This small volume of only twenty-seven poems was found richer and stronger than its predecessor.

Mezey's transition to open forms was fully evident in the selected poems published in 1970 as *The Door Standing Open.* Daniel Jaffe wrote that the twenty-six new poems in this collection "clutch at the heavens and scratch at the gravel. His tone is Jeremiah. He speaks out of anguish, out of anger, in the prophetic tradition, open and radical yet still somehow gentle." Indeed, E. L. Mayo has said that "a kind of passionate melancholy underlies most of his poetry," a quarrel "with the nature of things" skillfully expressed through "images which supply objective correlatives for his own moods," as in "There":

> . . . I see
> the Atlantic moving in slow
> contemplative fury
> against the rocks, the beaten

headlands, and the towns sunk deep
in a blind northern light. Here,
far inland, in the mountains
of Mexico, it is raining
hard, battering the soft mouths
of flowers. I am sullen, dumb,
ungovernable. I taste myself
and I taste those winds, uprisings
of salt and ice, of great trees
brought down, of houses and cries
lost in the storm; and what breaks
on that black shore breaks in me.

Mayo points out that for all his insistence nowadays on open forms, Mezey owes much of the force of his poetry to his tight control of rhythm, which gives an impression of great passion held in check by equally powerful restraints. Mayo also praises the unfailing clarity of Mezey's poetry, his "sharp, clear images," and his "frequent, unobtrusive, but effective employment of articulatory symbolism"—a device employed in several places in the poem quoted above and, for example, in "Touch It": "Past the thinning orchard the fields/ are on fire. A mountain of smoke/ climbs the desolate wind, and at its roots/ fire is eating dead grass with many small teeth." Reading that last line out loud obliges the reader to emulate the action it describes.

Mezey was the editor with Stephen Berg of *Naked Poetry,* an anthology of recent American poetry in open forms by the editors and by poets like Philip Levine, Denise Levertov, Robert Bly, Galway Kinnell, and James Wright, as well as such figures as Lowell, Roethke, and Berryman; *The New Naked Poetry* followed in 1976. Mezey's anthology, *Poems From the Hebrew,* included some of his own translations and was generally admired. He received an Ingram-Merrill Foundation grant in 1973 and a Guggenheim Fellowship in 1977. His recreations include "chess, tennis, any game in sight."

In *Naked Poetry* Mezey wrote: "When I was quite young I came under unhealthy influences —Yvor Winters, for example, and America, and my mother, though not in that order. Yvor Winters was easy to exorcize: all I had to do was meet him. My mother and America are another story and why, tell it in prose?" And in the 1975 edition of *Contemporary Poets* he says that he feels allegiance to no school of poetry, but especially admires Galway Kinnell, Bob Dylan, Philip Levine, Charles Simic, and Luis Salinas. He says: "My poems are largely mysterious to me—I don't want to analyze them. I have written love poems, poems of outrage at daily universal fraud and cruelty, expressions of gratitude to mountains and trees, jokes, messages, enig-

mas, obscenities. My theme is mortality and life everlasting. Influences: Catullus, Po Chu-i, Herbert (both George and Zbigniew), Ecclesiastes, Blake, Clare, Loren Eiseley, Cabeza de Vaca, Sam Cooke, Kenneth Rexroth, Issa, Archilochus, John Fowles, and a dog named Nina."

PRINCIPAL WORKS: *Poetry*—Berg-Goodman-Mezey, 1957; The Wandering Jew, 1960; Poems, 1961; The Lovemaker, 1961; White Blossoms, 1965; Favors, 1968; The Door Standing Open: New and Selected Poems 1954-1969, 1970; A Book of Dying, 1970; Couplets, 1977. *As Editor*—(with Stephen Berg) Naked Poetry: Recent American Poetry in Open Forms, 1969; Poems From the Hebrew, 1973; (with Stephen Berg) The New Naked Poetry, 1976. *As Translator* —The Mercy of Sorrow (poems by Uri Zvi Greenberg), 1965.

ABOUT: Contemporary Authors 57–60, 1976; Malkoff, K. Crowell's Handbook of Contemporary American Poetry, 1973; Penguin Companion to Literature 3, 1971; Vinson, J. (ed.) Contemporary Poets, 1975. *Periodicals*—American Poetry Review Fall 1974; Chicago Review Summer 1963; Hudson Review Winter 1960-1961, Winter 1961-1962; New Statesman September 25, 1970; Poetry December 1961, September 1962, December 1966, August 1971; Saturday Review April 3, 1971; Sewanee Review Summer 1962; Times Literary Supplement September 11, 1970; Virginia Quarterly Review Spring 1971.

MIDDLETON, STANLEY (August 1, 1919–), English novelist, writes: "I was born in Bulwell, Nottingham, the youngest child of working-class parents. My father was a railway goods-guard. As far as I recall I had a happy childhood, with two lots of adults at home, for my brother and sister, who were both much older than I, seemed grown up from the time I remember. I attended local elementary schools, won a scholarship to a secondary school and later to the University College of Nottingham, where I took an honours degree in English. Later, after war service and training as a teacher, I read for a research degree in education, and settled down to teach in Nottingham where I still live. I am married with two daughters.

"From the time I was at university I have wanted to write novels. As a child I remember running up and down the short garden path for hours making up stories or talking to myself. This tendency was further encouraged by a serious illness when I was thirteen which kept me in bed for some months with little to do but fantasize and read. By the time I was in the sixth form I was deliberately trying to copy the styles of authors who attracted me. I cannot think that these were altogether suitable models for a candidate for Higher Certificate and I remember getting into trouble for writing history essays in the manner of Hazlitt. Forster, Joyce, Shaw, H.C. Bailey, T.S. Eliot and the poets in Palgrave all added their mite, together with many others

Mark Gerson

STANLEY MIDDLETON

as I was a voracious reader, but the most powerful influence must have been that of D. H. Lawrence, who opened my eyes to the possibility that a major author could write about the sort of life I saw around me, using my own dialect and describing places that I had seen with my own eyes. Until that time literature for me had been written by people remote in time and/or social caste. I do not think my novels now are like those of Lawrence, nor am I pleased when critics compare my work with his, although I still greatly admire him, but he certainly was for me a liberating influence. The other major concern which must have affected my writing is my interest in music. I still get great pleasure from playing and singing and when I want to enjoy myself as I write (not a usual experience!) I describe a piece of music or its performance.

"Now I write about people who live in my part of the world, the midlands of England. Though I travelled extensively in India during my army service and have used this material in one of my novels, I concentrate on people whose material circumstances are not dissimilar from my own. The characters in my books struggle in states of crisis, on account of bereavements or partings or breakdowns of relationships, or perhaps because of the difficulties of their jobs. Their perplexities and successes in creating works of art (music, novels, poems) are also my subjects.

"My own life is rather quiet. I write and I teach; I look after my family, or they look after me. I do not usually pursue either excitement or exotic settings. A great deal of preparation for writing goes on in my head. I watch and I listen and I use these observations to stir my imagina-

tion. The actual writing I try to do as powerfully and steadily as I can, but often it's like handling fire; even with care one gets burnt. I am never certain how successful I am, but that is as it should be. I work carefully enough, writing slowly with a fountain-pen, but as an apostle of puzzlement I cannot think it's my place to come up with four-square solutions or cut-and-dried circumstances or fully graspable characters. I seem to write out of my own faults and failings. If at the end of one of my novels the reader has been gripped, with his emotions and sympathies aroused, and now feels slightly at a loss as at some calamity or stroke of good fortune in real life, then I have done my work properly.

"I sometimes write radio and stage plays, and enjoy this rather more than working on novels, insofar as I find the creation of dialogue easier. I write poems to please myself, but make no attempt to publish them, though editors have inveigled copies out of me and into print. I feel that I have been very fortunate in managing to write as I have wanted, and in spite of periods of depression am still optimistic enough to hope that I can continue for a few years longer."

Stanley Middleton is the son of Thomas Middleton and the former Elizabeth Ann Burdett. He was educated at High Pavement School in Nottingham and received his B.A. in 1940 from the University College of Nottingham (now Nottingham University). He served in the army from 1940 to 1946, first with the Royal Artillery and then with the Army Education Corps, which he left with the rank of warrant officer. Back at Nottingham University, he qualified as a teacher in 1947 and the same year returned to High Pavement School as a teacher of English. There he has remained, becoming head of the English department in 1958. Nottingham gave him his M.Ed. in 1952.

On the strength of his early novels, *A Short Answer* (1958) and *Harris's Requiem* (1960), Middleton was, as Shirley Toulson has pointed out, "grouped rather too quickly with the regional, kitchen sink novelists who set the trend in the late fifties." He is a subtler and less conventional writer than he seems, and is understandably irritated by critics who perceive no more than social realism or reportage in his work (which nevertheless includes these elements in abundance). He likes to take people at a moment of crisis or perplexity, and to imagine what might happen in that situation to his protagonists and to friends or relations who intervene, and what all these people might learn from the encounter. "My novels," he says in *Contemporary Novelists*, "are imaginative attempts to write down illuminating actions and talk from the lives of fictional people."

That this endeavor should be misunderstood is probably due to the fact that virtually all of Middleton's novels are set in the English midlands, the source of so much literature in the realistic tradition. However, by the time Middleton published his fourth novel, *The Just Exchange,* in 1962, some critics were beginning to grasp his larger intentions. The story centers on a Nottingham repertory theatre where Henrietta Angell is guest artist and her husband is the producer. After a quarrel she leaves her husband and takes refuge with the family of a fellow actor, son of a local solicitor. Before long, all the men of this family are in love with her. Everyone involved learns some painful but valuable lessons, and in the end Henrietta, matured by the experience, resumes her marriage more hopefully. A reviewer in the *Times Literary Supplement* admired the authenticity of Middleton's portrayal of Nottingham, and remarked that "it is nice to be reminded of other aspects" of the city than those presented by Alan Sillitoe, another Nottingham novelist. Nevertheless, for all its perception and delicacy of insight, it was felt that the novel never really "catches alight."

This was not the case with *Two's Company,* which followed a year later. It is about a young man from a middle-class family who utterly rejects his parents' values. He opts out of university, gets a job as a clerk, and spends his evenings playing a guitar at local dance halls. In the same spirit, he takes as his mistress a working-class girl, dim-witted and amoral, whom his parents then seize on as the bait with which they can lure him back to respectability. This novel was warmly praised, and Martin Seymour-Smith wrote of the "beautifully balanced tone of compassionate irony" with which Middleton handles this story of a "rebel without a cause or even much conviction."

A steady development is discernible throughout Middleton's prolific output, and *Terms of Reference* (1966) was not the first of his novels to be called his "most completely achieved work to date." It is a study of two of the affluent middle-class families that so interest Middleton —one the family of a self-made tycoon, the other of a university professor who has married money. The businessman's son marries the don's daughter, the marriage fails disastrously, and the parents find, when they try to mend the situation, that their "terms of reference" disqualify them from making any useful contribution whatever. On the other hand the old humanist James Mansfield in *Cold Gradations* (1972), a retired teacher, finds to his astonish-

ment that those around him need help that he can still give. "Every one of these characters," one reviewer wrote, "is done with that precise, meticulously exact sense of just how people think, talk, dress and behave which is Mr. Middleton's particular skill. . . . Yet once again, the book is something more than a very true and delicate re-creation of life in painfully accurate detail. As a novelist . . . [he] is examining, in his own distinctive and unobtrusively distinguished way, the whole question of human purpose. . . . He is a moral novelist in the same worried, intelligent, agnostic way as George Eliot . . . and the comparison does not utterly dwarf his own achievement."

James Mansfield is a characteristic Middleton hero—a man no longer young who is uncertain of his powers and his relevance in a world that is changing with bewildering speed around him. Jack Riley in *A Man Made of Smoke* (1973) is a somewhat younger and altogether less articulate character, but he is placed in a very similar situation. A widower, and formerly a noncommissioned officer in the army, he has become the reasonably successful manager of a small factory which may be "rationalized" out of existence. At the age of forty-five he is plunged into the kind of insecurity that has always secretly threatened him, and is driven to a reappraisal of his life and its significance for which nothing in his training or experience has equipped him. In the end, he hopes to survive, but has found no "solution." It was with this book that Middleton began to attract wide attention, and it seemed to some readers his first fully mature novel. It draws together all his concerns into a whole, and unlike some of its predecessors it "catches alight"—perhaps precisely because he had distanced himself from his own situation.

With *Holiday,* which followed, Middleton became joint winner with Nadine Gordimer of the important and valuable Booker Prize. The setting is not the midlands but an East Coast vacation resort. Edwin Fisher, a young university lecturer who has left his hysterical wife but still desires her, has gone there to consider what to do about his marriage, and is followed there by his wife's tactful parents. Martin Seymour-Smith, who believes that the English novel needs to be both "modernistic" and coherent, thought that *Holiday* went some considerable way towards fulfilling these requirements, while a reviewer in the *Sunday Times* wrote that "we need Stanley Middleton to remind us what the novel is about."

Middleton extended his territory in *Distractions* (1975) to include "the mansions of the rich and the estates of the landed gentry." Helen

Fielding, first the mistress and then the wife of a wealthy building contractor and property dealer, is desired by a number of other people as well, including her friend the Countess of Marcroft. Most critics thought that these relatively exotic characters were treated with exemplary sympathy and understanding, but Gay Clifford reprimanded Middleton for his "refusal to offer an authorial perspective," which created, she thought, "a situation where the [success-oriented] values of the characters appear also to underlie the novel. . . . Those who fail by being plain, inarticulate, undesired or (the greatest sin) mad, are viewed even more cursorily than the favoured." The same reviewer was also dissatisfied by Middleton's habit of building a novel "largely of summary conversations . . . the intervening narrative, with maximum punctuation, minimum nuance," being "as staccato as the dialogue, placing people, things, flatly, with little regard for the differences between them. The flatness is highly reductive." In the two novels that followed Middleton returned to his familiar middle-class Midlands world, the "unremarkable doings" of whose inhabitants, as Michael Irwin put it, "are given significance by the author's sensitivity and technical skill."

Shirley Toulson has commended Middleton's "rare and surprising gift of making all his characters at the same time both unlikeable and interesting. . . . What he has grasped is that people at the end of their tether do not become heroic and loveable through suffering. An emotional snarl-up makes people selfish, irritable and dull. The skill of the dialogue here is that, although the first two qualities are caught, the third is avoided because the reader is held by the way the remarks of one speaker rasp on those of the other. . . . Because all these people are caught in a crisis point of their lives, they lay aside the masks that make the usual run of social intercourse both possible and dull. . . . That despite it all these people do somehow get something over to each other is the surprising optimism of these bleak novels." It has puzzled British critics that none of Middleton's books has so far been published in the United States. His radio plays, several of them based on his novels, have been well received.

Stanley Middleton was married in 1951 to Margaret Welch. He is a Christian and a Socialist, and says that he enjoys music, walking, listening, and argument. He received an honorary M.A. from Nottingham University in 1975. In 1974, when Middleton went to collect his share of the Booker Prize, Philip Howard wrote in the London *Times* that "with his grey flannel suit, generally kempt appearance, and placid Not-tingham burr, he appears more like a provincial bank manager or a successful farmer than a novelist of psychological crisis." Middleton remarked "cheerfully" to Howard that "if you put me down as a social realist, I will be after you at *The Times* with a jack-knife."

PRINCIPAL WORKS: A Short Answer, 1958; Harris's Requiem, 1960; A Serious Woman, 1961; The Just Exchange, 1962; Two's Company, 1963; Him They Compelled, 1964; Terms of Reference, 1966; The Golden Evening, 1968; Wages of Virtue, 1969; Apple of the Eye, 1970; Brazen Prison, 1971; Cold Gradations, 1972; A Man Made of Smoke, 1973; Holiday, 1974; Distractions, 1975; Still Waters, 1976; Ends and Means, 1977.

ABOUT: Burgess, A. The Novel Today, 1963; Contemporary Authors 25-28 1st revision, 1971; Vinson, J. (ed.) Contemporary Novelists, 1976; Who's Who, 1978. *Periodicals*—Listener October 9, 1975; September 9, 1976; New Statesman August 9, 1968; Sunday Times (London) June 23, 1974; Times November 28, 1974; December 4, 1974; Times Educational Supplement December 6, 1974; Times Literary Supplement April 28, 1961; June 1, 1962; June 14, 1963; October 8, 1964; June 16, 1966; August 15, 1968; March 31, 1972; June 1, 1973; October 17, 1975; September 10, 1976; September 9, 1977.

"MILL, C.R." *See* CRNJANSKI, MILOŠ

MILLER, "JASON" (i.e. JOHN) (April 22, 1939–), American dramatist, was born in Long Island City, New York, the only child of John Miller, an electrician, and his wife Mary, a teacher of brain-damaged children. The family is an Irish Catholic one, Miller's ancestors on his mother's side being mostly miners, those on his father's side "sea people from New England." Jason Miller grew up in Scranton, in the Lackawanna Valley of Pennsylvania, where the family moved soon after he was born. He had a Catholic upbringing in that "poverty area," and says that his "whole frame of reference, even toward the theatre, was built on being an altar boy and on the ritual and on Midnight Mass."

At St. Patrick's High School, maintained in Scranton by the Sisters of the Immaculate Heart of Mary, Miller excelled at football, basketball, and baseball, but at little else. He says that he was not far from delinquency when Sister Celine, who taught public speaking and coached the debating team, "gave me encouragement, at a time when I might have stolen cars." Miller began to win prizes for elocution, and was soon acting in school productions. From St. Patrick's Miller went with an athletic scholarship to the University of Scranton, a Jesuit institution. There he soon switched his attention from sports to acting and writing for the theatre because, as he explained to an interviewer, "I didn't want to get my head bashed in." His first play, a one-acter about a prizefighter appropriately called

JASON MILLER

"The Winner," won the Jesuit Eastern Play Contest.

Miller graduated in 1961 and then, he says, "I suppose because I'd read *On the Road* by Jack Kerouac, wanderlust got in me. . . . I wanted to do Shakespeare, so I went to Washington to act with a touring Shakespeare company, in combination with graduate school." It was during his two years of drama training at Catholic University in Washington that Miller met Linda Gleason, daughter of the comedian Jackie Gleason. They were married in 1963, and for a while toured high schools in the Washington area with a program of Shakespeare selections. When children began to arrive they moved to New York, where Miller drudged as a messenger, driver, welfare investigator, and in other casual jobs while looking for work as an actor.

At first he could find nothing but occasional stints in television commercials and soap operas, or minor parts in short-lived Off-Broadway productions. Then he began to secure roles in regional resident theatres like the Champlain Shakespeare Festival in Burlington, New York, Baltimore's Center Stage, Cincinnati's Shakespeare Festival, and the Hartke Theatre at Catholic University. His first significant appearance in New York City was as Pip in Roy Richardson's *Pequod* (1961), and the following year he played the Assistant in Dennis Reardon's *The Happiness Cage*. His performance as Paryfon Rogozhin in Robert Montgomery's *Subject to Fits* (1971), inspired by Dostoevsky's *The Idiot,* was generally admired and led indirectly to greater things. Montgomery's play was presented at the New York Shakespeare Festival's Public Theatre and brought Miller to the atten-

tion of Joseph Papp, the Festival's protean founder and impresario. It also introduced him to the director A. J. Antoon, a recent graduate of Yale Drama School and an ex-Jesuit, who became a close friend.

Meanwhile, Miller's other career, as a dramatist, was beginning to gather momentum. Three of his short pieces were produced in 1967 at the Triangle Theatre, off-off-Broadway: "Perfect Son," "The Circus Lady," and "Lou Gehrig Did Not Die of Cancer." They sank without much of a trace, but Miller's first full-length play fared rather better. This was *Nobody Hears a Broken Drum,* in which he drew on his own family's history in a drama about the exploited Irish miners of Pennsylvania in the nineteenth century, and the uprising of the "Molly Maguires." Miller was careful to explain that "there is no central ideology in the play except the ideology of desperation; there are no politics in the play except the politics of survival. Finally, and most important, there are no heroes in the play. There is only that insatiable need in man which seeks to find a hero, almost any hero, so that his life might then appear to have purpose, appear to have some momentary yet obscure meaning which shelters his kind from the certainty of despair."

After a try-out at the Triangle Theatre, the play opened at the off-Broadway Fortune Theatre in March 1970, where its brief run drew mixed but generally favorable reviews. Edith Oliver, for example, found the play predictable but nevertheless impressive, given the author's lack of experience, and wrote: "There was so much that was good . . . that its weaknesses didn't seem to me to spoil it." Marilyn Stasio, on the other hand, concluded that "this is one to wring your hands over because it is at its core a good play, but one strangled by its flaws," despite Miller's "exceptional gift for tough yet lyrical language."

Jason Miller wrote his next play, *That Championship Season,* while appearing as one of the poker players in Neil Simon's *The Odd Couple* at a Fort Worth dinner theatre in 1970. "I'd swim all morning and write all afternoon," he told a *New Yorker* interviewer. "What else is there to do?" Elsewhere he has said: "I read a lot of Odets, Williams and Albee to see how to put a play together, but working three hours a day, it took me ten weeks to finish. . . . I didn't stop to think about it too much—it just came." Soon afterwards it nearly went, the manuscript blowing off the roof of the car while Miller was driving to Dallas airport at the end of his Fort Worth engagement. Airborne over Texas, the play formed "a beautiful cloud of what seemed like yellow sunflowers floating over a field." Every one of the play's one hundred and fifty-three pages was "recaptured," a fact which partly accounts for Miller's "special feeling" about it. Unfortunately, the Broadway producers who read the play had no such feeling, and balked at its all-male cast and small-town setting. Miller reluctantly began to revise the play but still found no takers until his friend A. J. Antoon showed it to Joseph Papp, who agreed to produce it. "A.J., Joe and I had lots of late-night Scotch-drinking over the script," Miller says. "It was very collaborative, very creative, and we finally got it back to the way I'd wanted it originally."

That Championship Season is set in the living room of a house in the Lackawanna Valley, the home of a retired high school basketball coach. Twenty years earlier, his "boys" had unexpectedly won the last game of the season to become the 1952 Pennsylvania State Champions. Four of the five heroes are gathered at their annual reunion to honor their old coach, to drink, and to reminisce about their victory, the high point of all their lives. One of them is now mayor of the town, but seems certain to be voted out of office at the next election. Another is a frustrated junior high school principal, dependent on the mayor (who is cuckolding him) for advancement. His brother is a cynical alcoholic, but the only one of the group capable of anything like honesty, and the last of the quartet is a totally unscrupulous and ruthless strip-miner.

Martin, the star of the team, is mysteriously absent. It finally emerges that in the crucial game Martin, on the coach's orders, had put the ablest of their opponents out of action by breaking his ribs. They had not earned the championship, they had stolen it, believing what the coach had told them—that winning is the only truth. No one had ever taught them a better creed and the play demonstrates the result. As Catharine Hughes puts it, "the coach's 'boys', his 'real trophy', are a microcosm of a declining, increasingly purposeless America. They are empty and self-important, insecure and ambitious, venally motivated and capable of almost any treachery or duplicity. . . . 'We are the country, boys,' says the coach."

That Championship Season opened at Papp's Estelle Newman Theatre in May 1972, moving the following September to the Booth Theatre on Broadway. After the avant-garde experiments of the 1960s, Glenn Loney wrote, reviewers and audiences "crushed this emphatically realistic play to their collective bosoms as though it were a long-lost teddy-bear." Clive Barnes reported in the London *Times* that the play "has really scored in New York in perhaps the way no serious drama has scored since Albee's *Who's Afraid of Virginia Woolf.* This is not to say that Mr. Miller's play is a masterpiece, but it is a great piece of popular Broadway theatre, and it deserves every millimetre of its success. . . . It is such a remarkably slick and telling play that at first sight it is easily underestimated. But at its heart there lies a most brilliant analysis of middle America, its conscience and mores." And John Simon could think of few plays "that are funnier, grimmer, truer and more needed in this losing season of our theatre, our politics, and our society."

Not quite everyone joined the chorus of praise. Stanley Kaufmann wrote that "the evening is only partially boring, and the division is not by segments, it's lateral, horizontal. At the same time that the pattern and purpose are tedious from the start, the dialogue is briskly speakable and the acting is good. So the performance has a contrapuntal effect: good surface against dull foundations and a dull overall form." Thomas J. McCormack found much to praise, but thought it "a somber comment on American theatre that one of the most promising plays of the early 1970s could have been written in the early 1950s."

That Championship Season carried off the New York Drama Critics Circle award as the best play of 1971–1972, the Antoinette Perry ("Tony") Award for 1972–1973, and the 1973 Pulitzer Prize for drama. Returning to acting, Miller scored another success with his performance in the title role of the Warner Brothers film *The Exorcist* (1973), which earned him an Oscar nomination as best supporting actor. He was seen more recently as Cooper, a professional criminal, in *The Nickel Ride* (1975) and as a sinister aesthete in *The Dain Curse* (1978). Asked about a successor to *That Championship Season,* Miller said: "The conclusion I came to —if I can use a sports metaphor—is that Ted Williams batted .400 only once in his lifetime. Every other season, he batted .350, which was still awfully good. I can't think qualitatively about my work: 'This play is better than that one'. . . . I may try to do something totally different . . . to test my own range. I'm a young writer, I'm not committed to any one style or vision—or one concept of the theatre."

The author has been described as "quick, lithe, small-boned, black-haired, sharp-featured, intense, jaunty." He and his ex-wife (he is divorced) have three children: Jennifer, Jason, and Jordan. Miller, who has often referred to the religious element in his plays, says that he is "beyond the institutional aspects of religion," but that "there's still an immense depth and mystery about it that appeals to me."

PRINCIPAL PUBLISHED WORKS: Nobody Hears a Broken Drum, 1970; That Championship Season, 1972.

ABOUT: Current Biography, 1975; Hughes, C. American Playwrights 1945-75, 1976; Magill, F. Survey of Contemporary Literature, 1977; Notable Names in the American Theatre, 1976; Vinson, J. (ed.) Contemporary Dramatists, 1977; Who's Who in America, 1976-1977; Who's Who in the Theatre, 1977. *Periodicals*—After Dark January 1973; America May 27, 1972; October 7, 1972; Commonweal October 20, 1972; Nation May 22, 1972; New Republic June 3, 1972; New York Times March 21, 1972; New Yorker March 28, 1970; May 13, 1972; May 20, 1972; Newsweek May 15, 1972; September 25, 1972; Saturday Review June 3, 1972; Seventeen September 1973; Time May 15, 1972; May 21, 1973; Times (London) May 18, 1972.

GASTON MIRON

*MIRON, GASTON (1928–), Canadian poet and editor, was born at Sainte-Agathe-des-Monts in the province of Québec. He began to write when he was about fourteen, and has been described by Robert Sutherland as one of those writers of working-class origin who have "taken over" French-Canadian poetry from "the clergy and upper classes." Miron went to Montréal in 1947, worked at an assortment of jobs, and published his first poems in *Le Devoir* and *Amérique française.* In 1953 he was one of the founders of the small but active publishing house Les Éditions de l'Hexagone, which over the years has issued about a hundred volumes of verse, and has greatly influenced Canadian poetry. The same year, 1953, Miron and the poet Olivier Marchand published a joint collection of poems, *Deux Sangs* (Two Bloods).

During the early 1950s, Miron began to write the three verse cycles that have been seen as the core of his work: "La Batèche," "La Marche à l'amour" (The March to Love), and "La Vie agonique" (The Anguished Life). From these developed two secondary sequences: "L'Amour et le militant" (Love and the Militant) and "Poèmes de l'amour en sursis" (Poems of Love Deferred). These poems were never published in their entirety, but appeared in fragments, along with other pieces, in such journals as *Liberté* and *Parti Pris,* and later in various anthologies. Miron read them at poetry recitals and gave away copies to friends and acquaintances, but had no wish to publish them in book form. Nevertheless, during the 1950s and 1960s, he became a legend in Québec and Montréal, where his friends included such leading figures in the French-Canadian renaissance as Jacques Ferron, Victor-Levy Beaulieu, Roland Giguère, and Jean-Guy Pilon, as well as Irving Layton, F.R. Scott, Louis Dudek, and other members of the
*mē rôN'

Canadian literary establishment. The Canadian-born poet Gael Turnbull gives this impression of Miron as he was in Montréal in October 1955:

... both your feet off the ground at each stride
both eyes following invisible sparrows,
your arms and hands moving like pennants
above a battlement of words—

in a nest of a room ...
woven with books and poems and letters
with an egg at the centre
that trembles, ready to burst—

... It will hatch, who knows when?
... and even you don't know what will come out
but whatever it is
it will have wings and a throat
and will soar over the chimneys
singing as it goes ...

In 1957 Miron ran, unsuccessfully, as candidate in Québec for the anti-nuclear, left-wing New Democratic Party. In October 1957 he suffered a heart attack due, in his own words, to "intellectual strain and physical exhaustion." Yet he stood again for the NDP in 1958. By January 1959 he was at his lowest ebb: "I have not recovered from this attack," he wrote (in French) to Gael Turnbull; "I am dragged down by nervous depression. ... My poetic work has been interrupted: I have written nothing for two years, not even a single poem." In the same letter he spoke of "a most terrible metaphysical crisis" that had overtaken him, and of his inability to communicate its nature to others. In August 1959 Miron went to Paris, where he lived for a year with the help of a grant from the Arts

Council of Canada. On his return he became a militant Québec separatist. During the 1960s he became increasingly active in the RIN (Rassamblement pour l'indépendance nationale), and in the crisis of October 1970 he was detained for a time, although not finally charged.

When Miron began to write, the French-Canadian language reflected the self-doubt, isolation, and subservience of the French Canadians themselves: it had suffered, he discovered, "semantic perversion on a national scale." Betty Bednarski has explained in an article in the *Times Literary Supplement* (October 26, 1973) how this discovery has affected Miron's work and his life. "Miron believes," she writes, "that the state of a language reflects the particular problems of a society; his poet's commitment to language has become automatically a commitment to French-Canadian society.... As long as language is undermined and the existence of his people threatened, he refuses to go to the limits of his individual potential, refuses to create for himself a privileged existence through poetry. Rather than personal liberation, he must seek to bring about the liberation of his people.

"Convinced that this liberation can only be achieved through political change, Miron has devoted much of his energy to political action, and was tempted for a time to give up writing altogether.... To the poems he has given us he assigns a specific role: to expose alienation, beginning with the alienation of language itself, and to help remove it by encouraging a new self-awareness.... For the moment he is obliged to write something less than the poetry he dreams of, obliged to write of the *non-poème* —his term for all the conditions which prevent him from fulfilling himself and his poetry from having autonomous life. The *non-poème* negates poetry by negating a people and its language. Poetry can only exist to the extent that the *non-poème* is eliminated. Miron therefore sets out to expose it, first by evoking its atmosphere in passages of nightmarish confusion, of 'raving alienation,' in which English words play a vital part, then by naming and analysing it in a language deliberately, laboriously, logical and exact.... His poetry thus carries the burden of all the destructive forces at work in his society. He cannot merely tell, he must demonstrate, and in so doing risks the life of his own work."

It seemed to Miron false under these circumstances to aspire to the creation of anything as composed and homogeneous as a book, and this is why his immensely influential poems, written "sporadically, in response to events and his own painfully evolving consciousness," remained for so many years uncollected. It was not until 1970 that his friends were able to persuade him to take this step. The result was *L'Homme rapaillé* (1970), "a book on the present impossibility of writing a book."

L'Homme rapaillé contains fifty-seven poems and some prose articles by or about Miron, including one by André Vachon which describes Miron as one of "the great contemporary poets of the French language." The collection includes poems in tight, neat quatrains, others in free forms reminiscent of Whitman, Claudel, and St.-John Perse. "Uniting common speech with the most modern and creative inventions of contemporary French poetry," wrote Naim Kattan, Miron "writes poems of sadness, longing, hope, and joy—nature and love poems and some emotion-filled separatist lyrics." Versatile as he is, Miron is probably most successful in such poems as "Héritage de la tristesse," a poignant expression of his love for Québec, and a separatist poem which never even mentions the word:

Sad and confused among the fallen stars
pale, silent, nowhere and afraid, a vast phantom,
here is this land alone with winds and rocks
a land forever lost to its natal sun
a beautiful body drowned in mindless sleep. . . .

The poem ends:

. . . with your river arms
embrace this face of a ruined people, give it the
    warmth
and the abundant light that rings the wake of
    swallows

(translated by Martin Seymour-Smith)

Betty Bednarski writes that "Miron's most significant achievement and his greatest victory over the *non-poème* has been to repatriate elements of French-Canadian usage which vary from the norm of standard French, and which acquire new dignity in the context of his poetry. He also stresses concrete terms, everyday words of nature and the land, which are the legacy of his mother tongue and enable him to possess at least part of his reality intact. These are the 'gnarled words of our endurance,' the 'bare chill words of our inheritance,' which he brought with him to Montréal from the country, and which bind him still to Québec, while the city, with its linguistic pollution, remains foreign, the bastion of the *non-poème*." With the publication of *L'Homme rapaillé,* according to Naim Kattan, Miron's work was "at last granted its importance"—in Canada, and to some extent in France. It brought him the Prix France-Canada and the prize offered by the review *Études fran-*

çaises in 1970, the literary prize of the city of Montréal in 1971, and the Prix littéraire Belgique-Canada in 1972. A second collection, *Courtepointes* (Counterpanes), followed in 1975.

Miron, as Claude Ryan has said, is now generally recognized to be in the forefront of those who have established the values in terms of which "the intellectual and creative activity of our society is gradually evolving." The dramatist Jean-Claude Germain has hailed him as one of the "vigilantes of Québec": "It is the unwearying dream of [such] creators which prevents the sky of Québec from beheading us." Betty Bednarski thinks him "probably the single most influential figure in French-Canadian literature today. His teachings have inspired a whole generation of militant young writers, passionately committed to social and political revolution, and to the urgent task of defending the national language of Québec."

JULIAN MITCHELL

PRINCIPAL WORKS IN ENGLISH TRANSLATION: *Poems in* Glassco, J. (ed.) The Poetry of French Canada in Translation, 1970; Edge Winter 1967-1968, Summer 1969.

ABOUT: Brault, J. Miron le magnifique, 1966; Toye, W. (ed.) Supplement to the Oxford Companion to Canadian History and Literature, 1973. *Periodicals*—Ellipse 5 1972; Times Literary Supplement October 26, 1973.

MITCHELL, (CHARLES) JULIAN (HUMPHREY) (May 1, 1935–), English novelist, dramatist, and television writer, was born in Epping, just outside London, the son of William Moncur Mitchell and the former Christine Mary Browne. Julian Mitchell was educated at Winchester College (1948-1953) and then did his national service as a midshipman in the Royal Naval Volunteer Reserve (1953-1955), serving for a time in an "ancient and very small submarine." In 1955 he resumed his education at Wadham College, Oxford, earning an honors degree in English in 1958. He went to the United States as a Harkness fellow in 1959 and received his M.A. from St. Antony's College, Oxford, in 1962. Mitchell's verse and short stories began to appear in magazines in the late 1950s, and some of the stories were collected in the anthology *Introduction.* Four novels followed in quick succession, all of them written before Mitchell was thirty.

Imaginary Toys (1961) is about university life in the mid-1950s, a talented romp reminiscent of the early Aldous Huxley in its "fanciful, essay-like speculations" and acute sense of period; critics found it promising, if superficial. *A Disturbing Influence* (1962), equally deft and professional, is set in a complacent but pleasant Berkshire village and describes the impact on the

inhabitants of an evil and destructive young outsider—a type with a particular fascination for Mitchell, as Bernard Bergonzi has pointed out, though the heroes of his novels tend to be characters of a very different sort, well-meaning, good-natured, intelligent, but rather weak and inept. One such is Harold Barlow in *As Far As You Can Go* (1963), who is sent to the United States to retrieve, on behalf of a banker, family portraits sold by an Edwardian ne'er-do-well. This is a well-observed "high-grade satirical frolic" which, most critics thought, does not quite transcend its purpose of exploiting an interesting background—the hipster subculture of California. But Mitchell's professional skill was growing, and this novel was called "more substantial and interesting" than its two predecessors.

The White Father (1964), which won both the Rhys Memorial Prize and the Somerset Maugham Award, is generally considered to be Mitchell's best, if not his most ambitious, novel. Hugh Shrieve is a British colonial official, a district officer in a remote part of Africa, responsible for the well-being of the primitive Ngulu tribe. Shrieve is fond of these peaceable people and goes to London to defend their interests at the forthcoming independence conference, since he fears for their safety at the hands of more sophisticated neighbors. In "swinging London," at the beginning of the pop era, he feels far more alien and disoriented than he ever did in Africa, but he struggles to come to terms with the new, and to give some meaning to the life of Edward, a talented but aimless young Oxford graduate. Edward is torn between idealism, which impels him to serve for a time as Shrieve's assistant, and a greedy hankering after wealth and fame as a pop star. Looming over the scene from his Piccadilly penthouse is Brachs, a tycoon of the entertainment industry and a megalomaniac with a rabid fear of communism.

One American reviewer called this "a very British sort of British novel, with lots of talk, lots of caricaturing, and a thin but clever plot, adroitly counterpointed." The *Times Literary Supplement* was worried about Brachs, whose "activities belong to the world of satirical fantasy," and with whom Mitchell "has to modulate into a key very remote from the one he uses for Edward and Shrieve." But the same reviewer found the book in general "colourful and exact" in its style, with "plentiful conversations . . . most adroitly managed. It is . . . thoroughly well organized and crowded with characters."

A Circle of Friends (1966), a relatively slight book in which a rather solitary young Englishman is taken up (and put down) by a circle of sophisticates in New York, was followed by *The Undiscovered Country* (1968), the most extraordinary of Mitchell's novels. The first part of the book is narrated by "Julian Mitchell," a novelist who resembles the real Julian Mitchell in many particulars. It describes the narrator's relationship with his friend and would-be seducer Charles Humphries, a homosexual intellectual dropout who becomes bisexual, sadistic, variously self-destructive, and eventually a suicide. The second part is "The New Satyricon," which purports to be a manuscript left by Charles, and is a satirical fantasy, an account in allegorical terms of the same relationship, seen from the point of view of the pursuer rather than the pursued. Webster Schott said that this was "an authentically homosexual novel. Loving, inoffensive. No catalogue of sodomy. Socially responsive. A marginal achievement." But, as Schott appears not to have noticed, "Charles" and "Humphrey" are Mitchell's own given names, and the author slyly remarks of Charles that "our lives were so close that they are, to me, almost inextricable." It is for the reader to decide whether or not the novel is "authentically homosexual" or a study of contending elements in the author's personality.

"Mitchell's style is elegant and fastidious," wrote Neil Millar, "yet fastidious readers may be tempted to reject his book because parts of it read like sexual fantasy. Other parts are parodies and burlesques of current social, political, and artistic follies. Much of the novel is a quiet tragedy, civilized, intelligent, flecked with doubt, pity, and sometimes bitter laughter. . . . *The Undiscovered Country* is a very accomplished work, conceivably the only one of its austere, tender,

comical sad kind." Other reviewers were less impressed, especially with "The New Satyricon," which Schott called "a grinding bore" with its "tedious variations of Nabokov, Kafka, Genet, etc."

Bernard Bergonzi has suggested that *The Undiscovered Country* demonstrated Mitchell's "dissatisfaction with his more conventional early novels," and asked whether, despite his "fluent, witty and ingenious" work in that form, his gifts are "those of a natural novelist." And Bergonzi points out that "Julian," in introducing "The New Satyricon," writes: "I think it unlikely that I shall write another book of my own for a long time, with the fact of this one before me. Charles said that all art comes from an inner need. He said that I began to write because I wanted to be a writer, and that was the wrong kind of need."

In fact, Mitchell has so far published no more novels, and has turned his attention instead to the theatre, television, and the cinema, most notably with his stage adaptations of two of the novels of the late Ivy Compton-Burnett, *A Heritage and Its History* and *A Family and a Fortune.* They were regarded as good theatre which sacrificed none of the subtlety of the originals. His own stage play, *Half-life* (1977), was moderately well received. He has written a number of television plays and adaptations, and a much-acclaimed series about the colorful life of Jennie, Lady Randolph Churchill, Winston Churchill's mother—the subject also of a biography written in collaboration with Peregrine Churchill, and based on her personal correspondence. His views on the novel are briefly stated in *Truth and Fiction.* Julian Mitchell is a dark, amiable, and rather reticent man, but a quietly amusing raconteur. He lives in London, but has made many visits to the United States, and has traveled a good deal in Europe. He is a governor of the Chelsea School of Art. His television play *Abide With Me* received the International Critics' Prize at Monte Carlo in 1977.

PRINCIPAL PUBLISHED WORKS: *Novels*—Imaginary Toys, 1961; A Disturbing Influence, 1962; As Far As You Can Go, 1963; The White Father, 1964; A Circle of Friends, 1966; The Undiscovered Country, 1968. *Stories in* Introduction, 1960. *Plays*—A Heritage and Its History, 1968; Shadow in the Sun (television play) *in* Trewin, J.C. (ed.) Elizabeth R., 1972; A Family and a Fortune, 1976; Half-life, 1978. *Criticism*—Truth and Fiction, 1972. *Biography*—(with Peregrine Churchill) Jennie: Lady Randolph Churchill: A Portrait With Letters, 1974. *As Editor*—(with others) Light Blue, Dark Blue: An Anthology of Recent Writing From Oxford and Cambridge, 1960.

ABOUT: B.B.C., Writers on Themselves, 1964; Burgess, A. The Novel Now, 1971; Contemporary Authors 5-8 1st revision, 1969; Moraes, D. (ed.) Voices for Life, 1974; Vinson,

MONTES DE OCA

J. (ed.) Contemporary Novelists, 1976; Who's Who, 1978.
Periodicals—Book Week February 14, 1965; Christian
Science Monitor January 24, 1970; Listener December 31,
1964; New Statesman February 16, 1968; New York Times
Book Review February 21, 1965; January 18, 1970; Times
(London) November 19, 1977; Times Literary Supplement
March 23, 1962; January 18, 1964; April 9, 1964; September 22, 1966; February 15, 1968.

*MONTES DE OCA, MARCO ANTONIO
(August 3, 1932–), Mexican poet, was born in
Mexico City. He recalls his father, a former
revolutionary, as a man of heroic stature, while
his mother seemed to him "the very essence of
giving." Montes de Oca wrote his first verses
while still at school, and soon made friends with
others who shared his love of literature. He was
a rebellious and adventurous child, and says that
he was devoted to football and the movies as well
as to poetry. At the National University he began his studies in the law faculty, but later transferred to humanities. After his graduation he
taught for a while, did some clerical and editorial work, and in 1957 opened a forge as a metal
worker. Less arduous but infinitely more humiliating were his painful experiences as a ghostwriter for radio programs. The uncertain income
derived in these ways was eked out by various
scholarships, but he experienced periods of real
poverty and hardship.

As a young man, Montes de Oca became
associated with the *Poeticismo* (Poeticization)
movement founded by Enrique González Fojo
and Eduardo Lizalde. Flamboyantly eccentric in
their determination to attract public attention
and to revitalize the Mexican literary scene, the
group defined *Poeticismo* as "a vigorous attempt
to rationalize the different approaches to poetry
and poetics, especially on the question of imagery. *Poeticismo* not only sets out to study how
images are created by the poet, but also to give
them a prominence within the poem in keeping
with their complexity, originality and clarity."

This preoccupation with imagery is evident in
the extravagant metaphors which characterize
Montes de Oca's early verse, beginning in 1953
with *Ruina de la infame Babilonia* (The Downfall of Infamous Babylon). This was followed
during the 1950s by several more collections of
long, surrealistic, and torrentially verbose poems, most of them inspired by Mexico's landscape, history, and mythology—dramatized
visions of "unique, resplendent, irresistible creation."

Like Octavio Paz, to whom he acknowledges
an enormous debt, Montes de Oca is intent upon
capturing the plenitude of the world, rich and
multitudinous to the point of insanity: "Damsels
*mon′ tes dā o′ ca

Ricardo Salazar

MARCO ANTONIO MONTES DE OCA

and gallants, stones and birds/ it is the beauty of
life that leaves us so poor/ the beauty of life/
which slowly turns us mad." There was a strong
religious element in this celebratory verse, an
ecstatic certainty that faith "pierces burial boxes
and fills anew the chewed grapeskins." Octavio
Paz has acknowledged the similarity between
the young poet's work and his own, especially in
the use of symbol and metaphor. However,
while Paz has praised not only the energy and
audacity of Montes de Oca's verse but also his
subtle perception of movement and sound, other
critics have been less impressed, considering that
the narcissism and uncontrolled histrionics of
his early work outweigh its virtues.

And indeed the poet himself is omnipresent in
his poems, especially in *Cantos al sol que no se
alcanza* (Hymns to the Sun Beyond Our Reach,
1959), the most "surrealist-baroque" of all his
books, filled with a furious excitement. Montes
de Oca has said that the book was an attempt to
make poetry out of the state of "psychic chaos"
in which it was composed—a state which was
evidently connected with a crisis in his religious
faith. In this and subsequent volumes, Christian
certainty has been replaced by doubt and self-questioning: "Never again for me, the soft
spongy white bread/ Jesus dispensed to me continuously for twenty-eight years." Gordon
Brotherston, writing in *Books Abroad* (Winter
1971), suggests that Montes de Oca's poetry
since that time "could be understood as an attempt to reemerge into an earlier sunlit landscape and to reconquer faith"; meanwhile he
looks less to God than to love—"a love which in
origin is perhaps Christian but which becomes a
force for and from itself."

Along with these self-explorations has come a deliberate progress towards greater discipline and control in his poetry. The poet's struggle with language is a recurrent theme in his later verse: "Words make their way along the tortuous road/ That goes from the throat to the infinite/ Words march in perfect order/ Into the twittering ambush of their own making." Some critics have found the poems in such collections as *Vendimia del juglar* (Minstrel's Vintage, 1965) uncomfortably close to anecdote, but most have welcomed their growing maturity and skill, the more careful matching of imagery to theme. The poet now sees himself as "the conscience of song," and identifies both the strength and the weakness of his work when he exclaims: "I enter my century/ through the palpitating door of myself."

In such later volumes as *Las fuentes legendarias* (Legendary Fountains, 1966) and *Pedir el fuego* (Pursuit of Fire, 1968), Montes de Oca (like Paz) turns frequently to the prose poem, a form which in his hands is "elusive, mysterious, a blend of children's stories, magic, and science fiction." Whether he writes in prose or verse, these more mature poems have retained the energy and excitement of his earliest works. There is the same passion to transform reality into words and words into images, the same surrealistic imagery and verbal orchestration. Metamorphoses abound, for he is convinced that "It is good that the world assumes ever-changing names/ And that suddenly it is called nest, willow, or pine tree dancing at noon." He has come to question or modify most of the precepts of *Poeticismo* except where they insist upon clarity.

Montes de Oca is fully conscious of the difficulty of reconciling art and propaganda, but his work has exhibited a growing social awareness even though it has generally avoided overt political commitment. A notable exception is the much quoted and admired "Ode Upon the Death of Che Guevara" which closes *Pedir el fuego,* a powerful and deeply felt tribute to the revolutionary hero.

In an autobiographical essay published in 1967, Montes de Oca speaks of the way in which his critical standing has been diminished by the excesses of his early work. Meditating upon Max Aub's statement that "Mexican poets have always been excessively ornate," he is prepared to agree only if this ornamentation is recognized to be not merely decorative but also metaphysical. He maintains with great conviction that poetry should be "something more than a lesson in philosophy enhanced by lyrical interjections. ... [It is] an essential ingredient of the living order, an element added to the order of existence which, once assimilated, augments its very existence." Reviewing Montes de Oca's *Poesía reunida* (1971), Manuel Durán wrote: "It is obvious now that ... [he] is a first-rank poet, a major figure in today's Mexican letters: there is unity within diversity, order and lucidity among the chaos and the ruins that populate his landscapes."

The author has served as secretary of the P.E.N. Club of Mexico, which he helped to resuscitate, as vice-president of the Association of Mexican Writers, editor of *La Pajarita de Papel* and director of *La Vida Literaria.* He has represented Mexico at a number of international literary congresses, and has taught as a visiting professor at the University of Essex in England. He was awarded the Villaurrutia Prize for poetry in 1959 and the Mazatlán Prize in 1966, and has received scholarships and grants from the College of Mexico (1955-1957), the Center for Mexican Writers (1956-1957 and 1960-1961), the Fondo de Cultura Económica (1963-1964) and the Guggenheim Foundation (1967-1968 and 1970-1971). Since the early 1960s he has lectured extensively and given many public readings of his work, in Mexico and abroad. Married, with four daughters, Montes de Oca is currently on the editorial staff of the publications department at the National University of Mexico.

PRINCIPAL WORKS IN ENGLISH TRANSLATION: *Poems in* Brotherston, G. Latin American Poetry, 1975; Caracciolo-Trejo, E. (ed.) Penguin Book of Latin American Verse, 1971; Cohen, J.M. (ed.) Latin American Writing Today, 1967; Donoso, J. and Henkin, W.A. (eds.) Triquarterly Anthology of Contemporary Latin American Literature, 1969; Strand, M. (ed.) New Poetry of Mexico, 1972.

ABOUT: Monsiváis, C. (ed.) La poesía mexicana del siglo XX, 1966; Marco Antonio Montes de Oca (autobiographical essay), 1967; Paz, O. and others (eds.) Poesía en movimiento, 1966; Sanchez, L.A. Sobre la nueva poesía mexicana, 1966; Xirau, R. Poetas de México y España, 1962. *Periodicals*—Books Abroad Winter 1971, January 1972.

*MORAES, VINÍCIUS DE (October 19, 1913–), Brazilian poet, songwriter, and film scenarist, was born in the district of Gávea, Rio de Janeiro, and grew up in that city. His father was Clodoaldo Pereira da Silva Moraes, son of the poet and essayist Mello Moraes Filho and grandson of the historian Alexandre José de Mello Moraes. His mother was Lydia Cruz de Moraes.

In 1924 Moraes began his secondary schooling at the College of St. Ignatius, where he sang in a choir and developed an early interest in music and composition. A biographical essay by

*mor aezh'

VINÍCIUS DE MORAES

Manchete, from Pictorial Parade

his sister Laetitia in his *Obra Poética* describes him as a frail and introspective child, remarkable nevertheless for his courage and sense of initiative. Graduating in 1929, Moraes embarked without enthusiasm upon legal studies at the Academy of Juridical and Social Studies, where he received his degree in 1933. The same year, encouraged by the writer Octávio de Faria, he published his first book of poems.

O Caminho para a Distância (The Path Into the Distance) was edited and published by his close friend Augusto Frederico Schmidt. Schmidt had rejected the strident rhetoric and fierce nationalism of the 1922 Generation of Brazilian Modernists, calling for a return to a more introspective poetry dealing with universal human concerns. Schmidt's neoromanticism had some influence on the immature and self-absorbed poems in Moraes's first book, but so did the French Parnassians and symbolists, many Brazilian poets, and such figures as Valéry, Claudel, Eliot, García Lorca, and Neruda. "I plagiarized a great deal in the beginning," Moraes has said. "Tentatively to begin with, then like someone possessed."

Growing technical assurance is evident in Moraes's subsequent books—*Forma e Exegese* (Form and Exegesis, 1935), *Ariana, a Mulher* (Ariana, the Woman, 1936), and *Novos Poemas* (New Poems, 1938)—but the prevailing mood is still of overdramatized loneliness and unhappiness, from which the poet seeks relief in religious speculations and, increasingly, in communion with nature. Human beings are viewed cynically and with mistrust. In 1936 Moraes joined the Ministry of Education as its representative on the Board of Film Censors. It was during this period also that Moraes began his lifelong friendships with two of Brazil's most distinguished poets, Manuel Bandeira and Carlos Drummond de Andrade.

In 1938, after the publication of *Novos Poemas,* Moraes received the first British Council scholarship ever awarded to a Brazilian. He went to Magdalen College, Oxford, where he read English, working in his spare time for the Brazilian section of the British Broadcasting Corporation. The outbreak of World War II brought him back to Brazil in 1939. By 1941 Moraes was film critic of the Rio newspaper *A Manhã* (Morning) and a contributor to the highly respected *Suplemento Literário* (Literary Supplement). His sphere of influence widened, and he came to be regarded as a leading authority on film and the film industry. In 1942 he made an extensive tour of Northeastern Brazil with the American writer Waldo Frank, meeting many of the region's most prominent writers and critics.

Cinco Elegias (Five Elegies, 1943) marked a turning point in Moraes's work, and this was confirmed by the publication three years later of *Poemas, Sonetos e Baladas* (Poems, Sonnets and Ballads). The much anthologized Sonnets of Fidelity and Separation, the "Balada do Mangue" (Ballad of the Red Light District), and the satirical "O Dia de Criação" (The Day of Creation) all belong to the latter collection. Now in full command of his technical resources, Moraes here experiments with a much greater variety of genres and techniques. Sonnets and shorter lyrics appear alongside alexandrines; traditional themes and forms are interspersed with "shaped" poems, with pastiches and parodies and poems that successfully employ slang and jargon without surrendering their lyricism. The introspection and mysticism of Moraes's early work have given way in this second phase to a mature commitment to the world of human affairs.

In 1943, meanwhile, Moraes had entered the Brazilian diplomatic service. Between then and 1946 he served also as editor of the *Suplemento Literário* and *O Jornal* (The Journal), doing a great deal to promote the work of avant-garde artists and writers. In 1946 he went as vice-consul to Los Angeles. During his five years in that post, Moraes was able to develop further his interest in the cinema, meeting many of Hollywood's most talented and influential figures and launching, in collaboration with Alex Vrony, the magazine *Review.*

Moraes returned to Brazil in 1950, when his father died, becoming film critic for *Última Hora* (Late Final). In 1951, in collaboration with his cousins Humberto and José Franceschi, he made a film about the colonial cities of Minas Gerais, with special emphasis upon the life and times of the sixteenth-century sculptor Aleijadinho. Moraes subsequently made a tour of the major European film festivals before organizing a similar event as part of São Paulo's fourth centenary celebrations.

In 1953 Moraes was appointed second secretary in his country's embassy in Paris. His *Antologia Poética* (Poetry Anthology)—the first of several—appeared the following year, containing what the author considered the best and most representative poems of his various phases. In the newer work in this collection Moraes, without losing anything of his innate lyricism and sensuousness, emerges as something of a social poet, observing the disintegration of bourgeois society and the exploitation of man by man, like those two brothers "June and July, coldly/ Preparing the catastrophes of August" ("May Sonnet"). It was in 1954 also that Moraes staged his prize-winning verse drama *Orfeu da Conceição* (Orpheus of Conceição) at Rio's Municipal Theatre, with music composed by Antonio Carlos Jobim. This was later adapted as the film *Orfeu Negro* (Black Orpheus, 1958), directed by Marcel Camus, receiving the Palme d'Or at the Cannes Film Festival and a Hollywood Oscar as the best foreign film of the year.

Moraes was transferred from Paris to Montevideo in 1957, but not before he had written a group of songs in collaboration with the noted French conductor Claudio Santoro. Soon after, a long-playing record, "Canção do Amor Demais" (The Song of Too Much Love), with lyrics by Moraes, music by Jobim, and the voice of Elizete Cardoso, marked the advent of the *bossa nova,* a samba-like dance. Moraes returned to the Ministry of Foreign Affairs in Rio in 1960.

The years that followed brought further notable collaborations with composers of popular music in Brazil, and appearances in many recitals and stage shows. Lyrics by Moraes won both the first and second prizes in the Festival of Popular Music held in São Paulo in 1965. The same year he started work on a movie based on one of his most famous lyrics, "Garota de Ipanema" (The Girl from Ipanema), directed by Leon Hirzman. In 1966 the poet himself became the subject of a documentary film produced jointly by American, French, German, and Italian television. Another of his popular lyrics, "Samba Saravah" was featured in the Oscar-winning French film *Un Homme et une femme* (A Man and a Woman). By that time, Moraes had become a much-loved national figure, actively involved in all the major festivals of films and of popular music held in Brazil.

Vinícius de Moraes has been married four times—in 1939 to Beatriz Azevedo de Mello, in 1951 to Maria Esquerdo e Bôscoli, in 1958 to Maria Lúcia Proença, and in 1963 to Nelita Abreu Rocha. He has three daughters and a son. Moraes has been spoken of as a modern counterpart of Villon, and has proclaimed his admiration for Rimbaud. The critic Sergio Milliet considered him the last and most brilliant of the poets of orthodox Brazilian modernism, but J. M. Cohen writes: "It is as an independent, with a light and sardonic lyrical gift, that he seems to hold his place in modern poetry." His versatility has been both his greatest strength and his greatest weakness. John Nist speaks of the constant warfare in his work between "the flesh and the spirit" and goes on: "Of the many voices he sings with—lyrically tender and nostalgic, boisterously humorous and plagiaristic, symbolically amorous, satirically bitter and ironic, popularly rhythmical and easy of imagic texture—it is the spiritual voice of Vinícius de Moraes that will prevail." Moraes himself has defined the poet as someone "in constant pursuit of the absolute and, in social terms, a permanent rebel."

PRINCIPAL WORKS IN ENGLISH TRANSLATION: *Poems in* Bishop, E. and Brasil, E. (eds.) An Anthology of Twentieth Century Brazilian Poetry, 1972; Caracciolo-Trejo, E. (ed.) The Penguin Book of Latin American Verse, 1971; Cohen, J.M. (ed.) Latin American Writing Today, 1967; Nist, J. (ed.) Modern Brazilian Poetry, 1962; Pontiero, G. (ed.) An Anthology of Brazilian Modernist Poetry, 1969.

ABOUT: Brotherston, G. Latin American Poetry, 1975; Faria, O. de. Dois Poetas: Augusto Frederico Schmidt and Vinícius de Moraes, 1935; International Who's Who, 1977-78; Moraes, V. de. Obra Poética (with introduction and critical statements by various hands), 1968; Nist, J. The Modernist Movement in Brazil, 1967; Penguin Companion to Literature 3, 1971; Pontiero, G. (ed.) An Anthology of Brazilian Modernist Poetry, 1969. *Periodicals*—New Directions 1974; Saturday Review World February 9, 1974.

MORGAN, EDWIN (GEORGE) (April 27, 1920–), Scottish poet, translator, and critic, writes: "I was born in Glasgow and have lived in and around the city most of my life. I identify strongly with it as a place and would be reluctant to live anywhere else. My father worked as a clerk with a local firm of iron and steel scrap merchants and eventually became a director in the firm. Both he and my mother were hard-working, conscientious, anxious persons, with a strong sense of what was ordered and right, and although there was nothing dour or oppressive in the family atmosphere—I remember the evening card games of whist and rummy and bezique, the dart board being set up, the gramophone being wound and the squat metal needles

EDWIN MORGAN

being picked from their little paper-lined boxes
—the Presbyterian work ethic was there and has
undoubtedly left its mark. I have short bursts of
hedonism, but can quickly feel uneasy and guilty
if there's an absence of work. In the same way,
because my parents were regular churchgoers
and I went to both church and Sunday school
and learned large parts of the Bible by heart,
there are recurring religious themes and images
in my writing which are part of the Scottish
grain as much as they may be signs of anything
in my own character.

"Most of my schooling was at Rutherglen
Academy, and then I went with a scholarship to
Glasgow High School for the last three years.
Art was one of my main subjects at school, and
I had planned to go on to art school but at the
last moment decided to go to Glasgow University instead, and took English Honours. I graduated in 1947, after a five-year interruption as a
private in the Royal Army Medical Corps.
These war years were spent in Egypt, Palestine,
and Lebanon. The Middle East and its people
made a deep impression on me, although I was
unable to write about this, or the war, at the
time. After graduating I taught English at Glasgow University, where I am now a titular
professor.

"Although I have published a good deal of
critical prose (essays and reviews both journalistic and academic), poetry has always been central, and in this I include translations, visual
poems, sound poems, and opera librettos as well
as ordinary verse. I have written poetry since my
schooldays, but have gone through various bad
patches when I was uncertain of my direction
and dissatisfied with what I was writing. The

war years in particular, when I wrote nothing,
seem to have had some kind of deadening or
inhibiting effect from which it took me a while
to recover. I remember the late 1940s and early
1950s with little affection. But the 1960s were for
me a great liberating period, and most of the
work which has been anthologized, or which I
use at poetry readings, was written after I was
forty. The climate of that time, its loosenings
and renewals and discoveries, musical, poetic,
sexual, and political, coincided with an unforeseen resurgence of joy and energy in my personal life; feeling absolutely at home in the
decade, I wrote productively and in a wide range
of styles.

"Because of its variety my poetry is hard to
generalize about. At the moment I see different
kinds of poems as different kinds of problems,
linked only by the fact that one person writes
them all and must therefore leave some fingerprints, even if he is not trying to do so. I recognize, of course, certain clear focal points or
preoccupations: Glasgow life, science fiction,
verbal experiment, themes of change and
rebirth. Yet even here there is not much
homogeneity except a desire to penetrate the immediate and forward point of life rather than the
past—and the fact that on the whole I have
negative feelings about 'tradition' does at least
confirm this interest if it does not explain it. I
like writing that takes risks. Poetry, for all the
intellect that can be applied to it creatively and
critically, retains a mysterious exploratory quality that one learns to respect. You have a good
poem when a combination of luck and hard
work strikes the right balance between exploration (which is the artist's part of the bargain) and
communication (which is the human parameter
—blessed parameter!): and best of all when the
reader or audience is aware of both aspects and
receives them. Poetry may well use, and use
well, modes and conventions and rhetorics, but
I like to think of it as being still in basis and
potential a frontier art—whether scouting for
chinaberries or megatheriums."

Edwin Morgan expresses above his dissatisfaction with his early verse, and none of it was
published in book form. His first small collection, *The Vision of Cathkin Braes,* appeared
when he was thirty-two. It showed many of the
characteristics of his later work—wit, humor,
great versatility, and delight in verbal experiment—but revealed little about his personality
or special concerns. There is far more self-revelation in the long, ambitious, but flawed poem
The Cape of Good Hope, published in a limited
edition in 1955. It examines various experiences

of isolation and alienation with a "sense of personal seriousness, a sense of urgency" that, as Robin Fulton has pointed out, is "frequently lacking in his more accomplished later verse."

Other booklets came from various small presses in the 1960s, but it was not until 1968, when Morgan was forty-eight, that Edinburgh University Press collected, in *The Second Life,* the fruits of his "great liberating period" of the 1960s, with "its loosenings and renewals and discoveries, musical, poetic, sexual, and political." This volume alone would be enough to establish Morgan as the most versatile of living British poets. It includes poems expressing affection for a human (even if imperfect) scale of values, poems of sympathy for human vulnerability (including three about great wounded *monstres sacrés*—Hemingway, Piaf, and Marilyn Monroe); a group of unsentimentally compassionate Glasgow poems; poems (some of them love poems) about renewal—about the idea of a "second life"—personal, urban, and cosmic; a group of science fiction poems; and several sections of sound, concrete, and found poems.

The book was generally recognized to be what Raymond Gardner called it, the product of a "profound eclecticism," sweeping "across the complete axis of poetic creation, from lyric to concrete, tragedy to farce, surrealist to home-spun philosophy," but not all of its reviewers would go so far as to agree that it was also the product of "an immense talent." The consensus was probably more in line with the verdict of a writer in the *Times Literary Supplement,* who concluded that, although Morgan can "write with a piercing directness and simplicity," he is also "very much a performer, and when he fails it is through an excess of virtuosity."

Further examples of Morgan's versatility followed. *Instamatic Poems* is a collection of fifty-two short poems, each carrying a dateline as title, which are imaginative and brilliantly concentrated reconstructions of news items—most of them sinister or even gruesome. *The Whittrick* is a series of eight imaginary dialogues, as for example between James Joyce and Hugh Mac-Diarmid, Hieronymus Bosch and Johan Faust, Charlotte and Emily Brontë.

From Glasgow to Saturn, Morgan's second major collection, and a Poetry Book Society choice, contains anecdotal and descriptive poems, science fiction fantasies, surrealistic poems, and a variety of pointed and often very funny typographical and phonic experiments. There was much praise for the ten *Glasgow Sonnets* reprinted in this volume. Tightly written in Morgan's own sonnet form, they form a grimly realistic but still affectionate portrait of the slum-ridden city and its people and, "like Sassoon's poems about war . . . at least say something intelligent and humane about an unbearable situation." Peter Porter, discussing the collection as a whole, complained that Morgan had too often "been content with an idea (and he gets more ideas than a dozen ordinary poets), and hasn't bothered to turn it into a poem," but concluded that the book's "flaws and inequalities are those of a poet of real originality." It seemed to Blake Morrison that in *The New Divan* (1977), Morgan's "perseverance with oral and visual experimentation" was "beginning to have important consequences for his work as a whole"—for example when some of the devices of visual poetry are effectively employed in an otherwise traditional lyric. The long title sequence was found interesting in its search for continuities, its preoccupation with renewal and resurrection (though the vision was thought bleaker than in earlier work).

Robin Fulton finds unclear in Morgan's work "the relation of his own personality to its protean but partial manifestations. He may not assume masks such as dramatis personae but his many different modes of expression seem to serve a like function: are they ways of *saying* or ways of *hiding*?" Fulton suggests that, at the heart of Morgan's poetry, is "an unresolved tension between a romantic desire for exotic distances and a particular human concern for local unromantic circumstances," and he quotes in evidence from "Floating Off to Timor," one of the poems in *From Glasgow to Saturn:*

> If only we'd been strangers
> we'd be floating off to Timor
> we'd be shimmering on the Trades
> in a blue jersey boat
> with shandies, flying fish,
> a pace of dolphins
> to the copra ports. . . .
>
> But here we are care
> of the black roofs.
> It's not hard to find
> with a collar turned up
> and a hoot from the Clyde. . . .
>
> We take in
> the dream, a cloth from the line
> the trains fling sparks on
> In our city. We're better awake.
> But you know I'd take
> you all the same,
> if you were my next stranger.

Morgan has translated poetry from Ancient Greek, Old English, Italian, Spanish, French,

569

German, Russian, and Hungarian. Much of it has been the work of politically committed poets —Brecht, Neruda, Lorca, Mayakovsky—whose example has encouraged him in his desire to make his own poetry, or some of it, accessible and relevant to a wide readership. He is also attracted, as a translator, to the challenges offered by the verbal fireworks and virtuosity of such poets as Sándor Weöres and Mayakovsky —his renderings of Mayakovsky into Scots are at least a tour de force. In *Rites of Passage* (1977), a collection of his translations, he explains that he has refused himself the freedom of approach employed by Pound and Lowell, "and have tried to work within a sense of close and deep obligation to the other poet." It is interesting that some of Morgan's translations—of Montale, for example—carry more emotional weight than most of his own original poetry. His success in this sphere suggests that he possesses more powerful resources than he has so far found access to in his own voice.

Morgan published a volume of perceptive critical essays in 1974, dealing with a characteristically wide range of subjects—from concrete poetry to the work of Mervyn Peake, from the Polish poet Zbigniew Herbert to Hugh MacDiarmid. The author, who is unmarried, is the son of Stanley and Margaret (Arnott) Morgan. He received the Cholmondely Award in 1968 and awards from the Scottish Arts Council in 1968, 1973, 1975, and 1977. His recreations include color photography, scrapbooks, and looking at cities.

In a *Guardian* interview, Edwin Morgan said "I am interested in the kind of poetry which British poets seem to find difficult to write. ... You might roughly describe it as political, although I don't like using that word. It is a poetry which really is aware of the poet and artist being a citizen with a place in society and duties and responsibilities in society. My poet is a man who looks at his society and feels that he has something to say about it."

PRINCIPAL WORKS: *Poetry*—The Vision of Cathkin Braes, 1952; The Cape of Good Hope, 1955; Starryveldt, 1965; Scotch Mist, 1965; Sealware, 1966; Emergent Poems, 1967; Gnomes, 1968; The Second Life, 1968; Proverbfolder, 1969; (with Alan Bold and Edward Brathwaite) Penguin Modern Poets 15, 1969; The Horseman's Word, 1970; Twelve Songs, 1970; Glasgow Sonnets, 1972; Instamatic Poems, 1972; The Whittrick, 1973; From Glasgow to Saturn, 1973; The New Divan, 1977. *Translations*—Beowulf, 1952; Poems from Eugenio Montale, 1959; Sovpoems, 1961; (with David Wevill) Sándor Weöres and Ferenc Juhász: Selected Poems, 1970; Wi the Haill Voice: Twenty-five Poems by Vladimir Mayakovsky Translated Into Scots, 1972; Rites of Passage: Selected Translations, 1977. *Prose* —Essays, 1974; Hugh MacDiarmid (Writers and Their Work series), 1976. *As Editor*—Collins Albatross Book of Longer Poems, 1963; Fifty Renascence Love Poems, 1975.

ABOUT: Contemporary Authors 5-8, 1st revision, 1969; Fulton, R. Contemporary Scottish Poetry, 1974; International Who's Who in Poetry, 1974-1975; King, C. (ed.) Twelve Modern Scottish Poets, 1971; Summerfield, G. (ed.) Worlds, 1974; Vinson, J. (ed.) Contemporary Poets, 1975; Who's Who, 1978. *Periodicals*—Eboracum (University of York) October 1971; Glasgow University Magazine February 1971; Guardian May 9, 1972; New Edinburgh Review August 1972; Poetry April 1974; Scottish Field June 1969; Scottish International Review August 1968; Stand 4 1969; Times Literary Supplement July 20, 1973; March 18, 1977; October 14, 1977.

MORRIS, IVAN (IRA ESME) (November 29, 1925–July 19, 1976), British scholar, translator, and writer of books on Japanese history and literature, was born in London, the only child of Ira Victor Morris, an American novelist, and the former Edit de Toll, also a writer, who was Swedish. The parents met in Sweden, where Ivan Morris's grandfather, Ira Nelson Morris, was at one time American ambassador. Morris's parents lived most of the time in Paris, but he had a cosmopolitan upbringing in Europe, Britain, and the United States. He attended Gordonstoun School in Scotland, the Putney School in Vermont, and Phillips Academy at Andover, Massachusetts. After serving with U.S. Naval Intelligence as a lieutenant, junior grade, Morris resumed his education at Harvard University, graduating *magna cum laude* in 1946. He went on to London University for graduate studies in oriental languages, receiving his doctorate in 1951.

Having opted for British citizenship, Morris began his career in England. He worked briefly for the British Broadcasting Corporation as a news editor (1951-1952), then joined the Foreign Office as a senior research assistant (1953-1956). For the next four years Morris lived in Japan. He fell in love with the country, its history, and its people, and began the work for which he will be remembered. His first book, edited in collaboration with Paul C. Blum, was indeed a labor of love—a comprehensive index to the papers appearing in the Asiatic Society's *Transactions* (1872-1957). This was published in 1958, and Morris's translations from the Japanese began to appear at about the same time. In 1960 Morris settled in the United States, joining the faculty of Columbia University in New York. He was an associate professor of Japanese history from 1960 to 1966 and a professor thereafter; from 1966 to 1969 he served as chairman of the department of East Asian languages and cultures.

Morris's first wholly original work was *Nationalism and the Right Wing in Japan: A Study of Post-War Trends* (1960). It marshals an immense amount of information about the rightist organizations that developed in Japan after

New York Times

IVAN MORRIS

World War II and their prewar connections, concluding that, if democracy failed in Japan, the dictatorship that followed would probably be of the Right rather than of the Left. Kazuo Kawai said in *Pacific Affairs* that he had "approached this book with misgivings but ended with admiration if not unqualified agreement—misgivings because the subject is one which is so easily susceptible to unbalanced and alarmist treatment, admiration because the author has so successfully combined detailed analysis with judicious evaluation in relation to a broad historical perspective." A reviewer in the *Times Literary Supplement* called Morris "a sharp observer of current social and political trends in Japan" and said "his book deserves to be called monumental. On its subject and period it can be welcomed and accepted as the standard work in the English language."

The World of the Shining Prince (1964) is an account of court life in Heian-Kyo (Kyoto) in the tenth century, when that city was Japan's capital. It draws a great deal on *The Tale of Genji* (Genji is the "shining prince" of the title), the famous novel written by Murasaki Shikibu, who was a member of the aristocratic society she described. Morris's book sketches the Heian period in general and goes on to deal in some detail with the setting in which the court lived; with politics, religion, and superstition; everyday life at court; the cult of beauty; and relations between men and women. Morris also discusses the author of *The Tale of Genji* and her views on fiction, and asks if the novel as we know it is complete.

Phoebe Adams wrote that "the study is specifically intended to help readers of *The Tale of Genji* who wish to know what realities underlie that old classic, but it is so full of antiquarian enthusiasm and bizarre information, and presents its ceremonious, inbred, melancholy world with such vividness, that it becomes highly interesting regardless of one's knowledge of Lady Murasaki's novel." One reader thought the book "too specialized for the general reader and insufficiently specialized for the expert," but Oliver Statler said that Morris "has made the tenth century come alive to the twentieth. . . . He has written a book which should delight anyone interested in Japan, a book which provides more background and insight than an armload of journalistic attempts to encompass the contemporary scene." It brought Morris the Duff Cooper Memorial Prize in 1965.

The third and last of his major books was *The Nobility of Failure,* which delves into Japan's long history to examine the peculiarly Japanese sympathy for the tragic hero, the brave failure. It was reportedly inspired by the suicide of Morris's friend Yukio Mishima. Morris wrote that "this predilection for heroes who were unable to achieve their concrete objectives can teach us more about Japanese values and sensibility." David Brudnoy agreed that the book might "serve as the English-language version of the Japanese history of Japan: the story as the Japanese best like it told." Morris devotes most of his space to accounts of nine heroes and their half-legendary exploits, and the Kamikaze pilots of World War II. Some academic critics regretted that he had given so much attention to narrative, but most readers were fascinated. R. J. Lifton said that "each chapter illuminates important subterranean byways of Japanese history, and no reader can finish the book without having greatly expanded his knowledge of this . . . nation and people."

Morris also compiled dictionaries of the grammatical forms used in classical Japanese literature and (at another extreme) collections of "diabolical" puzzles of which the following is an unusually simple example: "Two Abyssinians enter a bar: one Abyssinian is the father of the other Abyssinian's son. How are they related?" His translations from the Japanese included novels by such contemporary writers as Mishima, Ooka, and Osaragi, books on Japanese history and politics, and such works as Saikaku Ihara's *The Life of an Amorous Woman* (1686), a Japanese *Moll Flanders.* Donald Keene, reviewing the latter, noted that Morris had chosen to render Saikaku into an eighteenth-century idiom, and went on: "This practice might have resulted in an unconvincing pastiche, but in his hands the tour de force comes off beautifully."

The Pillow Book of Sei Shonagon (1967) is the diary of a tenth-century lady-in-waiting—a work which stands comparison with *The Tale of Genji*. Kenneth Rexroth, reviewing Morris's edition, wrote that Morris "has become with this work one of the historic orientalists. The second volume of exhaustively explanatory notes is as endlessly fascinating as the text itself." The *Times Literary Supplement*'s reviewer shared Rexroth's enthusiasm for Morris's scholarship and said of the translation that it "will stand for centuries; it is Sei Shonagon in English, and there can be no higher praise."

Ivan Morris was a member of the Royal Asiatic Society, the Asiatic Society of Japan, the Royal Institute of International Affairs, and the Association of Teachers of Japanese, of which he became chairman in 1962. The University of London gave him an honorary doctorate in 1964. Morris served on the executive committee of Amnesty International, the London-based organization that works for the release of "prisoners of conscience"—those imprisoned for political or religious reasons. He helped to found Amnesty's American section in 1966 and became its general secretary in 1973. Under his leadership the membership of the American section grew from three thousand to forty thousand members, and during the last few months of his life Morris devoted almost all his time to this work.

The author spoke eight languages, was an expert chess player and a fine performer on the tenor recorder. His friend Ved Mehta says that "he was truly an internationalist, with several cultures in his background . . . he knew everybody—Stephen Spender, the late Yukio Mishima, people like that. Yet I think his spiritual home was in medieval Japan." Morris was married three times, twice to Japanese women. He died of a heart attack in Bologna, Italy, at the age of fifty. His obituarist in the London *Times* wrote that he was "a loyal friend and ever-interesting companion who enjoyed a varied social and intellectual life. . . . But beneath a convivial exterior he was imbued with a deep pessimism about the human condition"; he was "one of the greatest of the present generation of interpreters of Japanese culture."

PRINCIPAL WORKS: Nationalism and the Right Wing in Japan: A Study of Post-War Trends, 1960; Japan (Reader's Guides series), 1960; Selected List of Bungo and Other Forms Found in Japanese Literature Until c.1330, 1960; The World of the Shining Prince: Court Life in Ancient Japan, 1964; Dictionary of Selected Forms in Classical Japanese Literature, 1966 (Corrigenda, Addenda, Substituenda, 1970); The Riverside Puzzles, 1969 (in England, The Pillow Book Puzzles); The Lonely Monk and Other Puzzles, 1970; (with Herbert Paul Varley and Nobuko Mor-

ris) The Samurai, 1970; Foul Play and Other Puzzles of All Kinds, 1974; The Nobility of Failure: Tragic Heroes in the History of Japan, 1975. *As Editor and Translator*—The Life of an Amorous Woman and Other Writings, by Saikaku Ihara, 1963; Thought and Behavior in Modern Japanese Politics, by Masao Maruyama, 1963; The Pillow Book of Sei Shonagon, 1967. *As Editor*—(with Paul C. Blum) Comprehensive Index: A Classified List Followed by Author and Subject Indexes, of Papers Appearing in the Transactions, 1872-1957, Asiatic Society of Japan, 1958; Modern Japanese Stories, 1961; Japan 1931-1945: Militarism, Fascism, Japanism?, 1963; Madly Singing in the Mountains: An Appreciation and Anthology of Arthur Waley, 1970. *As Translator*—Fires on the Plain, by Shohei Ooka, 1957; The Temple of the Golden Pavilion, by Yukio Mishima, 1959; The Journey, by Jiro Osaragi, 1960; As I Crossed a Bridge of Dreams: Recollections of a Woman in Eleventh Century Japan, 1971; The Tale of Genji Scroll, 1971.

ABOUT: Contemporary Authors 9-12 1st revision, 1974. *Periodicals*—American Historical Review January 1961; American Political Science Review December 1960; Atlantic October 1964; Book Week November 29, 1964; Encounter June 1976; Hudson Review Autumn 1968; Listener December 14, 1967; November 26, 1970; Nation November 1, 1975; New Republic December 20, 1975; New York Review of Books September 18, 1975; New York Times July 21, 1976; New York Times Book Review May 12, 1963; August 23, 1964; March 3, 1968; September 28, 1975; Observer December 10, 1967; Pacific Affairs September 1960; Political Science Quarterly September 1961; Punch January 24, 1968; Publishers Weekly August 16, 1976; Times (London) July 26, 1976; August 9, 1976; Times Literary Supplement August 5, 1960; August 29, 1968; January 16, 1976.

MOSLEY, NICHOLAS (LORD RAVENSDALE) (June 25, 1923–), English novelist, film scenarist, and writer on religious and historical subjects, writes: "I was born in London in 1923. My father was Oswald Mosley, then a Conservative M.P., later leader of the British Union of Fascists. My mother was Cynthia, daughter of the Conservative Foreign Secretary Lord Curzon. By 1929 both my father and my mother had become Labour M.P.s. My upbringing was upper class but not conventional. My parents' friends were fashionable, artistic. I grew up with the impression that I was not part of any society around me.

"My mother died in 1933. I went to school at Eton. In 1940 my father was imprisoned under the wartime regulations to do with people of fascist sympathies. In 1942 I joined the army and fought as an infantry platoon commander in Italy from 1943 to 1945. I was wounded, and won the Military Cross. This was important to me, since it seemed to make some nonsense of my father's imprisonment.

"In 1946 I went to Oxford and read philosophy for a year. Then I married and went to live on a hill farm in north Wales. I began to write novels.

"My early novels *(Spaces of the Dark, The*

NICHOLAS MOSLEY

Gerhard Cohn

Rainbearers, Corruption) were stories about young men at odds with life—somewhat tragic and rhapsodic. During the 1950's I became, in some sense or other, a christian: this now seems to me to have been an effort to get at some distance from myself. I edited a christian magazine—*Prism*—one of the purposes of which was to be critical of most forms of established religion. I wrote a biography of an Anglican monk, Raymond Raynes, who was the only holy man I have ever met. There seemed to be this conflict between the manifestations of religion, and what it was for.

"When I began writing novels again in the early 1960's *(Meeting Place, Accident)* I was trying to find some style by which life's riddles would not seem stultifying but would not be skated over either by rhapsody or religion. *Impossible Object* and *Natalie Natalia* were efforts to show how, by a person's being able to stand back and look at himself, there might be a style—in life, in art—by which circumstances even of tragedy or farce could be made lively. Conventional attitudes seemed to deny this.

"In the early 1970's I wrote the scripts for two films—Joseph Losey's *The Assassination of Trotsky* and John Frankenheimer's film of my novel *Impossible Object*. These excursions showed perhaps my own lack of aptitude for writing for actors and directors; also their difficulties in following a style which they said they wanted to follow.

"Since then I have been trying to get a better hold of this style by which a standing-back-from-oneself and coming-to-terms-with-oneself might seem lively. It seems to me that the political history of the last fifty years has shown that the pursuit of purely social ideals has gone as far as it can: circumstances have become too complex for people by these means to handle. I think people now have to be able to deal with more of their own complexities (and probably those of their children) before there can be any further social advancement.

"From the death of my mother in 1933 I have had sufficient private income to enable me not to worry too much about money: perhaps this has made it easy for me to feel not tied to society. Also in 1966 I inherited from my mother's sister the title of Lord Ravensdale; and this too has made me feel society's oddities. But this distancing has perhaps also enabled me to try to understand, and say something about, what I think is necessary for most people—the need to come to terms with oneself before one can make profitable terms with others.

"I married for the second time in 1974. I have four children by my first marriage and one by my second. In politics I am a Liberal. I hope to continue to write about how it might be possible to have a good life, even in some chaos, by keeping one's wits, amongst other things, about one."

———

Nicholas Mosley's first novel, *Spaces of the Dark* (1951), written on his Welsh hill farm, is a highly romantic and emotional story about a young Army officer's relations with the family and fiancée of his dead friend. "Written in at least half-a-dozen styles, badly constructed, and almost totally lacking in characterization," it nevertheless had for one reviewer "a force and feeling that suggests that Mr. Nicholas Mosley might do something with his talent by the application of rigid discipline." *The Rainbearers* (1955) and *Corruption* (1957) similarly deal with abortive love affairs, concentrating more on introspection than on action, and both are written in a baroque and overwrought prose, in an "eternal flux of run-on sentences monotonously checked by short final ones." Some critics were simply enraged by the stylistic perversities and pretensions of these books, but others found in them "a certain maddening fascination," and signs of real ability and of "a savage, slightly surreal wit that is not given enough air." By contrast, reviewers complained of a dry and unemotional style and almost excessive detachment in *African Switchback* (1958), Mosley's account of his journey by car through French Africa with his fellow novelist and Old Etonian the late Hugo Charteris.

Meanwhile, Mosley had met Raymond Raynes, the remarkable superior of an Anglican religious order, the Community of the Resurrection, and had been converted from a nostalgic agnosticism to a kind of commitment to Christianity (though not to the Christian establishment). When Raynes died in 1958, the Community commissioned Mosley to write his biography, and this was published in 1961 and welcomed as a good but necessarily exterior view of "a great religious." At the same time, during the late 1950s, Mosley served for a time as editor of *Prism,* a Christian journal critical, as he says, of "most forms of established religion." Although he believes that organized religions "skate over" life's riddles, and God is scarcely mentioned in his novels, the great themes and concerns of religion have continued to preoccupy him and underly his subsequent work.

Meeting Place (1962) tells the story of Harry Gates, who seeks escape from a wealthy and corrupt milieu (as well as self-fulfillment) in social work among dropouts and psychopaths. Some reviewers could find in it no "sense of direction," and thought it, though ambitious, obscure, intense, and pretentious, but Anastasia Leech has suggested that this novel gives the first hint that Mosley "might not be content with the novel as a mere chronological narration of events. In . . . [this] fragmented and impressionistic story . . . [he] is clearly making an attempt to expand the limits of what he might require a novel to do."

Mosley's concerns became somewhat clearer in *Accident* (1965), which is presented as the work of a novelist, Charlie, who is himself involved in the events he describes. Charlie chooses as his narrator his friend Stephen Jervis, an Oxford don—a double distancing reminiscent of the French antinovel. Charlie and Jervis have each in his own way exploited the enigmatic Anna, one of Jervis's students, and they are morally responsible for the car crash that, at the beginning of the book, kills William, another student, who had loved Anna; to that extent, the crash is not an accident at all. How much we are at the mercy of chance, and how much we can understand and control our own destinies, is one of the novel's concerns. Another is the role of the novelist in the modern world—a sophisticated and self-aware world in which traditional "stories of characters, action and society" provide no revelations because "we know all this now."

A reviewer in the *Times Literary Supplement* noted that *Accident* was "significantly shorter" than its predecessors, and "far more successful." Where the earlier books "seemed sometimes to be indulging in obscurity for the sake of obscurity . . . here . . . [Mosley] makes a fully coherent attempt to achieve a new form. The texture of the writing itself is deliberately simple; the complexity arises from the way in which the parts are put together." But this reviewer thought that a religious element was "conspicuously absent—almost as if it had been cut away with scissors." The novel was made into an excellent film, directed by Joseph Losey, with an enigmatic but extremely effective scenario by Harold Pinter (which, indeed, some reviewers preferred to the original text). *Assassins* (1966), about the abduction of the daughter of a British Foreign Secretary at a time when he is conducting delicate negotiations with a communist regime, explores the same sort of concerns as *Accident.*

Mosley says in *Impossible Object* (1968) that "society used to provide the difficulties that made love exciting and romantic. But in today's world, men and women must create the difficulties in order to perpetuate love at the level of ecstasy." The novel contains eight chapters or stories in which two lovers are shown creating such difficulties—they are described at different stages of their affair, by different narrators, in different settings. Interspersed among these stories are nine short fables on related themes—grotesque parables that, according to one reviewer, generate "an emotionally charged field of ideas and attitudes which then cluster around [and illuminate] the situations in the 'real' stories." *Time*'s critic thought that the lovers' problems "are scarcely the sort to elicit ecstasy—or belief," and called the novel self-indulgent, but this was a minority opinion. Vernon Scannell, describing Mosley as "one of the most interesting and gifted English novelists writing today," and "a truly experimental writer," found the book "moving, witty and continuously absorbing." Robert Scholes said it was "the best book by a young [sic] Englishman that I have read in recent years."

The paradox that love might thrive on its frustration is carried much further in *Natalie Natalia* (1971), whose epigraph is from Goethe: "Only in the impossible did . . . [he] seem to find pleasure, and the possible . . . [he] seemed to thrust from himself in contempt." Anthony Greville is a Conservative M.P., rich and powerful enough to be unsatisfied with "the possible." He is in love with Natalia Jones, wife of a colleague, and the narrative moves back and forth in time from their first meeting to the point where Natalia renounces him, apparently to avert their mutual destruction. Greville is sent to Africa to investigate a political crisis in a British colony, and there loses his increasingly shaky hold on objective reality. Recuperating from this breakdown (or breakthrough), he is able to "stand back and look at himself" and to "come to terms with himself." The letters he writes then to Natalia and to his wife discuss, among other things, a theory of fiction.

The novel evidently left many reviewers at a loss. One praised Mosley's "adventurousness," but thought that this "seems somehow to have gone to seed and we long for more definition, both of happening and circumstance, and of what the author wants us to feel about it all." Dudley Young believed that Mosley's "ultimate aim in this book is to convince us that in rejecting wife, lover and political power, his hero is not just crazy but is bearing witness to the contrary nature of human aspiration. . . . Like Nietzsche, and unlike most of us today, Mosley knows that man is a fundamentally religious animal." Young thought that the book was weakened by its author's romanticism but was nevertheless "a fruitfully disturbing experience, perhaps chiefly because Mosley is the master of an aggressively cubist prose style; which is to say that most of his meanings are in the montage, silently arising from juxtapositions of the discontinuous. . . . *Natalie Natalia* is a book full of gaps, syntactic gaps composed to register the fragmentary nature of contemporary experience, and above all the absence of God from all the centers he used to inhabit." Mosley himself has pointed out that the book "is stuffed with Christian images and a commitment to search for truth about human beings [that] I regard as intensely religious."

The research Mosley did in order to write his scenario for Losey's film *The Assassination of Trotsky* also provided the makings of a book on the same theme and with the same title; this was chiefly interesting for what it revealed about Mosley's own political views and philosophy. His earlier essay *Experience and Religion* (1965) is an attempt to discuss in theological terms such subjects as the relations between husband and wife, parents and children—sources of "the deepest hopes and fears of human life." A reviewer in the *Listener* welcomed in this essay "a genuinely new voice, not only in the sense that Nicholas Mosley has not before written in this field, nor merely that his strange, clipped, allusive style is unlike anyone else's, but in that he is really managing to say things which are new in areas where it would seem impossible."

In 1976 Mosley published *Julian Grenfell: His Life and the Times of His Death,* a biography of a brilliant young poet and sportsman—"the Philip Sidney of his day"—who was killed in World War I. It examines in particular his relationship with his mother, Lady Desborough, and a reviewer in the *Economist* wrote that "a crude paraphrase" of this "intricate and allusive" book "would say that it is the story of a mother's attempt to enslave her son, as she enslaved so many other males; and of the son's adoring resistance to that bewitchment. But it is a better book than that. It is in some ways perhaps over-subtle, especially on family relationships. . . . But for anyone who wants to know when and how the stuffing went out of the English upper classes, it is a must." Anthony Storr said that Mosley had "extrapolated from the Grenfells to condemn a whole society," and asked: "Is he justified in doing so? Yes, on the whole he is. . . . This brilliant, disturbing book is rich in psychological insight."

Sir Oswald Mosley's tragic career made his son "aware of the uselessness of social and political activity. I saw clearly that while the right hand dealt with grandiose ideas and glory, the left hand let the rat out of the sewer." Dudley Young has made the interesting suggestion that both father and son are "spiritual children" of Nietzsche: "Whereas the father got fouled up by trying to translate this demonic German's metaphors into political terms, the son has tried to shoulder the central legacy: an insight into the dialectical nature of human psychology and a determination to explore it at whatever cost."

Nicholas Mosley became the third Baron Ravensdale in 1966, as he says, and is also heir to his father's baronetcy. His 1947 marriage to Rosemary Laura Salmond, a painter, was dissolved in 1974. His present wife is the former Verity Elizabeth Bailey, and they live in Hampstead, London. Mosley is a tall man, absentminded, loquacious, and "immensely humorous," with "a mind that teases and plays with ideas," but that is fundamentally very serious indeed. In 1970 he was injured almost fatally in a car crash, an event which (as author of *Accident*) he finds of almost mystical significance.

"I am obsessed," Mosley told an interviewer, "by trying to understand how human beings work. This makes novels important for me, since they are the best records of man's attempts to describe what a human being is." When the interviewer suggested that he devotes too much attention to his characters' inner life, not enough to external action, Mosley replied in effect that life was like that and he had to write accordingly: "You go on and on, and one dark night or early morning you know this is what you ought to be writing, and you realise how hard it is. By now I have some sort of confidence that if one goes on and on one will get it right."

PRINCIPAL WORKS: *Novels*—Spaces of the Dark, 1951; The Rainbearers, 1955; Corruption, 1957; Meeting Place, 1962; Accident, 1965; Assassins, 1966; Impossible Object, 1968;

MPHAHLELE

Natalie Natalia, 1971. *Nonfiction*—African Switchback, 1958; The Life of Raymond Raynes, 1961; Experience and Religion: A Lay Essay in Theology, 1965; The Assassination of Trotsky, 1972; Julian Grenfell, 1976.

ABOUT: Vinson, J. (ed.) Contemporary Novelists, 1976; Who's Who, 1978. *Periodicals*—Book World October 3, 1971; Christian Science Monitor February 6, 1969; Commonweal December 17, 1971; Guardian June 29, 1971; Life January 24, 1969; London Magazine November 1958; New Statesman January 15, 1965; September 2, 1968; June 2, 1971; New York Times Book Review February 2, 1969; October 24, 1971; New Yorker July 12, 1969; Observer April 18, 1976; Saturday Review January 25, 1969; November 6, 1971; Spectator September 22, 1968; Time April 22, 1966; January 31, 1969; Times Literary Supplement February 2, 1951; October 7, 1955; September 1, 1961; November 16, 1962; January 14, 1965; October 27, 1966; July 9, 1971; August 11, 1972.

EZEKIEL MPHAHLELE

*MPHAHLELE, EZEKIEL (December 17, 1919–), South African essayist, memoirist, short story writer, and novelist, was born in Pretoria. His father worked as a messenger for a clothing store, his mother as a domestic servant in white homes. He has described the first part of his life in *Down Second Avenue* (1959), one of the most important African autobiographies. Though it is seldom specific about dates, it so candidly and vividly evokes the conditions of Mphahlele's early years that they take on the quality of archetypal experiences for countless black South Africans from a similarly impoverished background. Gerald Moore has commented on the way "in which the author cuts across a more or less sequential narrative by inserting freely-associative and directly-recalled flashes of experience here and there in the story. These 'Interludes,' as he calls them, are written in a more jagged and immediate style than the main stream of the narrative; they recreate instants of experience, while the narrative reconstructs a series of events. . . . The finished work lacks unity of style, but it does have organization." And another critic has said that the book "combines documentary precision with the structure and style of a novel."

Down Second Avenue begins: "I have never known why we—my brother, sister and I—were taken to the country when I was five." His earliest memories are of Maupaneng, a large village of about five thousand people where the children lived with their paternal grandmother. When Mphahlele was thirteen their mother reclaimed them and they returned to Pretoria. Soon afterwards their father, in a drunken rage, assaulted their mother so violently that she went to the hospital and he to prison. They never saw him again, and their mother was obliged to go back to work as a domestic servant. The children were

*əm paĸ′ lā lē

deposited with their other grandmother on Second Avenue, a squalid, noisy, and violent slum in the Marabastad location of Pretoria.

Mphahlele's grandmother and aunt supported this overcrowded household by brewing illicit beer and taking in white people's washing. The police raided the house frequently, and Mphahlele suffered his first assault by a white constable when he was fourteen. After sleepless nights in a bed which he shared with at least two others, he rose at four to cycle about the city, collecting and delivering washing for customers who very soon taught him the full ignominy of his position. He nevertheless showed such promise in his primary school studies that his mother somehow contrived to send him on at sixteen to St. Peter's Secondary School, a boarding school in a white suburb of Johannesburg, run on progressive and enlightened lines by the Community of the Resurrection. He left that excellent institution, as he says, "the personification of the African paradox, detribalized, Westernized, but still an African."

From St. Peter's Mphahlele went for teacher training to Adams College in Natal (1939–1940). From 1941 to 1945 he held a secretarial post in an institute for the African blind, and it was at this time that his first short stories appeared in such magazines as *Drum, New Age,* and *Africa South.* He was married in 1945 and in 1945–1952 taught English and Afrikaans at Orlando High School, Johannesburg, while continuing his education as an external student of the University of South Africa. He received his B.A. with honors in 1949 and his M.A. in 1956.

In 1952, meanwhile, Mphahlele had played an active role in the agitation against the deeply discriminatory Bantu Education Act, which closed St. Peter's Secondary School, Adams College, and all other such liberal institutions. As a result, he was forbidden to teach anywhere in South Africa. Between 1952 and 1955 Mphahlele eked out an existence as a messenger and (for a few months) as a teacher in Basutoland, and in 1955–1957 he worked as a reporter and later as fiction editor on the popular Johannesburg monthly *Drum*. He did not enjoy journalism and, as his children began to grow up, he became increasingly distressed by his lack of funds and by the humiliations imposed on all his people in South Africa. *Down Second Avenue* ends with his decision to leave his native country for a life of permanent exile.

In September 1957 Mphahlele went to Nigeria, where he taught English at the Church Missionary Society grammar school in Lagos until the end of 1958, and for the next three years was an English lecturer in the Extra-Mural Department of Ibadan University. From 1961 to 1963 he worked in Paris as director of the African programs of the International Association (formerly Congress) for Cultural Freedom. He went to Nairobi, Kenya, in 1963, serving in 1963–1965 as founder-director of Chem-chemi, a cultural center for writers and artists, and in 1965–1966 lecturing at University College, Nairobi. Mphahlele earned his Ph.D. in 1968 at the University of Denver, where he lectured in English literature in 1966–1968. After two years as senior lecturer in English at the University of Zambia, he returned to the United States. There he has remained, as an associate professor of English at the University of Denver (1970–1974), and since then as a professor of English at the University of Pennsylvania.

Mphahlele's first published work was a collection of rather slight short stories, *Man Must Live* (1946), which he later described as "escapist writing." The seven stories in *The Living and Dead*, published in Ibadan in 1961, seemed to Gerald Moore to straddle Mphahlele's stylistic development, "some obviously written earlier than the angry, jabbing prose of *Down Second Avenue*," others looking forward to the quality that Mphahlele has sought in his mature work, "the ironic meeting between protest and acceptance." The title story in *The Living and Dead* was particularly admired. It is a study of racial bigotry which begins with the thoughts and experiences of two apparently unconnected people —a black sweeper and a white civil servant—on a particular morning in South Africa. Moore wrote that "the way in which Mphahlele draws his apparently random, anonymous threads together into a significant pattern of unacknowl-

edged human relationship, unaccepted human responsibility, shows an altogether new power in his imaginative resources." A more substantial and technically sophisticated collection of stories, *In Corner B*, was published in Nairobi in 1967. There is an especially telling application of Mphahlele's brand of irony in "Mrs. Plum," in which we are given a black servant girl's view of her "liberal" white mistress.

The Wanderers (1971), so far Mphahlele's only novel, was written in lieu of a doctoral dissertation at Denver. It draws on his own experiences to offer a panoramic view of modern Africa, white and black. This is provided mostly through the wanderings of Timi Tabane, a South African teacher and journalist who publishes an article about kidnapping and murder on a slave farm, and as a result has to go into exile in Nigeria and Kenya. A reviewer in the *Times Literary Supplement* wrote that "what follows is full of perception concerning the situation of the black South African who escapes to other, independent black African countries; but simple political and racial debate rather than a strong story tends increasingly to take the centre of the stage. Timi is uneasy in his exiled freedom. . . . He wanders, unable to give of his talents and ideas under systems which restrict his scope in subtler ways. The accounts of these provide some insight into areas now being explored for virtually the first time in fiction." The same critic remarked that Mphahlele "writes a clear and serviceable, if unexciting—and sometimes too baldly didactic—prose, has a zest and a fair talent for the creation of a wide variety of characters from all races, and an occasional flair for narrative suspense which gives his story pace." The novel won first prize in a literary competition organized by the periodical *African Arts*.

There has been more positive enthusiasm, less clouded by reservations, for Mphahlele's work as an essayist and critic—Emile Snyder has gone so far as to call him "the most balanced literary critic of African literature." *The African Image*, his first volume of essays, was published in 1962 and extensively revised twelve years later. Mphahlele describes his travels in England, the United States, and Africa, and his reactions to the people he met. "He searches for his roots," as *Library Journal* put it, "examines his sense of values, and seeks to determine how and where he fits into the world." Two long essays, developed from his M.A. research, examine the image of the black man presented in white and in black literature. One anonymous reviewer concluded that Mphahlele "is the most interesting writer to emerge from South Africa for some time. It is not that he possesses a high degree of technical accomplishment. . . . What he does possess, to an extent unusual at the best of times and especially perhaps among exiles, is a capacity for combining passion with scrutiny."

A second collection of essays, *Voices in the Whirlwind,* appeared in 1972. Julius Lester thought that the book "could have been subtitled 'Toward a Black Esthetic,' because five of the six pieces are concerned with this difficult problem of definition. . . . The longest and most important essay, 'Voices in the Whirlwind: Poetry and Conflict in the Black World,' is concerned with 'the meaning and function of poetry' in situations of political and cultural conflict." "We have had few books by Africans or Europeans which dealt with these controversial topics," Robert Koester wrote, "and certainly none which so evidently manifest themselves as products of a lifetime of thought and passionate concern." Mphahlele's growing interest in the work of black American writers is reflected in his discussion here of Gwendolyn Brooks, Don L. Lee, Larry Neal, and Imamu Amiri Baraka, among others.

Mphahlele says, "I write poetry when I have nothing else to do," so it is not surprising that his verse is generally inferior to his prose, though it deals with similar themes of exile and quest. From June 1960 to November 1964 he was co-editor with Wole Soyinka and Ulli Beier of the influential African arts journal *Black Orpheus.* Critics of Mphahlele's work all recognize his central place among the chroniclers of the South African *malaise,* and Donald E. Herdeck has called him "probably Black Africa's leading literary intellectual using the English language." He is highly regarded as an essayist concerned to illuminate the metaphysical and aesthetic life of Africa, but his orientation is too quintessentially South African for him to immerse himself completely in either philosophical abstraction or total pan-Africanism. Gerald Moore has suggested that Mphahlele illustrates "the supreme irony of the South African situation . . . His whole life has been an unrelenting struggle to achieve the way of life for which his urban upbringing and liberal education had prepared him. But to achieve that life he has had finally to become an exile." Mphahlele and his wife Rebecca have five children.

PRINCIPAL WORKS: *Fiction*—Man Must Live and Other Stories, 1946; The Living and Dead, and Other Stories, 1961; In Corner B (stories), 1967; The Wanderers, 1971. *Nonfiction*—Down Second Avenue (autobiography), 1959; The African Image, 1962; A Guide to Creative Writing, 1966; Voices in the Whirlwind, 1972. *As Editor*—(with Ellis Ayitey Komey) Modern African Stories, 1964; African Writing Today, 1967.

ABOUT: Barnett, U. Ezekiel Mphahlele, 1976; Beier, U. (ed.) Introduction to African Literature, 1967; Dathorne, O.R. African Literature in the Twentieth Century, 1974; Duerden, D. and Pieterse, C. (eds.) African Writers Talking, 1972; Herdeck, D.E. (ed.) African Authors, 1974; International Who's Who, 1978–79; Lindfors, B. (and others, eds.) Palaver: Interviews With Five African Writers in Texas, 1972; Moore, G. Seven African Writers, 1962; Moore, G. The Chosen Tongue, 1969; Olney, J. Tell Me Africa, 1973; Penguin Companion to Literature 4, 1969; Pieterse, C. and Munro, D. (eds.) Protest and Conflict in African Literature, 1969; Vinson, J. (ed.) Contemporary Novelists, 1976; Who's Who in African Literature, 1972; Zell, H. and Silver, H. (eds.) A Reader's Guide to African Literature, 1972. *Periodicals*—Library Journal March 15, 1963; September 15, 1972; New York Review of Books September 23, 1971; New York Times Book Review October 22, 1972; New Yorker November 13, 1971; Saturday Review June 19, 1971; Times Literary Supplement April 27, 1963; March 10, 1972.

*MYKLE, AGNAR (August 8, 1915–), Norwegian novelist, short story writer, and puppet-theatre dramatist, was born in Trondheim and educated at the University of Economic and Political Sciences in Bergen. After World War II he went to Paris to study drama at the Académie des Compagnons de la Marionette (1947-1948), and later to England and the United States (where he held a Fulbright scholarship in 1951-1952). Returning to Norway, he settled in Oslo, working as a journalist, as a teacher, and then as head of the drama department and secretary of the Workers' Educational Association. He has been married three times, and has two sons and two daughters.

Mykle founded the Norwegian Puppet Theatre and has written a number of highly successful puppet plays, but he owes his international fame to four semi-autobiographical novels whose frank sexuality has caused much controversy. The same protagonist figures under various names in all four books, and appears as Ash Grande in the first of them, *Tyven, tyven skal du hete* (1951). It was translated as *The Hotel Room* by Maurice Michael, who is responsible for the English versions of all Mykle's novels. Ash Grande has assaulted a hotel night porter who entered a room where Ash and his girlfriend were making love. The novel is an account of Ash's trial for this offense and of his reflections upon his past as the court goes about its work.

Mykle has said that "the desire to censor, to play the tyrant and supervise sex is to be found in all people and in all countries." As the novel proceeds, the porter emerges as an embodiment of this desire, a moralistic busybody, a bigoted nay-sayer. Ash's explosion of violence against him is seen as a passionate defense of the individual's right to love and make love and—in the spirit of the Viking sagas—to hate those who

*mü′ klə

Gyldendal Norsk Forlag

AGNAR MYKLE

would deny his rights and revenge himself upon them.

The author himself now recognizes that the book "bears the unmistakable stamp of having been written for dear life: it is hurried, out of breath, desperate." Christopher Ricks wrote that, for him, it was also "trashy, brutal and infantile." But most reviewers of the English translation, if they found a certain stridency and shapelessness, were entirely won over by its passionate energy. There were comparisons with Joyce (because of the long stream-of-consciousness monologues), with Lawrence (because of the book's celebration of the mystique of sex), and with Thomas Wolfe (because of the "joyfully robust magic" of Mykle's language). The *Times Literary Supplement* concluded that the book was "morally good: it is for life."

Ash Grande is forty in *The Hotel Room;* he reappears, much younger, as Ash Burlefoot in *Lasso rundt fru luna* (1954, translated as *Lasso Round the Moon*). Burlefoot is a gauche, blundering young provincial teacher, emotionally intense, acutely sensitive, torn between lust and love in a series of sexual encounters that ends with two of his girlfriends becoming pregnant. He flees, but twelve years later, a famous composer, he returns to his small home town and recalls the tempestuous story of his youth.

Ben Ray Redman found in this novel evidence that Mykle's talent was "one of the greatest that I have encountered in forty years of reviewing. He is a passionate poet and a naked realist, and he can speak with the organ tones of a prophet." At the opposite extreme was an English critic who called the book "as dull and wholesome as a fiord." A more balanced assessment was provided by V. S. Naipaul: "Mykle is longwinded; he has certain rhetorical mannerisms, and his technique is clumsy. But the sensibility is true, the passion genuine. The book is likely to attract attention because of its frank sexual detail. But this detail is a necessary part of Mykle's theme, which is of development and discovery; it is of a piece with the intensity and honesty of the book."

Sangen om den rode rubin (1955, translated as *The Song of the Red Ruby*) deals with Burlefoot's life after his flight from home. A student in Oslo, slightly embittered by his experiences, he nevertheless embraces an idealistic socialism and a great gallery of sexual partners, while seeking to realize himself as a musician and as a man. It was Ash's sexual encounters, realistically described in great detail, that led to the book's prosecution for obscenity in 1957. Since no such charge had been brought in Norway for seventy years, the case became a *cause célèbre,* bringing Mykle immediate fame. After the entire novel had been read aloud in court, it was judged obscene, but this decision was reversed on appeal. Thanks to the trial, it became an international best-seller on such a scale as to make the violently mixed critical reception largely irrelevant.

The Grande/Burlefoot trilogy was followed in 1965 by *Rubicon* (translated under the same title), in which the same young man, now named Valemon Gristvag, motorcycles across Hitler's Germany to France in the summer of 1939, pouring out his raptures, his bewilderments, and his fears. It disappointed many reviewers and Richard Rhodes complained that the innocence of the earlier books had gone, leaving only "strained, hyperbolic comedy." *Largo* (1967) has not been translated. It contains two stories, one exploring the hopes and uncertainties of a deeply confused adolescent, the other focusing on a small but telling crisis in a man's life when he has to drown part of a litter of kittens. A reviewer in the *Times Literary Supplement* wrote that the book "moves like some solemn, slow Scandinavian film lingering on flesh, idyllic landscape and sinful man." The collection of short stories translated by Maurice Michael in 1968 as *A Man and His Sink* was not much noticed. Martin Seymour-Smith, although he regards Mykle as the most outstanding of the postwar Norwegian novelists, has suggested nevertheless that "he does not do as much with his energy as he should—it does not hide his rather simplistic bewilderment."

PRINCIPAL WORKS IN ENGLISH TRANSLATION: Lasso Round the Moon, 1960; The Song of the Red Ruby, 1961; The

MYRIVILIS

Hotel Room, 1963; Rubicon, 1966; A Man and His Sink (stories), 1968.

ABOUT: Cassell's Encyclopedia of World Literature, 1973; Contemporary Authors 13-16 1st revision, 1975; International Who's Who, 1977-78; Seymour-Smith, M. Guide to Modern World Literature, 1973. Periodicals—Best Sellers June 1, 1963; New Statesman April 26, 1963; Newsweek April 25, 1960; Times Literary Supplement April 26, 1965; October 13, 1966; January 4, 1968.

*"MYRIVILIS," STRATIS (pseudonym of Stratis Stamatopoulos) (June 30, 1892–July 19, 1969), Greek novelist, short story writer, and journalist, was born in the mountain village of Sykamia on the island of Mytilene (the ancient Lesbos) near the coast of Asia Minor. Until the end of his life he spent his summers by the small harbor below his birthplace, and this was the setting of his best-known novel.

Completing his secondary education on Mytilene, Myrivilis entered Athens University to study philosophy and law. In 1912, before he had graduated, he volunteered for service in the Balkan Wars against Turkey and later against Bulgaria. He remained in the army for the next ten years, fighting in World War I and in the Asia Minor campaign of 1922. He was twice wounded and received a number of military decorations. He married during the Asia Minor campaign, and after it left the army and returned to Mytilene, where from 1922 to 1930 he published a local newspaper. He then moved to Athens, where he contributed to national newspapers and the Greek radio. Apart from a tour as a war correspondent during the Albanian campaign of 1940, he remained there for the rest of his life.

Myrivilis had begun to write while still at school, and his first collection of short stories appeared in 1915 as Kokkines Istories (Red Stories). He attracted a measure of public attention when one of these stories was serialized in an Athens daily paper. But it was his first novel that fully established him as a major figure in modern Greek literature. I Zoi En Tafo (1924, translated by Peter Bien as Life in the Tomb), begun in the Serbian trenches during World War I, is written in the form of a soldier's letters home to his girl. It powerfully conveys the horrors and the longueurs of the war, but also evokes its moments of humor and pathos and the poignant beauty of the setting in which so many fought and died. A novel written as carefully as a poem, it is one of the best—certainly the best by a Greek writer—of the many books that have been written about World War I. Though he "writes as a humanist rather than as a Christian," C. M. Woodhouse

*my riv ē′ lēs

STRATIS MYRIVILIS

said, "there is no doubt that Myrivilis meant his title to symbolize the resurrection as well as the crucifixion." It seemed to Woodhouse that Peter Bien's translation had "turned a Greek masterpiece into something not much less than an English one," even though "there is no way of conveying in English the advance which Myrivilis made in transforming demotic Greek into a literary language without weakening its dynamism."

This was followed by I Daskala Me Ta Chrysa Matia (1933, translated by Philip Sherrard as The Schoolmistress With the Golden Eyes). The novel is set on Mytilene, where a young painter, his senses blunted by his experiences in the 1922 Anatolian campaign, is trying to rediscover beauty and feeling. He finds both in the widow of an army comrade, and the book describes the gradual growth of their love, as well as the idiosyncrasies of the prying villagers.

A reviewer in the Times Literary Supplement wrote that "the sun and the sea have for Myrivilis the sacramental mystery that snow and forest have for Pasternak. He is primarily a lyric writer, using myths with far less conscious artifice than Iris Murdoch or John Updike; the legends he recalls belong in a natural, instinctive way to the temper of his mind." The young schoolteacher is "a modern village Aphrodite," whose "central, half-legendary figure dominates the Aegean landscape that the author calls 'the most erotic countryside in the world' and describes with the intensity of an artist passionately attached to his own land." The love story was considered so realistic that the Greek government censored it, and from 1936 to 1944 it was banned.

Myrivilis's most famous novel is *I Panaghia I Gorgona* (1949, translated by Abbott Rick as *The Mermaid Madonna*). It gives a haunting picture of life in the Mytilene of an earlier day, in a small fishing village which is trying to cope with an influx of refugees fleeing from the Turks on the mainland. In the harbor is a chapel housing a painting of the Virgin as half human and half fish, a local icon of great importance to the villagers and especially to the beautiful and mysterious foundling girl Smaragthi. Her independence of spirit—she goes out fishing like a man—separates her from the hidebound villagers and drives her to live out the local legend of the mermaid's human child who brings disaster to those who love her. Mary Renault wrote that "one of the rarest and headiest scents a book can give off is the smell of authenticity. . . . [Here] a world is opened to us at all the levels of reality—visual, social, spiritual." And Edmund Fuller, commenting on the book's "rich paintings of a place and a way of life," points out that "the unresolved enigmas are deliberate. They create the mythic spell of the book."

The author published many short stories, combining detailed observation, shrewd psychology, and a delight in the absurdities of a rich gallery of characters. He served for four terms as president of the Greek National Writers' Society and in 1958 was elected to the Athens Academy. Myrivilis worked for a number of years as general program director of the Greek National Broadcasting Institute and as director of the Greek Parliament Library. He was considered the leading Greek novelist of his generation, and received many awards for his work as a writer and a journalist. He and his wife had three children.

PRINCIPAL WORKS IN ENGLISH TRANSLATION: The Mermaid Madonna, 1959; The Schoolmistress With the Golden Eyes, 1964; Life in the Tomb, 1977.

ABOUT: Dimaras, C. A History of Modern Greek Literature, 1973; Penguin Companion to Literature 2, 1969; Seymour-Smith, M. Guide to Modern World Literature, 1973. *Periodicals*—Nation November 21, 1959; New York Times Book Review September 13, 1959; Saturday Review October 3, 1959; Times (London) July 21, 1969; Times Literary Supplement November 6, 1959; August 20, 1964; July 22, 1977.

NETO, JOÃO CABRAL DE MELO. *See* MELO NETO, JOÃO CABRAL DE

"NEWTON, FRANCIS." *See* HOBSBAWM, ERIC JOHN

*****NEZVAL, VITĚZSLAV** (May 26, 1900–April 6, 1958), Czech poet, novelist, and dramatist, who also wrote music and painted, was born at Biskoupky, near Trěbíč, in western Moravia. He was the son of a schoolteacher, Bohumil Nezval, and of the former Emilie Mytisková. Nezval went to school in Brno, and studied literature and philosophy at the University Charles IV in Prague until 1923, but thereafter devoted himself entirely to literature and earned his living as a writer.

His early poetic development has been summed up by Alfred French in *The Poets of Prague:* "Nezval's poems document the secret life of his imagination, and from his own confessions we can trace the steps which led him to poetry. Among his most vivid early impressions was the feeling of terror induced by dreams, a terror lingering on when its cause had been forgotten with the dream. It was a feeling which could have no logical exposition nor be subjected to rational analysis, since the terror could not be related to any remembered experience: its compelling urgency existed, as it were, in the void, and could be rationalized within no context of incident. At first the young Nezval believed that such emotion, divorced from visualized action or logic, could adequately be expressed only through the medium of music; and it was when he became dissatisfied with the technical level of his own musical attainments that he turned to verse, as to a new field of improvisation in patterns of sound."

At first, however, Nezval did not yield himself in his poetry to the exploration of this dream world or to his great gift for fantasy. A natural revolutionary, with strong communist sympathies, he belonged as a young man to the Devětsil group, which was devoted to revolution in art, life, and politics, and which advocated a socially committed proletarian poetry. In fact, for Nezval, revolution was not so much a political program as a way of life—an expression of his own unruly nature and his hatred of authority and conformity. In 1922 he heard a lecture given by Jaroslav Seifert which argued that truly revolutionary poets could best reach the masses not through Marx but through fantasy. This theory, which fitted so well with his own instincts, gave him the justification he needed to break with the Devětsil group. He became a leading member of the important movement known as poetism, which called for a pure poetry that would have the same sort of direct emotional impact as music. Karel Teige, a leader of the Devětsil group who followed Nezval into the new movement, said that poetism should be

*nez' val

Foto ČTK

VÍTĚSLAV NEZVAL

"airy and playful, full of fantasy, unfettered and unheroic, with a bias towards love."

Poetism later developed into surrealism, in a way which is already adumbrated in Nezval's first collection *Most* (The Bridge, 1922). The volume shows the influence of the French poets, from Rimbaud to Apollinaire, whom Nezval had read in Karel Čapek's anthology of modern French poetry, and also draws on the rich heritage of Czech fantasy literature. Along with the social and proletarian concerns which always nagged at Nezval's conscience are chains of images, spontaneously and sometimes bizarrely associated, in a way which Martin Seymour-Smith has described as "proto-surrealistic." An example is the title poem of *Most,* in which the bridges across the Vltava River at Prague, seen by night as strings of lights reflected in the water, symbolize human life as a connection between two invisible and unknown points.

In the same year Nezval published the remarkable epic poem "Podivuhodny kouzelník" (The Amazing Magician), in which the poet is presented as a magician and a liberator—not simply a revolutionary political leader, but a liberator of the human spirit who, experiencing fantastic adventures and metamorphoses, dives deep into the unconscious, confronts the submerged fears and guilts that enslave the human imagination, and carries them up to the light.

The poet could also be a clown, as in Nezval's second collection *Pantomima* (1924), which is full of dadaistic irreverence, fantastic rhymes, and the slapstick of silent comedy films, and is enlivened by cheerful picture poems rather like comic strips. *Menší růžová zahrada* (The Smaller Rose Garden, 1926) shows him widening his range still further, including as it does ballets, elegies, and a section of pastorals and minuets inspired by a visit to the fashionable rococo spa at Marienbad. *Hra v kostky* (Dice, 1929), in which Nezval's verbal agility and versatility are most lavishly displayed, also sees him turning to traditional metrical verse forms.

Poetism had been criticized even by some of its adherents for declining into mere verbal acrobatics, but a darker note is heard in the collection *Básně noci* (Poems of the Night, 1930). Nezval's exaltation of life and the brotherhood of man had always been counterbalanced by an acute and even morbid consciousness of death, and these night poems, full of open graves and supernatural horror, reflect the influence of Edgar Allan Poe, whose "Raven" he had just translated. The collection includes a long impressionist poem conjuring up with mingled horror and fascination a vision of a drowned girl floating down the river in Paris, "Neznámá ze Seiny" (The Unknown Girl of the Seine). Another famous long poem in this collection is "Edison," an ode which was read by some critics as a hymn to modern technology, though in fact it is another celebration of the artist-liberator, able to transform darkness into light—a polarity that runs throughout the poem.

Sbohem a šáteček (A Farewell and a Handkerchief, 1934) is a series of poetic impressions, often strange and grotesque, of a journey to Vienna, then across the Alps to Paris, and back to Prague by way of the Riviera and Italy. In France Nezval had made friends with the Surrealist poets Aragon, Éluard, and Soupault, whose attempts to catch the flow of the subconscious in "automatic writing" resembled his own earlier exploitation of subconscious imagery in extreme and illogical juxtapositions. He founded a surrealist group in Prague, including painters and musicians as well as poets, and published his own surrealist poems in *Žena v množném čísle* (Woman in the Plural, 1936), *Praha s prsty deště* (Prague With Fingers of Rain, 1936) and *Absolutní Hrobař* (The Absolute Gravedigger, 1937).

All of the Nezval poems translated into English by Ewald Osers in *Three Czech Poets* (1971) are surrealistic evocations of the Czech capital selected from *Prague With Fingers of Rain,* like the very short poem "The Clock in the Old Jewish Ghetto":

While time is running away on Příkopy Street
Like a racing cyclist who thinks he can overtake
    death's machine
You are like the clock in the ghetto whose hands
    go backwards
If death surprised me I would die a six-year-old boy.

Graham Martin, in his introduction to these translations, suggests that Nezval was attracted to surrealism because it "provides a style for what is contradictory and paradoxical in experience. Prague's many-sided life—its glamorous history, various weathers, different kinds of people—becomes a general symbol of this contradictoriness, whose meaning has to be puzzled out 'as we divine the thoughts of a beloved woman.' "

Nezval had gone with the Czech delegation to the Congress of Soviet writers in Moscow in 1934, and to an international meeting of left-wing writers in Paris the following year. But his claim that surrealism had a positive revolutionary role as an expression of defiance against a corrupt order found few supporters. Under the impact of the Munich crisis and the Nazi occupation he turned to more directly political poetry, as in *Historický obraz* (A Historical Picture, 1939), expressing his grief at the fate of his country. After the war he committed himself to the new communist regime. He became head of a department in the Ministry of Information, while writing inferior propagandist poetry like *Stalin* (1949) and *Zpěv miru* (1950, translated by Jack Lindsay and Stephen Jolly as *Song of Peace*). Nezval soon became disillusioned with the communist government. He did his best to secure the release of writers imprisoned by the regime and was criticized for associating with elements hostile to "socialist realism." This change of heart is reflected in the darker and deeper tone of some of his later collections, especially *Chrpy a města* (Cornflowers and Town, 1955).

Nezval made excellent but very free translations from Rimbaud, Mallarmé, Heine, Pushkin, and Pablo Neruda. His prose works, such as *Pan Marat* (Citizen Marat, 1932), *Řetěz štěstí* (Chain of Fortune, 1936), and *Jak vejce vejci* (As Like as Two Peas, 1933), are loosely composed, often using the surrealist method of automatic writing. *Z meho života* (From My Life, 1959) is autobiographical, as is the trilogy comprising *Kronika z konce století* (Chronicle of the End of the Century, 1929), *Posedlost* (Obsession, 1930), and *Dolce far niente* (1931), though these were not intended to record the events of his life but rather "the forgotten regions of my soul."

His great versatility is perhaps best shown in his plays, for which he himself composed the music, including *Milenci z kiosku* (Kiosk Lovers, 1932) and *Manon Lescaut* (1940). These are verse dramas, as is *Dnes ještě zapada slunce nad Atlantidou* (The Sun Still Sets Over Atlantis, 1956), which gives a new and very modern twist to the myth of Atlantis by making the destruction of the continent a warning against nuclear war. The collected works of this immensely prolific author have been published in twenty-four volumes.

PRINCIPAL WORKS IN ENGLISH TRANSLATION: Song of Peace, 1951; (with others) Three Czech Poets, 1971. *Poems in* French, A. (ed.) A Book of Czech Verse, 1958; Osers, E. and Montgomery, J.K. (eds.) Modern Czech Poetry, 1945; Otruba, M. and Pešat, Z (eds.) The Linden Tree, 1962.

ABOUT: Ceskoslovensko Biografie, 1936; French, A. The Poets of Prague, 1969; Jelínek, A. Vítěslav Nezval, 1961 (in Czech); Kratochvil, L. Wolker a Nezval, 1936 (in Czech); Rechcigl, M. (ed.) The Czechoslovak Contribution to World Culture, 1964; Smith, H. (ed.) Columbia Dictionary of Modern European Literature, 1947; Soldan, F. O Nezvalovi a poválečné generaci, 1933; Svoboda, J. Prítel Vítěslav Nezval, 1966. *Periodicals*—Books Abroad 42:3 1968.

*NGUGI WA THIONG'O (formerly James Ngugi) (January 5, 1938–), Kenyan novelist, short story writer, essayist, and dramatist, was born in Limuru, near Nairobi, in Kenya's Central Province, into a large polygamous Kikuyu family. In 1946 his mother sent him to a local mission school, and in 1947 he went on to a Kikuyu school at Karinga. He studied there until 1955, except for the period between 1948 and 1950 when the school was closed because of the Mau Mau rebellion. In 1959 Ngugi graduated from Alliance High School. He wrote his first play there and in 1959 published three stories in the *Kenya Weekly News*.

Ngugi's play *The Black Hermit* was produced in Nairobi in 1962. Partly in verse, it tells the story of an educated young Kikuyu who is torn between his English girlfriend and life in Nairobi and his tribal responsibilities (including his brother's widow) in the village where he was born. Most reviewers found it less than compelling. Meanwhile Ngugi had entered Makerere University in Kampala, Uganda, where he received his B.A. in 1963, and edited the lively and influential student magazine *Penpoint*. After working for a few months on the Nairobi *Daily Nation*, he went to England for graduate study at Leeds University.

Returning to Africa in 1967, Ngugi became a lecturer in English at University College, Nairobi, now the University of Nairobi. He taught there until the students' strike in January 1969, when he resigned in protest at the authoritarianism displayed by the administration. At the same time, from 1967 to 1969, Ngugi was editor of the important English-language literary review *Zuka* (Emerge), published in Dar es Salaam, Tanzania. In 1970–1971 he worked in the United States as an associate professor of African literature at Northwestern University,

*ngōō' gĕ wä thē on' go

NGUGI

NGUGI WA THIONG'O

Lutfi Özkök

Evanston, Illinois. Thereafter, until his arrest on political charges at the beginning of 1978, he was head of the English department at the University of Nairobi.

Weep Not, Child (1964) the first published English-language novel by an East African writer, received awards from both the Dakar Festival of Negro Arts and the East African Literature Bureau. It is an account of the impact of the Mau Mau rebellion on a Kikuyu family, and there is a strong element of autobiography in the story of Njoroge, an ambitious young idealist whose plans are thwarted when the rebellion disrupts his education. The book was admired for its simple but expressive prose, and the ironic parallels that Ngugi draws between the white settlers' love of the land and the Kikuyus' literally religious attachment to the same soil. The novel's weaknesses, John Reed thought, "come from the need to make it at once a book about the Mau Mau rebellion and yet also a book written out of immediate and personal experience."

The River Between, published a year later, had in fact been written earlier than *Weep Not, Child,* and there is evidence of this in the relative simplicity of the novel's structure. It is set in Kenya before Mau Mau, and looks back to the origins of that conflict. The river of the title separates two villages inhabited by members of the same tribe, of whom half are christianized and half worship tribal gods and follow tribal ways. Waiyaki, an idealistic young man much like Njoroge in *Weep Not, Child,* falls in love with the Christian pastor's daughter across the river, and dreams of reconciling the two villages and leading his people to freedom. His leadership is re-

jected because he advocates a peaceful transition to racial equality through education, at a time when the country is ready for revolution. When he wrote this novel, Ngugi evidently shared Waiyaki's disapproval of political activism, and this has troubled some critics.

There is general agreement that *A Grain of Wheat* (1967) marked a major advance in Ngugi's work. It takes place just before Kenya's Independence Day, and explores the wounds left in Kenyan society by the bitter struggle against colonialism. Mugo, a hero of the rebellion, is to speak in honor of Kihika, a Mau Mau leader who had been executed by the British. Mugo's refusal of this role adds to his reputation as modest hero, but on the day itself he confesses before the crowd that it was he who had betrayed the dead man. The state of mind that leads to this confession is displayed with a convincing sobriety and exactness in which there is not one gratuitous or empty gesture. The novel is no less successful in its portraits of Karanja, who chooses the wrong side, and the well-meaning but weak Gikonyo, and we are shown each of these men painfully coming to terms with his own limitations.

Arthur Ravenscroft called this "an accomplished novel of mature outlook. . . . At last Ngugi is able to treat a messianic figure with detachment, but also with humane sympathy. . . . A great strength of this finely orchestrated novel is Ngugi's skilful use of disrupted time sequence to indicate the close inter-relatedness between the characters' behavior in the Rebellion and the state of their lives (and of the nation) at Independence. . . . Though *A Grain of Wheat* is a disturbing novel, it proclaims cautious, tempered hope for the regenerative capabilities of ordinary human nature." Eldred Jones thought the book had "the stature of art that changes and transforms our vision."

Excellent as they were, the reviews of this novel reportedly left Ngugi with "a general sense of futility," and it was some years before he wrote any more fiction. *Homecoming,* a collection of his essays on "African and Caribbean literature, culture and politics," appeared in 1972, and revealed how far he had come from the political inertia of his early novels. A reviewer in the *Times Literary Supplement* wrote that the first few essays "really show the shape of the ideological reformation that Ngugi underwent in England and after his return to Kenya. This reformation, along fairly orthodox Marxist lines with a strong dash of Fanon, has made his vision piercing and strong, though it does occasionally make for over-simplified explanations of problems which refuse to be so contained." The same writer thought that Ngugi's essays on Caribbean literature contain "some of the best and most penetrating African criticism yet published," and Angus Calder said much the same about the essays dealing with African writers. Calder thought that Ngugi was "immune to the fashionable trivialities of academic criticism. For him the bearing of a book towards society, the capacity it may lend us to cut down oppression, is all-important. . . . The clarity with which he writes stems from complete conviction."

Ngugi has said that revolutionary struggle "is sweeping through Africa. . . . The artist in his writings is not exempted from the struggle. By diving into the sources, he can give moral direction and vision to a struggle which, though suffering temporary reaction, is continuous and is changing the face of the twentieth century." His own novel *Petals of Blood,* published in 1977, takes a Marxist line in attacking not only colonialism but what he sees as its direct continuance, the oppression of the Kenyan poor a dozen years after independence by foreign capital and its local allies. The novel loops back and forth over twelve years in the recent history of a village, using the framework of a murder mystery to expose the sources of current social unrest in Kenya. The qualified optimism expressed in *A Grain of Wheat* appears in this phase of his work to have turned to anger and despair, and some reviewers found the book weakened by its passionate didacticism.

The 1966 radio play *This Time Tomorrow* had touched on a similar theme, and in a more recent play in Kikuyu, *Ngahika Ndenda,* Ngugi dramatized the two most explosive issues of modern Kenya, the ownership of land and the distribution of wealth. *Ngahika Ndenda* (I'll Marry When I Choose) was done in collaboration with Ngugi wa Mirii. It embodies a number of Kikuyu songs, and reflects Ngugi's disillusionment "with the use of foreign languages to express Kenya's soul or . . . social conditions." This play, or *Petals of Blood,* or both, led to Ngugi's arrest on January 1, 1978. He was held incommunicado for two weeks, then detained under Kenya's public security regulations in Kamiti Maximum Security Prison. Ngugi's arrest was surprising: he is generally regarded as the most distinguished East African writer, and his works are studied in Kenyan high schools. He was held until December 12, 1978, when President Moi marked a national holiday by releasing a number of detainees. According to Ngugi, no charges were ever brought against him. He was not beaten in prison, but was subjected to mental torture, he has told interviewers; however, he has no intention of leaving Kenya.

William Walsh has said that Ngugi's writing "is highly sensitive, plain and restrained, and most apt in the reconstruction of individual states of feeling, weaker in establishing them in a convincingly solid outer world. The characters in his novels do not develop or change greatly, but he manages beautifully to fix the emotions of a given moment. He has not, as yet, achieved an equal success in exhibiting the movement and confusion of social process, nor a comparable diagnostic skill in defining social structure. He seems to be writing historical novels when his main gift is for rendering with a nice balance and objectivity the inner life of the individual." Whether or not Ngugi would accept this criticism, he is unlikely to swerve from what he considers the artist's obligation to "dive into the sources" of the developing conflict "between the emergent African bourgeoisie and the African masses."

PRINCIPAL WORKS: *Fiction*—Weep Not, Child, 1964; The River Between, 1965; A Grain of Wheat, 1967; Secret Lives and Other Stories, 1975; Petals of Blood, 1977. *Plays*—The Black Hermit, 1963; This Time Tomorrow (contains The Rebels, The Wound in the Heart, This Time Tomorrow), 1970 (This Time Tomorrow also *in* Pieterse, C. (ed.) Short African Plays, 1972). *Other*—Homecoming: Essays on African and Caribbean Literature, Culture and Politics, 1972.

ABOUT: Cartey, W. Whispers From a Continent, 1971; Duerden, D. and Pieterse, C. (eds.) African Writers Talking, 1972; Gakwandi, S.A. The Novel of Contemporary Experience in Africa, 1977; Herdeck, D.E. African Authors, 1974; International Who's Who, 1978–79; Larson, C.R. The Emergence of African Fiction, 1972; Olney, J. Tell Me Africa, 1973; Palmer, E. An Introduction to the African Novel, 1972; Pieterse, C. and Munro, D. (eds.) Protest and Conflict in African Literature, 1969; Tucker, M. *introduction to* Weep Not, Child, 1969; Vinson, J. (ed.) Contemporary Dramatists, 1977; Vinson, J. (ed.) Contemporary Novelists, 1976; Wästberg, P. (ed.) The Writer in Modern Africa, 1969; Who's Who in African Literature, 1972; Wright, E. (ed.) The Critical Evaluation of African Literature, 1973; Zell, H.M. and Silver, H. A Reader's Guide to African Literature, 1972. *Periodicals*—African Forum Summer 1967; Books Abroad Autumn 1967; Cultural Events in Africa 50 1969; Guardian March 6, 1978; Journal of Commonwealth Literature September 1965, January 1969; New Statesman October 20, 1972; New York Times Book Review February 19, 1978; Times Literary Supplement November 3, 1972.

NICHOLS, PETER (RICHARD) (July 31, 1927–), English dramatist, writes: "As a boy growing up in Bristol, England, the two events of my year were the summer circus and the Christmas pantomime. The circus was in a field and the pantomime in the Prince's Theatre, an Edwardian house gutted early in the Second War by German incendiaries. The panto included most of the elements reckoned by the British to add up to a wholesome family show: women dressed as men, men dressed as women, scenery

PETER NICHOLS

David Farrell

showing trees and cottages, patriotism, little-girl fairies, love, smut, community singing, real animals and two tap-dancing comics in a horse's skin. But now, like the circus, it seems to be finished. London's only panto last year was a failure. As one who has played Back Legs of the Horse, I suppose I should be glad to see it go. Except that it was so beautiful. What can replace it?

"My boyhood hero wasn't Henry the Fifth or Lawrence of Arabia but Cary Grant, the local boy who made good by running away with a circus. Boys who went to the same school said his name was chiselled on a desk lid: Archie Leach. We all longed to do as he'd done but lacked the nerve.

"My father had left his home in London but not with the circus. He became a salesman of grocery sundries, the stock occupation for a prurient drunk, but wrong for him, an upright man, a total abstainer, who never left a room without making an exit. He could cry with rage over a broken shoelace. Perhaps family life might have been easier if he'd acted *on* the stage as well as off. As it was, fear of insecurity kept him in commerce.

"During the Second War, my mother and I did our bit by joining a concert-party. She sang 'Come, come, I love you only' to vast assemblies of servicemen. I recited comic verse in a breaking voice and couldn't take my eyes off the peroxide-blonde dancer who hoofed away on roller skates in satin bolero and briefs.

"As war ended, I was conscripted into the R.A.F. and soon left Britain for the first time, swaddled in blankets in the unheated bomb-bays of a Liberator. Within a day, we were under

canvas in sight of the Pyramids. From there I was posted for a year to Calcutta and, with the end of the Raj, for the rest of my time to Singapore. I elbowed my way into an entertainments unit, staying on as actor, scene-shifter, chorus-boy, till the failure of our shows led to the unit's overdue disbandment.

"Back in Bristol, I went to drama school, then struggled for five years to earn a living as an actor at a time when legit drama was run by a homosexual Mafia. After this I taught in primary schools in London. All the time, of course, I'd been writing plays, radio scripts, short stories, songs and sketches. None were produced or published because none had been submitted, until a BBC TV contest forced a play out of me. I sent it in and won a prize and a single showing. In this, I turned my back on colour, limiting myself to shades of grey, with an occasional startling flash of black or white. This was only partly due to the television of the time being monochrome. I was older, wiser, sadder, and determined to have no truck with the tatty apparatus of my stage-struck youth. I had my eye to the keyhole now and saw no transvestites, no tap-dancing blondes. This tone was dominant through twelve or so plays for television, though at the time I was writing them life became richer, more dramatic, for me. I married, went to live by the sea in Devon. We began a family with a helplessly handicapped daughter. Two more girls and a boy followed, all very healthy. I turned out four plays a year, many of which were not produced. We moved back to Bristol and put our spastic child into hospital care. I was asked to write a feature film script for a pop group and with the money I spent a year describing our life with the first child, Abigail. The play began as keyhole naturalism, but as I thought about the theatre and what it had meant to me, the form changed. I included sketches, monologues, front-cloth routines, song-and-dance, slapstick. Nobody would do it in London but my friend Michael Blakemore was directing at Citizens' Theatre, Glasgow, and said he would. A disciple of Tyrone Guthrie, he believes in the theatre as a means of celebrating life. His production of *A Day in the Death of Joe Egg* added jazz, pop-painting, stylish comedy, melodrama. It was perfect. Our collaboration continued with *The National Health* and *Forget-Me-Not Lane,* both of which developed further the use of entertainment which I'd first seen in the circus and the panto and the variety halls of my childhood.

"Abigail, our first child, died in hospital at the age of ten, without ever having spoken, sat up, fed herself or conveyed any but the most primitive symptoms of cognition. We now live, with our three other children, in London. I have learnt very little and know only what all writers know—that the work gets harder every year, that success and failure are fortuitous, that 'patient merit' is no more prized now than then. But a play may be all that survives of a life. Our daughter, who never really lived, has a sort-of existence wherever *Joe Egg* is played."

Though Nichols was attracted to the theatre by such live and lively forms as pantomime, music hall, and the circus, it was as a television dramatist that he learned his craft. In spite of this, and the fact that most of his stage plays have developed from pieces originally written for television, he has no great regard for the medium. He says that he has "always felt that on television I naturally work in a lighter register, don't go so deeply into my subjects, or don't in the first place pick subjects which require me to go really deeply into them."

In fact, Nichols's television plays received a good deal of critical attention, although (the memory of television audiences being notoriously short) they scarcely made his name a household word. The first of them to attract serious critical interest was *Ben Spray* (1961), an inventive and tough-minded comedy about a young teacher whose weakness for fantasy and capacity for being misunderstood are reminiscent of Waterhouse and Hall's Billy Liar. In *The Hooded Terror* (1963), two young couples meet a masked boxer at a local carnival and invite him home with them as a joke. The boxer turns out to be a truly good man; the real "hooded terror" is the jealousy and stifled violence underlying his hosts' apparently conventional lives.

This is a theme that Nichols has returned to in later plays. A related theme—the mutually destructive relations between parents and children—is explored in *The Continuity Man* (1963), originally written for the stage with an Arts Council bursary, and in *When the Wind Blows* (1965), a haunting piece about the bitterly damaging warfare between an intellectual young couple and the husband's parents, played out in the innocent setting of an English family tea party.

Nichols's first performed stage play was an adaptation of *The Hooded Terror*, produced in Bristol in 1964, but for all practical purposes his theatrical career began in 1967 with the transfer of *A Day in the Death of Joe Egg* from Glasgow to London's West End; it made his reputation overnight, and the following year repeated this operation on Broadway (where it was called simply *Joe Egg*). Of the New York production William Goldman wrote: "There is no way that *Joe Egg* can be warm and funny, which is why, since it is warm and funny, its achievement is so great."

As the father of a seriously handicapped child, Nichols had read a great deal on this theme and had been struck by the solemnity with which it was always treated: "Sort of hushed in the face of private grief. And that was not how I had experienced it at all. Nothing in my life has ever been really dignified . . . even the most serious moments of life always turn into grotesque comedy. That's why all my television plays are somehow or other comedies: I have used television as a sort of public diary into which I poured my observations as they occurred to me, and they always came up comic. The same here, except that no one, but no one, would countenance this subject in terms of comedy. So it had to be a stage play."

The play is in two acts. In the first, Bri and Sheila, most of the time addressing themselves directly to the audience, describe their ten years as parents of a spastic child whom they have nicknamed Joe Egg. Nichols says that the first act material was originally addressed to two other characters on stage, and that he then eliminated them and had Bri and Sheila speak to the audience instead: "Out of talking to the audience came the style of the play." This style is inseparable from its content. When Bri and Sheila present their experience as a series of vaudeville routines (taking it in turns to parody the ludicrous platitudes of clergymen and doctors), not only do they get the desperate facts of their situation across, they also reveal far more about the state of their marriage than they could in a naturalistic scene. It becomes clear that their jokes—and perhaps all jokes—are a by-product of pain.

The same process continues in the second act when they are visited by some old friends—a middle-class couple liberal, well-meaning, but uncomprehending—and by Bri's working-class mother, whose principal attitude is one of shame that such a tragedy should have occurred in her family. The comments and advice of these visitors only intensify the loneliness of the parents. Bri makes an unsuccessful attempt to kill Joe and then walks out, leaving Sheila to cope with a situation he can no longer face. In this act as well the use of direct address and compulsive joking enables Nichols to place the domestic situation in a wider social context. The method also serves to banish all trace of self-pity and leaves the audience entertained and thoughtful about the world they are living in rather than harrowed by a private hard-luck story. "It has to be described as a comedy," Ronald Bryden wrote, "one of the funniest and most touching I have ever seen."

In *The National Health* (1969), Nichols produced another wholly serious comedy about the incurable and the dying—and also, he says, about "the spiritual and moral health of the nation." It was based on a rejected television play, *The End Beds,* and like *Joe Egg* derives from personal experience—Nichols spent several long periods in a state hospital with an obstinately collapsing lung during his years as a teacher. In this case, the social dimension is evident from the start through the interaction of the assorted characters who happen to be thrown together in the Stafford Cripps Ward of a large hospital. There are the patients themselves, whose attitudes vary from half-educated bigotry to imperial nostalgia; and there is the power relationship between the patients and the doctors and nursing staff. Nichols also introduces the ambiguous figure of a ward orderly, a partly comic and partly sinister master of ceremonies who cheerfully acknowledges that "there is something bent about the healing arts." The relationships point up the contrast between the gross realities of suffering and its pseudo-cheerful institutional mask—a contrast which the play underlines by running (on a simulated television screen) a medical soap-opera in tandem with the main action, wafting the same patients and hospital staff from oxygen cylinders and bed-pans to the cosmetic world of "Nurse Norton's Affair."

One of the play's great merits is to promote a constantly shifting balance of sympathies between the patients and the staff, which led some reviewers to compare Nichols with Chekhov (though he himself likens the piece to an Agatha Christie thriller: "Who's going to die next?"). In Britain, *The National Health* carried off the Evening Standard award as the best new play of the year, as *Joe Egg* had done before it. In New York, where it had arrived in 1974, Walter Kerr disapproved, finding it "an essentially static venture," and the soap-opera interludes irrelevant and "uncomfortably broad." This was a minority view, however, and Clive James called it "a work of genius."

Although Nichols arrived by crashing the barriers of English good taste, this was more the result of autobiographical accident than of any wish to shock. An inescapably autobiographical artist, who claims that he has "no imaginative faculty" and who draws heavily on the diary he has kept most of his life, he is *par excellence* the dramatist of ordinary middle-class British life, as he demonstrated in his family comedy *Forget-Me-Not Lane* (1971). This play is built around the figure of a middle-aged man who is deserting

his wife, and sets up a dialogue between the immediate situation and the wartime memories (straight out of Nichols's Bristol boyhood) that throng Frank's mind while he is packing: the play is, among many other things, "a hymn to the 1940s."

Once again, the form was dictated by the material. There is nothing inherently dramatic about these recollections of a bickering home life and rowdy troop shows; and of the dominant character, the hero-narrator's father, Nichols says: "Real people don't, as a rule, mean anything. Our lives make no sense. His didn't. But I'm trying." The play achieves meaning by setting youth in middle-aged perspective: Frank "stands in a cage of doors from which the people in his past burst like members of a pierrot concert-party to do their turns on the stage of memory"—orderly chronology is relinquished and instead we are given the illusion of a continuous theatrical present. Frank discovers in the end that none of us can escape the genetic trap; we all become our parents.

John Russell Taylor found the result an extraordinary technical achievement, entirely built "on a pattern of ironies, brilliantly manipulated. An effect will be meticulously built up, and then cheerfully undercut with some deflating comment or absurd juxtaposition. But the deflation is not merely destructive, a cancelling-out; instead it always brings us into something deeper, stranger, another layer in Nichols's complex, many-layered reality." More than any other Nichols play, *Forget-Me-Not Lane* evokes what Frank Marcus called the "laughter of recognition," and Ronald Bryden concluded that "in trying to come to terms with his own past, Nichols has written a play which helps us to come to terms with our own."

In *Chez Nous* (1974) Nichols returned to the theme of the English liberal double-think he first explored in *Joe Egg.* The comic zone is defined by the stage set, a converted farmhouse in the Dordogne region of France with spotlights nesting in the rafters, typifying the latest affluent variation on the pastoral ideal. This folly is the work of Liz and Dick, who have moved there with their two children on the strength of Dick's best-selling book on sexual freedom. Two old friends, Phil and Diane, arrive to visit them and it emerges that Phil has sired a baby on Dick's fourteen-year-old daughter, and that Liz is passing off the child as her own. Sexual freedom, in short, is put to the test—not to mention the idea of the extended family, the flight from urban sprawl, and other topical issues which feed the ironic action.

The piece drew critical comparisons with

Pinero and certainly, besides resembling an Edwardian "problem play" in content, it is uncharacteristically traditional in construction. Nichols here discards direct address and presents long, fully articulated acts in place of the brief, kaleidoscopic scenes that he carried over from television in his previous stage plays. If some of the issues are transitory, the characters are drawn in great detail (Nichols is elsewhere not above employing stereotypes). The play aroused a chorus of almost unanimous critical praise, led by Robert Cushman who considered it "the best its author has written."

Nichols's run of critical acclaim remained unbroken until the National Theatre production of *The Freeway* (1974). In this piece he abandoned autobiography for impersonal social satire, examining British notions of freedom in terms of a vast three-day traffic jam. It appeared to some of his admirers that he had sacrificed the comedy of hard-won experience for the easier territory of detached mockery. The author himself thinks that "the message of the play is that we'd do better to stay where we are and make life work there. I suppose in a sense that's what I've tried to say in all my plays." There was a somewhat mixed reception also for *Privates on Parade,* staged by the Royal Shakespeare Company in 1977. Here Nichols draws on his army experience in a play about the misadventures of a wildly camp concert-party of soldiers touring Malaya in the late 1940s. The show was enjoyed for its jokes, songs, spoof dances, and nostalgia, but found rambling, shapeless, and rather aimless.

He has not entirely ceased to write for television. *The Gorge* (1968), about a family outing to Cheddar Gorge, examines the complex interactions between the generations through the perceptive eyes of the adolescent son. It was one of the most praised of British television plays and has been shown several times. *Daddy Kiss It Better* (1968) and *Hearts and Flowers* (1971) also turn on Nichols's preoccupation with the family as an inescapable trap. He has written scenarios for the films *Catch Us If You Can* (1965, called *Having a Wild Weekend* in the United States), *Georgy Girl* (1966), *Joe Egg* (1972), and *The National Health* (1973).

Nichols is too sympathetic a writer to be labeled a satirist, but he has the satirist's instinct for surveying the social facade and knowing which parts of it are going rotten and are due for the ax. His work is based on an immense gift for observation coupled with an ironically humane intelligence. His preeminence in modern English social comedy rests above all on his accuracy as a reporter. The class attitudes, sexual conventions, and left-wing hypocrisies he records have a documentary source in his notebooks; and, as for speech habits, "people say more surprising things than you could invent." When the middle-class theatregoing public took him to their hearts it was because they recognized their reflections in the mirror.

The author is the son of Richard George Nichols and the former Violet Annie Poole. He attended Bristol Grammar School from 1936 to 1944, served in the Royal Air Force from 1945 to 1948, and studied at the Bristol Old Vic Theatre School in 1948-1950, subsequently working for five years as an actor in repertory, on television, and in films (with interludes as a park-keeper, English language teacher in Italy, and clerk). He qualified as a teacher at Trent Park Teachers' Training College in Hertfordshire (1955-1957). Nichols is a governor of the Greenwich Theatre, London; served in 1973-1975 on the Arts Council Drama Panel; and was at one time a member of the Euthanasia Society. In 1976 he was playwright-in-residence at the Guthrie Theatre in Minneapolis. Nichols lives in Greenwich and (like the couple in *Chez Nous*) owns a farmhouse in the Dordogne. He lists his recreations as listening to jazz and looking at cities.

PRINCIPAL WORKS: *Television Plays*—Promenade *in* Six Granada Plays, 1960; Ben Spray *in* New Granada Plays, 1961; The Gorge *in* Muller, R. (ed.) The Television Dramatist, 1973; Hearts and Flowers *in* B.B.C. The Television Playwright, 1960. *Stage Plays*—A Day in the Death of Joe Egg, 1967 (U.S., Joe Egg); The National Health, or, Nurse Norton's Affair, 1970; Forget-Me-Not Lane, 1971; Chez Nous, 1974; The Freeway, 1975; Privates on Parade, 1977.

ABOUT: Hayman, R. Playback Two, 1973; Taylor, J.R. The Second Wave, 1971; Vinson, J. (ed.) Contemporary Dramatists, 1977; Who's Who, 1975; Who's Who in the Theatre, 1977. *Periodicals*—Encounter December 1974; Guardian January 26, 1970; December 2, 1971; New York Times October 18, 1974; November 10, 1974; Times (London) September 28, 1974.

NYE, ROBERT (March 15, 1939–), English poet and novelist, writes: "I was born in London in 1939 and educated at state schools and the Southend High School, 1944–1955. I had good language training at the last, a grammar school of the kind now extinct in England, but suspect that such general education as I have had dates really from the day—I must have been about twelve—when I discovered that I could get three tickets at the public library for every member of my family, and use them all myself since none of the others was much of a reader. My father Oswald Nye was a minor civil servant, a clerkly man who had worked his way up from being a telegram messenger boy on a bicycle to being in

Fay Godwin

ROBERT NYE

charge of a small General Post Office department in Essex for the selling of telephones. My mother Frances Weller was a farmer's daughter, the youngest of twenty-one brothers and sisters, of the best blood in England, yeoman stock. She had left school to earn her living as a lady's maid at the age of twelve. Consequently she never learned to read and write properly, but she was possessed of an innate peasant storytelling ability, and I believe that I have inherited as much from her, at least, as from my father. I started writing poems when I was nine. I left school as soon as the compulsory education system allowed—when I was sixteen. After that, I went through the motions of various non-jobs, always with a view to saving a little money to support myself while I got on with my writing. In this way, between the ages of sixteen and twenty-one, I was at different times a newspaper reporter, a milkman, a labourer in a market garden, and a ward orderly in a sanitorium. My true occupation was always writing—which at that time, for me, meant the writing of poems. My first poems were published in *The London Magazine* when I was sixteen, and I suppose I took this as a sort of confirmation that proceeding to a university was no part of my vocation. Besides, the writers I most admired at that point—Shakespeare, Rimbaud, Dylan Thomas—had all done well enough without benefit of a degree.

"Writing is my work. Writing is my life. Since 1961, it has also been my full-time occupation. I found a remote cottage in North Wales, without electricity or running water, but with a spring in the woods nearby. I rented this cottage for ten shillings a week. When my first book of poems was published it was quite well reviewed.

I had married by this time, and fathered a son. It occurred to me that here were three of us starving while the reviewers were paid to write about what I had written. So I sent off letters to the literary editors of journals where my book had been well received, asking if they could let me review for them. Two of these editors began to keep me supplied with reviewing work, although several years passed before I met either of them face to face. (I mention this to disabuse young writers who believe that there is an 'Establishment' anywhere, or that everything depends on who you know). For the next fifteen years or so, I subsidised my own creative work by a great deal of criticism in the form of review contributions to periodicals. There were two more sons by my first wife, Judith Pratt, but the marriage failed, and we were divorced in 1967. In 1968 I married again, my second wife being Aileen Campbell, who is a painter and a poet currently studying to become an analytical psychologist at the C. G. Jung Institute in Zürich. There is one daughter from this second marriage. We lived for ten years in Edinburgh. We live now in Ireland.

"Form has always interested me, which is why I have tried my hand at many different kinds of writing—short stories, books for children, plays for stage and radio, libretti, as well as poems and novels. My breakthrough came in the final form, with my novel *Falstaff* (1976), not merely in the sense that it became some kind of best-seller and got itself translated into various foreign languages, but that in writing it I found myself, my own voice and pitch, so that I feel entitled to call myself a novelist. As for poems: I hope never to write more of them than I have to.

"At the same time my stories are intended as a relief from the truth-telling which poetry requires of its adherents. The connection between fiction and lying interests me. As a matter of fact I do not write short stories so much as tall stories, fibs, lies, whoppers. The matter is traditional—it comes from the parish pump, not the well of personal experience. That is to say, my stories have their source in dreams which more than one person has dreamt, in ballads, jests, yarns, and in those folk tales which are as it were the dreams of the people coming to us without the interference of our own identity. I do not claim for them any importance on account of their origins. 'A Bach fugue is an obsession overcome,' as Simone Weil says in a sentence which I have always meant one day to use as an epigraph to my fictions, 'which is why the initial theme is not of so much importance.' The delight taken in *storying* in Chaucer, Nashe, Swift,

Sterne, Rabelais, and for that matter the *Arabian Nights* interests me."

Nye's first verse collection, published in 1961 as *Juvenilia,* was also his first book. The poems, including some written as early as 1952, were found at times elusive in meaning as well as permissibly immature in attitude, but admired for the author's innate lyrical gift, his poetic inventiveness and feeling for language. When *Juvenilia 2* appeared in 1963, earning Nye the Eric Gregory Award, a reviewer in the *Times Literary Supplement* welcomed his "Gravesian decorum, cool passion and judging concentration" and wrote: "Here is a proper poet." As he explains above, these excellent early reviews led to Nye's becoming a reviewer himself—one of great fluency and generous perception. He became poetry editor of the *Scotsman* in 1969 and poetry critic of the London *Times* in 1971, by which time he was turning out a hundred thousand words of literary journalism a year. This by no means exhausted Nye's creative energy, which he has channeled into most contemporary literary forms (and some that are not contemporary at all, like his masque of *The Seven Deadly Sins).*

An "indispensable" version of Beowulf for young readers, retellings of Welsh legends (in *March Has Horse's Ears* and *Taliesin*), and other books for children began to appear in the mid-1960s. Nye's startling (and no doubt autobiographical) first novel, *Doubtfire,* was published in 1967. It is set, more or less, in Southend, the Essex seaside resort where the author grew up, but one reviewer called this Southend "a country of metaphor, a fabulous kingdom by the sea. It is Arthur's Britain, it is fifteenth century France." In fact, as P. J. Kavanagh saw it, the action really takes place "within the troubled psyche of William Retz (alias Gilles de Retz) enduring a crisis of identity exacerbated by the unattainable nature of Joan Dark (Jeanne d'Arc). It consists of telephone calls into a dead receiver, fantasy playlets, conversations with anti-selves, descriptions of the natural world (a very good one of a spring of water), descriptions of the creative process, and of apothegms, also good: 'Seek simplicity and mistrust it.' " It seemed to Kavanagh that Nye had used in his novel "the sudden transitions, parallels, unexpected connections that were once the prerogatives of poetry, and for which, now, a vast audience has been prepared by the cinema. . . . *Doubtfire* is also a love affair with rhythms and language. . . . The effect is breathless, brilliant, but in the end uninvolving. The frequent

opacities give us too much time to notice that the Retz disease stays private, that this passionate caress of language sometimes has the effect of stifling it."

The short stories collected in *Tales I Told My Mother* (1969) were generally enjoyed. They were called Rabelaisian in their energy and their discursiveness, and sometimes in their content (as in the story about a man buried in a snowdrift who ploughs his way out using the only tool he has to hand, his penis). As well as vigorous tall tales like this one, the collection includes pieces that make fantastic or parodic intrusions into the lives of such heroes as Thomas Chatterton and Dante Gabriel Rossetti, and Nye says he wrote a whole "lost book" by Emily Brontë so that he could quote from it in the story called "The Amber Witch." The volume brought him the James Kennaway Memorial Award in 1970.

Darker Ends, Nye's third verse collection, also appeared in 1969. One critic thought the book altogether too reticent, a "well-mannered whisper," but most enjoyed its epigrammatic wryness and formal skill. Philip Hobsbaum, noting how Nye had purged and tightened some poems that had first appeared in the *Juvenilia* volumes, decided that he was "rising on the stepping-stones of his former romantic selves to finer things. After the baroque ambitions of his earlier years, he looks about to emerge as a poet of distinction, wit and epigram." Alan Brownjohn found Nye "still oddly and unconsciously, derived in places, quaintly metaphysical or even Victorian . . . and there are too many flimsy, imagistic fragments. But his poems about the dissatisfaction and coldness behind the conventional domestic emotions are modestly well judged." Brownjohn was thinking particularly of the title poem, "Darker Ends," in which the poet describes how he frightens his young son by making shadow pictures on the wall with his hands:

> Why do I scare him? Fearful of my love
> I'm cruelly comforted by his warm fear,
> Seeing the night made perfect on the wall
> In my handwriting, if illegible,
> Still full of personal beasts, and terrible.
>
> Abjure that art—it is no true delight
> To lie and turn the dark to darker ends
> Because my heart's dissatisfied and cold.
> To tell the truth, when he is safe asleep,
> I shut my eyes and let the darkness in.

There was another collection of poems in 1976, *Divisions on a Ground,* also found somewhat low-pressured, but respectfully received. And between 1969 and 1976 there were more children's books, several plays, editions of poetry by Sir Walter Raleigh, William Barnes, and Swinburne, and a great deal of reviewing. Nye was by then established as an energetic, versatile, and highly professional man of letters—an all-rounder of exceptional talent and promise, but not of major achievement. Nor were his books particularly successful financially—he says that up to 1976 none of them had earned him more than a few hundred pounds. All this changed with the publication of his novel *Falstaff,* in which, as he says, he found himself, his own "voice and pitch."

The novel purports to be Sir John Falstaff's own memoirs, set down in 1459 and subsequently lost (though not before Shakespeare had ransacked them for plots). In Nye's version, Falstaff survives his rejection by Prince Hal (only feigning death to escape his creditors), fights at Agincourt, makes his fortune in France, and retires to Norfolk. There, at the age of eighty-one, he appalls and fascinates a gang of scriveners with his recollections (and fabrications) of a long life almost wholly devoted to the lusts of the flesh. Alex Hamilton called the novel "a celebration of the giant of Englishness, whose heavy descendant is John Bull, not Merrie England but the pagan delight in the rich taste of the world. . . . It's about orthodoxy laughing at conformity. . . . It is a fable that takes the form of a *bildungsroman,* very noisy at the start, and through many a summer of futter and foin moves more quietly to the confession . . . made by a lonely old man alone with his belly." His qualities are summed up in his last words: "Bless me, father. Bugger all. Whoops. We're off then."

Paul West wrote that Falstaff's unflagging salaciousness "cannot disguise his relentless empty-headedness over four hundred and fifty-two pages" and Michael Wood also found the bawdy sometimes tiresome, though "generally it takes on a rather attractive pathos, for we are rarely allowed to forget that Falstaff is not bragging but *lying.*" Paul Bailey called the book "clever, original, and intermittently brilliant," but thought it went on too long. There were few other complaints, and it seemed to Michael Ratcliffe that the novel "will surely be regarded as one of the most ambitious and seductive novels of the decade. . . . If his first [master] is Shakespeare, his second is Rabelais. . . . *Falstaff* is rich in poetic synthesis, primitive superstition, ordinary and extraordinary English occasions—the great winters of Falstaff's boyhood on the Hundred River in Norfolk; the blood in the air after Shrewsbury and the drum that beat all night; the yellow-hammer drinking a drop of devil's blood on May morning to sing the sweeter thereby—and as generously endowed with opinionated and confidential observations." Nye's Falstaff lives for us, wrote J. I. M. Stewart, "because of the magic of the words in which he is bodied forth; they alone preserve the dirty old ruffian joyous hearted, scandalously irresistible, a gentleman as well as a pig. Mr. Nye gets away with his project—triumphantly, it must be roundly said—because he is a minor lord of language himself." Nye says he never enjoyed anything at all as much as he enjoyed writing *Falstaff,* and it won him the *Guardian* Fiction Prize and became a bestseller.

PRINCIPAL PUBLISHED WORKS: *Fiction*—Doubtfire, 1967; Tales I Told My Mother, 1969; Falstaff: Being the 'Acta domini Johannis Fastolfe'; or 'Life and Valiant Deeds of Sir John Faustoff'; or 'The Hundred Days War'; As Told by Sir John Fastolf, K.G., to His Secretaries William Worcester, Stephen Scrope, Fr. Brackley, Christopher Hanson, Luke Nanton, John Bussard, and Peter Bassett, 1976; Merlin, 1978. *Poetry*—Juvenilia 1, 1961; Juvenilia 2, 1963; Darker Ends, 1969; Divisions on a Ground, 1976. *Plays*—(with William Watson) Sawney Bean, 1970; The Seven Deadly Sins: A Mask, 1974; Penthesilea and Other Plays (with Fugue and Sisters), 1975. *Children's Books*—Taliesin, 1966; March Has Horse's Ears, 1966; Bee Hunter: Adventures of Beowulf, 1968; (U.S., Beowulf: A New Telling; republished in England in 1972 as Beowulf, the Bee Hunter); Wishing Gold, 1970; Poor Pumpkin, 1971 (U.S., The Mathematical Princess); Out of the World and Back Again, 1977; Once Upon Three Times, 1978 (U.S., Cricket: Three Stories). *As Editor*—A Choice of Sir Walter Raleigh's Verse, 1972; William Barnes of Dorset: A Selection of His Poems, 1973; A Choice of Swinburne's Verse, 1973; The English Sermon 1750–1850, 1976; The Faber Book of Sonnets, 1976.

ABOUT: Contemporary Authors 33–36, 1973; Tibble, A. The Story of English Literature, 1970; Vinson, J. (ed.) Contemporary Novelists, 1976; Vinson, J. (ed.) Contemporary Poets, 1975; Who's Who, 1979; Writers Directory, 1976–1978. *Periodicals*—Books and Bookmen August 1970; British Book News February 1970; Guardian January 26, 1969; November 6, 1969; November 25, 1976; London Magazine January 1977; New Fiction July 1976; New Statesman March 6, 1970; September 10, 1976; New York Review of Books January 20, 1977; New York Times Book Review November 7, 1976; Observer July 14, 1963; September 7, 1976; Poetry May 1971; Publishers Weekly August 2, 1976; Scotsman September 4, 1976; Time November 8, 1976; Times (London) January 27, 1968; June 24, 1976; September 9, 1976; September 14, 1978; Times Literary Supplement July 26, 1963; November 11, 1969; December 2, 1971; September 3, 1976; December 2, 1977; April 7, 1978.

OATES, JOYCE CAROL (June 16, 1938–), American novelist, short story writer, poet, dramatist, and critic, writes: "Literature in its various forms has been completely absorbing to me throughout my life. Apart from my writing, I am more or less dedicated to promoting and exploring literature—as a university professor and a critic and reviewer. I am not conscious of being in any particular literary tradition, though I share with many of my contemporaries an intense interest in the formal aspects of writing;

JOYCE CAROL OATES

each of my books is an experiment of a kind, an investigation of the relationship between a certain consciousness and its formal, aesthetic expression. My method has always been to combine the 'naturalistic' world and the 'symbolic' method of expression, so that I am always —or usually—writing about real people in a real society, but the means of expression may be naturalistic, realistic, surreal, or parodistic. In this way I have, to my own satisfaction at least, solved the old problem—should one be faithful to the 'real' world, or to one's imagination?"

Joyce Carol Oates was born in Lockport, New York, a small city near Buffalo on the Erie Canal. She is one of the three children of Frederic James Oates, a tool and die designer, and the former Carolina Bush. The family was Roman Catholic. Joyce Carol Oates grew up in what Alfred Kazin describes as "that colorless, often frozen and inhospitable lonely country in western New York, outside of Lockport," and began her education in a one-room schoolhouse. She dismisses her childhood as "dull, ordinary, nothing people would be interested in," but she has also said that "a great deal frightened me." This may be why she took refuge so early in the life of the imagination. Even before she could write she drew picture stories, and some of her later "books" ran to two hundred pages. One of these early stories, written when she was fifteen, describes the rehabilitation of a drug addict through the discipline of caring for a black stallion.

The author graduated from the Central High School in Williamsville, New York, in 1956 and went on to Syracuse University, where she majored in English and minored in philosophy. Although her family seems not to have experienced the acute poverty of some of her fictional characters, it was only with the aid of scholarships that she was able to go to college and, Kazin says, she has retained "frugality, simplicity, even academic solemnity." At Syracuse she was Phi Beta Kappa and class valedictorian. She published in the university literary magazine and in 1959 won a *Mademoiselle* college fiction award with her story "In the Old World." Other stories began to appear in such magazines as *Cosmopolitan, Prairie Schooner,* the *Literary Review,* the *Southwest Review,* and the *Arizona Quarterly.*

Syracuse gave Joyce Carol Oates her B.A. in 1960 and a Knapp Fellowship took her to the University of Wisconsin, where she received her M.A. in 1961. Earlier the same year she married a Wisconsin Ph.D. candidate, Raymond Joseph Smith, whom she accompanied to his first teaching post in Beaumont, Texas. It was there that she discovered, quite by chance, that one of her stories had been cited in the Honor Roll of Martha Foley's annual *Best American Short Stories.* With this encouragement, she devoted most of her year in Texas to assembling the fourteen stories in her first book, *By the North Gate* (1963).

According to the *Times Literary Supplement,* Oates territory is a "muddy pastoral" of "farmhouses, gas stations, dirt roads, empty shacks, places with names out of *Pilgrim's Progress,* or with no names at all," and she has never deserted it for long. In some of her books this territory, roughly the western New York counties of Niagara and Erie, is ironically named Eden County. Oates once told a *Commonweal* interviewer that she was "really a romantic writer in the tradition of Stendhal and Flaubert" but thought she shared with Melville a "certain clumsiness and bluntness and blindness toward excess." Some of these qualities have reminded others of Theodore Dreiser, while her determination "to know what poverty really means . . . to test herself against it" has suggested comparisons with Zola. Other writers that she admires and has learned from include Kafka and Sartre, Dostoevsky and Flannery O'Connor, Freud and Nietzsche, and an important early influence was William Faulkner (which may help to account for the fact that her upstate New York characters "burn with the kind of short-fused violence and curious pride of privacy that have always been the exclusive hallmark of writers from the South").

"Swamps," the opening story in *By the North Gate,* is about an old man living by himself, discarded by his married son, who takes in a pregnant girl and cares for her until the child is born. When the girl murders her baby and leaves him, the old man moans: "They robbed me. They robbed me." In the title story, another old man is shattered when some boys senselessly kill his dog. In "Boys at a Picnic," a gang of young thugs break up a country picnic, causing the death of a girl with a weak heart—a confrontation with mortality that has a telling effect on one of the boys. R. D. Spector wrote of the collection that it had "emotional consistency and thematic unity that produce a single, effective fictional experience. It is one that, at times, seems too painful to bear. Yet it is also too interesting to ignore, too perceptive to turn away from and too honest to reject."

Joyce Carol Oates's first novel, *With Shuddering Fall* (1964), was written at a time of intense religious questioning which led to her renunciation of Catholicism. She has said that the book was "very personal" and in many ways "very autobiographical," and that it has certain parallels with the biblical story of Abraham—the father in the novel is "the father of the Old Testament who gives a command, as God gave a command to Abraham." In this novel, as in so much of her writing, Oates addresses herself to extreme violence—a physical violence which here is perhaps a symbolic expression of remembered emotional violence. The father-dominated teenager Karen Hertz meets the half-mad racing driver Shar, and from this encounter, as Ellen Joseph succinctly reported, "follows rape, carwreck, murderous confrontations, enraged lovemaking, the death of a rival driver, miscarriage, race-riot, suicide and insanity." Stanley Kauffmann found the dialogue false and the motivations maneuvered, and thought the book "arty egoism" rather than art, "all effort, no effect."

Some reviewers also complained of excessive contrivance in the stories in Joyce Carol Oates's next collection, *Upon the Sweeping Flood* (1966), which rehearse what was by then familiar Oates material—murder, suicide, abortion—in the lives of "people, born guilty, spending their lives sinning to justify their guilt," their "legacy of spiritual disgust out of the rural past." Joyce Carol Oates's Freudian reading of life is sometimes not far from the Catholic one she put aside.

It was the "thematic trilogy" of novels that followed—connected by the characters' preoccupation with money—which fully established her reputation, though in the first two of them it was thought that their "account of real life" was still somewhat distorted by "patterning and inevitabilities" imposed by the author. In the first of them, *A Garden of Earthly Delights*

(1967), the daughter of a migrant worker goes up the social ladder as the mistress, then the wife, of a rich man. "Clara," wrote a reviewer in the *Times Literary Supplement,* "is one of those apparently dewy girls without resources Miss Oates is as good at as Zola is, girls endowed with a magical sturdiness to survive neglect and boredom. It is this sturdiness which is destroyed when she marries her rich lover and settles to uphold standards of expectation she has always believed distinguished the rich from the poor." Elizabeth Janeway saw in the novel evidence of "a big solid talent getting under way" and was reminded of Dreiser rather than Zola by the sometimes clumsy writing, the "strong, vivid characters—ordinary, unromantic, but thoroughly alive.... This is, in a way, a dreary book despite its excellences: dreary, powerful, determined, limited and true." It received the Rosenthal Award and was a strong contender for the National Book Award, as was its successor.

This was *Expensive People* (1968), in which the author surprisingly combines black humor with a satire of suburbia in the journal of a fat boy genius who explains why he found it necessary to murder his beloved, unloving mother. The novel includes a short story attributed to the dead mother, who is supposed to have been a minor writer of national reputation, and a batch of imaginary reviews of *Expensive People—* bonuses which delighted some critics but not those who agreed with Robert M. Adams that Oates lacked "the delicacy of touch required for satire."

The trilogy's last and best volume is *Them* (1969), which brought Joyce Carol Oates the National Book Award for fiction in 1970. It is set in Detroit, where she lived and taught from 1961 to 1967, and focuses upon Loretta, another of Oates's sturdy dumb bunnies, upon the men who drift in and out of her life, and upon her children, whose heritage is the culture of poverty. As Robert M. Adams wrote, emotions in "the murky, half-submerged world of which she writes. . . . are superficial, temporary, and violent; they don't really 'express' anything, and behind their emptiness one feels flowering an impulse toward the meaningless, consuming violence of the 1967 riots in Detroit, with which the book effectively comes to an end."

Adams found this book "psychologically more subtle" than its predecessors, "structurally less predictable, but with the same strong flow of verbal and imaginative energy. . . . Generally, the current of narrative runs swift and strong, the language is lean and muscular; passages like that describing the mental degeneration of Maureen [Loretta's daughter] have a hallucinatory particularity. Apart from individual scenes, many·of which are handled with real theatrical *éclat,* the novel is written for long stretches with great change of pace, fine control and that special fictional rhythm which balances a reader's expectations anxiously between the unpredictable and the inevitable." An English reviewer was particularly struck by the novel's "dependence on the real events in the lives of real people, its avoidance of solutions and endings, the way violence is used as a motif but not as a device for changing the direction of the narrative or pointing a moral—all this suggests a new approach to her material. What is less satisfactory in the end is the somewhat wayward elaboration of character from events, the determined search for depth and complexity of feeling and the overwrought and literary language in which such feeling is conveyed."

In *The Wheel of Love* (1970), Joyce Carol Oates offers a gallery of academic or city women variously broken on the wheel in stories that were found modestly experimental in form, "a little colder and harder" in mood, and somewhat less "literary" than in earlier collections; at their best, it was thought, they offered the shock not merely of recognition, but of discovery. And at this stage in her career, attempts were being made to assess the overall significance of her large output. Her virtues, Richard Gilman decided, were "a native gift for 'story-telling'; a more or less clean narrative line . . . a passion for, amounting to an obsession with, what we like to call inner life; a good, almost photographic eye and ear for the minutiae of ordinary existence; a concern with some central human issues and conditions: the myths of love, the nature of female morale, the oppressions of family life, the aridity of urban and suburban existence, the quest for communion, the struggle against 'others.' " These qualities, Gilman thought, should earn her "a minor, respectable place if we weren't so inflationary in our estimates"—if we were not so grateful to her for satisfying a "longing for familiar ground, for what literature is supposed 'to be about' "; but at about the same time P. S. Prescott in *Look* came right out and called her "one of the best living American writers."

After all that, there was a shaky reception for *Wonderland* (1971), another illustrated catalog of American horrors, this time taking in madness, drug addiction, the assassination of President Kennedy, phallic mutilation, incest, and cannibalism; and starting off with a father's murder of all his family except his son. The son becomes a brilliant, moody brain surgeon, and another example of Oates's awareness of how "one powerful and grotesque person can transform everyone into himself." Geoffrey Wolff found it "as entertaining as a fatal plane crash," and "a bad, a very bad, single performance from a brilliant writer." Nor was there unmixed enthusiasm for *Do With Me What You Will* (1973), recording "the dumb, dreamy, intermittently panicked progress of Elena Ross into existential risk, sexual aggression"—and Joyce Carol Oates's progress from the nihilism of her earlier books to a new faith in the possibility of regeneration. But on this evidence critics could not agree whether she was "a well-promoted middle-brow heavy with intellectual pretensions" or "a potent myth-maker in the drab guise of a social naturalist." The difference of opinion was not resolved by *The Assassins* (1975), a vivid but too-long novel examining the causes and effects of a politician's murder through the interior monologues of his two brothers and his widow. *Childwold* (1976), in which a lonely eccentric falls reluctantly and disastrously in love with a girl of fourteen, seemed to Josephine Hendin the author's best novel in years, but other reviewers found it rambling and uncompelling.

If none of Oates's recent novels has carried off quite as many laurels as *Them,* her short stories have continued to sustain her reputation as "one of the most formidable talents of the age." And stories have poured from her—twenty-four in *Marriages and Infidelities* (1972), twenty-five in *The Goddess and Other Women* (1974), and, in *The Hungry Ghosts* (1974), seven slashing satires on writers, critics, reviewers, academics, and others of that stripe. *The Poisoned Kiss* (1975) is an oddity, a collection of stories which buzzed around in her head until she felt obliged to write them down, but which she feels she picked up out of the ether rather than created; she has designated them "translations" from the work of an imaginary Portuguese author, Fernandes de Briao. Most of the fifteen tales in *Crossing the Border* (1976) concern Americans in Canada, but "the real borders," Anne Tyler wrote, "are personal: the boundaries by which each individual defines himself and . . . fends off other individuals." Her characters "stand out sharply in what appears to be a deliberately stark landscape, where the most ordinary event—a phone call from a friend, a boy wading in a river— looms and threatens, and calls for a doubling of the border patrol." It was followed by *Night-Side,* a collection of stories devoted, one reviewer wrote, "to mystery and imagination, to other-worlds of dreams and nightmares, mediums and odd happenings."

Not content with producing twenty volumes of fiction in the first dozen years of her writing

595

life, Joyce Carol Oates has also been prolific as a poet and moderately so as a dramatist and critic. Her verse has its admirers, but not many of them are professional critics. She writes in this form on the same themes that engage her in fiction—sex, unrequited love, wasted lives, murder, abortion, and brutality. Reviewing her second collection, *Anonymous Sins* (1969), Calvin Bedient said that "the most important of her gifts, her dramatic imagination, seems shut off. Though about emotional experience, the poems do not connect with it but lie on top of it, curious inorganic aggregations of words." Another reviewer, of *Love and Its Derangements* (1970), found her verse defective "not only in its rhythm but in the crucial relation of the sound of words to their meaning," and Helen Vendler dismissed *Angel Fire* (1973) thus: "These poems have an awkward gait and an ungainly structure, an incoherence of parts and a lack of conclusiveness in the whole."

Oates's plays have not attracted much favorable attention either, but as a critic she has been taken more seriously. *The Edge of Impossibility* (1972) contains nine essays about "tragic forms in literature," and defines tragic art, rather interestingly, as growing out of "a break between self and community, a sense of isolation. At its base is fear." C. C. Park found these to be "difficult essays on difficult works" (by Chekhov, Shakespeare, Beckett, Ionesco, Yeats, and Mann, among others). "They are sometimes obscure, often awkwardly phrased. A phrase like 'the actual valuelessness of the contextual world' does much to explain why in reading her fiction, the content holds our attention while the language encourages us to skim." But most reviewers admired her urgent, dogged drive to communicate her frequently acute and valuable responses to particular works.

Nine more essays, collected in *New Heaven, New Earth* (1974), consider "the visionary experience in literature" as exemplified in the work of Henry James, Virginia Woolf, Lawrence, Beckett, Harriet Arnow, Sylvia Plath, Flannery O'Connor, Norman Mailer, Kafka, and others. Her interest centers on the problems the visionary artist faces in reconciling his transcendent vision with society's demands upon him. A reviewer in *Library Journal* described this as literary criticism based on Taoism and other Oriental systems of thought, and as a "brilliantly eccentric collection"—"a mystic herself, she considers her subjects as standing, in varying degrees, between the 'real' world and another world." And another critic remarked that, in spite of Oates's heavily academic language, her essays can sometimes be read as "highly intellectualized poetry."

Since 1967 Joyce Carol Oates has been an associate professor of English at the University of Windsor in Canada, teaching courses in creative writing and modern European literature. Her husband teaches eighteenth-century English literature there, and together they edit a literary magazine, *The Ontario Review*. She does most of her writing on a back terrace of their house in Windsor, looking out over the Detroit River. There she sits, she says, daydreaming, doodling, miserably doing nothing, until at times "my head seems crowded; there is a kind of pressure inside it, almost a frightening physical sense of confusion, fullness, dizziness. Strange people appear in my thoughts and define themselves slowly to me: first their faces, then their personalities and quirks and personal histories, then their relationships with other people, who very slowly appear, and a kind of 'plot' then becomes clear to me as I figure out how all these people came together and what they are doing. . . . When the story is more or less coherent and has emerged from the underground, then I can begin to write quite quickly"—up to forty or fifty pages a day: "It occurs to me that I am really transcribing dreams."

The author is tall and slim, with enormous dark eyes "burning," as one writer put it, "in a dove's face." She gives an impression of great fragility, and interviewers frequently find it difficult to believe that she could bring herself even to read about the horrors with which she fills her books. She cannot explain her preoccupation with violence—"am I personally haunted by the fear of violence, the need for violence, or do I reflect everyone else's fears about it?" According to Alfred Kazin "she is shy, doesn't drink or smoke, has no small talk, no jokes, no anecdotes, no gossip, no malice, no verbal embroidery of the slightest kind. . . . Joyce Carol Oates is a square, a lovely schoolmarm, but her life is in her head, her life is all the stories she carries in her head." In her spare time she likes to paint and listen to music, and she also enjoys movies, travel, bicycling, and a little tennis. She won the O. Henry Prize in 1967 and held a Guggenheim fellowship in 1967-1968, among other awards and honors.

Kazin believes that Joyce Carol Oates is "radical," not programmatically but "in her sweetly brutal sense of what American experience is really like." His deepest feeling about her "is that her mind is unbelievably crowded with psychic existences"; writing to "relieve her mind of the people who haunt it," she is, he thinks, "not artistically ambitious enough"—the reader is involved in her work because of her own "intense connection with her material," but we "miss the perfectly suggestive shapes that modern art and fiction have taught us to venerate." It is a theory that accounts very well for the reservations that continue to be expressed about her fiction, even by those who consider her a major writer. She herself appears to be almost unbelievably humble about her work; she regards herself as no more than "a process recording phases of American life," with her most serious work yet to come.

PRINCIPAL WORKS: *Novels*—With Shuddering Fall, 1964; A Garden of Earthly Delights, 1967; Expensive People, 1968; Them, 1969; Wonderland, 1971; Do With Me What You Will, 1973; The Assassins: A Book of Hours, 1975; Childwold, 1976; The Triumph of the Spider Monkey, 1976; Son of the Morning, 1978. *Short Stories*—By the North Gate, 1963; Upon the Sweeping Flood, 1966; The Wheel of Love, 1970; Marriages and Infidelities, 1972; The Goddess and Other Women, 1974; Where Are You Going, Where Have You Been? Stories of Young America, 1974; The Hungry Ghosts: Seven Allusive Comedies, 1974; The Seduction, 1975; The Poisoned Kiss and Other Stories From the Portuguese, 1975; Crossing the Border, 1976; Night-Side: Eighteen Stories, 1977. *Poetry*—Women in Love, 1968; Anonymous Sins, 1969; Love and Its Derangements, 1970; Cupid and Psyche, 1970; Angel Fire, 1973; Dreaming America, 1973; The Fabulous Beasts, 1975; Women Whose Lives Are Food, Men Whose Lives Are Money, 1978. *Published Plays*—Miracle Play, 1974. *Criticism*—The Edge of Impossibility: Tragic Forms in Literature, 1972; The Hostile Sun: The Poetry of D.H. Lawrence, 1973; New Heaven, New Earth: The Visionary Experience in Literature, 1974. *As Editor*—Scenes From American Life: Contemporary Short Fiction, 1972.

ABOUT: Bellamy, J.D. (ed.) The New Fiction, 1975; Contemporary Authors 5-8 1st revision, 1969; Current Biography, 1970; Diamondstein, B. Open Secrets, 1972; Vinson, J. (ed.) Contemporary Novelists, 1976; Who's Who in America, 1976-1977. *Periodicals*—Biography News May 1974; Book World April 23, 1972; Commonweal December 5, 1969; Commentary June 1970; Harper's August 1971; Nation January 5, 1974; New Republic October 27, 1973; January 3, 1977; New York Review of Books December 17, 1964; February 12, 1970; October 21, 1971; January 24, 1974; New York Times Book Review November 10, 1963; September 10, 1967; September 28, 1969; October 25, 1970; October 24, 1971; June 4, 1972; October 1, 1972; April 1, 1973; October 14, 1973; September 1, 1974; November 24, 1974; August 31, 1975; July 18, 1976; November 28, 1976; Newsweek March 23, 1970; December 11, 1972; Publishers Weekly October 22, 1973; June 26, 1978; Saturday Review October 26, 1968; Time October 10, 1969; Times Literary Supplement March 9, 1973; January 11, 1974; Toronto Globe March 14, 1970.

OCA, MARCO ANTONIO MONTES DE.
See MONTES DE OCA

*OKIGBO, CHRISTOPHER (IFEANYICHUKWU) (1932–August 1967), Nigerian poet, was born in the small forest village of Ojoto in Onitsha province, Eastern Nigeria. He was

*o kē' bo

CHRISTOPHER OKIGBO

the fourth of the five children of Anna and James I. Okigbo. Like most members of the Igbo tribe, the family was Roman Catholic. Okigbo studied at Umulobia Catholic School, where his father was a teacher, and in 1945 went for his secondary education to Umuahia Government College. He is said to have been a restless child, intelligent, active, and argumentative. He was a good student, particularly enjoying mathematics, literature, and Latin, and was equally successful at such school sports as football and cricket.

From 1951 to 1956 Okigbo studied at the newly-founded University College at Ibadan, graduating in classics. His contemporaries there included Wole Soyinka, Chinua Achebe, and John Pepper Clark, men who, with Okigbo himself, went on to establish themselves as the principal luminaries of a brilliant generation of Nigerian writers. Okigbo edited the *University Weekly* at Ibadan and tried his hand as a poet and as a translator of Greek and Latin verse; at this time, however, he thought of himself primarily as a musician and composer. It was not until 1957, when he had left the University College, that he began to take himself seriously as a poet.

It was part of Okigbo's complex character that he was fascinated by the idea of big business and high finance (for which he showed not the slightest aptitude). He worked briefly for the Nigerian Tobacco Company and the United Africa Company before serving for two years as private secretary to the Federal Minister of Information in Lagos. In 1959–1960 he taught Latin at Fiditi College in Western Nigeria, then returned to the Eastern Region as assistant university librarian at the new University of Nigeria at Nsukka. He quit this post in 1962 to become West African representative for Cambridge University Press, later serving also as an editor with the Mbara Press of Ibadan and as West African editor of the literary magazine *Transition,* published in Kampala, Uganda.

At the outbreak of the Nigerian civil war in 1967, Okigbo was working for an Italian business organization called Wartrade and planning to found a small publishing house in Enugu in partnership with Chinua Achebe. He abandoned his job and the publishing venture in order to join the Biafran army as a volunteer. In late August 1967, fighting as a major against the invading forces of the Nigerian Federation, Okigbo was killed in action. He was decorated posthumously with the Biafran National Order of Merit.

In the future, when a better perspective on African literature has developed, Okigbo will probably be seen as a transitional poet who represents a special, unrepeatable moment of attempted synthesis. The generation of his parents, flourishing 1910–1940, undertook a general movement away from traditional African culture. This was the generation of Christian converts whose new religion was shallowly implanted but rigidly held, who were all the more straitlaced for fear of "backsliding" into the exuberant pagan life still continuing around them. By contrast, the ensuing generation felt drawn back, if at first only by curiosity, to rediscover and experience all those currents of traditional life from which they had been cut off by a combination of missionary prohibitions, Western education, and increasing social mobility.

The intellectual leaders of this new generation were concentrated in a few elite grammar schools, like Umuahia, and in the University College at Ibadan. Consequently they developed a new kind of national "age-grade" consciousness which did something to replace the old tribal initiation rituals that most of them were denied. As the most consciously alienated members of their generation, they felt it their particular duty to search for a way of uniting both strands of their divided heritage and achieving a synthesis of African and European cultures.

Okigbo may be seen as the representative voice of that search, to which he devoted his brief career in poetry. In his own family there were devout Catholics like his parents and devout followers of the tribal religion like his maternal grandfather, who had been a priest of the local river-goddess Idoto. Okigbo was considered to be a reincarnation of this grandfather and, though brought up as a practicing Catholic, was fully conscious that the groves, shrines, and life-giving stream of his village were all devoted to another, older, and perhaps stronger religion. But his academic training in classics and mathematics, and his own highly eclectic reading, gave him a point of entry to literature far removed from the verbal art of his own culture. Virgil, Ovid, Eliot, and Pound appear to have been stronger influences on his early poetry than the oral literature of the Igbo.

The mainstream of his poetic development, starting with *Heavensgate* (1962) and continuing through *Limits* (1962) to "Distances" (1964), may be seen as a steady progress towards an integration of his divided heritage. His recovery of the African part of this heritage is imagined as a moment of union with a goddess, the "watermaid" who appears to the poet in fleeting moments of vision: "So brief her presence—/ match-flare in wind's breath—"

These visionary moments must be earned by a process of ritual cleansing and spiritual preparation, which is first seen in terms of a prodigal son returning from the Western adventure to the shrine of his ancestors:

> Before you, Mother Idoto, naked I stand
> before your watery presence a prodigal
>
> leaning on an oilbean
> lost in your legend. . . .
>
> (from "Heavensgate")

Okigbo has himself written of this moment of return: "This goddess is the earth mother, and also the mother of the whole family. . . . And . . . when I started taking poetry very seriously, it was as though I had felt a sudden call to begin performing my full functions as the chief priest of Idoto." Gradually the poet realizes that a further initiation, a further cleansing, is needed to heal the "scar of the crucifix/ over the breast/ by red blade inflicted."

At the beginning of his second poetic sequence, "Siren Limits" (the first section of *Limits*), Okigbo declares that he is now reconciled to his sensual nature and recognizes that the goddess does not demand that he reject any part of himself in order to be united with her:

> Queen of the damp half-light,
> I have had my cleansing,
> Emigrant with air-borne nose,
> The he-goat-on-heat.

In the course of *Limits* the prodigal image is gradually abandoned and the search for self-renewal comes to be seen in terms of an operation in which the goddess wields the knife above the altar/operating-table and the white-robed poet/pilgrim/patient awaits wholeness with terror as well as joy:

> When you have finished
> and done up my stitches,
> Wake me near the altar,
> and this poem will be finished. . . .
>
> (from "Siren Limits")

The imagery of *Limits,* in which the Chapel Perilous becomes one with the operating theatre and the goddess must first be experienced as a blood-stained surgeon before she can be known as complement and love, is continued in "Distances." Of this sequence, Okigbo wrote in the introduction to his collected poems, *Labyrinths:* "The self that suffers, that experiences, ultimately finds fulfilment in a form of psychic union with the supreme spirit that is both destructive and creative. The process is one of sensual anesthesia, of total liberation from all physical and emotional tension; the end result, a state of aesthetic grace." Thus the goddess is first seen in her aspect as the ministrant of death—"at her feet rolled their heads like cut fruits;/ about her fell/ their severed members, numerous as locusts"—before she can be approached and finally known:

> I have fed out of the drum
> I have drunk out of the cymbal
>
> I have entered your bridal
> chamber; and lo,
>
> I am the sole witness to my homecoming.
>
> (from "Distances")

The maturing of Okigbo's art within this poetic sequence, which occupied him for some five years (1959–1964) is remarkable; having achieved this mastery of self and voice he was ready to turn his poetry towards more public concerns. This is already apparent in "Fragments out of the Deluge" (the concluding section of *Limits*) and in the "Lament of the Drums" (1964), which is certainly in part a lament for the imprisoned Chief Awolowo and for the crumbling political fortunes of Nigeria: "But distant seven winds invite us and our cannons/ To limber our membranes for a dance of elephants."

Already in these "Lament" poems Okigbo begins to develop a quality resembling that of traditional Igbo poetry. In place of the intense self-communion of his early work, there is a growing awareness of the poet as a singer-musician with a specific craft and a specific audience.

Using the traditional Igbo orchestra, the poet tunes his drums to lament the fallen leader. The refrains also are more like those of his own people, less reminiscent of Eliot's "Hollow Men," the early Pound, or the modern Spanish poets from whom he once borrowed liberally. This more authoritative and public voice grows stronger in his final sequence, "Path of Thunder," written in the last two years of his life. These poems are entirely concerned with the gathering Nigerian crisis and the ever-increasing threat of civil war. There is also a sense of readiness for the sacrifice which Okigbo was about to make at a time when most of his intellectual peers took refuge in public relations and information posts well behind the battle lines:

> The eagles are suddenly there,
> New stars of an iron dawn;
>
> So let the horn paw the air howling goodbye. . . .
>
> O mother mother Earth, unbind me; let this be
>   my last testament, let this be
> The ram's hidden wish to the sword the sword's
>   secret prayer to the scabbard—

Okigbo was killed in a skirmish with the invading forces near Nsukka, leaving behind a wife and daughter, Safinat and Ibrahimat, from whom he had recently been estranged but to whom he dedicated *Labyrinths,* published four years later. In this collection he omitted his early and heavily derivative "Four Canzones," as well as revising extensively his major sequences of 1960–1967. His death and the sudden flowering of his work in the last four years of his life made a profound mark on the poetry of his younger contemporaries. His influence is strong, often too strong, upon the work of such Nigerian poets as M.J.C. Echeruo, Okogbule Wonodi, Romanus Egudu, and Pol Ndu. But most of those named have also been typical of their generation in showing a specific interest in Igbo traditional verse. And precisely because of Okigbo's own journey towards cultural integration, they have been able to receive their greatest influence, not from alien literatures, but from a fellow African who had already blazed the trail towards a new kind of poetry.

A gregarious and hospitable man, Okigbo was an exuberant conversationalist who liked nothing better than literary discussion and argument. Regarding himself as a poet shaped not only by his African heritage and setting but by classical, English, and European literary traditions (as well as by both African and European music), he had little time for *négritude*—what he called the "black mystique"—and has been criticized for this by some of his contemporaries. On the other hand, in Ali A. Mazrui's fanciful novel *The Trial of Christopher Okigbo,* he is indicted for his partisan zeal in the Biafran cause, which is viewed as a lapse from his professed commitment to a more universal view of the role of the artist.

S. O. Anozie, author of a useful monograph about Okigbo, wrote that "the structure of Okigbo's personality as a man was complex. Possessed of a strong will and great independence of mind, he was temperamentally incapable ... of letting his personality suffer any form of eclipse. Yet he was sometimes shy and withdrawn ... [His] revolt was an essentially artistic one. ... Prophetic, menacing, terrorist, violent, protesting—his poetry was all of these. ... But in a society such as Okigbo lived and wrote in, where the few leaders could hardly afford the cheap luxury of reading their own writers, ... [his] scarring message was ... safely insulated, by its own shrewd and learned obscurity." It should be said that the obscurity referred to here is not impenetrable. It might be better to call Okigbo a difficult rather than an obscure poet. With few exceptions, the difficulties of his work disappear as the reader becomes more familiar with it and perceives the continuity of theme and structure. Okigbo's poems appeal to the memory and, once read, remain in the mind. "Pointed Arches," a prose work in which Okigbo set out to record the growth of his own creative impulse, remains unpublished.

PRINCIPAL WORKS: Heavensgate, Mbari Publications, 1962; Limits (first published in *Transition,* July-August 1962) Mbari Publications, 1964; Labyrinths (collected poems), 1971.

ABOUT: Anozie, S.O. Christopher Okigbo: Creative Rhetoric, 1972; Awoonor, K. The Breast of the Earth, 1975; Beier, U. (ed.) Introduction to African Literature, 1965; Cartey, W. Whispers From a Continent, 1969; Duerden D. and Pieterse, C. (eds.) African Writers Talking, 1972; Herdick, D.E. (ed.) African Authors I, 1973; King, B. (ed.) Introduction to Nigerian Literature, 1972; Moore, G. (ed.) African Literature and the Universities, 1965; Moore G. The Chosen Tongue, 1969; Wright, E. (ed.) The Critical Evaluation of African Literature, 1973. *Periodicals*—African Literature Today 1 1968, 3 1969, 6 1973; Black Orpheus August 1964, August 1966; Journal of Commonwealth Literature July 1970; Transition 18 1965, 22 1965.

*OKUDZHAVA, BULAT SHALVOVICH (May 9, 1924–), Russian poet, singer, novelist, and short story writer, writes: "Born 1924 in Moscow of Georgian father and Armenian mother. Was brought up in Moscow by-lanes. My mother tongue is Russian. In 1942 when seventeen years old voluntarily joined combat army. Served as a soldier. Was wounded. Got to

*o kōō dzhä vǝ

BULAT SHALVOVICH OKUDZHAVA

understand a lot. When the war was over, graduated from university and got a job in a village school teaching Russian language and literature. Was writing bad poetry and felt highly complacent. After a while started writing for a provincial paper. In 1956 went back to Moscow. Worked as an editor in the Young Guard Publishing House, then as poetry editor of *Literary Gazette.* In 1962 gave up this job to make writing my profession. My poetry became a little better, but I felt a growing dissatisfaction and in a few years changed over to prose. Published six poetry collections: *Lyrical Poems, Islands, On the Way to Tinatin, Gay Drummer, March the Generous, Arbat, My Arbat.* Also published a long story, *Lots of Luck, Kid,* and novels: *My Poor Avrosimov, Shipov's Adventures, Amateurs' Travels,* some books for children, some film scripts, a play.

"Set many of my poems to music and gave recitals—something that scandalized some of my pen-colleagues, composers, singers and guitar players.

"Records of my songs have been brought out in France, Poland, Italy, the United States, West Germany, Bulgaria, Sweden, Chile, Israel. Two records have been put out at home.

"My books have appeared in many countries: West Germany, Britain, France, Italy, Yugoslavia, Poland, the United States, DDR, Czechoslovakia, Hungary, Japan, Turkey.

"Literary critics have written rather a lot about my writings, but since I don't collect other people's opinions about me, making a list of these writings is a feat almost impossible for me.

"Whatever I have had the time to write was written about myself, since there is nobody in the world known to me better. It considerably facilitates my work.

"I believe my literary career to be a lucky one: I am always writing things that give me pleasure and earn me a living to boot."

It was at the University of Tbilisi (Tiflis) in Georgia that Okudzhava studied when he left the army. He graduated in 1950 and subsequently taught in a village near Kaluga before turning to journalism. His poems began to appear in magazines in the early 1950s and his first verse collections soon followed, *Lirika* (Lyrical Poems) in 1956 and *Ostrova* (Islands) in 1959. He was poetry editor of *Literaturnaya gazeta* (Literary Gazette) when it published Yevtushenko's famous and controversial poem "Babi Yar" in 1962, and lost his job on that account. His subsequent collections include *Vesely barabanshchik* (Gay Drummer, 1964) and *Mart velikodushny* (Generous March, 1967).

During the 1960s Okudzhava was an immensely popular participant with poets like Yevtushenko and Voznesensky in the public verse readings that were such a feature of the Russian literary scene in those years. Unlike his companions Okudzhava did not recite his verses, but set them to music and sang them, accompanying himself on the guitar. Patricia Blake, who attended one such performance, says that Okudzhava was "a small dark man . . . with fuzzy receding hair and a minute moustache"; his audience, made up mostly of young people, seemed to know all of his songs by heart and called for them by name. Okudzhava's "vulgar" songs displeased the party hacks, but his recordings, and unofficial tapes of his performances, have circulated all over the Soviet Union as well as in Europe and the United States. The film *WR: Mysteries of the Organism* by the Yugoslav director Makavejev ends with Okudzhava singing a typically ironic ballad.

Daniel Weissbort, in his anthology *Post-War Russian Poetry,* wrote of Okudzhava that his "romantic yet ironical vision of the everyday world of the city . . . updates and revitalizes the decadent, sentimental pre-Revolutionary ballad tradition. . . . Okudzhava is a master of light-serious verse whose great charm, unfortunately, cannot be adequately conveyed in translation." A number of his lyrics have appeared in English nevertheless; "Midnight Trolleybus," translated here by J.R. Rowland, is one of several in Weissbort's own anthology:

When I find that my troubles are too much, at last,
  And despair sets in
Then I catch a blue trolleybus as it drives past

The last one, the chance one. . . .

Late night trolleybus, open your door:
  I know at cold midnight
How your sailors, the passengers riding on board
  You, come to my rescue.

I've often escaped from my troubles with them
  Our shoulders touching—
Imagine, how much comfort there is
  In silence, their silence.

Through Moscow the midnight trolleybus sails
  Moscow flows like a river:
And the ache that has throbbed like a bird in my brain
  Dies away and is over.

Andrew Field, in *The Complection of Russian Literature,* gives his own version of the first poem in Okudzhava's early collection *Ostrova:*

"Goodbye, my hostess."
  And you're off, a wanderer,
And to your road there's no end.
And with you beyond the gate stretches,
Beyond the outskirts, far, far off
the song of a woman's
  "Goodbye now,"
warm as steaming milk.
Everything will pass,
  but it will stay. . . .

"This poem," Field writes, "can serve as a key to Okudzhava's lyricism. It is permeated with goodness and tenderness toward people, but it consists of little things, prosaic elements and half-confessions. Frequently the poet leads us to believe that his poems refer to only ordinary and insignificant things. He prefers appearing a bit foolish in order not to seem stilted and grandiloquent, and avoids significance, it seems, in favor of some chance, secondary matter . . . or he speaks about an important thing inadvertently, by chance ('And bullets? There were bullets. A lot went down. But what's to say about them?—war'), or he's silent and lets us guess everything ourselves. Although Okudzhava's poems are clear and simple in their language and form, there is complexity in the range of psychological and intonational shades and reflexes which they radiate." And Robin Milner-Gulland has said that Okudzhava stands in a place of his own among the poets of his generation: "Though he is the undisputed master of light verse in Russia, most of his written work has a fundamental basis of seriousness and pathos, and he is a true poet."

Although his verse showed a steady development in technical subtlety and skill, Okudzhava, as he says above, "felt a growing dissatisfaction" with his work in this form, and since the mid-

1960s has concentrated mainly on prose. His first published piece in this form was the short story "Bud' zdorov, shkolyar" (1961, translated by R. Szulkin as "Lots of Luck, Kid!" and by John Richardson as "Good Luck, Schoolboy!"). It is a series of impressionistic episodes based on Okudzhava's own war experiences. From the beginning, when the bewildered teen-age narrator finds himself lost and crying on his second day at the front, to the end, when he is lying wounded in a hospital, it is a disillusioned and disillusioning account of war as it really is. Not surprisingly, the story was criticized for its "infantile psychology" and "mawkish pacifism" when it first appeared in Konstantin Paustovsky's famous anthology *Tarusskiye stranitsy* (Pages From Tarusa, 1961), a mixture of work by young Soviet authors and by older emigré writers which were withdrawn from circulation because of its liberal tone.

As he says, Okudzhava has also written children's books, screenplays, and novels, the latter including *Bedny Avrosimov* (My Poor Avrosimov, 1970) and *Glotok svobody* (A Gulp of Freedom, 1973), about the Decembrist conspiracy of 1825 and its leader Pavel Pestel, portraying the rebels as recognizable human beings rather than as the heroic supermen of Soviet legend.

But Okudzhava's major prose work so far has been a novel which was published in Russian in the magazine *Druzhba narodov* (Friendship of Peoples) and first appeared in book form in translation as *The Extraordinary Adventures of Secret Agent Shipov in Pursuit of Count Leo Tolstoy in the Year 1862* (1973). This satirical fantasy about bureaucratic obtuseness is based on facts which are themselves fantastic enough. By 1862 Tolstoy had started a school for peasant children on his estate at Yasnaya Polyana, aided by radical young students, and the police sent a secret agent to investigate. This was Shipov, an engagingly seedy character from the Moscow underworld, who, without wasting too much time on what might be happening at Yasnaya Polyana, entertained himself lavishly at the state's expense in the nearby town of Tula. Arrested in due course for "indiscretion and drunkenness," the resourceful Shipov justified his expense account with a wholly fictional report claiming that Tolstoy was producing illegal manifestos on hidden printing presses in his house, which was riddled with secret doors and passages and guarded by a private army. The large force of police that raided the estate of course found nothing. Okudzhava uses police reports and Tolstoy's letters as a framework for a series of fantastic episodes in which Shipov is catapulted from trailing pickpockets into a world of high intrigue, wild journeys by sledge or carriage, pursuing wolves, involvement with a beautiful young widow, and final escape from the convoy taking him off to Siberia.

A reviewer in the *Times Literary Supplement,* discussing Heather Maisner's "rather stiff Americanised translation," objected that Okudzhava "has taken refuge from the real issues of the secret agent's work in farce and magic.... and the result is a disappointing pastiche of various classical styles which never comes to life on its own account." Reviewers of the original, however, generally admired the novel, which one placed in the tradition of Gogol; George Reavey found it "certainly one of the most refreshing literary phenomena of the past decade." *Nocturne* (1978), Antonina W. Bouis's translation of the novel Okudzhava refers to above as *Amateurs' Travels,* is also set in pre-revolutionary Russia and tells its story partly through letters and memoirs. Unless the translator has failed to convey some intended irony, this story is a romantic one, about the adventures and sad love affairs of Prince Myatlev of the Imperial Guard. It was found of "little more than passing interest."

PRINCIPAL WORKS IN ENGLISH TRANSLATION: *Novels*—The Extraordinary Adventures of Secret Agent Shipov in Pursuit of Count Leo Tolstoy in the Year 1862, 1973; Nocturne, 1978. *Poems in* Bosley, K. (and others, eds.) Russia's Other Poets, 1968; Reavey, G. (ed.) The New Russian Poets 1953-1968, 1968; Weissbort, D. (ed.) Post-War Russian Poetry, 1974. *Stories in* Blake, P. and Hayward, M. (eds.) Half-way to the Moon, 1964; Field, A. (ed.) Pages From Tarusa, 1963; Pomorska, K. (ed.) Fifty Years of Russian Prose, 1971.

ABOUT: Field, A. (ed.) The Complection of Russian Literature, 1971; International Who's Who, 1978–79; Moore, H.T. and Parry, A. Twentieth Century Russian Literature, 1974; Prominent Personalities in the USSR, 1968. *Periodicals*—Books and Bookmen November 1974; Times Literary Supplement June 29, 1973.

OLSEN, TILLIE (January 14, 1913–), American novelist and short story writer, was born in Omaha, Nebraska, the daughter of Samuel and Ida (Beber) Lerner. She turned early to books, and at fifteen was deeply inspired and influenced by Rebecca Harding Davis's grimly naturalistic story "Life in the Iron Mills." Tillie Lerner's formal education ended when she left high school. Her passion for writing survived, however, and she began her first novel when she was nineteen. In 1936, when she was twenty-three, she married Jack Olsen. They had four daughters, and during most of the twenty years it took to raise them, Tillie Olsen was contributing to the family income by working—mostly in San Francisco, mostly as a typist—in the warehouse, food processing, and service industries; she was

Thomas Victor © 1978

TILLIE OLSEN

once jailed for her participation in a longshore-men's strike.

During all those years, she has said, "the simplest circumstances for creation did not exist. Nevertheless writing, the hope of it, was 'the air I breathed.'" She snatched what time she could for reading, began stories and finished a few. In 1956-1957 she was able to accept a creative writing fellowship at Stanford University. In 1959, when she felt that her unborn stories were "festering" within her, a Ford grant bought her two years of freedom from office work. The reprieve came almost too late: "Always roused by the writing, always denied," she was by then, she says, "like a woman made frigid. I had to learn response, to trust this possibility for fruition that had not been before."

Her first book, *Tell Me a Riddle,* appeared in 1961, when she was forty-eight. It contains four stories—all she had completed by then. In the long title story, which brought her the 1961 O. Henry Award, an old married couple are torn by a quarrel whose "stubborn, gnarled roots" reach back further into their forty-seven years together than they can remember. It is only when the woman is drifting in and out of consciousness on her deathbed that she is able to relive the love and deep sexual attraction that had brought them together as young people in tsarist Russia. And her husband, listening reluctantly to her ramblings, is finally brought to acknowledge their truth, and remembers "all the heavy passion he had loved to rouse from her." Dorothy Parker said of this story that Tillie Olsen "can spend no word that is not the right one."

"Hey Sailor, What Ship?" is about a boozy, lonely, soft-hearted seaman whose only close re-

lationship is with a man whose life he once saved and his family, on whom he lavishes gifts and money. These people love him but are increasingly embarrassed by his rowdy and uncontrolled drinking, and in the end he walks away from them, knowing that he will not return. Another friendship ends just as painfully and helplessly in "O Yes," where a white girl, shocked and terrified by the raw emotion she witnesses during a baptismal service in a black church, miserably separates herself from the black girl who has been her best friend. And in "I Stand Here Ironing" a mother, musing about her teenage daughter as she irons, faces with unembittered sadness the fact that because of poverty and divorce and the way things are, the girl's potential will never be realized.

"What Mrs. Olsen sees and conveys to us so sharply," wrote Gene Baro, "is the essential tragedy of everyday human existence, the downward movement of life. In her effort to discover underlying and perhaps timeless meanings of existence, she confronts her subjects with a nakedness of feeling that is often painful. . . . These stories are not to be paraphrased; they are to be read, experienced, pondered. They go deep, perhaps because they are both deeply felt and controlled by a discriminating intelligence." It seemed to R. M. Elman that "occasionally the prose will get out of hand, or, in choosing to be on such intimate terms with her characters, Mrs. Olsen will descend to a literal-mindedness which is her humanity unrestrained. Even so, there are stories in this collection which are perfectly realized works of art." The author's own long struggle with silence had left its mark on the collection, as Annie Gottlieb pointed out: "These four stories reverberate with wonder at the human urge to creation and with pity and pain at its crushing, again and again, by the circumstances of life." By the time it was reprinted in paperback in 1971, *Tell Me a Riddle* had become an "underground classic."

In 1962-1964 Tillie Olsen was a fellow of the Radcliffe Institute for Independent Study. She received a grant in 1966 from the National Endowment for the Arts, and in 1969-1970 began a new phase of her life as a visiting professor at Amherst College, Massachusetts. Further academic appointments have followed: she was a visiting instructor at Stanford University in the spring of 1971, writer-in-residence at Massachusetts Institute of Technology in 1973, and visiting professor at the University of Massachusetts in 1974. She held a Guggenheim fellowship in 1975-1976.

Tillie Olsen thought she had lost or destroyed the novel she had begun in 1932 and worked on intermittently until her first child was born, but in 1973 she found parts of various drafts of it among other old papers. Working in the "solitude and protection" of the MacDowell Colony in New Hampshire, in "arduous partnership" with her younger self, she pieced together what she could of the book, with "no rewriting, no new writing." The nearly two hundred pages rescued in this way were published in 1974 as *Yonnondio: From the Thirties.* Jim Holbrook, a Wyoming coal miner, tries his luck as a tenant farmer in Wyoming and then, when the farm fails, goes to work in a slaughterhouse in a prairie town that might be Omaha. Sometimes the effort to support and sustain his family is too much for him: he drinks, he beats his wife or his children. Then he recovers himself, is tender and remorseful, and tries again. Anna Holbrook, herself exhausted and often embittered, sometimes (as once in an interlude of leisure following a miscarriage) glimpses the possibility of "happiness and farness and selfness." And Mazie, the oldest child, whose developing mind provides the novel's chief focus, hangs on as best she can to the dreams that drudgery and squalor are already threatening to stifle in her. The novel's title is from a poem by Walt Whitman—a lament for the aborigines, who left "no picture, poem, statement, passing them to the future."

The Holbrooks' struggle to get out from under, wrote Annie Gottlieb, "is a terrible losing battle. . . and Tillie Olsen portrays it with relentless compassion and with a stark, impressionistic vividness unlike the style of any other writer I know," though not, in the first part of the book, without passages of melodrama and sentimentality—reminders that the book was written by a very young author. These early pages contain some notable writing in the proletarian mode of the time, together with a prophetic but unstrident feminism which does not inhibit "a deep sympathy for the restlessness and degraded pride of the men." Later, Annie Gottlieb writes, *Yonnondio* "moves into myth, an odyssey indeed, and its style into incantation," and then develops again as "its archetypal figures—the shawled women waiting around a caved-in mine, the men slumped on the front porch . . . deepen into individuals." For a very few reviewers the novel's flaws outweighed its virtues, but for many, like Annie Gottlieb, it was "another victory over silence" for Tillie Olsen.

The author received an award in 1975 from the American Academy of Arts and Letters for her "distinguished contribution to American letters." She held a Guggenheim fellowship in 1975-1976.

PRINCIPAL WORKS: Tell Me a Riddle: A Collection, 1961 (enlarged edition published in U.K., 1964); Yonnondio: From the Thirties, 1974; Silences, 1978.

ABOUT: Contemporary Authors 1-4 1st revision, 1967; Vinson, J. (ed.) Contemporary Novelists, 1976; Who's Who in America, 1976-1977. *Periodicals*—Chicago Sunday Tribune October 29, 1961; Christian Science Monitor November 9, 1961; Commonweal December 8, 1961; Harper's October 1965; Nation November 30, 1974; New Republic November 13, 1961; March 30, 1974; New York Times Book Review November 12, 1961; March 31, 1974; Sewanee Review Winter 1963; Studies in Short Fiction Fall 1963; Time October 27, 1961.

*ONETTI, JUAN CARLOS (July 1, 1909–), Uruguayan novelist, short story writer, and journalist, was born and grew up in Montevideo, the second child of Carlos Onetti and the former Honoria Borges. His father was a civil servant in the customs and excise department. Onetti left high school before completing his studies and for the next few years moved from one job to another as porter, clerk, waiter, and salesman. He married for the first time in 1930; three more marriages were to follow in 1934, 1945, and 1955.

In 1932 Onetti moved to Buenos Aires in Argentina, where he lived for two years, publishing his first short stories in the literary supplements of *La Prensa* and *La Nación.* His literary interests developed alongside a preoccupation with the political and social issues of the 1930s. Fascinated even as a youth by the Soviet Union, he longed to visit Russia in order to study at close quarters a "nation genuinely engaged in pursuing a socialist program" but could find no way of doing so. A similar urge gripped him in 1936, when he tried but failed to make his way to Spain to join the Republican forces in the civil war.

His first novel, *El pozo* (The Well), appearing in 1939, broke completely with the literary conventions of the time and ushered in the Latin American "new novel." This deeply pessimistic book, plain and almost journalistic in style, introduced in Eladio Linacero the archetypal Onetti antihero, "sólo y entre la mugre" (alone amidst the grime). An inarticulate dreamer, in love with youth and innocence, he has come no closer to the expression of his vision than to rape the adolescent Ana María. Eladio's politically militant contemporary Lázaro has his ideals; the poet Cordes has his beautiful thoughts; but for Eladio himself there is nothing but an unassuageable sense of guilt and the certainty of isolation in a world of eternal darkness: "I feel that my life is nothing more than the passing of fractions of time, one after the other, like the sound

*o net′ i

JUAN CARLOS ONETTI

of a clock, running water, coins being counted. I'm lying flat and time is passing."

The same year, 1939, Onetti became editor of *Marcha,* a new weekly magazine which has since become one of the most respected and influential in Latin America. From the beginning, under Onetti's editorship, *Marcha* did a great deal to promote new literary trends in culture-starved Montevideo. He himself contributed humorous articles to the magazine, signing himself "Groucho Marx." Onetti left *Marcha* in 1942 to join the Reuter News Agency, serving first in Montevideo (1942-1943), then in Buenos Aires (1943-1946). He remained in Buenos Aires thereafter until 1955 as editor of the magazine *Vea y Lea.*

In 1941, meanwhile, Onetti had published his second novel, *Tierra de nadie* (No Man's Land). Set this time in Buenos Aires, it is, like its predecessor, a totally despairing portrait of a demoralized society and, in the author's own words, of a type of "morally indifferent individual who has lost faith and all interest in his own fate." Some contemporary critics were displeased by "the continual exhibition of sordid settings" in this novel, "of rooms in which the sexual act is repeatedly carried out," but there was also much praise for "the secure novelistic technique, the clarity of his observations, the authenticity of his portrayals, filled with the strength and conviction of one who has experienced the situations he portrays." This book, winning second prize in the important Ricardo Güiraldes competition, inaugurated a period of intense activity for Onetti. During the 1940s, while continuing his work as a journalist, he began work on several novels and made translations of a number of North American authors, including Faulkner, the principal influence on his own work.

Para esta noche (For Tonight, 1943), another despondent tale of lost innocence, was followed by *La vida breve* (1950, translated by Hortense Carpentier as *A Brief Life*), a longer novel which is something of a landmark in Onetti's development as a novelist. The narrator and central character is an alienated and introspective Buenos Aires publicist named Brausen, who has been described as a "tragic Walter Mitty." His wife loses a breast to cancer and Brausen is fired from his job. Unable to cope with his situation, he withdraws into a series of fantasies, seeking "to construct the appearance of confusion, to erase my tracks at each step, to discover that each moment leaps out, shines, and disappears like a newly minted coin." At times he is the thug Arce, living with a prostitute and peddling drugs. Or he may be the cynical physician Díaz Grey, for whom Brausen invents a lover (who is provided with her own history) and a whole environment, the dreary riverside town of Santa María. Thus Brausen conducts his battle against anomie, seeking to live (and to "die") "without memory or foresight."

Onetti returned to Montevideo in 1955, took a post as manager of an advertising firm, and began writing for the political journal *Acción.* In 1957 he became director of the Montevideo municipal libraries, while continuing to pour out a stream of despairing novels and short stories. Onetti finds an element of catharsis in the writing of his dark chronicles; referring to *Los adioses* (The Farewells, 1954), another tragic variation on the impossibility of communication, he said that he felt at peace with himself after writing it: "To narrate certain things is to understand and to understand is to create." The central theme in Onetti's work is that (as T.S. Eliot put it) "human kind cannot bear very much reality." Unable to accept that their lives are meaningless, his characters seek to amend reality and thus destroy themselves. All the same, Onetti seems to suggest, it may be better for human kind to gnaw on a bare bone of hope than on no bone at all.

This theme is most powerfully worked out in *El astillero* (1962, translated by Rachel Caffyn as *The Shipyard*), which most critics regard as Onetti's masterpiece. The novel is dominated by the personality of Junta Larsen, a tough, laconic, and resourceful former brothel owner who first appeared in *Tierra de nadie* and who also plays a part in *La vida breve.* The idealistic visions of Larsen's youth, his subsequent dreams of power and money, have all eluded him; he is at the end of his tether. He returns to Santa María (the

Santa María created before our eyes in *La vida breve*) and becomes the highly paid manager of a shipyard. In fact, the shipyard is derelict and the salary imaginary, but Larsen, like the other employees, enters with zest and apparent conviction into a Kafkaesque game, studying files twenty years old, discussing ships that no longer exist, vigorously courting his employer's insane daughter. A crisis is precipitated when one of the yard's employees rebels against these absurdities, and Larsen, having failed to murder him, goes mad and (probably) dies.

Larsen, like his creator, is an existentialist of sorts: "All one can do is precisely this: anything, do one thing after another, without interest or meaning. One thing, then another, then another, without it mattering whether they turn out well or badly, without it mattering what it may mean." G. R. Coulthard has pointed out that Larsen, in spite of failure and degradation, assumes almost heroic dimensions, "heroic in his constant struggle to find something positive and meaningful." For most of Onetti's characters, to grow up is to fail, since it is only the young who are capable of love and the illusion of hope. The reader is left with the assurance that death is the only release from life's absurdities, holding in his hand a book whose pages will turn yellow, whose "spongy, rotten" binding will decompose. An earlier phase of Larsen's life, when he established his brothel in Santa María, is the theme of *Juntacadáveres* (Pimps, 1964).

Onetti has been called an anti-novelist because of his lack of interest in a traditional plot. Action in his books is usually subordinated to "descriptive detail that emphasizes the drag of time." His style, plain in the first book, has developed gradually into a highly individual instrument, dense and oblique, full of overlapping (and sometimes contradictory) narratives, obsessive reiterations, and elliptical monologues, in keeping with his characters' complexity and confusion, and the static nature of his own vision of life. Some critics have objected that Onetti's reading of reality is a very partial one, limited by the author's own bitterly resigned view of mankind; he has replied: "The characters don't function unless you love them. Writing a novel is an act of love." Mario Benedetti has remarked that Onetti's "attitude is not destructive, not *even* destructive."

El astillero brought Onetti both the Uruguayan National Prize for Literature and the William Faulkner award. His reputation has spread steadily, with translations into French, English, German, and Italian; his complete works were published by Aguilar in Mexico in 1970. He is now generally considered the most important novelist to have emerged in Uruguay in the past half-century, and his influence on other Latin-American writers is said to be second only to that of Jorge Luis Borges. Onetti, who believes that profound human experience defies any adequate expression, is himself terrified of being misinterpreted as a writer, maintaining that he is generally more puzzled than reassured by critical assessments of his work. His image of himself, as of so many of his characters, is as "a lonely man smoking somewhere in the night . . . turning toward the shadow on the wall at night to dwell on nonsensical fantasies."

In 1974 Onetti was a member of a jury which awarded first prize in a literary competition to a short story by a young writer, Nelson Marra, in which a Uruguayan police inspector is presented as a rapist and torturer. The story, based on a real case, was published in *Marcha*. As a result, the Uruguayan police closed *Marcha* for ten weeks, and imprisoned Marra, Onetti, another member of the competition jury, and both the editor and the publisher of *Marcha*. According to Suzanne Jill Levine, Marra and the editor were beaten by the police "to prove that you cannot say the Uruguayan police resorts to beating." Onetti had a nervous breakdown, was incarcerated for a time in a mental institution, and subsequently went into exile in Madrid, where he has remained.

PRINCIPAL WORKS IN ENGLISH TRANSLATION: The Shipyard, 1968; A Brief Life, 1976. *Stories in* Cohen, J.M. (ed.) Latin American Writing Today, 1967; Fiction and Poetry From Latin America, 1972; Prize Stories From Latin America, 1963; Short Stories in Spanish I, 1966; Short Stories in Spanish II, 1972.

ABOUT: Ainsa, F. Las trampas de Onetti, 1970; Benedetti, M. Literatura uruguaya siglo xx, 1963; Coulthard, G.R. Spanish-American Novel: 1940-1965, 1966; Flores, A. (ed.) The Literature of Spanish America, 1967; Franco, J. An Introduction to Spanish American Literature, 1969; Franco, J. The Modern Culture of Latin America, 1970; Franco, J. Spanish American Literature Since Independence, 1973; Giacoman, H.F. (ed.) Homenaje a Juan Carlos Onetti, 1974; Harss, L. and Dohmann, B. (eds.) Into the Mainstream, 1967; International Who's Who, 1977-78; Jones, Y.P. The Formal Expression of Meaning in J.C. Onetti's Narrative Art, 1971; Ludmer, J. Onetti: Los procesos de construcción del relato, 1971; Monegal, E. R. Literatura uruguaya del medio siglo, 1966; Moreno Aliste, X. Origen y sentido de la farsa en la obra de Juan Carlos Onetti, 1973; Penguin Companion to Literature 3, 1971; Ramos, R.G. Recopilación de textos sobre Juan Carlos Onetti, 1967; Ruffinelli, J. Onetti, 1973; Schwartz, K. A New History of Spanish American Fiction, 1971.

OPPEN, GEORGE (April 24, 1908–), American poet, was born in New Rochelle, New York, the son of George A. Oppen and the former Elsie Rothfeld. He moved to San Francisco at the age of ten when his father remarried. Oppen attend-

GEORGE OPPEN

Ann Resor Laughlin, courtesy New Directions

ed California public schools and went on to the University of Oregon, but left when he was only nineteen and hitchhiked to New York with Mary Colby, whom he married in 1928. The following year they went to France, where in Toulon they formed a publishing house, To Publishers (1930–1933). Oppen had been one of the founders in 1931 of the Objectivist movement in poetry, and in 1932 To published *An "Objectivists" Anthology,* edited by Louis Zukofsky. The same year Oppen, with Zukofsky, Charles Reznikoff, and Carl Rakosi, founded the Objectivist Press, which survived until 1936 and published among other things Ezra Pound's *ABC of Reading* and William Carlos Williams's *Collected Poems 1921–1931.*

Williams was the acknowledged master of the Objectivists, who sought to extend or rather to clarify the precepts of imagism in a way that would be compatible with Williams's dictum: "No idea but in things." Short-lived as a movement, and with no great following, the Objectivist aesthetic provides a crucial link between imagism and the theories of projective verse propounded by Charles Olson in the 1950s. According to L. S. Dembo, "Objectivism begins for Oppen as an attempt to 'construct a method of thought for the imagist technique of poetry—for the imagist intensity of vision.' " Dembo says that imagist thought "is a form of nominalism in which appreciation of the existence of an object, in its tangibility or luminosity, is the primary poetic feeling. . . . Poetry, then, ought not to have a social or moral intention. . . . What matters is 'the sense of the poet's self among things.' not a display of 'right thinking and right sentiment.' " For Oppen, the problem was how the

poet can "communicate a realization of the concrete object *as object* without drawing the reader's attention to the *way* in which he communicates. How can we avoid the confusion of gesture and object? How can we focus the attention directly upon the apple without the reader thinking the hand is just as important as the apple?"

Oppen's first collection of poems, *Discrete Series,* was published in 1934 by the Objectivist Press. It had the benefit of a preface by Ezra Pound, who wrote: "I salute a serious craftsman, a sensibility which is not everyman's sensibility and which has not been got out of any other man's books." Michael Hamburger found these poems difficult "because they present objects, clusters of objects, situations, complex perceptions not linked by argument, narrative, or an easily recognisable subjective correlative." The title derives from mathematics, and refers to a series of terms each one of which is "empirically derived . . . empirically true." Oppen has explained that the fragmentary character of these poems results from the attempt "to construct a meaning by empirical statements, by imagist statements. . . . The poems are a series, yet each is separate."

In 1935 Oppen and his wife joined the Communist Party—not for philosophic reasons but out of a desire to do something about mass hunger. They lived in Brooklyn and during the late 1930s and early 1940s went from house to house, apartment to apartment, in Bedford-Stuyvesant and North Brooklyn, organizing the unemployed. Oppen worked during these years as a tool- and die-maker, mechanic, and building contractor, among other occupations, and he ceased to write poetry. As he explained in a 1963 issue of *Kulchur,* he "didn't believe in political poetry or poetry as being politically efficacious. . . . If you decide to do something politically, you do something that has political efficacy. And if you decide to write poetry, then you write poetry, not something that you hope, or deceive yourself into believing, can save people who are suffering. . . . In a way I gave up poetry because of the pressures of what for the moment I'll call conscience. But there were some things I had to live through, some things I had to think my way through, some things I had to try out—and it was more than politics, really; it was the whole experience of working in factories, of having a child, and so on."

In 1943–1945 Oppen served in the U.S. Army, receiving a Purple Heart among other "normal 'decorations' and condolences." He resumed his political activities after the war, but in 1950, harassed by the McCarthy House Un-American Activities Committee, "faced with the prospect of informing on friends or going to jail," he fled to Mexico with his wife and his daughter Linda. Oppen lived for eight years in Mexico, and with some difficulty set up a small business there, selling furniture designed and made by himself and a Mexican partner. In 1958, when McCarthy was dead and the hue and cry had died down, the Oppens returned to the United States. By this time George Oppen had begun to write again, and his most creative period now began. According to Dembo, "his return to poetry marked an exhaustion with politics."

The Materials, Oppen's second collection of poems, appeared in 1962, twenty-eight years after the first. These new poems, written in Mexico and New York, seemed to Michael Hamburger to throw fresh light on the apparent "alienation of subject from object" that had characterized *Discrete Series,* showing a "reciprocity, the process of perceiving a mode of self-discovery": "What I've seen/ Is all I've found: myself." William Carlos Williams was moved by "these clean constructions. . . . They fulfill what he has promised to do with the poetic line, to keep it clean and succinct. He has never varied in his direct approach to the word as the supreme burden of the final poetic image." The same process ("of perceiving a mode of self-discovery") continues in the collection called *This In Which* (1965), which takes its title from the poem "Psalm":

> The small nouns
> Crying faith
> In this in which the wild deer
> Startle, and stare out.

In a 1969 interview in *Contemporary Literature,* Oppen described his response to the reality of objects as one of faith and of reference to his own experience—a nominalist response. "All the little nouns are the ones that I like the most: the deer, the sun, and so on. You say these perfectly little words and you're asserting that the sun is ninety-three million miles away, and that there is shade because of shadows, and more, who knows? It's a tremendous structure to have built out of a few small nouns. . . . In 'Psalm' I was constructing what I felt to be a pretty emotional poem out of those few little words isolating the deer. . . . these little nouns are crying out a faith in 'this in which' the wild deer stare out." According to one reviewer of *This In Which,* Oppen showed himself to be not only a "poet of clearly denoted phenomena" but also "a rigorous thinker about the relations between individuals and society, between consciousness and environment."

The truth of this assertion was confirmed in the most discussed of Oppen's books, *Of Being Numerous* (1968), which brought him the Pulitzer Prize for poetry in 1969. This small volume consists of the title poem, a long meditation in forty parts on man in the city; a sequel called "Route"; and six short poems. The book had its disparagers, who complained of "cliché and excessive repetition" or, like Laurence Lieberman, thought that "the burden of a protracted structure seems to drain intensity" out of Oppen's line. However, most critics reacted very differently. David Ignatow described the poet's progress in the title poem "from self-doubt and self-searching through the artifacts of the city, to a moment in which his mind is revealed to itself as its own strength." In its emphasis on the anonymity, incoherence, and futility of city life, the poem affords striking parallels with William Carlos Williams's *Paterson,* Ignatow said, but Oppen does not share Williams's admiration for the man who makes his own way independent of these stresses. For Oppen, no one can divorce himself from "the kind of crisis the city represents. . . . Once he understands and accepts his own involvement with this crisis, however, he may rescue the self through the consistent exercise of consciousness which is the self in being." Ignatow thought that "stylistically, 'Of Being Numerous' goes far beyond Oppen's earlier works in the power evoked through condensation and ellipsis. . . . If the city is the expression of man, then Oppen's poem surely is its finest exponent, in its capacity to think and to take pride in its judgments"—"the work of a man who rests his faith in the mind as a value in itself on which the individual may depend."

" 'Route' reflects profound determinism that marks the whole range of Oppen's work," according to L.S. Dembo. "It has a vision of love, but love understood as a biological phenomenon. . . . [It] sees aesthetic clarity as the sum of knowledge." Oppen himself, referring to this poem, speaks of the "lesson" that "one is, after all, just oneself and in the end is rooted in the singular, whatever one's absolutely necessary connections with human history are." Dembo wrote that "Of Being Numerous" and its sequel are both major poems "which mingle autobiography and metaphysics in an objectivist style that is anything but confessional." And if they "can be called meditative poems, they are meditative according to the logic of 'imagistic thought.' That is, each is a mosaic of observations that might justly be considered a discrete series; they are phenomenological rather than psychological renditions of the poet's consciousness." Paul Zweig thought that the title poem "presents a difficult challenge to the reader, for the poem proceeds by side leaps and deft associations. Single words are caught up from a preceding stanza, and expanded into a constellation of images. Sharply evoked cityscapes issue into elusive statements of feeling or philosophy. . . . It is, I think, Oppen's major achievement to date, and one of the most important single poems to be written in recent years."

Oppen once wrote: "I have not and never did have any motive of poetry/ But to achieve clarity," and some reviewers of *Seascape: Needle's Eye* (1972) thought that he had succeeded and at a profound level. Michael Heller found in this collection "a heightened sense of the struggle to articulate; the language is starker, more primordial, as is the use of spacing, so that the poems have a feeling of resolution arrived at only *in extremis*"—the beauty and power of this poetry "derive from the simultaneous apperception of its radical construction and the depth at which it seeks to cohere in sense." Mark Perlberg, on the other hand, thought the volume so involved "with a kind of gnomic reticence that it moves towards silence. . . . Oppen seems here to distrust most of the processes of language. Perhaps in an attempt to achieve the purest kind of statement, perfect in its honesty, he seems wary of rhythm, of patterns of rhythm, of connections, of the music a poem can make. Even on his own terms, the poems in this book are puzzles, not mysteries."

Irvin Ehrenpreis offered similar criticisms of Oppen's work as a whole in his review of the *Collected Poems* (1975): "But sparseness has little power by itself. When Oppen rejects the common privileges of a poet, he . . . risks bathos. The elliptical character of his style barely distinguishes it from the cryptic. When one receives his insights, they often sound like those of Pound and W. C. Williams, and though truly felt are unsurprising. Even humor is rare: Oppen sounds averse to wit or satire. I wonder whether by resisting the lure of abundance he has not been left with a style that is pinched and thin." But for many readers, as for Michael Heller, "the poetry of George Oppen is one of our most sustained examinations of the characteristic themes of poetry (themes of love and death, and of a sense of history), an attempt to determine if the very meaning of such words as love or humanity can be retained in the light of what we have come to know and of what we have become. . . . Oppen stands alone in this regard: that his poetry is not composed of the effects of modern life upon the self, but is rather our most profound investigation of it." Oppen himself says: "I'm really concerned with the substantive, with

the subject of the sentence, with what we are talking about, and not riding over the subject-matter to make a comment about it. . . . I'm trying to describe how the test of images can be a test of whether one's thought is valid, whether one can establish in a series of images, of experiences . . . whether or not one will consider the concept of humanity to be valid, something that is, or else have to regard it simply as a word." It seems to L. S. Dembo that "Oppen has realized the full potential of his objectivist allegiance: he has become a poet of the first order."

The author has listed among the influences on his work Middle English poetry, the philosophy of Martin Heidegger, and the poetry of William Blake, Ezra Pound, William Carlos Williams, and Charles Reznikoff. An unpretentious man, soft-spoken and modest, he divides his time between San Francisco and his summer home in Maine. Mary Oppen has described their life together in her autobiography, *Meaning a Life* (1978).

PRINCIPAL WORKS: Discrete Series, 1934; The Materials, 1962; This In Which, 1965; Of Being Numerous, 1968; Alpine: Poems, 1969; Seascape: Needle's Eye, 1972; Collected Poems, 1973 (England only); Collected Poems 1929–1975, 1975.

ABOUT: Contemporary Authors 13–16 1st revision, 1975; Hamburger, M. Art As Second Nature, 1975; International Who's Who in Poetry, 1974–1975; Oppen, M. Meaning Life, 1978; Penguin Companion to Literature 3, 1971; Seymour-Smith, M. Guide to Modern World Literature, 1973; Vinson, J. (ed.) Contemporary Poets, 1975; Who's Who in America, 1976–1977. *Periodicals*—American Poetry Review March/April 1975; Antioch Review 2 1966; Choice July 1966, February 1969, February 1976; Contemporary Literature Spring 1969; Encounter August 1973; Hudson Review Summer 1976; Kulchur Summer 1963; Library Journal February 15, 1968; March 1, 1976; Nation November 24, 1969; New Leader July 8, 1968; New York Review of Books January 22, 1976; New York Times Book Review October 19, 1975; Observer May 6, 1973; Partisan Review 2 1973; Poetry August 1966, April 1969, June 1975, December 1976; The Review January 1964.

ORTON, "JOE" (i.e. JOHN KINGSLEY ORTON) (January 1, 1933–August 9, 1967), English dramatist, was born on a Leicester housing project, the first child of William and Elsie Mary (Bentley) Orton. He grew up in an atmosphere of threadbare gentility, precariously sustained by his father's earnings as a gardener and his mother's as a machinist. It was a world that he was to satirize mercilessly in his plays. An asthmatic and bookish child often absent from school, Orton failed the eleven plus examination that might have earned him entry into an academic high school. He was sent to a private secretarial college, after which he said, "I was sacked from all the jobs I had between sixteen

© Douglas H. Jeffery

JOE ORTON

and eighteen because I was never interested in any of them." At the same time he was building up his impressive physique, acting in amateur productions, and taking speech lessons, all of which led to his departure to London for the Royal Academy of Dramatic Art (1950-1953).

Orton dismissed his training there as "complete rubbish" and after six months in repertory at Ipswich he shed his acting ambitions. At the Academy, however, he met Kenneth Halliwell, a scholarly would-be writer seven years his senior with whom he set up a writing partnership and a homosexual marriage that lasted for the rest of their lives. It was an austere and reclusive arrangement with no distractions outside their three priorities of writing, reading, and sex. Under Halliwell's guidance, Orton read the Greek classics, Lewis Carroll, Swift, Voltaire, and (the author who influenced him most) Ronald Firbank. The couple worked at various casual jobs and collaborated in writing fantastic novels, none of which found a publisher. On one of the rare occasions when they ventured into literary society, it struck their hosts that the bald, ponderous Halliwell was the creative partner and that the mischievous, bright-eyed Orton was merely the pretty boyfriend. All this changed in 1962 when they were sentenced to six months in jail for stealing and defacing library books. Prison completed Orton's literary apprenticeship. "Being in the nick," he said later, "brought detachment to my writing. . . . Before, I had been vaguely conscious of something rotting somewhere: prison crystallized this. The old whore society really lifted up her skirts and the stench was pretty foul."

Within a year of his release, the BBC accepted his radio play, *The Ruffian on the Stair,* which has been called "an intricate 'revenger's tragedy' compressed into one act and played as farce." In May 1964 his first stage play, *Entertaining Mr. Sloane,* opened in the West End, London's Broadway. It showed a debt to the work of Harold Pinter (who came to admire Orton's plays as "brilliant and truly original"), though Orton is always far more concerned than Pinter to make it clear exactly what is happening, and why, in his elaborate plots. *Entertaining Mr. Sloane* provoked the clash of enthusiasm and outrage that generally heralds the arrival of a new kind of theatrical animal. On one side, Sir Terence Rattigan greeted it as "the best first play" he had seen in "thirty-odd years"; on the other, it became the prime target of a contemporary campaign against "dirty plays." Orton gleefully fanned the flames by writing to the *Daily Telegraph* under the pseudonym of Mrs. Edna Welthorpe, attacking *Mr. Sloane* as "a disgusting piece of filth." The play carried off the London Critics' Variety Award as the best play of the year.

Mr. Sloane concerns a seductive young psychopath who takes lodgings with a middle-aged brother and sister and is blackmailed into permanent sexual submission when he murders their father: the genteel suburban household he has invaded far outdoes him in ruthlessness and wickedness. The play at once defined the style that gave birth to the term *Ortonesque,* meaning a stark dissociation between what characters do and what they say. The plot turns on acts of cold brutality and rapacious sexuality, while the dialogue preserves a tone of suburban decorum which led Ronald Bryden to label Orton "the Oscar Wilde of Welfare State gentility." His rhythms and elegant antitheses derive from the English high comedy tradition, expanded to incorporate advertising jargon, official euphemisms, and twisted clichés, set in startling conjunction and enabling characters to escape from any situation by perversely irrefutable logic.

Orton's consistent posture was that of an amoral outsider who (as he said) found people "profoundly bad but irresistibly funny." He himself arrived in the West End like a ruffian on the stair, and (as his diary verifies) that was an impression he wished to make. What mortally offended some people was that such an apparent thug could also write like Congreve.

In *Loot* (which won the 1966 Evening Standard Award for the best play of the year) he moved on from personal to institutional satire, taking aim at the police through the form of a detective thriller. Characteristically, he turned the form inside out. The crimes, starting with a young bank robber hiding the loot in his mother's coffin while his bereaved father is succumbing to the sexual attentions of a homicidal nurse, are blatantly obvious. What mystery there is focuses on a self-styled official from the Water Board who invades the house of mourning and starts asking awkward questions. This is Truscott of the Yard, a walking anthology of stage police clichés, all converted to his own corrupt ends. Told that "the police are for the protection of ordinary people," he replies: "I don't know where you pick up these slogans, sir." There are no bounds to Truscott's ingenuity and ruthlessness, apart from his total blindness to the evidence lying under his nose. In the end he arrests the old husband, the only innocent character on stage, and appropriates the spoils. *Loot,* said the *Times,* is "a piece that comes to mind whenever the police get trapped on the wrong side of the law."

"In a world run by fools," Orton wrote, "the writer can only chronicle the doings of fools and their victims." This is the program he pursued in the rest of his work, which centers mostly on institutional tyranny. His television play *The Good and Faithful Servant* (1967) concerns an old worker thrown onto the Welfare State scrapheap after fifty years with the same firm. The compassion and social indignation of this piece are unique in Orton's work, which otherwise shows scant sympathy for victims. *The Erpingham Camp* (1967) displays his characteristic reversal technique, presenting a vacation camp as a fascist dictatorship which is overturned by a food mutiny in which Erpingham perishes ("Let us pray for guidance," says one of his underlings: "Your car has been pushed into the Experienced Swimmers Only.") By including a docile church ("You're interested in religion, then, Padre?") within this political allegory, Orton also found an apt outlet for the compulsive, giggling anticlericism that also runs through *Loot* and his feeblest television play, *Funeral Games* (1968).

In his final play, *What the Butler Saw* (1969), Orton turned another institution inside out by staffing a mental hospital with lunatics ("I represent Her Majesty's Government," announces Dr. Rance, "your immediate superiors in madness.") Set in the private clinic of Dr. Prentice, this farce (or parody of a farce) opens with the proprietor's attempt to seduce a new secretary under cover of a medical examination, while his wife is attending a meeting of her lesbian coven. Subsequent developments include the pursuit of a transvestite bellboy and the search for the missing private parts of a statue of Winston Churchill, a blood-stained hue and cry and a Euripidean finale where the cast ascend to the higher regions. Dr. Rance presides over these events as a psychiatric Truscott, translating innocent remarks into schizophrenic symptoms and finding cogent reasons for certifying everyone in sight.

To John Lahr, his biographer, this is Orton's masterpiece, and Frank Marcus ranks it as "a comedy classic of English literature." It was, however, generally dismissed when it first appeared; and when the Royal Court Theatre revived it during a 1975 Orton season, other reviewers complained that it was overloaded with gags and that it reduced the method of *Loot* to a mechanical formula. Another complaint was that it failed to provide what is thought essential in farce—a normative code of behavior against which to measure the outrageous antics on stage.

Orton did not live to see the play performed. His success had distanced him from his Pygmalion-like partner, but on the night of August 9, 1967, Halliwell secured his own niche in theatre history by beating Orton to death with a hammer and then killing himself with an overdose of barbiturates. Orton at the time was planning a new play called *Prick Up Your Ears.*

A manner of death so fearsomely compatible with his own plays much strengthened Orton's posthumous reputation. During his lifetime, critics like W.A. Darlington in the *Daily Telegraph* took repeated exception to his unfeeling jokes about death; once he was in the grave, the jokes began to look prophetic. Likewise, his mother's funeral was, according to his diary, uncannily reminiscent of *Loot,* and Orton returned to London with the old woman's false teeth in his pocket "to amaze the cast."

He was an obviously literary and artificial writer who insisted "I write the truth." Hence the failure of the first productions of *Loot* and *What the Butler Saw,* which presented the plays as comic fantasies peopled with consciously funny characters. Absolute realism was what Orton demanded from his actors: "No attempt to match the author's extravagance of dialogue with extravagance of direction." This is the golden rule of farce playing, and the companies that adopted it established Orton as one of the most brilliant and popular British farceurs of the century. His claims to be a writer who persuades audiences to reexamine the values of their society must be qualified by the fact that there is no invitation to identify with his characters. From the spectators' viewpoint, he is making fun of Them, not of Us.

Orton's posthumously published novel *Head*

to Toe, written years earlier when he was working by night in a chocolate factory, is an allegorical fantasy describing the pilgrimage of an innocent young man named Gumbold up and down a magical territory which (we discover) is the body of a giant some hundreds of miles high. Gumbold's adventures include his involvement with a male revolutionary group struggling against the territory's female government, and in the end we learn that the giant is dead. The book's bias "is that of the English homosexual Left," according to a reviewer in the *Times Literary Supplement,* who concluded that "there is a spirit of true religion struggling to express itself in this weird book. It is a rag-bag, a curiosity, but it helps to explain Orton's brief life and his handful of plays."

PRINCIPAL WORKS: *Plays*—The Ruffian on the Stair *in* B.B.C. New Radio Drama, 1960; Entertaining Mr. Sloane, 1965; Loot, 1967; Crimes of Passion (contains The Ruffian on the Stair *and* The Erpingham Camp), 1967; Loot *in* New English Dramatists, 1968; What the Butler Saw, 1969; Funeral Games *and* The Good and Faithful Servant, 1970; The Complete Plays of Joe Orton, 1976.

ABOUT: Lahr, J. Prick Up Your Ears, 1978; *introduction to* The Complete Plays of Joe Orton, 1976; McCrindle, J.F. (ed.) Behind the Scenes, 1971; Marowitz, C. Confessions of a Counterfeit Critic, 1973; Taylor, J.R. The Second Wave, 1971. *Periodicals*—Antiquarian Bookman September 4-11, 1967; Encounter May 1967; New Society April 17, 1975; New York Times August 10, 1967; Plays and Players October 1970; Spectator August 18, 1967; Sunday Times Magazine November 22, 1970; Times Literary Supplement January 29, 1971; Transatlantic Review Spring 1967.

"OSBORNE, DAVID." *See* SILVERBERG, ROBERT

OUSMANE, SEMBÈNE. *See* SEMBÈNE, OUSMANE

*ØVERLAND, ARNULF (April 27, 1889–March 25, 1968), Norwegian poet, was born in Kristiansund, a seaport built on three small islands on the west coast of Norway, principal town of the county of Möre og Romsdal. He was the son of Peter Øverland, a ship's engineer. His father died when Øverland was a boy, and his mother brought up the family in straitened circumstances. He went to school in Bergen and then moved to Oslo, where he matriculated in 1907. Øverland began the study of philology at the University of Oslo but left without a degree. His real interests were poetry and painting and, though he came to concentrate on the former, he continued to paint throughout his life. In 1917-

*û′ vər lan

ARNULF ØVERLAND

1924 he worked for the Oslo dailies *Verdens Gang* and *Arbeiderbladet* as a literary critic.

Øverland's first literary idols were Heinrich Heine and the Swedish fin-de-siècle writer Hjalmar Söderberg. Their influence is evident in his own earliest books, *Den ensomme fest* (The Lonely Feast, 1911) and *De hundrede violiner* (The Hundred Violins, 1912). The poems in these collections, full of youthful longing and loneliness, were acclaimed by the critics for their taut power, their fastidious restraint, and the absence of all rhetoric.

To Øverland, still in his twenties, it seemed that "there was nothing more that could happen." World War I proved him wrong, and he was roused to active social and political engagement by the victors' treatment of Germany at Versailles. In *Brød og vin* (Bread and Wine, 1919) he turned away from his own emotional problems to express his revulsion at man's inhumanity to man. Like many other Norwegian intellectuals of the time he reached the conclusion that communism offered the only solution to the world's ills, and he joined the party in 1923. In 1923-1928 he was also an active chairman of the Norwegian Writers' Union.

In *Brød og vin* Øverland uses religious language and symbolism, as the title indicates. He was a violent opponent of Christianity (and was unsuccessfully prosecuted for blasphemy in 1933), but he argued that the Bible provided a common tradition in Norway, a language and culture that were elevated yet truly popular. He also borrowed from the diction and style of folk song, a genre similarly combining poetic beauty with wide appeal. In the passionate though astringent verse of *Berget det blå* (The Mountain

Blue, 1927) he showed a developing capacity for combining the romantic longing of his early poetry with exhortations to the dispossessed to take what is rightfully theirs: "Fable-blue/ rises under foreign stars/ the mountain only your dream can view,/ the mountain blue."

Øverland's private and public concerns coalesce most effectively in *Hustavler* (House Rules, 1929), generally considered to be his finest collection of verse. He grapples with the problems of love and death and evil, and in "Til en misantrop" (To a Misanthrope) he rejects the man who turns his back on the imperfect human world. The misanthrope worries that his personal achievements will die with him, failing to see that salvation lies in submerging personal ambition in communal labor: "But if you share the lot of other men,/ so you may find as times goes by that then/ in humble toil and common hope and sighs/ love will reveal itself before your eyes." Øverland's verse at its best is monumentally simple in language, rhymed and traditional in form, concentrated and concise; though his poems are often hortative or moralistic, they are sometimes purely lyrical, like many in *Jeg besverger dig* (I Beseech You, 1934) that express the physical joys of love and the despair that comes when it ends.

Øverland was early aware of the menace of Nazism and urged his countrymen to political watchfulness in the famous poem "Du må ikke sove" (You Must Not Sleep) and others collected in *Den røde front* (The Red Front, 1937). The same year he left the Communist Party in protest at Stalin's purges. It was through his resistance to fascism that Øverland achieved his greatest popularity. During the German occupation of Norway he continued to call for resistance to the Nazis, in poetry that circulated illegally and anonymously. Since he could hardly disguise his distinctive style, he was arrested in 1941 and in 1942 was sent to the Sachsenhausen concentration camp in Germany. Poems from his four years of imprisonment are collected in *Vi overlever allt!* (We Shall Survive Everything, 1945), of which more copies were sold than of any other book of verse ever published in Norway. Øverland returned from his ordeal to find himself a national hero and was given possession of the Grotto, Norway's national "author's house," the former home of the great Norwegian poet Henrik Wergeland.

It may be that the adulation Øverland received affected his capacity for self-criticism; his postwar poetry, rather stridently antimodernist in manner, only occasionally achieved the power and tension of his earlier work. The main themes of this later verse are praise of family life, in *Fiskeren og hans sjel* (The Fisherman and His Soul, 1950), for example, and the calm acceptance of death, evident in *Sverdet bak døren* (The Sword Behind the Door) and in later collections. He was also the author of some not particularly successful plays and some excellent short stories, containing according to one critic "a curious and strangely haunting mixture of Freudianism and mysticism."

Øverland resumed his involvement in public affairs after the war; never afraid of controversy, he was not always particularly subtle in his attacks on his opponents. He remained bitterly opposed to Soviet imperialism and was a passionate defender of the official *riksmål* version of the Norwegian language (which he himself spoke and wrote) against attempts to bring it closer to the *landsmål* version, based on spoken dialects. The author was married three times.

PRINCIPAL WORKS IN ENGLISH TRANSLATION: *Poems* in Allwood, M.S. (ed.) Twentieth Century Scandinavian Poetry, 1950; Stork, C.W. (ed.) Anthology of Norwegian Lyrics, 1942; Life and Letters May 1950. *Story* in Hallmundsson, H. (ed.) An Anthology of Scandinavian Literature, 1965.

ABOUT: Gelsted, O. Arnulf Øverland, 1946; Haakonsen, D. Arnulf Øverland og den etiske realisme 1905-1940, 1966; Johnsen, E.E. Livets spiral, 1956; Jorgenson, T. History of Norwegian Literature, 1970; Penguin Companion to Literature 2, 1969; Smith, H. (ed.) Columbia Dictionary of Modern European Literature, 1947. *Periodicals*—American Scandinavian Review 1973.

OWENS, ROCHELLE (BASS) (April 2, 1936–), American dramatist and poet, writes: "I was born in Brooklyn, New York. My father was a Post Office clerk and my mother a housewife. Both parents were highly intense and remote. Their lower-middle-class expectations and values conflicted with a naive longing for self-fulfillment and individuality. Oppression, tension, and inhibition were the conditions of my childhood. I always felt as if there were huge blocks of invisible concrete hanging in the air that one could not avoid smashing into. I was told often that I was a disappointment to their lives. My older sister, younger brother and I were frequently reminded by mother that father had wanted to be a lawyer or a merchant seaman but the depression of 1929 and marriage and family obligations had forced him to forsake these preferences. As a youth he had had to support his brother and three sisters after the death of his parents.

"I left home when I was nineteen and married a poor artist who worked as a carpenter; he helped considerably to improve my self-esteem as a young poet who wanted to write better and more innovative poems. The marriage lasted

ROCHELLE OWENS

three years. Because my formal education ended with high school I held many low-paying clerical jobs. I wrote constantly and assumed that my life would always be a battle of sorts but at least I would have produced a body of work. This idea gave me great pleasure. Being suspended in the landscape of mental concentration when writing a poem or play has been and is one of the most exquisite clarifications of my existence.

"In the early 1960s I was part of the dynamic renaissance of poetry and theatre that happened in New York and San Francisco. During that time I met George Economou, a poet and scholar, and we married in 1962. We have been an effecting force on each other, personally and professionally.

"My plays have been performed throughout the world and presented at festivals in Paris, Berlin, Edinburgh, and Rome. I've given poetry readings and discussions on experimental theatre throughout the United States.

"About my work—it is a commitment to seeing and feeling, to the transmission of information, the essential nucleus of the sphere of human existence, data which represents primal reality. I shall not do without."

Rochelle Owens, whose small first collection of poems appeared in 1961, is a poet also in her plays, which use grotesque symbolic figures and violent imagery to expose archetypal impulses usually hidden away in the subconscious. The Eskimos in *The String Game,* staged in 1965 at Judson Poets' Theatre in New York, are unrepressed enough to confront their libidinous fantasies, whiling away the long Greenland winters by creating cheerfully obscene images out of string. Father Bontempo, who wants to stamp out this sinful practice, has dark fantasies of his own, centering on richly garnished spaghetti. The entrepreneur Cecil, seeking to exploit the Eskimos commercially, gains Bontempo's support by bribing him with food, but is so disgusted by the priest's gluttony that he strikes and kills him: Christian puritanism and Western capitalism are defeated, and innocent sensuality is preserved.

Istanbul (1965), set during the Crusades, and *Homo* (1966) also dramatize the ways in which racial differences influence sexuality, but *Futz,* Rochelle Owens's most famous play, narrows the focus to study the conflict within a small community between "civilization" and man's animal nature. Cyrus Futz in this "stark hillbilly parable" falls in love with his sow Amanda. The lecherous Marjorie Satz forces Futz to let her participate in his sexual dealings with Amanda and the scene that results is observed by Ann Fox and the repressed Oscar Loop. Deranged by lust and guilt, Loop murders Ann Fox (as a surrogate for Futz) and is eventually condemned to hang. Marjorie Satz tells all, Futz is imprisoned by the outraged community, and is stabbed to death by Marjorie's brother.

First presented in Minneapolis at the Tyrone Guthrie Workshop of the Minnesota Theatre Company in October 1965, *Futz* was staged by the La Mama Experimental Theatre Club in New York in March 1967 and began a long run at the Theatre de Lys in June 1968, receiving the Obie award as the best off-Broadway play of 1967. It impressed Jack Kroll as "a poem, a brief exultant paroxysm of energy that plows up, tosses aloft and swirls about all sorts of simple, funny and true feelings about people lost in the great space between animal and angel." Robert Brustein described it as "a pornographic version of *Under Milk Wood,* complete with an omniscient narrator, episodic structure, and radiostyle loquacity," and went on to say that the author's "intense imagination" and "feverish, surrealist imagery" marked her as "a dramatic poet of genuine, if circumscribed power." Other reviewers disliked the play, and Walter Kerr, who found the plot "hypothetical, undramatized, ungraphic, without immediacy" was "scandalized . . . that such slovenliness should have been permitted to masquerade as new art." It was presented by the La Mama group at the 1967 Edinburgh Festival where, as Clive Barnes wrote, it "incurred some charming legal judgments and journalistic opinions from the worthy Edinburgh burghers."

"More obscure, more obscene and more tantalizing" than *Futz,* in Barnes's opinion, *Beclch* arrived at the Gate Theatre in New York in December 1968 "belching fire, brimstone and bad taste." Beclch is a white woman who "goes native" in Africa, becomes an insanely sadistic jungle queen, and winds up voluptuously anticipating her own torture and death. Ruby Cohn thought the message was that "for civilized people, there is no simple return to animality because we have too much imagination." Clive Barnes, however, found the play ambiguous: "Miss Owens," he wrote, "can never decide satisfactorily whether she wants to emphasize the darkness of her human sacrifices, the grim terror of a world without conscience, and the insensitivity of the new human jungle, or whether she wants to play intellectual footsie with us. Thus at one moment she is all blood-serious, and the next she is sliding wildly into bathos with a feeble joke or a careless idiomatic anachronism."

The most discussed of Rochelle Owens's subsequent plays was *The Karl Marx Play,* staged at the American Place Theatre in 1973. A considerable departure from her earlier work, it is an attempt, according to the author, at "a theatrical experiencing of the extreme humanness of Karl Marx, a vision of the man's spirit and fate." Marx is shown beset by domestic problems, ill-health, and self-doubt, but drawing inspiration for *Das Kapital* from his encounters with the singer Leadbelly, a personification of the nascent black consciousness. There was a great deal of praise for Rochelle Owens's lively neo-Brechtian style in this play—her effective use of declamatory addresses, choral speech, and ballads (with music by Galt MacDermot) to lend variety and force to her vision of "historical inevitability and suffering." Barnes found the work as a whole flawed and untidy, but rewarding and memorable. Jack Kroll was harsher: he wrote that "Miss Owens is a true theater poet . . . and authentic member of a wised-out generation. That is the trouble—Miss Owens is so wised up she has no time to be wise. . . . Unlike Brecht, who structured his cynicism into a powerful esthetic and didactic form, Miss Owens finally has nothing to give us but the gleeful energy of disenchantment." Nominated for an Obie, the play won the ASCAP award in 1973. Productions in several European cities have been well received.

Catharine Hughes in 1976 placed Rochelle Owens with a number of other American playwrights of the same generation who, she thought, had "accomplished relatively little of continuing interest." Ross Wetzsteon has expressed a very different view: "The genius of her work . . . lies not in ideological commitments but

in her access to the subconscious, and so her plays are not simple studies of the conflicts between our outer and inner selves, but sublimely subtle examinations of the ways in which these two selves are inextricable (our nature itself)—and inextricable, furthermore, from the selves of others. By the very nature of her gifts, then, Miss Owens is unable to celebrate anything but life itself (certainly no complacent attacks on society's hypocrisy, certainly no advocacy of sentimental atavisms, the two most common misinterpretations of her work)—which makes her, not at all paradoxically . . . perhaps the most profoundly tragic playwright in the American theatre."

Rochelle Owens has said that her plays are an "organic evolution" from her poetry, which began to gain attention in 1968 with the publication of *Salt and Core.* Charles Stein found this "a strange collection for a 'lady' poet—strange because the energy of her poetry is so phallic and sharply outward. . . . She is at her best when the cute side of her combines with the more violent and guttural." Stein concluded that "her attention is neither upon history nor myth, but [as in her plays] she uses ancient persons or artifacts as opportunity for intense expressive display."

Jane Augustine, similarly, said in discussing *I Am the Babe of Joseph Stalin's Daughter* (1972) that Rochelle Owens relished "Old Testament themes and the Mediterranean arena of contrast between Jew and Christian, Turk and Greek, which metaphorically extends to other conflicts —black vs. white, male vs. female, always juxtaposing ancient and traditional faith and language with contemporary slang and secular thought." Some poems in this collection "create voices speaking fragments of plays," while others "fearlessly explore the psychic realities of deviant personae." *The Joe 82 Creation Poems* (1974) is a sequence of over a hundred poems which, according to Jane Augustine, "has strong biblical and epic qualities. In the voice of a primal couple, Wild-Man and Wild-Woman, Owens redesigns the myths of creation in terms of the immediate creativity of every mind confronting its own experience. It is an ambitious task, with impressive results. Still an innovator and still young, this poet is enlarging her originality of thought and exuberant language to create a new vision of the world which rests on the old virtues of praise and joy."

The "tall and grand-looking" author is the daughter of Maxwell Bass and the former Molly Adler. She graduated in 1953 from Lafayette High School in Brooklyn and since then has studied at the Herbert Berghof Studio, the New School for Social Research in New York, and the Yale School of Drama. A member of the Dramatists' Guild, the New Dramatists' Committee, and Actors' Studio, she helped to found New York Theatre Strategy and the Women's Theatre Council. She has received grants and fellowships from the Ford, Rockefeller, and Guggenheim foundations, and the National Endowment for the Arts. Among her recreations are swimming, painting, sculpture, collage-making, and archaeology.

PRINCIPAL PUBLISHED WORKS: *Plays*—Futz, 1961; The String Game, 1965; Futz, and What Came After (contains Futz, The String Game, Beclch, Istanboul, Homo), 1968; The Karl Marx Play, 1973; The Karl Marx Play and Others (contains The Karl Marx Play, Kontraption, He Wants Shih!, Farmer's Almanac, Coconut Folk Singer, O.K. Certaldo), 1974; Emma Instigated Me *in* Performance Arts Journal 1 1976; The Widow and Me Colonel *in* Best Short Plays 1977, edited by Stanley Richards, 1977. *Poetry*—Not Be Essence That Cannot Be, 1961; Salt and Core, 1968; I Am the Babe of Joseph Stalin's Daughter: Poems 1961–1971, 1972; Poems From Joe's Garage, 1973; The Joe 82 Creation Poems, 1974; The Joe Chronicles II, 1977. *As Editor*—Spontaneous Combustion: Eight New American Plays (includes her own He Wants Shih!), 1972.

ABOUT: Cohn, R. Dialogue in American Drama, 1971; Contemporary Authors 17–20 1st revision, 1976; Crowell's Handbook of Contemporary Drama, 1971; De Loach, A. The East Side Scene, 1972; Guernsey, O. Playwrights, Lyricists, Composers on Theatre, 1974; Kerr, W. Thirty Plays Hath November, 1970; Notable Names in the American Theatre, 1976; Poland, A. and Mailman, B. (eds.) The Off Off Broadway Book, 1973; Rothenberg, J. *introduction to* Futz, and What Came After, 1968; Schroeder, R.J. The New Underground Theatre, 1968; Vinson, J. (ed.) Contemporary Dramatists, 1977; Vinson, J. (ed.) Contemporary Poets, 1975; Who's Who in America, 1976–1977; Who's Who in the Theatre, 1977. *Periodicals*—Christian Science Monitor April 5, 1973; Commonweal June 28, 1968; Kulchur II 1963; Life July 12, 1968; Margins (Milwaukee) 24–26 1975; Massachusetts Review Winter 1972; New Republic July 13, 1968; New York Times June 14, 1968; June 30, 1968; July 21, 1968; December 17, 1968; December 20, 1968; February 27, 1973; April 3, 1973; New Yorker February 10, 1968; April 7, 1973; Newsweek July 1, 1968; April 16, 1973; Saturday Review January 7, 1967; June 22, 1968; Time February 10, 1967; June 21, 1968; Times (London) December 7, 1968.

OZ, AMOS (May 4, 1939–), Hebrew novelist and short story writer, writes (in Hebrew): "Shortly after the October Revolution, my grandfather Alexander Klausner, a Jewish businessman and poet, fled from Odessa in Southern Russia. He was one of the early New Zionists who believed wholeheartedly that the time had come for the Jews to return to the Land of Israel, where they should first become a normal people and then perhaps an exemplary nation as well. And yet, in fleeing from Odessa, grandfather didn't turn to Jerusalem for which he had yearned—in Russian—in all his poems, but rather preferred settling with his wife and two

AMOS OZ

sons in Vilna, Poland. Apart from his passion for the ancient land of his ancestors, grandfather was a most European gentleman in manners, habits and principles. He supposed that living conditions in Palestine were still not sufficiently European. And so, in Vilna as well, he divided his time between business and poetry, bringing up his sons in the spirit of his European and Zionist ideals. Only that in those years no one in Europe, except for grandfather and a few other Jews like him, were European. Everyone was a panslavist, or a communist, or a pangermanic, or just a Bulgarian patriot. In 1933, as his antisemitic or order-loving neighbors repeatedly taunted him 'go to Palestine, little Jew,' grandfather sadly resolved upon traveling to the Orient with his wife and younger son. As for the elder son, my uncle David, he refused to give in to chauvinists and barbarians, and went on lecturing about the literature of Europe at Vilna University, where the Nazis got him and his wife and child as they purged Europe of cosmopolitans and Jews.

"In Jerusalem Alexander Klausner went on dividing his time between business and poetry, in spite of the oppressive heat, the poverty, the hostile Arabs, the bizarre Oriental atmosphere. His son, my father, found himself a librarian's post and spent his nights writing research in comparative literature. He took for a wife the middle daughter of a miller from Poland who in Israel fulfilled his ideology by becoming a teamster. My parents set up in Jerusalem a simple but bookladen home with a black tea cart and a Russian-style tea set. They would tell one another that Jewish Jerusalem would blossom into a true city. I was born in 1939, four months before the outbreak of war, when my parents realized that there was no going back. They dreamed in Yiddish, they conversed in Russian and Polish, they read mainly German and English, but me they taught one language only: Hebrew. In me they turned over a new leaf—an Israeli, tough and simple, blond and cleansed of old Jewish neuroses.

"The Jerusalem of my childhood was a lunatic town flooded with conflicting dreams, a vague federation of communities, people, faiths, ideologies and hopes. There were orthodox Jews who sat and waited with prayers for the Messiah to come, and there were busy revolutionary Jews who intended to play the part of messiah themselves, and there were Oriental Jews who had lived in Jerusalem for generations upon generations, and there were fanatic Christians who came to Jerusalem to be born anew, and there were the Arabs who called us 'children of death' and threw stones at us. Apart from all these, there were in Jerusalem madmen who had come almost from the four corners of the earth, each with his personal formula for the redemption of the world. Many of them may have secretly yearned to crucify or be crucified. I, too, so my parents decided, would go to a religiously-nationalistically inclined school where I would be inspired with longing for all the glorious ancient kingdoms of Israel and for their resurrection in blood and fire.

"My childhood in Jerusalem rendered me an expert on comparative fanaticism. When I was nine years old the British left the country and Jewish Jerusalem endured a prolonged siege, during Israel's War of Independence. We all believed that with victory would emerge a free Jewish state, in which nothing would be as it had been before. Three years after Hitler's downfall these survivors believed they were indeed the Sons of Light engaged in the last battle against the Sons of Darkness, and that Jewish independence would constitute a final omen that universal salvation was at hand.

"The War of Independence ended with a military victory and over a million Jewish refugees came to Israel within a few years. But the siege and the suffering were not over and along with them came the petty agonies of a very tiny state. After the sound and the fury came the morning after. Jerusalem was not to be a true, that is a European, city. The Jews were not to become 'a race of peasants joyful and healthy.' Some kept waiting. In his old age grandfather still kept writing songs of yearning for Jerusalem; another Jerusalem, the true, the heavenly, already redeemed by the Messiah and freed from agony and injustice. To his dying day in October 1970,

my father maintained his literary comparisons in fifteen languages. Only mother could not bear her life; driven by disappointment or yearning she committed suicide in 1952. Something went wrong. Two years after her death, when I was fourteen, I left home, the manners and the wisdom, changed my surname from Klausner to Oz, and went to work and to study at Kibbutz Hulda. Yes, I hoped to turn over a new leaf, and not in Jerusalem. For a few years I worked in the fields and studied in a free socialistic class, where barefoot we sat the livelong day discussing the origin of human evil, the nature of Jewish mischief and the ways to overcome them by gradually improving human nature. These were collectivist-egalitarian principles, sound and solid. To this day I stick to them, though with a certain sadness and a mile smile. In their name I reject to this day any radical theory in World Socialism and in Israeli politics. Owing to these principles, perhaps, my wife Nily and my daughters Fania and Gallia, all three born and educated in the kibbutz, experience only the day by day joys and sorrows of the searching heart, but have been spared those Jewish and Jerusalemite sufferings which afflicted grandfather, father, mother and myself. To me this might be called an achievement.

"As a child I wrote biblical poems about the resurrection in blood and fire of the kingdom of David and about the terrible vengeance upon the enemies of Israel. After serving in the regular army I returned to the kibbutz, working by day in the cotton fields and writing, night by night, ironical stories about the distance between dreamers and their nightdreams. After a while I was sent by the kibbutz assembly to study literature and philosophy at the university, so that when I came back I would work as a teacher with the kibbutz children. At night I could hear the jackals howling in the fields and occasionally the kibbutz watchmen would fire at infiltrators or at a moving shadow. I could hear refugees who had come to Hulda from many countries screaming in their sleep. Some had seen the devil incarnate with their very eyes.

"And so I wrote about the haunting shadows, about yearnings, fears, hatreds, nightmares, messianic aspirations, longings for the absolute. I wrote to explore in words whence and why my family had come, and what we had hoped to find here and what we actually found, and why this hatred flowing toward us from different quarters at different times. I wrote in an effort to figure out what else could be done and what could not.

"Twice, in 1967 with the victorious Israeli armored divisions in the Sinai desert, and in 1973 amid the burning tanks on the Golan

Heights, I saw with my own eyes that there is no hope for the weak and the dead, and that there is but little hope for the strong and victorious. I returned from the wars to write about the closeness of death and the pressing yearnings for redemption, the energy of longing that feeds the life about me, the depth of fear and the thrust of determination to turn over a new leaf.

"I write so as not to despair and not to give in to the temptation of hate for hate. I have written against the backgrounds of Jerusalem and kibbutz, the Middle Ages under the crusaders, and Europe under Hitler. I have written about Jewish refugees and pioneers, and about the new Israelis. I have also written articles and essays advocating a nonprincipled and perhaps even unjust compromise between Israeli Jews and Palestinian Arabs. I have seen that he who seeks absolute justice seeks death. My stories and articles have often brought upon me a storm of public fury in Israel. Some say I dampen the enthusiasm of Israeli Zionism. Others say I touch an open nerve, causing unnecessary pain. Maybe.

"In my stories I am the conjuror of evil spirits. As Nathan Zach puts it in his poem—'This song is a song about people,/ About what they think and what they want/ And what they think they want./ Apart from this there are not many things worthy of our interest.' "

Amos Oz is well established as one of Israel's most gifted and original writers. His fiction has nevertheless been controversial as well as successful, challenging as it does the pioneering simplicities and messianic Zionism that underpin Israeli society with the guilt and disillusionment of the younger generation. Yet Oz himself was expressing one aspect of Zionist idealism when he left Jerusalem at fourteen to work on Kibbutz Hulda, where he still lives with his family, teaching in the school and contributing his growing income as a writer to kibbutz funds.

In the early story "Ha-nawad we ha-zepha" (The Nomad and the Viper), the kibbutz girl who meets a Bedouin in the desert is bitten by a poisonous snake because she throws herself to the ground in a rape fantasy, both terrified and ecstatic. The suppressed guilt of young Israelis at the injustice done by their elders to the Arabs frequently reveals itself in Oz's stories in nightmares or fantasies of sexual humiliation. The author has said that it would be bad enough if the early Zionists had simply ignored the Arabs: "It was in a way even worse. They confronted the Arabs with Tolstoyan attitudes. We shall cure the Arabs, we shall educate them, we'll build for them, we'll show them what modern

life is. We embrace them with a loving embrace, and they must love us."

"The Nomad and the Viper" was one of the stories collected in Oz's first book, *Artsot ha-tan* (Lands of the Jackal, 1965), along with others in which the conflicts and disasters of kibbutz life come not from outside the perimeter but from the fears and desires of the beleaguered inhabitants. This is the case also in Oz's first novel, *Makom aher* (1966, translated by Nicholas de Lange as *Elsewhere, Perhaps*). It is set in a mountain kibbutz where Reuven, a vague and ineffectual teacher and poet whose wife has left him to live in Germany, has taken as his mistress a married woman. Reuven's adolescent daughter Noga entices the husband of Reuven's mistress into a passionate affair, becomes pregnant, and insists on keeping the baby. While the kibbutz gossips are sharpening their beaks on these outrages, the satanic Uncle Zechariah Berger arrives from Germany, and sets out to lure Noga back to Munich with him. Noga's awakened sexuality and the demonic Uncle Zechariah release emotions that this tidy, rational society had sought to banish forever, and the primitive Asiatic land that surrounds them finds an ally in the shadowy world of the kibbutzniks' subconscious fears and lusts. This "coolly unsparing analysis of a few households in a small village" (which put one reviewer in mind of a "Levantine Jane Austen") was used, it was said, "with extraordinary deftness, as the basis for a comprehensive view of an entire society." Paul Zweig likewise praised "the extraordinary breadth of Oz's conception and his deceptively simple style, mingling subtle characterization with natural imagery that takes on increasing symbolic power." A reviewer in the *Times Literary Supplement* welcomed the novel as a "revelation of a major talent among modern Israeli writers."

In *Mikha'el sheli* (1968, translated by Nicholas de Lange as *My Michael*), the setting is Jerusalem just before the Six Day War, and the comparisons were with *Madame Bovary* rather than Jane Austen. The Michael of the title is a geologist at the Hebrew University—the perfect, pragmatic, optimistic Israeli, contentedly moving rung by rung up the academic ladder. Michael is at a loss to understand the gulf between himself and his beloved wife Hannah—scarcely recognizes that it exists. Hannah herself is drowning, fast losing her grip on the prosaic world in which Michael lives, sinking ever more deeply into a private world of dreams and fantasies. The Arabs around her loom large in these dreams, especially the twin boys she grew up with, and whom she imagines returning as terrorists to rape her—both a degradation and a "cool pleasure." Hannah, who narrates the novel, is in some sense a personification of the schizoid city of Jerusalem itself, and the city, conversely, is brilliantly rendered as "a correlative for isolation and alienation."

While some native critics welcomed *My Michael* both as a work of literature and for its perceptions about the Israeli character, others regarded it as little short of seditious; one wrote that it was more dangerous to Israel than all the Arab armies marching against it. It became a major bestseller and was filmed and widely translated, establishing Oz's international reputation. Robert Alter called it "the study of a minutely felt process of psychological erosion, rendered with uncompromising consistency in an imaginatively wrought prose rich with suggestive imagery."

The novella *'Ad mavet* (1969, translated by de Lange as "Crusade") is not about contemporary Israel but about some of the circumstances that produced it. In A.D. 1096 a French count leaves his debts and his blighted vineyard and sets out for the Holy Land with a ragged army, murdering every Jew he finds to the greater glory of God. He does not find Jerusalem or the spiritual peace it represents for him. "Crusade" was published in English first in the magazine *Commentary* and then in book form, together with another novella, as *Unto Death* (1975). This other story is *Ahabah meuhereth,* translated by de Lange as "Late Love." It tells the story of an old Israeli who goes tirelessly from kibbutz to kibbutz giving his one and only lecture, a tirade of hate and fear about the "Russian menace." Both stories, as Joseph McElroy pointed out, "take as their theme the hatred that surrounds Jews and that destroys the hated and the haters alike." A reviewer in the *New Yorker* thought the first "a smooth amalgamation of ideology, myth, and narrative," while "the second too often reads like a philosophical speculation to which a story has been added as an afterthought."

Many reviewers, including some who greatly admire Oz's earlier work, were puzzled and displeased by *La-ga'ath ba-mayim, la-ga'ath ba-ruah* (1973, translated by de Lange as *Touch the Water, Touch the Wind*). The novel's hero is Elisha Pomeranz, a Jewish math teacher in Poland. When the Germans invade, Pomeranz survives imprisonment, lives for a time in the forest, then levitates his way to Israel. After a period on a kibbutz, a mathematical discovery about the nature of infinity brings him world renown, and in the end he is reunited with his beautiful wife Stefa, who meanwhile has become head of Soviet Intelligence. Other characters are eaten by bears, emigrate to Argentina, turn into animals.

It is this attempt to deal with the Nazi Holocaust in terms of fantasy and comedy that so upset the critics. John Thompson, for example (though interestingly enough he was reminded of Chagall by the levitation scene), complained that "each crucial event of the story is fobbed off into what appear to me most inept bits of foolish and obscure legerdemain—to me this seems oddly and frivolously cruel." But Alfred Kazin decided that Oz "is an immensely clever, subtle, and mischievous writer whose new book is a brilliant scenario of all Jewish experience in our day. . . . The clipped, stony, enigmatic language lends itself to marvelous sentences, bursts of eloquent sound that leave you hanging on the cliff. . . . To the unusually sensitive and humorous mind of Amos Oz, the real theme of Jewish history—especially in Israel—is unreality. . . . Tight-lipped about the history but mocking and funny about the perennially abstract Jewish mind, Oz is writing here about the messianic transcendent unreality of Jewish cravings—contrasted with experiences so terrible that they are still inadmissable."

Amos Oz is the son of Yehuda Arieh Klausner and the former Fania Mussman. He received his B.A. from the Hebrew University in Jerusalem in 1963 and in 1969-1970 was a visiting fellow of St. Cross College, Oxford University (M.A., 1970). He was author in residence at the Hebrew University in 1975. He received the Holon Prize in 1966 and the B'nai B'rith annual literary award in 1972. Oz says that Hebrew resembles Elizabethan English in its exuberance and flexibility. It is a language in which "everything is possible," and "the temptation is always there to become a William Shakespeare"; by contrast, modern English is "an elderly lady with whom you cannot take too many liberties." A "mild-mannered" man, he nevertheless derives "a kind of pleasure" from the fact that his promotion in 1975 to second lieutenant in the reserve gave him command of a unit which includes a literary critic.

PRINCIPAL WORKS: My Michael, 1972; Elsewhere, Perhaps, 1973; Unto Death, 1975; Touch the Water, Touch the Wind, 1975; The Hill of Evil Counsel, 1978.

ABOUT: Contemporary Authors 53-56, 1975; Yudkin, L.I. Escape Into Siege, 1973. *Periodicals*—Guardian April 24, 1972; Israeli Writing Autumn 1970; Nation September 7, 1974; New Republic November 29, 1975; New Society April 25, 1974; New York Review of Books October 5, 1972; February 7, 1974; January 23, 1975; New York Times May 25, 1972; New York Times Book Review May 21, 1972; November 18, 1973; November 24, 1974; October 26, 1975; New Yorker August 7, 1978; Publishers Weekly May 21, 1973; December 9, 1974; Saturday Review November 2, 1974; Times (London) April 29, 1972; Times Literary

OZICK

Supplement February 22, 1974; March 21, 1975; April 16, 1976.

OZICK, CYNTHIA (April 17, 1928–), American novelist and short story writer, was born in New York City, the daughter of a pharmacist, William Ozick, and the former Celia Regelson. She received her B.A. in English *cum laude* in 1949 at New York University, where she was Phi Beta Kappa, and went on to teach from 1949 to 1951 at Ohio State University, earning her M.A. there in 1950. In 1952 she married a lawyer, Bernard Hallote, by whom she has a daughter. Cynthia Ozick returned to New York University as an English instructor in 1964-1965. Since then she has been a full-time writer.

Writing in *Library Journal* about her first novel, ironically named *Trust* (1966), she said "it is about betrayal, it is about the failure of trust ... and it is about the failure of trust under every possible guise, in every possible relation—in love, sex, marriage, fatherhood, motherhood, politics high and low, government, law, citizenship, espionage, money, power, poverty, exploitation, victimization willing and unwilling, and other categories I can't think of now. And I was not always prepared for these betrayals of trust. ... The book seemed to open out under my hands from level to level of treachery and faithlessness. ... I believed I had to write not just another book about something, but an entirely underivative book about Everything. ... a novel which would encompass everything necessary to its vision, even if that also meant the inclusion of eccentricities, individualistic crotchets, passages requiring patience or inducing impatience, dialogue rendered as it needed to be rendered, assumptions, tests, allusions, long scrutinies."

All this being so, the five hundred and sixty-eight pages of *Trust* are not easy to summarize. The novel centers on the anonymous young narrator, her wealthy and much-married mother, and her stepfather, Enoch Vand. The story encompasses the heroine's progress from childhood to maturity and Enoch's progress from worldly to spiritual ambition, along the way unfolding a panorama of the social, political, and intellectual life of the rich in Europe and New York from the 1930s to the 1960s.

"*Trust,*" wrote R. Z. Sheppard, "introduces a novelist of remarkable intelligence, learning, and inventiveness," but "for all its high-powered philosophizing, sparkling dialogue, fine characterization, literary allusions, symbolism, and cutting satire, *Trust* is a curiously old-fashioned bit of realism. The brilliant bits seem to be waiting for a vision potent enough to fuse them into an important work of the imagination." Elinor

CYNTHIA OZICK

Baumbach also thought this "an interesting and sometimes brilliant first novel," but also had serious reservations. She found it necessary to "dismiss, as a dismal bore, a great part of the pseudo-Jamesian concerns of ... [the] book." It seemed to her that the novel's "world of high finance and policy-making" was "not entirely supported by the author's craft," and that "in this densely populated book filled with characters and caricatures who insist upon their right to be endlessly clever with each other, only the heroine and her stepfather, Enoch Vand, achieve real life." Yet, "when Cynthia Ozick clears the Jamesian hurdles she has set for herself ... we realize that she has a voice of her own, and that it is direct, poetic, inventive, playful, and, more often than not, full of wisdom."

All such reservations vanished when Miss Ozick published her first collection of short stories, *The Pagan Rabbi* (1971), where, according to Johanna Kaplan, "all that was best in the novel—that relentless, passionate, discovering and uncovering intelligence—is present and instantly recognizable, but there is now a difference in the prose. It is sharpened, clarified, controlled and above all beautifully and unceasingly welcoming." Indeed, these seven stories, all of which had previously appeared in such journals as *Hudson Review* and *Commentary,* had a rapturous reception—striking John Gross, for example, as the work of "the most interesting new American-Jewish writer to have come my way in the past few years." The story that most impressed Gross (as it did several other reviewers) was the novella "Envy; or, Yiddish in America," which studies an elderly, mediocre, embittered Yiddish writer gnawed by his envy of a more successful colleague. Gross found it "sardonic, fierce, completely unsentimental, wholly convincing, and though it dramatizes many of the ironies and complexities of Yiddish, or Yiddish in America, with great intelligence, it is in no sense a tract: language is the medium through which the characters move, not merely the excuse for their presence."

A reviewer in *Library Journal* thought that the theme of all of these stories was self-realization, pursued at times in "very unorthodox ways ... usually in vain." Another critic noted a preoccupation with "living fraudulently, whether by ignorance or design," and to a third it seemed that Cynthia Ozick was struggling most often with the question of "what is holy"—the magical, like the dryad in "The Pagan Rabbi" or the sea-nymph in "The Dock-Witch," or the ordinary phenomena and procedures of everyday life. These concerns are not mutually exclusive, but such different readings are an indication of the richness of these stories and of the characters in them. "From their smallest idiosyncratic gestures," wrote Johanna Kaplan —"their ways of eating, dressing, moving and arguing—to their largest concerns, they are people whom one knows, and not because we have met them before, but because we are meeting them ... *now*. Cynthia Ozick is a kind of narrative hypnotist. Her range is extraordinary: there is seemingly nothing she cannot do. Her stories contain passages of intense lyricism and brilliant, hilarious, uncontainable inventiveness— jokes, lists, letters, poems, parodies, satires." And *Newsweek's* critic thought that three of these stories were "among the best written by Americans in recent years. . . . Cynthia Ozick works with fantasy or with engaging conceits. Her stories, nudged on to the track, accelerate, change gears, turn at alarming angles from their predicted courses. . . . Nearly all of them, for all their wit and absurdities, turn out to be both funnier and sadder than we expected at the start. She builds her stories carefully and she writes them very well. They will be with us, I think, for some time."

Paul Bailey, reviewing *Bloodshed and Three Novellas* (1976), wrote that the title piece "invokes the horrors of the holocaust with a literally shocking irony," and was reminded by this and the novella "A Mercenary" of those works of Isaac Bashevis Singer which "succeed by their very outrageousness," defying explication. "Usurpation," which according to the author is "about the dread of Moloch, the dread of lyrical faith, the dread of metaphysics," seemed to Bailey to fail by comparison with Cynthia Ozick's best work. He reserved his praise primarily for "An Education," which charts the spiritual progress of Una Meyer, a brilliant scholar possessed by a need to debase herself in the pursuit of edification. She is, Bailey writes, "the most energetic of masochists, shuffling happily from one grisly experience to another with a frightening incapacity to be properly humiliated. Miss Ozick never explains her character, with the result that she is a constant mystery, as such people are in life." Thomas R. Edwards preferred "A Mercenary," a "nearly perfect long short story" set in the world of international diplomacy, full of impersonations and identity changes, whose point is this: "It may be that every man at length becomes what he wishes to victimize. It may be that every man needs to impersonate what he first must kill."

Cynthia Ozick also contributes poetry, translations, essays, and reviews to a wide range of periodicals. She taught a fiction workshop at the Chautauqua Writers' Conference in 1966, and held the O'Connor Professorship at Colgate University in 1973. She gave the America-Israel Address on Cultural Affairs at the Weizmann Institute in Israel in 1970, and was the Elly Stolnitz Memorial Lecturer at Indiana University in 1972. She had a fellowship from the National Endowment for the Arts in 1968, and in 1972 *The Pagan Rabbi* brought her the B'nai B'rith Jewish Heritage Award, the Edward Lewis Wallant Memorial Award, the Jewish Book Council Award, and a nomination for a National Book Award. An award from the National Academy of Arts and Letters followed in 1973, an O. Henry Prize in 1975, and the Epstein award in 1977. Julian Moynahan says of her that her imagination is adventurous, her prose "is often richly colored and nuanced, owing something to Woolf and Lawrence, and she also has an acute ear. . . . Whenever American writing is going now, Cynthia Ozick is a distinctive and bright part of that movement into the future."

PRINCIPAL WORKS: Trust, 1966; The Pagan Rabbi and Other Stories, 1971; Bloodshed and Three Novellas, 1976.

ABOUT: Contemporary Authors 17-20 1st revision, 1976; Who's Who in America, 1976-1977. *Periodicals*—Atlantic May 1976; Book Week June 19, 1966; Christian Science Monitor September 9, 1971; August 2, 1976; Commonweal September 3, 1971; Library Journal February 1, 1966; New Republic August 13, 1966; June 5, 1976; New Statesman July 23, 1976; New York Review of Books April 1, 1976; New York Times Book Review July 17, 1966; June 13, 1972; April 11, 1976; Newsweek May 10, 1971; Saturday Review July 9, 1966; April 17, 1976; Times Literary Supplement July 21, 1972; July 23, 1976.

PALAZZESCHI

*"PALAZZESCHI," ALDO (pseudonym of
Aldo Giurlani) (February 2, 1885–August 17,
1974), Italian novelist, short story writer, and
poet, was born in Florence, the son of Alberto
Giurlani and the former Amalia Martinelli. His
father was a well-known Florentine businessman, and Palazzeschi early rebelled against his
prosperous but strictly conventional family
background. Educated for a business career, he
elected to become a poet, a satirist, and an intellectual anarchist.

His first collection of poems, *I cavalli bianchi*
(The White Horses, 1905), employed D'Annunzian rhythms while occasionally parodying
D'Annunzian rhetoric, and this was characteristic of him. In subsequent volumes he echoed the
nostalgic and delicately lyrical tones of the "cre-
puscular" poets and blithely embraced the
iconoclasm and typographical experiments of
the futurists, whom he defended for a time in
Lacerba (1913-1915), the journal he founded
with his friends Giovanni Papini and Ardengo
Soffici. At about the same time he was a contributor to the important revisionist magazine
La Voce (1908-1916). And all this without ever
relinquishing his right to parody and make fun
of any aspect of any of these groups and movements that seemed to him pompous or otherwise
unacceptable.

Taken to task for his eclecticism and lack of
commitment, Palazzeschi replied with a nonsense poem of meaningless syllables—all that
should be expected of the contemporary poet—
and the admonition "E lasciatemi divertire!"—
"let me amuse myself!" Yet his playful antiliterary, ironic verse expressed not superficiality but
a hypersensitivity carefully armored against exigencies both historical and personal. Moreover,
as one critic observed in the *Times Literary Supplement,* Palazzeschi "had from the beginning
his own manner, his own rhythms and his own
music. . . . Whether he writes like a child in the
magic atmosphere of a nursery fairy-tale or like
a clown balancing on a pogo stick, he is always
true to himself." Horrified by World War I, he
wrote little poetry after 1914 until late in his
long life.

The imaginative power seldom released in
Palazzeschi's poetry emerged, eventually, in his
fiction. His first novel appeared in 1908 as *rifles-
si,* and was reissued in 1943 as *Allegoria di
novembre* (November Allegory). It is the haunting story of a prince, demoralized by the suicide
of his mother, who falls deeply in love with a
young Englishman. He chooses to preserve in
solitude a pure vision of love and beauty rather
than to seek a physical consummation which

*pä lät tsâ′ skē

ALDO PALAZZESCHI

might tarnish or diminish his ideal. Martin Seymour-Smith regards this study of Oedipal,
homosexual, and narcissistic problems as Palazzeschi's most personal novel and makes this interesting diagnosis: "Palazzeschi fought shy of
returning to this delicate problem—it leaves this
immature first novel as his most interesting but
not his most accomplished—and instead elected
to become a sceptic in the best Italian tradition.
The decision lay between becoming a major
writer and a minor one; Palazzeschi became a
good minor one, and his choice may well have
been correct."

In *Il codice di Perelà* (1911, revised in 1920
and 1943, and again in 1954 as *Perelà uomi di
fumo*), Palazzeschi combined what he had
learned from Pirandello's fiction with his acute
awareness of the dangers implicit in the Italian
political situation. Perelà, "the man of smoke,"
having spent his first thirty-two years in a chim-
ney, emerges into modern society; through his
innocent eyes, it seems a very odd institution
indeed. Perelà has great success in the world,
followed by equally extreme danger, and disappears again into smoke. It has been suggested
that this nebulous and uncommitted figure
represents the author himself, while the "voluntary madman" Prince Zarlino is a prophetic vision of Mussolini. The novel succeeds both as
satire and as fantasy, and beyond that is a remarkable examination of the seminal problem of
art versus activism. Some Italian critics recognized the seriousness beneath the book's frothy
surface, and one called it "a document about the
crisis of values." *Perelà, the Man of Smoke,*
Peter M. Riccio's English adaptation of the 1920
version, was on the whole less respectfully re-

ceived, though Alfred Kazin called it "an Italian version of Gulliver standing on its head."

Palazzeschi's early novels were highly subjective. They contained very little in the way of plot, dialogue, dramatic incident, or convincing characterization, and were largely vehicles for the author's flamboyant poetic prose, his theories, his satire and dark humor. Most of this was equally true of *Due imperi . . . mancati* (Two Empires . . . That Came to Nothing, 1920), but here Palazzeschi strung on his sketchy plot not the extravagances of a youthful aestheticism but a passionately sincere attack on World War I and on war in general. It was in this transitional book that Palazzeschi came closest to a clear social and political commitment, opposing to the spirit of nationalism a blend of Marxist philosophy and Christian ethics which, he imagined, might bring a world without war, and without the social taboos and conventions (including marriage) that he detested.

His first fully mature novel was *Sorelle Materassi* (1934, translated by Angus Davidson as *The Sisters Materassi*). This is, in the opinion of most critics, his masterpiece. It is a perfect work of art in the Flaubertian sense that the author has detached himself entirely from the story he tells—and yet, as Flaubert wrote of his own novels, it is "nothing but the exposition of the personality of the author." The story, set in and beautifully redolent of Florence, is of two elderly unmarried sisters who are bewitched, exploited, and finally ruined by their young nephew, who then marries a rich woman and goes off to America. Remo is a scoundrel—though an ambiguous one—but Palazzeschi shows with great precision and confidence how the seeds of the sisters' ruin lie in themselves.

Sorelle Materassi, like Palazzeschi's other novels, is not a straightforward narrative. Instead, as G. Singh writes in *From Verismo to Experimentalism,* we are given "a series of scenes and situations which do not necessarily emerge one from the other and are not always organically linked. Palazzeschi provides these links by introducing numerous descriptions, anecdotes and digressions, which, besides holding our interest, enrich our comprehension and enjoyment of the characters' psychological, cultural, or social milieu." The way these elements are fused "makes for that architectonical unity, that rich and complex pattern of subtly orchestrated notes and intensities, that is undoubtedly Palazzeschi's forte as a creative novelist."

Notable among Palazzeschi's later novels are *I fratelli Cuccoli* (The Cuccoli Brothers, 1948), thematically related to *Sorelle Materassi,* which describes with "warm humor" and "generous wisdom" what happens when a wealthy bachelor adopts four teenage boys, and *Roma* (1965, translated under the same title by Mihaly Csikszentmihalyi), contrasting the bygone age of faith with the immorality and greed of the present. These more or less realistic novels were followed after an interval by *Il doge* (The Duke, 1967), which marked a startling return to the fantastic and surreal manner of *Il codice de Perelà*. At about the same time Palazzeschi published a new volume of poetry, *Cuor mio* (My Love, 1968). An English critic, reviewing *Via delle cento stelle* (The Way of a Hundred Stars), a subsequent collection of one hundred short poems published in 1972 when the author was eighty-seven, wrote that they had "a more spacious and a calmer air than their predecessors, though some have a waspish sting in the tail. There are no *ghiribizzi* (whimsical ornaments) and no more childlike or birdlike chatter. Instead, Palazzeschi uses a shrewd, wry, colloquial, almost prosaic, style to set out his unexpected findings and bizarre discoveries. The extraordinary freshness of these poems, their originality, their humour and disconcerting wisdom are amazing for a man of his age."

In his later years Palazzeschi divided his time between Venice, in summer, and Rome, in winter; he finally settled in Rome, though remaining, as his work showed, deeply attached to Florence. He received the Feltrinelli prize in 1957. Palazzeschi, a bachelor, was a collector of porcelain. Little information about him is available in English, despite the international success of *Sorelle Materassi,* which was serialized on Italian television, to immense acclaim, a few months after his death.

Palazzeschi was ironic, versatile, popular, and prolific, but he was not (as one critic has suggested) only a "highly successful entertainer." He was acutely sensitive to the sinister political undercurrents in Italy and their implications for human freedom, from the beginning of the century. Though many of his friends joined the fascists, he became, in Luigi Russo's words, "one of the sharpest, most reticent, and most sorrowful of the antifascists." Moreover, as *Sorelle Materassi* demonstrates, he was capable of depth of vision, psychological insight, and a kind of compassion. G. Singh has pointed out that "however grotesquely and ironically . . . [the sisters] may be represented, we are never allowed to lose sight of their basic humanity and individuality," and maintains that in Palazzeschi's mature novels "there is both involvement and detachment, a basic sympathy and consideration for what he has created and a subtle ironic laugh or grin at the follies or self-deception of those characters."

If many critics regard this brilliantly original writer as ultimately a minor figure, it is because they find altogether too much detachment in his work and not enough involvement or moral commitment. But how far he was from superficiality is suggested by this passage from his autobiographical *Piacere della memoria* (The Pleasure of Memory, 1964): "I love solitude as others love speed, height, power, agility, risk. . . . Even if I owe to friendship some of the most unforgettable hours of my life and maintain a very close link with my friends [they included Marino Moretti, with whom he went to school, and Eugenio Montale] . . . the hours of happiness which I owe to solitude constitute a different kind of joy . . . something I would even say too sad for a writer; something beyond words. . . . something that was too deeply mine for me to be able to tell others that it even existed."

PRINCIPAL WORKS IN ENGLISH TRANSLATION: Perelà, the Man of Smoke, 1936; The Sisters Materassi (England, The Materassi Sisters), 1953; Roma, 1965. *Poems in* Golino, C.L. (ed.) Contemporary Italian Poetry, 1962.

ABOUT: Chi Scrive, 1962; De Luca, J. Aldo Palazzeschi, 1941 (in Italian); Flora, F. Dal romanticismo al futurismo, 1925; Pacifici, S. (ed.) From Verismo to Experimentalism, 1969; Palazzeschi, A. Piacere della memoria, 1964; Pancrazi, P. Scrittori d'oggi, 1946; Penguin Companion to Literature 2, 1969; Pullini, G. Aldo Palazzeschi, 1965 (in Italian); Seymour-Smith, M. Guide to Modern Literature, 1973; Smith, H. (ed.) Columbia Dictionary of Modern European Literature, 1947; Who's Who in Italy, 1958. *Periodicals*— Books Abroad Winter 1972; Corriere della Sera June 13, 1968; Lettere Italiane XII 1961; L'immagine 11 1948; New York Times August 18, 1974; Times Literary Supplement April 30, 1970; December 22, 1972.

PALEY, GRACE (December 11, 1922–), American short story writer, was born and grew up in the Bronx, New York City, the daughter of Isaac Goodside, a doctor, and the former Mary Ridnyik. Her father, who retired at sixty and devoted himself to painting, was a "grand storyteller"; her mother was "a very puritanical woman" but "very fine, a first-class person. . . . They were both very political people. They were both exiled. My father was sent to Siberia when he was about nineteen or twenty, and she was exiled to Germany."

The author herself was a talkative child, "absolutely entranced by stories and family conversation." She studied for a time at Hunter College and later at New York University but left without a degree. Indeed, she says that she was "sort of thrown out" of Hunter, and that "actually after the sixth grade my interest in the academic routine was over." As a writer she began with poetry, and in the early 1940s studied with W. H. Auden at the New School for Social Re-

GRACE PALEY

Karl Bissinger

search. At about the same time, in 1942, she married Jess Paley, a movie cameraman, by whom she has two children, Nora and Dan.

The Little Disturbances of Man (1959), her first book, is a collection of eleven short stories, only three of which had previously appeared in magazines. All of them are set in New York and for the most part they deal with the author or someone very much like her, her marriage, her children, her parents, and her friends. They are funny, warmhearted, and cheerfully disillusioned, distinguished by an exceptionally accurate ear for dialogue, and by a highly individual use of language. The collection was received with something like universal admiration and pleasure. R. C. Healey was particularly impressed by a story called "The Loudest Voice," about Jewish children performing in a school Christmas play—"a perfect gem of a story that is simultaneously hilarious, poignant and philosophical." Philip Roth said that Grace Paley "has deep feelings, a wild imagination, and a style whose toughness and bumpiness arise not out of exasperation with the language, but the daring and heart of a genuine writer of prose. Though no blood-sister, she is as funny as Jane Austen. And at her best . . . she displays an understanding of loneliness, lust, selfishness, and fatigue that is splendidly comic and unladylike."

The book became the object of something like a cult, and ten years later, when "the few dog-eared copies around began to disintegrate," *The Little Disturbances of Man* was republished, releasing a new and perhaps more considered wave of admiration. It was noted that some of these stories contained an element of surrealism, in the way that the narrative was sometimes "deliberately telescoped into the absurd," and in the startling leaps and skids of the language, which *Time* thought "supple and colloquial, yet framed in the syntax of surprise." Donald Barthelme called Paley "a wonderful writer and troublemaker. We are fortunate to have her in this country."

During the early 1960s Grace Paley taught at Columbia and at Syracuse University. At the same time—influenced, it seems, by her children—she became increasingly involved in politics and social action in Greenwich Village, where she lived. A "somewhat combative pacifist," she was one of the founders of the Village Peace Center in 1961, and served on the board of Resist/Support in Action, a group that supported draft resisters and shared with them the risk of legal retaliation. "Have been in jail," she noted some years later, "and will go again."

This commitment severely curtailed her writing. Passages from an uncompleted novel were published during the late 1960s in *The Noble Savage* and *New American Review,* but her next book, when it appeared, was another collection of short stories, *Enormous Changes at the Last Minute* (1974). The setting is the same but the mood is bleaker, the social concern more dominant. These new stories are about women struggling to raise their children alone, about drug addicts, drunks, the old, the lonely, the losers. The milieu is one in which, as a small boy remarks, "mostly nobody has fathers." And the situation for many of the characters is one of "crummy days and crummy guys, and no money and broke all the time and cockroaches and nothing to do on Sundays but take the kids to Central Park and row on that lousy lake."

The surreal element noted in the first book emerges more strongly here—in "Wants," for example, in which a man talking to his ex-wife says: "I attribute the dissolution of our marriage to the fact that you never asked the Bertrams to dinner." She agrees, but reminds him that "first, my father was sick that Friday, then the children were born, then I had those Tuesday-night meetings, then the war began. Then we didn't seem to know them any more." And in "The Long-Distance Runner" a middle-aged woman jogs off in her running shorts in search of the Coney Island apartment where she grew up, spends three weeks with the black family she finds living there, and jogs back home again, where she is greeted quite without surprise. Other stories are "slices of life" in which "Paley's Jews, blacks, Italians, Puerto Ricans and Irishmen sound, in tone and syntax, exactly like Jews, blacks, Italians, Puerto Ricans and Irishmen."

The old Jewish immigrant who appears in several of these seventeen stories is specifically acknowledged to be Grace Paley's father, and it is difficult not to identify his story-writing daughter Faith with the author. The dialogues between these two are important in the collection: the dour, defeated, affectionate old man represents, it was suggested, "the whole immigrant past, 'the cruel history of Europe,' " just as Faith, unhappy as she often is, never loses her American optimism for long—the buoyancy she acquired growing up in "the summer sunlight of upward mobility." Developing out of this dialectical conflict, wrote Gabriele Annan, is a preoccupation with time, "the haunting of the present by the past. Mrs. Paley explores time and all its sad related themes: the transience of life, the sorrow of old age, the fear of death, the irreplaceability of one human being by another."

Lis Harris found the collection uneven, containing some stories that were disappointingly thin or slight, but she could not "think of another writer who captures the itch of the city, or the complexities of love between parents and children, or the cutting edge of sexual combat, as well as Grace Paley does." Gabriele Annan, who like Lis Harris was reminded of Chekhov, concluded that Paley "is a conscious and deliberate artist," while Walter Clemons went so far as to say that she is "one of the best writers alive."

Grace Paley incorporates into her stories snatches of conversation heard on the street, attempting to make her fiction an exercise in a community of voices. However, according to a *Nation* critic, "it makes little difference whether she speaks in the first person or the third, disguised as someone called Faith or Alexandra, or whether she tells her own troubles"—the manner in which she deploys her materials remains very much a solo feat, and a virtuoso one. Her favorite writer is Isaac Babel, who she says is "really writing about things he doesn't exactly know and yet he's trying to understand, he's using writing to understand the world and that's what I want to do. And that's what I do."

The author teaches literature at Sarah Lawrence College, Bronxville, New York, and nowadays divides her time between Vermont and her beloved New York City. She received a Guggenheim fellowship in 1961, a grant from the National Endowment for the Arts in 1966, and an award from the National Institute of Arts and Letters in 1970. She is a member of the executive board of P.E.N. Grace Paley still writes some verse but says "I'm not such a hot poet . . . it serves me more than I serve it." A small woman, not much over five feet tall, she is said to be irresistibly funny, charming, and "magnetic." She is now married to Robert Nichols, a poet and dramatist. She has visited Hanoi and Moscow as a member of peace delegations, and spent six weeks in Chile with Nichols, who was studying the literature of that country and its development under the Allende government. On September 4, 1978, she and ten other demonstrators broke away from a tour group in Washington, D.C., and unfurled an anti-nuclear banner on the White House lawn. The "White House Eleven" were subsequently convicted of unlawful entry, fined, and given suspended sentences of 180 days in prison.

PRINCIPAL WORKS: The Little Disturbances of Man, 1959; Enormous Changes at the Last Minute, 1974.

ABOUT: Contemporary Authors 25–28, 1st revision, 1977; Vinson, J. (ed.) Contemporary Novelists, 1976; Who's Who in America, 1976–1977. *Periodicals*—America June 8, 1974; Commentary July 1974; Commonweal October 25, 1968; Esquire November 1970; Harper's June 1974; Nation September 10, 1973; May 11, 1974; New Boston Review Fall 1976; New Leader June 24, 1974; New Republic March 16, 1974; New York Review of Books March 21, 1974; New York Times April 19, 1959; March 23, 1968; New York Times Book Review March 17, 1974; Newsweek March 11, 1974; Saturday Review April 11, 1959; Time May 3, 1968; Times Literary Supplement February 14, 1975; Village Voice March 14, 1974; Washington Post April 2, 1968; December 29, 1968; February 25, 1974.

*PANOFSKY, ERWIN (March 30, 1892– March 14, 1968), American art historian, was born in Hanover, Germany, the son of Arnold and Caecilie (Solling) Panofsky. He was educated at the universities of Berlin, Munich, and Freiburg/Breisgau, taking his doctorate at Freiburg in 1914. He worked at the Warburg Library in Hamburg and was professor of art history at Hamburg University from 1926 to 1933, acquiring a reputation as a brilliant teacher and an outstanding scholar. In 1931 he paid his first visit to the United States as a visiting professor at New York University.

Panofsky's early major work, *"Idea"; ein Beitrag zur Begriffsgeschichte der älteren Kunsttheorie* (1924), has been translated by J.J.S. Peake as *Idea, a Concept in Art Theory*. It traces the history of the neoplatonic theory of art, in which the artist aims not merely to imitate nature but to penetrate the innermost essence of reality, the Platonic "idea." The artist who works in this way is truly a creator, according to the neoplatonists, serving an ideal of beauty derived from his own inner life. An example is provided in Michelangelo's famous sonnet beginning "Non ha l'ottimo artista alcun concetto," which expresses the Platonic concept of the form pre-existing in the marble, waiting for the sculptor to release it.

*pan of´skē

ERWIN PANOFSKY

Albrecht Dürer also invokes this neoplatonic tradition in his description of an artist as "one who is inwardly full of images," and who can realize his conception in his material. Panofsky had written several essays on Dürer, such as *Dürers Kunsttheorie* (Dürer's Theory of Art, 1915) before his classic study with Fritz Saxl, *Dürers "Melencolia I"* (Dürer's Melancholia I, 1923). The latter marked the beginning of the "iconological" approach to art history of which Panofsky was the chief exponent. He defined it as "that branch of the history of art which concerns itself with the subject matter or meaning of works of art as opposed to their form," and he adopted the term iconology to distinguish his broad approach to the analysis of meaning from iconography, the mere identification of subject matter. In Ernst Gombrich's definition, iconology "investigates the function of images in allegory and symbolism and their reference to what might be called 'the invisible world of ideas.' "

The art historian who adopts this method must, as Panofsky said, "have insight into the manner in which, under varying historical conditions, essential tendencies in the human mind were expressed by specific themes and concepts." In *Hercules am Scheidewege* (Hercules at the Crossroads, 1930), Panofsky fruitfully applies this approach to a whole series of different iconological and iconographical problems in artists ranging from Raphael to Titian and Holbein. Needless to say, iconology has its critics, who point out that where art fails to communicate directly but needs an interpreter it is vulnerable to the most arid kind of scholasticism. Panofsky himself saw "some danger that iconology will behave, not like ethnology as opposed to ethnog-

Svenskt Pressfoto, courtesy Wolfgang Panofsky

raphy, but like astrology as opposed to astrography."

When Hitler came to power in 1933, Panofsky was one of the many European Jewish intellectuals who migrated to the United States. He taught for a time at New York University, and in 1935 became professor of art history at the Institute for Advanced Study, Princeton, where he taught for the rest of his life. Most of his later books were written in English, beginning with *Studies in Iconology: Humanistic Themes in the Art of the Renaissance* (1939). These six essays were originally delivered as the Mary Flexner Lectures at Bryn Mawr College and later repeated at Princeton University. The first combines methodology with a study of classical mythology in the Middle Ages, and these ideas are then applied to specific subjects such as "Blind Cupid" and "Father Time."

Wolfgang Stechow called the book "a masterly exemplar of a novel and fruitful viewpoint and method in art history." He went on to explain the significance of the iconological approach: "There is no denying the fact that the purely aesthetic formal approach to art history which prevailed during the last fifty years or so and produced a number of outstanding achievements, has reached its climax and, at the same time, its limits. A younger generation does not find complete satisfaction in it and has thought of many means of emphasizing the primary importance of 'subject matter' and 'content' in works of art (a distinction excellently put forward in the present book) without ignoring the necessity of formal interpretation." According to Millard Meiss, "only two or three other books in the literature of the history of art have had an effect comparable to *Studies in Iconology.* In it Erwin Panofsky showed that the knowledge of the meaning of a work of art of the past increased not only its relevance to us but also its beauty, and for the determination of this meaning he presented precise historical methods, subject to objective control. The book, however, is not only a landmark in the discipline and in the humanities as a whole. Zestful, illuminated by a rare intelligence and an even rarer learning, it is a great delight to read."

Following his many early studies of Dürer, Panofsky went on to produce a major two-volume work examining the artist's whole achievement, *Albrecht Dürer* (1943), later republished in one volume as *The Life and Art of Albrecht Dürer* (4th edition, 1955). His copiously annotated translation, *Abbot Suger on the Abbey Church of St. Denis and Its Art Treasures* (1946), made available, for the first time in any modern language, a famous Latin work of the twelfth-century renaissance, Abbot Suger's account of his rebuilding of the royal abbey just outside Paris as the first Gothic cathedral. The abbot, a great historian and chief minister of France, decorated the abbey with priceless works of art, and his book defends this practice against the criticisms of the ascetic St. Bernard. Suger maintains that God should be served with the most precious materials and the richest workmanship, whose lavish sensuous beauty would be anagogically invested with spiritual meaning. Panofsky's editorial introduction sets the book in its historical and philosophical background, including the controversies surrounding the tearing down and rebuilding of the great royal abbey, of which he says: "It was as if a President of the United States were to have had the White House rebuilt by Frank Lloyd Wright." It was generally recognized that the book was, and would remain, of prime importance in medieval studies.

In his 1948 Wimmer lecture, published as *Gothic Architecture and Scholasticism* (1951), Panofsky set out to relate Gothic architecture to the thought of its times, describing changes in the character of Gothic through the centuries, and showing how stylistic changes reflected developments in the philosophy of the same period. Jean Bony called this "a contribution of the first importance to the history and definition of Gothic architecture," but Arnold Hauser objected that "the exponents of the history of ideas readily fall into the error of giving philosophical thought precedence over artistic forms just because the former gives clearest expression to their 'ideas'. . . . Yet there are no grounds at all for thinking that in philosophy is to be found the true origin, or at least the paradigmatic form, of that medieval world-view which is also expressed in art."

In 1947–1948 Panofsky gave the Charles Eliot Norton lectures at Harvard, and these were published as *Early Netherlandish Painting: Its Origins and Character* (1953). Panofsky had set out to clarify the historical premises of the achievement of Jan and Hubert Van Eyck, the Master of Flémalle, and Rogier van der Weyden, to analyze their style, "and to chart . . . the course of those ensuing developments which may be said to constitute the mainstream of the Early Netherlandish tradition." As one reviewer observed in the *Times Literary Supplement,* this "impressive and immensely learned book" is thus "at once less and more than a formal history of Flemish painting. It is less in that Professor Panofsky does not feel compelled to record every fact or transcribe every document, and it is more in that he ranges wider and digs deeper than previous writers in this field." Millard Meiss commented that these "two handsome volumes do far more than fill a need. Together with the articles that their author has published over the past twenty years, they inaugurate a new era in the understanding and enjoyment of early Netherlandish painting. . . . the reviewer feels certain that it will take its place as one of the major works in the history of art."

With his first wife, Dora Mosse Panofsky, herself an art historian well known for her work on Poussin's mythological landscapes, Panofsky wrote *Pandora's Box: The Changing Aspects of a Mythical Symbol* (1956), a study of the literary heritage of the myth of Pandora ("the pagan Eve") and the ways in which it was adapted to serve the visual arts. Pandora is the first woman, to whom we owe all our ills but also our hope for better things. The box she opened was in Greek mythology actually a jar, and the Panofskys show how the meaning and connotation of both Pandora and her jar or box have constantly and endlessly varied. As E. H. Gombrich observed, "the myth, therefore, becomes an instance of that phenomenon which Professor Panofsky has so brilliantly explored in the past: the continued creativity of mythological invention after the official demise of paganism." The *Times Literary Supplement,* describing it as a "learned, brilliant and charming book," said: "With immense erudition and an unrivalled virtuosity in its application, . . . [the authors] have put together a series of generously illustrated iconological essays which give a history of the migrations of the classical myth in post-classical times."

Meaning in the Visual Arts (1955) is a selection of earlier papers and essays, including some in revised versions and others translated from German, offering a good cross section of Panofsky's work. This was followed by *Renaissance and Renascences in Western Art* (1960), an outstanding synthesis of his conception of the history of art in Western Europe. Panofsky begins by discussing the validity of speaking at all of an Italian Renaissance and then explores the renaissances of the Middle Ages, bringing out the uniqueness of the Italian Renaissance by comparing it with earlier attempts at classical revival—the Carolingian and the Twelfth-Century. Panofsky's *Tomb Sculpture* (1964) is a copiously illustrated study of funerary art from ancient Egypt and the classical world through the Middle Ages to the Renaissance and Baroque, once again relating the art to the ideas that shaped it. John Canaday called it "a work of analytical scholarship that also deals constantly with religious experience—our ways of reconciling the goals of life with the problems of mortality. Since these intertwined preoccupations have always been at the core of thought, they have also been at the core of art, and they are at the core of this superb (and lively) study."

Panofsky was widely regarded as the most eminent art historian of the century, but he also had many other interests, and was an authority on Mozart, the history of the detective novel, and the cinema. His famous essay "Style and Medium in the Motion Pictures," first published in *Critique* (Vol. 1 No. 3 1947), was reprinted in many books and anthologies, including Daniel Talbot's *Film: an Anthology* (1959) and C.T. Samuel's *A Casebook on Film* (1970). Panofsky begins by saying that "film art is the only art the development of which men now living have witnessed from the very beginnings; and this development is all the more interesting as it took place under conditions contrary to precedents. It was not an artistic urge that gave rise to the discovery and gradual perfection of a new technique; it was a technical invention that gave rise to the discovery and gradual perfection of a new art." Panofsky goes on to argue that film is an art form: "It might be said that a film, called into being by a cooperative effort in which all contributions have the same degree of permanence is the nearest modern equivalent of a mediaeval cathedral." But "in modern life the movies are what most other forms of art have ceased to be, not an adornment but a necessity. . . . It is the movies, and only the movies, that do justice to that materialistic interpretation of the universe which, whether we like it or not, pervades contemporary civilization."

Panofsky had two sons by his 1916 marriage to Dora Mosse. The Panofskys were part of a brilliant circle at Princeton. During World War II Mrs. Panofsky contracted a painful disease that made it impossible for her to sleep, and a three-man team of volunteers undertook to distract her by taking turns reading to her: they were Panofsky, Thomas Mann, and Albert Einstein. Dora Panofsky died in 1965, and Dr. Panofsky was married again, to Gerda Soergel, in 1966. Panofsky was a member of the American Academy of Arts and Sciences, the British Academy, and a number of other foreign academies. He received the Haskins Medal of the Mediaeval Academy of America in 1962, and his other awards included honorary doctorates from many universities.

According to his obituarist in the New York *Times,* Panofsky was "a short man with thinning dark hair and lively eyes sparkling behind thick-lensed spectacles. . . . He appeared to have total recall of an almost complete range of knowledge. . . . On the lecture platform he captivated audiences, obscuring his strong German accent with his wit, growing as absorbed in communicating his ideas and love of art that his animation seemed almost to set him to dancing." John Canaday wrote that "for many years now it has been obvious that he is one of the great writers on art without restriction as to generation or century. His brilliance never dimmed, nor did the sparkle of his personality. . . . Erwin Panofsky saw men denying or neglecting the humanistic values to which his life was dedicated, and he could speak of a 'deteriorating world.' But his greatness was that he proved the strength of the very values that seemed to be decaying. When he talked or lectured or wrote, the humanistic traditions were not merely preserved: they were continued and enlarged in their fullest life."

PRINCIPAL WORKS IN ENGLISH AND ENGLISH TRANSLATION: Studies in Iconology: Humanistic Themes in the Art of the Renaissance, 1939; The Codex Huygens and Leonardo da Vinci's Art Theory, 1940; Albrecht Dürer, 1943 (revised as The Life and Art of Albrecht Dürer, 1955); Abbot Suger on the Abbey Church of St. Denis and Its Art Treasures (edited, translated, and annotated by Panofsky), 1946; Gothic Architecture and Scholasticism, 1951; Early Netherlandish Painting: Its Origins and Character, 1953; Galileo as a Critic of the Arts, 1954; (with Dora Panofsky) Pandora's Box: The Changing Aspects of a Mythical Symbol, 1956; Meaning in the Visual Arts: Papers in and on Art History, 1955: Renaissance and Renascences in Western Art, 1960; The Iconography of Correggio's Camera di San Paolo, 1961; Tomb Sculpture: Four Lectures on Its Changing Aspects from Ancient Egypt to Bernini (edited by H.W. Janson), 1964; Idea: A Concept in Art Theory, 1968; Problems in Titian, Mostly Iconographic, 1969; Dr. Panofsky and Mr. Tarkington: An Exchange of Letters, edited by Richard M. Ludwig, 1974.

ABOUT: Gombrich, E. Art and Illusion, 1960; Gombrich, E. Meditations on a Hobby Horse, 1964; Hauser, A. The Philosophy of Art History, 1958; Meiss, M. (ed.) De artibus opuscula: Essays in Honor of Erwin Panofsky, 1961; Pickering, F.P. Literature and Art in the Middle Ages, 1970; Webster's American Biographies, 1964; Who's Who in America, 1968-1969. Periodicals—Book Week December 13, 1964; Burlington Magazine 62 1933, 78 1941, 88 1946, 89 1947, 95 1953, 103 1961; Christian Science Monitor June 24, 1954; Classical World May 1965; College Art Journal Spring 1955; Commonweal August 17, 1956; Nation July 17, 1954; National Review December 15, 1964; New Republic August 13, 1956; New York Review of Books December 3, 1964; July 2, 1970; New York Times March 7, 1954; March 16, 1968; New York Times Book Review December 6, 1964; Spectator September 7, 1956; Times Literary Supplement June 28, 1947; March 5, 1954; August 3, 1956; January 14, 1965; June 4, 1970.

*PARRA, NICANOR (September 5, 1914–), Chilean poet, was born in San Fabian, the son of Nicanor P. Parra, a schoolteacher, and the former Clara S. Navarrete. Parra has recalled how, as children, he and his four brothers and three

*par′ ra

Andres Sanchez, courtesy New Directions

NICANOR PARRA

sisters played among the tombstones at the local cemetery, the only playground available to them. They were gifted children: one sister is a notable painter; another, the late Violeta Parra, became a folksinger of international fame. Nicanor Parra was drawn equally to science and to literature. His first book of poems, Cancionero sin nombre (Unnamed Lyrics) was published in 1937; the following year, after five years of study in Santiago at the University of Chile's Pedagogical Institute, he received his degree in mathematics and physics, subsequently teaching in various secondary schools.

Cancionero sin nombre, published in Santiago, brought Parra the Municipal Prize and immediate recognition as a new voice in Chilean poetry. Gabriela Mistral predicted an international reputation for him. Parra has acknowledged the influence (later regretted) of García Lorca and Whitman on his early work, and has expressed his admiration for an assortment of other books and writers, including the medieval Spanish epic Poema de Mio Cid, Chaucer's Canterbury Tales, Don Quixote, the poetry of Quevedo and Bécquer and, among contemporary writers, the experiments of Vicente Huidobro, pioneer of creacionismo, the impassioned lyricism of Gabriela Mistral, and the prophetic opulence of Pablo Neruda. The cynical and boisterous ballads in his own first book seem to have been written in reaction against both the bombast and the hermeticism of earlier Latin American writers. In the opinion of Gordon Brotherston, they also represent an attempt to sidestep Neruda's "overwhelming influence"—a problem facing all Chilean poets of Parra's generation, and one that was particularly acute for Parra, to whom Neruda was friend, mentor, and father figure.

In 1943 Parra went to the United States to study advanced mathematics at Brown University, Rhode Island. He returned to Chile in 1946, holding a university lectureship there until in 1949 he went to Oxford University in England to study cosmology under the supervision of Professor E.A. Milne. In 1952 he became professor of theoretical mechanics at his *alma mater,* the University of Chile's Pedagogical Institute, where he has remained.

Meanwhile, in 1948, Parra had broken an eleven-year silence with a number of poems in Jorge Elliott's magazine *Pro-Arte.* In 1954 came *Poemas y antipoemas* (Poems and Antipoems), the book which established Parra's international reputation. These poems introduced a highly individual juxtaposition of anguish and farce, of eroticism and pseudo-innocent bewilderment, of slapstick comedy and sardonic observation, recording betrayals and self-betrayals and the horrors of modern civilization in a style that is raw, colloquial, and frequently surreal. Life is seen (in "Los Vicios del Mundo Moderno"—The Vices of the Modern World) as an "enormous sewer/ its fashionable restaurants stuffed with digesting corpses/ Birds swooping dangerously low./ What's more: the hospitals are full of imposters/ Without mentioning those spiritual heirs who establish their colonies in the anus of the newly operated."

Parra regards his fellow men as "inocentes culpables" (guilt-ridden innocents), floundering absurdly and boringly between good and evil, inclination and conscience: "I am tired of God and the devil/ How much is this pair of trousers worth?" God himself is assured that "the gods are not infallible/ And that we forgive them everything" ("Padre Nuestro"—Our Father). The harsh cynicism of these poems is that of an idealist, deeply wounded but not quite destroyed by experience. He can still recognize that "truth, like beauty, is neither created nor lost"; he can still search, with however little optimism, for meaning: "Gravedigger, tell me the truth/ Surely there must be some tribunal/ Or are the worms our judges?"

Poemas y antipoemas caused a furor in Chile, where a hostile minority described them as "obscene rubbish." With characteristic panache, Neruda called the book "a delight of morning gold ... a fruit devoured in darkness," and in spite of the controversy it aroused, it received both the Municipal Prize of Santiago and the much-coveted Writers' Union Prize. Parra's "antipoems" met with instant success abroad, notably among such poets of the American Beat generation as Allen Ginsberg and Lawrence Ferlinghetti.

La cueca larga (The Great Dance, 1958), which takes its title from Chile's national dance, and *Versos de salón* (Drawing-Room Verses, 1962), contain songs, burlesques, parodies, and other poems which on the whole strike a lighter note than that sounded in *Poemas y antipoemas,* and reviewers found something like serene melancholy in *Canciones rusas* (Russian Lyrics, 1967). Parra's complete works, excluding some early poems, were published in 1969 as *Obra gruesa* (Gross Writings), bringing him the Chilean National Prize for Literature. It incorporates the more aggressive and bitterly satirical *La camisa de fuerza y otros poemas* (The Straitjacket and Other Poems). In the closing poem of *Obra gruesa,* Parra sadly confides: "I take back everything I've said./ With the greatest bitterness in the world/ I take back everything I've said."

Offering advice to aspiring poets in "Jóvenes" ("Young Poets"), Parra tells them that

. . . . Too much blood has run under the bridge
To go on believing
That only one road is right.

In poetry everything is permitted.

With only one condition, of course:
You must improve upon the blank page.

(translated by Miller Williams)

Like the Nicaraguan poet Ernesto Cardenal, with whom he feels a certain affinity, Parra wants the ordinary reader to understand him and is prepared to risk becoming prosaic (he sometimes does). But his "antipoems" are not so much anti-poetical as anti-rhetorical. Announcing the demise of lovesick poets, the disappearance of perfumed gardens, he writes in "La montaña rusa" (The Roller Coaster):

For half a century
Poetry was the paradise
Of the solemn fool.
Until I came
And built my roller coaster.
Go up, if you feel inclined.
I'm not responsible if you come down
Bleeding from nose and mouth.

(translated by Giovanni Pontiero)

Although social and humanitarian concern is implicit in much of Parra's work, he is more preoccupied in his writing with existential problems than with politics, seeing his main task as a poet "to plunge into the depths of human essence in order to illuminate certain obscure zones." Neruda wrote that "among the earthy poets of South America, Nicanor Parra stands out with strange foliage and strong roots. . . . He dares the most difficult explorations. . . . His southern imprint will remain on the whole domain of poetry."

In recent years, Parra has presented and read his poetry in England, France, Sweden, Germany, Italy, Russia, Mexico, Cuba, and China. He has served as a visiting professor at several universities in the United States. He has recently been experimenting with a new type of poetry that he calls "artefactos" (artifacts), and describes as a kind of "pop" verse created from aphorisms, slang, graffiti, and slogans: "Death yes! Funerals no!" He does not rule out the possibility of editing and publishing the short stories, diaries, and other prose works that he wrote as a young man.

Parra was married in 1948 to Ana Troncoso, and subsequently made a second marriage to Inga Palmen. He has seven children. Miller Williams has described him as "quick-witted and amiable, generous with his time and his stories, and—like his antipoems—[he] seems to have been chiseled out of a stone that shifts when we are not looking. There is this solidity, firmness of intellect about him, and at the same time an incredible chameleon whimsicalness."

An article by Victor Perera in the New York *Times Magazine* (April 13, 1975) suggested that Parra had been "disillusioned with [President] Allende before the coup" which overthrew Allende's socialist government, and had chosen to remain in Chile and accommodate himself to the military dictatorship that followed. A letter from Patricio C. Lerzundi in the same journal (May 11, 1975) denied this, saying that Parra had greatly admired Allende, though not some members of his government. Far from accommodating himself to the dictatorship, Parra was in fact *persona non grata* with the junta, which had banned his latest book. Lerzundi had asked Parra, shortly before the coup, why he was returning to Chile in spite of the fact that he had been offered a post in an American university. Parra replied: "Just because; if the table doesn't go to the chair, the chair must go to the table; because I am a masochist, that is, because I am in love with my country; because I want to die there."

PRINCIPAL WORKS IN ENGLISH TRANSLATION: Anti-poems, translated by Jorge Elliott, 1960; Poems and Antipoems, edited by Miller Williams, translated by William Carlos Williams, W.S. Merwin, Allen Ginsberg, Denise Levertov, Thomas Merton, and others, 1967; Emergency Poems, translated by Miller Williams, 1972. *Poems in* Caracciolo-Trejo, E. (ed.) The Penguin Book of Latin American Verse, 1971; Cohen, J.M. (ed.) Latin American Writing Today, 1967; Williams, M. (ed.) Chile: An Anthology of New Writing, 1968.

ABOUT: Adams, M.I. Three Authors of Alienation, 1975; Brotherston, G. Latin American Poetry, 1975; Franco, J. The Modern Culture of Latin America, 1970; Franco, J. Spanish American Literature Since Independence, 1973; International Who's Who, 1978–79; Montes, H. and Rodríguez, M. Nicanor Parra, 1970; Morales T., L. La Poesía de Nicanor Parra, 1972; Penguin Companion to Literature 3, 1971; Rein, M. Nicanor Parra y la antipoesía, 1970; Williams, M. (ed.) Chile, 1968.

*PESSOA, FERNANDO (ANTÓNIO NOGUEIRA) (June 13, 1888–November 30, 1935), Portuguese poet who also wrote as Alberto Caeiro, Ricardo Reis, and Álvaro de Campos, was born in Lisbon. He was the son of Joaquim de Seabra Pessoa, a music critic, and the grandson of a senior army officer who was descended from a Jewish convert to Christianity. His father died of tuberculosis when Pessoa was five. His mother, Maria Madalena Pinheiro Nogueira, was a cultured woman who herself wrote verse. A year after her first husband's death she married João Miguel Rosa, Portuguese consul in Durban, South Africa. Pessoa grew up in Durban and was educated there at a convent school, at Durban High School, and at the Commercial School, becoming bilingual in Portuguese and English. The English essay he wrote as part of his entrance examination for the University of the Cape came first out of nearly nine hundred entries, winning him the Queen Victoria Memorial Prize in 1904.

The following year, when he was seventeen, he left the University of the Cape and returned to Lisbon, living at first with his two aunts and his paternal grandmother, Dionísia, who was insane—the source, perhaps, of his own fears of madness. He matriculated at the University of Lisbon in 1906 and began a course in literature, but left the following year to launch a small printing press, intending to publish his own and other poetry. This proved an expensive failure.

Pessoa spent the rest of his life in Lisbon as a commercial correspondent and translator for various business firms. Literature was all he really cared for, and he apparently did no more work than was necessary to support himself, and refused more lucrative posts. He was nevertheless an able businessman; his advice was sought on complicated financial transactions and in 1926 he founded a successful journal of commerce and accountancy.

Peter Rickard describes Pessoa in these terms: "A rather unusual gait, rather jerky movements of the hands, rimless or gold-rimmed spectacles,

*pess ô′ ə

PESSOA

FERNANDO PESSOA

Centro de Turismo de Portugal

a small moustache over a tiny mouth, neatness and even elegance of dress. Very gentlemanly, exquisitely courteous, chastened in speech, a good listener, a heavy smoker and an increasingly heavy drinker, this last the cause of his early death." He was liked and admired by the writers he met in the Lisbon literary cafes, and respected by his business acquaintances, many of whom did not know that he wrote poetry and had no idea of the complexity and introversion that his urbane manner masked. He was deeply interested in the occult and the supernatural, and at one time thought of becoming a professional astrologer. Pessoa never married. There is a homosexual element in some of his early poems, but no evidence whatever to suggest that he was ever a practicing homosexual or that he had much interest in sex at all, apart from a brief romance with a girl typist in 1920.

For some time after his return to Lisbon, Pessoa continued to study the writers to whom his British education had introduced him, especially Shakespeare, Milton, Dickens, Wordsworth, Shelley, and Poe. The poems he wrote at this time, between 1905 and 1909, were also in English, many of them signed "Alexander Search." The *Times Literary Supplement,* reviewing *35 Sonnets* in 1918, said that "the sonnets . . . probing into mysteries of life and death, of reality and appearance, will interest many by reason of their ultra-Shakespearian Shakespearianisms, and their Tudor tricks of repetition, involution and antithesis, no less than by the worth of what they have to say."

Pessoa began to write poetry in Portuguese in 1909, but for the next three years produced little, instead reading intensively in Portuguese,

French, and other poetry, and in the fields of occultism, theosophy, alchemy, astrology, and magic. He also studied Hegel, Schopenhauer, and Nietzsche, whose amoralism, cult of the superman, and strictures on Christianity especially interested him.

Portugal was at this time a literary backwater, its poetry characterized by nineteenth-century rhetoric and sentimentality. Pessoa was one of a group of young writers who, eagerly following such developments as French post-symbolism, cubism, and futurism, sought to renovate Portuguese poetry. They advocated and experimented with the new techniques in articles and poems characterized by a youthful tendency to shock and mystify their elders. Pessoa was at first a leader of this literary revolution, but after about 1917 ceased to write poetry according to the tenets of any particular school. He had by then found his own way, and one that is unique in literature.

"Ever since I was a child," Pessoa wrote in a famous letter, "I have tended to create around me a fictitious world, to surround myself with friends and acquaintances who never existed. (I don't know, of course, whether they *really* didn't exist, or whether I'm the one who doesn't exist.)" He goes on to describe his plans for creating two imaginary poets, one of whom suddenly sprang to life on March 8, 1914. On that day Pessoa, in a surge of inspiration, wrote more than thirty poems in a style quite unlike his own, ascribing them to an imaginary poet whom he called Alberto Caeiro. "I know it sounds absurd, but my master had appeared," he wrote afterwards. "It was the triumphant day of my life, and there will never be another like it."

Caeiro represented for Pessoa a kind of holiday from his own profound and subtle metaphysical doubts. He is a blinkered innocent, a pastoral existentialist, disdainful of metaphor and metaphysics, for whom an object is exactly and solely what it appears to be, and reality is only what is perceived by the senses: "Things have no meaning: they have being./ Things are the only hidden meaning of things." In the biography that Pessoa invented for him (as he did also for his other "heteronyms"), Caeiro is described as a countryman of limited education. His poetry is plain, direct, free from abstractions, sparing in its use of complicating adjectives, and often dull. Important as he was to Pessoa, he is as a poet the least successful of the heteronyms.

Pessoa (in an anonymous article) explained that "a pseudonymic work is, except for the name with which it is signed, the work of an author writing as himself; a heteronymic work is by an author writing outside his own personality: it is the work of a complete individuality made up by him, just as the utterances of some character in a drama of his would be." Pessoa believed that his genius was essentially dramatic, but that he wrote "a drama in people instead of in acts."

And so, close on Caeiro's heels—"released" by him—appeared a second heteronym, Ricardo Reis. He is a disciple of Caeiro, and like him achieves a stoic acceptance of life's sorrows and mysteries by resolutely closing his eyes to them. But there the resemblance ends, for Reis is a classicist, pagan in religion, epicurean in his tastes, elegiac in mood, and his poems are polished and intricate classical odes:

This thing you give me, is it love you feel,
Or love you feign? You give it: that suffices me.
. . .
The gods give us little, and that little is false.
Yet, if they give it, for all its falseness
The gift is real. I take it
And close my eyes: 'tis enough.
Why ask for more?

(translated by Peter Rickard)

Reis in turn generated his opposite, Álvaro de Campos, who is Pessoa's most prolific *alter ego*. First engineer on a tanker, he is in his early poetry a passionately emotional extrovert in the tradition of Whitman and of the futurist Marinetti, intoxicated by the modern world and the dynamism of machines. His "Ode triunfal" (Triumphal Ode) makes a clean sweep of the past and exalts violence and aggression. His equally Whitmanesque "Ode Maritime" was described by Roy Campbell as "the loudest poem ever written." Later (under the influence, according to Pessoa, of Caeiro), he becomes more introverted and pessimistic, increasingly inclined to withdraw into drunkenness and reverie, from a reality that seems to him ludicrously, mysteriously, impossibly inadequate. Campos shares with Caeiro and Reis the conviction that life is an unfathomable mystery, but unlike them cannot resist probing at the mystery:

Oh musical essence of my pointless verse,
If only I could find you as something I created,
Instead of forever facing the tobacco-shop over opposite,
And treading on the awareness of my own existence
As though it were a rug on which a drunkard stumbles
Or a doormat stolen by gypsies and not worth stealing.

But the Tobacconist comes to his door and stands there.

I look at him with my head uncomfortably half-turned
And my spirit uncomfortably half-comprehending.
He will die and I shall die.
He will leave his signboard: I shall leave my poetry.
In time the signboard will die too, and so will my poetry.
A time will come when the street the signboard was in will die too,

So will the language my poetry was written in.
Then the whirling planets will die, where all this took place.
In other satellites in other systems something resembling people
Will go on doing things like writing poetry and living under things like signboards,
Forever one thing facing another,
Forever one thing as pointless as the next,
Forever impossibility as stupid as reality,
Forever mystery deep down as certain as mystery sleeping on the surface,
Forever this, forever that, or neither one thing nor the other.

(from "Tabacaria," ["Tobacco-Shop"] translated by Peter Rickard)

In his chronic state of metaphysical uncertainty, and also in his recurrent invocations of the lost Eden of childhood, the poems of Campos resemble, most nearly of the heteronyms, those Pessoa wrote under his own name. These are mostly short, compressed lyrics, metrical and rhyming, whose surface simplicity masks great complexity. They are generally rather abstract in their concerns, lacking the human warmth of the Campos poems, but intellectually fascinating and, for all their irony, deeply moving. Michael Wood has called Pessoa "the poet not only of contradiction and paradox but of the categorically impossible. . . . Pessoa hears voices sounding from the Islands of the Blessed, but as soon as he listens, they stop. In order for them to continue, he would have to hear without hearing, and the oxymoron becomes the emblem and instrument of a magical, inconceivable communication."

Pessoa's oxymorons have been much discussed, and are central to his poetry. As Michael Wood says, they range from purely formal figures of rhetoric "through the expression of possibilities which can't find their way into ordinary language (shapes without shape, unthought thoughts, the dead body of a God who is alive, the king who dies but still lives) and into the expression of sheer impossibility (a door in a wall that has no door, the child you don't have sleeping peacefully at home)." Pessoa maintains, for example, that the music which stopped when he woke from dreaming of it endures "in what inhibits thought in me." He says that he is grieved not by "What lies within the heart,/ But those things of beauty/ Which can never be." And then he throws doubt on the sincerity of these transcendental yearnings in a poem like "Autopsicografia" ("Self-Analysis"):

> The poet's good at pretending,
> Such a master of the art
> He even manages to pretend
> The pain he really feels is pain.
>
> And those who read his written words
> Feel, as they read of pain,
> Not the two kinds that were his
> But only the kind that's not theirs.
>
> And so around its little track,
> To entertain the mind,
> Runs that clockwork train of ours,
> The thing we call the heart.
>
> (translated by Peter Rickard)

In all of the uniquely complex and diverse poetry that Pessoa wrote, under his own name, under his three principal heteronyms, and under several less significant ones, the dominant note remains, as Wood says, "the finality of failure, the clearly struck note of the impossibility of having anything you want."

Pessoa's early experiments with futurism and other fashionable developments, together with his literary essays, began to appear in about 1912 in such magazines as *A Águia* (The Eagle), *A Renascença* (The Renaissance), and *Orpheu* (Orpheus). The latter, published simultaneously in Portugal and Brazil, included in its first issue (April 1915) two startling poems by "Álvaro de Campos," together with many similarly exhibitionistic pieces by other young poets (including Fernando Pessoa). The magazine was meant to shock, and did so, some critics suggesting that the *Orpheu* poets were insane. Pessoa was co-editor of *Orpheu*'s equally sensational second issue (June 1915), and of a third issue which was never published.

In 1916, in another short-lived magazine, *Centauro*, Pessoa published under his own name a sequence of fourteen sonnets called *Passos da Cruz* (Stations of the Cross). Here for the first time, in the opinion of Peter Rickard, were "poems which revealed not just potential and promise, but real greatness. . . . The wilful mingling of concrete and abstract, so obtrusive and even systematic in the early poems, is here more selectively applied, and results in images of great beauty and suggestive power. . . . *Taedium vitae* finds prominent expression, but also the haunting awareness of something which is out of reach

and may not even exist, an impossible ideal." And so Pessoa, imagining a woman playing a harp, dreams of kissing "the movement of your hands, without the hands themselves." In the sixth sonnet he identifies himself with "the backward glance" of the last Moorish king as he fled from Granada forever, and says: "I am myself the loss I suffered."

As early as January 1915, Pessoa was losing interest in the literary fashions of the time. He said in a letter that, though he could "find people who are in agreement with literary activities which are merely on the fringe of my true feelings . . . that is not enough for me. And so, as my feelings deepen, as I become increasingly aware of the terrible, religious mission which every man of genius receives from God together with his genius, any kind of literary trifling, or art which is merely art, gradually sounds more and more hollow and repugnant to me." After about 1917, he largely relinquished his role in Portuguese literary polemics, and ceased to write poems inspired by "the crude desire to shine for the sake of shining, and that other even cruder desire to startle and shock."

Nevertheless, Pessoa's poetry and essays continued to appear from time to time in Portuguese literary reviews (though he was always more diffident about publishing his verse than his prose). He founded and edited with Ruy Vaz the literary review *Athena,* of which five issues appeared in 1924-1925. Although his first, youthful attempt to establish a printing press had failed, he had rather more success with Olisipo, the publishing house he founded in 1921, through which he published some of his English poems, as well as verse by others. He also made an occasional foray into politics—for example in 1935, when the government drafted a law banning secret societies and Pessoa published an article passionately defending freemasonry.

Pessoa's intense patriotism is very evident in *Mensagem* (Message, 1934), the only volume of his poetry in Portuguese published during his lifetime. It is a collection of poems, written at various times, which together give a kind of mystic interpretation of Portuguese history, full of nostalgia for the glorious past, but with an element of almost messianic hope for the nation's future. These dense and sometimes cryptic poems were assembled so that the volume could be entered in a national competition. It won in the "second category" (for short poems) and the prize was augmented in recognition of its merit.

In fact, Pessoa was not particularly satisfied with *Mensagem,* which is scarcely typical of his work. He was engaged in preparing the remainder of his poetry for publication when in 1935, at the age of forty-seven, he died of cirrhosis of the liver. Among his uncompleted works were a fragment of a projected five-act play on the Faust theme and drafts of a number of detective stories. His *Obras completas* (Complete Works) were published in Lisbon in eight volumes between 1942 and 1956, and a one-volume *Obra poética* appeared in Rio de Janeiro in 1960.

At the end of his life, Pessoa had a small and growing coterie of admirers, who recognized his contribution to the renovation of Portuguese poetic syntax and vocabulary. There seems to have been less understanding among his contemporaries for what he had to say. And indeed, in his "early existentialist" views, he was ahead of his time. As Peter Rickard says, "he is of our time in his *Angst,* in his desperate struggle to make sense of himself and of his surroundings. All his work revolves round the mystery of existence. ... Obviously, what Pessoa has to say about man and the universe is not constructive: it contains no lessons for living. Man's choice is a limited one. He can shut his eyes to all but appearances, like Caeiro; he can discipline himself to expect nothing, and delude himself that that is happiness, like Ricardo Reis; or he can continue to speculate and go round and round in a vicious circle, like Campos or Pessoa himself, convinced that there must be something there to know, but equally convinced that it is unknowable." Fernando Pessoa is now regarded as one of the major European poets of this century and as the greatest Portuguese poet since Camões.

PRINCIPAL WORKS IN ENGLISH AND IN ENGLISH TRANSLATION: Antinous, 1918; Thirty-five Sonnets, 1918; English Poems, 1921; Selected Poems, translated by Peter Rickard, 1971; Selected Poems by Fernando Pessoa, translated by Edwin Honig, 1971; Sixty Portuguese Poems, translated by F.E.G. Quintanilha, 1971; Fernando Pessoa I-IV, translated by Jonathan Griffin, 1971; Selected Poems, translated by Jonathan Griffin, 1974; The Tobacconist by Álvaro de Campos, translated by J.C.R. Green, 1975; The Keeper of Flocks by Alberto Caeiro, translated by J.C.R. Green, 1976. *Poems* in Burnshaw, S. (ed.) The Poem Itself, 1964; Campbell, R. Portugal, 1957; Campbell, R. Collected Poems III, 1960; Laughlin, J. (ed.) New Directions in Prose and Poetry, 1966; Parker, J.M. Three Twentieth-Century Portuguese Poets, 1960.

ABOUT: Burnshaw, S. (ed.) The Poem Itself, 1964; Casaes Monteiro, A. Estudos sobre a poesia de Fernando Pessoa, 1958; Casaes Monteiro, A. Fernando Pessoa e a crítica, 1952; Casaes Monteiro, A. Fernando Pessoa, o insincero verídico, 1954; Freitas da Costa, E. Fernando Pessoa: Notas a uma biografia romanceada, 1951; Griffin, J. *introduction to* Fernando Pessoa: Selected Poems, 1974; Guerra, M.L. Ensaios sobre Álvaro de Campos, 1969; Hamburger, M. The Truth of Poetry, 1969; Kujawski, G. de M. Fernando Pessoa o outro, 1967; Lind, G.R. Teoria poética de Fernando Pessoa, 1970; Lourenço, E.P. Fernando Pessoa revisitado, 1973; Parker, J.M. Three Twentieth-Century Portuguese Poets, 1960; Prado Coelho, J. do, Diversidade e unidade em Fernando Pessoa, 1963; Quintanilha, F.E.G. *introduction to* Fernando Pessoa: Sixty Portuguese Poems, 1971; Rickard, P. *introduction to* Fernando Pessoa: Selected Poems, 1971; Rosa, P. Uma interpretação de Fernando Pessoa, 1971; Sacramento M. Fernando Pessoa (in Portuguese), 1970; Simões, J.G. Heteropsicografia de Fernando Pessoa, 1973; Simões, J.G. Vida e obra de Fernando Pessoa (two volumes), 1950. *Periodicals*—Books Abroad Spring 1966; Bulletin of Hispanic Studies January 1969; New York Review of Books September 21, 1972; Plural (Mexico) April-May 1972; Poetry October 1955; Times Literary Supplement October 18, 1974.

*PICCOLO (DI CALANOVELLA), LUCIO** (October 27, 1901–May 26, 1969), Italian poet, was born in Palermo, Sicily, into an ancient and illustrious Sicilian family. Though he was always referred to in Sicily as the Baron di Calanovella, he was actually a knight, the barony belonging to his elder brother. Piccolo was a cousin of Giuseppe Tomasi di Lampedusa, who was his lifelong friend and literary rival—as children they fought and played together, and maliciously destroyed one another's manuscripts. According to Piccolo it was he, together with Lampedusa's wife, who persuaded the prince to write *Il gattopardo* (The Leopard), the novel which brought him posthumous international fame. Helen Barolini says that Piccolo and Lampedusa shared "wit which sharpened itself on irony and self-ridicule, sense of caste, an absent-mindedness and apathy to what happened 'on the outside,' a reserve which could have seemed either timidity or proud indifference."

Piccolo began to write when he was eight or nine years old—"librettos for my future operas, in which the characters were the dog ... or my love for the dog, my love for the valet and things like that. I can say that my artistic world started in a dramatic way." He began to write verse at about the same time, but as he grew up he became dissatisfied with his poetry. Then, he told Michael Ricciardelli, "I forced myself into a kind of exile, a hard exile from poetry, and studied philosophy. I studied everything that was contrary to my nature. I broke myself down."

It seems that Piccolo devoted most of his life to study at his estate at Capo d'Orlando near Messina. He lived there with his brother and his sister, both of them (like himself) unmarried, surrounded by dogs, canaries, and other pets, some of whom he believed to be inhabited by the spirits of great writers and philosophers. Piccolo became, according to Eugenio Montale, "an accomplished musician, a student of philosophy who could read Husserl and Wittgenstein in the original, trained Greek scholar, knowledgeable in the entire field of European poetry, old and new, a reader, for example, of Gerard Manley

*pēk′ kō lō

635

PICCOLO

LUCIO PICCOLO

Piccolo chose Montale as his patron because he had learned from him, as he had from Carducci, Pascoli, D'Annunzio, and Verga—especially Verga, who had been a friend of his father. Other influences were Mallarmé and the English poets, particularly Yeats. However, Piccolo's work is wholly his own, and unique. It is intense, evocative poetry, frequently capturing the "flight of time which is anguish" that may be experienced so powerfully in the hot ambiguous South. His poetry arises from constant metaphysical tension between the scene observed and its effect upon the observer:

Mutable world of gusty
rays, of hours without color, of perennial
flux, the pomp
of clouds: an instant and look—the changed
forms dazzle, millenniums sway.
And the low door's arch and the worn
sill of too many winters, are a fable in the abrupt
glory of the March sun.

(translated by Sonia Raiziss
and Alfredo de Palchi)

Hopkins and of Yeats." In the end, Piccolo discovered that he "could not escape from poetry through the study of literature, philosophy and sciences." Having fought with poetry, he said, "poetry came to me."

In April 1954 the great Italian poet Eugenio Montale received through the mail a pamphlet containing nine lyrics by Piccolo, privately (and vilely) printed, and bearing insufficient postage. In his covering letter, Piccolo explained that it had been his intention, especially in a group of gaudy and funereal "Canti barocchi" (Baroque Songs), "to re-evoke and fix a unique Sicilian world—more precisely that of Palermo. . . . I mean to speak of that world of baroque churches, of old convents, of souls suited to these places, who spent their lives here without leaving a trace. I have tried not so much to recall as to interpret it from my childhood memories."

Montale was "struck by an afflatus, a rapture" in these poems that reminded him both of Dino Campana and of Dylan Thomas, and at the same time by their "lean, intense, and sharpened" diction and a harmony which was that of "a modern polytonal composer." He introduced Piccolo to a literary symposium at San Pellegrino in 1954, and to the Italian public at large in his afterword to *Canti barocchi e altre liriche* (Baroque Songs and Other Lyrics), the collection of nineteen poems published by Mondadori in 1956, when Piccolo was fifty-five. Another edition of this collection, with nine additional poems, followed in 1960 as *Gioco a nascondere; canti barocchi* (Hide and Seek; Baroque Poems), and another nine—all the Piccolo poems that have so far appeared—were published in 1967 as *Plumelia*.

Glauco Cambon suggests that Piccolo "shares with his ancestors of Góngora's age that supreme concern for the instability of phenomena which makes life a phantasmagoria—an inexhaustible yet deceptive richness under which nothingness yawns. . . . Piccolo's writing . . . expresses a post-historical consciousness, because he seems to inhabit a world where everything already happened long ago, where history can only regress to folklore, shadow, sorcery."

The same critic has described Piccolo's "open, waving free rhythms which accumulate breathlessly to suggest trance" but points out that an "anguished lucidity" emerges from this rapturous verse. Cambon calls Piccolo "a syntactical poet; with him clause generates clause, sentences and images proliferate, and (particularly in the first book) hidden rhymes vie and interlock with standard end-rhymes to intone a symphony of multiple echoes, indeed to minimize the independence of individual lines and wrench the set patterns within which the musical stream sometimes flows. Piccolo's phrase overflows the dams of fixed meter; formal limits are there only to be transgressed. This exuberance, which asserts itself both on the rhythmical and on the iconic level, is Piccolo's signature."

During his lifetime, Piccolo attracted much attention abroad, and was translated into English, Russian, French, and Swedish. He had a more mixed reception in Italy, where his hermetic poems appeared at a time when the vogue was for politically committed verse. Piccolo attacked his uncomprehending critics in "Un Osso

Duro" (A Hard Bone), an article published posthumously in *Fiera Letteraria* (September 26, 1971). His reputation has grown steadily since his death, however—partly, no doubt, for the reasons suggested by Brian Swann and Ruth Feldman in their translators' introduction to his *Collected Poems* in English. "At first glance," they wrote, "however complex the syntax or elusive the thought, he seems old-fashioned, even *fin-de-siècle,* fantastically and arcanely baroque. And yet, further acquaintance reveals that his main thrust is post-existential ('anxiety' is a key word): that, for instance, in his constant search to distinguish outer and inner reality, he has affinities with such a conjurer as Nabokov. . . . Although Piccolo is typically solid and specific in his task, at times the Italian almost floats away in a Roethkean 'shift of things.' "

Michael Ricciardelli has described in *Books Abroad* (Spring 1973) his meeting with Piccolo at Capo d'Orlando, a year before the poet's death. The local people pointed out the recluse's villa with awe, as if it were "a house of ghosts." Piccolo was reputed to hold seances and to be devoted to esoteric sciences and magic. Helen Barolini, writing in *Yale Review* (Winter 1976), paints a similar portrait of the author, who was, she says, intensely superstitious. He kept some letters from Yeats in a small coffer and often regretted that he could not reread them; however, the lock of the coffer had jammed, and Piccolo took this as a sign that it was not to be reopened—not, at any rate, during this lifetime. Nevertheless, Ricciardelli found him, though highly eccentric, hospitable and kindly: "low in stature, hair in disorder, humbly dressed, a little dog on his right arm—a surrealistic vision." Piccolo identified himself as the central figure in one of his own poems, "the poet who has given up everything because of his search for pure poetry and who has isolated himself from other men, thus becoming not a poet but an inflammable puppet made of tow. His own blaze of desire for pure poetry has worn him out, has burnt him up."

According to Glauco Cambon, "Piccolo's poetry, of clearly consummate craftsmanship, did not change much through the final years, unless we want to take into account Plumelia's somewhat drier diction. In what sense it would have developed if Piccolo had lived longer, it is hard to say. We can only say that it was another of those improbable Sicilian gifts to the literature of Italy and Europe, a gift against the grain, from the island of Pirandello and Lampedusa and Quasimodo, the island of volcanic paradox."

PRINCIPAL WORKS IN ENGLISH TRANSLATION: Collected Po-ems, 1972. *Poems in* Barnstone, W. (ed.) Modern European Poetry, 1966.

ABOUT: Cambon, G. *introduction to* Collected Poems, 1972; Montale, E. *afterword to* Collected Poems, 1972; Sciascia, L. La corda pazza, 1970. *Periodicals*—Belfagor May 31, 1959; Books Abroad Spring 1973; Yale Review Winter 1976.

*PIERCY, MARGE (March 31, 1936–), American poet and novelist, writes: "I was born and grew up in a working-class family in Detroit, Michigan. The name Piercy represents the least strain in my background. My father was half Welsh, and I used to meet Welsh-speaking miners at funerals and weddings in Cambria County, Pennsylvania, where my father's family lived, who would tell me they were my first or second cousin twice removed. He was also one-quarter Scottish and one-quarter English. He identified mostly with his father and mostly with the English strain.

"My mother is from a large, warm, down-and-out Jewish family with radical and vaudeville traditions. Their misadventures filled my childhood. The only grandparent I knew well was my mother's mother, who spoke Yiddish. My mother's father was a union organizer, killed before I was born. My mother never got to finish the tenth grade but had to go to work to help support the six younger children (she was the third of nine). The age run of my mother's family was so broad that my favorite youngest uncle hung out with my older brother.

"I was the first person in my family to go to college. My mother was an emotional woman of vivid imagination and frustrated curiosity to whom I expect I owe being a writer. Although she gave me no emotional support (any other kind was simply not available in the family) when I wanted to define myself as a writer or in any unusual or rebellious choice I made, she was nevertheless my original muse. She trained and sharpened my senses in early childhood and she and my grandmother fed me stories, legends, Jewish history, mythology, family scandals, the gossip of radical causes. Early poverty made her frightened of unconventional choice, and after the closeness of childhood we wasted years fighting about everything I did.

"After I had put myself through college as far as a master's degree, I became afraid I was losing what I had been and what I wanted to be. I spent years then doing part-time jobs, all the dreary jobs women do, and writing novels no one would publish and poems no one would hear or read. I did not begin to make a living by my writing until 1967. I have lived off it since then. Al-

*pēr'sē

637

MARGE PIERCY

though I give workshops and readings a great deal, I teach only rarely. Once in a while I succumb to it. It seems to me a totally different vocation, one inimical to writing but seductive to other parts of my character, one of the lives I have (mostly) not lived.

"I had been involved in opposing urban renewal and in civil rights in Chicago, but it wasn't until 1965 when I joined Students for a Democratic Society after their march on Washington, that I began to be intensely involved in political work. For years I burned with the Indo-China war, I raged against it day-long and I dreamed its agonies at night. That was how it was for many people in the middle and late 1960s. From 1965 through 1969 I worked in the New Left, sometimes doing power structure research as in the North American Congress on Latin America, sometimes writing pamphlets, but mostly organizing. I especially worked to build a movement off-campus, in the cities.

"I had been attracted to feminism and many of the interests classified today as women's studies (witches, Amazons, the mother religions) in the late 1950s and early 1960s, but I had put these concerns aside. I could not then publish my stories and my novels about women. Until I learned to write male viewpoint, there was truly no place for my fiction. From 1967 I had taken part in women's caucuses, but in January 1969 I decided to work in the women's movement.

"Each succeeding movement has been more involving for me and has changed me further. I haven't converted from one to another, haven't given up an interest in radical or economic justice in pursuing feminism, but each has had more to do with who I am and how I write. I

lived all my life in the center of cities until my health broke. I had used myself like an old car I might abandon all through the 1960s and I had been injured again and again and suddenly I came against my own mortality and limitations, in the form of my lungs. I live in Wellfleet on Cape Cod now, although I travel a lot for readings, and everyone in my house goes back and forth from Boston most weeks. I like that taste of the city and solid work-time in the country. I am a passionate gardener. I am actively involved in feminism locally and nationally, but I put in a thirty-five hour week on my writing and work outside also."

As an adolescent in the 1950s, Marge Piercy wrote in a *Partisan Review* article, she found herself "isolated, stuck in the alienated pose." She felt out of place in the English department at the University of Michigan, "a garlic among the Anglican-convert lilies," and says that college for her was "a never-ending education in the finer distinctions of class insult and bias." She tried to express her anger and frustration in rebellious gestures which, she says, only trivialized her sense of alienation: "soapsuds in a fountain, a faked news story, refusing to use footnotes or keep hours, taking off my clothes." It seemed to her then that "the only choices were conformity or exile. I could not imagine a future."

Securing her B.A. in 1957, she was married in "graduation panic" to a graduate student in physics, Michael Schiff. She went on to Northwestern University, where she was somewhat happier, and received her M.A. there in 1958 with a record score. At that point she left college and went to work to support herself and her husband. The marriage broke down less than a year later.

Marge Piercy lived in a poor white neighborhood in Chicago, working as she says at various "dreary jobs," immersing herself in "women's studies," and trying to write: "I was laboring for a sense of my self, origins, prospects, antecedents, intentions, a renewed sense of a living language natural to my mouth, even a mythology I could use. . . . Not until the slow opening of the 1960s was I able to think I might begin to cease to be a victim, an internal exile, a madwoman."

Breaking Camp, her first book of poetry, appeared in 1968. These were poems, Richard M. Elman wrote, "about love, trust, comradeship; celebration of animals, objects as part of the real world she inhabits; they are in short and long lines, free and regular meters, using internal rhymes or no rhymes at all. Where others seem intolerant, she is compassionate. Where others give way to fashionable despair, she hopes by doing and observing." Another reviewer wrote that "the will to survive is at the heart of every poem, standing up to life, not bending but not breaking either."

There was equal praise for the less tolerant poems of love, betrayal, and social protest in *Hard Loving* and the feminist poems in *To Be of Use,* though the latter collection seemed to some reviewers weakened at times by propagandist rhetoric. Both books were admired most of all for the force and precision of their imagery, as in "Bronchitis on the 14th Floor" from *Hard Loving:*

... My fever has ripened like a pear.
A bubble of oxygen,
I percolate in clogged lungs,
I simmer in sweet fat
above the flickering city.
The shocked limb of Broadway
flutters spasmodically below.
My lungs shine, two lanterns.
I love the man who stands
at the foot of my bed,
whose voice tumbles like a bear
over the ceiling,
whose hands smell of tangerine and medicine.
Through nights of fire and grit
streaked with falling claws
he carries me golden with fever
safely, swiftly forward
on the galloping sleigh of our bed.

Living in the Open (1976) contains more directly autobiographical poems than earlier collections, and includes a section about the author's discovery of country life. Again there were complaints that her "political concern overwhelms the artistry" in some of these poems, but Erica Jong thought this her best book, "direct, powerful and accessible without being unsubtle." Country life through the seasons becomes central in *The Twelve-Spoked Wheel Flashing* (1978), which records Marge Piercy's griefs and grievances and also her pleasures—in people, and in such pursuits as walking the tide flats, planting her garden, baking bread, and making friends with animals. Suzanne Juhasz concluded that, "though there are some lovely pieces here," the author is "a better person than a poet. The sense of that personhood informs this book and makes it a moving experience."

Marge Piercy, a recipient of Avery Hopwood and Borestone Mountain poetry awards, is widely regarded as "one of the finest poets of the Left." She wrote in *Contemporary Poets* that she has "regularly been published with, read with, am friends with, the editors of *Hanging Loose* (Dick Lourie, Emmett Jarrett, Bob Hershon,

Ron Schreiber) and thus we are *de facto* a group, if not a school." She goes on: "I don't write in the traditional forms of English verse but in measures derived from spoken American. I use both the short line first taught us by William Carlos Williams and the long prophetic line rediscovered by Allen Ginsberg, but basically I use my ears. All my poems are supposed to be read aloud, and I do so as often as I can. I try to write an honest tough language. I am always trying to learn how to say what I mean, and how to mean more truthfully."

Her first novel, *Going Down Fast,* about Chicago during urban renewal, was followed by *Dance the Eagle to Sleep,* set in the near future. America has become even more rigidly structured than it is today, and young people are assigned—on the strength of tests, and regardless of their preferences—to work as scientists, as soldiers, or in urban renewal projects. The novel describes the struggle for freedom of the Indians, a group of young revolutionaries. One reviewer found the characterization superficial and the novel's message unconvincing, but most readers seemed wholly won over by the excitement and energy of the narrative. Raymond A. Sokolov called it "the best writing about the fantasies and style of militant youth I have seen and the first unembarrassing heroic narrative to appear in quite a while."

Small Changes is a history of the loves and careers, and the subtly altering perceptions, of Beth, a "good little girl" from Syracuse who drops out of Middle America into a succession of women's communes, and of Miriam, a mathematician moving from one man to another in search of security. A reviewer in *Library Journal* called this "the big rich novel that one hoped would emerge from the new women's consciousness, although its lesbian bias will bother many —but the revolutionary rhetoric comes naturally out of the mouths that speak it; and Piercy's fierce energy as a novelist redeems the rhetoric." Richard Todd was struck by "the extraordinary confidence that suffuses the prose. It is written with a moralistic insistence that recalls nineteenth-century novels."

Connie Ramos in *Woman on the Edge of Time* (1976) is a Harlem Chicana who escapes (if only in her tormented mind) from the brutal hospital to which she has been condemned as unstable. The serene androgynous Massachusetts village of the future to which she projects herself did not impress many reviewers, but the novel was praised nevertheless as a powerful "scream of anguish and rage." Roger Sale wrote: "It is a mark of the intensity with which ... [Marge Piercy] believes her polemics and her vision that finally she can tell a good story about it." *The High Cost of Living* studies the interaction between Leslie, a lesbian moralist; Honor, a pretentious and rather devious teenager; and Bernard, a lonely homosexual thief. According to a review in *Publishers Weekly,* "Piercy concentrates on areas of unrest, uneasy roles, goes over her subjects with a fine-tooth comb. She does not entertain, but as she pokes and probes and worries her material, she does provide food for thought about some of our directions, feelings and values."

The author is the daughter of Robert and Bert (Bunnin) Piercy. She made a second marriage in 1962 to Robert M. Shapiro, a systems analyst. "I am a committed radical," she wrote in *Contemporary Poets:* "I don't understand distinctions between private and social poetry: love is between people, or mere mental decoration. On the other hand, I consider the attempt to build new kinds of relationships as political as a picket line. Half the human race (my half) has been sat on under just about every form of economic organization. I want my poems to be useful to the people I read them to or who read them, and I think they get that way by being as truthful as I can make them."

In 1975 Marge Piercy was distinguished visiting lecturer at Thomas Jefferson College, Grand Valley State Colleges, Michigan. She served as a consultant to the New York State Council on the Arts in 1971, on the Board of Advisers to the Feminist Book Club in 1971–1972, and on the Massachusetts Foundation for the Humanities and Council on the Arts in 1974. The many groups in which she has been active include Students for a Democratic Society (1965–1969), North American Congress on Latin America (1966–1967), Women's Caucus of Students for a Democratic Society (1967–1968), Movement for a Democratic Society (1968–1969), W.I.T.C.H. (1969–1970), the New York Women's Center (1969–1971), Cape Cod Women's Liberation (1971), the Feminist Party (1971–), Cambridge Women's Education Center (1972–), and the Lower Cape Women's Center (1973–). She is a member of the Authors Guild, the Authors League, P.E.N., the Fortune Society, Amnesty International, the National Audubon Society, the Massachusetts Audubon Society, and the American Rose Society.

PRINCIPAL WORKS: *Poetry*—Breaking Camp, 1968; Hard Loving, 1969; (with Bob Hershon, Emmett Jarrett, and Dick Lourie) 4-Telling, 1971; To Be of Use, 1973; Living in the Open, 1976; The Twelve-Spoked Wheel Flashing, 1978. *Novels*—Going Down Fast, 1969; Dance the Eagle to Sleep, 1971; Small Changes, 1973; Woman on the Edge of Time, 1976; The High Cost of Living, 1978.

ABOUT: Contemporary Authors 21–24 1st revision, 1977; International Who's Who in Poetry, 1974–1975; Vinson, J. (ed.) Contemporary Poets, 1975; Who's Who in America, 1976–1977; Who's Who of American Women, 1975–1976. *Periodicals*—Commonweal March 28, 1969; Library Journal October 1, 1969; Minnesota Review 1 1969; Partisan Review 41 1974; Saturday Review World December 14, 1974; Time January 24, 1968; Virginia Quarterly Review Summer 1968.

*PIONTEK, HEINZ** (November 15, 1925–), German poet, novelist, and essayist, writes (in German): "I was born at Kreuzberg, Upper Silesia, a German border town in the East that has been part of Poland since 1945. My father was a poor devil. He contracted a lung disease in poison gas attacks in World War I, and died in 1928 at the age of thirty-seven. My mother, born on a small farm, did not remarry, but worked very hard to keep my sister and me alive and give us a decent education. From my school desk I was taken off to the war. I was old enough to serve for two years. My time as a prisoner of war was not long. But I could not return to the lost province of Silesia. So I stayed in Bavaria, where I have been living for thirty years—at first in small towns on the Danube, then in Munich, for quite a few years now.

"My literary studies, too, were brief. In 1948 I started living from pen to mouth. Since then I have written more than twenty books, including seven books of poems, such as *Klartext* (Blueprint) and *Gesammelte Gedichte* (Complete Poetry), and two novels—the more recent is called *Dichterleben* (Poet's Life). To my surprise, these books have won prizes again and again. I am also a member of two German academies. All that is part and parcel of a 'pro's' life—it would be wrong to get a swollen head about it.

"My progress as a professional has not been a well-upholstered, universally pampered career. That is why I am not arrogant enough to shrug my shoulders at favorable notices. On the other hand, attacks on my work prove to me that it does not meet with indifference. Altogether my experience has confirmed Goethe's judgement. He once remarked: 'Against criticism one can neither protect nor defend oneself. One must carry on in spite of it; and that, in the end, wins approval.' "

After the war, Piontek held an assortment of more or less casual jobs—he was a construction worker and a sign painter, and tried his hand at a variety of native arts and crafts—before deciding to continue his education. He spent two years at the University of Munich, studying literature, philosophy, and history of art. Since

*pi' on tek

HEINZ PIONTEK

thentic "dialectical tension between nature and history, being and time," and already "wholly himself" in a number of poems in the second book. The poems from both collections were reprinted in 1956 in a second edition of *Die Rauchfahne*.

Piontek's third collection, *Wassermarken* (Watermarks), appeared in 1957 and confirmed his reputation. Both in theme and manner these new poems marked an advance on the earlier work, and the beginning of this poet's maturity. One of the longer poems in the book, "Die Verstreuten" (translated by Christopher Middleton as "The Dispersion") stood out among many fine poems drawing on Piontek's keen awareness of his lost homeland, its landscapes, legends, and way of life. The elegiac mood noted by Holthusen had become dominant, but in poems like "Mit 30 Jahren" (At Thirty Years) Piontek had found a new, unromantic, and laconically disillusioned voice that was felt to be characteristic of his generation and of postwar German lyricism in the late 1940s and 1950s:

1948, as he says, he has lived "from pen to mouth," working as a literary critic for press and radio, and writing short stories and radio plays as well as poetry and essays. He was married in 1951 to Gisela Dallmann.

Piontek's first volume of verse was *Die Furt* (The Ford, 1952), which takes its title from a poem in which the author remembers a river crossing he made as a soldier, and implies that the passage through life as a whole is no less hard and perilous. Other poems in the collection include lyrics invoking the Silesian landscape that the poet has lost, or commenting ironically on aspects of postwar life. The earliest lyrics in the book are rhythmically regular and scrupulously rhymed; later poems are denser and more impressionistic, and often employ unrhymed lines of unequal length.

It is this style that predominates in *Die Rauchfahne* (The Wisp of Smoke, 1953), which includes harshly realistic poems about the lives of stableboys, road workers, and other "unpoetic" subjects. Critics were struck by the extreme impressionism of some of these poems, in which the reader's mind is jerked violently from one image to another that seems, at first, totally remote. Piontek's reputation was established at once when these first two collections were made the subject of an extended essay-review by Hans Egon Holthusen, included in Holthusen's widely read book of essays *Ja und Nein* in 1954. Together with Paul Celan, Walter Höllerer, A.A. Scholl, and Georg Forestier (who later turned out to be the invention of a publisher's reader), Piontek was hailed as one of the representative German poets of his generation—still partly derivative, to be sure, but writing out of an au-

> No visible scars,
> no medals,
> no titles—
> but the eye sharp, untameable
> as rage or as a rapture,
> memory crowded
> and sleep light. . . .
>
> (translated by Michael
> Hamburger and
> Christopher Middleton)

In that self-portrait Piontek fixed a stance of quiet defiance that was to distinguish him throughout his later years; and the "crowded memory" of the poems, going back to his Silesian childhood and adolescence, continued to provide him with rich material for later poetry and prose. Not all of it is grave or gloomy in tone; some of the later poems have a lightness of touch and an imaginative freedom that make them something other than confessional verse.

The professional vicissitudes to which Piontek alludes above became acute in the 1960s, when West German literature was politicized to a degree that left all literary reputations open to stricture on ideological rather than artistic grounds. What was held against Piontek was the absence of an explicit political commitment in his work, and a greater concern with religious themes than with responses to current political events and social conflicts; this was taken to mean that he was backward-looking, and his writing "irrelevant." His book of poems *Mit einer Kranichfeder* (With a Crane's Feather, 1962) was condemned because it included "old-fash-

641

ioned" rhymed lyrics. Piontek still had his readers and admirers, one of whom described him as "the classic of his generation," but the most vociferous critics had little use for classics. It was during this decade that Piontek came to see himself as an outsider, with a grim determination to continue in his own way.

As a prose writer Piontek had begun with the laconic short stories collected in *Vor Augen* (Before Your Eyes, 1955) and *Kastanien aus dem Feuer* (Chestnuts From the Fire, 1963), followed by a book of travel sketches, *Windrichtungen* (Wind Directions, 1963). He had also proved himself as an essayist and literary theorist with *Buchstab, Zauberstab* (Letter Magic, 1959), and showed that he could master yet another medium, the radio play, which flourished in West Germany during this period. His radio play *Weisser Panther* (White Panther) was published in 1962, and in 1967 came his first novel, *Die Mittleren Jahre* (The Middle Years, 1967).

The narrator of *Die Mittleren Jahre* is a burnt-out case, near-alcoholic and a failure as a teacher, novelist, husband, and father. After his wife dies in a road accident he retires to lick his wounds in rustic Bavaria, returning seven years later, sadder and possibly wiser, to search for the daughter he had left behind in Munich. A reviewer in the *Times Literary Supplement* wrote that Piontek "eschews the distancing effect of humour to his detriment and shows a weakness for contrivance . . . but he possesses undeniable talent. . . . seen in a certain light his colour-card of accidie—from black to tenebrous—can have an oddly elevating effect on the beholder." The novel does full justice to social realities and conflicts, and Piontek's sympathy with outsiders and with the victims of dominant pressure groups does not prevent him from rendering the trivia of everyday experience in the Munich he evokes so vividly. The book brought him that city's Literature Prize. An autobiographical second novel, *Dichterleben,* also set in Munich, followed in 1976.

Piontek's other works range from a volume of translations of the poems of Keats to his co-editorship of the notable anthology of international writing *ensemble,* published by the Bavarian Academy of Fine Arts, Munich, of which Piontek is a member (as he is of the German Academy for Language and Literature, Darmstadt). A collection of his poems, including most of his mature poetry up to 1974, was published for his fiftieth birthday; it leaves no doubt as to the variety and consistency of the work of this temporarily underrated poet. In 1976 he received the most coveted of German literary awards, the Büchner Prize.

It has been suggested that Piontek possesses "almost too much versatility"; he himself says that he has no wish to specialize in one medium or style but is happier breaking new ground and taking new risks. For much the same sort of reason, he says, he has "joined no group and no trend. I don't want to base any value judgement or recommendation on this fact. To be on one's own is a matter of personal disposition, temperament and practice. But I do feel closely bound to many dead and a few living poets by admiration and affinity." The admiration and affinity have been reciprocated by a sufficient number of discriminating critics and fellow poets.

PRINCIPAL WORKS IN ENGLISH TRANSLATION: Alive or Dead: Poems, translated by Richard Exner, 1975. *Poems in* Barnstone, W. (ed.) Modern European Poetry, 1966; Bridgwater, P. (ed.) The Penguin Book of Twentieth Century German Verse, 1963; Hamburger, M. and Middleton, C. (eds.) Modern German Poetry, 1962. *Story in* Middleton, C. (ed.) German Writing Today, 1967. *Radio Play in* Dimension 2 1969.

ABOUT: Bithell, J. Modern German Literature, 1959; Closs, A. Twentieth Century German Literature, 1969; Contemporary Authors 25–28 1st revision, 1977; Hohoff, C. (and others) Heinz Piontek, 1966; International Who's Who, 1978–79; Moore, H.T. Twentieth Century German Literature, 1967; Penguin Companion to Literature 2, 1969. *Periodicals*—Books Abroad Winter 1968; German Life and Letters 13 1 1959; Times Literary Supplement April 24, 1969.

*"PLATONOV, ANDREI" (Pen name of Andrei Platonovich Klimentov) (August 20, 1899–January 6, 1951), Russian novelist and short story writer, was born in Yamskaya Sloboda, near Voronezh, three hundred miles south of Moscow. He was the eldest of the eight children of Platon Klimentov, a metalworker in the railroad yards at Voronezh. At the age of fourteen, after five years in the village school and only two years in the town school at Voronezh, he had to start work at a series of odd jobs to help support the family.

"The working-class is my mother-land," he was to write later to Gorky. And in a letter to one of his editors in 1922 he wrote of himself: "Even ten years ago there was hardly any difference between Yamskaya and the country. I loved the country, too, enough to cry for it although I have not seen it since I was twelve. There were wattle fences in Yamskaya, and kitchen gardens, and vacant land filled with burdocks, huts instead of houses, chickens, shoemakers, and a great many peasants walking along the Zadonski highway. The bell in the church was listened to with deep feelings by the old folks, by beggars, and by me. . . . Then I

*plə ton' əf

ANDREI PLATONOV

learned to write in school. After that I started work. I worked in a lot of places, and for a lot of bosses. At one time there were ten in our family, and I was the eldest son—the only worker except for my father. My father was a metalworker, and he couldn't feed a horde like that. I forgot to say that besides the fields, the countryside, my mother, and the sound of bells ringing, I also loved—and the longer I live the more I love—steam engines, machines, shrill whistles, and sweaty work. I believed then that everything is man-made and nothing comes by itself; for a long time I thought they made children somewhere at the factory instead of by mothers producing them from their stomachs.

"There is some kind of link, some kinship, among burdocks and beggars, singing in the fields, electricity, a locomotive and its whistle, and earthquakes—there is the same birth mark on all of them and on some other things, too."

In 1913, the year he began work, Platonov also started to teach himself science. Through evening study he eventually qualified for entry into the Voronezh Polytechnical Institute, where he enrolled in 1918 to study land improvement. By then, however, the Civil War had begun and, as the fighting became more bitter he joined the Red Army, first as an engine-driver's mate, and later as a private in a special division where most of his time was spent writing war reports for a Voronezh newspaper. These reports, which started as accounts of actual engagements, became increasingly concerned with the nature of the Revolution itself and Russia's need for modern science and technology if the Revolution's purposes were to be fulfilled.

In 1921 Platonov returned to the Voronezh

Polytechnic, and after graduating in 1924 he worked in land reclamation and rural electrification. In 1927 he went to Moscow as trade union delegate to the Central Committee of Land and Forestry Workers, later becoming senior engineer on the National Commissariat for Agriculture. During these crowded years Platonov had also begun his literary career, starting with poems which he read aloud to his friends and published in *Golubaya glubina* (The Sky-Blue Depths, 1922). But these were little more than prose in verse rhythms, and he soon turned to fiction, making the difficult transition from journalism via a new kind of literature of fact.

In 1924 Platonov became a member of the Pereval (Mountain Pass) group of writers, formed under the leadership of Alexander Voronsky, editor of the journal *Krasnaya nov* (Red Virgin Soil), who argued that the attempt to "portray reality, people, events, in their lively dialectical flow and actuality" was the way along the "mountain pass" of a transitional period in literature, back to the nineteenth-century classical realists. Most of its members were young writers who had fought in the Civil War and felt they had something to say but needed to learn how to say it.

Platonov himself was strongly influenced by two great nineteenth-century writers, Gogol and Leskov, sharing with them a strong identification with the little man who struggles to maintain his identity and self-respect in a harsh and uncaring world. In his work in land reclamation Platonov saw the terrible effects of the Civil War and the subsequent struggle to build an industrialized communist society. As Vyacheslav Zavalishin has said: "Over and over again the same characters recur in Platonov's stories—the grandsons of Leskov's Levsha, that uncrowned king of self-taught men, the craftsman who shod a mechanical flea. His descendants have come down in life and become hoboes, tramps, drunkards, failures and crackpots of all sorts, but have inherited their grandfather's audacity, innate intelligence and conscience. . . . Levsha's descendants are not stupid or lazy, nor have they lost their skills, but they rebel against dull, senseless labor which calls only for muscular strength without intelligence. They refuse to be an appendage of the machine." Marc Slonim has pointed out that it is these "little men" in Platonov's stories, these "village philosophers, restless artisans, dreamy vagabonds . . . misfits, eccentrics and sufferers," who voice the author's "interest in the existential problems of life and death, our situation in the universe, and our relationship to nature and culture."

The earliest pieces in Platonov's first collection *Epifanskie shlyuzy* (Epiphany Locks, 1927) are still exercises in reportage, but the book also includes two of his most masterly tales. In the title story, which established Platonov's reputation, an English engineer comes to the Russia of Peter the Great to help in that earlier industrialization. He admires the great autocrat's organizing genius but is horrified by the ruthless methods used in constructing the canals which are to make the country a great naval power. And the engineer's compassion for the sufferings of thousands of peasants forcibly torn from the land to work for him brings him to the executioner's block for frustrating the Tsar's plans.

It was Platonov's use of language that gave these stories their impact—what Marc Slonim has called "his quaint mixture of vernacular and neologisms, the deliberate roughness of his ungrammatical sentences linking the folklore tradition with the verbal oddities of city idioms, and his metaphorical and oblique style which defies translation." The novel *Chevengur,* published only in part in the Soviet Union but translated in its entirety by Anthony Olcott under the same title, describes an attempt by poor and illiterate peasants to set up a communist society, simply by driving out the landlords and waiting for the glorious future to arrive.

All the warring literary factions of the 1920s were dissolved in 1932, after the militant left-wing school known as RAPP had mounted a fierce campaign against the Pereval group. Platonov himself was violently attacked in the Soviet press for such stories as "Usomnivshiisya Makar" (Doubting Makar, 1929), in which the countryman Makar goes to Moscow to seek his fortune. His simple and literal interpretation of communism as the right to such things as free transport provides an effective satirical commentary on the realities of industrial communism, with its crushing army of bureaucrats.

Kotlovan, written at about the same time, was translated during the 1970s as *The Foundation Pit.* It centers on Voshchev, one of those who "refuse to be an appendage of the machine." At the age of thirty Voshchev loses his machine shop job because he thinks too much. He wanders to a village where the people are digging the foundations of a great building that is intended to house the entire community (and obviously represents the process of collectivization). Few seem convinced that the new house is the best solution for them, and most put what faith they have in the generations to come. The community adopts an orphan girl who symbolizes this hope but before long she dies and is lovingly buried. Paul Theroux called it "obviously a masterpiece," and "a magnificent experiment in de-

based language," characterized by uncompromising skepticism. The language employed is bureaucratese, Theroux says, "the impersonal and contemptuous language of ministerial hacks," which Platonov uses "like a man speaking with a rising gorge, occasionally gasping with disgust."

"Vprok" (In Reserve, 1931) is another grotesque panorama of the Russian countryside during the early stages of forced collectivization, when peasants chose to slaughter farm animals rather than hand them over to the state, agriculture broke down, and famine and poverty swept the countryside. Alexander Fadeyev attacked this story as a slander on collective-farm leadership, and denounced the author as an agent of the kulaks. Stalin himself wrote "Scum!" in red pencil on the story. Platonov was virtually unable to publish throughout the 1930s though he did contribute pseudonymously to various periodicals; there are unconfirmable rumors that he was twice arrested and exiled from Moscow.

During this period, nevertheless, Platonov remade himself as a writer, abandoning his earlier stylization of popular speech in favor of brevity and utter simplicity. And at a time when the individual counted for less and less, and private needs were being sacrificed to "socialist reconstruction," he was writing stories of piercing intensity which make up an eloquent plea for compassion towards Russia's poorest and most insignificant people. Though few of these stories were published during his lifetime, those that were rank among his best, like "Bessmertie" (Immortality) and "Fro," which appeared in a magazine in 1936, and the collection *Reka Potudan* (The Potudan River, 1939).

"In place of his earlier flamboyant style, he now began to write in a new manner, apparently naive and artless, but in fact a marvellously expressive medium for his compassionate outlook," writes Boris Thomson. "Two types frequently recur in Platonov's writings: a cripple hideously mutilated and pathologically embittered as a result of the past; and an innocent orphan-child, equally a victim of the past, but ignorant, trusting and defenceless. The two are thrown together in a half-parental, half-tyrannical relationship; often it ends with the death of the child. Like Mayakovsky, Platonov did not believe that the past could be eradicated so easily; as he saw it, the dead hand of the past still lay over the present." But in 1937 a long critical article by A. Gurvich described Platonov as a writer obsessed by themes of misery, orphanhood, and death, and thus completely out of tune with what was expected of a Soviet writer.

Unlike other Pereval writers, Platonov by

some miracle survived the purges, but in 1938 his only son Platon was arrested and accused of taking part in an alleged counterrevolutionary conspiracy. The fifteen-year-old boy was sent to a camp in the far north. Though he was released after two years, reputedly because the novelist Sholokhov had pleaded with Stalin himself, he returned fatally ill with tuberculosis and died in his father's arms.

After Hitler's invasion, Platonov worked as a war correspondent on the paper *Red Star,* writing sketches and stories. He was at last able to publish again, and several collections of short stories appeared during the war—*Pod nebesami rodiny* (Beneath the Skies of Our Motherland, 1942), *Bronya* (Armored Vehicles, 1943), *V storonu zakata solntsa* (Towards the Setting Sun, 1945), and *Soldatskoe serdtse* (The Heart of a Soldier, 1946). These are his weakest stories, however—honest accounts of the psychology of ordinary Russian people at war, but marred by sentimentality and emotionalism.

In 1947, in spite of the intense patriotism of his wartime writing, Platonov again came under critical attack, and his last years were a struggle against both poverty and illness. He had returned from the war wounded and seriously ill with tuberculosis, to find that the only works he was permitted to publish were folk tales—and even these only appeared because of the persistent representations of Sholokhov. At the beginning of the war Platonov had been evacuated to Ufa, the capital of the Bashkir republic, and his first folk tale collection was *Bashkirskiye narodnye skazski* (Bashkir Folk Tales, 1947), which was followed in 1950 by *Volshebnoye koltso* (The Magic Ring).

Platonov's early stories had been criticized as "terrible fairy-tales rather than events from real life," and Marian Jordan has pointed out that these folk tales may be seen as a continuation of his earlier work: "There had always been in Platonov's work something of the legendary." She notes the resemblance of his early characters to the type-figures of fairy tales, and shows that the settings and manner of these stories were also in keeping with the folk tradition, so that from the vast wealth of Russian tales, ranging from the fantastic to the earthily humorous, "it was easy for Platonov to choose ... a world which was remarkably similar to the modern world he had already portrayed. These humble peasants are subject to the same deprivation as Platonov's earlier characters. The bulk of them are either very old or very young, and the old have lost their children and the young have lost their parents."

When he died in January 1951 the greater part of Platonov's work was still unpublished, including the novels *Chevengur* and *Kotlovan,* and a great many stories, unproduced plays, and film scripts. His "rehabilitation" began in the 1960s, when several collections of his stories were published in huge editions in the Soviet Union, and received with great critical enthusiasm. He is now generally regarded as one of the most original of Soviet writers. Konstantin Paustovsky, writing in 1967 of the distortion of Russian literature under Stalin, asked how it could happen that "excellent works ... lay hidden and only saw the light of day a quarter of a century after they were written? The damage done is irreparable. Had for instance the works of Andrei Platonov and Mikhail Bulgakov appeared when they were written, our contemporaries would have been immeasurably richer in spirit." Yevgeny Yevtushenko, speaking of Hemingway's admiration for the pithiness and expressiveness of Platonov's style, describes him as belonging "among the delayed-action writers, whose talent is like a safety fuse which runs many years in length." Yevtushenko says that his face "looking out from one of his last photographs" is "the face of a worker who thinks—the face of a master. The prose Platonov wrote has just this kind of face." Andrew Field has called him "Isaac Babel's chief rival as a master of the short story in post-Revolutionary literature."

PRINCIPAL WORKS IN ENGLISH TRANSLATION: The Fierce and Beautiful World (selected stories translated by J. Barnes), 1969; The Foundation Pit, translated by Thomas P. Whitney, 1973 (also translated under the same title by Mirra Ginsburg, 1975); Fro and Other Stories, 1975 (Moscow); Chevengur, translated by Anthony Olcott, 1978; Collected Works (a selection), translated by Thomas P. Whitney and others, 1978. *Stories in* Beame, C.G. (ed.) Modern Russian Short Stories II, 1969; Glenny, M. (ed.) Novy Mir 1925-1967, 1972; London Magazine 3 1967.

ABOUT: Jordan, M. Andrei Platonov, 1973; Mihailovich, V.D. A Library of Literary Criticism: Modern Slavic Literatures, 1972; Struve, G. Russian Literature Under Lenin and Stalin 1917-1953, 1972; Thomson, B. The Premature Revolution, 1972; Who Was Who in the USSR, 1972; Zavalishin, V. Early Soviet Writers, 1958. *Periodicals*—Books Abroad Spring 1975; Commonweal February 22, 1974; New York Review of Books January 1, 1970; New York Times Book Review November 16, 1969; March 17, 1974.

*POIRIER, (WILLIAM) RICHARD (September 9, 1925–), American literary critic and scholar, was born in Gloucester, Massachusetts, the son of Philip Poirier and the former Annie Kiley. After service in the U.S. Army from 1943 to 1946, Poirier went to Amherst College, where he received his B.A. in 1949. Yale gave him his M.A. in 1951, by which time Poirier had begun

*pwä′ rē ā

RICHARD POIRIER

his teaching career as an instructor in English and American literature at Williams College, Williamstown, Massachusetts (1950–1952). He spent 1952–1953 in England, pursuing postgraduate studies as a Fulbright fellow at Cambridge University. Poirier received his Ph.D. in 1959 at Harvard, where he was a graduate student from 1953 to 1958 and taught from 1958 until 1963—as an instructor until 1960 and then as an assistant professor of English. In 1963 he went as professor of English to Rutgers University in New Jersey, where he has served also as chairman of the English Department in 1963–1972 and as director of graduate studies in English since 1970. Poirier was editor of the annual volume in the O. Henry Prize Stories series from 1961 to 1964, and joint editor in 1965 and 1966. From 1963 to 1973 he was a member of the editorial board of *Partisan Review.*

In his first book, *The Comic Sense of Henry James* (1960), Poirier sets out to show how, in the early novels, James either used melodrama to comic effect or used comedy as "a way of rejecting melodrama." Most of his characters, moreover, can be divided into the "free," whom we see changing and developing, and the "fixed" —more or less stock characters who are exploited for comic purposes, and who provide yardsticks against which to measure the deviations of the heroes and heroines. The book, which was based on Poirier's doctoral thesis, was found scholarly, original, and unpedantic, though "colorless" in its prose. Marius Bewley wrote: "Mr. Poirier dislikes the generalising statement so much that he increases difficulties by shying away from a forthright or dogmatic description of his argument, which we arrive at obliquely.

... This study of James is filled with valuable insights, and is obviously the product of a fine critical intelligence. ... It is good to be brought back to James specifically as an artist, and it is especially gratifying that Mr. Poirier should reassert this emphasis in the field of the early novels, which are still underestimated."

Bewley found the work unique among recent studies of James—"the only one that has made a detailed scrutiny almost page by page, of James's technique as an artist." Poirier works very much in the current mode of close textual analysis. He is, as R.W.B. Lewis says, "articulately fed up with moral and psychological interpretations, and with archetypal and genre studies." For him, "stylistic analysis is not an additional tool for criticism. It must entirely supersede every other mode of analysis."

This it largely does in *A World Elsewhere* (1966), which established Poirier as "one of the ablest critics now writing under the banner of radical modernism." This book proposes that most major American writers have not sought to represent reality but to displace it—"to create in their works an environment freed of [social] restraints and congenial to the evolutionary expansion of human consciousness." And Poirier seeks to demonstrate that this environment of freedom is brought into being solely by these writers' use of literary style. This thesis is supported by the close analysis of passages from the work of Cooper, Emerson, Thoreau, Hawthorne, Melville, Mark Twain, and Henry James, among others. For example, Poirier quotes a sentence from Faulkner's famous story "The Bear" and analyzes it to show how Faulkner's technique of statement by negation dismisses both conventional ideas about hunting and the "literary myths" about hunting which the author invents on the spot, leaving the reader in a purely imaginary world whose only other inhabitant is Faulkner himself.

Poirier's examples, wrote Leo Marx, "tend to be the familiar ones in the over-interpreted texts, but he is such a master of close stylistic analysis, and his angle of vision is so unusual, that he often succeeds in giving them fresh significance." However, it troubled Marx that Poirier "uncritically accepts the idiom of our native literary anarchism. System, in his lexicon, is a dirty word. ... The chief value of literature, it seems, is compensatory; it leads one away from rather than toward the world. One cannot help feeling that this fashionable doctrine was tailored to fit our contemporary despair." R. W. B. Lewis also admired the brilliance of Poirier's analyses and the deft elaboration of his argument, but thought that his thesis "emerges from certain highly contemporary apprehensions, and ... does not work very well with the classical American authors." Lewis added that "one disconcerting feature of the current and productive concern with style ... is that it makes visible for us in the works explored a carefully wrought and often crowded imaginative scene in which nothing human or important or morally challenging ever seems to happen."

A World Elsewhere was very widely discussed, and so was *The Performing Self,* which followed in 1971. This is a collection of nine essays on contemporary culture, and on the difficulty of retaining one's humanity and identity at a time of very rapid and extreme cultural, moral, and social change. When he speaks of the "performing self," Poirier is referring to "any self-discovering self-watching, finally self-pleasing response to the pressures and difficulties" of the times—like the "literature of self-parody" produced by such writers as Nabokov, Borges, Pynchon, and Barth. There is an attack on the dangerous limitations of academic discourse, a long essay in praise of the Beatles, and another in praise of youth, with its creative "freedom from believing that the so-called 'necessities' of life and thought are in fact necessities." The argument, as Tony Tanner says, is everywhere "against fixity and for fluidity, dislocation, a continuous reinvention of the forms by which we live (and teach). To meet the challenge of youth 'the universities need to dismantle their entire academic structure.' There must be a 'rebellion against the disorder we call order.' "

It seemed to Tony Tanner that these essays "are written with a mobile and compact intelligence, and are so effortlessly allusive and stylistically elegant, that summaries can only do him ... an injustice. ... It is ... an impressive performance by one of the most original of our contemporary critics." John Seelye was amazed "to find someone like Poirier, early on a firm devotee at the altar of the Master, James, the Great Snob Himself, yielding to the pressure of the classroom," but he thought "Poirier's willingness to start anew should earn our admiration and attention." Alfred Kazin, on the other hand, was dismayed by "the ponderousness of style" the book "brings to the preciosity of its ideas. It seems only too eager to show that literature is obsolete, but is itself inevitably out of date in its heavy-handed praise of the Beatles and some vague social entity called the 'young.' "

Predictably, critics were almost equally divided over the merits of Poirier's study in the "Modern Masters" series of Norman Mailer, one of the heroes of *The Performing Self.* Mailer's work is a prime example of literature as "performance," and Poirier thinks him "the only writer of prominence in English who can be expected to deliver a book that deserves comparison with the best of Faulkner or James." Mailer treats writing as a "kind of combative enterprise analogous to war"; he welcomes disorder and contradiction, and finds his form in the struggle to master chaos. "He treats the self that existed in the past as another soul or spirit with which the present self can contend, and his work is at last a record of his continuous wars among the selves that are Mailer." While David Thorburn found the book "shrewd, trendy, and confused by turns," Richard Gilman called it "the most intelligent reading of Mailer I know of.... Poirier has afforded such insights, so lithe and open a way of looking at this very important writer (and so at writing in general), as to make one's final response nothing less than gratitude."

Robert Frost: The Work of Knowing (1977) had a much less equivocal reception. "In close readings of poem after poem," wrote Katha Pollitt, "Poirier elucidates the tensions between the strongly felt contraries that obsessed Frost: domesticity and a need for freedom, reticence and passion, the meaningless sounds of nature and the accents of the human voice." She concluded that "Poirier's central accomplishment is his reintegration of the popular and the literary Frost, so that we no longer choose sides between a poseur and a genius but see him whole, as one of those classically great writers for whom 'the surfaces are as important as the depths.' "

Poirier, a member of Phi Beta Kappa, received a Bollingen fellowship in 1962–1963. He lists among his leisure interests American painting, travel, films, and food.

PRINCIPAL WORKS: The Comic Sense of Henry James: A Study of the Early Novels, 1960; A World Elsewhere: The Place of Style in American Literature, 1966; The Performing Self: Compositions and Decompositions in the Languages of Contemporary Life, 1971; Norman Mailer, 1972; Robert Frost: The Work of Knowing, 1977. *As Editor—* (with Reuben A. Brower) In Defense of Reading: A Reader's Approach to Literary Criticism, 1962; (with William L. Vance) American Literature, 1970; (with Frank Kermode) The Oxford Reader: Varieties of Contemporary Discourse, 1971.

ABOUT: Contemporary Authors 1-4 1st revision, 1967; Directory of American Scholars II, 1974; Who's Who in America, 1976–1977. *Periodicals*—American Scholar Winter 1971–1972; Atlantic May 1971; Book Week November 6, 1966; Christian Science Monitor May 26, 1971; Commentary April 1973; Michigan Quarterly Review Fall 1968; Modern Fiction Studies Winter 1960–1961, Summer 1967; Nation July 17, 1967; National Review June 15, 1971; New England Quarterly March 1967; New Republic November 26, 1966; May 1, 1971; New Statesman June 11, 1960; New York Review of Books March 9, 1967; September 20, 1973; New York Times Book Review January 8, 1967; May 30, 1971; December 17, 1972; Saturday Review May 22, 1971;

POPA

December 10, 1977; Spectator May 6, 1960; Times Literary Supplement September 9, 1960; February 4, 1972; Virginia Quarterly Review Winter 1967; Yale Review March 1967.

*POPA, VASKO (June 29, 1922–), Yugoslav poet and anthologist, was born in Grebenac, near Bela Crkva, in the Serbian province of Vojvodina. He studied at the universities of Vienna, Bucharest, and Belgrade, receiving his degree in French and Yugoslav literature in Belgrade in 1949. Since then he has worked as an editor at the Nolit publishing house in Belgrade.

Popa's early poems were influenced by French surrealism, but, guided by the example of Momčilo Nastasijević (1894–1938), whose collected works he has edited, he soon found a richer and more relevant source of imagery in the Serbian folk tradition, which embraces gnomic proverbs and riddles and a wealth of humorous and fantastic "nonsense" poetry, as well as lyric and epic verse. He has published an anthology of Serbian folk literature, *Od zlata jabuka* (Among Golden Apples, 1958). Under these influences, Popa developed a highly individual style, radically simple, aphoristic, and concise in diction, but full of striking and complex metaphors, startling ellipses and transmutations, sad or ironic parables. His poems are brief, and are often gathered into cycles on a particular theme, which they examine from a variety of viewpoints. Ted Hughes says that Popa "will trust no phrase with his meaning for more than six or seven words at a time before he corrects his tack with another phrase from another direction. In the same way, he will trust no poem with his meaning for more than fifteen or so lines, before he tries again from a totally different direction with another poem."

These qualities are all present in Popa's first collection of poems, *Kora* (Bark, 1953), along with a preoccupation with simple objects and organisms—a sustained attempt, reminiscent of that of Francis Ponge, to pierce beneath the bark or crust of things and to jettison his own human preconceptions about them; to apprehend their real nature and look back at the human world as it might appear to them. It is as if the poet, caught in mid-adolescence in a war which conclusively demonstrated the fragility of human claims to reason and order, was trying to rediscover the world afresh. As Hughes says, "his poems are trying to find out what does exist, and what the conditions really are."

Thus Popa scrutinizes a plate, a chair, some papers, or a dandelion—"the yellow eye of loneliness/ On the edge of the pavement/ At the end of the world." In the cycle called "Spisak"

*pop′ ə

VASKO POPA

© Lutfi Özkök

he tries to enter into the minds and feelings of various domestic animals, as in this poem about a pig, translated by Anne Pennington in her edition of Popa's *Selected Poems:*

> Only when she felt
> The savage knife in her throat
> Did the red veil
> Explain the game
> And she was sorry
> She had torn herself
> From the mud's embrace
> And had hurried that evening
> From the field so joyfully
> Hurried to the yellow gate

It is a terrifying and desolate world that Popa discovers in these poems. The speaker in "Acquaintance" anticipates "the breath of the beast" and in his fear will not participate, will not "play"; as if in a dream he feels "the dark of the jaws/ That open my eyes/ I see/ I see/ I'm not dreaming." Love itself is constantly threatened: "do you hear the bullet/ That circles around our heads/ Lying in wait for our kiss?" But there are some gleams of light in these dark poems, and it is love that provides such hope as there is of joy and permanence:

> The streets of your glances
> Have no ending
>
> The swallows from your eyes
> Do not migrate south
>
> From the aspens in your breasts
> The leaves do not fall

In the heaven of your words
The sun does not set

(from "Far Within Us,"
translated by
Anne Pennington)

Some Yugoslav critics were puzzled and disturbed by the originality and obscurity of these poems, but Popa's intentions became clearer in *Nepočin-Polje* (Unrest-Field, 1956), which established him as one of the best and most admired of contemporary Yugoslav poets. It includes the bitterly ironical cycle "Igre" (Games) which, as Vasa D. Mihailovich points out, parodies the insane games of war. In one of these games, the player is to bite off an opponent's arm or leg and bury it; the others are to sniff around in search of the missing limb. A player who unearths his own limb is entitled to the next bite: "The game goes on briskly/ As long as there are arms/ As long as there are legs/ As long as there is anything whatever." In another cycle, "Kost kosti" (One Bone to Another), where people strip the flesh from their bones in the hope that this innovation will make for a better life, the implications are clearly political:

That's better
We've got away from the flesh

Now we will do what we will
Say something

Would you like to be
The backbone of a streak of lightning

Say something more. . . .

I don't know anything else
Ribs of the heavens

We are not anyone's bones
Say something different

(translated by
Anne Pennington)

But nothing changes man's nature, and at the end of the cycle: "I am a bone you are a bone/ Why have you swallowed me/ I can't see myself any more. . . ."

Popa's third collection, *Pesme* (Songs, 1965), includes a number of poems in a different vein, in which the poet visits the great monuments and relics of his country's bloody and tragic past, and considers their relevance for the present. And having broadened his range in this way—from his early scrutiny of small and simple things to a consideration of a whole nation and its history—his vision becomes nothing less than cosmic in *Sporedno Nebo* (Secondary Heaven, 1968). In the allegory that runs through all

seven cycles of poems in this book, though the sun still rules over the "secondary heaven" of the title, his reign is troubled by the struggle between the forces of light and the forces of nothingness—of zero, "the forgetful number," which is "pristine and round like a sun/ But alone much alone." And the sun's heir is blind, so that when the "Sun Father" dies, only night comes out "to meet the blind sun." It seems unlikely that light can survive, but the struggle goes on. As Vasa D. Mihailovich points out, this allegory is not a mythological interpretation of reality, but a reflection of human fate in the celestial mirror. In this critic's opinion, "the force of the poet's idiom, the familiar simplicity, the use of old legends and folklore, the original humor and charming irony make this collection Popa's highest achievement so far. Above all, it signifies that his poetic thought has completed a circle. By way of the universe he reaches his final destination—his own self."

Some of the historical poems from *Pesme* reappear in *Uspravna zemlja* (1970, translated by Anne Pennington as *Earth Erect)*, along with others on similar themes written as early as 1950. All of the poems in this collection, old and new, find their final places in five thematically separate cycles. The first cycle, drawing upon the poet's pilgrimage to a number of ancient Serbian shrines and monuments, is followed by one dedicated to a single holy place, the Spring of Sava, patron saint of Serbia, who in "Saint Sava, the Shepherd," milks the stones of the hillside to succor his wolves, the Serbs:

He guards the stone-herd
On the green meadow

Inside the ancestral red cave
He helps each stone
To give birth

Wherever he roams
The herd trails him
The hills echo with stone-steps

He halts in a clearing
Yellow and secluded
He milks stone after stone

Then he lets his wolves drink
This thick stone-milk that reflects
The seven colours of the rainbow

Strong teeth and secret wings
Grow when you drink stone-milk.

(translated by Charles Simic)

Popa has here dismantled the universal archetype of the shepherd caring for his flock, and reassembled it in the light of the harsh historical experience of the Serbs. There is tension not only in the dialectic of contradictory motifs and symbols but between the animistic and myth-making consciousness that long ago created the archetype and the contemporary idioms of the poem's language. Here as elsewhere in this book, the result, as Charles Simic says, "is a poetry which engages the deepest unconscious responses of the native reader, while possessing at the same time an ontological and epic appetite which give it the stature of one of the most complex and successful poetic works of our time."

Up to this point, Popa's output had been small, but in 1975 he published no less than three collections of poetry. *Vučja so* (Wolf's Salt) develops further the theme of "Saint Sava, the Shepherd." In Serbian mythology the wolf is a heroic figure, and Popa uses the tenacity and courage of the lame wolf to symbolize the Serbian people; Saint Sava, thirteenth-century prince and archbishop, is shepherd to these wolves because he founded the Serbian Orthodox Church. There are more personal poems in *Živo meso* (Live Flesh), in which Popa recalls his childhood, and the myths and superstitions of Vojvodina. *Kuća nasred druma* (The House in the Middle of the Highway) is a more varied collection, lacking the cyclical unity of the earlier books.

Some of Popa's poems have been set to music by Dušan Radić and Milko Kelemen. His work has been translated into a dozen languages, and he is internationally the best-known of living Yugoslav poets. Popa made a great impact at the Poetry International Festival in London in 1961; a recording of his reading is available. He received the Branko Radičević prize in 1953, the Zmaj prize in 1956, and the Austrian Lenau prize in 1967.

PRINCIPAL WORKS IN ENGLISH TRANSLATION: Selected Poems, translated by Anne Pennington, 1969; The Little Box, translated by Charles Simic, 1970; Earth Erect, translated by Anne Pennington, 1973; Collected Poems: 1943–1976, translated by Anne Pennington, 1978. *Poems in* Johnson, B. (ed.) New Writing in Yugoslavia, 1970; Lavrin, J. (ed.) An Anthology of Modern Yugoslav Poetry, 1963; Books Abroad Spring 1973.

ABOUT: Radić, A. Contemporary Serbian Literature, 1964; Lukić, S. Contemporary Yugoslav Literature, 1972; Penguin Companion to Literature 2, 1969; Seymour-Smith, M. A Guide to Modern World Literature, 1973; Who's Who in the Socialist Countries, 1978. *Periodicals*—Books Abroad Winter 1969, Spring 1970, Spring 1973, Autumn 1976; Times Literary Supplement November 23, 1973; TriQuarterly Spring 1967.

POPE-HENNESSY, SIR JOHN (WYNDHAM) (December 13, 1913–), English art historian, was born in London, the son of Major-General Ladislaus H. R. Pope-Hennessy, who besides his distinguished army career in Africa, Europe, and Mesopotamia, and as a British military attaché, also published articles and books on military subjects. His mother was Dame Una (Birch) Pope-Hennessy, a prolific author who wrote critical biographies of such writers as Sir Walter Scott, Charles Dickens, and Edgar Allan Poe; historical studies and works on art, including *Early Chinese Jades.* Under her influence both her sons were to become writers, John's younger brother being the well-known biographer and historian James Pope-Hennessy, who was murdered by thieves in 1974.

The family was a Roman Catholic one, and both sons were educated at the famous Catholic public school of Downside, except for three years at St. Albans Cathedral School in Washington, D.C., when their father was military attaché at the British Embassy there. It was then that John Pope-Hennessy took up art history, which he insists is "a vocation, not a profession in the conventional sense. I embraced it at thirteen, when I bought Crowe and Cavalcaselle's *History of Painting in North Italy* in Washington during the Christmas holidays, and for five years thereafter such prizes as I won at school were books about Italian painting: first, volume by volume, Crowe and Cavalcaselle's *History of Painting in Italy* and then Berenson's *Study and Criticism of Italian Art.* At the time this interest was an eccentric one. The term 'art-historian' was not yet in common use, and it was generally explained that I was destined to be a *Kunstforscher.* For better or worse there were no facilities in England for training in *Kunstforschung,* and in the absence of the academic curriculum of lectures and seminars I was compelled to look and read and think."

Pope-Hennessy went on to Balliol College, Oxford University, where, he says, "people called me Botticelli. The name meant, or was meant to mean, not just that I was interested in Italian art, but that the paintings I preferred were mannered, etiolated and non-realistic." As an art historian he has in fact specialized in Italian painters and sculptors of the Renaissance, to which all his books relate. Immediately after graduating from Oxford he went to Siena to continue his self-education in Italian art. He has explained that "the distinction between the autodidact and the trained art-historian is more fundamental than it may appear. The indoctrinated art-historian is trained to teach. From a comparatively early stage he is expected to have

Metropolitan Museum of Art

SIR JOHN POPE-HENNESSY

a working knowledge of the literature of great artists and a grasp of the methods by which they were studied in the past, and his prospects of professional success are in the ratio of his academic armament. The self-trained art-historian, on the other hand, forges his own weapons. Establishing a bridgehead in some subject, he develops outwards as taste and opportunity dictate. In my own case the bridgehead was at Siena, and at first I operated on what seems in retrospect to have been a dangerously narrow front. One reason for this was that I was conscious (as were most people who embarked on academic study in the years immediately before the war) that time was short. What mattered was to achieve results."

And his concentration on Sienese painting did achieve results, its immediate fruit being monographs on the two main painters of the fifteenth-century Sienese school: *Giovanni di Paolo* (1937) and *Sassetta* (1939). And having dealt thus with its two major figures, Pope-Hennessy then produced a book on the school as a whole, *Sienese Quattrocento Painting* (1947), not published until after the war. L. J. Wathen in the New York *Times* said that this was "more than [a] mere picture book. . . . Mr. Pope-Hennessy's introduction is the clear and discriminating account of Sienese fifteenth-century painting which one expects from the author of the definitive studies of Sassetta and Giovanni di Paolo."

In 1938 Pope-Hennessy joined the staff of the Victoria and Albert Museum in London. World War II began a year later, and the author served in the Air Ministry from 1939 to 1945. At a late stage in the war he was invited to take part in the cataloging of the drawings in the Royal Library

at Windsor Castle, and one result of this was *The Drawings of Domenichino at Windsor Castle* (1948). By choosing these drawings of the seventeenth-century Bolognese painter, Pope-Hennessy moved from the earliest to the closing stages of the Renaissance. This choice, he explained, "was dictated by the considerations, first that the painter was stylistically congenial —if one cohabits with an artist for a long period of time the importance of compatibility cannot be overstressed—and second that the corpus of Domenichino drawings in the Royal Collection was so large that one could hope to reconstruct his creative machinery almost in its entirety. The experience of this work confirmed me in a belief that I already held, that the art-historian's legitimate concern is with the creative process and that no display of learning, no intellectual sleight-of-hand is of avail if the creative process has not been understood. After the war I spent two barren years working on a monograph on Matteo de Giovanni, but the focus of my interests had changed, and the unpublished manuscript lies in my desk."

Instead, Pope-Hennessy followed his works on fifteenth-century Sienese painters with commissioned books on two of their Florentine contemporaries, beginning with *Uccello* (1950, second revised edition 1969). Modern criticism has tended to endorse Vasari's verdict that Uccello was a potentially great artist distracted by his study of perspective from generating his full force. But Pope-Hennessy insists that "the confusion which has dogged criticism of the painter from Vasari's time down to our own is due in part to misunderstanding of Uccello's contribution to the development of pictorial perspective and in part to the abuse of the term 'science,' for his originality is to be sought not in the novelty of his technique but in the use to which he put it." This argument is developed in Pope-Hennessy's long biographical and critical commentary, and all of the artist's paintings and drawings are reproduced.

When the first edition of *Uccello* appeared it was described as "antediluvian," since Pope-Hennessy had accepted as authentic only those few works traditionally associated with Uccello, and had explicitly rejected a number of minor paintings recently attributed to him. In the interval between the first and second editions, knowledge of Uccello was increased by a "highly responsible and admirably executed campaign of restoration" in Florence, and this confirmed Pope-Hennessy in his view. John Woodward in the *Spectator* described this as "certainly one of the most attractive and useful books" the Phaidon Press had yet published. And Howard Devree in the New York *Times* commented that Pope-Hennessy's "discussion of Uccello's innovations in perspective and of the peculiar interrelations of his work with that of his great contemporary Piero della Francesca, provides a fascinating insight into the art history of the fifteenth century."

Fra Angelico (1952, second revised edition 1974) examines the problem of this painter's enigmatic personality as well as the main characteristics of his work and the ideas which it expressed. Fra Angelico's religious images are perhaps the most familiar as well as the most harmonious of any Renaissance artist's, so that it is easy to overlook the fundamentally innovative nature of his painting. Pope-Hennessy points out that "the history of fifteenth-century Florentine art opens with an anomaly, that Renaissance style appears in painting later than it does in sculpture. . . . Not till the middle of the fourteen-twenties was it appreciated that the way lay open to a type of painting which was physically more convincing and might, as a didactic instrument, prove more potent and purposeful." The Dominicans were one of the first orders to recognize this possibility, and it was the Dominican painter Fra Angelico who evolved an idiom which has come to be regarded as the natural language of religious painting.

Bernard Berenson found the book "full of fascinating heresies," and Nicolaus Pevsner said of it that "Mr. Pope-Hennessy is a scholar of amazing energy. . . . In whatever he writes he has proved reliable as well as readable, and his treatment of Fra Angelico is no exception." Benedict Nicolson wrote: "The scrupulousness with which Mr. Pope-Hennessy has separated master from assistants; and sorted out the various hands for the decoration of the cells at San Marco, is one of the chief merits of the book. From this sifting process, and from the hundreds of remarkable reproductions . . . a new artist emerges, less picturesque but more dignified than the old."

Pope-Hennessy returned to the Victoria and Albert Museum in 1954, as Keeper of the Department of Architecture and Sculpture until 1966 and as Director of the Museum from 1967 to 1973. He served also as Slade Professor of Fine Art at Oxford University in 1956-1957, at Cambridge in 1964-1965. In 1961-1962 Pope-Hennessy taught at Williams College, Massachusetts, as Robert Sterling Clark Professor of Art, and in 1963 he was Mellon Lecturer at the National Gallery of Art, Washington, D.C. He lectured at New York University in 1965. Meanwhile, in the years immediately after World War II, he was making what he has called his "first

timid contributions to the study of Italian sculpture. . . . They were timid because the study of Italian sculpture was less highly developed than the study of Italian painting, and it was some years before I felt confident enough to start work, first on a large-scale introduction to Italian sculpture, and then on the catalogue of Italian sculptures in the Victoria and Albert Museum."

Pope-Hennessy's large-scale *Introduction to Italian Sculpture* is in the form of a trilogy, the first volume of which is *Italian Gothic Sculpture* (1955, second edition 1972). A general introduction traces the stylistic development of Italian Gothic sculpture as a whole, and this is then followed by biographies of each sculptor in turn. Despite its large size, Michael Ayrton predicted that "with this book in their luggage, perhaps a proportion of those annual visitors to Florence will pause longer in Pisa than it takes to see the leaning tower and halt their journey at Lucca for more than the lunch-hour." While the *Times Literary Supplement* said that "it is with a feeling of anticipation that the book is finally set down. . . . There is every promise that the usefulness of the present book, and the great pleasures that are already to be derived from it, will receive a more than threefold increase when the series is complete."

The second volume, *Italian Renaissance Sculpture* (1958, second edition 1971), deals with one of the great creative periods of sculpture, the fifteenth century, during which the return to classical Roman sculpture initiated by Brunelleschi and Donatello in Florence gradually spread throughout Italy. Pope-Hennessy stresses that the Renaissance in sculpture "expressed itself not in academic imitation of Roman art but in a revival of the naturalistic principles by which Roman art had been inspired." A new relation was thus established between the sculptor and the world about him, and from this there arose problems which have persisted to the present day. When the first edition of this book appeared it was acclaimed as the most important contribution to its subject in three decades, and the revised edition remains the most authoritative work in English on the subject.

Michael Kitson was typical in describing it as "a marvellous book. Highly intelligent, lucid, erudite and deft, the author wings his way with unerring accuracy across a field—the Quattrocento—which is beyond doubt richer in illustrious names than any other in the history of European sculpture." The trilogy was completed by *Italian High Renaissance and Baroque Sculpture* (1963, revised edition 1970), which is dominated by the personalities of the two greatest sculptors of the period—Michelangelo, in whose hands the art of sculpture became a language of unsuspected richness and profundity, and Bernini, who welded the artistic aspirations of his age into a coherent, universal style, the Baroque.

Shortly afterwards Pope-Hennessy finished the three-volume *Catalogue of Italian Sculpture in the Victoria and Albert Museum* (1964), the first two volumes containing the text and the final volume the plates. The museum's collection of sculpture is the largest in the world, with most of the great sculptors represented in it, often by masterpieces of the first rank. And since in no other museum is the whole field of Italian sculpture illustrated with such richness and variety, these three volumes not only form a comprehensive catalog of the collection but are themselves a major contribution to the study of Italian sculpture. Pope-Hennessy followed this with other catalogs, *Renaissance Bronzes From the Kress Collection* (1965) and the *Catalogue of Sculpture in the Frick Collection* (1970).

John Pope-Hennessy has had a lifelong interest in portraiture: "The first book I ever wrote—it has remained unpublished—dealt with the iconography of Sir Walter Scott. Years later, during the last war, I returned to portraiture, this time to Hilliard and the Elizabethan miniature" —an interest which led to *A Lecture on Nicholas Hilliard* (1949). Portraiture was the subject also of his 1963 Mellon Lectures. These appeared in book form, somewhat amplified, as *The Portrait in the Renaissance* (1966), and discuss the development of Renaissance portraiture in terms of the ideas by which it was inspired. The Renaissance cult of individuality brought with it the demand that the features of the individual should be perpetuated, and under the impact of humanist thinking the portrait as a record of appearance gave way in the hands of Titian and other sixteenth-century artists to the portrait as analysis of character. The book was criticized for its lecture format, but the *Times Literary Supplement* commented that "the reader whose wish, so seldom granted, is simply to enjoy a book about art is certain to enjoy this one; the reader who is more committed to the subject is just as certain to find himself rethinking the many issues raised in the text."

Raphael (1970) also originated in a series of lectures—the Wrightsman Lectures delivered under the auspices of the New York University Institute of Fine Arts. Pope-Hennessy proceeds from the assumption "that Raphael's reputation lies in the past, and that to us his works speak less directly than those of painters who were once looked on as his inferiors . . . the root cause lies in a tendency, evident from a very early time, to substitute for the real Raphael an abstraction behind which the author of the paintings is concealed." Pope-Hennessy sets out to recover the real Raphael by investigating how the artist worked and why his paintings took the form they did, using the wealth of evidence provided by the many drawings which relate to finished paintings. Robert Melville, describing his own admiration for Raphael's art as too often "invaded by lassitude at the mere thought of the unflagging nobility of it all," described the book as "designed to help everyone who, like me, suffers from a diminished response to Raphael's masterpieces," while the *Times Literary Supplement* found these lectures "no hasty compilation, with fact piled on fact. They are the distillation of some forty years' vocation as an art historian, and their strength lies in Sir John's remarkable insight into an artist's working methods, and his capacity to make that insight intelligible. . . . Despite the author's disclaimer, his work is a monograph, since it is a detailed and thorough investigation of Raphael's technical skill and his efforts to communicate—it is the exceptional nature of Raphael's mind, as demonstrated by these, that is to fire the readers' interest."

John Pope-Hennessy left the Victoria and Albert Museum in 1974 and from 1974 to 1976 was director of the British Museum. There was some speculation about his reasons for leaving the British Museum after only three years there. It was rumored that he had not got his way with an appointment that he had wanted to make and had in general found the bureaucracy there overwhelming. In an *Art News* interview with Judith Weinraub, Sir John himself said that he had gone to the British Museum "out of curiosity, because I knew so little about it. It was a highly mysterious place. I wanted to see how it functioned, and to see if it could be made more useful to people than it was." After two years there he saw "that by the end of three years, I would have accomplished everything I originally set out to do in five." Indeed, it is generally agreed that Pope-Hennessy accomplished a great deal in a short time at the museum, particularly on the educational side, broadening its scope to embrace a wider audience. He also reorganized the museum's committee system and made it a more corporate institution. Sir John went on to say that he found so much administrative work boring—he hardly ever confronted art at all—and that he wanted to be able to spend a part of each year in Florence, studying and writing. He was attracted to the New York art scene ("it really is abysmal here in London") and thought that

American art students were "brighter and more interesting than British." In 1977 Pope-Hennessy went to New York as consultative chairman of the Department of European Paintings at the Metropolitan Museum, New York, and professor of fine arts at New York University.

The author was a member of the Arts Council in 1968–1972 and of the Ancient Monuments Board in 1969–1972. He was made an M.B.E. in 1944 and a C.B.E. in 1959, and he was knighted in 1971. Sir John is a Fellow of the British Academy, of the Society of Antiquaries, and of the Royal Society of Literature. He has received many other distinctions, including the Serena Medal (1961) and the New York University Medal (1965), as well as a number of honorary doctorates and fellowships. Music is the only recreation he lists in *Who's Who,* and he was a director of the Royal Opera House, Covent Garden, from 1971 to 1976. Judith Weinraub has described him as "an urbane, articulate, applecheeked, immaculately dressed English gentleman," and says that in the museum world he is referred to "both irreverently and deferentially" as "the Pope."

PRINCIPAL WORKS: Giovanni di Paolo, 1937; Sassetta, 1939; Sienese Quattrocento Painting 1947; A Sienese Codex of the Divine Comedy, 1947; The Drawings of Domenichino at Windsor Castle, 1948; A Lecture on Nicholas Hilliard, 1949; Donatello's Ascension, 1949; The Virgin With the Laughing Child, 1949; (ed.) The Autobiography of Benvenuto Cellini, 1949; Paolo Uccello, 1950; Italian Gothic Sculpture in the Victoria and Albert Museum, 1952; Fra Angelico, 1952; Italian Gothic Sculpture, 1955; Italian Renaissance Sculpture, 1958; Italian High Renaissance and Baroque Sculpture, 1963; Catalogue of Italian Sculpture in the Victoria and Albert Museum, 1964; The Italian Plaquette, 1964; Renaissance Bronzes From the Kress Collection, 1965; The Portrait in the Renaissance, 1966; Essays on Italian Sculpture, 1968; Catalogue of Sculpture in the Frick Collection, 1970; Raphael (Wrightsman Lectures), 1970; (with others) Westminster Abbey, 1972.

ABOUT: Contemporary Authors 1-4 1st revision, 1967; International Who's Who, 1978–79; Who's Who, 1978; Who's Who in America, 1976–1977. *Periodicals*—Apollo March 1963; Art News December 1976; Book World December 8, 1968; Chicago Sunday Tribune December 17, 1950; Choice September 1967, May 1971, January 1972; Economist August 26, 1967; Guardian September 5, 1950; December 2, 1952; July 5, 1953; January 9, 1959; Journal of Aesthetics Fall 1971; Library Journal April 1, 1967; November 15, 1968; Nation December 21, 1970; New Republic December 8, 1958; New Statesman October 23, 1948; February 7, 1953; June 18, 1955; December 13, 1958; September 6, 1968; January 8, 1971; New York Review of Books September 28, 1967; New York Times November 26, 1950; April 5, 1953; February 8, 1959; New Yorker March 6, 1948; San Francisco Chronicle May 3, 1953; Saturday Review October 9, 1948; August 1, 1953; December 6, 1958; Spectator May 14, 1948; August 11, 1950; December 26, 1952; December 26, 1958; Times (London) Educational Supplement June 15, 1973; Times Literary Supplement May 29, 1948; November 17, 1950; February 6, 1953; August 5, 1955; April 10, 1959; October 19, 1967; November 12, 1971; Virginia Quarterly Review Autumn 1967; Yale Review June 1967.

PORTER, PETER (NEVILLE FREDERICK) (February 16, 1929–), Australian poet, critic, radio dramatist, and journalist, was born in Brisbane, Queensland, but has lived since 1951 in England. He is the son of William Porter and the former Marion Main—of English descent on his father's side, Scottish on his mother's. In an autobiographical article in the *Times Literary Supplement* (July 30, 1971), Porter recalls that, when he was a boy, his grandfather "still lived in an old colonial house, which had witnessed the family's decline." Porter himself grew up in a weatherboard house in the Brisbane suburb of Annerley, where the average temperature was eighty degrees and the humidity "barely left the hundred mark." His father kept his job during the Depression, "but the fear and shabby gentility of our middle-class poverty shaped my subsequent attitude to life." Half the children at Porter's first school had no shoes and if Brisbane in the 1930s "was hardly Calcutta, it wasn't so very different from Naples. . . . What remained with me is a private iconography of hell. This may seem hysterical . . . But each man makes his own images to be haunted by, and the combination of the rigours of the 1930s plus the death of my mother when I was nine fixed Queensland life for me in a mould I cannot forget or even be fair to."

Porter was educated at the Church of England Grammar School in Brisbane and at various boarding schools, including the Toowoomba Grammar School, which he has since ferociously criticized. He left school at seventeen, worked for eighteen months as a journalist on an Australian provincial newspaper and for a time in the clothing industry, meanwhile writing many poems, of which he says, "nothing could be salvaged from their wreck. . . . It was the growing feeling of being at an impasse, a dim recognition that the only way out was by learning the hard lessons of technique and competition, that moved me to come to England"—"It was not that the Australian Dream had failed, it was more that I had never dreamt it." In London during the 1950s Porter worked as a bookseller and as a clerk, and he was in advertising from 1960 to 1970, since when he has been a freelance writer, reviewer, and broadcaster.

For some years beginning in the mid-1950s, Porter was one of the poets who used to meet and discuss one another's work at Edward Lucie-Smith's house in London—the so-called "Group." The Group has long since dispersed but, as Anthony Thwaite suggests, Porter's par-

PETER PORTER

might otherwise appear too bitterly serious. A strong positive element is there, in his celebration of the high points of European culture (particularly in the field of music), though it is often mixed with reflections on the melancholy of human achievement in face of decline and death—and his very moving poems on these subjects are juxtaposed with sad, caustically humorous attacks on current *avant-garde* posturings and any kind of egocentric pretentiousness. Many of the poems . . . deal with personal themes: his *persona* here is wry, angry and humorously self-reproaching. The love poems present that emotion as a tarnished thing, pitiable and unsuccessful, unsuited for treatment in a sensuous or delicate style—there is very little in the lyric vein. . . . His entire style is formal and compressed, with moments of measured solemnity and a hint of the grand manner: he has never been tempted by, or impressed with, attempts at spontaneous ease of form or unmediated fluency."

A reviewer in the *Times Literary Supplement* of *A Porter Folio* said that Porter wrote as "the Australian alienated by a European intelligence" who "arrives in Europe in time to find the European inheritance being shouted down by a volunteer militia of variously clad trendies marching faultlessly in formation. It is a rich situation for satire, and it is quite possible that the desperation induced is the real reason for the streaks of dreadfully careless writing which continually turn up in Peter Porter's work, otherwise the product of a man with a genuine formal sense. . . . The role (Eliot's role) of the visitor who knows the place better than the inhabitants retains its power . . . the resulting poetry, even at its most clumsily rushed, pulls off the trick of staying in contact while conveying no sense whatever of belonging." Describing Porter as "the most prominent and gifted of the literary ex-Australians," the reviewer was reminded of the great Italian poet Eugenio Montale by his "use of the past, especially his debt to the heritage of European music." Martin Dodsworth found "something decadent in the denunciation of decadence," but said it was "hard to praise the book's verve and wit too highly."

The Last of England (1970) contains more of Porter's sardonic investigations of the way we live now, and the way we always die—he believes that "human beings cannot get over the basic injustice that they may die." The collection also includes more of his "ribald, wittily anachronistic versions" of the Roman poet Martial, some of which had appeared in earlier collections. "All this," wrote Anthony Thwaite, "though familiar, is not wearyingly so, for Mr. Porter's inventiveness is as robust as ever.

ticipation in it "perhaps gave him confidence to develop, particularly in the direction of argumentative and even polemical poems," even though "his stance as an Australian outsider, despite his long residence in England, has never made him an easy member of anything." Porter published his first poem in 1957, and his first collection, *Once Bitten, Twice Bitten,* appeared in 1961. It attracted some interest and favorable comment, introducing Porter, to quote Anthony Thwaite, as "primarily a satirist, a fierce neo-Jacobean demolisher of social aspirations, the rich, the smug, the phoney, 'the smoothies of our Elizabethan age.' " Some of Porter's poems were included in *Penguin Modern Poets 2* (1962), along with work by two other poets, and *Poems Ancient and Modern* followed in 1964, but it was not until the publication of *A Porter Folio* in 1969 that he became the object of closer critical attention.

Porter has said that from the beginning his poems "have polarized about the art and life of the past and the everyday world of the present." This account is usefully extended by Alan Brownjohn in *Contemporary Poets:* "An expatriate who does not intend to return, he looks back on his native Australia with uneasy sadness and ironic distrust . . . and casts a scathing and rueful eye on present-day English civilization, especially the garishness of fashionable urban living. His poems on both these recurring themes, as on Europe and its history, catalogue the follies of mankind with a satire that is grave, sometimes brutal, and always acutely observant. But his considerable flair for a kind of bitter, epigrammatic wit and for elaborate and entertaining fantasy . . . lightens the texture of a poetry that

... But the greatest advance is seen in poems in which, without becoming vapid or merely personal, he seems to speak most directly from his concerns ... [and with] a wonderful weightiness and richness. . . . . The grand manner—which Mr. Porter has seemed to admire in others but distrust in himself—is proper and sounds natural [in such poems] as it does in the typically pessimistic close to "There are too many of us":

> The mystery of our sacrifices, our
> Faustian bargains, the golden pledges
> of loves we've spent are only
> Pitch-pine on a fire: we world-eaters
> Are eaten in our turn and if we shout
> At the gods they send us the god of death
> Who is immortal and cannot read.

This development continues in *Preaching to the Converted* (1972). Its reviewer in the *Times Literary Supplement* wrote: "One thing that has become increasingly obvious in Peter Porter's work is that he is not primarily a satirist but an elegiac poet. Death broods above and behind his poems with a suffocating presence, and it is the horror of this that seems to determine his pessimistic, blackly humorous attitude to the things of this world. . . . Mr. Porter is thus a very serious poet, for all his skill as an entertainer. . . . the range of manner is very wide, from cryptic and oblique free verse to formal and even stately structures. *Preaching to the Converted* develops an oracular and riddling tone which has always been Porterish but which now moves in a more grandly stately way . . . and sometimes the stateliness sheds its runic quality and becomes straightforwardly sententious and poignant, as in 'Fossil Gathering,' which moves towards this exalted conclusion:

> *A Little Guide in Colour* tells us how
> These creatures sank in their unconscious time,
> That life in going leaves a husk the plough
> Or amateur collector can displace,
> That every feeling thing ascends from slime
> To selfhood and in dying finds a face.

After Martial (1972), collecting fifty of Porter's "versions" of Martial, was praised in very similar terms—indeed, as one critic pointed out, "the voice of Martial as mediated by Mr. Porter. . . . is a voice that often closely matches Porter's own—sardonic, wryly humorous, full of the names of things, often scabrous, always unseriously serious. . . . The anachronisms . . . put Martial's world in focus rather than distracting from it. The absurdities of fashion, sexual behavior, boasting meanness, hypochondria are con-

stants; the only variables are the names and faces. And underneath it all is the realization that 'death/ has the best of ever-bearing crops.' "

In 1973, working in collaboration with the Australian artist Arthur Boyd, Porter produced a modern version of the story of Jonah which received high praise in the *Times Literary Supplement:* "This book brings to life what it seems to destroy, and the process is painful. . . . The toughness, the obscenity and the caricature work visually because of the words, and the poetry compels because of the images. In so far as the sequence has a plot, it dissolves or becomes fragmentary in the last pages. You can follow it only if you know the story already. Everything gets abolished except God and the singing bone of raw nature, to which God listens. . . . This is visually the most memorable and successful book of poems to have appeared in England for a very long time." Another critic thought that "Mr. Porter has undoubtedly been through some mystifying experience himself, and been marked and inwardly digested." A second collaboration with Arthur Boyd produced *The Lady and the Unicorn* in 1975. The same year Porter published *Living in a Calm Country*. John Matthias wrote of it that "the satirist's scalpel, so frequently effective before in poems on social themes, goes to work here on the face he sees in the mirror. He will allow no delusions, no self-deception. . . . the "calm country" of Porter's title is really the human body. . . . Porter's seeking in this landscape produces something like a combination of historic disappointment and prehistoric dread."

Martin Seymour-Smith has dismissed Peter Porter as "a self-educated journalist with a tin ear and a mind indissolubly linked to fashion." This is a minority view—even an eccentric one. Alan Brownjohn says that "Porter's is an intellectual poetry with a fierce moral emphasis—though he never moralises—and a suggestion of constant personal conflict and struggle. At its best, it makes some of the most powerful and moving statements that any of the younger poets have achieved in the last decade, and has shown a steady strengthening in its unflinching treatment of major themes." Anthony Thwaite, again, considers that "the range of Porter's knowledge and concerns, the inventiveness and restless intelligence of his attack, are more startling and many-faceted than any other English poet of the past fifteen years," and Gavin Ewart regards him as one of the best poets of the century.

Porter is also the author of two radio plays—*The Siege of Munster* (1971) and *The Children's*

Crusade (1973)—and co-author with Anthony Thwaite of a travel book about Italy. He was Compton Lecturer in Poetry at the University of Hull in 1970–1971, and visiting lecturer in English at the University of Reading in Autumn 1972. He has made many educational broadcasts and has occasionally appeared on television in literary quiz programs. Porter has retained his Australian passport and accent but considers himself "an English poet with an Australian tang." Bespectacled, modest, affable, and gregarious, he lives in Chelsea, has a very wide circle of English literary friends, and is interested in music and painting (as his poetry reveals). Porter was married in 1961 to an Englishwoman, Jannice Henry, by whom he has two daughters; she died in 1974, and four years later, in the collection *The Cost of Seriousness,* Porter wrote about her absence, and her recurrent presence, in what seemed to some reviewers the most beautiful and moving poems he has produced.

In his autobiographical piece in the *Times Literary Supplement,* Porter writes: "After earning myself a reputation as a satirist, someone concerned with the 'thingyness' of contemporary life, a wielder of brand names and journalistic tags, I think I am moving away to a very different position, one that takes in Europe and not merely England. If you do not eat the past, it will eat you, and I find modern England a good springboard for the main ambitions I now have for my poetry. To go back deeper into English poetry. . . . and at the same time to put out feelers towards the European imagination: this is my only answer to the unattractive tenets of Modernism." And Porter ends by quoting the second stanza of the title poem of *The Last of England,* letting it "stand for the continuity of the living and the dead which is the only reality I can find in England":

> Sailing away from ourselves, we feel
> The gentle tug of water at the quay—
> Language of the liberal dead speaks
> From the soil of Highgate, tears
> Show a great water table is intact.
> You cannot leave England, it turns
> A planet majestically in the mind.

PRINCIPAL WORKS: *Poetry*—Once Bitten, Twice Bitten, 1961; (with others) Penguin Modern Poets 2, 1962; Poems Ancient and Modern, 1964; Solemn Adultery at Breakfast Creek: An Australian Ballad, 1968; Words Without Music, 1968; A Porter Folio: New Poems, 1969; The Last of England, 1970; Epigrams by Martial, 1971; After Martial, 1972; Preaching to the Converted, 1972; (with Arthur Boyd) Jonah, 1973; Living in a Calm Country, 1975; (with Arthur Boyd) The Lady and the Unicorn, 1975; The Cost of Seriousness, 1978. *Travel*—(with Anthony Thwaite) In Italy, 1974. *As Editor*—New Poems: A P.E.N. Anthology of Contemporary Poetry 1971–1972, 1972; A Choice of Pope's Verse, 1972; (with Anthony Thwaite) The English Poets: From Chaucer to Edward Thomas, 1974; (with Charles Osborne) New Poetry: An Anthology, 1975.

ABOUT: Elkin, P.K. (ed.) Australian Poems in Perspective, 1978; Orr, P. (ed.) The Poet Speaks, 1966; Schmidt, M. and Lindop, G. (eds.) British Poetry Since 1960, 1972; Thwaite, A. Poetry Today 1960–1973, 1973; Vinson, J. (ed.) Contemporary Poets, 1975; Who's Who, 1977. *Periodicals*—Critical Quarterly Spring 1974; Guardian January 2, 1965; January 6, 1971; New Review March 1977; Observer April 9, 1978; The Review December 1970, 24 1971; Times Literary Supplement June 9, 1961; April 20, 1962; September 18, 1969; October 10, 1970; July 7, 1971; August 11, 1972; November 3, 1972; May 7, 1976.

POTTER, DAVID M(ORRIS) (December 6, 1910–February 18, 1971), American historian, was born in Augusta, Georgia, the son of David Morris Potter and the former Katie Brown. Growing up in Georgia, he lived, as he later explained, "in the long backwash of the [Civil] War in a land that remembered the past very vividly and somewhat inaccurately." Robert W. Johannsen thinks it natural enough that Potter was "drawn to the one great event that not only dominated the Southern past but also seemed to give direction to Southern thought and attitudes in his own time." Receiving his A.B. from Emory University in 1932, he went on to Yale for his master's degree (1933), studying there with the distinguished Civil War historian Ulrich B. Phillips. His doctorate, also from Yale, followed in 1940.

Potter had meanwhile begun his teaching career as an instructor in history at the University of Mississippi (1936–1938). He went on to the Rice Institute, Houston, Texas (1938–1942), and then returned to Yale as an assistant professor of history (1942–1947), associate professor (1947–1949), professor (1949–1950), and finally as Coe Professor of American History (1950–1961). He was a fellow of Timothy Dwight College throughout his years at Yale, and editor of the *Yale Review* in 1949–1951. In 1961 he accepted the Coe Professorship at Stanford University, where he remained until his death in 1971. Potter was always much in demand as a visiting professor and lecturer. In 1947–1948 he went to England as Harmsworth Professor of American History and fellow of Queen's College, Oxford University. He gave the Walgreen Lectures at the University of Chicago in 1950; the Commonwealth Fund Lectures at University College, London, in 1963; and the Walter L. Fleming Lectures at Louisiana State University in 1968. He was visiting professor at Connecticut College (1947), the University of Delaware (1954), the University of Wyoming (1952 and 1955), Stanford University (1957, 1958), Stetson

News & Publications Service, Stanford University

DAVID M. POTTER

University (1959), and the State University of New York (1966).

Lincoln and His Party in the Secession Crisis (1942) established Potter's reputation at once. According to the *Journal of American History* it "exemplified the historical monograph at its best. Besides presenting the results of exhaustive research in lucid and graceful prose, it combined rich narrative with analytic power and revealed a subtle understanding of . . . the 'agonizing dilemmas of statesmanship.' " Studying the political background of the Civil War, but focusing in particular on the critical months between Lincoln's election and the attack on Fort Sumter, Potter concluded that blame for the War rested equally with the Northern leaders, who had lacked generosity and understanding, and the politicians of the lower South, who had lacked prudence and a sense of responsibility. Avery Craven thought the book would offend patriots of both camps, but would be welcomed by scholars as a "sound contribution to a better understanding of the Civil War crisis."

The book offers no opinion as to whether or not the Civil War could have been avoided, and Margaret Leech wrote that "Dr. Potter's position as the sworn enemy of hindsight lends a freshness and illumination to the treatment." This indeed was a central element in Potter's historiography; he wrote once that "the supreme task of the historian, and the one of most superlative difficulty, is to see the past through the imperfect eyes of those who lived it, and not with his omniscient twenty-twenty vision."

Another important and influential aspect of Potter's work was his commitment to an interdisciplinary approach to history. This is very evident in his second major book, *People of Plenty* (1954). Based on Potter's Walgreen Lectures, this is a study of the psychological effects of relative economic abundance on the development of the American character. Potter concluded that abundance had encouraged American tendencies toward generosity and gentleness, but had also increased feelings of insecurity and the hunger for status and prestige. By and large, he thought the effect had been more beneficial than not: "Democracy paced the growth of our abundance and abundance broadened the base of our democracy."

Gary MacEoin pointed out that Potter had utilized the tools of cultural anthropology and social psychology as well as of history in a work that is "less concerned with judging our society than with describing its characteristics. This is done with erudition, detachment and a fine sense of perspective." Karl W. Deutsch thought this the best book on the national character since David Riesman's *The Lonely Crowd,* and Robert W. Johannsen wrote in 1974, twenty years later, that this "widely acclaimed and highly influential work . . . still stands at the top of a growing body of literature on the American character."

The essays collected in *The South and the Sectional Conflict* (1968) are arranged in three sections. In the first Potter examines the "riddle: what is the essence of the nature of the South?"; in the second he discusses the evolution of historical writing about the South; and in the third he deals with an assortment of topics related to the Civil War. Eugene D. Genovese wrote that "Potter's review of the historical literature on the South and the nation during the nineteenth century is not only useful, it is unique. No other historian in the United States has his ability to present the arguments of others, including his opponents, with such conciseness, scrupulousness, and sensitivity to nuance." Genovese thought the book marred by Potter's failure to face the class question, and a reviewer in *Saturday Review* suggested that "when Potter the Southerner interprets the Southern experience he is limited by his own Southernism."

For Martin Duberman, on the other hand, this work confirmed his belief that "David Potter may be the greatest living historian of the United States." Duberman went on: "To some, Potter's confessed bafflement, his appreciation of divergent insights and his resort to paradox, may seem the equivalents of evasion. . . . far more often Potter's fine distinctions, his subtleties of perception, are what the complexities of historical evidence always require but almost never find. To read him is to become aware of a truth that only the greatest historians have been able to show us: that the chief lesson to be derived from a study of the past is that it holds no simple lesson, and that the historian's main responsibility is to prevent anyone from claiming that it does."

The South and the Sectional Conflict was the last of Potter's books to appear during his lifetime, but several have been edited and/or completed by his colleagues and published posthumously. *The South and the Concurrent Majority,* edited by Don E. Fehrenbacher and C.N. Degler, was based on Potter's Walter Lynwood Fleming Lecture; in it he maintains that, until the 1960s, the South was able to preserve a concurrent majority or negative power in national politics by its manipulation of the machinery of politics. This was followed by *History and American Society,* a second collection of essays, edited by Fehrenbacher. In each essay, wrote J.A. Garraty, "one is caught up by the first paragraph, then held to the last by Potter's argument, by the aptness of his illustrations, and by the felicity of his style." A critic in the *Yale Review* said that "Potter wrote history as philosophers write philosophy, always defining issues, making distinctions, clarifying muddled terms"; whether or not the reader always agrees with Potter, he "will find himself engaged throughout . . . in a dialogue with a conscientious, lucid, and tenacious thinker."

In *The Impending Crisis: 1848–1861,* edited and completed by Fehrenbacher, Potter examines the complex problems of slavery, expansion, and sectionalism in the thirteen years leading up to the Civil War, seeking to reassess these years as they were experienced by a people "preoccupied with their personal affairs, with no sense of impending disaster nor any fixation on the issue of slavery." Eric Foner wrote that Potter "displays a remarkable command of the vast literature of the period, as well as an acute sense of historic irony. . . . With its chronological ordering and emphasis on national politics, this may seem a curiously old-fashioned book. . . . Its concerns are philosophical; it asks questions which have been eclipsed by newer interests. It seeks to examine the nature of the political process and the underlying patterns of historical causation. On these subjects, Potter's insights are profound and original." W.Z. Schenck concluded that the book would serve "as a lasting memorial to a great historian," and it received the Pulitzer Prize in history.

Potter taught as well as he wrote. His courses were always crowded with students, drawn by his "intimate and reflective tone, which invited his auditors to share with him the pleasures and perplexities of studying the past." He was a fellow of the American Academy of Arts and Sciences, a member of the American Philosophical Society, and at the time of his death was president of both the American Historical Association and the Organization of American Historians. He received a second M.A., from Oxford, in 1947, and had honorary doctorates from Emory University and the University of Wyoming. Potter was married in 1939 to Ethelyn E. Henry. That marriage ended in divorce in 1945, and in 1948 Potter married Dilys Mary Roberts, who died in 1969. He had one daughter. Potter's one serious avocation was the study and observation of birds, and he became an expert in this subject, and the owner of an impressive ornithological library.

According to a tribute to Potter in the *Journal of American History* (September 1971), he had become increasingly interested in the connections between individual personality and the social order. One of the most admired essays in *History and American Society* was an analysis of modern alienation, and he was planning an extensive study of this when he died. He was an enemy of parochialism in American history, and himself always sought the meaning of the Civil War as a phenomenon of world significance. He was also concerned to make his colleagues aware of the "implicit assumptions" often concealed behind their use of "explicit data." "To the examination of these problems," his colleagues wrote in the *Journal of American History,* "David Potter brought a probing curiosity, a relentless rigor of mind, and a commitment to interdisciplinary thinking that influenced a generation of historians in the United States." Edwin S. Morgan called him "the wisest man I ever knew."

PRINCIPAL WORKS: Lincoln and His Party in the Secession Crisis, 1942; The Lincoln Theme and American National Historiography (inaugural lecture at Oxford), 1947; (with T.G. Manning and Wallace E. Davies) Government and the American Economy, 1870–Present, 1950; People of Plenty: Economic Abundance and the American Character, 1954; (with T.G. Manning) Nationalism and Sectionalism in America, 1775–1877, 1949; The Background of the Civil War, 1961; The South and the Sectional Conflict, 1968; The South and the Concurrent Majority, edited by D.E. Fehrenbacher and Carl N. Degler, 1972; History and American Society: Essays of David M. Potter, edited by D.E. Fehrenbacher, 1973; Division and the Stresses of Reunion, 1845–1876, edited by C.N. Degler, 1973; The Impending Crisis, 1848–1861, completed and edited by D.E. Fehrenbacher, 1976; Freedom and Its Limitations in American Life, edited by D.E. Fehrenbacher, 1976. *As Editor*—(with J.H. Croushore) A Union Officer in the Reconstruction, by J.W. De Forest, 1943; Trail to California, by V.E. Geiger, 1945.

ABOUT: Cunliffe, M. and Winks, R.W. (eds.) Pastmasters, 1969; Who's Who in America, 1972–1973. *Periodicals*—American March 13, 1976; American Historical Review October 1971, April 1973; Books September 27, 1942; Christian Century September 23, 1942; Civil War History

PURDY

March 1974; Commonweal October 22, 1954; Journal of American History September 1969, September 1971, June 1973; Journal of Southern History May 1971; Nation October 31, 1942; New York Review of Books September 11, 1969; New York Times November 14, 1954; February 19, 1971; New York Times Book Review January 12, 1969; April 1, 1973; February 22, 1976; Saturday Review April 5, 1969; Virginia Quarterly Review Winter 1973; Yale Review Winter 1955, June 1973.

AL PURDY

PURDY, AL(FRED WELLINGTON) (December 30, 1918–), Canadian poet, was born in Wooller, Ontario, the son of Alfred and Eleanor (Ross) Purdy. He is descended from English Loyalists who left the United States at the time of independence and settled in Canada as farmers. He was educated at Dufferin Public School, Trenton, Ontario; at Albert College, Belleville, Ontario; and at Trenton Collegiate Institute. For some years he wandered throughout Canada, riding the freights and living rough. During World War II he served with the Royal Canadian Air Force (1940–1945). He was married in 1941 to Eurithe Parkhurst, by whom he has a son.

While in the Air Force, Purdy published (at his own expense) his first volume of poems, *The Enchanted Echo* (1944)—technically conventional verses in tight stanza forms, patriotic and sentimental in content. He has since described his work of that period as "crap." After the war Purdy "submerged" again, taking a variety of factory jobs and for a time running a taxi service in Belleville. The poems of these years, collected in *Pressed on Sand* (1955) and *Emu, Remember!* (1956) still favored poetical archaisms but showed some signs of development—a sharper ear, and a growing awareness that poetry should derive from the poet's experience, not his reading.

Purdy's poetry came fully to life when, under the influence of William Carlos Williams, he turned to open forms. The transition began to be evident in *The Crafte So Longe to Lerne* (1959), which also (in "At Roblin Lake") introduced the setting of many future poems, and the sense of place which has been of great importance in his mature work. The development continued in *Poems for All the Annettes* (1962). Mike Doyle, to whose essay on Purdy in *Poets and Critics* this note is much indebted, says of this collection that its best poems have "a tension between energy and watchfulness, energy and diffidence, energy and skepticism." It is a tension that works best when the poet is exploring his relationship with one other person, like Anna, his "Helen of Illyria with the big behind" in "Archaeology of Snow." Anna has left him, but:

Day after next day
    I found her
        heavy buttocks
        in the snow
printed there
        like a Cambrian trilobite
Except the girl was not there
but was there also somehow

Come spring, when the snow melts, these monuments will disappear; nevertheless:

the form is HERE
        has to be
            must be
As if we were all immortal
in some way I've not fathomed.

Doyle described *Poems for All the Annettes* as "a landmark in . . . [Purdy's] career and in Canadian poetry," in which Purdy's "creative energies gathered into a cohesiveness which comes through, at its high points, as fierce joy."

Purdy's late arrival as an important Canadian poet was confirmed by *The Cariboo Horses* (1965). Doyle has called him "a poet of the verb," and thinks this especially true of this collection, in which "time and space . . . predominate." None of these poems, one reviewer complained, is the kind of "finished structure which focuses and holds attention," but, Doyle writes, his best pieces here have highly dramatic qualities "of presentness and movement. . . . We are immediately involved in the process of his responses" by his "participatory verb-forms." He seems to find a sufficient justification for life in the flux of things—to feel (like his grandfather in one of these poems) that "you don't dast stop/ or everything would fall down." Another critic pointed out that this was a very Canadian book —almost half of these poems refer specifically to Canada—and praised in particular "The Observer," a witty expression of human ambivalence, and "In the Wilderness" and "Hockey Players," both of which comment thoughtfully on the transforming power of uninhibited feeling. *The Cariboo Horses* brought Purdy the Governor-General's Award in 1966.

Purdy's later poems have been on the whole more static in form though not in content— many of them are poetic journals of his endless travels about the world. *North of Summer* (1967) is an unpretentious though sometimes visionary account of the summer he spent in 1965 in the Arctic, and *Wild Grape Wine* (1968) contains poems inspired by Mexico and Cuba as well as Canada, and by prehistory as well as the present. However, this notable collection also includes some poems in which, Doyle thought, Purdy "appeared to be establishing Canada's psychic bearings"—"Wilderness Gothic," "Roblin Mills," "The Runners," and "My Grandfather's Country," from which the following lines are quoted:

But the hill-red has no such violence of endings
the woods are alive
and gentle as well as cruel
unlike sand and sea
and if I must give my heart to anything
it will be here in the red glow
where failed farms sink back into earth
the clearings join and fences no longer divide
where the running animals gather their bodies
  together
and pour themselves upward
into the tips of falling leaves
with mindless faith that presumes a future. . . .

Subsequent books include *Hiroshima Poems* (1972) and the poems describing what Purdy saw and felt during a visit to South Africa, collected in *Sex and Death* (1973)—both volumes competent, humane, but unexceptional.

The significance of Al Purdy's work for Doyle is that he "seems as much as anyone writing today to sense what it is, the Canadian thing, the local thing"; and his work "may be seen as a slow unpeeling, a groping towards the core of that thing." Other critics have praised his vigor, humanity, and witty allusiveness, his "concept of the universal as seen in the commonplace." George Woodcock speaks of the "essentially oral impact" of his mature verse and says "it is free verse in the truest form: fluent, untrammelled by convention" (though opponents of open form poetry in Canada dismiss Purdy as prosy or diffuse).

Margaret Atwood calls Purdy a poet of "many over-lapping self-created versions," and Milton Wilson long ago pointed out that he "has to find his directions by indirections." He himself has written of his poetry: "Form? Pretty irregular, but generally with rhythm running somewhere. . . . Influences? Very many, including the usual big names (Pound, Eliot, Yeats); also César Vallejo, Neruda, Supervielle, Charles Bukowski, Robinson Jeffers, etc., etc. . . . I believe that when a poet fixes on one style or method he severely limits his present and future development."

Purdy is the author of a number of radio and television plays and of a stage play, "Point of Transfer," which was produced in Toronto in 1962. He is much in demand as a reader of his own poetry. He has edited anthologies of Canadian poetry and a controversial collection of candid Canadian opinions of the United States *(The New Romans)*. He taught for a semester at the Simon Fraser University in British Columbia in 1970 and was poet-in-residence at Loyola College, Montreal, in 1973. He received the Centennial Medal in 1967, and has had several awards and fellowships from the Canada Council. Mike Doyle describes him as "joker, traveler, mythographer, political commentator, wine-maker, common man, archaeologist. . . . avid bookstore browser and collector of Canadiana," with "groundings in Canadian history, ancient history, art, myth, psychology."

PRINCIPAL WORKS: *Poetry*—The Enchanted Echo, 1944; Pressed on Sand, 1955; Emu, Remember!, 1956; The Crafte So Longe to Lerne, 1959; Poems for All the Annettes, 1962; The Blur in Between: Poems 1960–1961, 1962; The Cariboo Horses, 1965; North of Summer: Poems From Baffin Island, 1967; Poems for All the Annettes (selected poems), 1968; Wild Grape Wine, 1968; Spring Song, 1968; Love in a Burning Building, 1970; (with others) Five Modern Canadian Poets, edited by Eli Mandel, 1970; The Quest for Ouzo, 1970; Selected Poems, 1972; Hiroshima Poems, 1972; On the Bearpaw Sea, 1973; Sex and Death, 1973; In Search of Owen Roblin, 1974; The Poems of Al Purdy, 1976; Sundance at Dusk, 1976. *As Editor*—The New Romans: Candid Canadian Opinions of the United States, 1968; Fifteen Winds: A Selection of Modern Canadian Poems, 1969; I've Tasted My Blood: Poems 1956–1968, by Milton Acorn, 1969; Storm Warning: The New Canadian Poets, 1971; Storm Warning 2, 1976.

ABOUT: Bowering, G. Al Purdy, 1970; Creative Canada Vol. 2, 1972; Oxford Companion to Canadian History and Literature, 1967; Vinson, J. (ed.) Contemporary Poets, 1975; Woodcock, G. (ed.) Poets and Critics, 1974. *Periodicals* —Canadian Literature Spring 1966; Canadian Forum January 1975; Dalhousie Review Summer 1971; Poetry June 1969; Queens Quarterly Autumn 1972.

PUZO, MARIO (October 15, 1920–), American novelist, essayist, journalist, and screenwriter, was born in New York City, the son of illiterate Italian immigrants, Antonio and Maria (Le Conti) Puzo. His father, a trackman for the New York City Railroad, deserted the family when Puzo was twelve, leaving his wife to raise five sons and two daughters in the vicious Manhattan slum known as Hell's Kitchen. Mrs. Puzo, a formidable and indomitable "family chief," succeeded very well, and in "Choosing a Dream," his contribution to *The Immigrant Experience,* Mario Puzo recalls his childhood with more affection than bitterness.

Puzo's boyhood centered on the Hudson Guild Settlement House near his home, where he captained the football team and headed a gang known as the Star Club. Reading his way through the Hudson Guild library, from Rafael Sabatini to Dostoevsky, he played with "the usual dreams"—to be handsome, to be a wartime hero, a footloose adventurer, a great artist, a great criminal. By the time he was sixteen he had settled on the idea of becoming a writer, but during the next few years, working as a messenger for the New York Central Railroad, this seemed a remote and unlikely ambition.

World War II rescued him. In the army he "drove a jeep, toured Europe, had love affairs, found a wife, and lived the material for my first novel." He spent the war in Germany as a soldier, and after it stayed on as a civilian public relations man for the United States Air Force, returning to New York several years later to work as a civil service administrator. At this time he enrolled at Columbia University and the New School for Social Research, taking classes in literature and creative writing and trying his hand at short stories and plays. His first published story, "The Last Christmas," appeared in *American Vanguard* in 1950.

Puzo's first novel, *Dark Arena* (1955), has a hero whose career parallels the author's own. Walter Mosca, a tough and embittered ex-GI, dissatisfied with postwar life in the United States, returns to the "dark arena" of occupied Bremen and to the German mistress he had left there, and takes a job with the military government. The novel provides a grim portrait of the squalor and degradation of the Occupation, the exploiters and the exploited, and allows Mosca a degree of emotional growth in his deepening feeling for his mistress. When she dies of an infection, denied the drugs that would have saved her, he avenges her and becomes a renegade, sickened by the hypocrisy of his own countrymen. One English reviewer found the novel predictable, marred by "dramatic posturing"

Michael Abramson, Susan Fowler-Gallagher

MARIO PUZO

and a "wide-screen approach," but most critics were impressed, commending its inventiveness, sincerity, and atmospheric richness, and placing it in the naturalistic tradition of James T. Farrell, Sinclair Lewis, and Dreiser. Maxwell Geismar wrote: "It is a very good novel indeed, and one reads it with the sense of discovery and pleasure that a new talent evokes."

In 1963 Puzo left the civil service and became an editor of and writer for men's magazines, among them *Stag* and *Male,* at the same time contributing book reviews, stories, and articles to such journals as *Redbook, Holiday, Book World,* and the New York *Times. The Fortunate Pilgrim* (1965), his second novel, is regarded by many critics as his best book to date. It is a chronicle of Italian immigrant life in New York City in the 1920s and 1930s, focusing on a single family and especially on its twice-widowed matriarch Lucia, from her arrival in the United States as a newly married peasant girl to her realization of the American dream—"a bungalow of her own in Long Island." Puzo's talent for "merging social history with fiction" and conveying a vivid impression of an entire milieu was widely praised, as was his "luminously visualized" portrait of Lucia. David Boroff called it "a small classic. . . . lifted into literature by its highly charged language, its penetrating insights, and its mixture of tenderness and rage," and Gay Talese thought it "perhaps the best novel ever written about Italian immigrants in America."

Such heady praise was not enough for Puzo, who needed a best-seller to subsidize "the other books I really wanted to do." It was in that spirit that he began a novel about the Mafia, receiving an advance from Putnam after his ten-page synopsis had been rejected by Atheneum, his regular publisher. Published in 1969, *The Godfather* became one of the most successful books in publishing history, selling nine million copies within two years. The "godfather" is Don Vito Corleone, a Mafia chieftain intent on fighting his way to the top of the crime syndicate, ruthlessly exterminating enemies and competitors but retaining a Sicilian bandit's sense of ethics and courtesy—a sentimentalist and an executioner, an Old Testament god and a twentieth-century scourge.

The book is highly readable, charged with liberal allowances of sex and violence, moving at breakneck speed, and offering a colorful account of a strange subculture, its mores and personalities and traditional rituals. One critic called it "the *Little Caesar* of this generation," and another thought it the work of an extremely talented storyteller and a genuine social historian. Others were less impressed, objecting to the florid and careless prose and the novel's failure to come to grips with the moral issues it raised—one called it "a voyeur's dream, a skillful fantasy of violent personal power without consequences." Puzo agrees with his detractors, believing that the book "has energy" and wishing that he had bothered to write it better. All the same, he sold the film rights to Paramount for $85,000, collaborated for a while on the screenplay with the movie's director, Francis Ford Coppola, and saw the resulting film win three Academy Awards and break attendance records all over the world. Puzo also collaborated with Coppola on the script for *The Godfather, Part II,* dealing with the reign of Don Vito's college-educated son Michael, and in conjunction with George Fox wrote the screenplay for *Earthquake* (1974).

Fools Die (1978) covers forty years in the life of a writer named Merlyn, in New York, Las Vegas, and Hollywood. Like his creator, Merlyn eventually writes a best-selling novel that becomes a hugely profitable movie. He has a friend called Osano, *enfant terrible* of the New York literary scene, seven times married and hell-bent on a Nobel Prize, and another friend who runs a hotel in Las Vegas, where they all like to gamble. They are "a company of heroes" who "ignore their wounds and fight on," very much like the heroes Puzo used to write about for *Stag* and *Male.* "People gaze at each other smilingly," Hermione Lee reported, "they shake their heads in wonderment. And then they see the tears in each other's eyes. And then they start to cry, their whole bodies flooded with unbearable pain. And one knows just how they

feel." All the same, the novel is addictively full of action, and it earned its place in history when the paperback rights were sold for something over two-and-a-half million dollars, a record.

Puzo is also the author of *The Runaway Summer of Davie Shaw* (1966), a children's book about a thirteen-year-old on the run across the United States. The "frank, often pungent, miscellany" of articles, stories, anecdotes, and diary entries collected in *The Godfather Papers* was generally enjoyed. "What emerges," wrote one reviewer, "is that Mr. Puzo is above all a man who loves stories . . . and who loves even more the act and art of telling them." He also loves gambling, especially in Las Vegas, and he has written an account of that peculiar institution which, it was said, "reveals much about Las Vegas, Puzo, Americans and human nature."

"A stocky man of average height," Puzo is said to look like "an out-of-shape middle-weight boxer, and he is usually either starting a diet or ending one." A diabetic, he is nonetheless a connoisseur of Italian food and an enthusiastic tennis player. Puzo was married in 1946 to Erika Broske; they have five children, and live in a large house in Bay Shore, Long Island. "I am another Italian success story," he said once. "Not as great as DiMaggio or Sinatra but quite enough. It will serve."

PRINCIPAL WORKS: *Fiction*—The Dark Arena, 1955; The Fortunate Pilgrim, 1965; The Runaway Summer of Davie Shaw (for children), 1966; The Godfather, 1969; Fools Die, 1978. *Nonfiction*—The Godfather Papers and Other Confessions, 1972; Inside Las Vegas, 1977.

ABOUT: Contemporary Authors 65-68, 1977; Current Biography, 1976; Green, R.B. The Italian-American Novel, 1974; Madden, D. (ed.) Rediscoveries, 1971; Puzo, M. The Godfather Papers, 1972; Vinson, J. (ed.) Contemporary Novelists, 1976; Wheeler, T.C. (ed.) The Immigrant Experience, 1971; Who's Who in America, 1976-1977. *Periodicals* —Book World March 9, 1969; Commonweal May 6, 1969; Esquire February 1971; Harper's August 1971; Life July 10, 1970; Nation July 9, 1955; New York Review of Books July 20, 1972; New York Times Book Review January 31, 1965; April 27, 1969; July 9, 1978; Newsweek March 10, 1970; Publishers Weekly June 12, 1978; Saturday Review February 26, 1955; January 23, 1965; Time March 13, 1972; April 14, 1975; Time August 28, 1978.

PYM, BARBARA (MARY CRAMPTON)

(June 2, 1913–), English novelist, writes: "I was born in Oswestry, Shropshire, a small country town on the borders of Wales. My father was a solicitor and my mother was of half Welsh descent. When I was twelve I went away to a boarding school, Huyton College, near Liverpool, where I stayed until I was eighteen. I then went up to St. Hilda's College, Oxford and read for my degree in English language and literature. I took my B.A. degree in 1934. As a schoolgirl

BARBARA PYM

I had wanted to be a writer and used to contribute to the school magazine; I even completed a novel when I was sixteen but did not attempt to get it published. After coming down from Oxford I started to write seriously and finished a novel but did not succeed in getting it published, nor did I have any better luck with the next one I wrote. I continued trying to write until the beginning of the war in 1939, but at this time I worked in the Postal and Telegraph Censorship in Bristol and then in the WRNS (Women's Royal Naval Service). In the WRNS I was sent to Naples and stayed here nearly a year until the end of the war when I returned to live in London. I got a job at the International African Institute, first as a research assistant and later as assistant editor of the journal, *Africa.* During this time I had written and published my first novel *(Some Tame Gazelle)* in 1950 and during the next few years I published five more novels, the last in 1961. After this I had a period of misfortune or bad luck when, although I continued to write, no publisher wanted the kind of novel I was writing. This continued until early in 1977 when the *Times Literary Supplement* celebrated seventy-five years of publication by asking various well-known authors and critics to name the writers they considered to be the most over- and under-rated during that period. Both Lord David Cecil and Philip Larkin named me as being under-rated and I was the only writer to be mentioned twice. From then on my fortunes began to change and I was able to get my work published again and my earlier novels reprinted.

"I retired from the International African Institute in 1974 and now live with my sister in a village about twelve miles west of Oxford. I work on my novels and engage in the usual country pursuits—church, gardening, local history and country walks. I lead a quiet but enjoyable life and I believe that this is reflected in some of my novels. I prefer to write about the kind of things I have experienced and to put into my novels the kind of details that amuse me in the hope that others will share in this. I like to think that what I write gives pleasure and makes my readers smile, even laugh. But my novels are by no means only comedies as I try to reflect life as I see it."

Barbara Pym's first novel, *Some Tame Gazelle,* is an amiable account of middle-class life in a small English town soon after World War II, centering on the archdeacon of the diocese, his wife, and his female parishioners. These include the sisters Harriet and Belinda, both of whom receive proposals of marriage in the course of the book and decline them in the unspoken belief that they will be happier spending their lives together. The novel is full of precise and gently ironic observation of such modest events, and was compared by one reviewer, unfavorably, with the early work of Angela Thirkell.

Excellent Women, scarcely more sensational, attracted rather more critical attention. The setting this time is London—a run-down area near Victoria Station—and again the local church provides some sort of focus for the events described. Indeed, as Anne Duchêne points out, Barbara Pym has always been an expert in High Church comedy: "The mild changes imposed on her temperate characters by the seasons march very closely with the Church's calendar, and the Church's consolations and distractions—habit, festivals, vestments, the social effects of uncertain commitment to celibacy, the dynamics of the jumble sale—benignly shore up the insignificant or, at best, modest existence of her characters." The novel's narrator is Mildred Lathbury, a spinster in her thirties, who has a private income and works for distressed gentlewomen. As one critic put it, she "rises blithely to embrace her singleness, endowed with graceful primness, natural piety, and an unconquerable scepticism (an anthropologist's room is littered with journals 'with the rather stark and surprising title of *Man.* I wondered what they could be about')." Certainly Mildred seems more amused than impressed by the pretensions of the men around her—Father Malory, who assumes that it would break her heart if he married; the charming naval officer downstairs; the anthropologist who sees in her a voluntary indexer for his books.

This seems to Anne Duchêne the most felicitous of all Barbara Pym's novels.

Jane Cleveden in *Jane and Prudence* is a former Oxford don, highly literate but not very competent as the wife of a country vicar. Her town mouse friend Prudence has a smart but rootless life in London and is constantly harrowed by emotional crises. By the end of the book, Jane has failed to equip Prudence with a husband, but has seen her safely established in a new love affair. This was followed by *Less Than Angels,* in which Barbara Pym draws on her years at the International African Institute to study the behavior patterns and rituals of a group of anthropologists. As one critic wrote, "their jargon, their ambitions and their intrigues are examined by an ironic young woman, Catherine Oliphant, who, in love with one of them, keeps a kindly eye on them all."

Town and country are again contrasted in *A Glass of Blessings,* which Philip Larkin regards as the subtlest of the author's books. Wilmet Forsyth is the wealthy but aimless wife (subject to "useless little longings") of a typical Pym husband—a man hopelessly stolid and unperceptive, though well-intentioned and reliable. Finding nothing to sustain her in her marriage or herself, she becomes excited by the possibility of a love affair and when this fails to materialize finds a different kind of consolation in religion. In *No Fond Return of Love,* the last of Barbara Pym's novels to appear before the hiatus she mentions above, two unmarried women seek to cure this condition by genteel maneuverings in the ambit of a fastidious litterateur named Aylwin Forbes. The *Times Literary Supplement's* reviewer thought that this "subtle and penetrating" book confirmed the author's place as "a witty chronicler of the shy and delicate."

All of these novels were respectfully received by the critics, but none was more than moderately successful and, as Barbara Pym says, she could after 1961 find no one willing to publish her. There were signs of reviving interest in the early 1970s, however, when there were limited reprints of two or three of her books, and this trend was confirmed by the remarkable tributes she received in 1977 from Philip Larkin and Sir David Cecil, leading to the republication of her books and a reassessment of their value.

Larkin himself, writing in the *Times Literary Supplement* for March 11, 1977, said that the first of these six novels "is as practised as the last, the observation, the social comedy, the interplay of themes equally expert." He pointed out their unobtrusive interdependence—the way characters from one novel tended to appear or to be referred to in others—and went on: "Their narratives have the air of being picked up almost at random: the characters have usually been living for some time in the circumstances in which we meet them, and yet some small incident . . . serves to set off a chain of modest happenings among interrelated groups of characters, watched or even recounted by a protagonist who tempers an ironic perception of life's absurdities with a keen awareness of its ability to bruise." Although "amusement is constantly foiling more pretentious emotion," emotion is there— the absolute need for "something to love." Larkin asks what stays longest with the reader, "once the amusement, the satire, the alert ear and the exact eye have all been acknowledged? Partly it is the underlying loneliness of life . . . then partly it is the virtue of enduring this, the unpretentious adherence to the Church of England, the absence of self-pity, the scrupulousness of one's relations with others, the small blameless comforts. . . . The sparkle . . . [these novels] had on first acquaintance has been succeeded by the deeper brilliance of established art; they are miniatures, perhaps, but they will not diminish."

The first of Barbara Pym's novels to be published after her resurrection was *Quartet in Autumn.* The quartet whose autumn she describes are two men and two women who work in the same office, are all in their sixties, and all live alone. Anne Duchêne found "the ties of consanguinity" between this novel and its predecessors very strong, though "the tone now is drier, more bleached. . . . Miss Pym has made a scrupulously detailed picture of people living like mice in the wainscoting of life, never invited to its table, contenting themselves with its crumbs. She has a marvellously acute eye for their solitary consolations, a marvellously acute ear for the periphrases with which they fend off desolation. . . . These inarticulate protagonists cannot speak for themselves, so Miss Pym must speak for them; and since what she has to say is often quite dreadful, she has to keep her distance. . . . The warm current of sympathy . . . has chilled into an angry, appalled contemplation of loneliness. It is a finely detailed, unflinching chronicle; but the temperature is more hibernal than autumnal."

The Sweet Dove Died (1978) is a history of the intense three-cornered friendship that develops between Leonora, an idle, cold, attractive Londoner in her late forties, an antique dealer named Humphrey, and his bisexual young nephew James. Leonora allows herself to become sufficiently involved with James for it to hurt when he takes up with a predatory young American, but her defenses are soon back in place; she is a woman who dislikes tea "because of the comfort it was said to bring to those whom she normally despised." Susannah Clapp, quoting this, wrote that "Leonora is not likeable, but it is one of the strengths of this graceful novel that her ability to make such points is not presented as being merely plucky." Philip Howard called the book "deceptively simple," and said it was "sharp, funny and sad in its bitchy observations of these people living and partly living their lives of quiet desperation."

PRINCIPAL WORKS: Some Tame Gazelle, 1950; Excellent Women, 1952; Jane and Prudence, 1953; Less Than Angels, 1955; A Glass of Blessings, 1958; No Fond Return of Love, 1961; Quartet in Autumn, 1977; The Sweet Dove Died, 1978.

ABOUT: Contemporary Authors (Permanent Series) 1, 1975; Writers Directory 1976–1978. *Periodicals*—Ariel October 1971; Times Literary Supplement March 11, 1977; September 30, 1977; July 7, 1978.

DAVID RABE

RABE, DAVID (WILLIAM) (March 10, 1940–), American dramatist, was born in Dubuque, Iowa, the son of William and Ruth (McCormick) Rabe, a Midwestern couple whose income increased when Rabe's father exchanged high school history teaching for a job as a meatpacker. Rabe's first ambition was to become a professional football player, and he still believes that "nothing, not even writing, is as completely fulfilling as being successful in athletics." Nevertheless, he made an early start as a writer, and from his boyhood in local Roman Catholic schools his interest centered on drama. He received his B.A. in 1962 from Loras College, a Catholic school in Dubuque, and went on to Villanova University, intending to take a master's degree in theatre. After two years he dropped out to become a full-time writer, supporting himself with odd jobs. In January 1965 Rabe was drafted for military service in Vietnam. He might have avoided the draft by applying for a teacher's certificate, but he decided to go into uniform because at that time, he says, "I thought of it as a cause." It was this experience, above all, that shaped his future as a dramatist.

For the last eleven months of his two years in the army, Rabe was attached to a hospital support unit in Long Binh, South Vietnam, where he served as a clerk, guard, driver, and construction worker. He never went into combat against the Vietcong, but he saw enough of the realities of war to experience an acute sense of dissociation from civilian America when he returned home in 1967. He found himself estranged both from those who saw Vietnam as a long-running television show and from those who used it to prop up political arguments, whether of the

Right or the Left. He tried to return to Vietnam as a newspaper correspondent but no newspaper would engage him, and he went back to finish his studies at Villanova, receiving his M.A. in 1968, and meanwhile pouring his accumulated feelings into two plays, *The Basic Training of Pavlo Hummel* and *Sticks and Bones,* written concurrently during 1967 and 1968.

Apart from a student staging of *Sticks and Bones* at Villanova, the plays lay unproduced for three years. In 1969 Rabe joined the New Haven (Connecticut) *Register* as a feature writer, the following year winning an Associated Press award for a series of articles on the rehabilitation of drug addicts at the Daytop Village center. Then *Pavlo Hummel* was accepted by Joseph Papp, director of the New York Shakespeare Festival's Public Theatre: it opened at the Public Theatre's Newman Stage in May 1971 and *Sticks and Bones* followed it to the Anspacher Stage in November of the same year.

These two plays together with *The Orphan,* staged at the Anspacher in April 1973, comprise a Vietnam trilogy of a kind more familiar to European than to American audiences. They are reminiscent in particular of the *heimkehrer* plays which flourished in Germany in the 1920s, voicing an obsession with the First World War from the viewpoint of the returning veteran. There were several types of *heimkehrer* drama, and a German counterpart exists for each of Rabe's variations on the theme: the reenactment of life at the front, the homecoming of the alienated veteran, and the transposition of contemporary experience onto the plane of myth. The stylistic implications of that sequence are duly carried out in Rabe's cycle, which moves from point-blank realism in *Pavlo Hummel* to the distanced classicism of *The Orphan*. At no point, however, can Rabe be described as a naturalist. The sting in *Pavlo Hummel* is expressed in its punning title, which refers both to the hero's military initiation at a basic training camp in Georgia and to the reshaping of his whole personality by the army and the war. Isolated realistic scenes alternate with ritualized drills and fantasy episodes involving Hummel's invisible guardian Ardell, in a fractured narrative which strives to hold detached events in simultaneous ironic focus. The form, in short, preserves the "double vision" that, Rabe says, "made everything too intense" for him to be able to write about the war while he was still in it.

The play is entirely free from partisan loyalties. Vietcong atrocities are shown alongside the brutalities of the American troops. No blame is laid on the dominating figure of Sergeant Tower, who bullies, cajoles, and flatters his boys into action. He is a superhuman military father-figure, but not an all-devouring Moloch of the kind Megan Terry depicted in *Viet Rock*. Hummel himself is not an innocent led to the slaughter; he is a quirkish, charming, fast talker who gets people's backs up and who wants to kill to achieve manhood. Three times wounded, he finally meets a meaningless death in a Saigon brothel. His essential characteristic is the impulse "to leap into the fire."

The one point that emerges with unmistakable clarity is the atrocious futility of war itself— although, as Rabe says, *Pavlo Hummel* is not an "anti-war" play in the usual sense: "A play in which a family looks bad is not called an 'anti-family' play. A play in which a marriage looks bad is not called an 'anti-marriage' play. A play in which young people seem not the most perfect of beings is not called an 'anti-youth' play. A play about criminals is not called an 'anti-crime' play. I think these labels do not exist because family, marriage, youth, and crime are all viewed as phenomena permanently a part of the eternal human pageant. I believe war to be an equally permanent part of that pageant."

Pavlo Hummel ran for eleven months and carried off an Obie Award as the best off-Broadway play of 1970-1971, as well as Drama Guild and Drama Desk awards. Among those who saluted its tragicomic qualities and its grasp of character, Edith Oliver wrote: "It makes everything else I've seen on the subject seem skimpy and slightly false," while Catharine Hughes called it "the best play yet spawned by the Vietnam War."

Sticks and Bones moves on from the front line to the homecoming. David, a blinded and embittered war veteran, returns to his family, violently disrupts their domestic harmony, and finally dies in the living room instead of the battlefield. The action this time is chronological and contained within a single set, but the piece is no more naturalistic than *Pavlo Hummel*. Rabe has expressed the imprisonment of his characters inside separate mental cages by writing the play in two unrelated styles. David, inhabiting a zone of nightmare and hatred, attended by the fantasy figure of a girl he loved but then abandoned in Vietnam, is an expressionist creation. His family —guitar-playing kid brother, ex–sporting hero father, and food-obsessed mother—are confined within a stereotype of Middle America, and in fact take their names from a vacuous and saccharine television series. The play functions as an *Oedipus*-like dialogue between two kinds of blindness: David is physically blind; his family, treasuring their "happiness" above everything else, blind themselves to their son's condition. "Just be happy and home like all the others— why can't you?" pleads his mother, cheerfully offering him Ezy Sleep pills when he goes berserk. And at the end, when in the friendliest possible way they help him to cut his wrists, they take due care that no blood touches the wall-to-wall carpet.

The Anspacher production moved to Broadway in March 1972, running for seven months and winning a New York Drama Critics citation and the Antoinette Perry (Tony) Award for the best play in the 1971-1972 Broadway season. Allan Wallach described it as "mordantly funny and shockingly serious," and Brendan Gill wrote: "In the gravity and acuteness of his intelligence and the elegance of his literary skills, Mr. Rabe is already a formidable figure." Even Stanley Kauffmann, who has not shared the general enthusiasm for Rabe's work, found *Sticks and Bones* more interesting than his other plays. "The mode of the play, the best of it, is pop art," he wrote, ". . . the effect is of trivia swollen into threat, like Claes Oldenburg's gigantic hamburgers. . . . When the play works in this vein, it has some frightening moments, spotlighting the frenzy with which coziness is defended." A 1973 CBS television adaptation was withdrawn on the grounds that the play might be "unnecessarily abrasive to the feelings of millions of Americans." On the other hand, Rabe discovered in March 1973 that a pirated version of the play had been running for months at the Sovremennik Theatre in Moscow, where it was being publicized as a realistic portrayal of American life. When Rabe complained about this distortion in an open letter to the New York *Times*, Soviet officials described his letter as further evidence of the lack of artistic freedom in the United States.

No such widespread success awaited the finale of Rabe's trilogy, *The Orphan,* a work of O'Neill-like complexity which has appeared in three separate versions. Developed from a one-act piece called *The Bones of Birds* (produced at Villanova in 1968), the 1973 and 1974 versions of *The Orphan* (produced respectively at the Public Theatre and at the Manning Street Actors' Theatre in Philadelphia) rework Aeschylus' *Oresteia* through the analagous horrors of the My Lai massacres and the Manson murders. Not content with this weight of material, Rabe also introduces the figure of a Speaker who supplies a scientific perspective on the events, and a framework (based on the theory of relativity) that includes a section on the creation of the universe.

Rabe's most important structural device is the "time pool," a zone where mythical and modern characters can coexist during the breathing spaces of the narrative. According to Barnet Kellmann, the play's Philadelphia director, the action proceeds throughout with "a narrative step, a time pool interruption . . . then a halting reminder of the culminating event towards which the characters are moving." It is a technique that enables Rabe to escape the fetters of chronology and achieve swift ironic links between distant events, as in the synchronized slaughters of Iphigenia and Agamemnon, or in the Speaker's dissertation on cardiac anatomy as a fork slips into the heart of Aegisthus.

The Orphan, in its final form, amounts to two separate plays, one centering on Agamemnon and the other on Orestes. The first establishes a parallel between the Trojan War and the war in Vietnam, and the second mirrors the parricidal reactions of American youth in the late 1960s to the generation responsible for the war. Shifting between timeless and modern speech, the characters combine the features of classical archetype and media stereotype: Aegisthus appears as a nervous little businessman, Apollo as Manson, and the Furies as members of the Manson "Family." The second play might be subtitled "The Basic Training of Orestes," since its hero first appears as an earnest innocent who grudgingly accepts his murderous mission only after having studied the relevant assigned books, and who carries it out only after Apollo has launched him on a drug trip.

Characteristically, Rabe takes no sides between the "gook" killers and the "pig" killers. But he departs in one vital respect from his classical model. From the arrival of the prophet Calchas as a smooth-talking courier carrying the auguries in a briefcase (another of Apollo's disguises), the play contests the notion of any divine inevitability determining the events. Much the most ambitious of Rabe's works, *The Orphan* was greeted with bewilderment by reviewers of the New York production. "In the past," Clive Barnes wrote in the New York *Times,* "[the playwright's] symbols have been moderately direct. . . . But in *The Orphan,* Mr Rabe, in trying to pull all his themes together, is going for bigger game. And not always succeeding." The production at the Anspacher Stage closed in just under a month.

In *In the Boom Boom Room* (Vivian Beaumont Theatre, November 1973), Rabe at last forsook Vietnam to tell the story of a Philadelphia go-go dancer named Chrissy who is "trying to get some goddam order into my stupid life." The piece chronicles her odyssey in search of self-respect, taking in her attachments to a father who spiked her milk with vodka, a homosexual who copies her bunny suit, a bisexual dance captain, and a racist truck driver whose machismo is the hardest drug to shake off. The essential factor about Chrissy is that in spite of her inarticulate confusion, she has a clear aesthetic goal: she is aiming for a "kind of dancing in which you tell a story and of which go-go is a poor facsimile." That phrase is typical, and it does much to offset the opinion of those New York reviewers who saw the play as a sentimentally shallow fairy tale. This was not the view of London critics for whom this play was their introduction to Rabe, and from one of whom it drew an interesting comparison with Franz Kroetz's Bavarian peasant dramas.

In 1976, Rabe returned to his former territory in *Streamers* (Long Wharf Theatre, New Haven) with a brutality surpassing that of *Pavlo Hummel.* The setting is a Virginia army barracks in 1965 and the theme is homosexuality. In the first act, the subject is teasingly discussed; in the second it passes savagely into action. A black and a white, making love, are interrupted by another member of the hut who orders them out. There follow two bloodily prolonged knife assaults which drove a substantial number of the first audience out of the theatre. As before, Rabe strengthens and deepens his work by his use of symbols: the title, for instance, refers to parachutes that fail to open.

"Mr. Rabe is a writer," said Walter Kerr in his review; "he is not yet an adequate *designer* of plays. He can do many things well. The speech he gives his actors is easy and authentic, though he does tend to build it into descriptive monologues rather than bristling give-and-take. . . . His characters have sensibilities that can be acted. . . . [and] Mr. Rabe has humor on call when he wants it . . . [but] Mr. Rabe, it would seem, is still searching for a stage metaphor—a structure, not simply a speech—that will figure forth his deeply felt responses not only to the Vietnamese war as such but to senseless death of any kind. He has not yet found one that will say to us precisely what he sees." Stanley Kauffmann, more harshly, suggests that Rabe "has seen very little that every member of the audience hasn't seen for himself . . . many of his theatrical devices are striking, but the gravamen of the play is quite familiar." Kauffmann believes that Rabe has suffered from his championship by Joseph Papp, having been encouraged to bring to the stage works not yet in their mature and final form. For many critics, however, Rabe is one of the most important dramatists of his generation—for Catherine Hughes "the most significant American playwright to appear since Albee."

Rabe returned to Villanova University in 1970, serving as playwright-in-residence and teaching courses in writing for the theatre and film history. Unlike many American dramatists of his generation, he is a slow, careful worker who is prepared to revise a play again and again. If he has any theatrical progenitor it is Eugene O'Neill, with whom he shares a combination of hard-won American experience and European stagecraft, and a style with the precarious clarity of visions glimpsed briefly through fog. Rabe was married in 1969 to Elizabeth Pan, a Chinese-born laboratory technician; they have a son, Jason. The author is very tall and powerfully built, with blue eyes and prematurely graying sandy hair. He is a member of the Philadelphia Rugby Club.

PRINCIPAL PUBLISHED WORKS: The Basic Training of Pavlo Hummel *and* Sticks and Bones, 1973; The Orphan, 1975; In the Boom Boom Room, 1975; Streamers, 1977.

ABOUT: Current Biography, 1973; Hughes, C. American Playwrights 1945-1975, 1976; Kauffmann, S. Persons of the Drama, 1976; Vinson, J. (ed.) Contemporary Dramatists, 1977; Who's Who in America, 1976-1977. *Periodicals*—After Dark August 1972; New York Post March 11, 1972; New York Times December 12, 1971; November 24, 1973; February 22, 1976; April 25, 1976; Newsweek December 20, 1971; New Yorker November 20, 1971; Theatre Quarterly 25 1977.

*RADNÓTI, MIKLÓS (May 5, 1909–November 4, 1944), Hungarian poet, translator, and novelist, was born in Budapest. His mother died giving birth to him and his twin brother, who also died. This double tragedy, of which he learned while still a boy, had a profound and lasting effect on him, and his own preservation from the forces of destruction is a recurrent

*rod′ nō tē

MIKLÓS RADNÓTI

Interfoto MTI

theme in his poetry. He was raised by various relatives, never living long in any one place.

Radnóti studied Hungarian and French literature at the University of Szeged, where he became the center of a literary circle and a member of such progressive organizations as the Szeged College of Art for the Young. With fellow students who shared his interest in folklore he explored the countryside around Szeged, making studies of rural and village life. Radnóti went to Budapest after his graduation, hoping to teach. However, although he was a Christian convert and a highly gifted poet with a teaching diploma, he was unable to obtain a teaching post because of his Jewish origins. He was obliged to earn his living as a private tutor, and from the poems and translations he published in literary periodicals.

It was as a translator that Radnóti first gained recognition, for his accomplished versions of works by Shelley, Shakespeare, La Fontaine, Nerval, Apollinaire, and Cocteau, among others. But he is best remembered as Hungary's finest poet of protest against the regime of Admiral Horthy and the rising tide of European fascism.

In his early collections, *Pogány Köszöntő* (Pagan Toast, 1930), *Ujmódi Pásztorok Éneke* (Song of Modern Shepherds, 1931), and *Lábadozó Szél* (Rising Wind, 1933), his jauntily defiant verse conveys the frustrations of his generation in expressionist imagery and fractured rhythms that owe much to the influence of the surrealists. Yet, as Klaniczay, Szarder, and Szabolcsi say in their *History of Hungarian Literature,* "already in some of the poems of *Rising Wind,* the poet's voice gains in richness and clarity—the development proceeds in several directions simultaneously; the poet's message is here more unequivocal, more revolutionary, matched by an ever bolder use of the elements of reality and a growing tendency for more polished, more classical forms."

This development towards a purer diction and stricter forms continued in *Újhold* (New Moon, 1935), *Járkálj Csak Halálraitélt* (Condemned Man, Keep Walking), and in the last collection published in Radnóti's lifetime, *Meredek Út* (Steep Road, 1938). The poet celebrates his love for his wife Fanni and for nature, and yearns to enjoy these blessings in peace and harmony, but cannot turn his back on the ugly realities of a Europe increasingly dominated by fascism, or evade his poetic duty to speak out against tyranny in the name of freedom and justice.

In 1937, Radnóti visited Paris, where he wrote the sequence of gentle and happy vignettes he called "Cartes postales." But the same year he was writing dark poems about the Spanish Civil War, including one on the death of Lorca: "Because Spain loved you,/ because lovers read your poems,/ what else could they do?/ You were a poet—*they* killed you." The preoccupation with death which pervades Radnóti's verse becomes in these prewar years increasingly a presentiment that his poetry and his views will cost him his life:

... Believe me, believe me, there's good reason
why suspicion keeps me going!
I am a poet whose works are burned.
I am a witness to the truth.

I am the one who knows snow is white,
blood and the poppy red,
the poppy's delicate, flaxen stem is green.

I am the one they'll kill finally,
because I myself never killed.

     (from "I am a poet and no one needs me,"
     translated by Steven Polgar,
     Stephen Berg, and S. J. Marks)

In 1941 Radnóti was arrested as an opponent of Hungarian fascism. After forced labor in the mines, he was sent to disarm explosives on the Ukrainian front. He survived all this, and in 1944 was taken to Lager Heidenau, a German concentration camp attached to the copper mines at Bor, Yugoslavia. As the Germans retreated, their prisoners began in August 1944 a long death march which ended in November, when they reached Abda, near Györ in northwest Hungary. Here the exhausted survivors were made to dig a mass grave before being beaten to death or shot.

When Radnóti's body was exhumed for reburial two years later, his wife Fanni found in his greatcoat pocket the poems he had written during his imprisonment. All but five written in the terrible last days of his life had already been copied and brought back by camp survivors, and were published along with the uncollected poems written before his arrest in *Tajtékos Ég* (1946, translated with additional poems as *Clouded Sky*). The five last poems were included in the collected edition of his poems, *Radnóti Miklós versei* (1948), and in the later complete edition, *Radnóti Miklós összes versei es műforditásai* (Complete Poems and Translations of Miklós Radnóti, 1963). Apart from poetry and translations, he also published a critical study of the Hungarian author Margit Kaffka (1934), and an autobiographical novel, *Ikrek Hava* (A Month of Twins, 1940).

As Steven Polgar points out in *Clouded Sky,* the title of that collection is an inadequate rendering of the Hungarian original, which implies a sky that is foaming at the mouth: "Radnóti used a strong, colorful and extremely imaginative word to give the feeling of impending disaster, of chaos, and of strange unknown evils." These late poems, combining the bold imagery of the twentieth century with the disciplines of classical verse, achieve a greater power and intensity than any of Radnóti's earlier work. They explore the situation of the individual, and of the poet himself, in a nightmare world where people are turned into beasts and herded like beasts to destruction. Yet amid the scenes and images of present horror there shines a marvelous confidence in the eventual victory of peace and love. Radnóti's wife Fanni appears often in verses which are among the finest love poems in the language.

Among the camp poems are the last two of Radnóti's eight eclogues which, despite their very varied content and dates of composition, do form a sequence, as B. S. Adams has shown: "The message that he seeks to transmit through the Eclogues is that when things are wrong, there must be someone who will not flinch from saying that they are wrong, if ever the former values are to be restored.... The length of time that elapsed between the composition of the First and Eighth Eclogues only serves to demonstrate how very deeply Radnóti felt this problem, how closely he must have lived it, letting his views mature slowly over the years, and recording for posterity the stages of this maturing. This cycle of poems must be considered the core of Radnóti's work."

Many of the last poems are full of death and blood, like the sequence about the march to

Abda called "Razglednicák" (Postcards), so dreadfully different from the "Cartes postales" written in Paris seven years before:

> I fell next to him. His body rolled over.
> It was tight as a string before it snaps
> Shot in the back of the head—"This is how
> you'll end." "Just lie quietly," I said to myself.
> Patience flowers into death now.
> "Der springt noch auf," I heard above me.
> Dark filthy blood was drying on my ear

(translated by Steven Polgar,
Stephen Berg, and S.J. Marks)

Yet the most extraordinary feature of these prisoner poems is that they are full of happy reminiscences, so that B. S. Adams can sum them up by saying: "The poetic power of the Lager verse is based on Radnóti's happiness, a happiness derived . . . from the satisfaction of seeing his life complete, drawing to the end that he had envisaged. It is the happiness of a man in love—in love with his wife, with his work, with humanity and with life itself. It is the happiness of a man who has lived life to the full and who, looking back, has the satisfaction of seeing the good times and the bad fall into place, make sense. Above all it is the sublime joy of the martyr who goes to the stake because he has no alternative, fearlessly joining the ranks of those who have gone before, rejoicing in his faith in the future of mankind." Denise Levertov has called Radnóti "a truly great poet, one in whom the lyrical image-maker and the critical human intelligence dealing with the tragic twentieth century are utterly fused. . . . I feel he is speaking directly to me, the reader, in my time and place, as if from Vietnam or out of my pillow into my ear."

PRINCIPAL WORKS IN ENGLISH TRANSLATION: Clouded Sky, translated by Steven Polgar, Stephen Berg, and S.J. Marks, 1973: Subway Stops: Fifty Poems, translated by Emery George, 1977. *Poems in* Haydu, G.C. Statements and Avowals, 1973; Colorado State Review Summer 1967; Delos 1 1968; London Magazine 1972; Modern Poetry in Translation 6 1970; Nation October 30, 1967; Slavonic Review June 1965, January 1967; Stand 4 1970; Stony Brook Fall 1968.

ABOUT: Encyclopaedia Judaica, 1971; Klaniczay, T., Szarder, J., and Szabolcsi, M. History of Hungarian Literature, 1964; Madácsi, L. Radnóti Miklós, 1954 (in Hungarian); Magyar Irodalmi Lexikon, 1965; Penguin Companion to Literature 2, 1969. *Periodicals*—Nation May 28, 1973; Slavonic Review June 1965, January 1967.

---

*RAMOS, GRACILIANO (October 27, 1892– March 20, 1953), Brazilian novelist, short story writer, and memoirist, was born in the small town of Quebrangulo, in the northeastern state

*ru´mo͞os

GRACILIANO RAMOS

Manchete, from Pictorial Parade

of Alagoas. In the west of Alagoas begin the vast, poverty-stricken backlands—the *sertão*— which have provided the setting for so much major literature since Euclydes da Cunha's classic *Os Sertões (Rebellion in the Backlands)* appeared in 1902.

Ramos was the first of the many children of Sebastião Ramos, a storekeeper of Portuguese extraction, and the former Maria Amélia Ferro. His father was a stern authoritarian and his mother veered between affectionate playfulness and irascibility. Ramos, an "awkward, unkempt, physically ugly boy" with a tendency to nervous illnesses, had a harsh childhood which left him with a profoundly pessimistic view of human nature.

When Ramos was still very small, his father tried his hand at cattleranching in the Pernambuco *sertão*, but was ruined by drought. In 1899 the family moved back to Alagoas and settled in the municipality of Viçosa, where Sebastião Ramos opened another store, prospered, and in due course became a municipal judge. These early experiences equipped Ramos with his principal themes—the hopeless poverty but also the animal innocence of life in the *sertão;* the wickedness, squalor, and corruption of the towns.

When he was twelve, Ramos completed his elementary education in Viçosa and began a brief period of secondary schooling in Maceió, the state capital of Alagoas, where his first sonnets appeared in local magazines. He wrote pseudonymously because his father disapproved of his literary ambitions. His formal education ended in his early teens, but he read widely, stealing money from his father's till to buy the works of Dostoevsky, Balzac, and Eça de Queiróz, all of whom influenced his own writing. Ramos went on to study the languages and literatures of England, France, and Italy, as well as of Portugal, making of himself a man of very considerable culture.

In 1910 the family moved to another town in Alagoas, Palmeira dos Índios, where Ramos worked in his father's new store. In 1914 he went off to Rio de Janeiro. He wrote his first short stories there and worked as a journalist—apparently without much success, since the following year he returned to Palmeira and settled down. In 1915 he married Maria Augusta Barros and opened a store of his own—a drygoods shop which was also the town's "stock market, forum, agora, cenacle, library, and casino." His first wife died in 1920, leaving him with four children to raise.

A few years later Ramos was elected president of the Palmeira school board, and in 1927 he became mayor of the town. His first novel, Caetés, begun in 1925, was completed in 1928. The same year he married Heloísa Medeiros, by whom he had four more children. As he said, Ramos might very well have spent the rest of his life in that "dusty little town"; might have continued "to play chess and backgammon, attending to my petty chores, listening to the endless arguments on the sidewalks, taking refuge in the afternoon in the hulking cathedral."

However, in 1929, Ramos wrote a report on social and economic problems in his prefecture which was so outspoken that his superiors in Maceió attempted to suppress it. Ramos sent a copy of the report directly to the governor of Alagoas, who published it. A newspaper controversy followed which made Ramos a national figure. In 1930 he was moved to Maceió as director of the state printing office. He went home to Palmeira the following year, founded a school there, and then became ill. After an operation from which he never fully recovered, he returned to Maceió as director of public education (1933–1936). These promotions were not the only result of the famous relatorio. It was read by the poet and publisher Augusto Frederico Schmidt, who recognized it as the work of a natural novelist and asked Ramos for his manuscripts.

Caetés, ironically named after an extinct northeastern tribe of cannibals, was published in 1933. It is a naturalistic novel in the nineteenth-century manner, written under the influence of Eça de Queiróz, and showing little of the psychological perception that distinguishes Ramos's best books. It is typical of him all the same in its preoccupation with the stifling atmosphere

of small-town life in the northeast, in the purity of its style, and in its pessimism: human beings, whatever their claims and hypocrisies, are shown to be simply clever animals, motivated solely by the survival instinct and the pleasure principle.

It seemed to the critic Otto Maria Carpeaux that if Caetés was the work of a "Brazilian Eça, São Bernardo is worthy of Balzac." Ramos's second novel, published in 1934 and translated under the same title by R.L. Scott-Buccleuch, is an account, given in the first person by the protagonist, of how Paulo Honório cheats and murders his way from obscurity to the ownership of a vast estate. When Honório's uncontrollable possessiveness and jealousy drive his idealistic wife to suicide and himself to the verge of madness, it becomes clear that he is as much a victim of the society that bred him as those he has exploited and destroyed. In its structure and in its psychological probings São Bernardo is a far more sophisticated book than its predecessor, and it established Ramos as a major novelist.

Ramos knew to what extent the ignorance, poverty, and hopelessness of the sertanejo were the result of social injustice. This made him a socialist, and his novels works of implicit social criticism. At the same time, his determinism made it difficult for him to believe that revolution or anything else would ever cure Brazil's social sickness—he would not have been surprised by the developments there since his death. It is not altogether clear in fact how active a part he played in Brazilian politics, and accounts differ as to the reason for his arrest by the Vargas regime in 1936. It was a period of repression, following an uprising by National Liberation Alliance forces, and Ramos's attempts at reform in Maceió had made him enemies. At any rate, he was shipped from Maceió to a penal island near Rio de Janeiro and imprisoned there under conditions which permanently damaged his already poor health.

It was during this period that Ramos published Angústia (1936, translated by L. C. Kaplan as Anguish). This is the darkest of his novels, and his fullest statement of the alienating and destructive effect of the city on those who belong to the sertão. It uses a form of interior monologue to evoke the increasingly dangerous distress and confusion of Luís Silva, who exchanges a despairing existence in the backlands for the bewildering pace of life in Maceió. He conceives an obsessive passion for the tantalizing girl next door, and when she is left pregnant by a more sophisticated lover, murder is inevitable.

Released in 1937, Ramos settled in Rio, where he completed Vidas Sêcas (1938, translated by

R.E. Dimmick as *Barren Lives*). It is a series of vignettes, written in the third person and with only a minimum of dialogue, forming a remarkable portrait of an inarticulate and illiterate half-breed cowboy. Fabiano and his family, powerless, exploited, hungry, herded back and forth like their own cattle by the excesses of their implacable environment, are driven at last out of the frying pan of the *sertão* into the fire of the city—and can only hope that life will be a little less intolerable for some later generation of the poor. Jean Franco wrote that in this novel Ramos had presented the development of his protagonist "not through thoughts nor even stream of consciousness, but through behavior." The result is a masterpiece of Dostoevskyan power. It was successfully filmed in 1963, and the same year its English translation received the William Faulkner prize.

Fearing further persecution by the Vargas regime, Ramos wrote no more novels after *Vidas Sêcas.* He spent the last part of his life in Rio, working as a proofreader for a large city newspaper and writing relatively inoffensive works like the excellent autobiographical sketches of *Infância* (Childhood, 1945) and the short stories of *Insônia* (Insomnia, 1947). An enigma to many of his contemporaries, he remained what his friend José Lins do Rêgo called him: "The quiet *sertanejo* with the unfriendly face, distrustful eyes, and bitter smile" and "the man who knew the most mythology of all the *sertão.*" Ramos joined the Communist Party in 1945, and in 1952–1953 he and his wife visited the USSR and Czechoslovakia. He became seriously ill there, and died soon after his return to Rio. *Viagem,* his glowing account of this last journey, has been called "a book of evasion."

The most remarkable product of these last years was the four-volume *Memórias do Cárcere,* published posthumously in 1953, a relentlessly honest account of his imprisonment by the Vargas regime and of his own feelings and behavior under the dreadful stresses of those months in the house of the dead. Wilson Martins maintains that this factual book is in fact closer to the novel Ramos might have written than any of his fictional works—that Ramos, having "prepared himself to be a classical and traditional writer, a respecter of the Portuguese language," had become a Modernist "because in the thirties one tried to be a Modernist or died.... He could not withstand the pressures of his literary milieu and abruptly altered the direction of his work, attempted to conquer his original propensities and the very nature of his mind."

It is an interesting point of view but highly speculative; it does not follow that Ramos would have written better if he had written differently. Ramos's sociological novels are distinguished from those of his lesser contemporaries by the accuracy and profundity of his psychological perceptions; instead of peopling his books with ciphers chosen to illustrate his social theories, he presents closely observed and fully drawn human beings and shows, convincingly and movingly, how they have been debased and misshapen by social forces. His style has been called "incomparable in its sobriety, elegance, and refinement." He is universally regarded as one of the masters of the Brazilian "novel of the northeast," along with Lins do Rêgo and Jorge Amado, and in the opinion of some critics he is his country's greatest writer of fiction since Machado de Assis.

PRINCIPAL WORKS IN ENGLISH TRANSLATION: Anguish, 1946; Barren Lives, 1965; Sao Bernardo, 1975.

ABOUT: Ellison, F. Brazil's New Novel, 1954; Franco, J. The Modern Culture of Latin America, 1970; Grieco, A. Homenagem a Graciliano Ramos, 1943; Martins, W. The Modernist Idea, 1970; Mazzara, R.A. Graciliano Ramos, 1974; Penguin Companion to Literature 3, 1971; Pinto, R.M. Graciliano Ramos: Autor e Ator, 1962; Times Literary Supplement, January 2, 1976; Twentieth Century Writing, 1969.

"RANDALL, ROBERT." *See* SILVERBERG, ROBERT

RAVENSDALE, LORD. *See* MOSLEY, NICHOLAS

READ, PIERS PAUL (March 7, 1941–), English novelist, is one of the five children of the very influential critic and poet Herbert Read, who was knighted in 1953. His mother was Read's second wife, the former Margaret Ludwig. Piers Paul Read was born in Beaconsfield, a town in Buckinghamshire some twenty miles northwest of London. He was educated at the famous Roman Catholic school Ampleforth College, and is a Catholic by religion. From Ampleforth he went on to St. John's College, Cambridge University, gaining his B.A. with honors in 1961 and his M.A. in the following year. In 1963 he went to Germany for a year as artist-in-residence at the Ford Foundation in Berlin, returning to London to work as a subeditor on the *Times Literary Supplement* (1964–1965).

Game in Heaven With Tussy Marx (1966), Read's first novel, introduces several themes that have continued to preoccupy him: religion, politics (especially the politics of the extreme Left), sin, and grace. It is set in an anteroom of heaven, where a duchess, a young Englishman, and Karl Marx's daughter discuss the revolu-

Sophie Baker

PIERS PAUL READ

tionary situation developing on earth. To entertain his companions, the Englishman improvises tales about two kinds of revolutionaries: one is a middle-aged degenerate who persuades himself that his dissolute life will hasten the collapse of capitalism; the other is Hereward, a leader who sells out for love, experiments with debauchery, then returns, purged of his weaknesses, to lead the revolution. David Craig wrote that this "experimental novel is an infuriating mixture of the trenchant and the perverse," but the *Times Literary Supplement* thought that Read had "adopted a frivolous pattern rather than a frivolous tone, to make a short but complicated statement about the nature of revolution in the modern world. . . . It makes an interesting if enigmatical first novel."

Read was married in 1967 to Emily Boothby, by whom he has a son and a daughter. In 1967–1968 he held a Commonwealth Fund Harkness Fellowship in New York and in Lexington, Massachusetts. His second novel, *The Junkers* (1968), won the Faber Memorial Prize, was successfully adapted for television, and established Read's reputation. It is narrated by a young British diplomat serving in Berlin in the 1960s. He falls in love with a German girl and then discovers a connection between her aristocratic old uncle and a notorious Nazi war criminal who is still at large. Vernon Scannell wrote that Read had provided (in flashbacks) "a vivid account of the rise of the Nazis before the Second World War, some scenes of SS bestiality described with a careful restraint that intensifies the horror, and a penetrating and sympathetic account of the type of brave and patriotic German soldier who was also a devout Christian,

agonised by his growing realisation that his Fuehrer was . . . the incarnation of total evil. The flashbacks mesh smoothly with the development of the narrator's affair with Suzi and the novel is organised with unobtrusive but masterly skill." Another reviewer, noting its "rejection of explicit moral judgements," thought the book might seem heartless to older readers but praised Read's "detachment from his material, his refusal to suspend the reader's disbelief," and his "pure, unaffected, pre-Victorian" style.

Sin and grace continued to preoccupy Read in *Monk Dawson* (1969), which brought him the Hawthornden Prize. It is the story of a monk, a teacher at the exclusive Roman Catholic school where he had been a student, who leaves his order and enters materialistic modern society. Through his own pursuit of hedonism and his observation of the bored and empty materialism of others—including his mistress, who deserts him—he comes to apprehend man's natural need for spiritual values and returns to the monastic life, which becomes a true vocation. The prose is lucid, restrained, and objective. This is the least melodramatic of Read's novels, and some critics found it psychologically the most convincing. To others, however, the restraint seemed excessive, and Mary Borg thought that Read's "inspiration seems to fail and his invention to falter" in his attempt to convey both religious faith and corruption.

The Professor's Daughter (1971), drawing on what Read had seen of America as a Harkness Fellow, is about the relationship between an intelligent and liberal professor of political theory at Harvard and his daughter, who is successively a conventional young wife, a sensualist, and a member of a revolutionary group whose activities cause her father's death. Its rather obtrusive thesis is that political idealism is useless unless the family, society's basic unit, is in proper order. Critics found the book gripping and skillful, but some noted a tendency towards melodrama and simplistic thinking.

In *The Upstart* (1973) Read, evidently influenced by his fellow-Catholic Julian Green, who provides the epigraph, tries to present in Hilary Fletcher a portrait of a great sinner who becomes a saint. Hilary's childhood as the son of a Yorkshire clergyman and his growing sense of social inferiority to richer friends are, most critics agreed, brilliantly described; his entry into a life of crime and of real depravity is absorbing if melodramatic (though one reviewer found "a grim, simple intensity in the writing which makes the story acceptable as a serious representation of evil"). But his conversion to Roman Catholicism in prison is, as Martin Seymour-

Smith wrote, "quite simply unbelievable." Another critic pointed out that "Mr. Read is not particularly concerned with everyday reality," but concluded that "a belief in the details of Hilary's progress" is necessary to the reader and that Read "just hasn't bothered to make those details plausible. Upon the whole a failure then, although still unmistakably the work of a talented, wholly serious writer."

There was an even more mixed reception for *Polonaise* (1976), which follows the fortunes of Stefan and Krystyna Kornowski, children of a Polish aristocrat, from 1914 to the late 1950s. Anne Tyler said in her review that Read is "a novelist who specializes in histories—not just the few isolated events that constitute his characters' turning points, but the entire range of their lives. His major plot elements are those brought about by the passage of time. And he is particularly concerned with the slow, inner changes in what people believe—their faiths, politics and moral stands." In the extravagance of its characters, its "gloomy and deeply textured" landscapes, and its "undertone of feverishness," it seemed to Tyler an extraordinarily "Polish" novel for an English writer to have produced, and "a marvelous, complicated, absorbing book." Other reviewers were disappointed, finding the characters unconvincing and the novel as a whole altogether too broad in its scope. Melvin Maddocks concluded that, "overextended as he is, Read writes for the most part with grace and economy. He has the exceptional novelist's gift for making a reader believe in a character's predicaments even when he may not believe in the character."

According to a reviewer in the London *Sunday Times,* Read is an uneven writer; "he has an uncomfortable intensity of vision which is expressed in narratives that move from realism to the edge of fantasy. Sometimes the fantastic element heightens the effect, and the result is very impressive. Sometimes the balance is lost, and then you get a book that may fascinate but doesn't convince." There is, all the same, general agreement that, as Paul A. Doyle has said, "even in his least successful works, his willingness to face vital themes and the crucial moral issues of good and evil, guilt and redemption proves that one is in the presence of a serious and significant artist."

Read has written a short stage play, *The Class War,* two radio plays, and three television plays. His biggest commercial success, however, has been the nonfiction book *Alive! The Story of the Andes Survivors* (1974). This tells the story of the crash in 1972 of a Uruguayan plane carrying a rugby football team and their relatives and sup-

porters. Some of the passengers died in the crash and others later; some survived by eating the dead. Rescued over two months later, they chose Piers Paul Read to tell their story and, after interviewing them all in depth, he did so with much-acclaimed journalistic aplomb; indeed, with the "matter-of-fact unaffectedness" which Paul A. Doyle has praised in his best novels. His "deceptively factual method," observed the *Times Literary Supplement,* "managed to bring home the life-and-death atmosphere of those horrid heights." And Walter Clemons wrote: "Amid instances of ignoble pilfering and despair, which Read wisely refuses to suppress, *Alive!* records a remarkable communal feat of heroism. It will become a classic in the literature of survival." Many have felt this inspired piece of reportage, which brought him the Thomas More Medal, to be the best of all Read's books.

The Train Robbers, another nonfictional book, followed in 1978. It is an account of "the crime of the century"—the 1963 train robbery by a gang of British criminals which netted a record haul of six million dollars. Most reviewers found it absorbing, but most also expressed some doubts about the accuracy of Read's facts.

Piers Paul Read received the Somerset Maugham Award in 1970. He served on the council of the Institute of Contemporary Arts in 1971–1975 and on the management committee of the Society of Authors in 1973–1976. He is a Fellow of the Royal Society of Literature. In 1976, in a letter to the *Times,* Read said that he had joined the Labour Party; he confessed in a later interview that he had previously thought of joining the Conservatives but had finally decided in favor of the moderate Left. He says that he thoroughly enjoys the business side of his activities (bids for *Alive* reached £27,000), and believes that he has inherited his dedication to hard work from his famous father.

PRINCIPAL WORKS: *Novels*—Game in Heaven With Tussy Marx, 1966; The Junkers, 1968; Monk Dawson, 1969; The Professor's Daughter, 1971; The Upstart, 1973; Polonaise, 1976. *Nonfiction*—Alive! The Story of the Andes Survivors, 1974; The Train Robbers, 1978.

ABOUT: Contemporary Authors 21–24 1st revision, 1977; Who's Who, 1978; Writers Directory, 1976–1978. *Periodicals*—Commentary August 1974; Commonweal November 12, 1971; Critic July-September 1974; Encounter October 1968; Listener June 27, 1974; Nation November 16, 1970; New Statesman June 3, 1966; June 14, 1968; November 7, 1969; September 24, 1971; May 10, 1974; New York Review of Books November 15, 1973; New York Times Book Review September 13, 1970; November 7, 1971; May 20, 1973; April 7, 1974; November 28, 1976; Newsweek June 30, 1975; Observer Magazine July 6, 1975; Punch July 17, 1968; January 1, 1969; Spectator June 12, 1968; Sunday Times (London) February 9, 1963; Time October 25, 1971; December 27, 1976; Times (London) May 11, 1978; Times

REANEY

Literary Supplement June 2, 1966; June 20, 1968; November 6, 1969; September 24, 1971; September 7, 1973; May 10, 1974; November 19, 1976.

REANEY, JAMES (CRERAR) (September 1, 1926–), Canadian poet, dramatist, critic, and editor, writes: "Reaney was born on his father's farm near Stratford, Ontario. The community he was brought up in is known as the Little Lakes and both his parents had already been involved in dramatic activity there; images drawn from this Southwestern Ontario setting range from farm, garden, seasons, farmhouse to bush, tramps, threshers, pedlars, a one-room country school, a non-sectarian Sunday school run by Charles Jones, dances, Gospel hymn singing, school plays, circuses, fall fairs, Foxe's *Martyrs*, Bunyan, Bible reading, teachers Helen Coveney and Evelyn Freeborne who read George Eliot and Coleridge to their students; neighbours who made cider, told stories and played the harmonica, fiddle, Jew's harp, etc.

"Later on, Stratford Collegiate continued some of these images with great and good teachers such as Rose McQueen who'd read *Ulysses*, Mr. Crawford who lent out *The Red and the Black, Sense & Sensibility*, etc., Frances Ross who taught Homer and Xenophon, Virgil and Horace. According to this writer, one unforgettable experience was moving into town for the last year of high school; the steadily roaring factory nearby (Imperial Rattan) only closed down about midnight. Sadly missed was the daily walk or bike ride through fields, down sideroads to high school; instead there was a street experience in a hostile neighbourhood. Piano lessons from Cora B. Ahrens included the usual Bach and Beethoven, but also Debussy preludes.

"Left Stratford for the University of Toronto on scholarships in classics and studied English honours with such teachers as A.S.P. Woodhouse, F. L. Priestley, Norman Endicott, Knox; University College with its endless ribbon of Gothic Revival ornament was a new source of images as was Toronto with innumerable landladies on Harbord Street until at last the subject of this sketch moved into the Grenville Street annex of Toronto's only Bohemia at the time.

"First poems with the Little Lakes world as their subject were published in *The Undergrad* under the guidance of such editors as Robert Weaver and Paul Arthur; fellow poets included Colleen Thibaudeau (now his wife, with two children, James Stewart and Susan) and Phyllis Gotlieb. A story published in the *Undergrad* first and then in the Canadian edition of *Liberty* won national horrified response; graduate career ended for a while with a thesis on Ivy Compton-

JAMES REANEY

Burnett and a job teaching creative writing at the University of Manitoba. After the intensively detailed foregrounds of Southwestern Ontario, Manitoba, with its flatness and whiteness and huge distances, came as a healthy shock; first book of poems came out under the guidance of Sybil Hutchinson, the editor then at McClelland & Stewart; she has remained mentor and agent.

"Studied classics again under Hugill and Berry and Johannson at Manitoba; then in 1956 determined to come East again and study with Northrop Frye at Toronto; completed a thesis under his guidance on Spenser and Yeats; published second volume of poetry—*A Suit of Nettles*, a set of twelve eclogues in imitation of Spenser's *Shepherd's Calendar*. Most critics regretted the classical shift, but not all; back in Manitoba with a doctorate and having such colleagues as Jack Woodbury, Victor Cowie, Reaney started writing plays and also printing and editing a little magazine called *Alphabet: The Iconography of the Imagination*—the last phrase a quote from Frye's book on Blake, *Fearful Symmetry*. This magazine, handset, got as far as nineteen issues; Pamela Terry, a Toronto director with the University Alumni Theatre, directed *The Killdeer* in 1959; other plays followed: *Easter Egg; Names & Nicknames* directed by John Hirsch at Manitoba Theatre Centre; the subject moved back to Ontario with a position in the English department at the University of Western Ontario, not far away from where he was born.

"Reaney's most recent plays include *Colours in the Dark*, premiered at the Stratford Festival (1967); *Listen to the Wind* (the beginning of a new style and also the association with director Keith Turnbull); and *The Donnellys,* a trilogy based on the fate of a family murdered in the county next to Reaney's. In the fall of 1975 the author toured with this trilogy from coast to coast; performances by the NDWT Company directed by Turnbull were regarded by some, not by all, as signs of a theatrical renaissance. Living in a world that is quickly growing more and more unlike the world he was born into, Reaney keeps sifting the hoard of metaphors Southwestern Ontario has given him. Recent rumours have it that he and his theatre friends have found a permanent refuge in whose shelter Art and Work assist them in their task of stopping Time from careening by so meaninglessly."

James Reaney is regarded not only as one of the few important poets currently writing in Canada, but as one of the most arresting and original dramatists the country has produced.

He is the son of James Nesbitt Reaney and the former Elizabeth Henrietta Crerar. He has a half brother and a half sister, both younger than himself. The "one-room country school" he attended from 1932 to 1939 was at South Easthope, near Stratford. After high school in Stratford (1939–1944), he went on to study English at University College, University of Toronto (1944–1948). Reaney received the Epstein Award for the poems and stories he wrote there, some of which appeared in *The Undergrad, Canadian Poetry Magazine, Canadian Forum,* and *Northern Review,* among other journals.

Although he has published only a handful of short stories, it was these that first attracted attention. They showed from the first some of the preoccupations that have persisted throughout his work—a fascination with the macabre and with the conflict between the romantic or artistic sensibility and the brutal insensitivities of small-town life in Canada. The most famous (or notorious) of these stories is "The Box-Social," which describes a young woman's elaborate care in decorating the lunch box she will put up for auction, its purchase by the man for whom it is intended, and his discovery that it contains "the crabbed corpse of a still-born child wreathed in bloody newspaper."

The Red Heart, Reaney's first book, was published in 1949, when he was twenty-three, and received the Governor General's Award as the year's best volume of poetry. Its five hundred copies sold out, and it is now a collector's piece. These forty-two lyrics, appearing at a time when Canadian poetry had been largely social and realistic in its concerns, were by contrast startlingly personal and romantic. They offer a high-

ly colored portrait of the artist in childhood and adolescence, daydreaming in a lush but moribund pastoral landscape which he sees as a kind of Eden after the fall. He is haunted by nightmares, by fears of death, by a bitter sense of loneliness and lovelessness, and a disgust at sexuality—"that foul deed that struck/ Me out of chaos, out of nothing" into a world filled "with blood, pus, horror, death, stepmothers, and lies."

Along with these fearful or unhappy lyrics are others that are witty or satiric, and it is hard to know how literally to take Reaney's evocations of a tormented childhood. In form, these precocious poems are erratic and adventurous, inventive in imagery and rhythm. Their quality is uneven but their promise is unmistakeable.

The same year, 1949, Reaney received his M.A. from Toronto, and for the next seven years taught creative writing at the University of Manitoba. During this period he read Northrop Frye's *Fearful Symmetry: A Study of William Blake,* and came under the influence of both Frye and Blake. It was this that brought him back to Toronto in 1956 to prepare his doctoral thesis under Frye's supervision. Frye's influence is evident in much of what he has written since, most obviously in his use of Frye's "archetypal symbolism" and in his constant return to a central myth of quest and salvation. These elements are of the greatest importance in Reaney's second book, *A Suit of Nettles* (1958).

These twelve eclogues, comprising Reaney's longest poem to date, give a history of a society of geese on an Ontario farm. The geese achieve an ideal civilization, composing splendid pastoral music, and then, threatened from within and without, decline into disorder and destruction. The book brought Reaney a second Governor General's Award for poetry. It had its detractors, who found it pretentious and academic, but most critics admired it as a satirical allegory encompassing passages of poignant beauty. Louis Dudek, who considers it Reaney's "most ambitious and satisfying book," calls it "a metrical tour-de-force. . . . Language is used with a good deal of archaizing arbitrariness and artificial word-placing, but the whole effect is one of great skill and virtuosity in satirical handling. The themes of . . . *[The Red Heart]* are formalized into what is now clearly a unifying vision. . . . The nature of this vision is thoroughly traditional and recognizably Christian."

Reaney returned to the University of Manitoba with his doctorate in 1958, remaining there until he moved on to Middlesex College, University of Western Ontario, in 1960. His opera *Night-blooming Cereus,* with music by John

Beckwith, was broadcast by the Canadian Broadcasting Corporation in 1959, and his play *The Killdeer* had its first performance the following year. It was in 1960 also that Reaney himself gave the first performance of his *One-Man Masque,* a densely-wrought suite of sixteen grimly ironic monologues originally presented as a companion piece to the life-affirming romanticism of *Night-blooming Cereus.* In September 1960 Reaney, who had been studying typesetting for this purpose, published the first issue of his semi-annual magazine *Alphabet,* which flourished until 1971.

In 1961 came CBC's production of *Twelve Letters to a Small Town,* a suite of lyrics, prose poems, dialogues, and verbal games written between about 1950 and 1960, and set to chamber music by John Beckwith. The small town is Stratford, Ontario, in the late 1930s and early 1940s, and the setting is essentially that of *The Red Heart,* but celebrated now as a harmonious world. Even the farmhouse, the haunted scene of his futile search for identity in *The Red Heart,* is here the serene center from which the farm-boy-poet adventures out to the excitements of the town. The general effect has been found reminiscent of Dylan Thomas's *Under Milk Wood.* Although the vision is that of a mature artist, the style is deliberately naive and childlike. This has irritated some critics, but has not prevented the piece from enjoying great popularity in Canada.

Twelve Letters, published in 1962, brought Reaney his third Governor General's Award for Poetry. The same year he received the Governor General's Award for Drama for *The Killdeer and Other Plays.* In *The Killdeer,* wrote Alvin Lee, "through a dazzling array of poetic language, excellent acting parts, and bizarre psychological unravellings, one soon realized that *The Red Heart,* that intensely private book of problems stated but not resolved, had come to the stage. . . . But several of the redemptive elements brought together in *A Suit of Nettles* had been combined with *The Red Heart,* and resolutions had been worked out."

The Killdeer's protagonist is young Harry Gardner, who rightly believes that marriage to the egg-girl Rebecca will redeem him from the destructive attentions of his dominating mother. The marriage is prevented, and appalling consequences ensue, until sudden revelations in the third act license a happy ending. Eli, son of the monstrous Madame Fay, makes a similar progress—from trauma-induced infantilism to the beginning of maturity. Alvin Lee has shown how, in this and other plays, Reaney has dramatized Jung's "division of the soul into four parts, represented by an old woman, an old man, a

young man, and a young girl. The younger two cannot come together until the young man has come to terms with the older pair. When this has happened, however, a new human soul is integrated or born."

The Killdeer has been called arbitrary and melodramatic, implausible in characterization, inadequate in exposition—an uneasy mingling of naturalism, fantasy, and symbolism. A number of critics have recognized its originality, however—its surprisingly successful attempt to establish in contemporary terms a mode reminiscent of Shakespearian comedy (which Northrop Frye regards as a deliberate departure from the conventions of reality). Charles Spenser, reviewing a British production of the play in 1965, praised it as a mythopoeic exploration and illumination of the "hungry gorge of the human heart," and its author as "a dramatic poet of uncommon and forcible gifts," while Mavor Moore, discussing the first production in the Toronto *Telegram,* said that "when the history of the Canadian theatre comes to be written, I should not be at all surprised to find *The Killdeer* listed as the first Canadian play of real consequence, and the first demonstration of genius among us. . . . The great thing is that the words Mr. Reaney has written . . . soar, spin, whirl and flash like nothing ever heard on our stage before. And he rips us open as a people with a sort of jolly whimsy which may forever mark the end of the myth of the stolid, sober, inarticulate Canadian."

Reaney has turned increasingly to the theatre in recent years, in plays, almost all of them in verse, which according to Louis Dudek "rather shyly gravitate toward a Christian affirmation." Some of them have been written for children, like *Names and Nicknames* (1963), which shows a characteristic delight in wordlists and verbal play, and *All the Bees and All the Keys,* supplied with music by John Beckwith. Reaney has also written the libretto for another opera, *The Shivaree,* and two puppet plays, among other works for the stage. Most of his plays, whether for adults or children, are marked or marred by passages of naively childish doggerel, reminiscent of similar lapses in the poetry of William Blake, which Louis Dudek regards as a deliberate attempt "to simplify and to reach an indiscriminate audience."

Dudek finds "an aura of amateur theatre about the whole thing," and this may very well be Reaney's intention. *Listen to the Wind* was first produced by an amateur company under Reaney's own direction in 1966, and Alvin Lee felt that a professional production could do nothing but "impair its freshness and spontaneity." The play, which borrows some of the conventions of Chinese opera, is set in an Ontario farmhouse in the 1930s, where four children—Owen and his three cousins—entertain themselves one summer by acting out plays. Owen is ill, perhaps fatally so, and desperately unhappy because his mother has deserted the family. The children present a play, "The Saga of Caresfoot Court," which is a Victorian melodrama based on a childhood favorite of Reaney's, H. Rider Haggard's early novel *Dawn.* In this inner play, a beautiful heroine threads "her way through a world of evil manorhouses and sinister Lady Eldreds" in a story analogous to Owen's problems. A chorus of children provide an audience for the inner play and participate in it as guests at a garden party, flowers in a garden, a pack of starving dogs, and much else.

Alvin Lee considers the play a theatrical tour de force whose quality cannot be grasped from a reading of the text. He says that it displays Reaney's "uncanny knowledge of the minds and emotions of imaginative children, his life-long fascination with the macabre and with perennial patterns of romance. It also displays as well as anything he has written his capacity to create a verbal world which has its own color and music, its own peculiar way of winning an aesthetic triumph over those things which bedevil the life of the imaginative innocent."

Reaney's trilogy *The Donnellys* is widely regarded as his finest achievement. The "Black" Donnellys were a family of Irish immigrants who were almost wiped out in a horrific massacre in Ontario in the 1880s. Reaney's research convinced him that the family had always been more sinned against than sinning. They were Catholics who, back home in Ireland, had suffered for the fact that they were considered insufficiently hostile to the Protestant English. They emigrated to Ontario and, when the persecution continued, repaid their enemies with interest, bringing down on themselves a terrible reckoning. D.D.C. Chambers in *Contemporary Dramatists* says that Reaney had created out of this story "a sort of Canadian Oresteia. . . . Each play differs in the ritual that forms its structure, but the pattern of knowing and remembering that we think of as Faulknerian . . . is common to all. The history of the family surrounds the central event—their final murder-massacre in the last play—like dust in a sunbeam. . . . We find ourselves endlessly going round events that are and must remain mysterious, with bits of evidence, voices, recollections." Songs and dances play an important part in the trilogy which, Chambers says, is "also a ritual. And that ritual, although Reaney intended it to be an ex-

orcism of the 'Black' Donnellys' reputation, is more a celebration of a mystery that cannot be explained, only understood."

Alvin Lee, discussing *Listen to the Wind,* found a "vital connection" between that play "and the fantasies 'dreamed out' thirty years ago in a lonely Gothic farmhouse near Stratford." The same might be said of virtually everything that Reaney has written; he has taken the scenes, events, daydreams, and nightmares of his Ontario boyhood, and sought to construct from them a universal myth.

PRINCIPAL WORKS: *Poetry*—The Red Heart, 1949; A Suit of Nettles, 1958; Twelve Letters to a Small Town, 1962; The Dance of Death at London, Ontario, 1963; Poems, 1972; Selected Shorter Poems, edited by Germaine Warkentin, 1975; Selected Longer Poems, edited by Germaine Warkentin, 1976. *Plays*—The Killdeer and Other Plays (includes Sun and Moon, One-Man Masque, Night-blooming Cereus), 1962; Let's Make a Carol: A Play With Music for Children, 1965; Names and Nicknames, 1969; Colours in the Dark, 1969; Masks of Childhood (includes The Killdeer, Three Desks, Easter Egg), 1972; Listen to the Wind, 1972; Apple Butter and Other Plays for Children (includes Names and Nicknames, Ignoramus, Geography Match, Apple Butter), 1973; All the Bees and All the Keys (for children), 1975; The Donnellys (trilogy comprising Sticks and Stones, The St. Nicholas Hotel, Handcuffs), 1975–1976. *Fiction* —The Boy With an R in His Hand: A Tale of the Type-Riot at William Lyon Mackenzie's Printing Office in 1826 (for children), 1965.

ABOUT: Contemporary Authors 41–44, 1974; Lee, A.A. James Reaney, 1968; Moore, M. Four Canadian Playwrights, 1973; New, W.H. Dramatists in Canada, 1972; Oxford Companion to Canadian History and Literature, 1967; Reaney, J.S. James Reaney, 1976; Vinson, J. (ed.) Contemporary Dramatists, 1977; Vinson, J. (ed.) Contemporary Poets, 1975; Woodcock, G. (ed.) Poets and Critics, 1974; Woodman, R.G. James Reaney, 1971. *Periodicals*—Canadian Forum October 1958; Canadian Literature Winter 1964, Summer 1969, Winter 1974; New York Times January 15, 1978; Poetry January 1960; Tamarack Review Winter 1963; University of Toronto Quarterly July 1959; Vancouver Sun October 17, 1975; Varsity January 18, 1960.

REED, ISHMAEL (SCOTT) (February 22, 1938–), American novelist and poet, was born in Chattanooga, Tennessee, the son of Bennie Stephen Reed, an auto worker, and the former Thelma Coleman. He grew up in Buffalo, New York, and in 1956, after high school, attended night classes at the University of Buffalo. A short story he wrote then so impressed his teachers that special arrangements were made for him to become a full-time student at the University. Reed was soon bored, however, and left in 1960 in his junior year. During the next five years he worked on newspapers in Buffalo and in Newark, N.J., and spent some time as a struggling writer in New York City. He says that he "learned to write in New York City and wised up in Berkeley, California," where he now lives.

ISHMAEL REED

Reed has taught intermittently at the University of California, Berkeley, since 1968. He lectured at the University of Washington, Seattle in 1969 and was a visiting professor at the State University of New York, Buffalo, in 1975. In 1971 he joined the Yardbird Publishing Corporation as editorial vice-president, and he is a director of the Reed, Cannon, and Johnson Communications Company.

It is with Reed that the *Norton Anthology of Poetry* concludes a survey that begins with Chaucer and, as Alan Friedman has observed, "whether he likes it or not, Ishmael Reed has for some time now occupied a black outpost in a white landscape." According to Addison Gayle Jr., "Reed is our most important black satirist, and his lineage may be traced to the satirists of the 1920s—to Rudolph Fisher, George Schuyler and Wallace Thurman. However, his milieu encompasses far more than theirs, his range is far greater. A warrior against rationalism, science and technology, he also inveighs against politics, religion, and schism in the ranks of Blacks." Indeed, as Robert Scholes points out, "whoever called him Ishmael picked the right name. His hand is against every man's—and every woman's too. . . . He is a black Juvenal."

Reed's first novel, *The Free-Lance Pallbearers* (1967), was originally conceived as a satire on politics in Newark, N.J., but ended by taking on the entire United States. The country of HARRY SAM is ruled by the obscene tyrant HARRY SAM, who is protected from his wretched subjects by a brutish police force and a vast moat of his own excrement. The hero of the story is Bukka Doopeyduk, hospital orderly and aspirant to the Nazarene priesthood, who is driven to rebellion when the rotting society he lives in destroys his marriage and robs him of his home and his job. He throws away his Nazarene (Christian) handbook and sets out to overthrow the tyrant. "The plot is thin to invisible," wrote Sara Blackburn, "but Reed's hero . . . serves as a weird telescope for a society that is terrifying for its violence and passive hypocrisy, yet somehow hilarious as well." And a reviewer in the *Times Literary Supplement* called the book "a series of wild, erratically linked hallucinations whose cumulative effect is unsettling and decidedly exhausting."

Reviewers of *Yellow Back Radio Broke-Down* (1969) differed as to whether it was a satire on Christianity, American rationalism, or both, but agreed that it was intensely funny and disturbing. The Loop Garoo Kid, a black desperado and voodoo worker with a cloven hoof, rides into the pioneer town of Yellow Back Radio, and finds that it has been taken over by its children; tired of being exploited by their elders, they have run them out of town. It is rather as if Adam and Eve had evicted God from the Garden of Eden, but their paradise is threatened by the powerful cattleman Drag Gibson (Jehovah?), and no one can save them but the Luciferean Loop Garoo Kid. L.E. Sissman found the book "often sloppy and adventitious," and was troubled by scenes of sadism and torture, but thought that Reed "writes splendidly in short and mainly expository spurts" and shows evidence of "uncommon talent and promise." Leonore Fleischer was convinced that "the elements of fragmentation, the puzzling shifts in language that Reed uses so brilliantly, the seemingly anarchic structure of the book are, in fact, part of a strictly disciplined whole." As the Kid himself remarks, "no one says a novel has to be one thing. It can be anything it wants to be, a vaudeville show, the six o'clock news, the mumblings of wild men saddled by demons."

The novel is all these things and much more in *Mumbo Jumbo* (1972), in which the preoccupations underlying the first two novels are spelled out in a worldwide, all-time myth. It seems that there are and always have been two opposed principles at work in the world. One is Atonism (from the worship of Aton, the sun god), which is rationalist, monotheistic, and militaristic; the other (deriving from the cults of Osiris and Dionysus) is animistic, magical, and intuitive. The latter has long been suppressed by the former, but in America in the 1920s a mysterious plague begins to spread upriver from New Orleans, threatening order, common sense, and the whole structure of Western civilization. The plague, known as Jes Grew, is jazz, black art, black magic. The Atonists mobilize their military arm, the Wallflower Order, under its chief agent Hinckle Van Vampton (Carl Van Vechten?), a villainous publisher who is also a thousand-year-old Crusader, and battle is joined.

Mumbo Jumbo, which was nominated for a National Book Award, is according to Alan Friedman "a book of deliberate unruliness and sophisticated incongruity, a dazzling maze of black-and-white history and fantasy, in-jokes and outrage, erudition and superstition. . . . though it's a novel, the author's method is not novelistic. Wholly original, his book is an unholy cross between the craft of fiction and witchcraft." And T.R. Edwards, pointing out how the cunning Van Vampton exploits the black intelligentsia's reluctance to value indigenous black culture during the Harlem Renaissance, wrote that "among all the other things it is, *Mumbo Jumbo* is an astringent commentary on an important and painful episode in the history of black consciousness."

Papa LaBas, the old hoodoo detective featured in *Mumbo Jumbo,* is brought in to fight the Moochers in *The Last Days of Louisiana Red* (1974). Louisiana Red is not a person but a metaphor for the way exploited people "oppressed one another, maimed and murdered one another" instead of working together against their exploiters. The Moochers are in the vanguard of Red's armies—the self-serving layabouts and hypocrites who grab and whine and lend substance to the lying history of blacks in America concocted by white men (with the connivance, Reed maintains, of black women). As Robert Scholes says, the novel is not only "a cartoonist's version of the last decade in Berkeley, California," but a sermon addressed by Reed to "other members of the Afro-American persuasion, telling them pretty much what Booker T. told them a while ago. He is not really speaking to the white middle-class. But he knows we are listening, and every now and then lets fly a verbal arrow in our direction." Robert Scholes called this Reed's best novel, but others thought it less amusing and more self-conscious than its predecessors, hitting out "in so many directions at once that it eventually self-destructs."

There was a very much warmer reception for *Flight to Canada* (1976), about Raven Quickskill, a black slave on the run in Civil War America from his remorseless master, Arthur Swille. This being a novel by Ishmael Reed, it would be foolish to look for a work of plodding or romantic historical reconstruction—Raven heads for freedom via Greyhound and Air Canada, and the past is fruitfully enmeshed with the

future and the wholly mythic. Reed's runaway slaves are scarcely more noble than the vile Swille—one of them, a pornographer and retired chicken thief, offers his services in newspaper ads as anybody's "slave-for-a-day." "The landscape Reed creates . . . is scintillatingly irreal," wrote J. D. Bellamy. "It is a world skillfully designed to allow the free play of a talent for hyperbole and downright yarning unequalled since Twain and for the impressive energy and stunning improvisations of an original and exciting comic imagination."

Ishmael Reed has said that one of the first important influences on his work was that of Nathanael West, but he has also learned from the techniques of television and the cartoon strip, vaudeville, detective stories, and the movies. He defends very seriously his notion of the black artist as black magician or "conjuror," working to lift the spell that holds his people in thrall in white America. For him, all art is a kind of magic, and can create reality as well as reflect it. Facts and arguments "can prove things forever, but most people live on the basis of the irrational."

The same aesthetic—black art as "Neo-Hoo-Doo"—is at the basis of Reed's verse. George Lamming, reviewing the selected poems published as *Conjure* (1972), wrote that his "tone and rhythm derive from the militant tradition of the black underground. But his is an unusual brand of militancy; it is much concerned with the politics of language. He argues for a clean, free struggle between the liberating anarchisms of the black tongue and the frozen esthetic of a conventional White Power: 'May the best church win/ shake hands now and come out conjuring.' " A later collection, *Chattanooga,* seemed to one reviewer "perfunctory, low-key, predictable, forgettable," but was enjoyed by Peter Meinke for its "engaging mixture of mythology, history, folklore, literary references and hip street argot." Meinke was reminded of Laurence Ferlinghetti, and thought that Reed was "not really as experimental or 'free' as he at first seems." *Nineteen Necromancers From Now,* the author's anthology of excerpts from experimental novels and plays by other "Neo-HooDooists," was received with a mixture of alarm and excitement.

Ishmael Reed has a daughter by his 1960 marriage to Priscilla Rose, which ended in divorce, and has since made a second marriage to Carla Blank. He has received awards from the National Endowment for the Arts (1974), the Guggenheim Foundation (1975), and the National Institute of Arts and Letters (1975). In 1978, having described his busy life as a publisher, teacher, and editor as well as writer, he told an interviewer that he was "becoming more and more non-ideological in that I believe work is an ideology; building things is an ideology. That is my ideology." A collection of Reed's essays, articles, and reviews was published in 1978 as *Shrovetide in Old New Orleans* and warmly welcomed by most critics.

PRINCIPAL WORKS: *Novels*—The Free-Lance Pallbearers, 1967; Yellow Back Radio Broke-Down, 1969; Mumbo Jumbo, 1972; The Last Days of Louisiana Red, 1974; Flight to Canada, 1976. *Poetry*—Catechism of D Neoamerican Hoodoo Church, 1970; Conjure: Selected Poems 1963-1970, 1972; Chattanooga, 1973; Secretary to the Spirits, 1975. *Essays*—Shrovetide in Old New Orleans, 1978. *As Editor*—Nineteen Necromancers From Now, 1970.

ABOUT: Bellamy, J.D. (ed.) The New Fiction, 1975; Contemporary Authors 21-24 1st revision, 1977; Conversations With Writers II, 1978; O'Brien, J. (ed.) Interviews With Black Writers, 1973; Vinson, J. (ed.) Contemporary Novelists, 1976; Vinson, J. (ed.) Contemporary Poets, 1975; Who's Who in America, 1976-1977. *Periodicals*—Black World December 1972, June 1975; Book World August 10, 1969; Books Abroad Spring 1973; Carolina Quarterly Winter 1974; Cavalier 70 1967; Commonweal January 26, 1968; Nation September 25, 1972; September 18, 1976; March 11, 1978; Negro Digest December 1969; New Leader December 23, 1974; New Republic November 24, 1973; November 23, 1974; New York Review of Books October 5, 1972; December 12, 1974; New York Times Book Review August 6, 1972; May 6, 1973; November 10, 1974; September 19, 1976; March 12, 1978; New Yorker October 11, 1969; Newsweek June 16, 1969; Partisan Review 2 1975; Poetry July 1973; Saturday Review October 14, 1972; November 15, 1975; October 2, 1976; March 4, 1978; Time October 21, 1974; Times Literary Supplement January 9, 1969; Twentieth Century Literature April 1974; Virginia Quarterly Review Winter 1973.

"REIS, RICARDO." *See* PESSOA, FERNANDO

*REVE, GERARD (KORNELIS VAN HET) (December 14, 1923–) Dutch poet, novelist, and translator, writes: "My life seems an odd mixture of a nightmare and a fairy tale. I was born in Amsterdam as the second child of Baltic-Russian (refugee) parents. After the nightmare of communist persecution—my lucky parents seem to be the only members of their respective families who escaped extermination in Lenin's starvation camps—soon followed the hardship of the Depression, while the darkening shadows of World War II forecasted new disasters. During the German occupation of Holland my father without hesitation joined the Resistance forces, was seized and got imprisoned, with both his sons, but by an odd mistake in the Nazi administration was never put to trial and, though next to starved to death in a German concentration camp, yet lived it through to see

*rā′ və

GERARD REVE

the Liberation of Holland. The Dutch queen honored his courage by awarding him, and therewith my mother, my brother, and me, the Dutch nationality.

"According to family tradition I should follow a military career. As though one revolution and one war were not enough, I was, as a young army officer, sent to the Dutch East Indies to fight the rebel forces, recruited from pure idealists and mere gangsters, which called itself the army of the Indonesian people. I did not like this war, either. Probably I was too human, or not human enough. Too tender an interest in the fate of a young Indonesian prince made captive by our forces but secretly released by me, an interest greatly increased by 'the love that does not' —or at least did not then—'speak its name,' cost me a seven year's hard labor sentence by a Dutch military court, to be served in a Dutch fortress in Holland. After one year I escaped to Belgium and remained hidden there in the monastery of the Frères de la Peine, where a former brother-in-arms had become a prior. It was there and then that I wrote my first, most revolutionary novel *De Avonden* (The Evenings), which upon publication in my country was attacked by the critics as revolting and immoral and nihilistic, but which met with overwhelming success then, and still is a best seller now, nearly twenty-eight years later.

"Reprieved by a revision of the court sentence, I could return to Holland, but I preferred to stay abroad, travelling, accepting odd jobs to stay alive, and taking up writing as a vocation.

"I do not know what literary school I belong to, though I am usually placed amongst the decadent-romantics, as I have often been compared to Gustave Flaubert, Jean Genet, or to Louis Céline; sometimes I have even been called 'the Dutch Nabokov,' or 'the Dutch Gombrowicz.'

"After derision and rejection, recognition nevertheless came during my life. Rightly or not, I am by now generally considered the leading Dutch writer of my time. Once kicked about and trampled under foot as a youth-corrupting queen, I lately was even bestowed a knighthood from the hands of her Majesty, our Queen Juliana.

"I do not know anything for certain, though I have my opinions. I hate the man-eating totalitarian madness of marxism, which seems so much in fashion today. I am a practicing Roman-Catholic, and I believe in God, but I do not know what He looks like or what is His specific gravity, nor what is His favorite religion. I hope to die while loving my friends, not hating my enemies, and detesting all superstition."

Most writers allow their biography to penetrate their fiction; Gerard Reve allows his fiction to penetrate his biography. The note he supplies above is a curious mixture of fact (date and place of birth) and fiction (the Balto-Russian parents, his experiences in the Dutch East Indies), and also a good example of the myth-making with which he deliberately surrounds his life and work. His frequent name changes are also bound up with this process. Born as Gerard Kornelis van het Reve, he published his first book under the semi-pseudonym of Simon van het Reve. Later he reverted to Gerard Kornelis—hyphenated for a while—until he was received into the Roman Catholic Church, when he added Franciscus to his given names. Shortly after this, with a sidelong glance at the Marquis de Sade, he also adopted the title of Marquess, and was known as Gerard Kornelis Franciscus, Marquess van het Reve. In 1973 he simplified this baroque name with one bold stroke to Gerard Reve.

In fact, Reve is the son of Gerard J. M. van het Reve and the former Jacoba Doornbusch. His father was a journalist, and author of *Mijn rode jaren* (My Red Years), a memoir of his years as a member of the Communist party. Gerard Reve was educated in Amsterdam at the Vossius-gymnasium, a well-known high school. He spent the war years at a school for graphic design and in an assortment of jobs, and from 1945 to 1947 was a reporter in Amsterdam with the national daily newspaper *Het Parool*.

Reve's first novel, *De Avonden* (The Evenings), caused a great stir when it was published in 1947 because of the frankness with which it depicted the shockingly negative and aimless attitude to life of its main character. It is a novel with a deceptively simple structure, entirely without plot or development. It is an account in ten chapters of the way in which a young clerk, Frits van Egters, passes ten dull evenings from just before Christmas to New Year's Eve. Against this colorless background, Reve projects a minutely detailed picture of a life spent in total emotional isolation—a loneliness intensified by the general mood of postwar gloom. Frits van Egters tries desperately but vainly to establish some kind of communication with his parents and acquaintances, and hides his vulnerability behind a mask of callousness, black humor, and oddly stilted phrase making. It is a harrowing book, but its grimness is often relieved by Reve's sardonic sense of humor. This is one of the qualities which distinguishes him from the nineteenth-century naturalists whom he resembles in the dreariness of his subject matter and the precision of his observation. He also differs from these literary ancestors in the directness of his presentation. As R.P. Meijer has written, Reve "offers no explanations, no comments, no psychic key. He presents Frits van Egters in what he does and what he says, and in the reactions to him of other people." *De Avonden*, "*the novel of the postwar generation,*" is already established as a modern classic.

A masterly autobiographical novella followed, *Werther Nieland* (1949), and then two volumes of short stories—*Vier Wintervertellingen* (Four Winter Tales, originally written and published in English as *The Acrobat and Other Stories,* 1956), and *Tien Vrolijke Verhalen* (Ten Cheerful Stories, 1961). Thereafter, for some years, Reve concentrated on a new form of his own invention—a cross between letter and story and between reality and fiction. He published two collections of such pieces, *Op Weg naar het Einde* (The Road Towards the End, 1963) and *Nader tot U* (Nearer to Thee, 1966), both brilliant excursions on the themes of life and death, fear and despair, religion and homosexuality. These two books not only assured Reve of a very wide readership, but contributed a great deal to the liberalization of attitudes to homosexuality in the Netherlands. It did nothing to diminish Reve's sales that in 1967, after the publication of *Nader tot U* and an article in the journal *Dialoog,* he was taken to court charged with blasphemy: he had depicted God as a donkey with whom he would like to have sexual intercourse. The case was eventually dismissed.

Homosexual love, more often than not with sadistic overtones, continued to preoccupy Reve in the group of books that followed, along with the acute awareness of death that pervades all his work. The first novel in this group, *De Taal der Liefde* (The Language of Love, 1972), is shaped like a triptych: two chapters of fiction; then a centerpiece consisting of a number of letters about the writing of the book, addressed to the author Simon Carmiggelt; and finally three more chapters of fiction. This was the first time that Reve had tried to express the interplay of fact and fiction through the structure of a full-length book, and some critics found the result lacking in unity (although not even this managed to dampen the enthusiasm of Reve's devoted readers).

Reve returned to straightforward narration in the novel that followed. This was *Lieve Jongens* (Dear Boys, 1973), in which the narrator tells his lover about a boy he wants to give him on the principle of *revism*—the pleasure to be derived from enjoying someone else's pleasure—and entertains him with stories. These stories are told as eagerly and desperately as Scheherezade must have told hers—not because the narrator fears for his life, but in order to fend off the death of love, the onset of loneliness. It is Reve's most melancholy book, and stylistically a virtuoso performance which he has not so far surpassed.

Henk van Galen Last, discussing Netherlands literature in the *Times Literary Supplement* (August 11, 1972), wrote that the Dutch literary scene over the previous fifteen years had been completely dominated by three writers: W.F. Hermans, Harry Mulisch, and Reve, whose popularity with the general public probably "has a lot to do with the pleasure . . . [the public] takes in seeing bourgeois morality undermined." That Reve "has recently left Hermans and Mulisch far behind him in the public's estimation" is, in Last's opinion, due partly to his virtuosity as a writer, and partly to his talent for self-promotion: he "falls in with the latent anti-intellectualism of the Dutch people. He satisfies his public's longing to see the writer as a pitiable being: his much-praised feeling for comic situations bears out the impression of helplessness. This man, to whom nothing seems to come more easily than making his readers laugh, is at once an unfortunate and a searcher: in search of God and love—the homosexual variety of which he describes in scenes which would probably have struck the common reader as pornographic if the author had not succeeded in giving the impression that all those erotic gymnastics, like his drinking habits, were a form of prayer."

Not even Last, however, denies Reve's ability, and he is generally acknowledged to be one of the writers who in the late 1940s and 1950s gave the Dutch novel its new direction. In 1968 he

was awarded the Dutch State Prize for literature.

PRINCIPAL WORKS IN ENGLISH: The Acrobat and Other Stories, 1956.

ABOUT: Fens, K. De gevestigde chaos, 1966; Fens, K. (and others) Literair lustrum, 1967; Meijer, M. and Beckman, K. Gerard Reve (bibliography), 1973; Meijer, R.P. Literature in the Low Countries, 1971; Speliers, H. Gerard Kornelis van het Reve en de Groene Anjelier, 1974; Vestdijk, S. Zuiverende kroniek, 1956. *Periodicals*—Criterium 1948; Dialoog 1969; Podium 1947; Times Literary Supplement August 11, 1972.

"REVE, SIMON VAN HET." *See* REVE, GERARD

REZNIKOFF, CHARLES (August 31, 1894–January 22, 1976) American poet, dramatist, and novelist, wrote: "I was born in Brooklyn, New York. When I was almost sixteen, I was graduated from Brooklyn Boys' High School, then one of the best high schools in the country. The high school periodical had published some of my verse and I was eager to spend the rest of my life writing. Two or three years before my graduation from high school the University of Missouri had established a School of Journalism and, against the wishes of my parents and the advice of my teachers, I went there. They were very good to me there and, although just a freshman, the head of the school let me run a column in the local newspaper run by the school, but I soon found out that the primary object of journalism is news and writing secondary.

"The remark always used to explain 'news' is that if a dog bites a man that is not news but if a man bites a dog it is. However, I was not interested in a man biting a dog but only in the man bitten by a dog and, though I might have concentrated on 'human interest stories' as when I wrote up—and the school's newspaper printed —a story I had written about a Negro cemetery in the town (many Negroes there were too poor to have gravestones on their dead and in their local cemetery on the grave of a little girl they would just put the doll she had played with and on that of a boy one of his toys) at the end of the term I did not go back to that School of Journalism, still one of the best in the country.

"I was then almost seventeen and wanted just to stay at home and write but my parents would not have that and wanted me to go to college and take the regular academic courses and then decide what I wanted to do. But I was not interested in, or good at, some of the courses I would have to take such as science or mathematics. One day, as I was walking past New York University's law school, I remembered that both

CHARLES REZNIKOFF

Goethe and Heine had studied law and it occurred to me that I might too. I went up to the law school's office and got a catalogue and saw that the courses in law had only a couple of hours each school day and it seemed to me that that would leave me plenty of time for my own writing. I was just eighteen and eligible for admission.

"The New York University Law School had adopted Harvard's method of teaching law—the case-book method. The students were not fed the instructor's lectures but had to reason about the law from their books of cases; in other words, learn at once to think like a lawyer. I was soon involved in the daily and interesting arguments in class—preparation for which took me about six hours daily—and I found out that I not only had no time for my own writing but not even time or energy for thinking about it. After two years I wanted to leave the law school, although I stood second in my class with two honorable mentions as proof of it; but my mother persuaded me to stay just another year and get my Bachelor of Laws degree and I did, and then was admitted to the bar of the state of New York in 1916.

"I thought that a young lawyer would get little business, if any, and if I did not work for another lawyer and just rented desk-room I should have plenty of time for my own writing and, indeed, was soon at work at my verse at a desk. Harriet Monroe, then editor of *Poetry*, the first magazine to devote itself completely to verse, accepted two or three of my poems but did not get around to printing them right away. In the meantime, the United States had entered the First World War and I was subject to draft but, because of defective eyesight corrected by glasses, was listed for 'limited service.' However, I expected to be in military service sooner or later, and thought I ought to gather whatever verse I had written and still thought well of and have it printed myself. And I did. Columbia University had established an officers' training-camp that would also admit those listed for 'limited service' and I then felt free to apply for admission. I was admitted but before I had any actual training the war was over. However, I was not going back to my desk as a lawyer because tiring as I had found the study of law the practice of it was much more so: I felt it my duty to do the best I could for my clients.

"My parents were then in business and I found that working for them as a salesman gave me plenty of time and energy: we sold hats to large department stores and I had little talking to do—the buyers knew much more than I about what I was selling—and, besides, I had to wait at times for hours before the buyer was free to see me and so I was free to sit and wait and write.

"I had found the publication of the first pamphlet of my verse satisfactory not because of any praise but simply because it helped get that verse 'off my chest' and I felt free to go ahead: write as I liked and print what I wrote. It then occurred to me that I might as well learn how to set type and print my own writing myself; buy a press and get out my own books. And so I went to a school where printing was taught and bought type and a press, operated by a treadle, and went to work in the basement of my father's house.

"My parents, in the meantime, had retired from their business and, after a while, the great Depression of that period began. I had to look for a job and finally got one on the editorial staff of a publisher of an encyclopedia of law for lawyers. I found this much easier than practicing law because I was in fact merely a sort of filing clerk listing cases correctly under the statements of the law and even such statements seldom composed by the editors: they were more effective as quotations from the printed opinions of the judges. At this time, too, I made the acquaintance of two poets who had the same opinions about the proper writing of our verse as I had—all derived from the articles by Ezra Pound in Harriet Monroe's magazine *Poetry*. We agreed to publish our own poetry and we did. And now that I was earning a salary regularly, I married Marie Syrkin in 1930.

"My immediate superior in the publishing firm was an able and intelligent man but when he was sick for a while his superior took over. He did not like my work and asked for my resignation. When my immediate superior was back, I was rehired but I had lost confidence in the job. A friend who had become a 'grade A' producer of motion-pictures asked me to come to Hollywood and do research for him. I went and stayed there three years. The work took all day and almost every evening but I did not find it strenuous and had time for my own work at my own desk. When my superior left his job and I lost mine, I went back to New York. Here I did editing and writing for magazines that paid for my verse, stories, and articles and found publishers for my books—or rather they found me.

"In 1962 the Jewish Book Council of America gave me their award for poetry in English and in 1971 the National Institute of Arts and Letters gave me the Morton Dauwen Zabel Award for Poetry."

Charles Reznikoff told an interviewer that "when I was twenty-one I was particularly impressed by the new kind of poetry being written by Ezra Pound, H.D., and others, with sources in French free verse. It seemed to me just right, not cut to patterns, however cleverly, nor poured into molds . . . but [with the] words or phrases flowing as the thought." Long after the Imagists had dispersed as a school, Reznikoff remained faithful to their doctrines, and showed that Imagism could encompass urban subjects.

From the publication of *Rhythms* in 1918 to *Five Groups of Verse* in 1927, Reznikoff's subject remained the loneliness, small ironies, deaths and joys of the immigrant, the urban tenement dweller in New York. He placed supreme value upon clarity and precise observation, as in this untitled poem from the *Poems* of 1920:

> Trees standing far off in winter
> Against a polished blue sky
> With boughs blown about like brown hair;
>
> The stiff lines of the twigs
> Blurred by the April buds. . . .

or as in his deeply felt but unsentimental narratives of ghetto life, like "A Deserter" in *Uriel Accosta,* in which a woman, entertaining the handsome landlord, is surprised by her husband:

> She thought, One of the neighbors must have told him.
> She smiled and opened her mouth to speak, but could say nothing.
> Her husband stood looking at the floor. He turned and went away.
>
> She lay awake all night waiting for him.
> In the morning she went to his store. It was closed.
> She sent for his brothers and told them he had not been home.

> They went to the police. Hospitals and morgues were searched. For weeks they were called to identify drowned men.
>
> His business had been prosperous; bank account and all were untouched. She and their baby girl were provided for.
> In a few years they heard of him. He was dead.
> He had been making a poor living in a far off city.
> One day he stepped in front of a street-car and was killed.
> She married again. Her daughter married and had children. She named none after her father.

As one critic has suggested, it is as though "uncertainty, ambiguity, a clouded perception, the admission of things which exhorted or transcended the real, were a betrayal of the poet's responsibility." He understood the Imagist doctrine of "direct treatment" of the "thing" to be a call for precision, and more precision. Michael Heller speaks of his humility, "a desire that 'we,' as Reznikoff notes, 'whose lives are only a few words,' meet in the thing seen and not in the personality of the seer." In a review in 1921, Harriet Monroe, editor of *Poetry,* said that Reznikoff's poems were "as incisive as hokku."

These qualities found their place in the "Objectivist" movement founded at the beginning of the 1930s by Reznikoff, Louis Zukofsky, George Oppen, and others who shared their dislike of overly subjective and emotive poetry. In "Objectivist" poetry, Reznikoff said, the images were to be clear "but the meaning not stated but suggested by the objective details and the music of the verse." Reznikoff was among the contributors to a special "Objectivist" number of *Poetry* which was edited by Zukofsky in 1931. Zukofsky contributed a long essay ("Sincerity and Objectification: With Special Reference to the Work of Charles Reznikoff") which Reznikoff did not find very helpful. A year later Zukofsky included Reznikoff's play *Rashi,* some prose, and a poem in An *"Objectivists" Anthology,* which he edited from France. In 1932, Zukofsky, with Oppen, Reznikoff, and Carl Rakosi, founded the Objectivist Press, choosing as their first publication the *Collected Poems* of William Carlos Williams.

By the late 1920s Reznikoff had begun a serious study of the Bible, as well as of the Hebrew language and Jewish history. Beginning in the 1930s he published some powerful translations and retellings of biblical stories as well as verse plays on biblical and Jewish themes and long verse narratives like "In Memoriam" (1934). This "dramatic and moving sequence" consists of scenes from the history of Jewish persecution from the fall of Samaria in 722 B.C. to the Russian pogroms. Also, like so many of his contemporaries, as the Depression deepened Reznikoff wrote poems on contemporary political and social themes. His first novel, *By the Waters of Manhattan* (1930), traces the history of a young Jewish immigrant from Russia, Sarah Volsky, who works in the New York garment industry, marries, and sees her son Ezekiel become a bookstore owner in Greenwich Village. It was praised for its "simple, unassuming candor," but reviewers found "no great powers of characterization."

Reznikoff's legal training and subsequent employment with the publisher of *Corpus Juris* gave him a unique body of material to work with. The first result was *Testimony* (1934), a prose volume in which he selected and summarized, without comment, reports of trials from every state and from every year "since this country became a nation." The quality of his prose is remarkable, but his critics were unprepared for what Babette Deutsch described as Reznikoff's "cold impartiality" before "a sometimes disturbing, sometimes terrifying picture of human callousness." Reznikoff wanted the material to speak for itself, and to avoid unnecessary moralizing.

In the 1940s and 1950s Reznikoff continued to write poems, and to publish them in small private editions. He also turned his hand to other matters. He wrote a second novel, *The Lionhearted,* a spare but shrewd and effective account of the persecution of the Jews in twelfth-century England, centering on the trials and travels of a young medical student. Reznikoff also co-authored a history of the Jewish community in Charleston, South Carolina (1950); published articles on Jewish life in various American cities in the newly-founded *Commentary;* edited a two-volume selection of the legal papers of Louis Marshall (1958); and translated the tales of the German Zionist and writer Emil Cohn (1961). In addition, he joined the editorial staff of the labor-Zionist *Jewish Frontier.*

A major selection of Reznikoff's verse, called (like his first novel) *By the Waters of Manhattan,* appeared in 1962 with an introduction by C.P. Snow. Reznikoff's critics were quick to note that his poems were not "complex," allusive, or confessional, and that they stood in sharp contrast to the dominant poetic styles of the day. One complained of "rhetorical obviousness," and Stephen Stepanchev observed that Reznikoff's verse line was "loose and prosaic" and lacked sonority. But others, particularly his fellow poets, rejoiced in the discovery of a unique and original talent. "I was captivated," wrote Hayden Carruth, "enthralled, swept away—what *is* the word? Delighted, awed." Denise

Levertov praised Reznikoff's "rare innocence" of vision which made him "unafraid to say the almost-ordinary, that which of all things is most seldom really said; and to say it in a language bare of ornament, revealing its intrinsic music." Charles Tomlinson suggested that "it is this unexaggerated truth to feeling or to perception that makes Reznikoff's poetry memorable."

Reznikoff's readers were surprised, and some dismayed, by the publication in 1965 of *Testimony: The United States 1885–1890.* This was intended as the first of a five-volume history of the United States between 1885 and 1915 based on legal case histories. With this project Reznikoff returned to the materials of his earlier prose *Testimony,* only now he was employing a free-verse "recitative." Reznikoff's point of view and lawyerly objectivity were imperfectly understood, as was the basic proposition that a history of life in America could be told through the court records of its common crimes, violence, and accidents. The picture of America thus presented, especially during the Vietnam war, displeased some of Reznikoff's readers. William Dickey sweepingly called the book dishonest, distorted, evasive, and misleading; and Hayden Carruth concluded regretfully that "the language of this book is not poetry at all, but prose printed in irregular lines, and rather lifeless prose at that." Other critics, however, were moved, and R.D. Spector wrote that "like some disenchanted Whitman, Reznikoff sweeps across the country, examining its people and their violent activities. Placing ordinary details of the real world against grotesque behavior—rape, theft, and murder—he seems intent on telling us how we have gotten to be what we are. Straightforward, direct, his simplicity itself has the effect of a brutal metaphor." A second volume, covering the years between 1891 and 1900, followed in 1968.

Reznikoff's last major work in verse, *Holocaust* (1975), draws with the same kind of "brutally straightforward prosaicism" upon the testimony given at the Nuremberg tribunal of Nazi war criminals. His collected poems and verse plays are being published in several volumes. A novel, *The Manner Music,* was discovered among Reznikoff's papers at his death, and appeared in 1977. It describes the three years he spent in Hollywood in the early 1930s. At the end of his life Reznikoff's work had begun to attract a discriminating readership which had seldom been his through a literary career which extended over fifty-five years. He was a "passionate moralist," in the words of David Ignatow, "but also an artist in control. In short, he was a poet of the classical tradition, blessed with great gifts." Harvey Shapiro, similarly, wrote of Reznikoff as "an urban man describing his dark streets with a classical restraint. . . . Now Charles has his place in the anthologies. More important than that, he is honored by all the young poets of New York, of whatever school. They understand the integrity of his lines, forged in . . . [the] years of neglect. They honor a rhetoric that honors the city and its people by not doing violence to them, not exploiting them as materials for language; in the care and precision of his lines, people and objects maintain their own lives." Michael Heller has said that Reznikoff's "restraint . . . before the possibilities of language seems at once spiritually felt and, paradoxically, modern. It is a modernity diverging sharply from the subjectivity of much contemporary verse practice, particularly from the more popular surrealistic and confessional modes, yet it is astonishing in its power to do justice, exact justice, to contemporary life." And for C.P. Snow, Reznikoff "conveys, as sharply as I have ever seen conveyed in any writing about New York, the feeling of the lonely soul in the great city."

PRINCIPAL WORKS: *Poetry*—Rhythms, 1918; Rhythms II, 1919; Poems, 1920; Uriel Accosta: A Play and a Fourth Group of Verse, 1921; Chatterton, The Black Death, and Meriwether Lewis: Three Plays, 1922; Coral, and Captive Israel: Two Plays, 1923; Five Groups of Verse, 1927; Nine Plays, 1927; Jerusalem the Golden, 1934; In Memoriam: 1933, 1934; Separate Way, 1936; Going To and Fro and Walking Up and Down, 1941; Inscriptions: 1944–1956, 1959; By the Waters of Manhattan: Selected Verse, 1962; Testimony: The United States 1885–1890: Recitative, 1965; Testimony: The United States 1891–1900: Recitative, 1968; By the Well of Living and Seeing: New and Selected Poems 1918–1973, edited by Seamus Cooney, 1974; Holocaust, 1975; Poems: 1918–1936, edited by Seamus Cooney (volume 1 of the Complete Poems), 1976; Poems: 1937–1975, edited by Seamus Cooney (volume 2 of the Complete Poems), 1977. *Prose*—By the Waters of Manhattan, 1930; Testimony, 1934; The Lionhearted: A Story About the Jews in Medieval England, 1944; (with Uriah Z. Engelman) The Jews of Charleston: A History of an American Jewish Community, 1950; (as translator) Stories and Fantasies From the Jewish Past, by Emil Cohn, 1961; (with Nathan and Sarah Reznikoff) Family Chronicle, 1963; The Manner Music, 1977.

ABOUT: Contemporary Authors 33–36, 1973; Cooney, S. *introduction to* By the Well of Living and Seeing, 1974; Encyclopaedia Judaica, 1971; Hindus, M. Charles Reznikoff, 1977; Homberger, E. The Art of the Real, 1977; Kenner, H. A Homemade World, 1975; Penguin Companion to Literature 3, 1971; Seymour-Smith, M. Guide to Modern World Literature, 1973; Vinson, J. (ed.) Contemporary Poets, 1975; Who's Who in America, 1976–1977. *Periodicals*—American Poetry Review 5, 1974; Christianity Today December 9, 1977; Commentary January 1966, February 1977; Contemporary Literature Spring 1969; European Judaism Winter 1974–1975; Hudson Review Spring 1966; Jewish Frontier February, April 1976; Nation November 10, 1962; New Leader February 18, 1963; New Mexico Quarterly Spring 1964; New York Times January 23, 1976; New York Times Book Review May 16, 1976; Partisan Review December 1977; Times Literary Supplement October 1, 1976.

RICKS, CHRISTOPHER (BRUCE) (September 18, 1933–), English critic and scholar, was born in London, the son of James Bruce Ricks and the former Gabrielle Roszak. He was educated at King Alfred's School, Wantage. Ricks did his compulsory national service as a second lieutenant in the famous Nottinghamshire infantry regiment, the Green Howards (1951–1953) and the following year entered Balliol College, Oxford University, which gave him his B.A. with first-class honors in 1956, his B. Litt. in 1958, and his M.A. in 1960. On finishing his B. Litt. thesis—later published, in revised form, as *Milton's Grand Style*—Ricks left Balliol though not Oxford, becoming fellow and tutor of Worcester College (1958–1968), and a university lecturer in English literature. Beginning in 1960 he served as co-editor of F.W. Bateson's renowned academic journal *Essays in Criticism*, and he subsequently became a regular contributor to Ian Hamilton's influential magazine of poetry and poetry criticism, *the Review*.

Milton's Grand Style appeared in 1963 and was greeted in the *Times Literary Supplement* as a work of "clarity and wit," and "one of the most interesting books on *Paradise Lost* to have been published in recent years." Ricks was not "strikingly original," the reviewer thought; rather he was returning to "the best in eighteenth-century criticism of Milton," especially the work of Richard Bentley. The book also showed the influence of F.T. Prince, it was thought, and (in its search for ambiguities of language) of William Empson. These two critics differ markedly in their estimation of Milton but, though Ricks's own attitude to Milton is not made clear, it was said that his book "enables us not only to respect but also to enjoy Milton."

For the next five years, as well as carrying a heavy teaching burden, Ricks worked on his monumental edition of Tennyson's poetry. This appeared in 1969, at a time when British critics badly needed a properly annotated text to facilitate a revaluation of Tennyson, much of whose work had been dismissed by the pioneers of modernism. Seldom has a modern edition of a major poet been so highly praised. Ricks had worked under some difficulties: Trinity College, Cambridge, held important manuscripts under conditions which they then interpreted as "forbidding copying or quotation in perpetuity." In spite of this, academic critics—even those hostile to Tennyson—unanimously applauded Ricks's scholarship, his accuracy, and his generous and judicious notes. Edmund Blunden called the edition "superb," and Sir Charles Tennyson, the poet's grandson, declared that Ricks had "raised Tennysonian scholarship to a new level."

Ricks's critical biography of Tennyson followed in 1972. Its three-fold purpose, according to the publisher, was "to show what went into the making of Tennyson, the man; to establish the distinct power, subtlety, and variety of his poems along with the artistic principles and preoccupations that shaped his work; and to suggest the relationships between the man and the poet." As in his Milton study, Ricks tends to appeal to the judgments of Tennyson's contemporaries, and to reilluminate them in the light of modern psychological discoveries. And this time he had been allowed to draw freely upon the manuscripts held by Trinity College, Cambridge. He ends with a convincing endorsement of "Tennyson's unclamorous claim to the central humanity of a great poet."

The book provoked and provokes some disagreement, but once again it was received with universal respect. *Choice*'s reviewer called it "a major work of criticism and by far the best book on Tennyson since Harold Nicolson's revaluation fifty years ago. Always Ricks has his eye on the language, on Tennyson's use of words in profoundly creative ways, or on his unsatisfactory manipulating of them in 'Tennysonian' ways. Ricks shows how, in the finest poems, Tennyson's is an 'art of the penultimate,' the poems not concluding themselves but hanging suspended in some compelling inconclusiveness. . . . The criticism never dwells on the obvious, and by reconsidering conventional wisdom about the poems discovers new truth about them." And a reviewer in the *Times Literary Supplement* wrote that Ricks's "shrewd and sympathetic record of the facts of Tennyson's life helps us to focus more sharply on the distinctive features of Tennyson's work. . . . [Ricks's] intimacy both with Tennyson's normal methods of composition and with the unique processes which yielded certain individual poems enables him freshly to illuminate works as different as *In Memoriam* and *Idylls of the King*. . . . This compact but comprehensive study seems likely to remain for the foreseeable future our most useful and stimulating general introduction to Tennyson's poetry and life."

Keats and Embarrassment (1974) is a much more unusual and controversial work, and provoked a great deal of interesting discussion—one writer thought that it had claims to be regarded as the first truly phenomenological examination of a poet to be written by an Englishman. Ricks had set out to show that Keats was "alert to embarrassment" but frequently and delicately rendered embarrassing scenes and situations in his poetry; this willingness to offend against the sensibilities of his time in order to deal with important areas of human experience was brave —evidence of "his special goodness as a man and as a poet." Ricks's point, according to one rather hostile critic, was that we "need Keats's warm wetness because we, collectively, are arid, middle-aged and dried up. Only by braving the prickly heat of embarrassment can we recapture each other's pleasure and our own."

Ricks did not persuade everyone to share his own admiration for Keats, but his attempt was itself very warmly admired. Karl Miller thought that "for a man who was honorably alert to embarrassment, Keats could be very embarrassing: he was not loath to risk the reproach of vulgarity, and he has frequently incurred it. I think there is a difficulty here for the argument pursued by the book." But Miller goes on: "The essay brings us close to the occasions of the poet's life, as they are described in the letters and biographies and as they were translated into art. The use of the blush as an instrument for testing and understanding his art delivers some excellent results. The book has great energy, and great ingenuity." Jonathan Raban, likewise, called this "a dazzling book. It takes the most awkward and ticklish aspects of the poems at their softest and pinkest, and floods them with insights drawn from literature, psychoanalysis, sociology and medicine. . . . But he has . . . produced an unnaturally heroic, high-minded and altruistic version of the poet."

In 1968 Ricks went to the University of Bristol as professor of English. He left there in 1975 to become professor of English in the University of Cambridge. Ricks has made a number of visits to the United States, teaching as visiting professor at Berkeley and Stanford (1965), at Smith (1967), at Harvard (1971), at Wesleyan (1974), and at Brandeis (1977). He became a Fellow of the British Academy in 1975 and is a vice-president of the Tennyson Society. Ricks is prolific both as a contributor to learned journals and as a book reviewer in such periodicals as the *New York Review of Books,* the *Listener,* and the *Sunday Times.* He is also general editor of three important series: the Penguin Critical Anthologies, Penguin English Poets, and the Sphere History of Literature in the English Language, of which he himself has edited the second and third volumes. Ricks has two sons and two daughters by his 1956 marriage to Kirsten Jensen, which has been dissolved. In term time he lives in Cambridge, between terms in a cottage in Gloucestershire. He is an atheist and a member of the Labour Party. Ricks is cheerful in disposition, admired and liked by his students, and a highly articulate talker.

PRINCIPAL WORKS: Milton's Grand Style, 1963; Tennyson's Methods of Composition, 1966; Tennyson, 1972; Keats and Embarrassment, 1974. *As Editor*—Poems and Critics (anthology), 1966; Twentieth Century Interpretations of Arthur Ransome, 1968; A.E. Housman: A Collection of Critical Essays, 1968; The Poems of Tennyson, 1969; The Brownings: Letters and Poetry, 1970; English Poetry and Prose 1540–1674 (Sphere History of Literature in the English Language, Volume 2), 1970; English Drama to 1710 (Sphere History of Literature in the English Language, Volume 3), 1971; Selected Criticism of Matthew Arnold, 1972.

ABOUT: Contemporary Authors 9–12 1st revision, 1974; Who's Who, 1978. *Periodicals*—Choice September 1972; New Statesman October 6, 1972; March 29, 1974; New York Review of Books November 2, 1972; October 3, 1974; Times Literary Supplement September 20, 1963; April 3, 1969; August 25, 1972; April 26, 1974.

Sam Lambert

E. V. RIEU

*RIEU, E(MILE) V(ICTOR) (February 10, 1887–May 11, 1972), English translator, editor, and poet, was born in London, the seventh child and youngest son of Dr. C.P.H. Rieu, the erudite Keeper of Oriental Manuscripts at the British Museum and Professor of Arabic at Cambridge University, who spoke or could read twenty languages. Rieu was educated at St. Paul's School in London and Balliol College, Oxford University, to both of which he won scholarships. At Oxford he read classics and in the first part of the B.A. examination secured first-class honors, but in 1908 his health broke down, and he was forced to leave the university without a degree. This failure to achieve the academic success that had been predicted for him was a bitter and lasting disappointment and, it has been suggested, accounted for the somewhat forbidding seriousness of his demeanor.

In 1912, at the age of twenty-four, Rieu was hired by the Oxford University Press to extend its operations to India. He was to establish a headquarters in Bombay and branch offices in Calcutta and Madras. And he was to travel to Bombay via the old Trans-Siberian Railroad and Shanghai, there to investigate the activities of an unsatisfactory representative of the Press. Rieu made the journey—halfway round the world—in about six weeks, and dismissed OUP's man in Shanghai. During the next seven years, in spite of his youth and the obstacles and complications created by World War I, he went on to carry out the rest of his instructions. In 1914 he was married to Nelly Lewis, daughter of Dr. H. T. Lewis of Pembrokeshire, by whom he had two sons

*rē ü

and two daughters. Rieu served briefly at the end of the war as an officer in the 105th Mahratta Light Infantry. By that time he had become a chronic sufferer from malaria. A year later, in 1919, his illness forced him to leave India and return to England.

Rieu lived in London for the rest of his life, and in 1923 became manager of the educational department of the London publishers Methuen & Co. His first publication for Methuen was a school text which he himself had edited, *A Book of Latin Poetry* (1925), an admirable introduction that has remained in print ever since and is widely used. The following year he edited *Essays by Modern Masters,* and this also was widely prescribed in school English courses, as was its successor, *More Essays by Modern Masters* (1934).

The Tryst, a volume of Rieu's early poems, had appeared in 1918, but was not much noticed. This was not the case with his verses for what he characteristically called "youthful people," a collection of which was published in 1933 as *Cuckoo Calling.* Although Rieu was said to be personally "tense and stiff through much of his business life," he had a playful and even facetious side to his nature. His humorous verses are lightweight, but their charm has not faded with the years, as was shown when they were reissued with additions as *The Flattered Flying Fish* (1962) with illustrations by E. H. Shephard. According to Eleanor Graham, Rieu found his subjects "in the domestic affairs of home, family, and pets—or in a more exotic and fanciful world of unicorns, penguins . . . or flying fish." He was fond of long titles and short poems—"Night Thoughts of a Tortoise Suffering From Insomnia on a Lawn" reads: "The world is very flat—/ There is no doubt of that." Occasionally, as in "Cat's Funeral," a more somber note is struck. A reviewer in the *Times Literary Supplement* drew attention to the warmth of these poems, their dexterity and "pleasing fancy," and their "many incidental felicities."

In 1933, against his better judgment, Rieu accepted the post of managing director of Methuen. The world of general, as distinct from educational, publishing did not interest him or suit his abilities, and he resigned three years later (though Methuen retained him as academic adviser). Rieu's devotion to the classics had deepened over the years, and it had become his habit to spend his evenings reading to his wife from the works of Homer, Lucretius, Aeschylus, or Plato, not in the original but in extempore oral translation. In 1936, when he left Methuen, he embarked upon a prose translation of Homer's *Odyssey.* The wartime labor shortage returned him to Methuen in 1940, and his translation was further interrupted by his service in the Home Guard (in which he became a major), but Rieu's *Odyssey* was published by Penguin in January 1946. It was an immediate success, selling more copies than any earlier Penguin book.

Rieu felt strongly that foreign poetry should be translated into modern English prose rather than into verse, believing that successful verse translations are rare and fortunate accidents. This was the general policy he pursued as editor from 1944 to 1964 of the Penguin Classics. In his *Odyssey,* the first volume in the series, he sought "not only to give what . . . [Homer] says but to give it in his own way." However, too "faithful a rendering defeats its own purpose . . . if we put Homer straight into English words, neither meaning nor manner survives." Rieu, who commissioned Robert Graves to translate Apuleius' *Golden Ass* for Penguin, much admired the style of Graves's historical novels and modeled his own prose on this.

It was agreed that Rieu's *Odyssey* brought the Greekless reader closer to Homer than Chapman's verse translation does, even if Chapman's version is a masterpiece in its own right. A reviewer in the *Times Literary Supplement* said that "Rieu has achieved a compromise, admirably adapted to commend to the Greekless novel-reader of today on this side of the Atlantic this eternally fresh story." And Desmond MacCarthy wrote: "I had forgotten how easy it was for the Greekless reader to enjoy the two epics . . . until Dr. Rieu's translation of *The Odyssey* reminded me." Rieu's equally smooth-reading and accurate *Iliad* followed in 1950, and it has been suggested that the majority of English-speaking people today who know Homer know him through Rieu.

A member of the Virgil Society for many years and its president in 1951, Rieu published his version of the *Eclogues* in 1949 as *Pastoral Poems.* This was less well received than his translations of Homer. It was objected that, whereas in Homer the poetry lies mostly in the story, in Virgil it lies mostly in the treatment, and that a prose translation was therefore inadequate. In his introduction to *The Voyage of Argo* (1959), the last of his classical translations, Rieu wrote of Apollonius of Rhodes: "It is as a novelist that we must read him and analyse the characters he has created." It was generally agreed that Rieu had done this "to stimulating effect" in his introduction and in the "fluent and quite unstuffy prose" of his translation.

Rieu had been an agnostic all his life, and when it became known that he intended to make a translation of the Four Gospels of the New Testament, one of his sons is reported to have said: "It will be very interesting to see what father makes of the Gospels. It will be still more interesting to see what the Gospels make of father." In fact they made of him a member of the Church of England. And reviewers of the translation, when it appeared in 1952, agreed that Rieu had made "a faithful rendering of the Greek text" in "honest, straightforward English." Wilson Harris wrote that "it varies from the Authorised and Revised Versions sufficiently for the differences to make an interest in themselves, and not sufficiently to sacrifice what is best in those translations." In 1951 Rieu became a member of the Joint Committee selected to produce the *New English Bible,* a work that has been commended by some for its clarity and bitterly attacked by many others for its lack of poetry.

Success and religious faith came late to Rieu, but not too late to effect a considerable change in his personality. His "nature burgeoned," according to his *Times* obituarist, "and colleagues who had found him intractable came to feel far stronger affection as well as admiration for him. His curious walk, a crab-like gait with the left shoulder advanced as if defensively, appeared in later years at odds with the new confidence and geniality of his manner and propensity to joke." In fact, Rieu never gave the impression of being a man without humor, though his manner in dealing with strangers was one of courteous reserve. His recreations he listed as "carpentry, mountains, petrology."

Rieu received an honorary doctorate from the University of Leeds in 1949 and in 1953 was created a Commander of the Order of the British

Empire. He became one of the vice-presidents of the Royal Society of Literature in 1958. Rieu received the Benson Medal in 1968 and the Golden Jubilee Medal of the Institute of Linguists in 1971.

PRINCIPAL WORKS: *Translations*—The Odyssey of Homer, 1945; The Pastoral Poems of Virgil, 1949; The Iliad of Homer, 1950; The Four Gospels, 1952; The Voyage of Argo (Apollonius of Rhodes), 1959; The Word: A Synthesis of the Four Gospels, 1965. *Poetry*—The Tryst and Other Poems, 1918; Cuckoo Calling (for children), 1933 (revised with additions as The Flattered Flying Fish, 1962); (with others) A Puffin Quartet of Poets, 1958. *As Editor*—A Book of Latin Poetry, 1925; Essays by Modern Masters, 1926; More Essays by Modern Masters, 1934; (with Peter Wait) Modern Masters of Wit and Laughter, 1938; Essays by Divers Hands, Volume 29 (Royal Society of Literature), 1957.

ABOUT: Contemporary Authors 1–4 1st revision, 1967; Ward, M.E. and Marquardt, D.A. Authors of Books for Young People, 1964; Who's Who, 1972. *Periodicals*—New York Times May 13, 1972; Times (London) January 8, 1964; May 13, 1972; Times Literary Supplement March 23, 1946; December 28, 1962.

Consulate General of Denmark

KLAUS RIFBJERG

*RIFBJERG, KLAUS (December 15, 1931–), Danish novelist, poet, dramatist, short story writer, essayist, and journalist, writes: "I was born in Copenhagen as the only son of two schoolteachers. There were, however, two older sisters in the family and I grew up in peaceful and pretty harmonious surroundings, especially since the housekeeper had been with the family for decades and acted as a second mother. Instead of creating a complex, I have a feeling that a double portion of tenderness made the ascent to consciousness smoother for me than for most kids. Constant employment kept the impending economic crisis at bay in my parents' case and even if the depression cast heavy shadows over life in Denmark during the 1930s, the photographic impression of my childhood is fair. A backyard, fruit trees in blossom, constant play—although too frequent visits to the hospital made certain nightmares loom up unexpectedly and uncalled for.

"Although the German occupation of Denmark in 1940 did not have the traumatic dimensions of terror and misery that many other countries experienced, a nightmare larger than any other I had known moved into my life. The five following years were black, and a feeling of intense longing for change collided with a seemingly endless exclusion from light, travel, love, maturity. The horrors of life in an occupied country were clandestine, like a constant threat, and above all they created a general feeling of discrepancy: on one hand the willingness to act and resist in general mutuality, on the other a

rēf′ bjâ

craving for self-preservation beyond all loyalty. Claustrophobic and expansive like puberty, unendurably conservative and revolutionary, a time of transition with fixed and barbed frontiers.

"The liberation brought relief, but also a feeling of insecurity. As a thirteen-year-old boy I had, of course, no real part in the resistance, but still the postwar years underlined a sense of disappointment. Hopes had been high, people had stood together, and now the reconstruction of a well-balanced, democratic society suddenly became harrassed by the spooklike machinations of the cold war era—even an untrained observer could not help noticing that the older powers of reaction and isolationism were ready to take over where they left off in 1939. The world lay open but scarred, the struggle went on, but under the auspices of martial blocks like NATO, which Denmark became a member of in 1949. What had looked like a positive transference from catastrophe to catharsis drowned in political turmoil and global suspicion. Adolescence for me meant the Korean war, Senator McCarthy and my own country's fumbling ascent to economic welfare and mental self-satisfaction, a necessary social equalization, and a lamentable rise in national egoism and individual depression.

"I don't think I've always wanted to write, but some very active and inspirational school years instituted a lust for expression which was sharpened by the local and worldwide political and human upheaval. It canalized itself in a series of revues and articles and poems written and produced in cooperation with some talented school pals, who later found their fields in journalism, fiction, and political activity. We wanted a change and I think the substance and nucleus of all my writing since then has been a strong desire to combat stagnation and through a perpetual attack on conventionalism and *Spiesbürgerlichkeit* not only to keep the waters ice-free, but also to create a possibility for getting on in human relationships, to move up, to formulate a confrontation in a progressive way, even with the chance of losing face.

"This led to extensive experimentation in the theatre, in films, in poetry and in prose, and since my magazine debut in 1952 I have been constantly on the go, involved in literally hundreds of different activities, primarily under my own steam, but often—as in earlier days—with fellow writers, directors, composers, etc.

"After graduating from high school I spent a year at Princeton University (1950–1951) and upon my return to Europe found myself a 'dangling man.' The Danish academic milieu was stifling, and following a few years at the University of Copenhagen I functioned as a director of documentary films until the good-hearted editor-in-chief of the Copenhagen daily *Information* took me on and made me a critic-columnist, which I have been since then in varying phases of intensity.

"But first and foremost I am a writer and a poet, and it may seem evident from this sketch that the clash between childhood and adolescence, the engagement in and unlimited exploration of artistic and aesthetic means and possibilities have been my *raison d'être*. I have often been accused of chronic puberty but always take this as a compliment. To me life is change and development without compromise—and without sacrificing and betraying what was there in childhood, in youth, in that beautiful and terrifying photographic past.

"I married in 1955 and live south of Copenhagen in an old village school with my wife and three children."

Klaus Rifbjerg is the best-known and most influential writer of his generation in Denmark. His productivity is extraordinary and in the opinion of many critics excessive: his first book appeared in 1956, and between then and the end of 1975 he had published seventeen novels, eleven volumes of poetry, six plays, four collections of short stories, and innumerable newspaper articles and essays, as well as several film scenarios and musical revues. Rifbjerg is as versatile as he is prolific. On the one hand his "perpetual attack on conventionalism" has involved him in all kinds of modernistic experiments, especially in his poetry; on the other, his passion

for communication, for "getting on in human relationships," has led him to explore such popular forms of expression as that involved in *Rifbjerg's lytterroman* (Rifbjerg's Listener Novel, 1972), which is based on conversations with radio listeners during a phone-in program. His own life-style is equally contradictory—according to his biographer Torben Brostrøm he is "a socialist with large profits, an anti-Franco demonstrator who vacations annually in inexpensive Spain, a pacifist and a bullfight lover, an unintelligible modernist and a bestselling author, a Puritan and a gastronome."

Rifbjerg's first collection of poetry was *Under vejr med mig selv* (Getting Wind of Myself, 1956), in which he describes his middle-class progress from conception to marriage in radical and entertaining terms—he was, he notes, a "poseur from the start." However, the mood of this first book was almost idyllic compared to *Efterkrig* (Postwar, 1957), in which a hunger for life conflicts with a fear of death, powerful sexual drives with anxieties about impotence—the kind of unresolved tension that has characterized all of Rifbjerg's work since.

Konfrontation (Confrontation), published in 1960, remains the most famous of his poetry collections. The intention in these poems and prose poems, Rifbjerg said, was "to stand up in front of things and let them work on you." An outsider in an unreal world, the poet seeks to apprehend reality through direct sensory experience of the Now (which, however, disappears into the past as it is grasped). According to Hans-Jørgen Nielsen, "confrontation" became a key word for Danish modernists: "It lacked the political undertones which it has since acquired, being taken to mean something like the encounter of an unprepared consciousness with every aspect of a fragmented and ravaged modern life. This confrontation was mirrored in complex poems, full of attitudes and experiences of conflict." The content of these poems is reflected in their style, in which words are linked in surprising and disturbing new combinations. *Konfrontation* is a major text in the development of Danish modernism.

Rifbjerg employs the same technique of "confrontation" in the private, obscure, and often apparently incomplete poems of *Camouflage* (1961) in an attempt to strip away the disguises of his childhood. Rifbjerg has said that in this collection he sought "through a conjuring, lyrical-ecstatic method to reestablish contact with the lost past and, taking as one's starting point inklings and suggestions about kindred connections, to construct a transcendental universe of greater reality than the one the contemporary

693

person experiences through his matter-of-fact relationship to the so-called ordinary world." This "transcendental universe of greater reality" Rifbjerg has never ceased to strive after.

Some of Rifbjerg's experiments evidently derive from his work as a film director. The poems collected in *Portraet* (1963), for example, are characterized by their abandonment of a central perspective, abrupt changes of angle, sudden close-ups. These troubled poems deal with the difficulty of relating to another human being, and the search for the true inner self that Jung called the *anima*. Full of images of the Fall, they mark a period of crisis in the poet's life, and for the moment an end to his modernistic experiments. When Rifbjerg returned to the theme of his childhood in the Copenhagen district of Amager in *Amagerdigte* (Amager Poems, 1965) he wrote under the influence of the Swedish *nya enkelheten* (new simplicity) in a style that was altogether more detached, direct, and even banal.

According to Charlotte Schiander Gray in *Books Abroad* (Winter 1975), "the basic subject for Rifbjerg's investigations is inevitably the identity problem—the origin of the human being, his formative stages and his further development into adulthood. Whereas Rifbjerg's poetry often goes back to prepuberty and to preconscious stages, his novels focus on puberty and adulthood. To Rifbjerg, the biological age of puberty coincides with the historical postwar period; this was partly Rifbjerg's own age of puberty and, furthermore, here two ages resemble each other in their uncertainty and their potential for damage. Many works take place in the late 1940s and 1950s. While childhood is normally described in positive terms as the age of openness, immediacy and authenticity of feeling, adulthood is the time when these values are lost."

This is true of Rifbjerg's lyrical first novel, *Den kroniske uskyld* (Chronic Innocence, 1958), a book which is already established as something of a classic. It is the story of two boys: Janus, the narrator, and Tore, his friend and idol. Janus enters the adult world of compromise and guilt, but Tore remains chaste and is an easy prey for the corrupting wiles of his girlfriend's "vampire-mother": he cannot bear the burden of goodness and innocence that Janus and others place upon him. Some critics have pointed out that the novel can be read in Jungian terms if the other main characters are seen as aspects of Janus's own psyche: the Tore aspect is destroyed because Janus fails to integrate these disparate elements within himself.

The pitfalls of adult life are explored in a num-

ber of Rifbjerg's novels. *Operaelskeren* (The Opera Lover, 1966) is presented as the diary of a mathematician who represses anything in his nature smacking of the irrational or intuitive. The title is ambiguous—the diarist is devoted to the opera and has a singer as a mistress, but as a lover he is himself operatical and artificial. *Anna (jeg) Anna* (Anna (I) Anna, 1969), which was written as a radio serial, is about an ambassador's wife from a working-class background who stifles her sense of guilt at living out an "imperialist" role. She becomes possessed by an urge to murder her small daughter—a disguised attempt to obliterate her own inner self—and is only made whole when she meets her *animus* in the shape of a young criminal and runs off with him. The book is written with great vigor and humor, with passages of lyrical beauty, and is one of the most successful of Rifbjerg's novels. Charlotte Schiander Gray found in it evidence that Rifbjerg "is moving from his earlier existentialism toward greater social and political involvement. The identity problem remains the core of Rifbjerg's writing ... but the lyrical 'I' from Rifbjerg's earlier production is now, with the novels, seen in a social and political context."

Indeed, several of Rifbjerg's recent novels are concerned with actual events and institutions in present-day Denmark, often with little or no attempt to disguise names or places. These may be seen as evidence of Rifbjerg's "chronic puberty," his vast enjoyment of his role as Denmark's *enfant terrible*. He has become something of a myth, a fact he does not hesitate to acknowledge in the poem collection *Mytologi* (Mythology, 1970), with its portraits of celebrated figures from history and literature. At the same time, Rifbjerg's growing concern for the anonymous masses is evident, for example, in the poems of *Scener fra det daglige liv* (Scenes From Daily Life, 1973), and in his novel about an ordinary middle-aged housewife whose name and address provide its title: *Lena Jørgensen, Klintevej 4, 2650 Hvidovre* (1971). Rifbjerg has also written a travel book about Spain, *Til Spanien* (To Spain, 1971) and a novel with a Spanish setting, *Dilettanterne* (The Dilettantes, 1973).

Rifbjerg began his theatrical career in the early 1960s, when with various collaborators he wrote a series of musical revues satirizing the commercialism of postwar Denmark and the failure of the Social Democratic Party to institute democratic socialism. His first major success in the theatre was *Udviklinger* (translated by Pat Shaw as *Developments*) and staged by Ingmar Bergman in 1965 at the Royal Dramatic Theatre in Stockholm. A play for "four jazz musicians, four actors, and a small theatre," it expresses Rifbjerg's conviction that the individual must reject preconceptions about life and about his own role in it, retaining his freedom to develop as events and relationships dictate. This message is underlined by the play's form, which calls for the audience's participation in its development and conclusion. The best of Rifbjerg's subsequent plays is *Narrene* (Fools, 1971), an allegory about the state of contemporary Denmark with a fairy-tale setting

The author, the son of Thorvald and Lilly Rifbjerg, is married to the former Inge Gerner. He wrote for *Information* in 1955-1957, and since 1959 has been a literary critic and columnist for another Copenhagen daily, *Politiken.* From 1959 to 1963 he was co-editor with Villy Sørensen of the influential literary journal *Vindrosen.* Rifbjerg has received most of the honors and awards available to Danish writers, including the Aarestrup Medal (1964), the Danish Critics' Award (1965), the Danish Academy Award (1966), and the Nordic Council Award (1970).

PRINCIPAL WORKS IN ENGLISH TRANSLATION: *Play*—Developments *in* Modern Nordic Plays, 1973. *Poetry*—Selected Poems, translated by Nadia Christensen and Alexander Taylor, 1976; *Poems in* Modern Poetry in Translation 15 1973.

ABOUT: Bredsdorff, T. Saere Fortaellere, 1967; Brostrøm, T. Klaus Rifbjerg: En digter i tiden, 1970; Crowell's Handbook of Contemporary Drama, 1971; International Who's Who, 1978-79; Thorbjornsen, L. Klaus Rifbjerg, 1975. *Periodicals*—Books Abroad Winter 1975; Times Literary Supplement September 10, 1971; World Literature Today Spring 1977, Winter 1978.

*RITSOS, YANNIS** (May 14, 1909–), Greek poet, was born in Monemvasia, an ancient Venetian fortress town in the south of Peloponnesos, into a family of wealthy landowners. In 1922, when he was thirteen, his father was ruined by the Greek defeat in Asia Minor. This financial disaster was only one factor in the total collapse of his childhood world; the atmosphere of the Ritsos' decaying mansion, which supplies the central image of his great poem "The Dead House," had become one of disease and death. His elder brother had died of tuberculosis in 1921 and his mother died of the same disease a few months later. As a result of these tragedies his father became insane and was confined in an asylum, a fate which was to be shared some years later by one of his two sisters.

Ritsos spent his adolescence with relatives in the nearby seaside town of Yithion. In 1926, when he had finished his secondary schooling, *rē′ tsos

Greek Press and Information Service

YANNIS RITSOS

he went to Athens, which was full of destitute refugees from Anatolia, all like himself looking for work. He found employment for a while as a clerk in a law firm and as a calligrapher copying law diplomas, before he too developed severe tuberculosis. Ritsos spent three years in the Athens public sanatorium and a convalescent year in Crete; there were occasional relapses in later years. After his recovery he returned to Athens, working unhappily with various theatrical troupes as a dancer or actor, and later in a publishing house.

Throughout these years of tragedy Ritsos had found two forces to sustain him: the revolutionary movement, in which he has remained active all his life, and poetry, which has been his unfailing redemption, even at the darkest moments of his life when, haunted by death, he has come close to madness and suicide. He wrote his first verses at the age of eight, but originally was equally interested in music and in painting; he has continued to paint and draw, and has illustrated some of his own poetry. Ritsos is modern Greece's most prolific poet, having by 1975 published—apart from translations—sixty-seven books, most of them collections of poetry but some of them plays or essays. Peter Levi has described him as "the old-fashioned kind of great poet. His output has been enormous, his life heroic and eventful, his voice is an embodiment of national courage, his mind is tirelessly active. . . . One of the most brilliant gifts of this poet is the sheer abundance, the striking force and consequential rhetoric of his imagination."

Ritsos' poetry, intensely personal and frequently autobiographical, is equally bound up with the history and landscape of Greece. The

695

early collections *Trakter* (Tractor, 1934) and *Pyramides* (Pyramids, 1934) mix personal poems about his tragic family and his own humiliations with socialist poems condemning the decadent society in which he lived and calling passionately for freedom, justice, and the brotherhood of man. He found his own distinctive personal voice in *O Epitafios* (Epitaphios, 1936), in which a mother laments the murder of her son by police during a demonstration by striking tobacco workers. This elegy, written in the rhymed couplets of the folk *mirolói*, has remained among the best-known of Ritsos' poems, and became even more popular after it was set to music by Mikis Theodorakis in the 1950s. *To tragoudi tis adelfes mou* (The Song of My Sister, 1936) is another long elegy, very different in tone, recording his sister's decline into madness. It is written not in rhyme, like Ritsos' earlier poems, but in the free verse he has mostly used since.

In 1936 the fascist dictatorship of Metaxas was established in Greece. *O Epitafios* was burned by the new regime along with many other books in front of the Temple of Zeus, in a grotesque ceremony modeled on the Nazi bookburnings in Germany. Ritsos was unable to publish freely again until 1954, his work being banned throughout most of the Metaxas dictatorship, the German occupation (1941–1944), the liberation, and the subsequent civil war. Through all these years of political upheaval and personal distress, Ritsos' extraordinary productivity continued unabated. Even in his darkest moods he drew strength from the Greek landscape, the source of many of his images, as in the long poems *Eariní simfonía* (Spring Symphony, 1938) and *To emvatírio tou okeanou* (The Musical March of the Ocean, 1940). Here, as in earlier work, he takes up the theme of poetry as a bulwark against misfortune, but recognizes that the poetic imagination is rooted in the constancy of nature, of sun or sea. His work then and since has alternated between long, discursive, Whitmanesque poems and others that are brief, cryptic, and symbolistic.

His health made it impossible for Ritsos to join the guerrillas who fought the German invaders in the mountains, but he was active politically and fought with his pen, producing many poems that circulated clandestinely. When the leftist-controlled resistance movement was destroyed at the liberation by right-wing forces, aided by British tanks, Ritsos went into hiding. A great quantity of unpublished poetry, correspondence, and his only novel were destroyed in panic by the friends to whom he had entrusted them. It was at this time that Ritsos wrote *Romi-*

osini (translated under the same title by O. Laos), a magnificent tribute to the resistance fighters and all previous fighters for Greek freedom. William V. Spanos, who has discussed *Romiosini* at considerable length in the *American Poetry Review* (September-October 1973), says that in it "Ritsos's demotic imagination . . . metamorphoses a series of dead pasts into a living *presence.*" This defiant poem, whose title means something like "Greekness," could not be published until 1954. Several sections of it were later set to music by Theodorakis, and in this form it has become a sort of national anthem of the left in Greece. Peter Levi has said of this "astonishing sequence" that "stripped of its music, in fact, the poems . . . are even stronger, more rigorous, more direct and more terrible. If he had written nothing else, Ritsos would still be an important and even a great poet."

Ritsos was captured in 1948 and spent the next four years in the notorious concentration camps on the islands of Lemnos, Makronisos, and Ayios Efstratios. Even in detention he went on writing furiously, scribbling his poems on scraps of paper and burying them in bottles or tin cans until he could smuggle them out. During this period he gradually moved forward from the deeply personal lyricism of his early work to a more objective assertion of humane values in opposition to political injustice and social misery. This development can be observed in such volumes as *Paliá mazúrka se rithmó vrokhís* (An Old Mazurka in the Rhythm of Rain, 1942), *Dokimasia* (Trial, 1943), *O sintrofos mas* (Our Comrade, 1945), *O anthropos me to garifallo: Nikos Beloyannis* (The Man With the Carnation: Nikos Beloyannis, 1952), and *Agrypnia* (Vigil, 1954). The work of these years, which made Ritsos a hero of the left, did not escape criticism on purely literary grounds. Linos Politis, for example, wrote that the "broad torrent of his lyric language, which is the most characteristic feature and the chief merit of his poetry, is also at the same time its weak point. This current is often disproportionately broad and confounds the necessary with the superfluous, insists too much and sometimes does not avoid rhetoric."

Ritsos' release in 1952 and his return to Athens, celebrated in *Anipotakhti politeia* (Unsubjugated City, 1958), began what Peter Bien calls "a crucial period of happiness in his personal life and development in his artistry." In 1954 he married Yaroufalia Yeoryiadou, a doctor, and welcomed the birth of his daughter in the same year with "a small encyclopaedia of diminutives" called *Proino astro* (Morning Star, 1955). In 1956 he at last received official recognition, when *I sonata tou selinófotos* (Moonlight

Sonata, 1956) won the National Prize for Poetry. His international reputation grew quickly, he traveled abroad, and Louis Aragon eulogized him as "one of the greatest and most original of today's poets."

His output seems actually to have increased during the late 1950s and early 1960s, while his poetry grew deeper and more reflective. He turned increasingly to dramatic monologue as the form most suitable to express the intense meditation of the years of imprisonment, and he began to make great use of myth. He became especially obsessed with the Trojan War, that other prolonged conflict involving internecine strife, and since 1962 he has written a series of long poems about the war and the personalities involved in it, such as *Philoctetes* (1965), *Orestes* (1966), and *I Eleni* (Helen, 1972). Peter Bien has shown that "myth leads his work neither to evasion nor diversion, but to revelation," pointing out that his occasional use of anachronisms underlines the contemporary relevance of these ancient stories. In general, the long poems Ritsos has written since 1956 have according to Kimon Friar "become more structural in composition, the esoteric and thematic movements are better planned, the diction is stripped to more naked expression, the idioms are more colloquial, the themes shift from purely humanitarian concerns to existentialist problems of wider range. . . . Loneliness, death and decay are now among his basic themes, the dynasty of chance, the tyranny of necessity, the acceptance of the totality of life in all its incomprehensibility."

Ritsos' selected poems began to appear in the large volumes of *Poiimata* in 1961. He continued his political activities and was arrested for taking part in an Easter peace march from Marathon. When his friend the parliamentary deputy Lambrakis was murdered by right-wing thugs at Thessaloniki, he joined Theodorakis and others in a night-long vigil for the dying man at which *Epitaphios* was sung. Ritsos was arrested on the very first night of the colonels' coup in 1967 and sent back to the concentration camps. He was subsequently released because of ill health, but his works were banned once more until the dictatorship was overthrown in 1972.

The brief, harsh poems Ritsos wrote during the dictatorship of the colonels and since, full of dry wells and withered trees, black-clad old women and images of torture, are regarded by many critics as his best. Some of them have been translated by Nikos Stangos in *Gestures,* with illustrations by the author, and in a *Selected Poems.* Peter Levi, reviewing the former volume in the *Times Literary Supplement,* wrote: "There was a time when he shared with Éluard, to name a poet of comparable importance, the temptation to draw his passion larger than life-size, but his poems were always alive at the core, and now they are like small, bitter trees that have flowered":

Experienced words, dense, determined,
vague, insistent, simple, suspicious—
useless memories, pretexts, pretexts,
emphasis on modesty,—stones supposedly,
residences supposedly, weapons supposedly—door
  handle,
pitcher handle, table with vase,
made bed—smoke. Words—
you hammer them on air, on wood, on marble,
you hammer them on paper—nothing; death.

You tighten your tie. Like this.
Keep quiet. Wait. Like this. Like this.
Slowly, slowly, in the narrow opening, there
behind the stairs, pushed against the wall.

("The Meaning Is One"
translated by Nikos Stangos)

"These are not poems on an enormous scale," Levi writes; "they are more like the *Three Secret Poems* of George Seferis. One has the impression that they were similarly difficult to translate, since at certain moments they seem to swivel on a sixpence, the tone suddenly closes or opens or becomes thunderous, images are sensed and then thrust forward in the scope of very few words. . . . In 'Gestures,' the principal subsection of this book, something has dropped away, the poems are about ten lines long, but there is a terrible, ragged eloquence, the sense of a winter leaf held together only by its veins. . . . It seems no exaggeration to acknowledge that in these years Yannis Ritsos has become at last a great poet."

Ritsos has himself made many translations—from the Russian poets Blok, Mayakovsky, and Ehrenburg, the Hungarian poet Attila Jozsef, the Turkish poet Nazim Hikmet, and from anthologies of Romanian and Czech verse. He is also the author of the plays *Pera ap ton ískio ton kiparission* (Beyond the Shadow of the Cypress Trees, 1958) and *Mia gynaika pláï sti thalassa* (A Woman by the Sea, 1959). He now lives with his wife and daughter in a poor neighborhood of Athens, in a street called Koraka (Crow), still closely observing the life going on around him and still writing at a prodigious rate. His many awards and distinctions include, beside the National Prize for Poetry, the Grand Prix International de la Biennale de Poésie de Knokke (Belgium, 1972), the International Prize "Georgi Dimitroff" (Bulgaria, 1974), and the Grand Prix français de la poésie "Alfred de Vigny" (France, 1975). He has been nominated four times for the Nobel Prize, in 1973 placing second after the winner, Patrick White.

PRINCIPAL WORKS IN ENGLISH TRANSLATION: Romiosini, 1969; Poems of Yannis Ritsos in English Versions by Alan Page, 1969; Gestures and Others Poems 1968–1970, 1971; Selected Poems, 1974; Eighteen Short Songs of the Bitter Motherland, translated by Amy Mims, 1974; Corridor and Stairs, translated by Nikos Germanacos, 1976; Chronicle of Exile, translated by Minas Savvas, 1977; The Fourth Dimension: Selected Poems, translated by Rae Dalven, 1977. *Poems in* Barnstone, W. (ed.) Modern European Poetry, 1966; Friar, K. (ed.) Modern Greek Poetry, 1973; Modern Poetry in Translation 4 1968; The Review 21 1969.

ABOUT: Bien, P. *introduction to* Selected Poems, 1974; Friar, K. Modern Greek Poetry, 1973; Gianos, M. P. Introduction to Modern Greek Literature, 1969; Politis, L. A History of Modern Greek Literature, 1973; Seymour-Smith, M. Guide to Modern World Literature, 1973. *Periodicals—* American Poetry Review September-October 1973; Books Abroad Winter 1974, Spring 1975, Winter 1976; Hudson Review Winter 1975–1976; London Magazine February-March 1977; Nation March 9, 1977; New York Times Book Review July 10, 1977; Times Literary Supplement July 18, 1975.

ROCHA, ADOLFO CORREIA DA. *See* "TORGA, MIGUEL"

*ROCHE, DENIS (November 21, 1937–), French poet, translator, critic, and editor, was born in Paris, of Auvergnat and Cévenol descent. When he was six months old, he was taken abroad by his parents to Venezuela (1938–1941), then to Trinidad and Barbados (1941–1945), and finally, in 1945, to Brazil, where Roche received his first education from the Dominicans of Bahia. The family returned to France in 1946 at the end of World War II, and settled in a village near Alès, northeast of Nîmes. Roche continued his education there and then, from 1948 to 1953, at the Oratorian School, Juilly. Both his mother and his grandmother were poets (the latter writing in Provençal), and it was at this time that Roche began to read their work and to write his own first poems. In 1953 Roche went to Paris, where he studied philosophy for a year at the Collège Stanislas before switching to dentistry. He was a dentistry student in Paris from 1954 to 1962 but in the end, instead of qualifying, decided to write. Since 1964 Roche has worked as an editor in the fine arts department of the Paris publishing house, Éditions Tschou.

Roche's first small collection of poems, "Forestière amazonide," appeared in the magazine *Écrire* (no. 11 1962). It reflected his progress from the romantic and traditional poems of his adolescence to something like automatic writing, and he has explained that he strongly

*rosh

DENIS ROCHE

desired to separate himself "from all that pursuit of beauty or nobility in matters of form." The same year, Roche became a member of the editorial committee of the influential journal *Tel Quel,* founded in 1960 with the novelist and critic Philippe Sollers as its chief theorist. Roche's antipoetry is the product of a rigorously polemical approach to literature. His ferocious experimentalism is remote from almost anything that is being written in the United States or Britain, but it makes perfect sense in the intensely ideological atmosphere of French writing, and especially against the background of *Tel Quel.* It is from the position taken by the *Tel Quel* group that Roche has developed his own deliberately more extremist position, and the group has by no means disowned him.

The members of the *Tel Quel* group differ considerably from one another in their theories and in their practice, and even the views they do share have developed and altered through the free interchange of ideas between them. What they have in common, however, is a sympathy with a modified but atheistic neo-Marxism, and a vehement hatred and scorn for the habits of mind generated by bourgeois capitalism. Their chief characteristic is a desire to "desacralize" literature. They regard as their precursors Sade, Lautréamont, Roussel, Artaud, and Rimbaud, and among contemporary writers admire Roland Barthes, Georges Bataille, and the psychoanalyst Jacques Lacan. They assert that ultimately "a book expresses only itself"; they are interested not in the "content" of books but in the nature of language, and this gives them some affinity with the structuralists. They are "subversive" because in studying—and producing—literature they seek to "reflect the attention back on ourselves and our capacities, instead of deflecting it towards entities or things outside." Old-fashioned humanism and anthropomorphism—the pathetic fallacy—are their chief targets. They do not preach conventional revolutionary action: they consider that their act of writing is in itself revolutionary.

Roche goes further than his associates, declaring that "poetry is inadmissible, besides it does not exist," but continuing to write and publish his antipoems. C. A. Hackett says that most of Roche's work, "which resembles a vast bewildering collage, can be read, and enjoyed, as a parody—and pastiche—of every known style and genre of French poetry from the seventeenth to the twentieth century. Love, or rather eroticism, the main element in it, is parodied on several levels and in a variety of styles; but the intention is serious, namely, to deprive of all mystique and glamour the king of love which is the obsession of modern man and to show that it, like poetry and literature, is a *product* of capitalist society."

A collection of deliberately incomplete and often aleatoric pieces was published in 1963 as *Récits complets* (Complete Narratives). One of these has been translated by Edward Lucie-Smith in *French Writing Today* as "From 12.03 p.m. to 12.15 p.m. 3 February 1961":

Hands plunge in there with an estuary's boldness
Searching for marten's hair all the glossaries
Stripped to where the mountains strip
Without hoarfrost and the uproar
Of the countryside
You will really find the way of hanging things in
The air without any more houses or buses
No more towns nor ebb-tides nor trees nor stewed
   fruit
Nor friends
I am discharged all alone into the corps of the
   battledresses
Of the sky
Where I am going to have to fight for the one I
   love
Balloons bombs buildings a genuine far-off castaway
For once in my life I'm alone in the world. . . .

"The space-time of a poem," Roche says, "is above all that of the reader; it unrolls itself from the top to the bottom of the page. . . . The reader effects the transfer of energy from the poet to the reader." This news was not welcomed by the reviewer in the *Times Literary Supplement* of *Les Idées centésimales de Miss Élanize* (The Centesimal Ideas of Miss Élanize). He wrote that the book consisted of "an uninterrupted flow of lines of more or less equal length and, in the case of

the title poem, thirty-three pages of twenty-one lines each"; and he implied that he had been left feeling de-energized. Roche says that these poems were "composed with a deliberate wish to investigate the problems of writing itself." They were of the same length and in the same form "so that the reader will be solely preoccupied with what is going on inside the poem itself and with the language itself, continuously folding back upon itself."

However, it seemed to the British authors of *French Writing Today* that Roche's "structuralist camouflage should not be allowed to blind the reader to the underlying humour, erotic provocation and sly mythological-historical and literary allusion." These qualities became much more evident in *Éros énergumène* (Eros Possessed, 1968)—especially a kind of deliberately pornographic texture reminiscent of the later novels of Robbe-Grillet, as in this passage from "Théâtre des agissements d'Éros" (Theatre of the Doings of Eros):

The more accessible wheat of the painters was thoroughly pillaged when we stood up again.
What poetry, finally shoved into a hole of
Clay, dislikes the skirts from which cork-
screws are made?—'Would you grant me one
Delight, milady?—Oh yes, oh yes.—
To yield that pair . . . —I know, I know . . .'

It doesn't matter if I add court manners,
Spheres, Pulcinellas, or if I needed the
Swing itself as a token of puritan bilge,
Poetry, concerning a dairymaid, or the leap that
A friar would make upon her. . . .

(translated by Harry Matthews)

It seemed to C.A. Hackett that "the deliberate misuse of literary themes, allusions, and devices" in *Éros énergumène* was "so obvious and systematic that it ceases to be effective as an instrument of subversion. Until now, Denis Roche, an intellectual dandy, has played an equivocal game of affirming while denying, exploiting while undermining bourgeois literature and values. There is a risk, however, that instead of creating a new and revolutionary technique, he may become the victim of his own virtuosity; and, like the surrealists he despises, ironically have to suffer the 'récupération' . . . of his best poems in bourgeois anthologies."

Roche's next collection, *Le Mécrit* (The Miswriting, 1972), was published with an introduction by Sollers. A reviewer in the *Times Literary Supplement,* while praising other equally difficult French poets, called Roche's obscurity "that of the empty"—"M. Roche is more extreme than most: he positively *wishes* the weapon to blow up in his hands; and we react with a shrug, as doubtless we were meant to."

G. D. Martin finds Roche's observations on poetry more convincing than his actual poems. There has also been a great deal of praise for Roche's translations of Pound, Cummings, Olson, and others—one British critic thought it "remarkable how well M. Roche has translated them, considering his avowed contempt for poetry." Roche's novel *Louve basse* (1976) seemed to Michael Bishop like his poetry in that it seeks "to reconcile destruction with continuing, the compulsion to kill and perform the death and rotting of a certain mode of language already diseased ... with the desperate and *frightened* need to live the full potentiality of his own life, his own language." This resemblance between Roche's poetry and his fiction is natural in view of his "determined desire to negate ... everything which could be considered as separating poetry from all other literary genres or directions of research." The author has been described in *French Poetry Today* as "one of the most intelligent (and least loved) members of the [French] poetic avant-garde."

PRINCIPAL WORKS IN ENGLISH TRANSLATION: *Poems in* Gavronsky, S. (ed.) Poems and Texts, 1969; Martin, G.D. Anthology of Contemporary French Poetry, 1972; Taylor, S.W. (ed.) French Writing Today, 1968; Taylor, S.W. and Lucie-Smith, E. (eds.) French Poetry Today, 1971; Locus Solus III–IV 1961.

ABOUT: Ackroyd, P. Notes for a New Culture, 1976; Foucault, M. (and others) Théorie d'ensemble, 1968; Gavronsky, S. (ed.) Poems and Texts, 1969; Hackett, C.A. (ed.) New French Poetry, 1973; Jouffroy, A. La Fin des alternances, 1970; Prigent, C. Denis Roche, 1977; Taylor, S.W. and Lucie-Smith, E. (eds.) French Poetry Today, 1971. *Periodicals*—Critique June 1963; French Review October 1977; Littérature de notre temps IV 1970; Manteia VI 1969; Mercure de France May 1965; Nouvelle Revue française July 1, 1963; Promesse 22 1968; La Quinzaine littéraire July 1968; Times Literary Supplement August 4, 1966; January 19, 1973.

ROCHELLE, PIERRE EUGÈNE DRIEU LA. *See* DRIEU LA ROCHELLE, PIERRE EUGÈNE

RODITI, EDOUARD (HERBERT) (June 6, 1910–), American poet, translator, literary and art critic, and biographer, is the son of Oscar Roditi and the former Violet Waldheim. Although his parents were American, Roditi was born in Paris and raised in France and England, where he was educated at Elstree School in Hertfordshire, at Charterhouse in Surrey, and for a year (1927–1928) at Balliol College, Oxford University. Sidney Rosenfeld has given an account in *Books Abroad* of Roditi's "venerable

EDOUARD RODITI

Thomas Victor © 1979

family, which in its diverse branches settled eventually in Italy, France, England, Germany, and America." His ancestry is Spanish and Portuguese on one side, Greek on the other. His great-grandmother, who lived in palatial splendor in Istanbul and was a close friend of the Sultana Walideh, was according to Rosenfeld a member of the ancient Belinfante family, "famous for its learning and piety throughout the lands where the Torah is studied."

Perhaps because of this background, Roditi demonstrated from early childhood an exceptional sensitivity to the nuances of language, and he was precocious both as a poet and a translator. He made Greek and Latin translations of Byron and of Gray's *Elegy* at the age of twelve, and published French versions of Gerard Manley Hopkins and Stephen Spender when he was fourteen. During adolescence Roditi suffered from asthma, anterior temporal lobe seizures, and other mysterious "allergies to reality" that, he says, "repeatedly condemned me for long periods of time to a somewhat lonely, withdrawn life." At sixteen or seventeen he was obliged to spend three months in a Swiss nursing home, and there made an English translation of Saint-John Perse's *Anabase*. When he discovered that T. S. Eliot had undertaken the same project, Roditi sent him his version, and says that Eliot "even adopted a few of my interpretations and suggestions." Eliot also commented enthusiastically and at length on some of Roditi's own poems, but by then Roditi had lost interest in this relatively conventional early work and had become a convert to surrealism.

Roditi's seizures were characterized not by convulsions and unconsciousness, but by "deeply rhythmic intense hallucinations of unusually vivid colors and symbols." When he met Robert Desnos and other French surrealists in Paris in 1927, he recognized certain connections between these hallucinations and the surrealists' explorations of the unconscious. Encouraged by Desnos and others, Roditi began to experiment with "automatic writing." According to Edward B. Germain, he "recorded and organized a mythic, metamorphic land beyond nightmare—for its images do not invade consciousness, rather the other way around: consciousness seems to invade the dream, opening its shifting symbols to daylight exploration":

> The memory of my prodigious hands is like green waters that flow on the surface of the elements, and the shadow of my deeds is like the smoke of a burning city.

> My hands have held the ocean and the stars: the ocean with all its ships, the stars with all their centuries of space; and I have been Leviathan that swallowed eternity . . .

(from "The Prophet Delivered")

At Oxford in 1928 Roditi wrote the first surrealist manifesto in English, "The New Reality," which appeared the following year in *The Oxford Outlook*. It had little impact, and neither British nor American literary journals were hospitable to surrealist writings during the late 1920s and early 1930s. Surrealism nevertheless continued to be an important element in Roditi's poetry, along with work of a more conventional nature.

Roditi first visited the United States when he was nineteen, but went on living in Europe until 1937, when he returned to America and settled there for ten years. He went back to college, receiving his B.A. from the University of Chicago in 1939 and going on for postgraduate study to the University of California at Berkeley. Roditi has lived or sojourned in all of those parts of the world where his family's "diverse branches" have spread themselves, and in some where they have not. This cosmopolitanism is reflected in his grasp of languages. He grew up speaking English, French, and Ladino-Spanish, studied classics at school, and went on to become familiar with the languages, the literatures, and the visual arts of Spain, Portugal, Italy, Greece, and Germany.

He went to Germany as a student in 1930 and it was in response to the anti-Semitism he found there that he began the study of Hebrew and Jewish history and culture. These studies led to the composition between 1931 and 1938 of three elegies on Jewish themes. The longest of them,

"The Complaint of Jehudah Abravanel," first appeared in *The Jewish Review* in 1932. It is based on the "Elegy on Destiny" written in 1504 by Leone Ebreo, and concerns a great Talmudic scholar who in exile suffers the death of his son, but who is able to regard his arduous life of study and lonely old age as justified sacrifices made to preserve the purity of the word of God: "Fate has twisted this race like a turban/ about her mad head . . ./ but the word still lives." The three elegies were published in 1941 as *Prison Within Prison*.

Roditi spent the war years in the United States, serving at the French desk of Voice of America in New York. During this period he was closely associated with the surrealist magazine *View* and prepared his translations of the poetry of André Breton, *Young Cherry Trees Secured Against Hares* (1946). In 1945 Roditi left the Voice of America and, after serving for a time as an interpreter at the Nuremberg trials, transferred—still in American uniform—to the Allied Control Council in Berlin. In 1947, together with Alexander Koval and Alain Bosquet, he founded in Berlin the magazine *Das Lot*. According to Sidney Rosenfeld, this "journal of writing . . . during its three-year span of publication became a byword for literary urbanity and international orientation in postwar Germany. . . . After the ravages of the Hitler years it successfully undertook to help link Germany's literary life with the mainstreams of modern writing."

A collection of the poems Roditi had written between 1928 and 1948 was published in 1949. Edward B. Germain suggests that Roditi "is two poets, both evolved from the exhausted European romanticism he grew up with. . . . The conventional Roditi, encouraged and goaded by Eliot, began and remains elegiac, in cadence typically iambic, often end-rimed, becoming over the years slightly more lyrical, more rhythmically varied, enjambing more: a poetry of loss, loneliness, moral outrage, nearly always with an echo of literature in the lines":

> Lady, there's nothing more to say
> About your beauty that has not been said
> By other men about their other loves . . .

(from "Amare est amarum")

William Jay Smith in his review preferred this kind of "straightforward poem of statement" to Roditi's "quaintly surrealistic poems," but complained of "a great deal of singularly infelicitous phrasing." He thought that Roditi's principal theme is that of "the rootlessness of men forced to travel from country to country, from birth to death, from being to non-being." John Holmes, writing in *Poetry,* said "Roditi sees with a photographic eye, and a mind a little cynical, a little more compassionate, the lonely men and women, the ironic outcomes of love and effort, and the vast swirl of blind power in Europe and America. . . . His later poems are more edged, impatient, with the sense of modern man's complex and unhappy predicament growing"; in the best poems, Roditi's "ironic spirit, his international and cosmopolitan attitude, [is] something like Rilke's." The prose poems Roditi had written under the influence of the Paris surrealists were published forty years later as *New Hieroglyphic Tales,* and a fuller collection of his surrealist verse and prose (1927–1973) appeared in 1974 as *Emperor of Midnight.*

Roditi earns his living, he says, "as a simultaneous interpreter for international conferences, as a prose-writer or art critic, as a lecturer on art and literature, etc." He is the art critic of the French Jewish magazine *L'Arche* and a contributing editor of *European Judaism* (Amsterdam), *Antaeus* (New York), *The Expatriate Review* (New York), and *Shantih* (New York). The prose works of which he writes include a study of Oscar Wilde; a lucid and readable biography (in the "Great Travelers" series) of Ferdinand Magellan (1973); and a volume of literary essays, *The Disorderly Poet* (1975). His *Dialogues on Art* (1960) is a collection of interviews with twelve contemporary painters and sculptors: Chagall, Marino Marini, Giorgio Morandi, Miro, Kokoschka, Barbara Hepworth, Pavel Tchelitchew, Gabrièle Münter, Paolozzi, Josef Herman, Moore, and Fahr-el-Nissa Zeid. The *Times Literary Supplement* found this "a strange group of names, some being world famous and others little known. . . . Perhaps the interviews would have been more interesting and more successful if the author had been more ready to listen and less inclined to bore the artists with his own (often irrelevant) theories." Another reviewer, agreeing that Roditi sometimes "swamps his subjects with his own interpolations," thought that "despite these Socratic annoyances, the dialogues contain significant and often profound material found in no other book."

It may be that Roditi's greatest achievement is as what Sidney Rosenfeld calls "a mediator between literature and peoples." According to Rosenfeld, Roditi contributed in some measure not only to Eliot's translation of *Anabase* but to Salvatore Quasimodo's Italian versions of E.E. Cummings and to Paul Celan's German translations of Fernando Pessoa (of whose work Roditi has also made English translations). In 1936 he collaborated with Maurice Sachs in making French translations of the work of Ronald Firbank, and in 1953 he was the first to introduce Constantine Cavafy to American audiences. Roditi has also published English translations of Italo Svevo's *Confessions of Zeno, Pillar of Salt* by the French-Algerian novelist Albert Memmi, and *Memed, My Hawk* by the Turkish novelist Yashar Kemal. He has translated the stories of Ambrose Bierce into German and was responsible for many of the translations in the 1967 *Literary Review* devoted to Italian poetry. From 1956 to 1958 he appeared weekly on a French radio discussion program about foreign literature, and he has written a great deal about the art and culture of Sephardic Jewry.

Roditi received a grant from the Gulbenkian Foundation in 1969. He has a house in Paris and another in Tangier, but generally spends his winters teaching or lecturing in the United States. "Originally a Surrealist," he says in *Contemporary Poets,* "I have sought to broaden the scope of Surrealist poetry so that it can include elegiac, didactic or metaphysical poetry in addition to more strictly lyrical poetry. . . . I feel that my work now illustrates a very clear and positive evolution in the course of which I have achieved, as a poet, almost all that I have proposed to achieve. I do not feel the need to add much more to what I have already written, though much of my poetry of recent years remains unpublished, partly because I still may wish to correct it before publication." Sidney Rosenfeld writes that "as a poet and translator, as a critic and a commentator, he works, despite his acute sense of life's absurdities, to keep the world intact by keeping language pure."

PRINCIPAL WORKS IN ENGLISH: *Poetry*—Prison Within Prison: Three Elegies on Hebrew Themes, 1941; (with Paul Goodman and Meyer Liben) Pieces of Three, 1942; Poems 1928–1948, 1949; New Hieroglyphic Tales: Prose Poems, 1968; Emperor of Midnight, 1974. *Fiction*—The Delights of Turkey, 1977. *Nonfiction*—Oscar Wilde, 1947; Dialogues on Art, 1960; (with Will Grohmann and V. Zavalichin) Philipp Weichberger, 1969; Magellan of the Pacific, 1972; The Disorderly Poet and Other Essays, 1975. *As Translator* —Selected Works of Peter Takal, 1945; Young Cherry Trees Secured Against Hares, by André Breton, 1946; The Pillar of Salt, by Albert Memmi, 1955; Memed, My Hawk, by Yashar Kemal, 1961; Confessions of Zeno, by Italo Svevo, 1962; Art Nouveau, by Robert Schmutzler, 1964.

ABOUT: Roditi, E. *preface to* Poems 1928–1948, 1949; Vinson, J. (ed.) Contemporary Poets, 1976; Who's Who in World Jewry, 1972. *Periodicals*—Antaeus Spring 1971; Books Abroad Summer 1972; Furioso Fall 1948; Judaism Spring 1969; Kenyon Review Spring 1948; Poetry January 1950; Poetry Quarterly Spring 1944; Sewanee Review July-September 1950; Times Literary Supplement January 12, 1973.

ROTHENBERG, JEROME (DENNIS)
(December 11, 1931–), American poet and
theorist of poetry, editor, and translator, was
born in New York City, the son of Morris Rothenberg and the former Estelle Lichtenstein.
He grew up in the Bronx and attended public
schools there (1937–1948), earned his B.A. at
the City College of New York (1952) and his
M.A. at the University of Michigan (1953). Rothenberg served for two years in the United
States Army (1953–1955), part of the time in
occupied Germany. Since then, apart from visits
to Mexico and Cuba and travel in Europe, he has
lived in New York City, working as a teacher,
translator, publisher, editor, and poet. He was
an instructor at City College in 1959–1960 and
a lecturer in English at the Mannes College of
Music from 1961 to 1970.

Rothenberg has described the development of
his poetic ideas in *Revolution of the Word* and
elsewhere. By 1948, the year in which he was
seventeen, he "had been coming into poetry for
two years. My head was filled with Stein & Cummings, later with Williams, Pound, the French
Surrealists, the Dada poets who made 'pure
sound' three decades earlier. Blues. American
Indian things from Densmore. Cathay. Bible,
Shakespeare, Whitman. Jewish liturgies. Dali &
Lorca were ferocious possibilities. Joyce . . . The
thing was to get off on it, to hear one's mind,
learn one's own voice."

But all that, Rothenberg says, was the view
from the Bronx during the Depression and
World War II—he and his friends were behind
the times. "To us the news hadn't yet filtered
that the age of the modern, the experimental &
visionary . . . had passed: to be replaced by a
return to the old forms, to conventional metrics,
diction, a responsible modernism, liberal & reformist, rational & refined, & goodbye to the
madmen of language. Those were the first lessons of college days. . . . The images must be
inherited & the inheritance must be along the
lines of what was called the 'great tradition.'
Western. Christian. White."

Rothenberg himself did not join the "academic middle-grounders" for very long, and welcomed such innovators as the Black Mountain
poets, the Beats, the New York poets, the concrete and aleatoric poets, and others who "re-
explored the idea of an avant garde. . . . Primitive & archaic, esoteric & subterranean, non-
western & foreign, each had a part to play in a
greater 'great tradition.' " Rothenberg regards
all these groups and movements as manifestations of "a fundamentally new view of the relationship between consciousness, language &
poetic structure." His own contribution to this

JEROME ROTHENBERG

counterpoetics has been a sustained campaign,
fought on several fronts, to re-establish forms of
visionary poetry for the modern world.

Central to Rothenberg's poetic theories is the
notion of the "deep image." He says that as early
as 1952 he had begun "to sense 'Image' as a
power (among several) by which the poem is
sighted & brought close—a concern that developed quickly after 1958 and later in close workings with [Robert] Kelly, [David] Antin,
[Armand] Schwerner, [Robert] Bly, others." In
creating "deep image" poetry, he says, "the
effort is to draw things from myself, to draw
from things that I've experienced . . . to draw
from objects that have a real meaning for me at
the deepest level I can reach." The assumption
is that men are fundamentally in tune with each
other and with the universe, and that if the poet
digs deep enough he can reopen the connections
sealed off by the closed and logical thought habits of modern man. The intention is "an exploration of the unconscious region of the mind in
such a way that the unconscious [of the poet] is
speaking to the unconscious [of the reader]."

These efforts, and discussions with his friends
and fellow poets, along with the sort of early
reading mentioned above and further discoveries
in "Blake, Rimbaud, Neruda, Whitman, New
American & German Poets, Ancient Texts of
Lost Tribes, Aztecs, Navahos, etc." continued
the development of Rothenberg's theories. He
was led to a "reconsideration of the poem's roots
in, e.g. shamanism & to a growing sense of powers, new & old, of word & song & image still here
as keys for any man who reaches for them to-his-
limits." The modern American poet nevertheless differs in some ways from the shamans and

singers of the past. He has to confront the changes in man's awareness of himself brought about by the contemporary "revolution in communications & . . . easing of cultural and psychic boundaries that together produce an 'assault' of alternative ideas & forms." To project this "rush of disparate ideas & images . . . [modern] poets turn to every means afforded by language." It became clear to Rothenberg, moreover, that "the function of poetry isn't to impose a single vision or consciousness but to liberate similar processes in others."

In 1959 Rothenberg established the magazine *Poems From the Floating World,* which acquired a good deal of influence during its five years of life. It set out "to show the inter-relation between poetry written by some young poets in America today and some of the major aspects of European poetry"—to show that "poetry, in some sense, is transnational and transtemporal." At about the same time Rothenberg founded the Hawk's Well Press to publish innovative new poetry of the sort he values.

Hawk's Well, which survived until 1965, published Rothenberg's own first collection of poetry, *White Sun Black Sun* (1960), a "modest pamphlet," according to James Wright, containing poems "marked by a deeper exploration of imagery than has recently been the case among American poets," and including several poems that "genuinely blossom." In *Sightings I–IX* (1964), it seemed to A. R. Ammons that Rothenberg's method was "to make minimal means reverberate to the maximum. This can seem like straining both ways. But in enough cases the reverberations asked for are granted."

The Gorky Poems (1966) include some in which Rothenberg attempts to "transliterate" into poetry certain paintings by Arshile Gorky. James L. Weil was impressed by these and other explorations of the deep image, saying "I believe Rothenberg even where I can't understand him," and quoting with approval "The Pirate I":

> Wireworld, grey, frozen
> Remnant
> Bleak in the sandlight
>
> A cabinet
>
> Letting the light go, the
> Hidden light
> More preciously hidden
>
> Gold green, indented
> A graingrowth of gold
> A gold moment

> Melts with the candle
> Floods
> & quickly subsides
>
> Into centuries

In *Conversations* (1968), single short lines alternate between two different speakers, a form from which Rothenberg derives a wide range of effects and surprises. *A Steinbook & More* is an act of homage to Gertrude Stein—"accomplished performances of Miss Stein's music on the instrument of Rothenberg's voice," one reviewer called it, though another found Rothenberg's sensibility "too weighty, and not shrewd enough, to fit a mandarin style." Several of these slim volumes were gathered into *Poems 1964–1967,* in which Bill Berkson found "a gravity of intention and reference . . . hard to relax with, harder to enjoy." Berkson does not admire the work of Rothenberg and his colleagues, and wanted to know "why, if the so-called 'deep image' is so carefully attended to, does it always sound so flat?"

There was a more respectful press for the larger collection of Rothenberg's poetry published as *Poems for the Game of Silence, 1960–1970* (1971). "Silence is Mr. Rothenberg's grail," one reviewer explained, "but he does not set out on a quest for it. Rather, he lives in it and makes surrealistic noises symptomatic of its beauty" in poems which have "the kind of serenity found in, say, Japanese prints. . . . Most of the poems stand amid vast fields of white page—emblematic constructions where the method becomes the matter." John R. Carpenter was impressed by Rothenberg's versions of American Indian poems—"total translations" in which he sets out "to present what's essentially a sound poem," distorting words if the original does so, matching " 'meaningless' syllables with equivalents in our very different English soundings." Rothenberg's technical range is very wide, as Karl Malkoff has pointed out—he has used all of the new forms, including concrete and sound poetry, and breath-determined units of rhythm—but, as Malkoff says, "the approach is always in the interest of what Blake called cleansing the doors of perception."

In 1969 Rothenberg published *Poland/1931,* a collection of poems honoring the uniqueness of Jewish experience. He continued to write on this theme, and five years later published under the same title a larger collection in seven sections, in which the new poems are integrated with the old. One reviewer found these poems "sometimes violent, sometimes obscure, and usually oracular," marred at times by a use of language which draws more attention to the words themselves than to the feelings they are meant to evoke. This was a minority view, however, and this is perhaps the most admired and successful of Rothenberg's books. Robert Mesey called it "one hundred and fifty pages of lyrics, portraits, spells and events, myths and histories, novel-fragments, laws, and hymns," creating "an imaginary Poland full of real Jews, Jews dripping with sexuality, superstition, tenderness, prejudice, violence and chicken-fat, bringing their tormented and magical lives to the New World." *Poland/1931* has been performed as a mixed media event in New York, San Diego, and elsewhere. The most notable of Rothenberg's subsequent collections, *A Seneca Journal* (1978), draws on the two years he spent on the Allegany Seneca Reserve in New York State, and finds many parallels between that American Indian culture and Rothenberg's own Jewish culture.

Rothenberg has also edited a number of large didactic anthologies in which he has sought to illustrate and promulgate his theories. *Technicians of the Sacred* (1968) is a selection of poems, riddles, and proverbs, ancient and modern, from Africa, Asia, Oceania, and the Americas, designed to show that primitive poetry has as profound a relation to modern poetry as primitive art to modern art. Some scholarly reviewers were appalled: John Greenway in the *Atlantic* wrote that it "outrageously distorts already questionable translations of primitive literature to facilitate specious analogies with the obscenities and idiocies published in the far-out journals." But Rothenberg's intentions in this anthology were not scholarly but inspirational, and Armand Schwerner in the *Nation* welcomed it warmly as "a modern attempt to nourish the sundered spirit" and "one of the significant aesthetic documents of the postwar period." *America, a Prophecy* (1973), which Rothenberg edited with George Quasha, is a rather similar work, juxtaposing ancient and modern writings from the Americas in an attempt to show that American poetry is essentially visionary or mythic.

A Summoning of the Tribes (1970) and *Shaking the Pumpkin* (1972) are both anthologies of American Indian poetry. A reviewer of the "total translations" in the latter admired the way in which all the elements of this often cultic or communal poetry are made evident on the page —"the dance, the vowel changes, the pauses, the movement, the interaction between speaker and audience." *Revolution of the Word* (1974) is "a new gathering of American avant garde poetry" written between 1914 and 1945. *A Big Jewish Book* translates poetry and prose from the whole history of Jewry, from tribal times to contemporary America. Jonathan Colt called it "an in-

spired jumble. . . . a continually surprising and energizing work that extends the possibilities of poetic praxis—at the same time hinting, in its ecumenical vision, at a profound secular mysticism."

"In general," Rothenberg writes in *Contemporary Poets,* "I think of myself as making poems that other poets haven't provided for me & for the existence of which I feel a deep need. I look for new forms & possibilities, but also for ways of presenting in my own language the oldest possibilities of poetry going back to the primitive & archaic cultures that have been opening up to us over the last hundred years. I believe that everything is now possible in poetry, & that our earlier 'western' attempts at closed definitions represent a failure of perception we no longer have to endure."

Rothenberg was Regents' Professor at the University of California, San Diego, in 1971, and visiting lecturer in anthropology at New York's New School for Social Research in 1971–1972. In 1974 he went to the University of Wisconsin's Center for Twentieth Century Studies as a visiting research professor. From 1965 to 1969 Rothenberg was co-editor with David Antin of the magazine *Some/Thing* (New York), from 1968 to 1971 he was ethnopoetics editor of *Stony Brook* (New York), and in 1970–1976 he was co-editor with Dennis Tedlock of *Alcheringa: A First Magazine of Ethnopoetics,* published by Boston University. His translation of Rolf Hochhuth's immensely controversial play *Der Stellvertreter* (The Deputy) was produced in New York in 1964. Rothenberg received a Longview Foundation Award in 1962 and has had grants from the National Endowment for the Arts (1969), the Wenner-Gren Foundation (1969), the Guggenheim Foundation (1974), and the National Education Association (1976). He was married in 1952 to Diane Brodatz, and has a son.

PRINCIPAL WORKS: *Poetry*—White Sun Black Sun, 1960; The Seven Hells of the Jigoku Zoshi, 1962; Sightings (published with Lunes, by Robert Kelly), 1964; The Gorky Poems, 1966; Between: Poems 1960-1963, 1967; Further Sightings, 1967; Conversations, 1968; Poems 1964-1967, 1968; A Steinbook & More, 1968; Sightings I–IX & Red Easy a Color, 1968; Poland/1931, 1969; Poems for the Game of Silence, 1960-1970, 1971; A Book of Testimony, 1971; Net of Moon, Net of Sun, 1971; A Valentine No a Valedictory for Gertrude Stein, 1972; Esther K. Comes to America, 1931, 1974; The Cards, 1974; The Pirke and the Pearl, 1974; Poland/1931 (complete edition), 1974; A Seneca Journal, 1978. As *Translator*—New Young German Poets, 1959; The Deputy, by Rolf Hochhuth, 1965; The Flight of Quetzalcoatl, 1967; The Book of Hours, and Constellations, by Eugen Gomringer, 1968; (with Michael Hamburger and the author) Poems for People Who Don't Read Poems, by Hans Magnus Enzensberger, 1968; The Seventeen Horse Songs of Frank Mitchell, Nos. X–XIII, 1969. *As Editor*—Ritual: A Book of Primitive Rites and Events (pamphlet), 1966; (with David Antin) A Vietnam Assemblage, 1966; Technicians of the Sacred: A Range of Poetries From Africa, America, Asia, & Oceania, 1968; A Summoning of the Tribes, 1970; Shaking the Pumpkin: Traditional Poetry of the Indian North Americas, 1972; (with George Quasha) America, a Prophecy: A New Reading of American Poetry From Pre-Columbian Times to the Present, 1973; Revolution of the Word: A New Gathering of American Avant-Garde Poetry 1914–1945, 1974; (with Harris Lenowitz and Charles Doria) A Big Jewish Book: Poems and Other Visions of the Jews From Tribal Times to the Present, 1978.

ABOUT: Contemporary Authors 45–48, 1974; Leary, P. and Kelly, R. (eds.) A Controversy of Poets, 1965; Malkoff, K. Crowell's Handbook of Contemporary American Poetry, 1973; Ossman, D. The Sullen Art, 1963; Packard, W. (ed.) The Craft of Poetry, 1974; Penguin Companion to Literature 3, 1971; Vinson, J. (ed.) Contemporary Poets, 1975; Who's Who in America, 1978–1979. *Periodicals*—Atlantic February 1969; Hudson Review Winter 1960–1961; Kulchur 6 1962, 11 1963; Nation May 12, 1969; July 28, 1969; New York Quarterly Winter 1970; Parnassus Fall-Winter 1972; Poems From the Floating World 4 1962; Poetry December 1961, July 1969, June 1972; Prairie Schooner Spring 1962, Spring 1973; Trobar 2 1961, 11 1963; Western Humanities Review Spring 1975.

TADEUSZ RÓŻEWICZ

*RÓŻEWICZ, TADEUSZ (October 9, 1921–), Polish poet, dramatist, and short story writer, was born in Radomsko, the son of a minor official. He published his first poems in his school magazine in 1938, but his formal education was interrupted in that year because his father could no longer afford to keep him at school. After the German invasion in September 1939, he worked variously as a private tutor, a laborer, a factory worker, and a town-hall messenger, at the same time undergoing clandestine military training and publishing his poems through an underground press. Różewicz became a partisan and a killer of Germans and, though he himself survived, some of his closest relations died in the Resistance.

These appalling experiences were the great formative influence on Różewicz's writing. They left him disgusted with man and his values, and art itself seemed to him a self-indulgence, an offense against human suffering. Indeed, he has said that the moving force behind his poetry is "a disgust with poetry," which "had survived the end of the world as though nothing had happened." In 1945 nevertheless he entered the University of Krakow to study the history of art, and this was "no accident. . . . I did it in order to rebuild the Gothic temple, to raise inside myself that church, brick by brick, in order to reconstruct man bit by bit. I was full of reverential wonder at works of art (the aesthetic experience replaced religious experience) but simultaneously I felt a growing contempt for all

*rü zhā′ vich

'aesthetic' values. I felt that something had come to an end for ever for me and for humanity. Too early I came to understand Mickiewicz's *dictum* that 'it is more difficult to spend a day well than to write a book.' So I tried to rebuild what seemed to me most important for life and for the life of poetry: ethics. And because from my earliest youth I associated ethics with politics rather than aesthetics, my work had a political tinge, and 'political' meant for me socially progressive. That is why, despite my attentive apprenticeship with the masters of the word, I never took any interest in the so-called poetic schools and their market-place biddings concerning versification and metaphor."

These attitudes produced a "naked poetry" or "antipoetry" which, ironically enough, rapidly established Różewicz as one of the best known and most influential of Polish poets in the years after the war. His contempt for "aesthetic values" led him to express his despairing view of man with a radical simplicity and honesty, in a diction similar to prose, eschewing rhyme, meter, and often even metaphor, as in this merciless description of what the war had made of him (translated here by Konstantin Bazarov): "I am twenty/ I am a murderer/ I am a tool/ as blind as a sword/ in the hand of the executioner."

And since so many of the other promising talents of his tragic generation had not survived, he took on himself the burden of a dialogue with the dead—an obsessive theme especially in his first two books, *Niepokój* (Anxiety, 1947) and *Czerwona rękawiczka* (The Red Glove, 1948). Auschwitz, where the Nazis methodically stored the hair, teeth, and clothes of those they murdered, inspired such poems as "Pigtail," translated in *Faces of Anxiety* by Adam Czerniawski, who is Różewicz's regular translator:

> . . . Behind clean glass
> the stiff hair lies
> of those suffocated in gas chambers
> there are pins and side combs
> in this hair
>
> The hair is not shot through with light
> is not parted by the breeze
> is not touched by any hand
> or rain or lips
>
> In huge chests
> clouds of dry hair
> of those suffocated
> and a faded plait
> a pigtail with a ribbon
> pulled at school
> by naughty boys.

Seeking to free himself of all the ideologies and creeds that had shaped a world in which Auschwitz was possible, seeking to reject his own conditioning and remake himself, he writes sometimes as if he were seeing things and naming them for the first time. This is the case in "W środku życia" ("In the Midst of Life"), translated by Czerniawski in *Faces of Anxiety:*

> After the end of the world
> after death
> I found myself in the midst of life
> creating myself
> building life
> people animals landscapes
>
> this is a table I said
> this is a table
> there is bread and a knife on the table
> knife serves to cut bread
> people are nourished by bread
>
> man must be loved
> I learnt by night by day
> what must one love
> I would reply man. . . .

Różewicz has said that "the historical experience I carried away from the war, from the occupation, from immediate contact with Hitlerism and Fascism, pushed me towards materialism, realism, socialism, rather than towards metaphysics." For a time he sincerely hoped for a socialist humanization of the world, and his horror at the possibility of atomic war and his longing for peace helped him to identify with the communist cause. This is reflected in the more optimistic (and often sentimental) verse he produced between 1949 and 1955. He received the State Prize for *Równina* (The Plains, 1954). However, by the time of the 1956 "thaw" Różewicz was in the forefront of those pressing for greater freedom for writers and artists.

After his disillusionment with communism, Różewicz's vision of life grew even darker. And in contrast to Zbigniew Herbert, whose travels in Italy led him to seek spiritual values in classical and Renaissance art, Różewicz's visits to Italy, West Germany, and France inspired only a reaction against a "normal" way of life which seemed to him no more than a mask concealing the hideous face of reality. After 1955 he turned his attention from politics to human relationships, human suffering, and human evil. According to Czeslaw Milosz, "Różewicz, by drawing the inference that man is alone in a universe without metaphysical justification and that the only reality is his exposure to other men, hit upon (without realizing it at first) the central theme of French existentialists. . . . Choosing the Second World War as a touchstone for European civilization, he went so far in his despair over modern man's condition that even Albert Camus's existentialist ethics struck him as unfounded . . . He would be a thoroughgoing nihilist if not for the juxtaposition which, though seldom stated directly, permeates his whole work: 'normal' existence is negated in the name of a postulated 'full and authentic' existence."

Having written two plays as early as 1950, Różewicz then abandoned the form for almost ten years. He returned to the theatre with *Kartoteka* (1960, translated as *The Card Index* by Czerniawski, who has made English versions of six of Różewicz's plays), and rapidly established himself as one of the most prolific and influential of Polish dramatists. Różewicz is usually described as a representative of the "theatre of the absurd" or "theatre of inconsequence." His plays are concerned with psychological rather than physical reality; funny, bizarre, and surrealistic as they are, they conjure up a landscape of the imagination as desolate as that of Samuel Beckett. In this and to some extent in their form they resemble his poetry, which itself often tends toward dramatic monologue and dialogue. *Kartoteka,* in which a Polish Everyman lies on his bed and confronts a series of visitants from his past life, is in fact something like a poem divided among a number of voices.

Różewicz is no more interested in the conventions of the drama than of verse, and his plays often have little in the way of plot or characterization. *Grupa Laokoona* (The Group of Laocoon, 1961), portrays a civilization at the end of its tether through the ridiculously banal and aimless conversations of random groups of characters—a device which Różewicz first employed in the humorous pieces he once wrote for the satirical weeklies. *Świadkowie* (1962, translated as *The Witnesses*) similarly consists of three dialogues. In one, spoken by a newly married couple as the husband gets ready for work, the wife prattles on brightly about the "lovely little girl" she can see through her window, and it only gradually emerges that this "little angel" is torturing a kitten, blinding it, and burying it alive. Another of the dialogues is in fact two monologues, since the two men who chat together are not really communicating at all. And when something—a dog or a man—is knocked down by a car and drags itself in agony to their feet, they discuss it casually but never think of helping. Martin Esslin compares this "brilliant play," which has been widely translated and performed, with such "poetic masterpieces" as Genet's *The Blacks,* Ionesco's *The Chairs,* and Pinter's *The Dumb Waiter,* and says: "Once again the language is not just a straight expression of the content it relates, it is in a dialectical relationship to that content and emphasizes its horror by seemingly denying it."

Danced scenes and other innovations are introduced in *Wyszedl z domu* (1964, translated as *Gone Out*), in which a man slips on a banana skin, bangs his head on a statue, and loses his memory—a state of innocence altogether preferable to the absurd and seedy realities to which he must eventually return. This play employs a relatively large cast of characters; by contrast, *Smieszny staruszek* (1964, translated as *The Funny Old Man*) is the pathetic monologue of an old schoolteacher on trial before a court of dummies for molesting little girls. Różewicz's most extreme experiment in "antitheatre" is *Akt przerywany* (1964, translated as *The Interrupted Act*), which consists mainly of stage directions and the author's reflections on the impossibility of writing plays in such a time as ours, illustrated by scenes in which various dramatic conventions are explored and demolished; it has been performed with considerable success. *Stara kobieta wysiaduje* (1968, translated as *The Old Woman Broods*) is an apocalyptic vision of the world ending in a mountain of garbage. It has been called "the author's most pessimistic work" which, "through its ambivalence of meanings and its synthesis of the tragic with the comic, seems to complete a phase in his dramatic writing." Różewicz has also published several collections of short stories and has written screenplays in collaboration with his brother Stanislaw, a noted film director.

This biographical sketch draws on a compilation of published statements by Różewicz prepared on his behalf by Czerniawski. It includes this statement on some of the influences that have helped to shape Różewicz's work: "I am very often initially drawn to a man's biography, and then suddenly I become interested in his work as well. I became fascinated 'at first sight' with Wittgenstein as a thinker and as a man. My encounter with his philosophy and his biography was one of the most valuable and beautiful encounters in my spiritual and intellectual life. I search books and poems for practical help. I hope they will help me overcome despair and doubt, and strangely enough, I sought help both in Dostoevsky and in Conrad. Similarly I sought help during the occupation, and even before, in poetry. And when this led to disappointment—after all, these were only books—I became angry and disillusioned with the greatest works. I felt I was muddling things up in some way and yet I couldn't face up to this. Because I myself have always searched, begged for help, I began to think that I too may be able to help, though of course I also have moments when I feel it's not worth anything. Occasionally someone writes to me in a way that strengthens my convictions about turning words into practice."

Różewicz received the Literary Prize of the City of Krakow in 1959, the Prize of the Minister of Culture in 1962, the State Prize (First Class) in 1966. He is a Commander of the Cross of the Order Polonia Restituta.

PRINCIPAL WORKS IN ENGLISH TRANSLATION: *Poetry*—Faces of Anxiety, 1969; Selected Poems, 1976; The Survivor and Other Poems (this selection translated not by Czerniawski but by M.J. Krynski and R.A. Maguire), 1977. *Poems in* Milosz, C. (ed.) Postwar Polish Poetry, 1965; Wieniewska, C. (ed.) Polish Writing Today, 1967; Modern Poetry in Translation Spring 1975. *Plays*—The Card Index and Other Plays (*with* The Interrupted Act *and* Gone Out), 1969; The Witnesses and Other Plays (*with* The Funny Old Man *and* The Old Woman Broods), 1970. *Stories in* Gillon, A. and Krzyzanowski, L. (eds.) Introduction to Modern Polish Literature, 1964; Mayewski, P. (ed.) The Broken Mirror, 1958.

ABOUT: Crowell's Handbook of Contemporary Drama, 1971; Esslin, M. The Theatre of the Absurd, 1968; Esslin, M. Brief Chronicles, 1970; Giergielewicz, M. Introduction to Polish Versification, 1970; Gömöri, G. Polish and Hungarian Poetry 1946–1956, 1966; Hamburger, M. The Truth of Poetry, 1969; International Who's Who, 1978–79; Milosz, C. The History of Polish Literature, 1969; Raban, J. The Society of the Poem, 1971; Seymour-Smith, M. A Guide to Modern World Literature, 1973; Vogler, H. Różewicz, 1969. *Periodicals*—Books Abroad Summer 1972; Chelsea August 1965; Listener July 22, 1971; New Review April 1976; Polish Review Spring 1967, Summer 1970, Autumn 1971, Winter 1975.

*RULFO, JUAN (PÉREZ) (May 16, 1918–), Mexican novelist and short story writer, was
*rōōl' fō

JUAN RULFO

Bunny Adler

born in the province of Jalisco. A thin man with haunting, bright eyes, Rulfo speaks to an interviewer in the same mystically telegraphic style that he uses to such startling effect in his work: "I was born in what is now a small village, an agglomeration that belongs to the district of Sayula. But I never lived in Sayula. I don't know Sayula. I couldn't say what it's like . . . my parents registered me there." The section of Jalisco that plays an important part in Rulfo's work is a wretchedly poor and isolated region devastated by winds and heat, a land of the dead and dying. Rulfo himself is obsessed with the dead: he is a fanatical genealogist of his own family, whose ancestors came from the north of Spain around 1790.

Rulfo's father was murdered during the revolt of the *Cristeros* (guerrilla bands dedicated to Christ the King) which followed the break with the Catholic Church under President Calles. Six years later his mother died, but in spite of the abundance of Rulfos in the region, no one adopted him, and he was sent to an orphanage. He became an accountant, moving to Mexico City in 1933. Here he studied law, worked for the immigration service, processed impounded German ships during World War II, and from 1947 to 1954 worked in the publicity department of Goodrich Rubber. During the late 1950s he worked on television scripts and adaptations. Since 1962 he has worked at the Instituto Indigenista, an organization devoted to protecting primitive Indian communities and helping them to integrate more fully into Mexican society.

Rulfo is self-taught and was a late starter. In a sense, he is a literary anachronism in Mexico today; he has little use for the "masterpieces" of Mexican literature and despises the vaunted Spanish "generation of 1898." He admires Faulkner but prefers above all European authors like the Scandinavians Hamsun, Laxness, and Lagerlöf, the Russians Korolenko and Andreyev, and also Jean Giono and C. F. Ramuz, both like himself regionalists with a difference. He began writing around 1940 with an enormous novel which he later destroyed, because "the book was written in a somewhat rhetorical language that I was perfectly well aware of myself. That wasn't the way I wanted to say things. I started cutting down, working with simpler characters. Of course I went over to the opposite extreme, into complete simplicity. But that was because I was using characters like the country people of Jalisco, who speak a pure brand of sixteenth-century Spanish. Their vocabulary is very spare. In fact, they practically don't speak at all."

El llano en llamas (1953, translated by G.D. Schade as *The Burning Plain*) is a collection of fifteen stories about the peasants and Indians of Jalisco. It is a violent and despairingly callous world, its inhabitants crippled by their poverty, their ignorance, the climate, and the landscape. No one chooses his path. The girl forced into prostitution, the adulterers who drag the cuckolded husband on a pilgrimage which will kill him, the peasant revolutionaries who take to the hills and feel a savage glee at their brief escape from their grinding labor—all are prey to forces beyond their control.

These desolate stories are far removed from the detailed realism of the social protest novels which came out of the Mexican Revolution. Cruelly impersonal in tone, they make no judgments, political or moral; hunters and hunted, winners and losers, are all equally victims of the burning plain itself. With Rulfo, the pity is in the poetry of his lapidary prose—in the bare, intense, ringing phrases which are all that the parched landscape can support. These stories established Rulfo as a master among modern prose writers in Spanish.

Rulfo's style can be studied at its best in *Pedro Páramo* (1955, translated by Lysander Kemp under the same title). In this, his only published novel, he abandons realism and enters a timeless world of magic and dream. The opening is worth quoting in the original, for the cadence of this prose cannot be described or adequately conveyed in translation. It is an illegitimate son searching for his father who speaks: "Vine a Comala porque me dijeron que acá vivía mi padre, un tal Pedro Páramo. Mi madre me lo dijo. Y lo le prometí que vendría a verlo en cuanto ella muriera. Le apreté sus manos en señal que lo haría; pues ella estaba por morirse y yo en plan de prometerio todo." (I came to Comala because they said my father lived here, Pedro Páramo. My mother told me so. And I promised her that I would come to see him as soon as she died. I squeezed her hands as a sign that I would do it; she was just about to die and I would have promised her anything.)

The son, Juan Preciado, finds that Comala is literally a ghost town, peopled only by the crowding voices of the dead. The speakers had all once lived in Comala, had loved, hated, and hurt one another. But in death, as in life, each remains locked inside himself, pursuing some exclusive, unattainable, illusion. Juan himself soon dies also, but his search, and the voices, continue, unfolding the whole story of Pedro Páramo—landowner, despot, murderer, and sensualist—and of the world in which he lived and died.

The novel does not ignore the social evils of the pre-Revolutionary *cacique* system Páramo represented, but it goes beyond politics into the myths that the people of Comala live by. Páramo brutally exploited the peasants, but he was no less a victim than they, tormented by his hopeless love for a childhood playmate, destroyed by the vicious tradition of machismo, which forced him to stifle all that was humane in himself.

Dan Wickenden wrote that "a book as truly original as this one is perhaps bound to make special demands on the reader; because the man who wrote it is so notably gifted, it rewards those demands. It exerts, throughout, a powerful fascination; its episodes are vivid and haunting, its style is a triumph. Encountering Pedro Páramo in this altogether admirable translation by Lysander Kemp, Americans will understand why Juan Rulfo is regarded by his fellow Mexicans as the most eminent writer among them." Martin Seymour-Smith calls the novel "one of the most important and original books in modern literature in the Spanish language."

Rulfo, who takes no part in Mexican literary life, is known to be at work on a second novel, *Le cordillera* (The Mountain Range), which begins in sixteenth-century Jalisco. His influence on Latin American fiction has been very great, but he characteristically denies this, conceding only that his work may have called attention to the literary possibilities of ordinary speech. "So the person who writes that way is not influenced by *Pedro Páramo,*" he says. "He simply stopped to listen to the language he was talking, and realized of what use it could be to him."

PRINCIPAL WORKS IN ENGLISH TRANSLATION: Pedro Pára-mo, 1959; The Burning Plain and Other Stories, 1967. *Story in* Cohen, J.M. (ed.) Latin American Writing Today, 1967.

ABOUT: Anderson Imbert, E. Spanish-American Literature, 1963; Brushwood, J.S. Mexico in Its Novel, 1966; Forster, M.H. Tradition and Renewal, 1975; Franco, J. An Introduction to Spanish-American Literature, 1969; Harss, L. and Dohmann, B. Into the Mainstream, 1967; Penguin Companion to Literature 3, 1971; Rodríguez-Alcalá, H. El arte de Juan Rulfo, 1965; Schwartz, K. A New History of Spanish-American Fiction, 1971; Seymour-Smith, M. Guide to Modern World Literature, 1973; Sommer, J. After the Storm, 1968. *Periodicals*—Américas January 1964; Hispanic Review July 1966; Modern Language Notes March 1966; Revista Mexicana de Literatura September-October 1955; Revista de la Universidad de México April 1955, July 1961, Symposium Fall 1974; Times Literary Supplement February 5, 1960.

RYAN, CORNELIUS (JOHN) (June 5, 1920–November 23, 1974), American journalist and war historian, was born in Dublin, Ireland, the son of John Joseph Ryan and the former Amelia Clohisey. He was educated in Dublin by the Christian Brothers, and studied the violin at the Irish Academy of Music, playing in Dublin salon orchestras. At the age of twenty, Ryan went to London as secretary to Garfield Weston, the Canadian-born politician and industrialist. His ambition was to write, however, and the following year, 1941, he joined the London staff of Reuter's News Agency. In 1943 Ryan moved on to become a war correspondent with the London *Daily Telegraph*. He covered the air war over Germany and observed the D-Day invasion of Normandy on June 6, 1944, though he said later that he "was too horrified and too young then to fully appreciate and understand what I saw." Ryan followed the advance of General Patton's Third Army, and after the fall of Berlin was sent to the Pacific. Late in 1945 he opened the *Daily Telegraph*'s bureau in Tokyo, covering among other things the atomic bomb tests in the Pacific. In 1946–1947 Ryan was the *Telegraph*'s Middle East bureau chief in Jerusalem, writing at the same time as a stringer for *Time* and for the St. Louis *Post Dispatch*. He went to the United States in 1947 as a contributing editor of *Time* and became an American citizen in 1950. Ryan left *Time* in 1949 and, after a stint with *Newsweek,* was associate editor of *Collier's* from 1950 until the magazine folded at the end of 1956.

Ryan's first books had meanwhile appeared, beginning with two written in collaboration with Frank Kelley, *Star-Spangled Mikado* (1947) and *MacArthur: Man of Action* (1950). The first was a study of the postwar American occupation of Japan, emphasizing the political aspects of the occupation and the role of General of the Army Douglas MacArthur; it was generally admired

John Phillips

CORNELIUS RYAN

actually interviewed a thousand of his respondents, from enlisted men to generals, and quoted from four hundred of the interviews in his book. In a rented Manhattan storeroom Ryan covered a wall with a large-scale map of the Normandy beachhead, on which hundreds of pins showed the position of hundreds of participants hour by hour throughout the battle. He used no detail or anecdote in the book unless it was confirmed by at least two participants.

The Longest Day was published in 1959 with enormous success, became an equally successful film, and brought Ryan the Benjamin Franklin Award and the Overseas Press Club Award. Though some critics preferred David Howarth's book about D-Day for its depth and literary quality, the *Atlantic Monthly* described *The Longest Day* as "incomparably the best of the war histories," and others praised it as a masterpiece of popular history. Alastair Buchan called it "one of the most brilliant pieces of reconstruction and detective work ever applied to 'old, unhappy far-off things and battles long ago.' " It seemed to Buchan that, though Ryan's style "sometimes verges on the corny, he does not romanticise the horror of modern battle: he has pitched his narrative at the participant's-eye-level of confusion, muddle, agony and achievement." The *New Yorker* agreed that, "for all the glibness of its author's approach, for all the familiar tricks of juxtaposing incidents . . . it is a good book. . . . His reporting is cogent military history, and it is also high drama."

A major best-seller, the book made Ryan a millionaire. He moved to a fifteen-room house in Ridgefield, Connecticut, and, according to the New York *Times,* "settled down to a life of live-in maids, entertainment of friends, and research on the next book project." This was *The Last Battle,* an account of the fall of Berlin published in 1966 after five years of interviews and research. Ryan even persuaded the Russians to allow him to consult their military records, a unique concession. During this period Ryan also worked for *Reader's Digest* as a staff writer (1962 –1965) and thereafter as a roving editor.

David Schoenbrun, in his review of *The Last Battle,* wrote: "We find all of Mr. Ryan's professional skills: the sure control over the minutiae of war; the broad strokes with which he deftly depicts a continental battlefield; the journalist's eye for the human-interest vignette; the simple but startling insights into the lunacy of war." On the other hand, S. L. A. Marshall accused Ryan of being "prone to improvise battle scenes out of his powerful imagination when dependable data is lacking," while other critics credited him with "solid research and reporting" but "little in-

as "a colorful and informative report." Ryan and Kelley's brief biography of the General had a much chillier reception. *Library Journal* called it "the picture of a paragon, not a man," and S.L.A. Marshall wrote: "Though much of it is inaccurate, and all is undocumented, this book will be loved by those who already revere the General."

Across the Space Frontier, a symposium on space travel which had originally appeared in *Collier's,* was published under Ryan's editorship with great success in 1952. "Here in reasonably non-technical language and exciting pictures is the world to come," wrote one reviewer, and there were similar encomiums for a sequel, *Conquest of the Moon* (1953). At the end of 1956, when his *Collier's* job died on him, Ryan temporarily abandoned journalism and settled down to complete his research on a major book about the D-Day invasion. The theme had fascinated him from the beginning, but he had begun serious work on it only in 1949, when a trip to Normandy on the fifth anniversary of the invasion had reawakened his interest. By 1956, when he left *Collier's,* his researches had already put him $20,000 in debt, and he was able to devote a further three years to the book only because his wife undertook to support the family. She is the former Kathryn Ann Morgan, an editor of *House and Home* and *Architectural Forum* who has also written novels.

Ryan read two hundred and eighty-three books about D-Day in the course of his research, but this was only one aspect of his investigations. He also advertised in American, English, Canadian, and German newspapers, seeking interviews with participants in the invasion; he

sight, scope or subtlety." Robert Kee preferred this book to *The Longest Day,* "not just because it covers an even more awesome range of human experience but also because the undeniable skill with which he has organised his material has enabled him to transcend still further the severe limitations of his style. . . . An unmistakable honesty accompanies his vulgarity." This critical dissension seems to have had little effect on the book's popularity; it was another best-seller, and sold to the movies for $175,000.

Ryan's last book, *A Bridge Too Far* (1974), is an account of the airborne Allied invasion of Arnhem, in Holland, in September 1944, an ill-planned operation which, according to A.J.P. Taylor "could have succeeded only if there had been no enemy," and which cost more Allied casualties than D-Day. According to Taylor, "the story is presented with absolute mastery of the situation. It is dramatic and clear at the same time. Ryan is a blow-by-blow historian, building up his details with a Pre-Raphaelite technique. He has assembled the recollections of individuals high and low. He comes near to cataloguing every shot that was fired. Yet he never loses his grip on the overall scene." Melvin Maddocks said that "Ryan's account reads like a Greek tragedy—written by a meticulous police reporter who wants to spell all the names right."

In 1970 it had been discovered that Cornelius Ryan had cancer of the marrow. *A Bridge Too Far* was completed despite several operations and continual pain; it was second on the nonfiction best-seller list when he died at the age of fifty-four, and was subsequently made into a major film. He was survived by his widow, a son, and a daughter. Ryan left notebooks in which he had been planning two new books, one about the Battle of the Bulge and the other about scientific efforts to discover a cure for cancer. In researching the latter he had visited five countries and interviewed more than seven hundred people—doctors, nurses, technicians, and cancer patients.

Ryan was a director of the Connecticut State National Bank and of the Ryan Holdings Company of Ireland, and served on the national board of the Boys Club of America. He received an award from the University of Illinois for the most distinguished magazine writing of 1956, and the Italian Bancarelia Prize in 1962. He held the Medaille de la France Liberée and was a member of the Légion d'Honneur. Malcolm Muggeridge called Ryan "perhaps the most brilliant reporter in the world," and his friend Theodore H. White said that he was "one of the great living masters of the well-told story." Ryan himself once remarked, "There's nothing new in what I'm doing. It's only old-fashioned reporting."

"Anyone who thinks I am writing histories of war has not really read my books," Ryan said in September 1974. "I don't write of the senseless tragedy of war but of the courage and spirit of men and women and children caught up in war. The academic historian writes: 'The general ordered the attack and three hours later the objective was taken.' I want to know what happened to the soldiers on both sides of the conflict in those three crucial hours. I want to know the civilians who were in the area of the battle. I want to know the weather, the conversations, the thoughts, the extra reserves of spirit and determination that played a part in the success or failure of each side." There is no doubt that Ryan's respect for the men and women he interviewed so meticulously was warmly reciprocated. Shortly before his death, scarcely able to walk, and flanked by Generals Ridgway and Gavin, he attended a special parachute formation drop at Fort Bragg arranged in his honor by the United States Air Force. And Maxwell D. Taylor, former chairman of the Joint Chiefs of Staff, said when Ryan died: "He was a man who showed enormous feeling for the fighting soldier and recorded his hardships with an accuracy and realism seldom found in contemporary writers. All of us who were in a soldier's uniform admired him deeply indeed and thought he was one of us."

PRINCIPAL WORKS: (with Frank Kelley) Star-Spangled Mikado, 1947; (with Frank Kelley) MacArthur: Man of Action, 1950; Minute to Ditch! (short stories), 1957; The Longest Day: June 6, 1944, 1959; The Last Battle, 1966; A Bridge Too Far, 1974. *As Editor*—Across the Space Frontier, 1952; Conquest of the Moon, 1953 (in England, Man on the Moon).

ABOUT: Who's Who in America, 1974–1975. *Periodicals*—Book Week March 27, 1966; Nation November 11, 1950; New Statesman April 9, 1960; May 6, 1966; New York Herald Tribune Book Review November 12, 1950; November 22, 1959; New York Times November 25, 1974; New York Times Book Review June 29, 1947; October 29, 1950; March 27, 1966; September 8, 1974; June 22, 1975; Observer September 15, 1974; Publishers Weekly December 2, 1974; Saturday Review March 26, 1966; Time April 1, 1966; December 9, 1974; September 23, 1974; Times Literary Supplement June 10, 1960; November 1, 1974; Washington Post November 25, 1974.

SAINT-DENYS GARNEAU, HECTOR DE. *See* GARNEAU, HECTOR DE SAINT-DENYS

SALKEY, (FELIX) ANDREW (ALEXANDER) (January 30, 1928–), Jamaican poet, novelist, children's writer, editor, and radio journalist, writes: "Like so very many of my Caribbean

ANDREW SALKEY

countrymen and women, I was born outside the Caribbean; in Colón, Panama, in my case. When I was two, I was sent to live with my grandmother (my mother's mother) and one of my three aunts (my mother's sister) in Jamaica, my father's birthplace. My mother was born of Jamaican parents in Port au Prince, Haiti. She was a teacher, and my father variously an engineering worker on the Panama Canal, part-owner of a barber shop, the senior partner in a small operation of fishing boats and the sole proprietor of a general store.

"My mother returned to Jamaica with my younger brother, in 1932; my father, in 1959. His reason for remaining on in Panama, in his own words, was 'That one horsepower country of mine has nothing for me.' Though he lived away from us for so many years, my lasting impression of him is that of a loving, caring, dutiful man of great integrity. All during my childhood, that regular monthly air mail envelope, with its bright red-white-and-blue zigzag border, symbolized my father's continuing love and affection for my mother, my brother and myself.

"Of course, the main emotional and intellectual wellspring of my brother's and my own life was our mother. It was she who introduced us to the then cryptically rich world of Anancy folk tales, duppy stories, country songs, mento music, household proverbs, memory gems, dialect poetry, and other deeply native cultural treasures we *never* got at school. We were all, at that time, being diligently educated in the British colonial tradition.

"I think the two outstanding family influences, responsible for my early attempts at writ-

ing and for those even now, were: the fact that my mother wrote poems (she called them 'prayers', but they were really personal verses of devotional poetry) to which I was usually asked to contribute rhyme-endings and the odd phrase or 'word for'; and the presence in our house of a library which my father had bought at an auction on the American side of the Canal Zone and had given to my mother as one of his wedding presents. For, after all, she was his much esteemed 'teacher-lady' and he was very much the dynamic 'immigrant-worker-businessman' and adoring husband! That unique boom-town type relationship between them sustained a whole world of benefits for my brother and myself, throughout our childhood, adolescence and youth in Jamaica.

"Of course, something else that certainly helped me along the way was the coincidence of actually being a part of the community of Caribbean writers in London in the very early Fifties (I got there in 1952 to read English at London University). There, then, were the struggling poets, Clifford Sealy and Ellsworth Keane; playwrights like Errol Hill and Errol John; novelists like the best-selling and prolific Edgar Mittelholzer, and George Lamming, Samuel Selvon, Jan Carew, John Hearne, Roger Mais and V.S. Naipaul, all at work on their first novels.

"My apprenticeship centred round frenzied reading, over-patient listening and churning out poems, short stories, book reviews, features, articles and commentaries for the domestic and overseas services of the BBC, as a fee-paid, outside contributor to most of its literary programmes.

"My very first piece of sustained writing was a long poem—'a kind of historical symposium in verse' as V.S. Naipaul called it at the time, because its form and idiosyncratic poetic diction and content quite baffled him. About twenty years later, it was published simply as *Jamaica.*

"It still baffles many of its Caribbean readers. One, a blunt and thoughtful academic, wrote to me saying: 'I think you've made a cardinal mistake in trying to match antagonistic opposites. History is very definitely history, and poetry is more or less something we've all conspired to call into existence as a sort of cultural object which we refer to as poetry. The two forced into a union, as you've done, must result in a hell of a confusion. I don't get what you're up to in your *Jamaica* thing.'

"My first novel, *A Quality of Violence,* largely written in a rural demotic, was published in 1959 and displeased a lot of my back-home 'critics'; their *dissensus* went something along the lines of 'You can't write a novel in dialect and hope to reach an intelligent readership . . . There's something very odd about a first novel that isn't autobiographical or even semi-autobiographical; this one isn't; it's set in 1900 . . . Surely, there isn't a future in writing about peasants and particularly in a language that can't carry much more than folk speech-rhythms and humour and so little serious content!'

"Left up to do my own 'perverse' thing, I've continued to do just that, in poetry and prose—in both, incidentally, becoming more and more committed to the understanding and consequent reflection of the lives and struggles of the people living in underdevelopment throughout the Third World. That commitment has brought me a great deal of personal pleasure and countless literary benefits over the years. For instance, I've discovered how very necessary it is for someone like myself (and for others in my position, too) to make of one's writing a people-centred activity, and I've come to realize how profoundly rewarding it is to write for children: rewarding, that is, in the way it shears and concentrates the woolly adult mind and its 'sense of style', and also in the way it has provided me with readers against whom I'm able to measure my own growth and development as a children's writer, step by step, during my school, library and holidaycamp visits.

"However, the study and writing of poetry, along with regular public readings and lectures, are the activities presently at the centre of most of my work, and they will be so for the foreseeable future. I like it that way.

"Living in voluntary exile in London as I have been since 1952, many of my poems are beginning to nag away at the memory *and* present-day actuality of home, and at the reality of the condition of my Caribbean home-people in Britain. I'm now working very slowly on *Land* and *Away,* two volumes of poems which will reflect respectively my pressing concern with those preoccupations.

"I'm married, with two young teenage sons who were born in London and who are both kicking around the idea of authorship. They've jointly written a children's picture book called *The Multi-Coloured Bear of Moscow Road,* a story about the travels in Britain of a heavily bearded, sugar-eating, cigar-smoking, missiles-loving bear who more than slightly resembles Fidel Castro."

Andrew Salkey is the son of Andrew Alexander Salkey and the former Linda Marshall. He was educated in Jamaica, at St. George's College in Kingston and Munro College in St. Elizabeth. In 1952, as he says, he went to England. He enrolled at the University of London, and became, as he has remained, a freelance contributor to the British Broadcasting Corporation. In 1955 the university awarded him its Thomas Helmore Poetry Prize, and the same year he graduated with a B.A. in English.

From 1957 to 1959 Salkey taught English in a London comprehensive school. His first novel was published in 1959, and since then he has been a full-time writer and journalist. Concentrating on West Indian themes, and especially on Caribbean literature, Salkey has been active as a BBC radio interviewer, book reviewer, and discussion leader, and is the author of many radio plays and features. He is also a prolific contributor of short stories, essays, and articles to newspapers and magazines. Salkey was married in 1957 to Patricia Verden.

A Quality of Violence is set in a remote area of Jamaica at the turn of the century. The people are Christians, but a prolonged drought has turned them away from religious orthodoxy towards the darker and more violent irrationalism of Pocomania, a syncretic voodoo cult. A white cock is strangled and later, possessed by masochistic frenzy in a ritual flagellation dance, two men whip one another to death. In the end Ma Johnson, leader of the cult, allows herself to be stoned to death by her own followers in order that the kind of power she represents may survive. The novel may have displeased Salkey's "back-home critics," but in England it was generally admired for its tension and excitement, and the "quiet, lyrical dignity" of its prose. Kenneth Ramchand wrote that "it is Salkey's exploration . . . of the irrational element in human existence that makes the work such a powerful one."

This was followed by a very different kind of novel, *Escape to an Autumn Pavement* (1960), about the adventures of a young Jamaican in London during the 1950s. Johnny Sobert tells his story in a tough, staccato, idiomatic interior monologue, but with almost none of the dialect favored by Samuel Selvon and other West Indian immigrant novelists. Indeed, Gerald Moore suggests, Johnny is in flight from the values of his own society: "He is spiky, alert, afraid of being judged by the standards of his fellow immigrants and therefore anxious to avoid involvement with them." Part of the reason for this, as several critics have pointed out, is that Johnny is a product of the Jamaican middle class, and this also affects his relations with the proletarian white Londoners around him, many of whom assume that they are his racial superiors.

Johnny works as a waiter in a club used mostly by American GIs. He is drawn into an affair with Fiona, his white landlady, which is at first gratifying and then intolerably demanding. Johnny escapes from this situation to share a flat with Dick, a white chauffeur. Dick is a homosexual, a gentle and patient man who is content to wait for some sign that Johnny reciprocates his feelings. Johnny is, or pretends to be, unaware that this is the case and, when he resumes his relationship with Fiona, Dick moves out. Johnny ends the book as he began it, alone. The book had a mixed reception. Some reviewers found it slick and artificial, and Gerald Moore said that the reader tires of Johnny's "wisecracking energy and lack of real feeling for others." All the same, Moore found it interesting that Johnny's "sexual ambiguity and stillborn rebelliousness are problems he must encounter as a man, an individual alone in a big city, but not specifically as a black immigrant." Bill Carr, on the other hand, called the novel "a classic exposition of the tense polarities of middle-class West Indianness when these are dramatized in an alien setting, a setting which imposes the responsibility of a personal quest."

Throughout most of the 1960s, Salkey occupied himself with a series of children's books, each of them dealing in fictional terms with some important event in recent Jamaican history. *Hurricane* (1964), the first of them, is a small boy's account of the hurricane that devastated the island in 1951. Bill Carr wrote that "all the lower-middle-class Kingston folklore—shops, people, streets, nicknames, and the Saturday morning matinée—is present in writing of uncontrived simplicity, and so is the blind apocalypse of the hurricane itself." Few of these books are merely descriptive—in *Riot,* for example, published in 1967, the reader is left to decide whether the trade unionists, whose demonstration leads to the riot, are villains, heroes, or confused men of good will. The series, rejected by the Jamaican Ministry of Education as unsuitable for children, has been brought out by a London publisher with considerable success.

It was not until 1968 that Salkey published his third novel. This was *The Late Emancipation of Jerry Stover,* set in Jamaica just before independence. It deals with a young man's disastrous attempt to find a role for himself and his friends, of whom Salkey writes: "They had no private philosophy, no binding discipline, no real faith in anything. All they had was their freedom, an emancipation that had come much too late. They had not had the time and the kind of society in which to use it intelligently, to benefit from it, to build on it." *The Adventures of Catullus Kelly* (1969), which was rather coolly received, is about another young and well-

educated Jamaican in London, where (as his creator had done) he works in a coffee bar, as a teacher, and as a freelance broadcaster. Kelly is involved with numberless white girls, but feels that he is prized as a black sex object rather than for himself; he fails to stir his fellow immigrants to militant *négritude* and winds up in a Jamaican mental hospital.

The hero of *Come Home, Malcolm Heartland* (1975) is a Jamaican barrister who, after years in England, decides to go home to Kingston. Heartland wants to live his own life—to sort out his own problems in his own place—but he becomes involved with a group of black revolutionaries who see his return home as a political sellout, and in the novel's "abrupt, violent, and depressing end," Heartland is assassinated. Reviewers seemed agreed that Salkey had made a serious attempt to deal with serious questions, but thought that "the idea of the book is better than its execution"—that it "too often trudges off into abstract cogitations."

There was a generally enthusiastic welcome for *Anancy's Score* (1973), a collection of twenty fables about the anarchic spider-man of African and Caribbean folklore, told by Salkey in a rich, ebullient, though sometimes difficult Jamaican-English dialect. He is also the author of two long poems, *Jamaica* (1973) and *Caribbea* (1975). The *Times Literary Supplement,* reviewing the former, called it "a loud cry for the island to reclaim its identity from the wrongs and sorrows of imperialism, ancient and present, and reassert Caribbea in myth, history and current blood. . . . a rhythmic tenacity, interweaving the elliptical island *patois* with solemn oratorical cadences, and above all a driving seriousness of purpose, sustain a work that deserves an audience." Of the many works of West Indian literature and folklore that Salkey has edited, the best known is probably *Breaklight* (1971), his anthology of Caribbean poetry.

Andrew Salkey received a Guggenheim fellowship in 1960 and the Deutscher Kinderbuchpreis in 1967. He lives near Hyde Park in London. Salkey collects antique furniture, fine editions of novels, and contemporary paintings by unestablished artists. He is a Roman Catholic.

PRINCIPAL WORKS: *Adult Fiction*—A Quality of Violence, 1959; Escape to an Autumn Pavement, 1960; The Late Emancipation of Jerry Stover, 1968; The Adventures of Catullus Kelly, 1969; Anancy's Score (short stories), 1973; Come Home, Malcolm Heartland, 1975. *Poetry*—Jamaica, 1973; Caribbea: With Songs of Cuba and Jamaica on Her Mind, 1976. *Nonfiction*—Havana Journal, 1971; Georgetown Journal: A Caribbean Writer's Journey From London via Port of Spain to Georgetown, Guyana, 1970, 1972. *For Children*—Hurricane, 1964; Earthquake, 1965; Drought,

1966; The Shark Hunters (school reader), 1966; Riot, 1967; Jonah Simpson, 1969; Joey Tyson, 1974. *As Editor*—West Indian Stories, 1960; Caribbean: Stories From the Caribbean, 1965 (U.S., Island Voices, 1970); Caribbean Prose, 1967; One Love, 1971; Breaklight: An Anthology of Caribbean Poetry, 1971 (U.S., subtitled The Poetry of the Caribbean); (with others) Savacou 3 and 4, 1972; Caribbean Essays, 1973; Caribbean Folk Tales and Legends, 1975; Writing in Cuba Since the Revolution, 1975.

ABOUT: Cassell's Encyclopedia of World Literature, 1973; Contemporary Authors 5–8 1st revision, 1969; Dathorne, O.R. The Black Mind, 1975; Dathorne, O.R. (ed.) Caribbean Narrative, 1966; James, L. (ed.) The Islands in Between, 1968; May, D. (ed.) British and Commonwealth Novels of the Sixties, 1970; Moore, G. The Chosen Tongue, 1969; Ngugi Wa Thiong'o Homecoming, 1972; Parekh, B. Colour, Culture and Consciousness, 1974; Penguin Companion to Literature 1, 1971; Ramchand, K. The West Indian Novel and Its Background, 1970; Ramchand, K. (ed.) West Indian Narrative, 1966; Searle, C. The Forsaken Lover: White Words and Black People, 1972; Van Sertima, I. Caribbean Writers, 1968; Vinson, J. (ed.) Contemporary Novelists, 1976; Walsh, W. Commonwealth Literature, 1973. *Periodicals*—Bim (Barbados) 1959; Journal of Commonwealth Literature September 1965; Journal of the Royal Society of Arts August 1972; Times Educational Supplement October 27, 1967.

VERNON SCANNELL

SCANNELL, VERNON (January 23, 1922–), English poet, novelist, and memoirist, writes: "I was born in Spilsby, Lincolnshire, but I have no recollection of the place because the family moved to Beeston in Nottinghamshire shortly after my birth and from there to Ballaghaderreen, Roscommon, Ireland. I left school at the age of fourteen and, from the age of eighteen to twenty-three, served in the Gordon Highlanders in World War II. After being wounded in Normandy I spent some months in hospital in Lancashire and was in a Scottish convalescent depot when the Germans surrendered in May 1945. I felt that, if I stayed in the mindless, brutal and brutalizing environment of camp and barrack life any longer, I would be finished as a human being and as the writer I hoped I could become. I deserted and was on the run for over two years before being apprehended, court-martialled and found to be mentally unstable, sent to a military mental hospital and finally discharged.

"During the period of my desertion I began to write my first, feeble and derivative poems and I managed to earn enough to keep myself by private coaching and by boxing in the professional ring. Lack of an early formal education and the intellectual and spiritual lacuna of the war years prolonged my apprenticeship beyond the point where some authors have already produced their best work, and it was not until I was in my thirties that I began to find my own voice.

"Although I have written in most literary forms it is poetry that has always been my primary interest and now, in middle age, I find that my poetic concerns and intentions have remained fairly constant and are unlikely to change in any crucial way. There has been a tendency in post-war poetry written in the English language to move closer and closer to the condition of, not music, but prose, and Ezra Pound's warning: 'Don't imagine that the art of poetry is any simpler than the art of music' has been increasingly ignored. Never before has there been so much talk about technique and such a slovenly lack of it among so many of the highly regarded poets on both sides of the Atlantic.

"My own practice remains unchanged: I write about things, people, events known in the real world, and I try to do so as honestly as I can, striving to avoid the temptation to fake or posture, to attempt to extract more emotional juice than in fact resides in the situation which is the subject of the poem, and I hope, however vainly, to make what Robert Frost has called 'a momentary stay against confusion,' and I believe that this can be done only through a loving knowledge of the achievements of the past and a deep understanding of the principles on which those achievements were based."

After two years in Ireland, Scannell's family lived for a time in Lancashire. It was not until he was nine that they put down roots in Aylesbury, in Buckinghamshire, where Scannell attended Queen's Park School. The only subject he showed much talent for (apart from boxing) was English composition, and it was this, and "a promiscuous love of reading," that gave him the idea of being a writer. At first it was prose that interested him; he was converted to poetry by

716

the chance discovery of Methuen's *Anthology of Modern Verse*—a collection of mostly Georgian writers which inspired him "to write verses that were like parodies of the worst poems in the anthology."

These early experiments more or less ended in 1940, when Scannell joined the Gordon Highlanders; the only way he could contrive a working relationship with his subliterate comrades was to "let the Caliban in me grow big, flex his muscles, and outroar the roaring boys." Scannell served for two years with the Eighth Army in North Africa. After a year in Britain, his regiment joined the Normandy invasion in June 1944. Three weeks later, in fighting near Caen, he received the machine-gun burst through both legs that led to his hospitalization. His subsequent desertion from the army, comprehensible in view of what he says above, was all the same highly precipitate, since the war was over and his discharge imminent.

Scannell spent most of the next two years in Leeds, surviving, as he says, with no ration book or identity card, by fighting professionally and by coaching children for examinations (teaching himself French, a little Latin, and some mathematics in order to do so). He gave his spare time to reading—Faulkner, Melville, Dostoevsky, Forster, Hopkins, Baudelaire, Rimbaud, Coleridge, Blake, Hart Crane, Auden, Empson, and on and on. He had at first hated Leeds for its "drab mediocrity," but it was there, in a "little room high in the decaying street," that he "came fully back to life." The process was aided by the courses he managed to take with Bonamy Dobrée and G. Wilson Knight at Leeds University. At the same time he began to write again, and one or two of his poems were published before he was tracked down, arrested, and eventually given an honorable discharge from the army.

After this Scannell freelanced for a time, and from 1955 to 1962 taught English at Hazlewood School, Limpsfield, in Surrey. Since then he has earned his living as a freelance writer and broadcaster.

Writing in *Contemporary Poets,* Scannell says that his major themes are "violence, the experience of war, the 'sense of danger' which is part of the climate of our times; these are contrasted with poems of a more private nature which affirm the continuity and indestructibility of the creative spirit. Some verse satire; the work is traditional, very direct and firmly rooted in recognizable human experience." His first two books of verse made no great impact, but *The Masks of Love* (1960) brought him the Heinemann Award for Literature, and praise for his "ability to speak through images" in neat, ironi-

cal, and for the most part "superbly integrated poems."

All the same, Anthony Thwaite believes that "it was not until the publication of *A Sense of Danger* in 1962 that he showed his real talent as a skilful memorialist of the aspirations, daydreams, lusts, disillusionments and ironies of a bruised, wry and incorrigible romantic. . . . The world of Scannell's incendiaries, suicides, psychopaths, adulterers—as well as telephone calls, pubs, insurance agents and radio interviews—is thoroughly mid-twentieth century urban, acutely and mordantly observed." Thwaite says that Scannell "works easily and fluently within received forms . . . but his language is less sure" and is liable to acquire an "overheated metaphorical glow." This is successfully avoided in the best poems in *A Sense of Danger*—for example, in "Dead Dog":

One day I found a lost dog in the street.
The hairs about its grin were spiked with blood,
And it lay still as stone. It must have been
A little dog, for though I only stood
Nine inches for each one of my four years
I picked it up and took it home. . . .

I can't remember any feeling but
A moderate pity, cool not swollen-eyed
Almost a godlike feeling now it seems.
My lump of dog was ordinary as bread.
I have no recollection of the school
Where I was taught my terror of the dead.

Walking Wounded (1965) was also warmly praised, but there was a less friendly reception for *Epithets of War* (1969). A reviewer in the *Times Literary Supplement* called it "an over-demonstrative display of what are, for the most part, stalely conventional responses to the [war]. . . . Too many of the poems read like bad Sassoon and the volume, lacking any consistent set of concerns, ekes out its sparse subject-matter . . . with a slack and careless use of rhythm."

The most admired of Scannell's books of poetry so far has been *The Winter Man* (1973). Peter Porter wrote that "Scannell has always been a poet of uneasiness, of the generous colours of life stained by autumn darkenings, and this tone is conveyed in his new book more effectively than ever before. Some poems here are too long-winded, some grindingly formal, and his besetting fault of over-use of adjectives has not abated entirely, but there is an amplitude of emotion and a power of statement which is very welcome." Elsewhere Porter has said that "nothing in Scannell's poetry would be foreign to Hardy or Edward Thomas, but he goes about tradition in his own way. He specialises in the scena from experience, which sometimes degenerates into the equivalent of an O. Henry ending banging into place, but truth to detail justifies his large poetical personifications and his affection for the full romantic line."

Scannell considers himself primarily a poet, and says that he has "not taken the writing of prose fiction nearly seriously enough. . . . I am painfully aware that this lack of respect for the medium shows clearly in the work." Some readers would consider this a harsh judgment, and his novels have on the whole been well received. The themes of Scannell's novels are the same as those of his poems: as he puts it, "the preoccupation—perhaps obsession, with war, physical violence, courage and its lack, ageing and the sense of mortality." All of these themes are present in what is probably his best novel, *The Face of the Enemy* (1961). It is about some of the men who fought and won World War II and got little thanks for it, and who, fifteen years on, meet to mull over past glories in a seedy little drinking club in London. The plot centers on the admission by one of them that he had been court-martialled for cowardice, and the club's response to this confession. Without ignoring the futility and bigotry of these fallen heroes, misfits in the postwar world, Scannell draws them with a deep affection and respect for what they have been.

The Dividing Night (1962) is an account of an adultery which becomes, for one of the participants, a hopeless love affair; "for all its sameness and predictability," the story was said to exercise "a strange compulsion." *The Fight* (1953) and *The Big Time* (1965) both deal with boxing, the latter with a tycoon who discovers a brilliant young amateur heavyweight and seeks to turn him into "a perfect fighting-machine" and world champion; he discovers that men are not machines. The story is told by a "hard-bitten, soft-at-the-centre boxing journalist capable of higher things"; this is the best-drawn character in the book, a man "whose exploitation of his woman friend Mary neatly counterpoints that of . . . [the tycoon] in respect of his boy-wonder, and whose blend of egotism and wry self-distaste is effectively communicated." *The Big Chance* (1960) and *The Shadowed Place* (1961) are suspense novels.

Scannell's "brilliantly entertaining" autobiography, *The Tiger and the Rose,* takes its title from Siegfried Sassoon: "In me the tiger sniffs the rose/ Look in my heart, kind friends, and tremble." It covers the twenty years from the beginning of the war until 1960. *A Proper Gentleman* (1977) is an absorbing account of the nine months Scannell spent in 1975–1976 as Resident Poet, under the auspices of the Southern Arts Association, in the Oxfordshire village of Berinsfield. This interesting experiment was not a success and Scannell left Berinsfield seething with angry contempt for the ignorant, loutish, and mostly hostile people he seems to have found there.

Scannell has also written radio plays and a children's book, and is a prolific reviewer. *Not Without Glory* (1976) surveys the British and American poetry of World War II, seeking to show that it was not inferior to the better-known work produced in World War I. Paul Fussell wrote that Scannell is "a good critic, although some will wish him more serious intellectually and analytically," and welcomed in particular "his analysis and celebration of Lincoln Kirstein's brilliant *Rhymes and More Rhymes of a PFC,* a book insufficiently known on either side of the Atlantic." Scannell received Arts Council grants in 1967 and 1970, and a Cholmondeley Award for poetry in 1974. He is a Fellow of the Royal Society of Literature. Scannell was married in 1954 to Josephine Higson, and has five children. He has described himself as a "romantic radical" in politics, and his recreations as listening to the radio (mainly music), drinking, watching boxing, going to the cinema, and reading.

PRINCIPAL WORKS: *Poetry*—Graves and Resurrections, 1948; A Mortal Pitch, 1957; The Masks of Love, 1960; A Sense of Danger, 1962; Walking Wounded, 1965; Epithets of War: Poems 1965–1969, 1969; Mastering the Craft, 1970; (with Jon Silkin) Pergamon Poets 8, 1970; Selected Poems, 1971; Company of Women, 1971; (with others) Corgi Modern Poets in Focus 4, 1971; The Winter Man, 1973; The Apple-Raid (for children), 1974; The Loving Game, 1975. *Novels*—The Fight, 1953; The Wound and the Scar, 1953; The Big Chance, 1960; The Shadowed Place, 1961; The Face of the Enemy, 1961; The Dividing Night, 1962; The Big Time, 1965; The Dangerous Ones (for children), 1970. *Other*—Edward Thomas (Writers and Their Work), 1963; The Tiger and the Rose: An Autobiography, 1971; Not Without Glory: Poets of the Second World War, 1976; A Proper Gentleman (autobiography), 1977. *As Editor*—(with others) New Poems 1962: A PEN Anthology, 1962.

ABOUT: Badham-Thornhill, D. (ed.) Three Poets, Two Children, 1975; BBC. Writers on Themselves, 1964; Contemporary Authors 5–8 1st revision, 1969; Orr, P. (ed.) The Poet Speaks, 1966; Robson, J. (ed.) Corgi Modern Poets in Focus 4, 1971; Scannell, V. A Proper Gentleman, 1977; Scannell, V. The Tiger and the Rose, 1971; Thwaite, A. Poetry Today 1960–1973, 1973; Vinson, J. (ed.) Contemporary Novelists, 1976; Vinson, J. (ed.) Contemporary Poets, 1976; Who's Who, 1978. *Periodicals*—Guardian August 10, 1970; Listener July 5, 1962; August 22, 1963; Times Literary Supplement February 3, 1961; September 29, 1961; September 7, 1962; April 15, 1965; September 17, 1971.

*SCHMIDT, ARNO (OTTO) (January 18, 1914–), German novelist, short story writer,
*shmit

German Information Center

ARNO SCHMIDT

translator, essayist, and literary critic, was born in Hamburg, the son of Otto Friedrich Schmidt, a professional soldier and police official, and the former Klara Ehrentraut. He went to school in Hamburg until 1928, when his family returned to their native Silesia. Schmidt was a mathematical prodigy, and in 1933, after graduating from the gymnasium in the Silesian town of Görlitz, he went on to study mathematics and astronomy at Breslau University. Forced to break off his education for political reasons soon after the Nazis came to power, he started work in the Silesian textile industry in Greiffenberg (1934–1939). From 1939 to 1945 he was a soldier in the German artillery, serving as a noncommissioned officer in the occupying forces in Norway and working for a long time as a cartographer. In 1945 he was taken prisoner by the British in Belgium, and after his release became an English interpreter at an auxiliary police college in Benefeld.

Although Schmidt had begun to write while he was still at Breslau University, none of this early work was published, and it was lost along with his library when his Silesian home became part of Poland. It was only in 1947 that he became a professional author. He has since been a consistently avant-garde writer, revealing a mind of exceptional originality and ingenuity in stories and novels which experiment with everything from narrative technique to the representation of consciousness. Schmidt is a master of mathematical puzzles, philological oddities, and language games. He is an acidly pessimistic satirist, yet also a humorist who can brilliantly parody the styles of other writers. His early writing

has much in common with that of other German postwar writers to whose work terms such as *Trümmerliteratur* (literature of the rubble) and *Nullpunkt-literatur* (literature of the "Year Nought") have been applied. Schmidt's irony, the skepticism of a man determined never to be fooled again by facile slogans, seems characteristic of the period: "The 'Lord,' without Whose willing it no sparrow falls from the roof, nor are ten million people gassed in concentration camps. He must be a strange sort—if He exists now at all."

Schmidt has used the term *Kurz-roman* (literally "short novel") to describe the impressionistic tales with which he began his literary career. *Leviathan* (1949) includes three stories, two set in antiquity and one in the contemporary world. All have in common the theme of a flight which leads only to death, like that of the elderly prisoner Pytheas of Massilia, whose imagined escape across the frontier is in reality the oncoming of death. The title story, which is set in the collapsing Germany of the last days of the war, is an acid picture of a curiously assorted group of people who commandeer a train in February 1945 and set off away eastward from the ruins of Berlin on a hopeless and illicit journey. The book gained the Grand Literature Prize of the Mainz Academy.

Schmidt's stories are often essentially monologues presented in the form of diary entries—a diary usually written by a down-at-heel and thoroughly disillusioned intellectual. The three short novels which were linked in 1963 in the trilogy *Nobodaddy's Kinder* (Nobodaddy's Children) were originally published separately in a different order. As finally grouped in the trilogy they make up a series of diary entries by progressively younger characters.

The first part of the trilogy, originally published in 1953, is *Aus dem Leben eines Fauns* (From the Life of a Faun). A savage satirical evocation of civilian provincial life in wartime Germany, it clearly implies that the destruction of that society by bombing in 1944 was no great loss. *Brand's Haide* (Brand's Heath, 1951) is the story of a disillusioned prisoner-of-war who, returning to a devastated Germany in 1946, settles down in the seclusion of the heath to become a writer. The interlude of happiness he briefly finds in love ends when his mistress deserts him for an American, leaving him "empty and dull grey," and only faintly cheered by her promise of food parcels. The trilogy's last and most blackly satirical volume is *Schwarze Spiegel* (Black Mirrors, 1951), which foresees a catastrophic atomic war in the early 1960s finishing the work of destruction begun in World War II.

In these early stories, Schmidt seeks to represent the disjointed and discontinuous nature of human consciousness by the use of a similarly disjunctive narrative. This is well seen in the novel *Die Gelehrtenrepublik* (The Republic of Letters, 1957), another of Schmidt's anti-utopias, in which excessive atomic radiation has produced grotesque monsters such as the "Never-nevers," giant spiders with human heads and terrible poison-claws, as well as more attractive mutants. A few pages of this novel have been translated into English by Michael Horovitz in Christopher Middleton's *German Writing Today* (1967)—a passage in which the hero Harry Winers meets and makes love to an attractive young centaur whom he at first mistakes for a naked girl astride a deer:

A fabulous ashblonde stand-up mane, which started above her forehead in an impudent forelock, amenable to fringe or back-swept styling: channelled down a sweet nape of neck, and on between the shoulder-blades: continued at hand-height along the back strait; till it finally tumbled over into her black-tasselled tail.

Rather like a Grant-gazelle from the rear: quite a tautly stretched close-cropped pelt; back and outer shanks of pale russet hue. Belly and inside legs white: 4 slim legs.

And up front—a naked girl, no less; with arms!—Now I stood facing her, she inclined her narrow high head, and laughed at me: ?/The nose: firmly joined to her forehead by its wide bridge. A long red mouth. Throat. Ivory shoulders, smooth and sleek. Teenage bubs. Slender hips. Long girl's legs (but imagine—hooves to boot: almost as if a contemporary, hard, lady's shoe had taken root at the ankle).

Back to the face (*wow;* large pointed, brown velvet ears as well; mobile, with a wind-resistant look about them). (About 5.5 tall: that figures). She smiled patiently; archly. And her tongue ran one lap round her lips: which were considerably larger than mine; (hence presumably the ponderous diction!)

'What's your name?' came to me.: 'Thalja' from her. And, persistently, 'You're no forester.' /No; I was none. Still stood, however, as if bewitched. The which I was, without a doubt!: Her tail flicked at her side, one lash.

A prominent part in many of Schmidt's books is played by the characteristic scenery of the Lüneburger Heide, the flat, sparsely-inhabited heathland between Hamburg and Hanover which Schmidt came to know after the war when he lived in Cordingen (in Lower Saxony) until 1950. In 1951 he had moved to Kastel, in the Saarland, then in 1955 to the city of Darmstadt, but in 1958 he returned to the Lüneburger Heide and settled near Bargfeld in the privacy and seclusion of an isolated wooden house.

Schmidt's later work has become increasingly unorthodox in its narrative structure as he experiments with various ways of building a truthful picture out of fragments of consciousness. He is extremely interested in recent discoveries about the functioning of the brain and the memory, and in his theoretical essays *Berechnungen I* (Calculations I, 1955) and *Berechnungen II* (Calculations II, 1959) he writes at some length about these matters and their relevance to experimental writing. Schmidt's essays include a blueprint for four forms of prose representing different kinds of consciousness. The first is the real world of direct observation, from which may develop the second category, wish-fulfilling fantasy. Thirdly Schmidt concerns himself with the act of memory, which he had already tried to convey linguistically and typographically in works like *Die Umsiedler* (The Settlers, 1953), and finally there is the world of dream.

Some of the typographical conventions that Schmidt has adopted to express these different kinds of consciousness may be seen in the novel *Kaff auch Mare Crisium* (1960), a story about two different worlds. One is the actual, observable world of *Kaff* (a word which literally means "chaff," but is also slang for a "poor village" and for "nonsense"). Passages dealing with this world are indented about ten spaces from the right margin, while a similar indentation at the left margin indicates the imagined activities which occur on the moon, the *Mare Crisium* of the title. In the "real" story, Karl Richter and his girlfriend Hertha are staying with Aunt Heete in a small village on the Lüneburger Heide. As Karl courts Hertha on long country walks across the heath, he tells her the apocalyptic fantasy set on the moon which is an intricate echo of their own story.

The stories in the collections *Rosen und Porree* (Roses and a Leek, 1959) and *Kühe in Halbtrauer* (Cows in Half-mourning, 1964) are, like much of Schmidt's work, strongly autobiographical in content, projecting the writer's own sensual and imaginative problems as he grows older, his craving both for isolation and for communion with his fellows, and his interest in mathematics, surveying, local history, and literature. *Trommler beim Zarem* (Drummer for the Tsar, 1966), another volume of quasi-autobiographical short stories, was later reissued in a pocket-sized version, as many of Schmidt's books have been, as

Sommermeteor (Summer Meteor, 1970). The title was changed because the later edition omitted a whole section of the earlier one—"Und es blitzen die Sterne" (And the Stars Shine)—which contained a number of essays on literary subjects, giving valuable insights into writers who have influenced Schmidt's own writing, especially English humorists such as Laurence Sterne and Lewis Carroll, whom he describes as "the father of modern literature," anticipating James Joyce.

About a third of Schmidt's large output consists of literary criticism and literary biography, including the essays originally written for radio and collected in *Dya na sore: Gespräche in einer Bibliothek* (Conversations in a Library, 1958); *Belphegor: Nachrichte von Büchern und Menschen* (Belphegor: News of Books and Men, 1961); and *Der Triton mit den Sonnenschirm* (The Triton with the Sunshade, 1969). The three essays on James Joyce in *Der Triton* include an attempt to guide readers through *Finnegans Wake,* in which Schmidt argues that "the secret of the content of *Finnegans Wake* is autobiographical."

Schmidt has also been attracted by many eighteenth- and nineteenth-century German writers, and has written a major study of the Romantic writer and fabulist Friedrich de la Motte Fouqué, the author of the famous literary fairy tale *Undine.* Another important critical and biographical work is *Sitara und der Weg dorthin* (1963), a study of the life and works of Karl May, who wrote books about American Indians in the manner of James Fenimore Cooper and—like Schmidt himself—was a pacifist, very much against the spirit of the imperialistic age in which he lived. *Die Ritter vom Geist—von vergessenen Kollegen* (The Knights of the Spirit—On Forgotten Colleagues, 1966) contains accounts of six German-language writers who Schmidt considers have been unfairly overlooked. Schmidt has also sought to extend his countrymen's familiarity with the Anglo-American literary heritage by making many translations of such writers as Poe, Cooper, and Faulkner, as well as more popular writers like Evan Hunter and Stanley Ellin.

Schmidt's masterpiece is *Zettels Traum* (Zettel's Dream, 1970), a mammoth novel in eight parts, each approaching the length of an ordinary novel, and published as a facsimile reproduction of Schmidt's original manuscript. It deals with twenty-four hours in the life of Pagenstecher, a literary scholar in his mid-fifties who lives on the heath and like Schmidt himself is an expert on Poe. He is visited by a married couple—professional translators working on a German-language edition of Poe—and their daughter Franziska, to whom Pagenstecher is attracted. Tension mounts between husband and wife and between mother and daughter. Each page of the novel is set up in three columns, of which the center column contains Pagenstecher's narrative and interior monologue. The first column is a critical analysis of the life and works of Edgar Allan Poe, with lengthy quotations, and the third column contains a variety of things ranging from footnotes to comments on major philosophical questions.

The work operates on many planes—vertical as well as horizontal—the girl Franziska, for example, is both a real teenager and a mythological figure, as well as an echo of Poe's child bride Virginia, so that the story throws light on Poe while Poe enriches it. The ambiguity of the book is reflected in the title: *Zettel* is the German for "index-card," of which Schmidt has more than a hundred thousand in his legendary card file. But *Zettel* is not only a clue to Schmidt's method of composition; it is also the German name for Bottom the Weaver in Shakespeare's *Midsummer Night's Dream,* and *Zettels Traum* is a book in which, as in the Shakespearean comedy, myth and magic intrude into the lives of ordinary people. Hans-Bernhard Moeller has summed up this complex book and its author by saying that "readers and reviewers may feel more comfortable with Hemingway or Thomas Mann than with the linguistic experimenter of *Zettels Traum.* But Böll's earlier judgment of Schmidt is still valid today; he praised Schmidt's 'passionate love for the German language which he is practising with a writer's true and poetic fervor'. . . . With *Zettels Traum* Schmidt may remain the most respected author of the avant-garde and the least likely to be a bestseller, but his linguistic and typographical enrichment of contemporary German literature has left and will leave its mark."

Die Schule der Atheisten (The School of Atheists, 1972), described as a "six-act Novellen-Comodie," is a delightful literary fantasy—a farcical fable about two West German atheists and a Marxist professor from East Germany who in 1969 set out on a crusade for atheism. An explosion on board ship strands two of them on a Pacific island with two American evangelists whose missionary zeal (and food) convert the professor, who is then paraded by the triumphant evangelists on a world tour. The story, however, is told in the year 2014 by the surviving atheist who has become the leader of an Indian-type reservation—all that remains of Europe after a nuclear holocaust has left America and China ruling the world.

Schmidt himself is an atheist as well as a pacifist, and there is an autobiographical element in this *novelle,* as there is in *Abend mit Goldrand* (Evening With Goldrand, 1975), which explores the dichotomy between the writer's orderly and pedantic existence and his compensatory and anarchic dreams. This dramatized, scenic novel, published like *Zettels Traum* as a facsimile of the typescript, is a fable about three men who reflect various facets of their author's personality. Sharing a house, the sexual frustrations of aging, and an obsession with literature, they quote profusely from their reading, providing evidence in support of Schmidt's own Etym Theory, which suggests that a writer's vocabulary and imagery reflect his repressed sexual obsessions. The trio's peaceful if frustrated existence is disrupted by a group of hippies who stay with them for three days on their way to a supposed utopia in Tasmania. Friedrich Olt comments that the scenes of unmitigated pansexualism which follow "read like a satyr play to the Edenic eroticism of Bosch's Garden of Earthly Delights, which has a central place in the novel. Pornography fails as a criterion; Schmidt is giving 'insights into the workings of poor human nature,' a concern that indeed informs his entire opus."

Schmidt's extreme originality and his virtual seclusion have meant that his work has not received a great deal of critical attention even in Germany, where he has been most appreciated by other writers like Heinrich Böll and Günter Grass; Walter Jansen has called him "the great lone wolf of contemporary German literature." He has nevertheless received many major awards and prizes, including the Grosser Literaturpreis der Akademie Darmstadt (1950), the Berlin Fontane Prize (1965), the Grosse Ehrengabe für Literatur des Kulturkreises der BRD (1963), and Frankfurt's highly esteemed Goethe Prize (1973). His works have attracted considerable attention in French translation, but despite his own interest in English-language writers, his reputation has until now penetrated only superficially into the English-speaking world. Schmidt was married in 1937 to Alice Murawski.

PRINCIPAL WORKS IN ENGLISH TRANSLATION: Extract from Zettels Traum *in* Middleton, C. (ed.) German Writing Today, 1967.

ABOUT: Closs, A. Twentieth Century German Literature, 1969; Deutsche Dichter der Gegenwart, 1973; International Who's Who, 1978–79; Oxford Companion to German Literature, 1976; Waidson, H.M. The Modern German Novel, 1959; Wer ist Wer, 1976–1977; West, P. The Modern Novel, 1963. *Periodicals*—Books Abroad Autumn 1966, Autumn 1967, Summer 1970, Autumn 1970, Winter 1971, Winter 1973, Spring 1976.

*SCHOLEM, GERSHOM G(ERHARD)
(December 5, 1897–), Jewish scholar, was born in Berlin, Germany, the son of a printer who owned his own printshop, Arthur Scholem, and the former Betty Hirsch. In his home there was only a minimum of Jewish religious observance, and cigars and cigarettes were casually lit from the Sabbath candles. Even the alien festival of Christmas was celebrated with a decorated tree: "I am a member of a family that had lived in Germany—in Silesia—for a long time, and came to Berlin at the beginning of the nineteenth century. I myself was a fourth-generation Berliner. The transition in our family from [Judaic] Orthodoxy at the beginning of the nineteenth century to almost total assimilation at the beginning of the twentieth was a matter of three generations—from my grandfather, through my father, to my own generation; in the third generation assimilation was complete—or so it seemed."

Scholem's various accounts of his childhood in Wilhelmine Germany tell the story of a revolt against this family background and its whole life-style. He was the youngest of four brothers, of whom the oldest two "took after my father. One of them was even more German than my father, a right-wing German nationalist." The third brother, two years older than Gershom, became a revolutionary, a radical socialist who was eventually killed in Buchenwald by the Nazis as a former Communist deputy in the Reichstag. Gershom Scholem himself was early attracted to the Zionist movement, which he joined as a schoolboy in 1911. He has explained that "a person living in a liberal-Jewish, German-assimilationist environment had the feeling that these people were devoting their entire lives to self-delusion . . . Some of us, to be sure, went on to become real political Zionists, but the Zionist choice was a moral decision, an emotional one, an honesty-seeking response. The honesty did not express itself in the desire for a state, but in a revolt against the lie that Jewish existence was." This decision naturally affronted Scholem's father and "resulted in our total estrangement from each other." Although his maternal grandfather had founded a synagogue in West Berlin, there was not a single practicing Jew in Scholem's family circle. But "I wanted to learn. That is how the awakening of my Jewish interest expressed itself. I wanted to know who the Jews were." He began to study Hebrew privately and attended classes in the Talmud and other aspects of Jewish religion.
*sho' lem

GERSHOM G. SCHOLEM

Scholem was one of the small minority in Germany who opposed the First World War, and in 1915 he was expelled from school for writing an antiwar letter to a newspaper. He was however accepted into Berlin University, and for four years studied mathematics with the intention of becoming a teacher in Israel after the war. Meanwhile his personal life was undergoing "all kinds of crises." In 1917, after his socialist brother was arrested for taking part in an antiwar demonstration, their father threw them both out of the house, saying, "It's all the same—socialism, Zionism—it's all antipatriotic." The father made Gershom Scholem a once-and-for-all gift of one hundred marks and "sent me a registered letter ordering me to leave his household by March 1, 1917." Scholem was then drafted into the army, but pretended to be insane. He spent six weeks in a lunatic asylum, successfully bluffed the doctors into pronouncing him an incurable schizophrenic, and was sent back home. He managed to transfer to Jena University and continued his mathematical studies (1917–1918), then spent a year in Switzerland at Bern University.

Today, when German Jewry is virtually extinct, no German university is complete without its faculty for Jewish studies; in Scholem's youth, as he ironically points out, there was no such provision. However, he had been continuing with his private study of Judaica, becoming increasingly fascinated by the mysticism of the Kabbalah. When it came to preparing a Ph.D. thesis he decided not to continue with mathematics, but went to Munich University, the only German institution with a large collection of kabbalistic manuscripts. He was at Munich

from 1919 to 1922, working on his thesis and seeking to master the full historical, religious, and cultural tradition of Judaism. In this way he discovered the work which was to occupy him for the rest of his life.

Scholem believed that if there was to be any regeneration of Judaism it would have to take place in Palestine, and he emigrated there in 1923; "I really thought that a Jew has to go to Eretz Yisrael, even if we were going to be a small sect there. We didn't know there would be millions. Who knew? The problem was a personal, not a national one." In Palestine he took up a post as librarian of the newly founded Hebrew University of Jerusalem. He became a lecturer at the Hebrew University in 1925, and from 1933 was professor of Jewish mysticism there. He retired as professor emeritus in 1965.

Jewish mysticism and the Kabbalah had been much misinterpreted or denigrated by the Jewish rationalist scholars of the nineteenth century. It was Scholem, with his strict historical and philological methods, who put the study and interpretation of the Jewish esoteric tradition on a solid scientific basis. His first book, which arose from his doctoral studies, was *Das Buch Bahir* (The Book of Bahir, 1923). This was a translation of and commentary on the earliest extant kabbalistic text, *Sefer ha-Bahir,* whose prime importance lies in its use of symbolic language. Scholem continued to explore this virtually forgotten tradition of Judaism—the history and documents of its mystic teaching—in a number of works in Hebrew and German, culminating in *Major Trends in Jewish Mysticism* (1941, revised edition 1946), which Leon Wieseltier described as "a masterful survey of the subject which has become a classic of Jewish and religious history." It is an expanded version of lectures some of which had been given at the Jewish Institute of Religion in New York while Scholem was visiting professor there in 1938.

The Kabbalah, literally "tradition" (that is, the tradition of things divine), is the sum of Jewish mysticism. The literary production of the Kabbalists ranges over a long period in a great number of books, many of them dating back to the late Middle Ages. The central and basic literary work of this mystical movement is the *Zohar* (The "Book of Splendor"), much of it an allegorical and mystical commentary on the Pentateuch. The authorship of the *Zohar* has usually been ascribed to Rabbi Simeon ben Yohai and his disciples in the second century A.D., though it became known through its publication by Moses de Leon of Spain towards the end of the thirteenth century. Scholem rejects the authorship of Rabbi Simeon, and maintains that it is

723

mostly the work of Moses de Leon himself, based on materials extending over many centuries and deriving from both Jewish and non-Jewish sources. All the works of the later Jewish mystics are based on it, and it has exerted great influence on Jewish popular beliefs and Jewish ritual. For several centuries it was widely revered as a sacred text of unquestionable value, ranking with the Bible and the Talmud, and in certain Jewish communities it remains so today.

This heritage was lost to European Jewry, which in the late eighteenth century turned resolutely to European culture. Jewish mysticism seemed alien and disturbing, and was soon forgotten. Some aspects of this tradition repelled Scholem, also; what attracted him to the Kabbalists is that they "were able to create symbols that expressed their personal situation as a world situation," and the mystery of this world as a reflection of the divine mysteries. The images into which they crystallized their experience were deeply involved with the historical experience of the Jewish people, and Scholem argues that these symbols are not subjective, but objective projections of "the inner side of a miserable, grotesque, and weird Jewish externality." It is this interweaving of two realms that gives the Kabbalah its unique character. No understanding of the kabbalistic tradition is possible without a grasp of the historical world of Jewry that gave it birth, a Jewry repressed from without and therefore forced to turn in on itself, and to find in symbolic speculation a freedom it was otherwise denied.

Scholem's other studies of this subject include *Zur Kabbala und ihrer Symbolik* (1960, translated by Ralph Mannheim as *On the Kabbalah and Its Symbolism*), which consists of five essays on different aspects of the Kabbalah. These range from a discussion of "religious authority and mysticism" to the idea of the Golem, showing how a kabbalistic legend became transformed into a folk story about a man created by magical art from a figure of clay, and then took on an even more horrific form in Gustav Meyrinck's novel *Der Golem,* which was made into a famous German expressionist film. Scholem says in his introduction that "the chief interest of the Kabbalah for us" lies "in the light it throws on the 'historical psychology' of the Jews. Here each individual was the totality. And this is the source of the fascination which the great symbols of the Kabbalah possess for a historian no less than a psychologist. . . . In a generation that has witnessed a terrible crisis in Jewish history, the ideas of these medieval Jewish esoterics no longer seem so strange. We see with other eyes, and the obscure symbols strike

us as worth clarifying." Scholem observes that "psychoanalysts of all schools whom I have met in my travels and in Jerusalem have said, 'What you're saying is pure psychoanalysis. . . .' What I was saying seemed to them to corroborate what they were saying."

The Messianic Idea in Judaism (1970) collects in English translation seventeen essays originally written in German, or in a few cases Hebrew, on a wide range of themes in Jewish spirituality, such as the concept of the thirty-six just men who by their good work, hidden from the sight of the people, uphold the world. However, the central theme of these essays is the crucial concept of Messianism, which arose in an age of catastrophe for the ancient Jewish people. The Prophets predicted a Messianic Age in which the world would be shaken to its foundations before entering a millennium in which people would live in justice, harmony, and full knowledge of the Lord. Scholem also studies the later history of this idea, when in response to subsequent disasters there were great bursts of Messianic expectation. One such began after the expulsion of the Jews from Spain in 1492, and this was nurtured by the kabbalists and finally exploded into the Messianic movements of Shabbatai Tzevi and Jacob Frank, from 1665 to 1765. The Sabbatian and Frankist movements created paradoxical versions of Messianism in which sin became the vehicle of redemption and the breaking of the law the way of fulfillment. Scholem finds both of these Messiahs ultimately nihilistic, but shows how many of their doctrines grew from the mystical Judaism of the Kabbalah.

Earlier, in his two-volume book *Shabbatai Tzevi* (1957–1958, translated by R. J. Zwi Werblowsky as *Sabbatai Sevi: The Mystical Messiah, 1626–1676*), Scholem had dealt at length with the career of the false Messiah from Smyrna and its effect on later generations. The English edition was considerably revised and enlarged to take into account important new sources, in particular documents from the archives of a secret group of the Messiah's followers which survived in Salonika into this century. Reviewers described it as an outstanding and fascinating work, and C. P. Walker commented: "Apart from the great importance of Sabbatianism in the history of the Jewish people and religion, it is of immense interest to the historian of Christianity. For the parallels and contrasts between the early phases of the two movements are striking and profound. . . . a monumental work of historical scholarship, which recounts in minute detail a moving tragedy of vast dimensions." For Cynthia Ozick, the book "presses down on the gasping consciousness with the strength not simply of its invulnerable, almost tidal, scholarship, but of its singular instruction in the nature of man."

The essays collected as *On Jews and Judaism in Crisis* (1977) show the breadth and range of Scholem's interests in Jewish history, religion, literature, and intellectual life. As Arthur A. Cohen observes, "the power of Scholem's work is not alone that he thinks magnificently, but that he makes necessary and vital considerations that, like his interest in the Kabbalah sixty years ago, run counter to the rueful, ironic, sarcastic view of such matters adopted by many Jewish thinkers and Jewish institutions of learning. Scholem brings to the center of his thought a notion of Jewish intellectuality to which no discipline is alien or irrelevant." Leon Wieseltier observed that "Scholem has been the most original and influential Jewish historian of this century. . . . The historian shoulders a terrible responsibility: he depletes the future if he truncates the past. It is to restore such a truncated past that Scholem has labored; his books and papers have been volleys discharged against an occluded view of the Jewish tradition, which, by egregiously dismissing some of its most vital features, would imperil it entirely. 'A discussion of our past', he once modestly remarked, 'has something to do with our future.' "

In his later years Scholem has turned his attention increasingly to the late Imperial and early Weimar Germany in which he grew up. In the lecture *Walter Benjamin* (1965, translated under the same title by L. Furtmueller), given in the Leo Baeck Institute in New York, and in *Walter Benjamin: die Geschichte einer Freundschaft* (Walter Benjamin: The History of a Friendship, 1971) he reminisces at length about the writer whom Hannah Arendt described as the most important German critic between the two world wars, and whom Scholem calls a "man of genius." Benjamin's letters were published in a two-volume collection, *Briefe* (1966), which Scholem edited in collaboration with Theodor Adorno.

Scholem's own intellectual autobiography, *Von Berlin nach Jerusalem* (From Berlin to Jerusalem, 1978), not only describes his own family background and early life but vividly evokes the now vanished world of German Jewry in which he grew up. He is convinced that there never was any real dialogue between Germans and Jews, and he records his own disillusionment with this society, and his discovery of his own vocation in helping to renew Judaism. Lionel Kochan observed that "Scholem emerges from this portrayal of the German Jewry of his youth as a man to whom the past ineradicably clings. For all the attempt to discard and break loose from those Wilhelmine and Weimar years, Scholem's patent honesty and self-revelation forbid any such pretence. The very struggle between past and present brings out Scholem's integrity all the more clearly and makes this work a monument to a man and his unalloyed Zionist allegiance."

Scholem has been a very prolific author, and the bibliography of his writings published in *Studies in Mysticism and Religion* (1967) lists over five hundred books and essays. He was visiting professor at the Jewish Institute of Religion, New York, in 1938 and 1949, at Brown University in 1956–1957, at Hebrew Union College, Cincinnati, in 1966, and at Boston University in 1975. From 1946 to 1950 he was an Israeli representative in salvaging Jewish cultural treasures plundered by the Nazis. He was president of the Israel Academy of Science and Humanities in 1968–1974 and is a member of the American Academy of Arts and Sciences, the American Academy for Jewish Research, and several foreign academies. Scholem holds honorary degrees from a number of universities and has received many other distinctions and awards, including the State Prize of Israel for Jewish studies (1958), the Rothschild Prize for Jewish studies (1962), the Reuchlin Prize (1969), the Harvey Prize (1974), and the Literature Prize of the Bavarian Academy of Arts.

In 1923, a month after he arrived in Palestine, Scholem was married to Elsa Burchhard, who had preceded him there six months earlier. They were divorced in 1936 and the same year he married Fania Freud. A combative man, who thoroughly enjoys an argument, Scholem is also "a great conversationalist and an extraordinarily gifted raconteur." Leon Wieseltier has referred to his "imperturbable—though never demagogic—self-assurance," and "the clarity and self-possession that have characterized Scholem's work throughout his long life." The same writer concludes that "Gershom Scholem's account of Judaism's religious development, including the interpretation of Zionism he drew from it, has been, for its quality of mind and unrivalled erudition, probably the strongest secular vision described by a contemporary Jew."

PRINCIPAL WORKS IN ENGLISH TRANSLATION: Major Trends in Jewish Mysticism, 1941; (editor) Zohar: The Book of Splendor, 1949; Jewish Gnosticism, Merkabah Mysticism, and Talmudic Tradition, 1960; Jewish Mysticism in the Middle Ages, 1964; On the Kabbalah and Its Symbolism, 1965; Walter Benjamin, 1965; The Messianic Idea in Judaism, 1971; Sabbatai Sevi: The Mystical Messiah, 1626–1676, 1973; Kabbalah (Library of Jewish Knowledge), 1974;

SCHULZ

On Jews and Judaism in Crisis, edited by Werner J. Dannhauser, 1976.

ABOUT: Bloom, H. Kabbalah and Criticism, 1975; Contemporary Authors, 45–48, 1974; International Who's Who, 1978–79; Scholem, G.G. On Jews and Judaism in Crisis, 1976; Scholem, G.G. Von Berlin nach Jerusalem, 1978; Werblowsky, R.J.Z. and Wirszubski, C. (eds.) Studies in Mysticism and Religion Presented to Gershom G. Scholem on His Seventieth Birthday, 1967. *Periodicals*—Choice February 1974; Christian Century June 16, 1965; June 2, 1971; Commentary April 1973, March 1977; New York Review of Books October 4, 1973; March 31, 1977; April 14, 1977; New York Times Book Review February 24, 1974; Times Literary Supplement July 15, 1965; February 24, 1974; September 20, 1974; April 21, 1978; Washington Post December 13, 1971.

BRUNO SCHULZ

*SCHULZ, BRUNO** (July 12, 1892–November 1942), Polish novelist and short story writer, was born in Rodzymin, near the Eastern Galician town of Drohobycz (Ukrainian Drogobych) in the Carpathians, forty miles southwest of Lvov. The area was then part of the Austrian Empire, between the wars belonged to Poland, and since 1939 has been attached to the Ukraine. The town was predominantly Jewish, but Schulz came from a family of dry goods merchants whose trade separated them from the ghetto, so that his natural language was Polish rather than Yiddish. His father Jacob, who inherited a clothing store, ran it himself until illness forced him to abandon it to the care of his wife, when he retired to ten years of enforced idleness and eccentricity.

Bruno Schulz trained as an architect and artist, studying at Lvov (Lwów, Lemberg) University, specializing in lithography and drawing. He then returned to Drohobycz, where from 1921 to 1939 he earned his living as an art teacher at the local boys' high school. His translator Celina Wieniawska describes him as "small, unattractive and sickly, with a thin angular body and brown, deep-set eyes in a pale triangular face." He seems to have been a deeply inhibited man, incapable of leaving home or marrying. After his literary success in the mid-1930s he did visit Warsaw for a time, and once ventured as far as Paris. But for most of his life he remained in Drohobycz, far from any literary or artistic center, working at a job he detested.

Schulz was therefore a very solitary artist, at first too modest and timid to approach publishers, writing and drawing obsessively for himself alone, to relieve a chronic boredom which amounted almost to melancholia. Under these circumstances he developed one of the most original literary imaginations of modern Europe. His transfigured universe has often been compared with that of Kafka, whom Schulz ad-

*shōolts

mired greatly, translating Kafka's novel *The Trial* into Polish in 1936. But Schulz's talent was not derivative and his kinship with Kafka—who was also born into a middle-class Jewish family on the Slav fringes of the declining Austro-Hungarian Empire—was something much deeper than a literary influence: it was a profound affinity of background and temperament. Isaac Bashevis Singer, another Jewish writer from a similar background, observes: "I would say that between Schulz and Kafka there is something that Goethe calls *Wahlverwandtschaft,* an affinity of souls which you have chosen for yourself."

Indeed, as Celina Wieniawska points out, it is not necessary to explain Schulz in terms of literary derivations or theories: he "was a solitary man, living apart, filled with his dreams, with memories of his childhood, with an intense, formidable inner life, a painter's imagination, a sensuality and responsiveness to physical stimuli which most probably could find satisfaction only in artistic creation—a volcano, smouldering silently in the isolation of a sleepy provincial town." His paintings and drawings have been compared with those of Utrillo, de Chirico, Henri Rousseau, and above all Chagall. A selection of his drawings was published along with a brief manuscript of his in *Druga jesień* (The Second Autumn, 1973). A recurring subject is female dominance and male submission, and Philip Roth says "there is an eerie, almost tawdry erotic suggestiveness to some of these pictures—small, supplicating men looking not unlike Schulz himself, and remote, half-naked adolescent girls, or statuesque, painted shopgirls —they remind me a little of the 'trashy' erotic world of another Polish writer, Witold Gombrowicz." Like Kafka, Schulz seems to have lived a good deal of his erotic life through long and intense correspondences with women, and his first book is said to have begun as a series of letters to a woman friend, the Yiddish poet Deborah Vogel, who urged him to see them as a literary work. A selection of Schulz's letters, edited by his biographer Jerzy Ficowski, has been published as *Księga listów* (A Book of Letters, 1975), well illustrated with photographs of the author's home, family, friends, and literary acquaintances.

In his early forties this unknown art teacher startled the Polish literary world with two books in which his drab provincial town was transformed into a magical and sometimes terrifying world of the imagination. Schulz had sent some of his stories to Zofia Nalkowska, a distinguished woman novelist whom he knew through friends, and she arranged their publication. His first book was *Sklepy cynamonowe* (1934, translated by Celina Wieniawska as *The Street of Crocodiles;* in England as *Cinnamon Shops*). This was followed three years later by *Sanatorium pod klipsydrą* (1937, translated by Wieniawska as *Sanatorium Under the Sign of the Hourglass*), illustrated with his own lively drawings. Both contain stories in which the obsessively observed realities of life in Drohobycz are projected through the prismatic imagination of a single unnamed narrator, so that these short story collections have something of the unity of novels, as well as a strong element of transmogrified autobiography. The central figure is Father, forced into early retirement by illness, like Schulz's real father, a nuisance and an embarrassment in both shop and home.

He is one of the great eccentrics of literature, an "incorrigible improviser" waging war "against the fathomless, elemental boredom that strangled the city." Floating "on the periphery of life, in half-real regions, on the margins of existence," he immerses himself in bizarre hobbies and strange obsessions, like his ornithological phase. At great cost in effort and money he imports from Hamburg, Holland, and Africa fertilized eggs of all sorts of exotic birds, and hatches them out in the attic under brooding hens. Soon, brightly plumaged peacocks, pheasants, woodcocks, and condors are perching on cupboards and curtains and lamps, their feathers carpeting the floor at feeding time. One sad, ascetic condor was specially privileged, being allowed to use Father's chamber pot. A huge thin bird with a naked neck and a warty, wrinkled face, he would sit dozing opposite Father, and the narrator "could not shake off the impression, seeing him thus asleep, that I had before me a mummy, a wizened and hence smaller mummy of my father." The attic becomes "a real birds' hotel," where Father arranges incongruous matings and raises strange mutant birds. The nemesis of this kingdom of the birds is the young maid Adela, whose power over Father is almost limitless: "It was enough for Adela to waggle her fingers at him to imitate tickling, for him to rush through all the rooms in a wild panic, banging the doors after him, to fall at last flat on the bed in the farthest room and wriggle in convulsions of laughter." Losing patience, Adela one day sweeps the birds out of the window. Father comes down from the empty attic "a broken man, a banished king who had lost his throne and kingdom."

Father is a great believer in metamorphosis. He loathes and is fascinated by cockroaches; finding black spots on his skin one day, he philosophically prepares for a magic transformation into the creature he dreads by lying naked on the floor, then by imitating its "ceremonial crawl." (In Kafka's more famous myth it is—significantly—the ineffectual son who is changed into a cockroach.) Father hides in closets, climbs the curtains, disappears for many days into remote and forgotten corners of the house, re-emerges to proclaim new marvels. Watching the seamstresses snipping and sewing to dress the tailor's dummy, he sees this "lady of horsehair and cloth with a black knot instead of a head" as a "Moloch ... unrelenting as only female deities can be." Father, entranced, lectures the seamstresses on mannequins: "There is no dead matter ... lifelessness is only a disguise behind which lurk unknown forms of life." And this inspired heretic becomes the author of the derisive "A Treatise on Mannequins or the Second Book of Genesis," conjuring up demiurges out of the darkness, and asking: "Have you heard at night the frightening wail of those wax dummies locked in the market stalls, the mournful chorus of those torsos of wood and porcelain beating their fists against the walls of their prison?"

But Father's one-man campaign against the banal and the mechanical cannot keep pace with reality (which, Father assures us, "is as thin as paper and betrays with all its cracks its imitative nature"). Oil is discovered in Galicia and Drohobycz becomes a boom town, a confused place where a modern industrial society mushrooms inside the crumbling structures of an obsolete patriarchal world. The order and dignity represented by the cinnamon shops, with their aromas of spices from far distant countries, give way to something brash and greedy and second-rate. In this world the people are themselves transformed into mannequins, deprived of their illusions and hopes.

Schulz's vision of Jewish life, with his pixilated Father at its center, is pervaded by an almost religious sense of the oddness and mystery of existence. Reviewing *The Street of Crocodiles,* V.S. Pritchett concluded that "Schulz's book is a masterpiece of comic writing: grave yet demented, domestically plain yet poetic, exultant and forgiving, marvellously inventive, shy and never raw. There is not a touch of whimsy in it." It seemed to Paul Hamel that the stories "illustrate and comment on not only life, but contemporary literary forms and, at center, the nature of reality and illusion." Czeslaw Milosz praised Schultz's ability to turn people into "mythological figures, the heroes of a parable on existence," and Cynthia Ozick, commenting that "the shock of Schulz's images brings us the authentic bedevilment of the Europe we are heir to," places him with Babel, Singer, and Kafka "among those writers who break our eyes with torches, and end by demonstrating the remarkable uses of a purposeful dark."

In 1938 Schulz was awarded a prize by the Polish Academy of Literature for his two published books, which represent all that survives of his original work apart from a few pieces published in magazines. The most important of these is the brief novella "Kometa" (The Comet, 1938), which first appeared in the well-known literary magazine *Wiadomości Literackie* (Literary News). At the beginning of the war he was working on a novel with the title *Mesjasz* (The Messiah) but nothing remains of this work; the manuscript was left for safekeeping with a friend, but neither friend nor manuscript survived the Holocaust. The mannequin world which Schulz had so prophetically described overtook the author himself when the Nazis occupied Drohobycz, and the cinnamon shop world was reduced to a ghetto. A Gestapo officer who liked Schulz's drawings is said to have secured for him a special pass out of the ghetto into the "Aryan" quarter. Venturing there one day towards the end of 1942, he was recognized by another officer, a rival of his protector, and shot dead in the street. His works were reissued in Polish in 1957, and have been translated into French and German. When Celina Wieniawska's English version of *Sanatorium Under the Sign of the Hourglass* appeared in 1978, Isaac Bashevis Singer wrote that what Schulz had accomplished in his short life "was enough to make him one of the most remarkable writers who ever lived."

PRINCIPAL WORKS IN ENGLISH TRANSLATION: The Street of Crocodiles, 1963 (in England, Cinnamon Shops); Sanatorium Under the Sign of the Hourglass, 1978. *Stories in* Gillon, A. and Krzyzanowski, L. (eds.) Introduction to Modern Polish Literature, 1964.

ABOUT: Ficowski, J. Regiony wielkiej herezji, 1967; Goślicki-Baur, E. Die Prosa von Bruno Schulz, 1975; Milosz, C. The History of Polish Literature, 1969; Penguin Companion to Literature 2, 1969. *Periodicals*—Book Week December 22, 1963; New York Review of Books April 14, 1977; New York Times Book Review March 29, 1964; February 13, 1977; July 9, 1978; Polish Perspectives June 1966; Saturday Review October 26, 1963.

*SCIASCIA, LEONARDO (January 8, 1921–), Italian novelist, short story writer, dramatist, essayist, and critic, was born at Racalmuto, a small town near the ancient southern city of Agrigento in Sicily. He was educated at the Istituto Magistrale in the central Sicilian town of Caltanissetta, and subsequently worked as a teacher and a journalist, editing the review *Galleria* and contributing to many other magazines and newspapers. He spent most of his life in his native region before moving in 1968 to the Sicilian capital of Palermo. He lives with his wife in an apartment whose walls are crowded with graphics by Braque, de Chirico, Picasso, and contemporary Sicilian artists. Once a month he goes back to visit his family and friends in Racalmuto, the well from which he has drawn most of his stories.

In fact, however, Sciascia first made his name in Italy with nonfictional books like *La Sicilia, il suo cuore* (The Heart of Sicily, 1952) and, much more important, *Le parrocchie di Regalpetra* (1956, translated by Judith Green as *Salt in the Wound*). The latter is an account of life in Sicily as it is typified by the history and social biography of "Regalpetra," which is clearly Sciascia's home town of Racalmuto thinly disguised. Days at the local club are contrasted with conditions in the nearby salt and sulphur mines, and set in the context of centuries of exploitation of the workers and peasants by the rich in unholy alliance with the Church—an alliance later joined by the Mafia, the Fascists, and the Christian Democrats. It is a penetrating and fearless indictment of greed, hypocrisy, violence, and waste, and of those aspects of the Sicilian character that sustain this "continual defeat of reason."

Luigi Barzini has described this book as the matrix of Sciascia's work: "All the principal themes he later developed are to be found in it." Many of his novels center upon crimes of violence and attempts to solve them, but these attempts are usually forlorn and hopeless searches for justice in an unjust society. Told that in the

*shyä′ shyä

LEONARDO SCIASCIA

United States his books generally "fall into the mystery bin," he was puzzled and saddened, saying: "At least I hope they will be regarded as metaphysical mysteries." As a Sicilian, Sciascia is aware of writing in a literary tradition that includes the social awareness and harsh realism of Verga, the historical sense of Lampedusa, and the psychological penetration of Pirandello, on whom he has written two important critical essays. He is also the author of a number of erudite studies of Sicilian history.

Sciascia's first fictional book, *Gli zii di Sicilia* (The Patriarchs of Sicily, 1958), contains four historical tales giving a bleak account of the island's social and spiritual health; they were warmly praised by the novelist Elio Vittorini among others. But it was his novella *Il giorno della civetta* (1961, translated by Archibald Colquhoun and Arthur Oliver as *Mafia Vendetta*) that made him famous. A man is shot dead as he steps onto the morning bus for Palermo. The investigation is assigned to a young police officer from northern Italy, whose commitment to the law is contrasted with the Sicilians' helpless submission to force. He eventually breaks through the conspiracy of silence, and discovers that the murder is part of a Mafia plot to dominate the building trade, a plot that also involves important members of the government. And there the investigation ends, since the government's official position is that the Mafia exists only in the imagination of communists.

The author's indignation is implicit rather than explicit in the cool, lucid prose he employs to describe violence and corruption. A reviewer in the *Times Literary Supplement* thought the book was "more a documentary account than a

study in character; but as a documentary it is in the highest class." Anthony Boucher similarly wrote that "the telling is clean and direct (aside from a few fuzzy passages obviously written with . . . libel laws in mind), and the evocation of Sicily is economic and masterly. Sicily is herself the protagonist, and the individual characters matter far less." It was no doubt this documentary quality that gave such authenticity to Sciascia's revelations, and the book, a bestseller in Italy, caused a public outcry, greatly embarrassed members of the government, and did much to awaken the Italian conscience to the moral, social, and political problems posed by the Mafia. Sciascia's work is far removed from the American cult of "Mafia chic," the boom in books and films glorifying the gangster families. He says: "I don't particularly like to write about the Mafia, because I don't care to join the pack dignifying them. Apologists who glamorize the Mafia don't know the Mafia."

The "continual defeat of reason" in Sicily is traced back to the eighteenth century in *Il Consiglio d'Egitto* (1963, translated by Adrienne Foulke as *The Council of Egypt*), which recounts in a single narrative two stories based on historical fact. An impoverished chaplain who scrapes a living as an interpreter of dreams carries out an impudent forgery of Maltese-Arabic documents. This deception, inspired by greed, inadvertently brings about a confrontation between crown and nobility. The imposter escapes virtually unscathed, but an idealistic young lawyer who tries to create a Free Republic of Sicily is executed with his companions, after tortures that turn the stomachs even of their judges.

Martin Levin thought that Sciascia's "intentions in assembling his two sketches of forger and martyr are obscure, and his novel is static," but most reviewers responded quite differently. Anthony West said it was plain in the end "that Sciascia has really been writing not about Vella and his imposture but about the responsibilities that the writer takes on when he sets out to satisfy himself by playing with the words and ideas from which sentences of death are made in the everyday world. It is a fine and disturbing book." A reviewer in the *Times Literary Supplement* wrote: "This witty, high-spirited and intensely gloomy novel, which starts with the techniques of comedy and ends, without noticeable change of manner, with appalling and unforgettable accounts of torture, does more to show up the soul of Sicily than a hundred tracts, however heartfelt." *Morte dell'inquistore* (1964, translated by Judith Green as *The Death of the Inquisitor*), also based on historical records, delves even deeper into the roots of Sicilian psychology, describing the solitary revolt of a heroic monk, Fra Diego La Matina, who was burnt by the Inquisition in 1658. Sciascia's "incandescent hatred of evil," wrote Luigi Barzini, "his love of liberty and reason, shine through his tranquil, spare prose."

L'Onorevole (The Honorable), a three-act play about modern Sicilian political life published in 1965, was followed a year later by another study of Mafia violence, *A ciascuno il suo* (translated by Adrienne Foulke as *A Man's Blessing*). A small-town pharmacist and his friend are murdered by a Mafia lawyer, and the timid Professor Laurana begins to investigate the crime. But Laurana, for all his learning about contemporary literature, is "un cretino" and that is his epitaph—who else but a cretin would go up against the Mafia? This "dry, elliptical, short" book was generally admired, and Herbert Mitgang called it "a rarity: a murder story on the surface that conceals a sociological view of a small town. It is a gem-like example of the difference between a mystery and a realized work of fiction that does not depend upon a tidy solution for its novelistic life."

Tired, perhaps, of being thought of as a "regional novelist," Sciascia set his next novel in "an entirely imaginary country . . . in which only power for the sake of power counts," and which is quite obviously the Italian mainland. In *Il contesto* (1971, translated by Adrienne Foulke as *Equal Danger*), the literate, principled, brilliant Inspector Rogas is assigned to investigate the murder of a district attorney and no less than six Supreme Court judges. The tangled web of clues that he slowly unravels leads him to a group of people of great power and wealth—people who should be but are not above suspicion. And in the end yet another of Sciascia's brave, honorable, but lonely heroes is marked for extinction. It seemed to P. S. Prescott that Sciascia was a "witty writer no longer entertained by his own satire"—whose "cynicism seems to have led him from amusement to despair" in this fable about the way in which "justice can be removed to a platform where it is concerned only with its own forms." The novel caused a furor among Italian politicians but disappointed some reviewers, one of whom wrote: "It may have been that to move from the limited, familiar and more or less clear-cut scene of Sicilian life to the vast conundrum of Italian politics was in itself an impossible amibition, or that Signore Sciascia's deliberate, utilitarian intention of castigating Italy's inane political parties . . . could not be reconciled with his essentially poetic imagination, but the fact is that *Il contesto* is far less telling than his two Mafia novels."

Il mare colore del vino (The Wine-Dark Sea, 1973) is an excellent collection of short stories published between 1959 and 1972, offering a kind of summary of Sciascia's work and preoccupations. It was followed by *Todo modo* (1974, translated by Adrienne Foulke as *One Way or Another*), another elegantly cynical study of the misuse of power, set this time in a hermitage used by the rich and powerful for annual crash courses in spiritual rejuvenation. Three of these men are murdered, and the police are guided in their efforts to find the killer by the narrator, a painter whose irony and detachment put several reviewers in mind of his creator. The crimes are never solved and "the despairingly ingenious hypotheses invented to account for them are no more than an extra, posthumous indictment of three rotten lives spent in deceiving and fixing to keep the rich rich and the poor poor." One critic found evidence in this book of "an increasing sense that to write about corruption is a peculiarly ambiguous way of countering it." The novel was filmed in 1976 by Francesco Rosi as *Cadaveri eccellenti* (Illustrious Corpses), and provoked intense political debate.

La scomparsa di Majorana (The Disappearance of Majorana, 1975) and *I pugnalatori* (The Knifers, 1976) investigate real-life mysteries. Ettore Majorana was a young Italian physicist who disappeared in 1938 and Sciascia goes over the case again, suggesting that Majorana had committed suicide when he realized that the work he was doing would lead inevitably to the production of atomic weapons. *I pugnalatori* reconsiders the stabbing of thirteen citizens of Palermo on a single day in October 1862, assembling evidence that suggests the conspiracy was led by a local nobleman who was secretly in the pay of the Bourbons. This book, so shockingly similar to one of Sciascia's fictional indictments of Sicilian corruption and violence, is written with similar simplicity and economy.

Leonardo Sciascia received the Crotone Prize in 1962 for *Mafia Vendetta,* and has since been awarded the Premio Libera Stampa and the Premio Prato, among other prizes. He is now widely regarded as one of Italy's major writers. A critic in the *Times Literary Supplement* has said that "his style shows how strongly, how single-mindedly and intelligently he has reacted against the candyfloss fluffiness of so much around him. What he has to say is compressed so tightly that his writing is rock-hard, sometimes dry; in contrast to the almost crazy carelessness in the use of words so often found in Italy, his words are picked so exactly that they form mosaics of their own, precise patterns of emotional or intellectual meaning beyond the precise sense of what they seem to be saying. For all this deliberation and exactness, there is no sense of slowness, though; rather an air of speed and urgency, of the neat disposal of thoughts already patterned in the mind." The themes that concern him—power and its misuse, justice and its absence—are universal ones, and whether or not it is proper to classify him as a regional writer is a matter of opinion. He himself quotes his friend Guttoso, who once said: "Even if I paint an apple, Sicily is there." And Sciascia adds: "And the worm that is eating the apple from within."

PRINCIPAL WORKS IN ENGLISH TRANSLATION: Mafia Vendetta, 1963; The Council of Egypt, 1966; A Man's Blessing, 1968; Salt in the Wound, *published with* The Death of the Inquisitor, 1969; Equal Danger, 1973; One Way or Another, 1977. *Stories in* Trevelyan, R. (ed.) Italian Writing Today, 1967; Waldman, G. (ed.) Penguin Book of Italian Short Stories, 1969.

ABOUT: Guidice, G. Pirandello, 1975; International Who's Who, 1978–79; Literatura Italiana: I Contemporanei 5 1974; Pacifici, S. A Guide to Contemporary Italian Literature, 1962; Seymour-Smith, M. Guide to Modern World Literature, 1973. *Periodicals*—Atlantic August 1973; Books Abroad Winter 1973, Summer 1974, Winter 1976; Book World July 13, 1969; Choice April 1969; Critic November-December 1973; Italian Quarterly Summer-Fall 1965; Library Journal March 1, 1968; New York Review of Books October 9, 1969; New York Times Book Review May 12, 1968; September 16, 1973; New Yorker March 1966; Newsweek July 16, 1973; Times Literary Supplement July 19, 1963; November 7, 1963; October 6, 1966; May 1, 1969; March 17, 1972; October 5, 1973; March 14, 1975; January 30, 1976; March 25, 1977.

SCOTT, F(RANCIS) R(EGINALD) (August 1, 1899–), Canadian poet and writer on law and politics, was born in Quebec City. His father was a clergyman, Archdeacon Frederick George Scott, who was also a popular minor poet. F.R. Scott was educated at Quebec High School (1908–1917) and at Bishop's College, Lennoxville (Quebec), where he received his B.A. in 1919; in 1919–1920 he taught for a while at each of these two institutions. From 1920 to 1923 Scott pursued his literary studies as a Rhodes Scholar at Magdalen College, Oxford, earning a second B.A. in 1922, a B. Litt. in 1923. Returning to Canada, he taught briefly at Lower Canada College, Montreal, before entering McGill University to read law (1923–1927). His poetry began to appear at that time, much of it in the *McGill Fortnightly Review* which Scott founded with his friend A. J. M. Smith, and which survived from 1925 to 1927. Scott had come back from England profoundly excited by the new poetry of Eliot and Pound and both as editor of

F. R. SCOTT

the *MFR* and through the example of his own verse was an early champion of modernism in Canada.

Scott received his law degree and was called to the Quebec Bar in 1927, but practiced for only a year before returning to McGill University. He was assistant professor (1928–1929) then associate professor (1929–1934) of federal and constitutional law, professor of civil law (1934–1955), and Macdonald Professor of Law (1955–1967), serving as dean of the law faculty in 1961–1964. Scott is a Queen's Counsel (Quebec) and a recognized authority on constitutional law. He has a special (and characteristic) interest in civil liberties, and between 1956 and 1964 served as counsel in several such cases before the Supreme Court of Canada, for example fighting and winning the legal battle against the censorship of *Lady Chatterley's Lover.* He was chairman of the Legal Research Committee of the Canadian Bar Association in 1954–1956 and adviser to the government of Saskatchewan at constitutional conferences in 1950 and 1960. In 1952 he spent a year in Burma as the United Nations Technical Assistance representative.

Frank Scott has also been an important figure in Canadian politics and public affairs. He was a co-founder in 1932 of the League for Social Reconstruction, from which developed the socialist Cooperative Commonwealth Federation Party (now the New Democratic Party); Scott was national chairman of the CCF from 1942 to 1950. He has also served as a national council member of the Penal Association of Canada (1935–1946), on the national executive of the Canadian Institute of International Affairs (1935–1950), and as a member of the Royal

731

Commission on Bilingualism and Biculturism (1963–1970). Scott is the author or co-author of a number of books on politics, economics, social planning, federalism, and civil liberties in Canada, as well as many articles on these subjects and on constitutional law.

He has been equally vigorous in the field of literature. A.J.M. Smith says that "for more than thirty years he has been a leader of groups of younger poets and a stimulating force in the poetry scene"—there is "hardly a poet in Canada who has not, passing through Montreal, made his pilgrimage to Clarke Avenue, Westmount, and been royally entertained and stimulated." Scott has been the editor (and usually the founder or co-founder) of a whole succession of influential magazines, including *The Canadian Mercury* (1928), *Canadian Forum* (1936–1939), *Preview* (1942–1945), and *Northern Review* (1945–1947). He was chairman of the Canadian Writers' Conference in 1955.

In spite of this immensely busy and successful public life, Scott's poetry never reads like that of a "public man." His first collection, *Overture,* did not appear until 1945, when he was already in his mid-forties. It includes social and political satires, love poems, and nature lyrics—the three kinds of poetry that he has continued to write—all of them direct in language and clear-cut in their ideas. *Events and Signals,* appearing nine years later, was thought less bitter in its satires, richer in technique and language. It includes the deep and witty love poem "Will to Win," which begins:

> Your tall French legs, my V for victory,
> My sign and symphony, Eroica,
> Uphold me in these days of my occupation
> And stir my underground resistance . . .

The satires in these first books, together with others not previously collected, were assembled to form the volume *The Eye of the Needle* (1957). The contents range from "The Canadian Authors Meet," one of the earliest and most famous (but not most subtle) of Scott's lampoons, directed against the stuffy provincialism of Canadian literature, to the later, wittier, gentler "Bonne Entente":

> The advantages of living with two cultures
> Strike one at every turn,
> Especially when one finds a notice in an office
> building:
> "This elevator will not run on Ascension Day."

It has been suggested that the success of Scott's satirical verse has distracted attention from his other poetry, whose steady refinement in technique and deepening in content is evident in the metaphysical and mythopoeic poems in *Signature* (1964) and *Selected Poems* (1966). A. J. M. Smith has discussed at some length the first poem in the latter volume, "Lakeshore." The poet stands by the "bevelled edge" of the lake, then dives into the dark water. This immersion in the element where life began becomes a journey into man's biological history, from which the poet rises again to "the prison of our ground," where we have "grown/ Upright in posture, false-erect." He ends on a "crowded street" where he feels "the sudden rain come down/ And in the old, magnetic sound" hears "the opening of a gate/ That loosens all the seven seas./ Watching the whole creation drown/ I muse, alone, on Ararat." This poem, in irregularly rhymed stanzas, seems to Smith characteristic of Scott's mature work in its themes and motives, in its fascination with water (as element and symbol), in the identification of the poet's self with Man, and in "the inescapable tendency to interchange the language and imagery of science . . . with the language and imagery of religion."

Robin Skelton has said that it is "the pressure of intelligence that dominates and moulds" Scott's poetry—"even the visionary poems rather suggest a disciplined contemplation than a blinding illumination. . . . He is a splendid versifier, an intensely intelligent writer, a wit, and a man of deep feeling; nevertheless, though his stated opinions are often radical, liberal, and sophisticated, his modes of operation are so dependent upon already established modes and attitudes that poetically . . . he must be regarded as a conservative. . . . But he is assured of a place upon the middle slopes [of Parnassus]." William Walsh has little time for Scott's satires, which he calls "indignant thumping," but credits him with "several exquisitely fine . . . poems, charged with response to the land and to the modern self, which can be not unfairly related to Ezra Pound." Scott's friend A.J.M. Smith, on the other hand, hazards a comparison with Marvell, and concludes: "Scott has managed, more successfully than most, to unify his public life of social responsibility with the private, perceptive and contemplative life of the poet. All his poems, from the gayest and lightest expression of delight in life through his witty and sometimes savage satires to the metaphysical lyrics, are informed and qualified by a sense of responsibility and an inescapable sincerity, serious but never solemn."

Scott has maintained close links with French-Canadian writers and intellectuals, and has published a volume of translations from the poetry of St.-Denys Garneau and of Anne Hébert. He has also published (in French) a dialogue with the latter on the problems of translation. *Trouvailles* is a collection of "found" poems—carefully selected prose pieces, including passages from scientific works, newspaper articles, and public announcements, laid out as if they were free verse; the effect is sometimes satirical, sometimes funny, and sometimes surprisingly beautiful. With A.J.M. Smith, Scott has edited two important anthologies: *New Provinces* (1936), an introduction to the work of a generation of poets younger than themselves; and *The Blasted Pine* (1957), which collects satirical and "disrespectful" poetry, mostly by Canadian writers.

The author has been a visiting professor at the University of Toronto (1953), at Michigan State University (1957), in the French Canada Studies Program at McGill (1967–1971), and at Dalhousie University (1969–1971). He has been loaded with honors and awards, including a Guggenheim fellowship (1940), *Poetry*'s Guarantor's Prize, the Lorne Pierce Medal of the Royal Society of Canada (1964), and the Canada Council's Molson Award (1967). He is a Companion of the Order of Canada (1967), a Fellow of the Royal Society of Canada (1947), and an honorary foreign member of the American Academy of Arts and Sciences. He holds fifteen honorary degrees.

Frank Scott was married in 1928 to the painter Marian Mildred Dale, who has been a lively influence on the graphic arts in Canada. They have a son, Peter Dale Scott, who is also a writer. The poet Ralph Gustafson has written of Scott: "To say/ that this man is fantastic/ is to be/ Frankly wrong./ Real/ is the right root/ for him/ . . . / Mortality/ moves him,/ he goes for wrong-doing,/ never lets bad enough/ alone. . . ."

PRINCIPAL WORKS: *Poetry*—Overture, 1945; Events and Signals, 1954; The Eye of the Needle: Satires, Sorties, Sundries, 1957; Signature, 1964; Selected Poems, 1966; Trouvailles: Poems From Prose, 1967; (with others) Poets Between the Wars, edited by M.T. Wilson, 1967; The Dance Is One, 1973. *Nonfiction*—(with H.M. Cassidy) Labour Conditions in the Men's Clothing Industry, 1935; Canada Today: A Study of Her National Interests and National Policy, 1938; Canada and the United States, 1941; (with David Lewis) Make This Your Canada: A Review of C.C.F. History and Policy, 1943; Cooperation for What? United States and Britain's Commonwealth, 1944; The World's Civil Service, 1954; (with others) Evolving Canadian Federalism, 1958; The Canadian Constitution and Human Rights (radio talks), 1959; Civil Liberties and Canadian Federalism, 1959; (with Anne Hébert) Dialogue sur la traduction, 1970; Essays on the Constitution: Aspects of Canadian Law and Politics, 1977. *As Editor*—(with A. J. M. Smith) New Provinces: Poems of Several Authors, 1936; (with A. J. M. Smith) The Blasted Pine: An Anthology of Satire, Invective

and Disrespectful Verse, Chiefly by Canadian Writers, 1957 (revised 1967). *As Translator*—St.-Denys Garneau and Anne Hébert: Translations, 1962.

ABOUT: Creative Canada Vol. 1, 1971; Klinck, C.F. (ed.) The Literary History of Canada, 1965; Oxford Companion to Canadian History and Literature, 1967; Pacey, D. Ten Canadian Poets, 1958; Penguin Companion to Literature 1, 1971; Vinson, J. (ed.) Contemporary Poets, 1975; Walsh, W. Commonwealth Literature, 1973; Who's Who, 1978; Woodcock, G. (ed.) Poets and Critics, 1974. *Periodicals*—Canadian Literature Winter 1967 (special Scott issue); Dalhousie Review Winter 1973–1974; Poetry April 1956, February 1968; Queen's Quarterly Autumn 1972, Winter 1973.

"SEARCH, ALEXANDER." *See* PESSOA, FERNANDO

"SEBASTIAN, LEE." *See* SILVERBERG, ROBERT

SELBY, HUBERT (JR.) (July 23, 1928–), American novelist, writes: "I was born in Brooklyn, New York. I graduated from P.S. 102. Have been restless most of my life, until a few years ago, and extremely so as a child. I always loved the water and dreamed of going to sea. When I was fifteen I started working in the New York Harbor, and elsewhere, on dredges and other harbor craft. Eventually I went to sea during the latter part of World War II, sailing in the black gang.

"In September of 1946 I was taken off a ship in Bremen, Germany, with tuberculosis. I was brought back to the States, on the hospital ship *Charles Stafford,* in October of that year, and started over three years of hospitalization, almost dying on several occasions.

"When I arrived in this country my family was told that I could not live more than six weeks and so they brought streptomycin, which was administered, and my condition improved enough for me to undergo a series of operations. Eventually ten ribs were removed and most of one lung was collapsed and a piece of the other one was removed.

"I left the hospital in November of 1950, and have not had any problem with tuberculosis since. Subsequently I developed bronchial asthma and so, all things considered, I was forced to give up playing football.

"While in the hospital I started reading for the first time in my life and eventually developed a desire to write. I met a fellow from the neighborhood who had been writing since he was a kid, Gilbert Sorrentino, and he became my literary mentor. I think of him as the most outstanding and brilliant Man of Letters of my generation. He is not only a great poet and prose writer, but an incredibly perspicacious critic. He has the

HUBERT SELBY

ability to read your work from your point of view and criticize it constructively. We have spent years talking about the art of literature, and living, and he has helped me find my way and develop my voice.

"I have come to believe a few things. I believe that an artist's only job is the perfection of his art.

"I believe that each piece of work has its own needs which make their own demands and it is up to the artist to understand these needs and subordinate his ego to the work. No one should have to struggle through the artist's ego to get to the work.

"My goal as a writer is to have the surface of the line so loaded and obvious that it not only creates a profundity and subtlety, but is so complete that the reader does not have to read the words, that they will sing off the page.

"I believe that it is absolutely true: in *His* will is our Peace.

"I believe that this can become a reality by *living* the Prayer for Peace of St. Francis of Asissi, one day at a time.

"I believe that I fail at all these things, sometimes just humanly, other times miserably, but I also believe that through the Grace of God I can continue to try to be the best I can be today.

"I now live in Hollywood, the land of fruits and nuts, with my wife Suzanne and my daughter Rachel, age ten, and my son William, age five. We have two cats: Pumpkin, age seven, and her second son, Meanie, age six. Her first son Isaac Babel, age six, moved across the alley to a quieter home. Our children visit him occasionally.

"We are very happy."

Selby is the son of Hubert Selby, an engineer, and the former Adalin Layne. As he says, he was a Merchant Marine oiler from 1944 to 1946, when his health collapsed. He spent most of the next four years in the hospital, beginning then to read and to make his own attempts at writing. Selby told a *Newsweek* interviewer: "I've known the people I write about all my life, and for a while when I was twenty-one I lived their life. I wasn't looking in. I *was* in." From 1950 to 1964 Selby worked as a clerk in various offices and as an insurance adjuster, and in 1965 he became a freelance copywriter for the *National Enquirer*. An assortment of other jobs followed, while Selby continued to write. He is the author of several screen plays.

Last Exit to Brooklyn was published in 1964 and made Selby famous. The book is made up of six stories, connected by common characters, and set mostly in the slums of waterfront Brooklyn. Some of these stories or episodes had already appeared in *Black Mountain Review, New Directions, Swank,* and the *Provincetown Review.* "Another Day, Another Dollar," the opening piece, describes a night in the life of a gang of teenagers, who for no reason whatever beat and stomp a young soldier. The same gang appears in "The Queen Is Dead," taking part in a joyless orgy of sex, drugs, and drink with a group of homosexuals. The scene is described by Georgette, a young transvestite addicted to drugs and Edgar Allan Poe who is eventually brutalized by the gang member he tries to seduce. "Tralala," which had involved the *Provincetown Review* in an obscenity trial in 1961, is about a psychopathic young prostitute who, in a drunken fury of sexual pride, takes on all comers in a parking lot and is physically destroyed. Other episodes fill out a Dantean vision of a hell on earth, of squalid streets and garish bars, of lovingly executed violence, and sex committed in hatred—a cold inferno in which there are no dialogues, only lying monologues, where action is always destruction, and a chorus of old women see, hear, and speak evil.

The book caused a furor, praised in some quarters as a major work of art, hysterically condemned in others. It was banned in Italy, and in England it was published in 1966, found criminally obscene and suppressed, then republished in 1968 when the original verdict was overturned on appeal. Even so enlightened a critic as Theodore Solotaroff thought it the work of "a man whom violence turns on." It seemed to Solotaroff that the most successful section of the book was "Tralala," where the title character is created "from the inside out, so that the language of the narrative and her own interior monologue merge in one long rush of flat, baleful expression." Selby is "utterly faithful to the brutality of her nature and to the strong attraction that her nihilism exerts upon his imagination. ... Tralala is Selby's ideal character. She has none of the normal emotions that would offer opposition, contradiction, even ambiguity to the simple, destructive point he wants to make with her. Otherwise, Selby's characters soon begin to reveal less of their lives than of the narrow, habitual grooves in which their author's sensibility runs."

Charles D. Peavy, on the other hand, places Selby in "the tradition of the religious-moralist-satirist that includes Swift and Pope, and which began with the medieval preachers who denounced lechery and gluttony by presenting repulsive portraits of the sins of the flesh. ... Selby has an almost obsessive concern with sin—not with the fact that it exists, but that it has become, as he says, 'an ambiguous thing in our society.' " Anthony Burgess, who found "a unity of intention as well as scene which makes the term 'novel' altogether applicable," was reminded by Selby's style of the *rapportage* technique of Dos Passos: "The fingers seem to pound the keys in a mad effort to record conversation and interior monologue white-hot"; Kenneth Allsop similarly spoke of "an urgent ticker-tape from hell."

One of the calmer reviews was that of Webster Schott in the New York *Times Book Review.* "Above all," he wrote, "Selby is writing about the distortion of love, the rottenness of its substitutes, and the horror and pathos of its perversion. The shock produces total recoil. . . . This would have been richer and perhaps even more terrifying fiction if it had explored love as well as its denial. . . . Selby's people do not know what love is and cannot express it, as [Paul] Goodman has said, because their society has given them no opportunity to find out. . . . We believe Selby's characters and will never be able to forget them. But they are not Everyman. In praising Selby's astonishing power to tear our sensibilities, one must remember that this is part, not all, of the world we would weep for."

In Selby's second novel, *The Room,* a man awaits trial for a crime he has apparently not committed. The book is given over largely to his fantasies of revenge on the two policemen who arrested him, either by humiliating them in court by the brilliance of his defense, or by years of physical torture. These tortures, described in exhaustive detail, reduce the policemen to the level of animals; they are finally forced to couple like dogs while their families watch.

The reviewers were divided much as they had been by *Last Exit.* Dotson Rader thought *The Room* "an exquisite, meticulous examination of the curious, piteous lust between oppressor and oppressed. It documents the sexual basis of power and criminality. As a work of the imagination, I think it assures Hubert Selby's place in the front rank of American novelists. His work has the power, the intimacy with suffering and morality, the honesty and moral urgency of Dostoevsky's." Other reviewers disagreed, like one in the *Times Literary Supplement,* who wrote: "Blood, mucus, slime and pus drip from the pages as the fantasies become more frenzied. The impression of a man crazed by an impotent fury and by a wild, hopeless need for revenge is intended and—undeniably—achieved; the problem is that what begins as an understandable emotional indulgence on the part of the main character begins to look increasingly like a technical indulgence on the part of the author. . . . The bludgeon of sadism is wielded so excessively and with such force that the reader is soon clubbed into insensibility."

Harry White, the central character in *The Demon* (1976), is possessed by something close to satyriasis, a fact on which his employer plays to turn him into a willing corporate robot. When concupiscence begins to interfere with his work, however, Harry is advised to marry. He does so, very happily, but soon the lunchtime itch begins again. Shocked by his own insatiable needs, driven by self-disgust to self-defilement, Harry goes down the slippery slope to pilfering, burglary, and eventually to sadism and murder. Eric Korn treated this novel as the work of a caricaturist, regarding "the hyperboles . . . [as] those of his characters" in this "shrewd, sour and captivatingly unwholesome novel." To Dean Flower, on the other hand, Harry's fall seemed a reversion to "the snarling, suffering, sado-masochistic underground man that has always been Selby's real hero. Harry White, it turns out, is really Harry Black" (the corrupt and deviant union man in *Last Exit to Brooklyn*). "This solemn farce," Flower went on, "comes equipped with moral gestures: two biblical epigraphs to start and no end of Christian symbolizing. . . . The real moral, however, lies in the obsessive grossness of Selby's style. No wit, irony, qualification, contingency, credibility, subtlety, social or moral complexity appears to distract the monologuist from his dreary exercise."

Selby has been married three times—to Inez Taylor in 1953, to Judith Lumino in 1964, and to Suzanne Shaw in 1967. He has four children. Selby's literary idol is Isaac Babel, but he believes that Beethoven has influenced him more.

SEMBÈNE

He says that he writes "by ear," and that "music of line" is important to him.

PRINCIPAL WORKS: Last Exit to Brooklyn, 1964; The Room, 1971; The Demon, 1976; Requiem for a Dream, 1978.

ABOUT: Burgess, A. introduction to post-trial edition of Last Exit to Brooklyn, 1968; Contemporary Authors 15–16, 1966; Hayman, D. and Rabkin, E. (eds.) Form in Fiction, 1974; Solotaroff, T. The Red Hot Vacuum, 1970; Vinson, J. (ed.) Contemporary Novelists, 1976; Who's Who in America, 1974–1975. Periodicals—Book Week December 20, 1964; Commentary January 1965; Critique 3 1969; Encounter March 1967; Literature and Psychology 4 1974; Nation December 7, 1964; New York Review of Books December 3, 1964; March 9, 1972; New York Times Book Review November 8, 1964; December 12, 1971; November 16, 1976; Newsweek December 28, 1964; September 25, 1978; Saturday Review November 7, 1964; January 23, 1954; April 3, 1965; December 11, 1971; Times Literary Supplement February 25, 1972.

OUSMANE SEMBÈNE

*SEMBÈNE, OUSMANE (January 8, 1923–), Senegalese novelist, short story writer, and film maker, was born in Ziguinchor, Casamance, in the south of Senegal. His family were Wolof-speaking fishermen but he wrote until recently in French. "I could have written . . . in Wolof," he said at a conference in 1965, "but then who would have read it?" On the same occasion he suggested that "all of us who are writers are also people who have to some extent lost their roots." For Sembène this deracination happened gradually. He had three years of education in a technical school in Marsassoum, not far from his home town, and thereafter worked variously as a fisherman, a plumber, a mechanic's helper, and a bricklayer in Dakar until he entered the Free French army in World War II. His unit took part in the invasion of Italy and he also served in France and Germany before his release in 1946.

As part of his military service Sembène had worked as a stevedore at the port of Marseilles. After a spell as a fisherman in Dakar he returned to Marseilles as a docker, and was soon representing other workers as a trade union leader, meanwhile continuing his education through wide reading. All this is reflected in his first book, Le Docker noir (The Black Docker, 1956), in which a white woman steals the manuscript of a black stevedore's novel and publishes it as her own. This apprentice work is flawed in a number of ways but is interesting, the author himself believes, in that "when I was writing it, I was already in exile from my home. . . . If you read Le Docker noir carefully, you will see that the problem was not merely the position of the Negroes; it was that of the Arabs and the Spanish exiles as well. All right, no comparison is

*sem ben′

possible between my sensibilities and those of the Whites: true enough, but do not say, because of that, that I support négritude."

Négritude was launched in the 1930s by, among others, Léopold Sédar Senghor, the poet who became president of Senegal. It set out to replace the sense of inferiority imposed on black people by colonialism with feelings of pride in Negro culture and sensibility. Necessary and important as the movement was, it was not free of sentimentality nor of tendencies to a narrow and arrogant racialism, and Sembène belongs to a generation of writers in French-speaking West Africa who consciously reacted against it. This does not alter his conviction that "it is, after all, the Africans who will ultimately bring about change in Africa—not the Americans or the French or the Russians or the Chinese."

Sembène's second novel was Ô Pays, mon beau peuple! (O My Country, My Beautiful People, 1957). Oumar Faye, its main character, is a young Senegalese who after a long absence returns to his native country with a white wife. His family rejects him, and in the course of the novel he also encounters opposition from the white community and from black farmers whose methods he attempts to modernize along cooperative lines. He is eventually murdered. A story of failure and defeat, reflecting the author's anxiety about the difficulties of effecting change in Africa, it is written nevertheless in a style of confident lyricism.

Sembène began to travel widely in the late 1950s, and since then he has visited many parts of Africa and Europe as well as Cuba, China, and the Soviet Union, where in the early 1960s he studied for a year at the Gorki Film Studios in Moscow. His third book, *Les Bouts de bois de Dieu* (1960, translated by Francis Price as *God's Bits of Wood*), established Sembène as a major figure among contemporary African novelists. It tells the story of the long, bitter, but ultimately successful railroad workers' strike on the Dakar to Niger line between October 1947 and March 1948. The book is an efficient piece of historical reconstruction as well as an imaginative achievement on a more panoramic scale than Sembène has attempted elsewhere in his fiction; it is also a more optimistic expression of his anticapitalist views than its predecessors. A. C. Brench called it a "serious attempt to synthesize a traditional African narrative form with an alien medium of expression and to use this synthesis to portray the evolution of modern Africa with its mixture of indigenous and Western technological elements."

Voltaïque, a collection of twelve short stories, appeared in 1962, and was subsequently translated by Len Ortzen as *Tribal Scars.* The volume is dominated by Sembène's characteristic concern for the rights of ordinary people, and especially for the rights of women, and this sometimes leads him to be critical of Muslim traditions. Not all of these pieces follow the formula of the modern short story; a few show that Sembène has also mastered the art of the Senegalese *griot,* or official storyteller. *Référendum,* a novel published in 1964 in the journal *Présence Africaine,* is the first volume of a projected but uncompleted trilogy, *L'Harmattan* (The Storm). It takes as its starting point the 1958 referendum in all the French West African territories when de Gaulle demanded a straight yes or no vote on the issue of France's continued rule.

Two novellas followed in 1965, *Véhi-Ciosane ou Blanche-genèse, suivi du Mandat,* translated by Clive Wake as *The Money-Order, with White Genesis.* These stories, the most admired of Sembène's shorter works, brought him the literature prize of the 1966 Festival of Negro Arts in Dakar. Sembène's first full-length film, *Mandabi,* was based on *The Money-Order,* in which a devout Muslim, illiterate and naive, receives a large money order from his nephew in Paris, and is tricked and finally ruined in his efforts to cash it. Sembène had set out to denounce "in a Brechtian manner the dictatorship of the bourgeoisie over the people. This is a bourgeoisie of a special kind which does not consist of well-off people ... but of intellectuals and civil servants." This comic morality won the special jury prize at the Venice Film Festival in 1968 and was chosen as best foreign film at the Atlanta Film Festival in 1970.

Mandabi was filmed in Wolof, and Donald Herdeck has explained that Sembène turned to the cinema "in order to reach an African popular audience, few of whom know French or have access to books in any language." Since then he has concentrated more on films than on novels, becoming the first black African film director of world stature, generally recognized as "the father of the African film." His other films include *Borom Sarret* (1964), a brief study of poverty and social division in Senegal; *Le Noire de . . .* (Black Girl, 1967), about the humiliations imposed on a servant girl by her French employers; and *Emitai* (1972), set in Casamance in World War II, which shows the dawning of political consciousness in a fetish-worshipping tribal people suddenly brought into contact with the military power of French colonialism.

Xala (1973, translated under the same title by Clive Wake) was created as a film and published almost simultaneously as a short novel. It is a satire on the survival of colonial attitudes in post-colonial Senegal. El Hadji, a greedy Europeanized businessman, adds a third wife to his collection, but discovers on his wedding night that he has the *xala,* the curse of impotence. When modern pharmacology fails, he spends a fortune on quacks and witch doctors. His business collapses, he is voted off the board of the Chamber of Commerce, and he is horribly humiliated by a man he once ruined. This "wickedly effective" satire was almost universally praised, both as a novel and as a movie. *Ceddo* (The Common People, 1977), Sembène's most ambitious film, is a two-hour epic in color dealing explicitly with a number of highly controversial topics, including African involvement in the slave trade, the low status of women, and "Islamic colonialism." Though there is very little censorship in Senegal, *Ceddo* has been banned there, ostensibly over the spelling of the Wolof title—government officials insist that it should have only one *d.* Sembène has defended his spelling in a three-page open letter, and says: "Some groups in Africa are intolerant of others. This is a real danger for the continent, and the artists— more than any other people—must have the courage to put their fingers on this danger and to point it out. If African film makers are to be as useful to our people as our teachers, doctors, farmers and carpenters, then we must create films that will help us to see ourselves from many different angles."

Mbella Sonne Dipoko has described Sembène as "the leader of the new dynamic realism which is developing in French African writing," and this is the view of most critics. Though he is now most widely known as a filmmaker, his novels and stories are regarded as crucial to an appreciation of the abrasive and often self-satirizing generation that succeeded Léopold Senghor and David Diop. Sembène lives in Dakar and, according to Donald Herdeck, often sits in the market there giving his services as a scribe to illiterate peasants and workers. He is the founder and editor of the first Wolof monthly, *Kaddu.*

PRINCIPAL WORKS IN ENGLISH TRANSLATION: God's Bits of Wood, 1962; The Money-Order, with White Genesis, 1972; Tribal Scars, 1974; Xala, 1976.

ABOUT: Brench, A.C. The Novelists' Inheritance in French Africa, 1967; Brench, A.C. (ed.) Writing in French From Senegal to Cameroon, 1967; Dathorne, O.R. African Literature in the Twentieth Century, 1976; Gakwandi, S.A. The Novel and Contemporary Experience in Africa, 1977; Herdeck, D.E. (ed.) African Authors Vol. 1, 1973; International Who's Who, 1977–78; Killam, G.D. (ed.) African Writers on African Writing, 1973; King, B.A. and Ogungbesan, K. (eds.) A Celebration of Black and African Writing, 1975; Penguin Companion to Literature 4, 1969; Wästberg, P. (ed.) The Writer in Modern Africa, 1969; Who's Who in African Literature, 1972; Zell, H. and Silver, S. (eds.) A Reader's Guide to African Literature, 1972. *Periodicals*— Africa Report February 1963; Black Orpheus November 1959; New York Times November 9, 1969; January 27, 1978.

*SERENI, VITTORIO (July 27, 1913–), Italian poet, was born in Luino, a small Lombard town in the lake district of northern Italy. He is the son of Enrico Sereni, a customs official, and of the former Maria Colombi. Sereni studied literature at the University of Milan and afterwards remained in that city to teach Italian and Latin in senior high schools from 1939 to 1952. From 1952 to 1958 he was art director and press officer for the Pirelli Group, and since then he has been literary director of Mondadori, the famous Milan publishing house. He has also served as co-editor of the literary magazine *Questo e Altro* and as literary columnist in *Milano Sera,* as well as contributing to many other journals.

When Sereni published his first collections, *Frontiera* (Frontier, 1941) and *Poesie* (Poems, 1942), Italian poetry was dominated by the hermeticism of Ungaretti and Montale. *Ermetismo,* deriving ultimately from symbolism, sought to purge Italian poetry of noisy rhetoric, exploring private worlds of association and evocation in pursuit of an inner truth. Sereni, who contributed a great deal to the later phase of hermeticism, was also strongly influenced by the resigned, wistful, death-haunted verse of the *crepuscolari* —"twilight" poets like Guido Gozzano, whom he profoundly admires.

In these first two books, Sereni's typical manner was one of elegiac reverie, in discursive poems in a minor key about (as Franco Fortini puts

*se rān′ ē

it) "the cloudy lakeside seasons, the memory of a death, the sense of his own transitoriness, the presentiment of a threat to the things and people most dear to him":

> With a last roar upon the rails
> you found your peace, where the city
> in a flight of boulevards and bridges
> leaps into the countryside
> and the passer-by is unaware
> of you as you are not aware
> of the fleeting echoes of the hunt.
>
> Yours perhaps is the true peace
> and those, your eyes, we closed
> for ever now reopened
> wonder
> that still for us
> you die a little each year
> upon this day.
>
> ("December 3,"
> translated by C. L. Golino)

What brought Sereni from this effective but rather easy melancholy to a true tragic awareness was World War II. This was reflected in the poems collected in *Diario d'Algeria* (Algerian Diary, 1947), the volume that established his reputation. Sereni served as an army officer in the campaigns in Greece, the Balkans, and later in Sicily, where he was captured, spending two years (1943-1945) in Allied prison camps in Algeria and Morocco. This bitter experience of battle and exile produced poetry of a new simplicity, in which the poet is saddened, enraged, almost stupefied by the injustice of a world that has made him, as one critic put it, successively "a reluctant conqueror in Greece and a predestined victim in Sicily," and has condemned him to two years of living death in the prison camps. "I am dead, dead to war and peace," he writes in "Field Hospital 127," the most celebrated poem in the *Diario.*

This sense of alienation, in Sereni's case as much social as existential, has continued to influence his poetry, though he has never become an *engagé* writer. The poems in *Gli strumenti umani* (Human Instruments, 1965) confirm the persistence of this mood, and suggest that his war experiences may have brought out the true nature of Sereni's poetic personality. For here also one finds, expressed more openly than formerly, although still with a lingering flavor of hermeticism, the enduring uneasiness, the simultaneous yearning for escape and for greater involvement:

> What am I waiting for?
> For the rising of some wind

of change to stir my pen
and open new horizons of hope?

Franco Fortini speaks of Sereni's "cold armistice with a world that grows ever more inhuman," and says of his recent poems that: "Even in their external form, respectful·. . . to the point of irony to the literary conventions of the nineteenth century, you discern a corrosive claw, as it were the deep wound of an incurable present."

One of the poems in *Gli strumenti umani,* "Una visita in fabbrica" (A Visit to the Factory), admired by Montale, seems to offer, at least thematically, a token of deeper commitment. Meanwhile Sereni's long period of inner debate is of itself an indication of his deep seriousness; although he has published little, he is one of the most important and interesting poets of the post-Montale generation in Italy. Reviewing *Un posto di vacanza* (A Holiday Job, 1975), Fortini wrote that Sereni is now regarded by many "as a 'classic' of modern Italian verse. His poetry, constructed from subtle differences on the linguistic plane, indeterminate in colour . . . faithful to an image of man bereft of paradise or illusions but also haunted by ghosts and obscure premonitions . . . has had a profound effect on the sensibility of the middle generation [of Italian poets]." Sereni received the Libera Stampa prize in 1956, the Montefeltro prize in 1965, and the Feltrinelli prize in 1972.

Sereni has also published a volume of essays, *Gli immediati dintorni* (The Immediate Surroundings, 1962), and another of prose pieces, *L'opzione* (The Option, 1964), and has translated works by Julian Green, Paul Valéry, and René Char, as well as a selection of poems by William Carlos Williams. Sereni was married in 1940 to Maria Luisa Bonfanti and has three daughters. The author, who lives in Milan, lists soccer as his principal leisure interest.

PRINCIPAL WORKS IN ENGLISH TRANSLATION: Sixteen Poems, tr. Paul Vangelisti, 1971. *Poems in* Barnstone, W. (ed.) Modern European Poetry, 1966; Bergin, T.G. (ed.) An Italian Sampler, 1964; Golino, C. (ed.) Contemporary Italian Poetry, 1962; Pacifici, S. Guide to Contemporary Italian Literature, 1962; Singh, G. (ed.) Contemporary Italian Verse, 1968; Trevelyan, R. (ed.) Italian Writing Today, 1967.

ABOUT: Antonielli, S. Aspetti e figure del novecento, 1955; International Who's Who, 1973–74; Manacorda, G. Storia della letteratura italiana contemporanea, 1967; Pacifici, S. Guide to Contemporary Italian Literature, 1962; Penguin Companion to Literature 2, 1969; Pozzi, G. La poesia italiana del novecento, 1965; Trevelyan, R. (ed.) Italian Writing Today, 1967. *Periodicals*—Books Abroad Summer 1966; Corriere della sera October 24, 1965; Menabò 2, 1960;

Times Literary Supplement October 5, 1973; October 31, 1975.

SEYMOUR-SMITH, MARTIN (April 24, 1928–), English poet, scholar, critic, editor, satirist, and writer on sex and society, writes: "I was born in Stoke Newington, London. My father was a well known librarian and general bibliographer who compiled several books. He died in 1972; my mother is still living. On my mother's side I am directly descended from Elizabeth Fry —but unfortunately through the one of her daughters who got cut off. I started to write as soon as I could read: my first poem began 'O life why hast thou cheated me/ In the very hour of my triumph?'

"I was educated at Highgate School and then, after service with the army as a sergeant, in the Middle East, at St. Edmund Hall, Oxford. After that I spent three years in Palma de Mallorca, as tutor to one of Robert Graves's sons. I had known Graves ever since I was a small boy, and later I wrote the first monograph on him. Janet de Glanville and I had been living together since 1950, and in 1952, she tells me, we were married at the British Consulate at Oxford, where I met her, and she helped Graves with the raw material for his *The Greek Myths.* For some time we lived in a flat above his; he had his work-room in our flat. Our first daughter, Miranda, was born in Spain in 1953; she is now married to Colin Britt, and like him, is reading for a Ph.D. at the University of East Anglia, where both graduated. Both are writers. Our second daughter, Charlotte, was born on the last day of 1955; she took a first in anthropology at the L.S.E. (1976), and is now studying at the School of Latin-American Studies in London.

"From 1954 until 1960 I was a teacher at various schools, the unhappiest period of my life. I liked the children well enough, but was unlucky with the headmasters under whom I worked. In 1960 I went freelance, and have been so ever since.

"I have lived in Fulham (for a few months) and in various parts of East Sussex. We have been in Bexhill-on-Sea since 1958. I was visiting professor of English at the University of Wisconsin (on the Parkside campus) in 1971–1972: I thoroughly enjoyed this. I travel as much as I can, mostly to Italy.

"I was poetry editor of the *Isis* at Oxford, of the now defunct weekly *Truth* (1955–1958) and of *The Scotsman* (1963–1967); I was also literary advisor to Hodder & Stoughton from 1963 until 1967. I have reviewed for most of the British papers and magazines at one time or another, especially for the *Spectator* from 1965 until 1971.

Freddie Lott

MARTIN SEYMOUR-SMITH

Since 1973 I have been writing regularly about poetry and fiction in the London *Financial Times*.

"I have never been a member of any political party or religious organisation. My emotional sympathies are, on the whole, with the left, but I have found their performance almost uniformly depressing. But I could never reconcile myself to voting Tory. In any case, current affairs now seem to me to be uncommentable upon except in phantasmogoric terms. I am neither an atheist nor a Christian; my approach is sceptical, but I should not call myself a sceptic. I hope I shall always remain independent and a heretic—if only because I function best in that way.

"Some of my early poems were over-influenced by Robert Graves and Norman Cameron (whom I knew well). But in the Fifties I found I had my own voice, and I have been trying to pursue this ever since. I think English poets have to remain English; but I have been much influenced by Hagiwara, Montale, Campana, and Vallejo. I have never known where the next poem was going to come from: poetry contains art, but cannot be manufactured. As I have never been interested in becoming part of the literary scene (as it is called), my poetry has received little attention—though my books seem to sell quite well, if only by the standards of slim volumes by non-heavyweights. I don't complain; but the interest shown in my poems by such as Charles Sisson and David Wright has been important to me. I write for I suppose about six people; but, of course, the more the merrier.

"As a critic I aim to illuminate writers and their works, and, above all, to stimulate people into reading authors new to them. My approach is wholly eclectic—I will use whatever facts are to hand—and anti-abstract. Accuracy is important to me, and I don't think there are any more errors in my one-man jobs than there are in composite surveys. Certainly I keep catching the others out in errors—but with the greatest sympathy, because I keep catching myself out, too. No critic can be 'right': all he can do is to try to be sure that his account of a writer is undistorted by such accidentals as envy, subjective irritation, theoretical or dogmatic preoccupation, and so on. Then his point of view may be valuable.

"I have never been nearly satisfied with anything I have written; but I wish that those who call me 'dotty,' 'fascist,' 'communist' (usually, as it happens, ill-read conformists or hard-line dogmatists) would give examples. I don't think I am any more dotty than anyone else, though I have never followed fashion; and I am certainly not a fascist or a communist—although I do think that right-wing extremism creates totalitarian 'communist' regimes. I would rather live in New York than Moscow.

"My critical approach has widened from an almost exclusively psychological one: now I am deeply concerned—I hope not too earnestly—with phenomenology, anthropology (much under the influence and guidance of my younger daughter), religion, myth and philosophy. Hence *Sex and Society*. I am interested in relationships, connections; but I agree with Heraclitus that 'an unapparent connection is stronger than an apparent one'—so that some find the connections I make disconcerting. This pleases me, since I enjoy disconcerting pompous or complacent conformists and didacts. I think I lack charity towards them, and this often distresses me.

"I have been called 'well read', even 'erudite'; and while it is true that I have read widely in many fields, my most abiding sense is of my own ignorance, which I vainly seek to diminish all the time. The key to *gnosis* seems to me to lie mostly in that very difficult subject, anthropology; it is there, too, that all the poetry that is not in oneself can be found.

"Except for the time I spent in America, I have always been broke; inflation has made the situation—and that of other writers who try to be serious—much more difficult. But I get up at 5 a.m., work—I usually enjoy this—until 6 p.m., and thus find less time for anxiety or for fantasising self-pityingly about the 'financial breakthrough' which I wrongly consider myself entitled to.

"Since such lists can be indicative, I give the names of some contemporaries (leaving out the obvious ones, such as Kafka), who have meant a great deal to me: Pareto, Durkheim, Henry Handel Richardson, Merleau-Ponty, Gramsci, Allende, Unamuno, Valle-Inclán, Bergson, Ortega, Machado, Luis Cernuda, Hart Crane, Hašek, Ford, Wyndham Lewis, Laura Riding and, above all, Vallejo.

"I am tense, malarial, 'angry as a bull when roused,' stooped, ugly, clownish, bearded, and a compulsive talker who seldom allows anyone else to get a word in. As a person I am often cheerful, and I should like this cheer to break through into my attitude towards life, which is probably too cynical and pessimistic."

The pessimism Seymour-Smith claims above was evident in the stately poems he published as a young man in the early 1950s, most of them gloomy or ironical lyrics on love or death or both. That he is also "independent and a heretic" was not at first so obvious, though there is a hint of his radical originality of mind even in "He Came to Visit Me," the first poem in his first collection (1952):

He came to visit me, my mortal messenger;
    I saw the sorrow stamped upon his face.
He bade me chide at him, for grief. "But sir,"
    I said, "you know your dominating place."

This poem seems to C.H. Sisson "close to the point of orientation of the poet's mind," and in this as in its theme reminds him of Edward Thomas's poem "The Other." It is reprinted in *Tea With Miss Stockport* (1963), his first important collection (though even that contained only twenty-four poems). The long title poem is a cautionary tale about the unwisdom of condescending to old ladies like Miss Stockport who (after all) may one day poison her patronizing guests and then, suddenly rejuvenated, rape the sole survivor of her tea party:

Her pearly dentures then took sudden root
Leapt into her gums with maidenly spring. . . .

A reviewer in the *Times Literary Supplement,* praising the "pliant, wieldy verse" of this piece, said it was "the kind of unexpected butterfly-bomb that Mr. Seymour-Smith is always dropping in the paths of his characters and his readers—or finding in his own path"; he is "a good-tempered anarchist among the younger English poets—and it should not be thought that a good temper makes him any less subversive." Elizabeth Jennings found the author "as skilful with tender love lyrics . . as with long ironic pieces" in this "mature and impressive collection," and she and others drew attention to the

several poems here which deal with the plight of the intelligent and sensitive individual in an increasingly collectivized society. Indeed, C.H. Sisson has written that "the awareness of the individual predicament dominates his perception of the public as of the private world, as if he believed that, in reality, there is only the latter; he is, even painfully, aware of how much the impact of events depends upon the sensitivity and sophistication of the receiving mind."

The poems Seymour-Smith wrote between 1963 and 1970, collected in 1971 as *Reminiscences of Norma,* had a more mixed reception. John Fuller found something "blurred and graceless" about some of these poems, and it seemed to Alan Brownjohn that the satires were "corny, parochial," and the title section of "bizarre love-poems . . . honest but full of lapses. . . . But his poems of unembittered wit . . . and one or two quiet love poems in the old vein, show the warmer side of his talent." Douglas Dunn disagreed, praising this as "a stylish book, mature and confident." And C.H. Sisson, suggesting that Seymour-Smith is "a poet of the kind, and sometimes of the quality, of Henry Vaughan," spoke of the technical advance between the early collections and these poems, "in which abstract form does not obtrude at all upon the rhythms of speech." A number of these points are illustrated in "To Miss Parfitt (1934) Sadly: This Poem About Dying," which it is interesting to compare with "He Came to Visit Me," the earlier poem on a similar theme quoted above:

I've had too much trouble in my life.
Why, writing those words, I went back to
An ancient kindergarten cursive.
When I cried I could not do it
Soft-breasted woolly-warm Miss Parfitt
Took me on her lap. (Now I can,
And anyway, she's old.) Yes! I want
To get away from life, say nothing of
The young magus, the all-intelligent hag
Or the demands of universal love:
There is the darkness in myself
Which for too long I've said was
Not honest to hide. Let me have less
Trouble, is what I ask. . . .

And so you, to whom I have always to speak,
Say with the smile I put on strict lips
"There'll be no poems, no answers,
No harrowing of hell without
The pain you know you want."

I know I'm speaking to you Adversary.
Must.
Let me as usual put the sentence
In your mouth: "For trouble you've got

741

Your less and less obscure aches hinting
At dying. You always have your dying:
The wish is permanent."

But need that be trouble?

It's what I wait for, wanting
To know.

Robert Nye believes that Seymour-Smith's concern in his poetry is "to 'test' the moment of self-knowledge by applying to it the resources of an intelligent imagination." That same "intelligent imagination" distinguishes his work as a scholar and critic, not least in his "interesting and vigorous" critical edition of Shakespeare's *Sonnets* (1963). It was much discussed, has gone through several editions, and has become a set book in many schools and universities.

Poets Through Their Letters (1969), the first part of a projected two-volume work, analyzes the letters of Wyatt, Sidney, Spenser, Dryden, Pope, Wordsworth, and others for the "information and insights they give . . . into the nature and art of poetry and into the . . . poets who create it." Paul West wrote that Seymour-Smith had brought "an intimate light to bear upon the poems. . . . There isn't, I think, a pedantic or pot-boiling sentence in the entire book . . . and the chronologically arranged chapters build into a consistent, responsibly evaluative view that will gratify specialists and general readers alike." Anthony Burgess went further, praising Seymour-Smith's "large and deep" scholarship in a work which seemed to him "to be major criticism."

Another critic, however, said that Seymour-Smith's "treatment is fine when his sympathies are engaged, less than adequate when they are not," and some such charge has been leveled at most of his critical works. Thus, a reviewer in the *Times Literary Supplement* found a certain lack of balance in Seymour-Smith's *Fallen Women* (1969), "a sceptical inquiry into the treatment of prostitutes, their clients and their pimps, in literature" (factual and fictional). The same critic was plainly worried by the author's "ultra-libertarian coda, with its proposals for the nationalization of prostitution, with 'attractive pensions' and 'expert training' for whores; for a brothel in the House of Commons, which would, we are told, 'improve the quality of debate'; and for a Ministry of Sex to organize these and similar benefits." The reviewer concluded all the same that this was "a thought-provoking popular survey of behaviour, attitudes, and fantasies."

Seymour-Smith's twelve-hundred-page *Guide*

to Modern World Literature (1973) "extends to writers, of all nationalities, who survived 31 December 1899," as well as a few who died before that. The book is arranged in sections, each dealing with a national or regional literature—African, Albanian, American, Arabic, and so on. Each section gives a history of the literature concerned from about 1880 to the present, and goes on to deal with novelists, dramatists, and poets, and the movements and ideas that influenced them. There are quotations in English from the writings of some of the authors discussed, and references to the sources of further translations.

Martin Dodsworth has drawn attention to "the very audacity of such an attempt, in an age when many writers and scholars take refuge in very limited specialisation indeed." He goes on: "Zest for the task is evident everywhere in the firm judgments and crisp style," and quotes as an example this entry: "JACK LONDON (1876–1916), bastard son of a wandering Irish astrologer whom he never saw, is wrongly regarded in Russia as a great writer. . . ." As Dodsworth says, "there can be few works of reference at once as entertaining and informative as this. . . . The usefulness of the information extends beyond gossip. . . . Furthermore, in its record of the strange lives of authors, it perpetuates the myth of the artist's otherness from the reader, and presents literature in the context of this marvellous alien quality—a quality which . . . is intimately related to the otherness of literature itself." The distinction of the book is that it "embodies both the myths of literature and a sense of what it is like to encounter the thing itself."

But the *Guide* and Seymour-Smith's later *Who's Who in Twentieth Century Literature* (1976) also received some more negative and even openly hostile reviews from critics who were troubled or angered by the very decisiveness of his judgments—his willingness to refute received opinions about writers even in obscure literatures which (it was argued) he could scarcely know well. "Yet," C. H. Sisson writes, "even where the criticism is decisive in tone, and looks destructive, it is in fact modest, for it pretends to no more than the authority due to the plain reaction of a subtle but uncompromising mind."

It is not only unusually wide reading, and a mind extraordinarily gifted for the handling of information, which equip Seymour-Smith for these large tasks. It is, even more, the nature of his interest in literature as a main branch of the study of human behavior and the human mind—a study in which he is organically and irresistibly engaged, aided by a useful acquaintance with current psychology and anthropology. These qualities are evident in *Sex and Society* (1975) in which, according to John Naughton, "his basic approach is to identify the works of anyone who has written anything important about sex in the last hundred years, to summarise their findings, and to 'compare and contrast' different authors as he goes along." Naughton found that this method produces "flashes of real insight" and "a kind of synthesis," which is nevertheless "unsatisfactory because it does not derive from an overall, worked-out conceptual framework." Eric Korn noted that Seymour-Smith's "consistent 'fairmindedness' . . . is at times endearingly betrayed by bursts of wrath," as when he describes the studies of Masters and Johnson as "grotesquely vulgar and/or comic," and Queen Victoria as "excessively stupid and unpleasant." But Korn, like Naughton, concluded that this "subtle, dense, epigrammatic and sometimes bawdy book" begs more questions than it answers.

It cannot be said that Martin Seymour-Smith has as yet made a place for himself in the literature of the century. His books are read, for the most part, not because readers have the habit of looking out for the next Seymour-Smith, but because he is saying something interesting about something interesting. But an increasing number of discerning readers value his work as part of a growing *oeuvre* which is without exact parallel for its range, penetration, and the singular, almost morbid, honesty of the imagination.

PRINCIPAL WORKS: *Poetry*—(with Rex Taylor and Terence Hards) Poems, 1952; [Poems by] Martin Seymour-Smith (The Fantasy Poets No. 10), 1953; All Devils Fading, 1954; Tea With Miss Stockport, 1963; Reminiscences of Norma: Poems 1963–1970, 1971. *Criticism*—Robert Graves, 1956; Poets Through Their Letters: From the Tudors to Coleridge, 1969; (with James Reeves) Inside Poetry, 1970; Guide to Modern World Literature, 1973 (U.S., Funk & Wagnall's Guide to Modern World Literature); Who's Who in Twentieth Century Literature, 1976. *Sociology*—Fallen Women, 1969; Sex and Society, 1975. *Satire*—Bluff Your Way in Literature, 1966 (U.S., Bluffer's Guide to Literature). *As Editor*—Poetry From Oxford, 1953; Shakespeare's Sonnets, 1963; A Cupful of Tears: Sixteen Victorian Novelettes, 1965; Ben Jonson's Every Man in His Humour, 1966; (with James Reeves) A New Canon of English Poetry, 1967; (with James Reeves) Poems of Andrew Marvell, 1969; Longer Elizabethan Poems, 1972; (with James Reeves) Selected Poems of Walt Whitman, 1976; The English Sermon, Volume 1: 1550–1650, 1976.

ABOUT: Bate, J. How to Find Out About Shakespeare, 1968; Contemporary Authors 7–8, 1963; International Who's Who in Poetry, 1974–1975; Vinson, J. (ed.) Contemporary Poets, 1975; Who's Who in the World, 1976; Writers Directory 1976–1978. *Periodicals*—Book World April 6, 1969; Contemporary Review September 1973; Country Life July 19, 1973; Daily Telegraph June 21, 1973; Encounter August 1971, July 1973; Glasgow Herald September 5, 1975; Listener March 25, 1971; New Statesman October 4, 1963; January 31, 1969; March 19, 1971; December 5, 1975; Nova August 1975; Observer June 10, 1973; September 30, 1975; June 6, 1976; Punch July 4, 1973; Scotsman November 9, 1963; September 1973; Spectator November 8, 1963; March 7, 1969; June 23, 1973; Sunday Telegraph May 27, 1973; Sunday Times (London) May 27, 1976; Times Educational Supplement June 22, 1973; Times Literary Supplement June 11, 1964; February 13, 1969.

SHEPARD, SAM(UEL) (November 5, 1943–), American dramatist and short story writer, writes: "I was born in the heart of the Cornbelt, Fort Sheridan, Illinois, in an Army hospital. This happened on November 5, 1943. My father was the son of a dairy farmer in Crystal Lake and was in the Air Force somewhere across the sea at the time of my birth. I never saw my father until I was five. My mother was a strong woman. She carted me from state to state in an old Plymouth. By the time I was six I had lived or spent time in: Illinois, Wisconsin, Florida, North and South Dakota, Iowa, Washington, Indiana, Idaho, Michigan, the Marianas Islands, and finally California, where I stayed more or less until the age of eighteen.

"After spending some time living with my aunt we moved to a small avocado ranch in Duarte, California, at the foot of the San Gabriel Mountains. It was in this place that I first began to smell the real adventure of my life. To the north of us were lush thoroughbred farms. Rolling green pastures, rainbird sprinklers, pick-up trucks and horse trailers. To the south, lined up along the highway, were staunch lower-middle-class tracts. To the east was a trailer camp for transient workers. Further south was a steaming, deep-country hovel of shacks and stucco boxes full of blacks and Mexicans only. (I still have nightmares of walking down the narrow dirt street that led into this section that all whites referred to as 'Rock Town'). To the west was 'civilization': Santa Anita Race Track, Arcadia, Pasadena and L.A., 'the home of the Angels.' Duarte was an absolute cross-section of everything American. This never struck me until later of course, when I hit the 'Big Apple.'

"My father was prone to violent bouts with various types of alcohol and his own bitter disappointment with his life. This culminated for me on a night when he decided to rip the front door off the house since my mother had locked him out, threatening to call the police. My sisters and I lived in a separate section of the house. The next morning I left home in my '51 Chevy with all my gear stuffed in cardboard boxes. For a while I lived at the Y.M.C.A., then got a job as an actor with the Bishop's Company out of Burbank. They gave me twenty bucks and a one-way

SAM SHEPARD

ticket to Bethlehem, Pennsylvania, where I joined the troop.

"That was one of the most exciting times of my life. Suddenly I was on my own. The company was endowed with a brand new red bus which I volunteered to drive. We never spent more than one or two nights in the same place and our stages were always the altars of churches. We were all housed by different families in the parish of each town. We criss-crossed New England, up into Maine and Vermont. The country amazed me, having come from a place that was brown and hot and covered with Taco stands. Finally we hit New York City and I couldn't believe it. I'd always thought of the 'big city' as Pasadena and the Rose Parade. I was mesmerized by this place.

"Through a series of coincidences I made contact with an old high school friend of mine who had also come to New York. His name was Charles Mingus Jr. and it wasn't until New York that I found out who his father was. We lived together in a railroad flat on Avenue C and Tenth Street. His influence on me was very strong in those days. He was a painter and surrounded himself with his art. Night after night we'd get in free to the Five Spot on St. Mark's Place, since his father played there often. It was hearing that music and seeing Charlie's paintings all over the walls that gradually moved me from acting into playwriting. I wanted to write something for the theatre that might have the same kind of vibrant, pulsing life that I was feeling all around me. I arrived at the right time. 'Off-off-Broadway' was just being spawned and places were hungry for scripts. Ralph Cook, the head waiter at the Village Gate, where I was

working as a busboy, was starting something called Theater Genesis at St. Mark's Church in the Bowery. He read a script of mine called *Cowboys* and decided to put it on. From then on I've been writing plays."

The son of Samuel Shepard and the former Jane Elaine (Schook) Rogers, Shepard was educated at Duarte High School and went on to Mount San Antonio Junior College, Walnut, California (1961-1962). He worked as a "hot walker" at the Santa Anita Race Track, as a stable hand, sheep shearer, herdsman, and orange picker in various parts of California, and as a car wrecker in Charlemont, Massachusetts. After he went to New York, he was a busboy at the Village Gate, a waiter at Marie's Crisis Cafe, and played drums and guitar with the Holy Modal Rounders.

Cowboys, Shepard's first performed play, was presented by Theater Genesis in October 1964. Commenting some years later on this lost text, Shepard said: "Cowboys are really interesting to me—these guys, most of them really young, about sixteen or seventeen, who decided they didn't want to have anything more to do with the East Coast . . . and took on that immense country, and didn't have any real rules." Despite his early attachment to the East Coast as off-off-Broadway's most prolific playwright, much the same could be said of Shepard himself, who took the continent of America as his subject and made up his rules as he went along.

In *The Unseen Hand,* he defined his territory as AZUSA ("everything from A to Z in the U.S.A.")—a multidimensional zone including America's history, mythology, subcultures, and environment as well as its geography. Some of his plays do span vast distances, but more often they occupy a junk-strewn waste or some neutral territory, like a woodland cabin or hotel bedroom, where myth and reality can meet on equal terms, events develop with the wild logic of science fiction, and authentic characters mingle with folk heroes and media constructs.

For Shepard, the all-important principle is freedom: total stylistic freedom to depict characters who are themselves in flight from all forms of social confinement. Imprisonment of various kinds recurs obsessively in his plays, either as an explicit plot mechanism or as a shadowy background threat. Not that Shepard goes far towards analyzing the threat or taking sides against it as a social critic, as that would again thrust him into the kind of fixed role which he consistently avoids. Spectators who expect drama to be rooted in moral discrimination have been baffled by Shepard, a writer who evidently says Yes to everything—drugs, astrology, rock music, old movies, and Western legend—and limits his function to making connections without passing any judgments. Another source of bewilderment (particularly for non-American audiences) is his creation of uncompromising experimental works out of the raw ingredients of pop culture, plus the fact that the plays appear to have been improvised at high speed and are apt to make more sense moment by moment than when viewed as a whole. "I like," Shepard says, "to start with as little information about where I'm going as possible"; Jack Gelber describes Shepard's plays as "trips."

In a necessarily incomplete survey of his torrential output, one can locate the starting point of the trip in *The Rock Garden* (Theater Genesis, 1964), a three-scene family piece showing a boy and girl enduring the agonizing boredom of American home life. For the first scenes, they are at the mercy of a man and woman who keep up an endless drone of suburban trivialities. In the finale, the boy turns the tables by capping the man's gardening monologue with a detailed description of his sexual techniques that literally knocks the man out. Incorporated in Kenneth Tynan's long-running erotic revue, *Oh! Calcutta!,* this has become Shepard's best-known scene. It also offers an introduction to his dramatic methods, including the habit of placing characters side by side rather than in direct relationship, and his fondness for volcanic tirades that punctuate the dialogue like jazz riffs, often transforming the character of the speaker.

These are among the trademarks of the short plays Shepard launched at other off-off-Broadway addresses over the next three years. Their other characteristic, as George Stambolian has pointed out, is "the startling way in which . . . [Shepard] juxtaposed powerful visual and verbal images, producing an . . . often disconcerting impact on the spectator's mind." The short plays are mainly one-incident pieces, presenting footloose kids of the author's generation against a background of undefined anxiety and violence. Usually the characters are on the move to somewhere else and treat each other with the detachment of accidental companions; their relationships are rarely specified. Typical of the group are *Icarus's Mother* (Caffé Cino, 1965), a picnic play in which two girls peeing on a deserted beach are buzzed by a passing aircraft which then crashes into the sea; and *Red Cross* (Judson Poets' Theater, 1966), in which three characters in a forest cabin enact a series of imagined disasters before the boy turns to one of the girls with real blood pouring down his face.

La Turista, Shepard's first full-length play, followed in 1967 (American Place Theater). Unrelated to any time sequence, its two acts are set respectively in a Mexican and an American hotel bedroom where Kent and Salem (both named after cigarette brands) repeat the same basic situation, summed up in the title pun on the Spanish word for "tourist," also an American word for the diarrhea that afflicts visitors to Mexico. In the first act, Kent is literally suffering from *la turista,* from which he dies despite the arrival of a witch doctor who tries to cure him by sacrificing a pair of live chickens. In the second act, Kent's malady has changed to encephalitic sleeping sickness and the doctor to a Civil War figure in string tie and suspenders. Instead of dying, Kent undergoes transformation into Frankenstein's monster and finally makes his escape with a flying exit through a wall of the set.

Sickness and death pervade the play, and, as Elizabeth Hardwick said of the original production, "It is amazing the number of 'deaths' that will fit the text: Vietnam, Santo Domingo, racial violence, drop-outs, colonialism." With Shepard, though, it is a waste of time to probe the work for symbols and buried meanings. As in Andy Warhol's paintings, the life of these plays is all on the surface, transmitted through spasms of imagery and characters who become unrecognizably altered by changes of mood and costume. The only distinct viewpoint that emerges from *La Turista* is a loaded contrast between the sickly white tourists and the surviving potency of older, folk-rooted American cultures.

The Unseen Hand, one of Shepard's most admired plays, followed in 1969 (La Mama Experimental Theater Club). Set in a more or less literal Azusa (a real community on the outskirts of Los Angeles), it takes place amid a pile of California debris including the skeleton of a '51 Chevrolet convertible. This is the home of Blue Morphan, the one-hundred-and-twenty-year-old survivor of the Morphan Brothers, who robbed trains in the area long before it was submerged under billboards and Coke cans. Blue's monologue is interrupted by Willie the space freak, who has escaped from the dread planet of Nogoland to recruit earthly allies against the regime there (which still exercises telepathic control over him by means of a handprint burnt into his skull). Willie restores Blue's youth and brings his brothers back from the dead—at which point the plot is again interrupted by the arrival of a high school cheerleader who eavesdrops on the conspirators and turns a gun against them in defense of his beloved birthplace. "I love Azusa! I love the foothills and the drive-in movies and the bowling alleys and the football games and the girls and the dough-nut shop and the High School and the Junior College and the outdoor track meets and the parades and the Junior Chamber of Commerce and the Key Club and the Letterman's Club and the Kiwanis and the Safeway Shopping Center. . . ."

Robert Brustein has described *The Unseen Hand* as a "hallucination based on fact . . . Shepard's approach is simply to place these disparate characters against a contemporary landscape, and let them work upon one another. Taken together, they mingle past, present, and future in a pastiche of legend and actuality which describes prole America more effectively than the most fastidious documentary." Brustein went on to complain that Shepard "continues to confront American popular culture with a kind of manic exuberance . . . considerably turned on, like many of his generation, even by its more brutalized expressions. In a degenerate time, this may be a strategy for survival, and it certainly sparks the energy of *The Unseen Hand;* but I miss that quality of aloofness that would make this play not only a creative act, but an act of moral resistance as well." To which it must be added that Shepard, in *The Unseen Hand,* succeeds better than he sometimes does in shaping diverse elements into a robustly coherent plot.

By this time Shepard had written more than a hundred plays, and had been described by Mel Gussow as "the most prolific and prominent playwright in the underground theater." His first encounter with establishment theatre came in 1970 with the Lincoln Center production of *Operation Sidewinder,* a scenically elaborate extravaganza whose special effects included displays of Hopi Indian sacred dances, and a computer in the form of a sidewinder rattlesnake. The property of the Air Force, the snake escapes into the desert where it wraps itself around an inquisitive tourist and becomes the center of a battle between the military and a Black Power group who plan to take over the country by doping the reservoirs. The snake then falls into the hands of the Hopis, to whom it represents fertility. It thus sheds its deathly Christian associations and becomes a symbol of rebirth.

Like *La Turista,* the play is laid out in disconnected episodes which John Lahr compares to the panels of a medieval triptych. But, with pop songs interpolated in the Brechtian manner, the scenes add up to a portrait of modern America as a madman's prison, with nothing to choose between the deranged military, the tourists, and the blacks. The exception is the central figure of the Young Man, an all-American draft-dodger

("I was made in America. . . . I have American scars on my brain. . . . I bleed American blood. I dream American dreams. . . . I devour the planet. I'm an earth eater. No. I'm a lover of peace. . . . A flower child, burned by the times") who commits a double murder at the start of the play and finds redemption at the end by joining the Hopis.

Shepard, a spare-time rock musician who once told an interviewer "I much prefer playing music really to theater," has repeatedly included rock stars in his gallery of national heroes, starting with Duke Durgens, the bogus songwriter in *Melodrama Play* (La Mama, 1967), and the treasure-hunting Kosmo in *Mad Dog Blues* (Theater Genesis, 1971). These are among his preliminary sketches for Hoss, the protagonist of what is commonly regarded as his best work, *The Tooth of Crime.* Written while Shepard was living in Britain and first performed at the Open Space Theatre in London in 1972, the play tells the story of an aging rock star's last battle with an upcoming young rival, Crow. But thanks to its structure and multi-associative language, it also takes on the qualities of folk ritual and classical tragedy.

Hoss is a tribal king, inhabiting a moated castle, attended by a voluptuous consort and a retinue of servile courtiers, including a doctor who drugs him into fighting trim, and a disc-jockey soothsayer who foretells his future from the charts. All this is conveyed in dialogue combining the idioms of crime, car-racing, astrology, and Western movies—Shepard has no need to resort to character transformation in this play, since all the alternative roles he could wish for are fused into the compound language. Based on the oldest ritual pattern in the world, the piece proceeds to a tribal leadership duel fought out with hand-mikes under the supervision of a National Basketball referee, and completes its tragic pattern with the defeated Hoss's suicide, "a gesture that can never cheat on itself as it is the last of its kind." Like his hero, Shepard engages in the battle of ephemeral styles to achieve something permanent.

The other main fruit of Shepard's British period was *Geography of a Horse Dreamer,* which he directed at the Royal Court's Theatre Upstairs in 1974. A melodrama set in a London hotel bedroom, it concerns the kidnapping of a young man who has the gift of dreaming race horse winners. In captivity, however, Cody the dreamer is losing his touch; and even when he switches successfully from horses to greyhounds, his captors are threatening a fatal operation which is averted when Cody's two Wyoming brothers burst in, guns blazing, to liberate the dreamer. Reflecting Shepard's enthusiasm for the British dog-track, the play has been described (in *Theatre Quarterly*) as "a parable of the 'artist' exploited by a corrupt society, and ... [containing] the recurrent Shepard images of cowboys, animals, the underworld and death and rebirth."

Since returning to the United States in the mid-1970s, Shepard has maintained his high output, breaking new ground most ambitiously in *Curse of the Starving Class* and *Angel City*. Commissioned by Lincoln Center but premiered at the Royal Court Theatre in London (1977), the first play resumes a theme Shepard has ignored since the early *Rock Garden: "Curse* is the first time I've ever tried to deal with my family." Employing some directly autobiographical material, it tells a story of domestic disintegration, from acts of parental treachery and violence to the departure of the teenage children. The clarity of the narrative and its apparent echoes of O'Neill blinded some reviewers to the play's complexity. However, Charles Marowitz suggested that "the underlying indictment" in the play lay in the fact "that the members of this forlorn, oddly Saroyanesque family are the inevitable victims of the consumer society." And John Elsom in *The Listener* noted that "the starvation is seen on many levels: emotional, cultural, physical, and psychological." *The Buried Child,* produced in New York in 1978, also deals with a disintegrating family.

Angel City (directed by Shepard at the San Francisco Magic Theater, 1976) applies the techniques of *The Tooth of Crime* to the film world, extending the old story of young-writer-meets-dream-factory into a mythical region of crime and magic. Rabbit, the hero, has the double role of hopeful writer and amateur shaman; and even the obligatory studio secretary undergoes transformation into a Kabuki warlord and warm-hearted Irish charlady. The piece also excels as a satire on the movie industry, inflicting multiple disasters on characters who are trying to make the ultimate disaster film. Film culture throughout is viewed as a disease of the population, "replacing their families. Replacing religion, politics, art, conversation. Replacing their minds. And I ask myself, how can I stay immune?" Michael Feingold summed up the piece in the *Village Voice* as Shepard's "most playful work, and one of his most accessible." It also offers further evidence that he appears to be developing positive social attitudes and values.

Richard Schechner believes that Shepard is at bottom "a humanist, an optimist: a person who believes not only in the future of Mankind but in the development of the individual person.

... Shepard's faith, like that of the Elizabethans, is not sentimental or theological—it is in fecundity, the proliferation of life by life, and of various life forms. ... Shepard's apparent pessimism is only skin-deep. His essence is a fascination for the worlds of science fiction, the movies, the rock star: the artificial, the projected, the futuristic, the popular, the now-mythic. ... His plays do not reflect life: they are naturalistic in the sense that nature is now media. ... Shepard sees where the species appears to be heading and he doesn't dread it. He finds joy in an old automobile, and nourishment in a hamburger." Stanley Kauffmann has described Shepard as "the Tennessee Williams of today," in that "he is the most talented of his generation, he relies heavily on language to make his drama, he has a vivid theatrical sense, his subjects tend to be non-urban, he strikes toward elemental passion, and he sometimes makes you impatient with his fooling around." But, Kauffmann wrote, "he has not yet worked hard enough to produce one fully realized play."

A collection of Shepard's short stories, poems, and monologues was published in 1973 as *Hawk Moon*. Joe David Bellamy found the book "curious and disturbing ... full of perverse, often gratuitous, blood-lust, moodiness, retribution fantasies, Indians, run-on sentences, pop mysticism, and intensely imagined fragments." At times, Shepard seemed "to have embraced the ghoulishness and sadism of media-distorted aspects of the culture he wishes to attack and rationalized it as Indian lore and the wisdom of savagery." *Rolling Thunder Logbook* is an account of Bob Dylan's "Rolling Thunder Revue" on its "secret" tour of the Northeast. A critic in *Library Journal* wrote that "the author's perceptions are keen and his style is crisp, as in the vignette of Dylan and Allen Ginsberg performing impromptu blues over Jack Kerouac's grave. But overall, too little of significance occurred during the swing, and Shepard, apparently overawed by the mythic potential of his subject, makes little meaningful contact with Dylan, who comes over as an aloof caricature."

The author won Obie awards in 1967 and in 1973. He has received grants from the Rockefeller and Guggenheim Foundations and from the Office for Advanced Drama Research, and a Yale University fellowship. Shepard has been the coauthor of a number of film scenarios, including *Me and My Brother* (1967), Antonioni's *Zabriskie Point* (1968), and *Ringaleevio* (1971). Described by Mel Gussow as "a lanky, loping figure, with the handsomeness and the style of a movie cowboy hero," Shepard was married in 1969 to the actress O-Lan Johnson Dark, who has appeared in some of his plays. They have a son, Jesse Mojo.

PRINCIPAL PUBLISHED WORKS: *Plays*—Five Plays (Chicago, Icarus's Mother, Red Cross, Fourteen Hundred Thousand, Melodrama Play), 1967; La Turista, 1968; Operation Sidewinder, 1970 (*also in* Lahr, J. and Price, J. (eds.) The Great American Life Show, 1974); The Unseen Hand and Other Plays (The Unseen Hand, 4-H Club, Forensic and the Navigators, Holy Ghostly, Shaved Splits, Back Bog Beast Bait), 1971; Mad Dog Blues and Other Plays (Mad Dog Blues, The Rock Garden, Cowboys #2, Cowboy Mouth), 1971; The Tooth of Crime *and* Geography of a Horse Dreamer, 1974; Action *and* The Unseen Hand, 1975; Angel City, Curse of the Starving Class, and Other Plays (includes also Killer's Head, Action, Mad Dog Blues, Cowboy Mouth, The Rock Garden, Cowboys #2), 1976. *Other*—Hawk Moon: A Book of Short Stories, Poems, and Monologues, 1973; Rolling Thunder Logbook, 1977.

ABOUT: Hughes, C. American Playwrights 1945–1975, 1976; Kauffmann, S. Persons of the Drama, 1976; Lahr, J. Astonish Me: Adventures in Contemporary Theater, 1973; Vinson, J. (ed.) Contemporary Dramatists, 1977; Weales, G. The Jumping-Off Place, 1969; Who's Who in America, 1976–1977. *Periodicals*—Commonweal May 8, 1970; Drama Autumn 1973; Journal of Popular Culture Spring 1974; New York Times November 12, 1969; May 15, 1977; Partisan Review Spring 1974; Plays and Players April 1974; Theatrefacts August-October 1974; Times (London) March 13, 1973.

Kodansha Ltd.

SHIMAZAKI TOSON

*"SHIMAZAKI TOSON" (pseudonym of Shimazaki Haruki)** (February 17, 1872–August 22, 1943), Japanese novelist, poet, and essayist, was born in Kamisaka, in the then still remote mountainous district of Nagano, on the main island of Japan. He was the fourth son of a country gentleman, a hereditary village headman whose house was also a *honjin,* an inn used by feudal lords and government officials traveling to and from the capital on one of the five great national highways of the Edo period, the Nakasendo. Most of his school years were spent in Tokyo, and in 1887 he entered the Meiji Gakuin, a Christian college where he soon became a convert.

In 1892, after trying his hand at journalism, Shimazaki became a teacher. The following year, while teaching at a Christian Women's College, he met the young poet Kitamura Tokoku, one of the great formative influences of his life. Kitamura was the leader of the Japanese romantic movement which centered around the immensely influential magazine *Bungakkai* (Literary World), launched in 1893 at a time when contact with the West had presented Japanese writers with a dazzling array of new ideas and new ways of exploring them.

Shimazaki contributed to *Bungakkai* his own early poems, in which he experimented with new forms and modern diction, influenced primarily

*shi ma zä' kē

by such English Romantics as Byron, Wordsworth, and Shelley. As Ninomiya and Enright put it in their anthology *The Poetry of Living Japan,* "Here was a receptive soul, confronted suddenly with a fresh and vast view of poetry's potentialities." The result was a kind of poetry that was unmistakably Japanese yet wholly modern in spirit, as in "The Crafty Fox" (here translated by Ninomiya and Enright):

There in the garden, a little fox
Steals out at night, when no one is about,
And under the shadow of the autumn vines
He eats in secret the dewy bunch.

Love is no fox,
Nor you a bunch of grapes.
But unbeknown my heart stole out
And plucked you in secret, when no one was about.

When Shimazaki's early poems were published in *Wakanashu* (A Bunch of Young Leaves, 1897), they made his reputation at once. The book has been regarded ever since as a milestone in the development of modern Japanese poetry.

After this brilliant beginning, Shimazaki withdrew from the Tokyo literary world and from poetry and for six years taught in a small school at Komoro, in his native province of Nagano. Turning to prose, he wrote the sketches of country life published years later as *Chikumagawa no suketchi* (Sketches of the River Chikuma, 1912). Meanwhile, in 1899, he married his first wife, Hata Fuyuko.

Shimazaki's first novel, *Hakai* (1906, translated by Kenneth Strong as *The Broken Commandment*), was a pioneering attempt at naturalistic fiction in the manner of Zola, and one of the first Japanese novels to deal with a social problem. Its central character, Ushimatsu, belongs to the *eta,* a class somewhat resembling the Indian untouchables, traditionally consigned to such despised trades as butchery, tanning, and sandal-making. Ushimatsu has sworn on his father's deathbed that he will never reveal his origins in this pariah caste. He keeps his secret, obtains a good education, and becomes a teacher. But he can never wholly stifle his sympathy for his class, and when an *eta* is asked to leave the inn where he lodges he arouses suspicion by moving out in protest. His sense of guilt is increased by the example of a young *eta* who, far from concealing his background, campaigns openly for *eta* rights. Finally Ushimatsu breaks his vow and confesses the truth about himself—and then emigrates to America to take up a good job.

This ending has been seen by some Western critics as an evasion of all the moral and social problems posed by the novel, but Donald Keene disagrees: "The ending vitiates the story for us, but it was perhaps the only possible one in Japan. I think it likely that in a European novel of the same date . . . the hero, offered the choice of a comfortable job in Texas or badly paid work as a battler for *eta* rights in Japan, would have chosen the latter. In this the Japanese novel is realistic as European works are not." Martin Seymour-Smith, who praises the "consummate subtlety and skill" with which Shimazaki portrays the ambivalent feelings of his hero, has called this "one of the best of all Japanese novels."

In fact *Hakai,* though it is Zola-esque in its social concerns and in its detailed observation of places and people, is not wholly a social novel. Its depiction of the loneliness of its hero, his "sorrow at his ill-starred birth," seems to reflect the author's own solitary childhood, his situation as an alienated artist, and above all, perhaps, the terrible tragedy which occurred during the writing of the book, when his three small daughters died.

The success of *Hakai* enabled Shimazaki to abandon teaching and to earn his living solely as a writer. The novels that followed were more overtly autobiographical, but nevertheless reflect the profound changes which accompanied Japan's rapid emergence from feudalism into the modern world. Thus *Haru* (Spring, 1908) is a loosely knit and lyrically impressionistic account of the *Bungakkai* movement, in which the author figures as Kishimoto, a young poet struggling with a sense of purposelessness, and Kitamura Tokoku appears as Aoki. Aoki commits suicide, as Kitamura did, hanging himself in his own garden at the age of twenty-five because he can not reconcile the ugliness and materialism of the new Westernized Japan with his own idealistic pursuit of beauty and social justice.

Iye (1911, translated by Cecilia Segawa Seigle as *The Family*) is about a feudalistic family modeled on the author's own. As the old traditions and certainties buckle and collapse under the impact of the West, and the family loses its money and social position, the older generation becomes an increasingly crushing burden to the young hero, Koizumi Sankichi. The strains of this claustrophobic family life, the hero's helpless sense of loss, are touchingly and beautifully conveyed through Shimazaki's quietly lyrical prose and delicate imagery. *Sakura no mi no juku suru toki* (When the Cherries Ripen, 1917) is an account of an earlier but no less troubled period in the author's life, when he was living with friends of his family while studying in Tokyo.

In 1911 Shimazaki's first wife died, and it was not until 1928 that he made a second marriage, to Kato Shizuko. Meanwhile a grown niece came to live with him as a housekeeper and became pregnant by him. The child was given away, and Shimazaki fled to France, living in Paris from 1913 to 1916, but resuming this incestuous relationship when he returned to Japan. *Shinsei* (A New Life, 1919) is a fascinating confessional novel about this affair. The author, adopting once more the persona of Kishimoto, gives a full (and, in the opinion of some critics, rather smug) account of his motives and feelings, but leaves moral judgments to the reader.

Shimazaki's last book, *Yoake mae* (Before the Dawn, 1929-1935), is a long historical novel set in the period of Meiji Restoration. It provides a meticulously detailed chronicle of the years between 1853, when Commander Perry opened Japan to the outside world, and 1886. The enormous upheavals of this period are viewed through the eyes of Hanzo, who like the author's own father is a scholarly and idealistic village headman. Hanzo, who greets the new society full of hope, is nevertheless quite unable to cope with it. He incurs the hostility of Meiji officialdom and, though he loves the peasants, loses their sympathy as well. He takes to drink, is dismissed as headman, and ends up insane, a sacrifice offered by the old Japan to the new.

Glenn Shaw, discussing *Yoake mae* in the Asaki English Supplement *Present-Day Nippon* in 1936, soon after the book was published, said that it was "considered by many the greatest novel of modern Japan. It is timely because Japan is today passing confusedly through another ill-defined crisis, and ... [Shimazaki], without using direct comparison, makes the parallels obvious. Its weakness lies in its lack of first-hand incident, especially in the first part, and its strength in a realistic faithfulness to detail characteristic of all ... [Shimazaki's] work and a vastness of scale seldom found in Japanese literature."

Shimazaki became the first president of the Japanese P.E.N., which was founded in 1935. Japanese critics have compared him with Turgenev as a lyrical realist, a poet in spirit but a realist in technique. He has come to be regarded, with Mori Ogai and Natsume Soseki, as one of the greatest of all modern Japanese writers.

PRINCIPAL WORKS IN ENGLISH TRANSLATION: The Broken Commandment, 1974; The Family, 1976. *Poems in* Keene, D. (ed.) Modern Japanese Literature, 1956 (which also includes one chapter of The Broken Promise); Ninomiya, T. and Enright, D.J. (eds.) The Poetry of Living Japan, 1956; Bownas, G. and Thwaite, A. (eds.) Penguin Book of Japanese Verse, 1964.

ABOUT: Keene, D. Japanese Literature, 1953; Kokusai Bunka Shinkokai, Introduction to Contemporary Japanese Literature 1, 1939; Kokusai Bunka Shinkokai, Introduction to Classic Japanese Literature, 1948; Lang, D.M. (ed.) Guide to Eastern Literatures, 1971; McLellan, E. Two Japanese Novelists, 1969; Morrison, J.W. Modern Japanese Fiction, 1955; Seymour-Smith, M. Guide to Modern World Literature, 1973; Varley, J.P. Japanese Culture, 1973. *Periodicals* —Harvard Journal of Asiatic Studies XXIV 1962–1963; Monumenta Nipponica VII 1951; P.E.N. International Autumn 1958.

SHIMAZAKI HARUKI. *See* "SHIMAZAKI TOSON"

*SHLONSKY, ABRAHAM (March 6, 1900– May 18, 1973), Hebrew poet, translator, and journalist, was born in the Ukrainian town of Kryukov, on the river Dnieper in Poltava province, Russia. His parents were Habad Hasidim, deeply attached to Judaism. They sent him to Palestine in 1912 to attend the newly founded Herzlia Gymnasium in Tel Aviv, and he was thus one of the first to acquire a Western secondary education in Hebrew. On vacation at home in Russia in 1914, he was prevented by the outbreak of World War I from returning to Palestine, and so completed his secondary studies in Ekaterinoslav (now Dnepropetrovsk).

Having lived through the horrors of the civil war in the Ukraine, Shlonsky returned to Palestine in 1921. There he joined other dedicated young men in reclaiming the malaria-infested Valley of Jezreel, draining swamps and building roads. A year in Paris followed, at the Sorbonne

*shlon′ skē

ABRAHAM SHLONSKY

Sifriat Poalim

(1924), after which he began his journalistic career on the Tel Aviv daily *Davar.* He moved to *Haaretz* in 1928, remaining on the staff of that newspaper until 1943. In 1925 he founded with Eliezer Steinman a literary periodical, *Ketuvim,* which introduced the first revolt against the trends that had become traditional in modern Hebrew literature, and he subsequently edited other modernist and progressive periodicals.

Shlonsky was greatly influenced by Russian Futurist poets like Mayakovsky, some of whose work he translated into Hebrew. With the appearance of his own first poems in the early 1920s, Hebrew literature entered its modernist phase. His stormy poems with their pounding rhythms are full of new terms and idioms, words invented or unearthed (though their imagery is borrowed often from the Bible). The poet Nathan Alterman said that Shlonsky had always been both a lodestone and pelting-stone to Hebrew, making the ancient language perform all sorts of undignified acrobatics and cramming it with inventions by the bushel.

This flamboyant manner was used to express a despairing nihilism which linked Shlonsky with tendencies prevalent in Europe. His poems rage against the purposelessness and monotony of life to a "waif of the generation without prayer or God." But nihilism does not prevent Shlonsky from taking the Creator to task in "At the End of the Nights":

Everything goes into hiding yet dazzles.
Everything screams "I exist not" yet stays.
Everything falters, too baffled to frazzle
Your x-raying gaze. ...

But you, too, are weary of playing acquitter
And once more ensnare us, hellbound.
And once more a steely-eyed boa constrictor
Is holding us riveted, spellbound.

(translated by A. Birman)

These startling poems had great influence, their style and mannerisms beginning something like a cult. But, according to Eisig Silberschlag, "gradually the novelty wore off: the shrill assonance and dissonance in form, the content of grief and grievance in perpetual disharmony with the social orders of the world sounded like an endless variation on a potent but limited theme."

Some critics maintain that Shlonsky is at his best in less violent, more traditional poems, like many which express his love for Palestine and its people, and celebrate the pleasures of hard physical labor in its service. His lyrics include exquisite miniature pictures of nature, which he tends to endow with human qualities. Often there are Biblical overtones, as in "Tiller of the Ground":

A camel and plough. The blade and its colter
Toiling hard to dissever clod from clod.
Never were the eternities so clasped in one moment,
The world so single in plot.

Here's the hint of murder,
Here's the blade pressing forward,
Here's Cain who the unity of clod dares defy.
Never was distance so gaugeable, finite,
Between man
And camel
And sky.

(translated by Dov Vardi)

Shlonsky was a founder and for many years chief editor of *Sifriat Poalim* (Workers' Library), the publishing house of the left wing of the Israeli Labor Movement. He also edited its literary quarterly, *Orlogin* (1950–1957). His poetry brought him a number of important awards, including the Israel Prize. Shlonsky was married to the former Miriam Levin and had one daughter. They lived in Tel Aviv.

When Shlonsky's poems were collected in two volumes in 1956, Eisig Silberschlag wrote: "Today he is securely established as one of the masters of the Hebrew language, as an innovator who vastly increased its potentialities. As a poet he will be remembered for his daring technique and pre-existential pessimism which influenced an entire generation of contemporary Hebrew poetry." Shlonsky also produced poetry for children, plays, and even advertising jingles. He was a prolific translator from Russian, French, and

English. With Leah Goldberg he compiled an excellent anthology of Russian verse in Hebrew, much of it in his own translation.

PRINCIPAL WORKS IN ENGLISH TRANSLATION: *Poems in* Birman, A. (ed.) An Anthology of Modern Hebrew Poetry, 1968; Burnshaw, S. (ed.) The Modern Hebrew Poem Itself, 1965; Wallenrod, R. The Literature of Modern Israel, 1956.

ABOUT: Birman, A. (ed.) An Anthology of Modern Hebrew Poetry, 1968; Burnshaw, S. (ed.) The Modern Hebrew Poem Itself, 1965; Encyclopaedia Judaica, 1971; Kravitz, N. Three Thousand Years of Hebrew Literature, 1972; Wallenrod, R. The Literature of Modern Israel, 1956; Waxman, M. A History of Jewish Literature, Vol. 4, Part I, 1941. *Periodicals*—Books Abroad 1 1957; New York Times May 19, 1973.

SILVERBERG, ROBERT (1936?–), American science fiction and non-fiction writer, was born in Brooklyn, New York, to Jewish parents of eastern European background. His father, Michael Silverberg, was a certified public accountant; his mother, Helen (Baim) Silverberg, a schoolteacher. In an autobiographical statement in *Hell's Cartographers,* edited by Brian Aldiss and Harry Harrison, Silverberg describes himself when young as "a nastily bright little boy who was reading at three, writing little stories at six, spouting learned stuff about European dynasties and the sexual habits of plants at seven or eight, publishing illegible magazines at thirteen and selling novels at eighteen." Lonely and undersized as the youngest among his classmates, he found compensation in museums, books, and hobbies, and in his parents' enthusiastic support. He was attracted from childhood by the alien and the exotic, becoming engrossed in paleontology and astronomy as well as in the world of science fiction he discovered in the works of Jules Verne and H. G. Wells. Although gifted with "a superb memory and a quick wit," he abandoned plans for a career in the pure sciences, realizing that he "lacked depth, originality and consistency; my mind was like a hummingbird, darting erratically over surfaces."

It was while he was at Columbia University, where he received a B.A. in 1956, that Silverberg started writing science fiction stories—"in the drab Eisenhower years, when no one was seeking out every youngster with a typewriter and stuffing publishers' contracts in his pockets." Nevertheless, before he graduated, he had published not only several short stories but also a novel, *Revolt on Alpha C* (1955), which the New York *Times* reviewer dismissed as "inept and unreal . . . a series of old-hat adventures." Silverberg found himself able to write with extraordinary speed. He put aside artistic ambition and became "a complete writing machine," churning out stories "from slam-bang adventure to cerebral pseudo-philosophy" at the rate of fifteen to twenty a month. Although Silverberg later regretted this outpouring of "the sort of thing I had openly scorned in my fan-magazine critical essays seven or eight years before," his productivity won him a special Hugo award at the World Science Fiction Convention in 1956 as the year's most promising newcomer.

The slackening demand for "junk" science fiction in the late 1950s turned Silverberg's attention to nonfiction. He proved equally prolific in this field, averaging an annual rate of well over a million words for publication in the early 1960s, more than a million-and-a-half in 1965. These books, many of them aimed at children or teenagers, deal with such diverse subjects as archaeology, history, prehistory, American Indian culture, botany, oceanography, and the histories of science, medicine, and engineering. Biographical subjects ranged from Akhnaten, Socrates, and Kublai Khan to Edison, Henry Rawlinson, and John Muir.

These books, which were neither overspecialized nor oversimplified, received high praise for their liveliness, clarity, and accuracy, the result of thorough research in primary and secondary sources, and travel to many actual sites. For instance, *Lost Cities and Vanished Civilizations* (1962), which M.S. Libby described as "a very readable, swift-paced, detailed narrative" about the discovery and history of six ancient cultures, was selected by the Junior Literary Guild and listed as one of the year's five best books for young people. Peter Farb, reviewing *The Auk, the Dodo, and the Oryx: Vanished and Vanishing Creatures* (1967), commented: "Each season brings at least one excellent new book by Robert Silverberg, and this is no exception. . . . Even the non-specialist adult will find this one fascinating. . . . The material is well thought through and conscientiously researched; the writing is deft and pointed; and Mr. Silverberg obviously feels passionately about his subject."

By way of diversion, Silverberg continued to dabble in science fiction during the 1960s, when the genre was making its slow comeback to literary respectability. His first taste of critical success came with *Lost Race of Mars* (1960), a novel about two children who make contact with the Old Martians. The New York *Times* chose it as one of the hundred best children's books of the year, and described it as "a winning blend of fact and imaginative conjecture and a welcome addition to the difficult catagory of juvenile science fiction." By 1967, when he published *Thorns* and *The Time-Hoppers,* among other notable novels,

he was rapidly establishing a new reputation as one of the ablest and most thoughtful science fiction writers of his generation.

The Time-Hoppers was a much-praised example of Silverberg's new manner. It is set in 2490 A.D. in the city of Appalachia, which covers the entire eastern seaboard of North America. The city is overpopulated, and its complex society is rigidly stratified, those who achieve first-class status being rewarded with extreme longevity. Some unworthy citizens are escaping from this computer-ruled utopia by slipping backwards in time, and Joseph Quellen of the Secretariat of Crime is ordered to stamp out this pernicious practice. However, he finds something oddly uncertain and ambiguous about his orders, and realizes that what is bothering his superiors is the fear that their own ancestors might be among the time-hoppers—and if their ancestors are excluded from their roles in the past, will they themselves not fail to exist? A reviewer in the *Times Literary Supplement* found the book "beautifully designed, deploying standard SF components in interesting new patterns." The excitements of following Quellen as he bluffs the dictator Kloof "are counterbalanced by the banalities of ordinary conversation, a decent human sympathy for the characters, and a pleasant melancholy under all."

Hawksbill Station (1968), published in England as *The Anvil of Time,* is about a party of political prisoners who have been exiled by time machine back in the Cambrian era, with only trilobites and each other for company. One reviewer admired this very strong central image, but thought that Silverberg had spoiled the effect he was presumably after by filling his prison camp "with a crowd of undifferentiated characters."

Simeon Krug in *Tower of Glass* (1970) is obsessed by the idea of communicating with the stars. He builds a huge transmitting tower of glass and waits to discover that "there's a whole world up there." Krug is worshipped as a god by his android workers—a fact which profoundly shocks Krug's son Manuel when he learns of it. The androids are "human" to the extent that they are capable of rational discourse, and Manuel, finding their subservience intolerable, enters into a taboo love affair with one of them. According to David Ketterer he thus makes Silverberg's point "that unlike intellectual or religious communication, which may be unreliable or evil, sex, however dangerous, holds the promise of true communication." Communication is the central theme of the novel, Ketterer says, and he praises in particular the way in which "every element in the book illustrates this theme." A somewhat similar theme is explored in *A Time of Changes* (1971), one of Silverberg's several Nebula Award–winners, which deals with the impact on a loveless and restrictive society of a drug that induces direct telepathic communication between the minds of its users.

As the critical acclaim for his science fiction grew, Silverberg found himself less and less willing to maintain the "lunatic work schedule" involved in turning out a flood of nonfiction books, and he decided in 1972 to write no more of these. Notable among his subsequent fiction are the three novellas published in 1974 as *Born With the Dead*, which brought him another Nebula, and *The Stochastic Man* (1975). The latter, about a probability expert who jumps at a chance to read the future in order to further his political career, had a mixed reception. Francis Goskowski complained of a "load of political detail of the most offensive sort" and "preposterous turns of plot," while Ursula Le Guin found it "convincing, strong in detail and structure, elegantly economical, carefully imagined." She concluded that it was "superbly professional and cold as ice. . . . The flat tone of this book may be that of a man bored to death by his own proficiency, the final product of professionalism considered as an end."

In the opinion of Ursula Le Guin, Silverberg is "probably the most intelligent science fiction writer in America." He described himself in *Hell's Cartographers* as "a man who is living his own adolescent fantasies," explaining: "When I was sixteen or so I yearned to win fame as a writer of science fiction, to become wealthy enough to indulge in whatever amusements I chose, to know the love of fair women, to travel widely, to live free from the pressures and perils of ordinary life. All these things have come to me, and more; I have fewer complaints to make about the hand destiny has dealt me than anyone I know." And Isaac Asimov gives this account of a colleague who "zoomed upward at rocket velocities:" "He is dark, handsome and slim, with somber, deep-set, burning eyes that seem to probe under skin and muscle and to bare your very soul with a skillful scalpel. . . . He is bearded; not with offensive profusion, but with neat literary flair. It gives him an almost satanic appearance." "On top of that," Asimov continues, "his conversation is not frivolous. Not for him the tossed-off quip. . . . From him, rather, the stately machete of a riposte, that efficiently, and without undue haste, strips your skin from head to toe."

The author was married in 1956 to Barbara Brown, an engineer. In 1972, the Silverbergs moved from New York City to California, where the writer gives his leisure to gardening, reading, music, and the cinema. The American Guest of Honor at the World Science Fiction Convention at Heidelberg, Germany, in 1970, he served as President of the Science Fiction Writers of America in 1967-1968. He is one of the most respected and prolific editors of science fiction anthologies.

In *Contemporary Science Fiction Authors* (1975), Silverberg wrote that he was fascinated by the experimental techniques of science fiction's "new wave" but that he felt "no impulse to make use of those techniques in my own work. I think sf must be brought to a state of functional literacy before we go bounding off into avant-gardery." His own chief goals, he said, were "to attain the sort of stylistic proficiency that is demanded of any writer in noncategory fiction, and to transform the standard material of science fiction through an emphasis on emotion, intensity of incident, and complexity of character." Silverberg noted that much of his recent work "has had a very strong erotic content; I see this as a useful corrective to the innocence of nearly all sf of the past."

PRINCIPAL WORKS (a representative selection): *Fiction*—Revolt on Alpha C, 1955; Invaders From Earth, 1956; Master of Life and Death, 1957; (with Randall Garrett as "Robert Randall") The Shrouded Planet, 1957; (as "David Osborne") Invisible Barriers, 1958; (as "Ivar Jorgenson") Starhaven, 1958; The Planet Killers, 1959; Lost Race of Mars, 1960; Collision Course, 1961; Next Stop the Stars, 1962; Regan's Planet, 1964; To Worlds Beyond (short stories), 1965; The Time-Hoppers, 1967; Thorns, 1967; Hawksbill Station, 1968 (in England, The Anvil of Time); The Masks of Time, 1968 (in England, Vornan-19); the Calibrated Alligator (short stories), 1969; Nightwings, 1969; Up the Line, 1969; The Man in the Maze, 1969; Dimension Thirteen, 1969; Parsecs and Parables (short stories), 1970; Tower of Glass, 1970; A Time of Changes, 1971; The World Inside, 1971; Dying Inside, 1972; Unfamiliar Territory (short stories), 1973; Born With the Dead: Three Novellas, 1974; The Stochastic Man, 1975; The Feast of St. Dionysus (short stories), 1975; The Best of Robert Silverberg, 1976; Shadrach in the Furnace, 1976; etc. *Nonfiction*—Treasures Beneath the Sea, 1960; Lost Cities and Vanished Civilizations, 1962; Sunken History: The Story of Underwater Archaeology, 1963; Home of the Red Man: Indian North America Before Columbus, 1963; Fifteen Battles That Changed the World, 1963; Empires in the Dust: Ancient Civilizations Brought to Light, 1963; The Man Who Found Nineveh: The Story of Austen Henry Layard, 1964; Akhnaten: The Rebel Pharaoh, 1964; (as "Walker Chapman") The Loneliest Continent: The Story of Antarctic Discovery, 1964; The World of Coral, 1965; Socrates, 1965; The Old Ones: Indians of the American Southwest, 1965; The Great Wall of China, 1965; (as "Lee Sebastian") Rivers, 1966; (as "Walker Chapman") Kublai Khan, 1966; The World of the Rain Forest, 1967; Men Against Time: Salvage Archaeology in the United States, 1967; The Auk, the Dodo, and the Oryx: Vanished and Vanishing Creatures, 1967; Ghost Towns of the American West, 1968; Wonders of Ancient Chinese Science, 1969; Vanishing Giants: The Story of the Sequoias, 1969; The Challenge of Climate, 1969; If I Forget Thee, O Jerusalem: American Jews and the State of Israel, 1970; To the

753

SIMIC

Western Shore: Growth of the United States, 1776–1853, 1971; The Realm of Prester John, 1972; John Muir: Prophet Among the Glaciers, 1972; The Longest Voyage: Circumnavigators in the Age of Discovery, 1972; etc. *As Editor* —Great Adventures in Archaeology, 1964; Earthmen and Strangers: Nine Stories of Science Fiction, 1966; Men and Machines: Ten Stories of Science Fiction, 1968; Alpha One, 1970; The Mirror of Infinity: A Critic's Anthology of Science Fiction, 1970; Science Fiction Hall of Fame, 1970; Mind to Mind: Nine Stories of Science Fiction, 1971; Beyond Control: Seven Stories of Science Fiction, 1972; Deep Space: Eight Stories of Science Fiction, 1973; Infinite Jests: The Lighter Side of Science Fiction, 1974; Sunrise on Mercury and Other Science Fiction Stories, 1975; Earth Is the Strangest Planet: Ten Stories of Science Fiction, 1977; etc.

ABOUT: Aldiss, B.W. and Harrison, H. (eds.) Hell's Cartographers, 1975; Contemporary Authors 1-4 1st revision, 1967; Ketterer, D. New Worlds for Old, 1974; Reginald, R. (ed.) Contemporary Science Fiction Authors, 1975; Who's Who in America, 1976-1977. *Periodicals*—Book Week May 7, 1967; New York Times Book Review May 8, 1960; August 24, 1975; Times Literary Supplement August 15, 1968; June 12, 1969; January 8, 1970; November 9, 1973; March 15, 1974; May 23, 1975; August 8, 1975; July 30, 1976.

*SIMIC, CHARLES (May 9, 1938–), American poet and translator, was born in Beograd, Yugoslavia, the son of George Simic, an engineer, and the former Helen Matijevic. He was brought to the United States in 1949 and was educated at Oak Park High School, near Chicago. He studied at the University of Chicago from 1956 to 1959 and at New York University from 1959 to 1961. From then until 1963 he served with the United States Army, and then returned to New York University, receiving his B.A. in 1964. According to one account Simic "spent several years in the New York Public Library reading all the folklore he could find," but whether this was while he was at the university or later is not clear. Simic worked for a time as a proofreader for the Chicago *Sun-Times* and from 1966 to 1969 was an editorial assistant with the New York photography magazine *Aperture*. In 1970–1973 he taught English at California State College, Hayward, and since 1974 he has been an associate professor of English at the University of New Hampshire, Durham.

Simic has translated extensively from French, Russian, and Yugoslav poetry, and has been greatly influenced by the Serbian poet Vasko Popa. His first book, *What the Grass Says,* appeared in 1967 and its reviewers were astonished by Simic's ability to take the commonest object —a stone, a pair of shoes, a knife—and, writing about it in the plainest phrases, to use it as a door into a world of disquieting strangeness:

> Go inside a stone
> That would be my way.

*sim′ ik

CHARLES SIMIC

> Let somebody else become a dove
> Or gnash with a tiger's tooth.
> I am happy to be a stone....
>
> I have seen sparks fly out
> When two stones are rubbed,
> So perhaps it is not dark inside after all,
> Perhaps there is a moon shining
> From somewhere, as though behind a hill—
> Just enough light to make out
> The strange writings, the star-charts
> On the inner walls.

(from "Stone")

"The poems often have the same general structure," wrote Michael Benedikt, "beginning quietly and even prosily, and closing with miraculous insights that break down simplistic vision." Simic, he thought, "has a kind of rock-bottomed simplicity, a simplicity that is spiritual enough to qualify ... as a unique clarity of heart."

There were similar "cryptic and fascinating" poems in *Somewhere Among Us a Stone Is Taking Notes* (1969), but *Dismantling the Silence* (1971) seemed to Robert B. Shaw a darker collection, unrelieved by even the tough and menacing humor of the earlier books. "Its landscapes are bleak and seem only accidentally touched by humanity," Shaw wrote, although Simic's "mordant focusings on common objects ... only lead him closer to the human essence. With a pitiless reductionism he strips away the artificialities of civilization, and often prophesies a return to a harsh natural existence": "Whoever swings an ax/ Knows the body of man/ Will again be covered with fur." Shaw concluded that he had "met with very few volumes as imaginatively fertile, in which so many of the poems are instantly memorable," and quoted as an example "Butcher Shop":

Sometimes walking late at night
I stop before a closed butcher shop.
There is a single light in the store
Like the light in which the convict digs his tunnel.

An apron hangs on the hook:
The blood on it smeared into a map
Of the great continents of blood,
The great rivers and oceans of blood. . . .

There is a wooden slab where bones are broken,
Scraped clean:—a river dried to its bed
Where I am fed,
Where deep in the night I hear a voice.

White, which followed in 1972, was Simic's first attempt at a long poem, "a more expansive architecture." White, as the absence of color which contains all colors, is made to represent that silent region from which a poet draws his images. This poem or sequence, made up of ten-line sections, records the poet's repeated forays into this mysterious region—an austere, abstract, even mystical meditation on the creative process.

There was something like universal praise for Simic's next collection, *Return to a Place Lit By a Glass of Milk* (1974), which brought him an Edgar Allan Poe Award. Reviewers welcomed with something like relief the warmer humanity they found here, the touches of humor, the greater variety in theme, the subtler modulations in the poet's voice. The volume includes some remarkable love poems which combine "slapstick and subtle feeling, awkwardness and sophistication," standing "in vivid, ungainly contrast to the conventional language of love." Elsewhere, according to a reviewer in the *Virginia Quarterly Review,* Simic continues his pursuit of "the initiation into a pre-verbal, pre-conceptual consciousness" through "childhood, folklore, eroticism, foods, animals, and plants," bringing to this quest an "uncommon level of imagination and gnarled wit." Although "fine lines are everywhere in these poems," this writer also found disappointing passages of hollow rhetoric, and thought that for all its excellences "it falls short of the greatest irrationalist poetry." James Atlas made a similar complaint, but concluded that Simic "has a great and original gift, the gift of awakening in us the sensation of being." There was warm praise also for *Charon's Cosmology* (1977), in which Simic continues

to succumb to "the old sweet temptation/ to find an equivalent/ for the ineffable."

James Atlas believes that Simic owes less to surrealism than to East European poetry, "with its emphasis on a condensed, somber, even ballad-like language." He shows "the same incantatory powers" as Vasko Popa, "the same cunning and story-telling art." Simic himself says that the poet should be an explorer "of all that which came before thought and emotion but without which these two could not exist. In the deepest sense the possibilities that allow us to create belong to our ancestors. We can do very little but great things can be done through us." Robert B. Shaw has said that, at his most serious, Simic "writes as if he were naming things for the first time," and believes that he is "one of the few truly considerable poets of his generation."

Charles Simic was married in 1965 to Helene Dubin, a dress designer, and has a daughter. He is a member of the Eastern Orthodox church, but has no political affiliation. He received a P.E.N. International award for his work as a translator in 1970, a Guggenheim fellowship in 1972, and a grant from the National Endowment for the Arts in 1974. *Another Republic* (1976), which Simic edited with Mark Strand, contains translations from the work of seventeen recent European and Latin American writers seen as representatives of a "new international style" deriving from surrealism (in the case of writers like Popa, Michaux, Ponge, Paz, and Calvino) or from the poetry of Constantine Cavafy (Celan, Herbert, Ritsos, Bobrowski, Holub).

PRINCIPAL WORKS: *Poetry*—What the Grass Says, 1967; Somewhere Among Us a Stone Is Taking Notes, 1969; Dismantling the Silence, 1971; White, 1972; Return to a Place Lit By a Glass of Milk, 1974; Charon's Cosmology, 1977. *As Translator*—Four Yugoslav Poets, 1970; (with C.W. Truesdale) Fire Gardens, by Ivan Lalic, 1970; The Little Box, by Vasko Popa, 1970. *As Editor*—(with Mark Strand) Another Republic: Seventeen European and South American Writers, 1976.

ABOUT: Contemporary Authors 29-32 1st revision, 1978; Vinson, J. (ed.) Contemporary Poets, 1975; Who's Who in America, 1978–1979. *Periodicals*—Chicago Review 20 1 1968; Hudson Review Summer 1971; New Republic January 24, 1976; Poetry March 1972, February 1975; Shenandoah Summer 1971; Village Voice April 4, 1974; Virginia Quarterly Review Spring 1975; Western Humanities Review Autumn 1974.

*SIMONOV, "KONSTANTIN" (actually KIRILL) MIKHAILOVICH** (November 28, 1915–August 28, 1979), Russian poet, novelist, and dramatist, writes (in Russian): "I was born in Petrograd (now Leningrad), spent my child-

*sē' mon of

755

SIMONOV

KONSTANTIN SIMONOV

hood and youth in Ryazan and Saratov. My mother worked as a typist and a clerk, while my father, who served in the Russo-Japanese War and the First World War, was an instructor in tactics at the military academy.

"My family lived in the barracks, in the midst of the soldiers, so that I was surrounded by military life, and family discipline was strict. Everything was done strictly by the clock, to be late was absolutely impossible, to raise objections unthinkable, you had to be as good as your word and disdain even the smallest lie.

"At home we were allotted tasks. Mine included dusting, sweeping the floor, helping to wash the dishes, peeling potatoes, looking after the oil stove, and going for milk and bread. The atmosphere of our home and of the military unit gave me an affection for the army and in general for everything military, an affection linked with respect. This childish, not fully realized feeling had, as it afterwards turned out, entered my flesh and blood.

"In 1930, after seven grades of ordinary school, I enrolled in the factory apprenticeship school, and after finishing the course I worked from 1935 as a lathe operator in various plants in Moscow, where I had moved together with my parents in 1931.

"I began to write my first poems and stories at the age of sixteen. In 1934 I started evening courses in the Literary University (later the Gorky Institute of Literature), graduating in 1938. For the first two years I carried on working while studying, but from the third year I studied full time. In 1938 I published my first two books of verse, was accepted as a member of the Writers' Union, and became a professional writer.

"In autumn 1939 I was the war correspondent for an army newspaper at the battle of Khalkhin-Gol in Mongolia against the Japanese. In 1940-1941 I studied on a year's course as a war correspondent. I finished it and received officer's rank a few days after the outbreak of the Second World War, my service in which began on the Western front. I worked first for an army and then for a front newspaper, at the same time sending dispatches to *Izvestia*. From July 20, 1941 until the end of the war I was a war correspondent for the *Red Star,* and I also often wrote for *Pravda.* In May 1942 I joined the Communist party.

"For my part in the war I was awarded the Order of the Red Banner, the Order of the Great Fatherland War with bar, the Czechoslovak War Cross and Order of the White Lion, and the Mongolian Order of Sukhe-Bator for my part in the battle of Khalkhin-Gol. During the war I was at various times at most of the fronts, but as well as my war reports I also wrote two books of poetry, the novel *Dni i nochi* (Days and Nights), three plays, and also, even though insufficiently, kept a diary which has been and still is a great help in my work.

"After the war I was sent abroad on foreign missions, for about three years in all. I went to Japan, North and South America, China, almost every European country, Vietnam, and the Near East. My observations and reflections on these journeys provided the themes of several of my books and plays as well as a series of journalistic articles. But the most important thing for me in the postwar years was my work on my novels about the war. I wanted to show how much incredible effort and sacrifice the victory over the fascists cost my people—not only the heroism of the Soviet people both in battle and on the home front, but the bitterness of war—to say to people: that's what war is like, strive to avert another one. These were the feelings aroused in my books *Zhivye i myortvye* (The Living and the Dead), *Soldatami ne rozhdayutsya* (Soldiers Are Made, Not Born) and *Posledneye leto* (The Last Summer), now united as a single novel in three books under the general title *The Living and the Dead.* I worked on this trilogy for fifteen years. I was pursuing the same aim in preparing my war diaries in book form, the chief of which, 'Raznye dni voyni' (Various Days of War), was published in the journal *Druzhba narodov* (Friendship of Peoples) in 1973–1975, and also the cycle of stories 'Iz zapisok Lopatina' (From the Diary of Lopatin).

"During 1958–1960 I lived in Tashkent,

working as *Pravda's* traveling correspondent in Central Asia, and so came to know the Tien Shan and Pamir Mountains, the Golodnaya (Hungry) Steppe and Karshi Steppe, the deserts of Kara Kum and Kyzyl Kum. From 1963 to 1967, again as special correspondent of *Pravda,* I went to Mongolia, the Taymyr peninsula, Yakutia, through the central Siberian regions of Krasnoyarsk and Irkutsk, the Kola Peninsula in the north, Kazakhstan, the Far East, Kamchatka, Magadan, and Chukotia.

"I have devoted a considerable amount of time to the cinema. I collaborated in a series of documentary films, in particular, *Normandia-Neman* (From Normandy to the Niemen), *Esli dorog tebe tvoy dom* (If Your Home Is Dear to You), *Chuzhogo gorya ne byvaet* (Grief Belongs to Everyone), *Shel soldat* (I Was a Soldier).

"I have been and still am engaged in public activities. I have been elected a delegate to party congresses, a member of the Central Committee of the Communist Party, and a deputy in the Supreme Soviet; I have been chief editor of the magazines *Novy mir* and *Literaturnaya gazeta.* From 1946 to 1959 and in 1967 I was secretary of the Writers' Union; and I have served as vice-president of the Soviet Committee for the Defense of Peace.

"In 1947 I was awarded a Lenin Prize for the trilogy *The Living and the Dead,* and the title Hero of Socialist Labor was conferred on me."

Love and war were the two central experiences of Simonov's life and provided the main themes of all his work, whose characteristic tone is already present in such early poetry collections as *Nastoyashchiye lyudi* (Real People, 1938) and *Dorozhniye stikhi* (Wayside Poems, 1939). Much of this early verse is extremely intimate love poetry—passionate and earthy, but also sensitive. Typical is "Pyat stranits" (Five Pages), a poetic account of the birth and death of a love affair, in the form of a letter left in a hotel room and never posted. Simonov's youthful romanticism also expressed itself in long poems on patriotic historical themes. *Ledovoye poboishche* (The Battle on the Ice, 1938) is an epic account of how Alexander Nevsky defeated an earlier German threat, the invasion of the Teutonic Knights, in the famous battle on the ice of Lake Peipus in 1240 A.D. Another long poem, *Suvorov* (1940), recreates the exploits of the great eighteenth-century field marshal of that name.

But it was the poetry Simonov wrote during his own war, while working as a correspondent at the front, that brought him his immense popularity. Poetry has always been read more

widely in Russia than anywhere else in the world, and was often published in convenient pocket-sized volumes that soldiers could carry at the battlefront. Simonov's verse has sometimes been criticized as shallow or sentimental, expressing unexceptional thoughts and feelings not through poetic imagery but with a prosy directness. Perhaps precisely because he voiced the emotions of millions in unsophisticated verse, Simonov rose to unprecedented popularity with such poems as "Ty pomnish, Alesha, dorogi Smolenshchiny" (You Remember, Alyosha, the Roads of Smolensk). The Alyosha addressed here is Simonov's friend and fellow poet Alexei Surkov, who also spent the greater part of the war at the front. The poem recalls poignant scenes as the Russians retreated before the German onslaught in the early part of the war, yet it also records the poet's discovery of an eternal Russia of "villages, villages, villages and churchyards," of the hut where an old peasant woman had laid out her dead husband in white burial robes, of the quiet courage of simple people. (It was Simonov's deep and nostalgic love of the country, quite free from any specifically Soviet patriotism, that made the poem so popular with Russian *émigrés* abroad.)

Another very popular poem, "Zhdi menya, i ya vernus" (Wait For Me, and I'll Return), is a sort of prayer or incantation to the mystical power of love. The soldier at the front believes he will be protected against wounds, danger, and even death, if only his beloved will remain faithful and believe in his eventual return. The collection *S toboy i bez tebya* (With You and Without You, 1944) is made up largely of purely personal love poems. Simonov's wartime verse, like all his work, is very uneven, and Gleb Struve suggests that though some of it is excellent, "in the final analysis Simonov seems to lack that indefinable something, that magic which turns merely good poetry into great poetry."

Simonov's most successful novels were also about the war, like *Dni i nochi* (1944, translated as *Days and Nights*), a fictional account of the battle for Stalingrad. Captain Saburov, at twenty-nine a veteran of the great retreat, arrives in the besieged city with a unit of reinforcements and is ordered to retake three buildings from the Germans. The entire novel deals with the struggle for these half-ruined houses. Saburov's love affair with the young nurse Anya has been thought trite by some critics, though Vera Alexandrova found her "awkward childish kiss" and the apple she receives as a gift from her mother on her "wedding" day particularly moving. The novel has also been criticized as too loosely composed, perhaps too hastily written, to do justice to the tremendous events it portrays, though reviewers welcomed its appealing absence of bombast and its understanding of the psychology of men under fire.

After the war, Simonov wrote several retrospective novels about it, including the trilogy *The Living and the Dead,* in which he was able to portray aspects of the war that would have been forbidden before Stalin's death in 1953. Thus the first book, *Zhivye i myortvye* (1959, translated as *The Living and the Dead*), subsequently filmed, deals with the catastrophic reverses immediately following the German invasion in 1941, the large-scale panics as the front collapsed, Stalin's blunders, and the deadly atmosphere of suspicion that was the legacy of his purge of the officer corps. Emanuel Salgaller said in *Books Abroad* that "the bitterness of the retreat, the tragedy of unequal battle, the suffering and endurance of the Russian people make this rather artless and at times slow-moving narrative absorbing and even exciting reading." Tom Wolfe, however, complained that Simonov, who had been "pro-Stalin at the right time" in *Days and Nights* was here being "anti-Stalin at the right time," and wrote that Simonov and others like him "have had their eyes on the directives of the Union of Soviet Writers too long to take a look at the human condition at this late date."

Marc Slonim, who describes Simonov's novels as "satisfactory second-rate literature," has also said that he revived in his work "the spirit of Tolstoy's *Sebastopol Tales* and of certain chapters of *War and Peace*." This is also true of the play which brought Simonov his greatest success as a dramatist, *Russkiye lyudi* (1942, translated as *The Russians* and also as *The Russian People*). Set on the southern front, and glorifying the simplicity, stamina, and courage of a well-characterized group of ordinary people, it was one of the most popular plays of the period and was staged in many countries.

The tensions of the cold war are reflected in such later plays as *Pod kashtanami Pragi* (1947, translated as *Beneath the Chestnuts of Prague*) and *Russki vopros* (The Russian Question, 1947). In the latter, a liberal American journalist sells out to the reactionary American press by consenting to write lies about the Soviet Union. This play has been performed in both England and America and was made into a film directed by Mikhail Romm. *Russkiye lyudi* has also been filmed, by no less a director than Pudovkin, and Simonov wrote scenarios for other movies derived from his own works, including *Dni i nochi* and *Zhdi menya,* expanded from the poem "Wait for Me" and made into a tender and appealing film by Stolper and Ivanov in 1943.

After the war, Simonov was particularly active as a journalist and critic. He attacked Ehrenburg's novel *The Thaw* but subsequently moved closer to the liberal camp. In 1957 he was dismissed from his post as editor of the magazine *Novy mir* for publishing such works as Dudintsev's challenging novel *Not by Bread Alone.*

PRINCIPAL WORKS IN ENGLISH TRANSLATION: *Poetry*— Friends and Foes, translated by I. Zhukovitskaya, 1952. *Poems in* Lindsay, J. (ed.) Russian Poetry 1917–1935, 1937; Markov, V. and Sparks, M. (eds.) Modern Russian Poetry, 1966. *Novels*—Days and Nights, translated by Joseph Barnes, 1945; Days and Nights, translated by J. Fineberg, 1945; The Living and the Dead (U.K., Victims and Heroes), translated by R. Ainsztein, 1962 (also translated as The Living and the Dead by Alex Miller, 1975). *Short Stories in* Soviet Short Stories 1942–1943, 1943; Soviet War Stories, 1969. *Plays*—The Whole World Over, translated by Thelma Schnee, 1949; The Russians, translated by Gerard Shelley *in* Seven Soviet War Plays, 1944; The Russian People *in* Soviet Plays, 1946; Beneath the Chestnuts of Prague *in* Soviet Literature 2 1946. *Nonfiction*—On the Petsamo Road: Notes of a War Correspondent, 1942; Stalingrad Fights On, 1942; No Quarter on Russia's Fighting Lines, 1943.

ABOUT: Alexandrova, V. A History of Soviet Literature, 1963; Brown, E.J. Russian Literature Since the Revolution, 1963; International Who's Who, 1978–79; Lavrin, J. A Panorama of Russian Literature, 1973; Mihailovich, V.D. (ed.) A Library of Literary Criticism: Modern Slavic Literature 1 1972; Prominent Personalities in the USSR, 1968; Slonim, M. Soviet Russian Literature, 1964; Struve, G. Russian Literature Under Lenin and Stalin, 1971; *Periodicals* —Books Abroad Winter 1962; New Yorker November 3, 1945; Soviet Literature August 1946, 11 1975; Times Literary Supplement November 10, 1945.

SISSON, C(HARLES) H(UBERT) (April 22, 1914–) English poet, novelist, critic, translator, and essayist, writes: "I am afraid that autobiography is a form of lying, but I will do my best to give a few indications. Of what? Place of birth: a working-class district of Bristol. Parentage? My father from Westmorland, my mother from Gloucestershire and Wiltshire; neither had much formal education. My mother's family of immemorial farming stock; my father's small manufacturers, established for several generations: but both families in a poor way in my parents' childhoods. My father ran a small one-man business in Bristol and trade was generally bad.

"I went to the local elementary school, grim and brutal in tone but not outrageous by the standards of those times; at eleven I won a scholarship to a middling sort of mixed secondary school, where my chief proficiency was in English, French and Latin and I was rotten at games. Went to the University of Bristol—usually on foot since my pocket-money consisted of what I could save from bus fares. Poverty was not unusual so a life with no travel and few

C. H. SISSON

"My early articles in the *New English Weekly* felt their way forward sentence by sentence, and there is a direct progression from them to the few intermittent poems I wrote when in the army overseas. I do not mean that there was endless polishing but that I had to wait before I could say anything. After the war I continued to cultivate my still unfluent prose; my first appearance in book form was as the translator of four short stories by Jules Supervielle. Generally what I wrote took a long time to get into print, sometimes ten years or more.

"I gave up writing poetry at the age of twenty but perhaps I may say that it has gradually been borne in upon me that it is the mode of expression which serves me best. My training has included a good deal of verse translation, particularly from the Latin poets. The range of my discursive writing has been such as an academic would consider a disgrace. My work is now found regularly in the magazine *Poetry Nation,* and occasionally in the *Times Literary Supplement.*

"I live in a minute town in Somerset, from which I issue occasionally to London, Provence or elsewhere."

diversions was not remarkable. Took a first class degree in philosophy and English literature at the age of twenty and, being unable to find an employer who would pay for my services, went abroad on post-graduate scholarships—first to Germany (the choice being determined by the rate of exchange) then, on a slightly larger grant, to France. In all, the best part of two academic years abroad—a profitable time not least because I did not write the thesis which was the pretext for these excursions. I then went into the Civil Service, since in those days they had to have you in the Administrative Class if you could pass the highly competitive and somewhat elaborate examination. I elected to go into the Ministry of Labour, where I thought crucial domestic events would be reflected. In 1937 I started writing for the *New English Weekly,* edited by Philip Mairet as successor to A.R. Orage —articles in the main of what I can only describe as political and social criticism. There was no question in the *New English Weekly* of rousing a mob or pleasing a party; and no payment. I married a girl I had known at school but who had then rejected my inept suit. My army career (1942–1945) started in Ireland and most of it was spent in India; I never applied for a commission. My first daughter was born in 1943; my second in 1949. My domestic life has been that of a middle-class bread-winner and, for years, commuter. It was a pleasure to be able to walk out of the civil service even though it was only a year or so before my time. However at no time did it occur to me that I could make my living by writing. It is not altogether a merit to write what people won't pay for but at least it is an error on the right side.

Although, as he says, Sisson wrote some verse in his youth, and a few more poems were wrung from him while he was in India with the British Army Intelligence Corps, his first published books were a novel, *An Asiatic Romance* (1953), and a volume of translations of Heine (1955). It was not until 1959 that his work attracted widespread attention, and that was for a very different sort of book, *The Spirit of British Administration.* In 1956–1957, with a Simon senior research fellowship from Manchester University, Sisson had investigated the administrative structures of France, Germany, Austria, Sweden, and Spain, comparing them with British practice, and his book was a succinct and extremely witty defense of the British tradition of intelligent amateurism in the civil service.

One reviewer found in Sisson's first verse collection, *The London Zoo,* published when he was forty-seven, "the inviting yet menacing ripeness of a bruised pear." These were the poems, it was said, of a hedonist and a "bitterly despairing Christian," whose recurrent themes included lust, self-contempt, contempt for others, age, decline, and death. The same "quirky, disillusioned vision" was recognized in *Numbers* and in *Metamorphoses,* but there were complaints of a prosy diction in some of these poems, and "a straitjacket of rhyme which forces a vague and abstract tone." Sisson's translations of Catullus were called "a decent piece of work."

There was something very different from this faint praise, however, when the whole body of Sisson's poetry (and a selection of his translations) was published in 1974 as *In the Trojan Ditch;* it was greeted by some critics as one of the most important volumes of collected poems published in England since World War II.

What is central in Sisson's poetry is the tension between his determined commitment to an uncompromising kind of Anglican Christianity and his sense of the hopeless absurdity of his and all men's attempts to transcend bestial carnality:

It is the nature of man that puzzles me
As I walk from Saint James's Square to Charing
　　Cross;
The polite mechanicals are going home,
I understand their condition and their loss.

Ape-like in that their box of wires
Is shut behind a face of human resemblance,
They favour a comic hat between their ears
And their monkey's tube is tucked inside their
　　pants.

(from "The Nature of Man")

This tension is reflected in Sisson's style. His language is for the most part plain, emphatic, and sometimes scatalogical; his meters conventional. But this surface simplicity is made to express deep ambiguities—mostly, as Kenneth Cox has pointed out, through the use of various degrees of irony and an acute sensitivity to slight variations of tone. Sisson's poems have been called abstract and intellectual, but this is not to say that they are not also powerfully felt. Often, as Robert Nye has said, they begin in the present and journey back into the past, concerning themselves with a "passionate and lucid explication of *what it is* that remembers, and what the person or consciousness may be said to be which is performing the act of remembering." Some of the poems, especially the early ones, express the author's self-disgust with a savage relish that some readers have found disagreeable.

It is Sisson's more recent work that has been most admired. These later poems are more concentrated and more complex than their predecessors, both in content and rhythm, and at times, according to Robert Nye, their "thinking becomes so intense and their rhythm so subtle that a fluid syntax of pure intuition emerges." Several of these poems deal with the "theme of a divine flux being all there is for us in the way of hope," and most critics would agree with Nye that this theme is "approached most memorably, urgently and originally" in the sixty-line poem called "The Usk":

Nothing is in my voice because I have not
Any. Nothing in my own name
Here inscribed on water, nothing but flow
A ripple, outwards. Standing beside the Usk
You flow like truth, river, I will get in
Over me, through me perhaps, river let me be
　　crystalline
As I shall not be, shivering upon the bank. . . .

Donald Davie, who regards this as "one of the great poems of our time," has called it "an extraordinary triumph of the plain style in poetry precisely because, even as it deploys that style, it convicts it of dishonesty." Davie considers Sisson to be "a poet who can be mentioned in the same breath as Dryden, who can sustain the comparison at least for a while. . . . It is years since there appeared a book of verse to equal this one for seriousness and accomplishment, and the unadvertised drama that is acted out on its pages." This view is not universally held, however. Peter Porter, reviewing the later small collection *Anchises* (1976), said that he could find in Sisson's work "no marks of greatness other than a vein of aristocratic misanthropy. . . . If Sisson were the rhetorical genius his supporters make him out to be, I should be happy to welcome his late recognition, but I can find no emotional core to him other than disappointment."

Christopher Homm, Sisson's second novel, begins with the death of its quintessentially nondescript hero and works backwards through his life—to the middle-aged clerk cursed with a shrewish wife, the awkward young man, clumsy schoolboy, sickly child—to end with his beginning as an infant who, "if he had known how bitter the journey was to be would not have come." It was found a depressing book but also a comic and extremely skillful one, an autopsy executed "with grim precision and an attention to quotidian detail which sets his unlikely subject in an almost painfully literal light."

Sisson has also published three collections of essays on literary, religious, and social themes, in which he "wears his dislike of the modern world in most of its manifestations proudly like a decoration for bravery." His distaste for modern democratic egalitarianism, which he associates with the decline of moral and religious standards, made his 1972 study of the economist and journalist Walter Bagehot a generally hostile one. Sisson's translation of Lucretius's *De Rerum Natura,* published in 1976, was called "a nice way of becoming acquainted with Lucretius, just because of its vigour and energy as a piece of English verse." He has been joint editor since 1976 of *PN Review.*

The author is the son of Richard Sisson and

the former Ellen Minnie Worlock. He was married in 1937 to Nora Gilbertson. He joined the Ministry of Labour with the grade of Assistant Principal in 1936, became a Principal in 1945, Assistant Secretary in 1953, Under Secretary and Director of Establishments in 1962. In 1968, by which time the Ministry of Labour had become the Department of Employment, Sisson became Assistant Under Secretary of State there, and spent his last year in the civil service (1972–1973) as Director of Occupational Safety and Health. Few senior civil servants have had the courage to publish their criticism of the service while still in office, as Sisson did in articles in the *Spectator* in February and March 1971.

Writing in *Contemporary Poets,* Sisson said: "My verse is about things that I am, at the moment of writing, just beginning to understand. When I have understood them, or have that impression, the subject has gone, and I have to find another.... As to verse forms, whether they are what is called regular, or not, it is a small matter: I have written in both kinds. What matters is the rhythm, which is the identifying mark of the poem.... What I aim at is to make plain statements, and not more of them than I need. 'It is the nature of man that puzzles me'; I should like to leave a few recognizable—not novel—indications. The man that was the same in Neolithic and in Roman time, as now, is of more interest than the freak of circumstances. This truth lies at the bottom of a well of rhythm."

PRINCIPAL WORKS: *Poetry*—The London Zoo, 1961; Numbers, 1965; Metamorphoses, 1968; In the Trojan Ditch, 1974; The Corridor, 1975; Anchises, 1976. *Translations*—Versions and Perversions of Heine, 1955; Catullus, 1966; The Poetic Art (translation of Horace's Ars poetica), 1975; The Poem on Nature (translation of Lucretius's De rerum natura), 1976. *Novels*—An Asiatic Romance, 1953; Christopher Homm, 1965. *Nonfiction*—The Spirit of British Administration, 1959; Art and Action (essays), 1965; Essays, 1967; English Poetry 1900–1950, 1971; The Case of Walter Bagehot, 1972; David Hume (New Assessments series), 1976; (editor) South African Album, by David Wright, 1976; (editor) The English Sermon, Volume 2: 1650–1750, 1976. (editor) Selected Poems of Jonathan Swift, 1977; The Avoidance of Literature: Collected Essays, 1978.

ABOUT: Contemporary Authors 1–4 1st revision, 1967; International Who's Who, 1978–79; Vinson, J. (ed.) Contemporary Poets, 1975; Who's Who, 1978. *Periodicals*—Agenda 3–4 1970, Autumn 1974; Listener May 9, 1974; New York Times Book Review December 18, 1977; Observer January 27, 1977. Poetry Nation V 1975; Times Literary Supplement November 29, 1974; X 2 1962.

*SJÖWALL, MAJ (September 25, 1935–) and **WAHLÖÖ, PER (i.e. Peter Fredrik) (August 5, 1926–June 22, 1975), Swedish novelists, set out in the books they wrote together to mirror a changing society through the medium of

*shû′ val **vä′ lûû

MAJ SJÖWALL AND PER WAHLÖÖ

the detective story. Maj Sjöwall was born in Malmö, southern Sweden, the daughter of Will Sjöwall and the former Margit Trobäck. She began her career as a reporter, working in this capacity and as an art director for several Swedish magazines. In 1959–1961 she was an editor with the publishing house of Wahlström and Widstrand.

Wahlöö was recognized as a young novelist of promise even before the collaboration with Maj Sjöwall began. He was born in Gothenburg, the son of Waldeman and Karin (Svensson) Wahlöö, and attended the University of Lund. He also began his career as a journalist, working during the late 1940s as a criminal and social reporter for several leading Swedish newspapers. Wahlöö held extreme left-wing political views, and in the 1950s was engaged in political activities in Spain which ended in his deportation in 1957. Returning to Sweden, he wrote a number of television and radio plays and was managing editor of several magazines before becoming a full-time writer in 1961. By that time, he had already published two novels, *Himmelsgeten* (Heaven's Goats, 1959, republished in 1967 as *Hövdingen* or Chieftains), and *Vinden och regnet* (Winds and Rains, 1961). A third, *Lastbilen,* followed in 1962. It was translated by Joan Tate and published in the United States as *A Necessary Action* and in Britain as *The Lorry.*

The first of Wahlöö's novels to attract much international attention was *Uppdraget* (1963, translated by Joan Tate as *The Assignment*), about the political, moral, and emotional problems of a diplomat who is assigned to administer a Latin American country after the assassination of the previous administrator. H. W. Mott found

Ortega "more of a symbol of a man than a credible human being," but thought the novel appealing as "a case study in revolution . . . [and] a carefully constructed philosophical thesis . . . [with] ample doses of sex and violence." James Kelly agreed that Wahlöö seemed less "concerned with human characterization than with the detailed tactics of modern ideological conflict," and complained that his literary style "steadfastly hews to the telegraphic, no-nonsense mannerisms of TV's *Dragnet.*"

There was a much warmer reception for Wahlöö's next novel, *Mord å 31* (1964), which Joan Tate translated as *The Thirty-First Floor* (*Murder on the Thirty-First Floor* in Britain). It is set in a northern country (which might be Sweden sometime in the future) where too many years of the welfare state have reduced the population to unthinking though neurotic ciphers. A powerful publishing combine which spoon-feeds the public with journalistic placebos is threatened with a bomb attack, and Chief Inspector Jensen is ordered to bring the culprit to book forthwith.

This "dysutopia in a minor key" was widely admired, and Anthony Boucher called it "something quite special and fascinating: a use of the detection form to present a brooding and biting forecast of the future. . . . It is related to Kafka and to science fiction, and it has a nice haunted feel to it, along with some vivid (if nameless) characters and a pretty final twist of plot." Alan Levensohn was reminded less of Kafka than of the French "new novel," suggesting that Wahlöö had created "an anti-detective novel. . . . At moments of taut suspense, when he knows the reader is bound to keep reading, he introduces exasperating passages of irrelevant detail, rendered in a tense, important tone. At moments of genuine revelation, on the other hand, the tone is likely to be somewhat monotonous and apologetic. . . . Despite this nihilistic technique, Wahlöö has not escaped from the genre. His book, while serious, remains an exceptionally intelligent detective novel."

Wahlöö had meanwhile met Maj Sjöwall in 1961, when they were both working for the same publisher—he on the picture magazine *Se* and she on the woman's magazine *Idun.* Both had for a long time been intrigued by the idea of using the detective story genre as a means of analyzing society in a form that might be widely read—*Mord å 31* was to be an early expression of that interest. "We were sitting in a restaurant during lunch one day," Wahlöö said, "and we suddenly started talking about this idea we had both been nursing." Instead of returning to work, they spent the afternoon planning their escape from the magazine business. The following year they were married.

It was in 1962 also that their plans for a series of detective novels began to take shape—very exact shape, since before they began to write they planned the entire series in detail. The ten short novels, each of thirty chapters, were conceived as one long novel of three hundred chapters. One book was to be published each year, and the series would cover ten years in the career of their police detective Martin Beck. In this way, Wahlöö said, they could hope to show "the man's personality changing under the years, the milieu and the atmosphere changing, the political climate, the economic climate changing, the crime rate, so you can get the picture as a whole.".

By the time they were ready to write the series, the Wahlöös had two children. Partly for that reason, partly because both functioned best at night, they never settled down to work until ten or eleven P.M. Living in a large rented apartment in Malmö, Maj Sjöwall's hometown, with an inspiring view of a graveyard from their window, they worked at opposite ends of the same table until the children woke in the morning. Their style, as McCandlish Phillips has noted, is a product of their journalistic training—"spare, disciplined, and full of sharply observed detail" —and they were so in accord that they were able "to write alternate chapters in seamless prose." Another result of their journalistic backgrounds was an extreme concern for accuracy of detail: "If you read of Martin Beck taking off on a certain flight," Maj Sjöwall says, "there was that flight, at that time, with those same weather conditions."

Roseanna, the first book they wrote together, was published in Sweden in 1965 and was translated by Lois Roth under the same title in 1967. It introduces First Detective Inspector Martin Beck of the Stockholm National Police as he investigates the murder of a woman whose naked body has been dredged from Lake Vattern. Not very widely reviewed in the United States, it nevertheless struck one critic as "a wonderfully tough and pleasantly chilling tale though told without a wasted word."

By the time the second Beck novel appeared, American reviewers were beginning to realise that they were dealing with a phenomenon of more than ordinary interest. In *Mannen som gick upp i rök* (1966, translated by Joan Tate as *The Man Who Went Up in Smoke*), Beck is sent to Budapest to look into the disappearance of a Swedish newspaperman and stumbles into the midst of some very unpleasant drug smugglers. Sara Blackburn wrote that "the events themselves have a hard time competing with the absorbing details of their setting, and particularly with the delightful personality of their hero. The authors have a fine talent for describing location, and here they succeed completely in making us nervous accomplices of Beck as he grumbles about his majestic, creaky hotel room on the Danube, watching the river traffic and mulling over the strange ingredients of the case. . . . There is something enormously satisfying about reading this book—paradoxically so, for it's not often in fiction that one not only identifies completely with the hero, but hopes fervently and protectively that he will cheer up."

Mannen på balkongen (1967, translated by Alan Blair as *The Man on the Balcony*) was followed by one of the best novels in the Beck series, *Den skrattande polisen* (1968, translated by Blair as *The Laughing Policeman*), an account of what happens after nine people have been shot dead on a Stockholm bus. A.J. Hubin called it "a tantalizing, intricate tale, not really a police procedural in the strictest sense but the splendid story of an apparently clueless crime and its investigation by Stockholm's entire homicide squad." It brought the Wahlöös the Edgar Allan Poe Award from the Mystery Writers of America as the best mystery novel of 1970, and was filmed in 1973, with the setting shifted to San Francisco and Walter Matthau in the lead.

Contrary to the impression given by most crime novels, a police detective is seldom involved in only one case at a time, and an act of arson and the murders that follow are solved amid a plethora of other cases in *Brandbilen som försvann* (1969, translated by Joan Tate as *The Fire Engine That Disappeared*). Haskel Frankel concluded in his review that the Wahlöös were "among the best—perhaps they are the best—writers of detective fiction today." H.R.F. Keating also enjoyed the book but was struck by its "alienation effect"—the fact that Beck himself "fades utterly from the end of the book and is much superseded elsewhere," and that certain characters and events are introduced which appear to be irrelevant and really *are* irrelevant; Alan Levensohn had called *Mord å 31* "an anti–detective novel" and Keating said much the same of this one.

Beck's melancholy personality, his relationship with his shrewish wife and boring children, his gourmet interest in food, and his wretched digestion are relatively prominent in *Polis, polis, potatismos!* (1970, translated by Amy and Ken Knoespel as *Murder at the Savoy*). This had a rather mixed press, but most reviewers thought that the Wahlöös had returned to peak form in

Den Vedervärdige mannen från såffle (1971, translated by Thomas Teal as *The Abominable Man*), about the hunt for the man who has bayoneted a bestial police inspector to death in his hospital room. *Publishers Weekly* called this "one of the most exciting Martin Beck mysteries yet and one which is especially timely and pertinent in what it reveals of the tensions under which the police in big cities everywhere operate these days. . . . The characterizations are excellent, the dogged police work convincingly realistic and the outcome a real shocker. . . . proof that the . . . mystery novel has more than come into its own as a brilliant device for probing the ills of society."

Det slutna rummet (1972, translated by Paul Britten Austin as *The Locked Room*) was marred, according to a critic in *Library Journal,* by authorial attacks on "the shortcomings of the welfare state and the incompetence of the Swedish police force which may well be true, but which introduce a worrying note of incoherence." There were similar complaints about *Polismördaren* (1974, translated by Thomas Teal as *Cop Killer*). Phoebe Adams said that "as usual, the deficiencies of Swedish society are denounced with a fury which—not as usual—gets rather out of hand. The authors are so disgusted by conditions that they come perilously close to sermonizing on points already made effectively by the story itself."

The tenth and last novel in the series, *Terroristerna,* was published in 1975 and translated by Joan Tate as *The Terrorists*. Beck's main worry in this story is a gang of mercenaries of uncertain political orientation who have infiltrated Stockholm to assassinate a visiting U.S. Senator, but he has much else on his hands as well, including a bank robbery, the murder of a pornographer, and the mendacity and authoritarianism of Swedish bureaucracy. Several critics thought this the most suspenseful and best organized novel in the entire series. Per Wahlöö died soon after it was completed, at the age of forty-eight. Apart from his collaborations with Maj Sjöwall he had published two more novels after he began work on the Martin Beck series, *Generalerna* (1965, translated by Joan Tate as *The Generals*) and *Stålsprånget* (1968, translated by Joan Tate as *The Steel Spring*). The first was called "a grim little parable loosely based on the political and social set-up in his native Sweden. Too loosely, as it happens, to make effective, specific satire." *Stålsprånget* reintroduces Chief Inspector Peter Jensen of *Mord å 31* in another investigation into the ills of the welfare state. L.J. Davis thought that Wahlöö had "burdened his tale with such a ponderous millstone of left-wing dogma that it sinks out of sight," but Melvin Maddocks wrote that "for all his coldness, for all his clinical remoteness, Wahlöö keeps the issue of moral responsibility squarely in the center of his novels. . . . 'The computer tempted me, and I did sin,' is the confession of Wahlöö's futurists. . . . One respects Wahlöö for his tough standards of guilt. One respects him even more for his demanding concept of innocence."

Per Wahlöö and Maj Sjöwall had two sons, Tetz and Jens. Apart from their fiction, they wrote a comparative study of police methods in Sweden, the United States, Russia, and England. They also edited the Swedish magazine of literature and poetry *Peripeo.* Wahlöö translated into Swedish Noel Behn's *The Kremlin Letter,* as well as several of Ed McBain's police procedural novels about New York's 87th Precinct. Julian Symons said of him that "it was impossible to know Per Wahlöö . . . even slightly without appreciating his vigorous and powerful mind. He was an extreme Left-winger with a taste for popular sport, and his interest in British football . . . was passionate. . . . The books he wrote with Maj Sjöwall represent an attempt to bring his political feelings into a literary form with a wide appeal. They are excellent of their kind, although Wahlöö's own personality was much more interesting than that of his rather lugubrious hero, Martin Beck."

PRINCIPAL WORKS IN ENGLISH TRANSLATION: (By Per Wahlöö) The Assignment, 1965; Murder on the Thirty-First Floor, 1966 (U.S., The Thirty-First Floor); The Lorry, 1968 (U.S., A Necessary Action); The Steel Spring, 1970; The Generals, 1974. (By Per Wahlöö and Maj Sjöwall)— Roseanna, 1967; The Man on the Balcony, 1968; The Man Who Went Up in Smoke, 1969; The Laughing Policeman, 1970; The Fire Engine That Disappeared, 1970; Murder at the Savoy, 1971; The Abominable Man, 1972; The Locked Room, 1973; Cop Killer, 1975; The Terrorists, 1976.

ABOUT: Contemporary Authors 61–64, 1976; Vemärdet: Svensk Biografisk Handbok, 1973. *Periodicals*—Atlantic June 1975; Book Week April 3, 1966; Book World August 17, 1969; November 15, 1970; November 21, 1971; Christian Science Monitor May 2, 1967; September 10, 1970; Harper's January 1968; Library Journal April 15, 1966; March 1, 1967; November 1, 1972; August 1973; New York Times May 5, 1971; June 24, 1975; New York Times Book Review March 13, 1966; February 26, 1967; March 8, 1970; January 31, 1971; January 9, 1972; November 19, 1972; July 20, 1975; November 21, 1976; New Yorker May 22, 1971; Publishers Weekly September 6, 1971; August 4, 1975; Saturday Review February 27, 1971; October 28, 1972; Time August 11, 1975; Times Literary Supplement April 19, 1970; September 26, 1975; May 27, 1977.

SKINNER, B(URRHUS) F(REDERIC) (March 20, 1904–), American psychologist, writes: "I was born in the small town of Susquehanna, Pennsylvania, the first child of William A. and Grace (Burrhus) Skinner. My father

B. F. SKINNER

was a lawyer. I attended grade and high schools in Susquehanna and went on to Hamilton College where I majored in English language and literature. A letter from Robert Frost commenting favorably on some short stories I had sent him led to the decision to become a writer. I spent two years discovering that I was not to be successful in that field and then went to Harvard for graduate work in psychology. I had been attracted to behaviorism by some papers of Bertrand Russell and books by Jacques Loeb, John B. Watson and, slightly later, Pavlov.

"In the department at Harvard we were free to do pretty much as we pleased and I worked out a method for studying what I later called operant behavior. I was able to continue this work during five years of postdoctoral fellowships, two under the National Research Council and three as a Junior Fellow in the Harvard Society of Fellows.

"In 1936 I went to the University of Minnesota, where I finished the manuscript of *The Behavior of Organisms,* published in 1938—a fairly comprehensive study of operant conditioning, including certain schedules of reinforcement and related behavioral processes. I taught small classes of sophomores selected from the large introductory course. Shortly after going to Minnesota I married Yvonne Blue. A daughter, now Julie Vargas, was born in 1938 and a second daughter, now Deborah Buzan, in 1944. During the war, with the support of General Mills, Inc. and the Office of Scientific Research and Development, I explored the possibility of pigeon-guided missiles. When this work was terminated because of progress on the atom bomb, I resumed a Guggenheim fellowship which I had relinquished at the beginning of the war and spent a year writing about verbal behavior. I also built the Aircrib, a special device for the care of infants in which our second daughter (and subsequently two granddaughters) were raised. During that year I accepted an invitation to become chairman of the department at Indiana, but before moving to Indiana I wrote *Walden Two*—a fictional application of the principles developed in *The Behavior of Organisms* in the design of an experimental community.

"Invited to give the William James Lectures at Harvard in 1947, I chose verbal behavior as my subject. The following year I became professor of psychology at Harvard, where I began to teach a general education course, for which I wrote *Science and Human Behavior.* Further research, conducted with the cooperation of Charles B. Ferster, was published in our *Schedules of Reinforcement* in 1957. In the same year I published my *Verbal Behavior.*

"In 1953, with the help of Dr. Harry Solomon of the Harvard Medical School, I set up a project to investigate operant conditioning in psychotic patients at the Metropolitan State Hospital, Waltham, Massachusetts. This was taken over by Dr. Ogden Lindsley. Operant principles have since been widely used in hospital ward management with psychotics and retardates. At about the same time I returned to an interest in the effects of drugs on behavior, some examples of which were published in *The Behavior of Organisms.*

"In 1954 at the University of Pittsburgh I gave a paper called 'The Science of Learning and the Art of Teaching' in which I described programmed instruction and demonstrated a teaching machine for use with programmed material. With the help of Dr. James G. Holland, teaching machines and materials were designed for use in my general education course, and our program was published jointly as *The Analysis of Behavior* in 1961. A number of papers in the field, together with original material, appeared in *The Technology of Teaching* in 1968. More advanced papers in the analysis of behavior, with a number of relevant notes, were brought together in *Contingencies of Reinforcement* in 1969.

"As far back as 1953, when I published a paper called 'Freedom and the Control of Men,' I had been concerned with the social implications of my work. Some of these were discussed in a debate with Carl Rogers in 1956. In 1964 a Career Award from the National Institute of Mental Health permitted me to devote my time to the relevance of behavioral processes in the field of cultural design, the main result of which was *Beyond Freedom and Dignity,* published in 1971. It was widely and not always favorably reviewed. It seemed to me that certain fundamental principles of behaviorism were seriously misunderstood and *About Behaviorism,* published in 1974, was written to clarify matters.

"For ten years beginning in 1950 my family and I spent our summers on the island of Monhegan, Maine, but we now spend the whole year in Cambridge. My chief avocation has been music. I no longer play the piano because of trouble with my eyes, but I still listen.

"The first volume of an autobiography *(Particulars of My Life)* is scheduled for publication in the spring of 1976. It recounts my life up to the point at which I began to study psychology. A shorter autobiographical sketch was published in *The History of Psychology in Autobiography* (1967). Two papers which appear in my *Cumulative Record* (1959, revised 1961, 1972) also contain autobiographical material: 'A Case History in Scientific Method' describes my work in operant conditioning and 'Pigeons in a Pelican' the development of the pigeon-guided missile."

In his first volume of autobiography, *Particulars of My Life* (1976), Skinner provides what one critic called an "oddly touching and almost continuously interesting" history of his first twenty-four years. Another reader described it as "an account of small-town life in America done in that admirable tradition of getting myriad details down right, best exemplified by Theodore Dreiser." The author's father was a lawyer without a degree but with a "craving for a sense of worth with which his mother had damned him"; it seemed to A. S. Byatt that Skinner was "aware of the relationship of his own desire to reform America, and mankind, to its American antecedents, and to his father's desire to improve Susquehanna and himself." In fact, his father wrote what became a standard legal textbook and became successful enough to move on from Susquehanna to the wider world of Scranton, and rich enough, eventually, to take his family on a European grand tour. B. F. Skinner (as he signed himself from the age of nine) nevertheless clerked after school in a shoe store, wrote for the Susquehanna newspaper, played the piano for silent movies and the saxophone in a dance band, while trying his hand as an inventor and earning excellent grades as a student.

The letter Skinner received from Robert Frost about the stories he wrote as a student at Hamilton College would have convinced any young hopeful that literary success was imminent: "I ought to say you have the touch of art. . . . You are worth twice anyone else I have seen in prose this year." However, a "dark year" of unrewarding literary effort followed in Scranton, and a more bohemian spell in Greenwich Village, leading Skinner to the dismal conclusion that he "had no reason to write anything. . . . I had nothing to say, and nothing about my life was making any change in that condition."

When Skinner turned his attention to psychology it was because he decided that he "was interested in human behavior but I had been investigating it the wrong way." His father, he recalled, "possibly because he never quite understood how to get on with people, was always watching them, and he frequently called my attention to their behavior." At this point, wrote A. S. Byatt, the reader of Skinner's autobiography "realizes that Skinner's accounts of his own gaucheries and embarrassments, like his father's and family's, have been heading this way. Understanding, and social improvement, are required, and observation of minute particulars of behavior is the way to these."

As he explains above, Skinner was from the outset drawn to behaviorism—that school of psychology which explains human behavior in terms of the individual's response to environmental stimuli. *The Behavior of Organisms* (1938), his first book, extended behaviorist theory by introducing the notion of "operant behavior"—behavior not elicited by particular external stimuli but undertaken voluntarily, to achieve a particular goal or reward. Skinner, who believes that most human behavior is operant rather than respondent, had experimented with operant conditioning of rats, using a box in which an animal could be trained to press a bar in return for a delivery of food. Skinner had designed this box himself, and it is still widely used. A critic in the *Times Literary Supplement* remarked that the title of *The Behavior of Organisms* seemed to some people "a trifle grandiose in view of the fact that it was concerned exclusively with the behavior of rats, and under very restricted conditions at that. None the less, it signalled the appearance on the psychological scene of a man with much experimental ingenuity and a powerful analytical mind."

Skinner will no doubt always be remembered by some as the man who taught pigeons to play ping-pong. In fact this is only one particularly colorful example of his many successes in the step-by-step training of animals, using a system of rewards (or, to use his own terminology, a schedule of reinforcement). Experiments of this kind led to Skinner's attempt during World War II to train pigeons to pilot bombs or torpedoes, a scheme that was apparently perfectly feasible, though never adopted. In this connection he said

years later that he thought there should be "more crackpot ideas among psychologists," since "the remarkable fertility of our discussions . . . was largely due to the fact that we all knew that, in the eyes of the man in the street, we were all crazy." It was at about this time that Skinner invented the Aircrib, a large, air-conditioned, germ-free, and soundproof box designed to provide an ideal environment in which a growing baby could sleep or play without covers or clothing. This artificial environment impressed some of Skinner's colleagues and appalled others.

It may have been the raising of his own children that turned Skinner's attention from animal to human behavior. Some of his views emerge in his novel *Walden Two* (1948), which describes a utopian community where traditional methods of child rearing and education have been replaced by "behavioral engineering." From earliest infancy, children are encouraged by a carefully planned system of rewards to favor kinds of behavior considered desirable by the community. The result is an ideal society where punishment and discipline have no place, and goodness, spontaneity, and happiness prevail. *Walden Two,* which has been very widely read and discussed, seemed to most critics well written, though too full of ethical abstractions; there agreement ended. Many readers were outraged by the idea of applying to human beings a training system developed in experiments with rats, and Joseph Wood Krutch spoke of an "attempt to perfect mankind by making individual men incapable of anything except habit and prejudice." However, another critic pointed out that "traditional liberal and humanist values" are not wanting in *Walden Two,* and said that what evidently exasperates Skinner "is that so few people who advocate such goals appear to have the least notion of how to set to work to attain them." In fact several experimental communities have been established on Skinnerian principles, and one of these is described in Kathleen Kinkade's *A Walden Two Experiment* (1973).

Science and Human Behavior (1953), which Skinner wrote for his general education course at Harvard, clearly explains his behaviorist psychology, while taking into account previous psychological and sociological theories of human behavior. A science of human behavior, Skinner maintains, could be expected to "discover that what man does is the result of specifiable conditions and that once these conditions have been discovered, we can anticipate and to some extent determine his actions." Admirers and detractors agreed that the book was invaluable as the first "strong, consistent, and all but exhaustive case for a natural science of human behavior."

A number of more technical articles and books followed in the 1950s and 1960s, including *Verbal Behavior* (1957). Arguing that language is merely a form of behavior, Skinner contended that control of all the "contingencies of reinforcement influencing an individual" would make possible the "prediction and control of speech." It was in the 1950s also that Skinner's research into "reinforced" or rewarded step-by-step learning led to his pioneer work in programmed instruction and the teaching machine—inventions whose value seems to be limited to fairly elementary rote learning but which have nevertheless brought about a revolution in "the technology of education."

The most controversial of Skinner's books, *Beyond Freedom and Dignity* (1971), extends the ideas adumbrated in *Walden Two* in ways that repelled and horrified many readers. If humanity is to survive, Skinner asserts, we must abandon such "pre-scientific" ideals as freedom and dignity, and set about controlling our environment and ourselves by means of "a technology of behavior" which will be "comparable in power and precision to physical and biological technology" and which will "induce people not to be good but to behave well." In the end, survival is "the only value according to which a culture . . . can be judged."

In a long review in the *New York Review of Books,* Noam Chomsky wrote that "Skinner confuses 'science' with technology. He apparently believes that if he rephrases commonplace 'mentalistic' expressions with terminology derived from the laboratory study of behavior, but deprived of whatever content this terminology has within this discipline, then he has achieved a scientific analysis of behavior. It would be hard to conceive of a more striking failure to comprehend even the rudiments of scientific thinking." For Chomsky, Skinner's proposals conjured up visions of "a well run concentration camp with inmates spying on one another and the gas ovens smoking in the distance." George Steiner, calling the book "the happening of the American literary and intellectual season," went on to complain that "we are given nothing whatever to chew on: no analyses of how the 'technology of behavior' will be applied to a specific case, no single example of how one of the current crises of society and politics would actually be viewed in the light of the new environmentalism." To Robert Claiborne it seemed that Skinner "knows almost nothing about human beings. . . . Beginning with dogma and progressing through vague generalities and naive misinformation, it is hardly surprising that . . . [he] fails

to make even the beginning of a credible case for his central thesis."

There was a more moderate response from the book's reviewer in the *Times Literary Supplement,* who said: "Although *Beyond Freedom and Dignity* is well-written, provocative and thoughtful, it is marred by the fact that the author suffers from a well-known occupational disease of psychologists, namely premature generalization from limited evidence. . . . Why should a book rather narrow in scholarship, philosophically naive and scientifically almost worthless attract such wide notice?. . . . Skinner's principles embody little more than is already known to parents, teachers and, for that matter, trainers of performing animals; all he has done is to formulate our knowledge more adequately and to provide experimental techniques designed to make it more precise. There is, further, no reason to believe that Skinner himself fails to uphold the traditional values of our culture. He is an enemy only to empty and spineless humanism, with its endless repetition of well-meaning precepts without any thought as to their translation into practice." Skinner set out to answer his critics in *About Behaviorism* (1974), which, however, made few converts.

Though it had its detractors, *Particulars of My Life* had the warmest reception of any of Skinner's books. P. D. Zimmerman called it "a remarkably vivid piece of social history and an illuminating self-portrait" in which Skinner "tells the story of his life with the grace, economy, wit and intelligence of a literary talent. . . . Throughout, he is determined to describe the world as it was and is—without 'subjective' distortion. To the extent that this goal is possible, Skinner achieves it. Rarely has an autobiography seemed less motivated by self-justification or rancor, less clouded by sentiment . . . more ruthlessly matter-of-fact about personal limitations. But Skinner's objectivity . . . also deprives his narrative of a crucial emotional dimension."

Skinner was Edgar Pierce Professor of Psychology at Harvard from 1958 to 1974, when he retired as professor emeritus. He is said to be an excellent lecturer. He is a member of the American Psychological Association, the National Academy of Sciences, the American Academy for the Advancement of Science, the American Academy of Arts and Sciences, and the American Philosophical Society. He also belongs to the psychological societies of Sweden, Britain, and Spain, and is a Fellow of the (British) Royal Society of Arts. He received the Howard Crosby Warren Medal in 1942, a Guggenheim fellowship in 1944, the National Medal for Science in 1968, the gold medal of the American Psychological Association in 1971, and the Joseph P. Kennedy Jr. Foundation Award, also in 1971. He has honorary degrees from many universities.

The author has been described by Spencer Klaw as "a slender, restless man, with finely-cut features and a noble expanse of forehead," and as a "cranky, stubborn, inventive iconoclast." In 1961 he was apotheosized on the cover of *Time* magazine, which said that he was then "the most influential living psychologist and the most controversial figure in the science of behavior." He has struck a number of observers as a peculiarly American figure, and an anonymous critic in the *Times Literary Supplement* wrote: "Masked by a powerful intelligence and sophisticated experimental acumen, one senses in Skinner . . . naive idealism . . . and the characteristic American belief in human goodness and perfectability, given only the creation of a benign environment. Skinner embodies not only the formidable technocracy of mid-twentieth-century America but also the simplicity and optimism—one might almost say innocence—of an earlier generation of American intellectuals, happily far from extinct."

PRINCIPAL WORKS: The Behavior of Organisms: An Experimental Analysis, 1938; Walden Two, 1948; Science and Human Behavior, 1953; (with P.B. Dews) Techniques for the Study of Behavioral Effects of Drugs, 1956; (with C.B. Ferster) Schedules of Reinforcement, 1957; Verbal Behavior, 1957; Cumulative Record: A Selection of Papers, 1959; (with J.G. Holland) The Analysis of Behavior: A Program for Self-Instruction, 1961; The Technology of Teaching, 1968; Earth Resources, 1969; Contingencies of Reinforcement: A Theoretical Analysis, 1969; Beyond Freedom and Dignity, 1971; About Behaviorism, 1974; Particulars of My Life, 1976.

ABOUT: American Men and Women of Science: The Social and Behavioral Sciences, 1973; Bolles, R.C., Learning Theory, 1975; Boring, E.G. and Lindzey, G. (eds) The History of Psychology in Autobiography, 1967; Bower, G.H. and Hilgard, E.R. Theories of Learning, 1975; Cohen, D.(ed.) Psychologists on Psychology, 1977; Contemporary Authors 9–12 1st revision, 1974; Current Biography, 1964; Dews, P.B. (ed.) Festschrift for B.F. Skinner, 1970; Evans, R.I. B.F. Skinner: The Man and His Ideas, 1968; International Who's Who, 1977–78; Robinson, D. Miracle Finders, 1976; Schultz, D. Theories of Personality, 1976; Skinner, B.F. Cumulative Record, 1959; Skinner, B.F. Particulars of My Life, 1976; Who's Who, 1978; Who's Who in America, 1976 –1977; Wiegel, J.A. B.F. Skinner, 1977. Periodicals—Atlantic October 1971; Book World October 10, 1971; Harper's April 1963, October 1973; Language 1 1959; National Review November 22, 1974; New Republic October 16, 1971; New York Review of Books December 30, 1971; New York Times Book Review October 24, 1971; July 14, 1974; April 11, 1976; New York Times Magazine September 25, 1960; March 17, 1968; March 15, 1970; New Yorker July 26, 1976; Newsweek October 19, 1959; August 26, 1968; September 20, 1971; April 5, 1976; Saturday Review September 21, 1968; October 9, 1971; Time March 24, 1961; September 20, 1971; January 3, 1972; Times (London) March 10, 1972; Times Literary Supplement May 12, 1972; February 28, 1975.

*SLONIMSKI, ANTONI (October 15, 1895– June 6, 1976), Polish poet, dramatist, and journalist, was born in Warsaw, son of a well-known Jewish physician, into a family of scholars and scientists. After high school in Warsaw he studied painting at the Academy of Fine Arts in Warsaw, and then in Munich and Paris. He made his literary debut in 1913, though it was not until 1918 that he finally gave up painting in favor of literature.

At the end of World War I Slonimski became with Julian Tuwim one of the founders and leaders of a poetry group who read their poems in a Warsaw literary café and published their own monthly review, *Skamander* (the river on which Troy stood). The appearance of this important literary group coincided with Poland's newly-won independence, and their poetry made a decisive break with the commitment that had tied earlier Polish writers to nationalistic and patriotic themes. Progressive and cosmopolitan in their views, bitter opponents of bigotry and racialism, the *Skamander* group also shared a desire to renew the language of poetry. And while they retained conventional forms, they adapted them to themes analogous to those of the Russian and Italian futurists, above all the life and landscape of the modern city.

In the year of the group's formation Slonimski published his first volume of poems, *Soniety* (Sonnets, 1918), and between this and the outbreak of war in 1939 there followed among other collections *Harmonje* (Harmonies, 1919), *Parada* (Parade, 1920), *Godzina poezji* (An Hour of Poetry, 1923), and *Okno bez krat* (Window Without Bars, 1935). Czeslaw Milosz has described Slonimski as "a poet of the Warsaw liberal intelligentsia, attuned to their taste for debating world problems and their lyrico-sarcastic attitudes." He differed from his colleagues, according to Milosz, in his temperament, "that of a pure intellectual, always maintaining a distance between his feelings and their expression in poetry or in prose." But Manfred Kridl disagrees, maintaining that behind Slonimski's air of self-possession can be discerned "a sense of pathos, mystery, and tragedy . . . a feeling of loneliness and 'de la tristesse de tout celà.' "

Many of Slonimski's early poems deal with such traditional themes as love, nature, and human sadness; some are reactions to the exotic landscapes he encountered on his travels—to Palestine in *Droga na wschód* (The Road to the East, 1924) and to Brazil in *Z dalekiej podrózy*

*swo něm′ sky

ANTONI SLONIMSKI

(From a Long Journey, 1926). These "sentimental" poems, generally conventional in style, blunt and simple in language in a manner reminiscent of Slonimski's master Mickiewicz, were extremely popular.

Other poems of this period were more social or philosophical in temper, and it was these that gained him his reputation for fierce intellectual honesty, wit, and biting sarcasm—a reputation reinforced by his work as a journalist, columnist, and drama reviewer for *Wiadomości literackie* (Literary News), where he trenchantly dissected all sorts of contemporary problems. He did not hesitate to introduce such problems into his poems, many of which expressed his pacifist views. The criminality and stupidity of war is exposed with scathing irony in such long poems as *Dialog o miłości ojczyzny* (Dialogue on the Love of the Fatherland, 1923) and *Oko w oko* (Eye to Eye, 1928), with its terrifying procession of crippled veterans of World War I.

The world economic crisis and the rise of aggressive fascism in Germany, coupled with the increasing power of the chauvinist, anti-Semitic rightists in Poland itself, transformed his vague liberal humanism into a more definite political commitment, reflected in his poetry of the 1930s. Much of this was a prophetic response to the first hints of impending catastrophe; *Palenie zboza* (The Burning of the Corn, 1931) is about the destruction—in a world where millions were starving—of surplus wheat for which there was no commercial market. "Rozmowa" (Conversation, 1937) is an anti-Franco poem about the Spanish Civil War and *Dokument epoki* (Document of the Age, 1937) is filled with horrified frustration at the apparently irreversible stampede towards world war as the Japanese march into Manchuria, the "fat jester" Mussolini invades Ethiopia, and newsreels are clamorous with military maneuvers. Slonimski's craftsmanship can be seen at its most inventive in these long poems on social themes, some of which dispense with regular rhythmical patterns, using instead "an approximate, not always equal, number of principal stresses" and assonantal rhymes. This "torn poetic method," as Kridl says, does not make for easy reading, "but once one is engrossed in it, this picture of ruined human existence is experienced very powerfully."

In 1932 Slonimski had visited the Soviet Union. The articles he wrote about that country and collected in *Moja prodróz do Rosji* (My Russian Journey, 1932) pleased neither the Communists and their sympathizers nor their opponents. Slonimski's own political doubts and uncertainties are summed up in his poem "Hamletyzm" ("Hamletism," 1933), translated by P.D. Scott and Czeslaw Milosz in *Postwar Polish Poetry*. It is the fruit of a meeting in Leningrad with a cousin of his who was an ardent Communist:

... Michal, Aunt Fanny's, Uncle Ludwik's son,
Names which awake the wistful taste of childhood,
Sternly and gravely concludes the discussion.
And yet he's my cousin. A very close relation.

Magnitogorsk and Urals. With us or against.
Stalin, the Party. Vast, incessant toil.
The Five-Year Plan. As children five years old
We used to exchange letters. Michal looks ill.

Light of young eyes, yet hair untimely grey.
Calm, but intent, faithful in what you do,
You serve and you want to serve your country well
And you say: "Good night, prince,"—"Good night, Horatio."

Milosz has pointed out that Slonimski's poetry loses in translation "the interesting contrast between the songlike, slightly melancholy fluidity of his rhymed lines and the logic of his discourse."

As a dramatist Slonimski has been compared to George Bernard Shaw, and indeed such satirical comedies as *Wieza Babel* (The Tower of Babel, 1927) and *Lekarz bezdomny* (The Homeless Doctor, 1931) are essentially conversation pieces, like Shaw's in that action and conflict are created mainly through brilliantly witty dialogue. *Murzyn warszawski* (The Warsaw Negro, 1928) mocks the pretensions and snobbery of the Warsaw Jewish society to which Slonimski himself belonged. And *Rodzina* (The Family, 1933) makes an ironic satire out of the clash between

769

totalitarian ideologies in a family in which one brother becomes a Communist zealot committed to the triumph of the working class, the other a bigoted Nazi devoted to the ideal of Aryan purity. Both receive a violent ideological shock in a climax which reveals them to be neither working-class nor Aryan, but the sons of a prosperous Jewish miller.

Slonimski also wrote satirical novels, *Teatr w więzieniu* (The Theatre in the Prison, 1922) and *Dwa końce świata* (Two Ends of the Earth, 1937), which prophetically envisions a second world war that unleashes the sort of devastation possible with the arrival of the atomic age. Warsaw is totally destroyed by the bombs of the dictator Retlich (Hitler). Amid the rubble there are only two survivors, a Jewish bookstore clerk and a shambling lout who speaks an unintelligible slang. They meet but cannot communicate, and both end up in a concentration camp as the ruined city is overrun by an army of Lapps in reindeer skins.

When Hitler actually did invade Poland, Slonimski himself managed to escape, fleeing first to Paris and then to London. He spent the war years in England editing the monthly periodical *New Poland.* Slonimski, like other members of the *Skamander* group, had sought to transcend his country's traditional national romanticism, but was returned to it by Poland's sufferings during the German occupation. During these years of exile, when Poland existed for him only in the kind of memories, dreams, and hopes reflected in such collections as *Popiól i wiatr* (Ashes and Wind, 1942), he was transformed from a European-oriented liberal into a Polish patriot. And despite his absence in England, he was one of the poets most widely read as underground literature in occupied Poland.

Returning to Poland in 1946, Slonimski was soon back in London as director of the Polish Cultural Institute there (1949–1951) and served as head of the literary section on the UNESCO preparatory commission. By 1951 he was settled in Warsaw, where his colleagues elected him president of the Polish P.E.N. Club and chairman of the Polish Writers' Union (1956–1959). Although his earlier satirical treatment of Communism had not endeared him to the new regime, and his first postwar poetry collection in 1946 was attacked for his "inability to master reality," this willingness to work hard in official and semi-official positions helped him to come through the Stalinist years unscathed. But as president of the Writers' Union during the 1956 Polish crisis he became one of the leading spokesmen of the "rebel writers," along with Jan Kott, Artur Sandauer, and Julian Przyboś. He

remained an outspoken champion of liberal reform, and in 1964 was one of the signatories of the "Letter of Three," which protested against censorship.

Slonimski's own work nevertheless continued to appear freely until 1968, when he criticized the purge of "Zionists" from government posts which followed the Six-Day War. In return he was criticized by the Communist leader Gomulka, and publication of an anthology of his early poems was held up for three years, until 1971. Official wrath appeared to be abating by then, however, and in 1972 he was elected as a delegate to a congress of Polish writers. He died in 1976 in his eighty-first year as the result of shock suffered in a car accident. Slonimski received a State Prize in 1955 and the Warsaw Literary Prize in 1956. Apart from his original work, he also published some admirable translations of Shakespeare. He was a Roman Catholic.

PRINCIPAL WORKS IN ENGLISH TRANSLATION: *Poems in* Dynowska, W. (ed.) The Scarlet Muse, 1944; Gillon, A. and Krzysanowski, L. (eds.) Introduction to Modern Polish Poetry, 1964; Milosz, C. (ed.) Postwar Polish Poetry, 1965; Notley, F. (ed.) The Years of Exile, 1943; East Europe November 1958.

ABOUT: Gömöri, G. Polish and Hungarian Poetry 1945–1956, 1966; International Who's Who, 1976–77; Kridl, M. A Survey of Polish Literature and Culture, 1956; Milosz, C. The History of Polish Literature, 1969; Sandauer, A. Poeci trzech pokoleń, 1955; Seymour-Smith, M. Guide to Modern World Literature, 1973; Smith, H. (ed.) Columbia Dictionary of Modern European Literature, 1947. *Periodicals*— New York Times July 6, 1976; New York Times Book Review December 22, 1940; Times (London) July 7, 1976.

*SLUTSKY, BORIS (ABRAMOVICH) (May 7, 1919–), Russian poet of Jewish origin, was born in the Ukrainian salt-mining and spa town of Slavyansk, in the industrial Donets Basin. He finished his schooling in the Ukraine's second city and chief industrial center, Kharkov. In his poem "The Thirties," translated by Elaine Feinstein in Daniel Weissbort's *Post-War Russian Poetry,* he looks back to the years of the Stalinist purges, when he was a schoolboy:

> . . . We are grown up, yes, we are adult now.
> But we grew old a long while ago.
> We endured more than we could bear
> of all we had to carry then.
> And yet, looking back on those years (I
> was not a child but adolescent)
> in some sense they were a time
> of privilege I now feel significant.
> Whatever good deed it was saved me,
> I was lucky to live in Kharkov,
> and to run to a quiet secondary
> school, or to evening classes.

*slōōt′ skē

BORIS SLUTSKY

Yes, I lived on cold soy beans, but
I could read the trials in the papers;
and try to understand without yet
imagining I had to be a prophet.
I was only a cog in that huge and
strangely clumsy machine, which
at that time forests disguised:
but now from an airstrip in the square
all the trees have taken off into the skies.

From 1937 to 1941 Slutsky was a student at the Institute of Jurisprudence in Moscow, at the same time studying literature at the Gorky Institute of Literature. It was at this time that he published his first poems in magazines. In 1941, when Hitler invaded Russia, Slutsky volunteered for the Red Army and fought at the front, first as a private and later as a political officer. He was awarded the Order of Patriotic War, classes 1 and 2, and the Order of the Red Star. After the war he worked from 1948 to 1952 for All-Union Radio.

Throughout these years Slutsky had been writing poetry, though it has been suggested that in the Stalinist years he was able to publish little or nothing because of the often defiantly Jewish tone of his verse. Certainly he did not become well known until 1956, three years after Stalin's death. In that year several of these unpublished poems were quoted in an article on the poet by Ilya Ehrenburg, and caused a sensation. Slutsky's first book, *Pamyat* (Memory), including many poems written much earlier, followed in 1957, and was quickly succeeded by three more collections: *Lyudi i bogi* (People and Gods, 1959), *Nashi letyat* (Our Boys Are Flying, 1959), and *Vremya* (Time, 1959). Most of this deeply probing early poetry is colored by Slutsky's war experiences, both as seen at the time and as preserved in his memory, as in "Moyi tovarishchi" ("My Comrades"):

> They were burnt in tanks, my comrades,
> burnt to embers, cinders, reduced to ash.
> Grass grew out of them, of course,
> grass that spreads over half the world.
> My comrades
>   were blown up
> on mines,
>   pitched high in the air,
> and many stars, remote and peaceful,
> were kindled
>   from them,
>   from my friends. . . .
>
>   (translated by
>   George Reavey)

Even in translation such a poem shows the straightforward, almost crude, directness and economy of means of a poet who insists on "sense" rather than the rhetorical embellishments or word-play favored by younger writers who had been spared the experience of war. Slutsky sees it as his function to serve as a "telegraph wire," carrying urgent messages in Morse. Robin Milner-Gulland has pointed out that the qualities of this tough and exact verse, based on concrete descriptions of small incidents, are close to those cultivated by English poets of the 1950s. In the original Russian, however, this terseness is combined with a great sensitivity to language, and a lyricism which charges many of his poems with deep emotion.

Some of Slutsky's finest work has been inspired by the Holocaust, the effects of which he saw firsthand in the devastated Jewish settlements of western Russia as he advanced with the Red Army, and in which his own family was caught up. Thus the poem "How Did They Kill My Grandmother?" describes the round-up of the Jews when his native Ukrainian town was occupied by the Germans:

> . . . the German *polizei* were
> herding the old people briskly;
> and their tin mugs clanked as
> the young men led them away
>   far away.
>
> But my small grandmother
> my seventy-year-old grandmother
> began to curse and
> scream at the Germans;
> shouting that I was a soldier.
> She yelled at them: My grandson
> is off at the front fighting!

Don't you dare
touch me!
Listen, you
          can hear our guns!

Even as she went off, my grandmother
cried abuse,
          starting all over again
with her curses.
From every window then
Ivanovnas and Andreyevnas
Sidorovnas and Petrovnas
sobbed: You tell them, Polina
Matveyevna, keep it up!
They all yelled together:
     'What can we do against
this enemy, the Hun?'
Which was why the Germans chose
to kill her inside the town.

A bullet struck her hair
and kicked her grey plait down.
My grandmother fell to the ground.
That is how she died there.

          (translated by
          Elaine Feinstein)

Slutsky became an important poetic influence during the period of the Thaw in Soviet literature—the late 1950s and the 1960s. He became firmly identified with the liberals in Soviet literature, standing for a humanistic cultural heritage in opposition not only to the political oppression of the Stalin era but also to the increasingly technocratic character of society. The title poem of his collection *Fiziki i liriki* (Physicists and Lyricists, 1959) contrasts the high standing of physicists with that of poets. But poetry has in fact remained enormously popular in the Soviet Union, and the Thaw especially was notable for the public poetry readings that drew vast crowds, mainly of young people. Slutsky was older than most of the new poets who were then first attracting attention, such as Yevtushenko, Voznesensky, and Akhmadulina, although the delay in publishing his poetry meant that it too was appearing for the first time. Though he was not an experimentalist, as some of the younger poets were, Slutsky's verse was a great success with this youthful audience: it was very much in the spirit of this time of reaction against overblown official rhetoric, being personal, small-scale, and unpretentious, but often finding large implications in apparently trivial everyday events and scenes.

Slutsky has never been afraid to face up to moral complexities, or to speak up boldly and plainly about the vital problems of the day. For example, at the "Day of Poetry" celebrated on December 1, 1962 in the Sports Palace in Moscow, which attracted an audience of ten thousand to readings by the luminaries of the time, ecstatic applause greeted his reading of two poems attacking the Stalin cult, "The Master" and "God," which try to understand how a great nation could be held in physical and spiritual thrall by such a monster:

     . . . There was nothing you could teach
     This God: he had it over
     The one they call Jehovah
     Whom he hurled from His place
     Burned to cinders, ignored,
     Then yanked from the abyss
     And gave Him bed and board.
     We were all under God
     And in his steps we trod.
     Once as I took the air
     God in five cars went by.
     His mousegrey escort were
     Hunchbacked in terror: I
     Could see their trembling fear.
     It was both late and early.
     Dawn glimmered in the skies.
     He peered out, cruel, wise
     With his all-seeing eyes
     All-penetrating gaze.
     We were all under God.
     Ours were the steps he trod.

          (translated by Keith Bosley
          with Dimitry Pospielovsky)

Considerable encouragement was given to the avant garde of the 1960s by the liberals of the older generation, such as Konstantin Paustovsky, whose anthology *Tarusskiye stranitsy* (1961, translated as *Pages From Tarusa*), included many of the younger poets alongside older ones like Zabolotsky. This collection, which became one of the cultural sensations of the Khrushschev era because of its liberalism, included a group of poems by Slutsky which, as Andrew Field said in his introduction, show his "extraordinary range of feeling and empathy. Slutsky's poetic voice, as the selections in this book well illustrate, leaps effortlessly from youthful exuberance to the dusk of old age"— from the harshly tragic "Old Women Without Their Men" to the ballad-like simplicity of his description of life in a high-rise Moscow apartment—a description which characteristically keeps its sting in its tail:

     . . . Up here where the windows are pale blue
          squares
     There's cleanness, quiet, perennial brightness.
     Too high for mice
     —Mice can't stand heights—

Clouds keep me company, purring
And rubbing their sides against my balcony.
After spring storms, in May, for instance,
The puddles light up like coins in the streets.
Look up from below and my floor is a birdhouse
Swaying four hundred fifty feet nearer to the sun,
Four hundred fifty feet nearer to heaven,
Where I live on a level with the moon.
Yes, it's a good life up here, I think,
(Especially when the lift's not on the blink).

> (from "It's not too bad, living twenty floors
> high" translated by Anne Stevenson)

After the bitter controversy over Yevtushenko's famous poem "Babi Yar," another long, impassioned poem about the tragic fate of Russia's Jews was widely circulated. Its author was said to be Slutsky, though this was neither confirmed nor denied by the poet himself. But some savage political satires by Slutsky have appeared in underground *samizdat* magazines—the 1965 *Sphinxes* included a poem by him that runs:

> . . . Under rule of law the folk
> Serve what gives them food and drink
> But rebellion has no book
> And revolt no pen and ink.
>
> When rebellion goes to press
> When revolt takes up a pen
> It has donned official dress
> Nourishes the sons of men
>
> Codifies its rights and wrongs
> Rids the aged of their qualms.
> Revolutionary songs
> Are replaced by hymns and psalms.
>
> (from "In the state there is a law"
> translated by Keith Bosley
> with Dimitry Pospielovsky)

The titles of many of Slutsky's later collections reflect his preoccupation with history and time—*Sevodnya i vchera* (Today and Yesterday, 1961), *Sevodnya i zavtra* (Today and Tomorrow, 1963), and *Godovaya strelka* (The Year Hand, 1971). The last title is explained by the title poem, in which a man in his fifties is acutely conscious of the passing of time, while a young man eagerly buys a watch, but comes to wish that instead of minute and second hands ticking life away it could have a year hand moving "as slowly as the sun or a boat."

Many of the poems in these later collections meditate on the nature of science or poetry, or the problems of the postwar generation. But some of them still look back to the war, like "The Fate of Children's Balloons," with its moving image of escaped balloons rising into the heavens to be received as gifts by dead airmen, one for each of those who "went out, blazing, in the fire."

Slutsky has dedicated himself to the memory of the young writers—his own contemporaries—who died in the war, and has done much to help secure the publication of their surviving work. He has also made translations from the poetry of other Soviet republics, has edited an anthology of Polish poetry in Russian translation, and is named as the editor of the first collection of Israeli poetry ever published in the Soviet Union (1963). Slutsky did not write the introduction to the Israeli anthology, however, and this departure from the usual Soviet practice may reflect his disapproval of the censors' treatment of some of its contents. Though he is still little known in the West, Slutsky is widely regarded as one of the most talented contemporary Russian poets—probably the most important poet of the war generation—and because of the nature and quality of his fresh, nonconformist poetic voice, a major influence on the post-Stalin generation of writers.

PRINCIPAL WORKS IN ENGLISH TRANSLATION: *Poems in* Bosley, K. (and others, eds.) Russia's Other Poets (U.S., Russia's Underground Poets), 1968; Field, A. (ed.) Pages From Tarusa, 1963; Markov, V. and Sparks, M. (eds.) Modern Russian Poetry, 1966; Milner-Gulland, R. and Dewhirst, M. (eds.) Russian Writing Today, 1977; Ognev, V. and Rottenberg, D. (eds.) Fifty Soviet Poets, 1969; Proffer, C. and E. (eds.) The Ardis Anthology of Recent Russian Literature, 1973; Reavey, G. (ed.) The New Russian Poets 1953–1968, 1969; Weissbort, D. (ed.) Post-War Russian Poetry, 1974.

ABOUT: Alexandrova, V. A History of Soviet Literature, 1963; Encyclopaedia Judaica, 1971; International Who's Who, 1978–79; Penguin Companion to Literature 2, 1969; Prominent Personalities in the U.S.S.R., 1968. *Periodicals*—Times Literary Supplement October 11, 1974.

SMITH, IAIN CRICHTON (IAIN MAC A'GHOBHAINN) (January 1, 1928–), Scottish poet, novelist, short story writer, and dramatist, writes: "I was born in the Island of Lewis which is in the Outer Hebrides off the west coast of Scotland. My native language is Gaelic though at the age of five or so when I went to school I had to learn English. I grew up in a small village, attending from the age of eleven a secondary school in the main town of the island about seven miles away. At the age of seventeen years I left the island and went to the University of Aberdeen where after four years I emerged with an Honours degree in English. I then spent a year in a teachers' training college but at the end of the year had to join the Army to do my period of National Service which I spent as a Sergeant in the Education Corps. After I left the Army I became a teacher, teaching for three years in

IAIN CRICHTON SMITH

Clydebank High School, not far from Glasgow, and thereafter and up till the present in Oban High School in the town of Oban where I live now. I have been here now for twenty years.

"I have been writing since about the age of eleven and have never felt that I wished to do anything else though for financial reasons I am not a fulltime writer. In any case, being a full-time writer has also its disadvantages. I am I think in a special position since I am bilingual. For this reason I have written in both Gaelic and English. In Gaelic I have written short stories, poems and some plays; in English I have written poems, novels, and short stories. Strangely enough, though Gaelic is my first language, I believe that my best work has been written in English and this I suppose is because Gaelic is and has been for a long time in decline, and thus unable to provide for me the concepts and linguistic athleticism that I need. Nevertheless I have found the bilingual situation difficult and the choices at times difficult and demanding. I think I should prefer to be monolingual.

"A lot of the work that I have written has been concerned with language. For instance I have written a long poem called "Shall Gaelic Die?" in which I examine somewhat ironically this whole question. I have also been interested in philosophers like Wittgenstein who have examined the question of language in depth and more abstractly. I have also translated poetry from the Gaelic language, especially that of Duncan Ban Macintyre, a major Gaelic poet of the eighteenth century, and that of Sorley Maclean, a major Gaelic poet of our own century. I have also experimented with introducing some modern ideas and styles into the Gaelic

language, and have even translated some writers from other cultures into Gaelic.

"Brought up as I was on the Island of Lewis, I was immersed not only in problems of language but also problems of religion, since the religion there has always appeared to me narrow and at times intolerant. Thus much of my work has been an examination and attack on a religion which is life-denying. For this reason I have not been an ideological writer, since I am hostile to all ideologies, especially those which are narrow and intolerant. Some years ago I wrote a book of poems called *The Law and the Grace* in which the Law is that of religion and the Grace that of religion. However I connected this theme with poetry since at another level Grace became inspiration and the Law the apparatus—such as metre—which poetry has sometimes to obey. What I was trying to do, I think now, was to set art over against religion as being meaningful and important. Also in a novel called *Consider the Lilies* I created the character of an old woman who living by the law found that it failed her and that henceforth she must depend on the grace of common humanity. It has seemed to me that I have always had to defend my art against the narrow intolerance of my upbringing and to praise humanity, flawed as it is, against ideology. Thus both in my poetry and my novels I have written about people, many of whom emerge from the broken history of our past since we have been defeated so often by a linguistic imperialism and in other less subtle ways.

"Apart from the themes of language and religion, I have also been obsessed by the theme of loneliness. It is possible that this theme obsesses me because I have felt lonely as a writer who writes mostly in a language different from his own, and as a human being, since language and art cannot be divorced from life. The theme of the old woman recurs in my work. Sometimes she is hard and embittered, and sometimes vulnerable. The most recent exploration of this theme and I suppose the furthest point to which I shall carry it occurs in my recent *The Notebooks of Robinson Crusoe,* where it is intertwined with musings about language.

"I have hardly ever been out of Britain but recently I spent some time in Canada and it is possible that this may have some effect on my future work."

Iain Crichton Smith's central concerns arise, as he implies, from the narrow Calvinistic religion of his childhood. His poetry records his struggle away from this Calvinism—away from dogma, away from his *liking* for solitude, and even for linguistic alienation—towards the achievement of spontaneity and a vital human warmth. His early poetry in English was admired for its imagery and technical skill, and for a quality of "granitic objectivity," but seemed to some critics excessively cerebral, too self-consciously clever in wit and phrasing. *Deer on the High Hills* (1960), inspired by Duncan Ban Macintyre's "Praise of Ben Dorain" (which Smith has translated), attracted some critical interest, and this was quickened by the appearance of *The Law and the Grace*. In these poems on Calvinism, life, and death, with their "clean and transparent" diction, "hard and formal" rhythms, Smith achieved a new directness and firmness of line.

From Bourgeois Land contains many poems concerned with the guilt of poets because of their impotence in the face of the horrors of modern life. Here Smith, though admirably humane, is at his weakest: indignation gets the better of the metaphysicality upon which even the most moving of his poems rests. But the two sequences published together as *Love Poems and Elegies,* in which the effects of the death of a mother (his recurring old woman figure) are counterpointed against the sudden sharp shock of falling in love, were much more warmly received. A reviewer in the *Times Literary Supplement* wrote that the sequence of love poems "has the pressure, momentum and sureness of a poet who knows that he has found his voice," while the twenty-two elegies were distinguished by "their variety and suppleness of tone and address"—a poem like "Argument," which "plots its closely charted path through a discourse on death and immortality," stands next to the baleful and expressionist "The Black Jar":

if I shall say I had a jar it would
be a black mountain in the Hebrides
and round it fly your blackbirds black as pitch
and in their centre with a holy book
a woman all in black reading the world
consisting of black crows in a black field.

The Notebooks of Robinson Crusoe returns to the obsessive theme of loneliness, the Crusoe of the title being a projection of the still socially guilty poet. Here Smith, though he does not completely sustain his ambitious project, reaches the height of his eloquence—the seriousness and complexity of his theme more often than not carry the weight of his deliberately solemn rhetoric. Anthony Thwaite felt that the title sequence, with its postulations of ways of confronting loneliness, was liberating: "A remote island childhood was something to be laughed at as well as to be glum about, before going back

into 'the vast cinema of sensation.' " It seemed to Gavin Ewart that the main theme of Smith's next collection, *In the Middle,* was "the idea of change, which at first seems frightening but must finally be accepted." Robert Nye, who thinks Smith an uneven and careless writer, said in his review that "at his best, he is authentic and inspired, and he writes poems possessed by an impressive self-awareness, and by an even more impressive awareness of the self's limitations as a source of awareness."

Robin Fulton, in a useful essay on Smith's poetic method in *Contemporary Scottish Poetry,* concludes that "the most characteristic effects of Iain Crichton Smith's poetry depend on his individual and at times idiosyncratic manner of juxtaposing images. . . . What surprises us is the ellipsis in the thought, the unexpected associations, often heightened indeed by the very orderliness of the syntax." It is not surprising that Smith does not "like poets who are in complete control of their poems, because it seems to me that they're making objects. I like the poetry where people are not in full control, because if you are in full control of a poem as a conscious object, then it's finished."

Smith's first novel, *Consider the Lilies* (1968), is set in the Scottish Highlands early in the last century, when many landowners ruthlessly evicted their crofters to make way for large-scale sheep farming. The book, centering on the eviction of one formidable old woman, was found more successful in the creation of mood and atmosphere than in characterization, and one reviewer thought it "too often colourless in an attempt to be timeless." It was followed by two autobiographical novels—*The Last Summer,* a recreation of schooldays that was coolly received, and *My Last Duchess,* about a young lecturer at a college of education who marries one of his students. The breakdown of this marriage is studied with considerable delicacy, and the result was called in the *Times Literary Supplement* "a worthy and plausible novel, never boring and thoroughly authentic, but not often much more than this," written in prose that "shows much of the sensitiveness and unobtrusive ingenuity of the poetry, yet . . . never quite catches fire with the wit, indignation and imaginative resource of his best work in the other medium." *Goodbye, Mr. Dixon,* about a young man writing a novel about a novelist, and discovering in the process that literature is not for him, seemed to some reviewers disconcertingly flat and even banal, but struck one critic as unexpectedly touching.

There has been less equivocal praise for Smith's short stories, many of which center on the conflict between "narrow simplicity and sophisticated awareness." The economy and subtlety of his prose, the delicacy and honesty of his perceptions—qualities that are not always enough to support the weight of a novel—are perfectly suited to the short story form, in which, it has been said, he "can do almost anything." There is a supernatural element in some of the pieces collected in *The Hermit and Other Stories* (1977)—for example in "The Brothers," about a Scottish writer whose typewriter suddenly starts translating his stories into Gaelic, a language he despises and has abandoned. Smith is also the author of *The Golden Lyric,* a brief but illuminating critical essay on Hugh MacDiarmid.

Iain Crichton Smith's work in Gaelic includes two volumes of poetry, four volumes of short stories, and a novel for children. Two plays in that language have been performed (and published) in Glasgow, and Smith contributes regularly to the Gaelic quarterly *Gairm.* In a number of instances, he has translated or adapted a poem or short story originally written in one language into the other, often with interesting results. *The Permanent Island* is a collection of Smith's Gaelic poems which he has translated into English. Most critics agree that Smith's main contribution to Gaelic literature is in the short story, his best English work in verse.

The author is the son of John Smith, a sailor, and the former Christine Campbell. He received Scottish Arts Council awards in 1968, 1969, and 1971, a Book Council award in 1970, and a Silver Pen award for poetry in 1971.

PRINCIPAL WORKS IN ENGLISH: *Poetry*—The Long River, 1955; The White Noon (*in* New Poets, 1959), 1959; Thistles and Roses, 1961; The Law and the Grace, 1965; From Bourgeois Land, 1969; Selected Poems, 1970; Love Poems and Elegies, 1972; Hamlet in Autumn, 1972; (with others) Penguin Modern Poets 21, 1972; The Notebooks of Robinson Crusoe, 1975; The Permanent Island: Gaelic Poems, 1975; In the Middle, 1977. *Novels*—Consider the Lilies, 1968 (U.S., The Alien Light); The Last Summer, 1969; My Last Duchess, 1971; Goodbye, Mr. Dixon, 1974. *Short Stories*—Survival Without Error, 1970; The Black and the Red, 1973; The Hermit and Other Stories, 1977. *Criticism*—The Golden Lyric, 1967. *As Translator*—Ben Dorain (translated from the Gaelic of Duncan Ban Macintyre), 1969; Poems to Eimhir (translated from the Gaelic of Sorley Maclean), 1971.

ABOUT: Contemporary Authors 21–24 1st revision, 1977; Fulton, R. Contemporary Scottish Poetry, 1974; Penguin Companion to Literature 1, 1971; Schmidt, M. and Lindop, G. (eds.) British Poetry Since 1960, 1972; Seymour-Smith, M. Guide to Modern World Literature, 1975; Thwaite, A. Poetry Today, 1960–1973, 1973; Vinson, J. (ed.) Contemporary Novelists, 1976; Vinson, J. (ed.) Contemporary Poets, 1975. *Periodicals*—Lines Review (Edinburgh) 29 1969, 42–43 1972; Scottish International Review (Edinburgh) May 1970, September 1971; Times Literary Supplement October 29, 1972; October 19, 1973; May 23, 1975.

*SÖDERBERG, HJALMAR (EMIL FREDRIK) (July 2, 1869–October 14, 1941), Swedish novelist, short story writer, dramatist, and essayist, was born in Stockholm, the son of a notary. The life of Stockholm, especially in his own upper-middle-class milieu at the turn of the century, is the background to almost all of his work. He spent his schooldays in Stockholm and studied for a short time at Uppsala University before taking a civil service post in the Customs Department. Söderberg turned to journalism in 1891 but, after some time as a provincial newspaperman, he tired of "serving caviar to the Boeotians" and returned to Stockholm, where he soon established himself as a writer, though he also worked for the newspaper *Svenska Dagbladet.* From 1917 until his death in 1941 he lived in Copenhagen with his Danish second wife, Emide Vos.

Söderberg's first novel, *Förvillelser* (Errors, 1895), showed how much he had learned from modern French prose and shocked his Swedish contemporaries with its frankness. His ironic and disillusioned view of life had much in common with that of the young Strindberg, as well as with Heine and Anatole France, both of whom he had translated. Söderberg was a determinist, as is very evident from his partly autobiographical novel *Martin Bircks ungdom* (1901, translated by C. W. Stork as *Martin Birck's Youth*), which begins with a lyrical evocation of a childhood largely modeled on the author's own.

The book shows how a sensitive idealist, who dreams of a glorious career and a grand passion, is gradually crushed by life until he resigns himself to the humdrum existence of a clerical drudge and a pallid relationship with a girl as defeated as himself. Martin's attempted revolt against the conventions of his society vividly reflects the intellectual unrest of the period, and Alrik Gustafson has described the book as "the classical Swedish literary incarnation of the melancholy *fin de siècle* mood," which "captures the local color of Stockholm in all its subtle gradations and moods. No Stockholm novel can approach Söderberg's in its miraculous evocation of the 'poetry' of the city, its streets and squares, its waterways and building complexes, especially as these urban externals are caught up in the dim lights and drifting mists and the unobtrusive fluctuations of the seasons."

Söderberg was one of the first fiction writers to learn from Freud's discoveries, and his next novel, *Doctor Glas* (1905, translated by P.B. Austin under the same title), is an exploration of morbid psychology—an analysis by a lonely

*sü′ dǝr berg

HJALMAR SÖDERBERG

Swedish Consulate

middle-aged doctor of his own motives for murder. Glas has been consulted by the attractive young wife of a repulsive elderly clergyman, whose energetic love-making seems to her no better than rape. The doctor, torn between his medical code of ethics and his own confused attraction to his patient, at first tries to frighten the husband out of the marriage bed with warnings of a weak heart. When this fails he takes more decisive action, and the pastor dies of poisoning. Though Dr. Glas is by then deeply in love with his patient, neither profits from the murder: she withdraws wanly when her young lover becomes engaged to an heiress, and Glas is left feeling that life has passed him by.

This short novel, cast in the form of a diary, caused a scandal with its apparent endorsement of murder. In translation it was described in the *Times Literary Supplement* as a "moving little book [which] conveys with powerful economy the period, the close, confined environment, and the articulate despair of a man who has missed love, let alone marriage. Now, in fairly successful middle life, he analyzes his situation without pity, in Freudian terms. Dr. Glas makes much of his dreams, and this must be one of the earliest novels to draw on *The Interpretation of Dreams.*" Martin Seymour-Smith has called *Doctor Glas* a "neglected masterpiece," and "one of the century's great novels."

Söderberg's skepticism was complete: "I believe in the lust of the flesh and the incurable loneliness of the soul," reads the epigraph to his extremely successful play *Gertrud* (1906). This play and the novel *Den allvarsamme leken* (The Serious Game, 1912) are both tragic love stories in which love itself is seen as the last illusion. But

Söderberg's detached irony is nowhere more effective than in his short stories and sketches. He published five collections of stories, beginning with *Historietter* (Little Stories) in 1898, and some of the best of them have been translated by C.W. Stork in *Selected Short Stories.*

Some of Söderberg's short pieces are tragedies in the manner of Maupassant, a few are simply droll, but most demonstrate their author's determinism in realistic character sketches, usually told in the first person, of people helplessly trapped by circumstances or by their own weaknesses. These stories depend for their effect on skillfully selected detail, economy of line, and wit. But beneath the brilliant surface are the tragic perceptions of a moralist probing far into the depths of human psychology.

After 1917, when he settled in Denmark, Söderberg did little creative work, and apart from his translations devoted most of the rest of his life to a sustained and systematic campaign against Christianity in such works as *Jahves eld* (Jehovah's Fire, 1918) and *Den förvandlade Messias* (The Transformed Messiah, 1932). He also made a prophetic and determined stand against Nazism from the 1930s until his death in German-occupied Copenhagen.

In both mentality and manner Söderberg was close to the French spirit, and his lucid and elegant prose has always been praised. He was a stylistic perfectionist, and neither his output nor his range was very large. He was himself aware of his strengths and limitations, and said, "My ray of light is narrow but clear." Some critics have accused him of a merely constitutional melancholy, but Martin Seymour-Smith comments: "It is said that he lacks 'robustness'; but this may well reflect a sly distaste for his unsensational and persuasive pessimism."

PRINCIPAL WORKS IN ENGLISH TRANSLATION: Martin Birck's Youth, 1930; Selected Short Stories, 1935; Doctor Glas, 1963.

ABOUT: Austin, P.B. introduction to Doctor Glas, 1963; Bergman, B. Minne av Hualmar Söderberg, 1951; Bredsdorff, E. An Introduction to Scandinavian Literature, 1951; Gustafson, A. A History of Swedish Literature, 1961; Penguin Companion to Literature 2, 1969; Seymour-Smith, M. A Guide to Modern World Literature, 1973; Smith, H. (ed.) Columbia Dictionary of Modern European Literature, 1947; Stolpe, S. Hjalmar Söderberg, 1934 (in Swedish); Stork, C.W. introduction to Martin Birck's Youth, 1930 and Selected Short Stories, 1935. Periodicals—New York Times Book Review May 24, 1964; New Yorker August 8, 1964; Times Literary Supplement October 25, 1963.

*SOSNORA, VIKTOR (ALEKSANDRO-VICH) (April 28, 1936–), Russian poet, writes (in Russian): "I ought to have been born
*so′ snə ra

SOSNORA

VIKTOR SOSNORA

in Leningrad, since my family are from that city. But my parents, passionate Darwinians of the 1930s, decided that a child ought to make its appearance in sunshine and favorable climatic conditions. They therefore went specially to Alupka, where I was born. The result was that, brought back from the exotic Crimea to commonplace swampy Leningrad, I at once became ill with tuberculosis of the bones. For three years I lay in hospital, where the doctors decided to amputate my right foot and left hand. My (paternal) grandfather was secretly engaged in folk medicine (which in those days was severely proscribed in our country). When he learnt of the doctors' decision he took me home and within a month I was already playing leapfrog with children of my own age.

"My genealogy is a very mixed one: my father's father was Polish, his mother Estonian, while on my mother's side my great-grandfather was a Jewish rabbi. Our stock includes Barclay de Tolly, general of Scottish descent, and the composer Scriabin.

"My childhood biography is also a very mixed one. Until the age of six I can't remember a single face or situation. My earliest childhood memories are of the smell and taste of shell fragments during the siege of Leningrad, for we children used to suck these still warm metal splinters, which tasted like sour lollipops. In the spring of 1942 I was evacuated across the 'Road of Life' to the Kuban, in the south, where my grandmother lived and my uncle was a regimental commissar.

"It was a case of 'out of the frying pan into the fire,' for the Germans soon arrived in the Kuban. Three times I fell into the hands of the

Gestapo and was tortured to find out whether I was a Jew. They tortured me by fastening my wrist to a beam, and then leaving me hanging from it. Thus for several hours my shoulder blades were twisted, my whole body becoming completely cramped, until I lost consciousness. Then I was taken down and they 'set right' my shoulder blades with wooden mallets and lashed my stomach and the lower part of my body with barbed wire. My uncle had become commander of a partisan detachment and they took me away with them into the steppe to live like moles in burrows. I became a go-between: going at night into the village, stealing food and bullets, passing on notes. The whole detachment, including my uncle, were eventually shot. I alone remained alive, because before the execution I had been wounded in the head by a shell fragment and the Germans thought I was dead.

"At the end of the war my father, a colonel in the Polish army, became the military commandant in Praga (a suburb of Warsaw). After the war my fate and my education were linked with his military career, as he moved from town to town. My education was therefore very mixed: under the Germans in the Kuban I studied at a German school, in Makhach-Kala at a Daghestani school, in Praga at a Polish school, and in Arkhangelsk at a musical one. I finished middle school—Ukrainian and sports-oriented—in Lvov, and returned to my own city, Leningrad, thus closing the circle.

"I have written at such length about my childhood not because it is so interesting but because it played a major role in shaping my creative work: my strange genealogy, many years of serious illness, the Gestapo and the execution, the migratory life. My literary work, perhaps as a result of all this, is mainly atavistic in character —preoccupied with history, with solving the riddle of the meaning of contemporary symbols, with a fatalistic world view, with surrealism.

"My literary work is also a struggle against the cruelty of literature to our family: my grandfather wrote a great deal (stories, novels, memoirs), but all his manuscripts have been lost, while my uncle was a talented poet whose manuscripts were destroyed by the fascists after he was shot.

"Therefore the struggle with and for literature means more to me than the 'struggle for life.' After school I served for three years in the army, then for six years was a metal worker in a factory, was an almost professional sportsman, studied in the philosophical faculty, and in 1970 gave lectures on Russian poetry in Paris at the University of Vincennes. But all this real life is only slightly, or not at all, reflected in my work, for as far as possible I have always kept my inner self apart from my outward life.

"I began to write poetry at the age of four, from the time when I learned to write the letters of the alphabet. I have been seriously engaged in literature since 1952. My first publication appeared in 1960, my first collected book of poems in 1962. I am grateful to Nikolai Aseyev, Lilya Brik, Dmitri Likhachev, and Boris Slutsky for their influence on my formation as a writer.

"The poems of my youth were on such themes as ancient Russia or the 'Lay of Igor'; all the rest are about the contemporary world, its farcical dramas and apocalyptic delights. There are writers who approve of the collectivization of life and literature. While there may be some justification for collectivization in life, collectivized literature is merely the shame of the animal herd, anti-art. In our literature, in which stock clichés and hypocrisy have been raised to the level of axiom, the writer has a duty to express the truth in his soul and his brain, even if he remains a minority of one. This isn't a pose, but a tragedy. For this reason I have by and large ceased to be published in the last few years.

"My four published books are verse collections, but they represent only a third of all my poetry. In my writing desk there are also prose works: a novel of the time of Catherine the Great (the assassination of her husband Peter III, the famous conspiracy of Mirovich), a book of tales from Russian history, a fantasy, and eight contemporary stories. My three plays are unpublished and unstaged. So it turns out that almost all my work lies silent in a drawer labeled 'my never'—a name that is no idle prophecy. Our present is monolithic and stable. 'My never' will never be published in my own country in my lifetime."

Sosnora has been described by Suzanne Massie as taut and spare, with "something of a bird" in his sharp features, and as "an ultra-sensitive, moody man. . . . whose intense nature glowed in his dark eyes." His melancholy spirit and his strange and at times surrealistic poetry were shaped, as he explains above, by his dramatic and terrible childhood, full of illness, suffering, war, and death. Before the war his father was part of a well-known team of acrobats in the Leningrad circus. When the circus was broken up by the war, his father enlisted in the army as a private, quickly became an officer, and was selected to join a special unit fighting behind the German lines. Of the five hundred members of this unit only three or four survived, one of them being Sosnora's father, who went on to become a war hero and a general. After the war he was

the deputy Warsaw Pact commander in Poland under Field Marshal Rokossovsky, and later district commander in Arkhangelsk.

After his initial severe illness, Viktor Sosnora, spending two years in besieged Leningrad, suffered like all the children in the blockaded city from malnutrition, scurvy, and dystrophy. His survival was partly due to the fact that his mother was able to keep him warm during the freezing winters in the metallurgical factory where she worked as an engineer. He was six when he was evacuated under the strafing of German planes across the Road of Life, the famous siege-breaking winter road across the frozen Lake Ladoga. He was, as he says, taken to the Kuban, a region north of the Caucasus populated mainly by Cossacks. Sosnora was only seven years old when he was tortured by the Gestapo and joined his uncle's partisans in the steppes. They dug holes under the long grass for cover, and it was on emerging from one of these that the boy, wounded by an exploding shell, watched through a veil of blood the slaughter by the Germans of his uncle and all his band.

Viktor Sosnora was enlisted in the army at the age of nineteen and served from 1956 to 1958 in Leningrad, Arkhangelsk, and Novaya Zemlya. Later he worked on a blast furnace in the metallurgical factory in which he had spent his childhood days during the siege of Leningrad. Sosnora joined a poetry circle in the factory. His first published poems appeared in the Moscow journal *Literatura i Zhizn* (Literature and Life) in 1960, and later his poems were included in the literary almanac *Molodoy Leningrad* (Young Leningrad). In 1964 he became the youngest member of the Leningrad Writers' Union and left the factory to become a full-time writer. His first book, *Yanvarsky liven* (A January Shower, 1962), was published with an introduction by the poet Nikolai Aseyev. This was followed by three other poetry collections, *Triptykh* (Triptych, 1965), *Vsadniki* (Horsemen, 1969), and *Aist* (Stork, 1972).

Sosnora's verse has been characterized from the beginning by its subtle verbal rhythms and its musicality. His early work evoked comparisons with Voznesensky on this account, and because of its use of images derived from industry and technology. In Sosnora's case, such images are drawn most often from his own experience as a foundry worker:

. . . And the fir trees clanged in green metal!
Like skates scraping on ice!
Like a railway station gong!

SOSNORA

The cupola of each fir was bent back
Like an iron worker's helmet,
like a castle perched above a rampart!
Though the fir trees clanged in green metal,
I knew for certain
they were wooden. . .

(from "And Fir Trees Clanged,"
translated by George Reavey)

This is not to suggest, however, that Sosnora
was ever a "socialist realist," earnestly celebrating the achievements of Soviet industry. On the
contrary, his poetry adumbrates a dreamlike and
hallucinatory world, at times surreal to the point
of self-indulgence, while his experiments with
language, his archaisms, neologisms, and word-
play, recall the work of Viktor Khlebnikov, the
founder of Russian futurism.

As he indicates above, not much of Sosnora's
verse "about the contemporary world, its farcical dramas and apocalyptic delights," has been
published. He is best known for poems which
draw on history and myth, though they do so
very often in search of answers to "the riddle of
the meaning of contemporary symbols." Thus
"The Bronze Owl," one of a cycle of thirteen owl
poems, recalls Pushkin's "The Bronze Horseman," about the equestrian statue of Peter the
Great in St. Petersburg, and like that great poem
uses the tyrannies of the past to comment on
those of the present:

Giant horses carry Russia along,
squiggles of owlish dogma beneath,
Byzantine owlish ikons beneath
And a tiny, tin horse.

(translated by Paul Roche)

All of the poems in Sosnora's third collection,
Vsadniki (Horsemen), are based on old Russian
themes, either historical or legendary, like the
tale of the invisible city of Kitezh, used by
Rimsky-Korsakov as the theme of one of his
operas—the story of a heroic city which, during
the Mongol invasion of the thirteenth century,
chose to vanish from sight in a mist rather than
submit to conquest. However, as Dmitri Likhachev observes in his introduction to *Vsadniki,*
the stark descriptions of war in these poems
come directly from Sosnora's own traumatic experiences as a child. Likhachev comments on the
way the poet delves into the language to create
a rich impasto of verbal effects: "He finds treasures extracted from the entrails of the Russian
language. Ideas are born from the very roots of
words."

In such poetry, Daniel Weissbort writes, Sos-

nora "seems to be discovering and assembling
what may become a modern mythology, drawing on the legendary and historical chronicles of
Kievan Russia (as for example in his cycle of
poems attributed to the warrior-minstrel Boyan
referred to in the 'Lay of Igor'), as well as on
Greek myths, and fairy tales more or less common to all cultures. . . . When . . . [Sosnora] is
able to anchor himself in legend or in history, or
strongly enough in the life of nature and the
animals (for which, like Zabolotsky, he has great
feeling), he is capable of evoking an archetypal
world underlying contemporary existence."

Rain without end, harder and harder,
nations without leader or sail.
Its sad tribe is scattered far,
each, every droplet of rain.

Where am I? Who am I? Where going?
Will I come to old suns or new traps?
Will you or will you not lose me
in the crowd of hurrying drops.

My sword is unsullied. To be on my own
is my mission, in the horde without aim.
I am alone, I stand alone
in the rain, the rain, the rain.

(from "The Last Songs of Boyan,"
translated by Daniel Weissbort)

Sosnora turned to history also in the unpublished novel he mentions above. Intended to deal
with the eighteenth-century poet Gavrila Derz-
havin, it became primarily a novel about Peter
III, assassinated by his wife Catherine the Great
and usually dismissed as feeble and inept, but
defended and admired by Sosnora. The poet has
also worked on documentary films and has written the libretto for a musical, based on a Polish
tale and using the music of *Hair.* He himself
sometimes acts, but otherwise has few distractions from his work.

Suzanne Massie, with whose family Sosnora
stayed for two months on one of his visits to
Paris, gives this account of him: "He lived mostly at night. Every day the routine was the same.
He would appear about noon, unshaven, at the
kitchen door for his breakfast, a startling mixture which never varied: a raw egg, a tomato, a
piece of Roquefort cheese, and a bottle of beer.
Then, breakfast over, he would go out into the
garden, where he would walk around and
around in precisely regular circles for half an
hour. Then he would sit for a while and listen to
the sounds of the air. In the afternoon, I would
find him in our garret typing and retyping on the
old Russian typewriter we had found for him.

After dinner, suitably mellowed, he recited poetry and sang plaintive songs in an oddly touching off-pitched voice."

Sosnora lives with his wife Marina in one of the new apartment districts in Leningrad. His health has never fully recovered from the ordeals of his childhood. Suzanne Massie describes him as "an intellectual without culture," who reads widely to remedy his educational deficiencies. He knows Polish, Ukrainian, and a little German, and has translated some Serbian poets into Russian. "He is a complex, original loner, rarely mixing, rarely seen. He has no imitators, no disciples, no emotional audiences. . . . Sosnora is . . . a sort of twentieth-century prophet, who senses in his imagination apocalypses yet unseen by ordinary mortals."

PRINCIPAL WORKS IN ENGLISH TRANSLATION: *Poems in* Massie, S. (ed.) The Living Mirror: Five Poets From Leningrad, 1972; Reavey, G. (ed.) The New Russian Poets 1953–1968, 1969; Weissbort, D. (ed.) Post-War Russian Poetry, 1974.

ABOUT: Massie, S. (ed.) The Living Mirror, 1972; Massie, R. and S. Journey, 1975; Weissbort, D. (ed.) Post-War Russian Poetry, 1974.

STAMATOPOULOS, STRATIS. *See* "MYRIVILIS," STRATIS

STEAD, C(HRISTIAN) K(ARLSON) (October 17, 1932–), New Zealand poet, critic, short story writer, and novelist, writes: "I was born in Auckland, New Zealand, and though I like to travel as often as possible, and have spent a number of years abroad, I regard New Zealand as my permanent home. My earliest forebears in New Zealand arrived in 1832. I have English, Irish and Scots blood, but I am said to be most like my maternal grandfather, a sea-captain who was half-Swedish, half-German, from whom my forenames derive. I have always felt a slight distance between myself and my social surroundings and I think I can now identify this as a distaste for what seems to me the muddle characteristic of the Anglo-Saxon social order which New Zealand inherits. I feel an affection for England which is different from loyalty or identification. I enjoy France, partly because French is the only foreign language I have learned, but I know I do not belong there. My feeling of belonging in New Zealand is habit, association with people and love of the natural scene which shaped my consciousness as a child and which I continue to enjoy. I inherited very little culture, except perhaps musical culture (my mother taught the piano and played it well). Literary culture came

C. K. STEAD

to me through formal education, which means it came late.

"The invitation to write about oneself is a trap. There is a temptation to find ways of seeing oneself as interesting. But as I set down the sentences above I recognize that there is a sense in which as a literary intelligence I float free, without binding attachments. Perhaps because my father was active in Labour politics I have gone through phases of intense political commitment and activity (always to the Left), the most protracted of which occurred during New Zealand's involvement on the American side in the Vietnam War; but I withdraw from these phases into sceptical detachment. What continues unbroken is my commitment to literature and the arts. I do not feel inclined to defend these on the grounds that they serve something larger or more worthy than themselves. They are associated in my mind with the highest moments of human consciousness and seem to me self-justifying.

"I have written in a number of modes and genres but in my own conception I am a poet and theoretician of poetry. My critical writings have been influenced in the form they have taken by my employment in a university English department, but they spring direct from my practical concerns as a poet. I have written some few short stories, one of which, "A Fitting Tribute," has had surprising circulation in four languages; but the stories remain uncollected. My only novel, *Smith's Dream,* a political fantasy set in New Zealand, was recently made into a film. I have also written a number of essays on New Zealand poets and fiction writers which wait to be collected. Recently I have edited a selection of Katherine Mansfield's letters and journals.

Mansfield's clarity of mind and style, her anarchic intelligence, her wit, and the fact that she belongs nowhere yet has her roots so clearly in New Zealand, all appeal to me far more than the soft Bloomsbury qualities for which she is best known.

"In poetry my roots are in the Modernist phase of the early years of this century. I have admired Yeats and written at length about Eliot; but it is Pound whose work still seems to me (for all its unevenness and imperfections) the least exhaustible source of technical lessons. He is also the poet who rises highest in the scale of poetic intensity.

"Although I work in a university I am sceptical about what happens to literature in most cases where attempts are made to 'teach' it. It is too much analysed, too little felt; and there must be many students who only slowly recover their ability to feel the work, or to believe in their feeling. But I am an optimist and trust the human spirit to throw up necessary rebellions against these constrictions.

"I married Kathleen Elizabeth Roberts, a librarian, in 1955, and we have three children, a boy and two girls, born in 1963, 1966 and 1970."

Stead is the son of James Stead, an accountant, and the former Olive Karlson. He was educated at Mount Albert Grammar School and Auckland University, where he received his B.A. in English with first-class honors in 1953, his M.A. with honors in 1955. In 1954 he went to England as Michael Hiatt Baker Scholar at Bristol University, where he began his doctoral studies (1954–1955), subsequently pursuing them for a further year in London. Stead began his teaching career in Australia, as a lecturer in English at the University of New England, New South Wales (1956–1957). He then resumed his studies in London, where he remained until he returned to New Zealand in 1959. Since then he has taught at Auckland University as a lecturer in English (1959–1961), senior lecturer (1962–1964), associate professor (1964–1968), and professor of English (1968–). He received his Ph.D. from Bristol University in 1961.

Stead is probably most widely known for *The New Poetic: Yeats to Eliot* (1964). It is divided into three sections: an examination of W.B. Yeats illustrating the problems of poets of the modern era; a study of the condition of English poetry during the years 1909–1916 (including, in particular, the reaction against an exhausted tradition initiated by the Georgians, and the much more radical experiments of Ezra Pound); and, lastly, an appraisal of the poetry and criticism of T. S. Eliot. Stead's basic thesis is an original,

productive, and attractive one (which incidentally gives valuable clues to his own poetic intentions). He argues that "a poem may be said to exist in a triangle, the points of which are, first, the poet, second, his audience, and, third, that area of experience which we call variously 'Reality,' 'Truth,' or 'Nature.' Between these points run lines of tension, and depending on the time, the place, the poet and the audience, these lines will lengthen or shorten. At one time we may find the poet and his audience close together, and 'Reality' a great distance from them. . . . At another time we may find the poet close to the point 'Reality'. . . . There are infinite variations but . . . the finest poems in any language are likely to be those which exist in an equilateral triangle, each point pulling equally in a moment of perfect tension."

Applying this judgment to the poetry of the past hundred years, Stead finds that the original Romantic movement became divided at the end of the last century. On the one hand there was Kipling, the "prophet" who would teach the reader nothing that he did not want to know (and was thus "degenerate" and a victim of "middle-class simplification"). On the other hand was Wilde, the "aesthete" who sought "Beauty" but who insisted that "his image may not be brought into the world of men, and survive there." One of the principal problems for the poets of our own time has been "to bring together these two extremes, each of which, apart, constitutes a heresy. . . . The best poets of this century have tried again to 'bring the whole soul of man into activity.' Unity has been the aim, fragmentation the enemy: Hence . . . Yeats's concern with 'Unity of Being' and Eliot's with the undivided sensibility." In Stead's view both Yeats and Eliot solved the problem, though Eliot did so fully only in *The Waste Land,* which Stead takes to be an essentially romantic poem. He concludes that it is towards the image that "the most vigorous poetic minds" have striven; but "there is, unformulated in this effort of the contemporary mind, a new poetic which requires of the poet's sensibility that it should draw into itself both moral and aesthetic qualities latent in the raw materials of the art, fusing these qualities into a form richer, more alive, more intensely expressive of the full human condition."

Roy Fuller on the whole welcomed Stead's theory, and Graham Hough called this "a more important book than it appears. . . . both illuminating and persuasive." Hough wrote that the book offers "what one would hardly have thought possible—a view of Mr. Eliot's poetry and thinking about poetry that is both unusual and just. This is achieved partly by paying attention to what was really going on instead of what is said to have been going on, and partly by making some generous and sensitive discriminations among disparate pronouncements." All the same, the immediate attention granted to Stead's "new poetic" was less than the influence it finally gained. It is not unusual to discover criticism that derives from it but that does not acknowledge it.

Stead's own early verse (1954–1962) was collected in *Whether the Will Is Free* (1964). These were mostly personal poems, traditional, meticulously wrought, sometimes rather literary and academic. Stead himself has referred to their "preoccupation with place, and identity in relation to place," their "wide variety of verse forms," and the influence on them of Pound, Yeats, Eliot, Auden, Wallace Stevens, and the New Zealand poets Allen Curnow and James K. Baxter. "A Natural Grace," a comparatively early love poem, shows him at his best and most original:

Under my eaves untiring all the spring day
Two sparrows have worked with stalks the mowers
    leave
While I have sat regretting your going away.
All day they've ferried straw and sticks to weave
A wall against the changing moods of air,
And may have worked into that old design
A thread of cloth you wore, a strand of hair,
Since all who make are passionate for line,
Proportion, strength, and take what's near, and
    serves.
All day I sat remembering your face,
And watched the sallow stalks, woven in curves
By a blind process, achieve a natural grace.

In the poems he wrote after 1964, Stead, as he says, "largely abandoned rhyme and regular forms. The lines are shorter and more dramatic, governed by the natural flow of speech. There is a good deal of internal rhyme and assonance. The tone is grimmer, the poet-persona less pleased with himself." He also believes that he has shed or absorbed the influence of other poets. He likes now "to write with as little punctuation as possible, accommodating line-length and syntax to one another in a free-flowing verse-sentence in which words echo one another and the pauses and runs of sound parallel the sense." One poem in his second collection, *Crossing the Bar* (1972), begins: "Poetry. Second best./ It represents. It speaks/ Truest from a broken house." The poem ends:

Poets at the last are deft.
I contract to that end

My second-best art.
It will serve to praise the first.
The first served only itself.

Altogether less eclectic and more original than Stead's earlier verse, these poems aimed to be (to quote one of them) "Hard. Bright. Clean. Particular." One reviewer, in the *Times Literary Supplement,* found a "reserved, laconic, rather cold note," and gained an impression "of aridity and costiveness." Kendrick Smithyman welcomed the development, however, saying that while the early poems "comment" on their subjects, "Stead's later poems do not offer us comment, but rather experience, very near direct experience."

Writing in *Contemporary Poets* (1975 edition), Stead acknowledges that his verse is "disciplined," but maintains that his poetic discipline is quite unlike that involved, for example, in writing critical prose. And he makes this odd and interesting statement: "My natural tone is secure but not definitive. I am a liberal, fitted neither for moralising nor command. But when I am able to burrow deep enough I discover another self who (though not very likable) is perhaps the best of the poet in me. I conceive of this person as German, romantic, authoritarian, detached yet full of passion, above all a musician."

Smith's Dream (1971), Stead's only novel, was described by Roy Frayne as "a gallant attempt to combine the commonplace with the magical in a coherent form"; it was given scant attention outside New Zealand. Stead received the Poetry Awards Incorporated prize (U.S.) in 1955, a Readers' Award from the New Zealand magazine *Landfall* in 1959, the Katherine Mansfield Prize (for both fiction and the essay) in 1960, and the Winn-Mansen Menton Fellowship and the Jessie McKay Award for Poetry in 1972. A Nuffield Travelling Fellowship in 1965 enabled him to revisit England, where he took part in poetry readings during the Commonwealth Arts Festival. He has served as chairman of the New Zealand Literary Fund Advisory Committee, and is a member of the New Zealand Labour Party.

PRINCIPAL WORKS: *Poetry*—Whether the Will Is Free: Poems 1954–1962, 1964; Crossing the Bar, 1972; Quesada: Poems 1972–1974, 1975; Walking Westward, 1978. *Novel* —Smith's Dream, 1971. *Criticism*—The New Poetic: Yeats to Eliot, 1964. *As Editor*—New Zealand Short Stories: Second Series, 1966; Measure for Measure: A Casebook, 1971; The Letters and Journals of Katherine Mansfield: A Selection, 1977.

ABOUT: Cameron, W.J. New Zealand, 1965; Contemporary Authors 57–60, 1976; Doyle, C. Recent Poetry in New

Zealand, 1965; Vinson, J. (ed.) Contemporary Poets, 1975. *Periodicals*—Islands Summer 1972; Landfall September 1964; Listener March 12, 1964; London Magazine July 1964; Times Literary Supplement April 16, 1964; April 27, 1973.

STOKES, ADRIAN (DURHAM) (October 27, 1902–December 15, 1972), English art critic, was born in London, the son of a stockbroker who had once stood as a Liberal candidate for Parliament. He was educated at Rugby School and at Magdalen College, Oxford, where he read philosophy, politics, and economics, gaining a second-class honors degree in 1923. He was a gifted athlete, and at the university developed into a tennis player "of Wimbledon standard." After Oxford, he visited India, China, and the United States, acquiring in this way "a sense of what is specific to the European tradition." Stokes was wealthy enough to devote his life to the study of art.

ADRIAN STOKES

His autobiographical books *Inside Out* and *Smooth and Rough* have been compared to Ruskin's *Praeterita* as illuminating portraits of an artist and aesthete in the making—of a child hungry for sensory experience and for the understanding of this experience. A crucial event was his discovery of Italy, where he first arrived on New Year's Eve 1921–1922; he returned repeatedly, sometimes staying for long periods. He traveled with the Sitwells, "the first to open my eyes," played tennis with Ezra Pound at Rapallo, shared a villa with Aldous Huxley at Sanary, and for a time lived in Venice. In Italy during the 1920s Stokes encountered the thirteenth-century architecture and stone carvings which he regarded as the basic expressions of the fantasies fundamental to his own dream of Western art. He was also reading Freud and beginning to sense the fascination of psychoanalysis, which crystallized in the early 1930s during his own seven years of analysis with Melanie Klein.

Because his style and ideas are difficult and elusive, Stokes never found a wide audience. Yet he has had a profound influence on an important circle of artists, critics, and philosophers, who regard him as one of the most original and creative writers on art in the twentieth century. Lawrence Gowing said of him: "His writing is the only criticism today that casts an imaginative spell like art," and John Golding places him in a nineteenth-century tradition of aesthetic writing. "He is in the line of direct succession from Ruskin and Pater, and he writes as evocatively, as creatively, as either.... What renders Stokes's writing unique is that a life lived at a level of extreme visual intensity has been informed by what is perhaps a profounder knowledge of psychoanalysis than that enjoyed by any other writer on art."

Seeking to explain the way in which objects reflect the state of mind of the person viewing them, Stokes decisively enlarged the definition of artistic form. One of his key ideas was that works of art are perceived as analogues of the human body. For Stokes the experience of art was always most profound, most satisfying, when art found expression in a corporeal form, or in a form sufficiently close to the corporeal for us to make the connection. Hence it was natural for him to become passionately devoted to ballet during the London seasons of the Diaghilev *ballet russe,* and to write: "If I were allowed but one generalization with which to explain the glamour of the theatre as a whole, I should say that it resided in this, the projection of man's interior physical and mental life into terms of the outside world, and particularly into terms of man's exterior, of the appearance and movement of his body."

Stokes originally formulated his views in relation to Italian Renaissance art, and it was in *The Quattro Cento* (1932) that he really began to evaluate and systematize his perceptions. The first characteristic of what Stokes meant by "Quattro Cento" art was that the artist should respect the inherent qualities of his medium, whether stone, wood, canvas, or paint. The artist works to achieve what Stokes called in relation to sculpture "the blossoming of the stone." This presupposes a sort of compact between artist and stone: on the artist's side there is the outward thrust of fantasy, which he projects onto the stone; complementary to this is the way in which the stone, in the hands of such an artist, pushes itself forward onto the surface.

This kind of art, which Stokes also described as "the carving tradition," was opposed in his mind to "the modeling tradition," in which the artist uses his medium to express his own will and his own fantasies—to Stokes this sort of expressionism was aggressive, and he at first deeply distrusted and feared it. The distinction between carving and modeling was fully worked out in *Stones of Rimini* (1934), while in *Venice: An Aspect of Art* (1945) Stokes tries to show that the city's architecture and its relationship to water is "a creation of the Quattro Cento" and "the crucial image of Mediterranean culture."

Stokes's "Quattro Centro" had been freed from any chronological reference by renaming it "the carving tradition," under which heading Stokes felt himself able to discuss the great sculptors and architects of ancient Athens, Piero della Francesca, Giorgione, Michelangelo, Vermeer, and Cézanne—all artists who seemed to him to have worked to reveal the underlying forms of nature. In *Colour and Form* (1937) Stokes set out to establish correspondences in painting for what he had called the carving tradition in sculpture and architecture. Stokes had himself by this time become a painter, studying with Adrian Kent. For a while he worked in Paris, where he met his first wife, the painter Margaret Mellis. In 1936 he returned to London and joined the Euston Road School. He spent the war years in Cornwall, growing vegetables and entertaining the artists who gathered around him. At this time, according to his friend Richard Wollheim, Stokes looked "rather like a great blond hawk"—he was very striking, and his "looks . . . made a very strong and enduring impression upon both sexes." In manner he was "intense, wayward, and shy."

After the war, Stokes was divorced from his wife, and in 1947 he married her sister Ann, settling for a time in Switzerland. It was to be a happy marriage, marred only by the chronic mental illness of the second of their three children. The experience of happy family life was reflected in a broadening of his response to art and a change in his views on certain key artists: Michelangelo, Rembrandt, Hogarth, Turner, Matisse. Family life also encouraged in him a social commitment, a deep concern with the environment and with public issues.

It was only after his second marriage that Stokes began to incorporate psychoanalysis into his interpretation of art. *Inside Out* (1947) is a study of his own childhood memories and aesthetic responses, and in *Smooth and Rough* (1951) he turned to an interpretation of works of art based on the theories of Freud and Melanie Klein. The basic aim of all of Stokes's later, psychoanalytically-influenced writings—*Michelangelo, Greek Culture and the Ego, Three Essays on the Painting of Our Time, Painting and the Inner World, The Invitation in Art* and *Reflections on the Nude*—is an attempt to associate his carving and modeling traditions with Melanie Klein's reconstruction of the development of the inner world of the infant.

In the first weeks of life, according to this theory, the infant lacks a sense of his body as a continuous subject: he is a subject in flux, and his consciousness is directed particularly towards the mother's breast. Gradually, however, he begins to experience himself as an entity separate from his mother; he begins, in what Klein called the depressive state, to perceive her as separate and whole. In sensing her wholeness he is forced to face the contradictory nature of his drives: that he at once loves and hates her. Stokes traces the origin of creativity to these early conflicts. He maintains that the carving tradition corresponds to the depressive state, because the carver, in respecting the integrity and the separateness of the stone, celebrates both the object with which he enters into relation and the integrated ego that he projects.

As Richard Wollheim points out, "perhaps the most intriguing element in Stokes's later writing is what he makes of the modelling tradition." The two traditions are now seen as complementary, each with characteristics which are those of the other in reverse. So the wholeness, separateness, and self-sufficiency of the carving tradition are complemented by the loss of separateness and the "enveloping" quality of the modeling tradition. This loss of separateness, which Stokes first called the "incantatory" element in art and later "the invitation in art," became increasingly important for him in his later work.

Stokes's books acquired their reputation with a small appreciative circle. It was only in 1972, when a selection of his writings was put together as *The Image in Form: Selected Writings of Adrian Stokes,* that his ideas began to reach a wider public. This selection was edited by Richard Wollheim, whose introductory essay is a lucid account of the way Stokes's vision developed and expanded. In September of the same year Stokes came home from the hospital with the knowledge that he was incurably ill with cancer. For the next three months he worked on a last group of eleven small paintings. He died quietly in his sleep after lunch on December 15, 1972.

Stokes had little to say about many of the elements that have contributed to artistic formulation in the West, but was consistently concerned with one particular aspect, the emotional effect of artistic forms and shapes. As Lawrence Gowing observes, Stokes "has isolated attitudes that are very likely basic to the emotional constitution which art allows us to share with the artist." His books are moreover full of ideas on such subjects as the connection between art and aggression, the relationship between mental health and the environment, the role and effects of advertising, and in general the way in which feelings about art might be related to the totality of experience. As Andrew Forge has put it: "One reason why he is such a good writer on art is the broad connections he makes between art and life at large. He makes these not by bullying art into a shape it cannot hold ... but by taking his starting-point in aesthetic experience of the outside world, of which he sees art as the condensation." His critical writings were republished in 1978 in three volumes.

Stokes's own paintings, according to his obituarist in the London *Times,* had an "irridescent objectivity" and developed "an extraordinary consistency and strength"; the several exhibitions of his work "made a deep impression." Towards the end of his life Stokes began to write poetry, and some of his work in this form appears in *Penguin Modern Poets 23* (1973). He was from 1960 to 1967 a trustee of the Tate Gallery. Generous and high-spirited as he was, Stokes would not tolerate falseness or pretension in art or in people, and could be formidable. He had, Wollheim says, "a most remarkable way of half-listening to someone which also involved the most total concentration upon the person that I have ever observed in any human being."

PRINCIPAL WORKS: The Thread of Ariadne, 1925; Sunrise in the West, 1926; The Quattro Cento, 1932; Stones of Rimini, 1934; To-night the Ballet, 1934; Russian Ballet, 1935; Colour and Form, 1937; Venice: An Aspect of Art, 1945; Inside Out, 1947; Cézanne, 1947; Art and Science: A Study of Alberti, Piero della Francesca and Giorgione, 1949; Smooth and Rough, 1951; Michelangelo, 1955; Raphael, 1956; Monet, 1958; Greek Culture and the Ego, 1958; Three Essays on the Painting of Our Time, 1961; Painting and the Inner World, 1963; The Invitation in Art, 1965; Reflections on the Nude, 1967; The Image in Form: Selected Writings of Adrian Stokes, edited by Richard Wollheim, 1972; A Game That Must Be Lost: Collected Papers, edited by Eric Rhode, 1973; (with others) Penguin Modern Poets 23, 1973; The Critical Writings of Adrian Stokes—Volume 1: 1930–1937; Volume 2: 1937–1958; Volume 3: 1955–1967, 1978.

ABOUT: Who's Who, 1972; Wollheim, R. *introductions to* The Invitation in Art, 1965 and The Image in Form, 1972. *Periodicals*—Listener December 13, 1973; New Statesman January 22, 1965; March 2, 1973; New York Times Book Review April 30, 1978; Studio International April 1973; Times (London) December 19, 1972; Times Literary Supplement February 1, 1934; October 6, 1945; March 29, 1947; November 9, 1967; September 29, 1972; February 12, 1978; Twentieth Century November 1956.

STONE, I(SIDOR) F(EINSTEIN) (December 24, 1907–), American journalist, was born in Philadelphia to Russian-Jewish immigrants, Bernard and Katherine (Novack) Feinstein; he legally changed his name from Isidor Feinstein in 1938. Raised in Haddonfield, New Jersey, where his father owned a dry goods store, he says that "it wasn't easy being a small Jewish boy named Isidor in an all-Gentile community." The strains and loneliness of his situation made him an avid reader, and reading inclined him to writing. He launched his first magazine in 1922 as a fourteen-year-old high school sophomore— a monthly called *The Progressive,* offering poetry, editorials, and advertising, and circulating to five hundred subscribers at a nickel apiece. It was shut down after three issues by the publisher's father, who was concerned about its effect on his studies.

The Progressive nevertheless led to assignments with the Camden (New Jersey) *Courier-Post* and the Haddonfield *Press,* and Stone's school work suffered anyway. Foiled in his ambition to attend Harvard because of his dismal class ranking, he went instead to the University of Pennsylvania (1924–1927). There he studied philosophy while working full-time for two Philadelphia newspapers, the *Inquirer* and the *Record.* "I thought for a time of teaching philosophy," he said later, "but the smell of a newspaper shop was more enticing than the spinsterish atmosphere of a college faculty."

Stone was married in 1929 to Esther M. Roisman, whom he met "on a blind date and a borrowed dollar." They have a daughter and two sons. He went on reporting for the *Inquirer* and the *Record* until 1933, when he served briefly as an editorial writer for the *Record* before moving on to a similar job with the New York *Post* (1933–1939). In 1938 he also took on the associate editorship of the *Nation,* and in 1940 he became the *Nation*'s Washington editor, a post he retained until 1946. He also found time, between 1942 and 1952, to contribute as a reporter, columnist, and editorial writer to the *Post,* and to such other liberal or left-wing New York newspapers as *P.M.,* the *Star,* and the *Daily Compass.*

The Court Disposes (1937) was the first in a series of books that established Stone as "a guerrilla warrior, swooping down in surprise attack on a stuffy bureaucracy where it least expected independent inquiry." It was an attack on the

I. F. STONE

United States Supreme Court for inconsistencies, ambiguities, and expansion of powers beyond Constitutional limits, as exemplified in the Court's decisions on the minimum wage law. This "pungent, effective, and even brilliant" polemic was followed by *Business As Usual* (1941), condemning the government's wasteful and inefficient defense program. A reviewer in the Springfield *Republican* found this "critique of America's efforts to become the arsenal of democracy" both disturbing and challenging: "Even those moderates and conservatives who will fume at his leftwing viewpoint and profess to see unfair distortions here and there, even these will admit he is extraordinarily well informed, not completely the captive of doctrinaire nonsense and, as a writer, able to handle refractory material and still make his book move with the speed and fascination of a prairie fire."

In 1945 Stone reported from Palestine on the Jewish struggle to establish a homeland there, and a year later he joined and described the clandestine exodus of Jewish refugees running the British blockade in the Mediterranean. His dispatches, originally written for *P.M.,* were published in book form as *Underground to Palestine* (1946), of which Meyer Berger wrote: "It was a dangerous assignment. In it were all the elements that might tempt a reporter to flood his pages with hysteria in type. He has escaped that temptation.... It is a notable journalistic achievement." There was a much cooler reception for *This Is Israel* (1948), Stone's first-hand account of the Israeli War of Independence, dismissed by F.H. Bullock as "a big, profusely illustrated propaganda picture book."

At about the same time, writing in the New York *Star* and *Daily Compass,* Stone broke with many of his liberal friends by opposing Truman's cold war policy and advocating peaceful coexistence with the Soviet Union. His *Hidden History of the Korean War* (1952) also embarrassed more moderate colleagues, claiming as it did that the war was the outcome of a deliberate conspiracy between South Korea and the United States, not of North Korean aggression. "Dissent is a tonic in an age of conformism," wrote Michael Straight in the *New Republic.* "But this is not reasoned dissent."

But conformism was rampant in the postwar years. *P.M.* folded in June 1948 and the *Daily Compass* in November 1952; it became increasingly difficult for Stone to publish his opinions or find work. Denied a forum, he created his own. *I. F. Stone's Weekly,* his four-page journal of fact and opinion, was launched on January 17, 1953. It cost five dollars a year, and had an initial mailing list of just over five thousand, drawn mostly from former subscribers to the *Compass.* The *Weekly,* Stone told an interviewer, was the "equivalent of the old-fashioned Jewish momma-and-poppa grocery store." Stone's office was a converted bedroom in his house in northwest Washington. His wife was circulation manager, and he was researcher, reporter, writer, editor, proofreader, and printer. "I am, I suppose, an anachronism," he said. "In this age of corporation men, I am an independent capitalist. ... a wholly independent newspaperman ... beholden to no one but my good readers."

Stone set out to make the *Weekly* readable, honest, and provocative—"it's important to get the readers mad; otherwise they will just put the *Weekly* aside." At the same time, it had to be a paper that "a campus reader ... could pass on to a conservative colleague without having it dismissed as just another hysterical rag." Over the years, Stone's incisive, witty, and audacious articles dealt with every conceivable current issue. His method, according to an account in the *Christian Science Monitor,* was to shake up, "like a kaleidoscope, the fixed patterns for looking at events. Typically he will start off with an unusual historical comparison ... which forces the reader out of the protection of the standard clichés, compelling him to see people and events from some fresh, oblique angle. ... Having introduced his novel frame of reference, I.F. Stone then follows up with a barrage of novel facts."

Oddly enough, the *Weekly* owed its success partly to Stone's deafness—in other respects a serious handicap that was finally cured by surgery in 1965. Unable to rely on press conferences or interviews, he turned instead to a close reading of press transcripts and Congressional records, in this way dredging up all kinds of "significant trifles" other newspapermen had overlooked or underestimated. Out of such molehills rose mountainous indictments of Pentagon budgets and nuclear tests. As Murray Kempton put it, Stone remembered faithfully "the official lie of last month which is contradicted by the official lie of today."

Stone soon became famous, especially in the heyday of McCarthyism, as the "Establishment's rebel, the Rebellion's favorite establishmentarian." And indeed he never hesitated to ruffle the sensibilities of his Old Left, New Left, or liberal subscribers. He once told Israel Shenker that "being dependent on one's readers is the subtlest kind of slavery. The real test of leadership is whether you're willing to take up causes unpopular with your readers." The *Weekly* defended the Warren Commission Report on the assassination of John F. Kennedy and criticized the shortcomings of both Soviet and Chinese communism; it condemned militant Zionism in Israel, and that country's callousness toward Arab refugees after the Six Day War of 1967. At the same time, Stone's early opposition to American military involvement in Vietnam made him an "exalted figure in the pantheon of the peace movement."

Regarded for years as a political wild man, Stone came in from the cold in the mid-1960s, when the accuracy, maturity, and integrity of the *Weekly* established him as a leading voice in responsible left-wing journalism. Stone still refused to surrender his independence, saying in 1970 that "you've really got to wear a chastity belt in Washington to preserve your journalistic integrity. Once the Secretary of State invites you to lunch and asks your opinion, you're sunk." Nevertheless, the *Weekly* quadrupled its circulation in its first ten years. Some forty subscriptions went to Capitol Hill offices alone, and it was one of the twenty-five journals regularly abstracted for the President's information.

In 1967, ill health forced Stone to transform the paper into a bi-weekly. By 1971 this was reaching some seventy-four thousand subscribers and grossing about three hundred and fifty thousand dollars a year. The *Weekly* ceased publication on January 1, 1972, when Stone was sixty-three. "I'm the youngest man my age I know," he said, "but I just figured it was better not to continue this one-man five-day bike race." At the same time he commented: "I've shown that if you want to be a stubborn damn fool, you can do it your way and get away with it and make a living. It was a form of self-indulgence, and I've had a wonderful time at it. With all due respect to the New York *Times,* I'd rather have

had these nineteen years being editor of this fly sheet than editor of the *Times.*" A movie about the *Weekly* by Jerry Bruck Jr. was shown at the Cannes Film Festival in 1974 and has been screened several times since by the Public Broadcasting Service.

At intervals during the lifespan of the *Weekly,* Stone assembled some of its contents into books. *The Haunted Fifties* (1963) covered the years from 1953 to 1961, centering upon such topics as McCarthyism and the Eisenhower administration. *In a Time of Torment* (1967) contained articles published between 1961 and 1967 in the *Weekly* and the *New York Review of Books,* dealing with the Kennedy and Johnson administrations, civil rights and black revolutionaries, and the escalating Vietnam war. *Polemics and Prophecies, 1967–1970* (1970) considered the youth rebellion, the armaments race, tensions in the Middle East, and war in Southeast Asia, among other topics. *I. F. Stone's Weekly Reader* is a selection of the best of Stone's articles, edited by Neil Middleton.

The Killings at Kent State (1971), which did not derive directly from the *Weekly,* includes the Justice Department's summary of the FBI's reports on the shooting of students at Kent State University, as well as Stone's description and analysis of the tragedy. According to Alan Rudrum, the book shows "how local, state and federal political pressures combined to force the moment to its crisis, and why murder will almost certainly go unpunished." Rudrum said "it is hard to imagine how the feel of . . . [Kent State] could be more immediately conveyed" than in Stone's account.

In his "retirement," I. F. Stone serves as a contributing editor of the *New York Review of Books,* for which he has been writing since 1964. He has resumed his education and as Distinguished Scholar in Residence at the American University in Washington is studying Greek philosophy, history, sociology, and literature while working on a book about the freedom of thought and expression. "Izzy" is a short, stocky man, whose steel-rimmed spectacles give him "an owlish resemblance to Benjamin Franklin." He told Israel Shenker that he is "gregarious, strongly biased, morally arrogant," and likes "people of all kinds." Although he is an atheist, he feels deeply Jewish. Politically he says he is a socialist and a radical—"a real radical: one who gets to the roots of problems." His recreations include reading, listening to music, and dancing with his wife at a local disco.

Stone received the George Polk Memorial Award and a journalism award from Columbia University in 1971, the A. J. Liebling Award in

1972, and the Eleanor Roosevelt Peace Award from the National Committee for a Sane Nuclear Policy in 1975. He has a number of honorary degrees. Variously described as a gadfly, a Cassandra, a maverick, and a muckraker, Stone has earned comparison with Tom Paine, Edmund Burke, Upton Sinclair, and Lincoln Steffens. Sol Stern says that he is "an eternal optimist, forever hoping that the system, for all its imperfections, may yet deliver on its promises of a good society," and that he has fulfilled "the painful role of watchdog at a time when most of his colleagues bark rarely and bite not at all." To Elizabeth Drew he seems "one of the finest fogcutters in Washington," and "a living lesson in the potential of the journalist as outsider."

PRINCIPAL WORKS: The Court Disposes, 1937; Business as Usual: The First Year of Defense, 1941; Underground to Palestine, 1946 (reissued 1978); This Is Israel, 1948; The Hidden History of the Korean War, 1952; The Truman Era, 1953; The Haunted Fifties, 1963; In a Time of Torment, 1967; The Killings at Kent State: How Murder Went Unpunished, 1971; Polemics and Prophecies, 1967–1970, 1970; I.F. Stone's Weekly Reader, edited by Neil Middleton, 1973 (in England, The Best of I.F. Stone's Weekly).

ABOUT: Contemporary Authors 61–64, 1976; Current Biography, 1972; Paterson, T.G. (ed.) Cold War Critics, 1971; Who's Who in America, 1976–1977. Periodicals—Book World February 14, 1971; Christian Century November 4, 1970; Christian Science Monitor November 30, 1967; Commonweal January 26, 1968; Life January 21, 1972; Listener October 24, 1968; October 31, 1968; May 13, 1971; McCall's September 1971; Media and Methods December 1976; New York Review of Books December 5, 1968; New York Times November 19, 1968; New York Times Magazine January 22, 1978; Newsday January 20, 1968; Newsweek January 22, 1968; February 8, 1971; December 20, 1971; Ramparts February 1968, May 1974; Time February 8, 1971; December 20, 1971; Wall Street Journal July 14, 1970; Washington Post June 3, 1970.

STOPPARD, TOM (July 3, 1937–), British dramatist, was born Thomas Straussler in Zlin, Czechoslovakia, the second son of Dr. Eugene and Martha Straussler. His father, a company doctor for the Bata shoe company, was transferred to a Singapore factory, taking his family with him, at the time of the 1939 German invasion. When the Japanese overran Singapore three years later, Mrs. Straussler and her children were evacuated to India by the British: her husband remained behind and was killed. His widow subsequently married Kenneth Stoppard, a British Army officer stationed in India, whose name was also adopted by the two boys.

In 1946 the family moved to England, settling eventually in Bristol. Tom Stoppard was sent to a Nottinghamshire prep school and then to a boarding–grammar school at Pocklington in Yorkshire, which left him "thoroughly bored by the idea of anything intellectual." His ambition

New York Times/William E. Sauro

TOM STOPPARD

then was to be a war correspondent, and at the age of seventeen he joined the staff of Bristol's *Western Daily Press* as a general reporter. He says that he "got a bigger thrill from seeing my first by-line . . . than I did from having my first play on at the National."

After four years with the *Press*, Stoppard moved on in 1958 to the Bristol *Evening World* as a feature writer and drama critic. By that time John Osborne and the English Stage Company had arrived on the scene and "everybody of my age who wanted to write, wanted to write plays . . . and it struck me that I was never going to start writing unless I did something active about it." Feeling there was no more time to be lost, he turned freelance in 1960, wrote his first play, *A Walk on the Water* (subsequently staged as *Enter a Free Man*), and moved to London as theatre critic of *Scene* magazine. Under various pseudonyms, Stoppard reviewed one hundred and thirty-two shows in the seven months that *Scene* survived during 1963. The *nom de plume* he most favored was "William Boot," and this name, originally the property of the innocent journalist in Evelyn Waugh's novel *Scoop*, has recurred in Stoppard's plays.

Enter a Free Man reworks the theme of the impractical dreamer and the long-suffering family. George Riley, a failed inventor whose home is booby-trapped with gadgets like an "indoor rain" machine, is pinning his hopes on the idea of a reversible envelope with gum on both sides of the flap. Simultaneously his daughter is pursuing her own fantasy of a romantic elopement. Both dreams collapse when George's backer fades from the scene and the daughter's lover is unmasked as a married man. Set on a divided stage accommodating both George's living room and a pub interior, the piece is a neat comic mechanism with exceptionally sharp and literate dialogue. With its echoes of *Death of a Salesman* and Robert Bolt's *Flowering Cherry,* what it does not suggest is the presence of a strongly individual talent. But by the time of its belated 1968 London premiere, Stoppard had already revealed such a talent in *Rosencrantz and Guildenstern Are Dead* (1967).

This play, which won the *Evening Standard* award and made Stoppard's name, began life in 1964 in Berlin, where Stoppard spent six months on a Ford Foundation grant. In its original form it struck Stoppard's sponsor, Charles Marowitz, as "a lot of academic twaddle." Viewing the revised version, which reached the National Theatre via a fringe production at the Edinburgh Festival, Marowitz duly ate his words, and Ronald Bryden in the *Observer* saluted the event as "the most brilliant début by a young playwright since John Arden's."

The central idea of the play (originally suggested by Stoppard's agent) was to retell the plot of *Hamlet* from the viewpoint of the two attendant lords. Summoned to Elsinore and receiving a hasty briefing from the King, they are left alone in anterooms to make sense of their enigmatic situation. Periodically the court sweeps onstage to conduct its incomprehensible business and sweeps off again, leaving the two interchangeable partners stranded like driftwood on the beach. Accompanying Hamlet to England, they discover the letter containing their death warrant, and choose to deliver it so as to emerge, if only for a second, into lives of their own. Up to that moment they have a great deal of blank time to fill, but at no point does Stoppard make things easier for himself by introducing new material, least of all by inventing individual personalities for the two partners. The essential thing about them is that they are ciphers with no memory of the past, no understanding of the present, and no idea where they are going.

Much was made by some reviewers of the play's alleged existentialism, though Stoppard says "I didn't know what the word 'existential' meant until it was applied to *Rosencrantz.*" More to the point (as other critics observed) was the affinity between Stoppard's characters and the two tramps in Beckett's *Waiting for Godot,* who are likewise left hanging about at the mercy of some inexplicable grand design. The coin-spinning and word games with which Rosencrantz and Guildenstern pass the time show a fascination with philosophical paradox which is one of Stoppard's trademarks as a writer. Here, the games relate to chance and probability, thus allowing the partners a tiny area of free will in the midst of preordained tragedy. In this way, as Marowitz puts it, the play "becomes a blinding metaphor about the absurdity of life. We are summoned, we come. We are given roles, we play them. We are dismissed, we go. Have we ever been? Has there been a point? If so, what?"

Rosencrantz, which was in the National Theatre repertory for four years, reached New York in October 1967, carrying off the Antoinette Perry Award and the New York Drama Critics Circle Award as the best play of the 1968 season. MGM bought the screen rights and commissioned Stoppard to write a screenplay. This was never used, but all in all, the play is said to have earned its author about £350,000. Amid the general chorus of praise that greeted the play in Europe and the United States, Robert Brustein (in the *New Republic*) struck a sour note by complaining of a lack of "felt knowledge" in the writing. It is true that Stoppard's work is characterized by a curious weightlessness and by a view of the human race as if through the wrong end of a telescope. It is a viewpoint sometimes shared by his characters, like the philosopher hero of his prizewinning radio piece, *Albert's Bridge* (1967), who takes the job of painting a suspension bridge so as to acquire an ordered perspective on the world below. For critics like Brustein, Stoppard's claims as a serious writer are compromised by his taste for the flamboyantly frivolous. Another stumbling block to criticism is the fact that his plays resist synopsis. This problem does not arise with those that rely on an existing plot framework, like *Rosencrantz* or his television spy melodrama *Neutral Ground* (1968), based on Sophocles' *Philoctetes.* But in his wholly original work, plot often functions solely as a means of drawing together the ideas and images in which the real meaning resides.

The same is true of Stoppard's novel *Lord Malquist and Mr. Moon* (1966), whose message is summed up in the line: "Since we cannot hope for order let us withdraw with style from the chaos." The ninth and last Lord Malquist drives around Swinging London in his private coach, flinging chocolate money and bad checks to the poor, and coining aphorisms to be recorded by Mr. Moon, a perplexed Boswell hired at ten guineas a day. Moon carries for reassurance a bomb with which to liberate himself from his bewildered life if and when it should become insupportable. Adding to his miseries is his delicious wife Jane, who welcomes the embraces of Malquist (and of two imaginary cowboys) but has no time or use for Moon. In the end, Moon is exploded by someone else's bomb, his own (quite predictably) having failed him. "Here again," wrote Melvin Maddocks, "is Mr. Stoppard's charming passion for word-play. Events are seen once more through a slightly romantic pessimism. . . . At the heart of it lies Mr. Stoppard's iron-butterfly determination to deal with the most serious questions in the most witty way." Mordecai Richler thought this "a clever, dotty performance, a book full of amusing invention, bringing together an engaging band of screwballs with diverting results"—but "the author seems finally too charming, too gentle, for the material he has chosen."

Stoppard once said that his final objective was to contrive the "perfect marriage between the play of ideas and farce"; but *en route* towards that goal he also turned out several "nuts and bolts" comedies whose main interest lies in their staggering theatrical ingenuity. In his one-acter *The Real Inspector Hound* (1968), two theatre critics arrive for the first night of a parodied Agatha Christie thriller ("Hello," says the charlady into the telephone, "the drawing-room of Lady Muldoon's country residence one morning in early Spring?"), and are drawn into the stage action where their professional rivalries are played out to the death. *After Magritte* (1970) opens with a surrealist tableau (Magritte is Stoppard's favorite painter) which the play proceeds to reduce to rational terms. The joke is even more basic in *Dirty Linen* (1976), which shows a parliamentary select committee on public morals falling victim *en masse* to a skirtless secretary called Miss Gotobed ("You do speedwriting I suppose?" "Yes, if I'm given enough time.") Stoppard's output also includes smaller radio and television plays, several screenplays, stage adaptations of Mrożek's *Tango* and Lorca's *The House of Bernarda Alba,* and some seventy episodes of a radio serial for the BBC's Arabic service. An ex-journalist, he has regarded himself, at least until recently, as a writer "for hire." And his first two major works after *Rosencrantz—Jumpers* (1972) and *Travesties* (1974)—were commissioned respectively by the National Theatre and the Royal Shakespeare Company.

Jumpers is set in the future, with England under a Radical-Liberal government which has converted the churches into gymnasiums and appointed a veterinarian as Archbishop of Canterbury. The first moon landing has given people a new perspective on the earth, and dismantled the traditional moral absolutes. Against this background we witness the convulsive efforts of George Moore, a professor of ethics, to make out a case for the existence of God. George's disintegrating universe is reflected in his immediate environment. His wife Dotty has given up her stage career (finding she can no longer sing songs about the moon) and taken Sir Archibald Jumpers, the head of the philosophy department, as her lover. Sir Archibald also manages a team of philosopher-gymnasts, including a professor of logic, who is shot dead while forming part of a human pyramid in the first scene of the play. The ensuing murder investigation develops along the farcical lines of *Inspector Hound,* while George remains in his study wrestling with his lecture in defense of a benevolent deity.

The obvious objection to *Jumpers* is that although its separate elements have their own spheres of vitality, they do not quite link up. But if the intended union of farce and ideas is not fully consummated, there is no question that they meet and embrace in the person of George himself, a compound of impotent kindliness and intellectual vanity who finally emerges from his metaphysical labyrinth with the declaration: "I don't claim to *know* that God exists, I only claim that he does without my knowing it." Both the character and the play exemplify the centrifugal nature of Stoppard's work: a quality that seems to stem from his sense that the world consists of such a multitude of interrelated phenomena that nothing can be treated in isolation.

Among the reviewers who admired Stoppard's wicked satire on logical positivism and his agility as an intellectual clown, Michael Billington in the *Guardian* also recognized *Jumpers* as a "deeply moral play." To others, like Stanley Kauffmann (in the *New Republic*) the author remained a "juvenile" performer who employed weighty themes simply as "trampolines for undergraduate acrobatics." Kauffmann objected similarly to Stoppard's *Travesties,* which sets out to debate the rival claims of artistic and political revolution. *Travesties,* which brought Stoppard his second Antoinette Perry Award in 1976, takes its cue from the historical fact that Lenin, James Joyce, and the Dadaist Tristan Tzara were all living in Zurich during World War I. With those three giants to call on, Stoppard chooses as his hero a minor British consular official named Henry Carr of whom history records nothing except that he once sued Joyce for the cost of a pair of trousers.

The facts of the case are that Joyce, as business manager of a short-lived theatre company, invited Carr to play in *The Importance of Being Earnest,* and then refused to meet Carr's expenses for Algy's wardrobe. From this obscure footnote to *Ulysses* Stoppard spins out a web to snare his three revolutionaries in the same play. The action is presented by Carr as an aged nonentity recalling a time when Joyce and Co. were equally unknown. And while there is no firm evidence that the three principals ever met,

Stoppard overcomes the problem by involving them in a rewritten version of Wilde's comedy. Reverting to youth, Carr figures as Algy, Tzara as Jack, and Joyce as Lady Bracknell; while the two girls, Gwendolen and Cecily, cultivate a serious-minded attachment to the works of Joyce and Lenin which forms an obstacle to their two frivolous suitors.

Like *Jumpers, Travesties* consists of a complex action built around a central monologue. In performance, it operates through manifold time changes and action recapitulations, with dialogue switching between musical comedy and Wildean pastiche, grey official prose from Lenin's widow, and artfully rambling reminiscence from old Henry Carr, whose faltering consciousness is allegedly conjuring the whole thing up. Stoppard does not succeed in absorbing Lenin into the Wildean substructure, but otherwise he has discovered a form that articulates his ideas. As it turns out, though, the ideas have less to do with art and politics than with the fallibility of history. Just as George in *Jumpers* demonstrates the impossibility of knowing whether God exists, so Carr in *Travesties* is a walking refutation of the possibility of any objective knowledge of the past.

To his unsympathetic critics, *Travesties* supplied further evidence against Stoppard as an "undergraduate prankster." But, aside from the brilliance of the pranks, it is clear from the whole body of his work that Stoppard is attracted to philosophy for the most serious reasons and that he has philosophical justification for adopting the mask of the clown. "My plays," he says, "are a lot to do with the fact that I just don't know. But I believe all political acts must be judged in moral terms, in terms of consequences. . . . One thing I feel sure about is that the materialistic view of history is an insult to the human race."

These concerns became central in the two plays that followed in 1977, so that critics wrote of the "politicizing" of Tom Stoppard and of a progress from intellectual acrobatics to moral commitment. Stoppard himself says that "it was really only a coincidence that both these plays about human rights should have been written about the same time." He explains that the television play *Professional Foul* was inspired by Amnesty International's Prisoner of Conscience Year, while *Every Good Boy Deserves Favour* was written at the request of André Previn, conductor of the London Symphony Orchestra. Previn wrote the score for this "play for actors and orchestra," though it was Stoppard who chose the theme.

Stoppard's musical experience was limited to playing the triangle in a kindergarten band, an accomplishment shared by one of the play's two central characters. He is an inmate of a Russian mental hospital who imagines, as he tinkles his triangle, that he is conducting a full orchestra. "I know what you're thinking," he says to his audience of one, ending a performance with a bang on the triangle. "The cellos are rubbish." The "bitter irony and deep indignation" critics detected beneath the play's surface brilliance proceed from the fact that the madman's cellmate has been incarcerated there not because he is insane but because he is a political dissident. It turns out that the two men have the same name, so that, as Mel Gussow wrote, "the plot turns on the cracked-mirror confusion of the two identities." The uniformed colonel in charge of the hospital, a semanticist rather than a psychiatrist, is the source of much Stoppardian wit.

Every Good Boy Deserves Favour had an elaborate one-night stand in July 1977 at the Royal Festival Hall in London, with the whole of the London Symphony Orchestra on stage. With the score revised for a smaller orchestra of about thirty players, it ran the following year at theatres in London, New York, and elsewhere. "The short script," Mel Gussow wrote, "is filled with the author's usual felicitous turns of phrase, his deviously manipulative conceits, his lunatic lexicon of puns, literary allusions and rodomontade wordplays. Furthermore, a man with an orchestra in his head is a spectacular notion, and Mr. Stoppard improvises deliriously on the theme." All the same, it seemed to Gussow, the work remains a hybrid, and is "less a play than a playful puzzle."

This was a fairly common critical response to *EGBDF;* there was a different kind of press for *Professional Foul,* first seen on British television in September 1977 and in the United States the following year. Influenced by a trip to Russia in 1976, his own Czech birth, and the arrest in January 1977 of the dissident Czech dramatist Vaclav Havel, as well as by his commitment to Amnesty International, Stoppard produced in *Professional Foul* a play that is as full of intellectual *tours de force* and ironic wit as anything he has written, but which is also emotionally involving and moving. It is about a Cambridge University professor of ethics who goes to Prague to participate in an academic convention (and to enjoy an important soccer match). A cold man, whose interest in ethics is professional rather than personal, he is not pleased when he is accosted by Pavel Hollar, a former student of his at Cambridge, who asks him to smuggle out to the West an essay attacking the denial of human rights in Czechoslovakia. Professor Anderson has no wish whatever to involve himself in other people's political problems and goes to Hollar's flat to refuse his request and return the essay. When he gets there he finds that Hollar has been arrested, and he is himself detained for a while by the political police who are searching the apartment. Shaken by this encounter and its implications, he discards the harmless technical paper he had prepared and splendidly embarrasses his hosts at the convention with a speech in defense of intellectual freedom, before smuggling Hollar's essay out of Czechoslovakia in an obnoxious colleague's soft-core porn magazine.

The stage play *Night and Day* (1978) is set in an imaginary African country where three British journalists go to cover a civil war. The plot is partly one of straight professional rivalry between Wagner, an old pro, and Milne, an ambitious freelance who has scooped an interview with the rebel leader. Wagner, a union militant, despises Milne as a "scab" who has defied a journalists' strike, and their conflict gains another dimension from the fact that they both want the same woman. Irving Wardle said that, unlike Evelyn Waugh in *Scoop,* "Stoppard writes as a man who still cherishes some ideals about journalism and even finds it glamorous, and therein lies both the strength and the weakness of the play. . . . Stoppard has always excelled in inventing theatrical forms for whatever he wants to talk about; but even for him, it is a signal triumph to have related . . . [an African war and the wars of Fleet Street] within the discipline of a nuts-and-bolts naturalistic play."

Tom Stoppard has two sons by his 1965 marriage to Jose Ingle, which ended in divorce, and two by his 1972 marriage to Dr. Miriam Moore-Robinson. She is a physician and the author of a book on child care who now works as managing director of the British branch of an international pharmaceutical company. Stoppard, a Fellow of the Royal Society of Literature, received a C.B.E. in 1978. Kenneth Tynan says that because Stoppard "has a loose, lanky build, a loose thatch of curly dark hair, loose, liver-tinted lips, dark, flashing eyes, and long, flashing teeth, you might mistake him for an older brother of Mick Jagger." He is very nearly as witty in conversation as he is on paper. Like Vladimir Nabokov, whom he greatly admires, he is addicted to puns, and has been known to describe himself as "a bounced Czech." In fact, no one could seem more English—in his command of the language, in his manner, and in his tastes, which include a passionate devotion to cricket, as spectator and player.

PRINCIPAL PUBLISHED WORKS: *Plays*—Rosencrantz and

Guildenstern Are Dead, 1967; Enter a Free Man, 1968; The Real Inspector Hound, 1968; A Separate Peace (in Playbill 2, edited by Alan Durband, 1969); Albert's Bridge (*with* If You're Glad I'll Be Frank), 1969; After Magritte, 1971; Jumpers, 1972; Artist Descending a Staircase (*with* Where Are They Now?): Two Plays for Radio, 1973; Travesties, 1975; The Real Inspector Hound (*with* After Magritte), 1975; Dirty Linen (*with* New-Found-Land), 1976; Every Good Boy Deserves Favour (*with* Professional Foul), 1978; Night and Day, 1978. *Fiction*—Lord Malquist and Mr. Moon, 1966. *Stories in* Introduction 2: Stories by New Writers, 1964; Evergreen Review July 1968. *As Adapter*—Tango, by Slawomir Mrozek, 1968.

ABOUT: Bigsby, C.W.E. Tom Stoppard (Writers and Their Work), 1976; Brustein, R. The Third Theatre, 1969; Current Biography, 1975; Kerr, W. Thirty Plays Hath November, 1969; Marowitz, C. Confessions of a Counterfeit Critic, 1973; McCrindle, J.F. (ed.) Behind the Scenes, 1971; Taylor, J.R. Anger and After, 1969; Taylor, J.R. The Second Wave, 1971; Vinson, J. (ed.) Contemporary Dramatists, 1977; Who's Who, 1978; Who's Who in the Theatre, 1977. *Periodicals*—Encounter November 1975; Guardian April 12, 1967; March 21, 1973; Horizon April 1978; London Magazine August-September 1976; New Review December 1974; Look December 26, 1967; New York Times April 23, 1974; October 19, 1975; January 9, 1977; April 23, 1978; August 6, 1978; New Yorker May 4, 1968; December 19, 1977; Newsweek August 7, 1967; November 10, 1975; Observer December 17, 1967; Philosophy January 1975; Saturday Review January 8, 1977; Sunday Times Magazine (London) June 9, 1974; Theatre Quarterly May-July 1974; Time May 6, 1974; November 10, 1975; Times (London) November 11, 1972; November 10, 1978; Times Literary Supplement July 12, 1974; Transatlantic Review Summer 1968; Vogue October 15, 1967; Village Voice May 1, 1978.

STRAND, MARK (April 11, 1934–), American poet, was born in Summerside, Prince Edward Island, Canada, the son of Robert Strand and the former Sonia Apter. He was educated at Antioch College, Ohio (B.A., 1957), and went on to study painting under Joseph Albers at Yale (B.F.A., 1959). Strand decided that he was not "destined to be a very good painter," and became a poet instead, winning the Cook and Bergen prizes at Yale. He spent 1960–1961 in Italy with a Fulbright scholarship to the University of Florence. Strand was married in 1961 to Antonia Ratensky, and has a daughter, Jessica. He says that the teachers who influenced him most were Nolan Miller at Antioch and Donald Justice at the State University of Iowa, where Strand went as a graduate student (M.A., 1962) and remained as an instructor (1962–1965). In 1965–1966 he taught at the University of Brazil as a Fulbright lecturer, returning in 1967 to take up an assistant professorship at Mount Holyoke College, Massachusetts. He was a visiting professor at the University of Washington, Seattle, in 1968 and 1970, and at Yale in 1969, when he joined the Columbia faculty as an adjunct associate professor. Strand left Columbia to become an associate professor at Brooklyn Col-

STRAND

MARK STRAND

lege (1970–1972), and since 1973 has been the Bain-Swiggett Lecturer at Princeton.

Sleeping With One Eye Open, his first book, appeared in 1964 and established him at once as an impressive and disturbing new voice in American poetry. These poems and prose poems were spare, compact, and at first sight seemed unfashionably simple. But beneath their translucent surfaces glide terrible shadows—panicky doubts about the identity of the poet and the reality he describes with such desperate calm, a sense of imminent disaster barely contained by the poems' orderly structures, and sneaking in through dark dreams, disquieting puns, the blank faces of mirrors:

> . . . . the dark has made us
> Wonder where we are, and where
> We were, and who we are
> Thinking of where we were
> And, even, if.
>
> (from "In the Mountains")

In 1968, having learned, according to Richard Howard, from Rafael Alberti (whom he has translated), from the Surrealist painter Magritte, and from Jorge Luis Borges, the Argentinian master of labyrinths and mirrors, Strand published his second book, *Reasons for Moving.* His themes had not much altered, Howard said, but here "the buried metaphors . . . are discarded in favor of the explicit ones of narrative, of anecdote"; there is a new grotesquerie and playfulness, and the delicacy and decorum of mere verse are decisively rejected: "Ink runs down from the corners of my mouth./ There is no happiness like mine./ I have been eating poetry!

. . ./ I am a new man." These poems, Howard thought, "tell one story and one story only: they narrate the moment when Strand makes Rimbaud's discovery, that . . . the self is someone else, even something else":

> In a field
> I am the absence
> of field.
> This is always the case.
> Wherever I am
> I am what is missing . . .
>
> We all have reasons
> for moving.
> I move
> to keep things whole.
>
> (from "Keeping
> Things Whole")

And if this is true of the poet, what of the poem?: "The poem that has stolen these words from my mouth/ may not be this poem." Howard adds that "a new and particular pleasure of these poems . . . is an observation of occurrence, a communication of the *quality* of an occasion. . . . It is justice to the visible world which Strand renders, though he walks 'in the morning sun/ invisible/ as anyone,' and the wonderful thing . . . about these paragraphs of hallucination where everyday emblems of conversational phrasing are lifted to sudden lyric intensity by syntax, by the 'sound of sentences,' is that in the richest possible acceptation they are *visionary poems.*" Marius Bewley was almost as much impressed. Noting the profound subjectivity of these poems, he said that they nevertheless, at their best, reflect "a subjective life which is *general*: that is, if these images are private they nonetheless find their corresponding reflections in the hidden inwardness of most men"; it is "in this exquisitely established correspondence" that such a poem as "The Man in the Tree" achieves "its meaning and its integrity as a work of art."

Darker (1970) was another virtuoso performance, in which Strand widened his range while sharpening his focus, and employed when he chose to a new opulence of imagery and diction. It includes some apocalyptic political poems in which, according to Richard Howard, "the poet conjugates the nightmares of Fortress America with his own stunned mortality," other poems on "the wars of filiation, marriage and paternity," and a series of "astonishing meditations . . . on the death our bodies create and court as the cost and the consequence of identity, as its reward." In "From a Litany" in this collection, Strand for the first time moves beyond the stanza form to experiment with a mode resembling chanted litanies—series of imagistic statements that look as if they might begin or end anywhere but which, in the words of Laurence Lieberman, inveigle the reader's ear "with a mastery of tonal resonance that . . . [leaves] the aftertaste of an organic unity all but impossible to locate or account for by conventional inspection of the structure."

At this stage in his career, Strand was one of the most admired and influential American poets of his generation—a much-emulated magician who could both terrify and delight, who could do marvelous tricks with mirrors, whose brilliant patter never faltered while he sawed himself in half before one's very eyes. In *The Story of Our Lives* (1973), everything was different; the virtuoso performer had been supplanted by an elegist, mourning the death of his father, of his mother and his childhood, of his marriage (he was divorced in 1973), of his former aesthetic convictions and procedures. In place of the taut and elegant poems of earlier books were sprawling and hypnotic dirges, austere in diction, like the long, slow, incantatory "Elegy for My Father," which draws on the litanistic mode introduced in *Darker*. Some poems about the end of the poet's marriage employ a "strategy of self-discovery" which in Lieberman's opinion "challenges the narrowness" of the confessional school of poetry.

The Story of Our Lives also contains "The Untelling," which most critics regard as Strand's finest poem so far. It is a very long poem in which the adult speaker struggles to recover an incident from his childhood, a moment of epiphany which at the time he was unable to use or share. As Lieberman says, "the persona tells the same story, again and again, in his struggle to reconcile—or reconnect—his adult identity with a missing part of himself locked in his past. The poem begins with maximum distance, remove, between the adult and the child . . . and by a cyclic progression—toward and away, toward and away—they finally coincide." Towards the end of the poem, Lieberman writes (in his very detailed review in *Poetry*, August 1974), the music of the poem "is prolongedly holding its breath, and in listening, a reader finds that if the tone of poetry is superbly well modulated, a poem can stop breathing, but its life continues." Then a different music imperceptibly emerges:

> he was alone in the dark,
> unable to speak.
> He stood still.
> He felt the world recede
> into the clouds,
> into the shelves of art.
> He closed his eyes. . . .
> He felt himself at that moment to be
> more than his need to survive,
> more than his losses,
> because he was less than anything.
> He swayed back and forth.
> The silence was in him
> and it rose like joy,
> like the beginning. . . .

Lieberman has called this "a Wordsworthian vision of self reborn." John N. Morris wrote that "the ending of the poem, its undoing, unravelling, is not really a surprise so much as it is a confirmation, a perfection; the pleasure it provides is repeatable and lasting"; " 'The Untelling' is one of the very few nearly permanent American poems of recent years."

The Monument (1978) showed that Strand had lost nothing of his brilliance as a prestidigitator. The book consists of fifty-two numbered sections, most of them less than a page in length, most of them in prose, meditating on artistic immortality, the nature of fictions, and the problems of translation. *The Monument* is addressed "to the translator of *The Monument* in the Future" and this seems arrogant until the reader is given to understand that what he is reading *is* the projected translation (but from what language?). Thus, in Section 26, the writer confesses to his future translator "a yearning to make prophetic remarks. . . . I know it is sad, even silly, this longing to say something that will charm or amaze others later on. But one little phrase is all I ask. Friend, say something amazing *for* me. It must be something you take for granted, something meaningless to you, but impossible for me to think of. Say I predicted it." The unnamed translator appends this note: "Though I wanted to obey the author's request, I could not without violating what I took to be his desire for honesty. I believe he not only wanted it this way, but might have predicted it."

"It is to defeat death that the work exists," wrote William Logan in his review of *The Monument,* "and the act of translation, of carrying across from one language into another, insures survival by metamorphosis. . . . I cannot suggest here the work's intriguing consistencies, its clever reversals, or its tone, which is both serious and insouciant. *The Monument* is a jeu d'esprit, but bears comparison to the haunted poems of . . . *The Story of Our Lives.*" The same year Strand published a collection of lyrics called *The Late Hour,* which was said to contain some of his "simplest and most extraordinarily beautiful poems." Logan concluded that "no poet his age has a more human voice or a more piercing melancholy. Strand's mature work, more than ever concerned with mortality, makes one feel alive."

Strand received an Ingram Merrill fellowship in 1966, a grant from the National Council for the Arts and Humanities in 1967, a Rockefeller award in 1968, and one from the National Institute of Arts and Letters in 1975, when he also held a Guggenheim fellowship.

PRINCIPAL WORKS: *Poetry*—Sleeping With One Eye Open, 1964; Reasons for Moving, 1968; Darker, 1970; The Story of Our Lives, 1973; The Sargeantville Notebook, 1973; The Monument, 1978; The Late Hour, 1978. *As Translator*—Eighteen Poems From the Quechua, 1971; The Owl's Insomnia (poems by Rafael Alberti), 1973. *As Editor*—The Contemporary American Poets, 1969; New Poetry of Mexico, 1970; (with Charles Simic) Another Republic: Seventeen European and South American Writers, 1976.

ABOUT: Contemporary Authors 21–24 1st revision, 1977; Howard, R. Alone With America, 1969; Malkoff, K. Crowell's Handbook of Contemporary American Poetry, 1973; Shaw, R.B. (ed.) American Poetry Since 1960, 1973; Vinson, J. (ed.) Contemporary American Poetry, 1975. *Periodicals*—Chicago Review Spring 1977; Hudson Review Winter 1968–1969, Winter 1970–1971, Spring 1973; Library Journal, March 15, 1978; Nation April 24, 1967; New Republic July 29, 1978; New Statesman June 16, 1967; Ohio Review Winter 1972; Poetry June 1966, August 1974; Saturday Review August 24, 1968; Seneca Review April 1971; Shenandoah Winter 1969, Summer 1971; Southern Review January 1972; Times Literary Supplement September 15, 1978; Yale Review Autumn 1968.

STRAUSSLER, THOMAS. *See* STOPPARD, TOM

STRAWSON, SIR P(ETER) F(REDERICK) (November 23, 1919–), English philosopher, writes: "I was born in London, the second of four children, and grew up in the suburb of Finchley, where I went to school. My father, a London schoolmaster, had indifferent health and died when I was sixteen. We were rather poor. Both my parents had studied English literature and I won a scholarship in that subject at Oxford in the year of my father's death. I decided, nevertheless, to read Philosophy, Politics and Economics at Oxford, being moved partly by the political and economic problems of the time, partly by the beginnings of an interest in philosophical ideas and partly by a distaste for the thought of treating literature as matter for academic study. Philosophy soon became my dominant intellectual interest. My old ambition —to be a poet—succumbed to it. I wanted instead to be a don and doubted whether I could be. After my six years of war service I was lucky enough to be appointed to a junior lectureship in Wales, whence, after a year, I returned to Oxford.

P. F. STRAWSON

"There, in those post-war years, philosophy flourished as it had not flourished in Oxford since the fourteenth century. There was a great release of intellectual energy; there were brilliant people and brilliant insights, a flame of wit and subtlety in which it seemed that vagueness, muddle and pretentious obscurity must be finally consumed. Even moderate talents were carried by the general surge of excitement to levels of performance they would scarcely have achieved in ordinary times. It seemed almost that we might soon clear up the whole ancient mess and finish philosophy. That intoxication wore off, of course; and, as it did, the old problems were seen to be still there, looking almost, but not quite, as obdurate as ever. Soberer efforts at more constructive and systematic thinking were resumed. Later still, more account began to be taken of the technicalities of formal or mathematical logic. But continuity was preserved, philosophy was still conceived of as a critical and analytical activity, distinct from, though not indifferent to, scholarship on the one hand and the formal and natural sciences on the other, but, like them, impersonal and subject to correction; and hence quite distinct, too, from creative literature.

"My own life as a writer and teacher is simply a part of this story. I taught, as Oxford dons do, across a wide range of philosophical issues, and enjoyed tutorial teaching; discussed enormously with colleagues in the earlier part of this period, less as time went on; and wrote my books and articles. Ideas and illumination come to one, certainly, in teaching and discussion; but it is in the solitary struggle with the problem in thought, and in the attempt to set things out clearly in writing, that the real test, the real labour and the sense of achievement are found. Or so it is for me. One cannot expect to get anything absolutely right in philosophy. In the nature of the case, the idea of the finally right answer is only a regulative idea, an ideal of reason. Neither can one expect so to express one's thought that the expression is proof against misunderstanding. But the impulse to defend, or explain, or correct, my productions, once they are out, is weak in me. Let them take care of themselves. There is always another task; and I generally have the sense of approaching every thing I attempt *de novo*.

"My private and personal life has been in no way unusual. I married in my twenty-sixth year and have two sons and two daughters. I count myself fortunate in my family. My tastes are conservative, my principles liberal. I have no religious beliefs. Philosophy has flourished in my time, as have academic studies in general. Most other developments characteristic of the period I have viewed without enthusiasm, many with dislike, some with dismay. Besides philosophy and English and French literature, I have greatly loved landscape, architecture, wine and the company of clever or beautiful women. I have travelled and taught in the United States and other countries. Most things I prize I associate with the now menaced civilization of the Mediterranean world and Western Europe. I count myself fortunate again to have lived while something of it still survives."

P. F. Strawson is the son of Cyril Walter Strawson and the former Nellie Dora Jewell. His younger brother is Major-General John Michael Strawson, C.B., O.B.E. He went to school at Christ's College, in the north London suburb of Finchley, and from there, as he says, won a scholarship to St. John's College, Oxford University (1937–1940). After graduating, the beginning of his career was delayed by the war, in which he served as an army officer in the Royal Artillery (1940–1942) and the Royal Electrical and Mechanical Engineers (1942–1946), ending with the rank of captain. In 1945 he married Grace Hall Martin. Of his year as a junior lecturer in philosophy at the University College of North Wales he is reported as saying: "I didn't know what provincialism was until I got there," so that he was delighted to get an appointment as John Locke Scholar (1947) in his own university of Oxford, where he has since continued to live and work, first as a lecturer in philosophy, then as fellow and praelector in philosophy at University College (1948–1968), and since August 1968 as Waynflete Professor of Metaphysical Philosophy.

Strawson therefore became really active as a professional philosopher in the Oxford of the immediate postwar years, when the philosophical ferment there was dominated by Austin and Ryle, both of whom greatly influenced him. Though they differed profoundly in style, their methods had something in common, both giving scrupulous attention to the actual logical properties of words, as exhibited in their everyday use, untainted by special philosophical definitions. And it was in this tradition of "ordinary language philosophy" that Strawson began, doing close, detailed work on a few concepts in philosophical logic.

He first made his mark with his famous criticism of Bertrand Russell's theory of definite descriptions in an article called "On Referring," published in *Mind* in 1950. Russell maintained that any sentence like "The *f* is *g*"—for example, "The king of France is bald"—is properly analyzed in these terms: "There is a king of France. There is not more than one king of France. There is nothing which is king of France and which is not bald." Strawson argued that this analysis confuses a *reference* to an entity with an *assertion* of its existence. And he suggested that this confusion derived from another —Russell's supposition that every sentence must be either true, false, or meaningless. Strawson pointed out that to say, for example, that the king of France is bald is certainly meaningful, but it is at present neither true nor false (since there is no king of France). The theory of definite descriptions never fully recovered from this attack, which Russell did not take kindly.

Introduction to Logical Theory (1952), Strawson's first book, attempted rather more than the title promised. What it says about the nature of formal logic is less striking and original than its comparison of formal logic and ordinary language. Contrasting the behavior of ordinary words with the behavior of logical symbols, Strawson shows that ideal systems fail to represent the great complexity of ordinary language —and indeed that they perform this function even less adequately than had been supposed.

In the mid-1950s, Strawson's interest shifted from ordinary language philosophy to what he called "descriptive metaphysics"—descriptive in that he was concerned to *describe* "the most general features of our conceptual structure" rather than to seek improvements in the way we think about the world. Strawson's "descriptive metaphysics" was introduced in *Individuals* (1959), the most important and influential of his writings. Seeking to understand how language works, he asks if some subjects are more easily identified and discussed than others. He concludes (with Aristotle) that a material object, such as a man or a horse, is a more basic object of reference than a nonmaterial entity like a number or a feeling or a taste. He goes on to argue that in our conceptual structure two kinds of particulars are basic: material bodies and persons, the latter being thought of as essentially, though not solely, corporeal beings.

Individuals argues against the whole tradition of classical British empiricism, which has it that the basic particulars of language are not objects but our sensory impressions of them. The book also breaks completely with the spirit of postwar Oxford philosophy, employing the piecemeal investigation of ordinary language only as an adjunct to the discussion of the sort of large metaphysical questions that Austin had ruled out of court. According to John R. Searle, "the notion of 'descriptive metaphysics' has been as influential as the actual theses advanced in *Individuals*. More than any other single work, this book has resurrected metaphysics (albeit descriptive metaphysics) as a respectable philosophical enterprise."

Searle suggests that in *Individuals* Strawson "employs essentially Kantian methods to arrive at Aristotelian conclusions." *The Bounds of Sense,* which followed in 1966, is a study of Kant and especially of *The Critique of Pure Reason.* In a radio discussion with Brian Magee, Strawson described himself as trying "to perform the intellectual equivalent of a surgical operation on the body of a great philosopher's greatest work." He wanted to rescue from the book Kant's doctrine concerning the necessary general structure of experience (which has much in common with that posited in *Individuals*), but to cut away a second and connected body of ideas which Strawson regards as false, and indeed nonsensical. This was the doctrine of "transcendental idealism," according to which we ourselves shape the world of appearance. Not all of the book's reviewers were fully persuaded by Strawson's arguments, but there was general agreement that this was a lucid and serious piece of philosophy.

Strawson has not abandoned his work in philosophical logic, and twelve essays on subjects in this area were collected in *Logico-Linguistic Papers* (1971). A second and more wide-ranging volume of essays was published in 1974 as *Freedom and Resentment.* It included pieces on ethics (for example, the title essay, which seeks to reconcile some conflicting positions on the issue of free will), on the mind-body problem, on perception, and on aesthetics. Densely argued and rather technical as they

were, these essays were "written with Strawson's well-known clarity and precision."

In the second part of *Individuals,* Strawson had concentrated on the distinction between particulars and universals, showing how this is connected with the distinction between subject and predicate in a sentence. This argument is developed in *Subject and Predicate in Logic and Grammar* (1974), which seeks to construct a program for a "perspicuous grammar"—a set of universal requirements that rules must satisfy to qualify as rules of grammar. *Choice*'s reviewer found the work "at Strawson's usual high standard of rigor and insight," but thought it did not "represent a significant step beyond what he has already said on the topic." On the other hand there was a generally hostile review from Peter Geach in the *Times Literary Supplement.* It seemed to Geach that there was "much of interest and value" in passages devoted to issues of an "epistemological or psychological or even sociological" nature, but that the material relating to Strawson's grammar was "opaque, and thick with new and ill-explained technical terms."

Brian Magee points out that Strawson may be seen in retrospect to have followed a very logical development in the nature and content of his thought. And Strawson himself has said that "anyone who's interested both in language and in general structural features of human thinking will surely find it natural enough to think about grammar, which is, if anything is, structured, however bizarrely and capriciously it may seem to be structured in particular cases, in particular languages." The author was visiting professor at Duke University, North Carolina, in 1955–1956, a fellow of the Humanities Council and visiting associate professor at Princeton in 1960–1961, and visiting professor there in 1972. He is a foreign honorary member of the American Academy of Arts and Sciences. According to Ved Mehta, Strawson is recognized "by both undergraduates and his colleagues to be the most high-powered and creative philosopher in England." He received a knighthood in 1977.

PRINCIPAL WORKS: Introduction to Logical Theory, 1952; Individuals: An Essay in Descriptive Metaphysics, 1959; The Bounds of Sense, 1966; Logico-Linguistic Papers, 1971; Freedom and Resentment, 1974; Subject and Predicate in Logic and Grammar, 1974. *As Editor*—Philosophical Logic, 1967; Studies in the Philosophy of Thought and Action, 1968.

ABOUT: Ayer, A.J. The Concept of a Person, 1963; Contemporary Authors 25–28 1st revision, 1977; Coval, S.C. Philosophy and Phenomenological Research, 1964; Edwards, P. (ed.) The Encyclopaedia of Philosophy, 1967; Magee, B. (ed.) Modern British Philosophy, 1971; Mehta, V. Fly and the Fly-Bottle, 1963; O'Connor, D.J. (ed.) A Critical History of Western Philosophy, 1963; Who's Who,

1978. *Periodicals*— Listener January 28, 1971; Mind January 1961, July 1971, July 1972; New Statesman July 19, 1974; Philosophical Quarterly July 1969; Philosophy October 1961; Times Literary Supplement June 1, 1967; June 28, 1974; February 28, 1975.

TATE, JAMES (VINCENT) (December 8, 1943–), American poet, was born in Kansas City, Missouri, the son of Robert Sears Tate, a banker, and the former Betty Whitsitt. His father, a wartime pilot, was killed in action over Germany in 1944, when Tate was five months old. Tate attended the University of Missouri in 1963–1964, and received his B.A. in 1965 at Kansas State College. In 1966 he went to the University of Iowa as a graduate student and instructor in creative writing, earning his M.F.A. in 1967. In 1967–1968 he was a visiting instructor at the University of California, Berkeley, and the following year he traveled in Europe, returning in 1969 to become an assistant professor of English at Columbia.

Tate's first significant collection, *The Lost Pilot* (1967), was published in the Yale Series of Younger Poets when he was still in his early twenties. It contains more than fifty poems— "lively fantasies that are mock-ingenuously presented through a deadpan tone," or lyrics dealing with what one reviewer called "the great simplicities—time, love, life, fate, and death." Harold Jaffe was reminded of Robert Lowell but wrote that Tate's "low-keyed, off-hand style is his own and counterpoints forcefully with the feelings of estrangement, anger, and self-abasing humor to be found in a good many of these poems." Many reviewers were moved by the title piece, about the poet's dead father, and several received an impression in some of these poems of emotional intensity, pain, or even despair only just held in check. Other poems were enjoyed for their "freshness, attractive eccentricity, winning irreverence," but seemed fragmentary or purposeless—scarcely surprising in view of the fact that most of the poems in the collection were written in the course of a single year.

The book was extremely popular, especially with young readers, and Tate maintained his remarkable output, publishing eight or nine slim volumes through small presses during the next two years, among them *The Torches, Notes of Woe,* and *Row With Your Hair.* By 1970 P. H. Marvin was able to write that Tate had "set a fashion in style for many of the young poets of the 1960s: short personal lyrics, most of which are wittily whimsical and surrealistic in progression of thought. Underneath this facade are discernible questions of identity, motive, friendship, and ennui. But cleverly arranged metaphors and verbal gyrations do not replace

© 1979 by Jill Krementz

JAMES TATE

profundity." This glum tone was shared by most of Tate's reviewers at the time. Ronald Moran, discussing *Notes of Woe* and *Row With Your Hair,* wrote that "the acute perception of image, the sure rhythmic touch, the lyric founded on narrative" that he had so admired in *The Lost Pilot* "have been sacrificed in favor of wild excursions in image, metaphor, and subject. Tate is apparently determined to be *new,* at whatever cost." That there were grounds for these complaints, as well as for Tate's continuing popularity, is demonstrated by a witty, self-conscious, rather mechanically disquieting poem, "Camping in the Valley," from the 1968 volume of that title:

> Here is a place for my gun.
> I need everything less and less,
> have you noticed?
> But I feel something, almost
>
> anything is having some effect
> on me. I think I believe
> what I'm saying.
> Are you having a little trouble
>
> keeping up, dear?
> Now I am ready to survive,
> though I suppose we are in danger
> sitting here, arms crossed,
>
> in the valley
> with the black pig on the spit,
> our little doggy.
> I have faith the air will
>
> soon cohere or speak,
> tomorrow morning as you are

pulling on your boots,
my love, by the fire.

... Yes, it behooves us
to close our eyelids again,
the cold front, the rain,
the sun rising around 5:17,

an important mission in the morning:
what was it? The juniper berries?
The death we thought we left
in the mountains like a child.

The critics were somewhat cheered by Tate's second major book, *The Oblivion Ha-Ha* (1970), containing sixty poems filled with what William H. Pritchard called "sporty surrealist moments" —"I am encouraged to swallow/ the Scotch tape which/ has nothing to do with *bliss*"; "Brown mice scuttle like soft/ flexible jeeps out of the pine trees." Pritchard wrote that "Tate can do this sort of thing all night and very well too; he is extremely assured, both within the poetic line, where he never seems to be straining or nervous or pompous, or at the poetry-reading lectern." James Atlas was worried by Tate's assaults on "the precision of symbolism," but allowed that he was sometimes brilliant "and writes as well as anyone under thirty. He has borrowed with a studied ease the style of poets like James Wright and Robert Bly, and echoes their [antiwar] politics." A reviewer in the *Virginia Quarterly Review* found signs in this book of a major talent: "The poems move freely to surprising and ultimately right conclusions. But the world they investigate is constricted, a world in which every generous gesture, even Tate's own, is suspect." And Chad Walsh said it was as though Tate "had been born without illusions and had disciplined his talent to an antiseptic purity of naysaying."

Absences (1972) also seemed to Vernon Young "unattractively negative" as well as uninteresting, but this collection was on the whole warmly received. Julian Moynihan called these poems "very orderly as well as very surprising and original. ... They are meditative, introverted, self-reliant, funny, alarming, strange, difficult, intelligent and beautifully crafted." Speaking of the eight sonnets called "The Blue Canyon" and the concluding sequence of nine poems called "Cycle of Dust," Moynihan made the interesting suggestion that Tate's surrealism, as it appears in these poems, has deep affinities with the "durable and enchanting surrealism" of Emily Dickinson (Tate has been poetry editor of the *Dickinson Review* since 1967). Moynihan seemed particularly impressed by the title sequence of twenty numbered poems, "working as

a series of post-Freudian dream recordings, or as a serial definition of peculiar states of psychic and spiritual emptiness in which chaotic, painful aspects of the poet's world are let loose, then made manageable and endurable by becoming coherent parts of discrete, cool, end-stopped poems":

Why do I bother to speak?
Make love to a moose, maybe.
I can imagine a wife
serving dinner
of light bulbs & garbage cans.
How do you like your mashed potatoes?
With pins in them? ...

Where do the words go
When I have done with them?
My mouth should chase them.

A child plots his life to the end;
and spends the rest of his days
trying to remember the plot.

Brian Swann likewise thought that Tate's best poems were not "the bizarre rather random hyperbolic ones his followers prefer, but the subtly ironic metaphysical ones." Norman Rosten admired Tate's willingness to take risks—"to get out on that real or metaphysical limb and keep cutting, not caring much whether the saw is between him and the tree or not. This is the heady spirit that encourages the adventure of poetry."

Tate left Columbia in 1970. He taught at Emerson College, Boston, in 1970–1971, and since then he has been at the University of Massachusetts, Amherst. In 1972 he was Phi Beta Kappa Poet at Brown University, Providence, Rhode Island. He has served as an associate editor at the Pym Randall Press in Cambridge, Massachusetts, and consultant to the Coordinating Council of Literary Magazines. Tate, who writes fiction as well as poems, received grants from the National Endowment for the Arts in 1968 and 1969, and a poetry award from the National Institute for Arts and Letters in 1974. He held a Guggenheim fellowship in 1976.

PRINCIPAL WORKS: *Poetry*—Cages, 1967; The Destination, 1967; The Lost Pilot, 1967; The Torches, 1968 (revised edition 1971); Notes of Woe, 1968; Mystics in Chicago, 1968; Camping in the Valley, 1968; Row With Your Hair, 1969; The Massacre (of) (by) the Innocents, 1969; Is There Anything, 1969; Shepherds of the Mist, 1969; The Oblivion Ha-Ha, 1970; Amnesia People, 1970; Deaf Girl Playing, 1970; Wrong Songs, 1970; Apology for Eating Geoffrey Movius's Hyacinth, 1971; Nobody Goes to Visit the Insane Anymore, 1971; Hints to Pilgrims, 1971; Absences, 1972; Viper Jazz, 1976. *Fiction*—Hottentot Ossuary (short stories), 1974; (with Bill Knott) Lucky Darryl: A Novel, 1977.

ABOUT: Contemporary Authors 21–24 1st revision, 1977; Shaw, R. B. (ed.) American Poetry Since 1960, 1973; Vinson, J. (ed.) Contemporary Poets, 1975; Who's Who in America, 1978–1979. *Periodicals*—Encounter December 1967; Hudson Review Summer 1967, Autumn 1970, Spring 1972, Winter 1972-1973; Nation April 24, 1967; New York Times Book Review November 12, 1972; Poetry February 1968, September 1969, March 1971; Saturday Review August 12, 1972; Southern Review Winter 1972; Virginia Quarterly Review Autumn 1970; Yale Review June 1967.

TCHICAYA, GÉRALD FÉLIX. *See* "UTAM'-SI," GÉRALD FÉLIX TCHICAYA

TERRY, MEGAN (July 22, 1932–), American dramatist, was born in Seattle, Washington, where from early childhood, she says, "I was brought up in community theatre." She trained as an actress and designer at the Seattle Repertory Playhouse and the Banff School of Fine Arts, Alberta, where she studied summers in 1950–1952 and in 1956. She also attended the University of Alberta in 1952–1953, and went on to complete her formal education at the University of Washington, Seattle, which gave her a B. Ed. in 1956. At the same time (1954–1956) she taught drama at the Cornish School of Allied Arts in Seattle, a private school designed to bring all the arts together under one roof.

It was at the Cornish School that Megan Terry directed her own first plays, which allegedly horrified her colleagues. Classroom experience turned her against school work and, still in her early twenties, she organized an acting troupe as an offshoot of the school—the Cornish Players—which toured the Northwest for two years. At the age of twenty-four she cut her educational and theatrical ties with the Northwest and moved to the East Coast. "I was driven out because of the times—the fifties. They just weren't ready for my work so I decided to go to New York because I assumed there would be a more receptive audience for what I was trying to do."

In New York she found acting parts in television serials. She still saw herself primarily as an actress and designer; her writing began as a by-product of the Seattle company's improvisations. "Sometimes the improvisations would be so beautiful that I wanted to find a way to save them, so I had to teach myself to write. I never took myself seriously as a playwright until I was thirty."

This change of attitude developed out of her association with Joseph Chaikin in founding the Open Theatre in February 1963. The Open Theatre was an actors' collective which functioned for ten years as an autonomous creative unit, making an incalculable contribution to the development of American theatre. Its members were in revolt not only against commercial

MEGAN TERRY

working conditions but also against the authoritarian figures of the dramatist and the director. Aiming to take all the means of production into their own hands, they bypassed the traditional artistic hierarchy so as to elevate the actor into the primary position. Terry describes her Open Theatre associates as idealists who "believed that the theatre could be your life and your life could be the theatre.... We wanted to create a theatre in which you were always in a state of becoming . . . where the process, and not the end product, was the main thing."

Any survey of her own writing, therefore, must acknowledge the fact that she is not speaking entirely for herself; and that it is sometimes impossible for an outsider to draw a line showing where her invention comes to a stop and the group mind takes over. She describes her role as follows: "The playwright experiments with the actors on movement and visual images, but then he goes home and writes the play, including the words." Or, as Richard Schechner puts it: "Megan Terry doesn't write plays, she wrights them."

This statement may be clarified by comparing her Open Theatre work with the plays she wrote before 1963. The early play *Ex–Miss Copper Queen on a Set of Pills* (1956) is about a provincial beauty queen adrift in New York. Set on a street on the Lower East Side where she spends the night, the play presents the Copper Queen's drug-befuddled encounter with two scavenging old women who exploit her obsession with babies to strip her of a fur coat and a bottle of wine. Terry uses this dialogue between down-and-outs to draw a sardonic contrast between pioneer and urban values, most effectively in her treatment of the two scavengers, who discuss their trade and the hovel they share in terms of big business and bourgeois domesticity. The play presages the attitudes of her later work (notably her affection for the American heartland) through a naturalistic action and a tone of Dickensian pathos.

This stylistic inheritance had been discarded by the time she wrote *The Magic Realists* (1960), a one-act extravaganza on capitalist America. T. P. Chester, its "ultra-successful businessman" hero, is encamped by a private lake where he is seen recruiting a young outlaw into his organization, falling prey to a beautiful girl agent, and being rescued by a gun-brandishing offspring (named, like all Chester's children, after a New York bank). The play incorporates passages of nonsense language, others of wordless pantomime and dream; it shows characters devouring checks as food, and reduces the all-powerful Chester to washing his clothes in a stream rather than face his fanged wife in the family residence. Such non-naturalistic devices demonstrate Terry's determination to escape from narrow personal themes and invent a form capable of reflecting the typical forces shaping American life. She defined this form as "magic realism"—any wild thing can happen, but still inside the continuum of a developing story.

Her association with the Open Theatre freed Terry from the prison of narrative and from any lingering traces of authorial vanity. As director from 1963 to 1968 of the Open Theatre's weekly writers' workshop, and a participant in the organization's other sessions as a resident writer, she wrote what the group required, and her work must be considered in the context of the Open Theatre's extensive vocabulary of acting exercises. These exercises embody the group's allegiance to a "theatre of abstraction and illusion" in which behavior counts for more than ideas and where "anybody can be anybody, provided he drops one mode of behavior and assumes another." Aiming to promote an acting style that depicts the individual's response to a depersonalized society, the improvisations drew a contrast between "inner" and "outer" experience by acting out the equivalent of the Stanislavskian sub-text—for example, in the group's Perfect People improvisation (for characters from television commercials) or the Unnoticed Actions exercise, in which a respectable social event takes place with unruffled verbal decorum while the participants are picking their noses or looking up women's skirts.

Of these exercises, much the most important to Terry was Transformation, which delivered her from continuity of character as well as continuity of story line. She describes it as a "process whereby the actor begins to invent within the ensemble new and exciting choices. You can create a transformation of the who (character), the where (the environment), the when (the time), and the what (the basic situation)." This technique is the mainspring of the short plays she wrote for the Open Theatre's public performances at the Sheridan Square Theatre and the off-Broadway Martinique Hotel (1963–1965). *Calm Down Mother,* subtitled a "Transformation for Three Women," consists of a series of variations on the mother-daughter-sister relationship, in which three actresses on a bare stage pass through a sequence of self-contained situations, changing character as if they were picking masks out of a property basket. Individually the situations and characters are specifically defined, like fragments of a naturalistic play; collectively they form a rhythmic collage with a life of its own.

Keep Tightly Closed in a Cool Dry Place, written as a companion piece for male actors, derives from a news story about three men convicted of a murder and sharing the same cell. The piece contains a realistic plot in which one of the trio tries to maneuver his cellmates into taking full blame for the crime. Within this framework, Terry introduces transformation scenes that articulate the motives of the basic plot in terms of history, gangster movies, and vaudeville routines, all of which develop their own reality. In performance, therefore, the piece is open to multiple readings, depending on what is played as fact and what as fantasy, and its effect can vary between nightmare and farce.

In *The Gloaming, Oh My Darling,* Terry employs this method less ambiguously by presenting a literal situation with transformational excursions. Two institutionalized old women (drawn from a scene in *Calm Down Mother*) sit together reminiscing and bickering, with periodic interruptions by actual and fantasy visitors. By this means we see them as senile relics (from the viewpoint of their caricatured families and the nursing staff), and as mothers, wives, and sweethearts in a perspective of the American past stretching back to the Indian wars, and asserting what Terry calls "the embrace of life, no matter how little of it there is left."

Comings and Goings, a virtuoso acting exercise for two anonymous characters, consists of a fluid sequence of archetypal male-female relationships, established in tiny dissolving scenes. A lovers' embrace turns into a dialogue between a faulty plug and a wall socket, thence to an argument between a male crash victim and a woman driver, thence to a shopping list with the actress as the pad and her partner as the pencil.

In performance, with replacement performers stepping into the game every thirty-five to ninety seconds, the piece conveys the sheer fun of improvisation. It is also Terry's purest exercise in the transformational style, as defined by her Open Theatre colleague Peter Feldman: "Whatever realities are established at the beginning are destroyed after a few minutes and replaced by others. Then these are in turn destroyed and replaced. These changes occur swiftly and almost without transition, until the audience's dependence upon any fixed reality is called into question."

The most ambitious product of Terry's alliance with the Open Theatre was *Viet Rock,* the first full-length piece evolved between a writer and the troupe, which opened at the La Mama Experimental Theatre Club in May 1966 and subsequently appeared at Yale and off-Broadway. Originating in her improvisation workshop, this "folk war movie" derives from Terry's belief that "not enough plays are written out of an observation of . . . current world problems. . . . Where are the plays about the teach-ins, academic freedom, grading men who are subject to the draft if they don't get high enough marks? There is so much material around I wish I were quintuplets."

The content of *Viet Rock* was drawn mainly from media coverage of the war, plus first-hand testimony. On the basis of this material, she says, "we acted out personal stories, and tried to get at the roots of our drives toward anger and aggression." The resultant script is a collage of America at war, opening with a transformation of the company into mothers and babies, and then into induction-center recruits, rookies undergoing basic training, and combat troops facing the Vietcong. The idiom shifts between naturalistic close-ups, choric speech and rock numbers, brutal caricature, and light satire—including a Senate investigation featuring thinly disguised portraits of Eleanor Roosevelt, Norman Mailer, and Jesus Christ. Transformation is repeatedly used to change assailants into victims, and to match the sufferings of one side with those of the other; it also has the advantage of packing in vastly more material than any naturalistic structure could accommodate. The one thing it does not incorporate is any discussion of the rights and wrongs of this particular war. The play's antimilitarism is entirely nonpolitical; and the only character allowed any continuous life is the Moloch-like figure of the Sergeant, who responds to victory and defeat alike with the demand for blood.

Ironically, it was the commercial showing of this pacifist work which led to Terry's break with the Open Theatre, over the vexed question of money and careerism. Terry believes in taking creative opportunities as they arise, even at the risk of making a financial profit. And she stunned her more puritanical colleagues by pointing out that the word *talent* is a synonym for money: "a means of exchange."

Since then, she has collaborated with the Minneapolis Firehouse Theatre, the Omaha Magic Theatre (as writer in residence), and the La Mama troupe, even making a death-bed return to the Open Theatre as a contributor to the company's final production, *Nightwalk* (1973). Over this period she has broadened her range of experimental work and strengthened her grasp of orthodox technique. Having produced the first rock musical in *Viet Rock,* she created a pioneer environmental event in the La Mama production of *Changes* (1968), in which spectators were led, one by one, through a mind-dissociating obstacle course. She elaborated on this technique in *Jack-Jack* (Minneapolis, 1968) and *The Tommy Allen Show* (Los Angeles, 1970), in which the audience witness the disintegration of a series of televisual Perfect People and then descend to a torture chamber where psychological self-torment is externalized by crucified and boxed-in actors delivering individual "speeches on the cross."

At the same time, Megan Terry was producing radio and television material, some of which does not at all suggest the work of an experimentalist. The radio play *Sanibel and Captiva* for example, broadcast in 1968, is a delicately organized duet for a retired couple who are out fishing for the day. They are expecting their son, who fails to arrive, and the woman gently informs her husband that he is being expelled from his club. Nothing else happens. But through the sound of birdsong and the sea, approaching and receding cars, and dialogue patterned on the obsessions and forgetfulness of the elderly, the piece makes a touching comment on the persistence of human affection into the shrinking world of old age. The statement echoes that of *The Gloaming, Oh My Darling,* but without exceeding a Chekhovian vocabulary.

Conversely, in her television play *Home: or Future Soap* (1967), Megan Terry may be seen using her experimental resources to expand the medium. The piece is a science fictional treatment of the population explosion, set in a desperately overcrowded future in which the only hope for human survival lies in the colonization of another galaxy. The universal crisis is presented through the experience of a typical family of nine people, who spend their entire lives in a narrow room under the surveillance of monitor screens. The piece asks the obvious question of how the primary human impulses of propagation and territorial defense function in this unnatural environment. And its great achievement is to answer the question in two ways: showing a violent personal plot developing towards its climax through a series of cool ceremonial tableaux illustrating work, exercise, prayer, law, marriage and other aspects of communal life. Jack Gould, in the New York *Times,* saluted the piece as "consistently fascinating," and, together with Terry's admonitory "mini-musical" *One More Little Drinkie,* it had a number of performances on educational television networks.

The People vs Ranchman (Minneapolis, 1967) examines mob oratory and the madness of crowds through the case of a man on trial for mass rape. Ranchman, the accused, appears between banners reading "Down with Capital Punishment" and "Burn the Sex Maniac," and the play proceeds as a savage tournament between the Crusader Crowd and the Burning Crowd, while their scapegoat successively bounces back to life from the electric chair, the gallows, and the firing squad. Comic indignation finally subsides into a penitential finale, where the two crowds join in harmonized chorus, "Forgive us Ranchman. We've used you for our sins." As in *Viet Rock,* Terry takes no sides; rather her concern is with the way in which all causes become defiled through the corruption of language.

This is a central thread in *Approaching Simone,* Terry's most ambitious play since *Viet Rock* and winner of an Obie Award for the best off-Broadway play of 1970. A chronicle of the life of Simone Weil, it employs the shorthand devices of the Open Theatre to transport its heroine from her precocious childhood and university career through her experiences as an unorthodox *lycée* teacher, factory worker, supporter of the Spanish Loyalists, and mystical Christian convert, to her death by self-imposed starvation at the age of thirty-four. Making free use of Weil's own writings, the play succeeds in two of the hardest tasks confronting any dramatist: it enacts a credible spiritual development, and it offers a believable portrait of a genius. It also memorably sums up Terry's own long-term preoccupation with the connection between language and violence. "For our contemporaries the role of Helen is played by words with capital letters. . . . When a word is properly defined, it loses its capital letter and can no longer serve either as a banner or as a hostile slogan." Jack Kroll, in *Newsweek,* called the piece "a truly serious play, filled with the light, shadow, and weight of human life, and the exultant agonies of

the ceaseless attempt to create one's humanity."

In 1974, Terry sprung another surprise on her public with *Hothouse* (Chelsea Theatre Center, New York), a blamelessly naturalistic three-act family drama, presenting—as Michael Feingold said in the *Village Voice*—"a feminist view of an American family situation by the simple device of reversing the genders. In a teetery cliff house in a Washington fishing village live three generations of two-fisted, hard-drinking—women!" Relating to the place and time of Terry's own adolescence, *Hothouse* struck some reviewers as an early autobiographical work arriving twenty years late. But in its frankness about female behavior and appetites, it is clearly a product of the liberationist era. Young Jody, experimentally attached to a stuffily disapproving boyfriend, her hell-raising mother, and her still man-hungry grandmother, form an Amazonian bulwark built to withstand the adulteries, desertions, betrayals, and marital batterings that comprise the action. Christopher Sharp, in *Women's Wear Daily,* read the piece as a translation of the black matriarchal family stereotype into a white idiom. For Martin Gottfried, in the New York *Post, Hothouse* exemplified Terry's "amazing combination of technique, poetry, intelligence, stage sense and most of all, soul."

Megan Terry's career up to this point conveys the impression of a vastly inventive and prolific artist (with some forty plays to her credit) whose work has only rarely stopped traffic. This is partly a matter of choice, as she has always been ready to sink her individuality in a collective enterprise, and work through others' actions rather than her own words if she believed they could do the job more satisfactorily. If one image arises from her work, it is that of America as an ice-cream smile concealing a mouthful of rotting teeth. Others have depicted the country in similar terms. What marks out Terry's work as special is the prodigious and hopeful energy she has brought to the task of diagnosing the sickness and holding out the possibility of a cure.

In 1971 the author became a founding member and treasurer of New York Theater Strategy and a founding member of Women's Theatre Council, New York. She serves on the theatre panels of the National Endowment for the Arts and the Rockefeller Foundation. A member of the American Theatre Association, she was co-chairman of its playwriting program in 1977 and chairman of its playwrights' project committee in 1978–1979. She received a Stanley Drama Award and an award from the Office of Advanced Drama Research in 1965, an ABC–Yale University Fellowship in 1966, and a Rockefeller grant in 1968. She held a fellowship from the

National Education Association in 1973 and a Guggenheim fellowship in 1978. She was writer in residence at the Yale School of Drama in 1966–1967 and at the Omaha Magic Theatre in 1977. Her recreations are the "study of the living American language" and fishing.

PRINCIPAL PUBLISHED WORKS: Calm Down Mother, 1966; Viet Rock: Four Plays (*with* Comings and Goings, Keep Tightly Closed in a Cool Dry Place, The Gloaming Oh My Darling), 1967; The People vs. Ranchman (*with* Ex–Miss Copper Queen on a Set of Pills), 1968; Three One-Act Plays (Sanibel and Captiva, The Magic Realists, One More Little Drinkie), 1970; The Tommy Allen Show *in* Scripts 2, 1971; Megan Terry's Home: or Future Soap, 1972; Massachusetts Trust *in* Poland, A. and Mailman, B. (eds.) The Off-Off Broadway Book, 1972; Couplings and Groupings, 1972; Approaching Simone, 1973; Hothouse, 1974; (with Sam Shepard and J.C. van Itallie) Nightwalk, 1975.

ABOUT: Cohn, R. Currents in Contemporary Drama, 1969; Crowell's Handbook of Contemporary Drama, 1971; Croyden, M. Lunatics, Lovers and Poets, 1974; Lewis, A. American Plays and Playwrights, 1970; Pasoli, R. A Book on the Open Theatre, 1970; Vinson, J. (ed.) Contemporary Dramatists, 1977; Who's Who in America, 1978–1979; Who's Who in the Theatre, 1977.

THEODORESCU, ION. *See* "ARGHEZI, TUDOR"

*THEROUX, PAUL (EDWARD) (April 10, 1941–), American novelist, short story writer, travel writer, and critic, was born in Medford, Massachusetts, the third of the seven children of Albert Eugene Theroux, who is of French-Canadian ancestry, and the former Anne Dittami. An article on the Theroux family by James Atlas in the New York *Times Magazine* (April 30, 1978) describes Paul Theroux as "only the most prominent member of a prolific clan." His eldest brother Eugene, a lawyer and an expert on Sino-American trade, is a spare-time painter and caricaturist; Alexander, a year older than Paul, is well-known as a novelist *(Three Wogs)*, children's writer *(The Schinocephalic Waif* and *The Great Wheadle Tragedy)*, essayist, and wit; Joseph, who was twenty-three when Atlas wrote his article, was then a Peace Corps volunteer in Western Samoa, at work on a volume of short stories; and Peter (twenty-one) had completed five unpublished novels by the time he started college. Only the two sisters—Ann Marie (a teacher before she married) and Mary (a nurse) —seem not to have artistic ambitions.

Atlas speculates at some length on the sources of all this creativity. The family home is on Belle Avenue, Medford—"a drab working-class neighborhood" in an unattractive suburb of Boston. Perhaps, as Paul Theroux suggests, "it's the uncongenial place that provides material for one's art." His father, a retired shoe salesman,

*the roō

Ronald Hoeben

PAUL THEROUX

read Dickens and Melville to the children and showed them around Boston's museums and historic sites, but their creative energies seem to have come from their mother, an amateur painter, and from her Italian-born father. He was a tailor, "a saintly, operatic man," devoted to education and tenaciously ambitious. Anne Theroux exhorted her children to be creative but, according to Atlas, "her most important legacy was the conviction that 'it is possible to climb'— away from a mediocre existence into the more expansive realm of the imagination." And to some extent, the literary generation of Therouxs is self-created: "Clannish and self-contained, the Therouxs are eager collaborators in one another's lives."

Paul Theroux attended Medford High School, described by Alexander as "a sink of mediocrity," was a Boy Scout, and twice the winner of the Medford Science Fair. He was at the University of Maine in 1959–1960, then transferred to the University of Massachusetts at Amherst, which he says "looked as if it was made out of Tupperware and poison ivy." He went there as a premed student but, increasingly disillusioned with the American medical profession ("they won't operate unless you've eaten money") and increasingly drawn to a literary career, he switched to English. Always the rebel of the family, he alienated the authorities at both of his universities by writing militantly pacifist and left-wing editorials in college newspapers.

Theroux graduated in 1963. He summered in Italy, picked up a little teaching at the University of Urbino, and afterwards studied briefly at Syracuse University, New York. Later the same year he joined the Peace Corps in order to avoid the draft (or out of idealism—he has given different explanations to different interviewers). From 1963 to 1965 he lectured in English at Soche Hill College in Limbe, Nyasaland, which became Malawi in 1964. From there he contributed articles to the *Christian Science Monitor* about the problems and privileges of teaching in the bush with inadequate materials. He also launched a magazine, *The Migraine,* enraging the American ambassador with an editorial denouncing the escalation of the Vietnam War.

Considerably more dangerous was the service he performed for David Rubadiri, his first headmaster in Malawi and a distinguished poet. Having become Malawi's ambassador to the United Nations, Rubadiri had then denounced Dr. Hastings Banda, the country's president, and decamped to Uganda. Theroux agreed to drive Mr. Rubadiri's aged mother and a much-prized dinner service two thousand five hundred miles to Uganda, on the way back carrying a few messages for a Mr. Chisiza. He turned out to be a leader of the anti-Banda guerillas. The plot was discovered, some guerillas were ambushed and killed, and Theroux was deported. After a series of interrogations in Washington, he was expelled from the Peace Corps.

Through the good offices of David Rubadiri, Theroux then took a job in pre-Amin Uganda; lecturing in English at Makerere University, Kampala (1965–1968). It was in Kampala that he met Anne Castle, the English woman he married in 1967. The novelist V.S. Naipaul, who was also teaching at Makerere, took an interest in Theroux's writings. According to Hugh Hebert, Naipaul "made Theroux look much more closely at what he was writing, slowed him down," and taught him that "a book needs a reason for being written"; Theroux repaid this kindness later by writing a useful introduction to Naipaul's work.

Theroux was depressed by the disintegration of tribal life in Uganda and increasingly alarmed by the political situation there. In 1968 he and his wife were caught in a student riot in Kampala. Their car was stoned and the Therouxs "were sort of cut pretty bad." It seemed time to leave Africa, and Paul Theroux answered an advertisement for someone to teach seventeenth-century English literature at the University of Singapore. He was quite unqualified for the post but got it anyway, teaching at Singapore from 1968 to 1971, with the English poet D.J. Enright as his department head. At the end of the contract Theroux and his wife went to England and settled in a cottage in Dorset, where he became a full-time writer and reviewer.

By that time Theroux had already published five novels, generally setting each book in the country he had lived in last. *Waldo* (1967) concerns the adventures—sexual and otherwise—of a contemporary Candide in beatnik America, the author of a very profitable first novel; it was found picaresque, surrealistic, and frequently funny, but uneven, notable mostly for some striking "images, phrases and moments." In *Fong and the Indians* (1968) the scene shifts to a newly independent East African nation where the innocent Chinese grocer of the title is fleeced and/or bullied by all. One reviewer called it "a small masterpiece" and another said it was "outrageously funny," with a funniness that comes so close to the frequent tragedy of the human condition that this reader found himself wincing."

Girls at Play, which followed in 1969, is by no means funny. Five schoolteachers—a Peace Corps recruit, an Afro-Indian, and three English women—are thrown together in a school for African girls in the Kenyan bush. The novel traces their growing dislike for each other and ends in a bloodbath of murder, suicide, and rape. It seemed to Laurence Lafore that Theroux "tells his tale of terror and cruelty with cold detachment dressed in wit and irony, and his cold-bloodedness is so relentless that it becomes in itself a sort of cruelty inflicted on the reader. He is out to instruct in the ways that life and death can be horrible, and he does so with such persuasiveness that quite trivial details become nightmares. . . . Mr. Theroux's intellectual edifice is stunningly logical and eerily lit by the appalling certainty of approaching doom."

L.J. Davis saw *Jungle Lovers* (1971) as "an audacious attempt to tell the other half of *The Heart of Darkness.*" The comparison with Joseph Conrad is one often made by Theroux's reviewers and, though he inevitably fails to measure up to that "very tall ghost," most critics find his attempts honorable and praiseworthy. The protagonist of *Jungle Lovers* is a Massachusetts insurance salesman trying to do business in a small African country torn by revolution. In the contest between insurance and chaos, chaos, of a peculiarly African sort, prevails. After one client has been beheaded, the salesman sets up house with the dead man's sister in a brothel housing a rich assortment of characters, black and white. L.J. Davis found this "a first-rate performance," both sociologically and politically—"informative, colorful, and insightful. . . . His portrait of modern Malawi is as good as one could want."

A volume of short stories, *Sinning With Annie,* appeared in 1972, dealing mostly with "grayly greedy" characters in colorful places, and then came a novel set in Singapore, *Saint*

Jack (1973). Jack Flowers is an Italian-American from the North End of Boston, a pimp in his fifties still ambitious for wealth, fame, and even sainthood. A "missionary manqué," he entices foreign clients to his Paradise Gardens by offering them a chance to "participate in a cultural secret" and take away from Singapore "the ultimate souvenir." Jack's memoirs, wrote Jonathan Raban, form "the testament of a man who has tried, in all humility, to love a world of junk and flotsam." His "poetic truthfulness, sustained against all odds in a society that is vicious, vain and chronically dishonest, makes even Singapore a place fit for saints to live in." And a critic in the *Times Literary Supplement* wrote that "Theroux's style gets sadder, funnier and more distinctive with each novel. Those clashes of culture and race that produce stultifying ritual displays of 'sensitiveness' in so many writers come out in his fiction as living, unpredictable farce. . . . He is tremendously good at the commercial dialects that are generated on the very edge of articulacy, where conversation is more like barter than anything else."

The Black House (1974) is about the various kinds of reverse culture shock experienced by a British anthropologist who returns to England after ten years in the African bush. Life at the heart of darkness, he finds, had been no darker than among the hostile natives of bewitched and haunted Dorset. Michael Mewshaw described the novel as "a hybrid composed of unequal parts of social satire, commentary on colonialism, anthropological insights, some randy sex and an inconclusive gothic tale"; he thought it did "a serious disservice" to Theroux's talents but other critics found the hybrid greatly to their taste, and more than one considers it Theroux's best novel.

Long before these very mixed reviews appeared, Theroux had moved dramatically on. "Ending a book is a very fruitful time for me," he says, and on the very day he delivered the manuscript of *The Black House* to his publisher he set out on the four-month train journey, from Victoria Station to the Siberian steppes, that is the subject of his first travel book, *The Great Railway Bazaar: By Train Through Asia* (1975). V.S. Pritchett said that "the railway offers what up-to-date forms of travel cut us off from: passengers. There is an instant meeting with the desperate, anxious, boasting, confessional, jabbering hopefuls and casualties of the modern world. . . . We see private life as it screams at this very hour, sweating out the universal anxiety, the conglomerate Absurd. This is what Paul Theroux, with the eyes and ears of the novelist and the avidity of the responsive traveller, brings home to us, awaking us to horror, laughter, compassion at the sight of the shameless private will to live. His book is the most vigorous piece of travel among people I have read for years." A number of reviewers commented on the very personal nature of Theroux's response to what he had heard and seen, and he himself views travel writing as a form of autobiography because, he says, travel always brings you "back to yourself."

The Great Railway Bazaar, the first of Theroux's books to become a bestseller, made him famous. Its success was repeated by his next novel, *The Family Arsenal* (1976). The story centers on Valentine Hood, a disillusioned but quirkily ethical young American who was once a consul in Vietnam. Sacked for assaulting an offensive government official, he is now lying low in seediest London. He lives with Mayo, "a barbarian with taste" who has stolen an Old Master to further the cause of the IRA, and two dim-witted teenaged terrorists: this is his "family." Other characters represent various levels of a decaying society, from Lady Arrow, a rich bisexual collector of violent people, to Mr. Gawber, as Dickensian as his name—a sad accountant, dreaming of a cleansing holocaust. Inspired by opium and vestigial idealism, Hood murders a drunken bully and finds himself in charge of the dead man's wife and of a cache of weapons sought by the IRA.

The novel was received with very great enthusiasm and pleasure. Lawrence Graver praised its "narrative verve, the brightly sketched collection of urban desperadoes, and the extraordinary vividness" of Theroux's London, with its pervasive sense "of urban rot edging toward ruin"; Michael Ratcliffe agreed that it was "one of the most brilliantly evocative novels of London that has appeared for years." Graver thought that the author's "efforts to provide by implication an analysis of a historical situation and an ample sense of personal motivation are finally less successful than his handling of narrative excitement, satiric portraiture and the evocation of urban violence and distress." Norman Snider disagreed; it seemed to him that Theroux had "achieved an intelligent, precisely structured novel of suspense while giving us the first major fictional portrait of British society in the 1970s from top to bottom." It might have been a more original and "a less Mandarin novel," Snider thought, if it was not for Theroux's "enormous reverence for the literary past. Joseph Conrad's *The Secret Agent,* Henry James's *The Princess Casamassima,* Graham Greene's London novels of the thirties—all are insistently

807

present." The novel was a Book-of-the-Month Club selection.

There was also much praise for the twenty short stories, all narrated by an American consul in a remote Malaysian village, collected in *The Consul's File* (1977). "The sharp underlying focus is on how uprooted individuals connect or fail to connect with each other and with the places where they have ended up." wrote Richard Nordell. "Sometimes bizarre calamity is the result, sometimes it is international social comedy." Nordell was one of a number of reviewers who were reminded by the book's "dry and lucid tone" (as well as its setting) of Somerset Maugham. Nicholas Delbanco liked best the several stories with touches of the supernatural, and noted that Theroux's "comic gift remains substantial—his sense of incongruity—of blasted aspiration and the daily duty-round, is keen." At the same time, Delbanco found and disliked in these stories evidence of a "large contempt" for their hapless characters.

Maude Coffin Pratt in *Picture Palace* (1978) is a portrait photographer of international fame, whose subjects have included such figures as Thomas Mann, Gertrude Stein, Marilyn Monroe, D.H. Lawrence, and Robert Frost. At the age of seventy, preparing for a major retrospective exhibition, she combs through her files and recalls (in generally caustic terms) her encounters with the great. And she relives in the "picture palace" of her mind the two great passions of her life—photography and her incestuous (and unrequited) love for her brother Orlando. In the end she realizes that her past is in "all the pictures . . . [she] never took"—that, as Theroux says elsewhere, "the world of the senses is much greater than the paltry world of the eye." Walter Clemons found the novel "purple and writery" in its prose and thought it had "turned out so badly" because Theroux saw his native New England, where the book is mainly set, much less precisely than the foreign places he has known. Other critics did not agree that the book had turned out badly. Elaine Feinstein, indeed, called it Theroux's "least fussy, least self-conscious novel to date," and admired his portrait of the photographer as "an honest eye who leaves no record of herself in her portraits of others." It brought Theroux the valuable and prestigious Whitbread Prize in England, and struck Terry Coleman as a masterpiece.

Theroux and his wife live with their two sons in Clapham, an unfashionable part of London, in a house full of the trophies of Theroux's travels. Anne Theroux, a teacher when they met, is now a BBC producer. According to *Current Biography,* the author is "a tall, lean, handsome man with thick dark brown hair worn modishly long, and dark eyes." He has been called urbane, confident, and "disarmingly candid"; rarer than any of these things, he is happy and knows it. In 1978 he traveled by train from the northeastern United States through Mexico and Central America to the tip of Argentina, gathering material for a second travel book called *The Old Patagonian Express.* Rights to several of his novels have been sold to the movies, and James Atlas, writing in 1978, thought that "a number of profitable transactions have made him a virtual millionaire." Theroux has reviewed for the *New Statesman,* the New York *Times Book Review, Commentary,* and the *Evergreen Review,* among other magazines, and has served as a contributing editor of *Transition* (Ghana). In 1972–1973 he was writer-in-residence at the University of Virginia. He received an award in literature from the American Academy of Arts and Letters in 1977 and *Playboy* editorial awards in 1972, 1976, and 1977.

Hugh Hebert says of Theroux that "his eye is steadfastly dry, but there is a kind of compassion at work behind it even when he seems to crucify the tattered remnants of the colonial English or the button-bright missionary Americans. . . . the whole post-colonial mish-mash is for him and his books less a political than a social and personal thing." Norman Snider quotes Theroux's fictional consul: "Other people's lives are so much more interesting than one's own. I am an unrepenting eavesdropper and I find anonymity a consolation." It may be, Snider suggests, that the consul is here speaking for Theroux, who "clearly reacting against the excesses of such writers as Norman Mailer and Hunter Thompson . . . is a throwback to the fifties, to the careful conscientious dependable poets of the New Criticism. His stories are dispassionately written, conventional in form, with Good Commercial Potential. Sad to say, he may well be, with Robert Stone, the most interesting American novelist to have emerged in recent years." Theroux himself is modest about his work, dismissing the comparisons with Conrad and James as "an impertinence," though he is obviously pleased when critics find resemblances between his work and that of his friend Graham Greene (who appears in *Picture Palace,* discussing with Maude Pratt the nature of art and reality). "I am not interested in symbolism, but form," Theroux says. "I guess I'm a very traditional writer; I'm just interested in persuading people that what I'm writing is the truth."

PRINCIPAL WORKS: Novels—Waldo, 1967; Fong and the Indians, 1968; Girls at Play, 1969; Murder in Mount Holly,

1969; Jungle Lovers, 1971; Saint Jack, 1973; The Black House, 1974; The Family Arsenal, 1976; Picture Palace, 1978. *Short Stories*—Sinning With Annie, 1972; The Consul's File, 1977. *Nonfiction*—V.S. Naipaul: An Introduction to His Work, 1972; The Great Railway Bazaar, 1975. *For Children*—A Christmas Card, 1978.

ABOUT: Contemporary Authors 33–36, 1973; Current Biography, 1979; Vinson, J. (ed.) Contemporary Novelists, 1976; Who's Who in America, 1978–1979. *Periodicals*—American Scholar Autumn 1967; Atlantic October 1973; Christian Science Monitor September 5, 1968; Encounter July 1973; Guardian April 17, 1973; December 13, 1978; National Observer September 4, 1976; New Republic September 25, 1976; September 10, 1977; New Statesman October 4, 1974; October 17, 1975; June 17, 1977; New York Post August 28, 1976; New York Review of Books September 23, 1971; September 30, 1976; August 17, 1978; New York Times July 28, 1976; New York Times Book Review November 3, 1968; September 28, 1969; August 8, 1971; September 9, 1973; September 8, 1974; July 11, 1976; August 21, 1977; June 18, 1978; New York Times Magazine April 30, 1978; Newsday February 1, 1976; Publishers Weekly July 26, 1976; Saturday Review September 28, 1968; September 3, 1977; July 8, 1978; Times Literary Supplement June 12, 1969; April 27, 1973; October 4, 1974; June 3, 1977.

THOMPSON, ARTHUR BELL. *See* "CLIFFORD, FRANCIS"

THWAITE, ANTHONY (SIMON) (June 23, 1930–), English poet, critic, and editor, writes: "I was born in Chester, but to parents whose families were almost entirely Yorkshire (North Riding and West Riding) as far back as they can be traced. I lived in Leeds and Sheffield as a child. In June 1940 I was sent by my parents to live with my aunt and uncle in the United States, and so was one of that significant minority of British children of the time who never experienced 'the people's war.' I went to grade school and junior high in and around Washington D.C. By the time I was thirteen, I felt that my proper place was back in my own country, and I was allowed to return, unaccompanied, in a British aircraft carrier which was in mid-Atlantic on D-Day in 1944. From 1944 to 1949 I was at boarding school at Kingswood School, Bath, from which I won an open scholarship in English to Christ Church, Oxford. Before taking this up, however, I had to do my national service: I was conscripted into the Rifle Brigade, but soon found myself in the Educational Corps. As a sergeant-instructor in the R.A.E.C., I managed to get myself posted to precisely the station I wanted, a mile from the ruins of Leptis Magna in Tripolitania, Libya. From a very early age, encouraged by my father (who was and is an indefatigable genealogist and local historian), I have had a strong feeling for the past and the things of the past; indeed, for many years I intended to be a professional archaeologist, and

ANTHONY THWAITE

am still actively concerned in an amateur way with archaeology. This first Libyan experience was very important to me, as was my return (1965–1967, when I was assistant professor of English at the University of Libya, Benghazi: both periods are dealt with in my *The Deserts of Hesperides,* which I subtitled 'An Experience of Libya,' as well as in many poems in *The Stones of Emptiness* and *Inscriptions*).

"At Oxford, I was part of a very various and productive group of student poets. I had begun to write poems when I was fourteen, but wrote nothing of any value at all until I was at least in my early twenties. The Oxford undergraduate poets of my day included Geoffrey Hill, George MacBeth, Adrian Mitchell, Alan Brownjohn and Edward Lucie-Smith. However, except for friendship and the accident of being in Oxford at the same time, I think nothing united us then or unites us now. But at least one had a small and intensely critical audience, which isn't necessarily a bad thing.

"Very soon after going down from Oxford, I married and we went out to Japan (1955–1957), where I had been offered a so-called 'visiting professorship' in English literature at Tokyo University. This gave me a continuing interest in Japanese culture and Japanese history, though I think neither has made much of a mark on my own poetry. Since my return from Japan, I have earned my living (apart from the two years in Libya in the 1960s) in the literary/editorial field, as a BBC radio producer, literary editor of *The Listener* and *New Statesman,* and since 1973 as co-editor of *Encounter.* I combine this with a good deal of reviewing, broadcasting, lecturing, and all the other ancillary bits and pieces a man of letters finds himself doing. I live with my wife and four daughters in a mill house by a small river in Norfolk, from which I make regular forays to London and more sporadic ones elsewhere (including Yugoslavia, Kuwait, Czechoslovakia and Italy in the past couple of years).

"These biographical facts naturally have some interest to me, but I see no reason why they should have any to most readers. Though my poems often draw on autobiography (in the sense that they appear to start from a position of 'I saw this . . .' or the like), I think that they are self-explanatory, even autonomous. The interior life of a poem either reveals itself to the reader or it doesn't."

There are a number of poems of disappointed love in *Home Truths,* and others drawn from Thwaite's two years in Japan. Unexceptional in subject matter, ironic and didactic in tone, they were found technically accomplished but rather lacking in urgency. The technical skill was greater, and also less obtrusive, in *The Owl in the Tree,* which centers on domestic life, the tensions of suburbia, and "common experiences" in a way that reminded some critics of the work of Philip Larkin. That "common experience" death is the subject of "Manhood End," a poem about a country church which, for all its quietness of tone, is one of the most powerful and disturbing in the book:

. . . Above the pews, I saw a monument,
A sixteenth-century carving, with the dead
Husband and wife kneeling together, meant

For piety and remembrance. But on their right
I grasped with sudden shock a scene less pure—
A naked woman, arms bound back and tight,
And breasts thrust forward to be gnawed by great
Pincers two men held out. I left, unsure
Of what that emblem meant; and towards the gate

The small mounds of the overcrowded dead
Shrank in the sun. The eastern wall seemed built
Of darker stone. I lay: and by my head
A starling with its neck snapped; nestling there,
A thrush's egg with yolk and white half split,
And one chafed bone a molehill had laid bare.

Frail pictures of the world at Manhood End—
How we are shifted, smashed, how stones display
The names and passions that we cannot mend.
The lych-gate stood and showed me, and I felt
The pebbles teach my feet. I walked away,
My head full of the smell my nostrils smelt.

The Owl in the Tree was well enough received, but there was still some feeling that Thwaite was one of those poets who (as M.L. Rosenthal put

it) "lose themselves in the effort to say interesting things about the well-known and the commonplace." Most readers felt that Thwaite had found his proper theme, and a new vigor and excitement, in *The Stones of Emptiness,* which, as he says, "deals with the experience of the past, change, ruin, continuity, survival, as felt during my time in Libya." There was particular praise for "The Letters of Synesius," a sequence of twelve meditations on North African civilization spoken by the fifth-century bishop; it seemed to Peter Porter a notable achievement, "written in a finely controlled free verse, and uniting the sensibilities of the ancient and modern worlds."

There were more poems about the history and geography of North Africa in *Inscriptions,* along with others about the past and present in England and in Japan. The sincerity and integrity of these unassuming poems, and the freshness of their music and imagery, were greatly admired. Martin Dodsworth suggested that Thwaite writes of a past "that has been domesticated by age. A broken dish, a lost arrow-head, a bone turned up in a dig, an entry in a parish register—such rubble as men leave behind them is what the poet takes his poems from. At one level his concern is to make new patterns from old junk—at another it is to understand his own relation to this elusive human past. A sense of the temporary underlies any pattern he makes, but cannot nullify its value." The book "pits the human voice, and this particular unflurried tone of it, against all attrition. It names; it contains; it does not plume itself. Thwaite's unpretentiousness is a positive force."

New Confessions is a sequence of poems, with some prose passages, in which Thwaite muses on the *Confessions* of St. Augustine, and on the connections and disparities between the views of the fourth-century theologian and his own. One reviewer found the book "fussy and lifeless," but another, in the *Times Literary Supplement,* felt on the contrary that "powers have broken out and are moving loose in this book which Mr. Thwaite had always seemed to possess but not to find a free use for. It is Ariel flying round the head of Prospero. There is a new fragmentary intensity, and a new breadth. . . . The sequence as a whole is a self-study of some profundity."

Thwaite's prose account of his "experience of Libya," *The Desert of Hesperides,* was called an entertaining piece of light reportage. *Contemporary English Poetry,* based on a book produced for Thwaite's Japanese students at Tokyo University, is a sound and useful introduction. It has been expanded and revised as *Twentieth Century English Poetry.* Thwaite, for whom "every step and every breath is a constant apprehension of the physical past," has also produced an imaginative and lucid if traditional portrait of Roman Britain for children, *Beyond the Inhabited World.* The author, the son of Hartley and Alice (Mallinson) Thwaite, was married in 1955 to Ann Harrop. Between 1972, when he left the *New Statesman* after four years as its literary editor, and 1973 when he went to *Encounter,* the author held the Henfield Writing Fellowship at the University of East Anglia. He received the Richard Hillary Memorial Prize in 1968.

PRINCIPAL WORKS: *Poetry*—Home Truths, 1957; The Owl in the Tree, 1963; The Stones of Emptiness, 1967; (with A. Alvarez and Roy Fuller) Penguin Modern Poets 18, 1970; Inscriptions, 1973; New Confessions, 1974; (with Dannie Abse and D.J. Enright) Penguin Modern Poets 26, 1975; A Portion for Foxes, 1977. *Nonfiction*—Contemporary English Poetry, 1959 (revised as Twentieth Century English Poetry, 1978); Japan in Colour (with photographs by Roloff Beny), 1968; The Deserts of Hesperides, 1969; Poetry Today 1960–1973, 1973; In Italy (with Roloff Beny and Peter Porter), 1974; Beyond the Inhabited World (for children), 1976. *As Editor*—(with Geoffrey Bownas) Penguin Book of Japanese Verse, 1964; (with Peter Porter) The English Poets From Chaucer to Edward Thomas, 1974.

ABOUT: Contemporary Authors 5–8 1st revision, 1969; International Who's Who in Poetry, 1974–1975; Vinson, J. (ed.) Contemporary Poets, 1975; Who's Who, 1978. *Periodicals*—Guardian June 28, 1973; Observer (London) May 6, 1973; Poetry (Chicago) December 1973; Times (London) January 4, 1969; Times Literary Supplement May 18, 1973; June 21, 1974; December 10, 1976; July 15, 1977.

*TIKHONOV, NIKOLAI (SEMENOVICH)
(December 3, 1896–February 8, 1979) Russian poet and prose writer, was born in St. Petersburg (now Leningrad). His father was a barber, his mother a dressmaker. "When I took up writing (I tried my hand at short stories and poetry very early) my parents considered it a passing craze, useless but harmless. . . . I completed a course at a commercial school, but instead of going on studying I had to help support my family, which could only just make ends meet." Tikhonov worked as a merchant shipping clerk from 1911 to 1914. At the outbreak of World War I he went to the front as a volunteer in a hussar regiment, with which he served until the October Revolution of 1917. Later (1918-1922), he fought in the Red Army as a cavalry officer. It was under the impact of the early months of the Revolution that he wrote his first sheaf of poems, which he could not bring himself to publish because they "were declamatory, naive and feeble. By the time I was able to select poems for my first book to be published I had already been through the Civil War and had firmly made up my mind to

*tē′ kən of

NIKOLAI TIKHONOV

take up writing seriously after demobilization."

He "plunged head first into the noisy, clashing literary world of the nineteen-twenties," as a founder member of the Serapion Brothers, a group of writers who stood for an independent art free from political commitment and "boredom," and whose members also included Fedin, Zoshchenko, and Vsevolod Ivanov. The poems in his first two books, *Orda* (The Horde, 1922) and *Braga* (The Mead, 1923) are usually considered his best. They are mostly narrative in content, many of them ballads whose evocations of war and revolution are all the more powerful for being presented in lean and concrete images— "simple, like an iron nail," to use one of his own favorite similes. In their cult of heroism as well as in their clarity and precision they resemble the Acmeist poetry of Gumilev, and in their objective treatment of horror, cruelty, and gratuitous death they are close, at least in spirit, to Babel. When war came, he says in one well-known poem, "Ogon, verevka, pulya i topor":

Fire, the rope, the bullet and the axe,
Like servants bowed and followed after us

In the mid-1920s Tikhonov came more and more under the influence of such avant-garde poets as Khlebnikov and Pasternak, and for a time experimented with complex associations and rhymes, abrupt shifts of meaning, bizarre alliterations, and other modernistic devices. In such collections as *Poiski geroya* (The Hero's Quest, 1927) he became in his poetry less of a romantic and more of a realist, increasingly concerned with social issues. His prose, however, remained romantic in spirit and style, reminding some critics of the work of Rudyard Kipling, as in his first collection of short stories, *Riskovanny chelovek* (The Reckless Man, 1927). According to Gleb Struve, Tikhonov in his fiction favors "sharp, definite outlines, bright colors, and dramatic situations, and he prefers to show his characters in action ... he has an aversion to psychological analysis." His style is "compact, robust, and picturesque," and his technique is distinguished "by his interest in the plot, his careful construction, and his orderly narrative."

Tikhonov always had a passion for the East, and as a boy he dreamed of visiting Ellora and Benares, the Yangtze and the Ganges. He traveled widely, and during the 1920s and 1930s journeyed especially in Turkestan and in the Caucasus, where he studied the customs and history of the people. His visits to Turkmenistan in 1926 and 1930 inspired the poems in the collection *Yurga* (1930), and the stories in *Kochevniki* (The Nomads, 1931), which described how the Turkmen were reacting to Soviet ideas and to the Five-Year Plan then in operation.

The mountains of the Caucasus have been a source of romantic inspiration to Russian writers from the time of Pushkin and Lermontov onwards, and the collection *Stikhi o Kakhetii* (Poems About Kakhetia, 1935) is a sort of poetic travel diary inspired by the magnificent scenery, the ancient customs, and the dangers and rewards of mountaineering in this part of Georgia. Tikhonov was also influenced by Titsian Tabidze and other members of a brilliant galaxy of Georgian poets whom he met and whose poetry he translated into Russian and published, along with other translations by Pasternak, as *Poety Gruzii.*

By the early 1930s Tikhonov had put himself and his pen entirely at the service of communism. In his novel *Voyna* (War, 1931), he contrasts Europe's gloom and despair with Russia's faith in the future. *Voyna* is about the use of gas in the First World War, but the drift towards the Second was already obvious a few years later when Tikhonov traveled in Western Europe and recorded his impressions of Paris, London, and Vienna—"the stifling air of fear and suspense that hovers over the cities and plains of the continent"—in another of his poetic travel diaries, the collection *Ten druga* (The Shadow of a Friend, 1936).

When the Germans invaded Russia he joined the army once again, and was in his home city of Leningrad as a war correspondent for *Pravda* throughout the agony of the three-year siege. *Kirov s nami* (Kirov Is With Us) is a long narrative poem about the heroic resistance put up by the people of the city in the early days of the siege, taking its title from the Leningrad party leader who was murdered in 1934 but inspired the city's defenders in World War II. Tikhonov once read the poem to weeping workers in the Kirov plant during a heavy artillery shelling.

He was tirelessly active during the war, giving talks over the radio, at factories, to army units, and on the ships of the Baltic Fleet, yet still finding time to turn out poems, stories, and articles. In 1942 the collections *Ognenny god* (The Fiery Year) and *Leningrad prinimaet boy* (Leningrad Accepts the Challenge) were published, together with the stories in *Leningradskiye rasskazy* (Leningrad Tales), a book which, in Alexander Kaun's description, "raises reportage to the peak of literary art."

In 1944 he was elected president of the Soviet Writers' Union, but when Stalin's henchman Zhdanov began the new repression of literary activity in 1946 with his infamous attack on Akhmatova and Zoshchenko, Tikhonov was demoted for not having sufficiently opposed their "formalism," though he remained on the executive committee of the Union.

"Old soldier that I am, I became an active partisan of peace," said Tikhonov; and during the 1950s and 1960s he was active in the World Peace Council, an interest reflected in *Na vtorom vsemirnom kongrese mira* (At the Second World Peace Congress, 1951). Otherwise, his postwar writing was mainly concerned with his travels, for during this period he was able to fulfill his childhood dream of visiting China and India, as well as many other parts of the world. He published cycles of poems about China and Yugoslavia, among other places, and collections of stories such as *Rasskazy o Pakistane* (Stories About Pakistan, 1951). In recent years a series of articles about his meetings with interesting people in many different countries appeared in literary magazines.

Tikhonov joined in the denunciation of Pasternak during the 1950s, and this damaged his standing with some Soviet writers, who viewed his devotion to the party line with distaste and believed that the quality of his work had deteriorated since World War II, impaired by what one critic termed "the boredom of heroism." Indeed, Tikhonov owed his important place in Soviet poetry largely to his early ballads, which critics agree are his best, and which had great influence on other young poets of the period. He has been called "the supreme lyric poet of the Civil War."

Tikhonov received the Stalin prize three times and the Order of Lenin twice, and he won the Lenin Peace Prize in 1957.

PRINCIPAL WORKS IN ENGLISH TRANSLATION: Tales of

Leningrad, 1942; The Defence of Leningrad: Eye-witness Accounts of the Siege (by Tikhonov and others), 1943; Leningrad, translated by Elizabeth Donnelly, 1944. *Poems in* Bowra, C.M. (ed.) A Second Book of Russian Verse, 1948; Lindsay, J. (ed.) Russian Poetry, 1917-1955, 1957; Lindsay, J. (ed.) Modern Russian Poetry, 1960; Markov, V. and Sparks, M. (eds.) Modern Russian Poetry, 1966; Obolensky, D. (ed.) The Penguin Book of Russian Verse, 1962; Reavey, G. and Slonim, M. (eds.) Soviet Literature, 1934; Yarmolinsky, A. (ed.) A Treasury of Russian Verse, 1949. *Stories in* Montagu, I. and Marshall, H. (eds.) Soviet Short Stories 2 and 3, 1943; Rodker, J. (ed.) Soviet Anthology, 1943. *Poems and Stories in* Soviet Literature 12 1956, 2 1958, 2 1961, 1 1963, 9 1964, 12 1966, 4 1967.

ABOUT: Grigson, G. (ed.) Concise Encyclopedia of Modern World Literature, 1963; International Who's Who, 1978–79; Kaun, A.S. Soviet Poets and Poetry, 1943; Poggioli, R. The Poets of Russia, 1960; Prominent Personalities in the USSR, 1968; Slonim, M. Modern Russian Literature, 1953; Slonim, M. Soviet Russian Literature, 1964; Smith, H. (ed.) Columbia Dictionary of Modern European Literature, 1947; Struve, G. Russian Literature Under Lenin and Stalin, 1971; Struve, G. Twenty-five Years of Soviet Russian Literature, 1944. *Periodical*—Soviet Literature 6 1974.

ROSEMARY TONKS

TONKS, ROSEMARY (D. BOSWELL)

(1932–), English poet and novelist, was born in England. Her father, a descendant of James Boswell, was an engineer who died of blackwater fever in Africa before she was born. Her mother, a great-great-niece of the composer Verdi, made a second marriage to a man whose work took him abroad. Rosemary Tonks stayed behind in England, spending her infancy in "baby-homes" and her childhood in boarding schools, including Wentworth. She was an inventive and talented child, academically top of the school year after year, good at games, a ringleader in ingenious mischief. At sixteen she published a children's book, *On Wooden Wings*. The same year she was expelled from Wentworth. According to one account this was "ostensibly for stealing tomatoes but actually for frivolity," but she told another and more sensitive interviewer that she did not know why, and "it never occurs to you you'll be rejected."

After that, Rosemary Tonks joined her mother and stepfather for a time in Lagos, where she suffered attacks of dysentery and malaria. At eighteen, after much traveling, she settled with her mother in a London flat, and the following year published a second book for children, *The Wild Sea Goose*. Rosemary Tonks did not attend a university but educated herself. She haunted public libraries, discovered London's literary bohemia, and wrote short stories, some of which were accepted by the BBC.

In 1952 she married a civil engineer and in 1954 went with him to Pakistan, where she soon contracted typhoid. She returned to England, recovered, went back to Karachi, and within two months was paralyzed with polio. She says that she did not despair: "I was perfectly happy. I was working" (on a free-verse epic which remains unpublished). Leaving her husband behind in Karachi, where he had business, she went to live in extreme but colorful poverty in Paris. There she made a full recovery from her illness and fell in love with French culture— especially with the Symbolist poets. She identifies in particular with Baudelaire, and on the centenary of his death visited his grave in Montparnasse, lying full-length on the poet's effigy to see if she was the same height: she was. Eventually she returned to London, and in 1963, at the age of thirty-one, published her first two novels and her first collection of poems.

Rosemary Tonks writes in *Contemporary Poets:* "I have developed a visionary modern lyric, and, for it, an idiom in which I can write lyrically, colloquially, and dramatically. My subject is city life—with its sofas, hotel corridors, cinemas, underworlds, cardboard suitcases, self-willed business, banknotes, soapy bathrooms, newspaper-filled parks; and its anguish, its enraged excitement, its great lonely joys." The city life she evokes is that of London, but her London is very much an imagined Paris—a vague Paris nearer, in fact, to Laforgue's than to Baudelaire's. The poems generally employ a long and often rhythmless line, and juxtapose exotic, dated, *symboliste* images with accounts of contemporary urban malaise and ennui.

Notes on Cafés and Bedrooms, her first book of poems, seemed to Burns Singer "daring." He wrote that she "conveys an impression of danger," but that her Rimbaudesque cultivation of hysteria leads her to be hysterical in her lan-

813

guage: "There is . . . an endemic inflation of language and metaphor." Anthony Thwaite responded similarly to *Iliad of Broken Sentences* (1967): "Cafés, bedrooms, hotels are put into the mixer to make London a sort of megapolitan Kasbah of the mind. . . . This building of a private country would not matter if Miss Tonks could manage it with less effusiveness and greater conviction." He called her poetry "rhapsodic stuff," and "overblown," and suggested that it was "really very English." Other critics have complained just as sourly about the lack of structure in her work—"a poetry of hysterical but random gesture." Edward Lucie-Smith, on the other hand, wrote that her work, influenced by her reading of "a vast range of French poets," reads occasionally "like a good translation." It did not bother him that it is "gaudy and exclamatory," and he quoted approvingly A. Alvarez's description of Rosemary Tonks as "an original sensibility in motion."

She herself told Christine Ross that she is "looking for an idiom that would enable me to do all the things I thought it was possible to do in poetry. An idiom that would let me introduce *ideas,* but running with life, never against the grain as an avant-garde exercise. My search has been for an ideal modern classical line":

I have lived it, and lived it,
My nervous, luxury civilization.
My sugar-loving nerves have battered me to
  pieces. . . .

It's quiet; just the fresh, chilly weather . . . and he
Gets up from his dead bedroom, and comes in here
And digs himself into the sofa.
He stays there up to two hours in the hole—and
  talks
—Straight into the large subjects, he faces up to
  everything.
It's . . . damnably depressing.
(That great lavatory coat . . . the cigarillo burning
In the little dish . . . And when he calls out: "Ha!"
Madness!—you no longer possess your own
  furniture.)

On my bad days (and I'm being broken
At this very moment) I speak of my ambitions . . .
  and he
Becomes intensely gloomy, with the look of
  something jugged,
Morose, sour, mouldering away, with lockjaw . . .

I grow coarse; and more modern (*I,* who am driven
  mad
By my ideas; who go nowhere;
Who dare not leave my front door, lest an
  idea . . .)
All right. I admit everything, everything! . . .

(from "The Sofas, Fogs and Cinemas")

Rosemary Tonks's early novels were very much like her poetry; John Lucas calls them "rather odd, almost hallucinatory journeys round the inside of one woman's skull." The first of the two that appeared in 1963 was *Opium Fogs,* which mixes fantasy with sometimes sharp satirical observation of the London literary world of the early 1960s. This was followed closely by *Emir,* about a young woman alone in London, and her running battle for dominance with an infatuated cosmopolitan. Rosemary Tonks herself believes that *Emir* is her best prose work, but most reviewers preferred *Opium Fogs.* John Lucas admired its "acid wit" and "free-flowing element of fantasy," and thought that it "allowed . . . [her] particular gifts a fine flowering." He was reminded of Stevie Smith, but added that "there is a good deal that is willed about her language, and unlike Stevie Smith at her best there are bad lapses from the successful control of tone that is so essential if writing of her sort is to succeed." Richard Newman also liked this novel better than *Emir,* but wrote that both were the products of "a highly individual imagination."

Five years later came *The Bloater,* in which Min, described by one reviewer as "a 1960s flapper," tries to choose between two lovers—the "bloater" of the title (a baritone) and a more ordinary and romantic young man named Billy. The *Times Literary Supplement* found "a coyness under all the brittle sophistication and, even with the engaging Min, too much sly knowingness can be somewhat tedious." But this novel had its champions, and John Lucas in *Contemporary Novelists* found it more "achieved" than its predecessors, "because it is the one where a genuine concern with her subject matter subdues the conscious mannerisms of her style to the point where they become a genuine contribution to the novel's meaning." There were some friendly reviews also of *Businessmen as Lovers* (1969), published in the United States as *Love Among the Operators,* though the more academic critics remained cool. Ian Hamilton wrote that in this brief tale of two "late thirty-ish heroines" traveling across France to an Italian holiday, the author "continues to dissipate a spry intelligence in smart, prattling facetiousness."

But her novels were becoming steadily less eccentric and more expert, and critical interest in them continued to increase with *The Way Out of Berkeley Square* (1970), though she still seemed to irritate more reviewers than she pleased. Arabella, the narrator of this novel, is thirty and unmarried, a "gilded slavey" for her widowed father. She is bothered by the narrowness of her existence, and worried about her younger brother, a poet who is suffering from polio in India. And her guilts and anxieties are compounded by the presence of an attractive married man who is indecisively pursuing her. Arabella's "heart-searching, whether on her own behalf or on behalf of others," seemed "a pretty pointless exercise" to a reviewer in the *Times Literary Supplement,* but Martin Levin disagreed. He wrote that the author had made "of this curious polarity a little poem of a novel filled with unexpected visions and slashes of wit. . . . Miss Tonks's protagonist is a fragile invention through which one views these clearly defined characters and sees, at the same time, reflections of a less certain and more intriguing personality."

The most praised of Rosemary Tonks's novels was *The Halt During the Chase* (1972). Sophie, a London girl in her thirties, begins to develop an interest in Eastern mysticism, and comes to realize that Philip, the ambitious young civil servant whom she deeply loves, will never be any good for her: "He didn't believe in the invisible world; and . . . I was getting ill without it." She tries to escape from him, and in the central (and most admired) section of the novel he runs her to earth in a French chateau. More economical and shapely than her earlier novels, and psychologically more precise, *The Halt* was enjoyed by most of its reviewers. Derwent May thought that the slender plot was "justified by the various kinds of sympathy the author brings to her main characters, and the amount she gets out of them. . . . Often very funny, mostly extremely well written, the book is buzzing with ideas, and full of details that stick because they are not ornament but belong."

Rosemary Tonks has published poetry in French and has had "musical dramatizations" of three of her poems broadcast by the BBC. She has experimented with prose poems and sound poems, and has tried her hand at plays, critical essays, and at least one film scenario. Her short stories have not yet been collected. She has been a book reviewer on the BBC's European Service, and has contributed to the *Times Literary Supplement* and other periodicals. Her favorite poet is Robert Lowell. Terry Coleman said of her that he had "never met a writer so single-minded, or so intolerant of her own weaknesses or of other people's. It is difficult to name anyone writing poetry in English, except Lowell, that she admires"; but neither had he ever "met anyone who was so hurt by critics."

As a person, Rosemary Tonks has struck interviewers as being exotic and "scatty," but also precise. She works amid a snowfall of notes and scribbles, but enjoys driving racing cars (a precise art), plans her novels meticulously, and likes her ideas "to have hard edges." A laureate of Baudelairean despair, she gives no evidence of poverty. She lives in a Queen Anne house in Hampstead, near the Heath, has a white Italian sports car, and owns a "crumbling shack" in Italy.

PRINCIPAL WORKS: *Poetry*—Notes on Cafés and Bedrooms, 1963; Iliad of Broken Sentences, 1967. *Novels*—Opium Fogs, 1963; Emir, 1963; The Bloater, 1968; Businessmen as Lovers, 1969 (U.S., Love Among the Operators, 1970); The Way Out of Berkeley Square, 1970; The Halt During the Chase, 1972. *For Children*—On Wooden Wings, 1948; The Wild Sea Goose, 1951.

ABOUT: Orr, P. (ed.) The Poet Speaks, 1966; Schmidt, M. and Lindop, G. (eds.) British Poetry Since 1960, 1972; Vinson, J. (ed.) Contemporary Novelists, 1976; Vinson, J. (ed.) Contemporary Poets, 1975. *Periodicals*—Guardian June 27, 1968; October 24, 1970; New Statesman April 12, 1963; April 14, 1972; New York Times Book Review June 21, 1964; March 28, 1971; Scotsman November 21, 1970; Times (London) May 12, 1976; Times Literary Supplement July 26, 1963; October 25, 1963; November 9, 1967; December 19, 1968; September 25, 1969; November 13, 1970; April 28, 1972.

*"TORGA, MIGUEL" (pseudonym of Adolfo Correia da Rocha) (August 12, 1907–), Portuguese poet, dramatist, novelist, and short story writer. His wife Andrée Rocha, Professor of Portuguese Literature at the University of Coimbra, writes (in French): "Miguel Torga is a writer who doesn't have much need of a biographer. Not that his life hasn't been full of experiences and events, far from it. But he is a man who has told his own story much better than anyone else could in his autobiographical novel *A criação do mundo* (The Creation of the World, 1938), and in the pages of his *Diario* (volumes 1–8, 1941–1959), where he transmits to us with boldness and originality his emotions, his ideas, his discouragements and his indignations.

"Nevertheless, when one reads his work as a poet, story writer, dramatist, and essayist, it is very relevant to know that he is a son of country people from Trás-os-Montes whose only means of sparing him the hard life of the Douro peasants was the traditional resource of sending him to Brazil, alone, when he was twelve years old. Faithful to the ancestral lessons of tenacity and perseverance of his parents, he succeeded, thanks to five years of work on a *fazenda* in the state of Minas Gerais, in putting aside enough money to enable him to study medicine at the
*tor′ ga

815

MIGUEL TORGA

ancient university of Coimbra. Since then his life has been divided between the duties of his demanding profession and the elaboration of a creative output which is now very extensive, including numerous collections of poetry, volumes of stories, plays, novels and essays.

"To know all this is not irrelevant because in fact these factors are very pertinent to his personality and consequently to what he writes.

"From his rural origin he has preserved, apart from his love of the land, the tenacity to make his way as citizen and as artist absolutely alone, outside literary factions, and also without compromise, in opposition to a gloomily hostile milieu, with the obstinacy which his father brought to protecting his vineyard against hail, mildew, and all the elements.

"The tropical vitality of Brazil was a dazzling world, where his adolescence could flower tumultuously; but it was also the scene of a painful exile which by contrast strengthened his love for his native village (São Martinho de Anta, near Vila Real). Miguel Torga is a countryman, a man of the earth. And his way of belonging to the whole earth consists precisely in being fundamentally of his own part of it.

"His profession, whether as a country doctor in the mountains of the Serra da Lousã, or as a specialist in ear, nose, and throat diseases in Coimbra, brings him constantly into contact with undisguised human reality, and this has given him a sense of fraternal solidarity with his fellow men, particularly with those who suffer. Conversely, when he expresses them in his books, his sympathy and compassion for humble people bear the marks of a realistic and active authenticity.

"If there is today in Portugal a writer who owes nothing to literature in the pejorative sense of the word, it is surely Miguel Torga. Nothing in him is superficial or feigned; everything is lived, discovered, conquered, before being expressed in writing. From whatever angle we approach this rich and diverse writer, what becomes immediately evident—quite apart from the direct, salty language, often charged with tenderness and lyricism—is the vigorous sincerity of a human presence, consumed by a thirst for the absolute, and struggling tirelessly to surpass itself.

" 'An artist cannot stand still,' he tells us. And the trajectory of his work bears this out. The feverish rhythm of his literary productivity has sometimes disconcerted both the critics and the wide public he has acquired. In fact, to take here only his poetry collections, his readers have no sooner finished meditating on the meaning of the dense and tragic symbolism of *O outro livro de Job* (The Second Book of Job, 1936), in which the poet tells us of his struggle with God, than *Lamentação* (Lamentation, 1943) extends the poet's despair to the temporal world. His cry, however, becomes that of all his brother men in *Libertação* (Liberation, 1944). But the flesh cannot yield itself totally to collective anguish, and is exalted by contact with the elements and the myths which Torga sings in *Odes* (1946). This pagan explosion is soon restrained, and the poet again finds an almost classic serenity in *Nihil Sibi* (1948). The years have only served to ripen this lyricism, which preserves, despite everything, an incomparable youthful fervor in *Orfeu rebelde* (Rebel Orpheus, 1958) and *Cantico do homem* (Song of Man, 1950).

"A similar curve can be established for his prose works, from the delightful stories of *Bichos* (1940) to the Bacchic fresco of *Vindima* (The Grape Harvest, 1945), the harsh truths of *Montanha* (Tales of the Highlands, 1941), and the subtle penetration of *Portugal* (1950).

"In fact, Miguel Torga is an artist who does not stand still, who constantly travels through Portugal, Spain, Europe, the world, who reads, studies, passes through the sieve of his nonconformist spirit the cultural, political and historical problems of his time.

"His lucidity with an aura of pessimism is, paradoxically, as the critic Armindo Blanco asserts, 'a permanent source of hope for all the young writers who believe in the Portugal of tomorrow. Because he shares with us the very humus of Portugal, Torga proves to us that the ancient land continues to be fertile and that the Lusitanian genius is not exhausted.' "

―――――

Torga has said that the events of an artist's life have no intrinsic importance—that it is the nature of his reactions to them that matters. But his autobiographical works reveal how deeply the harsh struggles of his youth and adolescence have marked his work. His basic pessimism however is balanced by a determination to assert the dignity of man and the importance of poetry and art. Constantly dissatisfied with his achievements in each genre, he has turned restlessly from autobiography to poetry to stories to plays, constantly revising and republishing his works.

The same restless search is manifest in a literary career which began while he was a medical student at Coimbra, moving even then from group to group and from one literary journal to the next. In his youth he was one of the young modernist poets associated with the periodical *Presença* from its foundation in 1927. But in 1930 he broke away and collaborated on the short-lived magazine *Sinal* and on *Manifesto,* and became a contributor to the periodical *Revista da Portugal* (1937-1938). Finally he emerged as a highly independent but rather isolated figure who, in the title of one of his poetry collections, calls himself an *Orfeu rebelde* (Rebel Orpheus, 1958). The need to find his own lonely path is a recurrent theme, for example in "Perplexidade" ("Perplexity"), translated here by Jean Longland in her *Selections From Contemporary Portuguese Poetry:*

... Arrive—I know I shall not arrive,
not by any means.
But at least I would like to go with lyrical calm,
keeping the true path without a qualm.

And I do not go.
More and more alone
in solitude,
I doubt the rightness of my steps.
I see the ancestral thirst of the multitude
turn away from the springs that I sense abide
and I remain in the mortal indecision
of affirming or denying the blind intuition
that serves me as staff and guide.

Torga is a poet of the mountains, and Denis Brass finds a key to the understanding of his work in a statement in one of his autobiographical books: "I am a kind of smuggler on the frontier of two worlds—Agarez [his native region] and the rest—a rest that, however much I may wish to ignore it, is also half of me." Some of his poetry is concerned with this notion, exploring the destiny of Portugal and the Iberian Peninsula as a whole in relation to the rest of the

world, as in his series of poems devoted to the great figures of Iberian history—St. Teresa, St. Ignatius Loyola, Cervantes, Camões. Torga's "Historia Trágico-Maritima" is a poem cycle about the great world-enlarging voyages of discovery by Portuguese navigators and seamen.

But above all Torga's is a poetry of protest against life's harshness and its brevity, and a record of the poet's battle against his own despairing view of humanity. Despite his transcendental language and imagery, Torga is an atheist who rejects God as an irrelevance, while struggling to believe in the integral humanism whose values his poetry constantly asserts. He returns repeatedly to an affirmation of the need to labor and produce, however uncertain the future or the results of one's efforts, finding examples of this almost existentialist commitment in the dogged perseverance of peasants and seamen, animals and plants. His despair at the false ideals mankind has followed reaches its height in *Lamentação* (Lamentation, 1943), a long cry of grief over human corruption, the decline from the original innocence of natural life.

This is the central theme of his most popular prose work, *Bichos* (1940, translated by Denis Brass as *Farrusco the Blackbird and Other Stories*), a collection of anthropomorphic animal stories, some humorous but most of them tensely dramatic and ending tragically with the animal's stoic acceptance of death. At the same time these stories are allegories of human predicaments and problems. The rooster Don Juan has been domesticated, and like man himself is cut off from the natural world of instinct. The story of Mago the cat is a tragicomedy on the same theme; the cat is spared the risks inherent in natural life but instead sacrifices itself to the love of an old maid. Morgado the mule, as he lies dying, is the lonely witness of the ultimate human infidelity, as his master stumbles off at the end of the story carrying on his shoulders the packsaddle that the mule is now too weak to bear. But the worst fate of all is reserved for Miura the fighting bull; unlike the others he has been encouraged to give free rein to his wild and combative instincts, only to discover in the end that it has all served to bring him to the brutal mockery of his death in the ring.

Torga's prose, with its short crisp sentences, has been called cinematic, relying as it does on vivid scenes expressed in only a few carefully chosen and powerfully revealing words. The stories in which he depicts the harsh life of his own backward and barren northeastern province of Trás-os-Montes, collected in *Montanha* (Tales of the Highlands, 1941) and *Novos contos da montanha* (New Tales of the Mountains, 1944) have been acclaimed by Portuguese critics as the most direct and vivid accounts of the area and its people. Like all his work, these stories show an intimacy with the nature and meaning of birth, death, and illness earned during his years as a country doctor.

"In my breast," Torga writes, "there is the anguish of desire which needs the aridity of Castile, the tenacity of the Basque country, the perfumes of the Levant and the moonlight of Andalusia. I am, by the grace of life, peninsular." He is an insatiable wanderer of his beloved Iberia, and especially of Portugal, and his deep knowledge of his country (and deep pessimism about it) is reflected in the impressionistic regional essays collected in *Portugal* (1950). The same kind of fatalism dominates his novel *Vindima* (The Grape Harvest, 1945), a harrowing tale of exploitation on a Douro port wine estate at the time of a disastrous harvest, in which one catastrophe succeeds another. Martin Seymour-Smith found this "genuine piece of late naturalism, in which the characterization is outstanding . . . reminiscent of Verga in its bright harshness and fatalism."

Another recurrent theme in Torga's work is that of the pilgrim, the wanderer, the prodigal who may or may not return. According to Denis Brass, this theme is worked out most powerfully in the two plays *Terra Firme* (Terra Firma) and *Mar* (Sea), which were published together in 1941. Torga's diary, which includes poems, short essays, and random jottings, continues to appear at the rate of a volume every two or three years, each new installment being welcomed in Portugal as a major literary event. He is Portugal's most distinguished man of letters, and that nation's automatic candidate for the Nobel Prize.

PRINCIPAL WORKS IN ENGLISH TRANSLATION: Farrusco the Blackbird, 1950. *Poems in* Longland, J.R. (ed.) Selections From Contemporary Portuguese Poetry, 1966.

ABOUT: Brass, D. *introduction to* Farrusco the Blackbird, 1950; Lopes, O. Cinco personalidades literárias, 1961; Lopes, O. O problema religioso em Miguel Torga, 1960; Lourenço, E. O desespero humanista de Miguel Torga, 1955; Melo, J. de, Miguel Torga, 1960; Moura, F. de, Homenagem a Miguel Torga, 1958; Seymour-Smith, M. Guide to Modern World Literature, 1973; Seymour-Smith, M. Who's Who in Twentieth Century Literature, 1976; Twentieth Century Writing, 1969. *Periodicals*—Dublin Review 470 1955.

"TOSON, SHIMAZAKI." *See* "SHIMAZAKI TOSON"

*TRANSTRÖMER, TOMAS (GÖSTA) (April 15, 1931–), Swedish poet, was born in Stockholm, the son of Gösta and Helmy Tranströmer, who were divorced when he was still a child. He comes from a long line of ship-pilots working in and around the Stockholm Archipelago, and since childhood has spent his summers on the small island of Runmarö. Transtömer graduated from the University of Stockholm in 1956 and began his career (1960–1966) as a psychologist at the Roxtuna youth prison near Linköping, in the heavily wooded heart of Sweden. Since 1967 he has lived in the city of Västerås, working part-time as an occupational psychologist dealing especially with the handicapped. Transtömer has traveled very widely, both on business and for pleasure. He was married in 1958 to Monica Bladh and they have two daughters. Robert Bly says "his face is thin and angular, and the swift, spare face reminds one of Hans Christian Anderson's or the young Kierkegaard's."

Transtömer achieved immediate success with his first volume of poetry, *17 dikter* (17 Poems, 1954), which had such an impact that, as one critic remarked, it seemed that for some years "everybody heard and saw the same as Tomas Transtömer." He was imitated not so much for his subject matter, which consists predominantly of scenes from nature (and often from the landscapes and seascapes of Runmarö), but for his style. These poems are classical in their meters and formal in their diction, but their imagery is often surreal, distinguished by strikingly apt but wholly unexpected metaphors. Gogol wears a jacket "threadbare as a pack of wolves." In the night the poet hears "the constellations stamping in their stalls." The fettered energy of the universe implied in this latter metaphor is an underlying theme of the collection, where rest and movement seem to be counterbalanced—the title of one poem is "In the foaming prow there is rest." For Transtömer the visible world is not the only world. Another, deeper insight can be achieved at special moments, as at the point of waking: "In the day's first hours consciousness can embrace the world/ as a hand grasps a sun-warmed stone." Another of Transtömer's themes is the way in which the past coexists with us in the present. Civilization is compared to a whaling station where the inhabitants are always aware of the dead giant's presence. Human progress through the ages is like a procession, forever changing shape and form, while God is unchanging and seldom seen, crossing sideways through the procession "as a vessel passes through the mist/ and the mist notices nothing."

*trän' strû mər

Swedish Information Service

TOMAS TRANSTRÖMER

Hemligheter på vägen (Secrets on the Road), which followed in 1958, continues the themes of *17 dikter* and indicates by its title the poet's preoccupation with our rare moments of insight into the pattern of the universe. In the title poem he is struck by darkness: "I stood in a room that contained all moments—/ a butterfly museum./ And yet the sun as strong as ever./ Its impatient brushes painted the world." The tension between rest and movement is expressed in other poems; on the one hand he can speak of "imprisoned eternity's hammering fists," and on the other of "God's energy/ curled up in the darkness."

In *Den halvfärdiga himlen* (The Half-Finished Heaven, 1962) Tranströmer is less absorbed in mysteries and more open to the everyday world. There are poems about earthly love, and several poems express a sense of delight in life and confidence in its possibilities, often using trees to symbolize these feelings. The poet is aware of the suffering in the world but does not allow this knowledge to overcome the cautious optimism of the title. In a poem about a visit to Egypt and the tragedy and poverty he witnessed there, he hears a voice in a dream saying: "There is one who is good./ There is one who can see everything without hate."

The relationship between the poet and the world about him is further explored in *Klanger och spår* (Echoes and Traces, 1966), where his subject matter derives from several countries—America, Portugal, the Congo, Algeria—and his poems lead into larger and more cohesive statements than in earlier collections. Tranströmer distances himself from the suffering about him: in retrospect, his glimpse of a political prisoner

gazing out of a window in Lisbon seems unreal. And he sees the present in a historical perspective. When he hears bulletins from the war in Algeria, he sees the face of Dreyfus, while an old newspaper, "full of events," rots gradually to become part of the earth and the future. He also seeks moments of isolation from human company. When he goes to bed he writes: "The smaller boat is launched from the bigger boat./ I am alone on the water./ Society's dark hulk drifts further and further away." In a poem about Edvard Grieg he imagines the composer withdrawing into an attic "to grapple with silence"—one of the many references to music in Tranströmer's works. By this time Tranströmer was firmly established as the finest Swedish poet of his generation, though in fourteen years and four collections he had published only fifty-two poems.

Mörkerseende (1970, translated by Robert Bly as *Night Vision*) does not extend Tranströmer's range, but emphasizes particularly the themes of the individual in relation to history and in relation to the political present. History is alive in the old volumes that view the poet from the bookcase, or in portraits where there is condensation from breathing on the *inside* of the glass. There is a strongly autobiographical element in these eleven poems, reflecting a crisis or series of crises in the poet's personal life, including that precipitated by the death of his mother, to whom he was particularly close. Deeply interested and emotionally involved as he is in world politics, Tranströmer here as elsewhere refuses to follow the fashionable cry for literary engagement and his contemporaries' "furious hunger for simplicity"—a view which has earned him much criticism in the New Left press. More than half of *Stigar* (Paths, 1973) consists of translations from Robert Bly and the Hungarian poet János Pilinszky. *Östersjöar* (1974, translated by Samuel Charters as *Baltics*) is a long poem in six parts, in which Tranströmer writes of different aspects of the Baltic, with the sea acting as a link between the past and the present (his grandfather was a Baltic pilot) and between Sweden and other countries—the East Baltic where "the citizens are under control."

Tranströmer's idiom has altered very little during his career. According to Eric Sellin, its principal evolution "has been to move slowly away from the metric rationale either toward a 'field' rationale—that is, letting words somehow stake out their own claims on the page on the basis of shape, respiration, and the general terms of each poem's needs and laws ... [or] toward the elimination of such concerns and the adoption of straight prose."

819

Now, as at the beginning, it is above all Tranströmer's imagery that distinguishes his poetry. Robert Bly, in a letter to Eric Sellin, wrote: "He really has an amazing gift for the image—he knows just how much room the image needs to expand and resonate, and he keeps everything quiet and spacious around it. The poem becomes like a violin body." Tranströmer's "cosmic image," according to Sellin, is characteristically "an open-ended, soaring image, usually involving nature and combining microcosm and macrocosm." Sellin draws attention to Tranströmer's capacity for defining the infinite in terms of the finite, and the way in which his images forge "ideal ramifications which together surpass the sum total of the image's explicable parts." And he quotes in evidence from "Resan" (Journey): "Houses, streets, skies,/ blue inlets, and mountains/ opened their windows"; and from "Vinterns formler" (Winter's Formulas): "I stand under the starry heavens/ and feel the world crawl/ in and out of my coat/ as in an anthill."

Tranströmer has said that he first became interested in poetry in his teens, when he read the work of the French surrealists, and he works with unconscious associations, leaving the reader great freedom to supply his own connections and imaginative leaps. He regards existence as "a great mystery, and this mystery has at certain moments a tremendous charge, so that it has a religious character, and it's often at such times I write. . . . I really do have the feeling—purely personally—that I fulfil some function here, in the service of something else." Eric Sellin has applied to Tranströmer a passage from Walt Whitman's preface to *Leaves of Grass:* "If he breathes into anything that was before thought small it dilates with the grandeur of life and the universe."

PRINCIPAL WORKS IN ENGLISH TRANSLATION: Twenty Poems (translated by Robert Bly), 1970; Night Vision (translated by Robert Bly), 1972; Windows and Stones (translated by May Swenson and Leif Sjöberg), 1972; Selected Poems of Paavo Haavikko and Tomas Tranströmer (Tranströmer's poems translated by Robin Fulton), 1974; (with Harry Martinson, Gunnar Ekelöf) Friends, You Drank Some Darkness: Three Swedish Poets (chosen and translated by Robert Bly), 1975; Baltics, translated by Samuel Charters, 1975.

ABOUT: Bly, R. introduction to Twenty Poems, 1970; Penguin Companion to Literature 2, 1969; Sjöberg, L. introduction to Windows and Stones, 1972. Periodicals—American-Scandinavian Review 1 1972; American Swedish Monthly 5 1966; Books Abroad Autumn 1963, Winter 1971; New York Times Book Review September 7, 1975; Scandinavian Studies August 1965, Summer 1971; Scandinavica Supplement May 1973; Times Literary Supplement October 31, 1975.

*TREMBLAY, MICHEL (June 25, 1942–) French-Canadian dramatist, fiction writer, and film scenarist, was born and raised in a working-class district in Montréal's East End, and grew up a leftist and a Québeç separatist. At the age of eleven he started to specialize in graphic arts; at thirteen he won a scholarship to a classical college, but left after three months "because our professors told us that we were the intellectual cream of society. This was more than I could stomach." So he returned to secondary school, resumed his study of graphic arts, and became a linotype operator, like his father and brother. When he was eighteen he wrote his first play, *Le Train* (unpublished), which in 1964 won first prize in the Concours des Jeunes Auteurs de Radio-Canada (Radio Canada's Young Authors' Competition). In 1966 Tremblay published a collection of fantastic stories, *Contes pour buveurs attardés* (Tales for Late Drinkers), several of which had been presented in 1965 in a recital program called *Messe noire* (Black Mass) by the Mouvement Contemporain. Their director then had been André Brassard, who was to become Tremblay's regular collaborator—the director of his plays and later of his films also.

Despite his political beliefs, Tremblay's plays are not directly propagandistic, and he has said: "I hate political theatre. I think it's boring. We don't have to say political things on stage, we just have to be what we are. When people come to see my plays and say 'My God, are we really like that?' it's much more political than having one of my characters say 'Vive Québec libre!' I think it's stupid to go on a stage and say 'We have to separate.' If we just demonstrate how different we are, it will be clear that we have to be independent." Tremblay's characters, Henry Popkin writes, are "not at peace with the world. They are the victims of greed, repression or loss of identity, and they are likely to take refuge in the tinsel world of Montreal's night clubs. . . . Corrupt values are evasions, whether in seedy homes or in night clubs." Tremblay's method is to put the ordinary Québecois on stage, confronting his audience with themselves, and so effecting a true interaction between stage and auditorium.

Thus in *Les belles-soeurs* (1968, translated by Bill Glassco and John Van Burek under the same title), a working-class housewife who has won a million trading stamps gathers her female friends and relations to help her stick them into books. All of these women are frustrated and vulnerable, catty towards each other, and contemptuous in their gossip about their men. In a funny yet sad climax they run off with all the

*träN blä′

MICHEL TREMBLAY

cepted, but the plan fell through because Québec's Minister of Culture refused to pay the company's expenses, apparently because the play did not offer a sufficiently attractive picture of Québec life, and because its language was found objectionable. Eventually, in 1973, the play did reach Paris, where it was warmly received by the French critics. In the same year it was given a successful production in English at the St. Lawrence Centre for the Arts in Toronto, again staged by André Brassard.

Apart from plays and stories, Tremblay's early work also includes the novel *La cité dans l'oeuf* (The City Inside the Egg, 1969), a fantasy about the discovery, exploration, and eventual destruction of a world enclosed in a glass egg. A later novel, *C't à ton tour, Laura Cadieux* (It's Your Turn, Laura Cadieux, 1973), is a more realistic story, reminiscent of *Les belles-soeurs,* about a group of women who pour out their life stories to each other in a doctor's waiting room. However, since the success of *Les belles-soeurs,* Tremblay has concentrated mainly on the theatre, producing not only original plays but a translation of Aristophanes' *Lysistrata* (1969) which was staged by Brassard at the National Arts Center in Ottawa and also in Montréal, and versions of plays by Paul Zindel and Tennessee Williams.

À toi pour toujours, ta Marie-Lou (1971, translated by Glassco and Van Burek as *Forever Yours, Marie-Lou,* is a harsh study of a Québécois family "ruled by the curé, crushed by ignorance." Léopold is an intelligent man frustrated by the pointlessness of his factory job and infuriated by his devout wife's acceptance of their lot. Thanks to her rigid adherence to a primitive interpretation of Catholic doctrine, the couple have made love four times since their marriage, and each time Léopold has been made to feel like a rapist. Finally, seeing no way out, he kills Marie-Lou and commits suicide. One of the daughters declines into religious mania, but the other girl, Carmen, manages to escape from her impoverished background to become a country-and-western singer. (She is the central figure in a later play, *Sainte Carmen de la Main,* translated by Van Burek as *St. Carmen of the Main.*) The break-up of the family in *Forever Yours, Marie-Lou* reflects the break-up of the monolithic social structure that had existed in Québec until the 1960s, when the power of the Catholic church was broken, bringing Québec into secular alignment with the rest of Canada.

The play was first staged by André Brassard at the Théâtre de Quat' Sous in 1971, and the English version followed in 1972 at Bill Glassco's Tarragon Theatre in Toronto. *Forever*

stamps—why should one woman escape while they remain trapped in poverty? Only the winner's sister tries to help her, and she is the black sheep of the family, having escaped the fate of the others by becoming a hostess in a dubious nightclub. This is a political play only implicitly, in the sense that these women are diminished and alienated by degrading social conditions, and because it is written in *joual,* the pungent, inelegant *patois* spoken in Québec. Tremblay's use of this dialect on the stage is a deliberate rejection of standard French culture in Québec, and an assertion of the existence of an independent Québec culture, reflecting the emergence of a colonized people from years of social and cultural oppression and discrimination.

Tremblay was made to pay for his boldness—the play, which was written in 1965, had to wait three years for a production. In 1966 it was unanimously rejected on a first reading by the jury of the Dominion Drama Festival. Tremblay then had to peddle the play round Montréal for two-and-a-half years before it received its first public reading at the Centre d'Essai des Auteurs Dramatiques. It was subsequently bought by the Théâtre du Rideau Vert, and finally staged there on August 28, 1968 in a production by André Brassard. This first production of a Tremblay play has been called "probably the most important single event in the history of Québec theatre." In 1971 a revival was seen in Montréal by the great French actor-producer Jean-Louis Barrault. Excited both by Tremblay's play and its performance, he invited the Rideau Vert company to perform it in Paris under the auspices of his international theatre festival, the Théâtre des Nations. The offer was eagerly ac-

Yours, Marie-Lou was nominated in 1972 for the Chalmers Award, which is given annually for the best Canadian play acted in English in Ontario, but the award actually went to David Freeman's *Creeps,* a play about spastics which was first staged by Glassco and which Tremblay has translated into French. He was not displeased at this turn of events, explaining that, had his own play won, he would have had to refuse the award, since a Québec separatist could scarcely be the author of a *Canadian* play. In 1971 Tremblay did accept an award from the Canada Council that enabled him to live and work in Paris for a year.

In the musical comedy *Demain matin, Montréal m'attend* (Tomorrow Morning Montréal Waits for Me, 1972), with music by François Dompierre, Louise, like Carmen in *Marie-Lou,* escapes from her crippling environment. Setting out on a career as a nightclub singer, she tells her mother: "You're just going to go on doing what you started doing fifty years ago. . . . You're going to go on moaning and not do anything till you take your dying breath." But such escapes are rarely true means of liberation in Tremblay's plays, and in *En pièces detachées* (1973, translated under the same title by Allan Van Meer), the escape ends in madness.

In *La Duchesse de Langeais* (1969, translated under the same title by Van Burek) and in *Hosanna* (1973, translated under the same title by Glassco and Van Burek), the attempted escape is into homosexuality. The couple in the latter play live together as husband and wife, one of them adopting an exaggerated masculinity while the other is a transvestite who goes to a nightclub party as Elizabeth Taylor in her film role as Cleopatra—a marvellously theatrical part. In the end both drop their poses and embrace their real identities. Henry Popkin received the impression "that Tremblay likes to think of *Hosanna* as an allegory about Québec, which, he would argue, must not pretend to be France, Canada or the United States but must be itself." The original French version was produced in Montréal by André Brassard, while the English translation was staged by Bill Glassco not only in Toronto but also, less successfully, on Broadway in New York's Bijou Theater, where it received mixed reviews and closed after twenty-eight performances.

Trois petits tours, a trilogy of plays written for television, was shown in Canada on December 21, 1969 and again on August 22, 1971. Tremblay has also written a number of films, of which the first was *Françoise Durocher, Waitress* (1972), a half-hour color film produced by the National Film Board of Canada and directed by André Brassard. Tremblay and Brassard then turned to full-length feature films, beginning with *Il était une fois dans l'est* (Once Upon a Time in the East, 1974), which Brassard directed in close collaboration with Tremblay. It brings together a group of characters very like those in the earlier stage plays, following the fortunes of two groups of characters in parallel: an old woman wins a fortune in trading stamps, her dreadful friends come in to help her with them, but the stamps all turn to dead leaves; meanwhile, a beauty contest staged in a transvestite nightclub brings to the surface frantic fears and jealousies.

The special virtue of film is that it can bring the seedy working-class home and the glossy nightclub into equally clear focus, and Tremblay has said: "We noticed a peculiar pattern emerging: all the characters we had given life to on the stage knew each other, but their inter-relationship was often vague and begged further definition. So it was partly to tie things together, to complete the group portrait, that we embarked on *Il était une fois dans l'est*—a work in which already-established characters now find themselves in fresh dramatic situations." The film replaced Mordecai Richler's *The Apprenticeship of Duddy Kravitz* as the Canadian entry at the 1974 Cannes Film Festival, and from there went to the Chicago Film Festival later the same year. David Robinson saw it there and called it "funny and violent and ferociously sad." Other films written by Tremblay are *Le soleil se lève encore sur la Rue Belanger* (The Sun Rises Again Over Rue Belanger, 1975), directed by Brassard, and *Parlez-nous d'amour* (Speak to Us of Love, 1975), directed by Jean-Claude Lord. By 1974 success had enabled Tremblay to move from an apartment to a house of his own, and in that year he received the Prix Victor-Morin awarded by the Société Saint-Jean-Baptiste de Montréal.

The play *Bonjour là, Bonjour* (1974, translated under the same title by Glassco and Van Burek) deals with four sisters whose lives revolve round the only boy in their family, their brother Serge. He is struggling to free himself from their stifling attentions, but is himself in love with one of the girls. Another of the sisters has degenerated into a pathetic pill-popper, a third is a good-humored "pal" with a self-destructive eating problem, while the fourth, the only member of the family to have escaped from the working-class milieu, is here a thoroughly unpleasant character, a greedy slut who has married a doctor. Serge's problem—how to discover and express his authentic self—is related to that dramatized in *Hosanna:* liberation from lies and disguises. Tremblay sees his own work as feminine, as against the "manliness" which previously ruled in Québec theatre. "The traditional theatre view in Québec pits the son against the father. In *Bonjour là, Bonjour* I'm saying that you can say 'I love you' to your father. Serge becomes a hero when he says it. He says nothing until the end and then breaks through to his father and has to yell when he does. And Bill Glassco has him say it to the audience which is very interesting." Love, as in all Tremblay's plays, is fleeting but precious.

The musical comedy *Les héros de mon enfance* (My Childhood Heroes), with music by Sylvain Lelièvre, was staged by Gaetan Labrèche at the Théâtre de la Marjolaine in 1976. Instead of transposing the social and cultural reality of a particular sector of the Québec population, Tremblay here fills the stage with such well-known fairy-tale characters as Red Riding Hood and the Wolf, Beauty and the wicked fairy Carabosse, Cinderella and the Prince. In his preface Tremblay gives a long list of his child-hood heroes, a mixture of European and American, traditional and modern, from Pinocchio to Batman, from the Hare and the Tortoise to Laurel and Hardy, Walt Disney, and Tintin. His characters here, however, all speak a very European French: "My characters suffer, as always, from nervous disorders, but this time they are very cultivated. They may shock good sense, but not the ear. Their problems and their quarrels are very 'cultural.' "

Tremblay is described by David McCaughna as "a stocky man with huge round glasses which make his eyes pop forward and . . . a sartorial penchant for flowing Indian shirts. He's certainly one of Quebec's most celebrated writers now. Both as a playwright and novelist, Tremblay has established himself as a voice of a new Quebec sensibility that has largely found its voice in movies to date." Martin Knelman suggests that the "revolution . . . [Tremblay] has made in Quebec theatre has to be compared to the shock-waves John Osborne caused when he put Jimmy Porter on the stage of the Royal Court in *Look Back in Anger* . . . to announce the death of aristocratic dictatorship in the arts. Like Osborne, Tremblay is insisting on the importance of the rough-edged, the deprived, the semi-educated, and the impoverished—on their right to be heard. His work does not imply that attention must be paid to these people because they're pathetic losers; it suggests instead that their lifestyle and their aspirations have an authenticity and vitality that make them more honest, more engaging, and more valuable than anything presented by the worn-out, established order." Tremblay received the Ontario Lieuten-

ant-Governor's Medal in 1976. He is regarded by many critics as Canada's leading dramatist.

PRINCIPAL PUBLISHED WORKS IN ENGLISH TRANSLATION: Les Belles-soeurs, 1974; Hosanna, 1974; Bonjour là, Bonjour, 1975; En pièces detachées, 1975; Forever Yours, Marie-Lou, 1975; La Duchesse de Langeais and Other Plays (Berthe; Johnny Mangano and His Astonishing Dogs; Gloria Star; Surprise, Surprise), translated by John Van Burek, 1976.

ABOUT: Anthony, G. Stage Voices, 1978; Belair, M. Michel Tremblay, 1972; Colombo, J.R. Colombo's Canadian References, 1976; Toye, W. (ed.) Supplement to The Oxford Companion to Canadian History and Literature, 1973. *Periodicals*—Motion November-December 1973, August 1975; New York Times October 13, 1974; Nord Autumn 1971 (Tremblay Issue); Performing Arts Summer 1973, Spring 1975; Saturday Night May 1975; Times (London) November 27, 1974; Times Literary Supplement October 26, 1973.

*TRIOLET, ELSA (September 25, 1896–June 16, 1970), French novelist, translator, and critic, was born in Moscow, one of the two talented daughters of the lawyer Yuri Kagan and the former Hélène Berman. Both of them were profoundly influenced by their father's love of literature and their mother's love of music. "Our house was a house of music," Elsa Triolet wrote later. "The walls, windows and furniture were all saturated, heavy with sounds. My mother, an excellent pianist, arranged quartets, trios, or concertos for two pianos. . . . All my childhood I fell asleep to music."

Elsa's elder sister Lydia (Lilya) was a beautiful redhead, a painter and sculptor who married the prominent formalist critic Osip Brik and became the mistress of the great futurist poet Vladimir Mayakovsky. It was, however, Elsa who first attracted Mayakovsky's attention, when she was still a fifteen-year-old schoolgirl at the Lycée Valitzki in Moscow. She recalls how he shocked her mother with his talk of climbing up to her room at night. Mayakovsky was at that time making his living as an artist, and his poetry, heard for the first time one summer evening during a country walk, came as a revelation to her: "I was wild with emotion over the fact that I had discovered something which had been so near for so long but of which I was totally unaware. I asked for more and more."

Elsa Kagan entered the Institute of Architecture and for a time "was interested only in mathematics and drawing." After her graduation she left Moscow amid the revolutionary cataclysm of 1918 and went to France. There she met and married André Triolet, a Frenchman with a passion for horses. In her early writing career she was helped by the critic Viktor Shklovsky and by

*trē ō lā

TRIOLET

ELSA TRIOLET

Maxim Gorky, who encouraged the publication of her early novels, the first three of which were written in Russian. Another writer, Ilya Ehrenburg, tells the story in his autobiography: "In the early days of the Revolution she married a Frenchman, André Triolet ... and she went with him to Tahiti. ... After their return from Tahiti André Triolet remained in Paris, while Elsa went on to Berlin. She was very young, attractive, with the pink colouring of a Renoir picture, and sad. Viktor Shklovsky included four or five of her letters in his book *Zoo*. When the book came out Gorky told Shklovsky that he liked the letters written by a woman. Two years later the Moscow publishing house Krug (The Circle) published Elsa Triolet's first book *Na Tahiti* (In Tahiti). Later Elsa lived in Paris where I saw her almost every day in Montparnasse."

Na Tahiti (1925) draws on the author's own experiences in Tahiti and her second novel, *Zemlyanichka* (Wild Strawberry, 1926), is also partly autobiographical—a story about two sisters which some Russian critics regard as her best book. Elsa Triolet's meeting on the night of November 4, 1928 in the bar of the Coupole in Montparnasse with the surrealist poet Louis Aragon was the turning point in both their lives. Aragon, whom she married in 1939, has written obsessively about her in such books as *Les Yeux d'Elsa* (Elsa's Eyes, 1942), *Elsa* (1959), and *Le Fou d'Elsa* (Elsa's Fool, 1963); it is extraordinary that her sister played a comparable role in the poetry of Mayakovsky, who lived with Lilya and her husband in a famous and scandalous *ménage à trois*.

In the long poem *Le Fou d'Elsa*, Aragon writes: "I am created by the one who loves me," and in fact he has repeatedly claimed that this is literally true of his relationship with his wife, whom he regards as a great woman and a great novelist. Twenty years before Sartre and Camus, he was denouncing the "absurdity" of the world and seeking a way forward from "nausea" to human solidarity. When he met Elsa in 1928 his spiritual nihilism had reached crisis point, and it was through her that he found a resolution both of his internal conflicts and of the artistic difficulties involved in moving from surrealism to realism—a realism that blended social responsibility with personal lyricism, so that the Catholic critic Jean Sur has called it the "realism of love."

Louis Aragon and Elsa Triolet both took a passionate interest in the social problems of their time. They visited Russia together in 1930, 1931, 1932, and 1936—the last time specifically to see Gorky, at his request, shortly before his death. With other writers they went to Spain and campaigned for the republican side against the fascists in the civil war. Meanwhile Elsa became a French rather than a Russian writer, beginning with *Bonsoir, Thérèse* (Good Evening, Therese, 1937) and *Mille Regrets* (A Thousand Regrets, 1942). These novels deal with the loves, hopes, and fears of men and women caught up in the anguish of the years leading up to and immediately following the defeat of France. And indeed, Elsa Triolet's novels as a whole make up a fictionalized chronicle of her own times and experiences. She was always a realist but, despite her commitment to communism, never accepted "socialist realism." She believed, as she explained in her critical work *L'Écrivain et le livre* (The Writer and the Book, 1948), that a committed work of art has value only to the extent that it expresses the "flesh and blood" of the artist.

The themes which recur most often in her work are the sense of alienation that comes with exile, and the similar loneliness of the artist. *Le Cheval blanc* (1943, translated by Gerrie Thielens as *The White Charger* and by Mervyn Savill as *The White Horse*) has as its rootless hero a young Frenchman. Michel has grown up in a succession of hotels all over Europe and as far away as the South Pacific. His search for love and friendship during the period of the Munich crisis involves him with several women and with Stanislas, son of a Russian-Jewish terrorist, who like himself is an exile, a cynical sentimentalist nostalgic for his lost Russia. Michel eventually finds himself by sacrificing himself in the "phony war." Immensely successful in France, the novel had a mixed reception in translation. Stephen Stepanchev found it "spirited and entertaining" but thought the author had herself been "taken in by the miraculous, if empty, charm of her hero" and that "the book needs a generous dose of irony."

During World War II Elsa Triolet played a very active part in the Resistance, of which her husband was a much-decorated hero. Her story *Les Amants d'Avignon* (The Lovers of Avignon, 1943), published clandestinely under the pseudonym "Laurent Daniel," provides a convincing impression of France during the German Occupation. It centers on Juliette Noël, a youthful heroine of touching simplicity and gaiety who sustains herself as a fugitive from the Vichy police with girlish fantasies about film stars.

This story was republished under the author's real name as one of the three wartime stories making up her collection *Le premier accroc coûte deux cents francs* (1945, translated by Francis Golffing as *A Fine of Two Hundred Francs*), which brought her the Goncourt Prize in 1945. The most subtle and interesting of these stories is the one about a painter, Alexis Slavsky, who does not fight and is almost completely apolitical, but who makes his contribution to the Resistance simply by treasuring his art and his privacy. "Here, it may be supposed," wrote a reviewer in the *Times Literary Supplement,* "Mme. Triolet has had to grope for understanding, and the result is a striking revelation of the sense of boredom, nervousness, confusion and waste which the Occupation must have given to so many ordinary Frenchmen."

L'inspecteur des ruines (1948, translated by Norman Cameron as *The Inspector of Ruins*) is a satirical novel about the disintegration of postwar French society. Its picaresque hero, orphaned during the Resistance, floats aimlessly through life until he meets a strange old man who suggests that he should appoint himself "Inspector of Ruins" and tour Europe, like Gogol's "Inspector General," seeing what could be picked up. Reviewers admired some individual scenes, but tended to feel that an excellent satirical idea had been inadequately exploited. Nor was there much enthusiasm for *Le Cheval roux* (The Red Horse, 1953), an apocalyptic fantasy advocating what seemed to one critic "a naively kind-hearted form of communism." The author herself appears in the story, embarrassing some readers with her references to the literary renown of herself and her husband.

Later novels include *Roses à crédit* (Roses on Credit, 1959), *Luna Park* (1959), and *L'Âme* (The Soul, 1963), a trilogy of considerable breadth and power about the increasing artificiality of postwar life in "L'Age de Nylon" (The

Age of Nylon). *Le Grand Jamais* (The Great Never, 1965) seemed to some critics her finest book, fusing as it does all her profoundest preoccupations. After the death of the artist whom she loved, Régis Lalande seeks to understand him more completely by going through his papers. But the man she finds there is quite different from the one she had known, and his public reputation seems to belong to yet another person; we can never really know another human being.

Le Grand Jamais may have been suggested by the widespread misunderstanding of Mayakovsky and his poetry; Elsa Triolet was deeply affected by his suicide in 1930. She wrote down her memories of him in the preface to her French translations of his works, *Vers et proses de Maïakovski* (1957). She also made excellent French versions of works by another old friend, Viktor Shklovsky, of the poetry of Marina Tsvetayeva, and of Chekhov's plays, and produced a bilingual anthology of Russian poetry. In addition, she wrote a number of critical works about Russian literature, including a useful study of Chekhov. She died of a heart attack at her home at Saint-Arnoult-en-Yvelines. Elsa Triolet was a gifted storyteller who left, according to Henri Peyre, a "vivid and attractive, if not profound" record of the exciting and anguished times through which she lived.

PRINCIPAL WORKS IN ENGLISH TRANSLATION: The White Charger, 1946; A Fine of Two Hundred Francs, 1947; The White Horse, 1951; The Inspector of Ruins, 1952.

ABOUT: Adereth, M. Commitment in Modern French Literature, 1967; Cruickshank, J. French Literature and its Background: The Twentieth Century, 1968; Ehrenburg, I. People and Life, volume 3, 1963; Garaudy, R. L'Itinéraire Aragon, 1961; Madaule, J. Ce que dit Elsa, 1960; Sur, J. Aragon: le réalisme de l'amour, 1966; Who's Who in France, 1969–1970. *Periodicals*—Europe 506 1971; Times Literary Supplement May 27, 1949; July 18, 1952.

"TROUT, KILGORE." *See* FARMER, PHILIP JOSE

"TUR-MALKA." *See* GREENBERG, URI ZVI

TURNBULL, COLIN (MACMILLAN) (November 23, 1924–), American anthropologist, was born in Harrow, England, the son of Scottish parents, John Rutherford Turnbull and the former Dorothy Chapman. He was educated at Westminster School (1938–1941) and served during World War II with the coastal forces of the Royal Navy Volunteer Reserve (1942–1945), in which he became a lieutenant. After the war Turnbull went to Magdalen College, Oxford

© 1979 by Jill Krementz, courtesy Jonathan Cape

COLIN TURNBULL

University, receiving his B.A. with honors in 1947, his M.A. in 1949. His education continued at London University's School of Oriental and African Studies (1948–1949), and in 1949–1951 he did research in Indian social philosophy at Banaras Hindu University in India. In 1951, shifting his field of specialization from India to Africa, he returned to Oxford and entered the Institute of Social Anthropology, of which he became a diplomate in 1956.

It was from there that Turnbull made his first visit (1951) to the Mbuti pygmies of the Ituri Forest, in the northeastern Congo, now Zaïre. What he saw so interested him that he returned in 1954 and lived for some time with a large band of pygmies. It is of course common nowadays for anthropologists to live among a people whose society they are studying, but Turnbull's achievement was considerable, the pygmies being notoriously shy and elusive. Earlier studies had depended largely on what could be learned about the pygmies from neighboring tribes, and this had given rise to serious misunderstandings, including the belief that the Congolese tribesmen exercised authority over the pygmies and used them as servants. This view of their relationship was not shared by the pygmies, though they were glad enough to exchange their meat and honey for their larger neighbors' pots and knives.

Turnbull managed to involve himself with extraordinary intimacy in the daily life of the band. It was one that hunted game with nets, a technique calling for the close cooperation of every able-bodied member, and this made it essential that everyone should remain on good terms. Quarrels did occur, but in every band there was

a kind of official buffoon, usually a poor hunter, whose task was to distract disputants by making them laugh. Turnbull himself, as a novice hunter, too tall to run easily through the forest, fulfilled this role for a while.

His ethnographic study of the pygmies, containing much important new information, brought him a B. Litt. from Oxford in 1956. In 1957–1958 he returned to study other pygmy bands, and in 1959 he joined the staff of the American Museum of Natural History in New York, where he was assistant curator in charge of African ethnography in 1959–1965, assistant curator from 1965 to 1969. His first book, *The Forest People* (1961), a personal and nontechnical account of his life among the pygmies, was greeted with universal enthusiasm by both laymen and fellow anthropologists. Simon Ottenberg said that the book was "about individuals and their perception of the world, but . . . is also concerned with their society and culture as they see it. . . . Throughout the book the author's search for the meaning of life in the Pygmies' rituals, their symbolism, and their social relations, is blended with an admirable description of their social life." Margaret Mead wrote that it added "an entirely new dimension to existing literature on primitive people," and J. Vansina called it "a masterpiece . . . the combined work of Mr. Turnbull anthropologist and Mr. Turnbull artist."

Some critics suggested that Turnbull was a little too partisan in his account of these peaceful, happy, and musical people—"too much of a pygmy." A more rigorously objective and technical study of the same subject was made available when the American Museum of Natural History published Turnbull's B. Litt. thesis as *The Mbuti Pygmies: An Ethnographic Survey* (1965). *Wayward Servants: The Two Worlds of the African Pygmies* (1965), also written for specialists rather than for the general reader, discusses in detail the relationship between the pygmies and their Congolese neighbors.

The Lonely African (1962) sets out to consider "Africa's emergence into our brave new world" from the point of view of the individual African himself. Chapters discussing the transitional problems of urban Africans alternate with chapters on village life, each in effect a biography of an Eastern Congo villager at a time when the country was still under Belgian rule. Turnbull's intention, he wrote, was to show "how the problems of transition reach down into the souls of individuals, creating conflicts and loneliness in all but a lucky few." The result was admired as a highly readable, informative, and well-documented study, and "a quietly personal, yet fervent plea for racial assimilation and enlightenment."

This was followed by *The Peoples of Africa* (1962), in which Turnbull distinguishes between hunters like the pygmies and the Bushmen, pastoralists like the Masai, and agriculturists like the Kikuyu of Kenya. The book was warmly welcomed as an excellent introduction which never condescends to the young people for whom it was written. *Tradition and Change in African Tribal Life* (1966), also intended for young readers, explains how life is lived in four tribal societies, all of which Turnbull knows at first hand: the Bushmen, the Mbuti pygmies, the BaNdaka, who live by fishing, and the Ik, a light-skinned mountain people of northern Uganda, who live by farming. David Hapgood said of it that "if your knowledge of Africa were to be limited to one book, I would recommend [this one]. More wisdom about the way most people live in Africa is contained within its covers than in any other book I know, for adults as well as for children. . . . Turnbull traces African life through the cycle from birth to death . . . and he writes with the clarity of a man who knows his subject so well he can make it simple."

Turnbull had lived with the Ik for two separate periods between 1964 and 1967, and they are the subject of his remarkable book, *The Mountain People* (1972). A nomadic hunting people, the Ik had been confined to northern Uganda by the hardening of national boundaries, and their hunting grounds had been taken over as a game reserve. Forced to become farmers, without training, in an arid mountain area, the Ik lived on the edge of starvation. Under these conditions, as one reviewer wrote, they "have discarded as superfluous most of the institutions and values often assumed essential to human society. The family, religion, affection, pity—all these are meaningless to the Ik, for whom individual survival has become the primary value." So in this wretched society, old people and small children are turned out to forage for themselves, children steal food literally out of the mouths of their grandparents, parents hide food from their starving children. The only source of entertainment and humor among the Ik is the suffering of others, including those closest to them, and they actively seek to bring about such suffering through cruel practical jokes. After two years of observation and much thought, Turnbull "learned not to hate the Ik. . . . The Ik clearly show that society itself is not indispensable for man's survival, that man is not the social animal he has always thought himself to be, and that he is perfectly capable of associating for purposes of survival without being social."

Turnbull saw in the Ik an example and a warning of what may happen in western societies where "technology removes the necessity for cooperation between humans." Some reviewers rejected this as a "foolish and inappropriate sermon," but others, as Robert Ardrey wrote, saw "hanging over every page . . . the vision of Ulster, of Bangladesh, of New York streets, of our debatable future." And even those who disagreed with Turnbull's conclusions were fascinated by his account of these strange people, whom he came to admire for their shocking but absolute honesty. Julian Huxley recommended the book "to all who are concerned with human suffering," Margaret Mead called it "a beautiful and terrifying book," and Carleton S. Coon said it was "a masterpiece. A magnificent if ghastly tale." It has been adapted for the theatre by Denis Cannan and Colin Higgins as *The Ik* (1975), and staged by Peter Brook in Paris and London.

Man in Africa (1976) provides a panoramic view of the peoples and cultures of Africa, derived from work done some years earlier when Turnbull was preparing a new permanent exhibit on that subject for the American Museum of Natural History. The book, like the exhibit, emphasizes the central importance to the peoples of Africa of their environment, of their bond with the natural world, which is the source of the powerful unity that runs through traditional African societies. Turnbull suggests that if Africa can move into the modern world while retaining something of this traditional harmony with land and wildlife, "it may once again show that order, in human society, is possible without law, that government is possible without abuse, and that the family of man is more than a myth." Welcomed by most critics as a useful introduction, it was marred for some by what John Pfeiffer called "a kind of colonialism in reverse," presenting African societies as Edens before the Fall and consistently belittling Europeans and Americans.

Turnbull's work has not been limited entirely to African themes. *Tibet, Its History, Religion, and People* (1969) was written in collaboration with Thubten Jigme Norbu, the elder brother of the Dalai Lama, and interweaves a history of the country and Norbu's recollections. *The Straits Settlements, 1826–1867* (1972), which describes fifty years in the history of Singapore, Malacca, and Penang, derives from Turnbull's Oxford doctoral thesis (D.Phil., 1964).

In 1969 Turnbull left the American Museum of Natural History to become professor of anthropology at Hofstra University, and in 1971 he went as professor of sociology and anthropology to the Virginia Commonwealth University. He has also taught at Hunter College (1966–1967) and Vassar (1968–1969), lectured in African anthropology at Columbia University, served as consultant on Africa to the U.S. State Department, and as consultant on Africa and India to the American University, Washington, D.C. Among his many awards are those of the Voss Fund and the National Science Foundation for research in Africa, and the Birla research fellowship in Indian religion and philosophy. Dr. Turnbull, "a lanky Scotsman," is now an American citizen. He says that he is "interested as an anthropologist generally in the ways different people live and think; and, as an individual, interested in the apparent deterioration in human relationships, interpersonal and intergroup . . . especially as exemplified in racism." His principal recreation is music, and he is especially interested in harpsichords, old and new.

ANNE TYLER

PRINCIPAL WORKS: The Forest People, 1961; The Lonely African, 1962; The Peoples of Africa, 1962; The Mbuti Pygmies: An Ethnographic Survey, 1965; Wayward Servants: The Two Worlds of the African Pygmies, 1965; Tradition and Change in African Tribal Life, 1966; (with Thubten Jigme Norbu) Tibet, Its History, Religion, and People, 1969; The Straits Settlements, 1826–1867: Indian Presidency to Crown Colony, 1972; The Mountain People, 1972; (as editor) Africa and Change, 1973; Man in Africa, 1976.

ABOUT: Contemporary Authors 1–4 1st revision, 1967; Mair, L. African Societies, 1974. Periodicals—American Anthropologist June 1962, June 1963, February 1970; Christian Science Monitor October 26, 1961; Economist April 11, 1970; Library Journal September 1, 1965; April 15, 1967; March 1, 1969; Man March 1967; Natural History April 1969, March 1973; New Statesman December 8, 1961; New York Herald Tribune Books January 7, 1962; August 5, 1962; New York Times Book Review September 24, 1961; August 5, 1962; January 26, 1969; November 12, 1972; April 11, 1976; Pacific Affairs Winter 1969–1970, Winter 1972–1973; Publishers Weekly November 6, 1972; Saturday Review November 17, 1962; January 25, 1969; Time October 14, 1972; Times Literary Supplement February 9, 1962; April 9, 1970; January 31, 1975.

TYLER, ANNE (October 25, 1941–), American novelist and short story writer, writes: "I was born in Minneapolis, Minnesota, but spent my early years traveling across midwestern and southern America with my parents, who were Quakers searching for some kind of peaceful, communal way of life. After their last experiment (five years in Celo Community, in the mountains of North Carolina) my family moved to Raleigh, and from the age of eleven on I grew up there with my three younger brothers in a more or less conventional fashion, although to this day I am surprised by the taste of Coca-Cola and have difficulty using the telephone.

"I started telling myself stories at around the age of three, when I couldn't sleep nights and wanted some way of amusing myself. While I was growing up, I listened very carefully to the tobacco-stringers and tenant farmers who lived around us, but it wasn't till I was in high school and first read Eudora Welty that I realized that the stories these people told could be literature.

"When I was sixteen I entered Duke University, where I was lucky enough to land in the English class taught by Reynolds Price, who was then just completing his first novel. I majored in Russian, and in 1961–1962 went on to do graduate work in Russian at Columbia University. In the fall of 1962 I returned to Duke to work as a Russian bibliographer in the library, and there I met an Iranian child psychiatrist, Taghi Modarressi, whom I married in 1963. We moved then to Montreal, and it was there that I wrote my first novel, If Morning Ever Comes, largely for something to do while I was waiting to find work.

"Since coming back to the U.S. in 1967, I have lived in Baltimore with my husband and our two daughters—Tezh, born in 1965, and Mitra, born in 1967. I am very happy with my insulated life, in which I write novels and short stories concocted entirely from imagination; I consider that what I am doing is not really so very different from what I did at age three."

Anne Tyler's first three books are all set in North Carolina and, as Clifford A. Ridley says, are "steeped in the physical details of that world —the flatness, the heat, the parochialism, the laconic and off-hand speech patterns—and steeped most of all in a sense of community and self-protectiveness that transcends race, class, age, and everything else." If Morning Ever

Comes, published in 1964 when the author was only twenty-two, centers on Ben Joe Hawkes, a Columbia law student. Desperately worried about the various crises facing his family of women back in Sandhill, North Carolina, he suddenly decides that he must go home and help. As a reviewer wrote in *Library Journal,* "his sojourn in Sandhill shows him that his grandmother, mother and six sisters love him but are not dependent on him, although he may have helped some of them to grow in awareness as he himself does. The echoes of his dead father's desertion of his mother for another local woman, his older sister's flight from her husband, his grandmother's encounter with the death of a childhood friend, and his own reunion with a high school sweetheart are the main ingredients of his long weekend. He finds that he can't really 'go home again,' but he can (and does) take a part of home with him back to the city."

K.G. Jackson called this "one of the most delightfully zany novels I have ever read—and at the same time one of the most serious and sane. A young man, an editor and critic, said to me about it: 'It scares me. How can a twenty-two-year-old girl know so much about how a man feels?' . . . [The story is] told with a monumental feminine indirectness that produces absolute clarity of purpose at the end. A triumph of humor and perception." Other reviewers admired the book but with reservations—R.W. Saal, for example, thought its pace too slow, and Julian Gloag, who managed to find the book as well as its hero totally humorless, thought that Anne Tyler should have taken more risks and "let herself go." The author herself says that she wrote the book "in a way out of curiosity, out of wondering how it would feel to be part of a huge Southern family. Oh, there were four kids in our family, but we were spread out in years. I always felt isolated from the South; I always envied everybody. I used to work at tying tobacco and listen to all the farm wives strung out along a long table, talking all day long; they fascinated me."

She herself dislikes her first novel, which she thinks too bland. She feels no happier about the second, *The Tin Can Tree* (1965), in which a little girl is killed in a tractor accident and her mother, stunned by grief, is unable to give her attention to her ten-year-old son Simon. The mother's grown-up niece, who lives with the family, tries to take care of Simon while at the same time dealing with her own problems. It is Simon himself, in the end, who rescues his mother from her preoccupation with the dead child. This novel, like its predecessor, addresses itself to "the question of caring for people—whether we can and whether we should"—the question which, as Clifford A. Ridley points out, "runs so strongly and sometimes so contradictorily through Miss Tyler's work." *The Tin Can Tree* was praised for its perception and its highly disciplined writing, and reminded Millicent Bell of "the Carson McCullers of twenty-five years ago—who . . . also wrote of human disconnection and the need for love in a stagnant community. . . . Life, the young writer seems to be saying, achieves its once-and-for-all shape and then the camera clicks. This view, which brings her characters back on the last page to where they started, does not make for that sense of development which is the true novel's motive force. Because of it, I think, her book remains a sketch, a description, a snapshot. But as such, it still has a certain dry clarity."

In fact, Anne Tyler recognizes that her books reveal her "utter lack of faith in change. I really don't think most people are capable of it, although they think they are." She said in 1972 that she likes her third novel, *A Slipping-Down Life* (1970), "because it's the one book of mine in which the characters do change. . . . I felt as I was writing it that I was being braver." It tells the story (derived from a newspaper report) of a plump and homely teenaged girl who slashes the name of a local rock singer on her forehead, becomes a freak attraction at his performances, and eventually marries him. Reynolds Price said that "it finds and studies a kind of girl and boy previously unknown to me but now, I suspect, unevictable tenants of my head, for sadness and pleasure."

The Clock Winder (1972) was the first of Anne Tyler's books to be set in Baltimore, her home since 1967. It is an account of ten years in the lives of the Emerson family of Roland Park, and of Elizabeth Abbott, the shy North Carolina girl who joins the family as Mrs. Emerson's "handyman." During this decade, one of the Emersons kills himself, Elizabeth is shot and wounded by another, and the matriarch has a stroke. Elizabeth stays on through it all to marry one of the Emerson sons and hold the family together. Sara Blackburn found her a "delightful heroine . . . in her ashamed passivity, her struggle against it, her bursts of energy and what prevents them, her wry, open humor . . . a recognizable and even memorable character who encompasses many of the contradictions that women are seeking to resolve today." Martin Levin found "gentle charm" if not much substance in the book, and the *New Republic*'s reviewer praised the author's "remarkable understanding of the intricacies of family life, a sympathy for odd-ball characters who never become merely southern grotesques." And it seemed to this critic (in spite of what Anne Tyler says about her lack of faith in the human capacity for development) that Elizabeth does change in the course of the novel, "while around her the seven Emerson children, already grown when the book begins, move in and out of her life, she finally unalterably affecting them, they in turn affecting her."

Anne Tyler's favorite among her books is *Celestial Navigation* (1974), whose central character, Jeremy Pauling, is perhaps the closest she has come to writing about herself. The resemblance is not physical, Jeremy being a pudgy and diffident bachelor in his late thirties, the owner of a rundown Baltimore rooming house. He spends most of his time making collages out of odds and ends, and he has not mustered the courage to leave his own block for years. An attractive, pragmatic, and motherly young woman rents one of Jeremy's rooms and recognizes that there is more to him than meets the eye. They establish a common-law marriage and have five children. In the end she leaves him, unable to cope with the distance that Jeremy creates around him: "He sees from a distance at all times, without trying, even trying not to. It is his condition. He *lives* at a distance." In emotional terms, then, the story is a sad one, sad enough to cause one reviewer "truly physical distress." But Jeremy's way of seeing, which destroys his marriage, is also what makes him (as the reader is gradually persuaded) a great artist; if he is ill-equipped for the ordinary exigencies of life, it is because he does not steer by ordinary instruments but by "celestial navigation."

This novel was very warmly praised. Eileen Kennedy called it "a portrait of the artist Jeremy and an unusual portrayal of how the artist sees, selects, and arranges. . . . Tyler has translated into words the mind that works with form, line, color. . . . penetrating the psyche of the artist who distances reality because that is the only way he can see reality." Gail Godwin wrote that "Anne Tyler is especially gifted in the art of freeing her characters and then keeping track of them as they move in their unique and often solitary orbits. . . . She has a way of transcribing their peculiarities with such loving wholeness that when we examine them we keep finding more and more pieces of ourselves." Katha Pollitt called the book "extraordinarily moving and beautiful."

There was no less praise for *Searching for Caleb* (1976), a study of individualism and conformity in a rich Baltimore family. As one reviewer wrote, in a phrase that could be applied to all of Anne Tyler's books, it "has as its primary theme the ways in which people influence and depend upon each other while remaining always alone." It impressed Robert Ostermann that the novel "relies on all the conventional elements and does not fiddle with form or perspective or any of the dislocations of sensibility that some current novelists . . . have adopted. And yet *Searching for Caleb* . . . is a fresh, rich, absorbing, and totally contemporary piece of fiction. Tyler pulls it off by locating all our late Twentieth Century disruptions and indeterminacy in her characters and in the narrative they embody, not in formal devices." Katha Pollitt wrote: "at the center of Tyler's characters is a private, mysterious core which is left, wisely, inviolate. Ultimately this wisdom is what makes Tyler more than a fine craftsman of realistic novels."

The least successful of Anne Tyler's recent books was *Earthly Possessions* (1977). "The marriage wasn't going well and I decided to leave my husband," it begins. "I went to the bank to get cash for the trip." Instead, Charlotte Emory is taken as a not unwilling hostage by an inept and innocent bank robber, Jake Simms, who needs money to retrieve his girlfriend from a home for unmarried mothers in Florida. All Jake and Charlotte have in common is a dislike of "closed-in spaces"—her household in Charlotte's case, prison in Jake's—but at least, Charlotte comes to realize, "we *are* traveling," and afterwards she goes home again and discovers that she always had been traveling: "We couldn't stay in one place if we tried." Nicholas Delbanco found the novel technically very skillful, but "the wheels are a touch too audibly clicking, and inspiration seems second-hand."

Anne Tyler has also published a number of short stories in the *New Yorker, Saturday Evening Post, McCall's,* and elsewhere, but not yet a collection. She enjoys writing short fiction, as a sort of "dessert" after finishing a novel. In general, she says, she writes "because I want more than one life; I insist on a wider selection. It's greed, plain and simple. When my characters join the circus, I am joining the circus. Although I am happily married, I spend a great deal of time mentally living with incompatible husbands." And she is still "waiting to see what I'll be when I grow up."

As she has explained to various interviewers, Anne Tyler gets up at about 6 A.M. to clean the house and feed the children and fix an evening meal. She then imprisons herself in her working room, "a stern white cubicle," from just after 8 A.M., when her children go to school, until they return at 3:30. "If things are going well, I feel a little drugged by the events in my story; I'm desperate to know what happens next. When the children ring the doorbell I have trouble sorting my lives out. . . . We bake cookies. Run the dog. Argue a lot. My characters grow paler and paler and finally slink away." Sometimes she imagines "retiring to a peaceful little town where everyone I've invented is living in houses on Main Street. There are worse retirement plans. After all, they're people I've loved, or I never would have bothered writing about them." Elsewhere, speaking of the preoccupations that recur in her books, she says "I'm very interested in day-to-day endurance. And I'm very interested in space around people. The real heroes to me in my books are first the ones who manage to endure and second the ones who somehow are able to grant other people the privacy of the space around them and yet still produce some warmth." When she is writing a novel, she begins with the story, "with my characters talking and surprising. But I still don't know what it's about, or what it means. The second part comes when I read it back, and suddenly it seems as if someone else is telling me the story and I say 'now I see' and I go all the way back and drop references to what it means." It matters to her that she "be considered a serious writer. Not necessarily important, but serious. A serious book is one that removes me to another life as I am reading it. It has to have layers and layers and layers, like life does. It has to be an extremely believable lie."

PRINCIPAL WORKS: If Morning Ever Comes, 1964; The Tin Can Tree, 1965; A Slipping-Down Life, 1970; The Clock Winder, 1972; Celestial Navigation, 1974; Searching for Caleb, 1976; Earthly Possessions, 1977.

ABOUT: Contemporary Authors 9–12 1st revision, 1974; Vinson, J. (ed.) Contemporary Novelists, 1976; Who's Who in America, 1978–1979; Writers Directory, 1976–1978. *Periodicals*—Book World May 14, 1972; Harper's November 1964; Library Journal November 15, 1964; October 15, 1965; December 15, 1975; National Observer July 22, 1972; May 4, 1974; January 24, 1976; New Republic May 13, 1972; May 28, 1977; New York Review of Books May 26, 1977; New York Times May 3, 1977; New York Times Book Review November 22, 1964; November 21, 1965; April 28, 1974; January 18, 1976; May 8, 1977; New Yorker March 29, 1976; June 6, 1977; Saturday Review December 26, 1964; November 20, 1965; June 17, 1972; Times Literary Supplement May 23, 1975; August 27, 1976; Washington Post August 15, 1978.

"U TAM'SI," GÉRALD FÉLIX TCHICAYA

(pseudonym of Gérald Félix Tchicaya) (August 25, 1931–), Congolese poet, was born in Mpili in what was then the French colony of Moyen Congo. (Moyen Congo became independent as Congo-Brazzaville and is now the Congo Republic.) He is the son of Jean Félix Tchicaya,

a much respected Congolese politician. The family moved to metropolitan France in 1946, when U Tam'si's father was elected as one of the first African deputies to the reformed French National Assembly. The boy was educated at a *lycée* in Orleans and at the Lycée Janson de Sailly in Paris. U Tam'si did a variety of jobs after he left school, working as a farm laborer in the Champagne, a draughtsman for a Paris construction company, a restaurant doorman, and a carrier in Les Halles, and writing poetry in his spare time. From 1957 to 1960 he was a producer for French radio, adapting over a hundred traditional African stories for broadcasting. A collection of these was published in 1968 as *Légendes Africaines*. U Tam'si has frequently revisited Africa, especially the Congo and Zaïre, but his home is in Paris. Gerald Moore, who has been the poet's principal champion in the English-speaking world, says that "this tension between childhood memories of Africa and everyday mundane experience in an alien capital, between his passionate presence in the suffering Congo and his physical absence from it, is one of the dominant themes of his poetry."

As a black poet writing about Africa in French, and often surrealistically, U Tam'si could scarcely avoid comparisons with the major poets of *négritude* Aimé Césaire and Léopold Sédar Senghor. However, Gerald Moore has suggested that U Tam'si is carrying *négritude*—a conscious pride in Blackness—"forward to the era when Africa's face is no longer just towards the white world, but towards itself," and the poet himself insists that "my *négritude* was unconscious, or at least involuntary." Though Césaire has influenced his poetry, U Tam'si seems to Moore "more inward, spiral, exploratory" in his invention, and totally undidactic. With Senghor, U Tam'si shares a strong vein of Roman Catholic imagery and a preoccupation with such fundamental symbols as rivers, trees, flowers, and blood. The River Congo itself, near which U Tam'si was born, is a recurring motif in his work, and so is the sea into which it flows. Since "every river goes wandering to the sea," the sea represents for him the mingling of all the races of the world in a common humanity. This insistence on the unity of all experience and the absurdity of racial divisions informs all of U Tam'si's writing.

U Tam'si maintains that his "is a spoken poetry, not a written poetry, even though it is on paper." And certainly his repetition of images within the poem and the sonorousness of his diction show his links with the traditions of African oral poetry. At the same time, he has said that "Rimbaud was my first master and he is still my master."

Le Mauvais Sang (Bad Blood, 1955), U Tam'si's first collection, did not arouse much interest. It was followed by *Feu de brousse* (1957, translated by Ulli Beier under the pseudonym "Sangodare Akanji" as *Brush Fire*). The second collection dwells on the sense of alienation produced in U Tam'si by his European education, and both contain poems in which Christ is seen not only as the victim but as the betrayer of mankind, a theme that recurs in the poet's later work:

> faked presence I shall be unfaithful
> for christ the god of armies
> has betrayed me
> when he allowed his skin to be pierced
> treacherous christ
> here is my flesh of bronze
> and my blood closed
> by the numberless—copper and zinc
> by the two stones of my brain
> eternal through my slow death
>
> ("Presence")

À Triche-coeur (To Cheat-Heart, 1958) is a more directly autobiographical collection, full of intimations of isolation and rejection. Gerald Moore has examined at some length the endlessly inventive use of tree imagery—religious, sexual, genealogical—in this volume and in *Épitomé*, which followed in 1962. In one poem in the latter collection, Moore writes, "the tree becomes not only an image of unknown growth and secret origin; of life, death and regeneration; but of cultural purity and impurity. At least I take this to be the meaning of these lines, where U Tam'si appears to re-enact the hate affair with 'assimilation' which Damas and Senghor have played out before him:

> it is likely enough
> false growths upon the roots of my tree
> poison my utmost branch
> I no longer know the essence of my soul
> all the doors open into shut houses
> my hands crinkle already
> like these dying flowers.
>
> ("The Dead")

"This particular group of images could be pursued much further through the strange landscape of U Tam'si's imagination," Moore goes on, "but I hope we have travelled far enough to establish that this young poet is distinguished not only by *élan* and energy and the startling power of his invention, but above all by the intensity with which he explores, eviscerates, rearranges his vocabulary of images."

Épitomé is subtitled *Les Mots de tête pour le sommaire d'une Passion* (Headings for the Summary of a Passion). It won the grand prize for poetry at the Dakar Festival in 1966, and is generally recognized to be U Tam'si's most important work. The poems in this volume reflect the terrible events that took place in the Congo in 1960. U Tam'si worked in Leopoldville from August to October 1960 as editor of a short-lived daily newspaper called *Le Congo*. Poems like the one quoted above express his anguish at the normality of the life he returned to in Paris while tragedy continued to unfold in his native land.

The dismemberment of the Congo and the martyrdom of Patrice Lumumba also pervade the autobiographical, introspective poems in *Le Ventre* (The Belly, 1964), even when neither is named. *Arc musical* (Bow Harp, 1970) is considerably less agonized and intense, but was much admired for its technical skill and a new quality of lyricism. U Tam'si is regarded by many critics as the leading poet of his generation from French-speaking Africa.

When U Tam'si returned to Paris in 1960 he served as cultural attaché at the Congo-Brazzaville embassy there. He has spent the 1970s working with UNESCO in Paris. U Tam'si is a frequent contributor to *Vie Africaine,* and is a member of several French literary societies and committees. Mercer Cook has described him as "small but solid, shy and stubborn, fierce in the bristle of his moustache, but tender; in short, a man of dreams and of passion." He is said to be a notable raconteur.

PRINCIPAL WORKS IN ENGLISH TRANSLATION: Brush Fire, 1964; Selected Poems, translated by Gerald Moore, 1970. *Poems in* Hughes, L. (ed.) Poems From Black Africa, 1966; Mphahlele, E. (ed.) African Writing Today, 1967; Moore, G. and Beier, U. (eds.) Modern Poetry From Africa, 1963; Reed, J. and Wake, C. (eds.) French African Verse With English Translations, 1972; Black Orpheus 15 1964; Transition (Kampala) 9 1963.

ABOUT: Beier, U. (ed.) Introduction to African Literature, 1966; Dathorne, O.R. African Literature in the Twentieth Century, 1976; Herdeck, D.E. (ed.) African Authors Vol. 1, 1973; Killam, G.D. (ed.) African Writers on African Writing, 1973; Moore, G. (ed.) African Literature and the Universities, 1965; Penguin Companion to Literature 4, 1969; Senghor, L.S. introduction to Épitomé, 1962; Zell, H. and Silver, H. (eds.) Reader's Guide to African Literature, 1971.

*VAN DUYN, MONA (JANE) (May 9, 1921–), American poet, writes: "I was born in Waterloo, Iowa, but my family moved to the village of Eldora, Iowa when I was a year old. I have three vivid memories of my first year of life: being weaned (my mother blackened her breasts with burnt cork); having my throat

*van dīn

MONA VAN DUYN

"Three things made my childhood bearable, a 'best friend,' who took the place of a sister, my maternal grandmother, and school. My grandmother, loving, illiterate, superstitious, had an inexhaustible supply of unjudging affection for me, and I flourished when I stayed with her or when, as she frequently did, she stayed with us. In school, which I adored, my teachers praised and encouraged the devoted, hard-working student they found in me. My education was the painfully limited one offered by a tiny, mid-west town of that time. Though I was forced to practice for hours each day on a saxophone (which I hated, but which my parents had bought as a second-hand bargain), I had never heard a piece of classical music until I went to college; nor had I seen a serious painting or print. I fell in love, very early, with poetry (my first poem, which rhymed, was written at age six) and, from the fifth grade, wrote notebooks full of poems, none of which were shown to parents or teachers. In my writing, and there only, I had freedom and power. I set myself the project of reading every novel and book of poetry, good or bad, in the town library, and succeeded. In adolescence my life was perhaps more than usually unhappy, since I was the tallest female in the town and, for all I knew, in the world, and I thought of myself as a freak.

"In college, to which my parents reluctantly allowed me to go on a scholarship (for they feared I would get 'big-headed,') I found one English professor, of extraordinary sympathy and perception, who intellectually adopted me, guided my reading and encouraged me to write poetry seriously. It is to him that I owe any sense of confidence in my work that I have. I graduated with three majors and received a scholarship to graduate school at the University of Iowa, which had the first writers' workshop in the country. There I made my own way, learned to teach, began to publish, and married Jarvis Thurston, a young writer from the Western United States.

"When my husband finished his Ph.D. (but before I finished mine) we left to teach at the University of Louisville, in Kentucky. While there, we began our literary magazine, *Perspective,* which we still edit and publish. After four years, having been recommended for promotion, I was informed by the dean that if I was 'that good' I would have to be fired, since the university could not have husbands and wives teaching in the same department. (How I wish I had had the support of the present day women's rights movement!) My husband resigned and we moved to St. Louis, Missouri, where he took a job in the English department of Washington

painted by a doctor; being terrified by the first Black I ever saw (I had been repeatedly warned that a 'big, black nigger' would 'get' me if I was not good). I was walking and talking in sentences by the age of one year and can remember several things I said at these moments. My father, a farmer before my birth, was a gas station manager. His father was an Iowa farmer, of Dutch ancestry. My mother, a hysterically nervous, driven, but gregarious woman was the daughter of German farmers.

"I was an only child, and all my mother's anxieties, fears and resentments focussed on me. Among her many needs was that of considering me to be a chronic invalid who would perish instantly if I showed any independence or even played as vigorously as the other children did. I was sent to bed at 7:30 every night until I entered high school, and kept home from school for weeks at the slightest sign of a cold or flu. Attempts at disobedience were quickly squashed by frightening threats that I would 'get sick and die,' since my parents would refuse to pay 'the doctor bills.' (It was not until I left home and lived on my own in college that I discovered, to my utter astonishment, that I was perfectly healthy and could do anything anyone else did without falling ill.) I was a 'good,' docile child, but nothing I achieved ever quite satisfied my mother. My father, an unimaginative man who had an unexpressed fondness for me, took no part in my rearing except for delivering the punishments my mother requested. I led, as a consequence of all this, a very inward life, finding that reading enormously was of great consolation (though my parents constantly warned that so much reading would cause me to lose my mind).

University and I (since here, too, the 'nepotism' rule was enforced) became a lecturer in the night school of adult education. And here we still are. I have stopped teaching and, since winning the Bollingen Prize and the National Book Award, have travelled about the United States giving readings of my poems at colleges and universities.

"Since the incident at Louisville I have had intermittent bouts of depression, with their attendant shock treatments and months-long stays in psychiatric hospitals. However, unlike Lowell, Berryman, Plath or Sexton, I have not found the subjects for my poems in my illness; it is the years of good health between depressions that I cherish, that seem to me most real, and that provide me with occasions for poems. My adult life, thanks to my husband, my friends and my writing, is a happy one, though I still regret that I was unable to have children."

James Vinson in *Contemporary Poets* has called Mona Van Duyn's work "homey and sophisticated, colloquial and formal, sincere and witty, charming and tough—all at the same time." She is indeed a poet difficult to classify, which may be why it took so long for her reputation to catch up with her achievement.

Her first book, *Valentines to the Wide World* (1959), was published by a small press in Iowa and not much reviewed, but the twenty-five poems in *A Time of Bees* attracted a good deal of serious attention. A critic in the *Virginia Quarterly Review* wrote that "there are few poets whose dedication to the art is more intense, whose craftsmanship is more meticulous, whose verbal effects are more stunning, and whose visions are more intrinsically meaningful and wonderful." Not all of the comment was wholly favorable: Robert Mazzocco, for example, spoke of her as a poet who was a "failed novelist"— "sprinkling summery particulars and sour afterthoughts, funny yet compassionate, working with slant rhymes, a sestina, couplets (end-stopped and enjambment), her poems, so rattlingly well assured, are less poems (they can all be easily paraphrased, for one thing) than a series of sketches, essayish anecdotes of experience."

These apparently quite contradictory views are resolved, perhaps, by something Vinson says: "The prime joy of reading these poems lies in the mixture of the casual and the precise. The subtlety of the 'attack' on the objects of the poems belies simplicity, and often the reader gasps in surprise at what the poem is doing. Here the basis of many of these poems is a complex image or analogy, often beautiful, sometimes ugly, reflecting the complexities of life which, once perceived, are obvious and unforgettable." And he cites as an example the title poem, "A Time of Bees," which is "about a domestic problem of a beehive in a wall [and] also about love and mystery."

To See, To Take brought Mona Van Duyn both a Bollingen Prize (shared with Richard Wilbur) and the National Book Award. It was called "a collection of remarkably tough-minded lyrics" by a poet who is "unspoiled by those abstractions which plague too many of her contemporaries." One of the most admired poems in the collection was "Leda," which quotes Yeats's "Did she put on his knowledge with his power/ Before the indifferent beak could let her drop?" and answers:

Not even for a moment. He knew, for one thing,
  what he was.
When he saw the swan in her eyes he could let her
  drop.
In the first look of love men find their great
  disguise,
  and collecting these rare pictures of himself was
  his life. . . .

In men's stories her life ended with his loss.
She stiffened under the storm of his wings to a
  glassy shape,
  stricken and mysterious and immortal. But the
  fact is,
  she was not, for such an ending, abstract enough.

She tried for a while to understand what it was
  that had happened, and then decided to let it
  drop.
She married a smaller man with a beaky nose,
  and melted away in the storm of everyday life.

Merciful Disguises selects poems from all of the previous volumes (including *Bedtime Stories,* a sequence of "haunting reconstructions of an old woman's stories" published in a limited edition in 1972), together with some new work. Herbert Leibowitz wrote that Mona Van Duyn is "a brainy poet," not a confessional one— "even when she writes about mental illness . . . she keeps the delicate propriety of distance," puts on the "merciful disguises of metaphor." Although her themes are often domestic and suburban, Leibowitz believes that "the center of gravity—and dread—lies elsewhere, in the trenches of marriage, where routine narrows possibility, and familiarity breeds an icy, stricken candor. Mona Van Duyn is a love poet, not of courtship or sexual windfalls, but of the bittersweet aftermath, the slow dying of feeling and its fitful replenishments. . . . In a fallen world, her poems contend, against 'brilliant wasting' and death, man can marshal 'shapes, storms of fresh possibilities.' By which she means the hilarious masks of Eros, the wry benedictions of love. And the power of words, 'both birthright and blessing.'"

Mona Van Duyn has published short stories, reviews, and critical articles as well as poems. She is the daughter of Earl Van Duyn and the former Lora Kramer. Apart from the awards already mentioned she has received the Eunice Tietjens Prize from *Poetry* (1956), the Helen Bullis Prize for Poetry from *Poetry Northwest* (1964), the Harriet Monroe Memorial Prize from *Poetry* (1968), and first prize in the Borestone Mountain Awards (1968). She has also received an award from the National Endowment for the Arts (1966–1967), a travel grant from the National Foundation on the Arts (1967), a Guggenheim fellowship (1972–1973), a Loines award (1976), and several honorary doctorates. She serves as poetry consultant to the modern literature collection of Washington University's Olin Library. She is interested, she says, "in flower and vegetable gardening, dogs, D.N.A., Mexico City, cooking, fishing, sewing, the poem, the short story, the novel, the causes and cures of mental illness, old movies, myself, and other human beings, particularly my friends."

PRINCIPAL WORKS: Valentines to the Wide World, 1959; A Time of Bees, 1964; To See, To Take, 1970; Bedtime Stories, 1972; Merciful Disguises: Published and Unpublished Poems, 1973.

ABOUT: Contemporary Authors 9-12, 1st revision, 1974; Vinson, J. (ed.) Contemporary Poets, 1975; Who's Who in America, 1978–1979. *Periodicals*—American Poetry Review November/December 1973; Book World (Washington Post) January 6, 1974; Nation May 4, 1970; New Republic October 6, 1973; New York Review of Books April 8, 1965; New York Times January 11, 1971; New York Times Book Review August 2, 1970; December 9, 1973; Parnassus Summer 1974; Poetry June 1975; Virginia Quarterly Review Spring 1965, Winter 1974.

"VAN HET REVE (MARQUESS)," GERARD KORNELIS FRANCISCUS. *See* REVE, GERARD (KORNELIS VAN HET)

*VAN ITALLIE, JEAN-CLAUDE (May 25, 1936–), American dramatist, writes: "I was born in Brussels in 1936. My parents were Belgian. My father's parents had been Dutch. My mother's parents were Jewish, one born in France, and one half-English. My father and his father were stockbrokers. When the war came my father was in the Belgian army at Dunkirk. My mother drove the family through France, where my father joined us, and we travelled

*van it'al lē'

JEAN-CLAUDE VAN ITALLIE

through Spain and Portugal and emigrated to the United States. French was my first language. My first words of English were learned at Estoril in Portugal ('No fish, no soup').

"Our first home in the United States was the Hotel Taft in Times Square. Then we moved to Forest Hills and then to Great Neck on Long Island where my family remained for twenty years. My father became a commuter and my mother remained a Belgian in an American suburb. As I grew up the contrast was great between the culture of my school and schoolmates and my bourgeois European home. I went to camp in New England for a couple of years and then after the age of eleven returned to Belgium with my parents each summer, and travelled in Europe as I grew older.

"I enjoyed Great Neck High School, learned a little there, and played the Sheridan Whiteside role in *The Man Who Came to Dinner*. I was made to go to Deerfield Academy for my senior year, and then I went to Harvard. I left Harvard halfway through my sophomore year to become a carhop and then a display assistant in a department store in Washington, D.C., and then to mope around Paris for three months. I was back at Harvard by the summer and graduated in 1958. At Harvard I began writing plays in Robert Chapman's class and short stories for John Hawkes.

"After Harvard I moved to Greenwich Village in New York, and I continued writing plays. It took me four years to realize that I was writing to try to suit a naturalistic outmoded (for me) local theatre, and it was only then that, with some anger, I was able to write anything of any value. In 1962 I wrote two short plays: *War* and

Motel. War was first performed at a theatrical workshop on December 22, 1963 in New York City. It was my mother's birthday; she had died that year. 1963 was also the year that the Open Theatre was founded and that I joined it. 1963 was the beginning of the off-off-Broadway theatre movement. The Caffe Cino was founded, the Cafe La Mama, etc.

"The Open Theatre and Joseph Chaikin permitted me to develop non-naturalistic plays and styles for a new company that was deeply committed to performing these. Ellen Stewart permitted me to see actual performance. *Motel* was first performed at Café La MaMa.

"In 1966 *America Hurrah* was produced off-Broadway, and much to the amazement of those of us working on it, it was the first nonmusical play to be a commercial and artistic success off-Broadway. It was intended as a personal and a political statement and I was fully prepared to see it booed off the boards by the critics, but it was not. A year later we took the first company to the Royal Court in London.

"*The Serpent* was the first 'collaborative' full-length play the Open Theatre and I attempted. It took nine months, and birthed in Rome. Since then I have written *Mystery Play, The King of the United States* and shorter plays. I wrote a new English version of *The Seagull* which was produced in New York in 1974.

"I continue to work off my disenchantment with the theatre by alternately writing plays alone and with a group, or not writing plays but writing poems and journals (I wrote a journal of a frightening journey to India in 1971), or making 'underground' films.

"I still live in Greenwich Village in the winter but I live in an old and beautiful farmhouse in the Berkshires for as much of the time as I can. I eat organically and grow organically when I can. I regularly do yoga and meditation. For the last few years I have taught playwrighting at Princeton University in New Jersey and at Naropa Institute in Boulder, Colorado at different times during the year."

———

The case of van Itallie is that of an immensely gifted verbal artist who has chosen to ally himself with a theatre that mistrusts words.

Like Megan Terry, he made his name through his work for the Open Theatre, and his reputation has remained bound up with that company and its innovative director, Joseph Chaikin. Van Itallie's plays, like Terry's, reflect the technical procedures and expressive preoccupations of the troupe; with the difference that, in his case, one is always conscious of a fastidious literary intelligence and a European cultural tradition underlying the harsh nonverbal New World imagery.

It is also clear from his first plays that van Itallie was searching for an escape from linear dialogue and naturalistic plot structure even before the Open Theatre supplied him with an alternative vocabulary. In *War* he is already employing the role-playing techniques that developed into the Open Theatre's transformation exercises. Two actors, one middle-aged and one young, meet by appointment for an improvisation duel, in the course of which they pass through a succession of generational conflicts (father and son, recruiting officer and recruit, etc.) before descending to an outright exchange of insults and a regression to infancy. The hostilities are twice interrupted by a dream-like Edwardian lady, to whom they both respond as to an unattainable mother-mistress figure, and who finally joins them in a tableau of the two-headed eagle of war. As Elmer Borklund has pointed out, this play employs the technique that has governed much of van Itallie's work: "A fundamental term or theme is introduced, then illustrated metaphorically and applied to a shifting series of particular instances. There is no plot or character development in any conventional sense; rather the essence of the theme is made manifest by an accumulation of poetic illustrations."

In *Motel*, visually the most stunning of van Itallie's plays, speech dwindles to a taped accompaniment to the brutal pantomime performed by three monstrous Artaudian dolls—the Motel-Keeper, and a man and woman who arrive, silhouetted by car headlights, couple, and then proceed to desecrate the room while the Motel-Keeper's prerecorded voice drones on about the merits of her establishment: "All modern here but, as I say, with the tang of home. . . . There's a button-push here for TV. The toilet flushes of its own accord. . . . The best stop on route six sixty-six." Finally, amid an excruciating crescendo of sirens and rock music, the couple dismember the Motel-Keeper, who still shows no sign of recognizing their presence. Presented as the finale of van Itallie's *America Hurrah* (Pocket Theatre, New York, 1966), *Motel* was saluted by Robert Brustein in the *New Republic* for its discovery of "the truest poetic function of the theatre . . . to invent metaphors which can poignantly suggest a nation's nightmares and afflictions."

As playwright in residence with the Open Theatre from 1963 to 1968, van Itallie supplied quantities of workshop material before arriving at the two other plays that made up Chaikin and Jacques Levy's production of *America Hurrah*. Some of the material was simply a basis for improvisation exercises. *The Odets Kitchen,* for instance, was a three-character domestic playlet in the naturalistic style of the 1930s; its purpose was to allow the actors to portray what was really going on inside the naturalistic shell. Other short plays took off from the point where exercises came to an end. *The Hunter and the Bird* derived from an abandoned series on the Fool (the primitive encountering a civilized environment). The Bird (like the Fool) trusts everything that happens to her, even when she is shot down by the Hunter. He, however, sees her from his civilized viewpoint as an object to be used, and tries to learn the secret of flying from her. At which point, already corrupted by his presence, she borrows the gun and shoots him.

Van Itallie also drew upon the group's Perfect People exercises (improvisations drawn from the wonderland of film romance and television commercials) to write the two "Doris plays," *Almost Like Being* and *I'm Really Here* (1964), parodying the clichés of the Doris Day–Rock Hudson movies. In the first of these the star ("I'm not a star . . . I'm really nothing but a television, radio, theatre and motion picture actress doing her best") falls for the lowly but masterful Rock as a boy from her home town; blissful union ensues once Doris has eliminated the wealthy Mr. Knockefeller and opened her heart to her black maid ("Sometimes life is like an angel-food cake that will never rise again"). In *I'm Really Here,* van Itallie dismantles the goddess by placing her in a love scene that lurches off into rape and murder, finally leaving her alone, mouthing a terrified jumble of cheerful song titles, to face the impossible fact of her own death ("Doris doesn't die").

The Open Theatre and van Itallie subsequently forsook this kind of satire as too facile, and moved on to weightier things. But the Doris plays have great comic zest, which lingers on into one of the plays making up *America Hurrah. TV* is set in a viewing room, and consists of two groups of characters: two men and a girl from a television rating service, and a group of actors who perform for them the television situation comedies, commercials, and newscasts being rated. The second group, their faces made up with video lines, exude the hygienic unreality of Perfect People; the raters, with their figure problems, stomach ailments, and sexual frustrations, belong to the world of here and now. With television material such as Luci Baines Johnson's views on the Vietnam War, or a policy statement by an American Nazi Party cheerleader, van Itallie the satirist still shows his claws. But many of the program extracts are no more fatuous than the real thing. Taken in isola-

tion, neither the television scenes nor the raters' dialogue would add up to very much. It is the relationship between the two that counts. By aligning two parallel banalities—the lethargic, habit-ridden imperfection of private life, and the bright idealized world of public cliché—the play achieves its statement on the human dislocation of American society. The statement, again, is predominantly visual; and it is by visual rather than rational logic that the gestures and speech of the raters finally merge with those of the performers they are watching.

Interview, the first play in the *America Hurrah* triptych, is the one most indebted to Open Theatre exercises. Moving from an employment agency through the streets, hospitals, and telephone switchboards of New York, it amounts to a series of variations on the question "Can you help me?" The answer, of course, is "No"—usually delivered with a gleaming toothpaste smile. Structurally, it is a transformation play, in which characters, setting, and situation repeatedly dissolve in an ever-changing thematic pattern. It also draws on the Inside-Outside exercise of *The Odets Kitchen;* on machine exercises (as where several actors link up to form a telephone circuit); on exercises based on Brecht's *gestus,* whereby character is compressed into a single shorthand trait; and on the Unnoticed Actions exercise which contrasts conventional speech with taboo-breaking physical behavior. Ordinary playgoers in New York and London, seeing this kind of work for the first time, were struck by its great enrichment of the actors' kinetic vocabulary.

Van Itallie's main achievement in the piece was to devise a form as impersonally mechanized as the society it depicted, yet carrying a great weight of personal suffering. The opening dialogue for job applicants and masked interviewers deliberately orchestrates the entry of different voices in a strict fugue; yet there is enough human substance there to launch the housepainter, the ex–bank president, and the other applicants into dramatic life, and to establish the four interviewers as authority figures who subsequently crop up as (equally unhelpful) analysts, priests, and politicians. The text also achieves a verbal equivalent of the *gestus* whereby the essential characteristics of a switchboard operator or a gym instructor are hit off in a couple of lines. The structure accommodates extraordinary expressionist heightenings—like that of the girl at the party who can get no one to talk to her because she has been killed on the way there—which illuminate the environment like flashes of lightning.

Van Itallie describes *Interview* as "a fugue"

and *Motel* as "a masque," and from this it is possible to deduce his stylistic dilemma—that for him each new play burns up its form as well as its content; and the process of writing another one necessitates re-inventing what a play ought to be. "Plays," he says, "should be instruments to get into people's dreams."

He has probably come closest to this ideal in *The Serpent: A Ceremony* (1968), an experiment in what he calls "vertical time," using myth to chart the relationship between past and present. The myth is that of Genesis, which the "ceremony" explores in thirteen sections, opening in the present with the assassinations of John F. Kennedy and Martin Luther King, and then retracing the fall of man from the temptation of Eve. The play derives from Open Theatre's Bible Workshop and Assassination Workshop rehearsals, and was well advanced by the time van Itallie arrived on the scene—he describes the published text as "only a skeleton" to be clothed in flesh by actors. Certainly, its key ideas—that man invented God to define his own limits, and that modern man remains the prisoner of beliefs he has rejected intellectually—find their full expression not in the dialogue but in stage imagery. It is Adam himself, lifted above the heads of the company, who delivers the everlasting curses on his mortal replica: and while the cast celebrates the discovery of sex with a copulative orgy, the text consists of a sober recital of Old Testament genealogy.

As in previous collaborations, van Itallie excels in structuring his material. Margaret Croyden compares it to "an abstract film collage, juxtaposing contemporary assassinations with the murder of Abel, contemporary sexual mores with the innocence of sexual discovery, and contemporary alienation with Paradisal harmony." To promote a continuous reverberation between past and present, van Itallie employs a chorus of four women who respond throughout as modern witnesses. He has also achieved a form of diction that is as appropriate for Adam awakening in the Garden as for bystanders at the Dallas motorcade. Designed for incantation, it couples Biblical cadences with plain modern speech, effecting climaxes of emphasis through repetition; as in the recurring lines accompanying the first murder: "And it occurred to Cain/ To kill his brother./ But it did not occur to Cain/ That killing his brother/ Would cause his brother's death."

As in *America Hurrah,* visual logic is paramount. The connection between Cain's murder and the killing of Kennedy (precisely duplicating the Zapruder film and then replayed backwards with guards counting the shots) is left for the spectators to establish; likewise the significance of a Serpent consisting of five actors who also represent the fruit-laden tree. The piece ends with the entire company parading as so many living ghosts, who abruptly snap into a chorus of "Moonlight Bay." For Margaret Croyden, this represents a mockery of "American sentimentalism." For John Lahr, the same moment is "a leap of faith." Mistrustful of language, the piece resists verbal assessments. What remains constant is its power to reactivate its parent myth. "Old stories," as the text puts it, "are a prison./ Someone is locked inside them./ Sometimes, when it's very quiet,/ I can hear him breathing"—an effect partly achieved through language.

Together with Sam Shepard and Megan Terry, van Itallie contributed to the Open Theatre's final production, *Nightwalk* (1973), an amorphous exploration of "the levels of sleep" which moved Robert Brustein, the troupe's former champion, to comment: "The Open Theatre used to provide us with images of American society in disintegration; now these metaphors seem to be disintegrating too." *Mystery Play,* in the same year, presents a Washington cocktail party in which a Harvard professor, a callgirl, a senator, and other assorted guests are murdered by high explosive, poison, and other colorful means. Catherine Hughes assessed this piece as "satirized mystery rather than actual mystery. . . . Van Itallie seemed to have in mind some political point-scoring to go with his farce, but it wound up not mattering."

In 1975 he resumed his collaboration with Joseph Chaikin in a new version of Chekhov's *The Seagull,* and a new collaborative piece, *A Fable,* in which a girl makes an allegorical journey with the support of an extremely spare text. "There are times," wrote Walter Kerr, "when a full line escapes one or another pulsing throat that reminds you of Mr. van Itallie's own natural powers as a writer. . . . A haunted voice calls out: 'In the middle of the night there is crying, but no child.' We are . . . being deprived of something. We can't afford that." Van Itallie himself says that he has found it necessary to move beyond the conventional use of dialogue in order to counteract the "understandable, but frightening mistrust of words everywhere, because they are used as the lying tools of the power forces. . . . One has to find a new way to use language . . . where each word is chosen with care for its importance in juxtaposition with the other words and in juxtaposition with the action that's going on on stage—so that the total *play* comes out being a new language."

The author, the son of Hugo Ferdinand van

Itallie and the former Marthe Levy, became a naturalized American citizen in 1952. He was an associate editor of *Transatlantic Review* in the early 1960s, joined CBS television as a researcher in 1962, and during his years with the Open Theatre also worked as a freelance writer on public affairs programs for CBS and NBC (1963 –1967). Van Itallie taught playwriting at the New School for Social Research, New York, in 1967–1968 and in 1972, and at the Yale School of Drama in 1969. From 1972 to 1976 he was writer in residence at the McCarter Theatre, Princeton, and he was visiting Mellon Professor at Amherst College in the fall of 1976. He has an honorary doctorate from Kent State University (1977). Van Itallie won the Vernon Rice Award and the Outer Circle Critics Award in 1967 for *America Hurrah,* and an Obie Award in 1969 for *The Serpent.* He has also received a Rockefeller grant (1962–1963), a Guggenheim fellowship (1963), and a Creative Artists' Public Service grant (1975). Van Itallie has served as a member of the Theatre Advisory Panel of the National Endowment for the Arts, as a member of the board of directors of the Theatre Communications Group, and as a governor of American Playwrights' Theatre. He describes himself as an anarchist-pacifist and a Buddhist.

PRINCIPAL PUBLISHED WORKS: America Hurrah and Other Plays (including America Hurrah: Interview, TV, Motel; War; Almost Like Being), 1967; War and Four Other Plays (Where Is de Queen?, Almost Like Being, The Hunter and the Bird, I'm Really Here), 1967; (with Sharon Thie) Thoughts on the Instant of Greeting a Friend on the Street, 1968; The Serpent: A Ceremony, 1969; Mystery Play: A Farce, 1973 (revised as The King of the United States, with music by Richard Peaslee, 1975); Seven Short and Very Short Plays (including Photographs, Eat Cake, The Girl and the Soldier, Take a Deep Breath, Rosary, Harold, Thoughts on the Instant of Greeting a Friend on the Street), 1973; The Seagull (adaptation), 1974; A Fable, 1976.

ABOUT: Brustein, R. The Third Theatre, 1969; Contemporary Authors 45–48, 1974; Crowell's Handbook of Contemporary Drama, 1971; Croyden, M. Lunatics, Lovers and Poets, 1974; Hughes, C. American Playwrights 1945–1975, 1976; Lahr, J. Up Against the Fourth Wall, 1970; Lewis, A. American Plays and Playwrights, 1970; Pasoli, R. A Book on the Open Theatre, 1970; Vinson, J. (ed.) Contemporary Dramatists, 1977; Weales, G. The Jumping-Off Place, 1969; Who's Who in America, 1978–1979. *Periodicals*—New York Times November 27, 1966; December 11, 1966; November 7, 1967; November 30, 1975; Serif Winter 1972; Tulane Drama Review Summer 1966.

*VARGAS LLOSA, (JORGE) MARIO (PEDRO) (March 28, 1936–), Peruvian novelist, short story writer, critic, and journalist, was born in the town of Arequipa in southern Peru, the son of Ernesto Vargas Maldonado and the former Dora Llosa Ureta. His parents were divorced before he was born, and he was taken by
vär′ gas ly ōs′ə

MARIO VARGAS LLOSA

Jonathan Kandell/New York Times

his mother to live at Cochabamba, Bolivia, with her parents, who pampered him. When he was nine, he and his mother moved to Piura in northwestern Peru. A year later, his parents having remarried, the family settled in Lima.

The spoiled and sensitive boy found himself no longer idolized. At the church schools he attended in Lima, he was younger than most of his classmates and suffered for it; at home, his artistic inclinations had to be hidden from his father who (like many Peruvians) regarded writing as no work for a man. Literature for Vargas Llosa became "an escape, a way of justifying my life, compensating for everything that saddened and disgusted me. . . . The road to . . . [literature] has always led through that type of experience—of alienation." If life was wretched at his Catholic schools, it became a nightmare when his father, determined to "make a man of him," sent him to the Lima military academy, the Leoncio Prado. The *machismo* and brutality he encountered there were for Vargas Llosa "like discovering Hell—an unknown reality, the opposite side of life. It marked me to the core."

This traumatic experience ended in 1952, when Vargas Llosa returned to Piura for his final year of secondary schooling. He worked part-time there on the newspaper *La Industria* and wrote a play called *La huida* (The Escape), a piece of juvenilia which was performed locally with gratifying success. Returning to Lima, Vargas Llosa studied for his degree in literature at the University of San Marcos, at the same time working as a journalist with Radio Panamericana and the newspaper *La Crónica*.

In 1958, Vargas Llosa made a brief visit to Paris and won a prize in a short story competition organized by *La Revue Française*. The winning piece, "El desafío" (The Challenge) was included in his first book, published the same year as *Los jefes* (The Leaders). These six short stories, set in the back streets of Lima, deal in a laconic style reminiscent of Hemingway with the violent lives of working-class youths undergoing the rites of passage prescribed by the cult of *machismo*. In one story, in which a boy is killed in a knife fight, it emerges at the end that one of those who arranged the duel is the dead youth's father. "I think in a country like mine, violence is at the root of all human relations," Vargas Llosa has said.

Los jefes was published in Spain in 1959, winning the Premio Leopoldo Alas. The same year, Vargas Llosa went with a scholarship to the University of Madrid, but moved on to Paris without completing his doctoral dissertation. He was to live there for seven years, working as a teacher for Berlitz, then as a journalist with Agence France-Presse, and finally with URTF, the French radio and television network. In Paris Vargas Llosa met other Latin American and French writers and intellectuals, but worked and wrote in relative obscurity until the publication of his first novel in 1963 caused a sensation throughout the Spanish-speaking world.

La ciudad y los perros (translated by Lysander Kemp as *The Time of the Hero*) is an account of life at the Leoncio Prado military academy, where the officers victimize the students, the stronger students persecute the weak, and the weak make do with tormenting animals—all in the name of a concept of patriotic virility which is "arbitrarily, even monstrously conceived." It is also entirely hypocritical, as the novel demonstrates. A plot to steal an examination paper is revealed by one of the most demoralized of the junior students, who for this unmanly act is "accidentally" killed during maneuvers. The whole institution then draws together to protect its "good" name. A student who voices his suspicions is bullied and blackmailed into silence; an officer who seeks to establish the truth is posted away. *La ciudad y los perros* portrays an educational institution that deliberately corrupts innocence and perverts idealism; it indicts both the Leoncio Prado and the Peruvian military regime of which it is an expression.

The novel is a documentary to the extent that it refers to an actual institution and to living individuals who can easily be identified. In style, however, it is highly experimental—dense in its prose texture, and making use of multiple focus, parallel sequences within chapters, and a pendular movement throughout as the action moves from college to city, from past to present, from third person narration to interior monologues that reveal the sensibilities the Leoncio Prado seeks to cauterize. Bernard Bergonzi indeed thought the novel was "swamped in places with unnecessary attempts at literary sophistication," but concluded that "despite its prolixity, it is still a harsh and honest piece of fiction," and remarkably mature. The military authorities in Peru were less subtle in their criticism, burning a thousand copies of the book on the grounds of the Leoncio Prado, and then attempting to dismiss it as the work of a sick and/or communist mind. In Spain it received the Premio de la Crítica Española, and it has been translated into more than a dozen languages.

La casa verde (translated by Gregory Rabassa as *The Green House*) followed three years later. The action is set partly in Piura and partly in the wild Amazonian region of Peru and along the River Marañón—the "green house" refers both to a Piura brothel and to the great rain forest. Many of the characters who link the two settings are based on real people. A lecture given by the author and published as *Historia secreta de una novela* (Secret History of a Novel, 1971) gives a detailed account of how the book evolved after an archaeological expedition in 1958 and a return visit in 1964 to the primitive settlement of Santa María de Nieva, a jungle outpost dominated by a military garrison and a tiny mission run by nuns.

The novel's main threads of development stem from the curious dynasty that owns the Green House and its inmates; from the adventures of Bonifacia, a prostitute who was raised at the Santa María mission; and from the story of Fushía, a Japanese renegade suffering from leprosy who traffics in stolen rubber and is establishing a kind of jungle kingdom. The book is further enriched (and complicated) by a huge cast of minor characters and innumerable subplots, shuffled and interwoven in a bewilderingly jumbled time sequence.

The contrast (and the similarity) between city and jungle in *La casa verde* belongs to a central tradition in Latin American literature, though it is explored here with greater subtlety in both form and content than in any previous novel. The same may be said of the book's despairing social message—its recording of connivance between army and church, the harsh treatment of the native *aguarunas* and *huambisas,* the endless chain of human exploitation, in a way which attributes the dog-eat-dog procedures of the Leoncio Prado to an entire nation. Unlike the stereotyped heroes and villains of earlier social fictions, however, Vargas Llosa's sheep are not easily separated from his wolves, and there is a degree of ingenuousness and vulnerability in the most depraved of his characters. The nuns, for example, are shown conniving with the uncouth military, who abduct young women to be "saved" at the mission (much as girls are recruited for the Green House); but we are also made aware of the nuns' inner conflicts, their struggle to observe the spirit of their religious vows in a godless region.

Vargas Llosa set out in *La casa verde* "to present collective personalities ... groups of people who belong to, and embody, various different realities." Some reviewers regretted the resultant flatness in characterization, and Alexander Coleman, while praising the book's "luxuriant and at times dazzling detail," found a "dreadful sense of disproportion between what seems to be the determinative surroundings and the wayward turns of what might be the individual personality. In fact, the characters don't really exist; they act with a grinding sense of their own fatal condemnation. For Vargas Llosa, a novel is above all a chronicle of action, and not at all an inner revelation of the forces that impel men to act." V. S. Pritchett, on the other hand, admired the novel. He found no discernible theme, receiving "very much the sense of a drifting traveller. But there is a purpose: to instill tolerance and get into the mind of the outcast or mass population which is culturally stagnant, dumb, and numerically dominant, to catch what they are saying. Vargas Llosa gives himself up to the habits of speech and narration of his people and abandons a good deal of the classic bourgeois belief in imposing an order. ... Faced by subject matter like this, a Latin American novelist does something important when he makes the voices of jungle or desert ghettos audible to us." *La casa verde* was awarded the Premio de la Crítica in Spain, the Premio Nacional de la Novela in Peru, and the coveted Premio Internacional de Literature Rómulo Gallegos.

In 1966, Vargas Llosa left Paris for London, taking up an appointment as a visiting lecturer in Latin American literature at the University of London, and traveling and lecturing extensively in Britain and Europe. He subsequently visited the United States, spending a semester as writer-in-residence at the University of Washington in Seattle.

His third novel, *Conversacíon en la Catedral* (1969, translated by Gregory Rabassa as *Conversation in the Cathedral*) is a massive, two-volume indictment of Peruvian life under the corrupt dictatorship of Manuel Udria (1948–1956). The abuses of this regime are seen through the public and private affairs of Udria's government minister Don Cayo Bermúdez, who was equally skilled as politician and policeman, manipulator and torturer. Parallel sequences deal with various aspects of Bermúdez' life—at home in the provincial town of Chincha, in his Lima office, and in his nocturnal adventures as an impotent voyeur.

This novel takes structural experiment even further than its predecessor. It is constructed around a long, drunken conversation in the Cathedral (a Lima bar and brothel) between Santiago Zavala, once a rebel, now a hack journalist, and his father's former chauffeur Ambrosio. This discussion fans out into a web of dialogues spanning many decades and the entire range of Peruvian society—what Emir Rodríguez Monegal called a "diachronic collage of dialogues." Praising the great skill with which Vargas Llosa records the rituals and behavior patterns of a whole society, a reviewer in the *Times Literary Supplement* wrote: "The various interlocking stories of the novel are told simultaneously at different stages of their development and from different points of view. The result is that at one level we contemplate an innocently progressive, well-ordered, democratic Peru ruled by a well-bred, generous oligarchy and government; on another level we contemplate a scheming and ruthless secret police ... or politicians and industrialists in masochistic intercourse with their negro chauffeurs, and spending their bribes on lesbian exhibitions." Suzanne Jill Levine remarked that "it would be a pity if the enormous but not insurmountable difficulties of reading this massive novel prevent readers from becoming acquainted with a book that reveals, as few others have, some of the ugly complexities of the real Latin America."

In 1969, Vargas Llosa lectured for a time at the University of Puerto Rico. The doctoral dissertation he had begun in 1959, a study of the fiction of his close friend the Colombian novelist Gabriel García Márquez, was finally published in 1971. Two years later a fourth novel appeared. Set in the year 1956, near the end of Udria's regime, it is another attack on the unholy trinity of church, army, and brothel, but in an unexpected mode. Reviewers of his earlier books had commented upon his lack of humor, but *Pantaleon y las visitadoras* (translated by Gregory Kolovakos and Ronald Christ as *Captain Pantoja and the Special Service*) is conceived in broadly farcical terms. It describes what happens when an "exemplary" army captain is selected to arrange the supply of female "visitors" to remote army barracks, a task to which he applies all he has learned about military efficiency. There are unmistakable shades of

García Márquez in this parade of human absurdity, which includes some notable parodies of the Peruvian popular press. It is as complex in its structure as Vargas Llosa's earlier works, however, employing "temporal dislocations, spatial shifts and displaced dialogue." One critic was reminded of Flaubert by the "use of several third-person narrators and the device of making a place his central character."

Vargas Llosa himself, discussing this departure, says in the New York *Times Book Review* (April 9, 1978) that he had believed "that humor was dangerous to the type of literature I wanted to write; that is, a literature giving the reader an impression of things lived. . . . I thought that humor always established a distance because it gives a quality of play to the work of literature. But the story I wanted to write was one that I discovered right away could be told only with humor. That was the way to make it acceptable, available to the reader. And so I arrived at humor, and it was a marvelous discovery; a whole world of possibilities for literature has been opened up to me." Acknowledging that some of his readers saw in this development an abandonment of social criticism, Vargas Llosa denied this, saying that humor had allowed his story to be told "at various levels of reality. . . . I think it can be interpreted as something more complex [than an antimilitary fable] . . . as a type of parable, yes, but of an intermediary man, a man capable of taking the trees for the forest. That is to say, a parable about the bureaucratic spirit itself." And in the same interview, he suggests that "in back of the demand for the writer to be politicized . . . there is a certain contempt for literature itself. The notion that literature must justify its existence by extraliterary motives, that it must be a didactic instrument for political and social instruction, can only be held by those who think that literature has no purpose of its own."

The comic vein is furthered explored in Vargas Llosa's next novel, *La tía Julia y el escribidor* (Aunt Julia and the Writer, 1977). Set in the 1950s, it presents a satirical account of the discovery of a Bolivian genius, Pedro Camacho, a writer of radio melodramas. Vargas Llosa says the character is based on a man he knew and worked for during his student days: "He was a genius in his genre, with an extraordinary facility to strike the emotional chords of his audience —their sentimentality, vanity and warmth. . . . He was a formative influence on me because he lived for his literature." The story of Camacho's downfall and eventual madness is told by Mario, a young news reporter, whose own life and unhappy love affair are described in much the same maudlin terms as Camacho's soap operas, many of which are summarized in the course of the novel.

Vargas Llosa is also the author of a novella, *Los cachorros* (The Pups, 1967), and a prolific reviewer and critic. He regards literary criticism as "a creative form . . . exactly equal to the novel or the short story. . . . The most interesting critics are those who explore a literary text with the same liberty an author takes with living reality, with experience, in order to create his fiction. The problem of fidelity to the text does not interest me in the least. I believe that the critic has the same right to arbitrariness and to fantasy that the narrator or poet has." His study of Flaubert was published in 1975. The same year Vargas Llosa was the Edward Laroque Tinker visiting professor at Columbia University, New York, and in 1977–1978 he held the Simon Bolivar chair in Latin American studies at Churchill College, Cambridge University, also lecturing at Queen Mary College, London University. Vargas Llosa was married at the age of nineteen to Julia Urquidi, a Bolivian. That marriage ended in divorce, and in 1965 he married his first cousin, Patricia Llosa; they have two sons and a daughter. Vargas Llosa acknowledges many influences on his work, in particular the work of Flaubert and of Faulkner, the medieval romances, the philosophical writings of Sartre, and the fiction of García Márquez, of the Argentinian Julio Cortázar, and of Isak Dinesen.

The author is a socialist, but one who did not hesitate to condemn the Soviet invasion of Czechoslovakia in 1968 and Castro's imprisonment of the poet Heberto Padilla in 1971. In these ways, and by his avoidance of overt and serious social criticism in his recent fiction, he has displeased some of his left-wing former admirers. On the other hand, as president since 1976 of PEN International, he has been accused of "facilitating a takeover bid of PEN by Marxist elements"—this because he appealed to the president of Argentina against the persecution of artists there and is sympathetic to the idea of a PEN center being established in the Soviet Union. None of his books has so far been set in contemporary Peru, ruled since 1968 by a left-wing military government. He has applauded the regime's efforts at agrarian reform, but he has resisted official attempts to identify him as a partisan supporter of the Peruvian revolution: "The worst thing that can happen to an artist is to be subsidized by the state. It leads to an intellectual and artistic castration." After prolonged consideration, a 1976 movie version of *Pantaleon y las visitadoras,* directed by Vargas Llosa himself, was banned in Peru.

PRINCIPAL WORKS IN ENGLISH TRANSLATION: The Time of the Hero, 1966; The Green House, 1968; Conversation in the Cathedral, 1975; Captain Pantoja and the Special Service, 1978. *Stories in* Howes, B. (ed.) The Eye of the Heart, 1973; Spanish Short Stories II, 1972.

ABOUT: Boldori, R. Mario Vargas Llosa, 1969; Coulthard, G.R. Spanish American Novel 1940–1965, 1966; Current Biography, 1977; Dorfman, A. Imaginación y violencia en América, 1970; Franco, J. The Modern Culture of Latin America, 1970; Franco, J. Spanish American Literature Since Independence, 1973; Gallagher, D. Modern Latin American Literature, 1973; Giacoman, H.F. and Oviedo, J.M. (eds.) Homenaje a Mario Vargas Llosa, 1971; Harss, L. and Dohmann, B. (eds.) Into the Mainstream, 1967; International Who's Who, 1978–79; Oviedo, J.M. Mario Vargas Llosa: La invención de una realidad, 1970; Schwartz, K. A New History of Spanish American Fiction, 1971. *Periodicals*—Américas October 1977; Books Abroad Winter 1970; Encounter September 1965; Guardian June 12, 1978; Modern Language Quarterly September 29, 1968; Mundo Nuevo 3 1966, 24 1968; Nation April 1, 1978; New York Review of Books October 6, 1966; May 22, 1969; New York Times March 22, 1977; New York Times Book Review January 12, 1969; April 9, 1978; Review 75 Spring 1975; Times Literary Supplement February 19, 1970; October 12, 1973; June 9, 1978.

"VEN, TON" *See* BORDEWIJK, FERDINAND

*VENNBERG, KARL (GUNNAR) (April 11, 1910–), Swedish poet, critic, and journalist, was born in Blädinge in the southeastern province of Småland, the son of a farmer, Olof Wennberg, and his wife Johanna. As a boy, Vennberg found himself deeply at odds with the narrowly religious and conservative farming community in which he was growing up, and he set himself to escape. He worked privately for the university matriculation examination and went on to study at the universities of Lund and Stockholm. Vennberg was greatly influenced by the epistemological investigations and the theory of justice of the Uppsala philosopher Axel Hägerström. He became ultra-radical in his politics and a convinced atheist. Vennberg worked as a literary critic for the syndicalist newspaper *Arbetaren* in 1941–1947, and thereafter for the social-democrat paper *Aftonbladet,* whose cultural editor he became in 1957.

Both as a poet and a critic, Vennberg showed from the beginning of his career a familiarity with the most advanced experiments in European literature. However, his own first collection of verse, *Hymn och hunger* (Hymn and Hunger, 1937), aroused little interest. In 1938 he completed a translation of T.S. Eliot's *Murder in the Cathedral* in collaboration with his close friend, the poet Erik Lindegren, whose sister Anna-Lisa Vennberg married the same year. Vennberg's own verse benefited from this prolonged expo-

*ven′ bâr yə

KARL VENNBERG

Swedish Consulate

sure to Eliot's classical and intellectual style, as is evident from the collection that established his reputation as a poet, *Halmfackla* (Straw Torch, 1944).

Many of the deeply pessimistic and bitterly ironic poems in *Halmfackla* deal with the war that was then raging around Sweden, a war that Vennberg viewed with a mixture of horror and detachment. In such a world, it seemed to him, the words *good* and *evil* had no meaning: "The image/ that's stamped upon the proper coins is/ the same the counterfeited ones display." *Tideräkning* (The Calculation of Time), which followed in 1945, is even more bleak: "To live is to choose/ O blessed choice/ between the indifferent/ and the impossible." In the title poem, Vennberg ironically defends himself against those who see him as an iconoclast, a man who overthrows the traditional calendar, insisting that he never undertakes important actions without first fixing "their position in relation to the creation of the world/ the founding of Rome/ the flight to Medina and so on."

According to S. A. Bergmann, the prevailing mood of Vennberg's poetry is "radical pessimism, a recurrent theme being the inadequacy of all beliefs and ideologies; but the tone which comes across to the reader can be positively exhilarating. . . . Pride in his dialectic powers is clearly discernible; but the controlled aridity and pungent irony are off-set by the intensely moral concern and the surprisingly exact perception of sensuous detail." *Halmfackla* and *Tideräkning,* with their dense, recondite, and sometimes incomprehensible imagery, had great influence, and established Vennberg as one of the two leading poets (with Erik Lindegren) of

843

the principal poetic movement of the time, the group centered upon the magazine *40-tal.* At the same time, as Alrik Gustafson has written, Vennberg's "intelligent, hard-hitting book reviews and critical essays spearheaded the radical fighting cause of the *40-talister* and gave to their program substance and a solid rationale."

A more controlled and positive mood prevails in *Fiskefärd* (The Fishing Trip, 1949), where the poet escapes from the problems of the world on an early morning fishing expedition, aided by tobacco and aquavit. In another poem in the same collection Vennberg exhorts the reader to struggle against the destructive forces of fear, disillusionment, and apathy, but he seems to express these feelings himself in the autumnal poems of *Gatukorsning* (Street Crossing, 1952): "The squares shiver round extinguished fires. . . . Do not desire too much at this moment."

In the books that followed, *Vårövning* (Spring Exercise, 1953), and *Synfält* (Field of Vision, 1954), the poet adumbrates the possibility that the winter of his (and the world's) discontent may somehow give way to a spring-like rebirth, but his skepticism and self-deprecating irony are never far away. Some of the poems in the latter collection reflect Vennberg's commitment to the belief that Sweden should adopt a "third standpoint" (a policy of nonalignment in the East-West political struggle)—a view that involved him in much controversy during the 1950s. There are also some sad poems about love in middle age: "This is my pain when you leave me/ an indifferent pain, like the movement of a hand." Other pieces in *Synfält* are concerned with man's longing for a god in whom he cannot believe, a theme resumed in *Vid det röda trädet* (By the Red Tree, 1955). "A scent of gods disturbs our race," Vennberg writes, but mankind must beware of transcendence, contenting ourselves with "village gods," "family gods," even "pocket gods," if we are to avoid "resting our heads against rocks from which a greater/ unrest proceeds."

Tillskrift (Address, 1960) is very much in the same spirit—poems about love and about God, full of reservations. Alrik Gustafson senses in the poetry Vennberg wrote during and after the 1950s a desire "to break out of the isolation of his irony into some kind of fruitful relation with society and his fellows." This desire is seldom fulfilled, and Vennberg in his later work retains "much of his early scorn for political pretentiousness and his refusal to believe in either God or man," finding what solace he can "in life's fleeting visions of beauty and man's open-eyed determination to endure and, when possible, to enjoy": "Like a low plant along the ground,

creeping, flowerless/ is my disbelief, my stronghold." *Sju ord på tunnelbanan* (Seven Words on the Underground), a volume whose principal theme is old age and its problems, followed after a long silence in 1971.

Vennberg's unmistakable style has never varied: unrhymed free verse, with concentrated and constantly changing imagery, and a sense of restraint and understatement. Gustafson says that Vennberg thinks abstractly, tending "to reduce poetry to a series of pronouncements, definitions, and syllogisms—pursuing and seeking to perfect what has been called 'the critical-analytical line' in modern Swedish poetry." Vennberg has been accused by some critics of a cerebral cold-bloodedness, but the guardedness and control of his poetry is, in fact, his way of dealing with the violence of his feeling—his anguish at the lack of absolute values in the world, his despair at the failure of love, his longing for God.

PRINCIPAL WORKS IN ENGLISH TRANSLATION: *Poems in* Literary Review Winter 1965–1966.

ABOUT: Gustafson, A. A History of Swedish Literature, 1961; Lagerlöf, K.E. Den unge Karl Vennberg (with German summary), 1967; Näsström, N.G. and Strömberg, M. (eds.) Den unga Parnassen, 1947; Penguin Companion to Literature 2, 1969; Printz-Påhlson, G. Solen i spegeln, 1959; Ramnefalk, M.L. Tre lärodiktare (with English summary), 1974. *Periodicals*—Western Humanities Review 15 1961.

*VINOKUROV, YEVGENY MIKHAILOVICH (October 22, 1925–), Russian poet, was born in Bryansk, a provincial city southwest of Moscow. He is the son of Evgenya Matveevna Vinokurova and Mikhail Nikolaevich Peregudov. His childhood was spent in many different parts of the Soviet Union, as his father, a professional soldier, was posted from place to place. At Brezhersk, his mother became supervisor of the woman workers at a local factory, where she was known as an ardent campaigner for equal rights. During World War II, Vinokurov entered the Sevastopol Anti-Aircraft Artillery School, graduated in 1943, and, still in his teens, fought in the last phase of the war as a platoon commander on the Ukrainian front. It was then that he wrote his first poems. After demobilization he studied geology for a time, but in 1948 some of his poems were published, along with an encouraging note by Ilya Ehrenburg. The same year he entered the Gorky Institute of Literature in Moscow, graduating in 1951.

The main theme of his early work was the war, of which he wrote: "I am glad that I had to experience real difficulties. One cannot say of my generation that it was born at a time when there was nothing for it to do." His first two

*vē n ə kōōr′ of

YEVGENY MIKHAILOVICH VINOKUROV

in a makeshift theatre behind the storehouse, with freckled, thickset Lance-corporal Dyadin as the prince:

> When he came on, he'd hang his head,
> Folding his arms mournfully, but
> Somehow, as soon as he said
> "To be or not to be?" everyone laughed.
>
> I have seen many Hamlets stepping out
> From the dark wings into the spotlight,
> Tragic, with booming voices, spindle-legged.
> At the first word, a hush descends,
>
> Hearts stop beating, opera-glasses tremble.
> These Hamlets have passion, power, art!
> But ours froze and shivered in the damp with us
> And shared our fire's warmth.

> (from "We Rigged Up a Theatre"
> translated by Daniel Weissbort)

books were *Stikhi o dolge* (Verses About Duty, 1951) and *Voyennaya lirika* (War Lyrics, 1956) —scrupulous accounts of wartime events and situations in distinct contrast to the declamatory patriotic verse of the time.

It was, however, with the nature poems of *Sineva* (Sky Blue, 1956) that he began to reach maturity as a poet. Since then he has been extremely prolific, and his verse has improved in quality and deepened in content as he has come to grips with the philosophical and psychological problems that are his true theme. His books include *Priznaniya* (Confessions, 1958), in which he turned to such personal subjects as love and childhood, *Litso chelovecheskoye* (The Human Face, 1960), and *Slovo* (The Word, 1962). *Lirika* (Lyrics, 1962), a collection which includes most of the poetry he had produced up to that time, was followed by *Muzika* (Music, 1964), *Stikhotvoreniya* (Poems, 1964), *Zemniye predeli* (Terrestrial Limits, 1965), *Izbrannaya lirika* (Selected Lyrics, 1965), *Kharakteri: Noviye Stikhi* (Characters: New Verse, 1965), *Ritm* (Rhythm, 1966), *Golos* (Voice, 1967), *Metafory* (Metaphors, 1972), and others.

Vinokurov is one of the most notable of the "quiet," nonpolitical poets who emerged in the post-Stalin period and who have concerned themselves more with human nature than with political ideologies. His free, unrhymed verse deliberately avoids dramatic and rhetorical flourishes; his diction is lyrical but unpretentious and precise. Vinokurov uses concrete, everyday detail to evoke, as Pierre Forgues says, "an object, a moment, a memory, a person, in a few words." In one poem, for example, he describes a wartime production of Shakespeare's *Hamlet*

As D. M. Thomas has remarked of this poem, "the attractive qualities of Vinokurov's poetry are well illustrated here: directness, honesty, humour, compassion. Many of his poems, like this one, end with that most surprising of surprises, a revelation of the ordinary. . . . The Hamlet poem is all the stronger for its leaving unsaid the danger of sudden death that surrounds Lance-corporal Dyadin."

Vinokurov has consistently defended the importance of the individual as a free, independent, and thinking being, and speculation about the nature of the self recurs in his later poems. In "Ya" (I), he says "There is no ache more/ Deadly than the striving to be oneself," and concludes:

> There's the word "I." No wonder,
> In me, it is hostile to non-being.
> It's deep within me. At one blow it was hammered
> Into me, right up to its head, like a nail.

> (translated by George Reavey)

Mihajlo Mihajlov has described him as "a solitary philosopher for whom the world is a complete and constant puzzle about which people know so little they do not dream that it is a wonder."

The poet lives quietly in Moscow with his family. According to Daniel Weissbort, he was formerly poetry editor of the important magazine *Oktyabr* and "did a lot to confirm the reputations of Zabolotsky and Slutsky among others, and to establish that of Akhmadulina." He is now poetry editor of *Novy Mir.* He has taken no part in the public readings that have helped to spread the fame of such poets as Yevtushenko and Voznesensky, and he is less well known than they are. Nevertheless, it is held by many that, although his verse is less "brilliant" than Voznesensky's and less "ambitious" than Brodsky's, his achievement may come to be seen as of no less value and importance than theirs.

PRINCIPAL WORKS IN ENGLISH TRANSLATION: The War Is Over: Selected Poems of Evgeny Vinokurov, 1976. *Poems in* Blake, P. and Hayward, M. (eds.) Halfway to the Moon, 1963; Bogojavlensky, M. and Bradley, S. (eds.) Three New Soviet Poets, 1967; Field, A. (ed.) Pages From Tarusa, 1964; Markov, V. and Sparks, M. (eds.) Modern Russian Poetry, 1966; Obolensky, D. (ed.) The Penguin Book of Russian Verse, 1965; Reavey, G. (ed.) The New Russian Poets, 1953-1966, 1966; Weissbort, D. (ed.) Post-War Russian Poetry, 1974; Encounter April 1963; Kenyon Review Summer 1964; Modern Poetry in Translation 18, Winter 1974.

ABOUT: Hayward, M. and Labedz, L. (eds.) Literature and Revolution in Soviet Russia, 1917–1962, 1963; Mihajlov, M. Moscow Summer, 1965; Mikhailov, A. Evgeny Vinokurov, 1975; Vinokurov, E. autobiographical note *in* The War Is Over, 1976. *Periodicals*—Times Literary Supplement August 6, 1976.

Thomas Victor © 1979

DIANE WAKOSKI

WAHLÖÖ, PER. *See* SJÖWALL, MAJ and WAHLÖÖ, PER

WAKOSKI, DIANE (August 3, 1937–), American poet, writes: "Perhaps the best explanation of my aesthetic would be the statement that I think everything which is important about my life is in my poems. By that, I do not mean that my poems are autobiographical or documentary. What I hope is that my poems avoid the trivial, round up the mythical—or at least embody whatever can be the personal mythology of my life—and present me with some human (humane) vision that transcends what I hate about real people and real life. Poetry, for me, is bigger, more exciting, more beautiful, more dramatic and powerful than we can ever be.

"Oddly, I do see poetry as the metaphor for the process of dynamic living. And thus I see poetry as being part of the living and breathing of my every day. I do not really understand people who don't write poetry, or at least read it, for it seems to me to be so integrally related to my life.

"I don't mind telling anyone that I was born in Whittier, California on August 3rd, 1937 or that I grew up in the orange groves of Southern California. Nor do I mind telling anyone I went to the University of California at Berkeley from 1956–1960 or that I moved to New York City after I graduated. That I've never had any job that meant anything to me, except reading, writing, and talking about poetry. I don't mind telling anyone that I've been married six times, though only twice legally, but I think you find out these things about me in a more lively and interesting way if you read my poetry. And what's more, you also understand how unimportant these things are until they are mythologized. Until the orange tree becomes the tree of life growing outside my sagging back porch door, with the dew-soaked oranges, cool before breakfast, dusty on the tree and there, as the sun is there, as life, energy, masculine fire is there waiting. Facts are only useful when there is imagination. And the only way in which I really want anyone to know me is through my poems. I feel an attraction for the sea. My father was a sailor. My mother a bookkeeper. I see allegory everywhere I look."

It is not easy to convey the unique flavor of Diane Wakoski's long, long-lined, often surrealistic poems, and more useful to quote an example, like this opening passage from "Coins and Coffins Under My Bed," the title poem from her first book:

Three children dancing around an orange tree,
not holding hands because the tree is too round and full,
and there are only three of them:
The spiders, making their webs in the orange tree
    talk to the children.
    Do you want silver coins?
    Do you want silver cups?
    Do you remember our names?
they ask.
One little boy answers.
    I want silver rings.
    I want silver keys.
    I remember my own name. It is John.
But the spiders are making their webs larger and larger.
A yellow spider says:

Do you hear us spinning?
The sound
is so loud it makes our legs vibrate.
Do you know that David is dead
and buried
under this tree?
Do you want silver coins
to buy death away?

Reviewing *Discrepancies and Apparitions,* which followed in 1966, a critic in the *Virginia Quarterly Review* wrote that "Miss Wakoski is often a very imaginative and lively poet of real freshness, and as often a very fake imitation of a pop art exhibition. There are apparitions in these poems, nightmares and visions, but there are discrepancies too—clumsy lines and stale dreams. Miss Wakoski, for all her being out of school for six years, still sounds like an undergraduate who treasures every syllable and refuses to revise." Similar things have continued to be said about her work, though reviewers have differed radically in their response to Miss Wakoski's poetry.

Hayden Carruth, for example, was delighted by her *George Washington Poems,* in which she resuscitates the Father of Our Country as a many-sided fictional personage and converses with him, "in the cheerfullest terms imaginable," about her life, her parents and her husband, her feelings about America, and anything else that crosses her mind. Vernon Young, on the other hand, is plainly irritated by Miss Wakoski's procedures. Reviewing one of the several slim volumes of *Greed,* a long poem or sequence which began to appear in sections in 1968, he speaks of her very crossly indeed as a "spoiled child" whose "sticky fingers are into everything, tearing pistils and stamens out of the calyx, prying open every oyster, unscrewing the back of every clock, fumbling at the tripes of the poor, carrying torches for negroes and dead women, permanently in a lather about *men*—which *she* spells with four letters. . . . In every slim volume she becomes more fatuous, more immodest, more importunate, as if she could repair the absence of talent by screaming it into life."

The themes that pervade Diane Wakoski's poetry have been identified by Paul Zweig as "the woman betrayed, the anger she feels at her frail body and her face which seems hard to love; the rescue performed by the imagination, which reaches around the bareness of her life to create the comfort of clearly expressed needs." Zweig praises a rare "intensity of simple speech" in *The Motorcycle Betrayal Poems,* quoting from "I Have Had to Learn to Live With My Face":

Tonight I move alone in my face;
want to forgive all the men whom I've loved
who've betrayed me.
After all the great betrayer is that one I
carry around each day,
which I sleep with at night. My own face,
angry building I've fought to restore
imbued with arrogance, pride, anger and scorn.
To love this face
would be to love a desert mountain,
a killer, rocky, water hard to find,
no trees anywhere/
perhaps I do not expect anyone
to be strange enough to love it;
but you.

It is the extraordinarily personal nature of her poetry that accounts for the extreme reactions it provokes; readers react to her work as to a voluble and eccentric acquaintance, charmed or appalled according to their tastes. Douglas Blazek, one of the charmed, acknowledges that her poems "*come close* to being terrible; some are almost soap operas, others the grotesque fantasies of some overly imaginative and underexperienced little girl. . . . Many of her poems sound as if they're constantly in trouble, falling into triteness, clumsiness, or indirection. She is constantly jumping into deep water to save a drowning stanza or into a burning building to recover disintegrating meaning." Hayden Carruth, who considers her "one of the most interesting poets of the past decade," means something similar when he writes (of a volume splendidly entitled *Dancing on the Grave of a Son of a Bitch*) that Diane Wakoski "has a way of beginning her poems with the most unpromising materials imaginable, then carrying them on, often on and on and on, talkily, until at the end they come into surprising focus, unified works. With her it is a question of thematic and imagistic control, I think; her poems are deeply, rather than verbally, structured."

Some reviewers found signs of development in *Virtuoso Literature for Two and Four Hands* (1975). In these poems, wrote Louis Sasso, "she no longer directs anger inward with the same intensity as before. She has begun to realize and to accept her own humanity. . . . One senses that Wakoski is at a pivotal point in her writing." Peter Meinke thought that the poet "uses more similes here than I remember in her earlier work, often with great skill and imagination. . . . Her statements about life are not remarkable, but many of these poems and parts of poems are, especially when she sticks to the visual and informative." Helen Vendler was less impressed, but felt that the book marks "something of a plateau in . . . [Wakoski's] work." Critics also found much to admire in the volume that followed, *Waiting for the King of Spain* (1976), including a sequence called "Fifteen Poems for a Lunar Eclipse None of Us Saw," which one reviewer found "as fine as anything she has ever published." *The Man Who Shook Hands* (1978) was on the whole less warmly received, seeming to a number of readers irritating in its preoccupation with the poet's grievances.

The poet is the daughter of John Joseph and Marie (Mengel) Wakoski. She was a clerk at the British Book Centre in New York in 1960–1963, and taught at Junior High School 22, also in New York, in 1963–1969; since then she has taught at the New School for Social Research. She is a former editor of *Dream Sheet* and *Software.* Since 1967 she has given readings on several hundred college campuses. Her awards include a prize from the National Council on the Arts, a Robert Frost Fellowship from the 1966 Bread Loaf Writers' Conference, and grants from the National Endowment for the Arts and the Guggenheim Foundation, among others. She has been poet-in-residence at a number of colleges and universities since 1971. Four of the *George Washington Poems* form the basis of David Lenfest's film *George Washington Sleeps Here.* She says that she has no political or religious affiliations, but is interested in astrology.

PRINCIPAL WORKS: Coins and Coffins, 1962; Discrepancies and Apparitions, 1966; The George Washington Poems, 1967; Inside the Blood Factory, 1968; The Diamond Merchant, 1968; Greed: Parts I and II, 1968; Greed: Parts III and IV, 1969; The Lament of the Lady Bank Dick, 1969; The Moon Has a Complicated Geography, 1969; Thanking My Mother for Piano Lessons, 1969; Some Poems for the Buddha's Birthday, 1969; Poems, 1969; Black Dream Ditty for Billy "the Kid," 1970; The Magellanic Clouds, 1970; Greed: Parts V–VII, 1971; The Motorcycle Betrayal Poems, 1971; Smudging, 1972; The Pumpkin Pie, 1972; Form Is an Extension of Content, 1972; Greed: Parts VIII, IX, XI, 1973; Dancing on the Grave of a Son of a Bitch, 1973; Trilogy (reprinting first three collections), 1974; Virtuoso Literature for Two and Four Hands, 1975; Waiting for the King of Spain, 1976; The Man Who Shook Hands, 1978. *Poems in* Jones, LeRoi (ed.) Four Young Lady Poets, 1962.

ABOUT: Contemporary Authors 13–16 1st revision, 1975; International Who's Who in Poetry, 1974–1975; Vinson, J. (ed.) Contemporary Poets, 1975. *Periodicals*—Chicago Review Summer 1977; Choice July-August 1977; Contemporary Literature Winter 1977; Hudson Review Winter 1973-1974, Summer 1974; Library Journal May 1, 1975; New Republic June 14, 1975; New York Times Book Review December 12, 1971; April 6, 1975; August 13, 1978; Parnassus Fall-Winter 1972, Spring-Summer 1973; Poetry June 1974; Prairie Schooner Spring 1973; Yale Review Autumn 1975.

WAMBAUGH, JOSEPH (ALOYSIUS) JR.

(January 22, 1937–), American novelist, was born in East Pittsburgh, Pennsylvania, the only

JOSEPH WAMBAUGH JR.

Larry Stevenson

child of Joseph A. Wambaugh, a washing machine repairman, and the former Anne Malloy. He grew up, according to one interviewer, surrounded by a raucous Irish Catholic family of "steelworkers, bar owners, and champion drinkers." The family moved to California in 1951 and three years later, when he left school, Wambaugh joined the United States Marine Corps. In 1955 he was married to Dee Allsup, whom he had met in high school. After his discharge from the Marines in 1957, Wambaugh and his wife returned to California. He worked at various jobs—for a time as a steelworker at the Kaiser Mill—while attending college part-time. Wambaugh majored in English, in 1958 receiving his A.A. (Associate in Arts) at Chaffey College, Ontario, California.

On May 2, 1960, Wambaugh joined the Los Angeles Police Department, because he had "nothing better to do" and because the starting salary "was more money than I had ever earned in my life." He fell in love with the job. "I do police work because it relaxes me and soothes my soul," he told one reviewer, and elsewhere says that in a single night's duty he "sometimes learned things that a man could not expect to learn in a month or a year" about himself and about mankind in general. Wambaugh continued his night school studies, securing his B.A. in 1960 and his M.A. in 1968 from California State University, Los Angeles. He says that his colleagues in the LAPD never learned of these studies, any more than his college friends knew that he was a policeman.

It was after the Watts riots that Wambaugh felt he "wanted to say something about it. What it was like for young men, young policemen, to grow up, on the streets, in that dreadful but fascinating era." He began with some short stories about police work—"realistic stories as differentiated from the cops and robbers fantasy." After many rejections, an *Atlantic* editor suggested that Wambaugh might do well to try a full-length novel, and the eventual result was *The New Centurions* (1971).

The novel follows the careers of three young Los Angeles policemen from the academy to their first foot patrols, from their first patrol-car duties to their first promotions. Reviewers complained that the three main characters share a single sensibility, that the book "wears its exposition on its sleeve," and had other faults not uncommon in first novels, but they agreed that it was also absorbingly interesting, exciting, and readable, and "does a thorough job in telling the story of one of America's most maligned professions." It was a Book-of-the-Month Club selection, reigned for eight months on the bestseller lists, and was filmed by Columbia in 1972 with George C. Scott in the lead, precipitating a deluge of police novels and movies.

The Blue Knight, published a year later, is a portrait of the kind of policeman that "demonstrators love to hate." Bumper Morgan is potbellied, flatulent, tough, and egotistic. The reader accompanies him on his rounds during his last two days before retirement, sharing his recollections of twenty years of confrontations with all kinds of Los Angeles criminals and characters. Wambaugh, it was recognized, had learned a great deal very quickly about his new craft as a novelist, writing with "great gusto, rough, tough language, affection and even reverence for Bumper and the law-and-order school that he represents. His characters, all of them, are vivid, colorful, and memorable." There was some feeling that an old-school "bull" of Morgan's type would not be likely to enjoy hard rock music or to date a black girl, as Bumper does, and in the end, according to a *Time* reviewer, "Wambaugh sentimentalizes Bumper as a sort of repellently lovable supercop. . . . Oddly, some most persuasive moments occur when Bumper sits down to consume one of the Lucullan meals he regularly cadges. Wambaugh's feeling for food is almost erotic." *The Blue Knight* was televised in four episodes in 1973 by NBC, bringing William Holden an Emmy award for his performance as Bumper Morgan. A weekly series based on the novel followed on CBS, with George Kennedy in the lead, and Wambaugh as production consultant.

The book that followed, *The Onion Field,* was in the nature of a labor of love for Wambaugh—a documentary novel reconstructing the kidnap-ping in 1963 of two Los Angeles policemen, the murder of one of them, and the public pillorying of the other during the inordinately lengthy trial that followed. In pursuit of accuracy, Wambaugh had interviewed over sixty people connected with the case, and read some sixty-five thousand pages of court transcripts. James Conaway in the New York *Times Book Review* found *The Onion Field* as compelling as Truman Capote's *In Cold Blood* which initiated the genre of the "non-fiction novel," and thought Wambaugh's book superior "in terms of scope, revealed depth of character, and dramatic coherence," demonstrating that the author "belongs to the tradition of Dreiser and Farrell." It received the Herbert Brean Memorial Award in 1974, and was sold to the movies for an undisclosed sum very much larger than the $165,000 Wambaugh had received for his first novel.

"The Choirboys" in Wambaugh's 1975 novel of that title are ten cops working the nightwatch in pairs out of Wilshire Division in Los Angeles. Their tours of duty completed, they meet in MacArthur Park, unwinding with extorted booze and sex (provided by a pair of cocktail waitresses). One such "choir practice" ends with a death that leads to the dismissal of several members of the group. Very little in Wambaugh's earlier novels, John Leonard thought, "prepares one for the scabrous humor and ferocity of *The Choirboys.* . . . Wambaugh comes on like a Céline derailed along the laugh-track. His characters are a brutalized M.A.S.H. unit. . . . Wambaugh seems to be waving goodbye to all his liberal pieties. . . . People, including cops, are garbage. . . . His is a funny book that makes one gag. He is on his way to rediscovering original sin." *The Choirboys* was later filmed.

The Black Marble, which followed in 1978, is a rather different matter. Philo Skinner, a seedy doghandler, kidnaps a prize animal belonging to an impoverished scion of Old Pasadena. The police detective who sallies forth to right this wrong is neither a "new centurion" nor a "choirboy," but Andrei Mikhailovich Valnikov. Jerome Charyn thought him "almost as touching, variable and bravely idiotic as Nabokov's Professor Pnin. 'A burly man with wild cinnamon hair and a slouchy walk,' Valnikov lives on Russian vodka, Chaliapin, and *Boris Godunov.* Like Pnin, Valnikov is utterly displaced. The son of a captain in the Czar's last army, Valnikov was born and reared in Los Angeles. But he dreams of Petrograd, nightingales in raspberry bushes, wounded rabbits in the Siberian snow. Absent-minded and incorrigibly old-fashioned. . . . he's the 'black marble,' the loser, the bad-luck piece. . . . His new partner, Natalie Zimmerman, thinks Valnikov is a lunatic. His pockets are held together with staples, he gets lost driving in Los Angeles." It seemed to Charyn that, "as the misadventures of a sad, unlikely cop, *The Black Marble* is a very funny book. The problem with the novel is that it strays from Valnikov much too often. Joseph Wambaugh hasn't found a story that can contain his fat, haunted detective."

Wambaugh is also the creator of and consultant to NBC's weekly "Police Story," in which he strives to present an image of the typical cop as "neither a Galahad nor a pig" but simply an ordinary man doing his best. His determination to preserve this kind of realism in "Police Story" has led him into some much-publicized arguments with his producers at NBC, and he says that he would rather tangle "with the toughest burglar in Los Angeles than with a television executive."

Interviewed in the New York *Times* in November 1973, when he was thirty-six, Wambaugh was described by Susan Lydon as "a medium-sized man with thinning, shiny black hair, a ruddy complexion, and eyes that sparkle green—looks that reveal the three-quarters Irish ancestry his German surname conceals. . . . Open and gregarious, he speaks energetically, with the glib gift of the born storyteller, with certainty and forthrightness." Wambaugh was at that time still a detective sergeant in the Hollenbeck Division of the LAPD, spending his days "driving an unmarked car through the poor, predominantly Mexican section of the city, working the burglary detail." He resigned from the police department on March 8, 1974: "So many people knew who I was," he explained, "so many came to the station trying to see me. There were so many telephone calls that the other detectives had to screen them for me. . . . I had to stop it all." Wambaugh believes that he is "one of the ten highest-paid writers in the country." He has two sons and two daughters. The author told an interviewer in 1978 that since he left the police department "I've been drinking too much and my morals have been deteriorating, so since I have no honor left I've decided to become a producer, and make a movie that's faithful to *The Black Marble.*"

PRINCIPAL WORKS: The New Centurions, 1971; The Blue Knight, 1972; The Onion Field, 1973; The Choirboys, 1975; The Black Marble, 1978.

ABOUT: Contemporary Authors 33–36, 1973; Who's Who in America, 1978–1979. *Periodicals*—Biography News January 1974; Esquire December 1973; Life April 14, 1972; Los Angeles Times June 27, 1971; January 19, 1975; National Review April 2, 1976; New York Times January 22, 1971; November 11, 1973; New York Times Book Review November 2, 1975; January 8, 15, 1978; Newsweek March 26, 1973; Publishers Weekly August 23, 1971; Times (London) August 22, 1975; Times Literary Supplement November 1, 1974; April 9, 1976; Writer's Digest December 1973.

WARD, DOUGLAS TURNER (May 5, 1930–), American dramatist, was born in Burnside, Louisiana, the only child of plantation field hands, Roosevelt Ward and the former Dorothy Short. When he was eight the family moved to New Orleans, where his father worked as a forklift operator and later as a foreman on the docks before joining his wife in running a tailoring business at home. From 1941 to 1946 Ward attended Xavier University Prep, a Roman Catholic high school for blacks where he played football and ran track, and decided on a career in journalism. After a year at Wilberforce University in Xenia, Ohio (1946–1947) and another at the University of Michigan (1947–1948), he went to New York. "Artistically and aesthetically," he explained in an *Esquire* article, "the college experience wasn't as important to me as my radical political involvements in the Fifties, and growing up on a Louisiana plantation," and elsewhere he has said: "I had my years of handing out leaflets on street corners, writing for the *Daily Worker.* "

Asked to write a political skit for one of the radical organizations he had joined, Ward found this exercise so much to his taste that he abandoned journalism and turned forthwith to the theatre. In 1955 he enrolled in Paul Mann's Actors' Workshop, where he studied for over two years. His first professional roles (as Douglas Turner) began to come along in the late 1950s, when he played Joe Mott in a revival of Eugene O'Neill's *The Iceman Cometh,* Matthew Kumalo in a revival of Maxwell Anderson's *Lost in the Stars,* and a moving-man in Lorraine Hansberry's *A Raisin in the Sun.* In 1960, when *A Raisin in the Sun* began its national tour, Ward went along in the lead part as Walter Lee Younger. Back in New York, he appeared as Archibald in Jean Genet's *The Blacks* (1961–1962), as a porter in Thornton Wilder's *Pullman Car Hiawatha* (1962), as Zachariah Peterson in *The Blood Knot* (1964), and as a Roman citizen in a New York Shakespeare Festival production of *Coriolanus* (1965), among other parts.

Ward first made his mark as a dramatist in 1965, when two of his one-act plays opened Off-Broadway at the St. Mark's Playhouse, produced (in the face of acute financial problems) by the black actor Robert Hooks. In *Happy Ending,* a militant young black visits his aunts, servants in a white household, and is outraged by their "Aunt Jemima" attitudes, their genuine anxiety

DOUGLAS TURNER WARD

over their employers' impending divorce. He changes his tune when he learns that his aunts have compensated for their meager wages by years of expert pilferage—the source of his own fashionable wardrobe—and he then joins them in their concern for their employers' marital stability. *Day of Absence,* which Ward calls "a reverse minstrel show," considers what might happen if all the blacks in a Southern town suddenly disappeared. The remaining residents (played by blacks in "whiteface" and blond wigs) are suddenly confronted by domestic chores and the mysteries of child care, and chaos and panic ensue. The town's cracker mayor broadcasts a nationwide television appeal to the missing blacks, brandishing the shoeshine equipment and other nostalgic items that can be theirs again if only they will return.

Howard Taubman called *Happy Ending* a "cheerfully savage vaudeville sketch"; *Day of Absence* seemed to him more ambitious and sharper in its satire, though less well written. Some black critics thought that both plays revealed a fundamentally conservative attitude towards race, but Tom Prideaux found them "a gust of fresh air among racial plays," while Wilfrid Sheed saw them rather as master-servant jokes in the tradition of Molière and Goldoni: "These are not race plays in the usual sense; race is treated mainly as a local aspect of a universal institution." The program ran for over five hundred performances, won the 1966 Vernon Rice–Drama Desk Award, and brought the author an Off-Broadway Obie award for his performance as the mayor in *Day of Absence.*

In an article in the New York *Times* for August 14, 1966, Ward put the case for "a theatre concentrating primarily on themes of Negro life, but also resilient enough to incorporate and interpret the best of world drama." Only a predominantly black audience, he maintained, could "readily understand, debate, confirm, or reject the truth or falsity" of plays by black writers. The article greatly impressed an executive at the Ford Foundation, and in May 1967 the Negro Ensemble Company was established with a three-year grant from the Foundation of $434,000, and with Ward as artistic director, Robert Hooks as executive director, and Gerald S. Krone as administrative director. Based in the small St. Mark's Playhouse in Manhattan's East Village, the repertory company aimed to provide "the unusual combination of an extensive training-program which interlocks with a professional theatre designed for the production of plays relevant to black life." Ward's work for the Negro Ensemble Company, both as a director and as an actor, was highly praised from the outset. He received a Vernon Rice–Drama Desk award for his performance as Russell B. Parker, the Harlem widower, in Lonnie Elder III's *Ceremonies in Dark Old Men* (1969), and Richard Watts wrote then that "in two seasons the Negro Ensemble Company has grown into a vital force in our theatre. It does excellent and enterprising things and does them with distinction."

The Reckoning, Ward's first full-length play, opened the Company's 1969–1970 season. The author himself starred as Scar, the black pimp who successfully blackmails a bigoted Southern governor into promoting racial equality. Most reviewers found the play engrossing but excessively verbose—smothered under an "avalanche of words and oratory," as Edith Oliver put it. She found this "a hateful show—no doubt deliberately so. Mr. Ward is not out to attract or enchant or lightly amuse us, but his play's passion is alive, and despite all its faults, it does exist, which is more than can be said for most plays Off Broadway." There was a distinctly mixed critical response to Ward's one-act satire *Brotherhood* (1970), in which a white couple try unsuccessfully to hide their prejudice from the well-to-do blacks they are entertaining. Walter Kerr found the piece acutely embarrassing, but Edith Oliver wrote that "Mr. Ward is incapable of putting together a bad line, even when he sacrifices his sharp, subtle wit to a bitter practical joke, as he does here."

By the mid-1970s, the Negro Ensemble Company was generally recognized as one of the most creative and accomplished repertory groups in the United States. As of November 1975 it had given tuition-free training in the technical, creative, and administrative aspects of theatre to about four thousand students. Moreover, as Ward told an *Ebony* interviewer in 1973, "when we started, we had a twenty percent black audience. Now it's sixty percent. They come regularly without regard to what the critics write because they know we are saying something relevant to their lives and experiences, and we do it in a well-presented, entertaining, stimulating way." Since the expiration of the Company's original Ford Foundation grant, Ward has added fund raising to his other responsibilities, and to notable effect. In 1973 he spoke optimistically about the future of the Company, and added that "even with its uneven quality, the overall black theatre movement is the most vital and muscular development in the theatre today."

Douglas Turner Ward, who nowadays acts as well as writes under his own name, achieved a personal triumph in Joseph Walker's *The River Niger,* about a Harlem family struggling to cope with the return of a son embittered by his war experiences. The play opened under Ward's direction at the St. Mark's Playhouse in December 1972 and later transferred to the Brooks Atkinson Theatre on Broadway, running for almost a year in all. Ward's performance as Johnny Williams—the returning veteran's father and a character of great depth and complexity—brought him a 1973 Obie award. He was also nominated for an Antoinette Perry ("Tony") award as best supporting actor, but objected to that categorization of the part, and withdrew his name. Ward has also appeared in films and on television.

The author, six feet tall and powerfully built, with a graying beard, has been described as "leonine" in appearance. He was married in 1966 to Diana Hoyt Powell, a white woman who is or was a freelance editor for Doubleday. They have two children, Douglas and Elizabeth, and live in an East Village brownstone near the St. Mark's Playhouse. Ward lists among his recreations sports, reading, and theatre-going.

PRINCIPAL PUBLISHED WORKS: Happy Ending; and, Day of Absence: Two Plays, 1966 (republished as Two Plays, 1971); The Reckoning: A Surreal Southern Fable, 1970; Brotherhood, 1970.

ABOUT: Abramson, D.E. Negro Playwrights in the American Theatre, 1967; Black American Writers: Past and Present, 1975; Current Biography, 1977; Harrison, P.C. The Drama of Nommo, 1972; Living Black American Authors: A Biographical Directory, 1973; Mitchell, L. Black Drama, 1967; Notable Names in the American Theatre, 1976; Oliver, C. and Sills, S. Contemporary Black Drama, 1971; Rush, S. *introduction to* Two Plays, 1966; Vinson, J. (ed.) Contemporary Dramatists, 1977; Who's Who in America, 1976–1977; Who's Who in the Theatre, 1977. *Periodicals* —America September 27, 1969; Commonweal July 8, 1966; Ebony June 1973; Esquire January 1973; Life January 28,

1966; Newsweek December 24, 1973; New Yorker December 25, 1965; September 13, 1969; March 28, 1970; New York Times August 14, 1966; March 15, 1967; March 2, 1975; Saturday Review June 25, 1966; November 15, 1975; Studies in Black Literature Autumn 1972.

*WAT, ALEKSANDER (1900–1967), Polish poet, short story writer, critic, and translator, was born of Jewish parents in Warsaw. In the early 1920s Wat was a prominent member of the Warsaw futurist group called Nowa Sztuka (New Art), whose theories had much in common with dadaism and surrealism. In opposition to the conventional and harmonious Polish verse of the time, centering on the magazine *Skamander,* they called for a deliberate debasement of language—for the liberation of words from the tyranny of logic and syntax (as when Wat wrote: "I at one side and I at another side of my pug-iron stove"). Wat became an active propagandist for this "New Art," co-editing its journals *Nowa Sztuka* (1921–1922) and the *Almanach Nowej Sztuki* (1924–1925).

Bezrobotny Lucyfer (Unemployed Lucifer, 1927) is a collection of satiric tales, mostly antiutopian in theme. "The Wandering Jew," for example, imagines the future worldwide triumph of the Roman Catholic church. Since all the Jews have been converted to Christianity, and now serve as priests of the church, anti-Semites are obliged to become opponents of the Papacy, learning Hebrew and eagerly studying the Cabala. These stories foreshadow Wat's later poetry, but the surrealistic revolt in Polish literature proved short-lived. After its demise Wat established himself as a provocatively intelligent literary critic and editor. He edited the literary monthly *Miesięcznik Literacki* from 1929 to 1932, and from 1932 to 1939 worked as an editor for the publishers Gebethner and Wolff.

Fleeing from the Nazis in 1939, Wat was arrested in Lvov by the Soviet secret police, accused of obstruction and hostility towards the authorities. His sufferings as a prisoner and deportee in Kazakhstan during World War II shattered his communist ideals. After the war, however, it seems to have been these experiences, combined with the equally painful and frightening effects of a serious heart disease, which rekindled his poetic imagination. After a trickle of religious poems during the 1940s, and the novel *Ucieczka Lotna* (Lot's Escape, 1948–1949), the poems he had written "for the drawer" during the Stalinist period were published as *Wiersze* (Poems, 1957).

These deeply pessimistic poems caused a sensation, and were received with particular enthusiasm by the young, who admired Wat's

*vät

wide-ranging scholarship, and shared the frustration and nihilism expressed in such poems as "A Flamingo's Dream":

Water water water. And nothing but water.
If only an inch of land! An inch of no-matter-what land!
To set one foot on! If only!

We begged the gods for that! All of them!
Water gods, land gods, southern gods, northern gods,
For an inch, a strip, a scrap of any kind of land!
No more than just to support a claw of one foot!
And nothing. Only water. Nothing except water.
Water water water.
If only a speck of land!
There is no salvation.

(translated by Czeslaw Milosz)

In 1959 Wat went for the sake of his health to the south of France, and from then until his death he lived abroad. His last poems were published in *Ciemne świecidło* (The Dark Spangle, 1968), a collection which appeared posthumously in Paris and includes the best of his entire poetic output. His late poems show a turning to religious feeling and mysticism—one critic has suggested that "he blends a Jewish prophet's despair with Christian peace and humility." Bright colors and deliberate inconsistencies and buffooneries lighten the prevailing pessimism in these poems, and recall Wat's earlier surrealism, leading Czeslaw Milosz to observe: "For a literary critic it is a curious example of belated fulfillment, and at the same time of a once-defeated movement taking its revenge." But, as Kazimierz Wyka says, beneath the surrealistic elements in the late verse can be heard a deeper prophetic note of savage power:

By a great, swift water
on a stony bank
a human skull was lying
and shouting: Allah la ilah.

And in that cry such horror
and such supplication
so great was its despair
that I asked the helmsman:

For what can it still cry out? Of what is it still afraid?
What divine judgment could strike it yet again?

Suddenly there came a wave
took hold of the skull
and tossing it about
smashed it against the bank. . . .

(from "From Persian Parables,"
translated by Czeslaw Milosz)

In Wat's last years of increasing illness, the poems mark a series of small triumphs over physical pain and existential anguish, victories for which the poet claimed "I have paid. For everything. With my body and soul." As George Gömöri put it in *Books Abroad,* "In his 'prison cell of pain,' Wat evokes anything that can alleviate suffering (which, in his view, is eternal): irony—applied mercilessly to a political fool's paradise—invectives and faith. The latter is the most powerful—faith in human beings close to him. Without the self-sacrificing help of his wife and the support of some friends, Wat would not have been able to create poems of such force and insight as he did in the intervals of his grave illness."

PRINCIPAL WORKS IN ENGLISH TRANSLATION: Mediterranean Poems, translated by Czeslaw Milosz (and his graduate students), 1977. *Poems in* Gillon, A. and Krzyzanowski, L. (eds.) Introduction to Modern Polish Literature, 1964; Milosz, Cz. Postwar Polish Poetry, 1965; Peterkiewicz, J., Singer, B., and Stallworthy, J. (eds.) Five Centuries of Polish Poetry, 1970; Tri-Quarterly Spring 1967.

ABOUT: Encyclopaedia Judaica, 1971; Gömöri, G. Polish and Hungarian Poetry 1945 to 1956, 1966; Milosz, Cz. The History of Polish Literature, 1969; Seymour-Smith, M. Guide to Modern World Literature, 1973. *Periodicals*—Books Abroad Spring 1970.

"WATSON, JOHN H." *See* FARMER, PHILIP JOSÉ

*WEN I-TO (November 24, 1899–July 15, 1946), Chinese poet and scholar, was born into a large and wealthy family in a small "fish-and-rice" village at the confluence of the Pa and Yangtze rivers, near Hsishui, in Hupeh province. His father was a scholar who practiced and enforced a puritanical Confucianism, against which Wen I-to spent his life rebelling.

The boy began his education in the traditional manner of his class, receiving private tuition in the Confucian classics, and displeasing his father by preferring the poetry to the books on ethics and philosophy. There are many stories about his utter absorption in his favorite poems—he was missing even on his own wedding day, and was eventually discovered quietly reading in a corner. At the age of eleven he was sent to a "modern" school, where English and mathematics were added to his curriculum. Two years later, with a scholarship sponsored by the new republican government, he went on to the American-style Tsinghua College in Peking (now Tsinghua University).

He was a hardworking student, and found time to direct college plays and edit some of the
*wen yē do

853

student publications in which his own first essays and poems appeared. He at first wrote in the classical language, and staunchly supported it until he was caught up in the May 4th Student Movement of 1919. This movement, which led to a literary revolution in favor of the vernacular language, began as a nationalist protest against China's failure at the Versailles Peace Conference to recover an area of Shantung Province which had been occupied by the Japanese. Deeply stirred, Wen I-to pasted on the door of the college dining hall a huge red banner bearing the inflammatory words of a medieval soldier-statesman: "O let all things begin afresh!/ Give us back our mountains and our rivers. . . ."

After that, while other students marched and demonstrated, Wen I-to was made responsible for drafting and copying propaganda leaflets. By the time he returned to his literary studies, he was a convert to the spoken language. His first vernacular poem, "Hsi-an" (West Coast) appeared in the *Tsinghua Weekly* in July 1920. The poem is a curious blend of foreign and native elements, in which Wen I-to's characteristically rich imagery and his preoccupation with the quest for beauty are already evident, as is the influence of the English Romantic poets, especially Keats. (It should be said, however, that Wen I-to's enthusiasm for some Western and modern poetry never diminished his love for Chinese classical literature.)

In the spring of 1922 Wen I-to went home to marry Kao Hsiao-chen, daughter of an old family friend and distant relative, before leaving for the United States. He was in America from 1922 to 1925, studying Western painting first at the Art Institute of Chicago (1922-1923), where he was lonely and homesick, and then at Colorado College (1923-1924), where he joined his friend Liang Shih-ch'ui. Though he was majoring in fine arts, Wen's real interest was literature, which he said was to him "a faith, a vision, and an ideal, not merely a medium for the expression of emotion." He immersed himself in English literature, particularly the Romantic, Victorian, and modern poets, with results which were apparent in his first collection of poems, written in America but published as *Hung-chu* (Red Candles, 1922) in China, where it was acclaimed for its technical skill and the richness of its imagery.

The classical language in which Chinese poetry was traditionally composed had very little stress, and Chinese prosody therefore relied on euphony rather than on scansion. The pioneering struggles of modern Chinese poets with the more strongly stressed vernacular resulted in an excessively free verse which seemed by comparison with classical poetry no more than prose divided artificially into lines. Wen I-to, who thought that poetry should be like "dancing in fetters," was one of the earliest to evolve and master appropriate new forms. The content of the poems in *Hung-chu* was equally revolutionary, traditional themes and images giving way to topical subjects, as in Wen I-to's famous "Laundry Song," an eloquent expression of his resentment of the constant humiliation he suffered in the United States, where it seemed to him to be assumed that the Chinese existed only to launder the dirty linen of Caucasians.

In 1924 Wen moved to New York. He became a dedicated theatre-goer, joined the Art Students League, and also the Ta-chiang-she (Great River Society), a political society organized by Chinese students in the United States to support the development of a strong Chinese state. An admirer of Sun Yat-sen, he became a fervent cultural nationalist, intent upon the rejuvenation of Chinese painting, poetry, and drama.

Returning to China in May 1925, Wen I-to became dean of the National Academy of Fine Arts in Peking. He was greatly distressed by the social and political conditions he found in China, and expressed his feelings in his poetry, but resisted the directly political and starkly realistic verse then in vogue, and joined the Crescent Society, a group of western-educated young symbolist poets. With Hsü Chih-mo and others he founded in 1926 the *Shih-chien*, a weekly poetry supplement to the *Peking Morning Post* which, though it survived only from April to June, had great influence. It was in 1926 also that Wen published his essay "The Form of Poetry," which made an important contribution to the development of modern Chinese poetry, showing how the shapeless free verse of the time could be given a more orderly structure. The essay stressed the need for metrical balance and a degree of uniformity in line lengths, and also argued in favor of stanzaic structure, which was rare in classical Chinese verse.

The title poem of Wen's second (and last) collection, *Su-shui* (Dead Water, 1928), is a supreme example of his mastery of style and structure, and of his Keatsian use of synaesthesia. As Julia C. Lin says, his work "opens up an extraordinarily lush world interwoven with dazzling colors, startling imageries and a luxurious sensuousness." He was by temperament a romantic poet, and his aestheticism earned him much criticism from more obviously *engagé* writers. Yet many of the poems in *Su-shui* are bitterly satirical, and Wen's natural lyricism is often employed in the exploration of serious social and moral problems. "Dead Water" is an indirect but powerful expression of his feelings about

China, fouled and disgraced by poverty, civil war, and foreign exploitation:

Here is a ditch of dead and hopeless water:
No breeze can raise a ripple on it.
Best to throw in it scraps of rusty iron and copper,
And pour out on it the refuse of meat and soup.

Perhaps the copper will turn green as emeralds,
Perhaps the rusty iron will assume the shape of
  peach-blossoms.
Let grease weave a layer of silky gauze
And bacteria puff patches of cloud and haze.

So let the dead water ferment into green wine
Littered with floating pearls of white foam.
Small pearls cackle aloud and become big pearls,
Only to be burst like gnats to rob the vintage.

And so this ditch of dead and hopeless water
May boast a touch of brightness:
If the toads cannot endure the deadly silence,
The water may burst out singing. . . .

(translated by Ho Yo Yung)

In 1926, meanwhile, Wen I-to had resigned from his Peking Academy post and become dean of students at National Political University in Shanghai. The following year, after working briefly in a minor post for Chiang Kai-shek's regime, he became chairman of the department of foreign languages and literature in National Fourth Chungshan University in Nanking, now National Central University. In 1928 he went to Wuhan University as dean of the school of arts and chairman of the department of Chinese language and literature. In 1930 he moved to Tsingtao University, and in 1932 he became professor of Chinese literature at Tsinghua University, his *alma mater,* remaining on the faculty of that university until his death.

After the publication of *Su-shui* in 1928, Wen I-to wrote little poetry. Increasingly depressed about political and social conditions in China, he gradually ended his connection with the Crescent Society and its literary monthly *Hsin-yueh.* He neglected his friends and immersed himself in the study of Chinese classical literature, and of philology, mythology, and the ancient arts, publishing a number of scholarly works.

When Japan invaded China in 1937, he was evacuated with his university from Peking to Changsha. Early in 1938 it was decided that the university must be moved again, this time to the province of Yunnan, on the Tibetan border, a distance of over a thousand miles. Wen I-to led the long march of some two hundred students who had decided to make the journey on foot. His interest in art revived during the march, which he recorded in over a hundred landscape drawings.

He was to spend the rest of his life with his students in the city of Kunming, living in increasing poverty as wartime inflation reduced the value of his salary. His family shared two rooms above a pack-horse station with the family of his brother, also a professor, and Wen I-to became famous for the seals he carved to eke out his income. He was every inch the Romantic poet, colorful and dramatic in speech, with long hair and a full beard, grown on the march, which he had sworn not to shave until the Japanese had been defeated.

During the first years in Kunming, Wen continued to devote himself to study and teaching. In 1943, however, he was visited by a nephew who had served as a student volunteer in the Nationalist forces, and received from him a firsthand account of the wretched condition of the army, the corruption and incompetence of Chiang Kai-shek's regime. Wen retired into seclusion for a week to consider what he had learned. When he emerged, he had resolved to give up his isolation and to work for social and political reform. He began to read leftist literature and to discuss current affairs with his students. In 1944 he became a leading member of the Democratic League, a third party ta^ling up a position between the Communists and the Nationalists. As editor of the *Min-chu chou-k'an* (Democratic Weekly) he denounced Confucianism and the feudal system it encouraged, and called on the government to adopt "democratic measures" and to mobilize "the masses of the people." He also reversed his previously critical attitude towards such committed writers as Lu Hsün and T'ien Chien, maintaining that the poet must be "the drummer of the age."

By 1946, the inhabitants of Kunming were living in terror of Chiang Kai-shek's murder squads. Wen I-to, already a marked man, made his assassination inevitable when, in a speech given on July 15, he accused the government of the murder of a fellow teacher. Just after 5 p.m. the same day he was shot to death as he left the office of the *Democratic Weekly.* He was survived by his wife and five children.

According to the *Biographical Dictionary of Republican China,* Wen I-to "contributed to the development of a new poetic form in China by fusing Western technique, Chinese and Western images, and classical Chinese poetic diction in a new vernacular style." As a scholar he combined orthodox Chinese and Western methodology. Kai-yu Hsu has shown in the *Harvard Journal of Asiatic Studies* how the gradual development of his social and aesthetic opinions reflects "basic changes in the prevailing intellectual moods" in China during the first half of this century.

PRINCIPAL WORKS IN ENGLISH TRANSLATION: Red Candle: selected poems translated by Tao Tao Sanders, 1972. *Poems in* Acton, H. and Ch'en Shih-Hsiang (eds.) Modern Chinese Poetry, 1936; Hsu, Kai-yu (ed.) Twentieth Century Chinese Poetry, 1963; Payne, R. (ed.) Contemporary Chinese Poetry, 1947; Payne, R. (ed.) The White Pony, 1947.

ABOUT: Boorman, H.L. (ed.) Biographical Dictionary of Republican China, 1970; Lin, J.C. Modern Chinese Poetry, 1970; Lai, Ming. A History of Chinese Literature, 1964; Lang, D.M. (ed.) Guide to Eastern Literatures, 1971. *Periodicals*—Harvard Journal of Asiatic Studies XXI 1958.

*WEÖRES, SÁNDOR (June 22, 1913–), Hungarian poet, was born into a family of small landowners in Szombathely, the economic and cultural center of Western Transdubia, close to the Austrian frontier. He received his elementary schooling in Pápa and Csönge and went on to gymnasia at Szombathely, Györ, and Sopron, where his promise as a poet was recognized in his early teens. Weöres entered the University of Pécs to study law, but after six months switched to geography and history. A year and a half later, in 1935, he switched again to philosophy and aesthetics, graduated, and went on to earn his doctorate in philosophy with a literary-psychological thesis on poetic creation, "A vers születése" (The Birth of Poetry). From 1941 to 1950 he worked as a librarian at Pécs, Székesfehérvár, and Budapest. He has been a full-time writer since 1951.

Long before then, Weöres had established a high reputation as a poet. As a very young man he was encouraged by the distinguished poet and critic Mihály Babits, who published his poems in the important literary review *Nyugat.* Weöres' first collection, *Hideg van* (It's Cold), appeared in 1934, and was followed a year later by *A kö és az ember* (The Stone and the Man). Romantic and dreamy as these early poems were, they exhibited features which, as George Gömöri points out, have remained constant in his work—"a definite philosophical bent, an awareness of the human predicament and the tragic antinomies of life, an extraordinary mimetic talent, and an urge to speak through different personae and play elaborate games with words." Weöres received the Baumgarten Prize, which was then Hungary's highest literary award, in both 1935 and 1936, while still in his early twenties.

Hungary has undergone profound political changes during Weöres' lifetime, but he has retained his own poetic vision despite the brutal repressions of Horthy's fascist regime, which took the lives of writers like György Bálint and
*ve′ û resh

© 1979 by Layle Silbert

SÁNDOR WEÖRES

Miklos Radnóti, and the censorship imposed by the communist government that came to power after World War II. As the first true Hungarian modernist, Weöres had nothing in common with the tradition of political poetry and romantic nationalism that dominated Hungarian literature from Petöfi (1823–1849) to Attila József (1905–1937). Indeed, having grown up during the Great War and the Depression of 1929–1931, he has never put the slightest faith in political ideals or remedies, and the bankruptcy of classical Western rationalism seemed to him clearly demonstrated in the catastrophic history of the twentieth century.

Weöres therefore turned away from the West, and in 1937 went to India and the Far East to study Eastern religion and philosophy. This experience is reflected both in the content and the increased maturity of *A teremtés dicsérete* (In Praise of Creation), the notable collection he published in 1938. Weöres has sought, through the exploration of his own subconscious processes, to tap what Jung called the "collective unconscious," and to participate imaginatively in the great human cycle of birth, love, and death. He believes that "if you want to possess truth . . . you have to find it in the depth of yourself," and that "there is no way to improve your nation and mankind except by improving yourself." He has been called a "macrocosmic poet," who creates his own poetic universe out of his relationship—as an artist and a human being—to the ultimate realities of life and death, time and space.

If Weöres is not a political poet, he is quite often an antipolitical one. He mocked the hysterical enthusiasm that greeted the wartime alliance with Hitler and the short-lived territorial gains it brought: "My country, paradise of petty politicizing/ drop the ballyhoo: you yell for empty winds." In *Medúza* (Medusa, 1942) he drew a powerfully realistic picture of an age of chaos from whose struggles he could nevertheless hope to see a "new man" arise. But as the war progressed this gave way to despair in the magnificent long poem *A reménytelenség könyve* (The Book of Hopelessness, 1944): "Horror has swept to the heart of existence . . . and no peace is left anywhere, not even in death."

The end of the war released Weöres from this all-embracing feeling of horror. His "Huszadik századi freskó" ("Twentieth-Century Fresco") nevertheless gives a grim picture of the disintegrating old world, coupled with a warning to those who are about to build a new one not to make the same mistakes. With the Cloud-Cuckoo Town of narrow self-interest collapsing, and its values ("Freedom for the Privileged") burnt to ashes, even true Hatred disappears, and only Disgust remains. And so the poet, adopting the role of the Angel of Disgust, sets himself on fire and runs through the streets as a human torch, shouting out his warnings:

Don't be officious! don't long to wave banners,
Don't make empty gestures of building, destroying, salvaging
Leave slogans, pompous principles, quaking ideas!

A fogak tornáca (The Colonnade of Teeth), one of Weöres' finest books, appeared in 1947 during the short-lived Hungarian democracy. Its visionary title poem explores the notion that all things meet in a circle, so that heaven can be found through a descent into the depths of hell:

The Colonnade of Teeth, where you have entered,
red marble hall: your mouth,
white marble columns: your teeth,
and the scarlet carpet you step on: your tongue.

You can look out of any window of time
and catch sight of still another face of God.
Lean out of the time of sedge and warblers:
God caresses.
Lean out of the time of Moses and Elias:
God haggles.
Lean out of the time of the Cross:
God's face is all blood, like Veronica's napkin.
Lean out of your own time:
God is old, bent over a book. . . .

No sugar left for the child:
he stuffs himself with hen-droppings and finds
what's sweet.

Every clod: lightless star!
Every worm: wingless cherub!

If you make hell, plunge to the bottom:
heaven's in sight there. Everything circles round.

Man lays down easy roads.
The wild beast stamps a forest track.
And look at the tree: depth and height raying from
it to every compass-point;
Itself a road, to everywhere!

Once you emerge from the glitter of the last two
columns
the cupola your hair skims is then infinity,
and a swirl of rose-leaves throws you down,
and all that lies below, your bridal bed: the whole
world.
Here you can declare:
"My God, I don't believe in you!"
And the storm of rose-leaves will smile:
"but I believe in you: are you satisfied?"

(translated by Edwin Morgan)

Even Marxist critics who oppose Weöres' views appreciated the technical perfection of the lyrics in this collection, in which the musical and rhythmical pattern becomes as important as the content. Weöres has always been a poet of great virtuosity, handling the most complex metrical and rhythmic devices as confidently as free verse. His interest in the rhythmic and musical organization of sound is in keeping with his interest in primitive and ancient folk-poetry, an art derived from incantation and allied to dance and ritual. Some of his poems have been written as texts to melodies by Kodály. His short lyrics are remarkable for the variety of their rhythmic and phonetic effects, his inventiveness sometimes leading him to create imaginary languages. George Gömöri, commenting on this musicality, virtuosity, and amazing vitality, has described him as a miraculous spider spinning out a brilliant net of words: "Weöres at his most popular is not the author of great 'archetypal' poems or of antipolitical satires. He is known and loved by many for his mastery of the Hungarian language, rarely surpassed. . . . Poems like this could be enjoyed by the five-year-old for their sheer musical excitement and by grown-ups for their linguistic inventiveness and grotesque humor."

Condemned by the party hacks as an escapist and a nihilist, Weöres was not permitted to publish his original work between 1948 and 1955. He established himself during these years as a translator of great range and sensitivity. In 1955 he published *Bóbita,* a book of verse for children which is still popular. During the Thaw that followed Stalin's death Weöres brought out *A hallgatás tornya* (The Tower of Silence, 1956), which finally established him as a major poet. This collection contains a selection of his best earlier work along with many new poems written during the 1950s. These latter include many pieces drawing on classical and other mythologies, and such remarkable poems as "Le Journal," a brilliant critique of Stalinist Hungary, and "Az elveszített napernyö" ("The Lost Parasol"), a highly original work making brilliant use of rhyme, half-rhyme, and assonance. It centers on a theme fundamental to Weöres' works, the idea of nature as endless change and metamorphosis; here a lost parasol slowly disintegrates under the action of wind and rain, torn by rocks and branches, until every particle of it has dissolved back into nature. Yet this is also an intensely human poem, for the parasol has been left behind in the grass by two lovers, and though they have long since forgotten it, the tiny assertive flash of scarlet silk is the one man-made thing in the landscape until it becomes completely a part of nature—a nature that the lovers themselves can never escape from. This long poem of thirty-eight stanzas ends with the poet comparing himself to the golden oriole, singing exultantly of love, change, and death, until it too dissolves back into nature:

> The red silk parasol was my song,
>   sung for my only one;
> this true love is the clearest spring,
>   I have smoothed its mirror with my breath,
> I have seen the two of us, the secret is known:
>   we shall moulder into one after death.
> Now I expend my life exultantly
> like the oriole in the tree:
> till it falls down on the old forest floor,
> singing with such full throat its heart must burst
>   and soar.

(translated by Edwin Morgan)

On a visit to London in 1963 Weöres was asked if he always understood his own poems. He replied that he did not, adding that it was not really necessary to understand a poem in the same way as a naturalistic short story. And he stressed that exploration and experiment are essential to his art: "I think one should explore everything. Including those things which will never be accepted, not even in the distant future. We can never know, at the start of an experiment, where it will lead. . . . It may take decades or centuries to prove whether it was a useful experiment or a useless one. It may never be proved at all."

Such explorations and experiments are very evident in Weöres' next collection, *Tüzkút* (Well of Fire, 1964), which the poet dedicates to the

Third Millennium—the future that he hopes will understand him better than the present does. He claims that what others have described as his nihilism is simply an attempt to pierce the void into the Unknown, and several of these poems evoke mystic experiences, or prophesy an eventual cosmic harmony: "Man always conquered other men in the past, but ah, quivering hope!—the man of the future will conquer himself and for this destiny itself, and the stars, will yield to him."

In this collection and in the following one, *Merülö Saturnus* (Saturn Sinking, 1968), there are experiments of many sorts, including poems where form may be said to take over the function of content. As George Gömöri describes it, "an action or a dream is not *told* but is *expressed* through the structural arrangement of certain evocative, acoustic, and other elements. It is a new type of poem where there is no logical connection between words or lines; all they do is create a certain field of association in the mind of the reader":

Holdra nap	After moon sun
körsugár	rayring
mély morajt	lifts up
fölemel	a deep rumble
szikla függ	Cliff hangs
napro hold	after sun moon
csillagok	stars
hideg ür	cold void

(translated by George Gömöri)

Hold és Sárkány (The Moon and the Dragon, 1967) contains the poet's two verse plays. "The Boatman in the Moon," first published in 1941, is a puppet play for children in which heroes from an assortment of mythologies are brought together in a fantastic (and often extremely funny) plot centering on the thwarted love of a Magyar princess for the Boatman in the Moon, a supernatural character who steers the moon like a boat across the sky. The second play, originally published in 1965, is a tragicomedy in blank verse called "Octopus, or the History of St. George and the Dragon." A black comedy of human frailty, it shows how myths can be as compelling in the life of society as economic and social forces. For the image of the victorious Saint George will dominate the life of the city as completely as that of the dragon had done—though the politicians who exploit both myths to further their own interests are here shown meeting a nasty end.

These plays were included in *Egybegyüjtött irások* (Collected Writings, 1970), along with all the previously published poems, the aphorisms, the doctoral thesis on poetic creation, and the prose epic *Boland Istók* (about the shaman of ancient Hungarian religion, who has deteriorated into the harmless village idiot of later folklore). Edited by Imre Bata with the cooperation of the poet himself, this was recognized as an important literary event, making available the entire output of a great poet whose early volumes had been unavailable for over twenty years. Many of the original titles of both poems and books had not been selected by Weöres, and this edition, while noting the titles under which they originally appeared, also gives those preferred by Weöres.

In the same year Weöres was introduced to English-speaking readers in a *Selected Poems,* a volume in which his work appeared with that of the younger and very different Hungarian poet Ferenc Juhász. The translations of Weöres are by Edwin Morgan, who describes him as "a protean poet of great virtuosity, writing in all forms, from complex metre and rhyme to free verse, keenly aware of the musical and rhythmical powers which poetry shares with song and dance and ritual, and from this delighting in the means which poetry particularly offers of uniting the sophisticated and the primitive." The Weöres selection is restricted to only twenty-four poems, which one reviewer called "an appetizer rather than a proper meal," adding however that the selection does manage to give a reasonably good idea of the poet's versatility and his preoccupation with myth. Edwin Morgan's translations were generally admired, and there was particular praise for his versions of Weöres' experiments with rhythm and sound in poems like "Moon and Farmstead":

> full moon slip swim
> wind fog foam chord hum
> the house empty
>
> rampant
> thorn fence
> eye blaze
>
> moon swim flame
> grass chord twang
> cloud fling
>
> the house empty
> door window
> fly up
>
> chimney run
> fog swirl
> full moon circle
>
> the house empty
>
> (translated by
> Edwin Morgan)

Love of all kinds plays a central role in the lyric verse of Weöres—physical love, celebrated with a frankness which has both shocked and stirred his readers, and love as one of the great links between everyday life and transcendental reality. In the book *Psyche* (1972), Weöres creates the life story and work of a fictional nineteenth-century woman poet with such insight, magic of language, and beautiful eroticism that even before the book had been published people were lining up to hear the actress Marian Csernus reciting it at the University Theatre in Budapest. Weöres' reputation increased enormously during the 1960s, and he is now widely regarded as Hungary's greatest living poet, a profound metaphysician who can nevertheless write exquisite songs and enchanting nursery rhymes. George Gömöri has called him "a master of Hungarian verse unequalled in this century." Weöres received the Kossuth Prize in 1970. In recent years he has traveled widely, visiting China, Britain, and the United States. He is married to the poet Amy Károlyi.

PRINCIPAL WORKS IN ENGLISH TRANSLATION: Selected Poems of Sándor Weöres and Ferenc Juhász, 1970. *Poems in* Gömöri, G. and Newman, C. (eds.) New Writing of East Europe, 1968.

ABOUT: Fleischmann, W.B. (ed.) Encyclopedia of World Literature in the Twentieth Century, 1971; Gömöri, G. Polish and Hungarian Poetry, 1945–1956, 1966; Tezla, A. Hungarian Authors, 1970. *Periodicals*—Books Abroad Winter 1969, Winter 1972; Modern Language Journal April 8, 1949; Tri-Quarterly Spring 1967.

WILLIAMS, HEATHCOTE (November 15, 1941–), English dramatist, novelist, and editor, writes: "Heathcote Williams was born in Helsby, Cheshire, and is the author of *The Speakers,* a documentary novel about four orators in Hyde Park which was dramatised by William Gaskill and Max Stafford-Clark for the Joint Stock Theatre Company, and toured Eastern Europe. His *Manifestoes, Manifesten* were published in English and Dutch by the Cold Turkey Press, Rotterdam, and he is the author of three plays: *The Local Stigmatic* was presented by the Traverse Theatre, Edinburgh, and the Royal Court, London, in 1966, and published in Penguin's Traverse Plays; *AC/DC* was completed in 1969 and presented at the Royal Court Theatre and the Chelsea Theatre in Brooklyn, and published by Calder and Boyars and Viking Press; and *Remember the Truth Dentist,* which was presented at the Royal Court Theatre in 1973, directed by Ken Campbell. He's also written a

HEATHCOTE WILLIAMS

© Chris Davies

film-script, *Malatesta,* about the Italian anarchist and the siege of Sydney Street from the anarchist point of view. It was filmed in 1968 by Peter Lilienthal.

"For the last two years, being homeless, he has lived in a squat in Westbourne Park Road, and runs a free agency for the homeless, publishing regular bulletins of empty houses all over the British Isles (and even abroad) suitable to be squatted, advising people who turn up on the legal and practical implications of squatting, and occasionally opening up places, the most recent and successful being the Palm Court Hotel, which is now a refuge for one hundred and fifty battered wives and their children.

"He is co-founder with Jim Haynes, Bill Levy and Germaine Greer of *Suck,* a journal of Reichian sex-pol, and *The Fanatic,* which he co-edits with John Michell, Bill Levy, Richard Adams, and anyone else who cares to produce one. He is a contributing editor of *Seed, the Voice of Natural Living,* and of *Wordworks,* a literary mag. He was an editor of *Transatlantic Review* for ten years.

"He has just completed a book entitled *The Free Feast* about Windsor Free Festival, perhaps the largest squat in English history, and together with Nicholas Albery and Diana Senior successfully sued the chief of Thames Valley Police for causing a riot at one of these seminal events, and beating up the descendants of William Blake, God's Rake, Gerrard Winstanley ("the world is a common treasure house to all"), and Wat Tyler.

"He's also compiled an anthology and celebration of squatting culture entitled *Squat Now While Stocks Last,* a full-length musical *The*

Supernatural Family, and a volume of essays, *Severe Joy,* which will be published by Calder and Boyars."

The son of a barrister, Harold Heathcote Williams, and himself intended for a career at the bar, Williams came down from Oxford before taking his law finals and exchanged a stable middle-class background for a life on the fringe of the Soho underworld. Such a beginning suggests a juvenile gesture of class-reversal, substituting Speakers' Corner for the Oxford Union and transferring loyalty to the kind of articulate vagrants he might have found himself prosecuting in Court. This was not a short-lived rebellion, however, but the first stage in a process which has increasingly distanced him from the social status quo and from the usual priorities of professional authorship.

When *The Speakers* appeared in 1964, Maurice Richardson described its effect as one of "continuously present Apocalypse." The book consists of profiles of four of the orators who regularly entertain and/or instruct the crowds who gather to hear and heckle them at Speakers' Corner in London's Hyde Park, with introductory and closing chapters presenting the scene in long-shot. The history and legalities of the subject are touched on, but only through the remarks of Park *habitués.* To have written a formal study of Speakers' Corner would have contradicted the impulse that drew Williams to the subject in the first place. Implicit in his book is the denial of all forms of orthodox authority: political, legal, or authorial. Williams himself figures in the third person as "Cafferty," a transparent observer, recording barroom conversations with old Park hands and focusing on his four principals as dispassionately as a camera lens. The only element of judgment lies in his decision to treat them with respect and really listen to what they are saying, instead of viewing them as performing monsters in a tourist menagerie.

The speakers are: Axel Ney Hoch, a stateless Central European; John Webster, an ex-fascist hypnotherapist; Jacobus van Dyn, a villainously tattooed old Boer; and William MacGuinness, a "fearless, filthy dirty, toothless, black Irishman" who calls himself the King of the Gypsies, and with whom Williams shared a room in Soho until MacGuinness died in 1967. Their platform topics range from idealistic causes to personal grievances, but jointly they emerge as a professional fraternity as jealously critical of each other as vaudeville artists or poets. They cannot be dismissed as cranks or madmen, since Williams has quietly dismantled the boundaries of normality, leaving an open zone in which any statement may be true. Perhaps van Dyn had worked for Al Capone. Perhaps the "man with the silent message" has something important to tell the world. Perhaps there are invisible people walking about. Powerful commonsense arguments, like Hoch's vegetarianism, mingle on equal terms with messianic prophesy, fringe medicine, and home-brewed ideologies.

From this, the book acquires some of its apocalyptic character. But ultimately this derives less from what the speakers say than from their force of personality. MacGuinness, the most charismatic of the quartet, is not there to persuade people but to turn their brains upside down with pronouncements like "Hitting people for money is sexy." Oratory for him amounts to a drug, along with purple hearts, coal gas and milk, smoking false eyelashes, and eating grass in the Park ("They nicked me for grazing on the Queen's Highway"). When *The Speakers* came out, MacGuinness cited it as "the only book worth reading since I myself wrote the Bible." Other, less biased commentators invoked comparisons with Sophocles and Blake, while the *Evergreen Review* saluted the book as "documentary novel freed from Zola." Philip Toynbee was more moderate. Because of Williams's mingling of fact and invention, he thought that "in the end nothing seems authentic"—that this was an entertaining book about "excellent entertainers" but no more than that. In any case, *The Speakers* was, quite obviously, the work of a born dramatist, as the Joint Stock Company demonstrated in their widely admired stage adaptation in 1974. And by then Williams had himself transferred his attention to the theatre.

He began with a one-act piece, *The Local Stigmatic* (1965), which owes something to Harold Pinter in its abrupt brutality and disdain for biographical characterization. In retrospect, you might label Graham and Ray as street terrorists. In performance, though, you merely observe them walking from place to place, chatting about their bets on the greyhounds, until they fall in with David, a film actor, whom they court with obsequious flattery before beating him to a pulp. The extreme stylistic precision which John Russell Taylor noted in the play intensifies the ferocity of its impact. But the assault is no arbitrary piece of sadism. In destroying a man they know only on film, the two assailants are revenging themselves on the celebrity system and on what Williams has described as "psychic capitalists." "Attention," he told an interviewer, "is a basic human need like food or sex. ... As the media stand now, .0001 percent of the popula-

tion is getting *crème brûlé* every day, and the rest are being ignored."

This idea forms a central thread in his full-length play, *AC/DC* (1970), a work of total and uncompromising originality which earns Williams his place in any survey of modern British drama. Previously he had shown a powerful sympathy with mental disorder, but now schizophrenia takes over completely, and the author figures as a psychic explorer who has voyaged to the limits of sanity to struggle back with a report. Writing the play, he subsequently acknowledged, became a nightmare—"I thought it would only be performed in a madhouse with me playing all the parts."

The play's basic metaphor is to present the human animal as an electrical circuit, convertible to any current. In the first act, "Alternating Current," a hippy couple wander into an all-night amusement arcade with a black girl, Sadie, to have group sex in one of the machines. They are joined by Maurice, the arcade technician, and his companion Perowne. Instead of throwing them out, Maurice embarks on a speech about Mia Farrow's babies coming out of his nipples and about picking up television programs in his head. Maurice and Perowne are evidently lunatics, but they exercise a powerful hold over Sadie and expose the two hippies as "Mr. and Mrs. Jones," the latest incarnation of pair-bonding bourgeois America. Sadie switches them off and converts to Maurice (who, she says, is "satirizing attitudes which haven't yet arisen.")

In the second act, "Direct Current," she has moved in with Maurice and Perowne in a room containing a bank of video screens and papered with celebrity photographs. Against this "cybernetic model" the trio engage in a combat against the psychic capitalists, envisaged as an Attila-like horde of actors, pop stars, and newscasters smashing into the consciousness of the defenseless population and taking possession of their heads. Television and radio are seen as carriers of a plague ("Roach," Maurice says, squashing a valve underfoot) which afflicts its sufferers with the physical symptom of "media rash." Perowne is its chief victim, and his cure is first undertaken by Maurice, who tries to "demagnetize" him and "clean up his tracks." Sadie then takes over and performs a double exorcism by ritually desecrating the celebrity collage and finally trepanning Perowne to expel the media demons and open his third eye.

Synopsis does not take one very far into the play, as its force resides mainly in the dialogue—a compound of biochemistry, electronics, astronomy, Tantric spells, Buddhism, and other recondite disciplines mixed in with pop culture and American and Cockney vernacular. All of which assists in showing individual mentalities being absorbed into a group mind, and escaping what Williams describes as the "hopelessly stratified" conventional treatment of dramatic character. Schizophrenics or seers, his characters are plugged into a source of energy inaccessible to the sane grey spectator. John Russell Taylor has said that the play, "despite its looseness, its occasional infatuation with words for their own sake . . . its dangerous hovering on the border of something so private as to be beyond communication at all . . . is a rare tour de force, without any close parallel in British or world theatre today." And for a critic in the *Times Literary Supplement,* it was "perhaps the most theatrically inventive and prophetic work of the past decade."

AC/DC brought Williams the *Evening Standard* award, the George Devine and John Whiting awards, and an "Obie" award. After it, he produced nothing more for the theatre for four years. And his next piece, *Remember the Truth Dentist,* was not a play but a "one-man revue" assembled mostly from his magazine writings and ranging from a hymn of hate to a famous model to manifestos on plant liberation and income tax ("I will not pay taxes until I have invented a pacifist toy which is as sexually satisfying as a gun"). Victoria Radin called it "a liturgy, ranging from Te Deum to Requiem, told by incantation, invocation and commandment."

Hancock's Last Half Hour (1977) plays out the final act in the life of a bankrupt "psychic capitalist," the brilliant English comedian Tony Hancock. Barricaded in his hotel bedroom in Sydney, washing down his overdose with draughts of the vodka that had lubricated his decline, Hancock blearily recalls his wrecked career and marriages, draws on his erratic autodidactic reading for speculations about the nature of comedy, and dreams up antic last-minute schemes for a comeback. Irving Wardle called it "a play by someone who knows about self-destructiveness, who knows and loves his subject, and who has the technical skills to cut across chronological time and create Hancock entire through the inflections, attitudes, and verbal shorthand he gave to English speech."

A television interview with a bronzed athlete who says he is two hundred and seventy-eight years old is the subject of *The Immortalist* (1977). Wardle, who called the play "an act of intellectual guerilla warfare," wrote that Heathcote Williams "has access to a vast store of curious information" and a "capacity for making lightning connexions between supposedly unrelated categories of knowledge and experience"—a talent he uses to cut the ground from under the skeptical interviewer's feet. "You can take your choice," Wardle says, "of regarding the play as a literal claim for prolonging human survival, or as a marvellous sustained metaphor on time as a capitalist conspiracy. Either way, the piece leaves you feeling more alive." *Playpen,* also staged in 1977, uses masks and an assortment of vaudeville techniques in an attack on the way adults conspire to turn their children into emotional cripples like themselves. It was found funny, coarse, and violent, though most critics (brainwashed conformists all) doubted that it represented the best way to liberate their brainwashed children.

Heathcote Williams has described himself as a "paradisiac"; and as a private individual he has acted out his own brand of utopian anarchy in episodes such as suing the police for breaking up the 1974 Windsor Pop Festival, and conducting a near-fatal experiment in fire-eating. As he says, he himself "squats" (occupies without paying rent) an empty property in West London, and he does all he can to help other homeless Londoners find similar accommodations. The walls in his street are decorated with slogans proclaiming the new Albion Free State, and he has tried to uproot the sidewalk in order to plant a hedge.

PRINCIPAL PUBLISHED WORKS: *Plays*—The Local Stigmatic, 1965 (also published *with* AC/DC, 1972) (also published *in* Gambit 18–19, 1971); AC/DC, 1972 (also published *in* Gambit 18–19, 1971); Hancock's Last Half Hour, 1977; The Immortalist, 1978. *Novel*—The Speakers, 1964 (also published in a dramatization by William Gaskill and Max Stafford-Clark *in* Gambit 25, 1974). *Essays*—Severe Joy, 1978.

ABOUT: Contemporary Authors 21–22, 1969; Vinson, J. (ed.) Contemporary Dramatists, 1977; Worth, K.J. Revolutions in Modern English Drama, 1973; Writers Directory, 1976–1978. *Periodicals*—Gambit 18–19, 1971; New Republic March 18, 1967; New York Times Book Review February 26, 1967; Newsweek February 13, 1967; Observer December 22, 1974; Times May 4, 1974; January 10, 1975; April 25, 1977; October 24, 1977; November 24, 1977; Times Literary Supplement December 29, 1972.

WILLIAMS, JONATHAN (March 8, 1929–), American poet, publisher, and essayist, writes: "I was born in Tom Wolfe's town (Asheville, North Carolina) twenty-nine years after he was and suffer some of the same gargantuan appetites, some of the same Buncombe County afflatus. My parents nurtured my childhood tastes in books, and so I was well versed in the Wonder Books that poets require: Tolkien, Baum, Grahame, Kipling, Lofting, though I was forty before Kate Greenaway and Beatrix Potter joined the pantheon.

"I was agreeably educated at St. Albans

JONATHAN WILLIAMS

School in Washington, D.C., where I developed an interest in painting with an excellent master (Dean Stambaugh), ran the school newspaper, was captain of the soccer team and the tennis team, won a prize for Latin, was voted 'Most Thorough Gentleman,' was a prefect, and rewarded for 'Having Done Most For the School' —much of which seems a harbinger of what followed. My three semesters at Princeton were querulous. Then in quick succession I painted with Karl Knaths, engraved with Stanley William Hayter, attended the Institute of Design in Chicago, and reverted back to Buncombe County, the uneasy home of Black Mountain College. I went to study photography with Harry Callahan and Aaron Siskind, but met a poet I had never heard of named Charles Olson. Much of the enkindling that began me on the way of writing and publishing was Olson's doing. He continues to appear in dreams (as he did just last night), offering no particular vatic messages perhaps, but standing for maximal energy and devotion to craft. Some of my other mentors have been Kenneth Rexroth, Paul Goodman, Edward Dahlberg, Ian Hamilton Finlay, Louis Zukofsky, Guy Davenport, Basil Bunting, Stefan Wolpe, Lou Harrison, Robert Creeley, and Frederick Sommer. To go back, the first 'grown-up' writer I revered was H.P. Lovecraft, followed (curiously enough) by Henry Miller, Kenneth Patchen, e.e. cummings, C.S. Lewis, Aldous Huxley and Robinson Jeffers. If it doesn't add up, why should it?

"At Black Mountain I began The Jargon Society, a poet's press, and for twenty-five years have remained its editor, publisher, and designer. The best thing ever said about Jargon was Hugh Kenner's perception that we are a 'Custodian of Snowflakes.' Some eighty titles have been issued, including first or early books by Olson, Creeley, Robert Duncan, Zukofsky, Buckminster Fuller, Mina Loy, Denise Levertov, Lorine Niedecker, Ronald Johnson, Paul Metcalf, James Broughton, Irving Layton, Russell Edson, Michael McClure, Doris Ulmann, Lyle Bongé, and Ralph Eugene Meatyard. The latter three being photographers, that indicates that poetry is not the whole story for *Jargon.*

"In 1961 I began hiking and sweated up the Appalachian Trail from Georgia to Connecticut. Since then I have spent months afoot in the English Lake District, along Hadrian's Wall, along the north coasts of Cornwall, Devon, and Somerset, up the length of the River Wye, the Pennine Way, the North York Moors, the Three Peaks, etc. The result has been to turn me from being a Black Mountain Poet (whatever that is) and High-Culture Poet into a poet of concrete particulars and findings. I now read more maps than books and am delighted to encounter such scrawled revelations as PEACHES HEAR on a fence in Nacoochee Valley, Georgia; or, ONAN'S AUTO SERVICE on a sign outside Lexington, Kentucky. Such gifts have honed my abiding interest in the epitaph. Almost everything I make is either an elegy or a celebration. Tomorrow, for instance, I set forth on a trip which will permit me to traverse the White Mountains of New Hampshire, see the Boston Red Sox at Fenway Park, pay my respects at the grave of Carl Ruggles, see the Shelburne Museum in Vermont, talk about Erik Satie with Roger Shattuck, and photograph the field of sculptures that David Smith left at Bolton Landing, New York.

"My companion in life is Tom Meyer, poet and translator. We divide our time between a house near Highlands, North Carolina, in the Blue Ridge Mountains; and Corn Close, a seventeenth century stone cottage in the Yorkshire Dales. I continue to do one semester of teaching somewhere every year and by now have given about eight hundred and twenty-five readings, lectures, and showings of my slide collection. I must figure out something in the State of Kansas, for I long to see S.P. Dinsmoor's 'Garden of Eden' in the town of Lucas—something that ranks with the 'Ideal Dream Palace' of the Postman Cheval in the estimation of those as interested in the home-made, eccentric, and caitiff as I am.

"When Zukofsky says that the function of poetry is to record and elate, I think he has said it for all time. Being a mountain man I am interested in the earthy and what has tang. The 'com-

863

mon' yields this most often and I am ever looking to raise the common to grace. I am concerned with at-one-ment and sound like the Episcopal minister I might well have become, except that I belong to too many non-existent organizations like the Cast-Iron Lawn-Deer Owners of America, the Macon County North Carolina Meshugga Sound Society, and Cottonmouth Heterosexuals for Wallace. I am probably the only human being to possess signed, inscribed photographs from both Mae West and Vladimir Horowitz."

The autobiographical statement above is characteristically thorough, efficient, and entertaining. Not much needs to be added to it apart from the names of the author's parents—Thomas Benjamin Williams and the former Georgette Chamberlain—and a few dates. His triumphant years at St. Albans School were from 1941 to 1947. He was at Princeton in 1947–1949, studied painting and engraving in 1949–1950, and attended Black Mountain College intermittently between 1951 and 1956. These were the college's last years, when Charles Olson, Williams's mentor, was rector of that yeasty institution. In 1952–1954 Williams, a conscientious objector, served in the U.S. Army Medical Corps.

The Jargon Society, which Williams founded in 1951, and has operated and sustained ever since, has, to quote Robert Creeley, "persistently published poetry and prose of a demonstrably high order against the criticism and, even worse, the silence of many people indeed." Donald Hall wrote that "Jargon designs the best looking books around, and it has also printed a number of the best poets before the publishers in New York knew they were there." Williams himself says: "There are certain kindred spirits in the country, and it is to make coherence of these that Jargon exists." Jargon has never made much money, and he and it are supported mainly by Williams's endless round of readings and lectures. He works from the family home, "which sits on a mountain" in Highlands, North Carolina, and says that this is "the requisite, occasional sanctuary. Without it, no such hopeless vocational mission as Jargon could persist."

The Empire Finals at Verona, Williams's first considerable collection, appeared in 1959. Henry Birnbaum wrote that Williams "has a biting talent and true verbal facility, and a range of interests (music, baseball, history) which will surely be realized." But Birnbaum thought that these poems were "too circumstantial and bound by a deliberate spontaneity," and that this "deftly crafted book. . . . earns a place in the Jargon Books series with some difficulty."

Williams himself thinks that he was "all there" in his own voice and style for the first time in his 1962 collection, *In England's Green &,* which contains (among other things) evocations of England written before their author had ever set foot in that country. Richard Howard commented that the book was "literary and learned, and gives pleasure," but that these poems were "often hurried and silly, and always insolent." Something of Williams's range is suggested by the contrast in this volume between his extremely witty "Blues for Lonnie Johnson," about the rape of the moon by space rockets, and this pastoral for the English visionary painter Samuel Palmer:

> I cannot put my hand into
> a cabbage to turn
> on the light, but
>
> the moon moves over
> the field of dark cabbage and an
> exchange fills
> all veins.
>
> The cabbage is also a globe
> of light, the two globes
>
> now two eyes in
> my saturated
>
> head!
>
> ("If the Night Could
> Get Up and Walk")

An Ear in Bartram's Tree (1969), selecting from the poems Williams had published between 1957 and 1967, was on the whole very warmly received. Herbert Leibowitz called this "a wildly exuberant sketch book of literary pranks, doodles, found objects, 'a certain seediness,' good-bad puns, riddling games and Southern nursery songs, sign boards, Blakean proverbs, and Mahler songs." Leibowitz described Williams as "our best poet of serious tomfoolery," and found in the selection "no traces of arch self-reference; he is too curious about people and too busy listening to their opinions and salty talk to fuss over his own sensibility." (Thus he discovers this poem in the prose judgment of Sam Cresswell, auto mechanic: "Your points is blue/ and your timing's/ a week off.") Geof Hewitt, similarly, concludes that "Williams writes of what he sees and hears, and if his descriptions fail to convey his actual feelings, the body of his work suggests a man of impeccable tastes, deep intellect, and occasional, profound disgust for the homogenization of his country-folk." It seemed to Ralph J. Mills, Jr., that "perhaps the most striking quality in Williams's work, aside from the erudition and bookishness (which are of the delightful, never the pedantic variety), is the extraordinary acuteness of his ear." The critics agreed that this was one of the handsomest books to have appeared for some time outside the field of limited editions.

Mahler (1969) is a sequence of forty poems written in May and June 1964 after listening to recordings of the forty movements of Mahler's ten symphonies. "Rather than place the music in poetic terms," wrote Jerome Cushman, "Williams allows the music to provide an aural and emotional base for his own aesthetic." Illustrated with line drawings by R. B. Kitaj, the book seemed to Guy Davenport "one of the really lovely things of our time." *Blues & Roots/ Rue and Bluets* (1971) is "a garland for the Appalachians" of a hundred poems (including many found poems) accompanied by a hundred photographs by Nicholas Dean. Eric Mottram wrote that "Jonathan Williams moves between landscape and city with a technique and wit unique in American poetry. . . . His drastic political humor is aimed at the annihilation of a society which has no respect for ecology or privacy or visionary experience." *The Loco Logodaedalist in Situ* (1972) contains poems written in 1968–1970. It struck James Whitehead as the work of "a brilliant bucolic dandy. . . . Too much Williams could give a soul caries." But Elizabeth Jennings in England thought that it represented "the worst trend of what is considered to be poetry which is now being written in English."

Williams was poet-in-residence at the Aspen Institute, Aspen, Colorado, in 1962 and scholar-in-residence there in 1967–1968. He was scholar-in-residence at the Maryland Institute College of Art, Baltimore, in 1968–1969 (when he received an honorary doctorate from the College), and poet-in-residence at the University of Kansas in 1971. He received a Guggenheim fellowship in 1957–1958 for poetry, a Longview Foundation grant in 1960 for his editing of Jargon Books, and grants in 1968, 1969, and 1970 for publishing National Endowment for the Arts projects.

"Like John Clare," Williams says, "I tend to find poetry in fields. I believe the two most important concerns of any man, poet and citizen, are social justice and the development of an ecological conscience. My poems are directed accordingly." Robert Morgan suggests that Williams "more than any other poet . . . has used the Objectivist principle, the idea that a poem is first of all a linguistic, phonetic, graphic object. . . . He takes the language eroding right now in our mouths and cultivates it, shapes it, and speaks it into life." Guy Davenport says of his poetry that "its weightlessness is that of thistledown and like the thistle it bites. Its coherence is that of clockwork, at once obvious and admirable. Its beauty is that of the times: Hard, elegant, loud, sweet, abrupt all together." And Buckminster Fuller, referring to Williams's peregrinations among and on behalf of an international fraternity of poets and writers, once said that he was "our Johnny Appleseed. We need him more than we know."

PRINCIPAL PUBLISHED WORKS: *Poetry*—The Empire Finals at Verona, 1959; Amen/Huzza/Selah (with photographs by the author), 1960; Elegies and Celebrations, 1962; In England's Green &, 1962; The Macon County North Carolina Meshugga Sound Society, Jonathan Williams, Musical Director, Presents: Lullabies, Twisters, Gibbers, Drags, 1963; Mahler Becomes Politics, Beisbol, 1967; The Lucidities, 1968; Sharp Tools for Catullan Gardens, 1968; An Ear in Bartram's Tree: Selected Poems 1957–1967, 1969; Mahler, 1969; Strung Out With Elgar on a Hill, 1969; Blues & Roots/Rue & Bluets, 1971; The Loco Logodaedalist in Situ, 1972; Imaginary Postcards, 1975; Pairidaeza, 1975; Hot What?, 1975; gAy BC's, 1976; Letters to the Great Dead, 1976; Adventures With a Twelve-Inch Pianist Beyond the Blue Horizon, 1976; Elite Elate Poems: Selected Poems 1971–1975, 1976. *Nonfiction*—Descant on Rawthey's Madrigal: Conversations With Basil Bunting, 1968; Clarence John Laughlin, 1973; An Aperture Festschrift, 1976; Selected Essays, edited by Herbert Leibowitz, 1976. *As Editor*—Edward Dahlberg: A Tribute, 1970; Epitaphs for Lorine, 1973; Madeira & Toasts for Basil Bunting's Seventy-Fifth Birthday, 1975; Untinears & Antennae for Maurice Ravel, 1977.

ABOUT: Contemporary Authors 9–12 1st revision, 1974; Davenport, G. *introduction to* An Ear in Bartram's Tree, 1969; Penguin Companion to Literature 3, 1971; Rexroth, K. Assays, 1962; Vinson, J. (ed.) Contemporary Poets, 1975. *Periodicals*—English Summer 1971; Guardian July 3, 1972; Hudson Review Autumn 1969; Kulchur 11 1963; Library Journal June 1, 1969; May 1, 1970; Nation June 2, 1962; August 16, 1971; September 6, 1971; National Review November 19, 1960; New York Times Book Review November 21, 1971; New Statesman September 12, 1969; Parnassus Fall-Winter 1972; Poetry November 1960, June 1963, February 1971; Saturday Review September 6, 1969; Studio International September 1972; Virginia Quarterly Review Autumn 1969; Vort Fall 1973.

"WITKACY." *See* WITKIEWICZ, STANISLAW IGNACY

*WITKIEWICZ, STANISLAW IGNACY ("WITKACY") (February 24, 1885–September 18, 1939), Polish novelist, dramatist, philosopher, and aesthetician, was born in Kraków, the only son of the most celebrated and influential painter and critic of turn-of-the-century Poland, also Stanislaw Witkiewicz. He grew up in the Carpathian resort town of Zakopane, which was then in effect the country's artistic capital. His famous father made Witkiewicz the subject of an educational experiment, insisting that the child

*vit kye' vich

865

STANISLAW IGNACY WITKIEWICZ

should be preserved from formal instruction and allowed to develop freely in whatever direction he chose, with minimal guidance from tutors and from Witkiewicz senior himself. By the time he was eight the boy had written a dozen plays and had printed one of them on his own press. He participated in his first art exhibition at the age of sixteen, when his paintings were singled out for special praise from among the work of adult exhibitors. The following year he was studying higher mathematics, working in languages (English, French, German, and Russian, as well as Polish), and writing treatises on Dualism and the philosophy of Schopenhauer.

In 1904 Witkiewicz entered the Academy of Fine Arts in Kraków, but soon dropped out. He later traveled in Western Europe, where he encountered and was impressed by the revolutionary art of the Fauves, the Cubists, and the Futurists. An ardent sensualist, and precocious in this as in everything else, Witkiewicz was by 1908 immersed in a prolonged affair with the celebrated actress Irena Solska, who on stage and off played the role of the demonic and man-devouring woman. He adopted the pseudonym "Witkacy" to assert his independence and distinguish his art from his father's, but he continued to feel overwhelmed by the great man, and unable to control or choose among his manifold talents. By 1913 he was in a state of emotional collapse, and underwent analysis at the hands of the first Polish Freudian. The following year his young fiancée killed herself.

It was arranged that Witkiewicz should accompany his friend Bronislaw Malinowski on the latter's first anthropological field trip to New Guinea, an expedition that was to have far-

reaching effects on the development of social anthropology. In fact, Witkiewicz went with Malinowski as far as Australia and was deeply and permanently impressed by what he saw of the tropics. Malinowski found Witkiewicz's delusions of grandeur increasingly hard to tolerate. "I respect his art and admire his intelligence and worship his individuality," he wrote in his diary in 1914, "but I cannot stand his character."

The expedition was ended for Witkiewicz by the outbreak of World War I. He took the first ship home, entered an officer's training school in St. Petersburg, and subsequently served with the Pawlowski Regiment. He was wounded in 1915 and decorated for bravery with the Order of St. Anne, but also experienced other aspects of life available to an officer in an elite Russian regiment of that period—prolonged debauches in St. Petersburg (where he first tried drugs) and a ringside view of the court intrigues revolving around Rasputin. At the outbreak of the 1917 Revolution, Witkiewicz was elected a commissar by his soldiers, but the Revolution was for him a traumatic event. He drew on his Russian experience in all his subsequent writings about decadent and crumbling societies and their destruction in apocalyptic revolutions.

By 1918, when Witkiewicz returned to Poland, his father was dead, and Daniel Gerould suggests that it was this fact, together with the violent experience of war and revolution, that "released and focussed" his creative forces. He settled in Zakopane, and in a little over twenty years produced over two hundred literary works and thousands of portraits and paintings. His portraits included both run-of-the-mill likenesses, which he churned out for money, and remarkable psychological portraits, often of friends and often painted under the influence of drugs. Witkiewicz described his experiments with hallucinogenic and other drugs in *Nicotine, Alcohol, Cocaine, Peyote, Morphine, Ether* (1932), in which he singled out cigarettes and vodka as the most harmful of all the drugs he used.

In Poland, Witkiewicz was oddly enough regarded as an old-fashioned painter, related to Art Nouveau and the Vienna Secession. This was because the Surrealists remained unknown in Poland, where painting was then postimpressionist, constructivist, or cubist. Jan Kott recalls that when he fell under the spell of Witkiewicz just before World War II, he shared the general opinion of the time that this "extraordinary and splendid" man really belonged to the past. "Witkacy as a man, writer and artist seemed to me like a dazzling relic from the beginning of the twentieth century who had strayed into contemporary times." It was only later, as Kott says, that he could be seen as "one of the most original precursors of what might be called the intellectual and artistic climate of the sixties, of its style of life and of thinking. . . . Witkacy, who came too early, seemed to his contemporaries to be a man who came too late." Even his painting anticipates much in the art of the 1960s: "Witkacy's portraits and compositions often strikingly call to mind the psychedelic posters which have become a new art form for collectors. Witkacy's faces, which emerge from a colorful mist with their magnified eyes, their grimacing mouths, and all their striking resemblance to their models, are first of all psychological portraits. There is always tension and anxiety in them, a kind of tragic absence; they are faces from a narcotic 'trip.' "

Witkiewicz was an exhibitionist and a dandy, who as a young man walked the streets of Zakopane in a harlequin's costume. He adored all forms of social and intellectual provocation, treating life as a game and a play, not at all like the engagé artists of the 1930s. The philosophical and aesthetic ideas which underlie his work are nevertheless entirely serious, as is evident in the book which most fully expresses them, *Pojęcia i twierdzenia implikowane przez pojęcie istnienia* (Concepts and Principles Implied by the Concept of Existence), 1935. Witkiewicz was acutely conscious of the strangeness of human existence, and of the millions of "particular existences," each of which arrives in the world wondering why it is like this rather than that, why here rather than there. This existential predicament is at the center of Witkiewicz's plays and novels, which explore loneliness and alienation, and the dehumanization resulting from the increasingly conformist pressures of all modern societies. He foresaw that these and other factors would soon bring European civilization to ruin and catastrophe.

In such essays as *Wstęp do teorii czystej formy w teatrze* (Introduction to the Theory of Pure Form in the Theatre, 1918) and *Teatr* (The Theatre, 1923), Witkiewicz applied his theories to the theatre, developing the idea of "a new kind of play which will be liberated from the confines of imitating life and instead make a synthesis of all the elements of the theatre—sound, setting, gesture, dialogue—for purely formal ends. Freed from the demands of consistent psychology and logic, the dramatist will be able to use his materials as the musician uses notes and the modern painter colors and shapes. The meaning of such a work lies in its internal construction, not in the discursive content of its subject matter." The results of these theories seemed to contemporary audiences both nonsensical and shocking. Witkiewicz was widely misunderstood and ridiculed, and those of his plays that were performed appeared almost exclusively in small experimental theatres. Nevertheless, twenty-three plays were performed or published during his lifetime, and a further nine survive in manuscript; others seem to have been lost.

Witkiewicz's plays create a world of strange dreams and grotesque nightmares, freely mingled with macabre humor, philosophical discussions, literary parodies, and political fables. All of them embody his catastrophist view of human existence and contemporary society, in which he anticipated only the triumph of technology and the destruction of individualism. Thus in *Wariat i zakonnica* (1923, published 1925; translated by D.C. Gerould and C.S. Durer as *The Madman and the Nun*), the world is reduced to a lunatic asylum, and the action takes place in a single bare cell. This is occupied by the young poet Walpurg, mad as a result of an overdose of drugs, who is guarded by psychiatrists and nuns, the representatives of science and religion. Desperate for freedom, he easily seduces Anna, the young nun nursing him, but when one of the doctors begins to flirt with her, Walpurg kills him. The hated psychiatrist is replaced by an even more pernicious character—a psychoanalyst. The Freudian sets out to restore Walpurg's sanity by resolving his "complex," but realizes this diagnosis is wrong when the love affair is discovered, and abandons the case. Unable to endure being put back in a straitjacket, Walpurg hangs himself. But violence seems to be liberating, for both the suicide and the psychiatrist he has murdered turn up again, and the play ends with a violent fight.

In the nonrational world of Witkiewicz's plays, death is not necessarily terminal, and the title character in *Kurka wodna* (1922, translated by D.C. Gerould and C.S. Durer as *The Water Hen*) is resurrected more than once. Edgar in this "spherical tragedy" is a tormented but untalented young man whose mistress, the Water Hen, persuades him to kill her, since she can no longer endure the triviality of their relationship. Making a fresh start, Edgar adopts the ten-year-old Tadzio, hoping to make of him the artist that he has failed to be himself. When Edgar is pushed by his insensitive old father into marriage with Lady Alice, the Water Hen reappears. She shows Edgar that his entire life has been a failure, thus driving him to punish himself with a medieval torture box, until he rejects the Water Hen and seeks refuge from life and art with

Alice. In Alice's palace Tadzio withdraws into a dream state, but after ten years the Water Hen returns and seduces the boy, who wants to marry her. Edgar desperately kills her again, but as he does so Tadzio wakes from his dream and flees from the palace. Alice runs away with her old lover, now a revolutionary, leaving Edgar to end his life of failure by shooting himself. Revolution breaks out, and as the fighting rages and civilization falls apart, Edgar's cynical father goes on playing cards with the same old gang of financiers.

It is by such means—by mingling different kinds of reality within a single play—that Witkiewicz sought to convey his sense of the metaphysical strangeness of human existence. Bizarre as they are, Witkiewicz's plays are also highly theatrical—even when they embody a "message" as obvious as that of *Szalona lokomotywa* (1923, translated by D.C. Gerould and C.S. Durer as *The Crazy Locomotive*). This takes place on a moving locomotive driven by two aristocratic criminals who are posing as engineer and fireman. They confess their identities to each other, and admit to being in love with the same "demonic" woman, Julie. With her encouragement, they agree to accelerate to a speed that can only end in disaster, with the survivor taking all—freedom, liberation from guilt, and Julie. The result is an apocalyptic crash as they drive head-on into a locomotive speeding from the opposite direction.

On the strength of what he had seen in Russia, Witkiewicz believed that revolution leads to dictatorship, totalitarianism, and the mechanization of man. This is the theme of a number of his plays, including *Bezimienne dzielo* (1921, translated by D.C. and E. Gerould as *The Anonymous Work*), *Gyubul Wahazar* (1921, translated by D.C. and E. Gerould), and *ONI* (1920, translated by D. C. Gerould and C. S. Durer as *They*). The latter combines the author's political catastrophism with his fears for the future of culture. An art connoisseur and his actress mistress lead a blissful life of erotic, gastronomic, and artistic experiment. This idyll is brutally interrupted by a gang whose aim is the destruction of all art, which they see as an obstacle to the realization of a totally impersonal, automatized society. "They" include the founder of the new religion of "Absolute Automatism," as well as a financier and a military man. The connoisseur's art gallery is ruthlessly destroyed, the actress is forced to appear in a show in which she is murdered by a frenzied actor, and the connoisseur is charged with her murder.

Some of Witkiewicz's plays are or include excellent parodies of the classics of Polish literature, and the full appreciation of these is naturally difficult abroad. He also parodied Shakespeare, and in *Matka* (1924, translated by D.C. Gerould and C.S. Durer as *The Mother*) he pokes fun at the psychological theatre of Ibsen and Strindberg with playful references to *Ghosts* and *The Ghost Sonata*. However, this play is basically an ironic portrayal of society's anomalies, since the impoverished mother has to drudge to support her parasitical son Leon and his equally lazy bride. Leon justifies his idleness by claiming that he alone gives "higher meaning" to life, since he spends all his time dreaming up plans to abolish those oppressors of mankind, the social order and mechanization, by promoting antisocial actions on a mass scale. The second act seems to reverse the situation, since Mother is now living in luxury and has become an alcoholic and a morphine addict, while her son and his bride are highly industrious. However, after the revelations that Leon is a pimp, a gigolo, and a spy, and his bride a prostitute, Mother goes blind with shock and then takes a fatal overdose. Leon and his friends mourn her with a cocaine orgy. However, in Act Three Mother reappears, twenty-three years old and pregnant with Leon. She reveals that the corpse over which he is still mourning is only a straw-filled mannequin. Leon collapses totally, and as he dazedly clutches the fragments of the mannequin a group of workers rush in and murder him.

Witkiewicz's plays were written mainly between 1918 and the mid-1920s, and only one, *Szewcy* (1931-1934, translated by Daniel C. Gerould and C.S. Durer as *The Shoemakers*), dates from the 1930s. This is an almost orgiastic portrayal of the end of Western civilization in two successive revolutions, one fantastic and the other Marxist. Witkiewicz's two novels are equally apocalyptic. The first, *Pożegnanie jesieni* (Farewell to Autumn, 1927), predicts a Communist dictatorship in an imaginary country that strongly resembles Poland. The hero, Atanazy, is an artist who, not realizing that revolutionaries are always puritanical, creates a degenerate art reflecting the sexual fantasies which dominate his life. (Sexuality and artistic creativity seemed to Witkiewicz closely related, and a number of his characters are devoted erotic fantasists). The revolution leads to dictatorship and universal dreariness, and Atanazy flees across the border. He later returns in a brave attempt to reverse the effects of the revolution, only to be caught and executed.

The second novel, *Nienasycenie* (1930, translated by Louis Iribarne as *Insatiability*), imagines a Chinese invasion of Europe, and parodies contemporary fiction about the supposed "yellow peril." Western Europe has gone through communist upheavals, Russia has renounced communism, and Poland is ruled by a great dictator who is presented as the man who will save communist Europe from the onslaught of communist China. But when the Chinese army has conquered Russia and is approaching the borders of Poland, the dictator surrenders to the invaders and is beheaded, though his execution is carried out with all the pomp and ceremony due to his position. Before the defeat, the doomed Polish society is fraught with forebodings of catastrophe, with people clutching at every kind of irrationality and mysticism, and such panaceas as the "oriental pills" which induce a feeling of blissful harmony with the universe and allay the will to resist—the novel's title refers to the insatiability of such metaphysical cravings. Witkiewicz refused to acknowledge the novel as an art form, but described it as a "bag" into which the author may stuff anything he pleases, including his opinions on a wide range of topics. Jerzy Peterkiewicz, reviewing *Insatiability*, found this approach self-indulgent. The novel, he wrote, "operates on a premise of historical inevitability. The narrative relies on incessant comments and factual asides (the latter in small print and headed simply 'Information'); the result is a kind of metaphysical contest between fact and fantasy, with human creatures in the way and getting stuck. Their haphazard existence in the novel reflects the author's arbitrary method."

The author's apocalyptic expectations were realized with the Nazi invasion of Poland, which led to the outbreak of the Second World War. Witkiewicz, a proud, lonely, eccentric man, escaped eastward with his mistress from the advancing German army, but was soon exhausted. He committed suicide on September 18, 1939, the day after the entry of Soviet troops into eastern Poland had finally sealed the doom of his country's independence. After the war his work was neglected in Poland for many years, but in the late 1950s critics recognized him as one of the most fascinating writers in modern Polish literature, and his plays began to take their place in the theatrical repertoire; a two-volume collection containing twenty plays was published in 1962. And Witkiewicz has been increasingly recognized in the West as a precursor of the Theatre of the Absurd. Martin Esslin has called him "one of the most brilliant figures of the European avant-garde of his time, whose importance is only now being discovered outside his native Poland," and Jan Kott writes that "today Witkacy is more and more often described as a

'Renaissance man,' as one of the most universal European minds."

PUBLISHED WORKS IN ENGLISH TRANSLATION: *Fiction*—Insatiability: A Novel in Two Parts, 1977. *Plays*—The Madman and the Nun, edited and translated by D.C. Gerould and C.S. Durer (also contains The Water Hen, The Crazy Locomotive, The Mother, They, The Shoemakers), 1968; Tropical Madness, translated by D.C. and E. Gerould (contains The Pragmatists, Mr. Price, Gyubal Wahazar, Metaphysics of a Two-Headed Calf), 1972; The Water Hen *in* Duhore, B.F. and Gerould, D.C. (eds.) Avant-Garde Drama, 1969; The Cuttlefish *in* Gassner, J. and Duhore, B.F. (eds.) A Treasury of the Theatre, 4th edition, volume 2, 1970; The Anonymous Work and an essay (The Role of the Actor in the Theatre of Pure Form) *in* Gerould, D.C. (ed.) Twentieth Century Polish Avant-Garde Drama, 1977; The Madman and the Nun *in* First Stage Winter 1965–1966.

ABOUT: Crowell's Handbook of Contemporary Drama, 1971; Esslin, M. The Theatre of the Absurd, 1974; Gassner, J. and Quinn, E. (eds.) The Reader's Encyclopaedia of World Drama, 1970; Gerould, D.C. and Durer, C.S. *introduction to* The Madman and the Nun, 1968; Gerould, D.C. *essay in* Tropical Madness, 1972; Gerould, D.C. *introduction to* Twentieth Century Polish Avant-Garde Drama, 1977; Iribarne, L. *introduction to* Insatiability, 1977; Kridl, M. A Survey of Polish Literature and Culture, 1956; Matlaw, M. Modern World Drama, 1972; McGraw-Hill Encyclopedia of World Drama, 1972; Milosz, C. The Captive Mind, 1950; Milosz, C. The History of Polish Literature, 1969. *Periodicals*—Art International February 1976; Poland (American edition) April 1965; Polish Perspectives June 1963, October 1965; Polish Review Winter 1967; Times Literary Supplement July 21, 1978; Tri-Quarterly Spring 1967.

***WITTIG, MONIQUE** (1935–), French novelist and dramatist, was born in the Haut Rhin department of Alsace. She studied in Paris and, until the publication of her first book, worked there in various semi-academic posts—for the Bibliothèque Nationale and as a proofreader for the publishing house Editions de Minuit. She dislikes publicity, but was thrust into immediate prominence with the appearance of *L'Opoponax* (1964, translated by Helen Weaver as *The Opoponax*). This first novel was awarded the 1964 Prix Médicis and enthusiastically praised by other French novelists like Marguerite Duras and Alain Robbe-Grillet—the latter described it as "one of the most interesting and exciting ventures in contemporary literature."

All that happens in *L'Opoponax* is that a French girl, Catherine Legrand, develops from a grubby child in kindergarten into a wistful adolescent experiencing her first deep emotional attachment to another girl. However, the novel's intense evocation of childhood is achieved in a way quite new to literature. The narrative voice is neither the first person *je* of completely subjective autobiography, nor the third person *elle* of an omniscient observer, but somewhere in be-

*vi' tēk

869

French Cultural Services

MONIQUE WITTIG

tween. The narrator generally refers to herself either by her full name—as Catherine Legrand —or as *on*—the third-person indefinite pronoun. Mary McCarthy called this "a technical experiment, asking an epistemological question about the nature and limits of memory, which has led to a genuine finding. . . . The author is not recounting the story but reliving it sharply in memory. But she is reliving it as if it had happened to *somebody else,* which in fact is always the case. Catherine Legrand is not a fictional alias or transparent disguise for Monique Wittig: she is a conjecture about an earlier Monique Wittig."

Mary McCarthy, who called this "the book I've argued for—and about—most this year," was unhappy about Helen Weaver's translation of *on* as "you," but this seemed to work well enough for Sally Beauman, who found that "the narrator is alternately drawn closer to us, associated with us in the inclusive 'you'—then distanced again by a reversion to proper names. . . . The constant shuffle between subjectivity and objectivity is, in fact, the essential theme of the novel—Monique Wittig's vision of childhood as a process in which only gradually does the child cease to be an impartial spectator and become involved with people and with events. . . . She has managed to concoct a novel of marvelous artifice, in which the illusion that this *is* the voice of childhood is almost complete. Its strength is in its clear, glass-like style: simple primer sentences; a narrative that skips without either temporal, logical or emotional links from a school nature ramble to the death of a fellow pupil to mass to holiday games in a hayloft. . . . It is only gradually (almost as imperceptibly

for the reader as for Catherine Legrand herself) that events impinge. Her friend's name is gradually more present; she makes a joke and when her friends do not laugh, notes for the first time the reaction of others to herself. With such tiny shiftings, we see her progress to adult identity."

L'Opoponax evidently owes a great deal to Robbe-Grillet and the other exponents of the *nouveau roman* whom Monique Wittig had studied as a proofreader, but demonstrates great skill, discipline, and originality in its exploration of similar concerns; Sally Beauman thought it avoided "many of the potential traps of the *nouveau roman.*" There was a more mixed response to Monique Wittig's second novel, *Les guérillères* (1971, translated under the same title by David Le Vay), though this seemed to some critics as revolutionary in its understanding of women as the earlier novel had been in its understanding of children.

Les guérillères is an epic celebration of women and the female principle, expressed in brief paragraphs resembling imagist or incantatory prose poems. The battle between the sexes has become war to the death. The women (one learns little about the men) are "pearl-tressed, two-breasted Amazons" who aim to be more barbarous than Attila the Hun and who live in fortified camps, armed with knives, guns, and rocket launchers. They dance, sing, and make love together; they worship the sun-goddess, the circle, the vulval ring; and they read to each other from ancient books about the great deeds of Boadicea, Penthesilea, and Hippolyta. For food they hunt animals but for sport they hunt men, whom they hack to pieces with their knives (though some are spared as pets and studs).

Phoebe Adams described the book as "flapdoodle" and Clive Jordan observed that "like patriotic verse it is likely to appeal to the converted [and] like patriotic verse, it is intense, humourless and occasionally absurd." Frank Kermode thought it demanded "a curious kind of submissiveness in the reader, perhaps especially in the male. But to so obviously remarkable a writer it's worth submitting." And almost no one denied that Monique Wittig was a writer of dazzling ability. Mary McCarthy indeed called her "the best *writer* anywhere of her generation," and this "the only work of beauty to have come out of Women's Lib."

Le Corps lesbien (translated by David Le Vay as *The Lesbian Body*), followed in 1973. It is, like its predecessor, a sequence of prose poems— short, violent invocations of the female body, and fantasies of ways in which one lesbian body might totally possess and be possessed by another. The scene, naturally, is the island of Lesbos, here inhabited only by butterflies, she-goats, and a more or less mute female chorus. Everything centers on the lovers' desperate attempt to become one flesh: "Round your neck you place m/y duodenum pale-pink well-veined with blue. You unwind m/y yellow small intestine. So doing you speak of the odor of m/y damp organs, you speak of their consistence, you speak of their movements, you speak of their temperature. At this point you attempt to wrench out m/y kidneys. They resist you. You touch m/y green gallbladder. I have a deathly chill, I moan, I fall into an abyss, m/y head is awhirl."

For the purposes of this novel, or poem, Monique Wittig has tried to invent a specifically female vocabulary and grammar. Her *j/e* and *m/on* and *m/a* are divided to indicate the alienation of the woman writer using a masculine language. Male names are ruthlessly translated into feminine forms: the tendon of "Achillea," the principle of "Archimedea." Wittig, who even rejects the idea that she can be called *un écrivain* (a writer) because of the masculine gender of the French word, wants to create an entire lesbian culture, and in her introduction to *Le Corps lesbien* argues that whereas male homosexuals have a long literary tradition, "the lesbians, for their part, are silent—just as all women are as women at all levels. When one has read the poems of Sappho, Radclyffe Hall's *Well of Loneliness,* the poems of Sylvia Plath and Anaïs Nin, *La Bâtarde* by Violette Leduc, one has read everything. Only the women's movement has proved capable of producing lesbian texts in a context of total rupture with masculine culture, texts written by women exclusively for women, careless of male approval."

Le Corps lesbien is, obviously, not an easy book to translate, and a reviewer in the *Times Literary Supplement,* after quoting the introductory statement that David Le Vay "has abandoned any male chauvinism long enough to translate this book," comments that "unfortunately for the de-chauvinized Mr. Vay you can't conveniently insert a stroke into 'I,' so the English reader only gets the lame assertiveness of *I* to go with the sharper claims of 'm/e' and 'm/y.' The English translation thus adds its own kind of continued daftness to Ms Wittig's already irritatingly dubious semantic and grammatical position." Another reviewer felt "like going down on bended knees to Ms Wittig and begging her no longer to deny that part of her nature and talent which found expression in her first and beautiful book, *L'Opoponax.*"

Monique Wittig is also the author of a number of radio plays.

PRINCIPAL WORKS IN ENGLISH TRANSLATION: The Opoponax, 1966; Les Guérillères, 1971; The Lesbian Body, 1975.

ABOUT: Crosland, M. *introduction to* The Lesbian Body, 1975; Crosland, M. Women of Iron and Velvet, 1976; McCarthy, M. The Writing on the Wall, 1970. *Periodicals—* Atlantic November 1, 1971; Book World October 17, 1971; Library Journal October 1, 1975; New Statesman May 20, 1966; July 15, 1966; July 2, 1971; New York Review of Books December 1, 1966; December 16, 1971; New York Times Book Review June 26, 1966; October 10, 1971; November 23, 1975; New Yorker July 2, 1966; Newsweek October 25, 1971; Observer (London) Review July 18, 1971; Saturday Review July 2, 1966; Times Literary Supplement May 19, 1966; August 15, 1975.

*WOLF, CHRISTA (March 19, 1929–), German novelist, essayist, and screenwriter, was born Christa Ihlenfeld in Landsberg an der Warthe (now Gorzów in Poland). Her father, Otto Ihlenfeld, was a grocer. She grew up in a typical middle-class family, a comfortable, circumscribed, narrow-minded and pro-Nazi household whose security was abruptly destroyed by World War II. The collapse of Germany in 1945 coincided with her own adolescent traumas, and like Vera in her first novel, *Moskauer Novelle* (Moscow Story, 1961), she became a "disturbed sixteen-year-old girl who had fled as a refugee before the Soviet Army from the extreme east of what had been the German Reich."

The family settled in Mecklenburg region of East Germany, and Christa Ihlenfeld completed her high school education in Schwerin and Bad Frankenhausen. In 1949–1953 she studied German literature and history at the universities of Jena and Leipzig. In 1954 she became chief of the literature department in the executive offices of the Writers' Union in East Berlin, subsequently serving as editor of the Writers' Union magazine *Neue Deutsche Literatur* (New German Literature) and then as a reader for a children's book publisher. In 1959–1962 she read for another publishing house in Halle, and at the same time, seeking to understand a kind of life from which her background had insulated her, she went to work in a plant manufacturing railroad freight cars. Since 1962 she has lived as a freelance writer in the East German town of Kleinmachnow, just outside Berlin. She is married to the writer Gerhard Wolf, with whom she has collaborated in writing film scripts. They have two children.

It was Christa Wolf's second novel, *Der geteilte Himmel* (1963, translated by Joan Becker as *Divided Heaven*), that made her famous. It describes the search for self-knowledge and self-fulfillment of Rita Seidel, a country girl who, in

*volf

© 1979 by Jill Krementz

CHRISTA WOLF

reaction against the "idiocy of country life," goes to the town to train as a teacher, at the same time working in just such a factory as her creator had done (and undergoing, it seems, very similar experiences). She falls in love with a chemist, Manfred Herrfurth, but their relationship is complicated by her dislike of his bourgeois family, and almost ends when he flees to booming, materialistic West Berlin. Eventually she visits him there, and in a decisive confrontation in a Berlin restaurant rejects the temptation to join him. Returning to the East, exhausted and ill, she falls as she is crossing the railroad line and is injured.

Recovering in a hospital from this accident, with which the novel opens, Rita Seidel remembers and reflects upon her life. In a number of ways, *Der geteilte Himmel* is reminiscent of Uwe Johnson's *Mutmassungen über Jakob* (1959, translated as *Speculations About Jakob*), and in the opinion of some critics is a deliberate reply to it from the point of view of a writer wholly committed to the German Democratic Republic. *Speculations About Jakob* also opens with an accident on a railroad line, makes symbolic use of the railroad itself, and brings into confrontation the life and culture of the two Germanys. Christa Wolf's novel is more simple and straightforward in its manner, however, and (from the East German point of view) far more positive. It was highly acclaimed by East German critics, and received the important Heinrich Mann prize there in 1963, the Nationalpreis in 1964. On the strength of it, Christa Wolf was elected an alternate member of the Central Committee of the SED (Socialist Unity Party), an honor she later relinquished in "a conflict over

literary freedom." The novel was a best-seller in both East and West Germany, and was made into an equally successful film from the author's own scenario. David Caute, in his review of the English version, concluded that "Christa Wolf is not a writer who penetrates deeply. ... Frequently *Divided Heaven* echoes the banal and trivial tone of the romantic novel. Yet there is a difference. Rita's loyal and difficult commitment to the proud and frustrated technician, Manfred, holds the attention mainly because it is rooted in a social milieu containing its own intelligently observed contradictions."

There was a very different reception for *Nachdenken über Christa T.* (1968, translated by Christopher Middleton as *The Quest for Christa T.*). Christa T., we are told, was a former classmate of the author. After a wartime childhood, she went to university, studied German literature, and became a schoolteacher. She moved restlessly around, had a number of affairs, then married a veterinarian, settled in Mecklenburg, and raised three children. The marriage was not particularly successful; nor was a postmarital love affair; nor were the sketches and poems Christa T. sometimes wrote. She designed a house by a lake. And at the age of thirty-seven she died of leukemia. Her story is told in the novel, with no obvious regard for chronology, partly as an objective narrative, partly through the author's memories of her friend, and partly through excerpts from Christa T.'s writings and letters. (A preface explains that these documents actually exist, although the characters and events in the novel have been fictionalized.)

This "brilliant, insidious novel" was denied publication in East Germany for two years, and finally published there in 1968 in a limited edition of four thousand copies not available to the general public. It was bitterly attacked at the Sixth East German Writers' Congress in 1969, and officially condemned for its pessimism, its attempt to "replace Marx with Freud." Some of the more independent writers and critics had the courage to disagree, however, praising it as "the literary event of the year." It was received with universal enthusiasm in the West, and reprinted in the German Democratic Republic in 1973.

It was not the novel's politics that so outraged the East German critics, but its relative lack of them. As an undergraduate, Christa T. had been an idealistic socialist, joining the narrator in "those glorious rambling nocturnal discussions about the paradise on whose doorstep we were sure we stood, hungry and wearing our wooden shoes." But her "dangerous wish for a pure and terrible perfection" could not be satisfied by the realities of the new socialist order, "the vehement overplayed words, the waving banners. . . . the frightful beaming heroes of newspapers, films and books," any more than it could be satisfied by the gross materialism she sees and literally spits on during a visit to West Germany. This "unexemplary" person, quietly and scrupulously committed to "conscience and imagination," is in fact, as John Coleman said, "emblematic of the questing spirit that both makes and humanises revolutions." Her character is sketched in, obliquely, delicately, and respectfully, in a novel which John Willett described as a "small masterpiece."

Till Eulenspiegel (1973), written by Christa Wolf in collaboration with her husband and originally conceived as a film scenario, offers a socialist perspective on the prankster of tradition, involving Till Eulenspiegel as a kind of Robin Hood in the peasant rebellions of the early sixteenth century. This was followed in 1974 by the "three improbable stories" published as *Unter den Linden*. The title piece gives a flattering picture of life in East Berlin by comparison with the consumer society of the West, but any assumption that Christa Wolf was moving towards the remorseless optimism of "socialist realism" was dispelled by the other two stories in the collection. "Neue Lebensansichten eines Katers" revives E.T.A. Hoffman's tomcat Murr to mock the computerized mentality of the modern citizen, while "Selbstversuch" is a satirical fantasy about a woman who is transformed into a man. "Only at the end," wrote W.V. Blomster, "does one realize that Wolf offers here a profound and provocative essay on the problematic nature of love and its role in interpersonal relationships. Perhaps the fundamental perversity of the background is a necessary condition for the strident observations with which the story concludes."

Christa Wolf has written a critical biography (1965) of the East German novelist Anna Seghers, who is important to her both as a literary antecedent and as an emancipated and independent woman who (like Christa Wolf's heroines) has followed her own path through life. She has also published a collection of essays, *Lesen und Schreiben* (1971, translated by Joan Becker as *The Reader and the Writer*), in which literature is viewed, characteristically, as "only one operation in a more complex process to which we give the splendid but simple name of 'living.'" According to a reviewer in the *Times Literary Supplement*, "the writers whom she treats —including Ingeborg Bachmann, Bertolt Brecht, Vera Inber and Anna Seghers—come to life first and foremost as people, as writers whose works are the expression of deeply committed

lives. . . . It is a notable tribute to the author's achievement in these pieces that they bear the same sense of vitality and purpose which Christa Wolf admires in so many of her subjects."

One essay in *The Reader and the Writer* describes the author herself as a schoolgirl—an uncomprehending witness to the ruin of the Third Reich. This theme is developed in *Kindheitsmuster* (Patterns of Childhood, 1976), a work of notable originality and considerable importance. About half the book is taken up by an account of the author's childhood between the ages of three and seventeen (1932–1946). Unable to identify herself with the person she had been then, she writes of herself, in the third person, as "Nelly." The child grows up under the ever-increasing influence of Hitler, whom she learns to love and revere. As a matter of course, her father joins the Nazi party and she herself progresses through the various Nazi youth organizations. She is taught to hate and fear the Jews and feels no pity when the local synagogue is burned down. No one in the family protests when the euthanasia program costs the life of her simple-minded Aunt Jette. The account ends in 1946, with "Nelly" trying to come to terms with the collapse of everything she had been taught to believe in.

Parallel with this narrative is a description of a brief visit to Landsberg-Gorzow in 1971, when Christa Wolf was accompanied by her husband and her fourteen-year-old daughter Lenka. As Peter Graves wrote, "it is a reckoning with a past that still haunts and, with the presence of Lenka, an attempt to explain to a contemporary teenager how these things could have happened. The confrontation of two epochs in the form of mother and daughter is one of the book's greatest strengths." The technical problems involved in writing the book and the problems of narrative form in general are also discussed at length and in detail. Peter Graves found some of this "a little wearisome" but thought *Kindheitsmuster* as a whole "a courageous book that breaks taboos and, as we have come to expect from Christa Wolf, is infused with an integrity and a deep moral concern that raise it far above the narrow and selfconscious partisanship of much GDR literature." The same critic points out that East Germans "have consistently maintained that the establishment of a socialist state created an entirely new order untainted by complicity in Nazi atrocities. . . . It is against this background that the measure of Christa Wolf's achievement in . . . *Kindheitsmuster* must be judged."

The author received the Fontane Prize in 1972 and the Bremen Literature Prize in 1978. She is a member of the presidium of the East

German PEN Centre. In May 1978 she was one of seven authors banned from a Writers' Union literary congress, apparently because they had signed a 1976 resolution protesting against the exiling to the West of the poet and singer Wolf Biermann.

PRINCIPAL WORKS IN ENGLISH TRANSLATION: Divided Heaven, 1965; The Quest for Christa T., 1970; The Reader and the Writer: Essays, Sketches, Memories, 1977.

ABOUT: Deutsche Dichter de Gegenwart, 1973; Keith-Smith, B. (ed.) Essays on Contemporary German Literature IV, 1966; Namen und Daten, 1973; Stephan, A. Christa Wolf, 1976; Waidson, H.M. The Modern German Novel, 1971; Who's Who in the Socialist Countries, 1978. *Periodicals*—Books Abroad Winter 1975, Spring 1975; Library Journal December 1, 1970; Nation February 13, 1967; New Leader May 31, 1971; New York Review of Books September 2, 1971; New York Times June 3, 1969; New York Times Book Review January 31, 1971; Saturday Review May 8, 1971; Times Literary Supplement July 24, 1969; August 13, 1971; April 7, 1978.

© 1979 by Jill Krementz

TOM WOLFE

WOLFE, TOM (i.e. THOMAS KENNERLY JR.) (March 2, 1931–), American journalist, was born in Richmond, Virginia, the son of Thomas Kennerly Wolfe and the former Helen Perkins Hughes. His father, before his retirement, was professor of agronomy at the Virginia Polytechnic Institute, editor of *The Southern Planter,* and distribution director for the Southern States Cooperative. As a child, Tom Wolfe rewrote the Arthurian legends and compiled biographies of other heroes; later he became co-editor of his high school newspaper. From St. Christopher's School in Richmond he went on to Washington and Lee University in Lexington, Virginia, where he majored in English and was one of the founders of the literary quarterly *Shenandoah.* He also pursued his ardent interest in sports, editing the sports section of the college newspaper and pitching on the baseball team. After receiving his B.A. *cum laude* in 1951, he tried out unsuccessfully as a pitcher with the old New York Giants before settling for a Ph.D. in American studies at Yale University.

Shortly before he collected his doctorate in 1957, Tom Wolfe went to work as a reporter for the Springfield (Massachusetts) *Union.* "I immediately found . . . [newspaper work] glamorous," he said later. "Nobody else did at that late date . . . but I looked at it like the original 1922 Chicago cub reporter." In June 1959 he joined the Washington *Post,* and in 1960 he won Washington Newspaper Guild awards for his coverage of Cuban affairs and for his satirical account, illustrated with his own pen-and-ink drawings, of the 1960 Senate civil rights filibuster. Seeking more freedom to choose assignments that interested him, he moved on in April 1962 to the New

York *Herald Tribune.* The following year, during the long New York newspaper strike, Wolfe went to California to research a freelance assignment for *Esquire* about custom-built cars. He greatly admired the cars, and was equally fascinated by the tribal customs of the West Coast teenagers who commissioned these baroque sculptures. After months of research, Wolfe was left with a mass of information and impressions that he found himself unable to organize into the shape and pattern of the traditional feature article, and in the end he was asked simply to jot down rough notes for someone else to write up. "I just started recording it all," he says, "and inside a couple of hours, typing along like a madman, I could tell that something was beginning to happen." His *Esquire* editor printed Wolfe's eighteen pages of compulsive impressionism as they came, which was like this:

"I went by one of the guitar booths, and there was a little kid in there, about thirteen, playing the hell out of an electric guitar. The kid was named Cranston something or other. He looked like he ought to be named Kermet or Herschel; all his genes were kind of horribly Okie. Cranston was playing away and a big crowd was watching. But Cranston was slouched back with his spine bent like a sapling up against a table, looking gloriously bored. At thirteen, this kid was being fanatically cool. They all were. They were all wonderful slaves to form. They have created their own style of life, and they are much more authoritarian about enforcing it than are adults. Not only that, but today these kids—especially in California—have *money,* which, needless to say, is why all these shoe merchants and guitar sellers and the Ford Motor Company were at a Teen Fair in the first place. I don't mind observing that it is this same combination —money plus slavish devotion to form—that accounts for Versailles or St. Mark's Square."

A whole series of similarly—and increasingly —unorthodox pieces followed in the *Herald Tribune*'s Sunday magazine *New York, Esquire,* and elsewhere. Wolfe wrote like a spaced-out anthropologist about the Las Vegas crime world, the socialite movie star Baby Jane Holzer, English nannies, Cassius Clay, stock-car racing, Cary Grant, pop, camp, and many other heroes and rituals of our culture. And the style of Wolfe's "New Journalism," which at first seemed to owe most to J.D. Salinger's *Catcher in the Rye,* borrowed ever more freely and shamelessly from comic-strip and copywriter's English:

> Girls are reeling this way and that in the aisle and through their huge black decal eyes, sagging with Tiger Tongue Lick Me brush-on eyelashes and black appliqués, sagging like display window Christmas trees, they keep staring at—her—Baby Jane—on the aisle. What the hell is this? She is gorgeous in the most outrageous way. Her hair rises up from her head in a huge hairy corona, a huge tan mane around a narrow face and two eyes opened—swock!— like umbrellas, with all that hair flowing down over a coat made of . . . zebra! Those motherless stripes! Oh, damn!

According to a writer in *Newsweek,* "For the who-what-where-when-why of traditional journalism he has substituted what he calls 'the wowie!' Wolfe's wowie is a seemingly anarchic barrage of metaphor explanations . . . neologisms, hip phrases, nonsense words, ellipses, onomatopoeia, learned references to Greek myths and the Pre-Raphaelites, and architectural, medical, and comic-strip allusions." Wolfe himself has explained that he uses these assorted vernaculars, and typographical devices like italics and exclamation marks, to simulate as closely as possible his own stream of consciousness or that of his subject.

By 1965, Tom Wolfe was famous. "As the most spectacular journalist in years," wrote Liz Smith in *Status,* "Wolfe caused severe jealousy and outrage pangs throughout the U.S. literary establishment when he sprang right out of Pop Culture's forehead to become a star practically overnight. Seldom has anyone seen such visceral envies, such backbiting bitchiness, such voodoo malevolence directed at any writer. . . . He was, by degrees, tasteless, brilliant, inaccurate, witty, perverse, undisciplined, electric, perceptively scary, exhibitionistic, and absolutely of the moment. . . . but there was no one else around who could touch him. The other 'soft' journalists just

stood tongue-tied atop Roget's Thesaurus and watched him, the *noirest* of the *bête noires,* absquatulate with most of the fame and fortune." And in April 1965 Wolfe threw gasoline on his opponents' fires when he attacked the *New Yorker* magazine as "mummified."

Twenty-three of Wolfe's articles, along with eighteen satiric drawings, were assembled into his first book, *The Kandy-Kolored Tangerine-Flake Streamline Baby* (1965), named after the pioneering article on custom cars. Emile Capouya found Wolfe's prose, like his drawings, "astonishingly mean-spirited. . . . One wants to say to Mr. Wolfe: you're so clever, you can talk so well, tell us something interesting." Others, however, like *Newsweek*'s reviewer, were impressed: "Partly, Wolfe belongs to the old noble breed of poet-journalists, like Ben Hecht, and partly he belongs to a new breed of supereducated hip sensibilities like Jonathan Miller and Terry Southern, who see the complete human comedy in everything from a hair-do to a holocaust." And Kurt Vonnegut called this an "excellent book by a genius who will do anything to get attention."

In 1968 Wolfe became a contributing editor of *New York,* which after the demise of the *Herald Tribune* had survived as an independent magazine. The same year he published *The Pump-House Gang,* a second collection of articles about the way some of us live now, and *The Electric Kool-Aid Acid Test.* The latter is an account of Wolfe's travels with the Merry Pranksters, Ken Kesey's freaked-out flock of wandering hippies. Lawrence Dietz found this "the most profound and insightful book that has been written about the psychedelic life"; Wolfe had brought to his reportage "a sense of historical perspective, and, more important, a willingness to let accuracy take the place of the hysterical imprecations that have passed for reportage in most magazine articles and books on the subject." Wilfred Sheed thought the book "may well be the best literary work to come out of the Beat Movement."

None of Wolfe's subsequent books has been received with such nearly unanimous admiration, and there was a very mixed press for *Radical Chic and Mau-Mauing the Flak Catchers* (1970). "Radical Chic," the first of the two essays making up the volume, describes the party given by the conductor Leonard Bernstein and his wife to raise funds for the defense of twenty-one Black Panthers indicted on bomb plot charges. Wolfe's assumption is that the Bernsteins and their friends were motivated not by a concern for justice but by curiosity and snobbery, *"nostalgie de la boue."* It was the meanness of this view that many reviewers found offensive, and unjustified by Wolfe's own account. "Wolfe's sin," wrote Jason Epstein, "is a lack of compassion and his intellectual weakness a tendency to panic when he finds himself beyond his depth." The second essay, "Mau-Mauing the Flak Catchers," deals with what one reviewer called "those ritual confrontations between militants and bureaucrats which have become a distinguishing trade-mark of the poverty program." It seemed to Thomas R. Edwards that Wolfe in these essays had taken on "a serious theme, the dynamics of confrontation between oppressed peoples and well-intentioned privilege. But in each case Wolfe finally achieves complacent if elegant minification."

Tom Wolfe believes that journalism in America became, during the 1960s, more interesting than fiction. The New Journalism abandoned the tradition of level-toned, detached reporting, and began to use all the devices of fiction—dialogue, scene-by-scene reconstruction, symbolic detail—to make fact vivid. In evidence he offers the articles by Norman Mailer, Gay Talese, Rex Reed, Jimmy Breslin, Dick Schaap, and others collected in his *The New Journalism* (1973). Not many reviewers wholly accepted Wolfe's thesis, however, and John Seelye wrote: "The New Journalism, like the Old, deals mostly in ephemera, already crumbling to yellow journalism dust in the files of yesteryear. . . . If there is a difference between the Old Fiction and the New Journalism [it is that] fiction is blessed with a grace, a power of ideality and a compassion that is missing from the materials collected here. What we have, mostly, is not manners but manner, and I say it's panache, and I say the hell with it."

The Painted Word (1975) is an attack on the whole New York art establishment—on avant-garde artists, their work, the museums which show it, and the critics who appraise it. As Ruth Berenson pointed out, the book must have delighted "those who have long harbored dark suspicions that modern art beginning with Picasso is a put-on, a gigantic hoax perpetrated on a gullible public by a mysterious cabal of artists, critics, dealers, and collectors." Most knowledgeable readers, however, seemed to agree with John Russell of the New York *Times Book Review,* who wrote that Wolfe "doesn't seem to know what he is talking about. Somewhere inside the book is a very good subject: the extent to which people can be bullied into accepting what they don't believe in. It is not the most rewarding aspect of art, but it is worth discussing. The trouble is that on the social level . . . Wolfe is still some way behind Molière, who died in 1673, and on the level at which art and ideas coalesce he doesn't exist." And Robert Hughes concluded: "It is not just wrong history; it is not even firsthand reportage. There has been a long fall from—remember it?—the New Journalism."

A selection from the articles Wolfe had written between 1967 and 1976 was published in 1976 as *Mauve Gloves & Madmen, Clutter & Vine.* A various collection, as the title suggests, it ranged for its subjects from sex and violence to manners and decorum, from the passion for denim to mini-computers and New York accents. Jack Beatty found here "a lively picture of the surface of our society" which however revealed "little of what lies beneath the surface." He was most impressed by Wolfe's ability to adjust his style to his subject: "To recreate the look and feel of a jet taking off from an aircraft carrier, Wolfe unleashes a forty-five line sentence that puts you as close to the horror, noise and confusion of the real thing as you are ever likely to get."

Tom Wolfe is six feet tall, and has blue eyes and brown hair. According to Kurt Vonnegut, he "sees himself as an Edwardian fop with a ploughboy's three-by-eight wrists, and loves him." Once famous for his "pseudo-Mod" haircut and his "piqué-lapelled, double-breasted-vested, ice-cream-colored suits," he has become a little less flamboyant with the passing years. A bachelor, he enjoys big cars and window-shopping. There were one-man shows of his drawings at New York galleries in 1965 and 1974. Wolfe has honorary degrees from the Minneapolis College of Art (1971) and Washington and Lee University (1974). He received an award from the Society of Magazine Writers in 1970, and the Frank Luther Mott Research Award in 1973.

Wolfe has been described variously as "the poet laureate of pop" and as the "Bugs Bunny of American journalism—a squeaky, impudent dandy with a glib eye for the lumbering victim." Garry Wills has described him as "that American kind of 'conservative' who is in love with change and all the explosive powers of capitalism. . . . Wolfe's love of style is like Goldwater's love of gadgets as the ornaments and trophies of capitalism." And Chilton Williamson has said of Wolfe that "he inhaled the expelled atmosphere of the Glorious Sixties—and promptly breathed it back into them: had the decade faltered and swooned, Tom Wolfe could have revived it by means of mouth-to-mouth resuscitation."

PRINCIPAL WORKS: The Kandy-Kolored Tangerine-Flake Streamline Baby, 1965; The Pump-House Gang, 1968 (in England, Mid-Atlantic Man and Other New Breeds in England and America); The Electric Kool-Aid Acid Test, 1968; Radical Chic and Mau-Mauing the Flak Catchers, 1970;

(with E.W. Johnson) The New Journalism, 1973; The Painted Word, 1975; Mauve Gloves & Madmen, Clutter & Vine, and Other Stories, Sketches, and Essays, 1976.

ABOUT: Biography News May 1975; Contemporary Authors 15–16, 1966; Current Biography, 1971; Hoggart, H.R. Speaking to Each Other, 1970; Who's Who in America, 1976–1977. *Periodicals*—Book World June 27, 1965; August 18, 1968; Commentary March 1971, May 1975; Commonweal September 17, 1965; May 7, 1971; October 24, 1975; Encounter August 1966; Harper's February 1971; Life July 2, 1965; Nation September 23, 1968; March 5, 1977; National Review August 27, 1968; January 12, 1971; January 26, 1971; August 1, 1975; February 18, 1977; New Republic July 24, 1965; December 19, 1970; August 11, 1973; October 25, 1975; Newsweek February 1, 1965; April 19, 1965; January 31, 1966; August 26, 1968; June 9, 1975; New Statesman September 24, 1971; New York August 19, 1968; June 8, 1970; New York Review of Books August 26, 1965; February 3, 1966; August 22, 1968; December 17, 1970; June 26, 1975; New York Times Book Review June 27, 1965; August 18, 1968; November 29, 1970; December 3, 1972; July 22, 1973; June 15, 1975; December 26, 1976; Partisan Review 3 1969; Publishers Weekly June 18, 1973; Ramparts January 1972; Saturday Review July 31, 1965; Time July 2, 1965; April 16, 1965; September 6, 1968; June 15, 1970; December 21, 1970; June 23, 1975; December 27, 1976; Vogue April 15, 1966.

JAN WOLKERS

*WOLKERS, JAN (HENDRIK)** (October 26, 1925–), Dutch novelist, was born at Oegstgeest, a village near Leiden, where his father owned a grocery. The father, Jan Hendrik Wolkers, was a strict Calvinist—a man, according to his son, "of almost exalted religiousness." Most of Wolkers's work is a kind of fictional declaration of independence from this dominant father figure, his religion, and the rigid values and conventions of his generation, to which Wolkers opposes an equally extreme amorality. His mother, "a very diplomatic person who never . . . [said] much," bore her husband eleven children, of whom Jan Wolkers was the third.

It was as a sculptor that Wolkers first made his name. He studied in Amsterdam and Salzburg, and in Paris under Ossip Zadkine, and is still as active in that medium as in literature. Wolkers did not start writing until he was in his thirties, but then published several books in rapid succession. He made his debut in 1961 with a volume of short stories called *Serpentina's Petticoat,* and it is significant that the first story in the book opens with the words: "I rarely pay a visit to my parental home." A few months later came Wolkers's first novel, *Kort Amerikaans* (Crew Cut, 1962). Both books combine autobiographical material with bizarre and gothic elements; both are fierce assertions of a self-liberation, celebrating sexual freedom and the overthrow of every kind of moral repression and inhibition. It is not surprising that reviewers in the early 1960s were taken aback by the loos-

*wŏŏl′ kərs

ening of so many bonds all at the same time, and that Wolkers met with a warmer response from his readers than from his critics.

Gesponnen Suiker (Candy Floss), another volume of short stories, followed in 1963 and continued the mixture of autobiography and *grand guignol.* "Dominee met Strooien Hoed" (Minister in a Straw Hat), perhaps the most admired of Wolkers's short stories, is a brilliantly executed portrait of one of his fearsomely dour father figures, a small masterpiece of realism. But the same collection contains such bizarre entertainments as "Gevederde Vrienden" (Feathered Friends), in which a man disposes of his murdered wife's corpse by feeding it in bite-sized portions to the sea gulls. Wolkers's realistic fiction generally carries a great deal more conviction than his horror stories, and he seems to recognize this: "Only one's own experiences can have the quality of genuineness. But this is not enough. A transformation has to take place. One must try to see things more sharply and then arrange them in such a way that they assume meaning. . . . Imagination is useless. Lunatic asylums are full of it."

In Wolkers's grim novel *Een Roos van Vlees* (1963, translated by John Scott as *A Rose of Flesh*), a little girl is fatally scalded in the bathroom while her parents are arguing downstairs. The tragedy ends the parents' marriage, and the father, Daniel, becomes a lonely asthmatic, eaten alive by guilt. It was agreed that Daniel's agonized sensibility and his preoccupation with death and disease had been sharply and convincingly conveyed, but most reviewers shared the opinion of Manfred Wolf, who wrote: "By insisting that there is no more than despair Wolkers weakens the effect his main character can have. And despair itself, when examined from so fixed a position, at such stiflingly close quarters, becomes all too often merely oppressive and dreary."

The same year, 1963, Wolkers published two plays, *De Babel* (The Babel) and *Wegens Sterfgeval Gesloten* (Closed Owing to Bereavement), and in 1964 came another book of short stories, *De Hond met de Blàuwe Tong* (The Dog With the Blue Tongue). *Terug naar Oegstgeest* (Oegstgeest Revisited, 1965), regarded by many critics as Wolkers's best novel, is like much of his earlier work an evocation of his claustrophobic youth. But the miseries and occasional pleasures of those years are recalled here with a new objectivity and freedom from bitterness. A great deal of the material Wolkers had previously drawn upon reappears in this novel, which thus functions as a key to his earlier stories. His characteristic combination of realistic observation with imaginative selection never before worked so well as in this book, in which Wolkers also kept rigorously in check his tendency to overstate and overwrite.

In *Terug naar Oegstgeest,* Wolkers seemed finally to have settled accounts with the fearsome father figure that had haunted him, but other ghosts lingered. In *Horribele Tango* (1967, translated by R. R. Symonds as *The Horrible Tango*), he returned to a theme that from time to time had appeared in the short stories: the relationship with a dominant elder brother. A young student in Amsterdam meets a poor French-speaking black from Guadeloupe, and is impelled to share both his flat and his girlfriend with him. This urge is revealed as an attempt to exorcize childhood sufferings at the hands of a sadistic brother, now dead. But the participants in this Freudian scenario are not equipped to play the violent roles assigned to them, except (it seems) in fantasy. *Horribele Tango* is a hallucinatory novel, in which the boundaries between past and present, dream and reality, are never clearly defined. A reviewer in the *Times Literary Supplement* praised its "sharply evocative passages" of descriptive writing and thought that Wolkers's "predilection for surrealist imagery" had been "kept in tune with the narrator's fevered awareness." Structurally, it is Wolkers's most ambitious book, but it is marred, in the opinion of several critics, by too artificially neat a denouement.

Two years later, in 1969, Wolkers had a tremendous popular success with *Turks Fruit* (translated by Greta Kilburn as *Turkish Delight*). The story is told by an unnamed sculptor-painter who recalls his meeting with a red-head named Olga, their ecstatic sexual union, their tumultuous marriage, the divorce and the years of self-destruction that followed for them both. "What is right with these two," wrote Martin Levin, "their delight in one another, is described with gusto and humor. ... What is wrong with them has a real sense of tragedy." And what is wrong can this time be traced not to a demonic father or brother, but to a satanic mother-in-law more dreadful by far. The novel's structure is a great deal simpler than that of its predecessor, and its style is direct, boisterous, and deliberately antiliterary. It took the Dutch public by storm. It went through seventeen printings in its first year, was translated into half-a-dozen languages, and was made into a successful film.

Melodrama, an important ingredient in *Turks Fruit,* dominates *De Walgvogel* (The Dodo), which followed in 1974. The narrator, having lost his great love, finds her in Indonesia, then loses her again, first to another man and then to death. The improbability of the story seems to suggest that Wolkers has taken leave of realism proper and is moving in the direction of a kind of symbolism, while retaining the accuracy of his observation and his sense of both the macabre and the comic. Or it may be, as one disillusioned former admirer has suggested, that Wolkers, possessor of "one of the most brilliant gifts of his generation," has "chosen the path of self-indulgence in sick neo-decadence."

PRINCIPAL WORKS IN ENGLISH TRANSLATION: A Rose of Flesh, 1967; The Horrible Tango, 1970; Turkish Delight, 1974. *Story in* Delta (Netherlands) Spring 1964.

ABOUT: Caspers, J.H. (and others) In contact met het werk van moderne schrijvers, 1970; Fens, K. (and others) Literair lustrum, 1967; Penguin Companion to Literature 2, 1969; Seymour-Smith, M. Guide to Modern World Literature, 1973; Wispelaere, P. de. Het Perzischetapijt, 1966. *Periodicals*—Saturday Review April 15, 1967; Times Literary Supplement March 2, 1967; August 11, 1972; Writing in Holland and Flanders 15 1963, 24 1968.

WOODCOCK, GEORGE

WOODCOCK, GEORGE (May 8, 1912–), Canadian critic, poet, biographer, historian, radio dramatist, and editor writes: "I was born at Winnipeg, then a booming small city of the Canadian prairies. My parents were English, immigrants who had failed, and when I was a few months old, I was taken back to England. My youth was divided between Buckinghamshire, where I went to school, and Shropshire where I spent my holidays; between the fragile intellectualism my father projected and the bucolic robustness of my grandfather's house among its orchards and horse-pastures. I did not attend any university, for my family was poor and the

GEORGE WOODCOCK

Depression clouded my youth; instead I left school to work in the London head office of the Great Western Railway, where I stayed from 1929 to 1940. I had begun to write verse of a kind when I was thirteen, and first began to publish in 1932, in the *New English Weekly.* Later in the 1930s my work began to appear in the typical Thirties magazines, *New Verse* and *Twentieth Century Verse.* My first book of poems appeared in 1940; it was *The White Island.*

"In the same year I abandoned office work, going first to live in Middleton Murry's agricultural community at Langham, continuing farm work for a period as a conscientious objector during World War II, and becoming active in the anarchist movement, in which, from 1942 to 1949, I was one of the editors, successively, of *War Commentary* and *Freedom.* Also, in 1940, I founded the literary quarterly, *NOW,* and remained editor until the journal came to an end in 1949.

"During the 1940s, my attention began to shift from verse to prose, particularly history, biography and criticism. I became an active reviewer and journalist, as I have been ever since, and in 1946 my first considerable prose work, *William Godwin,* appeared, combining criticism and biography. I did not cease to write poetry. Four volumes have appeared since *The White Island,* and in the 1960s and 1970s there were bursts of verse writing, both in the lyric genre and also in terms of verse drama; four of my verse plays, the most notable of them 'Maskerman,' have been produced by the Canadian Broadcasting Corporation, as well as an opera, 'The Brideship,' for which I wrote the libretto.

"In 1949 I returned to the Canadian west coast; it has been my base ever since, for I have found that its combination of mountains and sea, and its remoteness from literary ambiances, gives Vancouver a peculiar combination of inspiration and serenity that makes it an almost ideal setting for work, given my own temperament, which tends to combine pantheism and misanthropy. I have travelled long and far from Vancouver indeed: to Latin America and Asia, to most parts of Europe and to the South Pacific Islands. Out of these journeys has come a number of travel books and also of works of cultural history, particularly in relation to the Indian sub-continent. In 1954, at the University of Washington, I began to teach English, and later, up to 1966, I taught English and later Asian Studies at the University of British Columbia. Ill-health forced me to abandon teaching in that year, but not to abandon my links with the academic world, since I continued to edit from the University of British Columbia the critical quarterly devoted to Canadian writers and writing—*Canadian Literature*—which I founded in 1959.

"The most important books of my Canadian period reflect the continuation of basic interests: *Anarchism,* which was a history of libertarian movements and ideas; *The Crystal Spirit,* a study of George Orwell, who had been my friend in the 1940s; *Herbert Read, The Stream and the Source,* a discussion of the work of another writer who had been my friend; *Dawn and the Darkest Hour,* a study of Aldous Huxley; *Incas and Other Men,* a travel book on Peru; *Who Killed the British Empire?,* an inquest on imperial decline; and several books whose titles adequately describe their subjects—*Canada and the Canadians, Faces of India, The Greeks in India, Gandhi,* and *South Sea Journey.* The last book arose from a series of travels linked with my only incursion into film making, when I wrote the scripts for the CBC documentary programme, *In the South Seas,* which was shown extensively in Europe and Asia. Among the languages into which my books were translated during this period are French, Italian, German, Spanish, Swedish, Japanese and Malayalam. I also continued to write articles and book reviews in a wide variety of British, Canadian and American publications, as well as dramatic and documentary scripts for radio and television.

"In Canada I am generally described as a man-of-letters, but looking back over my career I would add another appellation: *moralist,* but understood in the French sense. Poetry has continued to interest me and I have used it over the years to express states of mind too elusive for prose to trap them. But in prose I have been inclined towards the discursive essay, varying in magnitude from the book review to the book, in which I use a work of literary or visual art, a personality, a place, a trend in history, as the armature for a many-faceted statement about the human condition. Perhaps it is because I have found this form so adequate for my purposes that I never returned, after three youthful novels which I rejected as failures, to the art of fiction. Poetry and the grand essay seemed sufficient. I contemplate a future in which the genres may change, but not the duality of the private and public examinations of the human condition complementing each other, the former henceforward in autobiography, the latter in massive cultural histories reflecting on the origins and interconnections of religions, philosophies and the arts that mirror them."

George Woodcock, an extraordinarily prolific and versatile writer, made his first reputation in England, as a poet and radical journalist. His verse is not now highly regarded but some critics feel that it deserves more attention than it has received, and question its omission from A. J. M. Smith's *Oxford Book of Canadian Verse.* Julian Symons, writing in *Contemporary Poets,* says that Woodcock's best poems fall into two groups: "The first, and more powerfully imaginative, deals with an invented scene or story in fabulous yet realistic terms." Thus, in his much-anthologized "The Island," marauders capture and torture an inhabitant of an island which they have raided in search of gold. Fire bursts from the prisoner's torn joints and

There lay before us on the rigid rack
Straw limbs and a horse's polished skull.
Gulls mocked as walked away across the sea
The man we hunted but could not keep or kill.

Other poems reflect more directly Woodcock's political views, and in these he "shows us much more clearly than most writers of his generation what it was like to be a particular kind of Left-wing intellectual in the years before and during the War." Symons concludes that "when the war ended and [the] social structure remained unchanged except in minor details, Woodcock survived as writer and social commentator, but his poetic vision faded."

In any case, as Woodcock says, his attention shifted during the 1940s to prose. His early books on the libertarian thinkers Godwin, Kropotkin (written with Ivan Avakumovic), and Proudhon are colored by his commitment to anarcho-pacifism but, because Woodcock was always as intellectually curious as he was politically committed, they remain useful guides to

their subject. The last two have appeared as paperbacks in the 1970s, and neither seems dated. In his later work, Woodcock has fruitfully developed from an "engaged" to a more eclectic and critical outlook. Few reading the authoritative and lively *Anarchism,* which is a standard text, would guess that the author was once a dedicated anarchist himself. *Anarchism* was described by Colin MacInnes as "penetrating, scholarly, and as immensely detailed as it is entirely readable."

The Crystal Spirit, Woodcock's book about George Orwell, is not a biography because Orwell had not wanted one. Instead, Woodcock supplies a study of his friend's work which "intelligently relates Orwell's life to his work without straining for false relevance." The book was found lucid, sound, and shrewd, but too long, sometimes boring, and marred at times by "a chiding, patronizing tone." There was in general a grateful reception also for *Herbert Read,* a careful critical biography of a figure about whom there is a surprising paucity of material. In *Dawn and the Darkest Hour,* Woodcock sees the "movement out of darkness towards light" as the sustaining image of Aldous Huxley's art as well as of his life, and organizes around this metaphor his very thorough and complete survey of Huxley's work, which benefits from the fact that it is "something of a personal testament."

Woodcock's years as an expatriate and his subsequent travels all over the world have produced another large body of writings—a number of zestfully written travel books, like *Faces of India* and *Asia, Gods and Cities;* such works as *Into Tibet,* a history of early travels to that mysterious place; and some thoughtful essays in cultural and social history. *The British in the Far East,* for example, is a lively account of the way in which a handful of British merchants, missionaries, soldiers, and administrators exerted an immense influence over a huge area of Asia beyond India. *The Greeks in India* surveys the whole history of Indo-Greek relations and "abounds with good things at every level: his eye for exotic detail is matched by a cool sense of perspective." Woodcock has also served as general editor of the Great Travellers series.

Canada and the Canadians provides both a history of the country and a portrait of what it had become by the late 1960s. A reviewer in the *Times Literary Supplement* wrote that "a combination of talent and experience has enabled [Woodcock] to write a really good book about Canada." He "writes with sufficient vividness and feeling to create in the reader a sense of what the various regions and cities of Canada look and feel like, and his wide-ranging travels and sensitive eye enable him to draw evocative comparisons." In *Who Killed the British Empire?*, which was found both learned and readable, Woodcock concludes that the only "conspiracy" involved in the empire's decline and fall was one of social and economic factors. His biography of Gabriel Dumont, leader of the Métis (a part-white, part-Indian people) in the Saskatchewan Rebellion of 1885 seemed to Margaret Laurence "one of the strongest and most moving books I have read in a long time."

George Woodcock is the son of Samuel Woodcock, a musician, and the former Margaret Lewis. He was married in 1949 to Ingeborg Linzer, who supplied the photographs that accompany his essay on the city of Victoria. He was educated at Sir William Borlase's School at Marlow, in Buckinghamshire (1924–1929) and attended Morley College in London in 1935–1936. Woodcock went to the University of Washington in 1954 as a lecturer in English, and in the same capacity two years later to the University of British Columbia, where he became an assistant professor (1958–1961) and then an associate professor (1961–1963). He returned as a lecturer in Asian studies in 1966–1967. Woodcock held a Guggenheim fellowship in 1950, a Canadian Government Overseas fellowship in 1957, and a Canada Council Killam fellowship in 1970, and he has received several Canada Council travel grants. He has honorary doctorates from four universities. Woodcock received the Governor-General's Award for nonfiction in 1967 and the Molson Prize in 1973. He is a Fellow of the Royal Society of Canada (1968) and of the Royal Geographical Society (1971).

Woodcock has written several hundred scripts for radio and television talks, plays, and documentaries. He was an advisory editor of *Tamarack Review* in 1956–1960 and a contributing editor of *Dissent* (1954–) and *Arts Magazine* (1962–1964). His work as editor of *Canadian Literature* has been of inestimable value in demonstrating the liveliness of a culture too often dismissed as sterile. He is a prolific reviewer and essayist, and one of the most esteemed of Canadian critics. Woodcock remains devoted to the practical problem of how human beings may attain to a condition of individual freedom and self-realization but, though he is sympathetic to peaceful dissent, he has become wary of movements.

PRINCIPAL WORKS: *Poetry*—The White Island, 1940; The Centre Cannot Hold, 1942; Imagine the South, 1949; Selected Poems, 1967; Notes on Visitations, 1975. *Plays*—Maskerman *in* Prism Winter 1961. *Biography and criticism*—William Godwin: a Biographical Study, 1946; The Incomparable Aphra, 1948; The Paradox of Oscar Wilde, 1950; (with Ivan Avakumovic) The Anarchist Prince: A Biographical Study of Peter Kropotkin, 1950; Pierre-Joseph Proudhon: A Biography, 1953; The Crystal Spirit: A Study of George Orwell, 1966; Hugh MacLennan, 1969; Mordecai Richler, 1970; Odysseus Ever Returning: Essays on Canadian Writing, 1970; Mohandas Gandhi, 1971; Dawn and the Darkest Hour: A Study of Aldous Huxley, 1972; Herbert Read: The Stream and the Source, 1972; Amor de Cosmos: Journalist and Reformer, 1975; Gabriel Dumont: The Métis Chief and His Lost World, 1975; Thomas Morton: Monk and Poet, 1978. *Travel*—Ravens and Prophets: An Account of Journeys in British Columbia, Alberta and Southern Alaska, 1952; To the City of the Dead: An Account of Travel in Mexico, 1957; Incas and Other Men: Travels in the Andes, 1959; Faces of India: A Travel Narrative, 1964; Asia, Gods and Cities: Aden to Tokyo, 1966; Kerala: A Portrait of the Malabar Coast, 1967; Henry Walter Bates: Naturalist of the Amazon, 1969; Into Tibet: The Early British Explorers, 1971; Victoria, 1971; South Sea Journey, 1976. *History and Politics*—The Writer and Politics (essays), 1948; Anarchism: A History of Libertarian Ideas and Movements, 1962; The Greeks in India, 1966; Civil Disobedience (radio talks), 1966; (with Ivan Avakumovic) The Doukhobors, 1968; The British in the Far East, 1969; The Hudson's Bay Company, 1970; Canada and the Canadians, 1970; The Rejection of Politics and Other Essays on Canada, Canadians, Anarchism and the World, 1972; Who Killed the British Empire?, 1974; Peoples of the Coast: The Indians of the Pacific Northwest, 1977. *As Editor*—A Hundred Years of Revolution, 1948; A Choice of Critics: Selections From "Canadian Literature," 1966; The Sixties: Canadian Writers and Writing of the Decade, 1969; Malcolm Lowry: The Man and His Work, 1971; Wyndham Lewis in Canada, 1971; Poets and Critics, 1974; Colony and Confederation: Early Canadian Poets and Their Backgrounds, 1974; The Canadian Novel in the Twentieth Century, 1975; The Anarchist Reader, 1977.

ABOUT: Contemporary Authors 1–4 1st revision, 1967; Davey, F. From Here to There, 1974; Hughes, P. George Woodcock, 1974; Nelles, V. and Rotstein, A. Nationalism or Local Control: Responses to George Woodcock, 1973; Vinson, J. (ed.) Contemporary Poets, 1975; Who's Who, 1978.

WOODS, JOHN (WARREN) (July 12, 1926–), American poet, was born in Martinsville, Indiana, a small farming community near Indianapolis. He is the son of Jefferson Blount Woods and the former Doris Underwood. He served with the United States Army Air Force in 1944–1946, part of the time in Panama, and then entered Indiana University, receiving his B.S. in 1949, his M.A.T. (Master of Arts in Teaching) in 1955. The same year he began his career at Western Michigan University, Kalamazoo, where he has remained as assistant professor (1955–1961), associate professor (1961–1965), and since 1965 professor of English. Woods was a graduate student at the University of Iowa in 1957–1958, and a visiting professor at the University of California, Irvine, in 1967–1968.

At Indiana University Woods had submitted a collection of poems in lieu of a thesis for his

WOODS

JOHN WOODS

There were more poems in this rhetorical mode, some of them successful, in the first section of *On the Morning of Color* (1961), a collection which takes its name from "Poem at Thirty"—strongly reminiscent of Dylan Thomas in manner as well as title:

.... On the morning of color,
On the morning of first-seen,
When every acorn rolled into place,
When every child seemed the final incident of poise,
When the great waters
Were one small stream carrying out to river
The reflective world,
We could not sing of love or loss,
Or count to thirty, holding our breath.

But now we say, God, sun,
Circumstance, whatever riddles us,
Send us one such morning to grow on.

The volume also contained some love poems and "poems of persons," and some pieces in a lighter vein. Mona Van Duyn wrote: "Formal, musical, sometimes a little 'soft' in image or rhyme, once in a while derivative (Frost, Stevens), intelligent, rooted in consistent feeling, Mr. Woods' poems have their excellence."

The Cutting Edge (1966), which includes many poems on the landscape of Indiana and the town-country duality, struck Laurence Lieberman as a transitional volume in which the poet was moving beyond his usual "close, tight-packed forms" and restricted subject matter to engage "the dimensions of dream and memory. ... To accommodate ... [this] widening scope of his vision, he loosens his rhythms, adopts a more elastic line, and opens up the field of the poem's form." *Keeping Out of Trouble* (1968) had its admirers but seemed to William Dickey an unsuccessful collection in which Woods constantly defeats his own poems, failing finally "to produce either a positive or an ironic vision that can be of use."

There was also a mixed press for Woods's collected poems, *Turning to Look Back* (1972). The first of its five sections deals with "death and rumors of death in the seasons, death of ideals, and deaths that are also rebirths." There is a group of love poems and one of lyrics, "Barley Tongues," a section of poems of social comment called "Red Telephones," and a final section concerned with identity and identities. It seemed to *Choice*'s reviewer that the book illustrated very effectively Woods's growing range—"from the heavy-handed flatness of the Paragon group, through the keenly felt and moving lyrics and love poems, to the Dickey-strenuous topicality of the 'socially-conscious' group.... Some of the

master's degree, preparing the collection under the guidance of John Crowe Ransom, who taught summers at Indiana's School of Letters. These poems were published by Indiana University Press in 1955 as *The Deaths at Paragon, Indiana*. The collection takes its title from a sequence of poems about a fatal auto crash in a small town as it affects a diner waitress who witnesses the crash, the ambulance driver, the doctor who tries to revive the five dead youths, and the junkman ("king/ Of bang and rattle, of fall apart/ And rust in weeds") who receives their flattened car—"The shape was fall and spin and blast./ The shape was death. I let it go." Other poems in the book deal with such subjects as a cop prematurely aged by the death of his girlfriend and the behavior of local youths towards a new girl in town.

William Arrowsmith wrote that the idiom of these poems "is one of the most austere I have ever met, adamantly anti-literary, without allusions to any countryside but what this modern pastoral of Indiana can generate, almost anti-rhetorical: its characteristic motion is through a steady succession of flat understatements, neat, restrained, almost leached of color or gesture, coming close to monotony, and then closing on a sudden leap which quite transfigures the preceding crawl of the language. It is very much a world of the commonplace—folksy, cluttered with things ... and the intent of the poetry is very clearly the commonplace transfigured." In this mode, Arrowsmith thought, Woods "writes poetry of a very high order," though some of the later poems in the collection were in a more rhetorical manner, "too wilfully lyric ... both mannered and false."

poems are mere comments; some are reports; a few are recollections: but three of the five sections contain excellent lyrics and are apparently Woods' essential voice." Robert Pinsky thought that Woods "writes movingly of vivid bucolic landscapes, and of a sense, arising from those nostalgic landscapes, of things that die and of things that do not," but also found some poems that seemed to him no more than "exasperated language."

Vernon Young has said that Woods, as a poet, is "at the crossroads where romantic irony, black humor and the sentimental meet." Young thinks that the principal influences on Woods, apart from his Midwestern environment, have been Dylan Thomas and World War II: "The War killed a root of expectation in him" and Thomas "enriched his own sweet faculty for recapturing nature on the move." Like many critics, Young understands but regrets Woods's compulsion to write poems of social protest against war and materialism: "He is too good for so easy a game when instead he can be exploring the maze of the feral self . . . writing memorably bleak Americana . . . moping with good grace in the mock-troubadour vein."

John Woods was married in 1951 to Emily Newbury and has two sons. He received the Robert Frost fellowship at the Bread Loaf Writers' Conference in 1962, and spent part of 1963 at the Yaddo artists' colony at Saratoga Springs, New York, winning the Yaddo Award. He has also received *Poetry Northwest*'s Theodore Roethke Award (1969) and a publication award from the National Endowment for the Arts (1970). Woods has served as poetry editor of Western Michigan University's Aural Press, which publishes educational recordings, and of Indiana University Press. He has written plays, short stories, and book reviews as well as poems.

PRINCIPAL WORKS: The Deaths at Paragon, Indiana, 1955; On the Morning of Color, 1961; The Cutting Edge, 1966; Keeping Out of Trouble, 1968; Turning to Look Back: Poems 1955-1970, 1972; (with James Hearst and Felix Pollack) Voyages to the Inland Sea II, 1972; Alcohol, 1973; A Bone Flicker, 1973; Striking the Earth, 1976.

ABOUT: Contemporary Authors 1st revision, 1975; Leary, P. and Kelly, R. (eds.) A Controversy of Poets, 1965; Penguin Companion to Literature 3, 1971; Vinson, J. (ed.) Contemporary Poets, 1975. *Periodicals*—Chicago Review Winter 1972; Hudson Review Summer 1956, Summer 1969, Winter 1972-1973; Library Journal October 1, 1966; Northwest Review Winter 1972; Poetry June 1956, September 1962, March 1967, June 1973, August 1977; Prairie Schooner Fall 1969; Voices December 1962.

WOODWARD, C(OMER) VANN (November 13, 1908–), American historian, was born in Vanndale, Arkansas, the son of Hugh Allison

C. VANN WOODWARD

Pach Bros., NY

Woodward, a teacher who later became head of Emory Junior College at Oxford, Georgia, and the former Bess Vann. After graduating from high school at Morrilton, he attended a small Arkansas college for two years before transferring to Emory University in Atlanta (Ph.B., 1930). An English instructor at the Georgia Institute of Technology in Atlanta in 1930–1931, Woodward then went to Columbia University as a Social Science Research Council fellow, securing his M.A. in 1932. After two more years at Georgia Tech (1932–1933), he began a doctorate in history at the University of North Carolina in Chapel Hill under a General Education Board fellowship.

At Atlanta and Chapel Hill Woodward moved in circles that shared his own views as a "liberal, even more, a southern white liberal." Among his friends were Glenn Rainey and Will W. Alexander, director of the Commission on Interracial Cooperation. He was also influenced by the sociologists Rupert B. Vance and Howard W. Odum—pragmatists who wanted the South to share in the nation's wealth and material progress without surrendering its own distinctive qualities and values.

Receiving his Ph.D. in 1937, Woodward became an assistant professor of history at the University of Florida in Gainesville. The following year he published his doctoral dissertation, *Tom Watson: Agrarian Rebel,* chronicling the fluctuating fortunes of the Georgia agitator who became a U.S. Congressman in 1890 and was twice the Populist candidate for President. Woodward skillfully contrasted Watson's initial efforts to draw Southern blacks and whites together against economic exploitation with his subsequent virulent rantings against blacks, Jews, and Catholics alike. Although Woodward scrupulously avoided psychological speculation, the book was soon ranked among the most perceptive psychological portraits in American historical literature, and as one of the best available studies of a Southerner living in the postbellum South. Henry Steele Commager wrote that "Mr. Woodward's biography is a model of its kind. It has all the obvious qualities of scholarship, thoroughness and impartiality. It has, in addition, a sympathetic understanding of broad social movements, a mature appreciation of character, an original interpretation of economic facts and factors, an incisive criticism of political techniques, and a literary style that is always vigorous and sometimes brilliant."

A visiting assistant professor of history at the University of Virginia in 1939–1940, Woodward then went to an associate professorship at Scripps College in Claremont, California (1940–1943). During World War II he served from 1943 to 1946 as a lieutenant in the U.S. Naval Reserve, working in the Office of Naval Intelligence and the Naval Office of Public Information. In 1946, he resumed his career as an associate professor at Johns Hopkins University. He became a full professor there in 1947. He remained at Hopkins until 1961, when he accepted the Sterling Professorship of History at Yale.

C. Vann Woodward's second book—his only departure from Southern history—was *The Battle for Leyte Gulf* (1947). Stemming from his intensive wartime research into naval operations in the Philippine seas during October 1944, this account of "the greatest naval battle and the largest engagement ever fought on the high seas" combined complex tactical minutiae and high drama in a way that appealed to both historians and general readers. P.J. Searles praised its "thoroughness, objectivity and sheer good writing," predicting that "the narrative may be amplified as further information is uncovered, but it should stand for a long time as authoritative in basic aspects." Robert Coles offered this concise summary: "The historian proved a born storyteller, a subtle and powerful narrator, a skillful chronicler, a careful researcher, and a man who obviously relished the task in hand."

After this victorious sortie into naval history, Woodward returned to his own territory. In 1951 he published two books which together provided what was immediately recognized as the most original and important reinterpretation of postbellum Southern history to have appeared in several decades. The first, *Reunion and Reaction: The Compromise of 1877 and the End of Reconstruction,* was a study of the Hayes-Tilden Presidential election contest of 1876–1877, giving for the first time a detailed account of the complicated and unsavory secret negotiations between Southern Democrats and Northern Republicans that eventually resulted in Hayes's presidency and the end of Reconstruction. R.D. Heffner in the *Nation* called Woodward's detective work "a major contribution to our understanding of Southern interests and issues. His penetrating and provocative analysis of this most far-reaching compromise of our national history indicates clearly the inadequacy and superficiality of long accepted myths."

The second book, *The Origins of the New South, 1877–1913,* embodies a whole series of significant insights into Southern history between Reconstruction and World War I. The first mature and comprehensive history of this neglected period, it closed a major gap in the historiography of the region. Building upon the Beardian concept of the Civil War as a conflict between Southern agrarianism and Northern industrialism, Woodward argued that the same dualism existed within the South itself: the defeat at Appomattox had already opened a Pandora's box of Whiggish elements in the South, anxious to embrace industrialism. Thus, he concluded, the long-accepted view of the end of Reconstruction as a major turning point was largely illusory. The book goes on to question or demolish the prevailing version of postbellum history at many other points—in its interpretations of Redeemer regimes, Populism, the rise of segregation, and the New South movement. The scope and detail of Woodward's arguments and his moderate but uncompromising tone left no doubt in critics' minds that this was a pioneer work with which all future historians exploring the Southern paradox would have to deal. Representative of this general opinion was B.I. Wiley's comment in the New York *Times:* "Its quality is such that henceforth no one who has not explored its pages can consider himself informed in any aspect of the so-called New South."

In 1954 Woodward delivered the James W. Richard Lectures in History at the University of Virginia, and these were published the following year as *The Strange Career of Jim Crow.* In them he traced the origins of the Jim Crow laws in the South, a topic made pertinent by the dismantling of legal segregation following the Supreme Court decision *Brown* vs. *the Board of Education* the preceding May. Seeking to forestall violent resistance by white Southerners who believed that segregation was a matter of instinct rather than a social policy, Woodward showed that legal segregation, far from being an immutable system, did not become widely established in the South until the late 1890s; poll taxes, property and literacy requirements, and white primaries likewise became widespread only well after Reconstruction, between 1895 and 1910. All the same, although blacks and whites had lived, worked, and traveled side by side in the years following the Civil War, "no golden age of race relations" existed: "The evidence of race conflict and violence, brutality and exploitation in this very period is overwhelming."

Lewis Gannett found this a "cool, sane and factual book [which] undercuts hot-headed arguments from both sides ... a significant and original contribution to one of the historic controversies of American history." But other reviewers, including some of Woodward's fellow historians, took exception to his thesis, misinterpreting it as an idyllic portrayal of a South free from racial strife until the twentieth century, and criticizing it for failing to take into account the existence of condescension and paternalism —and the role of Federal troops in imposing a temporary and "token" toleration of blacks and their rights.

The Burden of Southern History (1960) is a collection of eight essays in which Woodward argues that the South represents a deviation from the norm of the American experience: although part of a country uniquely characterized by wealth, success, and a kind of innocence, it has reaped poverty and failure, remaining "basically pessimistic in its social outlook and its moral philosophy." For R.N. Current—and many reviewers evidently agreed—the book confirmed Woodward's right to be regarded as "one of the finest minds and most humane spirits of our time." An equally warm reception was accorded Woodward's second collection of essays, published in 1971 as *American Counterpoint: Slavery and Racism in the North-South Dialogue,* in which he is concerned to "deflate many of the stereotypes and images that have arisen around race and regional identity."

Comer Vann Woodward was married to Glenn Boyd MacLeod in 1937. Their only child, Peter Vincent, is deceased. Besides lecturing extensively in the United States, Woodward was a visiting professor at the University of Tokyo in summer 1953, a Commonwealth lecturer at the University of London in 1954, and Harmsworth Professor of American History at Oxford University in 1954–1955. He holds honorary degrees from a number of universities and was a Guggenheim Foundation Fellow in 1946–1947 and 1960–1961. He received the Bancroft History Prize in 1952, an award from the National

Institute for Arts and Letters in 1954, and a prize from the American Council of Learned Societies in 1962. Woodward was a member of the Social Science Research Council in 1956–1961 and a member of the board of directors of the American Council of Learned Societies in 1963–1971. He has also served as president of the Southern Historical Association (1952–1953), the American Historical Association (1968–1969), and the Organization of American Historians (1968–1969).

In the *New Yorker* Robert Coles described C. Vann Woodward as "a rather old-fashioned historian" who does not rely on computers or turn to "related disciplines" but writes traditional chronological history. "He takes issue with certain people, but quietly, and with no relish. He does not want bland 'consensus,' but he gets no kick out of an attention-getting fight. His 'method' is to use his mind's sensibility."

Woodward regards history as both a key to the past and a source of guidance for the present. He believes that the historian can show and interpret for society diverse possibilities and potentialities, thereby enabling it to reject determinism and make the best possible choice. As he remarked in his December 1969 address as president of the American Historical Association: "The historian is peculiarly fitted ... to serve as a mediator between man's limitations and his aspirations, between his dream of what ought to be and the limits of what, in the light of what has been, can be. There is no other branch of learning better qualified to mediate between man's daydream of the future and his nightmare of the past, or, for that matter, between his nightmare of the future and his daydream of the past."

Woodward is himself the foremost American practitioner of this historical philosophy. In David M. Potter's words, "his work has shown that history can be used in this way, but only in the hands of a scholar of extraordinary maturity, humane understanding, breadth of mind, and capacity to combine tolerance with idealism. And his vicissitudes have shown that, even for a man with these qualities, this may be the most difficult as well as the most rewarding use of history."

PRINCIPAL WORKS: Tom Watson: Agrarian Rebel, 1938; The Battle for Leyte Gulf, 1947; Reunion and Reaction: The Compromise of 1877 and the End of Reconstruction, 1951; The Origins of the New South, 1877–1913, 1951; The Strange Career of Jim Crow, 1955; The Burden of Southern History, 1960; American Counterpoint: Slavery and Racism in the North-South Dialogue, 1971. *As Editor*—Cannibals All, by George Fitzhugh, 1960; (with others) The National Experience, 1963; A Southern Prophecy: The Prosperity of the South Dependent Upon the Elevation of the Negro, by Lewis Harvie Blair, 1964; After the War: A Tour of the

WRIGHT

Southern States (1865–1866), by Whitelaw Reid, 1965; The Comparative Approach to American History, 1968; Responses of the Presidents to Charges of Misconduct: A Study Undertaken for the Impeachment Inquiry Staff of the House Committee on the Judiciary, 1974.

ABOUT: Contemporary Authors 5–8 1st revision, 1969; Cunliffe, M. and Winks, R.W. (eds.) Pastmasters: Some Essays on American Historians, 1969; Potter, D.M. History and American Society: Essays of David M. Potter, edited by D.E. Fehrenbacher, 1973; Genovese, E.D. In Red and Black, 1971; Who's Who in America, 1976–1977. *Periodicals*—American Historical Review June 1973; New Yorker April 15, 1972; Newsweek June 6, 1977.

WRIGHT, CHARLES (STEVENSON) (June 4, 1932–), American novelist and journalist, writes: "Born inland, three miles from the Missouri river. My mother died when I was four. Her parents raised me. We were very poor black Americans and there were traumas, family tragedies. But looking back—I was extremely fortunate: a happy childhood. After all, my nickname was Sonny. I was not a bookish child. However at thirteen or fourteen, read Richard Wright's *Black Boy* (we are not related) and, almost by accident, Ernest Hemingway. This began my passion for books, crystalized my desire to become a writer. I had always done well writing school book reports, essays, short stories. Having entered the world of books, nothing else mattered, not even baseball. I quit high school in my second year. It was a third-rate school. Worked typical odd jobs, hitch-hiked across the United States.

"Later spent several summers at the late Lowney Turner Handy Writer's Colony at Marshall, Illinois. James Jones is an ex–colony member. After being released from the aftermath of the Korean war, have lived mostly in New York City. I hope to become a very good writer, would like each book to be different in theme and style. Am interested in all phases of the cinema and architecture.

"I do not believe mankind will make sufficient humane gains in my lifetime. Therefore, the perfect dream of the future: writing, living as a semi-recluse, occasionally seeing good friends. Living by the sea."

Wright was born in New Franklin, Missouri, the son of Stevenson Wright, a laborer, and the former Dorthey Hughes. He received his education at public schools in New Franklin and Sedalia, Missouri. Wright's literary career began when he was a teenager with a regular column in the *Kansas City Call,* a weekly newspaper for blacks. The paper paid him one dollar for his first published short story. Between 1952 and 1954 Wright served with the United States

CHARLES WRIGHT

Army, spending one year in the States and one year in Korea, "when ... all the fighting was over." Since leaving the Army, Wright has lived mostly in New York, working as a freelance writer and at various casual jobs, and contributing a column ("Wright's World") to the *Village Voice.*

Wright's first novel, *The Messenger* (1963), is the story of Charles Stevenson, a young Negro writer from Sedalia, Missouri. Having moved North to New York, Stevenson works by day for a messenger service and by night as a male prostitute, becoming familiar with all the diverse worlds of the city, from Wall Street to the underworld. He befriends his seven-year-old neighbor Maxine, and the old lady known as the Grand Duchess, and carries on a hopeless relationship with his black girlfriend despite the fact that all feeling between them has long since fled. A gallery of character sketches takes in the whole range of struggling humanity—homosexuals and transvestites, a divinity student and an Army buddy, white academics and stockbrokers. An added dimension is provided by flashbacks to Stevenson's small-town youth, his first encounters with whites, his early travels, his experiences in the Army, and his return to Missouri on the death of his grandmother.

Stevenson's experiences as a black in white America have locked him into a shell of cynicism and indifference which stands between him and the capacity for compassion and understanding that he needs if he is to succeed as a writer; he progresses so far as to become an "ironic but generous observer." The novel is assembled out of a series of vignettes, deliberately inconclusive and undeveloped, reflecting the fragmentary nature of the protagonist's experience; the style is appropriately laconic.

Wright has said that he was "very bitter" when he wrote the novel, which to him was "simply a money-roof. I was amused at its success. Mini-popular first published thing. A pleasant dream with the frame of reality." The critical reaction was generally favorable, though not universally so. Richard Kluger, indeed, thought that it failed "to wake passion or bring understanding; it inspires downright contempt. . . . Mr. Wright gives us no reason to care about the title character or any of the others. . . . [his] prose, furthermore, is without spark." David Littlejohn, on the other hand, was impressed by the author's "sad honesty" in presenting "a pure, calm, existentially true bit of self-assessment," and Richard Kiely found both "stylistic control and a consistently implied moral attitude. . . . There are repeated flashes of humor and compassion in . . . [the hero's] narration which convince us that he has remained a human being in the face of great odds. And that is something worth writing about."

If in *The Messenger* the line between the real and the fantastic is sometimes thin, Wright's second novel, *The Wig* (1966), stretches the imagination still further. A savagely satirical black comedy, it describes the attempts of its hero, Lester Jefferson, to join the Great (i.e. White) Society. Lester, like everyone else in the novel, is on the make; he straightens his hair with "long-lasting Silky Smooth Hair Relaxer with the Built-in Sweat-Proof Base" and with his yellow-dyed "wig" as passport sets out to conquer America. This ambition is shared by a motley crew of hustlers, losers, and pretenders, most of them black, much like those in the first novel. Shedding guilt, compassion, and even identity in their eagerness to sell themselves to anyone who will buy, they find not the Great Society but "chaos and death where the only sin is 'believing, hoping.' " At the end of *The Wig* Lester submits to castration because "having children is the greatest sin in this country." In contrast to his feelings about his first novel, Wright says that *The Wig* "was my life," and the twenty-nine days in which he wrote the final draft were "the best days of my life." He told J. O'Brien that "one of the interesting things about the novel is that all of it was pure imagination, yet they came to pass—the slang, the see-through plastic dresses, abortions, vibrators."

Like its predecessor, *The Wig* lacks plot: "a loud, frenetic, batty, bitty book," Martin Shuttleworth called it, while the *Nation*'s reviewer thought it "awkward" with its piled imagery, contrived comedy, heavy jokes, and shifts of tone in the narrative voice. Frank Campenni, who finds in Wright's novels the "mordant wit, yearning despair and surrealistic lunacy of vintage [Nathanael] West," prefers the first book: "Charles Stevenson of *The Messenger* had something to tell; he could communicate love to a little girl and an old lady, if not the girl friend with whom he only quarreled. Charles Stevenson Wright, in *The Wig,* is raucous and loud, but neither he nor his hero Lester tell us much we don't know or need to hear." There was praise, however, for the novel's encapsulation of "the awful distorting pressures of the ghetto." Wright's "matter-of-fact bitterness . . . never allows the comic and the horrific to drift too far apart. And it rings sickeningly true."

Absolutely Nothing to Get Alarmed About, which followed in 1973, is a collection of Wright's *Village Voice* columns. A reviewer in the *New Yorker* wrote that "in recent years, . . . [Wright] has been angry and unhappy a lot of the time, and this raw-nerved, bitter journal, begun in 1967, explains why, and is also probably the clearest picture to have emerged of what it feels like nowadays to be poor, black, and American . . . Mr. Wright has spent many hours drifting around New York observing and communing with the city's most godforsaken, especially on the lower East Side. These closeups of friends and strangers are sometimes cruel, sometimes wry . . . but always intimate—and, unquestionably, depressingly true to life."

PRINCIPAL WORKS: *Fiction*—The Messenger, 1963; The Wig: A Mirror Image, 1966. *Nonfiction*—Absolutely Nothing to Get Alarmed About, 1973.

ABOUT: Contemporary Authors 9–12 1st revision, 1974; Hughes, L. Black American Short Stories, 1968; O'Brien, J. (ed.) Interviews With Black Writers, 1973; Schulz, M.F. Black Humor Fiction of the Sixties, 1973; Vinson J. (ed.) Contemporary Novelists, 1976. *Periodicals*—Books and Bookmen May 1967; Ebony November 1957; Library Journal February 1963; New Yorker November 2, 1963; New York Times February 23, 1966; New York Times Book Review February 27, 1966; Punch February 15, 1967; Sepia December 1957; Times Literary Supplement May 14, 1964; March 9, 1967; Village Voice July 23, 1973; Vogue July 1973; Yardbird Journal Autumn 1974.

YOUNG, G(EORGE) M(ALCOLM) (April 29, 1882–November 18, 1959), English historian, was born at Charlton, Kent, the only son of George Frederick Young and the former Rosetta Jane Elizabeth Ross. His father, a waterman on the Thames at Greenhithe, Kent, rose to become master of a steamer there. A brilliant student, G.M. Young went with a scholarship to St. Paul's, a London public school noted for its rigorous academic standards. From there, another scholarship took him to Balliol College,

© The Warden and Fellows of All Souls College, Oxford

G. M. YOUNG

Oxford University (1900–1904), where he read *literae humaniores*. Young graduated in 1904 with a second-class honors degree. He was elected a fellow of All Souls College, Oxford, in 1905, and in 1906 became a tutor of St. John's College.

In 1908 Young left Oxford and joined the civil service as a junior examiner in the universities branch of the Board of Education. In 1911 he was appointed first secretary of what became the University Grants Committee, and further innovative posts followed—in the newly formed Cabinet Office (1916–1917) and then as joint secretary of the new (but shortlived) Ministry of Reconstruction. Young was created a Companion of the Bath in 1917. The same year he accompanied the socialist statesman Arthur Henderson, then a member of the War Cabinet, on his controversial visit to Russia just after the Revolution. There Young met Sir Francis Lindley, counselor to the British Embassy. He went with Lindley to Archangel and later accompanied him to Vienna when Lindley was appointed minister plenipotentiary there. Young served for a time in Vienna as a director of the newly established Anglo-Austrian Bank. He was at this time, according to the *Dictionary of National Biography*, "a curious anaemic-looking man," somewhat reserved in manner, but already recognized as "a great scholar with a wide range of knowledge and a wonderful command of the English language."

Soon after the war Young left public service to devote himself to study and writing. He settled in Wiltshire, in a house called the Old Oxyard at Oare, near Marlborough. His companion there was Mona Wilson, a lifelong friend, who was herself an author. According to the *DNB*,

"she took charge of all those details of everyday life in which Young himself was oddly helpless and dependent. Surrounded in this neighbourhood by many cronies, including a bevy of ex-ambassadors, Young became, alongside Miss Wilson with her short fireside pipe, the centre of intellectual gossip and a dispenser of fascinating talk drawn from the resources of an astonishing memory."

It was not until 1932, when he was fifty, that Young published his first book, a brief study of Edward Gibbon in the Appleton Biographies series. It was called "a very good biography indeed," lively and well-proportioned, and tracing clearly and succinctly the development of the scholar and of *The Decline and Fall of the Roman Empire*. Young next edited the two volumes of *Early Victorian England* (1934), which was most notable for his own contribution, a final summary chapter called "The Portrait of an Age." Undertaken partly in protest against the "preposterous misreading of the age" which Young attributed to Lytton Strachey and his imitators, it was received with such pleasure that Young enlarged it into the volume published in 1936 as *Victorian England: Portrait of an Age*.

This has remained the most admired of Young's books. He thought that what was important in history was "not what happened, but what people said about it when it was happening"; his advice to the historian was "to go on reading until you can hear people talking." Young himself had gone on reading until he could not only hear people talking, but knew which areas of discourse were fundamental to the Victorian ethos. P. W. Wilson wrote that "with unbounded enthusiasm . . . [Young] has read up the memoirs, absorbed the blue books, browsed over the newspapers, studied the sermons, perused the poetry and fiction of a prolific era. The text of a volume that is not quite so brief as it seems thus sparkles with anecdotes and allusions. Even the statistics scintillate." R. C. K. Ensor thought that "so flashing and frequent are its epigrams, that quite trivially-minded people might read it for amusement. So wide and accurate is its knowledge, so fair and temperate, yet so penetrating and subtle, are its fundamental judgements, that the most serious scholar must take off his hat to it."

Young's footnotes to *Victorian England* are informative and often amusing, but they do not refer to his sources or identify quotations or allusions. The late George Kitson Clark set out to repair these omissions, and in time involved other scholars in the task. The work began, he said, as "a game to be pursued by myself and my friends in the intervals of what seemed to be more important work"; it was a game to which he devoted the last years of his life, drawing on the knowledge of nearly forty experts on the Victorian period. His annotated edition of *Victorian England* appeared in 1977. It identifies almost all of Young's references and allusions, completes and corrects his quotations (for which Young too often relied on his imperfect memory), refers to relevant scholarly work that has appeared since Young's book was last revised, and in some cases questions Young's interpretations. The work was warmly welcomed by many scholars, most of whom felt, with John Clive, that *Victorian England* "triumphantly survives even the most rigorous procedures of forensic medicine."

Charles I and Cromwell (1935), which seeks to chart the labyrinthine paths that led to the king's astonishing death on the scaffold, is fundamentally a study in the psychology of three men: Charles, Cromwell, and Ireton. Arthur Bryant said in his review that "Mr. Young is one of the first writers in England. Nothing better of the kind has ever been done. The story is a familiar one, but by exquisite scholarship, and, what is far rarer these days, the force of independent thought, he has told it as almost something new."

A volume of essays and reviews followed, *Daylight and Champaign* (1937), in which (the blurb says) Young offers "such meditations as occur to him day by day as he walks about the estate [of English culture], with a sharp eye for such vermin as Liberals, Examiners, poets whose verses do not scan, and biographers who peep through keyholes." A reviewer in the *Times Literary Supplement* agreed with the blurb writer that Young's viewpoint was that of an "English country gentleman" in his "good-humoured conservatism, his distaste for crude extremisms, his sense of historical continuity, his background of tradition and classical letters, his respect for the chastity of grammar and verse." The book touches on subjects as varied as Sir Robert Peel, Disraeli, Charles I, Victorian religious conflicts, Dickens, Newman, and William Morris, and Young was commended for his "peculiar fertility in bringing the ages together or in detecting resemblances between those who apparently stood far apart as contemporaries."

Mona Wilson died shortly after World War II, and Young was obliged to sell his house. He never fully recovered from these blows, but, after his re-election in 1948 to a fellowship of All Souls, built himself a new and congenial life in these familiar surroundings. Thereafter, until his health failed, Young gave much time and energy to a variety of public services. He had become a trustee of the National Portrait Gallery in 1937, and from 1947 to 1957 he was also a trustee of the British Museum. He served from 1938 onwards on the Standing Commission on Museums and Galleries and from 1948 onwards on the Historical Manuscripts Commission. He was also a member of the Royal Commission on the Press in 1947–1949.

Today and Yesterday, a second collection of essays, appeared in 1948, and *Last Essays* in 1950. Young's biography of Stanley Baldwin (1952), undertaken somewhat reluctantly at Baldwin's request, was handicapped by the unhelpfulness or hostility of some of Baldwin's associates and by the extraordinary shortage of documents relating to the prime minister's career. Lindsay Rogers found the biography "sometimes a little precious" but "not without admirable qualities," though "it leaves a good many questions unanswered." It brought Young the James Tait Black Memorial Prize.

Young died in an Oxford nursing home in 1959. According to his entry in the *Dictionary of National Biography,* Young "was a slight figure with a scholarly stoop; he had a longish, inquisitive nose . . . an unusual manner of clearing his throat, a voice warm and vibrant. He was a shy man and because sensitive, somewhat sharp: an intellectual who lived by his deep if hidden affections." It was remarked of him that few writers have said so many good things upon so many subjects. The *DNB* says he lived up to his own definition of a historian as "one for whom the past keeps something of the familiar triviality of the present, and the present has already some of the shadowy magnificence of the past."

PRINCIPAL WORKS: Gibbon, 1932; Charles I and Cromwell: An Essay, 1935; Victorian England: Portrait of an Age, 1936 (annotated edition by George Kitson Clark, 1977); Daylight and Champaign, 1937; The Government of Britain (Britain in Pictures), 1941; Mr. Gladstone (Romanes Lecture), 1944; Today and Yesterday, 1948; Last Essays, 1950; Stanley Baldwin, 1952; Victorian Essays, edited by W.D. Handcock, 1962. *As Editor*—Early Victorian England, 1830–1865, 1934; Speeches by Lord Macaulay, 1935; Selected Poems of Thomas Hardy, 1940; Prose and Poetry of Thomas Macaulay, 1952; (with W.D. Handcock) English Historical Documents 1833–1874, 1956.

ABOUT: Clark, G. *biographical memoir in* Victorian England (annotated edition), 1977; Dictionary of National Biography, 1951-1960; Handcock, W.D. *introduction to* Victorian Essays, 1962; Lockhart, R.H.B. Retreat From Glory, 1934; Somervell, D.C. Stanley Baldwin, 1953; Who Was Who, 1951-1960. *Periodicals*—Books April 4, 1937; Illustrated London News November 28, 1959; Nation July 12, 1933; New Statesman December 10, 1932; December 12, 1936; New York Times March 21, 1937; Saturday Review October 3, 1953; Spectator November 14, 1952; December 25, 1936; Times (London) November 19, 24, 1959; Times Literary Supplement December 15, 1932; November 23, 1935;

YURICK

December 12, 1936; October 9, 1937; July 31, 1948; September 29, 1950; November 14, 1952; January 20, 1978; Yale Review Winter 1954.

YURICK, SOL (January 18, 1925–), American novelist and short story writer, was born in New York City, the son of Samuel and Florence (Weinstein) Yurick. He served in the army in 1944–1945, and for the next eight years worked in the library at New York University, at the same time studying for the B.A. he received there in 1950. From 1954 to 1959 he was a social investigator with the New York Department of Welfare, and since then he has been a full-time writer. Yurick received his M.A. from Brooklyn College in 1961. He was married in 1958 to Adrienne Lash, and has a daughter.

Yurick learned about urban poverty by growing up in the midst of it, and his five years with the Welfare Department made him a specialist. Christopher Lehmann-Haupt says that "rage is the fuel that makes Sol Yurick's fiction burn—a revolutionist's rage at the urban bureaucratic machine that flattens people into forgotten file drawers"; Yurick says that writing should "define the scream of the people."

These attitudes were implicit rather than explicit in Yurick's first novel, *The Warriors* (1965), an ingenious and stylish adventure story of great originality. Six black teenagers from a Coney Island fighting gang make their way to Van Cortlandt Park for an all-city gang congress. Stripped by misfortune of their weapons, the six have to return from the Bronx to Brooklyn through what is to them *terra incognita.* The novel's epigraph is from Xenophon's *Anabasis,* and Robert Hatch wrote that these warriors "are a tribal party, bound together by magic rites, disciplined by paternal authority. . . . bronze-age infantry tossed by some grotesque time trick into a twentieth-century metropolis," who must rely largely on cunning and bravado to bring them safe through the territories of rival gangs, "principalities whose customs and prowess are unknown." These youths, for whom the adult world is an irrelevance, and the police hostile deities, are, Hatch wrote, "ignorant, superstitious, lecherous, cruel and treacherous by society's standards. Yurick has set up a prism that allows one to judge them by their own."

It was Yurick's second novel, *Fertig* (1966), that for all its faults laid the foundations of his "cult reputation." Harry Fertig kills seven people connected with the hospital whose negligence cost his son's life—not in simple revenge but in order to publicize the evils of "the system." In the end "the system" closes around him, and he is locked away to be forgotten as a

SOL YURICK

© 1979 by Layle Silbert

madman. The *New Yorker* dismissed "this curious and tedious work" as "merely a hodgepodge of factual reporting, Freudian conjecture, anti-Freudian conjecture, detective talk, lawyer talk, and amateur moralizing." But a reviewer in *Best Sellers,* though distressed by Yurick's "punishing" account of life in psychiatric wards and prison, acknowledged the novel's "savage power and . . . Chaucerian detail." And Yurick's "brutally funny style," his "deadly serious . . . black comedy," put a *Newsweek* critic in mind of Nathanael West.

Sam Miller in *The Bag* (1968) is an idealistic young novelist who, disgusted by the greed and irrelevance of the modern American literature industry, refuses to publish his much-admired new book and instead takes a job with the Welfare Department. What he learns in his new life is recorded, one reviewer wrote, in "a montage of events and characters . . . black nationalists; slumlords; bohemia, both esthetic and political; the collision of the races socially, psychically and sexually . . . liberals, junkies, psychiatrists, politicos, businessmen, cops, carnivores and computers, all flailing about for identity and power." It involves characters who first appeared in *The Warriors* and others—corrupt manipulators of "the system"—introduced in *Fertig.*

And like *Fertig,* the novel outraged some readers, moved and excited others. R. M. Elman called it "a potpourri of failures posing as a novel of ideas"—a book "always asserting the observed, the real, that which is, and then doubling back with images out of literature and Hollywood, and the life of the work is in the real and the death of it is in the literature." Even so,

Elman recognized this as "a work of great energy and passion, an accurate depiction of the sociology of the contemporary despair." Jack Kroll went further, describing Yurick as "one of the rare writers who can synthesize the claims of art and of social feeling and thought. Despite a few touches of apocalyptic sentimentality (the slumlord with culture, the white Jewish welfare worker who is cleansed of spiritual sludge in the giant black embrace of one of his clients) this book is possibly the most powerful, intelligent and balanced novel in recent years about our diseased, embattled and explosive cities." And John Leonard concluded that Yurick's achievement in this novel is "stunning because it is multiple; he has created real characters, from every social stratum; mastered their life-styles and their prose styles; resisted caricature and risked sympathy. ... With rare responsibility he has brilliantly conceived and powerfully executed a portrait of the sight, sound, smell and taste of Urban Now, beneath the plastic; and he has renewed the novel as a social transaction."

Yurick's short stories had meanwhile been appearing in such journals as *Transatlantic Review* and the *Quarterly Review of Literature,* and thirteen of them were published in 1972 as *Some Just Like You.* Like *The Bag,* many of these stories come out of Yurick's experience as a social worker. "The Annealing" is a brutal piece in which "the system" gives a sour psychiatrist something like absolute power over the destiny of a splendidly life-affirming black woman. "The Siege" is about another welfare recipient, an old woman whose pathetic but to her vitally important secret is forced from her by welfare investigators. But not all of Yurick's characters allow the system to roll them flat: the old pensioner in "Not With a Whimper But . . ." refuses to resign gracefully from life, and has the temerity to fall in love. Other stories deal with a power struggle among a group of homosexuals, the happy defeat of a young weightlifter's puritanism, a ladies' literary discussion group in Larchmont earnestly pursuing Dionysian liberation. "And Not in Utter Nakedness" is an extraordinary fantasy in which a naked and derelict girl gives birth as a group happening, accompanied by trumpet, action-painting, and dance.

"Because Yurick's material is so solid," wrote Joyce Carol Oates, "even excursions into the fanciful and the 'surreal' seem, in his hands, somehow realistic. His characters have a way of bursting into song and dance, sometimes joyfully, but more often as an expression of suppressed, frustrated rage." Oates found such "musical and formless" stories on the whole less satisfying than "the kind of writing he can do so well, with his formidable knowledge of reality, his ability to synthesize facts into esthetic experiences." The realistic stories in this collection, she thought, "have a power to move us, urgently and deeply, that cannot be matched by any of the author's superficially sophisticated contemporaries."

An Island Death (1975) is a considerable departure from the realism that Oates favors in Yurick's work, and from the raw and raucous urban slums of his earlier books. The passionate ghetto-born idealist Trag grows up and changes his name. As the classical scholar Professor Targ he visits Greece to recover from an exhausting bout of academic infighting. There, in "the cradle of civilization," he meets Kairos, an avatar of Targ's old classics teacher (as Targ is an avatar of Trag). Targ and Kairos together visit an island rich in classical antiquities and timeless superstitions. Kairos kills himself and Targ, forbidden to bury the body on the island (where it would defile the harvest), harassed by a Kafkaesque official, haunted by voices from the island's past and his own, descends into dementia and death.

Doris Grumbach wrote that "the bare plot does not suggest the horrors, as well as the pleasures and the wit of this novel. And then there is an added pleasure: the richness of the prose. But meaning, under the wealth and weight of Yurick's language, blurs, becomes ambiguous, suggestive, fertile, elusive." All the same, although "this is Yurick's most intricate creation . . . because of its allusive and hallucinatory character, it does not stick to the ribs . . . and goes through the system without nourishing the imagination."

Yurick was the editor of *Voices of Brooklyn* (1973), an anthology of "powerfully evocative" writings by some sixty residents of Brooklyn whose work had not previously been published. According to Yurick, the writers had set out "to evoke—in many forms and for different purposes—a sense of urban life as it is experienced" by members of a great variety of ethnic groups. The anthology, which grew out of a series of programs arranged by the Brooklyn Public Library, proved to him "how many people there are around who can write." John Fuegi in *Contemporary Novelists* notes that Yurick "was involved for several years in attempting to construct a sound theoretical and practical basis for action on the American left." Fuegi believes that Yurick's novels, taken together, "make up the most compelling vision available to us (in fiction or in non-fiction) of the most nightmarish megalopolis of all: New York now. . . . In a deliberate and obviously self-conscious way, he consistently attempts to close the gap between the Biblical and classical Greek world so often alluded to in his works and the world of welfare, of murder, and of political power plays, the three major elements in his portrait of New York today."

PRINCIPAL WORKS: *Fiction*—The Warriors, 1965; Fertig, 1966; The Bag, 1968; Some Just Like You (short stories), 1972; An Island Death, 1975. *As Editor*—Voices of Brooklyn, 1973.

ABOUT: Contemporary Authors 13–16 1st revision, 1975; Vinson, J. (ed.) Contemporary Novelists, 1976. *Periodicals*—Commonweal October 14, 1966; October 4, 1968; Nation November 26, 1965; August 8, 1966; July 8, 1968; New York Times Book Review May 19, 1968; June 9, 1968; September 3, 1972; April 20, 1975; Newsweek May 9, 1966; June 17, 1968; North American Review September 1966; Saturday Review July 20, 1968; April 5, 1975; Wilson Library Bulletin May 1977.

Martha Swope

PAUL ZINDEL

ZINDEL, PAUL (May 15, 1936–), American dramatist and novelist, was born on Staten Island, the son of Paul Zindel, a New York City policeman, and the former Betty Beatrice Mary Frank. Because his parents were separated, the boy saw very little of his father. He and his older sister Betty were raised by their mother, a licensed practical nurse of Irish descent who supported them by boarding terminal patients and by working over the years as a caterer, a breeder of collie dogs, a shipyard laborer, a hatcheck girl, and a hot-dog vendor. The family moved often and Paul Zindel, denied sustained friendships with other children, lived a great deal in his imagination. He played with marionettes and cycloramas, kept aquariums, insectariums, and terrariums. "What a great love I had of microcosms," he wrote many years later, "of peering at other worlds, framed and separate from me." It may have been this that attracted him to the drama; though he never went to the theatre until he was in his twenties, his own first plays and skits were written in high school, and during the year-and-a-half he spent away from school, recovering from an attack of tuberculosis. After he left the sanatorium, Zindel wrote a play that won him a prize in a contest sponsored by the American Cancer Society.

Graduating from Port Richmond High School, Zindel went on to Wagner College, also on Staten Island, where he majored in chemistry, receiving his B.S. in 1958 and his M.Sc. the following year. In a creative writing course he took at Wagner one of Zindel's teachers was Edward Albee, under whose guidance he wrote a play called *Dimensions of Peacocks.* When he left college, Zindel worked for a time as a technical writer for a chemical company, but he found this unrewarding and resigned to become a teacher of chemistry and physics at Tottenville High School on Staten Island. There he remained from 1960 to 1969, writing plays in his spare time. One of these, *Euthanasia and the Endless Hearts,* was performed in a New York coffeehouse in 1960, and *A Dream of Swallows,* about waifs and old people boarding in a country house, lasted one night at the off-Broadway Jan Hus House in 1964. "If one dares to guess at what the author is driving at," Howard Taubman wrote of the latter, "the play means to be a mood piece, suffused with poetic aspiration. But Mr. Zindel's flights of fancy are pretentious, and the only mood he establishes is ennui."

The Effects of Gamma Rays on Man-in-the-Moon Marigolds, Zindel's best-known play, had its premiere in 1965 at the Alley Theatre in Houston, Texas (where Zindel went in 1967 as playwright-in-residence on a leave of absence from Tottenville). Howard Taubman, who saw the Alley Theatre production, found the new play a distinct improvement over *A Dream of Swallows;* despite its "elliptical, occasionally murky style," it seemed to him to have an "odd, cumulative power" and "flashes of perception and suspense"; it "created a tension of its own." Over the next few years *Marigolds* was seen on television and tightened up in productions in various regional theatres. In April 1970 it opened in New York at the Mercer–O'Casey Theatre off-Broadway.

The heroine of *Marigolds* is Tillie, a sensitive, withdrawn, and gifted teenager almost overwhelmed by the damaged spirits around her— her embittered, eccentric, domineering mother Beatrice; her epileptic sister; and Nanny, the moribund old woman whom Beatrice cares for. Encouraged by a sympathetic teacher, Tillie carries out a series of experiments with marigold seeds that have been exposed to various degrees of radiation; some of the seeds grow into giant flowers, some mutate in other ways, and some die—shaped, just as human beings are, by the external forces brought to bear upon them. Tillie, it is clear, is to be one of the survivors. Her experiments win first prize in a high school science fair, and this success gives her the courage to stand up at the prize-giving and deliver a lecture affirming the order and beauty of the universe. Zindel has said that the idea for the play came to him when he was preparing a class lecture and was struck by the idea "that all carbon atoms on earth had to come from the sun. The idea of being linked to the universe by these atoms, which really don't die, gave me a feeling of meaning."

Richard Roud found the play "nothing more than a rehash of the clichés of the Broadway plays of a decade ago—along the lines of William Inge or even of Tennessee Williams"; *Variety* made the same comparison more positively, calling it "the most compelling work of its kind since Tennessee Williams' *The Glass Menagerie.*" Most of the New York critics took the play to their hearts. "The play is 'old-fashioned,' " wrote Harold Clurman, "harking back to a slice-of-life realism rarely practiced any more, but the clarity of its writing, the health of its spirit, and the touching courage of its basic statement are most sympathetic." Walter Kerr said: "The play itself is one of the lucky blooms; it survives, and is beautiful. . . . With it, Mr. Zindel becomes one of our most promising new writers." *Marigolds,* which moved to the New Theatre on Broadway in 1971, carried off the Drama Critics Circle Award, an off-Broadway "Obie," the Vernon Rice–Drama Desk Award, and the 1971 Pulitzer Prize for drama—a clean sweep of the major awards. A movie version, directed by Paul Newman and starring Joanne Woodward, was released in 1972.

The character of Beatrice in *Marigolds* was based on the author's own mother "in nightmarish exaggeration," Zindel says, and his next play was also partly autobiographical. This was *And Miss Reardon Drinks A Little,* which opened at the Morosco Theatre on Broadway in February 1971. The three Reardon sisters, all schoolteachers, are all emotionally scarred by years of domination by their neurotic mother, now dead. Catherine drinks too much and Anna, in disgrace because of an affair with a young student, is on the verge of insanity. Into this troubled household comes the coolly efficient Ceil (who is married unhappily to Catherine's old boyfriend), determined that Anna should be committed to an institution. It is this proposal that supplies the play's frail plot—for which, most critics thought, neither the witty dialogue nor the strong characterization was sufficient compensation.

There was an even harsher reception for *The Secret Affairs of Mildred Wild* (1972), in which the movie-addicted wife of a candy store owner in Greenwich Village fantasizes her way through a succession of starring roles. Zindel himself says that the play failed "because it was shallow. It wasn't me." After that he felt "at loose ends," and even toyed with the idea of going back to Staten Island to teach chemistry. Instead, he joined the Actors' Studio, attending sessions on acting, directing, and playwriting, and for the first time learning that "I didn't have to be afraid of actors. . . . I could use them creatively." This he proceeded to do. He conducted "deep, private confessional interviews" with five Actors' Studio actresses, had the tapes transcribed, and built parts of these monologues into *Ladies at the Alamo,* in which five women struggle for the control of a theatre complex in Texas. Not all of the contributors were pleased by Zindel's use of their monologues, and the play itself, which opened on Broadway in April 1977 with an impressive cast, disappointed the reviewers. T.E. Kalem summed up the general reaction when he called it "weak in credibility and ramshackle in structure."

Meanwhile, beginning in the 1960s, Zindel had established himself as one of the most admired and successful of contemporary novelists writing for teenagers. His first book, *The Pigman* (1968), traces the relationship between Angelo Pignati, a widower whose collection of ceramic pigs is his chief remaining delight, and two restless adolescents. They become his friends but, during a drunken party they give at his house while he is in the hospital, smash his collection. John Weston said that Zindel "catches the bright, hyperbolic sheen of teen-ager language accurately and with humor," and the *Horn Book*'s reviewer wrote: "Few books that have been written for young people are as cruelly truthful about the human condition. Fewer still accord the elderly such serious consideration or perceive that what we term senility may be a symbolic return to youthful honesty and idealism." According to Jean F. Mercier the book "is well on its way to classic status." It was a bestseller, like all of Zindel's novels, and has been filmed.

My Darling, My Hamburger (1969) studies four high school seniors as they face the problems of growing up in general and sex in particular. "The teen-agers here are the most realistic of any in high-school novels to date," wrote M.R. Singer. "They have appropriate feelings and relationships; smoke, drink, swear; have refreshingly normal sexual thoughts and conflicts. The dialogue and description are so natural and entertaining (and often very funny) that the author disarms his audience . . . while planting mines of moralism: pot and sex are destructive." Attacked for "copping out" in this novel on the issues of sex, contraception, and abortion, Zindel was then accused of writing "a squalid little book" in *I Never Loved Your Mind* (1970), in which Dewey, a high school dropout, loves and eventually loses the flower child Yvette. Great quantities of teenagers nevertheless read and admired both books, as they did the two that followed: *Pardon Me, You're Stepping on My Eyeball!* (1976) and *Confessions of a Teenage Baboon* (1977).

As Jean F. Mercier wrote in *Publishers Weekly,* some adults object to Zindel's "bizarre situations, portraits of monstrous parents and what they regard as over-drawn descriptions of teen traumas. Thoughtful grownups, however, see the novels as genuine aids to adolescents trying to handle loneliness and other bugbears." The English critic Isabel Quigly, in her review of *Confessions of a Teenage Baboon,* acknowledged that "it is not the stuff that teenage novels used to deal with; but then the stuff of teenage life is not what it used to be, either, and what counts is the way Paul Zindel handles it, with a delicacy at once funny and heartfelt, outspoken and sensitive. He comments on the mess that adults have made of the world their children inherit by showing, with candour but a certain gentleness

as well, a young-eyed view of it. His children are never type-cast, nor are the situations he puts them in. They show the variety as well as the weirdness of behaviour and of life itself."

Zindel is slightly built, red-haired, and bearded. He was married in 1973 to Bonnie Hildebrand and has two children. In addition to his other awards he has an honorary doctorate from his alma mater, Wagner College. He is the author of several screenplays. His television play *Let Me Hear You Whisper* (1969), a touching piece about a dolphin, destined for vivisection, who is taught to speak by a lonely cleaning woman, was generally well received.

PRINCIPAL PUBLISHED WORKS: *Plays*—The Effect of Gamma Rays on Man-in-the-Moon Marigolds, 1970; And Miss Reardon Drinks a Little, 1971; The Secret Affairs of Mildred Wild, 1973; Let Me Hear You Whisper, and, The Ladies Should Be in Bed: Two Plays, 1973. *Novels*—The Pigman, 1968; My Darling, My Hamburger, 1969; I Never Loved Your Mind, 1970; Pardon Me, You're Stepping on My Eyeball!, 1976; Confessions of a Teenage Baboon, 1977; The Undertaker's Gone Bananas, 1978.

ABOUT: Current Biography, 1973; Hohenberg, J. The Pulitzer Prizes, 1974; McGraw-Hill Encyclopedia of World Drama, 1972; Vinson, J. (ed.) Contemporary Dramatists, 1977; Who's Who in America, 1976–1977; Who's Who in the Theatre, 1977. *Periodicals*—English Journal November 1972; October 1977; Life July 4, 1970; Nation April 20, 1970; March 15, 1971; December 4, 1972; New York Review of Books December 17, 1970; New York Times April 15, 1964; June 7, 1965; June 27, 1965; October 4, 1966; April 8, 1970; April 19, 1970; July 26, 1970; February 26, 1971; March 2, 1971; March 7, 1971; November 15, 1972; April 3, 1977; April 8, 1977; April 17, 1977; New York Times Book Review November 3, 1968; November 9, 1969; May 24, 1970; New Yorker April 18, 1970; March 6, 1971; November 25, 1972; Newsweek April 27, 1970; November 27, 1972; Publishers Weekly December 5, 1977; Saturday Review June 26, 1965; May 2, 1970; March 20, 1971; Time April 20, 1970; March 8, 1971; May 17, 1971; November 27, 1972; April 18, 1977.

NECROLOGY

Braudel, F. Nov. 28, 1985
Brautigan, R. Sept.(?) 1984
Drummond de Andrade, C. Aug. 17, 1987
Farb, P. Apr. 8, 1980
Filippo, E. de Nov. 1, 1984
Foucault, M. June 25, 1984
Fuller, R. B. July 1, 1983
Gardner, J. Sept. 14, 1982
Hayden, R. Feb. 25, 1980
Herbert, F. Feb. 11, 1986
Jakobson, R. July 18, 1982

Killens, J. O. Oct. 27, 1987
Lash, J. P. Aug. 22, 1987
Laurence, M. Jan. 5, 1987
Mandelstam, N. Dec. 29, 1980
Maugham, R. Mar. 13, 1981
Medawar, P. Oct. 2, 1987
Moraes, V. de July 9, 1980
Oppen, G. July 7, 1984
Pym, B. Jan. 11, 1980
Rulfo, J. Jan. 7, 1986
Schmidt, A. June 3, 1979
Scholem, G. G. Feb. 20, 1982
Scott, F. R. Jan. 31, 1985